The Sporting News
BASEBALL GUIDE

1 9 9 3 E D I T I O N

Editors / Baseball Guide
CRAIG CARTER
DAVE SLOAN

The Sporting News

── PUBLISHING CO. ──

Francis P. Pandolfi, Chairman and Chief Executive Officer; **Nicholas H. Niles,** Publisher and President; **John D. Rawlings,** Editorial Director; **Kathy Kinkeade,** Vice President / Production; **William N. Topaz,** Director / Information Development; **Gary Brinker,** Director of Electronic Information Development; **Gary Levy,** Editor; **Mike Nahrstedt,** Managing Editor; **Joe Hoppel,** Senior Editor; **Craig Carter, Tom Dienhart and Dave Sloan,** Associate Editors; **Mark Shimabukuro,** Assistant Editor; **Bill Bayer and George Puro,** Editorial Assistants; **Bill Perry,** Director of Graphic Presentation; **Mike Bruner,** Art Director / Yearbooks and Books; **Corby Dolan,** Database Analyst; **Vern Kasal,** Composing Room Supervisor.

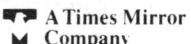 A Times Mirror
Company

World Series, A.L. Championship Series, N.L. Championship Series and All-Star Game highlights written by Joe Hoppel of THE SPORTING NEWS.

Major league statistics compiled by MLB-IBM Baseball Information System.

Minor league statistics compiled by Howe Sportsdata International Inc., Boston.

Additional assistance provided by STATS, Inc., Lincolnwood, Ill., and Elias Sports Bureau, New York.

ISBN: 0-89204-458-6 (perfect-bound)
        0-89204-459-4 (comb-bound)

10 9 8 7 6 5 4 3 2 1

CONTENTS

ON THE COVER: Minnesota's Kirby Puckett led the American League in hits and total bases in 1992, finishing with a .329 average, 19 homers and 110 RBIs. (Photo by The Sporting News)

1993
SEASON

MAJOR LEAGUE BASEBALL

COMMISSIONER'S OFFICE

Address
350 Park Avenue
New York, NY 10022
Telephone
212-339-7800
FAX
212-355-0007
Deputy commissioner
Steven D. Greenberg
(Resigning in April 1993)
Exec. director, broadcasting
David Alworth

Exec. dir., market development
Leonard Coleman
Director, special events
David Dziedzic
Exec. dir., security/facility management
Kevin Hallinan
Exec. dir., public relations
Richard Levin
Exec. dir., baseball operations
William Murray
General counsel
Thomas J. Ostertag

Director, minor league relations
Jimmie Lee Solomon
Director, broadcast administration
Leslie Sullivan
Chief financial officer
Jeffrey White
Exec. dir., licensing oper. and pres., MLBP
Rick White

AMERICAN LEAGUE

Address
350 Park Avenue
New York, NY 10022
Telephone
212-339-7600
President
Robert W. Brown, M.D.
Vice president
Gene Autry
Special assistant to baseball
Dick Wagner
Executive director of umpiring
Martin J. Springstead
Coordinator of umpire operations
Philip Janssen
Special assistant to the president
Richard Butler
V.p., admin. and media affairs
Phyllis Merhige
Director, waivers and player records
John G. Ricco

Assistant media affairs director
Joe Fitzgerald
Administrator of umpires/travel
Tess Basta
Administrative assistant
Carolyn Coen
Umpires
Lawrence Barnett
Joseph Brinkman
Alan Clark
Drew Coble
Terry Craft
Derryl Cousins
Donald Denkinger
James Evans
Dale Ford
Richard Garcia
Ted Hendry
John Hirschbeck
Mark Johnson
Jim Joyce

Kenneth Kaiser
Greg Kosc
Tim McClelland
Larry McCoy
James McKean
Chuck Meriwether
Durwood Merrill
Dan Morrison
Steve Palermo*
David Phillips
Rick Reed
Michael Reilly
John (Rocky) Roe
Dale Scott
John Shulock
Tim Tschida
Vic Voltaggio
Tim Welke
Larry Young
*Inactive status.

NATIONAL LEAGUE

Address
350 Park Avenue
New York, NY 10022
Telephone
212-339-7700
President and treasurer
William D. White
Senior vice president and secretary
Phyllis B. Collins
Vice president, media and public affairs
Katy Feeney
Director of umpire supervision
Ed Vargo
Asst. secretary and exec. dir., player records
Nancy Crofts
Executive secretary
Valerie Dietrich

Administrative assistant, umpires
Cathy Davis
Public relations assistant
Dorsey Parker
Umpires
Gregory Bonin
Gerald Crawford
Gary Darling
Robert Davidson
Gerald Davis
Dana DeMuth
Bruce Froemming
Eric Gregg
Thomas Hallion
Mark Hirschbeck
William Hohn
Jerry Layne
Randall Marsh

John McSherry
Edward Montague
Frank Pulli
James Quick
Edward Rapuano
Charles Reliford
Thomas Steven Rippley
Paul Runge
Terry Tata
Harry Wendelstedt
Joseph West
Charles Williams
Michael Winters

NOTE: Some additional umpires
will be hired at the completion
of spring training.

OTHER ORGANIZATIONS

NATIONAL BASEBALL
HALL OF FAME AND MUSEUM
Address
P.O. Box 590
Cooperstown, NY 13326
Telephone
607-547-9988
607-547-5980 (FAX)

President
Edward W. Stack
Director
Howard C. Talbot Jr.
Associate director
William J. Guilfoile
Curator
William T. Spencer

Registrar
Peter P. Clark
Merchandising director
Jeffrey D. Stevens
Controller
Fran Althiser
Librarian
Thomas R. Heitz

NATIONAL ASSOCIATION OF PROFESSIONAL BASEBALL LEAGUES

Address
P.O. Box A
St. Petersburg, FL 33731
Telephone
813-822-6937
813-821-5819 (FAX)
President
Mike Moore
General counsel
George E. Yund
Assistant general counsel
Ben Hayes
Exec. dir., special projects and events
Robert J. Sparks
Director of information and trade show
Larry Wiederecht
Exec. dir., business administration
Ann Perkins

MAJOR LEAGUE BASEBALL PLAYERS ASSOCIATION

Address
805 Third Ave.
New York, NY 10022
Telephone
212-826-0808
212-752-3649 (FAX)
Executive director and general counsel
Donald M. Fehr
Special assistant
Mark Belanger
Associate general counsel
Eugene D. Orza
Assistant general counsels
Lauren Rich
Michael Weiner
Doyle Pryor
Counsel
Arthur Schack
Director of licensing
Judy Heeter

PLAYER RELATIONS COMMITTEE

Address
350 Park Avenue
New York, NY 10022
Telephone
212-339-7400
212-371-2242 (FAX)
President and chief operating officer
Richard Ravitch
General counsel
Charles P. O'Connor
Associate counsels
Louis Melendez
John Westhoff
Contract administrator
Barbara Ernst
Director, public relations
Richard Levin

MAJOR LEAGUE BASEBALL UMPIRE DEVELOPMENT

Address
P.O. Box A
St. Petersburg, FL 33731
Telephone
813-823-1286 and 813-823-3729
813-821-5819 (FAX)
Executive director
Edwin W. Lawrence
Director of field supervision
Mike Fitzpatrick

HOWE SPORTSDATA INTERNATIONAL INC.

Address
Boston Fish Pier
West Building No. 2, Suite 306
Boston, MA 02210
Telephone
617-951-0070
617-951-1379 (stats request)
617-737-9960 (FAX)
President
Alan Goldfine
Executive vice president
Jay Virshbo

ELIAS SPORTS BUREAU

Address
500 Fifth Ave.
New York, NY 10110
Telephone
212-869-1530
212-354-0980 (FAX)
General manager
Seymour Siwoff

BASEBALL WRITERS' ASSOCIATION OF AMERICA

President
Neil Hohlfeld, Houston Chronicle
Vice president
Rick Hummel,
St. Louis Post-Dispatch
Secretary/treasurer
Jack O'Connell, Hartford Courant
Executive secretary
Jack Lang, SportsTicker
Board of directors
Bob Elliott, Toronto Sun
Gerry Fraley, Dallas Morning News
Bob Nightengale, Los Angeles Times
Pat Reusse,
Minneapolis Star Tribune

MAJOR LEAGUE SCOUTING BUREAU

Address
23712 Birtcher Dr., Suite A
El Toro, CA 92630
Telephone
714-458-7600
714-458-9454 (FAX)
Director
Donald F. Pries
Board of directors
Sandy Alderson
Dan Duquette
Lou Gorman
Roland Hemond
Joe McIlvaine
Bill Murray
Donald F. Pries
Art Stewart

MAJOR LEAGUE UMPIRES ASSOCIATION

Address
1735 Market St., Suite 3420
Philadelphia, PA 19103
Telephone
215-979-3220
General counsel
Richard G. Phillips

ASS'N OF PROFESSIONAL BASEBALL PLAYERS OF AMERICA

Address
12062 Valley View, Suite 211
Garden Grove, CA 92645
Telephone
714-892-9900
714-897-0233 (FAX)
President
John J. McHale
Secretary/treasurer
Chuck Stevens

BASEBALL ASSISTANCE TEAM INC.

Address
350 Park Avenue
New York, NY 10022
Telephone
212-339-7884
Chairman
Ralph Branca
President
Joe Garagiola
Vice presidents
Joe Black
Rusty Staub
Earl Wilson
Executive director
Frank Slocum
Secretary/treasurer
Tom Ostertag

MAJOR LEAGUE BASEBALL PLAYERS ALUMNI ASSOC.

Address
3637 4th St., North, Suite 101
St. Petersburg, FL 33704
Telephone
813-822-3399
813-822-6300 (FAX)
President
Brooks Robinson
Vice presidents
Hank Aguirre
Carl Erskine
Mike Hegan
Chuck Hinton
Al Kaline
Mike Schmidt
Rusty Staub
Billy Williams
Secretary/treasurer
Fred Valentine
Executive committee
Jerry Moses, Chairman
Jim Hannan, Vice chairman
Jim (Mudcat) Grant
Rich Hand
Lou Klimchock
Board of directors
Darrel Chaney
Jim (Mudcat) Grant
Rich Hand
Jim Hannan
Lou Klimchock
Tug McGraw
Bob Miller
Dick Radatz
Eddie Robinson
Ken Sanders
Fred Valentine
Carl Warwick
Bob Allison, Director emeritus

BALTIMORE ORIOLES
AMERICAN LEAGUE EAST DIVISION

1993 SCHEDULE

APRIL

SUN	MON	TUE	WED	THU	FRI	SAT
				1	2	3
4	5 TEX H	6	7 TEX H	8	9 N SEA	10 N SEA
11 SEA	12 TEX	13 N TEX	14 N TEX	15	16 N CAL	17 CAL H
18 CAL H	19	20 N CHI H	21 N CHI H	22	23 N KC	24 KC
25 KC	26 N CHI	27 CHI	28 N MIN H	29 N MIN H	30 N KC H	

MAY

SUN	MON	TUE	WED	THU	FRI	SAT
						1 KC H
2 KC H	3	4 N MIN	5 MIN	6 N TOR H	7 N TOR H	8 TOR
9 TOR	10 N BOS H	11 N BOS H	12 N BOS H	13	14 N DET	15 N DET
16 DET	17 N CLE H	18 N CLE H	19 N CLE H	20 N CLE H	21 N MIL H	22 MIL H
23 MIL H	24 N NY	25 N NY	26 N NY	27 N NY	28 N CAL	29 CAL
30 CAL	31 OAK					

JUNE

SUN	MON	TUE	WED	THU	FRI	SAT
		1 N OAK	2 OAK	3	4 N SEA	5 N SEA H
6 SEA H	7 OAK H	8 N OAK H	9 N OAK H	10 N BOS	11 N BOS	12 BOS
13 BOS	14 N MIL	15 N MIL	16	17	18 N CLE	19 N CLE
20 CLE	21	22 N DET H	23 N DET H	24 N DET H	25 N NY H	26 N NY H
27 NY H	28 N TOR H	29 N TOR H	30 N TOR H			

JULY

SUN	MON	TUE	WED	THU	FRI	SAT
				1 N CHI	2 N CHI	3 N CHI
4 CHI	5 N KC	6 N KC	7 N KC	8 N CHI H	9 N CHI H	10 CHI H
11 CHI H	12	13 * ALL-STAR GAME	14	15 N MIN	16 N MIN	17 N MIN
18 MIN H	19 N KC H	20 N KC H	21 N KC H	22 N MIN	23 N MIN	24 MIN
25 MIN	26	27 N TOR	28 N TOR	29	30 N BOS H	31 N BOS H

AUGUST

SUN	MON	TUE	WED	THU	FRI	SAT
1 BOS H	2 N MIL H	3 N MIL H	4 N MIL	5 N MIL	6 N CLE H	7 N CLE H
8 CLE H	9 N DET	10 N DET	11 N DET	12 DET	13 N NY	14 N NY
15 NY	16 N SEA	17 N SEA	18 SEA	19	20 N TEX H	21 N TEX H
22 TEX H	23 N TEX H	24 N CAL H	25 N CAL H	26	27 N CAL	28 TEX
29 TEX	30	31 N CAL				

SEPTEMBER

SUN	MON	TUE	WED	THU	FRI	SAT
			1 N CAL	2 N CAL	3 N OAK	4 N OAK
5 OAK	6 N OAK	7 N SEA H	8 N SEA H	9	10 N OAK H	11 N OAK H
12 N OAK H	13 N BOS	14 N BOS	15 N BOS	16	17 N MIL	18 N MIL
19 MIL	20 N CLE	21 N CLE	22 N CLE	23	24 N DET H	25 N DET H
26 DET H	27 N NY H	28 N NY H	29 N NY H	30 N TOR H		

OCTOBER

SUN	MON	TUE	WED	THU	FRI	SAT
					1 N TOR H	2 N TOR H
3 TOR H						

1993 SEASON

CLUB DIRECTORY

Chairman
Eli S. Jacobs
President
Lawrence Lucchino
Exec. vice president and general manager
Roland A. Hemond
Senior vice president/asst. to the chairman
Thomas A. Daffron
Vice president, administrative personnel
Calvin Hill
Vice president, business affairs
Robert R. Aylward
Vice president and club counsel
Lon Babby
Vice president, planning and development
Janet Marie Smith
Vice president
Sven Erik Holmes
Asst. g.m./dir. of player personnel
R. Douglas Melvin
Assistant to the general manager
Frank Robinson
Director of scouting
Gary Nickels
Special assistants to the vice president
Gordon Goldsberry
Fred Uhlman Sr.
Vice president, finance
Aric Holsinger
Director/ticket operations
Joseph R. Keough
Administrator/minor league operations
Andy Feffer
Assistant/player development and scouting
Leland MacPhail IV
Marketing coordinator
Michael Fiorelli
Traveling secretary
Philip E. Itzoe
Director of public relations
Richard L. Vaughn
Director of stadium services
Roy A. Sommerhof
Director of research and statistics
Eddie Epstein
Director of Orioles productions
Charles A. Steinberg, DDS
Director of sales operations
Vince Dunbar
Director, community relations
Julia A. Wagner
Director, computer services
James L. Kline
Special projects/baseball operations
Kenneth E. Nigro
Ticket office manager
Audrey Brown

Assistant director of public relations
Bob Miller
Director of marketing and advertising
David Cope
Assistant director of sales operations
Matt Dryer
Assistant director of scouting
Fred Uhlman Jr.
Assistant director of community relations
Stacey Beckwith
Assistant to director of public affairs
Amy Nelson
Assistant director/stadium operations
Scott Indorf
Assistant ticket office managers
Joseph B. Codd
Denise C. Addicks
Publishing coordinator
Stephanie Kelly
Club physicians
Dr. Sheldon Goldgeier
Dr. Charles E. Silberstein
Trainers
Richie Bancells
Jamie Reed
Strength and conditioning
Tim Bishop
Scouts
Rick Arnold
Carlos Bernhardt
Jesus Carmona
John Cox
Ray Crone
Lane Decker
Manny Estrada
Paul Fryer
Jim Gilbert
John Green
Jesus Halabi
Jim Howard
Deacon Jones
Leo Labossiere
Mike Ledna
Ed Liberatore
Earl Winn
Miguel Machado
Curt Motton
Lamar North
Camilo Nunez
Fred Petersen
Harry Shelton
Ed Sprague
John Stokoe
Mike Tullier
Jerry Zimmerman

SCHEDULE KEY

H—Home game.   N—Night game (any game starting after 5 p.m.).
*All-Star Game at Oriole Park at Camden Yards, Baltimore.

Manager—Johnny Oates (26).

Coaches—Greg Biagini (25), Dick Bosman (17), Mike Ferraro, Elrod Hendricks (44), Davey Lopes (15), Jerry Narron.

No.	PITCHERS	B/T	Ht./Wt.	Born	1992 clubs
49	Frohwirth, Todd	R/R	6-4/211	9-28-62	Baltimore
19	McDonald, Ben	R/R	6-7/213	11-24-67	Baltimore
75	Mills, Alan	B/R	6-1/192	10-18-66	Rochester, Baltimore
35	Mussina, Mike	R/R	6-2/185	12-8-68	Baltimore
	O'Donoghue, John	L/L	6-6/198	5-26-69	Hagerstown, Rochester
30	Olson, Gregg	R/R	6-4/212	10-11-66	Baltimore
56	Oquist, Mike	R/R	6-2/170	5-30-68	Rochester
47	Pennington, Brad	L/L	6-5/205	4-14-69	Frederick, Hagerstown, Rochester
45	Poole, Jim	L/L	6-2/203	4-28-66	Hagerstown, Rochester, Baltimore
53	Rhodes, Arthur	L/L	6-2/206	10-24-69	Rochester, Baltimore
40	Sutcliffe, Rick	L/R	6-7/239	6-21-56	Baltimore
50	Telford, Anthony	R/R	6-/189	3-6-66	Rochester
	Williams, Jeff	R/R	6-4/230	4-16-69	Hagerstown
32	Williamson, Mark	R/R	6-0/185	7-21-59	Baltimore, Hagerstown, Rochester

No.	CATCHERS	B/T	Ht./Wt.	Born	1992 clubs
23	Hoiles, Chris	R/R	6-/213	3-20-65	Baltimore, Hagerstown
27	Parent, Mark	R/R	6-5/220	9-16-61	Rochester, Baltimore
41	Tackett, Jeff	R/R	6-2/205	12-1-65	Baltimore

No.	INFIELDERS	B/T	Ht./Wt.	Born	1992 clubs
48	Alexander, Manny	R/R	5-10/165	3-20-71	Hagerstown, Rochester, Baltimore
	Carey, Paul	R/L	6-4/230	1-8-68	Frederick, Rochester, Hagerstown
37	Davis, Glenn	R/R	6-3/212	3-28-61	Baltimore
10	Gomez, Leo	R/R	6-/208	3-2-67	Baltimore
36	Hulett, Tim	R/R	6-/200	1-12-60	Baltimore
	Jennings, Doug	L/L	5-10/175	9-30-64	Rochester
	Lewis, T.R.	R/R	6-/180	4-17-71	Kane County, Frederick
6	Reynolds, Harold	B/R	5-11/165	11-26-60	Seattle
8	Ripken, Cal	R/R	6-4/220	8-24-60	Baltimore
43	Scarsone, Steve	R/R	6-2/191	4-11-66	Scranton/Wilkes-Barre, Philadelphia, Rochester, Baltimore
21	Segui, David	B/L	6-1/202	7-19-66	Baltimore

No.	OUTFIELDERS	B/T	Ht./Wt.	Born	1992 clubs
9	Anderson, Brady	L/L	6-1/190	1-18-64	Baltimore
	Baines, Harold	L/L	6-2/195	3-15-59	Oakland
	Buford, Damon	R/R	5-10/170	6-12-70	Hagerstown, Rochester
12	Devereaux, Mike	R/R	6-/195	4-10-63	Baltimore
14	Martinez, Chito	L/L	5-10/185	12-19-65	Baltimore
11	Mercedes, Luis	R/R	6-3/193	2-20-68	Rochester, Baltimore
	Obando, Sherman	R/R	6-4/215	1-23-70	Albany/Colonie
28	Voigt, Jack	R/R	6-1/175	5-17-66	Rochester, Baltimore

BALLPARK INFORMATION

Ballpark (capacity, surface)
Oriole Park at Camden Yards
(48,000, grass)

Address
333 W. Camden St.
Baltimore, MD 21201

Business phone
410-685-9800

Ticket information
410-685-9800

Ticket prices
$15 (lower boxes)
$14 (terrace boxes)
$12 (upper boxes)
$12 (left field lower boxes)
$11 (left field upper boxes)
$8 (reserved seats)
$6 (left field upper reserved)
$4 (bleachers)

Field dimensions (from home plate)
To left field at foul line, 333 feet
To center field, 400 feet
To right field at foul line, 318

First game played
April 6, 1992 (Orioles 2, Indians 0)

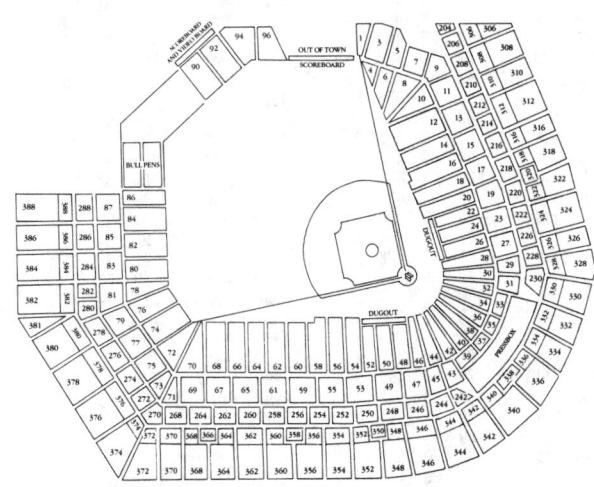

Class	Team	League	Manager
AAA	Rochester	International	Bob Miscik
AA	Bowie	Eastern	Don Buford
A	Frederick	Carolina	Pete Mackanin
A	Albany	South Atlantic	Mike O'Berry
Rookie	Sarasota	Gulf Coast	Oneri Fleita
Rookie	Bluefield	Appalachian	To be announced

Radio: WBAL-AM (1090). Broadcasters: Fred Manfra, Jon Miller, Chuck Thompson.
TV: WMAR-TV (Channel 2). Broadcasters: Scott Garceau, Jon Miller, Brooks Robinson.
Cable TV: Home Team Sports. Broadcasters: Mel Procter, John Lowenstein, Jim Palmer.

Ballpark (city): Twin Lakes Park (Sarasota, Fla.) from February 19 through March 4; then home games will be played at Al Lang Stadium (St. Petersburg, Fla.).
Ticket information: 813-822-3384.

Year	Pos.	W	L	Pct.	*GB
1901	8th	48	89	.350	35½
1902	2nd	78	58	.574	5
1903	6th	65	74	.468	26½
1904	6th	65	87	.428	29
1905	8th	54	99	.354	40½
1906	5th	76	73	.510	16
1907	6th	69	83	.454	24
1908	4th	83	69	.546	6½
1909	7th	61	89	.407	36
1910	8th	47	107	.305	57
1911	8th	45	107	.296	56½
1912	7th	53	101	.344	53
1913	8th	57	96	.373	39
1914	5th	71	82	.464	28½
1915	6th	63	91	.409	39½
1916	5th	79	75	.513	12
1917	7th	57	97	.370	43
1918	5th	58	64	.475	15
1919	5th	67	72	.482	20½
1920	4th	76	77	.497	21½
1921	3rd	81	73	.526	17½
1922	2nd	93	61	.604	1
1923	5th	74	78	.487	24
1924	4th	74	78	.487	17
1925	3rd	82	71	.536	15
1926	7th	62	92	.403	29
1927	7th	59	94	.336	50½
1928	3rd	82	72	.532	19
1929	4th	79	73	.520	26
1930	6th	64	90	.416	38
1931	5th	63	91	.409	45
1932	6th	63	91	.409	44
1933	8th	55	96	.364	43½
1934	6th	67	85	.441	33
1935	7th	65	87	.428	28½
1936	7th	57	95	.375	44½
1937	8th	46	108	.299	56
1938	7th	55	97	.362	44
1939	8th	43	111	.279	64½
1940	6th	67	87	.435	23
1941	T6th	70	84	.455	31
1942	3rd	82	69	.543	19½
1943	6th	72	80	.474	25
1944	1st	89	65	.578	+ 1
1945	3rd	81	70	.536	6
1946	7th	66	88	.429	38
1947	8th	59	95	.383	38
1948	6th	59	94	.386	37
1949	7th	53	101	.344	44

Year	Pos.	W	L	Pct.	*GB
1950	7th	58	96	.377	40
1951	8th	52	102	.338	46
1952	7th	64	90	.416	31
1953	8th	54	100	.351	46½
1954	7th	54	100	.351	57
1955	7th	57	97	.370	39
1956	6th	69	85	.448	28
1957	5th	76	76	.500	21
1958	6th	74	79	.484	17½
1959	6th	74	80	.481	20
1960	2nd	89	65	.578	8
1961	3rd	95	67	.586	14
1962	7th	77	85	.475	19
1963	4th	86	76	.531	18½
1964	3rd	97	65	.599	2
1965	3rd	94	68	.580	8
1966	1st	97	63	.606	+ 9
1967	T6th	76	85	.472	15½
1968	2nd	91	71	.562	12
1969	1st†	109	53	.673	+19
1970	1st†	108	54	.667	+15
1971	1st†	101	57	.639	+12
1972	3rd	80	74	.519	5
1973	1st‡	97	65	.599	+ 8
1974	1st‡	91	71	.562	+ 2
1975	2nd	90	69	.566	4½
1976	2nd	88	74	.543	10½
1977	T2nd	97	64	.602	2½
1978	4th	90	71	.559	9
1979	1st†	102	57	.642	+ 8
1980	2nd	100	62	.617	3
1981	2nd/4th	59	46	.562	§
1982	2nd	94	68	.580	1
1983	1st†	98	64	.605	+ 6
1984	5th	85	77	.525	19
1985	4th	83	78	.516	16
1986	7th	73	89	.451	22½
1987	6th	67	95	.414	31
1988	7th	54	107	.335	34½
1989	2nd	87	75	.537	2
1990	5th	76	85	.472	11½
1991	6th	67	95	.414	24
1992	3rd	89	73	.549	7

*Games behind winner. †Won Championship Series. ‡Lost Championship Series. §First half 31-23; second 28-23.

Name	Record	Years
Hugh Duffy	48-89	1901
Jimmy McAleer	551-632	'02-09
Jack O'Connor	47-107	1910
Bobby Wallace	57-134	'11-12
George Stovall	91-158	'12-13
Branch Rickey	139-179	'13-15
Fielder Jones	158-196	'16-18
Jimmy Austin	29-38	'18, '23
Jimmy Burke	172-180	'18-20
Lee Fohl	226-183	'21-23
George Sisler	218-241	'24-26
Dan Howley	220-239	'27-29
Bill Killefer	224-329	'30-33
Al Sothoron	2-6	1933
Rogers Hornsby	255-381	'33-37
		1952
Jim Bottomley	21-56	1937
Gabby Street	55-97	1938
Fred Haney	125-227	'39-41
Luke Sewell	432-410	41-46
Zack Taylor	235-410	1946
		'48-51
Marty Marion	96-161	'52-53
Jimmie Dykes	54-100	1954
Paul Richards	517-539	'55-61
Lum Harris	17-10	1961
Billy Hitchcock	163-161	'62-63
Hank Bauer	407-318	'64-68
Earl Weaver	1481-1060	'68-82
		'85-86
Cal Ripken Sr.	67-101	'87-88
Frank Robinson	230-285	88-91
Johnny Oates	143-144	'91-92

DAY BY DAY

Date	Opp.	Res.	Score (inn.*)	Hits	Opp. hits	Winning pitcher	Losing pitcher	Save	Record	Pos.	GB
4-6	Cle.	W	2-0	6	5	Sutcliffe	Nagy		1-0	T1st	...
4-8	Cle.	L	0-4	3	5	Otto	Milacki		1-1	T3rd	1
4-9	Cle.	W	2-0	6	2	McDonald	Armstrong		2-1	3rd	1
4-10	At Tor.	L	3-4	8	10	Hentgen	Olson		2-2	T3rd	2
4-11	At Tor.	L	2-7	8	13	Morris	Sutcliffe		2-3	T3rd	3
4-12	At Tor.	L	1-3	5	9	Wells	Mesa	Ward	2-4	T4th	4
4-13	At Bos.	W	8-6	12	9	Frohwirth	Fossas	Olson	3-4	3rd	3½
4-15	At Bos.	L	5-6	9	6	Harris	Davis	Reardon	3-5	5th	4½
4-17	Det.	W	8-0	13	4	Sutcliffe	Aldred		4-5	5th	4
4-18	Det.	W	6-1	11	8	Mussina	Tanana		5-5	3rd	4
4-19	Det.	W	3-2	5	5	Milacki	Terrell	Olson	6-5	3rd	3
4-20	Det.	W	12-4	16	6	Mills	King	Frohwirth	7-5	3rd	3
4-21	At K.C.	W	10-4	14	10	Mesa	Gubicza		8-5	3rd	3
4-22	At K.C.	W	2-1	6	6	Sutcliffe	Appier		9-5	3rd	2
4-23	At K.C.	W	8-1	12	6	Mussina	Davis		10-5	T2nd	2
4-24	At N.Y.	L	0-5	5	10	Cadaret	Milacki		10-6	3rd	3
4-25	At N.Y.	W	9-2	8	10	McDonald	Johnson		11-6	T2nd	3
4-26	At N.Y.	L	1-3	4	8	Howe	Mesa		11-7	3rd	3
4-27	At Min.	L	1-4	3	10	Krueger	Sutcliffe	Aguilera	11-8	3rd	3½
4-28	At Min.	W	10-5	10	8	Mussina	Erickson		12-8	3rd	2½
4-29	At Min.	W	5-4	8	8	Davis	Wayne	Olson	13-8	T2nd	2½
5-1	Sea.	W	15-1	11	5	McDonald	Johnson		14-8	T2nd	1
5-2	Sea.	W	4-2	9	6	Sutcliffe	Hanson	Olson	15-8	1st	...
5-3	Sea.	W	8-6	12	9	Mussina	DeLucia	Olson	16-8	1st	...
5-4	Tex.	W	8-5	7	10	Mills	Mathews		17-8	1st	...
5-5	Tex.	L	3-5	7	11	Robinson	Davis	Russell	17-9	2nd	1
5-6	Min.	W	6-2	11	6	McDonald	Tapani		18-9	2nd	1
5-7	Min.	W	5-4	9	9	Davis	Aguilera		19-9	2nd	1
5-8	Chi.	L	3-4 (10)	9	9	Leach	Olson	Thigpen	19-10	2nd	1
5-9	Chi.	W	5-2	10	9	Milacki	Fernandez	Olson	20-10	1st	...
5-10	Chi.	L	2-5	5	8	McDowell	Mesa	Thigpen	20-11	2nd	1
5-12	At Tex.	W	5-1	9	7	McDonald	Witt	Frohwirth	21-11	2nd	1
5-13	At Tex.	W	4-2	6	8	Sutcliffe	Brown	Olson	22-11	2nd	1
5-15	At Chi.	W	2-0	8	5	Mussina	Fernandez	Olson	23-11	2nd	½
5-16	At Chi.	W	7-2	14	7	McDowell	Milacki		24-11	1st	+½
5-17	At Chi.	L	10-14	17	14	Pall	McDonald		24-12	1st	+½
5-18	Oak.	L	4-8	7	10	Moore	Sutcliffe		24-13	1st	+½
5-19	Oak.	L	3-5	5	11	Slusarski	Mesa	Eckersley	24-14	1st	+½
5-20	Oak.	L	2-4	7	9	Welch	Mussina	Eckersley	24-15	2nd	½
5-22	Cal.	W	5-3	8	8	McDonald	Valera	Olson	25-15	2nd	...
5-23	Cal.	L	2-6	4	9	Langston	Sutcliffe		25-16	2nd	½
5-24	Cal.	W	6-4	12	11	Milacki	Finley	Olson	26-16	1st	+½
5-25	At Sea.	L	3-7	8	14	Fleming	Mesa	Schooler	26-17	1st	...
5-26	At Sea.	W	13-8	15	15	Sutcliffe	Johnson		27-17	1st	+1
5-27	At Sea.	L	1-7	5	10	Hanson	McDonald		27-18	1st	...
5-29	At Oak.	L	3-5	10	9	Moore	Milacki	Eckersley	27-19	2nd	1
5-30	At Oak.	W	7-6	12	9	Mesa	Slusarski	Olson	28-19	2nd	1
5-31	At Oak.	W	4-2	7	9	Sutcliffe	Darling	Olson	29-19	2nd	1
6-1	At Cal.	W	8-2	12	11	McDonald	Valera	Davis	30-19	2nd	1
6-2	At Cal.	W	4-2	10	6	Mussina	Langston	Olson	31-19	2nd	1
6-3	At Cal.	L	3-4 (10)	13	9	Bailes	Mills		31-20	2nd	1
6-5	Tor.	W	1-0	5	4	Sutcliffe	Key	Olson	32-20	1st	...
6-6	Tor.	L	3-4	7	5	Morris	McDonald	Henke	32-21	2nd	1
6-7	Tor.	W	7-1	10	8	Mussina	Stieb		33-21	1st	...
6-8	Bos.	W	5-2	9	7	Milacki	Gardiner	Olson	34-21	1st	...
6-9	Bos.	L	1-4	6	7	Dopson	Mesa	Reardon	34-22	2nd	1
6-10	Bos.	W	3-1	8	7	Sutcliffe	Bolton	Olson	35-22	2nd	1
6-11	At Det.	W	7-5	10	10	Mills	Gullickson	Olson	36-22	2nd	1
6-12	At Det.	W	6-0	8	6	Mussina	Aldred		37-22	1st	...
6-13	At Det.	L	1-15	9	16	Leiter	Milacki		37-23	1st	...
6-14	At Det.	L	4-7	8	10	Tanana	Mesa	Henneman	37-24	2nd	1
6-15	At Cle.	W	6-5	12	15	Davis	Cook	Olson	38-24	2nd	½
6-16	At Cle.	L	5-7	8	12	Armstrong	McDonald	Olin	38-25	2nd	½
6-17	At Cle.	L	2-3	13	5	Nagy	Mussina		38-26	2nd	1½
6-19	N.Y.	W	10-7	13	11	Mills	Hillegas	Olson	39-26	1st	...
6-20	N.Y.	L	5-9	10	15	Sanderson	Sutcliffe		39-27	2nd	1
6-21	N.Y.	L	2-8	7	6	Leary	McDonald		39-28	2nd	1
6-22	N.Y.	W	5-4	9	7	Olson	Burke		40-28	2nd	1
6-23	At Mil.	W	7-1	8	4	Mesa	Navarro	Davis	41-28	2nd	½
6-24	At Mil.	W	8-4	14	9	Mills	Holmes		42-28	2nd	½

Date	Opp.	Res.	Score	(inn.°)	Hits	Opp. hits	Winning pitcher	Losing pitcher	Save	Record	Pos.	GB
6-25	At Mil.	L	0-1		5	5	Bones	Sutcliffe	Henry	42-29	2nd	1
6-26	K.C.	W	6-5		13	10	Frohwirth	Meacham	Olson	43-29	2nd	1
6-27	K.C.	L	0-2		4	6	Appier	Mussina	Montgomery	43-30	2nd	1
6-28	K.C.	L	2-9		11	19	Pichardo	Mesa	Boddicker	43-31	2nd	1
6-29	Mil.	L	3-5		6	11	Bosio	Milacki	Fetters	43-32	2nd	2
6-30	Mil.	W	12-3		16	10	Sutcliffe	Bones		44-32	2nd	1
7-1	Mil.	W	7-4		12	10	McDonald	Wegman	Olson	45-32	2nd	1
7-3	At Min.	W	6-1		14	12	Mussina	Smiley		46-32	2nd	1
7-4	At Min.	L	2-3	(15)	12	11	Willis	Olson		46-33	2nd	2
7-5	At Min.	L	1-2		6	11	Tapani	Sutcliffe		46-34	2nd	3
7-6	Chi.	W	4-3	(14)	13	6	Mills	Hernandez		47-34	2nd	3
7-7	Chi.	L	4-8		8	13	Alvarez	Milacki		47-35	2nd	4
7-8	Chi.	W	5-3		8	9	Mills	Hough	Frohwirth	48-35	2nd	4
7-9	Min.	W	4-2		7	8	Rhodes	Erickson	Mills	49-35	2nd	4
7-10	Min.	L	2-5		5	8	Tapani	Sutcliffe	Aguilera	49-36	2nd	4
7-11	Min.	L	5-6		7	11	Krueger	McDonald	Aguilera	49-37	2nd	4
7-12	Min.	L	4-9		5	10	Edens	Milacki		49-38	2nd	4
7-16	At Tex.	L	2-5		3	9	Ryan	Sutcliffe	Russell	49-39	2nd	5
7-17	At Tex.	W	8-0		14	1	Mussina	Brown		50-39	2nd	4
7-18	At Tex.	W	7-0		8	2	McDonald	Guzman		51-39	2nd	4
7-19	At Tex.	W	3-2	(10)	8	3	Frohwirth	Mathews	Olson	52-39	2nd	4
7-20	At Chi.	W	3-2	(12)	8	11	Clements	Hernandez	Olson	53-39	2nd	3
7-21	At Chi.	L	7-10		10	12	Leach	Frohwirth		53-40	2nd	4
7-22	At Chi.	L	5-7		12	10	Pall	Olson	Radinsky	53-41	2nd	4
7-23	Tex.	L	2-4		9	8	Guzman	McDonald	Russell	53-42	2nd	5
7-24	Tex.	W	9-2	(8)	14	6	Rhodes	Burns		54-42	2nd	4
7-25	Tex.	L	8-10		12	10	Witt	Sutcliffe	Russell	54-43	2nd	4
7-26	Tex.	L	2-6		5	12	Ryan	Mussina	Nunez	54-44	2nd	4
7-28	At N.Y.	W	5-2		8	8	McDonald	Sanderson	Olson	55-44	2nd	4
7-29	At N.Y.	W	6-0		10	5	Rhodes	Kamieniecki		56-44	2nd	3
7-30	At N.Y.	L	3-6		8	11	Young	Sutcliffe	Farr	56-45	2nd	4
7-31 (1)	At Bos.	L	4-7		10	12	Hesketh	Frohwirth	Reardon	56-46	2nd	5
7-31 (2)	At Bos.	W	4-3	(5)	8	6	Lewis	Young		57-46	2nd	4 ½
8-1	At Bos.	W	9-3		10	12	Clements	Viola		58-46	2nd	4 ½
8-2	At Bos.	W	2-1		9	5	McDonald	Fossas	Olson	59-46	2nd	4 ½
8-3	Det.	W	6-3		9	8	Rhodes	Groom	Davis	60-46	2nd	3 ½
8-4	Det.	W	6-3		10	7	Sutcliffe	Knudsen	Olson	61-46	2nd	2 ½
8-5	Det.	W	4-0		7	5	Mussina	Kiely		62-46	2nd	2 ½
8-7	Cle.	L	4-5	(13)	9	12	Wickander	Mills		62-47	2nd	3
8-8	Cle.	L	0-6		1	13	Nagy	Rhodes		62-48	2nd	3
8-9	Cle.	W	3-2	(10)	10	7	Davis	Power		63-48	2nd	2
8-10	At Tor.	L	4-8		9	11	Stottlemyre	Mussina		63-49	2nd	3
8-11	At Tor.	W	3-0		8	8	Mills	Morris	Olson	64-49	2nd	2
8-12	At Tor.	W	11-4		15	9	McDonald	Key		65-49	2nd	1
8-13	At Tor.	L	2-4		3	8	Linton	Rhodes	Henke	65-50	2nd	2
8-14	At K.C.	W	3-1		5	10	Sutcliffe	Appier	Olson	66-50	2nd	2
8-15	At K.C.	L	4-5		10	11	Meacham	Olson		66-51	2nd	2 ½
8-16	At K.C.	L	2-15		8	17	Pichardo	Mills		66-52	2nd	3
8-18	Sea.	L	3-8		6	12	Fleming	McDonald	Nelson	66-53	2nd	4
8-19	Sea.	L	8-10		12	12	Grant	Rhodes	Swan	66-54	2nd	4
8-20	Sea.	W	2-1	(10)	5	11	Davis	Schooler		67-54	2nd	3
8-21	Oak.	W	4-2		5	9	Mussina	Downs	Mills	68-54	2nd	2
8-22	Oak.	L	3-5		8	10	Parrett	Lewis	Eckersley	68-55	2nd	3
8-23	Oak.	L	3-7		7	12	Moore	McDonald	Eckersley	68-56	2nd	3
8-24	Cal.	L	2-5		8	9	Abbott	Rhodes	Grahe	68-57	2nd	3
8-25	Cal.	W	9-1		14	4	Sutcliffe	Blyleven		69-57	2nd	2
8-26	Cal.	W	6-4		9	11	Frohwirth	Butcher	Olson	70-57	2nd	2
8-28	At Sea.	L	4-6		5	14	Leary	McDonald	Nelson	70-58	2nd	2 ½
8-29	At Sea.	W	4-0		11	5	Rhodes	Grant	Olson	71-58	2nd	1 ½
8-30	At Sea.	W	2-0		7	9	Sutcliffe	Fleming	Olson	72-58	2nd	1 ½
8-31	At Oak.	W	4-0		9	4	Mussina	Downs		73-58	2nd	1 ½
9-1	At Oak.	W	5-1		8	6	Milacki	Slusarski		74-58	2nd	1 ½
9-2	At Oak.	W	2-1	(10)	8	2	Mills	Honeycutt		75-58	2nd	½
9-4	At Cal.	W	8-7		11	6	Sutcliffe	Langston	Frohwirth	76-58	2nd	½
9-5	At Cal.	W	4-1		12	5	Mussina	Abbott	Olson	77-58	2nd	½
9-6	At Cal.	L	2-5		7	8	Blyleven	Lefferts	Grahe	77-59	2nd	1 ½
9-7	N.Y.	L	2-6	(13)	8	9	Monteleone	Mills		77-60	2nd	1 ½
9-8	N.Y.	L	4-16		7	20	Sanderson	Rhodes		77-61	2nd	2 ½
9-9	N.Y.	L	2-5		9	8	Wickman	Sutcliffe	Farr	77-62	2nd	3 ½
9-11	Mil.	W	3-2		10	6	Mussina	Wegman		78-62	2nd	3
9-12	Mil.	L	0-5		5	10	Navarro	Lefferts		78-63	2nd	4
9-13	Mil.	L	1-3		4	14	Eldred	McDonald		78-64	2nd	5
9-14	K.C.	W	2-1		6	4	Sutcliffe	Reed	Olson	79-64	2nd	4
9-15	K.C.	W	2-1	(14)	14	9	Davis	Sampen		80-64	2nd	4

Date	Opp.	Res.	Score	(inn.*)	Hits	Opp. hits	Winning pitcher	Losing pitcher	Save	Record	Pos.	GB
9-16	K.C.	W	3-0		13	4	Mussina	Haney		81-64	2nd	3
9-18	At Mil.	L	4-12		11	17	Eldred	Sutcliffe		81-65	2nd	4½
9-19	At Mil.	L	1-4		6	7	Bosio	McDonald	Holmes	81-66	3rd	5½
9-20	At Mil.	L	3-9		8	12	Austin	Davis		81-67	3rd	5½
9-21	At Mil.	W	4-1		6	7	Mussina	Wegman		82-67	3rd	5
9-22	Tor.	L	3-4		8	6	Stottlemyre	Sutcliffe	Henke	82-68	3rd	6
9-23	Tor.	W	4-1		7	4	Rhodes	Morris	Olson	83-68	3rd	5
9-24	Tor.	L	2-8		7	9	Key	McDonald		83-69	3rd	6
9-26 (1)	Bos.	L	3-7	(14)	9	9	Harris	Frohwirth		83-70	3rd	6½
9-26 (2)	Bos.	W	2-0		8	6	Lefferts	Dopson	Olson	84-70	3rd	6
9-27	Bos.	L	1-6		4	15	Hesketh	Sutcliffe		84-71	3rd	7
9-28	Bos.	W	7-3		9	8	Davis	Irvine		85-71	3rd	6½
9-29	At Det.	W	7-2		13	5	McDonald	Tanana		86-71	3rd	6½
9-30	At Det.	L	2-4		10	7	Doherty	Milacki	Henneman	86-72	3rd	6½
10-1	At Cle.	W	3-2	(10)	6	12	Mussina	Plunk	Olson	87-72	3rd	6
10-2	At Cle.	L	5-8		10	11	Nichols	Lefferts		87-73	3rd	7
10-3	At Cle.	W	7-1		14	10	Rhodes	Embree	Williamson	88-73	3rd	7
10-4	At Cle.	W	4-3	(13)	11	7	Mills	Plunk	Milacki	89-73	3rd	7

Monthly records: April (13-8), May (16-11), June (15-13), July (13-14), August (16-12), September (13-14), Oct. (3-1).

HIGHLIGHTS

High point: Trailing first-place Toronto by 2½ games August 28, Baltimore won seven straight games on a West Coast swing and jumped to a season-high 19 games over .500 (77-58) on September 5, only half a game behind the Blue Jays.

Low point: The Orioles tied a dubious club record by failing to score more than four runs in a game for 21 straight contests (September 5-27).

Turning point: The aforementioned offensive slumber. Baltimore went 8-13 in that span, tumbling seven games out of first and into third place.

Most valuable player: Center fielder Mike Devereaux. He had a breakthrough season, posting career-high home run (24) and RBI (107) figures.

Most valuable pitcher: Righthander Mike Mussina. At 18-5, he led the majors in winning percentage (.783) and ranked among the A.L. leaders in ERA (2.54), innings pitched (241), shutouts (four) and complete games (eight).

Most improved player: Left fielder Brady Anderson. Manager Johnny Oates handed him the full-time leadoff job out of spring training and he became the first player in league history to collect at least 20 home runs (21), 75 RBIs (80) and 50 stolen bases (53) in the same season.

Most pleasant surprise: Righthander Alan Mills. After coming to Baltimore in a seemingly insignificant February deal with the Yankees, Mills made the club and emerged as one of the game's most effective relievers (10-4, 2.61 ERA).

Biggest disappointment: Shortstop Cal Ripken. After winning A.L. MVP honors in 1991, he struggled at the plate all season, registering career lows in almost every offensive category.

Key injuries: First baseman/designated hitter Glenn Davis missed 25 games in the first half with a strained rib-cage muscle, and catcher Chris Hoiles missed two months with a fractured right wrist.

Notable: In its first season in Oriole Park at Camden Yards, Baltimore recorded the fifth-highest attendance figure in major league history (3,567,819) and shattered its all-time mark (2,552,753 in '91). . . . Baltimore went 10-1 in its first 11 games at Camden Yards, best start ever by a team playing in a new park. . . . The Orioles' 89-73 record was a 22-game improvement over 1991 (67-95). . . . Hoiles set a major league record for fewest RBIs (40) by a player who hit 20 or more home runs.

—PETER SCHMUCK

RECORDS

1992 regular-season record: 89-73 (3rd in A.L. East); 43-38 at home; 46-35 on road; 41-37 vs. East; 48-36 vs. West; 29-18 vs. LHP; 60-55 vs. RHP; 77-60 on grass; 12-13 on turf; 20-30 in daytime; 69-43 at night; 23-13 in one-run games; 9-6 in extra-inning games; 0-0-1 in doubleheaders.

Team record last five years: 373-435 (.462), ranks T11th in league in that span).

TEAM LEADERS

Batting average: Mike Devereaux (.276).
At-bats: Mike Devereaux (653).
Runs: Brady Anderson (100).
Hits: Mike Devereaux (180).
Total bases: Mike Devereaux (303).
Doubles: Mike Devereaux, Cal Ripken (29).
Triples: Mike Devereaux (11).
Home runs: Mike Devereaux (24).
Runs batted in: Mike Devereaux (107).
Stolen bases: Brady Anderson (53).
Slugging percentage: Mike Devereaux (.464).
On-base percentage: Randy Milligan (.383).
Wins: Mike Mussina (18).
Earned-run average: Mike Mussina (2.54).
Complete games: Mike Mussina (8).
Shutouts: Mike Mussina (4).
Saves: Gregg Olson (36).
Innings pitched: Mike Mussina (241).
Strikeouts: Ben McDonald (158).

GAMES BY POSITION

Catcher: Chris Hoiles 95, Jeff Tackett 64, Mark Parent 16, Rick Dempsey 8.
First base: Randy Milligan 129, David Segui 95, Glenn Davis 2.
Second base: Billy Ripken 108, Mark McLemore 70, Tim Hulett 10, Steve Scarsone 5.
Third base: Leo Gomez 137, Tim Hulett 27, Steve Scarsone 2, Jeff Tackett 1.
Shortstop: Cal Ripken 162, Tim Hulett 5, Manny Alexander 3, Steve Scarsone 1.
Outfield: Brady Anderson 158, Mike Devereaux 155, Joe Orsulak 110, Chito Martinez 52, David Segui 18, Luis Mercedes 16.
Designated hitter: Glenn Davis 103, Sam Horn 46, Mark McLemore 17, Tim Hulett 13, Luis Mercedes 7, Randy Milligan 6, Chito Martinez 4, Chris Hoiles 1, Joe Orsulak 1.

TOP 10 DRAFT CHOICES

1. **Jeffrey Hammonds**, OF, Stanford University.
2. **Brian Sackinsky**, RHP, Stanford University.
3. **Billy Owens**, 1B, University of Arizona.
4. **Hut Smith**, RHP, A.L. Brown High School, Kannapolis, N.C.
5. **Scott Klingenbeck**, RHP, Ohio State University.
6. **Robert Chancey**, OF, Stanhope Elmore High School, Millbrook, Ala.
7. **Keith Eaddy**, OF, William Paterson (N.J.) College.
8. **Cory Brown**, RHP/OF, Gibbs High School, St. Petersburg, Fla.
9. **Calvin Lee**, RHP, East St. John High School, Reserve, La.
10. **Roberto Lopez**, RHP, Wilcox High School, Santa Clara, Calif.

BOSTON RED SOX
AMERICAN LEAGUE EAST DIVISION

1993 SCHEDULE

APRIL

SUN	MON	TUE	WED	THU	FRI	SAT
				1	2	3
4	5 KC	6	7 N KC	8 N KC	9 N TEX	10 N TEX
11 TEX	12 CLE H	13	14 CLE H	15 N CLE H	16 N CHI H	17 N CHI H
18 CHI H	19 CHI H	20 N SEA	21 N SEA	22 N SEA	23 N CAL	24 N CAL
25 N CAL	26	27 OAK	28 OAK	29	30 N CAL H	

MAY

SUN	MON	TUE	WED	THU	FRI	SAT
						1 CAL H
2 CAL H	3 N SEA H	4 N SEA H	5 N OAK H	6 N OAK H	7 N MIL	8 MIL
9 MIL	10 N BAL	11 N BAL	12 N BAL	13	14 N MIN	15 MIN
16 MIN	17 N TOR H	18 N TOR H	19 N TOR H	20	21 N NY H	22 N NY H
23 N NY H	24 N DET	25 N DET	26	27	28 N TEX H	29 TEX H
30 TEX H	31 N KC H					

JUNE

SUN	MON	TUE	WED	THU	FRI	SAT
		1 N KC H	2 N KC H	3	4 N CHI	5 N CHI
6 CHI	7 N CLE	8 N CLE	9 N CLE	10 N BAL H	11 N BAL H	12 N BAL H
13 BAL H	14 N NY	15 N NY	16 N NY	17 TOR	18 N TOR	19 TOR
20 TOR	21 N MIN H	22 N MIN H	23 N MIN H	24	25 N DET H	26 DET H
27 DET H	28 N MIL H	29 N MIL H	30 N MIL H			

JULY

SUN	MON	TUE	WED	THU	FRI	SAT
				1	2 N SEA	3 N SEA
4 N SEA	5 CAL	6 N CAL	7 N CAL	8 OAK	9 N OAK	10 N OAK
11 OAK	12	13 * ALL-STAR GAME	14	15 N SEA H	16 N SEA H	17 N SEA H
18 SEA H	19 N CAL H	20 N CAL H	21 N CAL H	22 N OAK H	23 N OAK H	24 OAK H
25 OAK H	26 N MIL	27 N MIL	28 N MIL	29	30 N BAL	31 N BAL

AUGUST

SUN	MON	TUE	WED	THU	FRI	SAT
1 BAL	2	3 N MIN	4 N MIN	5 N MIN	6 N DET	7 DET
8 DET	9	10 N NY H	11 N NY H	12 N NY H	13 N TOR H	14 N TOR H
15 TOR H	16	17 N CHI H	18 N CHI H	19 N CHI H	20 N CLE H	21 N CLE H
22 CLE H	23	24 N TEX	25 N TEX	26 TEX	27 N KC	28 KC
29 KC	30 N TEX H	31 N TEX H				

SEPTEMBER

SUN	MON	TUE	WED	THU	FRI	SAT
			1 N TEX H	2	3 N KC H	4 N KC H
5 KC H	6 N CHI	7 N CHI	8 N CHI	9	10 N CLE	11 CLE
12 CLE	13 N BAL H	14 N BAL H	15 N BAL H	16 N NY	17 N NY	18 NY
19 NY	20	21 N TOR	22 N TOR	23 N TOR	24 N MIN H	25 MIN H
26 MIN H	27 N DET H	28 N DET H	29 N DET H	30 N DET H		

OCTOBER

SUN	MON	TUE	WED	THU	FRI	SAT
					1 N MIL H	2 MIL H
3 MIL H						

1993 SEASON

CLUB DIRECTORY

Owner/majority general partner
  JRY Corporation
President
  John L. Harrington
Vice president and treasurer
  William B. Gutfarb
Owner/general partner
  Haywood C. Sullivan
Senior vice president and general manager
  James (Lou) Gorman
Vice president and chief financial officer
  Robert C. Furbush
Vice president baseball development
  Edward M. Kasko
Assistant general manager
  Elaine W. Steward
Director of scouting
  W. Wayne Britton
Director of minor league operations
  Edward P. Kenney
Assistant to player dev. and scouting
  Erwin L. Bryant
Special assistant for player development
  John M. Pesky
Traveling secretary
  Steven W. August
Director of Florida Operations
  William A. MacKay
Medical director
  Arthur M. Pappas, M.D.
V.p., broadcasting and special projects
  James P. Healey
Vice president, public relations
  Richard L. Bresciani
Vice president, marketing
  Lawrence C. Cancro
Vice president, stadium operations
  Joseph F. McDermott
Director of baseball information
  James A. Samia
Dir. of comm. relations & personnel admin.
  Linda G. Ezell
Director of facilities management
  Thomas L. Queenan Jr.
Director of food services
  Patricia T. Flanagan

Dir. of parking and prop. maint.-buildings
  Michael L. Silva
Director of ticket operations
  Joseph P. Helyar
Superintendent of grounds and maintenance
  Joseph F. Mooney
Controller
  Stanley H. Tran
Staff accountant
  Robin R. Yeingst
Manager of advertising/promotions
  Lori T. McHugh
Manager of corporate sales
  Robert G. Capilli
Manager of publications
  Debra A. Matson
Manager of publicity
  Kevin J. Shea
Major league special assignment scouts
  Frank Malzone
  Sabath A. Mele
  Robert W. Schaefer
Scouts
  Rafael Batista
  Milton Bolling
  Charles (Buzz) Bowers
  Otho (Sonny) Bowers
  Clark Crist
  Ray Crone
  Luis Delgado
  Raymond Fagnant
  Jack Lee
  Howard McCullough
  Frank Malzone
  Sam Mele
  Willie Paffen
  Michael Rizzo
  Phillip Rossi
  Bob Schaefer
  Alex Scott
  Matt Sczesny
  Joe Stephenson
  Larry Thomas
  Fay Thompson
  Luke Wrenn
  Jeff Zona

SCHEDULE KEY

H—Home game.   N—Night game (any game starting after 5 p.m.).
*All-Star Game at Oriole Park at Camden Yards, Baltimore.

SPRING TRAINING ROSTER

Manager—Butch Hobson (17).

Coaches—Gary Allenson (32), Al Bumbry (37), Rick Burleson (7), Mike Easler (36), Rich Gale (35).

No.	PITCHERS	B/T	Ht./Wt.	Born	1992 clubs
29	Bankhead, Scott	R/R	5-10/185	7-31-63	Cincinnati
21	Clemens, Roger	R/R	6-4/220	8-4-62	Boston
54	Conroy, Brian	B/R	6-2/180	8-29-68	Pawtucket, New Britain
44	Darwin, Danny	R/R	6-3/205	10-25-55	Boston
40	Dopson, John	R/R	6-4/230	7-14-63	Pawtucket, Boston
27	Harris, Greg	B/R	6-0/175	11-2-55	Boston
55	Hesketh, Joe	L/L	6-2/173	2-15-59	Boston
59	Irvine, Daryl	R/R	6-3/210	11-15-64	Pawtucket, Boston
60	Livernois, Derek	L/R	6-1/185	4-17-67	New Britain, Pawtucket
51	Melendez, Jose	R/R	6-2/180	9-2-65	San Diego
57	Minchey, Nate	R/R	6-7/210	8-31-69	Greenville, Pawtucket
49	Quantrill, Paul	L/R	6-1/185	11-3-68	Pawtucket, Boston
50	Ryan, Ken	R/R	6-3/215	10-24-68	New Britain, Pawtucket, Boston
56	Taylor, Scott	L/L	6-1/190	8-2-67	Pawtucket, Boston
16	Viola, Frank	L/L	6-4/210	4-19-60	Boston
30	Young, Matt	L/L	6-3/210	8-9-58	Boston

No.	CATCHERS	B/T	Ht./Wt.	Born	1992 clubs
15	Flaherty, John	R/R	6-10/195	10-21-67	Boston, Pawtucket
20	Marzano, John	R/R	5-11/195	2-14-63	Pawtucket, Boston
3	Melvin, Bob	R/R	6-4/207	10-28-61	Kansas City
6	Pena, Tony	R/R	6-0/185	6-4-57	Boston

No.	INFIELDERS	B/T	Ht./Wt.	Born	1992 clubs
61	Byrd, Jim	R/R	6-1/185	10-3-68	Winter Haven, New Britain, Pawtucket
25	Clark, Jack	R/R	6-3/215	11-10-55	Boston
45	Cooper, Scott	L/R	6-3/205	10-13-67	Boston
5	Fletcher, Scott	R/R	5-11/173	7-30-58	Milwaukee
48	Garcia, Cheo	R/R	5-11/165	4-27-68	Orlando, Portland
11	Naehring, Tim	R/R	6-2/205	2-1-67	Boston, Pawtucket
18	Quintana, Carlos	R/R	6-2/220	8-26-65	DID NOT PLAY
2	Rivera, Luis	R/R	5-9/175	1-3-64	Boston
13	Valentin, John	R/R	6-0/180	2-18-67	Pawtucket, Boston
42	Vaughn, Mo	L/R	6-1/225	12-15-67	Boston, Pawtucket

No.	OUTFIELDERS	B/T	Ht./Wt.	Born	1992 clubs
38	Blosser, Greg	L/L	6-3/200	6-26-71	New Britain, Pawtucket
12	Calderon, Ivan	R/R	6-1/221	3-19-62	Montreal, West Palm Beach
10	Dawson, Andre	R/R	6-3/197	7-10-54	Chicago N.L.
39	Greenwell, Mike	L/R	6-0/205	7-18-63	Boston
22	Hatcher, Billy	R/R	5-10/190	10-4-60	Cincinnati, Boston
58	McNeely, Jeff	R/R	6-2/190	10-18-69	New Britain
43	Ross, Sean	L/L	6-2/185	10-21-67	Richmond, Pawtucket
28	Zupcic, Bob	R/R	6-4/225	8-18-66	Pawtucket, Boston

BALLPARK INFORMATION

Ballpark (capacity, surface)
Fenway Park (33,925, grass)
Address
4 Yawkey Way
Boston, MA 02215
Business phone
617-267-9440
Ticket information
617-267-8661
Ticket prices
$14 (upper box)
$10 (grandstand)
$7 (bleachers)
$7 (standing room)
Field dimensions (from home plate)
To left field at foul line, 315 feet
To center field, 420 feet
To right field at foul line, 302 feet
First game played
April 20, 1912 (Red Sox 7, New York Highlanders 6)

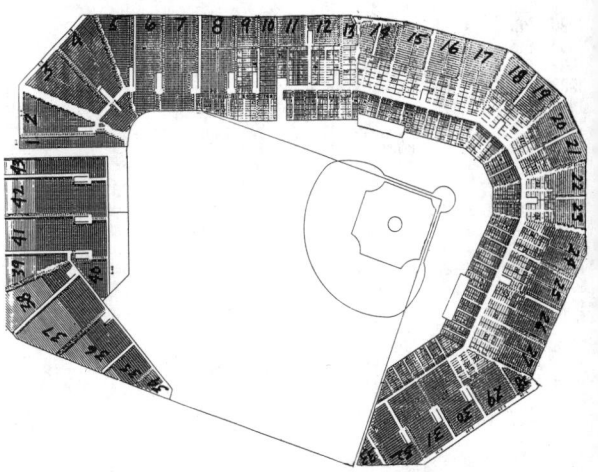

	MINOR LEAGUE AFFILIATES	
Class	**Team**	**League**	**Manager**
AAA	Pawtucket	International	Buddy Bailey
AA	New Britain	Eastern	Jim Pankovits
A	Lynchburg	Carolina	Mark Meleski
A	To be announced		Felix Maldonado
A	Utica	New York-Pennsylvania	Dave Holt
Rookie	Gulf Coast Red Sox	Gulf Coast	To be announced

BROADCAST INFORMATION

Radio: WRKO-AM (680). Broadcasters: Jerry Trupiano, Joe Castiglione.
TV: WSBK-TV (Channel 38). Broadcasters: Sean McDonough, Bob Montgomery.
Cable TV: New England Sports Network. Broadcasters: Bob Kurtz, Jerry Remy.

SPRING TRAINING

Ballpark (city): City of Palms Park (Ft. Myers, Fla.).
Ticket information: 813-334-4700.

HISTORY

YEAR-BY-YEAR RECORDS

Year	Pos.	W	L	Pct.	*GB	Year	Pos.	W	L	Pct.	*GB
1901	2nd	79	57	.581	4	1950	3rd	94	60	.610	4
1902	3rd	77	60	.562	6½	1951	3rd	87	67	.565	11
1903	1st	91	47	.659	+14½	1952	6th	76	78	.494	19
1904	1st	95	59	.617	+1½	1953	4th	84	69	.549	16
1905	4th	78	74	.513	16	1954	4th	69	85	.448	42
1906	8th	49	105	.318	45½	1955	4th	84	70	.545	12
1907	7th	59	90	.396	32½	1956	4th	84	70	.545	13
1908	5th	75	79	.487	15½	1957	3rd	82	72	.532	16
1909	3rd	88	63	.583	9½	1958	3rd	79	75	.513	13
1910	4th	81	72	.529	22½	1959	5th	75	79	.487	19
1911	5th	78	75	.510	24	1960	7th	65	89	.422	32
1912	1st	105	47	.691	+14	1961	6th	76	86	.469	33
1913	4th	79	71	.527	15½	1962	8th	76	84	.475	19
1914	2nd	91	62	.595	8½	1963	7th	76	85	.472	28
1915	1st	101	50	.669	+2½	1964	8th	72	90	.444	27
1916	1st	91	63	.591	+2	1965	9th	62	100	.383	40
1917	2nd	90	62	.592	9	1966	9th	72	90	.444	26
1918	1st	75	51	.595	+2½	1967	1st	92	70	.568	+1
1919	6th	66	71	.482	20½	1968	4th	86	76	.531	17
1920	5th	72	81	.471	25½	1969	3rd	87	75	.537	22
1921	5th	75	79	.487	23½	1970	3rd	87	75	.537	21
1922	8th	61	93	.396	33	1971	3rd	85	77	.525	18
1923	8th	61	91	.401	37	1972	2nd	85	70	.548	½
1924	7th	67	87	.435	25	1973	2nd	89	73	.549	8
1925	8th	47	105	.309	49½	1974	3rd	84	78	.519	7
1926	8th	46	107	.301	44½	1975	1st‡	95	65	.594	+4½
1927	8th	51	103	.331	59	1976	3rd	83	79	.512	15½
1928	8th	57	96	.373	43½	1977	T2nd	97	64	.602	2½
1929	8th	58	96	.377	48	1978	2nd§	99	64	.607	1
1930	8th	52	102	.338	50	1979	3rd	91	69	.569	11½
1931	6th	62	90	.408	45	1980	4th	83	77	.519	19
1932	8th	43	111	.279	64	1981	5th/T2nd	59	49	.546	*
1933	7th	63	86	.423	34½	1982	3rd	89	73	.549	6
1934	4th	76	76	.500	24	1983	6th	78	84	.481	20
1935	4th	78	75	.510	16	1984	4th	86	76	.531	18
1936	6th	74	80	.481	28½	1985	5th	81	81	.500	18½
1937	5th	80	72	.526	21	1986	1st‡	95	66	.590	+5½
1938	2nd	88	61	.591	9½	1987	5th	78	84	.481	20
1939	2nd	89	62	.589	17	1988	1st•	89	73	.549	+1
1940	T4th	82	72	.532	8	1989	3rd	83	79	.512	6
1941	2nd	84	70	.545	17	1990	1st•	88	74	.543	+2
1942	2nd	93	59	.612	9	1991	T2nd	84	78	.519	7
1943	7th	68	84	.447	29	1992	7th	73	89	.451	23
1944	4th	77	77	.500	12						
1945	7th	71	83	.461	17½						
1946	1st	104	50	.675	+12						
1947	3rd	83	71	.539	14						
1948	2nd†	96	59	.619	1						
1949	2nd	96	58	.623	1						

*Games behind winner. †Lost pennant playoff. ‡Won Championship Series. §Lost division playoff. *First half 30-26; second 29-23. • Lost Championship Series.

MANAGERS

Name	Record	Years
Jimmy Collins	455-376	'01-06
Chick Stahl	14-26	1906
George Huff	2-6	1907
Bob Unglaub	9-20	1907
Deacon McGuire	98-123	'07-08
Fred Lake	110-80	'08-09
Patsy Donovan	159-147	'10-11
Jake Stahl	144-88	'12-13
Bill Carrigan	489-500	'13-16
		'27-29
Jack Barry	90-62	1917
Ed Barrow	213-203	'18-20
Hugh Duffy	136-172	'21-22
Frank Chance	61-91	1923
Lee Fohl	160-299	'24-26
Heinie Wagner	52-102	1930
Shano Collins	73-134	'31-32
Marty McManus	95-153	'32-33
Bucky Harris	76-76	1934
Joe Cronin	1071-916	'35-47
Joe McCarthy	223-145	'48-50
Steve O'Neill	150-99	'50-51
Lou Boudreau	229-232	'52-54
Pinky Higgins	560-556	'55-59
		'60-62
Billy Jurges	59-63	'59-60
Johnny Pesky	147-179	'63-64
		1980
Billy Herman	128-182	'64-66
Pete Runnels	8-8	1966
Dick Williams	260-217	'67-69
Eddie Popowski	5-4	1969
Eddie Kasko	346-295	'70-73
Darrell Johnson	220-188	'74-76
Don Zimmer	411-304	'76-80
Ralph Houk	312-282	'81-84
John McNamara	297-273	'85-88
Joe Morgan	301-262	'88-91
Butch Hobson	73-89	1992

DAY BY DAY

Date	Opp.	Res.	Score	(inn.*)	Hits	Opp. hits	Winning pitcher	Losing pitcher	Save	Record	Pos.	GB
4-7	At N.Y.	L	3-4		7	8	Sanderson	Clemens	Farr	0-1	T4th	1
4-9	At N.Y.	L	2-3		6	6	Monteleone	Viola	Howe	0-2	T6th	2½
4-11	At Cle.	W	7-5	(19)	14	20	Gardiner	Bell		1-2	5th	3
4-12 (1)	At Cle.	L	1-2		9	0	Nagy	Young	Lilliquist	1-3	6th	4
4-12 (2)	At Cle.	W	3-0		9	2	Clemens	Scudder		2-3	3rd	3½
4-13	Bal.	L	6-8		9	12	Frohwirth	Fossas	Olson	2-4	T4th	4
4-15	Bal.	W	6-5		6	9	Harris	Davis	Reardon	3-4	4th	4
4-17	Tor.	W	1-0		4	3	Clemens	Wells	Reardon	4-4	4th	3½
4-18	Tor.	L	1-2		4	6	Stottlemyre	Viola	Henke	4-5	5th	4½
4-19	Tor.	W	5-4		9	10	Darwin	Henke		5-5	4th	3½
4-20	Tor.	L	4-6	(13)	10	13	MacDonald	Bolton		5-6	T4th	4½
4-21	At Mil.	W	3-1		6	3	Gardiner	Austin	Darwin	6-6	4th	4½
4-23	At Mil.	L	2-3		7	7	Wegman	Clemens	Henry	6-7	T4th	5
4-24	Tex.	W	3-1	(5½)	8	3	Viola	Guzman		7-7	T4th	5
4-26 (1)	Tex.	L	1-3		10	9	Witt	Young	Russell	7-8	5th	5½
4-26 (2)	Tex.	L	2-4		10	8	Mathews	Harris	Russell	7-9	5th	6
4-28	Chi.	W	6-3		8	11	Clemens	McCaskill	Reardon	8-9	T4th	5
4-29	Chi.	W	6-1		8	5	Viola	Fernandez	Reardon	9-9	T4th	5
5-1	K.C.	W	6-5		12	10	Darwin	Montgomery		10-9	5th	3½
5-2	K.C.	W	7-6		10	10	Harris	Pichardo	Reardon	11-9	5th	2½
5-3	K.C.	L	2-5		10	9	Appier	Hesketh		11-10	5th	3½
5-4	Min.	L	1-6		4	12	Smiley	Clemens		11-11	5th	4½
5-5	Min.	W	4-1		9	9	Viola	Mahomes	Reardon	12-11	4th	4½
5-6	At Chi.	L	5-7		12	8	Radinsky	Darwin	Thigpen	12-12	4th	5½
5-7	At Chi.	L	6-7		6	9	Pall	Harris	Thigpen	12-13	4th	6½
5-8	At K.C.	L	1-2		8	3	Appier	Hesketh	Montgomery	12-14	4th	6½
5-9	At K.C.	W	5-0		9	3	Clemens	Gordon		13-14	4th	5½
5-10	At K.C.	W	10-6		13	9	Viola	Magnante		14-14	3rd	5½
5-12	At Min.	L	3-6		9	11	Tapani	Gardiner	Aguilera	14-15	4th	6½
5-13	At Min.	L	3-4		6	12	Edens	Harris		14-16	4th	7½
5-15	Cal.	W	3-0		6	4	Clemens	Abbott		15-16	4th	7
5-16	Cal.	W	3-0		6	4	Viola	Valera	Reardon	16-16	4th	6½
5-17	Cal.	L	1-3		5	7	Langston	Dopson	Harvey	16-17	4th	6½
5-18	Sea.	W	3-2		7	7	Gardiner	Hanson	Reardon	17-17	4th	5½
5-19	Sea.	W	7-5		7	12	Bolton	Nelson	Reardon	18-17	4th	4½
5-20	Sea.	W	6-4		12	9	Clemens	Powell	Reardon	19-17	4th	4
5-22	Oak.	L	3-5		6	9	Stewart	Viola	Eckersley	19-18	4th	5
5-23	Oak.	W	5-1		12	8	Dopson	Moore		20-18	4th	4
5-24	Oak.	L	0-4		2	8	Darling	Gardiner		20-19	4th	4½
5-26	At Cal.	W	4-1		9	3	Clemens	Abbott	Reardon	21-19	4th	4
5-27	At Cal.	W	4-3	(10)	8	7	Reardon	Harvey	Darwin	22-19	4th	3
5-28	At Cal.	W	2-1		8	8	Hesketh	Langston	Reardon	23-19	4th	2½
5-29	At Sea.	L	3-7		9	10	Powell	Dopson		23-20	4th	3½
5-30	At Sea.	L	0-3		5	6	Fleming	Gardiner		23-21	4th	4½
5-31	At Sea.	W	7-1		12	6	Clemens	Johnson		24-21	4th	4½
6-1	At Oak.	L	7-10		13	8	Campbell	Darwin		24-22	4th	5½
6-2	At Oak.	L	4-5		7	5	Moore	Hesketh	Eckersley	24-23	4th	6½
6-3	At Oak.	L	6-7		12	10	Parrett	Gardiner	Eckersley	24-24	T4th	6½
6-6 (1)	Cle.	W	5-1		8	9	Clemens	Armstrong		25-24	4th	6
6-6 (2)	Cle.	L	1-3		6	8	Nagy	Viola	Olin	25-25	5th	6½
6-7	Cle.	W	4-0		11	7	Hesketh	Otto	Darwin	26-25	5th	5½
6-8	At Bal.	L	2-5		7	9	Milacki	Gardiner	Olson	26-26	5th	6½
6-9	At Bal.	W	4-1		7	6	Dopson	Mesa	Reardon	27-26	4th	6½
6-10	At Bal.	L	1-3		7	8	Sutcliffe	Bolton	Olson	27-27	4th	7½
6-11	At Tor.	L	0-4		4	7	Morris	Clemens		27-28	5th	8½
6-12	At Tor.	W	5-0		8	6	Viola	Stieb		28-28	4th	7½
6-13	At Tor.	W	5-3		10	6	Hesketh	Stottlemyre	Reardon	29-28	4th	6½
6-14	At Tor.	L	2-6		7	6	Guzman	Gardiner	Ward	29-29	T4th	7½
6-15	N.Y.	W	1-0		3	6	Dopson	Sanderson	Reardon	30-29	4th	7
6-16	N.Y.	W	4-3	(10)	8	11	Darwin	Cadaret		31-29	4th	6
6-17	N.Y.	W	4-3		8	5	Viola	Kamieniecki	Fossas	32-29	4th	6
6-18	N.Y.	L	4-5		10	10	Perez	Darwin	Farr	32-30	4th	6
6-19	At Tex.	L	1-4		6	7	Witt	Gardiner	Russell	32-31	4th	6
6-20	At Tex.	L	1-4		6	7	Brown	Dopson	Rogers	32-32	4th	7
6-21	At Tex.	L	2-3		8	6	Burns	Clemens	Russell	32-33	5th	7
6-22	At Det.	L	2-4	(11)	8	10	Knudsen	Darwin		32-34	5th	8
6-23	At Det.	L	7-11		15	15	Kiely	Hesketh		32-35	5th	8½
6-24	At Det.	L	1-5		8	10	Tanana	Gardiner		32-36	5th	9½
6-26	Mil.	W	8-4		13	11	Dopson	Robinson		33-36	5th	9½
6-27	Mil.	W	8-7	(13)	13	14	Darwin	Holmes		34-36	5th	8½

Date	Opp.	Res.	Score	(inn.*)	Hits	Opp. hits	Winning pitcher	Losing pitcher	Save	Record	Pos.	GB
6-28	Mil.	L	3-9		8	15	Navarro	Viola		34-37	5th	8½
6-29	Det.	L	3-8		5	15	Tanana	Hesketh	Knudsen	34-38	5th	9½
6-30	Det.	W	8-5		9	9	Irvine	Henneman		35-38	5th	8½
7-1	Det.	W	6-4		9	10	Dopson	Gullickson	Reardon	36-38	5th	8½
7-2	At Chi.	L	3-8		4	15	Alvarez	Clemens	Hernandez	36-39	5th	9
7-3	At Chi.	L	1-2	(10)	4	9	Thigpen	Harris		36-40	5th	10
7-4	At Chi.	W	2-1		8	4	Hesketh	McDowell	Reardon	37-40	5th	10
7-5	At Chi.	L	2-4		5	9	Hibbard	Gardiner	Radinsky	37-41	5th	11
7-6	K.C.	L	3-6		6	12	Reed	Dopson	Meacham	37-42	5th	12
7-7	K.C.	W	3-2	(11)	13	6	Darwin	Meacham		38-42	5th	12
7-8	K.C.	W	5-4		9	10	Fossas	Gordon	Reardon	39-42	5th	12
7-9	Chi.	L	3-10		7	17	McDowell	Hesketh		39-43	6th	13
7-10	Chi.	W	6-5		9	8	Reardon	Leach		40-43	5th	12
7-11	Chi.	W	11-2		14	6	Dopson	McCaskill		41-43	5th	11
7-12	Chi.	W	3-0		8	4	Viola	Alvarez	Harris	42-43	4th	10
7-16	At Min.	L	6-7		11	13	Willis	Gardiner	Aguilera	42-44	4th	11
7-17	At Min.	L	2-3	(10)	7	12	Kipper	Harris		42-45	4th	11
7-18	At Min.	W	1-0		5	2	Clemens	Erickson		43-45	4th	11
7-19	At Min.	L	5-7		12	14	Guthrie	Harris	Aguilera	43-46	4th	12
7-20	At K.C.	W	5-3		9	10	Quantrill	Shifflett	Reardon	44-46	4th	11
7-21	At K.C.	L	0-8		1	7	Pichardo	Hesketh		44-47	5th	12
7-22	At K.C.	L	4-6		9	7	Gordon	Viola	Montgomery	44-48	6th	12
7-24 (1)	Min.	L	0-5		1	7	Erickson	Clemens		44-49	6th	12½
7-24 (2)	Min.	W	5-4		13	12	Irvine	Willis		45-49	6th	12
7-25	Min.	L	2-3		8	3	Banks	Darwin	Aguilera	45-50	6th	12
7-26	Min.	L	2-8		7	16	Tapani	Hesketh	Guthrie	45-51	6th	12
7-27	Tex.	W	7-5		9	11	Viola	Brown	Reardon	46-51	5th	11½
7-28	Tex.	L	2-3	(10)	8	10	Leon	Quantrill	Russell	46-52	5th	12½
7-29	Tex.	W	6-5		10	10	Clemens	Burns	Reardon	47-52	4th	11½
7-31 (1)	Bal.	W	7-4		12	10	Hesketh	Frohwirth	Reardon	48-52	4th	12
7-31 (2)	Bal.	L	3-4	(5)	6	8	Lewis	Young		48-53	4th	12½
8-1	Bal.	L	3-9		12	10	Clemens	Viola		48-54	4th	13½
8-2	Bal.	L	1-2		5	8	McDonald	Fossas	Olson	48-55	4th	14½
8-3	Tor.	W	7-1		10	6	Clemens	Guzman		49-55	4th	13½
8-4	Tor.	W	9-4		11	10	Hesketh	Wells	Harris	50-55	4th	12½
8-5	Tor.	L	4-5		6	11	Eichhorn	Irvine	Henke	50-56	4th	13½
8-6	At N.Y.	W	3-1		9	4	Viola	Perez	Reardon	51-56	4th	13½
8-7	At N.Y.	L	5-7		8	9	Sanderson	Dopson	Farr	51-57	4th	13½
8-8	At N.Y.	W	4-2		9	6	Clemens	Kamieniecki	Reardon	52-57	4th	12½
8-9	At N.Y.	L	0-6		1	12	Militello	Hesketh	Farr	52-58	4th	12½
8-10	At Cle.	L	5-8		8	11	Armstrong	Quantrill	Olin	52-59	4th	13½
8-11	At Cle.	L	1-3		7	9	Otto	Viola	Lilliquist	52-60	5th	13½
8-12	At Cle.	L	5-8		11	12	Plunk	Irvine	Olin	52-61	5th	13½
8-13	At Cle.	W	4-2		8	9	Clemens	Nagy	Reardon	53-61	5th	13½
8-14 (1)	At Mil.	L	7-8	(13)	10	13	Austin	Reardon		53-62	5th	14½
8-14 (2)	At Mil.	L	0-1		3	7	Eldred	Harris	Holmes	53-63	5th	15
8-15	At Mil.	W	3-1		10	4	Darwin	Wegman		54-63	5th	14½
8-16	At Mil.	L	0-1		3	5	Navarro	Viola		54-64	5th	15
8-18	Cal.	W	8-0		13	4	Clemens	Langston		55-64	5th	15
8-19	Cal.	L	2-3		10	8	Abbott	Reardon	Grahe	55-65	T5th	15
8-20	Cal.	L	0-2		6	11	Blyleven	Darwin	Grahe	55-66	T6th	15
8-21	Sea.	L	2-5		5	12	Johnson	Viola		55-67	T6th	15
8-22	Sea.	W	10-8		14	13	Harris	Barton	Reardon	56-67	T6th	15
8-23	Sea.	L	3-9		8	13	Powell	Clemens		56-68	T6th	15
8-24	Oak.	L	3-9		7	14	Stewart	Dopson		56-69	7th	15
8-25	Oak.	W	5-4		12	8	Quantrill	Eckersley	Reardon	57-69	7th	14
8-26	Oak.	W	2-1	(10)	6	6	Viola	Campbell		58-69	7th	14
8-28	At Cal.	W	7-1		10	10	Clemens	Finley		59-69	T6th	13½
8-29	At Cal.	L	2-7		4	11	Langston	Dopson		59-70	T6th	13½
8-30	At Cal.	W	4-2	(10)	13	3	Darwin	Butcher	Harris	60-70	6th	13½
8-31	At Sea.	L	2-15		4	16	Johnson	Viola		60-71	T6th	14½
9-1	At Sea.	L	3-4		8	8	Schooler	Harris		60-72	T6th	15½
9-2	At Sea.	W	5-3		9	10	Clemens	Leary		61-72	6th	14½
9-4	At Oak.	W	8-3		11	9	Darwin	Stewart		62-72	6th	14½
9-5	At Oak.	W	7-3		9	6	Dopson	Darling		63-72	4th	14½
9-6	At Oak.	L	1-2	(10)	9	7	Eckersley	Quantrill		63-73	T6th	15½
9-7	At Tex.	W	3-0		9	4	Clemens	Ryan	Hesketh	64-73	T6th	14½
9-8	At Tex.	L	1-6		5	6	Brown	Young		64-74	6th	15½
9-9	At Tex.	L	2-3		8	9	Guzman	Darwin		64-75	T5th	16½
9-11	Det.	W	7-6		10	18	Gardiner	Doherty	Ryan	65-75	T5th	16
9-12	Det.	L	5-9		15	11	Terrell	Clemens		65-76	7th	17
9-13	Det.	L	2-7		9	11	Tanana	Dopson		65-77	7th	18
9-14	Mil.	L	0-6		4	11	Bosio	Darwin		65-78	7th	18
9-15	Mil.	L	2-7		8	11	Austin	Viola		65-79	7th	19

Date	Opp.	Res.	Score	(inn.*)	Hits	Opp. hits	Winning pitcher	Losing pitcher	Save	Record	Pos.	GB
9-16	Mil.	W	2-1	(15)	11	10	Irvine	Henry		66-79	7th	18
9-17	Mil.	L	4-10		14	15	Navarro	Clemens		66-80	7th	19
9-18	At Det.	L	3-10		7	13	Doherty	Dopson	King	66-81	7th	20
9-19	At Det.	L	2-3		4	4	Tanana	Harris		66-82	7th	21
9-20	At Det.	W	5-4		12	8	Viola	Gullickson	Fossas	67-82	7th	20
9-21	At Det.	L	5-6	(10)	9	7	Leiter	Irvine		67-83	7th	20½
9-22	Cle.	L	2-4		6	9	Power	Clemens	Lilliquist	67-84	7th	21½
9-23	Cle.	L	3-7		7	10	Nagy	Taylor		67-85	7th	21½
9-24	Cle.	W	6-4		9	11	Darwin	Scudder	Harris	68-85	7th	21
9-26 (1)	At Bal.	W	7-3	(14)	9	9	Harris	Frohwirth		69-85	7th	21
9-26 (2)	At Bal.	L	0-2		6	8	Lefferts	Dopson	Olson	69-86	7th	21½
9-27	At Bal.	W	6-1		15	4	Hesketh	Sutcliffe		70-86	7th	21½
9-28	At Bal.	L	3-7		8	9	Davis	Irvine		70-87	7th	22
9-29	At Tor.	L	2-5		7	9	Key	Darwin	Henke	70-88	7th	23
9-30	At Tor.	W	1-0		4	1	Viola	Cone		71-88	7th	22
10-2	N.Y.	L	3-6		9	11	Wickman	Dopson	Farr	71-89	7th	23
10-3	N.Y.	W	7-5		11	6	Taylor	Sanderson		72-89	7th	23
10-4	N.Y.	W	8-2		12	5	Hesketh	Kamieniecki	Quantrill	73-89	7th	23

Monthly records: April (9-9), May (15-12), June (11-17), July (13-15), August (12-18), September (11-17), Oct. (2-1).

HIGHLIGHTS

High point: Following a 2-1 win (Boston's 11th in the past 16 games) over California on May 28, the Red Sox were a season-high four games over .500 (23-19) and only 2½ games out of first place.

Low point: Boston lost 13 of 17 games from September 6-23, assuming permanent residence in last place, where the Red Sox finished for the first time in 60 years with a 73-89 record.

Turning point: The Red Sox lost seven games in a row from June 18-24, falling below .500 (32-36) for good.

Most valuable player: Right fielder Tom Brunansky. He led the Red Sox in batting average (.266), home runs (15) and RBIs (74).

Most valuable pitcher: Righthander Roger Clemens. He won 18 games, was 15-4 following a Red Sox loss, led the league in ERA (2.41) for the third straight year and struck out over 200 batters for the seventh straight year.

Most improved player: Infielder Scott Cooper. A third baseman his entire career, the rookie was moved to first base and performed exceptionally well. He got a chance to play regularly the last two months and batted .317.

Most pleasant surprise: Center fielder Bob Zupcic. He batted .276 in his first major league season. Two of his three homers were grand slams, tying a big-league rookie record.

Biggest disappointment: Designated hitter Jack Clark. Hampered by nagging injuries, he hit just five homers (none in Fenway Park), drove in only 33 runs and batted .210 in 81 games.

Key injuries: First baseman Carlos Quintana was lost for the year following an off-season automobile accident in Venezuela. He suffered a broken left arm and career-threatening nerve damage to his left wrist and left hand. By early July, two-thirds of the starting outfield was lost for the year when left fielder Mike Greenwell underwent right elbow and knee surgery and center fielder Ellis Burks suffered a recurrence of a back problem.

Notable: Righthander Jeff Reardon, who was traded to Atlanta on August 30, broke Rollie Fingers' all-time saves record when he notched his 342nd save 15 against the Yankees. . . . Lefthander Matt Young threw a no-hitter April 12 in the first game of a doubleheader in Cleveland—but lost, 2-1. He pitched eight innings. . . . Boston hit fewer than 100 home runs (84) for the first time in 46 years, excluding the strike-shortened 1981 season.

—JOE GIULIOTTI

RECORDS

1992 regular-season record: 73-89 (7th in A.L. East); 44-37 at home; 29-52 on road; 34-44 vs. East; 39-45 vs. West; 20-25 vs. LHP; 53-64 vs. RHP; 64-74 on grass; 9-15 on turf; 27-29 in daytime; 46-60 at night; 25-29 in one-run games; 9-8 in extra-inning games; 0-2-4 in doubleheaders.

Team record last five years: 417-393 (.515, ranks T4th in league in that span).

TEAM LEADERS

Batting average: Tom Brunansky (.266).
At-bats: Jody Reed (550).
Runs: Jody Reed (64).
Hits: Jody Reed (136).
Total bases: Tom Brunansky (204).
Doubles: Tom Brunansky (31).
Triples: Wade Boggs (4).
Home runs: Tom Brunansky (15).
Runs batted in: Tom Brunansky (74).
Stolen bases: Jody Reed (7).
Slugging percentage: Tom Brunansky (.445).
On-base percentage: Tom Brunansky (.354).
Wins: Roger Clemens (18).
Earned-run average: Roger Clemens (2.41).
Complete games: Roger Clemens (11).
Shutouts: Roger Clemens (5).
Saves: Jeff Reardon (27).
Innings pitched: Roger Clemens (246⅔).
Strikeouts: Roger Clemens (208).

GAMES BY POSITION

Catcher: Tony Pena 132, John Flaherty 34, John Marzano 18, Eric Wedge 5.
First base: Mo Vaughn 85, Scott Cooper 62, Tom Brunansky 28, Jack Clark 13, Steve Lyons 8.
Second base: Jody Reed 142, Tim Naehring 23, Tommy Barrett 2, Scott Cooper 1, Steve Lyons 1, Luis Rivera 1.
Third base: Wade Boggs 117, Scott Cooper 47, Tim Naehring 10, Luis Rivera 1.
Shortstop: Luis Rivera 93, John Valentin 58, Tim Naehring 30, Scott Cooper 1.
Outfield: Bob Zupcic 114, Tom Brunansky 92, Billy Hatcher 75, Phil Plantier 69, Herm Winningham 67, Ellis Burks 63, Mike Greenwell 41, Steve Lyons 5, Tim Naehring 1, Luis Rivera 1.
Designated hitter: Jack Clark 64, Phil Plantier 23, Wade Boggs 21, Mo Vaughn 20, Eric Wedge 20, Tom Brunansky 17, Mike Greenwell 6, Herm Winningham 6, Bob Zupcic 5, Tim Naehring 4, Scott Cooper 2, Luis Rivera 2, Ellis Burks 1, John Marzano 1, Jody Reed 1.

TOP 10 DRAFT CHOICES

1. **None.**
2. **Tony Sheffield**, OF, Tullahoma (Tenn.) High School.
3. **Doug Hecker**, 1B, University of Tennessee.
4. **Joe Hamilton**, 3B, Dighton-Rehoboth High School, North Dighton, Mass.
5. **Steve Rodriguez**, 2B, Pepperdine University.
6. **Derek Vinyard**, OF, San Diego State University.
7. **Joey DePastino**, LHP/OF, Riverview High School, Sarasota, Fla.
8. **John Bowles**, 3B, Richard Montgomery High School, Rockville, Md.
9. **Todd Carey**, SS, Brown University.
10. **Mark Senkowitz**, C, Ohio Wesleyan University.

CALIFORNIA ANGELS
AMERICAN LEAGUE WEST DIVISION

1993 SCHEDULE

APRIL

SUN	MON	TUE	WED	THU	FRI	SAT
				1	2	3
4	5	6 MIL H	7 N MIL H	8	9 N DET H	10 N DET H
11 DET H	12 MIL	13	14 N MIL	15 MIL	16 N BAL	17 BAL
18 BAL	19	20 N CLE	21 N CLE H	22 N CLE H	23 N BOS H	24 N BOS H
25 N BOS H	26	27 N NY H	28 N NY H	29	30 N BOS	

MAY

SUN	MON	TUE	WED	THU	FRI	SAT
						1 BOS
2 BOS	3 N CLE	4 N CLE	5 N NY	6 NY	7 N OAK H	8 N OAK H
9 OAK H	10 N MIN H	11 N MIN H	12 MIN H	13	14 N KC	15 N KC H
16 KC H	17 N CHI	18 N CHI	19 CHI	20	21 TEX	22 TEX
23 TEX	24 N SEA	25 N SEA	26 N SEA	27 N SEA	28 N BAL H	29 N BAL H
30 BAL H	31 TOR H					

JUNE

SUN	MON	TUE	WED	THU	FRI	SAT
		1 N TOR H	2 N TOR H	3	4 N DET	5 DET
6 DET	7 N TOR	8 N TOR	9 N TOR	10	11 N SEA H	12 N SEA H
13 SEA H	14 N TEX	15 N TEX H	16 N TEX H	17 N TEX H	18 N CHI H	19 N CHI H
20 CHI H	21 N KC	22 N KC	23 N KC	24 KC	25 N MIN	26 N MIN
27 MIN	28	29 N OAK	30 OAK			

JULY

SUN	MON	TUE	WED	THU	FRI	SAT
				1 OAK	2 N CLE H	3 N CLE H
4 N CLE H	5 N BOS H	6 N BOS H	7	8 N NY H	9 N NY H	10 N NY H
11 NY H	12	13 ★ ALL-STAR GAME	14	15 N CLE	16 N CLE	17 CLE
18 CLE	19 N BOS	20 N BOS	21 BOS	22 NY	23 N NY	24 NY
25 NY	26 N OAK H	27 N OAK H	28 N OAK H	29 N OAK H	30 N MIN H	31 N MIN H

AUGUST

SUN	MON	TUE	WED	THU	FRI	SAT
1 MIN H	2	3 N KC H	4 N KC H	5 N KC H	6 N CHI H	7 N CHI
8 CHI	9	10 N TEX	11 N TEX	12 N TEX	13 N SEA	14 N SEA
15 SEA	16 N DET H	17 N DET H	18 N DET H	19 N MIL H	20 N MIL H	21 N MIL H
22 MIL H	23	24 N BAL	25 N BAL	26 BAL	27 N MIL	28 MIL
29 MIL	30	31 N BAL H				

SEPTEMBER

SUN	MON	TUE	WED	THU	FRI	SAT
			1 N BAL H	2 N BAL H	3 N TOR H	4 N TOR H
5 TOR H	6	7 N DET	8 N DET	9 N DET	10 N TOR	11 TOR
12 TOR	13 N SEA H	14 N SEA H	15 SEA H	16	17 N TEX H	18 N TEX H
19 TEX H	20 N CHI H	21 N CHI H	22 N CHI H	23 N CHI H	24 KC	25 KC
26 KC	27 N MIN	28 N MIN	29 N MIN	30 MIN		

OCTOBER

SUN	MON	TUE	WED	THU	FRI	SAT
					1 N OAK	2 N OAK
3 OAK						

1993 SEASON

CLUB DIRECTORY

Chairman of the board
  Gene Autry
Board of directors
  Gene Autry
  Jackie Autry
  Richard M. Brown
  Stanley B. Schneider
  John P. Singleton
  Peter V. Ueberroth
President and chief executive officer
  Richard M. Brown
Executive vice president
  Jackie Autry
Senior vice president, baseball operations
  Daniel F. O'Brien
Senior vice president, player personnel
  Whitey Herzog
V.p., treasurer and chief financial officer
  Ronald C. Shirley
V.p., civic affairs and broadcasting
  Tom Seeberg
Asst. v.p. and director, facilities operations
  Kevin Uhlich
Assistant vice president, media relations
  Tim Mead
Assistant to the general manager
  Preston Gomez
Director, minor league operations
  Bill Bavasi
Traveling secretary
  Frank Sims
Manager, baseball information
  Larry Babcock
Director, sales and marketing
  Bob Wagner
Manager, publications
  Doug Ward
Controller
  Catherine Sullivan
Equipment manager
  Leonard Garcia
Visiting clubhouse
  Brian Harkins
Director, community relations
  Darrell Miller
Director, special projects
  Corky Lippert
Director, ticket department
  Carl Gordon
Supervisor, ticket services
  Susan Weiss
Medical director
  Dr. Robert K. Kerlan
Team physician, medicine
  Dr. Jules Rasinski
Team physician, orthopedics
  Dr. Lewis Yocum

Trainers
  Ned Bergert
  Rick Smith
Sportspsych
  Ken Ravizza
Director, scouting
  Bob Fontaine Jr.
Coordinator of scouting operations
  Tim Kelly
Director, international scouting
  Ray Poitevint
Supervisor, international scouting
  Lee Sigman
International cross-checker
  Harry Smith
Scouts
  Ted Brzenk
  Mike Cadahia
  Joe Caro
  Tom Davis
  Orv Franchuk
  Dave Garcia
  Red Gaskill
  Steve Gruwell
  Bob Harrison
  Fred Hatfield
  Rick Ingalls
  Bobby Johns
  Nick Kamzic
  Hal Keller
  Matt Keough
  Kris Kline
  Tom Kotchman
  Tony LaCava
  Joe Lewis
  Steve McAllister
  Jim McLaughlin
  John McNamara
  Bobby Myrick
  Jon Neiderer
  Tom Osowski
  Paul Robinson
  Rich Schlenker
  Moose Stubing
  Dale Sutherland
  Rip Tutor
  Jack Uhey
International scouts
  Pompeyo Davalillo
  Eusebio Perez
  Reuben Rodriguez
  Duk Jun Lee
  Lee Figueroa
  Wally Komatsubara
  David Schlenker
  Jorge Ortiz

SCHEDULE KEY

H—Home game.   N—Night game (any game starting after 5 p.m.).
*All-Star Game at Oriole Park at Camden Yards, Baltimore.

Manager—Buck Rodgers (7).

Coaches—Rod Carew (29), Chuck Hernandez (55), Bobby Knoop (2), Ken Macha (39), Jimmie Reese (50), Rick Turner (57), John Wathan (37).

No.	PITCHERS	B/T	Ht./Wt.	Born	1992 clubs
23	Butcher, Michael	R/R	6-1/200	5-10-65	Edmonton, California
32	Crim, Chuck	R/R	6-0/185	7-23-61	California
38	Farrell, John	R/R	6-4/210	8-4-62	DID NOT PLAY
31	Finley, Chuck	L/L	6-6/214	11-26-62	California
40	Fortugno, Tim	L/L	6-0/195	4-11-62	Edmonton, California
41	Frey, Steve	R/L	5-9/170	7-29-63	California
19	Grahe, Joe	R/R	6-0/200	8-14-67	California, Edmonton
48	Hathaway, Hilly	L/L	6-4/195	9-12-69	Palm Springs, Midland, California
42	Holzemer, Mark	L/R	6-0/165	8-20-69	Palm Springs, Midland, Edmonton
12	Langston, Mark	R/L	6-2/184	8-20-60	California
18	Lewis, Scott	R/R	6-3/178	12-5-65	California, Edmonton
45	Musset, Jose	R/R	6-3/173	9-18-68	Quad City
36	Nielsen, Jerry	L/L	6-3/188	8-5-66	Albany/Colonie, New York A.L., Columbus
27	Percival, Troy	R/R	6-3/200	8-9-69	Palm Springs, Midland
43	Scott, Darryl	R/R	6-1/185	8-6-68	Midland, Edmonton
51	Silverio, Victor	R/R	6-4/186	9-20-68	Palm Springs, Quad City
34	Springer, Russ	R/R	6-4/205	11-7-68	Columbus, New York A.L.
35	Swingle, Paul	R/R	6-0/185	12-21-66	Midland
45	Valera, Julio	R/R	6-2/215	10-13-68	Tidewater, California
46	Vasquez, Julian	R/R	6-3/165	5-24-68	Binghamton, Tidewater
47	Watson, Ron	L/R	6-5/240	9-12-68	Quad City

No.	CATCHERS	B/T	Ht./Wt.	Born	1992 clubs
21	Myers, Greg	L/R	6-2/206	4-14-66	Toronto, California
14	Orton, John	R/R	6-1/192	12-8-65	Edmonton, California
24	Tingley, Ron	R/R	6-2/194	5-27-59	California

No.	INFIELDERS	B/T	Ht./Wt.	Born	1992 clubs
5	Correia, Rod	R/R	5-11/170	9-13-67	Midland
33	DiSarcina, Gary	R/R	6-1/178	11-19-67	California
1	Easley, Damion	R/R	5-11/155	11-11-69	Edmonton, California
6	Flora, Kevin	R/R	6-0/180	6-10-69	Edmonton
3	Gaetti, Gary	R/R	6-0/200	8-19-58	California
17	Gruber, Kelly	R/R	6-0/185	2-26-62	Toronto
10	Lovullo, Torey	B/R	6-0/185	7-25-65	Columbus
6	Snow, J.T.	B/L	6-2/202	2-26-68	Columbus, New York A.L.
20	Van Burkleo, Ty	L/L	6-5/225	10-7-63	Edmonton

No.	OUTFIELDERS	B/T	Ht./Wt.	Born	1992 clubs
16	Curtis, Chad	R/R	5-10/175	11-6-68	California
44	Davis, Chili	B/R	6-3/219	1-17-60	Minnesota
25	Edmonds, Jim	L/L	6-1/190	6-27-70	Midland, Edmonton
22	Polonia, Luis	L/L	5-8/150	10-12-64	California
15	Salmon, Tim	R/R	6-3/200	8-24-68	Edmonton, California
11	Williams, Reggie	B/R	6-1/180	5-5-66	Edmonton, California

BALLPARK INFORMATION

Ballpark (capacity, surface)
Anaheim Stadium (64,593, grass)

Address
2000 Gene Autry Way
Anaheim, CA 92806

Business phones
714-937-7200
213-625-1123

Ticket information
714-634-2000

Ticket prices
$11 (field and club box)
$9 (terrace box)
$8 (center field box)
$7 (view level, reserved)
$4 (view level, unreserved)

Field dimensions (from home plate)
To left field at foul line, 333 feet
To center field, 404 feet
To right field at foul line, 333 feet

First game played
April 19, 1966 (White Sox 3, Angels 1)

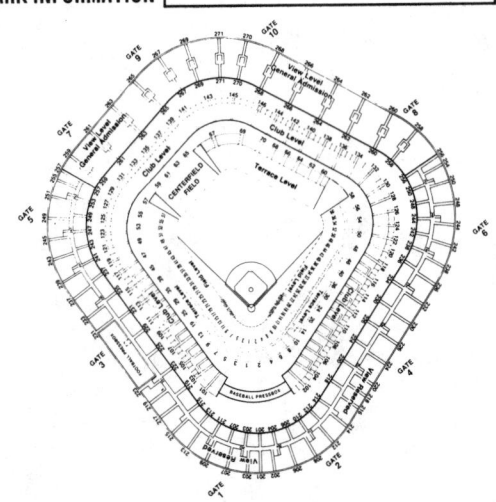

MINOR LEAGUE AFFILIATES

Class	Team	League	Manager
AAA	Vancouver	Pacific Coast	Max Oliveras
AA	Midland	Texas	Don Long
A	Palm Springs	California	Mario Mendoza
A	Quad City	Midwest	Mitch Seoane
A	Boise	Northwest	Tom Kotchman
Rookie	Mesa Angels	Arizona	Bill Lachemann

BROADCAST INFORMATION

Radio: KMPC-AM (710). Broadcasters: Bob Starr, Billy Sample. Spanish language station and broadcasters to be announced.
TV: KTLA-TV (Channel 5). Broadcasters: Ken Wilson, Ken Brett.
Cable TV: Prime Ticket. Broadcasters: To be announced.

SPRING TRAINING

Ballpark (city): Diablo Stadium (Tempe, Ariz.).
Ticket information: 602-678-2222 (Ticketron); 619-323-4143 (Angels Stadium).

HISTORY

YEAR-BY-YEAR RECORDS

Year	Pos.	W	L	Pct.	*GB	Year	Pos.	W	L	Pct.	*GB
1961	8th	70	91	.435	38½	1979	1st†	88	74	.543	+3
1962	3rd	86	76	.531	10	1980	6th	65	95	.406	31
1963	9th	70	91	.435	34	1981	4th/7th	51	59	.464	‡
1964	5th	82	80	.506	17	1982	1st†	93	69	.574	+3
1965	7th	75	87	.463	27	1983	T5th	70	92	.432	29
1966	6th	80	82	.494	18	1984	T2nd	81	81	.500	3
1967	5th	84	77	.522	7½	1985	2nd	90	72	.556	1
1968	8th	67	95	.414	36	1986	1st†	92	70	.568	+5
1969	3rd	71	91	.438	26	1987	T6th	75	87	.463	10
1970	3rd	86	76	.531	12	1988	4th	75	87	.463	29
1971	4th	76	86	.469	25½	1989	3rd	91	71	.562	8
1972	5th	75	80	.484	18	1990	4th	80	82	.494	23
1973	4th	79	83	.488	15	1991	7th	81	81	.500	14
1974	6th	68	94	.420	22	1992	T5th	72	90	.444	24
1975	6th	72	89	.447	25½						
1976	T4th	76	86	.469	14						
1977	5th	74	88	.457	28						
1978	T2nd	87	75	.537	5						

*Games behind winner. †Lost Championship Series. ‡First half 31-29; second 20-30.

MANAGERS

Name	Record	Years
Bill Rigney	625-707	'61-69
Lefty Phillips	222-225	'69-71
Del Rice	75-80	1972
Bobby Winkles	109-127	'73-74
Dick Williams	147-194	'74-76
Norm Sherry	76-71	'76-77
Dave Garcia	60-66	'77-78
Jim Fregosi	237-249	'78-81
Gene Mauch	379-332	'81-82
		'85-87
John McNamara	151-173	'83-84
Cookie Rojas	75-87	1988
Doug Rader	232-216	'89-91
Buck Rodgers	92-108	'91-92

DAY BY DAY

Date	Opp.	Res.	Score (inn.*)	Hits	Opp. hits	Winning pitcher	Losing pitcher	Save	Record	Pos.	GB
4-7	Chi.	L	4-10	8	14	McDowell	Langston	Alvarez	0-1	T5th	1½
4-8	Chi.	L	3-4	9	10	Hibbard	Abbott	Thigpen	0-2	T5th	2½
4-9	Chi.	L	6-7	11	12	McCaskill	Grahe	Radinsky	0-3	T5th	3½
4-10	Mil.	L	4-5	5	8	Plesac	Harvey	Henry	0-4	T6th	4
4-11	Mil.	W	4-1	10	8	Robinson	Wegman	Harvey	1-4	6th	4
4-12	Mil.	W	13-9	14	17	Langston	Bosio		2-4	6th	3½
4-13	At Tex.	W	3-0	9	6	Abbott	Guzman	Harvey	3-4	5th	3
4-14	At Tex.	W	8-1	13	4	Grahe	Robinson		4-4	4th	2
4-15	At Tex.	L	2-3	6	6	Witt	Valera	Russell	4-5	T4th	3
4-16	At Tex.	W	3-2	5	9	Crim	Russell	Harvey	5-5	4th	3
4-17	At K.C.	W	8-1	14	3	Lewis	Boddicker		6-5	4th	2
4-18	At K.C.	W	5-3 (10)	11	7	Frey	Montgomery		7-5	4th	2
4-20	At Oak.	L	3-4 (11)	7	7	Eckersley	Crim		7-6	4th	2½
4-21	At Oak.	W	3-2	5	6	Valera	Stewart	Harvey	8-6	4th	1½
4-22	At Oak.	L	4-10	11	10	Moore	Finley		8-7	4th	2½
4-24	Sea.	L	2-7	4	12	Fleming	Abbott		8-8	T3rd	2½
4-25	Sea.	L	6-10	8	14	Johnson	Grahe	Schooler	8-9	5th	3½
4-26	Sea.	W	7-5	11	10	Bailes	Nelson	Harvey	9-9	T4th	2½
4-28	At Tor.	W	9-5	14	7	Finley	Stieb		10-9	4th	2½
4-29	At Tor.	L	0-1	7	9	Stottlemyre	Abbott		10-10	4th	2½
4-30	At Cle.	W	8-5	9	10	Grahe	Shaw	Harvey	11-10	4th	2½
5-1	At Cle.	W	7-5	12	6	Langston	Scudder	Harvey	12-10	4th	2½
5-2	At Cle.	L	2-3	7	11	Lilliquist	Eichhorn	Olin	12-11	4th	2½
5-3	At Cle.	W	6-3	13	11	Bailes	Lilliquist	Harvey	13-11	4th	1½
5-4	At Det.	L	2-6	7	10	Gullickson	Abbott		13-12	4th	1½
5-5	At Det.	L	1-2	3	7	Doherty	Eichhorn		13-13	4th	2
5-6	N.Y.	W	3-2	10	5	Langston	Perez	Harvey	14-13	4th	2
5-7	N.Y.	W	6-0	10	5	Valera	Sanderson		15-13	3rd	2
5-8	Tor.	W	4-1	8	8	Eichhorn	Stieb		16-13	3rd	2
5-9	Tor.	W	2-1	6	6	Abbott	Stottlemyre	Harvey	17-13	3rd	1½
5-10	Tor.	L	1-4	4	7	Guzman	Grahe		17-14	3rd	2½
5-12	Det.	L	2-4	8	10	Tanana	Harvey	Henneman	17-15	3rd	2½
5-13	Det.	W	7-5	12	11	Frey	Terrell	Harvey	18-15	3rd	2
5-15	At Bos.	L	0-3	4	6	Clemens	Abbott		18-16	3rd	2
5-16	At Bos.	L	0-3	4	6	Viola	Valera	Reardon	18-17	T3rd	2½
5-17	At Bos.	W	3-1	7	5	Langston	Dopson	Harvey	19-17	T3rd	2
5-18	At N.Y.	L	2-7	8	9	Cadaret	Finley	Howe	19-18	4th	2½
5-19	At N.Y.	L	4-5 (10)	10	11	Monteleone	Eichhorn		19-19	5th	3½
5-20	At N.Y.	L	2-3 (12)	9	8	Habyan	Crim		19-20	5th	4½
5-22	At Bal.	L	3-5	8	8	McDonald	Valera	Olson	19-21	5th	5½
5-23	At Bal.	W	6-2	9	4	Langston	Sutcliffe		20-21	5th	4½
5-24	At Bal.	L	4-6	11	12	Milacki	Finley	Olson	20-22	5th	5½
5-26	Bos.	L	1-4	3	9	Clemens	Abbott	Reardon	20-23	5th	5
5-27	Bos.	L	3-4 (10)	7	8	Reardon	Harvey	Darwin	20-24	5th	5
5-28	Bos.	L	1-2	8	8	Hesketh	Langston	Reardon	20-25	5th	6
5-29	Cle.	L	2-14	8	18	Boucher	Finley		20-26	5th	7
5-30	Cle.	W	3-1	7	3	Blyleven	Armstrong	Harvey	21-26	5th	6
5-31	Cle.	L	3-4	4	7	Nagy	Abbott	Olin	21-27	5th	6½
6-1	Bal.	L	2-8	11	12	McDonald	Valera	Davis	21-28	T5th	6½
6-2	Bal.	L	2-4	6	10	Mussina	Langston	Olson	21-29	T5th	7½
6-3	Bal.	W	4-3 (10)	9	13	Bailes	Mills		22-29	5th	7½
6-5	At Mil.	L	1-7	5	12	Bosio	Abbott		22-30	5th	8½
6-6	At Mil.	L	3-4	8	8	Navarro	Harvey	Henry	22-31	5th	9½
6-7	At Mil.	L	3-10	6	10	Bones	Langston		22-32	T4th	9½
6-8	At Chi.	L	1-5	5	13	McDowell	Finley	Thigpen	22-33	6th	9½
6-9	At Chi.	L	2-4	7	9	Hibbard	Valera	Radinsky	22-34	7th	10½
6-10	At Chi.	L	2-3 (12)	8	12	Pall	Frey		22-35	7th	11½
6-11	At Chi.	W	4-0	7	9	Blyleven	Fernandez	Grahe	23-35	T6th	11
6-12	K.C.	W	5-0	8	7	Langston	Pichardo		24-35	T6th	11
6-13	K.C.	W	5-4	11	7	Finley	Reed	Eichhorn	25-35	5th	11
6-14	K.C.	W	5-1	10	6	Valera	Gubicza	Frey	26-35	5th	11
6-15	Tex.	L	2-5	4	13	Burns	Abbott	Russell	26-36	5th	12
6-16	Tex.	W	4-1	10	3	Blyleven	Guzman	Grahe	27-36	5th	11
6-17	Tex.	W	3-0	7	2	Langston	Ryan		28-36	5th	10
6-19	Oak.	L	8-12	15	15	Stewart	Finley	Eckersley	28-37	6th	11
6-20	Oak.	W	10-0	10	4	Valera	Welch		29-37	5th	10
6-21	Oak.	W	4-2	4	9	Abbott	Moore	Grahe	30-37	5th	9
6-22	At Min.	L	0-2	8	6	Smiley	Langston	Aguilera	30-38	5th	10
6-23	At Min.	L	3-5	8	8	Erickson	Blyleven	Aguilera	30-39	5th	11
6-24	At Min.	L	0-11	2	17	Tapani	Finley		30-40	5th	12

Date	Opp.	Res.	Score	(inn.*)	Hits	Opp. hits	Winning pitcher	Losing pitcher	Save	Record	Pos.	GB
6-25	At Sea.	L	4-13		11	14	DeLucia	Valera		30-41	5th	13
6-26	At Sea.	W	10-1		15	6	Abbott	Walker		31-41	5th	12
6-27	At Sea.	W	2-1		5	8	Langston	Johnson		32-41	5th	11
6-28	At Sea.	L	2-9		8	16	Hanson	Blyleven		32-42	5th	11
6-29	Min.	L	1-5		4	8	Tapani	Finley		32-43	6th	12
6-30	Min.	L	0-2		2	8	Krueger	Valera		32-44	6th	13
7-1	Min.	L	1-2		7	8	Banks	Abbott		32-45	6th	14
7-3	At Tor.	L	1-10		5	13	Key	Langston		32-46	6th	14
7-4	At Tor.	L	6-8		8	12	Morris	Eichhorn	Henke	32-47	7th	15
7-5	At Tor.	L	2-6		3	8	Wells	Valera		32-48	7th	16
7-6	At Tor.	L	0-3		4	7	Guzman	Abbott	Henke	32-49	7th	17
7-7	At Cle.	L	1-3		4	8	Cook	Finley	Olin	32-50	7th	17
7-8	At Cle.	L	4-8		7	9	Nagy	Langston		32-51	7th	18
7-9	At Det.	L	4-5		10	11	Tanana	Blyleven	Henneman	32-52	7th	18
7-10	At Det.	W	6-1		13	6	Valera	Groom		33-52	7th	18
7-11	At Det.	W	2-1		8	6	Crim	Gullickson	Grahe	34-52	7th	18
7-12	At Det.	W	5-4	(10)	11	7	Frey	Henneman		35-52	7th	18
7-16	N.Y.	W	3-2		8	5	Frey	Perez		36-52	6th	18
7-17	N.Y.	W	12-4		14	8	Crim	Sanderson	Grahe	37-52	6th	18
7-18	N.Y.	W	5-3		11	6	Langston	Kamieniecki	Eichhorn	38-52	6th	17
7-19	N.Y.	L	3-8		8	15	Young	Blyleven		38-53	6th	18
7-20	Tor.	W	5-3		10	6	Crim	Hentgen	Grahe	39-53	6th	17
7-21	Tor.	L	5-9		9	17	Morris	Crim	Ward	39-54	6th	17
7-22	Tor.	W	5-4		10	11	Grahe	Key		40-54	6th	17
7-23	Det.	L	2-5		5	6	Leiter	Langston	Doherty	40-55	6th	17½
7-24	Det.	W	6-3		8	5	Blyleven	Ritz	Grahe	41-55	6th	17
7-25	Det.	W	9-0		12	3	Fortugno	Terrell		42-55	6th	17
7-26	Det.	W	4-3		6	12	Crim	Doherty	Grahe	43-55	T5th	17
7-27	Sea.	W	3-0		7	6	Finley	Hanson	Grahe	44-55	5th	16
7-28	Sea.	L	1-8		8	18	Fleming	Langston		44-56	5th	16
7-29	Sea.	L	0-8		4	14	Fisher	Blyleven		44-57	6th	16
7-30	Sea.	W	6-5		7	9	Eichhorn	Swan	Grahe	45-57	5th	15½
7-31	At Tex.	W	5-3		9	11	Crim	Witt	Grahe	46-57	5th	15
8-1	At Tex.	W	6-1		10	7	Finley	Ryan		47-57	5th	15
8-2	At Tex.	L	1-5		6	7	Brown	Langston		47-58	5th	16
8-4 (1)	At K.C.	W	5-1		9	6	Blyleven	Appier	Crim	48-58	5th	15
8-4 (2)	At K.C.	L	1-4		8	5	Aquino	Fortugno		48-59	5th	15½
8-5	At K.C.	L	2-5		7	12	Gordon	Valera	Montgomery	48-60	6th	16½
8-6	At K.C.	L	6-7		12	10	Berenguer	Crim	Montgomery	48-61	6th	17½
8-7	Chi.	W	3-1		11	5	Langston	McDowell	Grahe	49-61	6th	17½
8-8	Chi.	L	2-8		4	11	Hernandez	Frey		49-62	6th	18½
8-9	Chi.	L	8-12	(14)	13	20	Pall	Bailes		49-63	6th	18½
8-10	Mil.	W	4-1		9	3	Valera	Wegman		50-63	6th	18½
8-11	Mil.	W	1-0	(10)	8	7	Grahe	Navarro		51-63	6th	17½
8-12	Mil.	W	2-1		4	2	Langston	Ruffin	Grahe	52-63	5th	17½
8-13	At Oak.	L	1-4		3	6	Moore	Abbott		52-64	5th	18½
8-14	At Oak.	W	2-1		4	6	Blyleven	Stewart	Grahe	53-64	5th	17½
8-15	At Oak.	L	5-9		9	14	Corsi	Crim		53-65	5th	18½
8-16	At Oak.	L	4-5		7	6	Eckersley	Grahe		53-66	6th	19½
8-18	At Bos.	L	0-8		4	13	Clemens	Langston		53-67	6th	18½
8-19	At Bos.	W	3-2		8	10	Abbott	Reardon	Grahe	54-67	6th	18½
8-20	At Bos.	W	2-0		11	6	Blyleven	Darwin	Grahe	55-67	6th	18½
8-21	At N.Y.	W	9-5		14	11	Butcher	Hillegas	Fortugno	56-67	6th	17½
8-22	At N.Y.	L	0-3		4	9	Perez	Finley	Farr	56-68	6th	18½
8-23	At N.Y.	W	7-3	(10)	13	7	Butcher	Monteleone		57-68	5th	18½
8-24	At Bal.	W	5-2		9	8	Abbott	Rhodes	Grahe	58-68	5th	18½
8-25	At Bal.	L	1-9		4	14	Sutcliffe	Blyleven		58-69	5th	18½
8-26	At Bal.	L	4-6		11	9	Frohwirth	Butcher	Olson	58-70	5th	18½
8-28	Bos.	L	1-7		10	10	Clemens	Finley		58-71	5th	19½
8-29	Bos.	W	7-2		11	4	Langston	Dopson		59-71	5th	19½
8-30	Bos.	L	2-4	(10)	3	13	Darwin	Butcher	Harris	59-72	5th	20½
8-31	Cle.	L	3-4		7	7	Nichols	Blyleven	Plunk	59-73	6th	20½
9-1	Cle.	W	7-6		14	10	Crim	Plunk	Grahe	60-73	6th	19½
9-2	Cle.	W	3-2	(15)	16	8	Lewis	Lilliquist		61-73	6th	19
9-4	Bal.	L	7-8		6	11	Sutcliffe	Langston	Frohwirth	61-74	5th	18½
9-5	Bal.	L	1-4		5	12	Mussina	Abbott	Olson	61-75	5th	18½
9-6	Bal.	W	5-2		8	7	Blyleven	Lefferts	Grahe	62-75	5th	18½
9-7	Oak.	W	3-2		8	10	Valera	Moore	Grahe	63-75	5th	17½
9-8	Oak.	L	2-14		7	19	Downs	Finley		63-76	5th	18½
9-9	Oak.	L	0-3		2	8	Stewart	Langston	Eckersley	63-77	5th	19½
9-11	At Min.	W	8-0		13	8	Abbott	Smiley		64-77	5th	20
9-12	At Min.	L	2-7		4	11	Trombley	Blyleven	Guthrie	64-78	5th	21
9-13	At Min.	L	2-6		6	9	Erickson	Valera		64-79	5th	22
9-15	At Sea.	W	9-0		14	4	Finley	Fleming		65-79	5th	22½

Date	Opp.	Res.	Score	(inn.*)	Hits	Opp. hits	Winning pitcher	Losing pitcher	Save	Record	Pos.	GB
9-16	At Sea.	W	2-1	(13)	5	8	Grahe	Jones	Frey	66-79	5th	22½
9-17	Min.	L	1-2		3	8	Trombley	Abbott	Aguilera	66-80	5th	23
9-18	Min.	L	1-4		5	10	Erickson	Blyleven	Aguilera	66-81	5th	24
9-19	Min.	W	5-1		9	5	Valera	Tapani		67-81	5th	23
9-20	Min.	L	5-7		10	11	Aguilera	Grahe		67-82	5th	24
9-22	At Mil.	L	2-3		8	6	Plesac	Langston	Holmes	67-83	T5th	24½
9-23	At Mil.	L	0-3		4	8	Eldred	Abbott		67-84	T5th	24½
9-24	At Mil.	L	0-4		5	11	Bosio	Blyleven		67-85	6th	25½
9-25	At Chi.	L	5-6		12	10	Hernandez	Grahe		67-86	6th	25½
9-26	At Chi.	W	1-0		7	5	Finley	Fernandez	Frey	68-86	6th	24½
9-27	At Chi.	L	2-3	(11)	8	7	Hernandez	Crim		68-87	6th	24½
9-28	K.C.	W	6-5	(11)	13	11	Lewis	Shifflett		69-87	T5th	24
9-29	K.C.	L	0-2		1	7	Rasmussen	Blyleven		69-88	6th	25
9-30	K.C.	L	0-4		7	16	Reed	Valera		69-89	6th	25
10-1	K.C.	W	5-2		10	11	Finley	Sampen	Frey	70-89	6th	24
10-2	Tex.	W	6-3		12	6	Langston	Chiamparino		71-89	T5th	23
10-3	Tex.	W	4-2		11	8	Lewis	Smith	Grahe	72-89	T5th	23
10-4	Tex.	L	5-9		8	17	Brown	Blyleven		72-90	T5th	24

Monthly records: April (11-10), May (10-17), June (11-17), July (14-13), August (13-16), September (10-16), Oct. (3-1).

HIGHLIGHTS

High point: Following a 2-1 win over Toronto on May 9, the team that nobody expected to be a factor in the A.L. West race was only 1½ games out of first place with a 17-13 record.

Low point: From June 28-July 9, the Angels lost 11 games in a row, then learned that Manager Buck Rodgers' recovery from injuries suffered in a team bus crash would take more than a month longer than anticipated.

Turning point: In the early-morning hours of May 21, California's team bus veered off the New Jersey Turnpike and overturned, injuring 13 passengers. Rodgers suffered multiple fractures in his arm, elbow and knee and was unable to manage the team for 100 days. Third-base coach John Wathan served as interim manager.

Most valuable player: Outfielder Luis Polonia. He hit below his career average of .302 but still managed to lead the club with a .286 mark and steal a career-high 51 bases.

Most valuable pitcher: Righthander Joe Grahe. He began the season as the Angels' third starter but lost his job after just seven starts. But after moving to the bullpen and replacing the injured Bryan Harvey as the closer, he amassed 21 saves with a 1.80 ERA.

Most improved player: Infielder Damion Easley. After hitting .289 with 26 steals as a shortstop at Class AAA, he was switched to third base and called up in mid-August. He proceeded to play spectacular defense while hitting .258.

Most pleasant surprise: Infielder Rene Gonzales. A non-roster invitee to spring training, he eventually started at second base and then third, hitting .277 with seven homers before a broken left arm ended his season August 11.

Biggest disappointment: Outfielders Von Hayes and Hubie Brooks. Signed to add punch to the middle of the lineup, the veterans hit .225 and .216, respectively, and combined for just 12 home runs. Brooks was injured much of the year; Hayes was waived August 20.

Key injuries: Lefthander Chuck Finley (left big toe) and catcher John Orton (sore right shoulder) didn't gain full strength until the second half of the season, and Harvey appeared in the fewest games of his career because of a strained right elbow.

Notable: Lefthander Jim Abbott had the best ERA on the team (2.77), yet led the staff in losses (15).... The Angels ranked last in the league in batting average (.243) and runs scored (579).... Third baseman Gary Gaetti led the Angels with 12 homers, the fewest by a club leader in the majors in 1992.

—DAVID CUNNINGHAM

RECORDS

1992 regular-season record: 72-90 (T5th in A.L. West); 41-40 at home; 31-50 on road; 38-46 vs. East; 34-44 vs. West; 13-22 vs. LHP; 59-68 vs. RHP; 65-75 on grass; 9-15 on turf; 23-24 in daytime; 49-66 at night; 23-25 in one-run games; 8-8 in extra-inning games; 0-0-1 in doubleheaders.

Team record last five years: 399-411 (.493), ranks 8th in league in that span).

TEAM LEADERS

Batting average: Luis Polonia (.286).
At-bats: Luis Polonia (577).
Runs: Luis Polonia (83).
Hits: Luis Polonia (165).
Total bases: Luis Polonia (190).
Doubles: Junior Felix (22).
Triples: Junior Felix (5).
Home runs: Gary Gaetti (12).
Runs batted in: Junior Felix (72).
Stolen bases: Luis Polonia (51).
Slugging percentage: Junior Felix (.361).
On-base percentage: Luis Polonia (.337).
Wins: Mark Langston (13).
Earned-run average: Jim Abbott (2.77).
Complete games: Mark Langston (9).
Shutouts: Mark Langston, Julio Valera (2).
Saves: Joe Grahe (21).
Innings pitched: Mark Langston (229).
Strikeouts: Mark Langston (174).

GAMES BY POSITION

Catcher: Mike Fitzgerald 74, Ron Tingley 69, John Orton 43, Lance Parrish 22, Greg Myers 8.
First base: Lee Stevens 91, Gary Gaetti 44, Alvin Davis 22, Rene Gonzales 13, Hubie Brooks 6, Von Hayes 4, Mike Fitzgerald 2, Ken Oberkfell 2, Bobby Rose 2.
Second base: Luis Sojo 96, Rene Gonzales 42, Bobby Rose 28, Ken Oberkfell 21, Mike Fitzgerald 1.
Third base: Gary Gaetti 67, Rene Gonzales 53, Damion Easley 45, Luis Sojo 9, Mike Fitzgerald 3.
Shortstop: Gary DiSarcina 157, Rene Gonzales 8, Luis Sojo 5, Damion Easley 3, Dick Schofield 1.
Outfield: Chad Curtis 135, Junior Felix 128, Luis Polonia 99, Von Hayes 85, Jose Gonzalez 22, Tim Salmon 21, Rob Ducey 20, John Morris 14, Reggie Williams 12, Mike Fitzgerald 1.
Designated hitter: Hubie Brooks 70, Luis Polonia 47, Gary Gaetti 17, Alvin Davis 9, Junior Felix 8, John Morris 6, Von Hayes 5, Ken Oberkfell 5, Lance Parrish 2, Lee Stevens 2, Reggie Williams 2, Chad Curtis 1, Rob Ducey 1, Mike Fitzgerald 1, Mark Langston 1, Greg Myers 1.

TOP 10 DRAFT CHOICES

1a. Pete Janicki, RHP, UCLA.
1b. Jeff Schmidt, RHP, U. of Minn.
2a. DeShawn Warren, LHP, Choctaw County High School, Butler, Ala.
2b. Chris Smith, SS/OF, Vallejo (Calif.) High School.
2c. Marquis Riley, OF, U. of Cent. Ark.
3. Brian Powell, RHP, Bainbridge (Ga.) High School.
4. Shawn Holcomb, RHP, El Dorado High School, Placentia, Calif.
5. Paxton Briley, RHP, Clemson Univ.
6. Billy Simas, RHP, Fresno (Cal.) C.C.
7. Larry Hingle, LHP, Stetson Univ.
8. John Lloyd, RHP, Englewood High School, Jacksonville, Fla.
9. Mickey Kerns, OF, Univ. of Alabama.
10. Travis Thurmond, RHP, Beaverton (Ore.) High School.

CHICAGO WHITE SOX
AMERICAN LEAGUE WEST DIVISION

1993 SCHEDULE

APRIL

SUN	MON	TUE	WED	THU	FRI	SAT
				1	2	3
4	5	6 N MIN	7 N MIN	8 N MIN	9 N NY H	10 N NY H
11 NY H	12 N MIN	13 N MIN	14 N MIN H	15	16 N BOS	17 BOS
18 BOS	19 BOS	20 N BAL	21 N BAL	22	23 N TOR	24 TOR
25 TOR	26 N BAL	27 N H BAL	28 N H MIL	29 N H MIL	30 N TOR H	

MAY

SUN	MON	TUE	WED	THU	FRI	SAT
						1 TOR H
2 TOR H	3	4 N MIL	5 N MIL	6	7 N CLE H	8 N CLE H
9 CLE H	10 N SEA	11 N SEA	12 N SEA	13	14 N TEX	15 N TEX
16 N TEX	17 N CAL	18 N CAL H	19 N CAL H	20	21 N OAK H	22 N OAK H
23 OAK H	24 N KC H	25 N KC H	26 N KC H	27 N H	28 N NY	29 NY
30 NY	31					

JUNE

SUN	MON	TUE	WED	THU	FRI	SAT
		1 N DET	2 N DET	3 N DET	4 N BOS H	5 N BOS H
6 BOS H	7 N DET H	8 N DET H	9 N DET H	10	11 N KC	12 N KC
13 KC	14 N OAK	15 N OAK	16 N OAK	17	18 N CAL	19 N CAL
20 CAL	21 N TEX H	22 N TEX H	23	24	25 N SEA H	26 N SEA H
27 SEA H	28 N CLE	29 N CLE	30 N CLE			

JULY

SUN	MON	TUE	WED	THU	FRI	SAT
				1 N BAL H	2 N BAL H	3 N BAL H
4 BAL H	5 N TOR	6 N TOR	7 N TOR	8 N BAL	9 N BAL	10 BAL
11 BAL	12	13 ✶ ALL-STAR GAME	14	15 N MIL	16 N MIL	17 N MIL
18 MIL	19 N TOR H	20 N TOR H	21 N TOR H	22 N MIL H	23 N MIL H	24 N MIL H
25 MIL H	26 N CLE H	27 N CLE H	28 N CLE H	29	30 SEA	31 SEA

AUGUST

SUN	MON	TUE	WED	THU	FRI	SAT
1 SEA	2 N TEX	3 N TEX	4 N TEX	5 N CAL	6 N CAL	7 N CAL H
8 CAL H	9 N OAK H	10 N OAK H	11 N OAK H	12 N KC H	13 N KC H	14 N KC H
15 KC H	16	17 N BOS	18 N BOS	19	20 N MIN	21 N MIN
22 MIN	23 N NY H	24 N NY H	25 N NY H	26	27 N MIN H	28 N MIN H
29 MIN H	30 N MIN H	31 N NY				

SEPTEMBER

SUN	MON	TUE	WED	THU	FRI	SAT
			1 N NY	2 N NY	3 N DET	4 N DET
5 DET	6 N BOS H	7 N BOS H	8 N BOS H	9	10 N DET H	11 N DET H
12 DET H	13 N KC	14 N KC	15 N KC	16	17 N OAK	18 OAK
19 OAK	20 N CAL	21 N CAL	22 N CAL	23 N OAK	24 N TEX H	25 N TEX H
26 TEX H	27 N SEA H	28 N SEA H	29 N SEA H	30 N		

OCTOBER

SUN	MON	TUE	WED	THU	FRI	SAT
					1 N CLE	2 N CLE
3 CLE						

1993 SEASON

CLUB DIRECTORY

Chairman
Jerry Reinsdorf
Vice chairman
Eddie Einhorn
Executive vice president
Howard Pizer
Senior v.p., major league operations
Ron Schueler
Senior v.p., marketing and broadcasting
Rob Gallas
Senior vice president, baseball
Jack Gould
Vice president, finance
Tim Buzard
Vice president, stadium operations
Terry Savarise
V.p., scouting and minor league operations
Larry Monroe
General counsel
Allan Muchin
Secretary
Gerald Penner
Director of baseball operations
Dan Evans
Special assistants to Ron Schueler
Ed Brinkman
Bart Johnson
Mike Squires
Dave Yoakum
Director of scouting
Duane Shaffer
Director of minor league operations
Steve Noworyta
Director of minor league instruction
Buddy Bell
Traveling secretary
Glen Rosenbaum
Assistant to the director of scouting
Grace Guerrero Zwit
Asst. to the director of baseball operations
Jeff Chaney
Major league computer scouting analyst
Mike Maziarka
Trainers
Herm Schneider
Mark Anderson
Director of conditioning
Steve Odgers
Team physicians
Dr. James Boscardin
Dr. Hugo Cuadros
Dr. Robert Daley
Dr. Bernard Feldman
Dr. David Orth
Dr. Scott Price
Dr. Lowell Scott Weil
Director of marketing and broadcasting
Mike Bucek

Director of advertising and promotions
Bob Grim
Director of p.r. and community affairs
Doug Abel
Director of ticket sales
Bob Voight
Director of ticket operations
Bob Devoy
Controller
Bill Waters
Director of park operations
David Schaffer
Director of purchasing
Don Esposito
Assistant director of public relations
Scott Reifert
Scouting national cross-checker
George Bradley
Scouting supervisors
Mark Bernstein
Doug Laumann
Ed Pebley
Marti Wolever
Full-time scouts
Steve Arnieri
Jose Bernhardt
Juan Ramon Bernhardt
Chuck Bizzell
Kevin Burrell
Joseph Butler
Scott Cerny
Alex Cosmidis
Warren Hughes
Miguel Ibarra
Reginald Lewis
Guy Mader
David Owen
Gary Pellant
Paul Provas
Victor Puig
Michael Sgobba
Ken Stauffer
John Tumminia
Part-time scouts
Alonzo Ganther
Nino Giarratano
Joe Ingalls
Jack Jolly
George Kachigian
Dario Lodigiani
John Nilmeyer
Larry O'Brien
Jose Ortega
Al Otto
Robert Rikeman Jr.
Tony Saladino
David Schlenker
Joe Thurman

SCHEDULE KEY

H—Home game.   N—Night game (any game starting after 5 p.m.).
*All-Star Game at Oriole Park at Camden Yards, Baltimore.

Manager—Gene Lamont (33).
Coaches—Terry Bevington (18), Jackie Brown (41), Walt Hriniak (6),
Doug Mansolino (17), Joe Nossek (15), Dewey Robinson (55).

No.	PITCHERS	B/T	Ht./Wt.	Born	1992 clubs
40	Alvarez, Wilson	L/L	6-1/235	3-24-70	Chicago A.L.
51	Bere, Jason	R/R	6-3/185	5-26-71	Sarasota, Birmingham, Vancouver
42	Bolton, Rodney	R/R	6-2/190	9-23-68	Vancouver
50	Drahman, Brian	R/R	6-3/231	11-7-66	Vancouver, Chicago A.L.
54	Dunne, Michael	L/R	6-4/212	10-27-62	Vancouver, Chicago A.L.
48	Ellis, Robert	R/R	6-5/215	12-25-70	South Bend, Gulf Coast White Sox
32	Fernandez, Alex	R/R	6-1/215	8-13-69	Chicago A.L., Vancouver
43	Garcia, Ramon	R/R	6-2/200	12-9-69	Vancouver
39	Hernandez, Roberto	R/R	6-4/235	11-11-64	Chicago A.L., Vancouver
34	Leach, Terry	R/R	6-0/194	3-13-54	Chicago A.L.
25	McCaskill, Kirk	R/R	6-1/205	4-9-61	Chicago A.L.
29	McDowell, Jack	R/R	6-5/188	1-16-66	Chicago A.L.
22	Pall, Donn	R/R	6-1/180	1-11-62	Chicago A.L.
31	Radinsky, Scott	L/L	6-3/204	3-3-68	Chicago A.L.
47	Ruffin, Johnny	R/R	6-3/172	7-29-71	Birmingham, Sarasota
49	Schwarz, Jeff	R/R	6-5/190	5-20-64	Birmingham, Vancouver
73	Stieb, Dave	R/R	6-1/195	7-22-57	Dunedin, Toronto
37	Thigpen, Bobby	R/R	6-3/222	7-17-63	Chicago A.L.

No.	CATCHERS	B/T	Ht./Wt.	Born	1992 clubs
36	Hemond, Scott	R/R	6-0/215	11-18-65	Oakland, Huntsville, Tacoma, Chicago A.L.
20	Karkovice, Ron	R/R	6-1/219	8-8-63	Chicago A.L.
5	Merullo, Matt	L/R	6-2/200	8-4-65	Chicago A.L., Vancouver

No.	INFIELDERS	B/T	Ht./Wt.	Born	1992 clubs
38	Beltre, Esteban	R/R	5-10/172	12-26-67	Vancouver, Chicago A.L.
28	Cora, Joey	B/R	5-8/155	5-14-65	Chicago A.L.
52	Cron, Chris	R/R	6-2/207	3-31-64	Vancouver, Chicago A.L.
53	Gilbert, Shawn	R/R	5-9/170	3-12-65	Portland
14	Grebeck, Craig	R/R	5-7/148	12-29-64	Chicago A.L.
13	Guillen, Ozzie	L/R	5-11/164	1-20-64	Chicago A.L.
7	Sax, Steve	R/R	5-11/189	1-29-60	Chicago A.L.
35	Thomas, Frank	R/R	6-5/257	5-27-68	Chicago A.L.
23	Ventura, Robin	L/R	6-1/198	7-14-67	Chicago A.L.
56	Wilson, Brandon	R/R	6-1/170	2-26-69	Sarasota, Birmingham

No.	OUTFIELDERS	B/T	Ht./Wt.	Born	1992 clubs
45	Abner, Shawn	R/R	6-1/196	6-17-66	Vancouver, Chicago A.L.
21	Bell, George	R/R	6-1/210	10-21-59	Chicago A.L.
10	Burks, Ellis	R/R	6-2/205	9-11-64	Boston
12	Huff, Michael	R/R	6-1/190	8-11-63	Chicago A.L., Vancouver, South Bend
8	Jackson, Bo	R/R	6-1/228	11-30-62	DID NOT PLAY
1	Johnson, Lance	L/L	5-11/160	7-6-63	Chicago A.L.
24	Newson, Warren	L/L	5-7/202	7-3-64	Chicago A.L., Vancouver
44	Pasqua, Dan	L/L	6-0/218	10-17-61	Chicago A.L., Birmingham
30	Raines, Tim	B/R	5-8/186	9-16-59	Chicago A.L.

BALLPARK INFORMATION

Ballpark (capacity, surface)
Comiskey Park (44,229, grass)
Address
333 W. 35th St.
Chicago, IL 60616
Business phone
312-924-1000
Ticket information
312-924-1000
Ticket prices
$18 (club level)
$15 (lower deck box)
$12 (upper deck box)
$11 (lower deck reserved)
$8 (upper deck reserved)
$8 (bleacher reserved)
Field dimensions (from home plate)
To left field at foul line, 347 feet
To center field, 400 feet
To right field at foul line, 347 feet
First game played
April 18, 1991 (Tigers 16, White Sox 0)

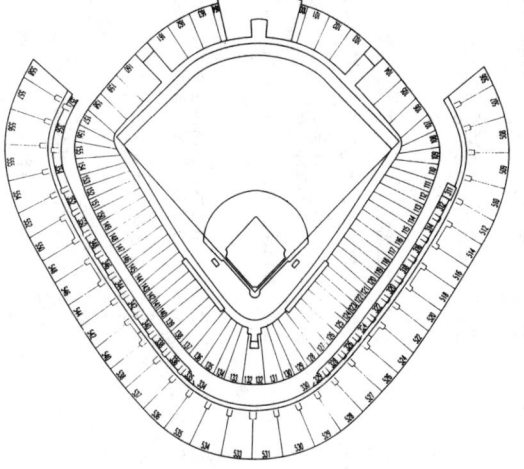

Class	Team	League	Manager
AAA	Nashville	American Association	Rick Renick
AA	Birmingham	Southern	Terry Francona
A	Sarasota	Florida State	Dave Huppert
A	South Bend	Midwest	Tony Franklin
A	Hickory	South Atlantic	Fred Kendall
Rookie	Sarasota	Gulf Coast	Mike Rojas

BROADCAST INFORMATION

Radio: WMAQ-AM (670). Broadcasters: John Rooney, Ed Farmer. WIND-AM (560, Spanish language). Broadcasters: Chico Carrasquel, Hector Molina.
TV: WGN-TV (Channel 9). Broadcasters: Ken Harrelson, Tom Paciorek.
Cable TV: SportsChannel. Broadcasters: Ken Harrelson, Tom Paciorek.

SPRING TRAINING

Ballpark (city): Ed Smith Stadium (Sarasota, Fla.).
Ticket information: 813-953-3388.

HISTORY

YEAR-BY-YEAR RECORDS

Year	Pos.	W	L	Pct.	*GB	Year	Pos.	W	L	Pct.	*GB
1901	1st	83	53	.610	+4	1949	6th	63	91	.409	34
1902	4th	74	60	.552	8	1950	6th	60	94	.390	38
1903	7th	60	77	.438	30½	1951	4th	81	73	.526	17
1904	3rd	89	65	.578	6	1952	3rd	81	73	.526	14
1905	2nd	92	60	.605	2	1953	3rd	89	65	.578	11½
1906	1st	93	58	.616	+3	1954	3rd	94	60	.610	17
1907	3rd	87	64	.576	5½	1955	3rd	91	63	.591	5
1908	3rd	88	64	.579	1½	1956	3rd	85	69	.552	12
1909	4th	78	74	.513	20	1957	2nd	90	64	.584	8
1910	6th	68	85	.444	35½	1958	2nd	82	72	.532	10
1911	4th	77	74	.510	24	1959	1st	94	60	.610	+5
1912	4th	78	76	.506	28	1960	3rd	87	67	.565	10
1913	5th	78	74	.513	17½	1961	4th	86	76	.531	23
1914	T6th	70	84	.455	30	1962	5th	85	77	.525	11
1915	3rd	93	61	.604	9½	1963	2nd	94	68	.580	10½
1916	2nd	89	65	.578	2	1964	2nd	98	64	.605	1
1917	1st	100	54	.649	+9	1965	2nd	95	67	.586	7
1918	6th	57	67	.460	17	1966	4th	83	79	.512	15
1919	1st	88	52	.629	+3½	1967	4th	89	73	.549	3
1920	2nd	96	58	.623	2	1968	T8th	67	95	.414	36
1921	7th	62	92	.403	36½	1969	5th	68	94	.420	29
1922	5th	77	77	.500	17	1970	6th	56	106	.346	42
1923	7th	69	85	.448	30	1971	3rd	79	83	.488	22½
1924	8th	66	87	.431	25½	1972	2nd	87	67	.565	5½
1925	5th	79	75	.513	18½	1973	5th	77	85	.475	17
1926	5th	81	72	.529	9½	1974	4th	80	80	.500	9
1927	5th	70	83	.458	29½	1975	5th	75	86	.466	22½
1928	5th	72	82	.468	29	1976	6th	64	97	.398	25½
1929	7th	59	93	.388	46	1977	3rd	90	72	.556	12
1930	7th	62	92	.403	40	1978	5th	71	90	.441	20½
1931	8th	56	97	.366	51	1979	5th	73	87	.456	14
1932	7th	49	102	.325	56½	1980	5th	70	90	.438	26
1933	6th	67	83	.447	31	1981	3rd/6th	54	52	.509	†
1934	8th	53	99	.349	47	1982	3rd	87	75	.537	6
1935	5th	74	78	.487	19½	1983	1st‡	99	63	.611	+20
1936	3rd	81	70	.536	20	1984	T5th	74	88	.457	10
1937	3rd	86	68	.558	16	1985	3rd	85	77	.525	6
1938	6th	65	83	.439	32	1986	5th	72	90	.444	20
1939	4th	85	69	.552	22½	1987	5th	77	85	.475	8
1940	T4th	82	72	.532	8	1988	5th	71	90	.441	32½
1941	3rd	77	77	.500	24	1989	7th	69	92	.429	29½
1942	6th	66	82	.446	34	1990	2nd	94	68	.580	9
1943	4th	82	72	.532	16	1991	2nd	87	75	.537	8
1944	7th	71	83	.461	18	1992	3rd	86	76	.531	10
1945	6th	71	78	.477	15						
1946	5th	74	80	.481	30						
1947	6th	70	84	.455	27						
1948	8th	51	101	.336	44½						

*Game behind winner. †First half 31-22; second 23-30. ‡Lost Championship Series.

MANAGERS

Name	Record	Years
Clark Griffith	157-113	'01-02
Nixey Callahan	309-329	'03-04
		'12-14
Fielder Jones	426-293	'04-08
Billy Sullivan	78-74	1909
Hugh Duffy	145-159	'10-11
Pants Rowland	339-247	'15-18
Kid Gleason	392-364	'19-23
Johnny Evers	66-87	1924
Eddie Collins	160-147	'25-26
Ray Schalk	102-125	'27-28
Lena Blackburne	99-133	'28-29
Donie Bush	118-189	'30-31
Lew Fonseca	120-196	'32-34
Jimmie Dykes	899-940	'34-46
Ted Lyons	185-245	'46-48
Jack Onslow	71-133	'49-50
Red Corriden	52-72	1950
Paul Richards	406-362	'51-54
		1976
Marty Marion	179-138	'54-56
Al Lopez	840-650	'57-65
		'68-69
Eddie Stanky	206-197	'66-68
Don Gutteridge	109-172	'69-70
Chuck Tanner	401-414	'70-75
Bob Lemon	124-112	'77-78
Larry Doby	37-50	1978
Don Kessinger	46-60	1979
Tony La Russa	522-510	'79-86
Jim Fregosi	193-226	'86-88
Jeff Torborg	250-235	'89-91
Gene Lamont	86-76	1992

DAY BY DAY

Date	Opp.	Res.	Score	(inn.*)	Hits	Opp. hits	Winning pitcher	Losing pitcher	Save	Record	Pos.	GB
4-7	At Cal.	W	10-4		14	8	McDowell	Langston	Alvarez	1-0	T2nd	½
4-8	At Cal.	W	4-3		10	9	Hibbard	Abbott	Thigpen	2-0	T1st	½
4-9	At Cal.	W	7-6		12	11	McCaskill	Grahe	Radinsky	3-0	T1st	½
4-10	At Oak.	L	5-6		9	12	Slusarski	Fernandez	Eckersley	3-1	T3rd	1
4-11	At Oak.	L	6-7	(10)	6	13	Parrett	Leach		3-2	T3rd	2
4-12	At Oak.	W	6-4		11	8	McDowell	Nelson	Thigpen	4-2	3rd	1½
4-13	Sea.	W	1-0		3	6	Hibbard	Swan	Thigpen	5-2	3rd	1
4-15	Sea.	L	0-6		7	6	Fleming	McCaskill		5-3	3rd	1½
4-16	Sea.	W	5-4		8	8	Fernandez	DeLucia		6-3	3rd	1½
4-17	Min.	L	0-7		5	10	Krueger	Hough		6-4	3rd	1½
4-18	Min.	W	4-3		6	10	McDowell	Erickson		7-4	2nd	1½
4-19	Min.	W	4-1		8	6	Hibbard	Smiley	Thigpen	8-4	2nd	½
4-21	N.Y.	L	3-4		7	9	Leary	McCaskill	Farr	8-5	2nd	1
4-22	N.Y.	L	3-4		10	13	Howe	Radinsky		8-6	3rd	2
4-24	At Det.	W	9-1		9	2	McDowell	Terrell		9-6	2nd	1
4-26	At Det.	W	7-6		12	5	Hibbard	King	Thigpen	10-6	2nd	½
4-28	At Bos.	L	3-6		11	8	Clemens	McCaskill	Reardon	10-7	2nd	1½
4-29	At Bos.	L	1-6		5	8	Viola	Fernandez	Reardon	10-8	3rd	1½
4-30	Tex.	W	12-1		13	3	McDowell	Ryan		11-8	2nd	1½
5-1	Tex.	L	4-8		7	12	Witt	Hibbard	Russell	11-9	3rd	2½
5-2	Tex.	L	1-4	(11)	5	8	Robinson	Thigpen		11-10	3rd	2½
5-3	Tex.	W	5-3		8	6	Radinsky	Brown		12-10	3rd	1½
5-4	Mil.	W	7-0		10	1	Fernandez	Bones		13-10	2nd	½
5-5	Mil.	W	12-2		11	7	McDowell	Bosio		14-10	1st	+½
5-6	Bos.	W	7-5		8	12	Radinsky	Darwin	Thigpen	15-10	1st	+½
5-7	Bos.	W	7-6		9	6	Pall	Harris	Thigpen	16-10	1st	+½
5-8	At Bal.	W	4-3	(10)	9	9	Leach	Olson	Thigpen	17-10	1st	+½
5-9	At Bal.	L	2-5		9	10	Milacki	Fernandez	Olson	17-11	2nd	½
5-10	At Bal.	W	5-2		8	5	McDowell	Mesa		18-11	2nd	½
5-12	At Mil.	L	2-6		10	13	Navarro	Hibbard		18-12	2nd	½
5-13	At Mil.	W	1-0		7	2	McCaskill	Wegman	Thigpen	19-12	1st	+½
5-15	Bal.	L	0-2		5	8	Mussina	Fernandez	Olson	19-13	1st	+½
5-16	Bal.	L	2-7		7	14	McDowell	Milacki		19-14	2nd	½
5-17	Bal.	W	14-10		14	17	Pall	McDonald		20-14	1st	+½
5-18	K.C.	L	1-6		6	10	Magnante	McCaskill		20-15	2nd	½
5-19	K.C.	W	2-1		5	6	Hough	Appier	Thigpen	21-15	2nd	½
5-20	K.C.	L	2-7		6	7	Pichardo	Fernandez	Boddicker	21-16	2nd	1½
5-22	Tor.	L	2-6		5	10	Guzman	McDowell	Ward	21-17	2nd	2½
5-23	Tor.	W	5-2		11	4	Hibbard	Key	Thigpen	22-17	2nd	1½
5-24	Tor.	W	8-1		10	8	McCaskill	Morris		23-17	2nd	1½
5-26	At Tex.	L	5-6		10	11	Guzman	Hough	Nunez	23-18	2nd	1
5-27	At Tex.	L	3-4	(11)	9	7	Bannister	Pall		23-19	3rd	1
5-28	At Tex.	L	2-4		3	7	Witt	McDowell	Russell	23-20	4th	2
5-29	At Tor.	L	0-3		4	10	Ward	Hibbard	Henke	23-21	4th	3
5-30	At Tor.	L	1-2	(11)	6	8	Wells	Pall		23-22	4th	3
5-31	At Tor.	L	2-3		3	5	Morris	Thigpen		23-23	4th	3½
6-1	At K.C.	W	5-3		8	7	Fernandez	Boddicker		24-23	4th	2½
6-2	At K.C.	L	1-2		5	6	Gubicza	Radinsky	Montgomery	24-24	4th	3½
6-3	At K.C.	L	1-3		6	8	Magnante	Hibbard	Montgomery	24-25	4th	4½
6-5	Oak.	L	3-10		9	13	Darling	McCaskill		24-26	4th	5½
6-6	Oak.	L	4-6		6	9	Stewart	Fernandez	Eckersley	24-27	4th	6½
6-7	Oak.	W	6-1		8	3	Hough	Moore		25-27	4th	5½
6-8	Cal.	W	5-1		13	5	McDowell	Finley	Thigpen	26-27	4th	4½
6-9	Cal.	W	4-2		9	7	Hibbard	Valera	Radinsky	27-27	4th	4½
6-10	Cal.	W	3-2	(12)	12	8	Pall	Frey		28-27	4th	4½
6-11	Cal.	L	0-4		9	7	Blyleven	Fernandez	Grahe	28-28	4th	5
6-12	At Min.	L	1-5		7	6	Smiley	Hough	Aguilera	28-29	4th	6
6-13	At Min.	W	4-2		7	9	McDowell	Erickson	Thigpen	29-29	4th	6
6-14	At Min.	L	7-8		15	9	Edens	Radinsky		29-30	4th	7
6-15	At Sea.	L	1-4		11	6	DeLucia	McCaskill	Swan	29-31	4th	8
6-16	At Sea.	L	6-9		5	14	Gunderson	Radinsky	Schooler	29-32	4th	8
6-17	At Sea.	L	1-2		5	4	Hanson	Hough	Schooler	29-33	4th	8
6-18	At Sea.	L	4-5	(11)	17	13	Gunderson	Alvarez		29-34	4th	8½
6-19	Det.	L	3-8	(13)	9	10	Terrell	Alvarez		29-35	4th	9½
6-20	Det.	W	3-1		5	7	McCaskill	Groom	Thigpen	30-35	4th	8½
6-21	Det.	W	6-5		9	8	Hernandez	Terrell	Thigpen	31-35	4th	7½
6-22	Cle.	W	7-1		9	7	Hough	Nagy		32-35	4th	7½
6-23	Cle.	W	7-1		12	8	McDowell	Otto		33-35	4th	7½
6-24	Cle.	W	4-3		8	7	Hernandez	Power		34-35	4th	7½
6-26	At N.Y.	W	2-1		5	3	McCaskill	Habyan	Radinsky	35-35	4th	7

Date	Opp.	Res.	Score	(inn.*)	Hits	Opp. hits	Winning pitcher	Losing pitcher	Save	Record	Pos.	GB
6-27	At N.Y.	L	7-8		11	10	Burke	Radinsky		35-36	4th	7
6-28	At N.Y.	W	6-3		8	6	Hough	Perez	Thigpen	36-36	4th	6
6-29	At Cle.	W	9-6		12	10	McDowell	Scudder	Thigpen	37-36	4th	6
6-30	At Cle.	L	4-5		12	14	Lilliquist	Leach		37-37	4th	7
7-1	At Cle.	W	8-5		16	11	McCaskill	Armstrong	Thigpen	38-37	4th	7
7-2	Bos.	W	8-3		15	4	Alvarez	Clemens	Hernandez	39-37	4th	6½
7-3	Bos.	W	2-1	(10)	9	4	Thigpen	Harris		40-37	4th	5½
7-4	Bos.	L	1-2		4	8	Hesketh	McDowell	Reardon	40-38	4th	6½
7-5	Bos.	W	4-2		9	5	Hibbard	Gardiner	Radinsky	41-38	4th	6½
7-6	At Bal.	L	3-4	(14)	6	13	Mills	Hernandez		41-39	4th	7½
7-7	At Bal.	W	8-4		13	8	Alvarez	Milacki		42-39	4th	6½
7-8	At Bal.	L	3-5		9	8	Mills	Hough	Frohwirth	42-40	4th	7½
7-9	At Bos.	W	10-3		17	7	McDowell	Hesketh		43-40	4th	6½
7-10	At Bos.	L	5-6		8	9	Reardon	Leach		43-41	4th	7½
7-11	At Bos.	L	2-11		6	14	Dopson	McCaskill		43-42	4th	8½
7-12	At Bos.	L	0-3		4	8	Viola	Alvarez	Harris	43-43	4th	9½
7-16	Mil.	W	5-4	(12)	14	10	Hernandez	Plesac		44-43	4th	9½
7-17	Mil.	L	3-4	(11)	3	9	Plesac	Radinsky	Henry	44-44	4th	10½
7-18	Mil.	L	1-3		7	7	Bones	McDowell	Henry	44-45	4th	10½
7-19	Mil.	L	3-6		11	7	Eldred	Hibbard	Henry	44-46	4th	11½
7-20	Bal.	L	2-3	(12)	11	8	Clements	Hernandez	Olson	44-47	4th	11½
7-21	Bal.	W	10-7		12	10	Leach	Frohwirth		45-47	4th	10½
7-22	Bal.	W	7-5		10	12	Pall	Olson	Radinsky	46-47	4th	10½
7-23	At Mil.	W	6-2		10	11	McDowell	Bones	Radinsky	47-47	4th	10
7-24	At Mil.	L	2-3		9	8	Fetters	Leach	Henry	47-48	4th	10½
7-25	At Mil.	L	0-3		7	6	Bosio	Hough		47-49	4th	11½
7-26	At Mil.	L	4-15		7	12	Wegman	McCaskill		47-50	4th	12½
7-28 (1)	At Det.	W	8-6		10	11	McDowell	Gullickson	Radinsky	48-50	4th	11
7-28 (2)	At Det.	W	5-3		12	10	Fernandez	Groom	Thigpen	49-50	4th	10½
7-29	At Det.	W	8-6		15	9	Leach	Munoz	Radinsky	50-50	4th	9½
7-31	Sea.	L	3-6		9	11	Johnson	Hough	Swan	50-51	4th	10
8-1	Sea.	W	8-1		11	6	McCaskill	Hanson	Hibbard	51-51	4th	10
8-2	Sea.	W	7-4		11	9	McDowell	Fleming	Radinsky	52-51	4th	10
8-4	Min.	W	19-11		19	19	Alvarez	Krueger	Pall	53-51	3rd	9
8-5	Min.	W	9-5		17	9	Hough	Tapani		54-51	3rd	9
8-6	Min.	W	5-3		11	7	McCaskill	Smiley	Hernandez	55-51	3rd	9
8-7	At Cal.	L	1-3		5	11	Langston	McDowell	Grahe	55-52	3rd	10
8-8	At Cal.	W	8-2		11	4	Hernandez	Frey		56-52	3rd	10
8-9	At Cal.	W	12-8	(14)	20	13	Pall	Bailes		57-52	3rd	9
8-10	At Oak.	L	3-5		5	7	Darling	Hough	Eckersley	57-53	3rd	10
8-11	At Oak.	W	10-6		14	7	Hernandez	Honeycutt	Radinsky	58-53	3rd	9
8-12	At Oak.	L	1-2		8	8	Eckersley	McDowell		58-54	3rd	10
8-14	N.Y.	W	6-2		9	11	Radinsky	Kamieniecki	Hernandez	59-54	3rd	9½
8-15	N.Y.	L	2-4		7	11	Militello	Hough	Farr	59-55	3rd	10½
8-16	N.Y.	W	4-2		7	7	McCaskill	Hillegas	Radinsky	60-55	3rd	10½
8-17	N.Y.	W	4-3		5	5	Hibbard	Perez	Radinsky	61-55	3rd	10
8-18	Tex.	W	3-0		9	6	McDowell	Brown		62-55	3rd	9
8-19	Tex.	W	3-2		7	5	Fernandez	Guzman	Radinsky	63-55	3rd	8
8-20	Tex.	L	1-6		6	13	Pavlik	Hough		63-56	3rd	9
8-21	K.C.	L	3-4		7	8	Meacham	McCaskill	Montgomery	63-57	3rd	9
8-22	K.C.	W	3-2		6	10	Hibbard	Pichardo	Radinsky	64-57	3rd	9
8-23	K.C.	W	3-1		6	5	McDowell	Reed		65-57	3rd	9
8-24	Tor.	W	8-4		11	10	Fernandez	Linton		66-57	3rd	9
8-25	Tor.	W	6-3		9	10	Hough	Wells	Hernandez	67-57	3rd	8
8-26	Tor.	L	0-9		1	11	Stottlemyre	McCaskill		67-58	3rd	8
8-28	At Tex.	L	1-4		5	11	Brown	Hibbard		67-59	3rd	9
8-29	At Tex.	W	6-4		9	7	McDowell	Witt	Hernandez	68-59	3rd	9
8-30	At Tex.	L	4-10		11	12	Guzman	Fernandez		68-60	3rd	10
8-31	At Tor.	L	2-9		5	9	Stottlemyre	Hough		68-61	3rd	10
9-1	At Tor.	L	3-9		4	11	Morris	McCaskill		68-62	3rd	10
9-2	At Tor.	W	3-2		5	12	Hibbard	Key	Hernandez	69-62	3rd	9
9-3	At K.C.	W	7-3		13	10	McDowell	Aquino		70-62	3rd	8½
9-4	At K.C.	W	8-0		14	6	Fernandez	Appier		71-62	3rd	7½
9-5	At K.C.	W	12-6	(8)	14	9	Alvarez	Berenguer		72-62	3rd	6½
9-6	At K.C.	L	2-3		8	7	Gordon	Hernandez	Montgomery	72-63	3rd	7½
9-8 (1)	Det.	W	4-3		6	9	McDowell	Tanana	Hernandez	73-63	3rd	7
9-8 (2)	Det.	W	4-3		4	5	Leach	Leiter	Radinsky	74-63	3rd	6½
9-9	Det.	W	6-4		9	4	Leach	Gullickson	Hernandez	75-63	3rd	6½
9-10	Det.	L	0-8		4	12	Haas	Fernandez		75-64	3rd	7½
9-11	Cle.	L	1-5		6	14	Nagy	Hibbard		75-65	3rd	8½
9-12	Cle.	L	3-5		7	10	Plunk	McCaskill	Olin	75-66	3rd	9½
9-13	Cle.	L	1-2	(13)	7	13	Plunk	Thigpen	Olin	75-67	3rd	10½
9-14	At N.Y.	W	8-6		12	8	Alvarez	Wickman	Hernandez	76-67	3rd	10½
9-15	At N.Y.	W	4-2		7	9	Fernandez	Monteleone	Thigpen	77-67	3rd	10½

— 30 —

Date	Opp.	Res.	Score	(inn.*)	Hits	Opp. hits	Winning pitcher	Losing pitcher	Save	Record	Pos.	GB
9-16	At N.Y.	W	9-6		18	12	Leach	Hitchcock	Hernandez	78-67	3rd	10½
9-18	At Cle.	W	8-7		9	10	McCaskill	Mlicki	Hernandez	79-67	3rd	10½
9-19	At Cle.	L	4-5		7	9	Plunk	McDowell	Olin	79-68	3rd	10½
9-20	At Cle.	W	10-8		13	11	Dunne	Mesa	Thigpen	80-68	3rd	10½
9-21	Oak.	L	5-6		12	10	Darling	Fernandez	Eckersley	80-69	3rd	11½
9-22	Oak.	W	8-3		13	9	Hough	Witt		81-69	3rd	10½
9-23	Oak.	W	17-6		15	8	McCaskill	Moore		82-69	3rd	9½
9-24	Oak.	L	1-4		5	6	Welch	McDowell	Eckersley	82-70	3rd	10½
9-25	Cal.	W	6-5		10	12	Hernandez	Grahe		83-70	3rd	9½
9-26	Cal.	L	0-1		5	7	Finley	Fernandez	Frey	83-71	3rd	9½
9-27	Cal.	W	3-2	(11)	7	8	Hernandez	Crim		84-71	3rd	8½
9-28	At Min.	W	9-4		16	9	McCaskill	Mahomes		85-71	3rd	8
9-29	At Min.	L	4-5		7	8	Edens	Radinsky		85-72	3rd	9
9-30	At Min.	W	4-3		13	8	Dunne	Erickson	Hernandez	86-72	3rd	8
10-1	At Min.	L	6-9		9	14	Willis	Leach	Aguilera	86-73	3rd	8
10-2	At Sea.	L	0-2		8	5	Fleming	Hough		86-74	3rd	8
10-3	At Sea.	L	2-7		4	11	Johnson	McCaskill		86-75	3rd	9
10-4	At Sea.	L	3-4		5	10	Fisher	McDowell	Nelson	86-76	3rd	10

Monthly records: April (11-8), May (12-15), June (14-14), July (13-14), August (18-10), September (18-11), Oct. (0-4).

HIGHLIGHTS

High point: A 6-4 win over Detroit on September 9 gave the White Sox seven wins in their last eight games and left them just 6½ games out of first place.

Low point: Chicago lost its next four games, falling 10½ games behind front-running Oakland.

Turning point: The White Sox posted a 2-14 record in back-to-back road trips in May-June and never recovered.

Most valuable player: First baseman Frank Thomas. He became just the eighth player in modern major league history to bat over .300 with 20 homers, 100 RBIs, 100 runs and 100 walks in consecutive seasons.

Most valuable pitcher: Righthander Jack McDowell. He won a career-high 20 games, paced the league in complete games (13) and ranked among the A.L. leaders in innings pitched (260⅔), strikeouts (178) and ERA (3.18).

Most improved player: Shortstop Craig Grebeck. He proved to be an everyday player in the wake of Ozzie Guillen's season-ending injury. Until he missed the last 54 games with a broken right foot, Grebeck hit .268 with 35 RBIs and just eight errors in 88 games.

Most pleasant surprise: Righthander Roberto Hernandez. Less than one year removed from life-threatening vein surgery on his right forearm, he led A.L. relievers (with 50 or more innings pitched) in opponents' batting average (.180), ranked third in ERA (1.65), fanned 68 batters in 71 innings and took over the closer's role.

Biggest disappointment: Righthander Bobby Thigpen. Baseball's single-season saves record holder struggled to notch a team-high 22 last year. Consequently, he lost his closer's role and finished with a 4.75 ERA.

Key injuries: Guillen's season ended April 21 when he injured his knee in a collision with Tim Raines. Carlton Fisk's foot injury kept the catcher out of the lineup until June 9.

Notable: The White Sox were just the eighth team ever, and the first since Toronto in 1985, to have three pitchers (Thigpen, Hernandez and lefthander Scott Radinsky) with 10 or more saves apiece. . . . Center fielder Lance Johnson, who led the league with 12 triples, registered the longest hitting streak in the majors (25 games). . . . Raines (45 steals) and Johnson (41) became the first White Sox duo to steal 40 bases each in a season since 1966, when Don Buford (51) and Tommie Agee (44) turned the trick.

—DAVE VAN DYCK

RECORDS

1992 regular-season record: 86-76 (3rd in A.L. West); 50-32 at home; 36-44 on road; 47-37 vs. East; 39-39 vs. West; 23-19 vs. LHP; 63-57 vs. RHP; 78-57 on grass; 8-19 on turf; 23-19 in daytime; 63-57 at night; 26-29 in one-run games; 6-10 in extra-inning games; 2-0-0 in doubleheaders.

Team record last five years: 407-401 (.504, ranks 6th in league in that span).

TEAM LEADERS

Batting average: Frank Thomas (.323).
At-bats: George Bell (627).
Runs: Frank Thomas (108).
Hits: Frank Thomas (185).
Total bases: Frank Thomas (307).
Doubles: Frank Thomas (46).
Triples: Lance Johnson (12).
Home runs: George Bell (25).
Runs batted in: Frank Thomas (115).
Stolen bases: Tim Raines (45).
Slugging percentage: Frank Thomas (.536).
On-base percentage: Frank Thomas (.439).
Wins: Jack McDowell (20).
Earned-run average: Jack McDowell (3.18).
Complete games: Jack McDowell (13).
Shutouts: Alex Fernandez (2).
Saves: Bobby Thigpen (22).
Innings pitched: Jack McDowell (260⅔).
Strikeouts: Jack McDowell (178).

GAMES BY POSITION

Catcher: Ron Karkovice 119, Carlton Fisk 54, Matt Merullo 16, Nelson Santovenia 2, Scott Hemond 1.

First base: Frank Thomas 158, Chris Cron 5, Dan Pasqua 5, Dale Sveum 2, Robin Ventura 2.

Second base: Steve Sax 141, Joey Cora 28.

Third base: Robin Ventura 157, Craig Grebeck 7, Joey Cora 5, Dale Sveum 2, Scott Hemond 1.

Shortstop: Craig Grebeck 85, Esteban Beltre 43, Dale Sveum 37, Ozzie Guillen 12, Joey Cora 6, Scott Hemond 3.

Outfield: Lance Johnson 157, Tim Raines 129, Shawn Abner 94, Dan Pasqua 81, Mike Huff 56, Warren Newson 50, George Bell 15, Shawn Jeter 8, Craig Grebeck 2, Scott Hemond 2, Chris Cron 1, Ron Karkovice 1.

Designated hitter: George Bell 140, Joey Cora 18, Tim Raines 14, Esteban Beltre 4, Scott Hemond 4, Warren Newson 4, Shawn Jeter 3, Carlton Fisk 2, Frank Thomas 2, Shawn Abner 1, Mike Huff 1, Matt Merullo 1, Dan Pasqua 1.

TOP 10 DRAFT CHOICES

1. Eddie Pearson, 1B, Bishop State Junior College (Ala.).

2. A.J. Hinch, C, Midwest City (Okla.) High School.

3. Byron Mathews, OF, University of Oklahoma.

4. Scott Patton, OF, Capistrano Valley High School, Mission Viejo, Calif.

5. Tim Moore, RHP, Stanford University.

6. Chris Snopek, 3B, University of Mississippi.

7. Mickey McKinion, RHP, Montgomery High School, Semmes, Ala.

8. Robert Theodile, RHP, San Jacinto College (Tex.).

9. Carmine Cappuccio, OF, Rollins College (Fla.).

10. Andres Levias, OF, El Camino College (Calif.).

CLEVELAND INDIANS
AMERICAN LEAGUE EAST DIVISION

1993 SCHEDULE

APRIL

SUN	MON	TUE	WED	THU	FRI	SAT
				1	2	3
4	5 NY H	6	7 N NY	8 N NY H	9 TOR	10 TOR
11 TOR	12 BOS	13	14 BOS	15 N BOS	16 N TOR H	17 TOR H
18 TOR H	19 H CAL	20 N CAL	21 N CAL	22 CAL	23 N OAK	24 OAK
25 OAK	26 N SEA	27 SEA	28 SEA	29	30 N OAK H	

MAY

SUN	MON	TUE	WED	THU	FRI	SAT
						1 OAK H
2 OAK H	3 CAL H	4 N CAL	5 N SEA H	6 SEA H	7 N CHI	8 N CHI
9 CHI	10	11 N KC H	12 N KC H	13 N KC H	14 N MIL	15 MIL
16 MIL	17 N BAL	18 N BAL	19 N BAL	20 N BAL	21 N DET H	22 DET H
23 DET H	24 N TEX H	25 N TEX H	26 N TEX H	27	28 N MIN	29 N MIN
30 MIN	31 NY					

JUNE

SUN	MON	TUE	WED	THU	FRI	SAT
		1 N NY	2 N NY	3	4 N MIN	5 MIN
6 MIN	7 N BOS	8 N BOS H	9 N BOS H	10	11 N TEX	12 N TEX
13 N TEX	14 DET	15 N DET	16 N DET	17 DET	18 N BAL H	19 BAL H
20 BAL H	21 MIL H	22 N MIL H	23 N MIL H	24 N MIL	25 N KC	26 N KC H
27 KC H	28 N CHI H	29 N CHI H	30 N CHI H			

JULY

SUN	MON	TUE	WED	THU	FRI	SAT
				1	2 N CAL	3 N CAL
4 N CAL	5 OAK	6 N OAK	7 OAK	8	9 N SEA	10 N SEA
11 SEA	12	13 * ALL-STAR GAME	14	15 N CAL H	16 N CAL H	17 N CAL H
18 CAL H	19 N OAK H	20 N OAK H	21 N OAK H	22 N SEA H	23 N SEA H	24 N SEA H
25 SEA H	26 N CHI	27 N CHI	28 N CHI	29	30 N KC	31 N KC

AUGUST

SUN	MON	TUE	WED	THU	FRI	SAT
1 KC	2	3 N DET H	4 N DET H	5 N DET H	6 N BAL	7 N BAL
8 BAL	9	10 N MIL	11 N MIL	12 MIL	13 N TEX H	14 N TEX H
15 TEX H	16 N TOR H	17 N TOR H	18 N TOR H	19 N BOS	20 N BOS	21 BOS
22 BOS	23 N TOR	24 N TOR	25 N TOR	26 N NY	27 N NY H	28 N NY H
29 NY H	30	31 N MIN				

SEPTEMBER

SUN	MON	TUE	WED	THU	FRI	SAT
			1 N MIN	2 MIN	3 N NY	4 N NY
5 NY	6	7 N MIN H	8 N MIN H	9 N MIN H	10 N BOS H	11 BOS H
12 BOS H	13 N TEX	14 N TEX	15 TEX	16	17 N DET	18 DET
19 DET	20 N BAL H	21 N BAL H	22 N BAL H	23	24 N MIL H	25 MIL H
26 MIL H	27 N KC	28 N KC	29 KC	30		

OCTOBER

SUN	MON	TUE	WED	THU	FRI	SAT
					1 N CHI H	2 CHI H
3 CHI H						

1993 SEASON

CLUB DIRECTORY

Board of directors
Richard E. Jacobs
Martin J. Cleary
Gary L. Bryenton
Chairman of the board and CEO
Richard E. Jacobs
Executive vice president, general manager
Rick Bay
Executive vice president, business
Dennis Lehman
V.p., marketing and communications
Jeff Overton
Vice president
Martin J. Cleary
Vice president, public relations
Bob DiBiasio
Vice president, finance
Gregg Olson
Dir. of baseball operations/asst. g.m.
Dan O'Dowd
Special assistant to the g.m./director of player procurement
Mickey White
Director, team travel
Mike Seghi
Manager, minor league operations
Mark Shapiro
Manager, scouting operations
Jay Green
Administrator, player personnel
Wendy Hoppel
Administrator, scouting
Murray Brunton
Manager, media relations
John Maroon
Assistant director, media relations
Susie Gharrity
Director, community relations
Glen Shumate
Coordinator, community relations
Eva Manning
Director, advertising
Valerie Arcuri
Director, promotions/sales
Jon Starrett
Manager, promotions/special events
Nadine Glinski
Coordinator, advertising/publications
Kim Carpinello
Controller
Ken Stefanov
Director, ticket services
Connie Minadeo
Manager, box office
Tom McGrane
Director, ticket sales
Vic Gregovits

Coordinator, season/group sales
Diane Stack
Director, ballpark operations
Jim Folk
Director, merchandising/licensing
Jayne Churchmack
Equipment and clubhouse manager
Cy Buynak
Assistant clubhouse manager
Jeff Sipos
Visiting clubhouse manager
Bill Sheridan
Medical director
Dr. William T. Wilder
Orthopedic specialist
Dr. Louis Keppler
Trainer
Jim Warfield
Assistant trainer
Paul Spicuzza
Team physicians
Dr. John Brantigan
Dr. Godofredo Domingo
Dr. K.V. Gopal
Dr. David Schultz
Dr. Zenos Vangelos
National cross-checker scout
Tony DeMacio
Director, East Coast scouting operations
Shawn Pender
Director, West Coast scouting operations
Jay Robertson
West Coast scouting supervisor
Jesse Flores
Scouts
Luis Aponte
Steve Avila
Mark Baca
Tom Chandler
Ramon Conde
Tom Couston
Jeff Datz
Joe Delucca
Mark Germann
Buzzy Keller
Jerry LaPenta
Alan Lewis
Winston Llenas
Rick Magnante
Bob Mayer
Buddy Mercado
Mark McKnight
Jim Richardson
Doug Takaragawa
Mark Weidemaier

SCHEDULE KEY

H—Home game.   N—Night game (any game starting after 5 p.m.).
*All-Star Game at Oriole Park at Camden Yards, Baltimore.

Manager—Mike Hargrove (21).
Coaches—Rick Adair (24), Ken Bolek (51), Dom Chiti (30), Ron Clark (6),
Jose Morales (34), Dave Nelson (14), Jeff Newman (55).

No.	PITCHERS	B/T	Ht./Wt.	Born	1992 clubs
59	Bryant, Shawn	R/L	6-2/190	6-10-69	Kinston
32	Christopher, Mike	R/R	6-5/205	11-3-63	Colorado Springs, Cleveland
39	Cook, Dennis	L/L	6-3/185	10-4-62	Cleveland
45	DiPoto, Jerry	R/R	6-2/203	5-24-68	Colorado Springs
56	Embree, Alan	L/L	6-2/185	1-23-70	Kinston, Cleveland, Canton/Akron
64	Kramer, Tom	B/R	6-0/190	1-9-68	Colorado Springs
28	Lilliquist, Derek	L/L	6-0/214	2-20-66	Cleveland
49	Mesa, Jose	R/R	6-3/222	5-22-66	Baltimore, Cleveland
36	Mlicki, Dave	R/R	6-4/185	6-8-68	Canton/Akron, Cleveland
50	Mutis, Jeff	L/L	6-2/185	12-20-66	Colorado Springs, Cleveland
41	Nagy, Charles	L/R	6-3/200	5-5-67	Cleveland
17	Ojeda, Bob	L/L	6-1/195	12-17-57	Los Angeles
31	Olin, Steve	R/R	6-2/190	10-4-65	Cleveland
38	Plunk, Eric	R/R	6-5/205	9-3-63	Canton/Akron, Cleveland
48	Power, Ted	R/R	6-4/220	1-31-55	Cleveland
47	Scudder, Scott	R/R	6-2/185	2-14-68	Cleveland, Colorado Springs
52	Shinall, Zak	R/R	6-4/212	10-14-68	Albuquerque
46	Wertz, William	R/R	6-6/220	1-15-67	Canton/Akron
53	Wickander, Kevin	L/L	6-3/200	1-4-65	Colorado Springs, Cleveland

No.	CATCHERS	B/T	Ht./Wt.	Born	1992 clubs
15	Alomar, Sandy	R/R	6-5/215	6-18-66	Cleveland
12	Levis, Jesse	L/R	5-9/180	4-14-68	Colorado Springs, Cleveland
4	Skinner, Joel	R/R	6-4/204	2-21-61	Canton/Akron

No.	INFIELDERS	B/T	Ht./Wt.	Born	1992 clubs
9	Baerga, Carlos	B/R	5-11/165	11-4-68	Cleveland
10	Espinoza, Alvaro	R/R	6-0/190	2-19-62	Colorado Springs
16	Fermin, Felix	R/R	5-11/170	10-9-63	Cleveland
2	Hernandez, Jose	R/R	6-1/180	7-14-69	Canton/Akron, Cleveland
44	Jefferson, Reggie	B/L	6-4/210	9-25-68	Colorado Springs, Cleveland
20	Lewis, Mark	R/R	6-1/190	11-30-69	Cleveland
42	Martinez, Carlos	R/R	6-5/175	8-11-65	Colorado Springs, Cleveland
11	Sorrento, Paul	L/R	6-2/223	11-17-65	Cleveland
25	Thome, Jim	L/R	6-4/215	8-27-70	Colorado Springs, Cleveland, Canton/Akron

No.	OUTFIELDERS	B/T	Ht./Wt.	Born	1992 clubs
8	Belle, Albert	R/R	6-2/200	8-25-66	Cleveland
1	Hill, Glenallen	R/R	6-2/210	3-22-65	Cleveland, Canton/Akron
33	Howard, Thomas	B/R	6-2/205	12-11-64	San Diego, Cleveland
35	Kirby, Wayne	L/R	5-10/185	1-22-64	Colorado Springs, Cleveland
7	Lofton, Kenny	L/L	6-0/180	5-31-67	Cleveland
58	Ramos, Ken	L/L	6-0/168	6-8-67	Canton/Akron
57	Sanders, Tracy	L/R	6-1/200	7-26-69	Canton/Akron
23	Whiten, Mark	B/R	6-3/215	11-25-66	Cleveland

BALLPARK INFORMATION

Ballpark (capacity, surface)
Cleveland Stadium (74,483, grass)
Address
Cleveland Stadium
Cleveland, OH 44114
Business phone
216-861-1200
Ticket information
216-241-5555
Ticket prices
$12 (box seats)
$9.50 (reserved seats)
$6 (general admission, adult)
$5 (g.a., youth 14 and under)
$5 (g.a., senior citizen 60 and older)
$5 (bleachers)
Field dimensions (from home plate)
To left field at foul line, 320 feet
To center field, 404 feet
To right field at foul line, 320 feet
First game played
July 31, 1932 (Philadelphia Athletics 1, Indians 0)

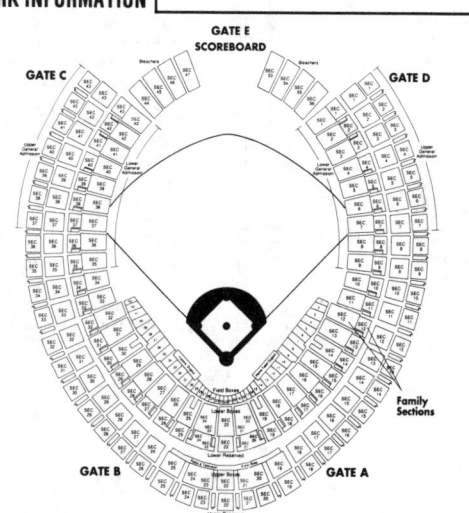

Class	Team	League	Manager
AAA	Charlotte	International	C. Manuel
AA	Canton/Akron	Eastern	Brian Graham
A	Kinston	Carolina	Dave Keller
A	Columbus, Ga.	South Atlantic	Mike Brown
A	Watertown	New York-Pennsylvania	Mike Young
Rookie	Burlington	Appalachian	Jim Gabella

BROADCAST INFORMATION

Radio: WKNR-AM (1220). Broadcasters: Tom Hamilton, Herb Score.
TV: WUAB-TV (Channel 43). Broadcasters: Mike Hegan, Jack Corrigan.
Cable TV: SportsChannel. Broadcasters: Rick Manning, John Sanders.

SPRING TRAINING

Ballpark (city): Chain O'Lakes (Winter Haven, Fla.).
Ticket information: 813-293-3900.

HISTORY

YEAR-BY-YEAR RECORDS

Year	Pos.	W	L	Pct.	*GB	Year	Pos.	W	L	Pct.	*GB
1901	7th	54	82	.397	29	1949	3rd	89	65	.578	8
1902	5th	69	67	.507	14	1950	4th	92	62	.597	6
1903	3rd	77	63	.550	15	1951	2nd	93	61	.604	5
1904	4th	86	65	.570	7½	1952	2nd	93	61	.604	2
1905	5th	76	78	.494	19	1953	2nd	92	62	.597	8½
1906	3rd	89	64	.582	5	1954	1st	111	43	.721 +	8
1907	4th	85	67	.559	8	1955	2nd	93	61	.604	3
1908	2nd	90	64	.584	½	1956	2nd	88	66	.571	9
1909	6th	71	82	.464	27½	1957	6th	76	77	.497	21½
1910	5th	71	81	.467	32	1958	4th	77	76	.503	14½
1911	3rd	80	73	.523	22	1959	2nd	89	65	.578	5
1912	5th	75	78	.490	30½	1960	4th	76	78	.494	21
1913	3rd	86	66	.566	9½	1961	5th	78	83	.484	30½
1914	8th	51	102	.333	48½	1962	6th	80	82	.494	16
1915	7th	57	95	.375	44½	1963	T5th	79	83	.488	25½
1916	6th	77	77	.500	14	1964	T6th	79	83	.488	20
1917	3rd	88	66	.571	12	1965	5th	87	75	.537	15
1918	2nd	73	54	.575	2½	1966	5th	81	81	.500	17
1919	2nd	84	55	.604	3½	1967	8th	75	87	.463	17
1920	1st	98	56	.636	+ 2	1968	3rd	86	75	.534	16½
1921	2nd	94	60	.610	4½	1969	6th	62	99	.385	46½
1922	4th	78	76	.507	16	1970	5th	76	86	.469	32
1923	3rd	82	71	.536	16½	1971	6th	60	102	.370	43
1924	6th	67	86	.438	24½	1972	5th	72	84	.462	14
1925	6th	70	84	.455	27½	1973	6th	71	91	.438	26
1926	2nd	88	66	.571	3	1974	4th	77	85	.475	14
1927	6th	66	87	.431	43½	1975	4th	79	80	.497	15½
1928	7th	62	92	.403	39	1976	4th	81	78	.509	16
1929	3rd	81	71	.533	24	1977	5th	71	90	.441	28½
1930	4th	81	73	.536	21	1978	6th	69	90	.434	29
1931	4th	78	76	.506	30	1979	6th	81	80	.503	22
1932	4th	87	65	.572	19	1980	6th	79	81	.494	23
1933	4th	75	76	.497	23½	1981	6th/5th	52	51	.504	‡
1934	3rd	85	69	.552	16	1982	T6th	78	84	.481	17
1935	3rd	82	71	.536	12	1983	7th	70	92	.432	28
1936	5th	80	74	.519	22½	1984	6th	75	87	.463	29
1937	4th	83	71	.539	19	1985	7th	60	102	.370	39½
1938	3rd	86	66	.566	13	1986	5th	84	78	.519	11½
1939	3rd	87	67	.565	20½	1987	7th	61	101	.377	37
1940	2nd	89	65	.578	1	1988	6th	78	84	.481	11
1941	T4th	75	79	.487	26	1989	6th	73	89	.451	16
1942	4th	75	79	.487	28	1990	4th	77	85	.475	11
1943	3rd	82	71	.536	15½	1991	7th	57	105	.352	34
1944	T5th	72	82	.468	17	1992	4th	76	86	.469	20
1945	5th	73	72	.503	11						
1946	6th	68	86	.442	36						
1947	4th	80	74	.519	17						
1948	1st†	97	58	.626 +	1						

*Games behind winner. †Won pennant playoff. ‡First half 26-24; second 26-27.

MANAGERS

Name	Record	Years
Jimmy McAleer	54-82	1901
Bill Armour	232-195	'02-04
Nap Lajoie	377-309	'05-09
Deacon McGuire	91-117	'09-11
George Stovall	74-62	1911
Harry Davis	54-71	1912
Joe Birmingham	170-191	'12-15
Lee Fohl	327-310	'15-19
Tris Speaker	617-520	'19-26
Jack McCallister	66-87	1927
Rog. Peckinpaugh	490-481	'28-33 1941
Walter Johnson	179-168	'33-35
Steve O'Neill	199-168	'35-37
Oscar Vitt	262-198	'38-40
Lou Boudreau	728-649	'42-50
Al Lopez	570-354	'51-56
Kerby Farrell	76-77	1957
Bobby Bragan	31-36	1958
Joe Gordon	184-19	'58-60
Jimmie Dykes	103-115	'60-61
Mel McGaha	80-82	1962
Birdie Tebbetts	269-298	'63-66
George Strickland	15-24	'66
Joe Adcock	75-87	1967
Alvin Dark	266-321	'68-71
Johnny Lipon	18-41	1971
Ken Aspromonte	220-260	'72-74
Frank Robinson	186-189	'75-77
Jeff Torborg	157-201	'77-79
Dave Garcia	247-244	'79-82
Mike Ferraro	40-60	1983
Pat Corrales	280-355	'83-87
Doc Edwards	173-207	'87-89
John Hart	8-11	1989
John McNamara	102-137	'90-91
Mike Hargrove	108-139	'91-92

DAY BY DAY

Date	Opp.	Res.	Score	(inn.*)	Hits	Opp. hits	Winning pitcher	Losing pitcher	Save	Record	Pos.	GB
4-6	At Bal.	L	0-2		5	6	Sutcliffe	Nagy		0-1	T5th	1
4-8	At Bal.	W	4-0		5	3	Otto	Milacki		1-1	T3rd	1
4-9	At Bal.	L	0-2		2	6	McDonald	Armstrong		1-2	T4th	2
4-11	Bos.	L	5-7	(19)	20	14	Gardiner	Bell		1-3	6th	3½
4-12 (1)	Bos.	W	2-1		0	9	Nagy	Young	Lilliquist	2-3	3rd	3½
4-12 (2)	Bos.	L	0-3		2	9	Clemens	Scudder		2-4	T4th	4
4-13	Det.	L	5-7		10	10	Leiter	Nichols	Henneman	2-5	4½	
4-14	Det.	W	8-7		15	8	Power	Lancaster	Olin	3-5	5th	4
4-15	Det.	L	1-8		9	10	King	Bell		3-6	6th	5
4-16	Det.	L	4-13		9	17	Gullickson	Cook		3-7	T6th	6
4-17	At N.Y.	W	11-1		15	6	Nagy	Sanderson		4-7	6th	5
4-18	At N.Y.	L	0-14		9	14	Cadaret	Otto		4-8	6th	6
4-19	At N.Y.	L	3-5		9	9	Johnson	Armstrong	Howe	4-9	6th	6
4-20	At N.Y.	W	3-1		5	5	Scudder	Perez	Olin	5-9	6th	6
4-21	At Tor.	L	1-2		5	5	Morris	Cook		5-10	6th	7
4-22	At Tor.	W	7-2		11	11	Nagy	Stieb	Power	6-10	6th	6
4-23	At Tor.	L	8-13		14	15	Stottlemyre	Otto		6-11	7th	7
4-24	Mil.	L	0-5		2	9	Plesac	Armstrong		6-12	T6th	8
4-26 (1)	Mil.	L	4-9		9	13	Bosio	Scudder		6-13	6th	8½
4-26 (2)	Mil.	W	3-1		8	7	Cook	Navarro	Power	7-13	6th	8
4-28	Oak.	L	1-3		7	7	Moore	Olin	Eckersley	7-14	7th	8
4-29	Oak.	W	5-2		13	10	Otto	Darling	Olin	8-14	6th	8
4-30	Cal.	L	5-8		10	9	Grahe	Shaw	Harvey	8-15	6th	8
5-1	Cal.	L	5-7		6	12	Langston	Scudder	Harvey	8-16	6th	8
5-2	Cal.	W	3-2		11	7	Lilliquist	Eichhorn	Olin	9-16	6th	7
5-3	Cal.	L	3-6		11	13	Bailes	Lilliquist	Harvey	9-17	7th	8
5-4	K.C.	L	6-11		8	15	Meacham	Nichols		9-18	7th	9
5-5	K.C.	W	8-6		10	10	Armstrong	Magnante	Olin	10-18	7th	9
5-6	At Tex.	W	7-2		9	6	Scudder	Witt	Wickander	11-18	7th	9
5-7	At Tex.	W	8-7		12	11	Nichols	Campbell	Olin	12-18	6th	9
5-8	At Min.	L	4-7		13	13	Erickson	Nagy	Aguilera	12-19	7th	9
5-9	At Min.	L	5-10		11	13	Smiley	Otto		12-20	7th	9
5-10	At Min.	L	6-10		12	13	Guthrie	Armstrong	Aguilera	12-21	7th	10
5-12	At K.C.	L	0-3		4	8	Gubicza	Scudder		12-22	7th	11
5-13	At K.C.	L	3-5		9	9	Appier	Cook	Montgomery	12-23	7th	12
5-15	Min.	W	5-0		9	6	Nagy	Erickson		13-23	7th	11½
5-16	Min.	L	6-8		13	11	Smiley	Armstrong	Aguilera	13-24	7th	12
5-17	Min.	L	5-9		11	15	Tapani	Cook	Aguilera	13-25	7th	12
5-18	Tex.	L	2-3		9	5	Brown	Lilliquist	Rogers	13-26	7th	12
5-19	Tex.	L	7-8		10	11	McCullers	Olin	Russell	13-27	7th	12
5-20	Tex.	L	0-1		5	7	Guzman	Nagy	Russell	13-28	6th	12½
5-22	At Sea.	L	1-2		5	5	Johnson	Scudder	Schooler	13-29	7th	13½
5-23	At Sea.	W	5-4		9	4	Lilliquist	Hanson	Olin	14-29	7th	12½
5-24	At Sea.	L	4-5		10	10	Jones	Olin		14-30	7th	13
5-25	At Oak.	W	10-6		16	11	Nagy	Slusarski	Power	15-30	7th	12
5-26	At Oak.	W	1-0		4	4	Otto	Welch	Olin	16-30	7th	12
5-27	At Oak.	W	4-2		6	8	Scudder	Stewart	Olin	17-30	7th	11
5-29	At Cal.	W	14-2		18	8	Boucher	Finley		18-30	7th	11
5-30	At Cal.	L	1-3		3	7	Blyleven	Armstrong	Harvey	18-31	7th	12
5-31	At Cal.	W	4-3		7	4	Nagy	Abbott	Olin	19-31	7th	12
6-2	Sea.	W	4-3		8	6	Otto	Hanson	Olin	20-31	7th	12½
6-3	Sea.	W	8-3		12	12	Scudder	Parker		21-31	7th	11½
6-4	Sea.	L	3-10		7	12	Fleming	Boucher		21-32	7th	12
6-6 (1)	At Bos.	L	1-5		9	8	Clemens	Armstrong		21-33	7th	12½
6-6 (2)	At Bos.	W	3-1		8	6	Nagy	Viola	Olin	22-33	7th	12
6-7	At Bos.	L	0-4		7	11	Hesketh	Otto	Darwin	22-34	7th	12
6-8	At Det.	L	2-9		11	11	Leiter	Scudder	Knudsen	22-35	7th	13
6-9	At Det.	W	6-1		11	5	Boucher	Tanana		23-35	7th	13
6-10	At Det.	W	4-2	(11)	9	6	Olin	Munoz		24-35	7th	13
6-12	N.Y.	W	3-0		5	5	Nagy	Kamieniecki		25-35	7th	12½
6-13	N.Y.	L	1-4		8	9	Perez	Otto		25-36	7th	12½
6-14	N.Y.	L	3-4	(10)	10	10	Monteleone	Power	Farr	25-37	7th	13½
6-15	Bal.	L	5-6		15	12	Davis	Cook	Olson	25-38	7th	14
6-16	Bal.	W	7-5		12	8	Armstrong	McDonald	Olin	26-38	7th	13
6-17	Bal.	W	3-2		5	13	Nagy	Mussina		27-38	7th	13
6-18	At Mil.	L	1-4		3	7	Wegman	Otto		27-39	7th	13
6-19	At Mil.	W	5-3		9	10	Scudder	Bones		28-39	7th	12
6-20	At Mil.	L	1-4		3	10	Bosio	Boucher	Henry	28-40	7th	13
6-21	At Mil.	L	2-4		8	7	Plesac	Armstrong	Henry	28-41	7th	13
6-22	At Chi.	L	1-7		7	9	Hough	Nagy		28-42	7th	14

Date	Opp.	Res.	Score	(inn.*)	Hits	Opp. hits	Winning pitcher	Losing pitcher	Save	Record	Pos.	GB
6-23	At Chi.	L	1-7		8	12	McDowell	Otto		28-43	7th	14½
6-24	At Chi.	L	3-4		7	8	Hernandez	Power		28-44	7th	15½
6-26	Tor.	L	1-6		4	10	Guzman	Armstrong		28-45	7th	16½
6-27	Tor.	W	6-4		13	8	Plunk	Ward		29-45	7th	15½
6-28	Tor.	W	7-6		12	8	Olin	Ward	Plunk	30-45	7th	14½
6-29	Chi.	L	6-9		10	12	McDowell	Scudder	Thigpen	30-46	7th	15½
6-30	Chi.	W	5-4		14	12	Lilliquist	Leach		31-46	7th	14½
7-1	Chi.	L	5-8		11	16	McCaskill	Armstrong	Thigpen	31-47	7th	15½
7-3	Oak.	W	8-1		15	5	Nagy	Darling		32-47	7th	15½
7-4	Oak.	W	8-1		18	7	Scudder	Downs	Power	33-47	7th	15½
7-5	Oak.	L	2-5		12	11	Welch	Armstrong	Eckersley	33-48	7th	16½
7-6	Oak.	L	4-13		10	17	Moore	Mutis		33-49	7th	17½
7-7	Cal.	W	3-1		8	4	Cook	Finley	Olin	34-49	7th	17½
7-8	Cal.	W	8-4		9	7	Nagy	Langston		35-49	7th	17½
7-9	At Tex.	L	4-14		10	12	Ryan	Scudder		35-50	7th	18½
7-10	At Tex.	L	5-6		7	14	Bohanon	Armstrong	Russell	35-51	7th	18½
7-11	At Tex.	L	1-5		6	12	Brown	Mutis		35-52	7th	18½
7-12	At Tex.	W	6-3		12	11	Olin	Rogers	Plunk	36-52	7th	17½
7-16	At K.C.	L	2-3		9	7	Pichardo	Mesa	Montgomery	36-53	7th	18½
7-17	At K.C.	L	3-4		5	8	Montgomery	Plunk		36-54	7th	18½
7-18	At K.C.	L	1-4		7	9	Appier	Armstrong	Meacham	36-55	7th	19½
7-19	At K.C.	W	4-3		11	7	Lilliquist	Shifflett	Olin	37-55	7th	19½
7-20	At Min.	W	5-1		8	11	Cook	Banks	Olin	38-55	7th	18½
7-21	At Min.	W	5-2		7	8	Mesa	Tapani	Olin	39-55	7th	18½
7-22	At Min.	L	1-2		3	10	Smiley	Nagy		39-56	7th	18½
7-23	K.C.	W	1-0	(14)	6	6	Wickander	Magnante		40-56	7th	18½
7-24	K.C.	L	3-8		11	16	Aquino	Scudder	Montgomery	40-57	7th	18½
7-25	K.C.	W	6-5		10	10	Olin	Meacham		41-57	7th	17½
7-26	K.C.	W	2-1	(13)	10	11	Olin	Shifflett		42-57	7th	16½
7-27	Mil.	L	0-4		3	13	Navarro	Nagy		42-58	7th	17
7-28	Mil.	W	4-2		12	6	Nichols	Bones	Lilliquist	43-58	7th	17
7-29	Mil.	W	4-3		10	7	Armstrong	Eldred	Lilliquist	44-58	7th	16
7-31	Det.	L	6-9		12	9	Kiely	Plunk	Henneman	44-59	7th	17½
8-1	Det.	W	8-5		13	7	Plunk	Lancaster	Lilliquist	45-59	7th	17½
8-2	Det.	L	4-5		11	5	Gullickson	Nagy	Henneman	45-60	7th	18½
8-3	At N.Y.	W	8-6	(12)	11	11	Olin	Habyan		46-60	7th	17½
8-4	At N.Y.	L	3-4		10	9	Young	Otto	Farr	46-61	7th	17½
8-5	At N.Y.	W	4-3	(11)	11	7	Lilliquist	Burke		47-61	7th	17½
8-7	At Bal.	W	5-4	(13)	12	9	Wickander	Mills		48-61	7th	17
8-8	At Bal.	W	6-0		13	1	Nagy	Rhodes		49-61	7th	16
8-9	At Bal.	L	2-3	(10)	7	10	Davis	Power		49-62	7th	16
8-10	Bos.	W	8-5		11	8	Armstrong	Quantrill	Olin	50-62	7th	16
8-11	Bos.	W	3-1		9	7	Otto	Viola	Lilliquist	51-62	T6th	15
8-12	Bos.	W	8-5		12	11	Plunk	Irvine	Olin	52-62	T6th	14
8-13	Bos.	L	2-4		9	8	Clemens	Nagy	Reardon	52-63	7th	15
8-14	Tor.	L	5-9		9	13	Wells	Nichols		52-64	7th	16
8-16 (1)	Tor.	W	4-2		11	7	Cook	Stottlemyre	Olin	53-64	7th	15½
8-16 (2)	Tor.	L	2-6		6	13	Morris	Otto		53-65	7th	16
8-18	Min.	W	8-1		11	9	Mesa	Erickson	Power	54-65	T6th	16
8-19	Min.	W	5-1		8	8	Nagy	Krueger		55-65	T5th	15
8-20	Min.	W	2-1	(10)	3	11	Plunk	Tapani		56-65	5th	14
8-21	Tex.	W	8-6		12	10	Cook	Ryan	Olin	57-65	5th	13
8-22	Tex.	W	6-1		13	5	Armstrong	Witt		58-65	4th	13
8-23	Tex.	L	4-14		12	15	Rogers	Olin		58-66	5th	13
8-25	At Sea.	L	0-6		2	11	Fleming	Nagy		58-67	5th	12½
8-26	At Sea.	W	6-3	(10)	11	11	Plunk	Swan	Olin	59-67	5th	12½
8-27	At Sea.	L	2-6		8	12	Fisher	Cook		59-68	6th	13½
8-28	At Oak.	L	6-7		13	8	Corsi	Armstrong	Eckersley	59-69	T6th	13½
8-29	At Oak.	L	1-4		4	7	Stewart	Mesa	Eckersley	59-70	T6th	13½
8-30	At Oak.	L	5-7		13	16	Darling	Nagy	Honeycutt	59-71	7th	14½
8-31	At Cal.	W	4-3		7	7	Nichols	Blyleven	Plunk	60-71	T6th	14½
9-1	At Cal.	L	6-7		10	14	Crim	Plunk	Grahe	60-72	T6th	15½
9-2	At Cal.	L	2-3	(15)	8	16	Lewis	Lilliquist		60-73	7th	15
9-4	Sea.	W	7-0		12	8	Mesa	Fleming		61-73	7th	15½
9-5	Sea.	W	5-4		9	6	Plunk	Swan		62-73	7th	15½
9-6	Sea.	W	12-9	(12)	14	16	Olin	Schooler		63-73	T6th	15½
9-7	At Mil.	L	0-2		5	6	Eldred	Cook	Henry	63-74	7th	15½
9-8	At Mil.	L	3-7		5	13	Bones	Armstrong	Fetters	63-75	7th	16½
9-9	At Mil.	W	5-4		9	8	Olin	Henry		64-75	6th	16½
9-11	At Chi.	W	5-1		14	6	Nagy	Hibbard		65-75	T5th	16
9-12	At Chi.	W	5-3		10	7	Plunk	McCaskill	Olin	66-75	5th	16
9-13	At Chi.	W	2-1	(13)	13	7	Plunk	Thigpen	Olin	67-75	5th	16
9-14	At Tor.	W	2-1		5	6	Mesa	Cone	Olin	68-75	5th	15
9-15	At Tor.	L	4-5		10	5	Guzman	Embree	Henke	68-76	5th	16

Date	Opp.	Res.	Score	(inn.*)	Hits	Opp. hits	Winning pitcher	Losing pitcher	Save	Record	Pos.	GB
9-16	At Tor.	W	6-3		13	7	Nagy	Stottlemyre	Power	69-76	4th	15
9-17	At Tor.	L	5-7	(10)	6	7	Ward	Plunk		69-77	T4th	16
9-18	Chi.	L	7-8		10	9	McCaskill	Mlicki	Hernandez	69-78	T4th	17
9-19	Chi.	W	5-4		9	7	Plunk	McDowell	Olin	70-78	T4th	17
9-20	Chi.	L	8-10		11	13	Dunne	Mesa	Thigpen	70-79	T4th	17
9-22	At Bos.	W	4-2		9	6	Power	Clemens	Lilliquist	71-79	5th	17
9-23	At Bos.	W	7-3		10	7	Nagy	Taylor		72-79	4th	16
9-24	At Bos.	L	4-6		11	9	Darwin	Scudder	Harris	72-80	5th	17
9-25	At Det.	L	5-6	(10)	14	11	Henneman	Olin		72-81	5th	18
9-26	At Det.	W	7-4		13	11	Armstrong	Knudsen	Olin	73-81	5th	17
9-27	At Det.	L	3-13		9	12	Terrell	Mesa		73-82	6th	18
9-28	N.Y.	W	6-4		11	11	Power	Militello	Olin	74-82	4th	17½
9-29	N.Y.	W	4-3		8	8	Nagy	Kamieniecki	Plunk	75-82	4th	17½
9-30	N.Y.	L	2-4		3	12	Perez	Mlicki	Farr	75-83	4th	17½
10-1	Bal.	L	2-3	(10)	12	6	Mussina	Plunk	Olson	75-84	T4th	18
10-2	Bal.	W	8-5		11	10	Nichols	Lefferts		76-84	T4th	18
10-3	Bal.	L	1-7		10	14	Rhodes	Embree	Williamson	76-85	T4th	19
10-4	Bal.	L	3-4	(13)	7	11	Mills	Plunk	Milacki	76-86	T4th	20

Monthly records: April (8-15), May (11-16), June (12-15), July (13-13), August (16-12), September (15-12), Oct. (1-3).

HIGHLIGHTS

High point: From August 1-September 23, the Indians posted a 28-20 record, putting themselves in position to make a run at fourth place in the A.L. East.
Low point: Cleveland possessed a 14-30 record May 24 and appeared destined for another 100-loss season.
Turning point: After Seattle took advantage of careless Cleveland defense to score three runs in the ninth inning of a 5-4 win over the Indians on May 24, Manager Mike Hargrove held a team meeting. The Indians finished their West Coast trip with a 5-1 record.
Most valuable player: Second baseman Carlos Baerga. He became only the second second baseman in history (Rogers Hornsby is the other) to bat .300 (.312), hit 20 homers, drive in 100 runs (105) and collect 200 hits (205) in a season.
Most valuable pitcher: Righthander Charles Nagy. In only his second full season in the big leagues, he posted a 17-10 record with a 2.96 ERA.
Most improved player: Lefthander Derek Lilliquist. At first, Hargrove trusted Lilliquist only against lefthanded hitters. However, by midseason he was a setup man and occasional closer. He finished with a 5-3 mark, six saves and a 1.75 ERA.
Most pleasant surprise: First baseman Paul Sorrento. When Reggie Jefferson suffered an elbow injury in spring training, the Indians acquired Sorrento from the Twins. Sorrento blossomed into a capable defensive player and a clutch hitter in 1992, batting .269 with 18 homers and 60 RBIs.
Biggest disappointment: Lefthander Dave Otto. He began the season in the rotation, but a 5-9 record and 7.06 ERA cost him his big-league job and probably any future work in Cleveland.
Key injuries: Cleveland was anxious to see its "infield of the future" work together, but injuries to third baseman Jim Thome and Jefferson kept them off the field for virtually the entire season. Catcher Sandy Alomar's season was ruined by a variety of nagging injuries.

Notable: Center fielder Kenny Lofton, who set a franchise record with 66 stolen bases, became the first rookie to lead the A.L. in steals since 1956. . . . The Indians completed a triple play at Baltimore on August 7, their first since 1981. . . . Cleveland's 19-game improvement over its 1991 record matched the third-biggest turnaround in team history. . . . After the All-Star break, the Indians compiled a 40-34 record, third best in the A.L. East and fifth best in the league.

—SHELDON OCKER

RECORDS

1992 regular-season record: 76-86 (T4th in A.L. East); 41-40 at home; 35-46 on road; 36-42 vs. East; 40-44 vs. West; 20-23 vs. LHP; 56-63 vs. RHP; 68-69 on grass; 8-17 on turf; 21-31 in daytime; 55-55 at night; 26-24 in one-run games; 10-8 in extra-inning games; 0-4 in doubleheaders.
Team record last five years: 361-449 (.446, ranks 14th in league in that span).

TEAM LEADERS

Batting average: Carlos Baerga (.312).
At-bats: Carlos Baerga (657).
Runs: Kenny Lofton (96).
Hits: Carlos Baerga (205).
Total bases: Carlos Baerga (299).
Doubles: Carlos Baerga (32).
Triples: Kenny Lofton (8).
Home runs: Albert Belle (34).
Runs batted in: Albert Belle (112).
Stolen bases: Kenny Lofton (66).
Slugging percentage: Albert Belle (.477).
On-base percentage: Kenny Lofton (.362).
Wins: Charles Nagy (17).
Earned-run average: Charles Nagy (2.96).
Complete games: Charles Nagy (10).
Shutouts: Charles Nagy (3).
Saves: Steve Olin (29).
Innings pitched: Charles Nagy (252).
Strikeouts: Charles Nagy (169).

GAMES BY POSITION

Catcher: Sandy Alomar 88, Junior Ortiz 86, Jesse Levis 21.
First base: Paul Sorrento 121, Carlos Martinez 37, Reggie Jefferson 15, Brook Jacoby 10, Felix Fermin 2.
Second base: Carlos Baerga 160, Felix Fermin 7, Tony Perezchica 4.
Third base: Brook Jacoby 111, Jim Thome 40, Carlos Martinez 28, Felix Fermin 17, Tony Perezchica 9, Craig Worthington 9, Dave Rohde 5, Mark Lewis 1.
Shortstop: Mark Lewis 121, Felix Fermin 55, Tony Perezchica 4, Jose Hernandez 3.
Outfield: Mark Whiten 144, Kenny Lofton 143, Thomas Howard 97, Glenallen Hill 59, Albert Belle 52, Alex Cole 24, Wayne Kirby 2.
Designated hitter: Albert Belle 100, Glenallen Hill 34, Paul Sorrento 11, Reggie Jefferson 7, Alex Cole 4, Wayne Kirby 4, Carlos Martinez 4, Thomas Howard 2, Mark Whiten 2, Sandy Alomar 1, Carlos Baerga 1, Jesse Levis 1, Tony Perezchica 1.

TOP 10 DRAFT CHOICES

1. Paul Shuey, RHP, University of North Carolina.
2. Michael Matthews, LHP, Montgomery-Rockville (Md.) College.
3. Jonathan Nunnally, OF, Miami-Dade (Fla.) Community College South.
4. Matt Williams, LHP, Virginia Commonwealth University.
5. Jamie Taylor, 3B, Ohio State University.
6. Jeff Liefer, OF, Upland (Calif.) High School.
7. John Thobe, RHP, Rancho Santiago College (Calif.).
8. Greg Gregory, LHP, Millikan High School, Long Beach, Calif.
9. Larry Schneider, C, Tulane University.
10. Ryan Ritter, SS, Wheeler High School, Marietta, Ga.

DETROIT TIGERS
AMERICAN LEAGUE EAST DIVISION

1993 SCHEDULE

APRIL

SUN	MON	TUE	WED	THU	FRI	SAT
				1	2	3
4	5 N OAK	6 N	7 N OAK	8 N OAK	9 N CAL	10 N CAL
11 CAL	12	13 OAK H	14	15 OAK H	16 N SEA	17 N SEA H
18 SEA H	19 SEA	20 N TEX H	21 TEX H	22	23 N MIN	24 N MIN
25 MIN	26 N KC	27 KC	28 N TEX	29 TEX	30 MIN H	

MAY

SUN	MON	TUE	WED	THU	FRI	SAT
						1 MIN H
2 MIN H	3	4 N KC H	5 KC H	6	7 N NY H	8 N NY H
9 NY H	10 N NY	11 N TOR	12 N TOR	13 TOR	14 N BAL H	15 N BAL H
16 BAL H	17 N MIL	18 N MIL	19 N MIL	20 MIL	21 N CLE	22 CLE
23 CLE	24 N BOS H	25 N BOS H	26 BOS H	27	28 N SEA	29 SEA
30 N SEA	31					

JUNE

SUN	MON	TUE	WED	THU	FRI	SAT
		1 N CHI H	2 N CHI H	3 N CHI H	4 N CAL H	5 N CAL H
6 CAL H	7 N CHI	8 N CHI	9 N CHI	10 N TOR H	11 N TOR H	12 N TOR H
13 TOR H	14 N CLE H	15 N CLE H	16 N CLE H	17 N CLE H	18 N MIL H	19 N MIL H
20 MIL H	21	22 N BAL	23 N BAL	24 N BAL	25 N BOS	26 BOS
27 BOS	28 N NY	29 N NY	30 N NY			

JULY

SUN	MON	TUE	WED	THU	FRI	SAT
				1 N TEX H	2 N TEX H	3 N TEX H
4 TEX H	5 N MIN	6 N MIN	7 N MIN	8 N KC	9 N KC	10 N KC
11 KC	12	13 ◦ AL-STAR GAME	14	15 N TEX	16 N TEX	17 N TEX
18 N TEX	19 N MIN H	20 N MIN H	21 N MIN H	22 N KC H	23 N KC H	24 N KC H
25 KC H	26 N NY H	27 N NY H	28 N NY H	29 N TOR	30 N TOR	31 TOR

AUGUST

SUN	MON	TUE	WED	THU	FRI	SAT
1 TOR	2	3 N CLE	4 N CLE	5 N CLE	6 N BOS H	7 N BOS H
8 BOS H	9 N BAL H	10 N BAL H	11 N BAL H	12 N BAL H	13 N MIL	14 N MIL
15 MIL	16 N CAL	17 N CAL	18 N OAK	19	20 N OAK H	21 N OAK H
22 OAK H	23 N OAK H	24 N SEA H	25 N SEA H	26	27 N OAK	28 OAK
29 OAK	30 SEA	31 N SEA				

SEPTEMBER

SUN	MON	TUE	WED	THU	FRI	SAT
			1 SEA	2	3 N CHI	4 N CHI H
5 CHI H	6	7 N CAL H	8 N CAL H	9 N CAL H	10 N CHI	11 N CHI
12 CHI	13	14 N TOR H	15 N TOR H	16	17 N CLE H	18 N CLE H
19 CLE H	20 N MIL H	21 N MIL H	22 N MIL H	23	24 N BAL	25 BAL
26 BAL	27 N BOS	28 N BOS	29 N BOS	30 N BOS		

OCTOBER

SUN	MON	TUE	WED	THU	FRI	SAT
					1 N NY	2 NY
3 NY						

1993 SEASON

CLUB DIRECTORY

Owners
Michael Ilitch
Marian Ilitch

Board of directors
Michael Ilitch, Chairman
Marian Ilitch
Charles P. Jones
Jay Bielfield
Denise Ilitch Lites
Ronald Ilitch
Michael Ilitch Jr.
Lisa Ilitch Murray
Atanas Ilitch
Christopher Ilitch
Carole Ilitch

Owner, chairman, president
Michael Ilitch

Owner, secretary treasurer
Marian Ilitch

General counsel
Jay Bielfield

Chief financial officer
Gerald Pasternak

League affairs
John Ziegler

Senior director, general manager
Jerry A. Walker

Senior director, assistant general manager
Gary Vitto

Senior director scouting
Joe Klein

Director minor league operations
Dave Miller

Director field operations
John Lipon

Assistant director equipment
Jim Schmakel

Asst. manager equipment and clubhouse
John Nelson

Traveling secretary
Bill Brown

Asst. director baseball operations
Kevin Qualls

Team physicians
Clarence S. Livingood, M.D.
David J. Collon, M.D.
Louis Saco, M.D. (Florida)

Head trainer
Russ Miller

Trainer
Pio DiSalvo

Strength and conditioning coach
Brad Andress

Scouting
Gary Blaylock
Gwen Keating

Minor league staff
Audrey Zielinski

Senior director administration
Alice Sloane

Senior director public relations
Daniel A. Ewald

Director of marketing
Michael Dietz

Director of sales
Len Perna

Director of stadium operations
John Pettit

Controller
Scott Fisher

Director of community relations
Jim Price

Director ticket operations
Ken Marchetti

Director ticket sales
Gino D'Ambrosio

Assistant director public relations
Greg Shea

Marketing coordinator
James Brylewski

Group sales coordinator
Jeff Dodge

Community relations coordinator
Jodi Schroeder

Scouts
Ruben Amaro
Arnie Beyeler
Wayne Blackburn
Gary Blaylock
Robert Curran
Andy Hancock
Jack Hays
Rich Henning
Lou Laslo
Joe Lewis
Dennis Lieberthal
Juan Lopez
Jeff Malinoff
Stan Meek
John Mirabelli
Mark Monahan
Ramon Pena
Dee Phillips
Joe Robinson
Don Rowland
Bill Schudlich
Steve Souchock
Clyde Weir
Dick Wiencek
Rob Wilfong

SCHEDULE KEY

H—Home game.   N—Night game (any game starting after 5 p.m.).
*All-Star Game at Oriole Park at Camden Yards, Baltimore.

SPRING TRAINING ROSTER

Manager—Sparky Anderson (11).

Coaches—Larry Herndon (31), Billy Muffett (56), Gene Roof (52), Dick Tracewski (53), Dan Whitmer (59).

No.	PITCHERS	B/T	Ht./Wt.	Born	1992 clubs
49	Bolton, Tom	L/L	6-3/185	5-6-62	Boston, Cincinnati
41	DeSilva, John	R/R	6-0/193	9-30-67	Toledo, London
44	Doherty, John	R/R	6-4/210	6-11-67	Detroit
34	Gohr, Greg	R/R	6-3/205	10-29-67	Toledo
48	Gonzales, Frank	R/L	6-0/185	3-12-68	London, Toledo
42	Groom, Buddy	L/L	6-2/200	7-10-65	Toledo, Detroit
36	Gullickson, Bill	R/R	6-3/220	2-20-59	Detroit
16	Haas, Dave	R/R	6-1/200	10-19-65	Toledo, Detroit
39	Henneman, Mike	R/R	6-4/205	12-11-61	Detroit
35	Hudek, John	B/R	6-1/200	8-8-66	Birmingham, Vancouver
46	Kiely, John	R/R	6-3/215	10-4-64	Toledo, Detroit
27	Knudsen, Kurt	R/R	6-3/200	2-20-67	Toledo, Detroit
30	Krueger, Bill	L/L	6-5/205	4-24-58	Minnesota, Montreal
23	Leiter, Mark	R/R	6-3/210	4-13-63	Detroit
37	Lumley, Mike	R/R	6-1/185	1-29-67	London
21	Moore, Mike	R/R	6-4/205	11-26-59	Oakland
43	Munoz, Mike	L/L	6-2/200	7-12-65	Detroit

No.	CATCHERS	B/T	Ht./Wt.	Born	1992 clubs
19	Kreuter, Chad	R/R	6-2/195	8-26-64	Detroit
12	Rowland, Rich	R/R	6-1/215	2-25-67	Toledo, Detroit
20	Tettleton, Mickey	B/R	6-2/212	9-16-60	Detroit

No.	INFIELDERS	B/T	Ht./Wt.	Born	1992 clubs
9	Barnes, Skeeter	R/R	5-10/180	3-7-57	Detroit
13	Brogna, Rico	L/L	6-2/200	4-18-70	Toledo, Detroit
30	Cruz, Ivan	L/L	6-3/210	5-3-68	London
45	Fielder, Cecil	R/R	6-3/250	9-21-63	Detroit
24	Fryman, Travis	R/R	6-1/194	3-25-69	Detroit
7	Livingstone, Scott	L/R	6-0/198	7-15-65	Detroit
4	Phillips, Tony	B/R	5-10/175	4-25-59	Detroit
3	Trammell, Alan	R/R	6-0/175	2-21-58	Detroit
1	Whitaker, Lou	L/R	5-11/180	5-12-57	Detroit

No.	OUTFIELDERS	B/T	Ht./Wt.	Born	1992 clubs
29	Bautista, Danny	R/R	5-11/170	5-24-72	Fayetteville
40	Clark, Phil	R/R	6-0/180	5-6-68	Toledo, Detroit
22	Cuyler, Milt	B/R	5-10/185	10-7-68	Detroit
28	Deer, Rob	R/R	6-3/225	9-29-60	Detroit
32	Gladden, Dan	R/R	5-11/184	7-7-57	Detroit
10	Hare, Shawn	L/L	6-1/200	3-26-67	Toledo, Detroit
25	Hurst, Jody	R/L	6-4/185	3-11-67	Toledo, London
17	Ingram, Riccardo	R/R	6-0/198	9-10-66	Toledo

BALLPARK INFORMATION

Ballpark (capacity, surface)
Tiger Stadium (52,416, grass)

Address
Tiger Stadium
Detroit, MI 48216

Business phone
313-962-4000

Ticket information
313-962-4000

Ticket prices
$14 (box seats)
$11 (reserved seats)
$7 (grandstand reserved seats)
$4 (bleacher seats)

Field dimensions (from home plate)
To left field at foul line, 340 feet
To center field, 440 feet
To right field at foul line, 325 feet

First game played
April 20, 1912 (Cleveland Naps 6, Tigers 5)

MINOR LEAGUE AFFILIATES

Class	Team	League	Manager
AAA	Toledo	International	Joe Sparks
AA	London, Ont.	Eastern	Tom Runnells
A	Fayetteville	South Atlantic	Mark Wagner
A	Lakeland	Florida State	Gerry Groninger
A	Niagara Falls	New York-Pennsylvania	Larry Parrish
Rookie	Bristol	Appalachian	Ruben Amaro

BROADCAST INFORMATION

Radio: WJR-AM (760). Broadcasters: Rick Rizzs, Bob Rathbun, Ernie Harwell. **TV:** WDIV-TV (Channel 4). Broadcasters: Al Kaline, George Kell. **Cable TV:** Pro Am Sports Systems. Broadcasters: Jim Northrup, Larry Osterman.

SPRING TRAINING

Ballpark (city): Marchant Stadium (Lakeland, Fla.). **Ticket information:** 813-682-1401.

HISTORY

YEAR-BY-YEAR RECORDS

Year	Pos.	W	L	Pct.	*GB	Year	Pos.	W	L	Pct.	*GB
1901	3rd	74	61	.548	8½	1950	2nd	95	59	.617	3
1902	7th	52	83	.385	30½	1951	5th	73	81	.474	25
1903	5th	65	71	.478	25	1952	8th	50	104	.325	45
1904	7th	62	90	.408	32	1953	6th	60	94	.390	40½
1905	3rd	79	74	.516	15½	1954	5th	68	86	.442	43
1906	6th	71	78	.477	21	1955	5th	79	75	.513	17
1907	1st	92	58	.613 +	1½	1956	5th	82	72	.532	15
1908	1st	90	63	.588 +	½	1957	4th	78	76	.506	20
1909	1st	98	54	.645 +	3½	1958	5th	77	77	.500	15
1910	3rd	86	68	.558	18	1959	4th	76	78	.494	18
1911	2nd	89	65	.578	13½	1960	6th	71	83	.461	26
1912	6th	69	84	.451	36½	1961	2nd	101	61	.623	8
1913	6th	66	87	.431	30	1962	4th	85	76	.528	10½
1914	4th	80	73	.523	19½	1963	T5th	79	83	.488	25½
1915	2nd	100	54	.649	2½	1964	4th	85	77	.525	14
1916	3rd	87	67	.565	4	1965	4th	89	73	.549	13
1917	4th	78	75	.510	21½	1966	3rd	88	74	.543	10
1918	7th	55	71	.437	20	1967	T2nd	91	71	.562	1
1919	4th	80	60	.571	8	1968	1st	103	59	.636 +12	
1920	7th	61	93	.396	37	1969	2nd	90	72	.556	19
1921	6th	71	82	.464	27	1970	4th	79	83	.488	29
1922	3rd	79	75	.513	15	1971	2nd	91	71	.562	12
1923	2nd	83	71	.539	16	1972	1st†	86	70	.551 +	½
1924	3rd	86	68	.558	6	1973	3rd	85	77	.525	12
1925	4th	81	73	.526	16½	1974	6th	72	90	.444	19
1926	6th	79	75	.513	12	1975	6th	57	102	.358	37½
1927	4th	82	71	.536	27½	1976	5th	74	87	.460	24
1928	6th	68	86	.442	33	1977	4th	74	88	.457	26
1929	6th	70	84	.455	36	1978	5th	86	76	.531	13½
1930	5th	75	79	.487	27	1979	5th	85	76	.528	18
1931	7th	61	93	.396	47	1980	5th	84	78	.519	19
1932	5th	76	75	.503	29½	1981	4th/T2d	60	49	.550	‡
1933	5th	75	79	.487	25	1982	4th	83	79	.512	12
1934	1st	101	53	.656 +	7	1983	2nd	92	70	.568	6
1935	1st	93	58	.616 +	3	1984	1st§	104	58	.642 +15	
1936	2nd	83	71	.539	19½	1985	3rd	84	77	.522	15
1937	2nd	89	65	.578	13	1986	3rd	87	75	.537	8½
1938	4th	84	70	.545	16	1987	1st†	98	64	.605 +	2
1939	5th	81	73	.526	26½	1988	2nd	88	74	.543	1
1940	1st	90	64	.584 +	1	1989	7th	59	103	.364	30
1941	T4th	75	79	.487	26	1990	3rd	79	83	.488	9
1942	5th	73	81	.474	30	1991	T2nd	84	78	.519	7
1943	5th	78	76	.506	20	1992	6th	75	87	.463	21
1944	2nd	88	66	.571	1						
1945	1st	88	65	.575 +	1½						
1946	2nd	92	62	.597	12						
1947	2nd	85	69	.552	12						
1948	5th	78	76	.506	18½						
1949	4th	87	67	.565	10						

*Games behind winner. †Lost Championship Series. ‡First half 31-26; second 29-23. §Won Championship Series.

MANAGERS

Name	Record	Years
George Stallings	74-61	1901
Frank Dwyer	52-83	1902
Ed Barrow	97-117	'03-04
Bobby Lowe	30-44	1904
Bill Armour	150-152	'05-06
Hugh Jennings	1131-972	'07-20
Ty Cobb	479-444	'21-26
George Moriarty	150-157	'27-28
Bucky Harris	516-557	'29-33
		'55-56
Del Baker	392-336	1933
		'38-42
Mickey Cochrane	379-278	'34-38
Steve O'Neill	509-414	'43-48
Red Rolfe	278-256	'49-52
Fred Hutchinson	155-235	'52-54
Jack Tighe	99-104	'57-58
Bill Norman	58-64	'58-59
Jimmie Dykes	118-115	'59-60
Joe Gordon	26-31	1960
Bob Scheffing	210-173	'61-63
Chuck Dressen	221-189	'63-65
Bob Swift	56-43	'65, '66
Frank Skaff	40-39	1966
Mayo Smith	363-285	'67-70
Billy Martin	248-204	'71-73
Joe Schultz	14-14	1973
Ralph Houk	366-443	'74-78
Les Moss	27-26	'1979
Sparky Anderson	1233-1025	'79-92

DAY BY DAY

Date	Opp.	Res.	Score (inn.*)	Hits	Opp. hits	Winning pitcher	Losing pitcher	Save	Record	Pos.	GB
4-6	Tor.	L	2-4	5	10	Morris	Gullickson		0-1	T5th	1
4-8	Tor.	L	9-10	10	12	Henke	Tanana	Ward	0-2	7th	2
4-9	Tor.	L	1-3	4	7	Guzman	Terrell	Ward	0-3	7th	3
4-10	N.Y.	L	3-7	6	15	Perez	King		0-4	7th	4
4-11	N.Y.	L	1-8	4	10	Leary	Gullickson		0-5	7th	5
4-12	N.Y.	L	1-5	6	11	Sanderson	Aldred	Habyan	0-6	7th	6
4-13	At Cle.	W	7-5	10	10	Leiter	Nichols	Henneman	1-6	7th	5½
4-14	At Cle.	L	7-8	8	15	Power	Lancaster	Olin	1-7	7th	6
4-15	At Cle.	W	8-1	10	9	King	Bell		2-7	7th	6
4-16	At Cle.	W	13-4	17	9	Gullickson	Cook		3-7	T6th	6
4-17	At Bal.	L	0-8	4	13	Sutcliffe	Aldred		3-8	7th	6
4-18	At Bal.	L	1-6	8	11	Mussina	Tanana		3-9	7th	7
4-19	At Bal.	L	2-3	5	5	Milacki	Terrell	Olson	3-10	7th	7
4-20	At Bal.	L	4-12	6	16	Mills	King	Frohwirth	3-11	7th	8
4-21	At Tex.	W	4-2	7	7	Gullickson	Witt	Henneman	4-11	7th	8
4-22	At Tex.	W	12-8	14	10	Leiter	Robinson		5-11	7th	7
4-23	At Tex.	W	11-5	15	10	Lancaster	Brown	Doherty	6-11	T6th	7
4-24	Chi.	L	1-9	2	9	McDowell	Terrell		6-12	T6th	8
4-26	Chi.	L	6-7	5	12	Hibbard	King	Thigpen	6-13	7th	8½
4-28	Sea.	W	4-1	6	5	Gullickson	Swan		7-13	6th	7½
4-30	Oak.	L	6-10	9	14	Horsman	Leiter	Eckersley	7-14	7th	8
5-1	Oak.	L	6-7	10	15	Parrett	Henneman	Eckersley	7-15	7th	8
5-2	Oak.	W	5-3	6	10	Tanana	Welch	Henneman	8-15	7th	7
5-3	Oak.	W	8-4	9	8	King	Moore	Henneman	9-15	6th	7
5-4	Cal.	W	6-2	10	7	Gullickson	Abbott		10-15	6th	7
5-5	Cal.	W	2-1	7	3	Doherty	Eichhorn		11-15	6th	7
5-6	At Oak.	L	2-5	4	7	Stewart	Terrell	Eckersley	11-16	6th	8
5-7	At Oak.	L	2-6	7	9	Welch	Tanana	Eckersley	11-17	7th	9
5-8	At Sea.	W	7-6	10	12	Lancaster	Schooler	Henneman	12-17	6th	8½
5-9	At Sea.	W	13-0	19	5	Gullickson	Swan		13-17	5th	7
5-10	At Sea.	L	2-6	7	6	Fleming	Aldred		13-18	6th	8
5-12	At Cal.	W	4-2	10	8	Tanana	Harvey	Henneman	14-18	6th	8
5-13	At Cal.	L	5-7	11	12	Frey	Terrell	Harvey	14-19	6th	9
5-15	At K.C.	W	8-2	12	10	Doherty	Young		15-19	6th	8½
5-16	At K.C.	W	7-2	12	9	Aldred	Gordon		16-19	6th	8
5-17	At K.C.	L	1-2	6	7	Gubicza	Terrell		16-20	6th	8
5-18	Mil.	L	1-9	4	13	Wegman	King		16-21	6th	8
5-19	Mil.	W	3-0	7	3	Tanana	Robinson	Henneman	17-21	6th	7
5-20	Mil.	W	4-3	5	12	Knudsen	Henry		18-21	6th	6½
5-21	Mil.	L	3-7	5	9	Nunez	Aldred		18-22	6th	7
5-22	Min.	W	6-3	8	7	Leiter	Smiley	Henneman	19-22	6th	7
5-23	Min.	L	5-6	9	13	Tapani	Doherty	Aguilera	19-23	6th	7
5-24	Min.	L	0-15	5	18	Krueger	Tanana		19-24	6th	7½
5-26	K.C.	W	8-1	8	6	Gullickson	Pichardo		20-24	6th	7
5-27	K.C.	W	11-2	12	8	Aldred	Boddicker		21-24	6th	6
5-28	K.C.	L	1-5	3	11	Gubicza	Leiter		21-25	6th	6½
5-29	At Min.	L	5-17	12	16	Tapani	Ritz	Willis	21-26	6th	7½
5-30	At Min.	L	5-7	10	10	Edens	Henneman	Aguilera	21-27	6th	8½
5-31	At Min.	L	1-4	5	8	Erickson	Gullickson	Guthrie	21-28	6th	9½
6-1	At Mil.	L	2-6	10	10	Navarro	Aldred		21-29	6th	10½
6-2	At Mil.	L	4-5	8	10	Orosco	Leiter	Henry	21-30	6th	11½
6-3	At Mil.	W	10-4	14	9	Ritz	Wegman		22-30	6th	10½
6-4	At N.Y.	W	6-2	9	7	Tanana	Sanderson		23-30	6th	10
6-6	At N.Y.	W	6-2	13	5	Gullickson	Kamieniecki		24-30	6th	9½
6-7	At N.Y.	L	5-6	11	9	Perez	Terrell	Farr	24-31	6th	9½
6-8	Cle.	W	9-2	11	11	Leiter	Scudder	Knudsen	25-31	6th	9½
6-9	Cle.	L	1-6	5	11	Boucher	Tanana		25-32	6th	10½
6-10	Cle.	L	2-4 (11)	6	9	Olin	Munoz		25-33	6th	11½
6-11	Bal.	L	5-7	10	10	Mills	Gullickson	Olson	25-34	6th	12½
6-12	Bal.	L	0-6	6	8	Mussina	Aldred		25-35	6th	12
6-13	Bal.	W	15-1	16	9	Leiter	Milacki		26-35	6th	11½
6-14	Bal.	W	7-4	10	8	Tanana	Mesa	Henneman	27-35	6th	11½
6-16	At Tor.	W	4-3	10	6	Gullickson	Key	Henneman	28-35	6th	10½
6-17	At Tor.	L	2-6	7	12	Morris	Ritz	Ward	28-36	6th	11½
6-18	At Tor.	W	14-10	16	15	Munoz	Timlin	Henneman	29-36	6th	10½
6-19	At Chi.	W	8-3 (13)	10	9	Terrell	Alvarez		30-36	6th	9½
6-20	At Chi.	L	1-3	7	5	McCaskill	Groom	Thigpen	30-37	6th	10½
6-21	At Chi.	L	5-6	8	9	Hernandez	Terrell	Thigpen	30-38	6th	10½
6-22	Bos.	W	4-2 (11)	10	8	Knudsen	Darwin		31-38	6th	10½
6-23	Bos.	W	11-7	15	15	Kiely	Hesketh		32-38	6th	10

Date	Opp.	Res.	Score	(inn.*)	Hits	Opp. hits	Winning pitcher	Losing pitcher	Save	Record	Pos.	GB
6-24	Bos.	W	5-1		10	8	Tanana	Gardiner		33-38	6th	10
6-25	Tex.	L	2-5		4	9	Brown	Groom		33-39	6th	10½
6-26	Tex.	W	4-2		7	7	Gullickson	Burns	Henneman	34-39	6th	10½
6-27	Tex.	L	8-10		13	11	Guzman	Ritz	Rogers	34-40	6th	10½
6-28	Tex.	L	4-8		11	9	Ryan	Leiter		34-41	6th	10½
6-29	At Bos.	W	8-3		15	5	Tanana	Hesketh	Knudsen	35-41	6th	10½
6-30	At Bos.	L	5-8		9	9	Irvine	Henneman		35-42	6th	10½
7-1	At Bos.	L	4-6		10	9	Dopson	Gullickson	Reardon	35-43	6th	11½
7-3 (1)	Sea.	W	6-4		6	9	Terrell	Johnson	Henneman	35-44	6th	12½
7-3 (2)	Sea.	L	0-11		10	5	Hanson	Lancaster		36-44	6th	12
7-4	Sea.	L	3-4	(10)	7	9	Schooler	Henneman	Swan	36-45	6th	13
7-5	Sea.	W	8-5		12	12	Terrell	DeLucia	Doherty	37-45	6th	13
7-6	Sea.	W	5-4	(14)	9	11	Kiely	Walker		38-45	6th	13
7-7	Oak.	W	3-2		9	6	Ritz	Darling	Henneman	39-45	5th	13
7-8	Oak.	W	6-3		12	6	Lancaster	Corsi	Henneman	40-45	5th	13
7-9	Cal.	W	5-4		11	10	Tanana	Blyleven	Henneman	41-45	5th	13
7-10	Cal.	L	1-6		6	13	Valera	Groom		41-46	6th	13
7-11	Cal.	L	1-2		6	8	Crim	Gullickson	Grahe	41-47	6th	13
7-12	Cal.	L	4-5	(10)	7	11	Frey	Henneman		41-48	6th	13
7-16	At Oak.	L	0-4		2	6	Downs	Tanana		41-49	6th	14
7-17	At Oak.	W	4-3		11	8	Gullickson	Welch	Knudsen	42-49	6th	13
7-18	At Oak.	W	5-2		12	9	Leiter	Moore	Groom	43-49	5th	13
7-19	At Oak.	L	2-6		9	8	Nelson	Ritz		43-50	6th	14
7-20	At Sea.	W	6-4		12	9	Terrell	Grant	Knudsen	44-50	6th	13
7-21	At Sea.	W	6-2		6	6	Tanana	Johnson		45-50	6th	13
7-22	At Sea.	W	3-2		5	5	Gullickson	Hanson	Knudsen	46-50	4th	12
7-23	At Cal.	W	5-2		6	5	Leiter	Langston	Doherty	47-50	4th	12
7-24	At Cal.	L	3-6		5	8	Blyleven	Ritz	Grahe	47-51	5th	12
7-25	At Cal.	L	0-9		3	12	Fortugno	Terrell		47-52	5th	12
7-26	At Cal.	L	3-4		12	6	Crim	Doherty	Grahe	47-53	5th	12
7-28 (1)	Chi.	L	6-8		11	10	McDowell	Gullickson	Radinsky	47-54	6th	13
7-28 (2)	Chi.	L	3-5		10	12	Fernandez	Groom	Thigpen	47-55	6th	13½
7-29	Chi.	L	6-8		9	15	Leach	Munoz	Radinsky	47-56	6th	13½
7-31	At Cle.	W	9-6		9	12	Kiely	Plunk	Henneman	48-56	6th	14
8-1	At Cle.	L	5-8		7	13	Plunk	Lancaster	Lilliquist	48-57	6th	15
8-2	At Cle.	W	5-4		5	11	Gullickson	Nagy	Henneman	49-57	5th	15
8-3	At Bal.	L	3-6		8	9	Rhodes	Groom	Davis	49-58	5th	15
8-4	At Bal.	L	3-6		7	10	Sutcliffe	Knudsen	Olson	49-59	6th	15
8-5	At Bal.	L	0-4		5	7	Mussina	Kiely		49-60	6th	16
8-6	Tor.	L	11-15		15	11	Morris	Tanana		49-61	6th	17
8-7	Tor.	W	7-2		9	8	Gullickson	Key		50-61	6th	16
8-8	Tor.	W	8-6		12	10	Kiely	Linton	Henneman	51-61	5th	15
8-9	Tor.	W	9-2		10	9	Haas	Wells		52-61	5th	14
8-10	N.Y.	W	10-5		16	14	Doherty	Hillegas		53-61	5th	14
8-11	N.Y.	W	5-1		9	6	Tanana	Perez		54-61	4th	13
8-12	N.Y.	L	0-10		2	16	Sanderson	Gullickson		54-62	4th	13
8-14	At Tex.	W	9-6		13	11	Haas	Pavlik	Henneman	55-62	4th	13½
8-15	At Tex.	W	10-3		11	9	Doherty	Witt	Munoz	56-62	4th	13
8-16	At Tex.	W	6-0		5	5	Tanana	Ryan		57-62	4th	12½
8-17	At K.C.	L	5-6		10	13	Meacham	Knudsen	Montgomery	57-63	4th	13
8-18	At K.C.	W	5-1		10	7	King	Berenguer		58-63	4th	13
8-19	At K.C.	L	2-7		5	8	Appier	Haas		58-64	4th	13
8-21	At Mil.	L	2-3		7	10	Navarro	Doherty	Henry	58-65	4th	12½
8-22	At Mil.	L	1-5		5	11	Eldred	Tanana		58-66	5th	13½
8-23	At Mil.	W	3-2		8	4	Henneman	Plesac		59-66	4th	12½
8-24	At Min.	W	6-2		10	8	King	Krueger		60-66	4th	11½
8-25	At Min.	W	4-3		8	11	Haas	Tapani	Henneman	61-66	4th	10½
8-26	At Min.	L	0-1		6	8	Smiley	Kiely		61-67	4th	11½
8-28	K.C.	W	4-2		6	10	Terrell	Meacham	Henneman	62-67	5th	13
8-29	K.C.	W	12-1		11	4	Gullickson	Berenguer		63-67	4th	10
8-30	K.C.	L	4-9		12	12	Appier	King		63-68	4th	11
8-31	Min.	L	3-5	(10)	10	10	Wayne	Henneman	Aguilera	63-69	4th	12
9-1	Min.	L	4-5		8	9	Willis	Lancaster	Aguilera	63-70	4th	13
9-2	Min.	L	2-4		7	8	Erickson	Terrell	Aguilera	63-71	4th	13
9-4	Mil.	L	3-6		9	14	Bosio	Gullickson	Plesac	63-72	4th	14
9-5	Mil.	L	3-10		6	16	Wegman	Haas		63-73	T4th	15
9-6	Mil.	W	6-2		12	9	Doherty	Navarro		64-73	T4th	15
9-8 (1)	At Chi.	L	3-4		9	6	McDowell	Tanana	Hernandez	64-74	T5th	15½
9-8 (2)	At Chi.	L	3-4		5	4	Leach	Leiter	Radinsky	64-75	6th	16
9-9	At Chi.	L	4-6		4	9	Leach	Gullickson	Hernandez	64-76	7th	17
9-10	At Chi.	W	8-0		12	4	Haas	Fernandez		65-76	5th	16½
9-11	At Bos.	L	6-7		18	10	Gardiner	Doherty	Ryan	65-77	7th	17
9-12	At Bos.	W	9-5		11	15	Terrell	Clemens		66-77	6th	17
9-13	At Bos.	W	7-2		11	9	Tanana	Dopson		67-77	6th	17

Date	Opp.	Res.	Score	(inn.*)	Hits	Opp. hits	Winning pitcher	Losing pitcher	Save	Record	Pos.	GB
9-15	Tex.	L	5-6		10	12	Guzman	Gullickson	Whiteside	67-78	6th	17½
9-16	Tex.	W	4-1		7	2	Haas	Pavlik	Henneman	68-78	6th	16½
9-18	Bos.	W	10-3		13	7	Doherty	Dopson	King	69-78	T4th	17
9-19	Bos.	W	3-2		4	4	Tanana	Harris		70-78	T4th	17
9-20	Bos.	L	4-5		8	12	Viola	Gullickson	Fossas	70-79	T4th	17
9-21	Bos.	W	6-5	(10)	7	9	Leiter	Irvine		71-79	4th	16½
9-22 (1)	At N.Y.	L	5-6	(12)	7	12	Farr	Aldred		71-80	6th	17½
9-22 (2)	At N.Y.	L	4-7		12	12	Habyan	King	Farr	71-81	6th	18
9-23	At N.Y.	W	10-8		15	10	Aldred	Hitchcock	Munoz	72-81	6th	17
9-24	At N.Y.	L	1-10		6	9	Kamieniecki	Tanana		72-82	6th	18
9-25	Cle.	W	6-5	(10)	11	14	Henneman	Olin		73-82	6th	18
9-26	Cle.	L	4-7		11	13	Armstrong	Knudsen	Olin	73-83	6th	18
9-27	Cle.	W	13-3		12	9	Terrell	Mesa		74-83	5th	18
9-29	Bal.	L	2-7		5	13	McDonald	Tanana		74-84	T5th	19
9-30	Bal.	W	4-2		7	10	Doherty	Milacki	Henneman	75-84	T5th	18
10-2	At Tor.	L	7-8		12	11	Morris	Gullickson	Henke	75-85	6th	19
10-3	At Tor.	L	1-3		3	9	Guzman	Haas	Ward	75-86	6th	20
10-4	At Tor.	L	4-7		7	9	Stottlemyre	Aldred	Timlin	75-87	6th	21

Monthly records: April (7-14), May (14-14), June (14-14), July (13-14), August (15-13), September (12-15), Oct. (0-3).

HIGHLIGHTS

High point: On August 29, the Tigers thumped Kansas City, 12-1, in the team's second home game under new Owner Mike Ilitch. Detroit won for the 14th time in 20 games and pulled within four games of .500 for the first time since early in the season.

Low point: On April 20, the Tigers lost, 12-4, in Baltimore and dropped to 3-11, eight games out of first place. They never were a factor in the race.

Turning point: Detroit's quest for .500 ended quickly following its 14-6 mark from August 7-29. The Tigers proceeded to drop six straight and nine of 10 en route to finishing at 75-87.

Most valuable player: Utilityman Tony Phillips. He showed his amazing defensive versatility again by starting games at five different positions. He also scored a league-leading 114 runs, drew 114 walks (third in the A.L.) and rapped 32 doubles.

Most valuable pitcher: Righthander Bill Gullickson. He led the Tigers in wins (14), starts (34) and innings (221⅔).

Most improved player: Right fielder Rob Deer. He improved his average 68 points (from .179 to .247) and hit 32 homers in just 393 at-bats.

Most pleasant surprise: Righthander John Kiely. After being sent down on the final day of spring training, the rookie battled his way up and went 4-2 with a team-best 2.13 ERA as a reliever.

Biggest disappointment: Center fielder Milt Cuyler. After a good rookie year, his '92 season ended in July with a right knee injury that required surgery. Consequently, he stole only eight bases, batted .241 and struggled afield.

Key injuries: Shortstop Alan Trammell suffered a broken right ankle May 15 and didn't play again. Cuyler's knee injury hurt, and Deer missed almost two months with hand and ankle injuries.

Notable: Ilitch bought the team August 26 from fellow pizza magnate Tom Monaghan. . . . Monaghan fired chairman Jim Campbell—who had been with the organization since 1949—and president Bo Schembechler. . . . First

baseman Cecil Fielder (124 RBIs) joined Babe Ruth as the only players to lead the majors in RBIs for three straight seasons. . . . Sparky Anderson passed Hughie Jennings (1907-20) on September 27 to became the winningest manager in Tigers history (1,133-1,025). His 1,996-1,611 all-time record makes him baseball's seventh all-time winningest manager.

—REID CREAGER

RECORDS

1992 regular-season record: 75-87 (6th in A.L. East); 38-42 at home; 37-45 on road; 35-43 vs. East; 40-44 vs. West; 23-20 vs. LHP; 52-67 vs. RHP; 63-75 on grass; 12-12 on turf; 21-35 in daytime; 54-52 at night; 15-25 in one-run games; 5-5 in extra-inning games; 0-3-1 in doubleheaders.

Team record last five years: 385-425 (.475, ranks 10th in league in that span).

TEAM LEADERS

Batting average: Lou Whitaker (.278).
At-bats: Travis Fryman (659).
Runs: Tony Phillips (114).
Hits: Travis Fryman (175).
Total bases: Travis Fryman (274).
Doubles: Tony Phillips (32).
Triples: Travis Fryman (4).
Home runs: Cecil Fielder (35).
Runs batted in: Cecil Fielder (124).
Stolen bases: Gary Pettis (13).
Slugging percentage: Mickey Tettleton (.469).
On-base percentage: Tony Phillips (.387).
Wins: Bill Gullickson (14).
Earned-run average: Bill Gullickson (4.34).
Complete games: Bill Gullickson (4).
Shutouts: Bill Gullickson, David Haas (1).
Saves: Mike Henneman (24).
Innings pitched: Bill Gullickson (221⅔).
Strikeouts: Frank Tanana (91).

GAMES BY POSITION

Catcher: Mickey Tettleton 113, Chad Kreuter 62, Rich Rowland 3.
First base: Cecil Fielder 114, Dave Bergman 55, Skeeter Barnes 17, Rico Brogna 8, Shawn Hare 4, Mickey Tettleton 3, Rich Rowland 1.
Second base: Lou Whitaker 119, Tony Phillips 57, Skeeter Barnes 7.
Third base: Scott Livingstone 112, Skeeter Barnes 39, Travis Fryman 26, Tony Phillips 3, Rich Rowland 1.
Shortstop: Travis Fryman 137, Alan Trammell 27, Tony Phillips 1.
Outfield: Dan Gladden 108, Rob Deer 106, Milt Cuyler 89, Mark Carreon 83, Tony Phillips 73, Gary Pettis 46, Skeeter Barnes 15, Phil Clark 13, Shawn Hare 9, Mickey Tettleton 2, Dave Bergman 1.
Designated hitter: Cecil Fielder 43, Mickey Tettleton 40, Tony Phillips 34, Mark Carreon 13, Dave Bergman 12, Lou Whitaker 10, Skeeter Barnes 7, Phil Clark 7, Rico Brogna 2, Rob Deer 2, Dan Gladden 2, Rich Rowland 2, Chad Kreuter 1.

TOP 10 DRAFT CHOICES

1. **Ricky Greene**, RHP, Louisiana State University.
2. **Yuri Sanchez**, SS, Lynn (Mass.) Technical School.
3. **Chris Gomez**, SS, Long Beach State University.
4. **Kenny Carlyle**, RHP, University of Mississippi.
5. **David Mysel**, RHP, University of Maryland.
6. **Malvin DeJesus**, SS, William Penn College (Ia.).
7. **Patrick Ahearne**, RHP, Pepperdine University.
8. **David Reinfelder**, LHP, Vassar (Mich.) High School.
9. **Lawrence Lopez**, RHP, University of Wyoming.
10. **Frank Catalanotto**, 2B, Smithtown East High School, St. James, N.Y.

KANSAS CITY ROYALS
AMERICAN LEAGUE WEST DIVISION

1993 SCHEDULE

APRIL

SUN	MON	TUE	WED	THU	FRI	SAT
				1	2	3
4	5 BOS H	6	7 N BOS H	8 N BOS H	9 N MIN H	10 MIN H
11 MIN H	12 NY	13	14 NY	15 N NY	16 N MIN	17 N MIN
18 MIN	19	20 TOR H	21 N TOR H	22 N TOR H	23 N BAL H	24 BAL H
25 BAL H	26 N DET H	27 N DET H	28 N TOR	29 TOR	30 BAL	

MAY

SUN	MON	TUE	WED	THU	FRI	SAT
						1 BAL
2 BAL	3	4 N DET	5 N DET	6	7 N TEX H	8 N TEX H
9 TEX H	10	11 N CLE	12 N CLE	13 N CLE	14 N CAL	15 N CAL
16 CAL	17	18 N OAK H	19 N OAK H	20 N OAK H	21 N SEA H	22 N SEA H
23 SEA H	24	25 N CHI	26 N CHI	27 N CHI	28 N MIL	29 N MIL
30 MIL	31 N BOS					

JUNE

SUN	MON	TUE	WED	THU	FRI	SAT
		1 N BOS	2 N BOS	3 N MIL H	4 N MIL H	5 N MIL H
6 MIL H	7 N NY H	8 N NY H	9 N NY H	10	11 N CHI H	12 N CHI H
13 CHI H	14 N SEA	15 N SEA	16 N SEA	17	18 N OAK	19 N OAK
20 OAK	21 N CAL H	22 N CAL H	23 N CAL H	24 N CAL H	25 N CLE	26 N CLE
27 CLE	28 N TEX	29 N TEX	30 N TEX			

JULY

SUN	MON	TUE	WED	THU	FRI	SAT
				1	2 N TOR H	3 N TOR H
4 N TOR H	5 N BAL H	6 N BAL H	7 N BAL H	8 N DET H	9 N DET H	10 N DET H
11 DET H	12	13 ○ ALL-STAR GAME	14	15 N TOR	16 N TOR	17 N TOR
18 TOR	19 N BAL	20 N BAL	21 N BAL	22 N DET	23 N DET	24 N DET
25 DET	26 N TEX H	27 N TEX H	28 N TEX H	29 N TEX H	30 N CLE H	31 N CLE H

AUGUST

SUN	MON	TUE	WED	THU	FRI	SAT
1 CLE H	2	3 N CAL	4 N CAL	5 N CAL	6 N OAK H	7 N OAK H
8 OAK H	9 N SEA H	10 N SEA H	11 N SEA H	12 N CHI	13 N CHI	14 N CHI
15 CHI	16	17 N MIN	18 N MIN	19 N MIN	20 N NY	21 NY
22 NY	23 N MIN H	24 N MIN H	25 N MIN H	26 N MIN H	27 N BOS H	28 N BOS H
29 BOS H	30 N MIL	31 N MIL				

SEPTEMBER

SUN	MON	TUE	WED	THU	FRI	SAT
			1 MIL	2	3 N BOS	4 BOS
5 BOS	6 MIL H	7	8 N MIL H	9	10 N NY H	11 N NY H
12 NY H	13 N CHI H	14 N CHI H	15 N CHI H	16 N SEA	17 N SEA	18 N SEA
19 SEA	20 N OAK	21 N OAK	22 N OAK	23 N OAK	24 N CAL H	25 N CAL H
26 CAL H	27 N CLE H	28 N CLE H	29 N CLE H	30		

OCTOBER

SUN	MON	TUE	WED	THU	FRI	SAT
					1 N TEX	2 TEX
3 TEX						

1993 SEASON

CLUB DIRECTORY

Board of directors
Spencer (Herk) Robinson
Charles Hughes
Ewing Kauffman
Mrs. Ewing Kauffman
Dale Rohr
Chairman of the board (owner)
Ewing Kauffman
Exec. vice president and general manager
Spencer (Herk) Robinson
Vice president, treasurer
Charles Hughes
Vice president, finance
Dale Rohr
Vice president, govt. and consumer affairs
Merle Wood
Vice president, public relations
Dean Vogelaar
Vice president, administration
Dennis Cryder
Director of scouting
Art Stewart
Assistant general manager
Jay Hinrichs
Director of minor league operations
Bob Hegman
Director of stadium operations
Tom Folk
Director of season ticket sales
Joe Grigoli
Director of group sales/Lancer coordinator
Chris Muehlbach
Director of data processing
Loretta Kratzberg
Director of benefits and compensation
Tom Pfannenstiel
Director of accounting
Ken Willeke
Traveling secretary
Dave Witty
Assistant directors of public relations
Steve Fink
Kevin Henderson
Assistant directors of marketing
Mike Behymer
Barry Holmes

Assistant director of stadium operations
John Johnson
Stadium engineers
Duane Robinson
Chris Frank
Production manager
Larry Magariel
Executive secretary/baseball
Peggy Mathews
Equipment manager
Mike Burkhalter
Team physician
Dr. Steve Joyce
Trainers
Nick Swartz
Steve Morrow
Scouts
Frank Baez
Allard Baird
Carl Blando
Bob Carter
Floyd Chandler
Balos Davis
Doug Deutsch
Steve Flores
Ken Gonzales
Dave Herrera
Ray Jackson
Gary Johnson
Al Kubski
Tony Levato
Ed Mathes
Jeff McKay
Chuck McMichael
Brian Murphy
Buck O'Neil
Herb Raybourn
Wil Rutenschroer
Steve Schryusr
Luis Silverio
Jerry Stephens
Jerry Terrell
Terry Wetzel
Stan Williams

SCHEDULE KEY

H—Home game.   N—Night game (any game starting after 5 p.m.).
*All-Star Game at Oriole Park at Camden Yards, Baltimore.

SPRING TRAINING ROSTER

Manager—Hal McRae (11).

Coaches—Steve Boros (43), Glenn Ezell (44), Guy Hansen (46), Bruce Kison (42), Lee May (45).

No.	PITCHERS	B/T	Ht./Wt.	Born	1992 clubs
55	Appier, Kevin	R/R	6-2/200	12-6-67	Kansas City
27	Aquino, Luis	R/R	6-1/195	5-19-65	Kansas City, Omaha
52	Boddicker, Mike	R/R	5-11/185	8-23-57	Kansas City
34	Brewer, Billy	L/L	6-1/175	4-15-68	West Palm Beach, Harrisburg
17	Cone, David	L/R	6-1/190	1-2-63	New York N.L., Toronto
37	Gardner, Mark	R/R	6-1/200	3-1-62	Montreal
36	Gordon, Tom	R/R	5-9/180	11-18-67	Kansas City
23	Gubicza, Mark	R/R	6-5/225	8-14-62	Kansas City
33	Haney, Chris	L/L	6-3/185	11-16-68	Montreal, Indianapolis, Kansas City
58	Harris, Doug	R/R	6-4/190	9-27-69	Baseball City
57	Magnante, Mike	L/L	6-1/180	6-17-65	Kansas City
28	Meacham, Rusty	R/R	6-2/165	1-27-68	Kansas City
21	Montgomery, Jeff	R/R	5-11/180	1-7-62	Kansas City
41	Morton, Kevin	R/L	6-2/185	8-3-68	Pawtucket
35	Pichardo, Hipolito	R/R	6-1/160	8-22-69	Memphis, Kansas City
54	Pierce, Ed	L/L	6-1/185	10-6-68	Memphis, Kansas City
47	Rasmussen, Dennis	L/L	6-7/235	4-18-59	Rochester, Iowa, Chicago N.L., Omaha, Kansas City
38	Reed, Rick	R/R	6-0/210	8-16-64	Omaha, Kansas City
50	Sampen, Bill	R/R	6-2/195	1-18-63	Indianapolis, Montreal, Kansas City
49	Shifflett, Steve	R/R	6-1/205	1-5-66	Omaha, Kansas City

No.	CATCHERS	B/T	Ht./Wt.	Born	1992 clubs
61	Jennings, Lance	R/R	6-0/190	10-3-71	Baseball City, Memphis
15	Macfarlane, Mike	R/R	6-1/205	4-12-64	Kansas City
24	Mayne, Brent	L/R	6-1/190	4-19-68	Kansas City

No.	INFIELDERS	B/T	Ht./Wt.	Born	1992 clubs
5	Brett, George	L/R	6-0/205	5-15-53	Kansas City
7	Gagne, Greg	R/R	5-11/172	11-12-61	Minnesota
48	Hamelin, Bob	L/L	6-0/230	11-29-67	Baseball City, Memphis, Omaha
60	Hiatt, Phil	R/R	6-3/190	5-1-69	Memphis, Omaha
13	Howard, David	B/R	6-0/165	2-26-67	Kansas City, Baseball City, Omaha
9	Jefferies, Gregg	B/R	5-10/185	8-1-67	Kansas City
12	Joyner, Wally	L/L	6-2/195	6-16-62	Kansas City
4	Lind, Jose	R/R	5-11/175	5-1-64	Pittsburgh
16	Miller, Keith	R/R	5-11/185	6-12-63	Kansas City
32	Rossy, Rico	R/R	5-10/175	2-16-64	Omaha, Kansas City
3	Shumpert, Terry	R/R	5-11/190	8-16-66	Kansas City, Omaha

No.	OUTFIELDERS	B/T	Ht./Wt.	Born	1992 clubs
14	Gwynn, Chris	L/L	6-0/210	10-13-64	Kansas City
40	Koslofski, Kevin	L/R	5-8/165	9-24-66	Omaha, Kansas City
56	McRae, Brian	B/R	6-0/185	8-27-67	Kansas City
22	McReynolds, Kevin	R/R	6-1/215	10-16-59	Kansas City
51	Pulliam, Harvey	R/R	6-0/210	10-20-67	Omaha, Kansas City
25	Thurman, Gary	R/R	5-10/175	11-12-64	Kansas City

BALLPARK INFORMATION

Ballpark (capacity, surface)
Royals Stadium (40,625, artificial)
Address
P.O. Box 419969
Kansas City, MO 64141
Business phone
816-921-2200
Ticket information
816-921-8000
Ticket prices
$13 (club box)
$12 (field box)
$10 (plaza reserved)
$9 (view upper box)
$8 (view upper reserved)
$4 (Royal nights)
$5 (general admission)
Field dimensions (from home plate)
To left field at foul line, 330 feet
To center field, 410 feet
To right field at foul line, 330 feet
First game played
April 10, 1973 (Royals 12, Rangers 1)

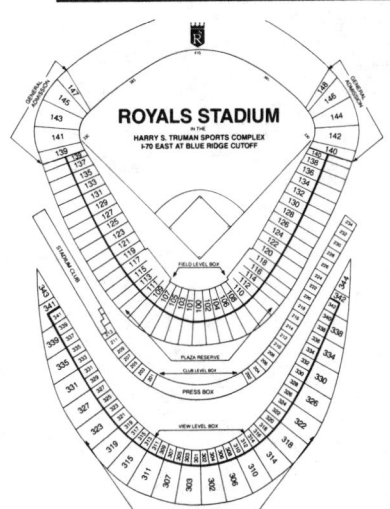

ROYALS STADIUM
HARRY S. TRUMAN SPORTS COMPLEX
I-70 EAST AT BLUE RIDGE CUTOFF

Class	Team	League	Manager
AAA	Omaha	American Association	Jeff Cox
AA	Memphis	Southern	Tom Poquette
A	Wilmington	Carolina	Ron Johnson
A	Rockford	Midwest	Mike Jirschele
A	Eugene	Northwest	John Mizerock
Rookie	Gulf Coast Royals	Gulf Coast	Bob Herold

BROADCAST INFORMATION

Radio: WIBW-AM (580). Broadcasters: Denny Matthews, Fred White.
TV: KSMO-TV (Channel 62). Broadcasters: Dave Armstrong, Paul Splittorff.
Cable TV: None.

SPRING TRAINING

Ballpark (city): Baseball City Stadium (Baseball City, Fla.).
Ticket information: 813-424-2500.

HISTORY

YEAR-BY-YEAR RECORDS

Year	Pos.	W	L	Pct.	*GB	Year	Pos.	W	L	Pct.	*GB
1969	4th	69	93	.426	28	1984	1st†	84	78	.519	+ 3
1970	T4th	65	97	.401	33	1985	1st‡	91	71	.562	+ 1
1971	2nd	85	76	.528	16	1986	T3rd	76	86	.469	16
1972	4th	76	78	.494	16½	1987	2nd	83	79	.512	2
1973	2nd	88	74	.543	6	1988	3rd	84	77	.522	19½
1974	5th	77	85	.475	13	1989	2nd	92	70	.568	7
1975	2nd	91	71	.562	7	1990	6th	75	86	.466	27½
1976	1st†	90	72	.556	+ 2½	1991	6th	82	80	.506	13
1977	1st†	102	60	.630	+ 8	1992	T5th	72	90	.444	24
1978	1st†	92	70	.568	+ 5						
1979	2nd	85	77	.525	3						
1980	1st‡	97	65	.599	+14						
1981	5th/1st	50	53	.485	§*						
1982	2nd	90	72	.556	3						
1983	2nd	79	83	.488	20						

*Games behind winner. †Lost Championship Series. ‡Won Championship Series. §First half 20-30; second 30-23. *Lost division playoff.

MANAGERS

Name	Record	Years
Joe Gordon	69-93	1969
Charlie Metro	19-33	1970
Bob Lemon	207-218	'70-72
Jack McKeon	215-205	'73-75
Whitey Herzog	410-304	'74-79
Jim Frey	127-105	'80-81
Dick Howser	404-365	'81-86
Mike Ferraro	36-38	1986
Billy Gardner	62-64	1987
John Wathan	288-270	'87-91
Hal McRae	138-148	'91-92

DAY BY DAY

Date	Opp.	Res.	Score	(inn.*)	Hits	Opp. hits	Winning pitcher	Losing pitcher	Save	Record	Pos.	GB
4-6	At Oak.	L	3-5		11	9	Honeycutt	Aquino	Eckersley	0-1	T6th	1
4-8	At Oak.	L	3-4	(13)	8	11	Parrett	Heaton		0-2	T5th	2½
4-9	At Oak.	L	2-5		7	10	Darling	Gubicza	Eckersley	0-3	T5th	3½
4-10	At Sea.	L	3-9		10	11	DeLucia	Davis		0-4	T6th	4
4-11	At Sea.	L	0-1		4	6	Johnson	Appier		0-5	7th	5
4-12	At Sea.	L	1-2		4	6	Hanson	Boddicker	Schooler	0-6	7th	5½
4-13	Oak.	L	1-6		5	10	Moore	Gordon		0-7	7th	6
4-14	Oak.	W	3-1		1	7	Heaton	Honeycutt	Montgomery	1-7	7th	5
4-15	Oak.	L	6-10		12	14	Parrett	Magnante		1-8	7th	6
4-16	Oak.	L	0-1	(10)	4	3	Stewart	Montgomery	Eckersley	1-9	7th	7
4-17	Cal.	L	1-8		3	14	Lewis	Boddicker		1-10	7th	7
4-18	Cal.	L	3-5	(10)	7	11	Frey	Montgomery		1-11	7th	8
4-21	Bal.	L	4-10		10	14	Mesa	Gubicza		1-12	7th	8
4-22	Bal.	L	1-2		6	6	Sutcliffe	Appier		1-13	7th	9
4-23	Bal.	L	1-8		6	12	Mussina	Davis		1-14	7th	9½
4-24	At Tor.	L	3-4		5	8	Guzman	Gordon	Henke	1-15	7th	9½
4-25	At Tor.	L	4-6		10	11	Hentgen	Young	Ward	1-16	7th	9½
4-26	At Tor.	W	9-0		13	4	Gubicza	Morris		2-16	7th	9½
4-28	At Mil.	W	3-2	(11)	6	3	Heaton	Orosco	Montgomery	3-16	7th	9½
4-29	At Mil.	L	3-5		5	9	Bones	Gordon	Henry	3-17	7th	9½
5-1	At Bos.	L	5-6		10	12	Darwin	Montgomery		3-18	7th	11
5-2	At Bos.	L	6-7		10	10	Harris	Pichardo	Reardon	3-19	7th	11
5-3	At Bos.	W	5-2		9	10	Appier	Hesketh		4-19	7th	10
5-4	At Cle.	W	11-6		15	8	Meacham	Nichols		5-19	7th	9
5-5	At Cle.	L	6-8		10	10	Armstrong	Magnante	Olin	5-20	7th	9½
5-6	Mil.	W	3-1		7	7	Gubicza	Navarro	Montgomery	6-20	7th	9½
5-7	Mil.	W	6-4		10	13	Young	Plesac	Montgomery	7-20	7th	9½
5-8	Bos.	W	2-1		3	8	Appier	Hesketh	Montgomery	8-20	7th	9½
5-9	Bos.	L	0-5		3	9	Clemens	Gordon		8-21	7th	10
5-10	Bos.	L	6-10		9	13	Viola	Magnante		8-22	7th	11
5-12	Cle.	W	3-0		8	4	Gubicza	Scudder		9-22	7th	10
5-13	Cle.	W	5-3		9	9	Appier	Cook	Montgomery	10-22	7th	9½
5-15	Det.	L	2-8		10	12	Doherty	Young		10-23	7th	9½
5-16	Det.	L	2-7		9	12	Aldred	Gordon		10-24	7th	10
5-17	Det.	W	2-1		7	6	Gubicza	Terrell		11-24	7th	9½
5-18	At Chi.	W	6-1		10	6	Magnante	McCaskill		12-24	7th	9
5-19	At Chi.	L	1-2		6	5	Hough	Appier	Thigpen	12-25	7th	10
5-20	At Chi.	W	7-2		7	6	Pichardo	Fernandez	Boddicker	13-25	7th	10
5-21	At Tex.	W	7-5		6	6	Meacham	Rogers	Montgomery	14-25	7th	9½
5-22	At Tex.	L	7-10		11	14	Witt	Gubicza		14-26	7th	10½
5-23	At Tex.	L	2-4		8	8	Brown	Magnante		14-27	7th	10½
5-24	At Tex.	L	3-4	(13)	12	10	Alexander	Gordon		14-28	7th	11½
5-26	At Det.	L	1-8		6	8	Gullickson	Pichardo		14-29	7th	11
5-27	At Det.	L	2-11		8	12	Aldred	Boddicker		14-30	7th	11
5-28	At Det.	W	5-1		11	3	Gubicza	Leiter		15-30	7th	11
5-29	Tex.	L	3-5		8	12	Brown	Montgomery		15-31	7th	12
5-30	Tex.	W	8-2		10	8	Appier	Jeffcoat		16-31	7th	11
5-31	Tex.	W	7-6		15	9	Meacham	Russell		17-31	6th	10½
6-1	Chi.	L	3-5		7	8	Fernandez	Boddicker		17-32	7th	10½
6-2	Chi.	W	2-1		6	5	Gubicza	Radinsky	Montgomery	18-32	7th	10½
6-3	Chi.	W	3-1		8	6	Magnante	Hibbard	Montgomery	19-32	7th	10½
6-5	Sea.	W	6-4		8	8	Appier	Jones	Montgomery	20-32	7th	10½
6-6	Sea.	W	4-3		11	7	Heaton	Schooler		21-32	7th	10½
6-7	Sea.	W	4-1		10	6	Reed	Hanson		22-32	T5th	9½
6-8	Min.	W	9-6		11	9	Gordon	Kipper	Montgomery	23-32	5th	8½
6-9	Min.	L	2-4		6	8	Krueger	Magnante	Aguilera	23-33	5th	9½
6-10	Min.	W	7-6		12	14	Meacham	Guthrie	Montgomery	24-33	5th	9½
6-12	At Cal.	L	0-5		7	8	Langston	Pichardo		24-34	5th	10½
6-13	At Cal.	L	4-5		7	11	Finley	Reed	Eichhorn	24-35	6th	11½
6-14	At Cal.	L	1-5		6	10	Valera	Gubicza	Frey	24-36	6th	12½
6-15	At Min.	W	7-0		13	4	Magnante	Krueger		25-36	6th	12½
6-16	At Min.	W	7-5		13	11	Appier	Kipper	Montgomery	26-36	6th	11½
6-17	At Min.	L	2-4		11	7	Aguilera	Gordon		26-37	7th	11½
6-18	At Min.	L	1-3		8	6	Erickson	Reed	Aguilera	26-38	7th	12
6-19	Tor.	W	11-4		12	10	Gubicza	Stottlemyre		27-38	7th	12½
6-20	Tor.	L	1-6		5	8	Guzman	Magnante		27-39	7th	12
6-21	Tor.	W	2-0		8	6	Appier	Key	Montgomery	28-39	7th	11
6-23	N.Y.	W	2-1		4	6	Pichardo	Perez	Montgomery	29-39	7th	11½
6-24	N.Y.	L	3-6		9	15	Johnson	Reed	Farr	29-40	6th	12½
6-25	N.Y.	L	3-4		7	13	Sanderson	Gubicza	Farr	29-41	7th	13½

Date		Opp.	Res.	Score	(inn.*)	Hits	Opp. hits	Winning pitcher	Losing pitcher	Save	Record	Pos.	GB
6-26		At Bal.	L	5-6		10	13	Frohwirth	Meacham	Olson	29-42	7th	13½
6-27		At Bal.	W	2-0		6	4	Appier	Mussina	Montgomery	30-42	6th	12½
6-28		At Bal.	W	9-2		19	11	Pichardo	Mesa	Boddicker	31-42	6th	11½
6-29		At N.Y.	W	7-3		14	5	Davis	Johnson	Montgomery	32-42	5th	11½
6-30		At N.Y.	L	0-6		4	12	Sanderson	Gubicza		32-43	5th	12½
7-1		At N.Y.	L	6-7		12	12	Cadaret	Gordon	Habyan	32-44	5th	13½
7-2		Mil.	W	8-2		13	6	Appier	Robinson		33-44	5th	13
7-3		Mil.	L	3-7		7	13	Navarro	Pichardo		33-45	5th	13
7-5	(1)	Mil.	L	1-2	(12)	10	7	Fetters	Montgomery	Henry	33-46	5th	14½
7-5	(2)	Mil.	L	7-9		11	9	Bones	Davis	Holmes	33-47	5th	15
7-6		At Bos.	W	6-3		12	6	Reed	Dopson	Meacham	34-47	5th	15
7-7		At Bos.	L	2-3	(11)	6	13	Darwin	Meacham		34-48	5th	15
7-8		At Bos.	L	4-5		10	9	Fossas	Gordon	Reardon	34-49	5th	16
7-9		At Mil.	W	3-2		10	9	Shifflett	Bosio	Montgomery	35-49	5th	15
7-10		At Mil.	W	3-1		13	9	Gordon	Bones	Montgomery	36-49	5th	15
7-11		At Mil.	L	1-5		13	9	Wegman	Reed		36-50	5th	16
7-12		At Mil.	W	5-1		7	7	Appier	Ruffin	Boddicker	37-50	5th	16
7-16		Cle.	W	3-2		7	9	Pichardo	Mesa	Montgomery	38-50	5th	16
7-17		Cle.	W	4-3		8	5	Montgomery	Plunk		39-50	5th	16
7-18		Cle.	W	4-1		9	7	Appier	Armstrong	Meacham	40-50	5th	15
7-19		Cle.	L	3-4		7	11	Lilliquist	Shifflett	Olin	40-51	5th	16
7-20		Bos.	L	3-5		10	9	Quantrill	Shifflett	Reardon	40-52	5th	16
7-21		Bos.	W	8-0		7	1	Pichardo	Hesketh		41-52	5th	15
7-22		Bos.	W	6-4		7	9	Gordon	Viola	Montgomery	42-52	5th	15
7-23		At Cle.	L	0-1	(14)	6	6	Wickander	Magnante		42-53	5th	15½
7-24		At Cle.	W	8-3		16	11	Aquino	Scudder	Montgomery	43-53	5th	15
7-25		At Cle.	L	5-6		10	10	Olin	Meacham		43-54	5th	16
7-26		At Cle.	L	1-2	(13)	11	10	Olin	Shifflett		43-55	6th	17
7-28		At Tor.	L	4-6		9	7	Key	Moeller	Henke	43-56	6th	16½
7-29		At Tor.	W	5-2		8	8	Appier	Timlin	Montgomery	44-56	6th	15½
7-30		At Tor.	L	0-3		3	8	Wells	Aquino	Henke	44-57	6th	16
7-31		Oak.	W	6-5	(10)	17	9	Meacham	Parrett		45-57	6th	15½
8-1		Oak.	W	8-4		12	9	Gordon	Downs		46-57	6th	15½
8-2		Oak.	L	4-8		13	13	Welch	Berenguer		46-58	6th	16½
8-4	(1)	Cal.	L	1-5		6	9	Blyleven	Appier	Crim	46-59	6th	16½
8-4	(2)	Cal.	W	4-1		5	8	Aquino	Fortugno		47-59	6th	16
8-5		Cal.	W	5-2		12	7	Gordon	Valera	Montgomery	48-59	5th	16
8-6		Cal.	W	7-6		10	12	Berenguer	Crim	Montgomery	49-59	5th	16
8-7		At Oak.	L	6-8		12	13	Welch	Moeller	Eckersley	49-60	5th	17
8-8		At Oak.	L	3-5		10	6	Eckersley	Montgomery		49-61	5th	18
8-9		At Oak.	W	5-2		8	5	Appier	Stewart	Montgomery	50-61	5th	17
8-10		At Sea.	L	1-3		3	6	Johnson	Aquino		50-62	5th	18
8-11		At Sea.	W	9-6		13	12	Pichardo	Hanson	Montgomery	51-62	5th	17
8-12		At Sea.	L	3-6		8	9	Fleming	Moeller	Nelson	51-63	6th	18
8-14		Bal.	L	1-3		10	5	Sutcliffe	Appier	Olson	51-64	6th	18½
8-15		Bal.	W	5-4		11	10	Meacham	Olson		52-64	6th	18½
8-16		Bal.	W	15-2		17	8	Pichardo	Mills		53-64	5th	18½
8-17		Det.	W	6-5		13	10	Meacham	Knudsen	Montgomery	54-64	5th	18
8-18		Det.	L	1-5		7	10	King	Berenguer		54-65	5th	18
8-19		Det.	W	7-2		8	5	Appier	Haas		55-65	5th	17
8-21		At Chi.	W	4-3		8	7	Meacham	McCaskill	Montgomery	56-65	5th	16½
8-22		At Chi.	L	2-3		10	6	Hibbard	Pichardo	Radinsky	56-66	5th	17½
8-23		At Chi.	L	1-3		5	6	McDowell	Reed		56-67	6th	18½
8-25		At Tex.	L	2-6		8	10	Guzman	Appier		56-68	6th	19
8-26		At Tex.	L	1-3		6	5	Pavlik	Sauveur	Russell	56-69	6th	19
8-27		At Tex.	W	7-2		9	6	Pichardo	Ryan		57-69	6th	18½
8-28		At Det.	L	2-4		10	6	Terrell	Meacham	Henneman	57-70	6th	19½
8-29		At Det.	L	1-12		4	11	Gullickson	Berenguer		57-71	6th	20½
8-30		At Det.	W	9-4		12	12	Appier	King		58-71	6th	20½
8-31		Tex.	W	5-2		11	5	Haney	Pavlik	Montgomery	59-71	5th	19½
9-1		Tex.	W	8-3		13	10	Boddicker	Burns		60-71	5th	18½
9-2		Tex.	L	2-6		6	11	Brown	Reed		60-72	5th	18½
9-3		Chi.	L	3-7		10	13	McDowell	Aquino		60-73	6th	19
9-4		Chi.	L	0-8		6	14	Fernandez	Appier		60-74	6th	19
9-5		Chi.	L	6-12	(8)	9	14	Alvarez	Berenguer		60-75	6th	19
9-6		Chi.	W	3-2		7	8	Gordon	Hernandez	Montgomery	61-75	6th	19
9-7		Tor.	W	5-4	(12)	12	14	Magnante	Wells		62-75	6th	18
9-8		Tor.	L	0-5		4	9	Key	Aquino		62-76	6th	19
9-9		Tor.	L	0-1		5	5	Cone	Appier	Henke	62-77	6th	20
9-11		At N.Y.	L	1-2		8	6	Monteleone	Magnante	Farr	62-78	6th	21½
9-12		At N.Y.	L	9-11		15	14	Habyan	Magnante	Farr	62-79	6th	22½
9-13		At N.Y.	W	3-0		9	6	Rasmussen	Perez	Montgomery	63-79	6th	22½
9-14		At Bal.	L	1-2		4	6	Sutcliffe	Reed	Olson	63-80	6th	23½
9-15		At Bal.	L	1-2	(14)	9	14	Davis	Sampen		63-81	6th	24½

Date	Opp.	Res.	Score	(inn.*)	Hits	Opp. hits	Winning pitcher	Losing pitcher	Save	Record	Pos.	GB
9-16	At Bal.	L	0-3		4	13	Mussina	Haney		63-82	6th	25½
9-18	N.Y.	W	3-2		8	9	Pichardo	Kamieniecki	Montgomery	64-82	6th	25½
9-19	N.Y.	W	7-4		13	8	Rasmussen	Perez	Montgomery	65-82	6th	24½
9-20	N.Y.	L	4-10		9	16	Wickman	Gordon	Cadaret	65-83	6th	25½
9-21	Sea.	W	3-0		8	4	Aquino	Fleming	Montgomery	66-83	6th	25½
9-22	Sea.	W	3-0		6	2	Haney	Johnson		67-83	T5th	24½
9-23	Sea.	L	1-6		5	14	Fisher	Pichardo		67-84	T5th	24½
9-24	Sea.	W	2-0		4	6	Rasmussen	Leary	Montgomery	68-84	5th	24½
9-25	At Min.	W	4-3		9	8	Meacham	Erickson	Montgomery	69-84	5th	23½
9-26	At Min.	L	2-9		7	13	Tapani	Aquino		69-85	5th	23½
9-27	At Min.	L	0-4		5	5	Smiley	Haney		69-86	5th	23½
9-28	At Cal.	L	5-6	(11)	11	13	Lewis	Shifflett		69-87	T5th	24
9-29	At Cal.	W	2-0		7	1	Rasmussen	Blyleven		70-87	5th	24
9-30	At Cal.	W	4-0		16	7	Reed	Valera		71-87	5th	23
10-1	At Cal.	L	2-5		11	10	Finley	Sampen	Frey	71-88	5th	23
10-2	Min.	L	1-5		4	11	Smiley	Haney		71-89	T5th	23
10-3	Min.	W	7-6	(11)	13	10	Meacham	Wayne		72-89	T5th	23
10-4	Min.	L	0-6		6	12	Trombley	Rasmussen		72-90	T5th	24

Monthly records: April (3-17), May (14-14), June (15-12), July (13-14), August (14-14), September (12-16), Oct. (1-3).

HIGHLIGHTS

High point: Designated hitter George Brett kept the Royals' season from being a complete disaster by getting his 3,000th career hit September 30 at California. Brett, who became the 18th player to reach the coveted milestone, finished the year with 3,005 hits.

Low point: The Royals started the year with a 1-16 mark, putting them 10½ games out of first by April 25. They were 71-74 after that but finished 24 games behind Oakland.

Turning point: Kansas City won 10 of 13 games from May 28 through June 10 to pull within nine games of .500. But then the Royals went 13-17 up to the All-Star break, and it was clear they were going nowhere.

Most valuable player: Brett. At age 39, he not only reached the 3,000-hit mark, but also tied third baseman Gregg Jefferies for the team lead in average (.285) and games played (152).

Most valuable pitcher: Righthander Kevin Appier. A Cy Young candidate until his season ended September 9 due to shoulder tendinitis, Appier finished 15-8 with a 2.46 ERA in 30 starts.

Most improved player: Righthander Rusty Meacham. In 64 games, the middle reliever was 10-4 with a 2.74 ERA.

Most pleasant surprise: Righthander Hipolito Pichardo. He was called up from Class AA Memphis on April 16 and developed into a solid starter, finishing at 9-6 with a 3.95 ERA in seven relief appearances and 24 starts.

Biggest disappointment: Left fielder Kevin McReynolds. Expected to provide run production from the cleanup spot, he played just 109 games due to injuries and knocked in only 49 runs with a .247 average and 13 homers.

Key injuries: Shortstop David Howard's back ailment sidelined him most of the first half, which hurt the heart of the defense. McReynolds, second baseman Keith Miller, outfielder Chris Gwynn and righthanders Mark Gubicza, Luis Aquino and Mike Boddicker also were out for extended periods.

Notable: The Royals' 90 losses were their most since 1970 (97), and their 28 road victories were their fewest ever. ... Jeff Montgomery recorded a career-high 39 saves, the third-highest total in club annals. ... The Royals hit just 75 homers, their lowest full-season total since 1976 (65).

—DICK KAEGEL

RECORDS

1992 regular-season record: 72-90 (T5th in A.L. West); 44-37 at home; 28-53 on road; 38-46 vs. East; 34-44 vs. West; 17-28 vs. LHP; 55-62 vs. RHP; 22-40 on grass; 50-50 on turf; 14-27 in daytime; 58-63 at night; 21-27 in one-run games; 4-10 in extra-inning games; 0-1-1 in doubleheaders.

Team record last five years: 405-403 (.501, ranks 7th in league in that span).

TEAM LEADERS

Batting average: George Brett, Gregg Jefferies (.285).
At-bats: Gregg Jefferies (604).
Runs: Gregg Jefferies, Wally Joyner (66).
Hits: Gregg Jefferies (172).
Total bases: Gregg Jefferies (244).
Doubles: Gregg Jefferies, Wally Joyner (36).
Triples: George Brett, Brian McRae (5).
Home runs: Mike Macfarlane (17).
Runs batted in: Gregg Jefferies (75).
Stolen bases: Gregg Jefferies (19).
Slugging percentage: Gregg Jefferies (.404).
On-base percentage: Wally Joyner (.336).
Wins: Kevin Appier (15).
Earned-run average: Kevin Appier (2.46).
Complete games: Kevin Appier (3).
Shutouts: Mark Gubicza, Chris Haney, Hipolito Pichardo, Dennis Rasmussen, Rick Reed (1).
Saves: Jeff Montgomery (39).
Innings pitched: Kevin Appier (208⅓).
Strikeouts: Kevin Appier (150).

GAMES BY POSITION

Catcher: Mike Macfarlane 104, Brent Mayne 62, Bob Melvin 21.
First base: Wally Joyner 145, George Brett 15, Jeff Conine 4, Bob Melvin 3.
Second base: Keith Miller 93, Curtis Wilkerson 39, Terry Shumpert 33, Juan Samuel 10, Rico Rossy 3, Gregg Jefferies 1.
Third base: Gregg Jefferies 146, Rico Rossy 9, Brent Mayne 8, Curtis Wilkerson 5, George Brett 3.
Shortstop: David Howard 74, Curtis Wilkerson 69, Rico Rossy 51, Terry Shumpert 1.
Outfield: Brian McRae 148, Kevin McReynolds 106, Jim Eisenreich 88, Gary Thurman 67, Kevin Koslofski 52, Jeff Conine 23, Chris Gwynn 19, Juan Samuel 18, Keith Miller 16, David Howard 2, Harvey Pulliam 1.
Designated hitter: George Brett 132, Mike Macfarlane 13, Gary Thurman 9, Jim Eisenreich 8, Wally Joyner 4, Chris Gwynn 2, Harvey Pulliam 2, Gregg Jefferies 1, Kevin McReynolds 1, Keith Miller 1, Terry Shumpert 1, Curtis Wilkerson 1.

TOP 10 DRAFT CHOICES

1a. Michael Tucker, SS, Longwood College (Va.).
1b. Jim Pittsley, RHP, Du Bois (Pa.) Area Senior High School.
1c. Sherard Clinkscales, RHP, Purdue U.
1d. Johnny Damon, OF, Dr. Phillips High School, Orlando, Fla.
2. Jon Lieber, RHP, U. of S. Alabama.
3. Chris Eddy, LHP, Texas Christian University.
4. Steve Murphy, OF, Birmingham-Southern College (Ala.).
5. Jeff Haas, LHP, Univ. of Houston.
6. Jelani Brandon, OF, Lloyd Memorial High School, Erlanger, Ky.
7. Justin Adam, RHP, Holy Names High School, Windsor, Ontario.
8. Mike Kern, OF, Culver City (Calif.) High School.
9. Bart Evans, RHP, Southwest Missouri State University.
10. John Dickens, LHP, Univ. of Texas.

1993 SCHEDULE

APRIL

SUN	MON	TUE	WED	THU	FRI	SAT
				1	2	3
4	5	6 CAL	7 N CAL	8 N	9 N OAK	10 N OAK
11 OAK	12 CAL H	13 CAL	14 N CAL H	15 N CAL H	16 N OAK H	17 OAK H
18 OAK H	19	20 N MIN	21 N MIN	22 MIN	23 N TEX	24 TEX H
25 TEX H	26 N MIN H	27 N MIN H	28 N CHI	29 N CHI	30 N TEX	

MAY

SUN	MON	TUE	WED	THU	FRI	SAT
						1 TEX
2 TEX	3 N TEX	4 N CHI H	5 N CHI H	6	7 N BOS H	8 BOS H
9 BOS H	10	11 NY	12 N NY	13 N CLE H	14 CLE H	15 CLE H
16 CLE H	17 N DET H	18 N DET H	19 N DET H	20 N DET H	21 N BAL	22 BAL
23 BAL	24 TOR	25 TOR	26 TOR	27 TOR	28 N KC H	29 KC H
30 KC H	31					

JUNE

SUN	MON	TUE	WED	THU	FRI	SAT
		1 N SEA	2 SEA	3 N KC	4 N KC	5 N KC
6 KC	7 N SEA	8 N SEA H	9 N SEA H	10 N NY	11 N NY H	12 N NY H
13 NY	14 N BAL H	15 N BAL H	16 BAL H	17	18 N DET	19 DET
20 DET	21 CLE	22 N CLE	23 CLE	24 CLE	25 TOR H	26 N TOR H
27 TOR H	28 N BOS	29 BOS	30 N BOS			

JULY

SUN	MON	TUE	WED	THU	FRI	SAT
				1	2 N MIN	3 MIN
4 MIN	5 1 6 N TEX H	7 N TEX H	8 N MIN H	9 N MIN H	10 N MIN H	
11 MIN H	12	13 ◇ ALL-STAR GAME	14	15 N CHI H	16 N CHI H	17 N CHI H
18 CHI H	19 N TEX	20 N TEX	21	22 N CHI	23 N CHI	24 N CHI
25 CHI	26 N BOS H	27 N BOS H	28 N BOS H	29 BOS H	30 N NY	31 NY

AUGUST

SUN	MON	TUE	WED	THU	FRI	SAT
1 NY	2 N BAL	3 N BAL	4 N BAL	5 N BAL	6 N TOR	7 TOR
8 N TOR	9	10 N CLE H	11 N CLE H	12 N CLE H	13 N DET	14 N DET
15 N DET H	16 N OAK	17 N OAK	18 OAK	19 N CAL	20 N CAL	21 N CAL
22 CAL	23	24 N OAK H	25 N OAK H	26 N OAK H	27 N CAL H	28 CAL H
29 CAL H	30 N KC	31 N KC H				

SEPTEMBER

SUN	MON	TUE	WED	THU	FRI	SAT
			1 KC H	2 N SEA	3 N SEA	4 N SEA
5 SEA	6 N KC	7	8 N KC	9	10 N SEA	11 SEA H
12 SEA H	13 N NY H	14 N NY H	15 N NY H	16	17 N BAL H	18 N BAL H
19 BAL H	20 N DET	21 N DET	22 DET	23	24 N CLE	25 CLE
26 CLE	27 N TOR H	28 N TOR H	29 N TOR H	30		

OCTOBER

SUN	MON	TUE	WED	THU	FRI	SAT
					1 N BOS	2 BOS
3 BOS						

1993 SEASON

CLUB DIRECTORY

President, chief executive officer
Allan H. (Bud) Selig
Senior vice president, baseball operations
Sal Bando
Senior vice president
Harry Dalton
Vice president, government affairs
Dick Hackett
Vice president, broadcast operations
Bill Haig
Vice president, finance
Dick Hoffmann
Vice president, stadium operations
Gabe Paul Jr.
Asst. vice president, baseball operations
Bruce Manno
Scouting director
Ken Califano
Senior consultant, baseball operations
Dee Fondy
Special assistants, baseball operations
Larry Haney
Chuck Tanner
General counsel
Wendy Selig-Prieb
Assistant general counsel
Eugene (Pepi) Randolph
Director of baseball administration
Brian Small
Director of communications
Laurel Prieb
Director of community relations
Michael Downs
Director of marketing
John Cordova
Director of stadium
Terry Ann Peterson
Director of grounds and maintenance
Gary Vandenberg
Director of media relations
Tom Skibosh
Director of player development
Fred Stanley
Director of player negotiations
Tom Gausden
Director of publications
Mario Ziino
Director of ticket operations
John Barnes
Director of ticket sales
Jeff Eisenberg
Traveling secretary
Steve Ethier
Trainers
John Adam
Al Price
Strength and conditioning coach
Toby Oldham

Team physicians
Dr. Paul Jacobs
Dr. Dennis Sullivan
Western crosschecker
Lou Snipp
Eastern crosschecker
Ed Durkin
Midwest supervisor
Fred Beene
Latin America supervisor
Felix Delgado
Northeast supervisor
Ron Rizzi
Northwest supervisor
Dick Foster
Southeast supervisor
Russ Bove
Southwest supervisor
Roland LeBlanc
Special assignment scout
Walter Youse
Scouts
Julio Blanco-Herrera
Tom Calvano
Kevin Christman
Miguel Flores
Bill Foley
Mark Garcia
Ramon Genoa
Dean Gruwell
Manola Hernandez
Ken Houp
Bob Hughes
Pete Jones
Harvey Kuenn Jr.
John Logan
Demie Mainieri
Frank Piet
Mike Powers
Cesar Presbott
Doug Reynolds
Pedro Rivera
Ron Rizzi
Phil Rizzo
Alexis Sakedo
Jerry Salzano
Richard Scarfia
Art Schuerman
Bob Sloan
Paul Tretiak
Fermin Ubri
Richard Waldt
Thomas Walsh
Red Whitsett
Ric Wilson
Brian York
David Young

SCHEDULE KEY

H—Home game.   N—Night game (any game starting after 5 p.m.).
*All-Star Game at Oriole Park at Camden Yards, Baltimore.

Manager—Phil Garner (3).
Coaches—Bill Castro (35), Gene Clines (12), Duffy Dyer (10), Tim Foli (14), Don Rowe (45).

No.	PITCHERS	B/T	Ht./Wt.	Born	1992 clubs
42	Austin, James	R/R	6-2/200	12-7-63	Milwaukee
25	Bones, Ricky	R/R	6-0/190	4-7-69	Milwaukee
57	Boze, Marshall	R/R	6-1/212	5-23-71	Beloit
21	Eldred, Cal	R/R	6-4/215	11-24-67	Denver, Milwaukee
36	Fetters, Mike	R/R	6-4/212	12-19-64	Milwaukee
58	Gamez, Francisco	R/R	6-2/185	4-2-70	Stockton
59	George, Chris	R/R	6-2/200	9-24-66	Denver
41	Green, Otis	L/L	6-2/192	3-11-64	Denver
28	Henry, Doug	R/R	6-4/185	12-10-63	Milwaukee
49	Higuera, Teddy	B/L	5-10/178	11-9-58	Beloit, El Paso, Denver
53	Ignasiak, Mike	B/R	5-11/175	3-12-66	Denver
43	Kiefer, Mark	R/R	6-4/175	11-13-68	Denver
37	Lloyd, Graeme	L/L	6-7/215	4-9-67	Knoxville
52	Maldonado, Carlos	R/R	6-1/215	10-18-66	Omaha
51	Manzanillo, Josias	R/R	6-0/190	10-16-67	Omaha, Memphis
38	Miranda, Angel	L/L	6-1/160	11-9-69	Denver
31	Navarro, Jaime	R/R	6-4/210	3-27-67	Milwaukee
55	Novoa, Rafael	L/L	6-1/180	10-26-67	El Paso
47	Orosco, Jesse	R/L	6-2/185	4-21-57	Milwaukee
33	Robinson, Ron	R/R	6-4/235	3-24-62	Stockton, Milwaukee, El Paso
39	Stanford, Larry	R/R	6-3/205	9-26-67	Columbus
46	Wegman, Bill	R/R	6-5/220	12-19-62	Milwaukee
61	Wishnevski, Rob	R/R	6-1/215	1-2-67	El Paso, Denver

No.	CATCHERS	B/T	Ht./Wt.	Born	1992 clubs
27	Kmak, Joe	R/R	6-0/185	5-3-63	Denver
26	McIntosh, Tim	R/R	5-11/195	3-21-65	Milwaukee
11	Nilsson, Dave	L/R	6-3/185	12-14-69	Denver, Milwaukee
5	Surhoff, B.J.	L/R	6-1/200	8-4-64	Milwaukee

No.	INFIELDERS	B/T	Ht./Wt.	Born	1992 clubs
	Doran, Bill	B/R	6-0/180	5-28-58	Cincinnati
32	Jaha, John	R/R	6-1/195	5-27-66	Denver, Milwaukee
16	Listach, Pat	B/R	5-9/170	9-12-67	Milwaukee
9	Spiers, Bill	L/R	6-2/190	6-5-66	Beloit, Milwaukee
54	Valentin, Jose	B/R	5-10/175	10-12-69	Denver, Milwaukee

No.	OUTFIELDERS	B/T	Ht./Wt.	Born	1992 clubs
	Brunansky, Tom	R/R	6-4/220	8-20-60	Boston
18	Diaz, Alex	B/R	5-11/175	10-5-68	Denver, Milwaukee
24	Hamilton, Darryl	L/R	6-1/180	12-3-64	Milwaukee
30	Mieske, Matt	R/R	6-0/185	2-13-68	Denver
60	O'Leary, Troy	L/L	6-0/175	8-4-69	El Paso
29	Reimer, Kevin	L/R	6-2/230	6-28-64	Texas
23	Vaughn, Greg	R/R	6-0/193	7-3-65	Milwaukee
19	Yount, Robin	R/R	6-0/180	9-16-55	Milwaukee

BALLPARK INFORMATION

Ballpark (capacity, surface)
County Stadium (53,192, grass)
Address
County Stadium
P.O. Box 3099 Milwaukee, WI
53201-3099
Business phone
414-933-4114
Ticket information
414-933-1818
Ticket prices
$15 (deluxe mezz. & mezzanine)
$14 (lower box)
$12 (upper box)
$11 (lower grandstand)
$8 (upper grandstand)
$7 (general admission)
$4 (bleachers)
Field dimensions (from home plate)
To left field at foul line, 315 feet
To center field, 402 feet
To right field at foul line, 315 feet
First game played
April 7, 1970 (Angels 12, Brewers 0)

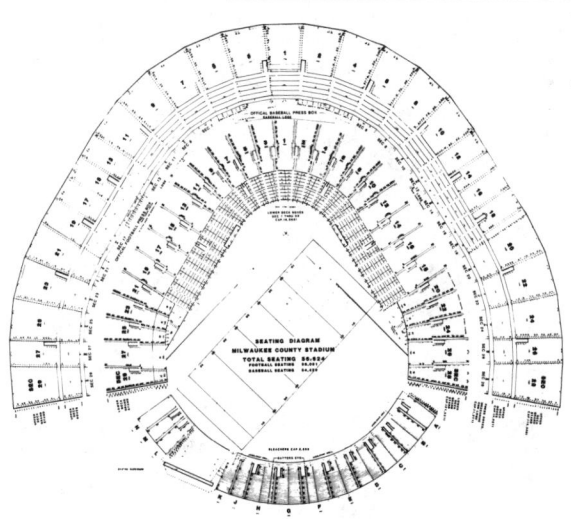

MINOR LEAGUE AFFILIATES

Class	Team	League	Manager
AAA	New Orleans	American Association	Chris Bando
AA	El Paso	Texas	Tim Ireland
A	Stockton	California	Lamar Johnson
A	Beloit	Midwest	Wayne Krenchicki
Rookie	Helena	Pioneer	Mike Epstein
Rookie	Chandler Brewers	Arizona	Ralph Dickenson

BROADCAST INFORMATION

Radio: WTMJ-AM (620). Broadcasters: Bob Uecker, Pat Hughes.
TV: WVTV-TV (Channel 24). Broadcasters: Rory Markus, Del Crandall.
Cable TV: None.

SPRING TRAINING

Ballpark (city): Compadre Stadium (Chandler, Ariz.).
Ticket information: 602-895-1200.

HISTORY

YEAR-BY-YEAR RECORDS

Year	Pos.	W	L	Pct.	*GB	Year	Pos.	W	L	Pct.	*GB
1969	6th	64	98	.395	33	1983	5th	87	75	.537	11
1970	T4th	65	97	.401	33	1984	7th	67	94	.416	36½
1971	6th	69	92	.429	32	1985	6th	71	90	.441	28
1972	6th	65	91	.417	21	1986	6th	77	84	.478	18
1973	5th	74	88	.457	23	1987	3rd	91	71	.562	7
1974	5th	76	86	.469	15	1988	T3rd	87	75	.537	2
1975	5th	68	94	.420	28	1989	4th	81	81	.500	8
1976	6th	66	95	.410	32	1990	6th	74	88	.457	14
1977	6th	67	95	.414	33	1991	4th	83	79	.512	8
1978	3rd	93	69	.574	6½	1992	2nd	92	70	.568	4
1979	2nd	95	66	.590	8						
1980	3rd	86	76	.531	17						
1981	3rd/1st	62	47	.569	†‡						
1982	1st§	95	67	.586 +	1						

*Games behind winner. †First half 31-25; second 31-22. ‡Lost division playoff. §Won Championship Series.

MANAGERS

Name	Record	Years
Joe Schultz	64-98	1969
Dave Bristol	144-209	'70-72
Del Crandall	271-338	'72-75
Alex Grammas	133-190	'76-77
George Bamberger	377-351	'78-80
		'85-86
Buck Rodgers	124-102	'80-82
Harvey Kuenn	160-118	'82-83
Rene Lachemann	67-94	1984
Tom Trebelhorn	422-397	'86-91
Phil Garner	92-70	1992

DAY BY DAY

Date	Opp.	Res.	Score (inn.*)	Hits	Opp. hits	Winning pitcher	Losing pitcher	Save	Record	Pos.	GB
4-6	Min.	L	2-4	6	11	Willis	Nunez	Aguilera	0-1	T5th	1
4-8	Min.	W	9-5	8	9	Ruffin	Aguilera		1-1	T3rd	1
4-9	Min.	L	1-3	4	11	Krueger	Navarro	Aguilera	1-2	T4th	2
4-10	At Cal.	W	5-4	8	5	Plesac	Harvey	Henry	2-2	T3rd	2
4-11	At Cal.	L	1-4	8	10	Robinson	Wegman	Harvey	2-3	T3rd	3
4-12	At Cal.	L	9-13	17	14	Langston	Bosio		2-4	T4th	4
4-14	At Min.	W	11-1	11	4	Navarro	Smiley		3-4	3rd	3½
4-15	At Min.	W	7-4	(10)	11	14	Austin	Willis		4-4	3rd	3½
4-17	Sea.	W	5-1	9	5	Wegman	Hanson		5-4	3rd	3
4-18	Sea.	L	3-5	6	12	Swan	Plesac	Schooler	5-5	T3rd	4
4-19	Sea.	L	9-12	15	15	Jones	Ruffin	Schooler	5-6	5th	4
4-21	Bos.	L	1-3	3	6	Gardiner	Austin	Darwin	5-7	5th	5½
4-23	Bos.	W	3-2	7	7	Wegman	Clemens	Henry	6-7	T4th	5
4-24	At Cle.	W	5-0	9	2	Plesac	Armstrong		7-7	T4th	5
4-26 (1)	At Cle.	W	9-4	13	9	Bosio	Scudder		8-7	4th	4½
4-26 (2)	At Cle.	L	1-3	7	8	Cook	Navarro	Power	8-8	4th	5
4-28	K.C.	L	2-3	(11)	3	6	Heaton	Orosco	Montgomery	8-9	T4th	5
4-29	K.C.	W	5-3	9	5	Bones	Gordon	Henry	9-9	T4th	5
4-30	Tor.	W	3-2	8	7	Bosio	Ward	Henry	10-9	4th	4
5-1	Tor.	W	4-3	8	7	Navarro	Key	Henry	11-9	4th	3
5-2	Tor.	W	5-4	8	7	Fetters	Morris	Henry	12-9	4th	2
5-3	Tor.	L	1-4	3	11	Stieb	Wegman		12-10	4th	3
5-4	At Chi.	L	0-7	1	10	Fernandez	Bones		12-11	4th	4
5-5	At Chi.	L	2-12	7	11	McDowell	Bosio		12-12	5th	5
5-6	At K.C.	L	1-3	7	7	Gubicza	Navarro	Montgomery	12-13	5th	6
5-7	At K.C.	L	4-6	13	10	Young	Plesac	Montgomery	12-14	5th	7
5-8	At Tex.	L	2-3	8	7	Brown	Wegman	Russell	12-15	5th	7
5-9	At Tex.	L	4-5	8	9	Robinson	Holmes	Russell	12-16	6th	7
5-10	At Tex.	W	6-2	11	8	Bosio	Guzman		13-16	5th	7
5-12	Chi.	W	6-2	13	10	Navarro	Hibbard		14-16	5th	7
5-13	Chi.	L	0-1	2	7	McCaskill	Wegman	Thigpen	14-17	5th	8
5-15	Tex.	W	7-3	(10)	15	11	Holmes	Robinson		15-17	5th	7½
5-16	Tex.	W	5-4	9	9	Holmes	Rogers		16-17	5th	7
5-17	Tex.	L	1-2	(10)	8	6	Russell	Navarro		16-18	5th	7
5-18	At Det.	W	9-1	13	4	Wegman	King		17-18	5th	6
5-19	At Det.	L	0-3	3	7	Tanana	Robinson	Henneman	17-19	5th	6
5-20	At Det.	L	3-4	12	5	Knudsen	Henry		17-20	6th	6½
5-21	At Det.	W	7-3	9	5	Nunez	Aldred		18-20	5th	6
5-22	At N.Y.	W	10-9	(14)	16	15	Henry	Monteleone		19-20	5th	6
5-23	At N.Y.	W	5-4	(10)	7	8	Wegman	Hillegas	Orosco	20-20	5th	5
5-24	At N.Y.	L	7-8	12	12	Habyan	Ruffin		20-21	5th	5½
5-25	At N.Y.	L	10-13	17	18	Guetterman	Austin		20-22	5th	5½
5-26	At Tor.	L	4-5	7	5	Stieb	Bones	Henke	20-23	5th	6½
5-27	At Tor.	W	8-4	13	7	Navarro	Stottlemyre	Henry	21-23	5th	5½
5-29	N.Y.	W	8-3	12	10	Wegman	Cadaret		22-23	5th	5½
5-30	N.Y.	L	1-8	5	11	Sanderson	Bosio		22-24	5th	6½
5-31	N.Y.	W	2-1	5	4	Orosco	Kamieniecki		23-24	5th	6½
6-1	Det.	W	6-2	10	10	Navarro	Aldred		24-24	5th	6½
6-2	Det.	W	5-4	10	8	Orosco	Leiter	Henry	25-24	5th	6½
6-3	Det.	L	4-10	9	14	Ritz	Wegman		25-25	T4th	6½
6-5	Cal.	W	7-1	12	5	Bosio	Abbott		26-25	4th	5½
6-6	Cal.	W	4-3	8	8	Navarro	Harvey	Henry	27-25	3rd	5½
6-7	Cal.	W	10-3	10	6	Bones	Langston		28-25	3rd	4½
6-8	Oak.	W	6-2	10	4	Wegman	Slusarski		29-25	3rd	4½
6-9	Oak.	L	1-6	4	15	Campbell	Robinson		29-26	3rd	5½
6-10	Oak.	L	2-5	9	7	Darling	Bosio	Eckersley	29-27	3rd	6½
6-12	At Sea.	L	1-4	7	7	Hanson	Navarro	Swan	29-28	3rd	7
6-13	At Sea.	W	8-7	13	11	Fetters	Gunderson	Henry	30-28	3rd	6
6-14	At Sea.	W	14-4	22	7	Bones	Fleming		31-28	3rd	6
6-15	At Oak.	W	2-3	(10)	9	7	Eckersley	Fetters		31-29	3rd	6½
6-16	At Oak.	W	10-0	12	3	Robinson	Darling		32-29	3rd	5½
6-17	At Oak.	W	10-2	12	5	Navarro	Moore		33-29	3rd	5½
6-18	Cle.	W	4-1	7	3	Wegman	Otto		34-29	3rd	4½
6-19	Cle.	L	3-5	10	9	Scudder	Bones		34-30	3rd	4½
6-20	Cle.	W	4-1	10	3	Bosio	Boucher	Henry	35-30	3rd	4½
6-21	Cle.	W	4-2	7	8	Plesac	Armstrong	Henry	36-30	3rd	3½
6-23	Bal.	L	1-7	4	8	Mesa	Navarro	Davis	36-31	3rd	4½
6-24	Bal.	L	4-8	9	14	Mills	Holmes		36-32	3rd	5½
6-25	Bal.	W	1-0	5	5	Bones	Sutcliffe	Henry	37-32	3rd	5
6-26	At Bos.	L	4-8	11	13	Dopson	Robinson		37-33	3rd	6

Date	Opp.	Res.	Score	(inn.*)	Hits	Opp. hits	Winning pitcher	Losing pitcher	Save	Record	Pos.	GB
6-27	At Bos.	L	7-8	(13)	14	13	Darwin	Holmes		37-34	3rd	6
6-28	At Bos.	W	9-3		15	8	Navarro	Viola		38-34	3rd	5
6-29	At Bal.	W	5-3		11	6	Bosio	Milacki	Fetters	39-34	3rd	5
6-30	At Bal.	L	3-12		10	16	Sutcliffe	Bones		39-35	3rd	5
7-1	At Bal.	L	4-7		10	12	McDonald	Wegman	Olson	39-36	3rd	6
7-2	At K.C.	L	2-8		6	13	Appier	Robinson		39-37	3rd	6½
7-3	At K.C.	W	7-3		13	7	Navarro	Pichardo		40-37	3rd	6½
7-5 (1)	At K.C.	W	2-1	(12)	7	10	Fetters	Montgomery	Henry	41-37	3rd	7
7-5 (2)	At K.C.	W	9-7		9	11	Bones	Davis	Holmes	42-37	3rd	6½
7-6	At Tex.	L	1-3		7	9	Brown	Wegman	Russell	42-38	3rd	7½
7-7	At Tex.	W	4-3		10	9	Austin	Burns	Henry	43-38	3rd	7½
7-8	At Tex.	W	4-3		11	6	Fetters	Guzman	Henry	44-38	3rd	7½
7-9	K.C.	L	2-3		9	10	Shifflett	Bosio	Montgomery	44-39	3rd	8½
7-10	K.C.	L	1-3		9	13	Gordon	Bones	Montgomery	44-40	3rd	8½
7-11	K.C.	W	5-1		9	13	Wegman	Reed		45-40	3rd	7½
7-12	K.C.	L	1-5		7	7	Appier	Ruffin	Boddicker	45-41	3rd	7½
7-16	At Chi.	L	4-5	(12)	10	14	Hernandez	Plesac		45-42	3rd	8½
7-17	At Chi.	W	4-3	(11)	9	3	Plesac	Radinsky	Henry	46-42	3rd	7½
7-18	At Chi.	W	3-1		7	7	Bones	McDowell	Henry	47-42	3rd	7½
7-19	At Chi.	W	6-3		7	11	Eldred	Hibbard	Henry	48-42	3rd	7½
7-20	Tex.	W	5-4		7	8	Holmes	Nunez		49-42	3rd	6½
7-21	Tex.	L	3-6	(10)	10	10	Mathews	Holmes	Russell	49-43	3rd	7½
7-22	Tex.	W	4-1		8	2	Navarro	Brown		50-43	3rd	6½
7-23	Chi.	L	2-6		11	10	McDowell	Bones	Radinsky	50-44	3rd	7½
7-24	Chi.	W	3-2		8	9	Fetters	Leach	Henry	51-44	3rd	6½
7-25	Chi.	W	3-0		6	7	Bosio	Hough		52-44	3rd	5½
7-26	Chi.	W	15-4		12	7	Wegman	McCaskill		53-44	3rd	4½
7-27	At Cle.	W	4-0		13	3	Navarro	Nagy		54-44	T2nd	4
7-28	At Cle.	L	2-4		6	12	Nichols	Bones	Lilliquist	54-45	3rd	5
7-29	At Cle.	L	3-4		7	10	Armstrong	Eldred	Lilliquist	54-46	3rd	5
7-30	At Min.	W	5-3		11	7	Bosio	Banks		55-46	3rd	5
7-31	At Min.	L	1-4		8	9	Tapani	Wegman	Edens	55-47	3rd	6
8-1	At Min.	L	6-9		7	11	Smiley	Navarro		55-48	3rd	7
8-2	At Min.	L	0-5		4	9	Erickson	Bones		55-49	3rd	8
8-4	Sea.	W	5-2		7	8	Bosio	Fisher	Henry	56-49	3rd	6½
8-5	Sea.	W	8-1		9	5	Wegman	Johnson		57-49	3rd	6½
8-6	Sea.	W	4-2		11	11	Navarro	Grant	Henry	58-49	3rd	6½
8-8 (1)	Min.	W	4-0		8	3	Eldred	Erickson		59-49	3rd	5
8-8 (2)	Min.	L	1-3		5	8	Krueger	Bones	Aguilera	59-50	3rd	5½
8-9	Min.	W	4-2		10	6	Bosio	West	Henry	60-50	3rd	4½
8-10	At Cal.	L	1-4		3	9	Valera	Wegman		60-51	3rd	5½
8-11	At Cal.	L	0-1	(10)	7	8	Grahe	Navarro		60-52	3rd	5½
8-12	At Cal.	L	1-2		2	4	Langston	Ruffin	Grahe	60-53	3rd	5½
8-14 (1)	Bos.	W	8-7	(13)	13	10	Austin	Reardon		61-53	3rd	6
8-14 (2)	Bos.	W	1-0		7	3	Eldred	Harris	Holmes	62-53	3rd	5½
8-15	Bos.	L	1-3		4	10	Darwin	Wegman		62-54	3rd	6
8-16	Bos.	W	1-0		5	3	Navarro	Viola		63-54	3rd	5½
8-18	Tor.	L	1-12		3	15	Key	Ruffin		63-55	3rd	6½
8-19	Tor.	W	10-5		12	10	Bosio	Linton		64-55	3rd	5½
8-20	Tor.	W	16-3		18	9	Wegman	Wells		65-55	3rd	4½
8-21	Det.	W	3-2		10	7	Navarro	Doherty	Henry	66-55	3rd	3½
8-22	Det.	W	5-1		11	5	Eldred	Tanana		67-55	3rd	3½
8-23	Det.	L	2-3		4	8	Henneman	Plesac		67-56	3rd	3½
8-24	At N.Y.	L	8-9		11	14	Nielsen	Henry	Farr	67-57	3rd	3½
8-25	At N.Y.	L	1-5		7	9	Militello	Wegman		67-58	3rd	3½
8-26	At N.Y.	L	3-4		7	7	Kamieniecki	Ruffin	Farr	67-59	3rd	4½
8-27	At Tor.	L	4-5		7	7	Morris	Navarro	Henke	67-60	3rd	5½
8-28	At Tor.	W	22-2		31	9	Eldred	Key		68-60	3rd	4½
8-29	At Tor.	W	7-2		9	6	Bosio	Cone	Holmes	69-60	3rd	3½
8-30	At Tor.	L	3-5		7	9	Ward	Wegman	Henke	69-61	3rd	4½
8-31	N.Y.	W	4-1		7	4	Bones	Kamieniecki	Henry	70-61	3rd	4½
9-1	N.Y.	L	1-7		8	16	Perez	Navarro		70-62	3rd	5½
9-2	N.Y.	W	7-0		9	6	Eldred	Sanderson		71-62	3rd	4½
9-4	At Det.	W	6-3		14	9	Bosio	Gullickson	Plesac	72-62	3rd	4½
9-5	At Det.	W	10-3		16	6	Wegman	Haas		73-62	3rd	4½
9-6	At Det.	L	2-6		9	12	Doherty	Navarro		73-63	3rd	5½
9-7	Cle.	W	2-0		6	5	Eldred	Cook	Henry	74-63	3rd	4½
9-8	Cle.	W	7-3		13	5	Bones	Armstrong	Fetters	75-63	3rd	4½
9-9	Cle.	L	4-5		8	9	Olin	Henry		75-64	3rd	5½
9-11	At Bal.	L	2-3		6	10	Mussina	Wegman		75-65	3rd	6
9-12	At Bal.	W	5-0		10	5	Navarro	Lefferts		76-65	3rd	6
9-13	At Bal.	W	3-1		14	4	Eldred	McDonald		77-65	3rd	6
9-14	At Bos.	W	6-0		11	4	Bosio	Darwin		78-65	3rd	5
9-15	At Bos.	W	7-2		11	8	Austin	Viola		79-65	3rd	5

Date	Opp.	Res.	Score	(inn.*)	Hits	Opp. hits	Winning pitcher	Losing pitcher	Save	Record	Pos.	GB
9-16	At Bos.	L	1-2	(15)	10	11	Irvine	Henry		79-66	3rd	5
9-17	At Bos.	W	10-4		15	14	Navarro	Clemens		80-66	3rd	5
9-18	Bal.	W	12-4		17	11	Eldred	Sutcliffe		81-66	3rd	5
9-19	Bal.	W	4-1		7	6	Bosio	McDonald	Holmes	82-66	2nd	5
9-20	Bal.	W	9-3		12	8	Austin	Davis		83-66	2nd	4
9-21	Bal.	L	1-4		7	6	Mussina	Wegman		83-67	2nd	4½
9-22	Cal.	W	3-2		6	8	Plesac	Langston	Holmes	84-67	2nd	4½
9-23	Cal.	W	3-0		8	4	Eldred	Abbott		85-67	2nd	3½
9-24	Cal.	W	4-0		11	5	Bosio	Blyleven		86-67	2nd	3½
9-25	Oak.	W	4-1		5	5	Bones	Stewart		87-67	2nd	3½
9-26	Oak.	W	2-1		6	6	Orosco	Darling	Henry	88-67	2nd	2½
9-27	Oak.	W	5-3		7	9	Navarro	Campbell	Henry	89-67	2nd	2½
9-29	At Sea.	W	7-4		12	11	Eldred	Fisher	Holmes	90-67	2nd	2½
9-30	At Sea.	L	4-7		10	10	Leary	Bosio	DeLucia	90-68	2nd	2½
10-1	At Sea.	W	7-2	(10)	13	4	Wegman	Nelson		91-68	2nd	2
10-2	At Oak.	W	3-2	(11)	6	7	Holmes	Corsi	Henry	92-68	2nd	2
10-3	At Oak.	L	3-10		6	13	Moore	Bones		92-69	2nd	3
10-4	At Oak.	L	1-7		6	7	Russell	Eldred		92-70	2nd	4

Monthly records: April (10-9), May (13-15), June (16-11), July (16-12), August (15-14), September (20-7), Oct. (2-2).

HIGHLIGHTS

High point: The Brewers won 21 of 28 games from September 1-October 1 to pull within two games of first-place Toronto entering the final weekend of the season.

Low point: With the Blue Jays struggling, the Brewers had a chance to reduce Toronto's 3½-game lead as they entered New York for a three-game series August 24-26. Toronto won just two of its three games, but the Yankees swept Milwaukee.

Turning point: When the Brewers called up righthander Cal Eldred from Class AAA Denver after the All-Star break and put him in the rotation. Before the All-Star break, Milwaukee was 45-41 with a 3.91 staff ERA. With Eldred, who went 11-2 with a 1.79 ERA in 14 big-league starts, the Brewers were 47-29 (tops in the A.L. East) with a 2.90 ERA.

Most valuable player: Shortstop Pat Listach. Recalled from Denver on April 7 to replace the injured Bill Spiers, the A.L. Rookie of the Year helped elevate the Brewers to bona fide contenders.

Most valuable pitcher: Eldred. The Brewers never would have gone as far as they did without Eldred, who—along with righthander Chris Bosio—notched a team-record 10 straight wins.

Most improved players: Second baseman Scott Fletcher and third baseman Kevin Seitzer. A non-roster invitee to spring training, Fletcher hit .275 after posting an abysmal .206 average with the White Sox in 1991. Seitzer, also a non-roster invitee, drove in a career-high 71 runs after collecting just 25 RBIs for Kansas City the year before.

Most pleasant surprise: Catcher Dave Nilsson. Known as a good hitter, the rookie did well defensively, throwing out 35 percent of would-be basestealers and posting a .992 fielding average.

Biggest disappointment: Left fielder Greg Vaughn. His numbers (23 homers, 78 RBIs) were respectable, but most of his production came in April, May and September. His lack of punch in the other months left a hole in the lineup.

Key injuries: Spiers, who was recovering from off-season back surgery, didn't play until the final month. Lefthander Teddy Higuera spent the season recovering from rotator cuff surgery. Righthander Ron Robinson was plagued by elbow problems.

Notable: On September 9, center fielder Robin Yount became the 17th player to register 3,000 career hits. ... The Brewers set a team record for fewest errors in a season (89). ... Milwaukee became the first A.L. East team to steal over 200 bases (256) in a season.

—BOB BERGHAUS

TEAM LEADERS

Batting average: Paul Molitor (.320).
At-bats: Paul Molitor (609).
Runs: Pat Listach (93).
Hits: Paul Molitor (195).
Total bases: Paul Molitor (281).
Doubles: Paul Molitor (36).
Triples: Darryl Hamilton, Paul Molitor (7).
Home runs: Greg Vaughn (23).
Runs batted in: Paul Molitor (89).
Stolen bases: Pat Listach (54).
Slugging percentage: Paul Molitor (.461).
On-base percentage: Paul Molitor (.389).
Wins: Jaime Navarro (17).
Earned-run average: Bill Wegman (3.20).
Complete games: Bill Wegman (7).
Shutouts: Jaime Navarro (3).
Saves: Doug Henry (29).
Innings pitched: Bill Wegman (261⅔).
Strikeouts: Bill Wegman (127).

RECORDS

1992 regular-season record: 92-70 (2nd in A.L. East); 53-28 at home; 39-42 on road; 45-33 vs. East; 47-37 vs. West; 30-12 vs. LHP; 62-58 vs. RHP; 79-59 on grass; 13-11 on turf; 31-24 in daytime; 61-46 at night; 26-22 in one-run games; 9-8 in extra-inning games; 2-0-2 in doubleheaders.
Team record last five years: 417-393 (.515, ranks T4th in league in that span).

GAMES BY POSITION

Catcher: B.J. Surhoff 109, Dave Nilsson 46, Tim McIntosh 14, Andy Allanson 9.
First base: Franklin Stubbs 68, Paul Molitor 48, John Jaha 38, B.J. Surhoff 17, Tim McIntosh 7, Dave Nilsson 3, Jim Gantner 2, Kevin Seitzer 1.
Second base: Scott Fletcher 106, Jim Gantner 68, William Suero 15, Bill Spiers 4, Kevin Seitzer 2, Pat Listach 1, Jose Valentin 1.
Third base: Kevin Seitzer 146, Jim Gantner 31, Jim Tatum 5, B.J. Surhoff 3, Scott Fletcher 1, Bill Spiers 1.
Shortstop: Pat Listach 148, Scott Fletcher 22, Bill Spiers 5, William Suero 1, Jose Valentin 1.
Outfield: Robin Yount 139, Greg Vaughn 131, Darryl Hamilton 124, Dante Bichette 101, Alex Diaz 11, Tim McIntosh 10, B.J. Surhoff 7, John Jaha 1, Pat Listach 1, Franklin Stubbs 1.
Designated hitter: Paul Molitor 108, Franklin Stubbs 16, Robin Yount 11, B.J. Surhoff 9, John Jaha 8, Greg Vaughn 7, Dante Bichette 4, Tim McIntosh 3, Alex Diaz 2, Jim Gantner 2, Dave Nilsson 2, William Suero 2, Bill Spiers 1.

TOP 10 DRAFT CHOICES

1a. Kenny Felder, OF, Florida State University.
1b. Gabby Martinez, SS, Santurce, Puerto Rico.
2. Bobby Hughes, C, University of Southern California.
3. Danan Hughes, OF, University of Iowa.
4. Kevin Kloek, RHP, California State University-Northridge.
5. Dan Kyslinger, RHP, Western Carolina University.
6. Scott Karl, LHP, University of Hawaii.
7. Chris Mayfield, OF, McNeese State University.
8. Jeff Droll, RHP, Allegany (Md.) Community College.
9. Wes Weger, SS, Stetson University.
10. Travis Wilson, C, Vista (Calif.) High School.

MINNESOTA TWINS
AMERICAN LEAGUE WEST DIVISION

1993 SCHEDULE

APRIL

SUN	MON	TUE	WED	THU	FRI	SAT
				1	2	3
4	5	6 N CHI	7 N CHI	8 N CHI H	9 N KC	10 KC
11 KC	12 N CHI	13 N CHI	14 N CHI	15	16 N KC	17 N KC H
18 KC H	19	20 N MIL H	21 N MIL H	22 N MIL H	23 N DET H	24 N DET H
25 DET H	26 N MIL	27 MIL	28 N BAL	29 BAL	30 DET	

MAY

SUN	MON	TUE	WED	THU	FRI	SAT
						1 DET
2 DET	3	4 N BAL H	5 N BAL H	6	7 N SEA	8 N SEA
9 SEA	10 N CAL	11 N CAL	12 N CAL	13	14 N BOS H	15 N BOS H
16 BOS H	17 N NY H	18 N NY H	19 N NY H	20	21 N TOR	22 TOR
23 TOR	24	25 N OAK	26 N OAK	27 OAK	28 N CLE H	29 N CLE H
30 CLE H	31 TEX H					

JUNE

SUN	MON	TUE	WED	THU	FRI	SAT
		1 N TEX H	2 N TEX H	3	4 N CLE	5 CLE
6 CLE	7 N TEX	8 N TEX	9 N TEX	10 N TEX	11 N OAK H	12 N OAK H
13 OAK H	14 N TOR H	15 N TOR H	16 N TOR H	17 N NY	18 N NY	19 NY
20 NY	21 N BOS	22 N BOS	23 N BOS	24	25 N CAL H	26 N CAL H
27 CAL H	28 N SEA H	29 N SEA H	30 N SEA H			

JULY

SUN	MON	TUE	WED	THU	FRI	SAT
				1 SEA H	2 N MIL	3 N MIL H
4 MIL H	5 N DET H	6 N DET H	7 N DET H	8 N MIL	9 N MIL	10 N MIL
11 MIL	12	13 ● ALL-STAR GAME	14	15 N BAL	16 N BAL	17 N BAL
18 BAL	19 N DET	20 N DET	21 N DET	22 N BAL H	23 N BAL H	24 N BAL H
25 BAL H	26	27 N SEA	28 N SEA	29 N SEA	30 N CAL	31 N CAL

AUGUST

SUN	MON	TUE	WED	THU	FRI	SAT
1 CAL	2	3 N BOS H	4 N BOS H	5 N BOS H	6 N NY H	7 N NY H
8 NY H	9	10 N TOR	11 N TOR	12 N TOR	13 N OAK	14 OAK
15 OAK	16	17 N KC H	18 N KC H	19 N KC H	20 N CHI H	21 N CHI H
22 CHI H	23 N KC	24 N KC	25 N KC	26 N KC	27 N CHI	28 N CHI
29 N CHI	30 N CHI	31 N CLE H				

SEPTEMBER

SUN	MON	TUE	WED	THU	FRI	SAT
			1 N CLE H	2 N CLE H	3 N TEX H	4 N TEX H
5 N TEX H	6	7 N CLE	8 N CLE	9 N CLE	10 N TEX	11 N TEX
12 TEX	13 N OAK H	14 N OAK H	15 N OAK H	16 N OAK H	17 N TOR H	18 TOR H
19 TOR H	20	21 N NY	22 N NY	23	24 N BOS	25 BOS
26 BOS	27 N CAL H	28 N CAL H	29 N CAL H	30		

OCTOBER

SUN	MON	TUE	WED	THU	FRI	SAT
					1 N SEA H	2 N SEA H
3 SEA H						

1993 SEASON

CLUB DIRECTORY

Owner
Carl R. Pohlad
President
Jerry Bell
Chairman of executive committee
Howard Fox
Directors
Donald E. Benson
Paul R. Christen
James O. Pohlad
Robert C. Pohlad
William M. Pohlad
Robert E. Woolley
Executive v.p., baseball operations/g.m.
Andy MacPhail
Vice president, player personnel
Terry Ryan
Vice president, marketing/sales
Bill Mahre
Chief financial officer
Kevin Mather
Vice president, stadium operations
Matt Hoy
Director of minor leagues
Jim Rantz
Director of scouting
Larry Corrigan
Assistant general manager
Bill Smith
Director of media relations
Rob Antony
Traveling secretary
Remzi Kiratli

Club physicians
Dr. Leonard J. Michienzi
Dr. John Steubs
Scouts
Floyd Baker
Vernon Borning
Ellsworth Brown
Gene DeBoer
Dan Durst
Cal Ermer
Marty Esposito
Vern Followell
Earl Frishman
Scott Groot
Joel Lepel
Bill Lohr
Kevin Murphy
Al Newman
Mike Radcliff
Clair Rierson
Eddie Robinson
Edwin Rodriguez
Mike Ruth
Jeff Schugel
Herb Stein
Ricky Taylor
Brad Weitzel
Steve Williams
John Wilson
International scouts
Enrique Brito
Howard Norsetter
Johnny Sierra

SCHEDULE KEY

H—Home game.   N—Night game (any game starting after 5 p.m.).
*All-Star Game at Oriole Park at Camden Yards, Baltimore.

Manager—Tom Kelly (10).

Coaches—Terry Crowley (46), Ron Gardenhire (35), Rocl Stelmaszek (43), Dick Such (42), Wayne Terwilliger (45).

No.	PITCHERS	B/T	Ht./Wt.	Born	1992 clubs
37	Abbott, Paul	R/R	6-3/194	9-15-67	Portland, Minnesota
38	Aguilera, Rick	R/R	6-5/205	12-31-61	Minnesota
23	Banks, Willie	R/R	6-1/202	2-27-69	Portland, Minnesota
56	Best, Jayson	R/R	6-0/170	9-9-68	Fort Myers, Orlando
48	Casian, Larry	R/L	6-0/170	10-28-65	Portland, Minnesota
44	Deshaies, Jim	L/L	6-4/222	6-23-60	Las Vegas, San Diego
19	Erickson, Scott	R/R	6-4/224	2-2-68	Minnesota
41	Garces, Richard	R/R	6-0/215	5-18-71	Orlando
53	Guthrie, Mark	B/L	6-4/206	9-22-65	Minnesota
49	Hartley, Mike	R/R	6-1/195	8-31-61	Scranton/Wilkes-Barre, Philadelphia
20	Mahomes, Pat	R/R	6-1/205	8-9-70	Minnesota, Portland
55	Munoz, Oscar	R/R	6-2/205	9-25-69	Orlando
54	Newman, Alan	L/L	6-6/212	10-2-69	Orlando
36	Tapani, Kevin	R/R	6-0/187	2-18-64	Minnesota
21	Trombley, Mike	R/R	6-2/200	4-14-67	Portland, Minnesota
30	Tsamis, George	R/L	6-2/175	6-14-67	Portland
47	Wayne, Gary	L/L	6-3/193	11-30-62	Minnesota, Portland
51	Willis, Carl	L/R	6-4/211	12-28-60	Minnesota

No.	CATCHERS	B/T	Ht./Wt.	Born	1992 clubs
12	Harper, Brian	R/R	6-2/206	10-16-59	Minnesota
59	Maksudian, Mike	L/R	5-11/220	5-28-66	Syracuse, Toronto
16	Parks, Derek	R/R	6-0/205	9-29-68	Portland, Minnesota
15	Webster, Lenny	R/R	5-9/191	2-10-65	Minnesota

No.	INFIELDERS	B/T	Ht./Wt.	Born	1992 clubs
39	Dunn, Steve	L/L	6-4/205	4-18-70	Visalia
57	Hocking, Dennis	B/R	5-10/165	4-2-70	Visalia
14	Hrbek, Kent	L/R	6-4/252	5-21-60	Minnesota
27	Jorgensen, Terry	R/R	6-4/213	9-2-66	Portland, Minnesota
11	Knoblauch, Chuck	R/R	5-9/180	7-7-68	Minnesota
9	Larkin, Gene	B/R	6-3/205	10-24-62	Minnesota
31	Leius, Scott	R/R	6-3/195	9-24-65	Minnesota
2	Meares, Pat	R/R	5-11/185	9-6-68	Orlando
17	Reboulet, Jeff	R/R	6-0/170	4-30-64	Portland, Minnesota
30	Russo, Paul	R/R	6-0/215	8-26-69	Orlando

No.	OUTFIELDERS	B/T	Ht./Wt.	Born	1992 clubs
26	Bruett, J.T.	L/L	5-11/175	10-8-67	Portland, Minnesota
40	Cordova, Marty	R/R	6-0/195	7-10-69	Visalia
1	Howell, Patrick	B/R	5-11/155	8-31-68	Tidewater, New York N.L.
52	Lee, Derek	L/R	6-0/195	7-28-66	Vancouver
24	Mack, Shane	R/R	6-0/188	12-7-63	Minnesota
5	Munoz, Pedro	R/R	5-10/207	9-19-68	Minnesota
34	Puckett, Kirby	R/R	5-8/226	3-14-61	Minnesota
32	Winfield, Dave	R/R	6-6/220	10-3-51	Toronto

Ballpark (capacity, surface)
Hubert H. Humphrey Metrodome
(55,883, artificial)

Address
501 Chicago Ave. South
Minneapolis, MN 55415

Business phone
612-375-1366

Ticket information
612-375-7444

Ticket prices
$14 (club level)
$12 (lower deck reserved)
$11 (upper deck club level)
$7 (g.a., lower left field)
$4 (g.a., upper deck outfield)

Field dimensions (from home plate)
To left field at foul line, 343 feet
To center field, 408 feet
To right field at foul line, 327 feet

First game played
April 6, 1982 (Mariners 11, Twins 7)

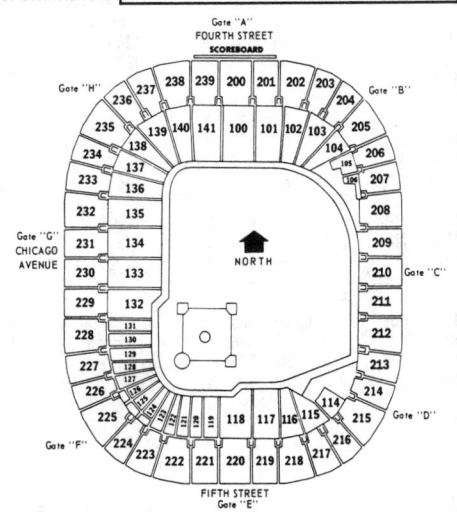

MINOR LEAGUE AFFILIATES

Class	Team	League	Manager
AAA	Portland	Pacific Coast	Scott Ullger
AA	Nashville	Southern	Phil Roof
A	Fort Myers	Florida State	Steve Liddle
A	Fort Wayne	Midwest	Jim Dwyer
Rookie	Elizabethton	Appalachian	Ray Smith
Rookie	Gulf Coast Twins	Gulf Coast	Jose Marzan

BROADCAST INFORMATION

Radio: WCCO-AM (830). Broadcasters: Herb Carneal, John Gordon.
TV: WCCO-TV (Channel 4). Broadcasters: Ted Robinson, Jim Kaat, Dick Bremer.
Cable TV: Midwest Sports Channel. Broadcasters: Jim Kaat, Dick Bremer, other to be announced.

SPRING TRAINING

Ballpark (city): Lee County Sports Complex (Fort Myers, Fla.).
Ticket information: 813-768-4200.

HISTORY

YEAR-BY-YEAR RECORDS

Year	Pos.	W	L	Pct.	*GB	Year	Pos.	W	L	Pct.	*GB
1901	6th	61	72	.459	20½	1950	5th	67	87	.435	31
1902	6th	61	75	.449	22	1951	7th	62	92	.403	36
1903	8th	43	94	.314	47½	1952	5th	78	76	.506	17
1904	8th	38	113	.251	55½	1953	5th	76	76	.500	23½
1905	7th	64	87	.421	29½	1954	6th	66	88	.429	45
1906	7th	55	95	.367	37½	1955	8th	53	101	.344	43
1907	8th	49	102	.325	43½	1956	7th	59	95	.383	38
1908	7th	67	85	.441	22½	1957	8th	55	99	.357	43
1909	8th	42	110	.276	56	1958	8th	61	93	.396	31
1910	7th	66	85	.437	36½	1959	8th	63	91	.409	31
1911	7th	64	90	.416	38½	1960	5th	73	81	.474	24
1912	2nd	91	61	.599	14	1961	7th	70	90	.438	38
1913	2nd	90	64	.584	6½	1962	2nd	91	71	.562	5
1914	3rd	81	73	.526	19	1963	3rd	91	70	.565	13
1915	4th	85	68	.556	17	1964	T6th	79	83	.488	20
1916	7th	76	77	.497	14½	1965	1st	102	60	.630 + 7	
1917	5th	74	79	.484	25½	1966	2nd	89	73	.549	9
1918	3rd	72	56	.563	4	1967	T2nd	91	71	.562	1
1919	7th	56	84	.400	32	1968	7th	79	83	.488	24
1920	6th	68	84	.447	29	1969	1st†	97	65	.599 + 9	
1921	4th	80	73	.523	18	1970	1st†	98	64	.605 + 9	
1922	6th	69	85	.448	25	1971	5th	74	86	.463	26½
1923	4th	75	78	.490	23½	1972	3rd	77	77	.500	15½
1924	1st	92	62	.597 + 2		1973	3rd	81	81	.500	13
1925	1st	96	55	.636 + 8½		1974	3rd	82	80	.506	8
1926	4th	81	69	.540	8	1975	4th	76	83	.478	20½
1927	3rd	85	69	.552	25	1976	3rd	85	77	.525	5
1928	4th	75	79	.487	26	1977	4th	84	77	.522	17½
1929	5th	71	81	.467	34	1978	4th	73	89	.451	19
1930	2nd	94	60	.610	8	1979	4th	82	80	.506	6
1931	3rd	92	62	.597	16	1980	3rd	77	84	.478	19½
1932	3rd	93	61	.604	14	1981	7th/4th	41	68	.376	†
1933	1st	99	53	.651 + 7		1982	7th	60	102	.370	33
1934	7th	66	86	.434	34	1983	T5th	70	92	.432	29
1935	6th	67	86	.438	27	1984	T2nd	81	81	.500	3
1936	4th	82	71	.536	20	1985	T4th	77	85	.475	14
1937	6th	73	80	.477	28½	1986	6th	71	91	.438	21
1938	5th	75	76	.497	23½	1987	1st§	85	77	.525 + 2	
1939	6th	65	87	.428	41½	1988	2nd	91	71	.562	13
1940	7th	64	90	.416	26	1989	5th	80	82	.494	19
1941	T6th	70	84	.455	31	1990	7th	74	88	.457	29
1942	7th	62	89	.411	39½	1991	1st§	95	67	.586 + 8	
1943	2nd	84	69	.549	13½	1992	2nd	90	72	.556	6
1944	8th	64	90	.416	25						
1945	2nd	87	67	.565	1½						
1946	4th	76	78	.494	28						
1947	7th	64	90	.416	33						
1948	7th	56	97	.366	40						
1949	8th	50	104	.325	47						

*Games behind winner. †Lost Championship Series. ‡First half 17-39; second 24-29. §Won Championship Series.

MANAGERS

Name	Record	Years
Jimmy Manning	61-72	1901
Tom Loftus	104-169	'02-03
Patsy Donovan	38-113	1904
Jake Stahl	119-182	'05-06
Joe Cantillon	158-297	'07-09
Jimmy McAleer	130-175	'10-11
Clark Griffith	693-646	'12-20
George McBride	80-73	1921
Clyde Milan	69-85	1922
Donie Bush	75-78	1923
Bucky Harris	1336-1416	'24-28
		'35-42
		'50-54
Walter Johnson	350-264	'29-32
Joe Cronin	165-139	'33-34
Ossie Bluege	375-394	'43-47
Joe Kuhel	106-201	'48-49
Chuck Dressen	116-212	'55-57
Cookie Lavagetto	271-384	'57-61
Sam Mele	524-436	'61-67
Cal Ermer	145-129	'67-68
Billy Martin	97-65	1969
Bill Rigney	208-184	'70-72
Frank Quilici	280-287	'72-75
Gene Mauch	378-394	'76-80
Johnny Goryl	34-38	'80-81
Billy Gardner	268-353	'81-85
Ray Miller	109-130	'85-86
Tom Kelly	527-468	'86-92

1992 REVIEW

DAY BY DAY

Date	Opp.	Res.	Score	(inn.*)	Hits	Opp. hits	Winning pitcher	Losing pitcher	Save	Record	Pos.	GB
4-6	At Mil.	W	4-2		11	6	Willis	Nunez	Aguilera	1-0	T1st	...
4-8	At Mil.	L	5-9		9	8	Ruffin	Aguilera		1-1	4th	1½
4-9	At Mil.	W	3-1		11	4	Krueger	Navarro	Aguilera	2-1	4th	1½
4-10	Tex.	W	7-1		12	8	Tapani	Witt		3-1	T3rd	1
4-11	Tex.	L	8-10	(10)	12	12	Russell	Aguilera	Rogers	3-2	T3rd	2
4-12	Tex.	L	3-4		6	5	Brown	Kipper		3-3	4th	2½
4-14	Mil.	L	1-11		4	11	Navarro	Smiley		3-4	5th	2½
4-15	Mil.	L	4-7	(10)	14	11	Austin	Willis		3-5	6th	3½
4-17	At Chi.	W	7-0		10	5	Krueger	Hough		4-5	5th	3
4-18	At Chi.	L	3-4		10	6	McDowell	Erickson		4-6	6th	4
4-19	At Chi.	L	1-4		6	8	Hibbard	Smiley	Thigpen	4-7	6th	4
4-20	At Sea.	L	0-2		4	5	Johnson	Tapani		4-8	6th	5
4-21	At Sea.	W	5-2		11	10	Mahomes	DeLucia	Aguilera	5-8	6th	4
4-22	At Sea.	W	8-1		14	8	Krueger	Hanson		6-8	6th	4
4-23	At Sea.	L	2-3		6	7	Swan	Erickson	Schooler	6-9	6th	4½
4-24	Oak.	W	6-5	(10)	11	9	Edens	Gossage		7-9	6th	3½
4-25	Oak.	L	4-8		11	18	Slusarski	Tapani	Eckersley	7-10	6th	4½
4-26	Oak.	W	8-4		12	6	Mahomes	Stewart	Aguilera	8-10	6th	3½
4-27	Bal.	W	4-1		10	3	Krueger	Sutcliffe	Aguilera	9-10	6th	3
4-28	Bal.	L	5-10		8	10	Mussina	Erickson		9-11	6th	4
4-29	Bal.	L	4-5		8	8	Davis	Wayne	Olson	9-12	6th	4
5-1	At N.Y.	L	3-5		5	8	Perez	Tapani	Farr	9-13	6th	5½
5-2	At N.Y.	W	7-6		12	14	Kipper	Guetterman	Aguilera	10-13	T5th	4½
5-3	At N.Y.	W	4-2		10	8	Erickson	Kamieniecki	Aguilera	11-13	5th	3½
5-4	At Bos.	W	6-1		12	4	Smiley	Clemens		12-13	5th	2½
5-5	At Bos.	L	1-4		9	9	Viola	Mahomes	Reardon	12-14	5th	3
5-6	At Bal.	L	2-6		6	11	McDonald	Tapani		12-15	5th	4
5-7	At Bal.	L	4-5		9	9	Davis	Aguilera		12-16	5th	5
5-8	Cle.	W	7-4		13	13	Erickson	Nagy	Aguilera	13-16	5th	5
5-9	Cle.	W	10-5		13	11	Smiley	Otto		14-16	5th	4½
5-10	Cle.	W	10-6		13	12	Guthrie	Armstrong	Aguilera	15-16	5th	4½
5-12	Bos.	W	6-3		11	9	Tapani	Gardiner	Aguilera	16-16	5th	3½
5-13	Bos.	W	4-3		12	6	Edens	Harris		17-16	4th	3
5-15	At Cle.	L	0-5		6	9	Nagy	Erickson		17-17	4th	3
5-16	At Cle.	W	8-6		11	13	Smiley	Armstrong	Aguilera	18-17	T3rd	2½
5-17	At Cle.	W	9-5		15	11	Tapani	Cook	Aguilera	19-17	T3rd	2
5-18	At Tor.	W	6-2	(11)	8	12	Wayne	Ward		20-17	3rd	1½
5-19	At Tor.	W	7-1		13	5	Mahomes	Stieb	Edens	21-17	3rd	1½
5-20	At Tor.	L	7-8	(10)	13	9	Henke	Aguilera		21-18	3rd	2½
5-22	At Det.	L	3-6		7	8	Leiter	Smiley	Henneman	21-19	3rd	3½
5-23	At Det.	W	6-5		13	9	Tapani	Doherty	Aguilera	22-19	3rd	2½
5-24	At Det.	W	15-0		18	5	Krueger	Tanana		23-19	3rd	2½
5-26	N.Y.	L	4-5		7	13	Leary	Mahomes	Howe	23-20	4th	2
5-27	N.Y.	W	5-1		7	8	Smiley	Perez		24-20	4th	1
5-29	Det.	W	17-5		16	12	Tapani	Ritz	Willis	25-20	3rd	1½
5-30	Det.	W	7-5		10	10	Edens	Henneman	Aguilera	26-20	2nd	½
5-31	Det.	W	4-1		8	5	Erickson	Gullickson	Guthrie	27-20	1st	+½
6-1	Tor.	L	3-5	(10)	9	9	Ward	Willis	Henke	27-21	1st	...
6-2	Tor.	L	5-7	(13)	13	14	Hentgen	Wayne	Henke	27-22	3rd	1
6-3	Tor.	W	11-3		11	14	Tapani	Guzman		28-22	3rd	1
6-4	At Tex.	W	15-12		14	16	Kipper	Nunez	Aguilera	29-22	2nd	½
6-5	At Tex.	L	4-5		10	9	Guzman	Banks	Russell	29-23	3rd	1½
6-6	At Tex.	W	6-1		9	4	Smiley	Ryan		30-23	2nd	1½
6-7	At Tex.	L	4-5		7	8	Witt	Guthrie	Russell	30-24	3rd	1½
6-8	At K.C.	L	6-9		9	11	Gordon	Kipper	Montgomery	30-25	3rd	1½
6-9	At K.C.	W	4-2		8	6	Krueger	Magnante	Aguilera	31-25	3rd	1½
6-10	At K.C.	L	6-7		14	12	Meacham	Guthrie	Montgomery	31-26	3rd	2½
6-12	Chi.	W	5-1		6	7	Smiley	Hough	Aguilera	32-26	3rd	2½
6-13	Chi.	L	2-4		9	7	McDowell	Erickson	Thigpen	32-27	3rd	3½
6-14	Chi.	W	8-7		9	15	Edens	Radinsky		33-27	2nd	3½
6-15	K.C.	L	0-7		4	13	Magnante	Krueger		33-28	3rd	4½
6-16	K.C.	L	5-7		11	13	Appier	Kipper	Montgomery	33-29	3rd	4½
6-17	K.C.	W	4-2		7	11	Aguilera	Gordon		34-29	2nd	3½
6-18	K.C.	W	3-1		6	8	Erickson	Reed	Aguilera	35-29	2nd	3
6-19	Sea.	L	0-1		4	4	Fleming	Tapani		35-30	2nd	4
6-20	Sea.	W	5-3		6	12	Krueger	DeLucia	Aguilera	36-30	2nd	3
6-21	Sea.	W	5-0		13	4	Banks	Walker	Edens	37-30	2nd	2
6-22	Cal.	W	2-0		6	8	Smiley	Langston	Aguilera	38-30	2nd	2
6-23	Cal.	W	5-3		6	8	Erickson	Blyleven	Aguilera	39-30	2nd	2
6-24	Cal.	W	11-0		17	2	Tapani	Finley		40-30	2nd	2

Date		Opp.	Res.	Score	(inn.*)	Hits	Opp. hits	Winning pitcher	Losing pitcher	Save	Record	Pos.	GB
6-25		At Oak.	L	1-5		11	12	Welch	Krueger	Eckersley	40-31	2nd	3
6-26		At Oak.	W	4-3		9	7	Banks	Moore	Aguilera	41-31	2nd	2
6-27		At Oak.	W	12-2		18	4	Smiley	Darling		42-31	2nd	1
6-28		At Oak.	W	10-2		14	10	Erickson	Campbell		43-31	T1st	...
6-29		At Cal.	W	5-1		8	4	Tapani	Finley		44-31	T1st	...
6-30		At Cal.	W	2-0		8	2	Krueger	Valera		45-31	T1st	...
7-1		At Cal.	W	2-1		8	7	Banks	Abbott		46-31	T1st	...
7-3		Bal.	L	1-6		12	14	Mussina	Smiley		46-32	1st	+1
7-4		Bal.	W	3-2	(15)	11	12	Willis	Olson		47-32	1st	+1
7-5		Bal.	W	2-1		11	6	Tapani	Sutcliffe		48-32	1st	+1
7-6		At N.Y.	W	10-5		13	8	Willis	Leary	Guthrie	49-32	1st	+1
7-7		At N.Y.	L	1-2		6	6	Monteleone	Banks	Habyan	49-33	1st	+1
7-8		At N.Y.	W	3-2		5	3	Smiley	Perez	Aguilera	50-33	1st	+2
7-9		At Bal.	L	2-4		8	7	Rhodes	Erickson	Mills	50-34	1st	+2
7-10		At Bal.	W	5-2		8	5	Tapani	Sutcliffe	Aguilera	51-34	1st	+2
7-11		At Bal.	W	6-5		11	7	Krueger	McDonald	Aguilera	52-34	1st	+2
7-12		At Bal.	W	9-4		10	5	Edens	Milacki		53-34	1st	+2
7-16		Bos.	W	7-6		13	11	Willis	Gardiner	Aguilera	54-34	1st	+2
7-17		Bos.	W	3-2	(10)	12	7	Kipper	Harris		55-34	1st	+3
7-18		Bos.	L	0-1		2	5	Clemens	Erickson		55-35	1st	+3
7-19		Bos.	W	7-5		14	12	Guthrie	Harris	Aguilera	56-35	1st	+3
7-20		Cle.	L	1-5		11	8	Cook	Banks	Olin	56-36	1st	+3
7-21		Cle.	L	2-5		8	7	Mesa	Tapani	Olin	56-37	1st	+3
7-22		Cle.	W	2-1		10	3	Smiley	Nagy		57-37	1st	+3
7-24	(1)	At Bos.	W	5-0		7	1	Erickson	Clemens		58-37	1st	+3½
7-24	(2)	At Bos.	L	4-5		12	13	Irvine	Willis		58-38	1st	+3
7-25		At Bos.	W	3-2		3	8	Banks	Darwin	Aguilera	59-38	1st	+3
7-26		At Bos.	W	8-2		16	7	Tapani	Hesketh	Guthrie	60-38	1st	+3
7-27		Oak.	L	1-9		5	10	Welch	Smiley		60-39	1st	+2
7-28		Oak.	L	10-12		12	19	Nelson	Edens	Eckersley	60-40	1st	+1
7-29		Oak.	L	4-5		14	7	Parrett	Aguilera	Eckersley	60-41	T1st	...
7-30		Mil.	L	3-5		7	11	Bosio	Banks		60-42	2nd	½
7-31		Mil.	W	4-1		9	8	Tapani	Wegman	Edens	61-42	1st	+½
8-1		Mil.	W	9-6		11	7	Smiley	Navarro		62-42	1st	+1½
8-2		Mil.	W	5-0		9	4	Erickson	Bones		63-42	1st	+1½
8-4		At Chi.	L	11-19		19	19	Alvarez	Krueger	Pall	63-43	T1st	...
8-5		At Chi.	L	5-9		9	17	Hough	Tapani		63-44	2nd	1
8-6		At Chi.	L	3-5		7	11	McCaskill	Smiley	Hernandez	63-45	2nd	2
8-8	(1)	At Mil.	L	0-4		3	8	Eldred	Erickson		63-46	2nd	3½
8-8	(2)	At Mil.	W	3-1		8	5	Krueger	Bones	Aguilera	64-46	2nd	3
8-9		At Mil.	L	2-4		6	10	Bosio	West	Henry	64-47	2nd	3
8-10		Tex.	W	7-5		11	9	Tapani	Witt	Aguilera	65-47	2nd	3
8-11		Tex.	W	3-2		8	4	Smiley	Rogers		66-47	2nd	2
8-12		Tex.	L	3-5		12	7	Brown	Aguilera	Russell	66-48	2nd	3
8-13		Tex.	L	1-6		6	12	Guzman	Erickson		66-49	2nd	4
8-14		At Sea.	W	9-6		14	9	West	Jones	Aguilera	67-49	2nd	3
8-15		At Sea.	L	2-3		4	7	Johnson	Edens		67-50	2nd	4
8-16		At Sea.	L	7-8		14	14	Nelson	Guthrie		67-51	2nd	5
8-18		At Cle.	L	1-8		9	11	Mesa	Erickson	Power	67-52	2nd	5
8-19		At Cle.	L	1-5		8	8	Nagy	Krueger		67-53	2nd	5
8-20		At Cle.	L	1-2	(10)	11	3	Plunk	Tapani		67-54	2nd	6
8-21		Tor.	W	5-1		7	7	Smiley	Stottlemyre		68-54	2nd	5
8-22		Tor.	L	2-4		9	8	Morris	West	Henke	68-55	2nd	6
8-23		Tor.	W	2-0		6	4	Erickson	Key		69-55	2nd	6
8-24		Det.	L	2-6		8	10	King	Krueger		69-56	2nd	7
8-25		Det.	L	3-4		11	8	Haas	Tapani	Henneman	69-57	2nd	7
8-26		Det.	W	1-0		8	6	Smiley	Kiely		70-57	2nd	6
8-27		N.Y.	L	0-5		6	8	Perez	West		70-58	2nd	6½
8-28		N.Y.	W	4-3	(14)	13	9	Willis	Cadaret		71-58	2nd	6½
8-29		N.Y.	L	3-6		6	8	Wickman	Krueger	Farr	71-59	2nd	7½
8-30		N.Y.	W	5-3		8	9	Tapani	Militello	Aguilera	72-59	2nd	7½
8-31		At Det.	W	5-3	(10)	10	10	Wayne	Henneman	Aguilera	73-59	2nd	6½
9-1		At Det.	W	5-4		9	8	Willis	Lancaster	Aguilera	74-59	2nd	5½
9-2		At Det.	W	4-2		8	7	Erickson	Terrell	Aguilera	75-59	2nd	4½
9-4		At Tor.	L	5-16		9	21	Cone	Tapani		75-60	2nd	4½
9-5		At Tor.	L	3-7		8	10	Guzman	Smiley		75-61	2nd	4½
9-6		At Tor.	L	2-4		7	8	Stottlemyre	Trombley	Henke	75-62	2nd	5½
9-7		Sea.	W	4-2		8	9	Erickson	Leary	Aguilera	76-62	2nd	4½
9-8		Sea.	W	8-4		13	9	Wayne	Jones		77-62	2nd	4½
9-9		Sea.	W	6-2		10	8	Tapani	Fleming	Guthrie	78-62	2nd	4½
9-11		Cal.	L	0-8		8	13	Abbott	Smiley		78-63	2nd	6
9-12		Cal.	W	7-2		11	4	Trombley	Blyleven	Guthrie	79-63	2nd	6
9-13		Cal.	W	6-2		9	6	Erickson	Valera		80-63	2nd	6
9-14		At Oak.	L	2-3		8	9	Corsi	Edens	Eckersley	80-64	2nd	7

Date	Opp.	Res.	Score	(inn.*)	Hits	Opp. hits	Winning pitcher	Losing pitcher	Save	Record	Pos.	GB
9-15	At Oak.	L	1-2		2	5	Darling	Mahomes	Eckersley	80-65	2nd	8
9-16	At Oak.	L	2-4		9	7	Witt	Smiley	Russell	80-66	2nd	9
9-17	At Cal.	W	2-1		8	3	Trombley	Abbott	Aguilera	81-66	2nd	8½
9-18	At Cal.	W	4-1		10	5	Erickson	Blyleven	Aguilera	82-66	2nd	8½
9-19	At Cal.	L	1-5		5	9	Valera	Tapani		82-67	2nd	8½
9-20	At Cal.	W	7-5		11	10	Aguilera	Grahe		83-67	2nd	8½
9-22	At Tex.	W	1-0	(13)	11	7	Casian	Rogers	Aguilera	84-67	2nd	8
9-23	At Tex.	L	3-5		10	10	Brown	Trombley		84-68	2nd	8
9-25	K.C.	L	3-4		8	9	Meacham	Erickson	Montgomery	84-69	2nd	8½
9-26	K.C.	W	9-2		13	7	Tapani	Aquino		85-69	2nd	7½
9-27	K.C.	W	4-0		5	5	Smiley	Haney		86-69	2nd	6½
9-28	Chi.	L	4-9		9	16	McCaskill	Mahomes		86-70	2nd	7
9-29	Chi.	W	5-4		8	7	Edens	Radinsky		87-70	2nd	7
9-30	Chi.	L	3-4		8	13	Dunne	Erickson	Hernandez	87-71	2nd	7
10-1	Chi.	W	9-6		14	9	Willis	Leach	Aguilera	88-71	2nd	6
10-2	At K.C.	W	5-1		11	4	Smiley	Haney		89-71	2nd	5
10-3	At K.C.	L	6-7	(11)	10	13	Meacham	Wayne		89-72	2nd	6
10-4	At K.C.	W	6-0		12	6	Trombley	Rasmussen		90-72	2nd	6

Monthly records: April (9-12), May (18-8), June (18-11), July (16-11), August (12-17), September (14-12), Oct. (3-1).

HIGHLIGHTS

High point: After a 9-13 start, the Twins were the best team in baseball for nearly three months, going 51-25. On July 26, the Twins had the best record in the major leagues (60-38) and led the A.L. West by three games.

Low point: The Twins collapsed in every phase of the game from August 4-20, going 4-12 and at one point losing five straight games to last-place teams.

Turning point: The Twins were swept at home by the Athletics July 27-29, losing leads in the second and third games of the series. In the series finale, Eric Fox's three-run, ninth-inning homer off Rick Aguilera wiped out a 4-2 lead.

Most valuable player: Center fielder Kirby Puckett. The league's best player in the first half of the season, Puckett hit .329 with 104 runs, 210 hits, 19 homers, 38 doubles and 110 RBIs.

Most valuable pitcher: Lefthander John Smiley. He won 16 games, led the club in innings (241) and strikeouts (163) and essentially contributed what Jack Morris provided in 1991.

Most improved player: Right fielder Pedro Munoz. He transformed himself from a role player into one of the league's best RBI men (71 in only 418 at-bats).

Most pleasant surprise: The Twins showed no signs of a World Series hangover. Even with the disappointing stretch in August, the Twins were one of seven teams to win 90 games.

Biggest disappointment: As General Manager Andy MacPhail said, "Our left-handed hitting just fell off the map." Among the culprits were Kent Hrbek, Chili Davis (a switch-hitter), Mike Pagliarulo and Randy Bush.

Key injuries: The Twins were relatively healthy all season, but Hrbek's shoulder problems hampered an offense that relied upon him too heavily. Pagliarulo was hit in the ear with a pitch in spring training. When he returned, he broke a bone in his hand April 22.

Notable: Tom Kelly became the club's all-time winningest manager, passing Sam Mele (522) and finishing the season with 527 victories. ... Aguilera saved 41 games, becoming one of only four relievers to attain the 40 plateau in consecutive seasons. He also supplanted Ron Davis as the club's all-time save leader with 109. ... Catcher Brian Harper hit better than .300 for the third time in four seasons with the Twins. ... Chuck Knoblauch, the A.L. Rookie of the Year in 1991, improved in almost every area in 1992 to steal only the fourth Twin ever to steal 30 bases.

—JEFF LENIHAN

RECORDS

1992 regular-season record: 90-72 (2nd in A.L. West); 48-33 at home; 42-39 on road; 48-36 vs. East; 42-36 vs. West; 22-12 vs. LHP; 68-60 vs. RHP; 34-28 on grass; 56-44 on turf; 38-15 in daytime; 52-57 at night; 22-24 in one-run games; 7-7 in extra-inning games; 0-2 in doubleheaders.

Team record last five years: 430-380 (.531, ranks 3rd in league in that span).

TEAM LEADERS

Batting average: Kirby Puckett (.329).
At-bats: Kirby Puckett (639).
Runs: Chuck Knoblauch, Kirby Puckett (104).
Hits: Kirby Puckett (210).
Total bases: Kirby Puckett (313).
Doubles: Kirby Puckett (38).
Triples: Chuck Knoblauch, Shane Mack (6).
Home runs: Kirby Puckett (19).
Runs batted in: Kirby Puckett (110).
Stolen bases: Chuck Knoblauch (34).
Slugging percentage: Kirby Puckett (.490).
On-base percentage: Shane Mack (.394).
Wins: John Smiley, Kevin Tapani (16).
Earned-run average: John Smiley (3.21).
Complete games: Scott Erickson, John Smiley (5).
Shutouts: Scott Erickson (3).
Saves: Rick Aguilera (41).
Innings pitched: John Smiley (241).
Strikeouts: John Smiley (163).

GAMES BY POSITION

Catcher: Brian Harper 133, Lenny Webster 49, Derek Parks 7.
First base: Kent Hrbek 104, Gene Larkin 55, Terry Jorgensen 13, Randy Bush 8, Chili Davis 1.
Second base: Chuck Knoblauch 154, Jeff Reboulet 13, Donnie Hill 7, Kirby Puckett 2.
Third base: Scott Leius 125, Mike Pagliarulo 37, Jeff Reboulet 22, Terry Jorgensen 9, Donnie Hill 5, Kirby Puckett 2, Luis Quinones 1.
Shortstop: Greg Gagne 141, Jeff Reboulet 36, Donnie Hill 10, Scott Leius 10, Terry Jorgensen 2, Chuck Knoblauch 1, Kirby Puckett 1, Luis Quinones 1.
Outfield: Shane Mack 155, Kirby Puckett 149, Pedro Munoz 122, J.T. Bruett 45, Gene Larkin 43, Jarvis Brown 31, Randy Bush 24, Darren Reed 13, Jeff Reboulet 7, Chili Davis 4, Bernardo Brito 3, Donnie Hill 1.
Designated hitter: Chili Davis 125, Randy Bush 24, Kirby Puckett 9, Kent Hrbek 8, Gene Larkin 4, J.T. Bruett 3, Pedro Munoz 3, Jarvis Brown 2, Brian Harper 2, Bernardo Brito 1, Chuck Knoblauch 1, Mike Pagliarulo 1, Luis Quinones 1, Jeff Reboulet 1, Darren Reed 1, Lenny Webster 1.

TOP 10 DRAFT CHOICES

1. Dan Serafini, LHP, Serra High School, San Mateo, Calif.
2a. Chad Roper, SS, Belton-Honea Path (S.C.) High School.
2b. Tom Knauss, SS, John Hersey High School, Arlington Heights, Ill.
3. G. Gandarillas, RHP, U. of Miami (Fla.).
4. Kevin Pearson, SS, Fergus Falls (Minn.) High School.
5. Aaron Thatcher, LHP, Mountain Crest High School, Hyrum, Utah.
6. Keith Linebarger, RHP, Columbus (Ga.) College.
7. Armann Brown, OF, Johnston High School, Austin, Tex.
8. Chad Cooley, SS/OF, Barbe High School, Lake Charles, La.
9. Rene Lopez, C, L.A. Harbor College.
10. Ben Jones, OF, Alexandria (La.) H.S.

NEW YORK YANKEES
AMERICAN LEAGUE EAST DIVISION

1993 SCHEDULE

APRIL

SUN	MON	TUE	WED	THU	FRI	SAT
				1	2 CHI	3
4	5 CLE	6	7 N CLE	8 N CLE	9 N CHI	10 N CHI
11 CHI	12 KC H	13	14 N KC	15 N KC	16 N TEX	17 TEX H
18 TEX H	19	20 N OAK	21 N OAK	22 OAK	23 N SEA	24 SEA
25 SEA	26	27 N CAL	28 N CAL	29	30 N SEA H	

MAY

SUN	MON	TUE	WED	THU	FRI	SAT
						1 SEA H
2 SEA H	3 OAK H	4 N OAK H	5 N CAL H	6 N CAL H	7 DET	8 N DET
9 DET	10 DET	11 N MIL H	12 N MIL H	13 N MIL H	14 N TOR H	15 TOR H
16 TOR H	17 N MIN	18 N MIN	19 MIN	20	21 N BOS	22 BOS
23 BOS	24 BAL H	25 BAL H	26 N BAL H	27 N BAL H	28 N CHI H	29 CHI H
30 CHI H	31 CLE H					

JUNE

SUN	MON	TUE	WED	THU	FRI	SAT
		1 N CLE H	2 N CLE H	3	4 N TEX	5 N TEX
6 N TEX	7 KC	8 N KC	9 N KC	10 N MIL	11 N MIL	12 N MIL
13 MIL	14 N BOS H	15 N BOS H	16 N BOS H	17 N MIN H	18 N MIN H	19 MIN H
20 MIN H	21	22 N TOR	23 N TOR	24 TOR	25 N BAL	26 BAL
27 BAL	28 N DET	29 N DET H	30 DET H			

JULY

SUN	MON	TUE	WED	THU	FRI	SAT
				1	2 N OAK	3 OAK
4 N OAK	5 N SEA	6 N SEA	7 SEA	8 N CAL	9 N CAL	10 CAL
11 CAL	12	13 * ALL-STAR GAME	14	15 N OAK H	16 N OAK H	17 OAK H
18 N OAK H	19 N SEA H	20 N SEA H	21 N SEA H	22	23 N CAL H	24 CAL H
25 CAL H	26 N DET	27 N DET	28 DET	29	30 N MIL H	31 N MIL H

AUGUST

SUN	MON	TUE	WED	THU	FRI	SAT
1 MIL H	2 N TOR H	3 N TOR H	4 N TOR H	5 N TOR H	6 N MIN	7 N MIN
8 MIN	9	10 N BOS	11 N BOS	12 N BAL	13 N BAL	14 BAL
15 BAL H	16 N TEX H	17 N TEX H	18 TEX H	19	20 N KC	21 KC H
22 KC H	23 N CHI	24 N CHI	25 CHI	26 N CLE	27 CLE	28 CLE
29 CLE	30	31 N CHI H				

SEPTEMBER

SUN	MON	TUE	WED	THU	FRI	SAT
			1 N CHI H	2 N CHI H	3 N CLE H	4 N CLE H
5 CLE H	6 N TEX	7 N TEX	8 N TEX	9	10 N KC	11 N KC
12 KC	13 N MIL	14 N MIL	15 MIL	16 N BOS H	17 N BOS H	18 BOS H
19 BOS H	20	21 N MIN H	22 N MIN H	23	24 N TOR	25 TOR
26 TOR	27 N BAL	28 N BAL	29 N BAL	30		

OCTOBER

SUN	MON	TUE	WED	THU	FRI	SAT
					1 N DET H	2 N DET H
3 DET H						

1993 SEASON

CLUB DIRECTORY

Principal owner
George M. Steinbrenner
General partner
Joseph A. Molloy
Executive vice president, general counsel
David W. Sussman
Senior vice president
Arthur Richman
Vice president and general manager
Gene Michael
Vice president, chief of operations
John C. Lawn
Vice president, marketing
John C. Fugazy
V.p., finance, chief financial officer
Barry Pincus
Vice president, community relations
Richard Kraft
Vice president
Ed Weaver
Controller
Steven M. Dauria
Director of office admin. and services
Harvey C. Winston
Vice president, ticket operations
Frank Swaine
V.p., player development and scouting
Bill Livesey
Senior advisor, baseball operations
Bill Bergesch
Asst. general manager, baseball operations
Tim McCleary
Asst. general manager, baseball admin.
Brian Cashman
Director of minor league operations
Mitch Lukevics
Coordinator of scouting
Kevin Elfering
Traveling secretary
David Szen
Director of stadium operations
Timothy D. Hassett
Director of customer services
Joel S. White
Director of video operations
John J. Franzone
Executive director of ticket operations
Jeff Kline
Ticket director
Ken Skrypek
Director of group and season sales
Debbie Tymon
Director of media relations and publicity
Jeff Idelson

Asst. dir. of media relations and publicity
Brian Walker
Director of special events
Bob Pelegrino
Director of publications
Tom Bannon
Team physician
Dr. Stuart Hershon
Head trainer
Gene J. Monahan
Assistant trainer
Steve Donohue
Major league scouts
Rick Cerone
Ron Hansen
Clyde King
Bob Lemon
Dick Tidrow
Scouting cross-checker
Jack Gills
Area supervisor scouts
Fernando Arango
Mark Batchko
Stephen Chandler
Joe DiCarlo
Lee Elder
Bill Geivett
Tim Kelly
Don Lindberg
Carl Moesche
Greg Orr
Joe Robison
Bill Schmidt
Jeff Taylor
Paul Turco
Leon Wurth
Foreign scouts
Joel Grampietro
Dick Groch
Rudy Santin
Luis Arroyo
Philip Elhage
Karl Heron
Pedro Ithier
Leo Lacle
Victor Mata
Raul Ortega
Arquimedes Rojas
Mike LaBossiere
Marc Pickard
Bruce Ross
Bill Saunders
Dennis Springenatic
Dale Tilleman

SCHEDULE KEY

H—Home game.   N—Night game (any game starting after 5 p.m.).
*All-Star Game at Oriole Park at Camden Yards, Baltimore.

SPRING TRAINING ROSTER

Manager—Buck Showalter (11).

Coaches—Clete Boyer (6), Tony Cloninger (40), Mark Connor (52), Dick Down (48), Frank Howard (46), Ed Napoleon (50).

No.	PITCHERS	B/T	Ht./Wt.	Born	1992 clubs
25	Abbott, Jim	L/L	6-3/210	9-19-67	California
65	Cook, Andy	R/R	6-5/205	8-30-67	Columbus
26	Farr, Steve	R/R	5-11/204	12-12-56	New York A.L.
42	Habyan, John	R/R	6-2/195	1-29-64	New York A.L.
35	Hitchcock, Sterling	L/L	6-1/192	4-29-71	Albany/Colonie, New York A.L.
57	Howe, Steve	L/L	5-11/196	3-10-58	New York A.L.
54	Hutton, Mark	R/R	6-6/225	1-20-68	Albany/Colonie, Columbus
62	Jean, Domingo	R/R	6-2/175	1-9-69	Fort Lauderdale, Albany/Colonie
43	Johnson, Jeff	R/L	6-3/200	8-4-66	New York A.L., Columbus
28	Kamieniecki, Scott	R/R	6-0/195	4-19-64	Fort Lauderdale, Columbus, New York A.L.
22	Key, Jimmy	R/L	6-1/185	4-22-61	Toronto
64	Martel, Ed	R/R	6-1/200	3-2-69	Columbus
34	Militello, Sam	R/R	6-3/195	11-26-69	Columbus, New York A.L.
55	Monteleone, Rich	R/R	6-2/214	3-22-63	New York A.L.
56	Munoz, Bobby	R/R	6-7/237	3-3-68	Albany/Colonie
33	Perez, Melido	R/R	6-4/210	2-15-66	New York A.L.
58	Rivera, Mariano	R/R	6-4/168	11-29-69	Fort Lauderdale
27	Wickman, Bob	R/R	6-1/212	2-6-69	Columbus, New York A.L.
39	Witt, Mike	R/R	6-7/208	7-20-60	Gulf Coast Yankees

No.	CATCHERS	B/T	Ht./Wt.	Born	1992 clubs
	Leyritz, Jim	R/R	6-0/195	12-27-63	New York A.L.
38	Nokes, Matt	L/R	6-1/210	10-31-63	New York A.L.
20	Stanley, Mike	R/R	6-0/192	6-25-63	New York A.L.

No.	INFIELDERS	B/T	Ht./Wt.	Born	1992 clubs
	Boggs, Wade	L/R	6-2/197	6-15-58	Boston
63	Davis, Russ	R/R	6-0/170	9-13-69	Albany/Colonie
59	Eenhoorn, Robert	R/R	6-3/170	2-9-68	Fort Lauderdale, Albany/Colonie
2	Gallego, Mike	R/R	5-8/175	10-31-60	Fort Lauderdale, New York A.L.
14	Kelly, Pat	R/R	6-0/182	10-14-67	New York A.L., Albany/Colonie
24	Maas, Kevin	L/L	6-3/204	1-20-65	New York A.L.
23	Mattingly, Don	L/L	6-0/200	4-20-61	New York A.L.
31	Meulens, Hensley	R/R	6-3/210	6-23-67	Columbus, New York A.L.
	Owen, Spike	B/R	5-10/170	4-19-61	Montreal
	Silvestri, Dave	R/R	6-0/196	9-29-67	Columbus, New York A.L.
17	Stankiewicz, Andy	R/R	5-9/165	8-10-64	New York A.L.
18	Velarde, Randy	R/R	6-0/192	11-24-62	New York A.L.

No.	OUTFIELDERS	B/T	Ht./Wt.	Born	1992 clubs
60	Humphreys, Mike	R/R	6-0/195	4-10-67	Columbus, New York A.L.
19	James, Dion	L/L	6-1/185	11-9-62	New York A.L.
21	O'Neill, Paul	L/L	6-4/215	2-25-63	Cincinnati
45	Tartabull, Danny	R/R	6-1/204	10-30-62	New York A.L.
51	Williams, Bernie	B/R	6-2/200	9-13-68	New York A.L., Columbus
29	Williams, Gerald	R/R	6-2/190	8-10-66	Columbus, New York A.L.

BALLPARK INFORMATION

Ballpark (capacity, surface)
Yankee Stadium (57,545, grass)
Address
Yankee Stadium
E. 161 St. and River Ave.
Bronx, NY 10451
Business phone
212-293-4300
Ticket information
212-293-6000
Ticket prices
$16 (lower and loge box seats)
$14.50 (tier box seats)
$13.50 (lower reserves)
$10.50 (tier reserves)
$1 (senior citizens)
$6.50 (bleachers)
Field dimensions (from home plate)
To left field at foul line, 312 feet
To center field, 410 feet
To right field at foul line, 310 feet
First game played
April 18, 1923 (Yankees 4, Red Sox 1)

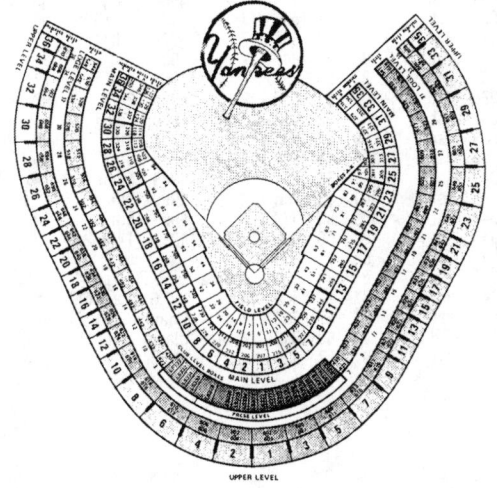

MINOR LEAGUE AFFILIATES

Class	Team	League	Manager
AAA	Columbus, O.	International	Rick Down
AA	Albany/Colonie	Eastern	Dan Radison
A	Prince William	Carolina	Mike Hart
A	Greensboro	South Atlantic	Trey Hillman
A	Oneonta	New York-Pennsylvania	To be announced
Rookie	Tampa Yankees	Gulf Coast	Gary Denbo

BROADCAST INFORMATION

Radio: WABC-AM (770). Broadcasters: John Sterling, Michael Kay.
TV: WPIX (Channel 11). Broadcasters: Bobby Murcer, Phil Rizzuto, Tom Seaver.
Cable TV: Madison Square Garden Network. Broadcasters: Dewayne Staats, Tony Kubek, Al Trautwig.

SPRING TRAINING

Ballpark (city): Fort Lauderdale Stadium (Fort Lauderdale, Fla.).
Ticket information: 305-776-1921.

HISTORY

YEAR-BY-YEAR RECORDS

Year	Pos.	W	L	Pct.	*GB	Year	Pos.	W	L	Pct.	*GB
1901	5th	68	65	.511	13½	1950	1st	98	56	.636	+ 3
1902	8th	50	88	.362	34	1951	1st	98	56	.636	+ 5
1903	4th	72	62	.537	17	1952	1st	95	59	.617	+ 2
1904	2nd	92	59	.609	1½	1953	1st	99	52	.656	+ 8½
1905	6th	71	78	.477	21½	1954	2nd	103	51	.669	8
1906	2nd	90	61	.596	3	1955	1st	96	58	.623	+ 3
1907	5th	70	78	.473	21	1956	1st	97	57	.630	+ 9
1908	8th	51	103	.331	39½	1957	1st	98	56	.636	+ 8
1909	5th	74	77	.490	23½	1958	1st	92	62	.597	+10
1910	2nd	88	63	.583	14½	1959	3rd	79	75	.513	15
1911	6th	76	76	.500	25½	1960	1st	97	57	.630	+ 8
1912	8th	50	102	.329	55	1961	1st	109	53	.673	+ 8
1913	7th	57	94	.377	38	1962	1st	96	66	.593	+ 5
1914	T6th	70	84	.455	30	1963	1st	104	57	.646	+10½
1915	5th	69	83	.454	32½	1964	1st	99	63	.611	+ 1
1916	4th	80	74	.519	11	1965	6th	77	85	.475	25
1917	6th	71	82	.464	28½	1966	10th	70	89	.440	26½
1918	4th	60	63	.488	13½	1967	9th	72	90	.444	20
1919	3rd	80	59	.576	7½	1968	5th	83	79	.512	20
1920	3rd	95	59	.617	3	1969	5th	80	81	.497	28½
1921	1st	98	55	.641	+ 4½	1970	2nd	93	69	.574	15
1922	1st	94	60	.610	+ 1	1971	4th	82	80	.506	21
1923	1st	98	54	.645	+16	1972	4th	79	76	.510	6½
1924	2nd	89	63	.586	2	1973	4th	80	82	.494	17
1925	7th	69	85	.448	30	1974	2nd	89	73	.549	2
1926	1st	91	63	.591	+ 3	1975	3rd	83	77	.519	12
1927	1st	110	44	.714	+19	1976	1st†	97	62	.610	+10½
1928	1st	101	53	.656	+ 2½	1977	1st†	100	62	.617	+ 2½
1929	2nd	88	66	.571	18	1978	1st†‡	100	63	.613	+ 1
1930	3rd	86	68	.558	16	1979	4th	89	71	.556	13½
1931	2nd	94	59	.614	13½	1980	1st§	103	59	.636	+ 3
1932	1st	107	47	.695	+13	1981	1st/6th	59	48	.551	†‡★
1933	2nd	91	59	.607	7	1982	5th	79	83	.488	16
1934	2nd	94	60	.610	7	1983	3rd	91	71	.562	7
1935	2nd	89	60	.597	3	1984	3rd	87	75	.537	17
1936	1st	102	51	.667	+19½	1985	2nd	97	64	.602	2
1937	1st	102	52	.662	+13	1986	2nd	90	72	.556	5½
1938	1st	99	53	.651	+ 9½	1987	4th	89	73	.549	9
1939	1st	106	45	.702	+17	1988	5th	85	76	.528	3½
1940	3rd	88	66	.571	2	1989	5th	74	87	.460	14½
1941	1st	101	53	.656	+17	1990	7th	67	95	.414	21
1942	1st	103	51	.669	+ 9	1991	5th	71	91	.438	20
1943	1st	98	56	.636	+13½	1992	T4th	76	86	.469	20
1944	3rd	83	71	.539	6						
1945	4th	81	71	.533	6½						
1946	3rd	87	67	.565	17						
1947	1st	97	57	.630	+12						
1948	3rd	94	60	.610	2½						
1949	1st	97	57	.630	+ 1						

*Games behind winner. †Won Championship Series. ‡Won division playoff. §Lost Championship Series. ★First half 34-22; second 25-26.

MANAGERS

Name	Record	Years
John McGraw	94-96	'01-02
Wilbert Robinson	24-57	1902
Clark Griffith	419-370	'03-08
Kid Elberfeld	27-71	1908
George Stallings	152-136	'09-10
Hal Chase	86-80	'10-11
Harry Wolverton	50-102	1912
Frank Chance	117-168	'13-14
Rog. Peckinpaugh	10-10	1914
Bill Donovan	220-239	'15-17
Miller Huggins	1067-719	'18-29
Art Fletcher	6-5	1929
Bob Shawkey	86-68	1930
Joe McCarthy	1460-867	'31-46
Bill Dickey	57-48	1946
Johnny Neun	8-6	1946
Bucky Harris	191-117	'47-48
Casey Stengel	1149-696	'49-60
Ralph Houk	944-806	'61-63
		'66-73
Yogi Berra	192-148	1964
		'84-85
Johnny Keane	81-101	'65-66
Bill Virdon	142-124	'74-75
Billy Martin	501-345	'75-78
		'79, '83
		'85, '88
Bob Lemon	99-73	'78-79
		'81-82
Dick Howser	103-59	1980
Gene Michael	92-76	'81, '82
Clyde King	29-33	1982
Lou Piniella	224-193	'86-87
		1988
Dallas Green	56-65	1989
Bucky Dent	36-53	'89-90
Stump Merrill	120-155	'90-91
Buck Showalter	76-86	1992

DAY BY DAY

Date	Opp.	Res.	Score (inn.*)	Hits	Opp. hits	Winning pitcher	Losing pitcher	Save	Record	Pos.	GB
4-7	Bos.	W	4-3	8	7	Sanderson	Clemens	Farr	1-0	T1st	...
4-9	Bos.	W	3-2	6	6	Monteleone	Viola	Howe	2-0	T1st	½
4-10	At Det.	W	7-3	15	6	Perez	King		3-0	T1st	½
4-11	At Det.	W	8-1	10	4	Leary	Gullickson		4-0	T1st	½
4-12	At Det.	W	5-1	11	6	Sanderson	Aldred	Habyan	5-0	T1st	½
4-13	At Tor.	W	5-2	6	6	Howe	Stottlemyre	Farr	6-0	1st	+½
4-14	At Tor.	L	6-12	13	14	Guzman	Johnson		6-1	2nd	½
4-15	At Tor.	L	0-2	3	8	Key	Perez	Henke	6-2	2nd	1½
4-16	At Tor.	L	6-7	7	11	Ward	Farr		6-3	2nd	2½
4-17	Cle.	L	1-11	6	15	Nagy	Sanderson		6-4	2nd	2½
4-18	Cle.	W	14-0	14	9	Cadaret	Otto		7-4	2nd	2½
4-19	Cle.	W	5-3	9	9	Johnson	Armstrong	Howe	8-4	2nd	1½
4-20	Cle.	L	1-3	5	5	Scudder	Perez	Olin	8-5	2nd	2½
4-21	At Chi.	W	4-3	9	7	Leary	McCaskill	Farr	9-5	2nd	2½
4-22	At Chi.	W	4-3	13	10	Howe	Radinsky		10-5	2nd	1½
4-24	Bal.	W	5-0	10	5	Cadaret	Milacki		11-5	2nd	2
4-25	Bal.	L	2-9	10	8	McDonald	Johnson		11-6	T2nd	3
4-26	Bal.	W	3-1	8	4	Howe	Mesa		12-6	2nd	2
4-27	Tex.	W	8-7	15	13	Habyan	Mathews	Farr	13-6	2nd	1½
4-28	Tex.	L	0-1	3	7	Brown	Leary	Russell	13-7	2nd	1½
4-29	Tex.	L	1-5	2	9	Guzman	Cadaret		13-8	T2nd	2½
5-1	Min.	W	5-3	8	5	Perez	Tapani	Farr	14-8	T2nd	1
5-2	Min.	L	6-7	14	12	Kipper	Guetterman	Aguilera	14-9	3rd	1
5-3	Min.	L	2-4	8	10	Erickson	Kamieniecki	Aguilera	14-10	3rd	2
5-4	At Sea.	W	7-5	7	6	Leary	Swan		15-10	3rd	2
5-5	At Sea.	L	4-7	8	10	Fleming	Cadaret		15-11	3rd	3
5-6	At Cal.	L	2-3	5	10	Langston	Perez	Harvey	15-12	3rd	4
5-7	At Cal.	L	0-6	5	10	Valera	Sanderson		15-13	3rd	5
5-8	At Oak.	L	6-8	11	12	Nelson	Habyan	Eckersley	15-14	3rd	5
5-9	At Oak.	L	3-5	7	5	Darling	Leary	Honeycutt	15-15	3rd	5
5-10	At Oak.	L	2-5	2	7	Slusarski	Cadaret	Eckersley	15-16	4th	6
5-12	Sea.	W	3-1	6	6	Perez	Johnson	Howe	16-16	3rd	6
5-13	Sea.	W	12-4	14	9	Sanderson	Hanson		17-16	3rd	6
5-15	Oak.	W	3-2	11	6	Kamieniecki	Welch	Farr	18-16	3rd	5½
5-16	Oak.	L	3-6	7	5	Darling	Leary	Eckersley	18-17	3rd	6
5-17	Oak.	W	11-2	10	7	Perez	Stewart		19-17	3rd	5
5-18	Cal.	W	7-2	9	8	Cadaret	Finley	Howe	20-17	3rd	4
5-19	Cal.	W	5-4 (10)	11	10	Monteleone	Eichhorn		21-17	3rd	3
5-20	Cal.	W	3-2 (12)	8	9	Habyan	Crim		22-17	3rd	2½
5-22	Mil.	L	9-10 (14)	15	16	Henry	Monteleone		22-18	3rd	3½
5-23	Mil.	L	4-5 (10)	8	7	Wegman	Hillegas	Orosco	22-19	3rd	3½
5-24	Mil.	W	8-7	12	12	Habyan	Ruffin		23-19	3rd	3
5-25	Mil.	W	13-10	18	17	Guetterman	Austin		24-19	3rd	2
5-26	At Min.	W	5-4	13	7	Leary	Mahomes	Howe	25-19	3rd	2
5-27	At Min.	L	1-5	8	7	Smiley	Perez		25-20	3rd	2
5-29	At Mil.	L	3-8	10	12	Wegman	Cadaret		25-21	3rd	3
5-30	At Mil.	W	8-1	11	5	Sanderson	Bosio		26-21	3rd	3
5-31	At Mil.	L	1-2	4	5	Orosco	Kamieniecki		26-22	3rd	4
6-1	At Tex.	W	7-1	7	7	Monteleone	Robinson		27-22	3rd	4
6-2	At Tex.	L	2-8	6	6	Witt	Leary		27-23	3rd	5
6-3	At Tex.	L	3-4 (13)	9	12	Rogers	Hillegas		27-24	3rd	5
6-4	Det.	L	2-6	7	9	Tanana	Sanderson		27-25	3rd	5½
6-6	Det.	L	2-6	5	13	Gullickson	Kamieniecki		27-26	4th	6
6-7	Det.	W	6-5	9	11	Perez	Terrell	Farr	28-26	4th	5
6-8	Tor.	L	3-16	6	21	Stottlemyre	Cadaret		28-27	4th	6
6-9	Tor.	L	1-2	4	5	Guzman	Leary	Henke	28-28	5th	7
6-10	Tor.	L	3-10	8	15	Key	Sanderson	Wells	28-29	5th	8
6-12	At Cle.	L	0-3	5	5	Nagy	Kamieniecki		28-30	5th	8½
6-13	At Cle.	W	4-1	9	8	Perez	Otto		29-30	5th	7½
6-14	At Cle.	W	4-3 (10)	10	10	Monteleone	Power	Farr	30-30	T4th	7½
6-15	At Bos.	L	0-1	6	3	Dopson	Sanderson	Reardon	30-31	5th	8
6-16	At Bos.	L	3-4 (10)	11	8	Darwin	Cadaret		30-32	5th	8
6-17	At Bos.	L	3-4	5	8	Viola	Kamieniecki	Fossas	30-33	5th	9
6-18	At Bos.	W	5-4	10	10	Perez	Darwin	Farr	31-33	5th	8
6-19	At Bal.	L	7-10	11	13	Mills	Hillegas	Olson	31-34	5th	8
6-20	At Bal.	W	9-5	15	10	Sanderson	Sutcliffe		32-34	5th	8
6-21	At Bal.	W	8-2	6	7	Leary	McDonald		33-34	4th	7
6-22	At Bal.	L	4-5	7	9	Olson	Burke		33-35	4th	8
6-23	At K.C.	L	1-2	6	4	Pichardo	Perez	Montgomery	33-36	4th	8½
6-24	At K.C.	W	6-3	15	9	Johnson	Reed	Farr	34-36	4th	8½

— 65 —

Date	Opp.	Res.	Score	(inn.*)	Hits	Opp. hits	Winning pitcher	Losing pitcher	Save	Record	Pos.	GB
6-25	At K.C.	W	4-3		13	7	Sanderson	Gubicza	Farr	35-36	4th	8
6-26	Chi.	L	1-2		3	5	McCaskill	Habyan	Radinsky	35-37	4th	9
6-27	Chi.	W	8-7		10	11	Burke	Radinsky		36-37	4th	8
6-28	Chi.	L	3-6		6	8	Hough	Perez	Thigpen	36-38	4th	8
6-29	K.C.	L	3-7		5	14	Davis	Johnson	Montgomery	36-39	4th	9
6-30	K.C.	W	6-0		12	4	Sanderson	Gubicza		37-39	4th	8
7-1	K.C.	W	7-6		12	12	Cadaret	Gordon	Habyan	38-39	4th	8
7-3	At Tex.	W	9-6		12	11	Perez	Guzman	Habyan	39-39	4th	8
7-4	At Tex.	L	1-4		3	8	Ryan	Kamieniecki		39-40	4th	9
7-5	At Tex.	W	5-4		11	11	Sanderson	Leon	Habyan	40-40	4th	9
7-6	Min.	L	5-10		8	13	Willis	Leary	Guthrie	40-41	4th	10
7-7	Min.	W	2-1		6	6	Monteleone	Banks	Habyan	41-41	4th	10
7-8	Min.	L	2-3		3	5	Smiley	Perez	Aguilera	41-42	4th	11
7-9	Sea.	W	7-6		5	13	Kamieniecki	Johnson	Habyan	42-42	4th	11
7-10	Sea.	L	2-5		5	11	Fleming	Sanderson	Swan	42-43	4th	11
7-11	Sea.	L	3-5	(12)	7	12	Swan	Habyan		42-44	4th	11
7-12	Sea.	L	6-7		8	14	Hanson	Cadaret	Swan	42-45	5th	11
7-16	At Cal.	L	2-3		5	8	Frey	Perez		42-46	5th	12
7-17	At Cal.	L	4-12		8	14	Crim	Sanderson	Grahe	42-47	5th	12
7-18	At Cal.	L	3-5		6	11	Langston	Kamieniecki	Eichhorn	42-48	6th	13
7-19	At Cal.	W	8-3		15	8	Young	Blyleven		43-48	5th	13
7-20	At Oak.	W	1-0		7	5	Hillegas	Darling		44-48	5th	12
7-21	At Oak.	W	5-1		12	4	Perez	Downs		45-48	4th	12
7-22	At Oak.	L	5-8		8	12	Parrett	Habyan	Eckersley	45-49	5th	12
7-23	At Sea.	W	5-4	(10)	11	9	Burke	Swan	Habyan	46-49	5th	12
7-24	At Sea.	W	8-7		15	15	Farr	Powell		47-49	4th	11
7-25	At Sea.	L	2-8		12	13	Grant	Hillegas	Nelson	47-50	4th	11
7-26	At Sea.	L	5-8		11	9	Johnson	Perez	Swan	47-51	4th	11
7-28	Bal.	L	2-5		8	8	McDonald	Sanderson	Olson	47-52	4th	12
7-29	Bal.	L	0-6		5	10	Rhodes	Kamieniecki		47-53	5th	12
7-30	Bal.	W	6-3		11	8	Young	Sutcliffe	Farr	48-53	4th	12
7-31	At Tor.	L	2-13		7	13	Stottlemyre	Hillegas		48-54	5th	13
8-1	At Tor.	L	1-3		8	6	Morris	Perez	Henke	48-55	5th	14
8-2	At Tor.	L	6-7		11	12	Eichhorn	Habyan	Ward	48-56	6th	15
8-3	Cle.	L	6-8	(12)	11	11	Olin	Habyan		48-57	5th	15
8-4	Cle.	W	4-3		9	10	Young	Otto	Farr	49-57	5th	14
8-5	Cle.	L	3-4	(11)	7	11	Lilliquist	Burke		49-58	5th	15
8-6	Bos.	L	1-3		4	9	Viola	Perez	Reardon	49-59	5th	16
8-7	Bos.	W	7-5		9	8	Sanderson	Dopson	Farr	50-59	5th	15
8-8	Bos.	L	2-4		6	9	Clemens	Kamieniecki	Reardon	50-60	6th	15
8-9	Bos.	W	6-0		12	1	Militello	Hesketh	Farr	51-60	6th	14
8-10	At Det.	L	5-10		14	16	Doherty	Hillegas		51-61	6th	15
8-11	At Det.	L	1-5		6	9	Tanana	Perez		51-62	T6th	15
8-12	At Det.	W	10-0		16	2	Sanderson	Gullickson		52-62	T6th	14
8-14	At Chi.	L	2-6		11	9	Radinsky	Kamieniecki	Hernandez	52-63	6th	15½
8-15	At Chi.	W	4-2		11	7	Militello	Hough	Farr	53-63	6th	15
8-16	At Chi.	L	2-4		7	7	McCaskill	Hillegas	Radinsky	53-64	6th	15½
8-17	At Chi.	L	3-4		5	5	Hibbard	Perez	Radinsky	53-65	T6th	16
8-18	Oak.	W	7-3		14	4	Sanderson	Moore	Farr	54-65	6th	16
8-19	Oak.	W	14-3		18	5	Kamieniecki	Stewart		55-65	T5th	15
8-20	Oak.	L	6-8		12	7	Parrett	Farr	Eckersley	55-66	T6th	15
8-21	Cal.	L	5-9		11	14	Butcher	Hillegas	Fortugno	55-67	T6th	15
8-22	Cal.	W	3-0		9	4	Perez	Finley	Farr	56-67	T6th	15
8-23	Cal.	L	3-7	(10)	7	13	Butcher	Monteleone		56-68	T6th	15
8-24	Mil.	W	9-8		14	11	Nielsen	Henry	Farr	57-68	6th	14
8-25	Mil.	W	5-1		9	7	Militello	Wegman		58-68	5th	13
8-26	Mil.	W	4-3		7	7	Kamieniecki	Ruffin	Farr	59-68	6th	13
8-27	At Min.	W	5-0		8	6	Perez	West		60-68	5th	13
8-28	At Min.	L	3-4	(14)	9	13	Willis	Cadaret		60-69	5th	13
8-29	At Min.	W	6-3		8	6	Wickman	Krueger	Farr	61-69	5th	12
8-30	At Min.	L	3-5		9	8	Tapani	Militello	Aguilera	61-70	5th	13
8-31	At Mil.	L	1-4		4	7	Bones	Kamieniecki	Henry	61-71	5th	14
9-1	At Mil.	W	7-1		16	8	Perez	Navarro		62-71	5th	14
9-2	At Mil.	L	0-7		6	9	Eldred	Sanderson		62-72	5th	14
9-4	Tex.	W	6-3		15	9	Wickman	Guzman	Farr	63-72	T4th	14
9-5	Tex.	L	3-7		10	8	Pavlik	Militello	Rogers	63-73	T5th	15
9-6	Tex.	W	7-0		9	3	Kamieniecki	Chiamparino		64-73	T4th	15
9-7	At Bal.	W	6-2	(13)	9	8	Monteleone	Mills		65-73	4th	14
9-8	At Bal.	W	16-4		20	7	Sanderson	Rhodes		66-73	4th	14
9-9	At Bal.	W	5-2		8	9	Wickman	Sutcliffe	Farr	67-73	4th	14
9-11	K.C.	W	2-1		6	8	Monteleone	Magnante	Farr	68-73	4th	13½
9-12	K.C.	W	11-9		14	15	Habyan	Magnante	Farr	69-73	4th	13½
9-13	K.C.	L	0-3		6	9	Rasmussen	Perez	Montgomery	69-74	4th	14½
9-14	Chi.	L	6-8		8	12	Alvarez	Wickman	Hernandez	69-75	4th	14½

Date	Opp.	Res.	Score (inn.*)	Hits	Opp. hits	Winning pitcher	Losing pitcher	Save	Record	Pos.	GB
9-15	Chi.	L	2-4	9	7	Fernandez	Monteleone	Thigpen	69-76	4th	15½
9-16	Chi.	L	6-9	12	18	Leach	Hitchcock	Hernandez	69-77	5th	15½
9-18	At K.C.	L	2-3	9	8	Pichardo	Kamieniecki	Montgomery	69-78	T4th	17
9-19	At K.C.	L	4-7	8	13	Rasmussen	Perez	Montgomery	69-79	6th	18
9-20	At K.C.	W	10-4	16	9	Wickman	Gordon	Cadaret	70-79	T4th	17
9-22 (1)	Det.	W	6-5 (12)	12	7	Farr	Aldred		71-79	T4th	17
9-22 (2)	Det.	W	7-4	12	12	Habyan	King	Farr	72-79	4th	16½
9-23	Det.	L	8-10	10	15	Aldred	Hitchcock	Munoz	72-80	5th	16½
9-24	Det.	W	10-1	9	6	Kamieniecki	Tanana		73-80	4th	16½
9-25	Tor.	L	1-3	4	9	Cone	Perez	Henke	73-81	4th	17½
9-26	Tor.	W	2-1	7	6	Wickman	Guzman	Farr	74-81	4th	16½
9-27	Tor.	L	2-12	8	19	Morris	Sanderson		74-82	4th	17½
9-28	At Cle.	L	4-6	11	11	Power	Militello		74-83	T5th	18
9-29	At Cle.	L	3-4	8	8	Nagy	Kamieniecki	Plunk	74-84	T5th	19
9-30	At Cle.	W	4-2	12	3	Perez	Mlicki	Farr	75-84	T5th	18
10-2	At Bos.	W	6-3	11	9	Wickman	Dopson	Farr	76-84	T4th	18
10-3	At Bos.	L	5-7	6	11	Taylor	Sanderson		76-85	T4th	19
10-4	At Bos.	L	2-8	5	12	Hesketh	Kamieniecki	Quantrill	76-86	T4th	20

Monthly records: April (13-8), May (13-14), June (11-17), July (11-15), August (13-17), September (14-13), Oct. (1-2).

HIGHLIGHTS

High point: The Yankees won their first six games en route to posting a modest half-game lead in the A.L. East.

Low point: New York lost eight of nine games from July 25-August 3, falling 15 games out of first place with a 48-57 record. Ironically, Manager Buck Showalter received a three-year contract extension during that skid.

Turning point: June 8, when lefthander Steve Howe was suspended from baseball for a seventh time due to substance abuse. The bullpen struggled in his absence.

Most valuable player: First baseman Don Mattingly. He led the club in batting (.288) and RBIs (86) while also collecting 40 doubles, 14 homers and his seventh Gold Glove.

Most valuable pitcher: Righthander Melido Perez. With better run support, he could have reversed his 13-16 record. He ranked among the A.L. leaders in innings (247⅔ innings), complete games (10) and strikeouts (218).

Most improved player: Third baseman Charlie Hayes. He established career highs in homers (18) and RBIs (66) and committed just 13 errors.

Most pleasant surprise: Infielder Andy Stankiewicz. After six years in the minors, he made the most of opportunities created by injuries. He played sound defense at second base and shortstop and was adept at reaching base.

Biggest disappointment: Center fielder Roberto Kelly. He hit .335 over the first two months but .242 thereafter. By August, he was playing left field and batting sixth.

Key injuries: Right fielder/DH Danny Tartabull missed 39 games because of various injuries and had two other furloughs to be with his pregnant wife. Infielder Mike Gallego played less than one-third of the season (heel, wrist), while right fielder Jesse Barfield was limited to 30 games (wrist).

Notable: New York's home attendance (1,748,737) was the lowest, excluding the '81 strike-shortened season, since Yankee Stadium was renovated in 1976. . . . George Steinbrenner was informed in late August by then-Commissioner Fay Vincent that he could resume active control of the club on March 1, 1993. Steinbrenner had been banished from everyday control August 20, 1990, for his association with gambler Howard Spira. . . . Righthander Pascual Perez was suspended for the season after testing positive for cocaine during spring training.

—JACK O'CONNELL

RECORDS

1992 regular-season record: 76-86 (T4th in A.L. East); 41-40 at home; 35-46 on road; 37-41 vs. East; 39-45 vs. West; 24-29 vs. LHP; 52-57 vs. RHP; 66-71 on grass; 10-15 on turf; 26-26 in daytime; 50-60 at night; 28-24 in one-run games; 6-9 in extra-inning games; 1-0-0 in doubleheaders.

Team record last five years: 373-435 (.462, ranks T11th in league in that span).

TEAM LEADERS

Batting average: Don Mattingly (.288).
At-bats: Don Mattingly (640).
Runs: Don Mattingly (89).
Hits: Don Mattingly (184).
Total bases: Don Mattingly (266).
Doubles: Don Mattingly (40).
Triples: Mel Hall (3).
Home runs: Danny Tartabull (25).
Runs batted in: Don Mattingly (86).
Stolen bases: Roberto Kelly (28).
Slugging percentage: Danny Tartabull (.489).
On-base percentage: Danny Tartabull (.409).
Wins: Melido Perez (13).
Earned-run average: Melido Perez (2.87).
Complete games: Melido Perez (10).
Shutouts: Greg Cadaret, Shawn Hillegas, Melido Perez, Scott Sanderson (1).
Saves: Steve Farr (30).
Innings pitched: Melido Perez (247⅔).
Strikeouts: Melido Perez (218).

GAMES BY POSITION

Catcher: Matt Nokes 111, Mike Stanley 55, Jim Leyritz 18.
First base: Don Mattingly 143, Kevin Maas 22, J.T. Snow 6, Charlie Hayes 4, Mike Stanley 4, Jim Leyritz 2.
Second base: Pat Kelly 101, Mike Gallego 40, Andy Stankiewicz 34, Randy Velarde 3, Jim Leyritz 1.
Third base: Charlie Hayes 139, Randy Velarde 26, Jim Leyritz 2, Hensley Meulens 2.
Shortstop: Andy Stankiewicz 81, Randy Velarde 75, Mike Gallego 14, Dave Silvestri 6.
Outfield: Roberto Kelly 146, Mel Hall 136, Danny Tartabull 69, Bernie Williams 62, Dion James 46, Jesse Barfield 30, Randy Velarde 23, Gerald Williams 12, Mike Humphreys 2, Jim Leyritz 2.
Designated hitter: Kevin Maas 62, Danny Tartabull 53, Jim Leyritz 31, Don Mattingly 15, Mel Hall 11, Mike Stanley 6, Dion James 5, Mike Humphreys 1, Pat Kelly 1, J.T. Snow 1, Andy Stankiewicz 1.

TOP 10 DRAFT CHOICES

1. **Derek Jeter,** SS, Kalamazoo (Mich.) Central High School.
2. **None.**
3. **None.**
4. **Mike Buddie,** RHP, Wake Forest University.
5. **Don Leshnock,** C, University of North Carolina.
6. **Ray Suplee,** OF, University of Georgia.
7. **Carlton Fleming,** 2B, Georgia Tech University.
8. **Matt Luke,** OF, University of California.
9. **Ryan Karp,** LHP, Florida International University.
10. **Robert Hinds,** 2B, UCLA.

OAKLAND ATHLETICS
AMERICAN LEAGUE WEST DIVISION

APRIL

SUN	MON	TUE	WED	THU	FRI	SAT
				1	2	3
4	5 N DET H	6	7 N DET H	8 N DET H	9 N MIL H	10 N MIL H
11 MIL H	12	13 DET	14	15 DET	16 N MIL	17 MIL
18 MIL	19	20 N NY H	21 N NY H	22 N NY H	23 N CLE H	24 CLE H
25 CLE H	26	27 N BOS H	28 BOS H	29	30 N CLE	

MAY

SUN	MON	TUE	WED	THU	FRI	SAT
						1 CLE
2 CLE	3 N NY	4 N NY	5 N BOS	6 N BOS	7 N CAL	8 N CAL
9 CAL	10 N TEX H	11 N TEX H	12 N TEX H	13 N TEX H	14 N SEA H	15 N SEA H
16 SEA H	17	18 N KC	19 N KC	20 N KC	21 N CHI	22 CHI
23 CHI	24	25 N MIN H	26 N MIN H	27 N MIN H	28 N TOR H	29 TOR H
30 TOR H	31 BAL H					

JUNE

SUN	MON	TUE	WED	THU	FRI	SAT
		1 N BAL H	2 N BAL H	3	4 N TOR	5 N TOR
6 TOR	7 N BAL	8 N BAL	9 N BAL	10	11 N MIN	12 N MIN
13 MIN	14 N CHI H	15 N CHI H	16 N CHI H	17 N CHI H	18 N KC H	19 N KC H
20 KC H	21 N SEA	22 N SEA	23 N SEA	24 N SEA	25 N TEX	26 N TEX
27 TEX	28	29 N CAL H	30 N CAL H			

JULY

SUN	MON	TUE	WED	THU	FRI	SAT
				1 N CAL H	2 N NY H	3 N NY H
4 N NY H	5 N CLE H	6 N CLE H	7 N CLE H	8 N BOS H	9 N BOS H	10 N BOS H
11 BOS H	12	13 ☆ ALL-STAR GAME	14	15 N NY	16 N NY	17 N NY
18 N NY	19 N CLE	20 N CLE	21 N CLE	22 N BOS	23 N BOS	24 BOS
25 BOS	26 N CAL	27 N CAL	28 N CAL	29 N CAL	30 N TEX H	31 TEX H

AUGUST

SUN	MON	TUE	WED	THU	FRI	SAT
1 TEX H	2	3 N SEA H	4 N SEA H	5 N SEA H	6 N KC	7 N KC
8 KC	9 N CHI	10 N CHI	11 CHI	12	13 N MIN H	14 N MIN H
15 MIN H	16 N MIL H	17 N MIL H	18 N MIL H	19	20 N DET	21 N DET
22 DET	23 N DET	24 N MIL	25 N MIL	26 MIL	27 N DET H	28 DET H
29 DET H	30 N TOR H	31 N TOR H				

SEPTEMBER

SUN	MON	TUE	WED	THU	FRI	SAT
			1 TOR H	2	3 N BAL H	4 N BAL H
5 BAL H	6	7 N TOR	8 N TOR	9 N TOR	10 N BAL	11 N BAL
12 N BAL	13 N MIN	14 N MIN	15 N MIN	16 N MIN	17 N CHI	18 CHI
19 CHI H	20 N KC H	21 N KC H	22 N KC H	23 N KC H	24 N SEA	25 N SEA
26 SEA	27	28 N TEX	29 N TEX	30 N TEX		

OCTOBER

SUN	MON	TUE	WED	THU	FRI	SAT
					1 N CAL H	2 N CAL H
3 CAL H						

CLUB DIRECTORY

Owner/managing general partner
Walter A. Haas Jr.
Chairman and chief operating officer
Walter J. Haas
President and general manager
Sandy Alderson
Executive vice president
Andy Dolich
Vice president, finance
Kathleen McCracken
Vice president, admin. and personnel
Raymond B. Krise Jr.
Asst. to the man. gen. partner, baseball
Bill Rigney
Director of player development
Keith Lieppman
Special assistant for baseball operations
Karl Kuehl
Director of scouting
Dick Bogard
Assistant director of scouting
Eric Kubota
Director of baseball administration
Walt Jocketty
Director of Latin American scouting
Juan Marichal
Director of team travel
Mickey Morabito
Director of baseball information
Jay Alves
Assistant director, baseball administration
Pamela Pitts
Administrative asst., baseball operations
Jennella Roark
Administrative assistant, baseball relations
Doreen Alves
Admin. asst., stats and desktop publishing
Mike Selleck
Director of broadcasting
Tom Cordova
Director of media relations
Kathy Jacobson
Dir. of community affairs/speakers bureau
Dave Perron
Director of stadium operations
Kevin Kahn
Director of broadcast operations
Bill King

Director of business administration
Alan Ledford
Dir. of corporate business and ticket sales
John Kamperschroer
Director of group sales and season tickets
Bettina Flores
Director of ticket operations
Shelley Landeros
Director of publications
Rob Kelly
Director of promotions
Sharon Kelly
Team physician
Dr. Allan Pont
Team orthopedist
Dr. Rick Bost
Trainers
Barry Weinberg
Larry Davis
Equipment manager
Frank Ciensczyk
Visiting clubhouse manager
Steve Vucinich
Scouts
Tony Arias
Billy Beane
Mark Conkin
Tim Corcoran
Ed Crosby
Grady Fuson
Bill Gayton
Michael Jones
Billy Merkel
Bill Meyer
Marty Miller
Steve Nichols
Chris Pittaro
J.P. Ricciardi
Dave Roberts
Rick Rodriguez
Will Schock
Jeff Scott
Mike Stafford
Ron Vaughn
Craig Wallenbrock

SCHEDULE KEY

H—Home game.   N—Night game (any game starting after 5 p.m.).
*All-Star Game at Oriole Park at Camden Yards, Baltimore.

Manager—Tony La Russa (10).

Coaches—Dave Duncan (18), Art Kusnyer (5), Greg Luzinski (19), Dave McKay (8), Tommie Reynolds (47).

No.	PITCHERS	B/T	Ht./Wt.	Born	1992 clubs
62	Baker, Scott	L/L	6-2/175	5-18-70	St. Petersburg
17	Darling, Ron	R/R	6-3/195	8-19-60	Oakland
15	Davis, Storm	R/R	6-4/225	12-26-61	Baltimore
31	Downs, Kelly	R/R	6-4/205	10-25-60	San Francisco, Oakland
43	Eckersley, Dennis	R/R	6-2/195	10-3-54	Oakland
41	Guzman, Johnny	R/L	5-10/155	1-21-71	Huntsville, Tacoma, Oakland
57	Hillegas, Shawn	R/R	6-2/223	8-21-64	Fort Lauderdale, Columbus, New York A.L., Oakland
40	Honeycutt, Rick	L/L	6-1/191	6-29-54	Oakland
26	Horsman, Vince	R/L	6-2/180	3-9-67	Oakland
58	Mohler, Mike	R/L	6-2/195	7-26-68	Huntsville
50	Ojala, Kirt	L/L	6-2/200	12-24-68	Albany/Colonie
56	Revenig, Todd	R/R	6-1/185	6-28-69	Huntsville, Oakland
61	Shaw, Curtis	L/L	6-1/190	8-16-69	Modesto
37	Slusarski, Joe	R/R	6-4/195	12-19-66	Oakland, Tacoma
23	Sturtze, Tanyon	R/R	6-5/190	10-12-70	Modesto
59	Van Poppel, Todd	R/R	6-5/210	12-9-71	Tacoma
35	Welch, Bob	R/R	6-3/198	11-3-56	Oakland
32	Witt, Bobby	R/R	6-2/205	5-11-64	Texas, Oakland
51	Zancanaro, David	B/L	6-1/170	1-8-69	Tacoma

No.	CATCHERS	B/T	Ht./Wt.	Born	1992 clubs
48	Helfand, Eric	L/R	6-0/195	3-25-69	Modesto, Huntsville
39	Mercedes, Henry	R/R	5-11/185	7-23-69	Tacoma, Oakland
45	Molina, Islay	R/R	6-1/200	6-3-71	Reno, Tacoma
36	Steinbach, Terry	R/R	6-1/195	3-2-62	Oakland

No.	INFIELDERS	B/T	Ht./Wt.	Born	1992 clubs
12	Blankenship, Lance	R/R	6-0/185	12-6-63	Tacoma, Oakland
14	Bordick, Mike	R/R	5-11/175	7-21-65	Oakland
7	Brosius, Scott	R/R	6-1/185	8-15-66	Oakland, Tacoma
30	Browne, Jerry	B/R	5-10/170	2-3-66	Tacoma, Oakland
25	McGwire, Mark	R/R	6-5/225	10-1-63	Oakland
20	Paquette, Craig	R/R	6-0/190	3-28-69	Huntsville, Tacoma
	Seitzer, Kevin	R/R	5-11/190	3-26-62	Milwaukee

No.	OUTFIELDERS	B/T	Ht./Wt.	Born	1992 clubs
60	Armas, Marcos	R/R	6-5/190	8-5-69	Huntsville
42	Henderson, Dave	R/R	6-2/220	7-21-58	Oakland, Modesto, Tacoma
24	Henderson, Rickey	R/L	5-10/190	12-25-58	Oakland
49	Lydy, Scott	R/R	6-5/190	10-26-68	Reno, Huntsville
16	Neel, Troy	L/R	6-4/210	9-14-65	Tacoma, Oakland
21	Sierra, Ruben	B/R	6-1/200	10-6-65	Texas, Oakland

Ballpark (capacity, surface)
Oakland-Alameda County Coliseum
(47,313, grass)

Address
Oakland A's
Oakland Coliseum
7000 Coliseum Way
Oakland, CA 94621-1918

Business phone
510-638-4900

Ticket information
510-568-5600

Ticket prices
$14 (field level)
$13 (plaza level)
$7 (upper reserved)
$4.50 (bleachers)

Field dimensions (from home plate)
To left field at foul line, 330 feet
To center field, 400 feet
To right field at foul line, 330 feet

First game played
April 17, 1968 (Orioles 4, Athletics 1)

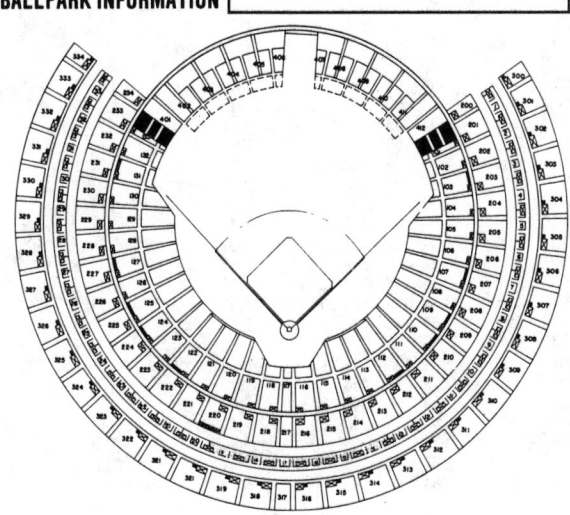

MINOR LEAGUE AFFILIATES

Class	Team	League	Manager
AAA	Tacoma	Pacific Coast	Bob Boone
AA	Huntsville	Southern	Casey Parsons
A	Modesto	California	Ted Kubiak
A	Madison	Midwest	Gary Jones
A	Southern Oregon	Northwest	Dick Scott
Rookie	Scottsdale Athletics	Arizona	Bruce Hines

BROADCAST INFORMATION

Radio: KNEW-AM (910). Broadcasters: Lon Simmons, Bill King, Ray Fosse. KNTA-AM (1430, Spanish language). Broadcasters: Amaury Pi-Gonzales, Erwin Higueros.
TV: KRON-TV (Channel 4). Broadcasters: To be announced.
Cable TV: SportsChannel. Broadcasters: To be announced.

SPRING TRAINING

Ballpark (city): Phoenix Stadium (Phoenix, Ariz.).
Ticket information: 602-392-0074.

HISTORY

YEAR-BY-YEAR RECORDS

Year	Pos.	W	L	Pct.	*GB	Year	Pos.	W	L	Pct.	*GB
1901	4th	74	62	.544	9	1950	8th	52	102	.338	46
1902	1st	83	53	.610	+ 5	1951	6th	70	84	.455	28
1903	2nd	75	60	.556	14½	1952	4th	79	75	.513	16
1904	5th	81	70	.536	12½	1953	7th	59	95	.383	41½
1905	1st	92	56	.622	+ 2	1954	8th	51	103	.331	60
1906	4th	78	67	.538	12	1955	6th	63	91	.409	33
1907	2nd	88	57	.607	1½	1956	8th	52	102	.338	45
1908	6th	68	85	.444	22	1957	7th	59	94	.386	38½
1909	2nd	95	58	.621	3½	1958	7th	73	81	.474	19
1910	1st	102	48	.680	+14½	1959	7th	66	88	.429	28
1911	1st	101	50	.669	+13½	1960	8th	58	96	.377	39
1912	3rd	90	62	.592	15	1961	T9th	61	100	.379	47½
1913	1st	96	57	.627	+ 6½	1962	9th	72	90	.444	24
1914	1st	99	53	.651	+ 8½	1963	8th	73	89	.451	31½
1915	8th	43	109	.283	58½	1964	10th	57	105	.352	42
1916	8th	36	117	.235	54½	1965	10th	59	103	.364	43
1917	8th	52	98	.359	44½	1966	7th	74	86	.463	23
1918	8th	52	76	.406	24	1967	10th	62	99	.385	29½
1919	8th	36	104	.257	52	1968	6th	82	80	.506	21
1920	8th	48	106	.312	50	1969	2nd	88	74	.543	9
1921	8th	53	100	.346	45	1970	2nd	89	73	.549	9
1922	7th	65	89	.422	29	1971	1st†	101	60	.627	+16
1923	6th	69	83	.454	29	1972	1st‡	93	62	.600	+ 5½
1924	5th	71	81	.467	20	1973	1st‡	94	68	.580	+ 6
1925	2nd	88	64	.579	8½	1974	1st‡	90	72	.556	+ 5
1926	3rd	83	67	.553	6	1975	1st†	98	64	.605	+ 7
1927	2nd	91	63	.591	19	1976	2nd	87	74	.540	2½
1928	2nd	98	55	.641	2½	1977	7th	63	98	.391	38½
1929	1st	104	46	.693	+18	1978	6th	69	93	.426	23
1930	1st	102	52	.662	+ 8	1979	7th	54	108	.333	34
1931	1st	107	45	.704	+13½	1980	2nd	83	79	.512	14
1932	2nd	94	60	.610	13	1981	1st/2nd	64	45	.587	§†*
1933	3rd	79	72	.523	19½	1982	5th	68	94	.420	25
1934	5th	68	82	.453	31	1983	4th	74	88	.457	25
1935	8th	58	91	.389	34	1984	4th	77	85	.475	7
1936	8th	53	100	.346	49	1985	T4th	77	85	.475	14
1937	7th	54	97	.358	46½	1986	T3rd	76	86	.469	16
1938	8th	53	99	.349	46	1987	3rd	81	81	.500	4
1939	7th	55	97	.362	51½	1988	1st‡	104	58	.642	+13
1940	8th	54	100	.351	36	1989	1st‡	99	63	.611	+ 7
1941	8th	64	90	.416	37	1990	1st‡	103	59	.636	+ 9
1942	8th	55	99	.357	48	1991	4th	84	78	.519	11
1943	8th	49	105	.318	49	1992	1st†	96	66	.593	+ 6
1944	T5th	72	82	.468	17						
1945	8th	52	98	.347	34½						
1946	8th	49	105	.318	55						
1947	5th	78	76	.506	19						
1948	4th	84	70	.545	12½						
1949	5th	81	73	.526	16						

*Games behind winner. †Lost Championship Series. ‡Won Championship Series. §First half 37-23; second 27-22. *Won division playoff.

MANAGERS

Name	Record	Years
Connie Mack	3582-3814	'01-50
Jimmie Dykes	198-254	'51-53
Eddie Joost	51-103	1954
Lou Boudreau	151-260	'55-57
Harry Craft	162-196	'57-59
Bob Elliott	58-96	1960
Joe Gordon	26-33	1961
Hank Bauer	187-226	'61-62
		1969
Eddie Lopat	90-124	'63-64
Mel McGaha	45-91	'64-65
Haywood Sullivan	54-82	1965
Alvin Dark	314-291	'66-67
		'74-75
Luke Appling	10-30	1967
Bob Kennedy	82-80	1968
John McNamara	97-78	'69-70
Dick Williams	288-190	'71-73
Chuck Tanner	87-74	1976
Jack McKeon	71-105	'77, '78
Bobby Winkles	61-86	'77-78
Jim Marshall	54-108	1979
Billy Martin	215-218	'80-82
Steve Boros	94-112	'83-84
Jackie Moore	163-190	'84-86
Tony La Russa	509-380	'86-92

DAY BY DAY

Date	Opp.	Res.	Score	(inn.*)	Hits	Opp. hits	Winning pitcher	Losing pitcher	Save	Record	Pos.	GB
4-6	K.C.	W	5-3		9	11	Honeycutt	Aquino	Eckersley	1-0	T1st	...
4-8	K.C.	W	4-3	(13)	11	8	Parrett	Heaton		2-0	T1st	½
4-9	K.C.	W	5-2		10	7	Darling	Gubicza	Eckersley	3-0	T1st	½
4-10	Chi.	W	6-5		12	9	Slusarski	Fernandez	Eckersley	4-0	1st	+½
4-11	Chi.	W	7-6	(10)	13	6	Parrett	Leach		5-0	1st	+½
4-12	Chi.	L	4-6		8	11	McDowell	Nelson	Thigpen	5-1	2nd	½
4-13	At K.C.	W	6-1		10	5	Moore	Gordon		6-1	1st	+½
4-14	At K.C.	L	1-3		7	1	Heaton	Honeycutt	Montgomery	6-2	1st	+½
4-15	At K.C.	W	10-6		14	12	Parrett	Magnante		7-2	1st	+½
4-16	At K.C.	W	1-0	(10)	3	4	Stewart	Montgomery	Eckersley	8-2	1st	+1½
4-17	At Tex.	L	5-6		10	11	Brown	Briscoe	Rogers	8-3	1st	+½
4-18	At Tex.	W	5-3		11	9	Moore	Mathews	Eckersley	9-3	1st	+1½
4-19	At Tex.	L	4-6		6	10	Manuel	Honeycutt	Russell	9-4	1st	+½
4-20	Cal.	W	4-3	(11)	7	7	Eckersley	Crim		10-4	1st	+1
4-21	Cal.	L	2-3		6	5	Valera	Stewart	Harvey	10-5	1st	+1
4-22	Cal.	W	10-4		10	11	Moore	Finley		11-5	1st	+1
4-24	At Min.	L	5-6	(10)	9	11	Edens	Gossage		11-6	1st	+1
4-25	At Min.	W	8-4		18	11	Slusarski	Tapani	Eckersley	12-6	1st	+1½
4-26	At Min.	L	4-8		6	12	Mahomes	Stewart	Aguilera	12-7	1st	+½
4-28	At Cle.	W	3-1		7	7	Moore	Olin	Eckersley	13-7	1st	+1½
4-29	At Cle.	L	2-5		10	13	Otto	Darling	Olin	13-8	1st	+1
4-30	At Det.	W	10-6		14	9	Horsman	Leiter	Eckersley	14-8	1st	+1½
5-1	At Det.	W	7-6		15	10	Parrett	Henneman	Eckersley	15-8	1st	+2
5-2	At Det.	L	3-5		10	6	Tanana	Welch	Henneman	15-9	1st	+1
5-3	At Det.	L	4-8		8	9	King	Moore	Henneman	15-10	1st	+1
5-4	Tor.	L	3-7		5	12	Stottlemyre	Darling		15-11	1st	+½
5-5	Tor.	L	1-5		5	12	Guzman	Slusarski	Ward	15-12	2nd	½
5-6	Det.	W	5-2		7	4	Stewart	Terrell	Eckersley	16-12	2nd	½
5-7	Det.	W	6-2		9	7	Welch	Tanana	Eckersley	17-12	2nd	½
5-8	N.Y.	W	8-6		12	11	Nelson	Habyan	Eckersley	18-12	2nd	½
5-9	N.Y.	W	5-3		5	7	Darling	Leary	Honeycutt	19-12	1st	+½
5-10	N.Y.	W	5-2		7	2	Slusarski	Cadaret	Eckersley	20-12	1st	+½
5-12	At Tor.	L	0-3		7	5	Key	Stewart	Henke	20-13	1st	+½
5-13	At Tor.	L	3-4		10	9	Morris	Moore	Henke	20-14	2nd	½
5-15	At N.Y.	L	2-3		6	11	Kamieniecki	Welch	Farr	20-15	2nd	½
5-16	At N.Y.	W	6-3		5	7	Darling	Leary	Eckersley	21-15	1st	+½
5-17	At N.Y.	L	2-11		7	10	Perez	Stewart		21-16	2nd	½
5-18	At Bal.	W	8-4		10	7	Moore	Sutcliffe		22-16	1st	+½
5-19	At Bal.	W	5-3		11	5	Slusarski	Mesa	Eckersley	23-16	1st	+½
5-20	At Bal.	W	4-2		9	7	Welch	Mussina	Eckersley	24-16	1st	+1½
5-22	At Bos.	W	5-3		9	6	Stewart	Viola	Eckersley	25-16	1st	+2½
5-23	At Bos.	L	1-5		8	12	Dopson	Moore		25-17	1st	+1½
5-24	At Bos.	W	4-0		8	2	Darling	Gardiner		26-17	1st	+1½
5-25	Cle.	L	6-10		11	16	Nagy	Slusarski	Power	26-18	1st	+1
5-26	Cle.	L	0-1		4	4	Otto	Welch	Olin	26-19	1st	+1
5-27	Cle.	L	2-4		8	6	Scudder	Stewart	Olin	26-20	1st	...
5-29	Bal.	W	5-3		9	10	Moore	Milacki	Eckersley	27-20	2nd	½
5-30	Bal.	L	6-7		9	12	Mesa	Slusarski	Olson	27-21	3rd	½
5-31	Bal.	L	2-4		9	7	Sutcliffe	Darling	Olson	27-22	3rd	1
6-1	Bos.	W	10-7		8	13	Campbell	Darwin		28-22	2nd	...
6-2	Bos.	W	5-4		5	7	Moore	Hesketh	Eckersley	29-22	1st	+½
6-3	Bos.	W	7-6		10	12	Parrett	Gardiner	Eckersley	30-22	1st	+½
6-5	At Chi.	W	10-3		13	9	Darling	McCaskill		31-22	1st	+1
6-6	At Chi.	W	6-4		9	6	Stewart	Fernandez	Eckersley	32-22	1st	+1½
6-7	At Chi.	L	1-6		3	8	Hough	Moore		32-23	1st	+1
6-8	At Mil.	L	2-6		4	10	Wegman	Slusarski		32-24	1st	...
6-9	At Mil.	W	6-1		15	4	Campbell	Robinson		33-24	1st	+1
6-10	At Mil.	W	5-2		7	9	Darling	Bosio	Eckersley	34-24	1st	+1
6-12	Tex.	W	6-5	(14)	13	10	Corsi	Nunez		35-24	1st	+2
6-13	Tex.	W	7-1		4	4	Stewart	Witt		36-24	1st	+3
6-14	Tex.	W	6-1		9	5	Welch	Brown		37-24	1st	+3½
6-15	Mil.	W	3-2	(10)	7	9	Eckersley	Fetters		38-24	1st	+4
6-16	Mil.	L	0-10		3	12	Robinson	Darling		38-25	1st	+4
6-17	Mil.	L	2-10		5	12	Navarro	Moore		38-26	1st	+3½
6-19	At Cal.	W	12-8		15	15	Stewart	Finley	Eckersley	39-26	1st	+4
6-20	At Cal.	L	0-10		4	10	Valera	Welch		39-27	1st	+3
6-21	At Cal.	L	2-4		9	4	Abbott	Moore	Grahe	39-28	1st	+2
6-22	Sea.	W	7-2		10	6	Darling	Hanson	Eckersley	40-28	1st	+2
6-23	Sea.	W	12-7		10	8	Slusarski	Kramer		41-28	1st	+2
6-24	Sea.	W	7-2		10	8	Stewart	Fleming		42-28	1st	+2

Date	Opp.	Res.	Score	(inn.*)	Hits	Opp. hits	Winning pitcher	Losing pitcher	Save	Record	Pos.	GB
6-25	Min.	W	5-1		12	11	Welch	Krueger	Eckersley	43-28	1st	+3
6-26	Min.	L	3-4		7	9	Banks	Moore	Aguilera	43-29	1st	+2
6-27	Min.	L	2-12		4	18	Smiley	Darling		43-30	1st	+1
6-28	Min.	L	2-10		10	14	Erickson	Campbell		43-31	T1st	...
6-29	At Sea.	W	5-4	(11)	10	17	Horsman	Schooler	Eckersley	44-31	T1st	...
6-30	At Sea.	W	4-2		11	6	Welch	Nelson	Eckersley	45-31	T1st	...
7-1	At Sea.	W	3-1		12	5	Moore	Grant	Eckersley	46-31	T1st	...
7-3	At Cle.	L	1-8		5	15	Nagy	Darling		46-32	T1st	...
7-4	At Cle.	L	1-8		7	18	Scudder	Downs	Power	46-33	2nd	1
7-5	At Cle.	W	5-2		11	12	Welch	Armstrong	Eckersley	47-33	2nd	1
7-6	At Cle.	W	13-4		17	10	Moore	Mutis		48-33	2nd	1
7-7	At Det.	L	2-3		6	9	Ritz	Darling	Henneman	48-34	2nd	1
7-8	At Det.	L	3-6		6	12	Lancaster	Corsi	Henneman	48-35	2nd	2
7-9	At Tor.	W	3-4		7	10	Henke	Gossage		48-36	2nd	2
7-10	At Tor.	W	5-1		9	5	Welch	Wells		49-36	2nd	2
7-11	At Tor.	W	3-1		8	2	Moore	Guzman	Eckersley	50-36	2nd	2
7-12	At Tor.	W	8-0		13	2	Darling	Hentgen		51-36	2nd	2
7-16	Det.	W	4-0		6	2	Downs	Tanana		52-36	2nd	2
7-17	Det.	L	3-4		8	11	Gullickson	Welch	Knudsen	52-37	2nd	3
7-18	Det.	L	2-5		9	12	Leiter	Moore	Groom	52-38	2nd	3
7-19	Det.	W	6-2		8	9	Nelson	Ritz		53-38	2nd	3
7-20	N.Y.	L	0-1		5	7	Hillegas	Darling		53-39	2nd	3
7-21	N.Y.	L	1-5		4	12	Perez	Downs		53-40	2nd	3
7-22	N.Y.	W	8-5		12	8	Parrett	Habyan	Eckersley	54-40	2nd	3
7-23	Tor.	L	3-9		9	12	Stieb	Moore		54-41	2nd	3½
7-24	Tor.	W	6-5		14	12	Eckersley	Henke		55-41	2nd	3
7-25	Tor.	W	6-0		7	2	Darling	Stottlemyre		56-41	2nd	3
7-26	Tor.	W	9-1		15	5	Downs	Morris		57-41	2nd	3
7-27	At Min.	W	9-1		10	5	Welch	Smiley		58-41	2nd	2
7-28	At Min.	W	12-10		19	12	Nelson	Edens	Eckersley	59-41	2nd	1
7-29	At Min.	W	5-4		7	14	Parrett	Aguilera	Eckersley	60-41	T1st	...
7-31	At K.C.	L	5-6	(10)	9	17	Meacham	Parrett		60-42	2nd	½
8-1	At K.C.	L	4-8		9	12	Gordon	Downs		60-43	2nd	1½
8-2	At K.C.	W	8-4		13	13	Welch	Berenguer		61-43	2nd	1½
8-3	At Tex.	W	4-1		8	5	Moore	Guzman	Eckersley	62-43	2nd	1
8-4	At Tex.	W	9-0		12	4	Stewart	Bohanon	Campbell	63-43	T1st	...
8-5	At Tex.	W	4-3		6	9	Darling	Witt	Eckersley	64-43	1st	+1
8-6	At Tex.	W	2-0		6	10	Downs	Ryan	Honeycutt	65-43	1st	+2
8-7	K.C.	W	8-6		13	12	Welch	Moeller	Eckersley	66-43	1st	+2½
8-8	K.C.	W	5-3		6	10	Eckersley	Montgomery		67-43	1st	+3
8-9	K.C.	L	2-5		5	8	Appier	Stewart	Montgomery	67-44	1st	+3
8-10	Chi.	W	5-3		7	5	Darling	Hough	Eckersley	68-44	1st	+3
8-11	Chi.	L	6-10		7	14	Hernandez	Honeycutt	Radinsky	68-45	1st	+2
8-12	Chi.	W	2-1		8	8	Eckersley	McDowell		69-45	1st	+3
8-13	Cal.	W	4-1		6	3	Moore	Abbott		70-45	1st	+4
8-14	Cal.	L	1-2		6	4	Blyleven	Stewart	Grahe	70-46	1st	+3
8-15	Cal.	W	9-5		14	9	Corsi	Crim		71-46	1st	+4
8-16	Cal.	W	5-4		6	7	Eckersley	Grahe		72-46	1st	+5
8-18	At N.Y.	L	3-7		4	14	Sanderson	Moore	Farr	72-47	1st	+5
8-19	At N.Y.	L	3-14		5	18	Kamieniecki	Stewart		72-48	1st	+5
8-20	At N.Y.	W	8-6		7	12	Parrett	Farr	Eckersley	73-48	1st	+6
8-21	At Bal.	L	2-4		9	5	Mussina	Downs	Mills	73-49	1st	+5
8-22	At Bal.	W	5-3		10	8	Parrett	Lewis	Eckersley	74-49	1st	+6
8-23	At Bal.	W	7-3		12	7	Moore	McDonald	Eckersley	75-49	1st	+6
8-24	At Bos.	W	9-3		14	7	Stewart	Dopson		76-49	1st	+7
8-25	At Bos.	L	4-5		8	12	Quantrill	Eckersley	Reardon	76-50	1st	+7
8-26	At Bos.	L	1-2	(10)	6	6	Viola	Campbell		76-51	1st	+6
8-28	Cle.	W	7-6		8	13	Corsi	Armstrong	Eckersley	77-51	1st	+6½
8-29	Cle.	W	4-1		7	4	Stewart	Mesa	Eckersley	78-51	1st	+7½
8-30	Cle.	W	7-5		16	13	Darling	Nagy	Honeycutt	79-51	1st	+7½
8-31	Bal.	L	0-4		4	9	Mussina	Downs		79-52	1st	+6½
9-1	Bal.	L	1-5		6	8	Milacki	Slusarski		79-53	1st	+5½
9-2	Bal.	L	1-2	(10)	2	8	Mills	Honeycutt		79-54	1st	+4½
9-4	Bos.	L	3-8		9	11	Darwin	Stewart		79-55	1st	+4½
9-5	Bos.	L	3-7		6	9	Dopson	Darling		79-56	1st	+4½
9-6	Bos.	W	2-1	(10)	7	5	Eckersley	Quantrill		80-56	1st	+5½
9-7	At Cal.	L	2-3		10	8	Valera	Moore	Grahe	80-57	1st	+4½
9-8	At Cal.	W	14-2		19	7	Downs	Finley		81-57	1st	+4½
9-9	At Cal.	W	3-0		8	2	Stewart	Langston	Eckersley	82-57	1st	+4½
9-10	Sea.	W	6-4		4	9	Darling	Johnson	Eckersley	83-57	1st	+5
9-11	Sea.	W	4-3		6	5	Russell	Nelson		84-57	1st	+6
9-12	Sea.	W	5-4		9	13	Moore	Leary	Eckersley	85-57	1st	+6
9-13	Sea.	W	3-1		4	2	Downs	Hanson	Russell	86-57	1st	+6
9-14	Min.	W	3-2		9	8	Corsi	Edens	Eckersley	87-57	1st	+7

Date	Opp.	Res.	Score	(inn.*)	Hits	Opp. hits	Winning pitcher	Losing pitcher	Save	Record	Pos.	GB
9-15	Min.	W	2-1		5	2	Darling	Mahomes	Eckersley	88-57	1st	+8
9-16	Min.	W	4-2		7	9	Witt	Smiley	Russell	89-57	1st	+9
9-18	At Sea.	W	7-4		10	10	Moore	Fisher	Eckersley	90-57	1st	+8½
9-19	At Sea.	L	4-6		8	8	Leary	Welch	Nelson	90-58	1st	+8½
9-20	At Sea.	W	4-2		13	7	Stewart	Hanson	Eckersley	91-58	1st	+8½
9-21	At Chi.	W	6-5		10	12	Darling	Fernandez	Eckersley	92-58	1st	+9
9-22	At Chi.	L	3-8		9	13	Hough	Witt		92-59	1st	+8
9-23	At Chi.	L	6-17		8	15	McCaskill	Moore		92-60	1st	+8
9-24	At Chi.	W	4-1		6	5	Welch	McDowell	Eckersley	93-60	1st	+8½
9-25	At Mil.	L	1-4		5	5	Bones	Stewart		93-61	1st	+8½
9-26	At Mil.	L	1-2		6	6	Orosco	Darling	Henry	93-62	1st	+7½
9-27	At Mil.	L	3-5		9	7	Navarro	Campbell	Henry	93-63	1st	+6½
9-29	Tex.	W	5-0		8	4	Moore	Brown		94-63	1st	+7
9-30	Tex.	L	3-7		7	7	Guzman	Welch	Whiteside	94-64	1st	+7
10-1	Tex.	L	3-4		5	6	Rogers	Horsman	Whiteside	94-65	1st	+6
10-2	Mil.	L	2-3	(11)	7	6	Holmes	Corsi	Henry	94-66	1st	+5
10-3	Mil.	W	10-3		13	6	Moore	Bones		95-66	1st	+6
10-4	Mil.	W	7-1		7	6	Russell	Eldred		96-66	1st	+6

Monthly records: April (14-8), May (13-14), June (18-9), July (15-11), August (19-10), September (15-12), Oct. (2-2).

HIGHLIGHTS

High point: A seven-game winning streak from August 2-8 propelled the Athletics into first place for the rest of the season.

Low point: Without left fielder Rickey Henderson (hamstring injury) and right fielder Jose Canseco (shoulder), the A's lost five of seven games from July 3-9 to fall from a first-place tie with Minnesota to a two-game deficit.

Turning point: Oakland won 13 of 15 games from July 24-August 8 to turn a 3½-game deficit into a three-game lead over the Twins. Included in that run was a three-game sweep of the Twins in Minnesota.

Most valuable player: Infielder Mike Bordick. Not only did he play well at shortstop and second base, but he became only the second infielder in Oakland history to bat .300 in a season.

Most valuable pitcher: Righthander Dennis Eckersley. The A.L. Most Valuable Player and Cy Young Award winner opened the year by recording a major league record 36 straight saves and finished with 51.

Most improved player: Utilityman Lance Blankenship. He played solid defense in the infield and outfield and had a .393 on-base percentage and 21 steals.

Most pleasant surprise: Utilityman Jerry Browne. A castoff from Cleveland, Browne started in the outfield and in the infield. He led the league with 16 sacrifice hits, was Oakland's best hitter (.308) after the All-Star break and went 7-for-15 as a pinch-hitter.

Biggest disappointment: Shortstop Walt Weiss. For the fourth straight year, he suffered injuries that limited his playing time. When he did play, he struggled, committing a career-high 19 errors and failing offensively (.212).

Key injuries: The A's had 16 players use the disabled list a team-record 22 times, including center fielder Dave Henderson, righthanders Bob Welch and Dave Stewart, Canseco, Rickey Henderson (twice), catcher Terry Steinbach, Weiss, outfielder Willie Wilson and first baseman Mark McGwire.

Notable: McGwire collected 42 homers and 104 RBIs after a dismal '91. . . . The A's lost five straight games only once, and that happened after they traded Canseco to Texas on August 31 for right fielder Ruben Sierra and righthanders Jeff Russell and Bobby Witt. . . . The A's have the best road record in the majors (229-176) over the last five seasons.

—KIT STIER

RECORDS

1992 regular-season record: 96-66 (1st in A.L. West); 51-30 at home; 45-36 on road; 42-42 vs. East; 54-24 vs. West; 28-6 vs. LHP; 68-58 vs. RHP; 80-57 on grass; 16-9 on turf; 38-25 in daytime; 58-41 at night; 23-21 in one-run games; 8-5 in extra-inning games; 0-0 in doubleheaders.

1992 postseason record: Lost to Blue Jays, 4 games to 2, in A.L. playoffs.

Team record last five years: 486-324 (.600, ranks 1st in league in that span).

TEAM LEADERS

Batting average: Mike Bordick (.300).
At-bats: Mike Bordick (504).
Runs: Mark McGwire (87).
Hits: Mike Bordick (151).
Total bases: Mark McGwire (273).
Doubles: Carney Lansford (30).
Triples: Willie Wilson (5).
Home runs: Mark McGwire (42).
Runs batted in: Mark McGwire (104).
Stolen bases: Rickey Henderson (48).
Slugging percentage: Mark McGwire (.585).
On-base percentage: Mark McGwire (.385).
Wins: Mike Moore (17).
Earned-run average: Ron Darling, Dave Stewart (3.66).
Complete games: Ron Darling (4).
Shutouts: Ron Darling (3).
Saves: Dennis Eckersley (51).
Innings pitched: Mike Moore (223).
Strikeouts: Dave Stewart (130).

GAMES BY POSITION

Catcher: Terry Steinbach 124, Jamie Quirk 59, Henry Mercedes 9, Scott Hemond 8.

First base: Mark McGwire 139, Carney Lansford 18, Jamie Quirk 9, Lance Blankenship 7, Terry Steinbach 5, Randy Ready 4, Scott Brosius 3, Troy Neel 2.

Second base: Mike Bordick 95, Lance Blankenship 78, Jerry Browne 19, Randy Ready 4.

Third base: Carney Lansford 119, Jerry Browne 58, Scott Brosius 12, Randy Ready 7, Scott Hemond 2, Jamie Quirk 2.

Shortstop: Walt Weiss 103, Mike Bordick 70, Scott Brosius 1, Jerry Browne 1, Carney Lansford 1.

Outfield: Willie Wilson 120, Rickey Henderson 108, Jose Canseco 77, Lance Blankenship 51, Jerry Browne 43, Eric Fox 43, Ruben Sierra 25, Randy Ready 24, Harold Baines 23, Scott Brosius 20, Dann Howitt 19, Dave Henderson 12, Mike Kingery 10, Troy Neel 9, Scott Hemond 2.

Designated hitter: Harold Baines 116, Randy Ready 24, Jose Canseco 20, Troy Neel 9, Rickey Henderson 6, Willie Wilson 5, Eric Fox 4, Dave Henderson 4, Lance Blankenship 3, Carney Lansford 2, Ruben Sierra 2, Terry Steinbach 2, Scott Brosius 1, Jerry Browne 1, Scott Hemond 1, Jamie Quirk 1.

TOP 10 DRAFT CHOICES

1. **Benji Grigsby,** RHP, San Diego St. U.
2. **Jason Giambi,** 3B, Long Beach St. U.
3a. **Gabe Alvarez,** SS, Bishop Amat High School, La Puente, Calif.
3b. **Scott Miller,** RHP, Clemson Univ.
4. **Don Wengert,** RHP, Iowa State U.
5. **Steve Cox,** 1B, Monache High School, Porterville, Calif.
6. **Clifton Foster,** RHP, U. of Oklahoma.
7. **Bob Bennett,** RHP, Dartmouth College.
8. **Troy Penix,** 1B, Univ. of California.
9. **Marcel Galligani,** OF, Iona College.
10. **William Urbina,** RHP, Pueblo High School, Tucson, Ariz.

SEATTLE MARINERS
AMERICAN LEAGUE WEST DIVISION

1993 SCHEDULE

APRIL

SUN	MON	TUE	WED	THU	FRI	SAT
				1	2	3
4	5	6 N TOR	7 N TOR H	8	9 N BAL H	10 N BAL H
11 BAL H	12	13 N TOR	14 N TOR	15 TOR	16 N DET	17 DET
18 DET	19	20 N BOS H	21 N BOS H	22 N BOS H	23 N NY H	24 N NY H
25 NY H	26 N CLE H	27 N CLE H	28 N CLE H	29	30 N NY	

MAY

SUN	MON	TUE	WED	THU	FRI	SAT
						1 N NY
2 NY	3 BOS	4 N BOS	5 N CLE	6 N CLE	7 N MIN H	8 N MIN H
9 MIN H	10 N CHI H	11 N CHI H	12 N CHI H	13	14 N OAK	15 OAK
16 OAK	17 N TEX	18 N TEX	19 N TEX	20 N TEX	21 N KC	22 KC
23 N KC	24 N CAL H	25 N CAL H	26 N CAL H	27 N CAL H	28 N DET H	29 N DET H
30 N DET H	31					

JUNE

SUN	MON	TUE	WED	THU	FRI	SAT
		1 N MIL H	2 N MIL H	3	4 N BAL	5 N BAL
6 BAL	7 N MIL	8 N MIL	9 N MIL	10	11 N TEX H	12 N TEX H
13 CAL	14 N KC H	15 N KC H	16 N KC H	17	18 N TEX	19 N TEX
20 TEX H	21 N OAK H	22 N OAK H	23 N OAK H	24 OAK	25 N CHI	26 CHI
27 CHI	28 MIN	29 N MIN	30 N MIN			

JULY

SUN	MON	TUE	WED	THU	FRI	SAT
				1 MIN	2 N BOS H	3 N BOS H
4 N BOS H	5 N NY H	6 N NY H	7 N NY H	8	9 N CLE	10 N CLE H
11 CLE H	12	13 * ALL-STAR GAME	14	15 N BOS	16 N BOS	17 BOS
18 BOS	19 NY	20 N NY	21 N NY	22 N CLE	23 N CLE	24 N CLE
25 CLE	26	27 N MIN H	28 N MIN H	29 N MIN H	30 N CHI	31 N CHI

AUGUST

SUN	MON	TUE	WED	THU	FRI	SAT
1 N CHI H	2	3 N OAK	4 N OAK	5 OAK	6 N TEX	7 N TEX
8 TEX	9 N KC	10 N KC	11 N KC	12	13 N CAL H	14 N CAL H
15 CAL	16 N BAL H	17 N BAL H	18 N BAL H	19	20 N TOR	21 TOR
22 TOR	23	24 N DET	25 DET	26 N TOR H	27 N TOR H	28 N TOR H
29 TOR H	30 N DET H	31 N DET H				

SEPTEMBER

SUN	MON	TUE	WED	THU	FRI	SAT
			1 DET H	2 N MIL H	3 N MIL H	4 N MIL H
5 MIL	6 N BAL	7 N BAL	8 N BAL	9	10 N MIL	11 MIL
12 MIL	13 N CAL	14 N CAL	15 N KC H	16 N KC H	17 N KC H	18 N CAL H
19 KC	20 N TEX	21 N TEX	22 N TEX H	23 TEX H	24 N OAK H	25 OAK H
26 OAK H	27 N CHI	28 N CHI	29 N CHI	30 CHI		

OCTOBER

SUN	MON	TUE	WED	THU	FRI	SAT
					1 N MIN	2 N MIN
3 MIN						

1993 SEASON

CLUB DIRECTORY

Chief Executive Officer
John Ellis
President and chief operating officer
Chuck Armstrong
Vice president, baseball operations
Woody Woodward
Vice president, communications
Randy Adamack
Vice president, finance and administration
Brian Beggs
Vice president, business development
Paul Isaki
Vice president, marketing and sales
Stuart Layne
V.p., scouting and player development
Roger Jongewaard
Director of baseball administration
Lee Pelekoudas
Assistant to v.p., baseball operations
George Zuraw
Minor league director
Jim Beattie
Coordinator of minor league instruction
George Zuraw
Director, team travel
Craig Detwiler
Director, community relations
Joe Chard
Director, corporate marketing
Greg Elliott
Director, promotions
Carl Weinstein
Director, public relations
Dave Aust
Director, stadium operations
Tony Perriera
Director of sales
Chris McCartney
Operations manager
Connie Zentner
Controller
Denise Podosek
Promotions manager
Kevin Martinez
Assistant director, public relations
Pete Vanderwarker
Exec. asst. to chairman and president
Shirley Ward
Payroll manager
Shirley Shreve
Player development and scouting assistant
Larry Beinfest
Public relations assistant
Molly Magan
Trainer
Rick Griffin
Home clubhouse and equipment manager
Henry Genzale

Club physicians
Dr. Larry Pedegana
Dr. Mitchel Storey
Club dentist
Dr. Richard Leshgold
Head groundskeeper
Wilbur Loo
Public address announcer
Tom Hutyler
Supervisor, international scouting
Gordon Blakely
Major league and special assignment scout
Bob Wadsworth
National supervisor and assignment scout
Benny Looper
Scouting supervisors
Ken Compton
Steve Pope
Chris Smith
Regular scouts
Maximo Alvarez
Fernando Arguelles
Brian Ballentine
Jeff Brisou
John Burden
Kendall Carter
Ramon de los Santos
Curtis Dishman
Miguel Escobar
Guy Gianni
Ron Hafner
Lewis Graham
Ron Hopkins
Gudalope Jabalera
Dan Jennings
Mark Jensen
Dave Karaff
John Leavitt
Gary McGraw
Jerry Marik
Omer Munoz
Glenn Murdock
Joe Nigro
Cotton Nye
Fran Oneto
Cliff Pastornicky
Mryon Pines
Don Poplin
Phil Pote
John Ramey
Louis Scheuermann
Douglas Scott
Roberto Valdez
Ray Vince
Jack Webber
Archie White
Bill Young

SCHEDULE KEY

H—Home game.   N—Night game (any game starting after 5 p.m.).
*All-Star Game at Oriole Park at Camden Yards, Baltimore.

— 74 —

Manager—Lou Piniella (14).

Coaches—Lee Elia (3), Sammy Ellis (32), Ken Griffey Sr. (30), John McLaren (7), Sam Mejias (16), Sam Perlozzo (2).

No.	PITCHERS	B/T	Ht./Wt.	Born	1992 clubs
29	Bosio, Chris	R/R	6-3/225	4-3-63	Milwaukee
37	Charlton, Norm	B/L	6-3/205	1-6-63	Cincinnati
34	Coffman, Kevin	R/R	6-3/206	1-19-65	Richmond, Greenville
47	Cummings, John	L/L	6-3/200	5-10-69	Peninsula
33	Darwin, Jeff	R/R	6-3/180	7-6-69	Peninsula
55	DeLucia, Rich	R/R	6-0/185	10-7-64	Seattle, Calgary
35	Fleming, Dave	L/L	6-3/200	11-7-69	Seattle
39	Hanson, Erik	R/R	6-6/215	5-18-65	Seattle
31	Harris, Reggie	R/R	6-1/190	8-12-68	Tacoma
36	Holman, Brian	R/R	6-4/190	1-25-65	DID NOT PLAY
51	Johnson, Randy	R/L	6-10/225	9-10-63	Seattle
54	Leary, Tim	R/R	6-3/220	12-23-58	New York A.L., Seattle
40	Nelson, Jeff	R/R	6-8/235	11-17-66	Calgary, Seattle
45	Nezelek, Andy	L/R	6-6/220	10-24-65	Greenville, Richmond
48	Powell, Dennis	R/L	6-3/227	8-13-63	Seattle
18	Remlinger, Mike	L/L	6-0/195	3-23-66	Calgary, Jacksonville
41	Salkeld, Roger	R/R	6-5/215	3-6-71	DID NOT PLAY
29	Schooler, Mike	R/R	6-3/210	8-10-62	Seattle, Calgary, Bellingham
17	Swan, Russ	L/L	6-4/210	1-3-64	Seattle
26	Wainhouse, Dave	L/R	6-2/185	11-7-67	Indianapolis
42	Woodson, Kerry	R/R	6-2/190	5-18-69	Jacksonville, Calgary, Seattle

No.	CATCHERS	B/T	Ht./Wt.	Born	1992 clubs
12	Deak, Brian	R/R	6-0/183	10-25-67	Richmond
15	Haselman, Bill	R/R	6-3/215	5-25-66	Oklahoma City, Calgary, Seattle
	Sasser, Mackey	L/R	6-1/210	8-3-62	New York N.L.
10	Valle, Dave	R/R	6-2/220	10-30-60	Seattle

No.	INFIELDERS	B/T	Ht./Wt.	Born	1992 clubs
8	Amaral, Rich	R/R	6-0/175	4-1-62	Calgary, Seattle
5	Boone, Bret	R/R	5-10/180	4-6-69	Calgary, Seattle
	Litton, Greg	R/R	6-0/187	7-13-64	Phoenix, San Francisco
11	Martinez, Edgar	R/R	5-11/190	1-2-63	Seattle
23	Martinez, Tino	R/R	6-2/210	12-7-67	Seattle
9	O'Brien, Pete	L/L	6-2/205	2-9-58	Seattle
20	Pirkl, Greg	R/R	6-5/225	8-7-70	Jacksonville, Calgary
6	Vina, Fernando	L/R	5-9/170	4-16-69	St. Lucie, Tidewater
13	Vizquel, Omar	B/R	5-9/165	4-24-67	Seattle, Calgary

No.	OUTFIELDERS	B/T	Ht./Wt.	Born	1992 clubs
1	Briley, Greg	L/R	5-8/180	5-24-65	Seattle
19	Buhner, Jay	R/R	6-3/210	8-13-64	Seattle
28	Cotto, Henry	R/R	6-2/180	1-5-61	Seattle
25	Felder, Mike	B/R	5-9/175	11-18-62	San Francisco
24	Griffey Jr., Ken	L/L	6-3/205	11-21-69	Seattle
27	Tinsley, Lee	B/R	5-10/185	3-4-69	Colorado Springs, Canton/Akron

Ballpark (capacity, surface)
  The Kingdome (59,702, artificial)
Address
  P.O. Box 4100
  411 First Ave. S.
  Seattle, WA 98104
Business phone
  206-628-3555
Ticket information
  206-628-3555
Ticket prices
  $12.50 (box)
  $11.50 (field)
  $9.50 (club)
  $6.50 (view)
  $5.50 (general admission)
  $5 (view, children 14 and under)
  $4 (g.a., children 14 and under)
Field dimensions (from home plate)
  To left field at foul line, 331 feet
  To center field, 405 feet
  To right field at foul line, 314 feet
First game played
  April 6, 1977 (Angels 7, Mariners 0)

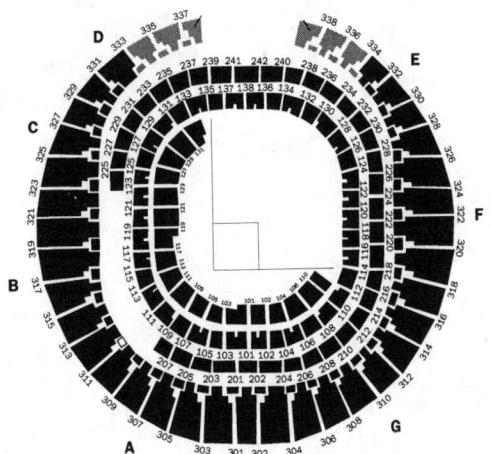

MINOR LEAGUE AFFILIATES

Class	Team	League	Manager
AAA	Calgary	Pacific Coast	Keith Bodie
AA	Jacksonville	Southern	Marc Hill
A	Riverside	California	Dave Myers
A	Appleton	Midwest	Carlos Lezcano
A	Bellingham	Northwest	Mike Goff
Rookie	Peoria Mariners	Arizona	Marty Martinez

BROADCAST INFORMATION

Radio: KIRO-AM (710). Broadcasters: Dave Niehaus; other(s) to be announced.
TV: KSTW-TV (Channel 11). Broadcasters: Dave Niehaus; other(s) to be announced.
Cable TV: None.

SPRING TRAINING

Ballpark: None.
Ticket information: 206-628-3555.
Spring training: The Mariners will play all of their spring games as visitors at other teams' facilities. They will not be handling the sales of any spring-training tickets.

HISTORY

YEAR-BY-YEAR RECORDS

Year	Pos.	W	L	Pct.	*GB	Year	Pos.	W	L	Pct.	*GB
1977	6th	64	98	.395	38	1987	4th	78	84	.481	7
1978	7th	56	104	.350	35	1988	7th	68	93	.422	35½
1979	6th	67	95	.414	21	1989	6th	73	89	.451	26
1980	7th	59	103	.364	38	1990	5th	77	85	.475	26
1981	6th/5th	44	65	.404	†	1991	5th	83	79	.512	12
1982	4th	76	86	.469	17	1992	7th	64	98	.395	32
1983	7th	60	102	.370	39						
1984	T5th	74	88	.457	10						
1985	6th	74	88	.457	17		*Games behind winner. †First half
1986	7th	67	95	.414	25		21-36; second 23-29.

MANAGERS

Name	Record	Years
Darrell Johnson	226-362	'77-80
Maury Wills	26-56	'80-81
Rene Lachemann	140-180	'81-83
Del Crandall	93-141	'83-84
Chuck Cottier	98-120	'84-86
Dick Williams	159-192	'86-88
Jimmy Snyder	45-60	1988
Jim Lefebvre	233-253	'89-91
Bill Plummer	64-98	1992

DAY BY DAY

Date	Opp.	Res.	Score (inn.*)	Hits	Opp. hits	Winning pitcher	Losing pitcher	Save	Record	Pos.	GB
4-6	Tex.	L	10-12	17	12	Fireovid	Schooler	Russell	0-1	T6th	1
4-7	Tex.	L	0-4	4	9	Brown	Hanson		0-2	7th	2
4-8	Tex.	L	1-13	8	17	Guzman	Swan		0-3	T5th	3
4-9	Tex.	L	1-9	8	12	Robinson	Fleming		0-4	T5th	4
4-10	K.C.	W	9-3	11	10	DeLucia	Davis		1-4	5th	3½
4-11	K.C.	W	1-0	6	4	Johnson	Appier		2-4	5th	3½
4-12	K.C.	W	2-1	6	4	Hanson	Boddicker	Schooler	3-4	5th	3
4-13	At Chi.	L	0-1	6	3	Hibbard	Swan	Thigpen	3-5	6th	3½
4-15	At Chi.	W	6-0	6	7	Fleming	McCaskill		4-5	T4th	3
4-16	At Chi.	L	4-5	8	8	Fernandez	DeLucia		4-6	5th	4
4-17	At Mil.	L	1-5	5	9	Wegman	Hanson		4-7	6th	4
4-18	At Mil.	W	5-3	12	6	Swan	Plesac	Schooler	5-7	5th	4
4-19	At Mil.	W	12-9	15	15	Jones	Ruffin	Schooler	6-7	5th	3
4-20	Min.	W	2-0	5	4	Johnson	Tapani		7-7	5th	3
4-21	Min.	L	2-5	10	11	Mahomes	DeLucia	Aguilera	7-8	5th	3
4-22	Min.	L	1-8	8	14	Krueger	Hanson		7-9	5th	4
4-23	Min.	W	3-2	7	6	Swan	Erickson	Schooler	8-9	5th	3½
4-24	At Cal.	W	7-2	12	4	Fleming	Abbott		9-9	T3rd	2½
4-25	At Cal.	W	10-6	14	8	Johnson	Grahe	Schooler	10-9	3rd	2½
4-26	At Cal.	L	5-7	10	11	Bailes	Nelson	Harvey	10-10	T4th	2½
4-28	At Det.	L	1-4	5	6	Gullickson	Swan		10-11	5th	3½
5-1	At Bal.	L	1-15	5	11	McDonald	Johnson		10-12	5th	4½
5-2	At Bal.	L	2-4	6	9	Sutcliffe	Hanson	Olson	10-13	T5th	4½
5-3	At Bal.	L	6-8	9	12	Mussina	DeLucia	Olson	10-14	6th	4½
5-4	N.Y.	L	5-7	6	7	Leary	Swan		10-15	6th	4½
5-5	N.Y.	W	7-4	10	8	Fleming	Cadaret		11-15	6th	4
5-6	Tor.	L	4-12	8	12	Key	Johnson		11-16	6th	5
5-7	Tor.	L	7-8	11	10	Hentgen	Schooler	Henke	11-17	6th	6
5-8	Det.	L	6-7	12	10	Lancaster	Schooler	Henneman	11-18	6th	7
5-9	Det.	L	0-13	5	19	Gullickson	Swan		11-19	6th	7½
5-10	Det.	W	6-2	6	7	Fleming	Aldred		12-19	6th	7½
5-12	At N.Y.	L	1-3	6	6	Perez	Johnson	Howe	12-20	6th	7½
5-13	At N.Y.	L	4-12	9	14	Sanderson	Hanson		12-21	6th	8
5-14	At Tor.	L	4-5	7	7	Stieb	Jones	Wells	12-22	6th	8½
5-15	At Tor.	W	2-1	5	8	Fleming	Stottlemyre	Schooler	13-22	6th	7½
5-16	At Tor.	W	7-6	10	8	Powell	Wells	Schooler	14-22	6th	7
5-17	At Tor.	W	3-2	8	7	Johnson	Key	Schooler	15-22	6th	6½
5-18	At Bos.	L	2-3	7	7	Gardiner	Hanson	Reardon	15-23	6th	7
5-19	At Bos.	L	5-7	12	7	Bolton	Nelson	Reardon	15-24	6th	8
5-20	At Bos.	L	4-6	9	12	Clemens	Powell	Reardon	15-25	6th	9
5-22	Cle.	W	2-1	5	5	Johnson	Scudder	Schooler	16-25	6th	9
5-23	Cle.	L	4-5	4	9	Lilliquist	Hanson	Olin	16-26	6th	9
5-24	Cle.	W	5-4	10	10	Jones	Olin		17-26	6th	9
5-25	Bal.	W	7-3	14	8	Fleming	Mesa	Schooler	18-26	6th	8
5-26	Bal.	L	8-13	15	15	Sutcliffe	Johnson		18-27	6th	8
5-27	Bal.	W	7-1	10	5	Hanson	McDonald		19-27	6th	7
5-29	Bos.	W	7-3	10	9	Powell	Dopson		20-27	6th	7½
5-30	Bos.	W	3-0	6	5	Fleming	Gardiner		21-27	6th	6½
5-31	Bos.	L	1-7	6	12	Clemens	Johnson		21-28	6th	7
6-2	At Cle.	L	3-4	6	8	Otto	Hanson	Olin	21-29	T5th	7½
6-3	At Cle.	L	3-8	12	12	Scudder	Parker		21-30	6th	8½
6-4	At Cle.	W	10-3	12	7	Fleming	Boucher		22-30	6th	8
6-5	At K.C.	L	4-6	8	8	Appier	Jones	Montgomery	22-31	6th	9
6-6	At K.C.	L	3-4	7	11	Heaton	Schooler		22-32	6th	10
6-7	At K.C.	L	1-4	6	10	Reed	Hanson	Montgomery	22-33	7th	10
6-8	At Tex.	L	3-14	7	18	Brown	Parker		22-34	7th	10
6-9	At Tex.	W	2-1	7	8	Fleming	Rogers	Schooler	23-34	6th	10
6-10	At Tex.	L	3-5	9	7	Guzman	Johnson	Russell	23-35	6th	11
6-12	Mil.	W	4-1	7	7	Hanson	Navarro	Swan	24-35	T6th	11
6-13	Mil.	L	7-8	11	13	Fetters	Gunderson	Henry	24-36	7th	12
6-14	Mil.	L	4-14	7	22	Bones	Fleming		24-37	7th	13
6-15	Chi.	W	4-1	6	11	DeLucia	McCaskill	Swan	25-37	7th	13
6-16	Chi.	W	9-6	14	5	Gunderson	Radinsky	Schooler	26-37	7th	12
6-17	Chi.	W	2-1	4	5	Hanson	Hough	Schooler	27-37	6th	11
6-18	Chi.	W	5-4	(11)	13	17	Gunderson	Alvarez		28-37	6th	10½
6-19	At Min.	W	1-0	4	4	Fleming	Tapani		29-37	5th	10½
6-20	At Min.	L	3-5	12	6	Krueger	DeLucia	Aguilera	29-38	6th	10½
6-21	At Min.	L	0-5	4	13	Banks	Walker	Edens	29-39	6th	10½
6-22	At Oak.	L	2-7	6	10	Darling	Hanson	Eckersley	29-40	6th	11½
6-23	At Oak.	L	7-12	8	10	Slusarski	Kramer		29-41	7th	12½

Date		Opp.	Res.	Score	(inn.*)	Hits	Opp. hits	Winning pitcher	Losing pitcher	Save	Record	Pos.	GB
6-24		At Oak.	L	2-7		8	10	Stewart	Fleming		29-42	7th	13½
6-25		Cal.	W	13-4		14	11	DeLucia	Valera		30-42	6th	13½
6-26		Cal.	L	1-10		6	15	Abbott	Walker		30-43	6th	13½
6-27		Cal.	L	1-2		8	5	Langston	Johnson		30-44	7th	13½
6-28		Cal.	W	9-2		16	8	Hanson	Blyleven		31-44	7th	12½
6-29		Oak.	L	4-5	(11)	17	10	Horsman	Schooler	Eckersley	31-45	7th	13½
6-30		Oak.	L	2-4		6	11	Welch	Nelson	Eckersley	31-46	7th	14½
7-1		Oak.	L	1-3		5	12	Moore	Grant	Eckersley	31-47	7th	15½
7-3	(1)	At Det.	L	4-6		9	6	Terrell	Johnson	Henneman	32-47	7th	14½
7-3	(2)	At Det.	W	11-0		5	10	Hanson	Lancaster		32-48	7th	15
7-4		At Det.	W	4-3	(10)	9	7	Schooler	Henneman	Swan	33-48	6th	15
7-5		At Det.	L	5-8		12	12	Terrell	DeLucia	Doherty	33-49	6th	16
7-6		At Det.	L	4-5	(14)	11	9	Kiely	Walker		33-50	6th	17
7-7		At Tor.	L	3-4		9	9	Ward	Nelson		33-51	6th	17
7-8		At Tor.	L	0-6		6	9	Key	Hanson		33-52	6th	18
7-9		At N.Y.	L	6-7		13	5	Kamieniecki	Johnson	Habyan	33-53	6th	18
7-10		At N.Y.	W	5-2		11	5	Fleming	Sanderson	Swan	34-53	6th	18
7-11		At N.Y.	W	5-3	(12)	12	7	Swan	Habyan		35-53	6th	18
7-12		At N.Y.	W	7-6		14	8	Hanson	Cadaret	Swan	36-53	6th	18
7-16		Tor.	L	2-7		6	10	Morris	Johnson		36-54	7th	19
7-17		Tor.	W	8-6		14	15	Hanson	Key	Swan	37-54	7th	19
7-18		Tor.	L	0-3		5	7	Guzman	Fleming	Henke	37-55	7th	19
7-19		Tor.	L	4-8		6	10	Wells	DeLucia		37-56	7th	20
7-20		Det.	L	2-6		9	12	Terrell	Grant	Knudsen	37-57	7th	20
7-21		Det.	L	2-6		6	6	Tanana	Johnson		37-58	7th	20
7-22		Det.	L	2-3		5	5	Gullickson	Hanson	Knudsen	37-59	7th	21
7-23		N.Y.	L	4-5	(10)	9	11	Burke	Swan	Habyan	37-60	7th	21½
7-24		N.Y.	L	7-8		15	15	Farr	Powell		37-61	7th	22
7-25		N.Y.	W	8-2		13	12	Grant	Hillegas	Nelson	38-61	7th	22
7-26		N.Y.	W	8-5		9	11	Johnson	Perez	Swan	39-61	7th	22
7-27		At Cal.	L	0-3		6	7	Finley	Hanson	Grahe	39-62	7th	22
7-28		At Cal.	W	8-1		18	8	Fleming	Langston		40-62	7th	21
7-29		At Cal.	W	8-0		14	4	Fisher	Blyleven		41-62	7th	20
7-30		At Cal.	L	5-6		9	7	Eichhorn	Swan	Grahe	41-63	7th	20½
7-31		At Chi.	W	6-3		11	9	Johnson	Hough	Swan	42-63	7th	20
8-1		At Chi.	L	1-8		6	11	McCaskill	Hanson	Hibbard	42-64	7th	21
8-2		At Chi.	L	4-7		9	11	McDowell	Fleming	Radinsky	42-65	7th	22
8-4		At Mil.	L	2-5		8	7	Bosio	Fisher	Henry	42-66	7th	22
8-5		At Mil.	L	1-8		5	9	Wegman	Johnson		42-67	7th	23
8-6		At Mil.	L	2-4		11	11	Navarro	Grant	Henry	42-68	7th	24
8-7		Tex.	L	6-7	(11)	16	11	Burns	Swan	Nunez	42-69	7th	25
8-8		Tex.	L	3-7		8	11	Guzman	Woodson		42-70	7th	25
8-9		Tex.	W	6-5	(14)	12	10	Jones	Whiteside		43-70	7th	25
8-10		K.C.	W	3-1		6	3	Johnson	Aquino		44-70	7th	25
8-11		K.C.	L	6-9		12	13	Pichardo	Hanson	Montgomery	44-71	7th	25
8-12		K.C.	W	6-3		9	8	Fleming	Moeller	Nelson	45-71	7th	25
8-14		Min.	L	6-9		9	14	West	Jones	Aguilera	45-72	7th	25½
8-15		Min.	W	3-2		7	4	Johnson	Edens		46-72	7th	25½
8-16		Min.	W	8-7		14	14	Nelson	Guthrie		47-72	7th	25½
8-18		At Bal.	W	8-3		12	6	Fleming	McDonald	Nelson	48-72	7th	24½
8-19		At Bal.	W	10-8		12	12	Grant	Rhodes	Swan	49-72	7th	23½
8-20		At Bal.	L	1-2	(10)	11	5	Davis	Schooler		49-73	7th	24½
8-21		At Bos.	W	5-2		12	5	Johnson	Viola		50-73	7th	23½
8-22		At Bos.	L	8-10		13	14	Harris	Barton	Reardon	50-74	7th	24½
8-23		At Bos.	W	9-3		13	8	Powell	Clemens		51-74	7th	24½
8-25		Cle.	W	6-0		11	2	Fleming	Nagy		52-74	7th	24
8-26		Cle.	L	3-6	(10)	11	11	Plunk	Swan	Olin	52-75	7th	24
8-27		Cle.	W	6-2		12	8	Fisher	Cook		53-75	7th	23½
8-28		Bal.	W	6-4		14	5	Leary	McDonald	Nelson	54-75	7th	23½
8-29		Bal.	L	0-4		5	11	Rhodes	Grant	Olson	54-76	7th	24½
8-30		Bal.	L	0-2		9	7	Sutcliffe	Fleming	Olson	54-77	7th	25½
8-31		Bos.	W	15-2		16	4	Johnson	Viola		55-77	7th	24½
9-1		Bos.	W	4-3		8	8	Schooler	Harris		56-77	7th	23½
9-2		Bos.	L	3-5		10	9	Clemens	Leary		56-78	7th	23½
9-4		At Cle.	L	0-7		8	12	Mesa	Fleming		56-79	7th	23½
9-5		At Cle.	L	4-5		6	9	Plunk	Swan		56-80	7th	23½
9-6		At Cle.	L	9-12	(12)	16	14	Olin	Schooler		56-81	7th	24½
9-7		At Min.	L	2-4		9	8	Erickson	Leary	Aguilera	56-82	7th	24½
9-8		At Min.	L	4-8		9	13	Wayne	Jones		56-83	7th	25½
9-9		At Min.	L	2-6		8	10	Tapani	Fleming	Guthrie	56-84	7th	26½
9-10		At Oak.	L	4-6		9	4	Darling	Johnson	Eckersley	56-85	7th	27½
9-11		At Oak.	L	3-4		5	6	Russell	Nelson		56-86	7th	28½
9-12		At Oak.	L	4-5		13	9	Moore	Leary	Eckersley	56-87	7th	29½
9-13		At Oak.	L	1-3		2	4	Downs	Hanson	Russell	56-88	7th	30½

Date	Opp.	Res.	Score	(inn.*)	Hits	Opp. hits	Winning pitcher	Losing pitcher	Save	Record	Pos.	GB
9-15	Cal.	L	0-9		4	14	Finley	Fleming		56-89	7th	32
9-16	Cal.	L	1-2	(13)	8	5	Grahe	Jones	Frey	56-90	7th	33
9-18	Oak.	L	4-7		10	10	Moore	Fisher	Eckersley	56-91	7th	34
9-19	Oak.	W	6-4		8	8	Leary	Welch	Nelson	57-91	7th	33
9-20	Oak.	L	2-4		7	13	Stewart	Hanson	Eckersley	57-92	7th	34
9-21	At K.C.	L	0-3		4	8	Aquino	Fleming	Montgomery	57-93	7th	35
9-22	At K.C.	L	0-3		2	6	Haney	Johnson		57-94	7th	35
9-23	At K.C.	W	6-1		14	5	Fisher	Pichardo		58-94	7th	34
9-24	At K.C.	L	0-2		6	4	Rasmussen	Leary	Montgomery	58-95	7th	35
9-25	At Tex.	W	4-3	(16)	14	16	Powell	Smith	Fisher	59-95	7th	34
9-26	At Tex.	W	8-4		11	11	Fleming	Pavlik		60-95	7th	33
9-27	At Tex.	L	2-3		9	7	Whiteside	Nelson		60-96	7th	33
9-29	Mil.	L	4-7		11	12	Eldred	Fisher	Holmes	60-97	7th	34
9-30	Mil.	W	7-4		10	10	Leary	Bosio	DeLucia	61-97	7th	33
10-1	Mil.	L	2-7	(10)	4	13	Wegman	Nelson		61-98	7th	33
10-2	Chi.	W	2-0		5	8	Fleming	Hough		62-98	7th	32
10-3	Chi.	W	7-2		11	4	Johnson	McCaskill		63-98	7th	32
10-4	Chi.	W	4-3		10	5	Fisher	McDowell	Nelson	64-98	7th	32

Monthly records: April (10-11), May (11-17), June (10-18), July (11-17), August (13-14), September (6-20), Oct. (3-1).

HIGHLIGHTS

High point: The Mariners recovered from a season-opening four-game home sweep administered by Texas to win 10 of their next 15 games. That streak moved Seattle into third place, 2½ games behind Oakland.

Low point: From September 2-18, Seattle endured a club-record 14-game losing streak that buried the Mariners deep in the A.L. West cellar, where they finished for the first time since 1988.

Turning point: On April 26 in Anaheim Stadium, third-place Seattle blew a 5-1 lead in the eighth inning to lose, 7-5, in a fight-scarred game. That started a streak of 13 losses in 15 games, dropping the Mariners to sixth place.

Most valuable player: Third baseman Edgar Martinez. He played through pain in his right shoulder to lead the league in hitting (.343) and went more than two games without a hit just once.

Most valuable pitcher: Dave Fleming. The rookie paced all A.L. lefthanders with 17 wins, collecting a team-record-tying nine straight victories after getting clobbered in his first start.

Most improved player: Shortstop Omar Vizquel. Once considered an all-field, no-hit player, Vizquel led all A.L. shortstops with a .294 batting average, 64 points above his career average.

Most pleasant surprise: Righthander Jeff Nelson. Scheduled to spend the season at Class AAA Calgary, he was forced to join Seattle in April and did a splendid job, appearing in 66 games and compiling a 3.44 ERA.

Biggest disappointment: Righthander Calvin Jones. Expected to become Seattle's setup man, he failed terribly. He allowed at least one earned run in 17 of his final 29 appearances, finishing with a 5.69 ERA.

Key injuries: The Mariners had 15 players use the disabled list a club-record 19 times. Among the key casualties were designated hitter Kevin Mitchell (twice), Vizquel, center fielder Ken Griffey, lefthander Randy Johnson and righthander Mike Schooler.

Notable: On July 1, the Mariners were officially sold to The Baseball Club of Seattle, a group of investors led by Hiroshi Yamauchi, the president of the Nintendo video games company of Japan. ... Bill Plummer was replaced by Lou Piniella as manager after the season. ... After never allowing a grand slam, Schooler tied a big-league record by yielding four. ... Against Baltimore on August 30, the Mariners turned their eighth triple play in club history.

—JIM STREET

RECORDS

1992 regular-season record: 64-98 (7th in A.L. West); 38-43 at home; 26-55 on road; 33-51 vs. East; 31-47 vs. West; 18-24 vs. LHP; 46-74 vs. RHP; 21-41 on grass; 43-57 on turf; 18-27 in daytime; 46-71 at night; 20-26 in one-run games; 5-9 in extra-inning games; 0-0-1 in doubleheaders.

Team record last five years: 365-444 (.451, ranks 13th in league in that span).

TEAM LEADERS

Batting average: Edgar Martinez (.343).
At-bats: Ken Griffey (565).
Runs: Edgar Martinez (100).
Hits: Edgar Martinez (181).
Total bases: Ken Griffey (302).
Doubles: Edgar Martinez (46).
Triples: Ken Griffey, Omar Vizquel (4).
Home runs: Ken Griffey (27).
Runs batted in: Ken Griffey (103).
Stolen bases: Henry Cotto (23).
Slugging percentage: Edgar Martinez (.544).
On-base percentage: Edgar Martinez (.404).
Wins: Dave Fleming (17).
Earned-run average: Dave Fleming (3.39).
Complete games: Dave Fleming (7).
Shutouts: Dave Fleming (4).
Saves: Mike Schooler (13).
Innings pitched: Dave Fleming (228⅓).
Strikeouts: Randy Johnson (241).

GAMES BY POSITION

Catcher: Dave Valle 122, Lance Parrish 34, Dave Cochrane 21, Matt Sinatro 18, Bill Haselman 5, Bert Heffernan 5, Scott Bradley 1.

First base: Pete O'Brien 81, Tino Martinez 78, Lance Parrish 16, Dann Howitt 4, Mike Blowers 3, Dave Cochrane 3, Rich Amaral 2, Edgar Martinez 2, Patrick Lennon 1.

Second base: Harold Reynolds 134, Bret Boone 32, Jeff Schaefer 7, Greg Briley 4, Rich Amaral 1, Dave Cochrane 1.

Third base: Edgar Martinez 103, Mike Blowers 29, Jeff Schaefer 21, Shane Turner 18, Rich Amaral 17, Dave Cochrane 10, Bret Boone 6, Greg Briley 4.

Shortstop: Omar Vizquel 136, Jeff Schaefer 33, Rich Amaral 17, Dave Cochrane 3.

Outfield: Jay Buhner 150, Ken Griffey 137, Henry Cotto 92, Kevin Mitchell 69, Greg Briley 42, Dave Cochrane 25, John Moses 18, Shane Turner 15, Dann Howitt 11, Rich Amaral 3, Bill Haselman 2, Harold Reynolds 1.

Designated hitter: Tino Martinez 48, Pete O'Brien 35, Edgar Martinez 28, Kevin Mitchell 26, Lance Parrish 14, Greg Briley 12, Henry Cotto 3, Ken Griffey 3, Dave Cochrane 2, Dann Howitt 1, Harold Reynolds 1.

TOP 10 DRAFT CHOICES

1. **Ron Villone**, LHP, U. of Mass.
2. **Bob Wolcott**, RHP, North Medford (Ore.) High School.
3. **Chris Widger**, C, George Mason U.
4. **Andy Sheets**, SS, LSU.
5. **John Vanhof**, LHP, Southgate (Mich.) Anderson High School.
6. **Tim Davis**, LHP, Florida State U.
7. **Chris Dessellier**, RHP, Ypsilanti (Mich.) High School.
8. **Brian Doughty**, RHP, Juanita High School, Kirkland, Wash.
9. **Ivan Montane**, RHP, Miami-Dade (Fla.) Community College South.
10. **Joe Pomierski**, 3B, Biloxi (Miss.) High School.

TEXAS RANGERS
AMERICAN LEAGUE WEST DIVISION

1993 SCHEDULE

APRIL

SUN	MON	TUE	WED	THU	FRI	SAT
				1	2	3
4	5 BAL	6	7 N BAL	8	9 N BOS H	10 BOS H
11 BOS H	12 N BAL H	13 N BAL H	14 N BAL H	15	16 N NY	17 N NY
18 NY	19	20 N DET	21 DET	22	23 N MIL	24 MIL
25 MIL	26 N TOR	27 N TOR	28 N DET H	29 N DET H	30 N MIL H	

MAY

SUN	MON	TUE	WED	THU	FRI	SAT
						1 MIL H
2 MIL H	3 N MIL H	4 N TOR H	5 N TOR H	6	7 N KC	8 KC
9 KC	10 N OAK	11 N OAK	12 N OAK	13	14 N CHI H	15 N CHI H
16 CHI H	17 N SEA H	18 N SEA H	19 N SEA H	20 N SEA H	21 N CAL H	22 N CAL H
23 CAL H	24 N CLE	25 N CLE	26 N	27	28 N BOS	29 BOS
30 BOS	31 MIN					

JUNE

SUN	MON	TUE	WED	THU	FRI	SAT
		1 N MIN	2 N MIN	3	4 N NY H	5 N NY H
6 N NY H	7 N MIN	8 N MIN	9 N MIN H	10 N MIN H	11 N CLE H	12 N CLE H
13 N CLE H	14 N CAL	15 N CAL	16 N CAL	17 N CAL	18 N SEA	19 N SEA
20 SEA	21 N CHI	22 N CHI	23 CHI	24	25 N OAK H	26 N OAK H
27 N OAK H	28 N KC	29 N KC H	30 N KC H			

JULY

SUN	MON	TUE	WED	THU	FRI	SAT
				1 N DET	2 N DET	3 DET
4 DET	5 MIL	6 N MIL	7 N MIL	8 N TOR	9 N TOR	10 TOR
11 TOR	12	13 * ALL STAR GAME	14	15 N DET H	16 N DET H	17 N DET H
18 N DET H	19 N MIL H	20 N MIL H	21	22 N TOR H	23 N TOR H	24 TOR H
25 N TOR H	26 N KC	27 N KC	28 N KC	29	30 N OAK	31 OAK

AUGUST

SUN	MON	TUE	WED	THU	FRI	SAT
1 OAK	2 N CHI H	3 N CHI H	4 N CHI H	5 N CHI H	6 N SEA H	7 N SEA H
8 N SEA H	9 N	10 CAL H	11 N CAL H	12 N CAL H	13 N CLE	14 N CLE
15 CLE	16 N NY	17 N NY	18 NY	19	20 N BAL	21 N BAL
22 BAL	23 N BAL	24 N BOS H	25 N BOS H	26 N BOS H	27 N BAL H	28 N BAL H
29 BAL H	30 N BOS	31 N BOS				

SEPTEMBER

SUN	MON	TUE	WED	THU	FRI	SAT
			1 N BOS	2	3 N MIN	4 N MIN
5 MIN	6 N NY H	7 N NY H	8 N MIN H	9	10 N MIN H	11 N MIN H
12 MIN H	13 N CLE H	14 N CLE H	15 N CLE H	16	17 N CAL	18 N CAL
19 CAL	20 N SEA	21 N SEA	22 N SEA	23	24 N CHI	25 N CHI
26 CHI	27	28 N OAK H	29 N OAK H	30 N OAK H		

OCTOBER

SUN	MON	TUE	WED	THU	FRI	SAT
					1 N KC	2 N KC H
3 KC H						

1993 SEASON

CLUB DIRECTORY

General partners
George W. Bush
Edward W. (Rusty) Rose
President
J. Thomas Schieffer
Vice president, general manager
Thomas A. Grieve
V.p., business operations/treasurer
John F. McMichael
Vice president, marketing
Matin B. Conway
Vice president, administration/secretary
Charles F. Wangner
Vice president, public relations
John C. Blake
Vice president, ballpark development
Jack W. Hill
General counsel
Gerald W. Haddock
Asst. g.m., player personnel and scouting
Sandy Johnson
Assistant general manager
Wayne Krivsky
Director, player development
Marty Scott
Dir., in-park entertainment/broadcasting
Chuck Morgan
Director, promotions
Dave Fendrick
Director, sales/customer service
Jay Miller
Director, stadium operations
Mat Stolley
Director, ticket operations
John Schriever
Traveling secretary
Dan Schimek
Controller
Steve McNeill
Director, community relations
Taunee Paur
Director, publications
Larry Kelly
Assistant director, ticket operations
Ben Marthaler
Assistant director, public relations
Luis R. Mayoral
Assistant director, community relations
Ashley Brown
Assistant director, promotions
Chuck Baugh
Assistant, special projects
Bobby Bragan
Major league scout/special assignments
Larry Hardy
Major league advance scout
Marc Sullivan

General manager, Charlotte Co. operations
Tim Murphy
Medical director
Dr. Mike Mycoskie
Field superintendent
Jim Anglea
Assistant field superintendent
Brad Richards
Spring training director
John Welaj
Equipment and home clubhouse manager
Joe Macko
Visiting clubhouse manager
Zack Minasian
Scouts
Hector Acevedo
Manuel Batista
Jim Benedict
Ray Blanco
Joe Branzell
Agustin Castro
Marco Cobos
Paddy Cottrell
Dick Coury
Mike Daughtry
Marc DelPlano
Amado Dinzey
Jim Dreyer
Bill Earnhart
Kip Fagg
Jim Fairey
Rene Gayo
Mike Grouse
Thoma Gushiken
Tim Hallgren
Larry Hardy
Bryan Lambe
Benny Latino
Robert Lavallee
John Littlefield
Omar Minaya
Mike Piatnik
Alan Regier
Antolin Reyes
Pat Rigby
Rodolfo Reyes
Don Shwery
Len Strelitz
Marc Sullican
Randy Taylor
Rudy Terrasas
Danilo Troncoso
George Urribarri
Juan Valera
Boris Villa

SCHEDULE KEY

H—Home game.   N—Night game (any game starting after 5 p.m.).
*All-Star Game at Oriole Park at Camden Yards, Baltimore.

— 80 —

SPRING TRAINING ROSTER

Manager—Kevin Kennedy (44).

Coaches—Mickey Hatcher (43), Perry Hill (47), Jackie Moore (42), Dave Oliver (26), Claude Osteen (48), Willie Upshaw (46).

No.	PITCHERS	B/T	Ht./Wt.	Born	1992 clubs
45	Bohanon, Brian	L/L	6-2/220	8-1-68	Oklahoma City, Texas, Tulsa
51	Bronkey, Jeff	R/R	6-3/210	9-18-65	Tulsa, Oklahoma City
54	Bross, Terry	R/R	6-9/230	3-30-66	Las Vegas
41	Brown, Kevin	R/R	6-4/195	3-14-65	Texas
28	Burns, Todd	R/R	6-2/195	7-6-63	Oklahoma City, Texas
53	Burrows, Terry	L/L	6-1/185	11-28-68	Charlotte, Tulsa, Oklahoma City
30	Fajardo, Hector	R/R	6-4/200	11-6-70	Gulf Coast Rangers, Charlotte, Tulsa, Oklahoma City
50	Henke, Tom	R/R	6-5/225	12-21-57	Toronto
	Lefferts, Craig	L/L	6-1/230	9-29-57	San Diego, Baltimore
32	Leibrandt, Charlie	R/L	6-3/200	10-4-56	Atlanta
49	Leon, Danny	R/R	6-1/175	4-3-67	Charlotte, Tulsa, Texas, Oklahoma City
36	Manuel, Barry	R/R	5-11/185	8-12-65	Oklahoma City, Texas, Tulsa
31	Nen, Robb	R/R	6-4/200	11-28-69	Tulsa
38	Patterson, Bob	R/L	6-2/192	5-16-59	Pittsburgh
59	Pavlik, Roger	R/R	6-2/220	10-4-67	Oklahoma City, Texas
37	Rogers, Kenny	L/L	6-1/205	11-10-64	Texas
34	Ryan, Nolan	R/R	6-2/212	1-31-47	Texas
35	Smith, Dan	L/L	6-5/190	8-20-69	Tulsa, Texas
27	Whiteside, Matt	R/R	6-0/185	8-8-67	Tulsa, Oklahoma City, Texas

No.	CATCHERS	B/T	Ht./Wt.	Born	1992 clubs
12	Petralli, Geno	B/R	6-1/190	9-25-59	Texas
7	Rodriguez, Ivan	R/R	5-9/205	11-30-71	Texas
24	Stephens, Ray	R/R	6-0/190	9-22-62	Scranton/Wilkes-Barre, Oklahoma City, Texas

No.	INFIELDERS	B/T	Ht./Wt.	Born	1992 clubs
4	Colon, Cris	B/R	6-2/180	1-3-69	Tulsa, Texas
14	Franco, Julio	R/R	6-1/190	8-23-61	Texas
1	Frye, Jeff	R/R	5-9/165	8-31-66	Oklahoma City, Texas
9	Huson, Jeff	L/R	6-3/180	8-15-64	Texas
2	Lee, Manuel	B/R	5-9/166	6-17-65	Toronto
39	Maurer, Rob	L/L	6-3/210	1-7-67	Oklahoma City, Texas
25	Palmeiro, Rafael	L/L	6-0/188	9-24-64	Texas
16	Palmer, Dean	R/R	6-2/195	12-27-68	Texas
52	Shave, Jon	R/R	6-0/185	11-4-67	Tulsa

No.	OUTFIELDERS	B/T	Ht./Wt.	Born	1992 clubs
33	Canseco, Jose	R/R	6-4/240	7-2-64	Oakland, Texas
29	Dascenzo, Doug	B/L	5-8/160	6-30-64	Chicago N.L.
19	Gonzalez, Juan	R/R	6-3/210	10-16-69	Texas
18	Harris, Donald	R/R	6-1/185	11-12-67	Tulsa, Texas
15	Hulse, David	L/L	5-11/170	2-25-68	Tulsa, Oklahoma City, Texas
20	Miller, Keith	B/R	5-11/175	3-7-63	Oklahoma City
17	Peltier, Dan	L/L	6-1/200	6-30-68	Oklahoma City, Texas
5	Redus, Gary	R/R	6-1/195	11-1-56	Pittsburgh

BALLPARK INFORMATION

Ballpark (capacity, surface)
Arlington Stadium (43,521, grass)
Address
1250 Copeland Road, 11th floor
Arlington, TX 76010
Business phone
817-273-5222
Ticket information
817-273-5000
Ticket prices
$14 (infield box)
$13 (reserved box)
$9 (plaza)
$7 (grandstand reserved)
$4 (general admission, adults)
$2 (g.a., children 13 and under)
Field dimensions (from home plate)
To left field at foul line, 330 feet
To center field, 400 feet
To right field at foul line, 330 feet
First game played
April 21, 1972 (Rangers 7, Angels 6)

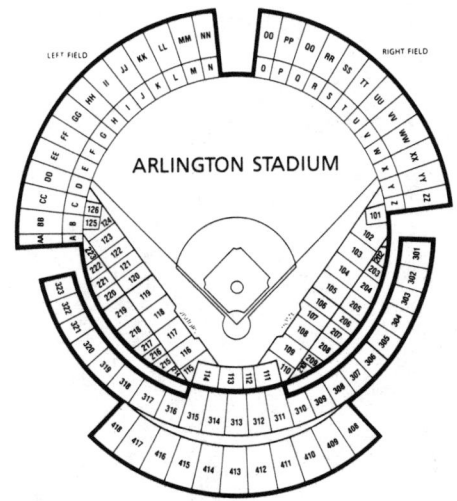

Class	Team	League	Manager
AAA	Oklahoma City	American Association	Bobby Jones
AA	Tulsa	Texas	Stan Cliburn
A	Charlotte	Florida State	Tommy Thompson
A	Charleston, S.C.	South Atlantic	Walt Williams
A	Erie	New York-Pennsylvania	Doug Sisson
Rookie	Gulf Coast Rangers	Gulf Coast	Chino Cadahia

BROADCAST INFORMATION

Radio: WBAP-AM (820). Broadcasters: Mark Holtz, Eric Nadel. KXEB-AM (910, Spanish language). Broadcasters: Mario Montez, Luis Mayoral.
TV: KTVT-TV (Channel 11). Broadcasters: Steve Busby, Jim Sundberg.
Cable TV: Home Sports Entertainment. Broadcasters: Greg Lucas, Norm Hitzges.

SPRING TRAINING

Ballpark (city): Charlotte County Stadium (Port Charlotte, Fla.).
Ticket information: 813-625-9500 or 813-624-2211.

HISTORY

YEAR-BY-YEAR RECORDS

Year	Pos.	W	L	Pct.	*GB	Year	Pos.	W	L	Pct.	*GB
1961	T9th	61	100	.379	47½	1979	3rd	83	79	.512	5
1962	10th	60	101	.373	35½	1980	4th	76	85	.472	20½
1963	10th	56	106	.346	48½	1981	2nd/3rd	57	48	.543	†
1964	9th	62	100	.383	37	1982	6th	64	98	.395	29
1965	8th	70	92	.432	32	1983	3rd	77	85	.475	22
1966	8th	71	88	.447	25½	1984	7th	69	92	.429	14½
1967	T6th	76	85	.472	15½	1985	7th	62	99	.385	28½
1968	10th	65	96	.404	37½	1986	2nd	87	75	.537	5
1969	4th	86	76	.531	23	1987	T6th	75	87	.463	10
1970	6th	70	92	.432	38	1988	6th	70	91	.435	33½
1971	5th	63	96	.396	38½	1989	4th	83	79	.512	16
1972	6th	54	100	.351	38½	1990	3rd	83	79	.512	20
1973	6th	57	105	.352	37	1991	3rd	85	77	.525	10
1974	2nd	84	76	.525	5	1992	4th	77	85	.475	19
1975	3rd	79	83	.488	19						
1976	T4th	76	86	.469	14						
1977	2nd	94	68	.580	8						
1978	T2nd	87	75	.537	5						

*Games behind winner. †First half 33-22; second 24-26.

MANAGERS

Name	Record	Years
Mickey Vernon	135-227	'61-63
Gil Hodges	321-444	'63-67
Jim Lemon	65-96	1968
Ted Williams	273-364	'69-72
Whitey Herzog	47-91	1973
Del Wilber	1-0	1973
Billy Martin	137-141	'73-75
Frank Lucchesi	142-149	'75-77
Eddie Stanky	1-0	1977
Connie Ryan	2-4	1977
Billy Hunter	146-108	'77-78
Pat Corrales	160-164	'78-80
Don Zimmer	95-106	'81-82
Darrell Johnson	26-40	1982
Doug Rader	155-200	'83-85
Bobby Valentine	581-605	'85-92
Toby Harrah	32-44	1992

DAY BY DAY

Date	Opp.	Res.	Score	(inn.*)	Hits	Opp. hits	Winning pitcher	Losing pitcher	Save	Record	Pos.	GB
4-6	At Sea.	W	12-10		12	17	Fireovid	Schooler	Russell	1-0	T1st	...
4-7	At Sea.	W	4-0		9	4	Brown	Hanson		2-0	1st	+½
4-8	At Sea.	W	13-1		17	8	Guzman	Swan		3-0	T1st	+½
4-9	At Sea.	W	9-1		12	8	Robinson	Fleming		4-0	T1st	+½
4-10	At Min.	L	1-7		8	12	Tapani	Witt		4-1	2nd	½
4-11	At Min.	W	10-8	(10)	12	12	Russell	Aguilera	Rogers	5-1	2nd	½
4-12	At Min.	W	4-3		5	6	Brown	Kipper		6-1	1st	+½
4-13	Cal.	L	0-3		6	9	Abbott	Guzman	Harvey	6-2	2nd	½
4-14	Cal.	L	1-8		4	13	Grahe	Robinson		6-3	3rd	½
4-15	Cal.	W	3-2		6	6	Witt	Valera	Russell	7-3	2nd	½
4-16	Cal.	L	2-3		9	5	Crim	Russell	Harvey	7-4	2nd	1½
4-17	Oak.	W	6-5		11	10	Brown	Briscoe	Rogers	8-4	2nd	½
4-18	Oak.	L	3-5		9	11	Moore	Mathews	Eckersley	8-5	3rd	1½
4-19	Oak.	W	6-4		10	6	Manuel	Honeycutt	Russell	9-5	3rd	½
4-21	Det.	L	2-4		7	7	Gullickson	Witt	Henneman	9-6	3rd	1
4-22	Det.	L	8-12		10	14	Leiter	Robinson		9-7	2nd	1
4-23	Det.	L	5-11		10	15	Lancaster	Brown	Doherty	9-8	4th	2½
4-24	At Bos.	L	1-3	(5½)	3	8	Viola	Guzman		9-9	T3rd	2½
4-26 (1)	At Bos.	W	3-1		9	10	Witt	Young	Russell	10-9	3rd	2
4-26 (2)	At Bos.	W	4-2		8	10	Mathews	Harris	Russell	11-9	3rd	1½
4-27	At N.Y.	L	7-8		13	15	Habyan	Mathews	Farr	11-10	3rd	2
4-28	At N.Y.	W	1-0		7	3	Brown	Leary	Russell	12-10	3rd	2
4-29	At N.Y.	W	5-1		9	2	Guzman	Cadaret		13-10	2nd	1
4-30	At Chi.	L	1-12		3	13	McDowell	Ryan		13-11	3rd	2
5-1	At Chi.	W	8-4		12	7	Witt	Hibbard	Russell	14-11	2nd	2
5-2	At Chi.	W	4-1	(11)	8	5	Robinson	Thigpen		15-11	2nd	1
5-3	At Chi.	L	3-5		6	8	Radinsky	Brown		15-12	2nd	1
5-4	At Bal.	L	5-8		10	7	Mills	Mathews		15-13	3rd	1
5-5	At Bal.	W	5-3		11	7	Robinson	Davis	Russell	16-13	3rd	½
5-6	Cle.	L	2-7		6	9	Scudder	Witt	Wickander	16-14	3rd	1½
5-7	Cle.	L	7-8		11	12	Nichols	Campbell	Olin	16-15	4th	2½
5-8	Mil.	W	3-2		7	8	Brown	Wegman	Russell	17-15	4th	2½
5-9	Mil.	W	5-4		9	8	Robinson	Holmes	Russell	18-15	4th	2
5-10	Mil.	L	2-6		8	11	Bosio	Guzman		18-16	4th	3
5-12	Bal.	L	1-5		7	9	McDonald	Witt	Frohwirth	18-17	4th	3
5-13	Bal.	L	2-4		8	6	Sutcliffe	Brown	Olson	18-18	5th	3½
5-15	At Mil.	L	3-7	(10)	11	15	Holmes	Robinson		18-19	5th	3½
5-16	At Mil.	L	4-5		9	9	Holmes	Rogers		18-20	5th	4
5-17	At Mil.	W	2-1	(10)	6	8	Russell	Navarro		19-20	5th	3½
5-18	At Cle.	W	3-2		5	9	Brown	Lilliquist	Rogers	20-20	5th	3
5-19	At Cle.	W	8-7		11	10	McCullers	Olin	Russell	21-20	4th	3
5-20	At Cle.	W	1-0		7	5	Guzman	Nagy	Russell	22-20	4th	3
5-21	K.C.	L	5-7		6	6	Meacham	Rogers	Montgomery	22-21	4th	3½
5-22	K.C.	W	10-7		14	11	Witt	Gubicza		23-21	4th	3½
5-23	K.C.	W	4-2		8	8	Brown	Magnante		24-21	4th	2½
5-24	K.C.	W	4-3	(13)	10	12	Alexander	Gordon		25-21	4th	2½
5-26	Chi.	W	6-5		11	10	Guzman	Hough	Nunez	26-21	3rd	1
5-27	Chi.	W	4-3	(11)	7	9	Bannister	Pall		27-21	2nd	...
5-28	Chi.	W	4-2		7	3	Witt	McDowell	Russell	28-21	1st	+½
5-29	At K.C.	W	5-3		12	8	Brown	Montgomery		29-21	1st	+½
5-30	At K.C.	L	2-8		8	10	Appier	Jeffcoat		29-22	1st	+½
5-31	At K.C.	L	6-7		9	15	Meacham	Russell		29-23	2nd	½
6-1	N.Y.	L	1-7		7	7	Monteleone	Robinson		29-24	3rd	½
6-2	N.Y.	W	8-2		6	6	Witt	Leary		30-24	2nd	½
6-3	N.Y.	W	4-3	(13)	12	9	Rogers	Hillegas		31-24	2nd	½
6-4	Min.	L	12-15		16	14	Kipper	Nunez	Aguilera	31-25	3rd	1
6-5	Min.	W	5-4		9	10	Guzman	Banks	Russell	32-25	2nd	1
6-6	Min.	L	1-6		4	9	Smiley	Ryan		32-26	3rd	2
6-7	Min.	W	5-4		8	7	Witt	Guthrie	Russell	33-26	2nd	1
6-8	Sea.	W	14-3		18	7	Brown	Parker		34-26	2nd	...
6-9	Sea.	L	1-2		8	7	Fleming	Rogers	Schooler	34-27	2nd	1
6-10	Sea.	W	5-3		7	9	Guzman	Johnson	Russell	35-27	2nd	1
6-12	At Oak.	L	5-6	(14)	10	13	Corsi	Nunez		35-28	2nd	2
6-13	At Oak.	L	1-7		4	4	Stewart	Witt		35-29	2nd	3
6-14	At Oak.	L	1-6		5	9	Welch	Brown		35-30	3rd	4
6-15	At Cal.	W	5-2		13	4	Burns	Abbott	Russell	36-30	2nd	4
6-16	At Cal.	L	1-4		3	10	Blyleven	Guzman	Grahe	36-31	2nd	4
6-17	At Cal.	L	0-3		2	7	Langston	Ryan		36-32	3rd	4
6-19	Bos.	W	4-1		7	6	Witt	Gardiner	Russell	37-32	3rd	4
6-20	Bos.	W	4-1		7	6	Brown	Dopson	Rogers	38-32	3rd	3

Date	Opp.	Res.	Score	(inn.*)	Hits	Opp. hits	Winning pitcher	Losing pitcher	Save	Record	Pos.	GB
6-21	Bos.	W	3-2		6	8	Burns	Clemens	Russell	39-32	3rd	2
6-22	Tor.	L	7-16		10	20	Morris	Guzman		39-33	3rd	3
6-24	Tor.	L	2-3		8	10	Wells	Witt	Henke	39-34	3rd	4½
6-25	At Det.	W	5-2		9	4	Brown	Groom		40-34	3rd	4½
6-26	At Det.	L	2-4		7	7	Gullickson	Burns	Henneman	40-35	3rd	4½
6-27	At Det.	W	10-8		11	13	Guzman	Ritz	Rogers	41-35	3rd	3½
6-28	At Det.	W	8-4		9	11	Ryan	Leiter		42-35	3rd	2½
6-29	At Tor.	L	4-11		9	8	Hentgen	Witt		42-36	3rd	3½
6-30	At Tor.	W	16-13		20	12	Brown	Wells		43-36	3rd	3½
7-1	At Tor.	L	2-3	(10)	5	6	Ward	Russell		43-37	3rd	4½
7-3	N.Y.	L	6-9		11	12	Perez	Guzman	Habyan	43-38	3rd	4½
7-4	N.Y.	W	4-1		8	3	Ryan	Kamieniecki		44-38	3rd	4½
7-5	N.Y.	L	4-5		11	11	Sanderson	Leon	Habyan	44-39	3rd	5½
7-6	Mil.	W	3-1		9	7	Brown	Wegman	Russell	45-39	3rd	5½
7-7	Mil.	L	3-4		9	10	Austin	Burns	Henry	45-40	3rd	5½
7-8	Mil.	L	3-4		6	11	Fetters	Guzman	Henry	45-41	3rd	6½
7-9	Cle.	W	14-4		12	10	Ryan	Scudder		46-41	3rd	5½
7-10	Cle.	W	6-5		14	7	Bohanon	Armstrong	Russell	47-41	3rd	5½
7-11	Cle.	W	5-1		12	6	Brown	Mutis		48-41	3rd	5½
7-12	Cle.	L	3-6		11	12	Olin	Rogers	Plunk	48-42	3rd	6½
7-16	Bal.	W	5-2		9	3	Ryan	Sutcliffe	Russell	49-42	3rd	6½
7-17	Bal.	L	0-8		1	14	Mussina	Brown		49-43	3rd	7½
7-18	Bal.	L	0-7		2	8	McDonald	Guzman		49-44	3rd	7½
7-19	Bal.	L	2-3	(10)	3	8	Frohwirth	Mathews	Olson	49-45	3rd	8½
7-20	At Mil.	L	4-5		8	7	Holmes	Nunez		49-46	3rd	8½
7-21	At Mil.	W	6-3	(10)	10	10	Mathews	Holmes	Russell	50-46	3rd	7½
7-22	At Mil.	L	1-4		2	8	Navarro	Brown		50-47	3rd	8½
7-23	At Bal.	W	4-2		8	9	Guzman	McDonald	Russell	51-47	3rd	8
7-24	At Bal.	L	2-9	(8)	6	14	Rhodes	Burns		51-48	3rd	8½
7-25	At Bal.	W	10-8		10	12	Witt	Sutcliffe	Russell	52-48	3rd	8½
7-26	At Bal.	W	6-2		12	5	Ryan	Mussina	Nunez	53-48	3rd	8½
7-27	At Bos.	L	5-7		11	9	Viola	Brown	Reardon	53-49	3rd	8½
7-28	At Bos.	W	2-1	(10)	10	8	Leon	Quantrill	Russell	54-49	3rd	7½
7-29	At Bos.	L	5-6		10	10	Clemens	Burns	Reardon	54-50	3rd	7½
7-31	Cal.	L	3-5		11	9	Crim	Witt	Grahe	54-51	3rd	8
8-1	Cal.	L	1-6		7	10	Finley	Ryan		54-52	3rd	9
8-2	Cal.	W	5-1		7	6	Brown	Langston		55-52	3rd	9
8-3	Oak.	L	1-4		5	8	Moore	Guzman	Eckersley	55-53	3rd	9½
8-4	Oak.	L	0-9		4	12	Stewart	Bohanon	Campbell	55-54	4th	9½
8-5	Oak.	L	3-4		9	6	Darling	Witt	Eckersley	55-55	4th	10½
8-6	Oak.	L	0-2		10	6	Downs	Ryan	Honeycutt	55-56	4th	11½
8-7	At Sea.	W	7-6	(11)	11	16	Burns	Swan	Nunez	56-56	4th	11½
8-8	At Sea.	W	7-3		11	8	Guzman	Woodson		57-56	4th	11½
8-9	At Sea.	L	5-6	(14)	10	12	Jones	Whiteside		57-57	4th	11½
8-10	At Min.	L	5-7		9	11	Tapani	Witt	Aguilera	57-58	4th	12½
8-11	At Min.	L	2-3		4	8	Smiley	Rogers		57-59	4th	12½
8-12	At Min.	W	5-3		7	12	Brown	Aguilera	Russell	58-59	4th	12½
8-13	At Min.	W	6-1		12	6	Guzman	Erickson		59-59	4th	12½
8-14	Det.	L	6-9		11	13	Haas	Pavlik	Henneman	59-60	4th	12½
8-15	Det.	L	3-10		9	11	Doherty	Witt	Munoz	59-61	4th	13½
8-16	Det.	L	0-6		5	5	Tanana	Ryan		59-62	4th	14½
8-18	At Chi.	L	0-3		6	9	McDowell	Brown		59-63	4th	14½
8-19	At Chi.	L	2-3		5	7	Fernandez	Guzman	Radinsky	59-64	4th	14½
8-20	At Chi.	W	6-1		13	6	Pavlik	Hough		60-64	4th	14½
8-21	At Cle.	L	6-8		10	12	Cook	Ryan	Olin	60-65	4th	14½
8-22	At Cle.	L	1-6		5	13	Armstrong	Witt		60-66	4th	15½
8-23	At Cle.	W	14-4		15	12	Rogers	Olin		61-66	4th	15½
8-25	K.C.	W	6-2		10	8	Guzman	Appier		62-66	4th	15
8-26	K.C.	W	3-1		5	6	Pavlik	Sauveur	Russell	63-66	4th	14
8-27	K.C.	L	2-7		6	9	Pichardo	Ryan		63-67	4th	14½
8-28	Chi.	W	4-1		11	5	Brown	Hibbard		64-67	4th	14½
8-29	Chi.	L	4-6		7	9	McDowell	Witt	Hernandez	64-68	4th	15½
8-30	Chi.	W	10-4		12	11	Guzman	Fernandez		65-68	4th	15½
8-31	At K.C.	L	2-5		5	11	Haney	Pavlik	Montgomery	65-69	4th	15½
9-1	At K.C.	L	3-8		10	13	Boddicker	Burns		65-70	4th	15½
9-2	At K.C.	W	6-2		11	6	Brown	Reed		66-70	4th	14½
9-4	At N.Y.	L	3-6		9	15	Wickman	Guzman	Farr	66-71	4th	14½
9-5	At N.Y.	W	7-3		8	10	Pavlik	Militello	Rogers	67-71	4th	13½
9-6	At N.Y.	L	0-7		3	9	Kamieniecki	Chiamparino		67-72	4th	14½
9-7	Bos.	L	0-3		4	9	Clemens	Ryan	Hesketh	67-73	4th	14½
9-8	Bos.	W	6-1		6	5	Brown	Young		68-73	4th	14½
9-9	Bos.	W	3-2		9	8	Guzman	Darwin		69-73	4th	14½
9-11 (1)	Tor.	L	5-7		13	15	Guzman	Chiamparino	Henke	69-74	4th	16
9-11 (2)	Tor.	W	4-3		10	6	Pavlik	Stottlemyre	Burns	70-74	4th	15½

Date	Opp.	Res.	Score	(inn.*)	Hits	Opp. hits	Winning pitcher	Losing pitcher	Save	Record	Pos.	GB
9-12	Tor.	L	2-4		7	9	Morris	Smith	Henke	70-75	4th	16½
9-13	Tor.	L	2-7		6	13	Key	Brown	Ward	70-76	4th	17½
9-15	At Det.	W	6-5		12	10	Guzman	Gullickson	Whiteside	71-76	4th	18
9-16	At Det.	L	1-4		2	7	Haas	Pavlik	Henneman	71-77	4th	19
9-18	At Tor.	L	0-13		9	13	Key	Brown		71-78	4th	20
9-19	At Tor.	L	0-1		4	4	Cone	Chiamparino	Henke	71-79	4th	20
9-20	At Tor.	W	7-5		13	7	Jo. Guzman	Ju. Guzman	Whiteside	72-79	4th	20
9-22	Min.	L	0-1	(13)	7	11	Casian	Rogers	Aguilera	72-80	4th	20½
9-23	Min.	W	5-3		10	10	Brown	Trombley		73-80	4th	19½
9-25	Sea.	L	3-4	(16)	16	14	Powell	Smith	Fisher	73-81	4th	20
9-26	Sea.	L	4-8		11	11	Fleming	Pavlik		73-82	4th	20
9-27	Sea.	W	3-2		7	9	Whiteside	Nelson		74-82	4th	19
9-29	At Oak.	L	0-5		4	8	Moore	Brown		74-83	4th	20
9-30	At Oak.	W	7-3		7	7	Guzman	Welch	Whiteside	75-83	4th	19
10-1	At Oak.	W	4-3		6	5	Rogers	Horsman	Whiteside	76-83	4th	18
10-2	At Cal.	L	3-6		6	12	Langston	Chiamparino		76-84	4th	18
10-3	At Cal.	L	2-4		8	11	Lewis	Smith	Grahe	76-85	4th	19
10-4	At Cal.	W	9-5		17	8	Brown	Blyleven		77-85	4th	19

Monthly records: April (13-11), May (16-12), June (14-13), July (11-15), August (11-18), September (10-14), Oct. (2-2).

HIGHLIGHTS

High point: From May 17-29, Texas won 11 of 12 games to leap from fifth (3½ games out of first) to first place (½-game lead). The Rangers held the top spot for the last time May 30.

Low point: From July 27-August 22, the Rangers lost 18 of 25 games, falling from third to fourth place, 15½ games out of first.

Turning point: Texas traveled to Oakland on June 12, trailing the division-leading Athletics by one game. But the Rangers were swept in the three-game set, leaving them four games behind Oakland. Texas was never a serious contender again.

Most valuable player: Outfielder Juan Gonzalez. The 22-year-old became the first Ranger ever to lead the league in home runs (43) while also driving in over 100 runs (109) for the second straight season.

Most valuable pitcher: Righthander Kevin Brown. He became just the second Ranger to record 20 wins, finishing with a 21-11 record, 3.32 ERA, 173 strikeouts and a league-leading 265⅔ innings pitched.

Most improved player: Utilityman Jeff Huson. He raised his batting average 48 points over his '91 mark (from .213 to .261) and played solid defense at both shortstop and second base.

Biggest disappointment: Second baseman Julio Franco. After leading the league in batting with a .341 average in '91, he hit a career-low .234. However, he was limited to just 35 games due to a right knee injury.

Most pleasant surprise: Third baseman Dean Palmer. In his first full big-league season, Palmer hit 26 homers and drove in 72 runs. His homer total ranked third among major league third basemen.

Key injuries: Franco's knee ailment forced him on the disabled list three times. Catcher Ivan Rodriguez missed three weeks because of a stress fracture in his lower back. Righthander Nolan Ryan missed most of the first month because of a strained calf muscle and inflamed Achilles tendon.

Notable: The Rangers acquired right fielder Jose Canseco from Oakland on August 31 for right fielder Ruben Sierra, righthanders Bobby Witt and Jeff Russell and cash. . . . Texas relievers compiled the highest ERA (4.53) in the majors. . . . The Rangers had the worst home record (36-45) in the majors. . . . After hitting .270 and scoring 829 runs in 1991, Texas managed to hit just .250 and score 682 runs.

—T.R. SULLIVAN

RECORDS

1992 regular-season record: 77-85 (4th in A.L. West); 36-45 at home; 41-40 on road; 38-46 vs. East; 39-39 vs. West; 20-26 vs. LHP; 57-59 vs. RHP; 63-73 on grass; 14-12 on turf; 17-14 in day-time; 60-71 at night; 25-22 in one-run games; 9-7 in extra-inning games; 1-0-1 in doubleheaders.

Team record last five years: 398-411 (.492), ranks 9th in league in that span).

TEAM LEADERS

Batting average: Ruben Sierra (.278).
At-bats: Rafael Palmeiro (608).
Runs: Rafael Palmeiro (84).
Hits: Rafael Palmeiro (163).
Total bases: Juan Gonzalez (309).
Doubles: Kevin Reimer (32).
Triples: Ruben Sierra (6).
Home runs: Juan Gonzalez (43).
Runs batted in: Juan Gonzalez (109).
Stolen bases: Jeff Huson (18).
Slugging percentage: Juan Gonzalez (.529).
On-base percentage: Rafael Palmeiro (.352).
Wins: Kevin Brown (21).
Earned-run average: Kevin Brown (3.32).
Complete games: Kevin Brown (11).
Shutouts: Kevin Brown (1).
Saves: Jeff Russell (28).
Innings pitched: Kevin Brown (265⅔).
Strikeouts: Jose Guzman (179).

GAMES BY POSITION

Catcher: Ivan Rodriguez 116, Geno Petralli 54, Russ McGinnis 10, Ray Stephens 6, John Russell 4, Doug Davis 1.
First base: Rafael Palmeiro 156, Jack Daugherty 8, Rob Maurer 4, Russ McGinnis 2, Monty Fariss 1.
Second base: Al Newman 72, Jeff Frye 67, Jeff Huson 47, Monty Fariss 17, Julio Franco 9, Mario Diaz 3, Geno Petralli 2.
Third base: Dean Palmer 150, Al Newman 28, Geno Petralli 4, Russ McGinnis 2, Mario Diaz 1.
Shortstop: Dickie Thon 87, Jeff Huson 82, Al Newman 20, Mario Diaz 16, Cris Colon 14.
Outfield: Juan Gonzalez 148, Ruben Sierra 119, Kevin Reimer 110, John Cangelosi 65, Monty Fariss 49, David Hulse 31, Jack Daugherty 26, Donald Harris 24, Jose Canseco 13, Dan Peltier 10, Julio Franco 4, Jeff Huson 2, John Russell 2, Al Newman 1.
Designated hitter: Brian Downing 93, Kevin Reimer 32, Julio Franco 15, Geno Petralli 14, Jack Daugherty 13, Jose Canseco 8, John Cangelosi 6, Monty Fariss 4, Juan Gonzalez 4, Ruben Sierra 4, Rafael Palmeiro 2, Ivan Rodriguez 2, Rob Maurer 1, John Russell 1, Ray Stephens 1.

TOP 10 DRAFT CHOICES

1. **Rick Helling,** RHP, Stanford Univ.
2. **Ritchie Moody,** LHP, Oklahoma State University.
3. **David Manning,** RHP, Palm Beach Community College (Fla.).
4. **Ramiro Martinez,** LHP, Los Angeles City College.
5. **Mike Smith,** SS, Indiana University.
6. **Cory Pearson,** OF, Logan (W.Va.) High School.
7. **Jeff Runion,** RHP, Riverdale (Ga.) High School.
8. **Kevin Dunivan,** RHP, Captain Shreve High School, Shreveport, La.
9. **Scott Malone,** OF, Texas Christian University.
10. **Scot Sealy,** C, U. of South Alabama.

TORONTO BLUE JAYS
AMERICAN LEAGUE EAST DIVISION

1993 SCHEDULE

APRIL

SUN	MON	TUE	WED	THU	FRI	SAT
				1	2	3
4	5	6 N SEA	7 N SEA	8	9 CLE H	10 CLE H
11 CLE H	12	13 N SEA	14 N SEA	15 H SEA	16 N CLE	17 CLE
18 CLE	19 CLE	20 N KC	21 N KC	22 N KC	23 N CHI	24 H CHI
25 CHI	26 H TEX	27 N TEX	28 H TEX	29 N KC	30 H CHI	

MAY

SUN	MON	TUE	WED	THU	FRI	SAT
						1 CHI
2 CHI	3	4 N TEX	5 N TEX	6 H BAL	7 N BAL	8 N BAL H
9 BAL H	10	11 N DET	12 H DET	13 N DET	14 H NY	15 NY
16 NY	17 N BOS	18 N BOS	19 BOS	20	21 N MIN	22 H MIN
23 MIN	24 H MIL	25 N MIL	26 H MIL	27 N MIL	28 N OAK	29 OAK
30 OAK	31 CAL					

JUNE

SUN	MON	TUE	WED	THU	FRI	SAT
		1 N CAL	2 N CAL	3	4 N OAK	5 N OAK H
6 OAK H	7 N CAL	8 N CAL	9 N DET	10 H DET	11 N DET	12 N DET
13 DET	14 N MIN	15 N MIN	16 MIN	17 N BOS	18 H BOS	19 BOS
20 BOS H	21	22 N NY	23 H NY	24 N NY	25 H MIL	26 N MIL
27 MIL	28 N BAL	29 N BAL	30 N BAL			

JULY

SUN	MON	TUE	WED	THU	FRI	SAT
				1	2 N KC	3 N KC
4 N KC	5 N CHI	6 N CHI	7 N CHI	8 N TEX	9 N TEX	10 H TEX
11 TEX H	12	13 ✱ ALL-STAR GAME	14	15 N KC	16 H KC	17 N KC
18 KC H	19 N CHI	20 N CHI	21 CHI	22 N TEX	23 H TEX	24 H TEX
25 TEX N	26	27 N BAL	28 H BAL	29 N DET	30 H DET	31 DET H

AUGUST

SUN	MON	TUE	WED	THU	FRI	SAT
1 DET	2 N NY	3 NY	4 N NY	5 N NY	6 N MIL	7 N MIL H
8 MIL H	9	10 MIN	11 N MIN	12 H MIN	13 N BOS	14 BOS
15 BOS	16 N CLE	17 N CLE	18 N CLE	19	20 SEA	21 N SEA H
22 SEA H	23 N CLE	24 H CLE	25 H CLE	26 N SEA	27 SEA	28 N SEA
29 SEA	30 N OAK	31 N OAK				

SEPTEMBER

SUN	MON	TUE	WED	THU	FRI	SAT
			1 OAK	2	3 N CAL	4 N CAL
5 CAL	6	7 N OAK	8 N OAK H	9 N OAK	10 H CAL	11 N CAL H
12 CAL H	13	14 N DET	15 N DET	16	17 N MIN	18 MIN
19 MIN	20	21 N BOS	22 H BOS	23 N BOS	24 H NY	25 NY
26 NY	27 N MIL	28 N MIL	29 H MIL	30 BAL		

OCTOBER

SUN	MON	TUE	WED	THU	FRI	SAT
				1 BAL	2 N BAL	3 N BAL
3 BAL						

1993 SEASON

CLUB DIRECTORY

Chairman
 P.N.T. Widdrington
President and chief executive officer
 Paul Beeston
Executive vice president, baseball
 Pat Gillick
Vice presidents, baseball
 Bob Mattick
 Al LaMacchia
Vice president, business
 Bob Nicholson
Special asst. to the exec. v.p., baseball
 Al Widmar
Assistant general manager
 Gord Ash
Director, public relations
 Howard Starkman
Director, stadium and ticket operations
 George Holm
Director, marketing
 Paul Markle
Director, finance
 Susie Quigley
Director, scouting
 Bob Engle
Director, international scouting
 Wayne Morgan
Director, player development
 Mel Queen
Director, Canadian scouting
 Bob Prentice
Director, minor league business
 Ken Carson
Administrator, player personnel
 Bob Nelson
Administrator, scouting
 Hank Zacharias
Assistant director, public relations
 Mark Leno
Asst. dir., tickets and box office manager
 Randy Low
Assistant director, operations
 Len Frejlich
Manager, group sales
 Maureen Haffey
Manager, team travel
 John Brioux
Manager, promotions and advertising
 Rick Amos
Manager, accounting
 Cathy McNamara
Manager, employee compensations
 Catharine Elwood
Manager, information systems
 Hans Frauenlob
Manager, ticket vault
 Paul Goodyear

Manager, ticket revenue
 Mike Maunder
Managers, ticket mail services
 Allan Koyanagi
 Doug Barr
Manager, security
 Fred Wootton
Manager, event personnel
 Mario Coutinho
Systems administrator
 Mark Graham
Supervisor, grounds
 Brad Bujold
Supervisor, office services
 Mick Bazinet
Trainers
 Tommy Craig
 Brent Andrews
Team physician
 Dr. Ron Taylor
Coord., Latin American scouting & develop.
 Epy Guerrero
Special assignment scouts
 Moose Johnson
 Gordon Lakey
 Tim Wilken
Director, international scouting
 Wayne Morgan
Advance scout
 Don Welke
Scouts
 David Blume
 Chris Bourjos
 Chris Buckley
 Ellis Clary
 John Cole
 Ellis Dungan
 Joe Ford
 Robert Campbell
 Tim Hewes
 Tom Hinkle
 Jim Hughes
 Duane Larson
 Ted Lekas
 Ben McLure
 Bill Moore
 Dave Nahabedian
 Andy Pienovi
 Alvin Rittman
 Red Robbins
 Joe Siers
 Mark Snipp
 Jerry Sobeck
 Neil Summers
 Ron Tostenson
 Ramon Webster

SCHEDULE KEY

H—Home game.   N—Night game (any game starting after 5 p.m.).
*All-Star Game at Oriole Park at Camden Yards, Baltimore.

Manager—Cito Gaston (43).

Coaches—Bob Bailor (3), Galen Cisco (42), Rich Hacker (7), Larry Hisle (39), John Sullivan (8), Gene Tenace (18).

No.	PITCHERS	B/T	Ht./Wt.	Born	1992 clubs
44	Brow, Scott	R/R	6-3/200	3-17-69	Dunedin
48	Eichhorn, Mark	R/R	6-3/210	11-21-60	California, Toronto
32	Flener, Huck	B/L	5-11/185	2-25-69	Dunedin
66	Guzman, Juan	R/R	5-11/195	10-28-66	Toronto, Syracuse
41	Hentgen, Pat	R/R	6-2/200	11-13-68	Toronto, Syracuse
28	Leiter, Al	L/L	6-3/215	10-23-65	Syracuse, Toronto
26	Linton, Doug	R/R	6-1/190	9-2-65	Syracuse, Toronto
45	MacDonald, Bob	L/L	6-3/208	4-27-65	Toronto, Syracuse
55	Menhart, Paul	R/R	6-2/190	3-25-69	Knoxville
47	Morris, Jack	R/R	6-3/210	5-16-55	Toronto
38	Small, Aaron	R/R	6-5/195	11-23-71	Knoxville
52	Steed, Rick	R/R	6-3/185	9-8-70	Dunedin
34	Stewart, Dave	R/R	6-2/200	2-19-57	Oakland
30	Stottlemyre, Todd	L/R	6-3/200	5-20-65	Toronto
21	Taylor, Bill	R/R	6-8/230	10-16-61	Richmond
40	Timlin, Mike	R/R	6-4/210	3-10-66	Dunedin, Syracuse, Toronto
35	Trlicek, Rick	R/R	6-3/200	4-26-69	Toronto, Syracuse
31	Ward, Duane	R/R	6-4/215	5-28-64	Toronto
36	Wells, David	L/L	6-4/225	5-20-63	Toronto

No.	CATCHERS	B/T	Ht./Wt.	Born	1992 clubs
10	Borders, Pat	R/R	6-2/200	5-14-63	Toronto
6	Delgado, Carlos	L/R	6-3/215	6-25-72	Dunedin
27	Knorr, Randy	R/R	6-2/218	11-12-68	Syracuse, Toronto
20	O'Halloran, Greg	L/R	6-1/190	5-21-68	Knoxville
33	Sprague, Ed	R/R	6-2/210	7-25-67	Syracuse, Toronto

No.	INFIELDERS	B/T	Ht./Wt.	Born	1992 clubs
12	Alomar, Roberto	B/R	6-0/185	2-5-68	Toronto
11	Coles, Darnell	R/R	6-1/185	6-2-62	Nashville, Cincinnati
19	Martinez, Domingo	R/R	6-2/215	8-4-67	Syracuse, Toronto
4	Molitor, Paul	R/R	6-0/185	8-22-56	Milwaukee
9	Olerud, John	L/L	6-5/220	8-5-68	Toronto
16	Quinlan, Tom	R/R	6-3/215	3-27-68	Syracuse, Toronto
5	Sojo, Luis	R/R	5-11/174	1-3-66	Edmonton, California
1	Zosky, Eddie	R/R	6-0/175	2-10-68	Syracuse, Toronto

No.	OUTFIELDERS	B/T	Ht./Wt.	Born	1992 clubs
14	Bell, Derek	R/R	6-2/205	12-11-68	Toronto, Dunedin
23	Bowers, Brent	L/R	6-3/190	5-2-71	Dunedin
29	Carter, Joe	R/R	6-3/225	3-7-60	Toronto
17	Perez, Robert	R/R	6-3/210	6-4-69	Knoxville
24	Ward, Turner	B/R	6-2/200	4-11-65	Toronto, Syracuse
25	White, Devon	B/R	6-2/195	12-29-62	Toronto

BALLPARK INFORMATION

Ballpark (capacity, surface)
SkyDome (50,516, artificial)
Address
One Blue Jay Way
Suite 3200
Toronto, Ontario M5V 1J1
Business phone
416-341-1000
Ticket information
416-341-1111
Ticket prices
$19.50 (esplanade IF, club level OF)
$15.00 (skydeck IF, esplanade OF)
$11 (skydeck)
$5 (skydeck outfield)
Field dimensions (from home plate)
To left field at foul line, 330 feet
To center field, 400 feet
To right field at foul line, 330 feet
First game played
June 5, 1989 (Brewers 5, Blue Jays 3)

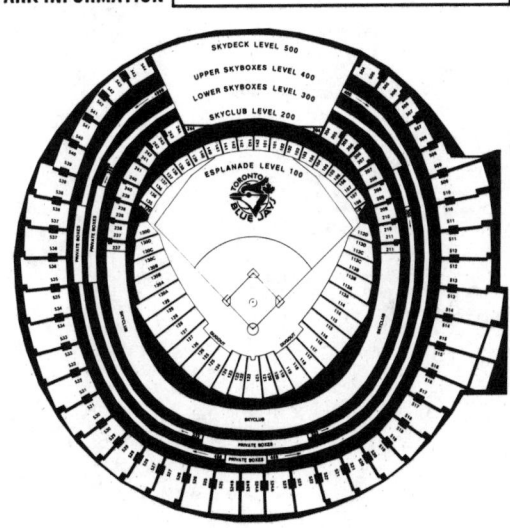

Class	Team	League	Manager
AAA	Syracuse	International	Nick Leyva
AA	Knoxville	Southern	Garth Iorg
A	Hagerstown	South Atlantic	Doug Ault
A	Dunedin	Florida State	Dennis Holmberg
A	St. Catharines	New York-Pennsylvania	J.J. Cannon
Rookie	Medicine Hat	Pioneer	Jim Nettles
Rookie	Gulf Coast Blue Jays	Gulf Coast	Omar Malave

☐ BROADCAST INFORMATION ☐

Radio: THE-FAN (1430). Broadcasters: Tom Cheek, Jerry Howarth.
TV: CFTO-TV (Channel 9). Broadcasters: Don Chevrier, Tommy Hutton, Fergie Olver. CBC-TV (Channel 6). Broadcasters: Don Chevrier, Tommy Hutton, Fergie Olver, Ken Daniels.
Cable TV: The Sports Network. Broadcasters: Jim Hughson, Buck Martinez.

SPRING TRAINING

Ballpark (city): Dunedin Stadium at Grant Field (Dunedin, Fla.).
Ticket information: 813-733-0429.

HISTORY

YEAR-BY-YEAR RECORDS

Year	Pos.	W	L	Pct.	*GB	Year	Pos.	W	L	Pct.	*GB
1977	7th	54	107	.335	45½	1988	T3rd	87	75	.537	2
1978	7th	59	102	.366	40	1989	1st‡	89	73	.549 + 2	
1979	7th	53	109	.327	50½	1990	2nd	86	76	.531	2
1980	7th	67	95	.414	36	1991	1st‡	91	71	.562 + 7	
1981	7th/7th	37	69	.349	†	1992	1st§	96	66	.593 + 4	
1982	T6th	78	84	.481	17						
1983	4th	89	73	.549	9						
1984	2nd	89	73	.549	15						
1985	1st‡	99	62	.615 + 2							
1986	4th	86	76	.531	9½						
1987	2nd	96	66	.593	2						

*Games behind winner. †First half 16-42; second 21-27. ‡Lost Championship Series. §Won Championship Series.

MANAGERS

Name	Record	Years
Roy Hartsfield	166-318	'77-79
Bobby Mattick	104-164	'80-81
Bobby Cox	355-292	'82-85
Jimy Williams	281-241	'86-89
Cito Gaston	350-262	'89-92

DAY BY DAY

Date	Opp.	Res.	Score	(inn.*)	Hits	Opp. hits	Winning pitcher	Losing pitcher	Save	Record	Pos.	GB
4-6	At Det.	W	4-2		10	5	Morris	Gullickson		1-0	T1st	...
4-8	At Det.	W	10-9		12	10	Henke	Tanana	Ward	2-0	1st	+½
4-9	At Det.	W	3-1		7	4	Guzman	Terrell	Ward	3-0	T1st	+½
4-10	Bal.	W	4-3		10	8	Hentgen	Olson		4-0	T1st	+½
4-11	Bal.	W	7-2		13	8	Morris	Sutcliffe		5-0	T1st	+½
4-12	Bal.	W	3-1		9	5	Wells	Mesa	Ward	6-0	1st	+½
4-13	N.Y.	L	2-5		6	6	Howe	Stottlemyre	Farr	6-1	2nd	½
4-14	N.Y.	W	12-6		14	13	Guzman	Johnson		7-1	1st	+½
4-15	N.Y.	W	2-0		8	3	Key	Perez	Henke	8-1	1st	+1½
4-16	N.Y.	W	7-6		11	7	Ward	Farr		9-1	1st	+2½
4-17	At Bos.	L	0-1		3	4	Clemens	Wells	Reardon	9-2	1st	+2½
4-18	At Bos.	W	2-1		6	4	Stottlemyre	Viola	Henke	10-2	1st	+2½
4-19	At Bos.	L	4-5		10	9	Darwin	Henke		10-3	1st	+1½
4-20	At Bos.	W	6-4	(13)	13	10	MacDonald	Bolton		11-3	1st	+2½
4-21	Cle.	W	2-1		5	5	Morris	Cook		12-3	1st	+2½
4-22	Cle.	L	2-7		11	11	Nagy	Stieb	Power	12-4	1st	+1½
4-23	Cle.	W	13-8		15	14	Stottlemyre	Otto		13-4	1st	+2
4-24	K.C.	W	4-3		8	5	Guzman	Gordon	Henke	14-4	1st	+2
4-25	K.C.	W	6-4		11	10	Hentgen	Young	Ward	15-4	1st	+3
4-26	K.C.	L	0-9		4	13	Gubicza	Morris		15-5	1st	+2
4-28	Cal.	L	5-9		7	14	Finley	Stieb		15-6	1st	+1½
4-29	Cal.	W	1-0		9	7	Stottlemyre	Abbott		16-6	1st	+2½
4-30	At Mil.	L	2-3		7	8	Bosio	Ward	Henry	16-7	1st	+2
5-1	At Mil.	L	3-4		7	8	Navarro	Key	Henry	16-8	1st	+1
5-2	At Mil.	L	4-5		7	8	Fetters	Morris	Henry	16-9	2nd	...
5-3	At Mil.	W	4-1		11	3	Stieb	Wegman		17-9	2nd	...
5-4	At Oak.	W	7-3		12	5	Stottlemyre	Darling		18-9	2nd	...
5-5	At Oak.	W	5-1		12	5	Guzman	Slusarski	Ward	19-9	1st	+1
5-6	At Sea.	W	12-4		12	8	Key	Johnson		20-9	1st	+1
5-7	At Sea.	W	8-7		10	11	Hentgen	Schooler	Henke	21-9	1st	+1
5-8	At Cal.	L	1-4		8	8	Eichhorn	Stieb		21-10	1st	+1
5-9	At Cal.	L	1-2		6	6	Abbott	Stottlemyre	Harvey	21-11	2nd	...
5-10	At Cal.	W	4-1		7	4	Guzman	Grahe		22-11	1st	+1
5-12	Oak.	W	3-0		5	7	Key	Stewart	Henke	23-11	1st	+1
5-13	Oak.	W	4-3		9	10	Morris	Moore	Henke	24-11	1st	+1
5-14	Sea.	W	5-4		7	7	Stieb	Jones	Wells	25-11	1st	+1½
5-15	Sea.	L	1-2		8	5	Fleming	Stottlemyre	Schooler	25-12	1st	+½
5-16	Sea.	L	6-7		8	10	Powell	Wells	Schooler	25-13	2nd	½
5-17	Sea.	L	2-3		7	8	Johnson	Key	Schooler	25-14	2nd	½
5-18	Min.	L	2-6	(11)	12	8	Wayne	Ward		25-15	2nd	½
5-19	Min.	L	1-7		5	13	Mahomes	Stieb	Edens	25-16	2nd	½
5-20	Min.	W	8-7	(10)	9	13	Henke	Aguilera		26-16	1st	+½
5-22	At Chi.	W	6-2		10	5	Guzman	McDowell	Ward	27-16	1st	...
5-23	At Chi.	L	2-5		4	11	Hibbard	Key	Thigpen	27-17	1st	+½
5-24	At Chi.	L	1-8		8	10	McCaskill	Morris		27-18	2nd	½
5-26	Mil.	W	5-4		5	7	Stieb	Bones	Henke	28-18	2nd	...
5-27	Mil.	L	4-8		7	13	Navarro	Stottlemyre	Henry	28-19	2nd	...
5-29	Chi.	W	3-0		10	4	Ward	Hibbard	Henke	29-19	1st	+1
5-30	Chi.	W	2-1	(11)	8	6	Wells	Pall		30-19	1st	+1
5-31	Chi.	W	3-2		5	3	Morris	Thigpen		31-19	1st	+1
6-1	At Min.	W	5-3	(10)	9	9	Ward	Willis	Henke	32-19	1st	+1
6-2	At Min.	W	7-5	(13)	14	13	Hentgen	Wayne	Henke	33-19	1st	+1
6-3	At Min.	L	3-11		14	11	Tapani	Guzman		33-20	1st	+1
6-5	At Bal.	L	0-1		4	5	Sutcliffe	Key	Olson	33-21	2nd	...
6-6	At Bal.	W	4-3		5	7	Morris	McDonald	Henke	34-21	1st	+1
6-7	At Bal.	L	1-7		8	10	Mussina	Stieb		34-22	2nd	...
6-8	At N.Y.	W	16-3		21	6	Stottlemyre	Cadaret		35-22	2nd	...
6-9	At N.Y.	W	2-1		5	4	Guzman	Leary	Henke	36-22	1st	+1
6-10	At N.Y.	W	10-3		15	8	Key	Sanderson	Wells	37-22	1st	+1
6-11	Bos.	W	4-0		7	4	Morris	Clemens		38-22	1st	+1
6-12	Bos.	L	0-5		6	8	Viola	Stieb		38-23	2nd	...
6-13	Bos.	L	3-5		6	10	Hesketh	Stottlemyre	Reardon	38-24	2nd	...
6-14	Bos.	W	6-2		6	7	Guzman	Gardiner	Ward	39-24	1st	+1
6-16	Det.	L	3-4		6	10	Gullickson	Key	Henneman	39-25	1st	+½
6-17	Det.	W	6-2		12	7	Morris	Ritz	Ward	40-25	1st	+1½
6-18	Det.	L	10-14		15	16	Munoz	Timlin	Henneman	40-26	1st	+1
6-19	At K.C.	L	4-11		10	12	Gubicza	Stottlemyre		40-27	2nd	...
6-20	At K.C.	W	6-1		8	5	Guzman	Magnante		41-27	1st	+1
6-21	At K.C.	L	0-2		6	8	Appier	Key	Montgomery	41-28	1st	+1
6-22	At Tex.	W	16-7		20	10	Morris	Guzman		42-28	1st	+1

Date	Opp.	Res.	Score (inn.*)	Hits	Opp. hits	Winning pitcher	Losing pitcher	Save	Record	Pos.	GB
6-24	At Tex.	W	3-2	10	8	Wells	Witt	Henke	43-28	1st	+½
6-26	At Cle.	W	6-1	10	4	Guzman	Armstrong		44-28	1st	+1
6-27	At Cle.	L	4-6	8	13	Plunk	Ward		44-29	1st	+1
6-28	At Cle.	L	6-7	8	12	Olin	Ward	Plunk	44-30	1st	+1
6-29	Tex.	W	11-4	8	9	Hentgen	Witt		45-30	1st	+2
6-30	Tex.	L	13-16	12	20	Brown	Wells		45-31	1st	+1
7-1	Tex.	W	3-2 (10)	6	5	Ward	Russell		46-31	1st	+1
7-3	Cal.	W	10-1	13	5	Key	Langston		47-31	1st	+1
7-4	Cal.	W	8-6	12	8	Morris	Eichhorn	Henke	48-31	1st	+2
7-5	Cal.	W	6-2	8	3	Wells	Valera		49-31	1st	+3
7-6	Cal.	W	3-0	7	4	Guzman	Abbott	Henke	50-31	1st	+3
7-7	Sea.	W	4-3	9	9	Ward	Nelson		51-31	1st	+4
7-8	Sea.	W	6-0	9	6	Key	Hanson		52-31	1st	+4
7-9	Oak.	W	4-3	10	7	Henke	Gossage		53-31	1st	+4
7-10	Oak.	L	1-5	5	9	Welch	Wells		53-32	1st	+4
7-11	Oak.	L	1-3	2	8	Moore	Guzman	Eckersley	53-33	1st	+4
7-12	Oak.	L	0-8	2	13	Darling	Hentgen		53-34	1st	+4
7-16	At Sea.	W	7-2	10	6	Morris	Johnson		54-34	1st	+5
7-17	At Sea.	L	8-15	15	14	Hanson	Key	Swan	54-35	1st	+4
7-18	At Sea.	W	3-0	7	5	Guzman	Fleming	Henke	55-35	1st	+4
7-19	At Sea.	W	8-4	10	6	Wells	DeLucia		56-35	1st	+4
7-20	At Cal.	L	3-5	6	10	Crim	Hentgen	Grahe	56-36	1st	+3
7-21	At Cal.	W	9-5	17	9	Morris	Crim	Ward	57-36	1st	+4
7-22	At Cal.	L	4-5	11	10	Grahe	Key		57-37	1st	+4
7-23	At Oak.	W	9-3	12	9	Stieb	Moore		58-37	1st	+5
7-24	At Oak.	L	5-6	12	14	Eckersley	Henke		58-38	1st	+4
7-25	At Oak.	L	0-6	2	7	Darling	Stottlemyre		58-39	1st	+4
7-26	At Oak.	L	1-9	5	15	Downs	Morris		58-40	1st	+4
7-28	K.C.	W	6-4	7	9	Key	Moeller	Henke	59-40	1st	+4
7-29	K.C.	L	2-5	8	8	Appier	Timlin	Montgomery	59-41	1st	+3
7-30	K.C.	W	3-0	8	3	Wells	Aquino	Henke	60-41	1st	+4
7-31	N.Y.	W	13-2	13	7	Stottlemyre	Hillegas		61-41	1st	+4½
8-1	N.Y.	W	3-1	6	8	Morris	Perez	Henke	62-41	1st	+4½
8-2	N.Y.	W	7-6	12	11	Eichhorn	Habyan	Ward	63-41	1st	+4½
8-3	At Bos.	L	1-7	6	10	Clemens	Guzman		63-42	1st	+3½
8-4	At Bos.	L	4-9	10	11	Hesketh	Wells	Harris	63-43	1st	+2½
8-5	At Bos.	W	5-4	11	6	Eichhorn	Irvine	Henke	64-43	1st	+2½
8-6	At Det.	W	15-11	11	15	Morris	Tanana		65-43	1st	+3
8-7	At Det.	L	2-7	8	9	Gullickson	Key		65-44	1st	+3
8-8	At Det.	L	6-8	10	12	Kiely	Linton	Henneman	65-45	1st	+3
8-9	At Det.	L	2-9	9	10	Haas	Wells		65-46	1st	+3
8-10	Bal.	W	8-4	11	9	Stottlemyre	Mussina		66-46	1st	+3
8-11	Bal.	L	0-3	8	8	Mills	Morris	Olson	66-47	1st	+2
8-12	Bal.	L	4-11	9	15	McDonald	Key		66-48	1st	+1
8-13	Bal.	W	4-2	8	3	Linton	Rhodes	Henke	67-48	1st	+2
8-14	At Cle.	W	9-5	13	9	Wells	Nichols		68-48	1st	+2
8-16 (1)	At Cle.	L	2-4	7	11	Cook	Stottlemyre	Olin	68-49	1st	+2½
8-16 (2)	At Cle.	W	6-2	13	6	Morris	Otto		69-49	1st	+3
8-18	At Mil.	W	12-1	15	3	Key	Ruffin		70-49	1st	+4
8-19	At Mil.	L	5-10	10	12	Bosio	Linton		70-50	1st	+4
8-20	At Mil.	L	3-16	9	18	Wegman	Wells		70-51	1st	+3
8-21	At Min.	L	1-5	7	7	Smiley	Stottlemyre		70-52	1st	+2
8-22	At Min.	W	4-2	8	9	Morris	West	Henke	71-52	1st	+3
8-23	At Min.	L	0-2	4	6	Erickson	Key		71-53	1st	+3
8-24	At Chi.	L	4-8	10	11	Fernandez	Linton		71-54	1st	+3
8-25	At Chi.	L	3-6	10	9	Hough	Wells	Hernandez	71-55	1st	+2
8-26	At Chi.	W	9-0	11	1	Stottlemyre	McCaskill		72-55	1st	+2
8-27	Mil.	W	5-4	7	7	Morris	Navarro	Henke	73-55	1st	+2½
8-28	Mil.	L	2-22	9	31	Eldred	Key		73-56	1st	+2½
8-29	Mil.	L	2-7	6	9	Bosio	Cone	Holmes	73-57	1st	+1½
8-30	Mil.	W	5-3	9	7	Ward	Wegman	Henke	74-57	1st	+1½
8-31	Chi.	W	9-2	9	5	Stottlemyre	Hough		75-57	1st	+1½
9-1	Chi.	W	9-3	11	4	Morris	McCaskill		76-57	1st	+1½
9-2	Chi.	L	2-3	12	5	Hibbard	Key	Hernandez	76-58	1st	+½
9-4	Min.	W	16-5	21	9	Cone	Tapani		77-58	1st	+½
9-5	Min.	W	7-3	10	8	Guzman	Smiley		78-58	1st	+½
9-6	Min.	W	4-2	8	7	Stottlemyre	Trombley	Henke	79-58	1st	+1½
9-7	At K.C.	L	4-5 (12)	14	12	Magnante	Wells		79-59	1st	+1½
9-8	At K.C.	W	5-0	9	4	Key	Aquino		80-59	1st	+2½
9-9	At K.C.	W	1-0	5	5	Cone	Appier	Henke	81-59	1st	+3½
9-11 (1)	At Tex.	W	7-5	15	13	Guzman	Chiamparino	Henke	82-59	1st	+3½
9-11 (2)	At Tex.	L	3-4	6	10	Pavlik	Stottlemyre	Burns	82-60	1st	+3
9-12	At Tex.	W	4-2	9	7	Morris	Smith	Henke	83-60	1st	+4
9-13	At Tex.	W	7-2	13	6	Key	Brown	Ward	84-60	1st	+5

Date	Opp.	Res.	Score	(inn.*)	Hits	Opp. hits	Winning pitcher	Losing pitcher	Save	Record	Pos.	GB
9-14	Cle.	L	1-2		6	5	Mesa	Cone	Olin	84-61	1st	+4
9-15	Cle.	W	5-4		5	10	Guzman	Embree	Henke	85-61	1st	+4
9-16	Cle.	L	3-6		7	13	Nagy	Stottlemyre	Power	85-62	1st	+3
9-17	Cle.	W	7-5	(10)	7	6	Ward	Plunk		86-62	1st	+3½
9-18	Tex.	W	13-0		13	9	Key	Brown		87-62	1st	+4½
9-19	Tex.	W	1-0		4	4	Cone	Chiamparino	Henke	88-62	1st	+5
9-20	Tex.	L	5-7		7	13	Jo. Guzman	Ju. Guzman	Whiteside	88-63	1st	+4
9-22	At Bal.	W	4-3		6	8	Stottlemyre	Sutcliffe	Henke	89-63	1st	+4½
9-23	At Bal.	L	1-4		4	7	Rhodes	Morris	Olson	89-64	1st	+3½
9-24	At Bal.	W	8-2		9	7	Key	McDonald		90-64	1st	+3½
9-25	At N.Y.	W	3-1		9	4	Cone	Perez	Henke	91-64	1st	+3½
9-26	At N.Y.	L	1-2		6	7	Wickman	Guzman	Farr	91-65	1st	+2½
9-27	At N.Y.	W	12-2		19	8	Morris	Sanderson		92-65	1st	+2½
9-29	Bos.	W	5-2		9	7	Key	Darwin	Henke	93-65	1st	+2½
9-30	Bos.	L	0-1		1	4	Viola	Cone		93-66	1st	+2½
10-2	Det.	W	8-7		11	12	Morris	Gullickson	Henke	94-66	1st	+2
10-3	Det.	W	3-1		9	3	Guzman	Haas	Ward	95-66	1st	+3
10-4	Det.	W	7-4		9	7	Stottlemyre	Aldred	Timlin	96-66	1st	+4

Monthly records: April (16-7), May (15-12), June (14-12), July (16-10), August (14-16), September (18-9), Oct. (3-0).

HIGHLIGHTS

High point: A 6-1 win June 20 in Kansas City propelled Toronto into first place for the rest of the season. The Blue Jays won 13 of 20 games and opened a five-game lead over Baltimore.

Low point: The Blue Jays began August with a 4½-game lead and ended it with a 1½-game edge after going 14-16.

Turning point: The August 27 acquisition of righthander David Cone from the New York Mets for rookie infielder Jeff Kent and a minor leaguer gave the Blue Jays a huge psychological boost. Toronto proceeded to register a 23-11 mark the rest of the season.

Most valuable player: Second baseman Roberto Alomar. He was the spark that made 100 RBI seasons possible for right fielder Joe Carter and designated hitter Dave Winfield. A Gold Glover and MVP of the League Championship Series, Alomar ranked among the league leaders in batting average (.310), on-base percentage (.405), runs (105), stolen bases (49) and hits (177).

Most valuable pitcher: Righthander Jack Morris. He became the first 20-game winner in club history, and the Blue Jays were 25-9 in games he started.

Most improved player: Catcher Pat Borders. En route to catching more games (136) than any catcher in the league, he set career highs in several offensive categories. He collected a hit in all 12 postseason games and was named World Series MVP.

Most pleasant surprise: Winfield. The 40-year-old solidified the team's DH spot and became the oldest player ever to drive in 100 runs (108).

Biggest disappointment: Third baseman Kelly Gruber. He hit just .229 with 43 RBIs and set a postseason record by going 23 at-bats without a hit.

Key injuries: Gruber missed 42 games because of neck, shoulder and leg injuries. Righthander Juan Guzman was 12-2 when a sore shoulder sidelined him almost a month.

Notable: The Blue Jays tied an A.L. record with 10 consecutive hits against the Twins on September 3. . . . Toronto finished over .500 for the 10th consecutive season. . . . The Toronto bullpen blew only 10 saves, none after July 24 until the final game of the World Series. . . . For the second straight year, Toronto set an all-time attendance record, breaking the mark it set in 1991 by drawing 4,028,318.

—NEIL MacCARL

RECORDS

1992 regular-season record: 96-66 (1st in A.L. East); 53-28 at home; 43-38 on road; 45-33 vs. East; 51-33 vs. West; 28-21 vs. LHP; 68-45 vs. RHP; 32-31 on grass; 64-35 on turf; 31-22 in daytime; 65-44 at night; 28-20 in one-run games; 7-2 in extra-inning games; 0-2 in doubleheaders.

1992 postseason record: Defeated A's, 4 games to 2, in A.L. playoffs; defeated Braves, 4 games to 2, in World Series.

Team record last five years: 449-361 (.554, ranks 2nd in league in that span).

TEAM LEADERS

Batting average: Roberto Alomar (.310).
At-bats: Devon White (641).
Runs: Roberto Alomar (105).
Hits: Roberto Alomar (177).
Total bases: Joe Carter (310).
Doubles: Dave Winfield (33).
Triples: Roberto Alomar (8).
Home runs: Joe Carter (34).
Runs batted in: Joe Carter (119).
Stolen bases: Roberto Alomar (49).
Slugging percentage: Joe Carter (.498).
On-base percentage: Roberto Alomar (.405).
Wins: Jack Morris (21).
Earned-run average: Juan Guzman (2.64).
Complete games: Jack Morris, Todd Stottlemyre (6).
Shutouts: Jimmy Key, Todd Stottlemyre (2).
Saves: Tom Henke (34).
Innings pitched: Jack Morris (240⅔).
Strikeouts: Juan Guzman (165).

GAMES BY POSITION

Catcher: Pat Borders 137, Greg Myers 18, Ed Sprague 15, Randy Knorr 8.
First base: John Olerud 133, Pat Tabler 34, Domingo Martinez 7, Joe Carter 4, Ed Sprague 4, Jeff Kent 3, Mike Maksudian 1.
Second base: Roberto Alomar 150, Jeff Kent 17, Alfredo Griffin 16.
Third base: Kelly Gruber 120, Jeff Kent 49, Tom Quinlan 13, Ed Sprague 1, Pat Tabler 1.
Shortstop: Manuel Lee 128, Alfredo Griffin 48, Eddie Zosky 8.
Outfield: Devon White 152, Candy Maldonado 132, Joe Carter 129, Derek Bell 56, Dave Winfield 26, Rob Ducey 13, Turner Ward 12, Pat Tabler 8.
Designated hitter: Dave Winfield 130, Joe Carter 24, Rob Ducey 4, Candy Maldonado 4, Rance Mulliniks 2, Ed Sprague 2, Pat Tabler 2, Roberto Alomar 1, Derek Bell 1, John Olerud 1, Devon White 1.

TOP 10 DRAFT CHOICES

1a. Shannon Stewart, OF, Miami Southridge Senior High School.
1b. Todd Steverson, OF, Arizona State University.
1c. Brandon Cromer, SS, Lexington (S.C.) High School.
2. Tim Crabtree, RHP, Michigan State University.
3. Levon Largusa, LHP, University of Hawaii.
4. Tom Evans, RHP/3B, Juanita High School, Kirkland, Wash.
5. Jeff Patzke, SS, Klamath Union High School, Klamath Falls, Ore.
6. Shea Morenz, OF, San Angelo (Tex.) Central High School.
7. Anthony Sanders, 3B/OF, Santa Rita High School, Tucson, Ariz.
8. Mike Kendzierski, RHP, Union-Endicott (N.Y.) Central School.
9. Tim Adkins, LHP, Wayne (W.Va.) High School.
10. Scott McCloughan, 3B, Wichita State University.

ATLANTA BRAVES
NATIONAL LEAGUE WEST DIVISION

1993 SCHEDULE

APRIL

SUN	MON	TUE	WED	THU	FRI	SAT
				1	2	3
4	5 CHI	6 CHI	7 CHI	8 N LA H	9 N LA H	10 N LA H
11 LA H	12 N CHI H	13 N CHI H	14 N CHI H	15 SF	16 SF	17 SF
18 SF	19	20 N FLA	21 N FLA	22 FLA	23 N STL	24 N STL
25 STL	26 N PIT H	27 N PIT H	28 N FLA H	29 N FLA H	30 N STL H	

MAY

SUN	MON	TUE	WED	THU	FRI	SAT
						1 STL H
2 STL H	3	4 N PIT	5 N PIT	6 N COL	7 N COL	8 COL
9 COL	10 N HOU	11 N HOU	12 N HOU	13	14 N PHI H	15 N PHI H
16 PHI H	17 N MON H	18 N MON H	19 N MON H	20	21 N NY	22 N NY
23 NY	24	25 N CIN	26 N CIN	27 N CIN	28 N SF H	29 N SF H
30 SF	31 N SD H					

JUNE

SUN	MON	TUE	WED	THU	FRI	SAT
		1 N SD H	2 N SD H	3 N SD H	4 N LA	5 N LA
6 LA	7 N SD	8 N SD	9	10 N CIN H	11 N CIN H	12 N CIN H
13 CIN	14 N NY H	15 N NY H	16 N NY H	17	18 N MON	19 N MON
20 MON	21 N PHI	22 N PHI	23 PHI	24	25 N HOU H	26 N HOU H
27 HOU H	28	29 N COL H	30 N COL H			

JULY

SUN	MON	TUE	WED	THU	FRI	SAT
				1 N COL H	2 N FLA H	3 N FLA H
4 FLA H	5 N FLA H	6 N STL	7 N STL	8 STL	9 N FLA	10 N FLA
11 N FLA	12	13 ∘ 14 ALL-STAR GAME		15 N PIT H	16 N PIT H	17 N PIT H
18 PIT	19 N STL H	20 N STL H	21 N STL H	22 PIT	23 N PIT	24 N PIT
25 PIT	26 N COL	27 COL	28 N COL	29 N HOU	30 N HOU	31 N HOU

AUGUST

SUN	MON	TUE	WED	THU	FRI	SAT
1 HOU	2	3 N PHI H	4 N PHI H	5 N PHI H	6 N MON H	7 N MON H
8 MON H	9	10 N NY	11 N NY	12 N NY	13 N CIN	14 CIN
15 CIN	16	17 N LA H	18 N LA H	19 N LA H	20 CHI	21 CHI
22 N CHI	23 N SF	24 SF	25 SF	26	27 N CHI H	28 H CHI H
29 CHI H	30	31 N SF H				

SEPTEMBER

SUN	MON	TUE	WED	THU	FRI	SAT
			1 N SF H	2 N SF H	3 N SD H	4 N SD H
5 SD H	6 N LA	7 N LA	8 N LA	9 N SD	10 N SD	11 N SD
12 SD	13	14 N CIN H	15 N CIN H	16 N CIN H	17 N NY	18 N NY
19 N NY H	20	21 N MON	22 N MON	23 N MON	24 PHI	25 PHI
26 PHI	27	28 N HOU H	29 H HOU H	30 N HOU H		

OCTOBER

SUN	MON	TUE	WED	THU	FRI	SAT
					1 N COL H	2 N COL H
3 COL H						

1993 SEASON

CLUB DIRECTORY

Chairman of the board
William C. Bartholomay
President
Stan Kasten
Sr. vice president and asst. to the president
Henry L. Aaron
Exec. vice president and general manager
John Schuerholz
Senior v.p., administration
Bob Wolfe
Director of player development and scouting
Chuck LaMar
Asst. v.p. and special asst. to the g.m.
Paul L. Snyder Jr.
Assistant general manager
Dean Taylor
Special assistant to general manager
Bill Lajoie
Assistant scouting director
Scott Proefrock
Assistant director of player development
Rod Gilbreath
Minor league field coordinator
Bobby Dews
V.p., director of marketing and broadcasting
Wayne Long
Dir. of team travel and equipment manager
Bill Acree
Sr. dir. of ticket sales and communications
Jack Tyson
Sr. dir. of promotions and special events
Miles McRea
Director of public relations
Jim Schultz
Director of community relations
Danny Goodwin
Director of ticket operations
Ed Newman
Advertising sales manager
Rodney Henderson
Director of merchandising
Robert A. Hope
Director of stadium operations and security
Larry Bowman
Controller
Chip Moore
Media relations manager
Glen Serra
Publications manager
Mike Ringering
Public relations assistant
Phil Civins
Trainer
Dave Pursley
Assistant trainer
Jeff Porter
Club physician
Dr. David T. Watson

Associate physicians
Dr. John Cantwell
Dr. Robert Crow
Club orthopedist
Dr. Joe Chandler
Scouts
Mike Arbuckle
Butch Baccala
Ray Belanger
Sonny Bowers
Bart Braun
James Buchert
Stu Cann
Joe Caputo
Bill Clark
Roy Clark
Ray Corbett
Harold Cronin
Bob Dunning
Rob English
John Flannery
Ralph Garr
Steve Givens
Pedro Gonzalez
John Hagemann
Bob Isabelle
Jim Johnson
Dean Jongewaard
Steve Jongewaard
Brian Kohlscheen
Deric Ladnier
Bill Lajoie
Scott Littlefield
Gerardo Lopez
Robert Lucas
Robyn Lynch
Scott Nethery
Ernie Pederson
Rolando Petit
Julian Perez
Jack Pierce
Rance Pless
Carlos Rios
Fred Shaffer
Alex Smith
Charlie Smith
Paul Snyder
Ted Sparks
John Stewart
Tony Stiel
Bob Turzilli
Wes Westrum
Bill Wight
Dave Wilder
Don Williams
Bobby Wine

SCHEDULE KEY

H—Home game.   N—Night game (any game starting after 5 p.m.).
*All-Star Game at Oriole Park at Camden Yards, Baltimore.

Manager—Bobby Cox (6).
Coaches—Jim Beauchamp (37), Pat Corrales (39), Clarence Jones (28), Leo Mazzone (54), Jimy Williams (22).

No.	PITCHERS	B/T	Ht./Wt.	Born	1992 clubs
33	Avery, Steve	L/L	6-4/190	4-14-70	Atlanta
57	Bark, Brian	L/L	5-9/160	8-26-68	Greenville, Richmond
51	Borbon, Pedro	L/L	6-1/205	11-15-67	Greenville, Atlanta
48	Davis, Mark	L/L	6-4/210	10-19-60	Kansas City, Atlanta
62	Elliott, Donnie	R/R	6-4/190	9-20-68	Clearwater, Reading, Greenville
40	Freeman, Marvin	R/R	6-7/222	4-10-63	Atlanta
47	Glavine, Tom	L/L	6-1/190	3-25-66	Atlanta
55	Holman, Shawn	R/R	6-1/200	11-10-64	Nuevo Laredo
31	Maddux, Greg	R/R	6-0/175	4-14-66	Chicago N.L.
50	Mercker, Kent	L/L	6-2/195	2-1-68	Atlanta
63	Murray, Matt	L/R	6-6/210	9-26-70	DID NOT PLAY
59	Potts, Michael	L/L	5-9/170	9-5-70	Durham
25	Smith, Pete	R/R	6-2/200	2-27-66	Richmond, Atlanta
29	Smoltz, John	R/R	6-3/185	5-15-67	Atlanta
30	Stanton, Mike	L/L	6-1/190	6-2-67	Atlanta
43	Wohlers, Mark	R/R	6-4/207	1-23-70	Richmond, Atlanta

No.	CATCHERS	B/T	Ht./Wt.	Born	1992 clubs
11	Berryhill, Damon	B/R	6-0/205	12-3-63	Atlanta
19	Cabrera, Francisco	R/R	6-4/193	10-10-66	Atlanta, Richmond
61	Houston, Tyler	L/R	6-2/210	1-17-71	Durham
8	Lopez, Javier	R/R	6-3/185	11-5-70	Greenville, Atlanta
10	Olson, Greg	R/R	6-0/200	9-6-60	Atlanta

No.	INFIELDERS	B/T	Ht./Wt.	Born	1992 clubs
2	Belliard, Rafael	R/R	5-6/160	10-24-61	Atlanta
4	Blauser, Jeff	R/R	6-0/170	11-8-65	Atlanta
12	Bream, Sid	L/L	6-4/220	8-3-60	Atlanta
65	Caraballo, Ramon	B/R	5-7/150	5-23-69	Greenville, Richmond
14	Hunter, Brian	R/R	6-0/195	3-4-68	Atlanta
18	Klesko, Ryan	L/L	6-3/220	6-12-71	Richmond, Atlanta
20	Lemke, Mark	B/R	5-9/167	8-13-65	Atlanta
45	Oliva, Jose	R/R	6-1/150	3-3-71	Tulsa
32	Pecota, Bill	R/R	6-2/195	2-16-60	New York N.L.
9	Pendleton, Terry	B/R	5-9/195	7-16-60	Atlanta
72	Roa, Hector	B/R	5-11/170	6-11-69	Durham, Greenville

No.	OUTFIELDERS	B/T	Ht./Wt.	Born	1992 clubs
5	Gant, Ron	R/R	6-0/172	3-2-65	Atlanta
66	Hughes, Troy	R/R	6-4/195	1-3-71	Durham
23	Justice, David	L/L	6-3/200	4-14-66	Atlanta
17	Mitchell, Keith	R/R	5-10/180	8-6-69	Richmond
7	Nieves, Melvin	B/R	6-2/186	12-28-71	Durham, Greenville, Atlanta
1	Nixon, Otis	B/R	6-2/180	1-9-59	Atlanta
24	Sanders, Deion	L/L	6-1/195	8-9-67	Atlanta
70	Tarasco, Tony	L/R	6-0/185	12-9-70	Greenville

Ballpark (capacity, surface)
Atlanta-Fulton County Stadium
(52,709, grass)
Address
P.O. Box 4064
Atlanta, GA 30302
Business phone
404-522-7630
Ticket information
404-522-7630
Ticket prices
$15 (club level)
$12 (field level)
$10 (lower pavilion)
$9 (upper level)
$4 (upper pavilion)
$1 (g.a., children under 12)
Field dimensions (from home plate)
To left field at foul line, 330 feet
To center field, 402 feet
To right field at foul line, 330 feet
First game played
April 12, 1966 (Pirates 3, Braves 2)

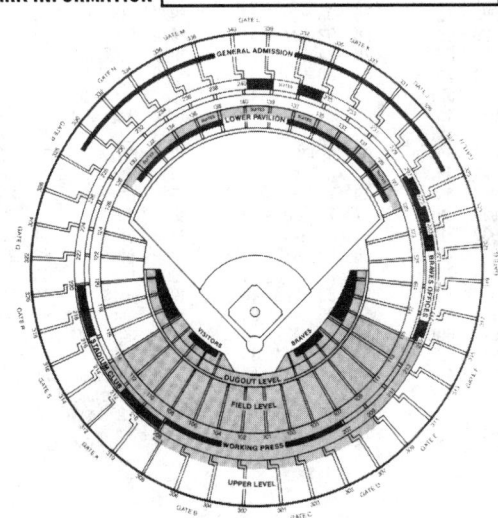

Class	Team	League	Manager
AAA	Richmond	International	Grady Little
AA	Greenville	Southern	Bruce Kimm
A	Durham	Carolina	Leon Roberts
A	Macon	South Atlantic	Randy Ingle
Rookie	Danville	Appalachian	Bruce Benedict
Rookie	Idaho Falls	Pioneer	Paul Runge
Rookie	Gulf Coast Braves	Gulf Coast	Jim Saul

BROADCAST INFORMATION

Radio: WGST-AM (640). Broadcasters: Skip Caray, Don Sutton, Pete Van Wieren, Joe Simpson. WPCH-FM (94.9). Broadcasters: Skip Caray, Don Sutton, Pete Van Wieren, Joe Simpson. **TV:** TBS-TV (Channel 17). Broadcasters: Skip Caray, Don Sutton, Pete Van Wieren, Joe Simpson. **Cable TV:** SportsSouth. Broadcasters: Chip Caray, Ernie Johnson.

SPRING TRAINING

Ballpark (city): Municipal Stadium (West Palm Beach, Fla.). **Ticket information:** 407-683-6100.

HISTORY

YEAR-BY-YEAR RECORDS

Year	Pos.	W	L	Pct.	*GB	Year	Pos.	W	L	Pct.	*GB
1901	5th	69	69	.500	20½	1950	4th	83	71	.539	8
1902	3rd	73	64	.533	29	1951	4th	76	78	.494	20½
1903	6th	58	80	.420	32	1952	7th	64	89	.418	32
1904	7th	55	98	.359	51	1953	2nd	92	62	.597	13
1905	7th	51	103	.331	54½	1954	3rd	89	65	.578	8
1906	8th	49	102	.325	66½	1955	2nd	85	69	.552	13½
1907	7th	58	90	.392	47	1956	2nd	92	62	.597	1
1908	6th	63	91	.409	36	1957	1st	95	59	.617	+8
1909	8th	45	108	.294	65½	1958	1st	92	62	.597	+8
1910	8th	53	100	.346	50½	1959	T2nd	86	70	.551	2
1911	8th	44	107	.291	54	1960	2nd	88	66	.571	7
1912	8th	52	101	.340	52	1961	4th	83	71	.539	10
1913	5th	69	82	.457	31½	1962	5th	86	76	.531	15½
1914	1st	94	59	.614	+10½	1963	6th	84	78	.519	15
1915	2nd	83	69	.546	7	1964	5th	88	74	.543	5
1916	3rd	89	63	.586	4	1965	5th	86	76	.531	11
1917	6th	72	81	.471	25½	1966	5th	85	77	.525	10
1918	7th	53	71	.427	28½	1967	7th	77	85	.475	24½
1919	6th	57	82	.410	38½	1968	5th	81	81	.500	16
1920	7th	62	90	.408	30	1969	1st†	93	69	.574	+ 3
1921	4th	79	74	.516	15	1970	5th	76	86	.469	26
1922	8th	53	100	.346	39½	1971	3rd	82	80	.506	8
1923	7th	54	100	.351	41½	1972	4th	70	84	.455	25
1924	8th	53	100	.346	40	1973	5th	76	85	.472	22½
1925	5th	70	83	.458	25	1974	3rd	88	74	.543	14
1926	7th	66	86	.434	22	1975	5th	67	94	.416	40½
1927	7th	60	94	.390	34	1976	6th	70	92	.432	32
1928	7th	50	103	.327	44½	1977	6th	61	101	.377	37
1929	8th	56	98	.364	43	1978	6th	69	93	.426	26
1930	6th	70	84	.455	22	1979	6th	66	94	.413	23½
1931	7th	64	90	.416	37	1980	4th	81	80	.503	11
1932	5th	77	77	.500	13	1981	4th/5th	50	56	.472	‡
1933	4th	83	71	.539	9	1982	1st†	89	73	.549	+ 1
1934	4th	78	73	.517	16	1983	2nd	88	74	.543	3
1935	8th	38	115	.248	61½	1984	T2nd	80	82	.494	12
1936	6th	71	83	.461	21	1985	5th	66	96	.407	29
1937	5th	79	73	.520	16	1986	6th	72	89	.447	23½
1938	5th	77	75	.507	12	1987	5th	69	92	.429	20½
1939	7th	63	88	.417	32½	1988	6th	54	106	.338	39½
1940	7th	65	87	.428	34½	1989	6th	63	97	.394	28
1941	7th	62	92	.403	38	1990	6th	65	97	.401	26
1942	7th	59	89	.399	44	1991	1st§	94	68	.580	+ 1
1943	6th	68	85	.444	36½	1992	1st§	98	64	.605	+ 8
1944	6th	65	89	.422	40						
1945	6th	67	85	.441	30						
1946	4th	81	72	.529	15½						
1947	3rd	86	68	.558	8						
1948	1st	91	62	.595	+6½						
1949	4th	75	79	.487	22						

*Games behind winner. †Lost Championship Series. ‡First half 25-29; second 25-27. §Won Championship Series.

MANAGERS

Name	Record	Years
Frank Selee	69-69	1901
Al Buckenberger	186-242	'02-04
Fred Tenney	202-402	'05-07
		1911
Joe Kelley	63-91	1908
Frank Bowerman	23-55	1909
Harry Smith	22-53	1909
Fred Lake	53-100	1910
Johnny Kling	52-101	1912
George Stallings	579-597	'13-20
Fred Mitchell	186-274	'21-23
Dave Bancroft	249-363	'24-27
Jack Slattery	11-20	1928
Rogers Hornsby	39-83	1928
Emil Fuchs	56-98	1929
Bill McKechnie	560-666	'30-37
Casey Stengel	394-516	'38-43
Bob Coleman	107-140	'44-45
Del Bissonette	25-34	1945
Billy Southworth	424-358	'46-51
Tommy Holmes	61-69	'51-52
Charlie Grimm	341-285	'52-56
Fred Haney	341-231	'56-59
Chuck Dressen	159-124	'60-61
Birdie Tebbetts	98-89	'61-62
Bobby Bragan	310-287	'63-66
Billy Hitchcock	110-100	'66-67
Ken Silvestri	0-3	1967
Lum Harris	379-373	'68-72
Eddie Mathews	149-161	'72-74
Clyde King	96-101	'74-75
Connie Ryan	9-18	1975
Dave Bristol	131-192	'76-77
Ted Turner	0-1	1977
Bobby Cox	498-512	'78-81
		'90-92
Joe Torre	257-229	'82-84
Eddie Haas	50-71	1985
Bobby Wine	16-25	1985
Chuck Tanner	153-208	'86-88
Russ Nixon	130-216	'88-90

DAY BY DAY

Date	Opp.	Res.	Score	(inn.*)	Hits	Opp. hits	Winning pitcher	Losing pitcher	Save	Record	Pos.	GB
4-7	At Hou.	W	2-0		7	2	Glavine	Harnisch		1-0	1st	+½
4-8	At Hou.	W	3-1		8	5	Smoltz	Kile	Pena	2-0	1st	+½
4-9	S.F.	L	4-11		8	15	Heredia	Avery		2-1	T1st	...
4-10	S.F.	W	5-3		8	9	Leibrandt	Burba	Stanton	3-1	1st	+½
4-11	S.F.	L	0-3		6	6	Swift	Bielecki		3-2	T2nd	½
4-12	S.F.	W	6-2		12	8	Glavine	Downs		4-2	2nd	½
4-13	At Cin.	L	4-5		9	7	Belcher	Smoltz	Charlton	4-3	2nd	1
4-14	At Cin.	L	4-5		7	6	Bankhead	Freeman		4-4	3rd	2
4-15	At Cin.	L	1-3		4	8	Hammond	Leibrandt	Charlton	4-5	T3rd	3
4-16	At L.A.	W	3-0		10	2	Bielecki	Ke. Gross		5-5	3rd	2
4-17	At L.A.	L	5-7		7	12	McDowell	Pena		5-6	5th	2
4-18	At L.A.	L	3-7		8	10	McDowell	Stanton		5-7	T5th	2
4-19	At L.A.	L	2-4		7	8	Candiotti	Avery		5-8	6th	2½
4-20	At S.D.	W	10-4		13	13	Freeman	Lefferts		6-8	T5th	2½
4-21	At S.D.	L	2-4		5	11	Rodriguez	Bielecki	Myers	6-9	6th	2½
4-22	At S.D.	L	4-9		7	15	Hurst	Glavine		6-10	6th	3½
4-24	Hou.	L	2-4		5	7	Kile	Smoltz	D. Jones	6-11	6th	4½
4-25	Hou.	W	2-0		5	4	Avery	Portugal		7-11	6th	3½
4-26	Hou.	W	3-2		9	8	Freeman	Harnisch	Pena	8-11	6th	2½
4-27	Chi.	W	5-0		7	2	Glavine	Boskie		9-11	T5th	2
4-28	Chi.	W	1-0		3	3	Leibrandt	Castillo	Pena	10-11	5th	1½
4-29	Chi.	W	8-0		12	7	Smoltz	Jackson		11-11	T4th	1
5-1	N.Y.	L	7-8		11	12	Burke	Berenguer	Franco	11-12	5th	1½
5-2	N.Y.	W	3-0		9	9	Glavine	Gooden		12-12	4th	1½
5-3	N.Y.	L	0-7		5	8	Cone	Leibrandt		12-13	5th	1½
5-4	At Chi.	W	6-1		12	5	Smoltz	Castillo		13-13	T3rd	1
5-5	At Chi.	L	3-4	(10)	9	7	McElroy	Pena		13-14	T4th	1
5-6	At Pit.	L	3-4	(16)	12	16	Patterson	Rivera		13-15	T4th	1½
5-7	At Pit.	W	4-2		10	8	Glavine	Neagle	Stanton	14-15	3rd	1½
5-8	At St.L.	W	2-1		9	7	Leibrandt	Tewksbury	Freeman	15-15	3rd	1½
5-9	At St.L.	L	11-12		13	15	Perez	Freeman	L. Smith	15-16	4th	1½
5-10	At St.L.	L	5-6		11	12	Agosto	Pena		15-17	4th	2½
5-11	At St.L.	L	3-8		9	13	DeLeon	Avery		15-18	5th	3
5-12	Pit.	W	4-2		10	6	Glavine	Tomlin	Freeman	16-18	4th	3
5-13	Pit.	L	10-11		15	21	Belinda	Pena		16-19	4th	4
5-14	Pit.	L	3-4		10	7	Palacios	Smoltz	Mason	16-20	4th	4½
5-15	Mon.	W	4-2		7	6	Mercker	Nabholz	Stanton	17-20	4th	3½
5-16	Mon.	L	1-7		6	11	Martinez	Avery	Rojas	17-21	4th	4½
5-17	Mon.	L	4-5		6	9	Hill	Glavine	Wetteland	17-22	4th	4½
5-18	St.L.	W	5-1		12	6	Leibrandt	Osborne		18-22	4th	4
5-19	St.L.	L	2-7		8	11	Tewksbury	Smoltz		18-23	4th	5
5-20	St.L.	W	6-3		10	5	Avery	Cormier		19-23	4th	5
5-22	At Mon.	L	1-7		2	9	Martinez	Glavine		19-24	4th	6½
5-23	At Mon.	L	6-7		13	14	Fassero	Stanton	Wetteland	19-25	4th	6½
5-24	At Mon.	W	2-1		7	6	Smoltz	Gardner		20-25	4th	5½
5-25	At Phi.	L	1-4		6	6	Mulholland	Avery	Mit. Williams	20-26	4th	6
5-26	At Phi.	L	2-5		2	11	Robinson	Bielecki	Mit. Williams	20-27	6th	7
5-27	At Phi.	W	9-3		15	7	Glavine	Brantley		21-27	5th	7
5-29	At N.Y.	W	5-1		10	7	Smoltz	Gooden		22-27	5th	5½
5-30	At N.Y.	W	6-1		14	6	Avery	Cone		23-27	5th	5
6-1	Phi.	W	7-6		11	9	Glavine	Brantley	Wohlers	24-27	5th	4
6-2	Phi.	W	5-3		10	11	Stanton	Mit. Williams		25-27	5th	4
6-3	Phi.	L	1-4		7	9	Schilling	Smoltz	Mit. Williams	25-28	5th	5
6-5	At S.D.	W	3-2		8	7	Berenguer	Lefferts	Wohlers	26-28	4th	4½
6-6	At S.D.	W	5-1		15	2	Glavine	Benes		27-28	4th	4½
6-7	At S.D.	W	9-4		10	6	Smoltz	Seminara		28-28	4th	3½
6-8	At L.A.	W	4-2		7	8	Leibrandt	R. Martinez		29-28	4th	3½
6-9	At L.A.	L	2-3		5	6	Hershiser	Stanton	McDowell	29-29	4th	4½
6-10	At L.A.	W	2-1		6	6	Avery	Ke. Gross	Stanton	30-29	4th	3½
6-12	S.D.	W	6-4		12	10	Berenguer	Maddux	Stanton	31-29	2nd	3½
6-13	S.D.	W	4-2		10	6	Smoltz	Seminara		32-29	4th	3½
6-14	S.D.	W	4-2		12	7	Leibrandt	Hurst	Wohlers	33-29	T3rd	3½
6-15	L.A.	W	2-0		4	5	Avery	Hershiser		34-29	2nd	3½
6-16	L.A.	W	9-8		12	10	Berenguer	Candelaria		35-29	2nd	3½
6-17	L.A.	W	4-3		8	5	Glavine	Ojeda		36-29	2nd	3½
6-18	Cin.	L	5-7	(10)	10	9	Bankhead	Stanton	Charlton	36-30	2nd	4½
6-19	Cin.	W	3-2	(10)	6	9	Mercker	Henry		37-30	2nd	3½
6-20	Cin.	W	2-1		9	11	Avery	Browning	Mercker	38-30	2nd	2½
6-21	Cin.	W	2-0		9	6	Bielecki	Rijo	Mercker	39-30	2nd	1½
6-23	S.F.	W	7-0		17	5	Glavine	Burkett		40-30	2nd	1

Date	Opp.	Res.	Score (inn.*)	Hits	Opp. hits	Winning pitcher	Losing pitcher	Save	Record	Pos.	GB
6-24	S.F.	W	5-0	7	2	Smoltz	Wilson		41-30	2nd	1
6-26	At Cin.	L	4-7	7	9	Browning	Avery		41-31	2nd	2
6-27	At Cin.	L	3-12	6	12	Rijo	Leibrandt		41-32	2nd	3
6-28	At Cin.	L	5-6	7	6	Charlton	Wohlers		41-33	2nd	4
6-30	At S.F.	W	4-3	7	8	Smoltz	Wilson		42-33	2nd	2½
7-1	At S.F.	L	1-2	6	5	Black	Avery	Beck	42-34	2nd	2½
7-3	Chi.	W	3-0	9	5	Glavine	Boskie		43-34	2nd	3
7-4	Chi.	W	4-2	6	7	Leibrandt	Jackson	Mercker	44-34	2nd	3
7-5	Chi.	L	0-8	6	10	Maddux	Smoltz		44-35	2nd	4
7-6	N.Y.	L	1-3	4	9	Cone	Freeman	Guetterman	44-36	2nd	5
7-7	N.Y.	L	4-5	5	8	Fernandez	Bielecki	Young	44-37	2nd	6
7-8	N.Y.	W	2-1	6	10	Glavine	Whitehurst	Pena	45-37	2nd	5
7-9	At Chi.	W	2-0 (12)	7	3	Stanton	Bullinger	Pena	46-37	2nd	5
7-10	At Chi.	W	4-0	10	4	Smoltz	Maddux		47-37	2nd	4
7-11	At Chi.	W	3-1	9	4	Avery	Scanlan	Pena	48-37	2nd	3
7-12	At Chi.	W	7-4 (10)	11	14	Mercker	Assenmacher	Pena	49-37	2nd	2
7-16	At Hou.	W	4-2	9	8	Avery	Williams	Pena	50-37	2nd	1
7-17	At Hou.	W	5-0	8	5	Smoltz	Harnisch		51-37	2nd	1
7-18	At Hou.	W	3-0	10	6	Glavine	J. Jones	Pena	52-37	2nd	1
7-19	At Hou.	W	3-2 (10)	9	6	Freeman	Hernandez	Pena	53-37	2nd	1
7-21	At St.L.	W	9-7 (12)	13	13	Pena	Perez		54-37	2nd	½
7-22	At St.L.	W	2-0	7	7	Smoltz	Olivares	Mercker	55-37	1st	+½
7-24	Pit.	W	4-3	7	4	Glavine	Walk	Pena	56-37	1st	+2
7-25	Pit.	W	1-0	1	5	Leibrandt	Jackson	Mercker	57-37	1st	+2
7-26	Pit.	L	4-5	8	9	Belinda	Wohlers		57-38	1st	+1
7-27	Hou.	L	1-5 (11)	8	12	D. Jones	Pena		57-39	1st	+1
7-28	Hou.	L	5-7	7	12	Harnisch	Freeman	D. Jones	57-40	1st	...
7-29	Hou.	W	5-3	9	9	Glavine	Blair	Pena	58-40	1st	+1
7-30	At S.F.	L	0-5	4	11	Burkett	Leibrandt		58-41	1st	+½
7-31	At S.F.	L	3-4	10	6	Jackson	Mercker		58-42	2nd	½
8-1	At S.F.	W	5-3	11	9	Smoltz	Black		59-42	2nd	½
8-2 (1)	At S.F.	W	3-0	6	5	Smith	Swift	Pena	60-42	1st	+½
8-2 (2)	At S.F.	W	8-5	11	10	Reynoso	Hickerson	Freeman	61-42	1st	+1
8-4	Cin.	W	7-5	7	11	Freeman	Charlton		62-42	1st	+1½
8-5	Cin.	W	5-1	9	10	Avery	Belcher		63-42	1st	+2½
8-6	Cin.	W	5-3	10	6	Smoltz	Swindell		64-42	1st	+3½
8-7	L.A.	W	6-2	10	6	Leibrandt	Ke. Gross		65-42	1st	+3½
8-8	L.A.	W	12-2	18	9	Smith	Candiotti		66-42	1st	+3½
8-9	L.A.	W	10-3	11	7	Glavine	Hershiser		67-42	1st	+4½
8-10	L.A.	L	3-5	6	15	R. Martinez	Avery	Gott	67-43	1st	+4
8-11	S.D.	L	4-8	8	12	Hurst	Smoltz	Maddux	67-44	1st	+4
8-13	S.D.	W	4-3	6	9	Davis	Andersen		68-44	1st	+4½
8-14	At Pit.	W	15-0	22	6	Glavine	Smith		69-44	1st	+5½
8-15	At Pit.	W	7-5	9	12	Avery	Jackson	Pena	70-44	1st	+5½
8-16	At Pit.	L	2-4	7	7	Wakefield	Smoltz		70-45	1st	+4½
8-17	At Pit.	W	5-4 (10)	12	5	Freeman	Patterson	Pena	71-45	1st	+5
8-18	At Mon.	W	5-1	9	4	Leibrandt	Hill		72-45	1st	+5½
8-19	At Mon.	W	4-2	7	7	Glavine	Nabholz	Stanton	73-45	1st	+6½
8-20	At Mon.	L	2-3	7	8	Fassero	Pena		73-46	1st	+6
8-21	St.L.	L	2-5 (10)	7	10	Perez	Mercker	L. Smith	73-47	1st	+6
8-22	St.L.	W	3-2	6	4	Smith	Clark		74-47	1st	+7
8-23	St.L.	L	3-8	11	13	Olivares	Leibrandt		74-48	1st	+6
8-25	Mon.	L	0-6	8	10	Nabholz	Glavine		74-49	1st	+4½
8-26	Mon.	L	4-5	7	13	Martinez	Avery	Wetteland	74-50	1st	+3½
8-28	At Phi.	L	3-7	7	7	Mulholland	Smoltz		74-51	1st	+4
8-29	At Phi.	W	7-6	13	7	Leibrandt	Schilling	Mercker	75-51	1st	+5
8-30	At Phi.	L	2-10	5	12	Rivera	Glavine		75-52	1st	+5
8-31 (1)	At N.Y.	W	8-6 (14)	15	9	Wohlers	Guetterman	Stanton	76-52	1st	+6
8-31 (2)	At N.Y.	W	7-5	12	13	Smith	Birkbeck	Reardon	77-52	1st	+6½
9-1	At N.Y.	W	4-1	9	8	Nied	Whitehurst	Reardon	78-52	1st	+7½
9-2	At N.Y.	L	5-6	11	9	Schourek	Smoltz	Young	78-53	1st	+7½
9-3	Mon.	L	2-11	7	14	Barnes	Leibrandt	Bottenfield	78-54	1st	+6½
9-4	Phi.	L	1-2	4	6	Schilling	Glavine	Mit. Williams	78-55	1st	+6½
9-5	Phi.	W	6-5	9	7	Reardon	Mit. Williams		79-55	1st	+6½
9-6	Phi.	W	4-3	6	12	Reardon	Hartley		80-55	1st	+6½
9-7	L.A.	W	7-1	16	5	Smoltz	Astacio		81-55	1st	+6½
9-8	L.A.	W	7-5	10	13	Freeman	Crews	Reardon	82-55	1st	+7½
9-9	Cin.	W	12-5	11	11	Glavine	Belcher		83-55	1st	+8½
9-10	Cin.	W	3-2	6	6	Stanton	Bankhead		84-55	1st	+9
9-11	At Hou.	W	7-0	13	4	Smith	Kile		85-55	1st	+9½
9-12	At Hou.	W	9-3	11	10	Nied	Williams		86-55	1st	+9½
9-13	At Hou.	W	9-2	10	7	Leibrandt	Harnisch		87-55	1st	+10½
9-15	At Cin.	L	2-4	4	7	Belcher	Avery	Dibble	87-56	1st	+9½
9-16	At Cin.	W	3-2	5	10	Stanton	Ruskin	Wohlers	88-56	1st	+10½

Date		Opp.	Res.	Score	(inn.*)	Hits	Opp. hits	Winning pitcher	Losing pitcher	Save	Record	Pos.	GB
9-17		At Cin.	L	2-3		6	9	Rijo	Smoltz	Foster	88-57	1st	+9 ½
9-18		Hou.	L	3-13		8	18	Harnisch	Leibrandt		88-58	1st	+8 ½
9-19		Hou.	L	2-3	(12)	10	8	D. Jones	Freeman		88-59	1st	+7 ½
9-20		Hou.	W	16-1		15	7	Avery	Bowen		89-59	1st	+7 ½
9-21		At L.A.	L	4-2		7	6	Smith	Hershiser	Stanton	90-59	1st	+8
9-22		At L.A.	L	1-4		5	7	Candiotti	Smoltz		90-60	1st	+6 ½
9-23		At S.F.	W	7-0		13	6	Leibrandt	Black		91-60	1st	+6 ½
9-24		At S.F.	L	0-4		3	7	Brantley	Glavine		91-61	1st	+5 ½
9-25		At S.D.	L	0-1		6	7	Gr. Harris	Avery	Myers	91-62	1st	+4 ½
9-26		At S.D.	W	2-1	(10)	9	3	Stanton	Rodriguez		92-62	1st	+5 ½
9-27		At S.D.	W	2-1	(10)	8	6	Reardon	Myers		93-62	1st	+5 ½
9-29		S.F.	W	6-0		8	8	Leibrandt	Black		94-62	1st	+6 ½
9-30		S.F.	L	0-1		5	6	Brantley	Glavine	Beck	94-63	1st	+5 ½
10-1		S.F.	W	6-5	(10)	11	8	Freeman	Jackson		95-63	1st	+6 ½
10-2	(1)	S.D.	W	4-1		7	4	Nied	Benes		96-63	1st	+7 ½
10-2	(2)	S.D.	W	7-2		10	10	Smith	Deshaies		97-63	1st	+8
10-3		S.D.	W	1-0	(5 ½)	3	4	Leibrandt	Maddux	Reynoso	98-63	1st	+8
10-4		S.D.	L	3-4	(12)	7	8	Myers	Borbon		98-64	1st	+8

Monthly records: April (11-11), May (12-16), June (19-6), July (16-9), August (19-10), September (17-11), Oct. (4-1).

HIGHLIGHTS

High point: From May 27-August 2, the Braves won 41 of 56 games to move from last place (seven games out) into first place (half-game lead) for good.

Low point: Before that stretch, Atlanta had lost 27 of its first 47 games and appeared to be falling out of the race.

Turning point: In May, when Manager Bobby Cox benched right fielder David Justice and center fielder Ron Gant and played Otis Nixon and Deion Sanders together in center and right field, respectively, for the first time. The two speedsters at the top of the batting order sparked the team.

Most valuable player: Third baseman Terry Pendleton. He proved that his 1991 N.L. MVP award was no fluke, batting .311 with 21 homers and a career-high 105 RBIs.

Most valuable pitcher: Lefthander Tom Glavine. He registered 20 wins for the second straight season, posting a team-record-tying 13-game winning streak in the process.

Most improved player: Shortstop Jeff Blauser. Despite hitting a career-high 14 homers, it was his defense that was particularly impressive. As a regular during the second half of the season, he proved to be a steady fielder.

Most pleasant surprise: Righthander Pete Smith. After replacing injured righthander Mike Bielecki in the rotation August 2, he recorded seven straight wins and a 2.05 ERA.

Biggest disappointment: Gant. After posting consecutive 32-homer seasons, he collected just 17 homers and 80 RBIs. Those are decent numbers, but they aren't the stats of a rising star.

Key injuries: Bielecki (elbow), righthander Alejandro Pena (elbow) and catcher Greg Olson, who broke a leg and dislocated an ankle in a home-plate collision, saw their seasons end in late July, late August and mid-September, respectively.

Notable: The Braves tied a franchise record by winning 13 consecutive games from July 8-25 and set a modern-day team record with 98 wins.

...Atlanta led the league in attendance with a franchise-record 3,077,400 fans.... The pitching staff led the majors with a club-record 24 shutouts.... Blauser became the fourth shortstop in major league history to hit three homers in a game when he victimized the Cubs on July 12 in Chicago.

—BILL ZACK

RECORDS

1992 regular-season record: 98-64 (1st in N.L. West); 51-30 at home; 47-34 on road; 40-32 vs. East; 58-32 vs. West; 34-17 vs. LHP; 64-47 vs. RHP; 76-44 on grass; 22-20 on turf; 27-18 in daytime; 71-46 at night; 28-26 in one-run games; 10-7 in extra-inning games; 3-0-0 in doubleheaders.

1992 postseason record: Defeated Pirates, 4 games to 3, in N.L. playoffs; lost to Blue Jays, 4 games to 2, in World Series.

Team record last five years: 374-432 (.464, ranks 11th in league in that span).

TEAM LEADERS

Batting average: Terry Pendleton (.311).
At-bats: Terry Pendleton (640).
Runs: Terry Pendleton (98).
Hits: Terry Pendleton (199).
Total bases: Terry Pendleton (303).
Doubles: Terry Pendleton (39).
Triples: Deion Sanders (14).
Home runs: David Justice, Terry Pendleton (21).
Runs batted in: Terry Pendleton (105).
Stolen bases: Otis Nixon (41).
Slugging percentage: Terry Pendleton (.473).
On-base percentage: David Justice (.359).
Wins: Tom Glavine (20).
Earned-run average: Tom Glavine (2.76).
Complete games: John Smoltz (9).
Shutouts: Tom Glavine (5).
Saves: Alejandro Pena (15).
Innings pitched: John Smoltz (246⅔).
Strikeouts: John Smoltz (215).

GAMES BY POSITION

Catcher: Greg Olson 94, Damon Berryhill 84, Javier Lopez 9, Francisco Cabrera 1, Jerry Willard 1.
First base: Sid Bream 120, Brian Hunter 92, Ryan Klesko 5.
Second base: Mark Lemke 145, Jeff Treadway 45, Jeff Blauser 21, Steve Lyons 2, Rafael Belliard 1.
Third base: Terry Pendleton 158, Mark Lemke 13, Vinny Castilla 4, Jeff Blauser 1, Jeff Treadway 1.
Shortstop: Rafael Belliard 139, Jeff Blauser 106, Vinny Castilla 4.
Outfield: Ron Gant 147, David Justice 140, Otis Nixon 111, Deion Sanders 75, Lonnie Smith 35, Tommy Gregg 9, Brian Hunter 6, Steve Lyons 6, Mel Nieves 6.

TOP 10 DRAFT CHOICES

1. **Jamie Arnold,** RHP, Kissimmee-Osceola High School, Kissimmee, Fla.
2. **Jamie Howard,** RHP, St. Thomas More High School, Lafayette, La.
3. **Carey Paige,** RHP, Cooper High School, Abilene, Tex.
4. **Damon Hollins,** OF, Vallejo (Calif.) High School.
5. **Sean Smith,** C, Oconomowoc (Wis.) High School.
6. **Justin Atcheley,** LHP, Walla Walla (Wash.) High School.
7. **Ken Warner,** SS, St. Helena Central High School, Greensburg, La.
8. **Maurice Christmas,** RHP, Lexington (Mass.) Christian Academy.
9. **Anthony Diieso,** OF, Copiague (N.Y.) High School.
10. **Brad Clontz,** RHP, Virginia Tech University.

CHICAGO CUBS
NATIONAL LEAGUE EAST DIVISION

1993 SCHEDULE

APRIL

SUN	MON	TUE	WED	THU	FRI	SAT
				1	2	3
4	5 ATL H	6 ATL H	7 ATL H	8	9 PHI	10 PHI N
11 PHI	12 ATL N	13 ATL N	14 ATL N	15	16 PHI H	17 PHI H
18 PHI H	19 HOU N	20 HOU N	21 HOU H	22	23 CIN H	24 CIN H
25 CIN N	26 COL H	27 COL N	28 HOU N	29 HOU N	30 CIN	

MAY

SUN	MON	TUE	WED	THU	FRI	SAT
						1 CIN
2 CIN	3	4 COL N	5 COL H	6	7 SD H	8 SD H
9 SD H	10 LA N	11 LA N	12 LA N	13	14 PIT H	15 PIT H
16 PIT H	17	18 STL N	19 STL N	20 STL N	21 FLA	22 FLA N
23 FLA	24	25 SF H	26 SF H	27 SF H	28 MON H	29 MON H
30 MON H	31 NY H					

JUNE

SUN	MON	TUE	WED	THU	FRI	SAT
		1 NY N	2 NY H	3 MON N	4 MON N	5 MON N
6 MON N	7 NY N	8 NY N	9 NY N	10	11 SF N	12 SF N
13 SF	14 FLA H	15 FLA H	16 FLA H	17	18 STL N	19 STL N
20 STL H	21 PIT	22 PIT N	23 PIT N	24	25 LA N	26 LA N
27 LA	28 SD N	29 SD N	30 SD N			

JULY

SUN	MON	TUE	WED	THU	FRI	SAT
				1	2 COL N	3 COL N
4 COL	5 COL	6 CIN N	7 CIN H	8 CIN H	9 HOU H	10 HOU H
11 HOU H	12	13 ★ ALL-STAR GAME	14	15 COL H	16 COL H	17 COL H
18 COL H	19 CIN	20 CIN N	21 CIN N	22 HOU N	23 HOU N	24 HOU N
25 HOU	26 SD N	27 SD H	28 SD H	29	30 LA N	31 LA H

AUGUST

SUN	MON	TUE	WED	THU	FRI	SAT
1 LA	2 PIT H	3 PIT H	4 PIT H	5 PIT H	6 STL N	7 STL H
8 STL H	9 FLA N	10 FLA N	11 FLA N	12 SF H	13 SF H	14 SF H
15 SF H	16	17 MON N	18 MON N	19 MON H	20 ATL H	21 ATL H
22 ATL N	23 MON H	24 MON N	25 MON H	26	27 ATL H	28 ATL
29 ATL	30 PHI N	31 PHI H				

SEPTEMBER

SUN	MON	TUE	WED	THU	FRI	SAT
			1 PHI H	2 NY N	3 NY H	4 NY H
5 NY H	6 PHI H	7 PHI N	8 PHI N	9 PHI N	10 NY N	11 NY H
12 NY H	13 STL N	14 SF N	15 SF H	16	17 FLA H	18 FLA H
19 FLA N	20 STL N	21 STL H	22 STL N	23	24 PIT N	25 PIT N
26 PIT	27 LA N	28 LA N	29 LA N	30		

OCTOBER

SUN	MON	TUE	WED	THU	FRI	SAT
				1 SD N	2 SD N	
3 SD						

SPRING TRAINING ROSTER

Manager—Jim Lefebvre (5).
Coaches—Billy Connors (4), Chuck Cottier (15), Jose Martinez (3), Tony Muser (40), Tom Trebelhorn (41).

No.	PITCHERS	B/T	Ht./Wt.	Born	1992 clubs
45	Assenmacher, Paul	L/L	6-3/210	12-10-60	Chicago N.L.
47	Boskie, Shawn	R/R	6-3/200	3-28-67	Chicago N.L., Iowa
52	Bullinger, Jim	R/R	6-2/185	8-21-65	Iowa, Chicago N.L.
49	Castillo, Frank	R/R	6-1/195	4-1-69	Chicago N.L.
33	Dickson, Lance	R/L	6-1/190	10-19-69	Iowa
42	Guzman, Jose	R/R	6-3/195	4-9-63	Texas
22	Harkey, Mike	R/R	6-5/235	10-25-66	Peoria, Iowa, Charlotte, Chicago N.L.
37	Hibbard, Greg	L/L	6-0/185	9-13-64	Chicago A.L.
32	Hollins, Jessie	R/R	6-3/215	1-27-70	Charlotte, Chicago N.L.
35	McElroy, Chuck	L/L	6-0/195	10-1-67	Chicago N.L.
36	Morgan, Mike	R/R	6-2/220	10-8-59	Chicago N.L.
28	Myers, Randy	L/L	6-1/225	9-19-62	San Diego
48	Plesac, Dan	L/L	6-5/215	2-4-62	Milwaukee
38	Robinson, Jeff D	R/R	6-4/195	12-12-60	Iowa, Chicago N.L.
30	Scanlan, Bob	R/R	6-8/210	8-9-66	Chicago N.L.
51	Slocumb, Heathcliff	R/R	6-3/220	6-7-66	Chicago N.L., Iowa
50	Stevens, Dave	R/R	6-3/210	3-4-70	Charlotte
46	Swartzbaugh, Dave	R/R	6-2/195	2-11-68	Charlotte
43	Wendell, Turk	B/R	6-2/180	5-19-67	Iowa

No.	CATCHERS	B/T	Ht./Wt.	Born	1992 clubs
10	Lake, Steve	R/R	6-1/195	3-14-57	Philadelphia
7	Pedre, George	R/R	6-0/205	10-12-66	Iowa, Chicago N.L.
9	Walbeck, Matt	B/R	5-11/195	10-2-69	Charlotte
2	Wilkins, Rick	L/R	6-2/215	6-4-67	Chicago N.L., Iowa

No.	INFIELDERS	B/T	Ht./Wt.	Born	1992 clubs
24	Buechele, Steve	R/R	6-2/200	9-26-61	Pittsburgh, Chicago N.L.
12	Dunston, Shawon	R/R	6-1/175	3-21-63	Chicago N.L.
17	Grace, Mark	L/L	6-2/190	6-28-64	Chicago N.L.
6	Sanchez, Rey	R/R	5-9/170	10-5-67	Chicago N.L., Iowa
23	Sandberg, Ryne	R/R	6-2/185	9-18-59	Chicago N.L.
1	Shields, Tommy	R/R	6-0/185	8-14-64	Rochester, Baltimore
53	Viera, Jose	R/R	6-1/205	2-23-70	Winston-Salem
16	Vizcaino, Jose	B/R	6-1/180	3-26-68	Chicago N.L.

No.	OUTFIELDERS	B/T	Ht./Wt.	Born	1992 clubs
29	Dauphin, Phil	L/L	6-1/185	5-11-69	Charlotte
25	Maldonado, Candy	R/R	6-0/205	9-5-60	Toronto
27	May, Derrick	L/R	6-4/205	7-14-68	Iowa, Chicago N.L.
39	Ramsey, Fernando	R/R	6-1/175	12-20-65	Iowa, Chicago N.L.
19	Roberson, Kevin	B/R	6-4/210	1-29-68	Iowa
18	Smith, Dwight	L/R	5-11/195	11-8-63	Chicago N.L., Iowa
21	Sosa, Sammy	R/R	6-0/185	11-12-68	Chicago N.L., Iowa
11	Wilson, Willie	B/R	6-3/200	7-9-55	Oakland

BALLPARK INFORMATION

Ballpark (capacity, surface)
Wrigley Field (38,710, grass)
Address
1060 W. Addison St.
Chicago, IL 60613
Business phone
312-404-2827
Ticket information
312-404-2827
Ticket prices
$17 (field box)
$12 (terrace box)
$12 (upper deck box)
$9 (terrace reserved)
$7 (adult upper deck reserved)
$5 (under 14 upper deck reserved)
$7 (bleachers)
All tickets are $1 less for weekday afternoon games
Field dimensions (from home plate)
To left field at foul line, 355 feet
To center field, 400 feet
To right field at foul line, 353 feet
First game played
April 20, 1916 (Cubs 7, Reds 6)

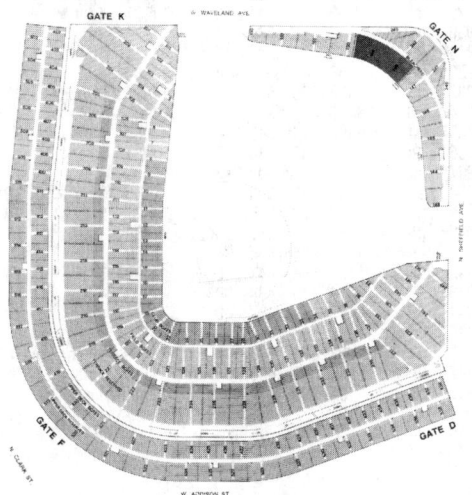

Class	Team	League	Manager
AAA	Iowa	American Association	Marv Foley
AA	Orlando	Southern	Tommy Jones
A	To be announced	Florida State	Bill Hayes
A	Peoria	Midwest	Steve Roadcap
A	Geneva	New York-Pennsylvania	Jerry Weinstein
Rookie	Huntington	Appalachian	Steve Kolinsky
Rookie	Gulf Coast Cubs	Gulf Coast	Butch Hughes

BROADCAST INFORMATION

Radio: WGN-AM (720). Broadcasters: Harry Caray, Thom Brennaman, Ron Santo.
TV: WGN-TV (Channel 9). Broadcasters: Harry Caray, Steve Stone, Thom Brennaman.
Cable TV: WGN subscription cable. Broadcasters: Harry Caray, Steve Stone.

SPRING TRAINING

Ballpark (city): HoHoKam Park (Mesa, Ariz.).
Ticket information: 602-964-4467.

HISTORY

YEAR-BY-YEAR RECORDS

Year	Pos.	W	L	Pct.	*GB	Year	Pos.	W	L	Pct.	*GB
1901	6th	53	86	.381	37	1949	8th	61	93	.396	36
1902	5th	68	69	.496	34	1950	7th	64	89	.418	26½
1903	3rd	82	56	.594	8	1951	8th	62	92	.403	34½
1904	2nd	93	60	.608	13	1952	5th	77	77	.500	19½
1905	3rd	92	61	.601	13	1953	7th	65	89	.422	40
1906	1st	116	36	.763	+20	1954	7th	64	90	.416	33
1907	1st	107	45	.704	+17	1955	6th	72	81	.471	26
1908	1st	99	55	.643	+ 1	1956	8th	60	94	.390	33
1909	2nd	104	49	.680	6½	1957	T7th	62	92	.403	33
1910	1st	104	50	.675	+13	1958	T5th	72	82	.468	20
1911	2nd	92	62	.597	7½	1959	T5th	74	80	.481	13
1912	3rd	91	59	.607	11½	1960	7th	60	94	.390	35
1913	3rd	88	65	.575	13½	1961	7th	64	90	.416	29
1914	4th	78	76	.506	16½	1962	9th	59	103	.364	42½
1915	4th	73	80	.477	17½	1963	7th	82	80	.506	17
1916	5th	67	86	.438	26½	1964	8th	76	86	.469	17
1917	5th	74	80	.481	24	1965	8th	72	90	.444	25
1918	1st	84	45	.651	+10½	1966	10th	59	103	.364	36
1919	3rd	75	65	.536	21	1967	3rd	87	74	.540	14
1920	T5th	75	79	.487	18	1968	3rd	84	78	.519	13
1921	7th	64	89	.418	30	1969	2nd	92	70	.568	8
1922	5th	80	74	.519	13	1970	2nd	84	78	.519	5
1923	4th	83	71	.539	12½	1971	T3rd	83	79	.512	14
1924	5th	81	72	.529	12	1972	2nd	85	70	.548	11
1925	8th	68	86	.442	27½	1973	5th	77	84	.478	5
1926	4th	82	72	.532	7	1974	6th	66	96	.407	22
1927	4th	85	68	.556	8½	1975	T5th	75	87	.463	17½
1928	3rd	91	63	.591	4	1976	4th	75	87	.463	26
1929	1st	98	54	.645	+10½	1977	4th	81	81	.500	20
1930	2nd	90	64	.584	2	1978	3rd	79	83	.488	11
1931	3rd	84	70	.545	17	1979	5th	80	82	.494	18
1932	1st	90	64	.584	+ 4	1980	6th	64	98	.395	27
1933	3rd	86	68	.558	6	1981	6th/5th	38	65	.369	†
1934	3rd	86	65	.570	8	1982	5th	73	89	.451	19
1935	1st	100	54	.649	+ 4	1983	5th	71	91	.438	19
1936	T2nd	87	67	.565	5	1984	1st‡	96	65	.596	+ 6½
1937	2nd	93	61	.604	3	1985	4th	77	84	.478	23½
1938	1st	89	63	.586	+ 2	1986	5th	70	90	.438	37
1939	4th	84	70	.545	13	1987	6th	76	85	.472	18½
1940	5th	75	79	.487	25½	1988	4th	77	85	.475	24
1941	6th	70	84	.455	30	1989	1st‡	93	69	.574	+ 6
1942	6th	68	86	.442	38	1990	T4th	77	85	.475	18
1943	5th	74	79	.484	30½	1991	4th	77	83	.481	20
1944	4th	75	79	.487	30	1992	4th	78	84	.481	18
1945	1st	98	56	.636	+ 3						
1946	3rd	82	71	.536	14½						
1947	6th	69	85	.448	25						
1948	8th	64	90	.416	27½						

*Games behind winner. †First half 15-37; second 23-28. ‡Lost Championship Series.

MANAGERS

Name	Record	Years
Tom Loftus	53-86	'01
Frank Selee	295-223	'02-05
Frank Chance	753-379	'05-12
Johnny Evers	130-121	'13, '21
Hank O'Day	78-76	1914
Roger Bresnahan	73-80	1915
Joe Tinker	67-86	1916
Fred Mitchell	308-269	'17-20
Bill Killefer	299-292	'21-25
Rabbit Maranville	23-30	1925
George Gibson	12-14	1925
Joe McCarthy	442-321	'26-30
Rogers Hornsby	141-114	'30-32
Charlie Grimm	946-784	'32-38
		'44-49
		1960
Gabby Hartnett	203-176	'38-40
Jimmy Wilson	213-258	'41-44
Roy Johnson	0-1	1944
Frank Frisch	141-196	'49-51
Phil Cavarretta	169-213	'51-53
Stan Hack	196-265	'54-56
Bob Scheffing	208-254	'57-59
Lou Boudreau	54-83	1960
Vedie Himsl*	10-21	1961
Harry Craft*	7-9	1961
Elvin Tappe*	46-69	'61-62
Lou Klein*	65-83	'61-62
		1965
Charlie Metro*	43-69	1962
Bob Kennedy	182-198	'63-65
Leo Durocher	535-526	'66-72
Whitey Lockman	157-162	'72-74
Jim Marshall	175-218	'74-76
Herman Franks	238-241	'77-79
Joe Amalfitano	66-116	1979
		'80-81
Preston Gomez	38-52	1980
Lee Elia	127-158	'82-83
Charlie Fox	17-22	1983
Jim Frey	196-182	'84-86
John Vukovich	1-1	1986
Gene Michael	114-124	'86-87
Frank Lucchesi	8-17	1987
Don Zimmer	265-259	'88-91
Jim Essian	59-63	1991
Jim Lefebvre	78-84	1992

*College of Coaches.

DAY BY DAY

Date		Opp.	Res.	Score	(inn.*)	Hits	Opp. hits	Winning pitcher	Losing pitcher	Save	Record	Pos.	GB
4-7		At Phi.	W	4-3		10	7	Maddux	Mulholland	McElroy	1-0	T1st	...
4-8		At Phi.	L	3-11		10	12	Greene	Jackson		1-1	T3rd	1
4-9		At Phi.	L	1-7		4	9	Cox	Morgan		1-2	T5th	1
4-10		St.L.	L	1-2	(11)	7	5	Carpenter	Assenmacher	L. Smith	1-3	6th	2
4-11		St.L.	W	5-1		10	4	Boskie	DeLeon	McElroy	2-3	5th	1
4-12		St.L.	W	4-2		6	11	Maddux	Olivares	Slocumb	3-3	T3rd	1
4-14		At Pit.	L	2-3		4	3	Walk	Jackson	Mason	3-4	5th	2
4-15		At Pit.	L	2-7		8	9	Tomlin	Morgan		3-5	6th	3
4-18		At St.L.	W	5-4		6	8	Boskie	Olivares	McElroy	4-5	4th	3½
4-19		At St.L.	L	3-4		9	8	DeLeon	Jackson	L. Smith	4-6	5th	4½
4-20		Phi.	W	8-3		9	5	Maddux	Abbott		5-6	5th	4½
4-21		Phi.	L	5-7	(10)	11	11	Mit. Williams	Slocumb	Schilling	5-7	5th	5½
4-22		Phi.	W	9-5		10	6	Boskie	Mulholland		6-7	3rd	5
4-23		Phi.	L	2-8		3	11	Greene	Castillo		6-8	4th	5½
4-24		Pit.	L	2-3		7	12	Mason	Scanlan	Belinda	6-9	6th	6½
4-25		Pit.	L	0-1		3	4	Tomlin	Maddux	Belinda	6-10	6th	6½
4-26		Pit.	W	5-4	(10)	10	7	McElroy	Mason		7-10	6th	6½
4-27		At Atl.	L	0-5		2	7	Glavine	Boskie		7-11	6th	7
4-28		At Atl.	L	0-1		3	3	Leibrandt	Castillo	Pena	7-12	6th	7
4-29		At Atl.	L	0-8		7	12	Smoltz	Jackson		7-13	6th	8
5-1		At Cin.	L	0-4		6	11	Swindell	Maddux	Dibble	7-14	6th	8
5-2		At Cin.	W	10-3		10	11	Morgan	Hammond		8-14	6th	8
5-3		At Cin.	L	1-7		7	8	Bankhead	Boskie		8-15	6th	8
5-4		Atl.	L	1-6		5	12	Smoltz	Castillo		8-16	6th	9
5-5		Atl.	W	4-3	(10)	7	9	McElroy	Pena		9-16	6th	9
5-6		Hou.	W	8-4		7	7	Maddux	Harnisch		10-16	6th	9
5-7		Hou.	W	9-2		11	7	Morgan	Bowen		11-16	6th	8
5-8		Cin.	L	7-10	(12)	19	16	Charlton	McElroy		11-17	6th	9
5-9		Cin.	W	3-1		10	5	Castillo	Browning	Assenmacher	12-17	6th	9
5-10		Cin.	L	0-6		2	9	Belcher	Jackson		12-18	6th	9
5-11		At Hou.	L	1-2	(10)	7	5	Hernandez	McElroy		12-19	6th	9½
5-12		At Hou.	W	3-2		5	5	Assenmacher	Boever		13-19	6th	8½
5-13		At Hou.	W	8-3		12	8	Boskie	Henry		14-19	5th	8½
5-15		At S.F.	W	5-3		8	8	Scanlan	Brantley	Assenmacher	15-19	5th	8
5-16		At S.F.	L	0-2		6	5	Burkett	Maddux	Beck	15-20	5th	8
5-17		At S.F.	W	4-3		8	5	Morgan	Burba	Scanlan	16-20	5th	7
5-18		At L.A.	W	3-0		5	5	Castillo	Ke. Gross	McElroy	17-20	4th	6½
5-19		At L.A.	L	2-5		9	9	Hershiser	Boskie	McDowell	17-21	4th	6½
5-20		At L.A.	L	3-5		10	9	Ojeda	Jackson	Candelaria	17-22	6th	6½
5-22		At S.D.	L	0-2		3	6	Benes	Maddux		17-23	6th	7
5-23		At S.D.	W	7-2		9	9	Morgan	Hurst		18-23	6th	6
5-24		At S.D.	W	6-4		10	7	Castillo	Melendez	McElroy	19-23	5th	5½
5-26		S.F.	L	2-3		9	11	Jackson	McElroy	Brantley	19-24	6th	6
5-27		S.F.	L	2-6		9	6	Burkett	Maddux		19-25	6th	6
5-28		S.F.	W	5-0		10	4	Morgan	Burba		20-25	6th	5½
5-29		L.A.	L	0-1		3	5	R. Martinez	Castillo		20-26	6th	6½
5-30		L.A.	L	2-3		7	12	Hershiser	Patterson	McDowell	20-27	6th	6½
5-31		L.A.	L	2-6		8	9	Ke. Gross	Jackson		20-28	6th	6½
6-1		S.D.	W	6-1		10	4	Maddux	Benes		21-28	6th	6
6-2		S.D.	W	3-2	(13)	10	9	Boskie	Ge. Harris		22-28	6th	5
6-3		S.D.	L	1-5		6	7	Hurst	Castillo		22-29	6th	6
6-5	(1)	At Mon.	W	10-4		15	10	Jackson	Gardner	Scanlan	23-29	5th	6½
6-5	(2)	At Mon.	L	2-6		10	8	Nabholz	Maddux	Wetteland	23-30	6th	7
6-7		At Mon.	L	2-3		6	10	Fassero	Scanlan		23-31	6th	7½
6-8	(1)	At St.L.	W	5-2	(13)	10	8	Robinson	Agosto	Scanlan	24-31	6th	7
6-8	(2)	At St.L.	W	6-4		13	14	Castillo	DeLeon	Bullinger	25-31	6th	6½
6-9		At St.L.	L	5-6	(11)	15	17	Carpenter	Scanlan		25-32	6th	7
6-10		At St.L.	W	4-2		7	3	Maddux	Clark		26-32	6th	7
6-12		Mon.	W	5-2		8	7	McElroy	Martinez	Bullinger	27-32	T3rd	7
6-13		Mon.	W	4-3		7	8	Castillo	Nabholz	Bullinger	28-32	6th	7
6-14		Mon.	W	5-1		9	5	Jackson	Hill		29-32	4th	7
6-15		St.L.	W	7-1		11	4	Maddux	Tewksbury		30-32	3rd	6
6-16		St.L.	W	2-1		7	4	Scanlan	Clark	Bullinger	31-32	T2nd	6
6-18		At Phi.	L	3-4		8	11	Hartley	Scanlan	Mit. Williams	31-33	3rd	6½
6-19		At Phi.	W	5-2		11	5	Jackson	Brink	Bullinger	32-33	T2nd	5½
6-20		At Phi.	L	1-4		3	6	Mulholland	Maddux	Mit. Williams	32-34	3rd	5½
6-21		At Phi.	W	5-2		11	7	Morgan	Abbott	Assenmacher	33-34	T2nd	5½
6-22		At N.Y.	L	2-8		8	10	Fernandez	Boskie		33-35	T2nd	6½
6-23		At N.Y.	L	1-4		6	10	Schourek	Castillo	Franco	33-36	T3rd	7½
6-24		At N.Y.	L	2-3		9	5	Gooden	Jackson	Franco	33-37	4th	7½

Date		Opp.	Res.	Score	(inn.*)	Hits	Opp. hits	Winning pitcher	Losing pitcher	Save	Record	Pos.	GB
6-25		At N.Y.	W	9-2		12	6	Maddux	Young		34-37	4th	7
6-26		Phi.	W	3-0		8	7	Morgan	Abbott	Bullinger	35-37	3rd	6
6-27		Phi.	L	4-5		9	13	Hartley	McElroy	Mit. Williams	35-38	4th	7
6-28		Phi.	W	5-3		10	4	Castillo	Schilling	Assenmacher	36-38	3rd	6
6-29		N.Y.	W	5-2		7	6	Jackson	Gooden	Assenmacher	37-38	3rd	5
6-30		N.Y.	W	3-1		11	4	Maddux	Young		38-38	2nd	5
7-1		N.Y.	L	4-6	(12)	10	14	Guetterman	Bullinger	Young	38-39	2nd	6
7-3		At Atl.	L	0-3		5	9	Glavine	Boskie		38-40	3rd	5½
7-4		At Atl.	L	2-4		7	6	Leibrandt	Jackson	Mercker	38-41	4th	5½
7-5		At Atl.	W	8-0		10	6	Maddux	Smoltz		39-41	T3rd	4½
7-6		Cin.	L	2-6		9	6	Ruskin	Morgan	Dibble	39-42	4th	5½
7-7		Cin.	L	2-3		8	7	Rijo	Castillo	Charlton	39-43	5th	6½
7-8		Cin.	W	3-2	(10)	11	5	Assenmacher	Dibble		40-43	4th	5½
7-9		Atl.	L	0-2	(12)	3	7	Stanton	Bullinger	Pena	40-44	4th	5½
7-10		Atl.	L	0-4		4	10	Smoltz	Maddux		40-45	5th	6½
7-11		Atl.	L	1-3		4	9	Avery	Scanlan	Pena	40-46	5th	7½
7-12		Atl.	L	4-7	(10)	14	11	Mercker	Assenmacher	Pena	40-47	5th	8½
7-16		At Pit.	L	1-2		4	7	Drabek	Boskie	Belinda	40-48	5th	9½
7-17		At Pit.	W	2-1		8	6	Maddux	Tomlin	Scanlan	41-48	5th	8½
7-18		At Pit.	L	0-4		7	6	Walk	Morgan	Patterson	41-49	5th	9½
7-19		At Pit.	W	4-2		9	5	Scanlan	Neagle		42-49	5th	8½
7-20		At Cin.	L	2-5		8	9	Ruskin	McElroy	Dibble	42-50	5th	8½
7-21		At Cin.	W	1-0		4	3	Patterson	Belcher	Scanlan	43-50	5th	7½
7-22		At Cin.	W	3-0		13	6	Maddux	Swindell		44-50	5th	7½
7-24		At Hou.	W	1-0		7	6	Morgan	D. Jones	Scanlan	45-50	5th	6½
7-25		At Hou.	L	2-3	(11)	8	11	Hernandez	McElroy		45-51	5th	6½
7-26		At Hou.	W	8-5		16	11	Harkey	Reynolds		46-51	5th	6½
7-27		Pit.	W	3-2		9	6	Maddux	Drabek	Robinson	47-51	T4th	5½
7-28		Pit.	W	11-1		18	8	Morgan	Tomlin		48-51	4th	4½
7-29		Pit.	W	6-4	(11)	10	9	Assenmacher	Belinda		49-51	3rd	3½
8-1	(1)	At N.Y.	L	0-3		7	7	Schourek	Maddux	Young	49-52	4th	5½
8-1	(2)	At N.Y.	W	6-1		12	2	Robinson	Whitehurst		50-52	3rd	5
8-2		At N.Y.	L	2-4		9	5	Cone	Morgan	Franco	50-53	4th	6
8-3		At Mon.	L	2-3		10	7	Martinez	Castillo	Wetteland	50-54	4th	6½
8-4		At Mon.	W	8-6		13	9	McElroy	Sampen	Assenmacher	51-54	T3rd	6½
8-5		At Mon.	L	3-5		8	12	Barnes	Patterson	Wetteland	51-55	T3rd	7½
8-6		N.Y.	W	5-2		10	6	Maddux	Whitehurst		52-55	3rd	7½
8-7		N.Y.	W	9-1		12	8	Morgan	Cone		53-55	3rd	7½
8-8		N.Y.	W	4-3		11	9	Bullinger	Guetterman		54-55	3rd	7½
8-9		N.Y.	W	6-2		12	10	Harkey	Fernandez		55-55	3rd	7½
8-10		Mon.	L	0-11		8	18	Barnes	Robinson		55-56	3rd	8½
8-11		Mon.	L	2-3	(17)	11	10	Sampen	Robinson		55-57	3rd	8½
8-12		Mon.	L	1-3		3	11	Nabholz	Morgan	Rojas	55-58	3rd	9½
8-13		Hou.	L	3-4		6	5	J. Jones	Castillo	D. Jones	55-59	3rd	10
8-14		Hou.	W	4-2		8	8	Harkey	Kile	Assenmacher	56-59	3rd	9
8-15		Hou.	L	0-5		8	12	Henry	Bullinger		56-60	3rd	9
8-16		Hou.	W	1-0		8	4	Maddux	Williams		57-60	3rd	9
8-18		At S.F.	W	4-1		6	11	Morgan	Black		58-60	3rd	8½
8-19		At S.F.	L	1-9		7	11	Swift	Castillo		58-61	3rd	9½
8-20		At S.F.	W	6-5		10	9	Harkey	Wilson	Scanlan	59-61	3rd	9½
8-21		At L.A.	W	3-2	(12)	15	12	Robinson	Howell	Scanlan	60-61	3rd	8½
8-22		At L.A.	W	5-4		9	7	Patterson	Candelaria	Scanlan	61-61	3rd	8½
8-23		At L.A.	W	4-2		11	8	Morgan	Astacio	McElroy	62-61	3rd	7½
8-24		At S.D.	W	6-3		11	7	Castillo	Gr. Harris	Scanlan	63-61	3rd	6½
8-25		At S.D.	L	4-7		10	9	Maddux	Patterson	Myers	63-62	3rd	7½
8-26		At S.D.	L	0-3		8	8	Lefferts	Maddux	Myers	63-63	3rd	8½
8-28		S.F.	W	3-2		8	11	Morgan	Jackson	Scanlan	64-63	3rd	7½
8-29		S.F.	W	7-2		13	6	Castillo	Burba	Scanlan	65-63	3rd	7½
8-30		S.F.	W	3-1		6	1	Bullinger	Wilson		66-63	3rd	7½
8-31		L.A.	W	2-0		2	5	Maddux	Candiotti		67-63	3rd	7
9-1		L.A.	L	4-5	(13)	12	16	McDowell	Slocumb	Candelaria	67-64	3rd	8
9-2		L.A.	W	5-1		11	3	Morgan	Ojeda		68-64	3rd	8
9-4		S.D.	L	5-7	(14)	12	14	Hernandez	Boskie		68-65	3rd	9½
9-5		S.D.	L	3-5		12	7	Melendez	Maddux	Myers	68-66	3rd	10½
9-6		S.D.	L	1-3		6	5	Benes	Bullinger	Myers	68-67	3rd	10½
9-7		At Pit.	W	6-5	(11)	21	10	Assenmacher	Belinda	Scanlan	69-67	3rd	9½
9-8		At Pit.	L	2-5		3	8	Drabek	Boskie		69-68	3rd	10½
9-9		At Pit.	L	8-13		14	13	Cox	Robinson		69-69	4th	11½
9-11		At St.L.	W	8-2		15	10	Maddux	Olivares		70-69	3rd	10½
9-12		At St.L.	L	3-11		10	13	Cormier	Morgan		70-70	4th	11½
9-13		At St.L.	L	3-10		10	14	Tewksbury	Bullinger		70-71	4th	11½
9-14		N.Y.	L	2-10		16	13	Innis	McElroy	Young	70-72	4th	12½
9-15		N.Y.	L	2-4	(7½)	8	6	Dewey	Boskie		70-73	4th	13½
9-16		Phi.	W	14-9		17	13	Maddux	Rivera		71-73	4th	12½

Date	Opp.	Res.	Score (inn.*)	Hits	Opp. hits	Winning pitcher	Losing pitcher	Save	Record	Pos.	GB
9-17	Phi.	W	3-0	7	2	Morgan	DeLeon		72-73	4th	12½
9-18	St.L.	W	9-7	14	7	Robinson	B. Smith		73-73	4th	12½
9-19 (1)	St.L.	W	6-5	10	14	Castillo	Osborne	Scanlan	74-73	3rd	12½
9-19 (2)	St.L.	L	10-11 (10)	11	14	L. Smith	Assenmacher		74-74	4th	13
9-20	St.L.	L	4-16	11	22	B. Smith	Boskie		74-75	4th	14
9-21	At N.Y.	W	10-1	16	8	Maddux	Hillman		75-75	4th	14
9-22	At N.Y.	L	7-8	11	11	Guetterman	Assenmacher	Young	75-76	4th	14
9-23	At Phi.	L	3-9	11	9	Ayrault	Bullinger		75-77	4th	14
9-24	At Phi.	L	2-3 (10)	7	7	Mit. Williams	Scanlan		75-78	4th	15
9-25	At Mon.	L	3-4 (10)	8	12	Wetteland	Slocumb		75-79	4th	16
9-26	At Mon.	L	0-12	4	16	Nabholz	Boskie		75-80	4th	17
9-27	At Mon.	L	0-1	5	3	Rojas	Morgan	Wetteland	75-81	4th	18
9-28	Pit.	L	3-10	5	13	Wakefield	Bullinger		75-82	4th	19
9-29	Pit.	L	0-3	2	7	Wagner	Castillo	Belinda	75-83	4th	20
9-30	Pit.	W	6-0	11	7	Maddux	Tomlin		76-83	4th	19
10-2	Mon.	W	3-1	10	5	Morgan	Nabholz		77-83	4th	18
10-3	Mon.	L	1-3	7	7	Bottenfield	Bullinger	Wetteland	77-84	4th	18
10-4	Mon.	W	3-2	7	8	Castillo	Gardner	Assenmacher	78-84	4th	18

Monthly records: April (7-13), May (13-15), June (18-10), July (11-13), August (18-12), September (9-20), Oct. (2-1).

HIGHLIGHTS

High point: After completing a three-game sweep of the Pirates on July 29, the Cubs moved to within 3½ games of first place in the N.L. East.

Low point: Following their sweep of Pittsburgh, Chicago fell four games in the standings in a week. A 9-20 mark in September sealed the Cubs' fate.

Turning point: The Cubs went into their final downward spiral after righthander Mike Harkey ruptured a knee tendon while doing a cartwheel during pregame warmups September 6. He had posted a 4-0 record with a 1.89 ERA after returning from a right shoulder operation. Without him the last 22 games, the staff's ERA was 5.06.

Most valuable player: Second baseman Ryne Sandberg. He led the team in homers (26), runs (100), stolen bases (17) and slugging percentage (.510) and finished second with a .304 batting average and 87 RBIs.

Most valuable pitcher: Righthander Greg Maddux. Despite being shut out seven times when he pitched, Maddux tied for the N.L. lead in victories with 20. He also pitched a league-high 268 innings, ranked third in the league with a 2.18 ERA and 199 strikeouts and won his third straight Gold Glove.

Most improved player: Outfielder Derrick May. He capitalized on a chance to play regularly in the second half of the season, hitting .303 in his final 44 starts.

Most pleasant surprise: Shortstop Rey Sanchez. Filling in for disabled Shawon Dunston, Sanchez hit .251 in 74 games. He batted .325 from August 5 on.

Biggest disappointment: Outfielder Kal Daniels. Obtained from the Dodgers on June 27 to provide power, he reported out of shape and with a bad knee. He hit .250 with four homers in 48 games.

Key injuries: A herniated disk in his lower back limited Dunston to just 18 games, and Sanchez missed the last month with a bulging disk in his back. Harkey's injury also hurt, and outfielder Sammy Sosa played in just 67 games due to a broken hand and ankle.

Notable: Maddux became the first Cub to win 20 games in a season since Rick Reuschel in 1977. ... Sandberg, who hasn't committed a throwing error in 389 straight games, joined Charlie Gehringer as the only second basemen in major league history to record at least 500 assists in six different seasons. ... The Cubs set team single-season records for highest fielding percentage (.982) and most errorless games (88). ... Chicago had a winning record against just one division rival (11-7 vs. St. Louis).

—JOE GODDARD

RECORDS

1992 regular-season record: 78-84 (4th in N.L. East); 43-38 at home; 35-46 on road; 44-46 vs. East; 34-38 vs. West; 28-33 vs. LHP; 50-51 vs. RHP; 58-56 on grass; 20-28 on turf; 45-40 in daytime; 33-44 at night; 23-27 in one-run games; 8-15 in extra-inning games; 1-0-3 in doubleheaders.

Team record last five years: 402-406 (.498, ranks 8th in league in that span).

TEAM LEADERS

Batting average: Mark Grace (.307).
At-bats: Ryne Sandberg (612).
Runs: Ryne Sandberg (100).
Hits: Ryne Sandberg (186).
Total bases: Ryne Sandberg (312).
Doubles: Mark Grace (37).
Triples: Ryne Sandberg (8).
Home runs: Ryne Sandberg (26).
Runs batted in: Andre Dawson (90).
Stolen bases: Ryne Sandberg (17).
Slugging percentage: Ryne Sandberg (.510).
On-base percentage: Mark Grace (.380).
Wins: Greg Maddux (20).
Earned-run average: Greg Maddux (2.18).
Complete games: Greg Maddux (9).
Shutouts: Greg Maddux (4).
Saves: Bob Scanlan (14).
Innings pitched: Greg Maddux (268).
Strikeouts: Greg Maddux (199).

GAMES BY POSITION

Catcher: Joe Girardi 86, Rick Wilkins 73, Hector Villanueva 28, George Pedre 4.
First base: Mark Grace 157, Hector Villanueva 6, Luis Salazar 5.
Second base: Ryne Sandberg 157, Doug Strange 12, Jose Vizcaino 5, Rey Sanchez 4, Jeff Kunkel 3, Steve Buechele 2, Chico Walker 2.
Third base: Steve Buechele 63, Luis Salazar 40, Doug Strange 33, Gary Scott 30, Jose Vizcaino 29, Chico Walker 2.
Shortstop: Rey Sanchez 68, Jose Vizcaino 50, Alex Arias 30, Shawon Dunston 18, Luis Salazar 12, Jeff Kunkel 6, Gary Scott 2.
Outfield: Andre Dawson 139, Doug Dascenzo 122, Derrick May 108, Sammy Sosa 67, Dwight Smith 63, Luis Salazar 34, Kal Daniels 28, Jerome Walton 24, Fernando Ramsey 15, Chico Walker 6, Jeff Kunkel 3.

TOP 10 DRAFT CHOICES

1. **Derek Wallace,** RHP, Pepperdine University.
2. **None.**
3. **Brant Brown,** 1B, Fresno State University.
4. **Brandon Pico,** OF, Rogers High School, Newport, R.I.
5. **Ryan Wilson,** C, Cerritos (Calif.) High School.
6. **Emilio Mendez,** SS, Miami Beach (Fla.) Senior High School.
7. **Chris Dreyer,** RHP, Southwest Texas State University.
8. **Mike Hubbard,** C, James Madison University.
9. **Chris Peterson,** SS, Georgia Southern University.
10. **Kris Hanson,** RHP, University of Wisconsin-Stevens Point.

CINCINNATI REDS
NATIONAL LEAGUE WEST DIVISION

1993 SCHEDULE

APRIL

SUN	MON	TUE	WED	THU	FRI	SAT
				1	2	3
4	5 MON H	6	7 N MON H	8 N MON H	9 N STL	10 N STL
11 N STL	12 N PHI	13 N PHI	14 N PHI	15	16 N NY	17 N NY H
18 NY H	19	20 N PIT	21 N PIT	22 N PIT	23 CHI	24 CHI
25 CHI	26 N FLA H	27 N FLA H	28 N PIT H	29 N PIT H	30 N CHI H	

MAY

SUN	MON	TUE	WED	THU	FRI	SAT
						1 CHI H
2 CHI H	3	4 N FLA	5 N FLA	6 N HOU	7 N HOU	8 N HOU
9 N HOU	10 N SD H	11 N SD H	12 N SD H	13 N COL H	14 N COL H	15 N COL H
16 N COL H	17 N LA	18 N LA	19 N LA	20 N SF	21 SF	22 SF
23 SF	24	25 N ATL H	26 N ATL H	27 N ATL H	28 N NY	29 NY
30 NY	31 N PHI H					

JUNE

SUN	MON	TUE	WED	THU	FRI	SAT
		1 N PHI H	2 N PHI H	3 N STL H	4 N STL H	5 N STL H
6 STL H	7 N MON	8 N MON	9 N MON	10 N ATL	11 N ATL	12 N ATL
13 ATL	14	15 N SF H	16 N SF H	17 N SF H	18 N LA H	19 N LA H
20 LA H	21 N COL	22 N COL	23 COL	24	25 N SD	26 N SD
27 SD	28	29 N HOU H	30 N HOU H			

JULY

SUN	MON	TUE	WED	THU	FRI	SAT
				1 N HOU H	2 N PIT H	3 N PIT H
4 PIT H	5 N PIT H	6 N CHI H	7 CHI	8 CHI	9 N PIT	10 N PIT
11 PIT	12	13 ◦ ALL-STAR GAME	14	15 N FLA H	16 N FLA H	17 N FLA H
18 FLA H	19 N CHI H	20 N CHI H	21 N CHI H	22 N FLA	23 N FLA	24 N FLA
25 N FLA	26 N HOU	27 N HOU	28 N HOU	29	30 N SD H	31 N SD H

AUGUST

SUN	MON	TUE	WED	THU	FRI	SAT
1 SD H	2 N COL H	3 N COL H	4 N COL H	5 N COL H	6 N LA	7 N LA
8 LA	9 N SF	10 N SF	11 SF	12	13 N ATL H	14 N ATL H
15 N ATL H	16 N NY H	17 N NY H	18 N NY H	19	20 N MON H	21 N MON H
22 MON H	23 N NY	24 N NY	25 N NY	26	27 N PHI	28 N PHI
29 PHI	30 N STL	31 N STL				

SEPTEMBER

SUN	MON	TUE	WED	THU	FRI	SAT
			1 N STL	2	3 N PHI H	4 N PHI H
5 PHI H	6	7 N STL H	8 N STL H	9	10 N MON	11 N MON
12 MON	13	14 N ATL	15 N ATL	16 N ATL	17 N SF H	18 N SF H
19 SF H	20 N LA H	21 N LA H	22 N LA H	23 N LA H	24 N COL	25 N COL
26 COL	27	28 N SD	29 N SD	30		

OCTOBER

SUN	MON	TUE	WED	THU	FRI	SAT
					1 N HOU H	2 N HOU H
3 HOU H						

1993 SEASON

CLUB DIRECTORY

General partner
Marge Schott
President and chief executive officer
Marge Schott
General manager
Jim Bowden
Director, player development
Sheldon Bender
Director, scouting
Julian Mock
Special assistant to the general manager
Gene Bennett
Senior advisor/player personnel
Tony Robello
Controller
Ernie Brubaker
Director, stadium operations
Tim O'Connell
Director, ticket department
John O'Brien
Director, season ticket sales
Pat McCaffrey
Director, group sales
Susan Toomey
Director, marketing
Chip Baker
Director, publicity
Jon Braude
Director, speakers bureau
Gordy Coleman
Traveling secretary
Joel Pieper
Assistant publicity director
Joe Kelley
Assistant ticket director
Ken Ayer
Assistant/baseball operations
Darrell Rodgers

Chief administrative assistant
Joyce Pfarr
Administrative assistant, business
Ginny Kamp
Administrative assistant, scouting
Wilma Mann
Admin. assistant, player development
Lois Schneider
Scouting secretary
Lois Hudson
Trainers
Greg Lynn
Doug Spreen
Field superintendent
To be announced
Equipment manager
Bernie Stowe
Scouts
Johnny Almarez
Jeff Barton
Larry Barton Jr.
Ray Bellino
Jack Bowen
George Brill
Dave Calaway
Clay Daniel
Paul Faulk
Les Houser
Eddie Kolo
Tom Severtson
Bob Szymkowski
Marion (Bo) Trumbo
Tom Wilson
Jeff Zimmerman
Scouting consultant
Paul Campbell

SCHEDULE KEY

H—Home game.   N—Night game (any game starting after 5 p.m.).
*All-Star Game at Oriole Park at Camden Yards, Baltimore.

Manager—Tony Perez (24).

Coaches—Dave Bristol (4), Don Gullett (35), Dave Miley (2), Ron Oester (3), Larry Rothschild (37).

No.	PITCHERS	B/T	Ht./Wt.	Born	1992 clubs
59	Ayala, Bobby	R/R	6-3/200	7-8-69	Chattanooga, Cincinnati
31	Belcher, Tim	R/R	6-3/220	10-19-61	Cincinnati
32	Browning, Tom	L/L	6-1/195	4-28-60	Cincinnati
25	Cadaret, Greg	L/L	6-3/215	2-27-62	New York A.L.
49	Dibble, Rob	L/R	6-4/230	1-24-64	Cincinnati
64	Ferry, Mike	R/R	6-3/185	7-26-69	Cedar Rapids
54	Foster, Steve	R/R	6-0/180	8-16-66	Cincinnati, Nashville
45	Hammond, Chris	L/L	6-1/195	1-21-66	Cincinnati
48	Henry, Dwayne	R/R	6-3/230	2-16-62	Cincinnati
39	Hill, Milton	R/R	6-0/180	8-22-65	Cincinnati, Nashville
62	Luebbers, Larry	R/R	6-6/190	10-11-69	Cedar Rapids, Chattanooga
55	Powell, Ross	L/L	6-0/180	1-24-68	Nashville, Chattanooga
40	Pugh, Tim	R/R	6-6/225	1-26-67	Nashville, Cincinnati
27	Rijo, Jose	R/R	6-2/210	5-13-65	Cincinnati
71	Robinson, Scott	R/R	6-2/195	11-15-68	Charleston, W.Va., Chattanooga
28	Ruskin, Scott	R/L	6-2/195	6-8-63	Cincinnati
41	Service, Scott	R/R	6-6/235	7-27-67	Indianapolis, Montreal, Nashville
57	Smiley, John	L/L	6-4/215	3-17-65	Minnesota
65	Spradlin, Jerry	B/R	6-7/230	6-14-67	Chattanooga, Cedar Rapids

No.	CATCHERS	B/T	Ht./Wt.	Born	1992 clubs
63	Cox, Darron	R/R	6-1/210	11-21-67	Chattanooga
9	Oliver, Joe	R/R	6-3/210	7-24-65	Cincinnati
6	Wilson, Dan	R/R	6-3/190	3-25-69	Nashville, Cincinnati

No.	INFIELDERS	B/T	Ht./Wt.	Born	1992 clubs
20	Branson, Jeff	L/R	6-0/180	1-26-67	Nashville, Cincinnati
18	Costo, Tim	R/R	6-5/230	2-16-69	Chattanooga, Cincinnati
15	Greene, Willie	L/R	5-11/180	9-23-71	Cedar Rapids, Chattanooga, Cincinnati
26	Gregg, Tommy	L/L	6-1/190	7-29-63	Richmond, Atlanta
11	Larkin, Barry	R/R	6-0/190	4-28-64	Cincinnati
23	Morris, Hal	L/L	6-4/215	4-9-65	Cincinnati, Nashville
10	Roberts, Bip	B/R	5-7/165	10-27-63	Cincinnati
17	Sabo, Chris	R/R	6-0/185	1-19-62	Cincinnati, Nashville

No.	OUTFIELDERS	B/T	Ht./Wt.	Born	1992 clubs
46	Brumfield, Jacob	R/R	6-0/180	5-27-65	Cincinnati, Nashville
29	Canate, Willie	R/R	6-0/170	12-11-71	Columbus
22	Espy, Cecil	B/R	6-3/195	1-20-63	Pittsburgh
72	Gordon, Keith	R/R	6-1/200	1-22-69	Cedar Rapids
58	Hernandez, Cesar	R/R	6-0/160	9-28-66	Chattanooga, Nashville, Cincinnati
36	Kelly, Roberto	R/R	6-2/190	10-1-64	New York A.L.
7	Mitchell, Kevin	R/R	5-11/210	1-13-62	Seattle
16	Sanders, Reggie	R/R	6-1/180	12-1-67	Cincinnati
42	Varsho, Gary	L/R	5-11/190	6-20-61	Pittsburgh

BALLPARK INFORMATION

Ballpark (capacity, surface)
Riverfront Stadium (52,952, artificial)

Address
100 Riverfront Stadium
Cincinnati, OH 45202

Business phone
513-421-4510

Ticket information
513-421-7337

Ticket prices
$11.50 (blue level box seats)
$10 (green level box seats)
$10 (yellow level box seats)
$9 (red level box seats)
$8 (green level reserved seats)
$6.50 (red level reserved seats)
$3.50 ("top six" reserved seats)

Field dimensions (from home plate)
To left field at foul line, 330 feet
To center field, 404 feet
To right field at foul line, 330 feet

First game played
June 30, 1970 (Braves 8, Reds 2)

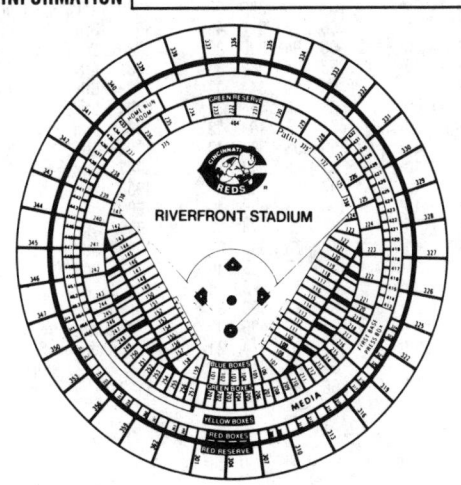

RIVERFRONT STADIUM

MINOR LEAGUE AFFILIATES

Class	Team	League	Manager
AAA	Indianapolis	American Association	Marc Bombard
AA	Chattanooga	Southern	Pat Kelly
A	Winston-Salem	Carolina	Mark Berry
A	Charleston, W.Va.	South Atlantic	Tom Nieto
Rookie	Billings	Pioneer	Donnie Scott
Rookie	Princeton	Appalachian	Sam Mejas

☐ BROADCAST INFORMATION ☐

Radio: WLW-AM (700). Broadcasters: Joe Nuxhall, Marty Brennaman.
TV: WLWT-TV (Channel 5). Broadcasters: Gordy Coleman, Steve LaMar, Marty Brennaman.
Cable TV: SportsChannel Cincinnati. Broadcasters: To be announced.

SPRING TRAINING

Ballpark (city): Plant City Stadium (Plant City, Fla.).
Ticket information: 813-752-7337.

HISTORY

YEAR-BY-YEAR RECORDS

Year	Pos.	W	L	Pct.	*GB	Year	Pos.	W	L	Pct.	*GB
1901	8th	52	87	.374	38	1950	6th	66	87	.431	24½
1902	4th	70	70	.500	33½	1951	6th	68	86	.442	28½
1903	4th	74	65	.532	16½	1952	6th	69	85	.448	27½
1904	3rd	88	65	.575	18	1953	6th	68	86	.442	37
1905	5th	79	74	.516	26	1954	5th	74	80	.481	23
1906	6th	64	87	.424	51½	1955	5th	75	79	.487	23½
1907	6th	66	87	.431	41½	1956	3rd	91	63	.591	2
1908	5th	73	81	.474	26	1957	4th	80	74	.519	15
1909	4th	77	76	.503	33½	1958	4th	76	78	.494	16
1910	5th	75	79	.487	29	1959	T5th	74	80	.481	13
1911	6th	70	83	.458	29	1960	6th	67	87	.435	28
1912	4th	75	78	.490	29	1961	1st	93	61	.604 +	4
1913	7th	64	89	.418	37½	1962	3rd	98	64	.605	3½
1914	8th	60	94	.390	34½	1963	5th	86	76	.531	13
1915	7th	71	83	.461	20	1964	T2nd	92	70	.549	1
1916	T7th	60	93	.392	33½	1965	4th	89	73	.549	8
1917	4th	78	76	.506	20	1966	7th	76	84	.475	18
1918	3rd	68	60	.531	15½	1967	4th	87	75	.537	14½
1919	1st	96	44	.686 +	9	1968	4th	83	79	.512	14
1920	3rd	82	71	.536	10½	1969	3rd	89	73	.549	4
1921	6th	70	83	.458	24	1970	1st†	102	60	.630 +	14½
1922	2nd	86	68	.558	7	1971	T4th	79	83	.488	11
1923	2nd	91	63	.591	4½	1972	1st†	95	59	.617 +	10½
1924	4th	83	70	.542	10	1973	1st‡	99	63	.611 +	3½
1925	3rd	80	73	.523	15	1974	2nd	98	64	.605	4
1926	2nd	87	67	.565	2	1975	1st†	108	54	.667 +	20
1927	5th	75	78	.490	18½	1976	1st†	102	60	.630 +	10
1928	5th	78	74	.513	16	1977	2nd	88	74	.543	10
1929	7th	66	88	.429	33	1978	2nd	92	69	.571	2½
1930	7th	59	95	.383	33	1979	1st‡	90	71	.559 +	1½
1931	8th	58	96	.377	43	1980	3rd	89	73	.549	3½
1932	8th	60	94	.390	30	1981	2nd/2nd	66	42	.611	§
1933	8th	58	94	.382	33	1982	6th	61	101	.377	28
1934	8th	52	99	.344	42	1983	6th	74	88	.457	17
1935	6th	68	85	.444	31½	1984	5th	70	92	.432	22
1936	5th	74	80	.481	18	1985	2nd	89	72	.553	5½
1937	8th	56	98	.364	40	1986	2nd	86	76	.531	10
1938	4th	82	68	.547	6	1987	2nd	84	78	.519	6
1939	1st	97	57	.630 +	4½	1988	2nd	87	74	.540	7
1940	1st	100	53	.654 +	12	1989	5th	75	87	.463	17
1941	3rd	88	66	.571	12	1990	1st†	91	71	.562 +	5
1942	4th	76	76	.500	29	1991	5th	74	88	.457	20
1943	2nd	87	67	.565	18	1992	2nd	90	72	.556	8
1944	3rd	89	65	.578	16						
1945	7th	61	93	.396	37						
1946	6th	67	87	.435	30						
1947	5th	73	81	.474	21						
1948	7th	64	89	.418	27						
1949	7th	62	92	.403	35						

*Games behind winner. †Won Championship Series. ‡Lost Championship Series. §First half 35-21; second 31-21.

MANAGERS

Name	Record	Years
Biddy McPhee	79-124	'01-02
Frank Bancroft	9-7	1902
Joe Kelley	275-230	'02-05
Ned Hanlon	130-174	'06-07
John Ganzel	73-81	1908
Clark Griffith	222-238	'09-11
Hank O'Day	75-78	1912
Joe Tinker	64-89	1913
Buck Herzog	165-226	'14-16
Chris. Mathewson	164-176	'16-18
Heinie Groh	7-3	1918
Pat Moran	425-329	'19-23
Jack Hendricks	469-450	'24-29
Dan Howley	177-285	'30-32
Donie Bush	58-94	1933
Bob O'Farrell	30-60	1934
Chuck Dressen	214-282	'34-37
Bobby Wallace	5-20	1937
Bill McKechnie	747-632	'38-46
Johnny Neun	117-137	'47-48
Bucky Walters	81-123	'48-49
Luke Sewell	176-234	'50-52
Rogers Hornsby	91-106	'52-53
Buster Mills	4-4	'1953
Birdie Tebbetts	372-357	'54-58
Jimmie Dykes	24-17	1958
Mayo Smith	35-45	1959
Fred Hutchinson	443-372	'59-64
Dick Sisler	121-94	'64-65
Don Heffner	37-46	1966
Dave Bristol	298-265	'66-69
Sparky Anderson	863-586	'70-78
John McNamara	279-244	'79-82
Russ Nixon	101-131	'82-83
Vern Rapp	51-70	1984
Pete Rose	426-388	'84-89
Tommy Helms	14-21	1989
Lou Piniella	255-231	'90-92

DAY BY DAY

Date	Opp.	Res.	Score (inn.*)	Hits	Opp. hits	Winning pitcher	Losing pitcher	Save	Record	Pos.	GB
4-6	S.D.	L	3-4	7	10	Melendez	Rijo	Myers	0-1	T5th	1
4-7	S.D.	W	4-2	11	5	Browning	Gr. Harris	Charlton	1-1	T2nd	½
4-8	S.D.	L	1-2	8	6	Benes	Belcher	Myers	1-2	5th	1½
4-9	At Hou.	L	5-6	(13)	11	11	Osuna	Ruskin		1-3	6th	1½
4-10	At Hou.	W	8-5	10	14	Hammond	Bowen	Charlton	2-3	5th	1½
4-11	At Hou.	L	1-2	6	9	Osuna	Rijo	D. Jones	2-4	6th	2
4-12	At Hou.	W	5-4	8	5	Browning	Harnisch	Charlton	3-4	4th	2
4-13	Atl.	W	5-4	7	9	Belcher	Smoltz	Charlton	4-4	T3rd	1½
4-14	Atl.	W	5-4	6	7	Bankhead	Freeman		5-4	2nd	1½
4-15	Atl.	W	3-1	8	4	Hammond	Leibrandt	Charlton	6-4	2nd	1½
4-17	At S.F.	L	3-7	4	9	Hickerson	Rijo	Beck	6-5	2nd	1
4-18	At S.F.	L	3-7	9	13	Wilson	Browning		6-6	4th	1
4-19	At S.F.	L	2-8	5	13	Burkett	Belcher		6-7	T4th	1½
4-20	At L.A.	L	0-6	9	9	Ojeda	Swindell		6-8	T5th	2½
4-21	At L.A.	W	4-3	8	8	Ruskin	Ke. Gross	Dibble	7-8	T4th	1½
4-22	At L.A.	W	4-3	9	12	Bankhead	Wilson	Charlton	8-8	4th	1½
4-24	At S.D.	W	7-6	(16)	15	11	Foster	Hernandez	Bankhead	9-8	T2nd	1½
4-25	At S.D.	W	11-5	17	11	Swindell	Benes		10-8	2nd	½
4-26	At S.D.	L	1-2	8	5	Lefferts	Hammond	Myers	10-9	T2nd	½
4-28	Pit.	W	3-2	9	6	Browning	Drabek	Charlton	11-9	T1st	...
4-29	Pit.	L	0-4	4	4	Smith	Belcher		11-10	T2nd	½
5-1	Chi.	W	4-0	11	6	Swindell	Maddux	Dibble	12-10	T1st	...
5-2	Chi.	L	3-10	11	10	Morgan	Hammond		12-11	2nd	1
5-3	Chi.	W	7-1	8	7	Bankhead	Boskie		13-11	T1st	...
5-4	At Pit.	L	5-12	12	15	Lamp	Henry		13-12	2nd	½
5-5	At Pit.	L	2-5	6	8	Miller	Belcher	Belinda	13-13	T2nd	½
5-6	N.Y.	W	5-3	6	7	Swindell	Young	Charlton	14-13	1st	+½
5-7	N.Y.	W	4-2	6	3	Hammond	Gooden	Dibble	15-13	1st	+½
5-8	At Chi.	W	10-7	(12)	16	19	Charlton	McElroy		16-13	1st	+½
5-9	At Chi.	L	1-3	5	10	Castillo	Browning	Assenmacher	16-14	1st	+½
5-10	At Chi.	W	6-0	9	2	Belcher	Jackson		17-14	1st	+½
5-12	At St.L.	L	4-6	9	10	Osborne	Swindell	L. Smith	17-15	2nd	1
5-13	At St.L.	L	2-4	8	7	Tewksbury	Bankhead	L. Smith	17-16	2nd	2
5-15	Phi.	L	0-8	5	12	Mulholland	Browning		17-17	3rd	2
5-16	Phi.	W	6-5	9	8	Belcher	Ritchie	Dibble	18-17	3rd	2
5-17	Phi.	L	4-5	8	13	Hartley	Dibble	Mit. Williams	18-18	3rd	2
5-18	At Mon.	W	2-1	9	4	Bankhead	Gardner	Charlton	19-18	3rd	1½
5-19	At Mon.	W	7-4	9	6	Henry	Wetteland	Dibble	20-18	3rd	1½
5-20	At Mon.	L	5-6	11	7	Rojas	Dibble		20-19	3rd	2½
5-22	At Phi.	L	2-8	7	10	Brantley	Belcher		20-20	3rd	4
5-23	At Phi.	W	10-0	14	6	Swindell	Brink		21-20	3rd	3
5-24	At Phi.	W	8-3	8	6	Rijo	Schilling		22-20	3rd	2
5-25	At N.Y.	W	3-0	10	5	Hammond	Schourek	Charlton	23-20	2nd	1½
5-27	At N.Y.	W	1-0	6	3	Belcher	Fernandez	Charlton	24-20	3rd	2
5-29	Mon.	W	3-2	(11)	8	8	Bankhead	Sampen		25-20	3rd	½
5-30	Mon.	W	9-4	13	9	Browning	Gardner		26-20	1st	+½
5-31	Mon.	L	2-6	7	10	Nabholz	Rijo		26-21	3rd	½
6-2	St.L.	W	2-1	6	7	Belcher	DeLeon	Dibble	27-21	1st	+1
6-3	St.L.	W	8-7	12	13	Ruskin	Carpenter	Charlton	28-21	1st	+1
6-4	At L.A.	L	4-7	7	11	Hershiser	Browning	McDowell	28-22	1st	+½
6-5	At L.A.	W	6-2	14	9	Rijo	Ke. Gross		29-22	1st	+1½
6-6	At L.A.	W	5-4	10	10	Bankhead	Wilson	Charlton	30-22	1st	+2½
6-7	At L.A.	L	0-1	6	3	Candiotti	Belcher		30-23	1st	+1½
6-8	At S.F.	W	4-1	9	8	Swindell	Heredia	Dibble	31-23	1st	+2½
6-9	At S.F.	W	3-2	7	8	Charlton	Beck		32-23	1st	+2½
6-10	At S.F.	L	2-6	3	9	Black	Rijo		32-24	1st	+1½
6-12	L.A.	W	4-3	6	9	Bankhead	McDowell	Charlton	33-24	1st	+2½
6-13	L.A.	W	11-1	14	4	Belcher	Candiotti		34-24	1st	+2½
6-14	L.A.	W	5-1	9	10	Swindell	R. Martinez	Dibble	35-24	1st	+3½
6-15	S.F.	W	7-5	10	10	Browning	Jackson	Charlton	36-24	1st	+3½
6-16	S.F.	W	5-3	7	7	Rijo	Heredia	Dibble	37-24	1st	+3½
6-17	S.F.	W	6-4	8	7	Hammond	Burkett	Dibble	38-24	1st	+3½
6-18	At Atl.	W	7-5	(10)	9	10	Bankhead	Stanton	Charlton	39-24	1st	+4½
6-19	At Atl.	L	2-3	(10)	9	6	Mercker	Henry		39-25	1st	+½
6-20	At Atl.	L	1-2	11	9	Avery	Browning	Mercker	39-26	1st	+2½
6-21	At Atl.	L	0-2	6	9	Bielecki	Rijo	Mercker	39-27	1st	+1½
6-22	Hou.	L	2-5	6	8	Williams	Hammond	Hernandez	39-28	1st	+1
6-23	Hou.	W	10-6	15	11	Belcher	Blair		40-28	1st	+1
6-24	Hou.	W	9-6	13	12	Swindell	Harnisch	Charlton	41-28	1st	+1
6-26	Atl.	W	7-4	9	7	Browning	Avery		42-28	1st	+2

Date	Opp.	Res.	Score	(inn.*)	Hits	Opp. hits	Winning pitcher	Losing pitcher	Save	Record	Pos.	GB
6-27	Atl.	W	12-3		12	6	Rijo	Leibrandt		43-28	1st	+3
6-28	Atl.	W	6-5		6	7	Charlton	Wohlers		44-28	1st	+4
6-29	At Hou.	L	3-4		7	7	Osuna	Dibble	D. Jones	44-29	1st	+3½
6-30	At Hou.	L	1-5		5	9	J. Jones	Hammond	Hernandez	44-30	1st	+2½
7-1	At Hou.	L	2-3		10	7	D. Jones	Bankhead		44-31	1st	+2½
7-2	At Pit.	W	2-1		9	7	Rijo	Robinson	Charlton	45-31	1st	+3
7-3	At Pit.	W	7-3		13	11	Belcher	Tomlin		46-31	1st	+3
7-4	At Pit.	W	5-2		10	5	Swindell	Cole		47-31	1st	+3
7-5	At Pit.	W	2-1		10	4	Menendez	Drabek	Charlton	48-31	1st	+4
7-6	At Chi.	W	6-2		6	9	Ruskin	Morgan	Dibble	49-31	1st	+5
7-7	At Chi.	W	3-2		7	8	Rijo	Castillo	Charlton	50-31	1st	+6
7-8	At Chi.	L	2-3	(10)	5	11	Assenmacher	Dibble		50-32	1st	+5
7-9	Pit.	W	5-2		8	6	Bankhead	Mason	Charlton	51-32	1st	+5
7-10	Pit.	L	0-4		6	11	Drabek	Hammond		51-33	1st	+4
7-11	Pit.	L	3-9		7	12	Smith	Brown		51-34	1st	+3
7-12	Pit.	L	6-7	(10)	8	12	Patterson	Belcher	Belinda	51-35	1st	+2
7-16	St.L.	L	1-5		9	11	Olivares	Belcher	Worrell	51-36	1st	+1
7-17	St.L.	W	8-1		12	12	Swindell	Cormier		52-36	1st	+1
7-18	St.L.	W	3-2		9	8	Rijo	Tewksbury	Charlton	53-36	1st	+1
7-19	St.L.	W	5-4		8	9	Henry	Carpenter	Charlton	54-36	1st	+1
7-20	Chi.	W	5-2		9	8	Ruskin	McElroy	Dibble	55-36	1st	+1½
7-21	Chi.	L	0-1		3	4	Patterson	Belcher	Scanlan	55-37	1st	+½
7-22	Chi.	L	0-3		6	13	Maddux	Swindell		55-38	2nd	½
7-23	At St.L.	L	2-3		9	7	Cormier	Rijo	L. Smith	55-39	2nd	1
7-24	At St.L.	L	2-8		10	13	Tewksbury	Hammond		55-40	2nd	2
7-25	At St.L.	W	9-1		15	11	Bolton	Clark		56-40	2nd	2
7-26	At St.L.	W	7-6	(10)	17	12	Dibble	Carpenter		57-40	2nd	1
7-27	At S.D.	L	1-2		7	7	Benes	Swindell	Myers	57-41	2nd	1
7-28	At S.D.	W	4-1		8	7	Rijo	Deshaies	Charlton	58-41	2nd	...
7-29	At S.D.	L	3-7		8	11	Seminara	Bolton		58-42	2nd	1
7-31	Hou.	W	6-1		9	4	Belcher	Henry		59-42	1st	+½
8-1	Hou.	W	9-0		13	6	Swindell	Williams		60-42	1st	+½
8-2	Hou.	L	4-5		8	7	Boever	Rijo	D. Jones	60-43	2nd	1
8-3	Hou.	W	4-0		12	5	Hammond	J. Jones		61-43	2nd	½
8-4	At Atl.	L	5-7		11	7	Freeman	Charlton		61-44	2nd	1½
8-5	At Atl.	L	1-5		10	9	Avery	Belcher		61-45	2nd	2½
8-6	At Atl.	L	3-5		6	10	Smoltz	Swindell		61-46	2nd	3½
8-7	S.F.	W	4-3		9	8	Rijo	Black	Dibble	62-46	2nd	3½
8-8	S.F.	W	4-3	(16)	10	15	Henry	Pena		63-46	2nd	3½
8-9	S.F.	L	1-7		3	12	Wilson	Bolton		63-47	2nd	4½
8-11	L.A.	L	4-8		6	15	Ojeda	Belcher		63-48	2nd	4
8-12	L.A.	W	3-2		4	6	Swindell	Ke. Gross	Dibble	64-48	2nd	3½
8-13	L.A.	L	3-4		9	4	McDowell	Henry	Howell	64-49	2nd	4½
8-14	S.D.	L	1-5		8	10	Deshaies	Hammond		64-50	2nd	5½
8-15	S.D.	W	5-4		11	5	Dibble	Myers		65-50	2nd	5½
8-16	S.D.	W	12-2		15	7	Belcher	Hurst		66-50	2nd	4½
8-18 (1)	At Phi.	W	6-0		12	7	Swindell	Mulholland		67-50	2nd	5
8-18 (2)	At Phi.	L	1-6		4	9	Schilling	Rijo		67-51	2nd	5½
8-19	At Phi.	L	3-9		6	10	Rivera	Hammond		67-52	2nd	6½
8-21	At Mon.	L	3-6		8	10	Wetteland	Belcher		67-53	2nd	6
8-22	At Mon.	L	1-3		5	10	Rojas	Swindell	Wetteland	67-54	2nd	7
8-23	At Mon.	W	1-0		7	5	Rijo	Hill	Dibble	68-54	2nd	6
8-24	Phi.	W	8-5		12	10	Hammond	Rivera	Charlton	69-54	2nd	5½
8-25	Phi.	W	7-1		10	4	Belcher	Mathews		70-54	2nd	4½
8-26	Phi.	W	4-3		8	12	Bolton	Ashby	Dibble	71-54	2nd	3½
8-28 (1)	At N.Y.	L	3-4		9	7	Jones	Bankhead	Young	71-55	2nd	3½
8-28 (2)	At N.Y.	L	1-12		5	15	Whitehurst	Foster	Guetterman	71-56	2nd	4
8-29	At N.Y.	L	5-6		11	9	Gooden	Hammond	Young	71-57	2nd	5
8-30	At N.Y.	L	3-4		6	4	Jones	Dibble		71-58	2nd	5
8-31	Mon.	L	4-8		7	11	Rojas	Bolton		71-59	2nd	6½
9-1	Mon.	L	2-5		9	11	Martinez	Pugh	Wetteland	71-60	2nd	7½
9-2	Mon.	L	3-7		9	12	Fassero	Charlton	Wetteland	71-61	2nd	7½
9-3	N.Y.	W	4-3		4	3	Dibble	Young		72-61	2nd	6½
9-4	N.Y.	L	2-5		5	6	Fernandez	Belcher		72-62	2nd	6½
9-5	N.Y.	W	6-5		11	10	Charlton	Young		73-62	2nd	6½
9-6	N.Y.	W	6-1		10	9	Pugh	Gibson	Dibble	74-62	2nd	6½
9-7	At Hou.	W	10-0		13	3	Rijo	Williams		75-62	2nd	6½
9-8	At Hou.	L	0-2		4	6	Harnisch	Hammond	Hernandez	75-63	3rd	7½
9-9	At Atl.	L	7-12		11	11	Glavine	Belcher		75-64	3rd	8½
9-10	At Atl.	L	2-3		6	6	Stanton	Bankhead		75-65	3rd	9½
9-11	At S.D.	W	4-1		12	6	Pugh	Benes	Dibble	76-65	2nd	9½
9-12	At S.D.	W	7-4		15	9	Rijo	Hurst		77-65	2nd	9½
9-13	At S.D.	L	1-3		4	9	Seminara	Ayala	Myers	77-66	2nd	10½
9-15	Atl.	W	4-2		7	4	Belcher	Avery	Dibble	78-66	2nd	9½

Date	Opp.	Res.	Score	(inn.*)	Hits	Opp. hits	Winning pitcher	Losing pitcher	Save	Record	Pos.	GB
9-16	Atl.	L	2-3		10	5	Stanton	Ruskin	Wohlers	78-67	2nd	10½
9-17	Atl.	W	3-2		9	6	Rijo	Smoltz	Foster	79-67	2nd	9½
9-18	S.D.	W	4-2		8	7	Pugh	Hurst	Dibble	80-67	2nd	8½
9-19	S.D.	W	5-2		6	9	Ayala	Seminara	Dibble	81-67	2nd	7½
9-20	S.D.	W	6-1		11	7	Belcher	Gr. Harris		82-67	2nd	7½
9-22 (1)	Hou.	W	6-3		10	5	Rijo	Scheid		83-67	2nd	7
9-22 (2)	Hou.	W	4-3		9	11	Bankhead	Reynolds	Hill	84-67	2nd	6½
9-23	At L.A.	W	3-0		13	5	Pugh	Astacio	Dibble	85-67	2nd	6½
9-24	At L.A.	W	8-4		15	9	Bolton	McDowell	Charlton	86-67	2nd	5½
9-25	At S.F.	W	4-2		11	6	Belcher	Rogers	Foster	87-67	2nd	4½
9-26	At S.F.	L	3-8		13	12	Burkett	Swindell		87-68	2nd	5½
9-27	At S.F.	W	3-2		9	10	Rijo	Carter	Dibble	88-68	2nd	5½
9-29	L.A.	L	0-5		3	10	Astacio	Pugh		88-69	2nd	6½
9-30	L.A.	W	3-1		8	5	Belcher	P. Martinez	Dibble	89-69	2nd	5½
10-1	L.A.	L	2-4		9	8	Ke. Gross	Swindell	Howell	89-70	2nd	6½
10-2	S.F.	L	1-4		4	8	Reed	Rijo	Beck	89-71	2nd	8
10-3	S.F.	W	6-1		10	5	Ayala	Carter		90-71	2nd	8
10-4	S.F.	L	2-6	(13)	9	12	Righetti	Ruskin		90-72	2nd	8

Monthly records: April (11-10), May (15-11), June (18-9), July (15-12), August (12-17), September (18-10), Oct. (1-3).

HIGHLIGHTS

High point: After a 20-20 start, the Reds won 30 of their next 41 games to take a six-game lead in the National League West on July 7.

Low point: On July 28, Cincinnati was 58-41 and percentage points behind first-place Atlanta. But the Reds proceeded to go 19-25, placing them 10½ games behind the Braves on September 13.

Turning point: On August 4 in Atlanta, the Reds carried a 5-2 lead into the eighth inning. With a win, they could have moved into first. But the Braves scored five runs against lefthander Norm Charlton to win, 7-5. Atlanta moved 1½ games ahead of the Reds and remained in first the rest of the year.

Most valuable player: Utilityman Bip Roberts. He hit a career-high .323, scored 92 runs and stole 44 bases. He also tied an N.L. record by becoming the first player since 1943 to collect 10 consecutive hits (from September 19-23).

Most valuable pitcher: Righthander Jose Rijo. After overcoming elbow problems early in the year, he led the staff in ERA (2.56) and strikeouts (171) while tying for the team lead in wins (15) despite not getting his first victory until May 24.

Most improved player: Catcher Joe Oliver. He set career highs in several offensive categories, including batting average (.270), hits (131), RBIs (57), doubles (25) and runs (42).

Most pleasant surprise: Righthander Scott Bankhead. His 10 wins equaled the most by a Cincinnati reliever since John Franco went 12-3 in 1985.

Biggest disappointment: Right fielder Paul O'Neill. After hitting 28 homers and driving in 91 runs in 1991, he failed to carry the load as the cleanup hitter, collecting just 14 homers and 66 RBIs.

Key injuries: Third baseman Chris Sabo sprained his right ankle in the second game of the season and was never the same. Lefthander Tom Browning suffered a season-ending injury to his left knee on July 1 in Houston, and the Reds could never adequately replace him.

Notable: Manager Lou Piniella resigned on October 6, and General Manager Bob Quinn was fired two days later. The Reds named director of player development Jim Bowden to replace Quinn, while first-base coach Tony Perez, a member of the great Big Red Machine teams, replaced Piniella. . . . Charlton (26 saves) and righthander Rob Dibble (25) became the first teammates in big-league history to each record 25 or more saves in the same season.

—JERRY CRASNICK

RECORDS

1992 regular-season record: 90-72 (2nd in N.L. West); 53-28 at home; 37-44 on road; 39-33 vs. East; 51-39 vs. West; 31-30 vs. LHP; 59-42 vs. RHP; 22-26 on grass; 68-46 on turf; 29-24 in daytime; 61-48 at night; 34-24 in one-run games; 6-5 in extra-inning games; 1-1 in doubleheaders.

Team record last five years: 417-392 (.515, ranks 3rd in league in that span).

TEAM LEADERS

Batting average: Bip Roberts (.323).
At-bats: Barry Larkin (533).
Runs: Bip Roberts (92).
Hits: Bip Roberts (172).
Total bases: Barry Larkin (242).
Doubles: Bip Roberts (34).
Triples: Barry Larkin, Bip Roberts, Reggie Sanders (6).
Home runs: Paul O'Neill (14).
Runs batted in: Barry Larkin (78).
Stolen bases: Bip Roberts (44).
Slugging percentage: Barry Larkin (.454).
On-base percentage: Bip Roberts (.393).
Wins: Tim Belcher, Jose Rijo (15).
Earned-run average: Jose Rijo (2.56).
Complete games: Greg Swindell (5).
Shutouts: Greg Swindell (3).
Saves: Norm Charlton (26).
Innings pitched: Tim Belcher (227⅔).
Strikeouts: Jose Rijo (171).

GAMES BY POSITION

Catcher: Joe Oliver 141, Troy Afenir 15, Rick Wrona 10, Dan Wilson 9, Jeff Reed 6, Scott Bradley 2.

First base: Hal Morris 109, Bill Doran 25, Dave Martinez 21, Darnell Coles 20, Tim Costo 12, Joe Oliver 1, Rick Wrona 1.

Second base: Bill Doran 104, Bip Roberts 42, Freddie Benavides 37, Jeff Branson 33.

Third base: Chris Sabo 93, Bip Roberts 36, Willie Greene 25, Darnell Coles 23, Jeff Branson 8, Freddie Benavides 1, Gary Green 1.

Shortstop: Barry Larkin 140, Freddie Benavides 34, Gary Green 6, Jeff Branson 1.

Outfield: Paul O'Neill 143, Dave Martinez 111, Reggie Sanders 110, Glenn Braggs 79, Bip Roberts 79, Billy Hatcher 23, Cesar Hernandez 18, Jacob Brumfield 16, Darnell Coles 5, Geronimo Berroa 3.

TOP 10 DRAFT CHOICES

1. Chad Mottola, OF, University of Central Florida.
2a. Chad Alexander, OF, Lufkin (Tex.) High School.
2b. Rick Magdelano, SS, Baldwin Park (Calif.) High School.
3. Todd Etler, RHP, Covington (Ky.) Catholic High School.
4. Eric Owens, SS, Ferrum (Va.) College.
5. Jason Angel, RHP, Clemson University.
6. Curtis Lyons, RHP, Madison Central High School, Richmond, Ky.
7. Martin Lister, LHP, Jefferson Davis Junior College (Ala.).
8. Mike Meggers, OF, University of Mary Hardin-Baylor (Tex.).
9. Brian Silvia, C, University of Mississippi.
10. Dan Kopriva, 3B, University of Louisville.

COLORADO ROCKIES
NATIONAL LEAGUE WEST DIVISION

1993 SCHEDULE

APRIL
SUN	MON	TUE	WED	THU	FRI	SAT
				1	2	3
4	5 N NY	6	7 N NY	8	9 N MON H	10 MON H
11 MON H	12 N NY H	13 N NY H	14 N NY H	15 N NY H	16 N MON	17 MON
18 MON	19	20 N STL	21 N STL	22 STL	23 N FLA	24 FLA H
25 FLA H	26 N CHI H	27 N CHI H	28 N STL H	29 N STL H	30 N FLA	

MAY
SUN	MON	TUE	WED	THU	FRI	SAT
						1 N FLA
2 N FLA	3	4 N CHI	5 N CHI	6 N ATL	7 N ATL H	8 N ATL H
9 ATL H	10 N SF	11 N SF	12 N SF	13 N SF	14 N CIN	15 N CIN
16 CIN	17 N SD	18 N SD	19 N SD	20 SD	21 N LA	22 N LA
23 LA	24	25 N HOU	26 N HOU	27 N HOU	28 N PHI	29 PHI H
30 PHI H	31 N PIT H					

JUNE
SUN	MON	TUE	WED	THU	FRI	SAT
		1 N PIT H	2 N PIT H	3 N	4 N PHI	5 N PHI
6 PHI	7	8 N PIT	9 N PIT	10	11 N HOU H	12 N HOU H
13 HOU H	14 N LA	15 N LA	16 N LA H	17	18 N SD H	19 N SD H
20 SD	21 N CIN H	22 N CIN H	23 N CIN H	24 SF	25 N SF	26 SF
27 SF	28	29 N ATL	30 N ATL			

JULY
SUN	MON	TUE	WED	THU	FRI	SAT
				1 N ATL	2 N CHI H	3 N CHI H
4 CHI H	5 N CHI H	6 N FLA	7 N FLA H	8 N FLA H	9 N STL	10 N STL
11 STL	12	13 * ALL-STAR GAME	14	15 N CHI	16 N CHI	17 CHI
18 CHI	19 FLA	20 N FLA	21 N FLA	22 N STL H	23 N STL H	24 N STL H
25 STL H	26 N ATL H	27 N ATL H	28 N ATL H	29	30 N SF	31 N SF H

AUGUST
SUN	MON	TUE	WED	THU	FRI	SAT
1 SF	2 N CIN	3 N CIN	4 N CIN	5 N CIN	6 DH N SD	7
8 SD	9 N LA	10 N LA	11 N LA	12 N LA	13 N HOU	14 N HOU
15 HOU	16	17 N PHI	18 N PHI H	19 N PHI H	20 N NY	21 NY
22 NY	23 N PHI	24 N PHI	25 PHI	26 N NY	27 N NY	28 N NY
29 NY	30 N MON H	31 N MON H				

SEPTEMBER
SUN	MON	TUE	WED	THU	FRI	SAT
			1 N MON H	2	3 N PIT	4 N PIT
5 PIT H	6 N MON	7 N MON	8 N MON	9 N PIT	10 N PIT	11 N PIT
12 PIT	13 N HOU H	14 N HOU H	15 N HOU H	16 N HOU H	17 N LA	18 N LA
19 LA	20 N SD H	21 N SD H	22 N SD H	23	24 N CIN H	25 N CIN H
26 CIN H	27	28 N SF	29 SF	30		

OCTOBER
SUN	MON	TUE	WED	THU	FRI	SAT
					1 N ATL	2 N ATL
3 ATL						

1993 SEASON

CLUB DIRECTORY

Chairman and chief executive officer
John Antonucci
President and chief operating officer
Steve Ehrhart
Exec. vice president, baseball operations
John McHale
Executive vice president/general counsel
Paul Jacobs
Senior vice president/general manager
Bob Gebhard
Special assistant to general manager
Larry Bearnarth
Senior vice president, business operations
Bernie Mullin
Vice president, finance
Michael Kent
Assistant general manager
Randy Smith
Director of scouting
Pat Daugherty
Assistant director of scouting
Paul Egins
Director of community relations
Roger Kinney
Director of ticket operations
Chuck Javernick
Director of corporate marketing
Dave Glazier
Director of merchandising
Mark Ehrhart
Special events coordinator
Alan Bossart
Executive administrator
Wendy Jobe
Assistant to chairman
Carolyn Shaffer

Assistant to president
Jennifer Moore
Asst. to senior v.p., business operations
Liz Stecklein
Administrators, baseball operations
Mary Cheney
Jeff Tamarkin
Administrative asst., baseball operations
Chris Rice
Administrative assistant, public affairs
Barb Maniscalco
Administrative assistant
Lisa Quarton
Secretary, scouting department
Penny Biever
Sales assistant
Jan Giovino
Scouting supervisors
Ty Coslow
Darwin Cox
Jimmy Lester
Lance Nichols
Ed Santa
Area scouting supervisor
Tom Wheeler
National cross-checker scout
Herb Hippauf
Regular scouts
Julian Gonzalez
Al Hargesheimer
Randy Johnson
Pat Jones
Danny Montgomery
Jorge Posada
Johnny Zizzo

SCHEDULE KEY
H—Home game.   DH—Doubleheader.
N—Night game (any game starting after 5 p.m.).
*All-Star Game at Oriole Park at Camden Yards, Baltimore.

SPRING TRAINING ROSTER

Manager—Don Baylor (25).

Coaches—Larry Bearnarth (36), Ron Hassey (29), Amos Otis (26), Jerry Royster (3), Don Zimmer (23).

No.	PITCHERS	B/T	Ht./Wt.	Born	1992 clubs
32	Aldred, Scott	L/L	6-4/215	6-12-68	Detroit, Toledo
43	Ashby, Andy	R/R	6-5/180	7-11-67	Philadelphia, Scranton/Wilkes-Barre
19	Blair, Willie	R/R	6-1/185	12-18-65	Tucson, Houston
50	Bochtler, Doug	R/R	6-3/185	7-5-70	Harrisburg
37	Boucher, Denis	R/L	6-1/195	3-7-68	Colorado Springs, Cleveland
47	Buckley, Travis	R/R	6-4/210	6-15-70	Harrisburg
49	Fredrickson, Scott	R/R	6-3/215	8-19-67	Wichita
48	Hawblitzel, Ryan	R/R	6-2/170	4-30-71	Charlotte
27	Henry, Butch	L/L	6-1/195	10-7-68	Houston
40	Holmes, Darren	R/R	6-0/199	4-25-66	Denver, Milwaukee
51	Jones, Calvin	R/R	6-3/185	9-26-63	Seattle, Calgary
35	Leskanic, Curt	R/R	6-0/180	4-2-68	Orlando, Portland
53	Merriman, Brett	R/R	6-2/180	7-15-66	Midland, Edmonton
54	Moore, Marcus	B/R	6-5/195	11-2-70	Knoxville
17	Nied, David	R/R	6-2/185	12-22-68	Richmond, Atlanta
28	Painter, Lance	L/L	6-1/195	7-21-67	Wichita
39	Reed, Steve	R/R	6-2/202	3-11-66	Shreveport, Phoenix, San Francisco
42	Reynoso, Armando	R/R	6-0/186	5-1-66	Richmond, Atlanta
31	Ritz, Kevin	R/R	6-4/220	6-8-65	Detroit
34	Sanford, Mo	R/R	6-6/225	12-24-66	Nashville, Chattanooga
44	Seanez, Rudy	R/R	5-10/185	10-20-68	DID NOT PLAY
52	Shepherd, Keith	R/R	6-2/197	1-21-68	Birmingham, Reading, Philadelphia

No.	CATCHERS	B/T	Ht./Wt.	Born	1992 clubs
11	Ausmus, Brad	R/R	5-11/185	4-14-69	Albany/Colonie, Columbus
7	Girardi, Joe	R/R	5-11/195	10-14-64	Chicago N.L.
33	Owens, J.	R/R	6-1/200	2-10-69	Orlando
22	Wedge, Eric	R/R	6-3/215	1-27-68	Pawtucket, Boston

No.	INFIELDERS	B/T	Ht./Wt.	Born	1992 clubs
12	Benavides, Freddie	R/R	6-2/185	4-7-66	Cincinnati
15	Castellano, Pedro	R/R	6-1/175	3-11-70	Iowa, Charlotte
9	Castilla, Vinny	R/R	6-1/175	7-4-67	Richmond, Atlanta
14	Galarraga, Andres	R/R	6-3/235	6-18-61	St. Louis, Louisville
13	Hayes, Charlie	R/R	6-0/207	5-29-65	New York A.L.
8	Mejia, Roberto	R/R	5-11/160	4-14-72	Vero Beach
20	Tatum, Jim	R/R	6-2/200	10-9-67	Denver, Milwaukee
21	Young, Eric	R/R	5-9/180	11-26-66	Albuquerque, Los Angeles

No.	OUTFIELDERS	B/T	Ht./Wt.	Born	1992 clubs
10	Bichette, Dante	R/R	6-3/225	11-18-63	Milwaukee
6	Boston, Daryl	L/L	6-3/195	1-4-63	New York N.L.
16	Castillo, Braulio	R/R	6-0/160	5-13-68	Scranton/Wilkes-Barre, Philadelphia
24	Clark, Jerald	R/R	6-4/205	8-10-63	San Diego
5	Cole, Alex	L/L	6-0/170	8-17-65	Cleveland, Pittsburgh

BALLPARK INFORMATION

Ballpark (capacity, surface)
Mile High Stadium (76,100, grass)
Address
1700 Broadway, Suite 2100
Denver, CO 80290
Business phone
303-292-0200
Ticket information
303-292-0200
Ticket prices
$10 (outfield mezz. and infield terr.)
$8 (outfield terr. and infield view)
$5 (outfield view)
$4 (reserved general admission)
$1 (rockpile reserved)
Field dimensions (from home plate)
To left field at foul line, 335 feet
To center field, 423 feet
To right field at foul line, 370
First game played
Scheduled for April 9, 1993

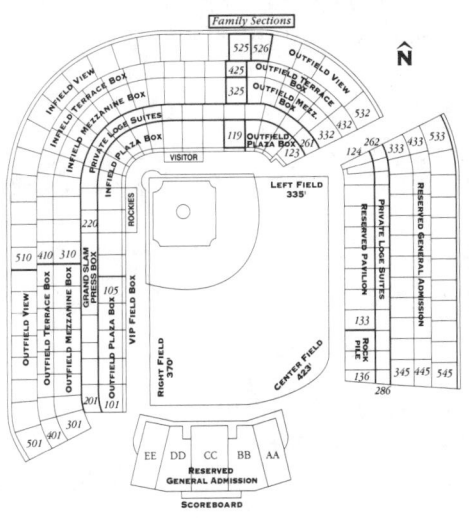

MINOR LEAGUE AFFILIATES

Class	Team	League	Manager
AAA	Colorado Springs	Pacific Coast	Brad Mills
AA	None		
A	Central Valley	California	Paul Zuvella
A	Bend	Northwest	Howie Bedell
Rookie	Mesa	Arizona	P.J. Carey

BROADCAST INFORMATION

Radio: KOA-AM (850). Broadcasters: Jeff Kingery, Wayne Hagin.
TV: KWGN-TV (Channel 2). Broadcasters: To be announced.
Cable TV: None.

SPRING TRAINING

Ballpark (city): Hi Corbett Field (Tucson, Ariz.).
Ticket information: 602-327-9467.

TOP 10 DRAFT CHOICES

1. **John Burke,** RHP, University of Florida.
2. **Mark Thompson,** RHP, University of Kentucky.
3. **Roger Bailey,** RHP, Florida State University.
4. **Lloyd Peever,** RHP, Louisiana State University.
5. **Ryan Freeburg,** 3B/OF, Grand Canyon University (Ariz.).
6. **Bill Scalzitti,** C, Miami-Dade (Fla.) Community College North.
7. **Jason Bates,** SS, University of Arizona.
8. **Chris Henderson,** RHP, Brevard Community College (Fla.).
9. **Mike Eiffert,** LHP, University of Texas-Pan American.
10. **Garvin Alston,** RHP, Florida International University.

FLORIDA MARLINS
NATIONAL LEAGUE EAST DIVISION

1993 SCHEDULE

APRIL

SUN	MON	TUE	WED	THU	FRI	SAT
				1	2	3
4	5 LA H	6 N LA H	7 N LA H	8 N	9 N SD H	10 N SD H
11 SD H	12 SF	13 SF	14 SF	15	16 N HOU	17 N HOU
18 HOU	19	20 N ATL H	21 N ATL H	22 N ATL H	23 N COL	24 COL
25 COL	26 CIN	27 CIN	28 N ATL	29 N ATL	30 N COL H	

MAY

SUN	MON	TUE	WED	THU	FRI	SAT
						1 N COL H
2 N COL H	3	4 N CIN H	5 N CIN H	6	7 N NY	8 N NY
9 NY	10 N NY	11 N MON	12 N MON	13 N MON	14 N STL	15 N STL
16 STL	17 N PHI H	18 N PHI H	19 N PHI H	20	21 N CHI H	22 N CHI H
23 CHI H	24	25 N PIT	26 N PIT	27 N PIT	28 N HOU H	29 N HOU H
30 HOU H	31 SF H					

JUNE

SUN	MON	TUE	WED	THU	FRI	SAT
		1 N SF H	2 N SF H	3	4 N SD	5 N SD
6 SD	7 N LA	8 N LA	9	10 N PIT H	11 N PIT H	12 N PIT H
13 PIT H	14 N CHI	15 N CHI	16	17 N PHI	18 N PHI	19 PHI
20 PHI	21 N STL H	22 N STL H	23 N STL H	24	25 N MON H	26 N MON H
27 MON H	28	29 N NY H	30 N NY H			

JULY

SUN	MON	TUE	WED	THU	FRI	SAT
				1 N NY H	2 N ATL	3 ATL
4 ATL	5 N ATL	6 N COL	7 N COL	8 COL	9 N ATL H	10 N ATL H
11 ATL H	12	13 ● ALL-STAR GAME	14	15 CIN	16 N CIN	17 N CIN
18 CIN	19 N COL H	20 N COL H	21 N COL H	22 N CIN H	23 N CIN H	24 N CIN H
25 CIN H	26	27 N NY	28 N NY	29 NY	30 N MON	31 N MON

AUGUST

SUN	MON	TUE	WED	THU	FRI	SAT
1 MON	2 N STL	3 N STL	4 STL	5 N STL	6 N PHI H	7 N PHI H
8 N PHI H	9 N CHI H	10 N CHI H	11 N CHI H	12 N CHI H	13 N PIT	14 N PIT
15 PIT	16	17 N HOU	18 N HOU	19 N HOU	20 N SF	21 N SF
22 SF	23	24 N HOU H	25 N HOU H	26 N HOU H	27 N SF H	28 N SF H
29 N SF H	30 N SD H	31 N SD H				

SEPTEMBER

SUN	MON	TUE	WED	THU	FRI	SAT
			1 N SD H	2 N SD H	3 N LA H	4 N LA H
5 LA H	6 N SD	7 N SD	8 N SD	9 N LA	10 N LA	11 N LA
12 LA	13	14 N PIT H	15 N PIT H	16 N PIT H	17 N CHI	18 CHI
19 CHI	20 N PHI	21 N PHI	22 N PHI	23	24 N STL H	25 N STL H
26 STL H	27 N MON H	28 N MON H	29 N MON H	30 N MON H		

OCTOBER

SUN	MON	TUE	WED	THU	FRI	SAT
					1 N NY H	2 N NY H
3 NY H						

1993 SEASON

CLUB DIRECTORY

Owner
H. Wayne Huizenga

Exec. vice president and general manager
David Dombrowski

Vice president of business operations
Richard Andersen

Vice president of communications
Dean Jordan

Vice president of finance
Jonathan Mariner

Vice president of sales and marketing
Donald Smiley

Assistant general manager
Frank Wren

Director of Latin American operations and special consultant to the general manager
Angel Vasquez

Asst. dir. of Latin American operations
Al Avila

Director of player development
John Boles

Senior adviser, player personnel
Whitey Lockman

Director of minor league administration
Dan Lunetta

Associate director of scouting and director of international operations
Orrin Freeman

Director of team travel
John Panagakis

Dir. of admin. and stadium operations
M. Bruce Schulze

Director of merchandising
Steve Stock

Director of ticket operations
Bill Galante

Director of group sales
William Beck

Dir. of corporate sales and sponsorships
Neal Bendesky

Director of media relations
Chuck Pool

Assistant director of media relations
Adolfo Salgueiro

Director of Brevard County operations
Ken Lehner

Equipment manager
Mike Wallace

Team physician
Dr. Dan Kanell

Head trainer
Larry Starr

Major league scouts
Ken Kravec
Scott Reid
John Young

National crosschecker
Jax Robertson

Regional crosscheckers
Dick Egan
Murray Cook
Greg Zunino

Scouts
Kelvin Bowles
Ty Brown
John Castleberry
Brad Del Barba
Lou Fitzgerald
William George
Jim Hendry
Joe Campise
Stan Saleski
Stan Zielinski
Ed Bockman
Richard Bordi
Al Geddes
Bill Serena
Charlie Silvera
Keith Snider
Matthew King
Robert Laurie
Grady Mack
Steve Minor
Francis Oneto
James Pentland
Bill Scherrer
Tim Schmidt
Bill Singer
George Tebbetts
Wally Walker
DeJon Watson
Jeff Wren

Director Dominican Republic operations
Jesus Alou

Dominican Republic scouts
Edmundo Borrome
Julian Camilo
Pablo Lantigua

Puerto Rico scout
Cucho Rodriguez

Venezuela scout
Levy Ochoa

SCHEDULE KEY

H—Home game. N—Night game (any game starting after 5 p.m.).
*All-Star Game at Oriole Park at Camden Yards, Baltimore.

SPRING TRAINING ROSTER

Manager—Rene Lachemann (15).

Coaches—Marcel Lachemann (53), Vada Pinson (28), Doug Rader (12), Frank Reberger (33), Cookie Rojas (1).

No.	PITCHERS	B/T	Ht./Wt.	Born	1992 clubs
77	Armstrong, Jack	R/R	6-5/215	3-7-65	Cleveland
29	Berumen, Andres	R/R	6-1/205	4-5-71	Appleton
46	Bowen, Ryan	R/R	6-0/185	2-10-68	Houston, Tucson
44	Carpenter, Cris	R/R	6-1/185	4-5-65	St. Louis
56	Carrasco, Hector	R/R	6-2/175	10-22-69	Asheville
43	Chiamparino, Scott	L/R	6-2/205	8-22-66	Gulf Coast Rangers, Charlotte, Tulsa, Oklahoma City, Texas
41	Corsi, Jim	R/R	6-1/220	9-9-61	Tacoma, Oakland
40	Griffiths, Brian	R/R	6-2/190	5-29-68	Jackson
34	Harvey, Bryan	R/R	6-2/212	6-2-63	California
51	Hoffman, Trevor	R/R	6-0/205	10-13-67	Chattanooga, Nashville
42	Johnstone, John	R/R	6-3/195	11-25-68	Binghamton
26	Lewis, Richie	R/R	5-10/175	1-25-66	Rochester, Baltimore
37	Martinez, Jose	R/R	6-2/155	1-1-71	St. Lucie, Binghamton
31	McAndrew, Jamie	R/R	6-2/190	9-2-67	Albuquerque, San Antonio
32	Myers, Mike	B/L	6-3/185	6-26-71	Clinton, San Jose
48	Rapp, Pat	R/R	6-3/195	7-13-67	Phoenix, San Francisco
36	Spencer, Stan	R/R	6-3/195	8-2-69	DID NOT PLAY
38	Tabaka, Jeff	R/L	6-2/195	1-17-64	El Paso
35	Weathers, Dave	R/R	6-3/205	9-25-69	Syracuse, Toronto
45	Yaughn, Kip	R/R	6-0/180	7-20-69	Hagerstown

No.	CATCHERS	B/T	Ht./Wt.	Born	1992 clubs
55	Decker, Steve	R/R	6-3/210	10-25-65	Phoenix, San Francisco
13	Natal, Bob	R/R	5-11/190	11-13-65	Indianapolis, Montreal
9	Santiago, Benito	R/R	6-1/185	3-9-65	San Diego, Las Vegas

No.	INFIELDERS	B/T	Ht./Wt.	Born	1992 clubs
24	Arias, Alex	R/R	6-3/185	11-20-67	Iowa, Chicago N.L.
8	Barberie, Bret	B/R	5-11/180	8-16-67	Montreal, Indianapolis
19	Conine, Jeff	R/R	6-1/220	6-27-66	Omaha, Kansas City
39	Destrade, Orestes	B/R	6-4/210	5-8-62	Seibu
18	Magadan, Dave	L/R	6-3/200	9-30-62	New York N.L.
27	Martinez, Ramon	B/R	6-2/165	9-8-69	Salem
20	Scott, Gary	R/R	6-0/175	8-22-68	Chicago N.L., Iowa
22	Weiss, Walt	B/R	6-0/175	11-28-63	Tacoma, Oakland

No.	OUTFIELDERS	B/T	Ht./Wt.	Born	1992 clubs
21	Carr, Chuck	B/R	5-10/165	8-10-68	Arkansas, Louisville, St. Louis
3	Everett, Carl	B/R	6-0/181	6-3-71	Fort Lauderdale, Prince William
4	Fariss, Monty	R/R	6-4/205	10-13-67	Texas, Oklahoma City
47	Felix, Junior	B/R	5-11/165	10-3-67	California
7	Moore, Kerwin	B/R	6-1/190	10-29-70	Baseball City, Memphis
2	Pose, Scott	L/R	5-11/165	2-11-67	Chattanooga
17	Tavarez, Jesus	R/R	6-0/170	3-26-71	Jacksonville
11	Whitmore, Darrell	L/R	6-1/210	11-18-68	Kinston
30	Wilson, Nigel	L/L	6-1/185	1-12-70	Knoxville

BALLPARK INFORMATION

Ballpark (capacity, surface)
Joe Robbie Stadium (48,000, grass)

Address
2269 N.W. 199th St.
Miami, Fla. 33056

Business phone
305-623-6100

Ticket information
305-930-7800

Ticket prices
$22* (club level section B)
$19* (club level section C)
$13 (terrace box)
$8.50 (mezzanine reserved)
$7 (outfield reserved, adult)
$3.50 (outfield res., 12 and under)
$4 (general admission, adult)
$1.50 (g.a., 12 and under)
* does not include $5 license fee

Field dimensions (from home plate)
To left field at foul line, 335 feet
To center field, 410 feet
To right field at foul line, 345

First game played
Scheduled for April 5, 1993

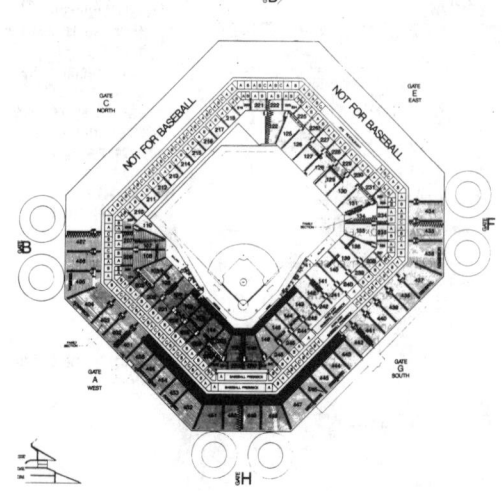

MINOR LEAGUE AFFILIATES

Class	Team	League	Manager
AAA	Edmonton	Pacific Coast	Sal Rende
AA	None		
A	High Desert	California	Fredi Gonzalez
A	Kane County	Midwest	Carlos Tosca
A	Elmira	New York-Pennsylvania	Lynn Jones
Rookie	Gulf Coast Marlins	Gulf Coast	Jim Hendry

BROADCAST INFORMATION

Radio: WQAM-AM (560). Broadcasters: Joe Angel, Dave O'Brien. WCMQ-AM (1210, Spanish language). Broadcasters: Felo Ramirez, Manolo Alvarez.
TV: WBFS-TV (Channel 13). Broadcasters: Jay Randolph, Gary Carter.
Cable TV: The Sunshine Network. Broadcasters: Jay Randolph, Gary Carter.

SPRING TRAINING

Ballpark (city): Cocoa Expo (Cocoa, Fla.).
Ticket information: 407-253-4433.

TOP 10 DRAFT CHOICES

1. **Charles Johnson.** C, University of Miami (Fla.).
2. **John Lynch.** RHP, Stanford University.
3. **Rich Ireland.** LHP, Crater High School, Central Point, Ore.
4. **Willie Brown.** OF, Florida A&M University.
5. **Alex Aranzamendi.** SS, Rio Piedras, Puerto Rico.
6. **Pat Leahy.** RHP, University of Notre Dame.
7. **Reynol Mendoza.** RHP, Incarnate Word College (Tex.).
8. **Dan Roman.** LHP, Brooklyn College.
9. **Scott Samuels.** OF, Arizona State University.
10. **Chris Sheff.** OF, Pepperdine University.

HOUSTON ASTROS
NATIONAL LEAGUE WEST DIVISION

1993 SCHEDULE

APRIL

SUN	MON	TUE	WED	THU	FRI	SAT
				1	2	3
4	5 N PHI H	6 N PHI H	7 N PHI H	8 N	9 N NY	10 N NY
11 NY	12	13 N MON	14 N MON	15 N MON	16 N FLA H	17 N FLA H
18 FLA H	19 N CHI	20 N CHI	21 N CHI	22	23 N PIT	24 N PIT
25 PIT	26 N STL H	27 N STL H	28 N CHI H	29 N CHI H	30 N PIT H	

MAY

SUN	MON	TUE	WED	THU	FRI	SAT
						1 N PIT H
2 PIT H	3	4 N STL	5 N STL	6 N CIN H	7 N CIN H	8 N CIN H
9 CIN H	10 N ATL H	11 N ATL H	12 N ATL H	13	14 N LA	15 N LA
16 LA H	17 SF	18 N SF	19 N SF	20	21 N SD	22 N SD
23 SD	24	25 N COL H	26 N COL H	27 N COL H	28 N FLA	29 N FLA
30 FLA	31 MON H					

JUNE

SUN	MON	TUE	WED	THU	FRI	SAT
		1 N MON H	2 N MON H	3	4 N NY	5 N NY
6 NY H	7 N PHI	8 N PHI	9 N PHI	10	11 N COL	12 N COL
13 COL	14	15 N SD H	16 N SD H	17 N SD H	18 N SF	19 N SF
20 SF H	21 N LA	22 N LA	23 N LA	24	25 N ATL	26 N ATL
27 ATL	28	29 N CIN	30 N CIN			

JULY

SUN	MON	TUE	WED	THU	FRI	SAT
				1 N CIN	2 N STL H	3 N STL H
4 STL H	5 N STL H	6 N PIT H	7 N PIT H	8 N PIT H	9 N	10
11 CHI	12	13 * ALL-STAR GAME	14	15 N STL	16 N STL	17 N STL
18 STL	19 N PIT	20 N PIT	21 N PIT	22 N CHI H	23 N CHI H	24 CHI H
25 CHI H	26 N CIN	27 N CIN H	28 N CIN H	29 N ATL H	30 N ATL H	31 N ATL H

AUGUST

SUN	MON	TUE	WED	THU	FRI	SAT
1 ATL H	2	3 N LA H	4 N LA H	5 N LA H	6 N SF	7 SF
8 SF	9 N SD	10 N SD	11 N SD	12 N SD	13 N COL H	14 N COL H
15 COL H	16	17 N FLA H	18 N FLA H	19 N FLA H	20 N PHI	21 N PHI
22 PHI H	23	24 N FLA	25 N FLA	26 N FLA	27 N MON	28 N MON
29 MON	30 NY	31 N NY				

SEPTEMBER

SUN	MON	TUE	WED	THU	FRI	SAT
			1 NY	2	3 N MON H	4 N MON H
5 MON H	6 N NY H	7 N NY H	8 N NY H	9	10 N PHI	11 N PHI
12 PHI	13 N COL	14 N COL	15 N COL	16	17 N SD H	18 N SD H
19 SD H	20 N SF H	21 N SF H	22 N SF H	23 N SF H	24	25 LA
26 LA	27	28 N ATL	29 N ATL	30 N		

OCTOBER

SUN	MON	TUE	WED	THU	FRI	SAT
					1 N CIN	2 CIN
3 CIN						

1993 SEASON

CLUB DIRECTORY

Owner and chairman of the board
  Drayton McLane Jr.
Senior vice president
  Sandy Sanford
Vice president
  Bob McClaren
General manager
  Bill Wood
Assistant general manager
  Bob Watson
Director of minor league operations
  Fred Nelson
Director of scouting
  Dan O'Brien
Director of public relations
  Rob Matwick
Director of Florida operations
  Pat O'Conner
Traveling secretary
  Barry Waters
Assistant to general manager
  Tim Hellmuth
Assistant director of public relations
  Tyler Barnes
Asst. to dir. of minor leagues and scouting
  Lew Temple
Asst. dir. of scouting and dir. of intl. dev.
  David Rawnsley
Coordinator of publications
  Kevin Guilfoile
Vice president, marketing
  Ted Haracz
Director of sales
  John Sorrentino
Director of broadcasting
  Jamie Hildreth
Director of advertising sales/promotions
  Norm Miller
Director of communications
  Pam Gardner
Director of season ticket services
  Andrew Huang
Director of group sales
  Debra Fulmer
Marketing operations manager
  Matt Kastel
Director of community services
  TBA
Scouts
  Bob Blair
  Stan Boroski
  Ralph Bratton

William Buck
Gerry Craft
Jug DeFord
Chuck Edmondson
Orlando Estevez
James Farrar
Ben Galante
Brian Granger
Carl Greene
Sterling Housley
Dan Huston
Marc Johnson
Don Kalkstein
Brian Keegan
Bill Kelso
Bob King
David Lakey
Julio Linares
Bobby Macias
Mike Maggert
Walt Matthews
Domingo Mercedes
Walter Millies
Tom Mooney
Carlos Muro
Hal Newhouser
Ramon Perez
Joe Pittman
Jim Pransky
Andres Reiner
Ramee Richards
Deron Rombach
Nelson Rood
Rich Schroeder
Mark Servais
Tad Slowik
Lynwood Stallings
Kevin Stein
Ronnie Stevens
Paul Weaver
Gene Wellman
Greg Whitworth
Advance scouts
  Stan Benjamin
  Jack Bloomfield
  George Brophy
  Charlie Fox
  Howie Haak
  Dick Hager
  Bob Skinner

SCHEDULE KEY

H—Home game.   N—Night game (any game starting after 5 p.m.).
*All-Star Game at Oriole Park at Camden Yards, Baltimore.

Manager—Art Howe (18).

Coaches—Bob Cluck (55), Matt Galante (48), Rudy Jaramillo (42), Ed Ott (14), Tom Spencer (52).

No.	PITCHERS	B/T	Ht./Wt.	Born	1992 clubs
15	Drabek, Doug	R/R	6-1/185	7-25-62	Pittsburgh
46	Edens, Tom	L/R	6-2/188	6-9-61	Minnesota
43	Grimsley, Jason	R/R	6-3/180	8-7-67	Tucson
27	Harnisch, Pete	R/R	6-0/207	9-23-66	Houston
31	Hernandez, Xavier	L/R	6-2/185	8-16-65	Houston
50	Hurta, Bob	L/L	6-0/190	11-17-65	Jackson, Tucson
23	Jones, Doug	R/R	6-2/195	6-24-57	Houston
59	Jones, Todd	R/R	6-3/200	4-24-68	Jackson, Tucson
44	Juden, Jeff	R/R	6-7/245	1-19-71	Tucson
57	Kile, Darryl	R/R	6-5/185	12-2-68	Houston, Tucson
56	Mallicoat, Rob	L/L	6-3/180	11-16-64	Tucson, Houston
29	Osuna, Al	L/L	6-3/200	8-10-65	Houston
51	Portugal, Mark	R/R	6-0/190	10-30-62	Houston
38	Reynolds, Shane	R/R	6-3/210	3-26-68	Tucson, Houston
21	Swindell, Greg	B/L	6-3/225	1-2-65	Cincinnati
53	Williams, Brian	R/R	6-2/195	2-15-69	Tucson, Houston

No.	CATCHERS	B/T	Ht./Wt.	Born	1992 clubs
10	Eusebio, Tony	R/R	6-2/180	4-27-67	Jackson
9	Servais, Scott	R/R	6-2/195	6-4-67	Houston
6	Taubensee, Eddie	L/R	6-4/205	10-31-68	Houston, Tucson
36	Tucker, Scooter	R/R	6-2/205	11-18-66	Tucson, Houston

No.	INFIELDERS	B/T	Ht./Wt.	Born	1992 clubs
5	Bagwell, Jeff	R/R	6-0/195	5-27-68	Houston
7	Biggio, Craig	R/R	5-11/180	12-14-65	Houston
11	Caminiti, Ken	B/R	6-0/200	4-21-63	Houston
1	Candaele, Casey	B/R	5-9/165	1-12-61	Houston
17	Cedeno, Andujar	R/R	6-1/168	8-21-69	Houston, Tucson
3	Donnels, Chris	L/R	6-0/185	4-21-66	Tidewater, New York N.L.
19	Guerrero, Juan	R/R	5-11/160	2-1-67	Houston
2	Miller, Orlando	R/R	6-1/180	1-13-69	Jackson, Tucson
28	Uribe, Jose	B/R	5-10/170	1-21-60	San Francisco

No.	OUTFIELDERS	B/T	Ht./Wt.	Born	1992 clubs
64	Ansley, Willie	R/R	6-2/200	12-15-69	Jackson, Gulf Coast Astros
24	Anthony, Eric	L/L	6-2/195	11-8-67	Houston
20	Bass, Kevin	B/R	6-0/190	5-12-59	San Francisco, New York N.L.
	Daugherty, Jack	B/L	6-0/190	7-3-60	Texas, Oklahoma City
12	Finley, Steve	L/L	6-2/180	3-12-65	Houston
26	Gonzalez, Luis	L/R	6-2/180	9-3-67	Houston, Tucson
60	Hatcher, Chris	R/R	6-3/220	1-7-69	Osceola
62	Hunter, Brian	R/R	6-2/170	3-5-71	Osceola
	James, Chris	R/R	6-1/190	10-4-62	San Francisco
63	Mota, Gary	R/R	6-0/195	10-6-70	Asheville
4	Rhodes, Karl	L/L	5-11/170	8-21-68	Tucson, Houston
22	Simms, Mike	R/R	6-4/185	1-12-67	Tucson, Houston

BALLPARK INFORMATION

Ballpark (capacity, surface)
The Astrodome (53,821, artificial)

Address
P.O. Box 288
Houston, TX 77001-0288

Business phone
713-799-9500

Ticket information
713-799-9555

Ticket prices
$12 (field box)
$10 (mezzanine)
$8 (loge)
$7 (upper box terrace)
$6 (upper box)
$5 (upper reserved)

Field dimensions (from home plate)
To left field at foul line, 330 feet
To center field, 400 feet
To right field at foul line, 330 feet

First game played
April 12, 1965 (Phillies 2, Astros 0)

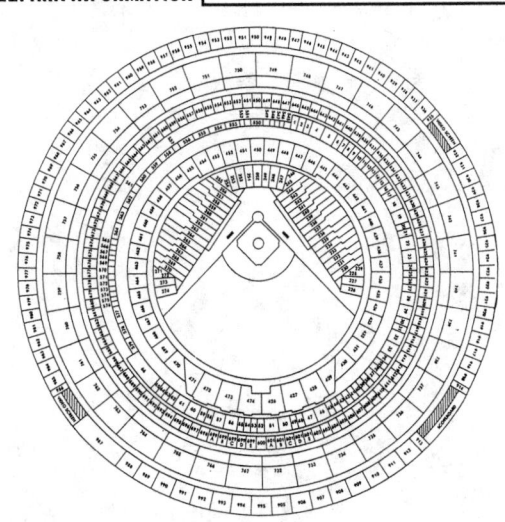

MINOR LEAGUE AFFILIATES

Class	Team	League	Manager
AAA	Tucson	Pacific Coast	Rick Sweet
AA	Jackson	Texas	Sal Butera
A	Osceola	Florida State	Tim Tolman
A	Asheville	South Atlantic	Bobby Ramos
A	Quad City	Midwest	Steve Dillard
A	Auburn	New York-Pennsylvania	Manny Aota
Rookie	Gulf Coast Astros	Gulf Coast	Julio Linares

BROADCAST INFORMATION

Radio: KPRC-AM (940). Broadcasters: Milo Hamilton, Larry Dierker, Bill Brown, Vince Cotroneo. KXYZ-AM (1320, Spanish language). Broadcasters: Rolando Becerra, Orlando Sanchez Diego.
TV: KTXH-TV (Channel 20). Broadcasters: Milo Hamilton, Larry Dierker, Bill Brown.
Cable TV: Home Sports Entertainment. Broadcasters: Milo Hamilton, Enos Cabell, Bill Worrell, Bill Brown.

SPRING TRAINING

Ballpark (city): Osceola County Stadium (Kissimmee, Fla.).
Ticket information: 407-933-2520.

HISTORY

YEAR-BY-YEAR RECORDS

Year	Pos.	W	L	Pct.	*GB	Year	Pos.	W	L	Pct.	*GB
1962	8th	64	96	.400	36½	1980	1st†‡	93	70	.571	+1
1963	9th	66	96	.407	33	1981	3rd/1st	61	49	.555	§*
1964	9th	66	96	.407	27	1982	5th	77	85	.475	12
1965	9th	65	97	.401	32	1983	3rd	85	77	.525	6
1966	8th	72	90	.444	23	1984	T2nd	80	82	.494	12
1967	9th	69	93	.426	32½	1985	T3rd	83	79	.512	12
1968	10th	72	90	.444	25	1986	1st‡	96	66	.593	+10
1969	5th	81	81	.500	12	1987	3rd	76	86	.469	14
1970	4th	79	83	.488	23	1988	5th	82	80	.506	12½
1971	T4th	79	83	.488	11	1989	3rd	86	76	.531	6
1972	2nd	84	69	.549	10½	1990	T4th	75	87	.463	16
1973	4th	82	80	.506	17	1991	6th	65	97	.401	29
1974	4th	81	81	.500	21	1992	4th	81	81	.500	17
1975	6th	64	97	.398	43½						
1976	3rd	80	82	.494	22						
1977	3rd	81	81	.500	17						
1978	5th	74	88	.457	21						
1979	2nd	89	73	.549	1½						

*Games behind winner. †Won division playoff. ‡Lost Championship Series. §Lost division playoff. *First half 28-29; second 33-20.

MANAGERS

Name	Record	Years
Harry Craft	191-280	'62-64
Lum Harris	70-105	'64-65
Grady Hatton	164-221	'66-68
Harry Walker	355-353	'68-72
Leo Durocher	98-95	'72-73
Preston Gomez	128-161	'73-75
Bill Virdon	544-522	'75-82
Bob Lillis	276-261	'82-85
Hal Lanier	254-232	'86-88
Art Howe	307-341	'89-92

DAY BY DAY

Date	Opp.	Res.	Score	(inn.*)	Hits	Opp. hits	Winning pitcher	Losing pitcher	Save	Record	Pos.	GB
4-7	Atl.	L	0-2		2	7	Glavine	Harnisch		0-1	6th	1
4-8	Atl.	L	1-3		5	8	Smoltz	Kile	Pena	0-2	6th	2
4-9	Cin.	W	6-5	(13)	11	11	Osuna	Ruskin		1-2	5th	1
4-10	Cin.	L	5-8		14	10	Hammond	Bowen	Charlton	1-3	6th	2
4-11	Cin.	W	2-1		9	6	Osuna	Rijo	D. Jones	2-3	T4th	1½
4-12	Cin.	L	4-5		9	8	Browning	Harnisch	Charlton	2-4	T5th	2½
4-13	L.A.	W	8-3		11	8	Kile	Hershiser	D. Jones	3-4	5th	2
4-14	L.A.	L	2-6		6	10	Candiotti	Henry		3-5	T5th	3
4-15	L.A.	W	5-4		9	7	Portugal	Ojeda	D. Jones	4-5	T3rd	3
4-17	S.D.	W	3-1		7	6	Harnisch	Hurst	D. Jones	5-5	T3rd	1½
4-18	S.D.	W	4-2	(10)	11	10	D. Jones	Myers		6-5	T2nd	½
4-19	S.D.	W	1-0	(11)	7	9	Hernandez	Rodriguez		7-5	T1st	...
4-20	S.F.	W	3-2		6	7	Portugal	Burba	D. Jones	8-5	1st	+1
4-21	S.F.	L	2-6		8	8	Swift	Bowen		8-6	T1st	...
4-22	S.F.	W	3-1	(12)	13	8	Hernandez	Jackson		9-6	1st	+½
4-24	At Atl.	W	4-2		7	5	Kile	Smoltz	D. Jones	10-6	1st	+1½
4-25	At Atl.	L	0-2		4	5	Avery	Portugal		10-7	1st	+½
4-26	At Atl.	L	2-3		8	9	Freeman	Harnisch	Pena	10-8	1st	+½
4-28	At N.Y.	L	0-4		2	8	Cone	Henry		10-9	3rd	½
4-29	At N.Y.	L	0-1		3	5	Saberhagen	Kile		10-10	T4th	1
4-30	At N.Y.	L	3-4		3	8	Innis	D. Jones	Franco	10-11	5th	1½
5-1	Pit.	W	10-4		13	9	Harnisch	Tomlin		11-11	4th	1
5-2	Pit.	L	0-6		4	8	Neagle	Bowen		11-12	5th	2
5-3	Pit.	W	1-0		7	4	Osuna	Mason	D. Jones	12-12	T3rd	1
5-4	N.Y.	L	1-5		6	9	Saberhagen	Kile		12-13	5th	1½
5-5	N.Y.	W	5-4		9	4	Portugal	Fernandez	D. Jones	13-13	T2nd	½
5-6	At Chi.	L	4-8		7	7	Maddux	Harnisch		13-14	3rd	1
5-7	At Chi.	L	2-9		7	11	Morgan	Bowen		13-15	T4th	2
5-8	At Pit.	L	3-6		7	6	Belinda	Osuna		13-16	5th	3
5-9	At Pit.	L	0-3		7	7	Smith	Kile		13-17	5th	3
5-10	At Pit.	W	6-4	(10)	10	8	D. Jones	Mason		14-17	5th	3
5-11	Chi.	W	2-1	(10)	5	7	Hernandez	McElroy		15-17	4th	2½
5-12	Chi.	L	2-3		5	5	Assenmacher	Boever		15-18	5th	3½
5-13	Chi.	L	3-8		8	12	Boskie	Henry		15-19	5th	4½
5-15	St.L.	L	5-7		7	15	McClure	D. Jones	L. Smith	15-20	5th	4½
5-16	St.L.	W	3-2		7	7	D. Jones	Agosto		16-20	5th	4½
5-17	St.L.	L	5-7		10	11	Carpenter	D. Jones	L. Smith	16-21	5th	4½
5-18	At Phi.	W	4-2		9	6	J. Jones	Abbott	Boever	17-21	5th	4
5-19	At Phi.	L	3-4		6	8	Schilling	Henry	Mit. Williams	17-22	5th	5
5-20	At Phi.	L	1-2		9	10	Mulholland	Kile	Mit. Williams	17-23	5th	6
5-22	At St.L.	W	3-1		8	2	Portugal	DeLeon	D. Jones	18-23	5th	7
5-23	At St.L.	L	4-10		6	14	Osborne	Harnisch	Carpenter	18-24	5th	6½
5-24	At St.L.	L	3-4		9	10	L. Smith	Osuna		18-25	5th	6½
5-25	At Mon.	W	10-8		14	14	Henry	Haney	D. Jones	19-25	5th	6
5-26	At Mon.	W	9-4		10	7	Boever	Nabholz	D. Jones	20-25	5th	5½
5-27	At Mon.	L	5-8		8	9	Martinez	Portugal	Wetteland	20-26	6th	7
5-29	Phi.	L	1-2	(12)	7	8	Jones	Osuna		20-27	6th	6½
5-30	Phi.	W	5-4		4	6	J. Jones	Mulholland	D. Jones	21-27	6th	6
5-31	Phi.	L	3-6	(11)	10	11	Jones	Murphy	Ritchie	21-28	6th	6½
6-1	Mon.	L	1-7		4	9	Martinez	Kile		21-29	6th	6½
6-2	Mon.	W	6-0		6	6	Portugal	Sampen		22-29	6th	6½
6-3	Mon.	W	5-3		9	8	Harnisch	Hill	D. Jones	23-29	6th	6½
6-4	At S.F.	W	12-6		12	8	J. Jones	Heredia		24-29	6th	5½
6-5	At S.F.	W	5-4		12	7	Hernandez	Brantley	D. Jones	25-29	6th	5½
6-6	At S.F.	L	6-12		9	14	Righetti	Boever		25-30	6th	6½
6-7	At S.F.	L	0-3		2	9	Wilson	Portugal		25-31	6th	6½
6-8	At S.D.	L	2-3		4	9	Hurst	Harnisch		25-32	6th	7½
6-9	At S.D.	L	4-5		10	12	Clements	Boever	Maddux	25-33	6th	8½
6-10	At S.D.	L	1-5		6	8	Lefferts	Henry		25-34	6th	8½
6-12	S.F.	L	2-3		7	8	Jackson	D. Jones	Beck	25-35	6th	9½
6-13	S.F.	W	4-1		7	8	Hernandez	Brantley	D. Jones	26-35	6th	9½
6-14	S.F.	W	15-7		14	12	Murphy	Righetti		27-35	6th	9½
6-15	S.D.	L	1-7		8	10	Lefferts	Henry		27-36	6th	10½
6-16	S.D.	W	11-0		15	7	Williams	Rodriguez	Hernandez	28-36	5th	10½
6-17	S.D.	L	0-5		4	8	Benes	Blair		28-37	5th	11½
6-19	L.A.	W	2-1	(12)	9	8	Boever	Gott		29-37	5th	11
6-20	L.A.	W	1-0		7	7	D. Jones	Hershiser		30-37	5th	10
6-21	L.A.	W	2-0		7	7	Henry	Ke. Gross	D. Jones	31-37	5th	9
6-22	At Cin.	W	5-2		8	6	Williams	Hammond	Hernandez	32-37	5th	8
6-23	At Cin.	L	6-10		11	15	Belcher	Blair		32-38	5th	9

— 119 —

Date	Opp.	Res.	Score	(inn.*)	Hits	Opp. hits	Winning pitcher	Losing pitcher	Save	Record	Pos.	GB
6-24	At Cin.	L	6-9		12	13	Swindell	Harnisch	Charlton	32-39	5th	10
6-25	At L.A.	L	5-8		12	14	R. Martinez	J. Jones		32-40	5th	10½
6-26	At L.A.	L	5-6		9	9	Candelaria	D. Jones	McDowell	32-41	5th	11½
6-27	At L.A.	W	5-1		9	3	Williams	Ke. Gross		33-41	5th	11½
6-28	At L.A.	L	2-8		9	10	Ojeda	Blair		33-42	5th	12½
6-29	Cin.	W	4-3		7	7	Osuna	Dibble	D. Jones	34-42	5th	11½
6-30	Cin.	W	5-1		9	1	J. Jones	Hammond	Hernandez	35-42	5th	10½
7-1	Cin.	W	3-2		7	10	D. Jones	Bankhead		36-42	5th	9½
7-4 (1)	At N.Y.	L	3-5		6	9	Gooden	Blair	Innis	36-43	5th	11½
7-4 (2)	At N.Y.	W	3-1		8	7	Osuna	Young	D. Jones	37-43	4th	11
7-5	At N.Y.	W	2-0	(10)	6	4	Murphy	Innis	D. Jones	38-43	4th	11
7-6	At Pit.	L	0-1		5	7	Smith	J. Jones	Belinda	38-44	5th	12
7-7	At Pit.	L	3-5		10	14	Walk	Boever		38-45	5th	13
7-8	At Pit.	W	3-2		8	6	D. Jones	Patterson		39-45	5th	12
7-9	N.Y.	W	4-0		8	5	Blair	Gooden		40-45	5th	12
7-10	N.Y.	L	6-7		9	10	Innis	D. Jones	Young	40-46	5th	12
7-11	N.Y.	L	2-8		9	10	Cone	J. Jones		40-47	5th	12
7-12	N.Y.	W	3-1		5	7	Henry	Fernandez	Hernandez	41-47	5th	11
7-16	Atl.	L	2-4		8	9	Avery	Williams	Pena	41-48	5th	11
7-17	Atl.	L	0-5		5	8	Smoltz	Harnisch		41-49	5th	12
7-18	Atl.	L	0-3		6	10	Glavine	J. Jones	Pena	41-50	5th	13
7-19	Atl.	L	2-3	(10)	6	9	Freeman	Hernandez	Pena	41-51	5th	14
7-20	Pit.	W	11-8		12	12	Blair	Mason	D. Jones	42-51	5th	14
7-21	Pit.	W	4-3	(12)	11	7	D. Jones	Mason		43-51	5th	13
7-22	Pit.	L	7-10	(13)	14	18	Belinda	Blair	Patterson	43-52	5th	13½
7-24	Chi.	L	0-1		6	7	Morgan	D. Jones	Scanlan	43-53	5th	14½
7-25	Chi.	W	3-2	(11)	11	8	Hernandez	McElroy		44-53	5th	14½
7-26	Chi.	L	5-8		11	16	Harkey	Reynolds		44-54	5th	14½
7-27	At Atl.	W	5-1	(11)	12	8	D. Jones	Pena		45-54	5th	13½
7-28	At Atl.	W	7-5		12	7	Harnisch	Freeman	D. Jones	46-54	5th	12½
7-29	At Atl.	L	3-5		9	9	Glavine	Blair	Pena	46-55	5th	13½
7-31	At Cin.	L	1-6		4	9	Belcher	Henry		46-56	5th	13½
8-1	At Cin.	L	0-9		6	13	Swindell	Williams		46-57	5th	14½
8-2	At Cin.	W	5-4		7	8	Boever	Rijo	D. Jones	47-57	5th	14½
8-3	At Cin.	L	0-4		5	12	Hammond	J. Jones		47-58	5th	15
8-4	At L.A.	L	2-7		5	7	R. Martinez	Reynolds		47-59	5th	16
8-5	At L.A.	W	7-6		13	7	Murphy	McDowell	D. Jones	48-59	5th	16
8-6	At S.D.	L	5-7		11	11	Benes	Williams	Myers	48-60	5th	17
8-7	At S.D.	L	2-4		6	13	Deshaies	Harnisch	Myers	48-61	5th	18
8-8	At S.D.	L	5-7		9	10	Rodriguez	Boever	Andersen	48-62	5th	19
8-9	At S.D.	L	3-4		8	8	Andersen	D. Jones	Myers	48-63	5th	20
8-10	At S.F.	L	1-4		6	9	Burkett	Henry		48-64	5th	20
8-11	At S.F.	W	6-3		12	7	Williams	Oliveras	D. Jones	49-64	5th	19
8-12	At S.F.	W	5-4	(10)	11	9	Hernandez	Brantley	D. Jones	50-64	5th	18½
8-13	At Chi.	W	4-3		5	6	J. Jones	Castillo	D. Jones	51-64	5th	18½
8-14	At Chi.	L	2-4		8	8	Harkey	Kile	Assenmacher	51-65	5th	19½
8-15	At Chi.	W	5-0		12	8	Henry	Bullinger		52-65	5th	19½
8-16	At Chi.	L	0-1		4	8	Maddux	Williams		52-66	5th	19½
8-18	At St.L.	W	7-6		9	7	J. Jones	Olivares	D. Jones	53-66	5th	20
8-19	At St.L.	L	1-12		4	17	Cormier	Kile		53-67	5th	21
8-20	At St.L.	L	1-3		4	9	Tewksbury	Henry	L. Smith	53-68	5th	21
8-21	At Phi.	W	6-1		8	6	Williams	Ashby		54-68	5th	20
8-22	At Phi.	W	14-9		18	13	Blair	Hartley		55-68	5th	20
8-23	At Phi.	W	3-1		4	8	J. Jones	Schilling	D. Jones	56-68	5th	19
8-25	St.L.	L	3-5	(13)	15	13	Carpenter	Boever	L. Smith	56-69	5th	19
8-26	St.L.	W	6-5	(10)	12	7	Hernandez	Perez		57-69	5th	18
8-27	St.L.	W	5-1		8	5	Williams	Osborne		58-69	5th	17½
8-28	Mon.	W	8-1		12	5	Harnisch	Gardner		59-69	T4th	16½
8-29	Mon.	W	8-2		10	5	J. Jones	Barnes		60-69	4th	16½
8-30	Mon.	L	0-4		4	7	Hill	Kile		60-70	4th	16½
8-31	Phi.	W	9-2		12	8	Henry	Ashby		61-70	4th	17
9-1	Phi.	W	5-3		9	8	Williams	Brantley	D. Jones	62-70	4th	17
9-2	Phi.	W	3-2		8	6	Harnisch	Mulholland	D. Jones	63-70	4th	16
9-4	At Mon.	L	2-5		7	6	Hill	J. Jones	Wetteland	63-71	4th	15½
9-5	At Mon.	W	5-2		8	7	Kile	Nabholz		64-71	4th	15½
9-6	At Mon.	W	3-1		6	4	Henry	Martinez	D. Jones	65-71	4th	15½
9-7	Cin.	L	0-10		3	13	Rijo	Williams		65-72	4th	16½
9-8	Cin.	W	2-0		6	4	Harnisch	Hammond	Hernandez	66-72	4th	16½
9-9	At S.F.	W	6-4		11	6	Blair	Swift	Hernandez	67-72	4th	16½
9-10	At S.F.	L	2-5		10	7	Burkett	Bowen	Beck	67-73	4th	17½
9-11	Atl.	L	0-7		4	13	Smith	Kile		67-74	4th	18½
9-12	Atl.	L	3-9		10	11	Nied	Williams		67-75	4th	19½
9-13	Atl.	L	2-9		7	10	Leibrandt	Harnisch		67-76	4th	20½
9-14	S.F.	W	5-0		8	4	Blair	Rogers	Hernandez	68-76	4th	20

Date	Opp.	Res.	Score	(inn.*)	Hits	Opp. hits	Winning pitcher	Losing pitcher	Save	Record	Pos.	GB
9-15	S.F.	W	9-6	(11)	15	10	D. Jones	Righetti		69-76	4th	19
9-16	S.F.	W	3-1		6	4	Kile	Carter	Boever	70-76	4th	19
9-18	At Atl.	W	13-3		18	8	Harnisch	Leibrandt		71-76	4th	17½
9-19	At Atl.	W	3-2	(12)	8	10	D. Jones	Freeman		72-76	4th	16½
9-20	At Atl.	L	1-16		7	15	Avery	Bowen		72-77	4th	17½
9-22 (1)	At Cin.	L	3-6		5	10	Rijo	Scheid		72-78	4th	18
9-22 (2)	At Cin.	L	3-4		11	9	Bankhead	Reynolds	Hill	72-79	4th	18½
9-23	At S.D.	W	7-6		11	11	D. Jones	Hernandez		73-79	4th	18½
9-24	At S.D.	L	1-7		3	10	Seminara	Blair		73-80	4th	18½
9-25	At L.A.	W	4-3		7	7	Portugal	Candelaria	D. Jones	74-80	4th	17½
9-26	At L.A.	W	5-4		15	8	Hernandez	Ki. Gross	D. Jones	75-80	4th	17½
9-27	At L.A.	W	4-2		14	14	Reynolds	Candelaria	D. Jones	76-80	4th	17½
9-29	S.D.	W	6-5		9	10	Osuna	Myers		77-80	4th	17½
9-30	S.D.	W	5-4		10	10	J. Jones	Hernandez	D. Jones	78-80	4th	16½
10-1	S.D.	L	2-3		5	7	Gr. Harris	Bowen	Myers	78-81	4th	17½
10-2	L.A.	W	6-1		10	5	Kile	Hershiser		79-81	4th	18
10-3	L.A.	W	3-2	(13)	16	10	J. Jones	Crews		80-81	4th	18
10-4	L.A.	W	3-0		8	5	Harnisch	Astacio	D. Jones	81-81	4th	17

Monthly records: April (10-11), May (11-17), June (14-14), July (11-14), August (15-14), September (17-10), Oct. (3-1).

HIGHLIGHTS

High point: From August 11 to the end of the year, the Astros won 33 of 50 games to finish 81-81, one game out of third place in the National League West.

Low point: On their first five road trips, the Astros went 10-24 and were outscored, 137-67, in the losses. Though they finished strong, this bad stretch put them in an inescapable hole.

Turning point: Oddly, it was a 26-game, 28-day road trip from July 27-August 23 that the Astros were forced to take because the Republican National Convention was being held in the Astrodome. The Astros went 12-14 on the trip and started their late-season turnaround. They went 21-20 on the road over the final half of the season.

Most valuable player: Center fielder Steve Finley. He hit a career-best .292, stole 44 bases and had 55 RBIs from the No. 2 spot in the batting order. He also established himself as one of the top defensive outfielders in the league.

Most valuable pitcher: Righthander Doug Jones. Pulled from the scrap heap in Cleveland, he paced the Astros with 11 wins and 36 saves, becoming the first pitcher in club history to lead the staff in both categories.

Most improved player: Right fielder Eric Anthony. After failing in three previous trials with the Astros, he had 19 homers and 80 RBIs in 440 at-bats.

Most pleasant surprise: Righthander Xavier Hernandez. Moved into a middle-relief role, he went 9-1 with seven saves and a 2.11 ERA.

Biggest disappointment: Shortstop Andujar Cedeno. After a promising 1991, he failed at the plate early in the season and spent most of 1992 in the minors.

Key injuries: Righthander Mark Portugal made only 15 starts before undergoing elbow surgery that put him on the disabled list from July 17-September 24. Third baseman Ken Caminiti missed nearly one month due to a right shoulder separation.

Notable: On July 24, John McMullen announced he was selling the club to Drayton McLane Jr., a businessman from Temple, Tex. ... Finley, first baseman Jeff Bagwell and second baseman Craig Biggio each played in all 162 games, the first three big-league teammates to do so since 1974. ... In a 13-inning game against St. Louis on August 25, Cedeno became the first Astro since 1977 to hit for the cycle. ... Houston relievers led the league with 39 wins and a 2.89 ERA.

—NEIL HOHLFELD

RECORDS

1992 regular-season record: 81-81 (4th in N.L. West); 47-34 at home; 34-47 on road; 36-36 vs. East; 45-45 vs. West; 32-32 vs. LHP; 49-49 vs. RHP; 20-28 on grass; 61-53 on turf; 20-28 in daytime; 61-53 at night; 32-21 in one-run games; 16-5 in extra-inning games; 0-1-1 in doubleheaders.

Team record last five years: 389-421 (.480, ranks 10th in league in that span).

TEAM LEADERS

Batting average: Ken Caminiti (.294).
At-bats: Craig Biggio (613).
Runs: Craig Biggio (96).
Hits: Steve Finley (177).
Total bases: Jeff Bagwell (260).
Doubles: Jeff Bagwell (34).
Triples: Steve Finley (13).
Home runs: Eric Anthony (19).
Runs batted in: Jeff Bagwell (96).
Stolen bases: Steve Finley (44).
Slugging percentage: Jeff Bagwell (.444).
On-base percentage: Craig Biggio (.378).
Wins: Doug Jones (11).
Earned-run average: Pete Harnisch (3.70).
Complete games: Butch Henry, Darryl Kile (2).
Shutouts: Butch Henry, Mark Portugal (1).
Saves: Doug Jones (36).
Innings pitched: Pete Harnisch (206⅔).
Strikeouts: Pete Harnisch (164).

GAMES BY POSITION

Catcher: Eddie Taubensee 103, Scott Servais 73, Scooter Tucker 19.
First base: Jeff Bagwell 159, Benny Distefano 6, Ernest Riles 4, Mike Simms 1.
Second base: Craig Biggio 161, Casey Candaele 9, Juan Guerrero 2, Ernest Riles 2.
Third base: Ken Caminiti 129, Casey Candaele 29, Juan Guerrero 12, Ernest Riles 5, Rafael Ramirez 1.
Shortstop: Andujar Cedeno 70, Casey Candaele 65, Rafael Ramirez 57, Juan Guerrero 19, Ernest Riles 6, Eric Yelding 2.
Outfield: Steve Finley 160, Eric Anthony 115, Luis Gonzalez 111, Pete Incaviglia 98, Gerald Young 57, Chris Jones 43, Casey Candaele 21, Benny Distefano 12, Mike Simms 9, Juan Guerrero 3, Eric Yelding 2, Karl Rhodes 1.

TOP 10 DRAFT CHOICES

1a. Phil Nevin, 3B, California State University-Fullerton.
1b. Kendall Rhine, RHP, University of Georgia.
2. David Landaker, SS, Royal High School, Simi Valley, Calif.
3. Chris Holt, RHP, Navarro College (Tex.).
4. Chad Sheffer, SS, Bloomingdale Senior High School, Valrico, Fla.
5. Sean Runyan, LHP, Urbandale (Ia.) School.
6. Jeff Tenbarge, RHP, University of Evansville.
7. Mike Rennhack, OF, Leland High School, San Jose, Calif.
8. Chris Thomas, OF, Boise State University.
9. Greg Elliott, 3B, Southeastern Louisiana University.
10. Jamie Walker, LHP, Austin Peay State University.

LOS ANGELES DODGERS
NATIONAL LEAGUE WEST DIVISION

1993 SCHEDULE

APRIL

SUN	MON	TUE	WED	THU	FRI	SAT
				1	2	3
4	5 N FLA	6 N FLA	7 N FLA	8 N ATL	9 N ATL	10 ATL
11 ATL	12	13 N STL H	14 N STL H	15 N STL H	16 N PIT H	17 N PIT H
18 PIT H	19	20 N MON	21 N MON	22 N MON	23 N PHI	24 N PHI
25 PHI	26 N NY	27 NY	28 N MON H	29 N MON H	30 N PHI H	

MAY

SUN	MON	TUE	WED	THU	FRI	SAT
						1 N PHI H
2 PHI H	3	4 N NY H	5 N NY H	6 N	7 N SF	8 SF
9 SF	10 N CHI	11 N CHI	12 CHI	13	14 N HOU	15 HOU
16 HOU	17 N CIN H	18 N CIN H	19 N CIN H	20	21 N COL H	22 N COL H
23 COL H	24 N SD H	25 N SD H	26 N SD H	27	28 N PIT	29 PIT
30 PIT	31 STL					

JUNE

SUN	MON	TUE	WED	THU	FRI	SAT
		1 N STL	2 N STL	3 N	4 N ATL H	5 N ATL H
6 ATL H	7 N FLA H	8 N FLA H	9 N FLA H	10 SD	11 N SD	12 N SD
13 SD	14 N COL	15 N COL	16 N COL	17	18 N CIN	19 N CIN
20 CIN	21 N HOU	22 N HOU	23 N HOU	24 HOU	25 N CHI	26 N CHI
27 CHI	28 N SF H	29 N SF H	30 N SF H			

JULY

SUN	MON	TUE	WED	THU	FRI	SAT
				1 N	2 N MON	3 MON
4 MON	5 N PHI	6 N PHI	7 N PHI	8 N NY	9 N NY	10 NY
11 N NY	12 N	13 ◆	14 ALL STAR GAME	15 N MON H	16 N MON H	17 N MON H
18 MON H	19 N PHI H	20 N PHI H	21 N PHI H	22 N NY H	23 N NY H	24 NY H
25 NY H	26 N SF	27 N SF	28 SF	29	30 CHI	31 CHI

AUGUST

SUN	MON	TUE	WED	THU	FRI	SAT
1 CHI	2	3 N HOU	4 N HOU	5 N HOU	6 N CIN H	7 N CIN H
8 CIN H	9 N COL H	10 N COL H	11 N COL H	12 N COL H	13 N SD	14 N SD
15 SD H	16	17 N ATL	18 N ATL	19 N ATL	20 N STL	21 N STL
22 STL	23 N PIT H	24 N PIT H	25 N PIT H	26	27 N STL H	28 N STL H
29 STL H	30	31 N PIT				

SEPTEMBER

SUN	MON	TUE	WED	THU	FRI	SAT
			1 N PIT	2 N PIT	3 N FLA	4 N FLA
5 FLA	6 N ATL H	7 N ATL H	8 N ATL H	9 N FLA H	10 N FLA H	11 N FLA H
12 FLA H	13 N SD	14 N SD	15 N	16	17 N COL	18 N COL
19 COL	20 N CIN	21 N CIN	22 N CIN	23 CIN	24 N HOU H	25 HOU H
26 HOU H	27 N CHI H	28 N CHI H	29 N CHI H	30 N SF H		

OCTOBER

SUN	MON	TUE	WED	THU	FRI	SAT
					1 N SF H	2 SF H
3 SF H						

1993 SEASON

CLUB DIRECTORY

Board of directors
Peter O'Malley
Harry M. Bardt
Roland Seidler
Mrs. Roland (Terry) Seidler
President
Peter O'Malley
Executive vice president
Fred Claire
Vice president, communications
Tom Hawkins
Vice president, finance
Bob Graziano
Vice president, marketing
Barry Stockhamer
Vice president, stadium operations
Bob Smith
Vice president, ticketing
Walter Nash
Vice president, treasurer
Roland Seidler
Vice president, Campo Las Palmas
Ralph Avila
Assistant secretary and general counsel
Santiago Fernandez
Director, accounting and finance
Bill Foltz
Director, advertising and special events
Paul Kalil
Director, broadcasting and publications
Brent Shyer
Director, community relations
Don Newcombe
Community relations
Roy Campanella
Dir., human resources and administration
Irene Tanji
Director, management information services
Mike Mularky
Director, minor league operations
Charlie Blaney
Director, scouting
Terry Reynolds
Director, publicity
Jay Lucas
Assistant director, publicity
Chuck Harris
Traveling secretary
Bill DeLury
Director, stadium operations
Jim Italiano
Director, ticket operations
Debra Duncan
Director, ticket marketing
Allan Erselius
Club physicians
Dr. Frank W. Jobe
Dr. Michael F. Mellman
Dr. Herndon Harding

Scouts
Eleodoro Arias
Eddie Bane
Bill Barkley
Gil Bassetti
Rick Birmingham
Bob Bishop
Gib Bodet
Flores Bolivar
Mike Brito
Joe Campbell
Jim Chapman
Bob Darwin
Eddie Fajardo Rodriguez
Lin Garrett
Ossie Alvarez Gonzalez
Rafael Gonzalez
Michael Hankins
Dick Hanlon
Dennis Haren
Gail Henley
Hank Jones
Lon Joyce
John Keenan
Gary LaRocque
Juan Latigua
Don LeJohn
Carl Lowenstine
Manuel Lunar
Teodoro Mata
Dale McReynolds
Bob Miske
Tommy Mixon
Victor Nazario
Alberto Osorio
Deni Pacini
Camilo Pasqual
Pablo Peguero
Cornelio Pena
Jose Pena
Claude Pelletier
Bill Pleis
Silvano Quesada
Mark Sheehy
Jim Stoeckel
Dick Teed
Tom Thomas
Glen Van Proyen

Special assignment scouts
Mel Didier
Phil Regan
Jerry Stephenson
Gary Sutherland

SCHEDULE KEY

H—Home game.   N—Night game (any game starting after 5 p.m.).
*All-Star Game at Oriole Park at Camden Yards, Baltimore.

Manager—Tom Lasorda (2).
Coaches—Joe Amalfitano (8), Mark Cresse (58), Joe Ferguson (13), Ben Hines (37),
Manny Mota (11), Ron Perranoski (16), Ron Roenicke (68).

No.	PITCHERS	B/T	Ht./Wt.	Born	1992 clubs
56	Astacio, Pedro	R/R	6-2/195	11-28-69	Albuquerque, Los Angeles
65	Bustillos, Albert	R/R	6-1/233	4-8-68	San Antonio, Albuquerque
49	Candiotti, Tom	R/R	6-2/228	8-31-57	Los Angeles
54	Clark, Dera	R/R	6-1/205	4-14-65	Gulf Coast Royals, Baseball City, Omaha
64	Daspit, James	R/R	6-7/210	8-10-69	Vero Beach
63	Delahoya, Javier	R/R	6-0/162	2-21-70	Vero Beach, San Antonio
35	Gott, Jim	R/R	6-4/229	8-3-59	Los Angeles
46	Gross, Kevin	R/R	6-5/227	6-8-61	Los Angeles
57	Gross, Kip	R/R	6-2/194	8-24-64	Albuquerque, Los Angeles
52	Hansell, Greg	R/R	6-5/213	3-12-71	San Antonio, Albuquerque
55	Hershiser, Orel	R/R	6-3/198	9-16-58	Los Angeles
59	James, Mike	R/R	6-3/182	8-15-67	Albuquerque, San Antonio
45	Martinez, Pedro	R/R	5-11/164	7-25-71	Albuquerque, Los Angeles
48	Martinez, Ramon	L/R	6-4/176	3-22-68	Los Angeles
17	McDowell, Roger	R/R	6-1/182	12-21-60	Los Angeles
62	Nichting, Chris	R/R	6-1/205	5-13-66	Albuquerque, San Antonio
50	Wilson, Steve	L/L	6-4/224	12-13-64	Los Angeles
38	Worrell, Todd	R/R	6-5/222	9-28-59	St. Louis

No.	CATCHERS	B/T	Ht./Wt.	Born	1992 clubs
41	Hernandez, Carlos	R/R	5-11/218	5-24-67	Los Angeles
31	Piazza, Mike	R/R	6-3/197	9-4-68	San Antonio, Albuquerque, Los Angeles
40	Wakamatsu, Don	R/R	6-2/200	2-22-63	Albuquerque

No.	INFIELDERS	B/T	Ht./Wt.	Born	1992 clubs
21	Bournigal, Rafael	R/R	5-11/165	5-12-66	Albuquerque, Los Angeles
51	Busch, Mike	R/R	6-5/241	7-7-68	San Antonio
5	Hansen, Dave	L/R	6-0/195	11-24-68	Los Angeles
29	Harris, Lenny	L/R	5-10/220	10-28-64	Los Angeles
23	Karros, Eric	R/R	6-4/213	11-4-67	Los Angeles
30	Offerman, Jose	B/R	6-0/165	11-8-68	Los Angeles
60	Pye, Eddie	R/R	5-10/175	2-13-67	Albuquerque
3	Reed, Jody	R/R	5-9/165	7-26-62	Boston
27	Sharperson, Mike	R/R	6-3/208	10-4-61	Los Angeles
28	Snyder, Cory	R/R	6-3/185	11-11-62	San Francisco
25	Wallach, Tim	R/R	6-3/202	9-14-57	Montreal

No.	OUTFIELDERS	B/T	Ht./Wt.	Born	1992 clubs
7	Ashley, Billy	R/R	6-7/227	7-11-70	San Antonio, Albuquerque, Los Angeles
22	Butler, Brett	L/L	5-10/161	6-15-57	Los Angeles
33	Davis, Eric	R/R	6-3/200	5-29-62	Los Angeles
47	Goodwin, Tom	L/R	6-1/170	7-27-68	Albuquerque, Los Angeles
43	Mondesi, Raul	R/R	5-11/202	3-12-71	Albuquerque, San Antonio
26	Rodriguez, Henry	L/L	6-1/200	11-8-67	Albuquerque, Los Angeles
44	Strawberry, Darryl	L/L	6-6/215	3-12-62	Los Angeles
20	Webster, Mitch	B/L	6-1/185	5-16-59	Los Angeles

BALLPARK INFORMATION

Ballpark (capacity, surface)
Dodger Stadium (56,000, grass)
Address
1000 Elysian Park Ave.
Los Angeles, CA 90012
Business phone
213-224-1500
Ticket information
213-224-1400
Ticket prices
$11 (box seats)
$8 (reserved seats)
$6 (top deck and pavilion)
$3 (g.a., youth 12 and under)
Field dimensions (from home plate)
To left field at foul line, 330 feet
To center field, 395 feet
To right field at foul line, 330 feet
First game played
April 10, 1962 (Reds 6, Dodgers 3)

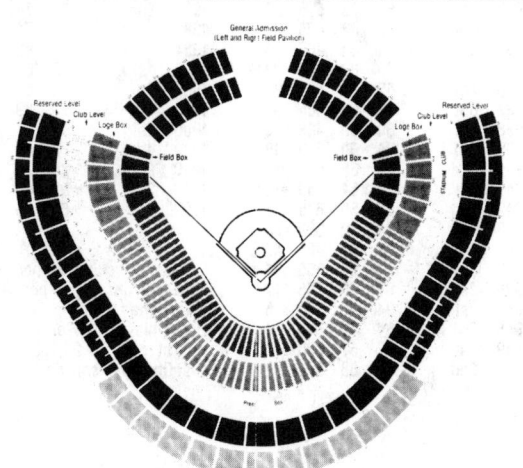

MINOR LEAGUE AFFILIATES

Class	Team	League	Manager
AAA	Albuquerque	Pacific Coast	Bill Russell
AA	San Antonio	Texas	Glenn Hoffman
A	Bakersfield	California	Rick Dempsey
A	Vero Beach	Florida State	Joe Vavra
A	Yakima	Northwest	John Shoemaker
Rookie	Great Falls	Pioneer	Jon Debus

BROADCAST INFORMATION

Radio: KABC-AM (790). Broadcasters: Vin Scully, Don Drysdale, Ross Porter. KWKW-AM (1330, Spanish language). Broadcasters: Jaime Jarrin, Rene Cardenas.
TV: KTLA-TV (Channel 5). Broadcasters: Vin Scully, Don Drysdale, Ross Porter.

SPRING TRAINING

Ballpark (city): Holman Stadium (Vero Beach, Fla.).
Ticket information: 407-569-4900.

HISTORY

YEAR-BY-YEAR RECORDS

Year	Pos.	W	L	Pct.	*GB	Year	Pos.	W	L	Pct.	*GB
1901	3rd	79	57	.581	9½	1951	2nd†	97	60	.618	1
1902	2nd	75	63	.543	27½	1952	1st	96	57	.627	+ 4½
1903	5th	70	66	.515	19	1953	1st	105	49	.682	+13
1904	6th	56	97	.366	50	1954	2nd	92	62	.597	5
1905	8th	48	104	.316	56½	1955	1st	98	55	.641	+13½
1906	5th	66	86	.434	50	1956	1st	93	61	.604	+ 1
1907	5th	65	83	.439	40	1957	3rd	84	70	.545	11
1908	7th	53	101	.344	46	1958	7th	71	83	.461	21
1909	6th	55	98	.359	55½	1959	1st‡	88	68	.564	+ 2
1910	6th	64	90	.416	40	1960	4th	82	72	.532	13
1911	7th	64	86	.427	33½	1961	2nd	89	65	.578	4
1912	7th	58	95	.379	46	1962	2nd†	102	63	.618	1
1913	6th	65	84	.436	34½	1963	1st	99	63	.611	+ 6
1914	5th	75	79	.487	19½	1964	T6th	80	82	.494	13
1915	3rd	80	72	.526	10	1965	1st	97	65	.599	+ 2
1916	1st	94	60	.610	+ 2½	1966	1st	95	67	.586	+ 1½
1917	7th	70	81	.464	26½	1967	8th	73	89	.451	28½
1918	5th	57	69	.452	25½	1968	7th	76	86	.469	21
1919	5th	69	71	.493	27	1969	4th	85	77	.525	8
1920	1st	93	61	.604	+ 7	1970	2nd	87	74	.540	14½
1921	5th	77	75	.507	16½	1971	2nd	89	73	.549	1
1922	6th	76	78	.494	17	1972	3rd	85	70	.548	10½
1923	6th	76	78	.494	19½	1973	2nd	95	66	.590	3½
1924	2nd	92	62	.597	1½	1974	1st§	102	60	.630	+ 4
1925	T6th	68	85	.444	27	1975	2nd	88	74	.543	20
1926	6th	71	82	.464	17½	1976	2nd	92	70	.568	10
1927	6th	65	88	.425	28½	1977	1st§	98	64	.605	+10
1928	6th	77	76	.503	17½	1978	1st§	95	67	.586	+ 2½
1929	6th	70	83	.458	28½	1979	3rd	79	83	.488	11½
1930	4th	86	68	.558	6	1980	2nd*	92	71	.564	1
1931	4th	79	73	.520	21	1981	1st/4th	63	47	.573	•§◆
1932	3rd	81	73	.526	9	1982	2nd	88	74	.543	1
1933	6th	65	88	.425	26½	1983	1st■	91	71	.652	+ 3
1934	6th	71	81	.467	23½	1984	4th	79	83	.488	13
1935	5th	70	83	.458	29½	1985	1st■	95	67	.586	+ 5½
1936	7th	67	87	.435	25	1986	5th	73	89	.451	23
1937	6th	62	91	.405	33½	1987	4th	73	89	.451	17
1938	7th	69	80	.463	18½	1988	1st§	94	67	.584	+ 7
1939	3rd	84	69	.549	12½	1989	4th	77	83	.481	14
1940	2nd	88	65	.575	12	1990	2nd	86	76	.531	5
1941	1st	100	54	.649	+ 2½	1991	2nd	93	69	.574	1
1942	2nd	104	50	.675	2	1992	6th	63	99	.389	35
1943	3rd	81	72	.529	23½						
1944	7th	63	91	.409	42						
1945	3rd	87	67	.565	11						
1946	2nd†	96	60	.615	2						
1947	1st	94	60	.610	+ 5						
1948	3rd	84	70	.545	7½						
1949	1st	97	57	.630	+ 1						
1950	2nd	89	65	.578	2						

*Games behind winner. †Lost pennant playoff. ‡Won pennant playoff. §Won Championship Series. *Lost division playoff. • Won division playoff. ◆First half 36-21; second 27-26. ■ Lost Championship Series.

MANAGERS

Name	Record	Years
Ned Hanlon	328-387	'01-05
Patsy Donovan	184-270	'06-08
Harry Lumley	55-98	1909
Bill Dahlen	251-355	'10-13
Wilbert Robinson	1375-1341	'14-31
Max Carey	146-161	'32-33
Casey Stengel	208-251	'34-36
Burleigh Grimes	131-171	'37-38
Leo Durocher	738-565	'39-46
		1948
Clyde Sukeforth	2-0	1947
Burt Shotton	326-215	1947
		'48-50
Chuck Dressen	298-166	'51-53
Walter Alston	2040-1613	'54-76
Tommy Lasorda	1341-1201	'76-92

DAY BY DAY

Date	Opp.	Res.	Score	(inn.*)	Hits	Opp. hits	Winning pitcher	Losing pitcher	Save	Record	Pos.	GB
4-6	S.F.	L	1-8		7	17	Swift	R. Martinez		0-1	T5th	1
4-7	S.F.	W	3-0		7	3	Hershiser	Downs	McDowell	1-1	T2nd	½
4-9	At S.D.	W	6-3		14	8	Candiotti	Lefferts	Gott	2-1	T1st	...
4-10	At S.D.	L	3-8		8	7	Melendez	Ojeda		2-2	T3rd	1
4-11	At S.D.	L	2-3	(10)	8	10	Melendez	McDowell		2-3	T4th	1½
4-12	At S.D.	L	4-5		6	8	Myers	McDowell		2-4	T5th	2½
4-13	At Hou.	L	3-8		8	11	Kile	Hershiser	D. Jones	2-5	6th	3
4-14	At Hou.	W	6-2		10	6	Candiotti	Henry		3-5	T5th	3
4-15	At Hou.	L	4-5		7	9	Portugal	Ojeda	D. Jones	3-6	6th	4
4-16	Atl.	L	0-3		2	10	Bielecki	Ke. Gross		3-7	6th	4
4-17	Atl.	W	7-5		12	7	McDowell	Pena		4-7	6th	3
4-18	Atl.	W	7-3		10	8	McDowell	Stanton		5-7	T5th	2
4-19	Atl.	W	4-2		8	7	Candiotti	Avery		6-7	T4th	1½
4-20	Cin.	W	6-0		9	9	Ojeda	Swindell		7-7	T3rd	1½
4-21	Cin.	L	3-4		8	8	Ruskin	Ke. Gross	Dibble	7-8	T4th	1½
4-22	Cin.	L	3-4		12	9	Bankhead	Wilson	Charlton	7-9	5th	2½
4-24	At S.F.	W	5-3		9	7	Hershiser	Wilson	McDowell	8-9	5th	2½
4-25	At S.F.	W	7-6	(10)	10	9	McDowell	Righetti	Gott	9-9	T3rd	1½
4-26	At S.F.	L	4-5	(11)	9	12	Heredia	Wilson		9-10	5th	1½
4-27	St.L.	L	4-5		9	13	Osborne	Ke. Gross	L. Smith	9-11	T5th	2
4-28	St.L.	L	1-2	(10)	9	9	Worrell	Gott	L. Smith	9-12	6th	2½
4-29	Phi.	L	3-7		9	8	Cox	Hershiser		9-13	6th	3
5-5	At Phi.	L	2-6		8	9	Mulholland	Candiotti		9-14	6th	3
5-6	At Phi.	W	3-1		11	6	R. Martinez	Cox	McDowell	10-14	6th	2½
5-8	At N.Y.	L	3-4		7	6	Innis	McDowell		10-15	6th	4
5-9	At N.Y.	L	2-5		5	9	Franco	McDowell		10-16	6th	4
5-10	At N.Y.	L	0-3		5	9	Fernandez	Candiotti	Franco	10-17	6th	5
5-11	At Mon.	L	5-6	(10)	9	13	Fassero	Wilson		10-18	6th	5½
5-12	At Mon.	W	2-0		8	3	Ke. Gross	Haney		11-18	6th	5½
5-13	At Mon.	L	1-5		3	10	Gardner	Hershiser	Wetteland	11-19	6th	6½
5-15	N.Y.	L	1-4		4	6	Saberhagen	Ojeda	Franco	11-20	6th	6½
5-16	N.Y.	W	2-0		6	6	Candiotti	Fernandez		12-20	6th	6½
5-17	N.Y.	W	6-3		9	9	R. Martinez	Young	McDowell	13-20	6th	5½
5-18	Chi.	L	0-3		5	5	Castillo	Ke. Gross	McElroy	13-21	6th	6
5-19	Chi.	W	5-2		9	9	Hershiser	Boskie	McDowell	14-21	6th	6
5-20	Chi.	W	5-3		9	10	Ojeda	Jackson	Candelaria	15-21	6th	6
5-22	Pit.	L	4-6		9	12	Tomlin	Candiotti		15-22	6th	7½
5-23	Pit.	W	5-2		10	9	Wilson	Belinda		16-22	6th	6½
5-24	Pit.	W	4-2		5	7	Ke. Gross	Drabek	McDowell	17-22	5th	5½
5-25	At St.L.	L	5-6		9	9	Worrell	McDowell		17-23	6th	6
5-26	At St.L.	W	5-2		9	7	Ojeda	Olivares	Candelaria	18-23	5th	6
5-27	At St.L.	W	9-2		12	5	Candiotti	DeLeon		19-23	4th	6
5-29	At Chi.	W	1-0		5	3	R. Martinez	Castillo		20-23	4th	4½
5-30	At Chi.	W	3-2		12	7	Hershiser	Patterson	McDowell	21-23	4th	4
5-31	At Chi.	W	6-2		9	8	Ke. Gross	Jackson		22-23	4th	3½
6-1	At Pit.	W	8-6		13	8	Gott	Neagle	Candelaria	23-23	4th	2½
6-2	At Pit.	L	0-1		6	7	Tomlin	Candiotti	Mason	23-24	4th	3½
6-3	At Pit.	L	5-6		9	8	Gleaton	R. Martinez	Belinda	23-25	4th	4½
6-4	Cin.	W	7-4		11	7	Hershiser	Browning	McDowell	24-25	4th	3½
6-5	Cin.	L	2-6		9	14	Rijo	Ke. Gross		24-26	5th	4½
6-6	Cin.	L	4-5		10	9	Bankhead	Wilson	Charlton	24-27	5th	5½
6-7	Cin.	W	1-0		3	6	Candiotti	Belcher		25-27	5th	4½
6-8	Atl.	L	2-4		8	7	Leibrandt	R. Martinez		25-28	5th	5½
6-9	Atl.	W	3-2		6	5	Hershiser	Stanton	McDowell	26-28	5th	5½
6-10	Atl.	L	1-2		6	6	Avery	Ke. Gross	Stanton	26-29	5th	5½
6-12	At Cin.	L	3-4		9	6	Bankhead	McDowell	Charlton	26-30	5th	8½
6-13	At Cin.	L	1-11		4	14	Belcher	Candiotti		26-31	5th	6½
6-14	At Cin.	L	1-5		10	9	Swindell	R. Martinez	Dibble	26-32	5th	7½
6-15	At Atl.	L	0-2		5	4	Avery	Hershiser		26-33	5th	9½
6-16	At Atl.	L	8-9		10	12	Berenguer	Candelaria		26-34	6th	10½
6-17	At Atl.	L	3-4		5	8	Glavine	Ojeda		26-35	6th	11½
6-19	At Hou.	L	1-2	(12)	8	9	Boever	Gott		26-36	6th	12
6-20	At Hou.	L	0-1		7	7	D. Jones	Hershiser		26-37	6th	12
6-21	At Hou.	L	0-2		7	7	Henry	Ke. Gross	D. Jones	26-38	6th	12
6-22	At S.D.	W	4-2		11	5	McDowell	Melendez		27-38	6th	11
6-23	At S.D.	L	4-8		10	8	Seminara	Candiotti		27-39	6th	12
6-25	Hou.	W	8-5		14	12	R. Martinez	J. Jones		28-39	6th	12
6-26	Hou.	W	6-5		9	9	Candelaria	D. Jones	McDowell	29-39	6th	12
6-27	Hou.	L	1-5		3	9	Williams	Ke. Gross		29-40	6th	13
6-28	Hou.	W	8-2		10	9	Ojeda	Blair		30-40	6th	13

Date		Opp.	Res.	Score	(inn.*)	Hits	Opp. hits	Winning pitcher	Losing pitcher	Save	Record	Pos.	GB
6-29		S.D.	W	6-5	(11)	9	11	Wilson	Clements		31-40	6th	12
6-30		S.D.	L	1-2		10	6	Hurst	R. Martinez	Maddux	31-41	6th	12
7-1		S.D.	L	2-6		7	13	Lefferts	Hershiser		31-42	6th	12
7-2		Phi.	W	9-4		11	9	Ke. Gross	Combs		32-42	6th	12
7-3	(1)	Phi.	W	5-1		7	7	Ojeda	Schilling		33-42	6th	12
7-3	(2)	Phi.	W	2-0		5	3	Astacio	Robinson		34-42	6th	11½
7-4		Phi.	L	2-3		7	6	Mulholland	Candiotti		34-43	6th	12½
7-5		Phi.	L	3-9		3	13	Mike Williams	R. Martinez		34-44	6th	13
7-6	(1)	Mon.	W	8-3		14	10	Ki. Gross	Martinez		35-44	6th	13½
7-6	(2)	Mon.	W	4-3		6	13	Hershiser	Fassero	Gott	36-44	6th	13
7-7	(1)	Mon.	L	1-4		8	5	Gardner	Ke. Gross	Wetteland	36-45	6th	14
7-7	(2)	Mon.	L	0-4		6	13	Hurst	Crews	Wetteland	36-46	6th	14½
7-8	(1)	Mon.	W	1-0	(11)	12	8	Candiotti	Valdez		37-46	6th	13½
7-8	(2)	Mon.	L	1-4		8	9	Risley	Astacio	Rojas	37-47	6th	14
7-9		St.L.	W	2-1		11	4	R. Martinez	Tewksbury	McDowell	38-47	6th	14
7-10		St.L.	L	1-3		7	8	Cormier	Candiotti	L. Smith	38-48	6th	14
7-11		St.L.	L	1-4		7	11	Clark	Hershiser	L. Smith	38-49	6th	14
7-12		St.L.	W	9-0		13	9	Ke. Gross	Osborne		39-49	6th	13
7-16		At Phi.	W	7-5		13	10	Candiotti	Mulholland	Gott	40-49	6th	12
7-17		At Phi.	L	3-11		6	13	Schilling	Hershiser		40-50	6th	13
7-18		At Phi.	L	3-14		10	17	Abbott	R. Martinez		40-51	6th	14
7-19		At Phi.	L	5-6		9	10	Ritchie	Howell	Mit. Williams	40-52	6th	15
7-20		At N.Y.	W	9-2		11	9	Candelaria	Innis	McDowell	41-52	6th	15
7-21		At N.Y.	L	2-5		11	7	Guetterman	Candelaria	Young	41-53	6th	15
7-22		At N.Y.	L	5-7		11	10	Cone	Hershiser	Young	41-54	6th	15½
7-24		At Mon.	L	3-4		6	9	D. Martinez	R. Martinez	Wetteland	41-55	6th	16½
7-25		At Mon.	L	1-4		4	10	Gardner	Ojeda	Wetteland	41-56	6th	17½
7-26		At Mon.	L	3-4		8	8	Rojas	Wilson		41-57	6th	17½
7-27		At S.F.	L	1-5		3	7	Black	Candiotti		41-58	6th	17½
7-28		At S.F.	L	3-5		11	8	Beck	McDowell		41-59	6th	17½
7-29		At S.F.	W	6-1		9	5	R. Martinez	Wilson		42-59	6th	17½
7-30		S.D.	W	6-5	(10)	8	11	Howell	Melendez		43-59	6th	16½
7-31		S.D.	L	3-4		10	7	Hurst	Ke. Gross	Myers	43-60	6th	17
8-1		S.D.	W	7-2		13	9	Candiotti	Benes		44-60	6th	17
8-2		S.D.	W	4-1		8	5	Hershiser	Deshaies		45-60	6th	17
8-4		Hou.	W	7-2		7	5	R. Martinez	Reynolds		46-60	6th	17
8-5		Hou.	L	6-7		7	13	Murphy	McDowell	D. Jones	46-61	6th	18
8-7		At Atl.	L	2-6		6	10	Leibrandt	Ke. Gross		46-62	6th	19½
8-8		At Atl.	L	2-12		9	18	Smith	Candiotti		46-63	6th	20½
8-9		At Atl.	L	3-10		7	11	Glavine	Hershiser		46-64	6th	21½
8-10		At Cin.	W	5-3		15	6	R. Martinez	Avery	Gott	47-64	6th	20½
8-11		At Cin.	W	8-4		15	6	Ojeda	Belcher		48-64	6th	19½
8-12		At Cin.	L	2-3		6	4	Swindell	Ke. Gross	Dibble	48-65	6th	20
8-13		At Cin.	W	4-3		4	9	McDowell	Henry	Howell	49-65	6th	20
8-14		S.F.	L	2-3		10	4	Hickerson	Candelaria	Beck	49-66	6th	21
8-15		S.F.	L	1-2		7	4	Wilson	R. Martinez	Beck	49-67	6th	22
8-16		S.F.	L	1-2		5	5	Burkett	Howell	Beck	49-68	6th	22
8-17		S.F.	W	2-0		8	0	Ke. Gross	Oliveras		50-68	6th	23
8-18		N.Y.	W	4-0		9	6	Astacio	Cone		51-68	6th	22
8-19		N.Y.	W	2-1		7	6	Hershiser	Gooden	Gott	52-68	6th	22
8-20		N.Y.	L	4-11		8	12	Fernandez	R. Martinez		52-69	6th	22
8-21		Chi.	L	2-3	(12)	12	15	Robinson	Howell	Scanlan	52-70	6th	22
8-22		Chi.	L	4-5		7	9	Patterson	Candelaria	Scanlan	52-71	6th	23
8-23		Chi.	L	2-4		8	11	Morgan	Astacio	McElroy	52-72	6th	23
8-24		Pit.	W	5-4		9	10	Gott	Neagle	Candelaria	53-72	6th	22½
8-25		Pit.	L	3-10		9	13	Cox	R. Martinez		53-73	6th	22½
8-26		Pit.	L	0-2		6	9	Wakefield	Candiotti		53-74	6th	22½
8-28		At St.L.	L	0-1		3	4	Clark	Ojeda	L. Smith	53-75	6th	22½
8-29		At St.L.	L	2-3		8	6	Olivares	Ke. Gross	L. Smith	53-76	6th	23½
8-30		At St.L.	L	0-3		6	9	Cormier	Hershiser	L. Smith	53-77	6th	23½
8-31		At Chi.	L	0-2		5	2	Maddux	Candiotti		53-78	6th	25
9-1		At Chi.	W	5-4	(13)	16	12	McDowell	Slocumb	Candelaria	54-78	6th	25
9-2		At Chi.	L	1-5		3	11	Morgan	Ojeda		54-79	6th	25
9-4		At Pit.	L	5-6		7	11	Patterson	Gott		54-80	6th	24½
9-5		At Pit.	L	1-6		6	10	Walk	Hershiser		54-81	6th	25½
9-6		At Pit.	W	7-5		13	9	Candiotti	Cox	Howell	55-81	6th	25½
9-7		At Atl.	L	1-7		5	16	Smoltz	Astacio		55-82	6th	26½
9-8		At Atl.	L	3-10		13	10	Freeman	Crews	Reardon	55-83	6th	27½
9-9		S.D.	W	4-1		8	4	Ke. Gross	Gr. Harris		56-83	6th	27½
9-10		S.D.	L	1-3		6	5	Deshaies	Hershiser	Myers	56-84	6th	28½
9-11		S.F.	L	3-7		8	12	Carter	Candiotti		56-85	6th	29½
9-12		S.F.	W	7-0		13	6	Astacio	Black		57-85	6th	29½
9-13		S.F.	L	3-7		8	12	Swift	Ojeda	Beck	57-86	6th	30½
9-14		At S.D.	W	5-4	(11)	12	10	Gott	Hernandez	McDowell	58-86	6th	30

Date	Opp.	Res.	Score	(inn.*)	Hits	Opp. hits	Winning pitcher	Losing pitcher	Save	Record	Pos.	GB
9-15	At S.D.	W	6-3		13	13	Hershiser	Deshaies	Howell	59-86	6th	29
9-16	At S.D.	L	1-3		5	6	Benes	Candiotti	Myers	59-87	6th	30
9-18	At S.F.	W	11-4		11	9	Astacio	Black	McDowell	60-87	6th	28½
9-19	At S.F.	L	0-3		5	11	Brantley	Ojeda	Swift	60-88	6th	28½
9-20	At S.F.	L	2-3		6	10	Beck	McDowell		60-89	6th	29½
9-21	Atl.	L	2-4		6	7	Smith	Hershiser	Stanton	60-90	6th	30½
9-22	Atl.	W	4-1		7	5	Candiotti	Smoltz		61-90	6th	29½
9-23	Cin.	L	0-3		5	13	Pugh	Astacio	Dibble	61-91	6th	30½
9-24	Cin.	L	4-8		9	15	Bolton	McDowell	Charlton	61-92	6th	30½
9-25	Hou.	L	3-4		7	7	Portugal	Candelaria	D. Jones	61-93	6th	30½
9-26	Hou.	L	4-5		8	15	Hernandez	Ki. Gross	D. Jones	61-94	6th	31½
9-27	Hou.	L	2-4		14	14	Reynolds	Candelaria	D. Jones	61-95	6th	32½
9-29	At Cin.	W	5-0		10	3	Astacio	Pugh		62-95	6th	32½
9-30	At Cin.	L	1-3		5	8	Belcher	P. Martinez	Dibble	62-96	6th	32½
10-1	At Cin.	W	4-2		8	9	Ke. Gross	Swindell	Howell	63-96	6th	32½
10-2	At Hou.	L	1-6		5	10	Kile	Hershiser		63-97	6th	34
10-3	At Hou.	L	2-3	(13)	10	16	J. Jones	Crews		63-98	6th	35
10-4	At Hou.	L	0-3		5	8	Harnisch	Astacio	D. Jones	63-99	6th	35

Monthly records: April (9-13), May (13-10), June (9-18), July (12-19), August (10-18), September (9-18), Oct. (1-3).

HIGHLIGHTS

High point: From May 16-June 1, the Dodgers won 12 of 15 games, including a season-high six in a row (May 26-June 1), to reach .500 (23-23) and climb within 2½ games of first place.

Low point: But from June 10-21, Los Angeles fell out of the race by losing a season-high 10 straight games. On June 19, the Dodgers dropped into last place for good.

Turning point: May 6, when right fielder Darryl Strawberry hurt his lower back in Philadelphia. He played only 19 games after that and eventually had back surgery. The Dodgers probably wouldn't have contended even if Strawberry had been healthy, but they also wouldn't have lost 40 games by one run, an L.A. Dodger record.

Most valuable player: First baseman Eric Karros. Lacking protection in the lineup, he still earned N.L. Rookie of the Year honors by collecting an L.A. Dodger rookie-record 88 RBIs and a team-high 20 homers.

Most valuable pitcher: Righthander Kevin Gross. Despite posting his sixth consecutive losing record (8-13), he registered a career-best 3.17 ERA, paced the team in strikeouts (158) and tossed a no-hitter against San Francisco on August 17.

Most improved player: Shortstop Jose Offerman. Yes, he led the majors with 42 errors (the highest total by a Dodger in 51 years), but he had only two errors in his last 20 games. And he batted .267 over the second half of the season.

Most pleasant surprise: Righthander Pedro Astacio. Recalled solely as an emergency starter July 2, he shut out Philadelphia in his big-league debut the next day. He returned to the minors July 8 but was recalled August 13 and pitched three more shutouts.

Biggest disappointment: Left fielder Eric Davis. Injured as early as spring training, he played in a career-low 76 games and batted .228 with five homers and 32 RBIs.

Key injuries: The injuries to Strawberry and Davis were devastating. Right-hander Jay Howell missed the first 33 games because of a tender shoulder. Righthander Ramon Martinez missed the last six weeks with a sore right elbow and won only eight games.

Notable: The Dodgers finished in last place for the first time in 87 years (1905), lost more games than any Dodger team since the 1908 club lost 101 times and finished 35 games out of first place, their biggest deficit since finishing 42 games out in 1944.

—GORDON VERRELL

RECORDS

1992 regular-season record: 63-99 (6th in N.L. West); 37-44 at home; 26-55 on road; 29-43 vs. East; 34-56 vs. West; 25-37 vs. LHP; 38-62 vs. RHP; 51-69 on grass; 12-30 on turf; 20-34 in daytime; 43-65 at night; 17-40 in one-run games; 6-7 in extra-inning games; 2-1-1 in doubleheaders.

Team record last five years: 413-394 (.512, ranks 4th in league in that span).

TEAM LEADERS

Batting average: Brett Butler (.309).
At-bats: Brett Butler (553).
Runs: Brett Butler (86).
Hits: Brett Butler (171).
Total bases: Eric Karros (232).
Doubles: Eric Karros (30).
Triples: Brett Butler (11).
Home runs: Eric Karros (20).
Runs batted in: Eric Karros (88).
Stolen bases: Brett Butler (41).
Slugging percentage: Eric Karros (.426).
On-base percentage: Brett Butler (.413).
Wins: Tom Candiotti (11).
Earned-run average: Tom Candiotti (3.00).
Complete games: Tom Candiotti (6).
Shutouts: Pedro Astacio (4).
Saves: Roger McDowell (14).
Innings pitched: Orel Hershiser (210⅔).
Strikeouts: Kevin Gross (158).

GAMES BY POSITION

Catcher: Mike Scioscia 108, Carlos Hernandez 63, Mike Piazza 16.
First base: Eric Karros 143, Todd Benzinger 42, Kal Daniels 8, Henry Rodriguez 1.
Second base: Lenny Harris 81, Mike Sharperson 63, Eric Young 43, Juan Samuel 38.
Third base: Dave Hansen 108, Mike Sharperson 60, Lenny Harris 33, Dave Anderson 26.
Shortstop: Jose Offerman 149, Lenny Harris 10, Rafael Bournigal 9, Dave Anderson 7, Mike Sharperson 2.
Outfield: Brett Butler 155, Mitch Webster 90, Eric Davis 74, Todd Benzinger 51, Henry Rodriguez 48, Tom Goodwin 45, Darryl Strawberry 42, Billy Ashley 27, Stan Javier 27, Kal Daniels 21, Lenny Harris 15, Juan Samuel 1.

TOP 10 DRAFT CHOICES

1a. Ryan Luzinski. C, Holy Cross High School, Delran, N.J.
1b. Michael Moore. OF, UCLA.
2a. Dwain Bostic. SS, Samuel F.B. Morse High School, San Diego.
2b. Dan Melendez. 1B, Pepperdine University.
3a. Dwight Maness. OF, William Penn High School, New Castle, Del.
3b. David Spykstra. RHP, Cherry Creek High School, Englewood, Colo.
4. Keith Johnson. SS, University of the Pacific.
5. Chris Abbe. C, University of Texas.
6. Jon Graves. RHP, Long Beach State University.
7. Brian Richardson. 3B, St. Bernard High School, Playa del Rey, Calif.
8. Dan Markham. LHP, Diablo Valley College (Calif.).
9. Ryan Henderson. RHP, University of Southern California.
10. David Post. 3B, Kingston (N.Y.) High School.

MONTREAL EXPOS
NATIONAL LEAGUE EAST DIVISION

1993 SEASON

APRIL

SUN	MON	TUE	WED	THU	FRI	SAT
				1	2	3
4	5 CIN	6	7 N CIN	8	9 COL	10 COL
11 COL	12	13	14 N HOU	15 HOU	16 N COL	17 H COL
18 COL	19 H	20 N LA	21 H LA	22 N LA	23 N SF	24 SF H
25 SF	26 N SD H	27 SD	28 N LA	29 N LA	30 N SF	

MAY

SUN	MON	TUE	WED	THU	FRI	SAT
						1 SF
2 SF	3	4 N SD	5 N SD H	6	7 PIT	8 N PIT
9 PIT	10	11 N FLA	12 N FLA H	13 N FLA H	14 N NY H	15 NY H
16 NY H	17 H ATL	18 N ATL	19 N ATL	20 N PHI	21 PHI H	22 N PHI
23 PHI	24 STL H	25 N STL H	26 N STL H	27	28 CHI	29 CHI
30 CHI	31 HOU					

JUNE

SUN	MON	TUE	WED	THU	FRI	SAT
		1 N HOU	2 N HOU	3 N CHI H	4 N CHI H	5 N CHI H
6 N CHI H	7 N CIN H	8 N CIN H	9 N CIN H	10 STL	11 N STL	12 N STL
13 STL	14 H PHI H	15 N PHI H	16 N PHI H	17	18 N ATL H	19 N ATL H
20 ATL H	21 NY H	22 N NY	23 N NY	24	25 N FLA	26 N FLA
27 FLA	28 N PIT H	29 N PIT H	30 N PIT H			

JULY

SUN	MON	TUE	WED	THU	FRI	SAT
				1 PIT H	2 N LA H	3 N LA H
4 LA H	5 N SF	6 N SF	7 N SF H	8 N SD	9 N SD H	10 N SD H
11 SD H	12	13 * ALL-STAR GAME	14	15 N LA	16 N LA	17 N LA
18 LA	19 N SF	20 SF	21 N SD	22 N SD	23 N SD	24 N SD
25 SD	26	27 N PIT	28 N PIT	29 N PIT	30 N FLA H	31 N FLA H

AUGUST

SUN	MON	TUE	WED	THU	FRI	SAT
1 FLA H	2 N NY H	3 N NY	4 N NY H	5 N NY H	6 N ATL H	7 N ATL
8 ATL	9	10 N PHI	11 N PHI	12 PHI	13 N STL H	14 N STL H
15 STL H	16	17 CHI	18 CHI	19 CHI	20 N CIN H	21 N CIN
22 CIN	23 N CHI H	24 N CHI H	25 N CHI H	26	27 HOU H	28 N HOU H
29 HOU H	30 N COL	31 N COL				

SEPTEMBER

SUN	MON	TUE	WED	THU	FRI	SAT
			1 COL	2	3 N HOU	4 N HOU
5 HOU	6 COL H	7 N COL H	8 N COL H	9	10 N CIN H	11 N CIN
12 CIN H	13	14 N STL	15 N STL	16 N STL	17 N PHI H	18 N PHI
19 PHI H	20	21 N ATL	22 N ATL	23 N ATL H	24 N NY	25 N NY
26 NY	27 N FLA	28 N FLA	29 N FLA	30 N		

OCTOBER

SUN	MON	TUE	WED	THU	FRI	SAT
					1 N PIT H	2 PIT H
3 PIT H						

CLUB DIRECTORY

President and general partner
  Claude R. Brochu
Chairman of the board
  Jacques Menard
Vice chairmen of the board
  Jacques Berube
  Claude Blanchet
  Jocelyn Proteau
V.p., player personnel and general manager
  Dan Duquette
Vice president, baseball operations
  Bill Stoneman
Director, scouting
  Kevin Malone
Director, minor league field operations
  Herm Starrette
Director, team travel
  Erik Ostling
Director, minor league operations
  Kent Qualls
International scouting supervisor
  Fred Ferreira
Executive advisor, baseball operations
  Eddie Haas
Special consultant, baseball operations
  Jim Fanning
General mgr., West Palm Beach operations
  Rob Rabenecker
Administrator, baseball operations
  Roberta Mazur
Administrative assistant, scouting
  Gregg Leonard
Admin. asst., minor league operations
  Neal Huntingdon
V.p., marketing and communications
  Richard Morency
Vice president, business operations
  Gerry Trudeau
Executive director, business operations
  Claude Delorme
Controller
  Raymond St-Pierre
Director, marketing and communications
  Carole Boivin
Director, events
  Claudine Cook
Director, promotions
  Luigi Carolo
Director, ticket office
  Chantal Dalpe
Director, media services
  Monique Giroux
Director, media relations
  Richard Griffin
Director, advertising
  Johanne Heroux

Director, stadium operations
  Monique Lacas
Director, retailing
  Susan LeBlanc
Director, ticket sales
  Ronald Martineau
Director, corporate affairs
  Pierre O. Touchette
Public relations representative
  Ron Piche
Assistant controller
  Michel Bussiere
Assistant director, stadium operations
  Pierre Touzin
Club physician
  Dr. Robert Brodrick
Club orthopedist
  Dr. Larry Coughlin
Scouts
  Dennis Cardoza
  Doug Carpenter
  Emilio Carrasquel
  Carl Cassell
  Ed Creech
  Arturo DeFreitas
  Richard DeHart
  Phil Favia
  Fred Ferreira
  Joe Ferrone
  Jim Fleming
  Joe Frisina
  Eddie Haas
  Jim Holden
  John Hughes
  Dave Jauss
  Bob Johnson
  Jeff Kahn
  Gregg Leonard
  Dave Littlefield
  Juan Loyola
  Bill MacKenzie
  Kevin Malone
  Dave Malpass
  Rene Marchand
  Roberto Mazur
  Roy McMillan
  Tomas Morales
  Carlos Moreno
  Mike Murphy
  Bob Oldis
  Rene Picota
  Hank Sargent
  Scott Stanley
  Pat Sullivan
  Fred Wright

SCHEDULE KEY

H—Home game.   N—Night game (any game starting after 5 p.m.).
*All-Star Game at Oriole Park at Camden Yards, Baltimore.

Manager—Felipe Alou (17).

Coaches—Tommy Harper (21), Tim Johnson (1), Joe Kerrigan (45), Jerry Manuel (6), Luis Pujols (31).

No.	PITCHERS	B/T	Ht./Wt.	Born	1992 clubs
73	Arteaga, Ivan	L/R	6-2/220	7-20-72	DID NOT PLAY
54	Ausanio, Joe	R/R	6-1/205	12-9-65	Buffalo
47	Barnes, Brian	L/L	5-9/170	3-25-67	Indianapolis, Montreal
4	Batista, Miguel	R/R	6-0/197	2-19-71	Pittsburgh, West Palm Beach
46	Bottenfield, Kent	B/R	6-3/225	11-14-68	Indianapolis, Montreal
49	Cornelius, Reid	R/R	6-0/200	6-2-70	Harrisburg
62	Eischen, Joe	L/L	6-1/190	5-25-70	West Palm Beach
13	Fassero, Jeff	L/L	6-1/195	1-5-63	Montreal
16	Gardiner, Mike	B/R	6-0/200	10-19-65	Boston, Pawtucket
34	Heredia, Gil	R/R	6-1/190	10-26-65	Phoenix, San Francisco, Indianapolis, Montreal
44	Hill, Ken	R/R	6-2/175	12-14-65	Montreal
37	Hurst, Jonathan	R/R	6-3/175	10-20-66	Indianapolis, Montreal
32	Martinez, Dennis	R/R	6-1/180	5-14-55	Montreal
60	Mathile, Mike	R/R	6-4/220	11-24-68	Harrisburg
43	Nabholz, Chris	L/L	6-5/212	1-5-67	Montreal
58	Picota, Len	R/R	6-1/100	7-23-66	Harrisburg
50	Risley, Bill	R/R	6-2/210	5-29-67	Indianapolis, Montreal
27	Rojas, Mel	R/R	5-11/185	12-10-66	Indianapolis, Montreal
65	Thomas, Mike	L/L	6-2/200	9-2-69	Rockford
26	Valdez, Sergio	R/R	6-1/190	9-7-65	Indianapolis, Montreal
57	Wetteland, John	R/R	6-2/195	8-21-66	Montreal
20	Young, Pete	R/R	6-0/225	3-19-68	Indianapolis, Montreal

No.	CATCHERS	B/T	Ht./Wt.	Born	1992 clubs
61	Fitzpatrick, Rob	R/R	5-11/190	9-14-68	West Palm Beach
24	Fletcher, Darrin	L/R	6-1/199	10-3-66	Montreal, Indianapolis
19	Laker, Tim	R/R	6-3/195	11-27-69	Harrisburg, Montreal
63	Santana, Raul	R/R	5-10/207	2-9-72	Rockford
2	Spehr, Tim	R/R	6-2/195	7-2-66	Omaha

No.	INFIELDERS	B/T	Ht./Wt.	Born	1992 clubs
5	Berry, Sean	R/R	5-11/210	3-22-66	Omaha, Montreal
55	Bolick, Frank	B/R	5-10/175	6-28-66	Jacksonville, Calgary
14	Cianfrocco, Archi	R/R	6-5/200	10-6-66	Montreal, Indianapolis
15	Colbrunn, Greg	R/R	6-0/190	7-26-69	Indianapolis, Montreal
12	Cordero, Wilfredo	R/R	6-2/185	10-3-71	Indianapolis, Montreal
4	DeShields, Delino	L/R	6-1/170	1-15-69	Montreal
59	Lansing, Mike	R/R	6-0/175	4-3-68	Harrisburg
7	Stevens, Lee	L/L	6-4/219	7-10-67	California

No.	OUTFIELDERS	B/T	Ht./Wt.	Born	1992 clubs
18	Alou, Moises	R/R	6-3/190	7-3-66	Montreal
9	Grissom, Marquis	R/R	5-11/190	4-17-67	Montreal
25	Stairs, Matt	R/R	5-9/175	2-27-69	Indianapolis, Montreal
23	Vander Wal, John	L/L	6-2/190	4-29-66	Montreal
33	Walker, Larry	L/R	6-3/215	12-1-66	Montreal

BALLPARK INFORMATION

Ballpark (capacity, surface)
  Olympic Stadium (46,400, artificial)
Address
  4549 Pierre-de-Coubertin Ave.
  Montreal, QC H1V 3N7
Business phone
  514-253-3434
Ticket information
  514-253-3434
Ticket prices
  $22 (VIP box seats)
  $15.25 (box seats)
  $9 (terrace)
  $5.50 (general admission)
  $4 (bleachers)
Field dimensions (from home plate)
  To left field at foul line, 325 feet
  To center field, 404 feet
  To right field at foul line, 325 feet
First game played
  April 15, 1977 (Phillies 7, Expos 2)

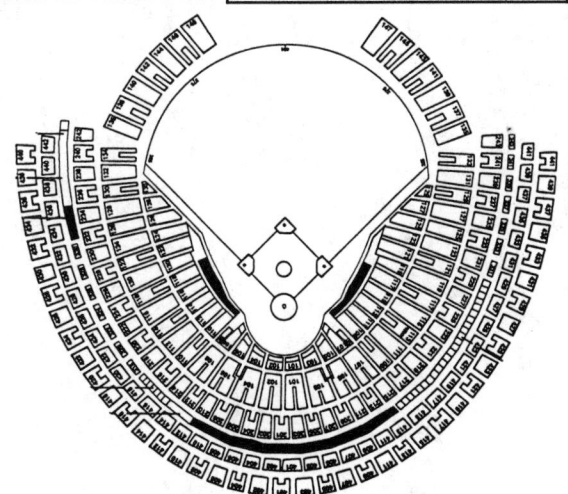

MINOR LEAGUE AFFILIATES

Class	Team	League	Manager
AAA	Ottawa	International	Mike Quade
AA	Harrisburg	Eastern	Jim Tracy
A	West Palm Beach	Florida State	Rob Leary
A	Burlington	Midwest	Lorenzo Bundy
A	Jamestown	New York-Pennsylvania	Tim Torricelli
Rookie	Gulf Coast Expos	Gulf Coast	Nelson Norman

☐ BROADCAST INFORMATION ☐

Radio: CICQ-AM (600). Broadcasters: Dave VanHorne, Ken Singleton, Bobby Winkles, Elliott Price. CKAC-AM (73, French language). Broadcasters: Rodger Brulotte, Jacques Doucet, Alain Chantelois.

TV: CFCF-TV (Channel 12). Broadcasters: Ken Singleton, Dave Van-Horne. CBFT (2, French language). Broadcasters: Claude Raymond, Raymond Lebrun.

Cable TV: The Sports Network. Broadcasters: Ken Singleton, Dave Van-Horne. RDS (French language). Broadcasters: Rodger Brulotte, Denis Casavant.

☐ SPRING TRAINING ☐

Ballpark (city): Municipal Stadium (West Palm Beach, Fla.).
Ticket information: 407-684-6801.

HISTORY

YEAR-BY-YEAR RECORDS

Year	Pos.	W	L	Pct.	*GB	Year	Pos.	W	L	Pct.	*GB
1969	6th	52	110	.321	48	1983	3rd	82	80	.506	8
1970	6th	73	89	.451	16	1984	5th	78	83	.484	18
1971	5th	71	90	.441	25½	1985	3rd	84	77	.522	16½
1972	5th	70	86	.449	26½	1986	4th	78	83	.484	29½
1973	4th	79	83	.488	3½	1987	3rd	91	71	.562	4
1974	4th	79	82	.491	8½	1988	3rd	81	81	.500	20
1975	T5th	75	87	.463	17½	1989	4th	81	81	.500	12
1976	6th	55	107	.340	46	1990	3rd	85	77	.525	10
1977	5th	75	87	.463	26	1991	6th	71	90	.441	26½
1978	4th	76	86	.469	14	1992	2nd	87	75	.537	9
1979	2nd	95	65	.594	2						
1980	2nd	90	72	.556	1						
1981	3rd/1st	60	48	.556	†‡§						
1982	3rd	86	76	.531	6						

*Games behind winner. †Won division playoff. ‡Lost Championship Series. §First half 30-25; second 30-23.

MANAGERS

Name	Record	Years
Gene Mauch	499-627	'69-75
Karl Kuehl	43-85	1976
Charlie Fox	12-22	1976
Dick Williams	350-322	'77-81
Jim Fanning	116-103	'81-82
		1984
Bill Virdon	146-147	'83-84
Buck Rodgers	520-499	'85-91
Tom Runnells	68-81	'91-92
Felipe Alou	70-55	1992

DAY BY DAY

Date	Opp.	Res.	Score	(inn.*)	Hits	Opp. hits	Winning pitcher	Losing pitcher	Save	Record	Pos.	GB
4-6	At Pit.	L	0-2		6	4	Drabek	Martinez	Mason	0-1	T5th	1
4-8	At Pit.	L	2-4		5	6	Smith	Gardner	Belinda	0-2	6th	2
4-9	At Pit.	W	8-3		14	7	Nabholz	Walk		1-2	T5th	1
4-10	At N.Y.	W	4-0		6	4	Hill	Gooden		2-2	T3rd	1
4-11	At N.Y.	W	9-2		12	6	Martinez	Cone		3-2	T1st	...
4-12	At N.Y.	W	8-2		7	6	Haney	Saberhagen		4-2	T1st	...
4-13	St.L.	W	3-2		8	11	Gardner	Cormier	Wetteland	5-2	1st	+½
4-14	St.L.	L	1-3		8	6	Osborne	Nabholz	L. Smith	5-3	2nd	½
4-15	St.L.	L	2-4		6	7	Tewksbury	Hill	L. Smith	5-4	2nd	1½
4-17	N.Y.	L	2-10		7	11	Cone	Martinez		5-5	T2nd	2½
4-18	N.Y.	W	8-6		11	9	Landrum	Innis	Wetteland	6-5	2nd	2
4-19	N.Y.	L	6-11		6	11	Young	Fassero		6-6	2nd	3½
4-20	Pit.	L	1-11		5	13	Tomlin	Hill		6-7	T3rd	4½
4-21	Pit.	L	7-8		11	10	Palacios	Haney	Mason	6-8	4th	5½
4-22	Pit.	L	0-2		5	4	Drabek	Martinez		6-9	5th	6½
4-23	Pit.	W	6-3		10	7	Gardner	Smith	Wetteland	7-9	5th	5½
4-24	At St.L.	L	3-4		8	10	Olivares	Wetteland		7-10	T4th	6½
4-25	At St.L.	L	1-2	(17)	8	15	Tewksbury	Rojas		7-11	T5th	7½
4-26	At St.L.	W	6-0		9	5	Haney	Cormier		8-11	T4th	6½
4-27	At S.F.	L	1-2		7	6	Burba	Martinez	Brantley	8-12	5th	7
4-28	At S.F.	L	1-2	(10)	5	9	Brantley	Sampen		8-13	5th	7
4-29	At S.D.	L	2-7		9	11	Gr. Harris	Nabholz		8-14	5th	8
4-30	At S.D.	W	9-3		15	8	Hill	Benes		9-14	5th	7½
5-5	S.D.	W	5-2		9	10	Martinez	Gr. Harris		10-14	5th	7½
5-6	S.D.	W	4-3		8	6	Hill	Benes	Wetteland	11-14	5th	7½
5-8	S.F.	L	3-6		5	9	Wilson	Fassero	Brantley	11-15	5th	8
5-9	S.F.	W	9-3		10	8	Nabholz	Black		12-15	4th	8
5-10	S.F.	L	3-8	(11)	7	9	Brantley	Landrum		12-16	5th	8
5-11	L.A.	W	6-5	(10)	13	9	Fassero	Wilson		13-16	4th	7½
5-12	L.A.	L	0-2		3	8	Ke. Gross	Haney		13-17	4th	7½
5-13	L.A.	W	5-1		10	3	Gardner	Hershiser	Wetteland	14-17	4th	7½
5-15	At Atl.	L	2-4		6	7	Mercker	Nabholz	Stanton	14-18	5th	8
5-16	At Atl.	W	7-1		11	6	Martinez	Avery	Rojas	15-18	4th	7
5-17	At Atl.	W	5-4		9	6	Hill	Glavine	Wetteland	16-18	4th	6
5-18	Cin.	L	1-2		4	9	Bankhead	Gardner	Charlton	16-19	5th	6½
5-19	Cin.	L	4-7		6	9	Henry	Wetteland	Dibble	16-20	5th	6½
5-20	Cin.	W	6-5		7	11	Rojas	Dibble		17-20	4th	5½
5-22	Atl.	W	7-1		9	2	Martinez	Glavine		18-20	4th	5
5-23	Atl.	W	7-6		14	13	Fassero	Stanton	Wetteland	19-20	4th	4
5-24	Atl.	L	1-2		6	7	Smoltz	Gardner		19-21	4th	4½
5-25	Hou.	L	8-10		14	14	Henry	Haney	D. Jones	19-22	4th	5½
5-26	Hou.	L	4-9		7	10	Boever	Nabholz	D. Jones	19-23	4th	6
5-27	Hou.	W	8-5		9	8	Martinez	Portugal	Wetteland	20-23	4th	4½
5-29	At Cin.	L	2-3	(11)	8	8	Bankhead	Sampen		20-24	5th	4½
5-30	At Cin.	L	4-9		9	13	Browning	Gardner		20-25	5th	5½
5-31	At Cin.	W	6-2		10	7	Nabholz	Rijo		21-25	5th	4½
6-1	At Hou.	W	7-1		9	4	Martinez	Kile		22-25	4th	4
6-2	At Hou.	L	0-6		6	6	Portugal	Sampen		22-26	4th	4
6-3	At Hou.	L	3-5		8	9	Harnisch	Hill	D. Jones	22-27	5th	5
6-5 (1)	Chi.	L	4-10		10	15	Jackson	Gardner	Scanlan	22-28	6th	6½
6-5 (2)	Chi.	W	6-2		8	10	Nabholz	Maddux	Wetteland	23-28	5th	6
6-7	Chi.	W	3-2		10	6	Fassero	Scanlan		24-28	5th	5½
6-8	N.Y.	W	6-0		11	1	Hill	Young		25-28	5th	4½
6-9	N.Y.	L	5-6		8	16	Franco	Fassero		25-29	5th	5½
6-10	N.Y.	W	8-2		13	8	Gardner	Cone		26-29	4th	5½
6-12	At Chi.	L	2-5		7	8	McElroy	Martinez	Bullinger	26-30	6th	8½
6-13	At Chi.	L	3-4		8	7	Castillo	Nabholz	Bullinger	26-31	5th	6½
6-14	At Chi.	L	1-5		5	9	Jackson	Hill		26-32	6th	7½
6-15	At N.Y.	W	4-1		9	3	Gardner	Young	Wetteland	27-32	6th	7½
6-16	At N.Y.	L	2-5		3	7	Cone	Hurst		27-33	6th	8½
6-17	At N.Y.	W	5-2		7	8	Martinez	Fernandez	Rojas	28-33	5th	8½
6-18	At Pit.	W	4-0		12	3	Nabholz	Palacios	Fassero	29-33	4th	7½
6-19	At Pit.	W	2-1		5	7	Hill	Drabek	Wetteland	30-33	4th	6½
6-20	At Pit.	W	4-3		5	8	Gardner	Smith	Wetteland	31-33	4th	5½
6-21	At Pit.	L	4-5		11	5	Robinson	Martinez	Belinda	31-34	4th	6½
6-22	Phi.	L	3-5		4	7	Combs	Barnes	Mit. Williams	31-35	5th	7½
6-23	Phi.	L	0-5		6	10	Schilling	Nabholz		31-36	6th	8½
6-24	Phi.	W	8-1		11	7	Hill	Weston		32-36	5th	7½
6-26	Pit.	W	6-2		11	6	Martinez	Smith	Rojas	33-36	5th	6½
6-27	Pit.	L	4-12		9	17	Robinson	Gardner	Belinda	33-37	5th	7½

Date		Opp.	Res.	Score	(inn.*)	Hits	Opp. hits	Winning pitcher	Losing pitcher	Save	Record	Pos.	GB
6-28		Pit.	W	9-0		10	5	Barnes	Tomlin		34-37	5th	6½
6-29		At Phi.	L	4-5		9	6	Mulholland	Fassero	Mit. Williams	34-38	5th	6½
6-30		At Phi.	W	7-2		12	5	Hill	Mike Williams		35-38	4th	6½
7-1		At Phi.	W	6-3		9	4	Martinez	Abbott	Wetteland	36-38	4th	6½
7-2		At S.D.	W	3-2		7	5	Gardner	Benes	Wetteland	37-38	4th	5½
7-3		At S.D.	L	4-6		7	12	Seminara	Barnes	Andersen	37-39	4th	5½
7-4		At S.D.	W	3-2	(10)	7	8	Wetteland	Melendez	Rojas	38-39	3rd	4½
7-5		At S.D.	W	4-3	(10)	8	6	Rojas	Scott		39-39	3rd	3½
7-6	(1)	At L.A.	L	3-8		10	14	Ki. Gross	Martinez		39-40	3rd	4½
7-6	(2)	At L.A.	L	3-4		13	6	Hershiser	Fassero	Gott	39-41	3rd	5
7-7	(1)	At L.A.	W	4-1		5	8	Gardner	Ke. Gross	Wetteland	40-41	3rd	5
7-7	(2)	At L.A.	W	4-0		13	6	Hurst	Crews	Wetteland	41-41	T2nd	4½
7-8	(1)	At L.A.	L	0-1	(11)	8	12	Candiotti	Valdez		41-42	3rd	4½
7-8	(2)	At L.A.	W	4-1		9	8	Risley	Astacio	Rojas	42-42	3rd	4
7-9		At S.F.	W	6-5	(12)	15	11	Wetteland	Righetti		43-42	2nd	3
7-10		At S.F.	W	3-2		7	8	Hill	Wilson	Rojas	44-42	2nd	3
7-11		At S.F.	L	0-3		8	6	Black	Martinez		44-43	3rd	4
7-12		At S.F.	L	0-4		7	12	Swift	Gardner		44-44	3rd	5
7-16		S.D.	W	7-4		10	7	Hill	Hurst	Wetteland	45-44	3rd	5
7-17		S.D.	W	3-0		9	7	Nabholz	Benes	Wetteland	46-44	2nd	4
7-18		S.D.	L	3-10		8	12	Seminara	Martinez		46-45	2nd	5
7-19		S.D.	L	2-9		10	16	Lefferts	Gardner		46-46	2nd	5
7-20		S.F.	W	2-1		5	4	Barnes	Rapp	Wetteland	47-46	2nd	4
7-21		S.F.	W	5-1		11	7	Hill	Black	Rojas	48-46	2nd	3
7-22		S.F.	L	1-4		8	10	Swift	Nabholz		48-47	2nd	4
7-24		L.A.	W	4-3		9	6	D. Martinez	R. Martinez	Wetteland	49-47	2nd	3
7-25		L.A.	W	4-1		10	4	Gardner	Ojeda	Wetteland	50-47	3rd	4
7-26		L.A.	W	4-3		8	8	Rojas	Wilson		51-47	2nd	2
7-27		At St.L.	W	6-4		9	12	Hill	Olivares	Wetteland	52-47	2nd	1
7-28		At St.L.	W	7-4		15	9	Fassero	Osborne		53-47	T1st	...
7-29		At St.L.	L	1-4		4	6	L. Smith	Martinez		53-48	T1st	...
7-30		Phi.	W	7-2		7	7	Gardner	Mathews		54-48	T1st	...
7-31		Phi.	L	0-2		5	7	Mulholland	Barnes		54-49	2nd	1
8-1		Phi.	L	2-4		6	9	Schilling	Hill	Mit. Williams	54-50	2nd	2
8-2		Phi.	W	1-0		4	5	Nabholz	Rivera	Wetteland	55-50	2nd	2
8-3		Chi.	W	3-2		7	10	Martinez	Castillo	Wetteland	56-50	2nd	1½
8-4		Chi.	L	6-8		9	13	McElroy	Sampen	Assenmacher	56-51	2nd	2½
8-5		Chi.	W	5-3		12	8	Barnes	Patterson	Wetteland	57-51	2nd	2½
8-6		At Phi.	W	7-4		12	12	Hill	Schilling	Wetteland	58-51	2nd	2½
8-7		At Phi.	L	1-3		4	10	Rivera	Nabholz	Mit. Williams	58-52	2nd	3½
8-8		At Phi.	W	6-1		11	4	Martinez	Abbott		59-52	2nd	3½
8-9		At Phi.	W	6-2		9	3	Gardner	Mathews	Rojas	60-52	2nd	3½
8-10		At Chi.	W	11-0		18	8	Barnes	Robinson		61-52	2nd	3½
8-11		At Chi.	W	3-2	(17)	10	11	Sampen	Robinson		62-52	2nd	2½
8-12		At Chi.	W	3-1		11	3	Nabholz	Morgan	Rojas	63-52	2nd	2½
8-14		St.L.	W	4-1		5	2	Martinez	Cormier	Wetteland	64-52	2nd	1½
8-15		St.L.	L	4-6		9	4	Tewksbury	Wetteland	L. Smith	64-53	2nd	1½
8-16		St.L.	L	2-5		5	4	Osborne	Barnes	L. Smith	64-54	2nd	2½
8-18		Atl.	L	1-5		4	9	Leibrandt	Hill		64-55	2nd	3
8-19		Atl.	L	2-4		7	7	Glavine	Nabholz	Stanton	64-56	2nd	4
8-20		Atl.	W	3-2		8	7	Fassero	Pena		65-56	2nd	4
8-21		Cin.	W	6-3		10	8	Wetteland	Belcher		66-56	2nd	3
8-22		Cin.	W	3-1		10	5	Rojas	Swindell	Wetteland	67-56	2nd	3
8-23		Cin.	L	0-1		5	7	Rijo	Hill	Dibble	67-57	2nd	3
8-25		At Atl.	W	6-0		10	8	Nabholz	Glavine		68-57	2nd	2½
8-26		At Atl.	W	5-4		13	7	Martinez	Avery	Wetteland	69-57	2nd	2½
8-28		At Hou.	L	1-8		5	12	Harnisch	Gardner		69-58	2nd	2½
8-29		At Hou.	L	2-8		5	10	J. Jones	Barnes		69-59	2nd	3½
8-30		At Hou.	W	4-0		7	4	Hill	Kile		70-59	2nd	3½
8-31		At Cin.	W	8-4		11	7	Rojas	Bolton		71-59	2nd	3
9-1		At Cin.	W	5-2		11	9	Martinez	Pugh	Wetteland	72-59	2nd	3
9-2		At Cin.	W	7-3		12	9	Fassero	Charlton	Wetteland	73-59	2nd	3
9-3		At Atl.	W	11-2		14	7	Barnes	Leibrandt	Bottenfield	74-59	2nd	3
9-4		Hou.	W	5-2		6	7	Hill	J. Jones	Wetteland	75-59	2nd	3
9-5		Hou.	L	2-5		7	8	Kile	Nabholz		75-60	2nd	4
9-6		Hou.	L	1-3		4	6	Henry	Martinez	D. Jones	75-61	2nd	4
9-7		St.L.	L	7-8	(10)	13	14	B. Smith	Wetteland	L. Smith	75-62	2nd	4
9-8		St.L.	W	6-1		11	6	Barnes	Clark	Rojas	76-62	2nd	4
9-9		St.L.	L	3-10		9	16	Magrane	Hill		76-63	2nd	5
9-11		N.Y.	W	4-3		12	5	Fassero	Saberhagen	Wetteland	77-63	2nd	4
9-12		N.Y.	W	4-1		8	5	Martinez	Schourek		78-63	2nd	4
9-13		N.Y.	W	7-5		14	8	Rojas	Young		79-63	2nd	3
9-14		At Phi.	L	2-6		8	8	Greene	Barnes	Shepherd	79-64	2nd	4
9-15		At Phi.	W	3-0		9	3	Hill	Schilling	Wetteland	80-64	2nd	4

Date	Opp.	Res.	Score	(inn.*)	Hits	Opp. hits	Winning pitcher	Losing pitcher	Save	Record	Pos.	GB
9-16	At Pit.	W	6-3		10	10	Nabholz	Walk	Wetteland	81-64	2nd	3
9-17	At Pit.	L	2-3	(13)	10	13	Cox	Bottenfield		81-65	2nd	4
9-18	At N.Y.	W	10-4		16	11	Gardner	Gooden		82-65	2nd	4
9-19	At N.Y.	L	5-7		8	8	Whitehurst	Fassero		82-66	2nd	5
9-20	At N.Y.	L	0-1		5	6	Fernandez	Hill		82-67	2nd	6
9-21	Phi.	L	2-9		4	11	Rivera	Nabholz		82-68	2nd	7
9-22	Phi.	L	2-5		6	8	Hartley	Bottenfield	Mit. Williams	82-69	2nd	7
9-23	Pit.	W	5-1	(14)	9	5	Fassero	Mason		83-69	2nd	6
9-24	Pit.	L	3-9		7	14	Drabek	Krueger		83-70	2nd	7
9-25	Chi.	W	4-3	(10)	12	8	Wetteland	Slocumb		84-70	2nd	7
9-26	Chi.	W	12-0		16	4	Nabholz	Boskie		85-70	2nd	7
9-27	Chi.	W	1-0		3	5	Rojas	Morgan	Wetteland	86-70	2nd	7
9-28	At St.L.	L	1-4		5	13	Olivares	Krueger	L. Smith	86-71	2nd	8
9-29	At St.L.	L	1-2	(10)	6	5	Perez	Valdez		86-72	2nd	9
9-30	At St.L.	L	2-3	(11)	10	7	B. Smith	Fassero		86-73	2nd	9
10-2	At Chi.	L	1-3		5	10	Morgan	Nabholz		86-74	2nd	9
10-3	At Chi.	W	3-1		7	7	Bottenfield	Bullinger	Wetteland	87-74	2nd	8
10-4	At Chi.	L	2-3		8	7	Castillo	Gardner	Assenmacher	87-75	2nd	9

Monthly records: April (9-14), May (12-11), June (14-13), July (19-11), August (17-10), September (15-14), Oct. (1-2).

HIGHLIGHTS

High point: The Expos won 22 of 33 games from June 24-July 28 to move from last place (8½ games back) into a first-place tie with Pittsburgh.

Low point: Seldom has a winning team looked as dispirited as Montreal did following a 6-5 comeback victory over the Reds on May 20. Most of the 9,651 fans left in the middle of a five-run Cincinnati seventh, booing Manager Tom Runnells and chanting for his firing. Two days later, Runnells was fired.

Turning point: Bench coach Felipe Alou put his stamp on a young, directionless club after taking over as manager of the 17-20 Expos on May 22. He created the right atmosphere in the clubhouse while adding a dash of baseball moxie in the dugout that had been sorely missing under Runnells. Montreal reached .500 (42-42) for good July 8 and finished 70-55 under Alou.

Most valuable player: Right fielder Larry Walker. The league's best defensive right fielder supplied the majority of the sock in the lineup, hitting 23 home runs and driving in 93 runs.

Most valuable pitcher: Righthander Mel Rojas. He was nothing short of dominant as Montreal's primary setup man and occasional long reliever, going 7-1 with a 1.43 ERA and 10 saves en route to stranding a league-high 82.8 percent of inherited runners.

Most improved player: Second baseman Delino DeShields. He rebounded from a .238 average in 1991 to hit .292. Alou's arrival helped him become consistent both offensively and defensively.

Most pleasant surprise: Left fielder Moises Alou. The manager's son filled in admirably for the injured Ivan Calderon, hitting .282 with nine homers, 28 doubles and 56 RBIs.

Biggest disappointment: Third baseman Tim Wallach. The veteran posted career lows in average (.223), homers (nine) and RBIs (59).

Key injuries: Most devastating was the pulled rib-cage muscle DeShields suffered in September that rendered him virtually useless. Calderon's three stints on the disabled list were offset by Moises Alou's surprising play. Walker and Alou also missed time.

Notable: Alou became the fifth person in big-league annals to manage his son. ... Wallach became the Expos' career hits leader with his 1,599th hit May 20 against the Reds. ... On August 22, center fielder Marquis Grissom recorded Montreal's first straight steal of home since 1988.

—JEFF BLAIR

RECORDS

1992 regular-season record: 87-75 (2nd in N.L. East); 43-38 at home; 44-37 on road; 47-43 vs. East; 40-32 vs. West; 32-27 vs. LHP; 55-48 vs. RHP; 24-18 on grass; 63-57 on turf; 32-22 in daytime; 55-53 at night; 25-21 in one-run games; 7-9 in extra-inning games; 1-1-2 in doubleheaders.

Team record last five years: 405-404 (.501, ranks 7th in league in that span).

TEAM LEADERS

Batting average: Larry Walker (.301).
At-bats: Marquis Grissom (653).
Runs: Marquis Grissom (99).
Hits: Marquis Grissom (180).
Total bases: Marquis Grissom (273).
Doubles: Marquis Grissom (39).
Triples: Marquis Grissom (8).
Home runs: Larry Walker (23).
Runs batted in: Larry Walker (93).
Stolen bases: Marquis Grissom (78).
Slugging percentage: Larry Walker (.506).
On-base percentage: Delino DeShields (.359).
Wins: Ken Hill, Dennis Martinez (16).
Earned-run average: Dennis Martinez (2.47).
Complete games: Dennis Martinez (6).
Shutouts: Ken Hill (3).
Saves: John Wetteland (37).
Innings pitched: Dennis Martinez (226⅓).
Strikeouts: Ken Hill (150).

GAMES BY POSITION

Catcher: Gary Carter 85, Darrin Fletcher 69, Rick Cerone 28, Tim Laker 28, Rob Natal 4.

First base: Tim Wallach 71, Archi Cianfrocco 56, Greg Colbrunn 47, Tom Foley 12, John Vander Wal 7, Gary Carter 5, Jerry Willard 5, Steve Lyons 1.

Second base: Delino DeShields 134, Bret Barberie 26, Tom Foley 13, Wilfredo Cordero 9, Todd Haney 5.

Third base: Tim Wallach 85, Bret Barberie 63, Sean Berry 20, Archi Cianfrocco 19, Tom Foley 4.

Shortstop: Spike Owen 116, Wilfredo Cordero 35, Tom Foley 33, Bret Barberie 1.

Outfield: Marquis Grissom 157, Larry Walker 139, Moises Alou 100, John Vander Wal 57, Ivan Calderon 46, Darren Reed 29, Matt Stairs 10, Steve Lyons 8, Archi Cianfrocco 5, Tom Foley 1.

TOP 10 DRAFT CHOICES

1. **B.J. Wallace**, LHP, Mississippi State University.
2. **Rod Henderson**, RHP, University of Kentucky.
3. **Everett Stull**, RHP, Tennessee State University.
4. **Scott Gentile**, RHP, Western Connecticut State University.
5. **Jon Saffer**, OF, Amphitheater High School, Tucson, Ariz.
6. **Jose Vidro**, 2B, Sabana Grande, Puerto Rico.
7. **Luis Martinez**, C, Santa Isabel, Puerto Rico.
8. **Tom Phelps**, RHP, Robinson High School, Tampa, Fla.
9. **John Geis**, 1B, P.V. Moore High School, Central Square, N.Y.
10. **Steve Falteisek**, RHP, University of South Alabama.

NEW YORK METS
NATIONAL LEAGUE EAST DIVISION

1993 SCHEDULE

APRIL

SUN	MON	TUE	WED	THU	FRI	SAT
				1	2	3
4	5 COL H	6	7 COL H	8	9 N HOU H	10 N HOU H
11 HOU H	12 N COL	13 N COL	14 N COL	15 COL	16 N CIN	17 CIN
18 CIN	19	20 N SF H	21 N SF H	22 N SF H	23 N SD H	24 N SD H
25 SD H	26 N LA H	27 N LA H	28 N SF	29 N SF	30 N SD	

MAY

SUN	MON	TUE	WED	THU	FRI	SAT
						1 N SD
2 SD	3	4 N LA	5 N LA	6	7 N FLA H	8 N FLA H
9 N FLA H	10 N FLA H	11 N STL	12 N STL	13 STL	14 N MON	15 N MON
16 MON	17 N PIT H	18 N PIT H	19 N PIT H	20	21 N ATL H	22 N ATL H
23 ATL H	24 N PHI	25 N PHI	26 N	27	28 N CIN H	29 N CIN H
30 CIN H	31 CHI					

JUNE

SUN	MON	TUE	WED	THU	FRI	SAT
		1 N CHI	2 N CHI	3	4 N HOU	5 N HOU
6 HOU	7 N CHI H	8 N CHI H	9 N CHI H	10 N PHI H	11 N PHI H	12 N PHI H
13 PHI H	14 N ATL	15 N ATL	16 N ATL	17 N PIT	18 N PIT	19 N PIT
20 N PIT	21 N MON H	22 N MON H	23 N MON H	24	25 N STL H	26 STL H
27 STL H	28	29 N FLA	30 N FLA			

JULY

SUN	MON	TUE	WED	THU	FRI	SAT
				1 N FLA	2 N SF H	3 N SF H
4 SF	5 N SD H	6 N SD H	7 N SD H	8 N LA H	9 N LA H	10 N LA H
11 N LA H	12	13 * ALL-STAR GAME	14	15 SF	16 N SF	17 SF
18 SF	19 N SD	20 N SD	21	22 N LA	23 N LA	24 LA
25 LA	26	27 N FLA H	28 N FLA H	29 N FLA H	30 N STL	31 N STL

AUGUST

SUN	MON	TUE	WED	THU	FRI	SAT
1 STL	2 N MON	3 N MON	4 N MON	5 N MON	6 N PIT H	7 N PIT H
8 PIT H	9	10 N ATL H	11 N ATL H	12 N ATL H	13 N PHI	14 N PHI
15 PHI	16 N CIN	17 N CIN	18 N CIN	19	20 N COL	21
22 COL	23 N CIN H	24 N CIN H	25 N CIN H	26	27 N COL H	28 N COL H
29 COL H	30 N HOU H	31 N HOU H				

SEPTEMBER

SUN	MON	TUE	WED	THU	FRI	SAT
			1 HOU H	2 N CHI	3 CHI	4 CHI
5 CHI	6 HOU	7 N HOU	8 N HOU	9 N	10 N CHI H	11 CHI H
12 CHI H	13 N PHI H	14 N PHI H	15 N PHI H	16	17 N ATL	18 N ATL
19 N ATL	20 N PIT	21 N PIT	22 N PIT	23	24 N MON H	25 N MON H
26 MON H	27 N STL H	28 N STL H	29 N STL H	30 N STL H		

OCTOBER

SUN	MON	TUE	WED	THU	FRI	SAT
					1 N FLA	2 N FLA
3 FLA						

1993 SEASON

CLUB DIRECTORY

Chairman of the board
Nelson Doubleday
President and chief executive officer
Fred Wilpon
Directors
Nelson Doubleday
Fred Wilpon
J. Frank Cashen
Saul Katz
Marvin Tepper
Special advisor to the board of directors
Richard Cummins
Senior vice president and consultant
J. Frank Cashen
Executive v.p. and general manager
Alan E. Harazin
General counsel
David Howard
Asst. vice president, baseball operations
Gerald H. Hunsicker
Vice president, operations
Bob Mandt
Vice president, treasurer and secretary
Harold W. O'Shaughnessy
Vice president, broadcasting
Mike Ryan
Director of public relations
Jay Horwitz
Promotions director
James Plummer
Executive assistant to the general manager
Jean Coen
Director of ticket operations
Bill Iannicielo
Controller
Rick Iandoli
Traveling secretary
Bob O'Hara
Director of minor leagues
Steve Phillips
Director of scouting, Northeast states and Latin America
Roland Johnson
Director of scouting, Southern states
Joe Mason

Direcotr of scouting, Western states
Bob Minor
Stadium manager
John McCarthy
Director of amateur baseball relations
Tommy Holmes
Assistant director, public relations
Craig Sanders
Club physician
Dr. David Altchek
Team trainer
Steve Garland
Scouts
Paul Baretta
Larry Chase
Dick Gernert
Mark Giegler
Dallas Green
Rob Guzik
Bud Harrelson
R.J. Harrison
Marty Harvat
Reginald Jackson
Darrell Johnson
Buddy Kerr
Andy Korenek
Craig Kornfeld
Jim Marshall
Jim Miller
Harry Minor
Carlos Pascual
Mark Ralston
Jim Reeves
Paul Ricciarini
Junior Roman
Tom Romenesko
Bob Rossi
Brad Sloan
Eddy Toledo
Terry Tripp
Bob Wellman
Jim Woodward

SCHEDULE KEY

H—Home game.   N—Night game (any game starting after 5 p.m.).
*All-Star Game at Oriole Park at Camden Yards, Baltimore.

SPRING TRAINING ROSTER

Manager—Jeff Torborg (10).

Coaches—Mike Cubbage (4), Barry Foote (26), Dave LaRoche (28), Tom McCraw (27), Mel Stottlemyre (30).

No.	PITCHERS	B/T	Ht./Wt.	Born	1992 clubs
63	Castillo, Juan	R/R	6-5/205	6-23-70	St. Lucie
43	Dewey, Mark	R/R	6-0/207	1-3-65	Tidewater, New York N.L.
47	Draper, Mike	R/R	6-2/180	9-14-66	Columbus
50	Fernandez, Sid	L/L	6-1/225	10-12-62	New York N.L.
31	Franco, John	L/L	5-10/188	9-17-60	New York N.L.
16	Gooden, Dwight	R/R	6-3/210	11-16-64	New York N.L.
53	Hillman, Eric	L/L	6-10/225	4-27-66	Tidewater, New York N.L.
40	Innis, Jeff	R/R	6-1/170	7-5-62	New York N.L.
32	Maddux, Mike	R/R	6-2/188	8-27-61	San Diego
18	Saberhagen, Bret	R/R	6-1/190	4-11-64	New York N.L.
48	Schourek, Pete	L/L	6-5/205	5-10-69	Tidewater, New York N.L.
29	Tanana, Frank	L/L	6-3/205	7-3-53	Detroit
38	Telgheder, David	R/R	6-3/212	11-11-66	Tidewater
49	Vitko, Joe	R/R	6-8/210	2-1-70	Binghamton, New York N.L.
19	Young, Anthony	R/R	6-2/190	1-19-66	New York N.L.

No.	CATCHERS	B/T	Ht./Wt.	Born	1992 clubs
64	Fordyce, Brook	R/R	6-1/185	5-7-70	Binghamton
9	Hundley, Todd	B/R	5-11/185	5-27-69	New York N.L.
22	O'Brien, Charlie	R/R	6-2/200	5-1-61	New York N.L.

No.	INFIELDERS	B/T	Ht./Wt.	Born	1992 clubs
36	Baez, Kevin	R/R	6-0/170	1-10-67	Tidewater, New York N.L.
23	Bogar, Timothy	R/R	6-2/198	10-28-66	Tidewater
1	Fernandez, Tony	B/R	6-2/175	6-30-62	San Diego
65	Huskey, Butch	R/R	6-3/244	11-10-71	St. Lucie
20	Johnson, Howard	B/R	5-10/195	11-29-60	New York N.L.
12	Kent, Jeff	R/R	6-1/185	3-7-68	Toronto, New York N.L.
61	Ledesma, Aaron	R/R	6-2/200	6-3-71	St. Lucie
7	McKnight, Jeff	B/R	6-0/180	2-18-63	Tidewater, New York N.L.
33	Murray, Eddie	B/R	6-2/222	2-24-56	New York N.L.
62	Navarro, Tito	B/R	5-10/165	9-12-70	DID NOT PLAY

No.	OUTFIELDERS	B/T	Ht./Wt.	Born	1992 clubs
25	Bonilla, Bobby	B/R	6-3/240	2-23-63	New York N.L.
5	Burnitz, Jeromy	L/R	6-0/190	4-15-69	Tidewater
11	Coleman, Vince	B/R	6-1/185	9-22-61	New York N.L., St. Lucie
8	Gallagher, Dave	R/R	6-0/185	9-20-60	New York N.L., Tidewater
6	Orsulak, Joe	L/L	6-1/205	5-31-62	Baltimore
21	Reed, Darren	R/R	6-1/205	10-16-65	Indianapolis, West Palm Beach, Montreal, Minnesota
44	Thompson, Ryan	R/R	6-3/200	11-4-67	Syracuse, New York N.L.
34	Walker, Chico	B/R	5-9/185	11-26-58	Chicago N.L., New York N.L.

BALLPARK INFORMATION

Ballpark (capacity, surface)
Shea Stadium (55,601, grass)
Address
Roosevelt Ave. and 126th St.
Flushing, NY 11368
Business phone
718-507-6387
Ticket information
718-507-8499
Ticket prices
$15 (box)
$12 (upper level box)
$12 (loge and mezzanine reserved)
$6.50 (bk. rows, loge & mezz. res.)
$6.50 (upper level reserved)
$1 (senior citizens)
Field dimensions (from home plate)
To left field at foul line, 338 feet
To center field, 410 feet
To right field at foul line, 338 feet
First game played
April 17, 1964 (Pirates 4, Mets 3)

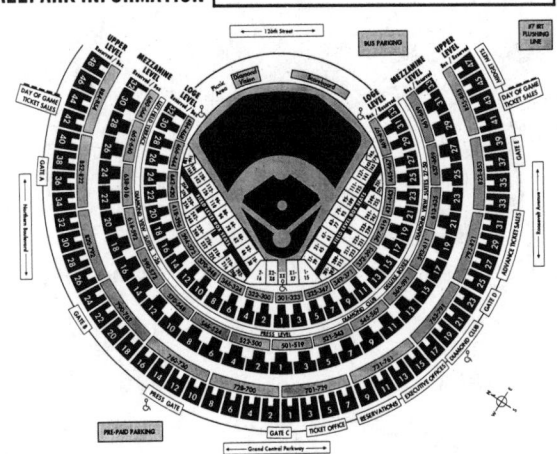

MINOR LEAGUE AFFILIATES

Class	Team	League	Manager
AAA	Norfolk	International	Clint Hurdle
AA	Binghamton	Eastern	Steve Swisher
A	St. Lucie	Florida State	John Tamargo
A	Columbia	South Atlantic	Ron Washington
A	Pittsfield	New York-Pennsylvania	Howie Freiling
Rookie	Kingsport	Appalachian	Ron Gideon
Rookie	Sarasota Mets	Gulf Coast	Junior Roman

BROADCAST INFORMATION

Radio: WFAN-AM (660). Broadcasters: Gary Cohen, Bob Murphy.
TV: WWOR-TV (Channel 9). Broadcasters: Ralph Kiner, Tim McCarver.
Cable TV: SportsChannel. Broadcasters: Ralph Kiner, Fran Healy, Rusty Staub.

SPRING TRAINING

Ballpark (city): St. Lucie County Stadium (Port St. Lucie, Fla.).
Ticket information: 407-871-2115.

HISTORY

YEAR-BY-YEAR RECORDS

Year	Pos.	W	L	Pct.	*GB	Year	Pos.	W	L	Pct.	*GB
1962	10th	40	120	.250	60½	1980	5th	67	95	.414	24
1963	10th	51	111	.315	48	1981	5th/4th	41	62	.398	‡
1964	10th	53	109	.327	40	1982	6th	65	97	.401	27
1965	10th	50	112	.309	47	1983	6th	68	94	.420	22
1966	9th	66	95	.410	28½	1984	2nd	90	72	.556	6½
1967	10th	61	101	.377	40½	1985	2nd	98	64	.605	3
1968	9th	73	89	.451	24	1986	1st†	108	54	.667	+21½
1969	1st†	100	62	.617	+ 8	1987	2nd	92	70	.568	3
1970	3rd	83	79	512	6	1988	1st§	100	60	.625	+15
1971	T3rd	83	79	.512	14	1989	2nd	87	75	.537	6
1972	3rd	83	73	.532	13½	1990	2nd	91	71	.562	4
1973	1st†	82	79	.509	+ 1½	1991	5th	77	84	.478	20½
1974	5th	71	91	.438	17	1992	5th	72	90	.444	24
1975	T3rd	82	80	.506	10½						
1976	3rd	86	76	.531	15						
1977	6th	64	98	.395	37						
1978	6th	66	96	.407	24						
1979	6th	63	99	.389	35						

*Games behind winner. †Won Championship Series. ‡First half 17-34; second 24-28. §Lost Championship Series.

MANAGERS

Name	Record	Years
Casey Stengel	175-404	'62-65
Wes Westrum	142-237	'65-67
Salty Parker	4-7	1967
Gil Hodges	339-309	'68-71
Yogi Berra	292-296	'72-75
Roy McMillan	26-27	1975
Joe Frazier	101-106	'76-77
Joe Torre	286-240	'77-81
George Bamberger	81-127	'82-83
Frank Howard	52-64	1983
Davey Johnson	595-417	'84-90
Bud Harrelson	145-129	'90-91
Mike Cubbage	3-4	1991
Jeff Torborg	72-90	1992

DAY BY DAY

Date	Opp.	Res.	Score	(inn.*)	Hits	Opp. hits	Winning pitcher	Losing pitcher	Save	Record	Pos.	GB
4-6	At St.L.	W	4-2	(10)	9	6	Innis	L. Smith	Franco	1-0	T1st	...
4-7	At St.L.	L	2-9		8	13	Olivares	Saberhagen		1-1	T3rd	½
4-8	At St.L.	L	7-15		7	15	Perez	Fernandez		1-2	5th	1½
4-9	At St.L.	W	7-1		13	6	Young	Agosto		2-2	T3rd	½
4-10	Mon.	L	0-4		4	6	Hill	Gooden		2-3	5th	1½
4-11	Mon.	L	2-9		6	12	Martinez	Cone		2-4	6th	1½
4-12	Mon.	L	2-8		6	7	Haney	Saberhagen		2-5	6th	2½
4-13	Phi.	L	2-3		7	10	Schilling	Fernandez	Mit. Williams	2-6	6th	3½
4-14	Phi.	W	8-5		8	14	Franco	Brantley		3-6	6th	3
4-15	Phi.	W	7-2		7	6	Gooden	Abbott		4-6	5th	3
4-17	At Mon.	W	10-2		11	7	Cone	Martinez		5-6	4th	3
4-18	At Mon.	L	6-8		9	11	Landrum	Innis	Wetteland	5-7	5th	4
4-19	At Mon.	W	11-6		11	6	Young	Fassero		6-7	4th	4
4-21	St.L.	W	4-2		7	6	Gooden	Cormier	Franco	7-7	2nd	4½
4-22	St.L.	W	3-2		9	5	Innis	Carpenter		8-7	2nd	4½
4-23	St.L.	W	1-0	(13)	6	8	Franco	Agosto		9-7	2nd	3½
4-24	At Phi.	L	3-4		8	10	Mit. Williams	Whitehurst		9-8	2nd	4½
4-25	At Phi.	W	3-2		7	4	Fernandez	Abbott	Franco	10-8	2nd	4½
4-26	At Phi.	L	4-5		6	12	Jones	Whitehurst	Mit. Williams	10-9	2nd	4½
4-28	Hou.	W	4-0		8	2	Cone	Henry		11-9	2nd	3½
4-29	Hou.	W	1-0		5	3	Saberhagen	Kile		12-9	2nd	3½
4-30	Hou.	W	4-3		8	3	Innis	D. Jones	Franco	13-9	2nd	2
5-1	At Atl.	W	8-7		12	11	Burke	Berenguer	Franco	14-9	2nd	2
5-2	At Atl.	L	0-3		9	9	Glavine	Gooden		14-10	2nd	3
5-3	At Atl.	W	7-0		8	5	Cone	Leibrandt		15-10	2nd	2
5-4	At Hou.	W	5-1		9	6	Saberhagen	Kile		16-10	2nd	2
5-5	At Hou.	L	4-5		4	9	Portugal	Fernandez	D. Jones	16-11	2nd	3
5-6	At Cin.	L	3-5		7	6	Swindell	Young	Charlton	16-12	2nd	4
5-7	At Cin.	L	2-4		3	6	Hammond	Gooden	Dibble	16-13	2nd	4
5-8	L.A.	W	4-3		6	7	Innis	McDowell		17-13	2nd	4
5-9	L.A.	W	5-2		6	5	Franco	McDowell		18-13	2nd	4
5-10	L.A.	W	3-0		9	5	Fernandez	Candiotti	Franco	19-13	2nd	3
5-11	S.D.	L	2-4		5	10	Benes	Young	Myers	19-14	2nd	3½
5-12	S.D.	W	7-3		8	10	Gooden	Melendez		20-14	2nd	2½
5-13	S.D.	L	0-7		6	12	Hurst	Cone		20-15	3rd	3½
5-15	At L.A.	W	4-1		6	4	Saberhagen	Ojeda	Franco	21-15	3rd	3
5-16	At L.A.	L	0-2		6	6	Candiotti	Fernandez		21-16	3rd	3
5-17	At L.A.	L	3-6		9	9	R. Martinez	Young	McDowell	21-17	3rd	3
5-18	At S.D.	L	0-3		1	12	Hurst	Gooden		21-18	3rd	3½
5-19	At S.D.	W	8-0		12	7	Cone	Melendez		22-18	3rd	2½
5-20	At S.D.	L	6-12		7	15	Lefferts	Burke		22-19	3rd	2½
5-21	At S.D.	W	8-3		14	6	Fernandez	Gr. Harris		23-19	3rd	1½
5-22	At S.F.	L	6-7		8	10	Downs	Burke	Righetti	23-20	3rd	2½
5-23	At S.F.	W	6-3		11	7	Gooden	Burba	Franco	24-20	3rd	1½
5-24	At S.F.	W	6-0		12	4	Cone	Wilson		25-20	3rd	1
5-25	Cin.	L	0-3		5	10	Hammond	Schourek	Charlton	25-21	3rd	2
5-27	Cin.	L	0-1		3	6	Belcher	Fernandez	Charlton	25-22	3rd	1½
5-29	Atl.	L	1-5		7	10	Smoltz	Gooden		25-23	3rd	1½
5-30	Atl.	L	1-6		6	14	Avery	Cone		25-24	3rd	2½
6-1	S.F.	W	14-1		16	7	Fernandez	Burkett		26-24	3rd	1½
6-2	S.F.	W	4-3		8	8	Whitehurst	Wilson	Franco	27-24	3rd	½
6-4	At Pit.	L	2-7		6	9	Drabek	Gooden	Patterson	27-25	3rd	2
6-5	At Pit.	L	4-5	(10)	14	10	Belinda	Innis		27-26	3rd	3
6-6	At Pit.	W	15-1		18	7	Fernandez	Neagle		28-26	2nd	2
6-7	At Pit.	L	0-3		6	8	Tomlin	Schourek		28-27	3rd	3
6-8	At Mon.	L	0-6		1	11	Hill	Young		28-28	3rd	3
6-9	At Mon.	W	6-5		16	8	Franco	Fassero		29-28	T2nd	3
6-10	At Mon.	L	2-8		8	13	Gardner	Cone		29-29	T2nd	4
6-12	Pit.	L	2-3		5	8	Tomlin	Fernandez	Patterson	29-30	T3rd	7
6-13	Pit.	L	2-3		10	15	Robinson	Whitehurst	Belinda	29-31	T2nd	5
6-14	Pit.	L	4-5		5	9	Neagle	Innis	Belinda	29-32	3rd	6
6-15	Mon.	L	1-4		3	9	Gardner	Young	Wetteland	29-33	4th	7
6-16	Mon.	W	5-2		7	3	Cone	Hurst		30-33	4th	7
6-17	Mon.	L	2-5		8	7	Martinez	Fernandez	Rojas	30-34	4th	8
6-18	St.L.	L	3-8		5	16	Olivares	Schourek		30-35	5th	8
6-19	St.L.	W	4-3		9	10	Franco	Perez		31-35	5th	7
6-20	St.L.	L	1-6		5	14	Tewksbury	Young		31-36	5th	7
6-21	St.L.	W	6-2		9	9	Cone	McClure		32-36	5th	7
6-22	Chi.	W	8-2		10	8	Fernandez	Boskie		33-36	4th	7
6-23	Chi.	W	4-1		10	6	Schourek	Castillo	Franco	34-36	2nd	7

Date		Opp.	Res.	Score	(inn.*)	Hits	Opp. hits	Winning pitcher	Losing pitcher	Save	Record	Pos.	GB
6-24		Chi.	W	3-2		5	9	Gooden	Jackson	Franco	35-36	2nd	6
6-25		Chi.	L	2-9		6	12	Maddux	Young		35-37	2nd	6½
6-26		At St.L.	L	3-4		3	11	L. Smith	Innis		35-38	4th	6½
6-27		At St.L.	W	2-1	(11)	5	8	Franco	L. Smith		36-38	2nd	6½
6-28		At St.L.	L	2-3	(11)	6	9	Perez	Franco		36-39	4th	6½
6-29		At Chi.	L	2-5		6	7	Jackson	Gooden	Assenmacher	36-40	4th	6½
6-30		At Chi.	L	1-3		4	11	Maddux	Young		36-41	5th	7½
7-1		At Chi.	W	6-4	(12)	14	10	Guetterman	Bullinger	Young	37-41	5th	7½
7-4	(1)	Hou.	W	5-3		9	6	Gooden	Blair	Innis	38-41	T4th	5½
7-4	(2)	Hou.	L	1-3		7	8	Osuna	Young	D. Jones	38-42	5th	6
7-5		Hou.	L	0-2	(10)	4	6	Murphy	Innis	D. Jones	38-43	5th	6
7-6		At Atl.	W	3-1		9	4	Cone	Freeman	Guetterman	39-43	5th	6
7-7		At Atl.	W	5-4		8	5	Fernandez	Bielecki	Young	40-43	4th	6
7-8		At Atl.	L	1-2		10	6	Glavine	Whitehurst	Pena	40-44	5th	6
7-9		At Hou.	L	0-4		5	4	Blair	Gooden		40-45	5th	6
7-10		At Hou.	W	7-6		10	9	Innis	D. Jones	Young	41-45	4th	6
7-11		At Hou.	W	8-2		10	9	Cone	J. Jones		42-45	4th	6
7-12		At Hou.	L	1-3		7	5	Henry	Fernandez	Hernandez	42-46	4th	7
7-16		S.F.	L	4-6		8	8	Black	Gooden	Beck	42-47	4th	8
7-17		S.F.	W	1-0		4	6	Cone	Swift		43-47	4th	7
7-18		S.F.	W	3-0		7	4	Fernandez	Wilson	Young	44-47	4th	7
7-19		S.F.	W	8-4		10	9	Schourek	Burkett		45-47	4th	6
7-20		L.A.	L	2-9		9	11	Candelaria	Innis	McDowell	45-48	4th	6
7-21		L.A.	W	5-2		7	11	Guetterman	Candelaria	Young	46-48	3rd	5
7-22		L.A.	W	7-5		10	11	Cone	Hershiser	Young	47-48	3rd	5
7-24		S.D.	W	3-0		9	3	Fernandez	Seminara		48-48	3rd	4
7-25		S.D.	L	0-2		6	7	Lefferts	Schourek	Myers	48-49	3rd	4
7-26		S.D.	L	0-1		7	6	Hurst	Whitehurst		48-50	3rd	5
7-27		At Phi.	L	0-5		6	6	Schilling	Saberhagen		48-51	3rd	5
7-28		At Phi.	W	8-6		13	7	Cone	Jones	Young	49-51	3rd	4
7-29		At Phi.	L	3-6		8	10	Mit. Williams	Innis		49-52	4th	4
8-1	(1)	Chi.	W	3-0		7	7	Schourek	Maddux	Young	50-52	3rd	5
8-1	(2)	Chi.	L	1-6		2	12	Robinson	Whitehurst		50-53	4th	5½
8-2		Chi.	W	4-2		5	9	Cone	Morgan	Franco	51-53	3rd	5½
8-4		At Pit.	L	2-3	(12)	8	10	Walk	Filer		51-54	T3rd	6½
8-5		At Pit.	L	2-6		7	7	Wakefield	Schourek		51-55	T3rd	7½
8-6		At Chi.	L	2-5		6	10	Maddux	Whitehurst		51-56	4th	8½
8-7		At Chi.	L	1-9		8	12	Morgan	Cone		51-57	4th	9½
8-8		At Chi.	L	3-4		9	11	Bullinger	Guetterman		51-58	4th	10½
8-9		At Chi.	L	2-6		10	12	Harkey	Fernandez		51-59	4th	11½
8-10		Pit.	L	2-4	(16)	9	17	Cooke	Guetterman		51-60	T4th	12½
8-11		Pit.	W	2-0		7	6	Hillman	Drabek	Franco	52-60	T4th	11½
8-12		Pit.	L	6-7	(10)	12	12	Neagle	Franco	Patterson	52-61	5th	12½
8-14		Phi.	L	2-6		7	10	Rivera	Gooden		52-62	5th	12½
8-15		Phi.	L	3-4		7	6	Hartley	Innis	Mit. Williams	52-63	5th	12½
8-18		At L.A.	L	0-4		6	9	Astacio	Cone		52-64	5th	13½
8-19		At L.A.	L	1-2		6	7	Hershiser	Gooden	Gott	52-65	5th	14½
8-20		At L.A.	W	11-4		12	8	Fernandez	R. Martinez		53-65	5th	14½
8-22		At S.D.	L	2-4		4	7	Hurst	Schourek	Myers	53-66	5th	15
8-23		At S.D.	L	3-4		5	4	Benes	Cone	Myers	53-67	5th	15
8-24		At S.F.	W	4-1		10	8	Gooden	Hickerson	Franco	54-67	5th	14
8-25		At S.F.	W	2-1		9	8	Fernandez	Wilson	Franco	55-67	5th	14
8-26		At S.F.	W	5-3		11	5	Hillman	Burkett	Young	56-67	5th	14
8-28	(1)	Cin.	W	4-3		7	8	Jones	Bankhead	Young	57-67	5th	13
8-28	(2)	Cin.	W	12-1		15	5	Whitehurst	Foster	Guetterman	58-67	5th	12½
8-29		Cin.	W	6-5		9	11	Gooden	Hammond	Young	59-67	5th	12½
8-30		Cin.	W	4-3		4	6	Jones	Dibble		60-67	5th	12½
8-31	(1)	Atl.	L	6-8	(14)	9	15	Wohlers	Guetterman	Stanton	60-68	5th	13
8-31	(2)	Atl.	L	5-7		13	12	Smith	Birkbeck	Reardon	60-69	5th	13½
9-1		Atl.	L	1-4		8	9	Nied	Whitehurst	Reardon	60-70	5th	14½
9-2		Atl.	W	6-5		9	11	Schourek	Smoltz	Young	61-70	5th	14½
9-3		At Cin.	L	3-4		3	4	Dibble	Young		61-71	5th	15½
9-4		At Cin.	W	5-2		6	5	Fernandez	Belcher		62-71	5th	15½
9-5		At Cin.	L	5-6		10	11	Charlton	Young		62-72	5th	16½
9-6		At Cin.	L	1-6		9	10	Pugh	Gibson	Dibble	62-73	5th	16½
9-7		At Phi.	W	6-3		6	12	Schourek	Mulholland	Young	63-73	5th	15½
9-8		At Phi.	L	1-2		9	6	Shepherd	Gooden	Mit. Williams	63-74	5th	16½
9-9		At Phi.	L	1-5		1	5	Schilling	Fernandez		63-75	5th	17½
9-11		At Mon.	L	3-4		5	12	Fassero	Saberhagen	Wetteland	63-76	5th	17½
9-12		At Mon.	L	1-4		5	8	Martinez	Schourek		63-77	5th	18½
9-13		At Mon.	L	5-7		8	14	Rojas	Young		63-78	5th	18½
9-14		At Chi.	W	10-8		13	16	Innis	McElroy	Young	64-78	5th	18½
9-15		At Chi.	W	4-2	(7½)	6	8	Dewey	Boskie		65-78	5th	18½
9-16		St.L.	L	4-10		7	12	Carpenter	Guetterman		65-79	5th	18½

Date	Opp.	Res.	Score	(inn.*)	Hits	Opp. hits	Winning pitcher	Losing pitcher	Save	Record	Pos.	GB
9-17	St.L.	L	2-3		5	7	Perez	Young	L. Smith	65-80	5th	19½
9-18	Mon.	L	4-10		11	16	Gardner	Gooden		65-81	5th	20½
9-19	Mon.	W	7-5		8	8	Whitehurst	Fassero		66-81	5th	20½
9-20	Mon.	W	1-0		6	5	Fernandez	Hill		67-81	5th	20½
9-21	Chi.	L	1-10		8	16	Maddux	Hillman		67-82	5th	21½
9-22	Chi.	W	8-7		11	11	Guetterman	Assenmacher	Young	68-82	5th	20½
9-23	At St.L.	W	3-2		4	6	Gooden	L. Smith		69-82	5th	19½
9-24	At St.L.	L	3-4	(14)	8	12	B. Smith	Whitehurst		69-83	5th	20½
9-25	At Pit.	L	2-3		9	8	Tomlin	Fernandez	Cox	69-84	5th	21½
9-26	At Pit.	L	2-19		10	20	Walk	Hillman		69-85	5th	22½
9-27	At Pit.	L	2-4		7	7	Jackson	Schourek	Belinda	69-86	5th	23½
9-28 (1)	Phi.	L	6-7	(10)	8	16	Mit. Williams	Innis		69-87	5th	24½
9-28 (2)	Phi.	L	6-7		12	13	Mathews	Vitko	Shepherd	69-88	5th	25
9-29	Phi.	L	3-5		6	7	Ayrault	Young	Mit. Williams	69-89	T5th	26
9-30	Phi.	W	6-2		10	8	Fernandez	Abbott		70-89	5th	25
10-2	Pit.	W	6-3		12	7	Schourek	Drabek	Jones	71-89	5th	24
10-3	Pit.	W	2-1		5	4	Gooden	Jackson		72-89	5th	23
10-4	Pit.	L	0-2		3	4	Wakefield	Saberhagen	Cooke	72-90	5th	24

Monthly records: April (13-9), May (12-15), June (11-17), July (13-11), August (11-17), September (10-20), Oct. (2-1).

HIGHLIGHTS

High point: On May 15, righthander Bret Saberhagen made a third straight impressive start as the Mets beat Los Angeles, 4-1, raising his record to 21-15 and moving three games behind first-place Pittsburgh. However, Saberhagen left the game after five innings with a finger injury that ruined his season. The Mets then began a steady decline.

Low point: On August 4, the Mets traveled to first-place Pittsburgh, which led New York by 5½ games. But they lost seven straight games and 12 out of their next 13 to fall 14½ games back.

Turning point: Entering that key series against the struggling Pirates on August 4, the Mets thought they still could catch the Bucs. But a 12-inning, 3-2 loss took the fight out of the Mets, and they never contended again.

Most valuable player: First baseman Eddie Murray. The 36-year-old Murray gave the Mets as much as they could have hoped for, hitting .261 with 16 homers and 93 RBIs.

Most valuable pitcher: Lefthander Sid Fernandez. Enjoying perhaps the best season of his career, he deserved better than the 14-11 record he posted.

Most improved player: Catcher Todd Hundley. Overmatched early, Hundley hit .243 over his final 193 at-bats.

Most pleasant surprise: Utilityman Chico Walker. Released by the Cubs in early May, Walker hit .308 with the Mets, 71 points above his career average.

Biggest disappointment: Outfielder Howard Johnson. Nagging injuries limited Johnson, whose season ended July 28 with a fractured right wrist. He had seven homers and 43 RBIs.

Key injuries: New York used the disabled list a team-record 18 times for 14 players. Among the key casualties were Saberhagen, Johnson, outfielder Vince Coleman (hamstring, rib cage), outfielder Bobby Bonilla (rib), righthander Dwight Gooden (shoulder) and lefthander John Franco (elbow).

Notable: The Mets' 72-90 record was their worst since 1983 (68-94). . . . Gooden posted the first losing record (10-13) of his pro career. . . . In two years as a Met, Coleman has played in only 143 of 323 games. . . . Righthander Anthony Young lost his final 14 decisions, the longest streak in the majors since 1980. . . . New York was shut out 16 times, its highest total since 1978 (16). . . . The Mets used 45 players, their most in a season since the '67 club used a league-record 54.

—JOHN HARPER

RECORDS

1992 regular-season record: 72-90 (5th in N.L. East); 41-40 at home; 31-50 on road; 34-56 vs. East; 38-34 vs. West; 25-31 vs. LHP; 47-59 vs. RHP; 57-57 on grass; 15-33 on turf; 21-27 in daytime; 51-63 at night; 24-30 in one-run games; 4-9 in extra-inning games; 1-2-2 in doubleheaders.

Team record last five years: 427-380 (.529, ranks 2nd in league in that span).

TEAM LEADERS

Batting average: Eddie Murray (.261).
At-bats: Eddie Murray (551).
Runs: Eddie Murray (64).
Hits: Eddie Murray (144).
Total bases: Eddie Murray (233).
Doubles: Eddie Murray (37).
Triples: Kevin Bass, Daryl Boston, Eddie Murray, Dick Schofield (2).
Home runs: Bobby Bonilla (19).
Runs batted in: Eddie Murray (93).
Stolen bases: Vince Coleman (24).
Slugging percentage: Bobby Bonilla (.432).
On-base percentage: Bobby Bonilla (.348).
Wins: Sid Fernandez (14).
Earned-run average: Sid Fernandez (2.73).
Complete games: David Cone (7).
Shutouts: David Cone (5).
Saves: John Franco, Anthony Young (15).
Innings pitched: Sid Fernandez (214⅔).
Strikeouts: David Cone (214).

GAMES BY POSITION

Catcher: Todd Hundley 121, Charlie O'Brien 64, Mackey Sasser 27.
First base: Eddie Murray 154, Mackey Sasser 12, Jeff McKnight 9, Bobby Bonilla 6, Dave Magadan 2, Bill Pecota 1.
Second base: Willie Randolph 79, Bill Pecota 38, Jeff Kent 34, Junior Noboa 16, Chico Walker 16, Jeff McKnight 14, Chris Donnels 12, Steve Springer 1.
Third base: Dave Magadan 93, Bill Pecota 48, Chico Walker 36, Chris Donnels 29, Jeff McKnight 3, Junior Noboa 3, Jeff Kent 1, Steve Springer 1.
Shortstop: Dick Schofield 141, Bill Pecota 39, Kevin Baez 5, Kevin Elster 5, Jeff McKnight 3, Junior Noboa 2, Jeff Kent 1.
Outfield: Bobby Bonilla 121, Howard Johnson 98, Daryl Boston 95, Dave Gallagher 76, Vince Coleman 61, Kevin Bass 39, Ryan Thompson 29, Pat Howell 28, D.J. Dozier 17, Chico Walker 15, Rodney McCray 13, Mackey Sasser 9, Jeff McKnight 1.

TOP 10 DRAFT CHOICES

1a. Preston Wilson, SS, Bamberg-Ehrhardt High School, Bamberg, S.C.
1b. Chris Roberts, LHP/OF, Florida State University.
1c. Jon Ward, RHP, Huntington Beach (Calif.) High School.
2. None.
3. None.
4. Steve Lyons, RHP, Old Dominion University.
5. Joe Petcka, RHP, Bradley University.
6. David Sumner, OF, Northport High School, East Northport, N.Y.
7. Chris Saunders, 3B, Fresno (Calif.) City College.
8. Robert Spang, RHP, William Horlick High School, Racine, Wis.
9. Andrew Trumpour, RHP, Cypress (Calif.) College.
10. Derek Baker, RHP, Glendale (Calif.) College.

PHILADELPHIA PHILLIES
NATIONAL LEAGUE EAST DIVISION

1993 SCHEDULE

APRIL
SUN	MON	TUE	WED	THU	FRI	SAT
				1	2	3
4	5 N HOU	6 N HOU	7 N HOU	8	9 H CHI	10 N CHI H
11 CHI H	12 N CIN H	13 N CIN	14 N CIN H	15	16 CHI	17 CHI
18 CHI	19	20 N SD	21 N SD H	22 N SD H	23 N LA H	24 N LA H
25 LA H	26 N SF H	27 SF H	28 N SD H	29 SD	30 N LA	

MAY
SUN	MON	TUE	WED	THU	FRI	SAT
						1 N LA
2 LA	3	4 N SF	5 SF	6	7 STL H	8 N STL H
9 STL H	10 N PIT H	11 N PIT H	12 N PIT H	13	14 N ATL	15 N ATL
16 ATL	17 N FLA	18 N FLA	19 N FLA	20 N MON H	21 N MON H	22 N MON H
23 MON H	24 N NY H	25 N NY H	26 N NY H	27	28 N COL	29 COL
30 COL	31 N CIN					

JUNE
SUN	MON	TUE	WED	THU	FRI	SAT
		1 N CIN	2 N CIN	3	4 N COL H	5 N COL H
6 COL H	7 N HOU H	8 N HOU H	9 N HOU H	10 N HOU H	11 N NY	12 N NY
13 NY	14 N MON	15 N MON	16 N MON	17 N FLA H	18 N FLA H	19 N FLA H
20 FLA H	21 N ATL H	22 N ATL H	23 N ATL H	24	25 N PIT	26 N PIT
27 PIT	28 N STL	29 N STL	30 N STL			

JULY
SUN	MON	TUE	WED	THU	FRI	SAT
				1 STL	2 N SD H	3 N SD H
4 N SD	5 N LA H	6 N LA H	7 N LA H	8 N SF H	9 N SF H	10 N SF H
11 SF H	12	13 * ALL-STAR GAME	14	15 SD	16 N SD	17 N SD
18 SD	19 LA	20 N LA	21 N SF	22 SF	23 N SF	24 SF
25 SF	26	27 N STL H	28 N STL H	29 N STL H	30 H PIT H	31 N PIT H

AUGUST
SUN	MON	TUE	WED	THU	FRI	SAT
1 PIT H	2	3 N ATL	4 N ATL	5 N ATL	6 N FLA	7 N FLA
8 N FLA	9	10 N MON H	11 N MON H	12 N MON H	13 N NY H	14 N NY H
15 NY H	16	17 N COL	18 N COL	19 N COL	20 N HOU	21 N HOU
22 HOU	23 N COL H	24 N COL H	25 N COL H	26	27 N CIN H	28 N CIN H
29 CIN H	30 N CHI	31 CHI				

SEPTEMBER
SUN	MON	TUE	WED	THU	FRI	SAT
		1 CHI	2	3 N CIN	4 N CIN	
5 CIN	6 N CHI H	7 N CHI H	8 N CHI H	9 N CHI H	10 N HOU H	11 N HOU H
12 HOU H	13 N NY	14 N NY	15 N NY	16	17 N MON	18 N MON
19 MON	20 N FLA H	21 N FLA H	22 N FLA H	23	24 N ATL H	25 N ATL H
26 ATL H	27 N PIT	28 N PIT	29 N PIT	30 N PIT		

OCTOBER
SUN	MON	TUE	WED	THU	FRI	SAT
					1 N STL	2 STL
3 STL						

1993 SEASON

CLUB DIRECTORY

President/CEO/general partner
Bill Giles
Partners
Claire S. Betz
Estate of John Drew Betz
Tri-Play Associates (Alexander K. Buck, J. Mahlon Buck Jr., William C. Buck)
Fitz Eugene Dixon Jr.
Mrs. Rochelle Levy
Executive v.p. and chief operating officer
David Montgomery
Executive secretary
Nancy Nolan
Secretary and general counsel
William Y. Webb
Dir., planning/develop. and super boxes
Tom Hudson
Senior vice president, general manager
Lee Thomas
Player personnel administrator
Ed Wade
Director, player development
Del Unser
Director, scouting
Mike Arbuckle
Assistant to the president
Paul Owens
Business manager, minor leagues
Bill Gargano
Traveling secretary
Eddie Ferenz
Senior vice president, finance and planning
Jerry Clothier
Vice president, public relations
Larry Shenk
Broadcaster/director speakers' bureau
Chris Wheeler
Director, community relations
Regina Castellani
Assistant director, community relations
Karen Howard
Manager, media relations
Gene Dias
Manager, publicity
Leigh Tobin
Vice president, marketing
Dennis Mannion
Director, promotions
Frank Sullivan
Manager, advertising and broadcasting
Jo-Anne Levy-Lamoreaux
Manager, entertainment
Chris Legault
Manager, marketing services
Kurt Funk
Manager, corporate marketing
Dave Buck

Vice president, ticket sales and operations
Richard Deats
Director, sales
Rory McNeil
Director, ticket department
Dan Goroff
Manager, group sales
Kathy Killian
Director, information systems
Brian Lamoreaux
Director, stadium operations
Mike DiMuzio
Club physician
Dr. Phillip Marone
Club trainers
Jeff Cooper
Mark Andersen
National supervisor
Mark Wolever
Regional cross-checker scouts
Larry Reasonover
Tony Reig
Dick Lawlor
Bob Reasonover
Special assignment, major league scouts
Ray Shore
Jimmy Stewart
Advance scout, major leagues
Hank King
Special assignment scouts
Jay Hankins
Larry Rojas
Regular scouts
Sal Agustinelli
Emil Belich
Jim Bierman
Tom Ferguson
Jim Fregosi Jr.
Eli Grba
Bill Harper
Ken Hultzapple
Jerry Jordan
John Kennedy
Jerry Lafferty
George Lauzerique
Terry Logan
Fred Mazuca
Willie Montanez
Arthur Parrack
Jack Pastore
Bob Poole
Larry Reasonover
David Sirak
Mitch Sokel
Roy Tanner
Scott Trcka

SCHEDULE KEY
H—Home game.   N—Night game (any game starting after 5 p.m.).
*All-Star Game at Oriole Park at Camden Yards, Baltimore.

Manager—Jim Fregosi (11).

Coaches—Larry Bowa (2), Denis Menke (14), Johnny Podres (46), Mel Roberts (26), Mike Ryan (25), John Vukovich (18).

No.	PITCHERS	B/T	Ht./Wt.	Born	1992 clubs
47	Abbott, Kyle	L/L	6-4/195	2-18-68	Philadelphia, Scranton/Wilkes-Barre
55	Ayrault, Bob	R/R	6-4/235	4-27-66	Scranton/Wilkes-Barre, Philadelphia
42	Borland, Toby	R/R	6-6/182	5-19-69	Scranton/Wilkes-Barre, Reading
51	Brantley, Cliff	R/R	6-1/215	4-12-68	Philadelphia, Scranton/Wilkes-Barre
31	Brink, Brad	R/R	6-2/203	1-20-65	Reading, Scranton/Wilkes-Barre, Philadelphia
21	Combs, Pat	L/L	6-4/213	10-29-66	Scranton/Wilkes-Barre, Philadelphia
54	DeJesus, Jose	R/R	6-5/213	1-6-65	DID NOT PLAY
50	DeLeon, Jose	R/R	6-3/226	12-20-60	St. Louis, Philadelphia
57	Farmer, Mike	B/L	6-1/175	7-3-68	Clearwater
	Fletcher, Paul	R/R	6-1/185	1-14-67	Reading, Scranton/Wilkes-Barre
49	Greene, Tommy	R/R	6-5/219	4-6-67	Philadelphia, Reading, Scranton/Wilkes-Barre
27	Jackson, Danny	R/L	6-3/205	1-5-62	Chicago N.L., Pittsburgh
45	Mulholland, Terry	R/L	6-2/215	3-9-63	Philadelphia
61	Parris, Steve	R/R	6-0/180	12-17-67	Reading, Scranton/Wilkes-Barre
34	Rivera, Ben	R/R	6-6/230	1-11-69	Atlanta, Philadelphia, Scranton/Wilkes-Barre
38	Schilling, Curt	R/R	6-4/215	11-14-66	Philadelphia
40	West, David	L/L	6-6/240	9-1-64	Portland, Minnesota
41	Williams, Mike	R/R	6-2/196	7-29-69	Reading, Scranton/Wilkes-Barre, Philadelphia
28	Williams, Mitch	L/L	6-4/205	11-17-64	Philadelphia

No.	CATCHERS	B/T	Ht./Wt.	Born	1992 clubs
10	Daulton, Darren	L/R	6-2/201	1-3-62	Philadelphia
35	Lindsey, Doug	R/R	6-2/200	9-22-67	Scranton/Wilkes-Barre
23	Pratt, Todd	R/R	6-3/227	2-9-67	Reading, Scranton/Wilkes-Barre, Philadelphia

No.	INFIELDERS	B/T	Ht./Wt.	Born	1992 clubs
5	Batiste, Kim	R/R	6-0/193	3-15-68	Philadelphia, Scranton/Wilkes-Barre
24	Bell, Juan	B/R	5-11/170	3-29-68	Rochester, Oklahoma City, Philadelphia
7	Duncan, Mariano	R/R	6-0/191	3-13-63	Philadelphia
15	Hollins, Dave	B/R	6-1/207	5-25-66	Philadelphia
17	Jordan, Ricky	R/R	6-3/205	5-26-65	Scranton/Wilkes-Barre, Philadelphia
29	Kruk, John	L/L	5-10/214	2-9-61	Philadelphia
60	Lockett, Ron	L/L	6-1/189	9-5-69	Reading
12	Morandini, Mickey	L/R	5-11/171	4-22-66	Philadelphia

No.	OUTFIELDERS	B/T	Ht./Wt.	Born	1992 clubs
33	Amaro, Ruben	B/R	5-10/175	2-12-65	Philadelphia, Scranton/Wilkes-Barre
44	Chamberlain, Wes	R/R	6-2/219	4-13-66	Philadelphia, Scranton/Wilkes-Barre
4	Dykstra, Lenny	L/L	5-10/193	2-10-63	Philadelphia
	Eisenreich, Jim	L/L	5-11/195	4-18-59	Kansas City
22	Incaviglia, Pete	R/R	6-1/230	4-2-64	Houston
59	Jackson, Jeff	R/R	6-2/185	1-2-72	Clearwater, Reading
16	Longmire, Tony	L/R	6-1/197	8-12-68	DID NOT PLAY
56	Nuneviller, Tom	R/R	6-3/210	5-15-69	Reading
25	Thompson, Milt	L/R	5-11/200	1-5-59	St. Louis
52	Williams, Cary	R/R	6-3/190	6-14-67	Scranton/Wilkes-Barre

BALLPARK INFORMATION

Ballpark (capacity, surface)
Veterans Stadium (62,382, artificial)

Address
P.O. Box 7575
Philadelphia, PA 19101

Business phone
215-463-6000

Ticket information
215-463-1000

Ticket prices
$12 (field box)
$10 (sections 258-274)
$10 (terrace box)
$10 (loge box)
$7 (reserved, 600 level)
$4 (reserved, 700 level)

Field dimensions (from home plate)
To left field at foul line, 330 feet
To center field, 408 feet
To right field at foul line, 330 feet

First game played
April 10, 1971 (Phillies 4, Expos 1)

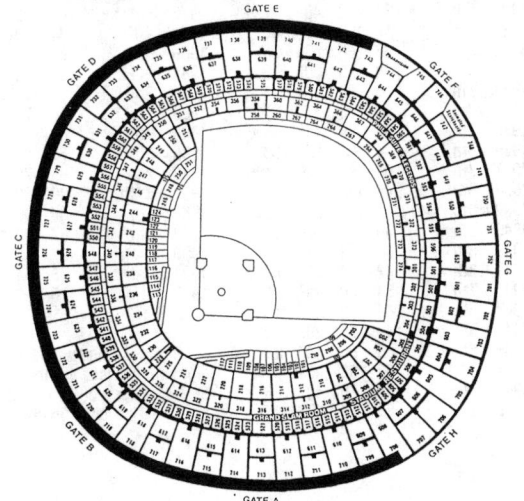

Class	Team	League	Manager
AAA	Scranton/Wilkes-Barre	International	George Culver
AA	Reading	Eastern	Don McCormack
A	Clearwater	Florida State	Bill Dancy
A	Spartanburg	South Atlantic	Roy Majtyka
A	Batavia	New York-Pennsylvania	Al LeBoeuf
Rookie	Martinsville	Appalachian	Ramon Henderson

BROADCAST INFORMATION

Radio: WOGL-AM (1210). Broadcasters: Harry Kalas, Richie Ashburn, Chris Wheeler, Andy Musser.
TV: WPHL-TV (Channel 17). Broadcasters: Andy Musser, Richie Ashburn, Harry Kalas.
Cable TV: PRISM, SportsChannel. Broadcasters: Garry Maddox, Chris Wheeler; Kent Tekulve, Andy Musser.

SPRING TRAINING

Ballpark (city): Jack Russell Stadium (Clearwater, Fla.).
Ticket information: 813-442-8496.

HISTORY

YEAR-BY-YEAR RECORDS

Year	Pos.	W	L	Pct.	*GB	Year	Pos.	W	L	Pct.	*GB
1901	2nd	83	57	.593	7½	1950	1st	91	63	.591	+ 2
1902	7th	56	81	.409	46	1951	5th	73	81	.474	23½
1903	7th	49	86	.363	39½	1952	4th	87	67	.565	9½
1904	8th	52	100	.342	53½	1953	T3rd	83	71	.539	22
1905	4th	83	69	.546	21½	1954	4th	75	79	.487	22
1906	4th	71	82	.464	45½	1955	4th	77	77	.500	21½
1907	3rd	83	64	.565	21½	1956	5th	71	83	.461	22
1908	4th	83	71	.539	16	1957	5th	77	77	.500	19
1909	5th	74	79	.484	36½	1958	8th	69	85	.448	23
1910	4th	78	75	.510	25½	1959	8th	64	90	.416	23
1911	4th	79	73	.520	19½	1960	8th	59	95	.383	36
1912	5th	73	79	.480	30½	1961	8th	47	107	.305	46
1913	2nd	88	63	.583	12½	1962	7th	81	80	.503	20
1914	6th	74	80	.481	20½	1963	4th	87	75	.537	12
1915	1st	90	62	.592	+ 7	1964	T2nd	92	70	.568	1
1916	2nd	91	62	.595	2½	1965	6th	85	76	.528	11½
1917	2nd	87	65	.572	10	1966	4th	87	75	.537	8
1918	6th	55	68	.447	26	1967	5th	82	80	.506	19½
1919	8th	47	90	.343	47½	1968	T7th	76	86	.469	21
1920	8th	62	91	.405	30½	1969	5th	63	99	.389	37
1921	8th	51	103	.331	43½	1970	5th	73	88	.453	15½
1922	7th	57	96	.373	35½	1971	6th	67	95	.414	30
1923	8th	50	104	.325	45½	1972	6th	59	97	.378	37½
1924	7th	55	96	.364	37	1973	6th	71	91	.438	11½
1925	T6th	68	85	.444	27	1974	3rd	80	82	.494	8
1926	8th	58	93	.384	29½	1975	2nd	86	76	.531	6½
1927	8th	51	103	.331	43	1976	1st†	101	61	.623	+ 9
1928	8th	43	109	.283	51	1977	1st†	101	61	.623	+ 5
1929	5th	71	82	.464	27½	1978	1st†	90	72	.556	+ 1½
1930	8th	52	102	.338	40	1979	4th	84	78	.519	14
1931	6th	66	88	.429	35	1980	1st‡	91	71	.562	+ 1
1932	4th	78	76	.506	12	1981	1st/3rd	59	48	.551	§*
1933	7th	60	92	.395	31	1982	2nd	89	73	.549	3
1934	7th	56	93	.376	37	1983	1st‡	90	72	.556	+ 6
1935	7th	64	89	.418	35½	1984	4th	81	81	.500	15½
1936	8th	54	100	.351	38	1985	5th	75	87	.463	26
1937	7th	61	92	.399	34½	1986	2nd	86	75	.534	21½
1938	8th	45	105	.300	43	1987	T4th	80	82	.494	15
1939	8th	45	106	.298	50½	1988	6th	65	96	.404	35½
1940	8th	50	103	.327	50	1989	6th	67	95	.414	26
1941	8th	43	111	.279	57	1990	T4th	77	85	.475	18
1942	8th	42	109	.278	62½	1991	3rd	78	84	.481	20
1943	7th	64	90	.416	41	1992	6th	70	92	.432	26
1944	8th	61	92	.399	43½						
1945	8th	46	108	.299	52						
1946	5th	69	85	.448	28						
1947	T7th	62	92	.403	32						
1948	6th	66	88	.429	25½						
1949	3rd	81	73	.526	16						

*Games behind winner. †Lost Championship Series. ‡Won Championship Series. §Lost division playoff. *First half 34-21; second 25-27.

MANAGERS

Name	Record	Years
Bill Shettsline	139-138	'01-02
Chief Zimmer	49-86	1903
Hugh Duffy	206-251	'04-06
Bill Murray	240-214	'07-09
Red Dooin	392-370	'10-14
Pat Moran	323-257	'15-18
Jack Coombs	18-44	1919
Gavvy Cravath	91-137	'19-20
Bill Donovan	31-71	1921
Kaiser Wilhelm	77-128	'21-22
Art Fletcher	231-378	'23-26
Stuffy McInnis	51-103	1927
Burt Shotton	370-439	'28-33
Jimmy Wilson	280-477	'34-38
Hans Lobert	42-111	'38, '42
Doc Prothro	138-320	'39-41
Bucky Harris	40-53	1943
Fred Fitzsimmons	102-179	'43-45
Ben Chapman	197-277	'45-48
Dusty Cooke	6-6	1948
Eddie Sawyer	390-424	'48-52
		'58-60
Steve O'Neill	182-140	'52-54
Terry Moore	35-42	1954
Mayo Smith	264-281	'55-58
Eddie Sawyer	94-132	'58-60
Andy Cohen	1-0	1960
Gene Mauch	645-684	'60-68
George Myatt	21-35	'68, '69
Bob Skinner	92-123	'68-69
Frank Lucchesi	166-233	'70-72
Paul Owens	161-158	1972
		'83-84
Danny Ozark	594-510	'73-79
Dallas Green	169-130	'79-81
Pat Corrales	132-115	'82-83
John Felske	190-194	'85-87
Lee Elia	111-142	'87-88
John Vukovich	5-4	1988
Nick Leyva	148-189	'89-91
Jim Fregosi	144-167	'91-92

DAY BY DAY

Date	Opp.	Res.	Score	(inn.*)	Hits	Opp. hits	Winning pitcher	Losing pitcher	Save	Record	Pos.	GB
4-7	Chi.	L	3-4		7	10	Maddux	Mulholland	McElroy	0-1	T5th	1
4-8	Chi.	W	11-3		12	10	Greene	Jackson		1-1	T3rd	1
4-9	Chi.	W	7-1		9	4	Cox	Morgan		2-1	T1st	...
4-10	Pit.	L	2-3		5	7	Tomlin	Abbott	Belinda	2-2	T3rd	1
4-11	Pit.	W	7-4		7	8	Ashby	Drabek		3-2	T1st	...
4-12	Pit.	L	1-6		5	7	Smith	Mulholland		3-3	T3rd	1
4-13	At N.Y.	W	3-2		10	7	Schilling	Fernandez	Mit. Williams	4-3	3rd	1
4-14	At N.Y.	L	5-8		14	8	Franco	Brantley		4-4	3rd	1½
4-15	At N.Y.	L	2-7		6	7	Gooden	Abbott		4-5	4th	2½
4-17	At Pit.	L	4-7		9	9	Drabek	Jones	Belinda	4-6	5th	3½
4-18	At Pit.	L	2-9		11	11	Smith	Greene		4-7	6th	4½
4-19	At Pit.	L	0-11		3	17	Patterson	Cox		4-8	6th	5½
4-20	At Chi.	L	3-8		5	9	Maddux	Abbott		4-9	6th	6½
4-21	At Chi.	W	7-5	(10)	11	11	Mit. Williams	Slocumb	Schilling	5-9	6th	6½
4-22	At Chi.	L	5-9		6	10	Boskie	Mulholland		5-10	6th	7½
4-23	At Chi.	W	8-2		11	3	Greene	Castillo		6-10	6th	6½
4-24	N.Y.	W	4-3		10	8	Mit. Williams	Whitehurst		7-10	T4th	6½
4-25	N.Y.	L	2-3		4	7	Fernandez	Abbott	Franco	7-11	T4th	7½
4-26	N.Y.	W	5-4		12	6	Jones	Whitehurst	Mit. Williams	8-11	T4th	6½
4-27	At S.D.	W	12-9		17	12	Schilling	Hurst	Mit. Williams	9-11	4th	6
4-28	At S.D.	L	6-7		7	14	Clements	Schilling		9-12	4th	6
4-29	At L.A.	W	7-3		8	9	Cox	Hershiser		10-12	4th	6
5-2	At S.F.	L	1-2		6	8	Swift	Abbott	Righetti	10-13	4th	6½
5-3	At S.F.	W	12-3		15	6	Brantley	Wilson	Schilling	11-13	4th	5½
5-5	L.A.	W	6-2		9	8	Mulholland	Candiotti		12-13	4th	6
5-6	L.A.	L	1-3		6	11	R. Martinez	Cox	McDowell	12-14	4th	7
5-8	S.D.	L	5-6		12	8	Melendez	Schilling	Myers	12-15	4th	7½
5-9	S.D.	L	1-5		7	11	Lefferts	Brantley	Myers	12-16	5th	8½
5-10	S.D.	W	9-3		8	11	Mulholland	Gr. Harris		13-16	4th	7½
5-11	S.F.	L	7-8	(10)	9	9	Burba	Mit. Williams		13-17	5th	8
5-12	S.F.	L	5-7		9	10	Hickerson	Jones	Jackson	13-18	5th	8
5-13	S.F.	L	3-5		6	8	Wilson	Abbott	Brantley	13-19	6th	9
5-15	At Cin.	W	8-0		12	5	Mulholland	Browning		14-19	6th	8½
5-16	At Cin.	L	5-6		8	9	Belcher	Ritchie	Dibble	14-20	6th	8½
5-17	At Cin.	W	5-4		13	8	Hartley	Dibble	Mit. Williams	15-20	6th	7½
5-18	Hou.	L	2-4		6	9	J. Jones	Abbott	Boever	15-21	6th	8
5-19	Hou.	W	4-3		8	6	Schilling	Henry	Mit. Williams	16-21	6th	7
5-20	Hou.	W	2-1		10	9	Mulholland	Kile	Mit. Williams	17-21	5th	6
5-22	Cin.	W	8-2		10	7	Brantley	Belcher		18-21	5th	5½
5-23	Cin.	L	0-10		6	14	Swindell	Brink		18-22	5th	5½
5-24	Cin.	L	3-8		6	8	Rijo	Schilling		18-23	6th	6
5-25	Atl.	W	4-1		6	6	Mulholland	Avery	Mit. Williams	19-23	T5th	5
5-26	Atl.	W	5-2		11	2	Robinson	Bielecki	Mit. Williams	20-23	4th	5
5-27	Atl.	L	3-9		7	15	Glavine	Brantley		20-24	5th	5
5-29	At Hou.	W	2-1	(12)	8	7	Jones	Osuna		21-24	4th	4
5-30	At Hou.	L	4-5		6	4	J. Jones	Mulholland	D. Jones	21-25	4th	4
5-31	At Hou.	W	6-3	(11)	11	10	Jones	Murphy	Ritchie	22-25	4th	4
6-1	At Atl.	L	6-7		9	11	Glavine	Brantley	Wohlers	22-26	5th	4½
6-2	At Atl.	L	3-5		11	10	Stanton	Mit. Williams		22-27	5th	4½
6-3	At Atl.	W	4-1		9	7	Schilling	Smoltz	Mit. Williams	23-27	3rd	1½
6-5	St.L.	W	7-5		11	10	Jones	Worrell	Mit. Williams	24-27	4th	5
6-6	St.L.	W	7-5		13	10	Hartley	McClure	Mit. Williams	25-27	4th	4
6-7	St.L.	L	4-5		9	12	Worrell	Ayrault	L. Smith	25-28	4th	5
6-8	Pit.	W	7-0		14	3	Schilling	Palacios		26-28	4th	4
6-9	Pit.	L	3-5		9	7	Drabek	Hartley	Neagle	26-29	4th	5
6-10	Pit.	L	1-2	(12)	8	4	Patterson	Jones	Mason	26-30	5th	6
6-12	At St.L.	W	8-5		12	11	Ritchie	Osborne	Mit. Williams	27-30	5th	6
6-13	At St.L.	L	1-4		8	4	Olivares	Schilling	L. Smith	27-31	5th	6
6-14	At St.L.	L	2-5		8	12	Cormier	Brink	L. Smith	27-32	5th	7
6-15	At Pit.	W	4-1		8	5	Mulholland	Smith		28-32	5th	7
6-16	At Pit.	L	5-6	(12)	10	11	Patterson	Brantley		28-33	5th	8
6-17	At Pit.	L	2-8		11	8	Tomlin	Robinson		28-34	6th	9
6-18	Chi.	W	4-3		11	8	Hartley	Scanlan	Mit. Williams	29-34	6th	8
6-19	Chi.	L	2-5		5	11	Jackson	Brink	Bullinger	29-35	6th	8
6-20	Chi.	W	4-1		6	3	Mulholland	Maddux	Mit. Williams	30-35	6th	7
6-21	Chi.	L	2-5		7	11	Morgan	Abbott	Assenmacher	30-36	6th	8
6-22	At Mon.	W	5-3		7	4	Combs	Barnes	Mit. Williams	31-36	5th	8
6-23	At Mon.	W	5-0		10	6	Schilling	Nabholz		32-36	5th	8
6-24	At Mon.	L	1-8		7	11	Hill	Weston		32-37	6th	8
6-26	At Chi.	L	0-3		7	8	Morgan	Abbott	Bullinger	32-38	6th	8

Date		Opp.	Res.	Score	(inn.*)	Hits	Opp. hits	Winning pitcher	Losing pitcher	Save	Record	Pos.	GB
6-27		At Chi.	W	5-4		13	9	Hartley	McElroy	Mit. Williams	33-38	6th	8
6-28		At Chi.	L	3-5		4	10	Castillo	Schilling	Assenmacher	33-39	6th	8
6-29		Mon.	W	5-4		6	9	Mulholland	Fassero	Mit. Williams	34-39	6th	7
6-30		Mon.	L	2-7		5	12	Hill	Mike Williams		34-40	6th	8
7-1		Mon.	L	3-6		9	9	Martinez	Abbott	Wetteland	34-41	6th	9
7-2		At L.A.	L	4-9		9	11	Ke. Gross	Combs		34-42	6th	9
7-3	(1)	At L.A.	L	1-5		7	7	Ojeda	Schilling		34-43	6th	9
7-3	(2)	At L.A.	L	0-2		3	5	Astacio	Robinson		34-44	6th	9½
7-4		At L.A.	W	3-2		6	7	Mulholland	Candiotti		35-44	6th	8½
7-5		At L.A.	W	9-3		13	3	Mike Williams	R. Martinez		36-44	6th	8
7-6		At S.F.	L	2-4		10	8	Black	Abbott	Beck	36-45	6th	8½
7-7	(1)	At S.F.	L	7-8		8	11	Hickerson	Hartley	Beck	36-46	6th	9½
7-7	(2)	At S.F.	L	6-10		8	15	Pena	Robinson		36-47	6th	10
7-8		At S.F.	L	3-4		10	8	Jackson	Hartley	Beck	36-48	6th	10
7-9		At S.D.	L	1-3		7	8	Deshaies	Mulholland	Myers	36-49	6th	10
7-10		At S.D.	L	7-8		12	15	Rodriguez	Jones	Myers	36-50	6th	11
7-11		At S.D.	L	2-3	(11)	8	9	Scott	Hartley		36-51	6th	12
7-12		At S.D.	L	2-8		7	12	Benes	Robinson		36-52	6th	13
7-16		L.A.	L	5-7		10	13	Candiotti	Mulholland	Gott	36-53	6th	14
7-17		L.A.	W	11-3		13	6	Schilling	Hershiser		37-53	6th	13
7-18		L.A.	W	14-3		17	10	Abbott	R. Martinez		38-53	6th	13
7-19		L.A.	W	6-5		10	9	Ritchie	Howell	Mit. Williams	39-53	6th	12
7-20		S.D.	L	1-2		6	6	Rodriguez	Jones	Myers	39-54	6th	12
7-21		S.D.	L	3-4		10	9	Hurst	Mulholland	Myers	39-55	6th	12
7-22		S.D.	W	4-0		7	5	Schilling	Benes		40-55	6th	12
7-24		S.F.	W	8-4		14	11	Jones	Jackson	Mit. Williams	41-55	6th	11
7-25		S.F.	L	2-6	(10)	6	11	Hickerson	Mit. Williams		41-56	6th	11
7-26		S.F.	W	7-2		6	7	Mulholland	Rapp		42-56	6th	11
7-27		N.Y.	W	5-0		6	6	Schilling	Saberhagen		43-56	6th	10
7-28		N.Y.	L	6-8		7	13	Cone	Jones	Young	43-57	6th	10
7-29		N.Y.	W	6-3		10	8	Mit. Williams	Innis		44-57	6th	9
7-30		At Mon.	L	2-7		7	7	Gardner	Mathews		44-58	6th	10
7-31		At Mon.	W	2-0		7	5	Mulholland	Barnes		45-58	6th	10
8-1		At Mon.	W	4-2		9	6	Schilling	Hill	Mit. Williams	46-58	6th	10
8-2		At Mon.	L	0-1		5	4	Nabholz	Rivera	Wetteland	46-59	6th	11
8-3		At St.L.	L	1-2		4	6	Tewksbury	Abbott	L. Smith	46-60	6th	11½
8-4		At St.L.	L	5-9		9	14	McClure	Mit. Williams		46-61	6th	12½
8-5		At St.L.	L	4-5		9	10	Osborne	Ayrault	L. Smith	46-62	6th	13½
8-6		Mon.	L	4-7		12	12	Hill	Schilling	Wetteland	46-63	6th	14½
8-7		Mon.	W	3-1		10	4	Rivera	Nabholz	Mit. Williams	47-63	6th	14½
8-8		Mon.	L	1-6		4	11	Martinez	Abbott		47-64	6th	15½
8-9		Mon.	L	2-6		3	9	Gardner	Mathews	Rojas	47-65	6th	16½
8-11		St.L.	L	6-7		8	15	Worrell	Mit. Williams	L. Smith	47-66	6th	17
8-12		St.L.	L	2-3	(10)	9	10	Worrell	Mit. Williams	L. Smith	47-67	6th	18
8-14		At N.Y.	W	6-2		10	7	Rivera	Gooden		48-67	6th	17
8-15		At N.Y.	W	4-3		6	7	Hartley	Innis	Mit. Williams	49-67	6th	16
8-18	(1)	Cin.	L	0-6		7	12	Swindell	Mulholland		49-68	6th	16
8-18	(2)	Cin.	W	6-1		9	4	Schilling	Rijo		50-68	6th	16½
8-19		Cin.	W	9-3		10	6	Rivera	Hammond		51-68	6th	16½
8-21		Hou.	L	1-6		6	8	Williams	Ashby		51-69	6th	17
8-22		Hou.	L	9-14		13	18	Blair	Hartley		51-70	6th	18
8-23		Hou.	L	1-3		6	4	J. Jones	Schilling	D. Jones	51-71	6th	18
8-24		At Cin.	L	5-8		10	12	Hammond	Rivera	Charlton	51-72	6th	18
8-25		At Cin.	L	1-7		4	10	Belcher	Mathews		51-73	6th	19
8-26		At Cin.	L	3-4		12	8	Bolton	Ashby	Dibble	51-74	6th	20
8-28		Atl.	W	7-3		7	7	Mulholland	Smoltz		52-74	6th	19
8-29		Atl.	L	6-7		7	13	Leibrandt	Schilling	Mercker	52-75	6th	20
8-30		Atl.	W	10-2		12	5	Rivera	Glavine		53-75	6th	20
8-31		At Hou.	L	2-9		8	12	Henry	Ashby		53-76	6th	20½
9-1		At Hou.	L	3-5		8	9	Williams	Brantley	D. Jones	53-77	6th	21½
9-2		At Hou.	L	2-3		6	8	Harnisch	Mulholland	D. Jones	53-78	6th	22½
9-4		At Atl.	W	2-1		6	4	Schilling	Glavine	Mit. Williams	54-78	6th	23
9-5		At Atl.	L	5-6		7	9	Reardon	Mit. Williams		54-79	6th	24
9-6		At Atl.	L	3-4		12	6	Reardon	Hartley		54-80	6th	24
9-7		N.Y.	L	3-6		12	6	Schourek	Mulholland	Mit. Williams	54-81	6th	24
9-8		N.Y.	W	2-1		6	9	Shepherd	Gooden	Mit. Williams	55-81	6th	24
9-9		N.Y.	W	2-1		5	1	Schilling	Fernandez		56-81	6th	24
9-11		Pit.	W	5-2		9	6	Rivera	Walk	Mit. Williams	57-81	6th	23
9-12		Pit.	L	7-9		11	12	Belinda	Mit. Williams		57-82	6th	23
9-13		Pit.	W	6-3		11	6	Mulholland	Patterson		58-82	6th	23
9-14		Mon.	W	6-2		8	8	Greene	Barnes	Shepherd	59-82	6th	23
9-15		Mon.	L	0-3		3	9	Hill	Schilling	Wetteland	59-83	6th	24
9-16		At Chi.	L	9-14		13	17	Maddux	Rivera		59-84	6th	24
9-17		At Chi.	L	0-3		2	7	Morgan	DeLeon		59-85	6th	25

Date	Opp.	Res.	Score	(inn.*)	Hits	Opp. hits	Winning pitcher	Losing pitcher	Save	Record	Pos.	GB
9-18	At Pit.	L	2-5	(5½)	6	8	Wakefield	Mulholland		59-86	6th	26
9-19	At Pit.	L	0-3		8	10	Drabek	Greene		59-87	6th	27
9-20	At Pit.	L	2-3	(13)	10	10	Mason	Shepherd		59-88	6th	28
9-21	At Mon.	W	9-2		11	4	Rivera	Nabholz		60-88	6th	28
9-22	At Mon.	W	5-2		8	6	Hartley	Bottenfield	Mit. Williams	61-88	6th	27
9-23	Chi.	W	9-3		9	11	Ayrault	Bullinger		62-88	6th	26
9-24	Chi.	W	3-2	(10)	7	7	Mit. Williams	Scanlan		63-88	6th	26
9-26 (1)	St.L.	W	3-1		7	4	Schilling	Magrane		64-88	6th	25½
9-26 (2)	St.L.	W	10-0		15	5	Rivera	Osborne		65-88	6th	26
9-27 (1)	St.L.	L	1-8		4	11	Cormier	Brink		65-89	6th	27
9-27 (2)	St.L.	W	6-5		15	9	Hartley	B. Smith	Mit. Williams	66-89	6th	26½
9-28 (1)	At N.Y.	W	7-6	(10)	16	8	Mit. Williams	Innis		67-89	6th	26½
9-28 (2)	At N.Y.	W	7-6		13	12	Mathews	Vitko	Shepherd	68-89	6th	26
9-29	At N.Y.	W	5-3		7	6	Ayrault	Young	Mit. Williams	69-89	T5th	26
9-30	At N.Y.	L	2-6		8	10	Fernandez	Abbott		69-90	6th	26
10-2	At St.L.	L	1-2		5	4	Osborne	Schilling	L. Smith	69-91	6th	26
10-3	At St.L.	W	3-2		9	7	Mathews	L. Smith	Mit. Williams	70-91	6th	25
10-4	At St.L.	L	3-6		10	12	Cormier	Greene	L. Smith	70-92	6th	26

Monthly records: April (10-12), May (12-13), June (12-15), July (11-18), August (8-18), September (16-14), Oct. (1-2).

HIGHLIGHTS

High point: If there was one, it was from September 8 to the end of the season, when the Phillies went 16-11. But by then, they were buried in last place.

Low point: The Phillies hit rock bottom at the All-Star break. The team staggered home from a 13-game, 11-day West Coast trip with a 2-11 record, concluding the journey with an eight-game losing streak. In last place, 13 games behind the division-leading Pirates, the Phillies were dead.

Turning point: July 1, when the club scheduled a night game (to accommodate a fireworks promotion) on the eve of the aforementioned West Coast trip. Catcher Darren Daulton and first baseman John Kruk publicly ripped the club for scheduling the night game before the trip and used the scheduling as an excuse for the team's bad play.

Most valuable player: Daulton, who became just the fourth catcher (and the first who hit lefthanded) in big-league annals to win an RBI title (109). He set career highs in homers (27), doubles (32) and runs (80).

Most valuable pitcher: Righthander Curt Schilling. Acquired from Houston on April 2 to be a middle reliever, he became the team's No. 1 starter due to injuries to other pitchers. He held foes to a big-league-low .201 batting average while notching 14 wins and a 2.35 ERA.

Most improved player: Third baseman Dave Hollins. In his first full season, he had 27 homers, 93 RBIs and 104 runs.

Most pleasant surprise: Righthander Ben Rivera. A bust in the first half after being acquired from Atlanta on May 28, the rookie harnessed his control to finish at 7-4 with a 3.07 ERA.

Biggest disappointment: Left fielder Wes Chamberlain. He reported to spring training out of shape and never recovered, finishing with a .258 average and nine homers.

Key injuries: The Phillies had 17 players use the disabled list 21 times (both club records). Among the key casualties were center fielder Lenny Dykstra, righthanders Ken Howell and Jose DeJesus, and Tommy Greene, right fielder Dale Murphy, infielder Wally Backman and Chamberlain.

Notable: Second baseman Mickey Morandini turned the ninth unassisted triple play in big-league history September 20 at Pittsburgh.... Lefthander Terry Mulholland picked off a major league record 16 runners. ... Hollins set a big-league mark for switch-hitters by getting hit by 19 pitches.

—BILL BROWN

RECORDS

1992 regular-season record: 70-92 (6th in N.L. East); 41-40 at home; 29-52 on road; 42-48 vs. East; 28-44 vs. West; 29-38 vs. LHP; 41-54 vs. RHP; 16-26 on grass; 54-66 on turf; 18-30 in daytime; 52-62 at night; 21-31 in one-run games; 5-7 in extra-inning games; 2-2-2 in doubleheaders.

Team record last five years: 357-452 (.441, ranks 12th in league in that span).

TEAM LEADERS

Batting average: John Kruk (.323).
At-bats: Dave Hollins (586).
Runs: Dave Hollins (104).
Hits: John Kruk (164).
Total bases: Dave Hollins (275).
Doubles: Mariano Duncan (40).
Triples: Mickey Morandini (8).
Home runs: Darren Daulton, Dave Hollins (27).
Runs batted in: Darren Daulton (109).
Stolen bases: Lenny Dykstra (30).
Slugging percentage: Darren Daulton (.524).
On-base percentage: John Kruk (.423).
Wins: Curt Schilling (14).
Earned-run average: Curt Schilling (2.35).
Complete games: Terry Mulholland (12).
Shutouts: Curt Schilling (4).
Saves: Mitch Williams (29).
Innings pitched: Terry Mulholland (229).
Strikeouts: Curt Schilling (147).

GAMES BY POSITION

Catcher: Darren Daulton 141, Steve Lake 17, Todd Pratt 11, Jeff Grotewold 2.

First base: John Kruk 121, Ricky Jordan 54, Dale Sveum 4, Jeff Grotewold 1, Dave Hollins 1.

Second base: Mickey Morandini 124, Mariano Duncan 52, Wally Backman 10, Steve Scarsone 3, Joe Millette 1.

Third base: Dave Hollins 156, Dale Sveum 5, Mariano Duncan 4, Joe Millette 3, Wally Backman 2.

Shortstop: Juan Bell 46, Mariano Duncan 42, Kim Batiste 41, Dale Sveum 34, Joe Millette 26, Mickey Morandini 3.

Outfield: Ruben Amaro 113, Lenny Dykstra 85, Stan Javier 74, Wes Chamberlain 73, Mariano Duncan 65, John Kruk 35, Tom Marsh 35, Braulio Castillo 23, Dale Murphy 16, Julio Peguero 14, Ricky Jordan 11, Jim Lindeman 9, Jeff Grotewold 2.

TOP 10 DRAFT CHOICES

1. **Chad McConnell**, OF, Creighton University.
2. **None.**
3. **Trevor Humphry**, RHP, Westark Community College (Ark.).
4. **Jason Moler**, C, California State University-Fullerton.
5. **Larry Mitchell**, RHP, James Madison University.
6. **Jamie Sepeda**, RHP, Stanford University.
7. **Steve Solomon**, OF, Stanford University.
8. **Jon McMullen**, 1B, Rio Mesa High School, Oxnard, Calif.
9. **Nate Brown**, RHP, University of California.
10. **Stan Evans**, OF, Seminole Community College (Fla.).

PITTSBURGH PIRATES
NATIONAL LEAGUE EAST DIVISION

1993 SCHEDULE

APRIL

SUN	MON	TUE	WED	THU	FRI	SAT
				1	2	3
4	5	6 N SD	7 H	8 SD	9 N SF	10 N SF H
11 SF H	12 N SD	13 N SD	14 N SD	15 N SD	16 LA	17 N LA
18 N LA	19	20 N CIN	21 N CIN H	22 N CIN H	23 N HOU	24 N HOU H
25 HOU	26 N ATL	27 N ATL	28 N CIN	29 N CIN	30 N HOU	

MAY

SUN	MON	TUE	WED	THU	FRI	SAT
					1 HOU	1 N HOU
2 HOU	3	4 N ATL H	5 N ATL H	6	7 N MON H	8 N MON H
9 MON N	10 N PHI	11 N PHI	12 N PHI	13	14 N CHI	15 N CHI
16 CHI	17 N NY	18 N NY	19 N NY	20	21 N STL	22 N STL H
23 STL H	24	25 N FLA	26 H FLA	27 N FLA	28 N LA	29 N LA H
30 LA H	31 N COL					

JUNE

SUN	MON	TUE	WED	THU	FRI	SAT
		1 N COL	2 N COL	3 N SF	4 N SF	5 SF
6 SF	7	8 N COL H	9 N COL H	10 N FLA	11 N FLA	12 N FLA
13 FLA	14 N STL	15 N STL	16 N STL	17 N NY	18 N NY H	19 N NY H
20 NY	21 N CHI	22 N CHI H	23 N CHI	24	25 N PHI	26 N PHI H
27 PHI	28 N MON	29 N MON	30 N MON			

JULY

SUN	MON	TUE	WED	THU	FRI	SAT
				1 MON	2 N CIN	3 N CIN
4 CIN	5 CIN	6 N HOU	7 HOU	8 N CIN	9 N CIN H	10 N CIN H
11 CIN N	12	13 ● ALL-STAR GAME	14 N ATL	15 N ATL	16 N ATL	17 N ATL
18 ATL	19 N HOU H	20 N HOU H	21 N ATL H	22 N ATL H	23 N ATL	24 N ATL
25 ATL H	26	27 N MON H	28 N MON H	29 N MON H	30 PHI	31 N PHI

AUGUST

SUN	MON	TUE	WED	THU	FRI	SAT
1 PHI	2 CHI	3 N CHI	4 CHI	5 N CHI	6 N NY	7 NY
8 NY	9 N STL	10 N STL H	11 N STL H	12 N STL	13 N FLA	14 N FLA H
15 FLA H	16	17 N SF H	18 N SF H	19 N SF	20 N SD	21
22 SD	23 N LA	24 N LA	25 N LA	26	27 N SD H	28 N SD H
29 DH SD H	30	31 N LA H				

SEPTEMBER

SUN	MON	TUE	WED	THU	FRI	SAT
			1 N LA H	2 N LA H	3 N COL	4 N COL
5 COL	6	7 N SF	8	9 N COL H	10 N COL H	11 N COL H
12 COL H	13	14 N NY	15 N FLA	16 N FLA	17 N STL	18 N STL
19 STL	20 N NY	21 N NY	22 N NY	23	24 N CHI	25 N CHI H
26 CHI H	27 N PHI	28 N PHI H	29 N PHI H	30 N PHI H		

OCTOBER

SUN	MON	TUE	WED	THU	FRI	SAT
					1 N MON	2 MON
3 MON						

1993 SEASON

CLUB DIRECTORY

Board of directors
Joe L. Brown
Frank V. Cahouet
Richard M. Cyert
Douglas D. Danforth
Eugene Litman
John Marous
Sophie Masloff
John H. McConnell
Thomas H. O'Brien
Paul H. O'Neill
David M. Roderick
Vincent A. Sarni
Mark Sauer
Harvey M. Walken
Chairman of the exec. comm. of the board
Vincent Sarni
President and chief executive officer
Mark Sauer
Sr. v.p. and g.m./baseball oper.
Ted Simmons
Sr. vice president for business operations
Doug Bureman
Assistant general manager
Cam Bonifay
Vice president, finance and administration
Kenneth C. Curcio
Vice president, public relations
Richard J. Cerrone
Vice president, marketing and operations
Steven N. Greenberg
Assistant vice president, finance
Patti Mistick
Exec. dir. of broadcasting and adv. sales
Mark Driscoll
Traveling secretary
Greg Johnson
Director of ticket operations
Gary Remlinger
Senior director of sales and marketing
Bob Derda
Senior account executive
Mark Ferraco
Director of baseball operations
John Sirignano
Director of Bradenton baseball operations
Jeff Podobnik
Director of broadcast administration
Declan Bolger
Director of community relations
Patty Paytas
Director of community services and sales
Al Gordon
Director of corporate sales
Nellie Briles
Director of Diamond Club
Chris Cronin

Director of finance
Jim Plake
Director of in-game entertainment
Mike Gordon
Director of media relations
Jim Trdinich
Director of merchandising
Joe Billetdeaux
Director of minor league operations
Chet Montgomery
Director of promotions
Kathy Guy
Director of publications and special projects
Jim Lachimia
Director of operations
Dennis DaPra
Director of scouting
Jack Zduriencik
Assistant director of public relations
Sally O'Leary
Club physician
Dr. Joseph Coroso
Team orthopedist
Dr. Jack Failla
Trainers
Kent Biggerstaff
Dave Tumbas
Equipment manager
Roger Wilson
Scouting coordinators
Bill Bryk
Ron King
Kevin Towers
Scouting supervisors
Tom Barnard
Pablo Cruz
Larry D'Amato
Steve Demeter
Angel Figueroa
Steve Fleming
Dave Holliday
Dave Klipstein
Carlos Loreto
Jose Luna
Leland Maddox
Rene Mons
Jim Nelson
Boyd Odom
Ed Roebuck
Paul Tinnell
Mike Williams
Major league scout
Lenny Yochim
Special assignment scout
Ken Parker

SCHEDULE KEY

H—Home game.   Doubleheader.
N—Night game (any game starting after 5 p.m.).
*All-Star Game at Oriole Park at Camden Yards, Baltimore.

Manager—Jim Leyland (10).

Coaches—Terry Collins (44), Rich Donnelly (45), Milt May (39), Ray Miller (31), Tommy Sandt (37), Bill Virdon (19).

No.	PITCHERS	B/T	Ht./Wt.	Born	1992 clubs
50	Belinda, Stan	R/R	6-3/187	8-6-66	Pittsburgh
54	Candelaria, John	R/L	6-6/225	11-6-53	Los Angeles
61	Cole, Victor	B/R	5-10/160	1-23-68	Buffalo, Pittsburgh
26	Cooke, Steve	R/L	6-6/220	1-14-70	Carolina, Buffalo, Pittsburgh
52	De Los Santos, Mariano	R/R	5-10/200	7-13-70	Augusta
56	Hope, John	R/R	6-3/195	12-21-70	Salem
64	Johnston, Joel	R/R	6-4/220	3-8-67	Kansas City, Omaha
66	Minor, Blas	R/R	6-3/195	3-20-66	Buffalo, Pittsburgh
24	Moeller, Dennis	R/L	6-2/195	9-15-67	Omaha, Kansas City
32	Neagle, Denny	L/L	6-2/215	9-13-68	Pittsburgh
34	Pena, Alejandro	R/R	6-1/203	6-25-59	Atlanta
58	Robertson, Rich	L/L	6-4/175	9-15-68	Salem, Carolina
42	Shouse, Brian	L/L	5-11/180	9-26-68	Carolina
41	Smith, Zane	L/L	6-1/205	12-28-60	Pittsburgh
29	Tomlin, Randy	L/L	5-10/170	6-14-66	Pittsburgh
43	Wagner, Paul	R/R	6-1/185	11-14-67	Carolina, Pittsburgh, Buffalo
49	Wakefield, Tim	R/R	6-2/195	8-2-66	Buffalo, Pittsburgh
17	Walk, Bob	R/R	6-3/217	11-26-56	Pittsburgh
15	Zimmerman, Mike	R/R	6-0/180	2-6-69	Carolina

No.	CATCHERS	B/T	Ht./Wt.	Born	1992 clubs
12	LaValliere, Mike	L/R	5-9/210	8-18-60	Pittsburgh
14	Prince, Tom	R/R	5-11/185	8-13-64	Pittsburgh, Buffalo
11	Slaught, Don	R/R	6-1/190	9-11-58	Buffalo, Pittsburgh

No.	INFIELDERS	B/T	Ht./Wt.	Born	1992 clubs
3	Bell, Jay	R/R	6-0/185	12-11-65	Pittsburgh
38	Bell, Mike	L/L	6-1/175	4-22-68	Greenville
16	Foley, Tom	L/R	6-1/175	9-9-59	Montreal
51	Garcia, Carlos	R/R	6-1/185	10-15-67	Buffalo, Pittsburgh
7	King, Jeff	R/R	6-1/180	12-26-64	Pittsburgh, Buffalo
6	Merced, Orlando	B/R	5-11/170	11-2-66	Pittsburgh
27	Richardson, Jeff	R/R	6-2/180	8-26-65	Buffalo
13	Sandoval, Jose	R/R	5-11/170	8-25-69	Mexico City Reds
22	Wehner, John	R/R	6-3/205	6-29-67	Buffalo, Pittsburgh
36	Young, Kevin	R/R	6-2/213	6-16-69	Buffalo, Pittsburgh

No.	OUTFIELDERS	B/T	Ht./Wt.	Born	1992 clubs
47	Bullett, Scott	L/L	6-2/190	12-25-68	Carolina, Buffalo
35	Clark, Dave	L/R	6-2/210	9-3-62	Buffalo, Pittsburgh
28	Martin, Al	L/L	6-2/220	11-24-67	Buffalo, Pittsburgh
23	McClendon, Lloyd	R/R	6-0/212	1-11-59	Pittsburgh
25	Pennyfeather, William	R/R	6-2/215	5-25-68	Buffalo, Carolina, Pittsburgh
2	Smith, Lonnie	R/R	5-9/170	12-22-55	Atlanta
55	Thomas, Keith	B/R	6-1/180	9-12-68	Salem, Carolina
18	Van Slyke, Andy	L/R	6-2/195	12-21-60	Pittsburgh

BALLPARK INFORMATION

Ballpark (capacity, surface)
Three Rivers Stadium (47,972, artificial)

Address
600 Stadium Circle
Pittsburgh, PA 15212

Business phone
412-323-5000

Ticket information
412-321-2827

Ticket prices
$14 (club boxes)
$10 (terrace boxes)
$8 (reserved seats)
$5 (general admission)
$2.50 (g.a., children 12 and under)

Field dimensions (from home plate)
To left field at foul line, 335 feet
To center field, 400 feet
To right field at foul line, 335 feet

First game played
July 16, 1970 (Reds 3, Pirates 2)

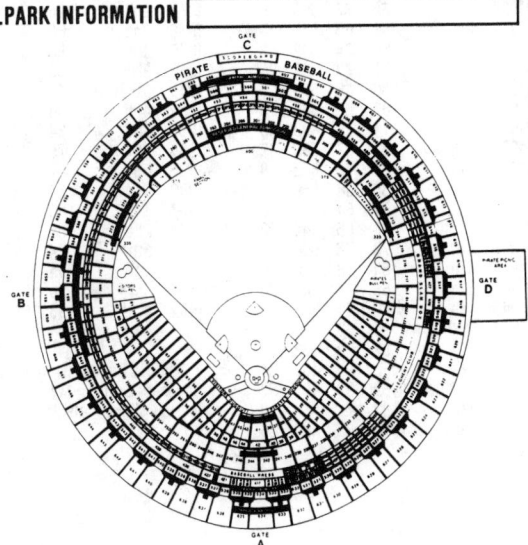

MINOR LEAGUE AFFILIATES

Class	Team	League	Manager
AAA	Buffalo	American Association	Doc Edwards
AA	Carolina	Southern	John Wockenfuss
A	Salem	Carolina	Scott Little
A	Augusta	South Atlantic	Trent Jewett
A	Welland, Ont.	New York-Pennsylvania	Larry Smith
Rookie	Bradenton Pirates	Gulf Coast	Woody Huyke

BROADCAST INFORMATION

Radio: KDKA-AM (1020). Broadcasters: Lanny Frattare, Jim Rooker, Kent Derdivanis, Steve Blass.
TV: KDKA-TV (Channel 2). Broadcasters: Lanny Frattare, Jim Rooker, Kent Derdivanis, Steve Blass.
Cable TV: KBL Sports Network. Broadcasters: Lanny Frattare, Jim Rooker, Kent Derdivanis, Steve Blass.

SPRING TRAINING

Ballpark (city): McKechnie Field (Bradenton, Fla.).
Ticket information: 813-748-4610.

HISTORY

YEAR-BY-YEAR RECORDS

Year	Pos.	W	L	Pct.	*GB	Year	Pos.	W	L	Pct.	*GB
1901	1st	90	49	.647	+ 7½	1950	8th	57	96	.373	33½
1902	1st	103	36	.741	+27½	1951	7th	64	90	.416	32½
1903	1st	91	49	.650	+ 6½	1952	8th	42	112	.273	54½
1904	4th	87	66	.569	19	1953	8th	50	104	.325	55
1905	2nd	96	57	.627	9	1954	8th	53	101	.344	44
1906	3rd	93	60	.608	23½	1955	8th	60	94	.390	38½
1907	2nd	91	63	.591	17	1956	7th	66	88	.429	27
1908	T2nd	98	56	.636	1	1957	T7th	62	92	.403	33
1909	1st	110	42	.724	+ 6½	1958	2nd	84	70	.545	8
1910	3rd	86	67	.562	17½	1959	4th	78	76	.506	9
1911	3rd	85	69	.552	14½	1960	1st	95	59	.617	+ 7
1912	2nd	93	58	.616	10	1961	6th	75	79	.487	18
1913	4th	78	71	.523	21½	1962	4th	93	68	.578	8
1914	7th	69	85	.448	25½	1963	8th	74	88	.457	25
1915	5th	73	81	.474	18	1964	T6th	80	82	.494	13
1916	6th	65	89	.422	29	1965	3rd	90	72	.556	7
1917	8th	51	103	.331	47	1966	3rd	92	70	.568	3
1918	4th	65	60	.520	17	1967	6th	81	81	.500	20½
1919	4th	71	68	.511	24½	1968	6th	80	82	.494	17
1920	4th	79	75	.513	14	1969	3rd	88	74	.543	12
1921	2nd	90	63	.588	4	1970	1st†	89	73	.549	+ 5
1922	T3rd	85	69	.552	8	1971	1st‡	97	65	.599	+ 7
1923	3rd	87	67	.565	8½	1972	1st†	96	59	.619	+11
1924	3rd	90	63	.588	3	1973	3rd	80	82	.494	2½
1925	1st	95	58	.621	+ 8½	1974	1st†	88	74	.543	+ 1½
1926	3rd	84	69	.549	4½	1975	1st†	92	69	.571	+ 6½
1927	1st	94	60	.610	+ 1½	1976	2nd	92	70	.568	9
1928	4th	85	67	.559	9	1977	2nd	96	66	.593	5
1929	2nd	88	65	.575	10½	1978	2nd	88	73	.547	1½
1930	5th	80	74	.519	12	1979	1st‡	98	64	.605	+ 2
1931	5th	75	79	.487	26	1980	3rd	83	79	.512	8
1932	2nd	86	68	.558	4	1981	4th/6th	46	56	.451	§
1933	2nd	87	67	.565	5	1982	4th	84	78	.519	8
1934	5th	74	76	.493	19½	1983	2nd	84	78	.519	6
1935	4th	86	67	.562	13½	1984	6th	75	87	.463	21½
1936	4th	84	70	.545	8	1985	6th	57	104	.354	43½
1937	3rd	86	68	.558	10	1986	6th	64	98	.395	44
1938	2nd	86	64	.573	2	1987	T4th	80	82	.494	15
1939	6th	68	85	.444	28½	1988	2nd	85	75	.531	15
1940	4th	78	76	.506	22½	1989	5th	74	88	.457	19
1941	4th	81	73	.526	19	1990	1st†	95	67	.586	+ 4
1942	5th	66	81	.449	36½	1991	1st†	98	64	.605	+14
1943	4th	80	74	.519	25	1992	1st†	96	66	.593	+ 9
1944	2nd	90	63	.588	14½						
1945	4th	82	72	.532	16						
1946	7th	63	91	.409	34						
1947	T7th	62	92	.403	32						
1948	4th	83	71	.539	8½						
1949	6th	71	83	.461	26						

*Games behind winner. †Lost Championship Series. ‡Won Championship Series. §First half 25-23; second 21-33.

MANAGERS

Name	Record	Years
Fred Clarke	1343-909	'01-15
Jimmy Callahan	85-129	'16-17
Honus Wagner	1-4	1917
Hugo Bezdek	166-187	'17-19
George Gibson	401-330	'20-22
		'32-34
Bill McKechnie	409-293	'22-26
Donie Bush	246-178	'27-29
Jewel Ens	176-167	'29-31
Pie Traynor	457-406	'34-39
Frank Frisch	539-528	'40-46
Spud Davis	1-2	1946
Billy Herman	61-92	1947
Bill Burwell	1-0	1947
Billy Meyer	317-452	'48-52
Fred Haney	163-299	'53-55
Bobby Bragan	102-155	'56-57
Danny Murtaugh	1115-950	'57-64
		1967
		'70-71
		'73-76
Harry Walker	224-184	'65-67
Larry Shepard	164-155	'68-69
Alex Grammas	4-1	1969
Bill Virdon	163-128	'72-73
Chuck Tanner	711-685	'77-85
Jim Leyland	592-540	'86-92

DAY BY DAY

Date	Opp.	Res.	Score (inn.*)	Hits	Opp. hits	Winning pitcher	Losing pitcher	Save	Record	Pos.	GB
4-6	Mon.	W	2-0	4	6	Drabek	Martinez	Mason	1-0	T1st	...
4-8	Mon.	W	4-2	6	5	Smith	Gardner	Belinda	2-0	1st	+½
4-9	Mon.	L	3-8	7	14	Nabholz	Walk		2-1	T1st	...
4-10	At Phi.	W	3-2	7	5	Tomlin	Abbott	Belinda	3-1	1st	+½
4-11	At Phi.	L	4-7	8	7	Ashby	Drabek		3-2	T1st	...
4-12	At Phi.	W	6-1	7	5	Smith	Mulholland		4-2	T1st	...
4-14	Chi.	W	3-2	3	4	Walk	Jackson	Mason	5-2	1st	+½
4-15	Chi.	W	7-2	9	8	Tomlin	Morgan		6-2	1st	+1½
4-17	Phi.	W	7-4	9	9	Drabek	Jones	Belinda	7-2	1st	+2½
4-18	Phi.	W	9-2	11	11	Smith	Greene		8-2	1st	+2½
4-19	Phi.	W	11-0	17	3	Patterson	Cox		9-2	1st	+3½
4-20	At Mon.	W	11-1	13	5	Tomlin	Hill		10-2	1st	+4
4-21	At Mon.	W	8-7	10	11	Palacios	Haney	Mason	11-2	1st	+4½
4-22	At Mon.	W	2-0	4	5	Drabek	Martinez		12-2	1st	+4½
4-23	At Mon.	L	3-6	7	10	Gardner	Smith	Wetteland	12-3	1st	+3½
4-24	At Chi.	W	3-2	12	7	Mason	Scanlan	Belinda	13-3	1st	+4½
4-25	At Chi.	W	1-0	4	3	Tomlin	Maddux	Belinda	14-3	1st	+4½
4-26	At Chi.	L	4-5 (10)	7	10	McElroy	Mason		14-4	1st	+4½
4-28	At Cin.	L	2-3	6	9	Browning	Drabek	Charlton	14-5	1st	+3½
4-29	At Cin.	W	4-0	4	4	Smith	Belcher		15-5	1st	+3½
5-1	At Hou.	L	4-10	9	13	Harnisch	Tomlin		15-6	1st	+2
5-2	At Hou.	W	6-0	8	4	Neagle	Bowen		16-6	1st	+3
5-3	At Hou.	L	0-1	4	7	Osuna	Mason	D. Jones	16-7	1st	+2
5-4	Cin.	W	12-5	15	12	Lamp	Henry		17-7	1st	+2
5-5	Cin.	W	5-2	8	6	Miller	Belcher	Belinda	18-7	1st	+3
5-6	Atl.	W	4-3 (16)	16	12	Patterson	Rivera		19-7	1st	+4
5-7	Atl.	L	2-4	8	10	Glavine	Neagle	Stanton	19-8	1st	+4
5-8	Hou.	W	6-3	6	7	Belinda	Osuna		20-8	1st	+4
5-9	Hou.	W	3-0	7	7	Smith	Kile		21-8	1st	+4
5-10	Hou.	L	4-6 (10)	8	10	D. Jones	Mason		21-9	1st	+3
5-12	At Atl.	L	2-4	6	10	Glavine	Tomlin	Freeman	21-10	1st	+2½
5-13	At Atl.	W	11-10	21	15	Belinda	Pena		22-10	1st	+3
5-14	At Atl.	W	4-3	7	10	Palacios	Smoltz	Mason	23-10	1st	+3½
5-15	S.D.	L	2-9	8	18	Lefferts	Neagle		23-11	1st	+2½
5-16	S.D.	L	9-10	13	12	Rodriguez	Walk	Myers	23-12	1st	+2½
5-17	S.D.	L	5-6	10	8	Benes	Tomlin	Myers	23-13	1st	+1½
5-19	At S.F.	L	2-7	6	10	Wilson	Drabek	Righetti	23-14	1st	+1
5-20	At S.F.	L	1-3	4	7	Black	Smith	Brantley	23-15	1st	+1
5-21	At S.F.	L	0-1	2	5	Burkett	Walk	Jackson	23-16	1st	+½
5-22	At L.A.	W	6-4	12	9	Tomlin	Candiotti		24-16	1st	+1
5-23	At L.A.	L	4-5	9	10	Wilson	Belinda		24-17	1st	+½
5-24	At L.A.	L	2-4	7	5	Ke. Gross	Drabek	McDowell	24-18	2nd	½
5-25	At S.D.	L	6-7	15	11	Lefferts	Smith	Myers	24-19	2nd	1½
5-26	At S.D.	L	3-6 (10)	7	13	Scott	Lamp		24-20	2nd	1½
5-27	At S.D.	L	7-8	14	16	Myers	Belinda		24-21	2nd	1½
5-29	S.F.	W	13-3	13	8	Palacios	Wilson	Patterson	25-21	2nd	½
5-30	S.F.	W	3-2 (10)	9	8	Neagle	Brantley		26-21	2nd	½
5-31	S.F.	L	3-5	8	9	Black	Smith	Brantley	26-22	2nd	½
6-1	L.A.	L	6-8	8	13	Gott	Neagle	Candelaria	26-23	2nd	1
6-2	L.A.	W	1-0	7	6	Tomlin	Candiotti	Mason	27-23	T1st	...
6-3	L.A.	W	6-5	8	9	Gleaton	R. Martinez	Belinda	28-23	1st	+1
6-4	N.Y.	W	7-2	9	6	Drabek	Gooden	Patterson	29-23	1st	+1½
6-5	N.Y.	W	5-4 (10)	10	14	Belinda	Innis		30-23	1st	+2½
6-6	N.Y.	L	1-15	7	18	Fernandez	Neagle		30-24	1st	+2
6-7	N.Y.	W	3-0	8	6	Tomlin	Schourek		31-24	1st	+2½
6-8	At Phi.	L	0-7	3	14	Schilling	Palacios		31-25	1st	+2½
6-9	At Phi.	W	5-3	7	9	Drabek	Hartley	Neagle	32-25	1st	+3
6-10	At Phi.	W	2-1 (12)	4	8	Patterson	Jones	Mason	33-25	1st	+4
6-12	At N.Y.	W	3-2	8	5	Tomlin	Fernandez	Patterson	34-25	1st	+5
6-13	At N.Y.	W	3-2	15	10	Robinson	Whitehurst	Belinda	35-25	1st	+5
6-14	At N.Y.	W	5-4	9	5	Neagle	Innis	Belinda	36-25	1st	+5
6-15	Phi.	L	1-4	5	8	Mulholland	Smith		36-26	1st	+5
6-16	Phi.	W	6-5 (12)	11	10	Patterson	Brantley		37-26	1st	+6
6-17	Phi.	W	8-2	8	11	Tomlin	Robinson		38-26	1st	+6½
6-18	Mon.	L	0-4	3	12	Nabholz	Palacios	Fassero	38-27	1st	+5½
6-19	Mon.	L	1-2	7	5	Hill	Drabek	Wetteland	38-28	1st	+5½
6-20	Mon.	L	3-4	8	5	Gardner	Smith	Wetteland	38-29	1st	+4½
6-21	Mon.	W	5-4	5	11	Robinson	Martinez	Belinda	39-29	1st	+5½
6-22	St.L.	W	5-2	10	7	Tomlin	Osborne	Walk	40-29	1st	+6½
6-23	St.L.	W	6-4	9	7	Mason	Worrell	Patterson	41-29	1st	+7

Date	Opp.	Res.	Score	(inn.*)	Hits	Opp. hits	Winning pitcher	Losing pitcher	Save	Record	Pos.	GB
6-24	St.L.	L	1-4		12	11	Tewksbury	Drabek		41-30	1st	+6
6-26	At Mon.	L	2-6		6	11	Martinez	Smith	Rojas	41-31	1st	+5½
6-27	At Mon.	W	12-4		17	9	Robinson	Gardner	Belinda	42-31	1st	+6½
6-28	At Mon.	L	0-9		5	10	Barnes	Tomlin		42-32	1st	+5½
6-29	At St.L.	L	1-3		7	9	Tewksbury	Cole		42-33	1st	+4½
6-30	At St.L.	W	2-0		9	3	Drabek	Cormier		43-33	1st	+5
7-1	At St.L.	W	1-0		6	5	Smith	Clark		44-33	1st	+6
7-2	Cin.	L	1-2		7	9	Rijo	Robinson	Charlton	44-34	1st	+5½
7-3	Cin.	L	3-7		11	13	Belcher	Tomlin		44-35	1st	+5
7-4	Cin.	L	2-5		5	10	Swindell	Cole		44-36	1st	+4½
7-5	Cin.	L	1-2		4	10	Menendez	Drabek	Charlton	44-37	1st	+3½
7-6	Hou.	W	1-0		7	5	Smith	J. Jones	Belinda	45-37	1st	+4½
7-7	Hou.	W	5-3		14	10	Walk	Boever		46-37	1st	+4½
7-8	Hou.	L	2-3		6	8	D. Jones	Patterson		46-38	1st	+3½
7-9	At Cin.	L	2-5		6	8	Bankhead	Mason	Charlton	46-39	1st	+3
7-10	At Cin.	W	4-0		11	6	Drabek	Hammond		47-39	1st	+3
7-11	At Cin.	W	9-3		12	7	Smith	Brown		48-39	1st	+3½
7-12	At Cin.	W	7-6	(10)	12	12	Patterson	Belcher	Belinda	49-39	1st	+4½
7-16	Chi.	W	2-1		7	4	Drabek	Boskie	Belinda	50-39	1st	+4½
7-17	Chi.	L	1-2		6	8	Maddux	Tomlin	Scanlan	50-40	1st	+4
7-18	Chi.	W	4-0		6	7	Walk	Morgan	Patterson	51-40	1st	+5
7-19	Chi.	L	2-4		5	9	Scanlan	Neagle		51-41	1st	+5
7-20	At Hou.	L	8-11		12	12	Blair	Mason	D. Jones	51-42	1st	+4
7-21	At Hou.	L	3-4	(12)	7	11	D. Jones	Mason		51-43	1st	+3
7-22	At Hou.	W	10-7	(13)	18	14	Belinda	Blair	Patterson	52-43	1st	+4
7-24	At Atl.	L	3-4		4	7	Glavine	Walk	Pena	52-44	1st	+3
7-25	At Atl.	L	0-1		5	1	Leibrandt	Jackson	Mercker	52-45	1st	+2
7-26	At Atl.	W	5-4		9	8	Belinda	Wohlers		53-45	1st	+2
7-27	At Chi.	L	2-3		6	9	Maddux	Drabek	Robinson	53-46	1st	+1
7-28	At Chi.	L	1-11		8	18	Morgan	Tomlin		53-47	T1st	...
7-29	At Chi.	L	4-6	(11)	9	10	Assenmacher	Belinda		53-48	T1st	...
7-30	St.L.	W	4-0		8	8	Jackson	Clark	Patterson	54-48	T1st	...
7-31	St.L.	W	3-2		5	6	Wakefield	DeLeon		55-48	1st	+1
8-1	St.L.	W	4-1		10	6	Drabek	Olivares		56-48	1st	+2
8-2	St.L.	W	2-1		7	6	Walk	L. Smith		57-48	1st	+2
8-4	N.Y.	W	3-2	(12)	10	8	Walk	Filer		58-48	1st	+2½
8-5	N.Y.	W	6-2		7	7	Wakefield	Schourek		59-48	1st	+2½
8-6	At St.L.	W	3-2	(13)	11	12	Mason	L. Smith	Neagle	60-48	1st	+2½
8-7	At St.L.	W	5-1		9	5	Tomlin	Cormier		61-48	1st	+3½
8-8	At St.L.	W	2-1		7	8	Walk	Tewksbury	Belinda	62-48	1st	+3½
8-9	At St.L.	W	7-5		9	12	Mason	Clark	Walk	63-48	1st	+3½
8-10	At N.Y.	W	7-5	(16)	17	9	Cooke	Guetterman		64-48	1st	+3½
8-11	At N.Y.	L	0-2		6	7	Hillman	Drabek	Franco	64-49	1st	+2½
8-12	At N.Y.	W	7-6	(10)	12	12	Neagle	Franco	Patterson	65-49	1st	+2½
8-14	Atl.	L	0-15		6	22	Glavine	Smith		65-50	1st	+1½
8-15	Atl.	L	5-7		12	9	Avery	Jackson	Pena	65-51	1st	+1½
8-16	Atl.	W	4-2		7	7	Wakefield	Smoltz		66-51	1st	+2½
8-17	Atl.	L	4-5	(10)	5	12	Freeman	Patterson	Pena	66-52	1st	+2
8-18	S.D.	W	5-1		6	8	Tomlin	Benes		67-52	1st	+3
8-19	S.D.	W	3-2		8	9	Walk	Deshaies	Cox	68-52	1st	+4
8-20	S.D.	W	7-1		12	5	Jackson	Lefferts		69-52	1st	+4
8-21	At S.F.	L	5-6		9	8	Burkett	Wakefield	Beck	69-53	1st	+3
8-22	At S.F.	W	9-2		13	5	Drabek	Oliveras		70-53	1st	+3
8-23	At S.F.	L	2-5		7	9	Black	Tomlin		70-54	1st	+3
8-24	At L.A.	L	4-5		10	9	Gott	Neagle	Candelaria	70-55	1st	+2½
8-25	At L.A.	W	10-3		13	9	Cox	R. Martinez		71-55	1st	+2½
8-26	At L.A.	W	2-0		9	6	Wakefield	Candiotti		72-55	1st	+2½
8-28	At S.D.	L	6-11		9	15	Maddux	Drabek		72-56	1st	+2½
8-29	At S.D.	W	3-2		8	7	Tomlin	Gr. Harris	Mason	73-56	1st	+3½
8-30	At S.D.	W	6-3		11	6	Walk	Deshaies		74-56	1st	+3½
9-1	S.F.	W	5-3		9	7	Jackson	Burkett	Mason	75-56	1st	+3
9-2	S.F.	W	3-2		9	9	Wakefield	Black	Patterson	76-56	1st	+3
9-3	S.F.	W	9-3		14	10	Drabek	Brantley		77-56	1st	+3
9-4	L.A.	W	6-5		11	7	Patterson	Gott		78-56	1st	+3
9-5	L.A.	W	6-1		10	6	Walk	Hershiser		79-56	1st	+4
9-6	L.A.	L	5-7		9	13	Candiotti	Cox	Howell	79-57	1st	+4
9-7	Chi.	L	5-6	(11)	10	21	Assenmacher	Belinda	Scanlan	79-58	1st	+4
9-8	Chi.	W	5-2		8	3	Drabek	Boskie		80-58	1st	+4
9-9	Chi.	W	13-8		13	14	Cox	Robinson		81-58	1st	+5
9-11	At Phi.	L	2-5		6	9	Rivera	Walk	Mit. Williams	81-59	1st	+4
9-12	At Phi.	W	9-7		12	11	Belinda	Mit. Williams		82-59	1st	+4
9-13	At Phi.	L	3-6		6	11	Mulholland	Patterson		82-60	1st	+3
9-14	At St.L.	W	5-4	(10)	14	9	Drabek	L. Smith	Belinda	83-60	1st	+4
9-15	At St.L.	W	4-2		8	7	Wagner	Clark	Cox	84-60	1st	+4

Date	Opp.	Res.	Score	(inn.*)	Hits	Opp. hits	Winning pitcher	Losing pitcher	Save	Record	Pos.	GB
9-16	Mon.	L	3-6		10	10	Nabholz	Walk	Wetteland	84-61	1st	+3
9-17	Mon.	W	3-2	(13)	13	10	Cox	Bottenfield		85-61	1st	+4
9-18	Phi.	W	5-2	(5½)	8	6	Wakefield	Mulholland		86-61	1st	+4
9-19	Phi.	W	3-0		10	8	Drabek	Greene		87-61	1st	+5
9-20	Phi.	W	3-2	(13)	10	10	Mason	Shepherd		88-61	1st	+6
9-21	St.L.	W	3-0		9	4	Cooke	Magrane		89-61	1st	+7
9-22	St.L.	L	4-5		8	10	Cormier	Jackson	L. Smith	89-62	1st	+7
9-23	At Mon.	L	1-5	(14)	5	9	Fassero	Mason		89-63	1st	+6
9-24	At Mon.	W	9-3		14	7	Drabek	Krueger		90-63	1st	+7
9-25	N.Y.	W	3-2		8	9	Tomlin	Fernandez	Cox	91-63	1st	+7
9-26	N.Y.	W	19-2		20	10	Walk	Hillman		92-63	1st	+7
9-27	N.Y.	W	4-2		7	7	Jackson	Schourek	Belinda	93-63	1st	+7
9-28	At Chi.	W	10-3		13	5	Wakefield	Bullinger		94-63	1st	+8
9-29	At Chi.	W	3-0		7	2	Wagner	Castillo	Belinda	95-63	1st	+9
9-30	At Chi.	L	0-6		7	11	Maddux	Tomlin		95-64	1st	+9
10-2	At N.Y.	L	3-6		7	12	Schourek	Drabek	Jones	95-65	1st	+9
10-3	At N.Y.	L	1-2		4	5	Gooden	Jackson		95-66	1st	+8
10-4	At N.Y.	W	2-0		4	3	Wakefield	Saberhagen	Cooke	96-66	1st	+9

Monthly records: April (15-5), May (11-17), June (17-11), July (12-15), August (19-8), September (21-8), Oct. (1-2).

HIGHLIGHTS

High point: A 14-3 start that carried the Pirates through an ensuing 39-45 tailspin that stretched to July 29. It marked the third consecutive year that the Pirates had ridden a hot start to a divisional title.

Low point: Losing 11 of 12 games from May 15-27, Pittsburgh was out of first place for more than two days for the first time since the opening weeks of the 1991 season.

Turning point: An 11-game winning streak from July 30 through August 10 broke a first-place tie with Montreal and sent the Pirates winging to a 43-18 finish.

Most valuable player: Left fielder Barry Bonds. He won the league's MVP honor for the second time, batting .311 with 39 stolen bases, 103 RBIs, a career-high 34 homers and a league-leading 109 runs scored. He also had the second 30-30 performance of his career and captured his third straight Gold Glove award.

Most valuable pitcher: Righthander Doug Drabek. His 15-11 record wasn't flashy, but he set career highs for innings pitched (256⅔), strikeouts (177) and complete games (10).

Most improved player: Center fielder Andy Van Slyke. His bad back forced him to alter his swing, and he proceeded to raise his average 59 points overall and hit .297 against lefthanders, 79 points better than his career average.

Most pleasant surprise: Righthander Tim Wakefield. A desperate search for starting pitchers led the Pirates to call up the knuckleball specialist July 31. He went 8-1 with a 2.15 ERA and won both of his playoff starts.

Biggest disappointment: For the third consecutive year, the Pirates lost in the playoffs. This time, defeat came with two out in the ninth inning of Game 7 after the Bucs had begun the inning with a 2-0 lead.

Key injuries: Zane Smith basically disappeared after the All-Star break with tendinitis in his left shoulder. The Pirates' shortage of pitching was aggravated by the absence of Vicente Palacios for most of the season with arm problems. Bob Walk spent two stretches on the disabled list with groin-muscle pulls.

Notable: The Pirates used 21 pitchers in 1992; 18 won at least one game. . . . The Pirates are the only N.L. team to post winning records in each season of the 1990s.

—JOHN MEHNO

RECORDS

1992 regular-season record: 96-66 (1st in N.L. East); 53-28 at home; 43-38 on road; 61-29 vs. East; 35-37 vs. West; 36-29 vs. LHP; 60-37 vs. RHP; 19-23 on grass; 77-43 on turf; 26-21 in daytime; 70-45 at night; 37-25 in one-run games; 14-8 in extra-inning games; 0-0 in doubleheaders.

1992 postseason record: Lost to Braves, 4 games to 3, in N.L. playoffs.

Team record last five years: 448-360 (.554, ranks 1st in league in that span).

TEAM LEADERS

Batting average: Andy Van Slyke (.324).
At-bats: Jay Bell (632).
Runs: Barry Bonds (109).
Hits: Andy Van Slyke (199).
Total bases: Andy Van Slyke (310).
Doubles: Andy Van Slyke (45).
Triples: Andy Van Slyke (12).
Home runs: Barry Bonds (34).
Runs batted in: Barry Bonds (103).
Stolen bases: Barry Bonds (39).
Slugging percentage: Barry Bonds (.624).
On-base percentage: Barry Bonds (.456).
Wins: Doug Drabek (15).
Earned-run average: Doug Drabek (2.77).
Complete games: Doug Drabek (10).
Shutouts: Doug Drabek (4).
Saves: Stan Belinda (18).
Innings pitched: Doug Drabek (256⅔).
Strikeouts: Doug Drabek (177).

GAMES BY POSITION

Catcher: Mike LaValliere 92, Don Slaught 79, Tom Prince 19.
First base: Orlando Merced 114, Gary Redus 36, Jeff King 32, Lloyd McClendon 18, John Wehner 13, Kevin Young 1.
Second base: Jose Lind 134, Jeff King 32, Carlos Garcia 14, John Wehner 5.
Third base: Steve Buechele 80, Jeff King 73, John Wehner 34, Kevin Young 7, Mike LaValliere 1, Tom Prince 1.
Shortstop: Jay Bell 159, Carlos Garcia 8, Jeff King 6.
Outfield: Andy Van Slyke 154, Barry Bonds 139, Cecil Espy 82, Lloyd McClendon 60, Alex Cole 53, Gary Varsho 44, Orlando Merced 17, Gary Redus 15, Kirk Gibson 13, William Pennyfeather 10, Dave Clark 8, Al Martin 7, Jeff King 1.

TOP 10 DRAFT CHOICES

1a. Jason Kendall, C, Torrance (Calif.) High School.
1b. Shon Walker, OF, Harrison County High School, Cynthiana, Ky.
2a. Danny Clyburn, OF, Lancaster (S.C.) Senior High School.
2b. Trey Beamon, OF, W.T. White High School, Dallas.
3. Jamie Keefe, SS, Spaulding High School, Rochester, N.H.
4. Tim Leger, OF, Acadiana High School, Lafayette, La.
5. Brett Backlund, RHP, University of Iowa.
6. Sean Lawrence, LHP, College of St. Francis (Ill.).
7. Dennis Konuszewski, RHP, University of Michigan.
8. Aaron Cannaday, C, Elon College (N.C.).
9. Rod Davidson, LHP, Rustburg (Va.) High School.
10. John Turlais, C, Illinois Mathematics and Science Academy, Aurora, Ill.

1993 SCHEDULE

APRIL

SUN	MON	TUE	WED	THU *	FRI	SAT
				1	2	3
4	5	6 N SF	7 N SF	8 N SF	9 N CIN	10 N H
11 N CIN	12	13 LA	14 N LA	15 N LA	16 N SD	17 N SD
18 N SD	19	20 N COL	21 N COL	22 N COL	23 N ATL	24 N ATL H
25 ATL H	26 N HOU	27 HOU	28 N COL	29 COL	30 ATL	

MAY

SUN	MON	TUE	WED	THU	FRI	SAT
						1 ATL
2 ATL	3	4 N HOU H	5 N HOU H	6	7 N PHI	8 N PHI H
9 PHI	10	11 N NY H	12 N NY H	13 N NY	14 N FLA H	15 N FLA H
16 FLA N	17	18 N CHI	19 N CHI H	20 N CHI H	21 N PIT	22 N PIT
23 PIT	24 N MON	25 N MON	26 N MON	27	28 N SD	29 N SD H
30 SD H	31 N LA H					

JUNE

SUN	MON	TUE	WED	THU	FRI	SAT
		1 N LA H	2 N LA H	3 N CIN	4 N CIN	5 N CIN
6 CIN	7	8 N SF	9 N SF	10 N MON H	11 N MON H	12 N MON H
13 MON H	14 N PIT H	15 N PIT H	16 N PIT H	17 N CHI	18 CHI	19 CHI
20 CHI	21 FLA	22 N FLA	23 N FLA	24	25 N NY	26 NY
27 NY	28 N PHI H	29 N PHI H	30 N PHI H			

JULY

SUN	MON	TUE	WED	THU	FRI	SAT
				1 N PHI	2 N HOU	3 N HOU
4 HOU	5 HOU	6 N ATL H	7 N ATL H	8 N ATL H	9 N COL H	10 N COL H
11 COL H	12	13 * ALL-STAR GAME	14	15 N HOU H	16 N HOU H	17 N HOU H
18 HOU H	19 N ATL	20 N ATL	21 N ATL	22 N COL	23 N COL	24 N COL
25 COL	26	27 N PHI	28 N PHI	29 N PHI	30 N NY H	31 N NY H

AUGUST

SUN	MON	TUE	WED	THU	FRI	SAT
1 NY H	2 N FLA H	3 N FLA H	4 N FLA H	5 N FLA H	6 N CHI H	7 N CHI H
8 CHI H	9 N PIT	10 N PIT	11 N PIT	12 N PIT	13 N MON	14 N MON
15 MON	16	17 N SD	18 N SD H	19 N SD H	20 N LA H	21 N LA H
22 LA H	23 N SD	24 N SD	25 SD	26	27 N LA	28 N LA
29 LA	30 N CIN	31 N CIN H				

SEPTEMBER

SUN	MON	TUE	WED	THU	FRI	SAT
			1 N CIN H	2 CIN	3 N SF H	4 N SF
5 SF H	6	7 N CIN	8 N CIN H	9 N SF	10 N SF	11 SF
12 SF	13	14 N MON H	15 N MON H	16 N MON H	17 N PIT H	18 N PIT H
19 PIT H	20 N CHI	21 N CHI	22 CHI	23	24 N FLA	25 N FLA
26 FLA	27 N NY	28 N NY	29 N NY	30 N NY		

OCTOBER

SUN	MON	TUE	WED	THU	FRI	SAT
					1 N PHI H	2 N PHI H
3 PHI H						

1993 SEASON

CLUB DIRECTORY

Chairman of the board
August A. Busch III
Vice chairman
Fred L. Kuhlmann
President and chief executive officer
Stuart F. Meyer
Vice president, business operations
Mark Gorris
Controller
Brad Wood
Vice president, general manager
Dal Maxvill
Admin. asst. to the president and CEO
Elaine Milo
Admin. asst. to the v.p., general manager
Judy Carpenter Barada
Admin. asst., business operations
Renee Garrett
Vice president, marketing
Marty Hendin
Admin. asst. to the v.p., marketing
Mary Ellen Edmiston
Director of promotions
Nancy Trammell
Director of player development
Mike Jorgensen
Director of scouting
Fred McAlister
Assistant director of scouting
Marty Maier
Asst. to player development and scouting
Scott Smulczenski
Director of public relations
Jeff Wehling
Public relations manager
Brian Bartow
Dir. of broadcasting and market develop.
Dan Farrell
Promotions supervisor
Thane Van Breusegen
Director of community relations
Joe Cunningham
Director of group sales
Joe Strohm
Director, target marketing
Ted Savage

Director, ticket systems
Josephine Arnold
Director, human resources
Marian Rhodes
Director, ticket services
Kevin Wade
Director, tickets and office administration
Colin Allsop
Manager, office services
Patti McCormick
Traveling secretary
C.J. Cherre
Club physician
Dr. Stan London
Scouting supervisors
Jorge Aranzamendi
Jim Bayens
Jim Belz
Randy Benson
Marty Keough
Tom McCormack
Joe Morlan
Joe Rigoli
Mike Roberts
Hal Smith
Special assignment scouts
Jack Hubbard
Rube Walker
Regular scouts
James Brown
Roy Cromer
Roberto Diaz
John DiPuglia
Manuel Espinosa
Cecil Espy
Manuel Guerra
Charles Menzhuber
Scott Nichols
Jay North
Ramon Ortiz
Jim Pamlanye
Joe Popek
Roger Smith
Kenneth Thomas

SCHEDULE KEY

H—Home game.　　N—Night game (any game starting after 5 p.m.).
*All-Star Game at Oriole Park at Camden Yards, Baltimore.

Manager—Joe Torre (9).

Coaches—Chris Chambliss (10), Joe Coleman (40), Dave Collins (15), Bucky Dent (30), Gaylen Pitts (4), Red Schoendienst (2).

No.	PITCHERS	B/T	Ht./Wt.	Born	1992 clubs
55	Clark, Mark	R/R	6-5/225	5-12-68	Louisville, St. Louis
65	Compres, Fidel	R/R	6-0/165	5-10-65	Arkansas
52	Cormier, Rheal	L/L	5-10/185	4-23-67	Louisville, St. Louis
35	Dixon, Steve	L/L	6-0/190	8-3-69	Arkansas, Louisville
62	Eversgerd, Bryan	R/L	6-1/190	2-11-69	St. Petersburg, Arkansas
	Lancaster, Les	R/R	6-2/200	4-21-62	Detroit
32	Magrane, Joe	R/L	6-6/230	7-2-64	St. Petersburg, Louisville, St. Louis
53	Milchin, Mike	L/L	6-3/190	2-28-68	Louisville
50	Murphy, Rob	L/L	6-2/215	5-26-60	Houston
00	Olivares, Omar	R/R	6-1/193	7-6-67	St. Louis
31	Osborne, Donovan	L/L	6-2/195	6-21-69	St. Louis
42	Perez, Mike	R/R	6-0/187	10-19-64	St. Louis
47	Smith, Lee	R/R	6-6/269	12-4-57	St. Louis
39	Tewksbury, Bob	R/R	6-4/208	11-30-60	St. Louis
41	Urbani, Tom	L/L	6-1/190	1-21-68	Arkansas, Louisville

No.	CATCHERS	B/T	Ht./Wt.	Born	1992 clubs
66	Ellis, Paul	L/R	6-2/205	11-12-68	St. Petersburg, Arkansas
25	Fulton, Ed	L/R	6-0/195	1-7-66	Arkansas, Louisville
19	Pagnozzi, Tom	R/R	6-1/190	7-30-62	St. Louis
67	Ronan, Marc	L/R	6-2/190	9-19-69	Springfield
29	Villanueva, Hector	R/R	6-1/220	10-2-64	Chicago N.L., Iowa

No.	INFIELDERS	B/T	Ht./Wt.	Born	1992 clubs
18	Alicea, Luis	B/R	5-9/177	7-29-65	Louisville, St. Louis
60	Andujar, Juan	B/R	6-0/150	8-14-71	St. Petersburg
33	Brewer, Rod	L/L	6-3/218	2-24-66	Louisville, St. Louis
44	Cromer, Tripp	R/R	6-2/165	11-21-67	Arkansas, Louisville
8	Jones, Tim	L/R	5-10/175	12-1-62	St. Louis
11	Oquendo, Jose	B/R	5-10/171	7-4-63	St. Louis, Arkansas, Louisville
21	Pena, Geronimo	B/R	6-1/195	3-29-67	St. Louis, Louisville
28	Perry, Gerald	L/R	6-0/201	10-30-60	St. Louis
5	Royer, Stan	R/R	6-3/221	8-31-67	Louisville, St. Louis
1	Smith, Ozzie	B/R	5-10/168	12-26-54	St. Louis
12	Wilson, Craig	R/R	5-11/208	11-28-64	St. Louis, Louisville
54	Woodson, Tracy	R/R	6-3/216	10-5-62	Louisville, St. Louis
27	Zeile, Todd	R/R	6-1/190	9-9-65	St. Louis, Louisville

No.	OUTFIELDERS	B/T	Ht./Wt.	Born	1992 clubs
46	Canseco, Ozzie	R/R	6-3/220	7-2-64	Louisville, St. Louis
61	Coleman, Paul	R/R	5-11/200	12-9-70	St. Petersburg
23	Gilkey, Bernard	R/R	6-0/190	9-24-66	St. Louis
3	Jordan, Brian	R/R	6-1/205	3-29-67	Louisville, St. Louis
34	Jose, Felix	B/R	6-1/221	5-8-65	Louisville, St. Petersburg, St. Louis
16	Lankford, Ray	L/L	5-11/198	6-5-67	St. Louis
51	Maclin, Lonnie	L/L	5-11/185	2-17-67	Louisville

Ballpark (capacity, surface)
Busch Stadium (56,627, artificial)

Address
250 Stadium Plaza
St. Louis, MO 63102

Business phone
314-421-3060

Ticket information
314-421-3060

Ticket prices
$12 (box)
$9.50 (reserved)
$5.50 (general admission)
$4 (bleachers)

Field dimensions (from home plate)
To left field at foul line, 330 feet
To center field, 402 feet
To right field at foul line, 330 feet

First game played
May 12, 1966 (Cardinals 4, Braves 3)

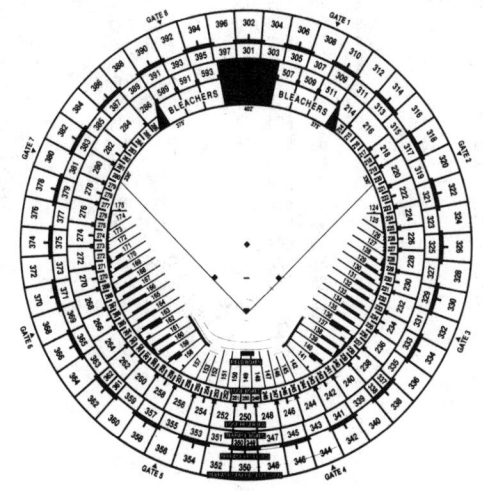

MINOR LEAGUE AFFILIATES

Class	Team	League	Manager
AAA	Louisville	American Association	Jack Krol
AA	Arkansas	Texas	Joe Pettini
A	St. Petersburg	Florida State	Terry Kennedy
A	Springfield	Midwest	Mike Ramsey
A	Savannah	South Atlantic	Chris Maloney
A	Glens Falls	New York-Pennsylvania	Steve Turco
Rookie	Johnson City	Appalachian	Joe Cunningham III
Rookie	Chandler Cardinals	Arizona	Roy Silver

BROADCAST INFORMATION

Radio: KMOX-AM (1120). Broadcasters: Jack Buck, Mike Shannon, Joe Buck.
TV: KPLR-TV (Channel 11). Broadcasters: Joe Buck, Al Hrabosky.
Cable TV: None.

SPRING TRAINING

Ballpark (city): Al Lang Stadium (St. Petersburg, Fla.).
Ticket information: 813-896-4641.

HISTORY

YEAR-BY-YEAR RECORDS

Year	Pos.	W	L	Pct.	*GB	Year	Pos.	W	L	Pct.	*GB
1901	4th	76	64	.543	14½	1949	2nd	96	58	.623	1
1902	6th	56	78	.418	44½	1950	5th	78	75	.510	12½
1903	8th	43	94	.314	46½	1951	3rd	81	73	.526	15½
1904	5th	75	79	.487	31½	1952	3rd	88	66	.571	8½
1905	6th	58	96	.377	47½	1953	T3rd	83	71	.539	22
1906	7th	52	98	.347	63	1954	6th	72	82	.468	25
1907	8th	52	101	.340	55½	1955	7th	68	86	.442	30½
1908	8th	49	105	.318	50	1956	4th	76	78	.494	17
1909	7th	54	98	.355	56	1957	2nd	87	67	.565	8
1910	7th	63	90	.412	40½	1958	T5th	72	82	.468	20
1911	5th	75	74	.503	22	1959	7th	71	83	.461	16
1912	6th	63	90	.412	41	1960	3rd	86	68	.558	9
1913	8th	51	99	.340	49	1961	5th	80	74	.519	13
1914	3rd	81	72	.529	13	1962	6th	84	78	.519	17½
1915	6th	72	81	.471	18½	1963	2nd	93	69	.574	6
1916	T7th	60	93	.392	33½	1964	1st	93	69	.574	+ 1
1917	3rd	82	70	.539	15	1965	7th	80	81	.497	16½
1918	8th	51	78	.395	33	1966	6th	83	79	.512	12
1919	7th	54	83	.394	40½	1967	1st	101	60	.627	+10½
1920	T5th	75	79	.487	18	1968	1st	97	65	.599	+ 9
1921	3rd	87	66	.569	7	1969	4th	87	75	.537	13
1922	T3rd	85	69	.552	8	1970	4th	76	86	.469	13
1923	5th	79	74	.516	16	1971	2nd	90	72	.556	7
1924	6th	65	89	.422	28½	1972	4th	75	81	.481	21½
1925	4th	77	76	.503	18	1973	2nd	81	81	.500	1½
1926	1st	89	65	.578	+ 2	1974	2nd	86	75	.534	1½
1927	2nd	92	61	.601	1½	1975	T3rd	82	80	.506	10½
1928	1st	95	59	.617	+ 2	1976	5th	72	90	.444	29
1929	4th	78	74	.513	20	1977	3rd	83	79	.512	18
1930	1st	92	62	.597	+ 2	1978	5th	69	93	.426	21
1931	1st	101	53	.656	+13	1979	3rd	86	76	.531	12
1932	T6th	72	82	.468	18	1980	4th	74	88	.457	17
1933	5th	82	71	.536	9½	1981	2nd/2nd	59	43	.578	‡
1934	1st	95	58	.621	+ 2	1982	1st§	92	70	.568	+ 3
1935	2nd	96	58	.623	4	1983	4th	79	83	.488	11
1936	T2nd	87	67	.565	5	1984	3rd	84	78	.519	12½
1937	4th	81	73	.526	15	1985	1st§	101	61	.623	+ 3
1938	6th	71	80	.470	17½	1986	3rd	79	82	.491	28½
1939	2nd	92	61	.601	4½	1987	1st§	95	67	.586	+ 3
1940	3rd	84	69	.549	16	1988	5th	76	86	.469	25
1941	2nd	97	56	.634	2½	1989	3rd	86	76	.531	7
1942	1st	106	48	.688	+ 2	1990	6th	70	92	.432	25
1943	1st	105	49	.682	+18	1991	2nd	84	78	.519	14
1944	1st	105	49	.682	+14½	1992	3rd	83	79	.512	13
1945	2nd	95	59	.617	3						
1946	1st†	98	58	.628	+ 2						
1947	2nd	89	65	.578	5						
1948	2nd	85	69	.552	6½						

*Games behind winner. †Won pennant playoff. ‡First half 30-20; second 29-23. §Won Championship Series.

MANAGERS

Name	Record	Years
Patsy Donovan	175-236	'01-03
Kid Nichols	94-108	'04-05
Jimmy Burke	17-32	1905
Stanley Robison	22-35	1905
John McCloskey	153-304	'06-08
Roger Bresnahan	255-352	'09-12
Miller Huggins	346-415	'13-17
Jack Hendricks	51-78	1918
Branch Rickey	458-485	'19-25
Rogers Hornsby	153-116	'25-26
Bob O'Farrell	92-61	1927
Bill McKechnie	129-88	'28-29
Billy Southworth	620-346	1929
		'40-45
Gabby Street	312-242	'30-33
Frank Frisch	458-354	'33-38
Mike Gonzalez	9-13	'38,'40
Ray Blades	106-85	'39-40
Eddie Dyer	446-325	'46-50
Marty Marion	81-73	1951
Eddie Stanky	260-238	'52-55
Harry Walker	51-67	1955
Fred Hutchinson	232-220	'56-58
Stan Hack	3-7	1958
Solly Hemus	190-192	'59-61
Johnny Keane	317-249	'61-64
Red Schoendienst	1028-944	'65-76
		1980
Vern Rapp	89-90	'77-78
Ken Boyer	166-190	'78-80
Whitey Herzog	835-739	1980
		'81-90
Joe Torre	191-191	'90-92

1992 REVIEW

DAY BY DAY

Date	Opp.	Res.	Score	(inn.*)	Hits	Opp. hits	Winning pitcher	Losing pitcher	Save	Record	Pos.	GB
4-6	N.Y.	L	2-4	(10)	6	9	Innis	L. Smith	Franco	0-1	T5th	1
4-7	N.Y.	W	9-2		13	8	Olivares	Saberhagen		1-1	T3rd	½
4-8	N.Y.	W	15-7		15	7	Perez	Fernandez		2-1	2nd	½
4-9	N.Y.	L	1-7		6	13	Young	Agosto		2-2	T3rd	½
4-10	At Chi.	W	2-1	(11)	5	7	Carpenter	Assenmacher	L. Smith	3-2	2nd	½
4-11	At Chi.	L	1-5		4	10	Boskie	DeLeon	McElroy	3-3	4th	½
4-12	At Chi.	L	2-4		11	6	Maddux	Olivares	Slocumb	3-4	5th	1½
4-13	At Mon.	L	2-3		11	8	Gardner	Cormier	Wetteland	3-5	5th	2½
4-14	At Mon.	W	3-1		6	8	Osborne	Nabholz	L. Smith	4-5	4th	2
4-15	At Mon.	W	4-2		7	6	Tewksbury	Hill	L. Smith	5-5	3rd	2
4-18	Chi.	L	4-5		8	6	Boskie	Olivares	McElroy	5-6	3rd	3½
4-19	Chi.	W	4-3		8	9	DeLeon	Jackson	L. Smith	6-6	2nd	3½
4-21	At N.Y.	L	2-4		6	7	Gooden	Cormier	Franco	6-7	3rd	5
4-22	At N.Y.	L	2-3		5	9	Innis	Carpenter		6-8	4th	6
4-23	At N.Y.	L	0-1	(13)	8	6	Franco	Agosto		6-9	5th	6
4-24	Mon.	W	4-3		10	8	Olivares	Wetteland		7-9	3rd	6
4-25	Mon.	W	2-1	(17)	15	8	Tewksbury	Rojas		8-9	3rd	6
4-26	Mon.	L	0-6		5	9	Haney	Cormier		8-10	3rd	6
4-27	At L.A.	W	5-4		13	9	Osborne	Ke. Gross	L. Smith	9-10	3rd	5½
4-28	At L.A.	W	2-1	(10)	9	9	Worrell	Gott	L. Smith	10-10	3rd	4½
4-29	At S.F.	W	2-1	(12)	11	9	Perez	Righetti	L. Smith	11-10	3rd	4½
4-30	At S.F.	L	3-9		6	11	Burkett	DeLeon		11-11	3rd	5
5-1	At S.D.	L	5-7		10	13	Rodriguez	Worrell	Myers	11-12	3rd	5
5-2	At S.D.	W	3-0		8	4	Osborne	Hurst	L. Smith	12-12	3rd	5
5-3	At S.D.	W	7-1		12	6	Tewksbury	Eiland		13-12	3rd	4
5-5	S.F.	W	7-5		11	9	Perez	Burba	L. Smith	14-12	3rd	4½
5-6	S.F.	W	5-4	(11)	13	9	Agosto	Righetti		15-12	3rd	4½
5-7	S.F.	L	0-2		4	7	Swift	Osborne		15-13	3rd	4½
5-8	Atl.	L	1-2		7	9	Leibrandt	Tewksbury	Freeman	15-14	3rd	5½
5-9	Atl.	W	12-11		15	13	Perez	Freeman	L. Smith	16-14	3rd	5½
5-10	Atl.	W	6-5		12	11	Agosto	Pena		17-14	3rd	4½
5-11	Atl.	W	8-3		13	9	DeLeon	Avery		18-14	3rd	4
5-12	Cin.	W	6-4		10	9	Osborne	Swindell	L. Smith	19-14	3rd	3
5-13	Cin.	W	4-2		7	8	Tewksbury	Bankhead	L. Smith	20-14	2nd	3
5-15	At Hou.	W	7-5		15	7	McClure	D. Jones	L. Smith	21-14	2nd	2½
5-16	At Hou.	L	2-3		7	7	D. Jones	Agosto		21-15	2nd	2½
5-17	At Hou.	W	7-5		11	10	Carpenter	D. Jones	L. Smith	22-15	2nd	1½
5-18	At Atl.	L	1-5		6	12	Leibrandt	Osborne		22-16	2nd	2
5-19	At Atl.	W	7-2		11	8	Tewksbury	Smoltz		23-16	2nd	1
5-20	At Atl.	L	3-6		5	10	Avery	Cormier		23-17	2nd	1
5-22	Hou.	L	1-3		2	8	Portugal	DeLeon	D. Jones	23-18	2nd	1
5-23	Hou.	W	10-4		14	6	Osborne	Harnisch	Carpenter	24-18	2nd	½
5-24	Hou.	W	4-3		10	9	L. Smith	Osuna		25-18	1st	+½
5-25	L.A.	W	6-5		9	9	Worrell	McDowell		26-18	1st	+1½
5-26	L.A.	L	2-5		7	9	Ojeda	Olivares	Candelaria	26-19	1st	+1½
5-27	L.A.	L	2-9		5	12	Candiotti	DeLeon		26-20	1st	+1½
5-29	S.D.	L	1-2		8	5	Hurst	L. Smith	Myers	26-21	1st	+½
5-30	S.D.	W	5-1		12	4	Tewksbury	Lefferts		27-21	1st	+½
5-31	S.D.	L	0-10		2	12	Gr. Harris	Cormier		27-22	1st	+½
6-2	At Cin.	L	1-2		7	6	Belcher	DeLeon	Dibble	27-23	T1st	...
6-3	At Cin.	L	7-8		13	12	Ruskin	Carpenter	Charlton	27-24	T2nd	1
6-5	At Phi.	L	5-7		10	11	Jones	Worrell	Mit. Williams	27-25	2nd	2½
6-6	At Phi.	L	5-7		10	13	Hartley	McClure	Mit. Williams	27-26	3rd	2½
6-7	At Phi.	W	5-4		12	9	Worrell	Ayrault	L. Smith	28-26	2nd	2½
6-8 (1)	Chi.	L	2-5	(13)	8	10	Robinson	Agosto	Scanlan	28-27	2nd	2
6-8 (2)	Chi.	L	4-6		14	13	Castillo	DeLeon	Bullinger	28-28	2nd	2½
6-9	Chi.	W	6-5	(11)	17	15	Carpenter	Scanlan		29-28	T2nd	3
6-10	Chi.	L	2-4		3	7	Maddux	Clark		29-29	T2nd	4
6-12	Phi.	L	5-8		11	12	Ritchie	Osborne	Mit. Williams	29-30	T2nd	5
6-13	Phi.	W	4-1		4	8	Olivares	Schilling	L. Smith	30-30	2nd	5
6-14	Phi.	W	5-2		12	8	Cormier	Brink	L. Smith	31-30	2nd	5
6-15	At Chi.	L	1-7		4	11	Maddux	Tewksbury		31-31	2nd	5
6-16	At Chi.	L	1-2		4	7	Scanlan	Clark	Bullinger	31-32	T2nd	6
6-18	At N.Y.	W	8-3		16	5	Olivares	Schourek		32-32	2nd	5½
6-19	At N.Y.	L	3-4		10	9	Franco	Perez		32-33	T2nd	5½
6-20	At N.Y.	W	6-1		14	5	Tewksbury	Young		33-33	2nd	4½
6-21	At N.Y.	L	2-6		9	9	Cone	McClure		33-34	T2nd	5½
6-22	At Pit.	L	2-5		7	10	Tomlin	Osborne	Walk	33-35	T2nd	6½
6-23	At Pit.	L	4-6		7	9	Mason	Worrell	Patterson	33-36	T3rd	7½
6-24	At Pit.	W	4-1		11	12	Tewksbury	Drabek		34-36	3rd	6½

Date	Opp.	Res.	Score	(inn.*)	Hits	Opp. hits	Winning pitcher	Losing pitcher	Save	Record	Pos.	GB
6-26	N.Y.	W	4-3		11	3	L. Smith	Innis		35-36	2nd	5½
6-27	N.Y.	L	1-2	(11)	8	5	Franco	L. Smith		35-37	3rd	6½
6-28	N.Y.	W	3-2	(11)	9	6	Perez	Franco		36-37	2nd	5½
6-29	Pit.	W	3-1		9	7	Tewksbury	Cole		37-37	2nd	4½
6-30	Pit.	L	0-2		3	9	Drabek	Cormier		37-38	3rd	5½
7-1	Pit.	L	0-1		5	6	Smith	Clark		37-39	3rd	6½
7-2	At S.F.	W	1-0		6	4	Osborne	Swift	L. Smith	38-39	T2nd	5½
7-3	At S.F.	L	1-4		5	6	Burkett	Olivares		38-40	2nd	5
7-4	At S.F.	W	1-0	(13)	6	9	Perez	Beck	L. Smith	39-40	2nd	4½
7-5	At S.F.	L	1-3		8	8	Wilson	Cormier		39-41	T3rd	4½
7-6	At S.D.	W	4-0		12	4	Clark	Lefferts		40-41	2nd	4½
7-7	At S.D.	W	6-3		11	10	Osborne	Benes	L. Smith	41-41	T2nd	4½
7-8	At S.D.	W	1-0		9	6	Olivares	Myers	L. Smith	42-41	2nd	3½
7-9	At L.A.	L	1-2		4	11	R. Martinez	Tewksbury	McDowell	42-42	3rd	3½
7-10	At L.A.	W	3-1		8	7	Cormier	Candiotti	L. Smith	43-42	3rd	3½
7-11	At L.A.	W	4-1		11	7	Clark	Hershiser	L. Smith	44-42	2nd	3½
7-12	At L.A.	L	0-9		9	13	Ke. Gross	Osborne		44-43	2nd	4½
7-16	At Cin.	W	5-1		11	9	Olivares	Belcher	Worrell	45-43	2nd	4½
7-17	At Cin.	L	1-8		12	12	Swindell	Cormier		45-44	3rd	4½
7-18	At Cin.	L	2-3		8	9	Rijo	Tewksbury	Charlton	45-45	3rd	5½
7-19	At Cin.	L	4-5		9	8	Henry	Carpenter	Charlton	45-46	3rd	5½
7-21	Atl.	L	7-9	(12)	13	13	Pena	Perez		45-47	4th	5
7-22	Atl.	L	0-2		7	7	Smoltz	Olivares	Mercker	45-48	4th	6
7-23	Cin.	W	3-2		7	9	Cormier	Rijo	L. Smith	46-48	4th	5½
7-24	Cin.	W	8-2		13	10	Tewksbury	Hammond		47-48	4th	4½
7-25	Cin.	L	1-9		11	15	Bolton	Clark		47-49	4th	4½
7-26	Cin.	L	6-7	(10)	12	17	Dibble	Carpenter		47-50	4th	5½
7-27	Mon.	L	4-6		12	9	Hill	Olivares	Wetteland	47-51	T4th	5½
7-28	Mon.	L	4-7		9	15	Fassero	Osborne		47-52	5th	5½
7-29	Mon.	W	4-1		6	4	L. Smith	Martinez		48-52	5th	4½
7-30	At Pit.	L	0-4		8	8	Jackson	Clark	Patterson	48-53	5th	5½
7-31	At Pit.	L	2-3		6	5	Wakefield	DeLeon		48-54	5th	6½
8-1	At Pit.	L	1-4		6	10	Drabek	Olivares		48-55	5th	7½
8-2	At Pit.	L	1-2		6	7	Walk	L. Smith		48-56	5th	8
8-3	Phi.	W	2-1		6	4	Tewksbury	Abbott	L. Smith	49-56	5th	8
8-4	Phi.	W	9-5		14	9	McClure	Mit. Williams		50-56	5th	8
8-5	Phi.	W	5-4		10	9	Osborne	Ayrault	L. Smith	51-56	5th	8
8-6	Pit.	L	2-3	(13)	12	11	Mason	L. Smith	Neagle	51-57	5th	9
8-7	Pit.	L	1-5		5	9	Tomlin	Cormier		51-58	5th	10
8-8	Pit.	L	1-2		8	7	Walk	Tewksbury	Belinda	51-59	5th	11
8-9	Pit.	L	5-7		12	9	Mason	Clark	Walk	51-60	5th	12
8-11	At Phi.	W	7-6		15	8	Worrell	Mit. Williams	L. Smith	52-60	T4th	11½
8-12	At Phi.	W	3-2	(10)	10	9	Worrell	Mit. Williams	L. Smith	53-60	4th	11½
8-14	At Mon.	L	1-4		2	5	Martinez	Cormier	Wetteland	53-61	4th	11½
8-15	At Mon.	W	6-4		4	9	Tewksbury	Wetteland	L. Smith	54-61	4th	10½
8-16	At Mon.	W	5-2		4	5	Osborne	Barnes	L. Smith	55-61	4th	10½
8-18	Hou.	L	6-7		7	9	J. Jones	Olivares	D. Jones	55-62	4th	11
8-19	Hou.	W	12-1		17	4	Cormier	Kile		56-62	4th	11
8-20	Hou.	W	3-1		9	4	Tewksbury	Henry	L. Smith	57-62	4th	11
8-21	At Atl.	W	5-2	(10)	10	7	Perez	Mercker	L. Smith	58-62	4th	10
8-22	At Atl.	L	2-3		4	6	Smith	Clark		58-63	4th	11
8-23	At Atl.	W	8-3		13	11	Olivares	Leibrandt		59-63	4th	10
8-25	At Hou.	W	5-3	(13)	13	15	Carpenter	Boever	L. Smith	60-63	4th	9½
8-26	At Hou.	L	5-6	(10)	7	12	Hernandez	Perez		60-64	4th	10½
8-27	At Hou.	L	1-5		5	8	Williams	Osborne		60-65	4th	11
8-28	L.A.	W	1-0		4	3	Clark	Ojeda	L. Smith	61-65	4th	10
8-29	L.A.	W	3-2		6	8	Olivares	Ke. Gross	L. Smith	62-65	4th	10
8-30	L.A.	W	3-0		9	6	Cormier	Hershiser	L. Smith	63-65	4th	10
8-31	S.D.	W	6-2		10	7	Tewksbury	Lefferts		64-65	4th	9½
9-1	S.D.	W	2-0		7	6	Osborne	Benes	L. Smith	65-65	4th	9½
9-2	S.D.	L	4-5		12	12	Hurst	Clark	Myers	65-66	4th	10½
9-4	S.F.	L	3-4	(10)	12	11	Beck	L. Smith		65-67	4th	12
9-5	S.F.	W	4-0		7	7	Cormier	Burkett	Worrell	66-67	4th	12
9-6	S.F.	W	5-3		9	6	Tewksbury	Carter	Worrell	67-67	4th	11
9-7	At Mon.	W	8-7	(10)	14	13	B. Smith	Wetteland	L. Smith	68-67	4th	10
9-8	At Mon.	L	1-6		6	11	Barnes	Clark	Rojas	68-68	4th	11
9-9	At Mon.	W	10-3		16	9	Magrane	Hill		69-68	3rd	11
9-11	Chi.	L	2-8		10	15	Maddux	Olivares		69-69	4th	11
9-12	Chi.	W	11-3		13	10	Cormier	Morgan		70-69	3rd	11
9-13	Chi.	W	10-3		14	10	Tewksbury	Bullinger		71-69	3rd	10
9-14	Pit.	L	4-5	(10)	9	14	Drabek	L. Smith	Belinda	71-70	3rd	11
9-15	Pit.	L	2-4		7	8	Wagner	Clark	Cox	71-71	3rd	12
9-16	At N.Y.	W	10-4		12	7	Carpenter	Guetterman		72-71	3rd	11
9-17	At N.Y.	W	3-2		7	5	Perez	Young	L. Smith	73-71	3rd	11

Date	Opp.	Res.	Score	(inn.*)	Hits	Opp. hits	Winning pitcher	Losing pitcher	Save	Record	Pos.	GB
9-18	At Chi.	L	7-9		7	14	Robinson	B. Smith		73-72	3rd	12
9-19 (1)	At Chi.	L	5-6		14	10	Castillo	Osborne	Scanlan	73-73	4th	13
9-19 (2)	At Chi.	W	11-10	(10)	14	11	L. Smith	Assenmacher		74-73	3rd	12½
9-20	At Chi.	W	16-4		22	11	B. Smith	Boskie		75-73	3rd	12½
9-21	At Pit.	L	0-3		4	9	Cooke	Magrane		75-74	3rd	13½
9-22	At Pit.	W	5-4		10	8	Cormier	Jackson	L. Smith	76-74	3rd	12½
9-23	N.Y.	L	2-3		6	4	Gooden	L. Smith		76-75	3rd	12½
9-24	N.Y.	W	4-3	(14)	12	8	B. Smith	Whitehurst		77-75	3rd	12½
9-26 (1)	At Phi.	L	1-3		4	7	Schilling	Magrane		77-76	3rd	14
9-26 (2)	At Phi.	L	0-10		5	15	Rivera	Osborne		77-77	3rd	14½
9-27 (1)	At Phi.	W	8-1		11	4	Cormier	Brink		78-77	3rd	14½
9-27 (2)	At Phi.	L	5-6		9	15	Hartley	B. Smith	Mit. Williams	78-78	3rd	15
9-28	Mon.	W	4-1		13	5	Olivares	Krueger	L. Smith	79-78	3rd	15
9-29	Mon.	W	2-1	(10)	5	6	Perez	Valdez		80-78	3rd	15
9-30	Mon.	W	3-2	(11)	7	10	B. Smith	Fassero		81-78	3rd	14
10-2	Phi.	W	2-1		4	5	Osborne	Schilling	L. Smith	82-78	3rd	13
10-3	Phi.	L	2-3		7	9	Mathews	L. Smith	Mit. Williams	82-79	3rd	13
10-4	Phi.	W	6-3		12	10	Cormier	Greene	L. Smith	83-79	3rd	13

Monthly records: April (11-11), May (16-11), June (10-16), July (11-16), August (16-11), September (17-13), Oct. (2-1).

HIGHLIGHTS

High point: Despite winning just three of eight games from May 24-June 2, the Cardinals enjoyed their only stay in first place.

Low point: From June 30-September 21, St. Louis lost 13 games in a row to the Pirates. Ironically, the Cardinals finished 13 games behind Pittsburgh.

Turning point: Eight consecutive losses to the Pirates in back-to-back weekend series from July 30-August 9. During that span, the Cardinals dropped from 4½ games behind Pittsburgh to 12 games back.

Most valuable player: Center fielder Ray Lankford. He hit .293 with 20 homers, 40 doubles, 86 RBIs and 42 steals.

Most valuable pitcher: Righthander Bob Tewksbury. He had the league's best winning percentage (.762, 16-5) and second-best ERA (2.16), while his walks-per-nine-innings-pitched ratio (0.77) was the lowest in the majors since 1933.

Most improved players: Left fielder Bernard Gilkey and righthander Mike Perez. Gilkey became a regular by batting .302. Perez, a long shot to make the team, pitched in a club-record 77 games and had a 1.84 ERA.

Most pleasant surprise: Lefthander Donovan Osborne. He had not pitched above the Class AA level before the '92 season, but he finished second on the team with 11 wins.

Biggest disappointment: Third baseman Todd Zeile. He was so unproductive that he was banished to Class AAA Louisville on August 2 for 21 games. After driving in 81 runs in '91, he collected just 48 RBIs and hit .214 with men in scoring position last year.

Key injuries: Second baseman Jose Oquendo (shoulder, heel) played in just 14 games. First baseman Andres Galarraga broke his wrist in the second game of the season. When he returned in late May, it took him several months to regain the form he had displayed in spring training.

Notable: En route to winning his second straight Gold Glove, catcher Tom Pagnozzi tied the N.L. record for highest fielding percentage (minimum 100 games) by a catcher with a .999 mark. He also tied an N.L. mark for fewest errors (one) by a catcher.... A September 5 save against the Giants was righthander Todd Worrell's 128th as a Cardinal, making him the franchise's all-time leader. ... The 37-year-old Ozzie Smith won his 13th straight Gold Glove and led the team in steals (43).

—RICK HUMMEL

RECORDS

1992 regular-season record: 83-79 (3rd in N.L. East); 45-36 at home; 38-43 on road; 42-48 vs. East; 41-31 vs. West; 28-28 vs. LHP; 55-51 vs. RHP; 22-20 on grass; 61-59 on turf; 20-26 in daytime; 63-53 at night; 34-31 in one-run games; 16-10 in extra-inning games; 0-2-2 in doubleheaders.

Team record last five years: 399-411 (.493, ranks 9th in league in that span).

TEAM LEADERS

Batting average: Felix Jose, Ozzie Smith (.295).
At-bats: Ray Lankford (598).
Runs: Ray Lankford (87).
Hits: Ray Lankford (175).
Total bases: Ray Lankford (287).
Doubles: Ray Lankford (40).
Triples: Luis Alicea (11).
Home runs: Ray Lankford (20).
Runs batted in: Ray Lankford (86).
Stolen bases: Ozzie Smith (43).
Slugging percentage: Ray Lankford (.480).
On-base percentage: Ray Lankford (.371).
Wins: Bob Tewksbury (16).
Earned-run average: Bob Tewksbury (2.16).
Complete games: Bob Tewksbury (5).
Shutouts: Mark Clark (1).
Saves: Lee Smith (43).
Innings pitched: Bob Tewksbury (233).
Strikeouts: Omar Olivares (124).

GAMES BY POSITION

Catcher: Tom Pagnozzi 138, Rich Gedman 40.
First base: Andres Galarraga 90, Gerald Perry 29, Pedro Guerrero 28, Rod Brewer 27, Rex Hudler 8, Stan Royer 4, Tracy Woodson 3.
Second base: Luis Alicea 75, Geronimo Pena 57, Tim Jones 28, Rex Hudler 16, Craig Wilson 11, Jose Oquendo 9, Bien Figueroa 3.
Third base: Todd Zeile 124, Tracy Woodson 26, Craig Wilson 18, Stan Royer 5, Tim Jones 2.
Shortstop: Ozzie Smith 132, Tim Jones 34, Bien Figueroa 9, Jose Oquendo 5, Luis Alicea 4.
Outfield: Ray Lankford 153, Felix Jose 127, Bernard Gilkey 111, Brian Jordan 53, Milt Thompson 45, Chuck Carr 19, Rex Hudler 12, Pedro Guerrero 10, Ozzie Canseco 8, Rod Brewer 4, Craig Wilson 3, Tim Jones 1.

TOP 10 DRAFT CHOICES

1. **Sean Lowe**, RHP, Arizona State University.
2. **Mike Gulan**, 3B, Kent State University.
3. **Steve Montgomery**, RHP, Pepperdine University.
4. **Mark Williams**, C, Coral Springs (Fla.) High School.
5. **Jeff Alkire**, LHP, University of Miami (Fla.).
6. **Keith Johns**, SS, University of Mississippi.
7. **Mike Corominas**, LHP, Diamond Bar (Calif.) High School.
8. **Brian Carpenter**, RHP, Baylor University.
9. **Donnie Bellum**, OF, Albertson College of Idaho.
10. **Bert Green**, SS, Lafayette High School, Ballwin, Mo.

SAN DIEGO PADRES
NATIONAL LEAGUE WEST DIVISION

CLUB DIRECTORY

APRIL

SUN	MON	TUE	WED	THU	FRI	SAT
				1	2	3
4	5	6 N PIT	7	8 N PIT	9 N FLA	10 N FLA
11 FLA	12 PIT	13 N PIT	14 N PIT	15 N PIT	16 N STL	17 N STL
18 STL H	19	20 N PHI	21 N PHI	22 PHI	23 N NY	24 NY
25 NY	26 N MON H	27 N MON H	28 N PHI	29 N PHI	30 N NY H	

MAY

SUN	MON	TUE	WED	THU	FRI	SAT
						1 N NY H
2 NY H	3	4 N MON	5 N MON	6 N	7 CHI	8 N CHI
9 CHI	10 N CIN	11 N CIN	12 N CIN	13 N CIN	14 N SF	15 N SF H
16 N SF H	17 N COL H	18 N COL H	19 N COL H	20 N COL H	21 HOU H	22 N HOU H
23 HOU H	24 N LA	25 N LA	26 N LA	27	28 STL	29 STL
30 STL	31 N ATL					

JUNE

SUN	MON	TUE	WED	THU	FRI	SAT
		1 N ATL	2 N ATL	3 N ATL	4 N FLA H	5 N FLA H
6 FLA H	7 N ATL H	8 N ATL H	9	10 N LA H	11 N LA H	12 N LA H
13 LA H	14	15 N HOU	16 N HOU	17 N HOU	18 N COL	19 N COL
20 COL	21 N SF	22 N SF	23 N SF	24 N CIN H	25 N CIN H	26 N CIN H
27 CIN H	28 N CHI H	29 N CHI H	30 N CHI H			

JULY

SUN	MON	TUE	WED	THU	FRI	SAT
				1	2 N PHI	3 N PHI
4 N PHI	5 N NY	6 N NY	7 N NY	8 N MON	9 N MON	10 N MON
11 MON	12	13 ● ALL-STAR GAME	14	15 N PHI H	16 N PHI H	17 N PHI H
18 PHI H	19 N NY H	20 N NY H	21 N NY H	22 N MON H	23 N MON H	24 N MON H
25 MON H	26 N CHI	27 CHI	28 CHI	29	30 N CIN	31 N CIN

AUGUST

SUN	MON	TUE	WED	THU	FRI	SAT
1 CIN	2	3 N SF	4 N SF H	5 N SF H	6 DH N COL H	7
8 COL H	9 N HOU	10 N HOU H	11 N HOU H	12 N HOU H	13 N LA	14 N LA
15 LA	16	17 N STL	18 N STL	19	20 N PIT H	21
22 PIT H	23 N STL H	24 N STL H	25 N STL H	26	27 N PIT	28 N PIT
29 DH PIT	30	31 N FLA				

SEPTEMBER

SUN	MON	TUE	WED	THU	FRI	SAT
			1 N FLA	2 N FLA	3 N ATL	4 N ATL
5 ATL	6 N FLA H	7 N FLA H	8 N FLA H	9 N ATL H	10 N ATL H	11 N ATL H
12 ATL H	13 N LA H	14 N LA H	15 N LA H	16	17 N HOU	18 N HOU
19 HOU	20 N COL	21 N COL	22 N COL	23	24 N SF	25 N SF
26 SF	27 N CIN H	28 N CIN H	29 N CIN H	30		

OCTOBER

SUN	MON	TUE	WED	THU	FRI	SAT
					1 N CHI H	2 N CHI H
3 CHI H						

Chairman
Tom Werner
Vice chairmen
Art Engel
Russell Goldsmith
Art Rivkin
Partners
Malin Burnham
Bruce Corwin
John Earhart
Jack Goodall
Keith Matson
Michael Monk
Leon Parma
Robert Payne
Peter Peckham
Ernest Rady
Scott Wolfe
President
Dick Freeman
Executive v.p./baseball operations and g.m.
Joe McIlvaine
Senior vice president, business operations
Bill Adams
Vice president/finance
Bob Wells
Vice president/public relations
Andy Strasberg
Assistant vice president/assistant g.m.
John Barr
Special assistant to the general manager
Larry Doughty
Major league scouts
Ken Bracey
Carmen Fusco
Advance scout
Steve Lubratich
Director/administrative services
Lucy Freeman
Director/broadcasting
Paul Phipps
Director/marketing
Don Johnson
Director/media relations
Jim Ferguson
Director/minor leagues
Ed Lynch
Director/promotions
Tom Ryba
Director/scouting
Reggie Waller
Director/stadium operations
Doug Duennes
Director/ticket operations
Dave Gilmore

Director/ticket sales
Jack Autry
Director/video and special events
Mark Guglielmo
Controller
Bob Croasdale
Traveling secretary
John Mattei
Club physician
Scripps Clinic
National supervisor
Ross Sapp
East Coast supervisor
Damon Oppenheimer
Midwestern supervisor
Logan White
Scouting coordinators
Larry Harper
Joe Henderson
Area scouts
Dave Finley
Denny Galehouse
Ronquito Garcia
Joe Henderson
John Kosciak
Scott Lovekamp
Donnie Lyle
Kasey McKeon
Bobby Malkmus
Patrick Murtaugh
Pete Peterson
Hosken Powell
Bruce Seid
Greg Smith
Van Smith
Mario Soto
Scipio Spinks
Craig Weissmann
Part-time scouts
Pedro Avila
Mike Becker
Howard Bowens
Billy Castell
Julio Coronado
James Ford
Ben Goodman
Timothy Harkness
Cesar Jarquin
William Killian
Darryl Milne
Charlie Ready
Earl Smith
Harry Stricklett

SCHEDULE KEY

H—Home game.   DH—Doubleheader.
N—Night game (any game starting after 5 p.m.).
*All-Star Game at Oriole Park at Camden Yards, Baltimore.

Manager—Jim Riggleman (8).

Coaches—Dave Bialas (32), Bruce Bochy (13), Rob Picciolo (5), Dan Radison (22), Merv Rettenmund (16), Mike Roarke (36).

No.	PITCHERS	B/T	Ht./Wt.	Born	1992 clubs
40	Benes, Andy	R/R	6-6/240	8-20-67	San Diego
49	Brocail, Doug	L/R	6-5/220	5-16-67	Las Vegas, San Diego
39	Gomez, Pat	L/L	5-11/185	3-17-68	Richmond, Greenville
33	Harris, Gene	R/R	5-11/190	12-5-64	Seattle, San Diego, Las Vegas
46	Harris, Greg	R/R	6-2/195	12-1-63	San Diego, High Desert, Las Vegas
50	Hernandez, Jeremy	R/R	6-6/195	7-7-66	San Diego, Las Vegas
47	Hurst, Bruce	L/L	6-3/220	3-24-58	San Diego
48	Mason, Roger	R/R	6-6/220	9-18-58	Pittsburgh
43	Pena, Jim	L/L	6-0/187	9-17-64	Phoenix, San Francisco
42	Rodriguez, Rich	L/L	6-0/200	3-1-63	San Diego
27	Sanders, Scott	R/R	6-4/210	3-25-69	Wichita, Las Vegas
52	Schullstrom, Erik	R/R	6-5/220	3-25-69	Hagerstown, Las Vegas
54	Scott, Tim	R/R	6-2/205	11-16-66	Las Vegas, San Diego
44	Seminara, Frank	R/R	6-2/205	5-16-67	Las Vegas, San Diego
37	Taylor, Kerry	R/R	6-2/195	1-25-71	Kenosha
41	Whitehurst, Wally	R/R	6-3/185	4-11-64	New York N.L.
58	Worrell, Tim	R/R	6-4/210	7-5-67	Wichita, Las Vegas

No.	CATCHERS	B/T	Ht./Wt.	Born	1992 clubs
55	Johnson, Brian	R/R	6-2/195	1-8-68	Wichita
25	Lampkin, Tom	L/R	5-11/185	3-4-64	Las Vegas, San Diego
11	Walters, Dan	R/R	6-4/230	8-15-66	Las Vegas, San Diego

No.	INFIELDERS	B/T	Ht./Wt.	Born	1992 clubs
31	Gainer, Jay	L/L	6-0/190	10-8-66	Wichita
12	Gardner, Jeff	L/R	5-11/175	2-4-64	Las Vegas, San Diego
7	Gutierrez, Ricky	R/R	6-1/175	5-23-70	Rochester, Las Vegas
53	Holbert, Ray	R/R	6-0/170	9-25-70	Wichita
14	Lopez, Luis	B/R	5-11/175	9-4-70	Las Vegas
29	McGriff, Fred	L/L	6-3/215	10-31-63	San Diego
10	Sheffield, Gary	R/R	5-11/190	11-18-68	San Diego
18	Shipley, Craig	R/R	6-1/190	1-7-63	San Diego
15	Stillwell, Kurt	B/R	5-11/185	6-4-65	San Diego
20	Teufel, Tim	R/R	6-0/175	7-7-58	San Diego
23	Velasquez, Guillermo	L/R	6-3/225	4-23-68	Las Vegas, San Diego

No.	OUTFIELDERS	B/T	Ht./Wt.	Born	1992 clubs
28	Dozier, D.J.	R/R	6-0/205	9-21-65	Tidewater, New York N.L.
19	Gwynn, Tony	L/L	5-11/215	5-9-60	San Diego
4	Jackson, Darrin	R/R	6-0/185	8-22-63	San Diego
9	Pegues, Steve	R/R	6-2/190	5-21-68	Las Vegas
24	Plantier, Phil	L/R	5-11/195	1-27-69	Boston, Pawtucket
3	Sherman, Darrell	L/L	5-9/160	12-4-67	Wichita, Las Vegas
26	Staton, Dave	R/R	6-5/215	4-12-68	Las Vegas
2	Vatcher, Jim	R/R	5-9/175	5-27-66	Las Vegas, San Diego

| BALLPARK INFORMATION |

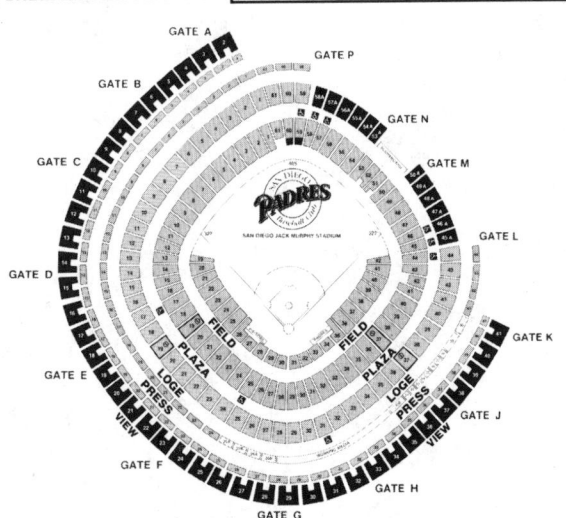

Ballpark (capacity, surface)
San Diego/Jack Murphy Stadium
(59,700, grass)
Address
P.O. Box 2000
San Diego, CA 92112-2000
Business phone
619-283-4494
Ticket information
619-283-4494
Ticket prices
$11 (field, plaza and press levels)
$9.50 (loge, view levels)
$7 (reserved grandstand)
$5 (general admission)
Field dimensions (from home plate)
To left field at foul line, 327 feet
To center field, 405 feet
To right field at foul line, 327 feet
First game played
April 8, 1969 (Padres 2, Astros 1)

MINOR LEAGUE AFFILIATES

Class	Team	League	Manager
AAA	Las Vegas	Pacific Coast	Russ Nixon
AA	Wichita	Texas	Dave Trembley
A	Rancho Cucamonga	California	Keith Champion
A	Waterloo	Midwest	Ed Romero
A	Spokane	Northwest	Tim Flannery
Rookie	Scottsdale Padres	Arizona	Ken Berry

BROADCAST INFORMATION

Radio: KFMB-AM (760). Broadcasters: Jerry Coleman, Bob Chandler, Ted Leitner. XEXX-AM (1420, Spanish language). Broadcasters: Mario Thomas, Eduardo Ortega.
TV: KUSI-TV (Channel 51). Broadcasters: Jerry Coleman, Bob Chandler.
Cable TV: San Diego Cable Sports Network. Broadcasters: Bob Chandler, Ted Leitner.

SPRING TRAINING

Ballpark (city): Desert Sun Stadium (Yuma, Ariz.).
Ticket information: 619-283-4494 (Padres' San Diego office).

HISTORY

YEAR-BY-YEAR RECORDS

Year	Pos.	W	L	Pct.	*GB	Year	Pos.	W	L	Pct.	*GB
1969	6th	52	110	.321	41	1983	4th	81	81	.500	10
1970	6th	63	99	.389	39	1984	1st‡	92	70	.568	+12
1971	6th	61	100	.379	28½	1985	T3rd	83	79	.512	12
1972	6th	58	95	.379	36½	1986	4th	74	88	.457	22
1973	6th	60	102	.370	39	1987	6th	65	97	.401	25
1974	6th	60	102	.370	42	1988	3rd	83	78	.516	11
1975	4th	71	91	.438	37	1989	2nd	89	73	.549	3
1976	5th	73	89	.451	29	1990	T4th	75	87	.463	16
1977	5th	69	93	.426	29	1991	3rd	84	78	.519	10
1978	4th	84	78	.519	11	1992	3rd	82	80	.506	16
1979	5th	68	93	.422	22						
1980	6th	73	89	.451	19½						
1981	6th/6th	41	69	.373	†						
1982	4th	81	81	.500	8						

*Games behind winner. †First half 23-33; second 18-36. ‡Won Championship Series.

MANAGERS

Name	Record	Years
Preston Gomez	180-306	'69-72
Don Zimmer	114-186	'72-73
John McNamara	224-310	'74-77
Alvin Dark	49-65	1977
Roger Craig	152-171	'78-79
Jerry Coleman	73-89	1980
Frank Howard	41-69	1981
Dick Williams	337-311	'82-85
Steve Boros	74-88	1986
Larry Bowa	81-127	'87-88
Jack McKeon	193-164	'88-90
Greg Riddoch	200-194	'90-92
Jim Riggleman	4-8	1992

1992 REVIEW

DAY BY DAY

Date	Opp.	Res.	Score	(inn.*)	Hits	Opp. hits	Winning pitcher	Losing pitcher	Save	Record	Pos.	GB
4-6	At Cin.	W	4-3		10	7	Melendez	Rijo	Myers	1-0	T1st	...
4-7	At Cin.	L	2-4		5	11	Browning	Gr. Harris	Charlton	1-1	T2nd	½
4-8	At Cin.	W	2-1		6	8	Benes	Belcher	Myers	2-1	2nd	½
4-9	L.A.	L	3-6		8	14	Candiotti	Lefferts	Gott	2-2	4th	½
4-10	L.A.	W	8-3		7	8	Melendez	Ojeda		3-2	2nd	½
4-11	L.A.	W	3-2	(10)	10	8	Melendez	McDowell		4-2	1st	+½
4-12	L.A.	W	5-4		8	6	Myers	McDowell		5-2	1st	+½
4-14	At S.F.	W	4-0		7	3	Benes	Burkett		6-2	1st	+1½
4-15	At S.F.	W	5-3		4	8	Lefferts	Hickerson	Myers	7-2	1st	+1½
4-16	At S.F.	L	1-6		8	12	Swift	Eiland		7-3	1st	+1
4-17	At Hou.	L	1-3		6	7	Harnisch	Hurst	D. Jones	7-4	1st	+1
4-18	At Hou.	L	2-4	(10)	10	11	D. Jones	Myers		7-5	1st	+½
4-19	At Hou.	L	0-1	(11)	9	7	Hernandez	Rodriguez		7-6	3rd	1½
4-20	Atl.	L	4-10		13	13	Freeman	Lefferts		7-7	T3rd	1½
4-21	Atl.	W	4-2		11	5	Rodriguez	Bielecki	Myers	8-7	3rd	½
4-22	Atl.	W	9-4		15	7	Hurst	Glavine		9-7	2nd	½
4-24	Cin.	L	6-7	(16)	11	15	Foster	Hernandez	Bankhead	9-8	T2nd	1½
4-25	Cin.	L	5-11		11	17	Swindell	Benes		9-9	T3rd	1½
4-26	Cin.	W	2-1		5	8	Lefferts	Hammond	Myers	10-9	T2nd	½
4-27	Phi.	L	9-12		12	17	Schilling	Hurst	Mit. Williams	10-10	4th	1
4-28	Phi.	W	7-6		14	7	Clements	Schilling		11-10	4th	½
4-29	Mon.	W	7-2		11	9	Gr. Harris	Nabholz		12-10	1st	+½
4-30	Mon.	L	3-9		8	15	Hill	Benes		12-11	3rd	½
5-1	St.L.	W	7-5		13	10	Rodriguez	Worrell	Myers	13-11	3rd	...
5-2	St.L.	L	0-3		4	8	Osborne	Hurst	L. Smith	13-12	3rd	1
5-3	St.L.	L	1-7		6	12	Tewksbury	Eiland		13-13	T3rd	1
5-5	At Mon.	L	2-5		10	9	Martinez	Gr. Harris		13-14	T4th	1
5-6	At Mon.	L	3-4		6	8	Hill	Benes	Wetteland	13-15	T4th	1½
5-8	At Phi.	W	6-5		8	12	Melendez	Schilling	Myers	14-15	4th	2
5-9	At Phi.	W	5-1		11	7	Lefferts	Brantley	Myers	15-15	3rd	1
5-10	At Phi.	L	3-9		11	8	Mulholland	Gr. Harris		15-16	3rd	2
5-11	At N.Y.	W	4-2		10	5	Benes	Young	Myers	16-16	3rd	1½
5-12	At N.Y.	L	3-7		10	8	Gooden	Melendez		16-17	3rd	2½
5-13	At N.Y.	W	7-0		12	6	Hurst	Cone		17-17	3rd	2½
5-15	At Pit.	W	9-2		18	8	Lefferts	Neagle		18-17	2nd	1½
5-16	At Pit.	W	10-9		12	13	Rodriguez	Walk	Myers	19-17	2nd	1½
5-17	At Pit.	W	6-5		8	10	Benes	Tomlin	Myers	20-17	2nd	½
5-18	N.Y.	W	3-0		12	1	Hurst	Gooden		21-17	2nd	...
5-19	N.Y.	L	0-8		7	12	Cone	Melendez		21-18	2nd	1
5-20	N.Y.	W	12-6		15	7	Lefferts	Burke		22-18	2nd	1
5-21	N.Y.	L	3-8		6	14	Fernandez	Gr. Harris		22-19	2nd	2
5-22	Chi.	W	2-0		6	3	Benes	Maddux		23-19	2nd	2
5-23	Chi.	L	2-7		9	9	Morgan	Hurst		23-20	2nd	2
5-24	Chi.	L	4-6		7	10	Castillo	Melendez	McElroy	23-21	2nd	2
5-25	Pit.	W	7-6		11	15	Lefferts	Smith	Myers	24-21	3rd	1½
5-26	Pit.	W	6-3	(10)	13	7	Scott	Lamp		25-21	2nd	1½
5-27	Pit.	W	8-7		16	14	Myers	Belinda		26-21	2nd	1½
5-29	At St.L.	W	2-1		5	8	Hurst	L. Smith	Myers	27-21	2nd	...
5-30	At St.L.	L	1-5		4	12	Tewksbury	Lefferts		27-22	3rd	½
5-31	At St.L.	W	10-0		12	2	Gr. Harris	Cormier		28-22	2nd	...
6-1	At Chi.	L	1-6		4	10	Maddux	Benes		28-23	3rd	...
6-2	At Chi.	L	2-3	(13)	9	10	Boskie	Ge. Harris		28-24	3rd	1
6-3	At Chi.	W	5-1		7	6	Hurst	Castillo		29-24	2nd	1
6-5	Atl.	L	2-3		7	8	Berenguer	Lefferts	Wohlers	29-25	2nd	1½
6-6	Atl.	L	1-5		2	15	Glavine	Benes		29-26	3rd	2½
6-7	Atl.	L	4-9		6	10	Smoltz	Seminara		29-27	3rd	2½
6-8	Hou.	W	3-2		9	4	Hurst	Harnisch		30-27	3rd	2½
6-9	Hou.	W	5-4		12	10	Clements	Boever	Maddux	31-27	2nd	2½
6-10	Hou.	W	5-1		8	6	Lefferts	Henry		32-27	2nd	1½
6-12	At Atl.	L	4-6		10	12	Berenguer	Maddux	Stanton	32-28	4th	4½
6-13	At Atl.	L	2-4		6	10	Smoltz	Seminara		32-29	3rd	2½
6-14	At Atl.	L	2-4		7	12	Leibrandt	Hurst	Wohlers	32-30	T3rd	3½
6-15	At Hou.	W	7-1		10	8	Lefferts	Henry		33-30	3rd	4½
6-16	At Hou.	L	0-11		7	15	Williams	Rodriguez	Hernandez	33-31	3rd	5½
6-17	At Hou.	W	5-0		6	4	Benes	Blair		34-31	3rd	5½
6-18	At S.F.	W	9-4		12	9	Seminara	Wilson	Maddux	35-31	3rd	5½
6-19	At S.F.	W	3-2	(10)	8	5	Melendez	Beck		36-31	3rd	4½
6-20	At S.F.	L	1-3		10	10	Black	Lefferts	Beck	36-32	3rd	4½
6-21	At S.F.	L	0-1	(11)	5	3	Jackson	Melendez		36-33	3rd	4½
6-22	L.A.	L	2-4		5	11	McDowell	Melendez		36-34	3rd	4½

Date	Opp.	Res.	Score	(inn.*)	Hits	Opp. hits	Winning pitcher	Losing pitcher	Save	Record	Pos.	GB
6-23	L.A.	W	8-4		8	10	Seminara	Candiotti		37-34	3rd	4½
6-25	S.F.	W	8-0		12	7	Hurst	Righetti		38-34	3rd	4½
6-26	S.F.	W	6-2		12	4	Lefferts	Black		39-34	3rd	4½
6-27	S.F.	L	3-5	(10)	10	14	Brantley	Myers		39-35	3rd	5½
6-28	S.F.	W	7-3		9	7	Seminara	Burkett	Maddux	40-35	3rd	5½
6-29	At L.A.	L	5-6	(11)	11	9	Wilson	Clements		40-36	3rd	5½
6-30	At L.A.	W	2-1		6	10	Hurst	R. Martinez	Maddux	41-36	3rd	5½
7-1	At L.A.	W	6-2		13	7	Lefferts	Hershiser		42-36	3rd	3½
7-2	Mon.	L	2-3		5	7	Gardner	Benes	Wetteland	42-37	3rd	4½
7-3	Mon.	W	6-4		12	7	Seminara	Barnes	Andersen	43-37	3rd	4½
7-4	Mon.	L	2-3	(10)	8	7	Wetteland	Melendez	Rojas	43-38	3rd	5½
7-5	Mon.	L	3-4	(10)	6	8	Rojas	Scott		43-39	3rd	6½
7-6	St.L.	L	0-4		4	12	Clark	Lefferts		43-40	3rd	7½
7-7	St.L.	L	3-6		10	11	Osborne	Benes	L. Smith	43-41	3rd	8½
7-8	St.L.	L	0-1		6	9	Olivares	Myers	L. Smith	43-42	3rd	8½
7-9	Phi.	W	3-1		8	7	Deshaies	Mulholland	Myers	44-42	3rd	8½
7-10	Phi.	W	8-7		15	12	Rodriguez	Jones	Myers	45-42	3rd	7½
7-11	Phi.	W	3-2	(11)	9	8	Scott	Hartley		46-42	3rd	6½
7-12	Phi.	W	8-2		12	7	Benes	Robinson		47-42	3rd	5½
7-16	At Mon.	L	4-7		7	10	Hill	Hurst	Wetteland	47-43	3rd	5½
7-17	At Mon.	L	0-3		7	9	Nabholz	Benes	Wetteland	47-44	3rd	6½
7-18	At Mon.	W	10-3		12	8	Seminara	Martinez		48-44	3rd	6½
7-19	At Mon.	W	9-2		16	10	Lefferts	Gardner		49-44	3rd	6½
7-20	At Phi.	W	2-1		6	6	Rodriguez	Jones	Myers	50-44	3rd	6½
7-21	At Phi.	W	4-3		9	10	Hurst	Mulholland	Myers	51-44	3rd	5½
7-22	At Phi.	L	0-4		5	7	Schilling	Benes		51-45	3rd	6
7-24	At N.Y.	L	0-3		3	9	Fernandez	Seminara		51-46	3rd	7
7-25	At N.Y.	W	2-0		7	6	Lefferts	Schourek	Myers	52-46	3rd	7
7-26	At N.Y.	W	1-0		6	7	Hurst	Whitehurst		53-46	3rd	6
7-27	Cin.	W	2-1		7	7	Benes	Swindell	Myers	54-46	3rd	5
7-28	Cin.	L	1-4		7	8	Rijo	Deshaies	Charlton	54-47	3rd	5
7-29	Cin.	W	7-3		11	8	Seminara	Bolton		55-47	3rd	5
7-30	At L.A.	L	5-6	(10)	11	8	Howell	Melendez		55-48	3rd	5
7-31	At L.A.	W	4-3		7	10	Hurst	Ke. Gross	Myers	56-48	3rd	4½
8-1	At L.A.	L	2-7		9	13	Candiotti	Benes		56-49	3rd	5½
8-2	At L.A.	L	1-4		5	8	Hershiser	Deshaies		56-50	3rd	6½
8-3	S.F.	W	6-5		10	15	Scott	Jackson		57-50	3rd	6
8-4	S.F.	L	1-7		8	14	Burkett	Lefferts		57-51	3rd	7
8-5	S.F.	W	4-1		10	9	Scott	Brantley	Myers	58-51	3rd	7
8-6	Hou.	W	7-5		11	11	Benes	Williams	Myers	59-51	3rd	7
8-7	Hou.	W	4-2		13	6	Deshaies	Harnisch	Myers	60-51	3rd	7
8-8	Hou.	W	7-5		10	9	Rodriguez	Boever	Andersen	61-51	3rd	7
8-9	Hou.	W	4-3		8	8	Andersen	D. Jones	Myers	62-51	3rd	7
8-11	At Atl.	W	8-4		12	8	Hurst	Smoltz	Maddux	63-51	3rd	5½
8-13	At Atl.	L	3-4		9	6	Davis	Andersen		63-52	3rd	6½
8-14	At Cin.	W	5-1		10	8	Deshaies	Hammond		64-52	3rd	6½
8-15	At Cin.	L	4-5		5	11	Dibble	Myers		64-53	3rd	7½
8-16	At Cin.	L	2-12		7	15	Belcher	Hurst		64-54	3rd	7½
8-18	At Pit.	L	1-5		8	6	Tomlin	Benes		64-55	3rd	9
8-19	At Pit.	L	2-3		9	8	Walk	Deshaies	Cox	64-56	3rd	10
8-20	At Pit.	L	1-7		5	12	Jackson	Lefferts		64-57	3rd	10
8-22	N.Y.	W	4-2		7	4	Hurst	Schourek	Myers	65-57	3rd	9½
8-23	N.Y.	W	4-3		4	5	Benes	Cone	Myers	66-57	3rd	8½
8-24	Chi.	L	3-6		7	11	Castillo	Gr. Harris	Scanlan	66-58	3rd	9
8-25	Chi.	W	7-4		9	10	Maddux	Patterson	Myers	67-58	3rd	8
8-26	Chi.	W	3-0		8	8	Lefferts	Maddux	Myers	68-58	3rd	7
8-28	Pit.	W	11-6		15	9	Maddux	Drabek		69-58	3rd	6
8-29	Pit.	L	2-3		7	8	Tomlin	Gr. Harris	Mason	69-59	3rd	7
8-30	Pit.	L	3-6		6	11	Walk	Deshaies		69-60	3rd	7
8-31	At St.L.	L	2-6		7	10	Tewksbury	Lefferts		69-61	3rd	8½
9-1	At St.L.	L	0-2		6	7	Osborne	Benes	L. Smith	69-62	3rd	9½
9-2	At St.L.	W	5-4		12	12	Hurst	Clark	Myers	70-62	3rd	8½
9-4	At Chi.	W	7-5	(14)	14	12	Hernandez	Boskie		71-62	3rd	7
9-5	At Chi.	W	5-3		7	12	Melendez	Maddux	Myers	72-62	3rd	7
9-6	At Chi.	W	3-1		5	6	Benes	Bullinger	Myers	73-62	3rd	7
9-7	At S.F.	W	7-5		9	10	Seminara	Black	Hernandez	74-62	3rd	7
9-8	At S.F.	L	5-6	(16)	13	13	Brantley	Ge. Harris		74-63	2nd	7½
9-9	At L.A.	L	1-4		4	8	Ke. Gross	Gr. Harris		74-64	3rd	9
9-10	At L.A.	W	3-1		5	6	Deshaies	Hershiser	Myers	75-64	2nd	9
9-11	Cin.	L	1-4		6	12	Pugh	Benes	Dibble	75-65	3rd	10
9-12	Cin.	L	4-7		9	15	Rijo	Hurst		75-66	3rd	11
9-13	Cin.	W	3-1		9	4	Seminara	Ayala	Myers	76-66	3rd	11
9-14	L.A.	L	4-5	(11)	10	12	Gott	Hernandez	McDowell	76-67	3rd	11½
9-15	L.A.	L	3-6		13	13	Hershiser	Deshaies	Howell	76-68	3rd	11½

Date	Opp.	Res.	Score	(inn.*)	Hits	Opp. hits	Winning pitcher	Losing pitcher	Save	Record	Pos.	GB
9-16	L.A.	W	3-1		6	5	Benes	Candiotti	Myers	77-68	3rd	11½
9-18	At Cin.	L	2-4		7	8	Pugh	Hurst	Dibble	77-69	3rd	11
9-19	At Cin.	L	2-5		9	6	Ayala	Seminara	Dibble	77-70	3rd	11
9-20	At Cin.	L	1-6		7	11	Belcher	Gr. Harris		77-71	3rd	12
9-21	S.F.	L	1-7		9	10	Jackson	Deshaies		77-72	3rd	13
9-22	S.F.	W	2-1		8	6	Benes	Carter	Myers	78-72	3rd	12
9-23	Hou.	L	6-7		11	11	D. Jones	Hernandez		78-73	3rd	13
9-24	Hou.	W	7-1		10	3	Seminara	Blair		79-73	3rd	12
9-25	Atl.	W	1-0		7	6	Gr. Harris	Avery	Myers	80-73	3rd	11
9-26	Atl.	L	1-2	(10)	3	9	Stanton	Rodriguez		80-74	3rd	12
9-27	Atl.	L	1-2	(10)	6	8	Reardon	Myers		80-75	3rd	13
9-29	At Hou.	L	5-6		10	9	Osuna	Myers		80-76	3rd	14
9-30	At Hou.	L	4-5		10	10	J. Jones	Hernandez	D. Jones	80-77	3rd	14
10-1	At Hou.	W	3-2		7	5	Gr. Harris	Bowen	Myers	81-77	3rd	14
10-2 (1)	At Atl.	L	1-4		4	7	Nied	Benes		81-78	3rd	15½
10-2 (2)	At Atl.	L	2-7		10	10	Smith	Deshaies		81-79	3rd	16
10-3	At Atl.	L	0-1	(5½)	4	3	Leibrandt	Maddux	Reynoso	81-80	3rd	17
10-4	At Atl.	W	4-3	(12)	8	7	Myers	Borbon		82-80	3rd	16

Monthly records: April (12-11), May (16-11), June (13-14), July (15-12), August (13-13), September (11-16), Oct. (2-3).

HIGHLIGHTS

High point: The Padres won 21 of 29 games from July 9 through August 11 to pull within 5½ games of first place in the N.L. West.

Low point: The Padres lost, 6-5, in 16 innings on September 8 at San Francisco and never recovered. Right fielder Tony Gwynn sustained a left knee injury in the game, and the Padres wound up losing 17 of their final 25 games.

Turning point: The Padres were only 8½ games behind first-place Atlanta on August 31 when they traded lefthander Craig Lefferts, who at the time was tied for the team lead with 13 wins, to Baltimore. The deal incensed the players, who accused management of giving up on the season. The team responded accordingly, posting a 13-19 mark from September 1 to the end of the year.

Most valuable player: Third baseman Gary Sheffield. Even though his bid for the Triple Crown fell short, he won the N.L. batting title (.330) and collected a career-high 33 homers and 100 RBIs.

Most valuable pitcher: Lefthander Randy Myers. He withstood some rough spots to save a career-high 38 games, the second-highest total in team history.

Most improved player: Sheffield. He bested his career homer total (21) and almost topped his lifetime RBI figure (133) while batting 71 points above his career average.

Most pleasant surprise: Catcher Dan Walters. When Benito Santiago broke a finger May 31, Walters was called up from Class AAA Las Vegas and responded by hitting .251 with four homers and 22 RBIs in 57 games.

Biggest disappointment: Second baseman Kurt Stillwell. The Padres believed the free agent could make the transition from shortstop to second base. Instead, he led N.L. second basemen in errors (16), batted a career-low .227 and was constantly nagged by injuries.

Key injuries: The Padres never fully recovered from the injuries to righthanders Ed Whitson and Greg Harris. Santiago missed over a month with his broken finger. For the third straight year, Gwynn's season was cut short due to injury.

Notable: San Diego fired Manager Greg Riddoch on September 23, replacing him with Las Vegas Manager Jim Riggleman. . . . The Padres again shook up their front office and farm system, firing 27 employees after the season. . . . After pacing the N.L. with 35 homers, first baseman Fred McGriff became the first player in baseball history to win homer titles in each league.

—BOB NIGHTENGALE

RECORDS

1992 regular-season record: 82-80 (3rd in N.L. West); 45-36 at home; 37-44 on road; 39-33 vs. East; 43-47 vs. West; 32-27 vs. LHP; 50-53 vs. RHP; 64-56 on grass; 18-24 on turf; 28-20 in day-time; 54-60 at night; 31-24 in one-run games; 6-14 in extra-inning games; 0-1-0 in doubleheaders.

Team record last five years: 413-396 (.511, ranks 5th in league in that span).

TEAM LEADERS

Batting average: Gary Sheffield (.330).
At-bats: Tony Fernandez (622).
Runs: Gary Sheffield (87).
Hits: Gary Sheffield (184).
Total bases: Gary Sheffield (323).
Doubles: Gary Sheffield (34).
Triples: Jerald Clark (6).
Home runs: Fred McGriff (35).
Runs batted in: Fred McGriff (104).
Stolen bases: Tony Fernandez (20).
Slugging percentage: Gary Sheffield (.580).
On-base percentage: Fred McGriff (.394).
Wins: Bruce Hurst (14).
Earned-run average: Andy Benes (3.35).
Complete games: Bruce Hurst (6).
Shutouts: Bruce Hurst (4).
Saves: Randy Myers (38).
Innings pitched: Andy Benes (231⅓).
Strikeouts: Andy Benes (169).

GAMES BY POSITION

Catcher: Benito Santiago 103, Dan Walters 55, Dann Bilardello 14, Tom Lampkin 7.

First base: Fred McGriff 151, Jerald Clark 11, Phil Stephenson 7, Tim Teufel 5, Guillermo Velasquez 3.

Second base: Kurt Stillwell 111, Tim Teufel 52, Jeff Gardner 11, Craig Shipley 11, Paul Faries 4.

Third base: Gary Sheffield 144, Tim Teufel 26, Craig Shipley 8, Paul Faries 2.

Shortstop: Tony Fernandez 154, Craig Shipley 23, Paul Faries 1.

Outfield: Darrin Jackson 153, Jerald Clark 134, Tony Gwynn 127, Kevin Ward 51, Oscar Azocar 37, Phil Stephenson 15, Gary Pettis 14, Jim Vatcher 13, Guillermo Velasquez 2, Tom Lampkin 1.

TOP 10 DRAFT CHOICES

1. None.
2. Todd Helton, OF, Central High School, Knoxville, Tenn.
3. Jared Baker, RHP, University of South Carolina.
4. Brett Laxton, RHP, Audubon (N.J.) High School.
5. Jimmy Baron, LHP, Humble (Tex.) High School.
6. Brad Gennaro, OF, San Diego State University.
7. Tom Kindler, RHP, Kent State University.
8. Rich Lawrence, SS, Barron Collier High School, Naples, Fla.
9. Todd Erdos, RHP, Meadville (Pa.) High School.
10. Ricky Talbott, 3B, Northview High School, Covina, Calif.

SAN FRANCISCO GIANTS
NATIONAL LEAGUE WEST DIVISION

1993 SCHEDULE

APRIL
SUN	MON	TUE	WED	THU	FRI	SAT
				1	2	3
4	5	6 N STL	7 N STL	8 N STL	9 N PIT	10 PIT
11 PIT	12 FLA H	13 N FLA H	14 N FLA H	15 ATL H	16 N ATL H	17 N ATL H
18 ATL H	19	20 N NY	21 N NY	22 N NY	23 N MON	24 MON
25 MON	26 N PHI	27 PHI	28 N NY H	29 N NY H	30 N MON H	

MAY
SUN	MON	TUE	WED	THU	FRI	SAT
						1 MON H
2 MON H	3	4 N PHI H	5 PHI H	6	7 N LA H	8 N LA H
9 LA H	10 N COL	11 N COL	12 N COL	13	14 N SD	15 N SD
16 SD	17 N HOU H	18 N HOU H	19 N HOU H	20 N CIN	21 N CIN	22 N CIN
23 CIN H	24	25 N CHI	26 N CHI	27 N CHI	28 N ATL	29 N ATL
30 ATL	31 FLA					

JUNE
SUN	MON	TUE	WED	THU	FRI	SAT
		1 N FLA	2 N FLA	3 N PIT H	4 N PIT H	5 N PIT H
6 PIT H	7	8 N STL H	9 N STL H	10	11 N CHI H	12 N CHI H
13 CHI H	14	15 N CIN	16 N CIN	17 N CIN	18 N HOU	19 N HOU
20 HOU	21 N SD	22 N SD	23 N SD	24	25 N COL	26 N COL
27 COL H	28 N LA	29 N LA	30 N LA			

JULY
SUN	MON	TUE	WED	THU	FRI	SAT
				1	2 N NY	3 N NY
4 NY	5 N MON	6 N MON	7 N MON	8 N PHI	9 N PHI	10 PHI
11 PHI	12	13 * ALL STAR GAME	14	15 N NY H	16 N NY H	17 N NY H
18 NY H	19 N MON H	20 N MON H	21 N MON H	22 PHI H	23 N PHI H	24 N PHI H
25 PHI H	26 N LA H	27 N LA H	28 LA H	29	30 N COL	31 N COL

AUGUST
SUN	MON	TUE	WED	THU	FRI	SAT
1 COL	2	3 N SD	4 N SD	5 N SD	6 N HOU H	7 N HOU H
8 HOU H	9	10 N CIN H	11 N CIN H	12	13 N CHI	14 N CHI
15 CHI	16	17 N PIT	18 N PIT	19 N PIT	20 N FLA H	21 N FLA H
22 FLA H	23 N ATL H	24 N ATL H	25 ATL H	26	27 N FLA	28 N FLA
29 N FLA	30	31 N ATL				

SEPTEMBER
SUN	MON	TUE	WED	THU	FRI	SAT
			1 N ATL	2 N ATL	3 N STL	4 N STL
5 STL	6 PIT H	7 N PIT H	8	9 N STL H	10 N STL H	11 N STL H
12 STL H	13 CHI H	14 N CHI H	15 CHI H	16	17 N CIN	18 N CIN
19 CIN	20 HOU	21 N HOU	22 N HOU	23 N HOU	24 N SD	25 SD H
26 SD H	27 SD H	28 N COL H	29 COL H	30 N LA		

OCTOBER
SUN	MON	TUE	WED	THU	FRI	SAT
					1 N LA	2 LA
3 LA						

1993 SEASON

CLUB DIRECTORY

President and managing general partner
Peter A. Magowan
Executive vice president
Larry Baer
Senior vice president and general manager
Bob Quinn
Senior vice president, business operations
Pat Gallagher
Asst. to the general manager and v.p. of scouting and player personnel
Brian Sabean
V.p./baseball admin. and operations
Tony Siegle
Vice president, finance
John Yee
Vice president, stadium operations
Jorge Costa
Director of communications
Robin Carr Locke
Director of community development
Jan Hutchins
Director of marketing
Mario Alioto
Director of retail operations
Robert Tolifson
Director of stadium operations
Gene Telucci
Director of travel
Dirk Smith
Director of legal and governmental affairs
Jack Bair
Media relations assistant
Jim Moorehead
Coordinator of scouting
Bob Hartsfield
National cross-checker
Randy Waddill
Western cross-checker
Doug Mapson

Eastern cross-checker
Mike Russell
Special assignments
Al Heist
Coordinator of Latin American operations
Luis Rosa
Scouts
Claudio Brito
Jose Cassino
Bob Cummings
Pablo Delgado
Nino Escalera
Bob Gardner
George Genovese
Herman Hannah
Chuck Hensley
Carlos Hernandez
Diego Herrera
Andres James
Elvio Jimenez
Mike Keenan
Tom Korenek
Jose Marcano
Alan Marr
Abraham Martinez
Doug McMillan
Tony Michalak
Rick Ragazzo
Hector Rivera
Gary Robinson
Milton Rosario
John Shafer
Joe Strain
Todd Thomas
Gene Thompson
Mike Toomey
Elanis Westbrooks
Tom Zimmer

SCHEDULE KEY
H—Home game.   N—Night game (any game starting after 5 p.m.).
*All-Star Game at Oriole Park at Camden Yards, Baltimore.

Manager—Dusty Baker (12).

Coaches—Bobby Bonds (16), Bob Brenly (15), Wendell Kim (20), Bob Lillis (5), Dick Pole (48).

No.	PITCHERS	B/T	Ht./Wt.	Born	1992 clubs
64	Ard, Johnny	R/R	6-5/220	6-1-67	Phoenix
47	Beck, Rod	R/R	6-1/236	8-3-68	San Francisco
40	Black, Bud	L/L	6-2/188	6-30-57	Phoenix, San Francisco
49	Brantley, Jeff	R/R	5-10/189	9-5-63	San Francisco
34	Burba, Dave	R/R	6-4/240	7-7-66	San Francisco, Phoenix
33	Burkett, John	R/R	6-2/211	11-28-64	San Francisco
53	Carlson, Dan	R/R	6-1/185	1-26-70	Shreveport
35	Carter, Larry	R/R	6-5/196	5-22-65	Phoenix, San Francisco
60	Hancock, Chris	L/L	6-3/175	9-12-69	San Jose, Shreveport
41	Hickerson, Bryan	L/L	6-2/203	10-13-63	San Francisco
55	Huisman, Rick	R/R	6-3/200	5-17-69	Shreveport, Phoenix
42	Jackson, Mike	R/R	6-2/223	12-22-64	San Francisco
57	McGehee, Kevin	R/R	6-0/190	1-18-69	Shreveport
19	Righetti, Dave	L/L	6-4/219	11-28-58	San Francisco
28	Rogers, Kevin	B/L	6-1/198	8-20-68	Shreveport, Phoenix, San Francisco
26	Swift, Bill	R/R	6-0/191	10-27-61	San Francisco
32	Wilson, Trevor	L/L	6-0/204	6-7-66	San Francisco

No.	CATCHERS	B/T	Ht./Wt.	Born	1992 clubs
54	Christopherson, Eric	R/R	6-0/195	4-25-69	Shreveport
46	Colbert, Craig	R/R	6-0/214	2-13-65	San Francisco, Phoenix
8	Manwaring, Kirt	R/R	5-11/203	7-15-65	San Francisco
30	McNamara, Jim	L/R	6-4/210	10-6-65	San Francisco, Phoenix

No.	INFIELDERS	B/T	Ht./Wt.	Born	1992 clubs
23	Anderson, Dave	R/R	6-2/184	8-1-60	Albuquerque, Los Angeles
18	Benjamin, Mike	R/R	6-0/169	11-22-65	San Francisco, Phoenix
22	Clark, Will	L/L	6-0/196	3-13-64	San Francisco
10	Clayton, Royce	R/R	6-0/183	1-2-70	San Francisco, Phoenix
21	Faries, Paul	R/R	5-10/170	2-20-65	Las Vegas, San Diego
7	Patterson, John	B/R	5-9/168	2-11-67	San Francisco, Phoenix
31	Phillips, J.R.	L/L	6-1/185	4-29-70	Midland
56	Santana, Andres	B/R	5-9/150	3-19-68	DID NOT PLAY
6	Thompson, Robby	R/R	5-11/173	5-10-62	San Francisco
9	Williams, Matt	R/R	6-2/216	11-28-65	San Francisco

No.	OUTFIELDERS	B/T	Ht./Wt.	Born	1992 clubs
14	Benzinger, Todd	B/R	6-1/192	2-11-63	Los Angeles
25	Bonds, Barry	L/L	6-1/190	7-24-64	Pittsburgh
29	Hosey, Steve	R/R	6-3/225	4-2-69	Phoenix, San Francisco
1	Leonard, Mark	L/R	6-0/212	8-14-64	San Francisco, Phoenix
2	Lewis, Darren	R/R	6-0/189	8-28-67	San Francisco, Phoenix
17	Martinez, Dave	L/L	5-10/180	9-26-64	Cincinnati
51	McGee, Willie	B/R	6-1/185	11-2-58	San Francisco
39	Wood, Ted	L/L	6-2/187	1-4-67	Phoenix, San Francisco

BALLPARK INFORMATION

Ballpark (capacity, surface)
 Candlestick Park (62,000, grass)
Address
 Candlestick Park
 San Francisco, CA 94124
Business phone
 415-468-3700
Ticket information
 415-467-8000
Ticket prices
 $12.25 (lower box)
 $11.25 (upper box)
 $10.25 (lower reserved)
 $6.25 (upper reserved)
 $5.25 (pavilion)
 $2.25 (general admission)
 $1.25 (g.a., under 15 with adult)
Field dimensions (from home plate)
 To left field at foul line, 335 feet
 To center field, 400 feet
 To right field at foul line, 330 feet
First game played
 April 12, 1960 (Giants 3, Cardinals
 1)

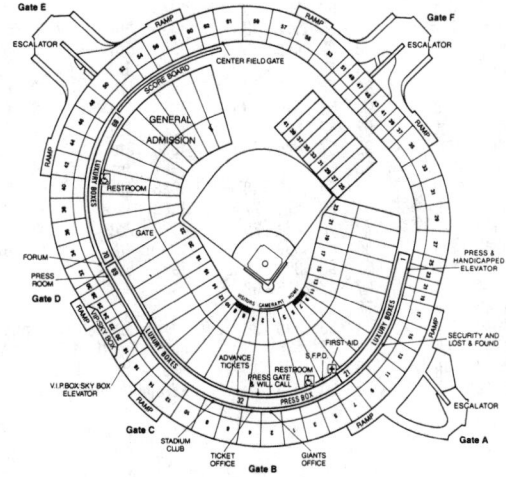

MINOR LEAGUE AFFILIATES

Class	Team	League	Manager
AAA	Phoenix	Pacific Coast	Carlos Alfonso
AA	Shreveport	Texas	Ron Wotus
A	San Jose	California	Dick Dietz
A	Clinton	Midwest	Jack Mull
A	Everett	Northwest	Norm Sherry
Rookie	Scottsdale	Arizona	Alan Bannister

BROADCAST INFORMATION

Radio: KNBR-AM (680). Broadcasters: Hank Greenwald, Ted Robinson. KLOK-AM (1170, Spanish language). Broadcasters: Tito Fuentes, Cesar Rivera.
TV: KTVU-TV (Channel 2). Broadcasters: Ted Robinson, TBA.
Cable TV: SportsChannel Pacific. Broadcasters: Joe Morgan, Ted Robinson.

SPRING TRAINING

Ballpark (city): Scottsdale Stadium (Scottsdale, Ariz.).
Ticket information: 602-990-7972.

HISTORY

YEAR-BY-YEAR RECORDS

Year	Pos.	W	L	Pct.	*GB	Year	Pos.	W	L	Pct.	*GB
1901	7th	52	85	.380	37	1950	3rd	86	68	.558	5
1902	8th	48	88	.353	53½	1951	1st†	98	59	.624 + 1	
1903	2nd	84	55	.604	6½	1952	2nd	92	62	.597	4½
1904	1st	106	47	.693	+13	1953	5th	70	84	.455	35
1905	1st	105	48	.686	+ 9	1954	1st	97	57	.630	+ 5
1906	2nd	96	56	.632	20	1955	3rd	80	74	.519	18½
1907	4th	82	71	.536	25½	1956	6th	67	87	.435	26
1908	T2nd	98	56	.636	1	1957	6th	69	85	.448	26
1909	3rd	92	61	.601	18½	1958	3rd	80	74	.519	12
1910	2nd	91	63	.591	13	1959	3rd	83	71	.539	4
1911	1st	99	54	.647	+ 7½	1960	5th	79	75	.513	16
1912	1st	103	48	.682	+10	1961	3rd	85	69	.552	8
1913	1st	101	51	.664	+12½	1962	1st†	103	62	.624	+ 1
1914	2nd	84	70	.545	10½	1963	3rd	88	74	.543	11
1915	8th	69	83	.454	21	1964	4th	90	72	.556	3
1916	4th	86	66	.566	7	1965	2nd	95	67	.586	2
1917	1st	98	56	.636	+10	1966	2nd	93	68	.578	1½
1918	2nd	71	53	.573	10½	1967	2nd	91	71	.562	10½
1919	2nd	87	53	.621	9	1968	2nd	88	74	.543	9
1920	2nd	86	68	.558	7	1969	2nd	90	72	.556	3
1921	1st	94	59	.614	+ 4	1970	3rd	86	76	.531	16
1922	1st	93	61	.604	+ 7	1971	1st‡	90	72	.556	+ 1
1923	1st	95	58	.621	+ 4½	1972	5th	69	86	.445	26½
1924	1st	93	60	.608	+ 1½	1973	3rd	88	74	.543	11
1925	2nd	86	66	.566	8½	1974	5th	72	90	.444	30
1926	5th	74	77	.490	13½	1975	3rd	80	81	.497	27½
1927	3rd	92	62	.597	2	1976	4th	74	88	.457	28
1928	2nd	93	61	.604	2	1977	4th	75	87	.463	23
1929	3rd	84	67	.556	13½	1978	3rd	89	73	.549	6
1930	3rd	87	67	.565	5	1979	4th	71	91	.438	19½
1931	2nd	87	65	.572	13	1980	5th	75	86	.466	17
1932	T6th	72	82	.468	18	1981	5th/3rd	56	55	.505	§
1933	1st	91	61	.599	+ 5	1982	3rd	87	75	.537	2
1934	2nd	93	60	.608	2	1983	5th	79	83	.488	12
1935	3rd	91	62	.595	8½	1984	6th	66	96	.407	26
1936	1st	92	62	.597	+ 5	1985	6th	62	100	.383	33
1937	1st	95	57	.625	+ 3	1986	3rd	83	79	.512	13
1938	3rd	83	67	.553	5	1987	1st‡	90	72	.556	+ 6
1939	5th	77	74	.510	18½	1988	4th	83	79	.512	11½
1940	6th	72	80	.474	27½	1989	1st★	92	70	.568	+ 3
1941	5th	74	79	.484	25½	1990	3rd	85	77	.525	6
1942	3rd	85	67	.559	20	1991	4th	75	87	.463	19
1943	8th	55	98	.359	49½	1992	5th	72	90	.444	26
1944	5th	67	87	.435	38						
1945	5th	78	74	.513	19						
1946	8th	61	93	.396	36						
1947	4th	81	73	.526	13						
1948	5th	78	76	.506	13½						
1949	5th	73	81	.474	24						

*Games behind winner. †Won pennant playoff. ‡Lost Championship Series. §First half 27-32; second 29-23. ★Won Championship Series.

MANAGERS

Name	Record	Years
George Davis	52-85	1901
Horace Fogel	18-23	1902
Heinie Smith	5-27	1902
John McGraw	2604-1801	'02-32
Bill Terry	823-661	'32-41
Mel Ott	464-530	'42-48
Leo Durocher	637-523	'48-55
Bill Rigney	406-430	'56-60
		1976
Tom Sheehan	46-50	1960
Alvin Dark	366-277	'61-64
Herman Franks	367-280	'65-68
Clyde King	109-95	'69-70
Charlie Fox	348-327	'70-74
Wes Westrum	118-129	'74-75
Joe Altobelli	225-239	'77-79
Dave Bristol	85-98	'79-80
Frank Robinson	264-277	'81-84
Danny Ozark	24-32	1984
Jim Davenport	56-88	1985
Roger Craig	586-566	'85-92

DAY BY DAY

Date	Opp.	Res.	Score	(inn.*)	Hits	Opp. hits	Winning pitcher	Losing pitcher	Save	Record	Pos.	GB
4-6	At L.A.	W	8-1		17	7	Swift	R. Martinez		1-0	T1st	...
4-7	At L.A.	L	0-3		3	7	Hershiser	Downs	McDowell	1-1	T2nd	½
4-9	At Atl.	W	11-4		15	8	Heredia	Avery		2-1	T1st	...
4-10	At Atl.	L	3-5		9	8	Leibrandt	Burba	Stanton	2-2	T3rd	1
4-11	At Atl.	W	3-0		6	6	Swift	Bielecki		3-2	T2nd	½
4-12	At Atl.	L	2-6		8	12	Glavine	Downs		3-3	3rd	1½
4-14	S.D.	L	0-4		3	7	Benes	Burkett		3-4	4th	2½
4-15	S.D.	L	3-5		8	4	Lefferts	Hickerson	Myers	3-5	5th	3½
4-16	S.D.	W	6-1		12	8	Swift	Eiland		4-5	T4th	2½
4-17	Cin.	W	7-3		9	4	Hickerson	Rijo	Beck	5-5	T3rd	1½
4-18	Cin.	W	7-3		13	9	Wilson	Browning		6-5	T2nd	½
4-19	Cin.	W	8-2		13	5	Burkett	Belcher		7-5	T1st	...
4-20	At Hou.	L	2-3		7	6	Portugal	Burba	D. Jones	7-6	2nd	1
4-21	At Hou.	W	6-2		8	8	Swift	Bowen		8-6	T1st	...
4-22	At Hou.	L	1-3	(12)	8	13	Hernandez	Jackson		8-7	3rd	1
4-24	L.A.	L	3-5		7	9	Hershiser	Wilson	McDowell	8-8	4th	2
4-25	L.A.	L	6-7	(10)	9	10	McDowell	Righetti	Gott	8-9	5th	2
4-26	L.A.	W	5-4	(11)	12	9	Heredia	Wilson		9-9	4th	1
4-27	Mon.	W	2-1		6	7	Burba	Martinez	Brantley	10-9	T2nd	½
4-28	Mon.	W	2-1	(10)	9	5	Brantley	Sampen		11-9	T1st	...
4-29	St.L.	L	1-2	(12)	9	11	Perez	Righetti	L. Smith	11-10	T2nd	½
4-30	St.L.	W	9-3		11	6	Burkett	DeLeon		12-10	1st	+½
5-2	Phi.	W	2-1		8	6	Swift	Abbott	Righetti	13-10	1st	+1
5-3	Phi.	L	3-12		6	15	Brantley	Wilson	Schilling	13-11	T1st	...
5-5	At St.L.	L	5-7		9	11	Perez	Burba	L. Smith	13-12	1st	+½
5-6	At St.L.	L	4-5	(11)	9	13	Agosto	Righetti		13-13	2nd	½
5-7	At St.L.	W	2-0		7	4	Swift	Osborne		14-13	2nd	½
5-8	At Mon.	W	6-3		9	5	Wilson	Fassero	Brantley	15-13	2nd	½
5-9	At Mon.	L	3-9		8	10	Nabholz	Black		15-14	2nd	½
5-10	At Mon.	W	8-3	(11)	9	7	Brantley	Landrum		16-14	2nd	½
5-11	At Phi.	W	8-7	(10)	9	9	Burba	Mit. Williams		17-14	T1st	...
5-12	At Phi.	W	7-5		10	9	Hickerson	Jones	Jackson	18-14	1st	+1
5-13	At Phi.	W	5-3		8	6	Wilson	Abbott	Brantley	19-14	1st	+2
5-15	Chi.	L	3-5		8	8	Scanlan	Brantley	Assenmacher	19-15	1st	+1½
5-16	Chi.	W	2-0		5	6	Burkett	Maddux	Beck	20-15	1st	+1½
5-17	Chi.	L	3-4		5	8	Morgan	Burba	Scanlan	20-16	1st	+½
5-19	Pit.	W	7-2		10	6	Wilson	Drabek	Righetti	21-16	1st	+1
5-20	Pit.	W	3-1		7	4	Black	Smith	Brantley	22-16	1st	+1
5-21	Pit.	W	1-0		5	2	Burkett	Walk	Jackson	23-16	1st	+2
5-22	N.Y.	W	7-6		10	8	Downs	Burke	Righetti	24-16	1st	+2
5-23	N.Y.	L	3-6		7	11	Gooden	Burba	Franco	24-17	1st	+2
5-24	N.Y.	L	0-6		4	12	Cone	Wilson		24-18	1st	+2
5-26	At Chi.	W	3-2		11	9	Jackson	McElroy	Brantley	25-18	1st	+1½
5-27	At Chi.	W	6-2		6	9	Burkett	Maddux		26-18	1st	+1½
5-28	At Chi.	L	0-5		4	10	Morgan	Burba		26-19	1st	+1
5-29	At Pit.	L	3-13		8	13	Palacios	Wilson	Patterson	26-20	1st	...
5-30	At Pit.	L	2-3	(10)	8	9	Neagle	Brantley		26-21	2nd	½
5-31	At Pit.	W	5-3		9	8	Black	Smith	Brantley	27-21	1st	...
6-1	At N.Y.	L	1-14		7	16	Fernandez	Burkett		27-22	2nd	...
6-2	At N.Y.	L	3-4		8	6	Whitehurst	Wilson	Franco	27-23	2nd	1
6-4	Hou.	L	6-12		8	12	J. Jones	Heredia		27-24	3rd	1½
6-5	Hou.	L	4-5		7	12	Hernandez	Brantley	D. Jones	27-25	3rd	2½
6-6	Hou.	W	12-6		14	9	Righetti	Boever		28-25	2nd	2½
6-7	Hou.	W	3-0		9	2	Wilson	Portugal		29-25	2nd	1½
6-8	Cin.	L	1-4		8	9	Swindell	Heredia	Dibble	29-26	2nd	2½
6-9	Cin.	L	2-3		8	7	Charlton	Beck		29-27	3rd	3½
6-10	Cin.	W	6-2		9	3	Black	Rijo		30-27	3rd	2½
6-12	At Hou.	W	3-2		8	7	Jackson	D. Jones	Beck	31-27	3rd	4½
6-13	At Hou.	L	1-4		8	7	Hernandez	Brantley	D. Jones	31-28	2nd	2½
6-14	At Hou.	L	7-15		12	14	Murphy	Righetti		31-29	2nd	3½
6-15	At Cin.	L	5-7		10	10	Browning	Jackson	Charlton	31-30	4th	5½
6-16	At Cin.	L	3-5		7	7	Rijo	Heredia	Dibble	31-31	4th	6½
6-17	At Cin.	L	4-6		7	8	Hammond	Burkett	Dibble	31-32	4th	7½
6-18	S.D.	L	4-9		9	12	Seminara	Wilson	Maddux	31-33	4th	8½
6-19	S.D.	L	2-3	(10)	5	8	Melendez	Beck		31-34	4th	8½
6-20	S.D.	W	3-1		10	10	Black	Lefferts	Beck	32-34	4th	7½
6-21	S.D.	W	1-0	(11)	3	5	Jackson	Melendez		33-34	4th	6½
6-23	At Atl.	L	0-7		5	17	Glavine	Burkett		33-35	4th	7
6-24	At Atl.	L	0-5		2	7	Smoltz	Wilson		33-36	4th	8
6-25	At S.D.	L	0-8		7	12	Hurst	Righetti		33-37	4th	8½

Date		Opp.	Res.	Score	(inn.*)	Hits	Opp. hits	Winning pitcher	Losing pitcher	Save	Record	Pos.	GB
6-26		At S.D.	L	2-6		4	12	Lefferts	Black		33-38	4th	9 ½
6-27		At S.D.	W	5-3	(10)	14	10	Brantley	Myers		34-38	4th	9 ½
6-28		At S.D.	L	3-7		7	9	Seminara	Burkett	Maddux	34-39	4th	10 ½
6-30		Atl.	L	3-4		8	7	Smoltz	Wilson		34-40	4th	10
7-1		Atl.	W	2-1		5	6	Black	Avery	Beck	35-40	4th	9
7-2		St.L.	L	0-1		4	6	Osborne	Swift	L. Smith	35-41	5th	10
7-3		St.L.	W	4-1		6	5	Burkett	Olivares		36-41	5th	10 ½
7-4		St.L.	L	0-1	(13)	9	6	Perez	Beck	L. Smith	36-42	5th	11
7-5		St.L.	W	3-1		8	8	Wilson	Cormier		37-42	5th	11
7-6		Phi.	W	4-2		8	10	Black	Abbott	Beck	38-42	4th	11
7-7	(1)	Phi.	W	8-7		11	8	Hickerson	Hartley	Beck	39-42	4th	11
7-7	(2)	Phi.	W	10-6		15	8	Pena	Robinson		40-42	4th	10 ½
7-8		Phi.	W	4-3		8	10	Jackson	Hartley	Beck	41-42	4th	9 ½
7-9		Mon.	L	5-6	(12)	11	15	Wetteland	Righetti		41-43	4th	10 ½
7-10		Mon.	L	2-3		8	7	Hill	Wilson	Rojas	41-44	4th	10 ½
7-11		Mon.	W	3-0		6	8	Black	Martinez		42-44	4th	9 ½
7-12		Mon.	W	4-0		12	7	Swift	Gardner		43-44	4th	8 ½
7-16		At N.Y.	W	6-4		8	8	Black	Gooden	Beck	44-44	4th	7 ½
7-17		At N.Y.	L	0-1		6	4	Cone	Swift		44-45	4th	8 ½
7-18		At N.Y.	L	0-3		4	7	Fernandez	Wilson	Young	44-46	4th	9 ½
7-19		At N.Y.	L	4-8		9	10	Schourek	Burkett		44-47	4th	10 ½
7-20		At Mon.	L	1-2		4	5	Barnes	Rapp	Wetteland	44-48	4th	11 ½
7-21		At Mon.	L	1-5		7	11	Hill	Black	Rojas	44-49	4th	11 ½
7-22		At Mon.	W	4-1		10	8	Swift	Nabholz		45-49	4th	11
7-24		At Phi.	L	4-8		11	14	Jones	Jackson	Mit. Williams	45-50	4th	12
7-25		At Phi.	W	6-2	(10)	11	6	Hickerson	Mit. Williams		46-50	4th	12
7-26		At Phi.	L	2-7		7	6	Mulholland	Rapp		46-51	4th	12
7-27		L.A.	W	5-1		7	3	Black	Candiotti		47-51	4th	11
7-28		L.A.	W	5-3		8	11	Beck	McDowell		48-51	4th	10
7-29		L.A.	L	1-6		5	9	R. Martinez	Wilson		48-52	4th	11
7-30		Atl.	W	5-0		11	4	Burkett	Leibrandt		49-52	4th	10
7-31		Atl.	W	4-3		6	10	Jackson	Mercker		50-52	4th	9 ½
8-1		Atl.	L	3-5		9	11	Smoltz	Black		50-53	4th	10 ½
8-2	(1)	Atl.	L	0-3		5	6	Smith	Swift	Pena	50-54	4th	11 ½
8-2	(2)	Atl.	L	5-8		10	11	Reynoso	Hickerson	Freeman	50-55	4th	12
8-3		At S.D.	L	5-6		15	10	Scott	Jackson		50-56	4th	12 ½
8-4		At S.D.	W	7-1		14	8	Burkett	Lefferts		51-56	4th	12 ½
8-5		At S.D.	L	1-4		9	10	Scott	Brantley	Myers	51-57	4th	13 ½
8-7		At Cin.	L	3-4		8	9	Rijo	Black	Dibble	51-58	4th	15
8-8		At Cin.	L	3-4	(16)	15	10	Henry	Pena		51-59	4th	16
8-9		At Cin.	W	7-1		12	3	Wilson	Bolton		52-59	4th	16
8-10		Hou.	W	4-1		9	6	Burkett	Henry		53-59	4th	15
8-11		Hou.	L	3-6		7	12	Williams	Oliveras	D. Jones	53-60	4th	15
8-12		Hou.	L	4-5	(10)	9	11	Hernandez	Brantley	D. Jones	53-61	4th	15 ½
8-14		At L.A.	W	3-2		4	10	Hickerson	Candelaria	Beck	54-61	4th	16
8-15		At L.A.	W	2-1		4	7	Wilson	R. Martinez	Beck	55-61	4th	16
8-16		At L.A.	W	2-1		5	5	Burkett	Howell	Beck	56-61	4th	15
8-17		At L.A.	L	0-2		0	8	Ke. Gross	Oliveras		56-62	4th	15
8-18		Chi.	L	1-4		11	6	Morgan	Black		56-63	4th	17
8-19		Chi.	W	9-1		11	7	Swift	Castillo		57-63	4th	17
8-20		Chi.	L	5-6		9	10	Harkey	Wilson	Scanlan	57-64	4th	17
8-21		Pit.	W	6-5		8	9	Burkett	Wakefield	Beck	58-64	4th	16
8-22		Pit.	L	2-9		5	13	Drabek	Oliveras		58-65	4th	17
8-23		Pit.	W	5-2		9	7	Black	Tomlin		59-65	4th	16
8-24		N.Y.	L	1-4		8	10	Gooden	Hickerson	Franco	59-66	4th	16 ½
8-25		N.Y.	L	1-2		8	9	Fernandez	Wilson	Franco	59-67	4th	16 ½
8-26		N.Y.	L	3-5		5	11	Hillman	Burkett	Young	59-68	4th	16 ½
8-28		At Chi.	L	2-3		11	8	Morgan	Jackson	Scanlan	59-69	T4th	16 ½
8-29		At Chi.	L	2-7		6	13	Castillo	Burba	Scanlan	59-70	5th	17 ½
8-30		At Chi.	L	1-3		1	6	Bullinger	Wilson		59-71	5th	17 ½
9-1		At Pit.	L	3-5		7	9	Jackson	Burkett	Mason	59-72	5th	19 ½
9-2		At Pit.	L	2-3		9	9	Wakefield	Black	Patterson	59-73	5th	19 ½
9-3		At Pit.	L	3-9		10	14	Drabek	Brantley		59-74	5th	19 ½
9-4		At St.L.	W	4-3	(10)	11	12	Beck	L. Smith		60-74	5th	18 ½
9-5		At St.L.	L	0-4		7	7	Cormier	Burkett	Worrell	60-75	5th	19 ½
9-6		At St.L.	L	3-5		6	9	Tewksbury	Carter	Worrell	60-76	5th	20 ½
9-7		S.D.	L	5-7		10	9	Seminara	Black	Hernandez	60-77	5th	21 ½
9-8		S.D.	W	6-5	(16)	13	13	Brantley	Ge. Harris		61-77	5th	22
9-9		Hou.	L	4-6		8	11	Blair	Swift	Hernandez	61-78	5th	22 ½
9-10		Hou.	W	5-2		7	10	Burkett	Bowen	Beck	62-78	5th	22 ½
9-11		At L.A.	W	7-3		12	8	Carter	Candiotti		63-78	5th	22 ½
9-12		At L.A.	L	0-7		6	13	Astacio	Black		63-79	5th	23 ½
9-13		At L.A.	W	7-3		12	8	Swift	Ojeda	Beck	64-79	5th	23 ½
9-14		At Hou.	L	0-5		4	8	Blair	Rogers	Hernandez	64-80	5th	24

Date	Opp.	Res.	Score	(inn.*)	Hits	Opp. hits	Winning pitcher	Losing pitcher	Save	Record	Pos.	GB
9-15	At Hou.	L	6-9	(11)	10	15	D. Jones	Righetti		64-81	5th	24
9-16	At Hou.	L	1-3		4	6	Kile	Carter	Boever	64-82	5th	25
9-18	L.A.	L	4-11		9	11	Astacio	Black	McDowell	64-83	5th	24½
9-19	L.A.	W	3-0		11	5	Brantley	Ojeda	Swift	65-83	5th	23½
9-20	L.A.	W	3-2		10	6	Beck	McDowell		66-83	5th	23½
9-21	At S.D.	W	7-1		10	9	Jackson	Deshaies		67-83	5th	23½
9-22	At S.D.	L	1-2		6	8	Benes	Carter	Myers	67-84	5th	23½
9-23	Atl.	L	0-7		6	13	Leibrandt	Black		67-85	5th	24½
9-24	Atl.	W	4-0		7	3	Brantley	Glavine		68-85	5th	23½
9-25	Cin.	L	2-4		6	11	Belcher	Rogers	Foster	68-86	5th	23½
9-26	Cin.	W	8-3		12	13	Burkett	Swindell		69-86	5th	23½
9-27	Cin.	L	2-3		10	9	Rijo	Carter	Dibble	69-87	5th	24½
9-29	At Atl.	L	0-6		8	8	Leibrandt	Black		69-88	5th	25½
9-30	At Atl.	W	1-0		6	5	Brantley	Glavine	Beck	70-88	5th	24½
10-1	At Atl.	L	5-6	(10)	8	11	Freeman	Jackson		70-89	5th	25½
10-2	At Cin.	W	4-1		8	4	Reed	Rijo	Beck	71-89	5th	26
10-3	At Cin.	L	1-6		5	10	Ayala	Carter		71-90	5th	27
10-4	At Cin.	W	6-2	(13)	12	9	Righetti	Ruskin		72-90	5th	26

Monthly records: April (12-10), May (15-11), June (7-19), July (16-12), August (9-19), September (11-17), Oct. (2-2).

HIGHLIGHTS

High point: After winning 13 of 18 games from May 7-27, the Giants boasted a 26-18 record and 1½-game lead in the National League West.

Low point: From August 24-September 3, the Giants lost nine games in a row, their longest streak since Roger Craig became manager in September 1985.

Turning point: There were two: On June 2, a ballot initiative for a new stadium in San Jose, Calif., was defeated. The Giants, 27-23 at the time, went 17-17 the rest of June. And on August 6, Owner Bob Lurie announced the team had been sold to investors from St. Petersburg, Fla. The Giants went 21-32 the rest of the season.

Most valuable player: First baseman Will Clark. It wasn't his greatest season, but he still hit .300 with 16 homers and 73 RBIs.

Most valuable pitcher: Righthander Bill Swift. He led the N.L. with a 2.08 ERA, the lowest by a title qualifier since 1985. Swift started the season 6-0 before developing shoulder problems that would plague him all season. He finished with a 10-4 record.

Most improved player: Catcher Kirt Manwaring. On the verge of being traded in 1991, Manwaring hit .244 while throwing out a league-best 43.9 percent of potential basestealers.

Most pleasant surprise: Righthander Rod Beck. He emerged by midseason as the closer, recording a team-high 17 saves with a 3-3 record and 1.76 ERA.

Biggest disappointment: Third baseman Matt Williams. After flourishing in 1990 and '91, Williams slumped last year, hitting .227 with 20 homers and 66 RBIs. Additionally, he led N.L. third basemen with 23 errors after winning a Gold Glove in '91.

Key injuries: Righthander Scott Garrelts didn't pitch for the Giants while spending the entire year rehabilitating from 1991 elbow surgery. Lefthander Trevor Wilson had a benign growth removed from a rib in March and was on the disabled list until April 17. He never fully recovered and went 8-14. Shoulder problems disabled Swift twice.

Notable: On November 10, N.L. owners rejected an attempt by Lurie to sell the Giants to a St. Petersburg, Fla., group. Lurie subsequently sold the team to a group of San Francisco investors, guaranteeing the Giants' presence in the Bay Area. ... The Giants posted their most losses (90) since dropping 100 games in 1985. ... The Dodgers' Kevin Gross threw a no-hitter against the Giants on August 17.

—LARRY STONE

RECORDS

1992 regular-season record: 72-90 (5th in N.L. West); 42-39 at home; 30-51 on road; 33-39 vs. East; 39-51 vs. West; 29-31 vs. LHP; 43-59 vs. RHP; 57-63 on grass; 15-27 on turf; 36-32 in day-time; 36-58 at night; 22-28 in one-run games; 10-12 in extra-inning games; 1-1-0 in doubleheaders.

Team record last five years: 407-403 (.502, ranks 6th in league in that span).

TEAM LEADERS

Batting average: Will Clark (.300).
At-bats: Matt Williams (529).
Runs: Will Clark (69).
Hits: Will Clark (154).
Total bases: Will Clark (244).
Doubles: Will Clark (40).
Triples: Kirt Manwaring, Matt Williams (5).
Home runs: Matt Williams (20).
Runs batted in: Will Clark (73).
Stolen bases: Darren Lewis (28).
Slugging percentage: Will Clark (.476).
On-base percentage: Will Clark (.384).
Wins: John Burkett (13).
Earned-run average: Bill Swift (2.08).
Complete games: John Burkett, Bill Swift (3).
Shutouts: Bill Swift (2).
Saves: Rod Beck (17).
Innings pitched: John Burkett (189⅔).
Strikeouts: John Burkett (107).

GAMES BY POSITION

Catcher: Kirt Manwaring 108, Craig Colbert 35, Jim McNamara 30, Steve Decker 15, Mark Bailey 7.
First base: Will Clark 141, Cory Snyder 27, Greg Litton 8.
Second base: Robby Thompson 120, Greg Litton 31, John Patterson 22, Cory Snyder 4, Mike Felder 3, Craig Colbert 2.
Third base: Matt Williams 144, Cory Snyder 14, Greg Litton 10, Craig Colbert 9, Mike Benjamin 2, Royce Clayton 1.
Shortstop: Royce Clayton 94, Jose Uribe 62, Mike Benjamin 33, Greg Litton 3, Cory Snyder 3.
Outfield: Willie McGee 119, Mike Felder 105, Darren Lewis 94, Kevin Bass 72, Cory Snyder 70, Chris James 62, Mark Leonard 37, Steve Hosey 18, Ted Wood 16, John Patterson 5, Greg Litton 1.

TOP 10 DRAFT CHOICES

1. **Calvin Murray**, OF, University of Texas.
2. **Jim Rosenbohm**, RHP, Hutchison (Kan.) Community College.
3. **Benji Simonton**, OF, Diablo Valley College (Calif.).
4. **Kurt Ehmann**, SS, Arizona State University.
5. **Doug Mirabelli**, C, Wichita State University.
6. **Aaron Fultz**, LHP, North Florida Junior College.
7. **Mark Pooschke**, 3B, Madison High School, Portland, Ore.
8. **Chris Wimmer**, SS, Wichita State University.
9. **Pete Roach**, 1B/OF, University of Nevada.
10. **Jamie Brewington**, RHP/OF, Virginia Commonwealth University.

1992
REVIEW

YEAR IN REVIEW

By STEVE GIETSCHIER

Despite the simple pleasures of a competitive regular season, an exciting postseason culminating in the first World Series truly deserving the name and several special achievements, baseball on the whole suffered more downs than ups in 1992. Economic uncertainty clouding the game's future stability stood at the heart of the sport's troubles, and at year's end no quick or easy solutions were at hand.

In mid-August, Commissioner Francis T. (Fay) Vincent, thoroughly soured by a job long since lacking much enjoyment, had summarized these dire straits when he declared in frustration that "we need about five major miracles in baseball."

Vincent, however, was not allowed the chance to be a miracle worker. Less than a month after making this pronouncement, he resigned under intense pressure from owners dissatisfied with his performance. Authority to govern the game passed to an Executive Council composed of the two league presidents and eight owners. The council in turn selected Milwaukee Brewers President Allan H. (Bud) Selig as chairman.

Selig announced that he would not make big decisions about baseball's problems alone. "The executive council with me as chairman will deal with any of these questions," he said. "I try to lead by consensus."

Still, it was quite apparent that the structure of baseball had been changed dramatically. When former President Jimmy Carter walked onto the field at Atlanta-Fulton County Stadium to throw out the ceremonial first pitch before Game 1 of the World Series, the Rawlings baseball he carried bore a blank space where the commissioner's signature normally is inscribed. To most observers, the symbolism of that void was inescapable.

Blue Jays rule majors

In a bid to avenge their defeat at the hands of the Minnesota Twins the previous fall, the Atlanta Braves captured the first game of the 89th World Series from the Toronto Blue Jays, 3-1. The Jays, however, went on to snare four of the next five games to win the first World Series championship in their history. While not quite as dramatic as the 1991 Series, the 1992 edition provided its own heroics. Four of the six contests were one-run affairs, and the decisive game went 11 innings before a verdict was rendered.

Toronto's advance to the Series marked the end of a skein of frustration dating to 1985. The Blue Jays captured their second consecutive American League East Division title, their third in four seasons and fourth in eight. But never before had Toronto journeyed through the A.L. Championship Series successfully.

Determined to lay to rest the derisive nickname "Blow Jays," Toronto Executive Vice President Pat Gillick had signed two veteran free agents, pitcher Jack Morris and outfielder/designated hitter Dave Winfield, in the off-season, hoping their experience would toughen the team's resolve. The Blue Jays charged out of the gate with six straight victories, never dropped more than half a game out of the division lead and held sole possession of first place from June 20 to the close of the season. Aided by a late-season trade that brought pitcher David Cone from the New York Mets, Toronto held off the hard-charging Milwaukee Brewers to clinch the pennant on the season's final Saturday.

In racking up 96 wins, the Blue Jays relied on superior offensive production from Joe Carter (34 home runs, 119 runs batted in), Roberto Alomar (.310 batting average, 76 RBIs) and Winfield (.290, 26 homers, 108 RBIs), who became the first player in major league history over the age of 40 to drive in 100 or more runs in a season. Morris became Toronto's first 20-game winner, Juan Guzman added 16 victories and reliever Tom Henke converted 34 of 37 save opportunities. Toronto drew a big-league-record 4,028,318 fans to SkyDome, with 68 sellouts in 81 home dates.

A's back on top in A.L. West

In the A.L. West, the Oakland Athletics regained the top spot they had occupied for three consecutive seasons before surrendering it to the Twins in 1991. Oakland also won 96 games, took over sole control of first place August 5 and sewed up the pennant September 28, an off-day for the A's, when the Twins lost to the Chicago White Sox. Minnesota defended its title valiantly, boasting a 53-34 record and a two-game lead over Oakland at the All-Star break. But the Twins went 37-38 after the break and wound up six games behind the A's.

Oakland Manager Tony La Russa had to deal with the effects of a spectacular trade (Jose Canseco going to the Texas Rangers for Ruben Sierra, Bobby Witt, Jeff Russell and cash) and extended injuries to outfielders Dave Henderson and Rickey Henderson, shortstop Walt Weiss, pitchers Bob Welch and Dave Stewart and first baseman Mark McGwire. La Russa often fashioned a makeshift lineup, using 45 different players overall (including 22 pitchers and 15 outfielders).

McGwire led the majors in home runs most of the season until he was sidelined in August with a muscle strain. He finished with 42 homers, one fewer than the major league leader, Juan Gonzalez of the Rangers. The A's best pitchers were Mike Moore, who won 17 games; Ron Darling, who pitched three two-hitters, and closer Dennis Eckersley, who recorded 51 saves and did not blow a save opportunity until August 8. For his performance, Eckersley won the A.L. Most Valuable Player honor and Cy Young Award and was named A.L. Fireman of the Year and A.L. Pitcher of the Year by THE SPORTING NEWS.

Braves again beat Pirates

The Braves reached the World Series for the second consecutive season by defeating the Pittsburgh Pirates, also for the second year in a row, in the National League Championship Series. Atlanta appeared out of the West Division race after the first two months of the season, standing in last place with a 20-27 record May 27. Thereafter, the Braves won 78 games against 37 losses (.678), reached first place for good August 2 and coasted home far in front of their rivals.

In winning 98 games, a franchise record, the Braves relied on a potent combination of speed, timely hitting and superb pitching. Tom Glavine won 20 games (including 13 in a row) for the second straight year, and John Smoltz (15-12) led the league in strikeouts with 215. Terry Pendleton hit .311 with 39 doubles, 21 home runs and 105 RBIs. Deion Sanders played in only 97 games, yet he led the league in triples with 14.

With their first-place finish in the N.L. East, the Pirates have now won three straight division titles on two occasions, 1970-72 and 1990-92. The Pirates dropped out of first place for only one eight-day span starting in late May and clinched the flag over the Montreal Expos with a week of the season to spare.

Manager Jim Leyland made up for the loss of free agent Bobby Bonilla by coaxing fine seasons out of several players, including Barry Bonds and Andy Van Slyke. Bonds (.311, 34 homers and 103 RBIs) won his second MVP award in three years. Van Slyke put together an outstanding season that included a .324 batting average, 199 hits and a league-leading 45 doubles. The Pirates' pitching was bolstered considerably by the promotion of Tim Wakefield from Class AAA Buffalo on July 31. His knuckleball consistently baffled rival hitters and propelled him to a record of 8-1 and an earned-run average of 2.15.

A.L. West reign ends

Toronto won the A.L. pennant by defeating Oakland in a six-game League Championship Series. The Jays thus snapped a streak of five straight West Division triumphs in the A.L. playoffs.

The teams split the first two games at SkyDome. The A's won Game 1 on a ninth-inning home run by Harold Baines, but Toronto evened the series with a 3-1 victory the next night.

In Oakland, the Blue Jays took Game 3, but they found themselves on the short end of a 6-1 score late in Game 4. Toronto scratched out three runs in the eighth inning and Alomar then hit a two-run homer off Eckersley to tie the game in the ninth. Pat Borders' sacrifice fly in the 11th sent Oakland to the brink of elimination.

The A's rebounded to win Game 5, but the Blue Jays put the series away with a 9-2 victory before their home fans in Game 6.

The margin by which the Braves defeated the Pirates in the N.L. Championship Series revivified the cliche that baseball is indeed a game of inches. In only the second repeat matchup of division winners in the 24-year history of the N.L. playoffs, the Braves squeaked out a 3-2 comeback victory in Game 7 to win their second straight N.L. pennant.

The series opened in Atlanta, and the Braves jumped out to a two-games-to-none lead behind the surprising baserunning of Sid Bream, the hitting of Ron Gant and the pitching of Smoltz and Steve Avery.

Wakefield helped Pittsburgh cut the deficit with a five-hitter in Game 3, but Smoltz beat Pirates ace Doug Drabek for the second time in five days to extend the Braves' lead to three games to one. Pittsburgh came back to tie the series with two decisive victories and was on the verge of sewing things up as Atlanta came to bat in the bottom of the ninth inning of the final game.

The Braves were down, 2-0, but they loaded the bases with none out. Gant's sacrifice fly drove in one run and, two batters later, pinch-hitter Francisco Cabrera singled to left to score David Justice and Bream, who slid home safely, barely eluding catcher Mike LaValliere's tag to bring the game to a stunning end.

As has happened so often in the past, the World Series provided an opportunity for lesser-known players to shine. Riding the emotional high of their dramatic victory over the Pirates, the Braves took Game 1 on a three-run homer by catcher Damon Berryhill, a reserve pressed into service by a late-season injury. Toronto evened the Series the next night on a pinch two-run homer in the ninth by utilityman Ed Sprague.

Game 2 was marred by an unfortunate mistake that nearly escalated into an international incident. The Marine color guard inadvertently carried the Canadian flag onto the field upside down, an error for which baseball officials quickly apologized. The off-day after the second game, however, gave this tempest time to percolate. The feelings of offended Canadians were assuaged by the Marines' offer to present the Canadian colors—right-side up—before Game 3.

The Blue Jays won the first two World Series games ever played outside the United States (the first of which featured a near triple play) and ousted Atlanta in Game 6. All of Toronto's four victories were by one run, and three came in the Jays' final at-bat. The Braves kept their hopes alive with a 7-2 triumph in Game 5 and very nearly pulled out Game 6. They tied the score, 2-2, in the ninth, surrendered a pair of runs on a Winfield double in the 11th and had the tying run poised on third base when Otis Nixon bunted out to pitcher Mike Timlin for the final out.

Each member of the Blue Jays voted a full share of the Series winnings received $114,962.16. Atlanta's full shares came to $84,259.13.

Yount, Brett attain 3,000

Baseball seems to be exhausting its supply of stars who play solely for a single team and last long enough to achieve significant career milestones. Robin Yount and George Brett defied this trend by reaching the 3,000-hit plateau late in the season without ever having switched uniforms.

Yount, a Milwaukee Brewer since 1974, got his 3,000th hit September 9 against the Cleveland Indians. With his single off Jose Mesa, Yount became the 17th player to attain 3,000 hits and the first since Rod Carew in 1985. Just a week short of his 37th birthday, he also was the third-youngest player to reach 3,000 behind Ty Cobb and Henry Aaron.

Brett, a Kansas City Royal since 1973, collected his 3,000th in a four-hit outburst against the California Angels on September 30. At 39, Brett had fought through an injury-filled career that nevertheless includes 59 games with four or more hits and batting titles in three decades, the latter a feat accomplished by no one else.

Dip in no-hitters

After two seasons in which major league pitchers hurled an inordinate number of no-hitters, 1992 saw only two such games recorded. On April 12, lefthander Matt Young of the Boston Red Sox no-hit the Indians in the first game of a doubleheader at Cleveland. Young pitched only eight innings, somewhat tainting his feat, because Cleveland did not have to bat in the ninth inning. The Indians took advantage of walks and errors to win the game, 2-1.

Kevin Gross of the Los Angeles Dodgers earned his no-hitter in more conventional fashion. The righthander shut out the San Francisco Giants in Los Angeles on August 17. Gross struck out six, walked two and hit one batter. He was aided by two fine fielding plays by Jose Offerman, the beleaguered shortstop who finished the year with an astounding 42 errors.

Other pitching accomplishments

Morris (21-6), Kevin Brown of the Rangers (21-11) and Jack McDowell of the Chicago White Sox (20-10) were the American League's 20-game winners. Boston's Roger Clemens led the league in shutouts with five and posted the league's lowest ERA (2.41) for the fourth time in seven years. The Seattle Mariners' Randy Johnson topped the league in strikeouts with 241. His victims included 18 Rangers on September 27, a total

that tied the league record for lefthanders held by Ron Guidry.

Greg Maddux of the Chicago Cubs (20-11) and Glavine (20-8) were the National League's only 20-game winners. Maddux finished third in ERA (2.18), third in strikeouts (199) and fourth in complete games (nine). For his achievements, Maddux won both the Cy Young and Gold Glove awards and was named N.L. Pitcher of the Year by THE SPORTING NEWS.

Bill Swift of the Giants captured the league's ERA title (2.08), and Terry Mulholland of the Philadelphia Phillies led in complete games with 12. Smoltz finished one strikeout ahead of Cone, who recorded 214 with the Mets before adding 47 more with Toronto.

Batting achievements

The A.L. batting crown went to Seattle's Edgar Martinez, who out-hit Kirby Puckett of the Twins, .343 to .329. The Detroit Tigers' Cecil Fielder surrendered the home run title to Gonzalez but drove in 124 runs to lead the league for the third year in a row.

Frank Thomas of the White Sox finished third in batting (.323) and RBIs (115), second in runs scored (108), tied for first in doubles (46) and first in on-base percentage (.439) and extra-base hits (72). He finished eighth in the MVP balloting.

For most of the season, Gary Sheffield of the San Diego Padres threatened to become the first N.L. player to win the Triple Crown since Joe Medwick in 1937. Sheffield's attempt died September 29 when he fractured his right index finger. At the time, he was leading the league in hitting and stood second in home runs and fourth in RBIs.

Sheffield's teammate, Fred McGriff, won the home run race, 35 to 34, over Bonds, and Philadelphia catcher Darren Daulton took the RBI crown with 109. Sheffield finished fifth in RBIs, third in homers and first in batting (.330), for which he was named Major League Player of the Year by THE SPORTING NEWS.

On September 23, Leon (Bip) Roberts of the Cincinnati Reds tied an N.L. record held by eight others when he got his 10th consecutive hit in a game against Los Angeles. The major league mark is 12, set by Mike Higgins of the Red Sox in 1938 and equaled by Detroit's Walt Dropo in 1952.

Unassisted triple play

Mickey Morandini of the Phillies made the first unassisted triple play in the National League since 1927 in the sixth inning of a September 20 game against the Pirates. Morandini's feat was the ninth unassisted triple play in major league history, the fourth in the National League and just the second ever by a second baseman.

Minnesota catcher Brian Harper pulled off an even rarer play, perhaps unique in baseball history, on June 27. Oakland's Mike Bordick hit a shot off the right foot of Twins pitcher Willie Banks. The ball caromed into foul territory, where Harper caught it in his bare hand and fired to first for a 1-2-3 groundout.

Cal Ripken of the Baltimore Orioles played in all 162 of his team's games, thereby extending to 1,735 his streak of consecutive games played.

Attendance drops

Major league attendance dropped for the second time in three years, to 55,872,271, a decline of more than 1 percent. National League attendance fell to 24,112,770, with only the Braves and Expos showing an increase. American League attendance also fell, to 31,759,501.

Besides Toronto, crowds were larger only in Baltimore (where Oriole Park at Camden Yards made its debut), Cleveland, Milwaukee and Minnesota.

Angels' bus crashes

California Angels Manager Buck Rodgers was seriously injured May 21 when one of the buses carrying the team from New York to Baltimore swerved out of control on the New Jersey Turnpike and crashed through a guardrail. Rodgers broke his right elbow, left knee and a rib.

Twelve others also were hurt in the mishap, less seriously. Coach John Wathan managed the Angels until Rodgers returned August 28.

Managerial merry-go-round

After prolonged selection processes, the National League's two expansion teams, scheduled to begin play in 1993, named their inaugural managers. The Florida Marlins selected Oakland's third-base coach, Rene Lachemann, and the Colorado Rockies picked St. Louis Cardinals hitting coach Don Baylor.

Three teams replaced their managers during the season, and another four made managerial changes before year's end. Tom Runnells of the Expos was fired May 22 and succeeded by Felipe Alou, the first Dominican to be named a major league manager. The Expos were 17-20 under Runnells and in fourth place in the N.L. East.

On July 9, the Rangers dumped Bobby Valentine despite their 45-41 record and appointed coach Toby Harrah as his interim replacement. Twelve games from the end of the season, on September 23, the Padres dismissed Greg Riddoch and gave the helm to Jim Riggleman, at 39 the youngest manager in the National League.

Two days after the close of the season, Lou Piniella resigned as manager of the Reds. Owner Marge Schott replaced him with Tony Perez, longtime Reds player and coach. Piniella's stay on the sidelines was brief. He was named to manage the Mariners on November 9 after Seattle fired Bill Plummer on October 13.

The Rangers decided not to retain Harrah; on October 26, they hired Montreal bench coach Kevin Kennedy as their new manager. Roger Craig of the Giants fell victim to a volatile ownership situation in San Francisco. He was discharged December 1 by prospective new owners, who acted before their purchase of the franchise was approved and replaced him December 16 with Giants coach Dusty Baker. This appointment brought the number of minority managers to six.

Move against Vincent

One of the first indications that Commissioner Vincent's continued tenure in office was in jeopardy came in early June at a meeting of the Player Relations Committee, baseball's collective bargaining arm. Several owners, apparently upset with Vincent for his intervention to end the 1990 lockout, proposed stripping the commissioner of any power in labor relations. Other owners came to the commissioner's defense, and Vincent himself refused to relinquish any authority.

After a heated debate, the commissioner emerged with his power intact, but some owners clearly had not been placated. When Vincent lashed out publicly at the owners, scolding them for their lack of cohesion and unity in the face of serious adversity, the stage was set for a protracted conflict between the commissioner and his critics.

In fact, Vincent already had incurred the wrath of several clubs when he testified earlier in June before a Senate subcommittee that copyright law should be amended to restrict cable television's easy access to games broadcast by local stations. Vincent was taking particular aim at the so-called superstations—WTBS of Atlanta, WGN of Chicago and WWOR of Secaucus, N.J.—each of which has its baseball broadcasts picked up by satellite and sent to significant numbers of cable subscribers.

Realignment issue

The issue that brought the Vincent controversy to a head seems to have been his insistence on National League divisional realignment over the objection of N.L. owners.

Realignment became important once the National League decided to expand to Denver and Miami and considered adopting an unbalanced schedule. In March, N.L. owners proposed placing the Rockies in the West and the Marlins in the East and shifting four existing franchises: St. Louis and Chicago to the West and Atlanta and Cincinnati to the East, thus giving the league geographic logic. Owners voted to approve this proposal, 10-2, but one of the two negative votes came from the Cubs, who as a directly affected party had to give assent.

In June, Vincent said he was taking the problem under advisement at the urging of several N.L. clubs and would render a decision by July 1, the date on which the league was bound to deliver the 1993 schedule to the Major League Baseball Players Association. Vincent said he would determine whether he could act under the best-interests-of-baseball clause in the major league rules.

With the schedule deadline extended a month, Vincent approved the proposed realignment July 6 and was immediately hit with a wave of opposition from owners, who believed he had exceeded his authority and overridden established N.L. procedures.

The Cubs sued the commissioner July 7 in U.S. District Court in Chicago and asked for a preliminary injunction barring Vincent from enforcing his decision. The injunction was granted July 23 by Judge Suzanne B. Conlon. Attorneys for the commissioner appealed her decision to the 7th Circuit U.S. Court of Appeals in Chicago and filed an emergency motion for an expedited appeal.

On August 10, the appeals court set September 30 as the date for oral arguments, but before any further court action transpired, Vincent had resigned. The National League, under pressure from the players association, scrapped realignment entirely September 24 and issued a balanced schedule for 1993. The Cubs dropped their suit, and Conlon lifted the injunction. Executive Council chairman Selig appointed a restructuring committee, composed of six owners plus the league presidents, to look into scheduling, divisional alignment and a possible third tier of postseason play. "We can move forward to resolve the realignment issue by consensus," Selig said, "rather than confrontation."

Proposed sale of Giants

Complicating the realignment debate was the proposed sale of the Giants. This unexpected turn began with the June 2 rejection of a referendum to build a new stadium in San Jose partially supported by public funds. Following the failure of this fourth initiative to build a stadium to replace Candlestick Park, Giants Owner Robert Lurie received permission from Vincent to consider moving or selling the team. On August 7, Lurie reached agreement in principle to sell the Giants for a reported $115 million to a group of Florida investors who would move the franchise to St. Petersburg.

San Francisco Mayor Frank Jordan organized a last-ditch attempt to keep the team in San Francisco despite Lurie's commitment to the Florida group not to seek other offers. For a while, George Shinn, owner of the National Basketball Association's Charlotte Hornets, was linked to Jordan's effort as a potential investor.

That effort, however, seemed to collapse in October when Shinn pulled out and refused to be part of a formal offer. Shortly thereafter, a group headed by Peter Magowan, chairman of Safeway Inc., announced a surprising bid of $95 million, later raised to $100 million, to buy the Giants and keep them in San Francisco, leaving the stadium question unresolved.

Since Lurie already had accepted the Florida offer, the Magowan proposal created a sticky situation. Lurie appeared to have permission to sell the team and let it be moved, but other factors—

including realignment, the reported opposition of the Florida Marlins to the move and the resignation of the commissioner—delayed a decision.

Owners gathered at a special November meeting in Phoenix to sort the matter out. The Executive Council took no position, but N.L. owners rejected the bid to transfer the team to Florida by a 9-4 vote. Later that month, Lurie accepted the Magowan group's offer, pending approval from the other club owners.

Other ownership changes

Other changes in ownership came with their own complications.

In serious financial difficulty, Mariners Owner Jeff Smulyan had put his team up for sale in December 1991, with an asking price of $100 million. Smulyan was committed to accepting local bids until March 27, but speculation suggested that his intention after that date would be to petition to move his club to St. Petersburg.

A local offer was announced January 23, but baseball officials generally were chagrined to learn that 60 percent of the money to buy the Mariners would come from Hiroshi Yamauchi, president of Nintendo Co. Ltd. of Kyoto, Japan. "It's unlikely foreign investors would receive the requisite baseball approvals," Vincent said initially.

Coming at a time when economic friction between the United States and Japan was quite sharp, the Nintendo offer flew hard in the face of the tradition that no major league team had ever been owned by interests outside the United States or Canada. Baseball's ownership committee, composed of eight owners, the two league presidents and the commissioner, nevertheless took the offer under study, and over the next few months opposition to the sale softened.

A revised proposal was finally approved June 11 by a 25-1 vote of all owners. Yamauchi, who contributed $75 million of the $125 million package, agreed to forgo control of the team except for decisions involving relocation or future sale. John Ellis, chairman of Puget Sound Power & Light Co., became chief executive officer of the Mariners.

Ownership of the Tigers changed hands as Thomas Monaghan of Domino's Pizza Inc. sold the team to Michael Ilitch of Little Caesars Enterprises Inc., a rival pizza company. The two reached agreement in late July, and the sale, for a reported $85 million, was approved by major league owners in September. In the interim, Monaghan fired club president Bo Schembechler and board chairman Jim Campbell.

About a year after announcing he wanted to sell the Houston Astros, John McMullen reached an agreement to sell the team and related properties to Drayton McLane, the second-largest stockholder in Wal-Mart Enterprises. The value of the club was estimated at about $90 million. Major league owners approved the sale in October.

Changes in the Yankees' hierarchy were a mere

backdrop to George Steinbrenner's attempt to re-gain active control of the team. Steinbrenner, principal owner of the club, had requested and received a lifetime ban August 20, 1990, for his involvement with gambler Howard Spira even though Vincent was prepared merely to suspend him for two years. Early in 1992, rumors circulated that Steinbrenner would seek reinstatement, but Vincent announced that he would hear no such petition until all three lawsuits relevant to Stein-brenner's ban were dropped.

The first of the three suits, filed by limited partners Daniel McCarthy and Howard Bowman, already had been dropped in December 1991. The Yankees then elected McCarthy to replace Robert Nederlander as managing general partner, but Vincent refused to approve this decision. He cited two reasons—McCarthy's willingness to sue the commissioner in the first place and McCarthy's refusal to relocate from Cleveland to New York. Subsequently, Vincent did approve the selection of Joseph Molloy, Steinbrenner's son-in-law, as managing general partner.

The second suit was settled in January, and the last of the three was dropped in April. Steinbrenner met with Vincent in May. Following some additional investigation, Vincent announced Stein-brenner's complete reinstatement on July 24, effective March 1, 1993.

Drug-abuse incidents

Baseball's continuing problem with drug abuse, albeit far less rampant than in previous years, reared its ugly head again in 1992. There were two incidents, both involving pitchers for the Yankees. Pascual Perez received a one-year suspension, the second of his career, on March 6 after testing positive for cocaine. Steve Howe also was suspended, for the seventh time in his career, and then permanently banned after he pleaded guilty to a drug charge. His penalty, however, was overturned by arbitrator George Nicolau.

Howe had been arrested in December 1991 in Kalispell, Mont., and charged with attempting to buy one gram of cocaine from a Drug Enforcement Agency informant. A second charge, possessing two grams of cocaine, was added later. On June 8, Howe pleaded guilty to the first charge, and Vincent suspended him indefinitely.

The players association filed a grievance over the suspension, arguing that Vincent had acted prematurely. At the grievance hearing, Nicolau urged Vincent to put a definite time limit on the suspension, and Vincent responded by making Howe's ban permanent.

Howe was sentenced to three years' probation August 18, but Nicolau overturned his suspension November 12. In his decision, the arbitrator supported the players association's contention that an underlying psychological problem, in this case Howe's childhood hyperactivity, should be a mitigating factor. Nicolau reinstated Howe, who sub-sequently signed a new contract with the Yankees, but recommended a lifetime ban if he fails an eighth time.

Take aim at commissioner

The players association filed an unfair-labor-practices charge against Vincent after he summoned three Yankees officials to his office in the wake of their testimony at the Howe grievance hearing. He threatened the three—Manager Buck Showalter, General Manager Gene Michael and Vice President Jack Lawn—with discipline for not supporting baseball's drug policy and caused Showalter to arrive late for a Yankees day game.

On August 17, three days after Vincent's plea for major miracles, A.L. President Bobby Brown and N.L. President Bill White wrote to him requesting a special owners meeting to discuss "the office and duties of the commissioner." Amid substantial rumors that owners wanted him to step down, Vincent rejected this request vigorously August 20.

"I will not resign—ever," Vincent said.

Major league owners decided to meet anyway, and they convened September 3 in suburban Chicago. There, they voted to approve a resolution of no confidence in the commissioner, 18-9, with the Cincinnati Reds abstaining, and urged Vincent to resign.

The resolution stated in part: "The major league clubs do not have confidence in the ability of the present commissioner . . . and that under his direction, it is impossible for baseball to move forward effectively and constructively." Owners who voted for the resolution cited nearly every controversial issue in which Vincent had become involved over the preceding three years. Those who voted against the resolution urged their colleagues to support stability in a time of crisis.

Vincent calls it quits

After several days of reflection, the commissioner resigned September 7, calling his decision "my final act as commissioner 'in the best interests of baseball.'"

The gloom that these events cast was alleviated somewhat by postseason play and later by November's expansion draft, in which the Rockies and Marlins stocked their rosters. Considerable speculation ensued when the lists of players protected by the established clubs were leaked to the press several days before the draft, revealing the decision by many teams to leave high-salaried players exposed. In the main, though, the new franchises shied away from assuming large contracts and focused on drafting young talent and prospects untried at the major league level.

Players' salaries jump

If baseball's troubles are fundamentally matters of economics, the salary figures and other financial data released at the end of the season provided little solace. The players association announced an average salary for 1992 of $1,028,667, an increase of 21 percent over 1991's $851,492 and 72 percent over 1990's $597,537.

The Player Relations Committee, which computes signing bonuses slightly differently, announced an average salary of $1,012,424.

The highest individual salary went to Bobby Bonilla of the New York Mets. He earned $6,100,000 in the first year of a five-year, $29 million contract.

Toronto was the team with the highest average salary, $1,719,694, and Cleveland's average, $326,537, was the lowest. Fourteen of the 26 teams paid an average salary in excess of $1 million.

Part of the increase in average salary can be attributed to several impressive contracts signed before and during the season and to 1992's round of salary-arbitration cases.

In January, free agent Danny Tartabull signed a five-year contract with the Yankees for $25.5 million, and Barry Larkin re-signed with the Reds for $25.6 million over five years. In March, Ryne Sandberg agreed to a four-year contract extension with the Cubs that could bring him $30.5 million. Spreading his $3.5 million signing bonus over the life of this contract made Sandberg baseball's first $7 million man. In August, Cal Ripken did nearly as well when he signed a five-year, $32.5 million deal with the Orioles.

A total of 149 players filed for salary arbitration in January, 10 fewer than in the previous year. The average salary for these players, plus those who accepted arbitration offered by their clubs, jumped from $710,095 in 1991 to $1,424,739 in 1992, an increase of 100 percent. In dollar terms, the average raise of $714,644 was the largest ever.

Several records were set during the arbitration process. Cecil Fielder topped the list of all players submitting salary requests by asking for an all-time-high $5.4 million. He avoided a hearing by signing a one-year contract for $4.5 million with the Tigers. Barry Bonds and Ruben Sierra asked for $5 million, and five other players asked for more than $4 million.

Twenty cases proceeded all the way through the hearing and award stages, with the clubs winning 11 times. David Cone surpassed Doug Drabek's record 1991 award of $3.35 million when an arbitrator granted him $4.25 million. Sierra bested Cone a few days later, winning the $5 million he had sought.

The largest percentage increase went to Jack McDowell of the White Sox—even though he lost his request for $2.3 million. His salary rose 814 percent from $175,000 to $1.6 million.

Schott faces racism charge

Three weeks before the start of the winter meetings in December, baseball's establishment was rocked by allegations of racism lodged against Marge Schott. Depositions taken for a suit filed by former Reds controller Tim Sabo against Schott alleged that the Reds' owner had engaged in discriminatory hiring practices and spoken of Jews and African Americans in derogatory terms.

In response, Schott denied the discrimination charge but admitted using words that many people consider racial and ethnic slurs. She said she did not think they were offensive. Henry Aaron, Atlanta Braves senior vice president, called upon baseball to investigate the allegations. "We won't stand for this," he said. "There is no place for it in the national pastime."

Schott issued a formal apology for all her comments December 9, but she also insisted that she "was not the cause of the problem. Minority issues have been present in baseball long before I came to the game."

Opportunity to act

The winter meetings in Louisville presented an unusual opportunity for baseball, now governed by the Executive Council and a series of committees, to demonstrate how the consensus Bud Selig earnestly sought could solve some of the sport's problems. But neither the ownership committee nor the restructuring committee nor the Schott committee moved its agenda to final resolution.

Also, a search committee to begin the process of hiring a new commissioner was not yet appointed by year's end.

Reopen Basic Agreement

What the assembled owners did decide in Louisville, by a 15-13 vote, was to reopen the collective bargaining agreement with the players association, one year short of its expiration. The 1990 Basic Agreement allowed for reopening by either side, and the Player Relations Committee, looking for some change in the player-compensation system, urged the owners to take this step.

Lurking behind this decision was the possibility of a lockout or other work stoppage sometime during 1993. Donald Fehr, executive director of the players association, called a lockout a "foregone conclusion," but Richard Ravitch, president of the Player Relations Committee, disagreed. "It is a legal option," he said, "but one I hope never comes to pass." Ravitch did get the owners to amend their rules so that approval of a lockout would require a three-fourths majority vote.

Enormous contracts

The stunning news emanating from Louisville concerned the enormous contracts many teams gave to free agents, this in the face of rather steady assertions by owners that their teams are not profitable and that the game is headed for economic calamity.

The bidding for free agents was as furious as ever, with pitcher John Smiley becoming the first premier player to reap its benefits when he signed a four-year deal with the Reds for $18.4 million.

Other prominent players who signed large contracts and moved to new teams included pitchers Doug Drabek (Houston, four years, $19.5 million), Greg Swindell (Houston, four years, $17 million), David Cone (Kansas City, three years, $18 million) and Greg Maddux (Atlanta, five years, $28 million) and designated hitter Paul Molitor (Toronto, three years, $13 million).

Some players chose to remain with their previous teams, including outfielders Kirby Puckett (Minnesota, five years, $30 million), Joe Carter (Toronto, three years, $19.5 million) and Ruben Sierra (Oakland, five years, $28 million) and shortstop Ozzie Smith (St. Louis, one year, $4.2 million with options).

The largest package of all went to Barry Bonds, who signed with the Giants for six years at $43.75 million, making him baseball's highest-salaried player.

Antitrust exemption re-examined

The antitrust subcommittee of the Senate Judiciary Committee reacted to the state of baseball in 1992 by opening hearings in December to re-examine the sport's exemption from antitrust regulation, which has stood since a 1922 decision by the U.S. Supreme Court. Sen. Howard Metzenbaum, chairman of the subcommittee, did not submit legislation to repeal the exemption, but he said, "The burden of proof is on baseball to show why it should continue."

A week after the winter meetings, which ended with tragic abruptness upon the death of Florida Marlins President Carl Barger, who succumbed to an aortic aneurysm, the Economic Study Committee on Baseball released its report. The group, created in 1990 by labor and management, criticized both players and owners for fostering a pattern of strikes and lockouts that has damaged the short-term and long-term interests of both parties. The committee called for elimination of salary arbitration, reduction of service eligibility for free agency from six years to three and revenue-sharing between large- and small-market clubs.

Whatever problems baseball has, the essence of the game still unfolds unhurriedly on the field between the white lines. In 1992, here's how that game wound up:

FINAL STANDINGS

AMERICAN LEAGUE

EAST DIVISION

Team	Tor.	Mil.	Bal.	Cle.	N.Y.	Det.	Bos.	Oak.	Min.	Chi.	Tex.	Cal.	K.C.	Sea.	W	L	Pct.	GB
Toronto	...	5	8	7	11	8	6	6	7	9	7	7	7	8	96	66	.593	—
Milwaukee	8	...	7	8	6	8	8	7	6	7	7	7	5	8	92	70	.568	4
Baltimore	5	6	...	7	5	10	8	6	6	6	7	8	8	7	89	73	.549	7
Cleveland	6	5	6	...	7	5	7	6	6	5	5	6	5	7	76	86	.469	20
New York	2	7	8	6	...	8	6	6	5	4	6	5	7	6	76	86	.469	20
Detroit	5	5	3	8	5	...	9	6	3	2	8	5	7	9	75	87	.463	21
Boston	7	5	5	6	7	4	...	5	3	6	4	8	7	6	73	89	.451	23

WEST DIVISION

Team	Oak.	Min.	Chi.	Tex.	Cal.	K.C.	Sea.	Tor.	Mil.	Bal.	Cle.	N.Y.	Det.	Bos.	W	L	Pct.	GB
Oakland	...	8	8	9	8	9	12	6	5	6	6	6	6	7	96	66	.593	—
Minnesota	5	...	5	6	11	7	8	5	6	6	7	9	9	6	90	72	.556	6
Chicago	5	8	...	5	10	7	4	5	5	6	7	8	10	6	86	76	.531	10
Texas	4	7	8	...	4	7	9	3	5	5	7	6	4	8	77	85	.475	19
California	5	2	3	9	...	8	7	5	5	4	6	7	7	4	72	90	.444	24
Kansas City	4	6	6	6	5	...	7	5	7	4	7	5	5	5	72	90	.444	24
Seattle	1	5	9	4	6	6	...	4	4	5	5	6	3	6	64	98	.395	32

NATIONAL LEAGUE

EAST DIVISION

Team	Pit.	Mon.	St.L.	Chi.	N.Y.	Phi.	Atl.	Cin.	S.D.	Hou.	S.F.	L.A.	W	L	Pct.	GB
Pittsburgh	...	9	15	10	14	13	5	6	5	6	6	7	96	66	.593	—
Montreal	9	...	6	11	12	9	8	7	8	4	5	8	87	75	.537	9
St. Louis	3	12	...	7	9	11	6	5	8	7	7	8	83	79	.512	13
Chicago	8	7	11	...	9	9	2	5	5	8	8	6	78	84	.481	18
New York	4	6	9	9	...	6	5	5	4	7	10	7	72	90	.444	24
Philadelphia	5	9	7	9	12	...	6	5	3	4	3	7	70	92	.432	26

WEST DIVISION

Team	Atl.	Cin.	S.D.	Hou.	S.F.	L.A.	Pit.	Mon.	St.L.	Chi.	N.Y.	Phi.	W	L	Pct.	GB
Atlanta	...	9	13	13	11	12	7	4	6	10	7	6	98	64	.605	—
Cincinnati	9	...	11	10	10	11	6	5	7	7	7	7	90	72	.556	8
San Diego	5	7	...	11	11	9	7	4	4	7	8	9	82	80	.506	16
Houston	5	8	7	...	12	13	6	8	5	4	5	8	81	81	.500	17
San Francisco	7	8	7	6	...	11	6	7	5	4	2	9	72	90	.444	26
Los Angeles	6	7	9	5	7	...	5	4	4	6	5		63	99	.389	35

NOTE: Read across for wins, down for losses.

A.L. CHAMPIONSHIP SERIES

GAME 1

HIGHLIGHTS

OAKLAND 4, TORONTO 3

Why the Athletics won: Old pros Harold Baines, Dave Stewart and Dennis Eckersley came through. Baines, a 13-season major league veteran, came to the plate in the ninth inning of a 3-3 game and drilled a Jack Morris pitch over the right-field wall. Stewart, who entered the fray with a 5-0 career record in League Championship Series play, was his usual intimidating self—at least for 7⅔ innings. His trademark glare and mix of pitches working well, Stewart took a 3-2 lead into the eighth inning before giving way to Jeff Russell, who was nicked for John Olerud's game-tying single up the middle. The 38-year-old Eckersley, coming off a 51-save season (the second-best performance in major league history), came on in the ninth and recorded his 10th save in 13 championship-series appearances.

Why the Blue Jays lost: Having dropped championship series in 1985, 1989 and 1991, Toronto merely was doing what comes naturally—or so it seemed. One thing was certain—the 51,000-plus fans provided no home-field advantage. The loss, after all, was the Blue Jays' sixth straight playoff setback at SkyDome, dating to 1989. As for a more tangible reason, Blue Jays Manager Cito Gaston may have stayed with his veteran, the 37-year-old Morris—a money pitcher, to be sure—one inning too long.

The turning points:

1. Stewart's ability to induce double-play grounders in each of the first two innings and then get Joe Carter on a fly ball in the third with runners on second and third base and two out. Stewart then settled down, remaining in command despite yielding bases-empty homers to Toronto's Pat Borders (fifth inning) and Dave Winfield (sixth inning).

2. Oakland's resilience. Having watched a 3-0 lead evaporate when the Blue Jays collected single runs in the fifth, sixth and eighth innings, the A's let Toronto revel in its comeback only briefly. Just minutes after Winfield doubled with two out in the eighth and raced home with the tying run on Olerud's hit, Baines strode to the plate as Oakland's leadoff hitter in the ninth and promptly took Morris deep.

Notable: The victory extended the Athletics' championship-series winning streak to seven games. ... The home run was Winfield's first in postseason play, which until 1992 had consisted of the 1981 playoffs and World Series with the Yankees. ... When Mark McGwire (a two-run shot) and Terry Steinbach rapped consecutive homers for Oakland in the second inning, it marked the first back-to-back blasts in the A.L. playoffs since Rick Cerone and Lou Piniella connected for the Yankees in 1980.

Quotable: "This one will be special for a long time," Baines said of his game-winning homer.... "This is my time of year," Stewart said of the playoff success that has marked his 13-year major league career. ... Oakland Manager Tony La Russa wasn't totally satisfied with the night's proceedings. "The only thing I didn't like," he said, "was that Stewart didn't get the win. He did the most for us." ... Gaston's reason for staying with Morris in the ninth after the Blue Jays had tied the score at 3-3: "I figured that Jack has pitched well enough for us this year to give him a shot to go out and win the game."

BOX SCORE

WEDNESDAY, OCTOBER 7, AT TORONTO

Oakland	AB	R	H	RBI	PO	A
R. Henderson, lf	2	0	0	0	2	0
Lansford, 3b	4	0	0	0	0	1
Sierra, rf	4	0	0	0	3	0
Baines, dh	4	2	3	1	0	0
McGwire, 1b	3	1	1	2	8	1
Steinbach, c	4	1	1	1	2	0
Wilson, cf	4	0	1	0	3	0
Bordick, ss	4	0	0	0	3	5
Blankenship, 2b	2	0	0	0	5	4
Stewart, p	0	0	0	0	1	1
Russell, p	0	0	0	0	0	0
Eckersley, p	0	0	0	0	0	0
Totals	31	4	6	4	27	12

Toronto	AB	R	H	RBI	PO	A
White, cf	3	0	1	0	1	0
Alomar, 2b	4	0	1	0	3	3
Carter, rf-1b	4	0	1	0	3	0
Winfield, dh	4	2	2	1	0	0
Olerud, 1b	3	0	1	1	11	0
Bell, pr-rf	0	0	0	0	1	0
Maldonado, lf	4	0	0	0	1	0
Gruber, 3b	4	0	0	0	1	4
Borders, c	4	1	1	1	5	0
Lee, ss	3	0	1	0	1	5
Sprague, ph	1	0	1	0	0	0
Griffin, pr	0	0	0	0	0	0
Morris, p	0	0	0	0	0	2
Totals	34	3	9	3	27	14

Oakland	0 3 0	0 0 0	0 0 1	—4
Toronto	0 0 0	0 1 1	0 1 0	—3

Oakland	IP	H	R	ER	BB	SO
Stewart	7⅔	7	3	3	3	2
Russell (W)	⅓	1	0	0	0	0
Eckersley (S)	1	1	0	0	0	0

Toronto	IP	H	R	ER	BB	SO
Morris (L)	9	6	4	4	4	4

E—R. Henderson. DP—Oakland 2, Toronto 2. LOB—Oakland 4, Toronto 7. 2B—Winfield. HR—McGwire, Steinbach, Borders, Winfield, Baines. SB—Wilson, Alomar. WP—Morris. U—Denkinger, plate; Young, first; Clark, second; Merrill, third; Brinkman, left field; Coble, right field. T—2:47. A—51,039.

HIGHLIGHTS

TORONTO 3, OAKLAND 1

Why the Blue Jays won: Their "hired gun," David Cone, triggered the victory with eight-plus innings of masterful pitching. Obtained in a late-August trade with the Mets for the express purpose of getting Toronto over the postseason hump, free agent-to-be Cone permitted only five hits and made clutch pitches time and again.

Why the Athletics lost: Twice in three innings they had runners on second and third base and could not score. Also, A's starter Mike Moore couldn't handle Toronto third baseman Kelly Gruber, who broke open a scoreless game with a two-run homer in the fifth inning and then doubled and scored the Blue Jays' final run (on Manny Lee's sacrifice fly) in the seventh.

The turning points:

1. With one out in the fifth and A's runners on first and second base, Cone threw a pitch into the dirt that bounced away from catcher Pat Borders. Willie Wilson, stationed on second, steamed around third and dashed home, apparently giving the A's a 1-0 lead. However, the ball rolled into the Toronto dugout. The rule book calls for an advancement of only one base in such a dead-ball situation, and Wilson was sent back to third and Mike Bordick was returned to second. Given a reprieve, Cone proceeded to strike out Walt Weiss and Rickey Henderson and the game remained 0-0.

2. Gruber's home run in the bottom of the fifth. Slowed with injuries and stymied by slumps over the last two years after enjoying a banner 1990 season, Gruber got back on the fans' good side with his timely smash.

Notable: After two games of the A.L. playoffs, the top third of the Oakland batting order—Henderson, Carney Lansford and Ruben Sierra—had one hit in 21 at-bats. That hit was a ninth-inning triple in Game 2 off the bat of Sierra, who scored the Athletics' only run of the night when Harold Baines followed with a single. . . . The A's stole six bases against Cone, equaling the A.L. Championship Series record, but none of the thefts figured in the scoring. . . . Oakland's baserunning wasn't entirely exemplary. After rapping a single and stealing second in the eighth (when the A's trailed 3-0), Weiss inexplicably tried to advance to third on a fly ball to left and was thrown out easily, Candy Maldonado to Gruber.

Quotable: "Naturally, you think about being called a hired gun and where you're going to be next year," Cone said of his impending free agency. "But you try to throw all of that out of your mind. Free agency will take care of itself. Right now, I have a chance to be on a team that will go all the way."

. . . Cone, on dodging the fifth-inning bullet when his errant pitch wound up in the dugout: "We got

the break, and you could feel the emotions lift." . . . "It's been rough," Gruber said of his tribulations of the last two years. ". . . When I ran around the bases (after his home run), it was a sigh of relief."

BOX SCORE

THURSDAY, OCTOBER 8, AT TORONTO

Oakland	AB	R	H	RBI	PO	A
R. Henderson, lf	4	0	0	0	4	0
Lansford, 3b	4	0	0	0	0	3
Sierra, rf	3	1	1	0	1	0
Baines, dh	4	0	2	1	0	0
Fox, pr-dh	0	0	0	0	0	0
McGwire, 1b	4	0	0	0	6	0
Steinbach, c	4	0	1	0	3	2
Wilson, cf	4	0	1	0	6	0
Bordick, 2b	2	0	0	0	2	2
Weiss, ss	2	0	1	0	2	1
Moore, p	0	0	0	0	0	1
Corsi, p	0	0	0	0	0	0
Parrett, p	0	0	0	0	0	0
Totals	31	1	6	1	24	9

Toronto	AB	R	H	RBI	PO	A
White, cf	3	0	0	0	2	0
Alomar, 2b	3	0	1	0	1	0
Carter, rf	3	0	0	0	2	0
Winfield, dh	3	0	0	0	0	0
Olerud, 1b	3	0	0	0	4	0
Maldonado, lf	2	1	0	0	3	1
Gruber, 3b	3	2	2	2	1	2
Borders, c	3	0	1	0	8	1
Lee, ss	2	0	0	1	6	1
Cone, p	0	0	0	0	0	1
Henke, p	0	0	0	0	0	0
Totals	25	3	4	3	27	6

Oakland	0 0 0	0 0 0	0 0 1—1			
Toronto	0 0 0	0 2 0	1 0 x—3			

Oakland	IP	H	R	ER	BB	SO
Moore (L)	7	4	3	3	4	3
Corsi	⅔	0	0	0	1	0
Parrett	⅓	0	0	0	0	0

Toronto	IP	H	R	ER	BB	SO
Cone (W)	8	5	1	1	3	6
Henke (S)	1	1	0	0	0	1

DP—Oakland 1, Toronto 1. LOB—Oakland 6, Toronto 4. 2B—Wilson, Gruber. 3B—Sierra. HR—Gruber. SB—Wilson 3, Weiss 2, Bordick, Alomar, Carter. CS—White, Sierra. SF—Lee. U—Young, plate; Clark, first; Merrill, second; Brinkman, third; Coble, left field; Denkinger, right field. T—2:58. A—51,114.

GAME 3

HIGHLIGHTS

TORONTO 7, OAKLAND 5

Why the Blue Jays won: They got a solid effort from righthander Juan Guzman and displayed a pesky—albeit hardly explosive—offense. Guzman, who missed most of August because of shoulder soreness and struggled at times after returning to the Blue Jays' rotation, permitted seven hits and two runs over six innings before giving way to Toronto's relief corps. Offensively, the Blue Jays scored in five of the game's final six innings.

Why the Athletics lost: They played very un-Oakland-like baseball, committing three errors, uncorking three wild pitches, yielding five bases on balls, leaving 11 men on base and having a runner thrown out at the plate.

The turning points:

1. Candy Maldonado's leadoff home run to left in the fifth inning, which snapped a 2-2 tie. While there were numerous ebbs and flows in the game thereafter, Maldonado's smash nevertheless gave Toronto the lead for good. A veteran of five previous League Championship Series (with the Dodgers, Giants and Blue Jays) in which he batted a composite .137, Maldonado also knocked home Toronto's first run with a second-inning single.

2. Having deadlocked the game with two fourth-inning runs, the Athletics had a chance to break it open in that frame when they loaded the bases with no one out. However, Mike Bordick flied out to Joe Carter in right field, a play on which the hulking Mark McGwire, a 6-foot-5, 225-pounder, tagged up at third base and was thrown out, Carter to catcher Pat Borders, as he attempted to score. The inning then ended when Walt Weiss grounded out.

Notable: The contest was the longest, in time, for a nine-inning game in A.L. Championship Series history, running three hours and 40 minutes. . . . Blue Jays shortstop Manny Lee, who had only one triple and just 14 extra-base hits overall in the regular season, gave his club some breathing room in the seventh when he belted a two-run triple into the right-field corner. The hit boosted Toronto's lead to 5-2. . . . Oakland's Ruben Sierra, Harold Baines and Terry Steinbach combined for seven hits and all five of the Athletics' RBIs.

Quotable: "We played awfully sloppy today," A's starter Ron Darling said. "It wasn't indicative of the type of ball we've played all year." . . . Guzman was disbelieving about McGwire's attempt to score on a bases-loaded fly ball in the fourth inning. "He's not a good runner," Guzman said. "That play picked me up. I told myself after that I had to go after them." . . . "I was surprised he tested me," Jays right fielder Carter said of McGwire.

BOX SCORE

SATURDAY, OCTOBER 10, AT OAKLAND

Toronto	AB	R	H	RBI	PO	A
White, cf	3	0	1	0	1	0
Alomar, 2b	5	1	1	1	2	3
Carter, rf	5	0	1	0	5	1
Winfield, dh	4	2	1	1	0	0
Olerud, 1b	5	1	1	0	10	1
Maldonado, lf	3	1	2	2	2	0
Gruber, 3b	4	0	0	0	0	2
Borders, c	4	1	1	0	5	0
Lee, ss	3	1	1	2	2	3
Guzman, p	0	0	0	0	0	0
Ward, p	0	0	0	0	0	0
Timlin, p	0	0	0	0	0	0
Henke, p	0	0	0	0	0	0
Totals	36	7	9	6	27	10

Oakland	AB	R	H	RBI	PO	A
R. Henderson, lf	4	1	1	0	2	0
Lansford, 3b	5	0	1	0	0	1
Sierra, rf	4	1	2	2	4	0
Baines, dh	5	2	2	1	0	0
McGwire, 1b	4	0	1	0	9	0
Steinbach, c	4	0	3	2	3	3
Wilson, cf	4	0	2	0	2	0
Bordick, 2b	2	0	0	0	3	2
Browne, ph	0	0	0	0	0	0
Blankenship, pr-2b	1	0	1	0	0	0
Weiss, ss	4	1	0	0	3	4
Darling, p	0	0	0	0	1	0
Downs, p	0	0	0	0	0	0
Corsi, p	0	0	0	0	0	0
Russell, p	0	0	0	0	0	0
Honeycutt, p	0	0	0	0	0	0
Eckersley, p	0	0	0	0	0	0
Totals	37	5	13	5	27	10

```
Toronto .......................... 0 1 0   1 1 0   2 1 1—7
Oakland .......................... 0 0 0   2 0 0   2 1 0—5
```

Toronto	IP	H	R	ER	BB	SO
Guzman (W)	6	7	2	2	3	3
Ward	1	3	2	2	1	1
Timlin	1/3	2	1	1	0	0
Henke (S)	1 2/3	1	0	0	0	0

Oakland	IP	H	R	ER	BB	SO
Darling (L)	6	4	3	2	2	3
Downs	1	2	2	0	0	0
Corsi	1/3	0	0	0	0	0
Russell	*2/3	1	2	2	3	0
Honeycutt	2/3	0	0	0	0	0
Eckersley	1/3	2	0	0	0	1

*Pitched to one batter in ninth.

E—Lee, Lansford, Blankenship 2. DP—Toronto 2, Oakland 1. LOB—Toronto 7, Oakland 11. 2B—White, Sierra. 3B—Lee. HR—Alomar, Maldonado. SB—Carter, Wilson 2, Henderson. CS—Maldonado, White. SF—Sierra. HBP—By Guzman (McGwire). WP—Darling 2, Russell. U—Clark, plate; Merrill, first; Brinkman, second; Coble, third; Denkinger, left field; Young, right field. T—3:40. A—46,911.

GAME 4

HIGHLIGHTS

TORONTO 7, OAKLAND 6

Why the Blue Jays won: They took the "choke" label that had been an albatross around the franchise's neck and flung it aside. League Championship Series losers in 1985, 1989 and 1991, the Blue Jays lost the opener in this series—on their home grounds—and many critics were ready to write them off again. While Manager Cito Gaston's team rebounded to win Games 2 and 3, Toronto faced a 6-1 deficit in the eighth inning of Game 4 and seemed headed for a series tie at two victories apiece. But these Jays, compared with earlier Toronto teams, demonstrated they were birds of a different feather, striking for three eighth-inning runs, two in the ninth and the game-winner in the 11th. The most telling blow was a two-run homer in the ninth by Toronto's Roberto Alomar, a shot off Oakland relief ace Dennis Eckersley that tied the game and punctuated the point that Eckersley was not Mr. Invincible.

Why the Athletics lost: In a rarity, Oakland's bullpen just didn't get the job done. Eckersley, Jeff Parrett, Jim Corsi and Kelly Downs were roughed up for 10 hits and five runs in four innings.

The turning points:

1. When Eckersley, entering a 6-2 game in the eighth (the Blue Jays had just scored in the inning on Joe Carter's RBI single), was greeted by run-scoring singles off the bats of John Olerud and Candy Maldonado. Toronto had whittled the lead to striking-distance proportions and, at the same time, proved that Eckersley was hittable.

2. After connecting for his tying homer in the top of the ninth, Alomar threw out a potential game-winning baserunner, Eric Fox, in the bottom half of the inning. Fox had entered the game as a pinch-runner for Harold Baines, who had reached base on Alomar's throwing error, and he proceeded to steal second base. After moving to third on a sacrifice, Fox tried to score on Terry Steinbach's grounder to Alomar but was thrown out easily.

Notable: Alomar hit two singles, a double (which ignited his team's eighth-inning rally) and the ninth-inning homer, extending his championship-series hitting streak to nine games, dating to the 1991 playoffs against Minnesota. . . . The triumph put Toronto ahead three games to one, the same lead they enjoyed—but squandered—in the '85 championship series against Kansas City.

Quotable: "Eck's Little League act came back to haunt him today, and we couldn't be happier about that," said Toronto starter Jack Morris, who was hammered in his 3⅓ innings of work. Morris was referring to Eckersley's fist-pumping gesture at the Toronto dugout when he finally extricated himself from the Jays' eighth-inning fireworks. . . . "With Eckersley making that gesture with his hand, it woke us up," said the Blue Jays' Derek Bell, who opened the 11th with a walk off Downs, motored to third on Maldonado's single and scored the game's decisive run on Pat Borders' sacrifice fly to left. . . . After allowing five hits and two runs in a 1⅔-inning stint, Eckersley lamented that he simply "couldn't stop the bleeding."

BOX SCORE

SUNDAY, OCTOBER 11, AT OAKLAND

Toronto	AB	R	H	RBI	PO	A
White, cf	6	1	2	0	2	0
Alomar, 2b	5	2	4	2	8	5
Carter, rf-1b	6	1	2	1	2	0
Winfield, dh	6	1	1	0	0	0
Olerud, 1b	5	1	4	2	11	0
Bell, pr-rf	0	1	0	0	0	0
Maldonado, lf	5	0	2	1	1	0
Gruber, 3b	5	0	0	0	2	4
Borders, c	5	0	1	1	5	1
Lee, ss	3	0	1	0	1	3
Sprague, ph	1	0	0	0	0	0
Griffin, ss	2	0	0	0	0	3
Morris, p	0	0	0	0	0	2
Stottlemyre, p	0	0	0	0	0	0
Timlin, p	0	0	0	0	0	0
Ward, p	0	0	0	0	1	0
Henke, p	0	0	0	0	0	0
Totals	49	7	17	7	33	18

Oakland	AB	R	H	RBI	PO	A
R. Henderson, lf	6	2	3	1	3	0
Browne, cf	2	1	0	0	3	0
Wilson, cf	2	0	0	0	3	0
Sierra, rf	4	0	2	2	0	0
Baines, dh	5	1	2	1	0	0
Fox, pr-dh	1	0	0	0	0	0
McGwire, 1b	4	0	0	0	10	0
Steinbach, c	4	0	0	1	9	0
Lansford, 3b	5	0	2	1	2	4
Bordick, ss	5	1	1	0	3	1
Blankenship, 2b	4	1	2	0	0	3
Welch, p	0	0	0	0	0	1
Parrett, p	0	0	0	0	0	0
Eckersley, p	0	0	0	0	0	0
Corsi, p	0	0	0	0	0	0
Downs, p	0	0	0	0	0	0
Totals	42	6	12	6	33	9

```
Toronto .............. 0 1 0   0 0 0   0 3 2   0 1—7
Oakland ............. 0 0 5   0 0 1   0 0 0   0 0—6
```

Toronto	IP	H	R	ER	BB	SO
Morris	3⅓	5	5	5	5	2
Stottlemyre	3⅔	3	1	1	0	1
Timlin	1	2	0	0	0	1
Ward (W)	2	1	0	0	0	0
Henke (S)	1	1	0	0	0	0

Oakland	IP	H	R	ER	BB	SO
Welch	*7	7	2	2	1	7
Parrett	†0	2	2	2	0	0
Eckersley	1⅔	5	2	2	0	1
Corsi	1	2	0	0	2	0
Downs (L)	1⅓	1	1	1	1	0

*Pitched to one batter in eighth.
†Pitched to two batters in eighth.

E—Lee 2, Borders, White, McGwire, R. Henderson. DP—Toronto 2. LOB—Toronto 14, Oakland 11. 2B—Alomar, Olerud, Sierra, Baines. HR—Olerud, Alomar. SB—Alomar, Blankenship, R. Henderson, Fox. SH—Browne, McGwire. SF—Borders, Sierra. U—Merrill, plate; Brinkman, first; Coble, second; Denkinger, third; Young, left field; Clark, right field. T—4:25. A—47,732.

GAME 5

HIGHLIGHTS

OAKLAND 6, TORONTO 2

Why the Athletics won: They sent money pitcher Dave Stewart to the mound. He responded with a complete-game seven-hitter, improving his League Championship Series record to 6-0. In eight championship-series appearances since 1988, Stewart has allowed only 44 hits in 62 innings and fashioned a 2.03 earned-run average.

Why the Blue Jays lost: Toronto righthander David Cone couldn't deliver a reasonable facsimile of his performance in Game 2. Particularly troublesome was the top third of the Athletics' batting order, with Rickey Henderson, Jerry Browne and Ruben Sierra collecting all eight of Oakland's hits and all five of its RBIs.

The turning points:

1. When Sierra followed Browne's one-out, first-inning single with a home run to right. It created a double whammy for the Blue Jays: an early deficit and Stewart on the mound. (Browne was just getting started. He delivered run-scoring singles in the third and fifth innings, helping Oakland to a 6-1 edge, and also contributed a single in the seventh.)

2. When, after Devon White had singled in a Toronto run in the seventh (reducing Oakland's lead to 6-2), Roberto Alomar lined into an inning-ending double play with two runners aboard. The twin killing dashed any Blue Jay hopes of a Game 4-like comeback.

Notable: Dave Winfield, Toronto's 41-year-old wonder, crashed his second homer of the series, a bases-empty drive leading off the fourth. ... Of Stewart's five strikeouts, three came against John Olerud. ... A's regular third baseman Carney Lansford, 3-for-18 in the series, was given the day off, which proved a boon to Manager Tony La Russa's A's. His replacement, Browne, went 4-for-4.

Quotable: "This was the greatest game I've ever had in my professional career," gushed Browne, who was signed by the Oakland organization in the spring after being released by the Cleveland Indians. ... After the Athletics' agonizing 7-6 setback in Game 4, Stewart offered this: "Hey, we've got a game tomorrow. When we get up, the sun's going to shine and if it doesn't, I'm going to shine, so don't worry about it." ... Toronto Manager Cito Gaston got his hopes up when Alomar strode to the plate in a two-on, one-out situation in the seventh and his team down by four runs. "For a moment, it looked pretty promising," Gaston said. "We had come back yesterday and the guys were pumped up. Robby hit the ball hard. If it goes through, who knows what might have happened." However, the ball didn't go through. Second baseman Lance Blankenship speared it and Jays baserunner Pat Borders was doubled off second.

BOX SCORE

MONDAY, OCTOBER 12, AT OAKLAND

Toronto	AB	R	H	RBI	PO	A
White, cf	4	0	3	1	6	0
Alomar, 2b	4	0	1	0	2	2
Carter, rf	3	0	0	0	1	0
Winfield, dh	3	1	2	1	0	0
Olerud, 1b	4	0	0	0	6	0
Maldonado, lf	4	0	0	0	1	0
Gruber, 3b	3	1	0	0	1	2
Borders, c	4	0	1	0	6	1
Lee, ss	3	0	0	0	1	2
Cone, p	0	0	0	0	0	0
Key, p	0	0	0	0	0	0
Eichhorn, p	0	0	0	0	0	0
Totals	32	2	7	2	24	7

Oakland	AB	R	H	RBI	PO	A
R. Henderson, lf	3	2	2	0	1	0
Fox, pr-lf	0	0	0	0	1	0
Browne, 3b	4	2	4	0	2	0
Sierra, rf	4	1	2	3	3	0
Baines, dh	3	0	0	0	0	0
McGwire, 1b	1	0	0	0	7	0
Steinbach, c	4	0	0	0	6	1
Wilson, cf	4	0	0	0	1	0
Bordick, ss	4	0	0	0	3	1
Blankenship, 2b	4	1	0	0	3	4
Stewart, p	0	0	0	0	0	0
Totals	31	6	8	5	27	6

Toronto	0 0 0	1 0 0	1 0 0—2
Oakland	2 0 1	0 3 0	0 0 x—6

Toronto	IP	H	R	ER	BB	SO
Cone (L)	*4	6	6	3	2	3
Key	3	2	0	0	2	1
Eichhorn	1	0	0	0	0	0

Oakland	IP	H	R	ER	BB	SO
Stewart (W)	9	7	2	2	3	5

*Pitched to four batters in fifth.

E—Cone, Gruber, Carter. DP—Oakland 1. LOB—Toronto 6, Oakland 6. 2B—White. HR—Sierra, Winfield. CS—Sierra, White. SH—Baines. PB—Borders. U—Brinkman, plate; Coble, first; Denkinger, second; Young, third; Clark, left field; Merrill, right field. T—2:51. A—44,955.

GAME 6

HIGHLIGHTS

TORONTO 9, OAKLAND 2

Why the Blue Jays won: Almost possessed in their determination to shed their "Blow Jays" tag once and for all, they pounced on Athletics starter Mike Moore for six runs in the first three innings and let righthander Juan Guzman and bullpen stalwarts Duane Ward and Tom Henke do the rest. Joe Carter and Candy Maldonado provided the heavy artillery, Carter belting a two-run home run in the first inning and Maldonado hitting a three-run shot in the third.

Why the Athletics lost: The A's couldn't solve Guzman, who yielded only five singles and one run over seven innings while improving his League Championship Series record to 3-0 over two seasons. Plus, Moore and the Athletics' relief corps couldn't contain the Toronto offense, which added to its early scoring spree by notching one run in the fifth and two more in the eighth.

The turning points:
1. Maldonado's home run in the third inning, which for all intents and purposes took the Athletics out of the ball game. With one out and Roberto Alomar on second base after a single and a stolen base, A's Manager Tony La Russa instructed Moore to issue an intentional base on balls to Dave Winfield. John Olerud foiled Oakland's strategy with an RBI double down the right-field line, giving the Jays a 3-0 edge, and Maldonado then supplied the coup de grace with a drive over the center-field wall.

2. Guzman's ability to thwart a big inning in the Oakland sixth. After pitching no-hit ball through the first four innings and then escaping unscathed after the A's began the fifth with two hits, Guzman ran into a jam in the sixth when Ruben Sierra, Harold Baines and Mark McGwire delivered consecutive one-out singles. However, he proceeded to strike out Terry Steinbach and Willie Wilson.

Notable: The Blue Jays established a League Championship Series record with 10 home runs. Alomar (the Most Valuable Player in this playoff), Maldonado and Winfield led the way with two each. ... The total of 15 errors by the Jays and A's tied a championship-series mark. ... Baines was the leading hitter in the series, batting .440, and

Alomar was next at .423. ... Guzman was the most effective pitcher in the '92 A.L. playoffs, going 2-0 with a 2.08 ERA.

Quotable: "It's so unbelievable," said Henke, who has been a member of the Jays since 1985, the season they blew a three-games-to-one lead in the playoffs. "I've put eight years of my life in up here, and I wanted to be a part of this. I don't know what will happen in the future. But you can't put into words what it feels like." ... "I talked to my mother and family last night," Guzman said. "I told them to pray for me, and I guess it worked." ... Alomar, who extended his championship-series hitting streak to 11 games, spoke for most of his teammates when he said, "I tried to do my best because everyone said we'd choke in the end, but we didn't, and the monkey is off our backs."

BOX SCORE

WEDNESDAY, OCTOBER 14, AT TORONTO

Oakland	AB	R	H	RBI	PO	A
R. Henderson, lf	4	0	0	0	3	0
Quirk, ph	1	0	0	0	0	0
Browne, 3b	4	0	0	0	1	0
Lansford, 3b	0	0	0	0	0	0
Sierra, rf	5	1	1	0	1	0
Baines, dh	4	1	2	0	0	0
McGwire, 1b	4	0	1	1	6	1
Steinbach, c	4	0	2	1	7	1
Wilson, cf	4	0	1	0	1	0
Bordick, ss	2	0	0	0	1	3
Fox, ph	0	0	0	0	0	0
Weiss, ss	0	0	0	0	0	1
Blankenship, 2b	2	0	0	0	3	2
Ready, ph	1	0	0	0	0	0
Moore, p	0	0	0	0	1	0

	AB	R	H	RBI	PO	A
Parrett, p	0	0	0	0	0	1
Honeycutt, p	0	0	0	0	0	0
Russell, p	0	0	0	0	0	0
Witt, p	0	0	0	0	0	0
Totals	35	2	7	2	24	9

Toronto	AB	R	H	RBI	PO	A
White, cf	4	1	1	1	4	0
Alomar, 2b	5	1	3	1	0	2
Carter, rf	5	1	1	2	3	0
Winfield, dh	4	1	0	0	0	0
Olerud, 1b	3	2	2	1	9	0
Maldonado, lf	4	1	2	3	1	0
Gruber, 3b	3	0	0	0	0	2
Borders, c	2	1	2	1	9	0
Lee, ss	4	1	2	0	1	1
Guzman, p	0	0	0	0	0	0
Ward, p	0	0	0	0	0	0
Henke, p	0	0	0	0	0	0
Totals	34	9	13	9	27	5

Oakland .... 0 0 0   0 0 1   0 1 0—2
Toronto .... 2 0 4   0 1 0   0 2 x—9

Oakland	IP	H	R	ER	BB	SO
Moore (L)	2⅔	7	6	5	1	4
Parrett	2	4	1	1	0	1
Honeycutt	1⅓	0	0	0	0	1
Russell	1	0	0	0	1	0
Witt	1	2	2	2	1	1

Toronto	IP	H	R	ER	BB	SO
Guzman (W)	7	5	1	1	2	8
Ward	1	2	1	1	0	1
Henke	1	0	0	0	2	1

E—R. Henderson. LOB—Oakland 10, Toronto 7. 2B—Baines, Olerud, Lee. HR—Carter, Maldonado. SB—Wilson, Sierra, Fox, Alomar 2. CS—White. SH—Gruber. SF—Borders, White. PB—Borders 2. U—Coble, plate; Denkinger, first; Young, second; Clark, third; Merrill, left field; Brinkman, right field. T—3:15. A—51,335.

STATISTICS

TORONTO BLUE JAYS' BATTING AND FIELDING AVERAGES

Player, position	G	AB	R	H	TB	2B	3B	HR	RBI	BB	IBB	SO	Avg.	PO	A	E	Avg.
Sprague, ph	2	2	0	1	1	0	0	0	0	0	0	1	.500	0	0	0	.000
Alomar, 2b	6	26	4	11	18	1	0	2	4	2	0	1	.423	16	15	0	1.000
Olerud, 1b	6	23	4	8	13	2	0	1	4	2	0	5	.348	51	1	0	1.000
White, cf	6	23	2	8	10	2	0	0	2	5	0	6	.348	16	0	1	.941
Borders, c	6	22	3	7	10	0	0	1	3	1	0	1	.318	38	3	1	.976
Lee, ss	6	18	2	5	8	1	1	0	3	1	0	2	.278	12	15	3	.900
Maldonado, lf	6	22	3	6	12	0	0	2	6	3	0	4	.273	9	1	0	1.000
Winfield, dh	6	24	7	6	13	1	0	2	3	4	1	2	.250	0	0	0	.000
Carter, rf-1b	6	26	2	5	8	0	0	1	3	2	0	4	.192	16	1	1	.944
Gruber, 3b	6	22	3	2	6	1	0	1	2	2	0	3	.091	5	16	1	.955
Bell, pr-rf	2	0	1	0	0	0	0	0	0	1	0	0	.000	1	0	0	1.000
Cone, p	2	0	0	0	0	0	0	0	0	0	0	0	.000	0	1	1	.500
Eichhorn, p	1	0	0	0	0	0	0	0	0	0	0	0	.000	0	0	0	.000
Guzman, p	2	0	0	0	0	0	0	0	0	0	0	0	.000	0	0	0	.000
Henke, p	4	0	0	0	0	0	0	0	0	0	0	0	.000	0	0	0	.000
Key, p	1	0	0	0	0	0	0	0	0	0	0	0	.000	0	0	0	.000
Morris, p	2	0	0	0	0	0	0	0	0	0	0	0	.000	0	4	0	1.000
Stottlemyre, p	1	0	0	0	0	0	0	0	0	0	0	0	.000	0	0	0	.000
Timlin, p	2	0	0	0	0	0	0	0	0	0	0	0	.000	0	0	0	.000
Ward, p	3	0	0	0	0	0	0	0	0	0	0	0	.000	1	0	0	1.000
Griffin, pr-ss	2	2	0	0	0	0	0	0	0	0	0	0	.000	0	3	0	1.000
Totals	6	210	31	59	99	8	1	10	30	23	1	29	.281	165	60	8	.966

OAKLAND ATHLETICS' BATTING AND FIELDING AVERAGES

Player, position	G	AB	R	H	TB	2B	3B	HR	RBI	BB	IBB	SO	Avg.	PO	A	E	Avg.
Baines, dh	6	25	6	11	16	2	0	1	4	0	0	3	.440	0	0	0	.000
Browne, ph-cf-3b	4	10	3	4	4	0	0	0	2	2	0	0	.400	6	0	0	1.000
Sierra, rf	6	24	4	8	15	2	1	1	7	2	0	1	.333	12	0	0	1.000

Player, position					BATTING										FIELDING		
	G	AB	R	H	TB	2B	3B	HR	RBI	BB	IBB	SO	Avg.	PO	A	E	Avg.
Steinbach, c	6	24	1	7	10	0	0	1	5	2	0	7	.292	30	7	0	1.000
R. Henderson, lf	6	23	5	6	6	0	0	0	1	4	0	4	.261	15	0	3	.833
Blankenship, 2b-pr	5	13	2	3	3	0	0	0	0	3	0	4	.231	11	13	2	.923
Wilson, cf	6	22	0	5	6	1	0	0	0	1	0	5	.227	16	0	0	1.000
Lansford, 3b	5	18	0	3	3	0	0	0	1	1	0	1	.167	2	9	1	.917
Weiss, ss	3	6	1	1	1	0	0	0	0	2	0	1	.167	5	6	0	1.000
McGwire, 1b	6	20	1	3	6	0	0	1	3	5	2	4	.150	46	2	1	.980
Bordick, ss-2b	6	19	1	1	1	0	0	0	0	1	0	2	.053	15	14	0	1.000
Corsi, p	3	0	0	0	0	0	0	0	0	0	0	0	.000	0	0	0	.000
Darling, p	1	0	0	0	0	0	0	0	0	0	0	0	.000	1	0	0	1.000
Downs, p	2	0	0	0	0	0	0	0	0	0	0	0	.000	0	0	0	.000
Eckersley, p	3	0	0	0	0	0	0	0	0	0	0	0	.000	0	0	0	.000
Honeycutt, p	2	0	0	0	0	0	0	0	0	0	0	0	.000	0	0	0	.000
Moore, p	2	0	0	0	0	0	0	0	0	0	0	0	.000	1	0	0	1.000
Parrett, p	3	0	0	0	0	0	0	0	0	0	0	0	.000	0	1	0	1.000
Russell, p	3	0	0	0	0	0	0	0	0	0	0	0	.000	0	0	0	.000
Stewart, p	2	0	0	0	0	0	0	0	0	0	0	0	.000	1	1	0	1.000
Welch, p	1	0	0	0	0	0	0	0	0	0	0	0	.000	0	1	0	1.000
Witt, p	1	0	0	0	0	0	0	0	0	0	0	0	.000	0	0	0	.000
Fox, pr-dh-lf	4	1	0	0	0	0	0	0	0	1	0	0	.000	1	0	0	1.000
Quirk, ph	1	1	0	0	0	0	0	0	0	0	0	0	.000	0	0	0	.000
Ready, ph	1	1	0	0	0	0	0	0	0	0	0	1	.000	0	0	0	.000
Totals	6	207	24	52	71	5	1	4	23	24	2	33	.251	162	55	7	.969

TORONTO BLUE JAYS' PITCHING RECORDS

Pitcher	G	GS	CG	IP	H	R	ER	HR	BB	IBB	SO	HB	WP	W	L	Pct.	ERA
Henke	4	0	0	4⅔	4	0	0	0	2	0	2	0	0	0	0	.000	0.00
Key	1	0	0	3	2	0	0	0	2	1	1	0	0	0	0	.000	0.00
Eichhorn	1	0	0	1	0	0	0	0	0	0	0	0	0	0	0	.000	0.00
Guzman	2	2	0	13	12	3	3	0	5	0	11	1	0	2	0	1.000	2.08
Stottlemyre	1	0	0	3⅔	3	1	1	0	0	0	1	0	0	0	0	.000	2.46
Cone	2	2	0	12	11	7	4	1	5	0	9	0	1	1	1	.500	3.00
Morris	2	2	1	12⅓	11	9	9	3	9	1	6	0	1	0	1	.000	6.57
Ward	3	0	0	4	5	3	3	0	1	0	2	0	0	1	0	1.000	6.75
Timlin	2	0	0	1⅓	4	1	1	0	0	0	1	0	0	0	0	.000	6.75
Totals	6	6	1	55	52	24	21	4	24	2	33	1	1	4	2	.667	3.44

No shutouts. Saves—Henke 3.

OAKLAND ATHLETICS' PITCHING RECORDS

Pitcher	G	GS	CG	IP	H	R	ER	HR	BB	IBB	SO	HB	WP	W	L	Pct.	ERA
Corsi	3	0	0	2	2	0	0	0	3	0	0	0	0	0	0	.000	0.00
Honeycutt	2	0	0	2	0	0	0	0	0	1	0	0	0	0	0	.000	0.00
Welch	1	1	0	7	7	2	2	1	1	0	7	0	0	0	1	.000	2.57
Stewart	2	2	1	16⅔	14	5	5	3	6	0	7	0	1	1	0	1.000	2.70
Darling	1	1	0	6	4	3	2	2	2	0	3	0	2	0	1	.000	3.00
Downs	2	0	0	2⅓	3	3	1	0	1	0	0	0	0	0	1	.000	3.86
Eckersley	3	0	0	3	8	2	2	1	0	0	2	0	0	0	0	.000	6.00
Moore	2	2	0	9⅔	11	9	8	3	5	1	7	0	0	0	2	.000	7.45
Russell	3	0	0	2	2	2	2	0	4	0	0	0	1	1	0	1.000	9.00
Parrett	3	0	0	2⅓	6	3	3	0	0	0	1	0	0	0	0	.000	11.57
Witt	1	0	0	1	2	2	2	0	1	0	1	0	0	0	0	.000	18.00
Totals	6	6	1	54	59	31	27	10	23	1	29	0	3	2	4	.333	4.50

No shutouts. Save—Eckersley.

COMPOSITE SCORE BY INNINGS

Toronto	2	2	4		2	5	1		4	7	3	0	1—31
Oakland	2	3	6		2	3	2		2	2	2	0	0—24

MISCELLANEOUS STATISTICS

Sacrifice hits—Browne, McGwire, Baines, Gruber.

Sacrifice flies—Sierra 2, Borders 2, Lee, White.

Stolen bases—Wilson 7, Alomar 5, Weiss 2, Carter 2, R. Henderson 2, Fox 2, Bordick, Blankenship, Sierra.

Caught stealing—White 4, Sierra 2, Maldonado.

Double plays—Lee, Alomar and Olerud 3; Bordick, Blankenship and McGwire 2; Morris, Lee and Olerud; Lansford, Bordick and McGwire; Maldonado and Gruber; Alomar, Lee and Olerud; Carter and Borders; Weiss, Bordick and McGwire; Blankenship and Bordick.

Left on bases—Toronto 7, 4, 7, 14, 6, 7—45; Oakland—4, 6, 11, 11, 6, 10—48.

Hit by pitcher—By Guzman (McGwire).

Passed balls—Borders 3.

Balks—None.

Time of games—First game, 2:47; second game, 2:58; third game, 3:40; fourth game, 4:25; fifth game, 2:51; sixth game, 3:15.

Attendance—First game, 51,039; second game, 51,114; third game, 46,911; fourth game, 47,732; fifth game, 44,955; sixth game, 51,335.

Umpires—Denkinger, Young, Clark, Merrill, Brinkman and Coble.

Official scorers—John Hickey, Hayward (Cal.) Daily Review; Joe Sawchuk, Toronto official scorer.

GAME 1

HIGHLIGHTS

ATLANTA 5, PITTSBURGH 1

Why the Braves won: John Smoltz pitched like, ah, well, John Smoltz. And Sid Bream ran the bases like, ah, well, Otis Nixon. Smoltz, who shut out the Pirates in Game 7 of the 1991 N.L. playoffs and entered this contest with a postseason earned-run average of 1.52, held Pittsburgh to four hits over eight innings. Bream, a painfully slow baserunner, did his best impersonation of fleet Braves teammate Nixon by scoring twice from second base on balls that didn't reach the outfield.

Why the Pirates lost: It's elementary—they could not score, at least not until Jose Lind poked a homer over the left-field fence to lead off the eighth inning. Before Lind muscled up, Pittsburgh had been held scoreless for 29 consecutive postseason innings, dating to Game 5 of the '91 League Championship Series.

The turning points:

1. The Braves' two-run fourth inning, which gave Atlanta a 3-0 edge and provided Smoltz (yet to allow a hit) with some breathing room. Bream doubled in one of the runs and then scored all the way from second base when Pirates first baseman Orlando Merced made an errant throw on Ron Gant's bunt. (In the second inning, Bream, who had singled and moved to second on a walk, huffed and puffed his way home on Mark Lemke's infield hit up the middle that second baseman Lind knocked down.)

2. Atlanta's ability to keep Pittsburgh's 1-2 punch in check—again. Andy Van Slyke (runner-up in the N.L. batting race) and Barry Bonds (second in the league in homers) went a combined 1-for-7 with three strikeouts. In the '91 championship series against the Braves, Van Slyke and Bonds flailed away at a .154 clip with a total of eight hits in 52 at-bats.

Notable: Braves second baseman Lemke, who batted .417 in the 1991 World Series, picked up where he left off in postseason play by rapping two singles in three at-bats. . . . Lind, who hadn't homered in 468 regular-season at-bats, also collected an infield single against Smoltz. The two-out, fifth-inning hit was Pittsburgh's first of the game.

Quotable: Smoltz said his performance in Game 7 of the '91 World Series—shutout pitching over 7⅓ innings—had helped prepare him for this championship series. "It gave me the confidence that there isn't any bigger game you could pitch in," Smoltz said. . . . Bream, discussing how he ran through a coach's stop sign on his second-inning mad dash, said: "I was running because I couldn't stop. If I did try to stop, my (reconstructed) knee would have gone up in the stands somewhere." . . .

Atlanta shortstop Jeff Blauser, used sparingly in 1991 postseason play, was thrilled over his starting role. "I didn't contribute much in last year's postseason," said Blauser, who cracked a fifth-inning homer off Doug Drabek, "so I'm like a little kid out there . . . playing stickball in the streets."

BOX SCORE

TUESDAY, OCTOBER 6, AT ATLANTA

Pittsburgh	AB	R	H	RBI	PO	A
Cole, rf	4	0	1	0	3	0
Bell, ss	3	0	0	0	3	0
Van Slyke, cf	4	0	1	0	4	0
Bonds, lf	3	0	0	0	0	0
King, 3b	4	0	1	0	1	2
Merced, 1b	3	0	0	0	6	1
LaValliere, c	3	0	0	0	7	0
Lind, 2b	3	1	2	1	0	3
Drabek, p	2	0	0	0	0	0
Patterson, p	0	0	0	0	0	0
Neagle, p	0	0	0	0	0	0
Varsho, ph	1	0	0	0	0	0
Cox, p	0	0	0	0	0	0
Totals	30	1	5	1	24	6

Atlanta	AB	R	H	RBI	PO	A
Nixon, cf	5	1	1	0	0	0
Blauser, ss	3	1	1	1	0	2
Belliard, pr-ss	0	0	0	0	0	1
Pendleton, 3b	4	0	1	1	2	2
Justice, rf	3	1	1	0	2	0
Bream, 1b	4	2	2	1	12	0
Gant, lf	3	0	0	0	2	0
Berryhill, c	3	0	0	0	7	2
Lemke, 2b	3	0	2	1	2	5
Smoltz, p	3	0	0	0	0	1
L. Smith, ph	1	0	0	0	0	0
Stanton, p	0	0	0	0	0	0
Totals	32	5	8	4	27	13

Pittsburgh	0 0 0	0 0 0	0 1 0—1
Atlanta	0 1 0	2 1 0	1 0 x—5

Pittsburgh	IP	H	R	ER	BB	SO
Drabek (L)	4⅔	5	4	3	2	4
Patterson	*1⅓	3	1	1	1	1
Neagle	1	0	0	0	0	0
Cox	1	0	0	0	1	1

Atlanta	IP	H	R	ER	BB	SO
Smoltz (W)	8	4	1	1	3	6
Stanton	1	1	0	0	0	2

*Pitched to three batters in seventh.

E—Merced. DP—Atlanta 1. LOB—Pittsburgh 5, Atlanta 8. 2B—King, Justice, Bream. HR—Blauser, Lind. SB—Gant, Nixon. CS—Merced. SH—Gant. WP—Smoltz. U—McSherry, plate; Marsh, first; Rippley, second; Darling, third; Davis, left field; Montague, right field. T—3:00. A—51,971.

GAME 2

HIGHLIGHTS

ATLANTA 13, PITTSBURGH 5

Why the Braves won: They put together the lethal combination of good hitting and good pitching. Ron Gant, coming off a subpar season, walloped the first bases-loaded home run of his big-league career, a fifth-inning shot off reliever Bob Walk that doubled Atlanta's 4-0 lead. Terry Pendleton and Dave Justice drove home two runs each for the Braves, who played big-inning baseball (four runs in the second, four in the fifth and five in the seventh). Lefthander Steve Avery, who mystified Pittsburgh in the 1991 N.L. playoffs by tossing 16 1/3 consecutive shutout innings, blanked the Pirates for six innings this time around and thereby set a League Championship Series record of 22 1/3 straight scoreless innings.

Why the Pirates lost: Another deadly tandem—poor hitting and poor pitching. Pittsburgh managed only seven hits off five Braves pitchers and didn't dent the scoring column until the game was out of hand at 8-0. Pirates starter Danny Jackson lasted only 1 2/3 innings, during which he yielded four runs on four hits and two bases on balls.

The turning points:

1. The Pirates' inability to mount any kind of threat while the game was still competitve. While the Pirates finally woke up from their offensive snooze—they had managed exactly one run in their last 37 innings of postseason play dating to 1991—and scored four runs in the seventh, their glimmer of hope was dashed when Atlanta retaliated with five runs in its half of the inning.

2. Gant's grand slam.

Notable: Every member of the Braves' starting lineup—with the exception of pitcher Avery—collected at least one hit. However, Avery chipped in offensively, delivering a sacrifice fly. Mark Lemke banged out three of Atlanta's 14 hits. . . . Pirate sluggers Barry Bonds and Andy Van Slyke endured more postseason blues, getting only one hit in eight at-bats. Bonds, a particular target of Braves fans, doffed his cap after hitting a leadoff single in the seventh and receiving a derisive response from the Atlanta throng. . . . Usually light-hitting Jose Lind, whose homer accounted for all of the Pirates' offense in Game 1, drilled a two-run triple to highlight Pittsburgh's seventh-inning uprising.

Quotable: "I told myself early to get ready for the playoffs to be able to display everything that I have," said Gant, who wanted to atone for a disappointing regular-season performance (17 homers/80 RBIs after a 1991 season of 32/105). Atone he did. . . . Pirates Manager Jim Leyland, assessing Bonds' postseason woes, said: "Barry Bonds is trying to hit a five-run home run." . . . "Eight runs (ahead), you find yourself relaxing a bit," said Avery, reflecting on the Bucs' breakthrough against him in the seventh.

BOX SCORE

WEDNESDAY, OCTOBER 7, AT ATLANTA

Pittsburgh	AB	R	H	RBI	PO	A
Redus, 1b	3	0	0	0	6	0
Merced, ph-1b	1	0	0	0	1	0
Bell, ss	4	0	1	0	0	2
Van Slyke, cf	5	0	0	0	2	0
Bonds, lf	3	2	1	0	1	0

	AB	R	H	RBI	PO	A
King, 3b	4	0	0	0	1	4
McClendon, rf	3	1	2	1	3	0
Cole, ph-rf	0	0	0	0	1	0
Slaught, c	3	1	1	1	6	0
Lind, 2b	4	1	1	2	2	2
Belinda, p	0	0	0	0	0	0
Jackson, p	0	0	0	0	0	0
Mason, p	0	0	0	0	1	0
Wehner, ph	1	0	0	0	0	0
Walk, p	1	0	0	0	0	1
Tomlin, p	0	0	0	0	0	1
Espy, ph	1	0	1	0	0	0
Neagle, p	0	0	0	0	0	0
Patterson, p	0	0	0	0	0	0
Garcia, 2b	1	0	0	0	0	0
Totals	34	5	7	4	24	11
Atlanta	AB	R	H	RBI	PO	A
Nixon, cf	4	2	1	0	4	0
Blauser, ss	2	1	1	1	0	3
Belliard, ss	1	1	0	0	1	2
Pendleton, 3b	5	1	2	2	0	3
Justice, rf	3	1	1	2	3	0
Hunter, 1b	2	1	1	0	4	0
L. Smith, ph	1	0	0	0	0	0
Bream, 1b	1	0	0	0	5	0
Gant, lf	4	3	2	4	2	0
Reardon, p	0	0	0	0	0	0
Berryhill, c	5	1	2	1	4	0
Lemke, 2b	5	1	3	1	3	0
Avery, p	2	0	0	1	0	0
Freeman, p	0	0	0	0	0	0
Stanton, p	1	1	1	1	0	1
Wohlers, p	0	0	0	0	0	0
Sanders, ph-lf	1	0	0	0	1	0
Totals	37	13	14	13	27	9

Pittsburgh	0 0 0	0 0 0	4 1 0 —	5
Atlanta	0 4 0	0 4 0	5 0 x —	13

Pittsburgh	IP	H	R	ER	BB	SO
Jackson (L)	1 2/3	4	4	4	2	0
Mason	1/3	0	0	0	0	0
Walk	2 2/3	3	4	4	2	4
Tomlin	1 1/3	2	0	0	1	0
Neagle	2/3	4	5	5	3	0
Patterson	1/3	0	0	0	0	0
Belinda	1	1	0	0	0	2
Atlanta	IP	H	R	ER	BB	SO
Avery (W)	6 1/3	6	4	4	2	3
Freeman	1/3	1	0	0	0	1
Stanton	*1/3	0	1	0	1	0
Wohlers	1	0	0	0	1	0
Reardon	1	0	0	0	1	0

*Pitched to one batter in eighth.

LOB—Pittsburgh 7, Atlanta 9. 2B—McClendon, Pendleton, Stanton. 3B—Lind, Blauser. HR—Gant. SB—Nixon. SF—Avery. WP—Avery. PB—Berryhill. U—Marsh, plate; Rippley, first; Darling, second; Davis, third; Montague, left field; McSherry, right field. T—3:20. A—51,975.

GAME 3

HIGHLIGHTS

PITTSBURGH 3, ATLANTA 2

Why the Pirates won: Rookie righthander Tim Wakefield seemed immune to big-game pressure. Called up from Class AAA Buffalo in July, knuckleballer Wakefield had proved his mettle by winning eight of nine decisions for Pittsburgh in the stretch run and again demonstrated his cool in the wake of Atlanta's two-games-to-none lead in the N.L.

playoffs. Despite throwing his sometimes-elusive knuckleball almost exclusively, he walked only one Braves batter and permitted just five hits (two of them home runs, bases-empty shots by Sid Bream and Ron Gant).

Why the Braves lost: Their pitchers' amazing post-season success at Three Rivers Stadium came to an end—or at least was tempered. Dating to Game 2 of the 1991 N.L. Championship Series, Atlanta hurlers had pitched 31 consecutive scoreless innings against the Pirates at Three Rivers—a streak that ended in the fifth inning of this contest when Don Slaught thrust the Bucs into a 1-1 tie with a home run to left-center off 20-game winner Tom Glavine.

The turning points:

1. Coming off a year in which he batted .324 with 89 RBIs, Andy Van Slyke shook off some of his postseason cobwebs—he was 12-for-80 (.150) in 26 previous championship-series and World Series games—and delivered not once but twice. With the game deadlocked in the sixth inning, Van Slyke doubled to right, moved to third on a fly ball and scored on Jeff King's two-base hit as Pittsburgh seized a 2-1 advantage. Then, with the score knotted at 2-2 in the seventh inning, he lofted what proved to be a game-winning sacrifice fly. The drive to right scored Gary Redus, who had singled and advanced to third base on Jay Bell's double.

2. The Pirates' ability to overcome a here-we-go-again start. With his team having dropped the first two games of this series, Redus got the Pirates off to a rousing start with a leadoff triple in the first inning. However, Glavine wriggled out of trouble—Redus wound up stranded at third base—when he induced ground balls off the bats of Bell, Van Slyke and Barry Bonds. Wakefield proceeded to keep the Bucs close (or in the lead), and Pittsburgh broke through against Glavine with single runs in the fifth, sixth and seventh innings.

Notable: Of Wakefield's 109 pitches, 104 were knuckleballs. . . . After three games of this championship series, Atlanta's Mark Lemke had twice as many hits (six) as any player on either team. . . . Pittsburgh slugger Bonds continued to struggle, going 0-for-3. To this point in the series, he had one hit (a single) and zero RBIs in nine at-bats.

Quotable: "To be able to be a rookie and get a chance to pitch in a game like this doesn't come along every day," Wakefield said. "I wanted to make the most of the opportunity." . . . "I was probably more nervous than he (Wakefield) was," said Pirates pitching coach Ray Miller, who, like virtually all other observers, was impressed with Wakefield's ability to throw his flutterball for strikes. . . . Van Slyke said he welcomes the challenge of batting in key situations. "And it's a lot more fun when you can get the job done," he emphasized.

BOX SCORE

FRIDAY, OCTOBER 9, AT PITTSBURGH

Atlanta	AB	R	H	RBI	PO	A
Nixon, cf	3	0	1	0	5	0
Blauser, ss	4	0	0	0	1	2
Pendleton, 3b	4	0	0	0	0	2
Justice, rf	4	0	1	0	2	0
Bream, 1b	4	1	1	1	10	1
Gant, lf	3	1	1	1	0	0
Berryhill, c	3	0	0	0	3	0
Lemke, 2b	3	0	1	0	2	3
Glavine, p	2	0	0	0	1	2
Stanton, p	0	0	0	0	0	0
L. Smith, ph	1	0	0	0	0	0
Wohlers, p	0	0	0	0	0	0
Totals	31	2	5	2	24	10

Pittsburgh	AB	R	H	RBI	PO	A
Redus, 1b	3	1	3	0	9	1
Bell, ss	4	0	1	0	2	0
Van Slyke, cf	3	1	1	1	2	0
Bonds, lf	3	0	0	0	2	0
King, 3b	4	0	1	1	3	3
McClendon, rf	2	0	0	0	0	0
Espy, ph-rf	1	0	1	0	0	0
Slaught, c	3	1	1	1	3	0
Lind, 2b	4	0	0	0	3	4
Wakefield, p	3	0	0	0	3	2
Totals	30	3	8	3	27	10

Atlanta	0 0 0	1 0 0	1 0 0—2			
Pittsburgh	0 0 0	0 1 1	1 0 x—3			

Atlanta	IP	H	R	ER	BB	SO
Glavine (L)	6⅓	7	3	3	3	2
Stanton	⅔	0	0	0	0	0
Wohlers	1	1	0	0	0	0

Pittsburgh	IP	H	R	ER	BB	SO
Wakefield (W)	9	5	2	2	1	3

E—Lind. DP—Atlanta 1, Pittsburgh 2. LOB—Atlanta 3, Pittsburgh 8. 2B—Nixon, Lemke, Redus, Bell, Van Slyke, King. 3B—Redus. HR—Bream, Slaught, Gant. SF—Van Slyke. HBP—By Glavine (Bonds). U—Rippley, plate; Darling, first; Davis, second; Montague, third; McSherry, left field; Marsh, right field. T—2:37. A—56,610.

GAME 4

HIGHLIGHTS

ATLANTA 6, PITTSBURGH 4

Why the Braves won: Otis Nixon, Atlanta's catalyst over the last two seasons, was at his make-things-happen best. He lashed three singles and a double, scored twice, knocked in two runs and figured prominently in all three of the innings in which the Braves scored.

Why the Pirates lost: For the second time in this League Championship Series, Pittsburgh ace Doug Drabek failed to get through the fifth inning. Also for the second time in this series, Atlanta starter John Smoltz, despite a bothersome muscle strain in his back, was more than a match for the Bucs' offense. After limiting Pittsburgh to four hits and one run over eight innings in Game 1, he yielded six hits and three earned runs over 6⅓ innings in Game 4. All told, he now had 15 strikeouts in 14⅓ innings of work against the Pirates.

The turning points:

1. Nixon's offensive handiwork. He singled home

a run in the Braves' two-run second, singled to ignite Atlanta's two-run fifth and doubled in a run in the West Division champions' two-run sixth.

2. Manager Jim Leyland's decision to start Drabek on three days' rest for the first time in three years. Obviously, Drabek was not up to the task.

Notable: Smoltz helped himself with the bat, going 2-for-3, driving in one run and scoring another. Shortstop Jeff Blauser had an identical line. . . . The victory was Smoltz's fourth in four championship-series starts over two years. . . . The '92 N.L. playoffs marked Nixon's first venture into post-season play. In October 1991, he was on the disqualified list because of drug use. . . . Pittsburgh's Andy Van Slyke continued to awaken offensively, whacking a double and a triple. Teammate Barry Bonds was still looking for a breakthrough, walking twice but striking out in both of his official at-bats. . . . Overall, the Pirates struck out 14 times against Smoltz and relievers Mike Stanton and Jeff Reardon. . . . Reardon earned a save, his first in postseason play since he was a member of the Minnesota Twins in 1987.

Quotable: "Nobody wants to win it (the championship series) as bad as I do because of what happened . . . of not being a part of it last year," the 33-year-old Nixon said. "I was going through a lot of pain." . . . "I like our chances (of wrapping up this series)—and I like my chances of not pitching again, not with Steve Avery and Tom Glavine ready," said Smoltz, whose Braves forged a 3-1 lead in the best-of-seven series. . . . "We scored four runs, and that should have been enough," Leyland moaned. "We just didn't pitch very well. We made some bad pitches at bad times."

BOX SCORE
SATURDAY, OCTOBER 10, AT PITTSBURGH

Atlanta	AB	R	H	RBI	PO	A
Nixon, cf	5	2	4	2	2	0
Blauser, ss	3	1	2	1	2	0
Belliard, ss	1	0	0	0	0	0
Pendleton, 3b	5	0	0	0	0	2
Justice, rf	4	0	1	1	2	1
Bream, 1b	2	0	0	0	3	0
Hunter, ph-1b	2	0	0	0	3	0
Gant, lf	4	1	1	0	2	0
Stanton, p	0	0	0	0	0	0
Reardon, p	0	0	0	0	0	0
Berryhill, c	3	0	1	0	13	1
Lemke, 2b	2	1	0	0	0	1
Smoltz, p	3	1	2	1	0	0
Sanders, lf	1	0	0	0	0	0
Totals	35	6	11	5	27	5

Pittsburgh	AB	R	H	RBI	PO	A
Cole, rf	4	1	1	1	2	1
Bell, ss	5	0	0	0	0	1
Van Slyke, cf	4	0	2	1	6	0
Bonds, lf	2	0	0	0	2	0
King, 3b	4	1	0	0	1	4
Merced, 1b	3	0	1	1	10	1
Redus, ph-1b	1	0	0	0	0	1
LaValliere, c	3	1	1	0	2	0
Slaught, ph-c	1	0	0	0	0	0
Lind, 2b	3	1	1	0	3	4
Drabek, p	1	0	0	0	0	0
Tomlin, p	0	0	0	0	0	0
Cox, p	0	0	0	0	0	0
Wehner, ph	1	0	0	0	0	0
Mason, p	0	0	0	0	1	0
Espy, ph	1	0	0	0	0	0
Totals	33	4	6	3	27	12

Atlanta .... 0 2 0 0 2 2 0 0 0—6
Pittsburgh .... 0 2 1 0 0 0 1 0 0—4

Atlanta	IP	H	R	ER	BB	SO
Smoltz (W)	6⅓	6	4	3	5	9
Stanton	1⅔	0	0	0	0	3
Reardon (S)	1	0	0	0	0	2

Pittsburgh	IP	H	R	ER	BB	SO
Drabek (L)	4⅓	7	4	3	2	1
Tomlin	1⅓	3	2	2	0	0
Cox	⅓	1	0	0	0	0
Mason	3	0	0	0	2	1

E—Blauser, King. DP—Pittsburgh 3. LOB—Atlanta 7, Pittsburgh 7. 2B—Nixon, Van Slyke, Merced. 3B—Van Slyke. SB—Nixon, Smoltz. SH—Blauser. U—Darling, plate; Davis, first; Montague, second; McSherry, third; Marsh, left field; Rippley, right field. T—3:10. A—57,164.

GAME 5
HIGHLIGHTS
PITTSBURGH 7, ATLANTA 1

Why the Pirates won: They entrusted journeyman Bob Walk with the job of keeping their hopes alive—and the 6-foot-4 righthander came through. Pitching in his eighth League Championship Series game, the 35-year-old Walk, cast into the playoff rotation because of Danny Jackson's poor outing in Game 2, shackled the Braves on three hits.

Why the Braves lost: Lefthander Steve Avery, who befuddled Pittsburgh in the 1991 playoffs and then beat the Pirates in Game 2 of this postseason matchup, was racked for four doubles, one single and four runs before leaving the premises with one out in the first inning.

The turning points:

1. Barry Bonds' contribution to the first-inning pyrotechnics. Bonds, 1-for-11 in the '92 N.L. playoffs entering Game 5, drilled one of the Bucs' doubles, a run-scoring hit that perhaps signaled the end of his postseason batting funk. By game's end, Bonds was 2-for-5 with two runs scored and one stolen base.

2. Bonds' sensational backhanded catch of a fourth-inning drive off the bat of Atlanta's Ron Gant. It kept the Braves off the scoreboard—Sid Bream was stationed at second with a double—and seemed to portend that this game belonged to the Pirates.

Notable: Walk's complete-game performance was his second of 1992. He had managed just one in 19 regular-season starts. (He also made 17 relief appearances in '92.) . . . The Pirates' No. 5 and No. 6 hitters, Jeff King and Lloyd McClendon, sizzled offensively, combining for six hits in seven at-bats, scoring two runs and driving in three. . . . The Pirates' crowd of 52,929 was approximately 4,000 under capacity.

Quotable: "The (starting) assignment was a surprise, but a pleasant surprise," Walk said. "He (Manager Jim Leyland) is a pretty good judge of talent. If he thinks I should be out there, I figure maybe I am pretty good." ... Avery offered no great insight into his short stint. "It's just something that happens," he said. "There isn't any explanation for it. If you don't have it, they're going to hit you." ... Free-agent-to-be Bonds, acknowledging he might well have played his last game as a Pirate in Three Rivers Stadium, said the night "was a very emotional time for me. I thought it would be easy. My father (Bobby) was traded so much, we moved all over the place." ... "Forget about the two hits," said Leyland, alluding to Bonds' offensive production. "That was the best catch (the fourth-inning grab of Gant's smash) I've ever seen."

SUNDAY, OCTOBER 11, AT PITTSBURGH

Atlanta	AB	R	H	RBI	PO	A
Nixon, cf	4	0	0	0	2	0
Blauser, ss	3	0	0	1	3	2
Pendleton, 3b	4	0	1	0	1	3
Justice, rf	2	0	0	0	1	0
Bream, 1b	4	0	1	0	8	0
Gant, lf	3	0	0	0	3	0
Berryhill, c	4	0	0	0	4	1
Lemke, 2b	3	0	0	0	2	4
Avery, p	0	0	0	0	0	0
P. Smith, p	1	0	0	0	0	1
Treadway, ph	1	0	0	0	0	0
Leibrandt, p	0	0	0	0	0	0
Freeman, p	0	0	0	0	0	1
L. Smith, ph	1	1	1	0	0	0
Mercker, p	0	0	0	0	0	0
Totals	30	1	3	1	24	12

Pittsburgh	AB	R	H	RBI	PO	A
Redus, 1b	4	1	2	1	10	1
Bell, ss	5	1	1	1	0	2
Van Slyke, cf	5	0	1	0	2	0
Bonds, lf	5	2	2	1	3	0
King, 3b	4	2	3	1	2	3
McClendon, rf	3	0	3	2	4	0
Slaught, c	1	1	1	1	3	1
Lind, 2b	4	0	0	0	2	4
Walk, p	4	0	0	0	1	1
Totals	35	7	13	7	27	12

Atlanta	0 0 0	0 0 0	0 1 0—1
Pittsburgh	4 0 1	0 0 1	1 0 x—7

Atlanta	IP	H	R	ER	BB	SO
Avery (L)	1/3	5	4	4	0	0
P. Smith	3 2/3	2	1	1	2	3
Leibrandt	1 2/3	2	1	1	1	0
Freeman	1 1/3	3	1	1	0	0
Mercker	1	1	0	0	1	0

Pittsburgh	IP	H	R	ER	BB	SO
Walk (W)	9	3	1	1	5	2

LOB—Atlanta 7, Pittsburgh 9. 2B—Bream, Redus 2, Bonds, King, McClendon. 3B—L. Smith. SB—Bonds. CS—King. SF—McClendon. U—Davis, plate; Montague, first; McSherry, second; Marsh, third; Rippley, left field; Darling, right field. T—2:52. A—52,929.

┌─────────────┐ **HIGHLIGHTS** ┌─────────────┐

PITTSBURGH 13, ATLANTA 4

Why the Pirates won: The real Barry Bonds surfaced once again—and so did the rest of Pittsburgh's offense. Bonds, coming off a banner season (a .311 batting average with 34 home runs and 103 RBIs) but another slow start in the N.L. playoffs, bashed the first postseason homer of his big-league career and thereby ignited Pittsburgh's eight-run explosion in the second inning. He added a second hit, a single, in that inning. And, for the second straight game, the Pirates collected 13 hits (three of which were homers).

Why the Braves lost: Tom Glavine recorded his second can-you-believe-this pitching line of 1992. Instead of showing the 20-victory form he exhibited in both 1991 and '92, lefthander Glavine pitched just about the way he did in the '92 All-Star Game—atrociously. In the midsummer classic, Glavine was hammered unmercifully as the National League starter, yielding an almost-unfathomable nine hits and five runs in 1 2/3 innings; in Game 6 of the '92 N.L. playoffs, he allowed six hits and eight runs (seven earned) while pitching one inning-plus.

The turning points:

1. When the Pirates put the Braves behind the eight ball with their second-inning salvo. Besides Bonds' two hits in that frame, the inning also featured a two-run double by Don Slaught and a three-run homer by Jay Bell.

2. Knuckleballer Tim Wakefield's solid pitching for the Bucs in the early going. Working in a ballpark (Atlanta's "Launching Pad") where even the largest of leads can dissipate quickly, Wakefield permitted only one run over the first six innings en route to his second complete game of the series.

Notable: Pittsburgh right fielder Lloyd McClendon enjoyed his second straight 3-for-3 game. ... Dave Justice cracked two home runs for the Braves, connecting in the seventh and ninth innings. The power display raised his homer output to five in 20 championship-series games over two years. ... By the seventh inning, approximately half of the Atlanta-Fulton County Stadium throng of 51,975 had headed for the exits.

Quotable: "It was pretty much a nightmare," said Glavine, perhaps understating his performance in Game 6. ... Did the Pirates' second straight victory, which squared the series at 3-3, mean the N.L. East Division titlists had momentum on their side? "To me, in baseball, there is no such thing as momentum," Pirates Manager Jim Leyland said. "Momentum is very simple. It's your next day's pitcher." ... "We really haven't accomplished anything. All we've done is bought ourself a Game 7," said McClendon, whose perfect night at the plate—it included a sixth-inning homer—boosted his series average to .727 (eight hits in 11 at-bats).

TUESDAY, OCTOBER 13, AT ATLANTA

Pittsburgh	AB	R	H	RBI	PO	A
Redus, 1b	5	2	2	2	6	0
Bell, ss	4	1	1	3	1	2
Van Slyke, cf	4	0	1	1	2	0
Bonds, lf	4	1	2	1	5	0
King, 3b	5	1	1	0	1	1
McClendon, rf	3	3	3	1	3	0
Varsho, ph-rf	1	0	1	0	0	0
Slaught, c	4	2	1	2	5	0
Lind, 2b	5	2	1	2	4	2
Wakefield, p	3	1	0	0	0	0
Totals	38	13	13	12	27	5

Atlanta	AB	R	H	RBI	PO	A
Nixon, cf	3	0	0	0	1	0
Mercker, p	0	0	0	0	0	0
Wohlers, p	0	0	0	0	1	0
Cabrera, ph	1	0	0	0	0	0
Blauser, ss	5	0	1	0	1	5
Pendleton, 3b	4	0	2	0	0	3
Treadway, 2b	1	1	1	0	0	1
Justice, rf	5	2	3	3	3	1
Bream, 1b	4	1	1	0	11	2
Gant, lf	3	0	0	0	3	0
Berryhill, c	3	0	0	0	4	1
Lopez, c	1	0	0	0	2	0
Lemke, 2b-3b	3	0	0	0	1	2
Glavine, p	0	0	0	0	0	0
Leibrandt, p	1	0	0	0	0	1
L. Smith, ph	1	0	1	1	0	0
Freeman, p	0	0	0	0	0	1
Sanders, ph-cf	2	0	0	0	0	0
Totals	37	4	9	4	27	17

Pittsburgh .... 0 8 0   0 4 1   0 0 0 — 13
Atlanta .... 0 0 0   1 0 0   1 0 2 — 4

Pittsburgh	IP	H	R	ER	BB	SO
Wakefield (W)	9	9	4	4	4	4

Atlanta	IP	H	R	ER	BB	SO
Glavine (L)	*1	6	8	7	0	0
Leibrandt	3	2	0	0	2	3
Freeman	2	4	5	5	2	0
Mercker	2	0	0	0	0	1
Wohlers	1	1	0	0	0	2

*Pitched to eight batters in second.

E—Bell, Blauser. DP—Atlanta 1. LOB—Pittsburgh 5, Atlanta 10. 2B—Redus, Slaught, Lind. HR—Bonds, Bell, Mc-Clendon, Justice 2. SH—Wakefield 2. HBP—By Glavine (Bell). WP—Wakefield. PB—Slaught 2. U—Montague, plate; McSherry, first; Marsh, second; Rippley, third; Darling, left field; Davis, right field. T—2:50. A—51,975.

GAME 7

HIGHLIGHTS

ATLANTA 3, PITTSBURGH 2

Why the Braves won: Pitching-wise, they threw everything but the kitchen sink at Pittsburgh and thereby were able to stay within striking distance until the end. Atlanta's John Smoltz came up with another big Game 7 performance—he had shut out the Pirates in the 1991 N.L. playoff finale and hurled 7⅓ scoreless innings against Minnesota in the final game of the '91 World Series—and the Braves got clutch relief work from Mike Stanton, usual starters Pete Smith and Steve Avery and closer Jeff Reardon. Smoltz allowed only four hits in six innings, yielding Pittsburgh's runs on Orlando Merced's first-inning sacrifice fly and Andy Van Slyke's RBI single in the sixth. Stanton, Smith, Avery and Reardon shut down the Pirates the rest of the way.

Why the Pirates lost: Some observers thought Manager Jim Leyland stayed with starter Doug Drabek too long. He didn't replace the feisty righthander until the bases were full with none out in the ninth.

The turning points:

1. After Atlanta's Terry Pendleton led off the ninth with a double—Pittsburgh was guarding a 2-0 lead at the time—Dave Justice reached base on second baseman Jose Lind's error. The misplay on a ground ball gave the Braves an extra out—and they made the most of it. Sid Bream followed by coaxing a walk off Drabek, loading the bases, and Stan Belinda was summoned from the Pirates' bullpen. Ron Gant then hit a sacrifice fly, making it a 2-1 game. Damon Berryhill walked to reload the bases. Pinch-hitter Brian Hunter popped to Lind for what should have been the third out. And then Francisco Cabrera, who saw action in only 12 big-league games in the regular season, lined a two-run, pennant-deciding single to left field.

2. With the bases loaded for Pittsburgh in the seventh and the Braves trying to stay within two runs, Avery came on to pitch and got Van Slyke to fly out to center.

3. With the score still 2-0 in the eighth, Pittsburgh's Merced was thrown out at the plate by right fielder Justice while trying to score from first base on Jeff King's double.

Notable: While Drabek had a creditable 3.71 earned-run average in three games, he set a championship-series record with three defeats. ... The Braves' back-to-back N.L. pennants were the first in the senior circuit since the Dodgers won league flags in 1977 and 1978. ... The Pirates achieved a hat trick of sorts, losing in the N.L. playoffs for the third consecutive season.

Quotable: "I made the pitch I wanted to make and he got me," said Belinda, alluding to Cabrera's ninth-inning at-bat. ... "I wasn't nervous. Not at all," said Cabrera, whose hit scored Justice and Bream. "I play in the Dominican League in the winter and lots of major leaguers play there, so I know I can hit." ... "It's the most dramatic baseball victory I've ever been associated with," Braves General Manager John Schuerholz said.

BOX SCORE

WEDNESDAY, OCTOBER 14, AT ATLANTA

Pittsburgh	AB	R	H	RBI	PO	A
Cole, rf	2	1	0	0	1	0
McClendon, ph-rf	0	0	0	0	0	0
Espy, pr-rf	0	0	0	0	0	0
Bell, ss	4	1	1	0	0	1

	AB	R	H	RBI	PO	A
Van Slyke, cf	4	0	2	1	2	0
Bonds, lf	3	0	1	0	4	0
Merced, 1b	3	0	0	1	10	0
King, 3b	4	0	1	0	2	2
LaValliere, c	4	0	1	0	5	0
Lind, 2b	4	0	1	0	2	4
Drabek, p	3	0	0	0	0	0
Belinda, p	0	0	0	0	0	0
Totals	31	2	7	2	26	7

Atlanta	AB	R	H	RBI	PO	A
Nixon, cf	4	0	1	0	2	0
Blauser, ss	4	0	0	0	0	1
Pendleton, 3b	4	1	1	0	1	3
Justice, rf	4	1	0	0	6	1
Bream, 1b	3	1	1	0	4	1
Gant, lf	2	0	0	1	4	0
Berryhill, c	3	0	1	0	8	0
Lemke, 2b	2	0	1	0	1	1
L. Smith, ph	1	0	0	0	0	0
Belliard, 2b	0	0	0	0	1	0
Hunter, ph	1	0	0	0	0	0
Smoltz, p	1	0	0	0	0	0
Treadway, ph	1	0	1	0	0	0
Stanton, p	0	0	0	0	0	0
P. Smith, p	0	0	0	0	0	0
Avery, p	0	0	0	0	0	0

	AB	R	H	RBI	PO	A
Sanders, ph	1	0	0	0	0	0
Reardon, p	0	0	0	0	0	0
Cabrera, ph	1	0	1	2	0	0
Totals	32	3	7	3	27	7

Pittsburgh .... 1 0 0 0 0 1 0 0 0—2
Atlanta .... 0 0 0 0 0 0 0 0 3—3

Two out when winning run scored.

Pittsburgh	IP	H	R	ER	BB	SO
Drabek (L)	*8	6	3	1	2	5
Belinda	2/3	1	0	0	1	0

Atlanta	IP	H	R	ER	BB	SO
Smoltz	6	4	2	2	2	4
Stanton	2/3	1	0	0	1	0
P. Smith	0	0	0	0	1	0
Avery	1 1/3	2	0	0	0	0
Reardon (W)	1	0	0	0	1	1

*Pitched to three batters in ninth.

E—Lind. DP—Pittsburgh 1. LOB—Pittsburgh 9, Atlanta 7. 2B—Bell, Van Slyke, King, Lind, Pendleton, Bream, Berryhill. SH—Drabek. SF—Merced, Gant. WP—Reardon. U—McSherry, plate; Marsh, first; Rippley, second; Darling, third; Davis, left field; Montague, right field (Note: McSherry left game after first inning due to illness and was replaced by Marsh behind plate). T—3:22. A—51,975.

STATISTICS

ATLANTA BRAVES' BATTING AND FIELDING AVERAGES

					BATTING										FIELDING		
Player, position	G	AB	R	H	TB	2B	3B	HR	RBI	BB	IBB	SO	Avg.	PO	A	E	Avg.
Stanton, p	5	1	1	1	2	1	0	0	1	0	0	0	1.000	0	1	0	1.000
Treadway, ph-2b	3	3	1	2	2	0	0	0	0	0	0	1	.667	0	1	0	1.000
Cabrera, ph	2	2	0	1	1	0	0	0	2	0	0	0	.500	0	0	0	.000
Lemke, 2b-3b	7	21	2	7	8	1	0	0	2	5	1	3	.333	11	17	0	1.000
L. Smith, ph	6	6	1	2	4	0	1	0	1	0	0	0	.333	0	0	0	.000
Nixon, cf	7	28	5	8	10	2	0	0	2	4	1	4	.286	16	0	0	1.000
Smoltz, p	3	7	1	2	2	0	0	0	1	0	0	2	.286	0	1	0	1.000
Justice, rf	7	25	5	7	14	1	0	2	6	6	1	2	.280	19	3	0	1.000
Bream, 1b	7	22	5	6	12	3	0	1	2	3	0	0	.273	53	4	0	1.000
Pendleton, 3b	7	30	2	7	9	2	0	0	3	0	0	2	.233	4	18	0	1.000
Blauser, ss	7	24	3	5	10	0	1	1	4	3	0	2	.208	7	15	2	.917
Hunter, 1b-ph	3	5	1	1	1	0	0	0	0	0	0	1	.200	7	0	0	1.000
Gant, lf	7	22	5	4	10	0	0	2	6	4	0	4	.182	16	0	0	1.000
Berryhill, c	7	24	1	4	5	1	0	0	1	3	0	2	.167	43	5	0	1.000
Freeman, p	3	0	0	0	0	0	0	0	0	0	0	0	.000	0	2	0	1.000
Mercker, p	2	0	0	0	0	0	0	0	0	0	0	0	.000	0	0	0	.000
Reardon, p	3	0	0	0	0	0	0	0	0	0	0	0	.000	0	0	0	.000
Wohlers, p	3	0	0	0	0	0	0	0	0	0	0	0	.000	1	0	0	1.000
Leibrandt, p	2	1	0	0	0	0	0	0	0	0	0	1	.000	0	1	0	1.000
Lopez, c	1	1	0	0	0	0	0	0	0	0	0	0	.000	2	0	0	1.000
P. Smith, p	2	1	0	0	0	0	0	0	0	0	0	0	.000	0	1	0	1.000
Avery, p	3	2	0	0	0	0	0	0	0	1	0	1	.000	0	0	0	.000
Belliard, pr-ss-2b	4	2	1	0	0	0	0	0	0	1	0	0	.000	2	3	0	1.000
Glavine, p	2	2	0	0	0	0	0	0	0	0	0	0	.000	1	2	0	1.000
Sanders, ph-lf-cf	4	5	0	0	0	0	0	0	0	0	0	3	.000	1	0	0	1.000
Totals	7	234	34	57	90	11	2	6	32	29	3	28	.244	183	74	2	.992

PITTSBURGH PIRATES' BATTING AND FIELDING AVERAGES

					BATTING										FIELDING		
Player, position	G	AB	R	H	TB	2B	3B	HR	RBI	BB	IBB	SO	Avg.	PO	A	E	Avg.
McClendon, rf-ph	5	11	4	8	13	2	0	1	4	4	1	1	.727	10	0	0	1.000
Espy, ph-rf-pr	4	3	0	2	2	0	0	0	0	0	0	1	.667	0	0	0	.000
Varsho, ph-rf	2	2	0	1	1	0	0	0	0	0	0	0	.500	0	0	0	.000
Redus, 1b-ph	5	16	4	7	13	4	1	0	3	2	0	3	.438	31	4	0	1.000
Slaught, c-ph	5	12	5	4	8	1	0	1	5	6	1	3	.333	17	1	0	1.000
Van Slyke, cf	7	29	1	8	13	3	1	0	4	1	0	5	.276	20	0	0	1.000
Bonds, lf	7	23	5	6	10	1	0	1	2	6	1	4	.261	17	0	0	1.000
King, 3b	7	29	4	7	11	4	0	0	2	0	0	1	.241	11	19	1	.968
Lind, 2b	7	27	5	6	13	2	1	1	5	1	1	4	.222	16	23	2	.951
Cole, rf-ph	4	10	2	2	2	0	0	0	1	3	0	2	.200	7	1	0	1.000

Player, position	G	AB	R	H	TB	2B	3B	HR	RBI	BB	IBB	SO	Avg.	PO	A	E	Avg.
					BATTING										FIELDING		
LaValliere, c	3	10	1	2	2	0	0	0	0	0	0	3	.200	14	0	0	1.000
Bell, ss	7	29	3	5	10	2	0	1	4	3	0	4	.172	6	8	1	.933
Merced, 1b-ph	4	10	0	1	2	1	0	0	2	2	0	4	.100	27	2	1	.967
Belinda, p	2	0	0	0	0	0	0	0	0	0	0	0	.000	0	0	0	.000
Cox, p	2	0	0	0	0	0	0	0	0	0	0	0	.000	0	0	0	.000
Jackson, p	1	0	0	0	0	0	0	0	0	0	0	0	.000	0	0	0	.000
Mason, p	2	0	0	0	0	0	0	0	0	0	0	0	.000	2	0	0	1.000
Neagle, p	2	0	0	0	0	0	0	0	0	0	0	0	.000	0	0	0	.000
Patterson, p	2	0	0	0	0	0	0	0	0	0	0	0	.000	0	0	0	.000
Tomlin, p	2	0	0	0	0	0	0	0	0	0	0	0	.000	0	1	0	1.000
Garcia, 2b	1	1	0	0	0	0	0	0	0	0	0	0	.000	0	0	0	.000
Wehner, ph	2	2	0	0	0	0	0	0	0	0	0	2	.000	0	0	0	.000
Walk, p	2	5	0	0	0	0	0	0	0	0	0	1	.000	1	2	0	1.000
Drabek, p	3	6	0	0	0	0	0	0	0	1	0	4	.000	0	0	0	.000
Wakefield, p	2	6	1	0	0	0	0	0	0	0	0	0	.000	3	2	0	1.000
Totals	7	231	35	59	100	20	3	5	32	29	4	42	.255	182	63	5	.980

ATLANTA BRAVES' PITCHING RECORDS

Pitcher	G	GS	CG	IP	H	R	ER	HR	BB	IBB	SO	HB	WP	W	L	Pct.	ERA
Stanton	5	0	0	4⅓	2	1	0	0	2	1	5	0	0	0	0	.000	0.00
Mercker	2	0	0	3	1	0	0	0	1	0	1	0	0	0	0	.000	0.00
Reardon	3	0	0	3	0	0	0	0	2	0	3	0	1	1	0	1.000	0.00
Wohlers	3	0	0	3	2	0	0	0	1	0	2	0	0	0	0	.000	0.00
Leibrandt	2	0	0	4⅔	4	1	1	0	3	0	3	0	0	0	0	.000	1.93
P. Smith	2	0	0	3⅔	2	1	1	0	3	0	3	0	0	0	0	.000	2.45
Smoltz	3	3	0	20⅓	14	7	6	1	10	2	19	0	1	2	0	1.000	2.66
Avery	3	2	0	8	13	8	8	0	2	0	3	0	1	1	1	.500	9.00
Glavine	2	2	0	7⅓	13	11	10	3	3	1	2	2	0	0	2	.000	12.27
Freeman	3	0	0	3⅔	8	6	6	1	2	0	1	0	0	0	0	.000	14.73
Totals	7	7	0	61	59	35	32	5	29	4	42	2	3	4	3	.571	4.72

No shutouts. Save—Reardon.

PITTSBURGH PIRATES' PITCHING RECORDS

Pitcher	G	GS	CG	IP	H	R	ER	HR	BB	IBB	SO	HB	WP	W	L	Pct.	ERA
Mason	2	0	0	3⅓	0	0	0	0	2	0	1	0	0	0	0	.000	0.00
Belinda	2	0	0	1⅔	2	0	0	0	1	0	2	0	0	0	0	.000	0.00
Cox	2	0	0	1⅓	1	0	0	0	1	0	1	0	0	0	0	.000	0.00
Wakefield	2	2	2	18	14	6	6	4	5	0	7	0	1	2	0	1.000	3.00
Drabek	3	3	0	17	18	11	7	1	6	1	10	0	0	0	3	.000	3.71
Walk	2	1	1	11⅔	6	5	5	1	7	1	6	0	0	1	0	1.000	3.86
Patterson	2	0	0	1⅔	3	1	1	0	1	0	1	0	0	0	0	.000	5.40
Tomlin	2	0	0	2⅔	5	2	2	0	1	0	0	0	0	0	0	.000	6.75
Jackson	1	1	0	1⅔	4	4	4	0	2	0	0	0	0	0	1	.000	21.60
Neagle	2	0	0	1⅔	4	5	5	0	3	1	0	0	0	0	0	.000	27.00
Totals	7	7	3	60⅔	57	34	30	6	29	3	28	0	1	3	4	.428	4.45

No shutouts or saves.

SCORE BY INNINGS

Atlanta	0	7	0	4	7	2	8	1	5—34
Pittsburgh	5	10	2	0	5	4	7	2	0—35

MISCELLANEOUS STATISTICS

Sacrifice hits—Wakefield 2, Gant, Blauser, Drabek.

Sacrifice flies—Avery, Van Slyke, McClendon, Merced, Gant.

Stolen bases—Nixon 3, Gant, Smoltz, Bonds.

Caught stealing—Merced, King.

Double plays—Pendleton, Lemke and Bream 2; King and Lind; King, Lind and Redus; King, Lind and Merced; Cole and Merced; King and Merced; Lemke, Blauser and Bream; King (unassisted).

Left on bases—Atlanta 8, 9 ,3, 7, 7, 10, 7—51; Pittsburgh 5, 7, 8, 7, 9, 5, 9—50.

Hit by pitcher—By Glavine 2 (Bonds, Bell).

Passed balls—Slaught 2, Berryhill.

Balks—None.

Time of games—First game, 3:00; second game, 3:20; third game, 2:37; fourth game, 3:10; fifth game, 2:52; sixth game, 2:50; seventh game, 3:22.

Attendance—First game, 51,971; second game, 51,975; third game, 56,610; fourth game, 57,164; fifth game, 52,929; sixth game, 51,975; seventh game, 51,975.

Umpires—McSherry, Marsh, Rippley, Darling, Davis and Montague.

Official scorers—Mark Frederickson, Atlanta official scorer; Nick Peters, San Francisco Chronicle; Bob Webb, Pittsburgh official scorer.

WORLD SERIES

HIGHLIGHTS

ATLANTA 3, TORONTO 1

Why the Braves won: Lefthander Tom Glavine displayed his regular-season form (40 victories, 19 losses) of the last two seasons and not his postseason form (a combined 1-5 record in the National League playoffs and the World Series). He permitted only four hits—three singles and Joe Carter's leadoff home run in the fourth inning—and did not issue a base on balls.

Why the Blue Jays lost: Big-game pitcher Jack Morris made one bad pitch—and Atlanta catcher Damon Berryhill, batting in the sixth inning with two men on base and two out, deposited it over the right-field wall.

The turning points:

1. When Glavine kept his cool after allowing Carter's homer. Since the lefthander had been hammered in Game 6 of the N.L. Championship Series (in the wake of other postseason disappointments), there were some questions about the condition of his psyche. Glavine, though, allayed any fears and kept the Blue Jays in check the rest of the way.

2. When Berryhill made the most of his chance to play. Thrust into full-time catching duty with the Braves after Greg Olson suffered an ankle fracture in mid-September, Berryhill, whose career has been waylaid by rotator cuff problems, stepped to the fore in his sixth-inning at-bat. Falling behind on the count at 1-2 with runners on second and third base, he proceeded to line a homer to right. Not only did the blast catapult the Braves into the lead, but it also showed that Blue Jays starter Jack Morris, 4-0 in World Series play entering this game, wasn't unbeatable in the fall classic.

Notable: Berryhill's home run snapped Morris' 18-inning scoreless streak in World Series competition. ... Carter's shot extended the Blue Jays' 1992 postseason homer streak to (all) seven games.

Quotable: "I look at this as an opportunity to show the people that I can play this game," said Berryhill, who was obtained from the Chicago Cubs in September 1991. "I generally try to stay out of the spotlight, but this is the World Series and you're in it. You just want to play well." ... Morris, discussing the pitch that Berryhill creamed: "Your basic hanging, 390-foot forkball." ... Atlanta Manager Bobby Cox, on the 28-year-old Berryhill: "He's come through for us. He's done everything we've asked of him. We're very comfortable with him handling our pitchers. Anything we get offensively is frosting on the cake." ... "To sit here the last few days and read about how terrible I've been, it's aggravating," Glavine said. "Everybody forgets that I've won 20 games for two straight years. I don't really care what people say about me, but it motivates me."

BOX SCORE

SATURDAY, OCTOBER 17, AT ATLANTA

Toronto	AB	R	H	RBI	PO	A
White, cf	4	0	0	0	2	0
Alomar, 2b	4	0	0	0	1	2
Carter, 1b	4	1	1	1	10	0
Winfield, rf	3	0	1	0	0	0
Maldonado, lf	3	0	0	0	0	0
Gruber, 3b	3	0	0	0	1	1
Borders, c	3	0	2	0	10	0
Lee, ss	3	0	0	0	0	3
Morris, p	2	0	0	0	0	1
Stottlemyre, p	0	0	0	0	0	0
aTabler	1	0	0	0	0	0
Wells, p	0	0	0	0	0	0
Totals	30	1	4	1	24	7

Atlanta	AB	R	H	RBI	PO	A
Nixon, cf	3	0	1	0	1	0
Blauser, ss	4	0	0	0	1	2
Belliard, ss	0	0	0	0	1	2
Pendleton, 3b	4	0	0	0	0	2
Justice, rf	2	1	0	0	3	0
Bream, 1b	3	0	1	0	12	0
Gant, lf	3	1	0	0	1	0
Berryhill, c	4	1	1	3	6	0
Lemke, 2b	3	0	1	0	2	3
Glavine, p	2	0	0	0	0	1
Totals	28	3	4	3	27	10

Toronto	0 0 0	1 0 0	0 0 0—1			
Atlanta	0 0 0	0 0 3	0 0 x—3			

Toronto	IP	H	R	ER	BB	SO
Morris (L)	6	4	3	3	5	7
Stottlemyre	1	0	0	0	0	2
Wells	1	0	0	0	1	1

Atlanta	IP	H	R	ER	BB	SO
Glavine (W)	9	4	1	1	0	6

Bases on balls—Off Morris 5 (Justice 2, Bream, Glavine, Nixon), off Wells 1 (Gant).
Strikeouts—By Morris 7 (Gant 2, Justice, Berryhill, Lemke, Pendleton, Blauser), by Stottlemyre 2 (Nixon, Blauser), by Wells 1 (Berryhill), by Glavine 6 (Maldonado 2, Morris 2, Gruber, Alomar.
aFlied out for Stottlemyre in eighth. DP—Atlanta 1. LOB—Toronto 2, Atlanta 7. HR—Carter, Berryhill. SB—Nixon, Gant. WP—Morris. U—Crawford (N.L.), plate; Reilly (A.L.), first; West (N.L.), second; Morrison (A.L.), third; Davidson (N.L.), left field; Shulock (A.L.), right field. T—2:37. A—51,763.

PLAY BY PLAY

FIRST INNING

Toronto—White and Alomar grounded to third. Carter grounded to second.

Atlanta—Nixon singled to center. Nixon stole second. Blauser popped to first. Pendleton grounded to third, Nixon went to third. Justice struck out.

SECOND INNING

Toronto—Winfield singled to third. Maldonado struck out. Gruber flied to right. Borders singled to left, Winfield went to second. Lee forced Borders at second, shortstop to second baseman.

Atlanta—Bream popped to first. Gant and Berryhill struck out.

THIRD INNING

Toronto—Morris struck out. White grounded to second. Alomar grounded to the pitcher.

Atlanta—Lemke struck out. Glavine grounded to short. Nixon grounded to the pitcher.

FOURTH INNING

Toronto—Carter homered to left-center. Winfield grounded to second. Maldonado grounded to short. Gruber struck out.

Atlanta—Blauser popped foul to first. Pendleton struck out. Justice and Bream walked. Justice went to third and Bream to second on a wild pitch. Gant struck out.

FIFTH INNING

Toronto—Borders grounded to first. Lee popped to short. Morris struck out.

Atlanta—Berryhill flied to center. Lemke grounded to second. Glavine and Nixon walked. Blauser struck out.

SIXTH INNING

Toronto—White popped to first. Alomar struck out. Carter flied to left.

Atlanta—Pendleton grounded to second. Justice walked. Bream singled to left, Justice went to second. Gant forced Bream at second, shortstop to second baseman, Justice went to third. Gant stole second. Berryhill homered to right, scoring Justice and Gant. Lemke singled to center. Glavine flied to center.

SEVENTH INNING

Toronto—Winfield popped to first. Maldonado struck out. Gruber flied to right.

Atlanta—Stottlemyre now pitching. Nixon and Blauser struck out. Pendleton grounded to short.

EIGHTH INNING

Toronto—Belliard now at short. Borders singled to center. Lee grounded into a double play, shortstop to first baseman. Tabler, pinch-hitting for Stottlemyre, flied to center.

Atlanta—Wells now pitching. Justice popped foul to third. Bream grounded to first. Gant walked. Berryhill struck out.

NINTH INNING

Toronto—White grounded to short. Alomar popped to second. Carter flied to right.

GAME 2

HIGHLIGHTS

TORONTO 5, ATLANTA 4

Why the Blue Jays won: They got big-time performances from their bullpen and their bench. After starter David Cone struggled for 4⅓ innings (three earned runs, five hits and five walks), David Wells, Todd Stottlemyre, Duane Ward and Tom Henke combined for 4⅔ innings of scoreless—and hitless—pitching. With the bullpen keeping the Jays in the ball game, reserves Derek Bell and Ed Sprague did the rest. Bell, pinch hitting for shortstop Manny Lee with one out in the ninth inning and Toronto down by a 4-3 score, drew a walk off Braves stopper Jeff Reardon. Sprague, who played only 22 games for the Jays in the regular season and hit one home run, then batted for Ward and, in a stunning moment in postseason history, rocketed Reardon's first offering over the left-field wall at Atlanta-Fulton County Stadium. Henke then protected the 5-4 lead in the bottom of

the ninth, getting Terry Pendleton to foul out with two Braves on base and two out.

Why the Braves lost: Reardon, obtained from the Boston Red Sox in late August to extricate the Braves from tight situations, just wasn't up to the job. The major leagues' all-time saves leader did come to the rescue in the eighth inning after the Braves' lead had been sliced from 4-2 to 4-3, striking out Kelly Gruber with runners at the corners. But then came the fateful—and fitful—ninth.

The turning points:

1. The fact that Sprague went to the plate hacking, not looking. Jumping on Reardon's first pitch, he forever established a place for himself in baseball lore.

2. Toronto Manager Cito Gaston's decision to use the hook on Cone before Atlanta had fashioned a sizable lead.

Notable: Braves starter John Smoltz continued to have bad luck in the World Series. Allowing only two earned runs and striking out eight batters in 7⅓ innings, Smoltz came away with a no-decision for his efforts and was still looking for his first Series victory. In the 1991 Series, he had a 1.26 earned-run average over 14⅓ innings but had two no-decisions. . . . Smoltz struck out five of the first six batters he faced. . . . Cone's biggest contribution to the Blue Jays in Game 2 was with his bat. He went 2-for-2 at the plate with one RBI. . . . A U.S. color guard committed a diplomatic gaffe, inadvertently flying the Canadian flag upside down in pregame ceremonies.

Quotable: "I had not done a lot of pinch-hitting," the 25-year-old Sprague said in the postgame bedlam. "I had been watching some of the other hitters, and they told me that he (Reardon) had been throwing some high fastballs. They said to wait until I got a fastball that I could hit." Wait, he didn't. . . . "You'll hear from this young man (Sprague) for a long time," Gaston said. "He studies the game, he works hard and he'll be around." . . . Smoltz, on his luckless World Series efforts (contrasted with his 4-0 career mark in League Championship Series play): "No, I don't feel that it's a scar on my record that I still don't have a World Series win. I pitched as well as I could, and I know I'll get another shot at them in the Series."

BOX SCORE

SUNDAY, OCTOBER 18, AT ATLANTA

Toronto	AB	R	H	RBI	PO	A
White, cf	5	0	1	1	5	0
Alomar, 2b	4	1	1	0	0	1
Carter, lf	3	0	1	0	2	0
Winfield, rf	4	0	1	1	5	0
Olerud, 1b	4	0	0	0	5	0
Gruber, 3b	4	0	0	0	1	1
Borders, c	3	1	1	0	6	0
Lee, ss	3	1	1	0	3	3
cBell	0	1	0	0	0	0
Griffin, ss	0	0	0	0	0	0
Cone, p	2	0	2	1	0	0

	AB	R	H	RBI	PO	A
Wells, p	0	0	0	0	0	0
bMaldonado	1	0	0	0	0	0
Stottlemyre, p	0	0	0	0	0	0
Ward, p	0	0	0	0	0	0
dSprague	1	1	1	2	0	0
Henke, p	0	0	0	0	0	0
Totals	34	5	9	5	27	5

Atlanta	AB	R	H	RBI	PO	A
Nixon, cf	5	0	0	0	2	0
Sanders, lf	3	1	1	0	0	0
Pendleton, 3b	4	1	1	0	2	2
Justice, rf	3	1	1	1	4	0
Bream, 1b	1	1	0	0	4	0
aHunter, 1b	1	0	0	1	3	0
Blauser, ss	3	0	1	0	1	2
Belliard, ss	0	0	0	0	0	0
Berryhill, c	3	0	0	0	8	2
Lemke, 2b	4	0	1	1	2	0
Smoltz, p	3	0	0	0	1	2
Stanton, p	0	0	0	0	0	0
Reardon, p	0	0	0	0	0	0
eL. Smith	0	0	0	0	0	0
fGant	0	0	0	0	0	0
Totals	30	4	5	3	27	8

Toronto .... 0 0 0 0 2 0 0 1 2—5
Atlanta .... 0 1 0 1 2 0 0 0 0—4

Toronto	IP	H	R	ER	BB	SO
Cone	4⅓	5	4	3	5	2
Wells	1⅔	0	0	0	1	2
Stottlemyre	1	0	0	0	0	0
Ward (W)	1	0	0	0	0	2
Henke (S)	1	0	0	0	1	0

Atlanta	IP	H	R	ER	BB	SO
Smoltz	7⅓	8	3	2	3	8
Stanton	⅓	0	0	0	0	0
Reardon (L)	1⅓	1	2	2	1	1

Bases on balls—Off Cone 5 (Justice, Berryhill, Sanders, Bream, Pendleton), off Wells 1 (Blauser), off Henke 1 (Sanders), off Smoltz 3 (Alomar, Borders, Carter), off Reardon 1 (Bell).

Strikeouts—By Cone 2 (Smoltz, Nixon), by Wells 2 (Berryhill, Smoltz), by Ward 2 (Blauser, Berryhill), by Smoltz 8 (Gruber 2, White, Carter, Winfield, Olerud, Lee, Maldonado), by Reardon 1 (Gruber).

aHit sacrifice fly for Bream in fifth. bStruck out for Wells in seventh. cWalked for Lee in ninth. dHomered for Ward in ninth. eHit by pitch for Reardon in ninth. fRan for L. Smith in ninth. E—Lee, Bream, Borders. DP—Toronto 2, Atlanta 1. LOB—Toronto 6, Atlanta 8. 2B—Borders, Alomar. HR—Sprague. SB—Sanders 2, Justice, Blauser, Gant. SF—Hunter. HBP—By Henke (L. Smith). WP—Smoltz 2, Cone. U—Reilly (A.L.), plate; West (N.L.), first; Morrison (A.L.), second; Davidson (N.L.), third; Shulock (A.L.), left field; Crawford (N.L.), right field. T—3:30. A—51,763.

PLAY BY PLAY

FIRST INNING

Toronto—White struck out. Alomar grounded to the pitcher. Carter struck out.

Atlanta—Nixon flied to left. Sanders flied to right. Pendleton grounded to short.

SECOND INNING

Toronto—Winfield, Olerud and Gruber struck out.

Atlanta—Justice walked. Bream flied to center. Justice stole second. Blauser reached on a fielder's choice as the shortstop threw wild to third for an error. Justice scored on a wild pitch and Blauser, who stole second on the play, went to third. Berryhill walked. Lemke grounded into a double play, shortstop to first baseman.

THIRD INNING

Toronto—Borders grounded to third. Lee flied to right. Cone singled to left. White lined to right.

Atlanta—Smoltz struck out. Nixon flied to center. Sanders walked. Sanders stole second. Pendleton singled to second, Sanders went to third. Justice flied to right.

FOURTH INNING

Toronto—Alomar walked. Alomar went to second on a wild pitch. Carter popped to third. Winfield grounded out to the pitcher, Alomar went to third. Alomar was tagged out trying to score on a ball which got away from the catcher, but the catcher recovered and threw to the pitcher for the out.

Atlanta—Bream walked. Blauser singled to right, Bream went to third. Berryhill lined to right. Lemke singled to right, scoring Bream as Blauser went to third. Smoltz grounded into a double play, shortstop to first baseman.

FIFTH INNING

Toronto—Olerud flied to right. Gruber grounded to third. Borders walked. Lee singled to right, Borders went to second. Cone singled to left, scoring Borders as Lee went to second. On the same play Lee advanced to third and Cone to second when the first baseman made a bad throw for an error. White singled to second, scoring Lee as Cone went to third. Alomar forced White at second, shortstop to second baseman.

Atlanta—Nixon struck out. Sanders singled to right. Sanders stole second and advanced to third on a wild throw by the catcher, who was charged with an error. Pendleton walked. Justice singled to left, scoring Sanders as Pendleton went to third. Wells now pitching. Hunter, pinch-hitting for Bream, hit a sacrifice fly to right, scoring Pendleton. Blauser walked. Berryhill struck out.

SIXTH INNING

Toronto—Hunter now at first. Carter walked. Winfield flied to center. Olerud lined into a double play, shortstop to first baseman.

Atlanta—Lemke flied to center. Smoltz struck out. Nixon fouled to right.

SEVENTH INNING

Toronto—Gruber struck out and was retired, catcher to first baseman, on the dropped third strike. Borders doubled to left. Lee struck out. Borders went to third on a wild pitch. Maldonado, pinch-hitting for Wells, struck out.

Atlanta—Stottlemyre now pitching. Sanders lined to short. Pendleton grounded to second. Justice flied to center.

EIGHTH INNING

Toronto—White flied to center. Alomar doubled to left. Carter singled to center, Alomar went to third. Winfield singled to right, scoring Alomar as Carter went to third. Stanton now pitching. Olerud popped to third. Reardon now pitching. Gruber struck out.

Atlanta—Ward now pitching. Hunter grounded to third. Blauser and Berryhill struck out.

NINTH INNING

Toronto—Belliard now at short. Borders flied to right. Bell, pinch-hitting for Lee, walked. Sprague, pinch-hitting for Ward, homered to left, scoring Bell. White grounded to first. Alomar popped to second.

Atlanta—Griffin now at short and Henke pitching. Lemke flied to left. L. Smith, pinch-hitting for Reardon, was hit by a pitch. Gant pinch ran for L. Smith. Nixon flied to center. Gant stole second. Sanders walked. Pendleton popped foul to third.

GAME 3

HIGHLIGHTS

TORONTO 3, ATLANTA 2

Why the Blue Jays won: A postseason bust (a .129 batting average on eight hits in 62 at-bats) entering 1992, veteran Candy Maldonado continued to find the range offensively. Coming off an American League Championship Series in which he poled two home runs and drove in six runs, Maldonado, batting in the ninth inning of a 2-2 game with the bases loaded and one out, lined a single over the head of drawn-in center fielder Otis Nixon. The hit, off Braves reliever Jeff Reardon, gave the Blue Jays a 3-2 victory and a lead of two games to one in the World Series.

Why the Braves lost: In a deadlocked game, they allowed Toronto's leadoff hitter to reach base in the ninth. That batsman, Roberto Alomar, proved a catalyst by rapping a single and stealing second base. Joe Carter was given an intentional base on balls, and Dave Winfield, to the surprise of many, advanced the runners to second and third with a bunt. Pinch-hitter Ed Sprague then was walked intentionally, bringing Maldonado to the plate and Reardon to the mound as the Braves' fourth pitcher of the inning. Maldonado stroked a 0-2 pitch over Nixon's head.

The turning points:

1. Toronto center fielder Devon White's dazzling catch against the wall of Dave Justice's fourth-inning drive. With Deion Sanders and Terry Pendleton on base with singles in a 0-0 game, Atlanta's Justice smashed a Juan Guzman pitch to deep center, over White's head. White sprinted toward the wall, leaped and made a sensational backhanded catch against the 400-foot sign. The catch was nearly turned into a triple play, with Pendleton passing Sanders on the basepaths for an automatic out and Jays third baseman Kelly Gruber just missing a tag on Sanders, who was caught in no man's land between second and third. Guzman then struck out Lonnie Smith, and Atlanta's hopes for a big inning were snuffed out.

2. Gruber's eighth-inning home run. Mired in a 0-for-23 slump in 1992 postseason play and having committed an error that led to Atlanta's go-ahead run in the top of the eighth, Gruber squared the game at 2-2 when he led off the bottom half of the inning with a homer to left off Steve Avery.

Notable: The game was the first World Series contest ever played in Canada. Some notable World Series happenings, Canadian version: first-ever batter: Nixon, first inning; first hit: Sanders, first inning; first home run: Carter, fourth inning; first winning pitcher: Duane Ward.

Quotable: "If I don't get the ball, two runs score, easy," said White, alluding to his grab of Justice's fourth-inning clout. "I guess I've made similar plays in the regular season. But this is the World Series. The whole world watched me make that catch." . . . Gruber, on his rundown of Sanders (toward second base) for what would have capped a triple play: "I definitely hit him on the back of the heel." Umpire Bob Davidson begged to differ, but after seeing a televised replay he later admitted that he blew the call. . . . Maldonado, reflecting on his game-winning at-bat: "He (Rear-

don) had made me look bad twice with sliders. There seemed to be no reason why he wouldn't come with the same thing again." . . . "I don't even throw a slider," was Reardon's rejoinder. "It was a curveball."

BOX SCORE

TUESDAY, OCTOBER 20, AT TORONTO

Atlanta	AB	R	H	RBI	PO	A
Nixon, cf	4	1	0	0	5	0
Sanders, lf	4	1	3	0	0	0
Pendleton, 3b	4	0	2	0	0	5
Justice, rf	3	0	1	1	0	0
L. Smith, dh	4	0	1	1	0	0
Bream, 1b	4	0	2	0	8	0
aHunter, 1b	0	0	0	0	0	1
Blauser, ss	4	0	0	0	0	1
Berryhill, c	4	0	0	0	9	0
Lemke, 2b	3	0	0	0	3	1
Avery, p	0	0	0	0	0	2
Wohlers, p	0	0	0	0	0	0
Stanton, p	0	0	0	0	0	0
Reardon, p	0	0	0	0	0	0
Totals	34	2	9	2	25	10

Toronto	AB	R	H	RBI	PO	A
White, cf	4	0	0	0	3	0
Alomar, 2b	4	1	1	0	0	3
Carter, rf	3	1	1	1	1	0
Winfield, dh	3	0	1	0	0	0
Olerud, 1b	3	0	0	0	5	2
bSprague	0	0	0	0	0	0
Maldonado, lf	4	0	1	1	0	1
Gruber, 3b	2	1	1	1	2	0
Borders, c	3	0	1	0	9	1
Lee, ss	3	0	0	0	5	0
Guzman, p	0	0	0	0	2	0
Ward, p	0	0	0	0	0	0
Totals	29	3	6	3	27	7

Atlanta	0 0 0	0 0 1	0 1 0—2
Toronto	0 0 0	1 0 0	0 1 1—3

One out when winning run scored.

Atlanta	IP	H	R	ER	BB	SO
Avery (L)	*8	5	3	3	1	9
Wohlers	⅓	0	0	0	1	0
Stanton	0	0	0	0	1	0
Reardon	0	1	0	0	0	0

Toronto	IP	H	R	ER	BB	SO
Guzman	8	8	2	1	1	7
Ward (W)	1	1	0	0	0	2

*Pitched to one batter in ninth.

Bases on balls—Off Avery 1 (Gruber), off Wohlers 1 (Carter), off Stanton 1 (Sprague), off Guzman 1 (Justice). Strikeouts—By Avery 9 (Alomar 2, Olerud 2, White 2, Maldonado, Borders, Winfield), by Guzman 7 (L. Smith 2, Blauser 2, Berryhill 2, Justice), by Ward 2 (Blauser, Berryhill). aRan for Bream in ninth. bWas walked intentionally for Olerud in ninth. E—Gruber. DP—Atlanta 1, Toronto 2. LOB—Atlanta 6, Toronto 5. 2B—Sanders. HR—Carter, Gruber. SB—Sanders, Gruber, Nixon, Alomar. CS—Hunter. SH—Winfield. U—West (N.L.), plate; Morrison (A.L.), first; Davidson (N.L.), second; Shulock (A.L.), third; Crawford (N.L.), left field; Reilly (A.L.), right field. T—2:49. A—51,813.

PLAY BY PLAY

FIRST INNING

Atlanta—Nixon flied to center. Sanders singled to right-center. Sanders stole second. Pendleton grounded to first, Sanders went to third. Justice struck out.

Toronto—White grounded to third. Alomar struck out. Carter flied to center.

SECOND INNING

Atlanta—L. Smith struck out. Bream popped to short. Blauser struck out.

Toronto—Winfield singled to short. Olerud struck out. Maldonado grounded into a double play, third baseman to second baseman to first baseman.

THIRD INNING

Atlanta—Berryhill struck out. Lemke grounded to first. Nixon flied to center.

Toronto—Gruber grounded to the pitcher. Borders singled to left. Lee grounded to third, Borders went to second. White struck out.

FOURTH INNING

Atlanta—Sanders singled to the pitcher. Pendleton singled to right, Sanders went to second. Justice flied into a double play as Pendleton was ruled out for passing Sanders on the basepaths, center fielder to shortstop (although the center fielder was not credited with an assist on the play). L. Smith struck out.

Toronto—Alomar grounded to third. Carter homered to left. Winfield popped to second. Olerud grounded to the pitcher.

FIFTH INNING

Atlanta—Bream singled to center. Blauser and Berryhill struck out. Lemke grounded to second.

Toronto—Maldonado struck out. Gruber walked. Borders struck out as Gruber stole second. Lee grounded to third.

SIXTH INNING

Atlanta—Nixon grounded to second. Sanders doubled to right. Pendleton singled to short, Sanders went to third. Justice singled to right, scoring Sanders as Pendleton went to second. L. Smith flied to right. Bream grounded to the first baseman, who tossed to the pitcher for the out.

Toronto—White flied to center. Alomar struck out. Carter flied to center.

SEVENTH INNING

Atlanta—Blauser grounded to the first baseman, who tossed to the pitcher for the out. Berryhill fouled to third. Lemke popped to short.

Toronto—Winfield and Olerud struck out. Maldonado flied to center.

EIGHTH INNING

Atlanta—Nixon reached first on an error by the third baseman. Nixon stole second. Sanders popped to short. Pendleton grounded to second, Nixon went to third. Justice was walked intentionally. L. Smith singled to left, scoring Nixon as Justice went to second. Justice tried to go to third on the play but was out, left fielder to third baseman.

Toronto—Gruber homered to left. Borders flied to center. Lee grounded to short. White struck out.

NINTH INNING

Atlanta—Ward now pitching. Bream singled to right. Hunter pinch ran for Bream. Blauser struck out into a double play as Hunter was caught stealing, catcher to shortstop. Berryhill struck out.

Toronto—Hunter now at first. Alomar singled to center. Wohlers now pitching. Alomar stole second. Carter was walked intentionally. Winfield advanced Alomar to third and Carter to second with a sacrifice hit, first baseman to second baseman. Stanton now pitching. Sprague, pinch-hitting for Olerud, was walked intentionally. Reardon now pitching. Maldonado singled to right-center, scoring Alomar as Carter went to third and Sprague to second.

— 199 —

HIGHLIGHTS

TORONTO 2, ATLANTA 1

Why the Blue Jays won: Lefthanded starter Jimmy Key escaped unscathed from first-inning trouble and went on to pitch masterfully, allowing only five hits and walking no one in his 7⅔-inning stint. In the first, he yielded a single to Braves leadoff man/catalyst Otis Nixon, but then picked Nixon off first base. Jeff Blauser then singled and stole second, but Terry Pendleton lined out and Lonnie Smith grounded out. Beginning with Pendleton's out, Key retired 16 consecutive Atlanta hitters.

Why the Braves lost: Tom Glavine pitched just well enough to lose. Having given up only six home runs in 225 regular-season innings, he was cuffed for his fifth home run of '92 postseason play—Pat Borders' leadoff shot in the third inning. Then, in the seventh, he committed the often-deadly sin of walking the leadoff batter. Down by a 1-0 score entering the inning, Glavine issued a base on balls to Kelly Gruber, who moved to second on a groundout and scampered home on Devon White's single. The "insurance" run proved to be just that, as the Braves scrambled for an eighth-inning run before being held in check by Toronto's relief corps.

The turning points:

1. With Braves runners on first and third base with none out in the eighth inning and Toronto nursing a 2-0 lead, Atlanta catcher Damon Berryhill, not exactly a gazelle, inexplicably tried to bunt—and popped out in the process. A potentially big inning was short-circuited.

2. With Braves runners now on second and third with two out in the eighth and Toronto's lead reduced to 2-1 (Atlanta scored earlier in the inning on Mark Lemke's groundout), Blauser rapped a hard grounder down the first-base line. First baseman John Olerud made a sliding, backhanded stop of the ball and beat Blauser to the bag, ending the inning.

Notable: Borders' smash extended Toronto's homer streak to 10 games (all six League Championship Series games and all four World Series games). . . . The start was Key's first since the final day of the regular season—a span of 17 days.

Quotable: "I have no idea what was going through Damon's mind," said Atlanta Manager Bobby Cox, alluding to Berryhill's decision to lay one down in the eighth inning. . . . Berryhill's view: "If I get a halfway decent one (bunt) down, we have a run in and a runner at second." . . . Cox, Toronto's manager from 1982 through 1985, embraced Key briefly outside the postgame interview room. "He gave me confidence when I needed it most," Key said of Cox. "Whatever I've accomplished in the major leagues, it's because of him. He put me in the bullpen my first year (1984) and stayed with me when I became a starter in 1985. I had a lot of rocky moments early on, but Bobby never lost faith.''

BOX SCORE
WEDNESDAY, OCTOBER 21, AT TORONTO

Atlanta	AB	R	H	RBI	PO	A
Nixon, cf	4	0	2	0	2	0
Blauser, ss	4	0	1	0	2	6
Pendleton, 3b	4	0	0	0	0	4
L. Smith, dh	4	0	0	0	0	0
Justice, rf	4	0	0	0	2	0
Gant, lf	3	1	0	0	1	1
Hunter, 1b	3	0	1	0	11	0
Berryhill, c	3	0	0	0	2	0
Lemke, 2b	3	0	0	1	4	4
Glavine, p	0	0	0	0	0	1
Totals	32	1	5	1	24	16

Toronto	AB	R	H	RBI	PO	A
White, cf	4	0	3	1	4	0
Alomar, 2b	3	0	0	0	1	0
Carter, rf	3	0	0	0	2	0
Winfield, dh	3	0	0	0	0	0
Olerud, 1b	3	0	2	0	8	1
Maldonado, lf	3	0	0	0	2	0
Gruber, 3b	2	1	0	0	0	3
Borders, c	3	1	1	1	7	1
Lee, ss	3	0	0	0	2	1
Key, p	0	0	0	0	1	3
Ward, p	0	0	0	0	0	0
Henke, p	0	0	0	0	0	1
Totals	27	2	6	2	27	10

Atlanta	0 0 0	0 0 0	0 1 0—1			
Toronto	0 0 1	0 0 0	1 0 x—2			

Atlanta	IP	H	R	ER	BB	SO
Glavine (L)	8	6	2	2	4	2

Toronto	IP	H	R	ER	BB	SO
Key (W)	7⅔	5	1	1	0	6
Ward	⅓	0	0	0	0	0
Henke (S)	1	0	0	0	0	1

Bases on balls—Off Glavine 4 (Alomar, Winfield, Carter, Gruber).
Strikeouts—By Glavine 2 (Olerud, Maldonado), by Key 6 (Hunter, Berryhill, Lemke, Blauser, Justice, L. Smith), by Ward 1 (Nixon), by Henke 1 (Pendleton).
DP—Atlanta 2. LOB—Atlanta 4, Toronto 5. 2B—White, Gant. HR—Borders. SB—Blauser, Alomar, Nixon. WP—Ward. U—Morrison (A.L.), plate; Davidson (N.L.), first; Shulock (A.L.), second; Crawford (N.L.), third; Reilly (A.L.), left field; West (N.L.), right field. T—2:21. A—52,090.

PLAY BY PLAY
FIRST INNING
Atlanta—Nixon singled to right. Nixon was picked off first, pitcher to first baseman. Blauser singled to center. Blauser stole second. Pendleton lined to short. L. Smith grounded to short.

Toronto—White singled to center. Alomar forced White at second, shortstop to second baseman. Carter grounded to third, Alomar went to second. Alomar stole third. Winfield grounded to second.

SECOND INNING
Atlanta—Justice grounded to the first baseman, who tossed to the pitcher for the out. Gant flied to right. Hunter struck out.

Toronto—Olerud struck out. Maldonado grounded to short. Gruber grounded to first.

THIRD INNING
Atlanta—Berryhill struck out and was retired, catcher to first baseman, on the dropped third strike. Lemke struck out. Nixon grounded to third.

Toronto—Borders homered to left. Lee grounded to second. White doubled to right. Alomar walked. Carter lined into a double play, shortstop to second baseman.

FOURTH INNING
Atlanta—Blauser struck out. Pendleton flied to right. L. Smith popped to short.

Toronto—Winfield walked. Olerud singled to right, Winfield went to second. Maldonado flied to left. Gruber grounded into a double play, shortstop to second baseman to first baseman.

FIFTH INNING
Atlanta—Justice struck out. Gant and Hunter flied to center.

Toronto—Borders grounded to short. Lee grounded to third. White flied to right.

SIXTH INNING
Atlanta—Berryhill grounded to the pitcher. Lemke flied to center. Nixon singled to center. Blauser forced Nixon at second, third baseman to second baseman.

Toronto—Alomar flied to center. Carter walked. Winfield forced Carter at second, third baseman to second baseman. Olerud singled to center, Winfield went to third. Maldonado struck out.

SEVENTH INNING
Atlanta—Pendleton flied to left. L. Smith struck out. Justice flied to center.

Toronto—Gruber walked. Borders flied to center. Lee grounded to the pitcher, Gruber went to second. White singled to left, scoring Gruber, but White was out trying for second, left fielder to third baseman to second baseman to first baseman.

EIGHTH INNING
Atlanta—Gant doubled to left. Hunter singled to third, Gant went to third. Berryhill fouled to the catcher. Lemke grounded the ball off the pitcher, but was thrown out by the third baseman, as Gant scored and Hunter went to second. Ward now pitching. Nixon struck out but reached first on a wild pitch third strike, as Hunter went to third. Nixon stole second. Blauser grounded to first.

Toronto—Alomar flied to right. Carter lined to short. Winfield grounded to short.

NINTH INNING
Atlanta—Henke now pitching. Pendleton struck out. L. Smith grounded to the pitcher. Justice flied to left.

GAME 5
HIGHLIGHTS
ATLANTA 7, TORONTO 2

Why the Braves won: Veteran Lonnie Smith, still haunted by his pivotal baserunning gaffe in Game 7 of the 1991 World Series, pretty much resolved the outcome of Game 5 of the '92 Series when he unloaded a grand slam off Jack Morris in the fifth inning.

Why the Blue Jays lost: Morris' reputation as a big-game pitcher was getting sullied. Boasting a 7-1 record in postseason play entering 1992, Morris endured all kinds of trouble against Oakland in the A.L. playoffs and Atlanta in the World Series. In 23 innings of '92 postseason pitching, he was now 0-3 with a 7.43 ERA.

The turning points:

1. When Atlanta's make-things-happen guy, Otis Nixon, singled with two out in the fifth inning of a 2-2 game. It seemed to be a harmless single— no one was on base at the time—but the blow triggered a big inning. Nixon stole second and then scored what proved to be the game-winning run on Deion Sanders' single up the middle. Terry Pendleton followed with a double, sending Sanders to third, and Dave Justice was given an intentional base on balls. Smith proceeded to foil the strategy.

2. The moment Smith's drive off Morris disappeared over the right-field wall.

Notable: Smith's grand slam was the first by a National Leaguer in World Series competition since St. Louis' Ken Boyer hit one in Game 4 of the 1964 fall classic. ... Game 5 marked the first time in 1992 postseason play that the Blue Jays failed to connect for a home run. ... Toronto's offense was a two-man show, with Pat Borders and John Olerud accounting for what little damage was done against Braves starter John Smoltz (who notched his first-ever Series triumph). Borders drove home Olerud with a second-inning double and then knocked in the Blue Jays' first baseman with a fourth-inning single.

Quotable: "I don't think I will ever get any retribution from that game (the '91 Series finale)," said Smith, whose grand slam was a salve but not a cure-all to the pain he had experienced 12 months earlier. "People all year brought it up (the baserunning mistake), and some people considered it one of the major blunders in World Series history. No, I didn't get retribution tonight." ... "I don't know how to describe it," Morris said of his pitching woes against the Braves. "I've pitched against the same team two years in a row, and they've seen me five times. I keep trying, but sometimes the advantage switches to their side." ... Smoltz said he "tried to give as much as I could, but I was obviously out of gas (after six innings)." No problem. Reliever Mike Stanton, summoned one batter into the seventh, hurled three innings of scoreless ball and permitted just one hit.

BOX SCORE

THURSDAY, OCTOBER 22, AT TORONTO

Atlanta	AB	R	H	RBI	PO	A
Nixon, cf	5	2	3	0	4	0
Sanders, lf	5	1	2	1	4	0
Pendleton, 3b	5	1	2	1	2	4
Justice, rf	3	2	1	1	3	0
L. Smith, dh	4	1	1	4	0	0
Bream, 1b	4	0	0	0	6	0
Blauser, ss	4	0	1	0	1	3
Belliard, ss	0	0	0	0	0	0
Berryhill, c	4	0	1	0	5	0
Lemke, 2b	4	0	2	0	2	1
Smoltz, p	0	0	0	0	0	0
Stanton, p	0	0	0	0	0	0
Totals	38	7	13	7	27	8

Toronto	AB	R	H	RBI	PO	A
White, cf	4	0	0	0	4	0
Alomar, 2b	3	0	0	0	0	4
Carter, rf	4	0	1	0	2	0
Winfield, dh	4	0	1	0	0	0
Olerud, 1b	3	2	2	0	7	0
aSprague, 1b	1	0	0	0	0	0
Maldonado, lf	2	0	0	0	3	1
Gruber, 3b	4	0	0	0	1	0
Borders, c	4	0	2	2	9	1
Lee, ss	3	0	0	0	1	1
Morris, p	0	0	0	0	0	0
Wells, p	0	0	0	0	0	0
Timlin, p	0	0	0	0	0	0
Eichhorn, p	0	0	0	0	0	0
Stottlemyre, p	0	0	0	0	0	0
Totals	32	2	6	2	27	7

```
Atlanta ........... 1 0 0   1 5 0   0 0 0—7
Toronto ........... 0 1 0   1 0 0   0 0 0—2
```

Atlanta	IP	H	R	ER	BB	SO
Smoltz (W)	*6	5	2	2	4	4
Stanton (S)	3	1	0	0	0	1

Toronto	IP	H	R	ER	BB	SO
Morris (L)	4⅔	9	7	7	1	5
Wells	1⅓	1	0	0	0	0
Timlin	1	0	0	0	0	0
Eichhorn	1	0	0	0	0	1
Stottlemyre	1	3	0	0	0	1

*Pitched to one batter in seventh.

Bases on balls—Off Smoltz 4 (Maldonado 2, Alomar, Lee), off Morris 1 (Justice).
Strikeouts—By Smoltz 4 (White 2, Carter, Gruber), by Stanton 1 (Winfield), by Morris 5 (Sanders, Justice, Blauser, Pendleton, Berryhill), by Eichhorn 1 (L. Smith), by Stottlemyre 1 (Berryhill).

aFlied out for Olerud in eighth. DP—Atlanta 1, Toronto 1. LOB—Atlanta 5, Toronto 7. 2B—Nixon, Pendleton 2, Borders. HR—Justice, L. Smith. SB—Nixon 2. CS—Blauser. U—Davidson (N.L.), plate; Shulock (A.L.), first; Crawford (N.L.), second; Reilly (A.L.), third; West (N.L.), left field; Morrison (A.L.), right field. T—3:05. A—52,268.

PLAY BY PLAY

FIRST INNING

Atlanta—Nixon doubled to left. Sanders struck out. Nixon stole third. Pendleton doubled to right, scoring Nixon. Justice struck out. L. Smith flied to right.

Toronto—White struck out. Alomar grounded to short. Carter struck out.

SECOND INNING

Atlanta—Bream flied to center. Blauser struck out. Berryhill fouled to third.

Toronto—Winfield lined to center. Olerud singled to center. Maldonado walked, Olerud went to second. Gruber struck out. Borders doubled to left, scoring Olerud as Maldonado went to third. Lee lined to third.

THIRD INNING

Atlanta—Lemke singled to center. Nixon grounded to short, Lemke went to second. Sanders grounded to second, Lemke went to third. Pendleton struck out.

Toronto—White flied to center. Alomar walked. Carter flied to right. Winfield forced Alomar at second, third baseman to second baseman.

FOURTH INNING

Atlanta—Justice homered to right. L. Smith flied to right. Bream flied to left. Blauser singled to left. Blauser caught stealing, catcher to shortstop.

Toronto—Olerud singled to right. Maldonado walked, Olerud went to second. Gruber flied to left. Borders singled to center, scoring Olerud as Maldonado went to second. Lee forced Maldonado at third, third baseman unassisted. White struck out.

FIFTH INNING

Atlanta—Berryhill struck out. Lemke grounded to second. Nixon singled to center. Nixon stole second. Sanders singled to center, scoring Nixon. Pendleton doubled to right, Sanders went to third. Justice was walked intentionally. L. Smith homered to right, scoring Sanders, Pendleton and Justice. Wells now pitching. Bream flied to left.

Toronto—Alomar and Carter flied to left. Winfield singled to center. Olerud flied to left.

SIXTH INNING

Atlanta—Blauser fouled to first. Berryhill singled to center. Lemke flied to center. Nixon lined to first.

Toronto—Maldonado flied to right. Gruber flied to center. Borders grounded to short.

SEVENTH INNING

Atlanta—Timlin now pitching. Sanders flied to center. Pendleton grounded out to the catcher, unassisted. Justice grounded to second.

Toronto—Lee walked. Stanton now pitching. White forced Lee at second, third baseman to second baseman. Alomar grounded into a double play, second baseman to shortstop to first baseman.

EIGHTH INNING

Atlanta—Eichhorn now pitching. L. Smith struck out. Bream flied to center. Blauser grounded to second.

Toronto—Belliard now at short. Carter singled to center. Carter reached second on defensive indifference. Winfield struck out. Sprague, pinch-hitting for Olerud, flied to right as Carter went to third. Maldonado grounded to third.

NINTH INNING

Atlanta—Sprague now at first and Stottlemyre pitching. Berryhill struck out. Lemke singled to right. Nixon singled to center, Lemke went to second. Sanders singled to center, Lemke went to third and Nixon to second. Pendleton flied into a double play, left fielder to catcher, who retired Lemke at the plate after the catch.

Toronto—Gruber flied to center. Borders grounded to third. Lee fouled to first.

GAME 6

HIGHLIGHTS

TORONTO 4, ATLANTA 3

Why the Blue Jays won: Veteran Dave Winfield picked an opportune time to collect his first World Series extra-base hit—with two on and two out in the 11th inning of a 2-2 game. The 41-year-old Winfield, who had managed only five singles in 43 career Series at-bats, rifled a grounder down the third-base line off Braves reliever Charlie Leibrandt. The double scored Devon White, who was aboard after being hit by a pitch, and Roberto Alomar, who had singled.

Why the Braves lost: Their lack of a true stopper out of the bullpen was exploited. With two men on base and one out in the Blue Jays' 11th, Braves Manager Bobby Cox elected to stay with lefthander Leibrandt (his fifth pitcher of the night) despite the fact that righthanded-hitting sluggers Joe Carter and Winfield were due up and righthander Jeff Reardon was throwing in the Atlanta bullpen. Reardon, though, had given up a game-winning homer in Game 2 and also had been tagged for the decisive hit in Game 3 and seemingly wasn't to be entrusted with the task of keeping the game dead-

locked. So, Leibrandt, who had pitched in relief only once in the regular season, remained in the game. He induced Carter to fly out but was victimized by Winfield's double, which thrust Toronto into a 4-2 lead.

The turning points:

1. With two Braves runners on base and one out and Toronto guarding a 2-1 lead in the bottom of the ninth, Blue Jays left fielder Candy Maldonado misjudged Francisco Cabrera's smash—but recovered in time to make a leaping stab of the drive. If the ball had sailed over Maldonado's head, the tying and winning runs would have scored. As it turned out, a two-strike single by Otis Nixon enabled the Braves to tie the score and force extra innings.

2. Nixon's bunt-attempt failure in the 11th. With the Braves having just moved within a run of the Blue Jays at 4-3 on Brian Hunter's RBI groundout, Nixon came to the plate with the potential tying run on third and two out. But reliever Mike Timlin reacted quickly on Nixon's bunt and threw out the Braves' speedster to end the game—and the Series.

Notable: Catcher Pat Borders had two hits for Toronto, extending his postseason hitting streak to 14 games over two years. ... When Atlanta scored off Tom Henke in the ninth inning, it ended a Series string of 15 1/3 scoreless innings by the Blue Jays' bullpen.

Quotable: "It was one measly hit, but it was the biggest hit of my career," Winfield said of his World Series-winning double. "I tell you, I said a couple of extra prayers when I went up there. Normally, you rely on your own skills. But I had to look upstairs for some extra help." ... Cox said that Reardon "would have come in the next inning (the 12th, if the game had remained tied). Charlie (Leibrandt) was throwing the ball well. He's effective against righthanders. He gave up a ground ball (Winfield's double down the line). You can't fault that."

BOX SCORE

SATURDAY, OCTOBER 24, AT ATLANTA

Toronto	AB	R	H	RBI	PO	A
White, cf	5	2	2	0	4	0
Alomar, 2b	6	1	3	0	3	2
Carter, 1b	5	0	2	1	10	1
Winfield, rf	5	0	1	2	2	0
Maldonado, lf	6	1	2	1	3	0
Gruber, 3b	4	0	1	0	0	0
Borders, c	4	0	2	0	7	2
Lee, ss	4	0	1	0	3	2
fTabler	1	0	0	0	0	0
Griffin, ss	0	0	0	0	0	1
Cone, p	2	0	0	0	0	0
Stottlemyre, p	0	0	0	0	0	0
Wells, p	0	0	0	0	0	0
cBell	1	0	0	0	0	0
Ward, p	0	0	0	0	0	0
Henke, p	0	0	0	0	0	1
Key, p	1	0	0	0	1	1
Timlin, p	0	0	0	0	0	1
Totals	44	4	14	4	33	11

Atlanta	AB	R	H	RBI	PO	A
Nixon, cf	6	0	2	1	4	0
Sanders, lf	3	1	2	0	1	1
bGant, lf	2	0	0	0	1	0
Pendleton, 3b	4	0	1	1	0	2
Justice, rf	4	0	0	0	3	0
Bream, 1b	3	0	0	0	12	1
Blauser, ss	5	2	3	0	2	8
Berryhill, c	4	0	0	0	2	1
gSmoltz	0	0	0	0	0	0
Lemke, 2b	2	0	0	0	6	3
dL. Smith	0	0	0	0	0	0
Belliard, 2b	0	0	0	0	1	0
Avery, p	1	0	0	0	0	0
P. Smith, p	1	0	0	0	0	0
aTreadway	1	0	0	0	0	0
Stanton, p	0	0	0	0	0	0
Wohlers, p	0	0	0	0	0	0
eCabrera	1	0	0	0	0	0
Leibrandt, p	0	0	0	0	1	0
hHunter	1	0	0	1	0	0
Totals	38	3	8	3	33	16

Toronto	1 0 0	1 0 0	0 0 0	0 2—4
Atlanta	0 0 1	0 0 0	0 0 1	0 1—3

Toronto	IP	H	R	ER	BB	SO
Cone	6	4	1	1	3	6
Stottlemyre	2/3	1	0	0	0	1
Wells	1/3	0	0	0	1	1
Ward	1	0	0	0	1	1
Henke	1 1/3	2	1	1	1	0
Key (W)	1 1/3	1	1	1	0	0
Timlin (S)	1/3	0	0	0	0	0

Atlanta	IP	H	R	ER	BB	SO
Avery	4	6	2	2	2	2
P. Smith	3	3	0	0	0	0
Stanton	1 2/3	2	0	0	1	0
Wohlers	1/3	0	0	0	0	0
Leibrandt (L)	2	3	2	2	0	0

Bases on balls—Off Cone 3 (Bream 2, Lemke), off Ward 1 (Justice), off Henke 1 (L. Smith), off Avery 2 (Winfield, Cone), off Stanton 1 (Borders).

Strikeouts—By Cone 6 (Avery, Justice, Berryhill, P. Smith, Pendleton, Blauser), by Stottlemyre 1 (Lemke), by Ward 1 (Pendleton).

aGrounded out for P. Smith in seventh. bAt plate for Sanders when runner caught stealing for third out of seventh. cHit into force play for Wells in eighth. dWalked for Lemke in ninth. eLined out for Wohlers in ninth. fPopped out for Lee in 10th. gRan for Berryhill in 11th. hGrounded out for Leibrandt in 11th. E—Justice, Griffin. DP—Atlanta 1. LOB—Toronto 13, Atlanta 10. 2B—Carter 2, Sanders, Winfield. HR—Maldonado. SB—Sanders 2, White, Alomar. CS—Nixon. SH—Gruber, Berryhill, Belliard. SF—Carter, Pendleton. HBP—By Leibrandt (White). U—Shulock (A.L.), plate; Crawford (N.L.), first; Reilly (A.L.), second; West (N.L.); third; Morrison (A.L.), left field; Davidson (N.L.), right field. T—4:07. A—51,763.

PLAY BY PLAY

FIRST INNING

Toronto—White singled to left. White stole second. Alomar grounded to second, White went to third. Carter hit a sacrifice fly to right and went to second when the right fielder dropped the ball for an error, White scored on the play. Winfield walked. Maldonado forced Winfield, shortstop to second baseman, as Carter went to third. Gruber forced Maldonado at second, shortstop to second baseman.

Atlanta—Nixon grounded to short. Sanders grounded to first. Pendleton singled to right-center. Justice popped to short.

SECOND INNING

Toronto—Borders singled to left-center. Lee flied to right.

Cone grounded into a double play, second baseman to shortstop to first baseman.

Atlanta—Bream walked. Blauser singled to left, Bream went to second. Berryhill flied to center, Bream went to third. Lemke flied to center. Avery struck out.

THIRD INNING

Toronto—White struck out and was retired, catcher to first baseman, on the dropped third strike. Alomar singled to right-center. Alomar stole second. Carter grounded to first, Alomar went to third. Winfield flied to right.

Atlanta—Nixon grounded to short. Sanders doubled to right. Sanders stole third. Pendleton hit a sacrifice fly to center, scoring Sanders. Justice struck out.

FOURTH INNING

Toronto—Maldonado homered to left-center. Gruber grounded to short. Borders doubled to left. Lee struck out. Cone walked. White singled to left but Borders was out trying to score, left fielder to catcher.

Atlanta—Bream flied to left. Blauser grounded to second. Berryhill struck out.

FIFTH INNING

Toronto—P. Smith now pitching. Alomar grounded to second. Carter doubled to left. Winfield lined to center. Maldonado grounded to short.

Atlanta—Lemke walked. P. Smith struck out. Nixon popped to short. Sanders singled to center, Lemke went to third. Sanders stole second. Pendleton struck out.

SIXTH INNING

Toronto—Gruber flied to left. Borders fouled to first. Lee singled to right. Cone forced Lee at second, shortstop to second baseman.

Atlanta—Justice lined to right. Bream walked. Blauser struck out. Berryhill popped to short.

SEVENTH INNING

Toronto—White flied to right. Alomar singled to short. Carter forced Alomar at second, third baseman to second baseman. Winfield flied to center.

Atlanta—Stottlemyre now pitching. Lemke struck out and was retired, catcher to first baseman, on the dropped third strike. Treadway, pinch-hitting for P. Smith, grounded to second. Nixon singled to left. Wells now pitching. With Gant at the plate, pinch-hitting for Sanders, Nixon was caught stealing, catcher to second baseman.

EIGHTH INNING

Toronto—Gant now in left field and Stanton pitching. Maldonado singled to left. Gruber sacrificed Maldonado to second, third baseman to second baseman. Borders was walked intentionally. Lee fouled to first. Bell, pinch-hitting for Wells, forced Borders at second, first baseman to shortstop.

Atlanta—Ward now pitching. Gant lined to right. Pendleton struck out. Justice walked. Bream flied to left.

NINTH INNING

Toronto—White lined to second. Alomar flied to center. Carter doubled to left. Wohlers now pitching. Winfield grounded to short.

Atlanta—Henke now pitching. Blauser singled to left. Berryhill sacrificed Blauser to second, pitcher to second baseman. L. Smith, pinch-hitting for Lemke, walked. Cabrera, pinch-hitting for Wohlers, lined to left. Nixon singled, scoring Blauser as L. Smith went to third and Nixon to second on the throw home. Gant flied to center.

10TH INNING

Toronto—Belliard now at second and Leibrandt pitching. Maldonado grounded to short. Gruber singled to center. Borders flied to left. Tabler, pinch-hitting for Lee, popped to the pitcher.

Atlanta—Griffin now at short. Pendleton grounded to first. Key now pitching. Justice grounded to short. Bream grounded to the first baseman, who tossed to the pitcher for the out.

11TH INNING

Toronto—Key fouled to first. White was hit by a pitch. Alomar singled to center, White went to second. Carter flied to center. Winfield doubled to left, scoring White and Alomar. Maldonado popped to second.

Atlanta—Blauser singled to left. Berryhill was safe at first and Blauser went to third on an error by the shortstop. Smoltz pinch-ran for Berryhill. Belliard sacrificed Smoltz to second, pitcher to second baseman. Hunter, pinch-hitting for Leibrandt, grounded to first, scoring Blauser as Smoltz went to third. Timlin now pitching. Nixon grounded to the pitcher.

STATISTICS

TORONTO BLUE JAYS' BATTING AND FIELDING AVERAGES

Player, position	G	AB	R	H	TB	2B	3B	HR	RBI	BB	IBB	SO	Avg.	PO	A	E	Avg.
Cone, p	2	4	0	2	2	0	0	0	1	1	0	0	.500	0	0	0	.000
Sprague, ph-1b	3	2	1	1	4	0	0	1	2	1	1	0	.500	0	0	0	.000
Borders, c	6	20	2	9	15	3	0	1	3	2	1	1	.450	48	5	1	.981
Olerud, 1b	4	13	2	4	4	0	0	0	0	0	0	4	.308	25	3	0	1.000
Carter, 1b-lf-rf	6	22	2	6	14	2	0	2	3	3	1	2	.273	27	1	0	1.000
White, cf	6	26	2	6	7	1	0	0	2	0	0	6	.231	22	0	0	1.000
Winfield, rf-dh	6	22	0	5	6	1	0	0	3	2	0	3	.227	7	0	0	1.000
Alomar, 2b	6	24	3	5	6	1	0	0	3	0	3	3	.208	5	12	0	1.000
Maldonado, lf-ph	6	19	1	3	6	0	0	1	2	2	0	5	.158	8	2	0	1.000
Gruber, 3b	6	19	2	2	5	0	0	1	1	2	0	5	.105	5	5	1	.909
Lee, ss	6	19	1	2	2	0	0	0	0	1	0	2	.105	14	10	1	.960
Eichhorn, p	1	0	0	0	0	0	0	0	0	0	0	0	.000	0	0	0	.000
Griffin, ss	2	0	0	0	0	0	0	0	0	0	0	0	.000	0	1	1	.500
Guzman, p	1	0	0	0	0	0	0	0	0	0	0	0	.000	2	0	0	1.000
Wells, p	4	0	0	0	0	0	0	0	0	0	0	0	.000	0	0	0	.000
Henke, p	3	0	0	0	0	0	0	0	0	0	0	0	.000	0	2	0	1.000
Timlin, p	2	0	0	0	0	0	0	0	0	0	0	0	.000	0	1	0	1.000
Stottlemyre, p	4	0	0	0	0	0	0	0	0	0	0	0	.000	0	0	0	.000
Ward, p	4	0	0	0	0	0	0	0	0	0	0	0	.000	0	0	0	.000
Bell, ph	2	1	1	0	0	0	0	0	0	1	0	0	.000	0	0	0	.000
Key, p	2	1	0	0	0	0	0	0	0	0	0	0	.000	2	4	0	1.000
Tabler, ph	2	2	0	0	0	0	0	0	0	0	0	0	.000	0	0	0	.000
Morris, p	2	2	0	0	0	0	0	0	0	0	0	2	.000	0	1	0	1.000
Totals	6	196	17	45	71	8	0	6	17	18	3	33	.230	165	47	4	.981

Bell—Walked for Lee in ninth inning of second game; grounded into force out for Wells in eighth inning of sixth game.

Maldonado—Struck out for Wells in seventh inning of second game.

Sprague—Homered for Ward in ninth inning of second game; walked intentionally for Olerud in ninth inning of third game; flied out for Olerud in eighth inning of fifth game.

Tabler—Flied out for Stottlemyre in eighth inning of first game; popped out for Lee in 10th inning of sixth game.

ATLANTA BRAVES' BATTING AND FIELDING AVERAGES

Player, position	G	AB	R	H	TB	2B	3B	HR	RBI	BB	IBB	SO	Avg.	PO	A	E	Avg.
Sanders, lf	4	15	4	8	10	2	0	0	1	2	0	1	.533	5	1	0	1.000
Nixon, cf	6	27	3	8	9	1	0	0	1	1	0	3	.296	18	0	0	1.000
Blauser, ss	6	24	2	6	6	0	0	0	0	1	0	9	.250	7	22	0	1.000
Pendleton, 3b	6	25	2	6	8	2	0	0	2	1	0	5	.240	4	19	0	1.000
Lemke, 2b	6	19	0	4	4	0	0	0	2	1	0	3	.211	18	12	0	1.000
Bream, 1b	6	15	1	3	3	0	0	0	0	4	0	0	.200	42	1	1	.977
Hunter, ph-1b	4	5	0	1	1	0	0	0	2	0	0	1	.200	14	1	0	1.000
L. Smith, ph-dh	5	12	1	2	5	0	0	1	5	1	0	4	.167	0	0	0	.000
Justice, rf	6	19	4	3	6	0	0	1	3	6	2	5	.158	15	0	1	.938
Gant, lf-pr-ph	4	8	2	1	2	1	0	0	0	1	0	2	.125	3	1	0	1.000
Berryhill, c	6	22	1	2	5	0	0	1	3	1	0	11	.091	32	3	0	1.000
Reardon, p	2	0	0	0	0	0	0	0	0	0	0	0	.000	0	0	0	.000
Belliard, ss-2b	4	0	0	0	0	0	0	0	0	0	0	0	.000	3	2	0	1.000
Wohlers, p	2	0	0	0	0	0	0	0	0	0	0	0	.000	0	0	0	.000
Stanton, p	4	0	0	0	0	0	0	0	0	0	0	0	.000	0	0	0	.000
Leibrandt, p	1	0	0	0	0	0	0	0	0	0	0	0	.000	1	0	0	1.000
Avery, p	2	1	0	0	0	0	0	0	0	0	0	1	.000	0	0	0	.000
P. Smith, p	1	1	0	0	0	0	0	0	0	0	0	1	.000	0	0	0	.000
Treadway, ph	1	1	0	0	0	0	0	0	0	0	0	0	.000	0	0	0	.000
Cabrera, ph	1	1	0	0	0	0	0	0	0	0	0	0	.000	0	0	0	.000
Glavine, p	2	2	0	0	0	0	0	0	0	1	0	0	.000	0	2	0	1.000
Smoltz, p-pr	3	3	0	0	0	0	0	0	0	0	0	2	.000	1	2	0	1.000
Totals	6	200	20	44	59	6	0	3	19	20	2	48	.220	163	68	2	.991

Cabrera—Lined out for Wohlers in ninth inning of sixth game.

Gant—Ran for L. Smith in ninth inning of second game; was at plate when runner caught stealing for third out in seventh inning of sixth game.

Hunter—Hit sacrifice fly for Bream in fifth inning of second game; ran for Bream in ninth inning of third game; grounded out for Leibrandt in 11th inning of sixth game.

L. Smith—Hit by pitch for Reardon in ninth inning of second game; walked for Lemke in ninth inning of sixth game.
Smoltz—Ran for Berryhill in 11th inning of sixth game.
Treadway—Grounded out for P. Smith in seventh inning of sixth game.

TORONTO BLUE JAYS' PITCHING RECORDS

Pitcher	G	GS	CG	IP	H	R	ER	HR	BB	IBB	SO	HB	WP	W	L	Pct.	ERA
Wells	4	0	0	4⅓	1	0	0	0	2	0	3	0	0	0	0	.000	0.00
Stottlemyre	4	0	0	3⅔	4	0	0	0	0	0	4	0	0	0	0	.000	0.00
Ward	4	0	0	3⅓	1	0	0	0	1	0	6	0	1	2	0	1.000	0.00
Timlin	2	0	0	1⅓	0	0	0	0	0	0	0	0	0	0	0	.000	0.00
Eichhorn	1	0	0	1	0	0	0	0	0	0	1	0	0	0	0	.000	0.00
Key	2	1	0	9	6	2	1	0	0	0	6	0	0	2	0	1.000	1.00
Guzman	1	1	0	8	8	2	1	0	1	1	7	0	0	0	0	.000	1.13
Henke	3	0	0	3⅓	2	1	1	0	2	0	1	1	0	0	0	.000	2.70
Cone	2	2	0	10⅓	9	5	4	0	8	0	8	0	1	0	0	.000	3.48
Morris	2	2	0	10⅔	13	10	10	3	6	1	12	0	1	0	2	.000	8.44
Totals	6	6	0	55	44	20	17	3	20	2	48	1	3	4	2	.667	2.78

No shutouts. Saves—Henke 2, Timlin.

ATLANTA BRAVES' PITCHING RECORDS

Pitcher	G	GS	CG	IP	H	R	ER	HR	BB	IBB	SO	HB	WP	W	L	Pct.	ERA
Stanton	4	0	0	5	3	0	0	0	2	2	1	0	0	0	0	.000	0.00
P. Smith	1	0	0	3	3	0	0	0	0	0	0	0	0	0	0	.000	0.00
Wohlers	2	0	0	⅔	0	0	0	0	1	1	0	0	0	0	0	.000	0.00
Glavine	2	2	2	17	10	3	3	2	4	0	8	0	0	1	1	.500	1.59
Smoltz	2	2	0	13⅓	13	5	4	0	7	0	12	0	2	1	0	1.000	2.70
Avery	2	2	0	12	11	5	5	3	3	0	11	0	0	0	1	.000	3.75
Leibrandt	1	0	0	2	3	2	2	0	0	0	0	0	0	0	1	.000	9.00
Reardon	2	0	0	1⅓	2	2	2	1	1	0	1	1	0	0	1	.000	13.50
Totals	6	6	2	54⅓	45	17	16	6	18	3	33	1	2	2	4	.333	2.65

No shutouts. Save—Stanton.

COMPOSITE SCORE BY INNINGS

Toronto	1	1	1	4	2	0	1	2	3	0	2—17
Atlanta	1	1	1	2	7	4	0	2	1	0	1—20

MISCELLANEOUS STATISTICS

Sacrifice hits—Winfield, Gruber, Berryhill, Belliard.
Sacrifice flies—Hunter, Carter, Pendleton.
Stolen bases—Nixon 5, Sanders 5, Alomar 3, Blauser 2, Gant 2, Justice, Gruber, White.
Caught stealing—Hunter, Blauser, Nixon.
Double plays—Lee and Olerud 2; Lemke, Blauser and Bream 2; Belliard and Bream; Blauser and Hunter; Pendleton, Lemke and Bream; White and Lee; Borders and Lee; Blauser and Lemke; Blauser, Lemke and Hunter; Maldonado and Borders.
Left on bases—Toronto 2, 6, 5, 5, 7, 13—38; Atlanta 7, 8, 6, 4, 5, 10—40.
Hit by pitcher—By Henke (L. Smith), by Leibrandt (White).
Passed balls—None.
Balks—None.
Time of games—First game, 2:37; second game, 3:30; third game, 2:49; fourth game, 2:21; fifth game, 3:05; sixth game, 4:07.
Attendance—First game, 51,763; second game, 51,763; third game, 51,813; fourth game, 52,090; fifth game, 52,268; sixth game, 51,763.
Umpires—Crawford (N.L.), Reilly (A.L.), West (N.L.), Morrison (A.L.), Davidson (N.L.) and Shulock (A.L.).
Official scorers—Red Foley, retired baseball writer; Neil Hohlfeld, Houston Chronicle; Paul Newberry, Atlanta official scorer; Joe Sawchuk, Toronto official scorer.

ALL-STAR GAME

HIGHLIGHTS

AMERICAN LEAGUE 13, NATIONAL LEAGUE 6

Why the American League won: The junior circuit staged a wild singles party at the National League's expense. Lacing seven consecutive first-inning singles, the American Leaguers bolted to a 4-0 lead before the N.L. placed a man in the batter's box.

Why the National League lost: Starter Tom Glavine and two of his successors, Bob Tewksbury and Doug Jones, worked a total of 4⅓ innings and were tagged for 17 hits and 12 runs. Glavine yielded nine hits before taking shelter with two out in the second inning.

The turning points:

1. When Barry Bonds, batting with the bases loaded in the third inning and his N.L. team trailing by a 6-0 score, hit an inning-ending foul popup.

2. When the American Leaguers struck for four sixth-inning runs, turning a safe lead into an insurmountable one. Ruben Sierra's two-run homer capped the uprising, which made it a 10-0 game.

Notable: Seattle center fielder Ken Griffey Jr., one of four American Leaguers with two runs batted in, went 3-for-3. He singled home a run in the first inning, homered in the third and triggered his team's sixth-inning outburst with a double. The performance netted the game's Most Valuable Player honor for the 22-year-old Griffey. . . . Besides Sierra and Griffey, other A.L. players with two RBIs were Mark McGwire, who singled in two runs in the first inning, and Roberto Kelly, who doubled home the Americans' final two runs in the eighth. . . . The All-Star triumph was the fifth straight for the suddenly dominant American League, which a decade earlier had suffered its 11th straight midsummer loss and its 19th defeat in 20 games.

Quotable: "What I've done up to this point (of the season) proves what I'm capable of doing, and that's the reason I'm here," said Atlanta's Glavine, who took a 13-3 record (which included five shutouts) and a 2.57 earned-run average into the game. . . . N.L. Manager Bobby Cox, commenting on Glavine's performance: "It wasn't like he was really ripped. A lot of balls were off the end of the bat.". . . The Braves' Cox, on Griffey's talents: "I saw Ken Griffey Jr. in high school at Moeller High in Cincinnati, and he was the best prospect I've ever seen in my life." . . . "Can you imagine having to face the pitchers we sent out there?" said Juan Guzman, the man who got into a sticky situation (bases full) in the third inning but proceeded to retire Bonds. The A.L. used one starting pitcher per inning through seven frames, then employed three relievers over the final two innings.

BOX SCORE

American League	AB	R	H	RBI	PO	A
R. Alomar, 2b (Blue Jays) .	3	1	1	0	0	1
Baerga, 2b (Indians)	1	1	1	0	1	2
Nagy, p (Indians)	1	1	1	0	0	0
Montgomery, p (Royals) ...	0	0	0	0	0	0
Aguilera, p (Twins)	1	0	0	0	0	0
Eckersley, p (A's)	0	0	0	0	0	0
Boggs, 3b (Red Sox)	3	1	1	0	1	0
Ventura, 3b (White Sox) ...	2	1	2	1	1	1
Puckett, lf (Twins)	3	1	1	0	2	0
Clemens, p (Red Sox)	0	0	0	0	0	0
Sierra, rf (Rangers)	2	2	1	2	1	0
Carter, rf (Blue Jays)	3	1	2	1	1	0
Fryman, ss (Tigers)	1	1	1	1	0	3
McGwire, 1b (A's)	3	1	1	2	4	0
cMolitor, 1b (Brewers)	2	0	1	0	5	0
Ripken, ss (Orioles)	3	0	1	1	1	1
Mussina, p (Orioles)	0	0	0	0	0	0
Kelly, cf (Yankees)	2	0	1	2	1	0
Griffey, cf (Mariners)	3	2	3	2	1	0
Rodriguez, c (Rangers)	2	0	0	0	4	0
S. Alomar, c (Indians)	3	0	1	0	3	0
Langston, p (Angels)	0	0	0	0	0	0
fKnoblauch, 2b (Twins)	1	0	0	0	0	0
Brown, p (Rangers)	1	0	0	0	0	0
McDowell, p (White Sox) ..	0	0	0	0	0	0
aE. Martinez (Mariners) ...	1	0	0	0	0	0
Guzman, p (Blue Jays)	0	0	0	0	0	0
Anderson, lf (Orioles)	3	0	0	0	1	0
Totals............................	44	13	19	13	27	8

National League	AB	R	H	RBI	PO	A
O. Smith, ss (Cardinals)	3	0	1	0	1	1
Fernandez, ss (Padres)	2	1	1	0	3	0
Gwynn, rf (Padres)	2	0	0	0	0	2
Kruk, rf (Phillies)	2	1	2	0	0	1
Bonds, lf (Pirates)	3	1	1	0	2	0
Roberts, lf (Reds)	2	1	2	2	0	0
McGriff, 1b (Padres)	3	0	2	1	7	1
D. Martinez, p (Expos)	0	0	0	0	0	0
Jones, p (Astros)	0	0	0	0	0	0
gPagnozzi (Cardinals)	1	0	0	0	0	0
Charlton, p (Reds)	1	0	0	0	0	0
Pendleton, 3b (Braves)	2	0	1	0	0	2
Tewksbury, p (Cardinals) .	0	0	0	0	0	0
Smoltz, p (Braves)	0	0	0	0	0	0
dClark, 1b (Giants)	2	1	1	3	1	0
Van Slyke, cf (Pirates)	2	0	0	0	0	0
eGant, cf (Braves)	2	0	0	0	1	0
Sandberg, 2b (Cubs)	2	0	0	0	2	3
Biggio, 2b (Astros)	2	0	0	0	0	2
Santiago, c (Padres)	1	0	0	0	3	0
Daulton, c (Phillies)	3	1	0	0	5	0
Glavine, p (Braves)	0	0	0	0	0	0
Maddux, p (Cubs)	0	0	0	0	1	0
bWalker (Expos)	1	0	1	0	0	0
Cone, p (Mets)	0	0	0	0	0	0
Sheffield, 3b (Padres)	2	0	0	0	0	0
Sharperson, 3b (Dodgers) .	1	0	0	0	1	0
Totals............................	39	6	12	6	27	12

American League 4	1	1	0	0	4	0 3 0—13
National League 0	0	0	0	0	1	0 3 2— 6

American League	IP	H	R	ER	BB	SO
Brown (Rangers)	1	0	0	0	0	1
McDowell (W. Sox).....	1	0	0	0	0	0
Guzman (Blue Jays) ...	1	2	0	0	1	2
Clemens (Red Sox)	1	2	0	0	0	0
Mussina (Orioles)	1	0	0	0	0	0

	IP	H	R	ER	BB	SO
Langston (Angels)	1	2	1	1	0	1
Nagy (Indians)	1	0	0	0	0	1
Montgomery (Royals)	⅔	2	2	2	0	0
Aguilera (Twins)	⅔	1	1	1	0	0
Eckersley (A's)	⅔	3	2	0	0	2

National League	IP	H	R	ER	BB	SO
Glavine (Braves)	1⅔	9	5	5	0	2
Maddux (Cubs)..........	1⅓	1	1	1	0	0
Cone (Mets)	1	0	0	0	0	1
Tewksbury (Cards) ...	1⅔	4	4	4	1	0
Smoltz (Braves).........	⅓	1	0	0	0	0
D. Martinez (Expos) ...	1	0	0	0	1	1
Jones (Astros)..........	1	4	3	3	0	2
Charlton (Reds)	1	0	0	0	0	1

Winning pitcher—Brown. Losing pitcher—Glavine.
aGrounded out for McDowell in third. bSingled for Maddux in third. cSingled for McGwire in sixth. dStruck out for Smoltz in sixth. eGrounded out for Van Slyke in sixth. fWalked for Langston in seventh. gFlied out for Jones in eighth. E—Kruk, Molitor. DP—A.L. 1. LOB—A.L. 6, N.L. 7. 2B—O. Smith, Griffey, Baerga, Ventura, Bonds, Kelly. HR—Griffey, Sierra, Clark. SB—R. Alomar 2. BB—Off Guzman 1 (Gwynn), off Tewksbury 1 (Fryman), off D. Martinez 1 (Knoblauch). SO—By Brown 1 (O. Smith), by Guzman 2 (Sandberg, Santiago), by Langston 1 (Clark), by Nagy 1 (Biggio), by Eckersley 2 (Sharperson, Charlton), by Glavine 2 (Brown, Puckett), by Cone 1 (Boggs), by D. Martinez 1 (Kelly), by Jones 2 (Molitor, Rodriguez), by Charlton 1 (Aguilera). U—Harvey (N.L.), plate; Garcia (A.L.), first; Wendelstedt (N.L.), second; Kosc (A.L.), third; Hallion (N.L.), left field; Tschida (A.L.), right field. Official scorers—Phil Collier (San Diego Union-Tribune), Pat Reusse (Minneapolis Star & Tribune), Bill Zavestoski (Padres official scorer). T—2:55. A—59,372.
Player listed on roster but not used: N.L.—L. Smith.

PLAY BY PLAY

FIRST INNING

A.L.—R. Alomar grounded to second. Boggs singled to center. Puckett singled to center, Boggs went to second. Carter singled to center, Boggs went to third and Puckett to second. McGwire singled to center, scoring Boggs and Puckett, and Carter went to second. Ripken singled to right, scoring Carter, and McGwire went to third. Ripken was out at second trying for a double, right fielder to shortstop. Griffey singled to center, scoring McGwire. S. Alomar singled to left, Griffey went to second. Brown struck out.

N.L.—O. Smith struck out. Gwynn and Bonds flied to left.

SECOND INNING

A.L.—R. Alomar singled to center. Boggs lined to left. R. Alomar stole second. Puckett struck out. R. Alomar stole third. Carter singled to center, scoring R. Alomar. Maddux now pitching. McGwire grounded to third.

N.L.—McDowell now pitching. McGriff flied to right. Pendleton grounded to second. Van Slyke flied to center.

THIRD INNING

A.L.—Ripken flied to left. Griffey homered to left. S. Alomar grounded to the first baseman, who tossed to the pitcher covering first. E. Martinez, pinch-hitting for McDowell, grounded to second.

N.L.—Guzman now pitching. Sandberg and Santiago struck out. Walker, pinch-hitting for Maddux, singled to third. O. Smith doubled to left, Walker went to third. Gwynn walked. Bonds fouled to third.

FOURTH INNING

A.L.—Cone now pitching. R. Alomar grounded to short. Boggs struck out. Puckett grounded to third.

N.L.—Clemens now pitching, Baerga at second, Ventura at third and Anderson in left. McGriff singled to center. Pendleton singled to left, McGriff went to second. Van Slyke grounded into a double play, second to short to first, as McGriff went to third. Sandberg grounded to second.

FIFTH INNING

A.L.—Tewksbury now pitching, Daulton catching and Sheffield at third. Carter and McGwire popped to second. Ripken called out for running into his batted ball which bounced in front of the plate.

N.L.—Mussina now pitching, Fryman at short and Sierra in right. Daulton popped to second. Sheffield lined to left. O. Smith grounded to short.

SIXTH INNING

A.L.—Fernandez now at short. Griffey doubled to right. S. Alomar grounded to second, Griffey went to third. Anderson grounded to first. Baerga doubled to left-center, scoring Griffey. Ventura doubled off the first baseman's glove, scoring Baerga. Sierra homered to right, scoring Ventura. Fryman walked. Smoltz now pitching. Molitor pinch-hitting for McGwire, singled to right but Fryman was out after overrunning second, right fielder to shortstop.

N.L.—Langston now pitching, Rodriguez catching, Molitor at first and Kelly in line. Gwynn grounded to short. Bonds hit a bad-hop double over the first baseman's shoulder. McGriff singled to left, scoring Bonds. Clark, pinch-hitting for Smoltz, struck out. Gant, pinch-hitting for Van Slyke, grounded to third.

SEVENTH INNING

A.L.—D. Martinez now pitching, Clark at first, Biggio at second, Roberts in left, Gant in center and Kruk in right. Kelly struck out. Rodriguez reached on a two-base error by the right fielder, but was out trying for third, right fielder to second baseman to third baseman. Knoblauch, pinch-hitting for Langston, walked. Anderson forced Knoblauch at second, shortstop unassisted.

N.L.—Nagy now pitching and Knoblauch at second. Biggio struck out. Daulton grounded to first. Sheffield grounded to short.

EIGHTH INNING

A.L.—Jones now pitching and Sharperson at third. Nagy singled over the pitcher's mound. Ventura singled to center, Nagy went to second. Sierra forced Ventura at second, second baseman to shortstop, as Nagy went to third. Fryman singled to right, scoring Nagy, as Sierra went to third. Molitor struck out. Kelly doubled to left, scoring Sierra and Fryman. Rodriguez struck out.

N.L.—Montgomery now pitching. Fernandez grounded to first. Kruk singled to center. Roberts singled to right, Kruk went to second. Pagnozzi, pinch-hitting for Jones, flied to right. Aguilera now pitching. Clark homered to left, scoring Kruk and Roberts. Gant fouled to third.

NINTH INNING

A.L.—Charlton now pitching. Knoblauch popped to first. Anderson flied to center. Aguilera struck out.

N.L.—Biggio lined to center. Eckersley now pitching. Daulton reached on an error by the first baseman. Sharperson struck out. Fernandez singled to right, Daulton went to second. Kruk singled to second, Daulton went to third and Fernandez went to second. Roberts singled to right-center, scoring Daulton and Fernandez, as Kruk went to second. Charlton struck out.

NOTABLE PERFORMANCES

MATT YOUNG

APRIL 12
Cleveland 2, Boston 1 (G1)

BOSTON	ab	r	h	bi	CLEVELAND	ab	r	h	bi
Boggs, 3b	5	0	2	0	Lofton, cf	1	1	0	0
Reed, 2b	5	0	1	0	Hill, dh	4	0	0	0
Greenwell, lf	4	0	0	0	Baerga, 2b	4	0	0	2
Burks, cf	3	1	2	0	Belle, lf	4	0	0	0
Plantier, rf	4	0	0	0	Whiten, rf	3	0	0	0
Clark, dh	3	0	0	0	Sorrento, 1b	3	0	0	0
Winningham, pr-dh	0	0	0	0	Jacoby, 3b	3	0	0	0
Vaughn, 1b	2	0	1	0	Ortiz, c	2	0	0	0
Rivera, ss	4	0	2	1	Lewis, ss	1	1	0	0
Flaherty, c	3	0	1	0					
Cooper, ph	0	0	0	0					
Brunansky, ph	0	0	0	0					
TOTALS	33	1	9	1	TOTALS	25	2	0	2

Boston ....0 0 0 1 0 0 0 0 0—1
Cleveland ....1 0 1 0 0 0 0 0 x—2

E—Rivera (1). DP—Cleveland 2. LOB—Boston 11, Cleveland 6. 2B—Flaherty (1). SB—Burks (1), Lofton 4 (4), Hill (2), Ortiz (1). CS—Burks (1), Whiten (1).

BOSTON	IP	H	R	ER	BB	K
Young (L 0-1)	8	0	2	2	7	6

CLEVELAND	IP	H	R	ER	BB	K
Nagy (W 1-1)	7	8	1	1	4	10
Arnsberg	1	0	0	0	1	1
Lilliquist (S 1)	1	1	0	0	1	0

T—2:37. A—20,480. Umpires—HP, Garcia. 1B, Morrison. 2B, Welke. 3B, Scott.

KEVIN GROSS

AUGUST 17
Los Angeles 2, San Francisco 0 (N)

SAN FRANCISCO	ab	r	h	bi	LOS ANGELES	ab	r	h	bi
Felder, lf	4	0	0	0	Offerman, ss	4	0	1	0
McGee, cf	4	0	0	0	Butler, cf	4	1	3	0
Clark, 1b	3	0	0	0	Rodriguez, rf	4	0	2	1
Snyder, rf	2	0	0	0	Karros, 1b	2	1	1	1
Thompson, 2b	3	0	0	0	Webster, lf	4	0	0	0
Williams, 3b	2	0	0	0	Scioscia, c	2	0	0	0
Manwaring, c	3	0	0	0	Hansen, 3b	2	0	0	0
Benjamin, ss	2	0	0	0	Young, 2b	3	0	0	0
Leonard, ph	0	0	0	0	Gross, p	3	0	1	0
Swift, pr	0	0	0	0					
Oliveras, p	1	0	0	0					
Wood, ph	1	0	0	0					
Brantley, p	0	0	0	0					
Righetti, p	0	0	0	0					
Litton, ph	1	0	0	0					
TOTALS	26	0	0	0	TOTALS	28	2	8	2

San Francisco ....0 0 0 0 0 0 0 0 0—0
Los Angeles ....0 1 0 1 0 0 0 0 2—2

DP—San Francisco 2, Los Angeles 1. LOB—San Francisco 2, Los Angeles 6. 2B—Butler (12). HR—Karros (17). CS—Butler (16).

SAN FRANCISCO	IP	H	R	ER	BB	K
Oliveras (L 0-2)	5	4	2	2	2	2
Brantley	2	2	0	0	0	1
Righetti	1	2	0	0	1	1

LOS ANGELES	IP	H	R	ER	BB	K
Gross (W 6-12)	9	0	0	0	2	6

HBP—Hansen by Brantley, Leonard by Gross. T—2:23. A—25,561. Umpires—HP, Winters. 1B, Froemming. 2B, Montague. 3B, Bell.

AMERICAN LEAGUE

ONE-HIT GAMES

Date Pitcher(s), Team, Opponent, Result—Player with hit

4-14 Ron Darling (7 innings) and Rick Honeycutt (1 inning), Oakland at Kansas City, L 3-1—Keith Miller (single in eighth)
5-4 Alex Fernandez, Chicago vs. Milwaukee, W 7-0—Dante Bichette (double in second)
7-17 Mike Mussina, Baltimore at Texas, W 8-0—Kevin Reimer (double in fifth)
7-21 Hipolito Pichardo, Kansas City vs. Boston, W 8-0—Luis Rivera (double in sixth)
7-24* Scott Erickson, Minnesota at Boston, W 5-0—Tom Brunansky (single in second)
8-8 Charles Nagy, Cleveland at Baltimore, W 6-0—Glenn Davis (single in seventh)
8-9 Sam Militello (7 innings) and Steve Farr (2 innings), New York vs. Boston, W 6-0—Tony Pena (single in second)
8-26 Todd Stottlemyre, Toronto at Chicago, W 9-0—Dan Pasqua (double in eighth)
9-29 Dennis Rasmussen, Kansas City at California, W 2-0—Damion Easley (single in fourth)
9-30 Frank Viola, Boston at Toronto, W 1-0—Devon White (single in ninth)

TWO-HIT GAMES

Date Pitcher(s), Team, Opponent, Result—Player(s) with hits

4-9 Ben McDonald, Baltimore vs. Cleveland, W 2-0—Mark Lewis (single in third), Glenallen Hill (single in fourth)
4-12† Roger Clemens, Boston at Cleveland, W 3-0—Carlos Baerga (single in first), Glenallen Hill (single in third)
4-24 Dan Plesac (5⅔ innings), Mike Fetters (1⅓ innings) and Edwin Nunez (2 innings), Milwaukee at Cleveland, W 5-0—Thomas Howard (single in first), Carlos Baerga (single in sixth)
4-24 Jack McDowell (7 innings), Donn Pall (1 inning) and Bobby Thigpen (1 inning), Chicago at Detroit, W 9-1—Mickey Tettleton (home run in fifth), Mark Carreon (single in fifth)
4-29 Jose Guzman, Texas at New York, W 5-1—Matt Nokes (home run in seventh), Kevin Maas (single in seventh)
5-10 Joe Slusarski (8 innings) and Dennis Eckersley (1 inning), Oakland vs. New York, W 5-2—Randy Velarde (single in third), Pat Kelly (home run in third)
5-13 Kirk McCaskill (7⅓ innings) and Bobby Thigpen (1⅔ innings), Chicago at Milwaukee, W 1-0—Kevin Seitzer (single in seventh), Jim Gantner (double in eighth)
5-24 Ron Darling, Oakland at Boston, W 4-0—Mike Greenwell (single in third), Phil Plantier (single in fourth)
6-17 Mark Langston, California vs. Texas, W 3-0—Al Newman (single in third), John Cangelosi (single in sixth)
6-24 Kevin Tapani, Minnesota vs. California, W 11-0—Rene Gonzales (single in first), Junior Felix (double in seventh)
6-30 Bill Krueger, Minnesota at California, W 2-0—Luis Sojo (single in fifth), Gary DiSarcina (single in sixth)

Date	Pitcher(s), Team, Opponent, Result—Player(s) with hits
7-11	Mike Moore (8 innings) and Dennis Eckersley (1 inning), Oakland at Toronto, W 3-1—John Olerud (home run in second), Roberto Alomar (double in sixth)
7-12	Ron Darling, Oakland at Toronto, W 8-0—Candy Maldonado (single in eighth), Manuel Lee (single in ninth)
7-16	Kelly Downs (7 innings), Jeff Parrett (1 inning) and Rich Gossage (1 inning), Oakland vs. Detroit, W 4-0—Milt Cuyler (single in sixth), Mickey Tettleton (double in seventh)
7-18	Ben McDonald, Baltimore at Texas, W 7-0—Dean Palmer (single in first), Ivan Rodriguez (single in second)
7-18	Roger Clemens, Boston at Minnesota, W 1-0—Shane Mack (single in second), Gene Larkin (single in fifth)
7-22	Jaime Navarro, Milwaukee vs. Texas, W 4-1—Jeff Huson (single in third), Jeff Frye (single in third)
7-25	Ron Darling, Oakland at Toronto, W 6-0—Candy Maldonado (single in seventh), Devon White (double in eighth)
8-12	Mark Langston (8 innings) and Joe Grahe (1 inning), California vs. Milwaukee, W 2-1—Pat Listach (double in fourth), Dante Bichette (single in fourth)
8-12	Scott Sanderson (7⅓ innings) and Rich Monteleone (1⅔ innings), New York at Detroit, W 10-0—Travis Fryman (single in first), Lou Whitaker (single in third)
8-25	Dave Fleming, Seattle vs. Cleveland, W 6-0—Kenny Lofton (double in sixth and single in ninth)
9-2	Ben McDonald (6 innings) and Alan Mills (4 innings), Baltimore at Oakland, W 2-1 (10 innings)—Mike Bordick (single in eighth), Dave Henderson (single in seventh)
9-9	Dave Stewart (7 innings), Jeff Russell (1 inning) and Dennis Eckersley (1 inning), Oakland at California, W 3-0—Luis Sojo (single in third), Ken Oberkfell (single in fourth)
9-13	Bob Welch (4 innings), Kelly Downs (4⅓ innings) and Jeff Russell (⅔ inning), Oakland vs. Seattle, W 3-1—Harold Reynolds (single in ninth), Greg Briley (double in ninth)
9-15	Ron Darling (8 innings) and Dennis Eckersley (1 inning), Oakland vs. Minnesota, W 2-1—Scott Leius (single in sixth), Kirby Puckett (single in sixth)
9-16	David Haas (7 innings) and Mike Henneman (2 innings), Detroit vs. Texas, W 4-1—Jose Canseco (double in fourth), Juan Gonzalez (single in fourth)
9-22	Chris Haney, Kansas City vs. Seattle, W 3-0—Henry Cotto (single in third), Dave Valle (single in ninth)

NATIONAL LEAGUE

ONE-HIT GAMES

Date	Pitcher(s), Team, Opponent, Result—Player with hit
5-18	Bruce Hurst, San Diego vs. New York, W 3-0—Chico Walker (single in sixth)
6-8	Ken Hill, Montreal vs. New York, W 6-0—Anthony Young (single in fifth)
7-25	Danny Jackson (7 innings) and Bob Patterson (1 inning), Pittsburgh at Atlanta, L 1-0—David Justice (home run in second)
8-30	Jim Bullinger, Chicago vs. San Francisco, W 3-1—Kirt Manwaring (home run in eighth)
9-9	Curt Schilling, Philadelphia vs. New York, W 2-1—Bobby Bonilla (home run in fifth)

TWO-HIT GAMES

Date	Pitcher(s), Team, Opponent, Result—Player(s) with hits
4-7	Tom Glavine, Atlanta at Houston, W 2-0—Steve Finley (single in first), Pete Incaviglia (single in second)
4-16	Mike Bielecki, Atlanta at Los Angeles, W 3-0—Brett Butler (single in sixth and double in ninth)
4-27	Tom Glavine, Atlanta vs. Chicago, W 5-0—Shawon Dunston (single in sixth), Ryne Sandberg (single in seventh)
4-28	David Cone, New York vs. Atlanta, W 4-0—Benny Distefano (single in eighth), Jeff Bagwell (single in ninth)
5-10	Tim Belcher, Cincinnati at Chicago, W 6-0—Dawson (single in fifth), Derrick May (single in fifth)
5-21	John Burkett (7 innings) and Mike Jackson (2 innings), San Francisco vs. Pittsburgh, W 1-0—Andy Van Slyke (singles in first and fourth)
5-22	Dennis Martinez, Montreal vs. Atlanta, W 7-1—David Justice (single in second), Damon Berryhill (home run in eighth)
5-22	Mark Portugal (8⅓ innings) and Doug Jones (⅔ inning), Houston at St. Louis, W 3-1—Ozzie Smith (singles in fourth and ninth)
5-26	Don Robinson (6 innings), Mike Hartley (⅓ inning), Wally Ritchie (⅔ inning) and Mitch Williams (2 innings), Philadelphia vs. Atlanta, W 5-2—Jeff Blauser (single in sixth), Mark Lemke (triple in ninth)
5-31	Greg Harris (5 innings), Mike Maddux (1 inning), Gene Harris (2 innings) and Rich Rodriguez (1 inning), San Diego at St. Louis, W 10-0—Andres Galarraga (single in second), Milt Thompson (single in fifth)
6-6	Tom Glavine, Atlanta at San Diego, W 5-1—Jerald Clark (triple in second), Kurt Stillwell (single in second)
6-7	Trevor Wilson, San Francisco vs. Houston, W 3-0—Rafael Ramirez (single in second), Luis Gonzalez (single in second)
6-24	John Smoltz, Atlanta vs. San Francisco, W 5-0—Will Clark (singles in first and ninth)
8-1†	Jeff D. Robinson (7 innings) and Chuck McElroy (2 innings), Chicago at New York (second game), W 6-1—Howard Johnson (double in first), Chris Donnels (double in second)
8-14	Dennis Martinez (7 innings), Mel Rojas (1 inning) and John Wetteland (1 inning), Montreal vs. St. Louis, W 4-1—Tracy Woodson (single in second), Felix Jose (single in seventh)
8-31	Tom Candiotti, Los Angeles at Chicago, L 2-0—Steve Buechele (single in seventh), Dwight Smith (single in seventh)
9-17	Mike Morgan, Chicago vs. Philadelphia, W 3-0—Ruben Amaro (single in fourth), Dave Hollins (single in seventh)
9-29	Zane Smith (3 innings), Paul Wagner (4 innings), Steve Cooke (1 inning) and Stan Belinda (1 inning), Pittsburgh at Chicago, W 3-0—Luis Salazar (single in second), Ryne Sandberg (single in fourth)

*First game of doubleheader.   †Second game of doubleheader.

15-STRIKEOUT GAMES

Date	Pitcher, Team, Opponent	IP	H	R	ER	BB	SO	Result
5-24	John Smoltz, Atlanta at Montreal	9	6	1	1	2	15	W 2-1
9-16	Randy Johnson, Seattle vs. California (13 inn.)	9	1	1	1	1	15	L 1-2
9-27	Randy Johnson, Seattle at Texas	8	6	2	2	4	18	L 2-3

10-STRIKEOUT GAMES

AMERICAN LEAGUE

Team	No.	Pitchers
Seattle	10	Randy Johnson 9, Erik Hanson 1.
California	6	Mark Langston 3, Jim Abbott 1, Chuck Finley 1, Tim Fortugno 1.
New York	4	Melido Perez 3, Sam Militello 1.
Texas	4	Jose Guzman 2, Nolan Ryan 2.
Boston	3	Roger Clemens 3.
Minnesota	3	Pat Mahomes 1, John Smiley 1, Kevin Tapani 1.
Cleveland	2	Charles Nagy 2.
Toronto	2	Juan Guzman 2.
Baltimore	1	Mike Mussina 1.
Kansas City	1	Kevin Appier 1.
Milwaukee	1	Cal Eldred 1.
Oakland	1	Dave Stewart 1.
Chicago	0	None.
Detroit	0	None.

NATIONAL LEAGUE

Team	No.	Pitchers
New York	13	David Cone 8, Sid Fernandez 5.
Cincinnati	5	Tim Belcher 3, Jose Rijo 2.
Houston	4	Pete Harnisch 2, Darryl Kile 2.
Montreal	4	Mark Gardner 1, Ken Hill 1, Dennis Martinez 1, Chris Nabholz 1.
Atlanta	3	John Smoltz 3.
Los Angeles	3	Kevin Gross 2, Pedro Astacio 1.
Pittsburgh	3	Doug Drabek 2, Tim Wakefield 1.
St. Louis	3	Rheal Cormier 2, Donovan Osborne 1.
San Diego	3	Andy Benes 2, Bruce Hurst 1.
Chicago	2	Greg Maddux 2.
Philadelphia	0	None.
San Francisco	0	None.

1-0 GAMES

AMERICAN LEAGUE

Date	Winner	Loser	Inn.*	Site
4-11	Randy Johnson, Seattle	†Kevin Appier, Kansas City	7	Seattle
4-13	†Greg Hibbard, Chicago	†Russ Swan, Seattle	3	Chicago
4-16	†Dave Stewart, Oakland	†Jeff Montgomery, Kansas City	10	Kansas City
4-17	†Roger Clemens, Boston	†David Wells, Toronto	4	Boston
4-28	†Kevin Brown, Texas	Tim Leary, New York	2	New York
4-29	Todd Stottlemyre, Toronto	Jim Abbott, California	9	Toronto
5-13	†Kirk McCaskill, Chicago	Bill Wegman, Milwaukee	1	Milwaukee
5-20	†Jose Guzman, Texas	Charles Nagy, Cleveland	6	Cleveland
5-26	†Dave Otto, Cleveland	†Bob Welch, Oakland	5	Oakland
6-5	†Rick Sutcliffe, Baltimore	†Jimmy Key, Toronto	8	Baltimore
6-15	†John Dopson, Boston	Scott Sanderson, New York	5	Boston
6-19	Dave Fleming, Seattle	†Kevin Tapani, Minnesota	1	Minnesota
6-25	†Ricky Bones, Milwaukee	Rick Sutcliffe, Baltimore	7	Milwaukee
7-18	Roger Clemens, Boston	Scott Erickson, Minnesota	1	Minnesota
7-20	Shawn Hillegas, New York	Ron Darling, Oakland	3	Oakland
7-23	†Kevin Wickander, Cleveland	†Mike Magnante, Kansas City	14	Cleveland
8-11	†Joe Grahe, California	†Jaime Navarro, Milwaukee	10	California
8-14‡	†Cal Eldred, Milwaukee	Greg Harris, Boston	1	Milwaukee
8-16	Jaime Navarro, Milwaukee	Frank Viola, Boston	3	Milwaukee
8-26	John Smiley, Minnesota	†John Kiely, Detroit	9	Minnesota
9-9	†David Cone, Toronto	†Kevin Appier, Kansas City	2	Kansas City
9-19	†David Cone, Toronto	†Scott Chiamparino, Texas	6	Toronto
9-22	†Larry Casian, Minnesota	Kenny Rogers, Texas	13	Texas
9-26	†Chuck Finley, California	†Alex Fernandez, Chicago	3	Chicago
9-30	Frank Viola, Boston	†David Cone, Toronto	4	Toronto

PLAYERS HITTING HOME RUNS IN 1-0 GAMES: 4-11—Pete O'Brien, Seattle; 5-26—Mark Lewis, Cleveland; 6-15—Phil Plantier, Boston; 6-19—Greg Briley, Seattle; 8-26—Brian Harper, Minnesota; 9-30—John Valentin, Boston.

*Inning in which run was scored.   †Did not pitch complete game.   ‡Second game of doubleheader.

NATIONAL LEAGUE

Date	Winner	Loser	Inn.*	Site
4-19	†Xavier Hernandez, Houston	†Rich Rodriguez, San Diego	11	Houston
4-23	†John Franco, New York	†Juan Agosto, St. Louis	13	New York
4-25	†Randy Tomlin, Pittsburgh	†Greg Maddux, Chicago	6	Chicago
4-28	†Charlie Leibrandt, Atlanta	†Frank Castillo, Chicago	7	Atlanta
4-29	Bret Saberhagen, New York	Darryl Kile, Houston	2	New York
5-3	†Al Osuna, Houston	†Roger Mason, Pittsburgh	8	Houston
5-21	†John Burkett, San Francisco	†Bob Walk, Pittsburgh	7	San Francisco
5-27	Tim Belcher, Cincinnati	Sid Fernandez, New York	7	New York
5-29	Ramon Martinez, Los Angeles	†Frank Castillo, Chicago	9	Chicago
6-2	†Randy Tomlin, Pittsburgh	†Tom Candiotti, Los Angeles	7	Pittsburgh
6-7	Tom Candiotti, Los Angeles	†Tim Belcher, Cincinnati	5	Los Angeles
6-20	†Doug Jones, Houston	†Orel Hershiser, Los Angeles	9	Houston
6-21	†Mike Jackson, San Francisco	†Jose Melendez, San Diego	11	San Francisco
7-1	Zane Smith, Pittsburgh	†Mark Clark, St. Louis	4	St. Louis
7-2	†Donovan Osborne, St. Louis	†Bill Swift, San Francisco	6	San Francisco
7-4	†Mike Perez, St. Louis	†Rod Beck, San Francisco	13	San Francisco
7-6	†Zane Smith, Pittsburgh	†Jimmy Jones, Houston	6	Pittsburgh
7-8	†Omar Olivares, St. Louis	†Randy Myers, San Diego	9	San Diego

Date	Winner	Loser	Inn.*	Site
7-8§	†Tom Candiotti, Los Angeles	†Sergio Valdez, Montreal	11	Los Angeles
7-17	David Cone, New York	†Bill Swift, San Francisco	1	New York
7-21	†Ken Patterson, Chicago	†Tim Belcher, Cincinnati	4	Cincinnati
7-24	†Mike Morgan, Chicago	†Doug Jones, Houston	9	Houston
7-25	†Charlie Leibrandt, Atlanta	†Danny Jackson, Pittsburgh	2	Atlanta
7-26	Bruce Hurst, San Diego	†Wally Whitehurst, New York	2	New York
8-2	†Chris Nabholz, Montreal	†Ben Rivera, Philadelphia	6	Montreal
8-16	Greg Maddux, Chicago	†Brian Williams, Houston	1	Chicago
8-23	†Jose Rijo, Cincinnati	†Ken Hill, Montreal	2	Montreal
8-28	†Mark Clark, St. Louis	†Bob Ojeda, Los Angeles	1	St. Louis
9-20	Sid Fernandez, New York	†Ken Hill, Montreal	2	New York
9-25	†Greg Harris, San Diego	†Steve Avery, Atlanta	2	San Diego
9-27	†Mel Rojas, Montreal	†Mike Morgan, Chicago	7	Montreal
9-30	†Jeff Brantley, San Francisco	†Tom Glavine, Atlanta	1	Atlanta
10-3	†Charlie Leibrandt, Atlanta	†Mike Maddux, San Diego	2	Atlanta

PLAYERS HITTING HOME RUNS IN 1-0 GAMES: 5-3—Steve Finley, Houston; 7-6—Orlando Merced, Pittsburgh; 7-8—Tom Pagnozzi, St. Louis; 7-21—Kal Daniels, Chicago; 7-24—Rick Wilkins, Chicago; 7-25—David Justice, Atlanta; 9-25—Jerald Clark, San Diego.

*Inning in which run was scored. †Did not pitch complete game. §First game of doubleheader.

FOUR OR MORE HITS IN ONE GAME

AMERICAN LEAGUE

Team	No.	Hitters
Kansas City	18	George Brett 5, Gregg Jefferies 5, Keith Miller 4, Wally Joyner 2, Jim Eisenreich 1, Curtis Wilkerson 1.
Minnesota	15	Kirby Puckett 4, Chili Davis 3, Chuck Knoblauch 3, Shane Mack 3, Greg Gagne 1, Brian Harper 1.
Cleveland	14	Carlos Baerga 3, Kenny Lofton 2, Paul Sorrento 2, Sandy Alomar 1, Albert Belle 1, Alex Cole 1, Felix Fermin 1, Thomas Howard 1, Reggie Jefferson 1, Mark Whiten 1.
New York	13	Don Mattingly 4, Mel Hall 2, Danny Tartabull 2, Roberto Kelly 1, Matt Nokes 1, Andy Stankiewicz 1, Randy Velarde 1, Bernie Williams 1.
Chicago	11	Tim Raines 3, Frank Thomas 3, George Bell 2, Robin Ventura 2, Craig Grebeck 1.
Milwaukee	11	Dante Bichette 3, Pat Listach 2, Paul Molitor 2, Scott Fletcher 1, Darryl Hamilton 1, Dave Nilsson 1, Kevin Seitzer 1.
Oakland	11	Mike Bordick 4, Carney Lansford 3, Terry Steinbach 2, Scott Brosius 1, Jose Canseco 1.
Seattle	11	Edgar Martinez 3, Ken Griffey Jr. 3, Dave Cochrane 1, Tino Martinez 1, Kevin Mitchell 1, Harold Reynolds 1, Dave Valle 1.
Baltimore	9	Mike Devereaux 3, Joe Orsulak 3, Mark McLemore 1, Randy Milligan 1, Bill Ripken 1.
Detroit	8	Travis Fryman 3, Mark Carreon 1, Rob Deer 1, Dan Gladden 1, Tony Phillips 1, Lou Whitaker 1.
Texas	7	Brian Downing 2, Rafael Palmeiro 2, Ruben Sierra 2, Al Newman 1.
Boston	6	Wade Boggs 3, Tom Brunansky 1, Scott Cooper 1, Billy Hatcher 1.
California	6	Gary Gaetti 2, Gary DiSarcina 1, Junior Felix 1, Rene Gonzales 1, Reggie Williams 1.
Toronto	5	Devon White 2, Joe Carter 1, Candy Maldonado 1, John Olerud 1.

NATIONAL LEAGUE

Team	No.	Hitters
Houston	18	Jeff Bagwell 5, Steve Finley 4, Ken Caminiti 3, Craig Biggio 2, Andujar Cedeno 1, Benny Distefano 1, Luis Gonzalez 1, Eddie Taubensee 1.
Atlanta	11	Ron Gant 2, Deion Sanders 2, Damon Berryhill 1, Jeff Blauser 1, Sid Bream 1, Brian Hunter 1, Mark Lemke 1, Otis Nixon 1, Lonnie Smith 1.
Chicago	11	Andre Dawson 5, Ryne Sandberg 3, Alex Arias 1, Derrick May 1, Rey Sanchez 1.
Pittsburgh	11	Andy Van Slyke 3, Barry Bonds 2, Alex Cole 2, Don Slaught 2, Jay Bell 1, Cecil Espy 1.
St. Louis	11	Bernard Gilkey 3, Rod Brewer 1, Ray Lankford 1, Geronimo Pena 1, Stan Royer 1, Ozzie Smith 1, Craig Wilson 1, Tracy Woodson 1, Todd Zeile 1.
Montreal	10	Delino DeShields 5, Larry Walker 2, Moises Alou 1, Archi Cianfrocco 1, Spike Owen 1.
Cincinnati	9	Barry Larkin 3, Darnell Coles 2, Reggie Sanders 2, Paul O'Neill 1, Bip Roberts 1.
San Francisco	8	Kevin Bass 2, Will Clark 2, Willie McGee 2, Mike Felder 1, Cory Snyder 1.
New York	7	Bobby Bonilla 2, Eddie Murray 2, Vince Coleman 1, Jeff Kent 1, Chico Walker 1.
San Diego	7	Tony Gwynn 2, Darrin Jackson 2, Fred McGriff 1, Benito Santiago 1, Gary Sheffield 1.
Philadelphia	6	Mariano Duncan 2, Lenny Dykstra 2, Mickey Morandini 2.
Los Angeles	3	Brett Butler 2, Mike Sharperson 1.

FIVE- AND SIX-HIT GAMES

Date	Player, Team, Opponent	AB	R	H	2B	3B	HR	RBI	Result
4-11	Carlos Baerga, Cleveland vs. Boston (18 inn.)	9	1	6	0	0	0	0	L 5-7
4-30	George Bell, Chicago White Sox vs. Texas	5	4	5	2	0	1	2	W 12-1
5-3	Mariano Duncan, Philadelphia at San Francisco	5	5	5	0	1	1	1	W 12-3
6-29	Tino Martinez, Seattle vs. Oakland (11 inn.)	6	0	5	0	0	0	2	L 4-5
7-1	Craig Grebeck, Chicago White Sox at Cleveland	5	2	5	3	0	0	2	W 8-5
7-3	Mike Devereaux, Baltimore at Minnesota	5	2	5	0	1	0	0	W 6-1
7-12	Rafael Palmeiro, Texas vs. Cleveland	5	2	5	0	1	0	1	L 3-6
7-26	Darnell Coles, Cincinnati at St. Louis (10 inn.)	6	2	5	1	1	0	0	W 7-6
8-14	Lonnie Smith, Atlanta at Pittsburgh	6	3	5	2	0	1	6	W 15-0
8-28	Scott Fletcher, Milwaukee at Toronto	6	3	5	0	0	0	5	W 22-2

Date	Player, Team, Opponent	AB	R	H	2B	3B	HR	RBI	Result
8-28	Kevin Seitzer, Milwaukee at Toronto	7	4	5	2	0	0	3	W 22-2
8-30	Scott Cooper, Boston at California (10 inn.)	5	1	5	3	0	0	3	W 4-2
9-4	Andre Dawson, Chicago vs. San Diego (14 inn.)	7	1	5	2	0	0	2	L 5-7
9-7	Alex Arias, Chicago at Pittsburgh (11 inn.)	5	0	5	1	0	0	1	W 6-5
9-8	Tony Gwynn, San Diego at San Francisco (16 inn.)	8	1	5	2	0	0	2	L 5-6
9-8	Carney Lansford, Oakland at California	6	3	5	1	0	0	5	W 14-2
9-8	Danny Tartabull, New York Yankees at Baltimore	5	3	5	1	0	2	9	W 16-4
9-15	Jeff Bagwell, Houston vs. San Francisco (11 inn.)	6	3	5	1	0	1	4	W 9-6
9-16	Frank Thomas, Chicago White Sox at N.Y. Yankees	5	3	5	2	0	0	2	W 9-6
9-19	Rod Brewer, St. Louis at Chicago	5	4	5	0	0	0	1	W 16-4

HITTING STREAKS OF 15 OR MORE GAMES

AMERICAN LEAGUE

G	Player, Team	Span of streak
25	Lance Johnson, Chicago	July 16-Aug. 11
22	Shane Mack, Minnesota	July 26-Aug. 18
19	Frank Thomas, Chicago	July 20-Aug. 9
18	Gregg Jefferies, Kansas City	May 13-June 1
17	Pat Listach, Milwaukee	Aug. 31-Sept. 18
	Edgar Martinez, Seattle	Aug. 12-Aug. 31
	Kevin McReynolds, Kansas City	May 24-June 12
	Cal Ripken, Baltimore	June 12-June 29
	Dave Winfield, Toronto	April 22-May 9
16	Roberto Alomar, Toronto	Aug. 24-Sept. 11
	Joe Carter, Toronto	April 6-April 23
	Gregg Jefferies, Kansas City	June 18-July 5
	Cal Ripken, Baltimore	May 20-June 7
15	Glenn Davis, Baltimore	July 17-July 31
	Darryl Hamilton, Milwaukee	June 8-June 24
	Kent Hrbek, Minnesota	May 24-June 10
	Candy Maldonado, Toronto	Aug. 6-Aug. 21
	Don Mattingly, New York	June 18-July 3
	Kirby Puckett, Minnesota	June 2-June 18

NATIONAL LEAGUE

G	Player, Team	Span of streak
22	Jay Bell, Pittsburgh	Aug. 24-Sept. 17
19	Brett Butler, Los Angeles	July 16-Aug. 5
	Tony Fernandez, San Diego	Sept. 14-Oct. 4
18	Gary Sheffield, San Diego	May 5-May 25
15	Barry Bonds, Pittsburgh	Sept. 12-Sept. 26
	Terry Pendleton, Atlanta	May 4-May 18

MULTI-HOMER GAMES

AMERICAN LEAGUE

Team	No.	Hitters
Cleveland	12	Albert Belle 5, Glenallen Hill 3, Paul Sorrento 2, Carlos Baerga 1, Carlos Martinez 1.
Detroit	11	Rob Deer 5, Cecil Fielder 4, Travis Fryman 2.
Texas	9	Juan Gonzalez 7, Rafael Palmeiro 1, Dean Palmer 1.
Baltimore	8	Mike Devereaux 2, Randy Milligan 2, Brady Anderson 1, Glenn Davis 1, Chris Hoiles 1, Cal Ripken 1.
Seattle	8	Jay Buhner 2, Ken Griffey Jr. 2, Kevin Mitchell 2, Edgar Martinez 1, Lance Parrish 1.
Oakland	7	Mark McGwire 5, Scott Brosius 1, Jose Canseco 1.
Toronto	5	Joe Carter 1, Kelly Gruber 1, John Olerud 1, Devon White 1, Dave Winfield 1.
New York	4	Mel Hall 1, Charlie Hayes 1, Matt Nokes 1, Danny Tartabull 1.
Boston	3	Wade Boggs 1, Tom Brunansky 1, Jack Clark 1.
Chicago	3	George Bell 1, Ron Karkovice 1, Frank Thomas 1.
California	2	Chad Curtis 1, Gary Gaetti 1.
Milwaukee	2	Paul Molitor 1, Kevin Seitzer 1.
Minnesota	2	Chili Davis 1, Kirby Puckett 1.
Kansas City	0	None.

NATIONAL LEAGUE

Team	No.	Hitters
San Diego	8	Gary Sheffield 3, Fred McGriff 2, Darrin Jackson 1, Benito Santiago 1, Tim Teufel 1.
Chicago	4	Ryne Sandberg 2, Derrick May 1, Sammy Sosa 1.
Houston	4	Eric Anthony 2, Jeff Bagwell 1, Pete Incaviglia 1.
Philadelphia	4	Darren Daulton 1, Mariano Duncan 1, Dave Hollins 1, John Kruk 1.
Montreal	3	Larry Walker 2, Delino DeShields 1.
San Francisco	3	Kevin Bass 1, Cory Snyder 1, Matt Williams 1.
Atlanta	2	Jeff Blauser 1, Dave Justice 1.
Cincinnati	2	Chris Sabo 1, Reggie Sanders 1.
New York	2	Bobby Bonilla 1, Ryan Thompson 1.
Los Angeles	1	Darryl Strawberry 1.
Pittsburgh	1	Barry Bonds 1.
St. Louis	0	None.

THREE-HOMER GAMES

Date	Player, Team, Opponent	AB	R	H	2B	3B	HR	RBI	Result
6-7	Juan Gonzalez, Texas vs. Minnesota	4	3	3	0	0	3	4	W 5-4
7-12	Jeff Blauser, Atlanta at Chicago (10 inn.)	4	3	3	0	0	3	5	W 7-4
9-6	Albert Belle, Cleveland vs. Seattle (12 inn.)	3	3	3	0	0	3	5	W 12-9

AMERICAN LEAGUE

Date	Batter	Pitcher	Inn.*	Site
4-8	B.J. Surhoff, Milwaukee	Rick Aguilera, Minnesota	9	Milwaukee
4-11	Dan Pasqua, Chicago	Dave Stewart, Oakland	3	Oakland
4-17	Randy Milligan, Baltimore	Les Lancaster, Detroit	7	Baltimore
4-22	Rafael Palmeiro, Texas	Scott Aldred, Detroit	4	Texas
4-25	Tino Martinez, Seattle	Joe Grahe, California	2	California
5-1	Mike Devereaux, Baltimore	Jim Acker, Seattle	5	Baltimore
5-4	Chris Hoiles, Baltimore	Todd Burns, Texas	7	Baltimore
5-5	George Bell, Chicago	Chris Bosio, Milwaukee	1	Chicago
5-7	Dave Winfield, Toronto	Mike Schooler, Seattle	9	Seattle
5-13	Matt Nokes, New York	Erik Hanson, Seattle	2	New York
5-15	Franklin Stubbs, Milwaukee	Kenny Rogers, Texas	10	Milwaukee
5-19	Mark Whiten, Cleveland	Jeff Robinson, Texas	7	Cleveland
5-20	Gregg Jefferies, Kansas City	Alex Fernandez, Chicago	5	Chicago
5-20	Ellis Burks, Boston	Mike Schooler, Seattle	8	Boston
5-24	Shane Mack, Minnesota	Frank Tanana, Detroit	4	Detroit
5-25	Danny Tartabull, New York	Jesse Orosco, Milwaukee	8	New York
5-29	Kirby Puckett, Minnesota	Les Lancaster, Detroit	4	Minnesota
6-3	Sandy Alomar, Cleveland	Jim Acker, Seattle	4	Cleveland
6-3	Kirby Puckett, Minnesota	Juan Guzman, Toronto	3	Minnesota
6-4	Kevin Mitchell, Seattle	Denis Boucher, Cleveland	1	Cleveland
6-4	Dean Palmer, Texas	Bill Krueger, Minnesota	2	Texas
6-7	Mickey Tettleton, Detroit	Melido Perez, New York	5	New York
6-8	Milt Cuyler, Detroit	Dennis Cook, Cleveland	1	Detroit
6-12	Wade Boggs, Boston	Dave Stieb, Toronto	5	Toronto
6-12	Leo Gomez, Baltimore	Scott Aldred, Detroit	4	Detroit
6-13	Mark McGwire, Oakland	Kenny Rogers, Texas	8	Oakland
6-16	Steve Sax, Chicago	Mike Walker, Seattle	6	Seattle
6-19	Mike Devereaux, Baltimore	Jeff Johnson, New York	2	Baltimore
6-23	Cecil Fielder, Detroit	Matt Young, Boston	4	Detroit
6-30	Bob Zupcic, Boston	Mike Henneman, Detroit	9	Boston
7-3†	Jay Buhner, Seattle	Les Lancaster, Detroit	5	Detroit
7-5	George Bell, Chicago	Mike Gardiner, Boston	5	Chicago
7-8	Albert Belle, Cleveland	Joe Grahe, California	7	Cleveland
7-9	Mike Stanley, New York	Randy Johnson, Seattle	1	New York
7-9	Dean Palmer, Texas	Ted Power, Cleveland	5	Texas
7-10	Bob Zupcic, Boston	Bobby Thigpen, Chicago	8	Boston
7-11	Tom Brunansky, Boston	Donn Pall, Chicago	6	Boston
7-27	Tom Brunansky, Boston	Kevin Brown, Texas	1	Boston
7-27	Randy Ready, Oakland	Bob Kipper, Minnesota	9	Minnesota
8-1	Cecil Fielder, Detroit	Ted Power, Cleveland	7	Cleveland
8-1	Brian Harper, Minnesota	Doug Henry, Milwaukee	8	Minnesota
8-7	Carney Lansford, Oakland	Dennis Moeller, Kansas City	5	Oakland
8-14	Kirby Puckett, Minnesota	Brian Fisher, Seattle	3	Seattle
8-19	Edgar Martinez, Seattle	Todd Frohwirth, Baltimore	4	Baltimore
8-20	Jose Canseco, Oakland	John Habyan, New York	7	New York
8-22	John Valentin, Boston	Mike Schooler, Seattle	6	Boston
8-26	Danny Tartabull, New York	Bruce Ruffin, Milwaukee	3	New York
8-29	Lou Whitaker, Detroit	Juan Berenguer, Kansas City	4	Detroit
9-1	Kelly Gruber, Toronto	Donn Pall, Chicago	7	Toronto
9-4	Lee Stevens, California	Rick Sutcliffe, Baltimore	4	California
9-6	Carlos Martinez, Cleveland	Mike Schooler, Seattle	12	Cleveland
9-8	Ken Griffey, Seattle	Pat Mahomes, Minnesota	6	Minnesota

*Inning in which grand slam was hit.   †Second game of doubleheader.

NATIONAL LEAGUE

Date	Batter	Pitcher	Inn.*	Site
4-10	Fred McGriff, San Diego	John Candelaria, Los Angeles	7	San Diego
4-20	Kirk Gibson, Pittsburgh	Bill Sampen, Montreal	9	Montreal
4-20	Gary Scott, Chicago	Kyle Abbott, Philadelphia	4	Chicago
5-16	Barry Bonds, Pittsburgh	Greg Harris, San Diego	2	Pittsburgh
5-17	Felix Jose, St. Louis	Pete Harnisch, Houston	3	Houston
5-19	Bill Doran, Cincinnati	John Wetteland, Montreal	9	Montreal
5-27	Todd Benzinger, Los Angeles	Jose DeLeon, St. Louis	3	St. Louis
6-1	Bobby Bonilla, New York	John Burkett, San Francisco	2	New York
6-2	Eddie Murray, New York	Trevor Wilson, San Francisco	3	New York
6-18	Gary Sheffield, San Diego	Trevor Wilson, San Francisco	4	San Francisco
6-26	Glenn Braggs, Cincinnati	Steve Avery, Atlanta	1	Cincinnati
7-5	Kal Daniels, Chicago	Juan Berenguer, Atlanta	7	Atlanta
7-27	Eric Anthony, Houston	Alejandro Pena, Atlanta	11	Atlanta
7-28	Darren Daulton, Philadelphia	David Cone, New York	1	Philadelphia
7-29	Dave Hollins, Philadelphia	Lee Guetterman, New York	8	Philadelphia

Date	Batter	Pitcher	Inn.*	Site
8-1	Wes Chamberlain, Philadelphia	Ken Hill, Montreal	1	Montreal
8-8	Terry Pendleton, Atlanta	Roger McDowell, Los Angeles	7	Atlanta
8-14	Gary Sheffield, San Diego	Chris Hammond, Cincinnati	2	Cincinnati
8-14	Lonnie Smith, Atlanta	Roger Mason, Pittsburgh	2	Pittsburgh
8-15	Andres Galarraga, St. Louis	John Wetteland, Montreal	8	Montreal
8-31	Eric Anthony, Houston	Jay Baller, Philadelphia	6	Houston
9-4	Eddie Murray, New York	Tim Belcher, Cincinnati	6	Cincinnati
9-4	Todd Benzinger, Los Angeles	Bob Patterson, Pittsburgh	9	Pittsburgh
9-7	Jerald Clark, San Diego	Bud Black, San Francisco	4	San Francisco
9-9	Ryne Sandberg, Chicago	Danny Cox, Pittsburgh	6	Pittsburgh
9-9	Jeff King, Pittsburgh	Ken Patterson, Chicago	6	Pittsburgh
9-13	Ray Lankford, St. Louis	Jim Bullinger, Chicago	5	St. Louis
9-21	Darren Daulton, Philadelphia	Gil Heredia, Montreal	4	Montreal
9-23	Tom Marsh, Philadelphia	Jeff Hartsock, Chicago	4	Philadelphia
9-23	Moises Alou, Montreal	Roger Mason, Pittsburgh	14	Montreal
9-26	Lloyd McClendon, Pittsburgh	Eric Hillman, New York	1	Pittsburgh
10-4	Mark Litton, San Francisco	Scott Ruskin, Cincinnati	13	Cincinnati

*Inning in which grand slam was hit.

TRANSACTIONS

JANUARY 2

Mets' Tidewater affiliate signed P Mike Birkbeck, a free agent.

Rangers organization signed P Danilo Leon, a free agent.

Red Sox signed P Frank Viola, a free agent.

JANUARY 3

Angels signed P Don Robinson, a free agent.

Astros' Tucson affiliate signed OF-1B Benny Distefano, a free agent.

JANUARY 7

Cardinals re-signed OF-1B Pedro Guerrero, a free agent.

Twins re-signed 3B Mike Pagliarulo, a free agent.

JANUARY 8

Braves signed IF-OF Steve Lyons, a free agent.

Padres signed IF Tim Teufel, a free agent.

Rangers' Oklahoma City affiliate signed C Doug Davis, a free agent.

Yankees signed OF Danny Tartabull, a free agent, and traded P Darrin Chapin to Phillies for a player to be named later; Phillies sent 3B Charlie Hayes to Yankees to complete deal (February 19).

JANUARY 9

Yankees signed IF Mike Gallego, a free agent formerly with Athletics.

JANUARY 10

Phillies' Scranton/Wilkes-Barre affiliate re-signed P Jay Baller, a free agent.

Yankees traded 2B Steve Sax to White Sox for P Melido Perez, P Robert Wickman and P Domingo Jean.

JANUARY 14

Athletics signed IF Randy Ready, a free agent.

JANUARY 15

Cardinals' Louisville affiliate signed OF Ozzie Canseco, a free agent.

Giants signed OF Chris James, a free agent.

JANUARY 17

Angels re-signed SS Dick Schofield, a free agent.

Athletics re-signed P Ron Darling, a free agent.

Red Sox' Pawtucket affiliate re-signed 2B Tommy Barrett, a free agent.

JANUARY 19

Yankees released P Dave Eiland.

JANUARY 21

Mariners re-signed C Matt Sinatro, a free agent.

JANUARY 22

Angels signed P Dave Johnson, a free agent.

Mets traded OF Mark Carreon and P Tony Castillo to Tigers for P Paul Gibson and P Randy Marshall.

Reds signed P Scott Bankhead, a free agent.

JANUARY 23

Brewers' Denver affiliate signed C Andy Allanson, a free agent.

Dodgers re-signed P Jay Howell, a free agent.

Mets' Tidewater affiliate released P Rich Sauveur.

JANUARY 26

Brewers' Denver affiliate signed IF Jeff Kunkel, a free agent.

JANUARY 27

Astros' Tucson affiliate signed OF Pete Incaviglia, a free agent.

Athletics organization signed P Goose Gossage and P Jim Deshaies, both free agents.

Mariners' Calgary affiliate signed P Mark Grant, a free agent.

JANUARY 29

Red Sox signed OF Herm Winningham, a free agent.

Tigers signed P Eric King, a free agent.

JANUARY 30

Giants' Phoenix affiliate signed C Steve Lake, a free agent.

JANUARY 31

Royals re-signed OF Jim Eisenreich, a free agent.

Orioles' Rochester affiliate signed P Dennis Rasmussen, a free agent.

FEBRUARY 2

Reds' Nashville affiliate signed IF Al Newman, a free agent.

FEBRUARY 7

Athletics organization signed P Jeff Parrett, a free agent.

FEBRUARY 8

Royals' Omaha affiliate signed P Rich Sauveur, a free agent.

FEBRUARY 10

Rangers' Oklahoma City affiliate signed P Lance McCullers, a free agent.

FEBRUARY 12

Angels' Edmonton affiliate signed P John Farrell, a free agent.

Expos' Indianapolis affiliate signed C Rick Cerone, a free agent.

Royals' Omaha affiliate signed P Curt Young, a free agent.

FEBRUARY 14

Angels signed 1B Alvin Davis, a free agent.

Expos' Indianapolis affiliate signed P Terry Leach, a free agent.

FEBRUARY 17

Orioles traded 3B Craig Worthington and P Tom Martin to Padres for P Jim Lewis and OF Steve Martin; Orioles assigned Steve Martin to Rochester of International League.

FEBRUARY 19

Mariners' Calgary affiliate signed IF-OF Shane Turner, a free agent.

FEBRUARY 23

Brewers' organization signed 2B Scott Fletcher, a free agent.

FEBRUARY 24

Angels' Edmonton affiliate signed C Mike Fitzgerald, a free agent.

Athletics' Tacoma affiliate re-signed P Mike Raczka, a free agent.

FEBRUARY 25

Indians' Colorado Springs affiliate signed P Brad Arnsberg, a free agent.

Mets re-signed OF Daryl Boston, a free agent.

FEBRUARY 27

Dodgers re-signed 2B Juan Samuel, a free agent.

FEBRUARY 28

Braves re-signed P Alejandro Pena, a free agent.

Padres signed SS Kurt Stillwell, a free agent.

FEBRUARY 29

Yankees traded P Alan Mills to Orioles for two minor league players to be named later; Orioles sent P Francisco DeLaRosa (March 5) and P Mark Carper (June 8) to Yankees to complete deal. Yankees assigned Carper to Albany/Colonie of Eastern League.

MARCH 5

Athletics released P Eric Show.

MARCH 9

Mariners' Calgary affiliate signed OF-1B John Moses, a free agent.

MARCH 10

Royals traded OF Kirk Gibson to Pirates for P Neal Heaton.

White Sox granted OF-DH Bo Jackson free agency, then re-signed him.

MARCH 11

Pirates' Buffalo affiliate signed P Dennis Lamp, a free agent.

MARCH 15

Orioles released OF-DH Dwight Evans.

MARCH 16

Athletics' Tacoma affiliate signed P Jim Corsi, a free agent.

MARCH 17

Angels released P Dave Johnson.

Pirates traded P John Smiley to Twins for P Denny Neagle and OF Midre Cummings.

Reds released C Bob Geren.

Yankees released SS Alvaro Espinoza.

MARCH 18

Athletics granted OF Doug Jennings free agency.

MARCH 19

Blue Jays' Syracuse affiliate signed SS Alfredo Griffin, a free agent.

Pirates released P Bill Landrum.

MARCH 20

Athletics claimed P Vince Horsman on waivers from Blue Jays.

Padres claimed OF Steve Pegues on waivers from Tigers.

MARCH 23

Athletics organization released P Jim Deshaies.

MARCH 24

Angels released OF Mark Davis.

Red Sox granted P Josias Manzanillo free agency.

MARCH 25

Angels released OF Shawn Abner.

MARCH 26

Royals released 3B Kevin Seitzer.

Brewers traded 3B Gary Sheffield and P Geoff Kellogg to Padres for P Ricky Bones, IF Jose Valentin and OF Matt Mieske; Brewers assigned Valentin to Denver of American Association.

Padres reacquired OF Darrell Sherman from Orioles, who had selected him from Las Vegas in 1991 Rule 5 major league draft.

MARCH 27

Blue Jays' Syracuse affiliate released P Eric Plunk.

MARCH 28

Twins traded 1B Paul Sorrento to Indians for P Oscar Munoz and P Curt Leskanic.

MARCH 29

Dodgers granted 2B Greg Smith free agency.

Expos organization sold contract of P Steve Frey to Angels organization.

Mariners' Calgary affiliate signed P Dave Schmidt, a free agent.

MARCH 30

Cubs traded OF George Bell to White Sox for OF Sammy Sosa and P Ken Patterson.

Mets traded P Terry Bross to Padres for 3B Craig Bullock; Padres assigned Bross to Las Vegas of Pacific Coast League.

Padres released 3B Craig Worthington.

Pirates granted P Mike Roesler free agency.

White Sox granted P Wayne Edwards free agency.

MARCH 31

Cubs released P Les Lancaster.

Expos released 1B George Canale.

Giants released P Eric Gunderson.

Indians released OF-1B Mike Aldrete, 2B Jerry Browne and P Shawn Hillegas.

Orioles released P Eric Hetzel.

Red Sox released P Dana Kiecker.

Reds released P Tim Layana.

Yankees reacquired P Rafael Quirico from Giants, who had selected him from Columbus in 1991 Rule 5 major league draft.

APRIL 1

Braves released C Mike Heath.

Brewers' Denver affiliate released IF Mario Diaz.

Expos signed P Bill Landrum, a free agent.

Phillies reacquired P Donnie Elliott from Mariners, who had selected him from Scranton/Wilkes-Barre in 1991 Rule 5 major league draft.

Reds' Nashville affiliate released IF Al Newman.

APRIL 2

Astros traded P Curt Schilling to Phillies for P Jason Grimsley; Astros assigned Grimsley to Tucson of the Pacific Coast League.

Expos' Indianapolis affiliate released P Terry Leach, and Expos reacquired P Mike Thomas from Indians, who had selected him from Indianapolis in 1991 Rule 5 major league draft.

Giants' Phoenix affiliate released C Steve Lake.

Mariners claimed P Kevin Brown on waivers from Brewers.

Mets traded P Doug Simons to Expos for OF Rob Katzaroff; Expos assigned Katzaroff to Binghamton of Eastern League.

APRIL 3

Blue Jays reacquired P Jesse Cross from Twins, who had selected him from Syracuse in 1991 Rule 5 major league draft, and claimed P Shawn Hillegas, a free agent, on waivers from Indians.

Indians claimed SS Jose Hernandez on waivers from Rangers, and assigned him to Canton/Akron of the Eastern League.

Pirates granted P Rick Reed free agency and Pirates' Buffalo affiliate released P Brian Fisher.

Rangers signed IF Al Newman, a free agent.

White Sox's Vancouver affiliate signed OF Shawn Abner, a free agent.

Yankees signed OF Dion James, a free agent.

APRIL 4

Blue Jays granted P Shawn Hillegas free agency.

Mariners' Calgary affiliate signed IF Mario Diaz, a free agent.

Royals reacquired P Matt Karchner from Expos, who had selected him from Omaha in 1991 Rule 5 major league draft, and Royals' Omaha affiliate signed P Rick Reed, a free agent.

APRIL 5

Brewers signed 3B Kevin Seitzer, a free agent.

Indians signed P Ted Power, a free agent.

Phillies signed C Steve Lake, a free agent.

Rangers signed P Floyd Bannister, a free agent, and Rangers' Tulsa affiliate signed C-OF John Russell, a free agent.

White Sox signed P Terry Leach, a free agent.

APRIL 6

Rangers released OF Gary Pettis.

Tigers signed P Les Lancaster, a free agent.

APRIL 7

Brewers granted P Narciso Elvira free agency.

APRIL 8

Padres organization traded 3B Tom Redington to White Sox

organization for P Lenny Brutcher and assigned Brutcher to High Desert of the California League.

Royals' Omaha affiliate released P Jerry Don Gleaton.

APRIL 9

Indians' Canton/Akron affiliate signed P Eric Plunk, a free agent.

Mariners released C Scott Bradley.

Pirates signed P Jerry Don Gleaton, a free agent.

Yankees' Fort Lauderdale affiliate signed P Shawn Hillegas, a free agent.

APRIL 10

Mariners' Jacksonville affiliate signed P Eric Gunderson, a free agent.

APRIL 11

Athletics' Tacoma affiliate signed 2B Jerry Browne, a free agent.

APRIL 12

Angels traded SS Dick Schofield to Mets for P Julio Valera and a player to be named later; Mets sent P Julian Vasquez to Angels to complete deal (October 6).

APRIL 14

Padres signed OF Gary Pettis, a free agent, and traded OF Thomas Howard to Indians for SS Jason Hardtke and a player to be named later; Indians sent C Christopher Maffett to Padres to complete deal (July 10), and Padres assigned him to Spokane of the Northwest League.

APRIL 16

Reds' Nashville affiliate signed P Brian Fisher, a free agent.

APRIL 18

Indians' Colorado Springs affiliate signed 3B Craig Worthington, a free agent.

APRIL 23

Expos reacquired P Miguel Batista from Pirates, who had selected him from Indianapolis in 1991 Rule 5 major league draft.

Royals released P Hector Wagner.

APRIL 24

Royals released P Dera Clark.

APRIL 28

Padres organization signed P Jim Deshaies, a free agent.

Reds' Nashville affiliate signed C Scott Bradley, a free agent.

APRIL 30

Braves released IF-OF Steve Lyons.

MAY 5

Pirates released OF Kirk Gibson.

MAY 7

Expos granted C Gil Reyes free agency.

Mets claimed IF-OF Chico Walker on waivers from Cubs.

MAY 8

Expos signed IF-OF Steve Lyons, a free agent.

MAY 11

Padres traded OF Will Taylor to Mariners for P Gene Harris; Mariners assigned Taylor to Calgary of the Pacific Coast League.

MAY 14

Angels released P Don Robinson.

MAY 19

Indians claimed P Mike Gardella on waivers from Yankees.

MAY 22

Phillies signed P Don Robinson, a free agent.

MAY 25

Brewers traded P Edwin Nunez to Rangers for a player to be named later; Rangers sent P Mark Hampton to Brewers to complete deal (September 15) and Brewers assigned him to Stockton of the California League.

MAY 28

Braves traded P Ben Rivera to Phillies for P Donnie Elliott.

MAY 29

Mariners claimed C Bill Haselman on waivers from Rangers and assigned him to Calgary of the Pacific Coast League; Mariners' Calgary affiliate released IF Mario Diaz.

JUNE 2

Orioles' Rochester affiliate released P Dennis Rasmussen and loaned SS Juan Bell to Rangers' Oklahoma City affiliate.

JUNE 5

Cubs' Iowa affiliate signed P Dennis Rasmussen, a free agent.

JUNE 6

Mariners released P Dave Schmidt.

JUNE 7

Phillies released P Danny Cox, and Phillies organization traded C Ray Stephens to Rangers organization for a player to be named later.

JUNE 8

Expos granted P Scott Service free agency.

Mets released OF Rodney McCray.

Rangers released P Lance McCullers.

JUNE 9

Mets traded P Tim Burke to Yankees for P Lee Guetterman.

Reds' Nashville affiliate signed P Scott Service, a free agent.

JUNE 10

Pirates claimed P Jeff M. Robinson on waivers from Rangers.

Royals released P Curt Young.

JUNE 11

Pirates released P Dennis Lamp.

JUNE 13

Cardinals released P Juan Agosto.

JUNE 15

Indians' Colorado Springs affiliate released P Brad Arnsberg.

JUNE 16

Yankees' Columbus affiliate signed P Curt Young, a free agent.

JUNE 17

Dodgers' Albuquerque affiliate signed P Lance McCullers, a free agent.

JUNE 19

Cubs' Iowa affiliate signed P Brad Arnsberg, a free agent.

Mariners signed P Juan Agosto, a free agent.

Pirates' Buffalo affiliate signed P Danny Cox, a free agent.

Rangers' Oklahoma City affiliate signed IF Mario Diaz, a free agent.

JUNE 21

Padres released OF Gary Pettis.

JUNE 22

Giants released P Kelly Downs.

Orioles signed C Rick Dempsey, a free agent.

JUNE 23

Angels released C Lance Parrish.

JUNE 26

Angels released 1B Alvin Davis.

JUNE 27

Expos sold contract of IF-OF Steve Lyons to Red Sox.

Dodgers traded OF-1B Kal Daniels to Cubs for a player to be named later; Cubs sent P Michael Sodders to Dodgers to complete deal (July 28), and Dodgers assigned him to Bakersfield of the California League.

Reds organization traded P Brian Fisher to Mariners organization for future considerations; deal later settled in cash.

JUNE 28

Mariners signed C Lance Parrish, a free agent.

JUNE 30
Athletics signed P Kelly Downs, a free agent.
JULY 2
Braves granted C Jerry Willard free agency.

Dodgers traded OF Stan Javier to Phillies for P Steve Searcy and a player to be named later; Dodgers assigned Searcy to Albuquerque of the Pacific Coast League. Phillies sent IF Julio Peguero to Dodgers to complete deal (July 28), and Dodgers assigned him to Albuquerque of the Pacific Coast League.
JULY 4
Indians traded OF Alex Cole to Pirates for OF Tony Mitchell and P John Carter.

Tigers' Toledo affiliate signed OF Gary Pettis, a free agent.

White Sox traded P Rich Scheid to Astros for a player to be named later; Astros assigned Scheid to Tucson of the Pacific Coast League. Astros sent OF Eric Yelding to White Sox to complete deal (July 10), and White Sox assigned him to Vancouver of the Pacific Coast League.
JULY 6
Padres traded IF Scott Coolbaugh to Reds for IF Lenny Wentz and assigned Wentz to Charleston (S.C.) of the South Atlantic League.
JULY 7
Cubs traded OF Ced Landrum to Brewers organization for IF Jeff Kunkel; Brewers assigned Landrum to Denver of the American Association.
JULY 8
Athletics granted 1B-OF Dann Howitt free agency.
JULY 9
Reds traded OF Billy Hatcher to Red Sox for P Tom Bolton.

Royals traded C Erik Pappas to White Sox organization for P Jose Ventura.
JULY 10
Mariners' Calgary affiliate signed 1B-OF Dann Howitt, a free agent.

Orioles claimed P Pat Clements on waivers from Padres.
JULY 11
Pirates traded 3B Steve Buechele to Cubs for P Danny Jackson.
JULY 14
Orioles traded P Jose Mesa to Indians for OF Kyle Washington.
JULY 15
Expos' Indianapolis affiliate signed C Jerry Willard, a free agent.
JULY 16
Expos released C Rick Cerone.

Giants granted P Dave Masters free agency.

Phillies released P Don Robinson.
JULY 17
Twins released IF Donnie Hill.
JULY 19
Rangers released OF John Cangelosi.
JULY 21
Cubs released P Dennis Rasmussen.

Mariners released P Jim Acker.

Royals traded P Mark Davis to Braves for P Juan Berenguer.
JULY 25
Pirates released P Jerry Don Gleaton and P Jeff M. Robinson.
JULY 27
Reds traded C Scott Bradley to Mets for a player to be named later; Mets assigned Bradley to Tidewater of the International League. Mets sent P Joe McCann to Reds to complete deal (September 15).

Royals' Omaha affiliate signed P Dennis Rasmussen, a free agent.
JULY 28
Tigers' Toledo affiliate signed OF John Cangelosi, a free agent.
JULY 30
Angels traded P Mark Eichhorn to Blue Jays for OF Rob Ducey and C Greg Myers.

Dodgers released 2B Juan Samuel.

Royals released P Neal Heaton.
JULY 31
Angels released OF Jose Gonzalez.

Orioles released C Rick Dempsey.

Tigers' Toledo affiliate signed P Jeff M. Robinson, a free agent.

Twins released P Bob Kipper.
AUGUST 3
Giants' Phoenix affiliate signed P Jerry Don Gleaton, a free agent.
AUGUST 6
Royals signed 2B Juan Samuel, a free agent.

White Sox claimed C-IF Scott Hemond on waivers from Athletics.
AUGUST 8
Giants traded OF Kevin Bass to Mets for a player to be named later; Mets sent OF Rob Katzaroff to Giants to complete deal (October 1), and Giants assigned him to Phoenix of the Pacific Coast League.

Phillies released P Barry Jones.
AUGUST 9
Astros released OF-1B Benny Distefano.
AUGUST 10
Angels released OF John Morris.

Phillies traded IF Dale Sveum to White Sox for P Keith Shepherd.
AUGUST 11
Athletics released P Gene Nelson.

Rangers' Oklahoma City affiliate returned SS Juan Bell, previously on loan, to Orioles organization.

Phillies traded IF Steve Scarsone to Orioles for SS Juan Bell.
AUGUST 12
Brewers' Denver affiliate signed P Neal Heaton, a free agent.
AUGUST 13
Rangers released P Floyd Bannister.
AUGUST 14
Mets signed P Barry Jones, a free agent.
AUGUST 15
Phillies' Scranton/Wilkes-Barre affiliate signed OF Jose Gonzalez, a free agent.
AUGUST 17
Indians released P Bruce Egloff.
AUGUST 18
Expos claimed P Gil Heredia on waivers from Giants and assigned him to Indianapolis of the American Association.
AUGUST 19
Mariners' Calgary affiliate signed OF-1B Benny Distefano, a free agent.
AUGUST 21
Angels released OF-IF Von Hayes.
AUGUST 22
Yankees released P Shawn Hillegas, and traded P Tim Leary and cash to Mariners for OF Sean Twitty.
AUGUST 27
Mets traded P David Cone to Blue Jays for IF Jeff Kent and a player to be named later; Blue Jays sent OF Ryan Thompson to Mets to complete deal (September 1).

AUGUST 29

Expos traded P Bill Sampen and P Chris Haney to Royals for 3B Sean Berry and P Archie Corbin; Expos assigned Corbin to Harrisburg of the Eastern League.

AUGUST 30

Red Sox traded P Jeff Reardon to Braves for P Nate Minchey and OF Sean Ross; Red Sox assigned Minchey and Ross to Pawtucket of the International League.

AUGUST 31

Athletics traded OF Jose Canseco to Rangers for OF Ruben Sierra, P Jeff Russell, P Bobby Witt and cash; Athletics' Tacoma affiliate signed P Shawn Hillegas, a free agent.

Cardinals released P Jose DeLeon.

Padres traded P Craig Lefferts to Orioles for P Erik Schullstrom and a player to be named later; Orioles sent IF Ricky Gutierrez to Padres to complete deal (September 4), and Padres assigned him to Las Vegas of the Pacific Coast League.

Twins traded P Bill Krueger to Expos for OF Darren Reed.

SEPTEMBER 7

Giants released C Mark Bailey.

SEPTEMBER 8

Cardinals released P John Ericks.

SEPTEMBER 9

Phillies signed P Jose DeLeon, a free agent.

SEPTEMBER 19

Cubs released IF Jeff Kunkel.

SEPTEMBER 21

Mariners claimed OF Lee Tinsley on waivers from Indians.

SEPTEMBER 22

Reds granted P Gino Minutelli free agency.

SEPTEMBER 23

Indians released 3B Craig Worthington.

SEPTEMBER 27

Orioles re-signed C Rick Dempsey, a free agent.

OCTOBER 2

Tigers released SS Victor Rosario.

OCTOBER 5

Astros granted SS Rafael Ramirez, IF Ernest Riles and OF Gerald Young free agency, and released IF-OF Denny Walling.

Braves granted P Randy St. Claire free agency.

Cubs released OF-1B Kal Daniels.

Mariners released OF-1B John Moses, C Matt Sinatro and P Juan Agosto.

Rangers released SS Dickie Thon.

Twins claimed OF Derek Lee on waivers from White Sox.

White Sox granted C Nelson Santovenia free agency.

OCTOBER 6

Expos released IF Tom Foley and C Jerry Willard.

OCTOBER 7

Padres granted OF-1B Oscar Azocar and OF-1B Kevin Ward free agency.

OCTOBER 8

Padres released 1B-OF Phil Stephenson.

Rangers granted OF-1B Jack Daugherty free agency.

Royals granted P Juan Berenguer free agency.

OCTOBER 9

Phillies granted OF Jim Lindeman free agency.

OCTOBER 10

Brewers granted P Mark Lee free agency.

OCTOBER 11

Phillies granted P Darrin Chapin free agency.

OCTOBER 13

Dodgers granted P Tim Crews free agency.

Giants granted P Francisco Oliveras free agency.

OCTOBER 14

Rangers granted P Mike Jeffcoat free agency.

OCTOBER 15

Angels released P Scott Bailes.

Brewers released P Neal Heaton and C Andy Allanson.

Orioles released C Rick Dempsey.

OCTOBER 16

Angels sold contract of IF Bobby Rose to Taiyo Whales of Japan Central League.

OCTOBER 21

Marlins organization signed P Matt Turner, a free agent.

Royals granted OF-2B Juan Samuel free agency and claimed P Kevin Morton on waivers from Red Sox.

OCTOBER 26

Padres traded SS Tony Fernandez to Mets for P Wally Whitehurst, OF D.J. Dozier and a player to be named later; Mets sent C Raul Casanova to Padres to complete deal (December 7).

Rockies signed IF Nelson Liriano, OF Chris Jones, P Dana Ridenour and P Scott Holcomb, all free agents.

Twins claimed C Mike Maksudian on waivers from Blue Jays.

OCTOBER 27

Padres released C Dann Bilardello.

OCTOBER 29

Rockies signed P Mark Knudson, P Jim Neidlinger, OF Patrick Lennon and OF Gerald Young, all free agents.

OCTOBER 30

Brewers signed P Jeff Tabaka, a free agent.

Rockies signed P Balvino Galvez, C Gilberto Reyes and IF Trent Hubbard, all free agents.

NOVEMBER 3

Yankees traded OF Roberto Kelly to Reds for OF Paul O'Neill and 1B Joe DeBerry.

NOVEMBER 6

Cubs released C-1B Hector Villanueva.

Marlins signed C Charles Johnson, a free agent.

Rockies signed OF Jim Olander, P Clint Zavaras and IF Elvin Paulino, all free agents.

Yankees sold contract of P Greg Cadaret to Reds.

NOVEMBER 9

Expos traded P Travis Buckley to Rockies for a player to be named later; Rockies organization sent P Matt Connolly to Expos organization to complete deal (December 8).

Marlins organization signed C Jim McNamara, a free agent.

NOVEMBER 12

Expos claimed P Joseph Ausanio on waivers from Pirates.

Indians re-signed P Eric Plunk, a free agent.

White Sox claimed IF Shawn Gilbert on waivers from Twins.

NOVEMBER 16

Reds organization signed IF Jeff Kunkel, IF Junior Noboa, OF Eric Yelding, OF Steve Carter, OF Keith Hughes, OF Tracy Jones and OF Greg Tubbs, all free agents.

Rockies signed 1B Andres Galarraga, a free agent.

Taiyo Whales of Japan Central League signed OF Glenn Braggs, a free agent, and Lotte Marines of Japan Pacific League signed OF Mel Hall, a free agent.

NOVEMBER 17

Athletics traded SS Walt Weiss to Marlins for C Eric Helfand and a player to be named later; Marlins sent P Scott Baker to A's to complete deal (November 20).

Mariners traded OF Kevin Mitchell to Reds for P Norm Charlton.

Marlins traded P Greg Hibbard to Cubs for 3B Gary Scott and SS Alex Arias; traded P Tom Edens to Astros for P Brian Griffiths and P Hector Carrasco; and traded P Danny Jackson to

Phillies for P Joel Adamson and P Matt Whisenant.

Rockies traded OF Kevin Reimer to Brewers for OF Dante Bichette, and traded 2B Jody Reed to Dodgers for P Rudy Seanez.

NOVEMBER 18

Pirates released P Vince Palacios.

Twins traded OF Darren Reed to Mets for OF Pat Howell.

NOVEMBER 19

Angels released OF Rob Ducey and signed IF Torey Lovullo, a free agent.

Mariners signed P Kevin Coffman, C Brian Deak and OF Mike Felder, all free agents.

Pirates traded 2B Jose Lind to Royals for P Joel Johnston and P Dennis Moeller, and released P Roger Mason.

Rangers re-signed C-OF John Russell, a free agent.

NOVEMBER 20

Braves released IF Jeff Treadway.

Brewers signed P Josias Manzanillo, a free agent.

Expos traded P Dave Wainhouse and P Kevin Foster to Mariners for IF Frank Bolick and a player to be named later; Mariners organization sent C Miah Bradbury to Expos organization to complete deal (December 8). Expos traded P Archie Corbin to Brewers for a player to be named later.

Indians granted IF Brook Jacoby free agency.

Marlins organization signed IF Luis de los Santos, a free agent.

Padres organization signed OF Jarvis Brown and OF Vince Harris, both free agents.

Pirates released P Bob Patterson and signed OF Keith Thomas, a free agent.

Reds released OF Geronimo Berroa and P Tom Bolton and signed P Chris Bushing and P Bo Kennedy, both free agents.

NOVEMBER 23

Orioles re-signed P Rick Sutcliffe, a free agent.

Red Sox claimed OF Cheo Garcia on waivers from Twins.

NOVEMBER 24

Rangers organization signed OF-1B Benny Distefano, a free agent.

NOVEMBER 25

Reds claimed OF Gary Varsho and OF Cecil Espy on waivers from Pirates.

Royals re-signed P Mark Gubicza, a free agent.

NOVEMBER 27

Blue Jays signed IF-OF Darnell Coles, a free agent.

Red Sox re-signed OF Billy Hatcher, a free agent.

NOVEMBER 29

Mariners signed OF Mike Felder, a free agent formerly with Giants.

NOVEMBER 30

Reds signed P John Smiley, a free agent formerly with Twins.

DECEMBER 1

Astros signed P Doug Drabek, a free agent formerly with Pirates.

Cubs signed P Jose Guzman, a free agent formerly with Rangers.

Dodgers re-signed OF Eric Davis, a free agent.

Red Sox signed 2B Scott Fletcher, a free agent formerly with Brewers.

Reds claimed 1B Tommy Gregg on waivers from Braves.

DECEMBER 2

Cubs signed C Steve Lake, a free agent formerly with Phillies.

Marlins organization signed IF Chuck Jackson, IF Gus Polidor and C-1B Mitch Lyden, all free agents.

Mets signed P Roger Mason, a free agent.

Padres organization signed C Bob Geren, a free agent.

Tigers re-signed SS Alan Trammell, a free agent.

Yomiuri Giants of Japan Central League signed OF Jesse Barfield, a free agent.

DECEMBER 3

Mariners signed P Chris Bosio, a free agent formerly with Brewers.

DECEMBER 4

Astros signed P Greg Swindell, a free agent formerly with Reds.

Brewers re-signed P Jesse Orosco, a free agent.

Dodgers re-signed OF Mitch Webster, a free agent.

Reds released OF Mickey Brantley.

Twins re-signed OF Kirby Puckett, a free agent.

Yankees signed SS Spike Owen, a free agent formerly with Expos.

DECEMBER 5

Dodgers re-signed P Roger McDowell, a free agent, and signed OF Cory Snyder, a free agent formerly with Giants.

Twins traded P David West to Phillies for P Mike Hartley.

DECEMBER 6

Angels traded P Jim Abbott to Yankees for 1B J.T. Snow, P Jerry Nielsen and P Russ Springer.

Cardinals re-signed SS Ozzie Smith, a free agent.

Mariners signed P Andy Nezelek, a free agent.

Phillies re-signed OF Dale Murphy and P Ken Howell, both free agents.

DECEMBER 7

Athletics re-signed P Rick Honeycutt and P Goose Gossage, both free agents, and signed P Curt Young, a free agent formerly with Yankees.

Blue Jays organization re-signed OF Joe Carter, a free agent, and signed DH-1B Paul Molitor, a free agent formerly with Brewers.

Cardinals released OF-IF Rex Hudler.

Expos organization signed P Adam Peterson, P Mike Capel, P David Rosario, P Bruce Walton, IF Hector Vargas, OF Lou Frazier and OF Curtis Pride, all free agents.

Mariners organization signed 1B-OF Mike Marshall, a free agent formerly with Nippon Ham Fighters of Japan Pacific League.

Phillies traded P Mike Grimes to Rockies for future considerations.

Rockies organization signed P Bryn Smith, a free agent formerly with Cardinals, and Bruce Ruffin, a free agent formerly with Brewers.

Tigers re-signed 2B Lou Whitaker and P Bill Gullickson, both free agents.

DECEMBER 8

Athletics signed P Storm Davis, a free agent formerly with Orioles.

Blue Jays traded 3B Kelly Gruber and cash to Angels for IF Luis Sojo; signed P Dave Stewart, a free agent formerly with Athletics, and Blue Jays organization signed P Danny Cox, a free agent formerly with Pirates.

Cardinals signed C-1B Hector Villanueva, a free agent.

Cubs signed P Dan Plesac, a free agent formerly with Brewers.

Expos traded OF Ivan Calderon to Red Sox for P Mike Gardiner and P Terry Powers.

Giants signed OF Barry Bonds, a free agent formerly with Pirates.

Indians re-signed C Junior Ortiz, a free agent, and signed P Bob Ojeda, a free agent formerly with Dodgers.

Marlins organization signed P Charlie Hough, a free agent formerly with White Sox, and IF Dave Magadan, a free agent formerly with Mets.

Phillies signed OF Pete Incaviglia, a free agent formerly with Astros, and traded P Graeme Lloyd to Brewers for P John Trisler.

Rangers organization signed P Bob Patterson, P Francisco Oliveras, P Mark Lee and P Willie Smith, all free agents.

Red Sox signed P Scott Bankhead, a free agent formerly with Reds.

Reds organization signed P Tim Burke, a free agent formerly with Yankees.

Royals signed P David Cone, a free agent formerly with Blue Jays, and SS Greg Gagne, a free agent formerly with Twins, and re-signed IF Curtis Wilkerson, a free agent.

White Sox signed P Dave Stieb, a free agent formerly with Blue Jays.

Yankees re-signed P Steve Howe, a free agent.

DECEMBER 9

Athletics re-signed P Kelly Downs, a free agent.

Braves signed P Greg Maddux, a free agent formerly with Cubs, and traded P Charlie Leibrandt and P Pat Gomez to Rangers for 3B Jose Oliva.

Cubs signed P Randy Myers, a free agent formerly with Padres.

Dodgers signed P Todd Worrell, a free agent formerly with Cardinals, and traded P Zak Shinall to Indians for P Alan Walden.

Expos traded P Mark Gardner and P Doug Piatt to Royals for C Tim Spehr and P Jeff Shaw.

Giants signed OF Dave Martinez, a free agent formerly with Reds.

Marlins signed OF Geronimo Berroa, a free agent.

Orioles traded IF Rod Lofton to Reds for P Jason Satre and P Reggie Leslie.

Phillies signed OF Milt Thompson, a free agent formerly with Cardinals.

Red Sox signed OF Andre Dawson, a free agent formerly with Cubs, and traded OF Phil Plantier to Padres for P Jose Melendez.

Tigers signed P Mike Moore, a free agent formerly with Athletics.

Twins signed P Jim Deshaies, a free agent formerly with Padres.

DECEMBER 10

Athletics organization signed OF Gary Pettis, a free agent formerly with Tigers.

Mets signed P Frank Tanana, a free agent formerly with Tigers.

Orioles organization re-signed P Brian DuBois and signed IF Edgar Alfonzo and P Rafael Chaves, all free agents.

Padres traded IF Paul Faries to Giants for P Jim Pena.

Pirates signed P Alejandro Pena, a free agent.

Reds organization re-signed C Troy Afenir and signed C Brian Dorsett, IF Gary Green and P Jeff Kaiser, all free agents.

Royals traded P Carlos Maldonado to Brewers for SS Mike Guerrero, and Royals organization signed C Nelson Santovenia, C Paul Williams, P Keith Brown, P Enrique Burgos, C-IF Russ McGinnis, OF Sil Campusano and OF Mike White, all free agents.

Tigers signed P Tom Bolton, a free agent.

Yankees signed P Jimmy Key, a free agent formerly with Blue Jays.

DECEMBER 11

Angels signed DH Chili Davis, a free agent formerly with Twins.

Cubs signed OF Candy Maldonado, a free agent formerly with Blue Jays.

Orioles signed 2B Harold Reynolds, a free agent formerly with Mariners, and released 2B Bill Ripken, and Orioles organization signed P Dave Miller and IF Tommy Hinzo, both free agents.

Red Sox released P Tony Fossas.

Reds organization signed IF Juan Samuel, a free agent.

Tigers signed P Bill Krueger, a free agent formerly with Expos.

DECEMBER 14

Athletics re-signed C Terry Steinbach, a free agent.

Indians signed P Mike Bielecki, a free agent formerly with Braves.

Orioles organization signed P Jamie Moyer and IF Scott Coolbaugh, both free agents.

Pirates organization signed IF Tom Foley, a free agent.

Red Sox signed C Bob Melvin, a free agent formerly with Royals.

DECEMBER 15

Marlins signed 1B Orestes Destrade, a free agent formerly with Seibu Lions of Japan Pacific League, and Marlins organization signed P Bob McClure, a free agent formerly with Cardinals.

Rangers signed P Tom Henke, a free agent formerly with Blue Jays.

Yankees signed 3B Wade Boggs, a free agent formerly with Red Sox.

DECEMBER 16

Indians organization signed IF Jeff Schaefer, a free agent.

Marlins signed C Benito Santiago, a free agent formerly with Padres.

Padres traded P Terry Bross to Rangers for P Pat Gomez.

Phillies organization signed IF Jeff Manto, a free agent.

Pirates signed P John Candelaria, a free agent formerly with Dodgers.

Reds organization signed P Bill Landrum, a free agent.

DECEMBER 17

Athletics re-signed P Ron Darling, a free agent.

Braves organization signed P Steve Bedrosian, a free agent.

Cubs organization released OF Phil Bradley and P Jerry Kutzler and signed P Jose Bautista, P Jimmy Williams, P Jim Czajkowski, P Blaise Ilsley, P Mike York, C Kelly Mann, C Orlando Mercado, IF Dan Lewis, IF Greg Smith, OF Eduardo Zambrano and OF Roberto Zambrano.

Giants claimed 1B J.R. Phillips on waivers from Angels.

Indians organization signed IF Jeff Treadway, a free agent.

Mets traded P Roger Mason and P Mike Freitas to Padres for P Mike Maddux.

Twins signed DH-OF Dave Winfield, a free agent formerly with Blue Jays.

DECEMBER 18

Angels re-signed 3B Rene Gonzales, a free agent.

Astros claimed 3B Chris Donnels on waivers from Marlins.

Cubs signed OF Willie Wilson, a free agent formerly with Athletics, and signed IF Tommy Shields, a free agent.

Mets signed OF Joe Orsulak, a free agent formerly with Orioles.

Orioles organization signed P Steve Searcy, P Mike Cook, P David Walters, P Wayne Edwards and P Don Schulze, all free agents.

Phillies organization signed P Larry Andersen, a free agent.

Rangers signed OF Rob Ducey, a free agent.

DECEMBER 19

Rangers signed OF Doug Dascenzo, a free agent formerly with Cubs, and SS Manuel Lee, a free agent formerly with Blue Jays.

DECEMBER 21

Athletics re-signed OF Ruben Sierra, a free agent.

Blue Jays signed 1B Craig Stone, a free agent.

Braves organization re-signed P Randy St. Claire, a free agent, and signed C Jerry Willard, a free agent.

Rockies signed OF Daryl Boston, a free agent formerly with Mets.

DECEMBER 22

Athletics re-signed P Kirk Dressendorfer, a free agent.

Chunichi Dragons of Japan Central League signed 3B Brook Jacoby, a free agent formerly with Indians.

Mets organization signed P Tom Filer, P Mauro Gozzo, P Brandy Vann, C Dann Bilardello, C Scott Bradley, C Andy Dziadkowiec, C Javier Gonzalez, IF Steve Springer, OF Wayne Housie and OF Bert Hunter, all free agents.

Padres organization re-signed OF Kevin Ward, a free agent.

DECEMBER 23

Mariners signed C Mackey Sasser, a free agent formerly with Mets.

DECEMBER 24

Athletics re-signed 1B Mark McGwire, a free agent.

Expos traded 3B Tim Wallach to Dodgers for SS Tim Barker.

DECEMBER 28

Mets organization signed OF Eric Bullock, a free agent.

DECEMBER 29

Mariners signed IF Greg Litton, a free agent formerly with Giants.

Twins re-signed 1B-OF Gene Larkin, a free agent.

AWARD WINNERS

THE SPORTING NEWS

AMERICAN LEAGUE

Pitcher of the Year: Dennis Eckersley, Oakland
Rookie Player of the Year: Pat Listach, Milwaukee, SS
Rookie Pitcher of the Year: Cal Eldred, Milwaukee
Fireman of the Year: Dennis Eckersley, Oakland
Manager of the Year: Tony LaRussa, Oakland

NATIONAL LEAGUE

Pitcher of the Year: Greg Maddux, Chicago
Rookie Player of the Year: Eric Karros, Los Angeles, 1B
Rookie Pitcher of the Year: Tim Wakefield, Pittsburgh
Fireman of the Year: Doug Jones, Houston
                        Lee Smith, St. Louis
Manager of the Year: Jim Leyland, Pittsburgh

MAJOR LEAGUE

Player of the Year: Gary Sheffield, San Diego
Executive of the Year: Dan Duquette, Montreal

MINOR LEAGUE

Player of the Year: Tim Salmon, Edmonton, Pacific Coast
Manager of the Year: Grady Little, Greenville, Southern
Executive of the Year: Lou Schwechheimer, Pawtucket, Int'l

BASEBALL WRITERS' ASSOCIATION OF AMERICA

AMERICAN LEAGUE

MOST VALUABLE PLAYER

Player, Team	1	2	3	4	5	6	7	8	9	10	Pts.
Dennis Eckersley, Oakland	15	5	1	5	-	1	-	1	-	-	306
Kirby Puckett, Minnesota	3	4	8	3	2	5	1	1	1	-	209
Joe Carter, Toronto	4	6	3	3	3	2	3	2	-	-	201
Mark McGwire, Oakland	1	-	5	4	3	4	5	4	1	1	155
Dave Winfield, Toronto	2	5	2	4	-	3	-	1	1	4	141
Roberto Alomar, Toronto	3	4	1	3	1	-	-	1	-	2	118
Mike Devereaux, Baltimore	-	1	3	3	2	2	5	3	1	2	109
Frank Thomas, Chicago	-	-	1	3	7	2	4	2	2	1	108
Cecil Fielder, Detroit	-	2	1	-	2	4	-	5	5	-	83
Paul Molitor, Milwaukee	-	-	1	-	4	1	2	3	4	1	63
Carlos Baerga, Cleveland	-	-	-	-	-	1	2	2	3	6	31
Edgar Martinez, Seattle	-	-	-	-	2	1	1	1	2	1	29
Jack Morris, Toronto	-	-	-	-	1	-	2	-	1	2	18
Roger Clemens, Boston	-	-	1	-	-	-	1	-	2	-	16
Brady Anderson, Baltimore	-	-	-	-	-	-	1	2	3	-	16
Juan Gonzalez, Texas	-	1	-	-	-	-	1	-	-	2	15
Ken Griffey, Seattle	-	-	1	-	1	-	-	-	-	-	13
Pat Listach, Milwaukee	-	-	-	-	1	-	-	-	-	2	8
Jack McDowell, Chicago	-	-	-	-	-	1	-	-	-	-	5
George Bell, Chicago	-	-	-	-	-	-	-	-	1	1	3
Mike Bordick, Oakland	-	-	-	-	-	-	-	-	-	2	2
Mike Mussina, Baltimore	-	-	-	-	-	-	-	-	1	-	2
Albert Belle, Cleveland	-	-	-	-	-	-	-	-	-	1	1

Fourteen points awarded for a first-place vote, nine for second and on down to one for 10th.

MANAGER OF THE YEAR

Manager, Team	1	2	3	Pts.
Tony La Russa, Oakland	25	2	1	132
Phil Garner, Milwaukee	2	21	3	76
Johnny Oates, Baltimore	-	4	15	27
Cito Gaston, Toronto	1	1	5	13
Mike Hargrove, Cleveland	-	-	4	4

Five points awarded for a first-place vote, three for second and one for third.

CY YOUNG AWARD

Pitcher, Team	1	2	3	Pts.
Dennis Eckersley, Oakland	19	3	3	107
Jack McDowell, Chicago	2	12	5	51
Roger Clemens, Boston	4	7	7	48
Mike Mussina, Baltimore	2	4	4	26
Jack Morris, Toronto	1	1	2	10
Kevin Brown, Texas	-	1	6	9
Charles Nagy, Cleveland	-	-	1	1

Five points awarded for a first-place vote, three for second and one for third.

ROOKIE OF THE YEAR

Player, Team	1	2	3	Pts.
Pat Listach, Milwaukee	20	7	1	122
Kenny Lofton, Cleveland	7	15	5	85
Dave Fleming, Seattle	-	3	14	23
Cal Eldred, Milwaukee	1	3	8	22

Five points awarded for a first-place vote, three for second and one for third.

MOST VALUABLE PLAYER

Player, Team	1	2	3	4	5	6	7	8	9	10	Pts.
Barry Bonds, Pittsburgh	18	4	2	-	-	-	-	-	-	-	304
Terry Pendleton, Atlanta	4	16	4	-	-	-	-	-	-	-	232
Gary Sheffield, San Diego	2	3	17	1	1	-	-	-	-	-	204
Andy Van Slyke, Pittsburgh	-	1	-	9	9	2	1	1	1	-	145
Larry Walker, Montreal	-	-	-	5	5	5	2	3	1	2	111
Darren Daulton, Philadelphia	-	-	1	2	5	5	1	4	3	1	100
Fred McGriff, San Diego	-	-	-	5	2	5	5	1	2	1	100
Bip Roberts, Cincinnati	-	-	-	2	-	2	6	1	6	1	64
Marquis Grissom, Montreal	-	-	-	-	1	3	3	5	2	2	54
Tom Glavine, Atlanta	-	-	-	-	-	2	2	1	2	18
Greg Maddux, Chicago	-	-	-	-	-	1	1	1	0	2	14
Ryne Sandberg, Chicago	-	-	-	-	-	-	1	2	-	2	12
Barry Larkin, Cincinnati	-	-	-	-	-	-	1	1	2	1	12
Doug Jones, Houston	-	-	-	-	-	-	1	-	1	2	8
John Kruk, Philadelphia	-	-	-	-	-	1	-	1	-	-	8
Mark Grace, Chicago	-	-	-	-	-	-	-	1	1	1	6
Delino DeShields, Montreal	-	-	-	-	1	-	-	-	-	-	6
Ray Lankford, St. Louis	-	-	-	-	-	-	-	-	1	3	5
Jeff Bagwell, Houston	-	-	-	-	-	-	-	1	-	1	4
Dave Hollins, Philadelphia	-	-	-	-	-	-	-	-	1	1	3
Brett Butler, Los Angeles	-	-	-	-	-	-	-	-	1	-	2
Ozzie Smith, St. Louis	-	-	-	-	-	-	-	-	1	-	2
Otis Nixon, Atlanta	-	-	-	-	-	-	-	-	-	1	1
John Wetteland, Montreal	-	-	-	-	-	-	-	-	-	1	1

Fourteen points awarded for a first-place vote, nine for second and on down to one for 10th.

CY YOUNG AWARD

Pitcher, Team	1	2	3	Pts.
Greg Maddux, Chicago	20	4	-	112
Tom Glavine, Atlanta	4	19	1	78
Bob Tewksbury, St. Louis	-	1	19	22
Lee Smith, St. Louis	-	-	3	3
Doug Drabek, Pittsburgh	-	-	1	1

Five points awarded for a first-place vote, three for second and one for third.

ROOKIE OF THE YEAR

Player, Team	1	2	3	Pts.
Eric Karros, Los Angeles	22	2	-	116
Moises Alou, Montreal	-	8	6	30
Tim Wakefield, Pittsburgh	2	4	7	29
Reggie Sanders, Cincinnati	-	7	2	23
Donovan Osborne, St. Louis	-	3	3	12
Mike Perez, St. Louis	-	-	2	2
Ben Rivera, Philadelphia	-	-	1	1
Frank Seminara, San Diego	-	-	1	1
Brian Williams, Houston	-	-	1	1
Mark Wohlers, Atlanta	-	-	1	1

Five points awarded for a first-place vote, three for second and one for third.

MANAGER OF THE YEAR

Manager, Team	1	2	3	Pts.
Jim Leyland, Pittsburgh	20	3	0	109
Felipe Alou, Montreal	3	15	5	65
Bobby Cox, Atlanta	1	4	12	29
Art Howe, Houston	0	1	6	9
Lou Piniella, Cincinnati	0	1	1	4

Five points awarded for a first-place vote, three for second and one for third.

MISCELLANEOUS

ATTENDANCE

AMERICAN LEAGUE

	Home	Road
Baltimore	3,567,819	2,189,075
Boston	2,468,574	2,359,528
California	2,065,444	2,117,538
Chicago	2,681,156	2,218,863
Cleveland	1,224,274	2,223,384
Detroit	1,423,963	2,325,797
Kansas City	1,867,689	2,219,240
Milwaukee	1,857,314	2,172,834
Minnesota	2,482,428	2,274,513
New York	1,748,733	2,411,142
Oakland	2,494,160	2,438,292
Seattle	1,651,398	2,160,309
Texas	2,198,231	2,347,974
Toronto	4,028,318	2,301,012
Totals	**31,759,501**	**31,759,501**

NATIONAL LEAGUE

	Home	Road
Atlanta	3,077,400	2,130,793
Chicago	2,126,720	2,129,595
Cincinnati	2,315,946	2,115,204
Houston	1,211,412	1,946,653
Los Angeles	2,473,266	2,193,934
Montreal	1,669,077	1,792,801
New York	1,779,534	2,120,154
Philadelphia	1,927,448	1,724,270
Pittsburgh	1,829,395	2,067,948
St. Louis	2,418,483	1,885,699
San Diego	1,722,102	1,978,070
San Francisco	1,561,987	2,027,649
Totals	**24,112,770**	**24,112,770**

DEBUTS

Player	Pos.	Team	Birth date	Birthplace	Debut
Alexander, Manuel DeJesus	SS	Baltimore	3-20-71	San Pedro de Macoris, D.R.	9-18
Arias, Alejandro	PR	Chicago N.L.	11-20-67	New York, N.Y.	8-28
Ashley, Billy Manual	PH	Los Angeles	7-11-70	Taylor, Mich.	9-1
Astacio, Pedro Julio	P	Los Angeles	11-28-69	Hato Mayor, D.R.	7-3
Ayala, Robert Joseph	P	Cincinnati	7- 8-69	Ventura, Calif.	9-5
Ayrault, Robert Cunningham	P	Philadelphia	4-27-66	Lake Tahoe, Calif.	6-7
Barton, Shawn Edward	P	Seattle	5-14-63	Los Angeles, Calif.	8-6
Batista, Miguel Jerez	P	Pittsburgh	2-19-71	Santo Domingo, D.R.	4-11
Boone, Bret Robert	2B	Seattle	4- 6-69	El Cajon, Calif.	8-19
Borbon, Pedro Felix	P	Atlanta	11-15-67	Mao, D.R.	10-2
Bottenfield, Kent Dennis	P	Montreal	11-14-68	Portland, Ore.	7-6
Bournigal, Rafael Antonio	SS	Los Angeles	5-12-66	Azua, D.R.	9-1
Branson, Jeffery Glenn	3B	Cincinnati	1-26-67	Waynesboro, Miss.	4-12
Brink, Bradford Albert	P	Philadelphia	1-20-65	Roseville, Calif.	5-17
Brito, Bernardo	PH	Minnesota	12- 4-63	San Cristobal, D.R.	9-15
Brocail, Douglas Keith	P	San Diego	5-16-67	Clearfield, Pa.	9-8
Brogna, Rico Joseph	1B	Detroit	4-18-70	Turner Falls, Mass.	8-8
Bruett, Joseph Timothy	OF	Minnesota	10- 8-67	Milwaukee, Wis.	6-3
Brumfield, Jacob Donnell	PR	Cincinnati	5-27-65	Bogalusa, La.	4-6
Bullinger, James Eric	P	Chicago N.L.	8-21-65	New Orleans, La.	5-27
Butcher, Michael Dana	P	California	5-10-65	Davenport, Ia.	7-6
Carter, Larry Gene	P	San Francisco	5-22-65	Charleston, W.Va.	9-6
Cianfrocco, Angelo Dominic	3B	Montreal	10- 6-66	Rome, N.Y.	4-13
Clark, Phillip Benjamin	DH	Detroit	5- 6-68	Crockett, Tex.	5-27
Colbert, Craig Charles	C	San Francisco	2-13-65	Iowa City, Ia.	4-6
Colbrunn, Gregory Joseph	1B	Montreal	7-26-69	Fontana, Calif.	7-9
Cole, Victor Alexander	P	Pittsburgh	1-23-68	Leningrad, Russia	6-6
Colon, Cristobal	SS	Texas	1- 3-69	LaGuaira, Venezuela	9-18
Cooke, Stephen Montague	P	Pittsburgh	1-14-70	Kanai, Haw.	7-28
Cordero, Wilfredo	SS	Montreal	10- 3-71	Mayaguez, P.R.	7-24
Costo, Timothy Roger	1B	Cincinnati	2-16-69	Melrose Park, Ill.	9-18
Curtis, Chad David	OF	California	11- 6-68	Marion, Ind.	4-8
Diaz, Alexis	PR	Milwaukee	10- 5-68	Brooklyn, N.Y.	7-25
Doherty, John H.	P	Detroit	6-11-67	Bronx, N.Y.	4-8
Dozier, William Henry III	PH	New York N.L.	9-21-65	Norfolk, Va.	5-6
Easley, Jacinto Damion	3B	California	11-11-69	New York, N.Y.	8-13
Embree, Alan Duane	P	Cleveland	1-23-70	Vancouver, Wash.	9-15
Figueroa, Bienvenido	SS	St. Louis	2- 7-64	Santo Domingo, D.R.	5-17
Flaherty, John Timothy	C	Boston	10-21-67	New York, N.Y.	4-12
Fortugno, Timothy Shawn	P	California	4-11-62	Clinton, Mass.	7-20
Fox, Eric Hollis	PR	Oakland	8-15-63	LeMoore, Calif.	7-7
Frye, Jeffrey Dustin	2B	Texas	8-31-66	Oakland, Calif.	7-9
Greene, Willie Louis	3B	Cincinnati	9-23-71	Milledgeville, Ga.	9-1
Groom, Wedsel Gary	P	Detroit	6-10-65	Dallas, Tex.	6-20
Grotewold, Jeffrey Scott	PH	Philadelphia	12- 8-65	Madera, Calif.	4-12
Guerrero, Juan Antonio	PH	Houston	2- 1-67	Los Llanos, D.R.	4-9
Haney, Todd Michael	2B	Montreal	7-30-65	Galveston, Tex.	9-9
Hartsock, Jeffrey Roger	P	Chicago N.L.	11-19-66	Hamilton, O.	9-12
Hathaway, Hillary Houston	P	California	9-12-69	Jacksonville, Fla.	9-8

Player	Pos.	Team	Birth date	Birthplace	Debut
Heffernan, Bertram Alexander	C	Seattle	3- 3-65	Centereach, N.Y.	5-13
Henry, Floyd Bluford III	P	Houston	10- 7-68	El Paso, Tex.	4-9
Hernandez, Cesar Dario Perez	PH	Cincinnati	9-28-66	Yamasa, D.R.	7-19
Hernandez, Jose Miguel	SS	Cleveland	7-24-73	Laguna Salada, D.R.	9-27
Hillman, John Eric	P	New York N.L.	4-27-66	Gary, Ind.	5-18
Hitchcock, Sterling Alex	P	New York A.L.	4-29-71	Fayetteville, N.C.	9-11
Hollins, Jessie Edward	P	Chicago N.L.	1-27-70	Conroe, Tex.	9-19
Hosey, Steven Bernard	PH	San Francisco	4- 2-69	Oakland, Calif.	8-29
Howell, Patrick O'Neal	OF	New York N.L.	8-31-68	Mobile, Ala.	8-4
Hoy, Peter Alexander	P	Boston	6-29-66	Brockville, Ont.	4-11
Hulse, David Lindsey	DH	Texas	2-25-68	San Angelo, Tex.	8-11
Hurst, Jonathan	P	Montreal	10-20-66	New York, N.Y.	6-9
Jaha, John Emile	1B	Milwaukee	5-27-66	Portland, Ore.	7-9
Jeter, Shawn Darrell	OF	Chicago A.L.	6-28-66	Shreveport, La.	6-13
Jordan, Brian O'Neil	OF	St. Louis	3-26-67	Baltimore, Md.	4-8
Kent, Jeffrey Franklin	3B	Toronto	3- 7-68	Bellflower, Calif.	4-12
Klesko, Ryan Anthony	PH	Atlanta	6-12-71	Westminster, Calif.	9-12
Knudsen, Kurt David	P	Detroit	2-20-67	Arlington Heights, Ill.	5-16
Koslofski, Kevin Craig	OF	Kansas City	9-24-66	Decatur, Ill.	6-28
Laker, Timothy John	C	Montreal	11-27-69	Encino, Calif.	8-18
Leon, Danilo Enrique	P	Texas	4- 3-67	La Concepcion, Venezuela	6-6
Levis, Jesse	PH	Cleveland	4-14-68	Philadelphia, Pa.	4-24
Lewis, Richie Todd	P	Baltimore	1-25-66	Muncie, Ind.	7-31
Linton, Douglas Warren	P	Toronto	9- 2-65	Santa Ana, Calif.	8-3
Listach, Patrick Alan	PR	Milwaukee	9-12-67	Natchitoches, La.	4-8
Lopez, Javier Torres	C	Atlanta	11- 5-70	Ponce, P.R.	9-18
Mahomes, Patrick Lavon	P	Minnesota	8- 9-70	Bryan, Tex.	4-12
Maksudian, Michael Bryant	PH	Toronto	5-28-66	Belleville, Ill.	9-2
Marsh, Thomas Owen	PH	Philadelphia	12-27-65	Toledo, O.	6-5
Martin, Albert Lee	PH	Pittsburgh	11-24-67	West Covina, Calif.	7-28
Martinez, Domingo Emelio	1B	Toronto	8- 4-67	Santo Domingo, D.R.	9-11
Martinez, Pedro Jaime	P	Los Angeles	7-25-71	Manoguayabo, D.R.	9-24
Maysey, Matthew Samuel	P	Montreal	1- 8-67	Hamilton, Ont.	7-8
McGinnis, Russell Brent	C	Texas	6-18-63	Coffeyville, Kan.	6-3
McNamara, James Patrick	C	San Francisco	6-10-65	Nashua, N.H.	4-9
Menendez, Anthony	P	Cincinnati	2-20-65	Havana, Cuba	6-22
Mercedes, Henry Felipe Perez	C	Oakland	7-23-69	Santo Domingo, D.R.	4-22
Militello, Sam Salvatore Jr.	P	New York A.L.	11-26-69	Tampa, Fla.	8-9
Millette, Joseph Anthony	SS	Philadelphia	8-12-66	Walnut Creek, Calif.	7-16
Minor, Blas Jr.	P	Pittsburgh	3-20-66	Merced, Calif.	7-28
Mlicki, David John	P	Cleveland	6- 8-68	Cleveland, O.	9-12
Moeller, Dennis Michael	P	Kansas City	9-15-67	Tarzana, Calif.	7-28
Natal, Robert Marcilino	PH	Montreal	11-13-65	Long Beach, Calif.	7-18
Neel, Troy Lee	OF	Oakland	9-14-65	Freeport, Tex.	5-30
Nelson, Jeffrey Allen	P	Seattle	11-17-66	Baltimore, Md.	4-16
Nied, David Glen	P	Atlanta	12-22-68	Dallas, Tex.	9-1
Nielsen, Gerald Arthur	P	New York A.L.	8- 5-66	Sacramento, Calif.	7-12
Nieves, Melvin Ramos	PH	Atlanta	12-28-71	San Juan, P.R.	9-1
Nilsson, David Wayne	C	Milwaukee	12-14-69	Queensland, Australia	5-18
Osborne, Donovan Alan	P	St. Louis	6-21-69	Roseville, Calif.	4-9
Parks, Derek Gavin	C	Minnesota	9-29-68	Covina, Calif.	9-11
Patterson, John Allen	2B	San Francisco	2-11-60	Key West, Fla.	4-6
Pavlik, Roger Allen	P	Texas	10- 4-67	Houston, Tex.	5-2
Peguero, Julio Cesar	OF	Philadelphia	9- 7-68	San Isidro, D.R.	4-8
Peltier, Daniel Edward	OF	Texas	6-30-68	Clifton Park, N.Y.	6-26
Pena, James Patrick	P	San Francisco	9-17-64	Los Angeles, Calif.	7-7
Pennyfeather, William Nathaniel	OF	Pittsburgh	5-25-68	Perth Amboy, N.J.	6-27
Piazza, Michael Joseph	C	Los Angeles	9- 4-68	Norristown, Pa.	9-1
Pichardo, Hipolito	P	Kansas City	8-22-69	Jicome Esperanza, D.R.	4-21
Pierce, Edward John	P	Kansas City	10- 6-68	Arcadia, Calif.	9-6
Pratt, Todd Alan	C	Philadelphia	2- 9-67	Bellevue, Neb.	7-29
Pugh, Timothy Dean	P	Cincinnati	1-26-67	Lake Tahoe, Calif.	9-1
Quantrill, Paul John	P	Boston	11- 3-68	London, Ont.	7-20
Raczka, Michael	P	Oakland	11-16-62	New Britain, Conn.	9-4
Ramsey, Fernando	PR	Chicago N.L.	12-20-65	Rainbow, Pan.	9-7
Rapp, Patrick Leland	P	San Francisco	7-13-67	Jennings, La.	7-10
Reboulet, Jeffrey Allen	DH	Minnesota	4-30-64	Dayton, O.	5-12
Reed, Steven Vincent	P	San Francisco	3-11-66	Los Angeles, Calif.	8-30
Revenig, Todd Michael	P	Oakland	6-28-69	Brainerd, Minn.	8-24
Reynolds, Richard Shane	P	Houston	3-26-68	Bastrop, La.	7-20
Risley, William Charles	P	Montreal	5-29-67	Chicago, Ill.	7-8
Rivera, Bienvenido Santana	P	Atlanta	1-11-69	San Pedro de Macoris, D.R.	4-9
Rodriguez, Henry Anderson	OF	Los Angeles	11- 8-67	Santo Domingo, D.R.	7-5
Rogers, Charles Kevin	P	San Francisco	8-20-68	Cleveland, Miss.	9-4
Ryan, Kenneth Frederick Jr.	P	Boston	10-24-68	Pawtucket, R.I.	8-31
Salmon, Timothy James	OF	California	8-24-68	Long Beach, Calif.	8-21
Scarsone, Steven	2B	Philadelphia	4-11-66	Anaheim, Calif.	5-15

Player	Pos.	Team	Birth date	Birthplace	Debut
Scheid, Richard Paul	P	Houston	2- 3-65	Staten Island, N.Y.	9-11
Seminara, Frank Peter	P	San Diego	5-16-67	Brooklyn, N.Y.	6-2
Shepherd, Keith Wayne	P	Philadelphia	1-21-68	Wabash, Ind.	9-6
Shields, Thomas Charles	PR	Baltimore	8-14-64	Fairfax, Va.	7-25
Shifflett, Stephen Earl	P	Kansas City	1- 5-66	Kansas City, Mo.	7-3
Silvestri, David Joseph	SS	New York A.L.	9-29-67	St. Louis, Mo.	4-27
Smith, Daniel Scott	P	Texas	8-20-69	St. Paul, Minn.	9-12
Snow, Jack Thomas Jr.	1B	New York A.L.	2-26-68	Long Beach, Calif.	9-20
Springer, Russell Paul	P	New York A.L.	11- 7-68	Alexandria, La.	4-17
Stairs, Matthew Wade	PH	Montreal	2-27-69	St. John, N.B., Can.	5-29
Stankiewicz, Andrew Neal	2B	New York A.L.	8-10-64	Inglewood, Calif.	4-11
Suero, William Urban	2B	Milwaukee	11- 7-66	Santo Domingo, D.R.	4-9
Tatum, James Ray Jr.	3B	Milwaukee	10- 9-67	Grossmont, Calif.	9-18
Taylor, Rodney Scott	P	Boston	8- 2-67	Defiance, O.	9-17
Thompson, Ryan Orlando	OF	New York N.L.	11- 4-67	Chestertown, Md.	9-1
Trlicek, Richard Alan	P	Toronto	4-26-69	Houston, Tex.	4-8
Trombley, Michael Scott	P	Minnesota	4-14-67	Springfield, Mass.	8-19
Tucker, Eddie Jack	C	Houston	11-18-66	Greenville, Miss.	6-14
Valentin, John William	SS	Boston	2-18-67	Mineola, N.Y.	7-27
Valentin, Jose Antonio	PR	Milwaukee	10-12-69	Manati, P.R.	9-17
Velasquez, Guillermo	PH	San Diego	4-23-68	Mexicali, Mex.	9-14
Vitko, Joseph John III	P	New York N.L.	2- 7-70	Somerville, N.J.	9-18
Voigt, John David	PR	Baltimore	5-17-66	Sarasota, Fla.	8-3
Wagner, Paul Alan	P	Pittsburgh	11-14-67	Milwaukee, Wis.	7-26
Wakefield, Timothy Stephen	P	Pittsburgh	8- 2-66	Melbourne, Fla.	7-31
Walker, Michael Aaron	P	Seattle	6-23-65	Houston, Tex.	6-16
Walters, Daniel Gene	C	San Diego	8-15-66	Brunswick, Me.	6-1
Whiteside, Matthew Christopher	P	Texas	8- 8-67	Sikeston, Mo.	8-5
Wickman, Robert Joe	P	New York A.L.	2- 6-61	Green Bay, Wis.	8-24
Williams, Gerald Floyd	PR	New York A.L.	8-10-66	New Orleans, La.	9-15
Williams, Michael Darren	P	Philadelphia	7-29-69	Radford, Va.	6-30
Williams, Reginald Bernard	OF	California	5- 5-66	Laurens, S.C.	9-8
Wilson, Daniel Allen	C	Cincinnati	3-25-69	Arlington Heights, Ill.	9-7
Woodson, Walter Browne IV	P	Seattle	5-18-69	Jacksonville, Fla.	7-19
Young, Bryan Owen	P	Montreal	3-19-68	Meadville, Miss.	8-7
Young, Eric Orlando	2B	Los Angeles	5-18-67	New Brunswick, N.J.	7-30
Young, Kevin Stacey	1B	Pittsburgh	6-16-69	Alpena, Mich.	7-12

SALARY ARBITRATION RESULTS

WINNERS

Player, Team	Salary awarded	Team's offer
Ruben Sierra, Texas	$5,000,000	$3,800,000
David Cone, New York Mets	$4,250,000	$3,000,000
Rafael Palmeiro, Texas	$3,850,000	$2,350,000
Benito Santiago, San Diego	$3,300,000	$2,500,000
Jose Lind, Pittsburgh	$2,000,000	$1,000,000
Jay Buhner, Seattle	$1,445,000	$750,000
Kevin Brown, Texas	$1,200,000	$750,000
Bob Milacki, Baltimore	$1,180,000	$700,000
Ken Patterson, Chicago White Sox	$640,000	$400,000

LOSERS

Player, Team	Salary awarded	Player's request
Greg Swindell, Cincinnati	$3,675,000	$2,500,000
Luis Polonia, California	$2,450,000	$1,650,000
Jack McDowell, Chicago White Sox	$2,300,000	$1,600,000
Jody Reed, Boston	$2,250,000	$1,600,000
Glenn Braggs, Cincinnati	$1,340,000	$1,000,000
Jay Bell, Pittsburgh	$1,450,000	$875,000
Kevin Elster, New York Mets	$1,350,000	$760,000
Kenny Rogers, Texas	$975,000	$620,000
Dale Sveum, Philadelphia	$720,000	$375,000
Jeff Innis, New York Mets	$650,000	$355,000
Dann Bilardello, San Diego	$235,000	$125,000

1992 FREE-AGENT FILINGS

AMERICAN LEAGUE

Baltimore: Pat Clements, Storm Davis, Mike Flanagan, Craig Lefferts, Joe Orsulak, Rick Sutcliffe.
Boston: Wade Boggs, Tom Brunansky, Billy Hatcher, Steve Lyons, Herm Winningham.
California: Bert Blyleven, Hubie Brooks, Mike Fitzgerald, Rene Gonzales, Ken Oberkfell.
Chicago: Charlie Hough, Dale Sveum.
Cleveland: Brook Jacoby, Junior Ortiz, Eric Plunk.
Detroit: Dave Bergman, Bill Gullickson, Eric King, Gary Pettis, Frank Tanana, Walt Terrell, Alan Trammell, Lou Whitaker.
Kansas City: Jim Eisenreich, Mark Gubicza, Bob Melvin, Curtis Wilkerson.
Milwaukee: Chris Bosio, Scott Fletcher, Jim Gantner, Paul Molitor, Jesse Orosco, Dan Plesac, Bruce Ruffin, Kevin

Seitzer, Robin Yount.
Minnesota: Randy Bush, Chili Davis, Greg Gagne, Mike Pagliarulo, Kirby Puckett, John Smiley.
New York: Jesse Barfield, Tim Burke, Mel Hall, Steve Howe, Pascual Perez, Scott Sanderson, Curt Young.
Oakland: Harold Baines, Ron Darling, Kelly Downs, Rich Gossage, Rick Honeycutt, Mark McGwire, Mark Moore, Jamie Quirk, Randy Ready, Jeff Russell, Ruben Sierra, Terry Steinbach, Dave Stewart, Willie Wilson.
Seattle: Henry Cotto, Mark Grant, Lance Parrish, Harold Reynolds.
Texas: Brian Downing, Jose Guzman, Al Newman, Edwin Nunez, John Russell.
Toronto: Joe Carter, David Cone, Mark Eichhorn, Alfredo Griffin, Tom Henke, Jimmy Key, Manuel Lee, Candy Maldonado, Rance Mulliniks, Dave Stieb, Pat Tabler, Dave Winfield.

NATIONAL LEAGUE

Atlanta: Mike Bielecki, Alejandro Pena, Jeff Reardon, Lonnie Smith.
Chicago: Andre Dawson, Greg Maddux, Jeff D. Robinson, Luis Salazar, Dave Smith.
Cincinnati: Scott Bankhead, Glenn Braggs, Darnell Coles, Dave Martinez, Jeff Reed, Greg Swindell.
Houston: Pete Incaviglia, Rob Murphy.
Los Angeles: Dave Anderson, John Candelaria, Eric Davis, Jay Howell, Roger McDowell, Bob Ojeda, Mike Scioscia, Mitch Webster.
Montreal: Gary Carter, Bill Krueger, Spike Owen.

New York: Kevin Bass, Daryl Boston, Lee Guetterman, Barry Jones, Dave Magadan, Willie Randolph, Dick Schofield.
Philadelphia: Wally Backman, Ken Howell, Stan Javier, Steve Lake, Dale Murphy.
Pittsburgh: Barry Bonds, Danny Cox, Doug Drabek, Gary Redus.
St. Louis: Frank DiPino, Andres Galarraga, Rich Gedman, Pedro Guerrero, Bob McClure, Bryn Smith, Ozzie Smith, Scott Terry, Milt Thompson, Todd Worrell.
San Diego: Larry Andersen, Jim Deshaies, Randy Myers, Benito Santiago.
San Francisco: Mike Felder, Scott Garrelts, Chris James, Cory Snyder, Jose Uribe.

EXPANSION DRAFT OF NOVEMBER 17, 1992

COLORADO ROCKIES

FIRST ROUND

Pick	Name, Position, Former team
1.	David Nied, RHP, Atlanta
2.	Charlie Hayes, 3B, New York Yankees
3.	Darren Holmes, RHP, Milwaukee
4.	Jerald Clark, OF, San Diego
5.	Kevin Reimer, OF/DH, Texas
6.	Eric Young, 2B, Los Angeles
7.	Jody Reed, 2B, Boston
8.	Scott Aldred, LHP, Detroit
9.	Alex Cole, OF, Pittsburgh
10.	Joe Girardi, C, Chicago Cubs
11.	Willie Blair, RHP, Houston
12.	Jay Owens, C, Minnesota
13.	Andy Ashby, RHP, Philadelphia

SECOND ROUND

14.	Fred Benavides, SS, Cincinnati
15.	Roberto Mejia, 2B, Los Angeles
16.	Doug Bochtler, RHP, Montreal
17.	Lance Painter, LHP, San Diego
18.	Butch Henry, LHP, Houston
19.	Ryan Hawblitzel, RHP, Chicago Cubs
20.	Vinny Castilla, SS, Atlanta
21.	Brett Merriman, RHP, California
22.	Jim Tatum, 3B, Milwaukee
23.	Kevin Ritz, RHP, Detroit
24.	Eric Wedge, C/1B, Boston
25.	Keith Shepherd, RHP, Philadelphia
26.	Calvin Jones, RHP, Seattle

THIRD ROUND

27.	Brad Ausmus, C, New York Yankees
28.	Marcus Moore, RHP, Toronto
29.	Armando Reynoso, RHP, Atlanta
30.	Steve Reed, RHP, San Francisco
31.	Mo Sanford, RHP, Cincinnati
32.	Pedro Castellano, 3B, Chicago Cubs
33.	Curtis Leskanic, RHP, Minnesota
34.	Scott Fredrickson, RHP, San Diego
35.	Braulio Castillo, OF, Philadelphia
36.	Denis Boucher, LHP, Cleveland

FLORIDA MARLINS

FIRST ROUND

Pick	Player, Position, Former team
1.	Nigel Wilson, OF, Toronto
2.	Jose Martinez, RHP, New York Mets
3.	Bret Barberie, SS, Montreal
4.	Trevor Hoffman, RHP, Cincinnati
5.	Pat Rapp, RHP, San Francisco
6.	Greg Hibbard, LHP, Chicago White Sox
7.	Chuck Carr, OF, St. Louis
8.	Darrell Whitmore, OF, Cleveland
9.	Eric Helfand, C, Oakland
10.	Bryan Harvey, RHP, California
11.	Jeff Conine, 1B/OF, Kansas City
12.	Kip Yaughn, RHP, Baltimore
13.	Jesus Tavarez, OF, Seattle

SECOND ROUND

14.	Carl Everett, OF, New York Yankees
15.	David Weathers, RHP, Toronto
16.	John Johnstone, RHP, New York Mets
17.	Ramon Martinez, SS, Pittsburgh
18.	Steve Decker, C, San Francisco
19.	Cris Carpenter, RHP, St. Louis
20.	Jack Armstrong, RHP, Cleveland
21.	Scott Chiamparino, RHP, Texas
22.	Tom Edens, RHP, Minnesota
23.	Andres Berumen, RHP, Kansas City
24.	Robert Person, RHP, Chicago White Sox
25.	Jim Corsi, RHP, Oakland
26.	Richie Lewis, RHP, Baltimore

THIRD ROUND

27.	Danny Jackson, LHP, Pittsburgh
28.	Rob Natal, C, Montreal
29.	Jamie McAndrew, RHP, Los Angeles
30.	Junior Felix, OF, California
31.	Kerwin Moore, OF, Kansas City
32.	Ryan Bowen, RHP, Houston
33.	Scott Baker, LHP, St. Louis
34.	Chris Donnels, 3B, New York Mets
35.	Monty Fariss, OF, Texas
36.	Jeff Tabaka, LHP, Milwaukee

MAJOR LEAGUE DRAFT

(Listed in order of selection)

Player	Pos.	Drafted by	Drafted from (major league organization)
Dera Clark	P	Los Angeles	Omaha, American Association (Royals)
Reggie Harris	P	Seattle	Tacoma, Pacific Coast League (Athletics)
Graeme Lloyd	P	Philadelphia	Syracuse, International League (Blue Jays)
Jim McNamara	C	San Francisco	Edmonton, Pacific Coast League (Marlins)
Billy Brewer	P	Kansas City	Indianapolis, American Association (Expos)
Mike Draper	P	New York N.L.	Columbus, International League (Yankees)
John Hudek	P	Detroit	Vancouver, Pacific Coast League (White Sox)
Kerry Taylor	P	San Diego	Portland, Pacific Coast League (Twins)

Player	Pos.	Drafted by	Drafted from (major league organization)
William Canate	OF	Cincinnati	Colorado Springs, Pacific Coast League (Indians)
Sherman Obando	OF	Baltimore	Columbus, International League (Yankees)
Mike Bell	1B	Pittsburgh	Richmond, International League (Braves)
Larry Stanford	P	Milwaukee	Columbus, International League (Yankees)
Kirt Ojala	P	Oakland	Columbus, International League (Yankees)
William Taylor	P	Toronto	Richmond, International League (Braves)
Stan Spencer	P	Florida	Indianapolis, American Association (Expos)
Fernando Vina	SS	Seattle	Tidewater, International League (Mets)
Michael Myers	P	Florida	Phoenix, Pacific Coast League (Giants)

NECROLOGY

Sandy Amoros, 62, at Miami, on June 27. A seven-year major leaguer, he made a sensational catch in Game 7 of the 1955 World Series against the Yankees that helped Brooklyn nail down its only Series championship. With the Dodgers guarding a 2-0 lead and two Yankees on base in the sixth inning, Amoros raced to the left-field line and snared a slicing drive off the bat of Yogi Berra. Two relay throws doubled up a runner off first base, thwarting the Yanks' threat.

Red Barber, 84, at Tallahassee, Fla., on October 22. Barber, a member of the broadcasters' wing of baseball's Hall of Fame, was known for his folksy and insightful radio play-by-play calls of major league games featuring the Cincinnati Reds, Brooklyn Dodgers and New York Yankees.

Carl Barger, 62, at Louisville, Ky., on December 9. President of the Pirates from October 1987 to July 1991, Barger was president of the expansion Florida Marlins at the time of his death.

Boze Berger, 82, at Bethesda, Md., on November 3. A light-hitting infielder, he played 343 games overall for three American League teams in the 1930s.

Lonnie Blair, 62, at Baldwin, Pa., on January 27. A Negro leagues player in 1949 and 1950, Blair pitched and played second base for the Homestead Grays.

Joe Burke, 68, at Kansas City, Kan., on May 12. Burke had been president of the Royals since 1981 and was an executive of the American League club since 1973.

Elio Chacon, 55, at Caracas, Venezuela, on April 24. Chacon was a key backup player for the 1961 National League champion Reds. In 1962, the infielder appeared in 118 games for the original Mets.

Harlond Clift, 79, at Yakima, Wash., on April 27. One of the top players in St. Louis Browns history, Clift scored more than 100 runs in each of his first five big-league seasons and put together back-to-back seasons of 29 home runs/118 runs batted in (1937) and 34 homers/118 RBIs (1938).

Chuck Connors, 71, at Los Angeles on November 10. Connors, a first baseman who appeared in 66 games for the 1951 Cubs, gained his greatest fame after his baseball career when he starred in "The Rifleman" television series.

Pat Creeden, 85, at Brockton, Mass., on April 20. Infielder Creeden's big-league career consisted of five games with the Red Sox in 1931.

Vern Curtis, 72, at Cairo, Ill., on June 24. This righthander pitched in 16 games overall for the Senators in 1943, 1944 and 1946.

Ron Davis, 50, at Houston on September 5. Davis saw outfield duty with three major league clubs—the Astros, Cardinals and Pirates. He started two games for the Cards in the 1968 World Series.

Otto Denning, 79, at Chicago on May 25. A catcher/first baseman, Denning played a total of 129 games for the Indians in 1942 and 1943. He batted .222.

Atley Donald, 82, at West Monroe, La., on October 19. Donald equaled the modern big-league record for consecutive victories by a rookie pitcher, winning 12 straight decisions in 1939 en route to a 13-3 mark for the Yankees. In eight seasons with the Yanks, Donald fashioned a 65-33 record.

Elmer (Red) Durrett, 70, at Waxahachie, Tex., on January 17. Outfielder Durrett played a total of 19 games for the Brooklyn Dodgers in 1944 and 1945.

Joe Dwyer, 88, at Glen Ridge, N.J., on October 21. Dwyer had 11 at-bats as a pinch-hitter for the 1937 Reds and collected three hits.

Sherman Edwards, 82, at El Dorado, Ark., on March 8. Edwards pitched in one big-league game—for the Reds, in relief, in 1934.

Fabian Gaffke, 78, at Milwaukee on February 8. This outfielder batted .227 in a six-season major league career. In 1937, he hit six home runs and drove in 34 runs while getting 184 at-bats for the Red Sox.

Charlie Gassaway, 73, at Miami on January 15. Gassaway won five of 14 decisions while appearing in a total of 39 games for the Cubs, Athletics and Indians from 1944 through 1946.

Bernice Gera, 61, at Pembroke Pines, Fla., on September 23. Gera, who for years battled the baseball establishment in her bid to umpire professionally, finally won her case in 1972 but wound up calling only one game, in Class A.

Andy Gilbert, 78, at Davis, Calif., on August 29. Gilbert played in only eight big-league games—as an outfielder for the Red Sox in the 1940s—before becoming a longtime minor league manager. From 1972 through 1975, he was a coach with the Giants.

George Giles, 82, at Manhattan, Kan., on March 3. Giles was a standout first baseman in the Negro leagues in the late 1920s and 1930s.

Tom Gorman, 67, at New York on December 26. This right-handed reliever appeared in both the 1952 and 1953 World Series for the Yankees. In eight big-league seasons with the Yanks and Athletics, he compiled a 36-36 record.

Orval Grove, 72, at Sacramento, Calif., on April 20. Grove pitched in at least one game for the White Sox in each season of the 1940s, with his 15-9 record in '43 proving his best performance.

Dick Hahn, 76, at Orlando, Fla., on November 5. Hahn, a catcher, played in one major league game, for the Senators, in 1940.

Bob (Hurricane) Hazle, 61, at Columbia, S.C., on April 25. Called up in late July 1957 from Class AAA Wichita, where he was batting a modest .279, outfielder Hazle hit at a .403 clip over 41 games for Milwaukee and helped the Braves to the National League pennant.

Billy Herman, 83, at West Palm Beach Fla., on September 5. The Hall of Fame second baseman collected 2,345 hits and batted .304 over 15 major league seasons, primarily with the Cubs and Dodgers. In 10 All-Star Games, he hit .433.

Bill Humphrey, 80, at Springfield, Mo., on February 13. Righthander Humphrey appeared in two games for the 1938 Red Sox.

David H. Jacobs, 71, at Westlake, O., on September 17. Jacobs was co-owner of the Indians. He and his brother, Richard E. Jacobs, bought the club in December 1986.

Deron Johnson, 53, at Poway, Calif., on April 23. Johnson slammed 245 homers in 16 big-league seasons, including 32 for the Reds in 1965 and 34 for the Phillies in 1971. He led the N.L. in RBIs in '65 with 130.

Orville Jorgens, 83, at Colorado Springs, Colo., on January 11. Jorgens compiled a 21-22 record while pitching for the Phillies in 1935, 1936 and 1937.

Glenn Liebhardt, 81, at Winston-Salem, N.C., on March 14. The son of a former big-league pitcher, Liebhardt was roughed up in a total of 31 bullpen appearances over three major league seasons in the 1930s. His career earned-run average was 8.96.

Eddie Lopat, 73, at Darien, Conn., on June 15. Lopat, a master at changing speeds, won 166 games in a 12-year major league career. In one five-year stretch with the Yankees, Lopat fashioned a 77-30 record (.720). He was a member of the starting rotation for Yankee teams that won five consecutive pennants and World Series from 1949 through 1953.

Aurelio Lopez, 44, in an automobile accident in central Mexico on September 22. Lopez made 71 relief appearances for the 1984 World Series champion Tigers, winning 10 of 11 regular-season decisions and going 1-0 in both the '84 A.L. playoffs and the World Series. He was 62-36 overall in 11 major league seasons.

Sam Lowry, 72, at Philadelphia on December 1. Lowry pitched in a total of six games for the 1942 and 1943 Athletics.

Sal Maglie, 75, at Niagara Falls, N.Y., on Dec. 28. Maglie, a big-game pitcher known as the "The Barber" for his strategy of pitching hitters tight (and thereby giving them close shaves), fashioned a winning percentage of .657 in his 10-season major league career with the Giants, Indians, Dodgers, Yankees and Cardinals. From 1950 through 1952, he compiled a 59-18 record for the Giants.

Jim Marquis, 91, at Jackson, Calif., on August 5. Marquis appeared twice in relief for the 1925 Yankees.

Walt Masters, 85, at Ottawa, Ont., on July 10. Masters was a relief pitcher for the Senators, Phillies and Athletics in three brief stints in the 1930s. He failed to gain a decision in eight appearances.

George Meyer, 82, at Hoffman Estates, Ill., on January 3. Second baseman Meyer batted .296 in 24 games for the 1938 White Sox.

Randy Moore, 86, at Mount Pleasant, Tex., on June 12. Moore, an outfielder/first baseman, batted .278 over 10 major league seasons. His best year was 1933, when he hit .302 with 70 RBIs for the Boston Braves.

Louis Nippert, 89, at Cincinnati on November 16. Nippert was owner of the Reds when the National League club won World Series championships in 1975 and 1976.

John O'Connell, 88, at Canton, O., on October 17. Catcher O'Connell appeared in a total of three games for the 1928 and 1929 Pirates.

Arthur (Red) Patterson, 83, at Fullerton, Calif., on February 10. A longtime public relations director in the major leagues, Patterson is credited with introducing the term "tape-measure homer" to baseball's lexicon by pacing off a monstrous smash (565 feet) by Mickey Mantle in 1953.

John Ostrowski, 75, at Chicago on November 13. A member of the Cubs, Red Sox, White Sox and Senators, this outfielder/third baseman played seven seasons in the majors, ending in 1950, and hit .232 in 215 games.

Salty Parker, 79, at Houston on July 27. Infielder Parker played briefly for the Tigers in 1936 and later saw longtime duty as a minor league manager and big-league coach.

Babe Phelps, 84, at Odenton, Md., on December 10. Phelps, a catcher, batted .310 in 726 major league games. He spent most of his career with the Dodgers, for whom he batted .367 in 115 games in 1936.

Earl Rapp, 70, at Swedesboro, N.J., on February 13. Outfielder Rapp divided each of his three major league seasons between two teams. In 1949, he played for the Tigers and White Sox; in 1951, he was a member of the Giants and Browns; in 1952, he was with the Browns and Senators. Overall, he batted .262 in 135 games.

Len Rice, 73, at Sonora, Calif., on June 13. Rice, a catcher, played 42 games in the majors—10 for the 1944 Reds and 32 for the 1945 Cubs.

Lou Rochelli, 73, at Victoria, Tex., on October 23. Infielder Rochelli played briefly for Brooklyn in 1944 and later became a manager in the Dodgers' farm system.

Larry Rosenthal, 79, at Woodbury, Minn., on March 4. An outfielder for the White Sox, Indians, Yankees and Athletics, he batted .263 in a big-league career that began in 1936, ended in 1945 and covered 579 games.

Allan Roth, 74, at Los Angeles on March 3. Roth became the first full-time statistician hired by a big-league team when he joined the Dodgers in the late 1940s. Roth moved with the Dodgers a decade later when the franchise relocated to Los Angeles, and he eventually did statistical work for network baseball telecasts.

Chuck Rowland, 92, at Raleigh, N.C., on January 21. Catcher Rowland appeared in five games for the 1923 Athletics.

Celerino Sanchez, 48, at Leon, Guanajuato, Mexico, on May 1. Sanchez, an infielder, played a total of 105 games for the Yankees in 1972 and 1973 and batted .242.

Karl Schnell, 92, at Palo Alto, Calif., on May 31. Schnell made a total of 11 relief appearances for the Reds in 1922 and 1923.

Rod Scurry, 36, at Reno, Nev., on November 5. Scurry pitched in 332 games, 325 of them in relief, during a major league career that started in 1980 with the Pirates and concluded in 1988 with the Mariners. He was 19-32 overall, with 39 saves.

Tom Seats, 80, at San Ramon, Calif., on May 10. Active for two major league seasons, Seats went 2-2 for the Tigers in 1940 and put together a 10-7 record for the Dodgers in 1945.

Wally Shannon, 58, at Creve Coeur, Mo., on February 8. Shannon, son of longtime Cardinals farm director Walter Shannon, was an infielder who appeared in a total of 65 games for the Cards in 1959 and 1960.

Ken Silvestri, 75, at Tallahassee, Fla., on March 31. He was a backup catcher for the 1941 World Series-winning Yankees and the 1950 N.L. champion Phillies and a former big-league coach.

C.C. Johnson Spink, 75, at St. Louis on March 26. The last of the family that founded The Sporting News in 1886, Spink was publisher of the St. Louis-based sports weekly from 1962 to 1981. His father, J.G. Taylor Spink, preceded him as publisher, serving from 1914 to 1962.

Tuck Stainback, 82, at Camarillo, Calif., on November 29. A starting outfielder for the Yankees in all five games of the 1943 World Series, Stainback played for seven teams and batted .259 in a big-league career that began in 1934 and ended in 1946.

George Staller, 76, at Harrisburg, Pa., on July 3. Staller was an Orioles coach for nine seasons in the 1960s and 1970s. His big-league career consisted of 21 games for the 1943 Athletics, for whom the outfielder hit .271.

Buck Stanton, 85, at San Antonio, Tex., on January 1. Stanton saw action in 13 games, mostly as a pinch-hitter, for the 1931 Browns.

Justin Stein, 80, at Creve Coeur, Mo., on May 1. Stein, an infielder, played a total of 22 games in 1938 for the Phillies and Reds.

Eddie Taylor, 90, at San Diego on January 30. Taylor, a longtime major league scout, was an infielder who played 92 games for the Braves in 1926.

Coaker Triplett, 80, at Boone, N.C., on January 30. A standout minor league hitter, Triplett batted .256 in 470 big-league games. The outfielder broke into the majors with the Cubs in 1938 and later played for the Cardinals and Phillies.

Chris Van Cuyk, 65, at Hudson, Fla., on November 3. He posted a 7-11 record while pitching for the Dodgers from 1950 through 1952.

Al (Rube) Walker, 66, at Morganton, N.C., on December 12. A longtime backup catcher and coach in the major leagues, he was catching for Brooklyn on October 3, 1951, when the New York Giants' Bobby Thomson hit his pennant-winning home run against the Dodgers.

Stan Wasiak, 72, at Mobile, Ala., on November 20. Wasiak won 2,570 minor league games, an all-time high, while managing a record 37 consecutive seasons (1950 through 1986).

Ralph Weigel, 70, at Memphis, Tenn., on April 15. A late-1940s catcher with the Indians, White Sox and Senators, Weigel batted .230 in 106 major league games.

Claude Wilborn, 80, at Roxboro, N.C., on November 13. Outfielder Wilborn appeared in five games for the 1940 Braves.

Dib Williams, 82, at Searcy, Ark., on April 2. A major league infielder for six seasons, Williams batted .320 for the Athletics in the 1931 World Series.

Jean R. Yawkey, 83, at Boston on February 26. Majority owner of the Boston Red Sox, she was the widow of Thomas A. Yawkey, who purchased the Red Sox franchise in 1933.

1992
A.L. STATISTICS

BATTING

TEAM

Team	Avg.	G	AB	R	H	TB	2B	3B	HR	RBI	SH	SF	HP	BB	Int. BB	SO	SB	CS	GI DP	LOB	ShO	Slg.	OBP
Minnesota	.277	162	5582	747	1544	2185	275	27	104	701	46	59	53	527	53	834	123	74	130	1183	8	.391	.341
Milwaukee	.268	162	5504	740	1477	2065	272	35	82	683	61	72	33	511	45	779	256	115	102	1101	5	.375	.330
Cleveland	.266	162	5620	674	1495	2151	227	24	127	637	42	44	45	448	46	885	144	67	140	1105	11	.383	.323
Seattle	.263	162	5564	679	1466	2239	278	24	149	638	52	51	38	474	47	841	100	55	148	1120	14	.402	.323
Toronto	.263	162	5536	780	1458	2292	265	40	163	737	26	54	47	561	41	933	129	39	123	1159	10	.414	.333
New York	.261	162	5593	733	1462	2268	281	18	163	703	26	55	42	536	51	903	78	37	138	1157	8	.406	.328
Chicago	.261	162	5498	738	1434	2105	269	36	110	686	47	69	31	622	48	784	160	57	134	1174	11	.383	.336
Baltimore	.259	162	5485	705	1423	2182	243	36	148	680	50	59	51	647	55	827	89	48	139	1218	6	.398	.340
Oakland	.258	162	5387	745	1389	2082	219	24	142	693	72	59	49	707	46	831	143	59	139	1225	8	.386	.346
Kansas City	.256	162	5501	610	1411	2004	284	42	75	568	45	46	51	439	30	741	131	71	121	1106	13	.364	.315
Detroit	.256	162	5515	791	1411	2245	256	16	182	746	43	53	24	675	42	1055	66	45	124	1188	9	.407	.337
Texas	.250	162	5537	682	1387	2176	266	23	159	646	56	45	50	550	36	1036	81	44	115	1172	14	.393	.321
Boston	.246	162	5461	599	1343	1896	259	21	84	567	60	43	31	591	46	865	44	48	118	1215	11	.347	.321
California	.243	162	5364	579	1306	1812	202	20	88	537	56	40	40	416	40	882	160	101	137	975	15	.338	.301
Totals	.259	1134	77147	9802	2006	29702	3596	386	1776	9222	682	749	585	7704	626	12196	1704	860	1808	16098	141	.385	.328

INDIVIDUAL

TOP 15 QUALIFIERS FOR BATTING CHAMPIONSHIP

Minimum 502 plate appearances.   *Lefthanded batter.   †Switch-hitter.

Player, Team	Avg.	G	AB	R	H	TB	2B	3B	HR	RBI	SH	SF	HP	BB	Int. BB	SO	SB	CS	GI DP	Slg.	OBP
Martinez, Edgar, Seattle	.343	135	528	100	181	287	46	3	18	73	1	5	4	54	2	61	14	4	15	.544	.404
Puckett, Kirby, Minnesota	.329	160	639	104	210	313	38	4	19	110	1	6	6	44	13	97	17	7	17	.490	.374
Thomas, Frank, Chicago	.323	160	573	108	185	307	46	2	24	115	0	11	5	122	6	88	6	3	19	.536	.439
Molitor, Paul, Milwaukee	.320	158	609	89	195	281	36	7	12	89	4	11	3	73	12	66	31	6	13	.461	.389
Mack, Shane, Minnesota	.315	156	600	101	189	280	31	6	16	75	11	2	15	64	1	106	26	14	8	.467	.394
Baerga, Carlos, Cleveland†	.312	161	657	92	205	299	32	1	20	105	2	9	13	35	10	76	10	2	15	.455	.354
Alomar, Roberto, Toronto†	.310	152	571	105	177	244	27	8	8	76	6	2	5	87	5	52	49	9	8	.427	.405
Griffey, Ken, Seattle*	.308	142	565	83	174	302	39	4	27	103	0	3	5	44	15	67	10	5	15	.535	.361
Harper, Brian, Minnesota	.307	140	502	58	154	206	25	0	9	73	1	10	7	26	7	22	0	1	15	.410	.343
Bordick, Mike, Oakland	.300	154	504	62	151	187	19	4	3	48	14	5	9	40	2	59	12	6	10	.371	.358
Hamilton, Darryl, Milwaukee*	.298	128	470	67	140	188	19	7	5	62	4	7	1	45	0	42	41	14	10	.400	.356
Knoblauch, Chuck, Minnesota	.297	155	600	104	178	215	19	6	2	56	2	12	5	88	1	60	34	13	8	.358	.384
Raines, Tim, Chicago†	.294	144	551	102	162	223	22	9	7	54	4	8	0	81	4	48	45	6	5	.405	.380
Vizquel, Omar, Seattle†	.294	136	483	49	142	170	20	4	0	21	9	1	2	32	0	38	15	13	14	.352	.340
Listach, Pat, Milwaukee†	.290	149	579	93	168	202	19	6	1	47	12	2	1	55	0	124	54	18	3	.349	.352

DEPARTMENTAL LEADERS: G—C. Ripken, Bal., 162; AB—Fryman, Det., 659; R—Phillips, Det., 114; H—Puckett, Min., 210; TB—Puckett, Min., 313; 1B—Baerga, Cle., 152; 2B—E. Martinez, Sea., Thomas, Chi., 46; 3B—Johnson, Chi., 12; HR—Gonzalez, Tex., 43; RBI—Fielder, Det., 124; SH—Browne, Oak., 16; SF—Carter, Tor., 13; HP—Macfarlane, K.C., Mack, Min., 15; BB—Tettleton, Det., Thomas, Chi., 122; IBB—Boggs, Bos., 19; SO—Palmer, Tex., 154; SB—Lofton, Cle., 66; CS—Polonia, Cal., 21; GIDP—Bell, Chi., 29; Slg. Pct.—McGwire, Oak., .585; OB. Pct.—Thomas, Chi., .439.

ALL PLAYERS

*Lefthanded batter.   †Switch-hitter.

Player, Team	Avg.	G	AB	R	H	TB	2B	3B	HR	RBI	SH	SF	HP	BB	Int. BB	SO	SB	CS	GI DP	Slg.	OBP
Abner, Shawn, Chicago	.279	97	208	21	58	73	10	1	1	16	2	3	3	12	2	35	1	2	3	.351	.323
Alexander, Manny, Baltimore	.200	4	5	1	1	1	0	0	0	0	0	0	0	0	0	3	0	0	0	.200	.200
Allanson, Andy, Milwaukee	.320	9	25	6	8	9	1	0	0	2	0	0	1	0	2	3	1	1	.360	.346
Alomar, Roberto, Toronto†	.310	152	571	105	177	244	27	8	8	76	6	2	5	87	5	52	49	9	8	.427	.405
Alomar, Sandy, Cleveland	.251	89	299	22	75	97	16	0	2	26	3	0	5	13	3	32	3	3	7	.324	.293
Amaral, Rich, Seattle	.240	35	100	9	24	30	3	0	1	7	4	0	0	5	0	16	4	2	4	.300	.276
Anderson, Brady, Baltimore*	.271	159	623	100	169	280	28	10	21	80	10	9	9	98	14	98	53	16	2	.449	.373
Baerga, Carlos, Cleveland†	.312	161	657	92	205	299	32	1	20	105	2	9	13	35	10	76	10	2	15	.455	.354
Baines, Harold, Oakland*	.253	140	478	58	121	187	18	0	16	76	0	6	0	59	6	61	1	3	11	.391	.331
Barfield, Jesse, New York	.137	30	95	8	13	21	2	0	2	7	0	1	0	9	2	27	1	1	5	.221	.210
Barnes, Skeeter, Detroit	.273	95	165	27	45	64	6	1	3	25	2	2	2	10	1	18	3	1	4	.388	.318
Barrett, Tommy, Boston†	.000	4	3	1	0	0	0	0	0	0	1	0	0	2	0	0	0	0	0	.000	.400
Bell, Derek, Toronto	.242	61	161	23	39	57	6	3	2	15	2	1	5	15	1	34	7	2	6	.354	.324
Bell, George, Chicago	.255	155	627	74	160	262	27	0	25	112	0	6	6	31	8	97	5	2	29	.418	.294
Belle, Albert, Cleveland	.260	153	585	81	152	279	23	1	34	112	1	8	4	52	5	128	8	2	18	.477	.320
Beltre, Esteban, Chicago	.191	49	110	21	21	26	2	0	1	10	2	1	4	3	0	18	1	0	3	.236	.211
Bergman, Dave, Detroit*	.232	87	181	17	42	48	3	0	1	10	1	2	0	20	1	19	1	0	4	.265	.305
Bichette, Dante, Milwaukee	.287	112	387	37	111	157	27	2	5	41	2	3	3	16	3	74	18	7	13	.406	.318
Blankenship, Lance, Oakland	.241	123	349	59	84	119	24	1	3	34	8	1	6	82	2	57	21	7	10	.341	.393
Blowers, Mike, Seattle	.192	31	73	7	14	20	3	0	1	2	1	0	0	6	0	20	0	0	3	.274	.253
Boggs, Wade, Boston*	.259	143	514	62	133	184	22	4	7	50	0	6	4	74	19	31	1	3	10	.358	.353
Boone, Bret, Seattle	.194	33	129	15	25	41	4	0	4	15	1	0	1	4	0	34	1	1	4	.318	.224
Borders, Pat, Toronto	.242	138	480	47	116	185	26	2	13	53	1	5	2	33	3	75	1	1	11	.385	.290
Bordick, Mike, Oakland	.300	154	504	62	151	187	19	4	3	48	14	5	9	40	2	59	12	6	10	.371	.358
Bradley, Scott, Seattle*	.000	2	1	0	0	0	0	0	0	0	0	0	0	1	0	1	0	0	0	.000	.500
Brett, George, Kansas City*	.285	152	592	55	169	235	35	5	7	61	0	4	6	35	6	69	8	6	15	.397	.330
Briley, Greg, Seattle*	.275	86	200	18	55	80	10	0	5	12	0	2	1	4	0	31	9	2	4	.400	.290
Brito, Bernardo, Minnesota	.143	8	14	1	2	3	1	0	0	2	0	0	0	0	0	4	0	1	0	.214	.133

Player, Team	Avg.	G	AB	R	H	TB	2B	3B	HR	RBI	SH	SF	HP	BB	Int. BB	SO	SB	CS	GI DP	Slg.	OBP
Brogna, Rico, Detroit*	.192	9	26	3	5	9	1	0	1	3	0	0	0	3	0	5	0	0	0	.346	.276
Brooks, Hubie, California	.216	82	306	28	66	103	13	0	8	36	0	1	1	12	3	46	3	3	10	.337	.247
Brosius, Scott, Oakland	.218	38	87	13	19	33	2	0	4	13	0	1	2	3	1	13	3	0	0	.379	.258
Brown, Jarvis, Minnesota	.067	35	15	8	1	1	0	0	0	0	0	0	1	2	0	4	2	2	0	.067	.222
Browne, Jerry, Oakland†	.287	111	324	43	93	118	12	2	3	40	16	6	4	40	0	40	3	3	7	.364	.366
Bruett, J.T., Minnesota*	.250	56	76	7	19	23	4	0	0	2	1	0	1	6	1	12	6	3	0	.303	.313
Brumley, Mike, Boston†	.000	2	1	0	0	0	0	0	0	0	0	0	0	0	0	0	0	0	0	.000	.000
Brunansky, Tom, Boston	.266	138	458	47	122	204	31	3	15	74	2	7	0	66	2	96	2	5	11	.445	.354
Buhner, Jay, Seattle	.243	152	543	69	132	229	16	3	25	79	1	8	6	71	2	146	0	6	12	.422	.333
Burks, Ellis, Boston	.255	66	235	35	60	98	8	3	8	30	0	2	1	25	2	48	5	2	5	.417	.327
Bush, Randy, Minnesota*	.214	100	182	14	39	55	8	1	2	22	0	3	2	11	3	37	1	1	5	.302	.263
Cangelosi, John, Texas†	.188	73	85	12	16	21	2	0	1	6	3	0	0	18	0	16	6	5	0	.247	.330
Canseco, Jose, Oak.-Tex.	.244	119	439	74	107	200	15	0	26	87	0	4	6	63	2	128	6	7	16	.456	.344
Carreon, Mark, Detroit	.232	101	336	34	78	121	11	1	10	41	1	4	1	22	2	57	3	1	12	.360	.278
Carter, Joe, Toronto	.264	158	622	97	164	310	30	7	34	119	1	13	11	36	4	109	12	5	14	.498	.309
Clark, Jack, Boston	.210	81	257	32	54	80	11	0	5	33	0	5	2	56	3	87	1	1	4	.311	.350
Clark, Phil, Detroit	.407	23	54	3	22	29	4	0	1	5	1	0	0	6	1	9	1	0	2	.537	.467
Cochrane, Dave, Seattle†	.250	65	152	10	38	49	5	0	2	12	2	0	1	12	0	34	1	0	3	.322	.309
Cole, Alex, Cleveland*	.206	41	97	11	20	21	1	0	0	5	0	1	1	10	0	21	9	2	2	.216	.284
Colon, Cris, Texas†	.167	14	36	5	6	6	0	0	0	1	1	0	0	1	0	8	0	0	2	.167	.189
Conine, Jeff, Kansas City	.253	28	91	10	23	32	5	2	0	9	0	0	0	8	1	23	0	0	1	.352	.313
Cooper, Scott, Boston*	.276	123	337	34	93	129	21	0	5	33	2	2	0	37	0	33	1	1	5	.383	.346
Cora, Joey, Chicago†	.246	68	122	27	30	39	7	1	0	9	2	3	4	22	1	13	10	3	2	.320	.371
Cotto, Henry, Seattle	.259	108	294	42	76	104	11	1	5	27	3	1	1	14	3	49	23	2	2	.354	.294
Cron, Chris, Chicago	.000	6	10	0	0	0	0	0	0	0	0	0	0	0	0	6	0	0	0	.000	.000
Curtis, Chad, California	.259	139	441	59	114	164	16	2	10	46	5	4	6	51	2	71	43	18	10	.372	.341
Cuyler, Milt, Detroit†	.241	89	291	39	70	92	11	1	3	28	8	0	4	10	0	62	8	5	4	.316	.275
Daugherty, Jack, Texas†	.205	59	127	13	26	35	9	0	0	9	0	2	1	16	1	21	2	1	3	.276	.295
Davis, Alvin, California*	.250	40	104	5	26	34	8	0	0	16	0	1	0	13	2	9	0	0	2	.327	.331
Davis, Chili, Minnesota†	.288	138	444	63	128	195	27	2	12	66	0	9	3	73	11	76	4	5	11	.439	.386
Davis, Doug, Texas	1.000	1	1	0	1	1	0	0	0	0	0	0	0	0	0	0	0	0	0	1.000	1.000
Davis, Glenn, Baltimore	.276	106	398	46	110	168	15	2	13	48	1	4	2	37	2	65	1	0	12	.422	.338
Deer, Rob, Detroit	.247	110	393	66	97	215	20	1	32	64	0	1	3	51	1	131	4	2	8	.547	.337
Dempsey, Rick, Baltimore	.111	8	9	2	1	1	0	0	0	1	0	0	0	2	0	1	0	0	1	.111	.273
Devereaux, Mike, Baltimore	.276	156	653	76	180	303	29	11	24	107	0	9	4	44	1	94	10	8	14	.464	.321
Diaz, Alex, Milwaukee†	.111	22	9	5	1	1	0	0	0	1	0	0	0	0	0	3	2	0	0	.111	.111
Diaz, Mario, Texas	.226	19	31	2	7	8	1	0	0	1	1	0	0	1	1	2	0	1	2	.258	.250
DiSarcina, Gary, California	.247	157	518	48	128	156	19	0	3	42	5	3	7	20	0	50	9	7	15	.301	.283
Downing, Brian, Texas	.278	107	320	53	89	137	18	0	10	39	0	1	8	62	2	58	1	0	7	.428	.407
Ducey, Rob, Tor.-Cal.*	.188	54	80	7	15	19	4	0	0	2	0	1	0	5	0	22	2	4	1	.238	.233
Easley, Damion, California	.258	47	151	14	39	47	5	0	1	12	2	1	3	8	0	26	9	5	2	.311	.307
Eisenreich, Jim, Kansas City*	.269	113	353	31	95	120	13	3	2	28	0	3	0	24	4	36	11	6	6	.340	.313
Fariss, Monty, Texas	.217	67	166	13	36	54	7	1	3	21	2	0	2	17	0	51	0	2	3	.325	.297
Felix, Junior, California†	.246	139	509	63	125	184	22	5	9	72	5	9	2	33	5	128	8	8	9	.361	.289
Fermin, Felix, Cleveland	.270	79	215	27	58	69	7	2	0	13	9	2	1	18	1	10	0	0	7	.321	.326
Fielder, Cecil, Detroit	.244	155	594	80	145	272	22	0	35	124	0	7	2	73	8	151	0	0	14	.458	.325
Fisk, Carlton, Chicago	.229	62	188	12	43	58	4	1	3	21	0	2	1	23	5	38	3	0	2	.309	.313
Fitzgerald, Mike, California	.212	95	189	19	40	60	2	0	6	17	3	0	0	22	0	34	2	2	4	.317	.294
Flaherty, John, Boston	.197	35	66	3	13	15	2	0	0	2	1	1	0	3	0	7	0	0	2	.227	.229
Fletcher, Scott, Milwaukee	.275	123	386	53	106	139	18	3	3	51	6	4	7	30	1	33	17	10	4	.360	.335
Fox, Eric, Oakland†	.238	51	143	24	34	52	5	2	3	13	6	1	0	13	0	29	3	4	1	.364	.299
Franco, Julio, Texas	.234	35	107	19	25	38	7	0	2	8	1	0	0	15	2	17	1	1	3	.355	.328
Frye, Jeff, Texas	.256	67	199	24	51	65	9	1	1	12	11	1	3	16	0	27	1	3	2	.327	.320
Fryman, Travis, Detroit	.266	161	659	87	175	274	31	4	20	96	5	6	6	45	1	144	8	4	13	.416	.316
Gaetti, Gary, California	.226	130	456	41	103	156	13	2	12	48	0	3	6	21	4	79	3	1	9	.342	.267
Gagne, Greg, Minnesota	.246	146	439	53	108	152	23	0	7	39	12	1	2	19	0	83	6	7	11	.346	.280
Gallego, Mike, New York	.254	53	173	24	44	62	7	1	3	14	3	1	4	20	0	22	0	1	5	.358	.343
Gantner, Jim, Milwaukee*	.246	101	256	22	63	80	12	1	1	18	3	2	0	12	2	17	6	2	9	.313	.278
Gladden, Dan, Detroit	.254	113	417	57	106	149	20	1	7	42	5	5	2	30	0	64	4	2	10	.357	.304
Gomez, Leo, Baltimore	.265	137	468	62	124	199	24	0	17	64	5	8	8	63	4	78	2	3	14	.425	.356
Gonzales, Rene, California	.277	104	329	47	91	131	17	1	7	38	5	1	4	41	1	46	7	4	17	.398	.363
Gonzalez, Jose, California	.182	33	55	4	10	12	2	0	0	2	1	1	0	7	1	20	0	1	2	.218	.270
Gonzalez, Juan, Texas	.260	155	584	77	152	309	24	2	43	109	0	8	5	35	1	143	0	1	16	.529	.304
Grebeck, Craig, Chicago	.268	88	287	24	77	111	21	2	3	35	10	3	3	30	0	34	0	3	5	.387	.341
Greenwell, Mike, Boston*	.233	49	180	16	42	50	2	0	2	18	0	2	2	18	1	19	2	3	8	.278	.307
Griffey, Ken, Seattle*	.308	142	565	83	174	302	39	4	27	103	0	3	5	44	15	67	10	5	15	.535	.361
Griffin, Alfredo, Toronto†	.233	63	150	21	35	42	7	0	0	10	3	2	0	9	0	19	3	1	3	.280	.273
Gruber, Kelly, Toronto	.229	120	446	42	102	157	16	3	11	43	1	4	4	26	3	72	7	7	14	.352	.275
Guillen, Ozzie, Chicago*	.200	12	40	5	8	12	4	0	0	7	1	1	0	1	0	5	1	0	1	.300	.214
Gwynn, Chris, Kansas City*	.286	34	84	10	24	34	3	2	1	7	1	2	0	3	0	10	0	0	1	.405	.303
Hall, Mel, New York*	.280	152	583	67	163	250	36	3	15	81	0	9	1	29	4	53	4	2	13	.429	.310
Hamilton, Darryl, Milwaukee*	.298	128	470	67	140	188	19	7	5	62	4	7	1	45	0	42	41	14	10	.400	.356
Hare, Shawn, Detroit*	.115	15	26	0	3	4	1	0	0	5	0	1	0	2	0	4	0	0	0	.154	.172
Harper, Brian, Minnesota	.307	140	502	58	154	206	25	0	9	73	1	10	7	26	7	22	0	1	15	.410	.343
Harris, Donald, Texas	.182	24	33	3	6	7	1	0	0	1	0	0	0	0	0	15	1	0	0	.212	.182
Haselman, Bill, Seattle	.263	8	19	1	5	5	0	0	0	0	0	0	0	0	0	7	0	0	1	.263	.263
Hatcher, Billy, Boston	.238	75	315	34	75	98	16	2	1	23	6	1	3	17	1	41	4	6	9	.311	.283
Hayes, Charlie, New York	.257	142	509	52	131	208	19	2	18	66	3	6	3	28	0	100	3	5	12	.409	.297
Hayes, Von, California*	.225	94	307	35	69	100	17	1	4	29	3	3	0	37	4	54	11	6	9	.326	.305
Heffernan, Bert, Seattle*	.091	8	11	0	1	2	1	0	0	1	0	0	0	1	0	2	0	0	0	.182	.091
Hemond, Scott, Oak.-Chi.	.225	25	40	8	9	11	2	0	0	2	0	0	0	4	0	13	1	0	2	.275	.289
Henderson, Dave, Oakland	.143	20	63	1	9	10	1	0	0	2	0	0	0	2	0	16	0	0	0	.159	.169
Henderson, Rickey, Oakland	.283	117	396	77	112	181	18	3	15	46	0	3	6	95	5	56	48	11	5	.457	.426
Hernandez, Jose, Cleveland	.000	3	4	0	0	0	0	0	0	0	0	0	0	0	0	2	0	0	0	.000	.000
Hill, Donnie, Minnesota†	.294	25	51	7	15	18	3	0	0	2	2	0	1	5	0	6	0	0	3	.353	.368
Hill, Glenallen, Cleveland	.241	102	369	38	89	161	16	1	18	49	0	1	4	20	0	73	9	6	11	.436	.287
Hoiles, Chris, Baltimore	.274	96	310	49	85	157	10	1	20	40	1	3	2	55	2	60	0	2	8	.506	.384

— 235 —

Player, Team	Avg.	G	AB	R	H	TB	2B	3B	HR	RBI	SH	SF	HP	BB	Int. BB	SO	SB	CS	GI DP	Slg.	OBP
Horn, Sam, Baltimore*	.235	63	162	13	38	65	10	1	5	19	0	1	1	21	2	60	0	0	8	.401	.324
Howard, David, Kansas City†	.224	74	219	19	49	62	6	2	1	18	8	2	0	15	0	43	3	4	3	.283	.271
Howard, Thomas, Cleveland†	.277	117	358	36	99	124	15	2	2	32	10	2	0	17	1	60	15	8	4	.346	.308
Howitt, Dann, Oak.-Sea.*	.188	35	85	7	16	28	4	1	2	10	1	3	0	8	1	9	1	1	6	.329	.250
Hrbek, Kent, Minnesota*	.244	112	394	52	96	161	20	0	15	58	2	3	0	71	9	56	5	2	12	.409	.357
Huff, Mike, Chicago	.209	60	115	13	24	29	5	0	0	8	2	2	1	10	1	24	1	2	2	.252	.273
Hulett, Tim, Baltimore	.289	57	142	11	41	58	7	2	2	21	0	1	1	10	1	31	0	1	7	.408	.340
Hulse, David, Texas*	.304	32	92	14	28	32	4	0	0	2	2	0	0	3	0	18	3	1	0	.348	.326
Humphreys, Mike, New York*	.100	4	10	0	1	1	0	0	0	0	0	0	0	0	0	1	0	0	2	.100	.100
Huson, Jeff, Texas*	.261	123	318	49	83	115	14	3	4	24	8	6	1	41	2	43	18	6	7	.362	.342
Jacoby, Brook, Cleveland	.261	120	291	30	76	95	7	0	4	36	3	4	1	28	2	54	0	3	13	.326	.324
Jaha, John, Milwaukee	.226	47	133	17	30	41	3	1	2	10	1	4	2	12	1	30	10	0	1	.308	.291
James, Dion, New York*	.262	67	145	24	38	55	8	0	3	17	0	2	1	22	0	15	1	0	3	.379	.359
Jefferies, Gregg, Kansas City*	.285	152	604	66	172	244	36	3	10	75	0	9	1	43	4	29	19	9	24	.404	.329
Jefferson, Reggie, Cleveland†	.337	24	89	8	30	43	6	2	1	6	0	0	1	1	0	17	0	0	2	.483	.352
Jeter, Shawn, Chicago*	.111	13	18	1	2	2	0	0	0	0	0	0	0	0	0	7	0	0	0	.111	.111
Johnson, Lance, Chicago*	.279	157	567	67	158	206	15	12	3	47	4	5	1	34	4	33	41	14	20	.363	.318
Jorgensen, Terry, Minnesota	.310	22	58	5	18	19	1	0	0	5	0	1	1	3	0	11	1	2	4	.328	.349
Joyner, Wally, Kansas City*	.269	149	572	66	154	221	36	2	9	66	0	2	4	55	4	50	11	5	19	.386	.336
Karkovice, Ron, Chicago	.237	123	342	39	81	134	12	1	13	50	4	2	3	30	1	89	10	4	3	.392	.302
Kelly, Pat, New York	.226	106	318	38	72	119	22	2	7	27	6	3	10	25	1	72	8	5	6	.374	.301
Kelly, Roberto, New York	.272	152	580	81	158	223	31	2	10	66	1	6	4	41	4	96	28	5	19	.384	.322
Kent, Jeff, Toronto	.240	65	192	36	46	85	13	1	8	35	0	4	6	20	0	47	2	1	3	.443	.324
Kingery, Mike, Oakland*	.107	12	28	3	3	3	0	0	0	1	0	0	1	1	0	3	0	0	1	.107	.138
Kirby, Wayne, Cleveland*	.167	21	18	9	3	7	1	0	1	0	0	0	0	3	0	2	0	3	1	.389	.286
Knoblauch, Chuck, Minnesota	.297	155	600	104	178	215	19	6	2	56	2	12	5	88	1	60	34	13	6	.358	.384
Knorr, Randy, Toronto	.263	8	19	1	5	8	0	0	1	2	0	0	0	1	1	5	0	0	1	.421	.300
Koslofski, Kevin, Kansas City*	.248	55	133	20	33	46	0	2	3	13	3	1	1	12	0	23	2	1	2	.346	.313
Kreuter, Chad, Detroit*	.253	67	190	22	48	63	9	0	2	16	3	2	0	20	1	38	0	1	8	.332	.321
Langston, Mark, California	.000	33	2	1	0	0	0	0	0	0	0	0	0	0	0	2	0	0	0	.000	.000
Lansford, Carney, Oakland	.262	135	496	65	130	183	30	1	7	75	7	8	7	43	0	39	7	2	14	.369	.325
Larkin, Gene, Minnesota†	.246	115	337	38	83	121	18	1	6	42	0	4	4	28	6	43	7	2	7	.359	.308
Lee, Manuel, Toronto†	.263	128	396	49	104	125	10	1	3	39	8	3	0	50	0	73	6	2	8	.316	.343
Leius, Scott, Minnesota	.249	129	409	50	102	130	18	2	2	35	5	0	1	34	0	61	6	5	10	.318	.309
Lennon, Pat, Seattle	.000	1	2	0	0	0	0	0	0	0	0	0	0	0	0	0	0	0	0	.000	.000
Levis, Jesse, Cleveland*	.279	28	43	2	12	19	4	0	1	3	0	0	0	0	0	5	0	0	1	.442	.279
Lewis, Mark, Cleveland	.264	122	413	44	109	145	21	0	5	30	1	4	3	25	1	69	4	5	12	.351	.308
Leyritz, Jim, New York	.257	63	144	17	37	64	6	0	7	26	0	3	6	14	1	22	0	1	2	.444	.341
Listach, Pat, Milwaukee†	.290	149	579	93	168	202	19	6	1	47	12	2	1	55	4	124	54	18	3	.349	.352
Livingstone, Scott, Detroit*	.282	117	354	43	100	133	21	0	4	46	3	4	0	21	1	36	1	3	8	.376	.319
Lofton, Kenny, Cleveland*	.285	148	576	96	164	210	15	8	5	42	4	1	2	68	3	54	66	12	7	.365	.362
Lyons, Steve, Boston*	.250	21	28	3	7	9	0	1	0	2	0	0	0	2	0	1	0	1	0	.321	.300
Maas, Kevin, New York*	.248	98	286	35	71	116	12	0	11	35	0	4	0	25	4	63	3	1	1	.406	.305
Macfarlane, Mike, Kansas City	.234	129	402	51	94	179	28	3	17	48	1	2	15	30	2	89	1	5	8	.445	.310
Mack, Shane, Minnesota	.315	156	600	101	189	280	31	6	16	75	11	2	15	64	1	106	26	14	8	.467	.394
Maksudian, Mike, Toronto*	.000	3	3	0	0	0	0	0	0	0	0	0	0	0	0	0	0	0	0	.000	.000
Maldonado, Candy, Toronto	.272	137	489	64	133	226	25	4	20	66	2	3	7	59	3	112	2	2	13	.462	.357
Martinez, Carlos, Cleveland	.263	69	228	23	60	86	9	1	5	35	1	4	1	7	0	21	1	2	5	.377	.283
Martinez, Chito, Baltimore*	.268	83	198	26	53	80	10	1	5	25	0	4	2	31	4	47	0	1	9	.404	.366
Martinez, Domingo, Toronto	.625	7	8	2	5	8	0	0	1	3	0	0	0	0	1	0	0	0	1	1.000	.625
Martinez, Edgar, Seattle	.343	135	528	100	181	287	46	3	18	73	1	5	4	54	2	61	14	4	15	.544	.404
Martinez, Tino, Seattle*	.257	136	460	53	118	189	19	2	16	66	1	8	2	42	9	77	2	1	24	.411	.316
Marzano, John, Boston	.080	19	50	4	4	8	2	1	0	1	1	0	1	2	0	12	0	0	1	.160	.132
Mattingly, Don, New York*	.288	157	640	89	184	266	40	0	14	86	0	6	1	39	7	43	3	0	11	.416	.327
Maurer, Rob, Texas*	.222	8	9	1	2	2	0	0	0	1	0	0	0	1	0	2	0	0	0	.222	.300
Mayne, Brent, Kansas City*	.225	82	213	16	48	58	10	0	0	18	2	3	0	11	0	26	0	4	5	.272	.260
McGinnis, Russ, Texas	.242	14	33	2	8	12	4	0	0	4	0	0	2	3	0	7	0	0	1	.364	.306
McGwire, Mark, Oakland	.268	139	467	87	125	273	22	0	42	104	0	9	5	90	12	105	0	1	10	.585	.385
McIntosh, Tim, Milwaukee	.182	35	77	7	14	17	3	0	0	6	1	1	2	3	0	9	1	3	1	.221	.229
McLemore, Mark, Baltimore†	.246	101	228	40	56	67	7	2	0	27	6	1	0	21	1	26	11	5	6	.294	.308
McRae, Brian, Kansas City†	.223	149	533	63	119	164	23	5	4	52	7	4	6	42	1	88	18	5	10	.308	.285
McReynolds, Kevin, Kansas City	.247	109	373	45	92	156	25	0	13	49	0	5	0	67	3	48	7	1	6	.418	.357
Melvin, Bob, Kansas City	.314	32	70	5	22	27	5	0	0	6	0	2	0	5	0	13	0	0	3	.386	.351
Mercedes, Henry, Oakland	.800	9	5	1	4	6	0	1	0	1	0	0	0	0	0	1	0	0	0	1.200	.800
Mercedes, Luis, Baltimore	.140	23	50	4	7	9	2	0	0	4	2	1	1	8	0	9	1	2	1	.180	.267
Merullo, Matt, Chicago*	.180	24	50	3	9	12	1	1	0	3	0	1	1	1	0	8	0	0	0	.240	.208
Meulens, Hensley, New York	.600	2	5	1	3	6	0	0	1	1	0	0	0	1	0	0	0	0	1	1.200	.667
Miller, Keith, Kansas City	.284	106	416	57	118	162	24	4	4	38	1	2	14	31	0	46	16	6	1	.389	.352
Milligan, Randy, Baltimore	.240	137	462	71	111	167	21	1	11	53	0	5	4	106	0	81	0	1	15	.361	.383
Mitchell, Kevin, Seattle	.286	99	360	48	103	154	24	0	9	67	0	4	3	35	4	46	0	2	4	.428	.351
Molitor, Paul, Milwaukee	.320	158	609	89	195	281	36	7	12	89	4	11	3	73	12	66	31	6	13	.461	.389
Morris, John, California*	.193	43	57	4	11	15	1	0	1	3	1	1	0	1	1	11	1	0	0	.263	.258
Moses, John, Seattle†	.136	21	22	3	3	4	1	0	0	1	2	0	0	5	0	4	0	0	0	.182	.296
Mulliniks, Rance, Toronto*	.500	3	2	1	1	1	0	0	0	0	0	0	0	0	0	0	0	0	0	.500	.667
Munoz, Pedro, Minnesota	.270	127	418	44	113	171	16	3	12	71	0	3	1	17	1	90	4	5	18	.409	.298
Myers, Greg, Tor.-Cal.*	.231	30	78	4	18	28	7	0	1	13	1	2	0	5	0	11	0	0	2	.359	.271
Naehring, Tim, Boston	.231	72	186	12	43	60	8	0	3	14	6	1	3	18	0	31	0	0	1	.323	.304
Neel, Troy, Oakland*	.264	24	53	8	14	26	3	0	3	9	0	0	1	5	0	15	0	1	1	.491	.339
Nelson, Gene, Oakland	.000	29	0	1	0	0	0	0	0	0	0	0	0	0	0	0	0	0	0	.000	.000
Newman, Al, Texas†	.220	116	246	25	54	59	5	0	0	12	8	0	1	34	0	26	9	6	5	.240	.317
Newson, Warren, Chicago*	.221	63	136	19	30	36	3	0	1	11	0	0	0	37	2	38	0	4	3	.265	.387
Nilsson, Dave, Milwaukee*	.232	51	164	15	38	58	8	0	4	25	2	0	0	17	1	18	2	2	1	.354	.304
Nokes, Matt, New York*	.224	121	384	42	86	163	9	1	22	59	0	6	3	37	11	62	0	1	13	.424	.293
Oberkfell, Ken, California*	.264	41	91	6	24	25	1	0	0	10	0	2	0	8	2	5	0	1	5	.275	.317
O'Brien, Pete, Seattle*	.222	134	396	40	88	147	15	1	14	52	1	7	0	40	8	27	2	1	9	.371	.289
Olerud, John, Toronto*	.284	138	458	68	130	206	28	0	16	66	1	7	1	70	11	61	1	0	15	.450	.375
Orsulak, Joe, Baltimore*	.289	117	391	45	113	149	18	3	4	39	4	1	4	28	5	34	5	4	3	.381	.342

Player, Team	Avg.	G	AB	R	H	TB	2B	3B	HR	RBI	SH	SF	HP	BB	Int. BB	SO	SB	CS	GI DP	Slg.	OBP
Ortiz, Junior, Cleveland	.250	86	244	20	61	68	7	0	0	24	2	0	4	12	0	23	1	3	7	.279	.296
Orton, John, California	.219	43	114	11	25	34	3	0	2	12	2	0	2	7	0	32	1	1	1	.298	.276
Pagliarulo, Mike, Minnesota*	.200	42	105	10	21	25	4	0	0	9	0	1	1	10	1	17	1	0	1	.238	.213
Palmeiro, Rafael, Texas*	.268	159	608	84	163	264	27	4	22	85	5	6	10	72	8	83	2	3	10	.434	.352
Palmer, Dean, Texas	.229	152	541	74	124	227	25	0	26	72	2	4	4	62	2	154	10	4	9	.420	.311
Parent, Mark, Baltimore	.235	17	34	4	8	15	1	0	2	4	2	0	1	3	0	7	0	0	0	.441	.316
Parks, Derek, Minnesota	.333	7	6	1	2	2	0	0	0	0	0	0	0	1	0	1	0	0	0	.333	.500
Parrish, Lance, Cal.-Sea.	.233	93	275	26	64	115	13	1	12	32	1	3	1	24	3	70	1	1	7	.418	.294
Pasqua, Dan, Chicago*	.211	93	265	26	56	92	16	1	6	33	1	3	1	36	1	57	0	1	4	.347	.305
Peltier, Dan, Texas*	.167	12	24	1	4	4	0	0	0	2	0	0	0	0	0	3	0	0	0	.167	.167
Pena, Tony, Boston	.241	133	410	39	99	125	21	1	1	38	13	2	1	24	0	61	3	2	11	.305	.284
Perezchica, Tony, Cleveland	.100	18	20	2	2	3	1	0	0	1	2	0	0	2	0	6	0	0	0	.150	.182
Petralli, Geno, Texas*	.198	94	192	11	38	53	12	0	1	18	1	0	0	20	2	34	0	0	8	.276	.274
Pettis, Gary, Detroit†	.202	48	129	27	26	39	4	3	1	12	3	1	0	27	0	34	13	4	3	.302	.338
Phillips, Tony, Detroit†	.276	159	606	114	167	235	32	3	10	64	5	7	1	114	2	93	12	10	13	.388	.387
Plantier, Phil, Boston*	.246	108	349	46	86	126	19	0	7	30	2	2	2	44	8	83	2	3	9	.361	.332
Polonia, Luis, California*	.286	149	577	83	165	190	17	4	0	35	8	4	1	45	6	64	51	21	18	.329	.337
Puckett, Kirby, Minnesota	.329	160	639	104	210	313	38	4	19	110	1	6	6	44	13	97	17	7	17	.490	.374
Pulliam, Harvey, Kansas City	.200	4	5	2	1	2	1	0	0	0	0	0	0	1	0	3	0	0	0	.400	.333
Quinlan, Tom, Toronto	.067	13	15	2	1	2	1	0	0	2	0	0	0	2	0	9	0	0	1	.133	.176
Quinones, Luis, Minnesota†	.200	3	5	0	1	1	0	0	0	1	0	1	0	0	0	0	0	0	0	.200	.167
Quirk, Jamie, Oakland*	.220	78	177	13	39	54	7	1	2	11	5	1	3	16	3	28	0	0	4	.305	.294
Raines, Tim, Chicago†	.294	144	551	102	162	223	22	9	7	54	4	8	0	81	4	48	45	6	5	.405	.380
Ready, Randy, Oakland	.200	61	125	17	25	36	2	0	3	17	2	2	0	25	1	23	1	0	1	.288	.329
Reboulet, Jeff, Minnesota	.190	73	137	15	26	38	7	1	1	16	7	0	1	23	0	26	3	2	0	.277	.311
Reed, Darren, Minnesota	.182	14	33	2	6	8	2	0	0	4	0	2	0	2	0	11	0	0	2	.242	.216
Reed, Jody, Boston	.247	143	550	64	136	174	27	1	3	40	10	4	0	62	2	44	7	8	17	.316	.321
Reimer, Kevin, Texas*	.267	148	494	56	132	216	32	2	16	58	0	1	10	42	5	103	2	4	10	.437	.336
Reynolds, Harold, Seattle†	.247	140	458	55	113	151	23	3	3	33	11	4	3	45	1	41	15	12	12	.330	.316
Ripken, Billy, Baltimore	.230	111	330	35	76	103	15	0	4	36	10	2	3	18	1	26	2	3	10	.312	.275
Ripken, Cal, Baltimore	.251	162	637	73	160	233	29	1	14	72	0	7	7	64	14	50	4	3	13	.366	.323
Rivera, Luis, Boston	.215	102	288	17	62	75	11	1	0	29	5	0	3	26	0	56	4	3	5	.260	.287
Rodriguez, Ivan, Texas	.260	123	420	39	109	151	16	1	8	37	7	2	1	24	2	73	0	0	15	.360	.300
Rohde, David, Cleveland†	.000	5	7	0	0	0	0	0	0	0	0	0	0	0	0	1	3	0	0	.000	.222
Rose, Bob, California	.214	30	84	10	18	29	5	0	2	10	1	1	2	8	1	9	1	1	2	.345	.295
Rossy, Rico, Kansas City	.215	59	149	21	32	45	8	1	1	12	7	1	1	20	1	20	0	3	6	.302	.310
Rowland, Rich, Detroit	.214	6	14	2	3	3	0	0	0	0	0	0	0	0	0	3	0	0	1	.214	.353
Russell, John, Texas	.100	7	10	1	1	1	0	0	0	2	0	1	0	1	0	4	0	0	0	.100	.231
Salmon, Tim, California	.177	23	79	8	14	21	1	0	2	6	0	1	1	11	1	23	1	1	1	.266	.283
Samuel, Juan, Kansas City	.284	29	102	15	29	40	5	3	0	8	0	0	0	7	1	27	6	1	2	.392	.336
Santovenia, Nelson, Chicago	.333	2	3	1	1	4	0	0	1	2	0	0	0	0	0	0	0	0	0	1.333	.333
Sax, Steve, Chicago	.236	143	568	74	134	180	26	4	4	47	12	6	2	43	4	42	30	12	17	.317	.290
Scarsone, Steve, Baltimore	.176	11	17	2	3	3	0	0	0	0	1	0	0	1	0	6	0	0	0	.176	.222
Schaefer, Jeff, Seattle	.114	65	70	5	8	13	2	0	1	3	6	0	0	2	0	10	0	1	2	.186	.139
Schofield, Dick, California	.333	1	3	0	1	1	0	0	0	0	0	0	0	0	0	0	0	0	0	.333	.500
Segui, David, Baltimore†	.233	115	189	21	44	56	9	0	1	17	2	0	0	20	3	23	1	0	4	.296	.306
Seitzer, Kevin, Milwaukee	.270	148	540	74	146	198	35	1	5	71	7	9	2	57	4	44	13	11	16	.367	.337
Shumpert, Terry, Kansas City	.149	36	94	6	14	24	5	1	1	11	2	0	3	0	1	17	2	2	2	.255	.175
Sierra, Ruben, Tex.-Oak.†	.278	151	601	83	167	266	34	7	17	87	0	10	0	45	12	68	14	4	11	.443	.323
Silvestri, Dave, New York	.308	7	13	3	4	8	0	2	0	1	0	0	0	0	0	3	0	0	1	.615	.308
Sinatro, Matt, Seattle	.107	18	28	0	3	3	0	0	0	0	2	0	0	5	0	5	0	0	1	.107	.107
Snow, J.T., New York†	.143	7	14	1	2	3	1	0	0	2	0	0	0	5	1	5	0	0	2	.214	.368
Sojo, Luis, California	.272	106	368	37	100	139	12	3	7	43	7	1	1	14	0	24	7	11	14	.378	.299
Sorrento, Paul, Cleveland*	.269	140	458	52	123	203	24	1	18	60	1	3	1	51	7	89	0	3	13	.443	.341
Spiers, Bill, Milwaukee*	.313	12	16	2	5	7	2	0	0	2	1	0	0	1	0	4	1	1	0	.438	.353
Sprague, Ed Jr., Toronto	.234	22	47	6	11	16	2	0	1	7	0	0	0	3	0	7	0	0	0	.340	.280
Stankiewicz, Andy, New York	.268	116	400	52	107	139	22	2	2	25	7	1	5	38	0	42	9	5	13	.348	.338
Stanley, Mike, New York	.249	68	173	24	43	74	7	0	8	27	0	0	1	33	0	45	0	0	6	.428	.372
Steinbach, Terry, Oakland	.279	128	438	48	122	180	20	1	12	53	0	3	1	45	3	58	2	3	20	.411	.345
Stephens, Ray, Texas	.154	8	13	0	2	2	0	0	0	1	0	1	0	0	0	5	0	0	1	.154	.154
Stevens, Lee, California	.221	106	312	25	69	109	19	0	7	37	1	2	1	29	6	64	1	4	4	.349	.288
Stubbs, Franklin, Milwaukee*	.229	92	288	37	66	106	11	1	9	42	5	1	1	27	3	68	11	8	2	.368	.297
Suero, William, Milwaukee	.188	18	16	4	3	4	1	0	0	0	0	0	1	2	0	1	1	1	2	.250	.316
Surhoff, B.J., Milwaukee*	.252	139	480	63	121	154	19	1	4	62	5	10	2	46	4	41	14	8	9	.321	.314
Sveum, Dale, Chicago†	.219	40	114	15	25	40	9	0	2	12	2	3	0	12	0	29	1	1	1	.351	.287
Tabler, Pat, Toronto	.252	49	135	11	34	39	5	0	0	16	0	1	0	11	0	14	0	0	6	.289	.306
Tackett, Jeff, Baltimore	.240	65	179	21	43	68	8	1	5	24	6	4	2	17	1	28	0	1	11	.380	.307
Tartabull, Danny, New York	.266	123	421	72	112	206	19	0	25	85	0	2	0	103	14	115	2	2	7	.489	.409
Tatum, Jim, Milwaukee	.125	5	8	0	1	1	0	0	0	0	0	0	0	0	0	2	0	0	0	.125	.222
Tettleton, Mickey, Detroit†	.238	157	525	82	125	246	25	0	32	83	0	6	1	122	18	137	0	6	5	.469	.379
Thomas, Frank, Chicago	.323	160	573	108	185	307	46	2	24	115	0	11	5	122	6	88	6	3	19	.536	.439
Thome, Jim, Cleveland*	.205	40	117	8	24	35	3	1	2	12	0	2	2	10	0	34	2	0	3	.299	.275
Thon, Dickie, Texas	.247	95	275	30	68	101	15	3	4	37	3	5	0	20	1	40	12	2	2	.367	.293
Thurman, Gary, Kansas City	.245	88	200	25	49	61	6	3	0	20	6	0	1	9	0	38	9	6	3	.305	.281
Tingley, Ron, California	.197	71	127	15	25	38	2	1	3	8	5	0	2	13	0	35	0	1	4	.299	.282
Trammell, Alan, Detroit	.275	29	102	11	28	40	7	1	1	11	1	1	1	15	0	4	2	2	6	.392	.370
Turner, Shane, California*	.270	34	74	8	20	25	5	0	0	5	2	0	0	9	0	15	2	1	4	.338	.341
Valentin, John, Boston	.276	58	185	21	51	79	13	0	5	25	4	1	2	20	0	17	1	0	5	.427	.351
Valentin, Jose, Milwaukee†	.000	4	3	1	0	0	0	0	0	0	1	0	0	0	0	0	0	0	0	.000	.000
Valle, Dave, Seattle	.240	124	367	39	88	133	16	1	9	30	7	1	8	27	1	58	0	0	7	.362	.305
Vaughn, Greg, Milwaukee	.228	141	501	77	114	205	18	2	23	78	2	5	5	60	1	123	15	15	8	.409	.313
Vaughn, Mo, Boston*	.234	113	355	42	83	142	16	2	13	57	0	3	3	47	7	67	3	3	9	.400	.326
Velarde, Randy, New York	.272	121	412	57	112	159	24	1	7	46	4	5	2	38	1	78	7	2	13	.386	.333
Ventura, Robin, Chicago*	.282	157	592	85	167	255	38	1	16	93	1	8	0	93	9	71	2	4	14	.431	.375
Vizquel, Omar, Seattle†	.294	136	483	49	142	170	20	4	0	21	9	1	2	32	0	38	15	13	14	.352	.340
Ward, Turner, Toronto†	.345	18	29	7	10	16	3	0	1	3	0	0	0	4	0	4	1	1	2	.552	.424
Webster, Lenny, Minnesota	.280	53	118	10	33	48	10	1	1	13	2	0	0	9	0	11	0	2	3	.407	.331

Player, Team	Avg.	G	AB	R	H	TB	2B	3B	HR	RBI	SH	SF	HP	BB	Int. BB	SO	SB	CS	GI DP	Slg.	OBP
Wedge, Eric, Boston	.250	27	68	11	17	34	2	0	5	11	0	0	0	13	0	18	0	0	0	.500	.370
Weiss, Walt, Oakland†	.212	103	316	36	67	76	5	2	0	21	11	4	1	43	1	39	6	3	10	.241	.305
Whitaker, Lou, Detroit*	.278	130	453	77	126	209	26	0	19	71	5	4	1	81	5	46	6	4	9	.461	.386
White, Devon, Toronto†	.248	153	641	98	159	250	26	7	17	60	0	3	5	47	0	133	37	4	9	.390	.303
Whiten, Mark, Cleveland†	.254	148	508	73	129	183	19	4	9	43	3	3	2	72	10	102	16	12	12	.360	.347
Wilkerson, Curtis, Kansas City†	.250	111	296	27	74	92	10	1	2	29	7	4	1	18	3	47	18	7	4	.311	.292
Williams, Bernie, New York†	.280	62	261	39	73	106	14	2	5	26	2	0	1	29	1	36	7	6	5	.406	.354
Williams, Gerald, New York	.296	15	27	7	8	19	2	0	3	6	0	0	0	0	0	3	2	0	0	.704	.296
Williams, Reggie, California†	.231	14	26	5	6	9	1	1	0	2	0	0	1	0	1	10	0	2	0	.346	.259
Wilson, Willie, Oakland†	.270	132	396	38	107	132	15	5	0	37	2	3	1	35	2	65	28	8	11	.333	.329
Winfield, Dave, Toronto	.290	156	583	92	169	286	33	3	26	108	1	3	1	82	10	89	2	3	10	.491	.377
Winningham, Herm, Boston*	.235	105	234	27	55	68	8	1	1	14	0	0	0	10	0	53	6	5	3	.291	.266
Worthington, Craig, Cleveland	.167	9	24	0	4	4	0	0	0	2	0	0	0	2	0	4	0	1	0	.167	.231
Yount, Robin, Milwaukee	.264	150	557	71	147	217	40	3	8	77	4	12	3	53	9	81	15	6	9	.390	.325
Zosky, Eddie, Toronto	.286	8	7	1	2	4	0	1	0	1	0	1	0	0	0	2	0	0	0	.571	.250
Zupcic, Bob, Boston	.276	124	392	46	108	138	19	1	3	43	7	4	4	25	1	60	2	2	6	.352	.322

AWARDED FIRST BASE ON OBSTRUCTION OR CATCHER'S INTERFERENCE—R. Kelly, New York 8 (Rodriguez 2, Borders, Marzano, Ortiz, Quirk, Steinbach, Tingley); P. Kelly, New York 2 (Quirk, Rodriguez); Belle, Cleveland (Hoiles); Brett, Kansas City (Hoiles); Cooper, Boston (Sprague); Felix, California (Morris); Hamilton, Milwaukee (Quirk); Macfarlane, Kansas City (Orton); Molitor, Milwaukee (Mayne); Schaefer, Seattle (Ortiz); Steinbach, Oakland (Levis); Whiten, Cleveland (McIntosh).

PLAYERS WITH TWO OR MORE TEAMS

Player, Team	Avg.	G	AB	R	H	TB	2B	3B	HR	RBI	SH	SF	HP	BB	Int. BB	SO	SB	CS	GI DP	Slg.	OBP
Canseco, Jose, Oakland	.246	97	366	66	90	167	11	0	22	72	0	4	3	48	1	104	5	7	15	.456	.335
Canseco, Jose, Texas	.233	22	73	8	17	33	4	0	4	15	0	0	3	15	1	24	1	0	1	.452	.385
Ducey, Rob, Toronto*	.048	23	21	3	1	2	1	0	0	0	0	0	0	0	0	10	0	1	0	.095	.048
Ducey, Rob, California*	.237	31	59	4	14	17	3	0	0	2	0	1	0	5	0	12	2	3	1	.288	.292
Eichhorn, Mark, California	.000	42	0	0	0	0	0	0	0	0	0	0	0	0	0	0	0	0	0	.000	.000
Eichhorn, Mark, Toronto	.000	23	0	0	0	0	0	0	0	0	0	0	0	0	0	0	0	0	0	.000	.000
Heaton, Neal, Kansas City*	.000	31	0	0	0	0	0	0	0	0	0	0	0	0	0	0	0	0	0	.000	.000
Heaton, Neal, Milwaukee*	.000	1	0	0	0	0	0	0	0	0	0	0	0	0	0	0	0	0	0	.000	.000
Hemond, Scott, Oakland	.222	17	27	7	6	7	1	0	0	1	0	0	0	3	0	7	1	0	2	.259	.300
Hemond, Scott, Chicago	.231	8	13	1	3	4	1	0	0	1	0	1	0	1	0	6	0	0	0	.308	.267
Hillegas, Shawn, New York	.000	21	0	0	0	0	0	0	0	0	0	0	0	0	0	0	0	0	0	.000	.000
Hillegas, Shawn, Oakland	.000	5	0	0	0	0	0	0	0	0	0	0	0	0	0	0	0	0	0	.000	.000
Howitt, Dann, Oakland*	.125	22	48	1	6	9	0	0	1	2	1	0	0	5	1	4	0	0	4	.188	.208
Howitt, Dann, Seattle*	.270	13	37	6	10	19	4	1	1	8	0	3	0	3	0	5	1	1	2	.514	.302
Leary, Tim, New York	.000	18	0	0	0	0	0	0	0	0	0	0	0	0	0	0	0	0	0	.000	.000
Leary, Tim, Seattle	.000	8	0	0	0	0	0	0	0	0	0	0	0	0	0	0	0	0	0	.000	.000
Mesa, Jose, Baltimore	.000	13	0	0	0	0	0	0	0	0	0	0	0	0	0	0	0	0	0	.000	.000
Mesa, Jose, Cleveland*	.000	15	0	0	0	0	0	0	0	0	0	0	0	0	0	0	0	0	0	.000	.000
Myers, Greg, Toronto*	.230	22	61	4	14	23	6	0	1	13	0	2	0	5	0	5	0	0	2	.377	.279
Myers, Greg, California*	.235	8	17	0	4	5	1	0	0	1	0	1	0	0	0	6	0	0	0	.294	.235
Nunez, Edwin, Milwaukee	.000	10	0	0	0	0	0	0	0	0	0	0	0	0	0	0	0	0	0	.000	.000
Nunez, Edwin, Texas	.000	39	0	0	0	0	0	0	0	0	0	0	0	0	0	0	0	0	0	.000	.000
Parrish, Lance, California	.229	24	83	7	19	33	2	0	4	11	1	1	0	5	1	22	0	0	1	.398	.270
Parrish, Lance, Seattle	.234	69	192	19	45	82	11	1	8	21	0	2	1	19	2	48	1	1	6	.427	.304
Russell, Jeff, Texas	.000	51	0	0	0	0	0	0	0	0	0	0	0	0	0	0	0	0	0	.000	.000
Russell, Jeff, Oakland	.000	8	0	0	0	0	0	0	0	0	0	0	0	0	0	0	0	0	0	.000	.000
Sierra, Ruben, Texas†	.278	124	500	66	139	223	30	6	14	70	0	8	0	31	6	59	12	4	9	.446	.315
Sierra, Ruben, Oakland†	.277	27	101	17	28	43	4	1	3	17	0	2	0	14	6	9	2	0	2	.426	.359
Witt, Bobby, Texas	.000	25	0	0	0	0	0	0	0	0	0	0	0	0	0	0	0	0	0	.000	.000
Witt, Bobby, Oakland	.000	6	0	0	0	0	0	0	0	0	0	0	0	0	0	0	0	0	0	.000	.000
Young, Curt, Kansas City	.000	10	0	0	0	0	0	0	0	0	0	0	0	0	0	0	0	0	0	.000	.000
Young, Curt, New York	.000	13	0	0	0	0	0	0	0	0	0	0	0	0	0	0	0	0	0	.000	.000

NOTE: The following players (with games played in parentheses) appeared only as pinch-runners and are not listed in any batting, pitching or fielding sections: Shields, Tommy, Baltimore (2); Voigt, Jack, Baltimore (1).

DESIGNATED HITTING

TEAM

Team	Avg.	AB	R	H	TB	2B	3B	HR	RBI	SH	SF	HP	BB	Int. BB	SO	SB	CS	GI DP	Slg.	OBP
Milwaukee	.290	621	76	180	255	31	4	12	88	2	13	2	79	11	88	34	7	10	.411	.365
Kansas City	.278	643	72	179	255	33	5	11	62	0	4	6	40	6	88	11	8	12	.397	.325
Seattle	.275	625	84	172	280	42	0	22	88	2	8	1	56	8	87	10	1	19	.448	.332
Minnesota	.271	591	82	160	233	33	2	12	80	0	11	6	91	15	104	11	5	16	.394	.368
Detroit	.271	584	83	158	257	21	0	26	96	3	5	1	111	13	136	4	5	11	.440	.385
Toronto	.267	619	95	165	288	32	2	29	112	1	5	6	78	9	101	2	3	13	.465	.352
Baltimore	.262	626	74	164	253	26	3	19	74	3	5	3	65	4	142	4	1	21	.404	.332
Texas	.252	614	92	155	251	39	0	19	70	3	4	12	87	2	119	4	0	12	.409	.354
California	.247	647	77	160	226	27	3	11	62	4	3	4	34	6	102	18	15	17	.349	.288
New York	.245	613	76	150	243	27	0	22	90	1	7	4	75	8	126	2	3	9	.396	.328
Oakland	.244	622	88	152	250	20	0	26	108	1	9	1	80	8	107	5	6	17	.402	.327
Cleveland	.241	632	78	152	263	24	3	27	93	1	9	6	52	6	147	7	6	25	.416	.300
Chicago	.238	668	76	159	258	29	2	22	104	1	8	7	38	9	108	7	3	29	.450	.283
Boston	.235	592	76	139	208	19	1	16	69	2	9	5	85	6	132	3	1	14	.351	.331
Totals	.258	8697	1134	2245	3520	403	25	274	1196	24	100	64	971	111	1587	122	64	225	.405	.334

INDIVIDUAL

TOP 15 DESIGNATED HITTERS

Minimum 100 at-bats.   *Lefthanded batter.   †Switch-hitter.

Player, Team	Avg.	G	AB	R	H	TB	2B	3B	HR	RBI	SH	SF	HP	BB	Int. BB	SO	SB	CS	GI DP	Slg.	OBP
Martinez, Edgar, Seattle	.392	28	120	22	47	68	9	0	4	17	0	1	0	10	0	9	5	0	5	.567	.435
Polonia, Luis, California*	.314	47	188	30	59	71	8	2	0	12	3	1	1	12	2	20	15	9	7	.378	.356
Canseco, Jose, Oak.-Tex.	.312	28	109	23	34	60	5	0	7	29	0	1	1	14	0	29	2	2	5	.550	.392
Mitchell, Kevin, Seattle	.304	26	102	17	31	49	6	0	4	27	0	1	1	11	1	22	0	1	1	.480	.374
Molitor, Paul, Milwaukee	.298	108	413	53	123	176	20	3	9	57	2	8	2	56	9	53	24	3	9	.426	.378
Tettleton, Mickey, Detroit†	.295	40	139	19	41	73	5	0	9	25	0	0	1	37	6	35	0	1	1	.525	.443
Downing, Brian, Texas	.285	93	309	53	88	136	18	0	10	38	0	1	7	60	1	52	1	0	7	.440	.411
Brett, George, Kansas City*	.282	132	521	54	147	202	26	4	7	53	0	4	6	30	5	62	8	6	12	.388	.326
Davis, Chili, Minnesota†	.280	125	428	59	120	182	25	2	11	60	0	8	3	72	11	73	4	5	11	.425	.382
Winfield, Dave, Toronto	.278	130	490	75	136	234	27	1	23	91	1	3	1	67	9	81	1	2	8	.478	.364
Davis, Glenn, Baltimore	.276	103	392	45	108	166	15	2	13	48	1	4	2	36	2	64	1	0	11	.423	.336
Tartabull, Danny, New York	.270	53	185	28	50	80	9	0	7	33	0	0	3	38	3	51	0	2	4	.432	.395
Belle, Albert, Cleveland	.258	100	380	52	98	171	14	1	19	75	1	8	3	39	4	95	5	1	14	.450	.326
Martinez, Tino, Seattle*	.249	48	169	20	42	76	13	0	7	25	1	3	0	13	3	23	2	0	7	.450	.297
Bell, George, Chicago	.247	140	570	59	141	230	23	0	22	98	0	5	6	26	8	90	2	2	27	.404	.285

ALL DESIGNATED HITTERS

*Lefthanded batter.   †Switch-hitter.

Player, Team	Avg.	G	AB	R	H	TB	2B	3B	HR	RBI	SH	SF	HP	BB	Int. BB	SO	SB	CS	GI DP	Slg.	OBP
Abner, Shawn, Chicago	.000	1	1	0	0	0	0	0	0	0	0	0	0	0	0	0	0	0	0	.000	.000
Alomar, Roberto, Toronto†	.500	1	4	2	2	7	0	1	1	4	0	0	0	1	0	0	0	0	1	1.750	.600
Alomar, Sandy, Cleveland	.000	1	3	0	0	0	0	0	0	0	0	0	0	1	1	0	0	0	0	.000	.250
Baerga, Carlos, Cleveland†	.000	1	3	0	0	0	0	0	0	0	0	0	0	0	1	1	0	0	0	.000	.000
Baines, Harold, Oakland*	.237	116	410	47	97	158	16	0	15	69	0	6	0	50	5	58	1	3	10	.385	.315
Barnes, Skeeter, Detroit	.500	7	14	4	7	12	2	0	1	5	0	0	0	4	0	1	1	1	1	.857	.611
Bell, Derek, Toronto	.000	1	2	0	0	0	0	0	0	0	0	0	0	1	0	0	0	0	0	.000	.333
Bell, George, Chicago	.247	140	570	59	141	230	23	0	22	98	0	5	6	26	8	90	2	2	27	.404	.285
Belle, Albert, Cleveland	.258	100	380	52	98	171	14	1	19	75	1	8	3	39	4	95	5	1	14	.450	.326
Beltre, Esteban, Chicago	.000	4	0	2	0	0	0	0	0	0	0	0	0	0	0	0	1	0	0	.000	.000
Bergman, Dave, Detroit*	.270	12	37	3	10	10	0	0	0	0	0	0	0	3	0	3	0	0	1	.270	.325
Bichette, Dante, Milwaukee	.000	4	6	0	0	0	0	0	0	0	0	1	0	0	0	3	0	0	0	.000	.000
Blankenship, Lance, Oakland	.000	3	0	2	0	0	0	0	0	0	0	0	0	2	1	0	0	0	0	.000	1.000
Boggs, Wade, Boston*	.263	21	76	13	20	26	1	1	1	2	0	1	0	11	3	4	0	0	5	.342	.352
Brett, George, Kansas City*	.282	132	521	54	147	202	26	4	7	53	0	4	6	30	5	62	8	6	12	.388	.326
Briley, Greg, Seattle*	.378	12	37	3	14	17	3	0	0	2	0	1	0	1	0	5	1	0	0	.459	.385
Brito, Bernardo, Minnesota	.000	1	2	0	0	0	0	0	0	0	1	0	0	0	0	1	0	0	0	.000	.000
Brogna, Rico, Detroit*	.500	2	2	2	1	1	0	0	0	0	0	0	0	3	0	1	0	0	0	.500	.800
Brooks, Hubie, California	.218	70	275	28	60	97	13	0	8	34	0	1	1	10	2	43	3	3	9	.353	.247
Brosius, Scott, Oakland	.000	1	0	1	0	0	0	0	0	0	0	0	0	0	0	0	0	0	0	.000	.000
Brown, Jarvis, Minnesota	.000	2	0	1	0	0	0	0	0	0	0	0	0	0	0	1	0	0	0	.000	.000
Browne, Jerry, Oakland†	.000	1	3	0	0	0	0	0	0	0	0	0	1	0	0	1	0	0	0	.000	.250
Bruett, J.T., Minnesota*	.000	3	0	1	0	0	0	0	0	0	0	0	0	0	0	0	0	0	0	.000	.000
Brunansky, Tom, Boston	.333	17	54	10	18	30	0	0	4	16	2	2	0	9	1	9	0	0	1	.556	.415
Burks, Ellis, Boston	.000	1	4	0	0	0	0	0	0	0	0	0	0	0	0	1	0	0	0	.000	.000
Bush, Randy, Minnesota*	.260	24	73	8	19	26	4	0	1	11	0	0	2	4	1	13	1	0	3	.356	.316
Cangelosi, John, Texas†	.000	6	1	1	0	0	0	0	0	0	0	0	0	0	0	1	0	0	0	.000	.000
Canseco, Jose, Oak.-Tex.	.312	28	109	23	34	60	5	0	7	29	0	1	1	14	0	29	2	2	5	.550	.392
Carreon, Mark, Detroit	.227	13	44	3	10	15	2	0	1	3	0	0	0	3	0	8	0	0	1	.341	.277
Carter, Joe, Toronto	.229	24	96	15	22	39	2	0	5	15	0	2	3	6	0	17	1	0	5	.406	.290
Clark, Jack, Boston	.184	64	212	23	39	57	9	0	3	24	0	5	2	44	1	72	1	1	4	.269	.323
Clark, Phil, Detroit	.500	7	20	1	10	12	1	0	0	1	0	0	0	2	0	3	0	0	1	.600	.545
Cochrane, Dave, Seattle†	.000	2	5	0	0	0	0	0	0	0	0	0	0	0	0	3	0	0	0	.000	.000

Player, Team	Avg.	G	AB	R	H	TB	2B	3B	HR	RBI	SH	SF	HP	BB	Int. BB	SO	SB	CS	GI DP	Slg.	OBP
Cole, Alex, Cleveland*	.182	4	11	2	2	2	0	0	0	1	0	1	0	2	0	2	0	0	0	.182	.286
Cooper, Scott, Boston*	.200	2	5	0	1	1	0	0	0	1	0	0	0	1	0	2	0	0	0	.200	.333
Cora, Joey, Chicago†	.000	18	9	3	0	0	0	0	0	1	1	0	1	1	0	1	1	0	1	.000	.182
Cotto, Henry, Seattle	.000	3	11	0	0	0	0	0	0	0	0	0	0	1	0	2	0	0	0	.000	.083
Curtis, Chad, California	.000	1	0	1	0	0	0	0	0	0	0	0	0	0	0	0	0	0	0	.000	.000
Daugherty, Jack, Texas†	.243	13	37	2	9	14	5	0	0	3	0	1	0	4	0	5	0	0	2	.378	.310
Davis, Alvin, California*	.208	9	24	0	5	6	1	0	0	1	0	0	0	5	0	2	0	0	0	.250	.345
Davis, Chili, Minnesota†	.280	125	428	59	120	182	25	2	11	60	0	8	3	72	11	73	4	5	11	.425	.382
Davis, Glenn, Baltimore	.276	103	392	45	108	166	15	2	13	48	1	4	2	36	2	64	1	0	11	.423	.336
Deer, Rob, Detroit	.333	2	9	4	3	12	0	0	3	5	0	0	0	1	0	2	0	0	0	1.333	.400
Diaz, Alex, Milwaukee†	.000	2	0	1	0	0	0	0	0	0	0	0	0	0	0	0	0	0	0	.000	.000
Downing, Brian, Texas	.285	93	309	53	88	136	18	0	10	38	0	1	7	60	1	52	1	0	7	.440	.411
Ducey, Rob, Tor.-Cal.*	.000	5	5	0	0	0	0	0	0	0	0	0	0	0	0	2	0	0	0	.000	.000
Eisenreich, Jim, Kansas City*	.344	8	32	6	11	15	4	0	0	3	0	0	0	3	0	4	1	0	0	.469	.400
Fariss, Monty, Texas	.000	4	5	0	0	0	0	0	0	0	0	0	0	1	0	2	0	0	0	.000	.167
Felix, Junior, California†	.267	8	30	4	8	11	1	1	0	6	0	1	0	2	1	8	0	0	0	.367	.303
Fielder, Cecil, Detroit	.234	43	167	20	39	65	5	0	7	30	0	1	0	21	5	51	0	0	4	.389	.317
Fisk, Carlton, Chicago	.167	2	6	0	1	2	1	0	0	0	0	0	0	0	0	2	0	0	0	.333	.167
Fitzgerald, Mike, California	.500	1	2	0	1	1	0	0	0	0	0	0	0	0	0	0	0	0	0	.500	.500
Fox, Eric, Oakland†	.000	4	1	2	0	0	0	0	0	0	0	0	0	1	0	0	0	0	0	.000	.500
Franco, Julio, Texas	.190	15	58	12	11	20	3	0	2	4	1	0	0	8	1	8	1	0	2	.345	.288
Gaetti, Gary, California	.230	17	61	6	14	24	1	0	3	4	0	0	1	3	0	15	0	1	0	.393	.277
Gantner, Jim, Milwaukee*	.500	2	2	0	1	1	0	0	0	0	0	0	0	0	0	1	0	0	0	.500	.500
Gladden, Dan, Detroit	.500	2	10	2	5	7	2	0	0	2	0	0	1	0	0	0	0	0	0	.700	.545
Gonzalez, Juan, Texas	.188	4	16	1	3	6	0	0	1	1	0	0	0	0	0	5	0	0	0	.375	.188
Greenwell, Mike, Boston*	.263	6	19	2	5	9	1	0	1	2	0	0	1	2	0	1	0	0	0	.474	.364
Griffey, Ken, Seattle*	.231	3	13	2	3	10	1	0	2	3	0	0	0	0	0	2	0	0	0	.769	.231
Gwynn, Chris, Kansas City*	.250	2	8	0	2	4	0	1	0	0	0	0	0	0	0	1	0	0	0	.500	.250
Hall, Mel, New York*	.238	11	42	5	10	12	2	0	0	2	0	0	0	2	0	5	1	0	0	.286	.273
Harper, Brian, Minnesota	.429	2	7	2	3	4	1	0	0	0	0	0	0	2	1	0	0	0	0	.571	.556
Hayes, Von, California*	.412	5	17	5	7	10	3	0	0	1	0	0	0	0	0	3	0	0	1	.588	.412
Hemond, Scott, Oak.-Chi.	.200	5	10	0	2	3	1	0	0	1	0	1	0	0	0	5	0	0	0	.300	.182
Henderson, Dave, Oakland	.133	4	15	1	2	3	1	0	0	2	0	0	0	0	0	6	0	0	0	.200	.133
Henderson, Rickey, Oakland	.105	6	19	1	2	2	0	0	0	1	0	0	1	5	1	3	1	0	0	.105	.280
Hill, Glenallen, Cleveland	.209	34	134	10	28	49	4	1	5	12	0	0	2	3	0	31	2	1	4	.366	.237
Hoiles, Chris, Baltimore	.250	1	4	0	1	1	0	0	0	0	0	0	0	0	0	2	0	0	0	.250	.250
Horn, Sam, Baltimore*	.238	46	151	13	36	62	9	1	5	16	0	1	1	17	2	55	0	0	8	.411	.318
Howard, Thomas, Cleveland†	.000	2	6	0	0	0	0	0	0	0	0	0	0	0	0	0	0	1	0	.000	.000
Howitt, Dann, Seattle*	.000	1	3	0	0	0	0	0	0	0	0	0	0	0	0	1	0	0	1	.000	.000
Hrbek, Kent, Minnesota*	.240	8	25	3	6	7	1	0	0	1	0	0	0	5	0	5	0	0	0	.280	.406
Huff, Mike, Chicago	.000	1	1	0	0	0	0	0	0	0	0	0	0	0	0	1	0	0	0	.000	.000
Hulett, Tim, Baltimore	.290	13	31	3	9	10	1	0	0	4	0	0	0	4	0	7	0	0	0	.323	.371
Humphreys, Mike, New York	.000	1	3	0	0	0	0	0	0	0	0	0	0	0	0	0	0	0	0	.000	.000
Jaha, John, Milwaukee	.045	8	22	1	1	1	0	0	0	1	0	1	0	2	0	4	2	0	0	.045	.120
James, Dion, New York*	.000	5	11	1	0	0	0	0	0	1	0	1	0	1	0	0	0	0	0	.000	.077
Jefferies, Gregg, Kansas City†	.500	1	2	0	1	1	0	0	0	0	0	0	0	0	0	0	0	0	0	.500	.500
Jefferson, Reggie, Cleveland†	.370	7	27	3	10	15	3	1	0	2	0	0	1	0	0	6	0	0	1	.556	.393
Jeter, Shawn, Chicago*	.000	3	2	1	0	0	0	0	0	0	0	0	0	0	0	2	0	0	0	.000	.000
Joyner, Wally, Kansas City*	.200	4	15	1	3	3	0	0	0	0	0	0	0	2	0	0	0	0	0	.200	.294
Kelly, Pat, New York	.000	1	0	1	0	0	0	0	0	0	0	0	0	0	0	0	0	0	0	.000	.000
Kirby, Wayne, Cleveland*	.167	4	6	5	1	2	1	0	0	0	0	0	0	2	0	1	0	1	1	.333	.375
Knoblauch, Chuck, Minnesota	.500	1	4	1	2	2	0	0	0	0	0	0	0	0	0	0	0	0	0	.500	.500
Kreuter, Chad, Detroit†	.000	1	3	0	0	0	0	0	0	0	0	0	0	0	0	0	0	0	0	.000	.000
Langston, Mark, California	.000	1	2	1	0	0	0	0	0	0	0	0	0	0	0	2	0	0	0	.000	.000
Lansford, Carney, Oakland	.000	2	2	0	0	0	0	0	0	0	0	0	0	0	0	2	0	0	0	.000	.000
Larkin, Gene, Minnesota*	.077	4	13	1	1	1	0	0	0	0	0	0	1	2	1	2	2	0	0	.077	.250
Levis, Jesse, Cleveland*	1.000	1	1	0	1	1	0	0	0	0	0	0	0	0	0	0	0	0	0	1.000	1.000
Leyritz, Jim, New York	.235	31	81	13	19	38	4	0	5	17	0	2	4	5	0	15	0	0	2	.469	.304
Maas, Kevin, New York*	.238	62	214	23	51	80	8	0	7	26	0	4	0	21	3	46	1	1	1	.374	.301
Macfarlane, Mike, Kansas City	.255	13	51	8	13	27	2	0	4	6	0	0	3	1	0	17	0	1	0	.529	.296
Maldonado, Candy, Toronto	.182	4	11	1	2	3	1	0	0	0	0	0	1	2	0	1	0	0	0	.273	.357
Martinez, Chito, Baltimore*	.083	4	12	1	1	4	0	0	1	2	0	0	0	0	0	2	0	0	0	.333	.083
Martinez, Carlos, Cleveland	.000	4	10	0	0	0	0	0	0	0	0	0	0	0	0	1	0	0	2	.000	.000
Martinez, Edgar, Seattle	.392	28	120	22	47	68	9	0	4	17	0	1	0	10	0	9	5	5	5	.567	.435
Martinez, Tino, Seattle*	.249	48	169	20	42	76	13	0	7	25	1	3	0	13	3	23	2	0	7	.450	.297
Marzano, John, Boston	.000	1	1	0	0	0	0	0	0	0	0	0	0	0	0	0	0	0	0	.000	.000
Mattingly, Don, New York*	.297	15	64	10	19	32	4	0	3	11	0	0	0	4	1	5	0	0	1	.500	.338
Maurer, Rob, Texas*	.000	1	1	0	0	0	0	0	0	0	0	0	0	1	0	1	0	0	0	.000	.000
McIntosh, Tim, Milwaukee	.333	3	12	0	4	5	1	0	0	1	0	0	0	0	0	1	0	0	0	.417	.333
McLemore, Mark, Baltimore†	.308	17	13	6	4	5	1	0	0	3	1	0	0	4	0	4	3	1	0	.385	.308
McReynolds, Kevin, Kansas City	.000	1	3	0	0	0	0	0	0	0	0	0	0	1	0	1	0	0	0	.000	.250
Mercedes, Luis, Baltimore	.000	7	4	3	0	0	0	0	0	0	0	0	0	2	0	2	0	0	0	.000	.333
Merullo, Matt, Chicago*	.500	1	2	0	1	1	0	0	0	0	0	0	0	0	0	1	0	0	0	.500	.500
Miller, Keith, Kansas City	.250	1	4	0	1	1	0	0	0	0	0	0	0	0	0	0	0	1	0	.250	.250
Milligan, Randy, Baltimore	.278	6	18	3	5	5	0	0	0	1	0	0	0	6	0	5	0	0	2	.278	.458
Mitchell, Kevin, Seattle	.304	26	102	17	31	49	6	0	4	27	0	1	1	11	1	22	0	1	1	.480	.374
Molitor, Paul, Milwaukee	.298	108	413	53	123	176	20	3	9	57	2	8	2	56	9	53	24	3	9	.426	.378
Morris, John, California*	.000	6	11	0	0	0	0	0	0	0	0	0	0	1	1	2	0	0	0	.000	.154
Mulliniks, Rance, Toronto*	1.000	2	1	1	1	1	0	0	0	0	0	0	0	1	0	0	0	0	0	1.000	1.000
Munoz, Pedro, Minnesota	.000	3	2	1	0	0	0	0	0	0	0	0	0	0	0	2	1	0	0	.000	.000
Myers, Greg, California*	.000	1	1	0	0	0	0	0	0	0	0	0	0	0	0	0	0	0	0	.000	.000
Naehring, Tim, Boston	.286	4	7	2	2	2	0	0	0	0	0	0	1	0	0	0	0	0	0	.286	.375
Neel, Troy, Oakland*	.357	9	28	7	10	20	1	0	3	6	0	0	0	2	0	7	0	0	1	.714	.400
Newson, Warren, Chicago*	.250	4	8	1	2	2	0	0	0	0	0	0	0	0	0	2	0	0	0	.250	.250
Nilsson, Dave, Milwaukee*	.000	2	5	0	0	0	0	0	0	0	0	0	0	0	0	2	1	0	0	.000	.286
Oberkfell, Ken, California*	.200	5	20	1	4	4	0	0	0	2	0	0	0	0	0	2	0	0	0	.200	.200
O'Brien, Pete, Seattle*	.220	35	118	15	26	43	5	0	4	13	1	2	0	14	3	9	1	0	4	.364	.299

Player, Team	Avg.	G	AB	R	H	TB	2B	3B	HR	RBI	SH	SF	HP	BB	Int. BB	SO	SB	CS	GI DP	Slg.	OBP
Olerud, John, Toronto*	.500	1	2	1	1	2	1	0	0	1	0	0	0	0	0	1	0	0	0	1.000	.500
Orsulak, Joe, Baltimore*	.000	1	1	0	0	0	0	0	0	0	0	0	0	0	0	0	0	0	0	.000	.000
Pagliarulo, Mike, Minnesota*	.000	1	1	0	0	0	0	0	0	0	0	0	0	0	0	0	0	0	0	.000	.000
Palmeiro, Rafael, Texas*	.333	2	3	1	1	4	0	0	1	1	0	0	0	2	0	0	0	0	0	1.333	.600
Parrish, Lance, Cal.-Sea.	.161	16	56	4	9	17	5	0	1	2	0	0	0	6	0	15	1	0	2	.304	.242
Pasqua, Dan, Chicago*	.000	1	1	0	0	0	0	0	0	0	0	0	0	0	0	0	0	0	0	.000	.000
Perezchica, Tony, Cleveland	.000	1	4	0	0	0	0	0	0	0	0	0	0	0	0	2	0	0	0	.000	.000
Petralli, Geno, Texas*	.200	14	25	2	5	6	1	0	0	1	1	0	0	1	0	6	0	0	1	.240	.231
Phillips, Tony, Detroit†	.209	34	115	20	24	37	1	0	4	17	3	4	0	27	1	29	3	3	1	.322	.349
Plantier, Phil, Boston*	.296	23	81	10	24	30	3	0	1	5	0	1	0	8	0	17	0	0	1	.370	.356
Polonia, Luis, California*	.314	47	188	30	59	71	8	2	0	12	3	1	1	12	2	20	15	9	7	.378	.356
Puckett, Kirby, Minnesota	.257	9	35	4	9	11	2	0	0	6	0	1	0	4	1	8	3	0	2	.314	.325
Pulliam, Harvey, Kansas City	.333	2	3	2	1	2	1	0	0	0	0	0	0	0	0	2	0	0	0	.667	.333
Quinones, Luis, Minnesota†	.000	1	0	0	0	0	0	0	0	0	1	0	1	0	0	0	0	0	0	.000	.000
Quirk, Jamie, Oakland*	.000	1	1	0	0	0	0	0	0	0	0	0	0	0	0	0	0	0	0	.000	.000
Raines, Tim, Chicago†	.212	14	52	10	11	18	3	2	0	2	0	1	0	10	1	5	3	1	1	.346	.333
Ready, Randy, Oakland	.233	24	43	5	10	16	0	0	2	7	1	1	0	8	0	7	0	0	3	.372	.346
Reboulet, Jeff, Minnesota	.000	1	1	0	0	0	0	0	0	0	0	0	0	0	0	1	0	0	0	.000	.000
Reed, Darren, Minnesota	.000	1	0	1	0	0	0	0	0	0	0	0	0	0	0	0	0	0	0	.000	.000
Reed, Jody, Boston	.000	1	0	0	0	0	0	0	0	0	0	0	0	0	0	0	1	0	0	.000	.000
Reimer, Kevin, Texas*	.212	32	113	12	24	40	7	0	3	8	0	0	4	6	0	28	1	0	0	.354	.276
Reynolds, Harold, Seattle†	.500	1	2	1	1	1	0	0	0	0	0	0	0	0	0	0	0	0	0	.500	.500
Rivera, Luis, Boston	.000	2	1	0	0	0	0	0	0	0	0	0	0	0	0	1	0	0	0	.000	.000
Rodriguez, Ivan, Texas	.000	2	1	0	0	0	0	0	0	0	0	0	0	1	0	0	0	0	0	.000	.500
Rowland, Rich, Detroit	.250	2	4	1	1	1	0	0	0	0	0	0	0	2	0	1	0	0	1	.250	.500
Russell, Jeff, Texas	.000	1	1	0	0	0	0	0	0	0	1	0	1	0	0	0	0	0	0	.000	.000
Shumpert, Terry, Kansas City	.000	1	2	0	0	0	0	0	0	0	0	0	0	0	0	1	0	0	0	.000	.000
Sierra, Ruben, Tex.-Oak.†	.350	6	20	5	7	12	2	0	1	6	0	1	0	1	1	0	0	0	0	.600	.364
Snow, J.T., New York†	.000	1	1	0	0	0	0	0	0	0	0	0	0	1	1	1	0	0	0	.000	.500
Sorrento, Paul, Cleveland*	.282	11	39	6	11	22	2	0	3	3	0	0	0	4	0	6	0	1	2	.564	.349
Spiers, Bill, Milwaukee*	.000	1	2	1	0	0	0	0	0	0	0	0	0	1	0	1	0	0	0	.000	.333
Sprague, Ed, Toronto	.200	2	5	0	1	2	1	0	0	1	0	0	0	0	0	1	0	0	0	.400	.200
Stankiewicz, Andy, New York	.000	1	0	0	0	0	0	0	0	0	0	1	0	0	0	0	0	0	0	.000	.000
Stanley, Mike, New York	.083	6	12	0	1	1	0	0	0	1	0	0	0	3	0	2	0	0	1	.083	.267
Steinbach, Terry, Oakland	.500	2	8	1	4	4	0	0	0	1	0	0	0	1	0	0	0	0	0	.500	.556
Stephens, Ray, Texas	.000	1	1	0	0	0	0	0	0	0	0	0	0	0	0	1	0	0	0	.167	.286
Stevens, Lee, California*	.167	2	6	1	1	1	0	0	0	1	0	0	0	1	0	1	0	0	0	.167	.286
Stubbs, Franklin, Milwaukee*	.278	16	54	6	15	19	1	0	1	9	0	1	0	5	0	12	4	4	0	.352	.333
Suero, William, Milwaukee	.500	2	2	0	1	1	0	0	0	0	0	0	0	1	0	1	1	0	0	.500	.667
Surhoff, B.J., Milwaukee*	.405	9	37	7	15	21	4	1	0	7	0	0	0	3	1	1	0	0	0	.568	.450
Tabler, Pat, Toronto	.000	2	2	0	0	0	0	0	0	0	0	0	0	0	0	0	0	0	0	.000	.000
Tartabull, Danny, New York	.270	53	185	28	50	80	9	0	7	33	0	0	0	38	3	51	0	2	4	.432	.395
Tettleton, Mickey, Detroit†	.295	40	139	19	41	73	5	0	9	25	0	0	0	37	6	35	0	1	1	.525	.443
Thomas, Frank, Chicago	.143	2	7	0	1	2	1	0	0	1	0	0	0	1	0	2	0	0	0	.286	.250
Thurman, Gary, Kansas City	.000	9	1	0	0	0	0	0	0	0	0	0	0	0	0	0	2	0	0	.000	.000
Vaughn, Greg, Milwaukee	.250	7	28	3	7	14	1	0	2	8	0	1	0	4	0	4	0	0	0	.500	.241
Vaughn, Mo, Boston*	.200	20	70	6	14	23	3	0	2	9	0	0	1	2	1	11	0	0	2	.329	.233
Wedge, Eric, Boston	.232	20	56	7	13	27	2	0	4	9	0	0	0	8	0	16	0	0	0	.482	.328
Whitaker, Lou, Detroit*	.350	10	20	4	7	12	2	0	1	7	0	0	0	1	1	2	0	0	0	.600	.536
White, Devon, Toronto†	.000	1	3	0	0	0	0	0	0	0	0	0	0	0	0	0	0	0	0	.000	.000
Whiten, Mark, Cleveland†	.125	2	8	0	1	1	0	0	0	1	0	0	0	1	0	2	0	1	0	.125	.222
Wilkerson, Curtis, Kansas City†	.000	1	2	0	0	0	0	0	0	0	0	0	0	1	0	0	0	1	0	.000	.333
Williams, Reggie, California†	.000	2	0	0	0	0	0	0	0	0	0	0	0	0	0	1	1	1	0	.000	.000
Wilson, Willie, Oakland†	.000	5	2	1	0	0	0	0	0	0	0	0	0	0	0	0	1	0	0	.000	.000
Winfield, Dave, Toronto	.278	130	490	75	136	234	27	1	23	91	1	3	1	67	9	81	1	2	8	.478	.364
Winningham, Herm, Boston*	.500	6	4	2	2	2	0	0	0	0	0	0	0	0	0	0	0	0	0	.500	.500
Yount, Robin, Milwaukee	.342	11	38	4	13	17	4	0	0	4	0	1	0	9	1	6	1	0	1	.447	.458
Zupcic, Bob, Boston	.500	5	2	1	1	1	0	0	0	0	0	0	0	0	0	0	1	0	0	.500	.500

DESIGNATED HITTERS WITH TWO OR MORE TEAMS

Player, Team	Avg.	G	AB	R	H	TB	2B	3B	HR	RBI	SH	SF	HP	BB	Int. BB	SO	SB	CS	GI DP	Slg.	OBP
Canseco, Jose, Oakland	.316	20	79	18	25	42	2	0	5	19	0	1	0	10	0	19	2	2	5	.532	.389
Canseco, Jose, Texas	.300	8	30	5	9	18	3	0	2	10	0	0	1	4	0	10	0	0	0	.600	.400
Parrish, Lance, California	.125	2	8	0	1	1	0	0	0	1	0	0	0	0	0	3	0	0	0	.125	.125
Parrish, Lance, Seattle	.167	14	48	4	8	16	5	0	1	1	0	0	0	6	0	12	1	0	2	.333	.259
Sierra, Ruben, Texas†	.385	4	13	3	5	7	2	0	0	3	0	1	0	0	0	0	0	0	0	.538	.357
Sierra, Ruben, Oakland†	.286	2	7	2	2	5	0	0	1	3	0	0	0	1	1	0	0	0	0	.714	.375
Hemond, Scott, Oakland	.000	1	1	0	0	0	0	0	0	0	0	1	0	0	0	4	0	0	0	.333	.200
Hemond, Scott, Chicago	.222	4	9	0	2	3	1	0	0	1	0	0	0	0	0	1	0	0	0	.000	.000
Ducey, Rob, Toronto*	.000	4	2	0	0	0	0	0	0	0	0	0	0	0	0	1	0	0	0	.000	.000
Ducey, Rob, California*	.000	1	3	0	0	0	0	0	0	0	0	0	0	0	0	0	0	0	0	.000	.000

The following designated hitters, each of whom appeared in at least one game, had no plate appearances: Lyons, Steve, Boston (2); Ripken, Bill, Baltimore (2); Schaefer, Jeff, Seattle (2); Darling, Ron, Oakland; Gonzalez, Jose, California; Heffernan, Bert, Seattle; Hulse, David, Texas; Huson, Jeff, Texas; Mayne, Brent, Kansas City; Moses, John, Seattle; Newman, Al, Texas; Sax, Steve, Chicago; Trammell, Alan, Detroit; Webster, Lenny, Minnesota.

PINCH-HITTING

TEAM

Team	Avg.	AB	R	H	TB	2B	3B	HR	RBI	SH	SF	HP	BB	Int. BB	SO	SB	CS	GI DP	Slg.	OBP
Boston	.281	139	11	39	49	4	0	2	13	0	0	0	17	3	27	2	2	1	.353	.359
Toronto	.273	55	8	15	20	5	0	0	9	0	0	0	7	1	10	0	0	1	.364	.355
Oakland	.270	115	13	31	37	3	0	1	13	0	2	1	16	4	24	5	0	1	.322	.358
Detroit	.266	94	6	25	36	6	1	1	20	2	4	2	9	2	16	0	0	4	.383	.330
Minnesota	.266	158	11	42	61	14	1	1	31	2	5	0	14	4	23	1	1	5	.386	.316
Kansas City	.250	112	11	28	35	3	2	0	10	2	3	2	10	1	22	0	0	3	.313	.315
Cleveland	.245	110	15	27	40	7	0	2	19	2	1	0	7	0	26	1	0	3	.364	.288
Chicago	.240	104	9	25	28	3	0	0	11	0	2	1	14	2	24	2	0	3	.269	.331
Seattle	.234	158	12	37	56	7	0	4	24	0	3	1	6	1	34	2	1	4	.354	.262
California	.233	133	11	31	44	4	0	3	22	1	3	0	17	4	31	1	0	5	.331	.314
Baltimore	.233	86	9	20	31	6	1	1	19	0	1	2	15	2	23	0	0	1	.360	.343
New York	.214	98	4	21	32	2	0	3	17	1	1	2	10	4	24	0	0	1	.327	.297
Texas	.196	179	15	35	51	5	1	3	26	1	1	1	26	5	56	0	2	4	.285	.300
Milwaukee	.173	52	5	9	10	1	0	0	8	0	3	0	8	2	14	1	2	5	.192	.270
Totals	.242	1593	140	385	530	70	6	21	242	11	29	10	176	35	354	15	8	42	.333	.316

INDIVIDUAL

TOP 15 PINCH-HITTERS

Minimum 20 at-bats. *Lefthanded batter. †Switch-hitter.

Player, Team	Avg.	G	AB	R	H	TB	2B	3B	HR	RBI	SH	SF	HP	BB	Int. BB	SO	SB	CS	GI DP	Slg.	OBP
Eisenreich, Jim, Kansas City*	.370	30	27	3	10	11	1	0	0	4	0	1	0	2	0	1	0	0	1	.407	.400
Larkin, Gene, Minnesota†	.333	26	24	1	8	11	3	0	0	5	0	0	0	2	1	3	0	1	1	.458	.385
Winningham, Herm, Boston*	.316	40	38	4	12	13	1	0	0	3	0	0	0	0	0	8	2	0	0	.342	.316
Briley, Greg, Seattle*	.276	31	29	3	8	15	1	0	2	2	0	0	1	0	0	3	0	1	1	.517	.300
Bergman, Dave, Detroit*	.273	28	22	2	6	9	0	0	1	2	0	1	0	3	1	5	0	0	1	.409	.346
Petralli, Geno, Texas*	.250	40	32	3	8	12	1	0	1	6	0	0	0	6	1	8	0	0	0	.375	.368
Bush, Randy, Minnesota*	.188	56	48	2	9	13	2	1	0	5	0	1	0	5	2	6	0	0	2	.271	.259
Martinez, Chito, Baltimore*	.182	31	22	2	4	4	0	0	0	4	0	0	0	8	1	4	0	0	1	.182	.400
O'Brien, Pete, Seattle*	.174	26	23	1	4	6	2	0	0	5	0	2	0	0	0	3	0	0	0	.261	.160
Morris, John, California*	.160	28	25	2	4	4	0	0	0	1	0	0	0	2	1	6	0	0	0	.160	.222
Daugherty, Jack, Texas†	.136	25	22	1	3	4	1	0	0	3	0	0	0	3	0	4	0	0	0	.182	.240

ALL PINCH-HITTERS

*Lefthanded batter. †Switch-hitter.

Player, Team	Avg.	G	AB	R	H	TB	2B	3B	HR	RBI	SH	SF	HP	BB	Int. BB	SO	SB	CS	GI DP	Slg.	OBP
Abner, Shawn, Chicago	.316	21	19	2	6	8	2	0	0	1	0	0	1	1	0	4	0	0	0	.421	.381
Alomar, Sandy, Cleveland	.000	1	1	0	0	0	0	0	0	0	0	0	0	0	0	0	0	0	0	.000	.000
Alomar, Roberto, Toronto†	.000	1	0	0	0	0	0	0	0	0	0	0	0	1	0	0	0	0	0	.000	1.000
Amaral, Rich, Seattle	.000	2	2	0	0	0	0	0	0	0	0	0	0	0	0	1	0	0	0	.000	.000
Anderson, Brady, Baltimore*	.000	1	1	0	0	0	0	0	0	0	0	0	0	0	0	0	0	0	0	.000	.000
Baines, Harold, Oakland*	.333	11	9	2	3	3	0	0	0	1	0	0	0	2	1	2	0	0	0	.333	.455
Barfield, Jesse, New York	.000	3	3	0	0	0	0	0	0	0	0	0	0	0	0	1	0	0	0	.000	.000
Barnes, Skeeter, Detroit	.188	20	16	3	3	5	1	0	0	5	1	1	1	0	0	0	0	0	1	.313	.222
Bell, Derek, Toronto	.000	3	2	0	0	0	0	0	0	0	0	0	0	1	0	0	0	0	0	.000	.333
Belle, Albert, Cleveland	.000	1	1	0	0	0	0	0	0	0	0	0	0	0	0	0	0	0	0	.000	.000
Bergman, Dave, Detroit*	.273	28	22	2	6	9	0	0	1	2	0	1	0	3	1	5	0	0	1	.409	.346
Bichette, Dante, Milwaukee	.100	11	10	0	1	1	0	0	0	3	0	1	0	0	0	5	0	0	1	.100	.091
Blankenship, Lance, Oakland	.000	7	4	2	0	0	0	0	0	0	0	0	1	2	1	1	0	0	1	.000	.429
Blowers, Mike, Seattle	.000	1	1	0	0	0	0	0	0	0	0	0	0	0	0	0	0	0	0	.000	.000
Boggs, Wade, Boston*	.000	7	4	0	0	0	0	0	0	0	0	0	0	3	2	0	0	0	0	.000	.429
Boone, Bret, Seattle	.000	1	1	0	0	0	0	0	0	0	0	0	0	0	0	1	0	0	0	.000	.000
Borders, Pat, Toronto	1.000	4	3	3	3	5	2	0	0	1	0	0	0	1	1	0	0	0	0	1.667	1.000
Bordick, Mike, Oakland	.000	1	1	0	0	0	0	0	0	0	0	0	0	0	0	0	0	0	0	.000	.000
Bradley, Scott, Seattle*	.000	2	1	0	0	0	0	0	0	0	0	0	0	1	0	1	0	0	0	.000	.500
Brett, George, Kansas City*	.000	3	3	0	0	0	0	0	0	0	0	0	0	0	0	0	0	0	1	.000	.000
Briley, Greg, Seattle*	.276	31	29	3	8	15	1	0	2	2	0	0	1	0	0	3	0	1	1	.517	.300
Brito, Bernardo, Minnesota	.000	4	4	0	0	0	0	0	0	0	0	0	0	0	0	2	0	0	0	.000	.000
Brooks, Hubie, California	.250	8	8	1	2	3	1	0	0	1	0	0	0	0	0	2	0	0	1	.375	.250
Brosius, Scott, Oakland	.000	2	2	0	0	0	0	0	0	0	0	0	0	0	0	0	0	0	0	.000	.000
Browne, Jerry, Oakland†	.467	15	15	3	7	7	0	0	0	0	0	0	0	0	0	2	0	0	0	.467	.467
Bruett, J.T., Minnesota*	.375	11	8	1	3	4	1	0	0	1	0	0	0	2	0	1	1	0	0	.500	.500
Brumley, Mike, Boston†	.000	1	1	0	0	0	0	0	0	0	0	0	0	0	0	0	0	0	0	.000	.000
Brunansky, Tom, Boston	.286	12	7	1	2	2	0	0	0	2	0	0	0	5	0	1	0	1	1	.286	.583
Buhner, Jay, Seattle	.333	3	3	1	1	4	0	0	1	3	0	0	0	0	0	0	0	0	0	1.333	.333
Burks, Ellis, Boston	.000	3	3	0	0	0	0	0	0	0	0	0	0	0	0	0	0	0	0	.000	.000
Bush, Randy, Minnesota*	.188	56	48	2	9	13	2	1	0	5	0	1	0	5	2	6	0	0	2	.271	.259
Cangelosi, John, Texas†	.400	6	5	0	2	2	0	0	0	1	0	0	0	1	0	2	0	0	0	.400	.500
Canseco, Jose, Oak.-Tex.	.000	3	3	0	0	0	0	0	0	0	0	0	0	0	0	1	0	0	0	.000	.000
Carreon, Mark, Detroit	.250	8	8	0	2	3	1	0	0	1	0	0	0	0	0	1	0	0	1	.375	.250
Carter, Joe, Toronto	.000	1	1	0	0	0	0	0	0	0	0	0	0	0	0	0	0	0	0	.000	.000
Clark, Jack, Boston	.500	7	6	1	3	3	0	0	0	1	0	0	0	1	0	0	0	0	0	.500	.571
Clark, Phil, Detroit	.500	7	6	0	3	3	0	0	0	1	1	0	0	0	0	1	0	0	0	.500	.500

Player, Team	Avg.	G	AB	R	H	TB	2B	3B	HR	RBI	SH	SF	HP	BB	Int. BB	SO	SB	CS	GI DP	Slg.	OBP
Cochrane, Dave, Seattle†	.235	19	17	0	4	5	1	0	0	2	0	0	0	2	0	7	0	0	0	.294	.316
Cole, Alex, Cleveland*	.077	14	13	2	1	1	0	0	0	1	0	0	0	1	0	5	0	0	0	.077	.143
Colon, Cris, Texas†	.000	1	1	0	0	0	0	0	0	0	0	0	0	0	0	1	0	0	0	.000	.000
Cooper, Scott, Boston*	.333	18	15	1	5	8	3	0	0	0	0	0	0	2	0	5	0	0	0	.533	.412
Cora, Joey, Chicago†	.222	12	9	1	2	2	0	0	0	1	0	0	0	3	0	3	1	0	0	.222	.417
Cotto, Henry, Seattle	.500	21	18	4	9	13	1	0	1	5	0	0	0	1	1	1	1	0	0	.722	.526
Cron, Chris, Chicago	.000	4	4	0	0	0	0	0	0	0	0	0	0	0	0	2	0	0	0	.000	.000
Curtis, Chad, California	.000	9	5	1	0	0	0	0	0	0	0	0	0	4	0	0	0	0	0	.000	.444
Cuyler, Milt, Detroit†	.000	1	0	0	0	0	0	0	0	0	0	0	1	0	0	0	0	0	0	.000	1.000
Daugherty, Jack, Texas†	.136	25	22	1	3	4	1	0	0	3	0	0	0	3	0	4	0	0	0	.182	.240
Davis, Alvin, California*	.545	12	11	1	6	7	1	0	0	2	0	0	0	1	0	1	0	0	1	.636	.583
Davis, Chili, Minnesota†	.313	20	16	1	5	9	1	0	1	6	0	1	0	3	0	2	0	0	1	.563	.400
Davis, Glenn, Baltimore	.400	6	5	2	2	5	0	0	1	3	0	0	0	1	0	0	0	0	1	1.000	.500
Deer, Rob, Detroit	.000	3	3	0	0	0	0	0	0	0	0	0	0	0	0	2	0	0	0	.000	.000
Devereaux, Mike, Baltimore	1.000	1	1	0	1	1	0	0	0	0	0	0	0	0	0	0	0	0	1	1.000	1.000
Diaz, Mario, Texas	.000	1	1	0	0	0	0	0	0	0	0	0	0	0	0	0	0	0	0	.000	.000
DiSarcina, Gary, California	.000	1	1	0	0	0	0	0	0	0	0	0	0	0	0	0	0	0	0	.000	.200
Downing, Brian, Texas	.000	15	12	0	0	0	0	0	0	1	0	0	1	2	1	7	0	0	0	.000	.200
Ducey, Rob, Tor.-Cal.*	.300	12	10	0	3	4	1	0	0	0	0	0	0	0	0	4	0	0	0	.400	.300
Easley, Damion, California	.250	4	4	1	1	4	0	0	1	3	0	0	0	0	0	1	0	0	0	1.000	.250
Eisenreich, Jim, Kansas City*	.370	30	27	3	10	11	1	0	0	4	0	1	0	2	0	1	0	0	1	.407	.400
Fariss, Monty, Texas	.071	19	14	2	1	3	0	1	0	1	0	0	0	5	0	7	0	0	0	.214	.316
Felix, Junior, California†	.143	8	7	0	1	1	0	0	0	0	0	0	0	0	0	3	0	0	0	.143	.143
Fermin, Felix, Cleveland	.500	4	2	1	1	2	1	0	0	2	1	0	0	1	0	0	0	0	0	1.000	.667
Fisk, Carlton, Chicago	.333	7	6	0	2	2	0	0	0	2	0	0	0	1	1	1	0	0	0	.333	.429
Fitzgerald, Mike, California	.100	12	10	0	1	1	0	0	0	1	0	0	0	1	0	3	0	0	0	.100	.182
Flaherty, John, Boston	.000	1	1	0	0	0	0	0	0	0	0	0	0	0	0	1	0	0	0	.000	.000
Fletcher, Scott, Milwaukee	.000	4	4	0	0	0	0	0	0	0	0	0	0	0	0	1	0	0	0	.000	.000
Fox, Eric, Oakland†	.000	6	4	0	0	0	0	0	0	1	0	0	0	2	0	1	0	0	0	.000	.333
Franco, Julio, Texas	.429	8	7	0	3	3	0	0	0	1	0	0	0	1	1	2	0	0	1	.429	.500
Gaetti, Gary, California	.286	7	7	1	2	5	0	0	1	3	0	0	0	0	0	1	0	0	0	.714	.286
Gagne, Greg, Minnesota	.000	1	1	0	0	0	0	0	0	0	0	0	0	0	0	0	0	0	0	.000	.000
Gantner, Jim, Milwaukee*	.167	7	6	0	1	1	0	0	0	1	0	0	0	1	0	1	0	0	0	.167	.286
Gladden, Dan, Detroit	.400	6	5	1	2	3	1	0	0	1	0	0	0	1	0	1	0	0	0	.500	.500
Gonzales, Rene, California	.500	2	2	0	1	1	0	0	0	2	0	0	0	0	0	0	0	0	0	.500	.500
Gonzalez, Jose, California	.125	11	8	1	1	1	0	0	0	1	0	0	0	2	0	3	0	0	0	.125	.300
Gonzalez, Juan, Texas	.167	7	6	1	1	4	0	0	1	3	0	0	0	1	1	1	0	0	0	.667	.286
Greenwell, Mike, Boston*	1.000	2	2	0	2	2	0	0	0	0	0	0	0	0	0	0	0	0	0	1.000	1.000
Griffey, Ken, Seattle*	.333	3	3	0	1	1	0	0	0	0	0	0	0	0	0	0	0	0	0	.333	.333
Griffin, Alfredo, Toronto†	.000	5	5	1	0	0	0	0	0	0	0	0	0	0	0	1	0	0	1	.000	.000
Gruber, Kelly, Toronto	.000	1	1	0	0	0	0	0	0	0	0	0	0	0	0	0	0	0	0	.000	.000
Gwynn, Chris, Kansas City*	.200	14	10	4	2	5	0	0	0	4	0	0	0	1	0	1	0	0	2	.333	.273
Hall, Mel, New York*	.333	12	12	0	4	4	0	0	0	4	0	0	0	0	0	2	0	0	0	.333	.333
Hamilton, Darryl, Milwaukee*	.333	6	3	1	1	1	0	0	0	2	0	1	0	2	0	1	1	1	1	.333	.500
Hare, Shawn, Detroit*	.750	4	4	0	3	4	1	0	0	4	0	0	0	0	0	0	0	0	0	1.000	.750
Harper, Brian, Minnesota	.125	9	8	0	1	1	0	0	0	1	0	0	0	0	0	1	0	0	0	.125	.111
Harris, Donald, Texas	.500	2	2	0	1	1	0	0	0	1	0	0	0	0	0	1	0	0	0	.500	.500
Haselman, Bill, Seattle	1.000	1	1	0	1	1	0	0	0	0	0	0	0	0	0	0	0	0	0	1.000	1.000
Hatcher, Billy, Boston	.000	1	1	0	0	0	0	0	0	0	0	0	0	0	0	1	0	0	0	.000	.000
Hayes, Charlie, New York	.000	1	1	0	0	0	0	0	0	0	0	0	0	0	0	0	0	0	0	.000	.000
Hayes, Von, California*	.500	6	4	1	2	2	0	0	0	1	0	1	0	1	0	0	0	0	0	.500	.500
Heffernan, Bert, Seattle*	.000	2	2	0	0	0	0	0	0	0	0	0	0	0	0	0	0	0	0	.333	.250
Hemond, Scott, Oak.-Chi.	.333	4	3	0	1	1	0	0	0	1	0	0	0	0	0	2	0	0	0	.000	.000
Henderson, Dave, Oakland	.000	6	6	0	0	0	0	0	0	0	0	0	0	0	0	2	0	0	1	.333	.500
Henderson, Rickey, Oakland	.333	4	3	0	1	1	0	0	0	0	0	0	0	1	0	1	0	0	0	.444	.333
Hill, Donnie, Minnesota	.333	9	9	2	3	4	1	0	0	0	0	0	0	0	0	0	0	0	0	.111	.200
Hill, Glenallen, Cleveland	.111	10	9	0	1	1	0	0	0	2	0	0	0	1	0	4	0	0	0	.273	.400
Horn, Sam, Baltimore*	.182	18	11	0	2	3	1	0	0	3	0	0	0	4	0	5	0	0	0	.368	.316
Howard, Thomas, Cleveland†	.316	20	19	1	6	7	1	0	0	2	1	0	0	0	0	3	1	0	0	.000	.000
Howitt, Dann, Seattle*	.000	2	2	0	0	0	0	0	0	0	0	0	0	0	0	1	0	0	0	.500	.500
Hrbek, Kent, Minnesota*	.500	2	2	0	1	1	0	0	0	1	0	0	0	0	0	0	0	0	0	.313	.400
Huff, Mike, Chicago	.313	20	16	2	5	5	0	0	0	3	0	1	0	3	1	4	0	0	1	.333	.300
Hulett, Tim, Baltimore	.222	11	9	2	2	3	1	0	0	2	0	0	0	1	0	4	0	0	1	.000	.000
Humphreys, Mike, New York	.000	1	1	0	0	0	0	0	0	0	0	0	0	0	0	3	0	0	0	.083	.083
Huson, Jeff, Texas*	.083	12	12	1	1	1	0	0	0	0	0	0	0	0	0	2	0	0	0	.667	.600
Jacoby, Brook, Cleveland	.556	10	9	2	5	6	1	0	0	3	0	0	0	1	0	2	0	0	0	.667	.667
Jaha, John, Milwaukee	.667	3	3	0	2	2	0	0	0	0	0	0	0	0	0	0	0	0	0	.667	.667
James, Dion, New York*	.118	20	17	1	2	5	0	0	1	3	0	0	0	1	0	3	0	0	1	.294	.167
Jefferies, Gregg, Kansas City†	.000	5	5	0	0	0	0	0	0	0	0	0	0	2	1	0	0	0	0	.000	.400
Jefferson, Reggie, Cleveland†	.500	2	2	0	1	1	0	0	0	0	0	0	0	0	0	0	0	0	0	.500	.500
Jeter, Shawn, Chicago*	.000	2	2	0	0	0	0	0	0	0	0	0	0	0	0	1	0	0	0	.000	.000
Johnson, Lance, Chicago*	.333	3	3	1	1	1	0	0	0	0	0	0	0	0	0	0	0	0	1	.333	.333
Jorgensen, Terry, Minnesota	.000	1	1	0	0	0	0	0	0	0	0	0	0	0	0	0	0	0	0	.000	.000
Joyner, Wally, Kansas City*	.000	1	1	0	0	0	0	0	0	0	0	0	0	0	0	0	0	0	0	.000	.000
Karkovice, Ron, Chicago	.000	4	4	0	0	0	0	0	0	0	0	0	0	0	0	1	0	0	0	.000	.000
Kelly, Roberto, New York	.000	7	5	0	0	0	0	0	0	1	0	1	0	0	0	1	0	0	0	.500	.500
Kent, Jeff, Toronto	.500	2	2	0	1	1	0	0	0	0	0	0	0	0	0	0	0	0	0	.500	.500
Kingery, Mike, Oakland*	.000	3	3	0	0	0	0	0	0	0	0	0	0	0	0	0	0	0	0	.556	.300
Kirby, Wayne, Cleveland*	.222	10	9	2	2	5	0	0	1	1	0	0	0	1	0	0	0	0	0	.000	.000
Knoblauch, Chuck, Minnesota	.000	1	1	0	0	0	0	0	0	0	0	0	0	0	0	0	0	0	0	.400	.500
Koslofski, Kevin, Kansas City*	.400	6	5	1	2	2	0	0	0	0	0	0	0	1	0	1	0	0	0	.667	.667
Kreuter, Chad, Detroit†	.667	3	3	0	2	2	0	0	0	0	0	0	0	0	0	0	0	0	0	.400	.200
Lansford, Carney, Oakland	.200	5	5	0	1	2	1	0	0	0	0	0	0	0	0	1	0	0	0	.458	.385
Larkin, Gene, Minnesota†	.333	26	24	1	8	11	3	0	0	5	0	0	0	2	1	3	0	1	1	.458	.385
Leius, Scott, Minnesota	.667	4	3	0	2	2	0	0	0	1	1	0	0	0	0	2	0	0	0	.667	.667
Levis, Jesse, Cleveland*	.083	12	12	0	1	1	0	0	0	0	0	0	0	0	0	1	0	0	0	.083	.083
Leyritz, Jim, New York	.100	14	10	0	1	2	1	0	0	3	0	0	1	2	1	2	0	0	0	.200	.308

Player, Team	Avg.	G	AB	R	H	TB	2B	3B	HR	RBI	SH	SF	HP	BB	Int. BB	SO	SB	CS	GI DP	Slg.	OBP
Listach, Pat, Milwaukee†	.000	1	1	0	0	0	0	0	0	0	0	0	0	0	0	0	0	0	0	.000	.000
Livingston, Scott, Detroit*	.231	16	13	0	3	6	3	0	0	1	0	1	0	1	1	0	0	0	0	.462	.267
Lofton, Kenny, Cleveland*	.000	3	2	1	0	0	0	0	0	0	0	0	0	1	0	1	0	0	0	.000	.333
Lyons, Steve, Boston*	.400	6	5	2	2	2	0	0	0	0	0	0	0	1	0	0	0	0	0	.400	.500
Maas, Kevin, New York*	.368	24	19	2	7	11	1	0	1	3	0	0	0	2	1	5	0	0	1	.579	.429
Macfarlane, Mike, Kansas City	.250	19	16	2	4	7	1	1	0	3	0	0	2	1	0	3	0	0	0	.438	.368
Mack, Shane, Minnesota	.500	2	2	1	1	2	1	0	0	2	0	0	0	0	0	0	0	0	0	1.000	.500
Maksudian, Mike, Toronto*	.000	3	3	0	0	0	0	0	0	0	0	0	0	0	0	0	0	0	0	.000	.000
Maldonado, Candy, Toronto	.000	3	2	0	0	0	0	0	0	0	0	0	0	1	0	1	0	0	0	.000	.333
Martinez, Chito, Baltimore*	.182	31	22	2	4	4	0	0	0	4	0	0	0	8	1	4	0	0	1	.182	.400
Martinez, Carlos, Cleveland	.333	11	9	2	3	5	2	0	0	3	0	1	0	1	0	0	0	0	0	.556	.364
Martinez, Domingo, Toronto	1.000	2	2	0	2	2	0	0	0	0	0	0	0	0	0	0	0	0	0	1.000	1.000
Martinez, Edgar, Seattle	.000	3	3	0	0	0	0	0	0	0	0	0	0	0	0	0	0	0	0	.000	.000
Martinez, Tino, Seattle*	.091	12	11	1	1	1	0	0	0	0	0	0	0	0	0	4	0	0	2	.091	.091
Marzano, John, Boston	.000	1	1	0	0	0	0	0	0	0	0	0	0	0	0	0	0	0	0	.000	.000
Mattingly, Don, New York*	.000	2	2	0	0	0	0	0	0	0	0	0	0	0	0	0	0	0	0	.000	.000
Maurer, Rob, Texas*	.200	5	5	0	1	1	0	0	0	1	0	0	0	0	0	2	0	0	0	.200	.200
Mayne, Brent, Kansas City*	.286	16	14	0	4	4	0	0	0	1	0	1	0	0	0	5	0	0	1	.286	.267
McGinnis, Russ, Texas	.000	2	2	0	0	0	0	0	0	0	0	0	0	0	0	1	0	0	0	.000	.000
McGwire, Mark, Oakland	.000	1	1	0	0	0	0	0	0	0	0	0	0	0	0	0	0	0	0	.000	.000
McIntosh, Tim, Milwaukee	.000	2	2	0	0	0	0	0	0	0	0	0	0	0	0	0	0	0	0	.000	.000
McLemore, Mark, Baltimore†	.364	13	11	3	4	9	3	1	0	6	0	1	0	1	0	2	0	0	0	.818	.385
McRae, Brian, Kansas City†	.400	5	5	0	2	2	0	0	0	0	0	0	0	0	0	1	0	0	0	.400	.400
McReynolds, Kevin, Kansas City	.000	4	4	0	0	0	0	0	0	0	0	0	0	0	0	1	0	0	0	.000	.000
Melvin, Bob, Kansas City	.250	11	8	0	2	3	1	0	0	2	0	1	0	1	0	1	0	0	0	.375	.300
Mercedes, Henry, Oakland	.500	2	2	0	1	1	0	0	0	0	0	0	0	0	0	1	0	0	0	.500	.500
Mercedes, Luis, Baltimore	.000	2	2	0	0	0	0	0	0	0	0	0	0	0	0	0	0	0	0	.000	.000
Merullo, Matt, Chicago*	.000	8	7	0	0	0	0	0	0	0	0	0	0	1	0	0	0	0	0	.000	.125
Miller, Keith, Kansas City	.000	2	2	0	0	0	0	0	0	0	0	0	0	0	0	0	0	0	0	.000	.000
Milligan, Randy, Baltimore	.000	3	3	0	0	0	0	0	0	0	0	0	0	0	0	0	0	0	0	.000	.000
Mitchell, Kevin, Seattle	.600	5	5	0	3	4	1	0	0	4	0	0	0	0	0	0	0	0	0	.800	.600
Molitor, Paul, Milwaukee	.000	2	2	0	0	0	0	0	0	0	0	0	0	0	0	0	0	0	1	.000	.000
Morris, John, California*	.160	28	25	2	4	4	0	0	0	1	0	0	0	2	1	6	0	0	0	.160	.222
Moses, John, Seattle†	.000	1	1	0	0	0	0	0	0	0	0	0	0	0	0	0	0	0	0	.000	.000
Mulliniks, Rance, Toronto*	.500	3	2	1	1	1	0	0	0	0	0	0	0	1	0	0	0	0	0	.500	.667
Munoz, Pedro, Minnesota	.167	6	6	0	1	1	0	0	0	0	0	0	0	0	0	2	0	0	0	.167	.167
Myers, Greg, California*	.250	4	4	0	1	1	0	0	0	1	0	0	0	0	0	2	0	0	0	.250	.250
Naehring, Tim, Boston	.000	10	8	0	0	0	0	0	0	0	0	0	0	1	0	2	0	0	0	.000	.111
Neel, Troy, Oakland*	.429	8	7	0	3	5	2	0	0	3	0	0	0	1	0	1	0	0	0	.714	.500
Newman, Al, Texas†	.400	6	5	1	2	2	0	0	0	0	1	0	0	0	0	2	0	0	0	.400	.400
Newson, Warren, Chicago*	.200	18	15	1	3	3	0	0	0	1	0	0	0	3	0	5	0	0	2	.200	.333
Nilsson, Dave, Milwaukee*	.000	1	1	0	0	0	0	0	0	0	0	0	0	0	0	0	0	0	0	.000	.000
Nokes, Matt, New York*	.308	16	13	1	4	7	0	0	1	2	0	0	1	1	1	4	0	0	0	.538	.400
Oberkfell, Ken, California*	.125	15	8	0	1	1	0	0	0	3	0	2	0	4	2	0	0	0	1	.125	.357
O'Brien, Pete, Seattle*	.174	26	23	1	4	6	2	0	0	5	0	2	0	0	0	3	0	0	0	.261	.160
Olerud, John, Toronto*	.400	10	10	2	4	6	2	0	0	6	0	0	0	0	0	1	0	0	0	.600	.400
Orsulak, Joe, Baltimore*	.125	9	8	0	1	2	1	0	0	0	0	0	0	0	0	1	0	0	0	.250	.125
Ortiz, Junior, Cleveland	.667	3	3	1	2	2	0	0	0	1	0	0	0	0	0	0	0	0	0	.667	.667
Pagliarulo, Mike, Minnesota*	.167	12	12	2	2	4	2	0	0	1	0	0	0	0	0	3	0	0	0	.333	.167
Palmeiro, Rafael, Texas*	.000	4	3	0	0	0	0	0	0	2	0	1	0	0	0	0	0	0	0	.000	.000
Palmer, Dean, Texas	.500	6	4	3	2	5	0	0	1	2	0	0	0	2	0	1	0	0	0	1.250	.667
Parent, Mark, Baltimore	.000	1	1	0	0	0	0	0	0	0	0	0	0	0	0	1	0	0	0	.000	.000
Parrish, Lance, Seattle	.000	12	11	0	0	0	0	0	0	0	0	0	0	0	0	5	0	0	0	.000	.000
Pasqua, Dan, Chicago*	.250	9	8	0	2	2	0	0	0	0	0	0	0	1	0	1	0	0	0	.250	.333
Peltier, Dan, Texas*	.000	3	3	0	0	0	0	0	0	0	0	0	0	0	0	1	0	0	0	.000	.000
Pena, Tony, Boston	1.000	1	1	0	1	1	0	0	0	0	0	0	0	0	0	0	0	1	0	1.000	1.000
Perezchica, Tony, Cleveland	1.000	1	1	0	1	2	1	0	0	1	0	0	0	0	0	0	0	0	0	2.000	1.000
Petralli, Geno, Texas*	.250	40	32	3	8	12	1	0	1	6	0	0	0	6	1	8	0	0	0	.375	.368
Pettis, Gary, Detroit†	.000	1	1	0	0	0	0	0	0	0	0	0	0	0	0	1	0	0	0	.000	.000
Phillips, Tony, Detroit†	.000	1	1	0	0	0	0	0	0	0	0	0	0	0	0	1	0	0	0	.000	.000
Plantier, Phil, Boston*	.333	14	12	1	4	7	0	0	1	2	0	0	0	1	1	4	0	0	0	.583	.385
Polonia, Luis, California*	.250	4	4	0	1	1	0	0	0	0	0	0	0	0	0	2	1	0	0	.250	.250
Puckett, Kirby, Minnesota	.500	3	2	0	1	1	0	0	0	0	0	0	0	1	0	1	0	0	0	.500	.667
Pulliam, Harvey, Kansas City	.000	1	0	0	0	0	0	0	0	0	0	0	0	1	0	0	0	0	0	.000	1.000
Quinlan, Tom, Toronto	.000	2	1	0	0	0	0	0	0	0	0	0	0	1	0	1	0	0	0	.000	.500
Quinones, Luis, Minnesota†	.000	2	1	0	0	0	0	0	0	0	0	0	0	0	0	0	0	0	0	.000	.000
Quirk, Jamie, Oakland*	.353	20	17	1	6	6	0	0	0	2	0	1	0	1	0	5	0	0	0	.353	.368
Raines, Tim, Chicago†	.750	5	4	2	3	4	1	0	0	2	0	0	0	1	0	0	0	0	0	1.000	.800
Ready, Randy, Oakland	.375	23	16	4	6	9	0	0	1	6	0	1	0	4	1	1	0	0	0	.563	.476
Reboulet, Jeff, Minnesota	.000	3	2	0	0	0	0	0	0	1	0	0	0	1	0	2	0	0	0	.000	.333
Reed, Darren, Minnesota	.000	3	2	0	0	0	0	0	0	1	0	1	0	0	0	1	0	0	0	.000	.000
Reimer, Kevin, Texas*	.333	20	15	1	5	7	2	0	0	4	0	0	0	3	1	6	0	1	1	.467	.444
Reynolds, Harold, Seattle†	.182	12	11	1	2	2	0	0	0	1	0	0	0	0	0	3	1	0	0	.182	.167
Rivera, Luis, Boston	.000	6	6	0	0	0	0	0	0	0	0	0	0	0	0	4	0	0	0	.000	.000
Rodriguez, Ivan, Texas	.111	10	9	0	1	1	0	0	0	0	0	0	0	1	0	1	0	0	1	.111	.200
Rohde, David, Cleveland†	.000	2	2	0	0	0	0	0	0	0	0	0	0	0	0	0	0	0	0	.000	.000
Rose, Bob, California	.500	3	2	1	1	4	0	0	1	2	1	0	0	0	0	0	0	0	0	2.000	.500
Russell, John, Texas	.000	4	4	0	0	0	0	0	0	0	0	0	0	0	0	0	0	0	0	.000	.000
Samuel, Juan, Kansas City	.000	2	2	0	0	0	0	0	0	0	0	0	0	0	0	1	0	0	0	.000	.000
Sax, Steve, Chicago	.000	1	1	0	0	0	0	0	0	0	0	0	0	0	0	0	0	0	0	.000	.000
Segui, David, Baltimore†	.364	11	11	0	4	4	0	0	0	1	0	0	0	0	0	3	0	0	0	.364	.364
Seitzer, Kevin, Milwaukee	.000	1	0	0	0	0	0	0	0	0	0	0	0	1	0	0	0	0	0	.000	1.000
Sierra, Ruben, Tex.-Oak.†	.333	3	3	1	1	1	0	0	0	0	0	0	0	0	0	0	0	0	0	.333	.333
Silvestri, Dave, New York	.000	1	1	0	0	0	0	0	0	0	0	0	0	0	0	0	0	0	0	.000	.000
Snow, J.T., New York†	.000	1	0	0	0	0	0	0	0	0	0	0	0	1	1	0	0	0	0	.000	1.000
Sojo, Luis, California	.250	4	4	1	1	1	0	0	0	0	0	0	0	0	0	0	0	0	0	.250	.250
Sorrento, Paul, Cleveland*	.143	14	14	2	2	5	0	0	1	3	0	0	0	0	0	6	0	0	0	.357	.143

Player, Team	Avg.	G	AB	R	H	TB	2B	3B	HR	RBI	SH	SF	HP	BB	Int. BB	SO	SB	CS	GI DP	Slg.	OBP
Spiers, Bill, Milwaukee*	.000	1	1	0	0	0	0	0	0	0	0	0	0	0	0	1	0	0	0	.000	.000
Sprague, Ed, Toronto	.667	3	3	0	2	3	1	0	0	1	0	0	0	0	0	1	0	0	0	1.000	.667
Stankiewicz, Andy, New York	.000	4	3	0	0	0	0	0	0	0	1	0	0	2	0	3	0	0	0	.000	.400
Stanley, Mike, New York	.200	7	5	0	1	1	0	0	0	0	0	0	0	2	0	2	0	0	0	.200	.429
Steinbach, Terry, Oakland	.000	5	5	0	0	0	0	0	0	0	0	0	0	0	0	2	0	0	0	.000	.000
Stephens, Ray, Texas	.000	3	3	0	0	0	0	0	0	0	0	0	0	0	0	0	0	0	0	.000	.000
Stevens, Lee, California*	.250	16	12	0	3	4	1	0	0	2	0	0	0	2	1	4	0	0	1	.333	.357
Stubbs, Franklin, Milwaukee*	.300	14	10	3	3	4	1	0	0	2	0	0	0	3	2	1	0	1	1	.400	.462
Surhoff, B.J., Milwaukee*	.250	5	4	1	1	1	0	0	0	0	0	0	0	1	0	1	0	0	1	.250	.400
Sveum, Dale, Chicago†	.000	4	4	0	0	0	0	0	0	0	0	0	0	0	0	3	0	0	0	.000	.000
Tabler, Pat, Toronto	.000	8	7	0	0	0	0	0	0	1	0	0	0	1	0	1	0	0	0	.000	.125
Tackett, Jeff, Baltimore	.000	1	1	0	0	0	0	0	0	0	0	0	0	0	0	0	0	0	0	.000	.000
Tartabull, Danny, New York	.000	4	3	0	0	0	0	0	0	0	0	0	0	1	0	1	0	0	0	.000	.250
Tettleton, Mickey, Detroit†	.250	5	4	0	1	1	0	0	0	1	0	0	0	0	0	0	0	0	0	.250	.250
Thomas, Frank, Chicago	.000	1	1	0	0	0	0	0	0	0	0	0	0	0	0	1	0	0	0	.000	.000
Thome, Jim, Cleveland*	.000	1	1	0	0	0	0	0	0	1	0	0	0	1	0	1	0	1	0	.000	.500
Thon, Dickie, Texas	.375	11	8	1	3	4	1	0	0	1	0	0	0	0	0	4	0	0	0	.500	.375
Thurman, Gary, Kansas City	.125	11	8	1	1	3	0	1	0	0	1	0	0	0	0	3	0	0	0	.375	.125
Tingley, Ron, California	.000	3	3	0	0	0	0	0	0	0	0	0	0	0	0	1	0	0	0	.000	.000
Turner, Shane, Seattle*	.200	7	5	0	1	2	1	0	0	1	0	0	0	2	0	0	0	0	0	.400	.429
Valentin, Jose, Milwaukee†	.000	1	0	0	0	0	0	0	0	1	0	1	0	0	0	0	0	0	0	.000	.000
Valle, Dave, Seattle	.667	3	3	1	2	2	0	0	0	1	0	0	0	0	0	2	0	0	1	.667	.667
Vaughn, Greg, Milwaukee	.000	4	4	0	0	0	0	0	0	0	0	0	0	0	0	1	0	0	0	.000	.000
Vaughn, Mo, Boston*	.308	14	13	1	4	7	0	0	1	3	0	0	0	1	0	1	0	0	0	.538	.357
Velarde, Randy, New York	.667	3	3	0	2	2	0	0	0	1	0	0	0	0	0	0	0	0	0	.667	.667
Vizquel, Omar, Seattle†	.000	5	5	0	0	0	0	0	0	0	0	0	0	0	0	1	0	0	0	.000	.000
Ward, Turner, Toronto†	.000	4	4	0	0	0	0	0	0	0	0	0	0	0	0	0	0	0	0	.000	.000
Webster, Lenny, Minnesota	.833	6	6	1	5	8	3	0	0	6	0	0	0	0	0	1	0	0	0	1.333	.833
Wedge, Eric, Boston	.400	6	5	0	2	2	0	0	0	1	0	0	0	1	0	0	1	0	0	.400	.500
Weiss, Walt, Oakland†	.000	2	1	0	0	0	0	0	0	0	0	0	0	1	0	0	1	0	0	.000	.333
Whitaker, Lou, Detroit†	.000	12	8	0	0	0	0	0	0	0	0	0	0	4	0	2	0	0	0	.000	.333
Whiten, Mark, Cleveland†	1.000	1	1	1	1	2	1	0	0	0	0	0	0	1	0	0	0	0	0	2.000	1.000
Wilkerson, Curtis, Kansas City†	.250	5	4	0	1	1	0	0	0	0	0	0	0	1	0	3	0	0	0	.250	.400
Wilson, Willie, Oakland†	.300	12	10	1	3	3	0	0	0	0	0	0	0	2	1	2	3	0	0	.300	.417
Winningham, Herm, Boston*	.316	40	38	4	12	13	1	0	0	3	0	0	0	0	0	8	2	0	0	.342	.316
Yount, Robin, Milwaukee	.000	1	1	0	0	0	0	0	0	0	0	0	0	0	0	0	0	0	0	.000	.000
Zosky, Eddie, Toronto	1.000	1	1	1	1	1	0	0	0	0	0	0	0	0	0	1	0	0	0	1.000	1.000
Zupcic, Bob, Boston	.200	11	10	0	2	2	0	0	0	1	0	0	0	1	0	1	0	0	0	.200	.273

PINCH-HITTERS WITH TWO OR MORE TEAMS

Player, Team	Avg.	G	AB	R	H	TB	2B	3B	HR	RBI	SH	SF	HP	BB	Int. BB	SO	SB	CS	GI DP	Slg.	OBP
Canseco, Jose, Oakland	.000	1	1	0	0	0	0	0	0	0	0	0	0	0	0	1	0	0	0	.000	.000
Canseco, Jose, Texas	.000	2	2	0	0	0	0	0	0	0	0	0	0	0	0	1	0	0	0	.000	.000
Ducey, Rob, Toronto*	.000	2	2	0	0	0	0	0	0	0	0	0	0	0	0	3	0	0	0	.500	.375
Ducey, Rob, California*	.375	10	8	0	3	4	1	0	0	0	0	0	0	0	0	2	0	0	0	.000	.000
Hemond, Scott, Oakland	.000	2	2	0	0	0	0	0	0	1	0	1	0	0	0	0	0	0	1	.000	.500
Hemond, Scott, Chicago	1.000	2	1	0	1	1	0	0	0	0	0	0	0	0	0	0	0	0	0	.500	.500
Sierra, Ruben, Texas†	.500	2	2	1	1	1	0	0	0	1	0	0	0	0	0	0	0	0	0	.500	.000
Sierra, Ruben, Oakland†	.000	1	1	0	0	0	0	0	0	0	0	0	0	0	0	0	0	0	0	.000	.000

PITCHING

TEAM

Team	W	L	ERA	G	CG	ShO	Sv.	IP	H	TBF	R	ER	HR	SH	SF	HB	BB	Int. BB	SO	WP	Bk.
Milwaukee	92	70	3.43	162	19	14	39	1457.0	1344	6040	604	556	127	47	42	47	435	33	793	37	8
Boston	73	89	3.58	162	22	13	39	1448.2	1403	6173	669	577	107	51	49	41	535	56	943	50	6
Minnesota	90	72	3.70	162	16	13	50	1453.0	1391	6086	653	598	121	50	49	36	479	30	923	52	5
Oakland	96	66	3.73	162	8	9	58	1447.0	1396	6204	672	599	129	56	56	41	601	46	843	67	4
Baltimore	89	73	3.79	162	20	16	48	1464.0	1419	6193	656	616	124	59	47	36	518	38	846	45	6
Kansas City	72	90	3.81	162	9	12	44	1447.1	1426	6171	667	613	106	50	67	39	512	50	834	42	10
Chicago	86	76	3.82	162	21	5	52	1461.2	1400	6244	690	621	123	43	45	55	550	48	810	35	6
California	72	90	3.84	162	26	13	42	1446.0	1449	6154	671	617	130	47	50	39	532	40	888	42	5
Toronto	96	66	3.91	162	18	14	49	1440.2	1346	6108	682	626	124	32	55	45	541	37	954	66	6
Texas	77	85	4.09	162	19	3	42	1460.1	1471	6325	753	663	113	44	64	48	598	30	1034	72	6
Cleveland	76	86	4.11	162	13	7	46	1470.0	1507	6330	746	671	159	56	56	34	566	31	890	53	12
New York	76	86	4.21	162	9	4	46	1452.2	1453	6256	746	679	129	39	53	35	612	49	851	52	7
Seattle	64	98	4.55	162	21	9	30	1445.0	1467	6349	799	730	129	56	53	60	661	50	894	61	6
Detroit	75	87	4.60	162	10	4	36	1435.2	1534	6254	794	733	155	52	63	29	564	88	693	57	3
Totals	1134	1134	3.94	1134	242	141	619	20329.0	20006	86887	9802	8899	1776	682	749	585	7704	626	12196	731	90

NOTE—Totals for earned runs for several clubs do not agree with the composite total for all pitchers of each respective club due to instances in which provisions of Section 10.18(i) of the Scoring Rules were applied. The following differences are to be noted: Baltimore pitchers add to 617; Boston pitchers add to 585; Chicago pitchers add to 623; Cleveland pitchers add to 672; Detroit pitchers add to 736; Minnesota pitchers add to 600; New York pitchers add to 681; Texas pitchers add to 665; Toronto pitchers add to 627.

INDIVIDUAL

TOP 15 QUALIFIERS FOR EARNED-RUN AVERAGE TITLE

Minimum 162 innings.   *Lefthanded pitcher.

Pitcher, Team	W	L	ERA	G	GS	CG	ShO	GF	Sv.	IP	H	TBF	R	ER	HR	SH	SF	HB	BB	Int. BB	SO	WP	Bk.
Clemens, Roger, Boston	18	11	2.41	32	32	11	5	0	0	246.2	203	989	80	66	11	5	5	9	62	5	208	3	0
Appier, Kevin, Kansas City	15	8	2.46	30	30	3	0	0	0	208.1	167	852	59	57	10	8	3	2	68	5	150	4	0
Mussina, Mike, Baltimore	18	5	2.54	32	32	8	4	0	0	241.0	212	957	70	68	16	13	6	2	48	2	130	6	0
Guzman, Juan, Toronto	16	5	2.64	28	28	1	0	0	0	180.2	135	732	56	53	6	5	3	1	72	2	165	14	2
Abbott, Jim, California*	7	15	2.77	29	29	7	0	0	0	211.0	208	874	73	65	12	8	4	4	68	3	130	2	0
Perez, Melido, New York*	13	16	2.87	33	33	10	1	0	0	247.2	212	1013	94	79	16	6	8	4	93	5	218	13	0
Nagy, Charles, Cleveland	17	10	2.96	33	33	10	3	0	0	252.0	245	1018	91	83	11	6	9	2	57	1	169	7	0
McDowell, Jack, Chicago	20	10	3.18	34	34	13	1	0	0	260.2	247	1079	95	92	21	8	6	7	75	9	178	6	0
Wegman, Bill, Milwaukee	13	14	3.20	35	35	7	0	0	0	261.2	251	1079	104	93	28	7	4	9	55	3	127	1	2
Smiley, John, Minnesota*	16	9	3.21	34	34	5	2	0	0	241.0	205	970	93	86	17	4	9	6	65	0	163	4	0
Brown, Kevin, Texas	21	11	3.32	35	35	11	1	0	0	265.2	262	1108	117	98	11	7	8	10	76	2	173	8	2
Navarro, Jaime, Milwaukee	17	11	3.33	34	34	5	3	0	0	246.0	224	1004	98	91	14	9	13	6	64	4	100	6	1
Fleming, Dave, Seattle*	17	10	3.39	33	33	7	4	0	0	228.1	225	946	95	86	13	3	2	4	68	1	112	8	1
Erickson, Scott, Minnesota*	13	12	3.40	32	32	5	3	0	0	212.0	197	888	86	80	18	9	7	8	83	3	101	6	1
Viola, Frank, Boston*	13	12	3.44	35	35	6	1	0	0	238.0	214	999	99	91	13	7	10	7	89	4	121	12	2

DEPARTMENTAL LEADERS: W—Brown, Tex., Morris, Tor., 21; L—Hanson, Sea., 17; G—Rogers, Tex., 81; GS—Moore, Oak., Sutcliffe, Bal., 36; CG—McDowell, Chi., 13; ShO—Clemens, Bos., 5; GF—Eckersley, Oak., 65; Sv.—Eckersley, Oak., 51; IP—Brown, Tex., 265.2; H—Brown, Tex., 262; TBF—Brown, Tex., 1108; R—Sutcliffe, Bal., 123; ER—Sutcliffe, Bal., 118; HR—Gullickson, Det., 35; SH—Mussina, Bal., 13; SF—Navarro, Mil., 13; HB—Johnson, Sea., 18; TBB—Johnson, Sea., 144; IBB—Lancaster, Det., Nelson, Sea., 12; SO—Johnson, Sea., 241; WP—Moore, Oak., 22; Bk.—Cook, Cle., 5.

ALL PITCHERS

*Lefthanded pitcher.

Pitcher, Team	W	L	ERA	G	GS	CG	ShO	GF	Sv.	IP	H	TBF	R	ER	HR	SH	SF	HB	BB	Int. BB	SO	WP	Bk.
Abbott, Jim, California*	7	15	2.77	29	29	7	0	0	0	211.0	208	874	73	65	12	8	4	4	68	3	130	2	0
Abbott, Paul, Minnesota	0	0	3.27	6	0	0	0	5	0	11.0	12	50	4	4	1	0	1	1	5	0	13	1	0
Acker, Jim, Seattle	0	0	5.28	17	0	0	0	3	0	30.2	45	148	19	18	4	1	2	0	12	1	11	1	0
Agosto, Juan, Seattle*	0	0	5.89	17	1	0	0	2	0	18.1	27	84	12	12	0	2	1	0	12	0	12	0	0
Aguilera, Rick, Minnesota	2	6	2.84	64	0	0	0	61	41	66.2	60	273	28	21	7	1	2	1	17	4	52	5	0
Aldred, Scott, Detroit*	3	8	6.78	16	13	0	0	0	0	65.0	80	304	51	49	12	4	3	3	33	4	34	1	0
Alexander, Gerald, Texas	1	0	27.00	3	0	0	0	1	0	1.2	5	12	5	5	1	0	1	0	1	0	1	0	0
Alvarez, Wilson, Chicago*	5	3	5.20	34	9	0	0	4	1	100.1	103	454	64	58	12	3	4	4	65	2	66	2	0
Appier, Kevin, Kansas City	15	8	2.46	30	30	3	0	0	0	208.1	167	852	59	57	10	8	3	2	68	5	150	4	0
Aquino, Luis, Kansas City	3	6	4.52	15	13	0	0	1	0	67.2	81	293	35	34	5	2	3	1	20	1	11	1	1
Armstrong, Jack, Cleveland	6	15	4.64	35	23	1	0	0	5	166.2	176	735	100	86	23	6	5	3	67	0	114	6	3
Arnsberg, Brad, Cleveland	0	0	11.81	8	0	0	0	1	0	10.2	13	54	14	14	6	0	0	2	11	0	5	2	0
Austin, James, Milwaukee	5	2	1.85	47	0	0	0	12	0	58.1	38	235	13	12	2	1	1	2	32	6	30	1	0
Bailes, Scott, California*	3	1	7.45	32	0	0	0	10	0	38.2	59	200	34	32	7	1	2	2	28	4	25	2	1
Banks, Willie, Minnesota	4	4	5.70	16	12	0	0	2	0	71.0	80	324	46	45	6	2	2	5	37	0	37	5	1
Bannister, Floyd, Texas*	1	1	6.32	36	0	0	0	8	0	37.0	39	173	27	26	3	3	7	3	21	6	30	3	0
Barton, Shawn, Seattle*	0	1	2.92	14	0	0	0	2	0	12.1	10	50	5	4	1	0	1	0	7	2	4	2	0
Bell, Eric, Cleveland*	0	2	7.63	7	1	0	0	2	0	15.1	22	75	13	13	1	1	1	1	9	0	10	1	0
Berenguer, Juan, K.C.	1	4	5.64	19	2	0	0	7	0	44.2	42	195	30	28	3	1	3	1	20	3	26	2	1
Blyleven, Bert, California	8	12	4.74	25	24	1	0	0	0	133.0	150	568	76	70	17	3	5	5	29	2	70	3	1
Boddicker, Mike, K.C.	1	4	4.98	29	8	0	0	8	0	86.2	92	382	50	48	5	2	3	8	37	3	47	2	0
Bohanon, Brian, Texas*	1	1	6.31	18	7	0	0	3	0	45.2	57	220	38	32	7	0	2	1	25	0	29	2	0
Bolton, Tom, Boston*	1	2	3.41	21	1	0	0	0	0	29.0	34	135	11	11	0	0	0	2	14	1	23	2	1
Bones, Ricky, Milwaukee	9	10	4.57	31	28	0	0	0	0	163.1	169	705	90	83	27	2	5	9	48	0	65	3	2

Pitcher, Team	W	L	ERA	G	GS	CG	ShO	GF	Sv.	IP	H	TBF	R	ER	HR	SH	SF	HB	BB	Int. BB	SO	WP	Bk.
Bosio, Chris, Milwaukee	16	6	3.62	33	33	4	2	0	0	231.1	223	937	100	93	21	6	5	4	44	1	120	8	2
Boucher, Denis, Cleveland*	2	2	6.37	8	7	0	0	0	0	41.0	48	184	29	29	9	1	3	1	20	0	17	1	0
Briscoe, John, Oakland	0	1	6.43	2	2	0	0	0	0	7.0	12	40	6	5	0	1	0	0	9	0	4	2	0
Brown, J. Kevin, Texas	21	11	3.32	35	35	11	1	0	0	265.2	262	1108	117	98	11	7	8	10	76	2	173	8	2
Brown, Kevin D., Seattle*	0	0	9.00	2	0	0	0	0	0	3.0	4	15	3	3	1	0	0	0	3	0	2	0	0
Burke, Tim, New York	2	2	3.25	23	0	0	0	10	0	27.2	26	122	14	10	2	2	0	1	15	4	8	2	0
Burns, Todd, Texas	3	5	3.84	35	10	0	0	9	1	103.0	97	433	54	44	8	2	4	4	32	1	55	5	0
Butcher, Mike, California	2	2	3.25	19	0	0	0	6	0	27.2	29	125	11	10	3	0	0	2	13	1	24	0	0
Cadaret, Greg, New York*	4	8	4.25	46	11	1	1	9	1	103.2	104	471	53	49	12	3	3	2	74	7	73	5	1
Campbell, Kevin, Oakland	2	3	5.12	32	5	0	0	6	1	65.0	66	297	39	37	4	3	2	0	45	3	38	2	0
Campbell, Mike, Texas	0	1	9.82	1	0	0	0	0	0	3.2	3	15	4	4	1	0	0	0	2	0	2	0	0
Carman, Don, Texas*	0	0	7.71	2	0	0	0	1	0	2.1	4	11	3	2	0	0	0	0	2	0	2	0	0
Casian, Larry, Minnesota*	1	0	2.70	6	0	0	0	1	0	6.2	7	28	2	2	0	0	0	1	1	0	2	0	0
Chiamparino, Scott, Texas	0	4	3.55	4	4	0	0	0	0	25.1	25	102	11	10	2	0	1	0	5	0	13	1	0
Christopher, Mike, Cleveland	0	0	3.00	10	0	0	0	4	0	18.0	17	79	8	6	2	1	1	0	10	1	13	2	0
Clemens, Roger, Boston	18	11	2.41	32	32	11	5	0	0	246.2	203	989	80	66	11	5	5	9	62	5	208	3	0
Clements, Pat, Baltimore*	2	0	3.28	23	0	0	0	4	0	24.2	23	105	10	9	0	2	1	2	11	0	9	1	0
Cone, David, Toronto	4	3	2.55	8	7	0	0	0	0	53.0	39	224	16	15	3	0	3	3	29	2	47	3	0
Cook, Dennis, Cleveland*	5	7	3.82	32	25	1	0	1	0	158.0	156	669	79	67	29	3	2		50	2	96	4	5
Corsi, Jim, Oakland	4	2	1.43	32	0	0	0	16	0	44.0	44	185	12	7	2	4	0	0	18	2	19	0	0
Crim, Chuck, California	7	6	5.17	57	0	0	0	16	1	87.0	100	383	56	50	11	3	4	6	29	6	30	4	0
Darling, Ron, Oakland	15	10	3.66	33	33	4	3	0	0	206.1	198	866	98	84	15	4	4	4	72	5	99	13	0
Darwin, Danny, Boston	9	9	3.96	51	15	2	0	21	3	161.1	159	688	76	71	11	7	5	5	53	9	124	5	0
Davis, Mark, Kansas City*	7	3	7.18	13	6	0	0	4	0	36.1	42	176	31	29	6	1	4	0	28	0	19	1	0
Davis, Storm, Baltimore	7	3	3.43	48	2	0	0	24	4	89.1	79	372	35	34	5	6	4	2	36	6	53	4	0
DeLucia, Rich, Seattle	3	6	5.49	30	11	0	0	6	1	83.2	100	382	55	51	13	2	2	2	35	1	66	1	0
Doherty, John, Detroit	7	4	3.88	47	11	0	0	9	3	116.0	131	491	61	50	4	3	2	4	25	5	37	5	0
Dopson, John, Boston	7	11	4.08	25	25	0	0	0	0	141.1	159	598	78	64	17	2	2	2	38	2	55	3	3
Downs, Kelly, Oakland	5	5	3.29	18	13	0	0	2	0	82.0	72	364	36	30	4	6	4	4	46	3	38	3	1
Drahman, Brian, Chicago	0	0	2.57	5	0	0	0	2	0	7.0	6	29	3	2	0	0	0	0	2	0	1	1	0
Dunne, Mike, Chicago	2	0	4.26	4	1	0	0	0	0	12.2	12	54	7	6	0	0	0	1	6	1	6	0	0
Eckersley, Dennis, Oakland	7	1	1.91	69	0	0	0	65	51	80.0	62	309	17	17	5	3	1	1	11	6	93	0	0
Edens, Tom, Minnesota	6	3	2.83	52	0	0	0	14	0	76.1	65	317	26	24	1	4	0	2	36	3	57	5	0
Eichhorn, Mark, Cal.-Tor.	4	4	3.08	65	0	0	0	26	2	87.2	86	372	34	30	3	3	5	2	25	8	61	9	1
Eldred, Cal, Milwaukee	11	2	1.79	14	14	2	1	0	0	100.1	76	394	21	20	4	1	0	2	23	0	62	3	0
Embree, Alan, Cleveland*	0	2	7.00	4	4	0	0	0	0	18.0	19	81	14	14	3	0	2	1	8	0	12	1	1
Erickson, Scott, Minnesota	13	12	3.40	32	32	5	3	0	0	212.0	197	888	86	80	18	9	7	8	83	3	101	6	1
Farr, Steve, New York	2	2	1.56	50	0	0	0	42	30	52.0	34	207	10	9	2	1	2	2	19	0	37	0	0
Fernandez, Alex, Chicago	8	11	4.27	29	29	4	2	0	0	187.2	199	804	100	89	21	6	4	8	50	3	95	3	0
Fetters, Mike, Milwaukee	5	1	1.87	50	0	0	0	11	2	62.2	38	243	15	13	3	5	2	7	24	2	43	4	1
Finley, Chuck, California*	7	12	3.96	31	31	4	1	0	0	204.1	212	885	99	90	24	10	10	3	98	2	124	6	0
Fireovid, Steve, Texas	1	0	4.05	3	0	0	0	0	0	6.2	10	31	5	3	0	0	0	0	4	2	0	0	0
Fisher, Brian, Seattle	4	3	4.53	22	14	0	0	2	1	91.1	80	394	49	46	9	1	3	1	47	1	26	3	1
Flanagan, Mike, Baltimore*	0	0	8.05	42	0	0	0	15	0	34.2	50	180	34	31	3	2	2	5	23	1	17	4	0
Fleming, Dave, Seattle*	17	10	3.39	33	33	7	4	0	0	228.1	225	946	95	86	13	3	2	4	60	3	112	8	1
Fortugno, Tim, California*	1	1	5.18	14	5	1	1	5	1	41.2	37	177	24	24	5	0	1	0	19	0	31	2	1
Fossas, Tony, Boston*	1	2	2.43	60	0	0	0	17	2	29.2	31	129	9	8	1	3	0	1	14	3	19	0	0
Frey, Steve, California*	4	2	3.57	51	0	0	0	20	4	45.1	39	193	18	18	6	2	3	2	22	3	24	1	0
Frohwirth, Todd, Baltimore	4	3	2.46	65	0	0	0	23	4	106.0	97	444	33	29	4	7	1	3	41	4	58	1	0
Gardiner, Mike, Boston	4	10	4.75	28	18	0	0	3	0	130.2	126	566	78	69	12	3	5	2	58	2	79	8	0
Gordon, Tom, Kansas City	6	10	4.59	40	11	0	0	13	0	117.2	116	516	67	60	9	2	6	4	55	4	98	5	2
Gossage, Goose, Oakland	0	2	2.84	30	0	0	0	13	0	38.0	32	163	13	12	5	1	2	2	19	4	26	0	0
Gozzo, Mauro, Minnesota	0	0	27.00	2	0	0	0	0	0	1.2	7	12	5	5	2	0	0	0	0	0	1	0	0
Grahe, Joe, California	5	6	3.52	46	7	0	0	31	21	94.2	85	399	37	37	5	4	4	6	39	2	39	3	0
Grant, Mark, Seattle	2	4	3.89	23	10	0	0	4	0	81.0	100	352	39	35	6	5	1	2	22	2	42	2	0
Groom, Buddy, Detroit*	0	5	5.82	12	7	0	0	3	1	38.2	48	177	28	25	4	2	0	2	22	4	15	0	1
Gubicza, Mark, Kansas City	7	6	3.72	18	18	2	1	0	0	111.1	110	470	47	46	8	5	3	1	36	3	81	5	1
Guetterman, Lee, New York*	1	1	9.53	15	0	0	0	7	0	22.2	35	114	24	24	5	0	2	0	13	0	7	1	0
Gullickson, Bill, Detroit	14	13	4.34	34	34	4	1	0	0	221.2	228	919	109	107	35	7	9	0	50	5	64	6	0
Gunderson, Eric, Seattle*	2	1	8.68	9	0	0	0	4	0	9.1	12	45	12	9	1	0	2	1	5	3	2	0	2
Guthrie, Mark, Minnesota*	2	3	2.88	54	0	0	0	15	5	75.0	59	303	27	24	7	4	2	0	23	7	76	2	0
Guzman, Johnny, Oakland*	0	0	12.00	2	0	0	0	2	0	3.0	8	18	4	4	0	0	0	1	0	0	0	0	0
Guzman, Jose, Texas	16	11	3.66	33	33	5	0	0	0	224.0	229	947	103	91	17	9	7	4	73	0	179	6	0
Guzman, Juan, Toronto	16	5	2.64	28	28	1	0	0	0	180.2	135	733	56	53	6	3	1	1	72	2	165	14	2
Haas, David, Detroit	5	3	3.94	12	11	1	1	0	0	61.2	68	264	30	27	8	1	0	1	16	1	29	2	0
Habyan, John, New York	5	6	3.84	56	0	0	0	20	7	72.2	84	316	32	31	6	5	3	2	21	5	44	2	1
Haney, Chris, Kansas City*	2	3	3.86	7	7	1	1	0	0	42.0	35	174	18	18	5	0	3	0	12	0	27	0	0
Hanson, Erik, Seattle	8	17	4.82	31	30	6	1	0	0	186.2	209	809	110	100	14	8	9	7	57	1	112	6	0
Harris, Greg A., Boston	4	9	2.51	70	2	1	0	22	4	107.2	82	459	38	30	6	8	3	4	60	11	73	5	0
Harris, Gene, Seattle	0	0	7.00	8	0	0	0	2	0	9.0	8	40	7	7	3	0	0	0	6	0	4	1	0
Harvey, Bryan, California	0	4	2.83	25	0	0	0	22	13	28.2	22	122	12	9	4	2	1	0	11	3	34	4	0
Hathaway, Hilly, California*	0	0	7.94	2	1	0	0	0	0	5.2	8	29	5	5	1	1	0	1	3	0	1	0	0
Heaton, Neal, K.C.-Mil.*	3	1	4.07	32	0	0	0	9	0	42.0	43	189	21	19	5	2	3	1	23	2	31	3	1
Henke, Tom, Toronto	3	6	2.26	57	0	0	0	50	34	55.2	40	228	19	14	5	3	0	3	22	2	46	4	0
Henneman, Mike, Detroit	2	6	3.96	60	0	0	0	53	24	77.1	75	321	36	34	6	8	2	5	20	10	58	7	0
Henry, Doug, Milwaukee	1	4	4.02	68	0	0	0	56	29	65.0	64	277	34	29	6	1	2	0	24	4	52	4	0
Hentgen, Pat, Toronto	5	2	5.36	28	2	0	0	10	0	50.1	49	229	30	30	7	2	0	2	32	5	39	2	1
Hernandez, Roberto, Chicago	7	3	1.65	43	0	0	0	27	12	71.0	45	277	15	13	4	0	3	4	20	1	68	2	0
Hesketh, Joe, Boston*	8	9	4.36	30	25	1	0	1	0	148.2	162	659	82	72	15	5	6	2	58	0	104	6	0
Hibbard, Greg, Chicago*	10	7	4.40	31	28	0	0	2	1	176.0	187	755	92	86	17	10	6	7	57	3	69	1	1
Hillegas, Shawn, N.Y.-Oak.	1	8	5.23	26	9	1	1	6	0	86.0	104	385	57	50	13	2	3	0	37	2	49	2	0
Hitchcock, Sterling, N.Y.*	0	2	8.31	3	0	0	0	0	0	13.0	23	68	12	12	2	0	0	1	6	0	6	0	0
Holmes, Darren, Milwaukee	4	4	2.55	41	0	0	0	25	6	42.1	35	173	12	12	1	0	4	3	11	3	32	2	0
Honeycutt, Rick, Oakland*	1	4	3.69	54	0	0	0	17	3	39.0	41	169	19	16	2	4	1	3	10	3	32	2	0
Horsman, Vince, Oakland*	2	1	2.49	58	0	0	0	9	1	43.1	39	180	13	12	3	1	0	0	21	4	18	1	0
Hough, Charlie, Chicago	7	12	3.93	27	27	4	0	0	0	176.1	160	751	88	77	19	2	6	7	66	2	76	10	1
Howe, Steve, New York*	3	0	2.45	20	0	0	0	10	6	22.0	9	79	7	6	1	1	1	0	3	1	12	1	0

Pitcher, Team	W	L	ERA	G	GS	CG	ShO	GF	Sv.	IP	H	TBF	R	ER	HR	SH	SF	HB	BB	Int. BB	SO	WP	Bk.
Hoy, Pete, Boston	0	0	7.36	5	0	0	0	2	0	3.2	8	19	3	3	0	0	0	0	2	1	2	0	0
Irvine, Daryl, Boston	3	4	6.11	21	0	0	0	8	0	28.0	31	128	20	19	1	1	3	2	14	2	10	3	0
Jeffcoat, Mike, Texas*	0	1	7.32	6	3	0	0	2	0	19.2	28	89	17	16	2	2	2	0	5	0	6	0	0
Johnson, Jeff, New York*	2	3	6.66	13	8	0	0	3	0	52.2	71	245	44	39	4	2	2	2	23	0	14	1	0
Johnson, Randy, Seattle*	12	14	3.77	31	31	6	2	0	0	210.1	154	922	104	88	13	3	8	18	144	1	241	13	1
Johnston, Joel, Kansas City	0	0	13.50	5	0	0	0	1	0	2.2	3	13	4	4	2	0	0	0	2	0	1	0	0
Jones, Calvin, Seattle	3	5	5.69	38	1	0	0	14	0	61.2	50	275	39	39	8	1	4	2	47	1	49	10	0
Kamienicki, Scott, N.Y.	6	14	4.36	28	28	4	0	0	0	188.0	193	804	100	91	13	3	5	5	74	9	88	9	1
Key, Jimmy, Toronto*	13	13	3.53	33	33	4	2	0	0	216.2	205	900	88	85	24	2	7	4	59	0	117	5	0
Kiely, John, Detroit	4	2	2.13	39	0	0	0	20	0	55.0	44	231	14	13	2	4	3	0	28	3	18	0	0
King, Eric, Detroit	4	6	5.22	17	14	0	0	2	1	79.1	90	348	47	46	12	1	2	1	28	1	45	3	0
Kipper, Bob, Minnesota*	3	3	4.42	25	0	0	0	12	0	38.2	40	168	23	19	8	2	0	3	14	3	22	1	0
Knudsen, Kurt, Detroit	2	3	4.58	48	1	0	0	14	5	70.2	70	313	39	36	9	4	2	1	41	9	51	5	0
Kramer, Randy, Seattle	0	1	7.71	4	4	0	0	0	0	16.1	30	84	14	14	2	1	0	1	7	0	6	0	0
Krueger, Bill, Minnesota*	10	6	4.30	27	27	2	2	0	0	161.1	166	684	82	77	18	4	1	3	46	2	86	11	0
Lancaster, Les, Detroit	3	4	6.33	41	1	0	0	17	0	86.2	101	404	66	61	11	2	4	3	51	12	35	2	0
Langston, Mark, California*	13	14	3.66	32	32	9	2	0	0	229.0	206	941	103	93	14	4	5	6	74	2	174	5	0
Leach, Terry, Chicago	6	5	1.95	51	0	0	0	21	0	73.2	57	292	17	16	2	2	1	4	20	5	22	0	0
Leary, Tim, N.Y.-Sea.	8	10	5.36	26	23	3	0	2	0	141.0	131	624	89	84	12	6	11	9	87	5	46	9	0
Lefferts, Craig, Baltimore	1	3	4.09	5	5	1	0	0	0	33.0	34	136	19	15	3	2	1	0	6	0	23	1	0
Leiter, Al, Toronto*	0	0	9.00	1	0	0	0	0	0	1.0	1	7	1	1	0	0	0	0	2	0	0	0	0
Leiter, Mark, Detroit	8	5	4.18	35	14	1	0	7	0	112.0	116	475	57	52	9	2	8	3	43	5	75	3	0
Leon, Danilo, Texas	1	1	5.89	15	0	0	0	3	0	18.1	18	84	14	12	5	0	3	3	10	0	15	0	0
Lewis, Richie, Baltimore	1	1	10.80	2	2	0	0	0	0	6.2	13	40	8	8	1	0	1	0	7	0	4	0	0
Lewis, Scott, California	4	0	3.99	21	2	0	0	7	0	38.1	36	160	18	17	3	0	3	2	14	1	18	1	1
Lilliquist, Derek, Cleveland*	5	3	1.75	71	0	0	0	22	6	61.2	39	239	13	12	5	5	4	2	18	6	47	2	0
Linton, Doug, Toronto	1	3	8.63	8	3	0	0	2	0	24.0	31	116	23	23	5	1	2	0	17	0	16	2	0
MacDonald, Bob, Toronto*	1	0	4.37	27	0	0	0	9	0	47.1	50	204	24	23	4	1	1	1	16	3	26	0	0
Magnante, Mike, K.C.*	4	9	4.94	44	12	0	0	11	0	89.1	115	403	53	49	5	5	7	2	35	5	31	2	0
Mahomes, Pat, Minnesota	3	4	5.04	14	13	0	0	1	0	69.2	73	302	41	39	5	0	3	0	37	0	44	2	1
Manuel, Barry, Texas	1	0	4.76	3	0	0	0	0	0	5.2	6	25	3	3	2	0	0	1	1	0	9	0	0
Mathews, Terry, Texas	2	4	5.95	40	0	0	0	11	0	42.1	48	199	29	28	4	1	3	1	31	3	26	2	1
McCaskill, Kirk, Chicago	12	13	4.18	34	34	0	0	0	0	209.0	193	911	116	97	11	7	7	6	95	5	109	6	2
McCullers, Lance, Texas	1	0	5.40	5	0	0	0	1	0	5.0	1	23	4	3	0	0	0	0	8	0	3	0	0
McDonald, Ben, Baltimore	13	13	4.24	35	35	4	2	0	0	227.0	213	958	103	107	32	6	6	9	74	5	158	3	2
McDowell, Jack, Chicago	20	10	3.18	34	34	13	1	0	0	260.2	247	1079	95	92	21	8	6	7	75	9	178	6	0
Meacham, Rusty, K.C.	10	4	2.74	64	0	0	0	20	2	101.2	88	412	39	31	5	3	9	1	21	5	64	4	0
Mesa, Jose, Bal.-Cle.	7	12	4.59	28	27	1	1	1	0	160.2	169	700	86	82	14	2	5	4	70	1	62	2	0
Milacki, Bob, Baltimore	6	8	5.84	23	20	0	0	1	1	115.2	140	525	78	75	16	3	3	2	44	2	51	7	1
Militello, Sam, New York	3	3	3.45	9	9	0	0	0	0	60.0	43	255	24	23	6	0	2	2	32	1	42	1	0
Mills, Alan, Baltimore	10	4	2.61	35	3	0	0	12	2	103.1	78	428	33	30	5	6	5	1	54	10	60	2	0
Mlicki, Dave, Cleveland	0	2	4.98	4	4	0	0	0	0	21.2	23	101	14	12	3	2	0	1	16	0	16	1	0
Moeller, Dennis, K.C.*	0	3	7.00	5	4	0	0	1	0	18.0	24	89	17	14	5	3	3	0	11	2	6	1	1
Monteleone, Rich, New York	7	3	3.30	47	0	0	0	15	0	92.2	82	380	35	34	7	3	1	0	27	3	62	6	3
Montgomery, Jeff, K.C.	1	6	2.18	65	0	0	0	62	39	82.2	61	333	23	20	5	4	2	3	27	2	69	2	0
Moore, Mike, Oakland	17	12	4.12	36	36	2	0	0	0	223.0	229	982	113	102	20	7	11	8	103	5	117	22	0
Morris, Jack, Toronto	21	6	4.04	34	34	6	1	0	0	240.2	222	1005	114	108	18	4	7	10	80	2	132	9	2
Munoz, Mike, Detroit*	1	2	3.00	65	0	0	0	15	2	48.0	44	210	16	16	3	4	2	0	25	6	23	2	0
Mussina, Mike, Baltimore	18	5	2.54	32	32	8	4	0	0	241.0	212	957	70	68	16	13	6	2	48	2	130	6	0
Mutis, Jeff, Cleveland*	0	2	9.53	3	2	0	0	0	0	11.1	24	64	14	12	4	0	2	0	6	0	8	2	0
Nagy, Charles, Cleveland	17	10	2.96	33	33	10	3	0	0	252.0	245	1018	91	83	11	6	9	2	57	1	169	7	0
Navarro, Jaime, Milwaukee	17	11	3.33	34	34	5	3	0	0	246.0	224	1004	98	91	14	9	13	6	64	4	100	6	0
Nelson, Gene, Oakland	3	1	6.45	28	2	0	0	8	0	51.2	68	234	37	37	5	4	5	0	22	5	23	2	0
Nelson, Jeff, Seattle	1	7	3.44	66	0	0	0	27	6	81.0	71	352	34	31	7	9	3	6	44	12	46	2	0
Nichols, Rod, Cleveland	4	3	4.53	30	9	0	0	5	0	105.1	114	456	58	53	13	1	5	2	31	1	56	3	0
Nielsen, Jerry, New York*	0	0	4.58	20	0	0	0	12	0	19.2	17	90	10	10	1	1	1	0	18	2	12	1	0
Nunez, Edwin, Mil.-Tex.	1	3	4.85	49	0	0	0	16	3	59.1	63	263	34	32	6	0	4	2	22	0	49	5	0
Olin, Steve, Cleveland	8	5	2.34	72	0	0	0	62	29	88.1	80	360	25	23	8	5	2	4	27	6	47	1	1
Olson, Gregg, Baltimore	1	5	2.05	60	0	0	0	56	36	61.1	46	244	14	14	3	0	2	0	24	0	58	4	0
Orosco, Jesse, Milwaukee*	3	1	3.23	59	0	0	0	14	1	39.0	33	158	15	14	5	0	2	1	13	1	40	2	0
Otto, Dave, Cleveland*	5	9	7.06	18	16	0	0	0	0	80.1	110	368	64	63	12	3	1	1	33	0	32	5	0
Pall, Donn, Chicago	5	2	4.93	39	0	0	0	12	1	73.0	79	323	43	40	9	1	3	2	27	8	27	1	2
Parker, Clay, Seattle	0	2	7.56	8	0	0	0	1	0	33.1	47	154	28	28	6	0	2	2	11	0	20	1	0
Parrett, Jeff, Oakland	9	1	3.02	66	0	0	0	14	0	98.1	81	410	35	33	7	4	4	2	42	3	78	13	0
Pavlik, Roger, Texas	4	4	4.21	13	12	1	0	0	0	62.0	66	275	32	29	3	0	2	3	34	0	45	9	0
Perez, Melido, New York	13	16	2.87	33	33	10	1	0	0	247.2	212	1013	94	79	16	6	8	5	93	5	218	13	0
Pichardo, Hipolito, K.C.	9	6	3.95	31	24	1	1	0	0	143.2	148	615	71	63	9	6	5	3	49	1	59	3	1
Pierce, Ed, Kansas City*	0	0	3.38	2	1	0	0	0	0	5.1	9	26	2	2	1	0	1	0	4	0	3	0	0
Plesac, Dan, Milwaukee*	5	4	2.96	44	4	0	0	13	1	79.0	64	330	28	26	5	8	4	3	35	5	54	3	1
Plunk, Eric, Cleveland	9	6	3.64	58	0	0	0	20	4	71.2	61	309	31	29	5	3	2	0	38	2	50	5	0
Poole, Jim, Baltimore*	0	0	0.00	6	0	0	0	1	0	3.1	3	14	3	0	0	0	0	0	1	0	3	0	0
Powell, Dennis, Seattle*	4	2	4.58	49	0	0	0	11	0	57.0	49	243	30	29	5	3	3	2	29	2	35	2	0
Power, Ted, Cleveland	3	3	2.54	64	0	0	0	16	6	99.1	88	409	33	28	7	7	8	4	35	9	51	2	1
Quantrill, Paul, Boston	2	3	2.19	27	0	0	0	10	1	49.1	55	213	18	12	1	4	2	1	15	5	24	1	0
Raczka, Michael, Oakland*	0	0	8.53	8	0	0	0	1	0	6.1	8	33	7	6	0	0	2	0	5	0	2	0	0
Radinsky, Scott, Chicago*	3	7	2.73	68	0	0	0	33	15	59.1	54	261	21	18	3	2	1	2	34	5	48	3	0
Rasmussen, Dennis, K.C.*	4	1	1.43	5	5	1	1	0	0	37.2	25	134	7	6	0	1	1	0	12	0	13	3	0
Reardon, Jeff, Boston	2	2	4.25	46	0	0	0	39	27	42.1	53	183	20	20	6	1	2	1	7	0	32	0	0
Reed, Rick, Kansas City	3	7	3.68	19	18	1	1	0	0	100.1	105	419	47	41	10	2	5	5	20	3	49	0	0
Revenig, Todd, Oakland	0	0	0.00	2	0	0	0	2	0	2.0	2	7	0	0	0	0	0	0	0	0	1	0	0
Rhodes, Arthur, Baltimore*	7	5	3.63	15	15	2	1	0	0	94.1	87	394	39	38	6	1	1	1	38	2	77	2	1
Ritz, Kevin, Detroit	2	5	5.60	23	11	0	0	4	0	80.1	88	368	52	50	4	1	3	4	44	4	57	7	1
Robinson, Don, California	1	0	2.20	3	3	0	0	0	0	16.1	19	69	4	4	1	1	0	0	3	0	9	1	0
Robinson, Jeff M., Texas	5	9	5.72	16	4	0	0	2	0	45.2	50	203	30	29	6	1	3	0	21	1	18	6	1
Robinson, Ron, Milwaukee	1	4	5.86	8	8	0	0	0	0	35.1	51	171	26	23	3	0	2	1	14	0	12	0	0
Rogers, Kenny, Texas*	3	6	3.09	81	0	0	0	38	6	78.2	80	337	32	27	7	4	1	0	26	8	70	4	1
Rosenthal, Wayne, Texas	0	0	7.71	6	0	0	0	2	0	4.2	7	24	4	4	1	1	0	0	2	0	1	1	0

Pitcher, Team	W	L	ERA	G	GS	CG	ShO	GF	Sv.	IP	H	TBF	R	ER	HR	SH	SF	HB	BB	Int. BB	SO	WP	Bk.
Ruffin, Bruce, Milwaukee*	1	6	6.67	25	6	1	0	6	0	58.0	66	272	43	43	7	3	3	0	41	3	45	2	0
Russell, Jeff, Tex.-Oak.	4	3	1.63	59	0	0	0	46	30	66.1	55	276	14	12	3	1	2	2	25	3	48	3	0
Ryan, Ken, Boston	0	0	6.43	7	0	0	0	6	1	7.0	4	30	5	5	2	1	0	0	5	0	5	0	0
Ryan, Nolan, Texas	5	9	3.72	27	27	2	0	0	0	157.1	138	675	75	65	9	6	7	12	69	0	157	9	0
Sampen, Bill, Kansas City	0	2	3.66	8	1	0	0	3	0	19.2	21	81	10	8	0	1	2	3	3	1	14	1	0
Sanderson, Scott, New York ..	12	11	4.93	33	33	2	1	0	0	193.1	220	851	116	106	28	3	11	4	64	5	104	4	1
Sauveur, Rich, Kansas City*..	0	1	4.40	8	0	0	0	2	0	14.1	15	65	7	7	1	0	0	2	8	1	7	0	1
Schmidt, Dave, Seattle	0	0	18.90	3	0	0	0	0	0	3.1	7	19	7	7	1	0	0	0	3	0	1	0	0
Schooler, Mike, Seattle	2	7	4.70	53	0	0	0	36	13	51.2	55	232	29	27	7	4	3	1	24	6	33	0	0
Scudder, Scott, Cleveland	6	10	5.28	23	22	0	0	0	0	109.0	134	509	80	64	10	6	4	2	55	0	66	7	0
Shaw, Jeff, Cleveland	0	1	8.22	2	1	0	0	1	0	7.2	7	33	7	7	2	2	0	0	4	0	3	0	1
Shifflett, Steve, Kansas City ..	1	4	2.60	34	0	0	0	15	0	52.0	55	221	15	15	6	4	1	2	17	6	25	2	1
Slusarski, Joe, Oakland	5	5	5.45	15	14	0	0	1	0	76.0	85	338	52	46	15	1	5	6	27	0	38	0	1
Smiley, John, Minnesota*	16	9	3.21	34	34	5	2	0	0	241.0	205	970	93	86	17	4	9	6	65	0	163	4	0
Smith, Dan, Texas*	0	3	5.02	4	2	0	0	1	0	14.1	18	67	8	8	1	2	1	0	8	1	5	0	0
Springer, Russ, New York	0	0	6.19	14	0	0	0	5	0	16.0	18	75	11	11	0	0	1	0	10	0	12	0	0
Stewart, Dave, Oakland	12	10	3.66	31	31	2	0	0	0	199.1	175	838	96	81	25	5	8	8	79	1	130	3	1
Stieb, Dave, Toronto	4	6	5.04	21	14	1	0	3	0	96.1	98	415	58	54	9	6	5	4	43	3	45	4	0
Stottlemyre, Todd, Toronto	12	11	4.50	28	27	6	2	0	0	174.0	175	755	99	87	20	2	11	10	63	4	98	7	0
Sutcliffe, Rick, Baltimore	16	15	4.47	36	36	5	2	0	0	237.1	251	1018	123	118	20	6	11	7	74	4	109	7	2
Swan, Russ, Seattle*	3	10	4.74	55	9	1	0	26	9	104.1	104	457	60	55	8	7	5	3	45	7	45	6	0
Tanana, Frank, Detroit*	13	11	4.39	32	31	3	0	0	0	186.2	188	818	102	91	22	7	10	7	90	9	91	11	1
Tapani, Kevin, Minnesota	16	11	3.97	34	34	4	1	0	0	220.0	226	911	103	97	17	8	11	5	48	2	138	4	0
Taylor, Scott, Boston*	1	1	4.91	4	1	0	0	1	0	14.2	13	57	8	8	4	0	0	0	4	0	7	0	0
Terrell, Walt, Detroit	7	10	5.20	36	14	1	0	7	0	136.2	163	611	86	79	14	6	7	3	48	10	61	3	0
Thigpen, Bobby, Chicago	0	1	4.75	55	0	0	0	40	22	55.0	58	253	29	29	4	2	4	3	33	5	45	0	0
Timlin, Mike, Toronto	0	2	4.12	26	0	0	0	14	1	43.2	45	190	23	20	0	2	1	1	20	5	35	0	0
Trlicek, Rick, Toronto	0	0	10.80	2	0	0	0	0	0	1.2	2	9	2	2	0	0	0	0	2	0	1	0	0
Trombley, Mike, Minnesota	3	2	3.30	10	7	0	0	0	0	46.1	43	194	20	17	5	2	0	1	17	0	38	0	0
Valera, Julio, California	8	11	3.73	30	28	4	2	0	0	188.0	188	792	82	78	15	6	2	2	64	5	113	5	0
Viola, Frank, Boston*	13	12	3.44	35	35	6	1	0	0	238.0	214	999	99	91	13	7	10	7	89	4	121	12	2
Walker, Mike, Seattle	0	3	7.36	5	3	0	0	1	0	14.2	21	74	14	12	4	1	1	0	9	3	5	1	0
Walton, Bruce, Oakland	0	0	9.90	7	0	0	0	2	0	10.0	17	49	11	11	1	0	1	0	3	0	7	0	1
Ward, Duane, Toronto	7	4	1.95	79	0	0	0	35	12	101.1	76	414	27	22	5	3	4	1	39	3	103	7	0
Wayne, Gary, Minnesota*	3	3	2.63	41	0	0	0	13	0	48.0	46	210	18	14	2	8	3	3	19	5	29	1	1
Weathers, Dave, Toronto	0	0	8.10	2	0	0	0	0	0	3.1	5	15	3	3	1	0	0	0	2	0	3	0	0
Wegman, Bill, Milwaukee	13	14	3.20	35	35	7	0	0	0	261.2	251	1079	104	93	28	7	4	9	55	3	127	1	2
Welch, Bob, Oakland	11	7	3.27	20	20	0	0	0	0	123.2	114	513	47	45	13	3	3	2	43	0	47	1	0
Wells, David, Toronto	7	9	5.40	41	14	0	0	14	2	120.0	138	529	84	72	16	3	4	8	36	6	62	3	1
West, David, Minnesota*	1	3	6.99	9	3	0	0	1	0	28.1	32	139	24	22	3	0	2	1	20	0	19	2	0
Whiteside, Matt, Texas	1	1	1.93	20	0	0	0	8	4	28.0	26	118	8	6	1	0	1	1	11	2	13	2	0
Wickander, Kevin, Cle.*	2	0	3.07	44	0	0	0	10	1	41.0	39	187	14	14	1	2	4	2	28	3	38	1	1
Wickman, Bob, New York	6	1	4.11	8	8	0	0	0	0	50.1	51	213	25	23	2	1	3	2	20	0	21	3	0
Williamson, Mark, Baltimore..	0	0	0.96	12	0	0	0	5	1	18.2	16	78	3	2	1	0	0	0	10	1	14	1	0
Willis, Carl, Minnesota	7	3	2.72	59	0	0	0	21	1	79.1	73	313	25	24	4	2	3	0	11	1	45	2	1
Witt, Bobby, Tex.-Oak.	10	14	4.29	31	31	0	0	0	0	193.0	183	848	99	92	16	7	10	2	114	2	125	9	1
Woodson, Kerry, Seattle	1	1	3.29	8	1	0	0	0	0	13.2	12	62	7	5	0	0	0	2	11	0	6	1	0
Young, Curt, K.C.-N.Y.*	4	2	3.99	23	7	0	0	5	0	67.2	80	295	35	30	2	3	2	2	17	2	20	0	0
Young, Matt, Boston*	0	4	4.58	28	8	1	0	4	0	70.2	69	321	42	36	7	4	3	3	42	2	57	2	0

PITCHERS WITH TWO OR MORE TEAMS

Pitcher, Team	W	L	ERA	G	GS	CG	ShO	GF	Sv.	IP	H	TBF	R	ER	HR	SH	SF	HB	BB	Int. BB	SO	WP	Bk.
Eichhorn, Mark, California	2	4	2.38	42	0	0	0	19	2	56.2	51	237	19	15	2	2	3	0	18	8	42	3	1
Eichhorn, Mark, Toronto	2	0	4.35	23	0	0	0	7	0	31.0	35	135	15	15	1	1	2	2	7	0	19	6	0
Heaton, Neal, Kansas City*	3	1	4.17	31	0	0	0	8	0	41.0	43	185	21	19	5	2	3	1	22	2	29	3	1
Heaton, Neal, Milwaukee*	0	0	0.00	1	0	0	0	1	0	1.0	0	4	0	0	0	0	0	0	1	0	2	0	0
Hillegas, Shawn, New York	1	8	5.51	21	9	1	1	4	0	78.1	96	351	52	48	12	1	3	0	33	1	46	2	0
Hillegas, Shawn, Oakland	0	2	2.35	5	0	0	0	2	0	7.2	8	34	5	2	1	1	0	0	4	1	3	0	0
Leary, Tim, New York	5	6	5.57	18	15	2	0	2	0	97.0	84	414	62	60	9	4	4	4	57	2	34	7	0
Leary, Tim, Seattle	3	4	4.91	8	8	1	0	0	0	44.0	47	210	27	24	3	2	5	5	30	3	12	2	0
Mesa, Jose, Baltimore	3	8	5.19	13	12	0	0	1	0	67.2	77	300	43	39	9	0	3	2	27	1	22	2	0
Mesa, Jose, Cleveland	4	4	4.16	15	15	1	1	0	0	93.0	92	400	45	43	5	2	2	4	43	0	40	0	0
Nunez, Edwin, Milwaukee	1	1	2.63	10	0	0	0	5	0	13.2	12	58	5	4	1	0	0	0	6	0	10	0	0
Nunez, Edwin, Texas	0	2	5.52	39	0	0	0	11	3	45.2	51	205	29	28	5	0	4	2	16	0	39	5	0
Russell, Jeff, Texas	2	3	1.91	51	0	0	0	42	28	56.2	51	241	14	12	3	1	2	2	22	3	43	3	0
Russell, Jeff, Oakland	2	0	0.00	8	0	0	0	4	2	9.2	4	35	0	0	0	0	0	0	3	0	5	0	0
Witt, Bobby, Texas	9	13	4.46	25	25	0	0	0	0	161.1	152	708	87	80	14	5	8	2	95	1	100	6	1
Witt, Bobby, Oakland	1	1	3.41	6	6	0	0	0	0	31.2	31	140	12	12	2	2	2	0	19	1	25	3	0
Young, Curt, Kansas City*	1	2	5.18	10	2	0	0	2	0	24.1	29	107	14	14	1	0	1	0	7	1	7	0	0
Young, Curt, New York*	3	0	3.32	13	5	0	0	3	0	43.1	51	188	21	16	1	3	1	2	10	1	13	0	0

NOTE—The following pitchers combined to pitch shutout games: Baltimore (7)—Sutcliffe and Olson 2; Mussina and Olson; Mills, Frohwirth and Olson; Rhodes, Frohwirth and Olson; Mussina and Frohwirth; Lefferts and Olson; Boston (7)—Clemens, Harris, Fossas and Reardon; Viola, Harris and Reardon; Hesketh and Darwin; Viola and Darwin; Dopson and Reardon; Viola and Harris; Clemens, Fossas, Quantrill and Hesketh; California (7)—Finley and Grahe 2; Abbott and Harvey; Blyleven, Bailes and Grahe; Blyleven, Bailes, Crim and Grahe; Abbott and Lewis; Finley, Lewis and Frey; Chicago (2)—Hibbard and Thigpen; McCaskill and Thigpen; Cleveland (3)—Otto and Nichols; Otto, Plunk, Wickander and Olin; Nichols, Lilliquist, Plunk and Wickander; Detroit (2)—Tanana, Doherty and Henneman; Tanana and Kiely; Kansas City (7)—Appier and Montgomery 2; Rasmussen and Montgomery 2; Gubicza, Pichardo and Montgomery; Magnante, Meacham and Montgomery; Aquino, Sampen and Montgomery; Milwaukee (8)—Plesac, Fetters and Nunez; Robinson and Plesac; Bones and Henry; Eldred, Austin and Orosco; Eldred and Holmes; Eldred and Henry; Eldred, Austin and Henry; Bosio and Henry; Minnesota (5)—Krueger, Willis and Kipper; Banks and Edens; Smiley and Aguilera; Smiley, Wayne, Edens, Casian and Aguilera; Trombley, Casian, Edens, Guthrie and Aguilera; New York (5)—Cadaret and Monteleone; Militello and Farr; Sanderson and Monteleone; Perez and Farr; Kamieniecki and Young; Oakland (6)—Stewart and Eckersley; Downs, Parrett and Gossage; Stewart and Campbell; Downs, Corsi and Honeycutt; Stewart, Russell and Eckersley; Moore and Parrett; Seattle (2)—Fleming, Harris, Powell and Schooler; Fisher and DeLucia; Texas (2)—Brown, Rogers and Russell; Guzman and Russell; Toronto (9)—Guzman, Ward and Henke 3; Key and Henke; Key, Ward and Henke; Wells, Ward and Henke; Cone and Henke; Key, Eichhorn, Ward and Henke; Cone, Ward and Henke.

FIELDING

TEAM

Team	Pct.	G	PO	A	E	TC	DP	TP	PB
Milwaukee	.986	162	4371	1741	89	6201	146	0	5
Baltimore	.985	162	4392	1708	93	6193	168	1	15
Minnesota	.985	162	4359	1776	95	6230	155	0	14
Toronto	.985	162	4322	1591	93	6006	109	0	15
Seattle	.982	162	4335	1763	112	6210	170	1	9
New York	.982	162	4358	1739	114	6211	165	0	16
Detroit	.981	162	4307	1766	116	6189	164	1	8
Kansas City	.980	162	4342	1748	122	6212	164	0	14
Chicago	.979	162	4385	1778	129	6292	134	0	13
Oakland	.979	162	4341	1576	125	6042	158	0	8
California	.979	162	4338	1811	134	6283	172	0	5
Boston	.978	162	4346	1871	139	6356	170	0	8
Cleveland	.978	162	4410	1727	141	6278	176	1	9
Texas	.975	162	4381	1692	154	6227	153	0	19
Totals	.981	1134	60987	24287	1656	86930	2204	4	158

INDIVIDUAL

FIRST BASEMEN

*Throws lefthanded.

Leader, Team	Pct.	G	PO	A	E	TC	DP
MATTINGLY, N.Y.*	.997	143	1209	116	4	1329	129

Player, Team	Pct.	G	PO	A	E	TC	DP
Amaral, Seattle	.000	2	0	0	0	0	0
Barnes, Detroit	.989	17	82	6	1	89	7
Bergman, Detroit*	.986	55	339	22	5	366	29
Blankenship, Oakland	.975	7	37	2	1	40	4
Blowers, Seattle	1.000	3	9	2	0	11	0
Brett, Kansas City	.987	15	137	12	2	151	9
Brogna, Detroit*	.982	8	48	6	1	55	9
Brooks, California	.986	6	64	4	1	69	4
Brosius, Oakland	1.000	3	39	0	0	39	2
Brunansky, Boston	.990	28	184	10	2	196	19
Bush, Minnesota*	1.000	8	16	1	0	17	3
Carter, Toronto	.968	4	27	3	1	31	1
Clark, Boston	.992	13	111	8	1	120	7
Cochrane, Seattle	1.000	3	20	0	0	20	1
Conine, Kansas City	1.000	4	36	2	0	38	1
Cooper, Boston	.990	62	446	33	5	484	44
Cron, Chicago	.923	5	10	2	1	13	1
Daugherty, Texas*	1.000	8	40	6	0	46	2
Davis, California	.995	22	191	13	1	205	20
Davis, Minnesota	1.000	1	1	0	0	1	0
G. Davis, Baltimore	1.000	2	19	1	0	20	1
Fariss, Texas	1.000	1	2	0	0	2	0
Fermin, Cleveland	1.000	2	1	0	0	1	0
Fielder, Detroit	.991	114	957	92	10	1059	98
Fitzgerald, California	1.000	2	1	0	0	1	0
Gaetti, California	.988	44	371	33	5	409	35
Gantner, Milwaukee	1.000	2	2	0	0	2	0
Gonzales, California	1.000	13	75	9	0	84	8
Hare, Detroit*	1.000	4	21	2	0	23	2
Hayes, New York	1.000	4	31	0	0	31	3
Hayes, California	1.000	4	21	2	0	23	2
Howitt, Seattle	1.000	4	3	1	0	4	0
Hrbek, Minnesota	.997	104	954	68	3	1025	75
Jacoby, Cleveland	1.000	10	45	2	0	47	7
Jaha, Milwaukee	1.000	38	286	22	0	308	22
Jefferson, Cleveland*	.993	15	129	12	1	142	9
Jorgensen, Minnesota	1.000	13	98	8	0	106	11
Joyner, Kansas City*	.993	145	1236	137	10	1383	138
Kent, Toronto	1.000	3	5	1	0	6	0
Lansford, Oakland	.983	18	112	5	2	119	13
Larkin, Minnesota	.992	55	456	30	4	490	49
Lennon, Seattle	1.000	1	5	0	0	5	1
Leyritz, New York	1.000	2	4	1	0	5	1
Lyons, Boston	1.000	8	45	5	0	50	3
Maas, New York*	.986	22	142	4	2	148	11

Player, Team	Pct.	G	PO	A	E	TC	DP
Maksudian, Toronto	.000	1	0	0	0	0	0
Martinez, Cleveland	.996	37	263	20	1	284	40
Martinez, Toronto	1.000	7	12	0	0	12	2
E. Martinez, Seattle	1.000	2	16	2	0	18	1
T. Martinez, Seattle	.995	78	678	58	4	740	62
Mattingly, New York*	.997	143	1209	116	4	1329	129
Maurer, Texas*	1.000	3	9	1	0	10	0
McGinnis, Texas	1.000	2	4	0	0	4	1
McGwire, Oakland	.995	139	1118	71	6	1195	118
McIntosh, Milwaukee	1.000	7	56	5	0	61	6
Melvin, Kansas City	.960	3	22	2	1	25	3
Milligan, Baltimore	.994	129	1009	76	7	1092	110
Molitor, Milwaukee	.996	48	461	26	2	489	44
Neel, Oakland	.857	2	6	0	1	7	0
Nilsson, Milwaukee	1.000	3	7	0	0	7	1
Oberkfell, California	1.000	2	9	0	0	9	0
O'Brien, Seattle*	.996	81	623	54	3	680	72
Olerud, Toronto*	.994	133	1057	81	7	1145	72
Palmeiro, Texas*	.995	156	1251	143	7	1401	131
Parrish, Seattle	.980	16	93	3	2	98	9
Pasqua, Chicago*	1.000	5	32	3	0	35	4
Quirk, Oakland	1.000	9	29	2	0	31	2
Ready, Oakland	.700	4	7	0	3	10	2
Rose, California	1.000	2	10	0	0	10	0
Rowland, Detroit	1.000	1	6	0	0	6	0
Segui, Baltimore*	.998	95	375	34	1	410	42
Seitzer, Milwaukee	1.000	1	1	0	0	1	0
Snow, New York*	1.000	6	43	2	0	45	7
Sorrento, Cleveland	.993	121	996	78	8	1082	108
Sprague, Toronto	1.000	4	18	2	0	20	1
Stanley, New York	1.000	4	21	1	0	22	2
Steinbach, Oakland	1.000	5	18	3	0	21	4
Stevens, California*	.995	91	764	49	4	817	88
Stubbs, Milwaukee*	.987	68	525	63	8	596	44
Surhoff, Milwaukee	1.000	17	143	13	0	156	18
Sveum, Chicago	1.000	2	3	1	0	4	0
Tabler, Toronto	1.000	34	281	21	0	302	20
Tettleton, Detroit	1.000	3	3	0	0	3	1
Thomas, Chicago	.992	158	1428	92	13	1533	112
Vaughn, Boston	.982	85	741	57	15	813	76
Ventura, Chicago	1.000	2	0	3	0	3	0

TRIPLE PLAYS: Fielder, Detroit; Milligan, Baltimore.

SECOND BASEMEN

Leader, Team	Pct.	G	PO	A	E	TC	DP
B. RIPKEN, Baltimore	.993	108	217	317	4	538	66

Player, Team	Pct.	G	PO	A	E	TC	DP
Alomar, Toronto	.993	150	287	378	5	670	66
Amaral, Seattle	1.000	1	1	0	0	1	0

Player, Team	Pct.	G	PO	A	E	TC	DP
Baerga, Cleveland	.979	160	400	475	19	894	138
Barnes, Detroit	1.000	7	2	3	0	5	1
Barrett, Boston	1.000	2	3	4	0	7	0
Blankenship, Oakland	.992	78	159	223	3	385	56
Boone, Seattle	.965	32	71	93	6	170	22
Bordick, Oakland	.987	95	201	266	6	473	57
Briley, Seattle	1.000	4	7	8	0	15	3
Browne, Oakland	1.000	19	13	18	0	31	3
Cochrane, Seattle	.000	1	0	0	0	0	0
Cooper, Boston	.000	1	0	0	0	0	0
Cora, Chicago	.984	28	51	71	2	124	19
Diaz, Texas	1.000	3	0	2	0	2	0
Fariss, Texas	1.000	17	14	13	0	27	5
Fermin, Cleveland	1.000	7	4	8	0	12	3
Fitzgerald, California	.000	1	0	0	0	0	0
Fletcher, Milwaukee	.992	106	207	319	4	530	70
Franco, Texas	.906	9	12	17	3	32	2
Frye, Texas	.978	67	120	196	7	323	43
Gallego, New York	.990	40	86	112	2	200	27
Gantner, Milwaukee	.994	68	136	180	2	318	42
Gonzales, California	.994	42	78	92	1	171	28
Griffin, Toronto	.917	16	16	28	4	48	4
Hill, Minnesota	.950	7	10	9	1	20	1
Hulett, Baltimore	1.000	10	7	18	0	25	2
Huson, Texas	1.000	47	69	83	0	152	22
Jefferies, Kansas City	.000	1	0	0	0	0	0
P. Kelly, New York	.978	101	203	296	11	510	64
Kent, Toronto	.984	17	24	37	1	62	1
Knoblauch, Minnesota	.992	154	306	415	6	727	104
Leyritz, New York	.000	1	0	0	0	0	0
Listach, Milwaukee	.000	1	0	0	0	0	0
Lyons, Boston	1.000	1	0	1	0	1	0
McLemore, Baltimore	.978	70	126	186	7	319	47
Miller, Kansas City	.971	93	189	250	13	452	60
Naehring, Boston	.992	23	54	66	1	121	11
Newman, Texas	.983	72	118	168	5	291	31
Oberkfell, California	.986	21	34	34	1	69	4
Perezchica, Cleveland	1.000	4	3	0	0	3	0
Petralli, Texas	.500	2	1	0	1	2	0
Phillips, Detroit	.986	57	109	167	4	280	41
Puckett, Minnesota	.000	2	0	0	0	0	0
Ready, Oakland	.941	4	8	8	1	17	1
Reboulet, Minnesota	.982	13	21	34	1	56	8
Reed, Boston	.982	142	304	472	14	790	113
Reynolds, Seattle	.982	134	303	362	12	677	88
B. Ripken, Baltimore	.993	108	217	317	4	538	66
Rivera, Boston	1.000	1	1	0	0	1	0
Rose, California	.953	28	48	94	7	149	19
Rossy, Kansas City	1.000	3	4	6	0	10	1
Samuel, Kansas City	.939	10	19	27	3	49	9
Sax, Chicago	.972	141	305	390	20	715	75
Scarsone, Baltimore	.889	5	5	3	1	9	3
Schaefer, Seattle	1.000	7	6	15	0	21	3
Seitzer, Milwaukee	1.000	2	2	4	0	6	0
Shumpert, K.C.	.969	33	50	77	4	131	17
Sojo, California	.985	96	187	267	7	461	72
Spiers, Milwaukee	1.000	4	5	5	0	10	0
Stankiewicz, N.Y.	.993	34	52	89	1	142	20
Suero, Milwaukee	.971	15	11	22	1	34	5
Valentin, Milwaukee	.667	1	1	1	1	3	0
Velarde, New York	.923	3	3	9	1	13	1
Whitaker, Detroit	.984	119	256	312	9	577	72
Wilkerson, K.C.	.989	39	71	107	2	180	28

TRIPLE PLAYS: Baerga, Cleveland; Reynolds, Seattle.

Player, Team	Pct.	G	PO	A	E	TC	DP
Briley, Seattle	.667	4	0	4	2	6	0
Brosius, Oakland	.957	12	8	14	1	23	0
Browne, Oakland	.965	58	40	70	4	114	8
Cochrane, Seattle	.913	10	1	20	2	23	2
Cooper, Boston	.970	47	26	103	4	133	5
Cora, Chicago	.889	5	0	8	1	9	0
Diaz, Texas	1.000	1	1	0	0	1	0
Easley, California	.970	45	28	100	4	132	13
Fermin, Cleveland	.946	17	10	25	2	37	3
Fitzgerald, California	1.000	3	0	1	0	1	0
Fletcher, Milwaukee	.000	1	0	0	0	0	0
Fryman, Detroit	.968	26	15	46	2	63	4
Gaetti, California	.927	67	52	163	17	232	18
Gantner, Milwaukee	.978	31	17	28	1	46	3
Gomez, Baltimore	.951	137	106	246	18	370	19
Gonzales, California	.954	53	32	114	7	153	9
Grebeck, Chicago	1.000	7	2	6	0	8	0
Gruber, Toronto	.949	120	104	215	17	336	10
Hayes, New York	.963	139	94	249	13	356	29
Hemond, Oak.-Chi.	.000	3	0	0	0	0	0
Hill, Minnesota	1.000	5	2	4	0	6	0
Hulett, Baltimore	.935	27	16	70	6	92	7
Jacoby, Cleveland	.957	111	46	175	10	231	17
Jefferies, K.C.	.939	146	96	304	26	426	22
Jorgensen, Minnesota	.950	9	4	15	1	20	3
Kent, Toronto	.915	49	33	74	10	117	3
Lansford, Oakland	.965	119	86	162	9	257	10
Leius, Minnesota	.955	125	58	257	15	330	12
Lewis, Cleveland	.750	1	0	3	1	4	0
Leyritz, New York	1.000	2	1	2	0	3	0
Livingston, Detroit	.962	112	67	189	10	266	15
Martinez, Cleveland	.943	28	13	37	3	53	6
E. Martinez, Seattle	.943	103	72	209	17	298	24
Mayne, Kansas City	1.000	8	4	10	0	14	1
McGinnis, Texas	1.000	2	1	1	0	2	0
Meulens, New York	1.000	2	0	3	0	3	2
Naehring, Boston	.957	10	4	18	1	23	1
Newman, Texas	.976	28	12	28	1	41	8
Pagliarulo, Minnesota	.962	37	11	64	3	78	3
Palmer, Texas	.945	150	124	254	22	400	24
Perezchica, Cleveland	.875	9	1	6	1	8	0
Petralli, Texas	1.000	4	0	1	0	1	0
Phillips, Detroit	.972	20	11	24	1	36	4
Puckett, Minnesota	.000	2	0	0	0	0	0
Quinlan, Toronto	.909	13	4	6	1	11	0
Quinones, Minnesota	.714	1	3	2	2	7	0
Quirk, Oakland	.000	2	0	0	0	0	0
Ready, Oakland	.933	7	4	10	1	15	2
Reboulet, Minnesota	1.000	22	11	31	0	42	3
Rivera, Boston	1.000	1	2	1	0	3	1
Rohde, Cleveland	.900	5	3	6	1	10	1
Rossy, Kansas City	.923	9	9	15	2	26	1
Rowland, Detroit	1.000	1	0	1	0	1	0
Scarsone, Baltimore	.833	2	0	5	1	6	1
Schaefer, Seattle	.917	21	2	9	1	12	0
Seitzer, Milwaukee	.969	146	99	273	12	384	18
Sojo, California	.960	9	5	19	1	25	0
Spiers, Milwaukee	.000	1	0	0	0	0	0
Sprague, Toronto	.000	1	0	0	0	0	0
Surhoff, Milwaukee	1.000	3	1	2	0	3	0
Sveum, Chicago	1.000	2	1	0	0	1	0
Tabler, Toronto	1.000	1	0	1	0	1	0
Tackett, Baltimore	.000	1	0	0	0	0	0
Tatum, Milwaukee	1.000	5	6	2	0	8	0
Thome, Cleveland	.882	40	21	61	11	93	3
Turner, Seattle	.881	18	8	29	5	42	5
Velarde, New York	.907	26	14	35	5	54	7
Ventura, Chicago	.957	157	141	372	23	536	29
Wilkerson, K.C.	.923	5	4	8	1	13	1
Worthington, Cle.	.857	9	6	18	4	28	2

TRIPLE PLAYS: Barnes, Detroit; Gomez, Baltimore; Thome, Cleveland.

THIRD BASEMEN WITH TWO OR MORE TEAMS

Player, Team	Pct.	G	PO	A	E	TC	DP
Hemond, Oakland	.000	2	0	0	0	0	0
Hemond, Chicago	.000	1	0	0	0	0	0

THIRD BASEMEN

Leader, Team	Pct.	G	PO	A	E	TC	DP
SEITZER, Milwaukee	.969	146	99	273	12	384	18

Player, Team	Pct.	G	PO	A	E	TC	DP
Amaral, Seattle	.955	17	10	32	2	44	3
Barnes, Detroit	.919	39	34	68	9	111	7
Blowers, Seattle	.984	29	19	42	1	62	8
Boggs, Boston	.952	117	70	229	15	314	23
Boone, Seattle	1.000	6	1	3	0	4	0
Brett, Kansas City	.875	3	2	5	1	8	1

Leader, Team	Pct.	G	PO	A	E	TC	DP
VIZQUEL, Seattle	.989	136	223	403	7	633	92

Player, Team	Pct.	G	PO	A	E	TC	DP
Alexander, Baltimore ..	1.000	3	3	3	0	6	1
Amaral, Seattle............	.981	17	17	36	1	54	7
Beltre, Chicago	.924	43	53	92	12	157	12
Bordick, Oakland..........	.967	70	110	183	10	303	50
Brosius, Oakland	1.000	1	1	0	0	1	0
Browne, Oakland	1.000	1	1	0	0	1	0
Cochrane, Seattle	1.000	3	2	1	0	3	0
Colon, Texas	.946	14	17	36	3	56	5
Cooper, Boston	.000	1	0	0	0	0	0
Cora, Chicago	1.000	6	9	5	0	14	3
Diaz, Texas	.975	16	15	24	1	40	2
DiSarcina, Cal..............	.967	157	250	486	25	761	109
Easley, California	.800	3	2	2	1	5	0
Fermin, Cleveland	.971	55	64	135	6	205	36
Fletcher, Milwaukee	.948	22	29	63	5	97	14
Fryman, Detroit	.970	137	205	443	20	668	91
Gagne, Minnesota	.973	141	208	438	18	664	83
Gallego, New York	.944	14	26	41	4	71	10
Gonzales, California	.952	8	6	14	1	21	4
Grebeck, Chicago	.980	85	110	277	8	395	47
Griffin, Toronto	.981	48	45	108	3	156	13
Guillen, Chicago	1.000	12	20	39	0	59	7
Hemond, Chicago	.500	3	1	0	1	2	0
Hernandez, Cleveland .	.857	3	3	3	1	7	0
Hill, Minnesota.............	.944	10	9	25	2	36	4
Howard, Kansas City...	.976	74	124	204	8	336	52
Hulett, Baltimore	.857	5	2	4	1	7	2
Huson, Texas	.968	82	109	167	9	285	44
Jorgensen, Minnesota.	1.000	2	1	2	0	3	0
Knoblauch, Minnesota	.000	1	0	0	0	0	0
Lansford, Oakland.......	1.000	1	1	0	0	1	0
Lee, Toronto.................	.987	128	187	331	7	525	67
Leius, Minnesota	1.000	10	5	4	0	9	1
Lewis, Cleveland..........	.954	121	184	333	25	542	71
Listach, Milwaukee	.966	148	238	449	24	711	89
Naehring, Boston.........	.992	30	36	86	1	123	19
Newman, Texas	.958	20	19	27	2	48	8
Perezchica, Cleveland .	.900	4	4	5	1	10	0
Phillips, Detroit............	1.000	1	0	1	0	1	0
Puckett, Minnesota	.000	1	0	0	0	0	0
Quinones, Minnesota ..	.000	1	0	0	0	0	0
Reboulet, Minnesota....	.971	36	37	98	4	139	20
C. Ripken, Baltimore....	.984	162	287	445	12	744	119
Rivera, Boston	.966	93	117	286	14	417	56
Rossy, Kansas City	.961	51	60	135	8	203	38
Scarsone, Baltimore....	1.000	1	1	0	0	1	0
Schaefer, Seattle	.922	33	28	67	8	103	7
Schofield, California	1.000	1	3	1	0	4	0
Shumpert, K.C..............	.000	1	0	0	0	0	0
Silvestri, New York	.889	6	4	12	2	18	3
Sojo, California	.917	5	4	7	1	12	1
Spiers, Milwaukee	1.000	5	1	1	0	2	0
Stankiewicz, N.Y.	.973	81	133	257	11	401	54
Suero, Milwaukee	.000	1	0	0	0	0	0
Sveum, Chicago	.944	37	39	97	8	144	19
Thon, Texas.................	.958	87	117	225	15	357	38
Trammell, Detroit	.977	27	46	80	3	129	16
Valentin, Boston	.963	58	79	182	10	271	45
Valentin, Milwaukee....	.000	1	0	0	0	0	0
Velarde, New York	.974	75	129	212	9	350	42
Vizquel, Seattle............	.989	136	223	403	7	633	92
Weiss, Oakland	.956	103	144	270	19	433	57
Wilkerson, K.C.............	.968	69	73	142	7	222	27
Zosky, Toronto	.923	8	2	10	1	13	2

TRIPLE PLAY: Vizquel, Seattle.

OUTFIELDERS

*Throws lefthanded.

Leader, Team	Pct.	G	PO	A	E	TC	DP
HAMILTON, Mil.............	1.000	124	279	10	0	289	0

Player, Team	Pct.	G	PO	A	E	TC	DP
Abner, Chicago............	1.000	94	155	2	0	157	0
Amaral, Seattle............	1.000	3	5	0	0	5	0
Anderson, Baltimore* .	.980	158	382	10	8	400	6
Baines, Oakland*	.964	23	27	0	1	28	0
Barfield, New York......	.966	30	54	3	2	59	0
Barnes, Detroit	.909	15	9	1	1	11	1
Bell, Toronto	1.000	56	105	4	0	109	1
Bell, Chicago	.964	15	27	0	1	28	0
Belle, Cleveland	.969	52	94	1	3	98	0
Bergman, Detroit*	.000	1	0	0	0	0	0
Bichette, Milwaukee	.990	101	188	6	2	196	2
Blankenship, Oakland .	.978	51	90	1	2	93	0
Briley, Seattle	.967	42	58	1	2	61	0
Brito, Minnesota..........	.750	3	3	0	1	4	0
Brosius, Oakland	1.000	20	20	1	0	21	0
Brown, Minnesota	.952	31	20	0	1	21	0
Browne, Oakland	.990	43	95	0	1	96	0
Bruett, Minnesota*.......	.979	45	46	1	1	48	0
Brunansky, Boston......	.980	92	189	6	4	199	3
Buhner, Seattle............	.994	150	314	14	2	330	4
Burks, Boston	.984	63	120	3	2	125	0
Bush, Minnesota*	1.000	24	35	0	0	35	0
Cangelosi, Texas*	.964	65	76	4	3	83	1
Canseco, Oak.-Tex.	.985	90	195	5	3	203	3
Carreon, Detroit*	.979	83	178	5	4	187	2
Carter, Toronto	.971	129	257	10	8	275	2
Clark, Detroit	.931	13	27	0	2	29	0
Cochrane, Seattle	.879	25	26	3	4	33	1
Cole, Cleveland*	.971	24	33	1	1	35	1
Conine, Kansas City	1.000	23	39	1	0	40	0
Cotto, Seattle	1.000	92	170	2	0	172	0
Cron, Chicago	.000	1	0	0	0	0	0
Curtis, California	.978	135	250	16	6	272	3
Cuyler, Detroit	.983	89	232	4	4	240	1
Daugherty, Texas*.......	.939	26	30	1	2	33	0
Davis, Minnesota	1.000	4	5	0	0	5	0
Deer, Detroit	.983	106	229	8	4	241	1
Devereaux, Baltimore..	.989	155	431	5	5	441	3
Diaz, Milwaukee	1.000	11	10	0	0	10	0
Ducey, Tor.-Cal...........	.957	33	43	2	2	47	0
Eisenreich, K.C.*	.995	88	180	1	1	182	0
Fariss, Texas	1.000	49	57	0	0	57	0
Felix, California	.983	128	340	9	6	355	3
Fitzgerald, California ..	1.000	11	5	0	0	5	0
Fox, Oakland*..............	.990	43	92	3	1	96	1
Franco, Texas..............	1.000	4	9	0	0	9	0
Gladden, Detroit..........	.987	108	227	9	3	239	2
Gonzalez, California	1.000	22	30	1	0	31	1
Gonzalez, Texas	.975	148	379	9	10	398	2
Grebeck, Chicago	1.000	2	0	0	0	0	0
Greenwell, Boston........	1.000	41	85	1	0	86	0
Griffey, Seattle*	.997	137	359	8	1	368	4
Gwynn, Kansas City* ..	1.000	19	33	0	0	33	0
Hall, New York*	.990	136	283	10	3	296	2
Hamilton, Mil...............	1.000	124	279	10	0	289	0
Hare, Detroit*	1.000	9	12	0	0	12	0
Harris, Texas...............	.974	24	36	1	1	38	1
Haselman, Seattle	1.000	2	3	0	0	3	0
Hatcher, Boston	.968	75	145	5	5	155	0
Hayes, California..........	.983	85	169	1	3	173	1
Hemond, Oak.-Chi.	1.000	4	4	1	0	5	0
D. Henderson, Oak.......	.950	12	19	0	1	20	0
R. Henderson, Oak.*	.984	108	231	9	4	244	2
Hill, Minnesota.............	.000	1	0	0	0	0	0
Hill, Cleveland.............	.956	59	126	5	6	137	1
Howard, Kansas City...	.000	2	0	0	0	0	0
Howard, Cleveland	.990	97	185	5	2	192	0
Howitt, Oak.-Sea.	.970	30	60	4	2	66	3
Huff, Chicago	1.000	56	68	2	0	70	0
Hulse, Texas*	.984	31	61	0	1	62	0
Humphreys, New York.	1.000	2	7	1	0	8	0
Huson, Texas...............	.000	2	0	0	0	0	0
Jaha, Milwaukee	.000	1	0	0	0	0	0
James, New York*.......	1.000	46	62	1	0	63	0
Jeter, Chicago..............	.909	8	10	1	0	11	0
Johnson, Chicago*......	.987	157	433	11	6	450	3
Karkovice, Chicago	1.000	1	3	0	0	3	0

Player, Team	Pct.	G	PO	A	E	TC	DP
R. Kelly, New York	.983	146	389	8	7	404	3
Kingery, Oakland*	1.000	10	14	0	0	14	0
Kirby, Cleveland	1.000	2	3	0	0	3	0
Koslofski, Kansas City	.991	52	107	5	1	113	0
Larkin, Minnesota	.983	43	53	5	1	59	1
Leyritz, New York	1.000	2	2	0	0	2	0
Listach, Milwaukee	.000	1	0	0	0	0	0
Lofton, Cleveland*	.982	143	420	14	8	442	3
Lyons, Boston	1.000	5	6	0	0	6	0
Mack, Minnesota	.988	155	322	9	4	335	2
Maldonado, Toronto	.978	132	260	12	6	278	1
Martinez, Baltimore*	.973	52	104	4	3	111	1
McIntosh, Milwaukee	1.000	10	13	0	0	13	0
McRae, Kansas City	.993	148	419	8	3	430	2
McReynolds, K.C.	.986	106	204	4	3	211	0
Mercedes, Baltimore	.956	16	41	2	2	45	0
Miller, Kansas City	.953	16	41	0	2	43	0
Mitchell, Seattle	1.000	69	130	4	0	134	0
Morris, California*	1.000	14	13	0	0	13	0
Moses, Seattle*	1.000	18	19	0	0	19	0
Munoz, Minnesota	.987	122	220	8	3	231	4
Naehring, Boston	1.000	1	1	0	0	1	0
Neel, Oakland	.846	9	10	1	2	13	0
Newman, Texas	.000	1	0	0	0	0	0
Newson, Chicago*	1.000	50	67	5	0	72	3
Orsulak, Baltimore*	.983	110	228	9	4	241	1
Pasqua, Chicago*	.963	81	153	4	6	163	0
Peltier, Texas*	.857	10	6	0	1	7	0
Pettis, Detroit	.993	46	144	2	1	147	0
Phillips, Detroit	.968	69	181	3	6	190	0
Plantier, Boston	.975	76	148	6	4	158	0
Polonia, California*	.980	99	192	8	4	204	1
Puckett, Minnesota	.993	149	394	9	3	406	3
Pulliam, Kansas City	1.000	1	3	0	0	3	0
Raines, Chicago	.994	129	312	12	2	326	0
Ready, Oakland	1.000	24	34	1	0	35	0
Reboulet, Minnesota	1.000	7	2	0	0	2	0
Reed, Minnesota	1.000	13	14	1	0	15	0
Reimer, Texas	.949	110	198	7	11	216	1
Reynolds, Seattle	.000	1	0	0	0	0	0
Rivera, Boston	.000	1	0	0	0	0	0
Jo. Russell, Texas	.000	2	0	0	1	1	0
Salmon, California	.953	21	40	1	2	43	1
Samuel, Kansas City	.903	18	26	2	3	31	0
Segui, Baltimore*	1.000	18	31	1	0	32	0
Sierra, Tex.-Oak.	.976	144	283	6	7	296	0
Stubbs, Milwaukee*	.000	1	0	0	0	0	0
Surhoff, Milwaukee	1.000	7	9	0	0	9	0
Tabler, Toronto	1.000	8	7	0	0	7	0
Tartabull, New York	.980	69	142	3	3	148	1
Tettleton, Detroit	1.000	2	3	0	0	3	0
Thurman, Kansas City	.986	67	138	5	2	145	0
Turner, Seattle	1.000	15	13	0	0	13	0
Vaughn, Milwaukee	.990	131	288	6	3	297	0
Velarde, New York	1.000	23	33	1	0	34	0
T. Ward, Toronto	1.000	12	18	1	0	19	0
White, Toronto	.985	152	443	8	7	458	2
Whiten, Cleveland	.980	144	321	14	7	342	1
B. Williams, New York	.995	62	187	5	1	193	2
G. Williams, New York	.913	12	20	1	2	23	0
Williams, California	1.000	12	26	0	0	26	0
Wilson, Oakland	.981	120	355	2	7	364	2
Winfield, Toronto	1.000	26	52	1	0	53	0
Winningham, Boston	.975	67	112	7	3	122	1
Yount, Milwaukee	.995	139	371	6	2	379	0
Zupcic, Boston	.977	114	241	11	6	258	3

TRIPLE PLAYS: Buhner, Seattle; Lofton, Cleveland.

Player, Team	Pct.	G	PO	A	E	TC	DP
Howitt, Oakland	.951	19	36	3	2	41	3
Howitt, Seattle	1.000	11	24	1	0	25	0
Sierra, Texas	.970	119	224	6	7	237	0
Sierra, Oakland	1.000	25	59	0	0	59	0

CATCHERS

Leader, Team	Pct.	G	PO	A	E	TC	DP	PB
TETTLETON, Det..	.996	113	475	47	2	524	10	4

Player, Team	Pct.	G	PO	A	E	TC	DP	PB
Allanson, Mil.	.943	9	30	3	2	35	0	0
Alomar, Cleveland	.996	88	477	39	2	518	6	3
Borders, Toronto	.991	137	784	88	8	880	7	11
Bradley, Seattle	1.000	1	1	2	0	3	0	0
Cochrane, Seattle	1.000	21	58	5	0	63	1	1
Davis, Texas	1.000	1	0	0	0	0	0	0
Dempsey, Bal.	1.000	8	13	1	0	14	0	1
Fisk, Chicago	.993	54	252	26	2	280	2	4
Fitzgerald, Cal.	.990	74	290	20	3	313	4	3
Flaherty, Boston	.982	34	102	7	2	111	2	0
Harper, Minnesota	.984	133	744	58	13	815	8	12
Haselman, Seattle	1.000	5	16	2	0	18	0	0
Heffernan, Seattle	1.000	5	19	1	0	20	0	1
Hemond, Oak.-Chi.	1.000	9	29	5	0	34	0	0
Hoiles, Baltimore	.994	95	500	31	3	534	6	4
Karkovice, Chi.	.990	119	533	53	6	592	8	6
Knorr, Toronto	1.000	8	33	3	0	36	0	1
Kreuter, Detroit	.983	62	271	22	5	298	6	4
Levis, Cleveland	.985	21	59	5	1	65	0	1
Leyritz, New York	.990	18	89	12	1	102	1	2
Macfarlane, K.C.	.993	104	527	43	4	574	7	9
Marzano, Boston	.968	18	81	9	3	93	1	0
Mayne, K.C.	.990	62	277	23	3	303	1	3
McGinnis, Texas	1.000	10	40	3	0	43	2	6
McIntosh, Mil.	.983	14	53	5	1	59	0	0
Melvin, K.C.	.990	21	77	7	0	84	2	2
Mercedes, Oak.	.875	9	7	0	1	8	0	0
Merullo, Chicago	.971	16	64	3	2	69	0	3
Myers, Tor.-Cal.	.993	26	125	16	1	142	1	2
Nilsson, Mil.	.992	46	224	16	2	242	1	0
Nokes, New York	.993	111	552	47	4	603	6	7.
Ortiz, Cleveland	.989	86	402	38	5	445	2	5
Orton, California	.981	43	238	23	5	266	3	1
Parent, Baltimore	.988	16	73	7	1	81	1	1
Parks, Minnesota	1.000	7	18	1	0	19	0	0
Parrish, Cal.-Sea.	.987	56	290	20	4	314	6	4
Pena, Boston	.993	132	786	57	6	849	12	7
Petralli, Texas	.990	54	263	23	3	289	6	3
Quirk, Oakland	.973	59	258	26	8	292	4	1
Rodriguez, Texas	.983	116	763	85	15	863	10	10
Rowland, Detroit	1.000	3	6	0	0	6	1	0
Jo. Russell, Texas	1.000	4	14	2	0	16	0	0
Santovenia, Chi.	1.000	2	3	0	0	3	0	0
Sinatro, Seattle	1.000	18	43	4	0	47	1	0
Sprague, Toronto	.985	15	64	3	1	68	0	1
Stanley, New York	.980	55	266	29	6	301	3	7
Steinbach, Oak.	.985	124	580	69	10	659	6	7
Stephens, Texas	1.000	6	12	2	0	14	0	0
Surhoff, Mil.	.990	109	546	59	6	611	7	5
Tackett, Baltimore	.997	64	311	32	1	344	5	9
Tettleton, Detroit	.996	113	475	47	2	524	10	4
Tingley, California	.990	69	270	35	4	309	2	0
Valle, Seattle	.990	122	606	62	7	675	10	4
Webster, Min.	.995	49	190	11	1	202	3	2
Wedge, Boston	1.000	5	19	2	0	21	1	1

TRIPLE PLAY: Alomar, Cleveland.

OUTFIELDERS WITH TWO OR MORE TEAMS

Player, Team	Pct.	G	PO	A	E	TC	DP
Canseco, Oakland	.988	77	163	5	2	170	3
Canseco, Texas	.970	13	32	0	1	33	0
Ducey, Toronto	1.000	13	11	0	0	11	0
Ducey, California	.944	20	32	2	2	36	0
Hemond, Oakland	1.000	2	2	0	0	2	0
Hemond, Chicago	1.000	2	2	1	0	3	0

CATCHERS WITH TWO OR MORE TEAMS

Player, Team	Pct.	G	PO	A	E	TC	DP	PB
Hemond, Oakland	1.000	8	29	5	0	34	0	0
Hemond, Chicago	.000	1	0	0	0	0	0	0
Myers, Toronto	.991	18	92	13	1	106	1	2
Myers, California	1.000	8	33	3	0	36	0	0
Parrish, California	.975	22	107	8	3	118	2	1
Parrish, Seattle	.995	34	183	12	1	196	4	3

PITCHERS

*Throws lefthanded.

Leader, Team	Pct.	G	PO	A	E	TC	DP
McDONALD, Bal.	1.000	35	22	29	0	51	2

Player, Team	Pct.	G	PO	A	E	TC	DP
Abbott, California*	1.000	29	11	35	0	46	1
Abbott, Minnesota	1.000	6	2	3	0	5	0
Acker, Seattle	1.000	17	0	5	0	5	0
Agosto, Seattle*	1.000	17	1	3	0	4	0
Aguilera, Minnesota	1.000	64	2	5	0	7	0
Aldred, Detroit*	1.000	16	5	10	0	15	1
Alexander, Texas	1.000	3	1	0	0	1	0
Alvarez, Chicago*	.900	34	4	14	2	20	0
Appier, Kansas City	.976	30	19	21	1	41	4
Aquino, Kansas City	1.000	15	4	16	0	20	1
Armstrong, Cleveland	.905	35	13	25	4	42	2
Arnsberg, Cleveland	1.000	8	2	0	0	2	0
Austin, Milwaukee	1.000	47	2	2	0	4	0
Bailes, California*	1.000	32	1	4	0	5	1
Banks, Minnesota	1.000	16	9	5	0	14	0
Bannister, Texas*	1.000	36	4	5	0	9	0
Barton, Seattle*	.833	14	2	3	1	6	0
Bell, Cleveland*	1.000	7	0	5	0	5	0
Berenguer, K.C.	.875	19	2	5	1	8	1
Blyleven, California	1.000	25	5	13	0	18	1
Boddicker, K.C.	.962	29	12	13	1	26	1
Bohanon, Texas*	.889	18	5	3	1	9	0
Bolton, Boston*	.857	21	0	6	1	7	1
Bones, Milwaukee	.938	31	17	13	2	32	1
Bosio, Milwaukee	1.000	33	20	26	0	46	5
Boucher, Cleveland*	1.000	8	3	3	0	6	0
Briscoe, Oakland	.500	2	0	1	1	2	0
Brown, Seattle*	1.000	2	0	1	0	1	0
Brown, Texas	.901	35	37	36	8	81	4
Burke, New York	1.000	23	1	9	0	10	0
Burns, Texas	.929	35	5	8	1	14	1
Butcher, California	1.000	19	0	3	0	3	0
Cadaret, New York*	1.000	46	5	18	0	23	2
Campbell, Oakland	1.000	32	1	6	0	7	0
Campbell, Texas	.000	1	0	0	0	0	0
Carman, Texas*	.000	2	0	0	0	0	0
Casian, Minnesota*	1.000	6	1	1	0	2	1
Chiamparino, Texas	.600	4	1	2	2	5	0
Christopher, Cleveland	1.000	10	1	2	0	3	0
Clemens, Boston	.978	32	19	25	1	45	0
Clements, Baltimore*	1.000	23	2	7	0	9	2
Cone, Toronto	1.000	8	2	2	0	4	0
Cook, Cleveland*	.947	32	3	15	1	19	0
Corsi, Oakland	1.000	32	6	10	0	16	0
Crim, California	.950	57	7	12	1	20	0
Darling, Oakland	.902	33	11	26	4	41	2
Darwin, Boston	.957	51	9	13	1	23	2
Davis, Kansas City*	1.000	13	2	6	0	8	0
S. Davis, Baltimore	1.000	48	3	14	0	17	3
DeLucia, Seattle	.933	30	8	6	1	15	0
Doherty, Detroit	.967	47	10	19	1	30	4
Dopson, Boston	.974	25	19	18	1	38	1
Downs, Oakland	.929	18	5	8	1	14	0
Drahman, Chicago	.500	5	1	0	1	2	0
Dunne, Chicago	1.000	4	1	2	0	3	1
Eckersley, Oakland	1.000	69	3	10	0	13	1
Edens, Minnesota	1.000	52	8	4	0	12	0
Eichhorn, Cal.-Tor.	.960	65	5	19	1	25	0
Eldred, Milwaukee	.941	14	4	12	1	17	0
Embree, Cleveland*	.500	4	1	0	1	2	0
Erickson, Minnesota	.981	32	18	34	1	53	3
Farr, New York	.750	50	2	4	2	8	0
Fernandez, Chicago	.956	29	10	33	2	45	5
Fetters, Milwaukee	1.000	50	3	11	0	14	1
Finley, California*	.870	31	3	17	3	23	1
Fireovid, Texas	1.000	3	1	2	0	3	2
Fisher, Seattle	.947	22	5	13	1	19	0
Flanagan, Baltimore*	.923	42	6	6	1	13	2
Fleming, Seattle*	.974	33	4	33	1	38	4
Fortugno, California*	1.000	14	0	4	0	4	0

Player, Team	Pct.	G	PO	A	E	TC	DP
Fossas, Boston*	1.000	60	2	6	0	8	0
Frey, California*	1.000	51	4	5	0	9	1
Frohwirth, Baltimore	.970	65	8	24	1	33	4
Gardiner, Boston	.966	28	13	15	1	29	2
Gordon, Kansas City	.962	40	11	14	1	26	1
Gossage, Oakland	1.000	30	2	4	0	6	0
Gozzo, Minnesota	.000	2	0	0	0	0	0
Grahe, California	.893	46	12	13	3	28	1
Grant, Seattle	.813	23	6	7	3	16	0
Groom, Detroit*	1.000	12	0	6	0	6	0
Gubicza, Kansas City	1.000	18	10	12	0	22	2
Guetterman, N.Y.*	1.000	15	2	4	0	6	1
Gullickson, Detroit	.979	34	21	26	1	48	3
Gunderson, Seattle*	1.000	9	1	2	0	3	0
Guthrie, Minnesota*	.909	54	4	6	1	11	0
Guzman, Oakland*	.000	2	0	0	0	0	0
Guzman, Texas	.974	33	16	22	1	39	3
Guzman, Toronto	1.000	28	12	11	0	23	0
Haas, Detroit	1.000	12	3	8	0	11	0
Habyan, New York	1.000	56	3	15	0	18	1
Haney, Kansas City*	1.000	7	1	1	0	2	0
Hanson, Seattle	.974	31	14	23	1	38	2
Harris, Boston	.905	70	3	16	2	21	0
Harris, Seattle	.333	8	1	0	2	3	0
Harvey, California	1.000	25	0	1	0	1	0
Hathaway, California*	.000	2	0	0	0	0	0
Heaton, K.C.-Mil.*	.875	32	5	2	1	8	0
Henke, Toronto	1.000	57	2	2	0	4	0
Henneman, Detroit	.947	60	9	9	1	19	1
Henry, Milwaukee	1.000	68	10	4	0	14	2
Hentgen, Toronto	1.000	28	0	4	0	4	1
Hernandez, Chicago	.917	43	7	4	1	12	1
Hesketh, Boston*	.875	30	6	22	4	32	1
Hibbard, Chicago*	.933	31	6	36	3	45	4
Hillegas, N.Y.-Oak.	.800	26	7	5	3	15	0
Hitchcock, New York*	1.000	3	0	2	0	2	0
Holmes, Milwaukee	.900	41	5	4	1	10	1
Honeycutt, Oakland*	.833	54	3	2	1	6	0
Horsman, Oakland*	1.000	58	1	5	0	6	0
Hough, Chicago	1.000	27	7	20	0	27	1
Howe, New York*	.900	20	2	7	1	10	0
Hoy, Boston	1.000	5	0	1	0	1	1
Irvine, Boston	1.000	21	2	5	0	7	0
Jeffcoat, Texas*	1.000	6	1	3	0	4	1
Johnson, New York*	1.000	13	1	8	0	9	0
Johnson, Seattle*	.893	31	5	20	3	28	0
Johnston, Kansas City	.000	5	0	0	0	0	0
Jones, Seattle	.769	38	3	7	3	13	1
Kamieniecki, N.Y.	1.000	28	15	19	0	34	3
Key, Toronto*	.978	33	18	27	1	46	2
Kiely, Detroit	1.000	39	8	15	0	23	3
King, Detroit	.917	17	6	5	1	12	0
Kipper, Minnesota*	1.000	25	0	6	0	6	1
Knudsen, Detroit	1.000	48	6	7	0	13	2
Kramer, Seattle	1.000	4	1	0	0	1	0
Krueger, Minnesota*	1.000	27	4	9	0	13	0
Lancaster, Detroit	.923	41	3	9	1	13	4
Langston, California*	.941	32	7	41	3	51	1
Leach, Chicago	.957	51	9	13	1	23	1
Leary, N.Y.-Sea.	1.000	26	10	18	0	28	3
Lefferts, Baltimore*	.750	5	1	2	1	4	0
Leiter, Toronto*	.000	1	0	0	0	0	0
Leiter, Detroit	.958	35	8	15	1	24	0
Leon, Texas	1.000	15	3	1	0	4	0
Lewis, Baltimore	1.000	2	1	1	0	2	0
Lewis, California	1.000	21	3	8	0	11	2
Lilliquist, Cleveland*	1.000	71	3	9	0	12	0
Linton, Toronto	1.000	8	0	2	0	2	1
MacDonald, Toronto*	1.000	27	2	2	0	4	0
Magnante, K.C.*	1.000	44	9	20	0	29	3
Mahomes, Minnesota	1.000	14	5	4	0	9	0
Manuel, Texas	.000	3	0	0	0	0	0
Mathews, Texas	1.000	40	5	4	0	9	1
McCaskill, Chicago	.965	34	24	31	2	57	0
McCullers, Texas	1.000	5	1	2	0	3	1
McDonald, Baltimore	1.000	35	22	29	0	51	2

Player, Team	Pct.	G	PO	A	E	TC	DP
McDowell, Chicago	.956	34	16	27	2	45	3
Meacham, K.C.	.969	64	13	18	1	32	1
Mesa, Bal.-Cle.	.943	28	12	21	2	35	0
Milacki, Baltimore	1.000	23	14	10	0	24	0
Militello, New York	.750	9	2	4	2	8	0
Mills, Baltimore	1.000	35	9	17	0	26	2
Mlicki, Cleveland	1.000	4	6	3	0	9	1
Moeller, Kansas City*	1.000	5	0	5	0	5	0
Monteleone, New York	1.000	47	6	7	0	13	1
Montgomery, K.C.	.962	65	12	13	1	26	2
Moore, Oakland	.929	36	17	22	3	42	5
Morris, Toronto	.979	34	20	26	1	47	1
Munoz, Detroit*	1.000	65	8	12	0	20	0
Mussina, Baltimore	.978	32	13	31	1	45	0
Mutis, Cleveland*	1.000	3	0	2	0	2	0
Nagy, Cleveland	.985	33	22	43	1	66	3
Navarro, Milwaukee	.897	34	17	18	4	39	1
Nelson, Oakland	1.000	28	3	4	0	7	0
Nelson, Seattle	.882	66	3	12	2	17	2
Nichols, Cleveland	1.000	30	4	14	0	18	0
Nielsen, New York*	1.000	20	1	4	0	5	0
Nunez, Mil.-Tex.	.875	49	3	4	1	8	0
Olin, Cleveland	1.000	72	4	17	0	21	1
Olson, Baltimore	1.000	60	5	9	0	14	2
Orosco, Milwaukee*	1.000	59	2	3	0	5	0
Otto, Cleveland*	.944	18	3	14	1	18	1
Pall, Chicago	.917	39	5	6	1	12	2
Parker, Seattle	.833	8	1	4	1	6	0
Parrett, Oakland	.923	66	5	7	1	13	2
Pavlik, Texas	.900	13	6	3	1	10	0
Perez, New York	.811	33	15	28	10	53	0
Pichardo, Kansas City.	.946	31	19	16	2	37	2
Pierce, Kansas City*	1.000	2	0	1	0	1	0
Plesac, Milwaukee*	1.000	44	1	8	0	9	1
Plunk, Cleveland	.933	58	7	7	1	15	0
Poole, Baltimore*	1.000	6	0	2	0	2	0
Powell, Seattle*	1.000	49	3	5	0	8	1
Power, Cleveland	1.000	64	4	14	0	18	1
Quantrill, Boston	.833	27	4	6	2	12	0
Raczka, Oakland*	1.000	8	1	0	0	1	0
Radinsky, Chicago*	1.000	68	2	9	0	11	1
Rasmussen, K.C.	.000	5	1	12	0	13	0
Reardon, Boston	1.000	46	2	3	0	5	1
Reed, Kansas City	.960	19	6	18	1	25	0
Revenig, Oakland	.000	2	0	0	0	0	0
Rhodes, Baltimore*	1.000	15	1	13	0	14	2
Ritz, Detroit	1.000	23	4	10	0	14	1
Robinson, California	.000	3	0	0	0	0	0
Robinson, Texas	1.000	16	6	2	0	8	2
Robinson, Milwaukee	.875	8	5	2	1	8	0
Rogers, Texas*	.913	81	4	17	2	23	0
Rosenthal, Texas	1.000	6	0	1	0	1	0
Ruffin, Milwaukee*	1.000	25	4	5	0	9	0
Je. Russell, Tex.-Oak.	1.000	59	8	8	0	16	0
Ryan, Boston	1.000	7	1	2	0	3	0
Ryan, Texas	.857	27	2	16	3	21	1
Sampen, Kansas City	1.000	8	1	3	0	4	0
Sanderson, New York	.917	33	4	18	2	24	1
Sauveur, Kansas City*	1.000	8	0	1	0	1	0
Schmidt, Seattle	.000	3	0	0	0	0	0
Schooler, Seattle	1.000	53	1	10	0	11	1

Player, Team	Pct.	G	PO	A	E	TC	DP
Scudder, Cleveland	1.000	23	14	11	0	25	0
Shaw, Cleveland	.667	2	0	2	1	3	0
Shifflett, Kansas City	.923	34	5	7	1	13	0
Slusarski, Oakland	1.000	15	2	6	0	8	0
Smiley, Minnesota*	1.000	34	4	35	0	39	2
Smith, Texas*	1.000	4	1	1	0	2	0
Springer, New York	1.000	14	0	1	0	1	0
Stewart, Oakland	.875	31	8	13	3	24	2
Stieb, Toronto	1.000	21	8	21	0	29	1
Stottlemyre, Toronto	.970	28	15	17	1	33	2
Sutcliffe, Baltimore	.921	36	11	24	3	38	2
Swan, Seattle*	.968	55	7	23	1	31	0
Tanana, Detroit*	.950	32	8	30	2	40	1
Tapani, Minnesota	.956	34	17	26	2	45	0
Taylor, Boston*	1.000	4	0	3	0	3	0
Terrell, Detroit	.972	36	13	22	1	36	0
Thigpen, Chicago	1.000	55	7	6	0	13	2
Timlin, Toronto	1.000	26	2	5	0	7	1
Trlicek, Toronto	.000	2	0	0	0	0	0
Trombley, Minnesota	1.000	10	1	6	0	7	0
Valera, California	.958	30	10	13	1	24	0
Viola, Boston*	.964	35	6	47	2	55	6
Walker, Cleveland	.667	5	1	3	2	6	0
Walton, Oakland	1.000	7	0	1	0	1	0
D. Ward, Toronto	.938	79	4	11	1	16	0
Wayne, Minnesota*	1.000	41	1	13	0	14	0
Weathers, Toronto	.000	2	0	0	0	0	0
Wegman, Milwaukee	.975	35	35	43	2	80	3
Welch, Oakland	.947	20	5	13	1	19	1
Wells, Toronto*	.958	41	9	14	1	24	1
West, Minnesota*	.714	9	0	5	2	7	0
Whiteside, Texas	.833	20	3	2	1	6	0
Wickander, Cle.*	1.000	44	0	5	0	5	1
Wickman, New York	1.000	8	4	6	0	10	3
Williamson, Baltimore	1.000	12	1	0	0	1	0
Willis, Minnesota	.923	59	6	6	1	13	1
Witt, Tex.-Oak.	.971	31	14	20	1	35	2
Woodson, Seattle	1.000	8	3	2	0	5	1
Young, K.C.-N.Y.*	.933	23	4	10	1	15	1
Young, Boston*	.625	28	2	8	6	16	0

PITCHERS WITH TWO OR MORE TEAMS

Player, Team	Pct.	G	PO	A	E	TC	DP
Eichhorn, California	.941	42	5	11	1	17	0
Eichhorn, Toronto	1.000	23	0	8	0	8	0
Heaton, Kansas City*	.875	31	5	2	1	8	0
Heaton, Milwaukee*	.000	1	0	0	0	0	0
Hillegas, New York	.786	21	6	5	3	14	0
Hillegas, Oakland	1.000	5	1	0	0	1	0
Leary, New York	1.000	18	7	10	0	17	1
Leary, Seattle	1.000	8	3	8	0	11	2
Mesa, Baltimore	.944	13	8	9	1	18	0
Mesa, Cleveland	.941	15	4	12	1	17	0
Nunez, Milwaukee	1.000	10	1	1	0	2	0
Nunez, Texas	.833	39	2	3	1	6	0
Je. Russell, Texas	1.000	51	8	8	0	16	0
Russell, Oakland	.000	8	0	0	0	0	0
Witt, Texas	.968	25	14	16	1	31	1
Witt, Oakland	1.000	6	0	4	0	4	1
Young, Kansas City*	.833	10	3	2	1	6	0
Young, New York*	1.000	13	1	8	0	9	1

MISCELLANEOUS

SHUTOUT GAMES

Read across for wins, down for losses.

Team	Mil.	Bal.	Min.	Oak.	Tor.	Bos.	N.Y.	K.C.	Cal.	Sea.	Cle.	Chi.	Det.	Tex.	W	L	Pct.
Milwaukee..........	..	2	1	1	0	3	1	0	2	0	3	1	0	0	14	5	.737
Baltimore	0	..	0	1	2	1	1	1	0	2	2	1	3	2	16	6	.727
Minnesota	1	0	..	0	1	1	0	2	3	1	0	1	2	1	13	8	.619
Oakland..............	0	0	0	..	2	1	0	1	1	0	0	0	1	3	9	6	.600
Toronto	0	0	0	1	..	1	1	3	2	2	0	2	0	2	14	10	.583
Boston	0	0	0	0	3	..	1	1	3	0	2	1	0	1	13	11	.542
New York.............	0	1	1	1	0	1	..	1	1	0	1	0	1	1	9	8	.529
Kansas City	0	1	1	0	2	1	1	..	2	3	1	0	0	0	12	13	.480
California	1	0	1	0	0	1	1	1	..	2	0	2	1	2	13	15	.464
Seattle................	0	0	2	0	0	1	0	1	1	..	1	2	1	0	9	14	.391
Cleveland	0	2	1	1	0	0	1	1	0	1	..	0	0	0	7	11	.389
Chicago...............	2	0	0	0	0	0	0	1	0	1	0	..	0	1	5	11	.313
Detroit	1	0	0	0	0	0	0	0	0	1	1	0	1	..	4	9	.308
Texas	0	0	0	0	0	0	1	0	0	1	1	0	0	..	3	14	.176
Lost..............	5	6	8	6	10	11	8	13	15	14	11	11	9	14	141	141	.500

HOME RECORD

Read across for home wins, down for road losses.

Team	Tor.	Mil.	Oak.	Chi.	Min.	K.C.	Bos.	Bal.	N.Y.	Cle.	Cal.	Det.	Sea.	Tex.	W	L	Pct.
Toronto	..	3	3	5	4	3	4	3	5	6	4	5	4	3	4	53	28	.654
Milwaukee..........	5	..	4	4	3	2	4	4	4	5	6¹	4	4	4	53	28	.654
Oakland..............	3	3	..	4	4	5	4	1	4	3	4	5	7	4	51	30	.630
Chicago...............	4	3	3	..	5	3	5	3	3	3	5	5	4	4	50	32	.610
Minnesota	3	3	2	4	..	4	5	3	3	4	5	4	5	3	48	33	.593
Kansas City	3	3	3	3	3	..	3	2	3	5	3	3	6	4	44	37	.543
Boston	4	3	3	5	2	4	..	2	5	3	3	3	4	4	44	37	.543
Baltimore	3	3	1	3	3	4	4	..	2	3	4	7	4	2	43	38	.531
New York.............	1	5	4	1	2	4	4	3	..	3	4	4	3	3	41	40	.506
Cleveland	3	3	3	2	4	4	4	3	3	..	3	2	5	2	41	40	.506
California	4	5	3	1	1	5	1	2	5	3	..	4	3	4	41	40	.506
Detroit	3	3	4	0	1	4	6	3	2	3	3	..	4	2	38	42	.475
Seattle................	1	2	1	7	4	5	4	3	3	4	2	1	..	1	38	43	.469
Texas	1	3	2	5	3	5	5	1	3	3	2	0	3	..	36	45	.444
Lost on road....	38	42	36	44	39	53	52	35	46	46	50	45	55	40	621	513	.548

ROAD RECORD

Read across for road wins, down for home losses.

Team	Bal.	Oak.	Tor.	Min.	Tex.	Mil.	Det.	Chi.	N.Y.	Cle.	Cal.	Bos.	K.C.	Sea.	W	L	Pct.
Baltimore	..	5	2	3	5	3	3	3	3	4	4	4	4	3	46	35	.568
Oakland..............	5	..	3	4	5	2	2	4	2	3	3	3	4	5	45	36	.556
Toronto	3	3	..	3	5	2	4	2	5	3	2	3	3	5	43	38	.531
Minnesota	3	3	3	..	3	3	5	1	4	2	6	4	3	4	42	39	.519
Texas	4	2	2	4	..	2	4	3	3	4	2	3	2	6	41	40	.506
Milwaukee..........	3	3	3	3	3	..	4	3	2	3	1	4	3	4	39	42	.481
Detroit	0	2	2	2	6	2	..	2	3	5	2	3	3	5	37	45	.451
Chicago...............	3	2	1	3	1	2	5	..	5	4	5	1	4	0	36	44	.450
New York.............	5	2	1	3	3	2	4	3	..	3	1	2	3	3	35	46	.432
Cleveland	3	3	3	2	3	2	3	4	..	3	3	1	2	3	35	46	.432
California	2	2	1	1	5	0	3	2	2	3	..	3	3	4	31	50	.383
Boston	3	2	3	1	1	2	1	1	2	3	5	..	3	2	29	52	.358
Kansas City	2	1	2	3	2	4	2	3	2	2	2	2	..	1	28	53	.346
Seattle................	2	0	3	1	3	2	2	2	3	1	4	2	1	..	26	55	.321
Lost at home ...	38	30	28	33	45	28	42	32	40	40	40	37	37	43	513	621	.452

PITCHING AGAINST EACH CLUB

BALTIMORE—89-73

Pitcher	Bos. W-L	Cal. W-L	Chi. W-L	Cle. W-L	Det. W-L	K.C. W-L	Mil. W-L	Min. W-L	N.Y. W-L	Oak. W-L	Sea. W-L	Tex. W-L	Tor. W-L	Totals W-L
Clements	1-0	0-0	1-0	0-0	0-0	0-0	0-0	0-0	0-0	0-0	0-0	0-0	0-0	2-0
S. Davis........	1-1	0-0	0-0	2-0	0-0	1-0	0-1	2-0	0-0	0-0	1-0	0-1	0-0	7-3
Frohwirth.....	1-2	1-0	0-1	0-0	0-0	1-0	0-0	0-0	0-0	0-0	0-0	1-0	0-0	4-3

Pitcher	Bos. W-L	Cal. W-L	Chi. W-L	Cle. W-L	Det. W-L	K.C. W-L	Mil. W-L	Min. W-L	N.Y. W-L	Oak. W-L	Sea. W-L	Tex. W-L	Tor. W-L	Totals W-L
Lefferts	1-0	0-1	0-0	0-1	0-0	0-0	0-1	0-0	0-0	0-0	0-0	0-0	0-0	1-3
Lewis	1-0	0-0	0-0	0-0	0-0	0-0	0-0	0-0	0-0	0-1	0-0	0-0	0-0	1-1
McDonald	1-0	2-0	0-1	1-1	1-0	0-0	1-2	1-1	2-1	0-1	1-3	2-1	1-2	13-13
Mesa	0-1	0-0	0-1	0-0	0-1	1-1	1-0	0-0	0-1	1-1	0-1	0-0	0-1	3-8
Milacki	1-0	1-0	2-1	0-1	1-2	0-0	0-1	0-1	0-1	1-1	0-0	0-0	0-0	6-8
Mills	0-0	0-1	2-0	1-1	2-0	0-1	1-0	0-0	1-1	1-0	0-0	1-0	1-0	10-4
Mussina	0-0	2-0	1-0	1-1	3-0	2-1	2-0	2-0	0-0	2-1	1-0	1-1	1-1	18-5
Olson	0-0	0-0	0-2	0-0	0-0	0-1	0-0	0-1	1-0	0-0	0-0	0-0	0-1	1-5
Rhodes	0-0	0-1	0-0	1-1	1-0	0-0	0-0	1-0	1-1	0-0	0-1	1-0	1-1	7-5
Sutcliffe	1-1	2-1	0-0	1-0	2-0	3-0	1-2	0-3	0-3	1-1	3-0	1-2	1-2	16-15
Totals	8-5	8-4	6-6	7-6	10-3	8-4	6-7	6-6	5-8	6-6	7-5	7-5	5-8	89-73

No-decisions—Flanagan, Poole, Williamson.

BOSTON—73-89

Pitcher	Bal. W-L	Cal. W-L	Chi. W-L	Cle. W-L	Det. W-L	K.C. W-L	Mil. W-L	Min. W-L	N.Y. W-L	Oak. W-L	Sea. W-L	Tex. W-L	Tor. W-L	Totals W-L
Bolton	0-1	0-0	0-0	0-0	0-0	0-0	0-0	0-0	0-0	0-0	1-0	0-0	0-1	1-2
Clemens	0-0	4-0	1-1	3-1	0-1	1-0	0-2	1-2	1-1	0-0	3-1	2-1	2-1	18-11
Darwin	0-0	1-1	0-1	1-0	0-1	2-0	2-1	0-1	1-1	1-1	0-0	0-1	1-1	9-9
Dopson	1-1	0-2	1-0	0-0	1-2	0-1	1-0	0-0	1-2	2-1	0-1	0-1	0-0	7-11
Fossas	0-2	0-0	0-0	0-0	0-0	0-0	0-0	0-0	0-0	0-0	0-0	0-0	0-0	1-2
Gardiner	0-1	0-0	0-1	1-0	1-1	0-0	1-0	0-2	0-0	0-2	1-1	0-1	0-1	4-10
Harris	2-0	0-0	0-2	0-0	0-1	1-0	0-1	0-3	0-0	0-0	1-1	0-1	0-0	4-9
Hesketh	2-0	1-0	1-1	1-0	0-2	0-3	0-0	0-1	1-1	0-1	0-0	0-0	2-0	8-9
Irvine	0-1	0-0	0-0	0-1	1-1	0-0	1-0	1-0	0-0	0-0	0-0	0-0	0-1	3-4
Quantrill	0-0	0-0	0-1	0-0	0-0	1-0	0-0	0-0	0-0	1-1	0-0	0-1	0-0	2-3
Reardon	0-0	1-1	1-0	0-0	0-0	0-0	0-1	0-0	0-0	0-0	0-0	0-0	0-0	2-2
Taylor	0-0	0-0	0-0	0-1	0-0	0-0	0-0	0-0	1-0	0-0	0-0	0-0	0-0	1-1
Viola	0-1	1-0	2-0	0-2	1-0	1-1	0-3	1-0	2-1	1-1	0-2	2-0	2-1	13-12
Young	0-1	0-0	0-0	0-1	0-0	0-0	0-0	0-0	0-0	0-0	0-0	0-2	0-0	0-4
Totals	5-8	8-4	6-6	6-7	4-9	7-5	5-8	3-9	7-6	5-7	6-6	4-8	7-6	73-89

No-decisions—Hoy, Ryan.

CALIFORNIA—72-90

Pitcher	Bal. W-L	Bos. W-L	Chi. W-L	Cle. W-L	Det. W-L	K.C. W-L	Mil. W-L	Min. W-L	N.Y. W-L	Oak. W-L	Sea. W-L	Tex. W-L	Tor. W-L	Totals W-L
Abbott	1-1	1-2	0-1	0-1	0-1	0-0	0-2	1-2	0-0	1-1	1-1	1-1	1-2	7-15
Bailes	1-0	0-0	0-1	1-0	0-0	0-0	0-0	0-0	0-0	0-0	1-0	0-0	0-0	3-1
Blyleven	1-1	1-0	1-0	1-1	1-1	1-1	0-1	0-3	0-1	1-0	0-2	1-1	0-0	8-12
Butcher	0-1	0-1	0-0	0-0	0-0	0-0	0-0	0-0	2-0	0-0	0-0	0-0	0-0	2-2
Crim	0-0	0-0	0-1	1-0	2-0	0-1	0-0	0-0	1-1	0-2	0-0	2-0	1-1	7-6
Eichhorn	0-0	0-0	0-0	0-1	0-1	0-0	0-0	0-1	0-0	0-0	1-0	0-0	1-1	2-4
Finley	0-1	0-1	1-1	0-2	0-0	2-0	0-0	0-2	0-2	0-3	2-0	1-0	1-0	7-12
Fortugno	0-0	0-0	0-0	0-0	1-0	0-1	0-0	0-0	0-0	0-0	0-0	0-0	0-0	1-1
Frey	0-0	0-0	0-2	0-0	2-0	1-0	0-0	0-0	1-0	0-0	0-0	0-0	0-0	4-2
Grahe	0-0	0-0	0-2	1-0	0-0	0-0	1-0	0-1	0-0	0-1	1-1	1-0	1-1	5-6
Harvey	0-0	0-1	0-0	0-0	0-1	0-0	0-2	0-0	0-0	0-0	0-0	0-0	0-0	0-4
Langston	1-2	2-2	1-1	1-1	0-1	1-0	2-2	0-1	2-0	0-1	1-1	2-1	0-1	13-14
Lewis	0-0	0-0	0-0	1-0	0-0	2-0	0-0	0-0	0-0	0-0	0-0	1-0	0-0	4-0
Robinson	0-0	0-0	0-0	0-0	0-0	0-0	1-0	0-0	0-0	0-0	0-0	0-0	0-0	1-0
Valera	0-2	0-1	0-1	0-0	1-0	1-2	1-0	1-2	1-0	3-0	0-1	0-1	0-1	8-11
Totals	4-8	4-8	3-10	6-6	7-5	8-5	5-7	2-11	7-5	5-8	7-6	9-4	5-7	72-90

No-decisions—Hathaway.

CHICAGO—86-76

Pitcher	Bal. W-L	Bos. W-L	Cal. W-L	Cle. W-L	Det. W-L	K.C. W-L	Mil. W-L	Min. W-L	N.Y. W-L	Oak. W-L	Sea. W-L	Tex. W-L	Tor. W-L	Totals W-L
Alvarez	1-0	1-1	0-0	0-0	0-1	1-0	0-0	1-0	1-0	0-0	0-1	0-0	0-0	5-3
Dunne	0-0	0-0	0-0	1-0	0-0	0-0	0-0	1-0	0-0	0-0	0-0	0-0	0-0	2-0
Fernandez	0-2	0-1	0-2	0-0	1-1	2-1	1-0	0-0	1-0	0-3	1-0	1-1	1-0	8-11
Hernandez	0-2	0-0	3-0	1-0	1-0	0-1	1-0	0-0	1-0	0-0	0-0	0-0	0-0	7-3
Hibbard	0-0	1-0	2-0	0-1	1-0	1-1	0-2	1-0	0-0	1-0	1-0	0-2	2-1	10-7
Hough	0-1	1-0	0-0	1-0	0-0	1-0	0-1	1-2	1-1	1-1	0-3	0-2	1-1	7-12
Leach	2-0	0-1	0-0	0-1	3-0	0-0	0-1	0-1	1-0	0-1	0-0	0-0	0-0	6-5
McCaskill	0-0	0-2	1-0	2-1	1-0	0-2	1-1	2-0	2-1	1-1	1-3	0-0	1-2	12-13
McDowell	1-1	1-1	2-1	2-1	3-0	2-0	2-1	2-0	0-0	1-2	1-1	3-1	0-1	20-10
Pall	2-0	1-0	2-0	0-0	0-0	0-0	0-0	0-0	0-0	0-0	0-0	0-1	0-1	5-2
Radinsky	0-0	1-0	0-0	0-0	0-0	0-0	0-1	0-1	0-2	1-2	0-1	1-0	0-0	3-7
Thigpen	0-0	1-0	0-0	0-1	0-0	0-0	0-0	0-0	0-0	0-0	0-0	0-1	0-1	1-3
Totals	6-6	6-6	10-3	7-5	10-2	7-6	5-7	8-5	8-4	5-8	4-9	5-8	5-7	86-76

No-decisions—Drahman.

CLEVELAND—76-86

Pitcher	Bal. W-L	Bos. W-L	Cal. W-L	Chi. W-L	Det. W-L	K.C. W-L	Mil. W-L	Min. W-L	N.Y. W-L	Oak. W-L	Sea. W-L	Tex. W-L	Tor. W-L	Totals W-L
Armstrong....	1-1	1-1	0-1	0-1	1-0	1-1	1-3	0-2	0-1	0-2	0-0	1-1	0-1	6-15
Bell	0-0	0-1	0-0	0-0	0-1	0-0	0-0	0-0	0-0	0-0	0-0	0-0	0-0	0-2
Boucher	0-0	0-0	1-0	0-0	1-0	0-0	0-1	0-0	0-0	0-0	0-1	0-0	0-0	2-2
Cook	0-1	0-0	1-0	0-0	0-1	0-1	1-1	1-1	0-0	0-0	0-1	1-0	1-1	5-7
Embree	0-1	0-0	0-0	0-0	0-0	0-0	0-0	0-0	0-0	0-0	0-0	0-0	0-1	0-2
Lilliquist	0-0	0-0	1-2	1-0	0-0	1-0	0-0	0-0	1-0	0-0	1-0	0-1	0-0	5-3
Mesa	0-0	0-0	0-0	0-1	0-1	0-1	0-0	2-0	0-0	0-1	1-0	0-0	1-0	4-4
Mlicki	0-0	0-0	0-0	0-1	0-0	0-0	0-0	0-0	0-1	0-0	0-0	0-0	0-0	0-2
Mutis	0-0	0-0	0-0	0-0	0-0	0-0	0-0	0-0	0-0	0-1	0-0	0-1	0-0	0-2
Nagy	2-1	3-1	2-0	1-1	0-1	0-0	0-1	2-2	3-0	2-1	0-1	0-1	2-0	17-10
Nichols	1-0	0-0	1-0	0-0	0-1	0-1	1-0	0-0	0-0	0-0	0-0	1-0	0-1	4-3
Olin	0-0	0-0	0-0	0-0	1-1	2-0	1-0	0-0	1-0	0-1	1-1	1-2	1-0	8-5
Otto	1-0	1-1	0-0	0-1	0-0	0-0	0-0	0-1	0-3	2-0	1-0	0-0	0-2	5-9
Plunk	0-2	1-0	0-1	3-0	1-1	0-1	0-0	1-0	0-0	0-0	2-0	0-0	1-1	9-6
Power	0-1	1-0	0-0	0-1	1-0	0-0	0-0	0-0	1-1	0-0	0-0	0-0	0-0	3-3
Scudder	0-0	0-2	0-1	0-1	0-1	0-2	1-1	0-0	1-0	2-0	1-1	1-1	0-0	6-10
Shaw	0-0	0-0	0-1	0-0	0-0	0-0	0-0	0-0	0-0	0-0	0-0	0-0	0-1	0-1
Wickander ...	1-0	0-0	0-0	0-0	0-0	1-0	0-0	0-0	0-0	0-0	0-0	0-0	0-0	2-0
Totals	6-7	7-6	6-6	5-7	5-8	5-7	5-8	6-6	7-6	6-6	7-5	5-7	6-7	76-86

No-decisions—Arnsberg, Christopher.

DETROIT—75-87

Pitcher	Bal. W-L	Bos. W-L	Cal. W-L	Chi. W-L	Cle. W-L	K.C. W-L	Mil. W-L	Min. W-L	N.Y. W-L	Oak. W-L	Sea. W-L	Tex. W-L	Tor. W-L	Totals W-L
Aldred	0-2	0-0	0-0	0-0	0-0	2-0	0-2	0-0	1-2	0-0	0-1	0-0	0-1	3-8
Doherty	1-0	1-1	1-1	0-0	0-0	1-0	1-1	0-1	0-1	0-0	0-0	1-0	0-0	7-4
Groom	0-1	0-0	0-1	0-2	0-0	0-0	0-0	0-0	0-0	0-0	0-0	0-1	0-0	0-5
Gullickson....	0-1	0-2	1-1	0-2	2-0	2-0	0-1	0-1	1-2	1-0	3-0	2-1	2-2	14-13
Haas	0-0	0-0	0-0	1-0	0-0	0-1	0-1	1-0	0-0	0-0	2-0	1-1	1-1	5-3
Henneman....	0-0	0-1	0-1	0-0	1-0	0-0	1-0	0-2	0-0	0-1	0-1	0-0	0-0	2-6
Kiely	0-1	1-0	0-0	0-0	0-0	0-0	0-0	0-1	0-0	0-0	1-0	0-0	1-0	4-2
King	0-1	0-0	0-0	0-1	1-0	1-1	0-1	1-0	0-2	1-0	0-0	0-0	0-0	4-6
Knudsen	0-1	0-0	0-0	0-0	0-1	0-1	1-0	0-0	0-0	0-0	0-0	0-0	0-0	2-3
Lancaster	0-0	0-0	0-0	0-0	0-2	0-0	0-0	0-0	0-0	1-0	1-1	1-0	0-0	3-4
Leiter	1-0	1-0	1-0	0-1	2-0	0-1	0-1	1-0	0-0	1-1	0-0	1-1	0-0	8-5
Munoz	0-0	0-0	0-0	0-1	0-1	0-0	0-0	0-0	0-0	0-0	0-0	0-0	1-0	1-2
Ritz	0-0	0-0	0-1	0-0	0-0	0-0	1-0	0-1	0-0	1-1	0-0	0-1	0-1	2-5
Tanana	1-2	4-0	2-0	0-1	1-0	0-0	1-1	0-1	2-1	1-2	1-0	1-0	0-2	13-11
Terrell	0-1	1-0	0-2	1-2	1-0	1-1	0-0	0-1	0-1	0-1	3-0	0-0	0-1	7-10
Totals	3-10	9-4	5-7	2-10	8-5	7-5	5-8	3-9	6-6	9-3	8-4	5-8		75-87

KANSAS CITY—72-90

Pitcher	Bal. W-L	Bos. W-L	Cal. W-L	Chi. W-L	Cle. W-L	Det. W-L	Mil. W-L	Min. W-L	N.Y. W-L	Oak. W-L	Sea. W-L	Tex. W-L	Tor. W-L	Totals W-L
Appier	1-2	2-0	0-1	0-2	2-0	2-0	2-0	1-0	0-0	1-0	1-1	1-1	2-1	15-8
Aquino	0-0	0-0	1-0	0-1	1-0	0-0	0-0	0-1	0-0	0-1	1-1	0-0	0-2	3-6
Berenguer	0-0	0-0	1-0	0-1	0-0	0-2	0-0	0-0	0-0	0-1	0-0	0-0	0-0	1-4
Boddicker	0-0	0-0	0-1	0-1	0-0	0-1	0-0	0-0	0-0	0-0	0-1	1-0	0-0	1-4
Davis	0-1	0-0	0-0	0-0	0-0	0-0	0-1	0-0	1-0	0-0	0-1	0-0	0-0	1-3
Gordon	0-0	1-2	1-0	1-0	0-0	0-0	1-1	1-1	0-2	1-1	0-0	0-1	0-1	6-10
Gubicza	0-1	0-0	0-0	1-0	1-0	2-0	1-0	0-0	0-2	0-1	0-0	0-1	2-0	7-6
Haney	0-1	0-0	0-0	0-0	0-0	0-0	0-0	0-2	0-0	0-0	1-0	1-0	0-0	2-3
Heaton	0-0	0-0	0-0	0-0	0-0	0-0	1-0	0-0	0-0	1-1	1-0	0-0	0-0	3-1
Magnante	0-0	0-1	0-0	2-0	0-2	0-0	0-0	0-0	1-0	0-1	0-0	0-1	1-1	4-9
Meacham	1-1	0-1	0-0	1-0	1-1	1-1	0-0	3-0	0-0	1-0	0-0	2-0	0-0	10-4
Moeller	0-0	0-0	0-0	0-0	0-0	0-0	0-0	0-0	0-0	0-1	0-1	0-0	0-1	0-3
Montgomery	0-0	0-1	0-1	0-0	1-0	0-0	0-0	0-1	0-0	0-2	0-0	0-1	0-0	1-6
Pichardo	2-0	1-1	0-1	1-1	0-0	1-0	0-1	0-1	2-0	0-0	1-1	1-0	0-0	9-6
Rasmussen ..	0-0	0-0	1-0	0-0	0-0	0-0	0-0	0-1	2-0	0-0	1-0	0-0	0-0	4-1
Reed	0-1	1-0	1-1	0-1	0-0	0-0	0-1	0-1	0-1	0-0	1-0	0-1	0-0	3-7
Sampen	0-1	0-0	0-1	0-0	0-0	0-0	0-0	0-0	0-0	0-0	0-0	0-1	0-0	0-2
Sauveur	0-0	0-0	0-0	0-0	0-0	0-0	0-0	0-0	0-0	0-0	0-1	0-0	0-0	0-1
Shifflett	0-0	0-1	0-1	0-0	0-2	0-0	1-0	0-0	0-0	0-0	0-0	0-0	0-0	1-4
Young	0-0	0-0	0-0	0-0	0-0	0-1	1-0	0-0	0-0	0-0	0-0	0-0	0-1	1-2
Totals	4-8	5-7	5-8	6-7	7-5	5-7	7-5	6-7	5-7	4-9	7-6	6-7	5-7	72-90

No-decisions—Johnston, Pierce.

MILWAUKEE—92-70

Pitcher	Bal. W-L	Bos. W-L	Cal. W-L	Chi. W-L	Cle. W-L	Det. W-L	K.C. W-L	Min. W-L	N.Y. W-L	Oak. W-L	Sea. W-L	Tex. W-L	Tor. W-L	Totals W-L
Austin	1-0	2-1	0-0	0-0	0-0	0-0	0-0	1-0	0-1	0-0	0-0	1-0	0-0	5-2
Bones	1-1	0-0	1-0	1-2	1-2	0-0	2-1	0-2	1-0	1-1	1-0	0-0	0-1	9-10

Pitcher	Bal. W-L	Bos. W-L	Cal. W-L	Chi. W-L	Cle. W-L	Det. W-L	K.C. W-L	Min. W-L	N.Y. W-L	Oak. W-L	Sea. W-L	Tex. W-L	Tor. W-L	Totals W-L
Bosio	2-0	1-0	2-1	1-1	2-0	1-0	0-1	2-0	0-1	0-1	1-1	1-0	3-0	16-6
Eldred	2-0	1-0	1-0	1-0	1-1	1-0	0-0	1-0	1-0	0-1	1-0	0-0	1-0	11-2
Fetters	0-0	0-0	0-0	1-0	0-0	0-0	1-0	0-0	0-0	0-1	1-0	1-0	1-0	5-1
Henry	0-0	0-1	0-0	0-0	0-1	0-1	0-0	0-0	1-1	0-0	0-0	0-0	0-0	1-4
Holmes	0-1	0-1	0-0	0-0	0-0	0-0	0-0	0-0	0-0	1-0	0-0	3-2	0-0	4-4
Navarro	1-1	3-0	1-1	1-0	1-1	2-1	1-1	1-2	0-1	2-0	1-1	1-1	2-1	17-11
Nunez	0-0	0-0	0-0	0-0	0-0	1-0	0-0	0-1	0-0	0-0	0-0	0-0	0-0	1-1
Orosco	0-0	0-0	0-0	0-0	0-0	1-0	0-1	0-0	1-0	1-0	0-0	0-0	0-0	3-1
Plesac	0-0	0-0	2-0	1-1	2-0	0-1	0-1	0-0	0-0	0-0	0-1	0-0	0-0	5-4
Robinson	0-0	0-1	0-0	0-0	0-0	0-0	0-1	0-1	0-0	1-1	0-0	0-0	0-0	1-4
Ruffin	0-0	0-0	0-1	0-0	0-0	0-0	0-1	1-0	0-2	0-0	0-1	0-0	0-1	1-6
Wegman	0-3	1-1	0-2	1-1	1-0	2-1	1-0	0-1	2-1	1-0	3-0	0-2	1-2	13-14
Totals	7-6	8-5	7-5	7-5	8-5	8-5	5-7	6-6	6-7	7-5	8-4	7-5	8-5	92-70

No-decisions—Heaton.

MINNESOTA—90-72

Pitcher	Bal. W-L	Bos. W-L	Cal. W-L	Chi. W-L	Cle. W-L	Det. W-L	K.C. W-L	Mil. W-L	N.Y. W-L	Oak. W-L	Sea. W-L	Tex. W-L	Tor. W-L	Totals W-L
Aguilera	0-1	0-0	1-0	0-0	0-0	0-0	1-0	0-1	0-0	0-1	0-0	0-2	0-1	2-6
Banks	0-0	1-0	1-0	0-0	0-1	0-0	0-0	0-1	0-1	1-0	1-0	0-1	0-0	4-4
Casian	0-0	0-0	0-0	0-0	0-0	0-0	0-0	0-0	0-0	0-0	0-0	1-0	0-0	1-0
Edens	1-0	1-0	0-0	2-0	0-0	1-0	0-0	0-0	0-0	1-2	0-1	0-0	0-0	6-3
Erickson	0-2	1-1	3-0	0-3	1-2	2-0	1-1	1-1	1-0	1-0	1-1	0-1	1-0	13-12
Guthrie	0-0	1-0	0-0	0-0	1-0	0-0	0-1	0-0	0-0	0-1	0-1	0-0	0-0	2-3
Kipper	0-0	1-0	0-0	0-0	0-0	0-0	0-2	0-0	1-0	0-0	1-1	0-0	0-0	3-3
Krueger	2-0	0-0	1-0	1-1	0-1	1-1	1-1	2-0	0-1	0-1	2-0	0-0	0-0	10-6
Mahomes	0-0	0-1	0-0	0-1	0-0	0-0	0-0	0-0	0-1	1-1	1-0	0-0	1-0	3-4
Smiley	0-1	1-1	1-1	1-2	3-0	1-1	2-0	1-1	2-0	1-2	0-0	2-0	1-1	16-9
Tapani	2-1	2-0	2-1	0-1	1-2	2-1	1-0	1-0	1-1	0-1	1-2	2-0	1-1	16-11
Trombley	0-0	0-0	2-0	0-0	0-0	0-0	1-0	0-0	0-0	0-0	0-1	0-1	0-0	3-2
Wayne	0-1	0-0	0-0	0-0	0-0	1-0	0-1	0-0	0-0	0-0	1-0	0-0	1-1	3-3
West	0-0	0-0	0-0	0-0	0-0	0-0	0-0	0-1	0-1	0-0	1-0	0-0	0-1	1-3
Willis	1-0	1-1	0-0	1-0	0-0	1-0	0-0	1-1	2-0	0-0	0-0	0-0	0-1	7-3
Totals	6-6	9-3	11-2	5-8	6-6	9-3	7-6	6-6	7-5	5-8	8-5	6-7	5-7	90-72

No-decisions—Abbott, Gozzo.

NEW YORK—76-86

Pitcher	Bal. W-L	Bos. W-L	Cal. W-L	Chi. W-L	Cle. W-L	Det. W-L	K.C. W-L	Mil. W-L	Min. W-L	Oak. W-L	Sea. W-L	Tex. W-L	Tor. W-L	Totals W-L
Burke	0-1	0-0	0-0	1-0	0-1	0-0	0-0	0-0	0-0	0-0	1-0	0-0	0-0	2-2
Cadaret	1-0	0-1	1-0	0-0	1-0	0-0	1-0	0-1	0-1	0-1	0-2	0-1	0-1	4-8
Farr	0-0	0-0	0-0	0-0	0-0	1-0	0-0	0-0	0-0	0-1	1-0	0-0	0-0	2-2
Guetterman	0-0	0-0	0-0	0-0	0-0	0-0	0-0	1-0	0-1	0-0	0-0	0-0	0-0	1-1
Habyan	0-0	0-0	1-0	0-1	0-1	1-0	1-0	1-0	0-0	0-2	0-1	1-0	0-1	5-6
Hillegas	0-1	0-0	0-1	0-1	0-0	0-1	0-0	0-1	0-0	1-0	0-1	0-1	0-1	1-8
Hitchcock	0-0	0-0	0-0	0-1	0-0	0-1	0-0	0-0	0-0	0-0	0-0	0-0	0-0	0-2
Howe	1-0	0-0	0-0	1-0	0-0	0-0	0-0	0-0	0-0	0-0	0-0	0-0	1-0	3-0
Johnson	0-1	0-0	0-0	0-0	1-0	0-0	1-1	0-0	0-0	0-0	0-0	0-0	0-1	2-3
Kamieniecki	0-1	0-3	0-1	0-1	0-2	1-1	0-1	1-2	0-1	2-0	1-0	1-1	0-0	6-14
Leary	1-0	0-0	0-0	1-0	0-0	0-0	1-0	0-0	1-1	0-2	1-0	0-2	0-1	5-6
Militello	0-0	1-0	0-0	1-0	0-1	0-0	0-0	1-0	0-1	0-0	0-1	0-0	0-0	3-3
Monteleone	1-0	1-0	1-1	0-1	1-0	0-0	1-0	0-1	1-0	0-0	0-0	1-0	0-0	7-3
Nielsen	0-0	0-0	0-0	0-0	0-0	0-0	0-0	1-0	0-0	0-0	0-0	0-0	0-0	1-0
Perez	0-0	0-1	1-2	0-2	2-1	2-1	0-3	1-0	2-2	2-0	1-1	1-0	0-3	13-16
Sanderson	2-1	2-2	0-2	0-0	0-1	2-1	2-0	1-1	0-0	1-0	1-1	1-0	0-2	12-11
Wickman	1-0	0-0	0-1	0-0	0-0	0-0	1-0	0-0	1-0	0-0	0-0	1-0	1-0	6-1
Young	1-0	0-0	1-0	0-0	1-0	0-0	0-0	0-0	0-0	0-0	0-0	0-0	0-0	3-0
Totals	8-5	6-7	5-7	4-8	6-7	8-5	7-5	7-6	5-7	6-6	6-6	6-6	2-11	76-86

No-decisions—Springer.

OAKLAND—96-66

Pitcher	Bal. W-L	Bos. W-L	Cal. W-L	Chi. W-L	Cle. W-L	Det. W-L	K.C. W-L	Mil. W-L	Min. W-L	N.Y. W-L	Sea. W-L	Tex. W-L	Tor. W-L	Totals W-L
Briscoe	0-0	0-0	0-0	0-0	0-0	0-0	0-0	0-0	0-0	0-0	0-0	0-1	0-0	0-1
Campbell	0-0	1-1	0-0	0-0	0-0	0-0	0-0	1-1	0-1	0-0	0-0	0-0	0-0	2-3
Corsi	0-0	0-0	1-0	0-0	1-0	0-1	0-0	0-1	1-0	0-0	0-0	1-0	0-0	4-2
Darling	0-1	1-1	0-0	3-0	1-2	0-1	1-0	1-2	1-1	2-1	2-0	1-0	2-1	15-10
Downs	0-2	0-0	1-0	0-0	0-1	1-0	0-1	0-0	0-0	0-0	1-0	1-0	1-0	5-5
Eckersley	0-0	1-1	2-0	1-0	0-0	0-0	1-0	1-0	0-0	0-0	0-0	0-0	1-0	7-1
Gossage	0-0	0-0	0-0	0-0	0-0	0-0	0-0	0-0	0-1	0-0	0-0	0-0	0-1	0-2
Honeycutt	0-1	0-0	0-0	0-1	0-0	0-0	1-1	0-0	0-0	0-0	0-0	0-0	0-0	1-4
Horsman	0-0	0-0	0-0	0-0	0-0	1-0	0-0	0-0	0-0	0-0	1-0	0-1	0-0	2-1
Moore	3-0	1-1	2-2	0-2	2-0	0-2	1-0	1-1	0-1	0-1	3-0	3-0	1-2	17-12

Pitcher	Bal. W-L	Bos. W-L	Cal. W-L	Chi. W-L	Cle. W-L	Det. W-L	K.C. W-L	Mil. W-L	Min. W-L	N.Y. W-L	Sea. W-L	Tex. W-L	Tor. W-L	Totals W-L
Nelson	0-0	0-0	0-0	0-1	0-0	1-0	0-0	0-0	1-0	1-0	0-0	0-0	0-0	3-1
Parrett	1-0	1-0	0-0	1-0	0-0	1-0	2-1	0-0	1-0	2-0	0-0	0-0	0-0	9-1
Russell	0-0	0-0	0-0	0-0	0-0	0-0	0-0	1-0	0-0	0-0	1-0	0-0	0-0	2-0
Slusarski	1-2	0-0	0-0	1-0	0-1	0-0	0-0	0-1	1-0	1-0	1-0	0-0	0-1	5-5
Stewart	0-0	2-1	2-2	1-0	1-1	1-0	1-1	0-1	0-1	0-2	2-0	2-0	0-1	12-10
Welch	1-0	0-0	0-1	1-0	1-1	1-2	2-0	0-0	2-0	0-1	1-1	1-1	1-0	11-7
Witt	0-0	0-0	0-0	0-1	0-0	0-0	0-0	0-0	1-0	0-0	0-0	0-0	0-0	1-1
Totals	6-6	7-5	8-5	8-5	6-6	6-6	9-4	5-7	8-5	6-6	12-1	9-4	6-6	96-66

No-decisions—Guzman, Hillegas, Raczka, Revenig, Walton.

SEATTLE—64-98

Pitcher	Bal. W-L	Bos. W-L	Cal. W-L	Chi. W-L	Cle. W-L	Det. W-L	K.C. W-L	Mil. W-L	Min. W-L	N.Y. W-L	Oak. W-L	Tex. W-L	Tor. W-L	Totals W-L
Barton	0-0	0-1	0-0	0-0	0-0	0-0	0-0	0-0	0-0	0-0	0-0	0-0	0-0	0-1
DeLucia	0-1	0-0	1-0	1-1	0-0	0-1	1-0	0-0	0-2	0-0	0-0	0-0	0-1	3-6
Fisher	0-0	0-0	1-0	1-0	1-0	0-0	1-0	0-2	0-0	0-0	0-1	0-0	0-0	4-3
Fleming	2-1	1-0	2-1	2-1	2-1	1-0	1-1	0-1	1-1	2-0	0-1	2-1	1-1	17-10
Grant	1-1	0-0	0-0	0-0	0-0	0-0	0-1	0-0	0-1	0-0	0-0	1-0	0-0	2-4
Gunderson	0-0	0-0	0-0	2-0	0-0	0-0	0-0	0-1	0-0	0-0	0-0	0-0	0-0	2-1
Hanson	1-1	0-1	1-1	1-1	0-2	1-1	1-2	1-1	0-1	1-1	0-3	0-1	1-1	8-17
Johnson	0-2	2-1	1-1	2-0	1-0	0-2	2-1	0-1	2-0	1-2	0-1	0-1	1-2	12-14
Jones	0-0	0-0	0-1	0-0	0-0	0-0	0-1	1-0	0-2	0-0	0-0	1-0	0-1	3-5
Kramer	0-0	0-0	0-0	0-0	0-0	0-0	0-0	0-0	0-0	0-0	0-1	0-0	0-0	0-1
Leary	1-0	0-1	0-0	0-0	0-0	0-0	0-1	1-0	0-1	0-0	1-1	0-0	0-0	3-4
Nelson	0-0	0-1	0-1	0-0	0-0	0-0	0-0	0-1	1-0	0-0	0-2	0-1	0-1	1-7
Parker	0-0	0-0	0-0	0-0	0-1	0-0	0-0	0-0	0-0	0-0	0-0	0-1	0-0	0-2
Powell	0-0	2-1	0-0	0-0	0-0	0-0	0-0	0-0	0-0	0-1	0-0	1-0	1-0	4-2
Schooler	0-1	1-0	0-0	0-0	0-1	1-1	0-1	0-0	0-0	0-0	0-1	0-1	0-1	2-7
Swan	0-0	0-0	0-1	0-1	0-2	0-2	0-0	1-0	1-0	1-2	0-0	0-2	0-0	3-10
Walker	0-0	0-0	0-1	0-0	0-0	0-1	0-0	0-0	0-1	0-0	0-0	0-0	0-0	0-3
Woodson	0-0	0-0	0-0	0-0	0-0	0-0	0-0	0-0	0-0	0-0	0-1	0-1	0-0	0-1
Totals	5-7	6-6	6-7	9-4	5-7	3-9	6-7	4-8	5-8	6-6	1-12	4-9	4-8	64-98

No-decisions—Acker, Agosto, Brown, Harris, Schmidt.

TEXAS—77-85

Pitcher	Bal. W-L	Bos. W-L	Cal. W-L	Chi. W-L	Cle. W-L	Det. W-L	K.C. W-L	Mil. W-L	Min. W-L	N.Y. W-L	Oak. W-L	Sea. W-L	Tor. W-L	Totals W-L
Alexander	0-0	0-0	0-0	0-0	0-0	0-0	1-0	0-0	0-0	0-0	0-0	0-0	0-0	1-0
Bannister	0-0	0-0	0-0	1-0	0-0	0-0	0-0	0-0	0-0	0-0	0-1	0-0	0-0	1-1
Bohanon	0-0	0-0	0-0	0-0	1-0	0-0	0-0	0-0	0-0	0-0	0-1	0-0	0-0	1-1
Brown	0-2	2-1	2-0	1-2	2-0	1-1	3-0	2-1	3-0	1-0	1-2	2-0	1-2	21-11
Burns	0-1	1-1	1-0	0-0	0-0	0-1	0-1	0-1	0-0	0-0	0-0	1-0	0-0	3-5
Campbell	0-0	0-0	0-0	0-0	0-1	0-0	0-0	0-0	0-0	0-0	0-0	0-0	0-0	0-1
Chiamparino	0-0	0-0	0-1	0-0	0-0	0-0	0-0	0-0	0-0	0-1	0-0	0-0	0-2	0-4
Fireovid	0-0	0-0	0-0	0-0	0-0	0-0	0-0	0-0	0-0	0-0	1-0	0-0	0-0	1-0
Guzman	1-1	1-1	0-2	2-1	1-0	2-0	1-0	0-2	2-0	1-2	1-1	3-0	1-1	16-11
Jeffcoat	0-0	0-0	0-0	0-0	0-0	0-0	0-1	0-0	0-0	0-0	0-0	0-0	0-0	0-1
Leon	0-0	1-0	0-0	0-0	0-0	0-0	0-0	0-0	0-0	0-1	0-0	0-0	0-0	1-1
Manuel	0-0	0-0	0-0	0-0	0-0	0-0	0-0	0-0	0-0	1-0	0-0	0-0	0-0	1-0
Mathews	0-2	1-0	0-0	0-0	0-0	0-0	0-0	1-0	0-0	0-1	0-1	0-0	0-0	2-4
McCullers	0-0	0-0	0-0	0-0	1-0	0-0	0-0	0-0	0-0	0-0	0-0	0-0	0-0	1-0
Nunez	0-0	0-0	0-0	0-0	0-0	0-0	0-0	0-1	0-1	0-0	0-0	0-0	0-0	0-2
Pavlik	0-0	0-0	0-0	1-0	0-0	0-2	1-1	1-0	0-0	1-0	0-0	0-1	1-0	4-4
Robinson	1-0	0-0	0-1	1-0	0-0	0-1	0-0	1-1	0-0	0-1	0-0	1-0	0-0	4-4
Rogers	0-0	0-0	0-0	0-0	1-1	0-0	0-1	0-1	0-2	1-0	1-0	0-1	0-0	3-6
Russell	0-0	0-0	0-1	0-0	0-0	0-0	0-1	1-0	1-0	0-0	0-0	0-0	0-1	2-3
Ryan	2-0	0-1	0-2	0-1	1-1	1-1	0-1	0-0	0-1	1-0	0-1	0-0	0-0	5-9
Smith	0-0	0-0	0-1	0-0	0-0	0-0	0-0	0-0	0-0	0-0	0-0	0-1	0-1	0-3
Whiteside	0-0	0-0	0-0	0-0	0-0	0-0	0-0	0-0	0-0	0-0	0-0	1-1	0-0	1-1
Witt	1-1	2-0	1-1	2-1	0-2	0-2	1-0	0-0	1-2	1-0	0-2	0-0	0-2	9-13
Totals	5-7	8-4	4-9	8-5	7-5	4-8	7-6	5-7	7-6	6-6	4-9	9-4	3-9	77-85

No-decisions—Carman, Rosenthal.

TORONTO—96-66

Pitcher	Bal. W-L	Bos. W-L	Cal. W-L	Chi. W-L	Cle. W-L	Det. W-L	K.C. W-L	Mil. W-L	Min. W-L	N.Y. W-L	Oak. W-L	Sea. W-L	Tex. W-L	Totals W-L
Cone	0-0	0-1	0-0	0-0	0-1	0-0	1-0	0-1	1-0	1-0	0-0	0-0	1-0	4-3
Eichhorn	0-0	1-0	0-0	0-0	0-0	0-0	0-0	0-0	0-0	1-0	0-0	0-0	0-0	2-0
Guzman	0-0	1-1	2-0	1-0	2-0	2-0	2-0	0-0	1-1	2-1	1-1	1-0	1-1	16-5
Henke	0-0	0-1	0-0	0-0	0-0	1-0	0-0	0-0	1-0	0-0	1-1	0-0	0-0	3-2
Hentgen	1-0	0-0	0-0	0-0	0-0	0-1	0-0	0-0	1-0	0-0	0-0	0-0	0-0	5-2
Key	1-2	1-0	1-1	0-2	0-0	0-2	2-1	1-2	0-1	2-0	1-0	2-2	2-0	13-13
Linton	1-0	0-0	0-0	0-1	0-0	0-1	0-0	0-1	0-0	0-0	0-0	0-0	0-0	1-3

Pitcher	Bal. W-L	Bos. W-L	Cal. W-L	Chi. W-L	Cle. W-L	Det. W-L	K.C. W-L	Mil. W-L	Min. W-L	N.Y. W-L	Oak. W-L	Sea. W-L	Tex. W-L	Totals W-L
MacDonald...	0-0	1-0	0-0	0-0	0-0	0-0	0-0	0-0	0-0	0-0	0-0	0-0	0-0	1-0
Morris..........	2-2	1-0	2-0	2-1	2-0	4-0	0-1	1-1	1-0	2-0	1-1	1-0	2-0	21-6
Stieb............	0-1	0-1	0-2	0-0	0-1	0-0	0-0	2-0	0-1	0-0	1-0	1-0	0-0	4-6
Stottlemyre..	2-0	1-1	1-1	2-0	1-2	1-0	0-1	0-1	1-1	2-1	1-1	0-1	0-1	12-11
Timlin..........	0-0	0-0	0-0	0-0	0-0	0-1	0-0	0-1	0-0	0-0	0-0	0-0	0-0	0-2
D. Ward.......	0-0	0-0	0-0	1-0	1-2	0-0	0-0	1-1	1-1	1-0	0-0	1-0	1-0	7-4
Wells...........	1-0	0-2	1-0	1-1	1-0	0-1	1-1	0-1	0-0	0-0	0-1	1-1	1-1	7-9
Totals........	8-5	6-7	7-5	7-5	7-6	8-5	7-5	5-8	7-5	11-2	6-6	8-4	9-3	96-66

No-decisions—Leiter, Trlicek, Weathers.

HOME RUNS BY PARKS

	At Bal.	At Bos.	At Cal.	At Chi.	At Cle.	At Det.	At K.C.	At Mil.	At Min.	At N.Y.	At Oak.	At Sea.	At Tex.	At Tor.	Totals 1992	1991
Baltimore	75	7	5	6	10	6	3	6	3	6	10	3	5	3	148	170
Boston...................	3	45	2	1	4	7	3	1	3	3	4	2	0	6	84	126
California	4	0	44	3	5	6	4	3	1	4	5	2	4	3	88	115
Chicago.................	6	3	4	54	7	5	1	2	5	6	6	4	4	3	110	139
Cleveland	5	3	4	0	62	11	3	2	3	7	8	4	6	9	127	79
Detroit..................	6	2	6	10	15	91	4	7	5	9	8	6	10	3	182	209
Kansas City	1	4	6	3	7	3	24	3	4	2	4	2	8	4	75	117
Milwaukee.............	1	4	4	4	4	10	1	35	7	3	3	1	5	82	116	127
Minnesota	4	2	2	1	3	3	5	3	56	6	5	7	4	3	104	140
New York..............	15	3	6	2	4	10	3	7	4	88	5	5	5	6	163	147
Oakland.................	5	3	3	8	5	4	7	4	8	4	76	5	4	6	142	159
Seattle..................	6	5	7	7	11	6	0	0	5	7	7	78	3	7	149	126
Texas	9	6	5	8	8	8	6	5	10	4	3	14	71	2	159	177
Toronto	4	4	6	9	11	11	1	8	5	5	5	6	9	79	163	133
1992 total..........	144	91	104	116	156	181	65	86	112	158	149	141	134	139	1776	....
1991 total..........	152	145	133	153	63	198	87	135	137	166	143	138	156	147	....	1953

AT BALTIMORE (144):

Baltimore (75)—Anderson 15, Devereaux 14, Hoiles 8, Milligan 7, Gomez 6, Davis 5, C. Ripken 5, Tackett 4, B. Ripken 3, Horn 2, Martinez 2, Orsulak 2, Hulett 1, Segui 1. Boston (3)—Boggs 1, Burks 1, Cooper 1. California (4)—Fitzgerald 1, Gaetti 1, Hayes 1, Stevens 1. Chicago (6)—Thomas 2, Karkovice 1, Pasqua 1, Sax 1, Ventura 1. Cleveland (5)—Lewis 2, Baerga 1, Belle 1, Sorrento 1. Detroit (6)—Tettleton 2, Fielder 1, Fryman 1, Trammell 1, Whitaker 1. Kansas City (1)—Brett 1. Milwaukee (1)—Stubbs 1. Minnesota (4)—Mack 2, Munoz 1, Puckett 1. New York (15)—Tartabull 4, Hall 3, Hayes 2, Mattingly 2, Gallego 1, R. Kelly 1, Stanley 1, Velarde 1. Oakland (5)—Baines 1, Canseco 1, R. Henderson 1, Lansford 1, McGwire 1. Seattle (6)—Buhner 2, Griffey 2, E. Martinez 1, T. Martinez 1. Texas (9)—Gonzalez 2, Downing 1, Frye 1, Huson 1, Palmer 1, Reimer 1, Rodriguez 1, Sierra 1. Toronto (4)—Maldonado 1, Olerud 1, White 1, Winfield 1.

AT BOSTON (91):

Baltimore (7)—Gomez 3, Davis 1, Devereaux 1, Hoiles 1, Parent 1. Boston (45)—Brunansky 10, Vaughn 8, Plantier 5, Boggs 4, Burks 4, Wedge 3, Zupcic 3, Cooper 2, Reed 2, Hatcher 1, Pena 1, Valentin 1, Winningham 1. Chicago (3)—Bell 1, Santovenia 1, Thomas 1. Cleveland (3)—Belle 1, Hill 1, Martinez 1. Detroit (2)—Fryman 2. Kansas City (4)—McReynolds 2, Brett 1, Jefferies 1. Milwaukee (4)—Bichette 1, Listach 1, Vaughn 1, Yount 1. Minnesota (2)—Bush 1, Davis 1. New York (3)—Gallego 1, Hall 1, Hayes 1. Oakland (3)—Steinbach 2, Canseco 1. Seattle (5)—O'Brien 2, Boone 1, Buhner 1, Mitchell 1. Texas (6)—Gonzalez 3, Downing 2, Palmeiro 1. Toronto (4)—Kent 1, Maldonado 1, White 1, Winfield 1.

AT CALIFORNIA (104):

Baltimore (5)—Hoiles 2, Milligan 1, C. Ripken 1, Tackett 1. Boston (2)—Valentin 1, Wedge 1. California (44)—Gaetti 8, Gonzales 6, Curtis 5, Felix 5, Fitzgerald 3, Brooks 2, DiSarcina 2, Hayes 2, Sojo 2, Stevens 2, Tingley 2, Easley 1, Orton 1, Parrish 1, Rose 1, Salmon 1. Chicago (4)—Thomas 3, Bell 1. Cleveland (4)—Belle 2, Baerga 1, Hill 1. Detroit (6)—Fryman 2, Carreon 1, Deer 1, Fielder 1, Phillips 1. Kansas City (6)—Macfarlane 3, Jefferies 2, Joyner 1. Milwaukee (4)—Vaughn 2, Molitor 1, Stubbs 1. Minnesota (2)—Gagne 1, Knoblauch 1. New York (6)—James 1, P. Kelly 1, Maas 1, Mattingly 1, Tartabull 1, Velarde 1. Oakland (3)—Blankenship 1, Canseco 1, Steinbach 1. Seattle (7)—T. Martinez 2, Amaral 1, Buhner 1, Griffey 1, Mitchell 1, O'Brien 1. Texas (5)—Gonzalez 3, Palmeiro 1, Palmer 1. Toronto (6)—Carter 2, Borders 1, Kent 1, Olerud 1, Winfield 1.

AT CHICAGO (116):

Baltimore (6)—Gomez 2, Hoiles 2, Davis 1, Milligan 1. Boston (1)—Brunansky 1. California (3)—Brooks 1, Felix 1, Orton 1. Chicago (54)—Bell 16, Thomas 10, Ventura 7, Karkovice 5, Raines 4, Fisk 2, Grebeck 2, Johnson 2, Pasqua 2, Beltre 1, Newson 1, Sax 1, Sveum 1. Detroit (10)—Deer 3, Fielder 3, Fryman 1, Livingston 1, Phillips 1, Whitaker 1. Kansas City (3)—Brett 1, Jefferies 1, Macfarlane 1. Milwaukee (4)—Seitzer 2, Surhoff 1, Vaughn 1. Minnesota (1)—Harper 1. New York (2)—Tartabull 1, B. Williams 1. Oakland (8)—Baines 2, McGwire 2, Browne 1, Canseco 1, R. Henderson 1, Howitt 1. Seattle (7)—T. Martinez 2, Briley 1, Griffey 1, O'Brien 1, Parrish 1, Schaefer 1. Texas (8)—Palmeiro 3, Gonzalez 2, Fariss 1, Huson 1, Palmer 1. Toronto (9)—Maldonado 2, Winfield 2, Alomar 1, Gruber 1, Lee 1, Olerud 1, White 1.

AT CLEVELAND (156):

Baltimore (10)—Davis 2, Devereaux 2, C. Ripken 2, Hoiles 1, Horn 1, Milligan 1, Parent 1. Boston (4)—Clark 1, Naehring 1, Reed 1, Vaughn 1. California (5)—Fitzgerald 2, Brooks 1, Felix 1, Sojo 1. Chicago (7)—Bell 3, Karkovice 1, Raines 1, Thomas 1, Ventura 1. Cleveland (62)—Belle 15, Sorrento 11, Baerga 9, Hill 7, Whiten 6, Jacoby 3, Lofton 3, Lewis 2, Martinez 2, Alomar 1,

Howard 1, Jefferson 1, Thome 1. **Detroit (15)**—Fielder 5, Deer 4, Tettleton 2, Carreon 1, Gladden 1, Phillips 1, Whitaker 1. **Kansas City (7)**—Gwynn 1, Jefferies 1, Joyner 1, Macfarlane 1, McReynolds 1, Miller 1, Rossy 1. **Milwaukee (4)**—Hamilton 1, Jaha 1, Molitor 1, Vaughn 1. **Minnesota (3)**—Puckett 2, Munoz 1. **New York (4)**—Hayes 1, Leyritz 1, Tartabull 1, G. Williams 1. **Oakland (5)**—Brosius 2, Baines 1, McGwire 1, Neel 1. **Seattle (11)**—Griffey 4, Buhner 2, Mitchell 2, Blowers 1, T. Martinez 1, Valle 1. **Texas (8)**—Gonzalez 3, Palmer 2, Sierra 2, Downing 1. **Toronto (11)**—Olerud 4, Winfield 2, Carter 1, Kent 1, Knorr 1, Maldonado 1, White 1.

AT DETROIT (181):

Baltimore (6)—Hoiles 2, Davis 1, Gomez 1, Hulett 1, Orsulak 1. **Boston (7)**—Naehring 2, Valentin 2, Boggs 1, Cooper 1, Vaughn 1. **California (6)**—Curtis 1, Felix 1, Morris 1, Sojo 1, Stevens 1, Tingley 1. **Chicago (5)**—Abner 1, Fisk 1, Grebeck 1, Thomas 1, Ventura 1. **Cleveland (11)**—Baerga 4, Hill 4, Belle 1, Jacoby 1, Levis 1. **Detroit (91)**—Fielder 18, Tettleton 18, Deer 13, Whitaker 11, Fryman 9, Carreon 5, Barnes 3, Gladden 3, Phillips 3, Kreuter 2, Livingston 2, Bergman 1, Brogna 1, Cuyler 1, Pettis 1. **Kansas City (3)**—McReynolds 2, Joyner 1. **Milwaukee (10)**—Molitor 2, Vaughn 2, Yount 2, Fletcher 1, Hamilton 1, Seitzer 1, Stubbs 1. **Minnesota (3)**—Mack 2, Davis 1. **New York (10)**—Hall 2, Hayes 2, Velarde 2, R. Kelly 1, Mattingly 1, Nokes 1, B. Williams 1. **Oakland (4)**—McGwire 3, Browne 1. **Seattle (6)**—Buhner 2, O'Brien 2, E. Martinez 1, Reynolds 1. **Texas (8)**—Reimer 2, Canseco 1, Downing 1, Gonzalez 1, Palmeiro 1, Palmer 1, Rodriguez 1. **Toronto (11)**—Borders 2, Winfield 2, Alomar 1, Carter 1, Gruber 1, Kent 1, Maldonado 1, Olerud 1, White 1.

AT KANSAS CITY (65):

Baltimore (3)—Gomez 2, Anderson 1. **Boston (3)**—Clark 2, Burks 1. **California (4)**—Parrish 2, DiSarcina 1, Gaetti 1. **Chicago (1)**—Karkovice 1. **Cleveland (3)**—Baerga 1, Hill 1, Sorrento 1. **Detroit (4)**—Gladden 2, Cuyler 1, Phillips 1. **Kansas City (24)**—Macfarlane 7, McReynolds 4, Jefferies 3, McRae 2, Wilkerson 2, Brett 1, Eisenreich 1, Howard 1, Joyner 1, Koslofski 1, Miller 1. **Milwaukee (1)**—Vaughn 1. **Minnesota (5)**—Hrbek 3, Davis 2. **New York (3)**—Maas 2, Tartabull 1. **Oakland (7)**—Canseco 2, Blankenship 1, Fox 1, R. Henderson 1, Lansford 1, McGwire 1. **Texas (6)**—Gonzalez 3, Palmer 2, Downing 1. **Toronto (1)**—Carter 1.

AT MILWAUKEE (86):

Baltimore (6)—C. Ripken 3, Devereaux 1, Hoiles 1, Orsulak 1. **Boston (1)**—Brunansky 1. **California (3)**—Brooks 1, Sojo 1, Stevens 1. **Chicago (2)**—Thomas 1, Ventura 1. **Cleveland (2)**—Belle 2. **Detroit (7)**—Deer 2, Fielder 2, Fryman 2, Tettleton 1. **Kansas City (3)**—McReynolds 2, Joyner 1. **Milwaukee (35)**—Vaughn 11, Molitor 4, Bichette 3, Stubbs 3, Surhoff 3, Yount 3, Fletcher 2, Seitzer 2, Gantner 1, Hamilton 1, Jaha 1, Nilsson 1. **Minnesota (3)**—Gagne 1, Mack 1, Puckett 1. **New York (7)**—Hayes 2, Mattingly 2, P. Kelly 1, R. Kelly 1, Maas 1. **Oakland (4)**—McGwire 2, Baines 1, Steinbach 1. **Texas (5)**—Palmeiro 2, Gonzalez 1, Huson 1, Thon 1. **Toronto (8)**—Carter 3, Borders 2, Maldonado 1, Olerud 1, Winfield 1.

AT MINNESOTA (112):

Baltimore (3)—Devereaux 1, Hoiles 1, C. Ripken 1. **Boston (3)**—Brunansky 3. **California (1)**—Sojo 1. **Chicago (5)**—Ventura 2, Bell 1, Raines 1, Thomas 1. **Cleveland (3)**—Howard 1, Thome 1, Whiten 1. **Detroit (5)**—Clark 1, Deer 1, Fielder 1, Fryman 1, Gladden 1. **Kansas City (4)**—Jefferies 1, Joyner 1, Macfarlane 1, McRae 1. **Minnesota (56)**—Hrbek 10, Mack 10, Puckett 9, Munoz 8, Davis 6, Larkin 5, Harper 3, Leius 2, Gagne 1, Reboulet 1, Webster 1. **New York (4)**—P. Kelly 1, Leyritz 1, Nokes 1, Tartabull 1. **Oakland (8)**—McGwire 3, Steinbach 2, Baines 1, Fox 1, Ready 1. **Seattle (5)**—Briley 1, Cochrane 1, Griffey 1, Valle 1. **Texas (10)**—Palmer 3, Gonzalez 2, Palmeiro 2, Reimer 1, Rodriguez 1, Sierra 1. **Toronto (5)**—White 2, Alomar 1, Carter 1, Olerud 1.

AT NEW YORK (158):

Baltimore (6)—Devereaux 2, Anderson 1, Gomez 1, Hoiles 1, B. Ripken 1. **Boston (3)**—Clark 1, Plantier 1, Vaughn 1. **California (4)**—Brooks 1, Rose 1, Salmon 1, Sojo 1. **Chicago (6)**—Ventura 3, Bell 1, Pasqua 1, Sveum 1. **Cleveland (7)**—Baerga 2, Alomar 1, Belle 1, Lofton 1, Sorrento 1, Whiten 1. **Detroit (9)**—Tettleton 3, Whitaker 3, Carreon 1, Deer 1, Livingston 1. **Kansas City (2)**—Joyner 1, Koslofski 1. **Milwaukee (7)**—Stubbs 2, Bichette 1, Molitor 1, Nilsson 1, Vaughn 1, Yount 1. **Minnesota (6)**—Bush 1, Davis 1, Hrbek 1, Mack 1, Munoz 1, Puckett 1. **New York (88)**—Nokes 18, Tartabull 11, Hall 7, Hayes 7, Maas 7, R. Kelly 6, Mattingly 6, Stanley 5, P. Kelly 3, Leyritz 3, B. Williams 3, Barfield 2, James 2, Stankiewicz 2, Velarde 2, G. Williams 2, Gallego 1, Meulens 1. **Oakland (4)**—Canseco 2, R. Henderson 1, Lansford 1. **Seattle (7)**—Buhner 4, Griffey 1, E. Martinez 1, Parrish 1. **Texas (4)**—Palmeiro 2, Palmer 1, Reimer 1. **Toronto (5)**—Carter 1, Kent 1, Maldonado 1, Myers 1, White 1.

AT OAKLAND (149):

Baltimore (10)—Anderson 3, Martinez 2, Devereaux 1, Hoiles 1, Horn 1, Milligan 1, C. Ripken 1. **Boston (4)**—Burks 1, Clark 1, Cooper 1, Greenwell 1. **California (5)**—Brooks 1, Curtis 1, Felix 1, Gonzales 1, Stevens 1. **Chicago (6)**—Bell 2, Karkovice 2, Pasqua 1, Thomas 1. **Cleveland (8)**—Belle 3, Martinez 2, Sorrento 2, Lewis 1. **Detroit (8)**—Deer 3, Carreon 1, Fielder 1, Fryman 1, Phillips 1, Tettleton 1. **Kansas City (4)**—Brett 1, Eisenreich 1, Jefferies 1, Macfarlane 1. **Milwaukee (3)**—Molitor 1, Nilsson 1, Vaughn 1. **Minnesota (5)**—Gagne 2, Harper 2, Puckett 1. **New York (5)**—Hayes 1, P. Kelly 1, Mattingly 1, Nokes 1, Tartabull 1. **Oakland (76)**—McGwire 24, Canseco 12, Baines 10, R. Henderson 10, Lansford 4, Bordick 3, Steinbach 3, Neel 2, Quirk 2, Sierra 2, Blankenship 1, Brosius 1, Browne 1, Ready 1. **Seattle (7)**—Buhner 3, Briley 1, Cochrane 1, Cotto 1, E. Martinez 1. **Texas (3)**—Gonzalez 2, Palmeiro 1. **Toronto (5)**—Maldonado 2, Borders 1, Carter 1, Gruber 1.

AT SEATTLE (141):

Baltimore (3)—Davis 2, Martinez 1. **Boston (2)**—Vaughn 2. **California (2)**—Curtis 2. **Chicago (4)**—Karkovice 1, Pasqua 1, Sax 1, Thomas 1. **Cleveland (4)**—Belle 4. **Detroit (6)**—Deer 2, Phillips 2, Tettleton 1, Whitaker 1. **Kansas City (2)**—Joyner 1, Macfarlane 1. **Milwaukee (3)**—Hamilton 1, Nilsson 1, Yount 1. **Minnesota (7)**—Puckett 2, Gagne 1, Harper 1, Knoblauch 1, Larkin 1, Munoz 1. **New York (4)**—Hayes 1, R. Kelly 1, Leyritz 1, Stanley 1, Velarde 1. **Oakland (5)**—McGwire 2, Canseco 1, Sierra 1, Steinbach 1. **Seattle (78)**—Griffey 16, E. Martinez 11, T. Martinez 10, Buhner 9, Valle 7, O'Brien 6, Parrish 6, Mitchell 5, Boone 2, Cotto 2, Reynolds 2, Briley 1, Howitt 1. **Texas (14)**—Palmer 3, Fariss 2, Gonzalez 2, Sierra 2, Cangelosi 1, Huson 1, Palmeiro 1, Petralli 1, Reimer 1. **Toronto (6)**—Winfield 2, Carter 1, Kent 1, Lee 1, Maldonado 1.

AT TEXAS (134):

Baltimore (5)—Gomez 2, Devereaux 1, Horn 1, C. Ripken 1. **California (4)**—Brooks 1, Gaetti 1, Hayes 1, Stevens 1. **Chicago (4)**—Thomas 2, Johnson 1, Raines 1. **Cleveland (6)**—Sorrento 2, Baerga 1, Belle 1, Lofton 1, Whiten 1. **Detroit (10)**—Fielder 3,

Tettleton 2, Carreon 1, Cuyler 1, Deer 1, Fryman 1, Whitaker 1. **Kansas City (8)**—Macfarlane 2, Brett 1, Joyner 1, Koslofski 1, McReynolds 1, Miller 1, Shumpert 1. **Milwaukee (1)**—Stubbs 1. **Minnesota (4)**—Puckett 2, Harper 1, Hrbek 1. **New York (5)**—Tartabull 3, Hayes 1, Nokes 1. **Oakland (4)**—Canseco 1, R. Henderson 1, McGwire 1, Steinbach 1. **Seattle (3)**—Boone 1, Buhner 1, Cotto 1. **Texas (71)**—Gonzalez 19, Palmer 11, Reimer 10, Palmeiro 8, Sierra 8, Downing 4, Rodriguez 4, Canseco 3, Franco 2, Thon 2. **Toronto (9)**—Olerud 2, White 2, Carter 1, Gruber 1, Maldonado 1, Ward 1, Winfield 1.

AT TORONTO (139):

Baltimore (3)—Anderson 1, Davis 1, Devereaux 1. **Boston (6)**—Boggs 1, Burks 1, Greenwell 1, Plantier 1, Valentin 1, Wedge 1. **California (3)**—Curtis 1, Gaetti 1, Parrish 1. **Chicago (3)**—Karkovice 2, Sax 1. **Cleveland (9)**—Hill 4, Belle 3, Baerga 1, Kirby 1. **Detroit (3)**—Tettleton 2, Deer 1. **Kansas City (4)**—Brett 1, McRae 1, McReynolds 1, Miller 1. **Milwaukee (5)**—Molitor 2, Vaughn 2, Hamilton 1. **Minnesota (3)**—Davis 1, Gagne 1, Harper 1. **New York (6)**—Hall 2, Leyritz 1, Mattingly 1, Stanley 1, Tartabull 1. **Oakland (6)**—McGwire 2, Brosius 1, Fox 1, Ready 1, Steinbach 1. **Seattle (7)**—E. Martinez 3, O'Brien 2, Cotto 1, Griffey 1. **Texas (2)**—Rodriguez 1, Thon 1. **Toronto (79)**—Carter 21, Winfield 13, Maldonado 8, Borders 7, Gruber 7, White 7, Alomar 5, Olerud 4, Bell 2, Kent 2, Lee 1, Martinez 1, Sprague 1.

1992
N.L. STATISTICS

BATTING

TEAM

Team	Avg.	G	AB	R	H	TB	2B	3B	HR	RBI	SH	SF	HP	BB	Int. BB	SO	SB	CS	GI DP	LOB	ShO	Slg.	OBP
St. Louis	.262	162	5594	631	1464	2096	262	44	94	599	68	41	32	495	49	996	208	118	96	1153	11	.375	.323
Cincinnati	.260	162	5460	660	1418	2084	281	44	99	606	66	52	21	563	83	888	125	65	123	1181	10	.382	.328
Pittsburgh	.255	162	5527	693	1409	2107	272	54	106	656	89	56	25	569	88	872	110	53	102	1177	9	.381	.324
San Diego	.255	162	5476	617	1396	2116	255	30	135	576	78	41	26	453	67	864	69	52	126	1082	12	.386	.313
Chicago	.254	162	5590	593	1420	2035	221	41	104	566	78	40	31	417	49	816	77	51	121	1148	20	.364	.307
Atlanta	.254	162	5480	682	1391	2124	223	48	138	641	93	50	26	493	58	924	126	60	82	1132	8	.388	.316
Philadelphia	.253	162	5500	686	1392	2073	255	36	118	638	64	46	52	509	45	1059	127	31	111	1172	9	.377	.320
Montreal	.252	162	5477	648	1381	2024	263	37	102	601	82	55	43	463	43	976	196	63	104	1087	11	.370	.313
Los Angeles	.248	162	5368	548	1333	1818	201	34	72	499	102	40	24	503	36	899	142	78	111	1138	15	.339	.313
Houston	.246	162	5480	608	1350	1969	255	38	96	582	88	40	48	506	65	1025	139	54	97	1162	18	.359	.313
San Francisco	.244	162	5456	574	1330	1937	220	36	105	532	101	39	39	435	53	1067	112	64	111	1087	18	.355	.302
New York	.235	162	5340	599	1254	1826	259	17	93	564	74	45	28	572	53	956	129	52	117	1098	16	.342	.310
Totals	.252	972	65748	7539	16538	24209	2967	459	1262	7060	983	545	395	5978	689	11342	1560	741	1301	13617	157	.368	.315

INDIVIDUAL

TOP 15 QUALIFIERS FOR BATTING CHAMPIONSHIP

Minimum 502 plate appearances.   *Lefthanded batter.   †Switch-hitter.

Player, Team	Avg.	G	AB	R	H	TB	2B	3B	HR	RBI	SH	SF	HP	BB	Int. BB	SO	SB	CS	GI DP	Slg.	OBP
Sheffield, Gary, San Diego	.330	146	557	87	184	323	34	3	33	100	0	7	6	48	5	40	5	6	19	.580	.385
Van Slyke, Andy, Pittsburgh*	.324	154	614	103	199	310	45	12	14	89	0	9	4	58	4	99	12	3	9	.505	.381
Kruk, John, Philadelphia*	.323	144	507	86	164	232	30	4	10	70	0	7	1	92	8	88	3	5	11	.458	.423
Roberts, Bip, Cincinnati†	.323	147	532	92	172	230	34	6	4	45	1	4	2	62	4	54	44	16	7	.432	.393
Gwynn, Tony, San Diego*	.317	128	520	77	165	216	27	3	6	41	0	3	0	46	12	16	3	6	12	.415	.371
Pendleton, Terry, Atlanta†	.311	160	640	98	199	303	39	1	21	105	5	7	0	37	8	67	5	2	16	.473	.345
Bonds, Barry, Pittsburgh*	.311	140	473	109	147	295	36	5	34	103	0	7	5	127	32	69	39	8	9	.624	.456
Butler, Brett, Los Angeles*	.309	157	553	86	171	216	14	11	3	39	24	1	3	95	2	67	41	21	4	.391	.413
Grace, Mark, Chicago*	.307	158	603	72	185	259	37	5	9	79	2	8	4	72	8	36	6	1	14	.430	.380
Larkin, Barry, Cincinnati	.304	140	533	76	162	242	32	6	12	78	2	7	4	63	8	58	15	4	13	.454	.377
Sandberg, Ryne, Chicago	.304	158	612	100	186	312	32	8	26	87	0	6	1	68	4	73	17	6	13	.510	.371
Walker, Larry, Montreal*	.301	143	528	85	159	267	31	4	23	93	0	8	6	41	10	97	18	6	9	.506	.353
Clark, Will, San Francisco*	.300	144	513	69	154	244	40	1	16	73	0	11	4	73	23	62	12	7	5	.476	.384
McGee, Willie, San Francisco†	.297	138	474	56	141	168	20	2	1	36	5	1	1	29	3	88	13	4	7	.354	.339
Smith, Ozzie, St. Louis†	.295	132	518	73	153	177	20	2	0	31	12	1	0	59	4	34	43	9	11	.342	.367

DEPARTMENTAL LEADERS: G—Bagwell, Hou., Biggio, Hou., Finley, Hou., 162; AB—Grissom, Mon., 653; R—Bonds, Pit., 109; H—Pendleton, Atl., Van Slyke, Pit., 199; TB—Sheffield, S.D., 323; 1B—Butler, L.A., 143; 2B—Van Slyke, Pit., 45; 3B—Sanders, Atl., 14; HR—McGriff, S.D., 35; RBI—Daulton, Phi., 109; SH—Butler, L.A., 24; SF—Bagwell, Hou., 13; HP—Hollins, Phi., 19; BB—Bonds, Pit., 127; IBB—Bonds, Pit., 32; SO—Lankford, St.L., 147; SB—Grissom, Mon., 78; CS—Lankford, St.L., 24; GIDP—Jackson, S.D., 21; Slg. Pct.—Bonds, Pit., .624; OB. Pct.—Bonds, Pit., .456.

ALL PLAYERS

*Lefthanded batter.   †Switch-hitter.

Player, Team	Avg.	G	AB	R	H	TB	2B	3B	HR	RBI	SH	SF	HP	BB	Int. BB	SO	SB	CS	GI DP	Slg.	OBP
Abbott, Kyle, Philadelphia*	.069	31	29	1	2	3	1	0	0	2	6	0	0	1	0	18	0	0	0	.103	.100
Afenir, Troy, Cincinnati	.176	16	34	3	6	11	1	2	0	4	1	0	0	5	0	12	0	0	0	.324	.282
Agosto, Juan, St. Louis*	.000	22	4	0	0	0	0	0	0	0	0	0	0	0	0	2	0	0	0	.000	.000
Alicea, Luis, St. Louis†	.245	85	265	26	65	102	9	11	2	32	2	4	4	27	1	40	2	5	5	.385	.320
Alou, Moises, Montreal	.282	115	341	53	96	155	28	2	9	56	5	5	1	25	0	46	16	2	5	.455	.328
Amaro, Ruben Jr., Philadelphia†	.219	126	374	43	82	130	15	6	7	34	4	2	9	37	1	54	11	5	11	.348	.303
Andersen, Larry, San Diego	.000	34	1	0	0	0	0	0	0	0	0	0	0	1	0	1	0	0	0	.000	.000
Anderson, Dave, Los Angeles	.286	51	84	10	24	37	4	0	3	8	1	2	0	4	0	11	0	4	3	.440	.311
Anthony, Eric, Houston*	.239	137	440	45	105	179	15	1	19	80	0	4	1	38	5	98	5	4	7	.407	.298
Arias, Alex, Chicago	.293	32	99	14	29	35	6	0	0	7	1	0	2	11	0	13	0	0	4	.354	.375
Ashby, Andy, Philadelphia	.091	10	11	0	1	2	1	0	0	1	0	0	0	0	0	7	0	0	0	.182	.091
Ashley, Billy, Los Angeles	.221	29	95	6	21	32	5	0	2	6	0	0	0	5	0	34	0	0	2	.337	.260
Assenmacher, Paul, Chicago*	.000	70	4	1	0	0	0	0	0	0	2	0	0	1	0	1	0	0	0	.000	.000
Astacio, Pedro, Los Angeles	.125	11	24	2	3	3	0	0	0	1	5	0	0	0	0	14	0	0	0	.125	.125
Avery, Steve, Atlanta*	.171	35	76	8	13	17	2	1	0	4	9	0	0	3	0	22	0	1	0	.224	.224
Ayala, Bobby, Cincinnati	.000	5	9	1	0	0	0	0	0	0	0	1	0	0	0	6	0	0	0	.000	.000
Azocar, Oscar, San Diego*	.190	99	168	15	32	38	6	0	0	8	4	1	0	9	1	12	1	0	3	.226	.230
Backman, Wally, Philadelphia*	.271	42	48	6	13	14	1	0	0	6	1	0	0	6	1	9	1	0	3	.292	.352
Baez, Kevin, New York	.154	6	13	0	2	2	0	0	0	0	0	0	0	0	0	0	1	0	0	.154	.154
Bagwell, Jeff, Houston	.273	162	586	87	160	260	34	6	18	96	2	13	12	84	13	97	10	6	17	.444	.368
Bailey, Mark, San Francisco†	.154	13	26	0	4	5	1	0	0	1	0	0	0	3	0	7	0	0	0	.192	.241
Bankhead, Scott, Cincinnati	.222	54	9	0	2	2	0	0	0	0	2	0	0	0	0	7	0	0	0	.222	.222
Barberie, Bret, Montreal†	.232	111	285	26	66	80	11	0	1	24	1	2	8	47	3	62	9	5	4	.281	.354
Barnes, Brian, Montreal*	.276	21	29	1	8	8	0	0	0	1	6	0	0	1	0	15	0	0	0	.276	.300
Bass, Kevin, S.F.-N.Y.†	.269	135	402	40	108	168	23	5	9	39	1	3	1	23	3	70	14	9	8	.418	.308
Batiste, Kim, Philadelphia	.206	44	136	9	28	35	4	0	1	10	2	3	0	4	1	18	0	0	7	.257	.224
Beck, Rod, San Francisco	.500	65	2	0	1	1	0	0	0	0	0	0	0	0	0	1	0	0	0	.500	.500
Belcher, Tim, Cincinnati	.105	35	76	3	8	12	1	1	0	4	7	0	0	0	0	28	0	0	1	.158	.105
Belinda, Stan, Pittsburgh	.667	59	3	1	2	3	1	0	0	0	2	0	0	0	0	0	0	0	0	1.000	.667
Bell, Jay, Pittsburgh	.264	159	632	87	167	242	36	6	9	55	19	2	4	55	0	103	7	5	12	.383	.326
Bell, Juan, Philadelphia†	.204	46	147	12	30	38	3	1	1	8	0	2	1	18	5	29	5	4	0	.259	.292

Player, Team	Avg.	G	AB	R	H	TB	2B	3B	HR	RBI	SH	SF	HP	BB	Int. BB	SO	SB	CS	GI DP	Slg.	OBP
Belliard, Rafael, Atlanta	.211	144	285	20	60	68	6	1	0	14	13	0	3	14	4	43	0	1	6	.239	.255
Benavides, Freddie, Cincinnati	.231	74	173	14	40	55	10	1	1	17	2	0	1	10	4	34	0	1	3	.318	.277
Benes, Andy, San Diego	.149	34	67	3	10	15	2	0	1	5	5	1	0	5	0	29	0	0	1	.224	.205
Benjamin, Mike, San Francisco	.173	40	75	4	13	20	2	1	1	3	3	0	0	4	1	15	1	0	1	.267	.215
Benzinger, Todd, Los Angeles†	.239	121	293	24	70	102	16	2	4	31	0	5	0	15	1	54	2	4	6	.348	.272
Berenguer, Juan, Atlanta	.000	28	2	0	0	0	0	0	0	0	0	0	0	0	0	1	0	0	0	.000	.000
Berroa, Geronimo, Cincinnati	.267	13	15	2	4	5	1	0	0	0	0	0	1	2	0	1	0	1	1	.333	.389
Berry, Sean, Montreal	.333	24	57	5	19	23	1	0	1	4	0	0	0	1	0	11	2	1	1	.404	.345
Berryhill, Damon, Atlanta†	.228	101	307	21	70	118	16	1	10	43	0	3	1	17	4	67	0	2	4	.384	.268
Bielecki, Mike, Atlanta	.125	19	24	1	3	3	0	0	0	0	4	0	0	0	0	13	0	0	1	.125	.125
Biggio, Craig, Houston	.277	162	613	96	170	226	32	3	6	39	5	2	7	94	9	95	38	15	5	.369	.378
Bilardello, Dann, San Diego	.121	17	33	2	4	5	1	0	0	1	3	0	0	4	1	8	0	0	1	.152	.216
Birkbeck, Mike, New York	.000	1	2	0	0	0	0	0	0	0	0	0	0	0	0	0	0	0	0	.000	.000
Black, Bud, San Francisco*	.056	28	54	1	3	4	1	0	0	2	10	0	0	2	0	16	0	0	0	.074	.089
Blair, Willie, Houston	.059	29	17	0	1	1	0	0	0	0	1	0	0	1	0	14	0	0	0	.059	.111
Blauser, Jeff, Atlanta	.262	123	343	61	90	157	19	3	14	46	7	3	4	46	2	82	5	5	2	.458	.354
Boever, Joe, Houston	.000	81	7	0	0	0	0	0	0	0	0	0	0	0	0	3	0	0	0	.000	.000
Bolton, Tom, Cincinnati*	.000	16	14	0	0	0	0	0	0	0	1	0	0	0	0	5	0	0	0	.000	.000
Bonds, Barry, Pittsburgh*	.311	140	473	109	147	295	36	5	34	103	0	7	5	127	32	69	39	8	9	.624	.456
Bonilla, Bobby, New York†	.249	128	438	62	109	189	23	0	19	70	0	1	1	66	10	73	4	3	11	.432	.348
Boskie, Shawn, Chicago	.185	23	27	1	5	6	1	0	0	1	3	0	0	2	0	9	0	0	0	.222	.241
Boston, Daryl, New York*	.249	130	289	37	72	123	14	2	11	35	0	4	3	38	6	60	12	6	5	.426	.338
Bottenfield, Kent, Montreal†	.375	10	8	1	3	3	0	0	0	0	1	0	0	0	0	3	0	0	0	.375	.375
Bournigal, Rafael, Los Angeles	.150	10	20	1	3	4	1	0	0	0	0	0	1	1	0	2	0	0	0	.200	.227
Bowen, Ryan, Houston	.111	15	9	1	1	1	0	0	0	0	0	0	0	0	0	3	0	1	0	.111	.111
Bradley, Scott, Cincinnati*	.400	5	5	1	2	2	0	0	0	1	0	0	0	1	0	0	0	0	0	.400	.500
Braggs, Glenn, Cincinnati	.237	92	266	40	63	109	16	3	8	38	1	2	2	36	5	48	3	1	10	.410	.330
Branson, Jeff, Cincinnati*	.296	72	115	12	34	43	7	1	0	15	2	1	0	5	2	16	0	1	4	.374	.322
Brantley, Cliff, Philadelphia	.214	28	14	1	3	5	0	1	0	1	7	0	0	1	0	4	0	0	0	.357	.267
Brantley, Jeff, San Francisco	.111	56	9	2	1	1	0	0	0	0	0	0	0	1	0	2	0	0	0	.111	.200
Bream, Sid, Atlanta*	.261	125	372	30	97	154	25	1	10	61	3	4	1	46	2	51	6	0	3	.414	.340
Brewer, Rod, St. Louis*	.301	29	103	11	31	37	6	0	0	10	0	1	1	8	0	12	0	1	1	.359	.354
Brink, Brad, Philadelphia	.083	8	12	0	1	1	0	0	0	0	1	0	1	0	0	5	0	0	0	.083	.154
Brocail, Doug, San Diego*	.200	3	5	0	1	1	0	0	0	0	0	0	0	0	0	0	0	0	0	.200	.200
Brown, Keith, Cincinnati†	.000	2	2	0	0	0	0	0	0	0	1	0	0	0	0	1	0	0	0	.000	.000
Browning, Tom, Cincinnati*	.226	16	31	4	7	8	1	0	0	2	2	1	0	1	0	6	0	0	1	.258	.242
Brumfield, Jacob, Cincinnati	.133	24	30	6	4	4	0	0	0	2	0	0	1	2	1	4	6	0	0	.133	.212
Buechele, Steve, Pit.-Chi.	.261	145	524	52	137	195	23	4	9	64	4	3	7	52	6	105	1	3	10	.372	.334
Bullinger, Jim, Chicago	.250	39	20	3	5	8	0	0	1	2	1	0	0	1	0	7	1	0	0	.400	.286
Bullock, Eric, Montreal*	.000	8	5	0	0	0	0	0	0	0	0	0	0	0	0	1	0	0	0	.000	.000
Burba, Dave, San Francisco	.067	23	15	0	1	1	0	0	0	1	3	0	0	1	0	8	0	0	0	.067	.125
Burkett, John, San Francisco	.018	32	55	2	1	2	1	0	0	2	8	0	0	4	0	24	0	0	1	.036	.085
Butler, Brett, Los Angeles*	.309	157	553	86	171	216	14	11	3	39	24	1	3	95	2	67	41	21	4	.391	.413
Cabrera, Francisco, Atlanta	.300	12	10	2	3	9	0	0	2	3	0	0	0	1	0	1	0	0	0	.900	.364
Calderon, Ivan, Montreal	.265	48	170	19	45	72	14	2	3	24	0	1	1	14	1	22	1	2	4	.424	.323
Caminiti, Ken, Houston†	.294	135	506	68	149	223	31	2	13	62	2	4	1	44	13	68	10	4	14	.441	.350
Candaele, Casey, Houston†	.213	135	320	19	68	85	12	1	1	18	7	6	3	24	3	36	7	1	5	.266	.269
Candelaria, John, Los Angeles	.000	50	0	0	0	0	0	0	0	0	0	0	0	1	0	0	0	0	0	.000	1.000
Candiotti, Tom, Los Angeles	.107	32	56	3	6	7	1	0	0	1	12	0	0	1	0	9	0	0	5	.125	.123
Canseco, Ozzie, St. Louis	.276	9	29	7	8	13	5	0	0	3	0	0	0	7	0	4	0	0	1	.448	.417
Carpenter, Cris, St. Louis	.333	73	3	0	1	1	0	0	0	2	1	0	0	0	0	1	0	0	0	.333	.333
Carr, Chuck, St. Louis†	.219	22	64	8	14	17	3	0	0	3	3	0	0	9	0	6	10	2	0	.266	.315
Carter, Gary, Montreal	.218	95	285	24	62	97	18	1	5	29	1	4	2	33	4	37	0	4	4	.340	.299
Carter, Larry, San Francisco	.200	6	10	1	2	2	0	0	0	0	1	0	1	0	0	5	0	0	0	.200	.273
Castilla, Vinny, Atlanta	.250	9	16	1	4	5	1	0	0	1	0	0	1	1	1	4	0	0	0	.313	.333
Castillo, Braulio, Philadelphia	.197	28	76	12	15	26	3	1	2	7	1	0	0	4	0	15	1	0	1	.342	.238
Castillo, Frank, Chicago	.092	33	65	3	6	6	0	0	0	1	5	0	0	3	0	21	0	0	2	.092	.132
Cedeno, Andujar, Houston	.173	71	220	15	38	61	13	2	2	13	0	0	3	14	2	71	2	0	1	.277	.232
Cerone, Rick, Montreal	.270	33	63	10	17	24	4	0	1	7	1	0	1	3	0	5	1	2	0	.381	.313
Chamberlain, Wes, Philadelphia	.258	76	275	26	71	116	18	0	9	41	1	2	1	10	2	55	4	0	7	.422	.285
Charlton, Norm, Cincinnati†	.200	64	5	0	1	1	0	0	0	0	2	0	0	0	0	3	0	0	0	.200	.200
Cianfrocco, Archi, Montreal	.241	86	232	25	56	83	5	2	6	30	1	2	1	11	0	66	3	0	2	.358	.276
Clark, Dave, Pittsburgh*	.212	23	33	3	7	13	0	0	2	7	0	1	0	6	0	8	0	0	0	.394	.325
Clark, Jerald, San Diego	.242	146	496	45	120	190	22	6	12	58	1	3	4	22	3	97	3	0	7	.383	.278
Clark, Mark, St. Louis	.139	20	36	0	5	5	0	0	0	1	4	0	0	0	0	18	0	0	0	.139	.139
Clark, Will, San Francisco*	.300	144	513	69	154	244	40	1	16	73	0	11	4	73	23	82	12	7	5	.476	.384
Clayton, Royce, San Francisco	.224	98	321	31	72	99	7	4	4	24	3	2	0	26	3	63	8	4	11	.308	.281
Clements, Pat, San Diego	.000	27	1	0	0	0	0	0	0	0	0	0	0	0	0	0	0	0	0	.000	.000
Colbert, Craig, San Francisco	.230	49	126	10	29	41	5	2	1	16	2	2	0	9	0	22	1	0	8	.325	.277
Colbrunn, Greg, Montreal	.268	52	168	12	45	59	8	0	2	18	0	4	2	6	1	34	3	2	1	.351	.294
Cole, Alex, Pittsburgh*	.278	64	205	33	57	74	3	7	0	10	1	1	0	18	1	46	7	4	2	.361	.335
Cole, Victor, Pittsburgh†	.000	8	4	0	0	0	0	0	0	0	1	0	0	0	0	0	0	0	0	.000	.000
Coleman, Vince, New York†	.275	71	229	37	63	82	11	1	2	21	2	1	2	27	3	41	24	9	1	.358	.355
Coles, Darnell, Cincinnati	.312	55	141	16	44	68	11	2	3	18	3	2	0	3	0	15	1	0	1	.482	.322
Combs, Pat, Philadelphia*	.125	4	8	1	1	2	1	0	0	2	1	0	0	1	0	1	0	0	0	.250	.222
Cone, David, New York*	.092	27	65	5	6	7	1	0	0	4	7	0	0	3	0	19	0	0	1	.108	.132
Cooke, Steve, Pittsburgh	.333	11	3	0	1	1	0	0	0	1	2	0	0	0	0	0	0	0	0	.333	.333
Cordero, Wil, Montreal	.302	45	126	17	38	50	4	1	2	8	1	0	1	9	0	31	0	0	3	.397	.353
Cormier, Rheal, St. Louis*	.102	31	59	3	6	8	2	0	0	2	10	0	0	0	0	13	0	0	0	.136	.102
Costo, Tim, Cincinnati	.222	12	36	3	8	10	2	0	0	2	0	1	0	5	0	6	0	0	4	.278	.310
Cox, Danny, Phi.-Pit.	.071	25	14	0	1	1	0	0	0	1	0	0	0	0	0	8	0	0	0	.071	.071
Crews, Tim, Los Angeles	.286	49	7	1	2	2	0	0	0	0	0	0	0	0	0	4	0	0	0	.286	.286
Daniels, Kal, L.A.-Chi.*	.241	83	212	21	51	80	11	0	6	25	0	2	2	22	0	54	0	2	10	.377	.315
Dascenzo, Doug, Chicago†	.255	139	376	37	96	117	13	4	0	20	4	2	0	27	2	32	6	8	3	.311	.304
Daulton, Darren, Philadelphia*	.270	145	485	80	131	254	32	5	27	109	0	6	6	88	11	103	11	2	3	.524	.385
Davis, Eric, Los Angeles	.228	76	267	21	61	86	8	1	5	32	0	2	3	36	2	71	19	1	9	.322	.325
Davis, Mark, Atlanta*	.000	14	1	0	0	0	0	0	0	0	0	0	0	0	0	1	0	0	0	.000	.000

Player, Team	Avg.	G	AB	R	H	TB	2B	3B	HR	RBI	SH	SF	HP	BB	Int. BB	SO	SB	CS	GI DP	Slg.	OBP
Dawson, Andre, Chicago	.277	143	542	60	150	247	27	2	22	90	0	6	4	30	8	70	6	2	13	.456	.316
Decker, Steve, San Francisco	.163	15	43	3	7	8	1	0	0	1	0	0	1	6	0	7	0	0	0	.186	.280
DeLeon, Jose, St.L-Phi.	.115	32	26	4	3	3	0	0	0	1	5	0	0	2	0	9	0	0	0	.115	.179
Deshaies, Jim, San Diego*	.207	15	29	3	6	6	0	0	0	0	5	0	0	1	0	9	0	0	0	.207	.233
DeShields, Delino, Montreal*	.292	135	530	82	155	211	19	8	7	56	9	3	3	54	4	108	46	15	10	.398	.359
Dewey, Mark, New York	.000	20	1	0	0	0	0	0	0	0	0	0	0	0	0	1	0	0	0	.000	.000
Dibble, Rob, Cincinnati*	.400	63	5	0	2	2	0	0	0	1	0	0	0	0	0	0	0	0	0	.400	.400
DiPino, Frank, St. Louis*	1.000	9	1	0	1	1	0	0	0	0	0	0	0	0	0	0	0	0	0	1.000	1.000
Distefano, Benny, Houston*	.233	52	60	4	14	18	0	2	0	7	0	0	1	5	1	14	0	0	1	.300	.303
Donnels, Chris, New York*	.174	45	121	8	21	25	4	0	0	6	1	0	0	17	0	25	1	0	1	.207	.275
Doran, Bill, Cincinnati†	.235	132	387	48	91	135	16	2	8	47	3	2	0	64	9	40	7	4	11	.349	.342
Downs, Kelly, San Francisco	.000	19	14	0	0	0	0	0	0	0	2	0	0	0	0	5	0	0	0	.000	.000
Dozier, D.J., New York	.191	25	47	4	9	11	2	0	0	2	1	1	1	4	0	19	4	0	0	.234	.264
Drabek, Doug, Pittsburgh	.157	35	89	5	14	17	3	0	0	6	8	0	0	2	0	28	0	0	0	.191	.176
Duncan, Mariano, Philadelphia	.267	142	574	71	153	223	40	3	8	50	5	4	5	17	0	108	23	3	15	.389	.292
Dunston, Shawon, Chicago	.315	18	73	8	23	28	3	1	0	2	0	0	0	3	0	13	2	3	0	.384	.342
Dykstra, Lenny, Philadelphia*	.301	85	345	53	104	140	18	0	6	39	0	4	3	40	4	32	30	5	1	.406	.375
Eiland, Dave, San Diego	.111	7	9	1	1	4	0	0	1	2	1	0	0	0	0	4	0	0	0	.444	.111
Elster, Kevin, New York	.222	6	18	0	4	4	0	0	0	0	0	0	0	0	0	2	0	0	1	.222	.222
Espy, Cecil, Pittsburgh†	.258	112	194	21	50	66	7	3	1	20	1	1	0	15	2	40	6	3	3	.340	.310
Faries, Paul, San Diego	.455	10	11	3	5	6	1	0	0	1	0	0	0	1	0	2	0	0	0	.545	.500
Fassero, Jeff, Montreal*	.143	70	7	0	1	2	1	0	0	0	1	0	0	0	0	3	0	0	0	.286	.143
Felder, Mike, San Francisco†	.286	145	322	44	92	123	13	3	4	23	3	3	2	21	1	29	14	4	3	.382	.330
Fernandez, Sid, New York*	.203	32	74	8	15	18	3	0	0	0	7	0	0	0	0	25	0	0	1	.243	.203
Fernandez, Tony, San Diego†	.275	155	622	84	171	223	32	4	4	37	9	3	4	56	4	62	20	20	6	.359	.337
Figueroa, Bien, St. Louis	.182	12	11	1	2	3	1	0	0	4	0	0	0	1	0	2	0	0	0	.273	.250
Filer, Tom, New York	.000	9	3	0	0	0	0	0	0	0	0	0	0	0	0	1	0	0	0	.000	.000
Finley, Steve, Houston*	.292	162	607	84	177	247	29	13	5	55	16	2	3	58	6	63	44	9	10	.407	.355
Fletcher, Darrin, Montreal*	.243	83	222	13	54	74	10	2	2	26	2	4	2	14	3	28	0	2	8	.333	.289
Foley, Tom, Montreal*	.174	72	115	7	20	25	3	1	0	5	3	2	1	8	2	21	3	0	6	.217	.230
Foster, Steve, Cincinnati	.200	31	5	0	1	1	0	0	0	0	0	0	0	0	0	1	0	0	0	.200	.200
Franco, John, New York*	.000	31	1	0	0	0	0	0	0	0	0	0	0	0	0	1	0	0	0	.000	.000
Freeman, Marvin, Atlanta	.500	58	4	0	2	2	0	0	0	0	0	0	0	0	0	2	0	0	0	.500	.500
Galarraga, Andres, St. Louis	.243	95	325	38	79	127	14	2	10	39	0	3	8	11	0	69	5	4	8	.391	.282
Gallagher, Dave, New York	.240	98	175	20	42	58	11	1	1	21	3	7	1	19	0	16	4	5	7	.331	.307
Gant, Ron, Atlanta	.259	153	544	74	141	226	22	6	17	80	0	6	7	45	5	101	32	10	10	.415	.321
Garcia, Carlos, Pittsburgh	.205	22	39	4	8	9	1	0	0	4	1	2	0	0	0	9	0	0	1	.231	.195
Gardner, Jeff, San Diego*	.105	15	19	0	2	2	0	0	0	0	0	0	0	1	0	8	0	0	0	.105	.150
Gardner, Mark, Montreal	.140	33	50	4	7	9	0	1	0	2	8	2	0	3	0	18	0	0	0	.180	.182
Gedman, Rich, St. Louis*	.219	41	105	5	23	30	4	0	1	8	0	1	0	11	1	22	0	0	0	.286	.291
Gibson, Kirk, Pittsburgh*	.196	16	56	6	11	17	0	0	2	5	1	0	0	3	0	12	3	1	1	.304	.237
Gibson, Paul, New York	.000	43	6	0	0	0	0	0	0	0	1	0	0	1	0	3	0	0	0	.000	.143
Gilkey, Bernard, St. Louis	.302	131	384	56	116	164	19	4	7	43	3	4	1	39	1	52	18	12	5	.427	.364
Girardi, Joe, Chicago	.270	91	270	19	73	81	3	1	1	12	0	1	1	19	3	38	0	2	8	.300	.320
Glavine, Tom, Atlanta*	.247	35	77	11	19	22	1	1	0	7	9	1	0	3	0	10	0	0	0	.286	.272
Gleaton, Jerry Don, Pittsburgh*	.000	23	2	0	0	0	0	0	0	0	1	0	0	1	0	1	0	0	0	.000	.333
Goff, Jerry, Montreal*	.000	3	3	0	0	0	0	0	0	0	0	0	0	0	0	3	0	0	0	.000	.000
Gonzalez, Luis, Houston*	.243	122	387	40	94	149	19	3	10	55	1	2	2	24	3	52	7	7	6	.385	.289
Gooden, Dwight, New York	.264	33	72	8	19	27	3	1	1	9	4	0	0	1	0	16	0	0	1	.375	.274
Goodwin, Tom, Los Angeles*	.233	57	73	15	17	20	1	1	0	3	0	0	0	6	0	10	7	3	0	.274	.291
Gott, Jim, Los Angeles	.500	68	2	0	1	1	0	0	0	0	0	0	0	0	0	1	0	0	0	.500	.500
Grace, Mark, Chicago*	.307	158	603	72	185	259	37	5	9	79	2	8	4	72	8	36	6	1	14	.430	.380
Green, Gary, Cincinnati	.333	8	12	3	4	5	1	0	0	0	0	0	0	0	0	2	0	0	0	.417	.333
Greene, Tommy, Philadelphia	.125	13	24	1	3	3	0	0	0	0	0	0	0	0	0	12	0	0	0	.125	.125
Greene, Willie, Cincinnati*	.269	29	93	10	25	40	5	2	2	13	0	1	0	10	0	23	0	2	1	.430	.337
Gregg, Tommy, Atlanta*	.263	18	19	1	5	8	0	0	1	1	0	0	0	1	0	7	1	0	1	.421	.300
Grissom, Marquis, Montreal	.276	159	653	99	180	273	39	6	14	66	3	4	5	42	6	81	78	13	12	.418	.322
Gross, Kevin, Los Angeles	.095	34	63	3	6	7	1	0	0	0	3	0	0	4	0	26	0	0	0	.111	.149
Gross, Kip, Los Angeles	1.000	16	2	1	2	2	0	0	0	1	1	0	0	0	0	0	0	0	0	1.000	1.000
Grotewold, Jeff, Philadelphia*	.200	72	65	7	13	24	2	0	3	5	0	0	1	9	0	16	0	0	4	.369	.307
Guerrero, Juan, Houston	.200	79	125	8	25	36	4	2	1	14	1	2	1	10	2	32	1	0	0	.288	.261
Guerrero, Pedro, St. Louis	.219	43	146	10	32	43	6	1	1	16	0	2	0	11	3	25	2	2	4	.295	.270
Guetterman, Lee, New York*	.000	43	2	0	0	0	0	0	0	0	0	0	0	0	0	2	0	0	0	.000	.000
Gwynn, Tony, San Diego*	.317	128	520	77	165	216	27	3	6	41	0	3	0	46	12	16	3	6	12	.415	.371
Hammond, Chris, Cincinnati*	.136	30	44	7	6	10	1	0	1	4	3	1	0	6	0	20	0	0	0	.227	.235
Haney, Chris, Montreal*	.222	10	9	1	2	2	0	0	0	3	1	0	0	0	0	1	0	0	0	.222	.222
Haney, Todd, Montreal	.300	7	10	0	3	4	1	0	0	1	1	0	0	0	0	0	0	0	1	.400	.300
Hansen, Dave, Los Angeles*	.214	132	341	30	73	102	11	0	6	22	0	2	1	34	3	49	0	2	9	.299	.286
Harkey, Mike, Chicago	.267	8	15	4	4	4	0	0	0	0	0	0	0	0	0	3	0	0	0	.267	.267
Harnisch, Pete, Houston	.164	34	67	7	11	16	5	0	0	8	5	0	0	2	0	12	0	1	1	.239	.188
Harris, Gene, San Diego	.333	15	3	0	1	1	0	0	0	0	0	0	0	0	0	1	0	0	0	.333	.333
Harris, Greg W., San Diego	.129	20	31	1	4	5	1	0	0	1	5	0	0	5	0	13	0	0	0	.161	.250
Harris, Lenny, Los Angeles*	.271	135	347	28	94	105	11	0	0	30	6	2	1	24	3	24	19	7	10	.303	.318
Hartley, Mike, Philadelphia	.000	47	4	0	0	0	0	0	0	0	0	0	0	0	0	1	0	0	0	.000	.000
Hartsock, Jeff, Chicago	.000	4	2	0	0	0	0	0	0	0	0	0	0	0	0	0	0	0	0	.000	.000
Hatcher, Billy, Cincinnati	.287	43	94	10	27	36	3	0	2	10	0	3	0	5	0	11	0	2	2	.383	.314
Henry, Butch, Houston*	.148	28	54	3	8	11	0	0	1	7	5	0	0	1	0	10	0	0	1	.204	.164
Henry, Dwayne, Cincinnati	.250	60	4	1	1	1	0	0	0	0	0	0	0	0	0	3	0	0	0	.250	.250
Heredia, Gil, S.F.-Mon.	.111	20	9	0	1	1	0	0	0	0	1	0	0	0	0	1	0	0	0	.111	.111
Hernandez, Carlos, Los Angeles	.260	69	173	11	45	58	4	0	3	17	0	2	4	11	1	21	0	1	8	.335	.316
Hernandez, Cesar, Cincinnati	.275	34	51	6	14	18	4	0	0	4	0	0	0	0	0	10	3	1	1	.353	.275
Hernandez, Jeremy, San Diego	.000	26	2	0	0	0	0	0	0	0	0	0	0	0	0	0	0	0	0	.000	.000
Hernandez, Xavier, Houston*	.000	77	9	1	0	0	0	0	0	0	0	0	0	0	0	5	0	0	0	.000	.000
Hershiser, Orel, Los Angeles	.221	35	68	6	15	20	5	0	0	5	6	1	0	1	0	10	1	0	0	.294	.229
Hickerson, Bryan, S.F.*	.000	61	4	0	0	0	0	0	0	0	0	0	0	0	0	3	0	0	0	.000	.000
Hill, Ken, Montreal	.177	33	62	10	11	19	3	1	1	4	10	0	0	8	0	13	0	0	0	.306	.271
Hillman, Eric, New York*	.077	11	13	0	1	1	0	0	0	0	5	0	0	0	0	7	0	0	0	.077	.077

Player, Team	Avg.	G	AB	R	H	TB	2B	3B	HR	RBI	SH	SF	HP	BB	Int. BB	SO	SB	CS	GI DP	Slg.	OBP
Hollins, Dave, Philadelphia†	.270	156	586	104	158	275	28	4	27	93	0	4	19	76	4	110	9	6	8	.469	.369
Hosey, Steve, San Francisco	.250	21	56	6	14	18	1	0	1	6	0	2	0	0	0	15	1	1	1	.321	.241
Howard, Thomas, San Diego†	.333	5	3	1	1	1	0	0	0	0	0	0	0	0	0	0	0	0	0	.333	.333
Howell, Pat, New York†	.187	31	75	9	14	15	1	0	0	1	1	0	1	2	0	15	4	2	0	.200	.218
Hudler, Rex, St. Louis	.245	61	98	17	24	37	4	0	3	5	1	1	1	2	0	23	2	6	0	.378	.265
Hundley, Todd, New York†	.209	123	358	32	75	113	17	0	7	32	7	2	4	19	4	76	3	0	8	.316	.256
Hunter, Brian, Atlanta	.239	102	238	34	57	116	13	2	14	41	1	8	0	21	3	50	1	2	2	.487	.292
Hurst, Bruce, San Diego*	.159	33	69	2	11	15	4	0	0	1	9	0	0	3	0	27	0	0	0	.217	.194
Hurst, Jonathan, Montreal	.000	3	4	0	0	0	0	0	0	0	2	0	0	0	0	2	0	0	0	.000	.000
Incaviglia, Pete, Houston	.266	113	349	31	93	150	22	1	11	44	0	2	3	25	2	99	2	2	6	.430	.319
Innis, Jeff, New York	.000	76	2	0	0	0	0	0	0	0	0	0	0	0	0	0	0	0	0	.000	.000
Jackson, Danny, Chi.-Pit.	.083	34	60	2	5	5	0	0	0	2	9	0	0	1	0	31	0	1	0	.083	.098
Jackson, Darrin, San Diego	.249	155	587	72	146	230	23	5	17	70	6	5	4	26	4	106	14	3	21	.392	.283
Jackson, Mike, San Francisco	.000	67	2	0	0	0	0	0	0	0	0	0	0	0	0	0	0	0	0	.000	.000
James, Chris, San Francisco	.242	111	248	25	60	93	10	4	5	32	0	3	2	14	2	45	2	3	2	.375	.285
Javier, Stan, L.A.-Phi.†	.249	130	334	42	83	105	17	1	1	29	3	2	3	37	2	54	18	3	4	.314	.327
Johnson, Howard, New York†	.223	100	350	48	78	118	19	0	7	43	0	3	2	55	5	79	22	5	7	.337	.329
Jones, Barry, Phi.-N.Y.	.000	61	2	0	0	0	0	0	0	0	0	0	0	0	0	1	0	0	0	.000	.000
Jones, Chris, Houston	.190	54	63	7	12	19	2	1	1	4	3	0	0	7	0	21	3	0	1	.302	.271
Jones, Doug, Houston	.000	80	4	0	0	0	0	0	0	0	0	0	0	0	0	2	0	0	0	.000	.000
Jones, Jimmy, Houston	.167	26	36	5	6	7	1	0	0	4	9	0	0	6	0	13	0	0	1	.194	.286
Jones, Tim, St. Louis*	.200	67	145	9	29	33	4	0	0	3	2	0	0	11	1	29	5	2	1	.228	.256
Jordan, Brian, St. Louis	.207	55	193	17	40	72	9	4	5	22	0	0	1	10	1	48	7	2	6	.373	.250
Jordan, Ricky, Philadelphia	.304	94	276	33	84	115	19	0	4	34	0	3	0	5	0	44	3	0	8	.417	.313
Jose, Felix, St. Louis†	.295	131	509	62	150	220	22	3	14	75	0	1	1	40	8	100	28	12	9	.432	.347
Justice, David, Atlanta*	.256	144	484	78	124	216	19	5	21	72	0	6	2	79	8	85	2	4	1	.446	.359
Karros, Eric, Los Angeles	.257	149	545	63	140	232	30	1	20	88	0	5	2	37	3	103	2	4	15	.426	.304
Kent, Jeff, New York	.239	37	113	16	27	46	8	1	3	15	0	0	1	7	0	29	0	2	2	.407	.289
Kile, Darryl, Houston	.156	22	32	2	5	5	0	0	0	2	5	0	0	3	0	15	0	0	0	.156	.229
King, Jeff, Pittsburgh	.231	130	480	56	111	178	21	2	14	65	8	5	2	27	3	56	4	6	8	.371	.272
Klesko, Ryan, Atlanta*	.000	13	14	0	0	0	0	0	0	1	0	0	1	0	0	5	0	0	0	.000	.067
Krueger, Bill, Montreal*	.000	9	3	0	0	0	0	0	0	1	0	0	0	0	0	2	0	0	0	.000	.000
Kruk, John, Philadelphia*	.323	144	507	86	164	232	30	4	10	70	0	7	1	92	8	88	3	5	11	.458	.423
Kunkel, Jeff, Chicago	.138	20	29	0	4	6	2	0	0	1	0	0	0	0	0	8	0	0	1	.207	.138
Lake, Steve, Philadelphia	.245	20	53	3	13	18	2	0	1	2	0	1	0	1	0	8	0	0	1	.340	.255
Laker, Tim, Montreal	.217	28	46	8	10	13	3	0	0	4	0	0	1	2	0	14	1	1	1	.283	.250
Lamp, Dennis, Pittsburgh	.000	21	1	0	0	0	0	0	0	0	0	0	0	0	0	0	0	0	0	.000	.000
Lampkin, Tom, San Diego*	.235	9	17	3	4	4	0	0	0	0	0	0	1	6	0	1	2	0	0	.235	.458
Lankford, Ray, St. Louis*	.293	153	598	87	175	287	40	6	20	86	2	5	5	72	6	147	42	24	5	.480	.371
Larkin, Barry, Cincinnati	.304	140	533	76	162	242	32	6	12	78	2	7	4	63	8	58	15	4	13	.454	.377
LaValliere, Mike, Pittsburgh*	.256	95	293	22	75	96	13	1	2	29	0	5	1	44	14	21	0	3	8	.328	.350
Lefferts, Craig, San Diego*	.077	27	52	0	4	4	0	0	0	0	9	0	0	0	0	21	0	0	0	.077	.077
Leibrandt, Charlie, Atlanta	.121	32	58	1	7	8	1	0	0	4	8	1	0	1	0	12	0	1	1	.138	.133
Lemke, Mark, Atlanta*	.227	155	427	38	97	130	7	4	6	26	12	2	0	50	11	39	0	3	9	.304	.307
Leonard, Mark, San Francisco*	.234	55	128	13	30	49	7	0	4	16	0	1	3	16	0	31	0	1	3	.383	.331
Lewis, Darren, San Francisco	.231	100	320	38	74	87	8	1	1	18	10	2	1	29	0	46	28	8	3	.272	.295
Lind, Jose, Pittsburgh	.235	135	468	38	110	126	14	1	0	39	7	4	1	26	12	29	3	1	14	.269	.275
Lindeman, Jim, Philadelphia	.256	29	39	6	10	14	1	0	1	6	0	0	0	3	0	11	0	0	1	.359	.310
Litton, Greg, San Francisco	.229	68	140	9	32	49	5	0	4	15	3	0	0	11	0	33	0	1	2	.350	.285
Lopez, Javier, Atlanta	.375	9	16	3	6	8	2	0	0	2	0	0	0	0	0	1	0	0	0	.500	.375
Lyons, Steve, Atl.-Mon.*	.148	27	27	2	4	6	0	1	0	1	0	1	0	1	0	7	1	2	2	.222	.179
Maddux, Greg, Chicago	.170	35	88	6	15	21	3	0	1	8	13	0	0	1	0	22	0	0	1	.239	.180
Maddux, Mike, San Diego*	.111	50	9	0	1	1	0	0	0	0	3	0	0	1	0	4	0	0	0	.111	.200
Magadan, Dave, New York*	.283	99	321	33	91	111	9	1	3	28	2	0	0	56	3	44	1	0	6	.346	.390
Magrane, Joe, St. Louis	.200	5	10	1	2	5	0	0	1	2	1	0	0	2	0	0	0	0	0	.500	.200
Mallicoat, Rob, Houston*	.000	25	1	1	0	0	0	0	0	0	0	0	0	0	0	0	0	0	0	.000	.000
Manwaring, Kirt, San Francisco	.244	109	349	24	85	117	10	5	4	26	6	0	5	29	0	42	2	1	12	.335	.311
Marsh, Tom, Philadelphia	.200	42	125	7	25	38	3	2	2	16	2	1	2	2	0	23	0	1	2	.304	.215
Martin, Al, Pittsburgh*	.167	12	12	1	2	4	0	1	0	2	0	1	0	0	0	5	0	0	0	.333	.154
Martinez, Dave, Cincinnati*	.254	135	393	47	100	139	20	5	3	31	6	4	0	42	4	54	12	8	6	.354	.323
Martinez, Dennis, Montreal	.189	32	74	3	14	14	0	0	0	2	10	0	0	0	0	20	0	0	1	.189	.189
Martinez, Pedro, Los Angeles	.000	2	2	0	0	0	0	0	0	0	0	0	0	0	0	0	0	0	0	.000	.000
Martinez, Ramon, Los Angeles*	.120	26	50	1	6	6	0	0	0	2	5	0	0	0	0	14	0	0	1	.120	.120
Mason, Roger, Pittsburgh	.000	65	10	0	0	0	0	0	0	0	1	0	0	1	0	5	0	0	1	.000	.091
Mathews, Greg, Philadelphia	.000	14	14	0	0	0	0	0	0	0	2	0	0	1	0	8	0	0	0	.000	.067
May, Derrick, Chicago*	.274	124	351	33	96	131	11	0	8	45	2	1	3	14	4	40	5	3	10	.373	.306
McClendon, Lloyd, Pittsburgh	.253	84	190	26	48	67	8	1	3	20	1	3	2	28	0	24	1	3	5	.353	.350
McCray, Rodney, New York†	1.000	18	1	3	1	1	0	0	0	1	0	0	0	0	0	0	2	0	0	1.000	1.000
McDowell, Roger, Los Angeles	.000	65	3	1	0	0	0	0	0	0	1	0	1	2	0	3	0	0	0	.000	.500
McElroy, Chuck, Chicago*	.667	72	6	2	4	8	2	1	0	1	0	0	0	0	0	1	0	0	0	1.333	.667
McGee, Willie, San Francisco†	.297	138	474	56	141	168	20	2	1	36	5	1	1	29	3	88	13	4	7	.354	.339
McGriff, Fred, San Diego*	.286	152	531	79	152	295	30	4	35	104	0	4	1	96	23	108	8	6	14	.556	.394
McKnight, Jeff, New York†	.271	31	85	10	23	34	3	1	2	13	0	0	0	2	0	8	0	1	2	.400	.287
McNamara, Jim, San Francisco*	.216	30	74	6	16	20	1	0	1	9	2	0	0	6	1	20	0	0	1	.270	.275
Melendez, Jose, San Diego	.000	56	5	0	0	0	0	0	0	0	0	0	0	0	0	5	0	0	0	.000	.000
Merced, Orlando, Pittsburgh†	.247	134	405	50	100	156	28	5	6	60	1	5	2	52	8	63	5	4	6	.385	.332
Mercker, Kent, Atlanta*	.000	53	5	0	0	0	0	0	0	0	0	0	0	0	0	5	0	0	0	.000	.000
Miller, Paul, Pittsburgh	.000	6	3	0	0	0	0	0	0	0	0	0	0	0	0	1	0	0	0	.000	.000
Millette, Joe, Philadelphia	.205	33	78	5	16	16	0	0	0	2	0	2	0	5	2	10	1	0	8	.205	.271
Morandini, Mickey, Phi.*	.265	127	422	47	112	145	8	8	3	30	6	2	0	25	2	64	8	3	4	.344	.305
Morgan, Mike, Chicago	.108	34	74	1	8	8	0	0	0	5	11	1	0	2	0	16	0	0	1	.108	.130
Morris, Hal, Cincinnati*	.271	115	395	41	107	152	21	3	6	53	2	2	2	45	8	53	6	6	12	.385	.347
Mulholland, Terry, Philadelphia	.096	32	83	1	8	9	1	0	0	3	6	0	0	3	0	35	0	0	0	.108	.128
Murphy, Dale, Philadelphia	.161	18	62	5	10	17	1	0	2	7	0	0	1	0	0	13	0	0	1	.274	.175
Murphy, Rob, Houston*	.000	59	1	1	0	0	0	0	0	0	0	0	0	0	0	0	0	0	0	.000	.000
Murray, Eddie, New York†	.261	156	551	64	144	233	37	2	16	93	0	8	0	66	8	74	4	2	15	.423	.336
Myers, Randy, San Diego*	.143	66	7	0	1	1	0	0	0	0	0	0	0	0	0	5	0	0	1	.143	.143

Player, Team	Avg.	G	AB	R	H	TB	2B	3B	HR	RBI	SH	SF	HP	BB	Int. BB	SO	SB	CS	GI DP	Slg.	OBP
Nabholz, Chris, Montreal*	.123	32	65	3	8	11	3	0	0	2	7	0	0	1	0	12	0	0	3	.169	.136
Natal, Rob, Montreal	.000	5	6	0	0	0	0	0	0	0	0	0	0	1	0	1	0	0	1	.000	.143
Neagle, Denny, Pittsburgh*	.000	56	11	0	0	0	0	0	0	0	2	0	0	0	0	2	0	1	0	.000	.000
Nied, David, Atlanta	.286	6	7	1	2	2	0	0	0	0	0	0	0	0	0	2	0	0	0	.286	.286
Nieves, Melvin, Atlanta†	.211	12	19	0	4	5	1	0	0	1	0	0	0	2	0	7	0	0	0	.263	.286
Nixon, Otis, Atlanta†	.294	120	456	79	134	158	14	2	2	22	5	2	0	39	0	54	41	18	4	.346	.348
Noboa, Junior, New York	.149	46	47	7	7	7	0	0	0	3	0	1	1	3	0	8	0	0	2	.149	.212
O'Brien, Charlie, New York	.212	68	156	15	33	51	12	0	2	13	4	0	1	16	1	18	0	1	4	.327	.289
Offerman, Jose, Los Angeles†	.260	149	534	67	139	178	20	8	1	30	5	2	0	57	4	98	23	16	5	.333	.331
Ojeda, Bob, Los Angeles*	.102	29	49	1	5	7	0	1	0	3	5	0	0	1	0	11	0	0	1	.143	.120
Olivares, Omar, St. Louis	.235	36	68	7	16	20	1	0	1	4	3	0	0	1	0	19	0	0	0	.294	.246
Oliver, Joe, Cincinnati	.270	143	485	42	131	188	25	1	10	57	6	7	1	35	19	75	2	3	12	.388	.316
Oliveras, Francisco, S.F.	.143	16	7	0	1	1	0	0	0	0	0	0	0	1	0	2	0	0	0	.143	.250
Olson, Greg, Atlanta	.238	95	302	27	72	99	14	2	3	27	1	2	1	34	4	31	2	1	8	.328	.316
O'Neill, Paul, Cincinnati*	.246	148	496	59	122	185	19	1	14	66	3	6	2	77	15	85	6	3	10	.373	.346
Oquendo, Jose, St. Louis†	.257	14	35	3	9	14	3	1	0	3	0	0	0	5	1	3	0	0	0	.400	.350
Osborne, Donovan, St. Louis*	.121	34	58	4	7	9	0	1	0	0	2	0	0	0	0	21	0	0	1	.155	.121
Owen, Spike, Montreal†	.269	122	386	52	104	147	16	3	7	40	4	6	0	50	3	30	9	4	10	.381	.348
Pagnozzi, Tom, St. Louis	.249	139	485	33	121	174	26	3	7	44	6	3	1	28	9	64	2	5	15	.359	.290
Palacios, Vince, Pittsburgh	.071	20	14	0	1	1	0	0	0	0	2	0	0	0	0	6	0	0	0	.071	.071
Patterson, Bob, Pittsburgh	.333	60	6	1	2	3	1	0	0	4	0	0	0	1	0	3	0	0	0	.500	.429
Patterson, John, San Francisco†	.184	32	103	10	19	22	1	1	0	4	0	0	1	5	0	24	5	1	2	.214	.229
Patterson, Ken, Chicago*	.000	32	1	0	0	0	0	0	0	0	1	0	0	0	0	1	0	0	0	.000	.000
Pecota, Bill, New York	.227	117	269	28	61	80	13	0	2	26	5	2	1	25	3	40	9	3	7	.297	.293
Pedre, George, Chicago	.000	4	4	0	0	0	0	0	0	0	0	0	0	0	0	0	0	0	0	.000	.000
Peguero, Julio, Los Angeles†	.222	14	9	3	2	2	0	0	0	0	0	0	1	0	0	3	0	0	0	.222	.417
Pena, Alejandro, Atlanta	.000	41	2	0	0	0	0	0	0	0	0	0	0	0	0	2	0	0	0	.000	.000
Pena, Geronimo, St. Louis†	.305	62	203	31	62	97	12	1	7	31	0	4	5	24	0	37	13	8	1	.478	.386
Pena, Jim, San Francisco*	.200	25	5	0	1	1	0	0	0	0	0	0	0	0	0	2	0	0	0	.200	.200
Pendleton, Terry, Atlanta†	.311	160	640	98	199	303	39	1	21	105	5	7	0	37	8	67	5	2	16	.473	.345
Pennyfeather, William, Pitts.	.222	15	9	2	2	2	0	0	0	0	1	0	0	0	0	0	0	1	.222	.222
Perez, Mike, St. Louis	.000	77	4	0	0	0	0	0	0	0	2	0	0	0	0	2	0	0	1	.000	.000
Perry, Gerald, St. Louis*	.238	87	143	13	34	45	8	0	1	18	0	2	1	15	4	23	3	6	3	.315	.311
Pettis, Gary, San Diego†	.200	30	30	0	6	7	1	0	0	0	0	0	2	0	11	1	0	0	.233	.250
Piazza, Mike, Los Angeles	.232	21	69	5	16	22	3	0	1	7	0	0	1	4	0	12	0	0	1	.319	.284
Portugal, Mark, Houston	.107	18	28	1	3	3	0	0	0	0	6	0	0	0	0	12	0	0	0	.107	.107
Pratt, Todd, Philadelphia	.283	16	46	6	13	20	1	0	2	10	0	0	4	0	12	0	0	2	.435	.340
Prince, Tom, Pittsburgh	.091	27	44	1	4	6	2	0	0	5	0	2	0	6	0	9	1	1	2	.136	.192
Pugh, Tim, Cincinnati	.077	7	13	0	1	1	0	0	0	0	1	0	0	1	0	4	0	0	0	.077	.143
Ramirez, Rafael, Houston	.250	73	176	17	44	53	6	0	1	13	1	0	1	7	1	24	0	0	5	.301	.283
Ramsey, Fernando, Chicago	.120	18	25	0	3	3	0	0	0	2	0	0	0	0	0	6	0	0	0	.120	.120
Randolph, Willie, New York	.252	90	286	29	72	91	11	1	2	15	6	0	4	40	1	34	1	3	6	.318	.352
Rapp, Pat, San Francisco	.000	3	2	0	0	0	0	0	0	0	1	0	0	0	0	1	0	0	0	.000	.000
Rasmussen, Dennis, Chicago*	.000	3	0	0	0	0	0	0	0	0	0	0	0	0	0	0	0	0	0	.000	.000
Redus, Gary, Pittsburgh	.256	76	176	26	45	67	7	3	3	12	0	0	0	17	0	25	11	4	1	.381	.321
Reed, Darren, Montreal	.173	42	81	10	14	31	2	0	5	10	0	0	1	6	2	23	0	0	3	.383	.239
Reed, Jeff, Cincinnati*	.160	15	25	2	4	4	0	0	0	2	0	0	0	1	1	4	0	0	1	.160	.192
Reynolds, Shane, Houston	.500	8	4	1	2	3	1	0	0	0	2	0	0	0	0	0	0	0	0	.750	.500
Reynoso, Armando, Atlanta	.000	3	2	0	0	0	0	0	0	0	1	0	0	0	0	1	0	0	0	.000	.000
Rhodes, Karl, Houston*	.000	5	4	0	0	0	0	0	0	0	0	0	0	0	0	0	0	0	0	.000	.000
Righetti, Dave, San Francisco*	.143	54	7	0	1	1	0	0	0	0	4	0	0	0	0	4	0	0	0	.143	.143
Rijo, Jose, Cincinnati	.194	33	72	3	14	16	2	0	0	6	6	0	0	0	0	18	0	0	0	.222	.194
Riles, Ernest, Houston*	.262	39	61	5	16	20	1	0	1	4	0	1	0	2	0	11	1	0	0	.328	.281
Risley, Bill, Montreal	.000	1	2	0	0	0	0	0	0	0	0	0	0	0	0	0	0	0	0	.000	.000
Ritchie, Wally, Philadelphia*	.000	40	1	0	0	0	0	0	0	0	0	0	0	1	0	1	0	0	0	.000	.500
Rivera, Ben, Atl.-Phi.	.091	28	33	1	3	3	0	0	0	2	2	0	0	2	0	11	0	0	0	.091	.143
Roberts, Bip, Cincinnati†	.323	147	532	92	172	230	34	6	4	45	1	4	2	62	4	54	44	16	7	.432	.393
Robinson, Don, Philadelphia	.389	10	18	0	7	10	3	0	0	1	0	0	0	0	0	5	0	0	1	.556	.389
Robinson, Jeff D., Chicago	.000	49	12	0	0	0	0	0	0	0	2	0	0	0	0	3	0	0	0	.000	.000
Robinson, Jeff M., Pittsburgh	.091	8	11	0	1	1	0	0	0	1	2	0	0	0	0	6	0	0	0	.091	.091
Rodriguez, Henry, Los Angeles*	.219	53	146	11	32	48	7	0	3	14	1	1	0	8	0	30	0	0	2	.329	.258
Rodriguez, Rich, San Diego*	.000	61	6	0	0	0	0	0	0	0	2	0	0	1	0	0	0	0	1	.000	.143
Rogers, Kevin, San Francisco*	.222	6	9	0	2	2	0	0	0	0	3	0	0	0	0	6	0	0	1	.222	.222
Rojas, Mel, Montreal	.067	68	15	0	1	1	0	0	0	0	0	0	0	0	0	10	0	0	0	.067	.067
Royer, Stan, St. Louis	.323	13	31	6	10	18	2	0	2	9	0	1	0	1	0	4	0	0	0	.581	.333
Ruskin, Scott, Cincinnati	.000	57	3	0	0	0	0	0	0	0	2	0	0	0	0	0	0	0	0	.000	.000
Saberhagen, Bret, New York	.107	17	28	0	3	3	0	0	0	0	3	0	0	1	0	9	0	0	0	.107	.138
Sabo, Chris, Cincinnati	.244	96	344	42	84	145	19	3	12	43	1	6	1	30	1	54	4	5	12	.422	.302
Salazar, Luis, Chicago	.208	98	255	20	53	79	7	2	5	25	3	4	0	11	2	34	1	1	10	.310	.237
Sampen, Bill, Montreal	.000	44	6	0	0	0	0	0	0	0	1	0	0	0	0	5	0	0	0	.000	.000
Samuel, Juan, Los Angeles	.262	47	122	7	32	37	3	1	0	15	4	1	2	7	3	22	2	2	0	.303	.303
Sanchez, Rey, Chicago	.251	74	255	24	64	87	14	3	1	19	5	2	3	10	1	17	2	1	7	.341	.285
Sandberg, Ryne, Chicago	.304	158	612	100	186	312	32	8	26	87	0	6	1	68	4	73	17	6	13	.510	.371
Sanders, Deion, Atlanta*	.304	97	303	54	92	150	6	14	8	28	1	1	2	18	0	52	26	9	5	.495	.346
Sanders, Reggie, Cincinnati	.270	116	385	62	104	178	26	6	12	36	0	1	4	48	2	98	16	7	6	.462	.356
Santiago, Benito, San Diego	.251	106	386	37	97	148	21	0	10	42	0	4	0	21	1	52	2	5	14	.383	.287
Sasser, Mackey, New York*	.241	92	141	7	34	46	6	0	2	18	0	5	0	3	0	10	0	0	4	.326	.248
Scanlan, Bob, Chicago	.000	69	4	1	0	0	0	0	0	0	0	0	0	0	0	1	0	0	0	.000	.000
Scarsone, Steve, Philadelphia	.154	7	13	1	2	2	0	0	0	0	0	0	0	0	0	6	0	0	0	.154	.214
Scheid, Rich, Houston*	.000	7	1	0	0	0	0	0	0	0	0	0	0	0	0	0	0	0	0	.000	.000
Schilling, Curt, Philadelphia	.156	42	64	3	10	11	1	0	0	3	8	0	0	1	0	22	0	0	0	.172	.169
Schofield, Dick, New York	.205	142	420	52	86	120	18	2	4	36	10	3	5	60	4	82	11	4	11	.286	.309
Schourek, Pete, New York*	.048	23	42	0	2	2	0	0	0	1	2	1	0	0	0	13	0	0	0	.048	.047
Scioscia, Mike, Los Angeles*	.221	117	348	19	77	98	6	3	3	24	5	3	1	32	4	31	3	2	9	.282	.286
Scott, Gary, Chicago	.156	36	96	8	15	23	2	0	2	11	1	0	0	5	1	14	0	1	3	.240	.198
Seminara, Frank, San Diego	.118	19	34	3	4	4	0	0	0	0	2	0	0	0	0	11	0	0	0	.118	.143
Servais, Scott, Houston	.239	77	205	12	49	58	9	0	0	15	6	0	5	11	2	25	0	0	7	.283	.294
Service, Scott, Montreal	.000	5	2	0	0	0	0	0	0	0	0	0	0	0	0	2	0	0	0	.000	.000

Player, Team	Avg.	G	AB	R	H	TB	2B	3B	HR	RBI	SH	SF	HP	BB	Int. BB	SO	SB	CS	GI DP	Slg.	OBP
Sharperson, Mike, Los Angeles..	.300	128	317	48	95	125	21	0	3	36	5	3	0	47	1	33	2	2	9	.394	.387
Sheffield, Gary, San Diego.........	.330	146	557	87	184	323	34	3	33	100	0	7	6	48	5	40	5	6	19	.580	.385
Shipley, Craig, San Diego..........	.248	52	105	7	26	32	6	0	0	7	1	0	0	2	1	21	1	1	2	.305	.262
Simms, Mike, Houston...............	.250	15	24	1	6	10	1	0	1	3	0	0	1	2	0	9	0	0	1	.417	.333
Slaught, Don, Pittsburgh.............	.345	87	255	26	88	123	17	3	4	37	6	5	2	17	5	23	2	2	6	.482	.384
Slocumb, Heathcliff, Chicago......	.000	30	4	0	0	0	0	0	0	0	0	0	0	0	0	3	0	0	0	.000	.000
Smith, Bryn, St. Louis.................	.000	13	3	0	0	0	0	0	0	0	1	0	0	0	0	0	0	0	0	.000	.000
Smith, Dwight, Chicago*.............	.276	109	217	28	60	85	10	3	3	24	0	2	1	13	0	40	9	8	1	.392	.318
Smith, Lonnie, Atlanta................	.247	84	158	23	39	69	8	2	6	33	0	4	3	17	1	37	4	0	1	.437	.324
Smith, Ozzie, St. Louis†.............	.295	132	518	73	153	177	20	2	0	31	12	1	0	59	4	34	43	9	11	.342	.367
Smith, Pete, Atlanta..................	.038	12	26	1	1	1	0	0	0	2	3	0	0	2	0	11	0	0	0	.038	.107
Smith, Zane, Pittsburgh*.............	.122	26	49	2	6	8	2	0	0	3	3	0	0	2	0	11	0	0	1	.163	.157
Smoltz, John, Atlanta.................	.160	36	75	7	12	15	0	0	1	4	10	0	0	6	0	32	0	1	1	.200	.222
Snyder, Cory, San Francisco......	.269	124	390	48	105	173	22	2	14	57	2	3	2	23	2	96	4	4	10	.444	.311
Sosa, Sammy, Chicago...............	.260	67	262	41	68	103	7	2	8	25	4	2	4	19	1	63	15	7	4	.393	.317
Springer, Steve, New York..........	.400	4	5	0	2	3	1	0	0	0	0	0	0	0	0	1	0	0	0	.600	.400
Stairs, Matt, Montreal*...............	.167	13	30	2	5	7	2	0	0	5	0	1	0	7	0	7	0	0	2	.233	.316
Stanton, Mike, Atlanta*..............	.500	65	2	1	1	1	0	0	0	0	0	0	0	0	0	0	0	0	0	.500	.500
Stephenson, Phil, San Diego*.....	.155	53	71	5	11	15	2	1	0	8	3	0	0	10	0	11	0	0	0	.211	.259
Stillwell, Kurt, San Diego†..........	.227	114	379	35	86	113	15	3	2	24	4	6	1	26	9	58	4	1	6	.298	.274
Strange, Doug, Chicago†............	.160	52	94	7	15	19	1	0	1	5	2	0	0	10	2	15	1	0	2	.202	.240
Strawberry, Darryl, L.A.*............	.237	43	156	20	37	60	8	0	5	25	0	1	1	19	4	34	3	1	2	.385	.322
Sveum, Dale, Philadelphia†........	.178	54	135	13	24	34	4	0	2	16	0	2	0	16	4	39	0	0	5	.252	.261
Swift, Bill, San Francisco............	.157	34	51	3	8	11	3	0	0	3	5	0	0	1	0	18	0	0	0	.216	.173
Swindell, Greg, Cincinnati..........	.125	31	80	2	10	12	2	0	0	4	5	1	0	1	0	15	0	0	0	.150	.134
Taubensee, Eddie, Houston*......	.222	104	297	23	66	96	15	0	5	28	0	1	2	31	3	78	2	1	4	.323	.299
Teufel, Tim, San Diego...............	.224	101	246	23	55	83	10	0	6	25	0	1	1	31	3	45	2	1	7	.337	.312
Tewksbury, Bob, St. Louis..........	.086	33	70	4	6	7	1	0	0	3	6	0	0	4	0	29	0	0	1	.100	.135
Thompson, Milt, St. Louis*.........	.293	109	208	31	61	84	9	1	4	17	0	2	1	16	3	39	18	6	3	.404	.350
Thompson, Robby, S.F...............	.260	128	443	54	115	184	25	1	14	49	7	4	8	43	1	75	5	9	8	.415	.333
Thompson, Ryan, New York........	.222	30	108	15	24	42	7	1	3	10	0	1	0	8	0	24	2	2	2	.389	.274
Tomlin, Randy, Pittsburgh*.........	.138	35	65	4	9	9	0	0	0	1	7	0	0	3	0	15	0	0	1	.138	.176
Treadway, Jeff, Atlanta*.............	.222	61	126	5	28	36	6	1	0	5	1	0	0	9	4	16	1	2	3	.286	.274
Tucker, Eddie, Houston..............	.120	20	50	5	6	7	1	0	0	3	1	0	2	3	0	13	1	1	2	.140	.200
Uribe, Jose, San Francisco†.......	.241	66	162	24	39	56	9	1	2	13	4	1	0	14	3	25	2	2	3	.346	.299
Valdez, Sergio, Montreal............	.000	27	3	0	0	0	0	0	0	0	0	0	0	0	0	2	0	0	0	.000	.000
Vander Wal, John, Montreal*.......	.239	105	213	21	51	75	8	2	4	20	0	0	2	24	2	36	3	0	2	.352	.316
Van Slyke, Andy, Pittsburgh*......	.324	154	614	103	199	310	45	12	14	89	0	9	4	58	4	99	12	3	9	.505	.381
Varsho, Gary, Pittsburgh*..........	.222	103	162	22	36	60	6	3	4	22	0	1	0	10	1	32	5	2	2	.370	.266
Vatcher, Jim, San Diego.............	.250	13	16	1	4	5	1	0	0	2	0	0	0	3	0	6	0	0	0	.313	.368
Velasquez, Guillermo, S.D.*.......	.304	15	23	1	7	10	0	0	1	5	0	0	0	1	0	7	0	0	0	.435	.333
Villanueva, Hector, Chicago........	.152	51	112	9	17	29	6	0	2	13	0	0	1	11	2	24	0	0	5	.259	.228
Vizcaino, Jose, Chicago†............	.225	86	285	25	64	85	10	4	1	17	5	1	0	14	2	35	3	4	4	.298	.260
Wagner, Paul, Pittsburgh............	.333	6	3	0	1	1	0	0	0	0	0	0	0	0	0	1	0	0	0	.333	.333
Wakefield, Tim, Pittsburgh	.071	14	28	0	2	2	0	0	0	0	4	0	0	1	0	9	0	0	0	.071	.103
Walk, Bob, Pittsburgh.................	.093	36	43	2	4	5	1	0	0	2	1	0	0	2	0	11	0	0	1	.116	.093
Walker, Chico, Chi.-N.Y.†............	.289	126	253	26	73	99	12	1	4	38	0	5	0	27	3	50	15	1	9	.391	.351
Walker, Larry, Montreal*.............	.301	143	528	85	159	267	31	4	23	93	0	8	6	41	10	97	18	6	9	.506	.353
Wallach, Tim, Montreal...............	.223	150	537	53	120	178	29	1	9	59	0	7	8	50	2	90	2	2	10	.331	.296
Walling, Denny, Houston*...........	.333	3	3	1	1	1	0	0	0	0	0	0	0	0	0	0	0	0	0	.333	.333
Walters, Dan, San Diego............	.251	57	179	14	45	70	11	1	4	22	1	2	2	10	0	28	1	0	3	.391	.295
Walton, Jerome, Chicago............	.127	30	55	7	7	9	0	1	0	1	3	0	2	9	0	13	1	2	1	.164	.273
Ward, Kevin, San Diego..............	.197	81	147	12	29	43	5	0	3	12	1	1	2	14	0	38	2	3	8	.293	.274
Webster, Mitch, Los Angeles†.....	.267	135	262	33	70	110	12	5	6	35	8	5	2	27	3	49	11	5	1	.420	.334
Wehner, John, Pittsburgh............	.179	55	123	11	22	28	6	0	0	4	2	0	0	12	2	22	3	0	4	.228	.252
Weston, Mickey, Philadelphia......	.000	1	0	0	0	0	0	0	0	0	0	0	0	0	0	0	0	0	0	.000	.000
Wetteland, John, Montreal..........	.200	67	5	0	1	1	0	0	0	0	0	0	0	0	0	4	0	0	0	.200	.200
Whitehurst, Wally, New York.......	.182	44	22	1	4	5	1	0	0	3	1	0	0	1	0	5	0	1	0	.227	.217
Wilkins, Rick, Chicago*...............	.270	83	244	20	66	101	9	1	8	22	1	1	0	28	7	53	0	2	6	.414	.344
Willard, Jerry, Atl.-Mon.*............	.229	47	48	2	11	18	1	0	2	8	0	0	0	2	1	10	0	0	5	.375	.260
Williams, Brian, Houston............	.133	20	30	2	4	5	1	0	0	4	5	1	0	0	0	13	0	0	1	.167	.129
Williams, Matt, San Francisco....	.227	146	529	58	120	203	13	5	20	66	0	2	6	39	11	109	7	7	15	.384	.286
Williams, Mike, Philadelphia........	.400	5	10	1	4	4	0	0	0	2	1	0	0	0	0	4	0	0	0	.400	.400
Williams, Mitch, Philadelphia*.....	.250	66	4	0	1	1	0	0	0	0	0	0	0	0	0	2	0	0	0	.250	.250
Wilson, Craig, St. Louis..............	.311	61	106	6	33	39	6	0	0	13	2	1	0	10	2	18	1	2	4	.368	.368
Wilson, Dan, Cincinnati..............	.360	12	25	2	9	10	1	0	0	3	0	0	0	3	0	8	0	0	2	.400	.429
Wilson, Steve, Los Angeles*.......	.333	60	3	0	1	1	0	0	0	0	0	0	0	0	0	2	0	0	0	.333	.333
Wilson, Trevor, San Francisco*..	.077	27	39	3	3	4	1	0	0	3	7	0	0	3	0	21	0	0	2	.103	.143
Wohlers, Mark, Atlanta...............	.000	32	2	0	0	0	0	0	0	0	0	0	0	0	0	2	0	0	0	.000	.000
Wood, Ted, San Francisco*........	.207	24	58	5	12	17	2	0	1	3	2	0	1	6	0	15	0	0	4	.293	.292
Woodson, Tracy, St. Louis..........	.307	31	114	9	35	46	8	0	1	22	1	0	1	3	0	10	0	0	2	.404	.331
Wrona, Rick, Cincinnati..............	.174	11	23	0	4	4	0	0	0	0	0	0	0	0	0	3	0	0	2	.174	.174
Yelding, Eric, Houston...............	.250	9	8	1	2	2	0	0	0	0	0	0	0	0	0	3	0	0	0	.250	.250
Young, Anthony, New York..........	.111	52	27	2	3	3	0	0	0	0	0	2	0	1	0	13	0	0	0	.111	.143
Young, Eric, Los Angeles...........	.258	49	132	9	34	38	1	0	1	11	4	0	0	8	0	9	6	1	3	.288	.300
Young, Gerald, Houston†............	.184	74	76	14	14	17	1	1	0	4	4	0	0	10	0	11	6	2	2	.224	.279
Young, Kevin, Pittsburgh............	.571	10	7	2	4	4	0	0	0	4	0	0	0	2	0	1	0	0	1	.571	.667
Zeile, Todd, St. Louis.................	.257	126	439	51	113	160	18	4	7	48	0	7	0	68	4	70	7	10	11	.364	.352

AWARDED FIRST BASE ON CATCHER'S INTERFERENCE—Amaro, Philadelphia (Villanueva); Bream, Atlanta (Hundley); Cedeno, Houston (Walters); Hansen, Los Angeles (O'Brien); Lind, Pittsburgh (Villanueva); Merced, Pittsburgh (Piazza); Van Slyke, Pittsburgh (Servais).

PLAYERS WITH TWO OR MORE TEAMS

Player, Team	Avg.	G	AB	R	H	TB	2B	3B	HR	RBI	SH	SF	HP	BB	Int. BB	SO	SB	CS	GI DP	Slg.	OBP
Bass, Kevin, San Francisco†	.268	89	265	25	71	109	11	3	7	30	1	2	1	16	1	53	7	7	6	.411	.310
Bass, Kevin, New York†	.270	46	137	15	37	59	12	2	2	9	0	1	0	7	2	17	7	2	2	.431	.303
Buechele, Steve, Pittsburgh	.249	80	285	27	71	111	14	1	8	43	2	2	2	34	4	61	0	2	5	.389	.331
Buechele, Steve, Chicago	.276	65	239	25	66	84	9	3	1	21	2	1	5	18	2	44	1	1	5	.351	.338
Cox, Danny, Philadelphia	.091	9	11	0	1	1	0	0	0	1	0	0	0	0	0	7	0	0	0	.091	.091
Cox, Danny, Pittsburgh	.000	16	3	0	0	0	0	0	0	0	0	0	0	0	0	1	0	0	0	.000	.000
Daniels, Kal, Los Angeles*	.231	35	104	9	24	35	5	0	2	8	0	1	1	10	0	30	0	0	7	.337	.302
Daniels, Kal, Chicago*	.250	48	108	12	27	45	6	0	4	17	0	1	1	12	0	24	0	2	3	.417	.328
DeLeon, Jose, St. Louis	.048	29	21	2	1	1	0	0	0	0	4	0	0	2	0	8	0	0	0	.048	.130
DeLeon, Jose, Philadelphia	.400	3	5	2	2	2	0	0	0	1	1	0	0	0	0	1	0	0	0	.400	.400
Heredia, Gil, San Francisco	.167	13	6	0	1	1	0	0	0	0	1	0	0	0	0	1	0	0	0	.167	.167
Heredia, Gil, Montreal	.000	7	3	0	0	0	0	0	0	0	0	0	0	0	0	0	0	0	0	.000	.000
Jackson, Danny, Chicago	.083	19	36	0	3	3	0	0	0	1	4	0	0	0	0	19	0	1	0	.083	.083
Jackson, Danny, Pittsburgh	.083	15	24	2	2	2	0	0	0	1	5	0	0	1	0	12	0	0	0	.083	.120
Javier, Stan, Los Angeles†	.190	56	58	6	11	17	3	0	1	5	1	0	1	6	2	11	1	2	0	.293	.277
Javier, Stan, Philadelphia†	.261	74	276	36	72	88	14	1	0	24	2	2	2	31	0	43	17	1	4	.319	.338
Jones, Barry, Philadelphia	.000	44	2	0	0	0	0	0	0	0	0	0	0	0	0	1	0	0	0	.000	.000
Jones, Barry, New York	.000	17	0	0	0	0	0	0	0	0	0	0	0	0	0	0	0	0	0	.000	.000
Lyons, Steve, Atlanta*	.071	11	14	0	1	3	0	1	0	1	0	0	0	0	0	4	0	0	1	.214	.071
Lyons, Steve, Montreal*	.231	16	13	2	3	3	0	0	0	1	1	0	0	1	0	3	1	2	1	.231	.286
Rivera, Ben, Atlanta	.000	8	1	0	0	0	0	0	0	0	0	0	0	0	0	1	0	0	0	.000	.000
Rivera, Ben, Philadelphia	.094	20	32	1	3	3	0	0	0	2	2	0	0	2	0	10	0	0	0	.094	.147
Walker, Chico, Chicago†	.115	19	26	2	3	3	0	0	0	2	0	1	0	3	0	4	1	0	0	.115	.200
Walker, Chico, New York†	.308	107	227	24	70	96	12	1	4	36	0	4	0	24	3	46	14	1	9	.423	.369
Willard, Jerry, Atlanta*	.348	26	23	2	8	15	1	0	2	7	0	0	0	1	1	3	0	0	3	.652	.375
Willard, Jerry, Montreal*	.120	21	25	0	3	3	0	0	0	1	0	0	0	1	0	7	0	0	2	.120	.154

PINCH-HITTING

TEAM

Team	Avg.	AB	R	H	TB	2B	3B	HR	RBI	SH	SF	HP	BB	Int. BB	SO	SB	CS	GI DP	Slg.	OBP
Chicago	.271	225	18	61	73	6	0	2	23	4	2	0	16	2	48	2	2	7	.324	.317
Los Angeles	.266	304	36	81	119	14	0	8	43	4	2	2	32	2	57	5	1	9	.391	.338
Cincinnati	.253	217	27	55	77	12	2	2	42	0	1	1	11	3	50	1	2	4	.355	.294
Pittsburgh	.237	253	26	60	79	8	4	1	39	1	3	1	32	2	61	1	0	6	.312	.322
Philadelphia	.233	219	26	51	69	6	0	4	30	3	2	0	23	2	61	1	0	6	.315	.303
St. Louis	.232	237	26	55	77	10	0	4	30	0	5	1	32	7	58	9	8	4	.325	.320
Montreal	.228	197	11	45	54	6	0	1	21	1	2	2	23	4	55	1	2	7	.274	.306
Atlanta	.222	234	24	52	86	7	0	9	35	1	2	4	35	3	56	2	1	8	.368	.331
San Francisco	.217	240	19	52	86	7	3	7	40	4	6	3	20	2	55	3	1	6	.358	.279
San Diego	.198	222	15	44	56	6	0	2	22	10	3	0	18	0	48	3	1	9	.252	.255
New York	.182	292	24	53	76	9	1	4	38	4	5	2	27	6	58	6	1	4	.260	.252
Houston	.157	268	15	42	61	3	2	4	35	3	3	1	30	3	77	3	1	4	.228	.242
Totals	.224	2908	267	651	913	94	12	48	394	39	36	16	299	37	690	43	23	74	.314	.296

INDIVIDUAL

TOP 15 PINCH-HITTERS

Minimum 20 at-bats.   *Lefthanded batter.   †Switch-hitter.

Player, Team	Avg.	G	AB	R	H	TB	2B	3B	HR	RBI	SH	SF	HP	BB	Int. BB	SO	SB	CS	GI DP	Slg.	OBP
McGee, Willie, San Francisco†	.524	23	21	1	11	16	3	1	0	7	0	0	0	2	0	4	0	0	0	.762	.565
Dascenzo, Doug, Chicago†	.429	26	21	3	9	9	0	0	0	2	2	0	0	3	0	2	0	0	1	.429	.500
Merced, Orlando, Pittsburgh†	.400	31	25	1	10	16	4	1	0	11	0	0	0	6	2	4	0	0	0	.640	.516
Lindeman, Jim, Philadelphia	.400	21	20	4	8	12	1	0	1	5	0	0	0	2	1	4	0	0	0	.600	.429
Branson, Jeff, Cincinnati*	.382	39	34	7	13	17	4	0	0	10	0	0	0	2	1	5	0	0	0	.500	.417
Barberie, Bret, Montreal†	.364	28	22	2	8	8	0	0	0	5	0	0	0	6	2	5	0	0	1	.364	.500
Webster, Mitch, Los Angeles†	.362	56	47	6	17	23	0	0	2	12	1	2	1	5	0	10	3	0	0	.489	.418
Backman, Wally, Philadelphia*	.345	36	29	6	10	11	1	0	0	6	1	0	0	6	1	7	1	0	0	.379	.457
Pecota, Bill, New York	.300	21	20	1	6	11	0	0	1	6	0	0	0	1	0	1	0	0	2	.550	.333
Daniels, Kal, L.A.-Chi.*	.292	28	24	2	7	8	1	0	0	4	0	0	0	3	0	8	0	0	0	.333	.370
May, Derrick, Chicago*	.286	25	21	1	6	9	0	0	1	1	0	0	0	3	0	8	1	2	0	.429	.348
Smith, Dwight, Chicago*	.286	53	49	7	14	21	4	0	1	6	0	1	0	2	0	7	0	0	1	.429	.327
Jordan, Ricky, Philadelphia	.286	31	28	2	8	9	1	0	0	5	0	0	0	2	0	7	0	0	1	.321	.323
Thompson, Milt, St. Louis*	.276	68	58	9	16	22	3	0	1	8	0	0	0	10	2	11	6	3	0	.379	.382
Benzinger, Todd, Los Angeles†	.271	51	48	4	13	23	4	0	2	8	0	0	0	3	0	11	0	1	0	.479	.314

ALL PINCH-HITTERS

*Lefthanded batter.   †Switch-hitter.

Player, Team	Avg.	G	AB	R	H	TB	2B	3B	HR	RBI	SH	SF	HP	BB	Int. BB	SO	SB	CS	GI DP	Slg.	OBP
Afenir, Troy, Cincinnati	1.000	1	1	1	1	1	0	0	0	0	0	0	0	0	0	0	0	0	0	1.000	1.000
Alicea, Luis, St. Louis†	.000	8	6	0	0	0	0	0	0	0	0	0	0	1	0	2	0	1	0	.000	.143
Alou, Moises, Montreal	.467	16	15	2	7	10	3	0	0	1	0	0	0	0	0	2	0	0	0	.667	.467
Amaro, Ruben Jr., Philadelphia†	.143	16	14	1	2	2	0	0	0	1	1	0	0	2	0	0	0	0	0	.143	.250
Anderson, Dave, Los Angeles	.462	14	13	2	6	11	2	0	1	4	1	0	0	0	0	3	1	0	1	.846	.462
Anthony, Eric, Houston*	.227	24	22	2	5	8	0	0	1	5	0	0	0	2	0	1	0	0	0	.364	.292
Ashley, Billy, Los Angeles	.500	5	4	0	2	3	1	0	0	0	0	0	0	1	0	1	0	0	0	.750	.500
Azocar, Oscar, San Diego*	.179	65	56	5	10	11	1	0	0	5	3	1	0	3	0	6	1	0	0	.196	.217
Backman, Wally, Philadelphia*	.345	36	29	6	10	11	1	0	0	6	1	0	0	6	1	7	1	0	0	.379	.457
Bagwell, Jeff, Houston	.500	4	4	1	2	5	0	0	1	3	0	0	0	1	0	2	0	0	0	1.250	.600
Bailey, Mark, San Francisco†	.000	6	5	0	0	0	0	0	0	0	0	0	0	1	0	2	0	0	0	.000	.167
Barberie, Bret, Montreal†	.364	28	22	2	8	8	0	0	0	5	0	0	0	6	2	5	0	0	1	.364	.500
Bass, Kevin, S.F.-N.Y.†	.241	33	29	3	7	10	1	1	0	3	0	1	1	1	0	4	0	0	1	.345	.303
Batiste, Kim, Philadelphia	.000	4	2	0	0	0	0	0	0	0	0	0	0	0	0	1	0	0	0	.000	.000
Bell, Juan, Philadelphia†	.000	1	1	0	0	0	0	0	0	0	0	0	0	0	0	0	0	0	0	.000	.000
Belliard, Rafael, Atlanta	.273	12	11	2	3	5	2	0	0	3	0	0	0	0	0	3	1	0	0	.455	.333
Benavides, Freddie, Cincinnati	.000	3	2	0	0	0	0	0	0	0	0	0	0	1	0	1	0	0	0	.000	.000
Benjamin, Mike, San Francisco	.000	3	2	0	0	0	0	0	0	0	0	0	0	0	0	1	0	0	0	.000	.000
Benzinger, Todd, Los Angeles†	.271	51	48	4	13	23	4	0	2	8	0	0	0	3	0	11	0	1	0	.479	.314
Berroa, Geronimo, Cincinnati	.111	10	9	1	1	1	0	0	0	0	0	0	0	0	0	3	0	0	0	.111	.200
Berry, Sean, Montreal	.600	5	5	1	3	3	0	0	0	0	0	0	0	0	0	1	0	0	0	.600	.600
Berryhill, Damon, Atlanta†	.250	20	16	2	4	7	0	0	1	3	0	0	0	0	0	0	0	0	0	.438	.400
Biggio, Craig, Houston	.000	2	1	0	0	0	0	0	0	0	0	0	0	1	0	0	0	0	0	.000	.500
Bilardello, Dann, San Diego	.250	5	4	0	1	1	0	0	0	2	0	0	0	1	0	0	0	0	0	.250	.400
Blauser, Jeff, Atlanta	.125	23	16	3	2	3	1	0	0	0	0	0	0	2	0	6	0	0	0	.188	.222
Bonds, Barry, Pittsburgh*	.000	2	2	0	0	0	0	0	0	0	0	0	0	2	0	0	0	0	0	.000	.500
Bonilla, Bobby, New York*	.500	4	4	0	2	2	0	0	0	2	0	0	0	0	0	1	0	0	1	.500	.500
Boston, Daryl, New York*	.175	50	40	6	7	18	2	0	3	7	1	0	0	5	1	11	1	0	1	.450	.261
Bournigal, Rafael, Los Angeles	.000	1	1	0	0	0	0	0	0	0	0	0	0	1	0	0	0	0	0	.000	.500
Bradley, Scott, Cincinnati*	.500	5	4	1	2	3	1	0	0	1	0	0	0	1	0	0	0	0	0	.750	.600
Braggs, Glenn, Cincinnati	.222	19	18	4	4	11	2	1	1	7	1	0	0	2	1	4	0	0	0	.611	.417
Branson, Jeff, Cincinnati*	.382	39	34	7	13	17	4	0	0	10	0	0	0	2	1	5	0	0	0	.500	.417
Bream, Sid, Atlanta*	.333	17	12	1	4	5	1	0	0	3	0	0	0	4	0	1	0	0	0	.417	.529
Brewer, Rod, St. Louis*	.000	1	1	0	0	0	0	0	0	0	0	0	0	0	0	1	0	0	0	.000	.000
Brumfield, Jacob, Cincinnati	.200	6	5	1	1	1	0	0	0	0	0	0	0	0	0	1	0	0	0	.200	.333

Player, Team	Avg.	G	AB	R	H	TB	2B	3B	HR	RBI	SH	SF	HP	BB	Int. BB	SO	SB	CS	GI DP	Slg.	OBP
Buechele, Steve, Chicago	1.000	1	1	0	1	1	0	0	0	1	0	0	0	0	0	0	0	0	0	1.000	1.000
Bullock, Eric, Montreal*	.000	5	5	0	0	0	0	0	0	0	0	0	0	0	0	1	0	0	0	.000	.000
Butler, Brett, Los Angeles*	.333	4	3	1	1	1	0	0	0	0	0	0	0	0	0	1	0	0	0	.000	.000
Cabrera, Francisco, Atlanta	.300	11	10	2	3	9	0	0	2	3	0	0	1	0	1	1	1	0	0	.900	.364
Calderon, Ivan, Montreal	.500	3	2	0	1	1	0	0	0	1	0	0	0	0	0	0	0	0	0	.500	.500
Caminiti, Ken, Houston†	.167	7	6	0	1	1	0	0	0	1	0	0	0	0	0	0	0	0	0	.167	.167
Candaele, Casey, Houston†	.120	33	25	2	3	3	0	0	0	3	1	2	0	4	0	6	1	0	2	.120	.226
Canseco, Ozzie, St. Louis	1.000	1	1	0	1	1	0	0	0	0	0	0	0	0	0	0	0	0	0	1.000	1.000
Carter, Gary, Montreal	.200	11	10	0	2	3	1	0	0	1	0	0	0	1	1	2	0	0	0	.300	.273
Castillo, Braulio, Philadelphia	.000	5	5	0	0	0	0	0	0	1	0	0	0	0	0	1	0	0	0	.000	.000
Cedeno, Andujar, Houston	.000	1	1	0	0	0	0	0	0	0	0	0	0	0	0	1	0	0	0	.000	.000
Cerone, Rick, Montreal	.000	7	6	0	0	0	0	0	0	0	0	0	1	0	0	1	0	0	0	.000	.000
Chamberlain, Wes, Philadelphia	.250	4	4	0	1	1	0	0	0	0	0	0	0	0	0	1	0	0	0	.250	.250
Cianfrocco, Archi, Montreal	.200	11	10	0	2	2	0	0	0	3	0	0	0	1	0	4	0	0	0	.200	.273
Clark, Dave, Pittsburgh*	.182	15	11	1	2	2	0	0	0	2	0	1	0	3	0	6	0	0	0	.182	.333
Clark, Jerald, San Diego	.222	10	9	1	2	2	0	0	0	2	0	1	0	0	0	0	0	0	0	.222	.222
Clark, Will, San Francisco*	.500	3	2	1	1	4	0	0	1	3	0	1	0	0	0	0	0	0	0	2.000	.333
Clayton, Royce, San Francisco	.000	1	1	0	0	0	0	0	0	0	0	0	0	0	0	0	0	0	0	.000	.000
Colbert, Craig, San Francisco	.000	12	11	0	0	0	0	0	0	2	0	1	0	0	0	1	0	0	0	.000	.000
Colbrunn, Greg, Montreal	.000	7	5	0	0	0	0	0	0	0	0	0	0	0	0	0	0	0	1	.000	.000
Cole, Alex, Pittsburgh*	.176	18	17	1	3	4	1	0	0	1	0	1	0	1	0	3	0	0	0	.235	.222
Coleman, Vince, New York†	.375	8	8	2	3	3	0	0	0	0	0	0	0	1	0	5	0	1	1	.375	.375
Coles, Darnell, Cincinnati	.300	11	10	0	3	3	0	0	0	2	0	0	0	0	0	2	1	0	0	.300	.300
Cordero, Wil, Montreal	1.000	2	2	1	2	2	0	0	0	1	0	0	0	0	0	3	0	0	0	.300	.300
Daniels, Kal, L.A.-Chi.*	.292	28	24	2	7	8	1	0	0	4	0	0	0	0	0	8	0	0	0	1.000	1.000
Dascenzo, Doug, Chicago†	.429	26	21	3	9	9	0	0	0	4	0	0	0	3	0	2	2	0	0	.333	.370
Daulton, Darren, Philadelphia*	.200	6	5	0	1	1	0	0	0	1	0	0	0	1	0	2	0	0	0	.429	.500
Davis, Eric, Los Angeles	.000	2	0	0	0	0	0	0	0	0	0	0	0	2	1	0	0	0	0	.200	.333
Dawson, Andre, Chicago	.167	6	6	0	1	1	0	0	0	0	0	0	0	0	0	1	0	0	1	.000	1.000
Distefano, Benny, Houston*	.188	36	32	1	6	8	0	0	0	4	0	0	1	2	0	10	0	0	1	.167	.167
Donnels, Chris, New York*	.000	5	4	0	0	0	0	0	0	0	1	0	0	1	0	0	0	0	0	.250	.257
Doran, Bill, Cincinnati†	.071	16	14	1	1	1	0	0	0	1	0	0	0	2	0	2	0	0	0	.000	.000
Dozier, D.J., New York	.000	5	5	1	0	0	0	0	0	0	0	0	0	0	0	4	0	0	0	.071	.188
Drabek, Doug, Pittsburgh	.000	1	1	0	0	0	0	0	0	0	0	0	0	0	0	0	0	0	0	.000	.000
Duncan, Mariano, Philadelphia	.333	3	3	1	1	1	0	0	0	0	0	0	0	0	0	1	0	0	0	.333	.333
Elster, Kevin, New York	.000	1	1	0	0	0	0	0	0	0	0	0	0	0	0	1	0	0	0	.000	.000
Espy, Cecil, Pittsburgh†	.226	58	53	5	12	15	1	1	0	10	0	0	0	5	0	14	2	0	1	.283	.293
Faries, Paul, San Diego	.750	4	4	1	3	4	1	0	0	0	0	0	0	0	0	0	0	0	1	1.000	.750
Felder, Mike, San Francisco†	.224	55	49	5	11	13	0	1	0	5	2	0	0	4	1	3	2	1	1	.265	.273
Figueroa, Bien, St. Louis	1.000	1	1	0	1	2	1	0	0	3	0	0	0	0	0	0	0	0	0	2.000	1.000
Finley, Steve, Houston*	.000	3	2	0	0	0	0	0	0	1	0	0	0	1	0	0	0	0	0	.000	.333
Fletcher, Darrin, Montreal*	.250	19	16	1	4	4	0	0	0	1	0	0	0	1	0	1	0	0	0	.250	.294
Foley, Tom, Montreal*	.273	13	11	1	3	3	0	0	0	1	0	0	0	1	0	5	0	0	0	.273	.273
Galarraga, Andres, St. Louis	.000	6	6	0	0	0	0	0	0	0	2	0	0	0	0	2	0	0	0	.000	.000
Gallagher, Dave, New York	.167	36	30	1	5	5	0	0	0	5	1	1	0	3	0	3	0	0	0	.167	.235
Gant, Ron, Atlanta	.222	11	9	1	2	2	0	0	0	2	0	0	0	1	0	3	1	1	0	.222	.300
Garcia, Carlos, Pittsburgh	.333	3	3	0	1	1	0	0	0	1	0	0	0	0	0	1	0	0	0	.333	.333
Gardner, Jeff, San Diego*	.000	5	4	0	0	0	0	0	0	0	0	0	0	1	0	1	0	0	0	.000	.200
Gedman, Rich, St. Louis*	.000	2	2	0	0	0	0	0	0	0	0	0	0	0	0	0	0	0	0	.000	.000
Gibson, Kirk, Pittsburgh*	.000	3	3	0	0	0	0	0	0	0	0	0	0	0	0	0	0	0	0	.000	.000
Gilkey, Bernard, St. Louis	.200	25	20	3	4	4	0	0	0	2	0	1	0	4	0	3	2	1	0	.200	.320
Girardi, Joe, Chicago	.500	11	10	1	5	5	0	0	0	2	1	0	0	1	0	5	0	0	0	.500	.545
Glavine, Tom, Atlanta*	.500	2	2	0	1	1	0	0	0	0	0	0	0	0	0	1	0	0	0	.500	.500
Goff, Jerry, Montreal*	.000	3	3	0	0	0	0	0	0	0	0	0	0	0	0	1	0	0	0	.500	.500
Gonzalez, Luis, Houston*	.294	20	17	2	5	9	1	0	1	7	0	0	0	3	0	3	0	0	0	.529	.400
Gooden, Dwight, New York	.500	2	2	0	1	1	0	0	0	0	0	0	0	3	1	3	0	0	0	.500	.500
Goodwin, Tom, Los Angeles*	.400	6	5	0	2	2	0	0	0	0	0	0	0	1	0	0	0	0	0	.400	.500
Grace, Mark, Chicago*	.000	1	1	0	0	0	0	0	0	0	0	0	0	0	0	0	0	0	0	.000	.000
Green, Gary, Cincinnati	.000	1	1	0	0	0	0	0	0	0	0	0	0	0	0	0	0	0	0	.000	.000
Greene, Willie, Cincinnati*	.000	4	4	0	0	0	0	0	0	0	0	0	0	0	0	3	0	0	0	.000	.000
Gregg, Tommy, Atlanta*	.250	9	8	0	2	2	0	0	0	0	0	0	0	0	0	3	0	0	0	.250	.333
Grissom, Marquis, Montreal	.000	11	10	0	0	0	0	0	0	0	0	0	0	1	0	4	0	0	0	.000	.000
Grotewold, Jeff, Philadelphia*	.213	69	61	7	13	24	2	0	3	13	0	0	0	7	0	15	0	0	4	.393	.294
Guerrero, Juan, Houston	.132	43	38	1	5	6	1	0	0	4	0	0	0	5	0	15	1	0	0	.158	.233
Guerrero, Pedro, St. Louis	.000	5	3	0	0	0	0	0	0	0	0	0	0	2	1	1	0	0	0	.000	.400
Gwynn, Tony, San Diego*	.000	1	1	0	0	0	0	0	0	0	0	0	0	0	0	0	0	0	0	.000	.000
Haney, Todd, Montreal	.000	2	1	0	0	0	0	0	0	0	1	0	0	0	0	0	0	0	0	.000	.000
Hansen, Dave, Los Angeles*	.200	32	25	3	5	5	0	0	0	1	0	0	0	4	0	7	0	0	0	.200	.310
Harris, Lenny, Los Angeles*	.207	33	29	3	6	6	0	0	1	2	0	0	0	4	0	7	0	1	0	.360	.310
Hatcher, Billy, Cincinnati	.263	21	19	1	5	5	0	0	0	1	0	0	0	3	1	4	0	0	2	.207	.281
Hernandez, Carlos, Los Angeles	.000	10	10	0	0	0	0	0	0	0	0	0	0	0	0	2	0	0	0	.263	.333
Hernandez, Cesar, Cincinnati	.333	18	18	3	6	7	1	0	0	1	0	0	0	0	0	5	3	1	0	.000	.000
Hershiser, Orel, Los Angeles	.500	2	2	0	1	1	0	0	0	0	0	0	0	0	0	0	0	0	0	.389	.333
Hosey, Steve, San Francisco	.000	3	3	0	0	0	0	0	0	0	0	0	0	0	0	1	0	0	0	.500	.500
Howard, Thomas, San Diego†	.000	3	3	0	0	0	0	0	0	0	0	0	0	0	0	2	0	0	0	.000	.000
Hudler, Rex, St. Louis	.241	31	29	4	7	14	1	0	2	3	0	0	0	0	0	6	0	2	0	.333	.333
Hundley, Todd, New York†	.143	8	7	0	1	2	1	0	0	1	0	1	0	0	0	2	0	0	0	.483	.143
Hunter, Brian, Atlanta	.238	24	21	3	5	13	2	0	2	6	0	1	0	2	0	7	0	0	1	.286	.292
Hurst, Bruce, San Diego*	.000	1	1	0	0	0	0	0	0	0	0	1	0	0	0	0	0	0	0	.619	.000
Incaviglia, Pete, Houston	.222	18	18	1	4	7	0	0	1	3	0	0	0	0	0	9	0	0	0	.389	.263
Jackson, Darrin, San Diego	.000	2	2	0	0	0	0	0	0	0	0	0	0	0	0	0	0	0	0	.000	.000
James, Chris, San Francisco	.205	50	44	4	9	18	1	1	2	5	0	0	1	5	1	11	1	0	1	.409	.300
Javier, Stan, L.A.-Phi.†	.233	33	30	5	7	12	2	0	1	4	1	0	0	2	0	5	1	0	0	.400	.281
Johnson, Howard, New York†	.000	3	3	0	0	0	0	0	0	0	0	0	0	0	0	1	0	0	0	.000	.000
Jones, Chris, Houston	.071	16	14	1	1	1	0	0	0	1	0	0	0	0	0	6	0	0	1	.071	.188
Jones, Jimmy, Houston	.000	1	0	0	0	0	0	0	0	0	0	0	0	2	0	6	0	0	0	.000	.000
Jones, Tim, St. Louis*	.000	2	1	0	0	0	0	0	0	0	0	0	0	0	0	0	0	0	0	.000	.000

Player, Team	Avg.	G	AB	R	H	TB	2B	3B	HR	RBI	SH	SF	HP	BB	Int. BB	SO	SB	CS	GI DP	Slg.	OBP
Jordan, Brian, St. Louis	.200	5	5	0	1	1	0	0	0	0	0	0	0	0	0	2	0	0	1	.200	.200
Jordan, Ricky, Philadelphia	.286	31	28	2	8	9	1	0	0	6	0	1	0	2	0	7	0	0	1	.321	.323
Jose, Felix, St. Louis†	.400	6	5	1	2	2	0	0	0	1	0	0	0	1	1	2	0	0	0	.400	.500
Justice, David, Atlanta*	.000	5	3	0	0	0	0	0	0	0	0	0	0	2	1	0	0	0	0	.000	.400
Karros, Eric, Los Angeles	.571	7	7	3	4	8	1	0	1	4	0	0	0	0	0	2	0	0	0	1.143	.571
Kent, Jeff, New York	.000	1	1	0	0	0	0	0	0	0	0	0	0	0	0	1	0	0	0	.000	.000
King, Jeff, Pittsburgh	.143	7	7	1	1	3	0	1	0	1	0	0	0	0	0	2	0	0	0	.429	.143
Klesko, Ryan, Atlanta*	.000	9	7	0	0	0	0	0	0	0	0	0	1	0	0	2	0	0	0	.000	.125
Kruk, John, Philadelphia*	.000	2	1	0	0	0	0	0	0	0	0	0	0	1	1	1	0	0	0	.000	.500
Kunkel, Jeff, Chicago	.125	9	8	0	1	1	0	0	0	0	0	0	0	0	0	4	0	0	1	.125	.125
Lake, Steve, Philadelphia	.000	3	3	0	0	0	0	0	0	0	0	0	0	0	0	0	0	0	0	.000	.000
Lampkin, Tom, San Diego*	.000	1	1	0	0	0	0	0	0	0	0	0	0	0	0	1	0	0	0	.000	.000
Lankford, Ray, St. Louis*	.000	1	1	0	0	0	0	0	0	0	0	0	0	0	0	1	0	0	0	.000	.000
LaValliere, Mike, Pittsburgh*	.000	2	1	0	0	0	0	0	0	0	0	0	0	1	0	1	0	0	0	.000	.500
Lemke, Mark, Atlanta†	.000	12	10	0	0	0	0	0	0	0	1	0	0	1	0	3	0	0	0	.000	.091
Leonard, Mark, San Francisco*	.214	19	14	3	3	7	1	0	1	3	0	1	1	2	0	6	0	0	1	.500	.333
Lewis, Darren, San Francisco	.167	6	6	0	1	1	0	0	0	1	0	0	0	0	0	2	0	0	0	.167	.167
Lind, Jose, Pittsburgh	.000	1	1	0	0	0	0	0	0	0	0	0	0	0	0	0	0	0	0	.000	.000
Lindeman, Jim, Philadelphia	.400	21	20	4	8	12	1	0	1	5	0	0	0	1	0	4	0	0	0	.600	.429
Litton, Greg, San Francisco	.250	17	16	2	4	10	0	0	2	6	1	0	0	0	0	3	0	0	0	.625	.250
Lopez, Javier, Atlanta	.500	2	2	0	1	2	1	0	0	0	0	0	0	0	0	0	0	0	0	1.000	.500
Lyons, Steve, Atl.-Mon.*	.143	7	7	0	1	1	0	0	0	0	0	0	0	0	0	2	0	1	0	.143	.143
Magadan, Dave, New York*	.000	7	5	0	0	0	0	0	0	0	0	0	0	2	1	2	0	0	1	.000	.286
Mallicoat, Rob, Houston*	.000	1	1	0	0	0	0	0	0	0	0	0	0	0	0	0	0	0	0	.000	.000
Manwaring, Kirt, San Francisco	.500	3	2	0	1	1	0	0	0	1	0	0	0	0	0	0	0	0	0	.500	.500
Marsh, Tom, Philadelphia	.250	8	8	1	2	2	0	0	0	0	0	0	0	0	0	1	0	0	0	.250	.250
Martin, Albert, Pittsburgh*	.167	6	6	0	1	1	0	0	0	1	0	0	0	0	0	4	0	0	0	.167	.167
Martinez, Dave, Cincinnati*	.000	15	12	1	0	0	0	0	0	2	0	1	0	1	0	2	0	0	0	.000	.071
May, Derrick, Chicago*	.286	25	21	1	6	9	0	0	1	1	0	0	0	2	2	7	0	0	0	.429	.348
McClendon, Lloyd, Pittsburgh	.313	20	16	2	5	5	0	0	0	4	0	1	1	1	0	3	0	0	0	.313	.368
McGee, Willie, San Francisco†	.524	23	21	1	11	16	3	1	0	7	0	0	0	2	0	4	0	0	0	.762	.565
McGriff, Fred, San Diego*	.000	1	1	0	0	0	0	0	0	0	0	0	0	0	0	0	0	0	0	.000	.000
McKnight, Jeff, New York†	.231	14	13	2	3	3	0	0	0	0	0	0	0	1	0	2	0	0	0	.231	.286
McNamara, Jim, San Francisco*	.000	1	1	0	0	0	0	0	0	0	0	0	0	0	0	0	0	0	0	.000	.000
Merced, Orlando, Pittsburgh†	.400	31	25	7	10	16	4	1	0	11	0	0	0	6	2	2	0	0	1	.640	.516
Millette, Joe, Philadelphia	.000	2	1	1	0	0	0	0	0	0	1	0	0	0	0	1	0	0	0	.000	.000
Morandini, Mickey, Phi.*	.500	8	6	2	3	3	0	0	0	0	0	0	0	2	0	1	0	0	0	.500	.625
Morris, Hal, Cincinnati*	.250	9	8	0	2	3	1	0	0	0	0	0	0	1	1	5	0	1	0	.375	.333
Murphy, Dale, Philadelphia	.000	1	1	0	0	0	0	0	0	0	0	0	0	0	0	0	0	0	0	.000	.000
Murray, Eddie, New York†	.333	3	3	0	1	1	0	0	0	2	0	0	0	0	0	0	0	0	0	.333	.333
Myers, Randy, San Diego*	.000	1	0	0	0	0	0	0	0	0	1	0	0	0	0	0	0	0	0	.000	.000
Natal, Bob, Montreal	.000	1	1	0	0	0	0	0	0	0	0	0	0	0	0	0	0	0	1	.000	.000
Nieves, Melvin, Atlanta†	.167	7	6	0	1	1	0	0	0	0	0	0	0	1	0	2	0	0	0	.167	.286
Nixon, Otis, Atlanta†	.444	10	9	2	4	4	0	0	0	2	0	0	0	1	0	1	0	0	0	.444	.500
Noboa, Junior, New York	.100	22	20	3	2	2	0	0	0	1	0	0	1	0	0	5	0	0	1	.100	.143
O'Brien, Charlie, New York	.000	5	4	0	0	0	0	0	0	0	0	0	0	1	1	2	0	0	0	.000	.200
Offerman, Jose, Los Angeles†	.000	1	0	0	0	0	0	0	0	0	0	0	0	0	0	0	0	0	0	.000	.000
Olivares, Omar, St. Louis	.333	3	3	1	1	1	0	0	0	0	0	0	0	0	0	1	0	0	0	.333	.333
Oliver, Joe, Cincinnati	.500	2	2	0	1	1	0	0	0	2	0	0	0	0	0	0	0	0	0	.500	.500
Olson, Greg, Atlanta	.000	2	1	0	0	0	0	0	0	0	0	0	0	1	0	0	0	0	0	.000	.500
O'Neill, Paul, Cincinnati*	.333	10	9	1	3	3	0	0	0	4	0	0	0	0	0	0	0	0	0	.333	.333
Oquendo, Jose, St. Louis†	.000	2	2	0	0	0	0	0	0	0	0	0	0	1	0	1	0	0	0	.000	.000
Owen, Spike, Montreal†	.200	7	5	1	1	1	0	0	0	0	0	0	0	1	0	0	0	0	0	.200	.333
Pagnozzi, Tom, St. Louis	.000	4	3	1	0	0	0	0	0	0	0	0	0	1	1	1	0	0	0	.000	.250
Patterson, John, San Francisco†	.167	6	6	0	1	1	0	0	0	0	0	0	0	0	0	4	0	0	0	.167	.167
Pecota, Bill, New York	.300	21	20	1	6	11	2	0	1	6	0	0	0	1	0	1	0	0	0	.550	.333
Pedre, Jorge, Chicago	.000	1	1	0	0	0	0	0	0	0	0	0	0	0	0	0	0	0	0	.000	.000
Pena, Geronimo, St. Louis†	.667	5	3	0	2	2	0	0	0	0	0	0	1	1	0	1	0	0	0	.667	.800
Pendleton, Terry, Atlanta†	.000	2	2	0	0	0	0	0	0	0	0	0	0	0	0	1	0	0	0	.000	.000
Pennyfeather, William, Pit.	.000	2	1	0	0	0	0	0	0	0	1	0	0	0	0	0	0	0	0	.000	.000
Perry, Gerald, St. Louis*	.222	63	54	4	12	18	3	0	1	10	0	1	0	7	2	12	0	1	2	.333	.306
Pettis, Gary, San Diego†	.231	15	13	0	3	4	1	0	0	0	0	0	0	2	0	6	1	0	0	.308	.333
Piazza, Mike, Los Angeles	.400	5	5	0	2	2	0	0	0	2	0	0	0	0	0	0	0	0	0	.400	.400
Pratt, Todd, Philadelphia	.000	5	4	0	0	0	0	0	0	0	0	0	0	1	0	2	0	0	0	.000	.200
Prince, Tom, Pittsburgh	.000	6	6	0	0	0	0	0	0	0	0	0	0	0	0	3	0	0	0	.000	.000
Ramirez, Rafael, Houston	.118	20	17	0	2	3	1	0	0	0	0	0	0	3	0	4	0	0	0	.176	.250
Ramsey, Fernando, Chicago	.000	1	1	0	0	0	0	0	0	0	0	0	0	0	0	0	0	0	0	.000	.000
Randolph, Willie, New York	.143	13	7	3	1	1	0	0	0	0	1	0	1	4	0	2	0	0	0	.143	.500
Redus, Gary, Pittsburgh	.188	24	16	4	3	3	0	0	0	1	0	0	0	7	0	2	2	1	0	.188	.435
Reed, Darren, Montreal	.083	13	12	0	1	2	1	0	0	0	0	0	0	0	0	5	0	0	1	.167	.083
Reed, Jeff, Cincinnati*	.000	9	9	0	0	0	0	0	0	0	0	0	0	0	0	3	0	0	0	.000	.000
Rhodes, Karl, Houston*	.000	4	4	0	0	0	0	0	0	0	0	0	0	0	0	2	0	0	0	.000	.000
Righetti, Dave, San Francisco*	1.000	1	1	0	1	1	0	0	0	0	0	0	0	0	0	0	0	0	0	1.000	1.000
Riles, Ernest, Houston*	.200	25	20	1	4	4	0	0	0	2	0	1	0	1	0	3	0	0	0	.200	.227
Roberts, Bip, Cincinnati†	.333	12	12	1	4	6	0	1	0	4	0	0	0	0	0	4	0	0	1	.500	.333
Robinson, Don, Philadelphia	.000	2	2	0	0	0	0	0	0	0	0	0	0	0	0	1	0	0	0	.000	.000
Rodriguez, Henry, Los Angeles*	.000	7	5	0	0	0	0	0	0	0	0	0	0	0	0	3	0	0	0	.000	.000
Rodriguez, Rich, San Diego*	.000	1	0	0	0	0	0	0	0	0	0	1	0	0	0	0	0	0	0	.000	.000
Royer, Stan, St. Louis	.333	4	3	1	1	2	1	0	0	1	0	0	0	0	0	0	0	0	0	.667	.250
Sabo, Chris, Cincinnati	.000	2	2	0	0	0	0	0	0	0	0	0	0	0	0	0	0	0	1	.000	.000
Salazar, Luis, Chicago	.235	18	17	2	4	4	0	0	0	2	0	1	0	0	0	2	0	0	3	.235	.222
Samuel, Juan, Los Angeles	.308	14	13	0	4	4	0	0	0	2	1	0	0	1	0	1	0	0	0	.308	.308
Sanchez, Rey, Chicago	.333	4	3	0	1	1	0	0	0	0	1	0	0	0	0	0	0	0	0	.333	.333
Sandberg, Ryne, Chicago	.000	1	1	0	0	0	0	0	0	0	0	0	0	0	0	0	0	0	0	.000	.000
Sanders, Deion, Atlanta*	.357	16	14	3	5	8	0	0	1	1	0	0	1	1	0	3	0	0	0	.571	.438
Sanders, Reggie, Cincinnati	.273	11	11	2	3	7	1	0	1	2	0	0	0	0	0	4	0	0	0	.636	.273
Santiago, Benito, San Diego	.250	4	4	0	1	1	0	0	0	0	0	0	0	0	0	1	0	0	1	.250	.250

Player, Team	Avg.	G	AB	R	H	TB	2B	3B	HR	RBI	SH	SF	HP	BB	Int. BB	SO	SB	CS	GI DP	Slg.	OBP
Sasser, Mackey, New York*	.145	61	55	0	8	9	1	0	0	7	0	3	0	1	0	6	0	0	2	.164	.153
Scarsone, Steve, Philadelphia	.200	5	5	1	1	1	0	0	0	0	0	0	0	0	0	4	0	0	0	.200	.200
Scioscia, Mike, Los Angeles*	.154	14	13	0	2	2	0	0	0	0	0	0	1	0	0	4	0	0	0	.154	.214
Scott, Gary, Chicago	.000	4	4	0	0	0	0	0	0	0	0	0	0	0	0	0	0	0	0	.000	.000
Servais, Scott, Houston	.143	7	7	0	1	1	0	0	0	0	0	0	0	0	0	1	0	0	0	.143	.143
Sharperson, Mike, Los Angeles	.211	48	38	8	8	11	3	0	0	2	0	0	0	9	0	4	0	0	3	.289	.362
Sheffield, Gary, San Diego	.500	2	2	0	1	1	0	0	0	1	0	0	0	0	0	0	0	0	0	.500	.500
Shipley, Craig, San Diego	.429	14	14	1	6	6	0	0	0	1	0	0	0	0	0	2	0	0	0	.429	.429
Simms, Mike, Houston	.167	8	6	0	1	1	0	0	0	1	0	0	0	1	0	3	0	0	1	.167	.286
Slaught, Don, Pittsburgh	.286	15	14	0	4	4	0	0	0	1	0	0	0	1	0	2	0	1	0	.286	.333
Smith, Dwight, Chicago*	.286	53	49	7	14	21	4	0	1	5	0	0	0	3	0	8	1	2	0	.429	.327
Smith, Lonnie, Atlanta	.190	51	42	6	8	15	1	0	2	8	0	1	1	7	0	8	0	0	1	.357	.314
Smith, Zane, Pittsburgh*	.000	3	2	0	0	0	0	0	0	0	0	0	0	1	0	2	0	0	0	.000	.333
Smoltz, John, Atlanta	.000	1	1	0	0	0	0	0	0	0	0	0	0	0	0	1	0	0	0	.000	.000
Snyder, Cory, San Francisco	.133	19	15	1	2	2	0	0	0	0	0	1	0	3	0	6	0	0	1	.133	.278
Springer, Steve, New York	.000	2	2	0	0	0	0	0	0	0	0	0	0	0	0	1	0	0	0	.000	.000
Stairs, Matt, Montreal*	.333	3	3	0	1	1	0	0	0	0	0	0	0	0	0	2	0	0	0	.333	.333
Stephenson, Phil, San Diego*	.172	37	29	2	5	7	2	0	0	6	3	0	0	3	0	6	0	0	0	.241	.250
Stillwell, Kurt, San Diego†	.200	5	5	0	1	1	0	0	0	0	0	0	0	0	0	1	1	0	0	.200	.200
Strange, Doug, Chicago†	.100	10	10	1	1	1	0	0	0	0	0	0	0	0	0	2	0	0	0	.100	.100
Strawberry, Darryl, L.A.*	.500	2	2	1	1	1	0	0	0	0	0	0	0	0	0	0	0	0	0	.500	.500
Sveum, Dale, Philadelphia†	.067	15	15	0	1	2	1	0	0	0	0	0	0	0	0	7	0	0	1	.133	.067
Taubensee, Eddie, Houston*	.000	5	4	0	0	0	0	0	0	0	0	0	0	1	0	3	0	0	0	.000	.200
Teufel, Tim, San Diego	.105	24	19	0	2	2	0	0	0	0	0	0	0	3	0	5	0	0	1	.105	.227
Thompson, Milt, St. Louis*	.276	68	58	9	16	22	3	0	1	5	0	0	0	10	2	11	6	3	0	.379	.382
Thompson, Ryan, New York	.000	1	1	0	0	0	0	0	0	0	0	0	0	0	0	0	0	0	0	.000	.000
Thompson, Robby, S.F.	.125	8	8	0	1	2	1	0	0	2	0	0	0	0	0	1	0	0	0	.250	.125
Treadway, Jeff, Atlanta*	.176	18	17	0	3	3	0	0	0	0	0	0	0	1	0	1	0	1	1	.176	.222
Tucker, Eddie, Houston	.000	1	1	0	0	0	0	0	0	0	0	0	0	0	0	0	0	0	0	.000	.000
Uribe, Jose, San Francisco†	.000	2	1	0	0	0	0	0	0	0	0	1	0	0	0	1	0	0	0	.000	.000
Vander Wal, John, Montreal*	.171	49	35	2	6	10	1	0	1	6	0	0	0	12	1	9	1	0	0	.286	.383
Varsho, Gary, Pittsburgh*	.236	62	55	10	13	19	1	1	1	6	0	1	0	6	0	12	2	1	2	.345	.345
Vatcher, Jim, San Diego	.000	1	0	0	0	0	0	0	0	0	0	0	0	1	0	0	0	0	0	.000	1.000
Velasquez, Guillermo, S.D.*	.182	11	11	1	2	5	0	0	1	3	0	0	0	0	0	5	0	0	0	.455	.182
Villanueva, Hector, Chicago	.250	18	16	0	4	5	1	0	0	2	0	0	0	1	0	6	0	0	1	.313	.294
Vizcaino, Jose, Chicago†	.167	7	6	1	1	1	0	0	0	1	0	0	0	1	0	2	1	0	0	.167	.286
Walker, Chico, Chi.-N.Y.†	.175	69	57	3	10	12	2	0	0	10	0	1	0	9	2	11	2	0	3	.211	.284
Walker, Larry, Montreal*	.333	4	3	0	1	1	0	0	0	2	0	1	0	0	0	0	0	0	0	.333	.250
Wallach, Tim, Montreal	.000	4	3	0	0	0	0	0	0	0	0	0	0	0	0	2	0	0	0	.000	.000
Walling, Denny, Houston*	.333	3	3	1	1	1	0	0	0	0	0	0	0	0	0	0	0	0	0	.333	.333
Walters, Dan, San Diego	.000	5	3	0	0	0	0	0	0	0	1	0	1	1	0	1	0	0	0	.000	.200
Walton, Jerome, Chicago	.000	9	5	0	0	0	0	0	0	1	1	0	0	3	0	2	0	0	0	.000	.375
Ward, Kevin, San Diego	.167	43	36	3	6	10	1	0	1	4	1	1	0	3	0	10	0	1	2	.278	.225
Webster, Mitch, Los Angeles†	.362	56	47	6	17	23	0	0	2	12	1	2	1	5	0	10	3	0	0	.489	.418
Wehner, John, Pittsburgh	.417	12	12	1	5	6	1	0	0	1	0	0	0	0	0	3	1	0	0	.500	.417
Wilkins, Rick, Chicago*	.333	15	15	0	5	5	0	0	0	1	0	0	0	0	0	3	0	0	0	.333	.333
Willard, Jerry, Atl.-Mon.*	.231	42	39	1	9	13	1	0	1	6	0	0	0	1	1	9	0	0	5	.333	.250
Williams, Matt, San Francisco	.200	5	5	0	1	1	0	0	0	1	0	0	0	0	0	1	0	0	1	.200	.200
Wilson, Craig, St. Louis	.240	33	25	2	6	7	1	0	0	5	0	1	0	4	0	8	1	0	1	.280	.333
Wilson, Dan, Cincinnati	.500	4	4	0	2	3	1	0	0	3	0	0	0	0	0	0	0	0	0	.750	.500
Wood, Ted, San Francisco*	.286	9	7	1	2	6	1	0	1	1	0	0	1	1	0	2	0	0	0	.857	.444
Woodson, Tracy, St. Louis	.500	2	2	0	1	1	0	0	0	0	0	0	0	0	0	1	0	0	0	.500	.500
Yelding, Eric, Houston	.000	5	5	0	0	0	0	0	0	0	0	0	0	0	0	2	0	0	0	.000	.000
Young, Gerald, Houston†	.050	25	20	2	1	3	0	1	0	0	1	0	0	3	0	5	0	0	0	.150	.174
Young, Kevin, Pittsburgh	.000	1	1	0	0	0	0	0	0	0	0	0	0	0	0	0	0	0	0	.000	.000
Zeile, Todd, St. Louis	.000	4	3	0	0	0	0	0	0	0	0	0	0	1	0	0	0	0	0	.000	.250

PINCH-HITTERS WITH TWO OR MORE TEAMS

Player, Team	Avg.	G	AB	R	H	TB	2B	3B	HR	RBI	SH	SF	HP	BB	Int. BB	SO	SB	CS	GI DP	Slg.	OBP
Bass, Kevin, San Francisco†	.150	23	20	1	3	3	0	0	0	3	0	1	0	2	0	4	0	0	1	.150	.217
Bass, Kevin, New York†	.444	10	9	2	4	7	1	1	0	0	0	0	0	1	1	0	0	0	0	.778	.500
Daniels, Kal, Los Angeles*	.000	7	4	0	0	0	0	0	0	0	0	0	0	2	0	2	0	0	1	.000	.333
Daniels, Kal, Chicago*	.350	21	20	2	7	8	1	0	0	4	0	0	0	1	0	6	0	0	1	.400	.381
Javier, Stan, Los Angeles†	.241	32	29	5	7	12	2	0	1	4	1	0	0	2	0	5	1	0	0	.414	.290
Javier, Stan, Philadelphia†	.000	1	1	0	0	0	0	0	0	0	0	0	0	0	0	0	0	0	0	.000	.000
Lyons, Steve, Atlanta*	.000	3	3	0	0	0	0	0	0	0	0	0	0	0	0	1	0	0	0	.000	.000
Lyons, Steve, Montreal*	.250	4	4	0	1	1	0	0	0	0	0	0	0	0	0	1	0	1	0	.250	.250
Walker, Chico, Chicago†	.111	11	9	0	1	1	0	0	0	2	0	1	0	1	0	0	0	0	0	.111	.182
Walker, Chico, New York†	.188	58	48	3	9	11	2	0	0	8	0	0	0	8	2	11	2	0	3	.229	.304
Willard, Jerry, Atlanta*	.318	25	22	1	7	11	1	0	1	6	0	0	0	1	1	3	0	0	3	.500	.348
Willard, Jerry, Montreal*	.118	17	17	0	2	2	0	0	0	0	0	0	0	0	0	6	0	0	2	.118	.118

PITCHING

Team	W	L	ERA	G	CG	ShO	Sv.	IP	H	TBF	R	ER	HR	SH	SF	HB	BB	Int. BB	SO	WP	Bk.
Atlanta	98	64	3.14	162	26	24	41	1460.0	1321	6072	569	510	89	53	37	26	489	55	948	58	10
Montreal	87	75	3.25	162	11	14	49	1468.0	1296	6139	581	530	92	77	35	50	525	41	1014	48	11
Pittsburgh	96	66	3.35	162	20	20	43	1479.2	1410	6162	595	551	101	80	48	30	455	61	844	52	9
St. Louis	83	79	3.38	162	10	9	47	1480.0	1405	6140	604	556	118	77	46	32	400	46	842	41	3
Chicago	78	84	3.39	162	16	11	37	1469.0	1337	6201	624	554	107	88	52	44	575	75	901	63	11
Los Angeles	63	99	3.41	162	18	13	29	1438.0	1401	6192	636	545	82	109	44	28	553	95	981	64	10
Cincinnati	90	72	3.46	162	9	11	55	1449.2	1362	6042	609	558	109	78	47	28	470	51	1060	54	6
San Diego	82	80	3.56	162	9	11	46	1461.1	1444	6132	636	578	111	93	43	21	439	53	971	25	15
San Francisco	72	90	3.61	162	9	12	30	1461.0	1385	6134	647	586	128	88	42	35	502	61	927	33	22
New York	72	90	3.66	162	17	13	34	1446.2	1404	6118	653	588	98	72	52	36	482	54	1025	34	9
Houston	81	81	3.72	162	5	12	45	1459.1	1386	6213	668	603	114	87	46	38	539	60	978	45	14
Philadelphia	70	92	4.11	162	27	7	34	1428.0	1387	6113	717	652	113	81	53	27	549	37	851	43	9
Totals	972	972	3.50	972	177	157	490	17500.2	16538	73658	7539	6811	1262	983	545	395	5978	689	11342	565	129

NOTE—Totals for earned runs for several clubs do not agree with the composite total for all pitchers of each respective club due to instances in which provisions of Section 10.18(i) of the Scoring Rules were applied. The following differences are to be noted: Houston pitchers add to 606; New York pitchers add to 591; Philadelphia pitchers add to 655; San Diego pitchers add to 581.

TOP 15 QUALIFIERS FOR EARNED-RUN AVERAGE TITLE

Minimum 162 innings.   *Lefthanded pitcher.

Pitcher, Team	W	L	ERA	G	GS	CG	ShO	GF	Sv.	IP	H	TBF	R	ER	HR	SH	SF	HB	BB	Int. BB	SO	WP	Bk.
Swift, Bill, San Francisco	10	4	2.08	30	22	3	2	2	1	164.2	144	655	41	38	6	5	2	3	43	3	77	0	1
Tewksbury, Bob, St. Louis	16	5	2.16	33	32	5	0	1	0	233.0	217	915	63	56	15	9	7	3	20	0	91	2	0
Maddux, Greg, Chicago	20	11	2.18	35	35	9	4	0	0	268.0	201	1061	68	65	7	15	3	14	70	7	199	5	0
Schilling, Curt, Philadelphia	14	11	2.35	42	26	10	4	10	2	226.1	165	895	67	59	11	7	8	1	59	4	147	4	0
Martinez, Dennis, Montreal*	16	11	2.47	32	32	6	0	0	0	226.1	172	900	75	62	12	12	5	9	60	3	147	2	0
Morgan, Mike, Chicago	16	8	2.55	34	34	6	1	0	0	240.0	203	966	80	68	14	10	5	3	79	10	123	11	0
Rijo, Jose, Cincinnati	15	10	2.56	33	33	2	0	0	0	211.0	185	836	67	60	15	9	4	3	44	1	171	2	1
Hill, Ken, Montreal	16	9	2.68	33	33	3	3	0	0	218.0	187	908	76	65	13	15	3	3	75	4	150	11	4
Swindell, Greg, Cincinnati*	12	8	2.70	31	30	5	3	0	0	213.2	210	867	72	64	14	9	7	2	41	4	138	3	2
Fernandez, Sid, New York*	14	11	2.73	32	32	5	2	0	0	214.2	162	865	67	65	12	12	11	4	67	4	193	0	0
Glavine, Tom, Atlanta*	20	8	2.76	33	33	7	5	0	0	225.0	197	919	81	69	6	2	6	2	70	7	129	5	0
Drabek, Doug, Pittsburgh	15	11	2.77	34	34	10	4	0	0	256.2	218	1021	84	79	17	8	8	6	54	8	177	11	1
Smoltz, John, Atlanta	15	12	2.85	35	35	9	3	0	0	246.2	206	1021	90	78	17	7	8	5	80	5	215	17	1
Cone, David, New York	13	7	2.88	27	27	7	5	0	0	196.2	162	831	75	63	12	6	6	9	82	5	214	9	1
Candiotti, Tom, Los Angeles	11	15	3.01	32	30	6	2	0	0	203.2	177	839	78	68	13	20	6	3	63	5	152	9	2

DEPARTMENTAL LEADERS: W—Glavine, Atl., Maddux, Chi., 20; L—Candiotti, L.A., Hershiser, L.A., 15; G—Boever, Hou., 81; GS—Avery, Atl., Maddux, Chi., Smoltz, Atl., 35; CG—Mulholland, Phi., 12; ShO—Cone, N.Y., Glavine, Atl., 5; GF—D. Jones, Hou., 70; Sv.—L. Smith, St.L., 43; IP—Maddux, Chi., 268; H—Benes, S.D., 230; TBF—Maddux, Chi., 1061; R—Belcher, Cin., 104; ER—Belcher, Cin., 99; HR—Black, S.F., 23; SH—Candiotti, L.A., 20; SF—Belcher, Cin., Fernandez, N.Y., 11; HB—Maddux, Chi., 14; TBB—Cone, N.Y., 82; IBB—Gott, L.A., Hershiser, L.A., McDowell, L.A., 13; SO—Smoltz, Atl., 215; WP—Smoltz, Atl., 17; Bk.—Black, S.F., Wilson, S.F., 7.

ALL PITCHERS

*Lefthanded pitcher.

Pitcher, Team	W	L	ERA	G	GS	CG	ShO	GF	Sv.	IP	H	TBF	R	ER	HR	SH	SF	HB	BB	Int. BB	SO	WP	Bk.
Abbott, Kyle, Philadelphia*	1	14	5.13	31	19	0	0	0	0	133.1	147	577	80	76	20	6	5	1	45	0	88	9	1
Agosto, Juan, St. Louis*	2	4	6.25	22	0	0	0	10	0	31.2	39	143	24	22	2	3	3	9	2	13	2	0
Andersen, Larry, San Diego	1	1	3.34	34	0	0	0	13	2	35.0	26	140	14	13	2	1	1	1	8	2	35	0	0
Ashby, Andy, Philadelphia	1	3	7.54	10	8	0	0	0	0	37.0	42	171	31	31	6	2	2	1	21	0	24	2	0
Assenmacher, Paul, Chi.*	4	4	4.10	70	0	0	0	23	8	68.0	72	298	32	31	6	1	2	3	26	5	67	4	0
Astacio, Pedro, Los Angeles	5	5	1.98	11	11	4	4	0	0	82.0	80	341	23	18	3	1	3	2	20	4	43	1	0
Avery, Steve, Atlanta*	11	11	3.20	35	35	2	2	0	0	233.2	216	969	95	83	14	12	8	0	71	3	129	7	3
Ayala, Bobby, Cincinnati	2	1	4.34	5	5	0	0	0	0	29.0	33	127	15	14	1	2	0	1	13	2	23	0	0
Ayrault, Bob, Philadelphia	2	2	3.12	30	0	0	0	7	0	43.1	32	178	16	15	5	0	4	3	17	1	27	0	0
Baller, Jay, Philadelphia	0	0	8.18	8	0	0	0	4	0	11.0	10	51	10	10	5	0	1	0	10	0	9	1	0
Bankhead, Scott, Cincinnati	10	4	2.93	54	0	0	0	10	1	70.2	57	299	26	23	4	3	3	3	29	5	53	6	0
Barnes, Brian, Montreal*	6	6	2.97	21	17	0	0	2	0	100.0	77	417	34	33	9	5	1	3	46	1	65	1	2
Batista, Miguel, Pittsburgh	0	0	9.00	1	0	0	0	1	0	2.0	4	13	2	2	1	0	0	0	3	0	1	0	0
Beck, Rod, San Francisco	3	3	1.76	65	0	0	0	42	17	92.0	62	352	20	18	6	4	2	2	15	2	87	5	2
Belcher, Tim, Cincinnati	15	14	3.91	35	34	2	1	1	0	227.2	201	949	104	99	17	12	11	3	80	2	149	3	1
Belinda, Stan, Pittsburgh	6	4	3.15	59	0	0	0	42	18	71.1	58	299	26	25	8	4	6	0	29	5	57	1	0
Benes, Andy, San Diego	13	14	3.35	34	34	2	2	0	0	231.1	230	961	90	86	14	19	6	5	61	6	169	1	1
Berenguer, Juan, Atlanta	3	1	5.13	28	0	0	0	8	1	33.1	35	148	22	19	7	1	0	1	16	4	19	2	2
Bielecki, Mike, Atlanta	2	4	2.57	19	14	1	1	0	0	80.2	77	336	27	23	2	3	2	1	27	1	62	4	0
Birkbeck, Mike, New York	0	1	9.00	1	1	0	0	0	0	7.0	12	33	7	7	3	1	0	1	1	2	1	0	0
Black, Bud, San Francisco*	10	12	3.97	28	28	2	1	0	0	177.0	178	749	88	78	23	8	4	1	59	11	82	3	7
Blair, Willie, Houston	5	7	4.00	29	8	0	0	1	0	78.2	74	331	47	35	5	4	3	2	25	2	48	2	0
Boever, Joe, Houston	3	6	2.51	81	0	0	0	26	2	111.1	103	479	38	31	3	10	4	4	45	9	67	4	0
Bolton, Tom, Cincinnati*	3	3	5.24	16	8	0	0	3	0	46.1	52	210	28	27	9	1	1	2	23	2	27	3	1
Borbon, Pedro, Atlanta*	0	1	6.75	2	0	0	0	2	0	1.1	2	7	1	1	0	0	0	0	1	1	0	0	0
Boskie, Shawn, Chicago	5	11	5.01	23	18	0	0	2	0	91.2	96	393	55	51	14	9	6	4	36	3	39	5	1
Bottenfield, Kent, Montreal	1	2	2.23	10	4	0	0	2	1	32.1	26	135	9	8	1	1	2	1	11	1	14	0	0

Pitcher, Team	W	L	ERA	G	GS	CG	ShO	GF	Sv.	IP	H	TBF	R	ER	HR	SH	SF	HB	BB	Int. BB	SO	WP	Bk.
Bowen, Ryan, Houston	0	7	10.96	11	9	0	0	2	0	33.2	48	179	43	41	8	3	0	2	30	3	22	5	0
Brantley, Cliff, Philadelphia	2	6	4.60	28	9	0	0	6	0	76.1	71	353	45	39	6	5	3	4	58	4	32	4	1
Brantley, Jeff, San Francisco	7	7	2.95	56	4	0	0	32	7	91.2	67	381	32	30	8	7	3	3	45	5	86	3	1
Brink, Brad, Philadelphia	0	4	4.14	8	7	0	0	0	0	41.1	53	187	27	19	2	1	0	1	13	2	16	0	0
Brocail, Doug, San Diego	0	0	6.43	3	3	0	0	0	0	14.0	17	64	10	10	2	2	0	0	5	0	15	0	0
Brown, Keith, Cincinnati	0	1	4.50	2	2	0	0	0	0	8.0	10	37	5	4	2	0	0	0	5	0	5	0	0
Browning, Tom, Cincinnati*	6	5	5.07	16	16	0	0	0	0	87.0	108	386	49	49	6	5	4	2	28	7	33	3	1
Bullinger, Jim, Chicago	2	8	4.66	39	9	1	0	15	7	85.0	72	380	49	44	9	9	4	4	54	6	36	4	0
Burba, Dave, San Francisco	2	7	4.97	23	11	0	0	4	0	70.2	80	318	43	39	4	2	4	2	31	2	47	1	1
Burke, Tim, New York	1	2	5.74	15	0	0	0	9	0	15.2	26	76	15	10	1	1	1	0	3	0	7	2	0
Burkett, John, S.F.	13	9	3.84	32	32	3	1	0	0	189.2	194	799	96	81	13	11	4	4	45	6	107	0	0
Candelaria, John, L.A.*	2	5	2.84	50	0	0	0	11	5	25.1	20	108	9	8	1	2	2	0	13	3	23	1	0
Candiotti, Tom, Los Angeles	11	15	3.00	32	30	6	2	1	0	203.2	177	839	78	68	13	20	6	3	63	5	152	9	2
Carpenter, Cris, St. Louis	5	4	2.97	73	0	0	0	21	1	88.0	69	355	29	29	10	8	3	4	27	8	46	5	0
Carter, Larry, San Francisco	1	5	4.64	6	6	0	0	0	0	33.0	34	147	17	17	6	2	1	0	18	0	21	2	0
Castillo, Frank, Chicago	10	11	3.46	33	33	0	0	0	0	205.1	179	856	91	79	19	11	5	6	63	6	135	11	0
Chapin, Darrin, Philadelphia	0	0	9.00	1	0	0	0	0	0	2.0	2	8	2	2	1	0	0	0	0	0	1	1	0
Charlton, Norm, Cincinnati*	4	2	2.99	64	0	0	0	46	26	81.1	79	341	39	27	7	7	3	3	26	4	90	8	0
Clark, Mark, St. Louis	3	10	4.45	20	20	1	1	0	0	113.1	117	488	59	56	12	7	4	0	36	2	44	4	0
Clements, Pat, San Diego*	2	1	2.66	27	0	0	0	7	0	23.2	25	105	9	7	0	2	0	2	12	4	11	0	0
Cole, Victor, Pittsburgh	0	2	5.48	8	4	0	0	2	0	23.0	23	104	14	14	1	1	1	0	14	0	12	1	0
Combs, Pat, Philadelphia*	1	1	7.71	4	4	0	0	0	0	18.2	20	88	16	16	0	3	1	0	12	0	11	1	0
Cone, David, New York	13	7	2.88	27	27	7	5	0	0	196.2	162	831	75	63	12	6	6	9	82	5	214	9	1
Cooke, Steve, Pittsburgh*	2	0	3.52	11	0	0	0	8	1	23.0	22	91	9	9	2	0	0	0	4	1	10	0	0
Cormier, Rheal, St. Louis*	10	10	3.68	31	30	3	0	1	0	186.0	194	772	83	76	15	11	3	5	33	2	117	4	2
Cox, Danny, Phi-Pit.	5	3	4.60	25	7	0	0	8	3	62.2	66	278	37	32	5	5	3	0	27	2	48	1	0
Crews, Tim, Los Angeles	0	3	5.19	49	2	0	0	13	0	78.0	95	339	46	45	6	6	5	2	20	9	43	3	0
Davis, Mark, Atlanta*	1	0	7.02	14	0	0	0	7	0	16.2	22	85	13	13	3	0	1	1	13	2	15	4	1
DeLeon, Jose, St.L.-Phi.	2	8	4.37	32	18	0	0	3	0	117.1	111	506	63	57	7	6	6	2	48	1	79	3	0
Deshaies, Jim, San Diego*	4	7	3.28	15	15	0	0	0	0	96.0	92	395	40	35	6	3	2	1	33	2	46	1	2
Dewey, Mark, New York	1	0	4.32	20	0	0	0	6	0	33.1	37	143	16	16	2	1	0	0	10	2	24	0	1
Dibble, Rob, Cincinnati	3	5	3.07	63	0	0	0	49	25	70.1	48	286	26	24	3	2	2	2	31	2	110	6	0
DiPino, Frank, St. Louis*	0	0	1.64	9	0	0	0	3	0	11.0	9	45	2	2	0	1	0	0	3	0	8	0	0
Downs, Kelly, San Francisco	1	2	3.47	19	7	0	0	5	0	62.1	65	272	27	24	4	7	2	3	24	0	33	4	0
Drabek, Doug, Pittsburgh	15	11	2.77	34	34	10	4	0	0	256.2	218	1021	84	79	17	8	8	6	54	8	177	11	1
Eiland, Dave, San Diego	0	2	5.67	7	7	0	0	0	0	27.0	33	120	21	17	1	0	0	0	5	0	10	0	1
Fassero, Jeff, Montreal*	8	7	2.84	70	0	0	0	22	1	85.2	81	368	35	27	1	5	2	2	34	6	63	7	1
Fernandez, Sid, New York*	14	11	2.73	32	32	5	2	0	0	214.2	162	865	67	65	12	12	11	4	67	4	193	0	0
Filer, Tom, New York	0	1	2.05	9	1	0	0	1	0	22.0	18	88	8	5	2	1	0	0	6	2	9	1	0
Foster, Steve, Cincinnati	1	1	2.88	31	1	0	0	7	2	50.0	52	209	16	16	4	5	2	0	13	1	34	1	0
Franco, John, New York*	6	2	1.64	31	0	0	0	30	15	33.0	24	128	6	6	1	0	2	0	11	2	20	0	0
Freeman, Marvin, Atlanta	7	5	3.22	58	0	0	0	15	3	64.1	61	276	26	23	7	2	1	1	29	7	41	4	0
Gardner, Mark, Montreal	12	10	4.36	33	30	0	0	1	0	179.2	179	778	91	87	15	12	7	9	60	2	132	2	0
Gibson, Paul, New York*	0	1	5.23	43	1	0	0	12	0	62.0	70	273	37	36	7	3	1	0	25	0	49	1	0
Glavine, Tom, Atlanta*	20	8	2.76	33	33	7	5	0	0	225.0	197	919	81	69	6	2	6	2	70	7	129	5	0
Gleaton, Jerry Don, Pittsburgh*	1	0	4.26	23	0	0	0	6	0	31.2	34	142	16	15	4	2	1	0	19	3	18	1	0
Gooden, Dwight, New York	10	13	3.67	31	31	3	0	0	0	206.0	197	863	93	84	11	10	7	3	70	7	145	3	1
Gott, Jim, Los Angeles	3	3	2.45	68	0	0	0	28	6	88.0	72	369	27	24	4	6	1	1	41	13	75	9	3
Greene, Tommy, Phi.	3	3	5.32	13	12	0	0	0	0	64.1	75	298	39	38	5	4	2	0	34	2	39	1	0
Gross, Kevin, Los Angeles	8	13	3.17	34	30	4	3	0	0	204.2	182	856	82	72	11	14	6	3	77	10	158	4	2
Gross, Kip, Los Angeles	1	1	4.18	16	1	0	0	7	0	23.2	32	109	14	11	1	0	0	0	10	1	14	1	1
Guetterman, Lee, New York*	3	4	5.82	43	0	0	0	15	2	43.1	57	196	28	28	5	2	3	1	14	5	15	3	0
Hammond, Chris, Cin.*	7	10	4.21	28	26	0	0	1	0	147.1	149	627	75	69	13	5	3	3	55	6	79	6	0
Haney, Chris, Montreal*	2	3	5.45	9	6	1	1	2	0	38.0	40	165	25	23	6	0	3	4	10	0	27	5	1
Harkey, Mike, Chicago	4	0	1.89	7	7	0	0	0	0	38.0	34	159	13	8	4	1	2	1	15	0	21	3	1
Harnisch, Pete, Houston	9	10	3.70	34	34	0	0	0	0	206.2	182	859	92	85	18	5	5	5	64	3	164	4	1
Harris, Gene, San Diego	0	2	2.95	14	1	0	0	2	0	21.1	15	90	8	7	0	3	0	1	9	0	19	1	1
Harris, Greg W., San Diego	4	8	4.12	20	20	1	0	0	0	118.0	113	496	62	54	13	8	3	2	35	2	66	2	1
Hartley, Mike, Philadelphia	7	6	3.44	46	0	0	0	15	0	55.0	54	243	23	21	5	5	1	2	23	6	53	4	0
Hartsock, Jeff, Chicago	0	0	6.75	4	0	0	0	0	0	9.1	15	46	7	7	2	1	1	0	4	0	6	2	0
Henry, Butch, Houston*	6	9	4.02	28	28	2	1	0	0	165.2	185	710	81	74	16	12	7	1	41	7	96	2	2
Henry, Dwayne, Cincinnati	3	3	3.33	60	0	0	0	11	0	83.2	59	352	31	31	4	7	3	1	44	6	72	12	0
Heredia, Gil, S.F.-Mon.	2	3	4.23	20	5	0	0	4	0	44.2	44	187	23	21	4	2	1	1	20	1	22	1	0
Hernandez, Jeremy, S.D.	1	4	4.17	26	0	0	0	11	1	36.2	39	157	17	17	4	6	5	1	11	5	25	0	0
Hernandez, Xavier, Houston	9	1	2.11	77	0	0	0	25	7	111.0	81	454	31	26	5	3	2	3	42	7	96	5	0
Hershiser, Orel, Los Angeles	10	15	3.67	33	33	1	0	0	0	210.2	209	910	101	86	15	15	6	8	69	13	130	10	0
Hickerson, Bryan, S.F.*	5	3	3.09	61	1	0	0	8	0	87.1	74	345	31	30	7	4	5	1	21	2	68	4	1
Hill, Ken, Montreal	16	9	2.68	33	33	3	3	0	0	218.0	187	908	76	65	13	15	3	3	75	4	150	11	4
Hill, Milt, Cincinnati	0	0	3.15	14	0	0	0	5	1	20.0	15	80	9	7	1	2	1	1	5	2	10	0	0
Hillman, Eric, New York*	2	2	5.33	11	8	0	0	2	0	52.1	67	227	31	31	9	3	1	2	10	2	16	1	0
Hollins, Jessie, Chicago	0	0	13.50	4	0	0	0	3	0	4.2	8	27	7	7	1	0	2	0	5	0	0	1	0
Howell, Jay, Los Angeles	1	3	1.54	41	0	0	0	26	4	46.2	41	203	9	8	2	5	1	1	18	5	36	3	1
Hurst, Bruce, San Diego*	14	9	3.85	32	32	6	4	0	0	217.1	223	902	96	93	22	12	4	0	51	3	131	4	3
Hurst, Jonathan, Montreal	1	1	5.51	3	3	0	0	0	0	16.1	18	72	10	10	1	0	0	1	7	0	4	1	0
Innis, Jeff, New York	6	9	2.86	76	0	0	0	28	1	88.0	85	373	32	28	4	7	4	6	36	4	39	1	0
Jackson, Danny, Chi.-Pit.*	8	13	3.84	34	34	0	0	0	0	201.1	211	883	99	86	6	17	10	4	77	6	97	2	2
Jackson, Mike, S.F.	6	6	3.73	67	0	0	0	24	2	82.0	76	346	35	34	7	5	2	4	33	10	80	1	0
Jones, Barry, Phi.-N.Y.	7	6	5.68	61	0	0	0	17	1	69.2	85	319	46	44	3	3	3	2	35	7	30	2	2
Jones, Doug, Houston	11	8	1.85	80	0	0	0	70	36	111.2	96	440	29	23	5	9	0	5	17	5	93	2	1
Jones, Jimmy, Houston	10	6	4.07	25	23	0	0	1	0	139.1	135	579	64	63	13	7	4	5	39	3	69	4	1
Kile, Darryl, Houston	5	10	3.95	22	22	2	0	0	0	125.1	124	554	61	55	8	5	6	4	63	4	90	3	4
Krueger, Bill, Montreal*	0	2	6.75	9	2	0	0	3	0	17.1	23	81	13	13	0	0	0	1	7	0	13	1	0
Lamp, Dennis, Pittsburgh	1	1	5.14	21	0	0	0	2	0	28.0	33	125	16	16	3	1	0	2	9	4	15	0	1
Landrum, Bill, Montreal	1	1	7.20	18	0	0	0	6	0	20.0	27	95	16	16	3	1	0	2	9	2	7	0	0
Lefferts, Craig, San Diego*	13	9	3.69	27	27	0	0	0	0	163.1	180	684	76	67	16	12	5	0	35	2	81	4	1
Leibrandt, Charlie, Atlanta*	15	7	3.36	32	31	5	2	0	0	193.0	191	799	78	72	9	7	4	5	42	4	104	3	2
Maddux, Greg, Chicago	20	11	2.18	35	35	9	4	0	0	268.0	201	1061	68	65	7	15	3	14	70	7	199	5	0

Pitcher, Team	W	L	ERA	G	GS	CG	ShO	GF	Sv.	IP	H	TBF	R	ER	HR	SH	SF	HB	BB	Int. BB	SO	WP	Bk.
Maddux, Mike, San Diego	2	2	2.37	50	1	0	0	14	5	79.2	71	330	25	21	2	2	3	0	24	4	60	4	1
Magrane, Joe, St. Louis*	1	2	4.02	5	5	0	0	0	0	31.1	34	143	15	14	2	3	1	2	15	0	20	4	0
Mallicoat, Rob, Houston*	0	0	7.23	23	0	0	0	6	0	23.2	26	120	19	19	2	3	1	5	19	2	20	2	0
Martinez, Dennis, Montreal	16	11	2.47	32	32	6	0	0	0	226.1	172	900	75	62	12	12	5	9	60	3	147	2	0
Martinez, Pedro, L.A.	0	1	2.25	2	1	0	0	1	0	8.0	6	31	2	2	0	0	0	0	1	0	8	0	0
Martinez, Ramon, L.A.	8	11	4.00	25	25	1	1	0	0	150.2	141	662	82	67	11	12	1	5	69	4	101	9	0
Mason, Roger, Pittsburgh	5	7	4.09	65	0	0	0	26	8	88.0	80	374	41	40	11	8	4	4	33	8	56	3	0
Mathews, Greg, Phi.*	2	3	5.16	14	7	0	0	1	0	52.1	54	228	31	30	7	2	1	1	24	2	27	1	2
Maysey, Matt, Montreal	0	0	3.86	2	0	0	0	1	0	2.1	4	12	1	1	1	0	0	1	0	0	1	0	0
McClure, Bob, St. Louis*	2	2	3.17	71	0	0	0	16	0	54.0	52	230	21	19	6	1	3	2	25	5	24	1	0
McDowell, Roger, L.A.	6	10	4.09	65	0	0	0	39	14	83.2	103	393	46	38	3	10	3	1	42	13	50	4	1
McElroy, Chuck, Chicago*	4	7	3.55	72	0	0	0	30	6	83.2	73	369	40	33	5	5	5	0	51	10	83	3	0
Melendez, Jose, San Diego	6	7	2.92	56	3	0	0	18	0	89.1	82	363	32	29	9	7	4	3	20	7	82	1	1
Menendez, Tony, Cincinnati	1	0	1.93	3	0	0	0	1	0	4.2	1	15	1	1	1	0	0	0	0	0	5	0	0
Mercker, Kent, Atlanta*	3	2	3.42	53	0	0	0	18	6	68.1	51	289	27	26	4	4	1	3	35	1	49	6	0
Miller, Paul, Pittsburgh	1	0	2.38	6	0	0	0	1	0	11.1	11	46	3	3	0	1	1	0	1	0	5	1	0
Minor, Blas, Pittsburgh	0	0	4.50	1	0	0	0	0	0	2.0	3	9	2	1	0	0	0	0	0	0	0	1	0
Morgan, Mike, Chicago	16	8	2.55	34	34	6	1	0	0	240.0	203	966	80	68	14	10	5	3	79	10	123	11	0
Mulholland, Terry, Phi.*	13	11	3.81	32	32	12	2	0	0	229.0	227	937	101	97	14	10	7	3	46	3	125	3	0
Murphy, Rob, Houston*	3	1	4.04	59	0	0	0	6	0	55.2	56	242	28	25	2	3	3	0	21	4	42	4	0
Myers, Randy, San Diego*	3	6	4.29	66	0	0	0	57	38	79.2	84	348	38	38	7	7	5	1	34	3	66	5	0
Nabholz, Chris, Montreal*	11	12	3.32	32	32	1	1	0	0	195.0	176	812	80	72	11	7	4	5	74	2	130	5	1
Neagle, Denny, Pittsburgh*	4	6	4.48	55	6	0	0	8	2	86.1	81	380	46	43	9	4	3	2	43	8	77	3	2
Nied, David, Atlanta	3	0	1.17	6	2	0	0	0	0	23.0	10	83	3	3	0	1	0	0	5	0	19	0	0
Ojeda, Bob, Los Angeles*	6	9	3.63	29	29	2	1	0	0	166.1	169	731	80	67	8	11	7	1	81	8	94	3	0
Olivares, Omar, St. Louis	9	9	3.84	32	30	1	0	1	0	197.0	189	818	84	84	20	8	7	4	63	5	124	2	0
Oliveras, Francisco, S.F.	0	3	3.63	16	7	0	0	3	0	44.2	41	179	19	18	11	2	2	1	10	2	17	0	0
Osborne, Donovan, St.L.*	11	9	3.77	34	29	0	0	2	0	179.0	193	754	91	75	14	7	4	2	38	2	104	6	0
Osuna, Al, Houston*	6	3	4.23	66	0	0	0	17	0	61.2	52	270	29	29	8	5	6	1	38	5	37	3	1
Palacios, Vince, Pittsburgh	3	2	4.25	20	8	0	0	4	0	53.0	56	232	25	25	1	4	1	0	27	1	33	7	0
Patterson, Bob, Pittsburgh*	6	3	2.92	60	0	0	0	26	9	64.2	59	268	22	21	7	3	2	0	23	6	43	3	0
Patterson, Ken, Chicago*	2	3	3.89	32	1	0	0	4	0	41.2	41	191	25	18	7	6	4	1	27	6	23	3	1
Pecota, Bill, New York	0	0	9.00	1	0	0	0	1	0	1.0	1	4	1	1	1	0	0	0	0	0	0	0	0
Pena, Alejandro, Atlanta	1	6	4.07	41	0	0	0	31	15	42.0	40	173	19	19	7	2	1	0	13	5	34	0	0
Pena, Jim, San Francisco*	1	1	3.48	25	2	0	0	4	0	44.0	49	204	19	17	4	8	1	1	20	5	32	0	0
Perez, Mike, St. Louis	9	3	1.84	77	0	0	0	22	0	93.0	70	377	23	19	4	7	4	1	32	9	46	4	0
Portugal, Mark, Houston	6	3	2.66	18	16	1	1	0	0	101.1	76	405	32	30	7	5	1	1	41	3	62	1	1
Pugh, Tim, Cincinnati	4	2	2.58	7	7	0	0	0	0	45.1	47	187	15	13	2	2	1	1	13	3	18	0	0
Rapp, Pat, San Francisco	0	2	7.20	3	2	0	0	1	0	10.0	8	43	8	8	0	2	0	1	6	1	3	0	0
Rasmussen, Dennis, Chi.*	0	0	10.80	3	1	0	0	1	0	5.0	7	24	6	6	2	0	1	1	2	1	0	0	0
Reardon, Jeff, Atlanta	3	0	1.15	14	0	0	0	11	3	15.2	14	62	2	2	0	1	0	1	2	1	7	0	0
Reed, Steve, San Francisco	1	0	2.30	18	0	0	0	2	0	15.2	13	63	5	4	2	0	0	1	3	0	11	0	0
Reynolds, Shane, Houston	1	3	7.11	8	5	0	0	0	0	25.1	42	122	22	20	2	6	1	0	6	1	10	1	1
Reynoso, Armando, Atlanta	1	0	4.70	3	1	0	0	1	1	7.2	11	32	4	4	2	1	0	1	2	1	2	0	0
Righetti, Dave, S.F.*	2	7	5.06	54	4	0	0	23	3	78.1	79	340	47	44	4	6	4	0	36	5	47	5	2
Rijo, Jose, Cincinnati	15	10	2.56	33	33	2	0	0	0	211.0	185	836	67	60	15	9	4	3	44	1	171	2	1
Risley, Bill, Montreal	1	0	1.80	1	1	0	0	0	0	5.0	4	19	1	1	0	1	0	0	1	0	2	0	0
Ritchie, Wally, Philadelphia*	2	1	3.00	40	0	0	0	13	1	39.0	44	174	17	13	3	4	0	0	17	3	19	0	0
Rivera, Ben, Atl.-Phi.	7	4	3.07	28	14	4	1	7	0	117.1	99	487	40	40	9	5	2	4	45	4	77	5	0
Robinson, Don, Philadelphia	1	4	6.18	8	8	0	0	0	0	43.2	49	183	32	30	6	3	6	1	4	0	17	0	0
Robinson, Jeff D., Chicago	4	3	3.00	49	5	0	0	12	1	78.0	76	335	29	26	5	2	2	2	40	7	46	8	1
Robinson, Jeff M., Pittsburgh	3	1	4.46	8	7	0	0	0	0	36.1	33	152	18	18	2	0	1	1	15	0	14	0	0
Rodriguez, Rich, San Diego*	6	3	2.37	61	1	0	0	15	0	91.0	77	369	28	24	4	2	2	0	29	4	64	1	1
Rogers, Kevin, S.F.*	0	2	4.24	6	6	0	0	0	0	34.0	37	148	17	16	4	2	0	1	13	1	26	2	0
Rojas, Mel, Montreal	7	1	1.43	68	0	0	0	26	10	100.2	71	399	17	16	2	4	2	2	34	8	70	2	0
Ruskin, Scott, Cincinnati*	4	3	5.03	57	0	0	0	19	0	53.2	56	234	31	30	6	7	2	1	20	4	43	1	0
Saberhagen, Bret, New York	3	5	3.50	17	15	1	1	0	0	97.2	84	397	39	38	6	3	3	4	27	1	81	1	2
St. Claire, Randy, Atlanta	0	0	5.87	10	0	0	0	1	0	15.1	17	68	11	10	1	0	0	0	8	3	7	0	0
Sampen, Bill, Montreal	1	4	3.13	44	1	0	0	10	0	63.1	62	267	22	22	4	5	1	1	29	6	23	1	2
Scanlan, Bob, Chicago	3	6	2.89	69	0	0	0	41	14	87.1	76	360	32	28	4	4	2	1	30	6	42	6	4
Scheid, Rich, Houston*	0	1	6.00	7	1	0	0	3	0	12.0	14	56	8	8	2	0	0	0	6	1	8	1	1
Schilling, Curt, Philadelphia	14	11	2.35	42	26	10	4	10	2	226.1	165	895	67	59	11	7	8	1	59	4	147	4	0
Schourek, Pete, New York*	6	8	3.64	22	21	0	0	0	0	136.0	137	578	60	55	9	4	4	2	44	6	60	4	2
Scott, Tim, San Diego	4	1	5.26	34	0	0	0	16	0	37.2	39	173	24	22	4	4	1	1	21	6	30	0	1
Searcy, Steve, Philadelphia*	0	0	6.10	10	0	0	0	3	0	10.1	13	50	9	7	0	1	1	0	8	0	5	0	0
Seminara, Frank, San Diego	9	4	3.68	19	18	0	0	0	0	100.1	98	435	46	41	5	3	2	3	46	3	61	1	1
Service, Scott, Montreal	0	0	14.14	5	0	0	0	0	0	7.0	15	41	11	11	1	0	0	0	5	0	11	0	0
Shepherd, Keith, Phi.	1	1	3.27	12	0	0	0	6	2	22.0	19	91	10	8	0	4	3	0	6	1	10	1	0
Simons, Doug, Montreal*	0	0	23.63	7	0	0	0	2	0	5.1	15	35	14	14	3	1	1	1	2	0	6	1	0
Slocumb, Heathcliff, Chicago	0	3	6.50	30	0	0	0	11	1	36.0	52	174	27	26	3	2	2	1	21	3	27	1	0
Smith, Bryn, St. Louis	4	2	4.64	13	1	0	0	3	0	21.1	20	91	11	11	3	2	0	3	5	1	9	1	0
Smith, Dave, Chicago	0	0	2.51	11	0	0	0	4	0	14.1	15	61	4	4	0	1	1	0	4	2	3	0	1
Smith, Lee, St. Louis	4	9	3.12	70	0	0	0	55	43	75.0	62	310	28	26	4	2	1	0	26	4	60	2	0
Smith, Pete, Atlanta	7	0	2.05	12	11	2	1	0	0	79.0	63	323	19	18	3	4	1	0	28	2	43	2	1
Smith, Zane, Pittsburgh*	8	8	3.06	23	22	4	3	0	0	141.0	138	566	56	48	8	12	4	2	19	3	56	0	0
Smoltz, John, Atlanta	15	12	2.85	35	35	9	3	0	0	246.2	206	1021	90	78	17	7	8	5	80	5	215	17	1
Stanton, Mike, Atlanta*	5	4	4.10	65	0	0	0	23	8	63.2	59	264	32	29	6	1	2	2	20	2	44	3	0
Swift, Bill, San Francisco	10	4	2.08	30	22	3	2	2	1	164.2	144	655	41	38	6	5	2	3	43	3	77	0	1
Swindell, Greg, Cincinnati*	12	8	2.70	31	30	5	3	0	0	213.2	210	867	72	64	14	9	7	2	41	4	138	3	2
Tewksbury, Bob, St. Louis	16	5	2.16	33	32	5	0	1	0	233.0	217	915	63	56	15	9	7	3	20	0	91	2	0
Tomlin, Randy, Pittsburgh*	14	9	3.41	35	33	1	1	0	0	208.2	226	866	85	79	11	13	5	5	42	4	90	7	2
Valdez, Sergio, Montreal	0	2	2.41	27	0	0	0	9	0	37.1	25	148	12	10	2	1	0	0	12	1	32	4	0
Vitko, Joe, New York	0	1	13.50	3	1	0	0	1	0	4.2	12	29	11	7	1	0	1	0	1	0	6	1	0
Wagner, Paul, Pittsburgh	2	0	0.69	6	1	0	0	1	0	13.0	9	52	1	1	0	0	0	0	5	0	5	1	0
Wakefield, Tim, Pittsburgh	8	1	2.15	13	13	4	1	0	0	92.0	76	373	26	22	3	6	4	1	35	1	51	3	1
Walk, Bob, Pittsburgh	10	6	3.20	36	19	1	0	7	2	135.0	132	567	54	48	10	5	1	6	43	5	60	7	2
Weston, Mickey, Phi.	0	1	12.27	1	1	0	0	0	0	3.2	7	19	5	5	1	0	0	1	1	0	0	0	0

Pitcher, Team	W	L	ERA	G	GS	CG	ShO	GF	Sv.	IP	H	TBF	R	ER	HR	SH	SF	HB	BB	Int. BB	SO	WP	Bk.
Wetteland, John, Montreal.....	4	4	2.92	67	0	0	0	58	37	83.1	64	347	27	27	6	5	1	4	36	3	99	4	0
Whitehurst, Wally, New York.	3	9	3.62	44	11	0	0	7	0	97.0	99	421	45	39	4	6	3	4	33	5	70	2	1
Williams, Brian, Houston	7	6	3.92	16	16	0	0	0	0	96.1	92	413	44	42	10	7	3	0	42	1	54	2	1
Williams, Mike, Philadelphia..	1	1	5.34	5	5	1	0	0	0	28.2	29	121	20	17	3	1	1	0	7	0	5	0	0
Williams, Mitch, Phi.*	5	8	3.78	66	0	0	0	56	29	81.0	69	368	39	34	4	8	3	6	64	2	74	5	3
Wilson, Steve, Los Angeles* ..	2	5	4.19	60	0	0	0	18	0	66.2	74	301	37	31	6	5	4	1	29	7	54	7	0
Wilson, Trevor, S.F.*	8	14	4.21	26	26	1	1	0	0	154.0	152	661	82	72	18	11	6	6	64	5	88	2	7
Wohlers, Mark, Atlanta..........	1	2	2.55	32	0	0	0	16	4	35.1	28	140	11	10	0	5	1	1	14	4	17	1	0
Worrell, Todd, St. Louis.........	5	3	2.11	67	0	0	0	14	3	64.0	45	256	15	15	4	3	0	1	25	5	64	1	1
Young, Anthony, New York	2	14	4.17	52	13	1	0	26	15	121.0	134	517	66	56	8	11	4	1	31	5	64	3	1
Young, Pete, Montreal...........	0	0	3.98	13	0	0	0	6	0	20.1	18	85	9	9	0	0	2	1	9	2	11	1	0

PITCHERS WITH TWO OR MORE TEAMS

Pitcher, Team	W	L	ERA	G	GS	CG	ShO	GF	Sv.	IP	H	TBF	R	ER	HR	SH	SF	HB	BB	Int. BB	SO	WP	Bk.
Cox, Danny, Philadelphia.......	2	2	5.40	9	7	0	0	0	0	38.1	46	178	28	23	3	3	2	0	19	1	30	0	0
Cox, Danny, Pittsburgh.........	3	1	3.33	16	0	0	0	8	3	24.1	20	100	9	9	2	2	1	0	8	1	18	1	0
DeLeon, Jose, St. Louis.........	2	7	4.57	29	15	0	0	3	0	102.1	95	443	56	52	7	5	6	2	43	1	72	3	0
DeLeon, Jose, Philadelphia	0	1	3.00	3	3	0	0	0	0	15.0	16	63	7	5	0	1	0	0	5	0	7	0	0
Heredia, Gil, San Francisco ...	2	3	5.40	13	4	0	0	3	0	30.0	32	132	20	18	3	0	1	0	16	1	15	1	0
Heredia, Gil, Montreal...........	0	0	1.84	7	1	0	0	1	0	14.2	12	55	3	3	1	2	1	0	4	0	7	0	0
Jackson, Danny, Chicago*	4	9	4.22	19	19	0	0	0	0	113.0	117	501	59	53	5	11	5	3	48	3	51	1	2
Jackson, Danny, Pit.*	4	4	3.36	15	15	0	0	0	0	88.1	94	382	40	33	1	6	5	1	29	3	46	1	0
Jones, Barry, Philadelphia.....	5	6	4.64	44	0	0	0	10	0	54.1	65	243	30	28	3	2	2	2	24	4	19	1	2
Jones, Barry, New York.........	2	0	9.39	17	0	0	0	7	1	15.1	20	76	16	16	0	1	1	0	11	3	11	1	0
Rivera, Ben, Atlanta	0	1	4.70	8	0	0	0	3	0	15.1	21	78	8	8	1	0	1	2	13	2	11	0	0
Rivera, Ben, Philadelphia	7	3	2.82	20	14	4	1	4	0	102.0	78	409	32	32	8	5	1	2	32	2	66	5	0

NOTE—The following pitchers combined to pitch shutout games: Atlanta (10) —Smoltz and Mercker 2; Leibrandt, Freeman and Pena; Bielecki, Freeman and Mercker; Leibrandt, Freeman, Stanton and Pena; Glavine, Freeman and Pena; Leibrandt, Pena and Mercker; Smith, Mercker and Pena; Glavine, St. Claire and Stanton; Leibrandt and Reynoso; Chicago (6) —Castillo, Assenmacher, Scanlan and McElroy; Morgan and Scanlan; Morgan, Assenmacher and Bullinger; Maddux, Assenmacher and Scanlan; Robinson, Patterson, Bullinger and Scanlan; Morgan, McElroy and Scanlan; Cincinnati (7) —Swindell and Dibble; Hammond, Bankhead and Charlton; Belcher and Charlton; Hammond, Dibble and Ruskin; Rijo and Dibble; Rijo, Swindell and Hill; Pugh and Dibble; Houston (10) —Henry, Osuna and Hernandez; Henry, Boever, Osuna and D. Jones; Williams and Hernandez; J. Jones and D. Jones; Henry and D. Jones; Harnisch, Hernandez, Murphy and D. Jones; Portugal and Blair; Harnisch and Hernandez; Blair and Hernandez; Harnisch and D. Jones; Los Angeles (2) —Hershiser, Wilson and McDowell; Ojeda, Candelaria, McDowell and Candiotti; Montreal (9) —Nabholz and Wetteland 2; Nabholz and Fassero; Barnes and Rojas; Hurst and Wetteland; Barnes, Sampen and Fassero; Nabholz and Rojas; Hill and Wetteland; Bottenfield, Rojas, Fassero and Wetteland; New York (5) —Saberhagen, Gibson, Innis and Franco; Fernandez, Gibson, Burke and Franco; Fernandez, Guetterman and Young; Saberhagen, Schourek and Young; Hillman and Franco; Philadelphia (0); Pittsburgh (11) —Drabek and Mason; Walk, Patterson and Mason; Tomlin and Belinda; Neagle, Lamp and Mason; Tomlin and Mason; Smith and Belinda; Walk and Patterson; Jackson and Patterson; Walk and Cooke; Smith, Wagner, Cooke and Belinda; Wakefield, Smith, Walk and Cooke; St. Louis (8) —Osborne, Worrell and L. Smith 2; Osborne and L. Smith; Tewksbury, Carpenter, Worrell, Perez and L. Smith; Olivares, McClure and L. Smith; Clark, Worrell and L. Smith; Cormier, Worrell and L. Smith; Cormier and Worrell; San Diego (5) —Benes, Andersen and Melendez; Gr. Harris, Maddux, Ge. Harris and Rodriguez; Lefferts, Andersen and Myers; Lefferts, Melendez and Myers; Ge. Harris and Myers; San Francisco (7) —Brantley, Swift and Beck 2; Burkett and Beck; Burkett and Jackson; Swift, Heredia and Jackson; Swift and Beck; Brantley and Swift.

FIELDING

TEAM

Team	Pct.	G	PO	A	E	TC	DP	TP	PB
St. Louis	.985	162	4440	1777	94	6311	146	0	8
Pittsburgh	.984	162	4439	1931	101	6471	144	0	11
Cincinnati	.984	162	4349	1665	96	6110	128	0	8
Atlanta	.982	162	4380	1703	109	6192	121	0	13
Chicago	.982	162	4407	1934	114	6455	142	0	14
San Francisco	.982	162	4383	1782	113	6278	174	0	17
San Diego	.982	162	4384	1719	115	6218	127	0	2
Houston	.981	162	4378	1621	114	6113	125	0	13
New York	.981	162	4340	1717	116	6173	134	0	10
Montreal	.980	162	4404	1774	124	6302	113	0	9
Philadelphia	.978	162	4284	1614	131	6029	128	1	13
Los Angeles	.972	162	4314	1827	174	6315	136	0	20
Totals	.981	972	52502	21064	1401	74967	1618	1	138

INDIVIDUAL

FIRST BASEMEN

*Throws lefthanded.

Leader, Team	Pct.	G	PO	A	E	TC	DP
MORRIS, Cincinnati*	.999	109	841	86	1	928	65

Player, Team	Pct.	G	PO	A	E	TC	DP
Bagwell, Houston	.995	159	1334	133	7	1474	110
Benzinger, L.A.	1.000	42	177	17	0	194	17
Bonilla, New York	.953	6	39	2	2	43	2
Bream, Atlanta*	.989	120	856	73	10	939	69
Brewer, St. Louis*	1.000	27	214	18	0	232	16
Carter, Montreal	1.000	5	26	1	0	27	2
Cianfrocco, Montreal	.993	56	375	39	3	417	25
Clark, San Diego	1.000	11	59	0	0	59	1
Clark, San Francisco*	.993	141	1275	105	10	1390	130
Colbrunn, Montreal	.992	47	363	29	3	395	24
Coles, Cincinnati	1.000	20	146	8	0	154	7
Costo, Cincinnati	1.000	12	84	8	0	92	15
Daniels, Los Angeles	.985	8	60	5	1	66	4
Distefano, Houston*	1.000	6	23	2	0	25	4
Doran, Cincinnati	1.000	25	136	8	0	144	5
Foley, Montreal	.963	12	24	2	1	27	4
Galarraga, St. Louis	.991	90	777	62	8	847	71
Grace, Chicago*	.998	157	1580	141	4	1725	119
Grotewold, Phi.	1.000	1	2	0	0	2	0
Guerrero, St. Louis	.988	28	242	6	3	251	17
Hollins, Philadelphia	.000	1	0	0	0	0	0
Hudler, St. Louis	1.000	8	9	0	0	9	0
Hunter, Atlanta*	.997	92	528	49	2	579	34
Jordan, Philadelphia	.995	54	415	27	2	444	34
Karros, Los Angeles	.993	143	1211	126	9	1346	98
King, Pittsburgh	.993	32	270	21	2	293	27
Klesko, Atlanta*	1.000	5	25	0	0	25	2
Kruk, Philadelphia*	.993	121	979	58	7	1044	76
Litton, San Francisco	1.000	8	26	5	0	31	5
Lyons, Montreal	1.000	1	6	2	0	8	2
Magadan, New York	1.000	2	13	1	0	14	1
Martinez, Cincinnati*	.977	21	156	11	4	171	20
McClendon, Pit.	1.000	18	56	9	0	65	3
McGriff, San Diego*	.991	151	1219	108	12	1339	95
McKnight, New York	.985	9	63	2	1	66	2
Merced, Pittsburgh	.995	114	882	73	5	960	73
Morris, Cincinnati*	.999	109	841	86	1	928	65
Murray, New York	.991	154	1283	96	12	1391	109
Oliver, Cincinnati	1.000	1	1	0	0	1	0
Pecota, New York	1.000	1	2	0	0	2	1
Perry, St. Louis	.987	29	221	11	3	235	23
Redus, Pittsburgh	1.000	36	280	16	0	296	14
Riles, Houston	.962	4	24	1	1	26	0
Rodriguez, L.A.*	1.000	1	3	1	0	4	0
Royer, St. Louis	.947	4	33	3	2	38	7
Salazar, Chicago	1.000	5	34	1	0	35	3

Player, Team	Pct.	G	PO	A	E	TC	DP
Sasser, New York	1.000	12	39	0	0	39	4
Simms, Houston	1.000	1	4	0	0	4	0
Snyder, San Francisco	.990	27	170	20	2	192	15
Stephenson, S.D.*	.971	7	31	3	1	35	2
Sveum, Philadelphia	1.000	4	20	5	0	25	1
Teufel, San Diego	1.000	5	29	4	0	33	2
Vander Wal, Mon.*	1.000	7	23	4	0	27	3
Velasquez, San Diego	.933	3	13	1	1	15	1
Villanueva, Chicago	1.000	6	26	4	0	30	3
Wallach, Montreal	.991	71	633	60	6	699	42
Wehner, Pittsburgh	.989	13	81	5	1	87	9
Willard, Montreal	.952	5	17	3	1	21	0
Woodson, St. Louis	1.000	3	26	3	0	29	0
Wrona, Cincinnati	1.000	1	2	0	0	2	0
Young, Pittsburgh	1.000	1	1	0	0	1	0

SECOND BASEMEN

Leader, Team	Pct.	G	PO	A	E	TC	DP
LIND, Pittsburgh	.992	134	311	428	6	745	78

Player, Team	Pct.	G	PO	A	E	TC	DP
Alicea, St. Louis	.989	75	130	227	4	361	36
Backman, Phi.	.968	10	10	20	1	31	4
Barberie, Montreal	.989	26	29	59	1	89	7
Belliard, Atlanta	1.000	1	1	2	0	3	1
Benavides, Cincinnati	1.000	37	47	61	0	108	8
Biggio, Houston	.984	161	344	413	12	769	81
Blauser, Atlanta	.937	21	32	42	5	79	8
Branson, Cincinnati	.946	33	45	61	6	112	19
Buechele, Chicago	1.000	2	1	1	0	2	0
Candaele, Houston	1.000	9	13	9	0	22	1
Colbert, San Francisco	1.000	2	1	1	0	2	0
Cordero, Montreal	.941	9	11	21	2	34	1
DeShields, Montreal	.976	134	251	360	15	626	71
Donnels, New York	.979	12	19	28	1	48	3
Doran, Cincinnati	.988	104	170	241	5	416	55
Duncan, Philadelphia	.969	52	94	126	7	227	27
Faries, San Diego	1.000	4	4	4	0	8	1
Felder, San Francisco	1.000	3	0	1	0	1	0
Figueroa, St. Louis	1.000	3	0	3	0	3	0
Foley, Montreal	1.000	13	13	13	0	26	2
Garcia, Pittsburgh	.977	14	19	24	1	44	8
Gardner, San Diego	1.000	11	11	20	0	31	3
Guerrero, Houston	1.000	2	0	3	0	3	0
T. Haney, Montreal	1.000	5	2	6	0	8	1
Harris, Los Angeles	.963	81	160	206	14	380	39
Hudler, St. Louis	.957	16	28	39	3	70	6
Jones, St. Louis	.988	28	36	47	1	84	15
Kent, New York	.980	34	60	84	3	147	18
King, Pittsburgh	1.000	32	49	68	0	117	16
Kunkel, Chicago	.900	3	5	4	1	10	1

Player, Team	Pct.	G	PO	A	E	TC	DP
Lemke, Atlanta	.984	145	236	325	9	570	56
Lind, Pittsburgh	.992	134	311	428	6	745	78
Litton, San Francisco	.992	31	53	71	1	125	18
Lyons, Atlanta	1.000	2	0	1	0	1	0
McKnight, New York	.980	14	18	31	1	50	5
Millette, Philadelphia	1.000	1	1	3	0	4	1
Morandini, Phi.	.991	124	236	333	5	574	64
Noboa, New York	.977	16	15	28	1	44	6
Oquendo, St. Louis	1.000	9	14	22	0	36	5
Patterson, S.F.	.960	22	43	54	4	101	16
Pecota, New York	.972	38	45	95	4	144	15
Pena, St. Louis	.984	57	125	184	5	314	40
Randolph, New York	.977	79	149	195	8	352	53
Riles, Houston	1.000	2	3	5	0	8	1
Roberts, Cincinnati	.993	42	51	83	1	135	7
Samuel, Los Angeles	.974	38	75	77	4	156	13
Sanchez, Chicago	1.000	4	5	4	0	9	0
Sandberg, Chicago	.990	157	283	539	8	830	94
Scarsone, Phi.	1.000	3	3	3	0	6	1
Sharperson, L.A.	.979	63	104	134	5	243	26
Shipley, San Diego	1.000	11	18	23	0	41	5
Snyder, San Francisco	1.000	4	2	4	0	6	0
Springer, New York	1.000	1	3	1	0	4	1
Stillwell, San Diego	.970	111	250	266	16	532	66
Strange, Chicago	1.000	12	6	15	0	21	2
Teufel, San Diego	.987	52	95	125	3	223	20
Thompson, S.F.	.978	120	296	382	15	693	101
Treadway, Atlanta	.993	45	53	83	1	137	24
Vizcaino, Chicago	1.000	5	2	1	0	3	0
Walker, Chi.-N.Y.	.902	18	11	26	4	41	4
Wehner, Pittsburgh	1.000	5	0	1	0	1	0
Wilson, St. Louis	.950	11	14	24	2	40	6
Young, Los Angeles	.957	43	85	114	9	208	19

TRIPLE PLAY: Morandini, Philadelphia.

SECOND BASEMEN WITH TWO OR MORE TEAMS

Player, Team	Pct.	G	PO	A	E	TC	DP
Walker, Chicago	1.000	2	2	2	0	4	0
Walker, New York	.892	16	9	24	4	37	4

THIRD BASEMEN

Leader, Team	Pct.	G	PO	A	E	TC	DP
Hansen, Los Angeles	.968	108	61	183	8	252	13

Player, Team	Pct.	G	PO	A	E	TC	DP
Anderson, L.A.	.974	26	13	24	1	38	3
Backman, Phi.	.000	2	0	0	0	0	0
Barberie, Montreal	.932	63	37	127	12	176	10
Benavides, Cincinnati	.000	1	0	0	0	0	0
Benjamin, S.F.	.000	2	0	0	0	0	0
Berry, Montreal	.879	20	10	19	4	33	1
Blauser, Atlanta	1.000	1	0	1	0	1	0
Branson, Cincinnati	.750	8	1	2	1	4	0
Buechele, Pit.-Chi.	.958	143	102	288	17	407	16
Caminiti, Houston	.966	129	102	210	11	323	19
Candaele, Houston	.950	29	24	52	4	80	3
Castilla, Atlanta	.875	4	2	5	1	8	0
Cianfrocco, Montreal	.872	19	7	27	5	39	1
Clayton, S.F.	1.000	1	1	0	0	1	0
Colbert, San Francisco	1.000	9	6	10	0	16	1
Coles, Cincinnati	1.000	23	8	34	0	42	1
Donnels, New York	.941	29	15	49	4	68	3
Duncan, Philadelphia	.833	4	2	3	1	6	0
Faries, San Diego	.000	2	0	0	0	0	0
Foley, Montreal	.000	4	0	0	0	0	0
Green, Cincinnati	1.000	1	0	2	0	2	0
Greene, Cincinnati	.948	25	15	40	3	58	6
Guerrero, Houston	.938	12	3	12	1	16	0
Hansen, Los Angeles	.968	108	61	183	8	252	13
Harris, Los Angeles	.884	33	12	26	5	43	5
Hollins, Philadelphia	.954	156	120	253	18	391	22
Jones, St. Louis	1.000	2	0	1	0	1	0
Kent, New York	1.000	1	1	6	0	7	1
King, Pittsburgh	.953	73	44	139	9	192	14
LaValliere, Pittsburgh	1.000	1	0	1	0	1	0
Lemke, Atlanta	1.000	13	0	10	0	10	0

Player, Team	Pct.	G	PO	A	E	TC	DP
Litton, San Francisco	.875	10	1	6	1	8	1
Magadan, New York	.941	93	41	135	11	187	10
McKnight, New York	.800	3	0	4	1	5	0
Millette, Philadelphia	1.000	1	0	1	0	1	0
Noboa, New York	.000	3	0	0	1	1	0
Pecota, New York	.926	48	12	51	5	68	6
Pendleton, Atlanta	.960	158	133	325	19	477	27
Prince, Pittsburgh	.000	1	0	0	0	0	0
Ramirez, Houston	1.000	1	0	1	0	1	0
Riles, Houston	1.000	5	1	6	0	7	0
Roberts, Cincinnati	.946	36	20	68	5	93	6
Royer, St. Louis	.900	5	1	8	1	10	2
Sabo, Cincinnati	.961	93	60	159	9	228	13
Salazar, Chicago	.935	40	19	68	6	93	7
Scott, Chicago	.922	30	17	42	5	64	3
Sharperson, L.A.	.927	60	15	86	8	109	5
Sheffield, San Diego	.961	144	99	299	16	414	25
Shipley, San Diego	1.000	8	5	10	0	15	1
Snyder, San Francisco	.935	14	7	22	2	31	2
Springer, New York	.000	1	0	0	0	0	0
Strange, Chicago	.900	33	18	36	6	60	2
Sveum, Philadelphia	1.000	5	2	4	0	6	1
Teufel, San Diego	.922	26	13	34	4	51	1
Treadway, Atlanta	1.000	1	0	2	0	2	1
Vizcaino, Chicago	.972	29	18	51	2	71	6
Walker, Chi.-N.Y.	.960	38	14	58	3	75	2
Wallach, Montreal	.964	85	56	184	9	249	17
Wehner, Pittsburgh	.961	34	15	58	3	76	8
Williams, S.F.	.945	144	105	289	23	417	33
Wilson, St. Louis	.970	18	9	23	1	33	2
Woodson, St. Louis	.945	26	17	35	3	55	4
Young, Pittsburgh	.750	7	2	1	1	4	0
Zeile, St. Louis	.960	124	80	235	13	328	19

THIRD BASEMEN WITH TWO OR MORE TEAMS

Player, Team	Pct.	G	PO	A	E	TC	DP
Buechele, Pittsburgh	.957	80	52	169	10	231	10
Buechele, Chicago	.960	63	50	119	7	176	6
Walker, Chicago	.800	2	0	4	1	5	0
Walker, New York	.971	36	14	54	2	70	2

SHORTSTOPS

Leader, Team	Pct.	G	PO	A	E	TC	DP
SCHOFIELD, New York	.988	141	205	391	7	603	78

Player, Team	Pct.	G	PO	A	E	TC	DP
Alicea, St. Louis	.800	4	6	6	3	15	2
Anderson, L.A.	.893	7	8	17	3	28	4
Arias, Chicago	.967	30	43	74	4	121	8
Baez, New York	.889	5	5	11	2	18	2
Barberie, Montreal	1.000	1	0	2	0	2	1
Batiste, Philadelphia	.922	41	69	85	13	167	17
Bell, Philadelphia	.972	46	82	129	6	217	22
Bell, Pittsburgh	.973	159	268	526	22	816	94
Belliard, Atlanta	.969	139	151	289	14	454	47
Benavides, Cincinnati	.944	34	33	68	6	107	18
Benjamin, S.F.	.991	33	34	71	1	106	13
Blauser, Atlanta	.968	106	87	182	9	278	26
Bournigal, L.A.	.967	9	12	17	1	30	6
Branson, Cincinnati	.000	1	0	0	0	0	0
Candaele, Houston	.968	65	79	135	7	221	30
Castilla, Atlanta	1.000	4	0	7	0	7	1
Cedeno, Houston	.959	70	82	175	11	268	27
Clayton, S.F.	.973	94	141	257	11	409	51
Cordero, Montreal	.949	35	40	71	6	117	11
Duncan, Philadelphia	.959	42	37	80	5	122	16
Dunston, Chicago	.986	18	28	42	1	71	9
Elster, New York	1.000	5	8	10	0	18	3
Faries, San Diego	.000	1	0	0	0	0	0
Fernandez, San Diego	.983	154	240	405	11	656	65
Figueroa, St. Louis	.938	9	7	8	1	16	0
Foley, Montreal	.967	33	37	82	4	123	14
Garcia, Pittsburgh	.944	8	6	11	1	18	3
Green, Cincinnati	1.000	6	1	3	0	4	0
Guerrero, Houston	.980	19	15	35	1	51	5
Harris, Los Angeles	.778	10	6	15	6	27	4

Player, Team	Pct.	G	PO	A	E	TC	DP
Jones, St. Louis	.972	34	40	66	3	109	17
Kent, New York	1.000	1	1	3	0	4	0
King, Pittsburgh	.909	6	4	6	1	11	1
Kunkel, Chicago	1.000	6	4	10	0	14	1
Larkin, Cincinnati	.983	140	233	408	11	652	67
Litton, San Francisco	.714	3	2	3	2	7	2
McKnight, New York	1.000	3	1	3	0	4	1
Millette, Philadelphia	.974	26	32	82	3	117	14
Morandini, Phi.	.857	3	3	3	1	7	1
Noboa, New York	.857	2	4	2	1	7	0
Offerman, Los Angeles	.935	149	208	398	42	648	74
Oquendo, St. Louis	.923	5	4	8	1	13	2
Owen, Montreal	.982	116	188	300	9	497	44
Pecota, New York	.972	39	33	72	3	108	11
Ramirez, Houston	.961	57	60	113	7	180	17
Riles, Houston	1.000	6	1	3	0	4	1
Salazar, Chicago	1.000	12	14	26	0	40	5
Sanchez, Chicago	.974	68	143	198	9	350	52
Schofield, New York	.988	141	205	391	7	603	78
Scott, Chicago	1.000	2	1	1	0	2	0
Sharperson, L.A.	1.000	2	1	0	0	1	0
Shipley, San Diego	.986	23	29	41	1	71	12
O. Smith, St. Louis	.985	132	232	420	10	662	82
Snyder, San Francisco	.500	3	1	0	1	2	0
Sveum, Philadelphia	.948	34	56	91	8	155	17
Uribe, San Francisco	.971	62	75	157	7	239	37
Vizcaino, Chicago	.969	50	73	143	7	223	28
Yelding, Houston	.000	2	0	0	0	0	0

OUTFIELDERS

*Throws lefthanded.

Leader, Team	Pct.	G	PO	A	E	TC	DP
O'NEILL, Cincinnati*	.997	143	291	12	1	304	2

Player, Team	Pct.	G	PO	A	E	TC	DP
Alou, Montreal	.978	100	170	6	4	180	1
Amaro, Philadelphia	.992	113	232	5	2	239	1
Anthony, Houston*	.973	115	173	6	5	184	0
Ashley, Los Angeles	.857	27	34	2	6	42	0
Azocar, San Diego*	.942	37	64	1	4	69	0
Bass, S.F.-N.Y.	.985	111	191	2	3	196	0
Benzinger, L.A.	.989	51	86	1	1	88	0
Berroa, Cincinnati	1.000	3	2	1	0	3	0
Bonds, Pittsburgh*	.991	139	310	4	3	317	0
Bonilla, New York	.992	121	238	7	2	247	1
Boston, New York*	.993	95	133	5	1	139	1
Braggs, Cincinnati	.946	79	102	3	6	111	0
Brewer, St. Louis*	1.000	4	6	1	0	7	1
Brumfield, Cincinnati	1.000	16	20	1	0	21	0
Butler, Los Angeles*	.995	155	353	9	2	364	3
Calderon, Montreal	.988	46	79	2	1	82	0
Candaele, Houston	1.000	21	14	0	0	14	0
Canseco, St. Louis	.889	8	8	0	1	9	0
Carr, St. Louis	1.000	19	39	1	0	40	0
Castillo, Philadelphia	.956	24	43	0	2	45	0
Chamberlain, Phi.	.971	73	132	3	4	139	1
Cianfrocco, Montreal	1.000	5	5	0	0	5	0
Clark, Pittsburgh	1.000	8	10	0	0	10	0
Clark, San Diego	.990	134	285	10	3	298	4
Cole, Pittsburgh*	.989	53	85	5	1	91	0
Coleman, New York	.991	61	112	2	1	115	2
Coles, Cincinnati	1.000	5	7	0	0	7	0
Daniels, L.A.-Chi.	.984	49	59	4	1	64	0
Dascenzo, Chicago*	.978	122	221	2	5	228	0
Davis, Los Angeles	.961	74	123	0	5	128	0
Dawson, Chicago	.992	139	223	11	2	236	3
Distefano, Houston*	1.000	12	16	1	0	17	0
Dozier, New York	.971	17	33	0	1	34	0
Duncan, Philadelphia	.976	65	123	1	3	127	0
Dykstra, Phi.*	.989	85	253	6	3	262	4
Espy, Pittsburgh	.955	82	83	1	4	88	0
Felder, San Francisco	.994	105	159	2	1	162	0
Finley, Houston*	.993	160	417	8	3	428	3
Foley, Montreal	.000	1	0	0	0	0	0

Player, Team	Pct.	G	PO	A	E	TC	DP
Gallagher, New York	.982	76	105	4	2	111	3
Gant, Atlanta	.986	147	277	5	4	286	1
Gibson, Pittsburgh*	1.000	13	25	1	0	26	0
Gilkey, St. Louis	.978	111	217	9	5	231	3
Gonzalez, Houston	.993	111	261	5	2	268	1
Goodwin, Los Angeles	1.000	45	43	0	0	43	0
Gregg, Atlanta*	1.000	9	15	0	0	15	0
Grissom, Montreal	.983	157	401	7	7	415	2
Grotewold, Phi.	1.000	2	1	0	0	1	0
Guerrero, Houston	1.000	3	1	0	0	1	0
Guerrero, St. Louis	.944	10	17	0	1	18	0
Gwynn, San Diego*	.982	127	270	9	5	284	2
Harris, Los Angeles	.917	15	21	1	2	24	0
Hatcher, Cincinnati	.967	23	29	0	1	30	0
Hernandez, Cincinnati	.952	18	18	2	1	21	1
Hosey, San Francisco	.960	18	24	0	1	25	0
Howell, New York	1.000	28	66	0	0	66	0
Hudler, St. Louis	1.000	12	7	0	0	7	0
Hunter, Atlanta*	.882	6	14	1	2	17	1
Incaviglia, Houston	.970	98	188	8	6	202	1
Jackson, San Diego	.996	153	436	18	2	456	9
James, San Francisco	.974	62	112	2	3	117	2
Javier, L.A.-Phi.	.987	101	229	7	3	239	1
Johnson, New York	.981	98	206	3	4	213	0
C. Jones, Houston	.931	43	27	0	2	29	0
Jones, St. Louis	.000	1	0	0	0	0	0
Jordan, St. Louis	.991	53	101	4	1	106	0
Jordan, Philadelphia	1.000	11	12	0	0	12	0
Jose, St. Louis	.979	127	273	11	6	290	1
Justice, Atlanta*	.976	140	313	8	8	329	2
King, Pittsburgh	1.000	1	1	0	0	1	0
Kruk, Philadelphia*	.983	35	58	0	1	59	0
Kunkel, Chicago	1.000	3	9	0	0	9	0
Lampkin, San Diego	.000	1	0	0	0	0	0
Lankford, St. Louis*	.996	153	438	5	2	445	0
Leonard, S.F.	.984	37	61	2	1	64	2
Lewis, San Francisco	1.000	94	225	3	0	228	2
Lindeman, Phi.	1.000	9	6	0	0	6	0
Litton, San Francisco	.000	1	0	0	0	0	0
Lyons, Atl.-Mon.	1.000	14	8	0	0	8	0
Marsh, Philadelphia	.971	35	66	0	2	68	0
Martin, Pittsburgh*	1.000	7	6	0	0	6	0
Martinez, Cincinnati*	.991	111	226	7	2	235	3
May, Chicago	.969	108	153	3	5	161	0
McClendon, Pit.	.964	60	80	0	3	83	0
McCray, Houston	1.000	13	6	0	0	6	0
McGee, San Francisco	.976	119	231	11	6	248	2
McKnight, New York	.000	1	0	0	0	0	0
Merced, Pittsburgh	1.000	17	24	2	0	26	1
Murphy, Philadelphia	.950	16	19	0	1	20	0
Nieves, Atlanta	.727	6	8	0	3	11	0
Nixon, Atlanta	.991	111	333	6	3	342	1
O'Neill, Cincinnati*	.997	143	291	12	1	304	2
Patterson, S.F.	1.000	5	23	0	0	23	0
Peguero, Los Angeles	1.000	14	10	0	0	10	0
Pennyfeather, Pit.	1.000	10	8	0	0	8	0
Pettis, San Diego	.952	14	20	0	1	21	0
Ramsey, Chicago	1.000	15	17	0	0	17	0
Redus, Pittsburgh	.955	15	21	0	1	22	0
Reed, Montreal	1.000	29	37	1	0	38	0
Rhodes, Houston*	.000	1	0	0	0	0	0
Roberts, Cincinnati	.993	79	138	1	1	140	0
Rodriguez, L.A.*	.960	48	65	7	3	75	2
Salazar, Chicago	1.000	34	47	3	0	50	1
Samuel, Los Angeles	.500	1	1	0	1	2	0
Sanders, Atlanta*	.983	75	174	4	3	181	0
Sanders, Cincinnati	.978	110	262	11	6	279	4
Sasser, New York	1.000	9	8	0	0	8	0
Simms, Houston	1.000	9	6	0	0	6	0
Dw. Smith, Chicago	.979	63	93	2	2	97	0
L. Smith, Atlanta	.954	35	60	2	3	65	0
Snyder, San Francisco	.992	70	121	7	1	129	1
Sosa, Chicago	.961	67	145	4	6	155	5
Stairs, Montreal	.933	10	14	0	1	15	0
Stephenson, S.D.*	1.000	15	17	0	0	17	0

Player, Team	Pct.	G	PO	A	E	TC	DP
Strawberry, L.A.*	.986	42	67	2	1	70	0
Thompson, St. Louis	.974	45	74	1	2	77	1
Thompson, New York	.988	29	77	2	1	80	0
Vander Wal, Mon.*	.981	57	99	2	2	103	0
Van Slyke, Pittsburgh	.989	154	421	11	5	437	3
Varsho, Pittsburgh	.984	44	62	1	1	64	0
Vatcher, San Diego	1.000	13	13	1	0	14	0
Velasquez, San Diego	1.000	2	2	0	0	2	0
Walker, Chi.-N.Y.	.968	21	29	1	1	31	0
Walker, Montreal	.993	139	269	16	2	287	2
Walton, Chicago	.944	24	34	0	2	36	0
Ward, San Diego	.946	51	68	2	4	74	0
Webster, L.A.*	.977	90	130	0	3	133	0
Wilson, St. Louis	1.000	3	1	0	0	1	0
Wood, San Francisco*	.972	16	35	0	1	36	0
Yelding, Houston	1.000	2	1	0	0	1	0
Young, Houston	.964	57	53	0	2	55	0

OUTFIELDERS WITH TWO OR MORE TEAMS

Player, Team	Pct.	G	PO	A	E	TC	DP
Bass, San Francisco	.983	72	116	1	2	119	0
Bass, New York	.987	39	75	1	1	77	0
Daniels, Los Angeles	.964	21	26	1	1	28	0
Daniels, Chicago	1.000	28	33	3	0	36	0
Javier, Los Angeles	1.000	27	17	0	0	17	0
Javier, Philadelphia	.986	74	212	7	3	222	1
Lyons, Atlanta	1.000	6	4	0	0	4	0
Lyons, Montreal	1.000	8	4	0	0	4	0
Walker, Chicago	1.000	6	10	0	0	10	0
Walker, New York	.952	15	19	1	1	21	0

CATCHERS

Leader, Team	Pct.	G	PO	A	E	TC	DP	PB
PAGNOZZI, St.L.	.999	138	688	53	1	742	10	6

Player, Team	Pct.	G	PO	A	E	TC	DP	PB
Afenir, Cincinnati	1.000	15	57	2	0	59	1	1
Bailey, S.F.	1.000	7	33	2	0	35	0	1
Berryhill, Atlanta	.998	84	426	31	1	458	5	9
Bilardello, S.D.	1.000	14	73	9	0	82	2	0
Bradley, Cin.	1.000	2	2	0	0	2	0	0
Cabrera, Atlanta	.000	1	0	0	0	0	0	0
Carter, Montreal	.989	85	481	52	6	539	3	1
Cerone, Montreal	1.000	28	106	7	0	113	0	1
Colbert, S.F.	.994	35	140	13	1	154	4	6
Daulton, Phi.	.987	141	760	69	11	840	8	12
Decker, S.F.	1.000	15	94	4	0	98	1	1
Fletcher, Montreal	.995	69	360	33	2	395	3	3
Gedman, St. Louis	.988	40	227	12	3	242	2	2
Girardi, Chicago	.991	86	369	51	4	424	6	8
Grotewold, Phi.	1.000	2	3	0	0	3	0	0
Hernandez, L.A.	.979	63	295	37	7	339	4	5
Hundley, N.Y.	.996	121	700	48	3	751	2	6
Lake, Philadelphia	.975	17	71	8	2	81	1	0
Laker, Montreal	.991	28	102	8	1	111	1	4
Lampkin, St. Louis	1.000	7	30	3	0	33	0	1
LaValliere, Pit.	.994	92	421	62	3	486	6	4
Lopez, Atlanta	1.000	9	28	2	0	30	0	0
Manwaring, S.F.	.994	108	564	68	4	636	12	8
McNamara, S.F.	.993	30	131	8	1	140	1	1
Natal, Montreal	.909	4	10	0	1	11	0	0
O'Brien, New York	.979	64	287	44	7	338	4	1
Oliver, Cincinnati	.992	141	925	64	8	997	8	6
Olson, Atlanta	.998	94	522	43	1	566	8	4
Pagnozzi, St.L.	.999	138	688	53	1	742	10	6
Pedre, Chicago	1.000	4	3	0	0	3	0	0
Piazza, L.A.	.990	16	94	7	1	102	1	1
Pratt, Phi.	.972	11	65	4	2	71	1	1
Prince, Pittsburgh	.977	19	76	8	2	86	0	1
Reed, Cincinnati	1.000	6	29	2	0	31	0	0
Santiago, S.D.	.982	103	584	53	12	649	6	0
Sasser, New York	.989	27	84	5	1	90	0	3
Scioscia, L.A.	.988	108	641	74	9	724	8	14
Servais, Houston	.995	73	386	27	2	415	5	3
Slaught, Pit.	.988	79	365	35	5	405	4	6

Player, Team	Pct.	G	PO	A	E	TC	DP	PB
Taubensee, Hou.	.992	103	557	66	5	628	6	9
Tucker, Houston	.976	19	75	6	2	83	0	1
Villanueva, Chi.	.978	28	155	20	4	179	1	3
Walters, S.D.	.992	55	329	25	3	357	5	2
Wilkins, Chicago	.993	73	408	47	3	458	5	3
Willard, Atlanta	1.000	1	2	0	0	2	0	0
Wilson, Cincinnati	1.000	9	42	4	0	46	0	0
Wrona, Cincinnati	.965	10	50	5	2	57	0	1

PITCHERS

*Throws lefthanded.

Leader, Team	Pct.	G	PO	A	E	TC	DP
OLIVARES, St. Louis	1.000	32	15	40	0	55	4

Player, Team	Pct.	G	PO	A	E	TC	DP
Abbott, Philadelphia*	1.000	31	3	15	0	18	0
Agosto, St. Louis*	1.000	22	0	12	0	12	1
Andersen, San Diego	.900	34	4	5	1	10	0
Ashby, Philadelphia	1.000	10	1	6	0	7	0
Assenmacher, Chi.*	1.000	70	3	6	0	9	1
Astacio, Los Angeles	.895	11	4	13	2	19	1
Avery, Atlanta*	.945	35	16	36	3	55	1
Ayala, Cincinnati	1.000	5	3	8	0	11	1
Ayrault, Philadelphia	1.000	30	1	8	0	9	0
Baller, Philadelphia	1.000	8	1	1	0	2	0
Bankhead, Cincinnati	.778	54	5	2	2	9	0
Barnes, Montreal*	1.000	21	5	18	0	23	0
Batista, Pittsburgh	.000	1	0	0	0	0	0
Beck, San Francisco	.938	65	2	13	1	16	0
Belcher, Cincinnati	.980	35	23	27	1	51	2
Belinda, Pittsburgh	1.000	59	4	4	0	8	1
Benes, San Diego	.980	34	14	34	1	49	1
Berenguer, Atlanta	1.000	28	2	4	0	6	0
Bielecki, Atlanta	1.000	19	5	14	0	19	0
Birkbeck, New York	.800	1	3	1	1	5	1
Black, San Francisco*	1.000	28	5	37	0	42	4
Blair, Houston	.846	29	4	7	2	13	0
Boever, Houston	.920	81	4	19	2	25	2
Bolton, Cincinnati*	1.000	16	3	8	0	11	0
Borbon, Atlanta*	.000	2	0	0	0	0	0
Boskie, Chicago	.967	23	8	21	1	30	2
Bottenfield, Montreal	1.000	10	2	2	0	4	0
Bowen, Houston	1.000	11	0	3	0	3	0
Brantley, Philadelphia	.870	28	6	14	3	23	1
Brantley, S.F.	1.000	56	4	9	0	13	0
Brink, Philadelphia	.667	8	0	2	1	3	0
Brocail, San Diego	.667	3	1	1	1	3	0
Brown, Cincinnati	.500	2	0	1	1	2	0
Browning, Cincinnati*	.952	16	6	14	1	21	3
Bullinger, Chicago	1.000	39	17	17	0	34	2
Burba, San Francisco	1.000	23	3	8	0	11	0
Burke, New York	.833	15	2	3	1	6	0
Burkett, S.F.	.967	32	11	18	1	30	0
Candelaria, L.A.*	1.000	50	0	5	0	5	0
Candiotti, Los Angeles	.980	32	16	32	1	49	3
Carpenter, St. Louis	1.000	73	7	10	0	17	1
Carter, San Francisco	1.000	6	4	1	0	5	0
Castillo, Chicago	.974	33	10	28	1	39	2
Chapin, Philadelphia	.000	1	0	0	0	0	0
Charlton, Cincinnati*	.786	64	3	8	3	14	1
Clark, St. Louis	.938	20	2	13	1	16	0
Clements, San Diego*	1.000	27	1	7	0	8	0
Cole, Pittsburgh	1.000	8	3	3	0	6	0
Combs, Philadelphia*	1.000	4	0	6	0	6	0
Cone, New York	.947	27	16	20	2	38	1
Cooke, Pittsburgh*	1.000	11	0	3	0	3	0
Cormier, St. Louis*	1.000	31	9	34	0	43	2
Cox, Phi.-Pit.	.895	25	8	9	2	19	1
Crews, Los Angeles	.938	49	5	10	1	16	0
Davis, Atlanta*	.500	14	1	0	1	2	0
DeLeon, St. Louis-Phi.	1.000	32	7	10	0	17	0
Deshaies, San Diego*	1.000	15	2	22	0	24	1
Dewey, New York	1.000	20	3	5	0	8	0
Dibble, Cincinnati	.889	63	5	3	1	9	0
DiPino, St. Louis*	1.000	9	1	3	0	4	0
Downs, San Francisco	1.000	19	4	3	0	7	0

Player, Team	Pct.	G	PO	A	E	TC	DP
Drabek, Pittsburgh	.956	34	29	36	3	68	4
Eiland, San Diego	1.000	7	1	5	0	6	0
Fassero, Montreal*	1.000	70	1	15	0	16	0
Fernandez, New York*	.962	32	4	21	1	26	1
Filer, New York	.875	9	3	4	1	8	0
Foster, Cincinnati	1.000	31	5	11	0	16	0
Franco, New York*	1.000	31	2	12	0	14	2
Freeman, Atlanta	.818	58	4	5	2	11	0
Gardner, Montreal	.947	33	14	22	2	38	0
Gibson, New York*	1.000	43	2	6	0	8	0
Glavine, Atlanta*	1.000	33	18	31	0	49	2
Gleaton, Pittsburgh*	1.000	23	0	6	0	6	0
Gooden, New York	.891	31	9	40	6	55	1
Gott, Los Angeles	1.000	68	11	15	0	26	0
Greene, Philadelphia	.769	13	3	7	3	13	0
Ke. Gross, Los Angeles	.973	34	11	25	1	37	2
Ki. Gross, Los Angeles	1.000	16	1	7	0	8	0
Guetterman, N.Y.*	1.000	43	2	4	0	6	0
Hammond, Cincinnati*	.939	28	9	22	2	33	1
C. Haney, Montreal*	1.000	9	1	5	0	6	0
Harkey, Chicago	1.000	7	1	6	0	7	1
Harnisch, Houston	.939	34	16	15	2	33	1
Ge. Harris, San Diego	.800	14	0	4	1	5	0
Gr. Harris, San Diego	.861	20	10	21	5	36	0
Hartley, Philadelphia	.889	46	2	6	1	9	0
Hartsock, Chicago	1.000	4	0	2	0	2	0
Henry, Houston*	.935	28	13	30	3	46	2
Henry, Cincinnati	.900	60	5	13	2	20	0
Heredia, S.F.-Mon.	1.000	20	0	5	0	5	0
Hernandez, San Diego	1.000	26	2	6	0	8	2
Hernandez, Houston	.941	77	9	7	1	17	0
Hershiser, L.A.	.958	33	28	41	3	72	2
Hickerson, S.F.*	1.000	61	1	5	0	6	0
Hill, Montreal	.934	33	21	36	4	61	3
Hill, Cincinnati	1.000	14	3	2	0	5	0
Hillman, New York*	1.000	11	1	7	0	8	0
Hollins, Chicago	1.000	4	1	0	0	1	0
Howell, Los Angeles	1.000	41	6	7	0	13	0
Hurst, San Diego*	.977	32	10	32	1	43	0
Hurst, Montreal	1.000	3	2	2	0	4	0
Innis, New York	1.000	76	13	21	0	34	1
Jackson, Chi.-Pit.*	.840	34	9	33	8	50	2
Jackson, S.F.	.938	67	6	9	1	16	0
Jones, Phi.-N.Y.	1.000	61	4	13	0	17	2
D. Jones, Houston	.895	80	5	12	2	19	0
J. Jones, Houston	1.000	25	9	17	0	26	1
Kile, Houston	.737	22	2	12	5	19	0
Krueger, Montreal*	1.000	9	0	2	0	2	0
Lamp, Pittsburgh	1.000	21	4	4	0	8	0
Landrum, Montreal	1.000	18	2	2	0	4	0
Lefferts, San Diego*	.971	27	7	26	1	34	0
Leibrandt, Atlanta*	.955	32	20	44	3	67	1
Maddux, Chicago	.969	35	30	64	3	97	1
Maddux, San Diego	.964	50	9	18	1	28	1
Magrane, St. Louis*	1.000	5	1	5	0	6	0
Mallicoat, Houston*	1.000	23	0	3	0	3	0
Martinez, Montreal	.942	32	20	45	4	69	3
P. Martinez, L.A.	.000	2	0	0	0	0	0
R. Martinez, L.A.	.933	25	10	18	2	30	1
Mason, Pittsburgh	.929	65	6	7	1	14	0
Mathews, Phi.*	1.000	14	1	6	0	7	0
Maysey, Montreal	.000	2	0	0	0	0	0
McClure, St. Louis*	1.000	71	2	8	0	10	1
McDowell, L.A.	.906	65	8	21	3	32	2
McElroy, Chicago*	.917	72	3	8	1	12	2
Melendez, San Diego	.909	56	2	8	1	11	1
Menendez, Cincinnati	.000	3	0	0	0	0	0
Mercker, Atlanta*	1.000	53	1	2	0	3	0
Miller, Pittsburgh	1.000	6	0	1	0	1	0
Minor, Pittsburgh	.500	1	0	1	1	2	1
Morgan, Chicago	.955	34	19	45	3	67	3
Mulholland, Phi.*	.946	32	6	47	3	56	0
Murphy, Houston*	1.000	59	2	12	0	14	0
Myers, San Diego*	1.000	66	2	12	0	14	0
Nabholz, Montreal*	.965	32	14	41	2	57	3
Neagle, Pittsburgh*	1.000	55	2	11	0	13	0
Nied, Atlanta	1.000	6	0	2	0	2	0
Ojeda, Los Angeles*	.955	29	5	37	2	44	0
Olivares, St. Louis	1.000	32	15	40	0	55	4
Oliveras, S.F.	.900	16	0	9	1	10	0
Osborne, St. Louis*	.923	34	6	18	2	26	2
Osuna, Houston*	1.000	66	2	11	0	13	0
Palacios, Pittsburgh	.923	20	5	7	1	13	1
Patterson, Pit.*	1.000	60	3	7	0	10	1
Patterson, Chicago*	.909	32	4	6	1	11	0
Pecota, New York	.000	1	0	0	0	0	0
Pena, Atlanta	1.000	41	2	1	0	3	0
Pena, San Francisco*	.800	25	1	11	3	15	1
Perez, St. Louis	1.000	77	9	15	0	24	2
Portugal, Houston	.906	18	16	13	3	32	1
Pugh, Cincinnati	1.000	7	2	6	0	8	0
Rapp, San Francisco	1.000	3	2	2	0	4	0
Rasmussen, Chicago*	1.000	3	0	1	0	1	0
Reardon, Atlanta	1.000	14	0	1	0	1	0
Reed, San Francisco	1.000	18	3	4	0	7	0
Reynolds, Houston	.875	8	0	7	1	8	0
Reynoso, Atlanta	1.000	3	0	2	0	2	1
Righetti, S.F.*	.889	54	3	5	1	9	0
Rijo, Cincinnati	.962	33	19	31	2	52	1
Risley, Montreal	1.000	1	0	1	0	1	0
Ritchie, Philadelphia*	1.000	40	1	5	0	6	0
Rivera, Atl.-Phi.	1.000	28	3	19	0	22	0
Robinson, Phi.	1.000	8	2	3	0	5	0
Robinson, Chicago	1.000	49	7	13	0	20	1
Robinson, Pittsburgh	1.000	8	2	7	0	9	0
Rodriguez, San Diego*	.955	61	4	17	1	22	2
Rogers, S.F.*	1.000	6	1	3	0	4	0
Rojas, Montreal	.913	68	9	12	2	23	1
Ruskin, Cincinnati*	1.000	57	2	10	0	12	0
Saberhagen, New York	1.000	17	7	26	0	33	2
St. Claire, Atlanta	1.000	10	0	4	0	4	0
Sampen, Montreal	1.000	44	9	12	0	21	1
Scanlan, Chicago	.931	69	5	22	2	29	0
Scheid, Houston*	1.000	7	1	1	0	2	0
Schilling, Philadelphia	.921	42	14	21	3	38	1
Schourek, New York*	.923	22	7	13	0	20	1
Scott, San Diego	1.000	34	0	4	0	4	0
Searcy, Philadelphia*	1.000	10	0	2	0	2	0
Seminara, San Diego	.941	19	9	23	2	34	1
Service, Montreal	.000	5	0	0	0	0	0
Shepherd, Phi.	1.000	12	0	5	0	5	0
Simons, Montreal*	.000	7	0	0	1	1	0
Slocumb, Chicago	.778	30	3	4	2	9	0
B. Smith, St. Louis	1.000	13	3	3	0	6	0
Da. Smith, Chicago	1.000	11	0	2	0	2	0
L. Smith, St. Louis	.889	70	1	7	1	9	1
P. Smith, Atlanta	.941	12	3	13	1	17	1
Smith, Pittsburgh*	1.000	23	6	29	0	35	2
Smoltz, Atlanta	.980	35	23	26	1	50	3
Stanton, Atlanta*	1.000	65	3	10	0	13	2
Swift, San Francisco	.981	30	18	33	1	52	3
Swindell, Cincinnati*	.975	31	6	33	1	40	2
Tewksbury, St. Louis	.982	33	14	42	1	57	2
Tomlin, Pittsburgh*	.985	35	12	52	1	65	3
Valdez, Montreal	1.000	27	9	3	0	12	0
Vitko, New York	.333	3	1	0	2	3	0
Wagner, Pittsburgh	1.000	6	2	2	0	4	0
Wakefield, Pittsburgh	1.000	13	6	19	0	25	1
Walk, Pittsburgh	.974	36	10	28	1	39	1
Weston, Philadelphia	.000	1	0	0	0	0	0
Wetteland, Montreal	.929	67	7	6	1	14	0
Whitehurst, New York	.958	44	6	17	1	24	1
Williams, Houston	.920	16	8	15	2	25	0
Mike Williams, Phi.	1.000	5	0	5	0	5	0
Mit. Williams, Phi.*	.800	66	1	11	3	15	0
Wilson, Los Angeles*	.917	60	2	9	1	12	1
Wilson, S.F.*	.949	26	7	30	2	39	2
Wohlers, Atlanta	1.000	32	2	7	0	9	0
Worrell, St. Louis	1.000	67	2	2	0	4	0
Young, New York	.933	52	13	15	2	30	1
Young, Montreal	1.000	13	3	1	0	4	0

PITCHERS WITH TWO OR MORE TEAMS

Player, Team	Pct.	G	PO	A	E	TC	DP
Cox, Philadelphia	.929	9	6	7	1	14	1
Cox, Pittsburgh	.800	16	2	2	1	5	0
DeLeon, St. Louis	1.000	29	7	9	0	16	0
DeLeon, Philadelphia	1.000	3	0	1	0	1	0
Heredia, S.F.	1.000	13	0	1	0	1	0
Heredia, Montreal	1.000	7	0	4	0	4	0
Jackson, Chicago*	.778	19	4	17	6	27	1
Jackson, Pittsburgh*	.913	15	5	16	2	23	1
Jones, Philadelphia	1.000	44	4	11	0	15	1
Jones, New York	1.000	17	0	2	0	2	1
Rivera, Atlanta	1.000	8	0	3	0	3	0
Rivera, Philadelphia	1.000	20	3	16	0	19	0

MISCELLANEOUS

SHUTOUT GAMES

Read across for wins, down for losses.

Team	Atl.	Pit.	Mon.	Cin.	S.D.	L.A.	St.L.	N.Y.	Phi.	S.F.	Hou.	Chi.	W	L	Pct.
Atlanta	..	2	0	1	1	2	1	1	0	5	5	6	24	8	.750
Pittsburgh	0	..	2	2	0	2	4	2	2	0	3	3	20	9	.690
Montreal	1	2	..	0	1	1	1	2	2	0	1	3	14	11	.560
Cincinnati	0	0	1	..	0	1	0	2	2	0	3	2	11	10	.524
San Diego	1	0	0	0	..	0	1	4	0	2	1	2	11	12	.478
Los Angeles	0	0	2	3	0	..	1	2	1	3	0	1	13	15	.464
St. Louis	0	0	0	0	4	2	..	0	0	3	0	0	9	11	.450
New York	1	1	1	0	2	1	1	..	0	3	2	1	13	16	.448
Philadelphia	0	1	2	1	1	0	1	1	..	0	0	0	7	9	.438
San Francisco	4	1	2	0	1	1	1	0	0	..	1	1	12	18	.400
Houston	0	1	1	1	2	3	0	2	0	1	..	1	12	18	.400
Chicago	1	1	0	2	0	2	0	0	2	1	2	..	11	20	.355
Lost	8	9	11	10	12	15	11	16	9	18	18	20	157	157	.500

HOME RECORD

Read across for home wins, down for road losses.

Team	Pit.	Cin.	Atl.	Hou.	St.L.	S.D.	Mon.	Chi.	S.F.	Phi.	N.Y.	L.A.	W	L	Pct.
Pittsburgh	..	2	2	4	7	3	4	6	5	8	8	4	53	28	.654
Cincinnati	2	..	8	7	5	6	2	3	6	4	5	5	53	28	.654
Atlanta	3	8	..	4	3	7	1	5	6	4	2	8	51	30	.630
Houston	4	6	0	..	3	6	4	2	7	4	3	8	47	34	.580
St. Louis	1	4	3	4	..	3	6	4	4	7	5	4	45	36	.556
San Diego	4	4	3	8	1	..	2	3	6	5	4	5	45	36	.556
Montreal	4	3	3	2	3	4	..	7	3	3	6	5	43	38	.531
Chicago	5	2	1	4	6	2	5	..	4	6	6	2	43	38	.531
San Francisco	5	5	4	4	3	4	4	2	..	5	1	5	42	39	.519
Philadelphia	4	3	4	2	5	2	3	6	2	..	6	4	41	40	.506
New York	3	4	1	4	5	2	3	6	5	3	..	5	41	40	.506
Los Angeles	3	3	5	4	2	5	3	2	3	3	4	..	37	44	.457
Lost on road	38	44	34	47	43	44	37	46	51	52	50	55	541	431	.557

ROAD RECORD

Read across for road wins, down for home losses.

Team	Atl.	Mon.	Pit.	St.L.	S.D.	Cin.	Chi.	Hou.	N.Y.	S.F.	Phi.	L.A.	W	L	Pct.
Atlanta	..	3	4	3	6	1	5	9	5	5	2	4	47	34	.580
Montreal	5	..	5	3	4	4	4	2	6	2	6	3	44	37	.543
Pittsburgh	3	5	..	8	2	4	4	2	6	1	5	3	43	38	.531
St. Louis	3	6	2	..	5	1	3	3	4	3	4	4	38	43	.469
San Diego	2	2	3	3	..	3	4	3	4	5	4	4	37	44	.457
Cincinnati	1	3	4	2	5	..	4	3	2	4	3	6	37	44	.457
Chicago	1	2	3	5	3	3	..	4	3	4	3	4	35	46	.432
Houston	5	4	2	2	1	2	2	..	2	5	4	5	34	47	.420
New York	4	3	1	4	2	1	3	3	..	5	3	2	31	50	.383
San Francisco	3	3	1	2	3	3	2	2	1	..	4	6	30	51	.370
Philadelphia	2	6	1	2	1	2	3	2	6	1	..	3	29	52	.358
Los Angeles	1	1	2	2	4	4	4	1	1	4	2	..	26	55	.321
Lost at home	30	38	28	36	36	28	38	34	40	39	40	44	431	541	.443

PITCHING AGAINST EACH CLUB

ATLANTA—98-64

Pitcher	Chi. W-L	Cin. W-L	Hou. W-L	L.A. W-L	Mon. W-L	N.Y. W-L	Phi. W-L	Pit. W-L	St.L. W-L	S.D. W-L	S.F. W-L	Totals W-L
Avery	1-0	2-2	3-0	2-2	0-2	1-0	0-1	1-0	1-1	0-1	0-2	11-11
Berenguer	0-0	0-0	0-0	1-0	0-0	0-1	0-0	0-0	0-0	2-0	0-0	3-1
Bielecki	0-0	1-0	0-0	1-0	0-0	0-1	0-1	0-0	0-0	0-1	0-1	2-4
Borbon	0-0	0-0	0-0	0-0	0-0	0-0	0-0	0-0	0-0	0-1	0-0	0-1
Davis	0-0	0-0	0-0	0-0	0-0	0-0	0-0	0-0	0-0	1-0	0-0	1-0
Freeman	0-0	1-1	2-2	1-0	0-0	0-1	0-0	1-0	0-1	1-0	1-0	7-5
Glavine	2-0	1-0	3-0	2-0	1-3	2-0	2-2	4-0	0-0	1-1	2-2	20-8

Pitcher	Chi. W-L	Cin. W-L	Hou. W-L	L.A. W-L	Mon. W-L	N.Y. W-L	Phi. W-L	Pit. W-L	St.L. W-L	S.D. W-L	S.F. W-L	Totals W-L
Leibrandt	2-0	0-2	1-1	2-0	1-1	0-1	1-0	1-0	2-1	2-0	3-1	15-7
Mercker	1-0	1-0	0-0	0-0	1-0	0-0	0-0	0-0	0-1	0-0	0-1	3-2
Nied	0-0	0-0	1-0	0-0	0-0	1-0	0-0	0-0	0-0	1-0	0-0	3-0
Pena	0-1	0-0	0-1	0-1	0-1	0-0	0-0	0-1	1-1	0-0	0-0	1-6
Reardon	0-0	0-0	0-0	0-0	0-0	0-0	2-0	0-0	0-0	1-0	0-0	3-0
Reynoso	0-0	0-0	0-0	0-0	0-0	0-0	0-0	0-0	0-0	0-0	1-0	1-0
Rivera	0-0	0-0	0-0	0-0	0-0	0-0	0-0	0-1	0-0	0-0	0-0	0-1
P. Smith	0-0	0-0	1-0	2-0	0-0	1-0	0-0	0-0	1-0	1-0	1-0	7-0
Smoltz	3-1	1-2	2-1	1-1	1-0	1-1	0-2	0-2	1-1	2-1	3-0	15-12
Stanton	1-0	2-1	0-0	0-2	0-1	0-0	1-0	0-0	0-0	1-0	0-0	5-4
Wohlers	0-0	0-1	0-0	0-0	0-0	1-0	0-0	0-1	0-0	0-0	0-0	1-2
Totals	10-2	9-9	13-5	12-6	4-8	7-5	6-6	7-5	6-6	13-5	11-7	98-64

No-decisions—St. Claire.

CHICAGO—78-84

Pitcher	Atl. W-L	Cin. W-L	Hou. W-L	L.A. W-L	Mon. W-L	N.Y. W-L	Phi. W-L	Pit. W-L	St.L. W-L	S.D. W-L	S.F. W-L	Totals W-L
Assenmacher	0-1	1-0	1-0	0-0	0-0	0-1	0-0	2-0	0-2	0-0	0-0	4-4
Boskie	0-2	0-1	1-0	0-1	0-1	0-2	1-0	0-2	2-1	1-1	0-0	5-11
Bullinger	0-1	0-0	0-1	0-0	0-1	1-1	0-1	0-1	0-1	0-1	1-0	2-8
Castillo	0-2	1-1	0-1	1-1	2-1	0-1	1-1	0-1	2-0	2-1	1-1	10-11
Harkey	0-0	0-0	2-0	0-0	0-0	1-0	0-0	0-0	0-0	0-0	1-0	4-0
Jackson	0-2	0-1	0-0	0-2	2-0	1-1	1-1	0-1	0-1	0-0	0-0	4-9
Maddux	1-1	1-1	2-0	1-0	0-1	4-1	3-1	3-1	4-0	1-3	0-2	20-11
McElroy	1-0	0-2	0-2	0-0	2-0	0-1	0-1	1-0	0-0	0-0	0-1	4-7
Morgan	0-0	1-1	2-0	2-0	1-2	1-1	3-1	1-2	0-1	1-0	4-0	16-8
Patterson	0-0	1-0	0-0	1-1	0-1	0-0	0-0	0-0	0-0	0-1	0-0	2-3
Robinson	0-0	0-0	0-0	1-0	0-2	1-0	0-0	0-1	2-0	0-0	0-0	4-3
Scanlan	0-1	0-0	0-0	0-0	0-1	0-0	0-2	1-1	1-1	0-0	1-0	3-6
Slocumb	0-0	0-0	0-0	0-1	0-1	0-0	0-1	0-0	0-0	0-0	0-0	0-3
Totals	2-10	5-7	8-4	6-6	7-11	9-9	9-9	8-10	11-7	5-7	8-4	78-84

No-decisions—Hartsock, Hollins, Rasmussen, D. Smith.

CINCINNATI—90-72

Pitcher	Atl. W-L	Chi. W-L	Hou. W-L	L.A. W-L	Mon. W-L	N.Y. W-L	Phi. W-L	Pit. W-L	St.L. W-L	S.D. W-L	S.F. W-L	Totals W-L
Ayala	0-0	0-0	0-0	0-0	0-0	0-0	0-0	0-0	0-0	1-1	1-0	2-1
Bankhead	2-1	1-0	1-1	3-0	2-0	0-1	0-0	1-0	0-1	0-0	0-0	10-4
Belcher	2-2	1-1	2-0	2-2	0-1	1-1	2-1	1-3	1-1	2-1	1-1	15-14
Bolton	0-0	0-0	0-0	1-0	0-1	0-0	1-0	0-0	1-0	0-1	0-1	3-3
Brown	0-0	0-0	0-0	0-0	0-0	0-0	0-0	0-1	0-0	0-0	0-0	0-1
Browning	1-1	0-1	1-0	0-1	1-0	0-0	0-0	1-0	0-0	1-0	1-1	6-5
Charlton	1-1	1-0	0-0	0-0	0-1	1-0	0-0	0-0	0-0	0-0	1-0	4-2
Dibble	0-0	0-1	0-1	0-0	0-1	1-1	0-1	0-0	1-0	1-0	0-0	3-5
Foster	0-0	0-0	0-0	0-0	0-0	0-1	0-0	0-0	0-0	1-0	0-0	1-1
Hammond	1-0	0-1	2-3	0-0	0-0	2-1	1-1	0-1	0-1	0-2	1-0	7-10
Henry	0-1	0-0	0-0	0-1	1-0	0-0	0-0	0-1	1-0	0-0	1-0	3-3
Hill	0-0	0-0	0-0	0-0	0-0	0-0	0-0	0-0	0-0	0-0	0-0	0-0
Menendez	0-0	0-0	0-0	0-0	0-0	0-0	0-0	1-0	0-0	0-0	0-0	1-0
Pugh	0-0	0-0	0-0	1-1	0-1	1-0	0-0	0-0	0-0	2-0	0-0	4-2
Rijo	2-1	1-0	2-2	1-0	1-1	0-0	1-1	1-0	1-1	2-1	3-3	15-10
Ruskin	0-1	2-0	0-1	1-0	0-0	0-0	0-0	0-0	1-0	0-0	0-1	4-3
Swindell	0-1	1-1	2-0	2-2	0-1	1-0	2-0	1-0	1-1	1-1	1-1	12-8
Totals	9-9	7-5	10-8	11-7	5-7	7-5	7-5	6-6	7-5	11-7	10-8	90-72

HOUSTON—81-81

Pitcher	Atl. W-L	Chi. W-L	Cin. W-L	L.A. W-L	Mon. W-L	N.Y. W-L	Phi. W-L	Pit. W-L	St.L. W-L	S.D. W-L	S.F. W-L	Totals W-L
Blair	0-1	0-0	0-1	0-1	0-0	1-1	1-0	1-1	0-0	0-2	2-0	5-7
Boever	0-0	0-1	1-0	1-0	1-0	0-0	0-0	0-1	0-1	0-2	0-1	3-6
Bowen	0-1	0-1	0-1	0-0	0-0	0-0	0-0	0-1	0-0	0-1	0-2	0-7
Harnisch	2-4	0-1	1-2	1-0	2-0	0-0	1-0	1-0	0-1	1-2	0-0	9-10
Henry	0-0	1-1	0-1	1-1	2-0	1-1	1-1	0-0	0-1	0-2	0-1	6-9
Hernandez	0-1	2-0	0-0	1-0	0-0	0-0	0-0	0-0	1-0	1-0	4-0	9-1
D. Jones	2-0	0-1	1-0	1-1	0-0	0-2	0-0	3-0	1-2	2-1	1-1	11-8
J. Jones	0-1	1-0	1-1	1-1	1-1	0-1	3-0	0-1	1-0	1-0	1-0	10-6
Kile	1-2	0-1	0-0	2-0	1-2	0-2	0-1	0-1	0-1	0-0	1-0	5-10
Murphy	0-0	0-0	0-0	1-0	0-0	1-0	0-1	0-0	0-0	0-0	1-0	3-1
Osuna	0-0	0-0	3-0	0-0	0-0	1-0	0-0	1-1	0-1	1-0	0-0	6-3
Portugal	0-1	0-0	0-0	2-0	1-1	1-0	0-0	0-0	1-0	0-0	1-1	6-3
Reynolds	0-0	0-1	0-1	1-1	0-0	0-0	0-0	0-0	0-0	0-0	0-0	1-3

Pitcher	Atl. W-L	Chi. W-L	Cin. W-L	L.A. W-L	Mon. W-L	N.Y. W-L	Phi. W-L	Pit. W-L	St.L. W-L	S.D. W-L	S.F. W-L	Totals W-L
Scheid	0-0	0-0	0-1	0-0	0-0	0-0	0-0	0-0	0-0	0-0	0-0	0-1
Williams	0-2	0-1	1-2	1-0	0-0	0-0	2-0	0-0	1-0	1-1	1-0	7-6
Totals	5-13	4-8	8-10	13-5	8-4	5-7	8-4	6-6	5-7	7-11	12-6	81-81

No-decisions—Mallicoat.

LOS ANGELES—63-99

Pitcher	Atl. W-L	Chi. W-L	Cin. W-L	Hou. W-L	Mon. W-L	N.Y. W-L	Phi. W-L	Pit. W-L	St.L. W-L	S.D. W-L	S.F. W-L	Totals W-L
Astacio	0-1	0-1	1-1	0-1	0-1	1-0	1-0	0-0	0-0	0-0	2-0	5-5
Candelaria	0-1	0-1	0-0	1-1	0-0	1-1	0-0	0-0	0-0	0-0	0-1	2-5
Candiotti	2-1	0-1	1-1	1-1	1-0	1-1	1-2	1-3	1-1	2-2	0-2	11-15
Crews	0-1	0-0	0-0	0-1	0-1	0-0	0-0	0-0	0-0	0-0	0-0	0-3
Gott	0-0	0-0	0-0	0-1	0-0	0-0	0-0	2-1	0-1	1-0	0-0	3-3
Ke. Gross	0-3	1-1	1-3	0-2	1-1	0-0	1-0	1-0	1-2	1-1	1-0	8-13
Ki. Gross	0-0	0-0	0-0	0-1	1-0	0-0	0-0	0-0	0-0	0-0	0-0	1-1
Hershiser	1-3	2-0	1-0	0-3	1-1	1-1	0-2	0-1	0-2	2-2	2-0	10-15
Howell	0-0	0-1	0-0	0-0	0-0	0-0	0-1	0-0	0-0	1-0	0-1	1-3
P. Martinez	0-0	0-0	0-1	0-0	0-0	0-0	0-0	0-0	0-0	0-0	0-0	0-1
R. Martinez	1-1	1-0	0-1	2-0	0-1	1-1	1-2	0-2	1-0	0-1	1-2	8-11
McDowell	2-0	1-0	1-2	0-1	0-0	0-2	0-0	0-0	0-0	1-2	1-2	6-10
Ojeda	0-1	1-1	2-0	1-1	0-1	0-1	1-0	0-0	1-1	0-1	0-2	6-9
Wilson	0-0	0-0	0-2	0-0	0-2	0-0	0-0	1-0	0-0	1-0	0-1	2-5
Totals	6-12	6-6	7-11	5-13	4-8	5-7	5-7	5-7	4-8	9-9	7-11	63-99

MONTREAL—87-75

Pitcher	Atl. W-L	Chi. W-L	Cin. W-L	Hou. W-L	L.A. W-L	N.Y. W-L	Phi. W-L	Pit. W-L	St.L. W-L	S.D. W-L	S.F. W-L	Totals W-L
Barnes	1-0	2-0	0-0	0-1	0-0	0-0	0-3	1-0	1-1	0-1	1-0	6-6
Bottenfield	0-0	1-0	0-0	0-0	0-0	0-0	0-1	0-1	0-0	0-0	0-0	1-2
Fassero	2-0	1-0	1-0	0-0	1-1	1-3	0-1	1-0	1-1	0-0	0-1	8-7
Gardner	0-1	0-2	0-2	0-1	3-0	3-0	2-0	2-2	1-0	1-1	0-1	12-10
Haney	0-0	0-0	0-0	0-1	0-1	1-0	0-0	0-1	1-0	0-0	0-0	2-3
Hill	1-1	0-1	0-1	2-1	0-0	2-1	4-1	1-1	1-2	3-0	2-0	16-9
Hurst	0-0	0-0	0-0	0-0	1-0	0-1	0-0	0-0	0-0	0-0	0-0	1-1
Krueger	0-0	0-0	0-0	0-0	0-0	0-0	0-0	0-1	0-1	0-0	0-0	0-2
Landrum	0-0	0-0	0-0	0-0	0-0	1-0	0-0	0-0	0-0	0-1	0-0	1-1
Martinez	3-0	1-1	1-0	2-1	1-1	3-1	2-0	1-3	1-1	1-1	0-2	16-11
Nabholz	1-2	3-2	1-0	0-2	0-0	0-0	1-3	3-0	0-1	1-1	1-1	11-12
Risley	0-0	0-0	0-0	0-0	1-0	0-0	0-0	0-0	0-0	0-0	0-0	1-0
Rojas	0-0	1-0	3-0	0-0	1-0	1-0	0-0	0-0	0-1	1-0	0-0	7-1
Sampen	0-0	1-1	0-1	0-1	0-0	0-0	0-0	0-0	0-0	0-0	0-1	1-4
Valdez	0-0	0-0	0-0	0-0	0-1	0-0	0-0	0-0	0-1	0-0	0-0	0-2
Wetteland	0-0	1-0	1-1	0-0	0-0	0-0	0-0	0-0	0-3	1-0	1-0	4-4
Totals	8-4	11-7	7-5	4-8	8-4	12-6	9-9	9-9	6-12	8-4	5-7	87-75

No-decisions—Heredia, Maysey, Service, Simons, Young.

NEW YORK—72-90

Pitcher	Atl. W-L	Chi. W-L	Cin. W-L	Hou. W-L	L.A. W-L	Mon. W-L	Phi. W-L	Pit. W-L	St.L. W-L	S.D. W-L	S.F. W-L	Totals W-L
Birkbeck	0-1	0-0	0-0	0-0	0-0	0-0	0-0	0-0	0-0	0-0	0-0	0-1
Burke	1-0	0-0	0-0	0-0	0-0	0-0	0-0	0-0	0-0	0-1	0-1	1-2
Cone	2-1	1-1	0-0	2-0	1-1	2-2	1-0	0-0	1-0	1-2	2-0	13-7
Dewey	0-0	0-0	0-0	0-0	0-0	0-0	0-0	0-0	0-0	0-0	0-0	1-0
Fernandez	1-0	1-1	1-1	0-2	2-1	1-1	2-2	1-2	0-1	2-0	3-0	14-11
Filer	0-0	0-0	0-0	0-0	0-0	0-0	0-0	0-1	0-0	0-0	0-0	0-1
Franco	0-0	0-0	0-0	0-0	1-0	1-0	1-0	0-1	3-1	0-0	0-0	6-2
Gibson	0-0	0-0	0-1	0-0	0-0	0-0	0-0	0-0	0-0	0-0	0-0	0-1
Gooden	0-2	1-1	1-1	1-1	0-1	0-2	1-2	1-1	2-0	1-1	2-1	10-13
Guetterman	0-1	2-1	0-0	0-0	1-0	0-0	0-0	0-1	0-1	0-0	0-0	3-4
Hillman	0-0	0-1	0-0	0-0	0-0	0-0	0-0	1-1	0-0	0-0	1-0	2-2
Innis	0-0	1-0	0-0	2-1	1-1	0-1	0-3	0-2	2-1	0-0	0-0	6-9
Jones	0-0	0-0	2-0	0-0	0-0	0-0	0-0	0-0	0-0	0-0	0-0	2-0
Saberhagen	0-0	0-0	0-0	2-0	1-0	0-2	0-1	0-1	0-1	0-0	0-0	3-5
Schourek	1-0	2-0	0-1	0-0	0-0	0-1	1-0	1-3	0-1	0-2	1-0	6-8
Vitko	0-0	0-0	0-0	0-0	0-0	0-0	0-1	0-0	0-0	0-0	0-0	0-1
Whitehurst	0-2	0-2	1-0	0-0	0-0	1-0	0-2	0-1	0-1	0-1	1-0	3-9
Young	0-0	0-2	0-3	0-1	0-1	1-3	0-1	0-0	1-2	0-1	0-0	2-14
Totals	5-7	9-9	5-7	7-5	7-5	6-12	6-12	4-14	9-9	4-8	10-2	72-90

No-decisions—Pecota.

PHILADELPHIA—70-92

Pitcher	Atl. W-L	Chi. W-L	Cin. W-L	Hou. W-L	L.A. W-L	Mon. W-L	N.Y. W-L	Pit. W-L	St.L. W-L	S.D. W-L	S.F. W-L	Totals W-L
Abbott	0-0	0-3	0-0	0-1	1-0	0-2	0-3	0-1	0-1	0-0	0-3	1-14
Ashby	0-0	0-0	0-1	0-2	0-0	0-0	0-0	1-0	0-0	0-0	0-0	1-3
Ayrault	0-0	1-0	0-0	0-0	0-0	0-0	1-0	0-0	0-2	0-0	0-0	2-2
Brantley	0-2	0-0	1-0	0-1	0-0	0-0	0-1	0-1	0-0	0-1	1-0	2-6
Brink	0-0	0-1	0-1	0-0	0-0	0-0	0-0	0-0	0-2	0-0	0-0	0-4
Combs	0-0	0-0	0-0	0-0	0-1	1-0	0-0	0-0	0-0	0-0	0-0	1-1
Cox	0-0	1-0	0-0	0-0	1-1	0-0	0-0	0-1	0-0	0-0	0-0	2-2
DeLeon	0-0	0-1	0-0	0-0	0-0	0-0	0-0	0-0	0-0	0-0	0-0	0-1
Greene	0-0	2-0	0-0	0-0	0-0	1-0	0-0	0-2	0-1	0-0	0-0	3-3
Hartley	0-1	2-0	1-0	0-1	0-0	1-0	1-0	0-1	2-0	0-1	0-2	7-6
Jones	0-0	0-0	0-0	2-0	0-0	0-0	1-1	0-2	1-0	0-2	1-1	5-6
Mathews	0-0	0-0	0-1	0-0	0-0	0-2	1-0	0-0	1-0	0-0	0-0	2-3
Mulholland	2-0	1-2	1-1	1-2	2-1	2-0	0-1	2-2	0-0	1-2	1-0	13-11
Ritchie	0-0	0-0	0-1	0-0	1-0	0-0	0-0	0-0	1-0	0-0	0-0	2-1
Rivera	1-0	0-1	1-1	0-0	0-0	2-1	1-0	1-0	1-0	0-0	0-0	7-3
Robinson	1-0	0-0	0-0	0-0	0-1	0-0	0-0	0-1	0-0	0-1	0-1	1-4
Schilling	2-1	0-1	1-1	1-1	1-1	2-2	3-0	1-0	1-2	2-2	0-0	14-11
Shepherd	0-0	0-0	0-0	0-0	0-0	0-0	1-0	0-1	0-0	0-0	0-0	1-1
Weston	0-0	0-0	0-0	0-0	0-0	0-1	0-0	0-0	0-0	0-0	0-0	0-1
Mit. Williams	0-2	2-0	0-0	0-0	0-0	0-0	3-0	0-1	0-3	0-0	0-2	5-8
Mike Williams	0-0	0-0	0-0	0-0	1-0	0-1	0-0	0-0	0-0	0-0	0-0	1-1
Totals	6-6	9-9	5-7	4-8	7-5	9-9	12-6	5-13	7-11	3-9	3-9	70-92

No-decisions—Baller, Chapin, Searcy.

PITTSBURGH—96-66

Pitcher	Atl. W-L	Chi. W-L	Cin. W-L	Hou. W-L	L.A. W-L	Mon. W-L	N.Y. W-L	Phi. W-L	St.L. W-L	S.D. W-L	S.F. W-L	Totals W-L
Belinda	2-0	0-2	0-1	2-0	0-1	0-0	1-0	1-0	0-0	0-1	0-0	6-4
Cole	0-0	0-0	0-1	0-0	0-0	0-0	0-0	0-0	0-1	0-0	0-0	0-2
Cooke	0-0	0-0	0-0	0-0	0-0	0-0	1-0	0-0	1-0	0-0	0-0	2-0
Cox	0-0	1-0	0-0	0-0	1-1	1-0	0-0	0-0	0-0	0-0	0-0	3-1
Drabek	0-0	2-1	1-2	0-0	0-1	3-1	1-2	3-1	3-1	0-1	2-1	15-11
Gleaton	0-0	0-0	0-0	0-0	1-0	0-0	0-0	0-0	0-0	0-0	0-0	1-0
Jackson	0-2	0-0	0-0	0-0	0-0	0-0	1-1	0-0	1-1	1-0	1-0	4-4
Lamp	0-0	0-0	1-0	0-0	0-0	0-0	0-0	0-0	0-0	0-1	0-0	1-1
Mason	0-0	1-1	0-1	0-4	0-0	0-1	0-0	1-0	3-0	0-0	0-0	5-7
Miller	0-0	0-0	1-0	0-0	0-0	0-0	0-0	0-0	0-0	0-0	0-0	1-0
Neagle	0-1	0-1	0-0	1-0	0-2	0-0	2-1	0-0	0-0	0-1	1-0	4-6
Palacios	1-0	0-0	0-0	0-0	0-0	1-1	0-0	0-1	0-0	0-0	1-0	3-2
Patterson	1-1	0-0	1-0	0-1	1-0	0-0	0-0	3-1	0-0	0-0	0-0	6-3
Robinson	0-0	0-0	0-1	0-0	0-0	2-0	1-0	0-0	0-0	0-0	0-0	3-1
Smith	0-1	0-0	2-0	2-0	0-0	1-3	0-0	2-1	1-0	0-1	0-2	8-8
Tomlin	0-1	2-3	0-1	0-1	2-0	1-1	3-0	2-0	2-0	2-1	0-1	14-9
Wagner	0-0	1-0	0-0	0-0	0-0	0-0	0-0	0-0	1-0	0-0	0-0	2-0
Wakefield	1-0	1-0	0-0	0-0	1-0	0-0	2-0	1-0	1-0	0-0	1-1	8-1
Walk	0-1	2-0	0-0	1-0	1-0	0-2	2-0	0-1	2-0	2-1	0-1	10-6
Totals	5-7	10-8	6-6	6-6	7-5	9-9	14-4	13-5	15-3	5-7	6-6	96-66

No-decisions—Batista, Minor.

ST. LOUIS—83-79

Pitcher	Atl. W-L	Chi. W-L	Cin. W-L	Hou. W-L	L.A. W-L	Mon. W-L	N.Y. W-L	Phi. W-L	Pit. W-L	S.D. W-L	S.F. W-L	Totals W-L
Agosto	1-0	0-1	0-0	0-1	0-0	0-0	0-2	0-0	0-0	0-0	1-0	2-4
Carpenter	0-0	2-0	0-3	2-0	0-0	0-0	1-1	0-0	0-0	0-0	0-0	5-4
Clark	0-1	0-2	0-1	0-0	2-0	0-1	0-0	0-0	0-4	1-1	0-0	3-10
Cormier	0-1	1-0	1-1	1-0	2-0	0-3	0-1	3-0	1-2	0-1	1-1	10-10
DeLeon	1-0	1-2	0-1	0-1	0-1	0-0	0-0	0-0	0-1	0-0	0-1	2-7
Magrane	0-0	0-0	0-0	0-0	0-0	1-0	0-0	0-1	0-1	0-0	0-0	1-2
McClure	0-0	0-0	0-0	1-0	0-0	0-0	0-1	1-1	0-0	0-0	0-0	2-2
Olivares	1-1	0-3	1-0	0-1	1-1	2-1	2-0	1-0	0-1	1-0	0-1	9-9
Osborne	0-1	0-1	1-0	1-1	1-1	2-1	0-0	2-2	0-1	3-0	1-1	11-9
Perez	2-1	0-0	0-0	0-1	0-0	1-0	3-1	0-0	0-0	3-0	0-0	9-3
B. Smith	0-0	1-1	0-0	0-0	0-0	2-0	1-0	0-1	0-0	0-0	0-0	4-2
L. Smith	0-0	1-0	0-0	1-0	0-0	1-0	1-3	0-1	0-3	0-1	0-1	4-9
Tewksbury	1-1	1-1	2-1	1-0	0-1	3-0	1-0	1-0	2-1	3-0	1-0	16-5
Worrell	0-0	0-0	0-0	0-0	2-0	0-0	0-0	3-1	0-1	0-1	0-0	5-3
Totals	6-6	7-11	5-7	7-5	8-4	12-6	9-9	11-7	3-15	8-4	7-5	83-79

No-decisions—DiPino.

SAN DIEGO—82-80

Pitcher	Atl. W-L	Chi. W-L	Cin. W-L	Hou. W-L	L.A. W-L	Mon. W-L	N.Y. W-L	Phi. W-L	Pit. W-L	St.L. W-L	S.F. W-L	Totals W-L
Andersen	0-1	0-0	0-0	1-0	0-0	0-0	0-0	0-0	0-0	0-0	0-0	1-1
Benes	0-2	2-1	2-2	2-0	1-1	0-4	2-0	1-1	1-1	0-2	2-0	13-14
Clements	0-0	0-0	0-0	1-0	0-1	0-0	0-0	1-0	0-0	0-0	0-0	2-1
Deshaies	0-1	0-0	1-1	1-0	1-2	0-0	0-0	1-0	0-2	0-0	0-1	4-7
Eiland	0-0	0-0	0-0	0-0	0-0	0-0	0-0	0-0	0-0	0-1	0-1	0-2
Gr. Harris	1-0	0-1	0-2	1-0	0-1	1-1	0-1	0-1	0-1	1-0	0-0	4-8
Ge. Harris	0-0	0-1	0-0	0-0	0-0	0-0	0-0	0-0	0-0	0-0	0-1	0-2
Hernandez	0-0	1-0	0-1	0-2	0-0	0-0	0-0	0-0	0-0	0-0	0-0	1-4
Hurst	2-1	1-1	0-3	1-1	2-0	0-1	4-0	1-1	0-0	2-1	1-0	14-9
Lefferts	0-2	1-0	1-0	2-0	1-1	1-0	2-0	1-0	2-1	0-3	2-2	13-9
Maddux	0-2	1-0	0-0	0-0	0-0	0-0	0-0	0-0	1-0	0-0	0-0	2-2
Melendez	0-0	1-1	1-0	0-0	2-2	0-1	0-2	1-0	0-0	0-0	1-1	6-7
Myers	1-1	0-0	0-1	0-2	1-0	0-0	0-0	0-0	1-0	0-1	0-1	3-6
Rodriguez	1-1	0-0	0-0	1-2	0-0	0-0	0-0	2-0	1-0	1-0	0-0	6-3
Scott	0-0	0-0	0-0	0-0	0-0	0-0	0-1	1-0	1-0	0-0	0-0	4-1
Seminara	0-2	0-0	2-1	1-0	1-0	2-0	0-1	0-0	0-0	0-0	3-0	9-4
Totals	5-13	7-5	7-11	11-7	9-9	4-8	8-4	9-3	7-5	4-8	11-7	82-80

No-decisions—Brocail.

SAN FRANCISCO—72-90

Pitcher	Atl. W-L	Chi. W-L	Cin. W-L	Hou. W-L	L.A. W-L	Mon. W-L	N.Y. W-L	Phi. W-L	Pit. W-L	St.L. W-L	S.D. W-L	Totals W-L
Beck	0-0	0-0	0-1	0-0	2-0	0-0	0-0	0-0	0-0	1-1	0-1	3-3
Black	1-3	0-1	1-1	0-0	1-2	1-2	1-0	1-0	3-1	0-0	1-2	10-12
Brantley	2-0	0-1	0-0	0-3	1-0	2-0	0-0	0-0	0-2	0-0	2-1	7-7
Burba	0-1	0-3	0-1	0-1	0-0	1-0	0-1	1-0	0-0	0-1	0-0	2-7
Burkett	1-1	2-0	2-1	2-0	1-0	0-0	0-3	0-0	2-1	2-1	1-2	13-9
Carter	0-0	0-0	0-2	0-1	1-0	0-0	0-0	0-0	0-0	0-1	0-1	1-5
Downs	0-1	0-0	0-0	0-0	0-1	0-0	1-0	0-0	0-0	0-0	0-0	1-2
Heredia	1-0	0-0	0-2	0-1	1-0	0-0	0-0	0-0	0-0	0-0	0-0	2-3
Hickerson	0-1	0-0	1-0	0-0	0-0	0-0	0-1	3-0	0-0	0-0	0-1	5-3
Jackson	1-1	1-1	0-1	1-1	0-0	0-0	0-0	1-1	0-0	0-0	2-1	6-6
Oliveras	0-0	0-0	0-0	0-1	0-1	0-0	0-0	0-0	0-1	0-0	0-0	0-3
Pena	0-0	0-0	0-1	0-0	0-0	0-0	0-0	1-0	0-0	0-0	0-0	1-1
Rapp	0-0	0-0	0-0	0-0	0-0	0-1	0-0	0-1	0-0	0-0	0-0	0-2
Reed	0-0	0-0	1-0	0-0	0-0	0-0	0-0	0-0	0-0	0-0	0-0	1-0
Righetti	0-0	0-0	1-0	1-2	0-1	0-1	0-0	0-0	0-0	0-2	0-1	2-7
Rogers	0-0	0-0	0-1	0-1	0-0	0-0	0-3	0-0	0-0	0-0	0-0	0-2
Swift	1-1	1-0	0-0	1-1	2-0	2-0	0-1	1-0	0-0	1-1	1-0	10-4
Wilson	0-2	0-2	2-0	1-0	1-2	1-1	0-4	1-1	1-1	1-0	0-1	8-14
Totals	7-11	4-8	8-10	6-12	11-7	7-5	2-10	9-3	6-6	5-7	7-11	72-90

HOME RUNS BY PARKS

	At Atl.	At Chi.	At Cin.	At Hou.	At L.A.	At Mon.	At N.Y.	At Phi.	At Pit.	At St.L.	At S.D.	At S.F.	Totals 1992	Totals 1991
Atlanta	72	7	8	6	4	5	12	2	5	5	6	6	138	141
Chicago	4	59	4	3	2	4	5	5	4	7	4	3	104	159
Cincinnati	8	0	60	4	2	1	2	5	2	7	6	2	99	164
Houston	6	0	10	49	4	4	3	2	5	0	7	6	96	79
Los Angeles	1	5	3	2	26	5	2	4	3	6	6	9	72	108
Montreal	5	4	9	2	4	50	5	7	3	5	6	2	102	95
New York	4	6	2	3	7	3	42	5	3	7	6	5	93	117
Philadelphia	4	8	2	2	3	4	3	67	4	6	7	8	118	111
Pittsburgh	3	4	5	8	1	7	7	4	51	4	6	6	106	126
St. Louis	1	6	3	5	2	6	4	4	2	55	3	3	94	68
San Diego	6	6	5	1	1	3	3	5	5	3	87	10	135	121
San Francisco	3	3	9	5	3	6	3	6	1	2	7	57	105	141
1992 total	117	108	120	90	59	98	91	116	88	107	151	117	1262	....
1991 total	156	168	181	71	103	68	112	114	116	73	137	131	....	1430

AT ATLANTA (117):

Atlanta (72)—Pendleton 13, Gant 10, Justice 10, Hunter 9, Berryhill 6, Blauser 5, Sanders 5, Bream 4, Lemke 4, L. Smith 3, Gregg 1, Nixon 1, Willard 1. **Chicago (4)**—Daniels 1, Dawson 1, Grace 1, Sandberg 1. **Cincinnati (8)**—Braggs 2, Hatcher 1, Larkin 1, O'Neill 1, Oliver 1, Roberts 1, Sanders 1. **Houston (6)**—Bagwell 2, Anthony 1, Caminiti 1, Gonzalez 1, Riles 1. **Los Angeles (1)**—Karros 1. **Montreal (5)**—Walker 2, Cianfrocco 1, Owen 1, Wallach 1. **New York (4)**—Boston 2, Murray 1, O'Brien 1. **Philadelphia (4)**—Daulton 2, Hollins 2. **Pittsburgh (3)**—Bell 2, King 1. **St. Louis (1)**—Galarraga 1. **San Diego (6)**—McGriff 2, Benes 1, Jackson 1, Sheffield 1, Teufel 1. **San Francisco (3)**—Clark 1, Thompson 1, Williams 1.

AT CHICAGO (108):

Atlanta (7)—Blauser 3, Bream 1, Justice 1, Olson 1, Sanders 1. **Chicago (59)**—Sandberg 16, Dawson 13, Grace 5, Sosa 4, May 3, Salazar 3, Smith 3, Wilkins 3, Daniels 2, Villanueva 2, Buechele 1, Girardi 1, Maddux 1, Sanchez 1, Scott 1. **Los Angeles (5)**—Karros 2, Anderson 1, Benzinger 1, Hansen 1. **Montreal (4)**—Berry 1, Carter 1, Walker 1, Wallach 1. **New York (6)**—Murray 3, Bonilla 1, Boston 1, McKnight 1. **Philadelphia (8)**—Hollins 3, Chamberlain 2, Batiste 1, Daulton 1, Kruk 1. **Pittsburgh (4)**—Van Slyke 2, Bonds 1, Varsho 1. **St. Louis (6)**—Galarraga 1, Lankford 1, Pena 1, Royer 1, Thompson 1, Zeile 1. **San Diego (6)**—McGriff 2, Clark 1, Fernandez 1, Jackson 1, Teufel 1. **San Francisco (3)**—Manwaring 2, Leonard 1.

AT CINCINNATI (120):

Atlanta (8)—Blauser 2, Hunter 2, Cabrera 1, Gant 1, Olson 1, Sanders 1. **Chicago (4)**—Dawson 2, Daniels 1, Grace 1. **Cincinnati (60)**—Larkin 8, Sabo 8, Oliver 7, Doran 6, O'Neill 6, Sanders 6, Braggs 4, Martinez 3, Morris 3, Roberts 3, Greene 2, Belcher 1, Benavides 1, Coles 1, Hammond 1. **Houston (10)**—Gonzalez 3, Caminiti 2, Bagwell 1, Biggio 1, Taubensee 1. **Los Angeles (3)**—Karros 1, Rodriguez 1, Webster 1. **Montreal (9)**—Reed 2, Carter 1, Cianfrocco 1, Colbrunn 1, Grissom 1, Owen 1, Walker 1, Wallach 1. **New York (2)**—Murray 1, Schofield 1. **Philadelphia (2)**—Daulton 1, Jordan 1. **Pittsburgh (5)**—Buechele 2, Espy 1, Merced 1, Redus 1. **St. Louis (3)**—Olivares 1, Pagnozzi 1, Pena 1. **San Diego (5)**—McGriff 2, Jackson 1, Sheffield 1, Ward 1. **San Francisco (9)**—Snyder 2, Felder 1, James 1, Litton 1, Manwaring 1, Thompson 1, Uribe 1, Williams 1.

AT HOUSTON (90):

Atlanta (6)—Justice 3, Berryhill 1, Cabrera 1, Gant 1. **Chicago (3)**—Dawson 1, Salazar 1, Wilkins 1. **Cincinnati (4)**—Larkin 1, O'Neill 1, Oliver 1, Sanders 1. **Houston (49)**—Anthony 9, Bagwell 8, Caminiti 6, Finley 5, Gonzalez 4, Biggio 3, Cedeno 2, Taubensee 2, Candaele 1, Guerrero 1, C. Jones 1. **Los Angeles (2)**—Davis 1, Hansen 1. **Montreal (2)**—Alou 1, Cianfrocco 1. **New York (3)**—Johnson 1, Murray 1, Walker 1. **Philadelphia (2)**—Hollins 2. **Pittsburgh (8)**—Bonds 3, King 2, Buechele 1, Slaught 1, Van Slyke 1. **St. Louis (5)**—Jose 2, Lankford 1, Pena 1, Thompson 1. **San Diego (1)**—McGriff 1. **San Francisco (5)**—Williams 2, Bass 1, Clark 1, Thompson 1.

AT LOS ANGELES (59):

Atlanta (4)—Justice 2, Gant 1, Smoltz 1. **Chicago (2)**—Dawson 1, Wilkins 1. **Cincinnati (2)**—O'Neill 1, Sanders 1. **Houston (4)**—Caminiti 2, Bagwell 1, Gonzalez 1. **Los Angeles (26)**—Karros 6, Strawberry 3, Ashley 2, Rodriguez 2, Sharperson 2, Benzinger 1, Butler 1, Daniels 1, Davis 1, Hansen 1, Hernandez 1, Javier 1, Offerman 1, Piazza 1, Scioscia 1, Webster 1. **Montreal (4)**—DeShields 2, Vander Wal 1, Walker 1. **New York (7)**—Bonilla 2, Murray 2, Pecota 1, Sasser 1, Walker 1. **Philadelphia (3)**—Daulton 1, Kruk 1, Sveum 1. **Pittsburgh (1)**—Van Slyke 1. **St. Louis (2)**—Thompson 1, Zeile 1. **San Diego (1)**—McGriff 1. **San Francisco (3)**—Williams 2, Snyder 1.

AT MONTREAL (98):

Atlanta (5)—Berryhill 1, Blauser 1, Gant 1, Justice 1, Olson 1. **Chicago (4)**—Sosa 2, Grace 1, Wilkins 1. **Cincinnati (1)**—Doran 1. **Houston (4)**—Anthony 1, Biggio 1, Caminiti 1, Incaviglia 1. **Los Angeles (5)**—Karros 2, Hansen 1, Strawberry 1, Webster 1. **Montreal (50)**—Walker 13, Grissom 8, Alou 6, Wallach 5, Cianfrocco 3, Owen 3, Calderon 2, Carter 2, Vander Wal 2, Cerone 1, Colbrunn 1, Cordero 1, DeShields 1, Hill 1, Reed 1. **New York (3)**—Bonilla 1, Hundley 1, Walker 1. **Philadelphia (4)**—Daulton 2, Chamberlain 1, Dykstra 1. **Pittsburgh (3)**—Bonds 3, Gibson 2, Buechele 1, Merced 1. **St. Louis (6)**—Lankford 2, Galarraga 1, Gilkey 1, Hudler 1, Woodson 1. **San Diego (3)**—McGriff 1, Stillwell 1, Walters 1. **San Francisco (6)**—Clark 1, Clayton 1, Felder 1, Snyder 1, Uribe 1, Williams 1.

AT NEW YORK (91):

Atlanta (12)—Pendleton 3, Justice 2, L. Smith 2, Berryhill 1, Blauser 1, Bream 1, Gant 1, Hunter 1. **Chicago (5)**—Salazar 1, Sandberg 1, Scott 1, Vizcaino 1, Wilkins 1. **Cincinnati (2)**—Morris 1, O'Neill 1. **Houston (3)**—Anthony 2, Ramirez 1. **Los Angeles (2)**—Butler 1, Webster 1. **Montreal (5)**—Alou 1, Calderon 1, Cordero 1, Grissom 1, Owen 1. **New York (42)**—Murray 7, Bonilla 5, Boston 5, Schofield 3, Thompson 3, Bass 2, Coleman 2, Hundley 2, Johnson 2, Kent 2, Magadan 2, Randolph 2, Gallagher 1, McKnight 1, O'Brien 1, Pecota 1, Sasser 1. **Philadelphia (3)**—Castillo 1, Daulton 1, Hollins 1. **Pittsburgh (7)**—Bonds 3, King 2, Van Slyke 2. **St. Louis (4)**—Gilkey 1, Lankford 1, Magrane 1, Zeile 1. **San Diego (3)**—Gwynn 1, Jackson 1, Sheffield 1. **San Francisco (3)**—Benjamin 1, Snyder 1, Thompson 1.

AT PHILADELPHIA (116):

Atlanta (2)—Bream 1, Justice 1. **Chicago (5)**—May 2, Sandberg 2, Grace 1. **Cincinnati (5)**—Sanders 2, Braggs 1, Coles 1, Sabo 1. **Houston (2)**—Bagwell 1, Incaviglia 1. **Los Angeles (4)**—Karros 2, Hernandez 1, Sharperson 1. **Montreal (7)**—DeShields 2, Grissom 2, Carter 1, Vander Wal 1, Walker 1. **New York (5)**—Johnson 2, Bonilla 1, Hundley 1, Magadan 1. **Philadelphia (67)**—Daulton 17, Hollins 14, Kruk 7, Amaro 5, Dykstra 5, Chamberlain 3, Duncan 3, Jordan 2, Morandini 2, Murphy 2, Pratt 2, Bell 1, Castillo 1, Lake 1, Lindeman 1, Marsh 1. **Pittsburgh (4)**—Bonds 3, Bell 1. **St. Louis (4)**—Gilkey 2, Galarraga 1, Pagnozzi 1. **San Diego (5)**—McGriff 3, Gwynn 1, Sheffield 1. **San Francisco (6)**—Williams 3, Felder 1, Litton 1, McGee 1.

AT PITTSBURGH (88):

Atlanta (5)—Lemke 2, Bream 1, Hunter 1, L. Smith 1. **Chicago (4)**—May 2, Sandberg 2. **Cincinnati (2)**—Sabo 2. **Houston (5)**—Bagwell 2, Anthony 1, Henry 1, Incaviglia 1. **Los Angeles (3)**—Anderson 1, Benzinger 1, Webster 1. **Montreal (3)**—DeShields 1, Fletcher 1, Grissom 1. **New York (3)**—Bonilla 1, Hundley 1, Walker 1. **Philadelphia (4)**—Duncan 2, Hollins 2. **Pittsburgh (51)**—Bonds 15, King 6, Van Slyke 6, Bell 5, Merced 4, Buechele 3, McClendon 3, Varsho 3, Clark 2, Slaught 2, LaValliere 1, Redus 1. **St. Louis (2)**—Lankford 1, Pagnozzi 1. **San Diego (5)**—McGriff 1, Santiago 1, Sheffield 1, Teufel 1, Ward 1. **San Francisco (1)**—Clark 1.

AT ST. LOUIS (107):

Atlanta (5)—Pendleton 2, Berryhill 1, Bream 1, Gant 1. **Chicago (7)**—Sandberg 2, Sosa 2, Bullinger 1, Dawson 1, Wilkins 1. **Cincinnati (7)**—Morris 2, O'Neill 2, Braggs 1, Coles 1, Larkin 1. **Los Angeles (6)**—Karros 2, Anderson 1, Benzinger 1, Daniels 1, Hansen 1. **Montreal (5)**—Reed 2, Alou 1, DeShields 1, Grissom 1. **New York (7)**—Bonilla 2, Johnson 2, Boston 1, Hundley 1, Kent 1. **Philadelphia (6)**—Daulton 2, Amaro 1, Chamberlain 1, Hollins 1, Marsh 1. **Pittsburgh (4)**—King 2, Bonds 1, Van Slyke 1. **St. Louis (55)**—Lankford 13, Jose 12, Galarraga 4, Pena 4, Zeile 4, Gilkey 3, Jordan 3, Pagnozzi 3, Alicea 2, Hudler 2, Gedman 1, Guerrero 1, Perry 1, Royer 1, Thompson 1. **San Diego (3)**—Jackson 1, McGriff 1, Teufel 1. **San Francisco (2)**—Clark 1, Williams 1.

AT SAN DIEGO (151):

Atlanta (6)—Blauser 1, Gant 1, Justice 1, Pendleton 1, Sanders 1, Willard 1. **Chicago (4)**—Sandberg 2, May 1, Strange 1. **Cincinnati (6)**—Doran 1, Hatcher 1, Larkin 1, O'Neill 1, Oliver 1, Sanders 1. **Houston (7)**—Anthony 3, Bagwell 2, Biggio 1, Taubensee 1. **Los Angeles (6)**—Davis 2, Scioscia 2, Butler 1, Karros 1. **Montreal (6)**—Walker 3, Fletcher 1, Owen 1, Wallach 1. **New York (6)**—Bonilla 4, Boston 1, Murray 1. **Philadelphia (7)**—Chamberlain 2, Duncan 2, Hollins 2, Morandini 1. **Pittsburgh (6)**—Bonds 4, King 1, Redus 1. **St. Louis (3)**—Galarraga 1, Jordan 1, Pagnozzi 1. **San Diego (87)**—Sheffield 23, McGriff 21, Jackson 11, Clark 9, Santiago 8, Gwynn 4, Fernandez 3, Walters 3, Teufel 2, Eiland 1, Stillwell 1, Velasquez 1. **San Francisco (7)**—Thompson 2, Bass 1, Colbert 1, James 1, Snyder 1, Wood 1.

AT SAN FRANCISCO (117):

Atlanta (6)—Pendleton 2, Blauser 1, Bream 1, Hunter 1, Nixon 1. **Chicago (3)**—Dawson 3. **Cincinnati (2)**—O'Neill 1, Sabo 1. **Houston (6)**—Anthony 2, Bagwell 1, Gonzalez 1, Simms 1, Taubensee 1. **Los Angeles (9)**—Karros 3, Davis 1, Hansen 1, Hernandez 1, Strawberry 1, Webster 1, Young 1. **Montreal (2)**—Barberie 1, Walker 1. **New York (5)**—Bonilla 2, Boston 1, Gooden 1, Hundley 1. **Philadelphia (8)**—Grotewold 3, Amaro 1, Duncan 1, Jordan 1, Kruk 1, Sveum 1. **Pittsburgh (6)**—Bell 1, Bonds 1, Buechele 1, LaValliere 1, Slaught 1, Van Slyke 1. **St. Louis (3)**—Galarraga 1, Jordan 1, Lankford 1. **San Diego (10)**—Sheffield 5, Clark 2, Jackson 1, Santiago 1, Ward 1. **San Francisco (57)**—Clark 11, Williams 9, Snyder 8, Thompson 8, Bass 5, Clayton 3, James 3, Leonard 3, Litton 2, Felder 1, Hosey 1, Lewis 1, Manwaring 1, McNamara 1.

HISTORY

ALL-TIME RESULTS

AMERICAN LEAGUE CHAMPIONS

Year	Team	Manager	Year	Team	Manager
1901	Chicago	Clark Griffith	1949	New York	Casey Stengel
1902	Philadelphia	Connie Mack	1950	New York	Casey Stengel
1903	Boston	Jimmy Collins	1951	New York	Casey Stengel
1904	Boston	Jimmy Collins	1952	New York	Casey Stengel
1905	Philadelphia	Connie Mack	1953	New York	Casey Stengel
1906	Chicago	Fielder Jones	1954	Cleveland	Al Lopez
1907	Detroit	Hugh Jennings	1955	New York	Casey Stengel
1908	Detroit	Hugh Jennings	1956	New York	Casey Stengel
1909	Detroit	Hugh Jennings	1957	New York	Casey Stengel
1910	Philadelphia	Connie Mack	1958	New York	Casey Stengel
1911	Philadelphia	Connie Mack	1959	Chicago	Al Lopez
1912	Boston	Jake Stahl	1960	New York	Casey Stengel
1913	Philadelphia	Connie Mack	1961	New York	Ralph Houk
1914	Philadelphia	Connie Mack	1962	New York	Ralph Houk
1915	Boston	Bill Carrigan	1963	New York	Ralph Houk
1916	Boston	Bill Carrigan	1964	New York	Yogi Berra
1917	Chicago	Pants Rowland	1965	Minnesota	Sam Mele
1918	Boston	Ed Barrow	1966	Baltimore	Hank Bauer
1919	Chicago	Kid Gleason	1967	Boston	Dick Williams
1920	Cleveland	Tris Speaker	1968	Detroit	Mayo Smith
1921	New York	Miller Huggins	1969	Baltimore (E)	Earl Weaver
1922	New York	Miller Huggins	1970	Baltimore (E)	Earl Weaver
1923	New York	Miller Huggins	1971	Baltimore (E)	Earl Weaver
1924	Washington	Bucky Harris	1972	Oakland (W)	Dick Williams
1925	Washington	Bucky Harris	1973	Oakland (W)	Dick Williams
1926	New York	Miller Huggins	1974	Oakland (W)	Al Dark
1927	New York	Miller Huggins	1975	Boston (E)	Darrell Johnson
1928	New York	Miller Huggins	1976	New York (E)	Billy Martin
1929	Philadelphia	Connie Mack	1977	New York (E)	Billy Martin
1930	Philadelphia	Connie Mack	1978	New York (E)	Billy Martin, Bob Lemon
1931	Philadelphia	Connie Mack	1979	Baltimore (E)	Earl Weaver
1932	New York	Joe McCarthy	1980	Kansas City (W)	Jim Frey
1933	Washington	Joe Cronin	1981	New York (E)	Gene Michael, Bob Lemon
1934	Detroit	Mickey Cochrane	1982	Milwaukee (E)	Buck Rodgers, Harvey Kuenn
1935	Detroit	Mickey Cochrane	1983	Baltimore (E)	Joe Altobelli
1936	New York	Joe McCarthy	1984	Detroit (E)	Sparky Anderson
1937	New York	Joe McCarthy	1985	Kansas City (W)	Dick Howser
1938	New York	Joe McCarthy	1986	Boston (E)	John McNamara
1939	New York	Joe McCarthy	1987	Minnesota (W)	Tom Kelly
1940	Detroit	Del Baker	1988	Oakland (W)	Tony La Russa
1941	New York	Joe McCarthy	1989	Oakland (W)	Tony La Russa
1942	New York	Joe McCarthy	1990	Oakland (W)	Tony La Russa
1943	New York	Joe McCarthy	1991	Minnesota (W)	Tom Kelly
1944	St. Louis	Luke Sewell	1992	Toronto (E)	Cito Gaston
1945	Detroit	Steve O'Neill			
1946	Boston	Joe Cronin			
1947	New York	Bucky Harris			
1948	Cleveland*	Lou Boudreau			

*Defeated Boston in one-game playoff.

NATIONAL LEAGUE CHAMPIONS

Year	Team	Manager	Year	Team	Manager
1876	Chicago	Albert Spalding	1892	Boston	Frank Selee
1877	Boston	Harry Wright	1893	Boston	Frank Selee
1878	Boston	Harry Wright	1894	Baltimore	Edward Hanlon
1879	Providence	George Wright	1895	Baltimore	Edward Hanlon
1880	Chicago	Adrian Anson	1896	Baltimore	Edward Hanlon
1881	Chicago	Adrian Anson	1897	Boston	Frank Selee
1882	Chicago	Adrian Anson	1898	Boston	Frank Selee
1883	Boston	John Morrill	1899	Brooklyn	Edward Hanlon
1884	Providence	Frank Bancroft	1900	Brooklyn	Edward Hanlon
1885	Chicago	Adrian Anson	1901	Pittsburgh	Fred Clarke
1886	Chicago	Adrian Anson	1902	Pittsburgh	Fred Clarke
1887	Detroit	William Watkins	1903	Pittsburgh	Fred Clarke
1888	New York	James Mutrie	1904	New York	John McGraw
1889	New York	James Mutrie	1905	New York	John McGraw
1890	Brooklyn	William McGunnigle	1906	Chicago	Frank Chance
1891	Boston	Frank Selee	1907	Chicago	Frank Chance

Year	Team	Manager		Year	Team	Manager
1908	Chicago	Frank Chance		1954	New York	Leo Durocher
1909	Pittsburgh	Fred Clarke		1955	Brooklyn	Walter Alston
1910	Chicago	Frank Chance		1956	Brooklyn	Walter Alston
1911	New York	John McGraw		1957	Milwaukee	Fred Haney
1912	New York	John McGraw		1958	Milwaukee	Fred Haney
1913	New York	John McGraw		1959	Los Angeles‡	Walter Alston
1914	Boston	George Stallings		1960	Pittsburgh	Danny Murtaugh
1915	Philadelphia	Pat Moran		1961	Cincinnati	Fred Hutchinson
1916	Brooklyn	Wilbert Robinson		1962	San Francisco§	Al Dark
1917	New York	John McGraw		1963	Los Angeles	Walter Alston
1918	Chicago	Fred Mitchell		1964	St. Louis	Johnny Keane
1919	Cincinnati	Pat Moran		1965	Los Angeles	Walter Alston
1920	Brooklyn	Wilbert Robinson		1966	Los Angeles	Walter Alston
1921	New York	John McGraw		1967	St. Louis	Red Schoendienst
1922	New York	John McGraw		1968	St. Louis	Red Schoendienst
1923	New York	John McGraw		1969	New York (E)	Gil Hodges
1924	New York	John McGraw		1970	Cincinnati (W)	Sparky Anderson
1925	Pittsburgh	Bill McKechnie		1971	Pittsburgh (E)	Danny Murtaugh
1926	St. Louis	Rogers Hornsby		1972	Cincinnati (W)	Sparky Anderson
1927	Pittsburgh	Donie Bush		1973	New York (E)	Yogi Berra
1928	St. Louis	Bill McKechnie		1974	Los Angeles (W)	Walter Alston
1929	Chicago	Joe McCarthy		1975	Cincinnati (W)	Sparky Anderson
1930	St. Louis	Gabby Street		1976	Cincinnati (W)	Sparky Anderson
1931	St. Louis	Gabby Street		1977	Los Angeles (W)	Tommy Lasorda
1932	Chicago	Charlie Grimm		1978	Los Angeles (W)	Tommy Lasorda
1933	New York	Bill Terry		1979	Pittsburgh (E)	Chuck Tanner
1934	St. Louis	Frank Frisch		1980	Philadelphia (E)	Dallas Green
1935	Chicago	Charlie Grimm		1981	Los Angeles (W)	Tommy Lasorda
1936	New York	Bill Terry		1982	St. Louis (E)	Whitey Herzog
1937	New York	Bill Terry		1983	Philadelphia (E)	Pat Corrales, Paul Owens
1938	Chicago	Gabby Hartnett		1984	San Diego (W)	Dick Williams
1939	Cincinnati	Bill McKechnie		1985	St. Loius (E)	Whitey Herzog
1940	Cincinnati	Bill McKechnie		1986	New York (E)	Dave Johnson
1941	Brooklyn	Leo Durocher		1987	St. Louis (E)	Whitey Herzog
1942	St. Louis	Billy Southworth		1988	Los Angeles (W)	Tommy Lasorda
1943	St. Louis	Billy Southworth		1989	San Francisco (W)	Roger Craig
1944	St. Louis	Billy Southworth		1990	Cincinnati (W)	Lou Piniella
1945	Chicago	Charlie Grimm		1991	Atlanta (W)	Bobby Cox
1946	St. Louis*	Eddie Dyer		1992	Atlanta (W)	Bobby Cox
1947	Brooklyn	Burt Shotton				
1948	Boston	Billy Southworth				
1949	Brooklyn	Burt Shotton				
1950	Philadelphia	Eddie Sawyer				
1951	New York†	Leo Durocher				
1952	Brooklyn	Charlie Dressen				
1953	Brooklyn	Charlie Dressen				

*Defeated Brooklyn, two games to none, in playoff for pennant. †Defeated Brooklyn, two games to one, in playoff for pennant. ‡Defeated Milwaukee, two games to none, in playoff for pennant. §Defeated Los Angeles, two games to one, in playoff for pennant.

WORLD SERIES

Year	Winner	Loser
1903	Boston A.L. over Pittsburgh N.L., 5 games to 3.	
1904	No Series.	
1905	New York N.L. over Philadelphia A.L., 4-1.	
1906	Chicago A.L. over Chicago N.L., 4-2.	
1907	Chicago N.L. over Detroit A.L., 4-0 with 1 tie.	
1908	Chicago N.L. over Detroit A.L., 4-1.	
1909	Pittsburgh N.L. over Detroit A.L., 4-3.	
1910	Philadelphia A.L. over Chicago N.L., 4-1.	
1911	Philadelphia A.L. over New York N.L., 4-2.	
1912	Boston A.L. over New York N.L., 4-3 with 1 tie.	
1913	Philadelphia A.L. over New York N.L., 4-1.	
1914	Boston N.L. over Philadelphia A.L., 4-0.	
1915	Boston A.L. over Philadelphia N.L., 4-1.	
1916	Boston A.L. over Brooklyn N.L., 4-1.	
1917	Chicago A.L. over New York N.L., 4-2.	
1918	Boston A.L. over Chicago N.L., 4-2.	
1919	Cincinnati N.L. over Chicago A.L., 5-3.	
1920	Cleveland A.L. over Brooklyn N.L., 5-2.	
1921	New York N.L. over New York A.L., 5-3.	
1922	New York N.L. over New York A.L., 4-0 with 1 tie.	
1923	New York A.L. over New York N.L., 4-2.	
1924	Washington A.L. over New York N.L., 4-3.	
1925	Pittsburgh N.L. over Washington A.L., 4-3.	
1926	St. Louis N.L. over New York A.L., 4-3.	
1927	New York A.L. over Pittsburgh, N.L., 4-0.	
1928	New York A.L. over St. Louis N.L., 4-0.	
1929	Philadelphia A.L. over Chicago N.L., 4-1.	
1930	Philadelphia A.L. over St. Louis N.L., 4-2.	
1931	St. Louis N.L. over Philadelphia A.L., 4-3.	
1932	New York A.L. over Chicago N.L., 4-0.	
1933	New York N.L. over Washington A.L., 4-1.	
1934	St. Louis N.L. over Detroit A.L., 4-3.	
1935	Detroit A.L. over Chicago N.L., 4-2.	
1936	New York A.L. over New York N.L., 4-2.	
1937	New York A.L. over New York N.L., 4-1.	
1938	New York A.L. over Chicago N.L., 4-0.	
1939	New York A.L. over Cincinnati N.L., 4-0.	
1940	Cincinnati N.L. over Detroit A.L., 4-3.	
1941	New York A.L. over Brooklyn N.L., 4-1.	
1942	St. Louis N.L. over New York A.L., 4-1.	
1943	New York A.L. over St. Louis, N.L., 4-1.	
1944	St. Louis N.L. over St. Louis A.L., 4-2.	
1945	Detroit A.L. over Chicago N.L., 4-3.	
1946	St. Louis N.L. over Boston A.L., 4-3.	
1947	New York A.L. over Brooklyn, N.L., 4-3.	
1948	Cleveland A.L. over Boston N.L., 4-2.	
1949	New York A.L. over Brooklyn N.L., 4-1.	
1950	New York A.L. over Philadelphia N.L., 4-0.	
1951	New York A.L. over New York N.L., 4-2.	
1952	New York A.L. over Brooklyn N.L., 4-3.	
1953	New York A.L. over Brooklyn N.L., 4-2.	
1954	New York N.L. over Cleveland A.L., 4-0.	

Year	Winner	Loser
1955—Brooklyn N.L. over New York A.L., 4-3.		
1956—New York A.L. over Brooklyn N.L., 4-3.		
1957—Milwaukee N.L. over New York A.L., 4-3.		
1958—New York A.L. over Milwaukee N.L., 4-3.		
1959—Los Angeles N.L. over Chicago A.L., 4-2.		
1960—Pittsburgh N.L. over New York A.L., 4-3.		
1961—New York A.L. over Cincinnati N.L., 4-1.		
1962—New York A.L. over San Francisco N.L., 4-3.		
1963—Los Angeles N.L. over New York A.L., 4-0.		
1964—St. Louis N.L. over New York A.L., 4-3.		
1965—Los Angeles N.L. over Minnesota A.L., 4-3.		
1966—Baltimore A.L. over Los Angeles N.L., 4-0.		
1967—St. Louis N.L. over Boston A.L., 4-3.		
1968—Detroit A.L. over St. Louis N.L., 4-3.		
1969—New York N.L. over Baltimore A.L., 4-1.		
1970—Baltimore A.L. over Cincinnati N.L., 4-1.		
1971—Pittsburgh N.L. over Baltimore A.L., 4-3.		
1972—Oakland A.L. over Cincinnati N.L., 4-3.		
1973—Oakland A.L. over New York N.L., 4-3.		

Year	Winner	Loser
1974—Oakland A.L. over Los Angeles N.L., 4-1.		
1975—Cincinnati N.L. over Boston A.L., 4-3.		
1976—Cincinnati N.L. over New York A.L., 4-0.		
1977—New York A.L. over Los Angeles N.L., 4-2.		
1978—New York A.L. over Los Angeles N.L., 4-2.		
1979—Pittsburgh N.L. over Baltimore A.L., 4-3.		
1980—Philadelphia N.L. over Kansas City A.L., 4-2.		
1981—Los Angeles N.L. over New York A.L., 4-2.		
1982—St. Louis N.L. over Milwaukee A.L., 4-3.		
1983—Baltimore A.L. over Philadelphia N.L., 4-1.		
1984—Detroit A.L. over San Diego N.L., 4-1.		
1985—Kansas City A.L. over St. Louis N.L., 4-3.		
1986—New York N.L. over Boston A.L., 4-3.		
1987—Minnesota A.L. over St. Louis N.L., 4-3.		
1988—Los Angeles N.L. over Oakland A.L., 4-1.		
1989—Oakland A.L. over San Francisco N.L., 4-0.		
1990—Cincinnati N.L. over Oakland A.L., 4-0.		
1991—Minnesota A.L. over Atlanta N.L., 4-3.		
1992—Toronto A.L. over Atlanta N.L., 4-2.		

CHAMPIONSHIP SERIES

AMERICAN LEAGUE

Year	Winner	Loser
1969—Baltimore (East) over Minnesota (West), 3 games to 0.		
1970—Baltimore (East) over Minnesota (West), 3-0.		
1971—Baltimore (East) over Oakland (West), 3-0.		
1972—Oakland (West) over Detroit (East), 3-2.		
1973—Oakland (West) over Baltimore (East), 3-2.		
1974—Oakland (West) over Baltimore (East), 3-1.		
1975—Boston (East) over Oakland (West), 3-0.		
1976—New York (East) over Kansas City (West), 3-2.		
1977—New York (East) over Kansas City (West), 3-2.		
1978—New York (East) over Kansas City (West), 3-1.		
1979—Baltimore (East) over California (West), 3-1.		
1980—Kansas City (West) over New York (East), 3-0.		
1981—New York (East) over Oakland (West), 3-0.		
1982—Milwaukee (East) over California (West), 3-2.		
1983—Baltimore (East) over Chicago (West), 3-1.		
1984—Detroit (East) over Kansas City (West), 3-0.		
1985—Kansas City (West) over Toronto (East), 4-3.		
1986—Boston (East) over California (West), 4-3.		
1987—Minnesota (West) over Detroit (East), 4-1.		
1988—Oakland (West) over Boston (East), 4-0.		
1989—Oakland (West) over Toronto (East), 4-1.		
1990—Oakland (West) over Boston (East), 4-0.		
1991—Minnesota (West) over Toronto (East), 4-1.		
1992—Toronto (East) over Oakland (West), 4-2.		

NATIONAL LEAGUE

Year	Winner	Loser
1969—New York (East) over Atlanta (West), 3 games to 0.		
1970—Cincinnati (West) over Pittsburgh (East), 3-0.		
1971—Pittsburgh (East) over San Francisco (West), 3-1.		
1972—Cincinnati (West) over Pittsburgh (East), 3-2.		
1973—New York (East) over Cincinnati (West), 3-2.		
1974—Los Angeles (West) over Pittsburgh (East), 3-1.		
1975—Cincinnati (West) over Pittsburgh (East), 3-0.		
1976—Cincinnati (West) over Philadelphia (East), 3-0.		
1977—Los Angeles (West) over Philadelphia (East), 3-1.		
1978—Los Angeles (West) over Philadelphia (East), 3-1.		
1979—Pittsburgh (East) over Cincinnati (West), 3-0.		
1980—Philadelphia (East) over Houston (West), 3-2.		
1981—Los Angeles (West) over Montreal (East), 3-2.		
1982—St. Louis (East) over Atlanta (West), 3-0.		
1983—Philadelphia (East) over Los Angeles (West), 3-1.		
1984—San Diego (West) over Chicago (East), 3-2.		
1985—St. Louis (East) over Los Angeles (West), 4-2.		
1986—New York (East) over Houston (West), 4-2.		
1987—St. Louis (East) over San Francisco (West), 4-3.		
1988—Los Angeles (West) over New York (East), 4-3.		
1989—San Francisco (West) over Chicago (East), 4-1.		
1990—Cincinnati (West) over Pittsburgh (East), 4-2.		
1991—Atlanta (West) over Pittsburgh (East), 4-3.		
1992—Atlanta (West) over Pittsburgh (East), 4-3.		

ALL-STAR GAME

Date	Site	Score (Winner)	Winning pitcher (Losing pitcher)	Winning manager (Losing manager)	Att.
7-6-33	Comiskey Park Chicago	4-2 (A.L.)	Lefty Gomez, Yankees (Bill Hallahan, Cardinals)	Connie Mack, Athletics (John McGraw, Giants)	47,595
7-10-34	Polo Grounds New York	9-7 (A.L.)	Mel Harder, Indians (Van Mungo, Dodgers)	Joe Cronin, Senators (Bill Terry, Giants)	48,363
7-8-35	Municipal Stadium Cleveland	4-1 (A.L.)	Lefty Gomez, Yankees (Bill Walker, Cardinals)	Mickey Cochrane, Tigers (Frankie Frisch, Cardinals)	69,831
7-7-36	Braves Field Boston	4-3 (N.L.)	Dizzy Dean, Cardinals (Lefty Grove, Red Sox)	Charlie Grimm, Cubs (Joe McCarthy, Yankees)	25,556
7-7-37	Griffith Stadium Washington	8-3 (A.L.)	Lefty Gomez, Yankees (Dizzy Dean, Cardinals)	Joe McCarthy, Yankees (Bill Terry, Giants)	31,391
7-6-38	Crosley Field Cincinnati	4-1 (N.L.)	Johnny Vander Meer, Reds (Lefty Gomez, Yankees)	Bill Terry, Giants (Joe McCarthy, Yankees)	27,067
7-11-39	Yankee Stadium New York	3-1 (A.L.)	Tommy Bridges, Tigers (Bill Lee, Cubs)	Joe McCarthy, Yankees (Gabby Hartnett, Cubs)	62,892
7-9-40	Sportsman's Park St. Louis	4-0 (N.L.)	Paul Derringer, Reds (Red Ruffing, Yankees)	Bill McKechnie, Reds (Joe Cronin, Red Sox)	32,373
7-8-41	Briggs Stadium Detroit	7-5 (A.L.)	Ed Smith, White Sox (Claude Passeau, Cubs)	Del Baker, Tigers (Bill McKechnie, Reds)	54,674
7-6-42	Polo Grounds New York	3-1 (A.L.)	Spud Chandler, Yankees (Mort Cooper, Cardinals)	Joe McCarthy, Yankees (Leo Durocher, Dodgers)	34,178
7-13-43	Shibe Park Philadelphia	5-3 (A.L.)	Dutch Leonard, Senators (Mort Cooper, Cardinals)	Joe McCarthy, Yankees (Billy Southworth, Cardinals)	31,938

Date	Site	Score (Winner)	Winning pitcher (Losing pitcher)	Winning manager (Losing manager)	Att.
7-11-44	Forbes Field Pittsburgh	7-1 (N.L.)	Ken Raffensberger, Phillies (Tex Hughson, Red Sox)	Billy Southworth, Cardinals (Joe McCarthy, Yankees)	29,589
1945	No game played.				
7-9-46	Fenway Park Boston	12-0 (A.L.)	Bob Feller, Indians (Claude Passeau, Cubs)	Steve O'Neill, Tigers (Charlie Grimm, Cubs)	34,906
7-8-47	Wrigley Field Chicago	2-1 (A.L.)	Frank Shea, Yankees (Johnny Sain, Braves)	Joe Cronin, Red Sox (Eddie Dyer, Cardinals)	41,123
7-13-48	Sportsman's Park St. Louis	5-2 (A.L.)	Vic Raschi, Yankees (Johnny Schmitz, Cubs)	Bucky Harris, Yankees (Leo Durocher, Dodgers)	34,009
7-12-49	Ebbets Field Brooklyn	11-7 (A.L.)	Virgil Trucks, Tigers (Don Newcombe, Dodgers)	Lou Boudreau, Indians (Billy Southworth, Braves)	32,577
7-11-50	Comiskey Park Chicago	4-3* (N.L.)	Ewell Blackwell, Reds (Ted Gray, Tigers)	Burt Shotton, Dodgers (Casey Stengel, Yankees)	46,127
7-10-51	Briggs Stadium Detroit	8-3 (N.L.)	Sal Maglie, Giants (Ed Lopat, Yankees)	Eddie Sawyer, Phillies (Casey Stengel, Yankees)	52,075
7-8-52	Shibe Park Philadelphia	3-2† (N.L.)	Bob Rush, Cubs (Bob Lemon, Indians)	Leo Durocher, Giants (Casey Stengel, Yankees)	32,785
7-14-53	Crosley Field Cincinnati	5-1 (N.L.)	Warren Spahn, Braves (Allie Reynolds, Yankees)	Chuck Dressen, Dodgers (Casey Stengel, Yankees)	30,846
7-13-54	Municipal Stadium Cleveland	11-9 (A.L.)	Dean Stone, Senators (Gene Conley, Braves)	Casey Stengel, Yankees (Walter Alston, Dodgers)	68,751
7-12-55	Milwaukee Co. Stadium Milwaukee	6-5‡ (N.L.)	Gene Conley, Braves (Frank Sullivan, Red Sox)	Leo Durocher, Giants (Al Lopez, Indians)	45,643
7-10-56	Griffith Stadium Washington	7-3 (N.L.)	Bob Friend, Pirates (Billy Pierce, White Sox)	Walter Alston, Dodgers (Casey Stengel, Yankees)	28,843
7-9-57	Busch Stadium St. Louis	6-5 (A.L.)	Jim Bunning, Tigers (Curt Simmons, Phillies)	Casey Stengel, Yankees (Walter Alston, Dodgers)	30,693
7-8-58	Memorial Stadium Baltimore	4-3 (A.L.)	Early Wynn, White Sox (Bob Friend, Pirates)	Casey Stengel, Yankees (Fred Haney, Braves)	48,829
7-7-59	Forbes Field Pittsburgh	5-4 (N.L.)	Johnny Antonelli, Giants (Whitey Ford, Yankees)	Fred Haney, Braves (Casey Stengel, Yankees)	35,277
8-3-59	Memorial Coliseum Los Angeles	5-3 (A.L.)	Jerry Walker, Orioles (Don Drysdale, Dodgers)	Casey Stengel, Yankees (Fred Haney, Braves)	55,105
7-11-60	Municipal Stadium Kansas City	5-3 (N.L.)	Bob Friend, Pirates (Bill Monbouquette, Red Sox)	Walter Alston, Dodgers (Al Lopez, White Sox)	30,619
7-13-60	Yankee Stadium New York	6-0 (N.L.)	Vernon Law, Pirates (Whitey Ford, Yankees)	Walter Alston, Dodgers (Al Lopez, White Sox)	38,362
7-11-61	Candlestick Park San Francisco	5-4§ (N.L.)	Stu Miller, Giants (Hoyt Wilhelm, Orioles)	Danny Murtaugh, Pirates (Paul Richards, Orioles)	44,115
7-31-61	Fenway Park Boston	1-1 (tie)		Paul Richards, Orioles (A.L.) Danny Murtaugh, Pirates (N.L.)	31,851
7-10-62	District of Col. Stad. Washington	3-1 (N.L.)	Juan Marichal, Giants (Camilo Pascual, Twins)	Fred Hutchinson, Reds (Ralph Houk, Yankees)	45,480
7-30-62	Wrigley Field Chicago	9-4 (A.L.)	Ray Herbert, White Sox (Art Mahaffey, Phillies)	Ralph Houk, Yankees (Fred Hutchinson, Reds)	38,359
7-9-63	Municipal Stadium Cleveland	5-3 (N.L.)	Larry Jackson, Cubs (Jim Bunning, Tigers)	Alvin Dark, Giants (Ralph Houk, Yankees)	44,160
7-7-64	Shea Stadium New York	7-4 (N.L.)	Juan Marichal, Giants (Dick Radatz, Red Sox)	Walter Alston, Dodgers (Al Lopez, White Sox)	50,850
7-13-65	Metropolitan Stadium Bloomington, Minn.	6-5 (N.L.)	Sandy Koufax, Dodgers (Sam McDowell, Indians)	Gene Mauch, Phillies (Al Lopez, White Sox)	46,706
7-12-66	Busch Stadium St. Louis	2-1§ (N.L.)	Gaylord Perry, Giants (Pete Richert, Senators)	Walter Alston, Dodgers (Sam Mele, Twins)	49,936
7-11-67	Anaheim Stadium Anaheim, Calif.	2-1★ (N.L.)	Don Drysdale, Dodgers (Jim Hunter, Athletics)	Walter Alston, Dodgers (Hank Bauer, Orioles)	46,309
7-9-68	Astrodome Houston	1-0 (N.L.)	Don Drysdale, Dodgers (Luis Tiant, Indians)	Red Schoendienst, Cardinals (Dick Williams, Red Sox)	48,321
7-23-69	R.F.K. Stadium Washington	9-3 (N.L.)	Steve Carlton, Cardinals (Mel Stottlemyre, Yankees)	Red Schoendienst, Cardinals (Mayo Smith, Tigers)	45,259
7-14-70	Riverfront Stadium Cincinnati	5-4‡ (N.L.)	Claude Osteen, Dodgers (Clyde Wright, Angels)	Gil Hodges, Mets (Earl Weaver, Orioles)	51,838
7-13-71	Tiger Stadium Detroit	6-4 (A.L.)	Vida Blue, Athletics (Dock Ellis, Pirates)	Earl Weaver, Orioles (Sparky Anderson, Reds)	53,559
7-25-72	Atlanta Stadium Atlanta	4-3§ (N.L.)	Tug McGraw, Mets (Dave McNally, Orioles)	Danny Murtaugh, Pirates (Earl Weaver, Orioles)	53,107
7-24-73	Royals Stadium Kansas City	7-1 (N.L.)	Rick Wise, Cardinals (Bert Blyleven, Twins)	Sparky Anderson, Reds (Dick Williams, Athletics)	40,849
7-23-74	Three Rivers Stadium Pittsburgh	7-2 (N.L.)	Ken Brett, Pirates (Luis Tiant, Red Sox)	Yogi Berra, Mets (Dick Williams, Athletics)	50,706
7-15-75	Milwaukee Co. Stadium Milwaukee	6-3 (N.L.)	Jon Matlack, Mets (Jim Hunter, Yankees)	Walter Alston, Dodgers (Alvin Dark, Athletics)	51,480
7-13-76	Veterans Stadium Philadelphia	7-1 (N.L)	Randy Jones, Padres (Mark Fidrych, Tigers)	Sparky Anderson, Reds (Darrell Johnson, Red Sox)	63,974
7-19-77	Yankee Stadium New York	7-5 (N.L.)	Don Sutton, Dodgers (Jim Palmer, Orioles)	Sparky Anderson, Reds (Billy Martin, Yankees)	56,683

Date	Site	Score (Winner)	Winning pitcher (Losing pitcher)	Winning manager (Losing manager)	Att.
7-11-78	San Diego Stadium San Diego	7-3 (N.L.)	Bruce Sutter, Cubs (Rich Gossage, Yankees)	Tommy Lasorda, Dodgers (Billy Martin, Yankees)	51,549
7-17-79	Kingdome Seattle	7-6 (N.L.)	Bruce Sutter, Cubs (Jim Kern, Rangers)	Tommy Lasorda, Dodgers (Bob Lemon, Yankees)	58,905
7-8-80	Dodger Stadium Los Angeles	4-2 (N.L.)	Jerry Reuss, Dodgers (Tommy John, Yankees)	Chuck Tanner, Pirates (Earl Weaver, Orioles)	56,088
8-9-81	Municipal Stadium Cleveland	5-4 (N.L.)	Vida Blue, Giants (Rollie Fingers, Brewers)	Dallas Green, Phillies (Jim Frey, Royals)	72,086
7-13-82	Olympic Stadium Montreal	4-1 (N.L.)	Steve Rogers, Expos (Dennis Eckersley, Red Sox)	Tommy Lasorda, Dodgers (Billy Martin, Athletics)	59,057
7-6-83	Comiskey Park Chicago	13-3 (A.L.)	Dave Stieb, Blue Jays (Mario Soto, Reds)	Harvey Kuenn, Brewers (Whitey Herzog, Cardinals)	43,801
7-10-84	Candlestick Park San Francisco	3-1 (N.L.)	Charlie Lea, Expos (Dave Stieb, Blue Jays)	Paul Owens, Phillies (Joe Altobelli, Orioles)	57,756
7-16-85	Metrodome Minneapolis	6-1 (N.L.)	LaMarr Hoyt, Padres (Jack Morris, Tigers)	Dick Williams, Padres (Sparky Anderson, Tigers)	54,960
7-15-86	Astrodome Houston	3-2 (A.L.)	Roger Clemens, Red Sox (Dwight Gooden, Mets)	Dick Howser, Royals (Whitey Herzog, Cardinals)	45,774
7-14-87	Oak.-Alameda Co. Col. Oakland	2-0 • (N.L.)	Lee Smith, Cubs (Jay Howell, Athletics)	Dave Johnson, Mets (John McNamara, Red Sox)	49,671
7-12-88	Riverfront Stadium Cincinnati	2-1 (A.L.)	Frank Viola, Twins (Dwight Gooden, Mets)	Tom Kelly, Twins (Whitey Herzog, Cardinals)	55,837
7-11-89	Anaheim Stadium Anaheim, Calif.	5-3 (A.L.)	Nolan Ryan, Rangers (John Smoltz, Braves)	Tony La Russa, Athletics (Tommy Lasorda, Dodgers)	64,036
7-10-90	Wrigley Field Chicago	2-0 (A.L.)	Bret Saberhagen, Royals (Jeff Brantley, Giants)	Tony La Russa, Athletics (Roger Craig, Giants)	39,071
7-9-91	SkyDome Toronto	4-2 (A.L.)	Jimmy Key, Blue Jays (Dennis Martinez, Expos)	Tony La Russa, Athletics (Lou Piniella, Reds)	52,383
7-14-92	Jack Murphy Stadium San Diego	13-6 (A.L.)	Kevin Brown, Rangers (Tom Glavine, Braves)	Tom Kelly, Twins (Bobby Cox, Braves)	59,372

* 14 innings.   †5 innings (rain).   ‡12 innings.   §10 innings.   ★15 innings.   •13 innings.

AWARD WINNERS

MOST VALUABLE PLAYER

AMERICAN LEAGUE

Year	Player, Team, Pos.	Points
1929—	Al Simmons, Philadelphia, OF	40
1930—	Joe Cronin, Washington, SS	52
1931—	Lou Gehrig, New York, 1B	40
1932—	Jimmie Foxx, Philadelphia, 1B	46
1933—	Jimmie Foxx, Philadelphia, 1B	49
1934—	Lou Gehrig, New York, 1B	51
1935—	Hank Greenberg, Detroit, 1B	64
1936—	Lou Gehrig, New York, 1B	55
1937—	Charley Gehringer, Detroit, 2B	78
1938—	Jimmie Foxx, Boston, 1B	304
1939—	Joe DiMaggio, New York, OF	280
1940—	Hank Greenberg, Detroit, OF	292
1941—	Joe DiMaggio, New York, OF	291
1942—	Joe Gordon, New York, 2B	270
1943—	Spud Chandler, New York, P	246
1944—	Bobby Doerr, Boston, 2B	
1945—	Eddie Mayo, Detroit, 2B	

NATIONAL LEAGUE

Year	Player, Team, Pos.	Points
1929—	No selection	
1930—	Bill Terry, New York, 1B	47
1931—	Chuck Klein, Philadelphia, OF	40
1932—	Chuck Klein, Philadelphia, OF	46
1933—	Carl Hubbell, New York, P	64
1934—	Dizzy Dean, St. Louis, P	57
1935—	Arky Vaughan, Pittsburgh, SS	42
1936—	Carl Hubbell, New York, P	61
1937—	Joe Medwick, St. Louis, OF	70
1938—	Ernie Lombardi, Cincinnati, C	229
1939—	Bucky Walters, Cincinnati, P	303
1940—	Frank McCormick, Cincinnati, 1B	274
1941—	Dolf Camilli, Brooklyn, 1B	300
1942—	Mort Cooper, St. Loius, P	263
1943—	Stan Musial, St. Louis, OF	267
1944—	Marty Marion, St. Louis, SS	
1945—	Tommy Holmes, Boston, OF	

PLAYER AND PITCHER OF THE YEAR

AMERICAN LEAGUE

Year Player, Team, Pos.
1948— Lou Boudreau, Cleveland, SS
      Bob Lemon, Cleveland, P
1949— Ted Williams, Boston, OF
      Ellis Kinder, Boston, P
1950— Phil Rizzuto, New York, SS
      Bob Lemon, Cleveland, P
1951— Ferris Fain, Philadelphia, 1B
      Bob Feller, Cleveland, P
1952— Luke Easter, Cleveland, 1B
      Bobby Shantz, Philadelphia, P
1953— Al Rosen, Cleveland, 3B
      Bob Porterfield, Washington, P
1954— Bobby Avila, Cleveland, 2B
      Bob Lemon, Cleveland, P
1955— Al Kaline, Detroit, OF
      Whitey Ford, New York, P
1956— Mickey Mantle, New York, OF
      Billy Pierce, Chicago, P
1957— Ted Williams, Boston, OF
      Billy Pierce, Chicago, P
1958— Jackie Jensen, Boston, OF
      Bob Turley, New York, P
1959— Nellie Fox, Chicago, 2B
      Early Wynn, Chicago, P
1960— Roger Maris, New York, OF
      Chuck Estrada, Baltimore, P
1961— Roger Maris, New York, OF
      Whitey Ford, New York, P
1962— Mickey Mantle, New York, OF
      Dick Donovan, Cleveland, P
1963— Al Kaline, Detroit, OF
      Whitey Ford, New York, P
1964— Brooks Robinson, Baltimore, 3B
      Dean Chance, Los Angeles, P
1965— Tony Oliva, Minnesota, OF
      Jim Grant, Minnesota, P
1966— Frank Robinson, Baltimore, OF
      Jim Kaat, Minnesota, P
1967— Carl Yastrzemski, Boston, OF
      Jim Lonborg, Boston, P
1968— Ken Harrelson, Boston, OF
      Denny McLain, Detroit, P
1969— Harmon Killebrew, Minnesota, 1B-3B
      Denny McLain, Detroit, P

NATIONAL LEAGUE

Year Player, Team, Pos.
1948— Stan Musial, St. Louis, OF-1B
      Johnny Sain, Boston, P
1949— Enos Slaughter, St. Louis, OF
      Howard Pollet, St. Louis, P
1950— Ralph Kiner, Pittsburgh, OF
      Jim Konstanty, Philadelphia, P
1951— Stan Musial, St. Louis, OF
      Preacher Roe, Brooklyn, P
1952— Hank Sauer, Chicago, OF
      Robin Roberts, Philadelphia, P
1953— Roy Campanella, Brooklyn, C
      Warren Spahn, Milwaukee, P
1954— Willie Mays, New York, OF
      Johnny Antonelli, New York, P
1955— Duke Snider, Brooklyn, OF
      Robin Roberts, Philadelphia, P
1956— Hank Aaron, Milwaukee, OF
      Don Newcombe, Brooklyn, P
1957— Stan Musial, St. Louis, 1B
      Warren Spahn, Milwaukee, P
1958— Ernie Banks, Chicago, SS
      Warren Spahn, Milwaukee, P
1959— Ernie Banks, Chicago, SS
      Sam Jones, San Francisco, P
1960— Dick Groat, Pittsburgh, SS
      Vern Law, Pittsburgh, P
1961— Frank Robinson, Cincinnati, OF
      Warren Spahn, Milwaukee, P
1962— Maury Wills, Los Angeles, SS
      Don Drysdale, Los Angeles, P
1963— Hank Aaron, Milwaukee, OF
      Sandy Koufax, Los Angeles, P
1964— Ken Boyer, St. Louis, 3B
      Sandy Koufax, Los Angeles, P
1965— Willie Mays, San Francisco, OF
      Sandy Koufax, Los Angeles, P
1966— Roberto Clemente, Pittsburgh, OF
      Sandy Koufax, Los Angeles, P
1967— Orlando Cepeda, St. Louis, 1B
      Mike McCormick, San Francisco, P
1968— Pete Rose, Cincinnati, OF
      Bob Gibson, St. Louis, P
1969— Willie McCovey, San Francisco, 1B
      Tom Seaver, New York, P

Year	Player, Team, Pos.
1970—	Harmon Killebrew, Minnesota, 3B
	Sam McDowell, Cleveland, P
1971—	Tony Oliva, Minnesota, OF
	Vida Blue, Oakland, P
1972—	Dick Allen, Chicago, 1B
	Wilbur Wood, Chicago, P
1973—	Reggie Jackson, Oakland, OF
	Jim Palmer, Baltimore, P
1974—	Jeff Burroughs, Texas, OF
	Jim Hunter, Oakland, P
1975—	Fred Lynn, Boston, OF
	Jim Palmer, Baltimore, P
1976—	Thurman Munson, New York, C
	Jim Palmer, Baltimore, P
1977—	Rod Carew, Minnesota, 1B
	Nolan Ryan, California, P
1978—	Jim Rice, Boston, OF
	Ron Guidry, New York, P
1979—	Don Baylor, California, OF
	Mike Flanagan, Baltimore, P
1980—	George Brett, Kansas City, 3B
	Steve Stone, Baltimore, P
1981—	Tony Armas, Oakland, OF
	Jack Morris, Detroit, P
1982—	Robin Yount, Milwaukee, SS
	Dave Stieb, Toronto, P
1983—	Cal Ripken Jr., Baltimore, SS
	LaMarr Hoyt, Chicago, P
1984—	Don Mattingly, New York, 1B
	Willie Hernandez, Detroit, P
1985—	Don Mattingly, New York, 1B
	Bret Saberhagen, Kansas City, P
1986—	Don Mattingly, New York, 1B
	Roger Clemens, Boston, P
1987—	George Bell, Toronto, OF
	Jimmy Key, Toronto, P
1988—	Jose Canseco, Oakland, OF
	Frank Viola, Minnesota, P
1989—	Ruben Sierra, Texas, OF
	Bret Saberhagen, Kansas City, P
1990—	Cecil Fielder, Detroit, 1B
	Bob Welch, Oakland, P
1991—	Cal Ripken Jr., Baltimore, SS
	Roger Clemens, Boston, P
1992—	No AL Player of the Year named.
	Dennis Eckersley, Oakland, P

Year	Player, Team, Pos.
1970—	Johnny Bench, Cincinnati, C
	Bob Gibson, St. Louis, P
1971—	Joe Torre, St. Louis, 3B
	Ferguson Jenkins, Chicago, P
1972—	Billy Williams, Chicago, OF
	Steve Carlton, Philadelphia, P
1973—	Bobby Bonds, San Francisco, OF
	Ron Bryant, San Francisco, P
1974—	Lou Brock, St. Louis, OF
	Mike Marshall, Los Angeles, P
1975—	Joe Morgan, Cincinnati, 2B
	Tom Seaver, New York, P
1976—	George Foster, Cincinnati, OF
	Randy Jones, San Diego, P
1977—	George Foster, Cincinnati, OF
	Steve Carlton, Philadelphia, P
1978—	Dave Parker, Pittsburgh, OF
	Vida Blue, San Francisco, P
1979—	Keith Hernandez, St. Louis, 1B
	Joe Niekro, Houston, P
1980—	Mike Schmidt, Philadelphia, 3B
	Steve Carlton, Philadelphia, P
1981—	Andre Dawson, Montreal, OF
	Fernando Valenzuela, Los Angeles, P
1982—	Dale Murphy, Atlanta, OF
	Steve Carlton, Philadelphia, P
1983—	Dale Murphy, Atlanta, OF
	John Denny, Philadelphia, P
1984—	Ryne Sandberg, Chicago, 2B
	Rick Sutcliffe, Chicago, P
1985—	Willie McGee, St. Louis, OF
	Dwight Gooden, New York, P
1986—	Mike Schmidt, Philadelphia, 3B
	Mike Scott, Houston, P
1987—	Andre Dawson, Chicago, OF
	Rick Sutcliffe, Chicago, P
1988—	Andy Van Slyke, Pittsburgh, OF
	Orel Hershiser, Los Angeles, P
1989—	Kevin Mitchell, San Francisco, OF
	Mark Davis, San Diego, P
1990—	Barry Bonds, Pittsburgh, OF
	Doug Drabek, Pittsburgh, P
1991—	Barry Bonds, Pittsburgh, OF
	Tom Glavine, Atlanta, P
1992—	No NL Player of the Year named.
	Greg Maddux, Chicago, P

ROOKIE OF THE YEAR

1946—Combined selection—Del Ennis, Philadelphia NL, OF
1947—Combined selection—Jackie Robinson, Brooklyn NL, 1B
1948—Combined selection—Richie Ashburn, Philadelphia NL, OF

AMERICAN LEAGUE

Year	Player, Team, Pos.
1949—	Roy Sievers, St. Louis, OF
1950—	Combined selection—Whitey Ford, New York, A.L., P
1951—	Minnie Minoso, Chicago, OF
1952—	Clint Courtney, St. Louis, C
1953—	Harvey Kuenn, Detroit, SS
1954—	Bob Grim, New York, P
1955—	Herb Score, Cleveland, P
1956—	Luis Aparicio, Chicago, SS
1957—	Tony Kubek, New York, IF-OF
	(No pitcher named)
1958—	Albie Pearson, Washington, OF
	Ryne Duren, New York, P
1959—	Bob Allison, Washington, OF
1960—	Ron Hansen, Baltimore, SS
1961—	Dick Howser, Kansas City, SS
	Don Schwall, Boston, P
1962—	Tom Tresh, New York, OF-SS
1963—	Pete Ward, Chicago, 3B
	Gary Peters, Chicago, P
1964—	Tony Oliva, Minnesota, OF
	Wally Bunker, Baltimore, P

NATIONAL LEAGUE

Year	Player, Team, Pos.
1949—	Don Newcombe, Brooklyn, P
1951—	Willie Mays, New York, OF
1952—	Joe Black, Brooklyn, P
1953—	Jim Gilliam, Brooklyn, 2B
1954—	Wally Moon, St. Louis, OF
1955—	Bill Virdon, St. Louis, OF
1956—	Frank Robinson, Cincinnati, OF
1957—	Ed Bouchee, Philadelphia, 1B
	Jack Sanford, Philadelphia, P
1958—	Orlando Cepeda, San Francisco, 1B
	Carlton Willey, Milwaukee, P
1959—	Willie McCovey, San Francisco, 1B
1960—	Frank Howard, Los Angeles, OF
1961—	Billy Williams, Chicago, OF
	Ken Hunt, Cincinnati, P
1962—	Ken Hubbs, Chicago, 2B
1963—	Pete Rose, Cincinnati, 2B
	Ray Culp, Philadelphia, P
1964—	Dick Allen, Philadelphia, 3B
	Billy McCool, Cincinnati, P

Year	Player, Team, Pos.		Year	Player, Team, Pos.

Year Player, Team, Pos.

1965— Curt Blefary, Baltimore, OF
      Marcelino Lopez, California, P
1966— Tommie Agee, Chicago, OF
      Jim Nash, Kansas City, P
1967— Rod Carew, Minnesota, 2B
      Tom Phoebus, Baltimore, P
1968— Del Unser, Washington, OF
      Stan Bahnsen, New York, P
1969— Carlos May, Chicago, OF
      Mike Nagy, Boston, P
1970— Roy Foster, Cleveland, OF
      Bert Blyleven, Minnesota, P
1971— Chris Chambliss, Cleveland, 1B
      Bill Parsons, Milwaukee, P
1972— Carlton Fisk, Boston, C
      Dick Tidrow, Cleveland, P
1973— Al Bumbry, Baltimore, OF
      Steve Busby, Kansas City, P
1974— Mike Hargrove, Texas, 1B
      Frank Tanana, California, P
1975— Fred Lynn, Boston, OF
      Dennis Eckersley, Cleveland, P
1976— Butch Wynegar, Minnesota, C
      Mark Fidrych, Detroit, P
1977— Mitchell Page, Oakland, OF
      Dave Rozema, Detroit, P
1978— Paul Molitor, Milwaukee, 2B
      Rich Gale, Kansas City, P
1979— Pat Putnam, Texas 1B
      Mark Clear, California, P
1980— Joe Charboneau, Cleveland, OF
      Britt Burns, Chicago, P
1981— Rich Gedman, Boston. C
      Dave Righetti, New York, P
1982— Cal Ripken Jr., Baltimore, SS-3B
      Ed Vande Berg, Seattle, P
1983— Ron Kittle, Chicago, OF
      Mike Boddicker, Baltimore, P
1984— Alvin Davis, Seattle, 1B
      Mark Langston, Seattle, P
1985   Ozzie Gullen, Chicago, SS
      Teddy Higuera, Milwaukee, P
1986— Jose Canseco, Oakland, OF
      Mark Eichhorn, Toronto, P
1987— Mark McGwire, Oakland, 1B
      Mike Henneman, Detroit, P
1988— Walt Weiss, Oakland, SS
      Bryan Harvey, California, P
1989— Craig Worthington, Baltimore, 3B
      Tom Gordon, Kansas City, P
1990— Sandy Alomar Jr., Cleveland, C
      Kevin Appier, Kansas City, P
1991— Chuck Knoblauch, Minnesota, 2B
      Juan Guzman, Toronto, P
1992— Pat Listach, Milwaukee, SS
      Cal Eldred, Milwaukee, P

Year Player, Team, Pos.

1965— Joe Morgan, Houston, 2B
      Frank Linzy, San Francisco, P
1966— Tommy Helms, Cincinnati, 3B
      Don Sutton, Los Angeles, P
1967— Lee May, Cincinnati, 1B
      Dick Hughes, St. Louis, P
1968— Johnny Bench, Cincinnati, C
      Jerry Koosman, New York, P
1969— Coco Laboy, Montreal, 3B
      Tom Griffin, Houston, P
1970— Bernie Carbo, Cincinnati, OF
      Carl Morton, Montreal, P
1971— Earl Williams, Atlanta, C
      Reggie Cleveland, St. Louis, P
1972— Dave Rader, San Francisco, C
      Jon Matlack, New York, P
1973— Gary Matthews, San Francisco, OF
      Steve Rogers, Montreal, P
1974— Greg Gross, Houston, OF
      John D'Acquisto, San Francisco, P
1975— Gary Carter, Montreal, OF-C
      John Montefusco, San Francisco, P
1976— Larry Herndon, San Francisco, OF
      Butch Metzger, San Diego, P
1977— Andre Dawson, Montreal, OF
      Bob Owchinko, San Diego, P
1978— Bob Horner, Atlanta, 3B
      Don Robinson, Pittsburgh, P
1979— Jeff Leonard, Houston, OF
      Rick Sutcliffe, Los Angeles, P
1980— Lonnie Smith, Philadelphia, OF
      Bill Gullickson, Montreal, P
1981— Tim Raines, Montreal, OF
      Fernando Valenzuela, Los Angeles, P
1982— Johnny Ray, Pittsburgh, 2B
      Steve Bedrosian, Atlanta, P
1983— Darryl Strawberry, New York, OF
      Craig McMurtry, Atlanta, P
1984— Juan Samuel, Philadelphia, 2B
      Dwight Gooden, New York, P
1985— Vince Coleman, St. Louis, OF
      Tom Browning, Cincinnati, P
1986— Robby Thompson, San Francisco, 2B
      Todd Worrell, St. Louis, P
1987— Benito Santiago, San Diego, C
      Mike Dunne, Pittsburgh, P
1988— Mark Grace, Chicago, 1B
      Tim Belcher, Los Angeles, P
1989— Jerome Walton, Chicago, OF
      Andy Benes, San Diego, P
1990— David Justice, Atlanta, OF
      Mike Harkey, Chicago, P
1991— Jeff Bagwell, Houston, 1B
      Al Osuna, Houston, P
1992— Eric Karros, Los Angeles, 1B
      Tim Wakefield, Pittsburgh, P

FIREMAN OF THE YEAR

AMERICAN LEAGUE

Year Player, Team
1960— Mike Fornieles, Boston
1961— Luis Arroyo, New York
1962— Dick Radatz, Boston
1963— Stu Miller, Baltimore
1964— Dick Radatz, Boston
1965— Eddie Fisher, Chicago
1966— Jack Aker, Kansas City
1967— Minnie Rojas, California
1968— Wilbur Wood, Chicago
1969— Ron Perranoski, Minnesota
1970— Ron Perranoski, Minnesota
1971— Ken Sanders, Milwaukee
1972— Sparky Lyle, New York
1973— John Hiller, Detroit
1974— Terry Forster, Chicago

NATIONAL LEAGUE

Year Player, Team
1960— Lindy McDaniel, St. Louis
1961— Stu Miller, San Francisco
1962— Roy Face, Pittsburgh
1963— Lindy McDaniel, Chicago
1964— Al McBean, Pittsburgh
1965— Ted Abernathy, Chicago
1966— Phil Regan, Los Angeles
1967— Ted Abernathy, Cincinnati
1968— Phil Regan, L.A.-Chicago
1969— Wayne Granger, Cincinnati
1970— Wayne Granger, Cincinnati
1971— Dave Giusti, Pittsburgh
1972— Clay Carroll, Cincinnati
1973— Mike Marshall, Montreal
1974— Mike Marshall, Los Angeles

Year	Player, Team	Year	Player, Team
1975—	Rich Gossage, Chicago	1975—	Al Hrabosky, St. Louis
1976—	Bill Campbell, Minnesota	1976—	Rawly Eastwick, Cincinnati
1977—	Bill Campbell, Boston	1977—	Rollie Fingers, San Diego
1978—	Rich Gossage, New York	1978—	Rollie Fingers, San Diego
1979—	Mike Marshall, Minnesota	1979—	Bruce Sutter, Chicago
	Jim Kern, Texas		
1980—	Dan Quisenberry, Kansas City	1980—	Rollie Fingers, San Diego
			Tom Hume, Cincinnati
1981—	Rollie Fingers, Milwaukee	1981—	Bruce Sutter, St. Louis
1982—	Dan Quisenberry, Kansas City	1982—	Bruce Sutter, St. Louis
1983—	Dan Quisenberry, Kansas City	1983—	Al Holland, Philadelphia
			Lee Smith, Chicago
1984—	Dan Quisenberry, Kansas City	1984—	Bruce Sutter, St. Louis
1985—	Dan Quisenberry, Kansas City	1985—	Jeff Reardon, Montreal
1986—	Dave Righetti, New York	1986—	Todd Worrell, St. Louis
1987—	Dave Righetti, New York	1987—	Steve Bedrosian, Philadelphia
	Jeff Reardon, Minnesota		
1988—	Dennis Eckersley, Oakland	1988—	John Franco, Cincinnati
1989—	Jeff Russell, Texas	1989—	Mark Davis, San Diego
1990—	Bobby Thigpen, Chicago	1990—	John Franco, New York
1991—	Dennis Eckersley, Oakland	1991—	Lee Smith, St. Louis
	Bryan Harvey, California		
1992—	Dennis Eckersley, Oakland	1992—	Doug Jones, Houston
			Lee Smith, St. Louis

MAJOR LEAGUE PLAYER OF THE YEAR

Year	Player, Team	Year	Player, Team	Year	Player, Team
1936—	Carl Hubbell, New York NL	1956—	Mickey Mantle, New York AL	1975—	Joe Morgan, Cincinnati NL
1937—	Johnny Allen, Cleveland AL	1957—	Ted Williams, Boston AL	1976—	Joe Morgan, Cincinnati NL
1938—	Johnny Vander Meer, Cin. NL	1958—	Bob Turley, New York AL	1977—	Rod Carew, Minnesota AL
1939—	Joe DiMaggio, New York AL	1959—	Early Wynn, Chicago AL	1978—	Ron Guidry, New York AL
1940—	Bob Feller, Cleveland AL	1960—	Bill Mazeroski, Pittsburgh NL	1979—	Willie Stargell, Pittsburgh NL
1941—	Ted Williams, Boston AL	1961—	Roger Maris, New York AL	1980—	George Brett, Kansas City AL
1942—	Ted Williams, Boston AL	1962—	Maury Wills, Los Angeles NL	1981—	Fernando Valenzuela, L.A. NL
1943—	Spud Chandler, New York AL		Don Drysdale, Los Angeles NL	1982—	Robin Yount, Milwaukee AL
1944—	Marty Marion, St. Louis NL	1963—	Sandy Koufax, Los Angeles NL	1983—	Cal Ripken Jr., Baltimore AL
1945—	Hal Newhouser, Detroit AL	1964—	Ken Boyer, St. Louis NL	1984—	Ryne Sandberg, Chicago NL
1946—	Stan Musial, St. Louis NL	1965—	Sandy Koufax, Los Angeles NL	1985—	Don Mattingly, New York AL
1947—	Ted Williams, Boston AL	1966—	Frank Robinson, Baltimore AL	1986—	Roger Clemens, Boston AL
1948—	Lou Boudreau, Cleveland AL	1967—	Carl Yastrzemski, Boston AL	1987—	George Bell, Toronto AL
1949—	Ted Williams, Boston AL	1968—	Denny McLain, Detroit AL	1988—	Orel Hershiser, Los Angeles NL
1950—	Phil Rizzuto, New York AL	1969—	Willie McCovey, San Fran. NL	1989—	Kevin Mitchell, San Fran. NL
1951—	Stan Musial, St. Louis NL	1970—	Johnny Bench, Cincinnati NL	1990—	Barry Bonds, Pittsburgh NL
1952—	Robin Roberts, Philadelphia NL	1971—	Joe Torre, St. Louis NL	1991—	Cal Ripken Jr., Baltimore AL
1953—	Al Rosen, Cleveland AL	1972—	Billy Williams, Chicago NL	1992—	Gary Sheffield, San Diego NL
1954—	Willie Mays, New York NL	1973—	Reggie Jackson, Oakland AL		
1955—	Duke Snider, Brooklyn NL	1974—	Lou Brock, St. Louis NL		

MAJOR LEAGUE MANAGER OF THE YEAR

Year	Manager, Team	Year	Manager, Team	Year	Manager, Team
1936—	Joe McCarthy, New York AL	1958—	Casey Stengel, New York AL	1980—	Bill Virdon, Houston NL
1937—	Bill McKechnie, Boston NL	1959—	Walter Alston, Los Angeles NL	1981—	Billy Martin, Oakland AL
1938—	Joe McCarthy, New York AL	1960—	Danny Murtaugh, Pit. NL	1982—	Whitey Herzog, St. Louis NL
1939—	Leo Durocher, Brooklyn NL	1961—	Ralph Houk, New York AL	1983—	Tony La Russa, Chicago AL
1940—	Bill McKechnie, Cincinnati NL	1962—	Bill Rigney, Los Angeles AL	1984—	Jim Frey, Chicago NL
1941—	Billy Southworth, St. Louis NL	1963—	Walter Alston, Los Angeles NL	1985—	Bobby Cox, Toronto AL
1942—	Billy Southworth, St. Louis NL	1964—	Johnny Keane, St. Louis NL	1986—	John McNamara, Boston AL
1943—	Joe McCarthy, New York AL	1965—	Sam Mele, Minnesota AL		Hal Lanier, Houston NL
1944—	Luke Sewell, St. Louis AL	1966—	Hank Bauer, Baltimore AL	1987—	Sparky Anderson, Detroit AL
1945—	Ossie Bluege, Washington AL	1967—	Dick Williams, Boston AL		Buck Rodgers, Montreal NL
1946—	Eddie Dyer, St. Louis NL	1968—	Mayo Smith, Detroit AL	1988—	Tony La Russa, Oakland AL
1947—	Bucky Harris, New York AL	1969—	Gil Hodges, New York NL		Tom Lasorda, L.A. NL (tie)
1948—	Bill Meyer, Pittsburgh NL	1970—	Danny Murtaugh, Pit. NL		Jim Leyland, Pitt. NL (tie)
1949—	Casey Stengel, New York AL	1971—	Charlie Fox, San Francisco NL	1989—	Frank Robinson, Baltimore AL
1950—	Red Rolfe, Detroit AL	1972—	Chuck Tanner, Chicago AL		Don Zimmer, Chicago NL
1951—	Leo Durocher, New York NL	1973—	Gene Mauch, Montreal NL	1990—	Jeff Torborg, Chicago AL
1952—	Eddie Stanky, St. Louis NL	1974—	Bill Virdon, New York AL		Jim Leyland, Pittsburgh NL
1953—	Casey Stengel, New York AL	1975—	Darrell Johnson, Boston AL	1991—	Tom Kelly, Minnesota AL
1954—	Leo Durocher, New York NL	1976—	Danny Ozark, Philadelphia NL		Bobby Cox, Atlanta NL
1955—	Walter Alston, Brooklyn NL	1977—	Earl Weaver, Baltimore AL	1992—	Tony La Russa, Oakland AL
1956—	Birdie Tebbetts, Cincinnati NL	1978—	George Bamberger, Mil. AL		Jim Leyland, Pittsburgh NL
1957—	Fred Hutchinson, St. Louis NL	1979—	Earl Weaver, Baltimore AL		

MAJOR LEAGUE EXECUTIVE OF THE YEAR

Year	Executive, Team	Year	Executive, Team	Year	Executive, Team
1936	Branch Rickey, St. Louis NL	1955	Walter O'Malley, Brooklyn NL	1974	Gabe Paul, New York AL
1937	Ed Barrow, New York AL	1956	Gabe Paul, Cincinnati NL	1975	Dick O'Connell, Boston AL
1938	Warren Giles, Cincinnati NL	1957	Frank Lane, St. Louis NL	1976	Joe Burke, Kansas City AL
1939	Larry MacPhail, Brooklyn NL	1958	Joe Brown, Pittsburgh NL	1977	Bill Veeck, Chicago AL
1940	Walter Briggs Sr., Detroit AL	1959	Buzzie Bavasi, L.A. NL	1978	Spec Richardson, San Fran. NL
1941	Ed Barrow, New York AL	1960	George Weiss, New York AL	1979	Hank Peters, Baltimore AL
1942	Branch Rickey, St. Louis NL	1961	Dan Topping, New York AL	1980	Tal Smith, Houston NL
1943	Clark Griffith, Washington AL	1962	Fred Haney, Los Angeles AL	1981	John McHale, Montreal NL
1944	Billy DeWitt, St. Louis AL	1963	Bing Devine, St. Louis NL	1982	Harry Dalton, Milwaukee AL
1945	Phil Wrigley, Chicago NL	1964	Bing Devine, St. Louis NL	1983	Hank Peters, Baltimore AL
1946	Tom Yawkey, Boston AL	1965	Cal Griffith, Minnesota AL	1984	Dallas Green, Chicago NL
1947	Branch Rickey, Brooklyn NL	1966	Lee MacPhail, Comm. Office	1985	John Schuerholz, K.C. AL
1948	Bill Veeck, Cleveland AL	1967	Dick O'Connell, Boston AL	1986	Frank Cashen, New York NL
1949	Bob Carpenter, Philadelphia NL	1968	Jim Campbell, Detroit AL	1987	Al Rosen, San Francisco NL
1950	George Weiss, New York AL	1969	John Murphy, New York NL	1988	Fred Claire, Los Angeles NL
1951	George Weiss, New York AL	1970	Harry Dalton, Baltimore AL	1989	Roland Hemond, Baltimore AL
1952	George Weiss, New York AL	1971	Cedric Tallis, Kansas City AL	1990	Bob Quinn, Cincinnati NL
1953	Lou Perini, Milwaukee NL	1972	Roland Hemond, Chicago AL	1991	Andy MacPhail, Minnesota AL
1954	Horace Stoneham, New York NL	1973	Bob Howsam, Cincinnati NL	1992	Dan Duquette, Montreal NL

GOLD GLOVE TEAMS

1957
MAJORS
P—Bobby Shantz, N.Y. AL
C—Sherm Lollar, Chicago AL
1B—Gil Hodges, Brooklyn NL
2B—Nellie Fox, Chicago AL
3B—Frank Malzone, Boston AL
SS—Roy McMillan, Cin. NL
OF—Minnie Minoso, Chicago AL
OF—Willie Mays, N.Y. NL
OF—Al Kaline, Detroit AL

NATIONAL LEAGUE
P—Harvey Haddix, Pittsburgh
C—Del Crandall, Milwaukee
1B—Gil Hodges, Los Angeles
2B—Charley Neal, Los Angeles
3B—Ken Boyer, St. Louis
SS—Roy McMillan, Cincinnati
OF—Jackie Brandt, San Fran.
OF—Willie Mays, San Francisco
OF—Hank Aaron, Milwaukee

NATIONAL LEAGUE
P—Bobby Shantz, Pittsburgh
C—John Roseboro, Los Angeles
1B—Bill White, St. Louis
2B—Bill Mazeroski, Pittsburgh
3B—Ken Boyer, St. Louis
SS—Maury Wills, Los Angeles
OF—Willie Mays, San Francisco
OF—Roberto Clemente, Pittsburgh
OF—Vada Pinson, Cincinnati

1958
AMERICAN LEAGUE
P—Bobby Shantz, New York
C—Sherm Lollar, Chicago
1B—Vic Power, Cleveland
2B—Frank Bolling, Detroit
3B—Frank Malzone, Boston
SS—Luis Aparicio, Chicago
OF—Norm Siebern, New York
OF—Jimmy Piersall, Boston
OF—Al Kaline, Detroit

NATIONAL LEAGUE
P—Harvey Haddix, Cincinnati
C—Del Crandall, Milwaukee
1B—Gil Hodges, Los Angeles
2B—Bill Mazeroski, Pitt.
3B—Ken Boyer, St. Louis
SS—Roy McMillan, Cin.
OF—Frank Robinson, Cin.
OF—Willie Mays, San Fran.
OF—Hank Aaron, Milwaukee

1959
AMERICAN LEAGUE
P—Bobby Shantz, New York
C—Sherm Lollar, Chicago
1B—Vic Power, Cleveland
2B—Nellie Fox, Chicago
3B—Frank Malzone, Boston
SS—Luis Aparicio, Chicago
OF—Minnie Minoso, Cleveland
OF—Al Kaline, Detroit
OF—Jackie Jensen, Boston

1960
AMERICAN LEAGUE
P—Bobby Shantz, New York
C—Earl Battey, Washington
1B—Vic Power, Cleveland
2B—Nellie Fox, Chicago
3B—Brooks Robinson, Baltimore
SS—Luis Aparicio, Chicago
OF—Minnie Minoso, Chicago
OF—Jim Landis, Chicago
OF—Roger Maris, New York

NATIONAL LEAGUE
P—Harvey Haddix, Pittsburgh
C—Del Crandall, Milwaukee
1B—Bill White, St. Louis
2B—Bill Mazeroski, Pittsburgh
3B—Ken Boyer, St. Louis
SS—Ernie Banks, Chicago
OF—Wally Moon, Los Angeles
OF—Willie Mays, San Francisco
OF—Hank Aaron, Milwaukee

1961
AMERICAN LEAGUE
P—Frank Lary, Detroit
C—Earl Battey, Chicago
1B—Vic Power, Cleveland
2B—Bobby Richardson, N.Y.
3B—Brooks Robinson, Baltimore
SS—Luis Aparicio, Chicago
OF—Al Kaline, Detroit
OF—Jimmy Piersall, Cleveland
OF—Jim Landis, Chicago

1962
AMERICAN LEAGUE
P—Jim Kaat, Minnesota
C—Earl Battey, Minnesota
1B—Vic Power, Minnesota
2B—Bobby Richardson, N.Y.
3B—Brooks Robinson, Baltimore
SS—Luis Aparicio, Chicago
OF—Jim Landis, Chicago
OF—Mickey Mantle, New York
OF—Al Kaline, Detroit

NATIONAL LEAGUE
P—Bobby Shantz, St. Louis
C—Del Crandall, Milwaukee
1B—Bill White, St. Louis
2B—Ken Hubbs, Chicago
3B—Jim Davenport, S.F.
SS—Maury Wills, Los Angeles
OF—Willie Mays, San Francisco
OF—Roberto Clemente, Pittsburgh
OF—Bill Virdon, Pittsburgh

1963
AMERICAN LEAGUE
P—Jim Kaat, Minnesota
C—Elston Howard, New York
1B—Vic Power, Minnesota
2B—Bobby Richardson, N.Y.
3B—Brooks Robinson, Baltimore
SS—Zoilo Versalles, Minnesota
OF—Al Kaline, Detroit
OF—Carl Yastrzemski, Boston
OF—Jim Landis, Chicago

NATIONAL LEAGUE
P—Bobby Shantz, St. Louis
C—Johnny Edwards, Cincinnati
1B—Bill White, St. Louis
2B—Bill Mazeroski, Pittsburgh
3B—Ken Boyer, St. Louis
SS—Bobby Wine, Philadelphia
OF—Willie Mays, San Francisco
OF—Roberto Clemente, Pittsburgh
OF—Curt Flood, St. Louis

1964
AMERICAN LEAGUE
P—Jim Kaat, Minnesota
C—Elston Howard, New York
1B—Vic Power, Los Angeles
2B—Bobby Richardson, N.Y.
3B—Brooks Robinson, Baltimore
SS—Luis Aparicio, Baltimore
OF—Al Kaline, Detroit
OF—Jim Landis, Chicago
OF—Vic Davalillo, Cleveland

NATIONAL LEAGUE
P—Bobby Shantz, Philadelphia
C—Johnny Edwards, Cincinnati
1B—Bill White, St. Louis
2B—Bill Mazeroski, Pittsburgh
3B—Ron Santo, Chicago
SS—Ruben Amaro, Philadelphia
OF—Willie Mays, San Francisco
OF—Roberto Clemente, Pittsburgh
OF—Curt Flood, St. Louis

1965
AMERICAN LEAGUE
P—Jim Kaat, Minnesota
C—Bill Freehan, Detroit
1B—Joe Pepitone, New York
2B—Bobby Richardson, N.Y.
3B—Brooks Robinson, Baltimore
SS—Zoilo Versalles, Minnesota
OF—Al Kaline, Detroit
OF—Tom Tresh, New York
OF—Carl Yastrzemski, Boston

NATIONAL LEAGUE
P—Bob Gibson, St. Louis
C—Joe Torre, Atlanta
1B—Bill White, St. Louis
2B—Bill Mazeroski, Pittsburgh
3B—Ron Santo, Chicago
SS—Leo Cardenas, Cincinnati
OF—Willie Mays, San Francisco
OF—Roberto Clemente, Pittsburgh
OF—Curt Flood, St. Louis

1966
AMERICAN LEAGUE
P—Jim Kaat, Minnesota
C—Bill Freehan, Detroit
1B—Joe Pepitone, New York
2B—Bobby Knoop, California
3B—Brooks Robinson, Balt.
SS—Luis Aparicio, Baltimore
OF—Al Kaline, Detroit
OF—Tommie Agee, Chicago
OF—Tony Oliva, Minnesota

NATIONAL LEAGUE
P—Bob Gibson, St. Louis
C—John Roseboro, Los Angeles
1B—Bill White, Philadelphia
2B—Bill Mazeroski, Pittsburgh
3B—Ron Santo, Chicago
SS—Gene Alley, Pittsburgh
OF—Willie Mays, San Francisco
OF—Curt Flood, St. Louis
OF—Roberto Clemente, Pittsburgh

1967
AMERICAN LEAGUE
P—Jim Kaat, Minnesota
C—Bill Freehan, Detroit
1B—George Scott, Boston
2B—Bobby Knoop, California
3B—Brooks Robinson, Balt.
SS—Jim Fregosi, California
OF—Carl Yastrzemski, Boston
OF—Paul Blair, Baltimore
OF—Al Kaline, Detroit

NATIONAL LEAGUE
P—Bob Gibson, St. Louis
C—Randy Hundley, Chicago
1B—Wes Parker, Los Angeles
2B—Bill Mazeroski, Pittsburgh
3B—Ron Santo, Chicago
SS—Gene Alley, Pittsburgh
OF—Roberto Clemente, Pittsburgh
OF—Curt Flood, St. Louis
OF—Willie Mays, San Francisco

1968
AMERICAN LEAGUE
P—Jim Kaat, Minnesota
C—Bill Freehan, Detroit
1B—George Scott, Boston
2B—Bobby Knoop, California
3B—Brooks Robinson, Balt.
SS—Luis Aparicio, Chicago
OF—Mickey Stanley, Detroit
OF—Carl Yastrzemski, Boston
OF—Reggie Smith, Boston

NATIONAL LEAGUE
P—Bob Gibson, St. Louis
C—Johnny Bench, Cincinnati
1B—Wes Parker, Los Angeles
2B—Glenn Beckert, Chicago
3B—Ron Santo, Chicago
SS—Dal Maxvill, St. Louis
OF—Willie Mays, San Francisco
OF—Roberto Clemente, Pittsburgh
OF—Curt Flood, St. Louis

1969
AMERICAN LEAGUE
P—Jim Kaat, Minnesota
C—Bill Freehan, Detroit
1B—Joe Pepitone, New York
2B—Dave Johnson, Baltimore
3B—Brooks Robinson, Balt.
SS—Mark Belanger, Baltimore
OF—Paul Blair, Baltimore
OF—Mickey Stanley, Detroit
OF—Carl Yastrzemski, Boston

NATIONAL LEAGUE
P—Bob Gibson, St. Louis
C—Johnny Bench, Cincinnati
1B—Wes Parker, Los Angeles
2B—Felix Millan, Atlanta
3B—Clete Boyer, Atlanta
SS—Don Kessinger, Chicago
OF—Roberto Clemente, Pittsburgh
OF—Curt Flood, St. Louis
OF—Pete Rose, Cincinnati

1970
AMERICAN LEAGUE
P—Jim Kaat, Minnesota
C—Ray Fosse, Cleveland
1B—Jim Spencer, California
2B—Dave Johnson, Baltimore
3B—Brooks Robinson, Balt.
SS—Luis Aparicio, Chicago
OF—Mickey Stanley, Detroit
OF—Paul Blair, Baltimore
OF—Ken Berry, Chicago

NATIONAL LEAGUE
P—Bob Gibson, St. Louis
C—Johnny Bench, Cincinnati
1B—Wes Parker, Los Angeles
2B—Tommy Helms, Cincinnati
3B—Doug Rader, Houston
SS—Don Kessinger, Chicago
OF—Roberto Clemente, Pittsburgh
OF—Tommie Agee, New York
OF—Pete Rose, Cincinnati

1971
AMERICAN LEAGUE
P—Jim Kaat, Minnesota
C—Ray Fosse, Cleveland
1B—George Scott, Boston
2B—Dave Johnson, Baltimore
3B—Brooks Robinson, Balt.
SS—Mark Belanger, Baltimore
OF—Paul Blair, Baltimore
OF—Amos Otis, Kansas City
OF—Carl Yastrzemski, Boston

NATIONAL LEAGUE
P—Bob Gibson, St. Louis
C—Johnny Bench, Cincinnati
1B—Wes Parker, Los Angeles
2B—Tommy Helms, Cincinnati
3B—Doug Rader, Houston
SS—Bud Harrelson, New York
OF—Roberto Clemente, Pittsburgh
OF—Bobby Bonds, San Francisco
OF—Willie Davis, Los Angeles

1972
AMERICAN LEAGUE
P—Jim Kaat, Minnesota
C—Carlton Fisk, Boston
1B—George Scott, Milwaukee
2B—Doug Griffin, Boston
3B—Brooks Robinson, Baltimore
SS—Ed Brinkman, Detroit
OF—Paul Blair, Baltimore
OF—Bobby Murcer, New York
OF—Ken Berry, California

NATIONAL LEAGUE
P—Bob Gibson, St. Louis
C—Johnny Bench, Cincinnati
1B—Wes Parker, Los Angeles
2B—Felix Millan, Atlanta
3B—Doug Rader, Houston
SS—Larry Bowa, Philadelphia
OF—Roberto Clemente, Pittsburgh
OF—Cesar Cedeno, Houston
OF—Willie Davis, Los Angeles

1973
AMERICAN LEAGUE
P—Jim Kaat, Chicago
C—Thurman Munson, New York
1B—George Scott, Milwaukee
2B—Bobby Grich, Baltimore
3B—Brooks Robinson, Baltimore
SS—Mark Belanger, Baltimore
OF—Paul Blair, Baltimore
OF—Amos Otis, Kansas City
OF—Mickey Stanley, Detroit

NATIONAL LEAGUE
P—Bob Gibson, St. Louis
C—Johnny Bench, Cincinnati
1B—Mike Jorgensen, Montreal
2B—Joe Morgan, Cincinnati
3B—Doug Rader, Houston
SS—Roger Metzger, Houston
OF—Bobby Bonds, San Francisco
OF—Cesar Cedeno, Houston
OF—Willie Davis, Los Angeles

1974
AMERICAN LEAGUE
P—Jim Kaat, Chicago
C—Thurman Munson, New York
1B—George Scott, Milwaukee
2B—Bobby Grich, Baltimore
3B—Brooks Robinson, Baltimore
SS—Mark Belanger, Baltimore
OF—Paul Blair, Baltimore
OF—Amos Otis, Kansas City
OF—Joe Rudi, Oakland

NATIONAL LEAGUE
P—Andy Messersmith, Los Angeles
C—Johnny Bench, Cincinnati
1B—Steve Garvey, Los Angeles
2B—Joe Morgan, Cincinnati
3B—Doug Rader, Houston
SS—Dave Concepcion, Cincinnati
OF—Cesar Cedeno, Houston
OF—Cesar Geronimo, Cincinnati
OF—Bobby Bonds, San Francisco

1975
AMERICAN LEAGUE
P—Jim Kaat, Chicago
C—Thurman Munson, New York
1B—George Scott, Milwaukee
2B—Bobby Grich, Baltimore
3B—Brooks Robinson, Baltimore
SS—Mark Belanger, Baltimore
OF—Paul Blair, Baltimore
OF—Joe Rudi, Oakland
OF—Fred Lynn, Boston

NATIONAL LEAGUE
P—Andy Messersmith, Los Angeles
C—Johnny Bench, Cincinnati
1B—Steve Garvey, Los Angeles
2B—Joe Morgan, Cincinnati
3B—Ken Reitz, St. Louis
SS—Dave Concepcion, Cincinnati
OF—Cesar Cedeno, Houston
OF—Cesar Geronimo, Cincinnati
OF—Garry Maddox, Philadelphia

1976
AMERICAN LEAGUE
P—Jim Palmer, Baltimore
C—Jim Sundberg, Texas
1B—George Scott, Milwaukee
2B—Bobby Grich, Baltimore
3B—Aurelio Rodriguez, Detroit
SS—Mark Belanger, Baltimore
OF—Joe Rudi, Oakland
OF—Dwight Evans, Boston
OF—Rick Manning, Cleveland

NATIONAL LEAGUE
P—Jim Kaat, Philadelphia
C—Johnny Bench, Cincinnati
1B—Steve Garvey, Los Angeles
2B—Joe Morgan, Cincinnati
3B—Mike Schmidt, Philadelphia
SS—Dave Concepcion, Cincinnati
OF—Cesar Cedeno, Houston
OF—Cesar Geronimo, Cincinnati
OF—Garry Maddox, Philadelphia

1977
AMERICAN LEAGUE
P—Jim Palmer, Baltimore
C—Jim Sundberg, Texas
1B—Jim Spencer, Chicago
2B—Frank White, Kansas City
3B—Graig Nettles, New York
SS—Mark Belanger, Baltimore
OF—Juan Beniquez, Texas
OF—Carl Yastrzemski, Boston
OF—Al Cowens, Kansas City

NATIONAL LEAGUE
P—Jim Kaat, Philadelphia
C—Johnny Bench, Cincinnati
1B—Steve Garvey, Los Angeles
2B—Joe Morgan, Cincinnati
3B—Mike Schmidt, Philadelphia
SS—Dave Concepcion, Cincinnati
OF—Cesar Geronimo, Cincinnati
OF—Garry Maddox, Philadelphia
OF—Dave Parker, Pittsburgh

1978
AMERICAN LEAGUE
P—Jim Palmer, Baltimore
C—Jim Sundberg, Texas
1B—Chris Chambliss, New York
2B—Frank White, Kansas City
3B—Graig Nettles, New York
SS—Mark Belanger, Baltimore
OF—Fred Lynn, Boston
OF—Dwight Evans, Boston
OF—Rick Miller, California

NATIONAL LEAGUE
P—Phil Niekro, Atlanta
C—Bob Boone, Philadelphia
1B—Keith Hernandez, St. Louis
2B—Dave Lopes, Los Angeles
3B—Mike Schmidt, Philadelphia
SS—Larry Bowa, Philadelphia
OF—Garry Maddox, Philadelphia
OF—Dave Parker, Pittsburgh
OF—Ellis Valentine, Montreal

1979
AMERICAN LEAGUE
P—Jim Palmer, Baltimore
C—Jim Sundberg, Texas
1B—Cecil Cooper, Milwaukee
2B—Frank White, Kansas City
3B—Buddy Bell, Texas
SS—Rick Burleson, Boston
OF—Dwight Evans, Boston
OF—Sixto Lezcano, Milwaukee
OF—Fred Lynn, Boston

NATIONAL LEAGUE
P—Phil Niekro, Atlanta
C—Bob Boone, Philadelphia
1B—Keith Hernandez, St. Louis
2B—Manny Trillo, Philadelphia
3B—Mike Schmidt, Philadelphia
SS—Dave Concepcion, Cincinnati
OF—Garry Maddox, Philadelphia
OF—Dave Parker, Pittsburgh
OF—Dave Winfield, San Diego

1980
AMERICAN LEAGUE
P—Mike Norris, Oakland
C—Jim Sundberg, Texas
1B—Cecil Cooper, Milwaukee
2B—Frank White, Kansas City
3B—Buddy Bell, Texas
SS—Alan Trammell, Detroit
OF—Fred Lynn, Boston
OF—Dwayne Murphy, Oakland
OF—Willie Wilson, Kansas City

NATIONAL LEAGUE
P—Phil Niekro, Atlanta
C—Gary Carter, Montreal
1B—Keith Hernandez, St. Louis
2B—Doug Flynn, New York
3B—Mike Schmidt, Philadelphia
SS—Ozzie Smith, San Diego
OF—Andre Dawson, Montreal
OF—Garry Maddox, Philadelphia
OF—Dave Winfield, San Diego

1981
AMERICAN LEAGUE
P—Mike Norris, Oakland
C—Jim Sundberg, Texas
1B—Mike Squires, Chicago
2B—Frank White, Kansas City
3B—Buddy Bell, Texas
SS—Alan Trammell, Detroit
OF—Dwayne Murphy, Oakland
OF—Dwight Evans, Boston
OF—Rickey Henderson, Oakland

NATIONAL LEAGUE
P—Steve Carlton, Philadelphia
C—Gary Carter, Montreal
1B—Keith Hernandez, St. Louis
2B—Manny Trillo, Philadelphia
3B—Mike Schmidt, Philadelphia
SS—Ozzie Smith, San Diego
OF—Andre Dawson, Montreal
OF—Garry Maddox, Philadelphia
OF—Dusty Baker, Los Angeles

NATIONAL LEAGUE
P—Joaquin Andujar, St. Louis
C—Tony Pena, Pittsburgh
1B—Keith Hernandez, New York
2B—Ryne Sandberg, Chicago
3B—Mike Schmidt, Philadelphia
SS—Ozzie Smith, St. Louis
OF—Dale Murphy, Atlanta
OF—Bob Dernier, Chicago
OF—Andre Dawson, Montreal

NATIONAL LEAGUE
P—Rick Reuschel, Pitt.-S.F.
C—Mike LaValliere, Pittsburgh
1B—Keith Hernandez, New York
2B—Ryne Sandberg, Chicago
3B—Terry Pendleton, St. Louis
SS—Ozzie Smith, St. Louis
OF—Eric Davis, Cincinnati
OF—Tony Gwynn, San Diego
OF—Andre Dawson, Chicago

1982
AMERICAN LEAGUE
P—Ron Guidry, New York
C—Bob Boone, California
1B—Eddie Murray, Baltimore
2B—Frank White, Kansas City
3B—Buddy Bell, Texas
SS—Robin Yount, Milwaukee
OF—Dwight Evans, Boston
OF—Dave Winfield, New York
OF—Dwayne Murphy, Oakland

1985
AMERICAN LEAGUE
P—Ron Guidry, New York
C—Lance Parrish, Detroit
1B—Don Mattingly, New York
2B—Lou Whitaker, Detroit
3B—George Brett, Kansas City
SS—Alfredo Griffin, Oakland
OF—Gary Pettis, California
OF—Dave Winfield, New York
OF—Dwight Evans, Boston (tie)
    Dwayne Murphy, Oakland (tie)

1988
AMERICAN LEAGUE
P—Mark Langston, Seattle
C—Bob Boone, California
1B—Don Mattingly, New York
2B—Harold Reynolds, Seattle
3B—Gary Gaetti, Minnesota
SS—Tony Fernandez, Toronto
OF—Kirby Puckett, Minnesota
OF—Devon White, California
OF—Gary Pettis, Detroit

NATIONAL LEAGUE
P—Phil Niekro, Atlanta
C—Gary Carter, Montreal
1B—Keith Hernandez, St. Louis
2B—Manny Trillo, Philadelphia
3B—Mike Schmidt, Philadelphia
SS—Ozzie Smith, St. Louis
OF—Andre Dawson, Montreal
OF—Dale Murphy, Atlanta
OF—Garry Maddox, Philadelphia

NATIONAL LEAGUE
P—Rick Reuschel, Pittsburgh
C—Tony Pena, Pittsburgh
1B—Keith Hernandez, New York
2B—Ryne Sandberg, Chicago
3B—Tim Wallach, Montreal
SS—Ozzie Smith, St. Louis
OF—Willie McGee, St. Louis
OF—Dale Murphy, Atlanta
OF—Andre Dawson, Montreal

NATIONAL LEAGUE
P—Orel Hershiser, Los Angeles
C—Benito Santiago, San Diego
1B—Keith Hernandez, New York
2B—Ryne Sandberg, Chicago
3B—Tim Wallach, Montreal
SS—Ozzie Smith, St. Louis
OF—Andy Van Slyke, Pittsburgh
OF—Eric Davis, Cincinnati
OF—Andre Dawson, Chicago

1983
AMERICAN LEAGUE
P—Ron Guidry, New York
C—Lance Parrish, Detroit
1B—Eddie Murray, Baltimore
2B—Lou Whitaker, Detroit
3B—Buddy Bell, Texas
SS—Alan Trammell, Detroit
OF—Dwight Evans, Boston
OF—Dave Winfield, New York
OF—Dwayne Murphy, Oakland

1986
AMERICAN LEAGUE
P—Ron Guidry, New York
C—Bob Boone, California
1B—Don Mattingly, New York
2B—Frank White, Kansas City
3B—Gary Gaetti, Minnesota
SS—Tony Fernandez, Toronto
OF—Gary Pettis, California
OF—Jesse Barfield, Toronto
OF—Kirby Puckett, Minnesota

1989
AMERICAN LEAGUE
P—Bret Saberhagen, Kansas City
C—Bob Boone, Kansas City
1B—Don Mattingly, New York
2B—Harold Reynolds, Seattle
3B—Gary Gaetti, Minnesota
SS—Tony Fernandez, Toronto
OF—Kirby Puckett, Minnesota
OF—Devon White, California
OF—Gary Pettis, Detroit

NATIONAL LEAGUE
P—Phil Niekro, Atlanta
C—Tony Pena, Pittsburgh
1B—Keith Hernandez, St.L.-N.Y.
2B—Ryne Sandberg, Chicago
3B—Mike Schmidt, Philadelphia
SS—Ozzie Smith, St. Louis
OF—Andre Dawson, Montreal
OF—Dale Murphy, Atlanta
OF—Willie McGee, St. Louis

NATIONAL LEAGUE
P—Fernando Valenzuela, L.A.
C—Jody Davis, Chicago
1B—Keith Hernandez, New York
2B—Ryne Sandberg, Chicago
3B—Mike Schmidt, Philadelphia
SS—Ozzie Smith, St. Louis
OF—Tony Gwynn, San Diego
OF—Dale Murphy, Atlanta
OF—Willie McGee, St. Louis

NATIONAL LEAGUE
P—Ron Darling, New York
C—Benito Santiago, San Diego
1B—Andres Galarraga, Montreal
2B—Ryne Sandberg, Chicago
3B—Terry Pendleton, St. Louis
SS—Ozzie Smith, St. Louis
OF—Andy Van Slyke, Pittsburgh
OF—Tony Gwynn, San Diego
OF—Eric Davis, Cincinnati

1984
AMERICAN LEAGUE
P—Ron Guidry, New York
C—Lance Parrish, Detroit
1B—Eddie Murray, Baltimore
2B—Lou Whitaker, Detroit
3B—Buddy Bell, Texas
SS—Alan Trammell, Detroit
OF—Dwight Evans, Boston
OF—Dave Winfield, New York
OF—Dwayne Murphy, Oakland

1987
AMERICAN LEAGUE
P—Mark Langston, Seattle
C—Bob Boone, California
1B—Don Mattingly, New York
2B—Frank White, Kansas City
3B—Gary Gaetti, Minnesota
SS—Tony Fernandez, Toronto
OF—Jesse Barfield, Toronto
OF—Kirby Puckett, Minnesota
OF—Dave Winfield, New York

1990
AMERICAN LEAGUE
P—Mike Boddicker, Boston
C—Sandy Alomar Jr., Cleveland
1B—Mark McGwire, Oakland
2B—Harold Reynolds, Seattle
3B—Kelly Gruber, Toronto
SS—Ozzie Guillen, Chicago
OF—Ken Griffey Jr., Seattle
OF—Ellis Burks, Boston
OF—Gary Pettis, Texas

NATIONAL LEAGUE
P—Greg Maddux, Chicago
C—Benito Santiago, San Diego
1B—Andres Galarraga, Montreal
2B—Ryne Sandberg, Chicago
3B—Tim Wallach, Montreal
SS—Ozzie Smith, St. Louis
OF—Barry Bonds, Pittsburgh
OF—Andy Van Slyke, Pittsburgh
OF—Tony Gwynn, San Diego

NATIONAL LEAGUE
P—Greg Maddux, Chicago
C—Tom Pagnozzi, St. Louis
1B—Will Clark, San Francisco
2B—Ryne Sandberg, Chicago
3B—Matt Williams, San Francisco
SS—Ozzie Smith, St. Louis
OF—Barry Bonds, Pittsburgh
OF—Andy Van Slyke, Pittsburgh
OF—Tony Gwynn, San Diego

NATIONAL LEAGUE
P—Greg Maddux, Chicago
C—Tom Pagnozzi, St. Louis
1B—Mark Grace, Chicago
2B—Jose Lind, Pittsburgh
3B—Terry Pendleton, Atlanta
SS—Ozzie Smith, St. Louis
OF—Barry Bonds, Pittsburgh
OF—Andy Van Slyke, Pittsburgh
OF—Larry Walker, Montreal

1991
AMERICAN LEAGUE
P—Mark Langston, California
C—Tony Pena, Boston
1B—Don Mattingly, New York
2B—Roberto Alomar, Toronto
3B—Robin Ventura, Chicago
SS—Cal Ripken, Baltimore
OF—Ken Griffey Jr., Seattle
OF—Kirby Puckett, Minnesota
OF—Devon White, Toronto

1992
AMERICAN LEAGUE
P—Mark Langston, California
C—Ivan Rodriguez, Texas
1B—Don Mattingly, New York
2B—Roberto Alomar, Toronto
3B—Robin Ventura, Chicago
SS—Cal Ripken, Baltimore
OF—Ken Griffey Jr., Seattle
OF—Kirby Puckett, Minnesota
OF—Devon White, Toronto

SILVER SLUGGER TEAMS

1980
AMERICAN LEAGUE
1B—Cecil Cooper, Milwaukee
2B—Willie Randolph, New York
3B—George Brett, Kansas City
SS—Robin Yount, Milwaukee
OF—Ben Oglivie, Milwaukee
OF—Al Oliver, Texas
OF—Willie Wilson, Kansas City
C—Lance Parrish, Detroit
DH—Reggie Jackson, New York

1982
AMERICAN LEAGUE
1B—Cecil Cooper, Milwaukee
2B—Damaso Garcia, Toronto
3B—Doug DeCinces, California
SS—Robin Yount, Milwaukee
OF—Dave Winfield, New York
OF—Willie Wilson, Kansas City
OF—Reggie Jackson, California
C—Lance Parrish, Detroit
DH—Hal McRae, Kansas City

1984
AMERICAN LEAGUE
1B—Eddie Murray, Baltimore
2B—Lou Whitaker, Detroit
3B—Buddy Bell, Texas
SS—Cal Ripken Jr., Baltimore
OF—Tony Armas, Boston
OF—Jim Rice, Boston
OF—Dave Winfield, New York
C—Lance Parrish, Detroit
DH—Andre Thornton, Cleveland

NATIONAL LEAGUE
1B—Keith Hernandez, St. Louis
2B—Manny Trillo, Philadelphia
3B—Mike Schmidt, Philadelphia
SS—Garry Templeton, St. Louis
OF—Dusty Baker, Los Angeles
OF—Andre Dawson, Montreal
OF—George Hendrick, St. Louis
C—Ted Simmons, St. Louis
P—Bob Forsch, St. Louis

NATIONAL LEAGUE
1B—Al Oliver, Montreal
2B—Joe Morgan, San Francisco
3B—Mike Schmidt, Philadelphia
SS—Dave Concepcion, Cincinnati
OF—Dale Murphy, Atlanta
OF—Pedro Guerrero, Los Angeles
OF—Leon Durham, Chicago
C—Gary Carter, Montreal
P—Don Robinson, Pittsburgh

NATIONAL LEAGUE
1B—Keith Hernandez, New York
2B—Ryne Sandberg, Chicago
3B—Mike Schmidt, Philadelphia
SS—Garry Templeton, San Diego
OF—Dale Murphy, Atlanta
OF—Jose Cruz, Houston
OF—Tony Gwynn, San Diego
C—Gary Carter, Montreal
P—Rick Rhoden, Pittsburgh

1981
AMERICAN LEAGUE
1B—Cecil Cooper, Milwaukee
2B—Bobby Grich, California
3B—Carney Lansford, Boston
SS—Rick Burleson, California
OF—Rickey Henderson, Oakland
OF—Dwight Evans, Boston
OF—Dave Winfield, New York
C—Carlton Fisk, Chicago
DH—Al Oliver, Texas

1983
AMERICAN LEAGUE
1B—Eddie Murray, Baltimore
2B—Lou Whitaker, Detroit
3B—Wade Boggs, Boston
SS—Cal Ripken Jr., Baltimore
OF—Jim Rice, Boston
OF—Dave Winfield, New York
OF—Lloyd Moseby, Toronto
C—Lance Parrish, Detroit
DH—Don Baylor, New York

1985
AMERICAN LEAGUE
1B—Don Mattingly, New York
2B—Lou Whitaker, Detroit
3B—George Brett, Kansas City
SS—Cal Ripken Jr., Baltimore
OF—Rickey Henderson, New York
OF—Dave Winfield, New York
OF—George Bell, Toronto
C—Carlton Fisk, Chicago
DH—Don Baylor, New York

NATIONAL LEAGUE
1B—Pete Rose, Philadelphia
2B—Manny Trillo, Philadelphia
3B—Mike Schmidt, Philadelphia
SS—Dave Concepcion, Cincinnati
OF—Andre Dawson, Montreal
OF—George Foster, Cincinnati
OF—Dusty Baker, Los Angeles
C—Gary Carter, Montreal
P—Fernando Valenzuela, L.A.

NATIONAL LEAGUE
1B—George Hendrick, St. Louis
2B—Johnny Ray, Pittsburgh
3B—Mike Schmidt, Philadelphia
SS—Dickie Thon, Houston
OF—Andre Dawson, Montreal
OF—Dale Murphy, Atlanta
OF—Jose Cruz, Houston
C—Terry Kennedy, San Diego
P—Fernando Valenzuela, L.A.

NATIONAL LEAGUE
1B—Jack Clark, St. Louis
2B—Ryne Sandberg, Chicago
3B—Tim Wallach, Montreal
SS—Hubie Brooks, Montreal
OF—Willie McGee, St. Louis
OF—Dale Murphy, Atlanta
OF—Dave Parker, Cincinnati
C—Gary Carter, New York
P—Rick Rhoden, Pittsburgh

1986
AMERICAN LEAGUE
1B—Don Mattingly, New York
2B—Frank White, Kansas City
3B—Wade Boggs, Boston
SS—Cal Ripken Jr., Baltimore
OF—George Bell, Toronto
OF—Kirby Puckett, Minnesota
OF—Jesse Barfield, Toronto
C—Lance Parrish, Detroit
DH—Don Baylor, Boston

NATIONAL LEAGUE
1B—Glenn Davis, Houston
2B—Steve Sax, Los Angeles
3B—Mike Schmidt, Philadelphia
SS—Hubie Brooks, Montreal
OF—Tony Gwynn, San Diego
OF—Tim Raines, Montreal
OF—Dave Parker, Cincinnati
C—Gary Carter, New York
P—Rick Rhoden, Pittsburgh

1987
AMERICAN LEAGUE
1B—Don Mattingly, New York
2B—Lou Whitaker, Detroit
3B—Wade Boggs, Boston
SS—Alan Trammell, Detroit
OF—George Bell, Toronto
OF—Dwight Evans, Boston
OF—Kirby Puckett, Minnesota
C—Matt Nokes, Detroit
DH—Paul Molitor, Milwaukee

NATIONAL LEAGUE
1B—Jack Clark, St. Louis
2B—Juan Samuel, Philadelphia
3B—Tim Wallach, Montreal
SS—Ozzie Smith, St. Louis
OF—Andre Dawson, Chicago
OF—Eric Davis, Cincinnati
OF—Tony Gwynn, San Diego
C—Benito Santiago, San Diego
P—Bob Forsch, St. Louis

1988
AMERICAN LEAGUE
1B—George Brett, Kansas City
2B—Julio Franco, Cleveland
3B—Wade Boggs, Boston
SS—Alan Trammell, Detroit
OF—Kirby Puckett, Minnesota
OF—Jose Canseco, Oakland
OF—Mike Greenwell, Boston
C—Carlton Fisk, Chicago
DH—Paul Molitor, Milwaukee

NATIONAL LEAGUE
1B—Andres Galarraga, Montreal
2B—Ryne Sandberg, Chicago
3B—Bobby Bonilla, Pittsburgh
SS—Barry Larkin, Cincinnati
OF—Darryl Strawberry, New York
OF—Andy Van Slyke, Pittsburgh
OF—Kirk Gibson, Los Angeles
C—Benito Santiago, San Diego
P—Tim Leary, Los Angeles

1989
AMERICAN LEAGUE
1B—Fred McGriff, Toronto
2B—Julio Franco, Texas
3B—Wade Boggs, Boston
SS—Cal Ripken Jr., Baltimore
OF—Kirby Puckett, Minnesota
OF—Ruben Sierra, Texas
OF—Robin Yount, Milwaukee
C—Mickey Tettleton, Baltimore
DH—H. Baines, Chicago-Texas

NATIONAL LEAGUE
1B—Will Clark, San Francisco
2B—Ryne Sandberg, Chicago
3B—Howard Johnson, New York
SS—Barry Larkin, Cincinnati
OF—Kevin Mitchell, San Francisco
OF—Tony Gwynn, San Diego
OF—Eric Davis, Cincinnati
C—Craig Biggio, Houston
P—Don Robinson, San Francisco

1990
AMERICAN LEAGUE
1B—Cecil Fielder, Detroit
2B—Julio Franco, Texas
3B—Kelly Gruber, Toronto
SS—Alan Trammell, Detroit
OF—Rickey Henderson, Oakland
OF—Jose Canseco, Oakland
OF—Ellis Burks, Boston
C—Lance Parrish, California
DH—Dave Parker, Milwaukee

NATIONAL LEAGUE
1B—Eddie Murray, Los Angeles
2B—Ryne Sandberg, Chicago
3B—Matt Williams, San Francisco
SS—Barry Larkin, Cincinnati
OF—Barry Bonds, Pittsburgh
OF—Bobby Bonilla, Pittsburgh
OF—Darryl Strawberry, New York
C—Benito Santiago, San Diego
P—Don Robinson, San Francisco

1991
AMERICAN LEAGUE
1B—Cecil Fielder, Detroit
2B—Julio Franco, Texas
3B—Wade Boggs, Boston
SS—Cal Ripken Jr., Baltimore
OF—Jose Canseco, Oakland
OF—Joe Carter, Toronto
OF—Ken Griffey Jr., Seattle
C—Mickey Tettleton, Detroit
DH—Frank Thomas, Chicago

NATIONAL LEAGUE
1B—Will Clark, San Francisco
2B—Ryne Sandberg, Chicago
3B—Howard Johnson, New York
SS—Barry Larkin, Cincinnati
OF—Barry Bonds, Pittsburgh
OF—Bobby Bonilla, Pittsburgh
OF—Ron Gant, Atlanta
C—Benito Santiago, San Diego
P—Tom Glavine, Atlanta

1992
AMERICAN LEAGUE
1B—Mark McGwire, Oakland
2B—Roberto Alomar, Toronto
3B—Edgar Martinez, Seattle
SS—Travis Fryman, Detroit
OF—Joe Carter, Toronto
OF—Juan Gonzalez, Texas
OF—Kirby Puckett, Minnesota
C—Mickey Tettleton, Detroit
DH—Dave Winfield, Toronto

NATIONAL LEAGUE
1B—Fred McGriff, San Diego
2B—Ryne Sandberg, Chicago
3B—Gary Sheffield, San Diego
SS—Barry Larkin, Cincinnati
OF—Barry Bonds, Pittsburgh
OF—Andy Van Slyke, Pittsburgh
OF—Larry Walker, Montreal
C—Darren Daulton, Philadelphia
P—Dwight Gooden, New York

MAJOR LEAGUE ALL-STAR TEAMS

1925
1B—Jim Bottomley, St. Louis NL
2B—Rogers Hornsby, St. Louis NL
SS—Glenn Wright, Pittsburgh NL
3B—Pie Traynor, Pittsburgh NL
OF—Kiki Cuyler, Pittsburgh NL
OF—Max Carey, Pittsburgh NL
OF—Goose Goslin, Washington AL
C—Mickey Cochrane, Phil. AL
P—Walter Johnson, Washington AL
P—Ed Rommel, Philadelphia AL
P—Dazzy Vance, Brooklyn NL

1926
1B—George Burns, Cleveland AL
2B—Rogers Hornsby, St. Louis NL
SS—Joe Sewell, Cleveland AL
3B—Pie Traynor, Pittsburgh NL
OF—Goose Goslin, Washington AL
OF—John Mostil, Chicago AL
OF—Babe Ruth, New York AL
C—Bob O'Farrell, St. Louis NL
P—Herb Pennock, New York AL
P—George Uhle, Cleveland AL
P—Grover Alexander, St. Louis NL

1927
1B—Lou Gehrig, New York AL
2B—Rogers Hornsby, New York NL
SS—Travis Jackson, New York NL
3B—Pie Traynor, Pittsburgh NL
OF—Babe Ruth, New York AL
OF—Al Simmons, Philadelphia AL
OF—Paul Waner, Pittsburgh NL
C—Gabby Hartnett, Chicago NL
P—Charley Root, Chicago NL
P—Ted Lyons, Chicago AL

1928

1B—Lou Gehrig, New York AL
2B—Rogers Hornsby, Boston NL
SS—Travis Jackson, New York NL
3B—Fred Lindstrom, New York NL
OF—Babe Ruth, New York AL
OF—Heinie Manush, St. Louis AL
OF—Paul Waner, Pittsburgh NL
C—Mickey Cochrane, Phil. AL
P—Lefty Grove, Philadelphia AL
P—Waite Hoyt, New York AL

1929

1B—Jimmie Foxx, Philadelphia AL
2B—Rogers Hornsby, Chicago NL
SS—Travis Jackson, New York NL
3B—Pie Traynor, Pittsburgh, NL
OF—Al Simmons, Philadelphia AL
OF—Hack Wilson, Chicago NL
OF—Babe Ruth, New York AL
C—Mickey Cochrane, Phil. AL
P—Lefty Grove, Philadelphia AL
P—Burleigh Grimes, Pittsburgh NL

1930

1B—Bill Terry, New York NL
2B—Frank Frisch, St. Louis NL
SS—Joe Cronin, Washington AL
3B—Fred Lindstrom, New York NL
OF—Al Simmons, Philadelphia AL
OF—Hack Wilson, Chicago NL
OF—Babe Ruth, New York AL
C—Mickey Cochrane, Phil. AL
P—Lefty Grove, Philadelphia AL
P—Wes Ferrell, Cleveland AL

1931

1B—Lou Gehrig, New York AL
2B—Frank Frisch, St. Louis NL
SS—Joe Cronin, Washington AL
3B—Pie Traynor, Pittsburgh NL
OF—Al Simmons, Philadelphia AL
OF—Earl Averill, Cleveland AL
OF—Babe Ruth, New York AL
C—Mickey Cochrane, Phil. AL
P—Lefty Grove, Philadelphia AL
P—George Earnshaw, Phil. AL

1932

1B—Jimmie Foxx, Philadelphia AL
2B—Tony Lazzeri, New York AL
SS—Joe Cronin, Washington AL
3B—Pie Traynor, Pittsburgh NL
OF—Lefty O'Doul, Brooklyn NL
OF—Earl Averill, Cleveland AL
OF—Chuck Klein, Philadelphia NL
C—Bill Dickey, New York AL
P—Lefty Grove, Philadelphia AL
P—Lon Warneke, Chicago NL

1933

1B—Jimmie Foxx, Philadelphia AL
2B—Charley Gehringer, Detroit AL
SS—Joe Cronin, Washington AL
3B—Pie Traynor, Pittsburgh NL
OF—Al Simmons, Chicago AL
OF—Wally Berger, Boston NL
OF—Chuck Klein, Philadelphia NL
C—Bill Dickey, New York AL
P—Alvin Crowder, Washington AL
P—Carl Hubbell, New York NL

1934

1B—Lou Gehrig, New York AL
2B—Charley Gehringer, Detroit AL
SS—Joe Cronin, Washington AL
3B—Mike Higgins, Philadelphia AL
OF—Al Simmons, Chicago AL
OF—Earl Averill, Cleveland AL
OF—Mel Ott, New York NL
C—Mickey Cochrane, Detroit AL
P—Lefty Gomez, New York AL
P—Schoolboy Rowe, Detroit AL
P—Dizzy Dean, St. Louis NL

1935

1B—Hank Greenberg, Detroit AL
2B—Charley Gehringer, Detroit AL
SS—Arky Vaughan, Pittsburgh NL
3B—Pepper Martin, St. Louis NL
OF—Joe Medwick, St. Louis NL
OF—Doc Cramer, Philadelphia AL
OF—Mel Ott, New York NL
C—Mickey Cochrane, Detroit AL
P—Carl Hubbell, New York NL
P—Dizzy Dean, St. Louis NL

1936

1B—Lou Gehrig, New York AL
2B—Charley Gehringer, Detroit AL
SS—Luke Appling, Chicago AL
3B—Mike Higgins, Philadelphia AL
OF—Joe Medwick, St. Louis NL
OF—Earl Averill, Cleveland AL
OF—Mel Ott, New York NL
C—Bill Dickey, New York AL
P—Carl Hubbell, New York NL
P—Dizzy Dean, St. Louis NL

1937

1B—Lou Gehrig, New York AL
2B—Charley Gehringer, Detroit AL
SS—Dick Bartell, New York NL
3B—Red Rolfe, New York AL
OF—Joe Medwick, St. Louis NL
OF—Joe DiMaggio, New York AL
OF—Paul Waner, Pittsburgh NL
C—Gabby Hartnett, Chicago NL
P—Carl Hubbell, New York NL
P—Red Ruffing, New York AL

1938

1B—Jimmie Foxx, Boston AL
2B—Charley Gehringer, Detroit AL
SS—Joe Cronin, Boston AL
3B—Red Rolfe, New York AL
OF—Joe Medwick, St. Louis NL
OF—Joe DiMaggio, New York AL
OF—Mel Ott, New York NL
C—Bill Dickey, New York AL
P—Red Ruffing, New York AL
P—Lefty Gomez, New York AL
P—Johnny Vander Meer, Cin. NL

1939

1B—Jimmie Foxx, Boston AL
2B—Joe Gordon, New York AL
SS—Joe Cronin, Boston AL
3B—Red Rolfe, New York AL
OF—Joe Medwick, St. Louis NL
OF—Joe DiMaggio, New York AL
OF—Ted Williams, Boston AL
C—Bill Dickey, New York AL
P—Red Ruffing, New York AL
P—Bob Feller, Cleveland AL
P—Bucky Walters, Cincinnati NL

1940

1B—Frank McCormick, Cin. NL
2B—Joe Gordon, New York AL
SS—Luke Appling, Chicago AL
3B—Stan Hack, Chicago NL
OF—Hank Greenberg, Detroit AL
OF—Joe DiMaggio, New York AL
OF—Ted Williams, Boston AL
C—Harry Danning, New York NL
P—Bob Feller, Cleveland AL
P—Bucky Walters, Cincinnati NL
P—Paul Derringer, Cincinnati NL

1941

1B—Dolf Camilli, Brooklyn NL
2B—Joe Gordon, New York AL
SS—Cecil Travis, Washington AL
3B—Stan Hack, Chicago NL
OF—Ted Williams, Boston AL
OF—Joe DiMaggio, New York AL
OF—Pete Reiser, Brooklyn NL
C—Bill Dickey, New York AL
P—Bob Feller, Cleveland AL
P—Whitlow Wyatt, Brooklyn NL
P—Thornton Lee, Chicago AL

1942

1B—Johnny Mize, New York NL
2B—Joe Gordon, New York AL
SS—Johnny Pesky, Boston AL
3B—Stan Hack, Chicago NL
OF—Ted Williams, Boston AL
OF—Joe DiMaggio, New York AL
OF—Enos Slaughter, St. Louis NL
C—Mickey Owen, Brooklyn NL
P—Mort Cooper, St. Louis NL
P—Tiny Bonham, New York AL
P—Tex Hughson, Boston AL

1943

1B—Rudy York, Detroit AL
2B—Billy Herman, Brooklyn NL
SS—Luke Appling, Chicago AL
3B—Billy Johnson, New York AL
OF—Dick Wakefield, Detroit AL
OF—Stan Musial, St. Louis NL
OF—Bill Nicholson, Chicago NL
C—Walker Cooper, St. Louis NL
P—Spud Chandler, New York AL
P—Mort Cooper, St. Louis NL
P—Rip Sewell, Pittsburgh NL

1944

1B—Ray Sanders, St. Louis NL
2B—Bobby Doerr, Boston AL
SS—Marty Marion, St. Louis NL
3B—Bob Elliott, Pittsburgh NL
OF—Stan Musial, St. Louis NL
OF—Dick Wakefield, Detroit AL
OF—Dixie Walker, Brooklyn, NL
C—Walker Cooper, St. Louis NL
P—Hal Newhouser, Detroit AL
P—Mort Cooper, St. Louis NL
P—Dizzy Trout, Detroit AL

1945

1B—Phil Cavarretta, Chicago NL
2B—George Stirnweiss, New York AL
SS—Marty Marion, St. Louis NL
3B—Whitey Kurowski, St. Louis NL
OF—Tommy Holmes, Boston NL
OF—Andy Pafko, Chicago NL
OF—Goody Rosen, Brooklyn NL
C—Paul Richards, Detroit AL
P—Hal Newhouser, Detroit AL
P—Boo Ferriss, Boston AL
P—Hank Borowy, Chicago NL

1946

1B—Stan Musial, St. Louis NL
2B—Bobby Doerr, Boston AL
SS—Johnny Pesky, Boston AL
3B—George Kell, Detroit AL
OF—Ted Williams, Boston AL
OF—Dom DiMaggio, Boston AL
OF—Enos Slaughter, St. Louis NL
 C—Aaron Robinson, New York AL
 P—Hal Newhouser, Detroit AL
 P—Bob Feller, Cleveland AL
 P—Boo Ferriss, Boston AL

1947

1B—Johnny Mize, New York NL
2B—Joe Gordon, Cleveland AL
SS—Lou Boudreau, Cleveland AL
3B—George Kell, Detroit AL
OF—Ted Williams, Boston AL
OF—Joe DiMaggio, New York AL
OF—Ralph Kiner, Pittsburgh NL
 C—Walker Cooper, New York NL
 P—Ewell Blackwell, Cincinnati NL
 P—Bob Feller, Cleveland AL
 P—Ralph Branca, Brooklyn NL

1948

1B—Johnny Mize, New York NL
2B—Joe Gordon, Cleveland AL
SS—Lou Boudreau, Cleveland AL
3B—Bob Elliott, Boston NL
OF—Ted Williams, Boston AL
OF—Joe DiMaggio, New York AL
OF—Stan Musial, St. Louis NL
 C—Birdie Tebbetts, Boston AL
 P—Johnny Sain, Boston NL
 P—Bob Lemon, Cleveland AL
 P—Harry Brecheen, St. Louis NL

1949

1B—Tommy Henrich, New York AL
2B—Jackie Robinson, Brooklyn NL
SS—Phil Rizzuto, New York AL
3B—George Kell, Detroit AL
OF—Ted Williams, Boston AL
OF—Stan Musial, St. Louis NL
OF—Ralph Kiner, Pittsburgh NL
 C—Roy Campanella, Brooklyn NL
 P—Mel Parnell, Boston AL
 P—Ellis Kinder, Boston AL
 P—Joe Page, New York AL

1950

1B—Walt Dropo, Boston AL
2B—Jackie Robinson, Brooklyn NL
SS—Phil Rizzuto, New York AL
3B—George Kell, Detroit AL
OF—Stan Musial, St. Louis NL
OF—Ralph Kiner, Pittsburgh NL
OF—Larry Doby, Cleveland AL
 C—Yogi Berra, New York AL
 P—Vic Raschi, New York AL
 P—Bob Lemon, Cleveland AL
 P—Jim Konstanty, Philadelphia NL

1951

1B—Ferris Fain, Philadelphia AL
2B—Jackie Robinson, Brooklyn NL
SS—Phil Rizzuto, New York AL
3B—George Kell, Detroit AL
OF—Stan Musial, St. Louis NL
OF—Ted Williams, Boston AL
OF—Ralph Kiner, Pittsburgh NL
 C—Roy Campanella, Brooklyn NL
 P—Sal Maglie, New York NL
 P—Preacher Roe, Brooklyn NL
 P—Allie Reynolds, New York AL

1952

1B—Ferris Fain, Philadelphia AL
2B—Jackie Robinson, Brooklyn NL
SS—Phil Rizzuto, New York AL
3B—George Kell, Boston AL
OF—Stan Musial, St. Louis NL
OF—Hank Sauer, Chicago NL
OF—Mickey Mantle, New York AL
 C—Yogi Berra, New York AL
 P—Robin Roberts, Philadelphia NL
 P—Bobby Shantz, Philadelphia AL
 P—Allie Reynolds, New York AL

1953

1B—Mickey Vernon, Washington AL
2B—Red Schoendienst, St. Louis NL
SS—Pee Wee Reese, Brooklyn NL
3B—Al Rosen, Cleveland AL
OF—Stan Musial, St. Louis NL
OF—Duke Snider, Brooklyn NL
OF—Carl Furillo, Brooklyn NL
 C—Roy Campanella, Brooklyn NL
 P—Robin Roberts, Philadelphia NL
 P—Warren Spahn, Milwaukee NL
 P—Bob Porterfield, Washington AL

1954

1B—Ted Kluszewski, Cincinnati NL
2B—Bobby Avila, Cleveland AL
SS—Alvin Dark, New York NL
3B—Al Rosen, Cleveland AL
OF—Willie Mays, New York NL
OF—Stan Musial, St. Louis NL
OF—Duke Snider, Brooklyn NL
 C—Yogi Berra, New York AL
 P—Bob Lemon, Cleveland AL
 P—Johnny Antonelli, New York NL
 P—Robin Roberts, Philadelphia NL

1955

1B—Ted Kluszewski, Cincinnati NL
2B—Nellie Fox, Chicago AL
SS—Ernie Banks, Chicago NL
3B—Ed Mathews, Milwaukee NL
OF—Duke Snider, Brooklyn NL
OF—Ted Williams, Boston AL
OF—Al Kaline, Detroit AL
 C—Roy Campanella, Brooklyn NL
 P—Robin Roberts, Philadelphia NL
 P—Don Newcombe, Brooklyn NL
 P—Whitey Ford, New York AL

1956

1B—Ted Kluszewski, Cincinnati NL
2B—Nellie Fox, Chicago AL
SS—Harvey Kuenn, Detroit AL
3B—Ken Boyer, St. Louis NL
OF—Mickey Mantle, New York AL
OF—Hank Aaron, Milwaukee NL
OF—Ted Williams, Boston AL
 C—Yogi Berra, New York AL
 P—Don Newcombe, Brooklyn NL
 P—Whitey Ford, New York AL
 P—Billy Pierce, Chicago AL

1957

1B—Stan Musial, St. Louis NL
2B—Red Schoendienst, N.Y.-Mil. NL
SS—Gil McDougald, New York AL
3B—Ed Mathews, Milwaukee NL
OF—Mickey Mantle, New York AL
OF—Ted Williams, Boston AL
OF—Willie Mays, New York NL
 C—Yogi Berra, New York AL
 P—Warren Spahn, Milwaukee NL
 P—Billy Pierce, Chicago NL
 P—Jim Bunning, Detroit AL

1958

1B—Stan Musial, St. Louis NL
2B—Nellie Fox, Chicago AL
SS—Ernie Banks, Chicago NL
3B—Frank Thomas, Pittsburgh NL
OF—Ted Williams, Boston AL
OF—Willie Mays, San Francisco NL
OF—Hank Aaron, Milwaukee NL
 C—Del Crandall, Milwaukee NL
 P—Bob Turley, New York AL
 P—Warren Spahn, Milwaukee NL
 P—Bob Friend, Pittsburgh NL

1959

1B—Orlando Cepeda, S.F. NL
2B—Nellie Fox, Chicago AL
SS—Ernie Banks, Chicago NL
3B—Ed Mathews, Milwaukee NL
OF—Minnie Minoso, Cleveland AL
OF—Willie Mays, San Francisco NL
OF—Hank Aaron, Milwaukee NL
 C—Sherm Lollar, Chicago AL
 P—Early Wynn, Chicago AL
 P—Sam Jones, San Francisco NL
 P—Johnny Antonelli, S.F. NL

1960

1B—Bill Skowron, New York AL
2B—Bill Mazeroski, Pittsburgh NL
SS—Ernie Banks, Chicago NL
3B—Ed Mathews, Milwaukee NL
OF—Minnie Minoso, Chicago AL
OF—Willie Mays, San Francisco NL
OF—Roger Maris, New York AL
 C—Del Crandall, Milwaukee NL
 P—Vernon Law, Pittsburgh NL
 P—Warren Spahn, Milwaukee NL
 P—Ernie Broglio, St. Louis NL

1961
AMERICAN LEAGUE

1B—Norm Cash, Detroit
2B—Bobby Richardson, New York
SS—Tony Kubek, New York
3B—Brooks Robinson, Baltimore
OF—Mickey Mantle, New York
OF—Roger Maris, New York
OF—Rocky Colavito, Detroit
 C—Elston Howard, New York
 P—Whitey Ford, New York
 P—Frank Lary, Detroit

NATIONAL LEAGUE

1B—Orlando Cepeda, San Francisco
2B—Frank Bolling, Milwaukee
SS—Maury Wills, Los Angeles
3B—Ken Boyer, St. Louis
OF—Willie Mays, San Francisco
OF—Frank Robinson, Cincinnati
OF—Roberto Clemente, Pittsburgh
 C—Smoky Burgess, Pittsburgh
 P—Joey Jay, Cincinnati
 P—Warren Spahn, Milwaukee

1962
AMERICAN LEAGUE

1B—Norm Siebern, Kansas City
2B—Bobby Richardson, New York
SS—Tom Tresh, New York
3B—Brooks Robinson, Baltimore
OF—Leon Wagner, Los Angeles
OF—Mickey Mantle, New York
OF—Al Kaline, Detroit
 C—Earl Battey, Minnesota
 P—Ralph Terry, New York
 P—Dick Donovan, Cleveland

NATIONAL LEAGUE

1B—Orlando Cepeda, San Francisco
2B—Bill Mazeroski, Pittsburgh
SS—Maury Wills, Los Angeles
3B—Ken Boyer, St. Louis
OF—Tommy Davis, Los Angeles
OF—Willie Mays, San Francisco
OF—Frank Robinson, Cincinnati
C—Del Crandall, Milwaukee
P—Don Drysdale, Los Angeles
P—Bob Purkey, Cincinnati

1963
AMERICAN LEAGUE

1B—Joe Pepitone, New York
2B—Bobby Richardson, New York
SS—Luis Aparicio, Baltimore
3B—Frank Malzone, Boston
OF—Carl Yastrzemski, Boston
OF—Albie Pearson, Los Angeles
OF—Al Kaline, Detroit
C—Elston Howard, New York
P—Whitey Ford, New York
P—Gary Peters, Chicago

NATIONAL LEAGUE

1B—Bill White, St. Louis
2B—Jim Gilliam, Los Angeles
SS—Dick Groat, St. Louis
3B—Ken Boyer, St. Louis
OF—Tommy Davis, Los Angeles
OF—Willie Mays, San Francisco
OF—Hank Aaron, Milwaukee
C—John Edwards, Cincinnati
P—Sandy Koufax, Los Angeles
P—Juan Marichal, San Francisco

1964
AMERICAN LEAGUE

1B—Dick Stuart, Boston
2B—Bobby Richardson, New York
SS—Jim Fregosi, Los Angeles
3B—Brooks Robinson, Baltimore
OF—Harmon Killebrew, Minnesota
OF—Mickey Mantle, New York
OF—Tony Oliva, Minnesota
C—Elston Howard, New York
P—Dean Chance, Los Angeles
P—Gary Peters, Chicago

NATIONAL LEAGUE

1B—Bill White, St. Louis
2B—Ron Hunt, New York
SS—Dick Groat, St. Louis
3B—Ken Boyer, St. Louis
OF—Billy Williams, Chicago
OF—Willie Mays, San Francisco
OF—Roberto Clemente, Pittsburgh
C—Joe Torre, Milwaukee
P—Sandy Koufax, Los Angeles
P—Jim Bunning, Philadelphia

1965
AMERICAN LEAGUE

1B—Fred Whitfield, Cleveland
2B—Bobby Richardson, New York
SS—Zoilo Versalles, Minnesota
3B—Brooks Robinson, Baltimore
OF—Carl Yastrzemski, Boston
OF—Jimmie Hall, Minnesota
OF—Tony Oliva, Minnesota
C—Earl Battey, Minnesota
P—Jim Grant, Minnesota
P—Mel Stottlemyre, New York

NATIONAL LEAGUE

1B—Willie McCovey, San Francisco
2B—Pete Rose, Cincinnati
SS—Maury Wills, Los Angeles
3B—Deron Johnson, Cincinnati
OF—Willie Stargell, Pittsburgh
OF—Willie Mays, San Francisco
OF—Hank Aaron, Milwaukee
C—Joe Torre, Milwaukee
P—Sandy Koufax, Los Angeles
P—Juan Marichal, San Francisco

1966
AMERICAN LEAGUE

1B—Boog Powell, Baltimore
2B—Bobby Richardson, New York
SS—Luis Aparicio, Baltimore
3B—Brooks Robinson, Baltimore
OF—Frank Robinson, Baltimore
OF—Al Kaline, Detroit
OF—Tony Oliva, Minnesota
C—Paul Casanova, Washington
P—Jim Kaat, Minnesota
P—Earl Wilson, Detroit

NATIONAL LEAGUE

1B—Felipe Alou, Atlanta
2B—Pete Rose, Cincinnati
SS—Gene Alley, Pittsburgh
3B—Ron Santo, Chicago
OF—Willie Stargell, Pittsburgh
OF—Willie Mays, San Francisco
OF—Roberto Clemente, Pittsburgh
C—Joe Torre, Atlanta
P—Sandy Koufax, Los Angeles
P—Juan Marichal, San Francisco

1967
AMERICAN LEAGUE

1B—Harmon Killebrew, Minnesota
2B—Rod Carew, Minnesota
SS—Jim Fregosi, California
3B—Brooks Robinson, Baltimore
OF—Carl Yastrzemski, Boston
OF—Al Kaline, Detroit
OF—Frank Robinson, Baltimore
C—Bill Freehan, Detroit
P—Jim Lonborg, Boston
P—Earl Wilson, Detroit

NATIONAL LEAGUE

1B—Orlando Cepeda, St. Louis
2B—Bill Mazeroski, Pittsburgh
SS—Gene Alley, Pittsburgh
3B—Ron Santo, Chicago
OF—Hank Aaron, Atlanta
OF—Jim Wynn, Houston
OF—Roberto Clemente, Pittsburgh
C—Tim McCarver, St. Louis
P—Mike McCormick, San Francisco
P—Ferguson Jenkins, Chicago

1968
AMERICAN LEAGUE

1B—Boog Powell, Baltimore
2B—Rod Carew, Minnesota
SS—Luis Aparicio, Chicago
3B—Brooks Robinson, Baltimore
OF—Ken Harrelson, Boston
OF—Willie Horton, Detroit
OF—Frank Howard, Washington
C—Bill Freehan, Detroit
P—Dave McNally, Baltimore
P—Denny McLain, Detroit

NATIONAL LEAGUE

1B—Willie McCovey, San Francisco
2B—Tommy Helms, Cincinnati
SS—Don Kessinger, Chicago
3B—Ron Santo, Chicago
OF—Billy Williams, Chicago
OF—Curt Flood, St. Louis
OF—Pete Rose, Cincinnati
C—Johnny Bench, Cincinnati
P—Bob Gibson, St. Louis
P—Juan Marichal, San Francisco

1969
AMERICAN LEAGUE

1B—Boog Powell, Baltimore
2B—Rod Carew, Minnesota
SS—Rico Petrocelli, Boston
3B—Harmon Killebrew, Minnesota
OF—Frank Howard, Washington
OF—Paul Blair, Baltimore
OF—Reggie Jackson, Oakland
C—Bill Freehan, Detroit
RHP—Denny McLain, Detroit
LHP—Mike Cuellar, Baltimore

NATIONAL LEAGUE

1B—Willie McCovey, San Francisco
2B—Glenn Beckert, Chicago
SS—Don Kessinger, Chicago
3B—Ron Santo, Chicago
OF—Cleon Jones, New York
OF—Matty Alou, Pittsburgh
OF—Hank Aaron, Atlanta
C—Johnny Bench, Cincinnati
RHP—Tom Seaver, New York
LHP—Steve Carlton, St. Louis

1970
AMERICAN LEAGUE

1B—Boog Powell, Baltimore
2B—Dave Johnson, Baltimore
SS—Luis Aparicio, Chicago
3B—Harmon Killebrew, Minnesota
OF—Frank Howard, Washington
OF—Reggie Smith, Boston
OF—Tony Oliva, Minnesota
C—Ray Fosse, Cleveland
RHP—Jim Perry, Minnesota
LHP—Sam McDowell, Cleveland

NATIONAL LEAGUE

1B—Willie McCovey, San Francisco
2B—Glenn Beckert, Chicago
SS—Don Kessinger, Chicago
3B—Tony Perez, Cincinnati
OF—Billy Williams, Chicago
OF—Bobby Tolan, Cincinnati
OF—Hank Aaron, Atlanta
C—Johnny Bench, Cincinnati
RHP—Bob Gibson, St. Louis
LHP—Jim Merritt, Cincinnati

1971
AMERICAN LEAGUE

1B—Norm Cash, Detroit
2B—Cookie Rojas, Kansas City
SS—Leo Cardenas, Minnesota
3B—Brooks Robinson, Baltimore
OF—Merv Rettenmund, Baltimore
OF—Bobby Murcer, New York
OF—Tony Oliva, Minnesota
C—Bill Freehan, Detroit
RHP—Jim Palmer, Baltimore
LHP—Vida Blue, Oakland

NATIONAL LEAGUE
1B—Lee May, Cincinnati
2B—Glenn Beckett, Chicago
SS—Bud Harrelson, New York
3B—Joe Torre, St. Louis
OF—Willie Stargell, Pittsburgh
OF—Willie Davis, Los Angeles
OF—Hank Aaron, Atlanta
C—Manny Sanguillen, Pittsburgh
RHP—Ferguson Jenkins, Chicago
LHP—Steve Carlton, St. Louis

1972
AMERICAN LEAGUE
1B—Dick Allen, Chicago
2B—Rod Carew, Minnesota
SS—Luis Aparicio, Boston
3B—Brooks Robinson, Baltimore
OF—Joe Rudi, Oakland
OF—Bobby Murcer, New York
OF—Richie Scheinblum, Kansas City
C—Carlton Fisk, Boston
RHP—Gaylord Perry, Cleveland
LHP—Wilbur Wood, Chicago

NATIONAL LEAGUE
1B—Willie Stargell, Pittsburgh
2B—Joe Morgan, Cincinnati
SS—Chris Speier, San Francisco
3B—Ron Santo, Chicago
OF—Billy Williams, Chicago
OF—Cesar Cedeno, Houston
OF—Roberto Clemente, Pittsburgh
C—Johnny Bench, Cincinnati
RHP—Ferguson Jenkins, Chicago
LHP—Steve Carlton, Philadelphia

1973
AMERICAN LEAGUE
1B—John Mayberry, Kansas City
2B—Rod Carew, Minnesota
SS—Bert Campaneris, Oakland
3B—Sal Bando, Oakland
OF—Reggie Jackson, Oakland
OF—Amos Otis, Kansas City
OF—Bobby Murcer, New York
C—Thurman Munson, New York
RHP—Jim Palmer, Baltimore
LHP—Ken Holtzman, Oakland

NATIONAL LEAGUE
1B—Tony Perez, Cincinnati
2B—Dave Johnson, Atlanta
SS—Bill Russell, Los Angeles
3B—Darrell Evans, Atlanta
OF—Bobby Bonds, San Francisco
OF—Cesar Cedeno, Houston
OF—Pete Rose, Cincinnati
C—Johnny Bench, Cincinnati
RHP—Tom Seaver, New York
LHP—Ron Bryant, San Francisco

1974
AMERICAN LEAGUE
1B—Dick Allen, Chicago
2B—Rod Carew, Minnesota
SS—Bert Campaneris, Oakland
3B—Sal Bando, Oakland
OF—Joe Rudi, Oakland
OF—Paul Blair, Baltimore
OF—Jeff Burroughs, Texas
C—Thurman Munson, New York
DH—Tommy Davis, Baltimore
RHP—Jim Hunter, Oakland
LHP—Mike Cuellar, Baltimore

NATIONAL LEAGUE
1B—Steve Garvey, Los Angeles
2B—Joe Morgan, Cincinnati
SS—Dave Concepcion, Cincinnati
3B—Mike Schmidt, Philadelphia
OF—Lou Brock, St. Louis
OF—Jim Wynn, Los Angeles
OF—Richie Zisk, Pittsburgh
C—Johnny Bench, Cincinnati
RHP—Andy Messersmith, Los Angeles
LHP—Don Gullett, Cincinnati

1975
AMERICAN LEAGUE
1B—John Mayberry, Kansas City
2B—Rod Carew, Minnesota
SS—Toby Harrah, Texas
3B—Graig Nettles, New York
OF—Jim Rice, Boston
OF—Fred Lynn, Boston
OF—Reggie Jackson, Oakland
C—Thurman Munson, New York
DH—Willie Horton, Detroit
RHP—Jim Palmer, Baltimore
LHP—Jim Kaat, Chicago

NATIONAL LEAGUE
1B—Steve Garvey, Los Angeles
2B—Joe Morgan, Cincinnati
SS—Larry Bowa, Philadelphia
3B—Bill Madlock, Chicago
OF—Greg Luzinski, Philadelphia
OF—Al Oliver, Pittsburgh
OF—Dave Parker, Pittsburgh
C—Johnny Bench, Cincinnati
RHP—Tom Seaver, New York
LHP—Randy Jones, San Diego

1976
AMERICAN LEAGUE
1B—Chris Chambliss, New York
2B—Bobby Grich, Baltimore
3B—George Brett, Kansas City
SS—Mark Belanger, Baltimore
OF—Joe Rudi, Oakland
OF—Mickey Rivers, New York
OF—Reggie Jackson, Baltimore
C—Thurman Munson, New York
DH—Hal McRae, Kansas City
RHP—Jim Palmer, Baltimore
LHP—Frank Tanana, California

NATIONAL LEAGUE
1B—Willie Montanez, San Fran.-Atl.
2B—Joe Morgan, Cincinnati
3B—Mike Schmidt, Philadelphia
SS—Dave Concepcion, Cincinnati
OF—George Foster, Cincinnati
OF—Cesar Cedeno, Houston
OF—Ken Griffey, Cincinnati
C—Bob Boone, Philadelphia
RHP—Don Sutton, Los Angeles
LHP—Randy Jones, San Diego

1977
AMERICAN LEAGUE
1B—Rod Carew, Minnesota
2B—Willie Randolph, New York
3B—Graig Nettles, New York
SS—Rick Burleson, Boston
OF—Jim Rice, Boston
OF—Larry Hisle, Minnesota
OF—Bobby Bonds, California
C—Carlton Fisk, Boston
DH—Hal McRae, Kansas City
RHP—Nolan Ryan, California
LHP—Frank Tanana, California

NATIONAL LEAGUE
1B—Steve Garvey, Los Angeles
2B—Joe Morgan, Cincinnati
3B—Mike Schmidt, Philadelphia
SS—Garry Templeton, St. Louis
OF—George Foster, Cincinnati
OF—Dave Parker, Pittsburgh
OF—Greg Luzinski, Philadelphia
C—Ted Simmons, St. Louis
RHP—Rick Reuschel, Chicago
LHP—Steve Carlton, Philadelphia

1978
AMERICAN LEAGUE
1B—Rod Carew, Minnesota
2B—Frank White, Kansas City
3B—Graig Nettles, New York
SS—Robin Yount, Milwaukee
OF—Jim Rice, Boston
OF—Larry Hisle, Milwaukee
OF—Fred Lynn, Boston
C—Jim Sundberg, Texas
DH—Rusty Staub, Detroit
RHP—Jim Palmer, Baltimore
LHP—Ron Guidry, New York

NATIONAL LEAGUE
1B—Steve Garvey, Los Angeles
2B—Dave Lopes, Los Angeles
3B—Pete Rose, Cincinnati
SS—Larry Bowa, Philadelphia
OF—George Foster, Cincinnati
OF—Dave Parker, Pittsburgh
OF—Jack Clark, San Francisco
C—Ted Simmons, St. Louis
RHP—Gaylord Perry, San Diego
LHP—Vida Blue, San Francisco

1979
AMERICAN LEAGUE
1B—Cecil Cooper, Milwaukee
2B—Bobby Grich, California
3B—George Brett, Kansas City
SS—Roy Smalley, Minnesota
OF—Jim Rice, Boston
OF—Fred Lynn, Boston
OF—Ken Singleton, Baltimore
C—Darrell Porter, Kansas City
DH—Don Baylor, California
RHP—Jim Kern, Texas
LHP—Mike Flanagan, Baltimore

NATIONAL LEAGUE
1B—Keith Hernandez, St. Louis
2B—Dave Lopes, Los Angeles
3B—Mike Schmidt, Philadelphia
SS—Garry Templeton, St. Louis
OF—Dave Kingman, Chicago
OF—Omar Moreno, Pittsburgh
OF—Dave Winfield, San Diego
C—Ted Simmons, St. Louis
RHP—Joe Niekro, Houston
LHP—Steve Carlton, Philadelphia

1980
AMERICAN LEAGUE
1B—Cecil Cooper, Milwaukee
2B—Willie Randolph, New York
3B—George Brett, Kansas City
SS—Robin Yount, Milwaukee
OF—Ben Oglivie, Milwaukee
OF—Al Bumbry, Baltimore
OF—Reggie Jackson, New York
DH—Reggie Jackson, New York
C—Rick Cerone, New York
RHP—Steve Stone, Baltimore
LHP—Tommy John, New York

NATIONAL LEAGUE
1B—Keith Hernandez, St. Louis
2B—Manny Trillo, Philadelphia
3B—Mike Schmidt, Philadelphia
SS—Garry Templeton, St. Louis
OF—Dusty Baker, Los Angeles
OF—Cesar Cedeno, Houston
OF—George Hendrick, St. Louis
C—Gary Carter, Montreal
RHP—Jim Bibby, Pittsburgh
LHP—Steve Carlton, Philadelphia

1981
AMERICAN LEAGUE
1B—Cecil Cooper, Milwaukee
2B—Bobby Grich, California
3B—Buddy Bell, Texas
SS—Rick Burleson, California
OF—Rickey Henderson, Oakland
OF—Dwayne Murphy, Oakland
OF—Tony Armas, Oakland
C—Jim Sundberg, Texas
DH—Richie Zisk, Seattle
RHP—Jack Morris, Detroit
LHP—Ron Guidry, New York

NATIONAL LEAGUE
1B—Pete Rose, Philadelphia
2B—Manny Trillo, Philadelphia
3B—Mike Schmidt, Philadelphia
SS—Dave Concepcion, Cincinnati
OF—George Foster, Cincinnati
OF—Andre Dawson, Montreal
OF—Pedro Guerrero, Los Angeles
C—Gary Carter, Montreal
RHP—Tom Seaver, Cincinnati
LHP—Fernando Valenzuela, Los Ang.

1982
AMERICAN LEAGUE
1B—Cecil Cooper, Milwaukee
2B—Damaso Garcia, Toronto
3B—Doug DeCinces, California
SS—Robin Yount, Milwaukee
OF—Dave Winfield, New York
OF—Gorman Thomas, Milwaukee
OF—Dwight Evans, Boston
C—Lance Parrish, Detroit
DH—Hal McRae, Kansas City
RHP—Dave Stieb, Toronto
LHP—Geoff Zahn, California

NATIONAL LEAGUE
1B—Al Oliver, Montreal
2B—Manny Trillo, Philadelphia
3B—Mike Schmidt, Philadelphia
SS—Ozzie Smith, St. Louis
OF—Lonnie Smith, St. Louis
OF—Dale Murphy, Atlanta
OF—Pedro Guerrero, Los Angeles
C—Gary Carter, Montreal
RHP—Steve Rogers, Montreal
LHP—Steve Carlton, Philadelphia

1983
AMERICAN LEAGUE
1B—Eddie Murray, Baltimore
2B—Lou Whitaker, Detroit
3B—Wade Boggs, Boston
SS—Cal Ripken, Baltimore
OF—Jim Rice, Boston
OF—Dave Winfield, New York
OF—Lloyd Moseby, Toronto
C—Carlton Fisk, Chicago
DH—Greg Luzinski, Chicago
RHP—LaMarr Hoyt, Chicago
LHP—Ron Guidry, New York

NATIONAL LEAGUE
1B—George Hendrick, St. Louis
2B—Glenn Hubbard, Atlanta
3B—Mike Schmidt, Philadelphia
SS—Dickie Thon, Houston
OF—Dale Murphy, Atlanta
OF—Andre Dawson, Montreal
OF—Tim Raines, Montreal
C—Tony Pena, Pittsburgh
RHP—John Denny, Philadelphia
LHP—Larry McWilliams, Pittsburgh

1984
AMERICAN LEAGUE
1B—Don Mattingly, New York
2B—Lou Whitaker, Detroit
3B—Buddy Bell, Texas
SS—Cal Ripken, Baltimore
OF—Tony Armas, Boston
OF—Dwight Evans, Boston
OF—Dave Winfield, New York
C—Lance Parrish, Detroit
DH—Dave Kingman, Oakland
RHP—Mike Boddicker, Baltimore
LHP—Willie Hernandez, Detroit

NATIONAL LEAGUE
1B—Keith Hernandez, New York
2B—Ryne Sandberg, Chicago
3B—Mike Schmidt, Philadelphia
SS—Ozzie Smith, St. Louis
OF—Dale Murphy, Atlanta
OF—Jose Cruz, Houston
OF—Tony Gwynn, San Diego
C—Gary Carter, Montreal
RHP—Rick Sutcliffe, Chicago
LHP—Mark Thurmond, San Diego

1985
AMERICAN LEAGUE
1B—Don Mattingly, New York
2B—Damaso Garcia, Toronto
3B—Wade Boggs, Boston
SS—Cal Ripken, Baltimore
OF—Rickey Henderson, New York
OF—Harold Baines, Chicago
OF—Phil Bradley, Seattle
C—Carlton Fisk, Chicago
DH—Don Baylor, New York
RHP—Bret Saberhagen, Kansas City
LHP—Ron Guidry, New York

NATIONAL LEAGUE
1B—Keith Hernandez, New York
2B—Tom Herr, St. Louis
3B—Tim Wallach, Montreal
SS—Ozzie Smith, St. Louis
OF—Dave Parker, Cincinnati
OF—Willie McGee, St. Louis
OF—Dale Murphy, Atlanta
C—Gary Carter, New York
RHP—Dwight Gooden, New York
LHP—John Tudor, St. Louis

1986
AMERICAN LEAGUE
1B—Don Mattingly, New York
2B—Tony Bernazard, Cleveland
3B—Wade Boggs, Boston
SS—Tony Fernandez, Toronto
OF—Jim Rice, Boston
OF—George Bell, Toronto
OF—Kirby Puckett, Minnesota
C—Rich Gedman, Boston
DH—Don Baylor, Boston
RHP—Roger Clemens, Boston
LHP—Teddy Higuera, Milwaukee

NATIONAL LEAGUE
1B—Keith Hernandez, New York
2B—Steve Sax, Los Angeles
3B—Mike Schmidt, Philadelphia
SS—Ozzie Smith, St. Louis
OF—Tim Raines, Montreal
OF—Tony Gwynn, San Diego
OF—Dave Parker, Cincinnati
C—Gary Carter, New York
RHP—Mike Scott, Houston
LHP—Fernando Valenzuela, Los Ang.

1987
AMERICAN LEAGUE
1B—Don Mattingly, New York
2B—Willie Randolph, New York
3B—Wade Boggs, Boston
SS—Alan Trammell, Detroit
OF—George Bell, Toronto
OF—Kirby Puckett, Minnesota
OF—Dwight Evans, Boston
C—Matt Nokes, Detroit
DH—Paul Molitor, Milwaukee
RHP—Roger Clemens, Boston
LHP—Jimmy Key, Toronto

NATIONAL LEAGUE
1B—Jack Clark, St. Louis
2B—Juan Samuel, Philadelphia
3B—Tim Wallach, Montreal
SS—Ozzie Smith, St. Louis
OF—Andre Dawson, Chicago
OF—Tony Gwynn, San Diego
OF—Eric Davis, Cincinnati
C—Benito Santiago, San Diego
RHP—Rick Sutcliffe, Chicago
LHP—Zane Smith, Atlanta

1988
AMERICAN LEAGUE
1B—George Brett, Kansas City
2B—Johnny Ray, California
3B—Wade Boggs, Boston
SS—Alan Trammell, Detroit
OF—Kirby Puckett, Minnesota
OF—Mike Greenwell, Boston
OF—Jose Canseco, Oakland
C—Ernie Whitt, Toronto
DH—Harold Baines, Chicago
RHP—Dave Stewart, Oakland
LHP—Frank Viola, Minnesota

NATIONAL LEAGUE
1B—Will Clark, San Francisco
2B—Ryne Sandberg, Chicago
3B—Bobby Bonilla, Pittsburgh
SS—Barry Larkin, Cincinnati
OF—Darryl Strawberry, New York
OF—Andy Van Slyke, Pittsburgh
OF—Kevin McReynolds, New York
C—Mike LaValliere, Pittsburgh
RHP—Orel Hershiser, Los Angeles
LHP—Danny Jackson, Cincinnati

1989
AMERICAN LEAGUE
1B—Fred McGriff, Toronto
2B—Julio Franco, Texas
3B—Carney Lansford, Oakland
SS—Cal Ripken, Baltimore
OF—Ruben Sierra, Texas
OF—Kirby Puckett, Minnesota
OF—Robin Yount, Milwaukee
C—Mickey Tettleton, Baltimore
DH—Harold Baines, Chicago-Texas
RHP—Bret Saberhagen, Kansas City
LHP—Chuck Finley, California

NATIONAL LEAGUE
1B—Will Clark, San Francisco
2B—Ryne Sandberg, Chicago
3B—Howard Johnson, New York
SS—Shawon Dunston, Chicago
OF—Tony Gwynn, San Diego
OF—Kevin Mitchell, San Francisco
OF—Eric Davis, Cincinnati
C—Benito Santiago, San Diego
RHP—Mike Scott, Houston
LHP—Mark Davis, San Diego

1990
AMERICAN LEAGUE
1B—Cecil Fielder, Detroit
2B—Julio Franco, Texas
3B—Kelly Gruber, Toronto
SS—Alan Trammell, Detroit
OF—Rickey Henderson, Oakland
OF—Jose Canseco, Oakland
OF—Ellis Burks, Boston
C—Carlton Fisk, Chicago
DH—Dave Parker, Milwaukee
RHP—Bob Welch, Oakland
LHP—Chuck Finley, California

NATIONAL LEAGUE
1B—Eddie Murray, Los Angeles
2B—Ryne Sandberg, Chicago
3B—Matt Williams, San Francisco
SS—Barry Larkin, Cincinnati
OF—Barry Bonds, Pittsburgh
OF—Bobby Bonilla, Pittsburgh
OF—Darryl Strawberry, New York
C—Mike Scioscia, Los Angeles
RHP—Doug Drabek, Pittsburgh
LHP—Frank Viola, New York

1991
AMERICAN LEAGUE
1B—Cecil Fielder, Detroit
2B—Julio Franco, Texas
3B—Wade Boggs, Boston
SS—Cal Ripken, Baltimore
OF—Jose Canseco, Oakland
OF—Joe Carter, Toronto
OF—Ken Griffey Jr., Seattle
C—Mickey Tettleton, Detroit
RHP—Roger Clemens, Boston
LHP—Jim Abbott, California

NATIONAL LEAGUE
1B—Will Clark, San Francisco
2B—Ryne Sandberg, Chicago
3B—Terry Pendleton, Atlanta
SS—Barry Larkin, Cincinnati
OF—Barry Bonds, Pittsburgh
OF—Bobby Bonilla, Pittsburgh
OF—Ron Gant, Atlanta
C—Benito Santiago, San Diego
RHP—Jose Rijo, Cincinnati
LHP—Tom Glavine, Atlanta

1992
AMERICAN LEAGUE
1B—Mark McGwire, Oakland
2B—Roberto Alomar, Toronto
3B—Edgar Martinez, Seattle
SS—Travis Fryman, Detroit
OF—Joe Carter, Toronto
OF—Mike Devereaux, Baltimore
OF—Kirby Puckett, Minnesota
C—Mickey Tettleton, Detroit
RHP—Jack McDowell, Chicago
LHP—Dave Fleming, Seattle

NATIONAL LEAGUE
1B—Fred McGriff, San Diego
2B—Ryne Sandberg, Chicago
3B—Gary Sheffield, San Diego
SS—Barry Larkin, Cincinnati
OF—Barry Bonds, Pittsburgh
OF—Andy Van Slyke, Pittsburgh
OF—Larry Walker, Montreal
C—Darren Daulton, Philadelphia
RHP—Greg Maddux, Chicago
LHP—Tom Glavine, Atlanta

MINOR LEAGUE PLAYER OF THE YEAR

Year	Player, Team, League
1936	John Vander Meer, Durham, Piedmont
1937	Charlie Keller, Newark, International
1938	Fred Hutchinson, Seattle, Pacific Coast
1939	Lou Novikoff, Tulsa-Los Angeles
1940	Phil Rizzuto, Kansas City, American Association
1941	John Lindell, Newark, International
1942	Dick Barrett, Seattle, Pacific Coast
1943	Chet Covington, Scranton, Eastern
1944	Rip Collins, Albany, Eastern
1945	Gil Coan, Chattanooga, Southern
1946	Sibby Sisti, Indianapolis, American Association
1947	Hank Sauer, Syracuse, International
1948	Gene Woodling, San Francisco, Pacific Coast
1949	Orie Arntzen, Albany, Eastern
1950	Frank Saucier, San Antonio, Texas
1951	Gene Conley, Hartford, Eastern
1952	Bill Skowron, Kansas City, American Association
1953	Gene Conley, Toledo, American Association
1954	Herb Score, Indianapolis, American Association
1955	John Murff, Dallas, Texas
1956	Steve Bilko, Los Angeles, Pacific Coast
1957	Norm Siebern, Denver, American Association
1958	Jim O'Toole, Nashville, Southern
1959	Frank Howard, Victoria-Spokane
1960	Willie Davis, Spokane, Pacific Coast
1961	Howie Koplitz, Birmingham, Southern
1962	Bob Bailey, Columbus, International
1963	Don Buford, Indianapolis, International
1964	Mel Stottlemyre, Richmond, International

Year	Player, Team, League
1965	Joe Foy, Toronto, International
1966	Mike Epstein, Rochester, International
1967	Johnny Bench, Buffalo, International
1968	Merv Rettenmund, Rochester, International
1969	Danny Walton, Oklahoma City, American Association
1970	Don Baylor, Rochester, International
1971	Bobby Grich, Rochester, International
1972	Tom Paciorek, Albuquerque, Pacific Coast
1973	Steve Ontiveros, Phoenix, Pacific Coast
1974	Jim Rice, Pawtucket, International
1975	Hector Cruz, Tulsa, American Association
1976	Pat Putnam, Asheville, Western Carolina
1977	Ken Landreaux, S.L.C., Pacific Coast-El Paso, Texas
1978	Champ Summers, Indianapolis, American Association
1979	Mark Bomback, Vancouver, Pacific Coast
1980	Tim Raines, Denver, American Association
1981	Mike Marshall, Albuquerque, Pacific Coast
1982	Ron Kittle, Edmonton, Pacific Coast
1983	Kevin McReynolds, Las Vegas, Pacific Coast
1984	Alan Knicely, Wichita, American Association
1985	Jose Canseco, Hunt., Southern-Tac., Pacific Coast
1986	Tim Pyznarski, Las Vegas, Pacific Coast
1987	Randy Milligan, Tidewater, International
1988	Sandy Alomar Jr., Las Vegas, Pacific Coast
	Gary Sheffield, Denver, American Association (tie)
1989	Sandy Alomar Jr., Las Vegas, Pacific Coast
1990	Jose Offerman, Albuquerque, Pacific Coast
1991	Pedro Martinez, Albuquerque, Pacific Coast
1992	Tim Salmon, Edmonton, Pacific Coast

MINOR LEAGUE MANAGER OF THE YEAR

Year	Manager, Team, League
1936	Al Sothoron, Milwaukee, American Association
1937	Jake Flowers, Salisbury, Eastern Shore
1938	Paul Richards, Atlanta, Southern

Year	Player, Team, League
1939	Bill Meyer, Kansas City, American Association
1940	Larry Gilbert, Nashville, Southern
1941	Burt Shotton, Columbus, American Association

Year	Manager, Team, League	Year	Manager, Team, League
1942	Eddie Dyer, Columbus, American Association	1968	Jack Tighe, Toledo, International
1943	Nick Cullop, Columbus, American Association	1969	Clyde McCullough, Tidewater, International
1944	Al Thomas, Baltimore, International	1970	Tom Lasorda, Spokane, Pacific Coast
1945	Lefty O'Doul, San Francisco, Pacific Coast	1971	Del Rice, Salt Lake City, Pacific Coast
1946	Clay Hopper, Montreal, International	1972	Hank Bauer, Tidewater, International
1947	Nick Cullop, Milwaukee, American Association	1973	Joe Morgan, Charleston, International
1948	Casey Stengel, Oakland, Pacific Coast	1974	Joe Altobelli, Rochester, International
1949	Fred Haney, Hollywood, Pacific Coast	1975	Joe Frazier, Tidewater, International
1950	Rollie Hemsley, Columbus, American Association	1976	Vern Rapp, Denver, American Association
1951	Charlie Grimm, Milwaukee, American Association	1977	Tommy Thompson, Arkan., Texas
1952	Luke Appling, Memphis, Southern	1978	Les Moss, Evansville, American Association
1953	Bobby Bragan, Hollywood, Pacific Coast	1979	Vern Benson, Syracuse, International
1954	Kerby Farrell, Indianapolis, American Association	1980	Hal Lanier, Springfield, American Association
1955	Bill Rigney, Minneapolis, American Association	1981	Del Crandall, Albuquerque, Pacific Coast
1956	Kerby Farrell, Indianapolis, American Association	1982	George Scherger, Indianapolis, American Association
1957	Ben Geraghty, Wichita, American Association	1983	Bill Dancy, Reading, Eastern
1958	Cal Ermer, Birmingham, Southern	1984	Bob Rodgers, Indianapolis, American Association
1959	Pete Reiser, Victoria, Texas	1985	Jim Fregosi, Louisville, American Association
1960	Mel McGaha, Toronto, International	1986	Joe Sparks, Indianapolis, American Association
1961	Kerby Farrell, Buffalo, International	1987	Terry Collins, Albuquerque, Pacific Coast
1962	Ben Geraghty, Jacksonville, International	1988	Joe Sparks, Indianapolis, American Association
1963	Rollie Hemsley, Indianapolis, International	1989	Bob Bailor, Syracuse, International
1964	Harry Walker, Jacksonville, International	1990	Sal Rende, Omaha, American Association
1965	Grady Hatton, Oklahoma City, Pacific Coast	1991	Chris Chambliss, Greenville, Southern
1966	Bob Lemon, Seattle, Pacific Coast	1992	Grady Little, Greenville, Southern
1967	Bob Skinner, San Diego, Pacific Coast		

MINOR LEAGUE EXECUTIVE OF THE YEAR (HIGHER CLASSIFICATIONS)

(Restricted to Class AAA starting in 1963)

Year	Executive, Team, League	Year	Player, Team, League
1936	Earl Mann, Atlanta, Southern	1965	Harold Cooper, Columbus, International
1937	Robert LaMotte, Savannah, Sally	1966	John Quinn Jr., Hawaii, Pacific Coast
1938	Louis McKenna, St. Paul, American Association	1967	Hillman Lyons, Richmond, International
1939	Bruce Dudley, Louisville, American Association	1968	Gabe Paul Jr., Tulsa, Pacific Coast
1940	Roy Hamey, Kansas City, American Association	1969	Bill Gardner, Louisville, International
1941	Emil Sick, Seattle, Pacific Coast	1970	Dick King, Wichita, American Association
1942	Bill Veeck, Milwaukee, American Association	1971	Carl Steinfeldt Jr., Rochester, International
1943	Clarence Rowland, Los Angeles, Pacific Coast	1972	Don Labbruzzo, Evansville, American Association
1944	William Mulligan, Seattle, Pacific Coast	1973	Merle Miller, Tucson, Pacific Coast
1945	Bruce Dudley, Louisville, American Association	1974	John Carbray, Sacramento, Pacific Coast
1946	Earl Mann, Atlanta, Southern	1975	Stan Naccarato, Tacoma, Pacific Coast
1947	William Purnhage, Waterloo, I.I.I.	1976	Art Teece, Salt Lake City, Pacific Coast
1948	Edward Glennon, Birmingham, Southern	1977	George Sisler Jr., Columbus, International
1949	Ted Sullivan, Indianapolis, American Association	1978	Willie Sanchez, Albuquerque, Pacific Coast
1950	Clearnce (Brick) Laws, Oakland, Pacific Coast	1979	George Sisler Jr., Columbus, International
1951	Robert Howsam, Denver, West	1980	Jim Burris, Denver, American Association
1952	Jack Cooke, Toronto, International	1981	Pat McKernan, Albuquerque, Pacific Coast
1953	Richard Burnett, Dallas, Texas	1982	A. Ray Smith, Louisville, American Association
1954	Edward Stumpf, Indianapolis, American Association	1983	A. Ray Smith, Louisville, American Association
1955	Dewey Soriano, Seattle, Pacific Coast	1984	Mike Tamburro, Pawtucket, International
1956	Robert Howsam, Denver American Association	1985	Patty Cox Hampton, Oklahoma City, Amer. Assoc.
1957	John Stiglmeier, Buffalo, International	1986	Bob Goughan, Rochester, International
1958	Edward Glennon, Birmingham, Southern	1987	Stu Kehoe, Vancouver, Pacific Coast
1959	Edward Leishman, Salt Lake City, Pacific Coast	1988	Bob Rich, Buffalo, American Association
1960	Ray Winder, Little Rock, Southern	1989	Larry Schmittou, Nashville, American Association
1961	Elten Schiller, Omaha, American Association	1990	Greg Corns, Phoenix, Pacific Coast
1962	George Sisler Jr., Rochester, International	1991	Tom Maloney, Denver, American Association
1963	Lewis Matlin, Hawaii, Pacific Coast	1992	Lou Schwechheimer, Pawtucket, International
1964	Edward Leishman, San Diego, Pacific Coast		

MINOR LEAGUE EXECUTIVE OF THE YEAR (LOWER CLASSIFICATIONS, 1950-1990)

(Separate awards for Class AA and Class A started in 1963; for Short Class A in 1988)

Year	Executive, Team, League	Year	Executive, Team, League
1950	H. Cooper, Hutch'son, West. A.	1960	Hubert Kittle, Yakima, Northwest
1951	O. W. (Bill) Hayes, Triple, B.S.	1961	David Steele, Fresno, California
1952	Hillman Lyons, Danville, MOV	1962	John Quinn Jr., San Jose, California
1953	Carl Roth, Peoria, I.I.I.	1963	Hugh Finnerty, Tulsa, Texas
1954	James Meagham, Cedar Rapids, I.I.I.		Ben Jewell, M. Valley, Pioneer
1955	John Petrakis, Dubuque, MOV	1964	Glynn West, Birmingham, Southern
1956	Marvin Milkes, Fresno, California		Jas. Bayens, Rock Hill, W. Car.
1957	Richard Wagner, Lincoln, West.	1965	Dick Butler, Dallas-Ft. Worth, Texas
1958	Gerald Waring, Macon, Sally		Ken. Blackman, Quad Cities, Midwest
1959	Clay Dennis, Des Moines, I.I.I.	1966	Tom Fleming, Evansville, Southern
			Cappy Harada, Lodi, California

Year	Executive, Team, League
1967—	Robert Quinn, Reading, Eastern
	Pat Williams, Spar'burg, W.C.
1968—	Phil Howser, Charlotte, Southern
	Merle Miller, Burlington, Midwest
1969—	Charlie Blaney, Albuquerque, Texas
	Bill Gorman, Visalia, California
1970—	Carl Sawatski, Arkansas, Texas
	Bob Williams, Bakersfield, California
1971—	Miles Wolff, Savannah, Dixie A.
	Ed Holtz, Appleton, Midwest
1972—	John Begzos, S. Antonio, Texas
	Bob Piccinini, Modesto, California
1973—	Dick Kravitz, Jacksonville, Southern
	Fritz Colschen, Clinton, Midwest
1974—	Jim Paul, El Paso, Texas
	Bing Russell, Portland, Northwest
1975—	Jim Paul, El Paso, Texas
	Cordy Jensen, Eugene, Northwest
1976—	Woodrow Reid, Chattanooga, Southern
	Don Buchheister, Cedar Rapids, Midwest
1977—	Jim Paul, El Paso, Texas
	Harry Pells, Quad Cities, Midwest
1978—	Larry Schmittou, Nashville, Southern
	Dave Hersh, Appleton, Midwest
1979—	Bill Rigney Jr., Midland, Texas
	Tom Romenesko, Greensboro, W.C.

Year	Executive, Team, League
1980—	Frances Crockett, Charlotte, Southern
	Tom Romenesko, Greensboro, W.C.
1981—	Allie Prescott, Memphis, Southern
	Dan Overstreet, Hagerstown, Caro.
1982—	Art Clarkson, Birmingham, Southern
	Bob Carruesco, Stockton, California
1983—	Edward Kenney, New Britain, Eastern
	Terry Reynolds, Vero Beach, Florida State
1984—	Bruce Baldwin, Greenville, Southern
	Dave Tarrolly, Beloit, Midwest
1985—	Ben Bernard, Albany-Colonie, Eastern
	Pete Vonachen, Peoria, Midwest
1986—	Bill Davidson, Midland, Texas
	Rob Dlugozima, Durham, Carolina
1987—	Joe Preseren, Tulsa, Texas
	Skip Weisman, Greensboro, South Atlantic
1988—	Bill Valentine, Arkansas, Texas
	Dennis Bastien, Charleston (W.Va.), South Atlantic
	Bob Beban, Eugene, Northwest
1989—	Chuck Domino, Reading, Eastern
	John Baxter, South Bend, Midwest
	Bill Pereira, Boise, Northwest
1990—	Joe Preseren, Tulsa, Texas
	Dan Chapman, Stockton, California
	Dave Baggott, Salt Lake City, Pioneer

BASEBALL WRITERS' ASSOCIATION OF AMERICA

MOST VALUABLE PLAYER

AMERICAN LEAGUE

Year	Player, Team, Pos.	Points
1931—	Lefty Grove, Philadelphia, P	78
1932—	Jimmie Foxx, Philadelphia, 1B	75
1933—	Jimmie Foxx, Philadelphia, 1B	74
1934—	Mickey Cochrane, Detroit, C	67
1935—	Hank Greenberg, Detroit, 1B	*80
1936—	Lou Gehrig, New York, 1B	73
1937—	Charley Gehringer, Detroit, 2B	78
1938—	Jimmie Foxx, Boston, 1B	305
1939—	Joe DiMaggio, New York, OF	280
1940—	Hank Greenberg, Detroit, OF	292
1941—	Joe DiMaggio, New York, OF	291
1942—	Joe Gordon, New York, 2B	270
1943—	Spud Chandler, New York, P	246
1944—	Hal Newhouser, Detroit, P	236
1945—	Hal Newhouser, Detroit, P	236
1946—	Ted Williams, Boston, OF	224
1947—	Joe DiMaggio, New York, OF	202
1948—	Lou Boudreau, Cleveland, SS	324
1949—	Ted Williams, Boston, OF	272
1950—	Phil Rizzuto, New York SS	284
1951—	Yogi Berra, New York, C	184
1952—	Bobby Shantz, Philadelphia, P	280
1953—	Al Rosen, Cleveland, 3B	*336
1954—	Yogi Berra, New York, C	230
1955—	Yogi Berra, New York, C	218
1956—	Mickey Mantle, New York, OF	*336
1957—	Mickey Mantle, New York, OF	233
1958—	Jackie Jensen, Boston, OF	233
1959—	Nellie Fox, Chicago, 2B	295
1960—	Roger Maris, New York, OF	225
1961—	Roger Maris, New York, OF	202
1962—	Mickey Mantle, New York, OF	234
1963—	Elston Howard, New York, C	248
1964—	Brooks Robinson, Baltimore, 3B	269
1965—	Zoilo Versalles, Minnesota, SS	275
1966—	Frank Robinson, Baltimore, OF	*280
1967—	Carl Yastrzemski, Boston, OF	275
1968—	Denny McLain, Detroit, P	*280
1969—	Harmon Killebrew, Minnesota, 1B-3B	294
1970—	Boog Powell, Baltimore, 1B	234
1971—	Vida Blue, Oakland, P	268
1972—	Dick Allen, Chicago, 1B	321

NATIONAL LEAGUE

Year	Player, Team, Pos.	Points
1931—	Frank Frisch, St. Louis, 2B	65
1932—	Chuck Klein, Philadelphia, OF	78
1933—	Carl Hubbell, New York, P	77
1934—	Dizzy Dean, St. Louis, P	78
1935—	Gabby Hartnett, Chicago, C	75
1936—	Carl Hubbell, New York, P	60
1937—	Joe Medwick, St. Louis, OF	70
1938—	Ernie Lombardi, Cincinnati, C	229
1939—	Bucky Walters, Cincinnati, P	303
1940—	Frank McCormick, Cincinnati, 1B	274
1941—	Dolf Camilli, Brooklyn, 1B	300
1942—	Mort Cooper, St. Louis, P	263
1943—	Stan Musial, St. Louis, OF	267
1944—	Marty Marion, St. Louis, SS	190
1945—	Phil Cavarretta, Chicago, 1B	279
1946—	Stan Musial, St. Louis, 1B	319
1947—	Bob Elliott, Boston, 3B	205
1948—	Stan Musial, St. Louis, OF	303
1949—	Jackie Robinson, Brooklyn, 2B	264
1950—	Jim Konstanty, Philadelphia, P	286
1951—	Roy Campanella, Brooklyn, C	243
1952—	Hank Sauer, Chicago, OF	226
1953—	Roy Campanella, Brooklyn, C	297
1954—	Willie Mays, New York, OF	283
1955—	Roy Campanella, Brooklyn, C	226
1956—	Don Newcombe, Brooklyn, P	223
1957—	Hank Aaron, Milwaukee, OF	239
1958—	Ernie Banks, Chicago, SS	283
1959—	Ernie Banks, Chicago, SS	232 ½
1960—	Dick Groat, Pittsburgh, SS	276
1961—	Frank Robinson, Cincinnati, OF	219
1962—	Maury Wills, Los Angeles, SS	209
1963—	Sandy Koufax, Los Angeles, P	237
1964—	Ken Boyer, St. Louis, 3B	243
1965—	Willie Mays, San Francisco, OF	224
1966—	Roberto Clemente, Pittsburgh, OF	218
1967—	Orlando Cepeda, St. Louis, 1B	*280
1968—	Bob Gibson, St. Louis, P	242
1969—	Willie McCovey, San Francisco, 1B	265
1970—	Johnny Bench, Cincinnati, C	326
1971—	Joe Torre, St. Louis, 3B	318
1972—	Johnny Bench, Cincinnati, C	263

Year	Player, Team, Pos.	Points
1973—	Reggie Jackson, Oakland, OF	*336
1974—	Jeff Burroughs, Texas, OF	248
1975—	Fred Lynn, Boston, OF	326
1976—	Thurman Munson, New York, C	304
1977—	Rod Carew, Minnesota, 1B	273
1978—	Jim Rice, Boston, OF	352
1979—	Don Baylor, California, OF	347
1980—	George Brett, Kansas City, 3B	335
1981—	Rollie Fingers, Milwaukee, P	319
1982—	Robin Yount, Milwaukee, SS	385
1983—	Cal Ripken Jr., Baltimore, SS	322
1984—	Willie Hernandez, Detroit, P	306
1985—	Don Mattingly, New York, 1B	367
1986—	Roger Clemens, Boston, P	339
1987—	George Bell, Toronto, OF	332
1988—	Jose Canseco, Oakland, OF	*392
1989—	Robin Yount, Milwaukee, OF	256
1990—	Rickey Henderson, Oakland, OF	317
1991—	Cal Ripken Jr., Baltimore, SS	318
1992—	Dennis Eckersley, Oakland, P	306

*Unanimous selection.

Year	Player, Team, Pos.	Points
1973—	Pete Rose, Cincinnati, OF	274
1974—	Steve Garvey, Los Angeles, 1B	270
1975—	Joe Morgan, Cincinnati, 2B	321½
1976—	Joe Morgan, Cincinnati, 2B	311
1977—	George Foster, Cincinnati, OF	291
1978—	Dave Parker, Pittsburgh, OF	320
1979—	Willie Stargell, Pittsburgh, 1B	216
	Keith Hernandez, St. Louis, 1B	216
1980—	Mike Schmidt, Philadelphia, 3B	*336
1981—	Mike Schmidt, Philadelphia, 3B	321
1982—	Dale Murphy, Atlanta, OF	283
1983—	Dale Murphy, Atlanta, OF	318
1984—	Ryne Sandberg, Chicago, 2B	326
1985—	Willie McGee, St. Louis, OF	280
1986—	Mike Schmidt, Philadelphia, 3B	287
1987—	Andre Dawson, Chicago, OF	269
1988—	Kirk Gibson, Los Angeles, OF	272
1989—	Kevin Mitchell, San Francisco, OF	314
1990—	Barry Bonds, Pittsburgh, OF	331
1991—	Terry Pendleton, Atlanta, 3B	274
1992—	Barry Bonds, Pittsburgh, OF	304

CY YOUNG MEMORIAL AWARD

Year	Pitcher, Team	Votes
1956—	Don Newcombe, Brooklyn	10
1957—	Warren Spahn, Milwaukee	15
1958—	Bob Turley, New York AL	5
1959—	Early Wynn, Chicago AL	13
1960—	Vernon Law, Pittsburgh	8
1961—	Whitey Ford, New York AL	9
1962—	Don Drysdale, Los Angeles NL	14
1963—	Sandy Koufax, Los Angeles NL	*20
1964—	Dean Chance, Los Angeles AL	17
1965—	Sandy Koufax, Los Angeles NL	*20
1966—	Sandy Koufax, Los Angeles NL	*20
1967—	A.L.—Jim Lonborg, Boston	18
	N.L.—Mike McCormick, San Francisco	18
1968—	A.L.—Denny McLain, Detroit	*20
	N.L.—Bob Gibson, St. Louis	*20
1969—	A.L.—Denny McLain, Detroit	10
	Mike Cuellar, Baltimore	10
	N.L.—Tom Seaver, New York	23
1970—	A.L.—Jim Perry, Minnesota	55
	N.L.—Bob Gibson, St. Louis	118
1971—	A.L.—Vida Blue, Oakland	98
	N.L.—Fergie Jenkins, Chicago	97
1972—	A.L.—Gaylord Perry, Cleveland	64
	N.L.—Steve Carlton, Philadelphia	*120
1973—	A.L.—Jim Palmer, Baltimore	88
	N.L.—Tom Seaver, New York	71
1974—	A.L.—Jim Hunter, Oakland	90
	N.L.—Mike Marshall, Los Angeles	96
1975—	A.L.—Jim Palmer, Baltimore	98
	N.L.—Tom Seaver, New York	98
1976—	A.L.—Jim Palmer, Baltimore	108
	N.L.—Randy Jones, San Diego	96

Year	Pitcher, Team	Votes
1977—	A.L.—Sparky Lyle, New York	56½
	N.L.—Steve Carlton, Philadelphia	*104
1978—	A.L.—Ron Guidry, New York	*140
	N.L.—Gaylord Perry, San Diego	116
1979—	A.L.—Mike Flanagan, Baltimore	136
	N.L.—Bruce Sutter, Chicago	72
1980—	A.L.—Steve Stone, Baltimore	100
	N.L.—Steve Carlton, Philadelphia	118
1981—	A.L.—Rollie Fingers, Milwaukee	126
	N.L.—Fernando Valenzuela, Los Angeles	70
1982—	A.L.—Pete Vuckovich, Milwaukee	87
	N.L.—Steve Carlton, Philadelphia	112
1983—	A.L.—LaMarr Hoyt, Chicago	116
	N.L.—John Denny, Philadelphia	103
1984—	A.L.—Willie Hernandez, Detroit	88
	N.L.—Rick Sutcliffe, Chicago	*120
1985—	A.L.—Bret Saberhagen, Kansas City	127
	N.L.—Dwight Gooden, New York	*120
1986—	A.L.—Roger Clemens, Boston	*140
	N.L.—Mike Scott, Houston	98
1987—	A.L.—Roger Clemens, Boston	124
	N.L.—Steve Bedrosian, Philadelphia	57
1988—	A.L.—Frank Viola, Minnesota	138
	N.L.—Orel Hershiser, Los Angeles	*120
1989—	A.L.—Bret Saberhagen, Kansas City	138
	N.L.—Mark Davis, San Diego	107
1990—	A.L.—Bob Welch, Oakland	107
	N.L.—Doug Drabek, Pittsburgh	118
1991—	A.L.—Roger Clemens, Boston	119
	N.L.—Tom Glavine, Atlanta	110
1992—	A.L.—Dennis Eckersley, Oakland	107
	N.L.—Greg Maddux, Chicago	112

*Unanimous selection.

ROOKIE OF THE YEAR

1947—Combined selection—Jackie Robinson, Brooklyn NL, 1B.
1948—Combined selection—Alvin Dark, Boston NL, SS.

AMERICAN LEAGUE

Year	Player, Team, Pos.	Votes
1949—	Roy Sievers, St. Louis, OF	10
1950—	Walt Dropo, Boston, 1B	15
1951—	Gil McDougald, New York, 3B	13
1952—	Harry Byrd, Philadelphia, P	9
1953—	Harvey Kuenn, Detroit, SS	23
1954—	Bob Grim, New York, P	15

NATIONAL LEAGUE

Year	Player, Team, Pos.	Votes
1949—	Don Newcombe, Brooklyn, P	21
1950—	Sam Jethroe, Boston, OF	11
1951—	Willie Mays, New York, OF	18
1952—	Joe Black, Brooklyn, P	19
1953—	Jim Gilliam, Brooklyn, 2B	11
1954—	Wally Moon, St. Louis, OF	17

Year	Player, Team, Pos.	Votes	Year	Player, Team, Pos.	Votes
1955	Herb Score, Cleveland, P	18	1955	Bill Virdon, St. Louis, OF	15
1956	Luis Aparicio, Chicago, SS	22	1956	Frank Robinson, Cincinnati, OF	*24
1957	Tony Kubek, New York, IF-OF	23	1957	Jack Sanford, Philadelphia, P	16
1958	Albie Pearson, Washington, OF	14	1958	Orlando Cepeda, San Francisco, 1B	*†21
1959	Bob Allison, Washington, OF	18	1959	Willie McCovey, San Francisco, 1B	*24
1960	Ron Hansen, Baltimore, SS	22	1960	Frank Howard, Los Angeles, OF	12
1961	Don Schwall, Boston, P	7	1961	Billy Williams, Chicago, OF	10
1962	Tom Tresh, New York, OF-SS	13	1962	Ken Hubbs, Chicago, 2B	19
1963	Gary Peters, Chicago, P	10	1963	Pete Rose, Cincinnati, 2B	17
1964	Tony Oliva, Minnesota, OF	19	1964	Dick Allen, Philadelphia, 3B	18
1965	Curt Blefary, Baltimore, OF	12	1965	Jim Lefebvre, Los Angeles, 2B	13
1966	Tommie Agee, Chicago, OF	16	1966	Tommy Helms, Cincinnati, 3B	12
1967	Rod Carew, Minnesota, 2B	19	1967	Tom Seaver, New York, P	11
1968	Stan Bahnsen, New York, P	17	1968	Johnny Bench, Cincinnati, C	10½
1969	Lou Piniella, Kansas City, OF	9	1969	Ted Sizemore, Los Angeles, 2B	14
1970	Thurman Munson, New York, C	23	1970	Carl Morton, Montreal, P	11
1971	Chris Chambliss, Cleveland, 1B	11	1971	Earl Williams, Atlanta, C	18
1972	Carlton Fisk, Boston, C	*24	1972	Jon Matlack, New York, P	19
1973	Al Bumbry, Baltimore, OF	13½	1973	Gary Matthews, San Francisco, OF	11
1974	Mike Hargrove, Texas, 1B	16½	1974	Bake McBride, St. Louis, OF	16
1975	Fred Lynn, Boston, OF	23	1975	John Montefusco, San Francisco, P	12
1976	Mark Fidrych, Detroit, P	22	1976	Butch Metzger, San Diego, P	11
				Pat Zachry, Cincinnati, P	11
1977	Eddie Murray, Baltimore, DH-1B	12½	1977	Andre Dawson, Montreal, OF	10
1978	Lou Whitaker, Detroit, 2B	21	1978	Bob Horner, Atlanta, 3B	12½
1979	John Castino, Minnesota, 3B	7	1979	Rick Sutcliffe, Los Angeles, P	20
	Alfredo Griffin, Toronto, SS	7			
1980	Joe Charboneau, Cleveland, OF	103	1980	Steve Howe, Los Angeles, P	80
1981	Dave Righetti, New York, P	127	1981	Fernando Valenzuela, Los Angeles, P	107
1982	Cal Ripken, Baltimore, SS-3B	132	1982	Steve Sax, Los Angeles, 2B	63
1983	Ron Kittle, Chicago, OF	104	1983	Darryl Strawberry, New York, OF	109
1984	Alvin Davis, Seattle, 1B	134	1984	Dwight Gooden, New York, P	118
1985	Ozzie Guillen, Chicago, SS	101	1985	Vince Coleman, St. Louis, OF	*120
1986	Jose Canseco, Oakland, OF	110	1986	Todd Worrell, St. Louis, P	118
1987	Mark McGwire, Oakland, 1B	*140	1987	Benito Santiago, San Diego, C	*120
1988	Walt Weiss, Oakland, SS	103	1988	Chris Sabo, Cincinnati, 3B	79
1989	Gregg Olson, Baltimore, P	136	1989	Jerome Walton, Chicago, OF	116
1990	Sandy Alomar Jr., Cleveland, C	*140	1990	Dave Justice, Atlanta, OF	118
1991	Chuck Knoblauch, Minnesota, 2B	136	1991	Jeff Bagwell, Houston, 1B	118
1992	Pat Listach, Milwaukee, SS	122	1992	Eric Karros, Los Angeles, 1B	116

*Unanimous selection. †Three writers did not vote.

MANAGER OF THE YEAR

AMERICAN LEAGUE

Year	Manager, Team	Points
1983	Tony La Russa, Chicago	17
1984	Sparky Anderson, Detroit	96
1985	Bobby Cox, Toronto	104
1986	John McNamara, Boston	95
1987	Sparky Anderson, Detroit	90
1988	Tony La Russa, Oakland	103
1989	Frank Robinson, Baltimore	125
1990	Jeff Torborg, Chicago	128
1991	Tom Kelly, Minnesota	138
1992	Tony La Russa, Oakland	132

NATIONAL LEAGUE

Year	Manager, Team	Points
1983	Tommy Lasorda, Los Angeles	10
1984	Jim Frey, Chicago	101
1985	Whitey Herzog, St. Louis	86
1986	Hal Lanier, Houston	108
1987	Buck Rodgers, Montreal	92
1988	Tommy Lasorda, Los Angeles	101
1989	Don Zimmer, Chicago	118
1990	Jim Leyland, Pittsburgh	99
1991	Bobby Cox, Atlanta	96
1992	Jim Leyland, Pittsburgh	109

EARLY MOST VALUABLE PLAYER AWARDS

CHALMERS AWARD

AMERICAN LEAGUE

Year	Player, Team, Pos.	Points
1911	Ty Cobb, Detroit, OF	64
1912	Tris Speaker, Boston, OF	59
1913	Walter Johnson, Washington, P	*54
1914	Eddie Collins, Philadelphia, 2B	63

NATIONAL LEAGUE

Year	Player, Team, Pos.	Points
1911	Frank Schulte, Chicago, OF	29
1912	Larry Doyle, New York, 2B	48
1913	Jake Daubert, Brooklyn, 1B	50
1914	Johnny Evers, Boston, 2B	50

AMERICAN LEAGUE

Year	Player, Team, Pos.	Points
1922	George Sisler, St. Louis, 1B	59
1923	Babe Ruth, New York, OF	64
1924	Walter Johnson, Washington, P	55
1925	Roger Peckinpaugh, Washington, SS	45
1926	George Burns, Cleveland, 1B	63
1927	Lou Gehrig, New York, 1B	56
1928	Mickey Cochrane, Philadelphia, C	53
1929	No selection	

NATIONAL LEAGUE

Year	Player, Team, Pos.	Points
1922	No selection	
1923	No selection	
1924	Dazzy Vance, Brooklyn, P	74
1925	Rogers Hornsby, St. Louis, 2B	73
1926	Bob O'Farrell, St. Louis, C	79
1927	Paul Waner, Pittsburgh, OF	72
1928	Jim Bottomley, St. Louis, 1B	76
1929	Rogers Hornsby, Chicago, 2B	60

HALL OF FAME

HALL OF FAME ROSTER OF MEMBERS

Name	Des.*	Elec. year	Votes rec.†	Votes cast‡	% of vote	Teams as player
Aaron, Hank	P	1982	406	415	97.8	Milwaukee NL, Atlanta NL, Milwaukee AL
Alexander, Grover C.	P	1938	212	262	80.9	Philadelphia NL, Chicago NL, St. Louis NL
Alston, Walter	M	1983	CV	—	—	St. Louis NL
Anson, Cap	P	1939	C1	—	—	Chicago NL
Aparicio, Luis	P	1984	341	403	84.6	Chicago AL, Baltimore AL, Boston AL
Appling, Luke	P	1964	189	225	84	Chicago AL
Averill, Earl	P	1975	CV	—	—	Cleveland AL, Detroit AL, Boston AL
Baker, Home Run	P	1955	CV	—	—	Philadelphia AL, New York AL
Bancroft, Dave	P	1971	CV	—	—	Philadelphia NL, New York NL, Boston NL, Brooklyn NL
Banks, Ernie	P	1977	321	383	83.8	Chicago NL
Barlick, Al	U	1989	CV	—	—	
Barrow, Ed	E	1953	CV	—	—	
Beckley, Jake	P	1971	CV	—	—	Pittsburgh NL, Pittsburgh PL, New York NL, Cincinnati NL, St. Louis NL
Bell, Cool Papa	P	1974	SCNL	—	—	Negro Leagues
Bench, Johnny	P	1989	431	447	96.4	Cincinnati NL
Bender, Chief	P	1953	CV	—	—	Philadelphia AL, Philadelphia NL, Chicago AL
Berra, Yogi	P	1972	339	396	85.6	New York AL, New York NL
Bottomley, Jim	P	1974	CV	—	—	St. Louis NL, Cincinnati NL, St. Louis AL
Boudreau, Lou	P	1970	232	300	77.3	Cleveland AL, Boston AL
Bresnahan, Roger	P	1945	C2	—	—	Washington NL, Chicago NL, Baltimore AL, New York NL, St. Louis NL
Brock, Lou	P	1985	315	395	79.7	Chicago NL, St. Louis NL
Brouthers, Dan	P	1945	C2	—	—	Troy NL, Buffalo NL, Detroit NL, Boston NL, Boston PL, Boston AA, Brooklyn NL, Baltimore NL, Louisville NL, Philadelphia NL, New York NL
Brown, Three Finger	P	1949	C2	—	—	St. Louis NL, Chicago NL, Cincinnati NL
Bulkeley, Morgan	E	1937	CC	—	—	
Burkett, Jesse	P	1946	C2	—	—	New York NL, Cleveland NL, St. Louis NL, St. Louis AL, Boston AL
Campanella, Roy	P	1969	270	340	79.4	Brooklyn NL
Carew, Rod	P	1991	401	447	89.7	Minnesota AL, California AL
Carey, Max	P	1961	CV	—	—	Pittsburgh NL, Brooklyn NL
Cartwright, Alexander	O	1938	CC	—	—	
Chadwick, Henry	O	1938	CC	—	—	
Chance, Frank	P	1946	C2	—	—	Chicago NL, New York AL
Chandler, Happy	E	1982	CV	—	—	
Charleston, Oscar	P	1976	SCNL	—	—	Negro Leagues
Chesbro, Jack	P	1946	C2	—	—	Pittsburgh NL, New York AL, Boston AL
Clarke, Fred	P	1945	C2	—	—	Louisville NL, Pittsburgh NL
Clarkson, John	P	1963	CV	—	—	Worcester NL, Chicago NL, Boston NL, Cleveland NL
Clemente, Roberto	P	1973	393	424	92.7	Pittsburgh NL
Cobb, Ty	P	1936	222	226	98.2	Detroit AL, Philadelphia AL
Cochrane, Mickey	P	1947	128	161	79.5	Philadelphia AL, Detroit AL
Collins, Eddie	P	1939	213	274	77.7	Philadelphia AL, Chicago AL
Collins, Jimmy	P	1945	C2	—	—	Boston NL, Louisville NL, Boston AL, Philadelphia AL
Combs, Earle	P	1970	CV	—	—	New York AL
Comiskey, Charley	F/P	1939	C1	—	—	St. Louis AA, Chicago PL, Cincinnati NL
Conlan, Jocko	U	1974	CV	—	—	Chicago AL
Connolly, Tommy	U	1953	CV	—	—	
Connor, Roger	P	1976	CV	—	—	Troy NL, New York NL, New York PL, Philadelphia NL, St. Louis NL
Coveleski, Stan	P	1969	CV	—	—	Philadelphia AL, Cleveland AL, Washington AL, New York AL
Crawford, Sam	P	1957	CV	—	—	Cincinnati NL, Detroit AL
Cronin, Joe	P	1956	152	193	78.8	Pittsburgh NL, Washington AL, Boston AL
Cummings, Candy	P	1939	C1	—	—	Hartford NL, Cincinnati NL
Cuyler, Kiki	P	1968	CV	—	—	Pittsburgh NL, Chicago NL, Cincinnati NL, Brooklyn NL
Dandridge, Ray	P	1987	CV	—	—	Negro Leagues
Dean, Dizzy	P	1953	209	264	79.2	St. Louis NL, Chicago NL, St. Louis AL
Delahanty, Ed	P	1945	C2	—	—	Philadelphia NL, Cleveland PL, Washington AL
Dickey, Bill	P	1954	202	252	80.2	New York AL
Dihigo, Martin	P	1977	SCNL	—	—	Negro Leagues
DiMaggio, Joe	P	1955	223	251	88.8	New York AL
Doerr, Bobby	P	1986	CV	—	—	Boston AL
Drysdale, Don	P	1984	316	403	78.4	Brooklyn NL, Los Angeles NL
Duffy, Hugh	P	1945	C2	—	—	Chicago NL, Chicago PL, Boston AA, Boston NL, Milwaukee AL, Philadelphia NL
Evans, Billy	U	1973	CV	—	—	
Evers, Johnny	P	1946	C2	—	—	Chicago NL, Boston NL, Philadelphia NL, Chicago AL
Ewing, Buck	P	1939	C1	—	—	Troy NL, New York NL, New York PL, Cleveland NL, Cincinnati NL

Name	Des.*	Elec. year	Votes rec.†	Votes cast‡	% of vote	Teams as player
Faber, Red	P	1964	CV	—	—	Chicago AL
Feller, Bob	P	1962	150	160	93.8	Cleveland AL
Ferrell, Rick	P	1984	CV	—	—	St. Louis AL, Boston AL, Washington AL
Fingers, Rollie	P	1992	349	430	81.2	Oakland AL, San Diego NL, Milwaukee AL
Flick, Elmer	P	1963	CV	—	—	Philadelphia NL, Philadelphia AL, Cleveland AL
Ford, Whitey	P	1974	284	365	77.8	New York AL
Foster, Rube	P	1981	CV	—	—	Negro Leagues
Foxx, Jimmie	P	1951	179	226	79.2	Philadelphia AL, Boston AL, Chicago NL, Philadelphia NL
Frick, Ford	E	1970	CV	—	—	
Frisch, Frank	P	1947	136	161	84.5	New York NL, St. Louis NL
Galvin, Pud	P	1965	CV	—	—	Buffalo NL, Pittsburgh AA, Pittsburgh NL, Pittsburgh PL, St. Louis NL
Gehrig, Lou	P	1939	SE	—	—	New York AL
Gehringer, Charley	P	1949	159	187	85.0	Detroit AL
Gibson, Bob	P	1981	337	401	84.0	St. Louis NL
Gibson, Josh	P	1972	SCNL	—	—	Negro Leagues
Giles, Warren	E	1979	CV	—	—	
Gomez, Lefty	P	1972	CV	—	—	New York AL, Washington AL
Goslin, Goose	P	1968	CV	—	—	Washington AL, St. Louis AL, Detroit AL
Greenberg, Hank	P	1956	164	193	85.0	Detroit AL, Pittsburgh NL
Griffith, Clark	M	1946	C2	—	—	St. Louis AA, Boston AA, Chicago NL, Chicago AL, New York AL, Cincinnati NL, Washington AL
Grimes, Burleigh	P	1964	CV	—	—	Pittsburgh NL, Brooklyn NL, New York NL, Boston NL, St. Louis NL, Chicago NL, New York AL
Grove, Lefty	P	1947	123	161	76.4	Philadelphia AL, Boston AL
Hafey, Chick	P	1971	CV	—	—	St. Louis NL, Cincinnati NL
Haines, Jesse	P	1970	CV	—	—	Cincinnati NL, St. Louis NL
Hamilton, Billy	P	1961	CV	—	—	Kansas City AA, Philadelphia NL, Boston NL
Harridge, Will	E	1972	CV	—	—	
Harris, Bucky	M	1975	CV	—	—	Washington AL, Detroit AL
Hartnett, Gabby	P	1955	195	251	77.7	Chicago NL, New York NL
Heilmann, Harry	P	1952	203	234	86.8	Detroit AL, Cincinnati NL
Herman, Billy	P	1975	CV	—	—	Chicago NL, Brooklyn NL, Boston NL, Pittsburgh NL
Hooper, Harry	P	1971	CV	—	—	Boston AL, Chicago AL
Hornsby, Rogers	P	1942	182	233	78.1	St. Louis NL, New York NL, Boston NL, Chicago NL, St. Louis AL
Hoyt, Waite	P	1969	CV	—	—	New York NL, Boston AL, New York AL, Detroit AL, Philadelphia AL, Brooklyn NL, Pittsburgh NL
Hubbard, Cal	U	1976	CV	—	—	
Hubbell, Carl	P	1947	140	161	87.0	New York NL
Huggins, Miller	M	1964	CV	—	—	Cincinnati NL, St. Louis NL
Hunter, Catfish	P	1987	315	413	76.3	Kansas City AL, Oakland AL, New York AL
Irvin, Monte	P	1973	SCNL	—	—	New York NL, Chicago NL, Negro Leagues
Jackson, Reggie	P	1993	396	423	93.6	Kansas City AL, Oakland AL, Baltimore AL, New York AL, California AL
Jackson, Travis	P	1982	CV	—	—	New York NL
Jenkins, Ferguson	P	1991	334	447	74.7	Philadelphia NL, Chicago NL, Texas AL, Boston AL
Jennings, Hugh	P	1945	C2	—	—	Louisville AA, Louisville NL, Baltimore NL, Brooklyn NL, Philadelphia NL, Detroit AL
Johnson, Ban	E	1937	CC	—	—	
Johnson, Judy	P	1975	SCNL	—	—	Negro Leagues
Johnson, Walter	P	1936	189	226	83.6	Washington AL
Joss, Addie	P	1978	CV	—	—	Cleveland AL
Kaline, Al	P	1980	340	385	88.3	Detroit AL
Keefe, Tim	P	1964	CV	—	—	Troy NL, New York AA, New York NL, New York PL, Philadelphia NL
Keeler, Willie	P	1939	207	274	75.5	New York NL, Brooklyn NL, Baltimore NL, New York AL
Kell, George	P	1983	CV	—	—	Philadelphia AL, Detroit AL, Boston AL, Chicago AL, Baltimore AL
Kelley, Joe	P	1971	CV	—	—	Boston NL, Pittsburgh NL, Baltimore NL, Brooklyn NL, Baltimore AL, Cincinnati NL
Kelly, George	P	1973	CV	—	—	New York NL, Pittsburgh NL, Cincinnati NL, Chicago NL, Brooklyn NL
Kelly, Mike	P	1945	C2	—	—	Cincinnati NL, Chicago NL, Boston NL, Boston PL, Cincinnati AA, Boston AA, New York NL
Killebrew, Harmon	P	1984	335	403	83.1	Washington AL, Minnesota AL, Kansas City AL
Kiner, Ralph	P	1975	273	362	75.4	Pittsburgh NL, Chicago NL, Cleveland AL
Klein, Chuck	P	1980	CV	—	—	Philadelphia NL, Chicago NL, Pittsburgh NL
Klem, Bill	U	1953	CV	—	—	
Koufax, Sandy	P	1972	344	396	86.9	Brooklyn NL, Los Angeles NL
Lajoie, Nap	P	1937	168	201	83.6	Philadelphia NL, Philadelphia AL, Cleveland AL
Landis, Kenesaw M.	E	1944	C2	—	—	
Lazzeri, Tony	P	1991	CV	—	—	New York AL, Chicago NL, Brooklyn NL, New York NL
Lemon, Bob	P	1976	305	388	78.6	Cleveland AL
Lindstrom, Fred	P	1976	CV	—	—	New York NL, Pittsburgh NL, Chicago NL, Brooklyn NL
Lloyd, John Henry	P	1977	SCNL	—	—	Negro Leagues
Lombardi, Ernie	P	1986	CV	—	—	Brooklyn NL, Cincinnati NL, Boston NL, New York NL
Lopez, Al	M	1977	CV	—	—	Brooklyn NL, Boston NL, Pittsburgh NL, Cleveland AL
Lyons, Ted	P	1955	217	251	86.5	Chicago AL
Mack, Connie	M	1937	CC	—	—	Washington NL, Buffalo PL, Pittsburgh NL
MacPhail, Larry	E	1978	CV	—	—	

Name	Des.*	Elec. year	Votes rec.†	Votes cast‡	% of vote	Teams as player
Mantle, Mickey	P	1974	322	365	88.2	New York AL
Manush, Heinie	P	1964	CV	—	—	Detroit AL, St. Louis AL, Washington AL, Boston AL, Brooklyn NL, Pittsburgh NL
Maranville, Rabbit	P	1954	209	252	82.9	Boston NL, Pittsburgh NL, Chicago NL, Brooklyn NL, St. Louis NL
Marichal, Juan	P	1983	313	374	83.7	San Francisco NL, Boston AL, Los Angeles NL
Marquard, Rube	P	1971	CV	—	—	New York NL, Brooklyn NL, Cincinnati NL, Boston NL
Mathews, Eddie	P	1978	301	379	79.4	Boston NL, Milwaukee NL, Atlanta NL, Houston NL, Detroit AL
Mathewson, Christy	P	1936	205	226	90.7	New York NL, Cincinnati NL
Mays, Willie	P	1979	409	432	94.7	New York (Giants)NL, San Francisco NL, New York (Mets)NL
McCarthy, Joe	M	1957	CV	—	—	
McCarthy, Tommy	P	1946	C2	—	—	Boston UA, Boston NL, Philadelphia NL, St. Louis AA, Brooklyn NL
McCovey, Willie	P	1986	346	425	81.4	San Francisco NL, San Diego NL, Oakland AL
McGinnity, Joe	P	1946	C2	—	—	Baltimore NL, Brooklyn NL, Baltimore AL, New York NL
McGowan, Bill	U	1992	CV	—	—	
McGraw, John	M	1937	CC	—	—	Baltimore AA, Baltimore NL, St. Louis NL, Baltimore AL, New York NL
McKechnie, Bill	M	1962	CV	—	—	Pittsburgh NL, Boston NL, New York AL, New York NL, Cincinnati
Medwick, Joe	P	1968	240	283	84.8	St. Louis NL, Brooklyn NL, New York NL, Boston NL
Mize, Johnny	P	1981	CV	—	—	St. Louis NL, New York NL, New York AL
Morgan, Joe	P	1990	363	444	81.8	Houston NL, Cincinnati NL, San Francisco NL, Philadelphia NL, Oakland AL
Musial, Stan	P	1969	317	340	93.2	St. Louis NL
Newhouser, Hal	P	1992	CV	—	—	Detroit AL, Cleveland AL
Nichols, Kid	P	1949	C2	—	—	Boston NL, St. Louis NL, Philadelphia NL
O'Rourke, Jim	P	1945	C2	—	—	Boston NL, Providence NL, Buffalo NL, New York NL, Washington NL, New York PL
Ott, Mel	P	1951	197	226	87.2	New York NL
Paige, Satchel	P	1971	SCNL	—	—	Cleveland AL, St. Louis AL, Kansas City AL, Negro Leagues
Palmer, Jim	P	1990	411	444	92.6	Baltimore AL
Pennock, Herb	P	1948	94	121	77.7	Philadelphia AL, Boston AL, New York AL
Perry, Gaylord	P	1991	342	447	76.5	San Francisco NL, Cleveland AL, Texas AL, San Diego NL, New York AL, Atlanta NL, Seattle AL, Kansas City AL
Plank, Eddie	P	1946	C2	—	—	Philadelphia AL, St. Louis AL
Radbourn, Hoss	P	1939	C1	—	—	Buffalo NL, Providence NL, Boston NL, Boston PL, Cincinnati NL
Reese, Pee Wee	P	1984	CV	—	—	Brooklyn NL, Los Angeles NL
Rice, Sam	P	1963	CV	—	—	Washington AL, Cleveland AL
Rickey, Branch	E	1967	CV	—	—	St. Louis AL, New York AL
Rixey, Eppa	P	1963	CV	—	—	Philadelphia NL, Cincinnati NL
Roberts, Robin	P	1976	337	388	86.9	Philadelphia NL, Baltimore AL, Houston NL, Chicago NL
Robinson, Brooks	P	1983	344	374	92.0	Baltimore AL
Robinson, Frank	P	1982	370	415	89.2	Cincinnati NL, Baltimore AL, Los Angeles NL, California AL, Cleveland AL
Robinson, Jackie	P	1962	124	160	77.5	Brooklyn NL
Robinson, Wilbert	M	1945	C2	—	—	Philadelphia AA, Baltimore AA, Baltimore NL, St. Louis NL, Baltimore AL
Roush, Edd	P	1962	CV	—	—	Chicago AL, New York NL, Cincinnati NL
Ruffing, Red	P	1967	266	306	86.9	Boston AL, New York AL, Chicago AL
Rusie, Amos	P	1977	CV	—	—	Indianapolis NL, New York NL, Cincinnati NL
Ruth, Babe	P	1936	215	226	95.1	Boston AL, New York AL, Boston NL
Schalk, Ray	P	1955	CV	—	—	Chicago AL, New York NL
Schoendienst, Red	P	1989	CV	—	—	St. Louis NL, New York (Giants)NL, Milwaukee NL
Seaver, Tom	P	1992	425	430	98.8	New York NL, Cincinnati NL, Chicago AL, Boston AL
Sewell, Joe	P	1977	CV	—	—	Cleveland AL, New York AL
Simmons, Al	P	1953	199	264	75.4	Philadelphia AL, Chicago AL, Detroit AL, Washington AL, Boston NL, Cincinnati NL, Boston AL
Sisler, George	P	1939	235	274	85.8	St. Louis AL, Washington AL, Boston NL
Slaughter, Enos	P	1985	CV	—	—	St. Louis NL, New York AL, Kansas City AL, Milwaukee NL
Snider, Duke	P	1980	333	385	86.5	Brooklyn NL, Los Angeles NL, New York NL, San Francisco NL
Spahn, Warren	P	1973	316	380	83.2	Boston NL, Milwaukee NL, New York NL, San Francisco NL
Spalding, Al	P	1939	C1	—	—	Chicago NL
Speaker, Tris	P	1937	165	201	82.1	Boston AL, Cleveland AL, Washington AL, Philadelphia AL
Stargell, Willie	P	1988	352	427	82.4	Pittsburgh NL
Stengel, Casey	M	1966	CV	—	—	Brooklyn NL, Pittsburgh NL, Philadelphia NL, New York NL, Boston NL
Terry, Bill	P	1954	195	252	77.4	New York NL
Thompson, Sam	P	1974	CV	—	—	Detroit NL, Philadelphia NL, Detroit AL
Tinker, Joe	P	1946	C2	—	—	Chicago NL, Cincinnati NL
Traynor, Pie	P	1948	93	121	76.9	Pittsburgh NL
Vance, Dazzy	P	1955	205	251	81.7	Pittsburgh NL, New York AL, Brooklyn NL, St. Louis NL, Cincinnati NL
Vaughan, Arky	P	1985	CV	—	—	Pittsburgh NL, Brooklyn NL
Veeck, Bill	E	1991	CV	—	—	
Waddell, Rube	P	1946	C2	—	—	Louisville NL, Pittsburgh NL, Chicago NL, Philadelphia AL, St. Louis AL
Wagner, Honus	P	1936	215	226	95.1	Louisville NL, Pittsburgh NL
Wallace, Bobby	P	1953	CV	—	—	Cleveland NL, St. Louis NL, St. Louis AL
Walsh, Ed	P	1946	C2	—	—	Chicago AL, Boston NL
Waner, Lloyd	P	1967	CV	—	—	Pittsburgh NL, Boston NL, Cincinnati NL, Philadelphia NL, Brooklyn NL
Waner, Paul	P	1952	195	234	83.3	Pittsburgh NL, Brooklyn NL, Boston NL, New York AL

Name	Des.*	Elec. year	Votes rec.†	Votes cast‡	% of vote	Teams as player
Ward, John Montgomery	P	1964	CV	—	—	Providence NL, New York NL, Brooklyn PL, Brooklyn NL
Weiss, George	E	1971	CV	—	—	
Welch, Mickey	P	1973	CV	—	—	Troy NL, New York NL
Wheat, Zack	P	1959	CV	—	—	Brooklyn NL, Philadelphia AL
Wilhelm, Hoyt	P	1985	331	395	83.8	New York NL, St. Louis NL, Cleveland AL, Baltimore AL, Chicago AL, California AL, Atlanta NL, Chicago NL, Los Angeles NL
Williams, Billy	P	1987	354	413	85.7	Chicago NL, Oakland AL
Williams, Ted	P	1966	282	302	93.4	Boston AL
Wilson, Hack	P	1979	CV	—	—	New York NL, Chicago NL, Brooklyn NL, Philadelphia NL
Wright, George	M	1937	CC	—	—	Boston NL, Providence NL
Wright, Harry	M	1953	CV	—	—	Boston NL
Wynn, Early	P	1972	301	396	76.0	Washington AL, Cleveland AL, Chicago AL
Yastrzemski, Carl	P	1989	423	447	94.6	Boston AL
Yawkey, Tom	E	1980	CV	—	—	
Young, Cy	P	1937	153	201	76.1	Cleveland NL, St. Louis NL, Boston AL, Cleveland AL, Boston NL
Youngs, Ross	P	1972	CV	—	—	New York NL

*Designation for which he was honored. Abbreviations: E—executive; F—founder; M—manager; O—organizer; P—player; U—umpire.

†Where an abbreviation is listed rather than a vote total, the enshrinee was selected by one of the following groups: Centennial Commission (CC), committee of old-time players and writers (C1), committee on old-timers (C2), Committee on Veterans (CV), special election by Baseball Writers' Association of America (SE) or Special Committee on Negro Leagues (SCNL).

‡Votes cast by eligible members of the Baseball Writers' Association of America.

League abbreviations: AA—American Association; AL—American League; NL—National League; PL—Players League; UA—Union Association.

MINOR LEAGUES

FARM SYSTEMS

BALTIMORE (6): AAA—Rochester. AA—Bowie. A—Frederick, Albany. Rookie—Sarasota, Bluefield.

BOSTON (6): AAA—Pawtucket. AA—New Britain. A—Lynchburg, Utica, TBA. Rookie—Gulf Coast Red Sox.

CALIFORNIA (6): AAA—Vancouver. AA—Midland. A—Palm Springs, Quad City, Boise. Rookie—Mesa Angels.

CHICAGO (6): AAA—Nashville. AA—Birmingham. A—Sarasota, South Bend, Hickory. Rookie—Gulf Coast White Sox.

CLEVELAND (6): AAA—Charlotte. AA—Canton/Akron. A—Kinston, Columbus (Ga.), Watertown. Rookie—Burlington.

DETROIT (6): AAA—Toledo. AA—London (Ont.). A—Fayetteville, Lakeland, Niagara Falls. Rookie—Bristol.

KANSAS CITY (6): AAA—Omaha. AA—Memphis. A—Wilmington, Rockford, Eugene. Rookie—Gulf Coast Royals.

MILWAUKEE (6): AAA—New Orleans. AA—El Paso. A—Stockton, Beloit. Rookie—Helena, Chandler Brewers.

MINNESOTA (6): AAA—Portland. AA—Nashville. A—Fort Myers, Fort Wayne. Rookie—Elizabethton, Gulf Coast Twins.

NEW YORK (6): AAA—Columbus (O.). AA—Albany/Colonie. A—Prince William, Greensboro, Oneonta. Rookie—Gulf Coast Yankees.

OAKLAND (6): AAA—Tacoma. AA—Huntsville. A—Modesto, Madison, Southern Oregon. Rookie—Scottsdale Athletics.

SEATTLE (6): AAA—Calgary. AA—Jacksonville. A—Riverside, Appleton, Bellingham. Rookie—Peoria Mariners.

TEXAS (6): AAA—Oklahoma City. AA—Tulsa. A—Charlotte, Charleston (S.C.), Erie. Rookie—Gulf Coast Rangers.

TORONTO (7): AAA—Syracuse. AA—Knoxville. A—Hagerstown, Dunedin, St. Catharines. Rookie—Medicine Hat, Gulf Coast Blue Jays.

ATLANTA (7): AAA—Richmond. AA—Greenville. A—Durham, Macon. Rookie—Danville, Idaho Falls, Gulf Coast Braves.

CHICAGO (7): AAA—Iowa. AA—Orlando. A—Peoria, Geneva, TBA. Rookie—Huntington, Gulf Coast Cubs.

CINCINNATI (6): AAA—Indianapolis. AA—Chattanooga. A—Winston-Salem, Charleston (W.Va.). Rookie—Billings, Princeton.

COLORADO (4): AAA—Colorado Springs. AA—None. A—Central Valley, Bend. Rookie—Mesa.

FLORIDA (5): AAA—Edmonton. AA—None. A—High Desert, Kane County, Elmira. Rookie—Gulf Coast Marlins.

HOUSTON (7): AAA—Tucson. AA—Jackson. A—Osceola, Asheville, Quad City, Auburn. Rookie—Gulf Coast Astros.

LOS ANGELES (6): AAA—Albuquerque. AA—San Antonio. A—Bakersfield, Vero Beach, Yakima. Rookie—Great Falls.

MONTREAL (6): AAA—Ottawa. AA—Harrisburg. A—West Palm Beach, Burlington, Jamestown. Rookie—Gulf Coast Expos.

NEW YORK (7): AAA—Norfolk. AA—Binghamton. A—St. Lucie, Columbia, Pittsfield. Rookie—Kingsport, Gulf Coast Mets.

PHILADELPHIA (6): AAA—Scranton/Wilkes-Barre. AA—Reading. A—Clearwater, Spartanburg, Batavia. Rookie—Martinsville.

PITTSBURGH (6): AAA—Buffalo. AA—Carolina. A—Salem, Augusta, Welland (Ont.). Rookie—Gulf Coast Pirates.

ST. LOUIS (8): AAA—Louisville. AA—Arkansas. A—St. Petersburg, Springfield, Savannah, Glens Falls. Rookie—Johnson City, Chandler Cardinals.

SAN DIEGO (6): AAA—Las Vegas. AA—Wichita. A—Rancho Cucamonga, Waterloo, Spokane. Rookie—Scottsdale Padres.

SAN FRANCISCO (6): AAA—Phoenix. AA—Shreveport. A—San Jose, Clinton, Everett. Rookie—Scottsdale.

AMERICAN ASSOCIATION

FINAL STANDINGS

EASTERN DIVISION

Team	W	L	T	Pct.	GB
Buffalo (Pirates)	87	57	0	.604	....
Indianapolis (Expos)	83	61	0	.576	4
Louisville (Cardinals)	73	70	0	.510	13½
Nashville (Reds)	67	77	0	.465	20

WESTERN DIVISION

Team	W	L	T	Pct.	GB
Oklahoma City (Rangers)	74	70	0	.514	....
Denver (Brewers)	73	71	0	.507	1
Omaha (Royals)	67	77	0	.465	7
Iowa (Cubs)	51	92	0	.357	22½

COMPOSITE

Team	Buf.	Ind.	O.C.	Lou.	Den.	Oma.	Nash.	Iowa	W	L	T	Pct.	GB
Buffalo (Pirates)	....	12	11	15	9	12	16	12	87	57	0	.604	....
Indianapolis (Expos)	12	....	9	10	15	12	14	11	83	61	0	.576	4
Oklahoma City (Rangers)	7	9	....	8	10	15	10	15	74	70	0	.514	13
Louisville (Cardinals)	9	14	10	....	9	10	13	8	73	70	0	.510	13½
Denver (Brewers)	9	3	14	9	....	12	9	17	73	71	0	.507	14
Omaha (Royals)	6	6	9	8	12	....	11	15	67	77	0	.465	20
Nashville (Reds)	8	10	8	11	9	7	....	14	67	77	0	.465	20
Iowa (Cubs)	6	7	9	9	7	9	4	....	51	92	0	.357	35½

Major league affiliations in parentheses.

Iowa club represented Des Moines, Ia.

Playoffs—Oklahoma City defeated Buffalo, four games to none, to win league championship.

Regular-season attendance—Buffalo, 1,117,867; Denver, 347,615; Indianapolis, 332,941; Iowa, 453,386; Louisville, 646,951; Nashville, 489,991; Oklahoma City, 362,394; Omaha, 407,249. Total, 4,158,394. Playoffs (4 games), 51,519. Class AAA All-Star Game at Richmond, 12,186.

Managers—Buffalo, Marc Bombard; Denver, Tony Muser; Indianapolis, Pat Kelly; Iowa, Brad Mills; Louisville, Jack Krol; Nashville, Pete Mackanin (thru June 27) and Dave Miley (from June 28); Oklahoma City, Tommy Thompson; Omaha, Jeff Cox. Managerial records of teams with more than one manager: Nashville, Mackanin, 35-41, Miley 32-36.

All-Star team: 1B—Jeff Conine, Omaha; 2B—Jeff Frye, Oklahoma City; 3B—Jim Tatum, Denver; SS—Carlos Garcia, Buffalo; OF—Al Martin, Buffalo; Geronimo Berroa, Nashville; Chuck Carr, Louisville; C—Bob Natal, Indianapolis; DH—Steve Balboni, Oklahoma City; RHP—Rene Arocha, Louisville; LHP—Dennis Moeller, Omaha; Reliever—David Wainhouse, Indianapolis; Rookie of the Year—Kevin Young, Buffalo; Most Valuable Player—Jim Tatum, Denver; Manager of the Year—Marc Bombard, Buffalo.

BATTING

TEAM

Team	Avg.	G	AB	R	OR	H	TB	2B	3B	HR	RBI	SH	SF	HP	BB	Int. BB	SO	SB	CS	LOB
Denver	.286	144	4965	767	704	1421	2160	259	69	114	717	54	62	50	465	13	789	162	99	992
Buffalo	.279	144	4810	717	600	1342	2124	274	59	130	671	63	44	58	454	28	808	129	67	985
Indianapolis	.264	144	4699	614	594	1239	1852	251	22	106	570	64	37	42	466	27	851	80	60	1004
Oklahoma City	.263	144	4799	710	686	1264	1951	278	29	117	664	37	40	48	654	19	890	59	57	1079
Louisville	.262	143	4628	615	606	1213	1838	221	34	112	569	56	37	37	448	25	775	96	41	928
Nashville	.261	144	4976	640	636	1300	1966	259	31	115	590	65	41	41	422	19	771	121	68	1012
Iowa	.260	143	4765	600	759	1241	1847	248	29	100	549	76	34	37	427	20	844	95	51	969
Omaha	.255	144	4722	572	650	1206	1804	200	25	116	536	54	43	40	475	26	714	82	59	1024

INDIVIDUAL

(Leading qualifiers for batting championship—389 or more plate appearances)

*Bats lefthanded.   †Switch-hitter.

Player, Team	Avg.	G	AB	R	H	TB	2B	3B	HR	RBI	SH	SF	HP	BB	Int. BB	SO	SB	CS
Tatum, Jim, Denver	.329	130	492	74	162	261	36	3	19	101	4	11	9	40	3	87	8	9
Berroa, Geronimo, Nashville	.328	112	461	73	151	254	33	2	22	88	0	4	8	32	1	69	8	9
Young, Kevin, Buffalo	.314	137	490	91	154	219	29	6	8	65	8	3	11	67	0	67	18	12
Morman, Russ, Nashville	.310	101	384	53	119	196	31	2	14	63	0	2	1	36	3	60	5	2
Carr, Chuck, Louisville†	.308	96	377	68	116	154	11	9	3	28	0	0	3	31	0	60	53	10
Casillas, Adam, Omaha*	.307	89	362	41	111	129	12	3	0	27	3	3	0	31	3	17	3	4
Martin, Al, Buffalo*	.305	125	420	85	128	234	16	15	20	59	3	5	6	35	4	93	20	5
Garcia, Carlos, Buffalo	.303	113	426	73	129	214	28	9	13	70	4	5	4	24	2	64	21	7
Conine, Jeff, Omaha	.302	110	397	69	120	214	24	5	20	72	2	6	2	54	5	67	4	5
Frye, Jeff, Oklahoma City	.300	87	337	64	101	137	26	2	2	28	8	0	11	51	0	39	11	9

Departmental leaders: G—Valentin, 139; AB—Mieske, 524; R—K. Young, 91; H—Tatum, 162; TB—Tatum, 261; 2B—Tatum, 36; 3B—Martin, 15; HR—Balboni, 30; RBI—Balboni, 104; SH—Santangelo, 13; SF—Tatum, 11; HP—Frye, Spehr, K. Young, 11; BB—K. Miller, 91; IBB—Balboni, Brewer, 6; SO—Maurer, 117; SB—Carr, 53; CS—Tubbs, 19.

Player, Team	Avg.	G	AB	R	H	TB	2B	3B	HR	RBI	SH	SF	HP	BB	Int. BB	SO	SB	CS
Abreu, Frank, Louisville	.133	7	15	0	2	2	0	0	0	1	0	0	0	0	0	4	0	0
Adkins, Steve, Iowa	.105	33	19	1	2	2	0	0	0	1	0	0	0	6	0	12	0	0
Afenir, Troy, Nashville	.254	42	130	15	33	59	6	1	6	24	1	1	0	11	1	22	5	0
Akerfelds, Darrel, 24 O.C. - 24 Buf.	.250	48	4	0	1	1	0	0	0	1	0	0	0	0	0	1	0	0
Aldrete, Rich, Louisville*	.111	10	18	0	2	2	0	0	0	0	0	0	0	1	0	4	0	0
Alicea, Luis, Louisville†	.282	20	71	11	20	28	8	0	0	6	0	1	0	16	1	6	0	0
Allanson, Andy, Denver	.297	72	266	42	79	113	16	3	4	31	3	1	1	23	0	29	9	4
Arias, Alex, Iowa	.279	106	409	52	114	158	23	3	5	40	7	0	6	44	1	27	14	3
Arnsberg, Brad, Iowa	.500	20	8	0	4	4	0	0	0	0	1	0	0	0	0	2	0	0
Arocha, Rene, Louisville	.061	25	33	2	2	3	1	0	0	0	3	0	0	1	0	15	0	0
Ashley, Shon, Indianapolis	.227	58	172	18	39	59	11	0	3	20	2	3	1	24	0	47	1	0
Ausanio, Joe, Buffalo	.167	53	6	0	1	1	0	0	0	0	0	0	0	0	0	4	0	0
Backlund, Brett, Buffalo	.000	4	8	0	0	0	0	0	0	0	0	0	0	0	0	4	0	0
Balboni, Steve, Oklahoma City	.251	117	454	75	114	234	26	2	30	104	0	6	3	55	6	100	0	0
Ballard, Jeff, Louisville*	.161	26	31	1	5	7	2	0	0	1	6	0	0	0	0	9	0	0
Barberie, Bret, Indianapolis†	.395	10	43	4	17	29	3	0	3	8	0	0	0	1	0	9	0	1
Barnes, Brian, Indianapolis*	.167	13	18	2	3	3	0	0	0	0	1	0	0	1	0	7	0	0
Bates, Billy, Iowa*	.241	90	257	30	62	75	8	1	1	19	6	3	0	27	2	13	2	2
Beanblossom, Brad, Louisville	.235	5	17	2	4	4	0	0	0	1	0	0	0	1	0	5	0	0
Beatty, Blaine, Indianapolis*	.158	26	19	2	3	3	0	0	0	0	2	0	0	1	0	6	0	0
Beeler, Pete, Buffalo	.282	34	85	6	24	33	3	0	2	9	0	1	1	0	0	10	0	0
Belcher, Kevin, Oklahoma City	.286	2	7	2	2	3	1	0	0	0	0	0	0	1	0	3	0	0
Bell, Juan, Oklahoma City*	.256	24	82	12	21	30	4	1	1	9	0	0	0	4	0	19	2	0
Berger, Mike, Oklahoma City	.300	8	20	2	6	9	0	0	1	2	0	0	0	3	0	5	0	0
Berroa, Geronimo, Nashville	.328	112	461	73	151	254	33	2	22	88	0	4	8	32	1	69	8	9
Berry, Sean, Omaha	.287	122	439	61	126	215	22	2	21	77	2	6	7	39	1	87	6	8
Bottenfield, Kent, Indianapolis†	.143	25	28	3	4	4	0	0	0	1	2	0	0	0	0	12	0	0
Bradley, Phil, Iowa	.248	42	133	13	33	41	8	0	0	6	3	0	1	19	0	16	3	1
Bradley, Scott, Nashville*	.254	24	59	7	15	18	3	0	0	6	0	0	2	3	0	4	1	0
Branson, Jeff, Nashville*	.325	36	123	18	40	64	6	3	4	12	1	0	0	9	1	19	0	3
Brantley, Mickey, Nashville	.317	62	230	47	73	109	13	1	7	31	0	0	0	25	0	19	1	2
Brennan, Bill, Iowa	.000	19	0	0	0	0	0	0	0	0	1	0	0	0	0	0	0	0
Brewer, Rod, Louisville*	.288	120	423	57	122	200	20	2	18	86	0	1	5	49	6	60	0	3
Brito, Mario, Indianapolis	.000	2	1	0	0	0	0	0	0	0	0	0	0	0	0	1	0	0
Brower, Bob, Oklahoma City	.210	75	238	25	50	69	8	1	3	27	4	0	0	24	0	53	11	7
Brown, Keith, Nashville†	.080	28	25	1	2	2	0	0	0	1	4	0	0	1	0	9	0	0
Brumfield, Jacob, Nashville	.284	56	208	32	59	90	10	3	5	19	3	0	2	26	0	35	22	11
Bryant, Scott, Iowa	.251	98	315	35	79	161	22	3	18	49	2	2	3	25	2	73	0	2
Buchanan, Bob, Nashville*	.111	10	9	1	1	2	1	0	0	0	1	0	0	0	0	3	0	0
Bullett, Scott, Buffalo*	.400	3	10	1	4	8	0	2	0	1	0	0	0	0	0	3	0	0
Bullinger, Jim, Iowa	.000	20	0	0	0	0	0	0	0	0	.0	0	0	0	0	0	0	0
Bullock, Eric, Indianapolis*	.305	90	305	50	93	133	19	3	5	40	0	2	3	34	2	49	21	11
Campbell, Jim, Omaha*	.000	20	0	0	0	0	0	0	0	0	1	0	0	0	0	0	0	0
Canseco, Ozzie, Louisville	.266	98	308	53	82	169	19	1	22	57	1	2	2	43	0	96	1	1
Capra, Nick, Nashville	.233	90	287	48	67	98	14	1	5	27	12	2	3	51	1	36	31	10
Carmona, Greg, Louisville†	.147	70	136	19	20	26	3	0	1	6	1	1	1	18	1	41	1	2
Carr, Chuck, Louisville†	.308	96	377	68	116	154	11	9	3	28	0	3	1	31	0	60	53	10
Casillas, Adam, Omaha*	.307	89	362	41	111	129	12	3	0	27	3	3	0	31	3	17	3	4
Castellano, Pedro, Iowa	.248	74	238	25	59	87	14	4	2	20	8	1	1	32	0	42	2	2
Cerutti, John, Buffalo*	.188	9	16	2	3	3	0	0	0	1	1	0	0	0	0	6	0	0
Chance, Tony, Iowa	.270	131	434	60	117	175	23	1	11	52	4	3	4	34	1	100	5	3
Christian, Rico, Indianapolis	.250	11	16	4	4	4	0	0	0	1	0	0	1	0	0	5	0	1
Cianfrocco, Archi, Indianapolis	.305	15	59	12	18	33	3	0	4	16	0	1	2	5	0	15	1	0
Clark, Dave, Buffalo*	.304	78	253	43	77	139	17	6	11	55	2	1	2	34	4	51	6	4
Clark, Mark, Louisville	.000	9	8	0	0	0	0	0	0	0	5	0	0	0	0	2	0	0
Colbrunn, Greg, Indianapolis	.306	57	216	32	66	120	19	1	11	48	0	2	3	7	2	41	1	0
Cole, Stu, Omaha	.195	63	205	30	40	60	8	0	4	17	6	0	3	25	0	27	3	5
Cole, Victor, Buffalo*	.063	21	16	3	1	1	0	0	0	0	3	0	0	2	0	4	1	0
Coles, Darnell, Nashville	.296	22	81	19	24	47	5	0	6	16	0	1	2	8	0	13	1	0
Conine, Jeff, Omaha	.302	110	397	69	120	214	24	5	20	72	2	6	2	54	5	67	4	5
Cook, Mike, Louisville*	.500	43	4	0	2	3	1	0	0	0	0	0	0	0	0	0	0	0
Cooke, Steve, Louisville*	.167	13	18	3	3	4	1	0	0	3	0	0	0	0	0	7	0	0
Coolbaugh, Scott, Nashville	.255	59	188	25	48	77	8	3	5	23	2	5	0	32	0	50	3	2
Cordero, Wil, Indianapolis	.314	52	204	32	64	95	11	1	6	27	1	1	0	24	2	54	6	7
Cormier, Rheal, Louisville*	.000	1	1	0	0	0	0	0	0	0	0	0	0	0	0	0	0	0
Cox, Danny, Buffalo	.143	8	7	0	1	1	0	0	0	0	0	0	0	1	0	3	0	0
Cromer, Tripp, Louisville	.200	6	25	5	5	1	1	1	1	7	0	1	0	1	0	6	0	0
Dalton, Mike, Buffalo	.333	56	3	1	1	1	0	0	0	0	0	0	0	0	0	1	0	0
Daugherty, Jack, Oklahoma City†	.278	9	18	3	5	7	2	0	0	2	0	0	0	3	0	3	0	0
Davis, Doug, Oklahoma City	.186	61	194	20	36	58	10	0	4	25	4	2	3	22	0	35	0	5
De Los Santos, Alberto, Buffalo	.160	10	25	1	4	6	0	1	0	3	0	0	0	1	0	9	0	0
Diaz, Alex, Denver*	.268	106	455	67	122	150	17	4	1	41	5	5	5	24	0	36	42	12
Diaz, Carlos, Omaha	.176	22	68	3	12	16	2	1	0	5	1	1	0	6	0	9	0	1
Diaz, Kiki, Nashville	.190	11	42	5	8	8	2	0	0	3	2	0	0	4	1	3	0	0
Diaz, Mario, Oklahoma City	.335	43	167	24	56	76	11	0	3	20	0	2	0	2	1	12	1	0
Dixon, Eddie, Buffalo	.000	26	4	0	0	0	0	0	0	0	0	0	0	1	0	3	0	0
Dobrolsky, Bill, Denver	.000	1	1	0	0	0	0	0	0	0	0	0	0	0	0	0	0	0
Dorsett, Brian, Buffalo	.289	131	492	69	142	240	35	0	21	102	2	5	6	38	4	68	1	0
Duffy, Darrin, Iowa	.211	31	71	8	15	17	2	0	0	3	1	0	7	0	0	15	0	2
Edge, Greg, Buffalo†	.195	38	118	11	23	33	8	1	0	10	4	0	0	5	0	10	1	2
Eppard, Jim, Indianapolis*	.267	97	258	38	69	97	15	2	3	27	3	6	2	46	1	22	5	2
Escalera, Ruben, Nashville*	.220	58	127	19	28	45	3	1	4	11	1	2	1	24	0	24	0	3
Fanning, Steve, Louisville	.184	19	49	8	9	14	1	2	0	4	0	0	1	7	1	14	0	0
Fariss, Monty, Oklahoma City	.299	49	187	28	56	102	13	3	9	38	0	1	0	31	1	42	5	4
Farmer, Howard, Indianapolis	.154	31	13	2	2	5	0	0	1	2	0	0	0	0	0	2	0	0
Fernandez, Joey, Louisville*	.107	20	28	2	3	5	2	0	0	3	0	0	0	3	0	6	0	0
Fernandez, Jose, Louisville*	.079	12	38	1	3	7	1	0	1	2	0	0	1	6	1	9	0	0
Figueroa, Bien, Louisville	.285	94	319	44	91	107	11	1	1	23	6	3	2	33	0	32	2	0
Fireovid, Steve, Oklahoma City†	.333	35	3	0	1	1	0	0	0	0	0	0	0	0	0	1	0	0
Fisher, Brian, Nashville	.000	29	2	0	0	0	0	0	0	0	0	0	0	0	0	0	0	0
Fletcher, Darrin, Indianapolis*	.255	13	51	2	13	18	2	0	1	11	0	0	0	4	0	10	0	0
Ford, Curt, Louisville*	.300	88	257	47	77	116	15	3	6	31	0	3	4	29	4	26	9	6

Player, Team	Avg.	G	AB	R	H	TB	2B	3B	HR	RBI	SH	SF	HP	BB	Int. BB	SO	SB	CS
Foster, Steve, Nashville	.000	17	9	1	0	0	0	0	0	0	1	0	0	0	0	1	0	0
Frye, Jeff, Oklahoma City	.300	87	337	64	101	137	26	2	2	28	8	0	11	51	0	39	11	9
Fulton, Ed, Louisville*	.201	77	234	19	47	88	5	0	12	29	2	2	0	22	1	56	0	0
Fulton, Greg, Indianapolis+	.216	92	292	29	63	93	10	1	6	29	2	1	6	20	4	53	1	4
Galarraga, Andres, Louisville	.176	11	34	3	6	14	0	1	2	3	0	0	1	0	0	8	1	0
Garcia, Carlos, Buffalo	.303	113	426	73	129	214	28	9	13	70	4	5	4	24	2	64	21	7
Garcia, Leo, Omaha*	.217	73	226	24	49	60	5	0	2	18	4	4	1	15	5	25	2	0
Gardner, John, Iowa	.125	39	8	0	1	1	0	0	0	0	0	2	0	0	0	3	0	0
Garner, Kevin, Nashville*	.333	8	24	4	8	17	3	0	2	7	1	0	0	4	0	8	0	1
Goff, Jerry, Indianapolis*	.239	94	314	37	75	136	17	1	14	39	1	3	2	32	3	97	0	1
Gonzalez, Denny, Nashville	.200	27	80	12	16	28	4	1	2	7	0	3	1	9	1	15	0	0
Grater, Mark, Louisville	.250	54	4	0	1	1	0	0	0	0	0	0	0	1	0	0	0	0
Green, Gary, Nashville	.193	101	316	23	61	84	12	1	3	27	8	2	2	22	1	44	0	1
Green, Tom, Buffalo	.208	13	24	4	5	7	2	0	0	2	0	0	0	5	0	9	0	0
Guerrero, Sandy, Denver*	.319	76	257	39	82	124	19	4	5	44	4	7	1	15	0	21	6	2
Guerrero, Pedro, Louisville	.255	18	55	5	14	28	5	0	3	7	0	0	0	6	1	7	0	0
Hall, Drew, Buffalo*	.167	16	6	1	1	1	0	0	0	0	0	0	0	1	0	4	0	0
Hamelin, Bob, Omaha*	.200	27	95	9	19	39	3	1	5	15	0	3	0	14	0	15	0	0
Hancock, Lee, Buffalo*	1.000	10	1	0	1	1	0	0	0	0	0	0	0	0	0	0	0	0
Haney, Chris, Indianapolis*	.100	15	10	1	1	1	0	0	0	0	1	0	0	0	0	4	0	0
Haney, Todd, Indianapolis	.265	57	200	30	53	85	14	0	6	33	3	2	1	37	0	34	1	0
Hanlon, Larry, Oklahoma City	.250	19	52	7	13	16	3	0	0	4	0	0	2	6	0	10	1	0
Harkey, Mike, Iowa	.000	4	4	0	0	0	0	0	0	0	0	0	0	0	0	2	0	0
Hartsock, Jeff, Iowa	.042	27	24	2	1	1	0	0	0	1	0	1	0	1	0	10	0	2
Haselman, Bill, Oklahoma City	.241	17	58	8	14	22	5	0	1	9	0	0	0	13	0	12	1	0
Heredia, Gil, Indianapolis	.200	3	5	0	1	1	0	0	0	0	0	0	0	0	0	3	0	1
Hernandez, Cesar, Nashville	1.000	1	2	0	2	2	0	0	0	0	0	0	0	0	0	0	0	1
Hiatt, Phil, Omaha	.214	5	14	3	3	9	0	0	2	4	0	0	0	2	0	3	1	0
Hill, Milt, Nashville	.000	53	3	0	0	0	0	0	0	0	0	0	0	0	0	2	0	0
Hillemann, Charlie, Denver	.217	15	46	6	10	16	1	1	1	7	0	0	3	9	0	21	0	0
Hinkle, Mike, Louisville	.000	38	4	0	0	0	0	0	0	0	0	0	0	0	0	2	0	0
Hoffman, Trevor, Nashville	.000	42	6	1	0	0	0	0	0	0	0	0	0	2	0	1	0	0
Howard, Dave, Omaha+	.118	19	68	5	8	9	1	0	0	5	2	2	0	3	0	8	1	0
Howie, Mark, Nashville	.246	105	346	35	85	120	21	1	4	42	3	3	1	22	3	28	4	3
Hulse, David, Oklahoma City*	.233	8	30	7	7	10	1	1	0	3	1	0	1	1	0	4	2	2
Hurst, Jon, Indianapolis	.120	23	25	0	3	3	0	0	0	0	4	0	0	0	0	7	0	0
Ilsley, Blaise, Louisville*	.154	34	13	0	2	2	0	0	0	2	1	0	0	0	0	5	0	0
Jackson, Chuck, Oklahoma City	.260	127	457	66	119	186	23	7	10	54	2	6	4	62	1	79	3	7
Jackson, Kenny, Denver	.260	94	338	49	88	148	24	0	12	53	4	4	6	26	1	79	6	8
Jaha, John, Denver	.321	79	274	61	88	164	18	2	18	69	1	2	6	50	1	60	6	4
Johnston, Joel, Omaha	.000	42	1	0	0	0	0	0	0	0	0	0	0	0	0	0	0	0
Jordan, Brian, Louisville	.290	43	155	23	45	62	3	1	4	16	0	2	4	8	1	21	13	2
Jose, Felix, Louisville+	.143	2	7	0	1	1	0	0	0	0	0	0	0	1	0	0	0	0
Kapano, Corey, Iowa	.313	5	16	2	5	5	0	0	0	1	0	0	0	3	0	6	0	0
Kilgus, Paul, Louisville*	.120	27	25	1	3	3	0	0	0	0	4	0	0	1	0	10	0	0
King, Jeff, Buffalo	.345	7	29	6	10	18	2	0	2	5	0	0	2	2	0	2	1	0
Kmak, Joe, Denver	.311	67	225	27	70	98	11	4	3	31	5	2	3	19	0	39	6	3
Knapp, Mike, Iowa	.246	54	138	16	34	48	5	0	3	15	0	0	3	10	0	28	2	2
Koslofski, Kevin, Omaha*	.311	78	280	29	87	121	12	5	4	32	7	1	2	21	3	47	8	3
Kremers, Jimmy, Indianapolis*	.215	60	144	14	31	49	10	1	2	15	0	1	0	19	0	46	1	1
Kunkel, Jeff, 69 Den.-6 Iowa	.275	75	291	44	80	128	13	4	9	51	4	4	1	12	1	56	5	5
LaCoss, Mike, Indianapolis	.000	7	1	0	0	0	0	0	0	0	0	0	0	1	0	1	0	0
Landrum, Ced, 8 Buf.-43 Den.*	.311	51	164	24	51	61	7	0	1	19	4	2	1	17	0	17	16	10
Landrum, Bill, Indianapolis	.500	14	2	1	1	1	0	0	0	0	1	0	0	0	0	1	0	0
Lane, Brian, Nashville	.239	19	67	8	16	28	3	0	3	8	1	1	0	2	0	14	0	1
Liddell, Dave, Denver	.195	47	123	14	24	35	6	1	1	11	0	4	1	9	0	22	2	1
Long, Kevin, Omaha*	.228	88	312	28	71	96	16	3	1	29	2	3	0	29	2	41	9	5
Loynd, Mike, Louisville	.333	11	3	0	1	2	1	0	0	2	0	0	0	0	1	1	0	0
Mack, Quinn, Indianapolis*	.282	103	301	33	85	116	19	0	4	36	2	2	1	20	2	44	5	4
Maclin, Lonnie, Louisville*	.324	111	290	29	94	120	17	3	1	38	4	7	5	22	1	31	4	7
Magrane, Joe, Louisville	.083	10	12	1	1	2	1	0	0	0	4	0	0	0	0	4	0	0
Maize, Dave, Buffalo+	.000	1	1	0	0	0	0	0	0	0	0	0	0	0	0	1	0	0
Marak, Paul, Iowa	.000	9	8	0	0	0	0	0	0	0	0	0	0	0	0	4	0	0
Martin, Al, Buffalo*	.305	125	420	85	128	234	16	15	20	59	3	5	6	35	4	93	20	5
Maurer, Rob, Oklahoma City*	.288	135	493	76	142	210	34	2	10	82	1	7	4	75	3	117	1	1
May, Derrick, Iowa*	.367	8	30	6	11	23	4	1	2	8	0	0	3	3	0	3	0	0
May, Scott, Iowa	.200	17	10	0	2	2	0	0	0	1	5	0	0	0	0	1	0	0
Maysey, Matt, Indianapolis	.333	35	6	0	2	3	1	0	0	3	2	0	0	0	0	3	0	0
McDaniel, Terry, Nashville+	.289	16	38	5	11	17	3	0	1	9	0	0	0	2	0	12	1	0
McGinnis, Russ, Oklahoma City	.264	99	330	63	87	162	19	1	18	51	2	2	7	79	1	52	0	6
Medina, Luis, Omaha	.276	91	341	39	94	160	16	1	16	49	2	2	0	23	4	71	1	1
Menendez, Tony, Nashville	.143	50	7	0	1	1	0	0	0	0	0	0	0	0	0	3	0	0
Mieske, Matt, Denver	.267	134	524	80	140	248	29	11	19	77	4	5	3	39	2	90	13	9
Milchin, Mike, Louisville*	.381	20	21	3	8	14	0	0	2	5	0	1	1	1	0	2	0	0
Miller, Keith, Oklahoma City+	.257	124	459	82	118	173	30	2	7	56	2	4	4	91	2	76	8	5
Miller, Paul, Buffalo	.286	8	7	0	2	2	0	0	0	1	1	0	0	0	0	3	0	0
Minor, Blas, Buffalo	.059	46	17	0	1	1	0	0	0	1	0	0	0	0	0	10	0	0
Minutelli, Gino, Nashville	.152	33	33	0	5	6	1	0	0	4	2	0	0	0	0	9	0	0
Montoyo, Charlie, Denver	.324	84	259	40	84	105	7	4	2	34	2	1	1	47	0	36	3	5
Morman, Russ, Nashville	.310	101	384	53	119	196	31	2	14	63	0	2	1	36	3	60	5	2
Morris, Hal, Nashville*	.167	2	6	1	1	2	1	0	0	0	0	0	0	2	0	1	0	0
Mota, Jose, Omaha+	.230	131	469	45	108	128	11	0	3	28	7	1	2	41	1	56	21	8
Munoz, Omer, Indianapolis	.251	116	375	33	94	111	12	1	1	30	9	4	4	10	0	32	7	2
Myers, Chris, Indianapolis*	.000	1	3	0	0	0	0	0	0	0	0	0	0	0	0	0	0	0
Natal, Bob, Indianapolis	.302	96	344	50	104	165	19	3	12	50	1	3	4	28	1	42	3	0
Nelson, Jerome, Indianapolis+	.270	24	74	9	20	29	2	3	1	5	2	0	0	5	0	10	2	4
Nilsson, Dave, Denver+	.317	66	240	38	76	115	16	7	3	39	2	5	0	23	2	19	10	4
Olander, Jim, Denver	.372	21	78	23	29	50	4	1	5	15	0	2	2	13	0	9	2	3
Oquendo, Jose, Louisville+	.266	20	64	8	17	19	2	0	0	6	0	1	0	11	0	3	0	1
Pappas, Erik, Omaha	.217	45	138	18	30	43	8	1	1	11	1	2	0	25	1	23	4	1
Paulino, Elvin, Iowa*	.217	59	157	15	34	42	3	1	1	16	2	0	0	13	2	28	0	3
Pavlas, Dave, Iowa*	.000	12	4	0	0	0	0	0	0	0	1	0	0	0	0	0	0	0
Pedre, George, Iowa	.253	98	296	31	75	112	17	1	6	34	5	1	1	26	1	62	2	0

Player, Team	Avg.	G	AB	R	H	TB	2B	3B	HR	RBI	SH	SF	HP	BB	Int. BB	SO	SB	CS
Pedrique, Al, Omaha	.212	66	198	11	42	45	3	0	0	9	3	1	2	10	0	25	5	3
Peltier, Dan, Oklahoma City*	.296	125	450	65	133	198	30	7	7	53	3	1	3	60	3	72	1	7
Pena, Geronimo, Louisville†	.248	28	101	16	25	51	9	4	3	12	0	1	1	13	1	27	4	3
Pennyfeather, William, Buffalo	.238	55	160	19	38	51	6	2	1	12	2	0	3	2	0	24	3	2
Petkovsek, Mark, Buffalo	.242	38	33	4	8	10	0	1	0	3	3	0	0	0	0	5	0	0
Piatt, Doug, Indianapolis*	.000	8	1	0	0	0	0	0	0	0	0	0	0	0	0	0	0	0
Postier, Paul, Oklahoma City	.206	29	97	9	20	24	4	0	0	11	1	1	1	8	0	17	0	0
Powell, Ross, Nashville*	.095	25	21	1	2	2	0	0	0	1	0	1	0	1	0	3	0	0
Presley, Jim, Oklahoma City	.237	48	173	16	41	61	8	0	4	28	2	3	1	18	0	42	3	0
Prince, Tom, Buffalo	.262	75	244	34	64	108	17	0	9	35	2	4	8	20	1	35	3	1
Pugh, Tim, Nashville	.176	27	34	2	6	6	0	0	0	2	5	0	0	0	0	8	0	0
Pulliam, Harvey, Omaha	.270	100	359	55	97	161	12	2	16	60	1	3	6	32	1	53	4	2
Ramsey, Fernando, Iowa	.269	133	480	62	129	151	9	5	1	38	11	0	2	23	0	78	39	12
Rasmussen, Dennis, 2 Iowa - 11 Oma.*	.000	13	1	0	0	0	0	0	0	0	0	0	0	1	0	0	0	0
Redfield, Joe, Buffalo	.224	94	214	28	48	71	13	2	2	21	1	3	4	29	2	40	16	3
Redman, Tim, Louisville	.308	7	13	0	4	4	0	0	0	2	0	0	0	0	0	2	0	0
Reed, Darren, Indianapolis	.333	1	3	0	1	2	1	0	0	0	0	0	0	0	0	1	0	0
Reed, Jeff, Nashville*	.240	14	25	1	6	10	1	0	1	2	1	0	2	1	1	7	0	0
Renfroe, Laddie, Iowa†	.000	61	3	0	0	0	0	0	0	0	0	0	0	0	0	2	0	0
Richardson, Jeff, Buffalo	.290	97	328	34	95	131	23	2	3	29	11	2	1	19	3	46	5	2
Ridenour, Dana, Indianapolis	.500	30	4	2	2	3	1	0	0	0	0	0	0	0	0	2	0	0
Risley, Bill, Indianapolis	.182	25	22	3	4	7	0	0	1	1	1	0	0	1	0	11	0	0
Roberson, Kevin, Iowa†	.305	51	197	25	60	101	15	4	6	34	1	1	2	5	1	46	0	0
Robinson, Jeff, Iowa	.000	10	2	0	0	0	0	0	0	0	0	0	0	0	0	2	0	0
Roesler, Mike, 34 Buf. - 11 Oma.	.200	45	5	0	1	1	0	0	0	0	0	0	0	0	0	4	0	0
Rohrmeier, Dan, Omaha	.241	8	29	4	7	11	1	0	1	5	0	0	0	3	0	4	0	1
Rossy, Rico, Omaha	.316	48	174	29	55	79	10	1	4	17	2	3	0	34	0	14	3	5
Royer, Stan, Louisville	.282	124	444	55	125	193	31	2	11	77	4	4	4	32	2	74	0	0
Ryal, Mark, Oklahoma City*	.094	12	32	0	3	5	2	0	0	2	0	1	0	1	0	4	0	1
Sabo, Chris, Nashville	.364	3	11	3	4	7	0	0	1	1	0	0	2	1	0	1	0	1
Salles, John, Iowa	.059	21	17	3	1	1	0	0	0	1	0	0	0	2	0	7	0	0
Sanchez, Rey, Iowa	.342	20	76	12	26	29	3	0	0	3	1	0	0	4	0	1	6	3
Sanford, Mo, Nashville	.160	25	25	1	4	5	1	0	0	3	1	0	1	1	0	12	0	0
Santangelo, F.P., Indianapolis†	.266	137	462	83	123	163	25	0	5	34	13	2	7	62	4	58	12	11
Schreiber, Bruce, Buffalo	.111	9	18	3	2	3	1	0	0	1	0	0	0	3	0	9	0	0
Schulz, Jeff, 37 Nash. -67 Iowa*	.269	104	308	38	83	113	14	2	4	43	0	2	0	21	5	46	2	4
Scott, Gary, Iowa	.263	95	354	48	93	149	26	0	10	48	4	5	6	37	1	48	3	1
Scruggs, Tony, Oklahoma City	.240	46	146	14	35	41	3	0	1	14	1	0	2	12	0	36	4	1
Sebra, Bob, 9 O.C. - 17 Iowa	.333	26	9	0	3	3	0	0	0	1	4	0	0	3	0	1	0	0
Service, Scott, 13 Ind. -39 Nash.	.000	52	9	0	0	0	0	0	0	0	1	0	0	0	0	6	0	0
Shamburg, Ken, Denver*	.281	18	57	9	16	23	1	0	2	9	0	0	0	5	0	4	1	1
Sherrill, Tim, Louisville*	.000	51	2	0	0	0	0	0	0	0	0	0	0	0	0	0	0	0
Shines, Razor, Indianapolis†	.251	71	179	25	45	59	6	1	2	22	1	2	3	24	3	26	2	1
Shireman, Jeff, Louisville†	.199	66	186	24	37	43	6	0	0	11	3	1	0	20	0	18	0	0
Shumpert, Terry, Omaha	.200	56	210	23	42	57	12	0	1	14	5	1	4	13	0	33	3	5
Simmons, Nelson, Denver†	.200	4	10	1	2	5	0	0	1	2	1	0	0	1	0	2	0	0
Simons, Doug, Indianapolis*	.222	32	18	0	4	5	1	0	0	2	0	0	0	0	0	6	0	0
Slaught, Don, Buffalo	.333	2	6	1	2	2	0	0	0	1	0	0	0	0	0	0	0	0
Slocumb, Heath, Iowa	.000	36	1	0	0	0	0	0	0	0	0	0	0	0	0	0	0	0
Small, Jeff, Nashville	.278	126	503	65	140	197	30	3	7	46	8	4	5	22	1	52	10	3
Smith, Bryn, Louisville	.500	2	2	1	1	2	1	0	0	0	0	0	0	0	0	0	0	0
Smith, Dwight, Iowa*	.250	3	8	1	2	3	1	0	0	1	0	0	0	2	0	1	0	0
Solis, Richardo, Indianapolis*	.000	2	3	0	0	0	0	0	0	0	0	0	0	1	0	1	0	0
Sosa, Sammy, Iowa	.316	5	19	3	6	8	2	0	0	1	0	0	0	1	1	2	5	0
Spehr, Tim, Omaha	.253	109	336	48	85	152	22	0	15	42	4	1	11	61	0	89	4	2
Stairs, Matt, Indianapolis	.267	110	401	57	107	171	23	4	11	56	4	2	4	49	3	61	11	11
Stephens, Ray, Oklahoma City	.304	54	191	22	58	84	8	0	6	32	3	2	0	15	1	39	0	1
Stone, Jeff, Nashville*	.216	35	102	9	22	25	1	1	0	7	0	1	3	8	0	26	7	2
Strange, Doug, Iowa†	.307	55	212	32	65	95	16	1	4	26	1	4	1	9	0	32	3	3
Strauss, Julio, Iowa	.000	22	2	0	0	0	0	0	0	0	0	0	0	0	0	2	0	0
Suero, William, Denver	.257	75	276	42	71	102	10	9	1	25	3	2	1	31	1	33	16	9
Tafoya, Dennis, Buffalo	.000	5	1	0	0	0	0	0	0	0	0	0	0	0	0	0	0	0
Tatum, Jim, Denver	.329	130	492	74	162	261	36	3	19	101	4	11	9	40	3	87	8	9
Taylor, Dwight, Nashville*	.260	81	223	22	58	70	8	2	0	13	1	0	2	11	0	32	16	7
Tolentino, Jose, Buffalo*	.301	78	209	39	63	105	16	1	8	34	1	5	3	24	4	28	0	1
Tovar, Edgar, Indianapolis	.000	1	4	0	0	0	0	0	0	0	0	0	0	0	0	0	0	0
Tracy, Jim, Buffalo	.211	29	19	1	4	5	1	0	0	3	0	0	0	6	0	0	0	0
Trafton, Todd, Nashville	.252	44	131	25	33	57	7	1	5	21	0	3	1	22	0	24	4	0
Trevino, Alex, Louisville	.206	80	199	15	41	64	11	0	4	23	4	1	1	29	2	33	1	0
Tubbs, Greg, Buffalo	.293	110	430	69	126	177	20	5	7	42	3	2	3	57	2	64	20	19
Urbani, Tom, Louisville*	.125	18	16	2	2	3	1	0	0	1	1	0	0	0	0	3	0	0
Valdez, Sergio, Indianapolis	.133	13	15	1	2	5	0	0	1	1	2	0	0	0	0	7	0	0
Valentin, Jose, Denver†	.240	139	492	78	118	168	19	11	3	45	9	6	5	53	2	99	9	4
Vierra, Joey, Nashville*	.250	53	8	1	2	2	0	0	0	0	1	0	0	0	0	8	0	0
Villanueva, Hector, Iowa	.239	49	159	21	38	73	8	0	9	35	1	2	0	20	0	36	0	1
Wade, Scott, Iowa	.238	72	227	38	54	110	14	0	14	38	3	7	4	28	2	57	5	3
Wagner, Paul, Buffalo	.000	8	13	0	0	0	0	0	0	0	2	0	0	1	0	7	0	0
Wainhouse, David, Indianapolis*	.000	44	2	0	0	0	0	0	0	0	0	0	0	0	0	2	0	0
Wakefield, Tim, Buffalo	.091	22	22	1	2	3	1	0	0	0	2	0	0	1	0	10	0	0
Walewander, Jim, Oklahoma City†	.210	44	124	20	26	33	7	0	0	10	3	2	2	17	0	18	5	2
Walton, Jerome, Iowa	.296	7	27	8	8	12	2	1	0	3	0	0	0	4	0	6	1	1
Watson, Allen, Louisville*	.000	2	3	0	0	0	0	0	0	0	1	0	0	0	0	1	0	0
Wehner, John, Buffalo	.269	60	223	37	60	98	13	2	7	27	1	3	2	29	0	30	10	7
Wendell, Turk, Iowa†	.000	4	3	0	0	0	0	0	0	0	1	0	0	0	0	0	0	0
Wilkins, Rick, Iowa*	.277	47	155	20	43	73	11	2	5	28	1	1	2	19	2	42	0	0
Willard, Jerry, Indianapolis*	.278	31	97	9	27	45	7	1	3	17	1	0	0	12	0	19	0	0
Williams, Kenny, Denver	.291	36	134	16	39	58	7	0	4	17	0	0	2	15	0	31	3	8
Wilson, Craig, Louisville	.296	20	81	13	24	31	5	1	0	5	1	0	0	5	0	8	3	2
Wilson, Dan, Nashville	.251	106	366	27	92	122	16	1	4	34	2	4	2	31	3	58	1	4
Woodson, Tracy, Louisville	.296	109	412	62	122	185	23	2	12	59	5	4	2	24	2	46	4	3
Wrona, Rick, Nashville	.246	40	118	16	29	47	8	2	2	10	1	0	1	5	0	21	1	1
York, Mike, Buffalo	.200	6	5	0	1	1	0	0	0	0	2	0	0	1	0	0	0	0
Young, Pete, Indianapolis	.000	36	1	0	0	0	0	0	0	0	0	1	0	0	0	1	0	0

Player, Team	Avg.	G	AB	R	H	TB	2B	3B	HR	RBI	SH	SF	HP	BB	Int. BB	SO	SB	CS
Young, Kevin, Buffalo	.314	137	490	91	154	219	29	6	8	65	8	3	11	67	0	67	18	12
Zambrano, Eddie, Buffalo	.284	126	394	47	112	190	22	4	16	79	3	5	4	51	2	75	3	2
Zeile, Todd, Louisville	.311	21	74	11	23	44	4	1	5	13	0	1	0	9	0	13	0	0

The following pitchers, listed alphabetically by club, with games in parentheses, had no plate appearances, primarily through use of designated hitters:

BUFFALO—Gleaton, Jerry Don (5); Lamp, Dennis (3); Rodriguez, Rosario (4).

DENVER—Eldred, Cal (19); George, Chris (12); Green, Otis (28); Heaton, Neal (6); Higuera, Ted (2); Holmes, Darren (12); Hunter, Jim (34); Ignasiak, Mike (62); Kiefer, Mark (27); Lee, Mark (48); McClellan, Paul (9); Miranda, Angel (28); Nolte, Eric (49); Ruffin, Bruce (4); Valdez, Efrain (36); Wishnevski, Bob (44).

INDIANAPOLIS—Diaz, Rafael (1); Grewal, Ranbir (1); Rojas, Mel (4); Sampen, Bill (2).

IOWA—Berrios, Hector (16); Boskie, Shawn (2); Dickson, Lance (1); Kutzler, Jerry (2); Melvin, Bill (18); Patterson, Ken (1); Taylor, Scott (1); Willis, Travis (3).

LOUISVILLE—DiPino, Frank (18); Dixon, Steve (18); Jones, Chris (3).

NASHVILLE—Alvarez, Jose (3); Bushing, Chris (5); Drummond, Timothy (3); Lynch, David (1); Segura, Jose (22).

OKLAHOMA CITY—Akerfelds, Darrel (24); Alexander, Gerald (38); Arner, Mike (4); Barfield, John (42); Blankenship, Kevin (32); Bohanon, Brian (9); Bronkey, Jeffery (13); Brown, Robert (7); Burns, Todd (8); Burrows, Terry (1); Campbell, Mike (11); Carman, Don (20); Chiamparino, Scott (5); Drees, Tom (12); Elvira, Narciso (19); Fajardo, Hector (1); Gore, Bryan (6); Jeffcoat, Mike (7); Leon, Danny (3); Manuel, Barry (27); Mathews, Terry (9); McCullers, Lance (13); Pavlik, Roger (19); Rosenthal, Wayne (57); Sebra, Bob (9); Shaw, Cedric (3); Whiteside, Matt (12).

OMAHA—Ahern, Brian (17); Aquino, Luis (2); Bautista, Jose (40); Clark, Dera (9); Huismann, Mark (29); Lambert, Reese (11); Maldonado, Carlos (47); Manzanillo, Josias (26); Moeller, Dennis (23); Rasmussen, Dennis (11); Reed, Rick (11); Roesler, Mike (11); Sauveur, Rich (34); Shifflett, Steve (32); Young, Curt (2).

GRAND SLAMS—Balboni, 3; Berry, Canseco, Morman, Tatum, 2 each; Brewer, Colbrunn, Coles, Conine, Dorsett, Fariss, E. Fulton, C. Garcia, G. Green, T. Haney, K. Jackson, Jaha, Maclin, Presley, Pulliam, Schulz, Scott, Stephens, Tolentino, Wade, K. Young, Zambrano, 1 each.

AWARDED FIRST BASE ON CATCHER'S INTERFERENCE—Medina 2 (Knapp 2); Stairs 2 (E. Fulton, McGinnis); Santangelo (Wrona).

PITCHING

TEAM

Team	ERA	G	CG	ShO	Sv.	IP	H	R	ER	HR	HB	BB	Int. BB	SO	WP	Bk.
Buffalo	3.59	144	12	12	53	1259.2	1193	600	503	93	33	467	26	655	63	7
Nashville	3.82	144	5	7	32	1295.0	1272	636	550	102	48	536	26	1033	46	12
Louisville	3.83	143	16	13	28	1221.0	1267	606	519	102	46	401	30	732	47	11
Indianapolis	3.95	144	11	14	44	1237.2	1237	594	543	99	30	416	27	849	43	11
Denver	4.13	144	11	8	26	1277.1	1318	704	586	123	42	500	26	885	47	22
Oklahoma City	4.24	144	7	4	37	1268.1	1303	686	598	112	52	487	11	739	62	17
Omaha	4.25	144	15	10	39	1240.0	1257	650	586	125	43	471	8	742	48	21
Iowa	4.91	143	7	5	29	1238.1	1379	759	675	154	67	533	22	807	59	14

INDIVIDUAL

(Leading qualifiers for earned-run average leadership—115 or more innings)

*Throws lefthanded.

Pitcher, Team	W	L	Pct.	ERA	G	GS	CG	GF	ShO	Sv.	IP	H	R	ER	HR	HB	BB	Int. BB	SO	WP
Moeller, Omaha*	8	5	.615	2.46	23	16	3	2	1	2	120.2	121	36	33	9	4	34	1	56	5
Ballard, Louisville*	12	8	.600	2.52	24	24	3	0	1	0	160.2	164	57	45	16	2	34	1	76	2
Arocha, Louisville	12	7	.632	2.70	25	25	3	0	1	0	166.2	145	59	50	8	6	65	0	128	3
Pavlik, Oklahoma City	7	5	.583	2.98	18	18	0	0	0	0	117.2	90	44	39	7	4	51	0	104	14
Eldred, Denver	10	6	.625	3.00	19	19	4	0	1	0	141.0	122	49	47	9	4	42	0	99	3
Wakefield, Buffalo	10	3	.769	3.06	20	20	6	0	1	0	135.1	122	52	46	10	3	51	1	71	9
Simons, Indianapolis*	11	4	.733	3.08	32	14	2	6	1	0	120.0	114	45	41	7	2	25	1	66	3
Cole, Buffalo	11	6	.647	3.11	19	19	3	0	1	0	115.2	102	46	40	8	4	61	0	69	8
Sauveur, Omaha*	7	6	.538	3.22	34	13	1	7	0	0	117.1	93	54	42	8	2	39	1	88	4
Bottenfield, Indianapolis	12	8	.600	3.43	25	23	3	1	1	0	152.1	139	64	58	12	2	58	1	111	2

Departmental leaders: G—Ignasiak, 62; W—Five pitchers tied with 12; L—Adkins, Kiefer, 13; Pct.—Service, .800; GS—Minutelli, 29; CG—Wakefield, 6; GF—Grater, 45; ShO—M. Clark, 3; Sv.—Grater, 24; IP—Hartsock, 173.1; H—Kilgus, 189; R—Adkins, 103; ER—Adkins, 92; HR—Kiefer, 25; HB—Gardner, 12; BB—Miranda, 77; IBB—Wishnevski, 7; SO—Kiefer, 145; WP—Adkins, 15.

(All pitchers—listed alphabetically)

Pitcher, Team	W	L	Pct.	ERA	G	GS	CG	GF	ShO	Sv.	IP	H	R	ER	HR	HB	BB	Int. BB	SO	WP
Adkins, Iowa*	7	13	.350	6.13	33	22	0	3	0	0	135.0	161	103	92	18	3	74	0	89	15
Ahern, Omaha	7	5	.583	4.02	17	17	1	0	0	0	103.0	94	50	46	11	5	38	0	45	3
Akerfelds, 24 O.C.-24 Buf.	3	6	.333	5.59	48	1	0	10	0	2	66.0	82	50	41	10	5	36	3	32	3
Alexander, Oklahoma City	7	5	.583	4.50	38	10	0	9	0	2	106.0	100	55	53	10	2	36	1	93	0
Alvarez, Nashville	0	1	.000	13.50	3	0	0	0	0	0	4.2	7	7	7	0	2	3	0	4	0
Aquino, Omaha	0	0	.000	2.61	2	2	0	0	0	0	10.1	13	3	3	1	0	4	0	3	1
Arner, Oklahoma City	2	1	.667	6.55	4	3	0	0	0	0	22.0	25	16	16	5	2	4	0	9	0
Arnsberg, Iowa	0	8	.000	6.51	20	11	1	5	0	1	74.2	95	60	54	13	3	27	0	33	6
Arocha, Louisville	12	7	.632	2.70	25	25	3	0	1	0	166.2	145	59	50	8	6	65	0	128	3
Ausanio, Buffalo	6	4	.600	2.90	53	0	0	39	0	15	83.2	64	35	27	5	1	40	6	66	4
Backlund, Buffalo	3	0	1.000	2.16	4	4	2	0	0	0	25.0	15	8	6	2	0	11	0	9	0
Ballard, Louisville*	12	8	.600	2.52	24	24	3	0	1	0	160.2	164	57	45	16	2	34	1	76	2
Barfield, Oklahoma City*	7	1	.875	4.14	42	0	0	12	0	2	71.2	75	39	33	6	2	26	0	26	1
Barnes, Indianapolis*	4	4	.500	3.69	13	13	2	0	1	0	83.0	69	35	34	8	1	30	1	77	2
Bautista, Omaha	2	10	.167	4.90	40	7	1	16	0	0	108.1	125	66	59	7	2	28	0	60	1
Beatty, Indianapolis*	7	5	.583	4.31	26	12	2	3	0	0	94.0	109	52	45	8	1	24	3	54	4
Berrios, Iowa*	1	1	.500	8.78	16	0	0	6	0	0	13.1	21	13	13	1	1	10	2	14	0
Blankenship, Oklahoma City	5	5	.500	4.57	32	15	2	4	0	1	106.1	112	59	54	7	9	52	2	53	5

Pitcher, Team	W	L	Pct.	ERA	G	GS	CG	GF	ShO	Sv.	IP	H	R	ER	HR	HB	BB	Int. BB	SO	WP
Bohanon, Oklahoma City*	4	2	.667	2.73	9	9	3	0	0	0	56.0	53	21	17	5	1	15	0	24	3
Boskie, Iowa	0	0	.000	3.68	2	2	0	0	0	0	7.1	8	4	3	0	0	3	0	3	0
Bottenfield, Indianapolis	12	8	.600	3.43	25	23	3	1	1	0	152.1	139	64	58	12	2	58	1	111	2
Brennan, Iowa	1	4	.200	6.37	19	1	0	9	0	0	29.2	43	27	21	4	2	12	1	34	3
Brito, Indianapolis	2	0	1.000	3.38	2	0	0	0	0	0	5.1	5	2	2	1	0	3	0	1	0
Bronkey, Oklahoma City	0	1	.000	7.47	13	0	0	8	0	3	15.2	26	13	13	1	2	5	0	10	1
Brown, Nashville	12	9	.571	3.61	26	23	1	1	0	0	149.2	157	74	60	6	4	43	0	102	3
Brown, Oklahoma City	1	2	.333	2.87	7	4	0	0	0	0	31.1	30	17	10	3	1	5	0	14	2
Buchanan, Nashville*	0	4	.000	4.96	10	9	0	0	0	0	49.0	63	34	27	3	1	21	1	19	1
Bullinger, Iowa	1	2	.333	2.45	20	0	0	20	0	14	22.0	17	6	6	0	0	12	3	15	2
Burns, Oklahoma City	3	2	.600	2.55	8	7	0	1	0	0	42.1	32	15	12	3	0	13	0	16	1
Burrows, Oklahoma City*	1	0	1.000	1.13	1	1	0	0	0	0	8.0	3	1	1	0	0	5	0	6	0
Bushing, Nashville	1	0	1.000	3.48	5	0	0	1	0	0	10.1	8	4	4	1	0	6	0	6	0
Campbell, Omaha*	5	7	.417	5.38	20	14	0	3	0	1	83.2	102	52	50	16	3	41	1	34	0
Campbell, Oklahoma City	2	3	.400	5.71	11	7	0	2	0	0	41.0	43	26	26	6	4	12	2	25	1
Capra, Nashville	1	0	1.000	0.00	1	0	0	1	0	0	2.0	1	0	0	0	0	0	0	1	0
Carman, Oklahoma City*	4	6	.400	4.02	20	12	1	1	1	1	80.2	80	39	36	5	3	31	0	43	5
Cerutti, Buffalo*	4	0	1.000	5.36	9	8	0	0	0	0	45.1	53	29	27	6	1	7	0	13	0
Chance, Iowa	0	0	.000	0.00	2	0	0	2	0	0	1.2	1	0	0	0	0	2	0	1	0
Chiamparino, Oklahoma City	2	1	.667	2.87	5	5	0	0	0	0	31.1	29	11	10	1	0	13	0	9	1
Clark, Omaha	1	6	.143	7.95	9	9	0	0	0	0	43.0	57	39	38	9	1	16	0	32	3
Clark, Louisville	4	4	.500	2.80	9	9	4	0	3	0	61.0	56	20	19	4	1	15	0	38	2
Cole, Buffalo	11	6	.647	3.11	19	19	3	0	1	0	115.2	102	46	40	8	4	61	0	69	8
Cook, Louisville	3	2	.600	4.60	43	0	0	8	0	0	58.2	58	31	30	5	1	31	4	56	3
Cooke, Buffalo*	6	3	.667	3.75	13	13	0	0	0	0	74.1	71	35	31	2	4	36	2	52	5
Cormier, Louisville*	0	1	.000	6.75	1	1	0	0	0	0	4.0	8	4	3	0	0	0	0	1	0
Cox, Buffalo	1	1	.500	1.70	8	8	0	0	0	0	42.1	28	11	8	0	0	18	0	30	3
Dalton, Buffalo*	3	3	.500	3.66	56	0	0	24	0	10	71.1	56	32	29	3	3	18	4	25	5
Diaz, Indianapolis	0	0	.000	4.50	1	1	0	0	0	0	4.0	3	2	2	0	1	3	0	2	0
Dickson, Iowa*	0	1	.000	19.29	1	1	0	0	0	0	2.1	6	5	5	1	0	2	0	2	1
DiPino, Louisville*	0	3	.000	3.97	18	0	0	5	0	0	22.2	28	15	10	3	0	8	0	10	2
Dixon, Louisville*	1	2	.333	5.03	18	0	0	8	0	2	19.2	20	12	11	0	1	19	2	16	0
Dixon, Buffalo	2	3	.400	5.57	26	2	0	3	0	0	42.0	60	31	26	8	0	8	3	10	0
Drees, Oklahoma City*	2	2	.500	5.20	12	5	0	3	0	0	36.1	43	25	21	2	2	13	0	22	1
Drummond, Nashville	0	0	.000	6.75	3	0	0	0	0	0	4.0	8	3	3	0	0	1	0	1	0
Edge, Buffalo	0	0	.000	0.00	1	0	0	0	0	0	0.0	1	1	1	0	0	1	0	0	0
Eldred, Denver	10	6	.625	3.00	19	19	4	0	1	0	141.0	122	49	47	9	4	42	0	99	3
Elvira, Oklahoma City*	4	5	.444	4.97	19	16	0	2	0	0	88.2	87	54	49	9	3	28	0	45	2
Eppard, Indianapolis*	0	0	.000	0.00	1	0	0	1	0	0	1.0	0	0	0	0	0	0	0	0	0
Fajardo, Oklahoma City	1	0	1.000	0.00	1	1	0	0	0	0	7.0	8	0	0	0	2	6	0	6	0
Farmer, Indianapolis	3	2	.600	3.75	30	6	0	9	0	0	84.0	89	41	35	8	1	24	2	64	10
Fireovid, Oklahoma City	7	2	.778	3.10	33	10	0	7	0	0	104.2	130	46	36	3	3	28	0	54	2
Fisher, Nashville	2	3	.400	4.11	29	6	0	7	0	0	50.1	52	23	23	3	3	15	0	42	0
Foster, Nashville	5	3	.625	2.68	17	7	0	6	0	1	50.1	53	20	15	3	1	22	0	28	1
Gardner, Iowa	5	7	.417	4.49	38	12	3	7	0	0	122.1	120	67	61	18	12	61	1	87	9
George, Denver	2	3	.400	4.64	12	8	0	2	0	0	42.2	54	30	22	2	4	10	0	20	2
Gleaton, Buffalo*	1	0	1.000	0.00	5	0	0	3	0	1	6.2	2	0	0	0	0	5	0	10	0
Gore, Oklahoma City*	1	0	1.000	3.43	6	3	0	2	0	0	21.0	23	10	8	4	0	5	0	10	0
Grater, Louisville	7	8	.467	2.13	54	0	0	45	0	24	76.0	74	26	18	2	3	15	2	46	2
Green, Denver*	11	8	.579	4.61	28	27	1	0	0	0	152.1	148	85	78	17	6	70	1	114	5
Grewal, Indianapolis	0	0	.000	16.20	1	1	0	0	0	0	1.2	1	4	3	0	0	3	0	2	0
Hall, Buffalo*	4	0	1.000	2.37	16	4	0	1	0	0	38.0	36	15	10	3	1	12	2	30	3
Hancock, Buffalo*	0	2	.000	2.00	10	0	0	7	0	0	9.0	9	2	2	0	0	3	1	5	2
Haney, Indianapolis*	5	2	.714	5.14	15	15	0	0	0	0	84.0	88	50	48	4	3	42	0	61	2
Harkey, Iowa	0	1	.000	5.56	4	4	0	0	0	0	22.2	21	15	14	3	4	13	0	16	3
Hartsock, Iowa	5	12	.294	4.36	27	27	2	0	0	0	173.1	177	91	84	13	10	61	2	87	3
Heaton, Denver*	2	1	.667	3.52	6	4	0	0	0	0	23.0	23	10	9	1	2	8	0	9	0
Heredia, Indianapolis	2	0	1.000	1.02	3	3	0	0	0	0	17.2	18	2	2	1	1	3	0	10	0
Higuera, Denver*	1	0	1.000	4.15	2	2	0	0	0	0	8.2	7	5	4	0	0	8	0	4	1
Hill, Nashville	0	5	.000	2.66	53	0	0	39	0	18	74.1	56	30	22	7	1	17	4	70	4
Hinkle, Louisville	2	5	.286	6.39	38	3	0	10	0	0	63.1	85	50	45	5	1	25	6	34	4
Hoffman, Nashville	4	6	.400	4.27	42	5	0	23	0	6	65.1	57	32	31	6	1	32	3	63	4
Holmes, Denver	0	0	.000	1.38	12	0	0	12	0	7	13.0	7	2	2	1	1	4	1	12	0
Huismann, Omaha	4	9	.308	5.17	29	17	3	7	0	0	123.2	139	80	71	10	6	34	0	58	8
Hunter, Denver	6	7	.462	3.68	34	18	3	9	0	2	134.2	144	68	55	13	4	46	2	56	2
Hurst, Indianapolis	4	8	.333	3.77	23	23	2	0	0	0	119.1	135	59	50	7	3	29	1	70	4
Ignasiak, Denver	7	4	.636	2.93	62	0	0	34	0	10	92.0	83	37	30	6	1	33	4	64	3
Ilsley, Louisville*	5	4	.556	4.30	33	10	1	10	0	1	98.1	114	56	47	15	4	23	2	56	3
Jackson, Oklahoma City	0	0	.000	13.50	1	0	0	1	0	0	2.0	4	3	3	1	0	1	0	1	0
Jeffcoat, Oklahoma City*	2	1	.667	4.22	7	5	1	1	0	0	32.0	33	20	15	3	0	6	0	20	1
Johnston, Omaha	5	2	.714	6.39	42	0	0	22	0	0	74.2	80	54	53	9	4	45	2	48	6
Jones, Louisville	0	0	.000	7.20	3	0	0	0	0	0	5.0	4	5	4	0	0	2	1	3	0
Kiefer, Denver	7	13	.350	4.59	27	26	1	0	0	0	162.2	168	95	83	25	9	65	1	145	8
Kilgus, Louisville*	9	8	.529	3.80	27	26	4	0	1	0	168.1	189	90	71	11	5	28	1	90	4
Kremers, Indianapolis	0	0	.000	0.00	1	0	0	0	0	0	1.0	0	0	0	0	0	1	0	0	0
Kunkel, Denver	0	0	.000	0.00	1	0	0	1	0	0	1.0	0	0	0	0	0	0	0	1	0
Kutzler, Iowa	0	0	.000	3.00	2	0	0	1	0	0	3.0	5	2	1	0	0	0	0	3	0
LaCoss, Indianapolis	0	3	.000	7.30	7	1	0	0	0	0	12.1	17	11	10	2	0	5	0	7	1
Lambert, Omaha*	2	2	.500	5.37	11	10	0	0	0	0	53.2	61	33	32	9	2	32	0	26	5
Lamp, Buffalo	0	0	.000	6.75	3	0	0	1	0	1	5.1	5	4	4	1	0	0	0	3	0
Landrum, Indianapolis	1	1	.500	3.95	14	5	0	0	0	0	27.1	27	15	12	4	1	4	0	23	1
Lee, Denver*	2	4	.333	4.19	48	0	0	14	0	1	68.2	78	45	32	5	0	26	4	57	1
Leon, Oklahoma City	1	0	1.000	0.00	3	0	0	1	0	0	4.2	2	0	0	0	0	3	0	4	0
Loynd, Louisville	0	0	.000	5.32	11	3	0	4	0	0	23.2	26	19	14	5	1	10	0	21	1
Lynch, Nashville*	0	0	.000	0.00	1	0	0	1	0	0	1.1	1	0	0	0	0	0	0	1	0
Magrane, Louisville*	3	4	.429	5.40	10	10	0	0	0	0	53.1	60	32	32	6	5	29	1	35	3
Maldonado, Omaha	7	4	.636	3.60	47	0	0	36	0	16	75.0	61	34	30	6	2	35	0	60	1
Manuel, Oklahoma City	1	8	.111	5.27	27	0	0	22	0	5	27.1	32	24	16	1	2	26	0	11	1
Manzanillo, Omaha	7	10	.412	4.36	26	21	0	2	0	0	136.1	138	76	66	12	7	71	0	114	9
Marak, Iowa	0	5	.000	4.68	9	9	1	0	0	0	57.2	69	33	30	9	1	22	1	24	1
Mathews, Oklahoma City	1	1	.500	4.32	9	2	0	4	0	0	16.2	17	8	8	1	1	7	0	13	2
May, Iowa	3	4	.429	4.80	17	8	0	3	0	0	65.2	78	44	35	11	4	23	0	52	1
Maysey, Indianapolis	5	3	.625	4.30	35	1	0	14	0	5	67.0	63	32	32	9	0	28	5	38	2
McClellan, Denver	1	1	.500	4.26	9	4	0	5	0	1	31.2	36	19	15	4	1	14	0	14	0

— 334 —

Pitcher, Team	W	L	Pct.	ERA	G	GS	CG	GF	ShO	Sv.	IP	H	R	ER	HR	HB	BB	Int. BB	SO	WP
McCullers, Oklahoma City	1	1	.500	5.33	13	0	0	2	0	1	25.1	26	22	15	3	1	11	1	10	4
Melvin, Iowa	3	0	1.000	4.62	18	0	0	7	0	0	39.0	32	20	20	9	1	27	2	31	1
Menendez, Nashville	3	5	.375	4.05	50	2	0	11	0	1	106.2	98	53	48	10	3	47	6	92	3
Milchin, Louisville*	2	6	.250	5.92	12	12	1	0	0	0	65.1	69	46	43	8	1	31	5	37	5
Miller, Buffalo	2	3	.400	3.90	8	7	0	0	0	0	32.1	38	23	14	3	1	16	0	18	0
Minor, Buffalo	5	4	.556	2.43	45	7	0	29	0	18	96.1	72	30	26	7	1	26	2	60	2
Minutelli, Nashville*	4	12	.250	4.27	29	29	1	0	0	0	158.0	177	96	75	18	5	76	1	110	11
Miranda, Denver*	6	12	.333	4.77	28	27	1	0	1	0	160.1	183	100	85	16	1	77	0	122	9
Moeller, Omaha*	8	5	.615	2.46	23	16	3	2	1	2	120.2	121	36	33	9	4	34	1	56	5
Myers, Indianapolis*	1	0	1.000	0.00	1	1	0	0	0	0	6.0	2	0	0	0	1	0	2	0
Nolte, Denver*	5	5	.500	5.13	49	2	0	22	0	3	72.0	74	53	41	7	4	31	4	45	4
Patterson, Iowa*	0	1	.000	21.60	1	0	0	0	0	0	1.2	4	4	4	2	1	1	0	1	0
Pavlas, Iowa	3	3	.500	3.38	12	4	0	6	0	0	37.1	43	20	14	5	1	8	0	34	0
Pavlik, Oklahoma City	7	5	.583	2.98	18	18	0	0	0	0	117.2	90	44	39	7	4	51	0	104	14
Pedrique, Omaha	0	0	.000	5.40	1	0	0	1	0	0	1.2	2	1	1	0	0	0	0	0	0
Petkovsek, Buffalo	8	8	.500	3.53	32	22	1	1	0	1	150.1	150	76	59	9	7	44	1	49	5
Piatt, Indianapolis	0	0	.000	4.22	8	0	0	7	0	3	10.2	13	6	5	0	0	3	0	6	1
Powell, Nashville*	4	8	.333	3.38	25	12	0	4	0	0	93.1	89	37	35	5	3	42	1	84	2
Pugh, Nashville	12	9	.571	3.55	27	27	3	0	2	0	169.2	165	75	67	10	8	65	3	117	4
Rasmussen, 2 Iowa - 11 Oma.*	4	4	.500	2.03	13	8	3	1	2	0	62.0	52	21	14	3	1	20	2	50	0
Reed, Iowa	5	4	.556	4.35	11	10	3	1	0	1	62.0	67	33	30	8	4	12	0	35	0
Renfroe, Iowa	3	10	.231	4.74	61	1	0	31	0	6	100.2	115	57	53	10	8	40	6	55	1
Ridenour, Indianapolis	1	1	.500	3.09	30	0	0	19	0	6	46.2	44	16	16	4	2	9	3	37	3
Risley, Indianapolis	5	8	.385	6.40	25	15	0	1	0	0	95.2	105	69	68	11	4	47	0	64	2
Robinson, Iowa	1	1	.667	4.61	10	0	0	2	0	0	13.2	12	8	7	2	5	0	12	1
Rodriguez, Buffalo*	0	1	.000	15.43	4	0	0	0	0	0	2.1	3	4	4	0	0	8	0	1	0
Roesler, 34 Buf. - 11 Oma.	4	6	.400	5.19	45	0	0	18	0	7	76.1	83	44	44	12	4	25	3	47	8
Rojas, Indianapolis	2	1	.667	5.40	4	0	0	1	0	0	8.1	10	5	5	0	0	3	0	7	1
Rosenthal, Oklahoma City	1	6	.143	5.69	57	0	0	33	0	11	61.2	72	42	39	5	2	29	3	54	11
Ruffin, Denver*	3	0	1.000	0.94	4	4	1	0	0	0	28.2	28	12	3	4	8	1	17	0
Salles, Iowa	4	9	.308	6.85	19	16	0	0	0	0	90.2	122	81	69	9	6	46	1	47	3
Sampen, Indianapolis	1	1	.500	6.00	2	0	0	0	0	0	3.0	3	5	2	0	3	0	4	0
Sanford, Nashville	8	8	.500	5.68	25	25	0	0	0	0	122.0	128	81	77	22	3	65	1	129	2
Sauveur, Omaha*	7	6	.538	3.22	34	13	1	7	0	0	117.1	93	54	42	8	2	39	1	88	4
Sebra, 9 O.C. - 17 Iowa	7	4	.636	5.03	26	15	0	5	0	1	91.1	115	54	51	14	8	35	1	61	2
Segura, Nashville	1	1	.500	3.98	22	0	0	11	0	1	31.2	33	16	14	0	1	18	1	16	3
Service, 13 Ind. - 39 Nash.	8	2	.800	1.89	52	2	0	22	0	6	95.0	66	25	20	2	5	44	3	112	2
Shaw, Oklahoma City*	2	5	.286	5.59	13	10	0	1	0	0	56.1	58	39	35	9	2	31	0	25	3
Sherrill, Louisville*	7	3	.700	3.90	51	0	0	36	0	1	62.1	61	28	27	4	2	22	4	28	2
Shifflett, Omaha	3	2	.600	1.65	32	0	0	29	0	14	43.2	30	8	8	0	0	15	1	19	0
Shireman, Louisville	0	0	.000	0.00	1	0	0	1	0	0	1.0	1	0	0	0	0	0	0	0	0
Simons, Indianapolis*	11	4	.733	3.08	32	14	2	6	1	0	120.0	114	45	41	7	2	25	1	66	3
Slocumb, Iowa	1	3	.250	2.59	36	1	0	23	0	1	41.2	36	13	12	0	0	16	1	47	4
Smith, Louisville	1	0	1.000	1.80	2	2	0	0	0	0	10.0	6	2	2	0	2	2	0	2	2
Solis, Indianapolis*	0	2	.000	3.75	2	2	0	0	0	0	12.0	11	6	5	1	0	2	0	5	0
Strauss, Iowa	2	2	.500	2.79	22	3	0	9	0	1	58.0	52	20	18	8	3	17	1	50	2
Tafoya, Buffalo	2	1	.667	4.35	5	0	0	1	0	0	10.1	13	5	5	1	0	3	0	5	0
Tracy, Buffalo	9	4	.692	4.27	29	16	0	2	0	0	116.0	115	64	55	12	2	34	0	51	5
Urbani, Louisville*	4	5	.444	4.67	16	16	0	0	0	0	88.2	91	50	46	9	7	37	1	46	5
Valdez, Denver*	1	1	.500	5.43	36	1	0	11	0	0	68.0	76	45	41	9	2	22	2	43	2
Valdez, Indianapolis	4	2	.667	3.75	13	8	0	1	0	0	62.1	59	29	26	3	1	13	1	41	2
Vierra, Nashville*	4	1	.800	2.98	52	3	0	19	0	0	81.2	65	29	27	6	2	28	2	62	6
Wagner, Buffalo	3	3	.500	5.49	8	8	0	0	0	0	39.1	51	27	24	1	1	14	0	19	2
Wainhouse, Indianapolis	5	4	.556	4.11	44	0	0	41	0	21	46.0	48	22	21	4	2	24	5	37	4
Wakefield, Buffalo	10	3	.769	3.06	20	20	6	0	1	0	135.1	122	52	46	10	3	51	1	71	9
Watson, Louisville*	1	0	1.000	1.46	2	2	0	0	0	0	12.1	8	4	2	1	0	5	0	9	2
Wendell, Iowa	2	0	1.000	1.44	4	4	0	0	0	0	25.0	17	7	4	3	0	15	0	12	1
Whiteside, Oklahoma City	1	0	1.000	0.79	12	0	0	12	0	8	11.1	7	1	1	1	0	3	1	13	0
Willis, Iowa	1	1	.500	7.71	3	0	0	2	0	0	7.0	9	6	6	4	0	3	0	1	1
Wishnevski, Denver	9	6	.600	5.03	44	1	0	27	0	3	77.0	87	49	43	4	3	39	7	64	7
York, Buffalo	4	1	.800	3.06	6	6	0	0	0	0	32.1	31	14	11	2	1	20	0	20	1
Young, Indianapolis	6	2	.750	3.51	36	0	0	20	0	7	48.2	53	19	19	5	1	21	3	34	0
Young, Omaha*	0	1	.000	5.40	2	2	0	0	0	0	10.0	15	6	6	1	0	2	0	6	0

BALKS—Miranda, 6; Gardner, 5; Drees, Fisher, Risley, Sauveur, 4 each; Barfield, K. Brown, J. Campbell, Huismann, Ignasiak, Kiefer, Milchin, Moeller, Salles, Shaw, 3 each; Arocha, Barnes, Cox, Farmer, Fireovid, Green, Hunter, Nolte, Shifflett, York, 2 each; Ahern, Akerfelds, Arnsberg, Ballard, Bautista, Beatty, Bullinger, Burns, Cook, Cooke, Dixon, Elvira, Foster, George, Hancock, Hartsock, Heredia, Hill, Hinkle, Johnston, Lambert, Lee, Magrane, Maldonado, Marak, May, Maysey, Minor, Minutelli, Pavlik, Powell, Rasmussen, Renfroe, Ruffin, Sebra, Urbani, E. Valdez, Vierra, York, 1 each.

COMBINATION SHUTOUTS—Cole-Akerfelds-Dalton, Cole-Ausanio, Cooke-Minor, Cox-Dalton-Minor, Hall-Dalton-Ausanio, Miller-Minor, Tracy-Akerfelds-Ausanio-Dalton, Tracy-Ausanio, Tracy-Minor, York-Akerfelds-Dalton, York-Akerfelds-Hall-Petkovsek, Buffalo; Eldred-Holmes, Green-Hunter, Green-Ignasiak, Green-Wishnevski-Kiefer-Valdez-Ignasiak, Kiefer-Holmes, Ruffin-Ignasiak-Lee-Wishnevski, Denver; Beatty-Young-Wainhouse, Bottenfield-Service, Bottenfield-Young, Haney-Farmer-Young, Landrum-Bottenfield, Myers-Maysey, Risley-Simons-Ridenour, Risley-Wainhouse, Simons-Maysey-Young, Simons-Service, Simons-Wainhouse, Indianapolis; Boskie-Pavlas, Hartsock-Renfroe, Hartsock-Renfroe-Melvin, Sebra-Slocumb, Sebra-Slocumb-Bullinger, Iowa; Arocha-Dixon, Arocha-Grater-Dixon-Sherrill, Arocha-Sherrill, Ballard-Cook, Kilgus-Grater, B. Smith-Hinkle-Sherrill, Urbani-Grater, Louisville; Hoffman-Hill, Minutelli-Fisher, Minutelli-Service, Service-Hoffman, Vierra-Bushing-Hill, Nashville; Fajardo-Barfield-Alexander-Bronkey, Pavlik-Blankenship, Pavlik-Blankenship-Rosenthal, Oklahoma City; Ahern-Moeller, Ahern-Roesler, Lambert-Manzanillo-Bautista-Shifflett, Manzanillo-Bautista, Manzanillo-Maldonado, Moeller-Maldonado-Shifflett, Sauveur-Johnston-Bautista, Omaha.

NO-HIT GAMES—None.

FIELDING

TEAM

Team	Pct.	G	PO	A	E	DP	PB	Team	Pct.	G	PO	A	E	DP	PB
Omaha	.977	144	3720	1595	123	144	17	Iowa	.974	143	3715	1527	139	139	21
Oklahoma City	.977	144	3805	1592	126	138	19	Louisville	.973	143	3663	1564	147	120	15
Indianapolis	.977	144	3721	1520	125	121	10	Denver	.973	144	3832	1671	155	137	13
Nashville	.975	144	3885	1540	137	146	9	Buffalo	.972	144	3779	1616	155	170	33

Triple plays—Oklahoma City, Omaha.

FIRST BASEMEN

*Throws lefthanded.

Player, Team	Pct.	G	PO	A	E	DP
Afenir, Nashville	.960	9	47	1	2	4
Aldrete, Louisville*	1.000	1	1	0	0	1
Allanson, Denver	1.000	9	72	7	0	10
Balboni, Oklahoma City	1.000	2	22	2	0	2
Beeler, Buffalo	1.000	3	21	0	0	1
Bradley, Nashville	.970	8	59	5	2	3
Brewer, Louisville*	.996	26	209	14	1	16
Bryant, Iowa	.991	52	414	32	4	42
Canseco, Louisville	1.000	1	5	0	0	0
Casillas, Omaha*	.994	18	158	21	1	14
Castellano, Iowa	1.000	1	9	0	0	4
Chance, Iowa	.983	7	56	1	1	4
Cianfrocco, Indianapolis	.954	8	59	3	3	4
Clark, Buffalo	.944	2	15	2	1	5
Colbrunn, Indianapolis	.992	50	441	27	4	34
Coles, Nashville	.983	6	52	5	1	7
Conine, Omaha	.995	92	813	60	4	81
Daugherty, Oklahoma City*	1.000	1	9	1	0	1
Dorsett, Buffalo	.986	52	400	33	6	52
Edge, Buffalo	1.000	1	1	0	0	0
Eppard, Indianapolis*	1.000	46	352	23	0	32
Escalera, Nashville*	1.000	5	27	2	0	2
Fernandez, Louisville	1.000	3	4	0	0	2
Fireovid, Oklahoma City	1.000	1	5	0	0	1
Galarraga, Louisville	.971	8	61	7	2	7
Goff, Indianapolis	1.000	7	53	2	0	3
Guerrero, Denver	.990	22	189	13	2	16
Hamelin, Omaha*	.988	25	230	13	3	20
Howie, Nashville	.988	9	72	7	1	6
Jaha, Denver	.990	75	652	50	7	50
King, Buffalo	1.000	3	17	1	0	1
Kremers, Indianapolis	1.000	2	7	0	0	2
Kunkel, 5 Den.-2 Iowa	1.000	7	68	7	0	6
Liddell, Denver	1.000	7	40	8	0	4
MAURER, Oklahoma City*	.994	123	1057	87	7	108
McGinnis, Oklahoma City	.992	13	111	7	1	4
Medina, Omaha*	1.000	12	113	12	0	16
Miller, Oklahoma City	.980	10	88	10	2	8
Montoyo, Denver	1.000	6	69	4	0	7
Morman, Nashville*	.990	97	771	54	8	80
Morris, Nashville*	1.000	2	13	3	0	3
Munoz, Indianapolis	1.000	2	11	0	0	1
Nilsson, Denver	.971	13	126	8	4	14
Pappas, Omaha	1.000	1	7	0	0	2
Paulino, Iowa	.981	50	375	34	8	34
Pedre, Iowa	1.000	5	16	3	0	3
Redfield, Buffalo	.991	26	219	5	2	26
Royer, Louisville	.992	107	947	70	8	80
Schulz, 6 Nash.-25 Iowa	.978	31	217	9	5	29
Shamburg, Denver	.980	16	134	11	3	9
Shines, Indianapolis	.994	44	330	18	2	27
Strange, Iowa	1.000	2	7	1	0	1
Tolentino, Buffalo*	.991	69	479	50	5	52
Trafton, Nashville	1.000	20	156	8	0	23
Trevino, Louisville	1.000	2	7	2	0	1
Villanueva, Iowa	.990	24	175	18	2	12
Wehner, Buffalo	1.000	11	118	3	0	5
Willard, Indianapolis	1.000	3	21	1	0	4
Williams, Denver	1.000	1	13	0	0	0
Wilson, Louisville	.941	3	15	1	1	0
Woodson, Louisville	1.000	2	15	1	0	1
Wrona, Nashville	1.000	2	16	0	0	2
Young, Buffalo	1.000	3	19	0	0	0

Triple plays—Conine, Maurer.

SECOND BASEMEN

Player, Team	Pct.	G	PO	A	E	DP
Abreu, Louisville	.833	1	3	2	1	0
Alicea, Louisville	.959	20	44	49	4	9
Arias, Iowa	.977	25	63	66	3	21
Barberie, Indianapolis	.944	7	21	13	2	4
Bates, Iowa	.988	75	163	167	4	52
Beanblossom, Louisville	1.000	1	0	5	0	0
Branson, Nashville	1.000	6	20	15	0	4
Capra, Nashville	1.000	5	4	4	0	0
Cole, Omaha	1.000	10	26	37	0	15
Coolbaugh, Nashville	1.000	1	0	0	0	0
Diaz, Denver	.967	10	29	29	2	11
Diaz, Oklahoma City	1.000	3	6	4	0	0
Duffy, Louisville	1.000	11	16	29	0	4
Edge, Buffalo	.959	27	55	61	5	17
Fanning, Iowa	1.000	5	5	3	0	2
Figueroa, Louisville	.981	39	70	84	3	15
Frye, Oklahoma City	.985	87	212	248	7	59
Fulton, Indianapolis	1.000	16	32	31	0	6
Garcia, Buffalo	1.000	9	21	22	0	8
Guerrero, Denver	1.000	6	12	13	0	4
Haney, Indianapolis	.975	55	113	161	7	32
Howie, Nashville	.976	25	50	70	3	19
Jackson, Oklahoma City	1.000	13	19	31	0	3
King, Buffalo	1.000	2	2	4	0	1
Kunkel, 26 Den.-3 Iowa	.963	29	63	91	6	14
Miller, Oklahoma City	.977	12	17	25	1	8
Montoyo, Denver	.975	39	61	93	4	19
Mota, Omaha	.983	94	172	232	7	53
Munoz, Indianapolis	.992	31	63	66	1	17
Oquendo, Louisville	1.000	6	12	13	0	4
Pedrique, Omaha	1.000	1	0	3	0	1
Pena, Louisville	.965	28	70	68	5	21
Redfield, Buffalo	.985	17	34	33	1	7
Richardson, Buffalo	.978	62	142	172	7	45
Sanchez, Iowa	1.000	5	9	17	0	4
Santangelo, Indianapolis	.990	50	99	100	2	24
Schreiber, Buffalo	.900	5	9	9	2	0
Shireman, Louisville	.970	46	93	101	6	31
Shumpert, Omaha	.981	44	94	115	4	32
SMALL, Nashville	.975	117	243	299	14	82
Strange, Iowa	.949	39	67	102	9	18
Suero, Denver	.975	74	178	214	10	53
Trevino, Louisville	1.000	1	1	0	0	0
Walewander, Oklahoma City	.972	40	68	107	5	18
Wehner, Buffalo	.967	41	101	102	7	34
Wilson, Louisville	.923	12	19	29	4	7
Woodson, Louisville	1.000	3	1	2	0	1

Triple plays—Cole, Frye.

THIRD BASEMEN

Player, Team	Pct.	G	PO	A	E	DP
Abreu, Louisville	1.000	2	0	1	0	0
Barberie, Indianapolis	1.000	2	3	4	0	0
Beanblossom, Louisville	.833	4	1	4	1	0
Beeler, Buffalo	1.000	1	0	1	0	0
BERRY, Omaha	.939	116	86	239	21	20
Branson, Nashville	.882	10	4	11	2	1
Castellano, Iowa	.943	67	34	132	10	9
Cianfrocco, Indianapolis	.867	7	3	10	2	0
Cole, Omaha	.897	10	4	22	3	1
Coles, Nashville	.922	17	17	30	4	3
Coolbaugh, Nashville	.927	56	36	116	12	11
Diaz, Oklahoma City	.842	6	7	9	3	0
Edge, Buffalo	.667	2	1	3	2	1
Figueroa, Louisville	.000	2	0	0	1	0
Fulton, Indianapolis	.944	63	27	125	9	7
Goff, Indianapolis	.896	71	50	139	22	10
Gonzalez, Nashville	.953	22	15	46	3	2
Guerrero, Denver	1.000	1	0	1	0	0
Hiatt, Omaha	.938	5	2	13	1	1
Howie, Nashville	.955	24	25	39	3	5
Jackson, Oklahoma City	.929	37	25	92	9	7
Kapano, Iowa	.917	5	6	5	1	0
King, Buffalo	1.000	4	2	7	0	0
Kunkel, Denver	.909	4	4	6	1	0
Lane, Nashville	.900	18	6	39	5	5
McGinnis, Oklahoma City	.890	55	28	117	18	8
Montoyo, Denver	.935	16	10	33	3	5
Morman, Nashville	1.000	4	2	5	0	0
Munoz, Indianapolis	.914	14	12	20	3	3
Nilsson, Denver	1.000	6	4	13	0	0
Pedre, Iowa	1.000	2	2	0	0	0
Pedrique, Omaha	.927	18	10	28	3	3
Postier, Oklahoma City	1.000	3	2	4	0	0
Presley, Oklahoma City	.937	47	39	95	9	10
Prince, Buffalo	.000	3	0	0	1	0
Redfield, Buffalo	.864	8	5	14	3	2
Royer, Louisville	.951	15	6	33	2	3
Santangelo, Indianapolis	.500	2	0	2	2	0
Schulz, Iowa	.885	6	4	19	3	0
Scott, Iowa	.964	56	34	100	5	5
Shines, Indianapolis	1.000	11	7	18	0	3
Shireman, Louisville	1.000	2	0	2	0	0
Small, Nashville	1.000	1	1	0	0	0
Spehr, Omaha	1.000	1	0	3	0	0
Strange, Iowa	.825	13	10	23	7	2
Tatum, Denver	.937	123	87	272	24	20
Trafton, Nashville	1.000	7	5	15	0	0
Walewander, Oklahoma City	1.000	1	1	1	0	0
Wehner, Buffalo	1.000	10	6	17	0	2
Wilson, Louisville	.889	3	0	8	1	0
Woodson, Louisville	.935	108	108	267	26	23
Wrona, Nashville	.500	2	0	1	1	0
Young, Buffalo	.927	127	104	300	32	41
Zeile, Louisville	.918	20	15	41	5	5

Triple play—Berry.

SHORTSTOPS

Player, Team	Pct.	G	PO	A	E	DP
Abreu, Louisville	.857	5	6	6	2	4
Alicea, Louisville	1.000	1	0	3	0	0
Arias, Iowa	.969	80	120	224	11	46
Barberie, Indianapolis	.800	1	1	3	1	0
Bell, Oklahoma City	.951	23	35	62	5	9
Branson, Nashville	.965	20	34	49	3	9
Carmona, Louisville	.932	59	40	138	13	15
Castellano, Iowa	1.000	1	0	1	0	0
Cianfrocco, Indianapolis	1.000	1	0	1	0	0
Cole, Omaha	.961	11	20	29	2	4
Cordero, Indianapolis	.948	52	75	146	12	26
Cromer, Louisville	1.000	6	13	20	0	4
Diaz, Denver	.900	2	4	5	1	2
Diaz, Nashville	.985	11	19	46	1	14
Diaz, Oklahoma City	.988	35	68	96	2	31
Duffy, Iowa	.913	11	18	24	4	9
Edge, Buffalo	.923	7	14	22	3	4
Fanning, Louisville	1.000	14	21	36	0	7
Fariss, Oklahoma City	1.000	1	1	2	0	0
Figueroa, Louisville	.965	63	92	185	10	22
Fulton, Indianapolis	.974	22	26	50	2	13
Garcia, Buffalo	.943	106	171	292	28	64
GREEN, Nashville	.961	101	134	289	17	60
Hanlon, Oklahoma City	.967	19	28	61	3	15
Howard, Omaha	.906	19	25	52	8	11
Howie, Nashville	.937	19	17	42	4	6
Jackson, Oklahoma City	.963	27	40	91	5	14
Kunkel, 6 Den.- 1 Iowa	.975	7	10	29	1	9
Miller, Oklahoma City	.922	25	36	71	9	7
Mota, Omaha	.962	32	36	116	6	23
Munoz, Indianapolis	.975	73	98	216	8	35
Oquendo, Louisville	.930	14	24	42	5	7
Pedrique, Omaha	.925	33	38	61	8	17
Postier, Oklahoma City	.972	26	38	68	3	14
Richardson, Buffalo	.975	36	53	102	4	18
Rossy, Omaha	.966	48	86	141	8	34
Sanchez, Iowa	.943	15	22	60	5	12
Santangelo, Indianapolis	1.000	4	3	7	0	1
Schreiber, Buffalo	.933	3	6	8	1	2
Scott, Iowa	.952	39	63	117	9	27
Shireman, Louisville	1.000	12	9	24	0	5
Shumpert, Omaha	.921	12	19	39	5	12
Small, Nashville	.919	9	13	21	3	4
Tovar, Indianapolis	1.000	1	2	4	0	1
Valentin, Denver	.941	138	187	414	38	70
Woodson, Louisville	1.000	1	1	1	0	0
Young, Buffalo	1.000	4	6	13	0	1

Triple play—Miller.

Player, Team	Pct.	G	PO	A	E	DP
Hillemann, Denver	1.000	15	25	0	0	0
Howie, Nashville	1.000	11	12	2	0	0
Hulse, Oklahoma City*	.929	8	13	0	1	0
Jackson, Oklahoma City	.992	56	120	2	1	2
Jackson, Denver	.965	83	127	9	5	0
Jaha, Denver	1.000	1	2	0	0	0
Jordan, Louisville	.989	41	89	3	1	0
Jose, Louisville	1.000	1	2	0	0	0
Koslofski, Omaha	.986	78	210	7	3	1
Kunkel, Denver	.981	25	49	2	1	1
Landrum, 4 Iowa - 38 Den.	.971	42	68	0	2	0
Long, Omaha*	.980	86	192	4	4	2
Mack, Indianapolis*	.994	85	163	4	1	2
Maclin, Louisville*	.967	70	115	1	4	0
Martin, Buffalo*	.967	113	222	10	8	6
May, Iowa	1.000	8	11	1	0	0
McDaniel, Nashville	1.000	6	2	0	0	0
Mieske, Denver	.955	131	252	23	13	4
Miller, Oklahoma City	.994	90	173	6	1	0
Montoyo, Denver	1.000	9	17	2	0	1
Mota, Omaha	1.000	4	7	0	0	0
Natal, Indianapolis	.941	10	15	1	1	0
Nelson, Indianapolis	.932	21	38	3	3	0
Olander, Denver	1.000	20	46	1	0	0
Pappas, Omaha	1.000	15	20	0	0	0
Pedrique, Omaha	1.000	5	6	0	0	0
Peltier, Oklahoma City*	.989	120	255	12	3	3
Pennyfeather, Buffalo	.979	48	92	3	2	0
Prince, Omaha	1.000	2	4	0	0	0
Pulliam, Omaha	.994	85	168	7	1	1
RAMSEY, Iowa	.997	130	342	6	1	0
Reed, Indianapolis	1.000	1	1	0	0	0
Roberson, Iowa	.957	51	87	1	4	1
Rohrmeier, Omaha	.944	7	17	0	1	0
Ryal, Oklahoma City*	1.000	4	3	0	0	0
Santangelo, Indianapolis	1.000	88	189	10	0	1
Schulz, 18 Nash.- 13 Iowa	.976	31	39	1	1	0
Scruggs, Oklahoma City	.970	44	94	2	3	1
Smith, Iowa	1.000	1	2	0	0	0
Sosa, Iowa	1.000	5	14	0	0	0
Stairs, Indianapolis	.985	104	188	11	3	2
Stone, Nashville	.949	25	36	1	2	0
Tatum, Denver	.750	2	3	0	1	0
Taylor, Nashville*	.976	65	118	4	3	2
Trafton, Nashville	1.000	13	19	1	0	1
Tubbs, Buffalo	.989	103	264	6	3	3
Wade, Iowa	.964	65	129	3	5	0
Walton, Iowa	1.000	6	10	0	0	0
Wehner, Buffalo	1.000	1	1	0	0	0
Williams, Denver	1.000	30	56	3	0	1
Wilson, Louisville	1.000	4	7	0	0	0
Woodson, Louisville	1.000	3	2	0	0	0
Wrona, Nashville	1.000	7	2	0	0	0
Zambrano, Buffalo	.996	114	235	15	1	5

OUTFIELDERS

Player, Team	Pct.	G	PO	A	E	DP
Afenir, Nashville	1.000	8	10	0	0	0
Allanson, Denver	.600	2	3	0	2	0
Ashley, Indianapolis	.964	55	104	3	4	0
Belcher, Oklahoma City	1.000	2	4	0	0	0
Berger, Oklahoma City	1.000	6	13	0	0	0
Berroa, Nashville	.977	108	194	16	5	0
Bradley, Iowa	1.000	33	62	4	0	2
Branson, Nashville	1.000	3	1	1	0	0
Brantley, Nashville	.972	56	99	4	3	1
Brewer, Louisville*	.981	94	190	13	4	4
Brower, Oklahoma City	.989	72	170	5	2	2
Brumfield, Nashville	.959	54	137	4	6	0
Bryant, Iowa	.941	31	44	4	3	2
Bullett, Buffalo*	1.000	3	7	0	0	0
Bullock, Indianapolis*	.960	82	140	4	6	1
Canseco, Louisville	.941	66	111	13	5	3
Capra, Nashville	.977	79	166	6	4	3
Carr, Louisville	.981	93	244	9	5	3
Casillas, Omaha*	.992	70	109	13	1	2
Chance, Iowa	.990	103	180	13	2	5
Christian, Louisville	.947	11	17	1	1	0
Clark, Buffalo	.970	70	156	4	5	2
Cole, Omaha	1.000	32	51	3	0	0
Conine, Omaha	.941	18	32	0	2	0
Daugherty, Oklahoma City*	1.000	6	7	0	0	0
Davis, Oklahoma City	.667	2	2	0	1	0
DeLosSantos, Buffalo	1.000	6	10	0	0	0
Diaz, Denver	.982	95	207	9	4	2
Eppard, Indianapolis*	1.000	18	24	1	0	0
Escalera, Nashville	.960	33	45	3	2	0
Fariss, Oklahoma City	1.000	41	113	3	0	0
Fernandez, Louisville	1.000	1	2	0	0	0
Ford, Louisville	.973	69	137	6	4	1
Garcia, Omaha*	.968	60	112	8	4	2
Green, Buffalo	1.000	5	8	0	0	0
Guerrero, Louisville	1.000	4	6	0	0	0
Haselman, Oklahoma City	.929	10	12	1	1	1
Hernandez, Nashville	.500	1	1	0	1	0

CATCHERS

Player, Team	Pct.	G	PO	A	E	DP	PB
Afenir, Nashville	.991	18	103	11	1	1	3
Allanson, Denver	.996	33	204	23	1	4	3
Beeler, Buffalo	.952	21	72	8	4	2	9
Bradley, Iowa	.952	5	20	0	1	0	0
Davis, Oklahoma City	.988	59	306	30	4	5	7
Diaz, Omaha	1.000	18	92	6	0	0	3
Dorsett, Buffalo	.994	64	289	36	2	9	14
Fernandez, Louisville	.987	12	67	7	1	2	2
Fletcher, Indianapolis	.986	11	65	7	1	0	2
Fulton, Louisville	.99272	75	374	35	3	5	6
Goff, Indianapolis	.949	8	33	4	2	0	0
Haselman, Oklahoma City	.951	8	33	6	2	0	2
Kmak, Denver	.993	63	351	54	3	6	7
Knapp, Iowa	.985	51	237	31	4	4	3
Kremers, Indianapolis	.975	45	210	25	6	1	2
Liddell, Denver	.986	29	128	11	2	3	3
McGinnis, Oklahoma City	.976	34	181	24	5	4	4
Natal, Indianapolis	.992	79	453	53	4	4	4
Nilsson, Denver	.992	36	220	30	2	1	0
Pappas, Omaha	.978	25	115	16	3	2	5
PEDRE, Iowa	.99277	78	361	51	3	7	13
Prince, Buffalo	.981	71	303	50	7	12	10
Redman, Louisville	.952	4	19	1	1	1	1
Reed, Nashville	1.000	7	47	4	0	0	0
Slaught, Buffalo	1.000	2	15	3	0	1	0
Spehr, Omaha	.989	106	577	62	7	10	9
Stephens, Oklahoma City	1.000	54	267	24	0	3	4
Taylor, Iowa	1.000	1	0	0	0	0	0
Trevino, Louisville	.988	70	303	29	4	4	6
Villanueva, Iowa	.973	11	64	8	2	0	2
Wilkins, Iowa	.990	29	177	18	2	5	3
Willard, Indianapolis	.976	20	114	10	3	3	2
Wilson, Nashville	.990	104	733	69	8	7	2
Wrona, Nashville	.977	27	162	11	4	1	4

Player, Team	Pct.	G	PO	A	E	DP
Adkins, Iowa*	.917	33	2	20	2	0
Ahern, Omaha	.966	17	10	18	1	1
Akerfelds, 24 O.C.-24 Buf.	.929	48	2	11	1	1
Alexander, Oklahoma City	.960	38	7	17	1	1
Alvarez, Nashville	1.000	3	1	1	0	0
Aquino, Omaha	1.000	2	0	2	0	0
Arner, Oklahoma City	1.000	4	2	4	0	0
Arnsberg, Iowa	.864	20	7	12	3	3
Arocha, Louisville	.909	25	8	22	3	1
Ausanio, Buffalo	.933	53	1	13	1	0
Backlund, Buffalo	1.000	4	0	1	0	0
BALLARD, Louisville*	1.000	24	10	23	0	3
Barfield, Oklahoma City*	1.000	42	3	15	0	0
Barnes, Indianapolis*	1.000	13	5	12	0	0
Bautista, Omaha	1.000	40	13	9	0	1
Beatty, Indianapolis*	1.000	26	4	15	0	2
Blankenship, Oklahoma City	.889	32	8	16	3	3
Bohanon, Oklahoma City*	1.000	9	1	6	0	0
Boskie, Iowa	1.000	2	1	0	0	0
Bottenfield, Indianapolis	.938	25	10	20	2	4
Brennan, Iowa	1.000	19	1	8	0	1
Brito, Indianapolis	1.000	2	0	2	0	0
Bronkey, Oklahoma City	1.000	13	2	4	0	2
Brown, Nashville	.974	26	10	27	1	2
Brown, Oklahoma City	.778	7	3	4	2	1
Buchanan, Nashville*	1.000	10	2	11	0	2
Bullinger, Iowa	1.000	20	4	4	0	0
Burns, Oklahoma City	1.000	8	3	1	0	0
Bushing, Nashville	1.000	5	1	1	0	1
Campbell, Omaha*	1.000	20	3	17	0	1
Campbell, Oklahoma City	.800	11	2	2	1	0
Capra, Nashville	1.000	1	0	1	0	0
Carman, Oklahoma City*	.857	20	6	6	2	1
Cerutti, Buffalo*	1.000	9	6	11	0	2
Chiamparino, Oklahoma City	1.000	5	2	2	0	1
Clark, Omaha	.867	9	4	9	2	1
Clark, Louisville	1.000	9	0	10	0	0
Cole, Buffalo	.929	19	6	20	2	2
Cook, Louisville	.900	43	6	3	1	0
Cooke, Buffalo*	.700	13	1	6	3	0
Cormier, Louisville*	1.000	1	0	2	0	0
Cox, Buffalo	1.000	8	4	5	0	0
Dalton, Buffalo*	.944	56	5	12	1	0
Diaz, Indianapolis	1.000	1	0	1	0	0
DiPino, Louisville*	.500	18	0	2	2	0
Dixon, Louisville	1.000	18	1	2	0	2
Dixon, Buffalo	1.000	26	4	11	0	1
Drees, Oklahoma City*	1.000	12	0	5	0	0
Drummond, Nashville	.000	3	0	0	1	0
ELDRED, Denver	1.000	19	13	20	0	0
Elvira, Oklahoma City*	1.000	19	5	17	0	0
Farmer, Indianapolis	1.000	30	3	16	0	2
Fireovid, Oklahoma City	1.000	33	4	19	0	1
Fisher, Nashville	1.000	29	5	6	0	0
Foster, Nashville	.889	17	3	5	1	1
Gardner, Iowa	.886	38	16	15	4	3
George, Denver	.750	12	4	5	3	1
Gleaton, Buffalo*	1.000	5	0	2	0	1
Gore, Oklahoma City*	1.000	6	1	4	0	1
Grater, Louisville	1.000	54	4	24	0	2
Green, Denver*	.962	28	7	18	1	0
Hall, Buffalo*	1.000	16	0	6	0	0
Hancock, Buffalo*	1.000	10	2	3	0	0
Haney, Indianapolis*	1.000	15	3	10	0	2
Harkey, Iowa	.833	4	0	5	1	0
Hartsock, Iowa	.949	27	8	29	2	2
Heaton, Denver*	1.000	6	3	1	0	1
Heredia, Indianapolis	1.000	3	1	0	0	0
Higuera, Denver*	1.000	2	0	3	0	0
Hill, Nashville	1.000	53	5	6	0	0
Hinkle, Louisville	.786	38	0	11	3	0
Hoffman, Nashville	1.000	42	0	9	0	2
Holmes, Denver	1.000	12	1	3	0	0
Huismann, Omaha	.949	29	8	29	2	1
Hunter, Denver	.939	34	12	19	2	2
Hurst, Indianapolis	1.000	23	3	21	0	0
Ignasiak, Denver	1.000	62	8	14	0	2
Ilsley, Louisville*	1.000	33	5	10	0	0
Jackson, Oklahoma City	1.000	1	1	0	0	0

Player, Team	Pct.	G	PO	A	E	DP	PB
Jeffcoat, Oklahoma City*	1.000	7	1	8	0	1	
Johnston, Omaha	1.000	42	1	14	0	1	
Jones, Louisville	1.000	3	0	2	0	0	
Kiefer, Denver	.959	27	18	29	2	1	
Kilgus, Louisville*	.953	27	10	31	2	1	
Kutzler, Iowa	1.000	2	1	1	0	0	
LaCoss, Indianapolis	1.000	7	0	4	0	0	
Lambert, Omaha*	1.000	11	1	12	0	0	
Landrum, Indianapolis	.667	14	1	1	1	0	
Lee, Denver*	1.000	48	3	11	0	0	
Leon, Oklahoma City	1.000	3	0	1	0	0	
Loynd, Louisville	1.000	11	1	3	0	0	
Lynch, Nashville*	1.000	1	1	0	0	0	
Magrane, Louisville*	1.000	10	4	13	0	0	
Maldonado, Omaha	.900	47	5	13	2	1	
Manuel, Oklahoma City	.857	27	1	5	1	0	
Manzanillo, Omaha	.975	26	11	28	1	3	
Marak, Iowa	.947	9	8	10	1	2	
Mathews, Oklahoma City	1.000	9	0	5	0	0	
May, Iowa	.667	17	3	5	4	0	
Maysey, Indianapolis	1.000	35	4	14	0	1	
McClellan, Denver	1.000	9	1	10	0	1	
McCullers, Oklahoma City	1.000	13	1	4	0	1	
Melvin, Iowa	1.000	18	1	3	0	0	
Menendez, Nashville	.966	50	7	21	1	1	
Milchin, Louisville*	1.000	12	2	3	0	0	
Miller, Buffalo	.875	8	3	4	1	0	
Minor, Buffalo	.962	45	6	19	1	1	
Minutelli, Nashville*	.933	29	6	22	2	2	
Miranda, Denver*	.860	28	9	28	6	3	
Moeller, Omaha*	.950	23	3	16	1	0	
Nolte, Denver*	.875	49	3	11	2	0	
Patterson, Iowa*	1.000	1	0	1	0	0	
Pavlas, Iowa	.833	12	2	3	1	0	
Pavlik, Oklahoma City	.955	18	9	12	1	0	
Petkovsek, Buffalo	.977	32	11	31	1	3	
Piatt, Indianapolis	1.000	8	2	2	0	0	
Powell, Nashville*	1.000	25	2	8	0	1	
Pugh, Nashville	1.000	27	13	17	0	0	
Rasmussen, 2 Iowa-11 Oma.*	.944	13	3	14	1	1	
Reed, Omaha	1.000	11	4	8	0	0	
Renfroe, Iowa	1.000	61	8	24	0	3	
Ridenour, Indianapolis	1.000	30	2	9	0	0	
Risley, Indianapolis	.933	25	5	9	1	1	
Robinson, Iowa	1.000	10	0	2	0	0	
Roesler, 34 Buf.-11 Oma.	1.000	45	5	9	0	0	
Rojas, Indianapolis	1.000	4	0	1	0	0	
Rosenthal, Oklahoma City	1.000	57	6	5	0	1	
Ruffin, Denver*	1.000	4	0	2	0	0	
Salles, Iowa	.950	19	4	15	1	0	
Sampen, Indianapolis	1.000	2	0	1	0	0	
Sanford, Nashville	1.000	25	5	16	0	0	
Sauveur, Omaha*	.967	34	4	25	1	1	
Sebra, 9 O.C.-17 Iowa	.941	26	8	8	1	0	
Segura, Nashville	1.000	22	1	3	0	0	
Service, 13 Ind.-39 Nash.	.941	52	4	12	1	1	
Shaw, Oklahoma City*	.909	13	5	15	2	0	
Sherrill, Louisville*	.923	51	6	6	1	0	
Shifflett, Omaha	.895	32	3	14	2	0	
Simons, Indianapolis*	1.000	32	7	22	0	0	
Slocumb, Iowa	1.000	36	0	10	0	1	
Smith, Louisville	1.000	2	0	4	0	0	
Solis, Indianapolis*	1.000	2	1	3	0	1	
Strauss, Iowa	1.000	22	3	4	0	0	
Tafoya, Buffalo	1.000	5	1	1	0	0	
Tracy, Buffalo	1.000	29	9	18	0	0	
Urbani, Louisville*	.933	16	3	11	1	0	
Valdez, Denver*	1.000	36	1	12	0	0	
Valdez, Indianapolis	.864	13	7	12	3	1	
Vierra, Nashville*	1.000	52	6	17	0	1	
Wagner, Buffalo	1.000	8	4	2	0	1	
Wainhouse, Indianapolis	.900	44	3	6	1	3	
Wakefield, Buffalo	.949	20	10	27	2	5	
Watson, Louisville*	1.000	2	0	2	0	0	
Wendell, Iowa	1.000	4	3	7	0	0	
Whiteside, Oklahoma City	1.000	12	0	1	0	0	
Willis, Iowa	1.000	3	1	4	0	1	
Wishnevski, Denver	1.000	44	6	9	0	2	
York, Buffalo	1.000	6	1	4	0	0	
Young, Indianapolis	1.000	36	3	10	0	0	
Young, Omaha*	1.000	2	0	2	0	1	

The following players did not have any fielding statistics at the positions indicated or appeared only as a designated hitter, pinch-hitter or pinch-runner: Berrios, p; Burrows, p; Chance, p; Dickson, p; Dobrolsky, ph; Edge, of, c, p; Eppard, p; Fajardo, p; Grewal, p; Kremers, p; Kunkel, p; Lamp, p; Maize, ph; Myers, p; Pedrique, p; Richardson, 3b; Rodriguez, p; Sabo, dh; Shireman, p; Simmons, dh, ph; Tolentino, of.

Year	Team	Pct.
1902—	Indianapolis	.683
1903—	St. Paul	.657
1904—	St. Paul	.646
1905—	Columbus	.658
1906—	Columbus	.615
1907—	Columbus	.584
1908—	Indianapolis	.601
1909—	Louisville	.554
1910—	Minneapolis	.637
1911—	Minneapolis	.600
1912—	Minneapolis	.636
1913—	Milwaukee	.599
1914—	Milwaukee	.590
1915—	Minneapolis	.597
1916—	Louisville	.605
1917—	Indianapolis	.588
1918—	Kansas City	.589
1919—	St. Paul	.610
1920—	St. Paul	.701
1921—	Louisville	.583
1922—	St. Paul	.641
1923—	Kansas City	.675
1924—	St. Paul	.578
1925—	Louisville	.635
1926—	Louisville	.629
1927—	Toledo	.601
1928—	Indianapolis	.593
1929—	Kansas City	.665
1930—	Louisville	.608
1931—	St. Paul	.623
1932—	Minneapolis	.595
1933—	Columbus*	.604
	Minneapolis	.562
1934—	Minneapolis	.570
	Columbus*	.556
1935—	Minneapolis	.591
1936—	Milwaukee†	.584
1937—	Columbus†	.584
1938—	St. Paul	.596
	Kansas City (2nd)‡	.556
1939—	Kansas City	.695
	Louisville (4th)‡	.490
1940—	Kansas City	.625
	Louisville (4th)‡	.500

Year	Team	Pct.
1941—	Columbus†	.621
1942—	Kansas City	.549
	Columbus (3rd)‡	.532
1943—	Milwaukee	.596
	Columbus (3rd)‡	.532
1944—	Milwaukee	.667
	Louisville (3rd)‡	.574
1945—	Milwaukee	.604
	Louisville (3rd)‡	.545
1946—	Louisville†	.601
1947—	Kansas City	.608
	Milwaukee (3rd)†	.513
1948—	Indianapolis	.649
	St. Paul (3rd)‡	.558
1949—	St. Paul	.608
	Indianapolis (2nd)‡	.604
1950—	Minneapolis	.584
	Columbus (3rd)‡	.549
1951—	Milwaukee†	.623
1952—	Milwaukee	.656
	Kansas City (2nd)‡	.578
1953—	Toledo	.584
	Kansas City (2nd)‡	.571
1954—	Indianapolis	.625
	Loiusville (2nd)‡	.556
1955—	Minneapolis†	.597
1956—	Indianapolis†	.597
1957—	Wichita	.604
	Denver (2nd)†	.584
1958—	Charleston	.589
	Minneapolis (3rd)‡	.536
1959—	Louisville§	.599
	Omaha§	.516
	Minneapolis (2nd)‡	.586
1960—	Denver	.571
	Louisville (2nd)‡	.556
1961—	Indianapolis	.573
	Louisville (2nd)‡	.533
1962—	Indianapolis	.605
	Louisville (4th)‡	.486
1963-1968—Did not operate.		
1969—	Omaha	.607
1970—	Omaha*	.529
	Denver	.504

Year	Team	Pct.
1971—	Indianapolis	.604
	Denver*	.521
1972—	Wichita	.621
	Evansville*	.593
1973—	Iowa	.610
	Tulsa*	.504
1974—	Indianapolis	.578
	Tulsa*	.567
1975—	Evansville*	.566
	Denver	.596
1976—	Denver*	.632
	Omaha	.574
1977—	Omaha	.563
	Denver*	.522
1978—	Indianapolis	.578
	Omaha*	.489
1979—	Evansville*	.574
	Oklahoma City	.533
1980—	Omaha	.676
	Springfield*	.551
1981—	Omaha	.581
	Denver*	.559
1982—	Indianapolis*	.551
	Omaha	.518
1983—	Louisville	.578
	Denver‡	.545
1984—	Denver	.513
	Louisville‡	.510
1985—	Oklahoma City	.556
	Louisville*	.521
1986—	Indianapolis*	.563
	Denver	.535
1987—	Denver	.564
	Indianapolis‡	.536
1988—	Indianapolis*	.627
	Omaha	.570
1989—	Indianapolis*	.596
	Omaha	.507
1990—	Omaha*	.589
	Nashville	.585
1991—	Buffalo	.566
	Denver*	.549
1992—	Buffalo	.604
	Oklahoma City*	.514

*Won playoff (East vs. West). †Won championship and four-team playoff. ‡Won four-team playoff. §Respective Eastern and Western division winners.

INTERNATIONAL LEAGUE

FINAL STANDINGS

EASTERN DIVISION

Team	W	L	T	Pct.	GB
Scranton-Wilkes Barre (Phillies)	84	58	0	.592	......
Pawtucket (Red Sox)	71	72	0	.497	13½
Rochester (Orioles)	70	74	0	.486	15
Syracuse (Blue Jays)	60	83	0	.420	24½

WESTERN DIVISION

Team	W	L	T	Pct.	GB
Columbus (Yankees)	95	49	0	.660	......
Richmond (Braves)	73	71	0	.507	22
Toledo (Tigers)	64	80	0	.444	31
Tidewater (Mets)	56	86	0	.394	38

COMPOSITE

Team	Col.	SWB	Rich.	Paw.	Roc.	Tol.	Syr.	Tide.	W	L	T	Pct.	GB
Columbus (Yankees)	...	14	16	12	16	11	14	12	95	49	0	.660	......
Scranton-Wilkes Barre (Phillies)	6	....	14	14	10	10	15	15	84	58	0	.592	10
Richmond (Braves)	4	6	....	9	13	13	14	14	73	71	0	.507	22
Pawtucket (Red Sox)	8	10	11	....	10	11	7	14	71	72	0	.497	23½
Rochester (Orioles)	4	10	7	10	....	14	13	12	70	74	0	.486	25
Toledo (Tigers)	13	10	7	9	6	....	10	9	64	80	0	.444	31
Syracuse (Blue Jays)	6	5	6	12	11	10	....	10	60	83	0	.420	34½
Tidewater (Mets)	8	3	10	6	8	11	10	....	56	86	0	.394	38

Tidewater club represented Norfolk and Portsmouth, Va.

Major league affiliations in parentheses.

Playoffs—Columbus defeated Richmond, three games to none; Scranton-Wilkes Barre defeated Pawtucket, three games to one; Columbus defeated Scranton-Wilkes Barre, three games to two, to win league championship.

Regular-season attendance—Columbus, 583,918; Pawtucket, 358,318; Richmond, 453,915; Rochester, 305,199; Scranton-Wilkes Barre, 560,464; Syracuse, 269,067; Tidewater, 174,362; Toledo, 242,442. Total—2,947,685. Playoffs (12 games)—70,723. Class AAA All-Star Game at Richmond—12,186.

Managers—Columbus, Rick Down; Pawtucket, Rico Petrocelli; Richmond, Chris Chambliss; Rochester, Jerry Narron; Scranton-Wilkes Barre, Lee Elia; Syracuse, Nick Leyva; Tidewater, Clint Hurdle; Toledo, Joe Sparks.

All-Star team: 1B—J.T. Snow, Columbus; 2B—Steve Scarsone, Scranton-Wilkes Barre/Rochester; 3B—Hensley Meulens, Columbus; SS—Dave Silvestri, Columbus; OF—Butch Davis, Syracuse; Bernie Williams, Columbus; Gerald Williams, Columbus; C—Rich Rowland, Toledo; DH—Torey Lovullo, Columbus; Starting Pitcher—Sam Militello, Columbus; Relief Pitcher—Mike Draper, Columbus; Most Valuable Player—J.T. Snow, Columbus; Most Valuable Pitcher—Sam Militello, Columbus; Rookie of the Year—J.T. Snow, Columbus; Manager of the Year—Lee Elia, Scranton-Wilkes Barre.

BATTING

TEAM

Team	Avg.	G	AB	R	OR	H	TB	2B	3B	HR	RBI	SH	SF	HP	BB	Int. BB	SO	SB	CS	LOB
Columbus	.274	144	4763	768	544	1305	2017	237	47	127	712	23	51	32	572	30	897	188	80	935
Rochester	.274	144	4750	686	618	1301	1865	225	33	91	623	37	44	40	509	18	869	152	67	1003
Richmond	.259	144	4757	611	553	1233	1829	230	27	104	553	47	35	40	446	26	869	82	62	986
Syracuse	.255	144	4792	580	717	1221	1889	220	35	126	541	38	37	39	476	27	870	63	31	1029
Tidewater	.255	142	4569	517	623	1163	1660	195	16	90	470	40	32	34	354	17	945	102	49	892
Toledo	.251	144	4683	557	673	1175	1708	184	23	101	518	39	36	31	388	24	830	118	65	895
Scranton WB	.250	142	4552	590	499	1136	1697	221	38	88	533	50	30	41	454	31	838	88	58	954
Pawtucket	.246	143	4652	581	663	1146	1753	226	30	107	537	49	38	30	505	28	876	66	47	986

INDIVIDUAL

(Leading qualifiers for batting championship—389 or more plate appearances)

*Bats lefthanded.   †Switch-hitter.

Player, Team	Avg.	G	AB	R	H	TB	2B	3B	HR	RBI	SH	SF	HP	BB	Int. BB	SO	SB	CS
Snow, J.T., Columbus†	.313	135	492	81	154	233	26	4	15	78	1	6	1	70	11	65	3	3
Mercedes, Luis, Rochester	.313	103	409	62	128	154	15	1	3	29	3	3	1	44	2	56	35	14
Schu, Rick, Scranton W.B.	.310	111	400	56	124	178	18	3	10	49	0	1	4	45	5	62	3	1
McKnight, Jeff, Tidewater†	.307	102	352	43	108	143	21	1	4	43	1	1	1	51	3	52	3	3
Williams, Bernie, Columbus†	.306	95	363	68	111	176	23	9	8	50	1	6	1	52	5	61	20	8
Shields, Tommy, Rochester	.302	121	431	58	130	189	23	3	10	59	4	4	6	30	1	72	13	7
Carter, Steve, Toledo*	.300	130	470	56	141	194	22	2	9	58	0	4	4	25	2	66	12	5
Lovullo, Torey, Columbus†	.295	131	468	69	138	238	33	5	19	89	2	6	3	64	4	65	9	4
Manto, Jeff, Richmond	.291	127	450	65	131	196	24	1	13	68	0	7	7	57	4	63	1	2
Twardoski, Mike, Pawtucket*	.290	121	389	55	113	183	23	4	13	49	9	6	1	92	4	56	1	5
Springer, Steve, Tidewater	.290	117	427	57	124	188	16	0	16	70	0	3	0	22	1	85	9	4

Departmental leaders: G—G. Williams, 142; AB—Davis, 550; R—Meulens, 96; H—G. Williams, 156; TB—Meulens, 257; 2B—Lovullo, 33; 3B—Davis, B. Williams, 9; HR—Meulens, 26; RBI—Meulens, 100; SH—Schunk, 12; SF—Manto, 7; HP—Quinlan, 10; BB—Twardoski, 92; IBB—Snow, 11; SO—Meulens, 168; SB—Humphreys, 37; CS—Caraballo, 16.

(All players—listed alphabetically)

Player, Team	Avg.	G	AB	R	H	TB	2B	3B	HR	RBI	SH	SF	HP	BB	Int. BB	SO	SB	CS
Abbott, Kyle, Scranton W.B.*	.000	5	4	0	0	0	0	0	0	0	0	0	0	0	0	3	0	0
Aguayo, Luis, Pawtucket	.255	80	231	31	59	92	16	1	5	36	3	4	7	30	2	36	1	1
Alexander, Gary, Scranton W.B.	.202	120	401	54	81	145	26	4	12	53	1	3	2	40	1	86	0	0
Alexander, Manny, Rochester	.292	6	24	3	7	8	1	0	0	3	1	0	0	1	0	3	2	2
Allaire, Karl, Toledo*	.255	137	479	68	122	160	18	1	6	45	7	3	1	60	3	68	11	6
Allison, Tom, Tidewater†	.400	5	10	4	4	7	1	1	0	1	0	0	0	2	0	0	0	0
Amaro, Ruben, Scranton W.B.†	.294	18	68	8	20	29	4	1	1	10	0	0	0	9	3	6	2	2
Ausmus, Brad, Columbus	.242	111	364	48	88	114	14	3	2	35	3	2	1	40	0	56	19	5
Baez, Kevin, Tidewater	.236	109	352	30	83	107	16	1	2	33	5	5	4	13	1	57	1	1

Player, Team	Avg.	G	AB	R	H	TB	2B	3B	HR	RBI	SH	SF	HP	BB	Int. BB	SO	SB	CS
Bark, Brian, Richmond*	.200	22	5	0	1	1	0	0	0	0	1	0	0	0	0	2	0	0
Barrett, Tom, Pawtucket†	.254	91	323	55	82	111	18	4	1	21	6	2	3	52	1	31	13	9
Batiste, Kim, Scranton W.B.	.260	71	269	30	70	100	12	6	2	29	2	0	1	7	1	42	6	5
Bell, Juan, Rochester†	.196	39	138	21	27	45	6	3	2	14	2	3	0	14	0	40	2	4
Bethea, Scott, Pawtucket*	.067	7	15	1	1	1	0	0	0	2	0	1	0	4	0	3	0	0
Birkbeck, Mike, Tidewater	.300	21	10	0	3	3	0	0	0	1	2	0	0	1	0	3	0	0
Blosser, Greg, Pawtucket*	.000	1	0	0	0	0	0	0	0	0	0	0	0	1	0	0	0	0
Bogar, Tim, Tidewater	.279	129	481	54	134	183	32	1	5	38	5	0	3	14	1	65	7	7
Bradley, Scott, Tidewater*	.207	35	111	8	23	27	1	0	1	7	0	0	1	7	1	9	0	1
Brady, Pat, Scranton W.B.	.000	3	9	0	0	0	0	0	0	1	0	0	0	2	0	1	0	0
Brink, Brad, Scranton W.B.	.125	17	8	0	1	1	0	0	0	0	0	0	0	1	0	2	0	0
Brogna, Rico, Toledo*	.261	121	387	45	101	158	19	4	10	58	4	5	1	31	2	85	1	1
Brumley, Mike, Pawtucket†	.263	101	365	50	96	134	16	5	4	41	3	6	1	37	0	76	14	6
Buford, Damon, Rochester	.284	45	155	29	44	61	10	2	1	12	2	1	1	14	0	23	23	4
Burnitz, Jeromy, Tidewater*	.243	121	445	56	108	159	21	3	8	40	2	3	3	33	2	84	30	7
Byrd, Jim, Pawtucket	.224	72	246	27	55	68	5	1	2	18	4	0	4	7	0	48	2	3
Cabrera, Francisco, Richmond	.272	81	301	30	82	120	11	0	9	35	0	1	0	17	2	49	0	1
Cangelosi, John, Toledo†	.270	27	74	9	20	23	3	0	0	6	0	0	4	7	0	13	11	4
Capra, Nick, Scranton W.B.	.286	18	56	12	16	22	3	0	1	3	1	0	0	10	1	7	3	2
Caraballo, Ramon, Richmond†	.281	101	405	42	114	146	20	3	2	40	7	1	3	22	1	60	19	16
Carey, Paul, Rochester*	.230	30	87	9	20	29	4	1	1	7	0	1	2	6	0	16	0	0
Carter, Steve, Toledo*	.300	130	470	56	141	194	22	2	9	58	0	4	4	25	2	66	12	5
Castilla, Vinny, Richmond	.252	127	449	49	113	165	29	1	7	44	3	6	4	21	1	68	1	2
Castillo, Braulio, Scranton W.B.	.246	105	386	59	95	165	21	5	13	47	2	4	4	40	1	96	8	4
Cedeno, Domingo, Syracuse†	.193	18	57	4	11	15	4	0	0	5	2	0	0	3	0	14	0	0
Chamberlain, Wes, Scranton W.B.	.331	34	127	16	42	64	6	2	4	26	1	2	2	11	0	13	6	2
Cinnella, Doug, Tidewater	.000	10	1	0	0	0	0	0	0	0	0	0	0	0	0	1	0	0
Clark, Phil, Toledo	.280	79	271	29	76	126	20	0	10	39	1	2	2	16	0	35	4	2
Clayton, Royal, Columbus	.000	37	1	0	0	0	0	0	0	0	0	0	0	0	0	1	0	0
Coffman, Kevin, Richmond	.250	16	12	0	3	4	1	0	0	0	1	0	0	0	0	4	0	0
Combs, Pat, Scranton W.B.*	.214	21	14	2	3	6	1	1	0	2	1	0	0	0	0	4	0	0
Cook, Andy, Columbus	.000	32	0	0	0	0	0	0	0	0	1	0	0	0	0	0	0	0
Crabbe, Bruce, Syracuse	.236	60	157	14	37	55	4	1	4	13	3	1	1	28	0	25	2	2
Cuevas, Johnny, Richmond	.000	3	6	1	0	0	0	0	0	0	0	0	0	2	0	3	0	0
Davis, Butch, Syracuse	.280	134	550	67	154	230	31	9	9	74	2	5	2	33	4	77	19	6
Deak, Brian, Richmond	.261	79	238	46	62	102	13	0	9	36	0	2	5	57	3	59	0	1
Decillis, Dean, Toledo	.246	86	268	23	66	79	7	0	2	16	3	0	2	15	2	37	0	3
DeJardin, Bobby, Columbus†	.238	124	416	51	99	128	14	3	3	42	8	6	1	40	1	80	13	6
Dellicarri, Joe, Tidewater	.250	5	16	1	4	7	0	0	1	1	0	0	0	1	0	3	0	0
Dickerson, Bobby, Rochester	.241	86	249	28	60	85	7	3	4	29	3	0	1	11	0	43	1	3
Donnels, Chris, Tidewater*	.301	81	279	35	84	120	15	3	5	32	3	2	0	58	1	45	12	1
Dostal, Bruce, Scranton W.B.*	.220	65	168	32	37	47	7	0	1	7	2	0	1	45	4	35	10	4
Dozier, D.J., Tidewater	.234	64	197	32	46	81	8	3	7	25	1	2	2	37	3	55	6	3
Draper, Mike, Columbus	.000	58	1	0	0	0	0	0	0	0	0	0	0	0	0	1	0	0
Dziadkowiec, Andy, Tidewater*	.243	11	37	2	9	10	1	0	0	2	0	0	1	0	0	10	0	1
Esasky, Nick, Richmond	.278	30	108	12	30	51	6	0	5	14	0	1	1	9	0	31	1	0
Eufemia, Frank, Tidewater	.000	11	3	0	0	0	0	0	0	0	0	0	0	0	0	1	0	0
Filer, Tom, Tidewater	.059	18	17	2	1	1	0	0	0	0	2	0	0	1	0	4	0	0
Flaherty, John, Pawtucket	.250	31	104	11	26	29	3	0	0	7	1	0	1	5	0	8	0	0
Fletcher, Paul, Scranton W.B.	.000	4	4	0	0	0	0	0	0	0	0	0	0	0	0	3	0	0
Gallagher, Dave, Tidewater	.250	3	12	1	3	3	0	0	0	0	0	0	0	3	0	2	0	1
Geren, Bob, Pawtucket	.207	66	213	28	44	78	7	0	9	25	0	0	3	17	3	53	0	2
Giannelli, Ray, Syracuse*	.229	84	249	23	57	85	9	2	5	22	0	2	0	48	2	44	2	2
Gomez, Pat, Syracuse*	.400	23	5	1	2	2	0	0	0	2	2	0	0	0	0	2	0	0
Gonzalez, Denny, Pawtucket	.191	18	47	2	9	14	2	0	1	3	0	1	0	6	0	18	0	0
Gonzalez, Javier, Tidewater	.208	39	120	9	25	41	4	0	4	12	2	0	2	4	0	33	0	0
Gonzalez, Jose, Scranton W.B.	.171	16	41	10	7	14	4	0	1	3	0	1	0	7	0	10	3	1
Gonzalez, Pedro, Toledo	.118	9	17	1	2	4	2	0	0	1	0	0	0	1	0	3	0	0
Greene, Tommy, Scranton W.B.	.500	5	2	0	1	1	0	0	0	0	1	0	0	0	0	0	0	0
Gregg, Tommy, Richmond*	.288	39	125	17	36	49	9	2	0	12	0	1	1	19	1	27	3	1
Grotewold, Jeff, Scranton W.B.*	.294	17	51	8	15	21	1	1	1	8	0	0	2	7	1	10	0	0
Gutierrez, Ricky, Rochester	.253	125	431	54	109	124	9	3	0	41	3	5	0	53	2	77	14	12
Hankins, Mike, Columbus†	.182	7	22	3	4	4	0	0	0	2	0	0	0	2	0	4	0	0
Hansen, Terrel, Tidewater	.248	115	395	43	98	152	18	0	12	47	1	4	7	24	1	96	4	2
Hare, Shawn, Toledo*	.330	57	203	31	67	98	12	2	5	34	0	4	0	31	2	28	6	1
Henderson, Derek, Syracuse	.143	7	14	0	2	3	1	0	0	0	0	0	0	2	0	1	0	0
Hillman, Eric, Tidewater*	.400	34	5	1	2	2	0	0	0	1	0	0	0	0	0	3	0	0
Housie, Wayne, Pawtucket†	.219	134	456	53	100	138	22	5	2	28	10	1	3	32	1	102	20	8
Howard, Steve, Richmond	.172	13	29	3	5	8	3	0	0	2	0	0	0	2	0	14	0	0
Howell, Pat, Columbus	.244	104	405	46	99	116	8	3	1	22	4	2	5	22	1	98	21	10
Humphreys, Mike, Columbus	.282	114	408	83	115	163	18	6	6	46	3	5	1	59	0	70	37	13
Hunter, Bert, Tidewater†	.500	1	4	1	2	3	1	0	0	0	0	0	0	0	0	0	0	1
Hurst, Jody, Toledo	.186	45	145	16	27	40	2	1	3	17	1	2	2	8	0	39	4	1
Ingram, Riccardo, Toledo	.251	121	410	45	103	154	15	6	8	41	4	5	5	31	4	52	8	6
Jennings, Doug, Rochester*	.275	119	396	70	109	184	23	5	14	76	0	4	9	68	5	80	11	4
Jordan, Ricky, Scranton W.B.	.263	4	19	1	5	5	0	0	0	2	0	0	0	0	0	2	0	0
Kelley, Dean, Tidewater*	.235	11	34	4	8	10	2	0	0	4	0	0	1	1	0	7	0	0
Kelly, Pat, Richmond	.467	6	15	1	7	7	0	0	0	4	0	0	0	3	0	2	0	0
King, Jason, Tidewater†	.500	1	2	2	1	1	0	0	0	0	0	0	0	0	0	0	0	0
Klesko, Ryan, Richmond*	.251	123	418	63	105	182	22	2	17	59	1	2	4	41	6	72	3	5
Kline, Doug, 16 Tide.- 11 Tol.	.000	27	1	0	0	0	0	0	0	1	0	0	0	0	0	0	0	0
Knoblauh, Jay, Columbus	.269	34	104	14	28	38	4	0	2	18	0	1	1	8	0	13	6	2
Knorr, Randy, Syracuse	.272	61	228	27	62	110	13	1	11	27	0	3	0	17	1	38	1	0
Legg, Greg, Scranton W.B.	.228	90	289	35	66	85	12	2	1	29	2	2	2	43	1	41	2	2
Lehman, Mike, Rochester	.190	8	21	3	4	5	1	0	0	1	0	0	1	0	0	4	1	0
Liddell, Dave, Rochester	.107	9	28	1	3	6	0	0	1	2	0	1	0	2	0	13	0	0
Lieberthal, Mike, Scranton W.B.	.200	16	45	4	9	10	1	0	0	4	1	1	0	7	1	11	0	0
Lindeman, Jim, Scranton W.B.	.302	15	53	5	16	18	0	1	0	8	0	0	1	1	1	10	0	0
Lindsey, Doug, Scranton W.B.	.208	87	274	28	57	78	9	0	4	27	1	2	1	37	4	66	0	2
Livesey, Jeff, Columbus	.111	3	9	0	1	1	0	0	0	1	0	0	0	0	0	2	0	0
Lofton, Rod, Rochester	.235	52	132	24	31	36	3	1	0	8	4	0	0	8	0	26	10	3
Lovullo, Torey, Columbus†	.295	131	468	69	138	238	33	5	19	89	2	6	3	64	4	65	9	4
Lyden, Mitch, Toledo	.258	91	299	34	77	132	13	0	14	52	0	4	3	12	0	95	1	2
Lyons, Steve, Pawtucket*	.259	37	135	14	35	59	14	2	2	12	0	1	8	2	3	18	3	1
Maksudian, Mike, Syracuse*	.280	101	339	38	95	153	17	1	13	58	0	1	1	32	6	63	4	1

Player, Team	Avg.	G	AB	R	H	TB	2B	3B	HR	RBI	SH	SF	HP	BB	Int. BB	SO	SB	CS
Manto, Jeff, Richmond	.291	127	450	65	131	196	24	1	13	68	0	7	7	57	4	63	1	2
Marsh, Tom, Scranton W.B.	.241	45	158	26	38	73	7	2	8	25	1	0	2	10	0	30	5	4
Marshall, Randy, Tidewater*	.083	26	12	0	1	1	0	0	0	0	0	0	0	3	0	2	0	0
Martinez, Domingo, Syracuse	.274	116	438	55	120	205	22	0	21	62	0	4	8	33	5	95	6	0
Marzano, John, Pawtucket	.290	18	62	5	18	25	1	0	2	12	0	0	2	3	0	11	0	0
Masse, Billy, Columbus	.266	110	357	52	95	148	13	2	12	60	2	3	5	51	0	51	7	6
Mathews, Greg, Scranton W.B.	.500	16	2	0	1	1	0	0	0	0	2	0	0	0	0	0	0	0
Mauser, Tim, Scranton W.B.	.000	45	5	0	0	0	0	0	0	0	0	0	0	1	0	4	0	0
May, Lee, Tidewater†	.213	87	235	28	50	66	10	0	2	15	6	4	2	21	0	74	4	4
McCarthy, Tom, Richmond	.000	48	3	0	0	0	0	0	0	0	0	0	0	0	0	2	0	0
McCray, Rodney, Tidewater	.000	8	10	1	0	0	0	0	0	0	0	0	0	1	0	5	3	0
McGriff, Terry, Tidewater	.250	21	56	4	14	22	2	0	2	7	0	1	0	9	0	11	1	0
McKnight, Jeff, Tidewater†	.307	102	352	43	108	143	21	1	4	43	1	1	1	51	3	52	3	3
McMichael, Greg, Richmond	.214	19	14	1	3	4	1	0	0	1	1	0	0	0	0	5	0	0
Meadows, Scott, Rochester	.264	65	216	23	57	67	7	0	1	9	1	0	4	34	0	47	6	0
Mercado, Orlando, Tidewater	.247	54	178	16	44	75	7	0	8	19	0	1	0	15	2	37	1	0
Mercedes, Luis, Rochester	.313	103	409	62	128	154	15	1	3	29	3	3	1	44	2	56	35	14
Meulens, Hensley, Columbus	.275	141	534	96	147	257	28	2	26	100	1	3	5	60	6	168	15	8
Millette, Joe, Scranton W.B.	.266	78	256	24	68	84	11	1	1	23	7	0	6	15	0	30	3	2
Milstien, Dave, Pawtucket	.248	85	266	29	66	82	11	1	1	34	0	2	1	13	0	23	2	2
Mitchell, Keith, Richmond	.226	121	403	45	91	124	19	1	4	50	2	4	4	66	2	55	14	9
Montalvo, Rob, Syracuse	.232	66	168	20	39	53	8	0	2	14	6	2	3	15	0	22	2	0
Monzon, Jose, Syracuse	.056	9	18	3	1	1	0	0	0	1	0	0	0	2	0	1	0	0
Moore, Bobby, Richmond	.250	92	316	41	79	98	13	3	0	25	6	3	0	21	0	26	14	6
Moore, Brad, Tidewater	.000	50	2	0	0	0	0	0	0	0	0	0	0	0	0	1	0	0
Mordecai, Mike, Richmond	.246	36	118	12	29	35	3	0	1	6	1	2	0	5	0	19	0	4
Moyer, Jamie, Toledo*	.000	21	0	0	0	0	0	0	0	0	0	0	0	1	0	0	0	0
Naehring, Tim, Pawtucket	.294	11	34	7	10	16	0	0	2	5	0	0	1	8	0	6	1	1
Nezelek, Andy, Richmond*	.250	3	4	0	1	1	0	0	0	0	0	0	0	0	0	1	0	0
Nied, Dave, Richmond	.100	26	10	0	1	1	0	0	0	0	5	0	0	0	0	3	0	0
Noboa, Junior, Tidewater	.200	6	20	1	4	4	0	0	0	0	0	0	0	0	0	4	0	0
Paredes, Johnny, Toledo	.193	23	83	6	16	23	1	0	2	5	0	0	0	5	0	14	3	2
Parent, Mark, Rochester	.287	101	356	52	102	177	24	0	17	69	0	3	0	35	1	64	4	3
Paris, Juan, Pawtucket	.182	44	110	8	20	27	2	1	1	10	2	0	0	5	0	20	1	1
Parris, Steve, Scranton W.B.	.500	11	2	1	1	1	0	0	0	0	0	0	0	0	0	0	0	0
Pederson, Stu, Syracuse*	.232	93	259	42	60	96	13	1	7	29	1	1	2	35	1	46	3	0
Peguero, Julio, Scranton W.B.†	.256	74	289	41	74	95	14	2	1	21	2	2	2	24	2	56	14	15
Pettis, Gary, Toledo†	.171	10	35	5	6	6	0	0	0	3	0	0	0	8	1	10	5	2
Pevey, Marty, Toledo*	.301	48	136	16	41	56	6	0	3	16	2	1	0	7	0	18	1	1
Plantier, Phil, Pawtucket*	.425	12	40	7	17	32	0	0	5	14	0	0	6	1	0	6	0	1
Plummer, Dale, Tidewater	.000	31	2	0	0	0	0	0	0	0	0	0	0	0	0	1	0	0
Polley, Dale, Richmond	.000	40	2	1	0	0	0	0	0	0	0	0	0	0	0	0	0	0
Pratt, Todd, Scranton W.B.	.320	41	125	20	40	72	9	1	7	28	1	2	0	30	0	14	1	0
Quinlan, Tom, Syracuse	.215	107	349	43	75	112	17	1	6	36	1	2	10	43	1	112	1	3
Ramos, John, Columbus	.172	18	64	5	11	20	4	1	1	12	0	1	0	8	0	14	1	0
Rauth, Chris, Tidewater	.167	26	12	0	2	2	1	0	0	1	1	0	0	3	0	1	0	1
Reimink, Bob, Toledo†	.328	19	58	8	19	22	3	0	0	2	1	0	0	9	0	12	1	3
Reynoso, Armando, Richmond	.154	28	13	0	2	2	0	0	0	0	2	0	0	0	0	2	0	0
Ritchie, Wally, Scranton W.B.*	.000	15	1	0	0	0	0	0	0	0	0	0	0	0	0	1	0	0
Robbins, Doug, Rochester	.306	93	288	45	88	126	18	1	6	46	7	3	4	43	0	50	8	5
Robertson, Rod, Toledo†	.207	70	222	23	46	69	6	1	5	22	3	2	2	15	2	41	8	5
Robinson, Nap, Richmond	.200	29	15	1	3	4	1	0	0	1	0	0	0	1	0	8	0	0
Rodriguez, Boi, Richmond*	.277	93	278	40	77	139	8	3	16	40	0	0	1	32	5	61	0	0
Rodriguez, Carlos, Columbus†	.000	1	4	0	0	0	0	0	0	0	0	0	0	0	0	1	0	0
Rodriguez, Ruben, Pawtucket	.227	17	44	3	10	13	3	0	0	1	0	0	0	2	1	11	0	0
Rodriguez, Victor, Scranton W.B.	.277	48	155	14	43	58	8	2	1	27	1	0	0	3	0	20	0	0
Rosado, Edwin, Scranton W.B.†	.000	4	10	0	0	0	0	0	0	0	0	0	0	0	0	1	0	0
Rosario, Victor, Tidewater	.202	102	337	26	68	85	9	1	2	16	6	1	1	9	0	72	6	6
Ross, Sean, 104 Rich.-2 Paw.*	.244	106	390	47	95	154	19	5	10	48	3	4	1	16	0	99	13	3
Roth, Greg, Rochester*	.217	18	46	5	10	14	1	0	1	2	0	0	1	6	0	13	1	0
Rowland, Rich, Toledo	.235	136	473	75	111	207	19	1	25	82	0	4	3	56	6	112	9	3
St. Claire, Randy, Richmond	.000	39	0	0	0	0	0	0	0	0	1	0	0	0	0	0	0	0
Sax, Dave, Columbus	.218	58	188	23	41	59	4	1	4	20	1	2	0	22	0	37	3	0
Scarsone, Steve, 89 S.W.B.-23 Roch.	.270	112	407	56	110	180	26	4	12	60	6	5	3	30	4	86	13	9
Schourek, Pete, Tidewater*	.000	8	3	0	0	0	0	0	0	0	1	0	0	0	0	0	0	0
Schu, Rick, Scranton W.B.	.310	111	400	56	124	178	18	3	10	49	0	1	4	45	5	62	3	1
Schunk, Jerry, Syracuse	.261	122	417	40	109	133	16	1	2	26	12	6	0	20	1	21	2	3
Scott, Shawn, Syracuse†	.321	7	28	2	9	13	2	1	0	1	0	0	1	0	0	5	0	0
Searcy, Steve, Scranton W.B.*	.000	8	2	0	0	0	0	0	0	0	0	0	0	0	0	2	0	0
Shamburg, Ken, Rochester	.209	58	191	22	40	64	9	0	5	34	1	4	0	12	0	30	2	0
Shelby, John, Pawtucket†	.205	127	468	56	96	182	27	4	17	64	5	3	0	47	3	125	6	3
Shields, Tommy, Rochester	.302	121	431	58	130	189	23	3	10	59	4	4	6	30	1	72	13	7
Silvestri, Dave, Columbus	.279	118	420	83	117	191	25	5	13	73	0	5	8	58	1	110	19	11
Sims, Mark, Scranton W.B.†	.000	44	1	0	0	0	0	0	0	0	0	0	0	0	0	0	0	0
Smith, Greg, Toledo†	.234	128	445	56	104	146	15	3	7	46	4	2	3	46	0	72	24	3
Smith, Keith, Tidewater†	.230	42	113	12	26	28	2	0	0	4	1	0	0	8	0	13	0	0
Smith, Pete, Tidewater	.250	15	8	1	2	3	1	0	0	0	1	0	0	0	0	3	0	0
Snider, Van, Pawtucket*	.234	116	384	44	90	150	22	1	12	51	1	5	1	23	5	91	2	1
Snow, J.T., Columbus†	.313	135	492	81	154	233	26	4	15	78	1	6	1	70	11	65	3	3
Sparks, Greg, Toledo*	.181	23	72	6	13	20	1	0	2	4	1	1	0	4	0	26	0	1
Sprague, Ed, Syracuse	.276	100	369	49	102	172	18	2	16	50	0	2	4	44	3	73	0	1
Springer, Steve, Tidewater	.290	117	427	57	124	188	16	0	16	70	0	3	0	22	1	85	9	4
Stanford, Don, Columbus	.000	40	1	0	0	0	0	0	0	0	0	0	0	0	0	0	0	0
Stephens, Ray, Scranton W.B.	.205	17	44	4	9	13	1	0	1	2	2	0	0	3	0	10	0	0
Stone, Jeff, 29 Tol.-14 S.W.B.*	.240	43	125	19	30	43	5	1	2	10	1	0	2	8	0	34	9	0
Szekely, Joe, Richmond*	.308	17	39	5	12	19	5	1	0	5	0	1	0	3	0	6	0	0
Taylor, Billy, Richmond†	.000	47	0	0	0	0	0	0	0	0	0	0	0	0	0	0	0	0
Telgheder, Dave, Tidewater	.000	28	12	0	0	0	0	0	0	0	0	0	0	0	0	4	0	0
Thompson, Ryan, Syracuse	.282	112	429	74	121	197	20	7	14	46	2	1	3	43	1	114	10	4
Tomberlin, Andy, Richmond*	.271	118	406	69	110	163	16	5	9	47	10	2	8	41	1	102	12	12
Twardoski, Mike, Pawtucket*	.290	121	389	55	113	183	23	4	13	49	9	6	1	92	4	56	1	5
Valentin, John, Pawtucket	.260	97	331	47	86	133	18	1	9	29	5	1	3	48	1	50	1	2
Vaughn, Mo, Pawtucket*	.282	39	149	15	42	66	6	0	6	28	0	1	1	18	1	35	1	0
Vina, Fernando, Tidewater*	.200	11	30	3	6	6	0	0	0	0	1	0	0	0	0	2	1	0
Voigt, Jack, Rochester	.284	129	443	74	126	205	23	4	16	64	2	3	0	4	58	3	102	9	2

Player, Team	Avg.	G	AB	R	H	TB	2B	3B	HR	RBI	SH	SF	HP	BB	Int. BB	SO	SB	CS
Wade, Scott, Syracuse	.156	18	45	3	7	9	2	0	0	3	0	1	2	5	0	12	0	0
Waggoner, Aubrey, Richmond*	.227	7	22	2	5	9	1	0	1	6	0	0	3	6	0	6	1	0
Waller, Casey, Scranton W.B.†	.295	23	61	11	18	22	4	0	0	8	0	3	0	6	3	11	1	1
Ward, Turner, Syracuse†	.239	81	280	41	67	111	10	2	10	29	2	1	2	44	3	43	7	5
Wearing, Melvin, Rochester	.326	58	187	33	61	93	16	2	4	45	0	5	3	33	1	45	2	1
Wedge, Eric, Pawtucket	.299	65	211	28	63	105	9	0	11	40	0	3	1	32	3	40	0	0
Weston, Mickey, Scranton W.B.	.000	27	15	1	0	0	0	0	0	0	3	0	0	0	0	4	0	0
White, Mike, Tidewater*	.000	1	3	0	0	0	0	0	0	0	0	0	0	0	0	0	0	0
Williams, Bernie, Columbus†	.306	95	363	68	111	176	23	9	8	50	1	6	1	52	5	61	20	8
Williams, Cary, Scranton W.B.	.223	112	373	38	83	128	18	3	7	40	4	7	15	0	66	7	4	0
Williams, Eddie, Richmond	.203	24	74	8	15	21	3	0	1	5	0	1	3	0	9	0	0	
Williams, Gerald, Columbus	.285	142	547	92	156	247	31	6	16	86	0	5	5	38	2	98	36	14
Williams, Mike, Scranton W.B.	.231	16	13	0	3	3	0	0	0	1	7	0	0	3	0	3	0	0
Wohlers, Mark, Richmond	.500	27	2	0	1	1	0	0	0	0	0	0	0	0	1	0	0	
Yacopino, Ed, Rochester†	.282	122	440	56	124	166	22	4	4	61	2	4	31	2	56	5	1	
Zosky, Eddie, Syracuse	.231	96	342	31	79	114	11	6	4	38	7	4	1	19	0	53	3	4
Zupcic, Bob, Pawtucket	.320	9	25	3	8	15	1	0	2	5	0	1	0	8	0	6	0	1

The following pitchers, listed alphabetically by club, with games in parentheses, had no plate appearances, primarily through use of designated hitters:

COLUMBUS—DeLaRosa, Francisco (48); Greer, Ken (1); Hillegas, Shawn (4); Holcomb, Scott (18); Hutton, Mark (1); Johnson, Jeff (11); Kamieniecki, Scott (2); Martel, Ed (26); Militello, Sam (22); Mmahat, Kevin (2); Nielsen, Gerald (4); Popplewell, Tom (4); Quirico, Rafael (1); Rosario, David (54); Rumer, Tim (1); Seiler, Keith (3); Springer, Russ (20); Stanford, Larry (2); Taylor, Wade (1); Wickman, Bob (23); Young, Curt (3).

PAWTUCKET—Cerutti, John (24); Conroy, Brian (15); Dixon, Colin (1); Dopson, John (6); Fischer, Tom (36); Gardiner, Mike (5); Hoy, Pete (45); Irvine, Daryl (36); Livernois, Derek (6); Minchey, Nathan (2); Morton, Kevin (26); Plympton, Jeff (58); Quantrill, Paul (19); Riley, Ed (1); Ryan, Ken (9); Shikles, Larry (29); Taylor, Scott (26); Walters, Dave (38).

RICHMOND—Johnson, Lloyd (1).

ROCHESTER—Drummond, Tim (2); Hall, Gardner (2); Jones, Stacy (2); Layana, Tim (41); Leinen, Patrick (17); Lewis, Jim (33); Lewis, Richie (27); Milacki, Bob (9); Miller, David (12); Mills, Alan (3); Moore, Daryl (1); O'Donoghue, John (13); Oquist, Mike (26); Pennington, Brad (29); Poole, Jim (32); Rasmussen, Dennis (9); Rhodes, Arthur (17); Sanchez, Israel (4); Stephan, Todd (44); Telford, Anthony (27); Williamson, Mark (4).

SCRANTON-WILKES BARRE—Ashby, Andy (7); Ayrault, Bob (20); Baller, Jay (44); Borland, Toby (27); Brantley, Cliff (5); Chapin, Darrin (40); Green, Tyler (2); Hartley, Mike (3); Patterson, Jeff (11); Rivera, Ben (2); Stevens, Matt (9); Wiegandt, Scott (1).

SYRACUSE—Alvarez, Jose (22); Blohm, Peter (37); Brown, Tim (4); Cross, Jesse (4); Dayley, Ken (4); Edwards, Wayne (41); Guzman, Juan (1); Hall, Darren (55); Hentgen, Patrick (4); Leiter, Al (27); Linton, Doug (25); MacDonald, Bob (17); Shea, John (25); Timlin, Mike (7); Trlicek, Richard (35); Walter, Gene (39); Ward, Anthony (20); Weathers, David (12); Williams, Greg (25).

TIDEWATER—Dewey, Mark (43); Dorn, Chris (1); Douma, Todd (6); Gibson, Paul (2); Pena, Hipolito (17); Valera, Julio (1); Vasquez, Julian (20); Wegmann, Tom (7).

TOLEDO—Aldred, Scott (16); August, Don (5); Brennan, Bill (12); Castillo, Tony (12); Corbett, Sherman (10); Cummings, Steve (5); DeSilva, John (7); Gakeler, Dan (3); Gohr, Greg (22); Gonzales, Francisco (18); Groom, Buddy (16); Haas, Dave (22); Johnson, Dave (25); Kaiser, Jeff (28); Kiely, Jim (1); King, Eric (3); Kline, Doug (11); Knudsen, Kurt (12); Lovelace, Vance (15); Pena, Hipolito (1); Rightnowar, Ron (34); Robinson, Jeff M. (13); Walker, Mike (42); Wolf, Steve (3).

GRAND SLAMS—G. Alexander, Rowland, Silvestri, 2 each; Allaire, Amaro, Geren, Knoblauh, Lyden, Maksudian, Scarsone, Schu, Shamburg, Snider, Waggoner, Wearing, 1 each.

AWARDED FIRST BASE ON CATCHER'S INTERFERENCE—DeJardin (Parent); Klesko (Ausmus); Ward (Sax); G. Williams (Sprague).

PITCHING

TEAM

Team	ERA	G	CG	ShO	Sv.	IP	H	R	ER	HR	HB	BB	Int. BB	SO	WP	Bk.
Scranton W.B.	3.23	142	16	12	46	1213.1	1099	499	436	83	27	431	31	907	59	9
Richmond	3.27	144	16	13	35	1246.0	1155	553	453	82	39	444	35	1004	52	9
Columbus	3.35	144	10	12	54	1269.0	1104	544	472	80	47	500	21	913	60	12
Rochester	4.11	144	12	10	30	1229.0	1195	618	561	112	29	490	20	945	70	6
Tidewater	4.17	142	14	11	26	1188.1	1212	623	550	106	29	407	23	799	61	8
Pawtucket	4.23	144	23	10	36	1234.2	1341	663	580	159	29	409	28	704	60	14
Toledo	4.36	144	16	6	29	1231.2	1276	673	596	107	41	471	19	877	79	3
Syracuse	4.56	143	13	6	35	1244.1	1298	717	631	105	46	552	24	845	93	8

INDIVIDUAL

(Leading qualifiers for earned-run average leadership—115 or more innings)

*Throws lefthanded.

Pitcher, Team	W	L	Pct.	ERA	G	GS	CG	GF	ShO	Sv.	IP	H	R	ER	HR	HB	BB	Int. BB	SO	WP
Militello, Columbus	12	2	.857	2.29	22	21	3	0	2	0	141.1	104	45	36	5	11	46	1	152	4
Reynoso, Richmond	12	9	.571	2.66	28	27	4	1	1	0	169.1	156	65	50	12	7	52	6	108	8
Springer, Columbus	8	5	.615	2.69	20	20	1	0	0	0	123.2	89	46	37	11	5	54	0	95	4
Nied, Richmond	14	9	.609	2.84	26	26	7	0	2	0	168.0	144	73	53	15	3	44	2	159	1
Moyer, Toledo*	10	8	.556	2.86	21	20	5	1	0	0	138.2	128	48	44	8	0	37	3	80	5
Wickman, Columbus	12	5	.706	2.92	23	23	2	0	1	0	157.0	131	61	51	12	5	55	0	108	10
Weston, Scranton W.B.	10	6	.625	3.11	26	24	2	1	1	1	170.2	165	65	59	12	3	29	2	79	4
Williams, Syracuse	6	8	.429	3.13	25	16	1	3	0	1	120.2	115	46	42	4	3	41	0	81	5
R. Lewis, Rochester	10	9	.526	3.28	24	23	6	1	1	0	159.1	136	63	58	15	3	61	2	154	13
Shikles, Pawtucket	13	8	.619	3.56	29	23	5	1	2	0	149.1	157	81	59	19	6	36	2	67	3

Departmental leaders: G—Plympton, 58; W—Nied, 14; L—Telgheder, 14; Pct.—M. Williams, .900; GS—N. Robinson, 28; CG—Linton, Nied, 7; GF—Draper, 50; ShO—Cerutti, 3; Sv.—Draper, 37; IP—Telford, 181.0; H—Telford, 183; R—Martel, 98; ER—Martel, 93; HR—Morton, Shikles, 19; HB—Militello, 11; BB—Edwards, 76; IBB—Rosario, 8; SO—Nied, 159; WP—Edwards, 22.

Pitcher, Team	W	L	Pct.	ERA	G	GS	CG	GF	ShO	Sv.	IP	H	R	ER	HR	HB	BB	Int. BB	SO	WP
Abbott, Scranton W.B.*	4	1	.800	1.54	5	5	1	0	1	0	35.0	20	6	6	0	0	16	0	34	3
Aldred, Toledo*	4	6	.400	5.13	16	13	3	1	0	0	86.0	92	57	49	13	2	47	0	81	6
Alvarez, Syracuse	1	4	.200	4.17	22	0	0	12	0	1	36.2	32	21	17	3	1	18	5	38	1
Ashby, Scranton W.B.	0	3	.000	3.00	7	7	1	0	0	0	33.0	23	13	11	4	3	14	0	18	4
August, Toledo	0	2	.000	8.59	5	3	0	2	0	0	14.2	25	17	14	2	0	7	0	6	1
Ayrault, Scranton W.B.	5	1	.833	4.97	20	0	0	14	0	6	25.1	19	15	14	4	1	15	3	30	0
Baller, Scranton W.B.	4	5	.444	1.42	44	0	0	36	0	22	63.1	48	13	10	0	1	25	6	67	8
Bark, Richmond*	1	2	.333	6.00	22	4	0	4	0	2	42.0	63	32	28	3	1	15	1	50	1
Birkbeck, Tidewater	4	10	.286	4.08	21	19	3	0	0	0	117.0	108	61	53	9	2	31	0	101	9
Blohm, Syracuse	7	6	.538	5.37	37	12	1	7	0	1	129.0	146	82	77	13	2	46	1	67	6
Bogar, Tidewater	0	0	.000	12.00	3	0	0	3	0	0	3.0	4	4	4	0	0	3	0	1	0
Borland, Scranton W.B.	0	1	.000	7.24	27	0	0	6	0	1	27.1	25	23	22	2	2	26	3	25	4
Brantley, Scranton W.B.	3	1	.750	1.76	5	5	0	0	0	0	30.2	19	7	6	1	2	14	0	26	2
Brennan, Toledo	0	4	.000	8.10	12	3	0	4	0	0	26.2	29	29	24	1	2	23	0	28	8
Brink, Scranton W.B.	8	2	.800	3.48	17	17	5	0	2	0	111.1	100	47	43	15	5	34	0	92	3
Brown, Syracuse	0	2	.000	6.32	4	3	0	1	0	0	15.2	19	12	11	2	0	4	0	13	0
Castillo, Toledo*	2	3	.400	3.63	12	9	0	3	0	2	44.2	48	23	18	3	0	14	0	24	4
Cerutti, Pawtucket*	7	7	.500	4.63	24	14	5	2	3	0	105.0	128	60	54	11	2	23	1	43	3
Chapin, Scranton W.B.	5	4	.556	5.11	40	0	0	16	0	4	61.2	72	39	35	5	0	33	5	67	7
Cinnella, Tidewater	0	3	.000	3.81	10	3	0	2	0	0	28.1	29	14	12	2	0	16	1	15	3
Clayton, Columbus	10	5	.667	3.58	36	15	1	10	1	1	130.2	132	62	52	5	3	45	2	72	6
Coffman, Richmond	6	5	.545	3.15	16	15	0	0	0	0	91.1	66	43	32	3	5	70	1	78	14
Combs, Scranton W.B.*	5	7	.417	3.61	21	21	0	0	0	0	124.2	123	62	50	9	0	41	0	77	3
Conroy, Pawtucket	7	5	.583	4.62	15	13	1	1	1	0	85.2	91	49	44	17	2	31	2	57	2
Cook, Columbus	7	5	.583	3.16	32	9	0	7	0	2	99.2	85	41	35	8	3	36	0	58	3
Corbett, Toledo*	0	0	.000	5.89	10	1	0	4	0	0	18.1	21	13	12	1	0	12	0	12	0
Cross, Syracuse	0	0	.000	9.45	4	0	0	1	0	0	6.2	11	8	7	3	0	3	1	3	0
Cummings, Toledo	0	2	.000	8.10	5	3	0	0	0	0	20.0	26	19	18	4	0	8	1	6	1
Dayley, Syracuse*	0	0	.000	17.18	4	0	0	1	0	0	3.2	3	7	7	1	2	6	0	4	0
DeLaRosa, Columbus	6	1	.857	3.72	48	0	0	18	0	3	55.2	47	26	23	5	2	18	1	43	2
DeSilva, Toledo	0	3	.000	8.53	7	2	0	3	0	0	19.0	26	18	18	5	0	8	0	21	0
Dewey, Tidewater	5	7	.417	4.31	43	0	0	32	0	9	54.1	61	29	26	5	0	18	6	55	5
Dopson, Pawtucket	1	2	.333	2.37	6	6	0	0	0	0	38.0	28	15	10	1	0	8	2	23	1
Dorn, Tidewater	0	0	.000	0.00	1	0	0	1	0	0	1.0	0	0	0	0	0	2	0	0	0
Douma, Tidewater*	0	1	.000	11.70	6	1	0	2	0	0	10.0	14	14	13	3	0	8	1	3	0
Draper, Columbus	5	6	.455	3.60	57	3	0	50	0	37	80.0	70	36	32	3	6	28	2	42	3
Drummond, Rochester	1	0	1.000	1.98	2	2	0	0	0	0	13.2	13	4	3	0	0	6	0	4	0
Edwards, Syracuse*	4	6	.400	4.48	41	12	0	10	0	3	130.2	127	71	65	13	4	76	3	108	22
Eufemia, Tidewater	1	3	.250	3.64	11	5	0	4	0	0	29.2	32	17	12	6	0	6	1	13	0
Filer, Tidewater	1	7	.125	2.78	18	17	3	0	1	0	100.1	106	45	31	2	2	28	1	47	6
Fischer, Pawtucket*	1	0	1.000	6.27	36	5	0	14	0	3	70.1	78	53*	49	9	2	41	4	46	5
Fletcher, Scranton W.B.	3	0	1.000	2.78	4	4	0	0	0	0	22.2	17	8	7	1	1	2	0	26	2
Gakeler, Toledo	0	1	.000	7.11	3	3	0	0	0	0	12.2	14	10	10	3	1	4	0	11	2
Gardiner, Pawtucket	1	3	.250	3.31	5	5	2	0	0	0	32.2	32	14	12	3	0	9	0	37	0
Gibson, Pawtucket*	0	0	.000	3.00	2	0	0	1	0	0	3.0	3	1	1	0	0	2	1	1	0
Gohr, Toledo	8	10	.444	3.99	22	20	0	0	0	0	130.2	124	65	58	9	3	46	1	94	5
Gomez, Richmond*	3	5	.375	5.45	23	11	0	3	0	0	71.0	79	47	43	10	2	42	2	48	3
Gonzales, Toledo*	4	6	.400	4.30	18	17	2	0	1	0	98.1	100	48	47	7	3	36	0	65	5
Green, Scranton W.B.	0	1	.000	6.10	2	2	0	0	0	0	10.1	7	7	7	1	1	12	0	15	0
Greene, Scranton W.B.	2	1	.667	2.49	5	5	1	0	1	0	21.2	15	7	6	3	1	4	0	21	0
Greer, Columbus	0	0	.000	9.00	1	0	0	1	0	0	1.0	3	2	1	0	0	1	0	1	0
Groom, Toledo*	7	7	.500	2.80	16	16	1	0	0	0	109.1	102	41	34	8	1	23	1	71	5
Guzman, Syracuse	0	0	.000	6.00	1	1	0	0	0	0	3.0	6	2	2	0	0	1	0	3	0
Haas, Toledo	9	8	.529	4.18	22	22	2	0	0	0	148.2	149	72	69	11	9	53	1	112	5
Hall, Syracuse	4	6	.400	4.30	55	0	0	26	0	5	69.0	62	36	33	5	2	35	2	49	11
Hall, Rochester*	0	0	.000	13.50	2	0	0	0	0	0	0.2	4	1	1	0	0	1	0	1	0
Hartley, Scranton W.B.	1	2	.333	4.09	3	3	0	0	0	0	11.0	9	6	5	2	0	7	0	10	0
Hentgen, Syracuse	1	2	.333	2.66	4	4	0	0	0	0	20.1	15	6	6	1	0	8	0	17	0
Hillegas, Columbus	2	0	1.000	3.29	4	4	0	0	0	0	27.1	24	10	10	2	10	0	20	2
Hillman, Tidewater*	9	2	.818	3.65	34	9	0	7	0	0	91.1	93	39	37	6	2	27	1	49	6
Holcomb, Columbus*	2	0	1.000	2.79	18	0	0	3	0	0	19.1	15	6	6	3	0	19	4	23	1
Hoy, Pawtucket	3	2	.600	4.79	45	0	0	22	0	5	73.1	83	41	39	9	3	25	5	38	5
Hutton, Columbus	0	1	.000	5.40	1	0	0	0	0	0	5.0	7	4	3	0	0	2	0	4	0
Irvine, Pawtucket	4	1	.800	1.54	36	0	0	31	0	18	41.0	32	10	7	0	0	10	3	25	3
Johnson, Toledo	4	4	.500	4.27	25	5	0	11	0	3	52.2	60	27	25	4	1	17	1	29	2
Johnson, Columbus*	2	1	.667	2.17	11	11	0	0	0	0	58.0	41	15	14	0	2	18	0	38	3
Johnson, Richmond*	0	0	.000	0.00	1	0	0	1	0	0	1.0	0	0	0	0	0	1	0	1	0
Jones, Rochester	0	0	.000	6.75	2	0	0	1	0	0	2.2	2	2	2	1	0	1	0	0	1
Kaiser, Toledo*	1	0	1.000	2.35	28	0	0	15	0	5	30.2	25	12	8	0	0	12	1	33	1
Kamieniecki, Columbus	1	0	1.000	0.69	2	2	0	0	0	0	13.0	6	1	1	0	0	4	0	12	0
Kiely, Toledo	1	1	.500	2.84	21	0	0	17	0	9	31.2	25	11	10	1	0	7	0	31	1
King, Toledo	1	2	.333	5.63	3	3	0	0	0	0	16.0	22	10	10	2	0	2	0	12	2
Kline, 16 Tide. - 11 Tol.	2	1	.667	4.08	27	1	0	11	0	1	46.1	34	21	21	6	0	21	0	38	2
Knudsen, Toledo	3	1	.750	2.08	12	0	0	8	0	1	21.2	11	5	5	1	1	6	0	19	1
Layana, Rochester	3	3	.500	5.35	41	3	0	28	0	4	72.1	79	45	43	4	4	38	6	48	14
Leinen, Rochester*	3	4	.429	5.86	17	8	0	3	0	0	55.1	76	36	36	7	2	19	0	19	1
Leiter, Syracuse*	8	9	.471	3.86	27	27	2	0	0	0	163.1	159	82	70	9	9	64	0	108	9
J. Lewis, Rochester	2	5	.286	4.92	33	2	0	15	0	1	60.1	67	45	33	5	1	32	3	38	3
R. Lewis, Rochester	10	9	.526	3.28	24	23	6	1	1	0	159.1	136	63	58	15	3	61	2	154	15
Linton, Syracuse	12	10	.545	3.74	25	25	7	0	1	0	170.2	176	83	71	17	7	70	3	126	12
Livernois, Pawtucket	3	2	.600	4.26	6	6	0	0	0	0	38.0	38	19	18	11	0	12	0	32	0
Lovelace, Toledo*	2	0	1.000	3.20	15	0	0	5	0	0	25.1	28	17	9	1	2	21	0	22	9
Lyons, Pawtucket	0	0	.000	0.00	1	0	0	1	0	0	2.0	3	0	0	0	0	1	0	0	0
MacDonald, Syracuse*	2	3	.400	4.63	17	0	0	11	0	2	23.1	25	13	12	2	0	12	1	14	2
Marshall, Tidewater*	7	13	.350	4.04	26	25	3	0	1	0	151.2	170	75	68	15	3	31	0	87	0
Martel, Columbus	10	9	.526	5.56	26	25	3	0	2	0	150.2	159	98	93	17	6	59	2	94	2
Mathews, Scranton W.B.*	3	7	.300	2.96	16	15	1	0	0	0	85.0	93	40	28	7	2	23	0	63	2
Mauser, Scranton W.B.	8	6	.571	2.97	45	5	0	15	0	4	100.0	87	37	33	6	0	45	4	75	4
McCarthy, Richmond	4	6	.400	3.21	48	3	0	34	0	4	92.2	91	45	33	2	4	21	5	52	5
McMichael, Richmond	6	5	.545	4.38	19	13	0	2	0	0	90.1	89	52	44	5	1	34	3	86	1
Milacki, Rochester	7	1	.875	4.57	9	9	3	0	0	0	61.0	57	33	31	9	2	21	0	35	3
Militello, Columbus	12	2	.857	2.29	22	21	3	0	2	0	141.1	104	45	36	5	11	46	1	152	4

Pitcher, Team	W	L	Pct.	ERA	G	GS	CG	GF	ShO	Sv.	IP	H	R	ER	HR	HB	BB	Int. BB	SO	WP
Miller, Rochester	4	0	1.000	3.81	12	9	0	1	0	0	49.2	60	22	21	1	1	17	0	21	1
Mills, Rochester	0	1	.000	5.40	3	0	0	3	0	1	5.0	6	3	3	1	0	2	0	8	0
Minchey, Pawtucket	2	0	1.000	0.00	2	0	0	2	0	0	7.0	3	0	0	0	0	0	0	4	0
Mmahat, Columbus*	0	0	.000	2.45	2	0	0	0	0	0	7.1	4	2	2	0	0	8	0	7	1
Moore, Tidewater	6	6	.500	5.45	50	1	0	24	0	6	79.1	80	55	48	5	5	52	4	55	14
Moore, Rochester*	0	0	.000	2.95	16	0	0	7	0	1	18.1	10	6	6	1	0	9	1	14	1
Morton, Pawtucket	2	12	.143	5.45	26	25	0	0	0	0	138.2	166	93	84	19	3	59	2	71	5
Moyer, Toledo*	10	8	.556	2.86	21	20	5	1	0	0	138.2	128	48	44	8	0	37	3	80	5
Nezelek, Richmond	0	0	.000	0.00	2	0	0	0	0	0	6.0	3	0	0	1	0	5	0	0	0
Nied, Richmond	14	9	.609	2.84	26	26	7	0	2	0	168.0	144	73	53	15	3	44	2	159	1
Nielsen, Columbus*	0	0	.000	1.80	4	0	0	2	0	1	5.0	2	1	1	0	1	2	0	5	1
O'Donoghue, Rochester*	5	4	.556	3.23	13	10	3	1	1	0	69.2	60	31	25	0	0	19	1	47	5
Oquist, Rochester	10	12	.455	4.11	26	24	5	0	0	0	153.1	164	80	70	17	5	45	1	111	6
Parris, Scranton W.B.	3	3	.500	4.03	11	6	0	2	0	1	51.1	57	25	23	1	4	17	1	29	6
Patterson, Scranton W.B.	2	1	.667	2.63	11	0	0	10	0	1	13.2	10	4	4	0	0	8	3	11	2
Pena, 1 Tol. - 17 Tide.*	0	0	.000	3.91	18	0	0	11	0	2	23.0	17	10	10	1	1	17	1	15	1
Pennington, Rochester*	1	3	.250	2.08	29	0	0	17	0	5	39.0	12	10	9	2	1	33	2	56	2
Plummer, Tidewater	4	0	1.000	3.57	31	0	0	14	0	2	58.0	59	26	23	8	4	19	1	29	0
Plympton, Pawtucket	6	9	.400	3.43	58	0	0	25	0	1	81.1	78	41	31	8	4	34	7	57	0
Polley, Richmond*	1	6	.143	2.88	39	0	0	12	0	2	56.1	54	20	18	1	1	24	5	42	2
Poole, Rochester	1	6	.143	5.31	32	0	0	19	0	10	42.1	40	26	25	8	1	18	1	30	3
Popplewell, Columbus	1	0	1.000	7.11	4	0	0	0	0	0	6.1	6	5	5	0	0	11	0	7	2
Quantrill, Pawtucket	6	8	.429	4.46	19	18	4	1	1	0	119.0	143	63	59	16	4	20	1	56	1
Quirico, Columbus*	1	0	1.000	3.00	1	1	0	0	0	0	6.0	6	3	2	0	0	4	0	1	1
Rasmussen, Rochester*	0	7	.000	5.67	9	9	1	0	0	0	46.0	49	33	29	3	0	22	0	33	1
Rauth, Tidewater	5	7	.417	5.12	26	19	0	4	0	0	121.1	132	76	69	16	6	44	1	72	3
Reynoso, Richmond	12	9	.571	2.66	28	27	4	1	1	0	169.1	156	65	50	12	7	52	6	108	8
Rhodes, Rochester*	6	6	.500	3.72	17	17	1	0	0	0	101.2	84	48	42	7	0	46	0	115	4
Rightnowar, Toledo	3	2	.600	6.16	34	0	0	20	0	3	57.0	68	43	39	10	5	18	4	33	5
Riley, Pawtucket*	0	0	.000	4.50	1	1	0	0	0	0	6.0	7	3	3	1	0	1	0	4	0
Ritchie, Scranton W.B.*	1	0	1.000	2.70	15	0	0	8	0	5	16.2	11	5	5	2	0	3	2	12	1
Rivera, Scranton W.B.	2	0	1.000	0.00	2	2	1	0	1	0	12.0	4	0	0	0	1	2	0	10	0
Robertson, Toledo	0	0	.000	9.00	1	0	0	1	0	0	1.0	0	1	1	0	0	1	0	1	2
Robinson, Toledo	1	2	.333	8.04	13	0	0	10	0	1	15.2	21	15	14	4	2	8	0	15	2
Robinson, Richmond	11	10	.524	3.57	29	28	1	0	0	0	163.2	149	73	65	9	10	52	2	106	9
Rosario, Columbus*	8	5	.615	2.33	54	1	0	19	0	6	73.1	67	22	19	1	1	41	8	65	7
Rumer, Columbus*	0	0	.000	0.00	1	1	0	0	0	0	1.0	0	0	0	0	0	1	0	0	0
Ryan, Pawtucket	2	0	1.000	2.08	9	0	0	9	0	7	8.2	6	2	2	1	0	4	0	6	0
St. Claire, Richmond	6	5	.545	3.52	39	0	0	24	0	4	71.2	82	33	28	6	0	21	2	62	1
Sanchez, Rochester*	0	0	.000	2.35	4	0	0	1	0	0	7.2	5	2	2	1	5	0	0	2	1
Schourek, Tidewater*	2	5	.286	2.73	8	8	2	0	1	0	52.2	46	20	16	2	0	23	0	42	3
Searcy, Scranton W.B.*	0	2	.000	3.46	8	3	0	1	0	1	26.0	19	10	10	0	0	12	0	22	2
Seiler, Columbus*	0	0	.000	4.15	3	0	0	2	0	0	4.1	5	2	2	0	0	2	0	2	1
Shea, Syracuse*	8	8	.500	6.18	25	21	1	2	1	0	118.0	151	92	81	8	5	49	1	50	8
Shikles, Pawtucket	13	8	.619	3.56	29	23	5	1	2	0	149.1	157	81	59	19	6	36	2	67	3
Sims, Scranton W.B.*	5	3	.625	3.04	44	2	0	13	0	0	53.1	53	23	18	3	3	14	0	26	0
Smith, Richmond	7	4	.636	2.14	15	15	4	0	1	0	109.1	75	27	26	6	4	24	0	93	1
Springer, Columbus	8	5	.615	2.69	20	20	1	0	0	0	123.2	89	46	37	11	5	54	0	95	4
D. Stanford, Columbus	5	3	.625	4.37	40	2	0	20	0	3	82.1	81	46	40	8	0	26	1	54	8
L. Stanford, Columbus	0	1	.000	4.50	2	0	0	2	0	1	2.0	2	3	1	0	0	1	0	5	2
Stephan, Rochester	5	6	.455	3.96	44	2	0	21	0	4	86.1	86	39	38	11	2	31	3	78	4
Stevens, Scranton W.B.	1	0	1.000	6.23	9	0	0	3	0	0	13.0	19	11	9	1	0	4	0	11	1
Taylor, Richmond	2	3	.400	2.28	47	0	0	27	0	12	79.0	72	27	20	5	0	27	3	82	0
Taylor, Pawtucket*	9	11	.450	3.67	26	26	0	0	0	0	162.0	168	73	66	16	2	61	1	91	17
Taylor, Columbus	0	0	.000	3.00	1	1	0	0	0	0	3.0	2	1	1	0	0	2	0	0	0
Telford, Rochester	12	7	.632	4.18	27	26	3	1	0	0	181.0	183	89	84	15	6	64	0	129	9
Telgheder, Tidewater	6	14	.300	4.21	28	27	3	1	2	0	169.0	173	87	79	16	0	36	4	118	1
Timlin, Syracuse	0	1	.000	8.74	7	1	0	4	0	0	11.1	15	11	11	3	0	5	1	7	0
Trlicek, Syracuse	1	1	.500	4.36	35	0	0	23	0	10	43.1	37	22	21	2	0	31	1	35	7
Valera, Tidewater	1	0	1.000	0.00	1	1	0	0	0	0	6.0	5	0	0	0	2	1	0	6	2
Vasquez, Tidewater	1	4	.200	5.56	20	0	0	18	0	6	22.2	22	14	14	3	1	8	0	22	2
Walker, Toledo	2	8	.200	5.83	42	1	0	16	0	1	78.2	102	62	51	5	8	44	6	44	7
Walter, Syracuse*	3	4	.429	2.83	39	0	0	26	0	9	57.1	51	25	18	2	4	28	3	46	5
Walters, Pawtucket	4	2	.667	5.28	38	1	0	11	0	2	76.2	100	46	45	18	1	34	0	45	6
Ward, Syracuse*	2	9	.182	6.87	20	11	1	3	0	0	73.1	100	69	56	14	5	34	0	46	2
Weathers, Syracuse	1	4	.200	4.66	12	10	0	1	0	0	48.1	48	29	25	3	2	21	2	30	2
Wegmann, Tidewater	2	3	.400	4.42	7	6	0	0	0	0	36.2	38	19	18	3	3	17	0	38	5
Weston, Scranton W.B.	10	6	.625	3.11	26	24	1	1	1	0	170.2	165	65	59	12	3	29	2	79	4
Wickman, Columbus	12	5	.706	2.92	23	23	2	0	1	0	157.0	131	61	51	12	5	55	0	108	10
Wiegandt, Scranton W.B.*	0	0	.000	0.00	1	0	0	1	0	0	1.0	0	0	0	0	0	2	0	0	0
Williams, Scranton W.B.	9	1	.900	2.43	16	16	3	0	1	0	92.2	84	26	25	4	0	30	2	59	2
Williams, Syracuse	6	8	.429	3.13	25	16	1	3	0	1	120.2	115	46	42	4	3	41	0	81	5
Williamson, Rochester	0	0	.000	0.00	4	0	0	3	0	2	3.2	2	0	0	0	0	0	0	1	0
Wohlers, Richmond	0	0	.000	3.93	27	2	0	20	0	9	34.1	32	16	15	0	0	17	3	33	6
Wolf, Toledo	2	0	1.000	3.12	3	3	0	0	0	0	17.1	16	6	6	0	1	13	0	18	0
Young, Columbus*	0	0	.000	3.38	3	3	0	0	0	0	16.0	16	6	6	1	0	6	0	2	0

BALKS—Reynoso, 5; Birkbeck, Clayton, Hoy, Mathews, D. Stanford, 3 each; Cerutti, Dopson, Gomez, Hillman, R. Lewis, Morton, Telford, Walter, 2 each; Bark, Castillo, Combs, Conroy, Fischer, Gohr, Green, Hentgen, Holcomb, J. Johnson, Linton, Martel, McMichael, Militello, Miller, Oquist, Parris, Patterson, Plympton, Quantrill, Rivera, Rosario, Schourek, Shea, Shikles, Telgheder, Trlicek, Walker, Ward, Wegmann, Weston, Wickman, G. Williams, 1 each.

COMBINATION SHUTOUTS—Clayton-Stanford, Cook-Rosario, Johnson-DeLaRosa-Draper, Johnson-Rosario-Draper, Militello-DeLaRosa-Rosario, Springer-Rosario-Draper, Columbus; Morton-Plympton-Irvine, Shikles-Ryan, Taylor-Plympton-Ryan, Pawtucket; Reynoso-Taylor 2, Bark-Polley-McCarthy, McCarthy-Taylor, McMichael-Bark, McMichael-St. Claire, Nied-Polley, Reynoso-Polley-McCarthy, Smith-McCarthy, Richmond; Drummond-Pennington, Leinen-Layana, Miller-Poole-Stephan-Pennington-Williamson, Oquist-Leinen, Oquist-Moore-Layana, Oquist-Pennington, Rhodes-Stephan-Layana, Stephan-Hall-Jones, Rochester; Abbott-Baller-Sims-Ayrault, Brantley-Mauser, Greene-Mauser-Ritchie, Hartley-Ayrault, Weston-Ayrault, Scranton-Wilkes Barre; Edwards-Hall, Leiter-Hall, Weathers-Hall, Williams-Dayley-Hall, Syracuse; Marshall-Dewey, Marshall-Hillman-Moore, Marshall-Moore-Dewey, Rauth-Plummer, Schourek-Plummer-Dewey, Wegmann-Moore, Tidewater; Gohr-Kiely, Groom-Castillo, Haas-Kaiser, Moyer-Rightnowar, Wolf-Corbett-Johnson, Toledo.

NO-HIT GAMES—Smith, Richmond, defeated Rochester, 1-0 (seven innings), May 3; Telgheder, Tidewater, defeated Pawtucket, 1-0, May 15; Rivera, Scranton-Wilkes Barre, defeated Pawtucket, 2-0 (seven innings, first game), July 25.

TEAM

Team	Pct.	G	PO	A	E	DP	PB	Team	Pct.	G	PO	A	E	DP	PB
Columbus	.979	144	3807	1461	115	138	22	Toledo	.973	144	3695	1544	145	131	13
Scranton-WB	.976	142	3640	1413	124	131	6	Pawtucket	.972	143	3704	1666	152	148	7
Tidewater	.973	142	3565	1516	140	131	14	Syracuse	.970	143	3733	1537	164	141	15
Rochester	.973	144	3687	1353	139	146	12	Richmond	.967	144	3738	1511	179	141	9

INDIVIDUAL

FIRST BASEMEN

*Throws lefthanded.

Player, Team	Pct.	G	PO	A	E	DP
Alexander, Scranton W.B.	.993	100	789	55	6	72
Bogar, Tidewater	1.000	1	5	1	0	2
Brogna, Toledo*	.991	114	896	76	9	77
Cabrera, Richmond	1.000	12	128	9	0	12
Carey, Rochester	.987	7	70	4	1	11
Crabbe, Syracuse	1.000	8	18	1	0	3
Decillis, Toledo	.994	19	145	8	1	20
Donnels, Tidewater	.984	13	111	10	2	13
Esasky, Richmond	.991	24	199	10	2	13
Grotewold, Scranton W.B.	1.000	6	42	2	0	6
Hansen, Tidewater	.994	80	648	45	4	68
Hare, Toledo*	1.000	11	80	4	0	7
Jennings, Rochester*	.982	49	363	14	7	49
Jordan, Scranton W.B.	1.000	4	47	3	0	4
Klesko, Richmond*	.989	109	947	51	11	96
Lovullo, Columbus	.989	12	79	12	1	9
Lyden, Tidewater	.991	31	216	12	2	24
Maksudian, Syracuse	.995	27	171	11	1	11
Manto, Richmond	1.000	1	9	0	0	2
Martinez, Syracuse	.990	109	918	64	10	97
McKnight, Tidewater	.975	30	212	21	6	12
Milstien, Pawtucket	.986	11	61	7	1	5
Pratt, Scranton W.B.	.947	3	18	0	1	2
Robbins, Rochester	.985	27	192	5	3	20
Rodriguez, Richmond	.935	3	26	3	2	5
Roth, Rochester	1.000	4	24	1	0	1
Sax, Columbus	1.000	8	46	3	0	5
Schu, Scranton W.B.	.991	34	292	25	3	34
Schunk, Syracuse	1.000	4	18	3	0	3
Shamburg, Rochester	.986	50	332	30	5	31
Snider, Pawtucket	.984	7	58	3	1	7
SNOW, Columbus*	.995	132	1097	93	6	107
Sparks, Toledo*	.985	16	124	6	2	12
Sprague, Syracuse	.991	11	101	4	1	9
Twardoski, Pawtucket*	.992	95	832	55	7	87
Vaughn, Pawtucket	.980	38	368	15	8	32
Voigt, Rochester	.977	19	118	11	3	12
Wearing, Rochester	1.000	3	21	1	0	2

SECOND BASEMEN

Player, Team	Pct.	G	PO	A	E	DP
Allison, Tidewater	.917	3	3	8	1	3
Barrett, Pawtucket	.979	82	183	234	9	50
Bell, Rochester	.984	15	30	31	1	6
Bethea, Pawtucket	1.000	1	0	1	0	0
Bogar, Tidewater	.986	80	155	198	5	40
Brumley, Pawtucket	.968	12	31	29	2	11
Byrd, Pawtucket	.958	38	94	87	8	28
Capra, Scranton W.B.	1.000	1	1	2	0	0
CARABALLO, Richmond	.973	100	217	284	14	69
Cedeno, Syracuse	1.000	10	21	16	0	7
Crabbe, Syracuse	.977	50	104	105	5	32
Decillis, Toledo	.973	18	36	37	2	8
DeJardin, Columbus	.970	92	153	234	12	56
Dellicarri, Tidewater	1.000	5	19	10	0	7
Dickerson, Rochester	1.000	3	3	4	0	0
Donnels, Tidewater	1.000	4	5	8	0	2
Giannelli, Syracuse	1.000	8	12	10	0	3
Gutierrez, Rochester	.986	82	171	175	5	50
Hankins, Columbus	.963	5	12	14	1	3
Kelley, Tidewater	.963	7	10	16	1	4
Kelly, Richmond	1.000	3	7	15	0	6
King, Tidewater	1.000	1	1	0	0	0
Legg, Scranton W.B.	.975	35	64	92	4	17
Lofton, Rochester	.986	38	59	81	2	27
Lovullo, Columbus	.981	56	94	160	5	39
Manto, Richmond	.967	13	29	29	2	10
McKnight, Tidewater	.985	17	27	39	1	11
Milstien, Pawtucket	1.000	10	20	21	0	7
Mitchell, Richmond	.000	1	0	0	1	0
Montalvo, Syracuse	.962	27	36	39	3	9
Mordecai, Richmond	.952	13	19	41	3	8
Naehring, Pawtucket	.953	10	22	39	3	12
Noboa, Tidewater	.895	4	9	8	2	5
Paredes, Toledo	1.000	4	5	11	0	5
Robertson, Toledo	1.000	5	13	8	0	5
Rodriguez, Columbus	1.000	1	2	5	0	1
Rodriguez, Scranton W.B.	.979	22	37	57	2	16
Rosario, Toledo	.970	13	31	34	2	5
Scarsone, 88 S.W.B.-20 Roch.	.952	108	209	304	26	77
Schunk, Syracuse	.957	77	169	166	15	45
Shields, Rochester	1.000	1	1	0	0	0
Smith, Toledo	.967	111	241	285	18	68
Smith, 21 Rich.-6 Tide.	.912	27	34	59	9	12
Springer, Tidewater	.963	21	53	51	4	14
Vina, Tidewater	.978	9	16	28	1	4

THIRD BASEMEN

Player, Team	Pct.	G	PO	A	E	DP
Aguayo, Pawtucket	.935	56	39	120	11	14
Allaire, Toledo	.951	80	46	168	11	21
Bethea, Pawtucket	1.000	3	0	12	0	0
Bogar, Tidewater	.891	18	12	37	6	6
Brumley, Pawtucket	.828	7	1	23	5	0
Byrd, Pawtucket	1.000	2	0	3	0	0
Crabbe, Syracuse	.926	7	6	19	2	3
Decillis, Toledo	.880	12	6	16	3	1
Dickerson, Rochester	1.000	4	1	9	0	3
Donnels, Tidewater	.929	65	44	138	14	8
Gonzalez, Pawtucket	.962	15	10	40	2	3
Hankins, Columbus	1.000	1	0	1	0	0
Legg, Scranton W.B.	.977	41	17	68	2	12
Lofton, Rochester	.870	9	5	15	3	2
Lovullo, Columbus	.959	21	13	34	2	6
Lyons, Pawtucket	.909	19	10	40	5	6
Manto, Richmond	.927	108	51	216	21	21
Martinez, Syracuse	.800	4	1	3	1	0
Meulens, Columbus	.920	128	88	255	30	25
Millette, Scranton W.B.	1.000	7	3	17	0	1
Milstien, Pawtucket	.918	51	33	102	12	8
Mitchell, Richmond	1.000	1	0	1	0	0
Montalvo, Syracuse	.960	6	3	21	1	3
Mordecai, Richmond	.867	5	2	11	2	0
Paredes, Toledo	.889	7	2	22	3	4
Quinlan, Syracuse	.940	106	71	276	22	27
Reimink, Toledo	.911	19	14	37	5	4
Robertson, Toledo	.953	38	24	78	5	8
Rodriguez, Richmond	.837	21	6	35	8	3
Rodriguez, Scranton W.B.	.973	21	12	24	1	2
Roth, Rochester	.867	5	4	9	2	1
Scarsone, Rochester	1.000	3	1	6	0	1
Schu, Scranton W.B.	.918	67	32	113	13	12
Schunk, Syracuse	.972	24	18	52	2	7
SHIELDS, Rochester	.954	121	84	265	17	27
Smith, Toledo	.000	2	0	0	1	0
Smith, Richmond	1.000	1	1	0	0	0
Snider, Pawtucket	.900	5	2	7	1	1
Sprague, Syracuse	.895	8	6	11	2	3
Springer, Tidewater	.959	62	38	150	8	13
Szekely, Richmond	1.000	1	0	3	0	2
Voigt, Rochester	.929	11	7	19	2	1
Waller, Scranton W.B.	1.000	14	8	23	0	1
Williams, Richmond	.868	20	7	26	5	3

SHORTSTOPS

Player, Team	Pct.	G	PO	A	E	DP
Alexander, Rochester	.974	6	12	25	1	6
Allaire, Toledo	.981	60	85	169	5	29
Baez, Tidewater	.960	109	147	305	19	60
Batiste, Scranton W.B.	.943	70	105	160	16	38
Bell, Rochester	.955	24	30	55	4	13
Bethea, Pawtucket	1.000	2	2	6	0	1
Bogar, Tidewater	.970	36	38	91	4	20
Brumley, Pawtucket	.905	10	13	25	4	1
Byrd, Pawtucket	.956	29	62	91	7	22
Castilla, Richmond	.944	125	162	357	31	72
Cedeno, Syracuse	1.000	8	15	27	0	2
DeJardin, Columbus	.978	38	54	121	4	25
Dickerson, Rochester	.955	75	83	172	12	43
Gutierrez, Rochester	.949	53	80	108	10	23
Henderson, Syracuse	.875	6	5	16	3	5
Millette, Scranton W.B.	.963	69	92	216	12	43
Milstien, Pawtucket	.857	9	8	22	5	3

Player. Team	Pct.	G	PO	A	E	DP
Montalvo, Syracuse	.957	32	43	90	6	15
Mordecai, Richmond	.938	17	27	49	5	19
Quinlan, Syracuse	1.000	2	2	3	0	1
Rodriguez, Scranton W.B.	.882	4	4	11	2	1
Rosario, Toledo	.939	82	135	247	25	45
Schunk, Syracuse	.970	26	31	67	3	9
SILVESTRI, Columbus	.977	114	195	265	11	61
Smith, Toledo	.891	11	16	33	6	9
Smith, 6 Rich.-6 Tide.	.940	12	17	30	3	8
Valentin, Pawtucket	.962	97	148	358	20	70
Zosky, Syracuse	.932	84	123	249	27	49

OUTFIELDERS

Player. Team	Pct.	G	PO	A	E	DP
Allaire, Toledo	1.000	1	1	0	0	0
Amaro, Scranton W.B.	1.000	18	35	1	0	1
Bradley, Tidewater	1.000	1	2	0	0	0
Brady, Scranton W.B.	1.000	3	7	1	0	0
Brumley, Pawtucket	.979	49	88	6	2	1
Buford, Rochester	.971	45	100	1	3	1
Burnitz, Tidewater	.967	118	222	11	8	2
Cangelosi, Toledo*	1.000	21	48	1	0	0
Capra, Scranton W.B.	1.000	16	31	0	0	0
Carey, Rochester	1.000	1	2	0	0	0
Carter, Toledo	.962	122	221	4	9	1
Castillo, Scranton W.B.	.974	100	216	7	6	4
Chamberlain, Scranton W.B.	1.000	29	51	4	0	1
Clark, Toledo	.932	39	65	4	5	0
Clayton, Columbus	1.000	1	1	0	0	0
Crabbe, Syracuse	1.000	1	1	0	0	0
Davis, Syracuse	.991	108	201	10	2	1
Decillis, Toledo	1.000	2	2	0	0	0
Dickerson, Rochester	1.000	1	2	0	0	0
Dostal, Scranton W.B.*	.988	47	83	2	1	0
Dozier, Tidewater	.952	56	76	4	4	0
Gallagher, Tidewater	1.000	3	13	1	0	1
Giannelli, Syracuse	.961	69	115	8	5	0
Gonzalez, Scranton W.B.	1.000	16	35	1	0	0
Gregg, Richmond*	.964	30	53	0	2	0
Hansen, Tidewater	1.000	26	33	2	0	0
Hare, Toledo	.970	49	93	3	3	1
Housie, Pawtucket	.967	133	313	11	11	2
Howard, Richmond	1.000	6	10	0	0	0
Howell, Tidewater	.982	101	259	10	5	0
HUMPHREYS, Columbus	.996	111	217	6	1	0
Hunter, Scranton W.B.	1.000	1	4	0	0	0
Hurst, Toledo*	1.000	45	94	0	0	0
Ingram, Rochester*	.970	99	155	5	5	0
Jennings, Rochester*	.975	47	75	3	2	0
Kelly, Pawtucket	1.000	1	1	0	0	0
Knoblauh, Columbus	.974	18	35	2	1	0
Lindeman, Scranton W.B.	1.000	8	9	0	0	0
Lovullo, Columbus	1.000	1	1	0	0	0
Lyons, Pawtucket	1.000	17	34	2	0	0
Maksudian, Scranton W.B.	1.000	1	2	0	0	0
Marsh, Scranton W.B.	.973	22	35	1	1	0
Masse, Columbus	.973	75	140	6	4	1
May, Tidewater	.980	74	144	6	3	2
McCray, Tidewater	1.000	4	6	0	0	0
McKnight, Tidewater	.982	60	102	7	2	1
Meadows, Rochester	.984	37	61	1	1	0
Mercedes, Rochester	.964	99	201	12	8	5
Mitchell, Richmond	.962	119	195	9	8	1
Moore, Richmond	.994	82	146	8	1	3
Paredes, Toledo	.968	14	28	2	1	0
Paris, Pawtucket	.961	30	45	4	2	0
Pederson, Syracuse*	.953	69	118	4	6	1
Peguero, Scranton W.B.	.989	71	185	0	2	0
Pettis, Toledo	1.000	10	20	0	0	0
Plantier, Pawtucket	1.000	12	23	1	0	0
Robertson, Toledo	.985	30	60	6	1	1
Ross, 101 Rich.-2 Paw.*	.960	103	190	2	8	1
Roth, Rochester	.929	5	12	1	1	1
Scott, Syracuse	.955	7	21	0	1	0
Shelby, Pawtucket	.994	95	152	12	1	0
Snider, Pawtucket	.990	83	192	13	2	3
Snow, Columbus*	.750	4	6	0	2	0
Stone, 22 Tol.-9 S.W.B.	.968	31	57	3	2	1
Thompson, Syracuse	.986	111	270	8	4	0
Tomberlin, Richmond*	.985	112	184	9	3	0
Twardoski, Pawtucket*	.971	18	31	2	1	0
Voigt, Rochester	.977	101	205	6	5	0
Wade, Rochester	.909	15	19	1	2	0
Waggoner, Richmond	1.000	7	13	0	0	0
Ward, Syracuse	.967	71	143	3	5	1
Wearing, Rochester	1.000	1	1	0	0	0
B. Williams, Columbus	.990	92	205	2	2	0
Williams, Scranton W.B.	.977	104	205	10	5	0
G. Williams, Columbus	.977	142	332	14	8	5
Yacopino, Rochester*	.975	120	261	12	7	5
Zupcic, Pawtucket	1.000	9	19	0	0	0

CATCHERS

Player. Team	Pct.	G	PO	A	E	DP	PB
Ausmus, Columbus	.988	107	666	63	9	6	8
Bradley, Tidewater	.986	24	129	10	2	1	2
Cabrera, Richmond	.974	55	413	41	12	3	7
Clark, Toledo	.978	16	80	9	2	0	2
Cuevas, Richmond	1.000	3	12	2	0	0	2
DEAK, Richmond	.995	78	527	43	3	6	2
Dziadkowiec, Tidewater	.942	8	42	7	3	0	0
Flaherty, Pawtucket	.978	27	158	17	4	2	2
Geren, Pawtucket	.996	55	257	23	1	2	1
Gonzalez, Tidewater	.992	38	209	26	2	2	6
Gonzalez, Toledo	.976	9	38	3	1	1	1
Grotewold, Scranton W.B.	.957	3	22	0	1	0	0
Knorr, Syracuse	.988	39	220	22	3	1	1
Lehman, Rochester	1.000	8	46	2	0	1	1
Liddell, Rochester	.982	8	55	1	1	0	0
Lieberthal, Scranton W.B.	.989	16	86	6	1	0	0
Lindsey, Scranton W.B.	.992	87	574	59	5	5	4
Livesey, Columbus	1.000	3	12	1	0	0	2
Lyden, Tidewater	.982	28	153	13	3	2	2
Maksudian, Syracuse	.996	44	226	19	1	3	5
Marzano, Pawtucket	.966	11	53	4	2	2	0
McGriff, Syracuse	.988	15	75	6	1	1	1
Mercado, Tidewater	.985	52	307	31	5	2	4
Monzon, Syracuse	1.000	9	27	4	0	1	0
Parent, Rochester	.994	91	588	49	4	8	4
Pevey, Toledo	.970	25	145	16	5	5	1
Pratt, Scranton W.B.	.980	22	134	16	3	0	2
Ramos, Columbus	.939	4	31	0	2	0	0
Robbins, Rochester	.994	53	295	20	2	4	7
Rodriguez, Pawtucket	.987	17	67	7	1	3	2
Rosado, Scranton W.B.	1.000	4	21	2	0	0	0
Rowland, Toledo	.991	107	628	68	6	5	9
Sax, Columbus	.992	35	229	16	2	3	12
Sprague, Syracuse	.976	50	331	29	9	5	8
Stephens, Scranton W.B.	.978	17	82	6	2	0	0
Szekely, Richmond	.976	11	71	9	2	1	0
Wedge, Pawtucket	.987	48	209	20	3	2	2

PITCHERS

Player. Team	Pct.	G	PO	A	E	DP
Abbott, Scranton W.B.*	1.000	5	2	1	0	0
Aldred, Toledo	1.000	16	4	14	0	1
Alvarez, Syracuse	1.000	22	2	8	0	1
Ashby, Scranton W.B.	.800	7	1	3	1	1
August, Toledo	1.000	5	0	1	0	0
Ayrault, Scranton W.B.	1.000	20	0	3	0	0
Baller, Scranton W.B.	.750	44	2	1	1	0
Bark, Richmond*	1.000	22	1	5	0	0
Birkbeck, Tidewater	.973	21	12	24	1	0
Blohm, Syracuse	.815	37	6	16	5	1
Bogar, Tidewater	1.000	3	1	0	0	0
Borland, Scranton W.B.	1.000	27	0	6	0	0
Brantley, Scranton W.B.	.667	5	1	1	1	1
Brennan, Toledo	.875	12	4	3	1	0
Brink, Scranton W.B.	.941	17	6	10	1	1
Brown, Syracuse	1.000	4	0	1	0	0
Castillo, Toledo*	1.000	12	0	13	0	0
Cerutti, Pawtucket*	1.000	24	6	25	0	2
Chapin, Tidewater	1.000	40	0	7	0	0
Cinnella, Tidewater	.875	10	0	7	1	1
CLAYTON, Columbus	1.000	36	10	23	0	1
Coffman, Richmond	.947	16	4	14	1	0
Combs, Scranton W.B.*	.897	21	6	20	3	1
Conroy, Pawtucket	.933	15	6	8	1	0
Cook, Columbus	.917	32	10	12	2	4
Corbett, Toledo*	1.000	10	0	6	0	0
Cross, Syracuse	1.000	4	1	1	0	0
Cummings, Toledo	1.000	5	0	5	0	0
DeLaRosa, Columbus	1.000	48	2	1	0	0
DeSilva, Toledo	1.000	7	1	3	0	1
Dewey, Tidewater	.900	43	2	7	1	0
Dopson, Pawtucket	1.000	6	3	8	0	0
Douma, Tidewater*	1.000	6	0	2	0	1
Draper, Columbus	1.000	58	4	13	0	3
Drummond, Rochester	.000	2	0	0	1	0
Edwards, Syracuse*	.909	41	7	23	3	4
Eufemia, Tidewater	1.000	11	2	3	0	0
Filer, Tidewater	.900	18	5	22	3	1
Fischer, Pawtucket*	1.000	36	2	8	0	1
Fletcher, Scranton W.B.	1.000	4	3	1	0	0
Gakeler, Toledo	1.000	3	2	0	0	0
Gardiner, Pawtucket	1.000	5	1	4	0	0
Gibson, Tidewater*	1.000	2	0	2	0	0
Gohr, Toledo	1.000	22	9	15	0	0
Gomez, Richmond*	.900	23	0	9	1	0
Gonzales, Toledo*	.938	18	2	13	1	0
Green, Scranton W.B.	1.000	2	1	2	0	0
Greene, Scranton W.B.	.750	5	1	2	1	0
Groom, Toledo*	.963	16	7	19	1	0
Haas, Toledo	1.000	22	10	18	0	0
Hall, Syracuse	.895	55	8	9	2	0
Hartley, Scranton W.B.	1.000	3	0	1	0	0

Player, Team	Pct.	G	PO	A	E	DP
Hentgen, Syracuse	1.000	4	1	3	0	0
Hillegas, Columbus	1.000	4	1	3	0	1
Hillman, Tidewater*	.929	34	2	11	1	4
Holcomb, Columbus*	1.000	18	0	2	0	0
Hoy, Pawtucket	1.000	45	1	20	0	3
Hutton, Columbus	1.000	1	1	1	0	0
Irvine, Pawtucket	1.000	36	1	7	0	2
Johnson, Toledo	1.000	25	2	12	0	1
Johnson, Columbus*	.929	11	3	10	1	2
Kaiser, Toledo*	1.000	28	1	5	0	0
Kamieniecki, Columbus	1.000	2	1	3	0	0
Kiely, Toledo*	1.000	21	1	1	0	0
King, Toledo	1.000	3	0	2	0	0
Kline, 16 Tide.- 11 Tol.	1.000	27	3	5	0	0
Knudson, Toledo	1.000	12	2	1	0	0
Layana, Rochester	.800	41	0	8	2	1
Leinen, Rochester*	1.000	17	4	12	0	0
Leiter, Syracuse*	.969	27	7	24	1	2
J. Lewis, Rochester	.900	33	3	6	1	0
R. Lewis, Rochester	.889	24	8	24	4	2
Linton, Syracuse	.920	25	16	30	4	2
Livernois, Pawtucket	.750	6	1	2	1	0
Lovelace, Toledo*	.833	15	2	3	1	0
MacDonald, Syracuse*	1.000	17	0	5	0	0
Marshall, Tidewater*	.862	26	4	21	4	0
Martel, Columbus	.815	26	11	11	5	0
Mathews, Scranton W.B.*	.909	16	2	8	1	0
Mauser, Scranton W.B.	.926	45	6	19	2	0
McCarthy, Richmond	.895	48	2	15	2	2
McMichael, Richmond	.938	19	6	9	1	0
Milacki, Rochester	1.000	9	6	7	0	0
Militello, Columbus	1.000	22	12	14	0	2
Miller, Rochester	1.000	12	2	5	0	0
Mills, Rochester	1.000	3	1	0	0	0
Minchey, Pawtucket	1.000	2	1	1	0	1
Mmahat, Columbus*	.500	2	1	0	1	0
Moore, Tidewater	.920	50	7	16	2	1
Moore, Rochester*	1.000	16	1	0	0	0
Morton, Pawtucket*	.968	26	6	24	1	0
Moyer, Toledo*	.971	21	9	24	1	1
Nezelek, Richmond	1.000	2	2	1	0	0
Nied, Richmond	.938	26	8	22	2	0
Nielsen, Columbus*	1.000	4	1	0	0	0
O'Donoghue, Rochester*	.857	13	4	8	2	1
Oquist, Rochester	1.000	26	7	23	0	3
Parris, Scranton W.B.	1.000	11	6	15	0	0
Patterson, Scranton W.B.	.875	11	3	4	1	1
Pena, 1 Tol.- 17 Tide.*	1.000	18	0	1	0	0
Pennington, Rochester*	.714	29	0	5	2	2
Plummer, Tidewater	.923	31	2	10	1	1
Plympton, Pawtucket	.867	58	5	8	2	1
Polley, Richmond*	.900	39	1	17	2	1
Poole, Rochester	.917	32	4	7	1	0
Popplewell, Columbus	1.000	4	1	0	0	0
Quantrill, Pawtucket	.973	19	8	28	1	5
Quirico, Columbus*	1.000	1	0	3	0	0
Rasmussen, Rochester*	.909	9	2	8	1	0
Rauth, Tidewater	1.000	26	9	13	0	1
Reynoso, Richmond	.906	28	14	34	5	3
Rhodes, Rochester*	.857	17	3	9	2	0
Rightnowar, Toledo	.929	34	8	5	1	2
Ritchie, Scranton W.B.*	1.000	15	1	1	0	0
Rivera, Scranton W.B.	1.000	2	1	0	0	0
Robinson, Toledo	1.000	13	1	3	0	0
Robinson, Richmond	.808	29	7	14	5	0
Rosario, Columbus*	.947	54	4	14	1	1
St. Claire, Richmond	.870	39	3	17	3	2
Sanchez, Rochester*	1.000	4	0	4	0	0
Schourek, Tidewater*	.909	8	6	4	1	1
Searcy, Scranton W.B.*	1.000	8	2	2	0	0
Shea, Syracuse*	.938	25	4	11	1	0
Shikles, Pawtucket	.929	29	14	25	3	3
Sims, Scranton W.B.*	.957	44	2	20	1	2
Smith, Richmond	1.000	15	8	15	0	2
Springer, Columbus	1.000	20	13	9	0	0
D. Stanford, Columbus	.875	40	5	2	1	0
Stephan, Rochester	1.000	44	4	3	0	1
Stevens, Scranton W.B.	1.000	9	0	3	0	0
Taylor, Pawtucket*	.944	26	4	30	2	1
Taylor, Richmond	.909	47	2	8	1	0
Telford, Rochester	.892	27	8	25	4	5
Telgheder, Tidewater	.942	28	14	35	3	4
Trlicek, Syracuse	1.000	35	6	7	0	0
Valera, Tidewater	1.000	1	0	1	0	0
Vasquez, Tidewater	.667	20	2	0	1	0
Walker, Toledo	.960	42	10	14	1	2
Walter, Syracuse*	.833	39	1	9	2	0
Walters, Pawtucket	1.000	38	2	6	0	0
Ward, Syracuse*	.833	20	2	8	2	0
Weathers, Syracuse	1.000	12	6	4	0	0
Wegmann, Tidewater	.818	7	4	5	2	0
Weston, Scranton W.B.	.962	26	27	24	2	2
Wickman, Columbus	.980	23	19	31	1	1
Wiegandt, Scranton W.B.*	1.000	1	0	1	0	0
Williams, Syracuse	.941	25	5	11	1	1
Williams, Scranton W.B.	.960	16	4	20	1	3
Wohlers, Richmond	1.000	27	3	3	0	0
Wolf, Toledo	1.000	3	0	2	0	0
Young, Columbus*	1.000	3	0	2	0	0

The following players did not have any fielding statistics at the positions indicated or appeared only as a designated hitter, pinch-hitter or pinch-runner: G. Alexander, of; Ausmus, of; Blosser, ph; Dayley, p; Dickerson, 1b; Dixon, pr; Dorn, p; Greer, p; Guzman, p; G. Hall, p; Humphreys, 3b; L. Johnson, p; Jones, p; Lyons, p; Meulens, 2b; Mordecai, of; Noboa, of; Pevey, 3b; Riley, p; Robertson, p; V. Rosario, 3b; Rowland, 1b; Rumer, p; Ryan, p; Sax, of; Schunk, of; Seiler, p; L. Stanford, p; Szekely, of; Wa. Taylor, p; Timlin, p; M. White, dh; Williamson, p.

LEAGUE CHAMPIONS

Year	Team	Pct.
1884 —	Trenton	.520
1885 —	Syracuse	.584
1886 —	Utica	.646
1887 —	Toronto	.644
1888 —	Syracuse	.723
1889 —	Detroit	.649
1890 —	Detroit	.617
1891 —	Buffalo (reg. season)	.727
	Buffalo (supplem'l)	.680
1892 —	Providence	.615
	Binghamton*	.667
1893 —	Erie	.606
1894 —	Providence	.696
1895 —	Springfield	.687
1896 —	Providence	.602
1897 —	Syracuse	.632
1898 —	Montreal	.586
1899 —	Rochester	.624
1900 —	Providence	.616
1901 —	Rochester	.642
1902 —	Toronto	.669
1903 —	Jersey City	.742
1904 —	Buffalo	.657
1905 —	Providence	.638
1906 —	Buffalo	.607
1907 —	Toronto	.619
1908 —	Baltimore	.593
1909 —	Rochester	.596
1910 —	Rochester	.601
1911 —	Rochester	.645
1912 —	Toronto	.595
1913 —	Newark	.625
1914 —	Providence	.617
1915 —	Buffalo	.632
1916 —	Buffalo	.586
1917 —	Toronto	.604
1918 —	Toronto	.693
1919 —	Baltimore	.671
1920 —	Baltimore	.719
1921 —	Baltimore	.717
1922 —	Baltimore	.689
1923 —	Baltimore	.677
1924 —	Baltimore	.709
1925 —	Baltimore	.633
1926 —	Toronto	.657
1927 —	Buffalo	.667
1928 —	Rochester	.549
1929 —	Rochester	.613
1930 —	Rochester	.629
1931 —	Rochester	.601
1932 —	Newark	.649
1933 —	Newark	.622
	Buffalo (4th)†	.494
	Toronto (3rd)†	.559
1934 —	Newark	.608
	Toronto (3rd)†	.559
1935 —	Montreal	.597
	Syracuse (2nd)†	.565
1936 —	Buffalo‡	.610
1937 —	Newark‡	.717
1938 —	Newark‡	.684
1939 —	Jersey City	.582
	Rochester (2nd)†	.556
1940 —	Rochester	.611
	Newark (2nd)†	.594
1941 —	Newark	.649
	Montreal (2nd)†	.584
1942 —	Newark	.601
	Syracuse (3rd)†	.513
1943 —	Toronto	.625
	Syracuse (3rd)†	.536
1944 —	Baltimore‡	.553
1945 —	Montreal	.621
	Newark (2nd)†	.582
1946 —	Montreal‡	.649
1947 —	Jersey City	.610
	Syracuse (3rd)†	.575
1948 —	Montreal‡	.614
1949 —	Buffalo	.584
	Montreal (3rd)†	.545
1950 —	Rochester	.609
	Baltimore (3rd)†	.556
1951 —	Montreal‡	.617
1952 —	Montreal	.629
	Rochester (3rd)†	.619
1953 —	Rochester	.630
	Montreal (2nd)†	.586
1954 —	Toronto	.630
	Syracuse (4th)§	.510
1955 —	Montreal	.617
	Rochester (4th)†	.497
1956 —	Toronto	.566
	Rochester (2nd)†	.553
1957 —	Toronto	.575
	Buffalo (2nd)†	.571
1958 —	Montreal‡	.588
1959 —	Buffalo	.582
	Havana (3rd)†	.523
1960 —	Toronto‡	.649
1961 —	Columbus	.597
	Buffalo (3rd)†	.559
1962 —	Jacksonville	.610
	Atlanta (3rd)†	.539
1963 —	Syracuse x	.533
	Indianapolis‡	.562

Year	Team	Pct.
1964—	Jacksonville	.589
	Rochester (4th)†	.532
1965—	Columbus	.582
	Toronto (3rd)†	.556
1966—	Rochester	.565
	Toronto (2nd-tied)†	.558
1967—	Richmond	.574
	Toledo (3rd)†	.525
1968—	Toledo	.565
	Jacksonville (4th)†	.514
1969—	Tidewater	.563
	Syracuse (3rd)†	.536
1970—	Syracuse‡	.600
1971—	Rochester‡	.614
1972—	Louisville	.563
	Tidewater (3rd)†	.545
1973—	Charleston	.586
	Pawtucket y†	.534

Year	Team	Pct.
1974—	Memphis	.613
	Rochester x‡	.611
1975—	Tidewater‡	.610
1976—	Rochester	.638
	Syracuse (2nd)†	.590
1977—	Pawtucket	.571
	Charleston (2nd)‡	.557
1978—	Charleston	.607
	Richmond (4th)†	.511
1979—	Columbus‡	.612
1980—	Columbus‡	.593
1981—	Columbus‡	.633
1982—	Richmond	.590
	Tidewater (3rd)†	.540
1983—	Columbus	.593
	Tidewater (4th)†	.511
1984—	Columbus	.590
	Pawtucket (4th)†	.536

Year	Team	Pct.
1985—	Syracuse	.564
	Tidewater (4th)†	.540
1986—	Richmond‡	.571
1987—	Tidewater	.579
	Columbus†	.550
1988—	Rochester z	.546
	Tidewater	.546
1989—	Syracuse	.572
	Richmond z	.555
1990—	Rochester z	.614
	Columbus	.596
1991—	Columbus z	.590
	Pawtucket	.552
1992—	Columbus z	.660
	Scranton-WB	.592

*Won split-season playoff. †Won four-team playoff. ‡Won championship and four-team playoff. §Defeated Havana in game to decide fourth place, then won four-team playoff. xLeague was divided into Northern, Southern divisions. yLeague divided into American, National divisions. zLeague divided into Eastern, Western divisions; won playoffs. (NOTE—Known as Eastern League in 1884, New York State League in 1885, International League in 1886-87, International Association in 1888, International League in 1889-90, Eastern Association in 1891 and Eastern League from 1892 until 1912.)

MEXICAN LEAGUE

FINAL STANDINGS

NORTHERN ZONE

Team	M.T.	M.R.	Min.	Yuc.	Cam.	Ver.	Tab.	Cor.	N.L.	U.L.	M.I.	Sal.	Ags.	M.S.	Mva.	Jal.	W	L	T	Pct.	GB
Mexico City Tigers	..	7	5	6	7	8	8	8	2	4	1	3	5	4	4	4	76	52	2	.594	....
Mexico City Reds	7	..	5	7	5	7	7	8	5	3	3	3	2	2	3	4	71	56	4	.559	4½
Minatitlan	6	6	..	8	7	10	9	7	3	3	2	2	1	3	3	2	72	58	3	.554	5
Yucatan	5	5	4	..	4	5	10	4	6	2	2	3	4	6	5		70	61	2	.534	7½
Campeche	5	5	4	7	..	5	8	8	3	6	2	2	3	4	6	5	64	64	3	.500	12
Veracruz	4	4	2	8	7	..	7	5	6	2	4	2	2	2	1		62	70	0	.470	16
Tabasco	4	3	7	4	7	..		7	5	2	4	1	2	3	3	4	56	75	2	.427	21½
Cordoba	2	3	7	2	4	7	6	..	2	3	3	1	3	3	1		50	79	1	.388	26½

SOUTHERN ZONE

Team	M.T.	M.R.	Min.	Yuc.	Cam.	Ver.	Tab.	Cor.	N.L.	U.L.	M.I.	Sal.	Ags.	M.S.	Mva.	Jal.	W	L	T	Pct.	GB
Nuevo Laredo	4	1	3	2	3	0	4	4	..	5	6	8	9	10	5	7	71	61	0	.538	....
Union Laguna	2	3	3	0	1	4	4	3	9	..	5	6	8	7	10	5	71	61	0	.538	....
Monterrey Ind.	3	3	4	4	2	2	4	3	6	6	..	7	7	9	10	5	70	63	0	.530	1
Saltillo	3	3	4	4	3	2	3	6	6	5	..	9	5	7	6	69	63	0	.523	2
Aguascalientes	1	4	3	4	4	2	5	4	6	7	3	..	6	9	7	69	64	0	.519	2½
Monterrey Sultans	2	4	5	2	4	3	5	3	5	3	9		8	..	8	67	66	1	.504	4½
Monclova	2	3	2	0	3	2	2	3	7	3	5	5	7		..	6	65	68	0	.489	6½
Jalisco	2	2	3	1	5	2	4	4	3	5	6	5	3		9	..	58	73	1	.443	12½

Playoffs—Mexico City Tigers defeated Yucatan, four games to none; Minatitlan defeated Mexico City Reds, four games to three; Nuevo Laredo defeated Saltillo, four games to two; Union Laguna defeated Monterrey Industrials, four games to three. Mexico City Tigers defeated Minatitlan, four games to two, in Southern Zone finals; Nuevo Laredo defeated Union Laguna, four games to two, in Northern Zone finals. Mexico City Tigers defeated Nuevo Laredo, four games to two, in final series to capture league championship.

(Compiled by Ana Luisa Talarico, League Statistician, Mexico, D.F.)

BATTING

TEAM

Team	Avg.	G	AB	R	OR	H	TB	2B	3B	HR	RBI	SH	SF	HP	BB	Int. BB	SO	SB	CS	LOB
Mexico City Reds	.303	131	4481	824	655	1357	2049	225	28	137	755	43	36		605	33	676	143	45	1063
Mexico City Tigers	.293	130	4257	690	570	1246	1829	205	27	108	637	69	38	48	492	45	574	90	49	954
Jalisco	.292	131	4418	642	738	1288	1803	204	46	73	578	57	58	44	421	38	656	94	53	939
Aguascalientes	.291	134	4580	702	714	1335	1959	198	33	120	645	94	46	27	480	43	637	64	54	989
Monclova	.289	132	4523	694	785	1309	1797	203	30	75	620	73	44	40	513	62	715	104	76	1052
Monterrey Ind.	.288	132	4398	641	593	1265	1873	214	20	118	593	49	34	36	398	29	578	47	47	873
Saltillo	.288	133	4393	672	680	1265	1814	235	43	76	623	61	49	40	554	51	704	113	73	990
Union Laguna	.288	133	4544	688	659	1308	1865	195	31	100	629	49	42	57	444	31	672	74	54	961
Yucatan	.278	133	4386	670	617	1219	1690	184	25	79	598	89	44	55	543	58	681	194	98	977
Nuevo Laredo	.277	133	4475	657	609	1241	1892	184	13	147	601	47	27	50	490	26	592	58	36	986
Minatitlan	.277	133	4307	618	592	1195	1742	190	18	107	572	76	38	35	511	37	575	51	50	940
Monterrey Sultans	.275	133	4389	612	641	1208	1696	178	23	88	565	55	27	27	547	50	693	42	51	1014
Campeche	.263	131	4288	575	550	1129	1596	159	10	96	524	71	36	32	522	38	590	54	53	979
Cordoba	.260	130	4123	496	589	1073	1513	171	16	79	438	66	34	48	402	36	775	74	47	897
Tabasco	.250	133	4261	539	656	1066	1558	170	35	84	476	77	30	50	472	39	750	99	80	896
Veracruz	.246	132	4161	467	539	1023	1353	151	19	47	396	56	25	33	505	36	605	84	48	942

INDIVIDUAL

(Leading qualifiers for batting championship—362 or more plate appearances)

Player, Team	Avg.	G	AB	R	H	TB	2B	3B	HR	RBI	SH	SF	HP	BB	Int. BB	SO	SB	CS
Perez Tovar, Raul, Monclova	.416	129	483	83	201	267	32	5	8	93	1	7	6	62	19	39	14	8
Garbey, Barbaro, Mexico City Tigers	.369	130	469	72	173	284	27	0	28	119	0	10	8	41	13	49	2	0
Alvarez, Chris, Monterrey Industrials	.368	111	378	55	139	197	19	0	13	70	1	3	3	60	3	29	2	1
Carrillo, Matias, Mexico City Tigers	.362	114	437	96	158	278	26	8	26	110	0	6	2	51	8	53	27	8
Castaneda, Nick, Monterrey Sultans	.361	124	407	79	147	262	28	0	29	95	0	2	1	94	10	73	2	0
Gainey, Ty, Mexico City Reds	.360	115	405	114	146	311	18	3	47	133	1	2	3	99	8	97	13	4
De Los Santos, Luis, Jalisco	.355	126	476	86	169	273	30	4	22	96	0	8	3	51	11	74	5	2
Fernandez, Daniel, Mexico City Tigers	.344	127	509	106	175	236	31	9	4	56	10	7	4	78	4	49	41	11
Smith, Gregory, Saltillo	.341	132	487	77	166	234	25	2	13	94	1	5	2	65	14	40	11	8
Garcia, Cornelio, Yucatan	.338	128	456	93	154	221	22	0	15	73	11	4	6	84	13	86	30	18

Departmental leaders: G—O. Sanchez, Wright, 133; AB—Hinzo, 544; R—Tatis, 195; H—Perez Tovar, 201; TB—Gainey, 311; 2B—Al. Sanchez, 38; 3B—Hinzo, 14; HR—Gainey, 47; RBI—Gainey, 133; SH—A. Castro, 19; SF—Sommers, 11; HP—Hinzo, 12; BB—E. Castro, 124; IBB—Perez Tovar, 19; SO—Iturbe, 116; SB—Hinzo, 80; CS—Hinzo, 31.

(All players—listed alphabetically)

Player, Team	Avg.	G	AB	R	H	TB	2B	3B	HR	RBI	SH	SF	HP	BB	Int. BB	SO	SB	CS
Abrego, Jesus, Yucatan	.265	123	385	47	102	141	26	2	3	50	12	5	5	59	8	57	12	12
Abril, Ramon, Monterrey Ind.	.215	51	65	9	14	15	1	0	0	2	0	5	5	59	8	57	12	12
Aganza, Ruben, Monclova	.189	62	169	13	32	53	4	1	5	24	0	1	1	10	1	35	0	1
Agramon, Antonio, Saltillo	.227	51	75	10	17	24	5	1	0	0	1	0	1	10	1	35	0	1
Aguilar, Enrique, Aguascalientes	.319	124	489	75	156	259	30	2	23	83	2	4	2	43	7	25	10	1
Aguilera, Antonio, Monterrey Sultans	.241	88	270	49	65	88	8	3	3	14	4	1	3	45	5	46	10	8
Alfaro, Jesus, Yucatan	.293	125	441	81	129	205	20	1	18	81	7	3	0	71	10	59	3	2
Alicea, Miguel, Union Laguna	.000	1	0	0	0	0	0	0	0	0	0	0	0	0	0	0	0	0
Allen, Rod, Yucatan	.000	3	8	0	0	0	0	0	0	0	0	0	0	0	0	1	0	0
Almeida, Shammar, Saltillo	.250	24	16	2	4	4	0	0	0	0	0	0	1	1		5	0	0
Almodobar, Ricardo, Jalisco	.244	107	303	40	74	89	7	1	2	20	12	0	2	12	0	45	7	5

Player, Team	Avg.	G	AB	R	H	TB	2B	3B	HR	RBI	SH	SF	HP	BB	Int. BB	SO	SB	CS
Alvarado, Ivan, Yucatan	.000	2	4	0	0	0	0	0	0	0	0	0	0	0	0	1	0	0
Alvarez, Chris, Monterrey Industrials	.368	111	378	55	139	197	19	0	13	70	1	3	3	60	3	29	2	1
Alvarez, Hector, Union Laguna	.241	105	369	50	89	122	19	1	4	49	3	3	5	32	0	55	1	2
Alvarez, Heriberto, Aguascalientes	.260	56	127	19	33	50	5	0	4	13	1	0	5	14	1	31	0	2
Arce, Francisco, Veracruz	.256	98	312	30	80	98	11	2	1	24	4	0	5	46	1	33	0	3
Arias, Everardo, Mexico City Tigers	.185	67	92	15	17	20	1	1	0	7	4	2	0	7	0	16	7	0
Arredondo, Luis, Jalisco	.305	106	383	69	117	151	10	9	2	22	5	1	1	46	0	57	28	12
Arzate, Martin, Minatitlan	.265	102	324	44	86	110	14	2	2	28	6	1	2	40	0	28	2	3
Avila, Ruben, Union Laguna	.280	126	446	57	125	167	16	1	8	55	7	2	2	40	3	83	4	2
Avina, Reyes, Minatitlan	.333	6	3	0	1	1	0	0	0	0	0	0	0	2	0	1	0	1
Baca, Manuel, Monterrey Sultans	.219	82	247	19	54	65	8	0	1	31	3	7	3	12	2	42	2	4
Barajas, Mario, Aguascalientes	.111	12	9	2	1	1	0	0	0	0	0	0	0	1	0	2	0	0
Barandica, Juan Carlos, Cordoba	.168	56	167	14	28	28	0	0	0	5	8	1	2	15	0	27	5	0
Barraza, Ernesto, Nuevo Laredo	.000	2	0	1	0	0	0	0	0	0	0	0	0	0	0	0	0	0
Barrera, Jesus, Tabasco	.224	110	339	28	76	86	8	1	0	30	6	2	5	24	1	30	5	5
Barrera, Nelson, Campeche	.275	130	484	74	133	222	12	1	25	87	3	9	6	44	1	96	3	5
Becerra, Juan, Nuevo Laredo	.140	38	50	5	7	8	1	0	0	4	0	0	4	0	7	1	0
Bellazetin, Jose Juan, M. City Tigers	.308	97	289	53	89	117	15	2	3	53	7	2	2	56	0	24	1	3
Bellino, Frank, Veracruz	.115	15	52	3	6	10	1	0	1	4	0	0	0	7	2	12	1	0
Beltran, Gerardo, Tabasco	.282	127	454	60	128	187	27	4	8	46	3	1	6	33	4	82	5	10
Beristain, Gregorio, Monterrey Sultans	.188	36	32	4	6	6	0	0	0	0	1	0	0	1	0	10	0	0
Blocker, Terry, Minatitlan	.318	114	406	61	129	181	22	6	6	49	2	5	2	55	7	47	23	8
Bocardo, Manuel, Monclova	.269	56	134	13	36	45	6	0	1	21	5	1	6	16	0	30	0	0
Brown, Todd, Tabasco	.334	95	320	52	107	160	15	1	12	53	1	3	0	54	7	39	8	8
Brown, Tony, Veracruz	.234	43	158	19	37	72	8	0	9	30	0	4	0	10	3	16	7	1
Burke, Norberto, Cordoba	.200	23	60	3	12	19	2	1	1	5	1	2	0	6	0	9	0	0
Burnet, Arturo, Tabasco	.111	8	9	0	1	1	0	0	0	0	0	0	0	2	0	5	0	1
Bustamante, Miguel, M. City Tigers	1.000	4	1	1	1	1	0	0	0	2	0	0	1	0	0	0	0	0
Camacho, Adulfo, Mexico City Tigers	.229	126	445	72	102	142	17	4	5	39	16	2	4	58	0	52	3	6
Camarero, Rolando, Minatitlan	.200	8	5	1	1	1	0	0	0	0	0	0	0	0	0	2	0	0
Camargo, Alonso, Veracruz	.250	30	68	4	17	24	4	0	1	3	0	0	0	3	0	22	0	1
Campusano, Sil, Saltillo	.283	61	233	46	66	110	15	4	7	40	1	0	4	33	2	47	9	7
Canizales, Juan Carlos, Mont. Sultans	.252	108	317	39	80	118	14	6	4	40	4	1	3	22	1	56	1	9
Cantu, Gerardo, Cordoba	.253	93	269	30	68	93	10	0	5	25	1	1	5	37	2	65	0	1
Carretero, Julio Alberto, Minatitlan	.067	21	15	2	1	1	0	0	0	0	0	0	1	0	1	0	1
Carrillo, Matias, Mexico City Tigers	.362	114	437	96	158	278	26	8	26	110	0	6	2	51	8	53	27	8
Castaneda, Nick, Monterrey Sultans	.361	124	407	79	147	262	28	0	29	95	0	2	2	94	10	73	2	0
Castaneda, Rafael, Mexico City Tigers	.269	122	391	54	105	135	19	1	3	46	8	2	3	52	1	63	2	2
Castelan, Miguel Angel, Yucatan	.245	100	310	40	76	98	9	2	3	37	2	4	0	23	2	61	6	3
Castellanos, Andres, Jalisco	.100	8	10	0	1	1	0	0	0	0	0	0	0	1	1	0	0
Castellanos, Humberto, Jalisco	.000	1	1	0	0	0	0	0	0	0	0	0	0	0	0	0	0	0
Castillo, Alfonso, Campeche	.667	2	3	2	2	3	1	0	0	0	0	0	0	1	0	1	0	0
Castillo, Carmelo, Tabasco	.265	85	309	45	82	143	11	4	14	50	2	2	2	28	2	57	3	5
Castillo, Raul, Tabasco	.182	14	22	1	4	6	0	1	0	5	2	0	0	2	0	3	0	0
Castro, Arnoldo, Minatitlan	.272	127	511	79	139	177	21	1	5	46	19	2	0	33	0	61	5	5
Castro, Eddie, Minatitlan	.310	129	403	84	125	228	26	1	25	94	4	4	3	124	14	89	4	3
Cazarin, Manuel, Minatitlan	.272	117	423	59	115	173	16	0	14	62	6	5	5	47	3	39	2	4
Cecena, Jose Isabel, Saltillo	.000	1	1	0	0	0	0	0	0	0	0	0	0	0	0	0	0	0
Cervera, Francisco, Cordoba	.271	114	377	51	102	139	16	0	7	36	12	3	5	46	2	78	13	6
Chan, Armando, Monclova	.204	48	108	12	22	37	6	0	3	16	0	2	0	8	0	31	0	1
Chan, Claudio, Union Laguna	.000	4	1	1	0	0	0	0	0	0	0	0	0	0	0	1	0	0
Chavez, Guadalupe, Monclova	.000	1	0	0	0	0	0	0	0	0	0	0	0	0	0	0	0	1
Chavez, Jose, Tabasco	.234	77	201	22	47	58	9	1	0	14	15	1	7	10	0	31	6	1
Contreras, Cuitlahuac, Union Laguna	.267	76	131	15	35	49	5	0	3	22	1	0	5	18	2	37	1	0
Contreras, Silvano, Cordoba	.180	40	111	13	20	41	3	0	6	12	2	0	0	7	0	38	0	0
Cornejo, Edgar, Saltillo	.000	3	2	0	0	0	0	0	0	0	0	0	0	0	0	2	0	0
Cruz, Fernando, Saltillo	.278	78	241	26	67	89	14	1	2	36	5	6	3	11	0	38	1	0
Cruz, Luis Alfonso, Union Laguna	.324	123	488	66	158	239	21	3	18	92	1	10	5	24	3	54	4	6
Cruz, Marco, Nuevo Laredo	.243	124	358	40	87	114	9	0	6	37	11	5	7	39	0	61	1	2
Cuevas, Angelo, Minatitlan	.323	62	186	41	60	94	15	2	5	22	2	3	2	39	3	15	4	3
Daut, Manuel, Monclova	.244	92	266	31	65	88	13	2	2	23	0	2	5	29	2	61	7	5
Davis, Mark, Tabasco	.293	116	416	70	122	204	24	8	14	58	7	4	7	61	6	111	23	15
Davis, Trench, Veracruz	.218	15	55	7	12	20	2	0	2	3	0	0	4	5	1	2	3
DeLeon, Luis, Minatitlan	.000	1	1	0	0	0	0	0	0	0	0	0	0	0	0	1	0	0
Delgado, Tomas, Aguascalientes	.000	6	6	2	0	0	0	0	0	0	0	0	0	4	1	3	0	0
De Los Santos, Luis, Jalisco	.355	126	476	86	169	273	30	4	22	96	0	8	3	51	11	74	5	2
Diaz, Luis Fernando, Nuevo Laredo	.262	112	382	62	100	172	19	1	17	53	2	3	1	73	3	94	2	2
Diaz, Remigio, Monterrey Sultans	.241	123	424	47	102	124	14	4	0	32	5	0	3	38	1	56	9	4
Diaz, Luna, Alejandro, Mex. City Reds	.000	3	1	2	0	0	0	0	0	0	0	0	0	2	0	1	0	0
Dojaquez, Omar, Monclova	.250	4	4	0	1	1	0	0	0	0	0	0	0	0	0	2	0	0
Dominguez, David, Veracruz	.284	126	450	54	128	204	20	4	16	66	1	2	0	63	4	71	5	1
Dominguez, Fausto, Jalisco	.250	29	64	6	16	22	6	0	0	8	0	2	1	0	0	14	0	0
Espinoza, Antonio, Jalisco	.235	39	102	18	24	36	6	0	2	8	3	0	7	0	25	0	1
Espinoza, Javier, Minatitlan	.271	114	350	46	95	133	17	3	5	39	12	2	3	33	3	58	4	6
Espinoza, Omar, Tabasco	.154	14	13	4	2	2	0	0	0	0	1	0	0	2	0	3	0	0
Esquer, Ramon, Union Laguna	.267	127	468	95	125	175	27	7	3	39	6	5	6	72	0	62	21	12
Estrada, Francisco, Minatitlan	.254	50	134	17	34	50	7	0	3	17	3	1	3	9	1	8	1	0
Estrada, Hector, Mexico City Reds	.299	89	298	33	89	122	18	0	5	46	2	5	1	15	1	37	3	0
Estrada, Ricardo, Veracruz	.000	2	2	0	0	0	0	0	0	0	0	0	0	0	0	2	0	0
Estrada, Roberto, Campeche	.209	54	134	19	28	35	2	1	1	13	0	0	1	18	0	7	4	1
Estrada, Ruben, Nuevo Laredo	.258	87	236	35	61	76	9	3	0	21	3	0	6	14	0	34	5	2
Felix, Jesus Arturo, Yucatan	.333	6	6	1	2	2	0	0	0	1	1	0	1	0	1	0	0
Fentanes, Oscar, Union Laguna	.344	15	32	5	11	11	0	0	0	5	1	0	0	0	3	0	1
Fernandez, Daniel, Mexico City Reds	.344	127	509	106	175	236	31	9	4	56	10	7	4	78	4	49	41	11
Ford, Curt, Union Laguna	.269	13	52	6	14	18	2	1	0	1	1	0	2	5	0	11	0	2
Franco, Manuel, Monterrey Sultans	.286	11	21	4	6	6	0	0	0	1	0	0	0	0	9	0	0
Francois, Manuel, Saltillo	.301	128	465	86	140	197	32	2	7	53	4	3	4	81	7	82	30	14
Gainey, Ty, Mexico City Reds	.360	115	405	114	146	311	18	3	47	133	1	2	3	99	8	97	13	4
Garbey, Barbaro, Mexico City Tigers	.369	130	469	72	173	284	27	0	28	119	0	10	8	41	13	49	2	0
Garcia, Carlos, Veracruz	.258	90	248	30	64	69	5	0	0	16	10	1	1	28	0	37	1	4
Garcia, Cornelio, Yucatan	.338	128	456	93	154	221	22	0	15	73	11	4	6	84	13	86	30	18
Garcia, Heriberto, Veracruz	.203	127	414	37	84	93	7	1	0	23	12	3	4	27	1	46	5	5
Garcia, Jose, Minatitlan	.364	14	11	2	4	5	1	0	0	1	0	0	0	0	2	0	0
Garcia, Jose Luis, Monterrey Sultans	.309	111	349	58	108	158	18	4	8	59	1	7	7	51	2	63	0	3

Player, Team	Avg.	G	AB	R	H	TB	2B	3B	HR	RBI	SH	SF	HP	BB	Int. BB	SO	SB	CS
Garcia, Jose, Campeche	.000	1	3	0	0	0	0	0	0	0	0	0	0	0	0	2	0	0
Garcia, Juan Manuel, Aguascalientes	.274	87	215	30	59	70	8	0	1	22	8	1	2	36	3	20	0	0
Garcia, Martin, Monclova	.259	101	316	36	82	110	15	2	3	36	6	2	2	34	2	61	3	4
Garcia, Porfirio, Tabasco	.297	25	37	5	11	12	1	0	0	2	0	0	0	5	0	8	1	1
Garibay, Luis, Mexico City Tigers	.284	44	88	16	25	36	2	0	3	9	1	0	2	13	0	35	1	1
Garibay, Roberto, Yucatan	.000	1	1	1	0	0	0	0	0	0	0	0	0	0	0	1	0	0
Garza, Gerardo, Monterrey Ind.	.281	125	424	51	119	150	22	0	3	43	10	2	1	24	0	39	7	2
Garzon, Eliseo, Tabasco	.193	112	332	42	64	110	11	1	11	42	6	3	4	62	4	77	2	1
Gassos, Genaro, Tabasco	.000	1	1	0	0	0	0	0	0	0	0	0	0	0	0	0	0	0
Gastelum, Carlos, Veracruz	.216	100	287	22	62	75	10	0	1	27	7	3	0	11	0	36	0	0
Gavia, Jesus, Veracruz	.288	74	156	14	45	50	5	0	0	12	5	1	2	11	0	18	0	1
Giles, Bryan, Tabasco	.275	25	91	17	25	43	3	3	3	16	1	2	0	13	1	20	0	1
Gomez, Alejandro, Campeche	.216	76	231	21	50	60	10	0	0	23	7	2	0	20	0	28	2	2
Gonzalez, Alfonso, Mexico City Reds	.100	28	10	8	1	1	0	0	0	0	0	0	1	2	0	5	0	0
Gonzalez, Jesus, Campeche	.286	131	503	64	144	193	26	1	7	48	14	3	2	32	3	40	2	2
Gonzalez, Mario Angel, Yucatan	.185	32	65	8	12	15	0	0	1	3	2	0	0	6	0	15	0	0
Gonzalez, Pedro, Yucatan	.233	60	120	16	28	44	7	0	3	18	0	0	1	24	2	34	2	2
Guerrero, Francisco, Mex. City Tigers	.225	119	409	59	92	133	12	1	9	45	6	3	3	40	0	79	7	7
Guerrero, Jaime, Aguascalientes	.249	120	393	54	98	138	16	6	4	36	13	7	4	43	2	72	17	5
Guerrero, Javier, Aguascalientes	.282	49	110	23	31	53	2	1	6	17	1	1	0	19	4	27	1	2
Guerrero, Leobardo, Minatitlan	.000	3	6	0	0	0	0	0	0	0	1	0	0	0	0	2	0	0
Gutierrez, Andres, Veracruz	.226	70	195	24	44	58	8	3	0	12	4	1	0	10	0	40	3	3
Gutierrez, Arnoldo Ivan, Union Laguna	.227	67	141	20	32	57	5	1	6	21	4	2	5	8	0	37	4	1
Gutierrez, Felipe, Campeche	.246	49	171	25	42	60	7	1	3	17	4	1	8	12	1	19	0	2
Gutierrez, Jose Luis, Jalisco	.248	59	109	8	27	29	2	0	0	12	2	2	2	14	2	22	1	1
Guzman, Marco, Campeche	.286	111	370	42	106	142	15	0	7	44	6	4	5	52	4	40	0	4
Hernandez, Eduardo, Saltillo	.262	21	42	5	11	13	2	0	0	8	0	0	0	4	0	5	0	0
Hernandez, Martin, Campeche	.187	34	75	9	14	22	5	0	1	9	0	0	1	4	1	13	1	1
Hernandez, Miguel, Monterrey Sultans	.234	114	286	26	67	75	6	1	0	24	9	1	2	33	0	30	1	5
Herrera, Isidro, Campeche	.296	102	331	47	98	112	7	2	1	30	7	4	6	62	4	24	18	8
Herrera, Ricardo, Jalisco	.300	118	426	84	128	177	19	12	2	39	11	3	4	54	1	45	19	9
Herrera, Roberto, Monterrey Ind.	.000	1	1	0	0	0	0	0	0	0	1	0	0	0	0	0	0	0
Hinzo, Tommy, Yucatan	.303	132	544	96	165	233	25	14	5	67	5	6	12	46	8	69	80	31
Howard, Steve, Aguascalientes	.288	18	66	14	19	22	3	0	0	6	0	0	0	12	2	26	0	1
Hurtado, Hector, Minatitlan	.250	7	20	1	5	5	0	0	0	1	0	0	0	0	0	5	0	0
Ibarra, Jose Alberto, Cordoba	.242	99	335	37	81	121	15	2	7	41	3	3	3	20	5	90	0	3
Iturbe, Pedro, Cordoba	.229	130	467	57	107	129	10	3	2	39	8	4	2	29	3	116	14	6
Jimenez, Jose Luis, Saltillo	.150	21	40	3	6	10	4	0	0	3	0	0	0	6	0	16	0	1
Jimenez, Leopoldo, Monterrey Ind.	.233	84	206	25	48	68	8	0	4	28	3	3	1	44	0	43	0	2
Johnson, Roy, Campeche	.282	123	401	70	113	184	12	1	19	65	0	4	0	105	13	44	3	3
Jones, Barry, Nuevo Laredo	.290	128	497	86	144	232	21	2	21	72	4	2	3	60	10	57	14	12
Jose, Manuel, Veracruz	.229	15	48	4	11	14	1	1	0	5	2	0	1	4	1	9	1	1
Jurak, Ed, Monclova	.252	27	103	18	26	44	7	1	3	19	0	1	0	16	1	13	1	2
Kerfeld, Charlie, Jalisco	.000	1	1	0	0	0	0	0	0	0	0	0	0	0	0	1	0	0
Knabenshue, Chris, Aguascalientes	.363	55	212	49	77	149	17	2	17	43	0	1	0	38	4	54	6	4
Kutcher, Randy, Monterrey Sultans	.138	9	29	3	4	4	0	0	0	0	0	0	0	6	0	11	0	0
Lagunes, Antonio, Monterrey Sultans	.267	19	30	4	8	12	2	1	0	1	0	0	0	4	0	7	0	0
Lara, Hugo, Campeche	.000	2	1	1	0	0	0	0	0	0	0	0	0	0	0	0	0	0
Leal, Guadalupe, Monclova	.285	108	354	52	101	166	19	2	14	46	2	4	1	29	10	69	5	3
Leon, Ramiro, Jalisco	.322	79	205	16	66	79	8	1	1	19	1	2	0	12	2	17	2	1
Leyva, German, Monclova	.293	126	499	79	146	168	14	1	2	42	13	3	2	78	8	24	14	16
Llanes, Juan, Tabasco	.217	27	69	1	15	16	1	0	0	4	0	1	0	5	3	6	0	4
Lopez, Alfredo, Jalisco	.260	26	73	12	19	36	2	3	3	11	1	0	0	6	0	15	1	1
Lopez, Emigdio, Cordoba	.000	2	0	2	0	0	0	0	0	0	0	0	0	0	0	0	0	0
Lopez, Gonzalo, Monclova	.273	106	363	58	99	128	6	7	3	53	14	4	1	41	2	58	9	6
Lopez, Jesus Manuel, Jalisco	.250	13	8	0	2	3	1	0	0	1	0	0	0	1	0	1	0	0
Lopez, Salvador, Aguascalientes	.308	130	523	82	161	204	20	4	5	60	16	5	3	30	1	50	14	9
Loredo, Jorge Luis, Campeche	.237	103	270	27	64	78	9	1	1	24	15	1	1	14	0	39	4	6
Luna, Jose Luis, Aguascalientes	.238	70	168	12	40	51	8	0	1	18	13	2	0	12	0	20	0	0
Machado, Victor, Tabasco	.000	2	2	0	0	0	0	0	0	0	0	0	0	0	0	1	0	0
Machiria, Pablo, Mexico City Tigers	.320	120	435	54	139	203	19	3	13	66	4	2	8	33	6	41	4	1
Magallanes, Wm. Jose, Union Laguna	.286	54	185	30	53	84	8	1	7	29	0	2	5	34	2	47	7	4
Magana, Gabriel, Yucatan	.159	52	69	12	11	13	0	1	0	5	4	0	1	13	0	13	1	4
Mangham, Eric, Mexico City Tigers	.330	95	364	69	120	161	19	5	4	42	5	3	8	49	1	37	27	16
Manriquez, Carlos, Monterrey Sultans	.000	2	4	0	0	0	0	0	0	0	0	0	0	0	0	3	0	0
Marquez, Victor, Union Laguna	.167	6	6	2	1	1	0	0	0	0	0	0	0	0	0	1	0	0
Marrufo, Hector, Tabasco	.000	10	0	3	0	0	0	0	0	0	0	0	0	0	0	0	0	0
Martinez, Asencion, Monterrey Ind.	.120	30	25	3	3	4	1	0	0	1	1	0	0	2	0	9	0	0
Martinez, Grimaldo, Monclova	.260	125	507	87	132	156	12	3	2	46	12	7	4	46	2	65	16	8
Martinez, Raul, Union Laguna	.267	118	408	55	109	157	15	0	11	58	4	7	6	42	1	40	2	3
Medina, Jose Ramon, Campeche	.150	62	107	13	16	19	1	1	0	3	0	1	1	13	0	38	5	3
Medina, Martin, Minatitlan	.444	7	9	1	4	7	3	0	0	2	0	0	0	0	0	3	0	0
Melendez, Francisco, Mexico City Reds	.320	131	488	88	156	222	24	0	14	107	0	6	4	79	4	59	1	4
Mendez, Ramon, Aguascalientes	.350	16	20	4	7	10	0	0	1	3	0	0	0	2	0	3	0	0
Mendez, Roberto, Mexico City Reds	.000	6	0	2	0	0	0	0	0	0	0	0	0	0	0	0	0	0
Mendoza, Eusebio, Jalisco	.500	6	4	0	2	2	0	0	0	0	0	0	0	1	0	1	0	0
Mere, Pedro, Nuevo Laredo	.284	128	429	78	122	187	20	0	15	69	5	2	9	69	3	67	7	0
Meza, Alfredo, Monterrey Sultans	.239	54	71	8	17	21	2	1	0	6	1	0	2	2	1	17	0	0
Meza, Evaristo, Veracruz	.000	1	0	1	0	0	0	0	0	0	0	0	0	0	0	0	0	0
Meza, Leobardo, Veracruz	.000	3	0	0	0	0	0	0	0	0	0	0	0	0	0	0	0	0
Michell, Domingo, Jalisco	.255	89	286	47	73	122	20	4	7	53	1	4	3	72	6	59	11	5
Molina, Jose Joaquin, Aguascalientes	.000	4	1	1	0	0	0	0	0	0	0	0	0	0	0	0	0	0
Monroy, Victor Hugo, Mex. City Tigers	.218	59	101	8	22	31	9	0	0	16	2	3	2	7	0	13	1	0
Montalvo, Ivan, Mexico City Tigers	.167	16	12	3	2	3	1	0	0	1	0	0	0	0	0	5	0	0
Mora, Andres, Nuevo Laredo	.247	98	332	32	82	134	19	0	11	39	0	4	1	33	1	34	1	2
Morales, Florentino, Union Laguna	.218	87	234	22	51	58	7	0	0	16	2	0	6	31	0	36	1	3
Moreno, Lorenzo, Monterrey Ind.	.000	1	0	0	0	0	0	0	0	0	0	0	0	0	0	0	0	0
Moreno, Roberto, Minatitlan	.213	60	164	15	35	40	5	0	0	4	4	0	2	4	0	27	2	3
Morones, Martin, Saltillo	.276	131	510	75	141	202	28	6	7	54	9	3	5	41	3	55	22	16
Motley, Darryl, Monterrey Sultans	.324	68	259	57	84	127	14	1	9	54	0	2	4	28	3	41	4	0
Munoz, Noe, Mexico City Reds	.270	77	196	21	53	65	4	1	2	28	3	0	0	17	0	31	0	1
Munoz, Ricardo, Jalisco	.000	1	1	0	0	0	0	0	0	0	0	0	0	0	0	0	0	0
Narvaez, Arquimedes, Monclova	.241	17	29	3	7	7	0	0	0	0	0	0	2	0	0	3	0	0
Navarro, Ruben, Cordoba	.277	98	314	29	87	129	11	2	9	41	4	1	3	28	2	53	1	3
Noriega, Luis Antonio, Jalisco	.198	41	81	9	16	21	2	0	1	6	0	1	0	11	0	20	1	1

Player, Team	Avg.	G	AB	R	H	TB	2B	3B	HR	RBI	SH	SF	HP	BB	Int. BB	SO	SB	CS
Noris, Rogelio, Mexico City Reds	.264	74	148	26	39	53	3	1	3	16	3	1	3	16	1	28	1	3
Nunez, Juan Jose, Jalisco	.000	1	0	0	0	0	0	0	0	0	0	0	0	0	0	0	0	0
Ontiveros, Juan, Monterrey Ind.	.000	1	1	0	0	0	0	0	0	0	0	0	0	0	0	0	0	0
Ortega, Roberto, Jalisco	.273	17	11	0	3	3	0	0	0	2	0	1	0	2	0	3	0	0
Ortiz, Alejandro, Nuevo Laredo	.304	126	464	79	141	234	7	1	28	83	0	2	4	77	4	75	1	3
Osuna, Antonio, Mexico City Tigers	.000	1	0	1	0	0	0	0	0	0	0	0	0	0	0	0	0	0
Osuna, Hector, Saltillo	.234	62	137	17	32	38	4	1	0	12	2	1	5	14	0	15	2	4
Pacho, Juan Jose, Yucatan	.276	129	456	69	126	148	12	2	2	34	15	4	2	40	1	57	19	2
Pacho, Luis Antonio, Veracruz	.344	18	32	6	11	12	1	0	0	2	0	0	0	2	0	4	0	1
Padron, Jorge Jesus, Veracruz	.125	2	8	0	1	1	0	0	0	0	0	0	0	0	0	0	0	0
Pardo, Victor, Cordoba	.215	75	200	25	43	53	10	0	0	11	4	1	2	13	1	21	4	2
Pena, Carlos, Monterrey Sultans	.296	27	27	6	8	8	0	0	0	2	0	0	1	2	0	10	0	0
Pena, Luis Alberto, Monterrey Ind.	.269	70	186	17	50	75	11	1	4	22	0	3	1	21	2	36	1	3
Peralta, Alfredo, Minatitlan	.000	2	2	0	0	0	0	0	0	0	0	0	0	0	0	1	0	0
Peralta, Amado, Saltillo	.262	127	381	55	100	142	19	1	7	65	3	5	7	76	13	80	4	8
Perez, Alfredo, Mexico City Tigers	.182	7	11	2	2	2	0	0	0	0	0	0	0	1	0	3	0	0
Perez, Carlos, Campeche	.500	16	2	3	1	1	0	0	0	1	0	0	0	1	0	1	0	1
Perez, Francisco, Monterrey Ind.	.274	55	124	20	34	54	7	2	3	15	1	0	3	7	1	38	0	2
Perez, Tovar Raul, Monclova	.416	129	483	83	201	267	32	5	8	93	1	7	6	62	19	39	14	8
Pina, John Joseph, Yucatan	.226	25	84	6	19	28	1	1	2	8	1	0	0	11	1	31	5	3
Plascencia, Obed, Nuevo Laredo	.257	79	187	17	48	56	3	1	1	19	1	2	2	15	0	24	2	1
Ponce, Hector, Campeche	.256	109	422	45	108	125	9	1	2	38	7	0	1	44	0	37	8	10
Pulido, Jesus, Mexico City Tigers	.263	15	19	2	5	5	0	0	0	1	1	0	0	0	0	3	0	0
Quintero, Guadalupe, Monclova	.200	5	5	2	1	1	0	0	0	0	0	0	0	5	0	2	0	0
Quintero, Guillermo, Monterrey Sult.	.125	24	8	10	1	1	0	0	0	0	1	0	0	0	0	1	0	0
Quiroz, Jose Julian, Tabasco	.195	51	82	7	16	24	3	1	1	6	3	0	0	14	0	22	0	1
Ramirez, Efren, Yucatan	.241	56	166	19	40	51	11	0	0	14	2	0	8	19	0	39	3	2
Ramirez, Enrique, Nuevo Laredo	.282	132	496	47	140	182	29	2	3	60	11	2	2	22	0	32	6	3
Ramirez, Gustavo, Monterrey Ind.	.190	18	21	3	4	5	1	0	0	1	1	0	2	5	0	1	0	0
Ramos, Enrique, Monterrey Sultans	.286	9	7	3	2	2	0	0	0	1	0	0	0	0	0	2	1	0
Renteria, Ricardo, Jalisco	.338	114	420	86	142	216	27	4	13	83	1	10	7	50	8	44	17	7
Reyes, Enrique, Aguascalientes	.208	31	72	7	15	16	1	0	0	6	3	0	2	5	0	12	0	0
Reyes, Juan, Monclova	.260	71	204	20	53	83	12	0	6	27	1	2	1	32	10	49	0	0
Reyna, Luis, Cordoba	.283	65	230	34	65	100	14	0	7	29	0	4	3	16	2	25	5	3
Reza, Hector, Union Laguna	.222	38	27	10	6	6	0	0	0	1	0	0	0	1	0	10	1	0
Riesgo, Nikco, Saltillo	.280	17	50	17	14	18	1	0	1	4	2	0	0	14	0	14	7	2
Rivera, Alberto, Jalisco	.241	87	187	27	45	53	6	1	0	17	4	2	7	21	0	38	3	4
Rivera, Eleazar, Aguascalientes	.234	82	214	21	50	60	4	0	2	20	6	4	2	11	0	37	0	0
Rivera, German, Monterrey Sultans	.296	127	463	65	137	191	14	2	12	70	3	3	2	53	6	59	4	7
Robles, Javier, Union Laguna	.268	118	336	59	90	119	12	4	3	36	11	1	3	33	0	78	6	3
Rodriguez, Cecilio, Veracruz	.234	40	94	4	22	22	0	0	0	10	2	2	0	13	1	8	1	3
Rodriguez, Genaro, Cordoba	.236	51	161	19	38	50	7	1	1	17	1	2	2	10	0	22	1	2
Rodriguez, Guillermo, Veracruz	.207	65	237	21	49	72	8	0	5	24	0	2	4	10	3	52	2	2
Rodriguez, Gustavo, Monclova	.252	49	111	19	28	38	3	2	1	11	4	0	1	13	0	30	1	1
Rodriguez, Hector, Mexico City Reds	.294	36	85	12	25	39	6	1	2	10	1	0	2	7	0	22	1	1
Rodriguez, Jose Luis, Saltillo	.291	89	275	38	80	116	17	2	5	28	7	1	4	14	3	48	3	4
Rodriguez, Juan Fco., Monterrey Sult.	.264	128	459	67	121	141	14	3	0	32	17	7	1	74	2	30	4	4
Rodriguez, Victor, Tabasco	.249	44	173	19	43	65	6	2	4	19	2	0	4	17	2	13	1	2
Rojas, Homar, Monterrey Industriales	.260	96	281	31	73	121	9	3	11	45	2	3	1	28	4	43	2	1
Romero, Marco, Nuevo Laredo	.298	123	480	78	143	230	19	1	22	67	2	3	4	36	4	49	7	5
Romero, Oscar, Cordoba	.279	129	448	67	125	211	17	3	21	69	3	6	10	62	4	76	10	6
Rosario, Melvin, Minatitlan	.273	4	11	2	3	3	0	0	0	2	0	0	1	3	0	6	0	0
Rubio, Marco, Minatitlan	.266	116	384	40	102	132	11	2	5	36	2	4	5	25	0	37	3	10
Rubio, Sergio, Yucatan	.207	24	29	9	6	6	0	0	0	1	0	0	0	1	0	8	1	0
Ruiz, Demetrio, Campeche	.271	72	170	17	46	56	8	1	0	19	4	0	0	11	2	14	1	1
Ruiz, Juan De Dios, Union Laguna	.293	126	529	91	155	228	23	4	14	76	5	2	8	28	1	56	21	11
Sabino, Miguel, Veracruz	.308	37	133	21	41	62	9	3	2	14	1	1	0	14	1	22	1	0
Saenz, Ricardo, Saltillo	.275	110	349	50	96	163	32	4	9	45	5	4	2	41	4	92	5	1
Sais, Herminio, Veracruz	.226	33	106	10	24	29	5	0	0	12	4	1	2	11	0	11	0	1
Salgado, Eduardo, Nuevo Laredo	.286	33	14	6	4	7	1	1	0	3	0	0	1	2	0	3	2	1
Samaniego, Manuel, Jalisco	.246	117	390	32	96	122	21	1	1	44	8	2	1	16	5	33	4	1
Sambo, Ramon, Veracruz	.273	119	444	73	121	136	13	1	0	18	1	1	3	79	4	44	45	11
Sanchez, Alejandro, Monclova	.306	127	496	89	152	269	38	2	25	107	1	6	9	32	7	100	20	12
Sanchez, Andres, Tabasco	.197	71	203	21	40	47	5	1	0	16	7	1	0	25	0	34	5	3
Sanchez, Armando, Mexico City Reds	.280	113	339	44	95	117	17	1	1	45	7	4	0	52	6	38	1	1
Sanchez, Gerardo, Nuevo Laredo	.296	132	527	88	156	253	26	1	23	72	8	2	10	61	1	49	9	3
Sanchez, Gilberto, Tabasco	.260	37	73	6	19	22	3	0	0	4	1	1	0	5	0	11	0	1
Sanchez, Martin, Monterrey Ind.	.000	1	0	0	0	0	0	0	0	0	0	0	0	0	0	0	0	0
Sanchez, Orlando, Monterrey Sultans	.307	133	492	53	151	213	26	0	12	77	1	1	1	56	8	56	1	3
Sandoval, Jose Luis, Mexico City Reds	.283	130	501	81	142	251	25	3	26	89	3	5	5	42	4	75	12	2
Santos, Julio, Jalisco	.400	7	5	1	2	2	0	0	0	0	0	0	0	0	0	1	0	0
See, Larry, Aguascalientes	.332	131	503	91	167	282	33	2	26	96	0	6	3	63	14	79	5	5
Sheperd, Ron, Monterrey Sultans	.276	82	322	43	89	142	14	0	13	55	1	1	1	28	2	79	3	3
Sievers, Carlos, Yucatan	.231	19	26	3	6	6	0	0	0	2	0	0	0	1	0	6	0	0
Simmons, Nelson, Jalisco	.403	69	253	38	102	150	16	1	10	59	0	4	0	37	8	34	1	1
Sinohui, David, Minatitlan	.000	1	0	0	0	0	0	0	0	0	0	0	0	0	0	0	0	0
Smith, Gregory, Saltillo	.341	132	487	77	166	234	25	2	13	94	1	5	2	65	14	40	11	8
Sommers, Jesus, Jalisco	.255	120	416	40	106	144	18	1	6	62	1	11	4	47	3	74	4	3
Stark, Matt, Veracruz	.329	64	210	27	69	98	12	1	5	29	0	1	3	46	4	21	0	1
Steels, James, Monterrey Industriales	.315	132	501	94	158	265	37	2	22	92	1	5	7	52	6	64	31	8
Stockstill, Dave, Union Laguna	.338	103	376	55	127	179	24	2	8	56	6	2	1	65	12	32	0	1
Tatis, Bernardo, Mexico City Reds	.305	131	491	123	150	227	27	4	14	82	1	2	2	96	4	87	53	12
Tejada, Wilfredo, Mexico City Tigers	.253	103	316	49	80	128	18	0	10	46	5	1	1	45	4	48	5	4
Tellez, Alonso, Monterrey Industriales	.324	132	521	77	169	246	27	4	14	64	3	0	2	22	2	41	4	6
Tillman, Rusty, Tabasco	.285	120	431	67	123	211	26	4	18	70	0	6	3	58	12	95	16	2
Tiquet, Lazaro, Cordoba	.303	119	366	40	111	145	16	3	4	36	13	3	6	37	1	57	3	6
Tirado, Federico, Cordoba	.175	66	166	12	29	33	4	0	0	4	7	0	0	9	2	21	1	1
Tirado, Victor, Tabasco	.171	41	70	7	12	14	0	1	0	5	3	0	3	6	0	11	0	1
Torres, Eduardo, Saltillo	.252	126	408	69	103	164	23	4	10	67	4	5	4	75	4	47	19	9
Torres, Eleuterio, Union Laguna	.000	15	5	0	0	0	0	0	0	0	0	0	0	0	0	3	0	0
Torres, Raymundo, Campeche	.267	86	303	61	81	165	18	0	22	63	0	5	3	53	3	70	2	0
Uzcanga, Ali, Aguascalientes	.198	48	162	22	32	38	3	0	1	10	6	1	0	13	0	25	0	0
Valdez, Baltazar, Yucatan	.262	125	458	53	120	183	21	0	14	84	6	7	11	43	2	51	7	6
Valdez, Edgar, Tabasco	.333	8	6	3	2	2	0	0	0	0	1	0	0	1	0	0	0	0

Player, Team	Avg.	G	AB	R	H	TB	2B	3B	HR	RBI	SH	SF	HP	BB	Int. BB	SO	SB	CS
Valdez, Francisco, Monterrey Ind.	.063	15	16	1	1	2	1	0	0	0	0	0	1	1	0	5	0	0
Valdez, Jesus, Union Laguna	.296	119	406	56	120	155	13	5	4	38	6	1	0	26	3	42	2	6
Valdez, Luis Alberto, Aguascalientes	.261	87	257	36	67	95	10	3	4	29	4	1	1	24	3	32	0	5
Valencia, Carlos, Aguascalientes	.323	120	467	64	151	231	15	4	19	99	4	1	4	22	0	35	3	7
Valencia, Fco. Javier, Monclova	.000	5	2	0	0	0	0	0	0	0	0	0	0	0	0	2	0	0
Valenzuela, Armando, Saltillo	.276	112	438	59	121	142	15	3	0	35	9	4	3	27	0	54	23	12
Valenzuela, Eduardo, Saltillo	.277	28	65	6	18	18	0	0	0	6	1	0	1	4	0	11	1	0
Valenzuela, Fernando, Jalisco	.000	2	2	0	0	0	0	0	0	0	0	0	0	0	0	1	0	0
Valenzuela, Horacio, Minatitlan	.281	125	420	57	118	216	9	1	29	99	0	5	4	59	4	68	0	1
Valenzuela, Jose Luis, Aguascalientes	.297	105	266	46	79	109	10	7	2	28	5	3	0	34	1	56	6	8
Valenzuela, Leonardo, Monterrey Sult.	.297	120	435	75	129	163	15	2	5	58	6	2	1	72	9	72	5	10
Valle, Jose Luis, Minatitlan	.262	116	366	44	96	122	17	0	3	36	14	6	3	21	0	41	1	1
Valverde, Aaron, Union Laguna	.292	54	120	10	35	40	5	0	0	16	2	1	2	14	0	21	0	0
Valverde, Raul, Jalisco	.317	86	281	30	89	118	16	5	1	39	7	5	2	15	1	38	1	2
Vargas, Hediberto, Campeche	.299	109	365	57	109	162	17	0	12	63	1	3	2	64	2	59	3	3
Vargas, Ignacio, Aguascalientes	.000	4	1	0	0	0	0	0	0	0	0	0	0	0	0	0	0	0
Vargas, Trinidad, Monterrey Sultans	.258	44	62	9	16	17	1	0	0	6	1	0	1	6	0	13	2	1
Velazquez, Armando, Veracruz	.204	27	49	7	10	11	1	0	0	7	1	1	0	7	0	11	1	2
Velazquez, Ernesto, Monclova	.000	2	1	0	0	0	0	0	0	0	0	0	0	0	0	0	0	0
Verdugo, Vicente, Mexico City Reds	.283	122	491	72	139	169	21	3	1	61	6	3	5	34	0	46	1	1
Villaescusa, Fernando, Yucatan	.316	95	320	51	101	119	13	1	1	43	18	6	2	29	1	19	13	3
Villagomez, David, Cordoba	.272	82	232	21	63	73	10	0	0	17	0	1	2	25	3	45	2	2
Villegas, Fernando, Saltillo	.000	4	3	0	0	0	0	0	0	0	0	0	0	1	0	1	0	0
Villela, Carlos, Monterrey Ind.	.270	121	466	73	126	146	14	3	0	43	8	2	0	30	0	82	1	1
Vizcarra, Marco, Monterrey Ind.	.259	85	174	23	45	53	6	1	0	12	6	3	3	19	0	23	4	2
Vizcarra, Roberto, Monterrey Ind.	.270	132	530	86	143	222	36	2	13	57	10	6	4	37	6	34	19	16
Vizcarra, Sergio Hugo, Aguascalientes	.269	78	227	28	61	72	9	1	0	34	13	2	2	29	0	22	0	4
Williams, Eddie, Union Laguna	.384	62	229	39	88	134	12	2	10	56	0	5	5	21	4	25	1	1
Wilson, James, Monterrey Ind.	.289	127	471	73	136	256	19	1	33	94	0	4	8	54	5	80	4	2
Wong, Julian, Tabasco	.277	123	444	61	123	174	16	10	5	53	15	6	3	49	1	62	5	4
Wright, George, Saltillo	.329	133	492	90	162	252	28	7	16	89	0	7	4	86	9	68	15	9
Wynne, Marvell, Yucatan	.241	14	54	3	13	18	2	0	1	5	0	0	0	4	1	10	1	1
Yong, Delwin, Mexico City Tigers	.222	14	45	6	10	17	1	0	2	4	0	0	0	8	3	12	1	0
Yuriar, Jesus, Monclova	.282	112	365	50	103	132	21	1	2	45	12	3	2	31	2	64	11	5
Zamudio, Rafael, Monterrey Sultans	.152	28	46	3	7	13	0	0	2	4	0	1	0	6	0	18	0	0
Zazueta, Mauricio, Mexico City Reds	.288	126	431	76	124	194	26	1	14	70	6	8	3	59	1	84	13	5
Zepeda, Alejandro, Monclova	.286	6	7	0	2	2	0	0	0	1	0	0	0	1	0	0	0	0
Zulueta, Felix, Yucatan	.270	77	159	23	43	56	4	0	3	35	2	2	6	22	1	33	5	4
Zuniga, Armando, Saltillo	.215	72	107	9	23	27	1	0	1	8	6	0	0	6	0	22	0	0

The following pitchers, listed alphabetically by club, with games in parentheses, had no plate appearances, primarily through use of designated hitters:

AGUASCALIENTES—Cano, Jose (27); Delgadillo, Gustavo (3); Enriquez, Martin (28); Granillo, Carlos (30); Jaime Granillo, Ismael (28); Jimenez, German (23); Lopez, Jonas (25); Miranda, Julio Cesar (64); Montalvo, Rafael (49); Neri, Braulio (29); Quinonez, Enrique (17); Velazquez, Ildefonso (18).

CAMPECHE—Browning, Mike (53); Corbette, Sherman (3); Dominguez, Herminio (23); Fuentes, David (4); Heinkel, Donald (29); Huerta, Luis (28); Ledon, Juan Carlos (37); Lopez, Jose Ramon (24); Lopez, Juan (2); Manzano, Fernando (4); Ocen, Victor (3); Raygoza, Martin (29); Rojo, Oscar (11); Sangeado, Juan Carlos (1); Sierra, Abel (3); Tejeda, Juan (20); Tinoco, Ruben (11); Toledo, Mario (3); Villegas, Ramon (22); Zamorano, Gabriel (2).

CORDOBA—Angulo, Julian (19); Araujo, Andy (29); Avendano, Rafael (5); Colorado, Salvador (25); Encarnacion, Luis (47); Jusaino, Martin (7); Macias, Abraham (31); Moreno, Juan de Dios (2); Perez, Joaquin (31); Puerto, Carlos (5); Pulido, Antonio (3); Ruelas, Hugo (1); Soto, Ernesto (4); Taylor, Terry (20); Veliz, Francisco (31).

JALISCO—Camacho, Ernie (1); Camacho, Ronaldo (8); Carranza, Javier (29); Castaneda, Aurelio (42); Cervantes, Lauro (28); Iniguez, Dario (12); Lugo, Urbano (27); Mojica, Hector (26); Moya, Ramon (4); Pavlas, Dave (12); Reyes, Jesus Manuel (11); Rivas, Martin (26).

MEXICO CITY REDS—Barojas, Salome (39); Cordoba, Francisco (16); Cruz, Javier (28); Hansen, Mike (15); Hilton, Howard (1); Jimenez, Saul (20); Leyva, Filiberto (25); Martinez, Ramon (18); Mendez, Luis Fernando (28); Moreno, Leobardo (32); Perez, Jorge (3); Pico, Jeff (12); Pineda, Gabriel (19); Ramirez, Roberto (19); Rivera, Hector (3); Valenzuela, Saul (25); Vazquez, Adrian (28).

MEXICO CITY TIGERS—Garcia, Juan (23); Garcia, Zenon (23); Gomez, Henry (4); Guajardo, Octavio (5); Hernandez, Jose Manuel (40); Marquez, Isidro (52); Mora, Eleazar (18); Moreno, Angel (28); Odekirk, Rick (2); Onofre, Jose (2); Perea, Juan Alberto (3); Rios, Jesus (28); Robles, Felix (6); Salas, Ernesto (40); Smith, Mike (10); Valdez, Ismael (5); Veres, Dave (14).

MINATITLAN—Aguilar, Miguel (22); Armenta, Jose (3); Cardenas, Benito (35); Castro, Rodrigo (29); Cerros, Alberto (1); Diaz, Alejandro (2); Diaz, Octavio (30); Hernandez, Julio (28); Martinez, Martin (4); Olivas, Anselmo (9); Purata, Julio (32); Sombra, Francisco (23); Soto, Fernando (34); Tejeda, Felix (15); Zavaleta, Marcelino (1).

MONCLOVA—Cosio, Mario (34); Eave, Gary (28); Espinoza, Carlos (10); Garcia, Miguel (5); Garza, Armando (11); Gracia, Anselmo (2); Ibarra, Jose (24); Jones, Odell (9); Malave, Benito (11); Mena, Evaristo (14); Morales, Isidro (45); Murillo, Felipe (29); Norman, Guy (27); Osuna, Roberto (44); Torres, Sotero (7); Valdez, Rodolfo (27); Valenzuela, Ramon Loreto (17); Vazquez, Florentino (9); Velazquez, Luis (3); Villarreal, Antonio (31).

MONTERREY INDUSTRIALS—Acosta, Carlos Emilio (3); Camarena, Martin (26); Flores, Jose Angel (5); Garza, Adrian (2); Hernandez, Martin (30); Hickey, Kevin (14); Jimenez, Isaac (18); Lara, Jorge (4); Noriega, Eduardo (7); Ochoa, Porfirio (59); Rodriguez, Ignacio (3); Solis, Jesus (28); Valdez, Armando (30).

MONTERREY SULTANS—Acosta, Aaron (41); Benitez, Francisco (7); Cano, Ezequiel (22); Garza, Alejandro (30); Gonzalez, Arturo (16); Heredia, Hector (54); Navarro, Adolfo (26); Orozco, Jaime (32); Ortiz, Gregorio (5); Pelcastregui, Leonardo (1); Perez, Leonardo (30); Pena, Jaime (4); Pruneda, Armando (8); Ruiz, Cecilio (18); Sandoval, Guillermo (3); Serna, Ramon (10); Villanueva, Luis (29).

NUEVO LAREDO—Alvarez, Juan (21); Castillo, Luis Trinidad (19); Couch, Enrique (37); Cruz, Miguel (22); Holman, Shawn (59); Moreno, Ricardo (14); Quiroz, Aaron (23); Rodriguez, Rene (19); Upshaw, Lee (24); Valdez, Jose (30); Valenzuela, Mario (4); Vega, Obed (3); Walsh, Dave (21).

SALTILLO—Alvarez, Martin (50); Barron, Avelino (36); Escamilla, Sergio (11); Lara, Eduardo (14); Lizarraga, Hugo (25); Medvin, Scott (27); Moreno, Jesus (31); Olmos, Arturo (11); Perry, Jeff (28); Pena, Ramon Arturo (8); Pulido, Alfonso (30); Rodriguez, Raul (31); Silva, Ramon (6); Solis, Ricardo (28).

TABASCO—Acosta, Martin (4); Chevez, Humberto (8); Diaz, Cesar (32); Flores, Julio (8); Garcia, Luna (4); Gomez, Martin (10); Herrera, Enrique (50); Ibarra, Carlos (19); McCament, Randy (3); Osuna, Ricardo (29); Retes, Lorenzo (30); Rodriguez, Mario (36); Rodriguez, Ulises (22); Romero, Hector (19); Romero, Juan (45); Saldana, Edgardo (14); Serafin, Hector (4); Sibate, Pedro (16); Sosa, Mario (37); Zamudio, Aurelio (11).

UNION LAGUNA—Alba, Gibson (6); Castro, Hugo (5); Garibay, Salvador (31); Grajales, Norberto (36); Herrera, Calixto (37); Medina, Eugenio (4); Mendez, Martin (12); Monson, Steve (5); Mosquera, David (3); Palafox, Juan Manuel (30); Pimentel, Roberto (21); Quintero, Victor Hugo (21); Renteria, Hilario (21); Richle, Darryn (49); Rincon, Ricardo (49); Sosa, Victor (2); Vespe, Will (10); Villegas, Jose Angel (40).

VERACRUZ—Arias, Daniel (5); Cabrales, Gabriel (38); Cazares, Juan (27); Contreras, Benjamin (17); Felix, Antonio (23); Garcia, Jorge Luis (33); Guzman, Benjamin (1); Hernandez, Manuel (26); Lopez, Raul (25); Luevano, Juan (25); Martinez, Victor (7); Munoz, Miguel (22); Sanchez, Hector (33); Sandoval, Carlos (3); Soto, Ramon (5); Torres, Martin (5); Valdez, Pedro (1); Valencia, Miguel Angel (1).

YUCATAN—Acosta, Villa Martin (5); Antunez, Martin (47); Burchan, Tim (17); Campos, Jorge (12); Chavarin, Jose (38); Cruz, Andres (22); Esquer, Mercedes (25); Gamboa, Ezequiel (5); Hernandez, Encarnacion (39); Merodio, Ramon (24); Montano, Francisco (26); Renteria, Manuel (6); Uribe, Juan Carlos (25); Velez, Arturo (16); Vizcarra, Rodrigo (7).

GRAND SLAMS—Carrillo, M. Davis, Gainey, Jones, Mere, Ge. Sanchez, R. Torres, C. Valencia, 2 each; Aganza, Aguilar, Hec. Alvarez, Castelan, C. Castillo, A. Chan, Cuevas, L. Diaz, J. Espinoza, Garbey, M. Garcia, J. Gonzalez, Iturbe, Johnson, Knabenshue, R. Martinez, Motley, G. Rivera, Jose Luis Rodriguez, Rojas, O. Sanchez, Shepherd, Tejada, Tellez, H. Vargas, Yuriar, 1 each.

AWARDED FIRST BASE ON CATCHER'S INTERFERENCE—Morones 2 (Daut, Luna); Almodobar (Luna); Todd Brown (R. Martinez); A. Chan (N. Munoz); M. Cruz (Ra. Mendez); Cuevas (M. Gonzalez); Ju. Garcia (A. Meza); J. Gonzalez (Abrego); Jav. Guerrero (Becerra); M. Hernandez (Luna); L. Valdez (Garzon); H. Osuna (R. Martinez); Ruiz (F. Cruz).

PITCHING

TEAM

Team	ERA	G	CG	ShO	Sv.	IP	H	R	ER	HR	HB	BB	Int. BB	SO	WP	Bk.
Veracruz	3.67	132	34	12	23	1122.0	1124	539	458	67	40	449	36	555	31	4
Campeche	3.73	131	27	9	33	1128.0	1163	550	468	87	34	389	37	618	53	3
Monterrey Industrials	3.77	132	25	4	32	1135.0	1160	593	475	87	53	490	46	722	85	3
Cordoba	3.95	130	41	8	17	1085.1	1159	589	476	94	43	434	53	556	45	8
Nuevo Laredo	4.08	132	18	8	35	1154.0	1130	609	523	103	41	575	24	819	71	3
Yucatan	4.08	133	34	9	19	1164.2	1145	617	528	87	38	566	38	675	78	6
Mexico City Tigers	4.22	130	23	15	29	1092.2	1156	570	512	103	52	475	24	774	53	5
Minatitlan	4.24	133	28	7	42	1137.1	1120	592	536	88	52	520	18	635	66	2
Monterrey Sultans	4.38	133	21	13	26	1139.0	1243	641	554	100	38	464	30	624	48	4
Union Laguna	4.43	134	21	8	35	1176.2	1317	659	579	106	33	484	58	684	55	2
Tabasco	4.59	133	10	5	26	1124.2	1237	656	574	99	46	516	59	562	50	2
Mexico City Reds	4.64	131	23	8	21	1118.0	1228	655	576	110	40	544	24	629	61	6
Aguascalientes	4.65	134	21	8	21	1186.1	1339	714	613	107	45	492	50	641	43	5
Saltillo	4.71	133	14	12	31	1145.1	1342	680	599	88	35	405	47	691	58	1
Jalisco	5.00	131	31	6	16	1132.1	1323	738	629	96	35	447	18	620	72	3
Monclova	5.16	132	14	5	26	1147.2	1341	785	658	112	37	649	81	640	73	4

INDIVIDUAL

(Leading qualifiers for earned-run average leadership— 107 or more innings)

Pitcher, Team	W	L	Pct.	ERA	G	GS	CG	GF	ShO	Sv.	IP	H	R	ER	HR	HB	BB	Int. BB	SO	WP
Esquer, Yucatan	18	4	.818	2.24	25	25	9	0	1	0	192.2	169	57	48	12	3	68	3	139	8
Munoz, Veracruz	13	7	.650	2.58	22	22	10	0	3	0	160.2	152	59	46	7	5	24	2	58	1
Cruz, Yucatan	11	4	.733	2.61	22	18	5	4	2	0	124.0	93	44	36	4	1	47	0	71	16
Walsh, Nuevo Laredo	7	6	.538	2.73	21	21	4	0	1	0	142.0	109	49	43	12	4	52	0	116	4
Purata, Minatitlan	20	9	.690	2.77	32	32	10	0	0	0	237.0	184	85	73	13	11	112	1	152	12
Rios, Mexico City Tigers	15	9	.625	2.80	28	27	11	1	6	0	189.2	156	66	59	15	6	63	3	186	3
Palafox, Union Laguna	18	5	.783	2.80	30	30	10	0	1	0	235.0	217	83	73	21	8	80	7	104	8
Valdez, Monterrey Industriales	18	9	.667	2.82	30	30	7	0	2	0	210.1	192	88	66	14	11	74	7	143	15
Montalvo, Aguascalientes	13	9	.591	2.94	49	1	1	48	0	11	107.0	115	40	35	5	3	26	7	63	1
Hernandez, Veracruz	12	8	.600	2.95	26	21	10	5	1	0	165.0	133	62	54	6	3	57	4	106	5

Departmental leaders: G—Miranda, 64; W—Purata, 20; L—E. Lopez, 17; Pct.—Esquer, .818; GS—Purata, F. Soto, 32; CG—Mar. Hernandez, F. Valenzuela, 13; GF—Miranda, 63; ShO—Rios, 6; Sv.—DeLeon, 34; IP—Purata, 237.0; H—R. Solis, 242; R—Cervantes, 125; ER—F. Soto, 111; HR—Heinkel, 24; HB—Merodio, 14; BB—Purata, 112; IBB—Ro. Osuna, 13; SO—Rios, 186; WP—Carranza, A. Cruz, 16.

(All pitchers—listed alphabetically)

Pitcher, Team	W	L	Pct.	ERA	G	GS	CG	GF	ShO	Sv.	IP	H	R	ER	HR	HB	BB	Int. BB	SO	WP
Acosta, Monterrey Sultans	6	9	.400	4.23	41	12	2	29	0	1	117.0	144	69	55	9	0	49	3	63	7
Acosta, Tabasco	0	1	.000	14.04	4	2	0	2	0	0	8.1	16	13	13	3	0	3	0	2	1
Acosta F., Monterrey Ind.	0	0	.000	4.91	3	0	0	3	0	0	3.2	3	2	2	1	2	2	0	1	0
Acosta Villa, Yucatan	0	0	.000	16.50	5	0	0	5	0	0	6.0	13	11	11	2	1	7	0	1	2
Aguilar, Minatitlan	3	3	.500	3.69	22	6	1	16	0	0	61.0	53	25	25	5	2	25	0	32	2
Aguilera, Monterrey Sultans	0	0	.000	9.00	1	0	0	1	0	0	1.0	2	1	1	0	0	0	0	0	1
Alba, Union Laguna	1	2	.333	6.75	6	6	1	0	0	0	26.2	33	23	20	5	2	16	0	18	3
Alicea, Union Laguna	6	5	.545	2.92	57	0	0	57	0	24	77.0	76	29	25	7	0	24	5	48	0
Alvarez, Nuevo Laredo	9	4	.692	3.55	21	16	2	5	0	0	116.2	120	54	46	8	3	57	2	86	4
Alvarez, Saltillo	1	1	.500	5.17	50	0	0	50	0	1	47.0	55	29	27	1	1	27	2	27	4
Angulo, Cordoba	0	3	.000	2.81	19	1	0	18	0	1	32.0	32	14	10	4	1	13	2	13	0
Antunez, Yucatan	2	5	.286	5.49	47	2	0	45	0	1	57.1	76	42	35	7	1	45	7	42	6
Araujo, Cordoba	10	11	.476	3.58	29	26	9	3	1	1	188.1	191	89	75	18	6	66	12	91	9
Arias, Veracruz	1	1	.500	4.70	5	1	0	4	0	0	7.2	8	5	4	3	1	2	0	3	1
Armenta, Minatitlan	0	0	.000	31.50	5	0	0	5	0	0	2.0	10	7	7	1	0	4	0	3	0
Avendano, Cordoba	1	0	1.000	7.36	5	0	0	5	0	0	7.1	13	6	6	1	0	4	0	1	0
Barojas, Mexico City Reds	6	4	.600	3.17	39	0	0	39	0	19	65.1	52	23	23	5	0	28	5	34	3
Barraza, Nuevo Laredo	13	8	.619	3.27	28	28	5	0	2	0	192.2	173	91	70	11	3	96	3	102	8
Barron, Saltillo	2	3	.400	5.30	36	7	0	29	0	0	93.1	106	59	55	8	2	38	3	49	7
Bellazetin, Mexico City Tigers	0	0	.000	18.00	1	0	0	1	0	0	1.0	2	2	2	0	0	2	0	0	0
Benitez, Monterrey Sultans	0	1	.000	10.80	7	0	0	7	0	0	6.2	13	8	8	1	2	5	0	1	0
Browning, Campeche	7	4	.636	1.43	53	0	0	53	0	31	75.1	61	14	12	2	1	23	5	39	5
Burchan, Yucatan	8	4	.667	3.94	17	16	5	1	1	0	112.0	113	57	49	7	3	36	3	72	3
Cabrales, Veracruz	5	3	.625	2.25	38	0	0	38	0	15	60.0	61	20	15	1	3	17	5	38	3
E. Camacho, Jalisco	0	0	.000	13.50	1	0	0	1	0	0	0.2	2	1	1	1	0	0	0	0	0
R. Camacho, Jalisco	0	0	.000	5.73	8	0	0	8	0	0	11.0	12	7	7	1	0	5	0	1	0
Camarena, Monterrey Ind.	4	7	.364	5.67	26	11	0	15	0	1	106.1	137	74	67	15	4	43	3	42	4
Campos, Yucatan	0	0	.000	4.97	12	0	0	12	0	0	12.2	15	8	7	1	0	16	1	2	0
Cano, Monterrey Sultans	5	7	.417	4.44	22	16	3	6	1	0	103.1	133	57	51	11	6	33	2	48	1
Cano, Aguascalientes	13	5	.722	3.55	27	27	8	0	0	0	210.1	203	99	83	16	7	80	6	114	5
Cardenas, Minatitlan	4	0	1.000	4.08	35	0	0	35	0	0	70.2	66	33	32	3	4	31	2	23	8
Carranza, Jalisco	12	11	.522	4.06	29	28	7	1	1	0	186.1	178	96	84	12	2	88	2	107	16
Castaneda, Jalisco	4	6	.400	5.50	42	2	0	40	0	6	73.2	84	47	45	4	2	31	5	48	9
Castellanos, Jalisco	3	8	.273	6.26	34	6	0	28	0	1	92.0	127	78	64	13	3	28	1	45	2
Castillo, Nuevo Laredo	5	7	.417	6.35	19	18	0	1	0	0	85.0	108	68	60	17	5	33	1	48	6
Castro, Union Laguna	0	0	.000	2.84	5	0	0	5	0	0	6.1	11	2	2	0	1	2	0	4	0

Pitcher, Team	W	L	Pct.	ERA	G	GS	CG	GF	ShO	Sv.	IP	H	R	ER	HR	HB	BB	Int. BB	SO	WP
Castro, Minatitlan	1	0	1.000	6.11	29	1	0	28	0	1	28.0	43	19	19	3	2	17	4	15	2
Cazares, Veracruz	2	5	.286	4.62	27	6	1	21	1	1	50.2	59	30	26	5	5	26	3	33	1
Cecena, Saltillo	6	5	.545	2.35	44	0	0	44	0	18	61.1	46	25	16	3	2	29	6	77	10
Cerros, Minatitlan	0	0	.000	81.00	1	0	0	1	0	0	0.1	0	3	3	0	0	2	0	0	0
Cervantes, Jalisco	8	13	.381	5.54	28	28	2	0	1	0	164.0	236	125	101	21	2	52	3	65	7
Chavarin, Yucatan	0	2	.000	5.94	38	0	0	38	0	2	47.0	51	37	31	6	1	30	4	18	6
Chavez, Monclova	1	2	.333	5.80	31	2	0	29	0	2	59.0	69	45	38	3	2	38	6	38	10
Chevez, Tabasco	1	0	1.000	27.00	8	0	0	8	0	0	2.2	9	9	8	1	0	4	0	1	0
Colorado, Cordoba	4	13	.235	4.18	25	22	3	3	1	0	118.1	159	75	55	10	4	29	6	36	1
Contreras, Veracruz	3	3	.500	3.34	17	2	0	15	0	0	35.0	43	18	13	0	2	19	1	13	2
Contreras, Union Laguna	0	0	.000	11.57	3	0	0	3	0	0	4.2	6	6	6	1	0	2	0	3	0
Corbette, Campeche	1	1	.500	8.04	3	3	0	0	0	0	15.2	18	14	14	1	0	11	0	5	0
Cordoba, Mexico City Reds	3	0	1.000	5.79	16	1	0	15	0	0	28.0	28	19	18	2	5	14	3	15	4
Cosio, Monclova	7	12	.368	6.24	34	19	0	15	0	1	131.1	162	102	91	17	3	68	9	43	6
Couoh, Nuevo Laredo	5	9	.357	4.34	37	7	1	30	0	2	103.2	85	54	50	14	1	61	2	109	6
Cruz, Yucatan	11	4	.733	2.61	22	18	5	4	2	0	124.0	93	44	36	4	1	47	0	71	16
Cruz, Mexico City Reds	0	2	.000	5.11	28	2	0	26	0	0	61.2	85	40	35	9	4	30	1	25	2
Cruz, Nuevo Laredo	2	0	1.000	5.54	22	0	0	22	0	0	37.1	32	24	23	1	3	29	3	28	6
DeLeon, Minatitlan	2	7	.222	3.32	57	1	0	56	0	34	65.0	58	29	24	7	2	14	1	57	0
Delgadillo, Aguascalientes	0	0	.000	7.71	3	0	0	3	0	0	2.1	8	5	2	1	0	0	0	0	0
A. Diaz, Minatitlan	0	0	.000	20.25	2	0	0	2	0	0	1.1	4	3	3	0	0	1	0	0	1
Diaz, Tabasco	2	6	.250	5.45	32	15	0	17	0	1	104.0	133	68	63	15	4	39	5	61	2
O. Diaz, Minatitlan	8	6	.571	4.51	30	22	2	8	0	0	123.2	118	66	62	11	6	58	1	71	4
Dojaquez, Monclova	0	0	.000	9.45	4	0	0	4	0	0	6.2	13	7	7	1	1	7	0	3	2
Dominguez, Campeche	7	13	.350	3.46	23	23	5	0	1	0	145.2	175	71	56	7	0	36	1	79	6
Eave, Monclova	10	10	.500	3.86	28	28	9	0	2	0	200.1	196	102	86	16	11	98	7	132	4
Encarnacion, Cordoba	6	6	.500	2.84	47	0	0	47	0	14	69.2	56	24	22	2	2	28	9	39	5
Enriquez, Aguascalientes	8	11	.421	3.58	28	28	3	0	0	0	186.0	185	95	74	16	4	81	9	126	8
Escamilla, Saltillo	0	2	.000	4.13	11	3	0	8	0	0	24.0	25	14	11	2	1	12	0	14	3
Espinoza, Monclova	0	0	.000	2.84	10	0	0	10	0	0	19.0	19	10	6	1	1	12	1	9	2
Esquer, Yucatan	18	4	.818	2.24	25	25	9	0	1	0	192.2	169	57	48	12	3	68	3	139	1
Felix, Veracruz	6	6	.500	4.21	23	18	1	5	0	0	102.2	87	55	48	6	6	97	1	70	8
Flores, Monterrey Industriales	0	0	.000	2.08	5	0	0	5	0	0	4.1	4	1	1	0	4	2	4	0	
Flores, Tabasco	0	0	.000	10.13	8	0	0	8	0	0	8.0	14	9	9	0	1	8	0	7	1
Fuentes, Campeche	0	0	.000	1.50	4	0	0	4	0	0	6.0	5	2	1	0	5	0	7	0	
Gamboa, Yucatan	0	0	.000	7.84	5	0	0	5	0	0	10.1	15	11	9	0	0	6	0	7	2
Garcia, Veracruz	3	6	.333	3.18	33	6	1	27	1	6	73.2	78	37	26	2	1	28	3	30	1
Ju. Garcia, Mexico City Tigers	6	7	.462	5.24	23	21	0	2	0	0	125.1	140	79	73	16	5	63	1	68	5
Garcia, Monclova	0	0	.000	0.00	5	0	0	5	0	0	3.1	1	0	0	0	0	2	0	1	0
Z. Garcia, Mexico City Tigers	1	2	.333	5.23	23	0	0	23	0	0	31.0	36	24	18	4	3	9	0	9	5
Garcia-Luna, Tabasco	0	0	.000	4.26	4	1	0	3	0	0	12.2	17	6	6	1	0	8	0	5	1
Garibay, Yucatan	3	7	.300	3.28	46	1	0	45	0	8	57.2	42	24	21	3	2	49	4	36	5
Garibay, Union Laguna	1	3	.250	5.04	31	8	0	23	0	1	80.1	95	53	45	8	3	30	4	41	6
Garza, Monterrey Industriales	0	0	.000	40.50	2	1	0	1	0	0	1.1	4	7	6	0	0	3	0	2	1
Garza, Monterrey Sultans	8	8	.500	4.38	30	20	6	10	2	0	152.0	153	88	74	16	9	76	3	108	12
Garza, Monclova	0	1	.000	12.27	11	1	0	10	0	0	14.2	25	20	20	1	1	16	2	11	1
Gomez, Mexico City Tigers	1	2	.333	8.36	4	3	0	1	0	0	14.0	17	13	13	0	0	14	0	6	1
Gomez, Tabasco	0	1	.000	7.80	10	0	0	10	0	0	15.0	23	14	13	2	0	6	0	7	0
Gonzalez, Monterrey Sultans	6	3	.667	4.75	16	16	1	0	1	0	85.1	99	51	45	8	3	35	1	39	2
Gracia, Monclova	0	0	.000	7.71	2	0	0	2	0	0	4.2	3	4	4	0	0	7	1	3	0
Grajales, Union Laguna	4	1	.800	3.18	36	0	0	36	0	1	70.2	70	32	25	6	1	34	5	45	1
Granillo, Aguascalientes	2	0	1.000	4.58	30	1	0	29	0	2	37.1	31	21	19	2	0	18	1	22	3
Guajardo, Mexico City Tigers	1	1	.500	6.00	5	2	0	3	0	0	9.0	9	7	6	0	3	7	0	5	3
Guzman, Veracruz	0	0	.000	27.00	1	0	0	1	0	0	1.0	4	3	3	0	0	1	0	1	1
Hansen, Mexico City Reds	3	4	.429	4.58	15	9	2	6	0	1	70.2	77	44	36	7	1	28	0	34	2
Heinkel, Campeche	12	15	.444	3.25	29	29	11	0	2	0	210.1	182	90	76	24	5	49	6	149	12
Heredia, Monterrey Sultans	10	6	.625	2.37	54	0	0	54	0	24	79.2	65	23	21	4	1	25	9	66	3
Hernandez, Yucatan	5	10	.333	4.92	39	13	3	26	0	4	117.0	126	69	64	11	1	43	7	57	4
Hernandez, Mexico City Tigers	1	1	.500	4.28	40	1	0	39	0	2	33.2	34	17	16	3	1	18	0	23	5
Hernandez, Minatitlan	6	10	.375	6.24	28	28	4	0	0	0	131.1	149	101	91	10	5	96	0	60	6
Hernandez, Veracruz	12	8	.600	2.95	26	21	10	5	1	0	165.0	133	62	54	6	3	57	4	106	5
Hernandez, Monterrey Ind.	14	13	.519	3.47	30	29	13	1	0	0	207.2	206	98	80	19	4	74	8	128	10
Herrera, Union Laguna	7	5	.583	7.53	37	7	0	30	0	0	75.1	96	67	63	10	4	43	3	50	12
Herrera, Tabasco	11	4	.733	2.14	50	0	0	50	0	14	92.2	78	29	22	2	4	40	8	61	8
Herrera, Monterrey Ind.	6	8	.429	4.27	33	19	3	14	2	0	128.2	126	74	61	10	9	70	3	65	14
Hickey, Monterrey Ind.	3	3	.500	3.35	14	6	1	8	0	1	53.2	57	22	20	2	0	16	2	41	4
Hilton, Mexico City Reds	1	0	1.000	2.57	1	1	0	0	0	0	7.0	8	3	2	1	0	3	0	3	0
Holman, Nuevo Laredo	12	7	.632	2.53	59	3	0	56	0	31	106.2	87	36	30	7	5	34	2	91	5
Huerta, Campeche	9	12	.429	3.96	28	27	3	1	1	0	166.0	168	85	73	12	8	53	3	78	5
Ibarra, Tabasco	3	7	.300	6.56	19	9	0	10	0	0	72.2	99	62	53	8	6	18	0	23	1
Ibarra, Monclova	0	0	.000	5.12	24	0	0	24	0	0	19.1	27	19	11	1	2	14	0	9	1
Iniguez, Jalisco	1	1	.500	6.35	12	3	0	9	0	0	28.1	32	20	20	1	1	14	1	12	3
Jaime Granillo, Aguascalientes	1	4	.200	7.25	28	2	0	26	0	0	49.2	62	43	40	6	3	35	4	21	2
Jimenez, Aguascalientes	7	8	.467	4.38	23	23	5	0	2	0	135.2	147	70	66	13	2	40	3	69	9
Jimenez, Monterrey Industriales	7	7	.500	3.64	18	18	0	0	0	0	108.2	123	64	44	3	8	50	6	65	4
Jimenez, Mexico City Reds	4	1	.800	3.98	20	0	0	20	0	3	31.2	34	15	14	7	2	21	1	16	0
Jones, Monclova	2	4	.333	5.85	9	9	0	0	0	0	47.2	51	33	31	7	2	23	0	42	2
Jusaino, Cordoba	0	0	.000	12.46	7	0	0	7	0	0	8.2	17	13	12	4	1	8	0	4	0
Kerfeld, Jalisco	2	1	.667	4.00	12	0	0	12	0	4	18.0	15	10	8	1	0	15	0	13	2
Lara, Saltillo	0	0	.000	8.71	14	1	0	13	0	0	20.2	33	25	20	3	2	16	2	8	5
Lara, Campeche	2	2	.500	4.21	8	5	0	3	0	0	25.2	34	15	12	0	2	14	1	9	1
Lara, Monterrey Industriales	0	0	.000	7.11	4	0	0	4	0	0	6.1	9	6	5	2	0	6	0	5	2
Ledon, Campeche	5	1	.833	6.37	37	0	0	37	0	1	41.0	61	33	29	2	2	25	5	23	3
Leon, Jalisco	0	0	.000	8.10	7	0	0	7	0	0	6.2	8	8	6	0	0	9	2	0	0
Leyva, Mexico City Reds	1	0	1.000	5.00	25	0	0	25	0	1	27.0	25	17	15	0	3	19	2	11	0
Lizarraga, Saltillo	1	2	.333	7.11	25	2	0	23	0	1	57.0	82	47	45	6	2	32	4	36	6
Lopez, Cordoba	9	17	.346	3.55	28	27	12	1	0	0	192.1	193	97	76	17	7	61	11	102	6
Lopez, Aguascalientes	5	4	.556	6.36	25	9	0	16	0	0	69.1	105	59	49	7	4	28	1	23	1
Jose Lopez, Campeche	3	1	.750	5.14	24	0	0	24	0	1	42.0	47	28	24	3	0	21	1	16	3
Juan Lopez, Campeche	1	0	1.000	1.35	2	0	0	2	0	0	6.2	2	1	1	0	0	5	0	3	2
Lopez, Veracruz	9	11	.450	4.00	25	25	6	0	1	0	153.0	162	79	68	17	0	57	9	82	3
Luevano, Veracruz	5	9	.357	4.48	25	22	3	3	1	0	148.2	161	83	74	12	8	47	2	58	1
Lugo, Jalisco	12	9	.571	3.65	27	27	8	0	1	0	187.1	186	84	76	13	8	67	1	121	6
Macias, Cordoba	0	2	.000	7.34	31	1	0	30	0	0	41.2	56	39	34	3	5	34	5	19	7

Pitcher, Team	W	L	Pct.	ERA	G	GS	CG	GF	ShO	Sv.	IP	H	R	ER	HR	HB	BB	Int. BB	SO	WP
Malave, Monclova	2	0	1.000	4.34	11	1	0	10	0	1	18.2	17	14	9	1	0	20	3	11	1
Manzano, Campeche	0	0	.000	4.50	4	0	0	4	0	0	2.0	2	1	1	0	0	2	0	1	0
Marquez, Mexico City Tigers	5	5	.500	3.49	52	0	0	52	0	25	87.2	75	39	34	5	7	40	8	57	1
Martinez, Minatitlan	0	2	.000	23.14	4	2	0	2	0	0	4.2	13	13	12	0	0	8	0	4	1
Martinez, Mexico City Reds	1	3	.250	6.57	18	3	0	15	0	0	37.0	45	29	27	8	0	18	0	13	2
Martinez, Veracruz	0	2	.000	4.15	7	1	0	6	0	0	8.2	9	7	4	1	1	6	1	2	0
McCament, Tabasco	1	1	.500	8.59	3	3	0	0	0	0	7.1	10	7	7	1	0	5	0	4	0
Medina, Union Laguna	1	0	1.000	22.09	4	0	0	4	0	0	3.2	11	11	9	3	1	2	0	3	0
Medvin, Saltillo	7	10	.412	3.33	27	18	2	9	0	3	127.0	118	68	47	5	8	63	1	129	12
Mena, Monclova	0	1	.000	6.82	14	1	0	13	0	0	33.0	46	30	25	6	5	20	3	14	2
Mendez, Mexico City Reds	8	9	.471	4.23	28	28	4	0	2	0	170.1	189	98	80	18	4	52	1	97	3
Mendez, Union Laguna	1	1	.500	6.27	12	0	0	12	0	0	18.2	21	14	13	2	1	11	0	17	2
Merodio, Yucatan	9	13	.409	4.24	24	23	5	1	1	0	150.2	122	82	71	11	14	98	3	77	11
E. Meza, Veracruz	0	0	.000	0.00	1	0	0	1	0	0	1.0	1	0	0	0	0	0	0	1	0
L. Meza, Veracruz	0	7	.000	5.04	21	7	2	14	0	0	64.1	71	38	36	4	2	32	1	37	2
Miranda, Aguascalientes	4	6	.400	4.70	64	1	0	63	0	8	113.0	113	70	59	13	4	46	8	89	3
Mojica, Jalisco	0	0	.000	7.17	26	0	0	26	0	1	42.2	58	43	34	3	1	28	4	26	7
Monson, Union Laguna	1	1	.500	6.84	5	4	0	1	0	0	25.0	34	20	19	2	0	15	2	14	5
Montalvo, Aguascalientes	13	9	.591	2.94	49	1	1	48	0	11	107.0	115	40	35	5	3	26	7	63	1
Montano, Yucatan	10	8	.556	4.26	26	26	5	0	0	0	177.2	198	104	84	9	6	67	2	88	7
Mora, Mexico City Tigers	1	1	.500	4.09	18	0	0	18	0	0	22.0	22	12	10	0	1	12	1	14	0
Morales, Monclova	4	3	.571	3.92	45	0	0	45	0	6	39.0	39	20	17	4	2	19	7	20	2
Moreno, Mexico City Tigers	18	7	.720	3.28	28	28	8	0	2	0	189.1	192	85	69	16	6	61	2	130	5
Moreno, Saltillo	11	13	.458	4.82	31	29	2	2	1	0	158.2	166	94	85	13	10	67	6	108	5
Moreno, Cordoba	0	0	.000	9.00	2	0	0	2	0	0	4.0	7	5	4	1	0	1	0	0	0
Moreno, Mexico City Reds	18	8	.692	3.48	32	30	11	2	1	0	214.2	200	97	83	10	3	106	3	178	9
Moreno, Nuevo Laredo	1	0	1.000	6.04	14	1	0	13	0	0	28.1	35	23	19	4	0	18	1	9	2
Mosquera, Union Laguna	1	2	.333	8.25	3	2	0	1	0	0	12.0	13	12	11	3	0	12	1	6	2
Moya, Jalisco	1	0	1.000	3.60	4	0	0	4	0	0	5.0	4	2	2	0	0	1	0	0	0
Munoz, Veracruz	13	7	.650	2.58	22	22	10	0	3	0	160.2	152	59	46	7	5	24	2	58	1
Munoz, Jalisco	0	0	.000	7.43	7	0	0	7	0	0	13.1	19	11	11	1	1	5	0	5	2
Murillo, Monclova	6	9	.400	6.10	29	21	1	8	1	0	124.0	162	98	84	15	2	55	5	41	12
Navarro, Monterrey Sultans	3	4	.429	6.72	26	9	0	17	0	0	76.1	94	59	57	11	2	48	1	42	5
Neri, Aguascalientes	7	3	.700	4.27	29	11	3	18	0	0	97.0	116	54	46	9	8	48	5	46	5
Noriega, Monterrey Industriales	0	0	.000	4.66	7	0	0	7	0	0	9.2	9	6	5	0	0	8	0	5	2
Norman, Monclova	11	7	.611	4.77	27	27	3	0	1	0	162.1	197	104	86	11	2	82	4	101	12
Ocen, Campeche	0	0	.000	12.00	3	0	0	3	0	0	3.0	4	4	4	2	0	1	0	0	0
Ochoa, Monterrey Industriales	5	3	.625	2.55	59	0	0	59	0	30	88.1	83	30	25	7	0	21	6	50	2
Odekirk, Mexico City Tigers	0	0	.000	6.75	2	2	0	0	0	0	5.1	10	4	4	1	2	3	0	1	1
Olivas, Minatitlan	0	0	.000	2.70	9	0	0	9	0	0	13.1	6	5	4	0	1	10	0	12	3
Olmos, Saltillo	2	1	.667	3.60	11	3	0	8	0	0	35.0	34	19	14	4	0	20	4	31	1
Onofre, Mexico City Tigers	0	0	.000	4.50	2	0	0	2	0	0	2.0	1	1	1	0	1	0	0	0	0
Ontiveros, Monterrey Ind.	6	1	.857	4.75	39	0	0	39	0	1	66.1	84	38	35	14	3	24	4	31	3
Orozco, Monterrey Sultans	16	13	.552	3.33	32	29	6	3	1	0	205.1	203	100	76	14	6	51	5	95	5
Ortiz, Monterrey Sultans	0	0	.000	2.57	5	0	0	5	0	0	7.0	10	3	2	0	0	7	0	0	0
Osuna, Mexico City Tigers	13	7	.650	4.05	28	26	3	2	1	0	166.2	181	80	75	16	6	74	2	129	10
Osuna, Tabasco	11	8	.579	3.33	29	28	11	1	5	0	184.0	155	78	68	8	1	65	7	117	5
Osuna, Monclova	5	12	.294	3.94	44	6	0	38	0	11	91.1	77	48	40	8	2	67	13	74	4
Palafox, Union Laguna	18	5	.783	2.80	30	30	10	0	1	0	235.0	217	83	73	21	8	80	7	104	8
Pavlas, Jalisco	1	4	.200	2.61	12	4	1	8	0	4	41.1	35	16	12	1	3	10	0	25	5
Pelcastregui, Monterrey Sultans	0	1	.000	54.00	1	1	0	0	0	0	0.2	3	4	4	1	0	4	0	0	1
Pena, Monterrey Sultans	0	0	.000	9.00	4	0	0	4	0	0	3.0	6	3	3	0	0	1	0	3	2
Pena, Saltillo	1	0	1.000	7.45	8	0	0	8	0	0	9.2	17	8	8	1	0	2	0	6	0
Perea, Mexico City Tigers	0	0	.000	0.00	3	0	0	3	0	0	3.2	2	0	0	0	0	2	0	1	0
Perez, Cordoba	4	8	.333	4.14	31	11	5	20	1	0	100.0	112	64	46	9	7	40	4	39	8
Perez, Mexico City Reds	0	0	.000	13.50	3	0	0	3	0	0	2.0	6	3	3	1	0	2	0	3	0
Perez, Monterrey Sultans	5	5	.500	3.11	30	9	2	21	1	0	101.1	76	37	35	6	3	30	1	50	0
Perry, Saltillo	5	5	.500	4.60	28	0	0	28	0	5	47.0	57	25	24	5	3	13	4	36	2
Pico, Mexico City Reds	5	4	.556	5.50	12	12	0	0	0	0	73.2	86	49	45	5	4	35	2	29	7
Pimentel, Union Laguna	1	0	1.000	6.89	21	0	0	21	0	1	15.2	28	13	12	1	0	15	3	9	1
Pineda, Mexico City Reds	0	0	.000	5.60	19	1	0	18	0	0	27.1	31	23	17	2	0	23	0	16	6
Pruneda, Monterrey Sultans	0	0	.000	9.98	8	1	0	7	0	0	15.1	25	17	17	5	2	11	0	8	3
Puerto, Cordoba	0	0	.000	0.00	5	0	0	5	0	0	6.1	2	1	0	0	0	2	0	1	0
Pulido, Saltillo	12	11	.522	3.55	30	29	3	1	2	0	177.2	207	78	70	9	1	33	5	51	0
Pulido, Cordoba	0	0	.000	0.00	3	0	0	3	0	2	3.0	4	0	0	0	0	1	0	0	0
Purata, Minatitlan	20	9	.690	2.77	32	32	10	0	0	0	237.0	184	85	73	13	11	112	1	152	12
Quinonez, Aguascalientes	1	5	.167	7.60	17	13	0	4	0	0	55.2	76	55	47	8	5	32	0	28	0
Quintero, Union Laguna	1	3	.250	5.50	21	9	0	12	0	0	52.1	70	34	32	11	2	28	1	29	1
Quiroz, Nuevo Laredo	4	5	.444	6.83	23	15	0	8	0	0	89.2	104	71	68	12	7	57	3	68	9
Quiroz, Tabasco	0	0	.000	6.75	3	0	0	3	0	0	4.0	6	3	3	0	1	0	0	1	1
Ramirez, Mexico City Reds	3	9	.250	5.98	19	13	0	6	0	0	81.1	102	61	54	6	4	47	0	57	8
Raygoza, Campeche	11	8	.579	3.48	29	29	7	0	3	0	209.2	210	96	81	16	8	61	6	117	7
Renteria, Union Laguna	8	12	.400	3.70	26	26	6	0	3	0	168.0	209	85	69	9	1	45	5	84	3
Renteria, Yucatan	0	0	.000	5.79	6	0	0	6	0	1	4.2	5	4	3	1	1	6	1	4	1
Retes, Tabasco	10	12	.455	4.50	30	30	2	0	0	0	170.0	175	93	85	14	5	84	4	74	2
Reyes, Jalisco	0	0	.000	7.02	11	0	0	11	0	0	16.2	33	15	13	0	0	6	0	10	1
Richle, Union Laguna	5	7	.417	3.94	13	13	2	0	0	0	91.1	76	41	40	8	1	41	4	67	1
Rincon, Union Laguna	6	5	.545	3.91	49	9	0	40	0	6	89.2	87	45	39	4	0	46	8	91	8
Rios, Mexico City Tigers	15	9	.625	2.80	28	27	11	1	6	0	189.2	156	66	59	15	6	63	3	186	3
Rivas, Jalisco	2	3	.400	5.74	26	0	0	26	0	4	31.1	33	22	20	3	0	11	2	23	1
Rivera, Mexico City Reds	0	1	.000	19.29	3	1	0	2	0	0	2.1	5	5	5	0	0	5	0	0	0
Robles, Mexico City Reds	0	0	.000	9.00	6	0	0	6	0	0	6.0	12	6	6	0	0	3	0	6	0
Rodriguez, Monterrey Ind.	1	3	.250	8.44	31	3	0	28	0	0	37.1	36	36	35	3	2	34	1	30	0
M. Rodriguez, Tabasco	7	6	.538	4.38	36	8	2	28	0	1	113.0	135	70	55	8	7	48	4	50	3
Rodriguez, Saltillo	10	9	.526	4.96	31	29	1	2	0	0	176.0	217	114	97	16	7	71	7	102	10
Rodriguez, Nuevo Laredo	1	0	1.000	3.55	19	0	0	19	0	0	25.1	27	10	10	3	2	18	1	7	3
U. Rodriguez, Tabasco	1	2	.333	3.19	22	4	0	18	0	0	31.0	38	16	11	2	0	10	1	7	1
Rojo, Campeche	0	2	.000	7.20	11	4	0	7	0	0	20.0	22	24	16	4	2	19	1	13	2
H. Romero, Tabasco	1	6	.143	3.94	19	9	0	10	0	0	61.2	51	30	27	0	5	49	6	30	6
J. Romero, Tabasco	4	4	.500	4.16	45	0	0	45	0	4	67.0	57	41	31	1	8	38	10	24	6
Ruelas, Cordoba	0	0	.000	.....	1	0	0	1	0	0	0.0	3	4	0	0	0	1	0	1	1
Ruiz, Monterrey Sultans	3	2	.600	3.98	18	10	0	8	0	0	61.0	70	34	27	4	0	33	0	23	1
Salas, Mexico City Tigers	4	1	.800	4.60	40	1	0	39	0	0	72.1	89	41	37	11	5	26	2	50	3
Saldana, Tabasco	6	5	.545	2.99	14	13	2	1	0	0	84.1	89	36	28	7	1	26	1	31	3

Pitcher. Team	W	L	Pct.	ERA	G	GS	CG	GF	ShO	Sv.	IP	H	R	ER	HR	HB	BB	Int. BB	SO	WP
Sanchez, Veracruz	3	1	.750	3.05	33	0	0	33	0	1	73.2	76	28	25	4	2	18	4	19	3
Sanchez, Monterrey Industriales	1	2	.333	3.42	26	1	0	25	0	0	50.0	56	24	19	1	0	25	6	27	10
Sandoval, Veracruz	0	0	.000	6.00	3	0	0	3	0	0	3.0	4	2	2	0	0	2	0	1	0
Sandoval, Monterrey Sultans	0	0	.000	4.50	3	0	0	3	0	0	2.0	3	1	1	0	0	2	0	1	0
Sangeado, Campeche	0	0	.000	0.00	1	1	0	0	0	0	3.0	1	0	0	0	0	3	0	1	0
Serafin, Tabasco	0	1	.000	3.38	4	1	0	3	0	0	13.1	19	11	5	1	0	4	3	12	2
Serna, Monterrey Industriales	2	6	.250	6.85	10	9	0	1	0	0	43.1	59	36	33	3	4	17	1	26	1
Sibate, Tabasco	0	2	.000	4.32	16	1	0	15	0	0	33.1	41	21	16	4	1	14	1	13	5
Sierra, Campeche	2	0	1.000	2.70	3	2	1	1	1	0	16.2	18	5	5	0	2	4	0	6	0
Silva, Saltillo	0	0	.000	10.50	6	1	0	5	0	0	6.0	7	7	7	0	1	4	0	3	1
Sinohui, Minatitlan	13	11	.542	3.90	44	10	1	34	0	6	127.0	133	63	55	5	10	55	7	93	8
Smith, Mexico City Tigers	5	3	.625	4.10	10	10	1	0	1	0	59.1	66	30	27	2	2	35	1	35	3
Solis, Monterrey Industriales	2	1	.667	7.99	28	0	0	28	0	0	32.2	42	33	29	3	9	27	1	14	5
Solis, Saltillo	15	12	.556	4.52	28	28	7	0	1	0	191.0	242	105	96	14	2	32	4	107	3
Sombra, Minatitlan	0	2	.000	9.35	23	0	0	23	0	0	17.1	36	22	18	6	1	4	0	13	5
Sosa, Tabasco	3	7	.300	5.19	37	14	2	23	0	1	95.1	114	59	55	14	2	44	5	50	0
Sosa, Union Laguna	0	0	.000	9.00	2	0	0	2	0	0	1.0	0	1	1	0	0	1	0	0	0
Soto, Cordoba	0	0	.000	1.08	4	0	0	4	0	0	8.1	5	1	1	0	2	6	0	1	0
Soto, Minatitlan	14	10	.583	4.32	34	32	9	2	1	1	231.1	240	122	111	22	9	84	3	91	12
Soto, Veracruz	0	1	.000	9.00	5	0	0	5	0	0	7.0	7	7	7	0	1	4	1	2	0
Taylor, Cordoba	5	7	.417	4.74	20	12	3	8	0	4	76.0	81	49	40	4	2	49	0	74	5
Tejeda, Minatitlan	2	1	.667	5.67	15	3	0	12	0	0	27.0	40	19	17	0	1	8	0	15	2
Tejeda, Campeche	1	1	.500	2.60	20	2	0	18	0	0	34.2	36	11	10	1	1	12	1	16	4
Tinoco, Campeche	0	0	.000	4.68	11	4	0	7	0	0	32.2	42	19	17	4	1	12	1	9	0
Toledo, Campeche	0	2	.000	5.97	33	1	0	32	0	0	31.2	33	22	21	6	2	18	3	27	2
Torres, Veracruz	0	0	.000	9.00	5	0	0	5	0	0	3.0	5	4	3	0	1	4	1	3	0
Torres, Monclova	0	0	.000	8.10	7	0	0	7	0	0	6.2	11	6	6	1	1	2	0	3	0
Upshaw, Nuevo Laredo	9	9	.500	3.24	24	23	6	1	1	0	153.0	153	70	55	8	1	68	4	128	14
Uribe, Yucatan	3	3	.500	4.42	25	11	0	14	0	3	59.0	63	30	29	6	4	34	2	43	1
Valdez, Monterrey Industriales	18	9	.667	2.82	30	30	7	0	2	0	210.1	192	88	66	14	11	74	7	143	15
Valdez, Mexico City Tigers	0	0	.000	19.64	5	0	0	5	0	0	3.2	15	9	8	1	0	1	0	2	0
Valdez, Nuevo Laredo	1	5	.167	7.23	30	0	0	30	0	2	37.1	47	37	30	4	4	23	0	13	2
Valdez, Veracruz	0	0	.000	9.00	1	0	0	1	0	0	1.0	1	1	1	0	1	0	0	0	0
Valdez, Monclova	9	12	.429	4.14	27	27	3	0	0	0	169.2	192	96	78	11	3	84	11	89	8
Valencia, Veracruz	0	0	.000	4.50	1	0	0	1	0	0	2.0	3	1	1	0	0	0	0	0	0
Valenzuela, Jalisco	10	9	.526	3.86	22	22	13	0	0	0	156.1	154	81	67	15	8	51	0	98	7
Valenzuela, Nuevo Laredo	0	0	.000	5.06	4	0	0	4	0	0	5.1	7	4	3	0	0	7	0	3	1
Valenzuela, Monclova	1	0	1.000	7.26	17	1	0	16	0	1	31.0	48	28	25	7	0	9	0	9	2
Valenzuela, Mexico City Reds	2	3	.400	3.51	25	0	0	25	0	3	33.1	42	15	13	3	1	14	1	14	3
Vargas, Aguascalientes	1	1	.500	6.19	15	0	0	15	0	0	32.0	53	22	22	1	1	14	0	6	4
Vazquez, Mexico City Reds	14	7	.667	4.73	28	27	3	1	0	0	167.1	192	95	88	21	7	82	4	72	8
Vazquez, Monclova	0	1	.000	12.75	9	0	0	9	0	0	12.0	15	17	17	4	1	16	5	9	0
Vega, Nuevo Laredo	0	0	.000	0.00	3	0	0	3	0	0	3.2	5	0	0	0	0	2	0	4	0
E. Velazquez, Monclova	3	1	.750	5.28	37	1	0	36	0	3	58.0	74	37	34	8	2	33	5	39	4
Velazquez, Aguascalientes	5	10	.333	6.67	18	18	1	0	0	0	87.2	119	75	65	10	3	41	6	33	2
L. Velazquez, Monclova	0	1	.000	14.73	3	1	0	2	0	0	3.2	4	9	6	1	1	10	1	0	1
Velez, Yucatan	0	1	.000	9.00	16	1	0	15	0	0	22.0	32	26	22	4	1	18	0	15	2
Veliz, Cordoba	2	3	.400	4.82	31	6	0	25	0	1	61.2	72	35	33	10	2	29	0	32	1
Veres, Mexico City Tigers	1	5	.167	8.10	14	1	0	13	0	1	23.1	29	21	21	5	2	12	2	12	2
Vespe, Union Laguna	3	6	.333	6.23	10	10	0	0	0	0	47.2	58	42	33	8	1	30	1	40	6
Villaescusa, Yucatan	0	0	.000	0.00	1	0	0	1	0	0	1.1	0	0	0	0	0	1	0	1	0
Villanueva, Monterrey Sultans	1	0	1.000	3.54	29	0	0	29	0	2	20.1	23	9	8	1	0	8	1	15	0
Villarreal, Monclova	2	5	.286	4.58	31	3	1	28	0	2	78.2	81	48	40	9	0	30	3	51	4
Villegas, Union Laguna	9	6	.600	4.64	40	16	3	24	2	2	118.1	145	69	61	4	7	36	8	52	5
Villegas, Campeche	3	2	.600	2.88	22	1	0	21	0	0	34.1	35	11	11	2	0	12	3	18	0
Vizcarra, Yucatan	0	0	.000	3.60	7	0	0	7	0	0	5.0	8	2	2	0	0	4	0	2	1
Walsh, Nuevo Laredo	7	6	.538	2.73	21	21	4	0	1	0	142.0	109	49	43	12	4	52	0	116	4
Zamorano, Campeche	0	0	.000	40.50	2	0	0	2	0	0	1.1	7	6	6	2	0	0	0	0	0
Zamudio, Tabasco	2	6	.250	6.20	11	11	0	0	0	0	45.0	64	36	31	6	1	24	4	18	3
Zavaleta, Minatitlan	0	0	.000	8.10	1	0	0	1	0	0	2.2	3	2	2	1	0	0	0	1	0
Zulueta, Yucatan	0	0	.000	15.43	1	0	0	1	0	0	2.1	6	4	4	0	0	2	0	1	2

BALKS—E. Soto, 5; J. Alvarez, O. Diaz, Enriquez, Man. Hernandez, L. Mendez, Ro. Osuna, Serna, 2 each; Antunez, Barron, Camarena, Castaneda, Castellanos, Castillo, Chavez, A. Cruz, Eave, Encarnacion, Esquer, Al. Garza, Heinkel, E. Herrera, Jaime Granillo, Leyva, Jonas Lopez, Juan Lopez, R. Lopez, Marquez, R. Martinez, M. Mendez, Merodio, Monson, Montano, A. Moreno, M. Munoz, Neri, Odekirk, Ontiveros, Orozco, A. Osuna, Ramirez, Raygoza, Reyes, Rios, M. Sanchez, J. Solis, Taylor, A. Vazquez, E. Velazquez, Veliz, 1 each.

COMBINATION SHUTOUTS—Enriquez-Miranda, Enriquez-Montalvo, Enriquez-Neri-Montalvo, Lopez-Montalvo, Velazquez-Granillo-Montalvo, Velazquez-Jaime Granillo-Miranda, Aguascalientes; Raygoza-Browning, Campeche; Colorado-Rodriguez-Veliz-Encarnacion, Colorado-Taylor, Veliz-Araujo, Cordoba; Carranza-Castaneda, Cervantes-Pavlas, Pavlas-Castaneda, Jalisco; Mendez-Leyva-Hansen, Vazquez-Barojas, Mexico City Reds; Moreno-Marquez 2, Osuna-Hernandez, Osuna-Marquez, Uribe-Salas-Marquez-Alicea, Mexico City Tigers; O. Diaz-DeLeon 2, Purata-DeLeon 2, Purata-Villanueva, Soto-DeLeon, Minatitlan; Norman-Osuna, Valdez-Cosio, Monclova; Gonzalez-Heredia, Orozco-Heredia, Orozco-Sandoval, Perez-Heredia, Ruiz-Acosta, Ruiz-Heredia, Serna-Heredia, Monterrey Sultans; Barraza-Holman, Castillo-Holman, Holman-Valdez, Upshaw-Holman, Nuevo Laredo; Moreno-Cecena 2, Barron-Perry, Moreno-Alvarez-Rivas, Moreno-Castro, Moreno-Rodriguez-Cecena, Pulido-Cecena, Rodriguez-Cecena, Saltillo; H. Romero-Herrera-Sosa-Encarnacion, Tabasco; Palafox-Alicea, Rincon-Alicea, Union Laguna; Garcia-Cazares, Lopez-Cabrales, Luevano-Hernandez, L. Meza-Sanchez, Veracruz; Esquer-Antunez, Esquer-Hernandez, Montano-Gamboa, Yucatan.

PERFECT GAME—Heinkel, Campeche, defeated Mexico City Reds, 7-0, June 2.

NO-HIT GAME—Barraza, Nuevo Laredo, defeated Cordoba, 5-0, March 31; Cruz, Yucatan, defeated Jalisco, 8-0, July18.

FIELDING

TEAM

Team	Pct.	G	PO	A	E	DP	PB	Team	Pct.	G	PO	A	E	DP	PB
Aguascalientes	.977	134	3559	1638	125	152	12	Minatitlan	.972	133	3412	1507	142	135	15
Union Laguna	.976	134	3530	1473	124	149	14	Tabasco	.972	133	3374	1326	136	115	11
Veracruz	.976	132	3366	1442	116	112	18	Nuevo Laredo	.971	132	3462	1605	150	169	22
Mexico City Reds	.975	131	3354	1482	125	150	12	Saltillo	.971	133	3436	1548	148	143	12
Mexico City Tigers	.975	130	3278	1320	116	136	5	Jalisco	.970	131	3397	1481	153	155	8
Yucatan	.975	133	3494	1628	133	140	19	Monterrey Industrials	.968	132	3405	1490	163	137	25
Monterrey Sultans	.973	133	3417	1474	137	139	10	Cordoba	.968	130	3256	1336	150	113	16
Campeche	.973	131	3384	1491	136	142	12	Monclova	.965	132	3443	1366	176	133	31

Triple plays—Tabasco, Union Laguna, Veracruz.

FIRST BASEMEN

*Throws lefthanded.

Player, Team	Pct.	G	PO	A	E	DP
Pardo, Cordoba	1.000	15	77	4	0	5
Reyna, Cordoba	1.000	41	367	24	0	30
Hernandez, Campeche	1.000	24	170	7	0	18
Camargo, Veracruz	1.000	14	106	10	0	14
Llanes, Tabasco	1.000	19	166	12	0	15
Steels, Monterrey Industriales	1.000	11	41	4	0	4
Garbey, Mexico City Tigers	.998	62	488	39	1	57
Valenzuela, Minatitlan	.996	55	514	35	2	47
Tillman, Tabasco	.996	83	683	36	3	56
Garcia, Monclova	.995	26	179	6	1	22
Melendez, Mexico City Reds	.994	129	1153	95	7	138
See, Aguascalientes	.994	102	979	51	6	103
Valdez, Yucatan	.994	117	1222	104	8	115
Carrillo, Mexico City Tigers	.994	59	481	14	3	50
Aganza, Monclova	.993	51	283	18	2	27
Valdez, Union Laguna	.993	23	140	9	1	20
Leon, Jalisco	.992	16	107	12	1	17
Campusano, Saltillo	.991	12	102	7	1	8
Vargas, Campeche	.991	74	698	55	7	67
Leal, Monclova	.990	25	196	4	2	20
Romero, Nuevo Laredo	.990	120	1185	85	13	135
Williams, Union Laguna	.990	25	183	8	2	16
Ibarra, Cordoba	.989	38	347	25	4	38
E. Castro, Minatitlan	.989	77	700	43	8	72
Quiroz, Tabasco	.989	14	87	4	1	8
Sanchez, Monterrey Sultans	.989	129	1174	50	14	124
Wilson, Monterrey Industriales	.989	85	730	56	9	75
C. Castillo, Tabasco	.989	21	162	10	2	17
Michell, Jalisco	.988	73	649	34	8	50
Stark, Veracruz	.988	27	248	5	3	25
Alvarez, Monterrey Industriales	.988	31	152	10	2	17
Pena, Monterrey Industriales	.988	28	223	18	3	27
Javier Guerrero, Aguascalientes	.988	20	143	16	2	11
Pacho, Veracruz	.988	11	73	6	1	2
Sommers, Jalisco	.988	53	445	29	6	47
Smith, Saltillo	.987	121	1089	54	15	113
Avila, Union Laguna	.986	93	820	56	12	93
G. Rodriguez, Veracruz	.985	21	185	12	3	19
Guzman, Campeche	.985	15	123	7	2	16
Diaz, Nuevo Laredo	.985	12	61	4	1	8
De Los Santos, Jalisco	.980	69	555	35	12	68
Jurak, Monclova	.980	26	231	9	5	24
Rodriguez, Cordoba	.980	32	266	21	6	26
Chan, Monclova	.979	32	176	7	4	23
Contreras, Cordoba	.972	30	237	10	7	25
Zulueta, Yucatan	.970	21	129	2	4	13
Sanchez, Monclova	.966	14	136	8	5	13

Player, Team	Pct.	G	PO	A	E	DP
Villela, Monterrey Industriales	1.000	3	6	1	0	0
Rivera, Monterrey Sultans	1.000	5	24	1	0	2
Zamudio, Monterrey Sultans	1.000	7	24	4	0	6
Valenzuela, Monterrey Sultans	1.000	1	3	0	0	2
Barrera, Campeche	.988	9	76	5	1	4
Villagomez, Cordoba	.986	6	69	4	1	7
Estrada, Nuevo Laredo	.973	8	69	4	2	7
Valverde, Jalisco	.968	5	29	1	1	2
Simmons, Jalisco	.929	3	12	1	1	0
Rojas, Monterrey Industriales	.864	4	18	1	3	2
Cantu, Cordoba	.833	1	3	2	1	0

Triple plays—Avila, Tillman.

SECOND BASEMEN

Player, Team	Pct.	G	PO	A	E	DP
Zuniga, Saltillo	1.000	16	14	19	0	4
C. Rodriguez, Veracruz	1.000	10	17	17	0	3
Valdez, Aguascalientes	.989	73	153	219	4	56
Morales, Veracruz	.988	52	114	128	3	24
Gonzalez, Campeche	.988	130	314	403	9	101
Giles, Tabasco	.988	15	41	38	1	9
Renteria, Jalisco	.985	22	61	69	2	20
C. Garcia, Veracruz	.984	77	150	212	6	41
Magana, Yucatan	.982	16	26	29	1	7
Garcia, Monclova	.980	10	23	27	1	8
Sanchez, Mexico City Reds	.979	12	22	25	1	7
Esquer, Union Laguna	.979	126	347	395	16	102
Uzcanga, Aguascalientes	.978	27	66	70	3	18
Camacho, Mexico City Tigers	.977	122	280	307	14	91
Martinez, Monclova	.977	124	310	357	16	96
A. Castro, Minatitlan	.976	126	382	400	19	111
Hinzo, Yucatan	.976	121	304	350	16	96
Herrera, Jalisco	.975	91	249	260	13	75
Noriega, Jalisco	.975	12	18	21	1	8
Rivera, Jalisco	.974	19	39	37	2	9
Rodriguez, Monterrey Sultans	.974	127	282	326	16	94
Vizcarra, Aguascalientes	.974	58	108	119	6	28
Villela, Monterrey Industriales	.972	120	286	338	18	80
Wong, Tabasco	.971	122	286	324	18	87
Barandica, Cordoba	.969	33	51	75	4	15
Pardo, Cordoba	.969	45	93	124	7	28
Mere, Nuevo Laredo	.967	126	281	402	23	132
Zazueta, Mexico City Reds	.964	118	290	320	23	94
Rodriguez, Tabasco	.963	18	29	50	3	6
Barrera, Tabasco	.962	33	75	77	6	13
Francois, Saltillo	.952	126	315	324	32	86
Arias, Mexico City Tigers	.949	21	21	16	2	4
Contreras, Union Laguna	.943	10	18	15	2	3
Abril, Monterrey Industriales	.943	39	41	58	6	18
Loredo, Campeche	.931	17	13	14	2	3

(Fewer Than Ten Games)

Player, Team	Pct.	G	PO	A	E	DP
Monroy, Mexico City Tigers	1.000	3	19	1	0	0
Alvarez, Union Laguna	1.000	1	10	1	0	1
Pulido, Mexico City Tigers	1.000	6	20	2	0	2
Sanchez, Mexico City Reds	1.000	1	1	1	0	0
Verdugo, Mexico City Reds	1.000	1	1	3	0	0
Tatis, Mexico City Reds	1.000	2	2	1	0	1
Diaz Luna, Mexico City Reds	1.000	1	4	0	0	1
Rubio, Minatitlan	1.000	3	7	1	0	3
Arzate, Minatitlan	1.000	6	20	2	0	0
Arce, Veracruz	1.000	4	27	1	0	2
Dominguez, Veracruz	1.000	2	7	0	0	1
Beltran, Tabasco	1.000	1	1	0	0	0
Burke, Cordoba	1.000	7	40	2	0	5
Medina, Campeche	1.000	1	2	0	0	0
Ramirez, Yucatan	1.000	2	7	0	0	0
Garcia, Yucatan	1.000	1	1	0	0	0
P. Gonzalez, Yucatan	1.000	4	7	0	0	0
Villaescusa, Yucatan	1.000	2	14	1	0	4
Garzon, Tabasco	1.000	1	1	0	0	0
Tirado, Tabasco	1.000	1	0	1	0	0
V. Rodriguez, Tabasco	1.000	2	10	0	0	2
A. Sanchez, Tabasco	1.000	1	2	0	0	1
Jimenez, Monterrey Industriales	1.000	1	11	0	0	0
R. Castillo, Tabasco	1.000	2	9	1	0	1
Giles, Tabasco	1.000	1	3	0	0	0
Burnet, Tabasco	1.000	4	26	0	0	2
Garcia, Aguascalientes	1.000	9	61	4	0	9
Ortega, Jalisco	1.000	4	9	0	0	1
Osuna, Saltillo	1.000	1	1	1	0	0
Almeida, Saltillo	1.000	7	15	1	0	3
Peralta, Saltillo	1.000	2	6	0	0	2
Riesgo, Saltillo	1.000	2	19	0	0	0
Valverde, Union Laguna	1.000	4	7	2	0	0
Cruz, Union Laguna	1.000	3	20	1	0	3
Marquez, Union Laguna	1.000	1	3	0	0	0

(Fewer Than Ten Games)

Player, Team	Pct.	G	PO	A	E	DP
Espinoza, Minatitlan	1.000	1	3	2	0	1
Perez, Mexico City Tigers	1.000	5	2	3	0	0
Verdugo, Mexico City Reds	1.000	6	16	16	0	7
Rubio, Minatitlan	1.000	3	7	10	0	1
Sais, Veracruz	1.000	2	3	4	0	0
Romero, Cordoba	1.000	1	2	0	0	0
Gutierrez, Campeche	1.000	1	1	0	0	0
Perez, Campeche	1.000	4	2	2	0	0
G. Sanchez, Tabasco	1.000	4	1	5	0	0
Chavez, Tabasco	1.000	1	1	3	0	1
Marrufo, Tabasco	1.000	3	2	1	0	0
See, Aguascalientes	1.000	1	0	2	0	0
Barajas, Aguascalientes	1.000	1	1	0	0	0
Santos, Jalisco	1.000	1	1	0	0	0
Nunez, Jalisco	1.000	1	0	0	0	0
Camarero, Minatitlan	1.000	2	1	2	0	0
Vargas, Monterrey Sultans	1.000	3	3	4	0	2
Quintero, Monterrey Sultans	1.000	3	7	3	0	3
Leyva, Monclova	1.000	1	1	1	0	0
Estrada, Nuevo Laredo	1.000	1	6	9	12	0	2
Arce, Veracruz	.966	8	11	17	1	2
Sanchez, Nuevo Laredo	.963	4	12	14	1	4
Jimenez, Saltillo	.955	9	8	13	1	6
Canizales, Monterrey Sultans	.944	5	8	9	1	2
Beristain, Monterrey Sultans	.938	6	5	10	1	4
A. Sanchez, Tabasco	.929	7	13	13	2	5
Fentanes, Union Laguna	.929	5	4	9	1	0
Reza, Union Laguna	.909	3	4	6	1	2
Moreno, Minatitlan	.889	2	4	4	1	1
Valle, Minatitlan	.833	2	4	1	1	0
Villaescusa, Yucatan	.833	3	1	4	1	1
Gutierrez, Veracruz	.818	2	4	5	2	1
Hernandez, Saltillo	.500	1	1	0	1	0

Triple plays—Barrera, Esquer, Morales.

THIRD BASEMEN

Player, Team	Pct.	G	PO	A	E	DP
Hernandez, Saltillo	1.000	11	3	15	0	1
Sais, Veracruz	.990	30	28	70	1	5
Alfaro, Yucatan	.977	124	83	377	11	25
Garbey, Mexico City Tigers	.974	15	17	20	1	3
Rivera, Jalisco	.963	11	8	18	1	2
Barrera, Tabasco	.962	48	36	92	5	7
Moreno, Minatitlan	.962	10	7	18	1	1
Zuniga, Saltillo	.960	29	6	18	1	0
Castaneda, Mex. City Tigers	.959	119	85	245	14	31
Renteria, Jalisco	.955	93	77	221	14	29
Aguilar, Aguascalientes	.954	123	78	295	18	29
Romero, Cordoba	.949	125	98	255	19	24
Peralta, Saltillo	.947	123	80	224	17	20
Ruiz, Union Laguna	.947	125	102	235	19	23
Rubio, Minatitlan	.944	101	67	235	18	20
Barrera, Campeche	.940	122	92	252	22	26
M. Vizcarra, Monterrey Ind.	.939	62	45	108	10	15
G. Sanchez, Tabasco	.938	21	16	29	3	2
Arce, Veracruz	.936	83	50	184	16	8
Leyva, Monclova	.936	124	141	251	27	28
Rodriguez, Mexico City Reds	.935	24	9	34	3	4
Verdugo, Mexico City Reds	.932	112	74	201	20	25
Beristain, Monterrey Sultans	.929	10	4	9	1	0
Rivera, Monterrey Sultans	.927	125	84	271	28	30
Ortiz, Nuevo Laredo	.927	120	81	260	27	30
Morales, Veracruz	.925	18	10	27	3	1
C. Rodriguez, Veracruz	.925	20	11	38	4	5
V. Rodriguez, Tabasco	.923	26	23	49	6	6
Alvarez, Monterrey Ind.	.918	37	18	94	10	14
Jimenez, Monterrey Ind.	.912	70	52	113	16	17
A. Sanchez, Tabasco	.902	20	11	35	5	1
Cazarin, Minatitlan	.887	23	15	71	11	8
Magana, Yucatan	.882	14	5	25	4	3
De Los Santos, Jalisco	.880	35	21	67	12	6
Loredo, Campeche	.853	16	8	21	5	1

(Fewer Than Ten Games)

Player, Team	Pct.	G	PO	A	E	DP
Tirado, Cordoba	1.000	4	1	3	0	1
Monroy, Mexico City Tigers	1.000	1	0	1	0	0
Camacho, Mexico City Tigers	1.000	4	0	2	0	0
Arias, Mexico City Tigers	1.000	1	4	3	0	2
Perez, Mexico City Tigers	1.000	2	2	0	0	0
Sanchez, Mexico City Reds	1.000	1	0	1	0	0
Valle, Minatitlan	1.000	3	2	2	0	0
C. Garcia, Veracruz	1.000	2	0	5	0	1
H. Garcia, Veracruz	1.000	1	2	3	0	0
Gutierrez, Campeche	1.000	1	1	0	0	0
Castillo, Campeche	1.000	1	1	1	0	0
Zulueta, Yucatan	1.000	2	0	3	0	0
Chavez, Tabasco	1.000	4	2	5	0	0
Llanes, Tabasco	1.000	4	4	12	0	0
Valencia, Aguascalientes	1.000	1	1	1	0	1
Valenzuela, Aguascalientes	1.000	1	0	1	0	0
Barajas, Aguascalientes	1.000	3	0	1	0	0
Noriega, Jalisco	1.000	2	0	3	0	1
Santos, Jalisco	1.000	6	1	1	0	0
Saenz, Saltillo	1.000	2	3	2	0	1
Guerrero, Mexico City Tigers	1.000	1	1	1	0	0
Cruz, Union Laguna	1.000	1	1	0	0	0
Chan, Union Laguna	1.000	1	1	0	0	0
Vargas, Monterrey Sultans	1.000	7	1	13	0	1
Canizales, Monterrey Sultans	1.000	2	0	2	0	1
Garcia, Monclova	1.000	4	1	6	0	1
Zepeda, Monclova	1.000	3	0	2	0	0
Sanchez, Nuevo Laredo	.955	8	2	19	1	1
Aganza, Monclova	.941	6	4	12	1	1
Contreras, Union Laguna	.938	6	5	10	1	0
Jimenez, Saltillo	.913	9	4	17	2	0
Vizcarra, Aguascalientes	.875	4	2	5	1	0
Fentanes, Union Laguna	.875	5	2	5	1	1
Abril, Monterrey Ind.	.875	5	2	5	1	1
Franco, Monterrey Sultans	.857	5	1	5	1	1
Rodriguez, Monclova	.857	7	2	4	1	0
Felix, Yucatan	.833	5	1	4	1	1
Tatis, Mexico City Reds	.800	4	1	3	1	2
See, Aguascalientes	.800	8	8	12	5	2
Estrada, Nuevo Laredo	.800	7	2	6	2	0
Sandoval, Mexico City Reds	.000	1	0	0	1	0
Pardo, Cordoba	.000	3	0	0	1	0
Perez, Campeche	.000	2	0	0	1	0
Salgado, Nuevo Laredo	.000	2	0	0	1	0

Triple plays—V. Rodriguez, Ruiz.

SHORTSTOPS

Player, Team	Pct.	G	PO	A	E	DP
Rivera, Jalisco	.973	53	56	125	5	25
Reza, Union Laguna	.973	16	12	24	1	5
Diaz, Monterrey Sultans	.969	122	206	416	20	82
Sandoval, Mexico City Reds	.967	127	210	441	22	93
Guerrero, Mexico City Tigers	.966	118	219	352	20	94

Player, Team	Pct.	G	PO	A	E	DP
Gomez, Campeche	.965	74	121	212	12	51
H. Garcia, Veracruz	.965	125	238	419	24	77
Ramirez, Nuevo Laredo	.964	131	194	480	25	105
Loredo, Campeche	.963	19	17	35	2	13
Uzcanga, Aguascalientes	.962	24	34	67	4	14
Pacho, Yucatan	.962	128	195	436	25	88
Almodobar, Jalisco	.958	103	162	274	19	71
A. Valenzuela, Saltillo	.957	111	174	398	26	71
Cervera, Cordoba	.954	113	201	344	26	65
Robles, Union Laguna	.952	112	185	309	25	60
Jaime Guerrero, Aguascalientes	.950	117	197	415	32	79
Magana, Yucatan	.950	10	6	13	1	2
Zuniga, Saltillo	.945	28	38	65	6	17
Valle, Minatitlan	.945	114	176	356	31	71
Garcia, Monclova	.944	42	66	85	9	24
Contreras, Union Laguna	.943	11	20	30	3	6
A. Sanchez, Tabasco	.943	37	73	92	10	9
R. Vizcarra, Monterrey Ind.	.942	130	239	398	39	75
Lopez, Monclova	.942	99	143	279	26	55
Barrera, Tabasco	.939	30	40	68	7	14
Moreno, Minatitlan	.938	30	33	57	6	11
Barandica, Cordoba	.937	18	28	46	5	8
Chavez, Tabasco	.927	66	119	188	24	45
Vizcarra, Aguascalientes	.926	10	10	15	2	3
Vargas, Monterrey Sultans	.906	16	16	32	5	4
Gutierrez, Campeche	.905	47	72	138	22	17
Arias, Mexico City Tigers	.900	35	38	61	11	18
M. Vizcarra, Monterrey Ind.	.870	10	9	11	3	3

(Fewer Than Ten Games)

Player, Team	Pct.	G	PO	A	E	DP
Alvarez, Union Laguna	1.000	1	0	1	0	0
Bustamante, Mex. City Tigers	1.000	2	0	1	0	0
Montalvo, Mexico City Tigers	1.000	3	1	5	0	1
Verdugo, Mexico City Reds	1.000	7	12	15	0	6
Arce, Veracruz	1.000	2	2	3	0	0
Padron, Veracruz	1.000	2	4	7	0	1
Perez, Campeche	1.000	1	1	0	0	0
Marrufo, Tabasco	1.000	2	1	0	0	0
Llanes, Tabasco	1.000	1	1	2	0	1
Munoz, Jalisco	1.000	1	1	2	0	1
Noriega, Jalisco	1.000	1	0	1	0	0
E. Valenzuela, Saltillo	1.000	2	2	10	0	4
Ruiz, Union Laguna	1.000	1	1	3	0	1
Beristain, Monterrey Sultans	1.000	6	2	8	0	3
Canizales, Monterrey Sultans	1.000	1	2	2	0	0
Leyva, Monclova	1.000	1	1	2	0	1
Romero, Cordoba	.933	4	5	9	1	2
Herrera, Jalisco	.917	6	2	9	1	1
Giles, Tabasco	.914	6	8	24	3	1
Hernandez, Saltillo	.892	7	11	22	4	6
C. Rodriguez, Veracruz	.889	3	2	6	1	0
Quintero, Monterrey Sultans	.818	2	3	6	2	2
Cornejo, Saltillo	.750	3	0	3	1	1
Alvarado, Yucatan	.600	1	0	3	2	1
Zazueta, Mexico City Reds	.500	2	0	1	1	0

OUTFIELDERS

Player, Team	Pct.	G	PO	A	E	DP
Garibay, Mexico City Tigers	1.000	33	20	1	0	0
Bellazetin, Mexico City Tigers	1.000	23	25	3	0	1
Gonzalez, Mexico City Reds	1.000	10	8	0	0	0
Carretero, Minatitlan	1.000	10	9	1	0	1
Michell, Jalisco	1.000	11	21	0	0	0
Davis, Veracruz	1.000	13	30	2	0	0
Velazquez, Veracruz	1.000	23	30	3	0	0
Yong, Mexico City Tigers	1.000	12	29	1	0	0
Bellino, Veracruz	1.000	14	33	0	0	0
Ibarra, Cordoba	1.000	12	19	2	0	0
Villagomez, Cordoba	1.000	33	34	2	0	0
Herrera, Campeche	1.000	101	169	5	0	0
Tillman, Tabasco	1.000	36	90	5	0	1
Garcia, Aguascalientes	1.000	26	28	2	0	0
Agramon, Saltillo	1.000	27	13	1	0	0
Riesgo, Saltillo	1.000	13	16	2	0	0
Contreras, Union Laguna	1.000	13	14	2	0	1
Stockstill, Union Laguna	1.000	47	87	7	0	1
Williams, Union Laguna	1.000	27	48	0	0	0
Martinez, Monterrey Ind.	1.000	21	21	0	0	0
Motley, Monterrey Sultans	1.000	65	128	4	0	0
Rodriguez, Monclova	1.000	10	16	0	0	0
Plascencia, Nuevo Laredo	1.000	48	60	4	0	2
Valencia, Aguascalientes	.995	106	208	13	1	3
Fernandez, Mexico City Reds	.994	125	323	11	2	4
Knabenshue, Aguascalientes	.994	54	151	10	1	2
Valverde, Jalisco	.993	80	133	5	1	1
Wright, Saltillo	.993	118	256	14	2	5
Alvarez, Union Laguna	.992	104	237	13	2	2
Carrillo, Mexico City Tigers	.992	63	114	6	1	0
Brown, Tabasco	.991	78	112	4	1	0
Espinoza, Minatitlan	.989	103	175	6	2	0
Aguilera, Monterrey Sultans	.987	65	153	4	2	0
Tellez, Monterrey Ind.	.987	131	297	15	4	3

— 360 —

Player, Team	Pct.	G	PO	A	E	DP
Mangham, Mexico City Tigers	.987	90	150	5	2	0
Espinoza, Jalisco	.986	35	67	6	1	1
P. Gonzalez, Yucatan	.986	43	66	2	1	0
Gainey, Mexico City Reds	.983	88	166	8	3	2
Cruz, Union Laguna	.983	120	278	11	5	2
Machiria, Mexico City Tigers	.983	106	160	11	3	1
Cuevas, Minatitlan	.981	59	104	1	2	0
Sambo, Veracruz	.981	115	251	7	5	0
Torres, Campeche	.981	53	97	4	2	1
Loredo, Campeche	.980	58	95	5	2	1
Blocker, Minatitlan	.980	112	245	4	5	0
Iturbe, Cordoba	.979	129	320	7	7	1
Baca, Monterrey Sultans	.979	71	137	3	3	0
Davis, Tabasco	.978	116	305	9	7	2
Arredondo, Jalisco	.977	101	254	6	6	0
Valenzuela, Aguascalientes	.977	83	122	7	3	1
Simmons, Jalisco	.976	62	115	8	3	0
Castaneda, Monterrey Sultans ...	.976	59	116	6	3	2
Castelan, Yucatan	.976	91	202	1	5	0
Steels, Monterrey Industriales	.976	128	221	21	6	2
Sabino, Veracruz	.974	35	69	6	2	1
Arzate, Minatitlan	.973	91	141	4	4	0
Diaz, Nuevo Laredo	.973	105	133	9	4	0
Dominguez, Veracruz	.972	121	237	8	7	1
Abrego, Yucatan	.972	48	66	4	2	0
Medina, Campeche	.971	53	60	8	2	2
Garcia, Monterrey Sultans	.970	91	151	13	5	1
Beltran, Tabasco	.970	114	182	14	6	2
Lopez, Aguascalientes	.970	129	247	11	8	2
Gutierrez, Jalisco	.970	53	63	1	2	1
Estrada, Nuevo Laredo	.970	24	31	1	1	0
Torres, Saltillo	.969	123	299	12	10	1
Perez, Monclova	.968	129	354	12	12	3
Jose, Veracruz	.967	15	28	1	1	2
Tiquet, Cordoba	.966	109	189	8	7	0
Morones, Saltillo	.964	101	211	6	8	1
Tatis, Mexico City Reds	.964	124	204	12	8	2
Gutierrez, Veracruz	.964	42	79	1	3	0
Jones, Nuevo Laredo	.964	124	250	16	10	2
Campusano, Saltillo	.963	48	98	5	4	1
Sheperd, Monterrey Sultans	.962	77	147	5	6	1
Alvarez, Monterrey Industriales .	.961	59	71	3	3	0
Sanchez, Nuevo Laredo	.960	121	188	5	8	2
Estrada, Campeche	.960	47	70	2	3	1
Leal, Monclova	.960	74	136	8	6	0
Valenzuela, Monterrey Sultans ...	.959	60	114	4	5	0
Yuriar, Monclova	.959	114	238	20	11	4
Saenz, Saltillo	.959	89	127	12	6	1
Wayne, Yucatan	.958	10	23	0	1	0
Magallanes, Union Laguna	.958	52	106	7	5	2
Navarro, Cordoba	.956	89	147	6	7	0
Valdez, Union Laguna	.956	97	143	10	7	1
Brown, Veracruz	.956	41	79	7	4	2
Sanchez, Monclova	.955	86	183	10	9	1
Johnson, Campeche	.953	31	58	3	3	1
Lagunes, Monterrey Sultans	.952	14	19	1	1	0
Gutierrez, Union Laguna	.951	45	76	2	4	0
Garcia, Yucatan	.950	124	183	7	10	0
Pina, Yucatan	.950	24	54	3	3	0
A. Lopez, Jalisco	.950	23	54	3	3	0
Ponce, Campeche	.947	109	242	10	14	0
Canizales, Monterrey Sultans	.944	85	148	5	9	1
Perez, Monterrey Industriales	.941	50	62	2	4	0
Alvarez, Aguascalientes	.935	28	58	0	4	0
Moreno, Minatitlan	.929	11	13	0	1	0
Zulueta, Yucatan	.929	24	26	0	2	0
Rubio, Yucatan	.917	14	11	0	1	0
Noris, Mexico City Reds	.915	32	42	1	4	0
De Los Santos, Jalisco	.892	18	31	2	4	0
See, Aguascalientes	.889	20	22	2	3	1
Leon, Jalisco	.889	15	16	0	2	0

(Fewer Than Ten Games)

Player, Team	Pct.	G	PO	A	E	DP
Montalvo, Mexico City Tigers	1.000	2	2	0	0	0
A. Castro, Minatitlan	1.000	1	2	1	0	0
Valdez, Tabasco	1.000	3	1	0	0	0
E. Castro, Minatitlan	1.000	5	2	0	0	0
Reyna, Cordoba	1.000	5	5	0	0	0
Hernandez, Campeche	1.000	1	2	0	0	0
M. Gonzalez, Yucatan	1.000	2	2	0	0	0
Hinzo, Yucatan	1.000	1	1	0	0	0
Sievers, Yucatan	1.000	2	2	0	0	0
A. Sanchez, Tabasco	1.000	3	7	1	0	0
Jimenez, Monterrey Industriales.	1.000	1	0	1	0	0
Quiroz, Tabasco	1.000	1	0	1	0	0
Giles, Tabasco	1.000	4	10	0	0	0
Espinoza, Tabasco	1.000	6	7	0	0	0
Vargas, Aguascalientes	1.000	1	2	0	0	0
Howard, Aguascalientes	1.000	5	4	0	0	0
Delgado, Aguascalientes	1.000	2	1	0	0	0
Almodobar, Jalisco	1.000	2	0	1	0	0
Noriega, Jalisco	1.000	5	7	0	0	0
Peralta, Saltillo	1.000	1	2	0	0	0

Player, Team	Pct.	G	PO	A	E	DP
Rodriguez, Saltillo	1.000	8	4	0	0	0
Valverde, Union Laguna	1.000	3	1	0	0	0
Pena, Monterrey Industriales	1.000	5	4	0	0	0
M. Vizcarra, Monterrey Ind.	1.000	5	1	0	0	0
Moreno, Monterrey Industriales..	1.000	1	1	0	0	0
Vargas, Monterrey Sultans	1.000	7	7	0	0	0
Manriquez, Monterrey Sultans....	1.000	2	6	0	0	0
Zamudio, Monterrey Sultans	1.000	7	11	0	0	0
Ramos, Monterrey Sultans	1.000	5	6	0	0	0
Kutcher, Monterrey Sultans	1.000	8	11	0	0	0
Chan, Monclova	1.000	2	1	1	0	0
Valencia, Monclova	1.000	2	1	0	0	0
Zazueta, Mexico City Reds	.913	8	19	2	2	0
Lopez, Monclova	.824	7	12	2	3	0
Salgado, Nuevo Laredo	.800	4	4	0	1	0
Ford, Union Laguna	.500	2	1	0	1	0
Guerrero, Minatitlan	.000	1	0	0	0	0
Ruiz, Campeche	.000	2	0	0	1	0
Hernandez, Saltillo	.000	1	0	0	2	0

CATCHERS

Player, Team	Pct.	G	PO	A	E	DP	PB
Garcia, Minatitlan	1.000	14	24	2	0	0	0
Garcia, Tabasco	1.000	21	44	6	0	0	2
J. Lopez, Jalisco	1.000	10	10	2	0	0	0
Torres, Union Laguna	1.000	13	12	0	0	0	0
Pena, Monterrey Sultans	1.000	23	36	4	0	1	2
Tirado, Tabasco	.993	31	131	13	1	0	2
Estrada, Mexico City Reds	.993	83	384	32	3	1	7
Osuna, Saltillo	.992	61	220	37	2	4	5
Reyes, Aguascalientes	.992	30	102	17	1	2	0
Estrada, Minatitlan	.991	42	195	34	2	2	6
Ramirez, Yucatan	.989	52	246	29	3	3	6
Rivera, Aguascalientes	.988	80	309	34	4	1	7
Tejada, Mexico City Tigers	.988	101	615	55	8	9	4
Guzman, Campeche	.986	89	442	54	7	6	11
Gastelum, Veracruz	.986	99	424	66	7	6	10
Cruz, Union Laguna	.985	124	686	81	12	9	16
Gavia, Veracruz	.984	56	156	27	3	2	5
Luna, Aguascalientes	.983	69	293	57	6	2	4
Avila, Union Laguna	.983	24	105	11	2	1	0
Garzon, Tabasco	.983	101	408	55	8	5	6
Garza, Monterrey Industriales	.983	125	706	80	14	7	22
Cazarin, Minatitlan	.981	86	414	63	9	6	5
Martinez, Union Laguna	.981	115	609	80	13	11	14
Ruiz, Campeche	.981	60	230	29	5	4	1
Hernandez, Mont. Sultans	.979	113	481	76	12	5	6
Ramirez, Mont. Industriales .	.977	15	40	3	1	1	1
Meza, Monterrey Industriales .	.977	53	153	17	4	1	2
Samaniego, Jalisco	.976	116	571	67	16	7	6
Stark, Veracruz	.974	12	36	2	1	0	2
Bocardo, Monclova	.973	54	221	31	7	1	6
Tirado, Cordoba	.972	58	253	28	8	2	4
Munoz, Mexico City Reds	.972	75	276	31	9	2	5
Narvaez, Monclova	.971	14	33	0	1	2	1
Cruz, Saltillo	.970	77	390	58	14	3	4
Daut, Monclova	.969	91	416	59	15	9	22
Dominguez, Jalisco	.968	29	77	13	3	2	2
E. Valenzuela, Saltillo	.965	23	77	6	3	1	3
Cantu, Cordoba	.965	86	365	17	14	2	11
Abrego, Yucatan	.965	75	389	46	16	1	13
M. Gonzalez, Yucatan	.962	21	90	10	4	2	0
Becerra, Nuevo Laredo	.961	37	114	10	5	0	5
Monroy, Mexico City Tigers	.959	33	87	7	4	1	0
Valdez, Mont. Industriales	.958	13	22	1	1	3	2

(Fewer Than Ten Games)

Player, Team	Pct.	G	PO	A	E	DP	PB
Rojas, Monterrey Industriales.	1.000	3	23	1	0	0	0
Medina, Minatitlan	1.000	7	23	0	0	0	1
Camargo, Veracruz	1.000	1	1	0	0	0	0
Zulueta, Yucatan	1.000	1	0	1	0	0	0
Tillman, Saltillo	1.000	1	1	0	0	0	0
R. Castillo, Tabasco	1.000	8	20	2	0	0	0
See, Aguascalientes	1.000	4	15	1	0	0	0
Mendoza, Jalisco	1.000	6	4	0	0	0	0
Marquez, Union Laguna	1.000	5	7	0	0	0	0
M. Vizcarra, Mont. Ind.	1.000	2	6	1	0	0	1
Vargas, Monterrey Sultans	1.000	1	3	0	0	0	0
Zepeda, Monclova	1.000	3	0	0	0	0	0
Dojaquez, Monclova	1.000	1	2	1	0	0	0
Cruz, Nuevo Laredo	1.000	1	12	1	0	0	0
Pulido, Mexico City Tigers	.957	5	20	2	1	0	0
Hurtado, Minatitlan	.949	7	32	5	2	0	2
Mendez, Aguascalientes	.900	9	9	0	1	0	2
Quintero, Monclova	.900	4	8	1	1	0	2
Sanchez, Monterrey Sultans ...	.857	4	5	1	1	0	0

PITCHERS

Player, Team	Pct.	G	PO	A	E	DP
Grajales, Union Laguna	1.000	36	1	6	0	1
Z. Garcia, Mexico City Tigers	1.000	23	5	5	0	1
Hernandez, Mexico City Tigers ...	1.000	38	3	4	0	1

Player, Team	Pct.	G	PO	A	E	DP	Player, Team	Pct.	G	PO	A	E	DP
Veres, Mexico City Tigers	1.000	14	0	4	0	0	Pulido, Saltillo	.964	30	6	48	2	3
Mendez, Mexico City Reds	1.000	28	10	26	0	0	Moreno, Mexico City Reds	.964	32	12	41	2	3
Martinez, Mexico City Reds	1.000	18	2	5	0	0	Moreno, Mexico City Tigers	.963	28	7	45	2	3
Jimenez, Mexico City Reds	1.000	20	0	3	0	0	Colorado, Cordoba	.963	25	10	16	1	2
Leyva, Mexico City Reds	1.000	25	4	16	0	1	Valdez, Monterrey Industriales	.963	30	12	40	2	2
Barojas, Mexico City Reds	1.000	39	8	19	0	1	Ramirez, Mexico City Reds	.962	19	1	24	1	0
Cruz, Mexico City Reds	1.000	27	1	10	0	2	Cruz, Yucatan	.962	22	5	20	1	2
Valenzuela, Monclova	1.000	17	3	5	0	0	Miranda, Aguascalientes	.962	64	7	18	1	1
Villanueva, Monterrey Sultans	1.000	29	0	6	0	0	Holman, Nuevo Laredo	.962	59	6	19	1	3
Munoz, Veracruz	1.000	22	12	16	0	2	Orozco, Monterrey Sultans	.959	32	9	38	2	2
Aguilar, Minatitlan	1.000	22	0	6	0	0	Marquez, Mexico City Tigers	.958	51	4	19	1	1
Luevano, Veracruz	1.000	25	7	17	0	0	Acosta, Monterrey Sultans	.958	41	8	15	1	2
Rodriguez, Mont. Industriales	1.000	31	4	5	0	1	Heredia, Monterrey Sultans	.958	54	4	19	1	2
Meza, Veracruz	1.000	21	2	8	0	0	Osuna, Tabasco	.956	29	9	34	2	1
Contreras, Veracruz	1.000	17	0	9	0	1	Sosa, Tabasco	.955	37	4	17	1	2
Angulo, Cordoba	1.000	19	0	4	0	0	Couoh, Nuevo Laredo	.955	37	4	17	1	0
Perez, Cordoba	1.000	31	5	14	0	1	Medvin, Saltillo	.952	27	9	11	1	0
Valenzuela, Mexico City Reds	1.000	23	2	4	0	0	Carranza, Jalisco	.951	29	6	33	2	1
Veliz, Cordoba	1.000	31	4	5	0	1	Sanchez, Veracruz	.947	33	5	13	1	1
Raygoza, Campeche	1.000	29	21	40	0	4	Herrera, Union Laguna	.947	37	8	10	1	0
Tinoco, Campeche	1.000	11	0	4	0	0	Taylor, Cordoba	.947	20	7	11	1	1
Jose Lopez, Campeche	1.000	24	3	3	0	0	Castillo, Nuevo Laredo	.947	19	6	12	1	0
Villegas, Campeche	1.000	22	1	10	0	0	Rodriguez, Saltillo	.946	31	5	30	2	3
Browning, Campeche	1.000	52	4	21	0	2	Cano, Aguascalientes	.944	27	10	41	3	6
Ledon, Campeche	1.000	36	1	8	0	0	Pico, Mexico City Reds	.941	11	5	11	1	1
Toledo, Campeche	1.000	33	1	5	0	0	Garcia, Veracruz	.941	32	7	9	1	1
Esquer, Yucatan	1.000	26	10	46	0	3	J. Romero, Tabasco	.941	44	3	13	1	0
Merodio, Yucatan	1.000	24	9	16	0	0	Ruiz, Monterrey Sultans	.941	18	4	12	1	2
Burchan, Yucatan	1.000	17	6	18	0	0	Cervantes, Jalisco	.939	27	11	20	2	1
Retes, Tabasco	1.000	30	4	30	0	0	Barraza, Nuevo Laredo	.939	28	22	40	4	5
Encarnacion, Corboda	1.000	46	1	17	0	0	Salas, Mexico City Tigers	.938	40	2	13	1	0
Zamudio, Tabasco	1.000	10	0	6	0	0	Soto, Minatitlan	.938	33	5	25	2	2
H. Romero, Tabasco	1.000	19	3	10	0	2	Montalvo, Aguascalientes	.938	49	9	21	2	3
Herrera, Tabasco	1.000	49	2	19	0	1	Hansen, Mexico City Reds	.933	15	6	8	1	1
Sibate, Tabasco	1.000	16	0	7	0	0	Huerta, Campeche	.933	28	7	21	2	1
Gomez, Tabasco	1.000	10	1	2	0	2	Vazquez, Mexico City Reds	.929	28	11	28	3	4
Diaz, Tabasco	1.000	31	5	14	0	1	Hernandez, Veracruz	.929	26	9	17	2	0
Saldana, Tabasco	1.000	14	6	7	0	0	Quinonez, Aguascalientes	.929	17	4	9	1	0
Velazquez, Aguascalientes	1.000	17	4	7	0	0	Richle, Union Laguna	.929	13	3	10	1	1
Enriquez, Aguascalientes	1.000	28	17	26	0	2	O. Diaz, Minatitlan	.923	30	1	11	1	0
Jimenez, Aguascalientes	1.000	23	5	28	0	2	Gonzalez, Monterrey Sultans	.923	16	2	10	1	0
Granillo, Aguascalientes	1.000	29	1	1	0	0	Villarreal, Monclova	.923	31	3	9	1	1
Jaime Granillo, Aguascalientes	1.000	27	3	6	0	1	Dominguez, Campeche	.921	23	6	29	3	1
Lopez, Aguascalientes	1.000	25	5	12	0	1	Jimenez, Monterrey Industriales	.921	18	4	31	3	2
Cardenas, Minatitlan	1.000	35	5	9	0	0	Cabrales, Veracruz	.917	38	3	8	1	1
Vargas, Aguascalientes	1.000	15	1	1	0	0	Araujo, Cordoba	.917	29	10	34	4	3
Reyes, Jalisco	1.000	11	0	2	0	0	Hernandez, Yucatan	.917	39	13	20	3	2
Pavlas, Jalisco	1.000	12	6	7	0	1	Montano, Yucatan	.917	26	18	26	4	6
Iniguez, Jalisco	1.000	12	0	7	0	0	Camarena, Mont. Industriales	.917	26	3	8	1	1
Moreno, Saltillo	1.000	30	4	27	0	4	Neri, Aguascalientes	.917	29	5	17	2	1
Castro, Minatitlan	1.000	28	0	2	0	0	Castellanos, Jalisco	.917	34	1	10	1	1
Barron, Saltillo	1.000	36	3	8	0	2	Hickey, Monterrey Industriales	.917	14	2	9	1	0
Lara, Saltillo	1.000	14	0	3	0	1	Hernandez, Minatitlan	.915	28	11	32	4	4
Lizarraga, Saltillo	1.000	25	5	2	0	0	Cano, Monterrey Industriales	.913	22	8	13	2	1
Rivas, Jalisco	1.000	26	2	4	0	0	Sinohui, Minatitlan	.912	44	10	21	3	5
Olmos, Saltillo	1.000	11	2	5	0	0	Alvarez, Saltillo	.909	50	2	8	1	1
Renteria, Union Laguna	1.000	26	6	26	0	3	Cecena, Saltillo	.909	44	3	7	1	1
Perry, Saltillo	1.000	28	2	3	0	0	Lopez, Veracruz	.905	25	4	15	2	0
Rincon, Union Laguna	1.000	49	2	9	0	1	Alicea, Union Laguna	.900	56	0	9	1	0
Villegas, Union Laguna	1.000	40	5	16	0	1	Macias, Cordoba	.900	31	2	7	1	0
Quintero, Union Laguna	1.000	20	1	6	0	1	Ibarra, Tabasco	.900	19	3	15	2	0
Pimentel, Union Laguna	1.000	21	1	2	0	1	Cosio, Minatitlan	.900	34	7	20	3	1
Garibay, Union Laguna	1.000	31	3	9	0	1	M. Rodriguez, Tabasco	.895	36	4	13	2	1
Mendez, Union Laguna	1.000	12	0	4	0	0	Sanchez, Monterrey Industriales	.889	26	3	5	1	0
Escamilla, Saltillo	1.000	11	0	2	0	1	Castaneda, Jalisco	.882	42	2	13	2	1
Ochoa, Monterrey Industriales	1.000	59	5	10	0	1	Alvarez, Nuevo Laredo	.880	21	7	15	3	2
Ontiveros, Mont. Industriales	1.000	39	1	7	0	1	Cordoba, Mexico City Reds	.875	16	3	4	1	0
U. Rodriguez, Tabasco	1.000	22	0	6	0	0	Pineda, Mexico City Reds	.875	18	3	4	1	0
Garza, Monterrey Sultans	1.000	30	7	27	0	5	Cazares, Veracruz	.875	27	1	6	1	0
Serna, Monterrey Sultans	1.000	10	2	6	0	1	Garibay, Yucatan	.875	45	2	5	1	1
Perez, Monterrey Sultans	1.000	30	2	12	0	0	Chavarin, Yucatan	.875	38	2	5	1	0
Norman, Monclova	1.000	27	3	16	0	2	Osuna, Monclova	.875	44	3	11	2	1
Valdez, Monclova	1.000	27	2	24	0	2	Morales, Monclova	.875	45	0	7	1	0
E. Velazquez, Monclova	1.000	37	0	3	0	0	Rodriguez, Nuevo Laredo	.875	18	6	8	2	1
Malave, Monclova	1.000	11	0	4	0	0	Rios, Mexico City Tigers	.871	28	10	17	4	1
Chavez, Monclova	1.000	31	1	11	0	0	Uribe, Yucatan	.867	24	1	12	2	0
Espinoza, Monclova	1.000	10	2	2	0	1	Antunez, Yucatan	.867	47	7	6	2	1
Mena, Monclova	1.000	14	1	1	0	0	Murillo, Monclova	.864	29	2	17	3	0
Solis, Monterrey Industriales	1.000	28	2	3	0	0	Mora, Mexico City Tigers	.857	18	0	6	1	0
Valdez, Nuevo Laredo	1.000	31	2	14	0	2	DeLeon, Minatitlan	.857	55	2	10	2	2
Cruz, Nuevo Laredo	1.000	22	1	3	0	0	Osuna, Mexico City Tigers	.842	28	7	25	6	2
Quiroz, Nuevo Laredo	1.000	22	3	7	0	1	Felix, Veracruz	.818	23	1	8	2	1
Moreno, Nuevo Laredo	1.000	14	1	2	0	0	Smith, Mexico City Tigers	.813	10	2	11	3	0
Walsh, Nuevo Laredo	1.000	21	6	21	0	3	Herrera, Monterrey Industriales	.793	33	4	19	6	2
Heinkel, Campeche	.986	29	21	52	1	4	Rojo, Campeche	.750	11	1	2	1	1
Purata, Minatitlan	.981	33	12	41	1	5	Tejeda, Campeche	.750	20	1	2	1	1
Lopez, Cordoba	.980	28	17	32	1	3	Vespe, Union Laguna	.750	10	1	5	2	0
Palafox, Union Laguna	.980	30	13	36	1	4	Mojica, Jalisco	.750	26	1	5	2	3
Hernandez, Mont. Industriales	.980	30	21	27	1	4	Navarro, Monterrey Sultans	.750	26	0	6	2	0
Solis, Saltillo	.978	28	7	38	1	2	Tejeda, Minatitlan	.667	15	0	2	1	0
Eave, Monclova	.975	28	6	33	1	2	Ibarra, Monclova	.600	24	0	3	2	0
Valenzuela, Jalisco	.974	22	9	29	1	4	Velez, Yucatan	.500	16	0	1	1	0
J. Garcia, Mexico City Tigers	.970	22	5	27	1	1	Kerfeld, Jalisco	.500	12	0	1	1	1
Upshaw, Nuevo Laredo	.970	24	4	28	1	4	Garza, Monclova	.500	11	0	1	1	0

(Fewer Than Ten Games)

Player, Team	Pct.	G	PO	A	E	DP
Gomez, Mexico City Tigers	1.000	4	0	3	0	0
Onofre, Mexico City Tigers	1.000	2	0	1	0	0
Perez, Mexico City Reds	1.000	3	0	1	0	0
Avendano, Corboda	1.000	5	0	2	0	0
Hilton, Mexico City Reds	1.000	1	0	1	0	0
Rivera, Mexico City Reds	1.000	2	1	1	0	0
Olivas, Minatitlan	1.000	8	2	1	0	0
Torres, Monclova	1.000	7	2	0	0	0
Zavaleta, Minatitlan	1.000	1	1	1	0	0
Soto, Veracruz	1.000	5	0	2	0	0
Sandoval, Veracruz	1.000	3	1	0	0	0
Arias, Veracruz	1.000	5	1	0	0	0
Puerto, Cordoba	1.000	5	0	2	0	0
Martinez, Veracruz	1.000	7	0	3	0	0
Moreno, Cordoba	1.000	2	1	1	0	0
Jusaino, Cordoba	1.000	7	1	0	0	0
Corbette, Campeche	1.000	3	2	4	0	1
Manzano, Campeche	1.000	4	0	1	0	0
Sierra, Campeche	1.000	3	1	3	0	0
Vizcarra, Yucatan	1.000	7	0	2	0	0
Chevez, Tabasco	1.000	8	0	1	0	0
Acosta, Yucatan	1.000	5	1	0	0	1
Renteria, Yucatan	1.000	6	0	3	0	0
Serafin, Tabasco	1.000	4	0	2	0	0
McCament, Tabasco	1.000	3	0	3	0	0

Player, Team	Pct.	G	PO	A	E	DP
Flores, Tabasco	1.000	8	0	2	0	0
Garcia, Tabasco	1.000	4	0	3	0	0
Munoz, Jalisco	1.000	7	4	0	0	0
Camacho, Jalisco	1.000	8	1	0	0	0
Pena, Saltillo	1.000	8	0	2	0	0
Silva, Saltillo	1.000	6	1	1	0	1
Mosquera, Union Laguna	1.000	3	2	1	0	0
Medina, Union Laguna	1.000	4	1	0	0	0
Monson, Union Laguna	1.000	5	1	7	0	1
Noriega, Monterrey Industriales	1.000	7	0	1	0	0
Lara, Monterrey Industriales	1.000	4	1	0	0	0
Pruneda, Monterrey Sultans	1.000	8	1	4	0	0
Ortiz, Monterrey Sultans	1.000	5	0	1	0	1
Pelcastregui, Monterrey Sultans	1.000	1	0	1	0	0
L. Velazquez, Monclova	1.000	3	0	1	0	0
Vazquez, Monclova	1.000	9	1	1	0	0
Garcia, Monclova	1.000	5	1	0	0	0
Dojaquez, Monclova	1.000	4	2	0	0	0
Valenzuela, Nuevo Laredo	1.000	4	2	0	0	0
Vega, Nuevo Laredo	1.000	3	0	1	0	0
Jones, Monclova	.933	9	1	13	1	0
Lara, Campeche	.875	8	2	5	1	1
Alba, Union Laguna	.857	6	0	6	1	0
Guajardo, Mexico City Tigers	.667	5	0	2	1	0
Leon, Jalisco	.500	7	1	0	1	0
Martinez, Minatitlan	.000	4	0	0	1	0
Flores, Monterrey Industriales	.000	5	0	0	1	0

LEAGUE CHAMPIONS

Year	Team	Pct.
1955—	Mexico City Tigers*	.539
1956—	Mexico City Reds	.692
1957—	Yucatan	.567
	Mex. C. Reds (2nd)†	.550
1958—	Nuevo Laredo	.625
1959—	Poza Rica	.575
	Mex. C. Reds (3rd)†	.507
1960—	Mexico City Tigers	.538
1961—	Veracruz	.575
1962—	Monterrey	.592
1963—	Puebla	.606
1964—	Mexico City Reds	.586
1965—	Mexico City Reds	.590
1966—	Mexico City Tigers‡	.614
	Mexico City Reds	.571
1967—	Jalisco	.607
1968—	Mexico City Reds	.586
1969—	Reynosa	.591
1970—	Aguila§	.580
	Mexico City Reds	.607
1971—	Jalisco§	.558
	Saltillo	.593

Year	Team	Pct.
1972—	Saltillo	.636
	Cordoba§	.541
1973—	Saltillo	.656
	Mexico City Reds x	.590
1974—	Jalisco	.627
	Mexico City Reds x	.551
1975—	Tampico x	.541
	Cordoba	.649
1976—	Mexico City Reds x	.543
	Union Laguna	.547
1977—	Mexico City Reds	.623
	Nuevo Laredo x	.507
1978—	Aguascalientes x	.589
	Union Laguna	.523
1979—	Saltillo	.704
	Puebla x	.628
1980—	No champion y	
1981—	Mexico City Reds	.615
	Reynosa	.492
1982—	Ciudad Juarez x	.570
	Mexico City Tigers	.508

Year	Team	Pct.
1983—	Campeche z	.614
	Ciudad Juarez	.535
1984—	Yucatan z	.560
	Ciudad Juarez	.509
1985—	Mexico City Reds z	.606
	Nuevo Laredo	.5275
1986—	Puebla z	.682
	Monclova	.598
1987—	Mexico City Reds z	.605
	Monterrey	.536
1988—	Mexico City Reds z	.646
	Nuevo Laredo	.602
1989—	Nuevo Laredo z	.621
	Yucatan	.539
1990—	Nuevo Laredo	.618
	Leon z	.565
1991—	Monterrey z	.683
	Mexico City Reds	.627
1992—	Mexico City Tigers z	.594
	Nuevo Laredo	.538

*Defeated Nuevo Laredo, two games to none, in playoff for pennant. †Won four-team playoff. ‡Won split-season playoff. §League divided into Northern, Southern divisions; won two-team playoff. xLeague divided into Northern, Southern zones; sub-divided into Eastern, Western divisions, won eight-team playoff. yA players strike on July 1 forced the cancellation of the regular season and playoff schedule. zLeague divided into Northern, Southern zones; four clubs from each zone qualified for postseason play. Won final series for league championship.

PACIFIC COAST LEAGUE

FIRST HALF

NORTHERN DIVISION

Team	W	L	T	Pct.	GB
Vancouver (White Sox)	44	28	0	.611	......
Portland (Twins)	42	30	0	.583	2
Edmonton (Angels)	38	33	1	.535	5½
Calgary (Mariners)	28	41	1	.406	14½
Tacoma (Athletics)	26	45	0	.366	17½

SOUTHERN DIVISION

Team	W	L	T	Pct.	GB
Las Vegas (Padres)	41	31	0	.569	......
Colorado Springs (Indians)	36	33	0	.522	3½
Phoenix (Giants)	35	37	0	.486	6
Tucson (Astros)	33	39	0	.458	8
Albuquerque (Dodgers)	33	39	0	.458	8

SECOND HALF

NORTHERN DIVISION

Team	W	L	T	Pct.	GB
Portland (Twins)	41	31	0	.569	......
Vancouver (White Sox)	37	33	0	.529	3
Edmonton (Angels)	36	36	0	.500	5
Calgary (Mariners)	32	37	0	.464	7½
Tacoma (Athletics)	30	42	0	.417	11

SOUTHERN DIVISION

Team	W	L	T	Pct.	GB
Colorado Springs (Indians)	48	24	0	.667	......
Tucson (Astros)	37	35	0	.514	11
Las Vegas (Padres)	33	39	0	.458	15
Albuquerque (Dodgers)	32	39	0	.451	15½
Phoenix (Giants)	31	41	0	.431	17

COMPOSITE

Team	C.S.	Port.	Van.	Edm.	L.V.	Tuc.	Phoe.	Alb.	Cal.	Tac.	W	L	T	Pct.	GB
Colorado Springs (Indians)	....	4	5	4	12	16	15	18	5	5	84	57	0	.596	......
Portland (Twins)	4	....	14	15	6	4	3	6	13	18	83	61	0	.576	2½
Vancouver (White Sox)	3	12	....	16	3	3	7	5	18	14	81	61	0	.570	3½
Edmonton (Angels)	4	11	10	....	4	5	5	5	17	13	74	69	1	.517	11
Las Vegas (Padres)	14	2	5	4	....	10	10	16	12	5	74	70	0	.514	11½
Tucson (Astros)	10	4	5	3	16	....	12	13	3	4	70	74	0	.486	15½
Phoenix (Giants)	11	5	1	5	3	10	14	....	11	5	6	66	78	0	.458	19½
Albuquerque (Dodgers)	8	2	3	3	14	13	15	....	3	4	65	78	0	.455	20
Calgary (Mariners)	1	13	6	8	3	5	3	4	....	17	60	78	1	.435	22½
Tacoma (Athletics)	2	8	12	13	2	4	2	4	9	....	56	87	0	.392	29

Major league affiliations in parentheses.

Playoffs—Colorado Springs defeated Las Vegas, three games to two; Vancouver defeated Portland, three games to two; Colorado Springs defeated Vancouver, three games to none, to win league championship.

Regular-season attendance—Albuquerque, 362,283; Calgary, 277,307; Colorado Springs, 187,645; Edmonton, 257,146; Las Vegas, 382,838; Phoenix, 278,798; Portland, 184,097; Tacoma, 329,000; Tucson, 300,134; Vancouver, 333,564. Total, 2,892,812. Playoffs (13 games)—36,427. Class AAA All-Star Game at Richmond—12,186.

Managers—Albuquerque, Bill Russell; Calgary, Keith Bodie; Colorado Springs, Charlie Manuel; Edmonton, Max Oliveras; Las Vegas, Jim Riggleman; Phoenix, Bill Evers; Portland, Scott Ullger; Tacoma, Bob Boone; Tucson, Bob Skinner; Vancouver, Rick Renick.

All-Star team: 1B—Guillermo Velasquez, Las Vegas; 2B—Bret Boone, Calgary; 3B—Mike Blowers, Calgary; SS—Alvaro Espinoza, Colorado Springs; OF—Tim Salmon, Edmonton; Wayne Kirby, Colorado Springs; Bernardo Brito, Portland; C—Mike Piazza, Albuquerque; DH—Troy Neel, Tacoma; RHP—Rod Bolton, Vancouver; LHP—Denis Boucher, Colorado Springs; Relief Pitcher—Brian Drahman, Vancouver; Most Valuable Player—Tim Salmon, Edmonton; Manager of the Year—Charlie Manuel, Colorado Springs.

BATTING

TEAM

Team	Avg.	G	AB	R	OR	H	TB	2B	3B	HR	RBI	SH	SF	HP	BB	Int. BB	SO	SB	CS	LOB
Colorado Springs	.298	141	4869	845	675	1450	2190	286	74	102	779	38	53	40	515	34	814	104	53	1041
Albuquerque	.297	143	4889	689	719	1454	2061	262	42	87	624	73	46	36	389	44	696	96	58	1016
Edmonton	.290	144	4731	823	769	1371	2055	295	52	95	762	47	56	56	663	36	821	163	82	1061
Tucson	.285	144	4942	707	702	1409	1979	251	77	55	641	69	50	32	498	32	880	164	70	1073
Las Vegas	.277	144	4859	706	709	1345	1899	236	48	74	642	57	54	41	505	40	823	117	49	1029
Calgary	.274	139	4552	662	827	1246	1854	244	50	88	598	25	43	34	558	27	898	175	104	1000
Vancouver	.270	142	4648	644	592	1256	1786	201	46	79	586	62	34	50	592	45	733	144	60	1054
Portland	.267	144	4853	691	593	1295	1914	239	40	100	627	34	49	35	527	41	672	111	43	1009
Phoenix	.266	144	4794	605	680	1277	1796	222	51	65	562	73	46	43	495	36	866	134	108	1005
Tacoma	.263	143	4786	618	724	1260	1781	256	35	65	565	48	43	31	536	34	760	96	63	1061

INDIVIDUAL

(Leading qualifiers for batting championship—389 or more plate appearances)

*Bats lefthanded.   †Switch-hitter.

Player, Team	Avg.	G	AB	R	H	TB	2B	3B	HR	RBI	SH	SF	HP	BB	Int. BB	SO	SB	CS
Neel, Troy, Tacoma*	.351	112	396	61	139	232	36	3	17	74	0	5	6	60	11	84	2	5
Salmon, Tim, Edmonton	.347	118	409	101	142	275	38	4	29	105	0	4	6	91	11	103	9	7
Kirby, Wayne, Colorado Springs*	.345	123	470	101	162	245	18	16	11	74	4	2	2	36	4	28	51	20
Piazza, Mike, Albuquerque	.341	94	358	54	122	202	22	5	16	69	0	1	2	37	4	57	1	3
Young, Eric, Albuquerque	.337	94	350	61	118	153	16	5	3	49	13	7	4	33	0	18	28	11
Gardner, Jeff, Las Vegas*	.335	120	439	82	147	190	30	5	1	51	7	2	2	67	6	48	7	2
Bournigal, Rafael, Albuquerque	.324	122	395	47	128	148	18	1	0	34	10	4	5	22	5	7	5	3
Aldrete, Mike, Colorado Springs*	.322	128	463	69	149	219	42	2	8	84	1	4	3	65	8	113	1	0
Amaral, Rich, Calgary	.318	106	403	79	128	165	21	8	0	21	2	2	1	67	1	69	53	16
Boone, Bret, Calgary	.314	118	439	73	138	213	26	5	13	73	1	6	5	60	7	88	17	12

Departmental leaders: G-B. Brito, Cron, 140; AB-B. Brito, 564; R—Kirby, Salmon, 101; H—Kirby, 162; TB—Salmon, 275; 2B—Velasquez, 44;

3B—Kirby, 16; HR—Salmon, 29; RBI—Salmon, 105; SH—Booker, 14; SF—Allred, Rodriguez, 10; HP—Cron, 17; BB—Cron, 94; IBB—Cron, 12; SO—B. Brito, 124; SB—Amaral, 53; CS—Kirby, 20.

(All players—listed alphabetically)

Player, Team	Avg.	G	AB	R	H	TB	2B	3B	HR	RBI	SH	SF	HP	BB	Int. BB	SO	SB	CS
Abbott, Kurt, Tacoma	.154	11	39	2	6	7	1	0	0	1	2	0	1	4	0	9	1	0
Abner, Shawn, Vancouver	.266	20	79	12	21	27	4	1	0	2	2	1	2	9	2	13	2	2
Aldrete, Mike, Colorado Springs*	.322	128	463	69	149	219	42	2	8	84	1	4	3	65	8	113	1	0
Allred, Beau, Colorado Springs*	.288	135	434	79	125	219	23	10	17	76	2	10	7	57	8	75	1	1
Amaral, Rich, Calgary	.318	106	403	79	128	165	21	8	0	21	2	2	1	67	1	69	53	16
Anderson, Dave, Albuquerque	.321	16	53	9	17	20	1	1	0	5	1	0	1	6	0	4	2	1
Anderson, Kent, Calgary	.226	71	208	36	47	53	6	0	0	15	5	5	3	36	2	21	6	4
Angotti, Don, Tucson	.000	1	1	0	0	0	0	0	0	0	0	0	0	0	0	1	0	0
Ard, Johnny, Phoenix	.000	22	14	0	0	0	0	0	0	0	4	0	0	0	0	6	0	0
Ashley, Billy, Albuquerque	.211	25	95	11	20	33	7	0	2	10	0	0	0	6	0	42	1	0
Astacio, Pedro, Albuquerque	.080	24	25	0	2	3	1	0	0	0	5	0	0	0	0	12	0	0
Baar, Bryan, Albuquerque	.257	19	74	6	19	30	8	0	1	11	0	0	2	0	0	19	0	0
Bailey, Mark, Phoenix†	.310	35	87	15	27	49	4	0	6	23	0	2	2	20	0	19	0	0
Barbara, Don, Edmonton*	.298	118	396	70	118	158	26	1	4	63	4	6	4	78	4	78	9	4
Barron, Tony, Albuquerque	.301	78	286	40	86	126	18	2	6	33	2	0	2	17	1	65	6	4
Basso, Mike, Las Vegas	.218	23	55	2	12	15	1	1	0	1	1	0	0	7	1	11	0	0
Bean, Billy, Edmonton*	.246	39	138	17	34	49	8	2	1	24	1	4	8	7	1	13	5	3
Beltre, Esteban, Vancouver	.267	40	161	17	43	52	5	2	0	16	5	1	1	8	1	27	4	4
Benjamin, Mike, Phoenix	.306	31	108	15	33	47	10	2	0	17	1	0	3	3	1	18	4	2
Bilardello, Dann, Las Vegas	.192	11	26	2	5	9	1	0	1	2	0	0	0	1	0	5	0	0
Billmeyer, Mick, Edmonton*	.240	9	25	1	6	10	1	0	1	5	2	0	0	0	0	5	0	0
Black, Bud, Phoenix*	.111	3	9	0	1	1	0	0	0	2	0	0	0	0	0	1	0	0
Blair, Willie, Tucson	.000	21	3	1	0	0	0	0	0	0	0	0	0	1	0	1	0	0
Blankenship, Lance, Tacoma	.158	5	19	3	3	6	0	0	1	5	0	1	0	2	0	7	0	0
Blowers, Mike, Calgary	.317	83	300	56	95	154	28	2	9	67	0	2	1	50	2	64	2	3
Bolick, Frank, Calgary†	.288	78	274	35	79	151	18	6	14	54	1	4	1	39	2	52	4	4
Booker, Rod, Tucson*	.254	92	283	37	72	85	6	2	1	21	14	3	0	34	2	43	6	3
Boone, Bret, Calgary	.314	118	439	73	138	213	26	5	13	73	1	6	5	60	7	88	17	12
Bournigal, Rafael, Albuquerque	.324	122	395	47	128	148	18	1	0	34	10	4	5	22	5	7	5	3
Bowen, Ryan, Tucson	.182	22	22	1	4	4	0	0	0	2	3	0	0	4	0	9	0	0
Bowie, Jim, Calgary*	.238	49	172	17	41	50	6	0	1	17	0	3	1	21	3	25	3	1
Bradley, Phil, Edmonton	.299	41	134	26	40	55	8	2	1	18	1	1	3	17	2	15	5	1
Brantley, Mickey, Tucson	.224	50	156	21	35	50	8	2	1	23	0	1	1	18	0	17	1	2
Brito, Bernardo, Portland	.270	140	564	80	152	271	27	7	26	96	0	5	6	32	6	124	0	1
Brito, Jorge, Tacoma	.143	18	35	4	5	7	2	0	0	1	0	0	0	2	0	17	0	0
Brocail, Doug, Las Vegas*	.276	35	29	5	8	9	1	0	0	2	1	0	0	2	0	8	3	0
Brooks, Hubie, Edmonton	.292	8	24	2	7	14	2	1	1	10	0	2	2	1	0	2	0	0
Brooks, Jerry, Albuquerque	.266	129	467	77	124	204	36	1	14	78	0	7	4	39	1	68	3	2
Brosius, Scott, Tacoma	.237	63	236	29	56	96	13	0	9	31	0	4	1	23	3	44	8	5
Bross, Terry, Las Vegas	.429	49	7	0	3	3	0	0	0	1	0	0	0	0	0	1	0	0
Brown, Adam, Albuquerque*	.444	6	9	3	4	8	1	0	1	3	0	0	0	0	0	1	0	0
Brown, Jarvis, Albuquerque	.250	62	224	25	56	74	8	2	2	16	1	1	5	20	0	37	17	1
Browne, Jerry, Tacoma†	.412	4	17	1	7	10	1	1	0	3	0	0	3	0	1	0	0	0
Bruett, J.T., Portland*	.250	77	280	41	70	86	10	3	0	17	3	3	1	60	3	27	29	12
Brummett, Greg, Edmonton	.000	3	0	0	0	0	0	0	0	0	0	0	0	1	0	0	0	0
Brundage, Dave, Calgary*	.241	95	315	44	76	100	15	3	1	35	1	3	0	68	0	66	7	7
Buccheri, Jim, Tucson	.299	46	127	24	38	50	6	3	0	13	0	0	2	27	1	25	10	5
Burba, Dave, Phoenix	.056	13	18	0	1	1	0	0	0	0	0	0	0	1	0	2	0	0
Bustillos, Albert, Albuquerque	1.000	26	1	0	1	1	0	0	0	0	0	0	0	0	0	0	0	0
Campbell, Darrin, Vancouver	.152	25	46	6	7	11	4	0	0	3	1	1	1	6	0	13	0	0
Canale, George, Colorado Springs*	.294	46	163	33	48	79	12	2	5	31	0	2	0	16	1	27	0	0
Capel, Mike, Tucson	.000	58	5	0	0	0	0	0	0	0	0	0	0	0	0	3	0	0
Carter, Jeff, Tacoma†	.269	123	379	60	102	129	14	5	1	36	9	5	5	70	0	63	22	9
Carter, Larry, Phoenix	.161	28	31	2	5	5	0	0	0	2	2	0	0	1	0	15	0	0
Cedeno, Andujar, Tucson	.293	74	280	27	82	126	18	4	6	56	1	6	1	9	3	49	6	4
Chimelis, Joel, Phoenix	.303	49	185	26	56	74	9	3	1	23	5	2	1	5	1	24	1	4
Clayton, Royce, Phoenix	.240	48	192	30	46	65	6	2	3	18	2	1	0	17	0	25	15	6
Coachman, Pete, 24 Pho.-37 Edm.	.239	61	209	35	50	78	12	2	4	28	0	2	5	16	0	21	8	1
Cockrell, Alan, Colorado Springs	.236	82	259	31	61	92	6	2	7	38	2	2	4	22	1	51	0	2
Colbert, Craig, Phoenix	.321	36	140	16	45	58	8	1	1	12	2	2	1	3	0	16	0	1
Coolbaugh, Scott, Las Vegas	.241	65	199	30	48	89	13	2	8	39	1	1	3	19	1	52	0	0
Coomer, Ron, Vancouver	.237	86	262	29	62	99	10	0	9	40	3	4	0	16	3	36	3	0
Cooper, Gary, Phoenix	.300	127	464	66	139	203	31	3	9	73	3	7	3	47	0	86	8	6
Cooper, Jamie, Phoenix	.223	75	197	23	44	52	4	2	0	9	8	1	0	12	2	61	25	6
Cron, Chris, Vancouver	.278	140	500	76	139	216	29	0	16	81	2	3	17	94	12	111	12	4
Crosby, Todd, Phoenix†	.167	14	36	3	6	9	1	0	0	2	0	0	0	5	0	3	0	1
Crowe, Ron, Phoenix	.192	9	26	1	5	6	1	0	0	0	0	0	0	1	0	3	0	0
Davidson, Mark, Colorado Springs	.282	112	309	57	87	128	17	3	6	44	5	4	1	31	1	59	2	0
Davis, Butch, Las Vegas	1.000	1	1	0	1	1	0	0	0	0	0	0	0	0	0	0	0	0
Davis, Kevin, Edmonton†	.388	23	80	21	31	49	9	3	1	16	2	0	0	5	0	11	0	2
Davis, Matt, Phoenix†	.292	6	24	3	7	8	1	0	0	4	0	0	0	0	0	4	0	0
Davis, Rick, Las Vegas	.000	33	1	0	0	0	0	0	0	0	0	0	0	0	0	1	0	0
Dean, Kevin, Tucson	.219	35	73	8	16	25	4	1	1	4	2	1	1	10	2	21	2	1
Decker, Steve, Phoenix	.282	125	450	50	127	177	22	2	8	74	0	9	3	47	2	64	2	4
Denson, Drew, Vancouver	.276	105	340	43	94	146	7	3	13	70	0	7	3	36	3	58	1	0
Deshaies, Jim, Las Vegas*	.143	18	7	1	1	1	0	0	0	1	1	0	0	0	0	6	0	0
Diaz, Mario, Albuquerque	.269	18	52	8	14	18	4	0	0	11	1	1	0	0	0	6	0	1
Distefano, Benny, 14 Tuc.-18 Cal.*	.291	32	110	13	32	42	6	2	0	15	0	1	2	12	0	15	1	1
Easley, Damion, Edmonton	.289	108	429	61	124	157	18	3	3	44	3	6	5	31	0	44	26	10
Edmonds, Jim, Edmonton*	.299	50	194	37	58	95	15	2	6	36	2	2	0	14	2	55	3	1
Eiland, Dave, Las Vegas	.091	15	11	0	1	1	0	0	0	0	0	0	0	0	0	3	0	0
Epley, Daren, Colorado Springs	.264	29	87	9	23	31	8	0	0	14	0	1	0	13	0	14	0	0
Espinoza, Alvaro, Colorado Springs	.300	122	483	64	145	220	36	6	9	79	4	3	4	21	0	55	2	5
Faries, Paul, Las Vegas	.293	125	457	77	134	164	15	6	1	40	4	2	3	40	1	53	28	9
Flora, Kevin, Edmonton	.324	52	170	35	55	80	8	4	3	19	4	2	1	29	0	25	9	8
Foster, Lindsay, Vancouver†	.667	1	3	0	2	2	0	0	0	1	0	0	0	0	0	1	0	0
Fox, Eric, Tacoma†	.198	37	121	16	24	32	3	1	1	7	2	2	0	16	1	25	5	0
Galvez, Balvino, Albuquerque	.000	30	1	0	0	0	0	0	0	0	0	0	0	0	0	0	0	0
Garcia, Cheo, Portland	.333	3	6	0	2	2	0	0	0	0	0	0	0	0	0	0	0	0

Player, Team	Avg.	G	AB	R	H	TB	2B	3B	HR	RBI	SH	SF	HP	BB	Int. BB	SO	SB	CS
Gardner, Chris, Tucson	.278	21	18	0	5	8	1	1	0	3	1	0	0	0	0	5	0	0
Gardner, Jeff, Las Vegas*	.335	120	439	82	147	190	30	5	1	51	7	2	2	67	6	48	7	2
Garrelts, Scott, Phoenix	.500	4	4	1	2	3	1	0	0	0	0	0	0	0	0	0	0	0
Garrison, Webster, Tacoma	.241	33	116	15	28	41	5	1	2	17	1	2	0	2	0	12	1	1
Gilbert, Shawn, Portland	.245	138	444	60	109	139	17	2	3	52	5	2	4	36	2	55	31	8
Gleaton, Jerry Don, Phoenix*	.000	15	0	0	0	0	0	0	0	0	1	0	0	0	0	0	0	0
Gonzales, Larry, Edmonton	.328	80	241	37	79	98	10	0	3	47	3	4	4	38	0	24	2	1
Gonzalez, Jose, Edmonton	.326	26	86	16	28	45	7	2	2	14	0	1	0	18	0	18	9	5
Gonzalez, Luis, Tucson*	.432	13	44	11	19	30	4	2	1	9	0	1	1	5	2	7	4	1
Goodwin, Tom, Albuquerque*	.301	82	319	48	96	120	10	4	2	28	6	3	1	37	2	47	27	10
Grimsley, Jason, Tucson	.167	26	18	0	3	3	0	0	0	1	3	0	0	0	0	6	0	0
Gross, Kip, Albuquerque	.105	31	19	0	2	3	1	0	0	2	3	0	0	1	0	7	0	0
Grunhard, Dan, Tacoma*	.266	86	267	38	71	107	15	3	5	29	3	0	1	28	2	35	5	3
Guinn, Brian, Vancouver+	.270	53	89	14	24	31	5	1	0	4	0	0	0	17	0	10	0	0
Gutierrez, Ricky, Las Vegas	.167	3	6	0	1	1	0	0	0	1	0	1	0	1	0	3	0	0
Hale, Chip, Portland*	.285	132	474	77	135	179	25	8	1	53	4	6	0	73	11	45	3	3
Hall, Joe, Vancouver	.283	112	367	46	104	155	19	7	6	56	10	3	4	60	1	44	11	5
Hamilton, Jeff, Albuquerque	.302	55	159	21	48	75	12	0	5	30	0	4	1	13	3	20	0	1
Hansell, Greg, Albuquerque	.100	13	10	1	1	1	0	0	0	0	0	0	0	0	0	3	0	0
Harris, Gene, Las Vegas	.000	18	1	0	0	0	0	0	0	0	0	0	0	0	0	1	0	0
Harris, Greg, Las Vegas	.000	2	3	0	0	0	0	0	0	0	0	0	0	0	0	0	0	0
Haselman, Bill, Calgary	.255	88	302	49	77	152	14	2	19	53	1	3	2	41	4	89	3	3
Heath, Mike, Tacoma	.209	88	234	17	49	63	6	1	2	22	13	0	0	14	2	39	1	0
Heffernan, Bert, Calgary*	.304	15	46	8	14	19	2	0	1	4	0	0	0	7	0	7	1	1
Hemond, Scott, Tacoma	.242	8	33	6	8	11	3	0	0	3	0	0	0	5	0	6	1	0
Henderson, Dave, Tacoma	.182	3	11	0	2	2	0	0	0	1	0	0	0	0	0	3	0	0
Hengel, Dave, Phoenix	.127	27	55	1	7	9	2	0	0	6	0	1	0	7	0	17	0	1
Heredia, Gil, Phoenix	.111	22	9	0	1	1	0	0	0	0	4	0	0	0	0	2	0	0
Hernandez, Jeremy, Las Vegas	.000	42	2	0	0	0	0	0	0	0	1	0	0	0	0	0	0	0
Higgins, Kevin, Las Vegas*	.254	124	355	49	90	108	12	3	0	40	5	7	3	41	3	31	6	4
Hill, Orsino, Tacoma*	.246	118	378	56	93	144	25	4	6	44	0	2	7	54	6	86	5	8
Holton, Brian, Albuquerque	.000	29	2	0	0	0	0	0	0	0	0	0	0	0	0	1	0	0
Hosey, Steve, Phoenix	.286	125	462	64	132	204	28	7	10	65	0	5	6	39	4	98	15	15
Howard, Chris, Calgary	.238	97	319	29	76	116	16	0	8	45	3	2	5	14	0	73	3	7
Howard, Matt, Albuquerque	.293	36	116	14	34	37	3	0	0	8	2	0	0	9	0	7	1	2
Howitt, Dann, 43 Tac. -50 Cal.*	.299	93	318	54	95	150	22	6	7	60	2	6	3	35	1	58	9	3
Hubbard, Trent, Tucson	.310	115	420	69	130	160	16	4	2	33	9	2	4	45	1	68	34	10
Huff, Mike, Vancouver	.250	1	4	1	1	1	0	0	0	0	0	0	0	1	0	0	0	0
Hughes, Keith, Portland*	.271	89	221	37	60	92	11	3	5	26	0	1	0	25	2	39	6	4
Huisman, Rick, Phoenix	.083	9	12	0	1	1	0	0	0	0	0	0	0	0	0	4	0	0
Hurta, Bob, Tucson*	.000	20	1	0	0	0	0	0	0	0	0	0	0	0	0	0	0	0
Ingram, Linty, Las Vegas	.000	2	2	0	0	0	0	0	0	0	0	0	0	0	0	0	0	0
James, Mike, Albuquerque	.200	18	5	1	1	2	1	0	0	0	1	0	0	0	0	2	0	0
Jaster, Scott, Vancouver	.267	20	60	8	16	25	2	2	1	8	1	0	1	11	0	12	2	0
Jefferson, Reggie, Colorado Springs+	.312	57	218	49	68	120	11	4	11	44	0	2	0	29	3	50	1	0
Jelic, Chris, Las Vegas	.227	80	203	34	46	66	8	3	2	19	2	2	0	30	1	36	4	1
Jeter, Shawn, Vancouver*	.301	96	379	61	114	148	18	5	2	34	6	1	2	38	6	63	26	11
Johnson, Brian, Colorado Springs	.281	69	167	24	47	65	13	1	1	24	0	1	2	8	0	41	0	1
Johnson, Erik, Phoenix	.240	90	229	24	55	62	5	1	0	19	5	1	2	20	2	38	8	10
Jones, Chris, Tucson	.324	45	170	25	55	89	9	8	3	28	1	2	0	18	2	34	7	1
Jones, Tracy, Vancouver	.283	66	219	30	62	76	9	1	1	23	0	3	2	36	4	27	4	2
Jorgensen, Terry, Portland	.295	135	505	74	149	227	32	2	14	71	3	5	4	54	3	58	2	0
Juden, Jeff, Tucson	.310	26	29	2	9	12	0	0	1	4	3	0	0	1	0	14	0	0
Kile, Darryl, Tucson	.067	9	15	0	1	1	0	0	0	1	2	0	0	1	0	6	0	0
Kingery, Mike, Tacoma*	.306	99	363	44	111	140	18	4	1	37	1	4	0	33	3	27	8	9
Kirby, Wayne, Colorado Springs*	.345	123	470	101	162	245	18	16	11	74	4	2	2	36	4	28	51	20
Knudson, Mark, Las Vegas	.074	37	27	1	2	3	1	0	0	2	1	0	0	0	0	8	0	0
Komminsk, Brad, Vancouver	.275	120	415	72	114	182	24	7	10	68	2	3	1	65	1	79	9	8
Kvasnicka, Jay, Portland*	.163	26	80	12	13	16	1	1	0	5	2	1	0	15	0	17	4	3
Lampkin, Tom, Las Vegas*	.306	108	340	45	104	138	17	4	3	48	1	3	6	53	7	27	15	8
Lee, Derek, Vancouver*	.273	115	381	58	104	157	20	6	7	50	4	2	6	56	7	65	17	7
Lee, Terry, 24 C.S. -79 Por.	.283	103	367	68	104	148	22	2	6	56	0	4	5	36	2	41	8	0
Lennon, Pat, Calgary	.354	13	48	8	17	23	3	0	1	9	0	0	1	6	0	10	4	1
Leonard, Mark, Phoenix*	.338	39	139	17	47	68	4	1	5	25	0	2	3	21	1	29	1	2
Levis, Jesse, Colorado Springs*	.364	87	253	39	92	132	20	1	6	44	3	2	1	37	0	25	1	3
Lewis, Dan, Phoenix*	.270	70	244	32	66	115	15	2	10	41	1	4	2	24	5	42	0	8
Lewis, Darren, Phoenix	.228	42	158	22	36	45	5	2	0	6	2	0	2	11	0	15	9	6
Liriano, Nelson, Colorado Springs+	.305	106	361	73	110	162	19	9	5	52	3	7	1	48	4	50	20	8
Litton, Greg, Phoenix	.306	25	85	14	26	45	7	0	4	19	1	1	0	8	1	21	0	1
Lockhart, Keith, Tacoma*	.278	107	363	44	101	147	25	3	5	37	2	4	3	29	1	21	5	3
Lopez, Luis, Las Vegas+	.233	120	395	44	92	119	8	8	1	31	7	3	3	19	1	65	6	4
Lyons, Barry, Tucson	.300	71	277	32	83	119	24	0	4	45	1	3	0	9	2	35	1	0
Magallanes, Ever, Vancouver*	.230	93	243	32	56	80	9	3	3	23	4	3	1	29	1	24	2	1
Mallicoat, Rob, Tucson*	.500	37	2	1	1	1	0	0	0	0	1	0	0	0	0	0	0	0
Martin, Norberto, Vancouver+	.288	135	497	72	143	169	12	7	0	29	14	2	2	29	1	44	29	12
Martinez, Carlos, Colorado Springs	.313	9	32	7	10	11	1	0	0	5	0	2	1	1	1	5	0	0
Martinez, Luis, Albuquerque	.281	84	171	27	48	60	7	1	1	18	3	2	3	13	2	20	3	2
Martinez, Pedro, Albuquerque	.217	20	23	1	5	5	0	0	0	0	2	0	0	3	0	11	0	0
Martinez, Ray, Edmonton	.302	88	285	42	86	119	20	2	3	35	2	4	6	27	0	50	6	5
Massarelli, John, Tucson	.238	50	143	21	34	38	4	0	0	6	1	0	1	14	1	27	14	3
Masters, Dave, 26 Pho. -13 Cal.	.200	39	10	0	2	4	0	1	0	2	1	0	0	0	0	6	0	0
McAndrew, Jamie, Albuquerque	.250	5	4	1	1	2	1	0	0	0	0	0	0	0	0	2	0	0
McCarty, Dave, Portland	.500	7	26	7	13	18	2	0	1	8	1	0	1	5	0	3	1	0
McClellan, Paul, Phoenix	.000	20	4	1	0	0	0	0	0	0	1	2	0	1	0	1	0	0
McConnell, Walt, Edmonton*	.265	51	147	21	39	51	9	0	1	22	0	1	1	19	2	19	1	0
McCullers, Lance, Albuquerque+	.000	29	1	1	0	0	0	0	0	0	1	0	0	0	0	1	0	0
McDonald, Mike, Calgary*	.239	15	46	3	11	16	2	0	1	4	0	0	0	5	0	7	0	0
McDowell, Oddibe, Edmonton*	.214	6	14	1	3	4	1	0	0	0	0	0	0	5	1	4	0	1
McMurtry, Craig, Phoenix	.091	40	11	0	1	2	1	0	0	2	4	0	0	2	0	5	0	0
McNamara, Jim, Phoenix*	.209	23	67	5	14	17	3	0	0	3	0	0	0	14	3	13	0	0
Mercedes, Henry, Tacoma	.232	85	246	36	57	70	9	2	0	20	4	0	0	26	0	60	1	3
Merullo, Matt, Vancouver	.178	14	45	2	8	14	1	1	1	4	0	0	0	1	0	4	0	0
Mikulik, Joe, Tucson	.248	59	161	22	40	59	10	3	1	18	3	3	0	7	2	22	1	1
Miller, Orlando, Tucson	.243	10	37	4	9	15	0	0	2	8	0	1	0	1	0	2	0	0

Player, Team	Avg.	G	AB	R	H	TB	2B	3B	HR	RBI	SH	SF	HP	BB	Int. BB	SO	SB	CS
Mimbs, Mark, Albuquerque*	.000	12	3	1	0	0	0	0	0	0	0	0	0	0	0	0	0	0
Molina, Islay, Tacoma	.194	10	36	3	7	9	0	1	0	5	0	0	0	2	0	6	1	0
Mondesi, Raul, Albuquerque	.312	35	138	23	43	73	4	7	4	15	0	0	1	9	4	35	2	3
Morris, John, Edmonton*	.118	4	17	3	2	3	1	0	0	0	0	0	0	1	0	5	0	0
Morrow, Chris, Albuquerque*	.284	24	67	6	19	26	2	1	1	7	0	0	0	5	2	9	1	0
Moses, John, Calgary†	.254	67	248	41	63	92	15	4	2	31	3	3	0	33	2	32	5	9
Mota, Andy, Tucson	.240	96	317	33	76	111	14	6	3	32	1	3	6	16	0	53	7	8
Mota, Carlos, Colorado Springs	.233	8	30	1	7	8	1	0	0	6	0	0	0	4	0	9	1	0
Munoz, Jose, Albuquerque†	.304	131	450	48	137	169	20	3	2	45	7	0	1	25	6	46	7	4
Musolino, Mike, Edmonton*	.252	43	127	15	32	46	8	0	2	19	1	0	0	20	1	33	0	1
Myers, Jim, Phoenix	.000	25	1	0	0	0	0	0	0	0	0	0	0	0	0	0	0	0
Naveda, Ed, Portland	.243	115	374	34	91	120	20	0	3	31	3	3	1	25	0	51	2	0
Neel, Troy, Tacoma*	.351	112	396	61	139	232	36	3	17	74	0	5	6	60	11	84	2	5
Neidlinger, Jim, Albuquerque	.250	35	16	3	4	4	0	0	0	2	0	0	2	0	0	9	0	0
Nelson, Rob, 31 Por. - 53 Pho.*	.214	84	234	35	50	91	11	0	10	28	1	1	1	55	5	70	1	0
Newson, Warren, Vancouver*	.254	19	59	7	15	15	0	0	0	9	0	0	1	16	1	21	3	2
Nichting, Chris, Albuquerque	.100	10	10	1	1	2	1	0	0	1	0	0	0	0	0	4	0	0
Nixon, Donell, Colorado Springs	.257	49	70	23	18	28	5	1	1	7	1	1	0	4	0	13	7	0
Oberkfell, Ken, Edmonton*	.282	61	202	33	57	78	14	2	1	34	2	2	0	32	4	18	2	4
Oliveras, Francisco, Phoenix	.250	22	4	0	1	1	0	0	0	0	2	0	0	0	0	2	0	1
Opperman, Dan, Albuquerque	.000	6	6	0	0	0	0	0	0	0	0	0	0	0	0	1	0	0
Ortiz, Ray, Portland*	.328	42	134	17	44	67	12	1	3	22	0	3	1	7	2	17	0	1
Orton, John, Edmonton	.255	49	149	28	38	62	9	3	3	25	4	2	3	28	0	32	3	5
Pappas, Erik, Vancouver	.276	37	98	17	27	43	4	0	4	17	1	2	2	14	0	17	4	0
Paquette, Craig, Tacoma	.273	17	66	10	18	31	7	0	2	11	0	0	2	0	0	16	3	1
Parker, Rick, Tucson	.323	105	319	51	103	147	10	11	4	38	3	0	3	28	0	36	20	3
Parks, Derek, Portland	.245	79	249	33	61	109	12	0	12	49	4	6	4	25	0	47	0	2
Patterson, Dave, Phoenix	.256	117	367	34	94	119	13	6	0	35	8	1	4	56	2	62	6	5
Patterson, John, Phoenix†	.301	93	362	52	109	147	20	6	2	37	0	2	5	33	4	45	22	18
Peguero, Julio, Albuquerque†	.263	30	76	13	20	27	4	0	1	8	2	1	2	13	0	13	1	1
Pegues, Steve, Las Vegas	.263	123	376	51	99	155	21	4	9	56	3	9	6	7	1	64	12	3
Perezchica, Tony, Colorado Springs	.171	20	70	8	12	19	1	0	2	9	3	0	1	4	0	20	1	1
Peters, Reed, Phoenix	.288	29	59	10	17	22	2	0	1	4	2	1	0	7	0	6	0	0
Peterson, Adam, Las Vegas	.000	21	21	0	0	0	0	0	0	0	3	0	0	1	0	13	0	0
Piazza, Mike, Albuquerque	.341	94	358	54	122	202	22	5	16	69	0	1	2	37	4	57	1	3
Pirkl, Greg, Calgary	.266	79	286	30	76	121	21	3	6	32	0	2	3	14	0	64	4	3
Polidor, Gus, Tacoma	.278	99	363	23	101	120	16	0	1	43	4	3	1	22	0	24	4	4
Powell, Alonzo, Calgary	.343	10	35	7	12	18	1	1	1	7	0	0	1	5	0	10	0	1
Pye, Eddie, Albuquerque	.302	72	222	30	67	85	11	2	1	25	5	2	2	13	0	41	6	4
Quinones, Luis, Portland†	.243	88	276	45	67	118	7	4	12	49	1	6	2	41	5	42	1	0
Rambo, Dan, Phoenix	.000	20	4	0	0	0	0	0	0	0	1	0	0	0	0	1	0	0
Rapp, Pat, Phoenix	.133	40	15	1	2	2	0	0	0	0	1	0	0	0	0	5	0	0
Reboulet, Jeff, Portland	.286	48	161	21	46	65	11	1	2	21	4	1	1	35	0	18	3	3
Reed, Steve, Phoenix	.000	29	1	0	0	0	0	0	0	0	0	0	0	0	0	0	0	0
Reynolds, Shane, Tucson	.111	26	18	3	2	2	0	0	0	1	6	0	0	2	0	7	0	0
Rhodes, Karl, Tucson*	.289	94	332	62	96	138	16	10	2	54	4	7	2	55	5	63	8	8
Riles, Ernest, Tucson*	.307	60	202	37	62	88	17	3	1	35	1	4	0	30	4	33	2	1
Ritchie, Gregg, Phoenix*	.268	92	183	25	49	61	5	2	1	13	4	2	0	43	1	34	11	5
Rodriguez, Henry, Albuquerque*	.304	94	365	59	111	184	21	5	14	72	2	10	1	31	5	57	1	5
Rogers, Kevin, Phoenix†	.188	11	16	0	3	3	0	0	0	2	2	0	0	0	0	4	0	0
Rohde, Dave, Colorado Springs†	.295	121	448	85	132	189	17	14	4	55	8	2	4	57	1	60	13	8
Rose, Bob, Edmonton	.270	20	74	11	20	33	1	3	2	11	2	0	0	6	1	13	1	0
Sager, A.J., Las Vegas	.250	30	4	0	1	2	1	0	0	0	1	0	0	0	0	3	0	0
Salmon, Tim, Edmonton	.347	118	409	101	142	275	38	4	29	105	0	4	6	91	11	103	9	7
Sanders, Scott, Las Vegas	.000	14	12	0	0	0	0	0	0	0	1	0	0	0	0	4	0	0
Santiago, Benito, Las Vegas	.308	4	13	3	4	7	0	0	1	2	0	0	1	1	1	0	0	0
Santovenia, Nelson, Vancouver	.263	91	281	24	74	108	16	0	6	42	3	3	0	37	2	49	0	0
Schaefer, Jeff, Calgary	.300	12	40	4	12	16	1	0	1	5	0	1	0	2	0	10	1	3
Scheid, Rich, 29 Van. - 12 Tuc.*	.250	41	4	0	1	1	0	0	0	0	1	0	0	0	0	2	0	0
Schullstrom, Erik, Las Vegas	.000	1	1	0	0	0	0	0	0	0	0	0	0	0	0	1	0	0
Scott, Charles, Calgary	.500	18	2	1	1	1	0	0	0	0	0	0	0	0	0	0	0	0
Scott, Tim, Las Vegas	1.000	24	1	0	1	1	0	0	0	0	0	0	0	0	0	0	0	1
Searcy, Steve, Albuquerque*	.000	12	10	0	0	0	0	0	0	0	0	0	0	0	0	4	0	0
Seminara, Frank, Las Vegas	.222	13	18	1	4	5	1	0	0	1	1	0	0	0	0	5	1	0
Sheaffer, Danny, Portland	.276	116	442	54	122	168	23	4	5	56	3	4	2	21	3	36	3	5
Sherman, Darrell, Las Vegas*	.286	71	269	48	77	96	8	1	3	22	1	1	3	42	0	41	26	6
Shinall, Zak, Albuquerque	.000	64	1	0	0	0	0	0	0	0	0	0	1	0	0	1	0	0
Simms, Mike, Tucson	.282	116	404	73	114	181	22	6	11	75	0	3	4	61	3	107	7	1
Simon, Richie, Tucson	.000	9	1	0	0	0	0	0	0	0	0	0	0	0	0	1	0	0
Siwa, Joe, Tucson	.000	1	4	0	0	0	0	0	0	0	0	0	0	0	0	0	0	0
Smiley, Reuben, Phoenix*	.216	17	37	5	8	11	3	0	0	2	1	0	1	3	0	9	0	2
Smith, D.L., Colorado Springs	.242	13	33	6	8	15	2	1	1	7	0	2	2	2	0	4	0	0
Smith, Jack, Tacoma	.251	100	287	44	72	102	12	0	6	41	5	2	2	32	1	53	3	0
Sojo, Luis, Edmonton	.297	37	145	22	43	57	9	1	1	24	4	2	1	9	0	4	4	2
Springer, Dennis, Albuquerque	.083	11	12	0	1	1	0	0	0	0	1	0	0	1	0	4	0	0
Staton, Dave, Las Vegas	.281	96	335	47	94	171	20	0	19	76	0	5	6	34	2	95	0	0
Stephenson, Phil, Las Vegas*	.332	63	205	51	68	106	10	2	8	43	2	5	0	34	3	28	1	1
Taubensee, Eddie, Tucson*	.338	20	74	13	25	38	8	1	1	10	1	0	0	8	1	17	0	1
Taylor, Rob, Phoenix	.333	20	3	0	1	1	0	0	0	0	1	0	0	0	0	0	0	0
Taylor, Will, 21 L.V. - 4 Cal.†	.193	25	83	8	16	18	0	1	0	2	1	0	0	8	0	20	4	5
Tejero, Fausto, Edmonton	.235	8	17	0	4	5	1	0	0	2	0	0	2	1	0	3	0	0
Thomas, Andres, Phoenix	.270	39	115	10	31	44	8	1	1	11	2	2	0	3	0	19	0	0
Thome, Jim, Colorado Springs*	.313	12	48	11	15	27	4	1	2	14	0	0	1	5	0	16	0	0
Tinsley, Lee, Colorado Springs†	.235	27	81	19	19	23	2	1	0	4	1	1	1	16	0	19	3	1
Traxler, Brian, Albuquerque*	.303	127	393	58	119	186	26	4	11	58	1	5	1	36	9	34	1	1
Tucker, Scooter, Tucson	.302	83	288	36	87	107	15	1	1	29	1	2	3	28	1	35	5	1
Turner, Matt, Tucson	.000	63	6	0	0	0	0	0	0	0	0	0	0	0	0	3	0	0
Turner, Shane, Calgary*	.281	76	242	31	68	91	17	3	0	26	2	1	3	35	1	46	10	8
Valdez, Rafael, Las Vegas	.000	8	0	0	0	0	0	0	0	0	1	0	0	0	0	0	0	0
Van Burkleo, Ty, Edmonton*	.273	135	458	83	125	224	28	7	19	88	0	3	5	75	6	100	20	5
Vanderweele, Doug, Phoenix	.000	1	0	0	0	0	0	0	0	0	0	0	0	0	0	0	0	0
Vatcher, Jim, Las Vegas	.275	111	280	41	77	122	15	3	8	35	6	2	3	39	4	60	2	6
Velasquez, Guillermo, Las Vegas*	.309	136	512	68	158	231	44	4	7	99	0	9	1	44	8	94	3	1
Veres, Dave, Tucson	.200	29	5	0	1	2	1	0	0	0	0	0	0	1	0	2	0	0

Player, Team	Avg.	G	AB	R	H	TB	2B	3B	HR	RBI	SH	SF	HP	BB	Int. BB	SO	SB	CS
Vesling, Don, Las Vegas*	.000	8	1	0	0	0	0	0	0	0	0	0	0	0	0	0	0	0
Vizquel, Omar, Calgary†	.273	6	22	0	6	7	1	0	0	2	0	0	1	1	0	3	0	1
Wakamatsu, Don, Albuquerque	.323	60	167	22	54	70	10	0	2	15	1	0	4	15	0	23	0	1
Walters, Dan, Las Vegas	.394	35	127	16	50	65	9	0	2	25	1	2	2	10	1	12	0	0
Wasinger, Mark, Edmonton	.184	40	103	19	19	31	7	1	1	11	1	0	2	10	0	12	0	1
Wassenaar, Rob, Portland	1.000	60	1	0	1	1	0	0	0	1	0	0	0	0	0	0	0	0
Weber, Weston, Tacoma	.000	52	2	0	0	0	0	0	0	0	0	0	0	0	0	0	0	0
Weiss, Walt, Tacoma†	.231	4	13	2	3	4	1	0	0	3	0	1	0	2	0	1	0	1
Wetherby, Jeff, Calgary*	.245	70	245	28	60	84	9	3	3	28	0	3	0	25	2	48	5	4
Wilkins, Dean, Las Vegas	.000	8	2	0	0	0	0	0	0	0	0	0	0	1	0	2	0	0
Wilkins, Mike, Albuquerque	.125	46	8	1	1	1	0	0	0	0	0	0	0	0	0	1	0	0
Williams, Brian, Tucson	.333	12	12	1	4	7	1	1	0	0	0	0	1	0	0	4	0	0
Williams, Reggie, Edmonton†	.272	139	519	96	141	194	26	9	3	64	7	8	3	88	1	110	44	14
Williams, Ted, Calgary†	.244	92	250	36	61	79	5	5	1	17	3	0	5	12	0	58	41	13
Witkowski, Matt, Las Vegas	.188	5	16	1	3	5	0	1	0	0	0	0	0	3	0	2	0	0
Witmeyer, Ron, Tacoma*	.236	134	499	55	118	162	25	2	5	54	2	4	0	55	3	76	5	3
Wood, Ted, Phoenix*	.304	110	418	70	127	186	24	7	7	63	2	5	4	48	4	74	9	9
Worrell, Tim, Las Vegas	.000	10	15	0	0	0	0	0	0	0	0	0	0	1	0	13	0	0
Worthington, Craig, Colorado Springs	.295	90	319	47	94	137	25	0	6	57	1	3	4	33	1	67	0	1
Yelding, Eric, 57 Tuc.-36 Van.	.263	93	338	47	89	110	11	5	0	29	6	3	0	26	0	67	32	11
York, Mike, Las Vegas	.059	19	17	0	1	1	0	0	0	0	2	0	0	0	0	8	0	0
Young, Eric, Albuquerque	.337	94	350	61	118	153	16	5	3	49	13	7	4	33	0	18	28	11
Young, Gerald, Tucson†	.311	20	74	15	23	27	2	1	0	2	1	0	1	14	1	4	13	6

The following pitchers, listed alphabetically by club, with games in parentheses, had no plate appearances, primarily through use of designated hitters:

ALBUQUERQUE—Berrios, Hector (15); Brosnan, Jason (8); Daal, Omar (12); Hall, Gardner (12); Magnusson, Brett (1).

CALGARY—Acker, Jim (2); Agosto, Juan (10); Barton, Shawn (30); Brown, Kevin (32); Costello, John (4); DeLucia, Rich (8); Drees, Tom (17); Fisher, Brian (2); Grant, Mark (4); Gunderson, Eric (21); Hawkins, Andy (24); Jones, Calvin (21); Kramer, Randy (27); Nelson, Jeff (2); Newlin, Jim (30); Nunez, Jose (10); Parker, Clay (3); Remlinger, Mike (21); Rice, Pat (22); Schmidt, Dave (13); Schooler, Mike (1); Vande Berg, Ed (31); Walker, Mike (12); Woodson, Kerry (9); Zavaras, Clint (4).

COLORADO SPRINGS—Arnsberg, Brad (16); Bell, Eric (26); Boucher, Denis (20); Bruske, Jim (7); Christopher, Mike (49); Clark, Terry (9); Dipoto, Gerald (50); Kramer, Tom (38); Mutis, Jeff (25); Nichols, Rod (9); Otto, Dave (6); Roscoe, Greg (27); Scudder, Scott (1); Shaw, Jeff (25); Smith, Willie (19); Soper, Mike (10); Wells, Terry (5); Wickander, Kevin (8).

EDMONTON—Bair, Doug (7); Beasley, Chris (26); Blyleven, Bert (2); Butcher, Mike (26); Erb, Mike (2); Fortugno, Tim (26); Fraser, Bill (44); Grahe, Joe (3); Holzemer, Mark (17); James, Todd (7); Johnson, Dave (1); Jones, Odell (5); Kraemer, Joe (34); Lewis, Scott (22); Merriman, Brett (22); Pawlowski, John (20); Ridenour, Dana (5); Scott, Darryl (31); Searage, Ray (34); Soff, Ray (24); Vidmar, Don (16); Young, Cliff (28); Zappelli, Mark (10).

LAS VEGAS—Bryand, Renay (6); Perry, Pat (16); Wernig, Pat (17); Wood, Brian (7).

PHOENIX—Pena, Jim (33); Veres, Randolf (12).

PORTLAND—Abbott, Paul (7); Banks, Willie (11); Casian, Larry (58); Dyer, Mike (27); Gozzo, Mauro (37); Johnson, Greg (53); Klonoski, Jason (1); Leskanic, Curtis (5); Lind, Orlando (48); Mahomes, Pat (17); Schwabe, Mike (6); Trombley, Mike (25); Tsamis, George (40); Wayne, Gary (14); West, David (19).

TACOMA—Allison, Dana (19); Bittiger, Jeff (9); Briscoe, John (33); Campbell, Kevin (10); Chitren, Steve (29); Corsi, Jim (26); Guzman, Johnny (20); Harris, Reggie (29); Latter, Dave (5); Millay, Keith (2); Musselman, Jeff (19); Osteen, Gavin (4); Peek, Tim (57); Raczka, Mike (31); Schmidt, Dave (14); Slusarski, Joe (11); Smith, Tim (2); Van Poppel, Todd (9); Walton, Bruce (8); Wilkinson, Bill (8); Zancanaro, Dave (23).

TUCSON—Hartgraves, Dean (5); Helton, Keith (3); Jones, Todd (3); Lewis, Jim (1); Wall, Donnell (2); Windes, Rodney (20).

VANCOUVER—Bere, Jason (1); Bolton, Rodney (27); Carter, Jeff (30); Drahman, Brian (48); Dunne, Mike (21); Fernandez, Alex (4); Garcia, Ramon (8); Hernandez, Roberto (9); Howard, Christian (20); Hudek, John (39); Kennedy, Bo (4); Perschke, Greg (29); Scheid, Rich (29); Schwarz, Jeff (23); Stephens, Ron (32); Wapnick, Steve (39).

GRAND SLAMS—Denson, Espinoza, Hall, Van Burkleo, 2 each; Allred, Bailey, Cedeno, Coolbaugh, Coomer, Davidson, Decker, Haselman, Hill, Chris Howard, Howitt, Leonard, A. Mota, Naveda, Rhodes, Simms, Staton, 1 each.

AWARDED FIRST BASE ON CATCHER'S INTERFERENCE—Cedeno (Orton); Cron (Sheaffer); Epley (Walters); Heath (Santovenia); Heffernan (Baar); Kingery (Musolino); Van Burkleo (Chris Howard); Witmeyer (Baar).

PITCHING

TEAM

Team	ERA	G	CG	ShO	Sv.	IP	H	R	ER	HR	HB	BB	Int. BB	SO	WP	Bk.
Vancouver	3.54	142	11	13	39	1240.2	1159	592	488	61	25	528	35	772	62	11
Portland	3.82	144	16	15	37	1275.1	1276	593	542	83	29	523	32	932	56	9
Tucson	4.10	144	4	5	41	1268.0	1339	702	578	54	55	558	29	957	91	25
Phoenix	4.12	144	9	6	40	1272.1	1348	680	582	69	24	512	41	831	59	15
Colorado Springs	4.38	141	21	3	36	1225.2	1365	675	596	69	38	417	23	674	68	18
Las Vegas	4.44	144	9	9	45	1263.2	1407	709	623	81	42	464	43	799	56	20
Tacoma	4.53	143	5	7	26	1239.2	1272	724	624	98	50	696	59	769	77	20
Albuquerque	4.67	143	8	7	33	1236.1	1342	719	642	94	29	517	48	816	58	10
Edmonton	5.02	144	21	5	27	1226.0	1446	769	684	106	62	512	33	834	69	9
Calgary	5.48	139	15	7	27	1175.0	1409	827	715	95	44	551	26	579	68	11

INDIVIDUAL

(Leading qualifiers for earned-run average leadership—115 or more innings)

*Throws lefthanded.

Pitcher, Team	W	L	Pct.	ERA	G	GS	CG	GF	ShO	Sv.	IP	H	R	ER	HR	HB	BB	Int. BB	SO	WP
Dunne, Vancouver	10	6	.625	2.78	21	21	2	0	0	0	132.2	128	61	41	4	2	46	2	78	6
Bolton, Vancouver	11	9	.550	2.93	27	27	3	0	2	0	187.1	174	72	61	9	1	59	2	111	9
Rapp, Phoenix	7	8	.467	3.05	39	12	2	17	1	3	121.0	115	54	41	2	2	40	3	79	1
Gozzo, Portland	10	9	.526	3.35	37	19	3	11	2	1	155.2	155	61	58	11	3	50	3	108	2
Boucher, Colorado Springs*	11	4	.733	3.48	20	18	6	1	0	0	124.0	119	50	48	4	2	30	1	40	7
Trombley, Portland	10	8	.556	3.65	25	25	2	0	0	0	165.0	149	70	67	18	6	58	1	138	1
Reynolds, Tucson	9	8	.529	3.68	25	22	2	1	0	1	142.0	156	73	58	4	4	34	2	106	4
Garcia, Vancouver	9	11	.450	3.71	28	28	2	0	1	0	170.0	165	83	70	11	5	56	2	79	2
Bell, Colorado Springs*	10	7	.588	3.73	26	18	5	8	0	0	137.2	161	64	57	10	0	30	1	56	6
Perschke, Vancouver	12	7	.632	3.76	29	28	1	0	1	0	165.0	159	83	69	13	7	44	0	82	4

Departmental leaders: G—Shinall, 64; W—Shinall, Tsamis, 13; L—R. Harris, 16; Pct.—Walton, .800; GS—L. Carter, Garcia, R. Harris, Perschke, 28; CG—Boucher, 6; GF—Christopher, 45; ShO—Mahomes, 3; Sv.—Drahman, 30; IP—Bolton, 187.1; H—Tsamis, 195; R—R. Harris, 108; ER—R. Harris, 95; HR—Trombley, 18; HB—Chitren, Shaw, 10; BB—R. Harris, 117; IBB—Wassenaar, 12; SO—Trombley, 138; WP—R. Harris, 20.

(All pitchers—listed alphabetically)

Pitcher, Team	W	L	Pct.	ERA	G	GS	CG	GF	ShO	Sv.	IP	H	R	ER	HR	HB	BB	Int. BB	SO	WP
Abbott, Portland	4	1	.800	2.33	7	7	0	0	0	0	46.1	30	13	12	2	0	31	0	46	0
Acker, Calgary	0	0	.000	3.00	2	0	0	0	0	0	3.0	5	1	1	0	0	0	0	1	0
Agosto, Calgary*	1	0	1.000	4.98	10	0	0	4	0	1	21.2	20	12	12	2	2	13	0	12	1
Allison, Tacoma*	2	3	.400	4.84	19	4	0	6	0	0	44.2	63	32	24	6	1	17	2	17	0
Ard, Phoenix	5	8	.385	4.46	22	19	0	1	0	0	113.0	130	67	56	5	0	69	2	56	7
Arnsberg, Colorado Springs	1	1	.500	7.56	16	0	0	10	0	0	25.0	34	25	21	4	2	13	0	11	4
Astacio, Albuquerque	6	6	.500	5.47	24	15	1	4	0	0	98.2	115	68	60	8	2	44	1	66	6
Bair, Edmonton	3	2	.600	6.62	7	6	0	0	0	0	35.1	51	26	26	4	0	7	2	14	5
Banks, Portland	6	1	.857	1.92	11	11	2	0	1	0	75.0	62	20	16	2	0	34	0	41	5
Barton, Calgary*	3	5	.375	4.25	30	0	0	17	0	4	53.0	57	31	25	4	2	24	4	31	1
Basso, Las Vegas	0	0	.000	0.00	2	0	0	2	0	0	2.0	0	0	0	0	0	0	0	0	0
Beasley, Edmonton	2	1	.667	4.05	25	1	0	16	0	3	33.1	44	19	15	4	4	11	2	28	1
Bell, Colorado Springs*	10	7	.588	3.73	26	18	5	8	0	1	137.2	161	64	57	10	0	30	1	56	6
Bere, Vancouver	0	0	.000	0.00	1	0	0	0	0	0	1.0	2	0	0	0	1	0	0	2	0
Berrios, Albuquerque*	1	2	.333	4.38	15	0	0	6	0	0	12.1	10	6	6	0	0	11	5	12	1
Bittiger, Tacoma	3	3	.500	2.72	9	9	0	0	0	0	46.1	51	15	14	2	2	28	1	24	3
Black, Phoenix*	2	0	1.000	0.86	3	3	1	0	1	0	21.0	21	3	2	0	0	5	0	7	1
Blair, Tucson	4	4	.500	2.39	21	2	1	8	0	2	52.2	50	20	14	2	4	12	2	35	2
Blyleven, Edmonton	2	0	1.000	6.17	2	2	0	0	0	0	11.2	16	8	8	1	0	3	0	7	0
Bolton, Tucson	11	9	.550	2.93	27	27	3	0	2	0	187.1	174	72	61	9	1	59	2	111	9
Boucher, Colorado Springs*	11	4	.733	3.48	20	18	6	1	0	0	124.0	119	50	48	4	2	30	1	40	7
Bowen, Tucson	7	6	.538	4.12	21	20	1	0	1	0	122.1	128	68	56	7	5	64	1	94	8
Bowie, Calgary*	0	0	.000	0.00	1	0	0	1	0	0	1.0	0	0	0	0	0	0	0	1	0
Briscoe, Tacoma	2	5	.286	5.88	33	6	0	11	0	0	78.0	78	62	51	7	1	68	5	66	6
Brocail, Las Vegas	10	10	.500	3.97	29	25	4	2	0	0	172.1	187	82	76	7	6	63	5	103	6
Brosnan, Albuquerque*	0	0	.000	8.31	8	0	0	3	0	1	8.2	13	9	8	2	1	4	0	12	2
Bross, Las Vegas	7	3	.700	3.26	49	0	0	12	0	0	85.2	83	36	31	4	0	30	3	42	5
Brown, Calgary*	6	10	.375	4.84	32	20	4	2	0	0	150.2	163	97	81	13	4	64	2	49	5
Brummett, Phoenix	0	1	.000	7.71	3	1	0	2	0	0	4.2	8	4	4	0	0	1	0	2	1
Brundage, Calgary*	0	0	.000	6.75	5	0	0	4	0	0	6.2	7	5	5	1	1	4	0	5	0
Bruske, Colorado Springs	2	0	1.000	4.58	7	0	0	1	0	0	17.2	24	11	9	2	2	6	1	8	2
Bryand, Las Vegas*	0	0	.000	9.00	6	0	0	1	0	0	8.0	12	8	8	2	0	3	0	5	0
Burba, Phoenix	5	5	.500	4.72	13	13	0	0	0	0	74.1	86	40	39	5	3	24	2	44	3
Bustillos, Albuquerque	1	2	.333	4.50	26	0	0	13	0	3	37.2	41	20	20	4	0	16	5	23	2
Butcher, Edmonton	5	2	.714	3.07	26	0	0	16	0	4	29.1	24	12	10	2	2	18	2	32	1
Campbell, Tacoma	2	2	.500	4.05	10	0	0	3	0	0	13.1	16	6	6	2	0	8	2	14	3
Capel, Tucson	6	6	.500	2.19	58	0	0	44	0	18	82.1	68	29	20	3	3	36	9	70	7
Carter, Vancouver	9	6	.600	4.92	30	22	0	2	0	0	126.1	133	73	69	7	2	56	2	61	10
Carter, Phoenix	11	6	.647	4.37	28	28	2	0	0	0	185.1	188	95	90	17	3	62	3	126	9
Casian, Portland*	4	0	1.000	2.32	58	0	0	23	0	11	62.0	54	16	16	1	1	13	5	43	2
Chitren, Tacoma	4	7	.364	6.82	29	7	0	3	0	0	62.0	64	53	47	5	10	46	5	37	4
Christopher, Colorado Springs	4	4	.500	2.91	49	0	0	45	0	26	58.2	59	21	19	2	0	13	6	39	3
Clark, Colorado Springs	4	4	.500	3.77	9	9	2	0	0	0	59.2	62	30	25	3	1	13	0	33	3
Corsi, Tucson	0	0	.000	1.23	26	0	0	22	0	12	29.1	22	8	4	0	1	10	3	21	2
Costello, Calgary	0	1	.000	13.50	4	0	0	1	0	0	5.1	11	9	8	1	0	2	0	0	1
Cron, Vancouver	0	0	.000	27.00	1	0	0	1	0	0	1.0	4	3	3	0	0	1	0	1	0
Daal, Albuquerque*	0	2	.000	7.84	12	0	0	4	0	0	10.1	14	9	9	1	0	11	1	9	0
Davis, Las Vegas	3	3	.500	3.22	33	0	0	18	0	9	44.2	41	19	16	3	0	9	3	31	0
DeLucia, Calgary	4	2	.667	2.45	8	5	2	3	1	1	40.1	32	11	11	2	0	14	0	38	2
Deshaies, Las Vegas*	6	3	.667	4.03	18	8	0	2	0	1	58.0	68	28	26	6	2	17	0	46	3
Dipoto, Colorado Springs	9	9	.500	4.94	50	9	0	21	0	2	122.0	148	78	67	6	6	66	3	62	9
Drahman, Vancouver	2	4	.333	2.01	48	0	0	44	0	30	58.1	44	16	13	5	0	31	1	34	2
Drees, Calgary*	7	7	.500	5.18	17	16	2	0	0	0	92.0	108	61	53	10	1	37	1	38	9
Dunne, Vancouver	10	6	.625	2.78	21	21	0	0	0	0	132.2	128	61	41	4	2	46	2	78	6
Dyer, Portland	7	6	.538	5.06	27	16	0	4	0	1	105.0	119	62	59	7	7	56	2	85	14
Eiland, Las Vegas	4	5	.444	5.23	14	14	0	0	0	0	63.2	78	43	37	4	0	11	2	31	0
Erb, Edmonton	0	0	.000	27.00	4	0	0	0	0	0	2.2	6	8	8	2	0	6	0	3	1
Fernandez, Vancouver	2	1	.667	0.94	4	3	2	0	1	0	28.2	15	8	3	0	0	6	1	27	0
Fisher, Calgary	0	0	.000	1.69	2	0	0	1	0	0	5.1	6	1	1	1	0	0	0	1	0
Fortugno, Edmonton*	6	4	.600	3.56	26	7	0	4	0	1	73.1	69	36	29	5	2	33	0	82	3
Fraser, Edmonton	7	6	.538	4.90	44	7	0	19	0	6	90.0	110	59	49	8	3	24	4	49	5
Galvez, Albuquerque	5	3	.625	3.90	30	0	0	12	0	0	43.2	32	17	15	2	0	20	1	28	1
Garcia, Vancouver	9	11	.450	3.71	28	28	0	0	1	0	170.0	165	83	70	11	5	56	2	79	2
Gardner, Tucson	6	9	.400	5.69	20	20	0	0	0	0	110.2	141	80	70	1	5	63	1	49	6
Garrelts, Phoenix	0	0	.000	8.49	4	0	0	0	0	0	11.2	14	14	11	2	0	5	0	7	1
Gleaton, Phoenix*	1	1	.500	3.26	15	0	0	7	0	0	19.1	22	11	7	0	0	4	2	11	1
Gonzales, Edmonton	0	0	.000	13.50	2	0	0	2	0	0	1.1	1	2	2	1	0	1	0	1	0
Gozzo, Portland	10	9	.526	3.35	37	19	3	11	2	1	155.2	155	61	58	11	3	50	3	108	2
Grahe, Edmonton	1	0	1.000	3.20	3	3	0	0	0	0	19.2	18	7	7	0	0	5	2	12	1
Grant, Calgary	1	3	.250	4.15	4	3	1	0	0	0	26.0	32	15	12	2	2	4	1	11	2
Grimsley, Tucson	8	7	.533	5.05	26	20	1	0	0	0	124.2	152	79	70	4	9	55	0	90	14
Gross, Albuquerque	6	5	.545	3.51	31	14	2	16	0	8	107.2	96	48	42	1	2	36	5	58	3
Gunderson, Calgary*	0	2	.000	6.02	27	1	0	12	0	0	52.1	57	37	35	6	5	31	3	50	5
Guzman, Tacoma*	3	6	.333	5.11	20	9	0	4	0	0	68.2	70	43	39	6	0	24	4	45	1
Hale, Portland	0	0	.000	18.00	1	0	0	1	0	0	1.0	5	4	2	0	0	0	0	1	0
Hall, Albuquerque*	0	0	.000	8.38	12	0	0	2	0	0	9.2	21	10	9	0	0	5	4	3	0
Hansell, Albuquerque	1	5	.167	5.24	13	13	0	0	0	0	68.2	84	46	40	9	1	35	3	38	4
Ge. Harris, Las Vegas	0	2	.000	3.67	18	0	0	9	0	4	34.1	36	15	14	4	1	16	5	35	4
Gr. Harris, Las Vegas	2	0	1.000	0.56	5	2	0	0	0	0	16.0	8	1	1	0	0	1	0	15	0
Harris, Tacoma	6	16	.273	5.71	29	28	0	0	0	0	149.2	141	108	95	12	6	117	0	111	20
Hartgraves, Tucson*	0	1	.000	24.75	5	1	0	0	0	0	8.0	26	24	22	1	0	9	0	6	4
Hawkins, Calgary	10	9	.526	4.87	24	23	3	0	2	0	129.1	155	77	70	8	3	49	0	49	3
Helton, Tucson*	0	0	.000	9.00	2	0	0	0	0	0	4.0	7	5	4	0	0	1	0	1	0
Heredia, Phoenix	5	5	.500	2.01	22	7	1	7	1	1	80.2	83	30	18	3	1	13	1	37	3
Hernandez, Las Vegas	2	4	.333	2.91	42	0	0	33	0	11	55.2	53	19	18	2	4	20	4	38	3
Hernandez, Vancouver	3	3	.500	2.61	9	0	0	0	0	0	20.2	13	9	6	0	1	11	1	23	0
Higgins, Las Vegas	0	1	.000	6.75	3	0	0	3	0	0	2.2	4	2	2	1	0	2	1	0	0
Hill, Tacoma	0	0	.000	6.00	2	0	0	2	0	0	3.0	2	2	2	1	2	2	0	1	0

Pitcher, Team	W	L	Pct.	ERA	G	GS	CG	GF	ShO	Sv.	IP	H	R	ER	HR	HB	BB	Int. BB	SO	WP
Holton, Albuquerque	2	3	.400	5.75	29	0	0	7	0	1	40.2	50	26	26	1	0	13	1	28	3
Holzemer, Edmonton*	5	7	.417	6.67	17	16	4	1	0	0	89.0	114	69	66	12	7	55	1	49	6
Howard, Vancouver*	3	1	.750	2.92	20	0	0	5	0	0	24.2	18	9	8	3	0	22	3	23	0
Hudek, Vancouver	8	1	.889	3.16	39	3	1	19	1	2	85.1	69	36	30	4	4	45	9	61	6
Hughes, Portland*	0	0	.000	4.50	2	0	0	1	0	0	2.0	2	1	1	1	0	2	0	0	1
Huisman, Phoenix	3	2	.600	2.41	9	8	0	0	0	0	56.0	45	16	15	3	1	24	0	44	1
Hurta, Tucson*	3	1	.750	2.61	20	0	0	6	0	0	20.2	14	8	6	1	4	17	0	22	1
Ingram, Las Vegas	0	0	.000	9.00	2	0	0	0	0	0	6.0	8	9	6	1	0	5	0	5	0
James, Albuquerque	2	1	.667	5.59	18	6	0	3	0	1	46.2	55	35	29	4	2	22	0	33	4
James, Edmonton*	1	6	.143	10.19	7	7	0	0	0	0	32.2	50	44	37	5	7	26	0	12	6
Johnson, Edmonton	0	0	.000	22.50	1	1	0	0	0	0	2.0	8	6	5	0	1	1	0	1	0
Johnson, Portland	2	5	.286	4.73	53	0	0	38	0	10	51.1	65	32	27	4	1	27	4	44	1
Jones, Calgary	2	0	1.000	3.86	21	1	0	13	0	3	32.2	23	15	14	3	0	22	0	32	4
Jones, Edmonton	1	0	1.000	5.79	5	2	0	3	0	0	9.1	10	8	6	0	0	6	0	8	0
Jones, Tucson	0	1	.000	4.50	3	0	0	2	0	0	4.0	1	2	2	0	0	10	1	4	1
Juden, Tucson	9	10	.474	4.04	26	26	0	0	0	0	147.0	149	84	66	11	7	71	1	120	12
Kennedy, Vancouver	1	2	.333	6.32	4	4	0	0	0	0	15.2	21	20	11	1	0	9	0	15	2
Kile, Tucson	4	1	.800	3.99	9	9	0	0	0	0	56.1	50	31	25	3	3	32	0	43	4
Klonoski, Portland*	0	0	.000	0.00	1	0	0	0	0	0	1.0	1	2	0	0	0	2	0	2	0
Knudson, Las Vegas	11	7	.611	4.47	37	20	1	8	1	3	147.0	184	90	73	6	4	47	0	79	4
Kraemer, Edmonton*	1	0	1.000	4.35	34	2	0	8	0	2	41.1	42	22	20	6	3	28	2	32	2
Kramer, Calgary	1	4	.200	6.05	27	6	0	6	1	1	64.0	87	57	43	5	4	30	1	30	10
Kramer, Colorado Springs	8	3	.727	4.88	38	3	0	11	0	3	75.2	88	43	41	2	1	43	2	72	0
Latter, Tacoma	0	1	.000	3.38	5	0	0	0	0	0	10.2	9	5	4	1	1	13	0	5	2
Leskanic, Portland	1	2	.333	9.98	5	3	0	2	0	0	15.1	16	17	17	1	0	8	0	14	0
Lewis, Tucson	0	0	.000	0.00	1	1	0	0	0	0	1.0	0	0	0	0	0	2	0	0	0
Lewis, Edmonton	10	6	.625	4.17	22	22	5	0	0	0	146.2	159	74	68	9	7	40	2	88	7
Lind, Portland	3	3	.500	4.68	47	3	1	9	0	2	84.2	87	50	44	3	2	38	1	77	5
Mahomes, Portland	9	5	.643	3.41	17	16	3	1	3	1	111.0	97	43	42	7	1	43	1	87	4
Mallicoat, Tucson*	1	3	.250	2.68	37	0	0	15	0	3	50.1	36	17	15	0	2	21	3	53	3
Martinez, Albuquerque	7	6	.538	3.81	20	20	3	0	1	0	125.1	104	57	53	10	9	57	0	124	2
Masters, 26 Pho. - 13 Cal.	2	8	.200	6.08	39	9	0	17	0	1	90.1	107	71	61	3	2	71	4	70	9
McAndrew, Albuquerque	1	3	.250	5.83	5	5	0	0	0	0	29.1	41	20	19	1	0	14	0	9	0
McClellan, Phoenix	2	6	.250	5.88	20	7	0	4	0	1	64.1	85	46	42	9	1	21	0	43	7
McCullers, Albuquerque	4	1	.800	1.84	29	0	0	20	0	12	44.0	34	9	9	0	1	10	1	35	4
McMurtry, Phoenix	5	8	.385	4.23	40	14	1	10	1	1	129.2	140	71	61	5	4	59	4	83	6
Merriman, Edmonton	1	3	.250	1.42	22	0	0	14	0	4	31.2	31	10	5	0	2	10	3	15	2
Millay, Tacoma	0	0	.000	14.73	2	0	0	0	0	0	3.2	5	6	6	2	0	6	0	3	0
Mimbs, Albuquerque*	0	4	.000	6.10	12	7	0	0	0	0	48.2	58	34	33	4	0	19	1	32	4
Musselman, Tacoma*	7	7	.500	3.50	19	19	1	0	0	0	105.1	100	51	41	8	1	40	5	75	5
Mutis, Colorado Springs*	9	9	.500	5.08	25	24	0	0	0	0	145.1	177	99	82	8	5	57	1	77	8
Myers, Phoenix	0	4	.000	5.70	25	0	0	19	0	10	23.2	32	20	15	1	0	13	5	11	0
Neel, Tacoma	0	0	.000	6.75	3	0	0	0	0	0	4.0	8	3	3	0	0	4	0	0	0
Neidlinger, Albuquerque	8	9	.471	4.39	34	20	1	1	0	0	145.2	153	75	71	12	1	45	4	81	3
Nelson, Tacoma	1	0	1.000	0.00	2	0	0	2	0	0	3.2	0	0	0	0	0	1	0	0	0
Newlin, Calgary	1	1	.500	5.77	30	0	0	13	0	3	43.2	60	33	28	1	2	29	2	24	1
Nichols, Colorado Springs	3	3	.500	5.67	9	9	1	0	0	0	54.0	65	39	34	6	1	16	1	35	4
Nichting, Albuquerque	1	3	.250	7.93	10	9	0	0	0	0	42.0	64	42	37	2	0	23	1	25	5
Nunez, Calgary	1	1	.500	5.63	10	8	0	1	0	0	38.1	42	26	24	3	0	20	1	29	3
Oliveras, Phoenix	3	2	.600	3.38	22	5	1	4	0	0	61.1	51	24	23	4	1	21	2	26	3
Opperman, Albuquerque	2	3	.400	3.60	6	6	0	0	0	0	25.0	25	12	10	1	2	12	0	15	0
Ortiz, Portland*	0	0	.000	0.00	1	0	0	1	0	0	1.0	0	0	0	0	0	2	0	2	0
Osteen, Tacoma*	0	2	.000	10.05	4	4	0	0	0	0	14.1	21	18	16	4	2	13	0	7	1
Otto, Colorado Springs*	3	2	.600	2.89	6	6	1	0	0	0	43.2	35	14	14	0	1	10	1	11	3
Parker, Calgary	2	1	.667	4.00	3	3	0	0	0	0	18.0	20	9	8	0	0	3	0	11	0
Pawlowski, Edmonton	0	1	.000	6.35	20	1	0	7	0	0	34.0	51	27	24	4	0	22	2	18	2
Peek, Tacoma	4	3	.571	2.98	57	0	0	23	0	3	87.2	87	38	29	7	4	37	9	52	1
Pena, Phoenix*	7	3	.700	4.15	33	2	0	12	0	1	39.0	45	22	18	4	0	20	6	27	0
Perry, Las Vegas*	0	0	.000	6.39	16	0	0	2	0	0	12.2	19	11	9	0	1	1	1	3	4
Perschke, Vancouver	12	7	.632	3.76	29	28	1	0	1	0	165.0	159	83	69	13	7	44	0	82	4
Peterson, Las Vegas	6	3	.667	3.75	21	18	1	1	1	0	100.2	99	48	42	9	3	37	5	67	2
Raczka, Tacoma*	0	1	.000	3.51	31	1	0	11	0	1	48.2	38	22	19	3	0	24	6	26	2
Rambo, Phoenix	1	2	.333	5.93	20	1	0	4	0	1	41.0	42	28	27	1	3	15	2	32	0
Rapp, Phoenix	7	8	.467	3.05	39	12	2	17	1	3	121.0	115	54	41	2	2	40	3	79	1
Reed, Phoenix	0	1	.000	3.48	29	0	0	28	0	20	31.0	27	13	12	2	0	10	3	30	1
Remlinger, Calgary*	1	7	.125	6.65	21	11	0	1	0	0	70.1	97	65	52	7	4	48	1	24	9
Reynolds, Tucson	9	8	.529	3.68	25	22	2	1	0	1	142.0	156	73	58	4	4	34	2	106	4
Rice, Calgary	3	8	.273	8.21	21	15	0	1	0	0	83.1	133	81	76	7	6	47	1	27	3
Ridenour, Edmonton	1	0	1.000	6.10	5	0	0	1	0	0	10.1	12	7	7	0	0	8	2	7	2
Ritchie, Phoenix*	0	0	.000	4.50	1	0	0	1	0	0	2.0	4	2	1	1	0	2	0	1	1
Rogers, Phoenix*	3	3	.500	4.00	11	11	1	0	1	0	69.2	63	34	31	0	1	22	1	62	2
Roscoe, Colorado Springs	6	5	.545	4.30	27	20	1	2	1	0	127.2	141	70	61	5	4	34	2	78	9
Sager, Las Vegas	1	7	.125	7.95	30	3	0	7	0	1	60.0	89	57	53	8	1	17	3	40	3
Sanders, Las Vegas	3	6	.333	5.50	14	12	1	1	1	0	72.0	97	49	44	7	3	31	1	51	6
Scheid, 29 Van. - 12 Tuc.*	3	5	.375	2.63	41	8	0	7	0	1	92.1	78	36	27	4	1	51	6	58	7
Schmidt, 13 Cal. - 14 Tac.	5	4	.556	4.41	27	8	0	14	0	4	69.1	75	35	34	5	3	20	5	43	3
Schooler, Calgary	0	0	.000	0.00	1	1	0	0	0	0	2.0	2	0	0	0	0	0	0	0	0
Schullstrom, Las Vegas	1	0	1.000	0.00	1	1	0	0	0	0	5.0	3	0	0	0	0	3	0	4	0
Schwabe, Portland	1	2	.333	8.02	6	4	0	2	0	0	21.1	32	21	19	3	0	11	1	9	1
Schwarz, Vancouver	1	3	.250	3.00	23	0	0	17	0	3	36.0	26	18	12	0	3	31	4	42	5
Scott, Calgary	5	6	.455	4.78	16	14	2	2	1	0	84.2	95	51	45	8	0	28	1	32	1
Scott, Edmonton	0	2	.000	5.20	31	0	0	17	0	6	36.1	41	21	21	1	0	21	1	48	4
Scott, Las Vegas	1	2	.333	2.25	24	0	0	23	0	15	28.0	20	8	7	1	1	3	0	28	2
Scudder, Colorado Springs	0	1	.000	6.00	1	1	0	0	0	0	3.0	4	3	2	0	0	2	0	1	1
Searage, Edmonton*	3	3	.500	5.33	34	1	1	10	0	1	49.0	65	35	29	6	1	22	3	23	4
Searcy, Albuquerque*	3	6	.333	6.48	12	12	0	0	0	0	58.1	79	50	42	7	1	31	1	40	6
Seminara, Las Vegas	6	4	.600	4.13	13	13	1	0	1	0	80.2	92	46	37	2	3	33	3	48	2
Shaw, Colorado Springs	10	5	.667	4.76	25	24	1	0	0	0	155.0	174	88	82	11	10	45	2	84	5
Shinall, Albuquerque	13	5	.722	3.29	64	0	0	32	0	6	82.0	91	38	30	7	1	37	11	46	4
Simon, Tucson	0	1	.000	5.03	9	0	0	6	0	0	19.2	26	13	11	2	0	11	2	12	1
Slusarski, Tacoma	2	4	.333	3.77	11	10	0	0	0	0	57.1	67	30	24	6	1	18	1	26	1
J. Smith, Tacoma	0	0	.000	6.00	2	0	0	2	0	0	3.0	2	2	2	0	0	0	0	1	0
T. Smith, Tacoma	1	1	.500	7.15	2	2	1	0	0	0	11.1	10	9	9	1	0	4	0	7	0
Smith, Colorado Springs	3	0	1.000	4.75	19	0	0	9	0	1	41.2	39	24	22	4	1	25	2	30	3

Pitcher, Team	W	L	Pct.	ERA	G	GS	CG	GF	ShO	Sv.	IP	H	R	ER	HR	HB	BB	Int. BB	SO	WP
Soff, Edmonton	11	9	.550	3.89	24	24	5	0	0	0	166.2	177	85	72	14	7	65	2	115	10
Soper, Colorado Springs	0	0	.000	6.61	10	0	0	4	0	1	16.1	26	13	12	2	2	6	0	16	1
Springer, Albuquerque	2	7	.222	5.66	11	11	1	0	0	0	62.0	70	45	39	7	4	22	0	36	3
Stephens, Vancouver	5	3	.625	5.09	32	6	0	6	0	1	81.1	84	50	46	3	0	35	1	50	10
Taylor, Phoenix	4	1	.800	2.40	20	0	0	7	0	0	30.0	33	14	8	2	2	10	2	28	2
Traxler, Albuquerque*	0	0	.000	9.00	1	0	0	1	0	0	1.0	3	1	1	0	0	0	0	0	0
Trombley, Portland	10	8	.556	3.65	25	25	2	0	0	0	165.0	149	70	67	18	6	58	1	138	1
Tsamis, Portland*	13	4	.765	3.90	39	22	4	6	1	1	163.2	195	78	71	12	5	51	1	71	2
Turner, Tucson	2	8	.200	3.51	63	0	0	38	0	14	100.0	93	52	39	2	2	40	3	84	5
Valdez, Las Vegas	2	0	1.000	6.14	8	0	0	0	0	0	14.2	19	10	10	2	0	7	1	12	0
Van Poppel, Tacoma	4	2	.667	3.97	9	9	0	0	0	0	45.1	44	22	20	1	1	35	0	29	1
Vande Berg, Calgary*	1	3	.250	8.93	31	2	0	12	0	3	43.1	78	54	43	3	6	17	2	29	0
Vanderweele, Phoenix	0	0	.000	10.80	1	0	0	0	0	0	1.2	3	2	2	0	0	0	0	1	0
Veres, Tucson	2	3	.400	5.30	29	1	0	10	0	0	52.2	60	36	31	1	0	17	1	46	6
Veres, Phoenix	0	2	.000	8.10	12	0	0	4	0	1	13.1	14	12	12	1	0	13	1	13	2
Vesling, Las Vegas*	0	0	.000	5.06	8	0	0	0	0	0	5.1	7	3	3	1	0	9	1	4	0
Vidmar, Edmonton	0	5	.000	6.97	16	12	1	1	0	0	72.1	98	60	56	5	7	29	1	35	3
Walker, Calgary	5	1	.833	5.27	12	6	1	1	0	0	41.0	50	26	24	5	1	19	1	24	2
Wall, Tucson	0	0	.000	1.13	2	2	0	0	0	0	8.0	11	1	1	0	0	1	0	2	0
Walton, Tacoma	8	2	.800	2.77	35	7	2	22	1	8	81.1	76	29	25	6	3	21	4	60	1
Wapnick, Vancouver	4	2	.667	4.42	39	0	0	22	0	1	71.1	75	38	35	1	2	48	3	59	3
Wasinger, Edmonton	0	0	.000	0.00	2	0	0	2	0	0	3.0	2	0	0	0	0	0	0	1	0
Wassenaar, Portland	6	8	.429	3.50	60	0	0	22	0	5	90.0	96	41	35	4	1	33	12	60	9
Wayne, Portland*	0	1	.000	2.35	14	0	0	7	0	5	23.0	23	11	6	1	0	1	0	20	1
Weber, Tacoma	4	5	.444	4.12	52	0	0	23	0	2	94.0	95	45	43	6	8	53	9	51	10
Wells, Colorado Springs*	1	0	1.000	1.17	5	0	0	4	0	0	7.2	5	1	1	0	0	2	0	3	0
Wernig, Las Vegas*	0	0	.000	8.74	17	0	0	5	0	1	11.1	10	12	11	0	3	6	1	7	2
West, Portland*	7	6	.538	4.43	19	18	1	0	0	0	101.2	88	51	50	6	2	65	1	87	7
Wickander, Colorado Springs*	0	0	.000	1.64	8	0	0	4	0	2	11.0	4	2	2	0	0	6	0	18	0
Wilkins, Las Vegas	0	1	.000	7.43	8	1	0	3	0	0	13.1	16	15	11	2	0	9	3	9	4
Wilkins, Albuquerque	0	2	.000	3.57	46	3	0	11	0	1	88.1	89	42	35	11	2	30	3	63	1
Wilkinson, Tacoma*	0	3	.000	10.00	8	1	0	0	0	0	18.0	26	20	20	4	1	19	0	11	4
Williams, Tucson	6	1	.857	4.50	12	12	0	0	0	0	70.0	78	37	35	3	6	26	0	58	5
Windes, Tucson*	1	1	.500	4.93	20	0	0	8	0	1	34.2	44	20	19	5	0	14	1	28	4
Witmeyer, Tacoma*	0	0	.000	9.00	1	0	0	1	0	0	2.0	2	2	2	0	0	2	0	1	0
Wood, Las Vegas	0	0	.000	8.03	7	0	0	3	0	0	12.1	17	13	11	1	0	10	1	12	2
Woodson, Calgary	1	4	.200	3.43	10	0	0	5	0	2	21.0	20	15	8	1	0	12	1	9	1
Worrell, Las Vegas	4	2	.667	4.26	10	10	1	0	1	0	63.1	61	32	30	4	3	19	0	32	3
York, Las Vegas	5	7	.417	4.79	19	17	0	0	0	0	88.1	96	54	47	5	8	55	0	54	2
Young, Edmonton*	10	8	.556	5.59	28	20	5	2	1	0	143.1	174	94	89	14	4	42	4	104	2
Zancanaro, Tacoma*	2	11	.154	4.26	23	19	0	0	0	0	105.2	108	61	50	3	2	75	0	47	7
Zappelli, Edmonton	5	3	.625	3.65	10	10	0	0	0	0	61.2	73	30	25	3	5	28	1	51	2
Zavaras, Calgary	1	2	.333	13.17	4	4	0	0	0	0	13.2	24	22	20	1	0	12	0	5	2

BALKS—Juden, 7; Dipoto, R. Harris, 6 each; Knudson, Seminara, 5 each; Mutis, Williams, 4 each; Dunne, Gardner, Guzman, McClellan, Oliveras, Scheid, Turner, 3 each; Ard, Banks, Bell, Bolton, Boucher, Brown, Burba, Chitren, Daal, Dreshaies, Drees, G. Johnson, Kile, S. Lewis, Mallicoat, Opperman, Perschke, Roscoe, Sager, D. Scott, Trombley, Woodson, York, Young, Zancanaro, 2 each; Acker, Astacio, Barton, Bross, Brummett, J. Carter, Corsi, Dyer, Fortugno, Garcia, Gleaton, Gross, E. Harris, R. Hernandez, Holzemer, Howard, R. Kramer, Latter, Leskanic, McAndrew, McCullers, Musselman, Nichols, Nichting, Nunez, Osteen, Otto, Raczka, Rambo, Rapp, Reynolds, Rogers, Searcy, Soff, Vande Berg, Van Poppel, Wernig, West, Wilkinson, Worrell, 1 each.

COMBINATION SHUTOUTS—Astacio-Shinall-Gross, Gross-Wilkins-McCullers, James-Galvez-Shinall-McCullers, Martinez-Gross, Martinez-McCullers, Martinez-Wilkins-Shinall-McCullers, Albuquerque; Hawkins-Gunderson, Calgary; Clark-Kramer, Kramer-Christopher, Colorado Springs; Lewis-Merriman, Lewis-Merriman-Kraemer-Fraser, Young-Butcher, Zappelli-Scott, Edmonton; Deshaies-Bross, Eiland-Bross-Scott, Harris-Hernandez, Knudson-Perry-Davis, Las Vegas; Black-McClellan, Phoenix; Abbott-Tsamis-Wassenaar-Dyer-Lind, Abbott-Wassenaar-Casian-Johnson, Banks-Casian, Banks-Wassenaar-Johnson, Gozzo-Wassenaar-Wayne, Mahomes-Johnson, West-Casian-Johnson, West-Wassenaar, Portland; Allison-Chitren-Peek, Bittiger-Walton, Musselman-Wilkinson-Corsi, Schmidt-Peek-Guzman, Schmidt-Weber-Guzman, Zancanaro-Peek, Tacoma; Bowen-Mallicoat-Grimsley, Juden-Hurta-Turner, Juden-Mallicoat-Capel, Reynolds-Blair-Hurta-Turner, Tucson; Garcia-Drahman 2, Bolton-Drahman, Garcia-Scheid-Drahman, Hudek-Wapnick, Stephens-Bere-Howard-Wapnick-Drahman, Stephens-Drahman, Vancouver.

NO-HIT GAMES—West, Casian and Johnson, Portland, defeated Vancouver, 5-0, June 7; Worrell, Las Vegas, defeated Phoenix, 2-0, September 5.

FIELDING

TEAM

Team	Pct.	G	PO	A	E	DP	PB	Team	Pct.	G	PO	A	E	DP	PB
Portland	.980	144	3826	1623	110	140	12	Calgary	.973	139	3525	1590	141	139	30
Phoenix	.976	144	3817	1567	130	145	14	Albuquerque	.973	143	3709	1646	149	172	10
Edmonton	.975	144	3678	1580	134	137	12	Colorado Springs	.971	141	3677	1697	161	199	12
Tacoma	.974	143	3719	1589	141	181	16	Vancouver	.970	142	3722	1410	161	118	16
Las Vegas	.974	144	3791	1686	149	142	13	Tucson	.967	144	3804	1573	184	142	16

INDIVIDUAL

*Throws lefthanded.

FIRST BASEMEN

Player, Team	Pct.	G	PO	A	E	DP
Aldrete, Colorado Springs*	.995	63	529	35	3	64
Bailey, Phoenix	1.000	6	35	3	0	5
Barbara, Edmonton*	.983	70	600	53	11	55
Bilardello, Las Vegas	.933	1	13	1	1	1
Blowers, Calgary	1.000	8	49	1	0	4
Bowie, Calgary*	.991	49	408	56	4	50
Brooks, Edmonton	1.000	2	16	0	0	1
Canale, Colorado Springs	.990	21	186	11	2	34
Cooper, Tucson	.988	19	149	13	2	11
Cron, Vancouver	.988	131	1098	94	14	90
Decker, Phoenix	1.000	3	24	2	0	1
Denson, Vancouver	.952	12	92	7	5	9
Distefano, 14 Tuc.-2 Cal.*	1.000	16	123	11	0	13
Epley, Colorado Springs*	.979	16	129	12	3	18
Gonzales, Edmonton	1.000	1	3	0	0	0
Guinn, Vancouver	1.000	2	3	0	0	0
Haselman, Calgary	.923	1	11	1	1	1
Heath, Tacoma	.900	1	6	3	1	0
Hengel, Phoenix	1.000	1	10	2	0	0
Higgins, Las Vegas	1.000	8	43	3	0	5
Howitt, Tacoma	.974	4	37	0	1	4
Hughes, Portland*	.950	2	16	3	1	2
Jefferson, Colorado Springs*	.988	38	363	34	5	51
Jelic, Las Vegas	1.000	3	25	1	0	0
Jorgensen, Portland	.996	35	208	17	1	21
Kingery, Tacoma*	1.000	5	32	1	0	3
Lee, 9 C.S.-78 Por.	.995	87	706	69	4	75

Player, Team	Pct.	G	PO	A	E	DP
Lewis, Phoenix*	.981	56	499	27	10	39
Lyons, Tucson	.997	35	273	21	1	32
Magallanes, Vancouver	1.000	1	1	0	0	0
Martinez, Colorado Springs	.938	6	57	4	4	8
McCarty, Portland*	1.000	3	33	3	0	4
Merullo, Vancouver	1.000	2	9	2	0	1
Moses, Calgary*	1.000	5	44	4	0	10
Mota, Tucson	.938	2	13	2	1	2
Nelson, 28 Por.-50 Pho.*	.990	78	601	61	7	69
Oberkfell, Edmonton	.947	6	17	1	1	2
Ortiz, Portland*	.875	1	7	0	1	0
Parker, Tucson	1.000	2	4	2	0	2
Patterson, Phoenix	1.000	38	278	16	0	32
Pegues, Las Vegas	1.000	1	1	0	0	0
Piazza, Albuquerque	.969	11	87	7	3	11
Pirkl, Calgary	.990	76	625	44	7	67
Quinones, Portland	.978	5	45	0	1	4
Riles, Tucson	.995	41	337	31	2	35
Rodriguez, Albuquerque*	.987	54	419	35	6	57
Rohde, Colorado Springs	1.000	4	19	3	0	2
Rose, Edmonton	1.000	1	6	1	0	0
Santovenia, Vancouver	1.000	1	2	2	0	0
Sheaffer, Portland	1.000	3	22	4	0	3
Simms, Tucson	.983	45	374	27	7	33
Smith, Tacoma	.960	6	23	1	1	5
Staton, Las Vegas	.994	19	140	18	1	11
Stephenson, Las Vegas*	1.000	8	53	6	0	3
Traxler, Albuquerque*	.994	95	733	84	5	88
Turner, Calgary	.947	2	18	0	1	2
Van Burkleo, Edmonton*	.990	75	639	34	7	67
VELASQUEZ, Las Vegas	.994	120	1034	91	7	98
Witmeyer, Tacoma*	.992	133	1171	77	10	152
Wood, Phoenix*	.974	14	102	10	3	4

SECOND BASEMEN

Player, Team	Pct.	G	PO	A	E	DP
Amaral, Calgary	.981	30	66	92	3	16
Anderson, Calgary	1.000	2	3	5	0	0
Benjamin, Phoenix	1.000	1	3	2	0	0
Blankenship, Tacoma	1.000	3	6	9	0	2
Boone, Calgary	.9855	106	260	353	9	90
Browne, Vancouver	1.000	4	9	16	0	4
Buccheri, Tacoma	.926	9	7	18	2	5
Carter, Tacoma	.930	16	21	32	4	10
Chimelis, Phoenix	.955	18	41	44	4	7
Coachman, 17 Pho.-22 Edm.	.987	39	81	139	3	32
Colbert, Phoenix	.889	1	4	4	1	2
Crosby, Phoenix	.977	12	21	22	1	8
Davis, Edmonton	.983	11	21	36	1	9
Faries, Las Vegas	.991	22	45	66	1	8
Flora, Edmonton	.954	51	111	118	11	30
Gardner, Las Vegas	.980	114	233	391	13	77
Garrison, Tacoma	1.000	1	3	4	0	1
Gilbert, Portland	.944	9	13	21	2	6
Guinn, Vancouver	1.000	3	1	1	0	1
Gutierrez, Las Vegas	1.000	2	1	6	0	1
HALE, Portland	.9860	124	273	361	9	81
Hemond, Tacoma	.917	6	8	14	2	1
Higgins, Las Vegas	.966	7	14	14	1	1
Howard, Albuquerque	.994	34	53	106	1	27
Hubbard, Tucson	.974	109	238	353	16	70
Johnson, Phoenix	.964	33	43	89	5	15
Kirby, Colorado Springs	1.000	1	0	1	0	0
Liriano, Colorado Springs	.978	61	130	186	7	71
Litton, Phoenix	.977	8	20	22	1	4
Lockhart, Tacoma	.979	92	195	224	9	79
Magallanes, Vancouver	.981	14	22	31	1	5
Martin, Vancouver	.971	133	266	395	20	68
Martinez, Edmonton	.967	48	77	128	7	33
Mota, Tucson	.961	41	75	123	8	28
Munoz, Albuquerque	.968	16	21	40	2	8
Naveda, Portland	1.000	1	1	3	0	1
Oberkfell, Edmonton	1.000	11	19	26	0	1
D. Patterson, Phoenix	1.000	1	1	2	0	1
J. Patterson, Phoenix	.976	72	133	236	9	54
Perezchica, Colorado Springs	.927	16	27	49	6	11
Polidor, Tacoma	1.000	1	2	1	0	0
Pye, Albuquerque	.947	19	33	38	4	12
Quinones, Portland	.981	21	42	59	2	13
Rohde, Colorado Springs	.975	72	155	231	10	55
Rose, Edmonton	.955	5	9	12	1	4
Schaefer, Calgary	1.000	1	4	3	0	1
Smith, Tacoma	.980	34	62	82	3	28
Sojo, Edmonton	1.000	5	7	16	0	3
Turner, Calgary	1.000	3	5	9	0	2
Wasinger, Edmonton	1.000	5	2	3	0	0
Witkowski, Las Vegas	1.000	5	18	19	0	4
Young, Albuquerque	.961	91	207	287	20	77

THIRD BASEMEN

Player, Team	Pct.	G	PO	A	E	DP
Anderson, Albuquerque	.889	3	0	8	1	0
Anderson, Calgary	.875	10	6	15	3	1

Player, Team	Pct.	G	PO	A	E	DP
Blowers, Calgary	.968	57	36	85	4	7
Bolick, Calgary	.918	64	36	121	14	10
Booker, Tucson	.910	42	23	68	9	9
Brosius, Tacoma	.955	63	47	167	10	24
Carter, Tacoma	.774	11	8	16	7	1
Chimelis, Phoenix	.925	27	16	33	4	4
Coachman, Edmonton	1.000	13	14	36	0	2
Colbert, Phoenix	.938	23	26	34	4	1
Coolbaugh, Las Vegas	.938	56	29	77	7	7
Coomer, Vancouver	.927	77	49	115	13	10
Cooper, Tucson	.899	96	52	153	23	23
Cron, Vancouver	.824	8	3	11	3	2
Davis, Edmonton	.833	3	2	3	1	1
Easley, Edmonton	.957	6	6	16	1	1
Faries, Las Vegas	.961	72	37	111	6	14
Garcia, Portland	1.000	1	1	1	0	0
Garrison, Tacoma	.879	31	14	44	8	5
Gilbert, Portland	1.000	5	0	3	0	1
Gonzales, Edmonton	.923	17	10	26	3	2
Gonzalez, Edmonton	1.000	1	0	1	0	0
Guinn, Vancouver	1.000	4	0	2	0	0
Hall, Vancouver	.912	62	48	97	14	9
Hamilton, Albuquerque	.951	36	27	51	4	8
Heath, Tacoma	1.000	8	4	6	0	1
Heffernan, Calgary	.769	3	0	10	3	2
Higgins, Las Vegas	.925	42	25	74	8	9
Howitt, Tacoma	.750	6	1	5	2	0
Hubbard, Tucson	.000	1	0	0	1	0
Jelic, Las Vegas	.821	12	8	15	5	3
Johnson, Phoenix	.857	9	0	6	1	2
JORGENSEN, Portland	.972	105	91	225	9	24
Lee, Colorado Springs	1.000	7	4	15	0	3
Liriano, Colorado Springs	.979	17	9	38	1	1
Litton, Phoenix	.951	17	8	31	2	7
Lockhart, Tacoma	.857	5	3	3	1	1
Magallanes, Vancouver	.909	11	7	13	2	1
Martinez, Albuquerque	.889	22	8	32	5	5
Martinez, Edmonton	1.000	3	3	4	0	0
McConnell, Edmonton	.979	42	21	73	2	10
Mota, Tucson	.864	12	8	11	3	2
Munoz, Albuquerque	.923	71	46	121	14	14
Naveda, Portland	.947	8	6	12	1	0
Oberkfell, Edmonton	.971	13	7	26	1	1
Paquette, Tacoma*	.940	16	14	33	3	2
Parker, Tucson	1.000	2	3	2	0	0
D. Patterson, Phoenix	.978	82	51	127	4	19
J. Patterson, Phoenix	1.000	1	1	2	0	0
Perezchica, Colorado Springs	1.000	1	1	2	0	1
Polidor, Tacoma	1.000	1	0	1	0	0
Pye, Albuquerque	.912	40	19	74	9	13
Quinones, Portland	.973	33	25	48	2	7
Reboulet, Portland	1.000	1	1	2	0	1
Riles, Tucson	.864	10	6	13	3	2
Rohde, Colorado Springs	.962	27	21	54	3	8
Rose, Edmonton	1.000	5	2	12	0	1
Smith, Colorado Springs	.857	8	1	11	2	0
Smith, Tacoma	.984	25	17	44	1	4
Sojo, Edmonton	.965	32	25	85	4	7
Taylor, Calgary	1.000	1	1	3	0	0
Thomas, Phoenix	1.000	5	3	5	0	0
Thome, Colorado Springs	.784	11	9	20	8	3
Turner, Calgary	.828	9	4	20	5	3
Wasinger, Edmonton	.904	25	13	34	5	4
Worthington, Colorado Springs	.927	81	47	169	17	21

SHORTSTOPS

Player, Team	Pct.	G	PO	A	E	DP
Abbott, Tacoma	.930	11	21	32	4	10
Amaral, Calgary	.950	71	121	237	19	56
Anderson, Albuquerque	.944	12	20	32	3	9
Anderson, Calgary	.951	36	54	102	8	23
Beltre, Vancouver	.986	30	48	90	2	24
Benjamin, Phoenix	.921	45	57	119	15	21
Booker, Tucson	.955	4	8	13	1	4
Boone, Calgary						
BOURNIGAL, Albuquerque	.984	122	201	368	9	99
Carter, Tacoma	.857	1	2	4	1	1
Cedeno, Tucson	.936	74	112	211	22	47
Clayton, Phoenix	.971	48	81	150	7	40
Colbert, Phoenix	1.000	4	4	8	0	2
Davis, Edmonton	1.000	5	7	8	0	0
Davis, Phoenix	.967	6	3	26	1	4
Diaz, Calgary	.925	13	23	26	4	5
Easley, Edmonton	.942	102	146	326	29	62
Espinoza, Colorado Springs	.959	120	191	414	26	112
Faries, Las Vegas	.933	37	47	92	10	21
Foster, Vancouver	1.000	1	1	2	0	0
Garrison, Tacoma	.833	3	5	0	1	0
Gilbert, Portland	.949	93	131	275	22	63
Guinn, Vancouver	.939	35	53	54	7	11
Gutierrez, Las Vegas	1.000	1	0	2	0	0
Johnson, Phoenix	.951	41	50	104	8	20
Liriano, Colorado Springs	.917	4	5	6	1	2
Lockhart, Tacoma	.750	1	1	2	1	0

Player, Team	Pct.	G	PO	A	E	DP
Lopez, Las Vegas	.949	117	200	358	30	70
Magallanes, Vancouver	.953	59	89	136	11	29
Martinez, Albuquerque	.909	20	27	44	7	10
Martinez, Edmonton	.945	38	51	120	10	26
Miller, Tucson	.973	10	10	26	1	6
Munoz, Albuquerque	1.000	4	1	3	0	0
Naveda, Portland	.875	4	4	3	1	0
Parker, Tucson	.750	1	2	4	2	0
Perezchica, Colorado Springs	1.000	4	8	11	0	3
Polidor, Tacoma	.957	97	136	291	19	72
Pye, Albuquerque	1.000	3	0	3	0	0
Quinones, Portland	1.000	8	11	16	0	2
Reboulet, Portland	.968	47	71	139	7	28
Riles, Tucson	1.000	4	4	3	0	1
Rohde, Colorado Springs	.924	17	26	59	7	18
Schaefer, Calgary	.976	11	17	24	1	8
Smith, Colorado Springs	1.000	5	5	10	0	1
Smith, Tacoma	.944	35	66	101	10	30
Sojo, Edmonton	1.000	2	0	5	0	0
Thomas, Phoenix	.928	30	37	66	8	14
Turner, Calgary	.977	9	15	28	1	6
Vizquel, Calgary	.972	6	14	21	1	5
Wasinger, Edmonton	1.000	4	8	6	0	1
Weiss, Tacoma	.957	4	8	14	1	4
Yelding, 16 Tuc.-29 Van.	.950	45	59	112	9	23

OUTFIELDERS

Player, Team	Pct.	G	PO	A	E	DP
Abner, Vancouver	1.000	20	64	1	0	1
Aldrete, Colorado Springs*	1.000	36	38	3	0	1
Allred, Colorado Springs*	.976	131	273	12	7	1
Amaral, Calgary	1.000	3	5	0	0	0
Anderson, Calgary	1.000	16	29	1	0	0
Ashley, Albuquerque	.952	25	39	1	2	0
Barron, Albuquerque	.976	76	155	4	4	1
Bean, Edmonton*	1.000	29	35	3	0	0
Blankenship, Tacoma	1.000	2	5	0	0	0
Blowers, Calgary	.938	6	14	1	1	0
Bradley, Edmonton	1.000	39	62	3	0	2
Brantley, Tucson	.981	32	50	3	1	2
Brito, Portland	.949	55	87	6	5	1
Brooks, Albuquerque	.967	121	196	9	7	2
Brosius, Tacoma	1.000	1	3	0	0	0
Brown, Portland	.972	60	135	4	4	2
Bruett, Portland*	1.000	76	204	11	0	2
Brundage, Calgary*	.974	77	172	12	5	0
Buccheri, Tacoma	.989	37	89	0	1	0
Carter, Tacoma	.978	60	130	6	3	0
Chimelis, Phoenix	1.000	8	8	0	0	0
Cockrell, Colorado Springs	.957	66	87	2	4	0
Colbert, Phoenix	1.000	3	1	0	0	0
Cooper, Tucson	1.000	12	17	1	0	0
Cooper, Phoenix	.960	69	165	4	7	1
Cron, Vancouver	1.000	3	3	0	0	0
Crowe, Phoenix	1.000	8	9	0	0	0
Davidson, Colorado Springs	.974	107	175	10	5	0
Dean, Tucson	1.000	33	44	3	0	0
Distefano, Calgary*	1.000	14	26	1	0	0
Edmonds, Edmonton*	.988	48	79	5	1	0
Epley, Colorado Springs*	1.000	1	1	0	0	0
Fox, Tacoma*	1.000	35	78	4	0	2
Gilbert, Portland	.987	29	70	4	1	0
Gonzalez, Edmonton	1.000	23	47	0	0	0
Gonzalez, Tucson	.963	13	26	0	1	0
Goodwin, Albuquerque	.995	79	184	5	1	2
Grunhard, Tacoma*	.980	70	92	6	2	2
Hale, Portland	1.000	7	5	0	0	0
Hall, Vancouver	.988	45	80	1	1	0
Haselman, Calgary	.923	11	11	1	1	0
Heath, Tacoma	.967	19	28	1	1	0
Henderson, Tacoma	1.000	2	2	0	0	0
Hengel, Phoenix	1.000	6	5	0	0	0
Higgins, Las Vegas	.987	56	74	4	1	1
Hill, Tacoma	.967	96	169	8	6	2
Hosey, Phoenix	.958	123	268	6	12	1
Howitt, 31 Tac.-50 Cal.	.990	81	183	7	2	1
Huff, Vancouver	1.000	1	4	0	0	0
Hughes, Portland*	.959	79	86	7	4	0
Jaster, Vancouver	.957	18	42	3	2	1
Jelic, Las Vegas	.986	48	63	8	1	1
Jeter, Vancouver	.992	89	235	8	2	1
Jones, Tucson	.979	45	86	7	2	1
Jones, Vancouver	.980	50	90	7	2	2
Kingery, Tacoma*	.985	90	186	12	3	5
Kirby, Colorado Springs	.976	119	274	13	7	2
KOMMINSK, Vancouver	.99078	101	208	7	3	2
Kvasnicka, Portland*	.975	24	39	0	1	0
Lee, Vancouver	.985	96	188	6	3	4
Lennon, Calgary	.923	9	12	0	1	0
Leonard, Phoenix	.985	36	62	2	1	0
Dar. Lewis, Phoenix	1.000	38	93	2	0	1
Massarelli, Tucson	.946	23	32	3	2	0
McCarty, Portland*	.875	4	7	0	1	0

Player, Team	Pct.	G	PO	A	E	DP
McDonald, Calgary	1.000	8	19	1	0	0
McDowell, Edmonton*	1.000	3	5	0	0	0
Mikulik, Tucson	.979	51	92	3	2	0
Mondesi, Albuquerque	.933	35	89	8	7	2
Morris, Edmonton*	1.000	2	4	0	0	0
Morrow, Albuquerque*	.929	20	24	2	2	0
Moses, Calgary*	.994	61	169	3	1	0
Mota, Tucson	.946	21	32	3	2	0
Munoz, Albuquerque	.959	31	43	4	2	0
Naveda, Portland	.981	102	192	16	4	3
Neel, Tacoma	.964	31	49	4	2	0
Newson, Vancouver*	.977	17	42	1	1	0
Nixon, Colorado Springs	1.000	12	17	1	0	0
Ortiz, Portland*	.974	23	36	2	1	0
Parker, Tucson	.946	27	52	1	3	0
Patterson, Phoenix	1.000	17	51	1	0	0
Peguero, Albuquerque	1.000	24	59	1	0	0
Pegues, Las Vegas	.962	114	202	24	9	5
Peters, Phoenix	1.000	18	23	1	0	0
Powell, Calgary	1.000	7	10	2	0	0
Rhodes, Tucson*	.974	92	210	13	6	4
Ritchie, Phoenix*	.972	41	67	2	2	0
Rodriguez, Albuquerque*	.947	47	65	6	4	0
Rohde, Colorado Springs	1.000	5	11	0	0	0
Rose, Edmonton	1.000	3	3	1	0	0
Salmon, Edmonton	.988	110	231	14	3	2
Sheaffer, Portland	1.000	18	16	0	0	0
Sherman, Las Vegas*	.995	68	171	14	1	6
Simms, Tucson	.963	73	102	2	4	0
Smiley, Phoenix*	.958	12	21	2	1	0
Staton, Las Vegas	.982	45	46	9	1	3
Stephenson, Las Vegas*	.980	56	92	4	2	0
Taylor, 21 L.V.-3 Cal.	.962	24	50	0	2	0
Tinsley, Colorado Springs	.977	24	42	1	1	0
Turner, Calgary	.986	44	60	9	1	0
Van Burkleo, Edmonton*	1.000	47	56	3	0	0
Vatcher, Las Vegas	.970	96	178	13	6	3
Velasquez, Las Vegas	.938	10	15	0	1	0
Wasinger, Edmonton	1.000	4	9	2	0	2
Wetherby, Calgary*	.981	64	156	3	3	1
Williams, Edmonton	.99074	139	313	8	3	1
Williams, Calgary	.972	76	170	4	5	0
Wood, Phoenix*	.983	98	173	3	3	0
Yelding, 40 Tuc.-7 Van.	.960	47	95	1	4	0
Young, Albuquerque	1.000	3	3	0	0	0
Young, Tucson	.980	20	43	5	1	4

CATCHERS

Player, Team	Pct.	G	PO	A	E	DP	PB
Baar, Albuquerque	.978	19	116	19	3	1	1
Bailey, Phoenix	.956	15	80	6	4	0	2
Basso, Las Vegas	.990	19	93	11	1	2	2
Bilardello, Las Vegas	1.000	3	9	2	0	0	0
Billmeyer, Edmonton	.980	9	45	4	1	1	0
Brito, Tacoma	.976	18	65	16	2	0	1
Brown, Albuquerque	1.000	2	10	0	0	0	1
Campbell, Tacoma	.991	25	102	9	1	1	2
Cockrell, Colorado Springs	1.000	11	49	9	2	2	3
Colbert, Phoenix	1.000	5	26	4	0	0	2
Decker, Phoenix	.993	112	626	63	5	10	10
Gonzales, Edmonton	.990	58	275	37	3	4	6
Hall, Vancouver	.972	12	32	3	1	0	2
Haselman, Calgary	.983	43	205	21	4	0	7
Heath, Tacoma	.996	61	215	26	1	3	1
Heffernan, Calgary	.979	10	38	8	1	0	4
Hemond, Tacoma	1.000	4	27	2	0	2	1
Higgins, Las Vegas	1.000	7	16	6	0	0	1
Howard, Calgary	.975	91	383	53	11	2	19
Johnson, Colorado Springs	.970	68	240	23	8	7	9
Lampkin, Las Vegas	.979	97	506	64	12	11	7
Levis, Colorado Springs	.991	86	375	47	4	5	0
Lyons, Tucson	.990	37	276	29	3	1	4
Massarelli, Tucson	.986	14	67	5	1	1	1
McNamara, Phoenix	1.000	22	137	11	0	0	0
Mercedes, Tacoma	.984	85	476	62	9	10	10
Merullo, Vancouver	.959	9	45	2	2	0	1
Molina, Tacoma	1.000	10	52	4	0	0	3
Mota, Colorado Springs	.963	8	44	8	2	1	0
Musolino, Edmonton	.985	41	242	19	4	6	5
Orton, Edmonton	.993	44	265	31	2	2	1
Pappas, Vancouver	.951	37	181	12	10	0	3
Parks, Portland	.986	63	377	53	6	4	3
Piazza, Albuquerque	.988	79	463	43	6	4	5
Santiago, Las Vegas	1.000	3	13	2	0	0	1
Santovenia, Vancouver	.974	87	439	57	13	9	8
SHEAFFER, Portland	.994	89	567	62	4	3	9
Siwa, Portland	1.000	1	13	0	0	0	0
Taubensee, Tucson	.972	20	127	10	4	0	2
Tejero, Edmonton	.978	8	40	4	1	0	0
Tucker, Tucson	.991	83	517	56	5	6	9
Wakamatsu, Albuquerque	.987	55	264	41	4	4	4
Walters, Las Vegas	.974	35	200	23	6	3	2

Player, Team	Pct.	G	PO	A	E	DP
Abbott, Portland	1.000	7	4	6	0	0
Acker, Calgary	1.000	2	1	0	0	0
Agosto, Calgary*	1.000	10	2	6	0	2
Allison, Tacoma*	.818	19	1	8	2	0
Ard, Phoenix	.952	22	6	14	1	2
Arnsberg, Colorado Springs	.818	16	2	7	2	0
Astacio, Albuquerque	.944	24	7	11	1	1
Bair, Edmonton	1.000	7	2	6	0	0
Banks, Portland	.929	11	7	6	1	0
Barton, Calgary*	1.000	30	4	14	0	1
Beasley, Edmonton	1.000	25	3	4	0	0
Bell, Colorado Springs*	1.000	26	7	23	0	2
Berrios, Albuquerque*	1.000	15	1	3	0	0
Bittiger, Tacoma	1.000	9	0	4	0	0
Black, Phoenix*	1.000	3	0	3	0	0
Blair, Tucson	1.000	21	4	7	0	0
Blyleven, Edmonton	1.000	2	1	2	0	0
Bolton, Vancouver	.926	27	17	33	4	1
Boucher, Colorado Springs*	.969	20	7	24	1	0
Bowen, Tucson	.926	21	9	16	2	1
Briscoe, Tacoma	.833	33	0	10	2	0
Brocail, Las Vegas	.981	29	17	36	1	4
Bross, Las Vegas	.870	49	9	11	3	0
Brown, Calgary*	.978	32	8	37	1	4
Brummett, Phoenix	1.000	3	0	1	0	1
Bruske, Colorado Springs	.667	7	0	2	1	0
Burba, Phoenix	1.000	13	1	8	0	0
Bustillos, Albuquerque	1.000	26	7	8	0	0
Butcher, Edmonton	1.000	26	1	4	0	0
Campbell, Tacoma	1.000	10	0	3	0	0
Capel, Tucson	.900	58	5	13	2	0
Carter, Vancouver	1.000	30	12	16	0	0
Carter, Phoenix	.914	28	9	23	3	1
Casian, Portland*	.950	58	6	13	1	0
Chitren, Tacoma	1.000	29	2	13	0	1
Christopher, Colorado Springs	1.000	49	2	11	0	0
Clark, Colorado Springs	.929	9	5	8	1	3
Corsi, Tacoma	1.000	26	4	5	0	0
Cron, Vancouver	1.000	1	1	0	0	0
Daal, Albuquerque*	1.000	12	0	2	0	0
Davis, Las Vegas	.929	33	4	9	1	0
DeLucia, Calgary	.727	8	4	4	3	0
Deshaies, Las Vegas*	1.000	18	1	8	0	2
Dipoto, Colorado Springs	.941	50	8	24	2	1
Drahman, Vancouver	.900	48	4	5	1	1
Drees, Calgary*	.952	17	4	16	1	2
Dunne, Vancouver	.913	21	7	14	2	2
Dyer, Portland	1.000	27	8	12	0	2
Eiland, Las Vegas	.895	14	6	11	2	0
Erb, Edmonton	1.000	2	0	1	0	0
Fernandez, Vancouver	.875	4	3	4	1	0
Fortugno, Edmonton*	.929	26	0	13	1	1
Fraser, Edmonton	.923	44	4	8	1	0
Galvez, Albuquerque	1.000	30	5	6	0	0
Garcia, Vancouver	.973	28	14	22	1	1
Gardner, Tucson	.957	20	16	28	2	4
Garrelts, Phoenix	1.000	4	1	0	0	0
Gleaton, Phoenix*	1.000	15	1	3	0	0
Gozzo, Portland	.933	37	9	19	2	1
Grahe, Edmonton	1.000	3	1	3	0	0
Grant, Calgary	1.000	4	2	2	0	1
Grimsley, Tucson	.938	26	8	22	2	1
Gross, Albuquerque	.914	31	12	19	3	0
Gunderson, Calgary*	.846	27	0	11	2	0
Guzman, Tacoma*	1.000	20	1	12	0	1
Hall, Albuquerque*	1.000	12	0	4	0	0
Hansell, Albuquerque	1.000	13	10	9	0	1
Ge. Harris, Las Vegas	1.000	18	1	2	0	0
Gr. Harris, Las Vegas	1.000	2	1	0	0	0
Harris, Tacoma	.929	29	10	18	0	3
Hartgraves, Tucson*	1.000	5	1	0	0	0
Hawkins, Calgary	1.000	24	13	17	0	1
Helton, Tucson*	1.000	2	0	2	0	0
Heredia, Phoenix	1.000	22	5	15	0	2
Hernandez, Las Vegas	1.000	42	3	11	0	2
Hernandez, Vancouver	1.000	9	1	2	0	1
Higgins, Las Vegas	1.000	3	1	2	0	0
Holton, Albuquerque	1.000	29	2	4	0	0
Holzemer, Edmonton*	1.000	17	1	13	0	0
Howard, Vancouver*	.875	20	1	6	1	1
Hudek, Vancouver	.867	39	3	10	2	0
Huisman, Phoenix	.917	9	7	4	1	0
Hurta, Tucson*	1.000	20	0	2	0	1
Ingram, Las Vegas	.000	2	0	0	1	0
James, Albuquerque	1.000	18	1	10	0	2
James, Edmonton*	.875	7	2	5	1	0
Johnson, Portland	.833	53	3	2	1	1
Jones, Calgary	1.000	21	0	6	0	0
Jones, Edmonton	1.000	5	0	1	0	0
Jones, Tucson	1.000	3	0	1	0	0
Juden, Tucson	.882	26	7	23	4	0
Kennedy, Vancouver	1.000	4	0	2	0	0
Kile, Tucson	1.000	9	2	5	0	0
Knudson, Las Vegas	.962	37	16	9	1	0
Kraemer, Edmonton*	1.000	34	0	6	0	0
Kramer, Calgary	.950	27	5	14	1	0
Kramer, Colorado Springs	1.000	38	6	12	0	4
Latter, Tacoma	1.000	5	2	1	0	0
Leskanic, Portland	.800	5	2	2	1	0
Lewis, Edmonton	.923	22	17	19	3	5
Lind, Portland	.923	47	2	10	1	0
Mahomes, Portland	1.000	17	7	13	0	1
Mallicoat, Tucson*	.857	37	1	5	1	0
Martinez, Albuquerque	.857	20	5	7	2	1
Masters, 26 Pho.-13 Cal.	.952	39	8	12	1	1
McAndrew, Albuquerque	.750	5	2	4	2	0
McClellan, Phoenix	1.000	20	1	11	0	0
McCullers, Albuquerque	1.000	29	7	2	0	1
McMurtry, Phoenix	.968	40	11	19	1	3
Merriman, Edmonton	.750	22	4	2	2	1
Millay, Tacoma	1.000	2	0	2	0	1
Mimbs, Albuquerque*	1.000	12	1	7	0	0
Musselman, Tacoma*	1.000	19	1	24	0	2
Mutis, Colorado Springs*	.946	25	11	24	2	6
Myers, Phoenix	1.000	25	0	6	0	0
Neidlinger, Albuquerque	.971	35	14	19	1	1
Nelson, Calgary	1.000	2	0	1	0	0
Newlin, Calgary	.750	30	4	2	2	0
Nichols, Colorado Springs	.929	9	6	7	1	1
Nichting, Albuquerque	.818	10	5	4	2	0
Nunez, Calgary	.917	10	7	4	1	0
Oliveras, Phoenix	.941	22	2	14	1	1
Opperman, Albuquerque	.857	6	2	4	1	0
Osteen, Tacoma*	.000	4	0	0	1	0
Otto, Colorado Springs*	1.000	6	3	12	0	1
Pawlowski, Edmonton	.500	20	0	1	1	0
Peek, Tacoma	1.000	57	3	17	0	1
Pena, Phoenix*	.889	33	1	7	1	1
Perry, Las Vegas*	1.000	16	4	4	0	0
Perschke, Vancouver	.931	29	10	17	2	1
Peterson, Las Vegas	.947	21	4	14	1	1
Raczka, Tacoma*	1.000	31	3	11	0	3
Rambo, Phoenix	1.000	20	2	7	0	0
Rapp, Phoenix	.947	39	10	26	2	0
Reed, Phoenix	.833	29	0	5	1	1
Remlinger, Calgary*	.958	21	5	18	1	0
Reynolds, Tucson	.963	25	4	22	1	0
Rice, Calgary	.947	21	7	11	1	0
Ridenour, Edmonton	1.000	5	2	0	0	0
Rogers, Phoenix*	.955	11	6	15	1	0
Roscoe, Colorado Springs	.917	27	11	11	2	1
Sager, Las Vegas	1.000	30	7	3	0	0
Sanders, Las Vegas	.857	14	2	4	1	2
Scheid, 29 Van.-12 Tuc.*	.909	41	7	13	22	0
Schmidt, 13 Cal.-14 Tac.	.917	27	4	7	12	0
Schullstrom, Las Vegas	1.000	1	0	1	0	0
Schwabe, Portland	.917	6	2	9	1	0
Schwarz, Vancouver	.889	23	3	5	1	0
Scott, Calgary	.955	16	10	11	1	0
Scott, Edmonton	1.000	31	0	5	0	1
Scott, Las Vegas	1.000	24	1	2	0	0
Searage, Edmonton*	.846	34	7	4	2	1
Searcy, Albuquerque*	1.000	12	2	9	0	0
Seminara, Las Vegas	.952	13	10	10	1	0
Shaw, Colorado Springs	.971	25	13	20	1	2
Shinall, Albuquerque	.920	64	5	17	2	0
Simon, Tucson	.600	9	1	2	2	0
Slusarski, Tacoma	.875	11	3	4	1	0
T. Smith, Tacoma	1.000	2	1	2	0	0
Smith, Colorado Springs	.900	19	5	4	1	1
Soff, Edmonton	.891	24	9	32	5	3
Soper, Colorado Springs	1.000	10	0	2	0	0
Springer, Albuquerque	1.000	11	3	11	0	0
Stephens, Vancouver	1.000	32	10	13	0	1
Taylor, Phoenix	.667	20	0	2	1	0
Trombley, Portland	.886	25	15	16	4	0
Tsamis, Portland*	.932	39	9	32	3	3
Turner, Tucson	.850	63	6	11	3	0
Vande Berg, Calgary*	1.000	31	6	7	0	1
Van Poppel, Tacoma	1.000	9	2	3	0	0
Veres, Tucson	.833	29	5	5	2	0
Veres, Phoenix	1.000	12	1	1	0	0
Vidmar, Edmonton	.933	16	6	8	1	0
Walker, Calgary	.818	12	2	7	2	0
Wall, Tucson	1.000	2	1	0	0	0
Walton, Tacoma	1.000	35	3	11	0	2
Wapnick, Vancouver	1.000	39	10	4	0	1
Wassenaar, Portland	1.000	60	6	13	0	0
Wayne, Portland*	1.000	14	0	2	0	0
Weber, Tacoma	1.000	52	5	19	0	2
Wernig, Las Vegas*	.500	17	0	1	1	0
West, Portland*	1.000	19	5	11	0	0
Wickander, Colorado Springs*	.000	8	0	0	1	0
Wilkins, Las Vegas	1.000	8	1	0	0	0
Wilkins, Albuquerque	.000	46	6	10	0	2
Wilkinson, Tacoma*	1.000	8	2	1	0	0
Williams, Tucson	1.000	12	4	8	0	0
Windes, Tucson*	1.000	20	6	8	0	3
Wood, Las Vegas	.000	7	0	1	0	0
Woodson, Calgary	1.000	10	0	1	0	0

Player, Team	Pct.	G	PO	A	E	DP		Player, Team	Pct.	G	PO	A	E	DP
Worrell, Las Vegas	1.000	10	7	10	0	0		Zancanaro, Tacoma*	.909	23	5	15	2	1
York, Las Vegas	.882	19	7	8	2	0		Zappelli, Edmonton	.867	10	3	10	2	2
YOUNG, Edmonton*	1.000	28	11	23	0	1		Zavaras, Calgary	1.000	4	1	1	0	0

The following players did not have any fielding statistics at the positions indicated or appeared only as a designated hitter, pinch-hitter or pinch-runner: Angotti, ph; Basso, p; Bere, p; Bilardello, 3b; Bowie, p; Brosnan, p; Brundage, 1b; Bryand, p; Coachman, of; Costello, p; W. Davis, ph; Diaz, of; Distefano, c; Faries, of; Fisher, p; J. Garcia, 2b; Gonzales, p; Hale, p; J. Hall, 1b; Heffernan, of; Hill, p; Hughes, p; D. Johnson, p; Klonoski, p; Lennon, 3b; Dan. Lewis, of; J. Lewis, p; Lopez, of; Magnusson, pr; Neel, p; Ortiz, p; Orton, 3b; C. Parker, p; Ritchie, p; Schooler, p; Scudder, p; J. Smith, p; Traxler, p; Valdez, p; Vanderweele, p; Vesling, p; Wasinger, p; Wells, p; Witmeyer, p.

LEAGUE CHAMPIONS

Year	Team	Pct.
1903 — Los Angeles		.630
1904 — Tacoma		.589
	Tacoma§	.571
	Los Angeles§	.571
1905 — Tacoma		.583
	Los Angeles*	.604
1906 — Portland		.657
1907 — Los Angeles		.608
1908 — Los Angeles		.585
1909 — San Francisco		.623
1910 — Portland		.567
1911 — Portland		.589
1912 — Oakland		.591
1913 — Portland		.559
1914 — Portland		.574
1915 — San Francisco		.570
1916 — Los Angeles		.601
1917 — San Francisco		.561
1918 — Vernon		.569
	Los Angeles (2nd) x	.548
1919 — Vernon		.613
1920 — Vernon		.556
1921 — Los Angeles		.574
1922 — San Francisco		.638
1923 — San Francisco		.617
1924 — Seattle		.545
1925 — San Francisco		.643
1926 — Los Angeles		.599
1927 — Oakland		.615
1928 — San Francisco*		.630
	Sacramento§§	.626
	San Francisco§§	.626
1929 — Mission		.643
	Hollywood*	.592
1930 — Los Angeles		.576
	Hollywood*	.650
1931 — Hollywood		.626
	San Francisco*	.608
1932 — Portland		.587
1933 — Los Angeles		.610
1934 — Los Angeles z		.786
	Los Angeles z	.689
1935 — Los Angeles		.648
	San Francisco*	.608
1936 — Portland‡		.549
1937 — Sacramento		.573

Year	Team	Pct.
	San Diego (3rd)†	.545
1938 — Los Angeles		.590
	Sacramento (3rd)†	.537
1939 — Seattle		.589
	Sacramento (4th)†	.500
1940 — Seattle‡		.629
1941 — Seattle‡		.598
1942 — Sacramento		.590
	Seattle (3rd)†	.539
1943 — Los Angeles		.710
	S. Francisco (2nd)†	.574
1944 — Los Angeles		.586
	S. Francisco (3rd)†	.509
1945 — Portland		.622
	S. Francisco (4th)†	.525
1946 — San Francisco‡		.628
1947 — Los Angeles††		.567
1948 — Oakland‡		.606
1949 — Hollywood‡		.583
1950 — Oakland		.590
1951 — Seattle‡		.593
1952 — Hollywood		.606
1953 — Hollywood		.589
1954 — San Diego y		.604
1955 — Seattle		.552
1956 — Los Angeles		.637
1957 — San Francisco		.601
1958 — Phoenix		.578
1959 — Salt Lake City		.552
1960 — Spokane		.601
1961 — Tacoma		.630
1962 — San Diego		.604
1963 — Spokane		.620
	Oklahoma City a	.632
1964 — Arkansas		.609
	San Diego a	.576
1965 — Oklahoma City a		.628
	Portland	.547
1966 — Seattle a		.561
	Tulsa	.578
1967 — San Diego a		.574
	Spokane	.541
1968 — Tulsa a		.642
	Spokane	.586
1969 — Tacoma a		.589
	Eugene	.603

Year	Team	Pct.
1970 — Spokane a		.644
	Hawaii	.671
1971 — Salt Lake City		.534
	Tacoma	.545
1972 — Albuquerque		.622
	Eugene	.534
1973 — Tucson		.583
	Spokane a	.563
1974 — Spokane a		.549
	Albuquerque	.535
1975 — Salt Lake City		.556
	Hawaii a	.611
1976 — Salt Lake City		.625
	Hawaii a	.531
1977 — Phoenix a		.579
	Hawaii	.541
1978 — Tacoma b		.584
	Albuquerque b	.557
1979 — Albuquerque		.581
	Salt Lake City c	.541
1980 — Albuquerque		.578
	Hawaii	.539
1981 — Albuquerque*		.712
	Tacoma	.561
1982 — Albuquerque*		.594
	Spokane	.545
1983 — Albuquerque		.594
	Portland*	.528
1984 — Hawaii		.621
	Edmonton*	.486
1985 — Vancouver*		.522
	Phoenix	.563
1986 — Vancouver		.616
	Las Vegas*	.563
1987 — Calgary		.596
	Albuquerque*	.542
1988 — Vancouver		.599
	Las Vegas*	.529
1989 — Albuquerque		.563
	Vancouver*	.514
1990 — Albuquerque*		.641
	Edmonton	.553
1991 — Albuquerque		.580
	Tucson*	.564
1992 — Colorado Springs*		.596
	Portland	.576

*Won split-season playoff. †Won four-team playoff. ‡Won pennant and four-team playoff. §Tied for second-half title with Tacoma winning playoff. §§Tied for second-half title, with Sacramento winning playoff. ††Ended regular season in tie with San Francisco and won one-game playoff for pennant, then won four-club playoff. xWon playoff from first-place Vernon and awarded championship. yDefeated Hollywood in one-game playoff for pennant. zWon both halves, no playoff. aLeague was divided into Northern, Southern divisions in 1963, 1969-70-71, and Eastern, Western divisions in 1964 through 1968 and 1972 through 1977, won two-team playoff. bLeague divided into Eastern and Western divisions, Tacoma and Albuquerque declared co-champions following cancellation of four-team playoff due to continuing rain and wet grounds. cWon second-half title and defeated Hawaii in four-team playoff.

PACIFIC COAST LEAGUE

CLASS AAA

PACIFIC COAST LEAGUE

EASTERN LEAGUE

FINAL STANDINGS

Team	C.A.	Bing.	Har.	Alb.	Lon.	Read.	Hag.	N.B.	W	L	T	Pct.	GB
Canton-Akron (Indians)	....	7	12	9	14	17	8	13	80	58	0	.580	....
Binghamton (Mets)	13	...	9	8	11	12	16	10	79	59	1	.572	1
Harrisburg (Expos)	6	10	....	12	8	14	11	17	78	59	0	.569	1½
Albany (Yankees)	11	12	8	...	11	9	10	10	71	68	0	.511	9½
London (Tigers)	6	8	12	9	....	9	11	12	67	70	1	.489	12½
Reading (Phillies)	3	8	6	11	9	....	12	12	61	77	0	.442	19
Hagerstown (Orioles)	12	4	9	9	9	8	...	8	59	80	0	.424	21½
New Britain (Red Sox)	7	10	3	10	8	8	12	....	58	82	0	.414	23

London club represented London, Ontario, Can.

Major league affiliations in parentheses.

Playoffs—Binghamton defeated Harrisburg, three games to one; Canton-Akron defeated Albany, three games to one; Binghamton defeated Canton-Akron, three games to two, to win league championship.

Regular-season attendance—Albany, 145,936; Binghamton, 259,183; Canton-Akron, 194,362; Hagerstown, 130,331; Harrisburg, 209,159; London, 112,913; New Britain, 125,393; Reading, 287,078. Total—1,464,355. Playoffs (12 games)—31,664. Class AA All-Star Game at Charlotte, N.C.—4,009.

Managers—Albany, Dan Radison; Binghamton, Steve Swisher; Canton-Akron, Brian Graham; Hagerstown, Don Buford; Harrisburg, Mike Quade; London, Mark DeJohn; New Britain, Jim Pankovits; Reading, Don McCormack.

All-Star team: 1B—Ivan Cruz, London; 2B—Hector Vargas, Albany; 3B—Russ Davis, Albany; SS—Mike Lansing, Harrisburg; OF—Ken Ramos, Canton-Akron; Mark Smith, Hagerstown; Tracy Sanders, Canton-Akron; C—Mike Lieberthal, Reading; DH—Greg Sparks, London; RHP—Bobby Jones, Binghamton; LHP—Ed Riley, New Britain; Relief Pitcher—Len Picota, Harrisburg; Most Valuable Player—Russ Davis, Albany; Pitcher of the Year—Bobby Jones, Binghamton; Manager of the Year—Steve Swisher, Binghamton.

BATTING

TEAM

Team	Avg.	G	AB	R	OR	H	TB	2B	3B	HR	RBI	SH	SF	HP	BB	Int. BB	SO	SB	CS	LOB
Canton-Akron	.273	138	4536	630	559	1238	1716	188	31	76	566	42	41	38	514	27	820	111	74	999
Albany	.262	139	4524	612	555	1184	1749	233	40	84	561	28	40	46	409	11	802	112	65	910
London	.260	138	4547	646	614	1184	1710	206	19	94	582	25	36	29	554	11	927	151	76	992
Hagerstown	.252	139	4558	519	652	1150	1520	208	33	32	459	27	35	34	376	25	774	183	82	898
Reading	.251	138	4505	531	601	1133	1574	193	34	60	484	48	27	52	399	19	738	98	49	934
Harrisburg	.246	137	4388	539	470	1078	1521	181	35	64	476	32	38	59	406	18	808	157	50	900
Binghamton	.245	139	4501	565	488	1103	1597	191	36	77	492	44	36	34	461	21	920	87	63	956
New Britain	.228	140	4427	501	604	1009	1432	184	28	61	449	47	26	46	457	26	949	71	77	891

INDIVIDUAL

(Leading qualifiers for batting championship—378 or more plate appearances)

*Bats lefthanded.   †Switch-hitter.

Player, Team	Avg.	G	AB	R	H	TB	2B	3B	HR	RBI	SH	SF	HP	BB	Int. BB	SO	SB	CS
Ramos, Ken, Canton-Akron*	.339	125	442	93	150	198	23	5	5	42	5	1	0	82	6	37	14	11
Sparks, Don, Albany	.313	134	505	64	158	235	31	2	14	72	0	8	2	30	2	71	2	2
Vargas, Hector, Albany	.300	116	417	64	125	172	26	9	1	41	2	0	2	48	0	73	25	13
Reimink, Rob, London†	.296	118	412	56	122	157	24	1	3	46	0	2	1	66	4	77	7	6
Smith, Mark, Hagerstown	.288	128	472	51	136	192	32	6	4	62	0	6	4	45	5	55	15	5
Davis, Russ, Albany	.285	132	491	77	140	237	23	4	22	71	0	5	7	49	0	93	3	3
Tinsley, Lee, Canton-Akron†	.287	96	349	65	100	140	9	8	5	38	5	2	2	42	4	82	18	5
Kingwood, Tyrone, London	.284	108	377	57	107	145	15	1	7	47	0	3	1	28	1	63	22	8
Katzaroff, Rob, Binghamton*	.282	119	450	65	127	159	18	7	0	29	6	4	5	40	1	45	24	18
Cairo, Sergio, Hagerstown	.281	121	409	43	115	142	13	4	2	46	3	5	1	33	1	53	5	8
Obando, Sherman, Albany	.281	109	381	71	107	183	19	3	17	56	2	4	8	32	1	67	3	1

Departmental leaders: G—Butterfield, 138; AB—Cruz, 524; R—Ramos, 93; H—D. Sparks, 158; TB—Davis, 237; 2B—Smith, 32; 3B—Howard, Vargas, 9; HR—Sparks, 25; RBI—Cruz, 104; SH—DeKneef, 12; SF—Howard, 9; HP—Hirtensteiner, 13; BB—Frazier, 95; IBB—Blosser, 9; SO—Butterfield, 126; SB—Frazier, 58; CS—Frazier, 23.

(All players—listed alphabetically)

Player, Team	Avg.	G	AB	R	H	TB	2B	3B	HR	RBI	SH	SF	HP	BB	Int. BB	SO	SB	CS
Adamson, Joel, Reading*	.143	10	7	0	1	1	0	0	0	1	3	0	0	0	0	1	0	0
Alborano, Pete, Reading*	.232	52	142	16	33	47	6	1	2	9	0	1	1	8	1	26	2	1
Alexander, Manny, Hagerstown	.259	127	499	69	129	174	23	8	2	41	4	4	6	25	0	62	43	12
Allen, Ron, Reading	.333	3	3	0	1	1	0	0	0	0	0	0	0	0	0	0	0	0
Allison, Tom, Binghamton†	.248	59	117	19	29	39	4	0	2	14	3	1	1	18	0	37	1	2
Alvarez, Tavo, Harrisburg	.000	7	3	0	0	0	0	0	0	0	2	0	0	0	0	1	0	0
Ausmus, Brad, Albany	.167	5	18	0	3	5	0	0	1	0	0	0	2	0	0	3	2	1
Barfield, Jesse, Albany	.375	2	8	2	3	6	0	0	1	2	0	0	0	1	0	1	0	0
Barnwell, Richard, Albany	.260	123	434	80	113	152	26	5	1	31	4	3	11	48	1	102	42	18
Beams, Mike, New Britain	.221	87	262	34	58	107	15	2	10	44	4	1	7	22	1	65	2	4
Bethea, Scott, New Britain*	.236	99	313	39	74	80	6	0	0	16	4	2	2	51	0	37	5	11
Bieser, Steve, Reading†	.273	33	139	20	38	51	5	4	0	8	4	0	4	6	0	25	8	3
Billmeyer, Mick, Hagerstown*	.162	16	37	2	6	7	1	0	0	3	0	0	0	2	0	9	0	0
Blackwell, Juan, Albany	.281	15	32	2	9	9	0	0	0	5	0	0	0	1	0	13	0	0
Blosser, Greg, New Britain*	.242	129	434	59	105	202	23	4	22	71	0	3	1	64	9	122	0	2
Bochtler, Doug, Harrisburg	.000	13	2	0	0	0	0	0	0	0	2	0	0	0	0	2	0	0
Brady, Pat, Reading*	.262	67	233	40	61	94	10	1	7	44	0	1	2	37	2	39	5	1

Player, Team	Avg.	G	AB	R	H	TB	2B	3B	HR	RBI	SH	SF	HP	BB	Int. BB	SO	SB	CS
Brewer, Billy, Harrisburg*	.000	20	1	0	0	0	0	0	0	0	0	0	0	0	0	0	0	0
Brito, Mario, Harrisburg	.000	46	1	1	0	0	0	0	0	0	1	0	1	0	0	0	0	0
Buckley, Travis, Harrisburg	.150	26	20	1	3	3	0	0	0	0	0	0	0	0	0	5	0	0
Buford, Damon, Hagerstown	.239	101	373	53	89	115	17	3	1	30	7	3	1	42	0	62	41	12
Bushing, Chris, Reading	.250	22	4	1	1	1	0	0	0	0	1	0	0	0	0	2	0	0
Butterfield, Chris, Binghamton†	.224	138	483	59	108	176	20	3	14	51	4	3	3	57	8	126	9	4
Byrd, Jim, New Britain	.222	20	63	5	14	19	1	2	0	6	0	0	1	3	0	13	2	3
Cabrera, Basilio, London	.209	36	86	8	18	21	0	0	1	3	2	0	0	10	0	27	2	1
Cairo, Sergio, Hagerstown	.281	121	409	43	115	142	13	4	2	46	3	5	1	33	1	53	5	8
Canale, George, Canton-Akron*	.304	54	194	47	59	116	10	1	15	49	0	1	1	30	1	37	2	1
Carey, Paul, Hagerstown*	.270	48	163	17	44	64	8	0	4	18	0	1	2	15	5	37	3	2
Carpenter, Bubba, Albany*	.231	60	221	24	51	84	11	5	4	31	0	1	2	25	0	41	2	3
Carter, Andy, Reading*	.000	7	3	0	0	0	0	0	0	0	0	0	0	0	0	0	0	0
Chapman, Mark, Harrisburg	.000	34	0	0	0	0	0	0	0	0	0	0	1	0	0	0	0	0
Chick, Bruce, New Britain	.220	128	436	52	96	142	19	0	9	51	3	5	2	28	3	122	8	5
Colombino, Carlo, Canton-Akron	.258	87	306	33	79	111	14	0	6	38	2	1	6	25	0	37	1	8
Cooper, Craig, Canton-Akron	.151	23	86	5	13	21	5	0	1	8	0	1	2	9	0	19	0	0
Cornelius, Brian, London*	.260	103	300	34	78	118	14	4	6	39	2	3	0	23	1	63	1	7
Cornelius, Reid, Harrisburg	.000	4	1	0	0	0	0	0	0	0	0	0	0	0	0	0	0	0
Crowley, Terry, Canton-Akron†	.264	76	242	15	64	70	6	0	0	18	5	2	0	9	1	31	4	4
Cruz, Ivan, London*	.273	134	524	71	143	212	25	1	14	104	0	6	4	37	1	102	1	1
Davis, Russ, Albany	.285	132	491	77	140	237	23	4	22	71	0	5	7	49	0	93	3	3
DeButch, Mike, London	.267	95	318	64	85	107	11	1	3	25	3	3	3	53	0	44	16	10
DeKneef, Mike, New Britain	.227	118	409	51	93	122	10	5	3	33	12	2	3	27	0	61	10	13
Dellicarri, Joe, Binghamton	.250	109	328	32	82	103	11	2	2	29	2	1	6	33	1	52	1	5
Demus, Joe, New Britain†	.194	23	62	5	12	15	0	0	1	3	1	0	0	6	1	15	0	0
Devarez, Cesar, Hagerstown	.226	110	319	20	72	88	8	1	2	32	2	2	6	17	0	49	2	5
Dixon, Colin, New Britain	.211	83	266	24	56	69	8	1	1	26	1	1	3	15	1	62	1	0
Dorn, Chris, Binghamton	.000	35	2	0	0	0	0	0	0	0	0	0	0	0	0	1	0	0
Dostal, Bruce, Reading*	.238	33	122	19	29	40	3	1	2	6	0	1	0	17	2	20	9	4
Douma, Todd, Binghamton*	.143	25	14	0	2	2	0	0	0	1	0	0	1	0	0	3	0	0
Dziadkowiec, Andy, Binghamton*	.237	25	76	5	18	22	2	1	0	9	0	0	0	4	0	17	0	0
Eenhoorn, Robert, Albany	.235	60	196	24	46	64	11	2	1	23	3	3	1	10	1	17	2	1
Eiterman, Tom, Canton-Akron	.227	75	181	22	41	52	6	1	1	16	1	5	1	18	1	29	0	2
Elli, Rocky, Reading*	.000	12	6	0	0	0	0	0	0	0	1	0	0	1	0	3	0	0
Epley, Daren, Canton-Akron*	.327	80	294	42	96	123	19	1	2	58	0	7	2	37	4	57	6	4
Escobar, John, Reading	.237	96	304	30	72	97	14	1	3	28	3	0	1	19	1	61	1	2
Fermin, Carlos, London	.150	14	40	3	6	6	0	0	0	3	0	4	0	0	1	10	0	2
Ferretti, Sam, Hagerstown	.257	81	210	27	54	68	9	1	1	17	1	0	4	13	0	35	2	7
Fletcher, Paul, Reading	.100	22	10	1	1	1	0	0	0	0	0	0	0	1	0	6	0	0
Flores, Miguel, Canton-Akron	.272	126	456	45	124	155	20	4	1	43	3	5	5	35	3	39	25	11
Fordyce, Brook, New Britain	.278	118	425	59	118	181	30	0	11	61	3	6	4	37	1	78	1	2
Frazier, Lou, London†	.252	129	477	85	120	142	16	3	0	34	2	2	0	95	1	107	58	23
Fulton, Greg, Harrisburg†	.249	50	177	13	44	66	7	0	5	17	0	1	3	15	1	34	2	1
Gardella, Mike, 15 Alb.-33 C.A.*	.000	48	1	0	0	0	0	0	0	0	0	0	0	0	0	2	0	0
Giles, Brian, Canton-Akron*	.216	23	74	6	16	20	4	0	0	3	0	0	0	10	1	10	3	1
Gillette, Mike, London	.179	71	195	23	35	49	5	0	3	17	2	2	3	23	0	61	1	0
Goedhart, Darrell, Reading	.267	16	15	1	4	4	0	0	0	1	0	0	0	0	0	4	0	0
Gomez, Chris, London	.268	64	220	20	59	79	13	2	1	19	0	3	0	20	0	34	1	3
Graham, Greg, New Britain†	.225	104	347	32	78	86	6	1	0	19	5	1	3	30	1	62	9	10
Green, Tyler, Reading	.250	12	4	1	1	1	0	0	0	1	2	0	0	0	0	0	0	0
Harriger, Denny, Binghamton	.000	11	1	0	0	0	0	0	0	0	0	0	0	0	0	1	0	0
Hatteberg, Scott, New Britain*	.232	103	297	28	69	89	13	2	1	30	1	3	2	41	2	49	1	3
Hecht, Steve, Harrisburg*	.257	100	269	46	69	95	13	5	1	17	8	0	5	31	0	35	17	7
Hernandez, Kiki, Albany	.280	99	328	46	92	122	18	0	4	40	2	3	3	38	1	45	0	0
Hernandez, Jose, Canton-Akron.	.255	130	404	56	103	136	16	4	3	46	3	5	1	37	0	108	7	2
Hill, Eric, Reading	.286	25	14	0	4	6	2	0	0	3	1	0	0	2	0	6	0	0
Hill, Glenallen, Canton-Akron	.111	3	9	1	1	2	1	0	0	1	0	0	0	3	0	4	0	0
Hines, Tim, Harrisburg*	.163	18	49	5	8	12	1	0	1	8	0	1	0	2	0	17	1	0
Hirtensteiner, Rick, Harrisburg*	.263	127	449	68	118	161	18	5	5	50	2	6	13	33	3	95	18	4
Hoffner, Jamie, Binghamton*	.271	72	181	22	49	80	13	0	6	31	0	2	1	10	0	42	0	0
Hoiles, Chris, Hagerstown	.458	7	24	7	11	15	1	0	1	5	0	0	0	2	0	5	0	0
Holland, Tim, Hagerstown	.236	86	263	29	62	80	9	3	1	22	1	2	0	15	0	63	8	3
Horne, Tyrone, Harrisburg*	1.000	1	1	0	1	1	0	0	0	0	0	0	0	0	0	0	0	0
Horowitz, Ed, Harrisburg	.226	11	31	1	7	8	1	0	0	2	0	0	0	0	0	2	0	0
Howard, Tim, Binghamton*	.273	130	505	68	138	191	20	9	5	77	1	9	3	40	3	54	12	6
Hunter, Bert, Binghamton†	.236	117	407	61	96	141	19	4	6	35	10	2	2	39	0	93	16	3
Hurst, Jody, London	.316	76	269	48	85	139	17	2	11	53	0	4	3	38	1	58	17	3
Hyde, Mickey, Reading	.263	73	236	23	62	81	12	2	1	27	4	2	5	13	1	30	1	1
Jackson, Jeff, Reading	.185	36	108	12	20	25	1	2	0	6	0	0	4	12	0	34	9	4
Johnson, Chris, Harrisburg	.154	28	13	0	2	2	0	0	0	0	1	0	0	0	0	6	0	0
Johnstone, John, Binghamton	.000	24	10	0	0	0	0	0	0	0	5	0	0	0	0	4	0	0
Jones, Bobby, Binghamton	.067	24	15	1	1	1	0	0	0	0	0	0	0	0	0	6	0	0
Katzaroff, Rob, Binghamton*	.282	119	450	65	127	159	18	7	0	29	6	4	5	40	1	45	24	18
Kelly, Pat, Albany	.000	2	6	1	0	0	0	0	0	0	0	0	0	2	0	4	0	0
King, Jason, Binghamton†	.143	10	28	2	4	6	2	0	0	3	2	0	0	2	0	4	1	0
Kingwood, Tyrone, London	.284	108	377	57	107	145	15	1	7	47	0	3	3	28	1	63	22	8
Knoblauh, Jay, Albany	.237	68	236	29	56	91	7	2	8	39	3	3	3	20	2	36	6	7
Kosco, Bryn, Harrisburg†	.229	106	341	35	78	110	17	0	5	41	1	5	1	31	2	75	2	0
Laker, Tim, Harrisburg	.242	117	409	55	99	169	19	3	15	68	0	5	5	39	2	89	3	1
Lane, Nolan, Canton-Akron	.277	15	47	6	13	22	3	0	2	5	0	1	1	7	0	12	4	1
Lansing, Mike, Harrisburg	.280	128	483	66	135	185	20	6	6	54	1	3	4	52	3	64	46	9
Lehman, Mike, Hagerstown	.135	14	37	3	5	7	2	0	0	2	0	0	1	3	0	2	0	0
Lieberthal, Mike, Reading	.285	86	309	30	88	112	16	1	2	37	1	4	10	19	0	26	4	1
Limbach, Chris, Reading*	.000	53	3	0	0	0	0	0	0	0	0	0	0	0	0	1	0	0
Livesey, Jeff, Albany	.190	18	42	1	8	11	3	0	0	5	2	0	0	6	0	13	0	0
Lockett, Ron, Reading*	.228	116	400	42	91	127	17	2	5	36	1	1	2	17	1	91	12	4
Lofton, Rod, Hagerstown	.250	50	172	17	43	50	7	0	0	3	0	2	7	22	0	22	11	6
Lopez, Luis, Canton-Akron	.256	20	82	4	21	22	1	0	0	7	0	0	0	3	0	8	1	0
Malinoski, Chris, Harrisburg	.216	32	88	9	19	20	1	0	0	10	1	2	4	15	0	21	2	0
Marchok, Chris, Harrisburg*	.000	43	3	0	0	0	0	0	0	0	0	0	0	0	0	2	0	0
Martin, Chris, Harrisburg	.227	125	383	39	87	126	22	1	5	31	1	3	2	49	1	67	8	6
Martin, Steve, Hagerstown	.164	21	55	4	9	12	3	0	0	2	3	0	1	4	0	14	2	2
Martinez, Jose, Binghamton	.000	9	3	0	0	0	0	0	0	0	0	0	0	0	0	2	0	0

Player, Team	Avg.	G	AB	R	H	TB	2B	3B	HR	RBI	SH	SF	HP	BB	Int. BB	SO	SB	CS
Mathile, Mike, Harrisburg	.133	26	15	1	2	3	1	0	0	2	0	0	0	0	0	1	0	0
Mayo, Todd, Harrisburg*	.083	5	12	1	1	1	0	0	0	0	0	0	0	2	0	4	0	0
McDonald, Chad, Harrisburg	.197	64	188	18	37	56	9	2	2	18	0	2	3	17	0	43	1	1
McDougal, Julius, Reading†	.282	13	39	2	11	13	2	0	0	2	1	0	0	3	0	12	0	1
McNeely, Jeff, New Britain	.218	85	261	30	57	79	8	4	2	11	4	0	2	26	0	78	10	5
Meadows, Scott, Hagerstown	.317	45	164	25	52	66	4	2	2	14	0	0	0	21	0	32	2	2
Mendenhall, Kirk, London	.240	105	362	54	87	120	17	2	4	36	4	2	4	52	0	61	9	7
Miller, Brent, Hagerstown*	.259	125	440	47	114	156	28	1	4	51	0	5	0	23	8	74	5	3
Mota, Carlos, Canton-Akron	.210	59	181	14	38	49	8	0	1	6	2	0	1	10	0	46	3	2
Mouton, Lyle, Albany	.215	64	214	25	46	68	12	2	2	27	0	1	1	24	2	55	1	1
Myers, Chris, Harrisburg*	.000	19	6	0	0	0	0	0	0	0	0	0	0	0	0	3	0	0
Neitzel, R.A., Reading*	.188	75	266	31	50	57	7	0	0	18	6	4	2	34	0	45	11	5
Nelson, Jerome, Harrisburg†	.230	63	204	28	47	59	3	3	1	16	4	1	3	22	1	34	10	3
Nixon, Donell, Canton-Akron	.224	12	49	9	11	18	2	1	1	7	0	1	0	4	0	9	5	1
Noriega, Rey, Albany†	.103	22	78	2	8	10	2	0	0	3	0	0	0	5	0	31	1	0
Norris, Bill, New Britain*	.208	122	384	36	80	98	15	0	1	24	5	1	4	29	2	83	5	5
Nuneviller, Tom, Reading	.303	47	165	31	50	72	6	2	4	21	2	2	2	14	0	25	3	4
Obando, Sherman, Albany	.281	109	381	71	107	183	19	3	17	56	2	4	8	32	1	67	3	1
Oster, Paul, Albany†	.209	12	43	8	9	10	1	0	0	7	0	1	0	3	0	5	1	1
Parris, Steve, Reading	.111	18	9	2	1	1	0	0	0	0	3	0	1	0	0	3	0	0
Paulsen, Troy, Reading	.234	22	94	9	22	31	6	0	1	7	0	1	0	4	2	20	0	1
Pennye, Darwin, Harrisburg	.273	101	311	38	85	109	9	6	1	24	3	3	0	21	1	51	20	9
Piatt, Doug, Harrisburg*	.000	39	2	0	0	0	0	0	0	0	0	0	0	0	0	1	0	0
Picota, Len, Harrisburg	.000	53	1	0	0	0	0	0	0	0	0	0	0	0	0	0	0	0
Pollack, Chris, Harrisburg*	.125	25	8	0	1	2	1	0	0	0	3	0	1	0	0	2	0	0
Pratt, Todd, Reading	.333	41	132	20	44	70	6	1	6	26	0	0	0	24	0	28	2	0
Pride, Curtis, Binghamton*	.227	118	388	54	88	139	15	3	10	42	0	1	4	47	1	110	14	11
Quintell, John, Albany*	.143	4	7	0	1	1	0	0	0	0	0	0	0	1	0	0	0	0
Ramos, Ken, Canton-Akron*	.339	125	442	93	150	198	23	5	5	42	5	1	0	82	6	37	14	11
Reich, Andy, Binghamton	.000	41	2	0	0	0	0	0	0	0	0	0	0	1	0	1	0	0
Reimink, Rob, London†	.296	118	412	56	122	157	24	1	3	46	0	2	1	66	4	77	7	6
Robertson, Jason, Albany*	.216	55	204	18	44	67	12	1	3	33	2	2	2	10	0	44	9	3
Robertson, Rod, London	.239	64	243	26	58	91	12	0	7	34	4	1	3	15	0	34	13	5
Rodriguez, Carlos, Albany†	.262	112	381	37	100	128	18	2	2	38	5	3	4	29	0	26	3	4
Rodriguez, Ruben, New Britain	.252	39	119	10	30	44	14	0	0	14	4	1	3	3	0	15	1	0
Rogers, Bryan, Binghamton	.000	22	1	0	0	0	0	0	0	0	0	0	0	0	0	0	0	0
Rosado, Ed, Reading†	.310	60	197	23	61	85	9	3	3	26	4	0	3	16	2	21	4	1
Roseboro, Jaime, Harrisburg	.139	25	72	4	10	14	2	1	0	5	0	1	0	2	0	17	0	1
Roth, Greg, Hagerstown*	.146	53	130	13	19	28	6	0	1	11	0	1	1	17	2	40	4	1
Ryan, Ken, New Britain	.000	44	1	0	0	0	0	0	0	0	0	0	0	0	0	0	0	0
Ryan, Sean, Reading†	.268	107	354	29	95	137	19	1	7	57	0	0	0	38	2	49	0	1
Sanchez, Gordon, Albany*	.237	24	59	10	14	20	3	0	1	7	1	0	0	9	1	12	1	1
Sanders, Tracy, Canton-Akron*	.241	114	381	66	92	172	11	3	21	87	4	3	3	77	3	113	3	4
Sarbaugh, Mike, Canton-Akron	.233	38	120	7	28	39	5	0	2	18	3	0	2	8	0	21	1	2
Saunders, Doug, Binghamton	.248	130	435	45	108	143	16	2	5	38	5	4	1	52	0	68	8	12
Sellers, Rick, London*	.267	103	329	38	88	134	17	1	9	51	2	4	2	36	0	67	2	0
Shepherd, Keith, Reading	1.000	4	2	1	2	3	1	0	0	0	0	0	0	1	0	0	0	0
Siddall, Joe, Harrisburg†	.236	95	288	26	68	86	12	0	2	27	1	3	3	29	1	55	4	4
Skinner, Joel, Canton-Akron	.300	8	20	2	6	9	0	0	1	5	0	0	0	0	0	3	0	0
Smith, Mark, Hagerstown	.288	128	472	51	136	192	32	6	4	62	0	6	4	45	5	55	15	5
Sparks, Don, Albany	.313	134	505	64	158	235	31	2	14	72	0	8	2	30	2	71	2	2
Sparks, Greg, London*	.232	106	384	57	89	185	19	1	25	73	0	3	2	57	2	114	1	0
Stinnett, Kelly, Canton-Akron	.284	91	296	37	84	112	10	0	6	32	5	3	4	16	0	43	7	6
Stocker, Kevin, Reading†	.250	62	240	31	60	76	9	2	1	13	3	0	2	22	1	30	17	4
Strickland, Ricky, Albany*	.174	11	23	2	4	6	2	0	0	3	0	1	0	1	0	6	0	0
Sullivan, Mike, Reading	.000	34	0	0	0	0	0	0	0	0	0	0	0	1	0	0	0	0
Tallman, Troy, Hagerstown	.192	13	26	5	5	8	3	0	0	7	1	1	0	5	0	10	0	0
Tatum, Willie, New Britain†	.242	133	446	65	108	162	25	4	7	54	2	2	9	88	4	119	17	11
Taylor, Sam, Reading*	.246	98	349	42	86	144	18	5	10	55	3	4	4	34	1	40	5	6
Thomas, Tim, London	.364	3	11	1	4	5	1	0	0	1	0	1	0	0	0	5	0	0
Thome, Jim, Canton-Akron*	.336	30	107	16	36	52	9	2	1	14	0	0	1	24	3	30	0	2
Thoutsis, Paul, New Britain*	.242	108	327	31	79	118	21	3	4	47	1	4	4	24	2	46	0	5
Tinsley, Lee, Canton-Akron†	.287	96	349	65	100	140	9	8	5	38	5	2	2	42	4	82	18	5
Trevino, Tony, Reading	.228	83	281	32	64	81	10	2	1	21	3	2	7	24	1	40	2	2
Tyler, Brad, Hagerstown*	.223	83	256	41	57	74	9	1	2	21	1	0	2	34	2	45	23	6
Vargas, Hector, Albany*	.300	116	417	64	125	172	26	9	1	41	2	0	2	48	0	73	25	13
Viera, John, Albany*	.249	56	185	24	46	67	8	2	3	26	1	2	0	15	0	40	9	6
Vitko, Joe, Binghamton	.000	26	18	0	0	0	0	0	0	0	1	0	0	0	0	12	0	0
Walker, Larry, Albany	.067	6	15	1	1	1	0	0	0	2	0	0	0	0	0	0	0	0
Walker, Pete, Binghamton	.167	24	6	0	1	1	0	0	0	0	0	0	0	0	0	1	0	0
Waller, Casey, Reading*	.255	91	314	42	80	105	14	3	5	31	1	4	3	31	2	49	5	3
Washington, Kyle, 67 C.A. - 47 Hag.	.280	114	389	42	109	132	13	2	2	41	5	4	7	37	0	70	16	11
Wearing, Melvin, Hagerstown	.258	83	275	27	71	105	15	2	5	46	0	3	2	38	2	72	8	2
Wegmann, Tom, Binghamton	.000	27	5	0	0	0	0	0	0	0	0	0	0	1	0	1	0	0
White, Derrick, Harrisburg	.277	134	495	63	137	199	19	2	13	81	0	2	7	40	3	73	17	3
White, Mike, Binghamton*	.224	62	170	10	38	46	8	0	0	22	1	3	0	9	1	46	0	0
White, Rondell, Harrisburg	.303	21	89	22	27	42	7	1	2	7	0	0	4	6	0	14	6	1
Wiegandt, Scott, Reading*	.000	56	1	0	0	0	0	0	0	0	1	0	0	0	0	1	0	0
Williams, Paul, Hagerstown	.138	14	29	3	4	6	2	0	0	3	0	1	0	6	0	5	0	1
Woods, Tyrone, Harrisburg	.000	14	1	0	0	0	0	0	0	0	0	0	0	0	0	0	0	0
Zinter, Alan, Binghamton†	.223	128	431	63	96	167	13	5	16	50	0	0	4	70	5	117	0	0

The following pitchers, listed alphabetically by club, with games in parentheses, had no plate appearances, primarily through use of designated hitters:

ALBANY—Batchelor, Rich (58); Carper, Mark (20); Gardella, Mike (15); Gogolewski, Doug (6); Greer, Ken (40); Hitchcock, Sterling (24); Hodges, Darren (15); Hoffman, Jeff (35); Holcomb, Scott (36); Hutton, Mark (25); Jean, Domingo (1); Manon, Ramon (8); Munoz, Roberto (22); Nielsen, Jerry (36); Ojala, Kirt (24); Popplewell, Tom (28).

BINGHAMTON—Langbehn, Greg (52); Proctor, Dave (1); Vasquez, Julian (24).

CANTON-AKRON—Allen, Chad (12); Byrd, Paul (24); Charland, Colin (15); Embree, Alan (12); Garcia, Victor (29); Gideon, Brett (19); Kiser, Garland (40); Mlicki, Dave (27); Morgan, Scott (3); Ogea, Chad (7); Otto, Dave (1); Plunk, Eric (9); Smith, Willie (9); Soper, Mike (43); Trice, Walter (32); Turek, Joe (14); Wertz, Bill (57).

HAGERSTOWN—Blumberg, Robert (4); Bumgarner, Jeff (14); Carper, Mark (11); Drummond, Tim (26); Hall, Gardner (11); Hook, Michael (6); Jones, Stacy (11); Miller, Dave (25); Moore, Daryl (5); O'Donoghue, John (17); Pawlowski, John (15); Pennington, Brad (19); Pico, Jeff (14);

Polasek, John (22); Poole, Jim (7); Ricci, Charles (20); Schullstrom, Erik (23); Taylor, Tom (1); Williams, Jeff (36); Williamson, Mark (6); Wood, Brian (21); Yaughn, Kip (18).

HARRISBURG—Corbin, Archie (1); Haynes, Heath (3).

LONDON—August, Don (11); Bergman, Sean (14); Braley, Jeff (64); Coppeta, Greg (19); Corbett, Sherman (35); DeSilva, John (9); Freed, Dan (14); Gakeler, Dan (1); Garcia, Mike (27); Gonzales, Francisco (10); Henry, Jim (15); King, Eric (1); Lumley, Mike (55); Ramos, Jose (16); Rojas, Ricardo (32); Torres, Leonardo (5); Vesling, Don (12); Warren, Brian (26); Willis, Marty (27); Wolf, Steve (21).

NEW BRITAIN—Conroy, Brian (11); Donovan, Bret (1); Finnvold, Gar (25); Florence, Don (58); Glaze, Gettys (2); Livernois, Derek (20); Mosley, Anthony (49); Painter, Gary (20); Riley, Ed (19); Sanders, Alan (36); Sele, Aaron (7); Smith, Tim (27); Uhrhan, Kevin (43).

READING—Agostinelli, Salvatore (1); Borland, Toby (32); Brink, Brad (3); Elliott, Don (6); Gaddy, Bob (12); Greene, Tommy (1); Patterson, Jeff (26); Stevens, Matt (46); Wells, Bob (3); Williams, Mike (3).

GRAND SLAMS—Sanders, G. Sparks, 2 each; Davis, Dixon, Hecht, Norris, Obando, J. Robertson, Waller, 1 each.

AWARDED FIRST BASE ON CATCHER'S INTERFERENCE—Ramos 5 (Tallman 2, Demus, E. Hernandez, Lieberthal); Hirtensteiner 3 (Sellers 2, Gillette); C. Martin (Sellers).

PITCHING

TEAM

Team	ERA	G	CG	ShO	Sv.	IP	H	R	ER	HR	HB	BB	Int. BB	SO	WP	Bk.
Binghamton	3.12	139	22	17	38	1196.0	1103	488	414	62	48	364	6	802	31	7
Harrisburg	3.19	137	12	13	37	1169.1	1092	470	414	54	49	381	21	817	42	7
Canton-Akron	3.51	138	8	13	42	1193.0	1079	559	465	64	46	502	22	873	60	11
Albany	3.57	139	7	12	32	1174.2	1061	555	466	52	45	533	16	873	84	9
New Britain	3.86	140	18	12	30	1192.2	1215	604	511	67	39	411	25	756	59	19
Reading	3.89	138	6	8	39	1181.0	1175	601	510	96	29	416	29	855	61	5
London	3.92	138	13	12	31	1186.0	1221	614	516	82	35	421	32	812	46	9
Hagerstown	3.96	139	17	5	26	1193.1	1133	652	525	71	47	548	7	950	83	26

INDIVIDUAL

(Leading qualifiers for earned-run average leadership—112 or more innings)

*Throws lefthanded.

Pitcher, Team	W	L	Pct.	ERA	G	GS	CG	GF	ShO	Sv.	IP	H	R	ER	HR	HB	BB	Int. BB	SO	WP
Jones, Binghamton	12	4	.750	1.88	24	24	4	0	4	0	158.0	118	40	33	5	8	43	0	143	3
O'Donoghue, Hagerstown*	7	4	.636	2.24	17	16	2	1	0	0	112.1	78	37	28	6	4	40	1	87	7
Riley, New Britain*	10	8	.556	2.45	19	19	1	0	1	0	121.0	108	38	33	7	2	38	1	63	1
Hitchcock, Albany*	6	9	.400	2.58	24	24	2	0	0	0	146.2	116	51	42	6	9	42	0	155	9
Douma, Binghamton*	8	8	.500	2.82	25	20	3	4	1	0	137.0	136	51	43	7	2	43	0	76	2
Fletcher, Reading	9	4	.692	2.83	22	20	2	0	1	0	127.0	103	45	40	10	5	47	2	103	7
Carper, 11 Hag.-20 Alb.	9	7	.563	2.84	31	19	1	4	0	0	133.1	121	45	42	6	3	67	1	74	12
Mathile, Harrisburg	12	5	.706	2.86	26	26	7	0	3	0	185.2	175	61	59	6	5	28	0	89	6
Buckley, Harrisburg	7	7	.500	2.87	26	26	0	0	0	0	160.0	146	58	51	8	12	64	2	123	4
Byrd, Canton-Akron	14	6	.700	3.01	24	24	4	0	0	0	152.1	122	68	51	4	4	75	2	118	10

Departmental leaders: G—Braley, 64; W—Byrd, 14; L—T. Smith, 20; Pct.—Wegmann, .818; GS—Micki, 27; CG—Mathile, 7; GF—Braley, 45; ShO—R. Jones, 4; Sv.—Picota, 26; IP—Mathile, 185.2; H—T. Smith, 186; R—T. Smith, 104; ER—T. Smith, 91; HR—Livernois, 13; HB—Buckley, Vitko, 12; BB—Micki, Ojala, 80; IBB—Wertz, 6; SO—Hitchcock, 155; WP—V. Garcia, J. Williams, 15.

(All pitchers—listed alphabetically)

Pitcher, Team	W	L	Pct.	ERA	G	GS	CG	GF	ShO	Sv.	IP	H	R	ER	HR	HB	BB	Int. BB	SO	WP
Adamson, Reading*	3	6	.333	4.27	10	10	2	0	0	0	59.0	68	36	28	10	0	13	1	35	3
Allen, Canton-Akron	2	2	.500	5.54	12	5	0	1	0	0	37.1	50	27	23	3	2	15	0	11	0
Allen, Reading	1	3	.250	4.94	5	5	1	0	0	0	31.0	35	18	17	2	1	9	1	17	0
Alvarez, Harrisburg	4	1	.800	2.85	7	7	2	0	1	0	47.1	48	15	15	3	2	9	0	42	0
August, London	3	2	.600	2.72	11	6	1	0	1	0	53.0	47	16	16	5	0	10	2	39	2
Batchelor, Albany	4	5	.444	4.20	58	0	0	34	0	7	70.2	79	40	33	5	6	34	3	45	4
Bergman, London	4	7	.364	4.28	14	14	1	0	0	0	88.1	85	52	42	2	6	45	2	59	4
Bethea, New Britain	0	0	.000	0.00	1	0	0	1	0	0	1.0	1	0	0	0	0	0	0	2	0
Blumberg, Hagerstown*	0	0	.000	10.38	4	0	0	2	0	0	8.2	10	12	10	2	0	8	0	4	0
Bochtler, Harrisburg	6	5	.545	2.32	13	13	2	0	1	0	77.2	50	25	20	1	0	36	1	89	4
Borland, Reading	2	4	.333	3.43	32	0	0	18	0	5	42.0	39	23	16	2	1	32	3	45	3
Braley, London	3	6	.333	2.53	64	0	0	45	0	15	81.2	81	27	23	2	1	29	3	41	0
Brewer, Harrisburg*	2	0	1.000	5.01	20	0	0	4	0	0	23.1	25	15	13	1	1	18	1	18	5
Brink, Reading	1	1	.500	3.29	3	3	0	0	0	0	13.2	14	6	5	0	0	3	0	12	0
Brito, Harrisburg	6	4	.600	2.21	46	0	0	15	0	3	77.1	65	25	19	3	3	24	4	66	4
Buckley, Harrisburg	7	7	.500	2.87	26	26	0	0	0	0	160.0	146	58	51	8	12	64	2	123	4
Bumgarner, Hagerstown*	3	4	.429	6.51	14	1	0	8	0	1	27.2	26	23	20	4	1	18	0	30	2
Bushing, Reading	3	6	.333	4.35	22	8	0	2	0	1	70.1	68	38	34	9	2	30	0	72	4
Byrd, Canton-Akron	14	6	.700	3.01	24	24	4	0	0	0	152.1	122	68	51	4	4	75	2	118	10
Carper, 11 Hag.-20 Alb.	9	7	.563	2.84	31	19	1	4	0	0	133.1	121	45	42	6	3	67	1	74	12
Carter, Reading*	0	4	.000	9.24	7	6	0	0	0	0	25.1	37	28	26	3	1	15	0	17	3
Chapman, Harrisburg	4	2	.667	2.91	34	4	0	13	0	0	55.2	53	19	18	3	1	18	2	45	3
Charland, Canton-Akron*	5	3	.625	4.52	15	14	0	0	0	0	71.2	71	42	36	6	2	34	0	52	1
Colombino, Canton-Akron	0	0	.000	0.00	2	0	0	1	0	0	2.0	0	0	0	0	0	1	0	1	0
Conroy, New Britain	4	6	.400	3.82	11	11	3	0	1	0	75.1	70	33	32	9	0	17	0	40	1
Coppeta, London*	1	1	.500	2.31	19	0	0	3	0	0	23.1	24	8	6	0	0	10	1	18	2
Corbett, London*	0	4	.000	4.58	35	0	0	21	0	4	37.1	38	19	19	4	0	12	5	33	1
Corbin, Harrisburg	0	0	.000	0.00	1	1	0	0	0	0	3.0	2	0	0	0	0	3	0	3	0
Cornelius, London	0	0	.000	0.00	2	0	0	2	0	0	2.0	2	0	0	0	1	0	0	0	0
Cornelius, Harrisburg	1	0	1.000	3.13	4	4	0	0	0	0	23.0	11	8	8	0	6	8	0	17	1
DeSilva, London	2	4	.333	4.13	9	9	1	0	1	0	52.1	51	24	24	4	1	13	0	53	2
Donovan, New Britain*	0	1	.000	9.95	1	1	0	0	0	0	6.1	6	7	7	1	1	4	0	1	1
Dorn, Binghamton	3	1	.750	3.58	35	1	0	15	0	4	70.1	65	31	28	3	1	25	1	39	1
Douma, Binghamton*	8	8	.500	2.82	25	20	3	4	1	0	137.0	136	51	43	7	2	43	0	76	2
Drummond, Hagerstown	5	8	.385	3.87	26	11	2	13	1	4	111.2	108	59	48	8	5	33	1	62	3
Eiterman, Canton-Akron	0	0	.000	2.45	3	0	0	3	0	0	3.2	1	1	1	0	3	0	0	5	0
Elli, Reading*	2	6	.250	4.68	12	12	0	0	0	0	65.1	77	41	34	5	3	23	0	20	2
Elliott, Reading	3	3	.500	2.52	6	6	0	0	0	0	35.2	37	10	10	2	0	11	1	23	0

Pitcher, Team	W	L	Pct.	ERA	G	GS	CG	GF	ShO	Sv.	IP	H	R	ER	HR	HB	BB	Int. BB	SO	WP
Embree, Canton-Akron*	7	2	.778	2.28	12	12	0	0	0	0	79.0	61	24	20	2	2	28	1	56	2
Ferretti, Hagerstown	0	0	.000	0.00	1	0	0	1	0	0	1.1	0	0	0	0	1	0	2	0
Finnvold, New Britain	7	13	.350	3.49	25	25	3	0	0	0	165.0	156	69	64	6	6	52	4	135	6
Fletcher, Reading	9	4	.692	2.83	22	20	2	0	1	0	127.0	103	45	40	10	5	47	2	103	7
Florence, New Britain*	3	1	.750	2.41	58	0	0	30	0	6	74.2	65	23	20	0	3	27	3	51	4
Freed, London	2	0	1.000	3.24	14	0	0	4	0	0	16.2	16	8	6	2	0	8	1	10	1
Gaddy, Reading*	0	2	.000	2.92	12	1	0	5	0	1	24.2	15	8	8	2	3	13	1	19	0
Gakeler, London	0	0	.000	0.00	1	1	0	0	0	0	2.0	3	0	0	0	0	1	0	1	0
Garcia, London	8	8	.500	3.89	27	20	1	3	1	0	136.2	149	69	59	10	4	35	1	92	2
Garcia, Canton-Akron*	5	6	.455	6.07	29	9	0	6	0	1	102.1	115	73	69	9	5	57	2	56	15
Gardella, 15 Alb.-33 C.A.*	5	3	.625	3.21	48	3	0	27	0	12	73.0	61	34	26	6	4	42	1	63	4
Gideon, Canton-Akron	4	1	.800	3.38	19	0	0	14	0	5	24.0	25	10	9	2	0	7	3	23	2
Glaze, New Britain	0	1	.000	1.80	2	1	1	1	0	0	10.0	5	2	2	1	0	5	0	6	0
Goedhart, Reading	4	8	.333	4.27	16	16	0	0	0	0	86.1	95	48	41	5	2	24	2	56	3
Gogolewski, Albany	0	0	.000	9.45	6	0	0	3	0	1	6.2	9	7	7	0	0	2	0	6	1
Gonzales, London*	5	4	.556	3.02	10	10	0	0	0	0	65.2	64	25	22	5	1	10	0	37	2
Green, Reading	6	3	.667	1.88	12	12	0	0	0	0	62.1	46	16	13	2	1	20	0	67	5
Greene, Reading	0	0	.000	9.00	1	1	0	0	0	0	2.0	3	2	2	1	0	2	0	2	0
Greer, Albany	4	1	.800	1.83	40	1	0	18	0	4	68.2	48	19	14	1	0	30	4	53	6
Hall, Hagerstown*	3	4	.429	2.73	11	9	3	1	0	0	69.1	59	30	21	3	1	16	0	43	4
Harriger, Binghamton	2	2	.500	3.80	11	0	0	5	0	0	21.1	22	11	9	2	1	7	0	8	0
Haynes, Harrisburg	2	0	1.000	1.93	3	0	0	1	0	0	4.2	2	1	1	0	1	0	1	6	0
Henry, London*	5	5	.500	4.82	15	15	3	0	1	0	80.1	87	56	43	5	0	47	0	47	5
Hill, Reading	5	4	.556	4.78	25	15	1	1	0	0	98.0	111	61	52	11	4	24	1	61	5
Hitchcock, Albany*	6	9	.400	2.58	24	24	2	0	0	0	146.2	116	51	42	6	9	42	0	155	9
Hodges, Albany	4	7	.364	6.05	15	13	0	0	0	0	64.0	78	54	43	4	2	38	0	43	10
Hoffman, Albany	6	9	.400	4.09	35	14	0	14	0	3	121.0	130	64	55	5	2	37	0	42	10
Holcomb, Albany*	1	2	.333	3.18	36	0	0	11	0	1	34.0	21	14	12	3	3	23	2	45	2
Holland, Hagerstown	0	0	.000	0.00	1	0	0	0	0	0	1.0	0	0	0	0	0	0	0	1	0
Hook, Hagerstown*	0	2	.000	5.04	6	6	0	0	0	0	30.1	26	19	17	2	2	24	0	30	4
Horowitz, Hagerstown	0	0	.000	0.00	1	0	0	1	0	0	0.1	0	0	0	0	0	0	0	0	0
Hutton, Albany	13	7	.650	3.59	25	25	1	0	0	0	165.1	146	75	66	6	11	66	1	128	2
Jean, Albany	0	0	.000	2.25	1	1	0	0	0	0	4.0	3	2	1	0	0	3	0	6	1
Johnson, Harrisburg	9	10	.474	3.98	28	23	0	1	0	0	142.1	149	71	63	9	4	43	1	95	7
Johnstone, Binghamton	7	7	.500	3.74	24	24	2	0	0	0	149.1	132	66	62	8	9	36	0	121	3
Jones, Hagerstown	2	5	.286	3.49	11	9	0	0	0	0	69.2	62	30	27	1	1	25	0	45	0
Jones, Binghamton	12	4	.750	1.88	24	24	4	0	4	0	158.0	118	40	33	5	8	43	0	143	3
King, London	0	0	.000	2.25	1	1	0	0	0	0	4.0	2	1	1	0	0	0	0	4	0
Kiser, Canton-Akron*	3	2	.600	3.54	39	1	0	19	0	2	53.1	52	25	21	6	0	18	1	36	1
Langbehn, Binghamton*	5	5	.500	3.17	52	1	0	30	0	5	71.0	63	31	25	2	4	41	3	45	3
Limbach, Reading*	1	3	.250	3.14	53	0	0	22	0	5	83.0	70	35	29	8	0	17	2	57	5
Livernois, New Britain	11	7	.611	3.63	20	20	3	0	1	0	121.1	109	67	49	13	2	37	0	86	7
Lumley, London	8	3	.727	2.52	55	0	0	21	0	3	75.0	63	28	21	2	4	22	1	49	6
Manon, Albany	1	4	.200	5.23	8	4	1	3	0	0	32.2	34	23	19	0	2	19	0	22	3
Marchok, Harrisburg*	6	0	1.000	3.09	43	0	0	19	0	1	58.1	56	22	20	3	2	17	4	34	3
Martinez, Binghamton	5	2	.714	1.71	9	8	3	1	1	0	58.0	47	16	11	1	1	13	1	38	0
Mathile, Harrisburg	12	5	.706	2.86	26	26	7	0	3	0	185.2	175	61	59	6	5	28	0	89	6
Miller, Hagerstown	4	7	.364	3.72	25	7	0	5	0	0	75.0	76	40	31	3	3	25	0	47	1
Mlicki, Canton-Akron	11	9	.550	3.60	27	27	2	0	0	0	172.2	143	77	69	8	3	80	3	146	9
Moore, Hagerstown*	1	1	.500	3.12	5	0	0	3	0	1	8.2	7	4	3	0	0	7	0	12	0
Morgan, Canton-Akron	0	0	.000	4.05	3	0	0	1	0	0	6.2	11	4	3	0	0	0	0	1	0
Mosley, New Britain*	2	4	.333	5.00	49	2	0	26	0	1	90.0	105	67	50	7	3	35	4	44	5
Munoz, Binghamton	7	5	.583	3.28	22	22	0	0	0	0	112.1	96	55	41	2	4	70	0	66	8
Myers, Harrisburg*	4	3	.571	4.15	19	7	0	4	0	0	52.0	60	29	24	3	0	13	0	29	0
Nielsen, Albany*	3	5	.375	1.19	36	0	0	21	0	11	53.0	38	8	7	1	1	15	2	59	5
O'Donoghue, Hagerstown*	7	4	.636	2.24	17	16	2	1	0	0	112.1	78	37	28	6	4	40	0	87	7
Ogea, Canton-Akron	6	1	.857	2.20	7	7	0	0	1	0	49.0	38	12	12	2	4	12	0	40	3
Ojala, Albany*	12	8	.600	3.62	24	23	2	0	1	0	151.2	130	71	61	10	0	80	0	116	10
Otto, Canton-Akron*	0	0	.000	0.00	1	1	0	0	0	0	3.0	1	0	0	0	0	1	0	1	0
Painter, New Britain	7	2	.778	3.19	20	14	0	3	0	0	93.0	102	39	33	1	2	24	1	55	3
Parris, Reading	5	7	.417	4.64	18	14	0	0	0	0	85.1	94	55	44	9	3	21	1	60	2
Patterson, Reading	3	1	.750	4.60	26	0	0	21	0	13	31.1	30	16	16	2	0	14	2	22	2
Pawlowski, Hagerstown	1	1	.500	6.97	15	1	0	9	0	1	31.0	47	33	24	3	1	11	1	23	4
Pennington, Hagerstown*	1	2	.333	2.54	19	0	0	16	0	7	28.1	20	9	8	0	3	17	0	33	4
Piatt, Harrisburg	5	9	.357	3.45	39	5	0	24	0	7	62.2	55	26	24	2	4	32	2	65	0
Pico, Hagerstown	0	1	.000	2.63	14	0	0	9	0	1	27.1	27	13	8	6	1	6	0	29	1
Picota, Harrisburg	4	3	.571	1.88	53	0	0	41	0	26	72.0	56	21	15	2	5	23	4	38	0
Plunk, Canton-Akron	1	2	.333	1.72	9	0	0	3	0	0	15.2	11	4	3	0	1	5	0	19	2
Polasek, Hagerstown*	1	2	.333	6.04	22	1	0	12	0	1	44.2	52	36	30	4	4	24	3	35	8
Pollack, Harrisburg*	6	10	.375	4.71	25	21	1	3	1	0	124.1	139	74	65	9	4	46	0	58	5
Poole, Hagerstown*	0	1	.000	2.77	7	3	0	0	0	0	13.0	14	4	4	0	2	4	1	10	1
Popplewell, Albany	2	1	.667	7.28	28	2	0	11	0	0	50.2	52	46	41	4	3	34	2	33	4
Proctor, Binghamton	0	1	.000	23.63	1	1	0	0	0	0	2.2	8	7	7	2	0	2	0	1	0
Ramos, London*	1	0	1.000	3.14	16	0	0	5	0	4	14.1	12	8	5	1	0	16	4	8	0
Reich, Binghamton	4	4	.500	2.67	41	0	0	24	0	6	64.0	63	27	19	2	2	14	0	33	4
Ricci, Binghamton	1	4	.200	5.77	20	6	0	4	0	0	57.2	58	40	37	4	3	47	1	58	8
Riley, New Britain*	10	8	.556	2.45	19	19	1	0	1	0	121.0	108	38	33	7	2	38	1	63	1
Rodriguez, Albany	0	0	.000	0.00	1	0	0	1	0	0	1.0	1	0	0	0	0	0	0	0	0
Rogers, Binghamton	3	2	.600	4.33	22	0	0	10	0	1	35.1	37	21	17	4	1	7	0	20	0
Rojas, London	5	5	.500	4.87	32	0	0	17	0	5	40.2	49	32	22	6	2	17	5	33	3
Roth, New Britain	0	0	.000	36.00	1	0	0	0	0	0	1.0	4	4	4	0	0	3	0	0	0
Ryan, New Britain	1	4	.200	1.95	44	0	0	42	0	22	50.2	44	17	11	0	1	24	2	51	4
Sanders, New Britain	5	9	.357	4.51	36	13	2	5	1	0	113.2	121	66	57	12	3	48	2	69	14
Sarbaugh, Canton-Akron	0	0	.000	0.00	1	0	0	1	0	0	1.0	0	0	0	0	0	0	0	0	0
Schullstrom, Hagerstown	5	9	.357	3.61	23	22	2	0	0	0	127.0	120	66	51	7	3	63	0	128	7
Sele, New Britain	2	1	.667	6.27	1	1	0	0	0	0	33.0	43	29	23	2	5	15	0	29	4
Shepherd, Reading	0	1	.000	2.78	4	3	0	1	0	0	22.2	17	7	7	1	1	4	1	9	0
Smith, New Britain	3	20	.130	5.32	27	25	2	1	1	0	154.0	186	104	91	5	8	53	3	71	7
Smith, Canton-Akron	1	4	.200	4.68	9	7	0	0	0	0	32.2	33	18	17	0	1	14	0	28	2
Soper, Canton-Akron	3	2	.600	3.02	43	0	0	38	0	19	47.2	39	21	16	4	6	18	1	43	1
Stevens, Reading	4	4	.500	3.99	46	0	0	37	0	12	58.2	65	31	26	3	0	16	4	43	3
Sullivan, Reading	2	1	.667	4.84	34	0	0	13	0	0	44.2	56	34	24	5	1	18	2	27	3
Taylor, Hagerstown	0	0	.000	13.50	1	0	0	0	0	0	0.2	1	1	1	0	0	1	0	0	0
Torres, London	0	0	.000	10.80	5	0	0	1	0	0	5.0	12	6	6	1	1	4	1	6	0

Pitcher, Team	W	L	Pct.	ERA	G	GS	CG	GF	ShO	Sv.	IP	H	R	ER	HR	HB	BB	Int. BB	SO	WP
Trice, Canton-Akron*	5	7	.417	4.04	32	14	1	5	0	0	111.1	127	69	50	7	6	44	2	67	6
Turek, Canton-Akron	3	5	.375	3.70	14	14	0	0	0	0	75.1	60	38	31	4	3	28	1	56	0
Uhrhan, New Britain	3	5	.375	4.20	43	3	0	13	0	1	83.2	94	42	39	3	3	32	5	53	2
Vasquez, Binghamton	2	1	.667	1.35	24	0	0	23	0	17	26.2	17	5	4	1	0	7	0	24	0
Vesling, London*	4	3	.571	6.49	12	9	0	1	0	0	52.2	64	47	38	3	3	28	2	33	4
Vitko, Binghamton	12	8	.600	3.49	26	26	4	0	3	0	165.0	163	76	64	11	12	53	0	89	7
Walker, Binghamton	7	12	.368	4.12	24	23	4	1	0	0	139.2	159	77	64	9	3	46	0	72	5
Warren, London	7	9	.438	3.30	25	25	3	0	2	0	147.1	146	66	54	10	5	32	1	83	7
Wegmann, Binghamton	9	2	.818	2.58	27	11	2	4	0	1	97.2	73	29	28	5	4	27	1	93	3
Wells, Reading	0	1	.000	1.17	3	3	0	0	0	0	15.1	12	2	2	0	0	5	0	11	0
Wertz, Canton-Akron	8	4	.667	1.20	57	0	0	24	0	48	97.1	75	16	13	1	3	30	6	69	3
Wiegandt, Reading*	6	3	.667	2.98	56	0	0	12	0	2	81.2	66	31	27	3	1	48	5	65	8
Williams, Hagerstown	8	10	.444	4.83	36	15	3	16	0	6	123.0	148	91	66	9	6	70	0	82	15
Williams, Reading	1	2	.333	5.17	3	3	0	0	0	0	15.2	17	10	9	1	0	7	0	12	3
Williamson, Hagerstown	0	1	.000	4.91	6	5	0	0	0	0	14.2	13	9	8	1	0	2	0	8	0
Willis, London	1	5	.167	5.99	27	12	1	2	1	0	103.2	128	73	69	12	5	32	1	73	2
Wolf, London	8	4	.667	3.46	19	16	2	0	0	0	104.0	98	49	40	8	2	49	2	93	3
Wood, Hagerstown	6	3	.667	3.48	21	0	0	19	0	4	33.2	28	19	13	0	0	36	1	43	7
Yaughn, Hagerstown	7	8	.467	3.48	18	18	5	0	0	0	116.1	88	52	45	6	6	33	0	106	4

BALKS—Henry, T. Smith, 5 each; Finnvold, Hodges, O'Donoghue, Riley, 4 each; Schullstrom, Yaughn, 3 each; Drummond, Gardella, Hitchcock, Hook, S. Jones, Miller, Mosley, Plunk, Pollack, Ricci, Sullivan, Trice, Walker, Wegmann, Williamson, Wood, 2 each; Bethea, Buckley, Carper, Chapman, Charland, DeSilva, Douma, Elli, Embree, V. Garcia, Hill, Hutton, Johnson, R. Jones, Martinez, Mathile, Mlicki, Myers, Painter, Popplewell, Ramos, Sanders, Sele, W. Smith, Turek, Vesling, Wiegandt, J. Williams, Willis, 1 each.

COMBINATION SHUTOUTS—Carper-Holcomb-Hoffman, Hitchcock-Greer, Hitchcock-Hodges-Nielsen-Gardella, Hitchcock-Nielsen-Gardella, Hodges-Greer-Batchelor, Hoffman-Gardella, Hutton-Batchelor, Munoz-Batchelor-Nielsen-Gardella, Munoz-Greer, Ojala-Batchelor-Nielsen, Ojala-Nielsen, Albany; Jones-Langbehn 2, Walker-Langbehn 2, Johnstone-Vasquez, Vitko-Dorn-Harriger, Vitko-Vasquez, Wegmann-Vasquez, Binghamton; Mlicki-Soper 2, Byrd-Kiser, Byrd-Soper, Charland-Soper, Charland-Wertz, Charland-Wertz-Soper, Embree-Wertz, Gardella-Wertz, Otto-Garcia-Kiser-Wertz-Gideon, Smith-Kiser-Gideon, Turek-Plunk, Canton-Akron; Carper-Pennington, Carper-Williams, Poole-Ricci-Pennington, Williams-O'Donoghue, Hagerstown; Bochtler-Brito-Picota, Buckley-Piatt, Chapman-Piatt-Picota, Johnson-Myers, Mathile-Picota-Piatt, Myers-Chapman-Brito, Myers-Picota, Harrisburg; Gonzales-Freed, Warren-August-Lumley-Corbett, Warren-Garcia, Warren-Lumley-Braley, Warren-Lumley-Torres, London; Livernois-Mosley, Painter-Florence-Uhrhan-Ryan, Riley-Ryan, Riley-Sanders-Florence, Sanders-Florence, Sanders-Ryan, Smith-Ryan, New Britain; Brink-Wiegandt-Stevens, Bushing-Wiegandt, Fletcher-Wiegandt-Stevens, Goedhart-Hill-Wiegandt, Goedhart-Limbach-Patterson, Green-Bushing, Hill-Wiegandt-Patterson, Reading.

NO-HIT GAMES—None.

FIELDING

TEAM

Team	Pct.	G	PO	A	E	DP	PB	Team	Pct.	G	PO	A	E	DP	PB
Harrisburg	.975	137	3508	1455	127	123	20	Binghamton	.969	139	3588	1436	162	138	13
Albany	.973	139	3524	1485	140	136	19	Hagerstown	.967	139	3580	1291	168	117	26
New Britain	.970	140	3578	1450	134	123	31	Reading	.966	138	3543	1392	175	142	11
London	.969	138	3558	1435	159	120	27	Canton-Akron	.965	138	3579	1323	178	110	12

INDIVIDUAL

*Throws lefthanded.

FIRST BASEMEN

Player, Team	Pct.	G	PO	A	E	DP
Canale, Canton-Akron	.982	40	304	22	6	31
Carey, Hagerstown	.978	30	250	23	6	15
Colombino, Canton-Akron	1.000	2	13	3	0	1
Cooper, Canton-Akron	.980	20	139	11	3	11
Cornelius, London	.966	8	27	1	1	0
Cruz, London*	.986	68	549	35	8	47
Dixon, New Britain	.984	29	236	18	4	24
Eiterman, Canton-Akron	1.000	3	7	0	0	0
Epley, Canton-Akron*	.985	67	534	49	9	44
Hernandez, Albany	1.000	1	4	1	0	0
Hoffner, Binghamton	.997	38	305	22	1	37
Holland, Hagerstown	1.000	1	4	1	0	1
Lockett, Reading*	.990	86	659	60	7	69
Lopez, Canton-Akron	1.000	2	13	1	0	1
Meadows, Hagerstown	1.000	2	15	0	0	1
Miller, Hagerstown	.989	95	734	64	9	71
Obando, Albany	.977	49	430	32	11	32
Pratt, Reading	.947	3	18	0	1	2
Ryan, Reading	.990	56	448	35	5	49
Sarbaugh, Canton-Akron	.992	13	113	6	1	12
Siddall, Harrisburg	1.000	7	36	7	0	4
Sparks, Albany*	.991	92	822	60	8	89
Sparks, London	.993	69	663	34	5	66
Tatum, New Britain	.986	112	978	98	15	78
Trevino, Reading	1.000	1	3	0	0	0
Vargas, Albany	1.000	2	3	2	0	1
Wearing, Hagerstown	.980	15	95	4	2	9
WHITE, Harrisburg	.992	134	1178	106	10	110
Williams, Hagerstown	1.000	7	20	4	0	1
Zinter, Binghamton	.988	105	963	51	12	86

SECOND BASEMEN

Player, Team	Pct.	G	PO	A	E	DP
Allison, Binghamton	1.000	10	15	21	0	5
Bethea, New Britain	.989	36	74	107	2	23
Blackwell, Albany	.933	7	7	7	1	4
Crowley, Canton-Akron	.978	21	34	54	2	14
DeButch, London	.954	27	48	77	6	22

Player, Team	Pct.	G	PO	A	E	DP
DeKneef, New Britain	.970	113	183	309	15	61
Escobar, Reading	.974	27	56	56	3	20
Fermin, London	.947	11	21	33	3	4
Ferretti, Hagerstown	1.000	19	17	33	0	4
Flores, Canton-Akron	.957	122	241	296	24	67
Frazier, London	.800	3	2	6	2	1
Fulton, Harrisburg	.941	9	15	17	2	2
Hecht, Harrisburg	.981	18	20	32	1	9
Howard, Binghamton	1.000	3	4	0	0	0
Kelly, Albany	1.000	2	4	8	0	3
King, Binghamton	1.000	1	0	2	0	0
Lofton, Hagerstown	.966	49	94	106	7	25
Malinoski, Harrisburg	.979	11	12	35	1	6
Martin, Harrisburg	.965	113	190	309	18	64
Mendenhall, London	.976	37	60	104	4	18
Neitzel, Reading	.958	72	140	202	15	43
Robertson, London	.966	64	130	209	12	40
Rodriguez, Albany	.965	34	50	86	5	12
Roth, Hagerstown	1.000	6	5	8	0	2
Sarbaugh, Canton-Akron	1.000	3	4	6	0	0
Saunders, Binghamton	.971	130	272	365	19	94
Sparks, London	1.000	2	1	0	0	0
Thomas, London	1.000	3	10	4	0	3
Trevino, Reading	.987	43	61	86	2	20
Tyler, Hagerstown	.953	82	118	203	16	40
VARGAS, Albany	.975	104	172	336	13	70

THIRD BASEMEN

Player, Team	Pct.	G	PO	A	E	DP
Allison, Binghamton	1.000	3	0	3	0	1
Bethea, New Britain	1.000	2	1	0	0	1
Brady, Reading	.893	10	5	20	3	1
Butterfield, Binghamton	.908	137	108	299	41	29
Byrd, New Britain	1.000	3	1	9	0	0
Colombino, Canton-Akron	.936	76	52	138	13	15
Crowley, Canton-Akron	.940	40	17	61	5	5
Davis, Albany	.920	114	78	185	23	15
DeButch, London	.950	11	8	11	1	1
Dixon, New Britain	.941	35	33	47	5	7
Escobar, Reading	.957	11	9	13	1	1
Fermin, London	1.000	3	0	3	0	0

— 381 —

Player, Team	Pct.	G	PO	A	E	DP
Ferretti, Hagerstown	.908	33	16	53	7	8
Flores, Canton-Akron	1.000	1	0	1	0	0
Fulton, Harrisburg	.880	9	5	17	3	1
Holland, Hagerstown	.907	84	46	140	19	14
Kingwood, London	1.000	1	0	2	0	1
Kosco, Harrisburg	.918	85	51	139	17	9
Lopez, Canton-Akron	.667	1	0	2	1	0
Malinoski, Harrisburg	.846	18	12	32	8	3
Martin, Harrisburg	.000	2	0	0	1	0
McDonald, Harrisburg	.913	37	17	56	7	6
McDougal, Reading	.909	6	3	7	1	0
Mendenhall, London	.867	15	10	16	4	2
Miller, Hagerstown	.839	21	16	31	9	1
Mota, Canton-Akron	1.000	2	1	0	0	0
Norris, New Britain	.930	113	94	160	19	20
REIMINK, London	.942	111	68	207	17	21
Rosado, Reading	.884	14	11	27	5	3
Roth, Hagerstown	.925	24	11	38	4	3
Sarbaugh, Canton-Akron	.882	9	5	10	2	0
Sparks, Albany	.944	29	23	61	5	2
Thome, Canton-Akron	.920	23	11	35	4	3
Trevino, Reading	.886	14	12	19	4	1
Waller, Reading	.922	90	74	163	20	21

SHORTSTOPS

Player, Team	Pct.	G	PO	A	E	DP
Alexander, Hagerstown	.929	127	216	253	36	59
Allison, Binghamton	.887	36	32	54	11	18
Bethea, New Britain	.949	50	87	138	12	27
Blackwell, Albany	.947	5	10	8	1	2
Byrd, New Britain	.929	10	22	30	4	8
Crowley, Canton-Akron	.917	14	13	31	4	4
DeButch, London	.945	36	43	78	7	13
Dellicarri, Binghamton	.940	107	143	296	28	67
Eenhoorn, Albany	.949	58	88	153	13	29
Escobar, Reading	.926	55	87	163	20	35
Fermin, London	1.000	1	2	7	0	0
Ferretti, Hagerstown	.970	19	22	43	2	11
Flores, Canton-Akron	.905	5	10	9	2	2
Gomez, London	.951	64	100	174	14	37
Graham, New Britain	.928	91	117	232	27	40
Hernandez, Canton-Akron	.932	130	226	320	40	64
King, Binghamton	.786	9	7	15	6	3
LANSING, Harrisburg	.966	128	189	373	20	76
Malinoski, Harrisburg	1.000	2	2	1	0	1
Martin, Harrisburg	.922	12	18	29	4	10
McDougal, Reading	1.000	1	5	1	0	3
Mendenhall, London	.941	49	86	139	14	27
Paulsen, Reading	.881	22	34	62	13	14
Rodriguez, Albany	.980	81	144	252	8	71
Stocker, Reading	.951	62	100	172	14	39
Vargas, Albany	1.000	2	0	2	0	0

OUTFIELDERS

Player, Team	Pct.	G	PO	A	E	DP
Alborano, Reading*	.944	32	32	2	2	0
Barfield, Albany	1.000	2	4	1	0	0
Barnwell, Albany	.947	116	190	7	11	1
Beams, New Britain	.969	75	147	11	5	2
Bethea, New Britain	1.000	2	1	0	0	0
Bieser, Reading	.944	24	68	0	4	0
Blosser, New Britain*	.966	116	189	9	7	0
Brady, Reading	1.000	58	119	5	0	3
Buford, Hagerstown	.993	101	264	13	2	3
Cabrera, London	.981	31	53	0	1	0
Cairo, Harrisburg	.942	98	173	7	11	1
Carpenter, Albany*	.970	45	91	5	3	0
Chick, New Britain	.968	115	224	17	8	5
Cornelius, London	.939	84	144	9	10	0
DeButch, London	.975	24	35	4	1	0
Devarez, Hagerstown	1.000	1	2	0	0	0
Dostal, Reading*	.954	33	83	0	4	0
Eiterman, London	.987	47	75	0	1	0
Epley, Canton-Akron*	1.000	4	5	0	0	0
Frazier, London	.970	125	253	6	8	0
Fulton, Harrisburg	.970	32	30	2	1	0
Giles, Canton-Akron*	1.000	22	45	0	0	0
Gillette, London	1.000	1	1	0	0	0
Hecht, Harrisburg	.980	57	96	0	2	0
Hill, Canton-Akron	.800	1	4	0	1	0
Hirtensteiner, Harrisburg*	.992	126	246	11	2	3
Horne, Harrisburg	1.000	1	2	0	0	0
Howard, Binghamton	.987	99	136	11	2	1
Hunter, Binghamton	.966	115	218	6	8	2
Hurst, London*	.937	73	127	6	9	0
Hyde, Reading	.993	68	130	11	1	7
Jackson, Reading	.953	33	60	1	3	0
Katzaroff, Binghamton	.982	106	213	11	4	3
Kingwood, London	.987	103	212	10	3	1
Knoblauh, Albany	.947	62	86	3	5	0
Kosco, Harrisburg	1.000	1	2	0	0	0
Lane, Canton-Akron	.958	15	43	3	2	1
Lockett, Reading*	.915	26	43	0	4	0

Player, Team	Pct.	G	PO	A	E	DP
Lopez, Canton-Akron	1.000	3	2	0	0	0
Malinoski, Harrisburg	1.000	2	3	0	0	0
Martin, Hagerstown	.958	20	22	1	1	0
Mayo, Harrisburg*	1.000	3	5	0	0	0
McNeely, New Britain	.983	72	174	2	3	2
Meadows, Hagerstown	1.000	36	67	2	0	1
Mouton, Albany	1.000	63	102	1	0	0
Nelson, Harrisburg	.983	54	110	4	2	1
Nixon, Canton-Akron	1.000	2	3	0	0	0
Noriega, Albany	.971	17	32	1	1	1
Nuneviller, Reading	1.000	46	83	1	0	0
Oster, Albany*	1.000	12	20	1	0	1
PENNYE, Harrisburg	1.000	94	184	5	0	2
Pride, Binghamton	.964	107	214	3	8	1
Ramos, Canton-Akron*	.959	104	158	6	7	1
Robertson, Albany*	.967	55	116	3	4	3
Rosado, Reading	1.000	1	2	0	0	0
Roseboro, Harrisburg	1.000	16	36	1	0	0
Sanders, Canton-Akron	.974	91	183	8	5	2
Siddall, Harrisburg	.973	43	69	3	2	0
Smith, Harrisburg	.983	123	226	9	4	1
Sparks, London*	1.000	2	5	0	0	0
Strickland, Albany	1.000	3	2	0	0	0
Taylor, Reading*	.986	95	206	6	3	2
Thoutsis, New Britain	.992	65	125	6	1	1
Tinsley, Canton-Akron	.979	94	226	5	5	2
Trevino, Reading	.969	15	28	3	1	1
Viera, Albany*	.989	54	91	1	1	1
Washington, 62 C.A.-45 Hag.	.933	107	204	6	15	1
Wearing, Hagerstown	1.000	6	5	0	0	0
White, Harrisburg	.938	15	29	1	2	0
White, Binghamton	1.000	12	12	0	0	0

CATCHERS

Player, Team	Pct.	G	PO	A	E	DP	PB
Agostinelli, Reading	1.000	1	3	0	0	0	0
Ausmus, Albany	.970	5	30	2	1	0	1
Bieser, Reading	.978	8	38	6	1	2	0
Billmeyer, Hagerstown	.989	14	88	1	1	0	3
Demus, New Britain	.967	21	108	9	4	2	7
Devarez, Hagerstown	.989	108	653	82	8	11	19
Dziadkowiec, Binghamton	1.000	24	140	14	0	0	4
FORDYCE, Binghamton	.996	117	713	79	3	6	9
Gillette, London	.982	69	382	50	8	1	14
Hattebery, New Britain	.979	93	473	44	11	3	17
Hernandez, Albany	.992	98	579	62	5	7	11
Hines, Harrisburg	1.000	6	24	2	0	0	4
Hoiles, Harrisburg	1.000	4	16	5	0	0	0
Horowitz, Hagerstown	1.000	7	51	7	0	0	0
Laker, Harrisburg	.980	104	630	62	14	4	12
Lehman, Hagerstown	.986	13	67	5	1	0	1
Lieberthal, Reading	.988	76	524	48	7	5	7
Livesey, Albany	.990	18	86	16	1	1	4
Mota, Canton-Akron	.992	54	318	33	3	1	4
Pratt, Hagerstown	.975	12	72	6	2	0	1
Quintell, Albany	1.000	3	12	2	0	0	0
Rodriguez, New Britain	.988	37	208	34	3	4	7
Rosado, Reading	.964	43	241	30	10	7	3
Sanchez, Albany	.994	24	160	10	1	4	3
Sellers, London	.986	82	453	48	7	2	13
Siddall, Harrisburg	.996	34	199	28	1	4	8
Skinner, Canton-Akron	1.000	5	18	0	0	0	0
Stinnett, Canton-Akron	.979	90	560	57	13	3	8
Tallman, Hagerstown	.938	12	55	5	4	2	2
Walker, Albany	1.000	6	22	1	0	0	0
Williams, Hagerstown	.978	5	40	4	1	1	1

PITCHERS

Player, Team	Pct.	G	PO	A	E	DP
Adamson, Reading*	1.000	10	3	13	0	0
Allen, Canton-Akron	1.000	12	2	5	0	1
Allen, Reading	1.000	5	4	3	0	0
Alvarez, Harrisburg	1.000	7	4	10	0	1
August, London	1.000	11	1	5	0	1
Batchelor, Albany	.882	58	4	11	2	1
Bergman, London	.913	14	8	13	2	1
Blumberg, Hagerstown*	1.000	1	0	1	0	0
Bochtler, Harrisburg	.900	13	2	7	1	0
Borland, Reading	1.000	32	3	7	0	1
Braley, Reading	1.000	64	4	18	0	4
Brewer, Harrisburg*	1.000	20	4	6	0	0
Brink, Reading	.750	3	1	2	1	0
Brito, Harrisburg	.905	46	9	10	2	1
Buckley, Harrisburg	.917	26	13	20	3	4
Bumgarner, Hagerstown	1.000	14	1	2	0	1
Bushing, Reading	.909	22	6	14	2	1
Byrd, Canton-Akron	.862	24	10	15	4	2
Carper, 11 Hag.-20 Alb.	1.000	31	10	24	0	4
Carter, Reading*	.750	7	0	6	2	0
Chapman, Harrisburg	1.000	34	7	13	0	1
Charland, Canton-Akron*	1.000	15	3	9	0	0
Colombino, Canton-Akron	1.000	2	1	0	0	0
Conroy, New Britain	1.000	11	9	6	0	1

Player, Team	Pct.	G	PO	A	E	DP
Coppeta, London*	1.000	19	1	2	0	0
Corbett, London*	1.000	35	0	2	0	0
Corbin, Harrisburg	1.000	1	0	1	0	0
Cornelius, London	1.000	2	0	2	0	0
Cornelius, Harrisburg	1.000	4	1	5	0	0
DeSilva, London	1.000	9	5	7	0	0
Donovan, New Britain*	.500	1	0	1	1	0
Dorn, Binghamton	1.000	35	9	5	0	1
Douma, Binghamton*	.833	25	5	20	5	1
Drummond, Hagerstown	1.000	26	10	16	0	1
Elli, Reading*	.895	12	6	11	2	2
Elliott, Reading	.833	6	2	3	1	0
Embree, Canton-Akron*	.900	12	3	15	2	0
Finnvold, New Britain	.946	25	19	16	2	1
Fletcher, Reading	.938	22	9	6	1	2
Florence, New Britain*	.966	58	9	19	1	2
Freed, London	1.000	14	2	4	0	0
Gaddy, Reading*	.923	12	3	9	1	3
Garcia, London	1.000	27	4	9	0	2
Garcia, Canton-Akron*	1.000	29	4	12	0	3
Gardella, 15 Alb.-33 C.A.*	1.000	48	6	13	0	1
Gideon, Canton-Akron	1.000	19	0	5	0	0
Glaze, New Britain	1.000	2	1	2	0	0
Goedhart, Reading	.857	16	4	8	2	1
Gogolewski, Albany	1.000	6	1	0	0	0
Gonzales, London*	1.000	10	0	7	0	0
Green, Reading	.750	12	9	12	7	2
Greene, Reading	1.000	1	0	1	0	0
Greer, Albany	.929	40	3	10	1	2
Hall, Hagerstown*	1.000	11	8	21	0	1
Harriger, Binghamton	.750	11	0	3	1	1
Haynes, Harrisburg	1.000	3	1	0	0	0
Henry, London*	.893	15	5	20	3	0
Hill, Reading	1.000	25	7	14	0	1
Hitchcock, Albany*	.875	24	3	32	5	1
Hodges, Albany	1.000	15	4	14	0	1
Hoffman, Albany	1.000	35	6	24	0	3
Holcomb, Albany*	1.000	36	1	0	0	0
Hook, Hagerstown*	1.000	6	0	2	0	0
Hutton, Albany	.889	25	7	17	3	3
Jean, Albany	.000	1	0	0	1	0
Johnson, Harrisburg	.958	28	6	17	1	1
Johnstone, Binghamton	1.000	24	9	20	0	3
Jones, Hagerstown	.909	11	5	5	1	1
Jones, Binghamton	.852	24	10	13	4	1
King, London	1.000	1	1	0	0	0
Kiser, Canton-Akron*	1.000	39	3	5	0	0
Langbehn, Binghamton*	1.000	52	10	18	0	4
Limbach, Reading*	1.000	53	2	11	0	0
Livernois, New Britain	1.000	20	13	10	0	1
Lumley, London	.792	55	3	16	5	0
Manon, Albany	1.000	8	3	4	0	0
Marchok, Harrisburg*	1.000	43	7	12	0	0
Martinez, Binghamton	1.000	9	1	9	0	1
MATHILE, Harrisburg	1.000	26	20	18	0	2
Miller, Hagerstown	.957	25	11	11	1	1
Mlicki, Canton-Akron	.925	27	12	25	3	2
Morgan, Canton-Akron	1.000	3	2	0	0	0

Player, Team	Pct.	G	PO	A	E	DP
Mosley, New Britain*	.966	49	11	17	1	1
Munoz, Albany	.889	22	13	19	4	1
Myers, Harrisburg*	1.000	19	2	9	0	0
Nielsen, Albany*	.889	36	3	5	1	0
O'Donoghue, Hagerstown*	1.000	17	9	13	0	1
Ogea, Canton-Akron	.889	7	4	4	1	1
Ojala, Albany*	1.000	24	8	18	0	1
Painter, New Britain	.955	20	8	13	1	1
Parris, Reading	1.000	18	7	21	0	2
Patterson, Reading	1.000	26	3	5	0	1
Pawlowski, Hagerstown	1.000	15	5	2	0	0
Pennington, Hagerstown*	.500	19	0	1	1	0
Piatt, Harrisburg	1.000	39	6	7	0	1
Pico, Hagerstown	1.000	14	2	4	0	0
Picota, Harrisburg	.958	53	6	17	1	0
Plunk, Canton-Akron*	.750	9	2	1	1	0
Polasek, Hagerstown*	1.000	22	1	10	0	0
Pollack, Harrisburg*	.976	25	10	31	1	0
Poole, Hagerstown*	.800	7	2	2	1	0
Popplewell, Albany	.714	28	1	4	2	1
Proctor, Binghamton	1.000	1	1	0	0	0
Ramos, London*	1.000	16	1	2	0	0
Reich, Binghamton	.952	41	7	13	1	1
Ricci, Hagerstown	.857	20	5	7	2	1
Riley, New Britain*	1.000	19	5	22	0	0
Rodriguez, Albany	1.000	1	0	1	0	0
Rogers, Binghamton	1.000	22	2	11	0	1
Rojas, London	.833	32	3	7	2	1
Ryan, New Britain	.909	44	2	8	1	0
Sanders, New Britain	.955	36	8	13	1	1
Schullstrom, Hagerstown	.800	23	4	12	4	0
Sele, New Britain	1.000	7	1	8	0	0
Shepherd, Reading	1.000	4	2	2	0	0
Smith, New Britain	1.000	27	9	28	0	1
Smith, Canton-Akron	.833	9	0	5	1	0
Soper, Canton-Akron	1.000	43	6	6	0	0
Stevens, Reading	1.000	46	3	13	0	0
Sullivan, Reading	1.000	34	2	2	0	0
Trice, Canton-Akron*	.842	32	8	8	3	0
Turek, Canton-Akron	1.000	14	4	5	0	0
Uhrhan, New Britain	.938	43	8	7	1	1
Vasquez, Binghamton	1.000	24	1	2	0	0
Vesling, London*	1.000	12	0	5	0	1
Vitko, Binghamton	.918	26	18	27	4	1
Walker, Binghamton	.923	24	13	35	4	4
Warren, London	.950	25	17	21	2	1
Wegmann, Binghamton	1.000	27	7	8	0	1
Wells, Reading	1.000	3	2	2	0	1
Wertz, Canton-Akron	.920	57	5	18	2	3
Wiegandt, Reading*	1.000	56	6	16	0	2
Williams, Hagerstown	.952	36	10	10	1	0
Williams, Reading	1.000	3	2	6	0	2
Williamson, Hagerstown	1.000	6	6	2	0	0
Willis, London	1.000	27	4	8	0	1
Wolf, London	1.000	19	7	14	0	3
Wood, Hagerstown	1.000	21	2	5	0	0
Yaughn, Hagerstown	1.000	18	11	11	0	1

The following players did not have any fielding statistics at the positions indicated or appeared only as a designated hitter, pinch-hitter or pinch-runner: Allison, of; Bethea, p; Canale, 3b; Colombino, of; DeKneef, c; Eiterman, p; Ferretti, of, p; Flores, of; Gakeler, p; Gomez, 3b; Hatteberg, 1b; Hoffner, 2b; Holland, p; Horowitz, p; Moore, p; Mota, of; Otto, p; Roth, of, p; Sarbaugh, p; T. Taylor, p; Torres, p; Vargas, of; Woods, of.

LEAGUE CHAMPIONS

Year	Team	Pct.
1923—	Williamsport	.661
1924—	Williamsport	.654
1925—	York§	.583
	Williamsport§	.583
1926—	Scranton	.627
1927—	Harrisburg	.630
1928—	Harrisburg	.603
1929—	Binghamton	.597
1930—	Wilkes-Barre	.572
1931—	Harrisburg	.597
1932—	Wilkes-Barre	.561
1933—	Binghamton	.690
1934—	Binghamton	.694
	Williamsport*	.603
1935—	Scranton	.657
	Binghamton*	.580
1936—	Scranton*	.609
	Elmira	.629
1937—	Elmira†	.622
1938—	Binghamton	.622
	Elmira (3rd) ‡	.522
1939—	Scranton†	.571
1940—	Scranton	.568
	Binghamton (2nd) ‡	.554
1941—	Wilkes-Barre	.630
	Elmira (3rd) ‡	.514
1942—	Albany	.600
	Scranton (2nd) ‡	.593

Year	Team	Pct.
1943—	Scranton	.630
	Elmira (2nd) ‡	.568
1944—	Hartford	.723
	Binghamton (4th) ‡	.474
1945—	Utica	.615
	Albany (3rd) ‡	.564
1946—	Scranton†	.691
1947—	Utica†	.652
1948—	Scranton†	.636
1949—	Albany	.664
	Binghamton (4th) ‡	.500
1950—	Wilkes-Barre‡	.652
1951—	Wilkes-Barre‡	.612
	Scranton (2nd) †	.562
1952—	Albany	.603
	Binghamton (2nd) ‡	.562
1953—	Reading	.682
	Binghamton (2nd) ‡	.636
1954—	Wilkes-Barre	.576
	Albany (3rd) ‡	.540
1955—	Reading	.613
	Allentown (3rd) ‡	.565
1956—	Schenectady†	.609
1957—	Binghamton	.607
	Reading (3rd) ‡	.529
1958—	Lancaster x	.568
	Binghamton (6th) ‡	.493
1959—	Springfield†	.607

Year	Team	Pct.
1960—	Williamsport y	.551
	Springfield (3rd) y	.496
1961—	Springfield	.612
1962—	Williamsport	.593
	Elmira (2nd) ‡	.514
1963—	Charleston	.593
1964—	Elmira	.586
1965—	Pittsfield	.607
1966—	Elmira	.633
1967—	Binghamton z	.586
	Elmira	.532
1968—	Pittsfield	.604
	Reading (2nd) ‡	.579
1969—	York	.640
1970—	Waterbury a	.560
	Reading a	.553
1971—	Three Rivers	.569
	Elmira b	.561
1972—	West Haven b	.600
	Three Rivers	.559
1973—	Reading b	.551
	Pittsfield	.551
1974—	Thetford Miners (2nd) c	.536
	Pittsfield (2nd)	.496
1975—	Reading	.613
	Bristol*	.587
1976—	Three Rivers	.601
	West Haven d	.576

Year	Team	Pct.
1977—	West Haven e	.623
	Three Rivers	.551
1978—	Reading	.642
	Bristol*	.580
1979—	West Haven f	.597
1980—	Holyoke*	.561
	Waterbury	.540
1981—	Glens Falls	.615
	Bristol*	.577
1982—	West Haven*	.614
	Lynn	.590

Year	Team	Pct.
1983—	Lynn	.554
	New Britain†	.518
1984—	Waterbury	.543
	Vermont‡	.536
1985—	Albany	.540
	Vermont‡	.514
1986—	Reading	.566
	Vermont‡	.554
1987—	Pittsfield	.630
	Harrisburg‡	.550

Year	Team	Pct.
1988—	Glens Falls	.584
	Albany‡	.522
1989—	Albany‡	.657
	Harrisburg	.522
1990—	Albany	.568
	London†	.547
1991—	Harrisburg	.621
	Albany‡	.543
1992—	Canton-Akron	.580
	Binghamton†	.572

*Won split-season playoff. †Won championship and four-team playoff. ‡Won four-team playoff. §Tied for pennant, York winning playoff. xLeague was divided into Northern, Southern divisions and played a split season; Lancaster over-all season leader. yPlayoff finals canceled after one game because of rain with Williamsport and Springfield declared playoff co-champions. zLeague was divided into Eastern, Western divisions; Binghamton won playoff. aTied for pennant, Waterbury winning playoff. bLeague was divided into American, National divisions; won playoff. cLeague was divided into American and National divisions; won four-team playoff. dLeague was divided into Northern, Southern divisions, won playoff. eLeague was divided into New England and Canadian-American divisions; won playoff. fWon both halves of split season (no playoffs). (NOTE—Known as New York-Pennsylvania League prior to 1938.)

SOUTHERN LEAGUE

FINAL STANDINGS

FIRST HALF

EASTERN DIVISION						WESTERN DIVISION					
Team	W	L	T	Pct.	GB	Team	W	L	T	Pct.	GB
Greenville (Braves)	49	23	0	.681	......	Chattanooga (Reds)	46	25	0	.648	......
Jacksonville (Mariners)	38	34	0	.528	11	Huntsville (Athletics)	43	29	0	.597	3½
Charlotte (Cubs)	35	36	0	.493	13½	Memphis (Royals)	34	37	0	.479	12
Orlando (Twins)	29	42	0	.408	19½	Birmingham (White Sox)	31	41	0	.431	15½
Carolina (Pirates)	24	48	0	.333	25	Knoxville (Blue Jays)	27	41	0	.397	17½

SECOND HALF

EASTERN DIVISION						WESTERN DIVISION					
Team	W	L	T	Pct.	GB	Team	W	L	T	Pct.	GB
Greenville (Braves)	51	20	0	.718	......	Chattanooga (Reds)	44	28	1	.611	......
Charlotte (Cubs)	35	37	0	.486	16½	Birmingham (White Sox)	37	33	2	.529	6
Orlando (Twins)	31	40	2	.437	20	Huntsville (Athletics)	38	34	0	.528	6
Jacksonville (Mariners)	30	41	2	.423	21	Memphis (Royals)	37	36	0	.507	7½
Carolina (Pirates)	28	44	1	.389	23½	Knoxville (Blue Jays)	29	47	0	.382	17

COMPOSITE

Team	Grn.	Chat.	Hunt.	Mem.	Char.	Birm.	Jack.	Orl.	Knox.	Caro.	W	L	T	Pct.	GB
Greenville (Braves)	....	7	9	9	13	9	9	11	19	14	100	43	0	.699	......
Chattanooga (Reds)	6	....	6	8	9	20	10	8	14	9	90	53	1	.629	10
Huntsville (Athletics)	5	10	....	17	6	10	5	8	10	10	81	63	0	.563	19½
Memphis (Royals)	5	8	9	....	8	7	6	8	10	10	71	73	0	.493	29½
Charlotte (Cubs)	3	5	8	6	....	7	6	11	7	17	70	73	0	.490	30
Birmingham (White Sox)	5	6	6	9	7	....	9	8	10	8	68	74	2	.479	31½
Jacksonville (Mariners)	7	4	6	8	9	5	....	15	6	8	68	75	2	.476	32
Orlando (Twins)	5	6	6	6	5	4	11	....	8	9	60	82	2	.423	39½
Knoxville (Blue Jays)	5	2	6	6	7	6	8	6	....	10	56	88	0	.389	44½
Carolina (Pirates)	2	5	4	4	9	6	11	7	4	....	52	92	1	.361	48½

Carolina's home games played in Zebulon, N.C.

Major league affiliations in parentheses.

Playoffs—Greenville defeated Charlotte, three games to none; Chattanooga defeated Huntsville, three games to one; Greenville defeated Chattanooga, three games to two, to win league championship.

Regular-season attendance—Birmingham, 263,323; Carolina, 263,141; Charlotte, 338,047; Chattanooga, 269,688; Greenville, 247,798; Huntsville, 252,010; Jacksonville, 226,273; Knoxville, 90,387; Memphis, 212,448; Orlando, 154,965. Total, 2,318,080. Playoffs (12 games)—25,269. Class AA All-Star Game at Charlotte, N.C.—4,009.

Managers—Birmingham, Tony Franklin; Carolina, Don Werner; Charlotte, Marv Foley; Chattanooga, Dave Miley (through June 26), Tom Nieto (June 27 through June 29), Ron Oester (June 30 through end of season); Greenville, Grady Little; Huntsville, Casey Parsons; Jacksonville, Bob Hartsfield; Knoxville, Garth Iorg; Memphis, Brian Poldberg; Orlando, Phil Roof. Managerial records of team with more than one manager: Chattanooga, Miley (51-25), Nieto (2-1), Oester (37-27-1).

All-Star team: 1B—(tie) Marcos Armas, Huntsville, and Tim Costo, Chattanooga; 2B—Brian Turang, Jacksonville; 3B—Phil Hiatt, Memphis; SS—Chipper Jones, Greenville; OF—Scott Pose, Chattanooga; Juan De La Rosa, Knoxville; Melvin Nieves, Greenville; Scott Lydy, Huntsville; C—Javier Lopez, Greenville; DH—Nigel Wilson, Knoxville; RHP—Nate Minchey, Greenville; LHP—Larry Thomas, Birmingham; Player of the Year—Javier Lopez, Greenville; Pitcher of the Year—(tie) Jim Converse, Jacksonville, and Jerry Spradlin, Chattanooga; Manager of the Year—Grady Little, Greenville.

BATTING

TEAM

Team	Avg.	G	AB	R	OR	H	TB	2B	3B	HR	RBI	SH	SF	HP	BB	Int. BB	SO	SB	CS	LOB
Greenville	.266	143	4722	709	451	1258	1991	237	53	130	643	30	27	526	23	923	168	96	956
Chattanooga	.264	144	4680	631	507	1235	1836	229	30	104	580	36	43	49	505	28	1007	102	93	1004
Huntsville	.260	144	4821	654	605	1254	1802	218	39	84	578	33	46	30	521	21	1015	144	71	1030
Jacksonville	.259	145	4720	566	586	1221	1777	196	24	104	521	33	45	76	439	11	815	142	93	997
Orlando	.258	144	4603	611	684	1187	1747	221	24	97	543	35	46	56	434	9	896	120	73	932
Knoxville	.256	144	4643	504	662	1188	1732	209	55	75	442	60	33	46	277	15	967	82	89	858
Charlotte	.247	143	4592	593	551	1134	1662	210	18	94	523	60	42	58	479	18	840	64	58	973
Carolina	.243	145	4618	483	622	1123	1531	175	34	55	428	26	38	45	442	20	895	151	116	930
Memphis	.242	144	4651	526	592	1125	1654	215	31	84	485	45	37	55	383	14	823	77	90	886
Birmingham	.232	144	4672	524	541	1082	1489	195	22	56	464	41	38	37	438	21	1001	87	53	946

INDIVIDUAL

(Leading qualifiers for batting championship—389 or more plate appearances)

*Bats lefthanded.   †Switch-hitter.

Player, Team	Avg.	G	AB	R	H	TB	2B	3B	HR	RBI	SH	SF	HP	BB	Int. BB	SO	SB	CS
Pose, Scott, Chattanooga*	.342	136	526	87	180	224	22	8	2	45	4	3	4	63	5	66	21	21
De La Rosa, Juan, Knoxville	.329	136	508	68	167	259	32	12	12	53	2	5	8	15	0	94	16	12
Rohrmeier, Dan, Memphis	.323	123	433	54	140	195	33	2	6	69	0	4	4	26	2	46	3	7
Lopez, Javy, Greenville	.321	115	442	63	142	224	28	3	16	60	1	2	5	24	1	47	7	3
Lydy, Scott, Huntsville	.305	109	387	64	118	171	20	3	9	65	0	4	4	67	5	95	16	5
Walbeck, Matt, Charlotte†	.301	105	385	48	116	161	22	1	7	42	3	2	2	33	3	56	0	7
Vice, Darryl, Huntsville†	.295	131	481	75	142	160	13	1	1	38	4	2	1	86	5	89	9	2

Player, Team	Avg.	G	AB	R	H	TB	2B	3B	HR	RBI	SH	SF	HP	BB	Int. BB	SO	SB	CS
Tarasco, Tony, Greenville*	.286	133	489	73	140	211	22	2	15	54	3	7	1	27	2	84	33	19
Maynard, Tow, Jacksonville	.283	122	406	55	115	138	12	4	1	29	5		13	32	1	85	38	18
Armas, Marcos, Huntsville	.283	132	509	83	144	237	30	6	17	84	0	6	3	41	4	133	9	1

Departmental leaders: G—R. Perez, 139; AB—R. Perez, Pose, 526; R—Pose, 87; H—Pose, 180; TB—N. Wilson, 269; 2B—De La Nuez, N. Wilson, 34; 3B—De La Rosa, 12; HR—Costo, 28; RBI—Cepicky, 87; SH—Henderson, 11; SF—De La Nuez, Jensen, 8; HP—Crockett, 21; BB—Vice, 86; IBB—Yan, 6; SO—M. Kelly, 162; SB—Maynard, 38; CS—Pose, 27.

(All players—listed alphabetically)

Player, Team	Avg.	G	AB	R	H	TB	2B	3B	HR	RBI	SH	SF	HP	BB	Int. BB	SO	SB	CS
Abbott, Kurt, Huntsville	.254	124	452	64	115	166	14	5	9	52	4	3	3	31	0	75	16	5
Adams, Tommy, Jacksonville	.220	17	50	4	11	13	2	0	0	5	0	0	1	2	0	13	1	0
Alicea, Ed, Greenville†	.235	102	315	49	74	118	13	8	5	33	2	4	1	47	4	55	13	10
Allen, Rick, 7 Chat.-84 Orl.	.194	91	232	15	45	61	9	2	1	18	2	2	1	15	0	44	5	3
Alvarez, Clemente, Birmingham	.142	57	169	7	24	35	8	0	1	10	3	0	2	10	0	52	1	1
Anderson, Mike, Chattanooga	.000	28	15	0	0	0	0	0	0	0	1	0	0	1	0	10	0	0
Armas, Marcos, Huntsville	.283	132	509	83	144	237	30	6	17	84	0	6	3	41	4	133	9	1
Aude, Rich, Carolina	.200	6	20	4	4	11	1	0	2	3	0	0	0	1	0	3	0	0
Ayala, Bobby, Chattanooga	.267	27	15	2	4	8	1	0	1	1	2	0	0	0	0	6	0	0
Backlund, Brett, Carolina	.000	3	3	0	0	0	0	0	0	0	0	0	0	0	0	1	0	0
Bark, Brian, Greenville*	.000	12	6	0	0	0	0	0	0	0	0	0	0	0	0	1	0	0
Beasley, Tony, Carolina	.259	49	158	12	41	55	5	3	1	13	1	1	0	8	0	33	13	8
Beeler, Pete, Carolina	.198	36	116	7	23	34	5	0	2	18	0	2	0	7	0	14	0	0
Bell, Mike, Greenville*	.254	121	421	57	107	167	23	5	9	63	0	6	1	55	2	75	1	5
Bernhardt, Cesar, 24 Bir.-42 Mem.	.179	66	240	24	43	50	4	0	1	11	3	1	1	14	0	34	5	4
Bird, Dave, Carolina	.111	28	18	2	2	2	0	0	0	0	0	0	0	0	0	5	0	0
Bishop, Jim, Birmingham	.245	90	310	26	76	104	13	0	5	44	0	1	1	30	0	100	2	2
Bolick, Frank, Jacksonville†	.268	63	224	32	60	108	9	0	13	42	0	4	1	42	1	38	1	4
Borbon, Pedro, Greenville	.143	39	7	0	1	2	1	0	0	0	1	0	1	0	0	4	0	0
Borrelli, Dean, Huntsville	.202	85	238	20	48	56	5	0	1	23	3	2	2	26	0	45	3	3
Bowie, Jim, Jacksonville*	.286	80	276	36	79	125	16	0	10	43	1	2	3	41	2	40	0	1
Bradford, Troy, Charlotte	.000	2	1	0	0	0	0	0	0	0	0	0	0	0	0	0	0	0
Bridges, Tony, Memphis†	.138	24	58	7	8	10	2	0	0	4	2	0	0	8	0	19	1	1
Brito, Jorge, Huntsville	.208	33	72	10	15	23	2	0	2	6	3	0	1	13	0	21	2	0
Brito, Tilzon, Knoxville	.208	7	24	2	5	10	1	2	0	2	0	0	0	0	0	6	0	0
Brooks, Eric, Knoxville	.000	6	8	0	0	0	0	0	0	0	0	0	0	0	0	3	0	0
Bryant, Scott, Charlotte	.150	6	20	3	3	9	1	1	1	2	0	0	0	1	0	9	0	0
Buccheri, Jim, Huntsville	.150	20	60	8	9	16	2	1	1	5	1	1	0	9	0	18	5	3
Buckholz, Steve, Carolina	.200	20	5	0	1	1	0	0	0	1	0	0	0	0	0	0	0	0
Bullard, Jason, Carolina	.000	19	2	0	0	0	0	0	0	0	0	0	0	0	0	2	0	0
Bullett, Scott, Carolina*	.270	132	518	59	140	194	20	3	8	45	2	7	10	28	0	98	29	21
Burgos, Paco, Memphis†	.201	92	278	23	56	73	8	0	3	23	3	4	1	8	0	16	6	7
Burlingame, Dennis, Greenville	.133	26	15	1	2	2	0	0	0	0	3	0	0	0	0	4	0	0
Busby, Wayne, Birmingham	.163	62	178	20	29	36	5	1	0	12	0	1	1	23	0	72	6	3
Campanis, Jim, Jacksonville	.262	89	286	30	75	103	11	1	5	29	3	2	13	22	0	38	2	3
Campbell, Darrin, Birmingham	.223	66	202	27	45	71	11	0	5	24	1	4	1	17	3	47	4	3
Capellan, Carlos, Orlando	.167	4	6	3	1	1	0	0	0	0	0	0	0	0	0	0	0	0
Caraballo, Gary, Memphis	.210	58	195	17	41	60	6	2	3	17	3	1	5	7	0	37	1	3
Caraballo, Ramon, Greenville†	.312	24	93	15	29	44	4	4	1	8	0	1	0	14	0	13	10	6
Carcione, Tom, Huntsville	.167	17	48	3	8	11	0	0	1	4	1	0	1	5	0	11	0	0
Casarotti, Rich, Charlotte†	.203	68	192	20	39	58	5	4	2	22	6	1	1	12	2	38	3	3
Casillas, Adam, Memphis*	.327	49	168	25	55	77	12	2	2	23	1	0	2	32	2	6	1	4
Castellano, Pedro, Charlotte	.224	45	147	16	33	39	3	0	1	15	3	2	4	19	0	21	0	1
Castleberry, Kevin, Birmingham*	.257	104	382	57	98	123	9	5	2	26	0	1	3	48	1	59	13	10
Cedeno, Domingo, Knoxville*	.226	106	337	31	76	103	7	7	2	21	7	0	4	18	0	88	8	9
Cepicky, Scott, Birmingham*	.247	138	502	56	124	198	30	1	14	87	3	5	5	44	5	140	1	2
Coffman, Kevin, Greenville	.333	6	3	0	1	1	0	0	0	0	0	0	0	0	0	0	0	0
Cole, Stu, Memphis	.236	49	174	19	41	51	8	1	0	12	2	1	2	18	2	23	7	7
Colvard, Benny, Chattanooga	.257	108	366	46	94	158	20	1	14	47	1	6	4	26	3	85	6	7
Conte, Mike, Huntsville	.238	97	290	32	69	88	10	3	1	26	5	5	2	38	0	42	6	5
Cooke, Steve, Carolina	.000	6	2	0	0	0	0	0	0	0	0	0	0	0	0	2	0	0
Cooley, Fred, Orlando	.310	42	126	15	39	56	2	0	5	24	0	1	2	13	0	28	1	0
Costo, Tim, Chattanooga	.241	121	424	63	102	208	18	2	28	71	1	2	11	48	1	128	4	5
Cox, Darron, Chattanooga	.254	98	331	49	84	108	19	1	1	38	1	6	5	15	0	63	8	3
Crockett, Rusty, Charlotte	.239	107	314	33	75	89	9	1	1	26	7	2	21	24	0	47	9	6
Cromwell, Nate, Knoxville*	.500	37	2	0	1	1	0	0	0	1	0	0	0	0	0	0	0	0
Dattola, Kevin, Huntsville†	.247	103	324	31	80	107	15	3	2	34	4	3	3	39	0	65	14	9
Dauphin, Phil, Charlotte*	.254	136	515	63	131	191	24	3	10	43	6	4	6	55	2	71	17	10
David, Greg, Memphis*	.220	92	232	21	51	67	11	1	1	24	3	2	2	38	2	50	1	4
De La Nuez, Rex, Orlando	.268	132	437	70	117	191	34	2	12	59	6	8	12	69	0	88	13	10
De La Rosa, Juan, Knoxville	.329	136	508	84	167	259	32	12	12	53	2	5	8	15	0	94	16	12
Delarwelle, Chris, Orlando	.264	94	296	29	78	99	11	2	2	32	3	3	2	29	0	54	5	2
Delgado, Tim, Charlotte	.000	6	1	0	0	0	0	0	0	0	0	0	0	0	0	0	0	0
Delima, Rafael, Orlando*	.167	19	36	8	6	7	1	0	0	2	3	0	0	0	0	10	1	1
De Los Santos, Alberto, Carolina	.262	108	355	34	93	115	9	5	1	24	0	3	0	17	0	46	17	9
Diaz, Carlos, Memphis	.188	37	101	9	19	27	5	0	1	12	1	3	3	0	0	15	1	1
Diaz, Kiki, Chattanooga	.258	129	472	72	122	137	11	2	0	45	6	7	3	71	2	45	7	3
Dixon, Eddie, Carolina	.000	25	1	0	0	0	0	0	0	0	0	0	0	0	0	0	0	0
Duffy, Darrin, Charlotte	.132	17	53	9	7	9	2	0	0	1	0	1	0	2	1	12	1	0
Durso, Joe, Knoxville	.188	6	16	0	3	3	0	0	0	2	0	0	0	2	1	8	0	0
Ebright, Chris, Charlotte*	.255	123	404	61	103	180	22	2	17	77	4	3	3	52	4	98	7	3
Edge, Greg, Carolina†	.235	75	251	21	59	66	7	0	0	9	3	2	0	22	1	19	12	13
Edge, Tim, Carolina	.111	4	9	1	1	1	0	0	0	0	0	0	0	1	0	5	0	0
Elliott, Donnie, Greenville	.111	19	9	0	1	1	0	0	0	0	0	0	0	0	0	5	0	0
Escalera, Ruben, Chattanooga*	.270	50	141	22	38	47	7	1	0	15	2	2	5	22	1	19	6	4
Estep, Chris, 28 Car.-40 Chat.	.245	68	163	14	40	54	9	1	1	12	1	0	1	25	2	38	6	5
Fansler, Stan, Carolina	.083	25	12	0	1	1	0	0	0	0	0	0	0	0	0	4	0	0
Foster, Lindsay, Birmingham†	.218	76	211	24	46	56	6	2	0	22	5	1	1	12	1	53	8	6
Fox, Eric, Huntsville*	.271	59	240	42	65	100	16	2	5	14	0	3	0	27	4	43	16	5
Franco, Matt, Charlotte*	.283	108	343	35	97	127	18	3	2	31	0	3	1	26	1	46	3	3
Garber, Jeff, Memphis	.221	108	326	37	72	114	17	2	7	38	4	3	7	29	1	66	9	3
Garcia, Cheo, Orlando	.258	135	488	54	126	169	27	2	4	44	2	5	4	30	0	60	32	23

Player, Team	Avg.	G	AB	R	H	TB	2B	3B	HR	RBI	SH	SF	HP	BB	Int. BB	SO	SB	CS
Garner, Kevin, 13 Bir.-51 Chat.*	.300	64	213	36	64	116	10	0	14	53	1	1	1	23	5	48	0	2
Garrison, Webster, Huntsville	.276	91	348	50	96	153	25	4	8	61	3	5	0	30	0	59	8	6
Gillis, Tim, Greenville	.429	2	7	1	3	5	0	1	0	3	0	1	0	1	0	2	0	0
Giovanola, Ed, Greenville*	.267	75	270	39	72	92	5	0	5	30	1	2	0	29	2	40	4	1
Gomez, Pat, Greenville*	.500	8	6	1	3	3	0	0	0	1	0	0	0	0	0	0	0	0
Grace, Mike, Charlotte	.249	89	321	41	80	123	16	3	7	35	1	2	4	27	1	28	4	2
Grayum, Richie, Charlotte*	.243	116	334	46	81	145	25	0	13	52	5	5	1	45	2	84	4	2
Green, Tom, Carolina	.129	21	62	3	8	9	1	0	0	3	2	0	0	13	0	17	0	3
Greene, Willie, Chattanooga*	.278	96	349	47	97	165	19	2	15	66	1	5	3	46	3	90	9	9
Griffin, Ty, Chattanooga†	.239	114	347	44	83	120	16	3	5	38	2	4	0	66	2	85	8	9
Grifol, Pedro, Orlando	.275	14	40	2	11	13	2	0	0	5	0	1	0	2	0	9	0	1
Grunhard, Dan, Huntsville*	.286	23	84	11	24	35	4	2	1	9	0	1	0	5	1	20	1	1
Gustafson, Ed, Orlando	.000	34	1	0	0	0	0	0	0	0	0	0	0	0	0	1	0	0
Hamelin, Bob, Memphis*	.333	35	120	23	40	66	8	0	6	22	0	0	0	26	2	17	0	1
Harmes, Kris, Knoxville	.304	7	23	2	7	8	1	0	0	4	0	0	1	0	1	4	0	0
Harris, Robert, Birmingham	.248	86	282	40	70	94	13	1	3	24	4	3	3	10	0	60	13	5
Hartung, Andy, Charlotte	.333	2	9	1	3	7	1	0	1	3	0	0	0	0	0	1	0	0
Hawblitzel, Ryan, Charlotte	.214	29	28	4	6	7	1	0	0	3	0	0	0	0	0	8	0	0
Heath, Lee, Greenville†	.250	2	4	2	1	4	0	0	1	3	0	0	1	1	0	1	1	1
Heffernan, Bert, Jacksonville*	.286	58	196	16	56	71	9	0	2	23	2	2	2	29	0	28	4	7
Helfand, Eric, Huntsville*	.228	37	114	13	26	39	7	0	2	9	0	1	5	0	0	32	0	0
Hemond, Scott, Huntsville	.333	9	27	3	9	9	0	0	0	2	0	0	0	4	0	8	2	0
Henderson, Derek, Knoxville	.252	127	425	37	107	133	12	4	2	39	11	2	6	25	0	72	6	9
Hernandez, Cesar, Chattanooga	.277	93	328	50	91	132	24	4	3	27	2	0	4	19	1	65	12	9
Hiatt, Phil, Memphis	.244	129	487	71	119	230	20	5	27	83	1	3	5	25	1	157	5	10
Hoffman, Trevor, Chattanooga	.250	6	4	0	1	1	0	0	0	1	0	0	0	0	0	1	0	0
Holley, Bobby, Jacksonville	.276	124	402	51	111	164	19	2	10	45	2	4	8	39	1	66	4	8
Hostetler, Mike, Greenville	.125	16	8	1	1	1	0	0	0	1	1	0	0	2	0	1	0	0
Hunter, Bobby, Carolina†	.000	32	1	0	0	0	0	0	0	0	0	0	0	0	0	0	0	0
Hunter, Greg, Jacksonville*	.209	14	43	4	9	12	0	0	1	5	0	0	1	6	1	8	1	0
Imes, Rodney, Chattanooga	.500	45	4	1	2	3	1	0	0	0	0	0	0	0	0	1	0	0
Jacas, Dave, Huntsville	.265	116	441	62	117	161	21	4	5	48	2	5	5	43	2	80	18	10
Jaques, Eric, Charlotte*	.000	46	1	0	0	0	0	0	0	0	0	0	0	1	0	1	0	0
Jaster, Scott, Birmingham	.279	96	326	45	91	129	13	2	7	33	0	3	8	45	3	65	3	0
Jenkins, Bernie, Chattanooga	.313	22	48	7	15	22	3	2	0	4	0	0	2	6	0	12	2	1
Jennings, Lance, Memphis	.145	52	145	5	21	29	5	0	1	8	1	1	1	6	0	33	0	0
Jensen, John, Charlotte*	.261	116	399	64	104	162	16	0	14	54	0	8	5	55	1	86	5	7
Johnson, Judd, Greenville	.250	43	4	0	1	1	0	0	0	1	0	0	0	0	0	1	0	0
Johnson, Mark, Carolina*	.232	122	383	40	89	128	16	1	7	45	1	0	3	55	4	94	16	11
Jones, Chipper, Greenville†	.346	67	266	43	92	158	17	11	9	42	4	4	0	11	1	32	14	1
Kelly, Mike, Greenville	.229	133	471	83	108	209	18	4	25	71	0	3	6	65	2	162	22	11
Kelly, Pat, Greenville	.249	98	325	44	81	97	12	2	0	36	1	1	2	26	1	55	11	3
Kilgo, Rusty, Chattanooga*	.000	24	3	0	0	0	0	0	0	0	0	0	0	0	0	0	0	0
Kizziah, Daren, Knoxville	.000	38	1	0	0	0	0	0	0	0	0	0	0	0	0	0	0	0
Knabenshue, Chris, Huntsville*	.197	21	71	9	14	21	4	0	1	11	0	1	0	10	0	24	1	2
Kowitz, Brian, Greenville*	.286	21	56	9	16	20	4	0	0	6	0	0	0	6	0	10	1	4
Kremblas, Frank, Chattanooga	.230	100	282	29	65	83	16	1	0	28	5	2	1	18	1	58	4	5
Kutzler, Jerry, Charlotte*	.000	12	2	0	0	0	0	0	0	0	0	0	0	0	0	0	0	0
Kvasnicka, Jay, Orlando*	.236	51	165	19	39	52	1	3	2	12	1	2	2	15	1	39	3	1
Lane, Brian, Chattanooga	.282	38	142	21	40	56	7	0	3	23	0	1	1	19	1	32	3	1
Lawton, Marcus, Memphis†	.143	14	42	4	6	6	0	0	0	1	2	0	0	7	1	9	1	1
Leiper, Tim, Memphis*	.256	73	246	37	63	83	10	2	2	21	4	4	1	31	0	29	4	1
Letterio, Shane, Jacksonville	.156	46	90	5	14	16	2	0	0	5	3	0	1	8	0	20	1	2
Lewis, Mica, Orlando	.271	128	380	61	103	137	13	3	5	36	5	1	0	48	0	99	36	9
Liebert, Al, Birmingham*	.251	72	219	18	55	77	13	0	3	25	1	4	0	19	0	41	0	1
List, Paul, Carolina	.208	9	24	3	5	6	1	0	0	1	0	0	0	3	1	3	0	0
Lonigro, Greg, 12 Chat.-67 Bir.	.212	79	255	21	54	74	11	0	3	21	2	0	4	16	2	44	3	3
Lopez, Javy, Greenville	.321	115	442	63	142	224	28	3	16	60	1	2	5	24	1	47	7	3
Luebbers, Larry, Chattanooga	.000	14	7	0	0	0	0	0	0	0	2	0	0	0	0	4	0	0
Lydy, Scott, Huntsville	.305	109	387	64	118	171	20	3	9	65	0	4	4	67	5	95	16	5
Lynch, David, Chattanooga	.000	37	1	0	0	0	0	0	0	0	0	0	0	0	0	1	0	0
Manahan, Anthony, Jacksonville	.257	134	505	70	130	190	24	6	8	49	3	3	2	39	1	76	24	11
Manahan, Austin, Carolina	.221	107	340	44	75	120	18	6	5	33	1	0	4	29	1	101	7	6
Marak, Paul, Charlotte	.000	17	0	0	0	0	0	0	0	0	0	0	0	0	0	0	0	0
Masteller, Dan, Orlando*	.263	116	365	42	96	152	24	4	8	42	3	1	4	23	0	36	2	4
Matos, Francisco, Huntsville	.220	44	150	11	33	43	5	1	1	14	1	1	2	11	0	27	4	4
Maynard, Tow, Jacksonville	.283	122	406	55	115	138	12	4	1	29	5	3	13	32	1	85	38	18
McCarty, Dave, Orlando	.272	129	456	75	124	198	16	2	18	79	1	6	8	55	5	89	6	6
McCreary, Bob, Orlando†	.333	21	6	1	2	2	0	0	0	0	0	0	0	0	0	1	0	0
McDaniel, Terry, Chattanooga†	.263	6	19	1	5	6	1	0	0	3	0	0	0	2	0	3	1	0
McDonald, Mike, Jacksonville*	.258	92	310	49	80	127	17	3	8	33	3	2	4	32	0	58	5	6
McMichael, Greg, Greenville	.000	15	1	0	0	0	0	0	0	0	1	0	0	0	0	1	0	0
Meares, Pat, Orlando	.253	81	300	42	76	104	19	0	3	23	0	2	7	11	1	57	5	5
Melvin, Bill, Charlotte	.000	28	7	0	0	0	0	0	0	0	2	0	0	1	0	3	0	0
Mengel, Brad, Knoxville	.238	89	294	20	70	83	8	1	1	22	9	1	7	9	0	52	5	1
Menhart, Paul, Knoxville	.333	28	3	1	1	2	1	0	0	0	0	0	0	0	0	1	0	0
Merchant, Mark, Jacksonville†	.244	109	381	42	93	143	9	1	13	47	1	6	2	37	2	91	3	2
Minchey, Nate, Greenville	.105	28	19	1	2	2	0	0	0	3	0	0	0	0	0	5	0	0
Montalvo, Rob, Greenville	.167	32	72	7	12	13	1	0	0	4	5	0	0	12	0	19	1	1
Monzon, Jose, Knoxville	.230	65	178	17	41	52	9	1	0	10	3	1	2	12	0	42	3	2
Moore, Kerwin, Memphis†	.235	58	179	27	42	64	4	3	4	17	1	1	2	24	0	39	16	4
Mordecai, Mike, Greenville	.261	65	222	31	58	85	13	1	4	31	1	2	0	29	2	31	9	6
Mota, Domingo, Memphis	.265	119	430	46	114	142	16	0	4	23	9	1	4	19	1	67	14	17
Mulliniks, Rance, Knoxville*	.308	8	26	2	8	12	4	0	0	2	0	0	1	0	1	3	0	1
Neill, Mike, Huntsville*	.313	5	16	4	5	5	0	0	0	2	1	1	0	2	0	3	1	0
Newfield, Marc, Jacksonville	.247	45	162	15	40	64	12	0	4	19	1	1	3	12	0	34	1	5
Nezelek, Andy, Greenville*	.143	46	7	0	1	1	0	0	0	0	1	0	0	0	0	4	0	0
Nieves, Melvin, Greenville†	.283	100	350	61	99	186	23	5	18	76	2	4	6	52	2	98	6	4
Norman, Les, Memphis	.273	72	271	32	74	107	14	5	3	20	1	1	2	22	0	37	4	4
O'Halloran, Greg, Knoxville*	.271	117	409	44	111	147	20	5	2	34	2	5	0	31	2	64	7	7
Ohlms, Mark, Knoxville	1.000	52	1	0	1	2	1	0	0	2	0	0	0	0	0	0	0	0
Olmeda, Jose, Greenville†	.246	106	341	54	84	120	22	4	2	33	1	0	6	38	3	50	12	6
Ortiz, Ray, Orlando*	.263	78	266	40	70	118	16	1	10	47	0	2	1	21	1	46	0	1
Osik, Keith, Carolina	.259	129	425	41	110	144	17	1	5	45	0	4	15	52	1	69	2	9

Player, Team	Avg.	G	AB	R	H	TB	2B	3B	HR	RBI	SH	SF	HP	BB	Int. BB	SO	SB	CS
Osteen, Gavin, Huntsville	.000	16	2	0	0	0	0	0	0	0	0	0	0	0	0	1	0	0
Owens, Jay, Orlando	.267	102	330	50	88	124	24	0	4	30	0	5	11	36	0	67	10	2
Paquette, Craig, Huntsville	.258	115	450	59	116	200	25	4	17	71	1	3	2	29	0	118	13	10
Parker, Tim, Charlotte	.000	2	2	0	0	0	0	0	0	0	0	0	0	0	0	2	0	0
Pasqua, Dan, Birmingham*	.125	3	8	1	1	1	0	0	0	0	0	0	0	2	0	2	0	0
Patrick, Bronswell, Huntsville	.000	29	1	0	0	0	0	0	0	0	0	0	0	0	0	0	0	0
Paulino, Elvin, Charlotte†	.225	45	142	18	32	52	8	0	4	21	0	3	0	13	0	23	1	2
Pennyfeather, William, Carolina	.337	51	199	28	67	100	13	1	6	25	0	3	0	9	1	34	7	6
Perez, Eduardo, Charlotte	.229	91	275	28	63	97	16	0	6	41	1	4	2	24	0	41	3	3
Perez, Pedro, Charlotte	.000	1	1	0	0	0	0	0	0	0	0	0	0	0	0	0	0	0
Perez, Robert, Charlotte	.260	139	526	59	137	199	25	5	9	59	3	7	2	13	0	87	11	10
Perna, Bobby, Chattanooga†	.400	3	10	3	4	7	1	1	0	1	0	0	3	1	0	1	0	0
Pezzoni, Ron, Jacksonville	.226	27	93	10	21	24	3	0	0	15	0	3	1	7	0	19	3	0
Pirkl, Greg, Jacksonville	.291	59	227	25	66	109	11	1	10	29	0	4	7	9	1	45	0	0
Pledger, Kinnis, Birmingham*	.178	60	191	18	34	46	5	2	1	14	5	3	0	19	3	65	2	4
Plemmons, Ron, Birmingham*	.118	15	34	7	4	7	1	1	0	1	0	1	1	6	0	7	0	0
Polcovich, Kevin, Carolina	.171	13	35	1	6	6	0	0	0	1	0	0	2	4	0	4	0	2
Pose, Scott, Chattanooga*	.342	136	526	87	180	224	22	8	2	45	4	3	4	63	5	66	21	27
Powell, Ross, Chattanooga	.000	14	1	0	0	0	0	0	0	0	0	0	0	0	0	1	0	0
Raabe, Brian, Orlando	.278	32	108	12	30	42	6	0	2	6	3	0	0	2	0	2	0	4
Ratliff, Daryl, Carolina	.240	124	413	45	99	118	13	3	0	26	5	4	0	41	0	50	25	11
Ray, Johnny, Chattanooga	.000	24	0	0	0	0	0	0	0	0	1	0	0	0	0	0	0	0
Redington, Tom, Birmingham	.231	88	255	21	59	81	7	0	5	29	2	2	3	26	0	41	0	1
Riesgo, Nikco, Memphis	.103	13	29	6	3	5	0	1	0	4	0	1	1	9	0	12	0	0
Ritter, Darren, Greenville	.000	1	1	0	0	0	0	0	0	0	0	0	0	0	0	0	0	0
Roa, Hector, Greenville	.333	2	9	1	3	3	0	0	0	2	0	0	0	0	0	3	0	0
Roberts, Lonell, Knoxville	.000	5	14	1	0	0	0	0	0	0	0	0	0	1	0	4	1	0
Robertson, Mike, Birmingham*	.189	27	90	6	17	30	8	1	1	9	1	1	0	10	1	19	0	1
Robertson, Richard, Carolina*	.250	20	16	0	4	4	0	0	0	2	0	1	0	2	0	3	0	1
Robinson, Darryl, Memphis	.240	107	354	40	85	142	18	3	11	42	3	4	5	18	0	38	0	4
Robinson, Jim, Charlotte	.253	63	182	19	46	55	6	0	1	23	4	1	2	29	0	22	0	0
Robinson, Scott, Chattanooga	.200	13	10	2	2	2	0	0	0	1	1	0	0	0	0	4	0	0
Rodriguez, Roman, Carolina	.209	28	86	7	18	21	3	0	0	9	1	2	1	6	1	19	1	0
Rohrmeier, Dan, Memphis	.323	123	433	54	140	195	33	2	6	69	0	4		26	2	46	3	7
Romero, Mandy, Carolina†	.216	80	269	28	58	83	16	0	3	27	1	2	1	29	0	39	0	3
Roper, John, Chattanooga	.222	20	9	0	2	2	0	0	0	0	1	0	1	0	1	4	0	0
Roth, Greg, Birmingham*	.500	1	2	1	1	1	0	0	0	0	0	0	0	1	0	0	0	0
Russo, Paul, Orlando	.255	126	420	63	107	190	13	2	22	74	2	5	1	48	0	122	0	1
Salles, John, Charlotte	.333	9	3	0	1	2	1	0	0	0	1	0	0	0	0	1	0	0
Sanford, Mo, Chattanooga	.000	4	2	0	0	0	0	0	0	0	0	0	0	0	0	1	0	0
Satre, Jason, Chattanooga	.400	14	5	1	2	3	1	0	0	0	1	0	2	0	2	0	0	
Schreiber, Bruce, Carolina	.266	81	256	14	68	81	5	4	0	15	4	2	0	10	0	39	5	7
Scott, Shawn, Knoxville†	.224	99	321	31	72	90	4	4	2	26	6	3	0	26	0	60	5	14
Shelton, Ben, Carolina	.234	115	368	57	86	133	17	0	10	51	0	3	8	68	1	117	4	3
Shields, Doug, Memphis	.161	20	31	0	5	5	0	0	0	1	2	0	1	2	0	11	0	0
Shouse, Brian, Carolina*	.000	59	2	0	0	0	0	0	0	0	0	0	0	0	0	1	0	0
Siwa, Joe, Orlando	.198	54	126	9	25	30	3	1	0	11	3	2	1	7	0	40	0	1
Smith, Jack, Orlando	.138	11	29	1	4	4	0	0	0	0	1	0	1	0	0	8	1	0
Sodders, Mike, Charlotte	.250	23	8	1	2	3	1	0	0	1	0	0	0	0	0	2	0	0
Spradlin, Jerry, Chattanooga†	.000	59	2	0	0	0	0	0	0	0	0	0	0	0	0	1	0	0
Stevens, Dave, Charlotte	.059	26	17	1	1	1	0	0	0	1	0	2	0	1	1	4	0	0
Strange, Don, Greenville	.000	48	2	0	0	0	0	0	0	0	0	0	0	0	0	2	0	0
Strauss, Julio, Charlotte	.000	10	1	0	0	0	0	0	0	0	0	0	0	0	0	0	0	0
Sutko, Glenn, Chattanooga	.187	64	198	24	37	71	4	0	10	27	1	2	1	17	1	90	3	2
Swail, Steve, Greenville	.214	5	14	0	3	3	0	0	0	0	0	0	0	0	0	5	0	0
Swartzbaugh, Dave, Charlotte	.111	27	18	0	2	2	0	0	0	0	5	0	0	0	0	11	0	0
Swope, Mark, Orlando	1.000	5	1	1	1	1	0	0	0	0	0	0	0	0	0	0	0	0
Tafoya, Dennis, Carolina	.000	41	2	1	0	0	0	0	0	0	0	1	0	1	0	0	0	0
Tarasco, Tony, Greenville*	.286	133	489	73	140	211	22	2	15	54	3	7	1	27	2	84	33	19
Tatar, Kevin, Chattanooga	.000	9	4	1	0	0	0	0	0	0	0	0	0	0	0	1	0	0
Tavarez, Jesus, Jacksonville	.258	105	392	38	101	123	9	2	3	25	4	4	1	23	0	54	29	14
Taylor, Dwight, Chattanooga*	.211	16	57	6	12	18	3	0	1	9	0	1	1	1	0	12	4	2
Taylor, Mike, Knoxville	.000	14	17	2	0	0	0	0	0	1	1	0	0	1	0	4	0	1
Taylor, Scott, Greenville	.000	22	2	0	0	0	0	0	0	0	0	0	0	1	0	1	0	0
Tedder, Scott, Birmingham*	.235	126	430	54	101	125	15	3	1	47	4	7	2	65	2	34	2	6
Tellers, Dave, Carolina	.000	16	1	0	0	0	0	0	0	0	0	0	0	0	0	0	0	0
Thomas, Keith, Carolina†	.295	22	78	13	23	45	2	4	4	15	0	0		7	0	23	9	1
Timmons, Ozzie, Charlotte	.213	36	122	13	26	42	7	0	3	13	1	0	1	12	0	26	2	2
Todd, Theron, Jacksonville*	.176	23	85	7	15	23	3	1	1	6	2	1	0	4	0	22	4	3
Tollison, David, Knoxville	.226	105	340	37	77	101	15	3	1	22	5	2	3	35	1	77	4	8
Torres, Jessie, Carolina	.203	26	74	10	15	21	3	0	1	9	1	2	0	9	0	22	0	0
Townley, Jason, Knoxville	.232	56	185	7	43	60	11	0	2	20	4	0	1	14	0	48	1	1
Trachsel, Steve, Charlotte	.192	29	26	2	5	6	1	0	0	0	2	0	1	1	0	6	0	0
Trafton, Todd, Chattanooga	.281	67	242	34	68	117	18	2	9	38	0	3		28	2	47	1	1
Treadway, Jeff, Greenville*	.455	4	11	1	5	7	2	0	0	0	1	0	0	1	0	1	0	1
Tunison, Rich, Memphis†	.223	43	130	7	29	44	10	1	1	10	1	2	3	9	0	44	1	3
Turang, Brian, Jacksonville	.251	129	483	67	121	190	21	3	14	63	2	3	12	44	1	61	19	9
Vasquez, Marcos, Greenville	.125	14	8	0	1	1	0	0	0	1	1	0	0	0	0	2	0	0
Vice, Darryl, Huntsville	.295	131	481	75	142	160	13	1	1	38	4	2	1	86	5	89	9	2
Vierra, Joey, Chattanooga*	.000	1	2	0	0	0	0	0	0	0	0	0	0	0	0	0	0	0
Waggoner, Aubrey, Greenville*	.270	90	237	51	64	126	14	3	14	45	0	3	1	70	1	81	21	12
Waggoner, Jimmy, Huntsville*	.063	6	16	0	1	1	0	0	0	0	0	0	0	0	0	3	0	0
Wagner, Paul, Carolina	.231	19	13	1	3	3	0	0	0	0	0	0	0	1	0	5	0	0
Walbeck, Matt, Charlotte†	.301	105	385	48	116	161	22	1	7	42	3	2	2	33	3	56	0	7
Walker, Hugh, Memphis*	.203	23	74	9	15	24	4	1	1	5	0	4		9	0	31	0	5
Washington, U.L., Memphis†	.000	1	2	0	0	0	0	0	0	0	0	0	0	0	0	0	0	0
Watson, Preston, Greenville	.000	48	5	0	0	0	0	0	0	0	0	0	1	0	0	0	0	0
Webb, Ben, Carolina	.000	30	2	0	0	0	0	0	0	0	0	0	0	0	0	1	0	0
Weiss, Scott, Charlotte	.000	5	1	0	0	0	0	0	0	0	0	0	0	0	0	0	0	0
Welch, Doug, Charlotte	.210	52	124	12	26	44	6	0	4	18	2	1	0	8	1	27	0	1
Wetherby, Jeff, Jacksonville*	.250	11	40	5	10	18	5	0	1	7	0	0	1	4	0	6	1	0
White, Billy, Charlotte	.253	121	403	57	102	126	12	0	4	33	6	4	3	46	0	90	10	8
White, Charlie, Birmingham	.213	75	263	29	56	73	10	2	1	17	10	0	0	16	0	40	17	5
White, Rick, Carolina	.000	10	6	0	0	0	0	0	0	0	0	0	0	0	0	2	0	0

Player, Team	Avg.	G	AB	R	H	TB	2B	3B	HR	RBI	SH	SF	HP	BB	Int. BB	SO	SB	CS
Williams, Jerrone, Charlotte†	.203	19	64	6	13	22	3	0	2	8	2	1	0	3	0	16	2	1
Willis, Travis, Charlotte	.000	46	2	0	0	0	0	0	0	0	0	0	0	0	0	1	0	0
Wilson, Brandon, Birmingham	.271	27	107	10	29	33	4	0	0	4	0	0	0	4	0	16	5	0
Wilson, Craig, Jacksonville	.203	25	69	5	14	16	2	0	0	2	1	1	1	7	0	13	0	1
Wilson, Nigel, Knoxville*	.274	137	521	85	143	269	34	7	26	69	2	2	7	33	5	137	13	8
Wolak, Jerry, Birmingham	.296	46	169	18	50	65	13	1	0	13	1	0	2	8	0	25	5	2
Woodall, Brad, Greenville†	.000	21	1	0	0	0	0	0	0	0	0	0	0	0	0	1	0	0
Yan, Julian, Knoxville	.270	111	392	51	106	185	23	4	16	49	0	5	6	28	6	93	1	5
Zimmerman, Mike, Carolina	.357	27	14	0	5	6	1	0	0	1	1	0	2	0	0	3	1	0

The following pitchers, listed alphabetically by club, with games in parentheses, had no plate appearances, primarily through use of designated hitters:

BIRMINGHAM—Bere, Jason (8); Campos, Frank (31); Dabney, Fred (25); Fritz, Greg (1); Hudek, John (5); Johnson, Earnie (16); Kennedy, Bo (18); Keyser, Brian (28); Merigliano, Frank (24); Mongiello, Mike (44); Olsen, Steve (12); Ruffin, Johnny (10); Schrenk, Steve (2); Schwarz, Jeff (21); Shepherd, Keith (40); Stowell, Steve (21); Thomas, Larry (17); Ventura, Jose (18).

CAROLINA—Hancock, Leland (23); Toliver, Fred (15).

CHARLOTTE—Harkey, Mike (1); Hollins, Jessie (63); Tidwell, Mike (1).

CHATTANOOGA—Freed, Dan (10); Grott, Matt (32); Leslie, Reginald (4); Odekirk, Rich (2).

HUNTSVILLE—Allison, Dana (22); Ariola, Anthony (2); Bittiger, Jeff (17); Cormier, Russ (6); Erwin, Scott (23); Garland, Chaon (9); Guzman, Johnny (14); Jiminez, Miguel (1); Johns, Doug (3); Kuhn, Chadwick (19); Latter, Dave (47); Mohler, Mike (44); Phoenix, Steve (32); Revenig, Todd (53); Smith, Todd (5); Smithberg, Roger (20); Strebeck, Rich (30); Wernig, Pat (8); Wilkinson, Bill (15).

JACKSONVILLE—Bond, Daven (18); Borski, Jeff (11); Converse, Jim (27); Czarkowski, Mark (16); Erb, Mike (3); Figueroa, Fernando (53); Garcia, Marcos (5); Grant, Mark (5); Gunderson, Eric (15); Gutierrez, Jim (15); Hampton, Mike (2); Helton, Keith (7); Holman, Brad (35); Kent, Troy (59); Knackert, Brent (21); Newlin, Jim (12); Perkins, Paul (21); Pitcher, Scott (23); Remlinger, Mike (5); Walker, Mike (11); Wiggs, Johnny (8); Woodson, Kerry (11); Zavaras, Clint (21).

KNOXVILLE—Brown, Daren (43); Brown, Tim (24); Crabtree, Tim (3); Cross, Jesse (26); Lloyd, Graeme (49); Moore, Marcus (36); Ogliaruso, Mike (9); Small, Aaron (27); Ward, Anthony (6).

MEMPHIS—Ahern, Brian (11); Alvarez, Evelio (1); Bautista, Jose (1); Campbell, Jim (9); Centala, Scott (9); Corbin, Archie (27); Curry, Steve (27); Duncan, Calvin (33); Givens, Brian (7); Harvey, Greg (6); Karchner, Matt (33); Manzanillo, Josias (2); Miceli, Dan (32); Parnell, Mark (26); Perez, Vladimir (32); Pichardo, Hipolito (2); Pierce, Ed (25); Puig, Benito (68); Sanchez, Alex (1); Ventura, Jose (19); Wiley, Warren (39).

ORLANDO—Best, Jayson (11); Garces, Rich (58); Henry, Jon (28); Klonoski, Jason (54); Leskanic, Curt (26); Lipson, Marc (31); Munoz, Oscar (14); Newman, Alan (18); Pulido, Carlos (19); Richards, Rusty (15); White, Fred (16); Wissler, Bill (13).

GRAND SLAMS—Cepicky, Ortiz, 2 each; Alicea, Armas, Beeler, Dauphin, David, Ebright, Garcia, Garner, Greene, Jacas, M. Johnson, An. Manahan, Merchant, Moore, E. Perez, Redington, Tarasco, A. Waggoner, N. Wilson, 1 each.

AWARDED FIRST BASE ON CATCHER'S INTERFERENCE—Jensen 3 (Owens, Romero, Sutko); Casillas 2 (Campanis, Romero); Beasley (E. Perez); Beeler (Swail); Bell (Heffernan); C. Diaz (Romero); G. Hunter (Cox); Jacas (E. Perez); Ratliff (J. Robinson); Redington (J. Robinson); Turang (Jennings).

PITCHING

TEAM

Team	ERA	G	CG	ShO	Sv.	IP	H	R	ER	HR	HB	BB	Int. BB	SO	WP	Bk.
Greenville	2.64	143	14	24	33	1255.0	1022	451	368	77	50	422	22	1010	69	5
Chattanooga	3.08	144	12	16	48	1246.0	1158	507	427	86	37	418	28	966	88	21
Birmingham	3.27	144	29	17	25	1248.2	1123	541	454	65	28	480	26	896	83	9
Charlotte	3.42	143	20	14	31	1224.2	1148	551	466	100	32	360	21	834	67	8
Memphis	3.57	144	12	9	38	1251.2	1193	592	496	75	58	466	6	942	68	7
Jacksonville	3.67	145	7	15	36	1248.0	1217	586	509	100	59	505	25	923	67	8
Carolina	3.69	145	8	7	22	1235.1	1200	622	506	76	58	449	32	957	70	8
Huntsville	3.69	144	14	42	1263.2	1237	605	518	108	39	425	5	862	48	15
Knoxville	4.08	144	13	7	33	1216.2	1240	662	552	88	67	455	9	888	104	16
Orlando	4.40	144	18	10	22	1198.0	1269	684	586	108	51	464	6	904	80	22

INDIVIDUAL

(Leading qualifiers for earned-run average leadership—115 or more innings)

*Throws lefthanded.

Pitcher, Team	W	L	Pct.	ERA	G	GS	CG	GF	ShO	Sv.	IP	H	R	ER	HR	HB	BB	Int. BB	SO	WP
Thomas, Birmingham*	8	6	.571	1.94	17	17	3	0	0	0	120.2	102	32	26	4	1	30	2	72	5
Minchey, Greenville	13	6	.684	2.30	28	25	5	1	4	0	172.0	137	51	44	7	7	40	2	115	9
Kennedy, Birmingham	10	7	.588	2.38	18	18	6	0	1	0	128.2	117	48	34	5	1	30	2	65	5
Anderson, Chattanooga	13	7	.650	2.52	28	26	4	1	4	0	171.2	155	59	48	4	7	61	1	149	15
Converse, Jacksonville	12	7	.632	2.66	27	26	2	0	0	0	159.0	134	61	47	9	5	82	1	157	4
Ventura, 18 Bir.-9 Mem.	8	15	.348	2.73	27	27	9	0	4	0	184.1	153	73	56	13	9	68	1	123	5
Phoenix, Huntsville	11	5	.688	2.79	32	24	0	1	0	0	174.0	179	68	54	8	7	36	1	124	5
Robertson, Carolina*	6	7	.462	3.03	20	20	1	0	1	0	124.2	127	51	42	7	4	41	2	107	4
Wagner, Carolina	6	6	.500	3.03	19	19	2	0	1	0	121.2	104	52	41	3	3	47	1	101	6
Trachsel, Charlotte	13	8	.619	3.06	29	29	5	0	2	0	191.0	180	76	65	19	4	35	3	135	7

Departmental leaders: G—Puig, 68; W—Anderson, Minchey, Patrick, Trachsel, 13; L—Ventura, Zimmerman, 15; Pct.—Nezelek, .818; GS—Patrick, Trachsel, 29; CG—Ventura, 9; GF—Puig, 59; ShO—Anderson, Minchey, Ventura, 4; Sv.—Spradlin, 34; IP—Trachsel, 191.0; H—Patrick, 187; R—Gustafson, 96; ER—Gustafson, 85; HR—Patrick, 20; HB—T. Brown, Fansler, 13; BB—Converse, 82; IBB—Kent, 8; SO—Converse, 157; WP—Gustafson, 18.

(All pitchers—listed alphabetically)

Pitcher, Team	W	L	Pct.	ERA	G	GS	CG	GF	ShO	Sv.	IP	H	R	ER	HR	HB	BB	Int. BB	SO	WP
Ahern, Memphis	6	2	.750	2.54	11	11	1	0	1	0	71.0	56	23	20	3	6	21	0	51	6
Allen, Orlando	0	0	.000	54.00	1	0	0	0	0	0	0.1	2	2	2	0	0	2	0	0	0
Allison, Huntsville*	4	1	.800	2.93	22	6	0	6	0	1	61.1	51	24	20	8	1	5	0	40	1
Alvarez, Memphis	1	0	1.000	0.00	1	0	0	1	0	0	2.0	1	0	0	0	0	1	0	1	1
Anderson, Chattanooga	13	7	.650	2.52	28	26	4	1	4	0	171.2	155	59	48	4	7	61	1	149	15
Ariola, Huntsville*	2	0	1.000	2.57	2	2	1	0	1	0	14.0	9	4	4	1	0	7	0	7	0
Ayala, Chattanooga	12	6	.667	3.54	27	27	3	0	3	0	162.2	152	75	64	14	11	58	0	154	9
Backlund, Carolina	1	1	.500	1.89	3	3	0	0	0	0	19.0	11	6	4	0	0	3	0	17	0

— 389 —

Pitcher, Team	W	L	Pct.	ERA	G	GS	CG	GF	ShO	Sv.	IP	H	R	ER	HR	HB	BB	Int. BB	SO	WP
Bark, Greenville*	5	0	1.000	1.15	11	11	2	0	1	0	55.0	36	11	7	1	3	13	0	49	3
Bautista, Memphis	1	0	1.000	4.50	1	1	0	0	0	0	6.0	6	3	3	1	0	2	0	7	1
Bell, Greenville*	0	0	.000	0.00	1	0	0	1	0	0	1.0	2	2	0	0	0	1	0	0	1
Bere, Birmingham	4	4	.500	3.00	8	8	4	0	2	0	54.0	44	22	18	1	1	20	1	45	1
Best, Orlando	0	0	.000	0.79	11	0	0	11	0	4	11.1	6	4	1	0	2	5	0	12	2
Bird, Carolina*	5	11	.313	4.41	27	23	1	1	1	0	132.2	149	75	65	9	4	41	3	89	1
Bittiger, Huntsville	10	5	.667	3.09	17	17	0	0	0	0	102.0	89	42	35	2	2	44	0	94	4
Bond, Jacksonville	3	2	.600	4.80	18	4	0	4	0	0	50.2	59	27	27	3	3	19	0	28	5
Borbon, Greenville*	8	2	.800	3.06	39	10	0	14	0	3	94.0	73	36	32	6	3	42	1	79	2
Borski, Jacksonville	1	4	.200	4.98	11	5	0	5	0	0	34.1	39	23	19	2	5	19	2	25	5
Bradford, Charlotte	1	1	.500	3.18	2	2	0	0	0	0	11.1	16	5	4	0	0	3	0	8	1
D. Brown, Knoxville	5	4	.556	3.73	43	1	0	9	0	1	82.0	79	36	34	10	3	22	1	105	8
T. Brown, Knoxville	8	11	.421	3.72	24	24	2	0	0	0	152.1	159	77	63	10	13	32	0	82	6
Buckholz, Carolina	1	4	.200	7.38	20	4	0	2	0	0	46.1	62	47	38	4	3	26	0	32	8
Bullard, Carolina	0	2	.000	7.40	19	0	0	10	0	3	24.1	37	25	20	3	2	11	1	23	3
Burlingame, Greenville	9	9	.500	3.09	26	25	3	0	0	0	151.2	137	65	52	11	5	62	0	84	14
Campbell, Memphis*	4	2	.667	0.86	9	9	1	0	0	0	63.0	48	14	6	1	1	12	0	49	1
Campos, Birmingham	5	3	.625	5.37	31	2	0	15	0	0	53.2	56	37	32	4	0	41	3	31	9
Casillas, Memphis*	1	0	1.000	0.00	1	0	0	1	0	0	2.0	0	0	0	0	0	2	1	2	0
Centala, Memphis	3	3	.500	2.91	9	7	0	1	0	0	43.1	45	17	14	1	6	18	0	30	0
Coffman, Greenville	6	0	1.000	2.13	6	6	1	0	0	0	38.0	23	9	9	1	1	16	0	33	2
Conte, Huntsville	1	0	1.000	7.71	5	0	0	4	0	0	4.2	7	6	4	1	0	1	0	3	1
Converse, Jacksonville	12	7	.632	2.66	27	26	0	1	0	0	159.0	134	61	47	9	5	82	1	157	8
Cooke, Carolina*	2	2	.500	3.00	6	6	0	0	0	0	36.0	31	13	12	1	3	12	1	38	1
Cooley, Orlando	0	1	.000	0.00	1	0	0	1	0	0	0.1	2	1	0	0	0	0	0	0	0
Corbin, Memphis	7	8	.467	4.73	27	20	2	1	0	0	112.1	115	64	59	7	1	73	0	100	11
Cormier, Huntsville	1	1	.500	5.01	6	4	0	1	0	0	23.1	31	15	13	3	2	7	0	13	0
Crabtree, Knoxville	0	2	.000	0.95	3	3	1	0	0	0	19.0	14	8	2	0	2	4	0	13	0
Cromwell, Knoxville*	5	5	.500	5.17	37	10	0	11	0	0	101.0	102	68	58	4	5	69	1	101	17
Cross, Knoxville	8	13	.381	3.54	26	24	2	1	1	0	147.1	136	69	58	12	3	44	1	126	4
Curry, Memphis	8	12	.400	3.95	27	27	2	0	1	0	161.2	156	79	71	9	5	72	0	110	12
Czarkowski, Jacksonville*	7	4	.636	2.74	16	16	2	0	0	0	98.2	105	35	30	5	2	29	0	33	2
Dabney, Birmingham*	2	8	.200	3.84	25	14	0	5	0	0	105.1	116	57	45	9	1	41	1	86	6
Dattola, Huntsville	0	0	.000	9.00	1	0	0	1	0	0	1.0	4	1	1	0	0	0	0	0	1
De La Nuez, Orlando	0	0	.000	6.75	2	0	0	2	0	0	1.1	3	1	1	0	0	0	0	1	0
Delgado, Charlotte	0	0	.000	4.76	6	0	0	1	0	0	11.1	13	7	6	0	1	4	0	7	1
Dixon, Carolina	2	2	.500	3.21	25	0	0	20	0	4	28.0	25	14	10	0	2	3	1	17	0
Duncan, Memphis	0	3	.000	4.66	33	2	1	12	0	3	73.1	72	49	38	7	2	24	1	51	3
Ebright, Charlotte*	0	0	.000	0.00	1	0	0	1	0	0	1.0	0	0	0	0	0	2	0	0	0
Elliott, Greenville	7	2	.778	2.08	19	17	0	0	0	0	103.2	76	28	24	8	5	35	1	100	4
Erb, Jacksonville	0	0	.000	10.38	3	0	0	0	0	0	4.1	12	5	5	0	1	0	0	2	1
Erwin, Huntsville	3	5	.375	3.28	23	0	0	9	0	1	35.2	25	14	13	2	0	27	0	39	2
Fansler, Carolina	7	12	.368	4.17	25	24	2	0	0	0	140.1	127	73	65	17	13	54	0	107	6
Figueroa, Jacksonville*	4	5	.444	2.96	53	1	0	19	0	7	94.1	72	33	31	7	5	33	2	65	9
Freed, Chattanooga	3	2	.600	2.48	10	5	1	3	1	0	40.0	39	13	11	4	0	8	1	35	2
Fritz, Birmingham*	0	0	.000	7.71	1	1	0	0	0	0	7.0	9	6	6	1	0	4	0	3	5
Garces, Orlando	3	3	.500	4.54	58	0	0	42	0	13	73.1	76	46	37	6	2	39	1	72	6
Garcia, Orlando	0	0	.000	32.40	2	0	0	1	0	0	1.2	5	6	6	1	0	5	0	1	0
Garcia, Jacksonville	2	1	.667	1.59	5	3	0	1	0	1	22.2	13	4	4	1	3	8	1	21	1
Garland, Huntsville	3	4	.429	6.59	9	8	0	0	0	0	42.1	49	33	31	7	2	24	0	25	2
Givens, Memphis*	0	0	.000	3.24	7	0	0	1	0	0	8.1	5	5	3	0	0	7	0	9	1
Gomez, Greenville*	7	0	1.000	1.13	8	8	1	0	1	0	47.2	25	8	6	1	0	19	0	38	3
Grant, Jacksonville	1	2	.333	1.93	5	5	0	0	0	0	32.2	25	10	7	2	1	4	0	21	0
Grott, Chattanooga*	1	2	.333	2.68	32	0	0	20	0	6	40.1	39	16	12	4	0	25	4	44	5
Gunderson, Jacksonville*	2	0	1.000	2.31	15	0	0	8	0	2	23.1	18	10	6	2	0	7	0	23	0
Gustafson, Orlando	6	12	.333	5.30	32	23	3	3	1	0	146.0	170	96	86	18	6	61	1	98	18
Gutierrez, Jacksonville	1	5	.167	5.00	15	11	0	1	0	0	54.0	58	34	30	7	3	17	0	44	0
Guzman, Huntsville*	8	2	.800	3.71	14	14	2	0	1	0	89.2	87	43	37	8	8	26	0	55	8
Hampton, Jacksonville*	0	1	.000	4.35	2	2	1	0	0	0	10.1	13	5	5	0	0	1	0	6	1
Hancock, Carolina*	1	1	.500	2.23	23	1	0	6	0	0	40.1	32	13	10	2	0	12	4	40	0
Harkey, Charlotte	0	1	.000	5.63	1	1	0	0	0	0	8.0	9	5	5	2	0	0	0	5	0
Harvey, Memphis	0	3	.000	7.43	6	6	0	0	0	0	23.0	27	25	19	1	2	20	0	12	4
Hawblitzel, Charlotte	12	8	.600	3.76	28	28	3	0	1	0	174.2	180	84	73	18	4	38	3	119	8
Helton, Jacksonville*	1	1	.500	3.86	7	0	0	3	0	0	11.2	8	5	5	2	1	7	1	6	0
Henry, Orlando	10	9	.526	4.12	28	22	1	5	0	0	135.1	147	77	62	10	8	28	0	87	8
Hoffman, Chattanooga	3	0	1.000	1.52	6	6	0	0	0	0	29.2	22	6	5	1	1	11	1	31	3
Hollins, Charlotte	3	4	.429	3.20	63	0	0	56	0	25	70.1	60	28	25	4	1	32	0	73	14
Holman, Jacksonville	3	3	.500	2.57	35	0	0	15	0	4	73.2	67	24	21	6	4	21	3	76	3
Hostetler, Greenville	6	2	.750	3.90	16	13	1	0	0	0	80.2	78	37	35	11	4	23	1	57	3
Hudek, Birmingham	0	1	.000	2.31	5	0	0	4	0	1	11.2	9	4	3	0	0	11	2	9	0
Hunter, Carolina	4	4	.500	2.54	32	5	0	10	0	0	63.2	58	27	18	5	1	21	1	31	3
Imes, Chattanooga	7	2	.778	4.04	45	1	0	12	0	3	89.0	112	49	40	11	1	24	4	51	1
Jaques, Charlotte*	2	5	.286	3.53	46	0	0	16	0	0	66.1	65	36	26	5	2	22	4	50	4
Jimenez, Huntsville	1	0	1.000	1.80	1	1	0	0	0	0	5.0	3	1	1	0	3	0	0	8	0
Johns, Huntsville*	0	0	.000	3.94	3	1	0	1	0	0	16.0	21	11	7	0	0	5	0	4	1
Johnson, Birmingham*	1	1	.500	5.49	16	0	0	9	0	0	19.2	29	12	12	2	1	7	0	24	0
Johnson, Greenville*	6	0	1.000	1.71	43	0	0	16	0	2	68.1	56	21	13	6	2	14	3	40	1
Karchner, Memphis	8	8	.500	4.47	33	18	2	2	0	1	141.0	161	83	70	5	11	35	0	88	8
Kennedy, Birmingham	10	7	.588	2.38	18	18	6	0	1	0	128.2	117	48	34	5	1	30	2	65	5
Kent, Jacksonville	2	6	.250	3.03	59	0	0	50	0	21	68.1	70	30	23	5	3	30	8	62	6
Keyser, Birmingham	9	10	.474	3.73	28	27	1	3	0	0	183.1	173	86	76	12	4	60	1	99	9
Kilgo, Chattanooga*	1	3	.250	3.13	24	0	0	10	0	0	31.2	22	16	11	3	0	11	1	11	2
Kizzian, Huntsville	1	5	.167	5.12	38	3	2	11	0	0	82.2	108	55	47	9	6	28	0	41	7
Klonoski, Orlando*	5	7	.417	3.00	54	0	0	19	0	3	93.0	85	37	31	8	2	29	1	68	3
Knackert, Jacksonville	7	8	.467	4.08	21	19	2	1	1	0	117.0	123	62	53	15	3	41	0	74	0
Kremblas, Chattanooga	0	0	.000	0.00	2	0	0	2	0	0	2.0	2	0	0	0	0	2	0	1	0
Kuhn, Huntsville*	2	6	.250	4.47	19	6	0	5	0	0	50.1	50	29	25	6	2	27	2	37	7
Kutzler, Charlotte	1	2	.333	2.11	12	2	0	3	0	0	38.1	33	12	9	2	0	4	0	28	2
Latter, Huntsville	8	1	.889	3.03	47	0	0	17	0	0	77.1	66	31	26	5	2	27	0	64	2
Leskanic, Orlando	9	11	.450	4.30	26	23	3	1	0	0	152.2	158	84	73	15	9	64	0	126	10
Leslie, Chattanooga	0	0	.000	6.75	4	0	0	2	0	0	5.1	8	4	4	1	0	4	1	2	0
Lipson, Orlando	3	3	.500	5.45	31	0	0	14	0	1	36.1	44	26	22	6	4	16	1	20	1
Lloyd, Knoxville*	4	8	.333	1.96	49	7	1	33	0	14	92.0	79	30	20	2	3	25	2	65	8
Luebbers, Chattanooga	6	5	.545	2.27	14	14	1	0	0	0	87.1	86	34	22	5	4	34	1	56	5

Pitcher, Team	W	L	Pct.	ERA	G	GS	CG	GF	ShO	Sv.	IP	H	R	ER	HR	HB	BB	Int. BB	SO	WP
Lynch, Chattanooga*	3	1	.750	3.00	37	0	0	12	0	2	51.0	39	19	17	4	1	15	2	44	5
Manzanillo, Memphis	0	2	.000	7.36	2	0	0	0	0	0	7.1	6	6	6	0	1	6	0	8	2
Marak, Charlotte	2	4	.333	3.23	17	2	1	6	0	0	39.0	32	15	14	3	2	10	2	29	0
McCreary, Orlando	4	5	.444	3.51	16	8	2	0	0	0	66.2	73	29	26	6	1	18	1	35	2
McMichael, Greenville	4	2	.667	1.36	15	4	0	4	0	1	46.1	37	14	7	2	0	13	2	53	2
Melvin, Charlotte	4	4	.500	2.38	28	6	0	7	0	0	68.0	49	27	18	2	1	38	1	47	3
Mengel, Knoxville	0	0	.000	0.00	1	0	0	1	0	0	0.2	0	0	0	0	0	0	0	0	0
Menhart, Knoxville	10	11	.476	3.85	28	28	2	0	1	0	177.2	181	85	76	14	11	38	0	104	12
Merigliano, Birmingham	6	3	.667	3.08	24	12	1	4	1	1	90.2	67	33	31	5	4	41	2	71	2
Miceli, Memphis	3	0	1.000	1.91	32	0	0	16	0	4	37.2	20	10	8	5	1	13	0	46	1
Minchey, Greenville	13	6	.684	2.30	28	25	5	1	4	0	172.0	137	51	44	7	7	40	2	115	9
Mohler, Huntsville*	3	8	.273	3.59	44	6	0	19	0	3	80.1	72	41	32	5	3	39	1	56	2
Mongiello, Birmingham	5	2	.714	3.83	44	3	0	25	0	8	82.1	76	38	35	3	5	38	3	73	12
Monzon, Knoxville	0	0	.000	0.00	1	0	0	1	0	0	0.2	2	0	0	0	0	0	0	1	0
Moore, Knoxville	5	10	.333	5.59	36	14	1	18	0	0	106.1	110	82	66	10	5	79	0	85	17
Munoz, Orlando	3	5	.375	5.05	14	12	1	1	0	0	67.2	73	44	38	10	4	32	1	74	6
Newlin, Jacksonville	1	1	.500	2.05	12	0	0	11	0	1	22.0	22	5	5	1	2	10	0	13	3
Newman, Orlando*	4	8	.333	4.15	18	18	2	0	1	0	102.0	94	54	47	3	4	67	0	86	9
Nezelek, Greenville	9	2	.818	2.26	46	0	0	8	0	1	107.2	87	36	27	2	12	23	1	114	4
Odekirk, Chattanooga*	0	0	.000	20.25	2	0	0	0	0	0	1.1	5	4	3	0	0	3	0	1	1
Ogliaruso, Knoxville	1	4	.200	8.00	9	4	0	2	0	0	27.0	46	28	24	2	2	15	0	11	3
Ohlms, Knoxville	3	2	.600	1.55	52	0	0	43	0	18	69.2	49	15	12	2	6	26	4	50	5
Olsen, Birmingham	6	4	.600	3.03	12	12	1	0	0	0	77.1	68	28	26	5	0	29	1	46	2
Osik, Carolina	0	0	.000	0.00	2	0	0	2	0	0	2.2	2	0	0	0	0	0	0	3	0
Osteen, Huntsville*	5	5	.500	3.61	16	16	1	0	0	0	102.1	106	45	41	9	1	27	0	56	2
Parker, Charlotte	0	2	.000	12.46	2	2	0	0	0	0	8.2	17	12	12	3	0	3	0	6	2
Parnell, Memphis	4	7	.364	6.14	26	2	0	15	0	1	48.1	58	36	33	5	6	14	0	40	2
Patrick, Huntsville	13	7	.650	3.76	29	29	3	0	0	0	179.1	187	84	75	20	4	46	0	98	3
Perez, Charlotte	0	0	.000	7.71	1	0	0	0	0	0	2.1	4	3	2	0	0	1	0	3	0
Perez, Memphis	3	3	.500	2.57	32	1	0	6	0	1	70.0	71	26	20	3	2	24	0	48	3
Perkins, Jacksonville	2	3	.400	5.57	21	0	0	14	0	0	32.1	29	20	20	5	1	15	2	17	0
Phoenix, Huntsville	11	5	.688	2.79	32	24	0	1	0	0	174.0	179	68	54	8	7	36	1	124	5
Pichardo, Memphis	0	0	.000	0.64	2	2	0	0	0	0	14.0	13	2	1	0	0	1	0	10	0
Pierce, Memphis*	10	10	.500	3.81	25	25	1	0	1	0	153.2	159	74	65	11	3	51	1	131	8
Pitcher, Jacksonville	5	2	.714	3.41	23	6	0	4	0	0	63.1	62	27	24	1	1	23	1	32	1
Powell, Chattanooga*	4	1	.800	1.26	14	5	0	2	0	1	57.1	43	9	8	2	0	17	1	56	3
Puig, Memphis*	4	2	.667	2.02	68	0	0	59	0	25	75.2	45	17	17	4	1	21	1	64	1
Pulido, Orlando*	6	2	.750	4.40	52	5	0	20	0	1	100.1	99	52	49	7	3	37	0	87	4
Raabe, Orlando	0	0	.000	0.00	1	0	0	1	0	0	0.2	0	0	0	0	0	0	0	0	0
Ray, Chattanooga	4	1	.800	3.63	24	1	0	11	0	1	57.0	61	27	23	4	3	14	4	30	0
Redington, Birmingham	0	1	.000	27.00	1	0	0	1	0	0	0.1	2	1	1	0	0	1	0	1	0
Remlinger, Jacksonville*	1	1	.500	3.46	5	5	0	0	0	0	26.0	25	15	10	1	0	11	0	21	2
Revenig, Huntsville	1	1	.500	1.70	53	0	0	48	0	33	63.2	33	14	12	8	0	11	0	49	1
Richards, Orlando	4	7	.364	5.12	15	15	1	0	0	0	84.1	89	52	48	4	2	29	0	64	4
Ritter, Greenville	1	0	1.000	4.50	1	0	0	0	0	0	4.0	3	2	2	1	0	6	0	0	0
Robertson, Carolina*	6	7	.462	3.03	20	20	1	0	1	0	124.2	127	51	42	7	4	41	2	107	4
Robinson, Memphis	0	0	.000	4.50	2	0	0	2	0	0	2.0	1	3	1	1	0	3	0	1	0
Robinson, Chattanooga	7	2	.778	3.80	13	13	1	0	1	0	83.0	82	38	35	7	2	26	0	51	4
Roper, Chattanooga	10	9	.526	4.10	20	20	1	0	1	0	120.1	115	57	55	11	4	37	2	99	15
Ruffin, Birmingham	0	7	.000	6.04	10	10	0	0	0	0	47.2	51	48	32	3	1	34	0	44	9
Salles, Charlotte	6	2	.750	2.41	9	9	2	0	1	0	59.2	55	19	16	2	1	8	1	32	3
Sanchez, Memphis	0	1	.000	6.00	1	1	0	0	0	0	6.0	4	4	4	0	1	2	0	6	0
Sanford, Chattanooga	4	0	1.000	1.35	4	4	1	0	1	0	26.2	13	5	4	2	2	6	0	28	1
Satre, Chattanooga	3	5	.375	5.43	14	11	0	2	0	0	58.0	56	42	35	7	1	26	1	36	4
Schrenk, Birmingham	1	1	.500	3.65	2	2	0	0	0	0	12.1	13	5	5	0	1	11	0	9	1
Schwarz, Birmingham	2	1	.667	1.16	21	0	0	16	0	6	38.2	16	5	5	1	4	9	2	53	2
Scott, Knoxville	0	0	.000	162.00	1	0	0	0	0	0	0.1	2	7	6	0	0	4	0	1	2
Shepherd, Birmingham	3	3	.500	2.14	40	0	0	30	0	7	71.1	50	19	17	1	1	20	2	64	7
Shouse, Carolina*	5	6	.455	2.44	59	0	0	33	0	4	77.1	71	31	21	3	2	28	4	79	4
Small, Knoxville	5	12	.294	5.27	27	24	2	0	1	0	135.0	152	94	79	13	6	61	0	79	14
Smith, Huntsville	0	1	.000	5.63	5	0	0	1	0	0	8.0	13	5	5	2	0	2	0	6	1
Smithberg, Huntsville	3	3	.500	4.00	20	0	0	8	0	1	36.0	42	17	16	4	2	12	1	19	1
Sodders, Charlotte*	4	5	.444	3.57	23	8	2	4	2	0	68.0	65	28	27	5	1	20	1	39	3
Spradlin, Chattanooga	3	3	.500	1.38	59	0	0	53	0	34	65.1	52	11	10	1	0	13	3	35	3
Stevens, Charlotte	9	13	.409	3.91	26	26	2	0	0	0	149.2	147	79	65	16	5	53	1	89	8
Stowell, Birmingham*	1	2	.333	3.00	21	0	0	5	0	2	21.0	20	9	7	1	0	11	2	20	4
Strange, Greenville	5	3	.625	2.40	48	0	0	41	0	18	60.0	43	19	16	3	1	19	3	58	3
Strauss, Charlotte	0	1	.000	3.38	10	0	0	4	0	0	18.2	19	9	7	3	0	4	0	17	1
Strebeck, Huntsville	1	6	.143	6.79	30	4	0	10	0	2	51.2	67	43	39	2	1	31	0	32	2
Sutko, Chattanooga	0	0	.000	1.69	4	1	0	2	0	1	5.1	5	1	1	0	0	3	0	4	2
Swartzbaugh, Charlotte	7	10	.412	3.65	27	27	5	0	2	0	165.0	134	78	67	13	9	62	2	111	5
Swope, Orlando	1	0	1.000	4.50	4	4	0	0	0	0	16.0	26	15	8	2	1	6	0	6	3
Tafoya, Carolina	3	5	.375	3.11	41	2	0	17	0	2	75.1	72	32	26	2	5	17	5	51	3
Tatar, Chattanooga	5	4	.556	3.13	9	9	0	0	0	0	54.2	45	22	19	1	0	20	1	46	8
Taylor, Knoxville	0	1	.000	2.70	1	0	0	1	0	0	3.1	3	1	1	0	0	2	0	3	0
Taylor, Carolina	1	1	.500	6.69	22	4	0	6	0	1	39.0	44	31	29	6	3	18	0	20	3
Tellers, Carolina	2	1	.667	3.55	16	0	0	6	0	2	25.1	23	11	10	2	2	9	2	23	1
Thomas, Birmingham*	8	6	.571	1.94	17	17	3	0	0	0	120.2	102	32	26	4	1	30	2	72	5
Tidwell, Charlotte*	0	0	.000	0.00	1	0	0	0	0	0	1.0	0	0	0	0	0	0	0	1	0
Toliver, Carolina	1	2	.333	4.19	15	0	0	10	0	3	19.1	22	11	9	2	2	10	1	24	2
Trachsel, Charlotte	13	8	.619	3.06	29	29	5	0	2	0	191.0	180	76	65	19	4	35	3	135	7
Vasquez, Greenville	6	4	.600	4.30	14	14	1	0	0	0	73.1	81	38	35	6	2	30	0	38	7
Ventura, 18 Bir.-9 Mem.	8	15	.348	2.73	27	27	9	0	4	0	184.1	153	73	56	13	9	68	1	123	5
Vice, Huntsville	0	0	.000	0.00	1	0	0	1	0	0	1.0	1	0	0	0	0	0	0	0	0
Vierra, Chattanooga*	1	0	1.000	0.00	1	1	0	0	0	0	6.0	5	0	0	0	0	3	0	5	0
Wagner, Carolina	6	6	.500	3.03	19	19	2	0	1	0	121.2	104	52	41	3	3	47	1	101	6
Walker, Jacksonville	3	3	.500	4.79	11	11	0	0	0	0	62.0	63	38	33	6	3	18	0	40	3
Ward, Huntsville*	1	0	1.000	2.75	6	2	0	0	0	0	19.2	18	7	6	0	2	6	0	21	1
Watson, Greenville	4	6	.400	1.96	48	1	0	28	0	6	73.1	58	28	16	3	1	36	6	81	5
Webb, Charlotte	1	4	.200	4.34	30	1	0	19	0	4	47.2	47	27	23	3	2	21	3	23	3
Weiss, Charlotte	1	0	1.000	3.86	5	1	0	3	0	0	11.2	14	5	5	0	0	5	0	2	0
Wernig, Huntsville*	1	2	.333	5.28	8	6	0	1	0	0	29.0	28	19	17	4	1	11	0	18	0
White, Orlando	2	1	.667	5.13	15	0	0	5	0	0	26.1	43	22	15	3	0	10	1	10	6
White, Carolina	1	7	.125	4.21	10	10	1	0	0	0	57.2	59	32	27	8	3	18	1	45	6

Pitcher, Team	W	L	Pct.	ERA	G	GS	CG	GF	ShO	Sv.	IP	H	R	ER	HR	HB	BB	Int. BB	SO	WP
Wiggs, Jacksonville*	2	1	.667	11.32	8	0	0	2	0	0	10.1	17	14	13	4	0	6	1	14	0
Wiley, Memphis	5	2	.714	3.41	39	3	0	15	0	3	68.2	76	30	26	6	3	18	2	37	2
Wilkinson, Huntsville*	0	0	.000	6.32	15	0	0	5	0	1	15.2	17	15	11	2	1	13	0	15	2
Willis, Charlotte	5	3	.625	2.92	46	0	0	22	0	4	61.2	55	23	20	2	1	16	3	34	5
Wissler, Orlando	3	8	.273	3.72	13	13	5	0	1	0	82.1	74	36	34	9	2	18	0	56	2
Woodall, Greenville*	3	4	.429	3.20	21	1	0	10	0	1	39.1	26	15	14	1	0	17	2	45	4
Woodson, Jacksonville	5	4	.556	3.57	11	11	0	0	0	0	68.0	74	31	27	4	5	36	0	55	11
Zavaras, Jacksonville	3	11	.214	5.28	20	20	0	0	0	0	109.0	109	68	64	12	9	67	3	88	7
Zimmerman, Carolina	4	15	.211	3.82	27	27	1	0	0	0	153.0	141	82	65	10	7	75	2	107	13

BALKS—Gustafson, 7; T. Brown, 6; Moore, Roper, Wissler, 5 each; Merigliano, Zimmerman, 4 each; Anderson, Henry, Hollins, Newman, Tatar, Wilkinson, 3 each; Campbell, Coffman, Grott, Imes, Latter, Luebbers, Lynch, Nezelek, Osteen, V. Perez, Stowell, Wernig, Woodson, 2 each; Allison, Backlund, Bittiger, Burlingame, Converse, Cromwell, Dabney, Duncan, Fansler, Figueroa, Guzman, Jaques, E. Johnson, Karchner, Kizziah, Klonoski, Kuhn, Leskanic, Menhart, Mohler, Ohlms, Phoenix, Pierce, Powell, Pulido, Ray, Remlinger, Robertson, Salles, Scott, Shepherd, Shouse, Stevens, Swartzbaugh, Swope, Trachsel, Walker, Wiggs, Zavaras, 1 each.

COMBINATION SHUTOUTS—Kennedy-Merigliano, Kennedy-Schwarz, Keyser-Shepherd, Merigliano-Stowell-Mongiello, Olsen-Campos-Shepherd, Olsen-Mongiello, Thomas-Keyser, Birmingham; Fansler-Tafoya, Zimmerman-Hancock-Webb, Zimmerman-Tafoya, Zimmerman-Toliver, Carolina; Marak-Jaques, Melvin-Willis-Hollins, Salles-Willis, Stevens-Hollins, Stevens-Marak, Trachsel-Willis, Charlotte; Ayala-Lynch-Grott, Hoffman-Lynch-Spradlin, Roper-Lynch-Imes, Sanford-Imes, Tatar-Spradlin, Chattanooga; Elliott-Borbon 2, Bark-McMichael-Watson-Nezelek-Johnson, Borbon-Watson, Burlingame-McMichael-Strange, Burlingame-Watson, Coffman-Watson, Elliott-Nezelek-Strange, Elliott-Watson-Strange, Gomez-Nezelek, Gomez-Nezelek-Borbon, Gomez-Watson-Woodall, Minchey-Johnson-Nezelek-Taylor, Minchey-McMichael-Johnson, Taylor-Watson, Vasquez-Nezelek-McMichael, Greenville; Allison-Strebeck-Revenig, Allison-Smithberg-Revenig, Bittiger-Latter-Mohler, Bittiger-Revenig, Osteen-Revenig, Patrick-Erwin-Revenig, Patrick-Strebeck, Patrick-Strebeck-Allison, Phoenix-Latter-Wilkinson-Erwin, Phoenix-Mohler-Revenig, Phoenix-Revenig, Wernig-Latter-Kuhn, Huntsville; Woodson-Gunderson 2, Converse-Figueroa-Kent, Converse-Gunderson-Kent, Converse-Kent-Figueroa, Converse-Pitcher, Czarkowski-Kent-Figueroa, Grant-Kent, Gutierrez-Figueroa-Helton-Gunderson-Kent, Gutierrez-Figueroa-Kent, Pitcher-Figueroa-Kent, Pitcher-Perkins, Remlinger-Pitcher-Holman-Kent, Walker-Holman-Kent, Jacksonville; Cross-Ohlms 2, D. Brown-Lloyd, Lloyd-Kizziah-D. Brown, Knoxville; Centala-Miceli, Centala-Miceli-Puig, Corbin-Miceli-Duncan, Curry-Miceli, Pierce-Miceli, Memphis; Gustafson-Pulido, Henry-Garces, Leskanic-Garces, Leskanic-Garces-Pulido-Lipson, McCreary-Klonoski-Best, Newman-Garces, Richards-Garces, Orlando.

NO-HIT GAMES—Zimmerman-Tafoya, Carolina, defeated Chattanooga, 1-0 (eight innings, first game), May 8; Allison-Smithberg-Revenig, Huntsville, defeated Birmingham, 1-0 (10 innings, second game), August 3; Roper, Chattanooga, defeated Birmingham, 1-0 (first game), August 28.

FIELDING

TEAM

Team	Pct.	G	PO	A	E	DP	PB	Team	Pct.	G	PO	A	E	DP	PB
Greenville	.975	143	3765	1634	141	118	25	Memphis	.971	144	3755	1508	157	126	12
Chattanooga	.974	144	3738	1444	139	129	16	Charlotte	.971	144	3674	1475	155	115	7
Jacksonville	.972	145	3744	1510	151	128	16	Huntsville	.968	144	3791	1554	174	154	11
Orlando	.972	144	3594	1435	146	104	23	Carolina	.967	145	3706	1499	175	99	34
Birmingham	.972	144	3746	1508	154	120	15	Knoxville	.963	144	3650	1500	197	109	22

INDIVIDUAL

*Throws lefthanded.

FIRST BASEMEN

Player, Team	Pct.	G	PO	A	E	DP
Armas, Huntsville	.985	132	1177	75	19	122
Aude, Carolina	1.000	2	17	0	0	1
BELL, Greenville*	.997	116	1007	76	3	78
Bishop, Birmingham	1.000	16	105	8	0	8
Bolick, Jacksonville	1.000	1	2	1	0	0
Borrelli, Huntsville	1.000	2	25	0	0	6
Bowie, Jacksonville*	.993	80	641	60	5	58
Busby, Birmingham	1.000	1	11	0	0	0
Campanis, Jacksonville	.983	6	57	1	1	6
Casillas, Memphis*	.980	6	48	2	1	3
Cepicky, Birmingham	.990	110	953	63	10	73
Conte, Huntsville	.991	16	100	6	1	9
Cooley, Orlando	1.000	1	0	1	0	1
Costo, Chattanooga	.993	119	973	62	7	85
David, Memphis	1.000	4	29	2	0	1
Delarwelle, Orlando	1.000	51	418	47	0	32
Ebright, Charlotte*	.985	90	786	49	13	61
Escalera, Chattanooga*	.982	8	53	2	1	4
Franco, Charlotte	.991	25	211	14	2	20
Garner, Chattanooga	1.000	2	10	0	0	2
Gillis, Greenville	1.000	1	3	0	0	0
Hamelin, Memphis*	.989	21	173	9	2	21
Hiatt, Memphis	1.000	2	14	2	0	1
Holley, Jacksonville	1.000	7	26	4	0	1
Johnson, Carolina*	.988	67	610	41	8	38
Kelly, Greenville	1.000	1	6	0	0	0
Kremblas, Chattanooga	.981	17	146	5	3	15
Leiper, Memphis	.976	5	37	4	1	2
Masteller, Orlando*	.984	40	275	26	5	20
McCarty, Orlando*	.995	26	185	16	1	17
McDonald, Jacksonville	1.000	1	2	1	0	1
Mengel, Knoxville	.980	17	129	16	3	14
O'Halloran, Knoxville	.985	8	56	8	1	5
Paulino, Charlotte	.991	34	303	14	3	21
Perez, Greenville	.991	35	317	22	3	26
Pirkl, Jacksonville	.990	57	459	32	5	44
Robertson, Birmingham*	.987	24	213	21	3	19
Robinson, Memphis	.992	83	670	54	6	61
Rohrmeier, Memphis	.990	13	90	5	1	4

Player, Team	Pct.	G	PO	A	E	DP
Russo, Orlando	.983	40	268	28	5	24
Schreiber, Carolina	1.000	1	7	1	0	1
Shelton, Carolina*	.990	75	698	56	8	46
Townley, Knoxville	.989	11	78	9	1	7
Trafton, Chattanooga	.976	5	36	4	1	4
Tunison, Memphis	1.000	24	206	10	0	15
Walbeck, Charlotte	1.000	1	1	1	0	0
Wilson, Jacksonville	1.000	1	3	0	0	0
Yan, Knoxville	.990	111	920	89	10	68

SECOND BASEMEN

Player, Team	Pct.	G	PO	A	E	DP
Alicea, Greenville	.924	20	25	48	6	7
Allen, 4 Chat.-24 Orl.	.942	28	36	45	5	6
Beasley, Carolina	1.000	29	33	79	0	8
Bernhardt, 21 Bir.-7 Mem.	.979	28	53	87	3	14
Bridges, Memphis	.833	2	0	5	1	0
Burgos, Memphis	.960	7	18	6	1	1
Busby, Birmingham	.926	15	20	30	4	6
Capellan, Orlando	1.000	1	2	2	0	0
Caraballo, Greenville	.946	24	32	74	6	9
Casarotti, Greenville	.950	55	89	121	11	27
Castleberry, Birmingham	.969	102	195	272	15	56
Cedeno, Knoxville	.971	64	116	153	8	23
Crockett, Charlotte	.977	62	131	167	7	31
De La Nuez, Orlando	.667	1	0	2	1	0
Edge, Carolina	.933	4	6	8	1	2
Foster, Birmingham	1.000	1	0	1	0	0
Garber, Memphis	.978	21	38	49	2	7
Garcia, Orlando	.976	53	110	130	6	30
Garrison, Huntsville	.978	73	150	201	8	48
Griffin, Chattanooga	.949	110	203	262	25	68
Hemond, Huntsville	1.000	2	4	0	0	1
Holley, Jacksonville	1.000	8	17	17	0	4
Kelly, Greenville	.964	14	22	32	2	4
Kremblas, Chattanooga	.976	38	57	107	4	27
Letterio, Jacksonville	.988	20	35	44	1	10
Lewis, Orlando	.946	43	82	77	9	13
Lonigro, Birmingham	.983	13	25	32	1	6
Manahan, Carolina	.953	92	151	259	20	42
Matos, Huntsville	.966	26	61	80	5	29

Player, Team	Pct.	G	PO	A	E	DP
McCreary, Orlando	.833	2	4	1	1	1
Mengel, Knoxville	.973	25	44	66	3	16
Montalvo, Knoxville	.941	14	23	41	4	8
Mota, Memphis	.968	116	229	279	17	67
Olmeda, Greenville	.978	95	196	252	10	64
Osik, Carolina	1.000	3	4	2	0	0
Raabe, Orlando	.992	32	47	83	1	21
Roa, Greenville	1.000	1	2	5	0	0
Schreiber, Carolina	.980	21	41	55	2	9
Scott, Knoxville	.957	24	38	50	4	11
Smith, Orlando	1.000	6	18	20	0	6
Tarasco, Greenville	1.000	2	0	1	0	0
Taylor, Orlando	.700	4	1	6	3	1
Tollison, Knoxville	.965	31	46	64	4	13
Treadway, Greenville	1.000	3	8	10	0	1
TURANG, Jacksonville	.976	127	283	323	15	75
Vice, Huntsville	.949	46	87	119	11	30
Waggoner, Huntsville	.952	5	7	13	1	1
White, Charlotte	.958	36	62	96	7	13

THIRD BASEMEN

Player, Team	Pct.	G	PO	A	E	DP
Allen, Orlando	1.000	3	3	14	0	3
Aude, Carolina	1.000	1	0	1	0	0
Beasley, Carolina	.875	4	1	6	1	0
Bishop, Birmingham	.893	59	37	96	16	8
Bolick, Jacksonville	.972	63	49	125	5	6
Busby, Birmingham	.769	15	3	7	3	1
Caraballo, Memphis	.974	54	47	104	4	3
Castellano, Charlotte	.915	31	24	73	9	3
Conte, Huntsville	.500	2	0	1	1	1
Crockett, Charlotte	1.000	1	1	0	0	0
Delarwelle, Orlando	.885	24	17	37	7	4
Edge, Carolina	.963	8	3	23	1	0
Franco, Charlotte	.876	37	23	55	11	5
Garber, Memphis	.956	22	10	55	3	5
Garcia, Orlando	.977	67	45	128	4	14
Garrison, Huntsville	1.000	5	7	11	0	1
Gillis, Greenville	1.000	2	1	1	0	0
Giovanola, Greenville	.919	74	35	168	18	18
Grace, Charlotte	.952	81	70	150	11	11
Green, Carolina	.833	2	1	4	1	1
GREENE, Chattanooga	.947	96	77	174	14	24
Harmes, Knoxville	.895	5	5	12	2	3
Henderson, Knoxville	.888	30	19	52	9	6
Hiatt, Memphis	.928	68	50	144	15	14
Holley, Jacksonville	.940	66	41	116	10	11
Hunter, Jacksonville	.882	12	11	19	4	1
Kelly, Greenville	.932	72	51	128	13	9
Kremblas, Chattanooga	.909	9	5	15	2	0
Lane, Chattanooga	.951	37	36	61	5	6
Letterio, Jacksonville	.933	11	10	18	2	2
Lewis, Orlando	1.000	3	1	1	0	1
Lonigro, Birmingham	.927	19	14	24	3	3
Manahan, Carolina	.850	11	5	12	3	0
McDonald, Jacksonville	1.000	2	0	2	0	1
Mengel, Knoxville	.946	46	37	102	8	5
Montalvo, Knoxville	.923	20	11	25	3	2
Mulliniks, Knoxville	1.000	3	3	1	0	0
Olmeda, Greenville	.941	6	2	14	1	1
Osik, Carolina	.933	103	61	176	17	17
Paquette, Huntsville	.908	111	69	248	32	21
Perna, Chattanooga	1.000	3	2	6	0	2
Redington, Birmingham	.928	71	37	104	11	10
Roa, Greenville	1.000	1	0	2	0	0
Robinson, Memphis	.842	7	5	11	3	0
Romero, Carolina	1.000	1	0	1	0	0
Russo, Orlando	.965	59	33	103	5	6
Schreiber, Carolina	.950	18	10	28	2	0
Smith, Orlando	1.000	1	0	4	0	1
Taylor, Knoxville	1.000	5	0	4	0	0
Tollison, Knoxville	.896	49	28	84	13	10
Torres, Carolina	1.000	1	0	6	0	0
Trafton, Chattanooga	1.000	2	2	2	0	0
Vice, Huntsville	.919	31	26	65	8	7

SHORTSTOPS

Player, Team	Pct.	G	PO	A	E	DP
ABBOTT, Huntsville	.949	121	196	342	29	87
Allen, 1 Chat.-56 Orl.	.963	57	72	163	9	26
Beasley, Carolina	.940	12	18	29	3	5
Bernhardt, Memphis	.750	2	1	2	1	0
Bridges, Memphis	.963	7	11	15	1	3
Brito, Knoxville	.833	7	6	19	5	3
Burgos, Memphis	.948	82	128	217	19	41
Busby, Birmingham	.887	36	39	94	17	19
Caraballo, Memphis	.750	1	1	2	1	0
Castellano, Charlotte	.977	11	12	31	1	4
Cedeno, Knoxville	.902	44	73	111	20	25
Cole, Memphis	.978	40	66	113	4	29
Crockett, Charlotte	.952	37	55	83	7	10

Player, Team	Pct.	G	PO	A	E	DP
Diaz, Chattanooga	.948	129	173	333	28	62
Duffy, Charlotte	.926	17	27	48	6	9
Edge, Carolina	.963	60	95	162	10	26
Foster, Birmingham	.922	56	88	148	20	28
Garber, Memphis	.952	30	21	78	5	9
Garcia, Orlando	.964	20	36	45	3	6
Garrison, Huntsville	.957	14	26	41	3	9
Henderson, Knoxville	.942	97	135	255	24	40
Holley, Jacksonville	.932	10	17	38	4	6
Jones, Greenville	.945	64	92	218	18	30
Kelly, Greenville	.927	8	10	28	3	6
Kremblas, Chattanooga	.931	6	10	17	2	4
Letterio, Jacksonville	.667	2	1	3	2	0
Lonigro, 12 Chat.-37 Bir.	.966	49	70	128	7	18
Manahan, Jacksonville	.942	134	227	370	37	73
Matos, Huntsville	.956	13	12	31	2	3
McCreary, Orlando	1.000	1	1	0	0	0
Meares, Orlando	.889	74	91	190	35	31
Mordecai, Greenville	.964	65	93	204	11	33
Olmeda, Greenville	1.000	8	13	20	0	3
Polcovich, Carolina	.968	12	16	45	2	9
Rodriguez, Carolina	.919	28	41	84	11	9
Schreiber, Carolina	.926	39	46	80	10	17
Smith, Orlando	1.000	1	0	1	0	0
Washington, Memphis	.833	1	2	3	1	2
White, Charlotte	.948	86	110	254	20	48
Wilson, Birmingham	.965	27	33	76	4	15

OUTFIELDERS

Player, Team	Pct.	G	PO	A	E	DP
Adams, Jacksonville	.957	17	20	2	1	1
Alicea, Greenville	.985	42	59	7	1	1
Bernhardt, Memphis	.986	33	67	1	1	0
Bridges, Memphis	.950	12	19	0	1	0
Bryant, Charlotte	1.000	6	2	0	0	0
Buccheri, Huntsville	1.000	17	48	1	0	0
Bullett, Carolina*	.978	130	260	7	6	1
Campanis, Jacksonville	1.000	2	1	0	0	0
Capellan, Orlando	1.000	2	3	0	0	0
Casillas, Memphis*	.936	36	41	3	3	0
Colvard, Chattanooga	.973	69	136	10	4	1
Conte, Huntsville	.980	76	137	9	3	4
Crockett, Charlotte	.947	8	17	1	1	1
Dattola, Huntsville	.960	79	142	3	6	2
Dauphin, Charlotte*	.990	135	300	5	3	2
De La Nuez, Orlando	.986	121	198	9	3	0
De La Rosa, Knoxville	.978	126	297	17	7	4
Delima, Orlando*	1.000	16	30	0	0	0
De Los Santos, Carolina	.937	82	109	9	8	2
Edge, Carolina	1.000	3	1	0	0	0
Escalera, Chattanooga*	.984	34	60	1	1	0
Estep, 23 Car.-30 Chat.	.966	53	78	8	3	3
Foster, Birmingham	1.000	7	15	1	0	0
Fox, Huntsville*	1.000	59	125	4	0	1
Franco, Charlotte	1.000	8	14	0	0	0
Garber, Memphis	.980	33	47	1	1	0
Garner, Chattanooga	1.000	3	3	0	0	0
Grace, Charlotte	.909	7	10	0	1	0
Grayum, Charlotte	.972	94	166	7	5	1
Green, Carolina	1.000	19	23	4	0	1
Grunhard, Huntsville*	.947	20	35	1	2	0
Harris, Birmingham	1.000	73	138	9	0	2
Heffernan, Jacksonville	1.000	1	2	0	0	0
Hernandez, Chattanooga	.962	93	242	14	10	5
Hiatt, Memphis	.940	56	75	4	5	1
Holley, Jacksonville	.976	31	39	1	1	0
Jacas, Huntsville	.963	95	220	11	9	3
Jaster, Birmingham	.975	92	188	7	5	0
Jenkins, Chattanooga	.970	14	29	3	1	0
Jensen, Charlotte	.962	109	199	6	8	0
Johnson, Carolina*	.951	21	35	4	2	0
M. Kelly, Carolina	.988	125	244	7	3	0
P. Kelly, Greenville	1.000	4	7	0	0	0
Knabenshue, Huntsville	1.000	14	20	1	0	0
Kowitz, Greenville*	.970	16	29	3	1	0
Kremblas, Chattanooga	1.000	7	8	1	0	0
Kvasnicka, Orlando*	.990	47	99	2	1	0
Lawton, Memphis	1.000	14	18	1	0	1
Leiper, Memphis	1.000	46	78	3	0	0
Letterio, Jacksonville	1.000	9	8	1	0	0
Lewis, Orlando	.974	80	144	5	4	0
List, Carolina	.900	5	9	0	1	0
Lydy, Huntsville	.953	83	137	4	7	1
Masteller, Orlando*	.989	58	85	2	1	1
Maynard, Jacksonville	.961	121	262	10	11	2
McCarty, Orlando*	.959	96	172	16	8	3
McDaniel, Chattanooga	1.000	3	3	0	0	0
McDonald, Jacksonville	.979	81	130	12	3	2
Merchant, Jacksonville	1.000	22	36	1	0	0
Moore, Memphis	.986	57	141	2	2	0
Neill, Huntsville*	1.000	4	8	0	0	0
Newfield, Jacksonville	1.000	15	17	1	0	0
Nieves, Greenville	.965	85	127	9	5	1

Player, Team	Pct.	G	PO	A	E	DP
Norman, Memphis	.971	64	124	9	4	4
O'Halloran, Knoxville	1.000	1	1	0	0	0
Ortiz, Orlando*	.976	46	77	4	2	2
Owens, Orlando	1.000	1	1	0	0	0
Pasqua, Birmingham*	1.000	2	3	0	0	0
Pennyfeather, Carolina	.988	46	79	2	1	0
Perez, Knoxville	.973	133	241	13	7	2
Pezzoni, Jacksonville	1.000	24	41	1	0	0
Pledger, Birmingham	.968	57	115	5	4	2
Plemmons, Birmingham	1.000	3	4	1	0	0
POSE, Chattanooga	.996	136	216	10	1	2
Ratliff, Carolina	.975	104	153	5	4	2
Riesgo, Memphis	.917	6	10	1	1	0
Roberts, Knoxville	1.000	5	15	1	0	0
Rohrmeier, Memphis	.983	72	113	6	2	0
Russo, Orlando	1.000	4	2	1	0	0
Scott, Knoxville	.976	59	110	12	3	2
Shields, Memphis	.964	19	25	2	1	0
Smith, Orlando	1.000	2	1	0	0	0
Tarasco, Greenville	.978	126	209	16	5	2
Tavarez, Jacksonville	.977	104	208	7	5	1
Taylor, Chattanooga*	.969	16	31	0	1	0
Tedder, Birmingham*	.983	115	211	17	4	3
Thomas, Carolina	.974	20	35	2	1	0
Timmons, Charlotte	.978	34	41	3	1	0
Todd, Jacksonville*	.944	23	33	1	2	0
Tollison, Knoxville	1.000	1	1	0	0	0
Trafton, Chattanooga	1.000	58	116	8	0	2
Turang, Jacksonville	1.000	4	3	0	0	0
Waggoner, Greenville	1.000	47	62	2	0	0
Walker, Memphis	.949	23	36	1	2	0
Welch, Charlotte	.980	34	49	0	1	0
Wetherby, Jacksonville*	.913	10	20	1	2	0
White, Birmingham	.975	60	115	4	3	2
Williams, Charlotte	.971	15	34	0	1	0
Wilson, Jacksonville	1.000	2	3	0	0	0
Wilson, Knoxville*	.957	116	192	6	9	1
Wolak, Birmingham	.979	45	90	5	2	1

CATCHERS

Player, Team	Pct.	G	PO	A	E	DP	PB
Alvarez, Birmingham	1.000	57	353	57	0	8	4
Beeler, Carolina	.960	29	159	13	7	2	5
Borrelli, Huntsville	.982	82	478	60	10	4	7
Brito, Huntsville	.980	28	125	22	3	4	2
Brooks, Knoxville	1.000	6	16	2	0	0	0
Campanis, Jacksonville	.984	75	534	74	10	3	13
Campbell, Birmingham	.978	58	355	43	9	3	6
Carcione, Huntsville	1.000	17	103	13	0	3	0
COX, Chattanooga	.992	95	654	91	6	11	9
David, Memphis	.986	79	497	49	8	5	9
Diaz, Memphis	.978	36	199	19	5	4	0
Durso, Knoxville	.971	5	31	2	1	0	0
Edge, Carolina	1.000	2	9	3	0	0	0
Grifol, Orlando	.962	11	45	6	2	0	0
Harmes, Knoxville	1.000	2	9	0	0	0	0
Heffernan, Jacksonville	.989	50	311	36	4	6	3
Helfand, Huntsville	.990	33	180	21	2	0	2
Hemond, Huntsville	1.000	5	20	1	0	0	0
Jennings, Memphis	.994	51	287	33	2	5	3
Liebert, Birmingham	1.000	41	210	22	0	4	5
Lopez, Greenville	.990	96	680	75	8	8	19
Monzon, Knoxville	.988	41	219	28	3	1	8
O'Halloran, Knoxville	.982	78	491	49	10	12	13
Osik, Orlando	.989	23	157	17	2	0	2
Owens, Orlando	.981	97	655	62	14	4	17
Perez, Greenville	.970	51	314	42	11	3	6
Pirkl, Jacksonville	1.000	2	14	3	0	1	0
Robinson, Charlotte	.992	55	318	43	3	6	2
Romero, Carolina	.976	72	523	42	14	1	17
Siwa, Orlando	.993	50	247	30	2	2	6
Sutko, Chattanooga	.980	58	337	53	8	4	7
Swail, Greenville	.975	5	37	1	1	0	0
Tollison, Knoxville	1.000	1	4	0	0	0	0
Torres, Carolina	.988	23	152	12	2	4	10
Townley, Knoxville	.994	26	156	17	1	0	1
Walbeck, Charlotte	.984	93	551	79	10	8	5
Wilson, Jacksonville	.983	20	106	13	2	1	0

PITCHERS

Player, Team	Pct.	G	PO	A	E	DP
Ahern, Memphis	.952	11	5	15	1	1
Allison, Huntsville*	1.000	22	2	9	0	1
Anderson, Chattanooga	.909	28	6	14	2	0
Ariola, Huntsville*	1.000	2	1	3	0	1
Ayala, Chattanooga	.905	27	6	13	2	1
Backlund, Carolina	1.000	3	1	2	0	0
Bark, Greenville*	.833	11	2	8	2	0
Bautista, Memphis	1.000	1	0	1	0	0
Bell, Greenville*	1.000	1	0	1	0	0

Player, Team	Pct.	G	PO	A	E	DP
Bere, Birmingham	1.000	8	5	5	0	1
Best, Orlando	1.000	11	0	4	0	0
Bird, Carolina*	.909	27	6	24	3	3
Bittiger, Huntsville	1.000	17	8	9	0	0
Bond, Jacksonville	.938	18	6	9	1	1
Borbon, Greenville*	1.000	39	4	16	0	2
Borski, Jacksonville	1.000	11	2	7	0	0
Bradford, Charlotte	.833	2	2	3	1	1
D. Brown, Knoxville	1.000	43	6	8	0	0
T. Brown, Knoxville	.946	24	11	24	2	3
Buckholz, Carolina	.952	20	7	13	1	0
Bullard, Carolina	1.000	19	1	9	0	0
Burlingame, Greenville	.938	26	13	17	2	1
Campbell, Memphis*	.923	9	2	10	1	1
Campos, Birmingham	1.000	31	4	13	0	3
Casillas, Memphis*	1.000	1	0	1	0	0
Centala, Memphis	1.000	9	3	3	0	0
Coffman, Greenville	.923	6	6	6	1	0
Converse, Jacksonville	.833	27	7	13	4	1
Cooke, Carolina*	.600	6	1	2	2	0
Cooley, Orlando	.000	1	0	0	1	0
Corbin, Memphis	.813	27	5	21	6	1
Cormier, Huntsville	1.000	6	0	2	0	0
Crabtree, Knoxville	.500	3	0	2	2	0
Cromwell, Knoxville*	.958	37	5	18	1	0
Cross, Huntsville	.844	26	16	11	5	0
Curry, Memphis	.909	27	13	27	4	2
Czarkowski, Jacksonville*	.947	16	9	27	2	1
Dabney, Birmingham*	.923	25	5	19	2	1
Delgado, Charlotte	1.000	6	0	2	0	0
Dixon, Carolina	1.000	25	3	4	0	0
Duncan, Memphis	.875	33	7	21	4	1
Elliott, Greenville	.929	19	4	9	1	1
Erwin, Huntsville	.750	23	2	1	1	0
Fansler, Carolina	.976	25	15	26	1	1
Figueroa, Jacksonville*	.926	53	9	16	2	0
Freed, Chattanooga	1.000	10	1	3	0	0
Fritz, Birmingham*	1.000	1	0	1	0	0
Garces, Orlando	.867	58	5	8	2	0
Garcia, Carolina	1.000	5	1	1	0	0
Garland, Huntsville	1.000	9	3	2	0	0
Givens, Memphis*	.800	7	2	2	1	0
Gomez, Greenville*	1.000	8	2	13	0	1
Grant, Jacksonville	1.000	5	3	3	0	0
Grott, Chattanooga*	.889	32	3	5	1	0
Gunderson, Jacksonville*	1.000	15	2	4	0	0
Gustafson, Orlando	.967	32	12	17	1	0
Gutierrez, Jacksonville	1.000	15	4	5	0	0
Guzman, Huntsville*	1.000	14	9	16	0	0
Hampton, Jacksonville*	1.000	2	2	2	0	0
Hancock, Carolina*	1.000	23	3	4	0	0
Harvey, Memphis	1.000	6	1	1	0	0
Hawblitzel, Charlotte	.929	28	6	20	2	1
Helton, Knoxville*	1.000	7	1	2	0	0
Henry, Orlando	.964	28	13	14	1	1
Hoffman, Chattanooga	1.000	6	3	4	0	1
Hollins, Charlotte	1.000	63	7	11	0	3
Holman, Jacksonville	.750	35	3	3	2	0
Hostetler, Greenville	1.000	16	5	7	0	1
Hudek, Birmingham	1.000	5	2	6	0	1
Hunter, Carolina	.882	32	3	12	2	2
Imes, Chattanooga	1.000	45	2	11	0	0
Jaques, Charlotte*	1.000	46	2	8	0	1
Jimenez, Huntsville	1.000	1	0	1	0	0
Johns, Huntsville*	1.000	3	0	3	0	0
Johnson, Birmingham*	.833	16	0	5	1	0
Johnson, Greenville*	1.000	43	3	11	0	0
Karchner, Memphis	.946	33	9	26	2	3
Kennedy, Birmingham	.976	18	8	33	1	2
Kent, Jacksonville	.889	59	3	5	1	0
Keyser, Birmingham	.978	28	13	31	1	1
Kilgo, Chattanooga*	.909	24	4	6	1	1
Kizziah, Knoxville	.920	38	6	17	2	1
Klonoski, Orlando*	1.000	54	13	21	0	1
Knackert, Jacksonville	.920	21	6	17	2	2
Kuhn, Huntsville*	1.000	19	2	6	0	0
Kutzler, Charlotte	.889	12	0	8	1	1
Latter, Huntsville	.727	47	2	6	3	0
Leskanic, Orlando	.969	26	14	17	1	1
Lipson, Orlando	1.000	31	6	4	0	0
Lloyd, Knoxville*	.905	49	5	14	2	0
Luebbers, Chattanooga	.889	14	5	11	2	0
Lynch, Chattanooga*	.909	37	4	6	1	0
Manzanillo, Memphis	1.000	2	1	1	0	1
Marak, Charlotte	.933	17	5	9	1	2
McCreary, Orlando	1.000	16	6	6	0	1
McMichael, Greenville	.889	15	2	6	1	0
Melvin, Charlotte	.917	28	5	6	1	0
Menhart, Knoxville	.967	28	25	33	2	1
Merigliano, Birmingham	.938	24	5	10	1	0
Miceli, Memphis	1.000	32	2	2	0	0
Minchey, Greenville	.903	28	8	20	3	2
Mohler, Huntsville*	1.000	44	4	12	0	1
Mongiello, Birmingham	.929	44	3	10	1	2
Moore, Knoxville	.722	36	7	19	10	0
Munoz, Orlando	1.000	14	4	2	0	0

Player, Team	Pct.	G	PO	A	E	DP
Newlin, Jacksonville	.750	12	0	3	1	0
Newman, Orlando*	.900	18	2	16	2	0
Nezelek, Greenville	1.000	46	10	14	0	0
Ogliaruso, Knoxville	.857	9	4	2	1	0
Ohlms, Knoxville	.941	52	7	9	1	0
Olsen, Birmingham	.923	12	6	6	1	0
Osteen, Huntsville*	.926	16	5	20	2	3
Parker, Charlotte*	1.000	2	0	1	0	0
Parnell, Memphis	.857	26	3	3	1	0
Patrick, Huntsville	.907	29	16	23	4	0
Perez, Charlotte	1.000	1	0	1	0	0
Perez, Memphis	.857	32	7	5	2	0
Perkins, Jacksonville	1.000	21	4	5	0	0
Phoenix, Huntsville	1.000	32	3	29	0	2
Pierce, Memphis*	1.000	25	5	18	0	0
Pitcher, Jacksonville	1.000	23	3	8	0	0
Powell, Chattanooga*	1.000	14	0	6	0	0
Puig, Memphis*	.950	68	2	17	1	1
Pulido, Orlando*	.923	52	1	11	1	1
Ray, Chattanooga	1.000	24	3	4	0	0
Remlinger, Jacksonville*	.800	5	1	3	1	0
Revenig, Huntsville	1.000	53	3	10	0	4
Richards, Orlando	.944	15	8	9	1	0
Robertson, Carolina*	.882	20	7	23	4	0
Robinson, Chattanooga	.929	13	8	18	2	1
Roper, Chattanooga	.957	20	5	17	1	0
Ruffin, Birmingham	.846	10	7	4	2	0
Salles, Charlotte	1.000	9	2	7	0	2
Sanchez, Memphis	.000	1	0	0	2	0
Sanford, Chattanooga	1.000	4	0	3	0	0
Satre, Chattanooga	1.000	14	3	13	0	0
Schrenk, Birmingham	1.000	2	2	2	0	0
Schwarz, Birmingham	.875	21	4	3	1	0
Shepherd, Birmingham	.938	40	5	10	1	0
Shouse, Carolina*	.960	59	7	17	1	2
Small, Knoxville*	.906	27	6	23	3	1
Smith, Huntsville	1.000	5	0	1	0	0
Smithberg, Huntsville	1.000	20	3	7	0	0
Sodders, Charlotte*	.786	23	4	7	3	0
Spradlin, Chattanooga	1.000	59	2	12	0	0
Stevens, Charlotte	.966	26	10	18	1	1
Stowell, Birmingham*	1.000	21	1	0	0	0
Strange, Greenville	1.000	48	4	3	0	1
Strauss, Charlotte	1.000	10	1	2	0	0
Strebeck, Huntsville	.818	30	4	5	2	1
Swartzbaugh, Charlotte	.976	27	9	31	1	2
Swope, Orlando	1.000	4	1	3	0	1
Tafoya, Carolina	.962	41	9	16	1	0
Tatar, Chattanooga	1.000	9	3	8	0	0
Taylor, Knoxville	1.000	1	0	1	0	0
Taylor, Greenville	1.000	22	6	8	0	1
Tellers, Carolina	1.000	16	4	4	0	0
THOMAS, Birmingham*	1.000	17	7	29	0	0
Toliver, Carolina	1.000	15	2	3	0	0
Trachsel, Charlotte	.980	29	11	37	1	7
Vasquez, Greenville	.941	14	5	11	1	0
Ventura, 18 Bir. -9 Mem.	.875	27	11	17	4	0
Wagner, Carolina	.857	19	9	15	4	1
Walker, Jacksonville	1.000	11	1	9	0	1
Ward, Knoxville*	1.000	6	1	5	0	2
Watson, Greenville	.944	48	5	12	1	0
Webb, Carolina	.778	30	0	7	2	0
Weiss, Charlotte	1.000	5	1	0	0	0
Wernig, Huntsville*	1.000	8	1	2	0	0
White, Orlando	.714	15	2	3	2	0
White, Carolina	.923	10	2	10	1	0
Wiggs, Jacksonville*	1.000	8	1	8	0	0
Wiley, Memphis	.900	39	2	7	1	0
Willis, Charlotte	.929	46	3	10	1	1
Wissler, Orlando	1.000	13	8	9	0	2
Woodall, Greenville*	1.000	21	3	6	0	0
Woodson, Jacksonville	.941	11	3	13	1	1
Zavaras, Jacksonville	.875	20	4	10	2	0
Zimmerman, Carolina	.942	27	18	31	3	1

The following players did not have any fielding statistics at the positions indicated or appeared only as a designated hitter, pinch-hitter or pinch-runner: Alicea, 3b; Allen, of, p; E. Alvarez, p; Bell, of; Cole, of; Conte, p; Dattola, p; De La Nuez, p; Delarwelle, 2b; Ebright, p; Erb, p; Foster, 3b; J. Garcia, of, p; Garrison, of; Harkey, p; Hartung, dh; Heath, of; G. Hunter, of; Kremblas, p; Leslie, p; Lewis, ss; Mengel, of, p; Montalvo, ss; Monzon, p; Odekirk, p; Osik, p; Pichardo, p; Raabe, p; Redington, p; Ritter, p; Roa, ss; D. Robinson, p; Roth, 3b; Scott, p; Siwa, 1b; Sutko, p; Tidwell, p; Vice, p; Vierra, p; Welch, 3b; Wilkinson, p.

LEAGUE CHAMPIONS

Year	Team	Pct.	Year	Team	Pct.	Year	Team	Pct.
1904—	Macon	.598		Augusta (2nd)†	.597	1971—	Did not operate as league--clubs were members of Dixie Association.	
1905—	Macon	.625	1940—	Savannah	.627			
1906—	Savannah	.637		Columbus (2nd)†	.583	1972—	Asheville	.583
1907—	Charleston	.620	1941—	Macon	.643		Montgomery§	.561
1908—	Jacksonville	.694		Columbia (2nd)†	.636	1973—	Montgomery§	.580
1909—	Chattanooga*	.738	1942—	Charleston	.620		Jacksonville	.559
	Augusta	.702		Macon (2nd)†	.585	1974—	Jacksonville	.565
1910—	Columbus	.588	1943-45—	Did not operate.			Knoxville§	.533
1911—	Columbus*	.681	1946—	Columbus	.568	1975—	Orlando	.587
	Columbia	.710		Augusta (4th)†	.547		Montgomery§	.545
1912—	Jacksonville*	.679	1947—	Columbus	.575	1976—	Montgomery x	.591
	Columbus	.632		Savannah (2nd)†	.563		Orlando	.540
1913—	Savannah	.754	1948—	Charleston	.572	1977—	Montgomery x	.628
	Savannah	.593		Greenville (3rd)†	.549		Jacksonville	.522
1914—	Savannah*	.667	1949—	Macon‡	.623	1978—	Knoxville x	.611
	Albany	.650	1950—	Macon‡	.588		Savannah	.500
1915—	Macon	.588	1951—	Montgomery	.607	1979—	Columbus	.587
	Columbus*	.686	1952—	Columbia	.649		Nashville x	.576
1916—	Augusta*	.617		Montgomery (3rd)†	.558	1980—	Memphis	.576
	Columbia	.631	1953—	Jacksonville	.679		Charlotte x	.500
1917—	Charleston	.741		Savannah (2nd)†	.571	1981—	Nashville	.566
	Columbia*	.667	1954—	Jacksonville	.593		Orlando x	.556
1918—	Did not operate.			Savannah (2nd)†	.571	1982—	Jacksonville	.576
1919—	Columbia	.585	1955—	Columbia	.636		Nashville x	.535
1920—	Columbia	.633		Augusta (3rd)†	.543	1983—	Birmingham x	.628
1921—	Columbia	.642	1956—	Jacksonville‡	.621		Jacksonville	.531
1922—	Charleston	.625	1957—	Augusta	.636	1984—	Charlotte x	.510
1923—	Charlotte*	.653		Charlotte (2nd)†	.562		Knoxville	.483
	Macon	.580	1958—	Augusta	.550	1985—	Charlotte	.545
1924—	Augusta	.612		Macon (3rd)†	.500		Huntsville x	.542
1925—	Spartanburg	.620	1959—	Knoxville	.557	1986—	Huntsville	.553
1926—	Greenville	.662		Gastonia (4th)†	.504		Columbus x	.500
1927—	Greenville	.622	1960—	Columbia	.597	1987—	Charlotte	.586
1928—	Asheville	.664		Savannah (3rd)†	.561		Birmingham x	.476
1929—	Asheville	.605	1961—	Asheville	.635	1988—	Greenville	.604
	Knoxville*	.634	1962—	Savannah	.662		Chattanooga x	.566
1930—	Greenville*	.620		Macon (3rd)†	.576	1989—	Birmingham x	.615
	Macon	.643	1963—	Augusta*	.661		Greenville	.504
1931-35—	Did not operate.			Lynchburg	.662	1990—	Orlando	.590
1936—	Jacksonville	.652	1964—	Lynchburg	.579		Memphis x	.507
	Columbus*	.650	1965—	Columbus	.572	1991—	Greenville	.611
1937—	Columbus	.572	1966—	Mobile	.629		Orlando x	.535
	Savannah (3rd)†	.565	1967—	Birmingham	.604	1992—	Greenville x	.699
1938—	Savannah	.574	1968—	Asheville	.614		Chattanooga	.629
	Macon (2nd)†	.570	1969—	Charlotte	.579			
1939—	Columbus	.601	1970—	Montgomery	.569			

*Won split season playoff. †Won four-club playoff. ‡Won championship and four-club playoff. §League was divided into Eastern and Western divisions; won playoff. xLeague was divided into Eastern and Western divisions and played split season; won playoff.

TEXAS LEAGUE

FIRST HALF

EASTERN DIVISION

Team	W	L	T	Pct.	GB
Shreveport (Giants)	42	25	0	.627	......
Tulsa (Rangers)	36	30	0	.545	5 ½
Jackson (Astros)	31	35	0	.470	10 ½
Arkansas (Cardinals)	27	35	0	.435	12 ½

WESTERN DIVISION

Team	W	L	T	Pct.	GB
Wichita (Padres)	39	29	0	.574	......
El Paso (Brewers)	36	32	0	.529	3
Midland (Angels)	27	38	0	.415	10 ½
San Antonio (Dodgers)	27	41	0	.397	12

SECOND HALF

EASTERN DIVISION

Team	W	L	T	Pct.	GB
Tulsa (Rangers)	41	29	0	.586	......
Shreveport (Giants)	35	34	0	.507	5 ½
Arkansas (Cardinals)	32	38	0	.457	9
Jackson (Astros)	30	39	0	.435	10 ½

WESTERN DIVISION

Team	W	L	T	Pct.	GB
El Paso (Brewers)	37	31	0	.544	......
San Antonio (Dodgers)	35	33	0	.515	2
Midland (Angels)	34	34	0	.500	3
Wichita (Padres)	31	37	0	.456	6

COMPOSITE

Team	Tul.	Shrv.	E.P.	Wich.	Mid.	S.A.	Jax.	Ark.	W	L	T	Pct.	GB
Tulsa (Rangers)	...	17	6	6	6	8	21	15	77	59	0	.566	......
Shreveport (Giants)	15	...	5	5	2	6	20	24	77	59	0	.566	......
El Paso (Brewers)	4	5	....	16	20	19	2	7	73	63	0	.537	4
Wichita (Padres)	6	5	16	....	15	17	15	5	70	66	0	.515	7
Midland (Angels)	4	8	12	15	....	17	15	4	3	61	72	0	.459	14 ½
San Antonio (Dodgers)	2	4	13	17	17	...	5	4	62	74	0	.456	15
Jackson (Astros)	11	12	8	4	6	5	....	15	61	74	0	.452	15 ½
Arkansas (Cardinals)	17	8	3	5	4	6	16	....	59	73	0	.447	16

Arkansas club represented Little Rock, Ark.

Major league affiliations in parentheses.

Playoffs—Shreveport defeated Tulsa, two games to none; Wichita defeated El Paso, two games to one; Wichita defeated Shreveport, four games to none, to win league championship.

Regular-season attendance—Arkansas, 265,984; El Paso, 262,727; Jackson, 140,040; Midland, 195,629; San Antonio, 177,365; Shreveport, 207,925; Tulsa, 290,393; Wichita, 210,990. Total—1,751,053. Playoffs (9 games)—17,755. Class AA All-Star Game at Charlotte, N.C.—4,009. Texas League All-Star Game at Jackson—5,115.

Managers—Arkansas, Joe Pettini; El Paso, Chris Bando; Jackson, Rick Sweet; Midland, Don Long; San Antonio, Jerry Royster; Shreveport, Bill Robinson; Tulsa, Bobby Jones; Wichita, Bruce Bochy.

All-Star team: 1B—Jay Gainer, Wichita; 2B—Jon Shave, Tulsa; 3B—Adell Davenport, Shreveport; SS—Edgar Caceras, El Paso; OF—Troy O'Leary, El Paso; Billy Ashley, San Antonio; Jeff Kipila, Midland; C—Tony Eusebio, Jackson; DH—Jose Oliva, Tulsa; Pitchers—Dan Smith, Tulsa; Dan Carlson, Shreveport; Todd Jones, Jackson; Kevin Meier, Arkansas; Rick Huisman, Shreveport; Tim Worrell, Wichita. Most Valuable Player—Troy O'Leary, El Paso; Pitcher of the Year—Dan Smith, Tulsa; Manager of the Year—Bobby Jones, Tulsa.

BATTING

TEAM

Team	Avg.	G	AB	R	OR	H	TB	2B	3B	HR	RBI	SH	SF	HP	BB	Int. BB	SO	SB	CS	LOB
El Paso	.274	136	4461	649	649	1224	1689	229	64	36	570	51	52	49	488	40	755	151	93	932
Wichita	.259	136	4556	619	603	1182	1718	187	38	91	562	40	37	58	469	27	953	212	104	917
Tulsa	.258	136	4433	520	479	1143	1688	202	44	85	486	29	31	48	402	21	1026	67	57	939
San Antonio	.257	136	4429	541	560	1140	1688	194	39	92	493	46	32	54	310	25	942	119	76	831
Midland	.256	133	4525	624	647	1159	1720	230	35	87	563	32	30	44	480	21	1012	89	58	925
Shreveport	.248	136	4417	527	494	1094	1589	176	44	77	462	55	29	43	365	42	804	92	73	883
Jackson	.246	135	4422	509	531	1089	1518	188	29	61	454	58	39	50	392	26	920	99	59	920
Arkansas	.232	132	4046	397	423	937	1339	188	23	56	355	44	34	20	334	19	878	51	55	788

INDIVIDUAL

(Leading qualifiers for batting championship—367 or more plate appearances)

*Bats lefthanded.   †Switch-hitter.

Player, Team	Avg.	G	AB	R	H	TB	2B	3B	HR	RBI	SH	SF	HP	BB	Int. BB	SO	SB	CS
O'Leary, Troy, El Paso*	.334	135	506	92	169	227	27	8	5	79	3	8	1	59	6	87	28	16
Caceres, Edgar, El Paso†	.312	114	378	50	118	150	14	6	2	52	5	1	2	23	4	41	9	2
Eusebio, Tony, Jackson	.307	94	339	33	104	134	9	3	5	44	1	1	4	25	2	58	1	2
Byington, John, El Paso	.306	130	468	60	143	202	39	4	4	64	1	11	7	32	2	54	5	9
Correia, Ron, Midland	.290	123	482	73	140	183	23	1	6	56	5	6	8	28	2	72	20	11
Castaldo, Vince, El Paso*	.289	119	412	61	119	181	33	10	3	50	1	2	3	48	8	77	12	6
Davenport, Adell, Shreveport	.288	124	441	54	127	225	31	5	19	88	1	2	8	28	6	78	2	4
Weber, Pete, Shreveport*	.288	118	417	64	120	172	23	10	3	33	2	4	5	42	2	97	14	8
Shave, Jon, Tulsa	.287	118	453	57	130	169	23	5	2	36	7	5	4	37	1	59	6	7
Makarewicz, Scott, Jackson	.287	105	345	39	99	135	15	0	7	39	3	5	6	23	3	62	2	2

Departmental leaders: G—O'Leary, 135; AB—O'Leary, 506; R—O'Leary, 92; H—O'Leary, 169; TB—O'Leary, 227; 2B—Byington, 39; 3B—Castaldo, Weber, 10; HR—Ashley, 24; RBI—Davenport, 88; SH—Howard, 16; SF—Byington, 11; HP—Ingram, 12; BB—Dodson, 72; IBB—Castaldo, Smiley, 8; SO—Phillips, 165; SB—Noland, 40; CS—Noland, 23.

Player, Team	Avg.	G	AB	R	H	TB	2B	3B	HR	RBI	SH	SF	HP	BB	Int. BB	SO	SB	CS
Aldrete, Rich, Arkansas*	.214	23	70	6	15	24	4	1	1	6	0	0	0	8	0	15	1	0
Alfonzo, Edgar, Midland	.295	61	220	39	65	88	9	1	4	30	1	0	5	26	0	30	2	2
Allen, Harold, Jackson*	.227	27	22	2	5	8	3	0	0	1	4	0	0	2	0	10	0	0
Allen, Steve, San Antonio	.200	43	5	1	1	2	1	0	0	0	1	0	0	0	0	3	0	0
Alvarez, Jorge, San Antonio	.243	103	305	33	74	108	11	4	5	32	4	3	2	21	1	64	8	4
Anderson, Garret, Midland*	.274	39	146	16	40	51	5	0	2	19	0	0	0	9	2	30	2	1
Anderson, Paul, Arkansas	.182	22	22	0	4	6	2	0	0	1	2	0	0	1	0	10	0	0
Ansley, Willie, Jackson	.242	35	120	18	29	39	8	1	0	3	2	1	2	22	0	33	10	5
Ashley, Billy, San Antonio	.279	101	380	60	106	203	23	1	24	66	0	2	6	16	3	111	13	7
August, Sam, Jackson	.000	4	5	0	0	0	0	0	0	0	0	0	0	0	0	1	0	0
Aversa, Joe, Arkansas†	.236	49	106	16	25	31	4	1	0	3	2	0	0	21	0	20	3	2
Baar, Bryan, San Antonio	.137	39	131	11	18	33	6	0	3	11	0	0	1	3	0	47	0	0
Baldwin, Jeff, Jackson*	.285	55	179	33	51	70	13	0	2	27	0	4	3	19	2	24	0	1
Ball, Jeff, Jackson	.191	93	278	27	53	84	14	1	5	24	2	1	10	20	1	58	5	3
Barker, Tim, San Antonio	.271	97	350	47	95	121	17	3	1	26	6	1	5	33	2	91	25	9
Barron, Tony, San Antonio	.402	28	97	18	39	66	4	1	7	22	0	1	2	6	1	22	7	3
Basso, Mike, Wichita	.500	2	4	1	2	2	0	0	0	0	0	0	0	1	0	2	0	0
Beanblossom, Brad, Arkansas	.224	113	384	46	86	102	10	3	0	13	4	0	3	33	1	53	3	3
Beck, Wynn, El Paso*	.174	11	23	2	4	6	2	0	0	5	0	0	0	2	0	3	0	0
Belcher, Kevin, Tulsa	.244	122	381	55	93	172	19	3	18	60	3	4	6	71	1	121	6	6
Bellinger, Clay, Shreveport	.208	126	433	45	90	153	18	3	13	50	4	4	3	36	1	82	7	8
Bellomo, Kevin, Shreveport	.077	7	13	2	1	1	0	0	0	0	0	0	0	0	0	3	0	1
Bene, Bill, San Antonio	.000	18	2	0	0	0	0	0	0	0	0	0	0	0	0	1	0	0
Bethea, Steve, Wichita†	.249	93	253	32	63	84	12	3	1	32	2	2	6	35	2	66	11	4
Billmeyer, Mick, Midland*	.130	21	69	5	9	15	4	1	0	9	1	2	0	4	0	15	0	0
Brannon, Cliff, Arkansas	.212	112	340	32	72	110	16	2	6	35	1	6	0	25	1	88	2	1
Brosnan, Jason, San Antonio*	.000	8	3	0	0	0	0	0	0	0	0	0	0	0	0	2	0	0
Brown, Adam, San Antonio*	.211	31	76	4	16	26	4	0	2	9	0	0	0	3	0	16	0	0
Brown, Tony, Midland*	.257	48	183	22	47	72	9	2	4	18	0	2	0	9	1	40	3	1
Bruske, Jim, Jackson	.200	14	15	1	3	4	1	0	0	1	0	1	0	0	0	3	0	0
Bryand, Renay, Wichita*	.000	49	1	0	0	0	0	0	0	0	0	0	0	0	0	0	0	0
Burton, Mike, Tulsa	.236	20	72	11	17	25	2	0	2	13	0	0	1	5	0	18	0	1
Busch, Mike, San Antonio	.238	115	416	58	99	171	14	2	18	51	0	3	4	36	2	111	3	2
Byington, John, El Paso†	.306	130	468	60	143	202	39	4	4	64	1	11	7	32	2	54	5	9
Caceres, Edgar, El Paso†	.312	114	378	50	118	150	14	6	2	52	5	1	2	23	4	41	9	2
Calhoun, Ray, San Antonio	.333	32	3	0	1	1	0	0	0	0	0	0	0	0	0	0	0	0
Carlson, Dan, Shreveport	.121	27	33	1	4	5	1	0	0	3	5	0	0	5	0	6	0	0
Carr, Chuck, Arkansas†	.261	28	111	17	29	39	5	1	1	6	0	0	0	8	1	23	8	2
Carter, Mike, El Paso	.255	50	165	20	42	57	4	4	1	15	3	1	0	16	2	31	10	8
Cassidy, David, Arkansas	.000	8	3	1	0	0	0	0	0	0	0	0	0	0	0	1	0	0
Castaldo, Vince, El Paso*	.289	119	412	61	119	181	33	10	3	50	1	2	3	48	8	77	12	6
Chimelis, Joel, Shreveport	.319	75	279	47	89	131	13	1	9	32	4	1	1	18	3	34	6	6
Christian, Rico, Arkansas	.234	52	141	8	33	38	5	0	0	7	1	0	1	5	0	33	3	7
Christopherson, Eric, Shreveport	.252	80	270	36	68	98	10	1	6	34	0	2	1	37	0	44	1	6
Cisarik, Brian, El Paso*	.048	9	21	1	1	1	0	0	0	0	1	0	1	2	0	6	2	1
Clemens, Troy, Shreveport*	.167	3	6	0	1	1	0	0	0	1	0	0	0	0	0	2	0	0
Coachman, Pete, 9 Shr.-33 Mid.	.177	42	141	30	25	40	4	1	3	13	2	1	3	18	0	24	6	1
Collier, Anthony, San Antonio*	.227	46	141	12	32	46	5	3	1	13	4	2	0	5	0	35	0	1
Colon, Cris, Tulsa†	.263	120	415	35	109	134	16	3	1	44	3	5	0	16	3	72	7	4
Cooper, Jamie, Shreveport	.243	49	181	27	44	51	5	1	0	4	3	0	3	12	1	49	13	8
Correia, Ron, Midland	.290	123	482	73	140	183	23	1	6	56	5	6	8	28	2	72	20	11
Couture, Mike, El Paso	.267	5	15	3	4	5	1	0	0	0	0	0	2	1	0	5	1	0
Cromer, Tripp, Arkansas	.239	110	339	30	81	130	16	6	7	29	4	2	4	22	1	82	4	6
Crosby, Todd, Shreveport†	.200	71	195	13	39	44	3	1	0	14	9	1	0	17	1	31	0	3
Crowe, Ron, Shreveport	.242	81	256	26	62	85	12	1	3	25	0	1	1	10	1	40	4	4
Daal, Omar, San Antonio*	.000	35	4	0	0	0	0	0	0	0	0	0	0	0	0	1	0	0
Davenport, Adell, Shreveport	.288	124	441	54	127	225	31	5	19	88	1	2	8	28	6	78	2	4
Davis, Doug, Tulsa	.205	14	39	3	8	10	2	0	0	1	0	0	0	3	0	6	0	0
Dean, Kevin, Jackson	.183	79	208	26	38	62	8	2	4	20	1	2	2	28	1	66	8	4
Delahoya, Javier, San Antonio	.000	5	4	0	0	0	0	0	0	0	0	0	0	1	0	1	0	0
Deutsch, John, San Antonio*	.206	68	214	28	44	73	11	0	6	16	0	1	4	19	3	50	1	1
Diggs, Tony, El Paso†	.217	107	281	47	61	73	6	3	0	20	7	3	3	29	2	48	31	8
Dodson, Bo, El Paso*	.248	109	335	47	83	126	19	6	4	46	0	1	0	72	6	81	3	7
Doffek, Scott, San Antonio*	.288	81	205	26	59	78	7	3	2	28	3	4	1	6	1	22	2	2
Easley, Mike, Arkansas*	.206	88	194	20	40	47	3	2	0	11	2	1	0	24	6	27	2	5
Edmonds, Jim, Midland*	.313	70	246	42	77	120	15	2	8	32	1	0	1	41	1	83	3	4
Ellis, Paul, Arkansas*	.228	25	79	9	18	26	2	0	2	8	0	1	1	13	2	14	0	1
Ericks, John, Arkansas	.154	13	13	0	2	3	1	0	0	0	2	1	0	1	0	5	0	0
Ettles, Mark, Wichita	.000	54	1	0	0	0	0	0	0	0	1	0	0	0	0	0	0	0
Eusebio, Tony, Jackson	.307	94	339	33	104	134	9	3	5	44	1	4	4	25	2	58	1	2
Fanning, Steve, Arkansas	.222	58	117	17	26	37	5	0	3	12	2	14	1	3	0	10	0	37
Faulkner, Craig, El Paso	.272	103	324	38	88	126	19	2	5	51	2	5	8	20	1	67	1	7
Fernandez, Dan, Shreveport	.216	60	185	18	40	48	2	0	2	22	5	1	1	16	2	34	2	0
Fernandez, Jose, Arkansas*	.157	49	115	7	18	26	5	0	1	8	0	1	0	3	1	20	0	1
Finken, Steve, Shreveport	.231	37	91	8	21	35	5	0	3	6	2	0	3	12	1	20	0	2
Finn, John, El Paso	.276	124	439	83	121	148	12	6	1	47	9	7	11	71	3	44	30	12
Fredrickson, Scott, Wichita	.500	56	2	0	1	1	0	0	0	0	0	0	0	0	0	1	0	0
Fulton, Ed, Arkansas*	.261	9	23	3	6	8	2	0	0	5	0	0	0	3	1	8	0	0
Gainer, Jay, Wichita*	.261	105	376	57	98	181	12	1	23	67	1	6	0	46	6	101	4	2
Galvez, Balvino, San Antonio	.000	19	2	0	0	0	0	0	0	0	0	0	0	0	0	0	0	0
Garrelts, Scott, Shreveport	.000	2	2	0	0	0	0	0	0	0	0	0	0	0	0	0	0	0
Gash, Darius, Wichita†	.288	15	52	2	15	18	1	1	0	8	1	0	0	4	0	13	7	2
Gieseke, Mark, Wichita†	.246	83	240	30	59	89	11	2	5	36	0	2	6	24	4	48	0	4
Gonzalez, Freddy, San Antonio	.250	17	52	3	13	17	2	1	0	5	0	0	0	5	0	9	1	0
Gonzalez, Paul, Wichita*	.255	120	432	59	110	177	18	2	15	54	0	3	4	48	3	124	7	3
Greer, Rusty, Tulsa*	.267	106	359	47	96	141	22	4	5	37	0	4	5	60	6	63	2	2
Griffiths, Brian, Jackson	.111	17	9	0	1	1	0	0	0	0	3	0	0	1	0	6	0	0
Guerrero, Mike, El Paso	.245	96	257	36	63	85	11	4	1	28	12	3	1	31	2	38	6	6
Guerrero, Sandy, El Paso*	.200	9	20	2	4	8	1	0	1	3	0	1	0	0	0	4	0	0
Hajek, Dave, Jackson	.270	103	326	36	88	109	12	3	1	18	10	3	0	31	2	25	8	3
Hamilton, Joey, Wichita	.000	6	6	0	0	0	0	0	0	0	1	0	0	0	0	4	0	0
Hancock, Chris, Shreveport*	.000	8	10	0	0	0	0	0	0	0	0	0	0	0	0	4	0	0
Hansell, Greg, San Antonio	.143	14	14	2	2	3	1	0	0	0	3	0	0	1	2	0	5	0

Player, Team	Avg.	G	AB	R	H	TB	2B	3B	HR	RBI	SH	SF	HP	BB	Int. BB	SO	SB	CS
Hanselman, Carl, Shreveport*	.000	11	13	1	0	0	0	0	0	0	1	0	0	0	0	4	0	0
Harris, Donald, Tulsa	.254	83	303	39	77	129	15	2	11	39	3	1	7	9	0	85	4	3
Harris, Rusty, Jackson†	.221	29	95	18	21	25	4	0	0	10	0	2	1	13	0	14	4	1
Harris, Vince, Wichita†	.281	80	242	36	68	85	12	1	1	20	4	0	1	35	0	36	38	13
Hartgraves, Dean, Jackson	.111	22	27	1	3	4	1	0	0	3	1	0	0	0	0	8	0	0
Helton, Keith, Jackson	.000	34	10	0	0	0	0	0	0	0	1	0	0	1	0	7	0	0
Herring, Vince, Shreveport*	.000	23	2	0	0	0	0	0	0	0	1	0	0	0	0	1	0	0
Hillemann, Charlie, El Paso	.216	44	116	15	25	41	7	3	1	10	0	3	3	9	0	39	4	1
Hoeme, Steve, Wichita	.000	20	0	0	0	0	0	0	0	0	1	0	0	0	0	0	0	0
Holbert, Ray, Wichita	.283	95	304	46	86	105	7	3	2	23	3	1	1	42	2	68	26	8
Hosey, Dwayne, Wichita†	.253	125	427	56	108	168	23	5	9	68	1	7	10	40	3	70	16	11
Howard, Matt, San Antonio	.270	95	345	40	93	121	12	5	2	34	16	1	4	28	1	38	18	15
Howell, David, Arkansas*	.170	28	47	3	8	10	2	0	0	4	1	0	0	6	0	10	0	0
Huisman, Rick, Shreveport	.136	17	22	0	3	3	0	0	0	1	0	0	0	1	0	8	0	0
Hulse, David, Tulsa*	.285	88	354	40	101	130	14	3	3	20	1	0	3	20	2	86	17	10
Hurta, Bob, Jackson*	.000	38	4	0	0	0	0	0	0	0	0	0	0	0	0	3	0	0
Ingram, Garey, San Antonio	.288	65	198	34	57	82	9	5	2	17	2	1	12	28	2	43	11	6
Jackson, John, Midland*	.291	40	151	19	44	54	4	3	0	16	3	0	3	17	0	20	12	5
James, Mike, San Antonio	.125	11	8	0	1	1	0	0	0	0	3	0	0	0	0	7	0	0
Jelic, Chris, Wichita	.295	27	95	14	28	39	3	1	2	18	1	2	1	11	0	13	4	0
Johnson, Brian, Wichita	.290	75	245	30	71	100	20	0	3	26	1	1	3	22	1	32	3	0
Jones, Bobby, Midland†	.231	100	316	45	73	99	15	1	3	30	5	2	0	50	1	69	5	4
Jones, Dax, Shreveport	.303	19	66	10	20	27	0	2	1	7	1	2	1	4	0	6	2	0
Jones, Jimmy, Jackson	.250	3	4	0	1	1	0	0	0	0	0	0	0	0	0	1	0	0
Jones, Ron, Shreveport*	.242	66	198	20	48	77	9	4	4	25	0	3	2	21	1	24	3	2
Jones, Todd, Jackson*	.000	61	1	0	0	0	0	0	0	0	0	0	0	0	0	1	0	0
Kapano, Corey, Midland	.182	13	44	5	8	12	4	0	0	5	0	0	1	9	1	12	1	3
Kappesser, Bob, El Paso	.236	88	233	32	55	67	7	1	1	33	2	2	3	22	0	49	6	7
Kasper, Kevin, Shreveport	.206	28	68	7	14	21	5	1	0	7	2	1	0	2	1	8	0	1
Kellner, Frank, Jackson†	.238	125	474	45	113	150	18	5	3	48	4	2	3	42	5	89	8	7
Kennedy, Darryl, Tulsa	.224	30	98	6	22	24	2	0	0	9	2	1	2	8	0	18	0	0
Kipila, Jeff, Midland	.259	115	417	63	108	199	22	3	21	76	0	1	9	48	1	104	3	4
Kliafas, Steve, San Antonio	.257	13	35	1	9	11	2	0	0	4	1	0	0	1	0	8	0	0
Kuld, Pete, Tulsa	.228	68	224	24	51	92	8	3	9	30	0	0	4	11	1	78	1	0
Lambert, Layne, Jackson*	.234	23	64	7	15	17	0	1	0	1	1	0	0	1	0	12	0	1
LaRose, Steve, Jackson*	.000	18	1	0	0	0	0	0	0	0	0	0	0	0	0	1	0	0
Lawton, Marcus, Midland†	.300	32	120	15	36	50	7	2	1	11	1	1	0	8	0	14	0	5
Lewis, Alan, El Paso*	.271	112	328	41	89	133	20	6	4	44	5	3	3	39	4	50	2	2
Lewis, Dan, Shreveport*	.312	50	170	28	53	65	3	0	3	25	0	2	3	18	2	24	2	3
Lewis, Jim, Jackson	.105	12	19	0	2	2	0	0	0	0	2	0	0	0	0	7	0	0
Lifgren, Kelly, Wichita*	.167	37	6	0	1	1	0	0	0	0	1	0	0	1	0	1	0	0
Linskey, Mike, Wichita*	.095	26	21	0	2	2	0	0	0	0	1	0	0	1	0	6	0	0
List, Paul, Tulsa	.292	34	130	17	38	50	7	1	1	14	0	0	0	13	0	30	1	1
Lopez, Pedro, Wichita	.245	96	319	35	78	112	8	4	6	48	2	6	7	13	0	68	4	3
Luckham, Ken, Jackson	.286	17	7	1	2	2	0	0	0	1	4	0	0	2	0	1	0	0
Madsen, Lance, Jackson	.229	109	332	40	76	135	16	2	13	40	5	1	6	36	1	105	2	6
Majer, Steffen, Arkansas	.000	22	7	0	0	0	0	0	0	0	1	0	0	0	0	4	0	0
Makarewicz, Scott, Jackson	.287	105	345	39	99	135	15	0	7	39	3	5	6	23	3	62	2	2
Marrero, Oreste, El Paso*	.185	18	54	8	10	17	2	1	1	8	0	1	0	4	0	13	1	0
Martin, Steve, Wichita	.213	61	183	20	39	60	8	2	3	17	1	0	2	12	1	41	15	11
Martinez, Julian, Arkansas	.165	94	297	19	49	73	13	1	3	21	1	4	0	28	3	80	2	6
Martinez, Pedro, Wichita*	.136	26	22	0	3	4	1	0	0	2	3	0	0	1	0	8	0	0
Martinez, Ray, Midland	.225	30	111	16	25	44	4	3	3	14	0	0	2	6	0	31	1	0
Massarelli, John, Jackson	.276	27	98	15	27	36	4	1	1	10	1	0	0	5	0	20	10	2
Maurer, Ron, San Antonio	.272	82	224	29	61	74	13	0	0	14	4	0	5	15	3	32	4	3
McAndrew, Jamie, San Antonio	.400	11	10	2	4	5	1	0	0	3	0	0	0	0	0	4	0	0
McConnell, Walt, Midland*	.260	48	169	19	44	52	8	0	0	16	0	1	0	26	1	26	1	0
McCoy, Trey, Tulsa	.192	15	52	5	10	16	0	0	2	6	0	0	0	8	0	15	0	1
McFarlin, Jason, Shreveport*	.208	28	106	13	22	34	3	3	1	3	2	0	4	5	0	20	10	1
McGehee, Kevin, Shreveport	.111	26	27	2	3	3	0	0	0	0	3	0	0	0	0	9	0	0
McWilliam, Tim, Wichita	.233	48	146	18	34	53	5	1	4	14	0	1	1	21	1	31	0	2
Meier, Kevin, Arkansas	.294	27	34	3	10	12	2	0	0	2	4	0	0	1	0	9	1	0
Mendez, Jesus, Arkansas*	.286	111	297	36	85	125	18	2	6	37	4	3	2	19	3	20	4	2
Meury, Bill, Wichita	.250	24	8	0	2	2	0	0	0	1	0	0	0	0	0	4	0	0
Mikulik, Joe, Jackson	.262	46	168	20	44	64	7	2	3	20	1	1	0	7	0	30	4	4
Miller, Orlando, Jackson	.264	115	379	51	100	151	26	5	5	53	2	4	4	16	0	75	7	5
Mimbs, Mark, San Antonio*	.154	13	13	1	2	3	1	0	0	0	1	0	0	0	0	7	0	0
Mimbs, Mike, San Antonio*	.100	24	20	1	2	2	0	0	0	1	1	0	0	0	0	7	0	0
Mondesi, Raul, San Antonio	.265	18	68	8	18	30	2	2	2	14	0	3	2	0	0	24	3	2
Montgomery, Ray, Jackson	.209	51	148	13	31	40	4	1	1	10	1	1	0	7	2	27	4	1
Morris, Rod, Tulsa*	.262	100	366	37	96	127	13	9	0	29	3	1	2	28	2	63	9	10
Morrow, Chris, San Antonio*	.233	84	245	22	57	85	5	4	5	30	1	3	1	6	0	41	4	3
Morrow, Timmie, Tulsa	.133	7	30	2	4	5	1	0	0	3	0	0	0	2	0	11	1	1
Musolino, Mike, Midland*	.273	7	22	2	6	7	1	0	0	4	0	0	0	2	0	5	0	0
Nelson, Jerome, Shreveport†	.167	5	6	1	1	1	0	0	0	1	0	0	0	0	0	1	0	0
Nichting, Chris, San Antonio	.143	15	14	2	2	3	1	0	0	0	0	0	0	1	0	4	0	0
Niethammer, Darren, Tulsa	.206	34	107	21	22	37	4	1	3	13	1	1	1	18	0	28	3	2
Noland, J.D., Wichita*	.270	118	452	59	122	170	21	6	5	52	4	0	3	36	0	80	40	23
O'Leary, Troy, El Paso*	.334	135	506	92	169	227	27	8	5	79	3	8	1	59	6	87	28	16
Oliva, Jose, Tulsa	.270	124	445	57	120	208	28	6	16	75	2	7	2	40	3	135	4	0
Oquendo, Jose, Arkansas†	.429	2	7	3	3	3	0	0	0	0	1	0	0	0	0	0	0	0
Ortiz, Hector, San Antonio	.203	26	59	1	12	13	1	0	0	5	1	0	1	11	0	13	0	0
Ozuna, Gab, Arkansas	.000	57	2	0	0	0	0	0	0	0	0	0	0	0	0	0	0	0
Painter, Lance, Wichita*	.040	27	25	1	1	2	1	0	0	1	3	0	0	1	0	14	0	0
Palacios, Rey, Midland	.261	29	92	14	24	46	5	1	5	10	1	0	2	7	2	24	0	1
Parra, Jose, San Antonio	.000	3	2	0	0	0	0	0	0	0	0	0	0	1	0	1	0	0
Perez, Eduardo, Midland	.230	62	235	27	54	73	8	1	3	23	1	3	1	22	1	49	19	7
Petagine, Roberto, Jackson*	.300	21	70	8	21	37	4	0	4	12	0	2	2	6	1	15	1	0
Peters, Reed, Shreveport	.312	71	231	30	72	103	13	3	4	29	0	3	1	20	0	25	4	5
Phillips, J.R., Midland*	.237	127	497	58	118	200	32	4	14	77	1	4	2	32	4	165	5	3
Piazza, Mike, San Antonio	.377	31	114	18	43	75	11	0	7	21	0	0	0	13	2	18	0	0
Piotrowicz, Brian, San Antonio	.000	16	1	0	0	0	0	0	0	0	0	0	0	0	0	1	0	0
Ponte, Ed, Jackson	.500	33	4	1	2	2	0	0	0	1	0	0	0	0	0	0	0	0
Postier, Paul, Tulsa	.231	45	130	8	30	38	4	2	0	12	2	0	1	11	0	30	0	1

Player, Team	Avg.	G	AB	R	H	TB	2B	3B	HR	RBI	SH	SF	HP	BB	Int. BB	SO	SB	CS
Pote, Lou, Shreveport	.000	20	5	1	0	0	0	0	0	0	0	0	0	1	0	3	0	0
Prager, Howard, Jackson*	.258	113	326	36	84	112	13	0	5	48	2	3	6	45	4	75	1	4
Proctor, Murph, San Antonio†	.302	64	235	32	71	99	17	1	3	37	4	4	2	22	1	30	2	5
Prybylinski, Don, Arkansas	.194	74	196	10	38	49	8	0	1	10	6	1	2	20	2	45	2	2
Rambo, Dan, Shreveport	.250	28	8	0	2	3	1	0	0	1	1	0	0	0	0	4	0	0
Rambo, Matt, Jackson*	.000	5	6	0	0	0	0	0	0	0	2	0	0	1	0	5	0	0
Reid, Derek, Shreveport	.167	2	6	1	1	2	1	0	0	0	1	0	0	0	0	1	0	0
Rice, Lance, San Antonio†	.232	75	194	17	45	60	9	0	2	18	6	2	1	17	3	34	0	1
Richards, Dave, 41 Ark.-6 E.P.*	.000	47	2	0	0	0	0	0	0	0	0	0	0	0	0	1	0	0
Rodriguez, Albert, Shreveport	.241	27	79	7	19	22	3	0	0	3	0	0	0	6	0	12	0	0
Rogers, Kevin, Shreveport†	.105	16	19	1	2	2	0	0	0	1	2	1	0	3	0	6	0	0
Roman, Vince, Jackson	.222	11	36	4	8	11	3	0	0	3	0	0	0	0	0	8	0	2
Romero, Jonathan, Midland	.106	15	47	4	5	5	0	0	0	2	0	0	0	3	0	11	0	0
Ross, Mike, Arkansas	.274	121	401	40	110	156	28	0	6	42	3	6	4	31	2	64	4	4
Rumsey, Dan, Midland*	.271	65	218	39	59	101	10	7	6	32	1	1	0	36	0	52	5	1
Russell, John, Tulsa	.258	46	163	26	42	83	11	0	10	27	0	1	5	17	1	42	0	4
Sable, Luke, Tulsa	.243	85	268	27	65	83	8	2	2	16	2	1	3	22	0	56	3	3
Sammons, Lee, Jackson	.227	89	273	33	62	77	5	2	2	16	4	4	1	38	2	61	24	6
Sanders, Earl, Jackson	.000	4	2	0	0	0	0	0	0	0	1	0	0	0	0	2	0	0
Sanders, Scott, Wichita	.091	14	11	1	1	1	0	0	0	0	0	0	0	0	0	3	0	0
Savinon, Odalis, Arkansas	.171	35	105	10	18	21	3	0	0	3	1	0	1	9	0	28	3	5
Scruggs, Tony, Tulsa	.279	12	43	3	12	15	3	0	0	2	0	2	3	0	0	10	3	1
Sellick, John, Arkansas	.256	105	301	27	77	122	19	1	8	41	0	3	0	29	2	71	5	6
Shackle, Rick, Arkansas	.063	18	16	0	1	1	0	0	0	0	2	0	0	0	0	7	0	0
Shave, Jon, Tulsa	.287	118	453	57	130	169	23	5	2	36	7	5	4	37	1	59	6	7
Shaw, Cedric, Tulsa*	.000	12	1	0	0	0	0	0	0	0	0	0	0	0	0	0	0	0
Sherman, Darrell, Wichita*	.332	64	220	60	73	106	11	2	6	25	2	2	9	40	2	25	26	7
Simon, Richie, Jackson	.250	34	4	1	1	1	0	0	0	0	0	0	0	0	0	3	0	0
Smiley, Reuben, Shreveport*	.256	93	316	38	81	121	12	5	6	35	1	1	4	21	8	71	19	6
Smith, Ed, El Paso	.291	22	86	11	25	36	5	0	2	15	0	1	1	8	0	20	0	1
Smith, Ira, San Antonio	.364	6	11	3	4	6	0	1	0	1	0	0	0	1	0	2	0	0
Spearman, Vernon, San Antonio*	.281	48	185	24	52	61	3	3	0	11	6	1	1	15	0	16	18	9
Springer, Dennis, San Antonio	.143	18	21	1	3	3	0	0	0	0	1	0	0	0	0	5	0	0
Stark, Matt, Midland	.377	16	53	10	20	29	3	0	2	10	0	0	2	10	0	6	1	0
Taylor, Rob, Shreveport	.000	34	2	0	0	0	0	0	0	0	1	0	0	0	0	2	0	0
Taylor, Terry, Midland*	.256	82	250	37	64	88	22	1	0	22	4	1	1	55	3	61	0	2
Tejero, Fausto, Midland	.188	84	266	21	50	67	11	0	2	30	5	3	4	11	0	63	1	2
Thomas, John, Arkansas*	.272	115	408	49	111	169	18	5	10	49	0	3	1	21	0	91	3	6
Thomas, Royal, Wichita	.000	41	16	0	0	0	0	0	0	0	0	0	0	0	0	5	0	0
Torres, Salomon, Shreveport	.135	25	37	3	5	7	0	1	0	1	1	0	1	0	0	18	0	0
Treadwell, Jody, San Antonio	.286	30	14	2	4	5	1	0	0	1	0	0	0	0	0	3	0	0
Urbani, Tom, Arkansas*	.250	10	8	2	2	5	0	0	1	3	0	0	0	3	0	3	1	0
Wall, Donnie, Jackson	.136	18	22	0	3	3	0	0	0	0	1	0	1	0	0	3	0	0
Ward, Ricky, Shreveport	.000	1	3	0	0	0	0	0	0	0	0	0	0	0	0	1	0	0
Wasinger, Mark, Midland	.357	18	56	6	20	27	5	1	0	8	1	2	1	6	1	11	0	1
Watson, Allen, Arkansas*	.346	14	26	3	9	12	0	1	0	5	2	1	0	0	0	1	0	0
Weber, Pete, Shreveport*	.288	118	417	64	120	172	23	10	3	33	2	4	5	42	2	97	14	8
Wengert, Bill, San Antonio	.167	10	6	0	1	1	0	0	0	0	0	0	0	0	0	5	0	0
Wilkins, Dean, 13 E.P. - 13 Wich.	.000	26	0	0	0	0	0	0	0	0	1	0	0	0	0	0	0	0
Williams, Todd, San Antonio	.000	39	3	0	0	0	0	0	0	0	0	0	0	0	0	2	0	0
Windes, Rodney, Jackson*	1.000	30	2	0	2	2	0	0	0	0	0	0	0	0	0	0	0	0
Wiseman, Dennis, Arkansas	.034	24	29	0	1	1	0	0	0	0	3	0	0	0	0	15	0	0
Witkowski, Mat, Wichita	.271	125	431	61	117	156	13	4	6	48	2	4	4	33	2	80	11	11
Worrell, Tim, Wichita	.000	19	16	1	0	0	0	0	0	0	1	0	0	1	0	10	0	0
Yockey, Mark, Shreveport*	.000	42	1	0	0	0	0	0	0	0	0	0	0	0	0	1	0	0

The following pitchers, listed alphabetically by club, with games in parentheses, had no plate appearances, primarily through use of designated hitters:

ARKANSAS—Compres, Fidel (54); Dixon, Steve (40); Eversgerd, Bryan (7); Plemel, Lee (13); Rivera, Lino (2).

EL PASO—Carter, Larry (4); Carter, Glenn (15); Czajkowski, Jim (57); Dell, Tim (36); Farrell, Mike (14); Fitzgerald, Dave (24); Hancock, Brian (1); Higuera, Ted (1); Hunter, Jim (3); Knox, Kerry (13); Lienhard, Steve (7); Martinez, Dave (15); McGraw, Tom (11); Novoa, Rafael (22); Richards, Dave (6); Robinson, Ron (1); Sparks, Steve (29); Tabaka, Jeff (50); Taylor, Scott (11); Vann, Brandy (42); Wilkins, Dean (13); Wishnevski, Bob (13).

JACKSON—Costello, Fred (36).

MIDLAND—Acosta, Clemente (12); Adams, Dave (26); Bennett, Erik (7); Blyleven, Bert (5); Cobb, Marvin (17); Edenfield, Ken (31); Hathaway, Hilly (14); Holzemer, Mark (7); James, Todd (25); Kraemer, Joe (12); Leftwich, Phil (21); Merriman, Brett (38); Peck, Steve (43); Percival, Troy (20); Scott, Darryl (27); Swingle, Paul (25); Vidmar, Don (21); Zappelli, Mark (27).

SAN ANTONIO—Bustillos, Albert (6); Snedeker, Sean (3).

SHREVEPORT—McCament, Randy (6); Myers, Jim (33); Reed, Steve (27); Sharko, Gary (14).

TULSA—Arner, Mike (15); Bohanon, Brian (6); Bronkey, Jeff (45); Brown, Bob (38); Burrows, Terry (14); Carman, Don (12); Chiamparino, Scott (3); Fajardo, Hector (5); Gies, Chris (17); Goetz, Barry (10); Gore, Bryan (23); Hurst, Jim (8); Leon, Danny (12); Manuel, Barry (16); Miller, Kurt (16); Moody, Ritchie (7); Nen, Robb (4); Oliver, Darren (3); Perez, Dave (16); Romero, Brian (13); Rowley, Steve (3); Sellers, Jeff (7); Shifflett, Chris (11); Smith, Dan (24); Whiteside, Matt (33).

WICHITA—Hilton, Howard (7); Wood, Brian (17).

GRAND SLAMS—Davenport, P. Gonzalez, Greer, Kipila, Niethammer, O'Leary, Oliva, Prager, Witkowski, 1 each.

AWARDED FIRST BASE ON CATCHER'S INTERFERENCE—Ashley 2 (Stark 2); Faulkner (Lopez); Finn (Lopez); Hosey (Baar); D. Jones (Ellis); Kapano (Lopez); A. Lewis (Rice); Lopez (Faulkner); Martin (Makarewicz); Mikulik (J. Fernandez); Perez (Johnson); Prager (D. Fernandez); S. Sanders (Baar); Witkowski (Piazza).

PITCHING

TEAM

Team	ERA	G	CG	ShO	Sv.	IP	H	R	ER	HR	HB	BB	Int.BB	SO	WP	Bk.
Arkansas	2.89	132	13	13	35	1092.0	998	423	351	76	29	312	45	799	34	9
Tulsa	3.00	136	10	11	44	1171.2	1051	479	390	78	37	364	18	888	63	19
Shreveport	3.10	136	17	14	44	1177.0	1080	494	406	53	31	351	26	994	56	9
Jackson	3.37	135	10	9	38	1170.2	1089	531	438	62	52	489	23	948	71	9
San Antonio	3.66	136	8	9	35	1164.2	1086	560	474	63	35	520	37	887	64	14
Wichita	3.91	136	5	17	34	1215.2	1160	603	528	90	50	448	32	1074	66	12
Midland	4.24	133	7	5	26	1179.1	1261	647	556	92	63	339	16	835	59	7
El Paso	4.34	136	17	8	39	1177.2	1243	649	568	71	69	417	24	865	62	14

INDIVIDUAL

(Leading qualifiers for earned-run average leadership— 109 or more innings)

*Throws lefthanded.

Pitcher, Team	W	L	Pct.	ERA	G	GS	CG	GF	ShO	Sv.	IP	H	R	ER	HR	HB	BB	Int.BB	SO	WP
Smith, Tulsa*	11	7	.611	2.52	24	23	4	0	3	0	146.1	110	48	41	4	6	34	0	122	3
Meier, Arkansas	11	6	.647	2.58	27	27	2	0	1	0	171.0	156	63	49	15	2	37	3	107	8
Hartgraves, Jackson*	9	6	.600	2.76	22	22	3	0	1	0	146.2	127	54	45	7	3	40	1	92	9
Worrell, Wichita	8	6	.571	2.86	19	19	1	0	1	0	125.2	115	46	40	8	2	32	0	109	1
Wiseman, Arkansas	9	12	.429	2.90	24	24	3	0	1	0	146.0	146	59	47	6	2	28	3	83	3
McGehee, Shreveport	9	7	.563	2.96	25	24	1	0	0	0	158.1	146	61	52	10	5	42	0	140	8
Martinez, Wichita*	11	7	.611	2.99	26	26	1	0	0	0	168.1	153	66	56	12	3	52	0	142	3
Carlson, Shreveport	15	9	.625	3.19	27	27	4	0	1	0	186.0	166	85	66	15	1	60	3	157	4
Novoa, El Paso*	10	7	.588	3.26	22	21	6	1	0	0	146.1	143	63	53	6	9	48	3	124	8
Anderson, Arkansas	4	11	.267	3.37	22	20	2	0	0	0	123.0	117	49	46	13	3	27	4	73	7

Departmental leaders: G—T. Jones, 61; W—Carlson, 15; L—H. Allen, Wiseman, 12; Pct.—Painter, .667; GS—Carlson, Meier, Painter, 27; CG—Novoa, 6; GF—Compres, 49; ShO—Smith, 3; Sv.—Compres, 28; IP—Carlson, 186.0; H—Adams, 187; R—Thomas, 104; ER—Thomas, 88; HR—Carlson, Linskey, Meier, 15; HB—Painter, 10; BB—H. Allen, 82; IBB—Ozuna, 11; SO—Carlson, 157; WP—H. Allen, 19.

(All pitchers—listed alphabetically)

Pitcher, Team	W	L	Pct.	ERA	G	GS	CG	GF	ShO	Sv.	IP	H	R	ER	HR	HB	BB	Int.BB	SO	WP
Acosta, Midland*	0	1	.000	4.50	12	0	0	3	0	0	12.0	17	7	6	1	0	3	1	15	0
Adams, Midland	6	11	.353	4.48	26	26	1	0	1	0	168.2	187	98	84	12	6	51	1	86	11
Allen, Jackson*	6	12	.333	3.97	27	24	1	2	1	0	122.1	127	70	54	3	2	82	4	94	19
Allen, San Antonio	5	2	.714	2.62	43	0	0	22	0	5	79.0	62	31	23	2	7	17	4	64	5
Anderson, Arkansas	4	11	.267	3.37	22	20	2	0	0	0	123.0	117	49	46	13	3	27	4	73	7
Arner, Tulsa	2	0	1.000	3.54	15	0	0	7	0	1	28.0	32	11	11	2	2	8	4	19	1
August, Jackson	1	1	.500	1.83	4	4	0	0	0	0	19.2	15	6	4	1	2	0	0	16	0
Bene, San Antonio	0	2	.000	3.09	18	1	0	5	0	0	32.0	19	15	11	1	0	34	1	25	10
Bennett, Midland	1	3	.250	3.91	7	7	0	0	0	0	46.0	47	22	20	3	7	16	0	36	1
Bethea, Wichita	0	1	.000	10.80	2	0	0	2	0	0	1.2	4	2	2	0	0	0	0	0	0
Blyleven, Midland	2	3	.400	2.73	5	5	0	0	0	0	33.0	27	10	10	3	1	3	0	23	0
Bohanon, Tulsa*	1	1	.667	1.27	6	6	1	0	0	0	28.1	25	7	4	0	3	9	0	25	4
Bronkey, Tulsa	2	7	.222	2.55	45	0	0	34	0	13	70.2	51	27	20	0	3	25	4	58	6
Brosnan, San Antonio*	1	7	.125	7.79	8	8	0	0	0	0	32.1	44	33	28	9	1	21	1	27	4
Brown, Tulsa	5	4	.556	3.73	38	1	0	12	0	0	70.0	75	34	29	6	0	18	1	60	3
Bruske, Jackson	4	3	.571	2.63	13	9	1	1	0	0	61.2	54	23	18	2	4	14	1	48	1
Bryand, Wichita*	2	3	.400	4.27	49	0	0	17	0	1	52.2	59	27	25	3	4	19	2	39	4
Burrows, Tulsa*	6	3	.667	2.13	14	13	1	0	0	0	76.0	66	22	18	3	0	35	0	59	4
Bustillos, San Antonio	1	0	1.000	0.69	6	0	0	2	0	2	13.0	8	3	1	0	0	3	0	10	0
Calhoun, San Antonio	1	4	.200	2.51	32	0	0	26	0	5	43.0	37	19	12	2	1	33	4	25	3
Carlson, Shreveport	15	9	.625	3.19	27	27	4	0	1	0	186.0	166	85	66	15	1	60	3	157	4
Carman, Tulsa*	3	3	.500	2.68	12	7	0	1	0	0	57.0	45	23	17	2	3	12	1	36	2
G. Carter, El Paso	6	5	.545	4.73	15	14	2	1	0	0	78.0	91	47	41	7	4	23	2	40	5
L. Carter, El Paso	0	1	.000	6.23	4	2	0	1	0	0	13.0	15	12	9	0	0	3	0	9	0
Cassidy, Arkansas*	0	3	.000	5.16	8	5	0	1	0	0	29.2	33	18	17	6	1	6	0	9	0
Chiamparino, Tulsa	0	0	.000	1.93	3	3	0	0	0	0	18.2	17	5	4	0	0	5	0	18	1
Cobb, Midland	1	1	.500	6.28	17	0	0	2	0	0	28.2	46	29	20	3	3	17	1	21	6
Compres, Arkansas	4	3	.571	3.28	54	0	0	49	0	28	57.2	55	26	21	3	2	23	3	39	1
Costello, Jackson	2	2	.500	2.70	36	0	0	10	0	0	53.1	51	22	16	3	0	13	3	35	2
Crowe, Shreveport	0	0	.000	0.00	3	0	0	3	0	0	3.1	1	0	0	0	0	2	0	3	0
Czajkowski, El Paso	5	7	.417	4.88	57	0	0	28	0	10	79.1	92	44	43	8	7	26	4	62	1
Daal, San Antonio	2	6	.250	5.02	35	5	0	16	0	5	57.1	60	39	32	3	4	33	1	52	7
Delahoya, San Antonio	2	1	.667	2.84	5	5	0	0	0	0	25.1	20	11	8	1	1	17	0	24	1
Dell, San Antonio	5	5	.500	5.65	36	12	0	10	0	2	87.2	98	61	55	6	9	26	1	61	13
Dixon, Arkansas*	1	1	.500	1.84	40	0	0	20	0	2	49.0	34	11	10	2	0	15	4	65	2
Edenfield, Midland	1	5	.167	5.98	31	0	0	17	0	2	49.2	60	35	33	5	4	24	3	43	4
Ericks, Arkansas	2	6	.250	4.08	13	13	1	0	0	0	75.0	69	36	34	4	3	29	1	71	6
Ettles, Wichita	3	8	.273	2.77	54	0	0	43	0	22	68.1	54	23	21	6	4	23	6	86	8
Eversgerd, Arkansas*	0	1	.000	6.75	6	0	0	2	0	0	5.1	7	4	4	0	0	2	1	4	0
Fajardo, Tulsa	2	1	.667	2.16	5	4	0	0	0	0	25.0	19	6	6	2	0	7	0	26	1
Farrell, El Paso	7	6	.538	2.62	14	14	5	0	0	0	106.1	95	42	31	5	7	25	4	66	0
Fitzgerald, El Paso*	3	1	.750	6.59	24	1	0	0	0	0	42.1	54	36	31	3	5	15	1	23	2
Fredrickson, Wichita	4	7	.364	3.19	56	0	0	22	0	5	73.1	50	29	26	9	2	38	3	66	11
Galvez, San Antonio	0	6	.000	5.72	19	5	0	7	0	3	45.2	53	31	29	2	0	22	2	42	2
Garrelts, Shreveport	0	0	.000	1.86	2	2	0	0	0	0	9.2	4	2	2	0	0	3	0	15	1
Gies, Tulsa	6	8	.429	3.56	17	16	2	0	0	0	98.2	101	43	39	7	6	31	2	36	4
Gieseke, Wichita*	1	0	1.000	0.00	2	2	0	0	0	0	3.0	0	0	0	0	0	1	0	5	0
Goetz, Tulsa	2	1	.667	0.63	10	0	0	5	0	1	14.1	10	2	1	0	0	6	0	7	1
Gore, Tulsa*	6	5	.545	2.49	23	5	0	5	0	0	72.1	68	34	20	3	3	15	1	43	2
Griffiths, Jackson	3	9	.250	3.80	17	17	0	0	0	0	97.0	96	52	41	6	6	42	0	91	6
Hajek, Jackson	0	0	.000	3.00	2	0	0	2	0	0	3.0	3	1	1	0	0	0	0	3	0
Hamilton, Wichita	3	0	1.000	2.86	34	0	0	14	0	0	34.2	33	12	11	2	1	11	0	26	1
Hancock, El Paso*	1	0	1.000	3.18	1	1	0	0	0	0	5.2	9	2	2	1	0	2	0	5	0
Hancock, Shreveport*	2	4	.333	3.10	8	8	2	0	0	0	49.1	37	22	17	0	4	18	0	30	3
Hansell, San Antonio	6	4	.600	2.83	14	14	0	0	0	0	92.1	80	40	29	6	3	33	2	64	1

Pitcher, Team	W	L	Pct.	ERA	G	GS	CG	GF	ShO	Sv.	IP	H	R	ER	HR	HB	BB	Int. BB	SO	WP
Hanselman, Shreveport	6	4	.600	2.48	11	11	2	0	1	0	80.0	73	31	22	1	1	17	1	42	2
Hartgraves, Jackson*	9	6	.600	2.76	22	22	3	0	2	0	146.2	127	54	45	7	3	40	1	92	9
Hathaway, Midland*	7	2	.778	3.21	14	14	1	0	0	0	95.1	90	39	34	2	8	10	0	69	2
Helton, Jackson*	6	3	.667	2.49	34	4	0	9	0	2	61.1	53	21	17	2	3	25	5	58	4
Herring, Shreveport*	0	1	.000	4.06	23	0	0	9	0	1	31.0	37	16	14	2	0	14	2	26	1
Higuera, El Paso*	0	1	.000	3.60	1	1	0	0	0	0	5.0	4	2	2	0	0	2	0	3	0
Hilton, Wichita	0	1	.000	7.88	7	0	0	3	0	0	8.0	16	8	7	0	0	5	1	7	0
Hoeme, Wichita	1	1	.500	6.31	20	1	0	6	0	0	35.2	48	27	25	1	1	19	1	24	3
Holzemer, Midland*	2	5	.286	3.83	7	7	2	0	0	0	44.2	45	22	19	4	1	13	0	36	3
Huisman, Shreveport	7	4	.636	2.35	17	16	1	0	1	0	103.1	79	33	27	3	5	31	1	100	3
Hunter, El Paso	1	1	.500	3.00	3	3	0	0	0	0	18.0	18	6	6	0	1	3	0	9	0
Hurst, Tulsa*	1	0	1.000	0.57	8	0	0	2	0	0	15.2	10	2	1	0	0	3	0	12	0
Hurta, Jackson*	3	1	.750	2.33	38	1	0	16	0	3	46.1	33	16	12	2	4	31	1	52	3
James, San Antonio	2	1	.667	2.67	8	8	0	0	0	0	54.0	39	16	16	3	1	20	0	52	1
James, Midland*	2	3	.400	7.18	25	1	0	7	0	0	26.1	35	24	21	4	0	17	0	16	1
J. Jones, Jackson	1	2	.333	2.50	3	3	1	0	0	0	18.0	20	9	5	1	3	6	0	20	1
T. Jones, Jackson	3	7	.300	3.14	61	0	0	48	0	25	66.0	52	28	23	3	2	44	3	60	5
Knox, El Paso*	0	1	.000	6.89	13	1	0	2	0	0	15.2	16	14	12	1	2	12	1	12	1
Kraemer, Midland*	2	3	.400	4.89	12	5	1	2	0	0	38.2	44	24	21	4	3	10	1	28	0
Larose, Jackson	0	2	.000	7.61	17	0	0	5	0	0	23.2	39	21	20	2	4	15	1	20	2
Leftwich, Midland	6	9	.400	5.88	21	21	0	0	0	0	121.0	156	90	79	10	4	37	1	85	2
Leon, Tulsa	5	0	1.000	0.60	12	0	0	4	0	1	30.0	15	4	2	0	1	8	1	34	3
Lewis, Jackson	3	5	.375	4.11	12	12	2	0	1	0	70.0	64	33	32	4	2	30	0	43	4
Lienhard, El Paso	0	1	.000	6.90	7	5	0	0	0	0	30.0	44	23	23	2	0	7	0	21	0
Lifgren, Wichita	1	6	.143	4.10	37	5	0	11	0	0	85.2	89	50	39	4	3	32	3	65	2
Linskey, Wichita*	10	6	.625	4.22	26	24	2	1	2	0	136.1	121	73	64	15	8	53	0	128	10
Luckham, Jackson	3	6	.333	5.45	16	13	0	1	0	0	72.2	77	48	44	5	3	41	1	47	3
Majer, Arkansas	2	3	.400	3.83	22	6	0	5	0	0	47.0	42	26	20	4	1	26	3	34	1
Manuel, Tulsa	2	0	1.000	4.00	16	1	0	8	0	2	27.0	28	12	12	4	1	16	0	28	0
Martinez, El Paso	5	4	.556	4.80	15	13	0	1	0	0	80.2	95	47	43	4	5	26	1	75	10
Martinez, Wichita*	11	7	.611	2.99	26	26	1	0	0	0	168.1	153	66	56	12	3	52	0	142	3
McAndrew, San Antonio	3	4	.429	3.58	11	8	0	1	0	0	50.1	50	26	20	2	1	19	2	35	0
McCament, Shreveport	2	1	.667	10.80	6	0	0	3	0	0	5.0	11	6	6	1	0	7	0	1	2
McGehee, Shreveport	9	7	.563	2.96	25	24	1	0	0	0	158.1	146	61	52	10	5	42	0	140	8
McGraw, El Paso*	6	0	1.000	2.73	11	10	1	1	0	0	69.1	75	24	21	2	0	26	1	53	2
Meier, Arkansas	11	6	.647	2.58	27	27	2	0	1	0	171.0	156	63	49	15	2	37	3	107	8
Merriman, Midland	3	4	.429	2.70	38	0	0	27	0	9	53.1	49	26	16	3	3	10	1	32	7
Miller, Tulsa	7	5	.583	3.68	16	15	0	0	0	0	88.0	82	42	36	9	2	35	1	73	7
Ma. Mimbs, San Antonio*	1	5	.167	3.61	13	13	0	0	0	0	82.1	78	43	33	3	2	22	4	55	3
Mi. Mimbs, San Antonio*	10	8	.556	4.23	24	22	2	2	0	1	129.2	132	65	61	11	3	73	1	87	7
Moody, Tulsa*	0	0	.000	1.42	7	0	0	7	0	2	6.1	3	2	1	0	1	2	0	6	1
Myers, Shreveport	2	4	.333	4.78	33	0	0	32	0	18	32.0	39	17	17	0	2	10	1	15	1
Nen, Tulsa	1	1	.500	2.16	4	4	1	0	0	0	25.0	21	7	6	1	1	2	0	20	4
Nichting, San Antonio	4	5	.444	2.52	13	13	0	0	0	0	78.2	58	25	22	3	1	37	0	81	4
Novoa, El Paso*	10	7	.588	3.26	22	21	6	1	0	0	146.1	143	63	53	6	9	48	3	124	8
Oliver, Tulsa*	0	1	.000	3.14	3	3	0	0	0	0	14.1	15	9	5	1	0	4	0	14	0
Ozuna, Arkansas	3	6	.333	2.08	57	0	0	22	0	4	78.0	64	22	18	5	4	27	11	63	1
Painter, Wichita*	10	5	.667	3.53	27	27	0	0	1	0	163.1	138	74	64	11	10	55	1	137	6
Parra, San Antonio	2	0	1.000	6.14	3	3	0	0	0	0	14.2	22	12	10	0	1	7	0	7	0
Peck, Midland	8	6	.571	3.96	43	7	0	16	0	0	111.1	105	53	49	9	4	22	1	87	6
Percival, Midland	3	0	1.000	2.37	20	0	0	17	0	5	19.0	18	5	5	1	1	11	1	21	1
Perez, Tulsa	4	3	.571	4.68	15	11	1	1	0	0	59.2	61	36	31	5	2	26	1	30	6
Peters, Shreveport	0	0	.000	27.00	1	0	0	1	0	0	1.0	3	3	3	0	0	1	0	0	1
Piotrowicz, San Antonio	2	0	1.000	3.03	16	0	0	8	0	0	29.2	28	12	10	3	0	3	2	14	0
Plemel, Arkansas	1	1	.500	3.86	13	0	0	3	0	0	21.0	31	11	9	5	2	6	3	9	0
Ponte, Jackson	1	1	.500	2.54	33	0	0	9	0	0	46.0	49	17	13	4	2	19	0	38	0
Postier, Tulsa	0	0	.000	0.00	1	0	0	1	0	0	2.0	1	0	0	0	0	0	0	2	0
Pote, Shreveport	4	2	.667	0.96	20	3	0	9	0	0	37.2	20	7	4	1	1	15	2	26	3
Rambo, Shreveport	6	3	.667	2.85	28	2	0	11	0	1	60.0	56	23	19	2	2	19	5	45	6
Rambo, Jackson*	1	0	1.000	2.16	5	5	0	0	0	0	33.1	19	8	8	2	0	8	0	39	0
Reed, Shreveport	1	0	1.000	0.62	27	0	0	25	0	23	29.0	18	3	2	1	1	0	0	33	0
Richards, 41 Ark.-6 El Paso*	4	5	.444	2.86	47	2	0	16	0	1	63.0	55	24	20	4	2	34	3	71	2
Rivera, Arkansas	1	0	1.000	20.25	2	0	0	1	0	0	1.1	2	3	3	0	0	3	2	1	0
Robinson, El Paso	0	0	.000	10.80	1	1	0	0	0	0	5.0	8	6	6	1	0	1	0	0	0
Rogers, Shreveport*	8	5	.615	2.58	16	16	2	0	2	0	101.0	87	34	29	3	4	29	0	110	7
Romero, Tulsa*	2	5	.286	4.47	13	11	0	0	0	0	52.1	62	31	26	10	0	20	0	44	2
Rowley, Tulsa	0	0	.000	7.71	3	1	0	0	0	0	7.0	7	6	6	1	0	7	0	8	1
Sanders, Jackson	0	1	.000	4.50	4	2	0	0	0	0	10.0	7	6	5	0	1	10	0	10	2
Sanders, Wichita	7	5	.583	3.49	14	14	0	0	0	0	87.2	85	35	34	7	3	37	2	95	4
Scott, Midland	1	1	.500	1.82	27	0	0	22	0	9	29.2	20	9	6	0	2	14	1	35	4
Sellers, Tulsa	1	0	1.000	3.46	7	1	0	2	0	0	13.0	14	6	5	0	1	8	1	9	2
Shackle, Arkansas	4	4	.500	2.50	18	11	0	2	0	0	72.0	68	28	20	2	3	15	2	45	2
Sharko, Shreveport	1	1	.500	5.09	14	0	0	3	0	0	17.2	22	13	10	1	1	4	1	9	1
Shaw, Tulsa*	6	2	.750	3.75	12	11	0	0	0	0	69.2	64	37	29	9	0	18	0	49	1
Shiflett, Tulsa	1	1	.500	4.37	11	0	0	5	0	1	22.2	18	14	11	5	1	7	0	20	2
Simon, Jackson	3	4	.429	3.88	34	1	0	12	0	4	48.2	40	27	21	8	6	25	1	30	2
Smith, Tulsa*	11	7	.611	2.52	24	23	4	0	3	0	146.1	110	48	41	4	6	34	0	122	3
Snedeker, San Antonio	2	0	1.000	0.69	3	2	0	1	0	0	13.0	13	1	1	0	0	1	0	4	1
Sparks, El Paso	9	8	.529	5.37	28	22	3	3	0	1	140.2	159	99	84	11	8	50	1	79	6
Springer, San Antonio	6	7	.462	4.35	18	18	4	0	0	0	122.0	114	61	59	6	4	49	3	73	4
Swingle, Midland	8	10	.444	4.69	25	25	2	0	0	0	149.2	158	88	78	14	6	51	1	104	8
Tabaka, El Paso*	9	5	.643	2.52	50	0	0	23	0	10	82.0	67	23	23	1	4	38	1	75	5
Taylor, Shreveport	4	2	.667	2.54	34	1	1	10	0	1	60.1	60	22	17	1	0	17	4	56	3
Taylor, El Paso	4	2	.667	3.48	11	9	0	0	0	0	54.1	45	21	21	5	0	19	1	37	2
Thomas, Wichita	7	7	.500	6.32	41	14	0	6	0	2	125.1	151	104	88	12	6	51	3	91	8
Torres, Shreveport	6	10	.375	4.21	25	25	4	0	2	0	162.1	167	93	76	10	2	34	2	151	9
Treadwell, San Antonio	3	5	.375	4.14	29	4	0	7	0	1	76.0	74	40	35	3	4	40	4	68	6
Urbani, Arkansas*	4	6	.400	1.93	10	10	2	0	1	0	65.1	49	23	14	3	2	15	1	41	1
Vann, El Paso	1	8	.111	5.14	42	3	0	21	0	7	77.0	87	53	44	5	6	43	2	72	3
Vidmar, Midland	1	4	.200	3.35	21	1	0	9	0	0	53.2	53	25	20	4	5	11	2	39	1
Wall, Midland	9	6	.600	3.54	18	18	2	0	0	0	114.1	114	51	45	6	2	26	2	99	4
Watson, Arkansas*	8	5	.615	2.15	14	14	3	0	1	0	96.1	77	24	23	4	2	23	1	93	0
Wengert, San Antonio	2	3	.400	3.22	10	7	0	0	0	0	50.1	48	20	18	3	0	13	0	43	2
Whiteside, Tulsa	0	1	.000	2.41	33	0	0	32	0	21	33.2	31	9	9	2	1	3	1	30	2

Pitcher, Team	W	L	Pct.	ERA	G	GS	CG	GF	ShO	Sv.	IP	H	R	ER	HR	HB	BB	Int. BB	SO	WP
Wilkins, 13 El Paso-13 Wich........	1	2	.333	5.80	26	1	0	7	0	0	40.1	37	28	26	3	2	24	6	41	5
Williams, San Antonio.................	7	4	.636	3.27	39	0	0	34	0	13	44.0	47	17	16	0	1	23	6	35	3
Windes, Jackson*......................	3	3	.500	2.22	30	0	0	10	0	4	56.2	49	18	14	1	3	10	0	53	2
Wiseman, Arkansas....................	9	12	.429	2.90	24	24	3	0	1	0	146.0	143	59	47	6	2	28	3	83	3
Wishnevski, El Paso....................	1	0	1.000	1.04	13	0	0	13	0	9	17.1	7	2	2	0	1	4	0	16	2
Witkowski, Wichita.....................	0	0	.000	9.00	1	0	0	1	0	0	1.0	1	1	1	0	1	0	0	2	0
Wood, Wichita............................	1	1	.500	7.20	17	0	0	13	0	4	20.0	23	16	16	0	1	10	4	25	1
Worrell, Wichita..........................	8	6	.571	2.86	19	19	1	0	1	0	125.2	115	46	40	8	2	32	0	109	1
Yockey, Shreveport*...................	4	2	.667	4.14	42	1	0	13	0	0	50.0	53	23	23	2	2	28	4	35	1
Zappelli, Midland........................	7	1	.875	3.19	27	14	0	4	0	1	98.2	104	41	35	10	5	19	1	59	2

BALKS—Bronkey, Miller, Shaw, 4 each; Daal, Dell, Painter, Smith, Sparks, Watson, Worrell, 3 each; S. Allen, Brown, Bryand, Hansell, Hatha-way, Herring, Majer, D. Rambo, Swingle, Treadwell, 2 each; Adams, August, Bene, Bruske, G. Carter, Cassidy, Ettles, Farrell, Fitzgerald, Galvez, Gore, Griffiths, C. Hancock, Hartgraves, Hilton, Holzemer, Huisman, Hunter, M. James, T. Jones, Knox, Leftwich, Leon, Linskey, McGehee, Meier, Mike Mimbs, Novoa, Ozuna, Parra, Ponte, Simon, R. Taylor, S. Taylor, Thomas, Torres, Vann, Wall, Windes, Wiseman, 1 each.

COMBINATION SHUTOUTS—Anderson-Compres, Ericks-Shackle-Richards-Ozuna-Compres, Majer-Compres-Ozuna, Meier-Dixon-Ozuna, Meier-Majer-Dixon, Shackle-Compres; Urbani-Dixon-Compres, Watson-Dixon-Compres, Wiseman-Compres, Arkansas; Novoa-Czajkowski 2, Farrell-Czajkowski, Hunter-Tabaka, McGraw-Tabaka-Czajkowski, Sparks-Wishnevski, El Paso; August-Sanders-Ponte-T. Jones, Bruske-Hurta-Costello-T. Jones, Bruske-Simon-T. Jones, Luckham-Windes, Wall-Simon, Jackson; Blyleven-Merriman-Acosta, Hathaway-Merriman, Holzemer-Peck-Scott, Zappelli-Merriman-Scott, Midland; Hansell-Williams, McAndrew-Daal-Allen, Mike Mimbs-Williams, Nichting-Bustillos, Nichting-Piotrowicz-Daal, Nichting-Williams, Snedeker-Treadwell, Wengert-Williams, San Antonio; Carlson-Reed, Huisman-Rambo-Reed, Huisman-Yockey-Reed, McGehee-Herring, Pote-Herring, Pote-Reed, Rogers-Taylor-Pote, Shreveport; Bohanon-Bronkey-Whiteside, Burrows-Bronkey, Chi-amparino-Perez-Goetz-Gore, Gies-Whiteside, Miller-Brown-Perez, Perez-Goetz-Moody, Shaw-Whiteside, Smith-Goetz, Tulsa; Hamilton-Fredrickson-Ettles, Linskey-Fredrickson, Martinez-Lifgren-Ettles, Martinez-Lifgren-Wilkins-Fredrickson-Ettles-Gieseke, Martinez-Wood, Paint-er-Bryand, Painter-Fredrickson-Wood, Painter-Wilkins-Ettles, Sanders-Thomas-Ettles, Worrell-Ettles, Worrell-Ettles-Thomas, Worrell-Fredrickson, Worrell-Lifgren, Wichita.

NO-HIT GAMES—None.

FIELDING

TEAM

Team	Pct.	G	PO	A	E	DP	PB	Team	Pct.	G	PO	A	E	DP	PB
Arkansas....................	.974	132	3276	1322	125	98	6	Shreveport....................	.969	136	3531	1343	156	121	15
Wichita......................	.972	136	3647	1411	146	105	30	Midland	.968	133	3538	1502	168	131	18
Jackson.....................	.971	135	3512	1512	151	140	14	Tulsa	.968	136	3515	1453	166	113	7
El Paso......................	.971	136	3533	1543	153	119	27	San Antonio.................	.968	136	3494	1473	166	133	16

INDIVIDUAL

*Throws lefthanded.
FIRST BASEMEN

Player, Team	Pct.	G	PO	A	E	DP
Aldrete, Arkansas*..................	.973	20	166	12	5	11
Ashley, San Antonio.................	1.000	1	5	1	0	1
Baldwin, Jackson*...................	1.000	1	8	2	0	0
Ball, Jackson..........................	.978	35	242	22	6	34
Beck, El Paso.........................	1.000	1	1	0	0	0
Burton, Tulsa..........................	1.000	20	174	8	0	18
Busch, San Antonio.................	.977	10	80	6	2	8
Byington, El Paso....................	.962	3	24	1	1	3
Caceres, El Paso.....................	.983	9	56	1	1	1
Castaldo, El Paso....................	1.000	6	35	3	0	3
Crowe, Shreveport...................	.983	7	53	5	1	2
Davenport, Shreveport..............	.978	47	295	17	7	42
Deutsch, San Antonio*..............	.989	61	487	51	6	51
DODSON, El Paso*..................	.998	102	868	68	2	77
Easley, Shreveport...................	.992	82	494	29	4	42
Faulkner, El Paso.....................	.986	20	122	14	2	12
Gainer, Wichita.......................	.986	85	709	67	11	50
Gieseke, Wichita*....................	.997	48	356	30	1	30
Gonzalez, San Antonio..............	1.000	1	7	0	0	2
Gonzalez, Wichita....................	1.000	1	8	0	0	2
Greer, Tulsa*..........................	.987	98	808	50	11	61
Howell, Arkansas*...................	1.000	11	79	4	0	8
Jelic, Wichita..........................	.988	10	75	4	1	7
Kipila, Wichita........................	1.000	6	36	3	0	5
Lewis, El Paso........................	1.000	1	8	0	0	0
Lewis, Shreveport*..................	.984	40	298	10	5	22
Makarewicz, Jackson...............	.989	31	245	20	3	26
Marrero, El Paso*....................	1.000	5	41	0	0	0
Maurer, San Antonio................	1.000	1	2	0	0	0
McConnell, Midland..................	.857	1	6	0	1	0
McCoy, Tulsa..........................	1.000	1	7	1	0	2
Mendez, Arkansas*..................	.990	59	371	25	4	24
Niethammer, Tulsa...................	.965	8	69	13	3	7
Perez, Midland........................	.667	1	2	0	1	0
Petagine, Jackson*..................	1.000	18	151	15	0	7
Phillips, San Antonio................	.987	127	1222	100	17	106
Piazza, San Antonio.................	1.000	1	10	0	0	0
Postier, Tulsa.........................	1.000	13	106	14	0	12
Prager, Jackson*.....................	.993	67	509	36	4	53
Proctor, San Antonio*...............	.995	64	540	64	3	54
Ross, Arkansas.......................	1.000	11	77	8	0	8
Sellick, Arkansas.....................	.984	63	461	27	8	29
Smith, El Paso........................	.982	10	100	10	2	12
Wasinger, Midland...................	.917	1	11	0	1	0
Witkowski, Wichita...................	1.000	1	6	2	0	2

Triple play—Makarewicz.

SECOND BASEMEN

Player, Team	Pct.	G	PO	A	E	DP
Alfonzo, Midland	.973	48	74	144	6	18
Alvarez, San Antonio................	.977	43	67	106	4	26
Aversa, Arkansas....................	.978	20	27	63	2	8
Ball, Jackson..........................	.885	7	11	12	3	2
Beanblossom, Arkansas	.979	111	167	295	10	58
Bethea, Wichita.......................	1.000	14	21	33	0	6
Byington, El Paso....................	.931	18	26	28	4	6
Caceres, El Paso.....................	.987	49	64	87	2	16
Chimelis, Shreveport................	1.000	35	55	91	0	17
Coachman, 1 Shr.-4 Mid...........	.963	5	11	15	1	1
Crosby, Shreveport	.981	61	114	143	5	29
Doffek, San Antonio	.875	9	9	12	3	2
Fanning, Arkansas...................	1.000	5	9	9	0	1
Finken, Shreveport	.987	15	31	43	1	8
Finn, El Paso..........................	.982	87	147	225	7	45
E. Guerrero, El Paso.................	.905	6	8	11	2	3
M. Guerrero, El Paso................	1.000	4	10	13	0	2
Hajek, Jackson.......................	.974	48	100	129	6	35
Harris, Jackson.......................	.968	24	51	70	4	14
Harris, Wichita........................	.971	22	31	35	2	9
HOWARD, San Antonio	.989	94	167	268	5	49
Kappesser, El Paso..................	1.000	1	1	0	0	0
Kasper, Shreveport	.979	21	47	45	2	20
Kellner, Jackson......................	.988	71	127	203	4	51
Martinez, Midland....................	1.000	19	31	68	0	12
Oquendo, Arkansas..................	1.000	2	3	2	0	1
Postier, Tulsa.........................	1.000	1	3	5	0	3
Rodriguez, Shreveport..............	.987	21	37	41	1	13
Romero, Midland.....................	1.000	6	10	14	0	4
Ross, Arkansas.......................	1.000	2	2	2	0	0
Sable, Tulsa...........................	.975	38	77	80	4	19
Shave, Tulsa...........................	.964	107	233	278	19	63
Taylor, Midland	.975	63	133	183	8	44
Ward, Shreveport	1.000	1	0	1	0	0
Witkowski, Wichita...................	.984	120	214	279	8	58

THIRD BASEMEN

Player, Team	Pct.	G	PO	A	E	DP
Alfonzo, Midland	.800	6	3	5	2	1
Alvarez, San Antonio................	.872	21	12	29	6	2
Aversa, Arkansas....................	1.000	18	7	19	0	3
Ball, Jackson..........................	.836	46	14	78	18	10
Bethea, Wichita.......................	1.000	26	11	40	0	4
Busch, San Antonio..................	.888	81	61	154	27	14
Byington, El Paso....................	.929	34	18	60	6	4
Caceres, El Paso.....................	.923	9	6	18	2	0
Chimelis, Shreveport................	.915	31	14	40	5	6

— 402 —

Player, Team	Pct.	G	PO	A	E	DP
Coachman, 7 Shr.-2 Mid.	.909	9	4	6	1	1
Crowe, Shreveport	.873	25	12	36	7	3
Davenport, Shreveport	.907	77	38	137	18	7
Dean, Jackson	1.000	1	0	1	0	0
Doffek, San Antonio	1.000	11	3	8	0	1
Easley, Shreveport	1.000	3	0	7	0	0
Fanning, Arkansas	.853	20	6	23	5	0
Faulkner, El Paso	1.000	1	1	0	0	0
Finken, Shreveport	.879	14	10	19	4	5
Finn, El Paso	.889	3	0	8	1	0
Gonzalez, Wichita	.904	114	59	213	29	13
Guerrero, El Paso	1.000	4	2	6	0	0
Hajek, Jackson	.974	47	23	88	3	8
Jelic, Wichita	.800	6	1	7	2	0
Johnson, Wichita	1.000	2	0	1	0	0
Kapano, Midland	.825	13	14	19	7	2
Kellner, Jackson	1.000	2	0	3	0	0
Lambert, Jackson	.880	18	12	32	6	1
LEWIS, El Paso	.937	92	58	194	17	15
Madsen, Jackson	.890	49	36	77	14	5
Martinez, Arkansas	.865	30	10	35	7	1
Martinez, Midland	.786	9	2	9	3	2
Maurer, San Antonio	.941	36	30	50	5	9
McConnell, Midland	.942	40	26	55	5	5
Meury, Wichita	.800	2	3	1	1	0
Oliva, Tulsa	.915	113	75	225	28	15
Palacios, Midland	1.000	1	2	3	0	0
Perez, Midland	.918	52	39	96	12	6
Postier, Tulsa	1.000	6	2	7	0	0
Rodriguez, Shreveport	.800	1	0	4	1	0
Romero, Midland	1.000	7	6	15	0	1
Ross, Arkansas	.936	88	60	129	13	6
Sable, Tulsa	.867	25	13	39	8	1
Smith, El Paso	.881	14	4	33	5	0
Taylor, Midland	1.000	2	1	1	0	1
Wasinger, Midland	.900	7	8	10	2	3
Witkowski, Wichita	.875	4	0	7	1	0

SHORTSTOPS

Player, Team	Pct.	G	PO	A	E	DP
Alvarez, San Antonio	.750	1	0	3	1	0
Aversa, Arkansas	.944	5	8	9	1	0
Barker, San Antonio	.945	92	181	281	27	65
Beanblossom, Arkansas	1.000	1	1	0	0	0
Bellinger, Shreveport	.928	125	183	346	41	75
Bethea, Wichita	.960	52	63	155	9	22
Caceres, El Paso	.972	54	93	150	7	34
Chimelis, Shreveport	.936	13	15	29	3	7
Colon, Tulsa	.940	119	157	364	33	77
Correia, Midland	.948	121	204	385	32	72
CROMER, Arkansas	.962	107	135	315	18	56
Fanning, Arkansas	.964	22	23	57	3	12
Finken, Shreveport	.500	1	1	0	1	0
Finn, El Paso	.889	4	2	6	1	1
Guerrero, El Paso	.955	83	119	221	16	38
Hajek, Jackson	.933	4	5	9	1	3
Holbert, Wichita	.956	92	150	217	17	40
Kellner, Jackson	.935	60	75	170	17	31
Kliafas, San Antonio	.961	13	14	35	2	4
Lewis, El Paso	.962	14	16	35	2	4
Martinez, Arkansas	.810	8	6	11	4	3
Martinez, Midland	.895	3	5	12	2	1
Maurer, San Antonio	.928	36	48	68	9	17
Meury, Wichita	1.000	2	0	5	0	0
Miller, Jackson	.946	84	132	254	22	57
Postier, Tulsa	1.000	6	11	17	0	3
Rodriguez, Shreveport	1.000	4	2	8	0	1
Romero, Midland	1.000	1	3	3	0	1
Sable, Tulsa	.750	1	1	2	1	0
Shave, Tulsa	.964	15	18	36	2	5
Taylor, Midland	.965	9	28	27	2	4

Triple play—Miller.

OUTFIELDERS

Player, Team	Pct.	G	PO	A	E	DP
Alfonzo, Midland	1.000	1	2	0	0	0
Alvarez, San Antonio	.880	20	21	1	3	0
Anderson, Midland*	.986	39	62	6	1	1
Ansley, Jackson	.964	34	52	1	2	1
Ashley, San Antonio	.978	88	124	8	3	2
Baldwin, Jackson*	.986	51	66	4	1	1
Barron, San Antonio	.977	27	42	1	1	0
Belcher, Tulsa	.962	106	199	5	8	1
Bellomo, Shreveport*	1.000	5	2	0	0	0
Brannon, Arkansas	.962	105	166	13	7	4
Brown, Midland	.979	27	44	3	1	0
Busch, San Antonio	.952	26	39	1	2	0
Byington, El Paso	.600	3	2	1	2	0
Carr, Arkansas	.986	28	70	3	1	1
Carter, El Paso	.952	50	96	4	5	1
Castaldo, El Paso	.960	74	113	6	5	2
Christian, Arkansas	.953	44	79	2	4	1
Cisarik, El Paso*	1.000	8	12	1	0	0

Player, Team	Pct.	G	PO	A	E	DP
Collier, San Antonio*	.938	44	72	3	5	0
Cooper, Shreveport	.970	49	94	4	3	1
Couture, El Paso	.857	5	6	0	1	0
Crowe, Shreveport	.983	47	57	2	1	1
Dean, Jackson	.975	70	106	12	3	5
Diggs, El Paso	.964	101	174	14	7	3
Dodson, El Paso*	1.000	2	1	0	0	0
Doffek, San Antonio	.978	36	43	1	1	0
Edmonds, Midland*	.967	70	139	6	5	2
Finn, El Paso	.960	45	68	4	3	2
Gash, Wichita	.963	14	23	3	1	1
Gieseke, Wichita*	1.000	6	6	0	0	0
Gonzalez, San Antonio	.957	16	21	1	1	1
Greer, Tulsa*	1.000	6	6	0	0	0
Hajek, Jackson	1.000	12	12	0	0	0
Harris, Tulsa	.981	83	196	7	4	1
Harris, Wichita	1.000	45	64	3	0	1
Hillemann, El Paso	.980	41	49	1	1	0
Hosey, Wichita	.962	107	195	9	8	3
Hulse, Tulsa*	.956	60	84	2	4	0
Ingram, San Antonio	.967	61	112	4	4	0
Jackson, Midland*	.986	39	71	2	1	1
Jelic, Wichita	1.000	3	4	0	0	0
D. Jones, Shreveport	.900	15	24	3	3	0
Jones, Midland	.946	98	153	21	10	3
R. Jones, Shreveport	1.000	31	49	2	0	0
Kipila, Midland	.966	59	108	5	4	1
Kuld, Tulsa	.750	3	6	0	2	0
Lawton, Midland	.980	31	48	1	1	0
List, Tulsa	1.000	30	43	0	0	0
Madsen, Jackson	.955	45	57	7	3	0
Marrero, El Paso*	1.000	4	1	0	0	0
Martin, Wichita	.992	54	115	4	1	2
Martinez, Arkansas	.973	60	106	3	3	1
Massarelli, Jackson	.900	23	26	1	3	0
McFarlin, Shreveport*	.932	25	53	2	4	0
McWilliam, Shreveport	.983	37	52	5	1	0
Mendez, Arkansas*	.955	49	75	9	4	1
Mikulik, Jackson	.988	45	81	1	1	0
Mondesi, San Antonio	.974	18	31	6	1	3
Montgomery, Jackson	.975	46	76	3	2	0
Morris, Tulsa*	.975	98	192	3	5	2
Morrow, San Antonio*	.942	62	92	5	6	2
Morrow, Tulsa	.944	7	17	0	1	0
Nelson, Shreveport	1.000	1	3	0	0	0
Noland, Shreveport	.945	110	163	10	10	3
O'Leary, El Paso*	.955	133	220	11	11	1
Perez, Midland	1.000	7	12	1	0	0
Peters, Shreveport	.969	67	124	3	4	0
Phillips, Midland*	1.000	1	1	0	0	0
Postier, Tulsa	1.000	6	8	1	0	1
Prager, Jackson*	.950	35	53	4	3	1
Reid, Shreveport	1.000	3	3	0	0	0
Roman, Jackson	.947	10	16	2	1	0
Rumsey, Midland	.975	45	72	5	2	0
Sable, Tulsa	.870	10	16	4	3	0
Sammons, Jackson	.958	81	159	2	7	1
Savinon, Arkansas	.972	30	66	4	2	1
Scruggs, Tulsa	1.000	8	18	0	0	0
Sherman, Wichita*	.986	63	135	7	2	1
Smiley, Shreveport*	.956	91	166	7	8	2
Smith, Shreveport	1.000	1	1	0	0	0
Spearman, San Antonio*	.970	48	126	5	4	1
Thomas, Arkansas	.977	114	201	8	5	0
WEBER, Shreveport*	.995	111	190	5	1	0

CATCHERS

Player, Team	Pct.	G	PO	A	E	DP	PB
Baar, San Antonio	.987	32	209	20	3	3	9
Basso, Wichita	1.000	2	10	0	0	0	0
Beck, El Paso	.917	3	10	1	1	0	0
Billmeyer, Midland	.978	20	122	11	3	2	0
Brown, San Antonio	1.000	7	27	1	0	0	0
Christopherson, Shreveport	.994	80	604	66	4	10	10
Clemens, Shreveport	.987	2	11	0	0	1	1
Davis, Tulsa	1.000	14	96	9	0	0	0
Ellis, Arkansas	.993	22	128	13	1	2	1
EUSEBIO, Jackson	.9963	75	493	51	2	12	7
Faulkner, El Paso	.991	76	396	48	4	6	7
Fernandez, Shreveport	.987	60	400	43	6	2	4
Fernandez, Arkansas	.987	39	212	20	3	1	2
Fulton, Arkansas	1.000	7	36	1	0	0	0
Johnson, Wichita	.994	64	472	39	3	5	14
Kappesser, El Paso	.980	84	475	65	11	1	20
Kennedy, Tulsa	.970	30	200	27	7	2	1
Kuld, Tulsa	.991	46	295	29	3	1	2
Lopez, Wichita	.972	84	618	66	20	8	16
Makarewicz, Jackson	.994	68	488	47	3	7	5
Massarelli, Jackson	1.000	3	18	2	0	0	2
Musolino, Midland	1.000	6	33	3	0	1	1
Niethammer, Tulsa	.957	14	62	4	3	0	1
Ortiz, San Antonio	.982	25	140	23	3	2	1
Palacios, Midland	.989	26	162	23	2	4	1
Piazza, San Antonio	.980	25	179	22	4	2	0

Player, Team	Pct.	G	PO	A	E	DP	PB
Prybylinski, Arkansas	.9960	72	443	51	2	6	3
Rice, San Antonio	.986	65	376	57	6	9	6
Russell, Tulsa	.997	37	264	27	1	5	3
Stark, Midland	.964	11	50	4	2	1	1
Tejero, Midland	.976	84	503	75	14	9	15

PITCHERS

Player, Team	Pct.	G	PO	A	E	DP
Acosta, Midland*	.500	12	0	1	1	0
Adams, Midland	.914	26	11	21	3	1
Allen, Jackson*	.952	27	3	17	1	1
Allen, San Antonio	.944	43	5	12	1	1
Anderson, Arkansas	.917	22	12	21	3	4
Arner, Tulsa	1.000	15	1	4	0	0
August, Jackson	.800	4	2	2	1	0
Bene, San Antonio	.750	18	1	2	1	0
Bennett, Midland	.923	7	5	7	1	1
Blyleven, Midland	1.000	5	0	7	0	0
Bohanon, Tulsa*	1.000	6	0	5	0	0
Bronkey, Tulsa	.913	45	2	19	2	0
Brosnan, San Antonio*	1.000	8	2	5	0	1
Brown, Tulsa	1.000	38	5	10	0	2
Bruske, Jackson	.933	13	8	6	1	0
Bryand, Wichita	.909	49	9	11	2	0
Burrows, Tulsa*	1.000	14	2	14	0	0
Bustillos, San Antonio	.833	6	4	1	1	0
Calhoun, San Antonio	1.000	32	7	13	0	5
Carlson, Shreveport	.844	27	8	19	5	4
Carman, Tulsa*	.833	12	3	7	2	0
G. Carter, El Paso	1.000	15	7	5	0	1
L. Carter, El Paso	.800	4	2	2	1	0
Cassidy, Arkansas*	1.000	8	2	7	0	0
Chiamparino, Tulsa	1.000	3	1	1	0	0
Cobb, Midland	1.000	17	0	8	0	0
Compres, Arkansas	.818	54	3	6	2	1
Costello, Jackson	1.000	36	2	5	0	0
Czajkowski, El Paso	.944	57	6	11	1	3
Daal, San Antonio*	.923	35	7	17	2	1
Delahoya, San Antonio	.857	5	4	2	1	0
Dell, El Paso	.950	36	6	13	1	0
Dixon, Arkansas*	1.000	40	1	5	0	0
Edenfield, Midland	1.000	31	3	4	0	1
Ericks, Arkansas	.909	13	3	7	1	0
Ettles, Wichita	.857	54	3	9	2	0
Eversgerd, Arkansas*	1.000	6	4	2	0	0
Fajardo, Tulsa	1.000	5	1	4	0	0
Farrell, El Paso*	.963	14	3	23	1	1
Fitzgerald, El Paso*	1.000	24	4	6	0	1
Fredrickson, Wichita	.800	56	0	4	1	0
Galvez, San Antonio	.923	19	2	10	1	2
Garrelts, Shreveport	1.000	2	0	1	0	0
Gies, Tulsa	.893	17	10	15	3	1
Gieseke, Wichita*	1.000	2	0	1	0	0
Goetz, Tulsa	1.000	10	1	4	0	0
Gore, Tulsa*	1.000	23	4	9	0	1
Griffiths, Jackson	1.000	17	1	7	0	0
Hamilton, Wichita	.909	6	4	6	1	1
Hancock, Shreveport*	.818	8	2	7	2	0
Hansell, San Antonio	.857	14	9	9	3	2
Hanselman, Shreveport	.889	11	7	9	2	1
Hartgraves, Jackson*	.944	22	9	25	2	2
Hathaway, Midland*	.963	14	7	19	1	1
Helton, Jackson*	.909	34	1	9	1	1
Herring, Shreveport*	1.000	23	0	8	0	0
Higuera, El Paso*	1.000	1	1	1	0	0
Hilton, Wichita	1.000	7	2	1	0	0
Hoeme, Wichita	.778	20	1	6	2	0
Holzemer, Midland*	.857	7	2	4	1	1
Huisman, Shreveport	1.000	17	5	4	0	0
Hunter, El Paso	1.000	3	0	4	0	1
Hurst, Tulsa*	.500	8	0	1	1	0
Hurta, Jackson*	1.000	38	2	2	0	0
James, San Antonio	1.000	8	2	0	1	0
James, Midland*	.833	25	0	5	1	0
J. Jones, Jackson	1.000	3	2	0	0	0
T. Jones, Jackson	1.000	61	3	9	0	0
Knox, El Paso*	1.000	13	1	4	0	0
Kraemer, Midland*	.857	12	1	5	1	0
LaRose, Jackson	1.000	17	0	4	0	0
Leftwich, Midland	.966	21	9	19	1	1
Leon, Tulsa	.909	12	3	7	1	0
Lewis, Jackson	1.000	12	6	8	0	0
Lienhard, El Paso	.857	7	0	6	1	0
Lifgren, Wichita	.955	37	12	9	1	0
Linskey, Wichita*	1.000	26	4	11	0	0
Luckham, Jackson	1.000	17	5	10	0	1
Majer, Arkansas	1.000	22	4	6	0	0
Manuel, Tulsa	.889	16	2	6	1	0
Martinez, El Paso	.750	15	5	7	4	0
Martinez, Wichita*	.907	26	10	29	4	1
McAndrew, San Antonio	.917	11	7	4	1	0
McCament, Shreveport	1.000	6	3	1	0	0
McGEHEE, Shreveport	1.000	25	6	22	0	0
McGraw, El Paso*	.850	11	3	14	3	2
Meier, Arkansas	.971	27	9	24	1	1
Merriman, Midland	.923	38	2	10	1	2
Miller, Tulsa	1.000	16	3	9	0	2
Ma. Mimbs, San Antonio*	1.000	13	4	6	0	1
Mi. Mimbs, San Antonio*	.951	24	14	25	2	4
Moody, Tulsa*	1.000	7	0	1	0	0
Myers, Shreveport	1.000	33	2	8	0	0
Nen, Tulsa	.750	4	0	3	1	0
Nichting, San Antonio	.778	13	7	7	4	1
Novoa, El Paso*	.875	22	5	16	3	2
Oliver, Tulsa*	.833	3	1	4	1	0
Ozuna, Arkansas	.905	57	9	10	2	1
Painter, Wichita*	.964	27	10	43	2	1
Parra, San Antonio	1.000	3	1	3	0	0
Peck, Midland	.962	43	9	16	1	3
Percival, Midland	1.000	20	3	1	0	0
Perez, Tulsa	1.000	15	2	11	0	0
Piotrowicz, San Antonio	1.000	16	5	4	0	0
Plemel, Arkansas	1.000	13	0	6	0	0
Ponte, Jackson	.923	33	6	6	1	0
Pote, Shreveport	.750	20	1	5	2	0
Rambo, Shreveport	1.000	28	1	13	0	0
Rambo, Jackson*	1.000	5	0	4	0	0
Reed, Shreveport	1.000	27	2	2	0	0
Richards, 41 Ark.-6 E.P.*	.900	47	1	8	1	0
Robinson, El Paso	1.000	1	0	1	0	0
Rogers, Shreveport*	.929	16	3	10	1	0
Romero, Tulsa*	.923	13	2	10	1	0
Sanders, Jackson	.875	4	2	5	1	1
Sanders, Wichita	1.000	14	5	7	0	0
Scott, Midland	1.000	27	3	2	0	0
Sellers, Tulsa	.857	7	1	5	1	1
Shackle, Arkansas	1.000	18	7	6	0	0
Sharko, Shreveport	.833	14	1	4	1	1
Shaw, Tulsa*	1.000	12	3	13	0	0
Shiflett, Tulsa	1.000	11	3	0	0	0
Simon, Jackson	.923	34	4	8	1	0
Smith, Tulsa*	.976	24	7	33	1	3
Snedeker, San Antonio	1.000	3	3	3	0	0
Sparks, El Paso	.967	28	16	42	2	5
Springer, San Antonio	.973	18	19	17	1	0
Swingle, Midland	.933	25	7	21	2	2
Tabaka, El Paso*	.957	50	5	17	1	3
Taylor, Shreveport	1.000	34	1	8	0	0
Taylor, El Paso	.923	11	6	6	1	1
Thomas, Wichita	.964	41	14	13	1	0
Torres, Shreveport	.920	25	4	19	2	0
Treadwell, San Antonio	.941	29	5	11	1	2
Urbani, Arkansas*	1.000	10	6	10	0	0
Vann, El Paso	.864	42	8	11	3	3
Vidmar, Midland	.846	21	4	7	2	1
Wall, Jackson	1.000	18	8	12	0	0
Watson, Arkansas*	1.000	14	9	15	0	0
Wengert, San Antonio	1.000	10	7	8	0	1
Whiteside, Tulsa	.750	33	2	1	1	0
Wilkins, 13 E.P.-13 Wich.	.909	26	6	4	1	0
Williams, San Antonio	1.000	39	1	11	0	2
Windes, Jackson*	1.000	30	4	15	0	3
Wiseman, Arkansas	.893	24	6	19	3	2
Wishnevski, El Paso	1.000	13	0	4	0	0
Wood, Wichita	1.000	17	0	3	0	0
Worrell, Wichita	.944	19	5	12	1	3
Yockey, Shreveport*	.917	42	3	8	1	1
Zappelli, Midland	.893	27	12	13	3	0

The following players did not have any fielding statistics at the positions indicated or appeared only as a designated hitter, pinch-hitter or pinch-runner: Bethea, of, p; Crowe, p; Fanning, of; Hajek, p; B. Hancock, p; Kipila, 2b; Lambert, 2b; LaRose, of; A. Lewis, c; D. Lewis, of; Mendez, 3b; Niethammer, 3b; Peters, p; Postier, p; Rice, 3b; L. Rivera, p; Rowley, p; Wasinger, 2b; Weber, 1b; Witkowski, p.

LEAGUE CHAMPIONS

Year	Team	Pct.	Year	Team	Pct.	Year	Team	Pct.
1888 —	Dallas	.671		Fort Worth*	.750	1898 —	League disbanded.	
1889 —	Houston	.551	1896 —	Fort Worth	.757	1899 —	Galveston	.632
1890 —	Galveston	.705		Houston†	.679		Galveston	.762
1892 —	Houston	.741		Galveston	.548	1900-01 —	Did not operate.	
	Houston	.613	1897 —	San Antonio†	.657	1902 —	Corsicana	.866
1895 —	Dallas	.754		Galveston†	.717		Corsicana	.682

Year	Team	Pct.
1903—	Paris-Waco	.615
	Dallas*	.648
1904—	Corsicana*	.615
	Fort Worth	.800
1905—	Fort Worth	.545
1906—	Fort Worth	.677
	Cleburne x	.609
1907—	Austin	.629
1908—	San Antonio	.664
1909—	Houston	.601
1910—	Dallas†	.586
	Houston†	.586
1911—	Austin	.575
1912—	Houston	.626
1913—	Houston	.620
1914—	Houston†	.671
	Waco†	.671
1915—	Waco	.592
1916—	Waco	.587
1917—	Dallas	.600
1918—	Dallas	.584
1919—	Shreveport*	.677
	Fort Worth	.651
1920—	Fort Worth	.703
	Fort Worth	.750
1921—	Fort Worth	.691
	Fort Worth	.662
1922—	Fort Worth	.694
	Fort Worth	.711
1923—	Fort Worth	.632
1924—	Fort Worth	.689
	Fort Worth	.763
1925—	Fort Worth	.711
	Fort Worth y	.653
1926—	Dallas	.574
1927—	Wichita Falls	.654
1928—	Houston*	.679
	Wichita Falls	.731
1929—	Dallas*	.588
	Wichita Falls	.620
1930—	Wichita Falls	.697
	Fort Worth*	.632
1931—	Houston a	.625
	Houston	.734
1932—	Beaumont*	.640
	Dallas	.727
1933—	Houston	.623
	San Antonio (4th)§	.523
1934—	Galveston‡	.579
1935—	Oklahoma City‡	.590
1936—	Dallas	.604
	Tulsa (3rd)§	.519
1937—	Oklahoma City	.635
	Fort Worth (3rd)§	.535
1938—	Beaumont	.635
1939—	Houston	.606
	Fort Worth (4th)§	.540
1940—	Houston‡	.652
1941—	Houston	.673
	Dallas (4th)§	.519
1942—	Beaumont	.605
	Shreveport (2nd)§	.576
1943-44-45—Did not operate.		
1946—	Fort Worth	.656
	Dallas (2nd)§	.591
1947—	Houston‡	.623
1948—	Fort Worth‡	.601
1949—	Fort Worth	.649
	Tulsa (2nd)§	.584
1950—	Beaumont	.595
	San Antonio (4th)§	.513
1951—	Houston‡	.619
1952—	Dallas	.571
	Shreveport (3rd)§	.522
1953—	Dallas‡	.571
1954—	Shreveport	.559
	Houston (2nd)§	.553
1955—	Dallas	.581
	Shreveport (3rd)§	.540
1956—	Houston‡	.623
1957—	Dallas	.662
	Houston (2nd)§	.630
1958—	Fort Worth	.582
	Cor. Christi (3rd)§	.507
1959—	Victoria	.589
	Austin (2nd)§	.548
1960—	Rio Grande Valley	.590
	Tulsa (3rd)	.528
1961—	Amarillo	.643
	San Antonio (3rd)§	.532
1962—	El Paso	.571
	Tulsa (2nd)§	.550
1963—	San Antonio	.564
	Tulsa (3rd)§	.529
1964—	San Antonio‡	.607
1965—	Tulsa	.574
	Albuquerque b	.550
1966—	Arkansas	.579
1967—	Albuquerque	.557
1968—	Arkansas	.586
	El Paso b	.562
1969—	Amarillo	.593
	Memphis b	.504
1970—	Albuquerque a	.615
	Memphis	.507
1971—	Did not operate as league—clubs were members of Dixie Association.	
1972—	Alexandria	.600
	El Paso b	.557
1973—	San Antonio	.590
	Memphis b	.558
1974—	Victoria b	.581
	El Paso	.555
1975—	Lafayette c	.558
	Midland c	.604
1976—	Amarillo b	.600
	Shreveport	.515
1977—	El Paso	.600
	Arkansas d	.485
1978—	El Paso d	.593
	Jackson	.567
1979—	Arkansas d	.571
	Midland	.563
1980—	Arkansas d	.596
	San Antonio	.544
1981—	San Antonio	.571
	Jackson d	.507
1982—	El Paso	.559
	Tulsa	.515
1983—	Jackson	.507
	Beaumont d	.500
1984—	Beaumont	.654
	Jackson d	.610
1985—	El Paso	.632
	Jackson d	.537
1986—	El Paso d	.630
	Jackson	.533
1987—	Wichita d	.515
	Jackson	.515
1988—	El Paso	.552
	Tulsa d	.522
1989—	Arkansas d	.585
	Wichita	.537
1990—	San Antonio	.582
	Shreveport d	.489
1991—	Shreveport d	.632
	El Paso	.596
1992—	Shreveport	.566
	Wichita d	.515

*Won split-season playoff. †Won playoff for title. ‡Finished first and won four-club playoff. §Won four-club playoff. xTitle to Cleburne by default. yTied with Dallas in second half and won playoff for championship. zFort Worth disbanded. aTied with Beaumont at end of first half and won title in best-of-five series played as part of second-half schedule. bLeague divided into Eastern, Western divisions; won two-team playoff. cLeague divided into Eastern, Western divisions; declared co-champions when playoffs were not completed. dLeague divided into Eastern and Western divisions and played split-season; won playoffs. NOTE—Championship awarded to winner of four-team playoff, 1933-51; first-place team and playoff winner co-champions, 1952-64.

CALIFORNIA LEAGUE

FINAL STANDINGS

FIRST HALF

NORTHERN DIVISION

Team	W	L	T	Pct.	GB
Stockton (Brewers)	40	28	0	.588	......
Reno (Athletics)	39	29	0	.574	1
Modesto (Athletics)	39	29	0	.574	1
San Jose (Giants)	37	31	0	.544	3
Salinas (Independent)	19	49	0	.279	21

SOUTHERN DIVISION

Team	W	L	T	Pct.	GB
Palm Springs (Angels)	38	30	0	.559	......
Bakersfield (Dodgers)	37	31	0	.544	1
Visalia (Twins)	33	35	0	.485	5
High Desert (Padres)	30	38	0	.441	8
San Bernardino (Mariners)	28	40	0	.412	10

SECOND HALF

NORTHERN DIVISION

Team	W	L	T	Pct.	GB
Stockton (Brewers)	43	25	0	.632	......
San Jose (Giants)	41	27	1	.603	2
Modesto (Athletics)	40	28	0	.588	3
Reno (Athletics)	26	42	0	.382	17
Salinas (Independent)	17	50	0	.254	25½

SOUTHERN DIVISION

Team	W	L	T	Pct.	GB
Visalia (Twins)	42	26	1	.618	......
High Desert (Padres)	41	27	0	.603	1
Palm Springs (Angels)	34	33	0	.507	7½
Bakersfield (Dodgers)	31	37	0	.456	11
San Bernardino (Mariners)	24	44	0	.353	18

COMPOSITE

Team	Sto.	Mod.	S.J.	Vis.	P.S.	H.D.	Bak.	Reno	S.B.	Sal.	W	L	T	Pct.	GB
Stockton (Brewers)	....	9	9	4	7	8	8	12	8	18	83	53	0	.610	......
Modesto (Athletics)	10	....	8	6	8	7	6	11	7	16	79	57	0	.581	4
San Jose (Giants)	10	10	....	7	4	8	5	11	9	14	78	58	1	.574	5
Visalia (Twins)	8	6	5	....	10	5	13	7	10	11	75	61	1	.551	8
Palm Springs (Angels)	5	4	8	8	....	11	9	6	13	8	72	63	0	.533	10½
High Desert (Padres)	4	5	4	15	9	....	9	9	5	12	71	65	0	.522	12
Bakersfield (Dodgers)	4	6	7	7	9	9	....	6	12	8	68	68	0	.500	15
Reno (Athletics)	6	9	9	5	6	7	6	....	6	11	65	71	0	.478	18
San Bernardino (Mariners)	4	5	3	8	7	6	8	6	....	5	52	84	0	.382	31
Salinas (Independent)	2	3	5	1	3	4	4	7	7	....	36	99	0	.267	46½

Major league affiliations in parentheses.

Playoffs—Stockton defeated Modesto, three games to two; Visalia defeated Palm Springs, three games to one; Stockton defeated Visalia, three games to one, to win league championship.

Regular-season attendance—Bakersfield, 158,714; High Desert, 218,444; Modesto, 104,671; Palm Springs, 89,645; Reno, 105,346; Salinas, 54,256; San Bernardino, 106,481; San Jose, 135,891; Stockton, 112,347; Visalia, 86,209. Total, 1,172,004. Playoffs (13 games)—18,797. All-Star Game—1,554.

Managers—Bakersfield, Tom Beyers; High Desert, Bryan Little; Modesto, Ted Kubiak; Palm Springs, Mario Mendoza; Reno, Gary Jones; Salinas, Hide Koga; San Bernardino, Ivan DeJesus; Stockton, Tim Ireland; Visalia, Steve Liddle.

All-Star team: 1B—Steve Dunn, Visalia; 2B—Brent Gates, Modesto; 3B—Fabio Gomez, Reno; SS—Denny Hocking, Visalia; OF—Rich Becker, Visalia; Marty Cordova, Visalia; Mike Neill, Reno; C—Mike Durant, Visalia, and Eric Helfand, Modesto; DH—Billy Hall, High Desert; P—Rafael Chaves, High Desert; Mike Farrell, Stockton; Joe Rosselli, San Jose; Curtis Shaw, Modesto; Tim Smith, Reno; Most Valuable Player—Marty Cordova, Visalia; Pitcher of the Year—Joe Rosselli, San Jose; Rookie of the Year—Mike Neill, Reno; Manager of the Year—Tim Ireland, Stockton.

BATTING

TEAM

Team	Avg.	G	AB	R	OR	H	TB	2B	3B	HR	RBI	SH	SF	HP	BB	Int. BB	SO	SB	CS	LOB
Visalia	.295	137	4664	846	728	1377	2072	269	39	116	763	21	49	57	645	23	872	224	103	1041
Reno	.292	136	4703	855	916	1371	1942	223	51	82	757	40	46	48	717	28	816	138	96	1129
Palm Springs	.286	135	4492	734	671	1286	1658	199	31	37	646	34	40	37	562	28	717	143	86	988
High Desert	.273	136	4544	727	677	1242	1781	189	46	86	638	29	50	45	537	26	871	189	89	948
Modesto	.265	136	4552	728	639	1206	1800	228	21	108	647	43	44	72	668	36	1034	149	72	1096
Bakersfield	.264	136	4485	616	674	1184	1725	223	27	88	556	64	55	44	468	39	819	162	100	932
San Jose	.264	137	4612	689	566	1217	1670	212	44	51	593	60	55	59	566	38	893	148	90	1044
San Bernardino	.262	136	4583	629	771	1199	1693	207	19	83	540	37	35	43	464	13	824	161	112	920
Stockton	.253	136	4549	726	562	1151	1708	203	60	78	616	36	38	54	642	24	982	238	105	988
Salinas	.248	135	4466	526	872	1107	1459	145	42	41	464	70	34	46	523	22	934	132	109	965

INDIVIDUAL

(Leading qualifiers for batting championship—367 or more plate appearances)

*Bats lefthanded. †Switch-hitter.

Player, Team	Avg.	G	AB	R	H	TB	2B	3B	HR	RBI	SH	SF	HP	BB	Int. BB	SO	SB	CS
Hall, Billy, High Desert†	.356	119	495	92	176	214	22	5	2	39	1	3	1	54	2	77	49	27
Cordova, Marty, Visalia	.341	134	513	103	175	302	31	6	28	131	3	5	9	76	5	99	13	5
Neill, Mike, Reno*	.336	130	473	101	159	214	26	7	5	76	6	2	5	81	2	96	23	11
Grebeck, Brian, Palm Springs	.336	91	289	71	97	115	14	2	0	39	8	3	0	83	2	55	6	5
Hocking, Denny, Visalia†	.331	135	550	117	182	255	34	9	7	81	2	2	8	72	1	77	38	18
Gates, Brent, Modesto†	.321	133	505	94	162	235	39	2	10	88	2	7	2	85	9	60	9	7
Cruz, Fausto, Reno	.319	127	489	86	156	227	22	11	9	90	3	7	7	70	1	66	8	7
Becker, Rich, Visalia*	.316	136	506	118	160	246	37	2	15	82	1	6	4	114	2	122	29	13
Waggoner, Jimmy, Reno*	.309	93	317	75	98	149	18	0	11	57	1	3	4	87	2	50	2	5
Stahoviak, Scott, Visalia*	.308	110	409	62	126	173	26	3	5	68	0	2	3	82	2	66	17	6

Departmental leaders: G—Becker, 136; AB—Hocking, 550; R—Becker, 118; H—Hocking, 182; TB—Cordova, 302; 2B—Ricker, 41; 3B—Luka-chyk, 14; HR—Cordova, 28; RBI—Cordova, 131; SH—Castro, 20; SF—Adams, Spann, 10; HP—Hart, 18; BB—Becker, 114; IBB—Miller, 14; SO—Mashore, 136; SB—Hall, 49; CS—Hall, 27.

(All players—listed alphabetically)

Player, Team	Avg.	G	AB	R	H	TB	2B	3B	HR	RBI	SH	SF	HP	BB	Int. BB	SO	SB	CS
Adams, Tommy, San Bernardino	.280	94	339	56	95	155	21	0	13	75	2	10	5	38	4	68	20	9
Alfonzo, Ed, Palm Springs	.358	65	257	52	92	123	18	2	3	42	0	3	2	31	3	25	1	4
Anderson, Garret, Palm Springs*	.323	81	322	46	104	126	15	2	1	62	0	0	1	21	3	61	1	1
Arai, Kiyoshi, Salinas†	.250	128	400	47	100	115	9	3	0	31	12	1	6	47	1	62	25	26
Arredondo, Roberto, High Desert*	.264	70	216	23	57	74	9	1	2	18	2	2	3	16	1	25	2	5
Baar, Bryan, Bakersfield	.204	16	54	4	11	19	5	0	1	8	0	1	0	3	0	14	0	0
Balthazar, Doyle, San Bernardino	.292	82	284	27	83	98	10	1	1	23	0	3	2	26	0	47	5	6
Barns, Jeff, Modesto	.281	76	221	27	62	71	7	1	0	21	5	2	0	21	4	17	3	0
Basse, Mike, Stockton*	.270	115	407	77	110	138	16	3	2	37	4	2	3	62	1	87	36	15
Beard, Garrett, Modesto	.270	98	348	55	94	140	12	2	10	59	4	5	9	51	1	84	4	6
Becker, Rich, Visalia†	.316	136	506	118	160	246	37	2	15	82	1	6	4	114	2	122	29	13
Bellomo, Kevin, San Jose	.258	48	151	16	39	50	3	1	2	14	1	3	2	11	0	23	3	3
Benjamin, Bobby, Stockton*	.193	25	57	8	11	16	3	1	0	2	0	0	0	20	1	16	6	0
Bernhardt, Cesar, Stockton	.306	47	173	34	53	75	13	3	1	16	0	2	2	26	2	22	6	3
Bish, Brent, High Desert	.307	96	319	53	98	122	11	5	1	34	2	5	8	31	2	60	11	12
Bishop, Jim, Stockton	.000	2	3	0	0	0	0	0	0	0	0	0	0	1	0	2	0	0
Blanco, Henry, Bakersfield	.234	124	401	42	94	134	21	2	5	52	10	9	9	51	3	91	10	6
Booker, Eric, Modesto	.218	47	142	25	31	51	6	1	4	22	1	1	5	39	0	35	1	3
Boyzuick, Mike, Bakersfield	.321	42	134	32	43	85	13	1	9	30	0	0	3	33	2	24	2	2
Bradish, Mike, Salinas	.287	30	108	11	31	38	3	2	0	17	2	2	0	10	0	25	0	1
Brannon, Paul, San Bernardino	.199	44	141	17	28	42	2	0	4	11	0	2	2	15	1	40	2	0
Brewer, Matt, San Jose*	.232	47	155	15	36	47	7	2	0	19	0	0	2	27	0	29	0	2
Brown, Matt, Visalia	.267	37	101	8	27	33	3	0	1	7	0	0	0	0	0	23	0	1
Bruno, Julio, High Desert	.278	118	418	57	116	157	22	5	3	62	5	3	1	33	4	92	2	3
Bryant, Craig, San Bernardino	.191	31	94	9	18	31	2	1	3	10	1	3	8	0	21	4	1	
Buccheri, Jim, Reno	.367	63	259	65	95	125	14	2	4	38	2	2	56	3	40	33	13	
Butcher, Art, Salinas*	.179	21	28	2	5	8	0	0	1	2	0	0	2	0	6	0	3	
Calcagno, Dan, San Jose	.167	39	96	8	16	17	1	0	0	7	7	0	1	13	0	14	2	0
Carcione, Tom, Modesto	.271	84	269	47	73	101	11	1	5	45	3	4	3	68	1	60	2	2
Carter, Mike, Stockton	.262	67	252	38	66	86	9	1	3	26	3	5	2	17	1	26	31	8
Carter, Tim, Stockton	.236	84	237	25	56	83	5	2	6	26	0	2	7	23	1	76	3	3
Casper, Tim, San Jose†	.227	43	75	17	17	21	4	0	0	10	2	0	0	16	0	19	4	0
Castro, Juan, Bakersfield	.260	113	446	56	116	151	15	4	4	42	20	7	1	37	2	64	14	11
Cervantes, Manuel, San Bernardino*	.261	115	371	46	97	125	16	3	2	39	6	3	1	52	0	51	5	7
Charles, Frank, San Jose	.290	87	286	27	83	101	16	1	0	34	1	0	4	11	2	61	4	4
Cirillo, Jeff, Stockton	.222	7	27	2	6	7	1	0	0	5	0	0	2	2	0	0	0	0
Cisarik, Brian, San Jose*	.323	27	99	16	32	38	2	2	0	6	2	1	2	14	2	22	7	4
Clayton, Craig, San Bernardino	.249	63	217	21	54	78	14	2	2	20	0	4	0	19	0	21	1	5
Clemens, Troy, San Jose*	.264	65	159	12	42	52	8	1	0	20	0	3	1	12	2	27	0	0
Cohick, Emmitt, Palm Springs*	.301	117	402	69	121	174	17	6	8	78	2	7	3	49	2	91	15	12
Cole, Mark, Stockton	.254	111	389	51	99	128	9	7	2	53	7	2	4	33	1	60	19	9
Colon, David, Palm Springs	.229	92	292	42	67	87	12	1	2	27	4	3	2	38	0	28	2	4
Cookson, Brent, San Jose	.290	68	255	44	74	126	8	4	12	49	0	2	3	25	0	69	9	5
Cordova, Marty, Visalia	.341	134	513	103	175	302	31	6	28	131	3	5	9	76	5	99	13	5
Cruz, Fausto, Reno	.319	127	489	86	156	227	22	11	9	90	3	7	7	70	1	66	8	7
Dalesandro, Mark, Palm Springs	.297	126	492	72	146	203	30	3	7	92	0	6	5	33	6	50	6	2
Davis, Kevin, Salinas	.291	72	234	38	68	96	6	5	4	31	2	4	1	26	1	37	4	2
Davis, Matt, San Jose†	.275	123	415	67	114	146	17	6	1	67	2	6	1	84	4	75	9	10
DeFrancesco, Tony, Reno	.133	14	30	3	4	5	1	0	0	4	1	1	2	8	0	6	0	0
Demetral, Chris, Bakersfield*	.275	90	306	38	84	112	14	1	4	36	4	3	1	33	7	45	7	8
Dempsey, John, Salinas*	.301	51	146	13	44	51	2	1	1	14	1	2	0	8	0	25	1	0
Deutsch, John, Bakersfield*	.343	44	178	31	61	104	10	0	11	36	0	1	0	14	2	33	0	0
Diaz, Eddy, San Bernardino	.273	114	436	80	119	165	15	2	9	39	12	2	6	38	0	46	33	16
Dodge, Tom, Palm Springs†	.270	79	244	27	66	79	9	2	0	26	1	1	4	38	4	34	10	8
Dotel, Angel, Bakersfield*	.214	98	318	40	68	104	14	1	10	45	4	7	2	21	1	63	14	6
Duncan, Andres, San Jose	.231	109	308	46	71	87	7	3	1	32	13	4	9	35	2	76	19	9
Dunn, Steve, Visalia*	.305	125	492	93	150	270	36	3	26	113	0	4	7	41	6	103	8	3
Duplessis, Dave, Salinas*	.242	69	211	25	51	90	10	4	7	28	0	0	5	18	2	53	1	2
Durant, Mike, Visalia	.285	119	418	61	119	159	18	2	6	57	3	8	5	55	0	35	19	15
Fabregas, Jorge, Palm Springs*	.283	70	258	35	73	86	13	0	0	40	1	3	1	30	1	27	0	4
Faneyte, Rikkert, San Jose	.263	94	342	69	90	134	13	2	9	43	4	3	6	73	3	65	17	9
Fernandez, Julio, San Bernardino*	.244	54	176	26	43	58	7	1	2	16	6	0	0	23	0	43	8	3
Florez, Tim, San Jose	.244	38	131	15	32	43	6	1	1	17	4	4	0	4	0	21	3	3
Francisco, David, Reno	.200	7	15	5	3	3	0	0	0	0	1	0	0	3	0	5	1	0
Frias, Pepe, San Jose	.111	8	9	2	1	1	0	0	0	0	0	0	0	0	0	2	1	0
Garrett, Clifton, Palm Springs*	.280	111	410	91	115	132	8	3	1	34	7	3	1	73	2	68	37	20
Garrigan, Pat, San Bernardino	.255	95	282	35	72	88	13	0	1	27	3	0	1	42	0	55	10	6
Gash, Darius, High Desert†	.238	111	387	58	92	124	11	6	3	36	3	5	0	51	3	70	33	5
Gates, Brent, Modesto†	.321	133	505	94	162	235	39	2	10	88	2	9	2	85	9	60	9	7
Gill, Steve, High Desert*	.293	128	471	82	138	212	23	6	13	83	4	4	6	38	4	63	23	4
Glenn, Darrin, Stockton*	.207	88	275	36	57	103	12	2	10	36	1	2	0	40	0	86	17	8
Gomez, Fabio, Reno	.306	130	503	101	154	251	16	12	19	115	2	5	2	62	6	92	7	9
Gonzalez, Cliff, Salinas*	.244	118	381	53	93	127	14	4	4	41	4	2	3	59	6	47	18	7
Gray, Dan, Bakersfield	.193	18	57	7	11	15	1	0	1	4	3	0	1	6	1	11	2	1
Grebeck, Brian, Palm Springs	.336	91	289	71	97	115	14	2	0	39	8	3	0	83	2	55	6	5
Griffin, Tim, Bakersfield	.138	8	29	1	4	4	0	0	0	0	1	0	0	1	0	9	1	0
Guillen, Jose, Reno†	.216	28	74	6	16	16	0	0	0	4	0	0	0	10	0	13	2	2
Hall, Billy, High Desert†	.356	119	495	92	176	214	22	5	2	39	1	3	1	54	2	77	49	27
Hara, Hidefumi, Salinas*	.188	88	197	22	37	50	8	1	1	22	3	4	2	37	1	56	1	2
Hardtke, Jason, High Desert†	.268	10	41	9	11	18	1	0	2	8	0	1	1	4	0	4	1	1
Harris, Mike, Stockton*	.267	40	101	15	27	44	6	4	1	16	0	0	0	11	0	21	6	1
Hart, Chris, Modesto	.284	120	450	76	128	193	20	3	13	86	0	2	18	35	4	135	15	9
Helfand, Eric, Modesto*	.289	72	249	40	72	117	15	0	10	44	1	3	6	47	4	46	0	1
Helms, Tommy, Salinas	.000	12	11	1	0	0	0	0	0	0	1	0	0	0	0	5	0	0
Henderson, Dave I., Modesto	.308	3	13	3	4	8	1	0	1	2	0	0	0	0	0	2	0	0
Henderson, Dave S., San Bernardino	.250	4	12	3	3	7	1	0	1	2	0	0	0	0	0	3	0	0
Henderson, Lee, High Desert	.275	76	229	25	63	84	10	1	3	29	2	1	1	18	1	40	1	1
Hendley, Brett, Modesto*	.214	109	350	46	75	104	14	0	5	47	1	0	2	75	5	112	10	5
Henry, Scott, Reno*	.297	105	316	59	94	126	22	5	0	49	2	6	2	73	4	65	4	3
Heredia, Julian, Palm Springs	.000	30	1	0	0	0	0	0	0	0	0	0	0	0	0	0	0	0

Player, Team	Avg.	G	AB	R	H	TB	2B	3B	HR	RBI	SH	SF	HP	BB	Int. BB	SO	SB	CS
Hirsch, Chris, Palm Springs	.182	7	22	1	4	4	0	0	0	2	0	0	1	7	0	4	0	1
Hocking, Denny, Visalia†	.331	135	550	117	182	255	34	9	7	81	2	2	8	72	1	77	38	18
Holdridge, David, Palm Springs	.000	28	3	0	0	0	0	0	0	0	0	0	0	0	0	2	0	0
Hollandsworth, Todd, Bakersfield*	.258	119	430	70	111	183	23	5	13	58	0	2	3	50	5	113	27	13
Horowitz, Ed, High Desert	.260	46	150	14	39	47	6	1	0	18	1	2	1	9	1	14	1	1
Houk, Tom, Visalia	.230	93	278	42	64	88	7	1	5	35	3	3	1	47	0	55	7	4
House, Ken, Salinas	.059	22	51	6	3	4	1	0	0	2	0	0	4	5	0	12	1	0
Hunter, Greg, San Bernardino*	.212	29	99	12	21	24	3	0	0	6	0	1	1	1	0	17	2	3
Hyzdu, Adam, San Jose	.278	128	457	60	127	189	25	5	9	60	1	8	1	55	4	134	10	5
Jenkins, Brett, San Jose	.115	8	26	1	3	4	1	0	0	2	0	1	1	3	0	5	0	0
Johns, Doug, Reno	.000	27	2	1	0	0	0	0	0	0	0	0	0	0	0	0	0	0
Johnson, Herman, Reno	.167	2	6	0	1	1	0	0	0	2	0	1	0	2	0	1	0	0
Johnson, Jack, Bakersfield	.229	49	153	15	35	54	10	0	3	21	3	0	3	9	2	32	0	2
Kasper, Kevin, San Jose	.216	65	213	37	46	58	6	3	0	14	2	0	5	26	1	27	10	7
Kato, Hideki, Salinas	.183	99	240	22	44	57	9	2	0	16	11	1	2	28	0	49	5	3
Kliafas, Steve, Bakersfield	.248	50	133	19	33	45	9	0	1	11	2	1	3	9	1	24	1	4
Kluge, Matt, San Bernardino	.173	39	104	8	18	23	2	0	1	11	0	1	0	5	0	33	1	0
Kobza, Greg, Stockton*	.198	57	126	26	25	45	6	1	4	18	1	3	0	28	0	43	4	2
Kounas, Tony, San Bernardino	.262	111	378	51	99	156	23	2	10	55	1	1	1	40	1	43	2	5
Kuehl, John, High Desert†	.173	22	75	10	13	24	3	1	2	12	0	0	1	12	0	14	1	3
Laboy, Carlos, Salinas	.273	109	337	34	92	146	15	3	11	50	3	2	5	28	2	102	9	6
Lawn, Mike, 33 Sal. -56 Sto.	.276	89	225	28	62	78	11	1	1	25	6	0	2	3	0	61	10	5
Logan, Todd, Visalia*	.132	20	53	0	7	7	0	0	0	3	0	0	1	8	0	18	0	0
Love, Will, Reno*	.000	22	4	0	0	0	0	0	0	0	1	0	0	0	0	2	0	0
Lukachyk, Rob, Stockton*	.276	105	359	77	99	193	21	14	15	81	0	5	9	53	3	86	44	15
Lydy, Scott, Reno	.395	33	124	29	49	72	13	2	2	27	0	0	0	26	2	30	9	4
MacArthur, Mark, Visalia	.210	25	62	5	13	13	0	0	0	4	1	1	1	10	0	15	4	2
Marrero, Oreste, Stockton*	.276	76	243	35	67	105	17	0	7	51	1	1	1	44	6	49	3	2
Martinez, Manny, Modesto	.253	121	495	70	125	177	23	1	9	45	12	5	4	39	3	75	17	13
Martinez, Pablo, High Desert†	.239	126	427	60	102	118	8	4	0	39	2	4	1	50	0	74	19	14
Mashore, Damon, Modesto	.282	124	471	91	133	215	22	3	18	64	5	1	6	73	3	136	29	17
Matheny, Mike, Stockton†	.219	106	333	42	73	108	13	2	6	46	5	3	3	35	1	81	2	2
McCutchen, James, Salinas	.286	16	7	2	2	2	0	0	0	0	0	0	0	4	0	2	0	1
McDavid, Ray, High Desert*	.276	123	428	94	118	222	22	5	24	94	3	6	7	94	1	126	43	9
McFarlin, Jason, San Jose*	.304	70	276	61	84	100	7	3	1	24	5	1	9	27	1	43	32	11
McGonnigal, Brett, San Jose†	.204	48	142	19	29	38	5	2	0	13	6	1	0	8	1	35	5	4
McGough, Greg, Salinas*	.209	92	282	21	59	76	5	3	2	20	2	0	6	25	3	68	0	3
McMurray, Brock, Bakersfield	.258	76	267	38	69	107	12	1	8	38	1	3	2	24	2	51	17	4
Melendez, Dan, Bakersfield*	.267	39	146	18	39	54	11	2	0	11	0	1	0	22	5	18	1	0
Mercado, Rafael, Reno	.231	113	416	51	96	150	17	2	11	77	6	6	8	23	3	87	2	2
Meury, Bill, High Desert	.205	35	73	13	15	26	0	1	3	11	1	0	2	11	0	15	0	1
Meyers, Don, Bakersfield	.161	20	62	2	10	17	4	0	1	11	0	0	4	0	0	17	0	0
Miller, Barry, San Jose*	.281	124	420	69	118	188	32	4	10	70	4	6	6	72	14	76	4	1
Minik, Tim, Reno	.000	20	2	0	0	0	0	0	0	0	0	0	0	0	0	2	0	0
Mirabelli, Doug, San Jose	.232	53	177	30	41	54	11	1	0	21	2	2	4	24	0	18	1	3
Molina, Islay, Reno	.259	116	436	71	113	164	17	2	10	75	7	6	7	39	0	57	8	7
Montgomery, Don, San Jose	.000	2	7	0	0	0	0	0	0	0	0	0	0	0	0	1	0	0
Moore, Tim, Visalia†	.444	4	9	2	4	9	1	2	0	4	0	0	0	0	0	2	1	0
Mulligan, Sean, High Desert	.161	35	118	14	19	35	4	0	4	14	0	1	3	11	1	38	0	0
Munoz, Orlando, Palm Springs†	.234	103	329	50	77	88	9	1	0	43	4	2	4	50	1	53	21	4
Musolino, Mike, Palm Springs	.250	25	84	10	21	30	6	0	1	13	0	0	1	12	2	19	0	0
Neill, Mike, Reno*	.336	130	473	101	159	214	26	7	5	76	6	2	5	81	2	96	23	11
Nishijima, Takayuki, Salinas*	.271	135	414	62	112	126	3	4	1	39	7	5	6	74	0	96	16	22
Norton, Rick, Modesto*	.268	35	112	16	30	42	6	0	2	15	0	2	1	22	0	26	2	2
Ortiz, Hector, Bakersfield	.282	63	206	19	58	71	8	1	1	31	3	2	5	21	0	16	2	3
Ostermeyer, Bill, High Desert	.159	26	82	10	13	21	2	0	2	10	0	1	0	15	0	34	0	0
Pennington, Ken, San Bernardino	.285	58	214	28	61	90	9	1	6	34	0	1	4	16	0	30	6	4
Perez, Eduardo, Palm Springs	.314	54	204	37	64	89	8	4	3	35	0	3	3	23	0	33	14	3
Pezzoni, Ron, San Bernardino	.285	60	239	45	68	103	17	0	6	31	2	0	2	18	0	36	20	7
Picketts, Bill, Reno†	.241	83	216	21	52	64	10	1	0	22	1	1	2	37	0	27	2	1
Pozo, Arquimedez, San Bernardino	.261	54	199	33	52	77	8	4	3	19	1	0	2	20	0	41	13	8
Proctor, Murph, Bakersfield†	.318	71	261	38	83	114	15	2	4	42	1	9	0	23	1	33	0	2
Ramirez, Roberto, Reno	.342	55	190	31	65	105	13	3	7	29	2	2	2	15	2	45	3	5
Raven, Luis, Palm Springs	.288	107	378	59	109	156	16	2	9	55	0	4	2	24	2	81	18	7
Richardson, Dave, Salinas*	.000	5	1	0	0	0	0	0	0	0	0	0	0	0	0	1	0	0
Ricker, Troy, Salinas	.295	131	488	95	144	201	41	5	14	78	3	5	13	37	4	110	26	8
Rivera, David, Visalia	.282	87	298	60	84	104	12	1	2	31	5	2	1	37	1	46	48	20
Rivera, Rafael, Salinas	.212	31	52	7	11	15	1	0	1	4	0	0	0	5	0	13	0	0
Robertson, Tommy, San Bernardino*	.261	112	376	46	98	122	12	0	4	43	0	2	3	35	5	82	15	5
Rolen, Steve, San Jose	.282	23	78	9	22	37	5	2	2	18	0	1	1	8	0	9	0	0
Romay, Willie, Bakersfield	.222	16	54	4	12	20	2	0	2	4	0	0	0	2	0	10	3	2
Romero, Jonathan, Palm Springs	.197	46	132	9	26	30	4	0	0	14	1	0	0	13	0	29	1	3
Rose, Bobby, Palm Springs	.380	18	71	21	27	40	8	1	1	14	1	1	4	10	0	7	3	1
Rubiera, Jose, Palm Springs	.213	24	75	11	16	20	4	0	0	4	2	0	3	5	0	14	6	4
Rumsey, Dan, Palm Springs*	.310	25	84	17	26	33	2	1	1	11	2	0	0	7	0	14	2	0
Salazar, Carlos, Modesto	.223	75	220	17	49	73	12	0	4	27	4	4	6	26	0	65	0	0
Salazar, Julian, Stockton	.174	24	46	6	8	8	0	0	0	5	1	0	4	6	0	14	0	0
Sheppard, Don, Salinas	.255	114	377	50	96	127	17	4	2	43	7	3	0	40	0	101	27	14
Simmons, Enoch, Reno	.260	74	246	46	64	81	10	2	1	45	1	2	4	43	1	37	7	7
Singleton, Duane, 19 Sal. -97 Sto.*	.291	116	461	79	134	196	20	12	6	59	3	6	3	45	0	77	38	16
Skeels, Andy, Salinas*	.244	20	45	6	11	12	1	0	0	3	0	0	2	11	0	11	0	1
Smith, Ed, Stockton	.262	99	355	57	93	155	21	4	11	57	0	1	4	49	0	72	6	6
Smith, Ira, Bakersfield	.288	118	413	79	119	165	17	4	7	45	8	6	6	48	3	56	26	4
Spann, Tookie, High Desert	.265	123	423	80	112	197	28	0	19	103	0	10	9	66	5	89	2	3
Speakman, Willie, Palm Springs†	.237	18	59	8	14	18	2	1	0	4	2	0	1	4	0	7	0	0
Stahoviak, Scott, Visalia*	.308	110	409	62	126	173	26	3	5	68	0	2	3	82	1	66	17	6
Sutherland, Alex, San Bernardino	.256	31	90	10	23	30	1	0	2	17	0	1	5	0	28	0	1	1
Todd, Theron, San Bernardino*	.336	40	134	23	45	69	10	1	4	17	0	2	1	14	0	17	7	5
Turner, Ryan, Visalia	.266	118	413	70	110	165	22	6	7	62	0	9	4	49	2	71	14	8
Twitty, Sean, San Bernardino	.287	49	164	12	47	78	11	1	6	22	2	1	4	17	0	35	4	13
Uchinokura, Tokashi, Salinas	.215	135	414	34	89	113	13	1	3	44	8	3	2	53	0	80	5	5
Urso, Joe, Palm Springs	.250	28	84	6	21	29	4	0	0	11	1	0	0	11	0	14	0	2
Vorbeck, Eric, Bakersfield	.336	45	131	12	44	57	6	2	1	14	3	0	1	9	0	27	14	5
Waggoner, Jimmy, Reno*	.309	93	317	75	98	149	18	0	11	57	1	3	4	87	2	50	2	5

Player, Team	Avg.	G	AB	R	H	TB	2B	3B	HR	RBI	SH	SF	HP	BB	Int. BB	SO	SB	CS
Waldenberger, Dave, San Bernardino†..	.235	73	234	30	55	74	10	0	3	31	1	1	4	32	2	67	3	8
Walker, Dane, Reno*	.279	31	122	24	34	40	6	0	0	3	0	0	1	23	1	23	8	7
Ward, Ricky, San Jose	.299	88	335	49	100	139	28	1	3	53	4	9	3	21	2	34	6	8
Webb, Lonnie, Bakersfield	.258	82	302	51	78	99	13	1	2	20	2	2	4	47	2	66	21	14
Weger, Wesley, Stockton	.258	32	120	26	31	45	7	2	1	18	0	0	3	20	0	17	3	3
Whalen, Shawn, High Desert*	.313	58	192	33	60	86	7	5	3	28	3	1	0	24	1	36	1	0
Whitford, Eric, Stockton	.217	91	295	39	64	89	12	2	3	33	3	4	1	47	1	71	9	10
Wolfe, Joel, Reno	.255	122	463	80	118	149	18	5	1	44	4	2	0	59	1	72	19	13
Wong, Kevin, Salinas	.296	115	355	49	105	134	17	3	2	39	6	5	4	33	3	50	9	6
Wood, Jason, Modesto	.231	128	454	66	105	157	28	3	6	49	3	5	4	40	1	106	5	4
Wrona, Rick, Stockton†	.267	81	240	46	64	78	12	1	0	24	3	0	3	74	6	48	4	2
Young, Ernie, Modesto	.249	74	253	55	63	116	12	4	11	33	2	1	6	47	1	74	11	3
Zahner, Kevin, Bakersfield	.250	3	4	0	1	1	0	0	0	0	0	0	0	1	0	2	0	0
Zerilla, Torry, Visalia†	.162	30	74	10	12	13	1	0	0	7	0	0	2	17	0	30	0	0

The following pitchers, listed alphabetically by club, with games in parentheses, had no plate appearances, primarily through use of designated hitters:

BAKERSFIELD—Aronetz, Cameron (9); Brady, Mike (30); Calhoun, Ray (7); Castillo, Carlos (9); Farnsworth, Ross (25); Freeman, Scott (32); Gorecki, Rich (25); Henderson, Ryan (3); Howell, Jay (4); Lavigne, Martin (18); Maldonado, Albert (43); McFarlin, Terric (6); Parra, Jose (24); Salcedo, Jose (12); Sharp, Mike (33); Smith, Joe (26); Sodders, Mike (9); Sweeney, Bob (37); Tipton, Gordon (5); Vogelgesang, Joe (17); Walkden, Mike (27); Williams, Todd (13).

HIGH DESERT—Andersen, Larry (5); Bensching, Bruce (1); Brown, Jeff (2); Brutcher, Lenny (16); Chaves, Rafael (68); Devore, Ed (3); Felix, Nicholas (35); Florie, Bryce (26); Galindez, Luis (27); Hamilton, Joe (9); Harris, Greg W. (1); Hilton, Howard (13); Hoeme, Steve (7); Hyson, Cole (7); Ingram, Linty (7); Kellogg, Geoff (24); Lebron, Jose (24); Lifgren, Kelly (5); Martin, Tom (11); McKeon, Brian (15); Mortensen, Anthony (15); Soltero, Saul (15); Thibault, Ryan (44); Zinter, Ed (47).

MODESTO—Callahan, Steve (49); Cormier, Russ (4); Dillon, Jim (31); Dressendorfer, Kirk (3); Fermin, Ramon (14); Garland, Chaon (16); Grimes, Mike (16); Hokuf, Ken (35); Kuhn, Chadwick (6); Martinez, Jose (37); Millay, Keith (8); Nerat, Dan (21); Raczka, Mike (6); Shaw, Curtis (27); Shoemaker, Steve (10); Sturtze, Tanyon (25); Sudbury, Craig (46); Wojciechowski, Steve (14).

PALM SPRINGS—Bennett, Erik (6); Edenfield, Ken (13); Gamez, Bob (38); Hathaway, Hilly (3); Holzemer, Mark (5); Johnson, Dominick (22); Keling, Korey (30); Mitchell, Glenn (8); Mitchelson, Mark (7); Montoya, Norm (14); Percival, Troy (11); Purdy, Shawn (26); Robinson, Chris (24); Saitz, Bob (36); Santiago, Cedric (3); Silverio, Victor (14); Stroud, Derek (30); Van Dyke, Rod (41); Wylie, John (4).

RENO—Acre, Mark (35); Brock, Russ (25); Connolly, Craig (21); Gulledge, Hugh (44); Ingram, Todd (41); Jewell, Mike (5); McCarty, Scott (3); Mejia, Delfino (37); Misa, Joe (12); Myers, Tom (11); Pierce, Bob (15); Rose, Scott (20); Smith, Tim (28); Smithberg, Roger (10); Smock, Greg (36).

SALINAS—Agemy, Jim (1); Arola, Bruce (30); Carrasco, Carlos (9); Fritz, Greg (5); Green, Derek (8); Hooper, Mike (22); Hooper, Troy (17); Ito, Hiroyuki (11); Kohno, Takayuki (14); Kubicki, Marc (6); Law, Joe (3); Okoshi, Motoi (11); Powers, Randy (9); Sample, Deron (14); Samuels, Goeff (18); Sontag, Alan (32); Stephens, Mark (26); Suzuki, Makato (17); Tolar, Kevin (14); Toliver, Fred (20); Trautwein, Dave (49); Yamada, Tsutomu (47).

SAN BERNARDINO—Adam, Dave (26); Borski, Jeff (17); Duke, Kyle (34); Glinatsis, George (28); Hampton, Mike (25); King, Kevin (27); Lodding, Rich (35); Mecir, Jim (14); Nickell, Julian (13); Perkins, Paul (15); Phillips, Anthony (37); Rosenbaum, Marc (6); Schanz, Scott (38); Urso, Salvatore (37); Witte, Larry (21).

SAN JOSE—Benavides, Alvaro (8); Brummett, Greg (19); Castillo, Mariano (10); Flanagan, Dan (57); Garrelts, Scott (1); Grundt, Ken (11); Hancock, Chris (18); Hanselman, Carl (16); Henrikson, Dan (7); Herring, Vince (19); Huffman, Rodney (3); Hyde, Richard (37); McCament, Randy (11); McLeod, Brian (29); Myers, Mike (8); Peltzer, Kurt (46); Pote, Louis (4); Rosselli, Joe (22); Sharko, Gary (16); Vanderweele, Doug (16); Van Landingham, Bill (6); Whitaker, Steve (26).

STOCKTON—Archer, Kurt (55); Bush, Chuck (38); Carter, Larry (21); Christopher, Terry (7); Correa, Ramser (35); Farrell, Mike (13); Gamez, Francisco (23); Hancock, Brian (24); Knox, Kerry (5); McNeill, Randy (12); McGraw, Tom (15); McKeon, Brian (12); Mikkelsen, Lincoln (20); Miller, Pat (31); Pruitt, Don (13); Robinson, Ron (4); Rogers, Tom (54).

VISALIA—Acevedo, Juan (12); Bigham, Dave (54); Castillo, Carlos (27); Connolly, Matt (30); Dixon, Roger (27); Ericson, Mike (35); Guardado, Ed (7); Lewis, Mike (28); Mansur, Jeff (17); McCreary, Bob (14); Morris, Marc (11); Persing, Tim (10); Ritchie, Todd (28); Robinson, Bob (51); Thelen, Jeff (24).

GRAND SLAMS—Dunn, Spann, 3 each; Cordova, Hocking, Molina, 2 each; Adams, Beard, Booker, Boyzuick, Cohick, Diaz, Gates, Gomez, Gonzalez, Hart, Houk, McDavid, Mercado, Miller, Neill, Pezzoni, C. Salazar, E. Smith, Waldenberger, 1 each.

AWARDED FIRST BASE ON CATCHER'S INTERFERENCE—Miller 6 (Helfand 2, Carcione, Gray, McGough, Picketts); Gill 2 (Dodge, Kluge); Hocking 2 (Calcagno, Mulligan); E. Smith 2 (Calcagno, Dempsey); Whitford 2 (Calcagno 2); Becker (Mirabelli); Cordova (Dodge); Dunn (Carcione); Henry (Mirabelli); Norton (Matheny); Ortiz (Clemens); Wong (L. Henderson).

PITCHING

TEAM

Team	ERA	G	CG	ShO	Sv.	IP	H	R	ER	HR	HB	BB	Int. BB	SO	WP	Bk.
San Jose	3.29	137	15	11	36	1218.0	1114	566	445	44	74	556	21	806	64	19
Stockton	3.49	136	12	9	34	1215.2	1162	562	471	57	40	522	29	765	57	23
Modesto	4.02	136	6	5	34	1194.1	1112	639	534	78	59	622	24	946	72	10
Bakersfield	4.21	136	3	7	43	1191.0	1201	674	557	94	43	573	40	941	66	20
High Desert	4.25	136	4	4	40	1182.2	1100	677	558	90	49	726	30	870	91	22
Visalia	4.29	137	10	8	35	1193.1	1357	728	569	90	44	450	33	812	77	21
Palm Springs	4.42	135	20	11	29	1149.1	1218	671	564	48	51	537	31	935	95	19
San Bernardino	4.75	136	7	3	24	1188.1	1311	771	627	102	47	561	11	920	110	23
Salinas	5.25	135	17	2	17	1187.2	1335	872	693	70	57	611	16	909	83	23
Reno	5.29	136	5	5	27	1186.2	1430	916	697	97	41	634	42	858	92	22

INDIVIDUAL

(Leading qualifiers for earned-run average leadership— 109 or more innings)

*Throws lefthanded.

Pitcher, Team	W	L	Pct.	ERA	G	GS	CG	GF	ShO	Sv.	IP	H	R	ER	HR	HB	BB	Int. BB	SO	WP
Rosselli, San Jose*	11	4	.733	2.41	22	22	4	0	0	0	149.2	145	50	40	7	2	46	1	111	2
Hancock, Stockton*	14	4	.778	2.92	24	23	2	1	0	0	160.1	136	63	52	13	3	85	1	87	7
Shaw, Modesto*	13	4	.765	3.05	27	27	2	0	0	0	177.1	146	71	60	5	8	98	0	154	12
Hampton, San Bernardino*	13	8	.619	3.12	25	25	6	0	2	0	170.0	163	75	59	8	3	66	1	132	10
Johns, Reno*	13	10	.565	3.26	27	26	4	1	1	0	179.1	194	98	65	11	4	64	3	101	5
Lebron, High Desert	10	5	.667	3.30	24	24	1	0	0	0	144.2	133	70	53	10	7	53	2	79	8
Saitz, Palm Springs	7	7	.500	3.41	36	13	2	13	1	4	116.0	109	63	44	7	10	56	2	111	4
Toliver, Salinas	5	8	.385	3.49	20	20	3	0	1	0	123.2	125	63	48	5	4	43	1	104	3
McKeon, 15 H.D. - 12 Sto.	11	5	.688	3.55	27	15	3	5	0	0	116.2	105	57	46	7	6	54	0	76	2
Parra, Bakersfield	7	8	.467	3.59	24	23	3	0	0	0	143.0	151	73	57	5	4	47	4	107	5

(All pitchers—listed alphabetically)

Pitcher, Team	W	L	Pct.	ERA	G	GS	CG	GF	ShO	Sv.	IP	H	R	ER	HR	HB	BB	Int. BB	SO	WP
Acevedo, Visalia	3	4	.429	5.43	12	12	1	0	0	0	64.2	75	46	39	2	3	33	0	37	1
Acre, Reno	4	4	.500	4.56	35	8	0	11	0	2	77.0	67	56	39	5	1	50	1	65	13
Adam, San Bernardino	7	12	.368	5.63	26	26	0	0	0	0	155.0	178	110	97	17	4	64	1	112	16
Agemy, Salinas	0	1	.000	27.00	1	0	0	1	0	0	0.1	1	1	1	0	0	2	0	0	1
Andersen, High Desert	0	1	.000	2.25	5	2	0	1	0	0	8.0	7	5	2	1	0	2	0	10	0
Archer, Stockton	11	3	.786	1.88	55	0	0	42	0	15	76.2	60	19	16	2	5	32	8	49	2
Arola, Salinas	4	3	.571	4.89	30	0	0	21	0	3	38.2	47	26	21	2	0	24	3	36	5
Aronetz, Bakersfield*	0	2	.000	5.51	9	1	0	2	0	0	16.1	15	10	10	2	0	8	0	14	0
Benavides, San Jose	0	3	.000	9.00	8	0	0	3	0	0	7.0	8	8	7	0	3	8	0	4	0
Bennett, Palm Springs	4	2	.667	3.64	6	6	1	0	0	0	42.0	27	19	17	0	4	15	0	33	2
Bensching, High Desert	0	0	.000	0.00	1	0	0	0	0	0	0.0	2	1	1	0	0	1	0	0	0
Bigham, Visalia*	4	2	.667	3.68	53	0	0	24	0	5	58.2	48	30	24	7	3	19	1	53	4
Borski, San Bernardino	5	9	.357	3.71	17	16	0	0	0	0	104.1	100	62	43	6	3	44	0	76	10
Brady, Bakersfield*	2	5	.286	2.82	30	0	0	17	0	9	44.2	31	21	14	3	1	27	6	35	0
Brock, Reno	3	10	.231	4.40	25	23	0	0	0	0	90.0	109	61	44	10	5	34	3	72	3
Brown, High Desert*	1	0	1.000	3.86	2	2	0	0	0	0	11.2	13	6	5	2	0	4	0	10	0
Brown, Visalia	0	0	.000	13.50	1	0	0	1	0	0	2.0	3	3	3	0	1	0	0	1	0
Brummett, San Jose	10	4	.714	2.61	19	13	2	1	2	0	100.0	74	32	29	2	4	21	0	68	1
Brutcher, High Desert	1	1	.500	5.33	16	0	0	5	0	0	25.1	19	16	15	2	1	22	0	16	3
Bush, Stockton	3	2	.600	5.22	38	4	0	10	0	0	79.1	98	53	46	1	5	37	2	43	14
Calhoun, Bakersfield	0	0	.000	7.36	7	0	0	2	0	0	7.1	17	6	6	0	1	3	0	4	2
Callahan, Modesto*	9	3	.750	3.53	49	0	0	18	0	7	81.2	75	39	32	5	8	43	0	83	4
Carrasco, Salinas	0	1	.000	7.55	9	5	0	1	0	0	31.0	40	29	26	6	2	15	0	24	1
L. Carter, Stockton	8	4	.667	4.17	21	20	1	0	0	0	121.0	121	65	56	2	0	51	1	57	3
T. Carter, Stockton	0	0	.000	0.00	2	0	0	2	0	0	1.1	0	0	0	0	1	0	0	0	0
Castillo, 9 Bak.-27 Vis.	1	1	.500	4.70	36	1	0	17	0	2	59.1	65	37	31	3	2	34	4	52	4
Castillo, San Jose	3	0	.000	4.29	10	1	0	2	0	0	21.0	19	15	10	1	0	10	0	10	2
Chaves, High Desert	4	5	.444	1.83	68	0	0	53	0	34	88.1	64	28	18	5	3	36	3	67	2
Christopher, Stockton	3	1	.750	4.32	7	0	0	3	0	0	8.1	4	4	4	1	1	9	1	8	0
Clemens, San Jose	0	0	.000	3.86	3	0	0	3	0	0	2.1	3	1	1	0	0	0	0	1	1
Connolly, Reno	4	2	.667	3.91	21	0	0	10	0	2	46.0	39	20	20	2	4	20	1	56	0
Connolly, Visalia	5	1	.833	3.33	30	2	0	12	0	1	67.2	70	35	25	3	5	26	1	42	3
Cormier, Modesto	2	1	.667	4.26	4	4	0	0	0	0	25.1	26	13	12	0	3	8	0	15	0
Correa, Stockton	3	2	.600	3.58	35	4	0	9	0	1	70.1	71	31	28	2	2	38	2	55	5
Davis, San Jose	0	1	.000	13.50	2	0	0	2	0	0	2.0	5	1	3	0	0	0	0	1	0
Devore, High Desert	2	7	.222	6.60	23	13	0	6	0	0	75.0	96	66	55	7	3	47	3	47	14
Dillon, Modesto	5	1	.833	3.84	31	1	0	11	0	3	58.2	43	28	25	1	3	28	2	45	2
Dixon, Visalia*	12	6	.667	4.73	27	19	2	3	0	0	133.1	154	87	70	8	9	55	3	79	11
Dodge, Palm Springs	0	0	.000	27.00	2	0	0	1	0	0	1.1	4	4	4	1	0	0	0	0	0
Dressendorfer, Modesto*	0	2	.000	4.85	3	3	0	0	0	0	13.0	8	7	7	1	1	6	0	18	1
Duke, San Bernardino*	3	1	.750	6.10	34	4	0	16	0	1	62.0	67	48	42	6	3	46	1	56	6
Duplessis, Salinas*	0	0	.000	11.57	1	0	0	0	0	0	2.1	3	3	3	0	0	2	0	3	0
Edenfield, Palm Springs	0	0	.000	0.49	13	0	0	13	0	7	18.1	12	1	1	0	0	7	0	20	0
Ericson, Visalia	2	5	.286	2.90	35	0	0	21	0	9	62.0	77	27	20	2	1	19	8	70	3
Farnsworth, Bakersfield*	4	4	.500	5.17	25	12	0	5	0	1	94.0	103	63	54	14	3	37	3	60	2
Farrell, Stockton*	8	4	.667	2.33	13	13	3	0	1	0	92.2	82	28	24	6	5	21	0	67	1
Felix, High Desert*	5	3	.625	2.89	35	0	0	4	0	1	46.2	43	21	15	1	3	20	1	62	3
Fermin, Modesto	2	3	.400	5.70	14	5	0	4	0	1	42.2	50	31	27	5	2	19	1	18	3
Flanagan, San Jose	5	5	.500	3.04	57	0	0	31	0	16	80.0	66	36	27	2	16	45	7	44	5
Florie, High Desert	9	7	.563	4.12	26	24	0	0	0	0	137.2	99	79	63	8	12	114	2	106	10
Freeman, Bakersfield	5	9	.357	5.43	32	15	0	9	0	5	107.2	131	74	65	12	6	43	4	86	10
Fritz, Salinas*	0	4	.000	6.65	5	4	0	1	0	0	23.0	36	22	17	1	1	13	0	9	5
Galindez, High Desert	11	6	.647	3.87	26	26	1	0	0	0	158.0	123	79	68	10	1	93	1	111	12
Gamez, Palm Springs*	8	8	.500	4.94	38	13	0	8	0	3	98.1	106	63	54	4	2	44	5	70	10
Gamez, Stockton	9	5	.643	3.63	23	23	2	0	0	0	134.0	134	64	54	5	1	69	1	95	4
Garland, Modesto	7	3	.700	2.74	16	16	2	0	0	0	105.0	79	39	32	7	5	46	1	86	5
Garrelts, San Jose	0	0	.000	2.25	1	0	0	0	0	0	4.0	3	1	1	0	0	3	0	1	0
Gill, High Desert*	0	0	.000	0.00	2	0	0	2	0	0	1.2	1	0	0	0	0	3	0	0	0
Glinatsis, San Bernardino	3	12	.200	4.58	28	18	1	5	0	2	125.2	123	83	64	14	3	67	1	117	19
Gorecki, Bakersfield	11	7	.611	4.05	25	24	0	1	0	0	129.0	122	68	58	11	7	90	2	115	17
Green, Salinas	0	0	.000	9.64	9	0	0	4	0	0	14.0	20	20	15	0	1	14	0	6	2
Grimes, Modesto	5	6	.455	5.44	16	16	0	0	0	0	89.1	98	67	54	10	4	43	1	83	4
Grundt, San Jose*	1	0	1.000	1.02	11	0	0	5	0	3	17.2	9	3	2	1	2	7	1	17	0
Guardado, Visalia*	7	0	1.000	1.64	7	7	1	0	1	0	49.1	47	13	9	1	0	10	0	39	0
Gulledge, Reno	3	6	.333	6.34	44	3	0	16	0	2	88.0	126	78	62	9	3	62	8	44	6
Hamilton, High Desert	4	3	.571	2.74	9	8	0	0	0	0	49.1	46	20	15	0	4	18	0	43	2
Hampton, San Bernardino*	13	8	.619	3.12	25	25	6	0	2	0	170.0	163	75	59	8	3	66	1	132	10
Hancock, Stockton*	14	4	.778	2.92	24	23	2	1	0	0	160.1	136	63	52	13	3	85	1	87	7
Hancock, San Jose*	7	4	.636	4.04	18	17	0	1	0	0	111.1	104	60	50	2	6	55	1	80	8
Hanselman, San Jose	8	5	.615	2.54	16	16	5	0	2	0	106.1	102	44	30	3	5	32	0	62	5
Harris, High Desert	0	0	.000	0.00	1	1	0	0	0	0	5.1	2	0	0	0	1	0	0	5	2
Harris, Stockton*	0	0	.000	4.50	1	0	0	0	0	0	2.0	2	1	1	0	2	0	0	0	0
Hathaway, Palm Springs*	2	1	.667	1.50	3	3	2	0	1	0	24.0	25	5	4	0	3	3	0	17	0
Henderson, Bakersfield	0	2	.000	5.06	3	3	0	0	0	0	16.0	17	10	9	1	0	9	1	15	0
Hendley, Modesto	0	0	.000	0.00	1	0	0	1	0	0	2.0	3	0	0	0	0	0	0	1	0
Henrikson, San Jose*	0	2	.000	3.18	7	1	0	1	0	0	11.1	16	6	4	0	0	3	0	6	0
Henry, Reno	0	1	.000	2.79	3	0	0	7	0	0	9.2	10	3	3	0	0	4	2	6	0
Heredia, Palm Springs	3	1	.750	4.76	30	0	0	27	0	10	28.1	28	16	15	2	1	9	3	36	3
Herring, San Jose*	2	0	1.000	1.23	19	0	0	9	0	2	29.1	19	4	4	2	2	12	0	26	2
Hilton, High Desert	2	1	.667	3.86	13	1	0	8	0	0	28.0	32	17	12	3	0	14	0	17	1
Hoeme, High Desert	2	0	1.000	2.00	7	0	0	5	0	0	9.0	10	2	2	0	0	5	2	6	1
Hokuf, Modesto	7	2	.778	4.17	35	6	0	13	0	2	101.1	98	57	47	10	8	62	3	67	5
Holdridge, Palm Springs	12	12	.500	4.25	28	27	3	0	2	0	159.0	169	99	75	5	8	87	4	135	21
Holzemer, Palm Springs*	3	2	.600	3.00	5	5	2	0	0	0	30.0	23	10	10	2	3	13	0	32	2
M. Hooper, Salinas	3	9	.250	5.10	21	11	1	3	0	0	90.0	84	61	51	4	3	37	1	66	2
T. Hooper, Salinas	3	0	.000	10.58	17	3	0	7	0	0	41.2	59	60	49	5	2	36	0	40	9
Howell, Bakersfield	0	1	.000	6.00	4	4	0	0	0	0	6.0	6	5	4	0	0	1	0	6	0
Huffman, San Jose	0	0	.000	2.45	3	0	0	2	0	0	3.2	2	1	1	0	0	5	0	3	0

Pitcher, Team	W	L	Pct.	ERA	G	GS	CG	GF	ShO	Sv.	IP	H	R	ER	HR	HB	BB	Int. BB	SO	WP
Hyde, San Jose	6	2	.750	4.03	37	4	0	12	0	1	82.2	81	42	37	4	3	33	2	43	2
Hyson, High Desert	0	0	.000	19.80	7	0	0	3	0	1	5.0	10	12	11	2	0	12	0	6	3
Ingram, High Desert	1	1	.500	4.64	7	3	0	1	0	0	21.1	25	14	11	3	1	12	1	9	1
Ingram, Reno	1	7	.125	7.22	41	9	0	23	0	9	67.1	91	69	54	8	3	40	4	44	12
Ito, Salinas	1	1	.500	8.79	11	0	0	7	0	0	14.1	14	14	14	1	3	12	1	2	1
Jewell, Reno*	1	1	.500	9.00	5	0	0	1	0	0	10.0	20	21	10	3	1	14	2	9	2
Johns, Reno	13	10	.565	3.26	27	26	4	1	1	0	179.1	194	98	65	11	1	64	3	101	5
Johnson, Palm Springs	0	4	.000	6.75	22	4	0	6	0	1	40.0	44	32	30	4	3	35	1	23	10
Keling, Palm Springs	7	6	.538	4.79	30	18	0	2	0	0	124.0	138	72	66	4	4	53	0	107	15
Kellogg, High Desert	7	9	.438	4.94	24	23	1	1	0	0	120.1	120	77	66	12	5	89	2	77	10
King, San Bernardino*	7	16	.304	5.32	27	27	0	0	0	0	165.2	226	118	98	14	2	55	0	101	10
Kliafas, Bakersfield	0	0	.000	0.00	3	0	0	3	0	0	2.2	1	0	0	0	0	1	0	2	0
Knox, Stockton*	1	1	.500	2.19	5	4	0	0	0	0	24.2	26	6	6	1	0	5	0	15	1
Kubicki, Salinas	0	0	.000	15.43	6	0	0	2	0	0	9.1	13	20	16	0	1	20	0	12	10
Kuhn, Modesto*	1	0	1.000	4.70	6	1	0	4	0	1	15.1	13	9	8	0	1	10	0	17	0
Lavigne, Bakersfield*	7	6	.538	3.87	18	16	0	2	0	1	95.1	81	45	41	6	4	48	2	83	2
Law, Salinas	1	2	.333	6.55	3	2	0	0	0	0	11.0	16	9	8	0	2	5	0	15	1
Lebron, High Desert	10	5	.667	3.30	24	24	1	0	0	0	144.2	133	70	53	10	7	53	2	79	8
Lewis, Visalia*	6	6	.500	3.70	28	11	1	5	1	2	97.1	115	64	40	4	4	37	4	70	3
Lifgren, High Desert	0	0	.000	7.71	5	0	0	0	0	0	7.0	10	6	6	1	1	5	1	6	0
Lodding, San Bernardino	0	4	.000	5.40	35	0	0	10	0	0	55.0	60	47	33	5	10	40	0	43	13
Love, Reno*	10	4	.714	4.68	20	18	0	0	0	0	98.0	132	74	51	4	3	53	0	73	11
MacNeill, Stockton	0	0	.000	1.08	12	0	0	4	0	0	16.2	8	3	2	1	1	5	0	7	2
Maldonado, Bakersfield*	7	3	.700	3.24	43	0	0	21	0	4	80.2	69	42	29	4	0	37	9	55	5
Mansur, Visalia*	5	7	.417	4.11	17	16	0	0	0	0	100.2	130	67	46	11	1	25	3	61	6
Martin, High Desert*	0	2	.000	9.37	11	0	0	8	0	0	16.1	23	19	17	4	0	16	0	12	2
Martinez, Modesto	2	4	.333	4.33	37	0	0	18	0	2	62.1	66	40	30	8	2	33	8	41	5
McCament, San Jose	2	0	1.000	1.20	11	0	0	7	0	3	15.0	9	2	2	0	0	5	1	11	0
McCarty, Reno*	0	0	.000	5.79	3	3	0	0	0	0	9.1	7	8	6	1	1	18	0	4	1
McCreary, Visalia	8	3	.727	4.81	14	14	0	0	0	0	86.0	102	56	46	6	6	25	3	41	4
McCutchen, Salinas	0	4	.000	5.93	13	4	0	4	0	0	41.0	40	35	27	1	2	33	1	35	2
McFarlin, Bakersfield	2	0	1.000	2.63	6	5	0	1	0	0	27.1	16	10	8	2	1	19	0	30	1
McGraw, Stockton*	6	4	.600	2.68	15	15	1	0	0	0	97.1	97	44	29	1	2	31	5	70	5
McKeon, 15 H.D. - 12 Sto.	11	5	.688	3.55	27	15	3	5	0	0	116.2	105	57	46	7	6	54	0	76	2
McLeod, San Jose	2	4	.333	6.66	29	4	0	5	0	0	52.2	54	51	39	1	8	60	0	36	8
Mecir, San Bernardino	4	5	.444	4.67	14	11	0	1	0	0	61.2	72	40	32	8	5	26	0	53	5
Mejia, Reno	6	3	.667	3.70	37	7	0	15	0	7	90.0	89	54	37	0	6	41	5	77	5
Mikkelsen, Stockton	0	4	.000	5.51	20	5	0	3	0	0	47.1	49	32	29	2	1	24	1	31	3
Millay, Modesto	0	4	.000	7.75	8	7	0	0	0	0	36.0	37	31	31	4	5	28	0	24	5
Miller, Stockton	2	4	.333	4.94	31	0	0	13	0	1	47.1	47	30	26	4	1	25	4	25	2
Minik, Reno	0	2	.000	13.50	20	1	0	12	0	0	34.2	57	56	52	4	4	36	0	19	11
Misa, Reno	0	1	.000	7.04	12	0	0	1	0	1	23.0	26	19	18	2	1	13	0	23	2
Mitchell, Palm Springs	0	0	.000	6.75	8	0	0	1	0	0	9.1	12	11	7	0	0	4	1	7	3
Mitchell, Palm Springs*	0	0	.000	1.54	7	0	0	1	0	0	11.2	7	2	2	0	0	4	1	9	0
Montoya, Palm Springs*	2	3	.400	3.71	14	6	2	6	0	0	43.2	42	21	18	3	1	19	1	46	2
Morris, Visalia	0	0	.000	8.79	11	0	0	4	0	0	14.1	14	20	14	1	0	29	0	8	7
Mortensen, High Desert*	2	0	1.000	6.28	15	1	0	4	0	0	28.2	36	22	20	4	0	17	2	25	4
Myers, San Jose*	5	1	.833	2.30	8	8	0	0	0	0	54.2	43	20	14	1	2	17	0	40	3
Myers, Reno*	0	0	.000	9.18	11	0	0	2	0	1	16.2	23	26	17	2	0	13	1	17	1
Nerat, Modesto	0	1	.000	7.11	21	2	0	13	0	0	38.0	38	38	30	4	2	35	1	23	8
Nickell, San Bernardino	0	4	.000	6.98	13	4	0	4	0	0	40.0	45	33	31	8	4	23	0	30	3
Okoshi, Salinas	1	1	.500	3.42	11	2	0	4	0	0	23.2	19	12	9	3	0	17	0	19	1
Parra, Bakersfield	7	8	.467	3.59	24	23	3	0	0	0	143.0	151	73	57	5	4	47	4	107	5
Peltzer, San Jose*	2	2	.500	2.58	46	0	0	22	0	5	83.2	74	35	24	4	7	35	4	66	3
Percival, Palm Springs	1	1	.500	5.06	11	0	0	9	0	2	10.2	6	7	6	0	2	8	1	16	1
Perkins, San Bernardino	4	2	.667	1.80	15	0	0	13	0	5	25.0	18	6	5	2	0	8	4	17	0
Persing, Visalia	3	5	.375	5.52	10	7	0	0	0	0	44.0	54	34	27	4	1	19	0	29	3
Phillips, San Bernardino	4	3	.571	3.18	37	0	0	29	0	12	51.0	44	23	18	1	2	28	2	40	1
Picketts, Reno	0	0	.000	0.00	7	0	0	6	0	0	10.0	7	0	0	0	1	3	0	5	0
Pierce, Reno	0	1	.000	7.34	15	1	0	4	0	0	30.2	45	33	25	2	1	22	0	22	4
Pote, San Jose	0	1	.000	4.66	4	3	0	1	0	0	9.2	11	5	5	0	0	7	0	8	3
Powers, Salinas	2	5	.286	9.19	9	6	0	1	0	0	31.1	49	36	32	2	2	21	1	19	3
Pruitt, Stockton	2	7	.222	7.20	13	10	0	2	0	0	55.0	77	50	44	5	4	23	0	24	6
Purdy, Palm Springs	13	8	.619	4.13	26	26	7	0	0	0	168.0	203	90	77	7	5	51	3	113	5
Raczka, Modesto*	1	1	.500	6.75	6	0	0	3	0	0	9.1	13	9	7	1	1	3	0	5	1
Ramirez, Reno	0	0	.000	0.00	1	0	0	1	0	0	0.2	0	0	0	0	0	1	0	0	0
Raven, Palm Springs	0	0	.000	0.00	1	1	0	0	0	0	1.0	0	0	0	0	0	1	0	0	0
Richardson, Salinas*	0	0	.000	0.00	4	0	0	1	0	0	5.1	4	0	0	0	0	2	0	5	0
Ritchie, Visalia	11	9	.550	5.06	28	28	3	0	1	0	172.2	193	113	97	13	7	65	2	129	16
Robinson, Visalia	0	3	.000	2.50	51	0	0	44	0	16	57.2	62	21	16	2	1	21	3	29	6
Robinson, Palm Springs	1	1	.500	5.40	24	0	0	7	0	0	43.1	47	28	26	4	0	27	5	22	3
Robinson, Stockton	1	1	.500	3.57	4	4	1	0	0	0	22.2	17	10	9	3	1	4	0	11	0
Rogers, Stockton*	4	4	.500	2.81	54	0	0	34	0	17	80.0	65	28	25	3	2	26	3	64	2
Romero, Palm Springs	0	0	.000	0.00	1	0	0	1	0	0	2.0	1	0	0	0	0	0	0	1	0
Rose, Reno	2	4	.333	8.44	20	9	0	2	0	0	64.0	97	73	60	11	0	37	3	29	4
Rosenbalm, San Bernardino	0	1	.000	3.68	6	0	0	4	0	0	7.1	7	3	3	0	1	0	0	8	4
Rosselli, San Jose*	11	4	.733	2.41	22	22	4	0	0	0	149.2	145	50	40	7	2	46	1	111	4
Saitz, Palm Springs	7	7	.500	3.41	36	13	2	13	1	4	116.0	109	63	44	7	10	56	2	111	4
Salazar, Stockton	0	0	.000	0.00	1	0	0	1	0	0	1.0	1	0	0	0	1	1	0	1	1
Salcedo, Bakersfield	1	0	1.000	4.00	12	3	0	1	0	0	27.0	18	16	12	0	2	17	0	25	0
Sample, Salinas	1	4	.200	6.80	14	7	0	2	0	1	49.0	53	43	37	6	3	38	0	37	6
Samuels, Salinas	1	5	.167	5.17	18	9	1	4	0	0	69.2	100	57	40	8	3	24	2	31	1
Santiago, Palm Springs*	0	0	.000	27.00	1	0	0	1	0	0	1.0	4	3	3	0	0	1	0	0	0
Schanz, San Bernardino	1	5	.167	5.33	38	5	0	16	0	2	77.2	84	53	46	8	4	51	1	68	8
Sharko, San Jose	2	1	.667	0.96	16	0	0	15	0	8	18.2	11	2	2	1	0	3	1	16	1
Sharp, Bakersfield	5	4	.556	4.42	33	0	0	20	0	7	55.0	66	33	27	4	1	26	2	49	4
Shaw, Modesto*	13	4	.765	3.05	27	27	0	0	0	0	177.1	146	71	60	5	6	98	0	154	12
Shoemaker, Modesto	4	2	.667	3.08	10	9	1	0	0	0	61.1	59	25	21	6	2	15	0	50	0
Silverio, Palm Springs	2	5	.286	7.22	14	10	1	1	0	0	52.1	61	42	42	7	7	41	1	32	3
Smith, Bakersfield*	1	1	.500	4.22	26	0	0	3	0	1	49.0	40	37	23	2	3	39	1	20	5
Smith, Reno	11	10	.524	5.01	28	26	0	1	0	0	158.0	192	107	88	14	3	62	5	131	9
Smithberg, Reno	2	1	.667	3.24	10	0	0	5	0	2	16.2	23	10	6	0	0	10	3	11	2
Smock, Reno*	5	4	.556	5.27	36	2	0	12	0	1	66.2	73	47	39	8	1	37	1	49	1
Sodders, Bakersfield*	0	2	.000	9.00	9	1	0	3	0	0	10.0	19	13	10	2	1	8	1	10	0

Pitcher, Team	W	L	Pct.	ERA	G	GS	CG	GF	ShO	Sv.	IP	H	R	ER	HR	HB	BB	Int. BB	SO	WP
Soltero, High Desert	2	0	1.000	4.42	15	0	0	2	0	0	18.1	21	10	9	3	1	11	2	17	1
Sontag, Salinas	6	11	.353	4.30	28	28	4	0	1	0	178.0	188	110	85	9	14	71	2	137	9
Stephens, Salinas*	3	12	.200	4.88	26	19	2	2	0	0	121.2	157	86	66	7	3	49	2	92	1
Stroud, Palm Springs*	2	1	.667	2.21	30	0	0	10	0	1	40.2	36	13	10	1	0	17	1	37	3
Sturtze, Modesto	7	11	.389	3.75	25	25	1	0	0	0	151.0	143	72	63	6	4	78	1	126	5
Sudbury, Modesto	8	6	.571	4.32	46	0	0	45	0	17	58.1	57	31	28	3	2	30	6	36	7
Suzuki, Salinas	0	0	.000	0.00	1	0	0	0	0	0	1.0	0	0	0	0	0	0	0	1	0
Sweeney, Bakersfield	3	4	.429	4.96	37	1	0	14	0	1	69.0	71	44	38	12	1	33	1	68	6
Thelen, Visalia	8	9	.471	5.10	24	21	2	0	0	0	137.2	166	90	78	17	1	42	2	85	6
Thibault, High Desert*	4	5	.444	4.81	44	4	0	4	0	1	76.2	76	45	41	5	5	56	3	68	6
Tipton, Bakersfield	0	0	.000	0.00	5	0	0	1	0	0	8.2	4	1	0	0	2	0	0	4	6
Tolar, Salinas*	1	8	.111	6.08	14	8	3	3	0	0	53.1	55	43	36	4	5	46	0	24	6
Toliver, Salinas	5	8	.385	3.49	20	20	3	0	1	0	123.2	125	63	48	5	3	47	2	104	3
Trautwein, Salinas	3	6	.333	3.84	49	0	0	17	0	4	86.2	103	50	37	3	1	26	0	60	5
Urso, Palm Springs	0	0	.000	0.00	1	0	0	1	0	0	1.2	1	0	0	0	0	1	0	1	2
Urso, San Bernardino*	0	1	.000	5.08	37	0	0	21	0	1	51.1	66	34	29	2	1	32	0	40	4
Van Dyke, Palm Springs	5	1	.833	5.11	41	4	0	10	0	0	75.2	92	53	43	1	3	36	1	58	8
Vanderweele, San Jose	6	4	.600	3.71	16	15	1	0	0	0	87.1	77	49	36	7	8	50	1	51	4
Van Landingham, San Jose	1	3	.250	5.57	6	6	0	0	0	0	21.0	22	18	13	1	0	13	0	18	4
Vogelgesang, Bakersfield	2	0	1.000	3.09	17	0	0	11	0	4	23.1	27	10	8	0	0	20	2	22	2
Walkden, Bakersfield*	11	10	.524	4.10	27	27	0	0	0	0	149.1	165	75	68	13	4	54	2	108	5
Whalen, High Desert*	0	0	.000	0.00	1	0	0	1	0	0	1.0	0	0	0	0	0	0	0	0	0
Whitaker, San Jose*	8	9	.471	4.19	26	26	3	0	0	0	148.1	157	80	69	7	6	86	2	83	10
Williams, Bakersfield	0	0	.000	2.30	13	0	0	13	0	9	15.2	11	4	4	1	0	7	1	11	0
Witte, San Bernardino	1	1	.500	6.63	21	0	0	10	0	1	36.2	58	36	27	3	2	11	0	27	3
Wojciechowski, Modesto*	6	3	.667	3.53	14	14	0	0	0	0	66.1	60	32	26	2	1	27	0	53	5
Wolfe, Reno	0	0	.000	27.00	1	0	0	1	0	0	1.0	3	3	3	1	0	1	0	0	0
Wylie, Palm Springs	0	0	.000	11.88	4	0	0	1	0	0	8.1	21	17	11	0	1	5	1	10	0
Yamada, Salinas	4	11	.267	4.30	47	7	3	34	0	9	127.2	109	72	61	4	6	57	1	132	9
Zinter, High Desert	1	7	.125	4.33	47	0	0	20	0	3	60.1	51	35	29	5	1	54	4	53	4

BALKS—Samuels, 9; Love, 8; Nickell, Zinter, 6 each; Bush, L. Carter, Dixon, 5 each; Acre, Hampton, Lavigne, Rogers, Rosselli, 4 each; Adam, C. Castillo, Farrell, Freeman, Henderson, Keling, Kellogg, McCutchen, Phillips, Purdy, 3 each; Acevedo, Aronetz, Bigham, M. Castillo, Devore, Felix, Florie, Galindez, Hamilton, Hanselman, Herring, T. Ingram, Ito, Johns, King, Lebron, Martinez, Mejia, Mikkelsen, T. Myers, Nerat, Okoshi, Saitz, Sharp, Silverio, Sontag, Thelen, Vanderweele, Wojciechowski, Wylie, 2 each; Bennett, Callahan, M. Connolly, Correa, Duke, Ericson, Fermin, Flanagan, Fritz, F. Gamez, R. Gamez, Garland, Glinatsis, Guardado, C. Hancock, M. Harris, Henrikson, Heredia, M. Hooper, Hyde, Johnson, Law, Lewis, MacNeill, Maldonado, Mansur, McCreary, Mecir, Montoya, M. Myers, Parra, Peltzer, Percival, Persing, Ritchie, Salcedo, Santiago, Shaw, J. Smith, Smock, Stephens, Sweeney, Thibault, S. Urso, Van Landingham, Witte, Wolfe, Yamada, 1 each.

COMBINATION SHUTOUTS—Gorecki-Freeman, Gorecki-Lavigne, Howell-Freeman, McFarlin-Maldonado-Sweeney, McFarlin-Sharp, Parra-Brady-Sharp, Walkden-Vogelgesang-Sweeney, Bakersfield; Devore-Felix-Soltero-Chaves, Devore-Thibault-Ingram-McKeon, Florie-Chavez, Hamilton-Chaves, High Desert; Cormier-Callahan-Sudbury, Shaw-Martinez-Sudbury, Shoemaker-Martinez, Sturtze-Callahan, Sturtze-Dillon, Modesto; Purdy-Heredia 2, Holzemer-Robinson-Saitz-Edenfield, Johnson-Van Dyke, Keling-Heredia, Purdy-Edenfield, Purdy-Johnson, Palm Springs; Brock-Acre-Ingram, Johns-Smithberg-Smock, Smith-Mejia, Smith-Smock, Reno; Mecir-Perkins-Schanz, San Bernardino; Brummett-Peltzer-Sharko, Hancock-Flanagan-Hyde, Hancock-Peltzer-Flanagan, Henrikson-Hyde-Grundt, Rosselli-Grundt, Rosselli-Peltzer, Rosselli-Sharko, San Jose; Carter-Archer, Carter-Rogers, Correa-Miller, Farrell-Mikkelsen-Rogers, Hancock-Correa-MacNeill, Knox-MacNeill-Bush-Pruitt, McKeon-Archer, Mikkelsen-Archer-Rogers-Bush, Stockton; Dixon-Ericson-Robinson, Guardado-Castillo, Thelen-Robinson, Visalia.

NO-HIT GAMES—None.

FIELDING

TEAM

Team	Pct.	G	PO	A	E	DP	PB	Team	Pct.	G	PO	A	E	DP	PB
Stockton	.970	136	3647	1603	160	150	22	Visalia	.963	137	3580	1563	196	141	23
San Jose	.967	137	3654	1610	180	147	24	Modesto	.963	136	3583	1474	196	142	24
Bakersfield	.966	136	3573	1461	175	133	25	Reno	.957	136	3560	1494	228	135	33
Palm Springs	.965	135	3448	1432	176	116	30	San Bernardino	.957	136	3565	1607	235	130	44
High Desert	.965	136	3548	1610	187	160	34	Salinas	.953	135	3563	1374	243	124	37

Triple plays—San Jose, Stockton, Visalia.

INDIVIDUAL

*Throws lefthanded.

FIRST BASEMEN

Player, Team	Pct.	G	PO	A	E	DP	Player, Team	Pct.	G	PO	A	E	DP
Arredondo, High Desert*	.982	64	551	55	11	65	Horowitz, High Desert	1.000	1	3	1	0	0
Barns, Modesto	.987	20	138	9	2	15	Houk, Visalia	.993	14	125	8	1	14
Boyzuick, Bakersfield	1.000	5	40	1	0	6	House, Salinas	.949	9	53	3	3	2
Bradish, Salinas	.986	23	203	14	3	15	Johnson, Bakersfield	1.000	1	0	2	0	0
Brannon, San Bernardino	.975	25	219	17	6	23	Kobza, Stockton	1.000	1	1	0	0	1
Brewer, San Jose	1.000	8	49	4	0	4	Kounas, San Bernardino	.990	25	177	13	2	15
Brown, Visalia	1.000	1	6	0	0	1	Kuehl, High Desert	.987	8	78	0	1	8
Carcione, Modesto	.982	33	257	11	5	30	Laboy, Salinas*	.900	2	9	0	1	1
Carter, Stockton	.985	53	369	29	6	42	Lawn, Stockton	1.000	1	1	0	0	0
Cervantes, San Bernardino*	.992	100	876	97	8	77	Love, Reno*	1.000	1	6	0	0	0
Charles, San Jose	.966	22	134	7	5	16	Marrero, Stockton*	.977	6	43	0	1	5
Dalesandro, Palm Springs	.992	71	559	41	5	51	Melendez, Bakersfield*	.997	37	317	28	1	30
Davis, San Jose	1.000	9	43	3	0	6	Mercado, Reno	.982	112	925	86	19	95
DeFrancesco, Reno	1.000	2	4	0	0	0	Meury, Bakersfield	.932	9	40	1	3	5
Dempsey, Salinas	1.000	3	20	1	0	1	Meyers, Bakersfield	.960	14	109	11	5	10
Deutsch, Bakersfield*	.956	25	221	17	11	30	MILLER, San Jose*	.993	115	1030	112	8	101
Dotel, Bakersfield*	1.000	1	5	0	0	0	Ostermeyer, High Desert	.983	22	200	26	4	24
Dunn, Visalia*	.990	124	1125	106	13	117	Picketts, Reno	.979	12	86	7	2	12
Duplessis, Salinas*	.964	34	285	12	11	23	Proctor, Bakersfield*	.993	60	508	40	4	46
Glenn, Stockton	.985	79	667	67	11	61	Raven, Palm Springs	.992	68	572	45	5	50
Hara, Salinas*	.967	28	191	12	7	16	Rivera, Salinas	1.000	1	9	0	0	2
Harris, Stockton*	.989	14	85	8	1	6	Salazar, Modesto	.992	17	104	13	1	13
Helfand, Modesto	1.000	1	5	0	0	0	Smith, Stockton	1.000	9	63	5	0	9
Hendley, Modesto	.980	82	637	40	14	71	Spann, High Desert	.984	49	381	43	7	49
Henry, Reno	.979	21	131	6	3	10	Uchinokura, Salinas	1.000	3	7	1	0	1
							Waldenberger, San Bernardino	1.000	1	3	1	0	1
							Whalen, High Desert*	1.000	1	7	1	0	2

Player, Team	Pct.	G	PO	A	E	DP
Wolfe, Reno	1.000	4	14	0	0	0
Wong, Salinas	.978	54	360	44	9	44

Triple plays—Dunn, Glenn, Miller.

SECOND BASEMEN

Player, Team	Pct.	G	PO	A	E	DP
Barns, Modesto	.943	14	21	29	3	10
Bernhardt, Stockton	.978	11	21	24	1	6
Bish, High Desert	.974	18	19	55	2	13
Buccheri, Reno	.667	1	1	1	1	0
M. Carter, Stockton	1.000	2	2	2	0	0
T. Carter, Stockton	.750	1	2	1	1	0
Casper, San Jose	1.000	11	21	26	0	10
Cervantes, San Bernardino*	.889	1	0	8	1	1
Clayton, San Bernardino	1.000	1	1	0	0	0
COLE, Stockton	.973	108	204	300	14	63
Colon, Palm Springs	1.000	1	0	1	0	0
Davis, Salinas	.938	53	70	126	13	24
Davis, San Jose	1.000	4	10	9	0	1
Demetral, Bakersfield	.970	63	110	179	9	31
Diaz, San Bernardino	.966	81	159	268	15	59
Florez, San Jose	.959	36	87	101	8	23
Frias, San Jose	1.000	3	0	3	0	2
Garrigan, San Bernardino	.977	11	15	27	1	4
Gates, Modesto	.970	131	293	420	22	105
Gomez, Reno	.944	34	57	77	8	16
Guillen, San Bernardino	.951	21	42	56	5	11
Hall, High Desert	.964	115	239	348	22	97
Helms, Salinas	.875	3	3	4	1	0
Houk, Visalia	.928	33	61	81	11	19
Kasper, San Jose	1.000	12	18	31	0	6
Kato, Salinas	.947	55	69	109	10	25
Kliafas, Bakersfield	.925	10	16	21	3	4
Lukachyk, Stockton	1.000	1	1	2	0	1
MacArthur, Visalia	.868	9	12	21	5	2
Meury, High Desert	.968	7	15	15	1	5
Munoz, Palm Springs	.973	85	176	217	11	49
Picketts, Reno	.897	17	13	22	4	4
Pozo, San Bernardino	.946	53	105	157	15	29
Rivera, Visalia	.968	85	156	234	13	51
Romero, Palm Springs	1.000	5	12	14	0	5
Rose, Palm Springs	.956	6	22	21	2	6
Salazar, Stockton	1.000	1	1	1	0	0
Urso, Palm Springs	.981	23	48	57	2	14
Waggoner, Reno	.960	83	148	239	16	52
Waldenberger, San Bernardino...	1.000	1	2	5	0	0
Ward, San Jose	.969	82	173	238	13	55
Webb, Bakersfield	.935	67	116	201	22	42
Whitford, Stockton	.986	30	57	85	2	12
Wong, Salinas	.947	55	75	139	12	28
Zerilla, Visalia	.926	20	27	60	7	17

Triple plays—Davis, Whitford.

THIRD BASEMEN

Player, Team	Pct.	G	PO	A	E	DP
Alfonzo, Palm Springs	.921	17	6	29	3	3
Arai, Salinas	1.000	1	0	1	0	0
Barns, Modesto	.920	24	15	31	4	4
Beard, Modesto	.858	78	38	113	25	15
Bernhardt, Stockton	.929	37	23	55	6	8
Bish, High Desert	.940	23	14	49	4	7
Bishop, Stockton	1.000	2	3	2	0	0
BLANCO, Bakersfield	.959	123	95	236	14	34
Boyzuick, Bakersfield	.700	6	1	6	3	0
Bruno, High Desert	.927	117	70	224	23	19
Casper, San Jose	.938	14	3	12	1	3
Cirillo, Stockton	1.000	7	7	10	0	0
Clayton, San Bernardino	.810	48	28	70	23	8
Cole, Stockton	.800	1	2	2	1	1
Dalesandro, Palm Springs	.915	54	35	73	10	10
Davis, Salinas	1.000	3	0	2	0	0
Davis, San Jose	.955	83	58	152	10	23
Dodge, Palm Springs	1.000	1	3	2	0	1
Garrigan, San Bernardino	.891	39	26	56	10	7
Glenn, Stockton	1.000	1	1	0	0	0
Gomez, Reno	.884	84	50	133	24	9
Griffin, Bakersfield	.889	4	0	8	1	0
Henry, Reno	.905	65	41	93	14	4
Horowitz, High Desert	1.000	1	0	1	0	0
Houk, Visalia	.935	26	10	33	3	1
Jenkins, San Jose	1.000	7	4	19	0	1
Kasper, San Jose	.979	35	24	70	2	8
Kato, Salinas	.857	20	10	26	6	4
Kliafas, Bakersfield	.867	8	3	10	2	1
Kounas, San Bernardino	.929	5	1	12	1	0
Lawn, Stockton	1.000	3	2	3	0	0
MacArthur, Visalia	1.000	9	3	18	0	3
Meury, High Desert	1.000	2	1	3	0	0
Meyers, Bakersfield	1.000	1	1	0	0	1
Munoz, Palm Springs	1.000	6	4	18	0	1
Perez, Palm Springs	.879	51	29	87	16	9
Picketts, Reno	1.000	4	3	2	0	0
Raven, Palm Springs	.500	1	0	1	1	0

Player, Team	Pct.	G	PO	A	E	DP
Rolen, San Jose	.892	20	19	47	8	4
Romero, Palm Springs	.880	11	10	12	3	3
Rose, Palm Springs	1.000	2	2	5	0	1
Salazar, Modesto	.945	41	26	78	6	6
Salazar, Stockton	.833	15	10	20	6	2
Smith, Stockton	.864	52	42	85	20	6
Stahoviak, Visalia	.872	110	92	181	40	16
Uchinokura, Salinas	.927	128	90	191	22	24
Waldenberger, San Bernardino...	.899	62	39	121	18	17
Ward, San Jose	1.000	1	0	1	0	0
Whitford, Stockton	.960	41	39	57	4	9
Zerilla, Visalia	.625	5	3	2	3	0

Triple plays—Rolen, Smith.

SHORTSTOPS

Player, Team	Pct.	G	PO	A	E	DP
Alfonzo, Palm Springs	.972	25	33	73	3	17
Arai, Salinas	.913	124	193	287	46	64
Barns, Modesto	.907	12	22	27	5	10
Bish, High Desert	.947	6	6	12	1	3
Bryant, San Bernardino	.924	29	47	86	11	13
Casper, San Jose	1.000	1	0	1	0	1
Castro, Bakersfield	.928	112	180	309	38	73
Cole, Stockton	1.000	1	0	1	0	0
Cruz, Reno	.924	127	278	382	54	91
Davis, Salinas	.950	9	16	22	2	6
Davis, San Jose	.956	35	46	105	7	18
Diaz, San Bernardino	.947	37	55	105	9	22
Duncan, San Jose	.932	108	191	289	35	68
Frias, San Jose	.833	3	0	5	1	0
Garrigan, San Bernardino	.922	57	86	140	19	30
Grebeck, Palm Springs	.942	82	109	235	21	34
Guillen, San Bernardino	1.000	6	6	8	0	2
Helms, Salinas	1.000	3	1	1	0	0
Henderson, San Bernardino	.789	4	6	9	4	0
Hocking, San Bernardino	.947	135	214	469	38	97
Hunter, San Bernardino	.910	27	51	71	12	18
Kasper, San Jose	.929	16	17	22	3	1
Kato, Salinas	.950	20	24	33	3	7
Kliafas, Bakersfield	.955	26	39	68	5	16
MacArthur, Visalia	.875	5	4	10	2	2
MARTINEZ, High Desert	.951	124	209	408	32	103
Meury, High Desert	.870	13	14	26	6	8
Munoz, Palm Springs	.941	5	14	18	2	3
Perez, Palm Springs	1.000	1	1	3	0	0
Picketts, Reno	.800	1	1	3	1	0
Romero, Palm Springs	.893	29	29	63	11	13
Rose, Palm Springs	1.000	2	3	5	0	1
Salazar, Stockton	.900	5	3	6	1	2
Waggoner, Reno	.923	7	10	14	2	3
Weger, Stockton	.950	32	55	96	8	21
Whitford, Stockton	.925	24	43	55	8	13
Wood, Modesto	.938	128	203	360	37	86
Wrona, Stockton	.966	81	149	244	14	57
Zerilla, Visalia	.833	6	3	2	1	0

Triple play—Hocking.

OUTFIELDERS

Player, Team	Pct.	G	PO	A	E	DP
Adams, San Bernardino	.954	77	99	4	5	1
Anderson, Palm Springs*	.959	79	137	4	6	2
Barns, Modesto	1.000	4	9	0	0	0
BASSE, Stockton*	.985	111	182	11	3	4
Becker, Visalia*	.983	132	332	17	6	4
Bellomo, San Jose*	.959	38	68	3	3	1
Benjamin, Stockton	.950	10	18	1	1	0
Bish, High Desert	1.000	1	17	0	0	0
Booker, Modesto	.970	22	31	1	1	1
Brewer, San Jose	.867	24	25	1	4	0
Buccheri, Reno	.986	61	135	1	2	0
Butcher, Salinas*	1.000	12	14	0	0	0
M. Carter, Stockton	.974	65	143	9	4	0
T. Carter, Stockton	1.000	3	2	1	0	0
Cervantes, San Bernardino*	1.000	8	7	0	0	0
Cisarik, San Jose*	1.000	12	17	1	0	0
Clayton, San Bernardino	.667	10	3	1	2	0
Cohick, Palm Springs*	.967	111	169	8	6	2
Colon, Palm Springs	.966	92	166	7	6	0
Cookson, San Jose	.952	51	96	3	5	0
Cordova, Visalia	.984	109	173	10	3	0
Davis, San Jose	1.000	1	1	0	0	0
Dodge, Palm Springs	1.000	2	1	0	0	0
Dotel, Bakersfield*	.952	88	153	6	8	0
Faneyte, San Jose	.984	89	172	13	3	2
Fernandez, San Bernardino*	.950	52	88	7	5	1
Francisco, Reno	1.000	5	11	0	0	0
Garrett, Palm Springs*	.962	92	171	5	9	0
Gash, High Desert	.962	108	167	12	7	2
Gill, High Desert*	.969	126	233	16	8	3
Gonzalez, Salinas	.954	98	198	11	10	1
Hara, Salinas	.984	43	58	2	1	0
Harris, Stockton*	.946	23	32	3	2	1
Hart, Modesto	.959	104	180	8	8	1

Player, Team	Pct.	G	PO	A	E	DP
Henderson, Modesto	1.000	3	4	0	0	0
Hendley, Modesto	1.000	7	4	0	0	0
Hollandsworth, Bakersfield*	.975	119	230	8	6	1
Houk, Visalia	1.000	7	9	0	0	0
House, Salinas	1.000	8	11	1	0	0
Hunter, San Bernardino	1.000	2	3	0	0	0
Hyzdu, San Jose	.976	112	193	8	5	2
Kasper, San Jose	1.000	1	1	1	0	0
Kliafas, Bakersfield	1.000	2	2	0	0	0
Kluge, San Bernardino	1.000	2	3	0	0	0
Kounas, San Bernardino	.500	5	1	0	1	0
Laboy, Salinas*	.833	13	10	0	2	0
Lawn, 27 Sal.-43 Sto.	.980	70	142	5	3	0
Lukachyk, Stockton	.983	77	160	14	3	2
Lydy, Reno	.922	29	41	6	4	1
MacArthur, Visalia	1.000	3	2	0	0	0
Marrero, Stockton*	1.000	10	15	1	0	0
Martinez, Modesto	.961	110	232	12	10	3
Mashore, Modesto	.966	106	212	12	8	1
McCutchen, Salinas	.600	3	3	0	2	0
McDavid, High Desert	.981	119	206	4	4	0
McFarlin, San Jose*	.966	64	135	5	5	1
McGonnigal, San Jose*	.989	44	85	5	1	1
McMurray, Bakersfield	.970	63	89	7	3	0
Moore, Visalia*	.833	4	5	0	1	0
Munoz, Palm Springs	1.000	5	9	0	0	0
Neill, Reno*	.980	113	184	13	4	2
Nishijima, Salinas*	.968	128	234	8	8	2
Pennington, San Bernardino	.903	43	55	1	6	0
Pezzoni, Salinas	.980	35	49	1	1	0
Picketts, Reno	1.000	5	6	0	0	0
Proctor, Bakersfield*	1.000	10	10	1	0	0
Ramirez, Reno	.894	27	41	1	5	0
Raven, Palm Springs	1.000	13	16	2	0	0
Ricker, Visalia	.958	125	237	13	11	3
Robertson, San Bernardino	.913	107	172	6	17	0
Romay, Bakersfield	.974	16	35	2	1	0
Rubiera, Palm Springs	.974	20	37	1	1	0
Rumsey, Palm Springs	.900	11	9	0	1	0
Sheppard, Salinas	.944	109	227	11	14	0
Simmons, Reno	.965	62	105	6	4	0
Singleton, 18 Sal.-90 Sto.	.965	108	227	20	9	5
Smith, Stockton	.944	27	31	3	2	1
Smith, Bakersfield	.963	104	200	7	8	2
Spann, High Desert	.982	41	52	4	1	0
Todd, San Bernardino*	1.000	39	66	5	0	0
Turner, Visalia	.976	43	77	4	2	0
Twitty, Visalia	.971	48	98	2	3	0
Vorbeck, Bakersfield	.958	37	65	4	3	1
Waldenberger, San Bernardino...	.917	9	11	0	1	0
Walker, Reno	.953	31	80	1	4	0
Whalen, High Desert*	.971	23	33	1	1	0
Wolfe, Reno	.973	95	170	10	5	1
Young, Modesto	.958	68	126	11	6	1

CATCHERS

Player, Team	Pct.	G	PO	A	E	DP	PB
Baar, Bakersfield	1.000	13	76	16	0	1	3
Balthazar, San Bernardino	.982	53	294	32	6	2	13
Beard, Modesto	1.000	11	72	9	0	0	1
Brown, Visalia	.988	33	138	31	2	2	5
Calcagno, San Jose	.973	39	215	34	7	1	7
Carcione, Modesto	.988	45	289	40	4	6	4
Charles, San Jose	.976	49	253	26	7	6	11
Clemens, San Jose	.964	18	50	3	2	0	2
DeFrancesco, Reno	.967	11	73	15	3	1	3
Dempsey, Salinas	.971	43	220	18	7	3	9
Dodge, Palm Springs	.970	42	252	35	9	1	3
Durant, Visalia	.982	116	672	79	14	3	18
Fabregas, Palm Springs	.967	60	436	63	17	7	16
Gray, Bakersfield	.992	18	112	7	1	1	7
Helfand, Modesto	.973	60	417	47	13	3	8
Henderson, High Desert	.986	75	444	53	7	4	14
Henry, Reno	.875	1	7	0	1	0	1
Hirsch, Palm Springs	1.000	5	30	5	0	0	1
Horowitz, High Desert	.982	46	292	37	6	5	10
Johnson, Reno	1.000	2	11	2	0	0	0
Johnson, Bakersfield	.992	47	321	47	3	2	7
Kluge, San Bernardino	.981	38	183	23	4	2	7
Kobza, Stockton	.977	54	221	30	6	5	10
Kounas, San Bernardino	.981	57	375	45	8	1	21
Logan, Visalia	1.000	2	7	0	0	0	0
MATHENY, Stockton	.989	104	582	114	8	20	12
McGough, Salinas	.984	91	566	94	11	7	23
Meyers, Bakersfield	1.000	1	2	0	0	0	1
Mirabelli, San Jose	.973	53	321	38	10	3	4
Molina, Reno	.982	115	716	139	16	13	28
Montgomery, San Jose	.875	2	7	0	1	0	0
Mulligan, High Desert	.966	32	153	17	6	0	10
Musolino, Palm Springs	.979	16	125	12	3	1	6
Norton, Bakersfield	.984	27	168	19	3	1	11
Ortiz, Bakersfield	.994	63	428	44	3	2	7
Picketts, Reno	.939	16	67	10	5	0	1
Rivera, Salinas	.980	24	87	11	2	0	4
Salazar, Modesto	1.000	3	13	3	0	0	0

Player, Team	Pct.	G	PO	A	E	DP	PB
Skeels, Salinas	.953	14	74	7	4	2	1
Speakman, Palm Springs	.962	17	106	20	5	1	4
Sutherland, San Bernardino	.988	13	72	7	1	0	3
Zahner, Bakersfield	1.000	3	8	1	0	0	0

PITCHERS

Player, Team	Pct.	G	PO	A	E	DP
Acevedo, Visalia	.895	12	8	9	2	0
Acre, Reno	.870	35	10	10	3	0
Adam, San Bernardino	.946	26	11	24	2	1
Andersen, High Desert	1.000	5	0	1	0	0
Archer, Stockton	.960	55	6	18	1	1
Arola, Salinas	1.000	30	1	6	0	1
Aronetz, Bakersfield*	1.000	9	1	0	0	0
Benavides, San Jose	1.000	8	1	0	0	0
Bennett, Palm Springs	.889	6	5	3	1	0
Bigham, Visalia*	1.000	54	6	9	0	0
Borski, San Bernardino	.971	17	13	21	1	0
Brady, Bakersfield*	1.000	30	5	11	0	3
Brock, Reno	.960	25	12	12	1	0
Brown, High Desert*	.000	2	0	0	1	0
Brummett, San Jose	.931	19	11	16	2	1
Brutcher, High Desert	1.000	16	1	4	0	0
Bush, Stockton	.944	38	7	10	1	0
Callahan, Modesto*	.800	49	0	8	2	0
Carrasco, Salinas	.714	9	2	3	2	0
L. Carter, Stockton	.969	21	12	19	1	4
Castillo, 9 Bak.-27 Vis.	.777	36	6	8	4	2
Castillo, San Jose	.833	10	3	2	1	0
Chaves, High Desert	.935	68	9	20	2	1
Christopher, Stockton	1.000	7	1	2	0	1
Clemens, San Jose	1.000	3	0	1	0	0
Connolly, Reno	1.000	21	2	6	0	1
Connolly, Visalia	.909	30	6	4	1	1
Cormier, Modesto	.750	4	0	3	1	0
Correa, Stockton	1.000	35	5	12	0	1
Devore, High Desert	.727	23	2	6	3	1
Dillon, Modesto	1.000	31	3	9	0	0
Dixon, Visalia*	.889	27	5	19	3	1
Dodge, Palm Springs	1.000	2	1	0	0	0
Dressendorfer, Modesto	1.000	3	2	2	0	0
Duke, San Bernardino*	1.000	34	5	8	0	0
Edenfield, Palm Springs	1.000	13	1	2	0	0
Ericson, Visalia	.857	35	1	5	1	1
Farnsworth, Bakersfield*	.895	25	5	12	2	1
FARRELL, Stockton*	1.000	13	10	22	0	1
Felix, High Desert*	.667	35	2	4	3	0
Fermin, Modesto	1.000	14	4	6	0	0
Flanagan, San Jose	.923	57	7	17	2	0
Florie, High Desert	.900	26	16	29	5	3
Freeman, Bakersfield	.871	32	10	17	4	1
Fritz, Salinas*	.857	5	0	6	1	1
Galindez, High Desert*	.882	26	13	54	9	0
Gamez, Stockton	.938	23	10	20	2	2
Gamez, Palm Springs*	.967	38	4	25	1	1
Garland, Modesto	.889	16	12	12	3	1
Garrelts, San Jose	1.000	1	1	0	0	0
Gill, High Desert*	1.000	2	1	0	0	0
Glinatsis, San Bernardino	.906	28	9	20	3	0
Gorecki, Bakersfield	.892	25	11	22	4	1
Green, Salinas	1.000	8	0	2	0	0
Grimes, Modesto	.938	16	8	7	1	0
Grundt, San Jose*	.800	11	1	3	1	0
Guardado, Visalia*	1.000	7	6	8	0	2
Gulledge, Reno	.857	44	9	9	3	0
Hamilton, High Desert	.909	9	5	5	1	0
Hampton, San Bernardino*	.964	25	11	42	2	1
Hancock, San Jose*	.938	18	9	21	2	2
Hancock, San Jose*	.895	24	5	29	4	3
Hanselman, San Jose	.958	16	8	15	1	1
Harris, High Desert	.667	1	1	1	1	0
Hathaway, Palm Springs*	1.000	3	0	4	0	0
Henderson, Bakersfield	.667	3	0	2	1	0
Henrikson, San Jose*	.833	7	2	3	1	0
Henry, Reno	1.000	8	1	0	0	0
Heredia, Palm Springs	.889	30	4	4	1	1
Herring, San Jose*	1.000	19	1	1	0	0
Hilton, High Desert	1.000	13	3	4	0	0
Hokuf, Modesto	.952	35	3	17	1	2
Holdridge, Palm Springs	.925	28	12	25	3	1
Holzemer, Palm Springs*	.875	5	2	5	1	0
M. Hooper, Salinas	1.000	21	9	10	0	3
T. Hooper, Salinas	.750	17	7	5	4	1
Howell, Bakersfield	1.000	4	0	1	0	0
Hyde, San Jose	.789	37	7	8	4	0
Ingram, High Desert	1.000	7	2	3	0	0
Ingram, Reno	.867	41	8	5	2	0
Ito, Salinas	.500	11	0	1	1	0
Jewell, Reno	.333	5	1	0	2	0
Johns, Reno*	.957	27	17	50	3	2
Johnson, Palm Springs	1.000	22	1	5	0	0
Keling, Palm Springs	1.000	30	8	19	0	2
Kellogg, Bakersfield	1.000	24	8	21	0	1
King, San Bernardino*	.927	27	8	30	3	1
Knox, Stockton*	1.000	5	2	3	0	1

Player, Team	Pct.	G	PO	A	E	DP
Kubicki, Salinas	.667	6	1	1	1	0
Kuhn, Modesto*	.800	6	1	3	1	0
Lavigne, Bakersfield*	1.000	18	4	20	0	0
Law, Salinas	1.000	3	1	0	0	0
Lebron, High Desert	.941	24	20	28	3	3
Lewis, Visalia*	.966	28	4	24	1	2
Lifgren, High Desert	1.000	5	2	1	0	0
Lodding, San Bernardino	.864	35	7	12	3	0
Love, Reno*	.800	20	3	9	3	0
MacNeill, Stockton	1.000	12	1	1	0	0
Maldonado, Bakersfield*	.952	43	10	10	1	3
Mansur, Visalia*	.920	17	5	18	2	1
Martin, High Desert*	1.000	11	1	0	0	0
Martinez, Modesto	.900	37	1	8	1	0
McCament, San Jose	1.000	11	2	5	0	2
McCarty, Reno*	1.000	3	1	3	0	0
McCreary, Visalia	1.000	14	7	14	0	0
McCutchen, Salinas	.900	13	6	3	1	0
McFarlin, Bakersfield	.900	6	3	6	1	0
McGraw, Stockton*	.897	15	7	28	4	3
McKeon, 15 H.D. - 12 Sto.	.944	27	12	22	2	3
McLeod, San Jose	1.000	29	3	10	0	1
Mecir, San Bernardino	1.000	14	7	3	0	0
Mejia, Reno	.867	37	6	7	2	0
Mikkelsen, Stockton	.950	20	4	15	1	1
Millay, Modesto	.750	8	2	4	2	0
Miller, Stockton	1.000	31	3	7	0	1
Minik, Reno	1.000	20	3	2	0	0
Misa, Reno	1.000	12	0	5	0	0
Mitchell, Palm Springs	.500	8	0	1	1	0
Mitchelson, Palm Springs*	1.000	7	1	2	0	0
Montoya, Palm Springs*	1.000	14	4	5	0	0
Morris, Visalia	1.000	11	0	2	0	0
Mortensen, High Desert*	.500	15	0	1	1	0
Myers, San Jose*	.938	8	3	12	1	1
Myers, Reno*	.667	11	0	2	1	0
Nerat, Modesto	.750	21	1	2	1	0
Nickell, San Bernardino	.917	13	4	7	1	0
Okoshi, Salinas	.833	11	3	2	1	1
Parra, Bakersfield	.871	24	11	16	4	1
Peltzer, San Jose*	.913	46	7	14	2	2
Percival, Palm Springs	1.000	11	0	2	0	0
Perkins, San Bernardino	1.000	15	2	1	0	1
Persing, Visalia	.917	10	3	8	1	0
Phillips, San Bernardino	.941	37	3	13	1	1
Picketts, Reno	1.000	7	0	1	0	0
Pierce, Reno	1.000	15	0	3	0	0
Pote, San Jose	1.000	4	1	1	0	0
Powers, Salinas	1.000	9	1	2	0	0
Pruitt, Stockton	.938	13	5	10	1	0
Purdy, Palm Springs	.896	26	9	34	5	2
Raczka, Modesto*	1.000	6	1	2	0	0
Raven, Palm Springs	1.000	1	1	0	0	0
Richardson, Salinas*	1.000	4	0	1	0	0
Ritchie, Visalia	.930	28	19	34	4	5
Robinson, Palm Springs	1.000	24	1	9	0	1
Robinson, Visalia	.933	51	3	11	1	0
Robinson, Stockton	1.000	4	1	4	0	0
Rogers, Stockton*	.963	54	3	23	1	3
Rose, Reno	1.000	20	4	10	0	2
Rosenbalm, San Bernardino	1.000	6	0	2	0	0
Rosselli, San Jose*	.963	22	6	20	1	2
Saitz, Palm Springs	.923	36	7	17	2	1
Salcedo, Bakersfield	1.000	12	1	2	0	1
Sample, Salinas	.833	14	3	7	2	1
Samuels, Salinas	.826	18	2	17	4	1
Santiago, Palm Springs*	1.000	3	0	1	0	1
Schanz, San Bernardino	.909	38	3	7	1	0
Sharko, San Jose.	1.000	16	1	5	0	0
Sharp, Bakersfield	.929	33	4	9	1	1
Shaw, Modesto*	.959	27	8	39	2	3
Shoemaker, Modesto	.929	10	8	5	1	0
Silverio, Palm Springs	.857	14	1	5	1	0
Smith, Bakersfield*	.917	26	4	7	1	0
Smith, Reno	.944	28	16	18	2	2
Smithberg, Reno	1.000	10	2	3	0	1
Smock, Reno*	1.000	36	2	6	0	1
Sodders, Bakersfield*	1.000	9	0	2	0	0
Soltero, High Desert	1.000	15	3	1	0	0
Sontag, Salinas	.955	28	14	28	2	4
Stephens, Salinas*	.933	26	8	20	2	2
Stroud, Palm Springs	1.000	30	5	7	0	0
Sturtze, Modesto	.971	25	9	25	1	1
Sudbury, Modesto	.895	46	2	15	2	1
Sweeney, Bakersfield	1.000	37	7	5	0	1
Thelen, Visalia	.955	24	9	12	1	1
Thibault, High Desert*	1.000	44	7	8	0	2
Tipton, Bakersfield	.667	5	0	2	1	0
Tolar, Salinas*	.786	14	1	10	3	0
Toliver, Salinas	.935	20	9	20	2	1
Trautwein, Salinas	.917	49	4	18	2	2
Urso, San Bernardino*	.900	37	3	15	2	1
Vanderweele, San Jose	.792	16	6	13	5	1
Van Dyke, Palm Springs	1.000	41	7	8	0	0
Van Landingham, San Jose	.800	6	1	3	1	0
Vogelgesang, Bakersfield	1.000	17	1	8	0	3
Walkden, Bakersfield*	1.000	27	2	18	0	2
Whitaker, San Jose*	.960	26	6	42	2	3
Williams, Bakersfield	1.000	13	1	5	0	0
Witte, San Bernardino	.909	21	4	6	1	0
Wojciechowski, Modesto*	1.000	14	2	14	0	1
Wylie, Palm Springs	1.000	4	0	1	0	1
Yamada, Salinas	.917	47	6	16	2	0
Zinter, High Desert	1.000	47	4	2	0	0

Triple play—Dixon.

The following players did not have any fielding statistics at the positions indicated or appeared only as a designated hitter, pinch-hitter or pinch-runner: Agemy, p; Beard, of; Bensching, p; M. Brown, p; Calhoun, p; T. Carter, p; M. Davis, p; Demetral, of; Duplessis, p; Guillen, 3b; Hardtke, dh; M. Harris, p; Helms, 3b; Hendley, p; Hoeme, p; Huffman, p; Hyson, p; Jenkins, 2b; Kliafas, p; Kohno, pr; Lawn, 2b, ss; Lukachyk, 3b; Pennington, 3b; E. Perez, of; Ramirez, p; Romero, p; J. Salazar, p; Suzuki, p; J. Urso, p; Whalen, p; Wolfe, p; Wong, ss.

LEAGUE CHAMPIONS

Year	Team	Pct.	Year	Team	Pct.	Year	Team	Pct.
1914—	Fresno	.571		Reno	.643	1977—	Salinas	.564
1915—	Modesto	.857	1962—	San Jose§	.686		Lodi§	.579
1916-40—	Did not operate.			Reno	.587	1978—	Visalia§	.698
1941—	Fresno	.643	1963—	Modesto	.589		Lodi	.607
	S. Barbara (2nd)*	.597		Stockton§	.687	1979—	San Jose§	.636
1942—	Santa Barbara†	.642	1964—	Fresno	.638		Reno	.525
1943-44-45—	Did not operate.			Fresno	.600	1980—	Stockton§	.638
1946—	Stockton‡	.600	1965—	San Jose	.586		Visalia	.507
1947—	Stockton‡	.679		Stockton§	.614	1981—	Visalia	.621
1948—	Fresno	.607	1966—	Modesto	.577		Lodi§	.521
	S. Barbara (3rd)*	.529		Modesto	.671	1982—	Modesto§	.671
1949—	Bakersfield	.612	1967—	San Jose§	.676		Visalia	.586
	San Jose (4th)*	.543		Modesto	.586	1983—	Visalia	.621
1950—	Ventura	.607	1968—	San Jose	.629		Redwood§	.529
	Modesto (2nd)*	.586		Fresno§	.623	1984—	Modesto§	.597
1951—	Santa Barbara‡	.599	1969—	Stockton§	.600		Bakersfield	.486
1952—	Fresno‡	.629		Visalia	.614	1985—	Fresno§	.575
1953—	San Jose‡	.664	1970—	Bakersfield	.667		Stockton	.566
1954—	Modesto‡	.623		Bakersfield	.671	1986—	Palm Springs	.613
1955—	Stockton	.733	1971—	Visalia§	.583		Stockton§	.585
	Fresno§	.718		Fresno	.500	1987—	Fresno§	.559
1956—	Fresno§	.650	1972—	Modesto§	.547		Reno	.535
1957—	Visalia x	.622		Bakersfield	.629	1988—	Stockton	.657
	Salinas (4th)*	.504	1973—	Lodi§	.657		Riverside§	.599
1958—	Fresno*	.639		Bakersfield	.571	1989—	Stockton	.627
	Bakersfield	.672	1974—	Fresno§	.607		Bakersfield§	.577
1959—	Bakersfield	.592		San Jose	.579	1990—	Visalia	.638
	Modesto§	.643	1975—	Reno	.614		Stockton§	.582
1960—	Reno	.614		Reno	.614	1991—	San Jose	.676
	Reno	.657	1976—	Salinas	.650		High Desert§	.537
1961—	Reno	.743		Reno§	.547	1992—	Stockton§	.610
							Visalia	.551

*Won four-club playoff. †League disbanded June 28. ‡Won championship and four-club playoff. §Won split-season playoff. xWon both halves of split season.

CAROLINA LEAGUE

FINAL STANDINGS

FIRST HALF

NORTHERN DIVISION

Team	W	L	T	Pct.	GB
Lynchburg (Red Sox)	39	30	0	.565	....
Frederick (Orioles)	35	34	0	.507	4
Salem (Pirates)	33	36	0	.478	6
Prince William (Yankees)	31	38	0	.449	8

SOUTHERN DIVISION

Team	W	L	T	Pct.	GB
Peninsula (Mariners)	37	32	0	.536	....
Durham (Braves)	37	32	0	.536	....
Kinston (Indians)	35	34	0	.507	2
Winston-Salem (Cubs)	29	40	0	.420	8

SECOND HALF

NORTHERN DIVISION

Team	W	L	T	Pct.	GB
Lynchburg (Red Sox)	38	30	0	.576	....
Prince William (Yankees)	38	33	0	.535	2 ½
Frederick (Orioles)	34	37	0	.479	6 ½
Salem (Pirates)	31	40	0	.437	9 ½

SOUTHERN DIVISION

Team	W	L	T	Pct.	GB
Peninsula (Mariners)	37	32	0	.536	....
Winston-Salem (Cubs)	37	33	0	.529	½
Durham (Braves)	33	38	0	.465	5
Kinston (Indians)	30	37	0	.448	6

COMPOSITE

Team	Lyn.	Pen.	Dur.	P.W.	Fre.	Kin.	W.S.	Sal.	W	L	T	Pct.	GB
Lynchburg (Red Sox)	....	13	8	7	13	10	14	12	77	58	0	.570	....
Peninsula (Mariners)	6	....	11	11	9	12	13	12	74	64	0	.536	4 ½
Durham (Braves)	12	9	....	7	5	13	14	10	70	70	0	.500	9 ½
Prince William (Yankees)	13	9	13	....	12	8	7	7	69	71	0	.493	10 ½
Frederick (Orioles)	7	11	15	8	....	10	9	9	69	71	0	.493	10 ½
Kinston (Indians)	6	8	7	12	10	....	8	14	65	71	0	.478	12 ½
Winston-Salem (Cubs)	6	6	6	13	11	12	....	12	66	73	0	.475	13
Salem (Pirates)	8	8	10	13	11	6	8	....	64	76	0	.457	15 ½

Peninsula club represented Hampton, Va.

Major league affiliations in parentheses.

Playoffs—Peninsula defeated Lynchburg, three games to two, to win league championship.

Regular-season attendance—Durham, 280,994; Frederick, 329,592; Kinston, 105,090; Lynchburg, 92,778; Peninsula, 59,093; Prince William, 208,416; Salem, 134,598; Winston-Salem, 159,316. Total, 1,369,877. Playoffs (5 games)—6,567. All-Star Game—4,219.

Managers—Durham, Leon Roberts; Frederick, Bobby Miscik; Kinston, Dave Keller; Lynchburg, Buddy Bailey; Peninsula, Marc Hill; Prince William, Mike Hart; Salem, John Wockenfuss; Winston-Salem, Bill Hayes.

All-Star team: 1B—Bubba Smith, Peninsula; 2B—Kevin Jordan, Prince William; 3B—Jose Viera, Winston-Salem; SS—Ramon Martinez, Salem. OF—Darren Bragg, Peninsula; Stanton Cameron, Frederick; Brian Kowitz, Durham; C—Miah Bradbury, Peninsula; DH—Andy Hartung, Winston-Salem; Starting Pitcher—John Cummings, Peninsula; Relief Pitcher—Joe Caruso, Lynchburg; Most Valuable Player—Bubba Smith, Peninsula; Manager—Marc Hill, Peninsula.

BATTING

TEAM

Team	Avg.	G	AB	R	OR	H	TB	2B	3B	HR	RBI	SH	SF	HP	BB	Int. BB	SO	SB	CS	LOB
Salem	.259	140	4692	589	645	1213	1833	220	44	104	524	27	30	62	396	10	966	193	69	952
Kinston	.255	136	4531	662	627	1157	1692	182	25	101	580	38	40	68	527	21	885	124	62	978
Durham	.253	140	4647	615	621	1177	1814	217	36	116	542	67	43	23	417	23	1010	165	101	921
Frederick	.248	140	4578	641	607	1135	1719	211	32	103	591	36	59	75	540	24	922	78	57	1018
Winston-Salem	.247	139	4517	624	626	1116	1703	208	26	109	559	68	39	52	477	12	860	98	56	945
Prince William	.244	140	4503	640	632	1098	1620	199	46	77	562	47	51	36	525	14	997	131	73	928
Lynchburg	.242	135	4504	558	568	1088	1612	210	25	88	499	46	30	28	387	26	944	68	51	880
Peninsula	.241	138	4455	563	566	1073	1542	183	26	78	489	43	30	51	452	21	794	188	113	860

INDIVIDUAL

(Leading qualifiers for batting championship—378 or more plate appearances)

*Bats lefthanded.   †Switch-hitter.

Player, Team	Avg.	G	AB	R	H	TB	2B	3B	HR	RBI	SH	SF	HP	BB	Int. BB	SO	SB	CS
Kapano, Corey, Winston-Salem	.318	93	314	63	100	175	27	3	14	65	0	1	5	54	1	52	14	12
Jordan, Kevin, Prince William	.311	112	438	67	136	205	29	8	8	63	1	5	3	27	3	54	6	4
Wawruck, Jim, Frederick*	.309	102	350	61	108	158	18	4	8	46	1	5	2	47	2	69	11	8
Malzone, John, Lynchburg*	.306	117	386	49	118	166	24	6	4	52	2	2	2	29	0	53	1	2
Cummings, Midre, Salem†	.305	113	420	55	128	200	20	5	14	75	0	3	4	35	2	67	23	9
Kowitz, Brian, Durham*	.301	105	382	53	115	164	14	7	7	64	6	7	2	44	4	53	22	11
Ramirez, Omar, Kinston	.299	110	411	73	123	192	20	5	13	49	8	2	3	38	1	53	19	12
Santana, Ruben, Peninsula	.294	113	401	54	118	169	19	4	8	61	6	1	9	21	0	54	17	16
Ortiz, Luis, Lynchburg	.290	94	355	43	103	162	27	1	10	61	0	5	2	22	3	55	4	2
Martinez, Ramon, Salem	.289	131	533	73	154	204	17	12	3	30	5	2	2	29	0	139	35	17

NOTE: Under Section 10.23 of the Official Baseball Rules, Corey Kapano of Winston-Salem qualifies for the batting championship. He batted .318 in 374 plate appearances. By adding four more at-bats to Kapano's actual total of 314, he would have an adjusted batting average of .314 in an adjusted total of 378 plate appearances, thereby making him the leading qualifier.

Departmental leaders: G—Gillis, C. Smith, 137; AB—Martinez, 533; R—Bragg, 83; H—Martinez, 154; TB—C. Smith, 246; 2B—Vierra, 32; 3B—Martinez, 12; HR—C. Smith, 32; RBI—Hartung, 94; SH—Heath, 20; SF—Millares, 10; HP—Sondrini, 14; BB—Bragg, 105; IBB—C. Smith, 7; SO—Martinez, 139; SB—Heath, 50; CS—Bragg, 19.

Player, Team	Avg.	G	AB	R	H	TB	2B	3B	HR	RBI	SH	SF	HP	BB	Int. BB	SO	SB	CS
Albornoz, Rodolfo, Prince William	.207	37	121	19	25	27	2	0	0	9	2	1	1	24	0	22	0	3
Albrecht, Andrew, Prince William*	.209	92	287	43	60	93	9	3	6	31	4	0	6	36	2	78	11	2
Alstead, Jason, Frederick*	.234	77	269	37	63	82	4	3	3	18	1	1	2	29	3	49	17	12
Anderson, Steve, Prince William*	.225	11	40	6	9	11	2	0	0	5	1	0	0	1	0	5	0	2
Arace, Pascuale, Salem*	.291	87	278	48	81	125	20	3	6	26	1	2	1	32	0	51	7	3
Aude, Rich, Salem	.286	122	447	63	128	189	26	4	9	60	0	1	8	50	2	79	11	2
Audley, Jim, Frederick†	.174	50	149	15	26	33	4	0	1	9	1	2	2	20	0	37	3	0
Bailey, Robert, Salem†	.261	108	353	56	92	123	15	2	4	31	4	1	1	61	1	78	44	16
Bates, Tommy, Kinston	.246	86	264	35	65	98	15	3	4	28	3	3	9	22	0	51	8	5
Beasley, Tony, Salem	.262	72	237	34	62	97	10	2	7	25	2	1	3	16	0	44	12	4
Bell, David, Kinston	.252	123	464	52	117	156	17	2	6	47	2	7	1	54	1	66	2	4
Berni, Denny, Lynchburg*	.217	52	138	10	30	41	8	0	1	7	3	0	0	7	1	28	0	0
Biasucci, Joe, Winston-Salem	.237	30	93	13	22	35	6	2	1	9	2	0	1	9	0	22	1	1
Bonifay, Ken, Salem*	.201	71	209	20	42	51	6	0	1	20	1	2	3	28	0	36	1	2
Bradbury, Miah, Peninsula	.280	111	396	33	111	151	17	1	7	53	3	2	4	29	4	49	2	8
Bragg, Darren, Peninsula*	.273	135	428	83	117	179	25	5	9	58	5	5	5	105	6	76	44	19
Brittain, Grant, Durham*	.144	44	90	12	13	20	4	0	1	4	0	0	0	13	0	42	1	1
Burnett, Roger, Prince William	.188	101	341	38	64	84	11	3	1	32	5	8	6	23	0	81	1	3
Cameron, Stanton, Frederick	.247	127	409	76	101	206	16	1	29	92	2	5	11	90	3	121	2	3
Campusano, Genaro, Salem	.074	20	54	1	4	8	1	0	1	5	0	0	1	0	0	30	0	0
Carey, Paul, Frederick*	.301	41	136	24	41	74	6	0	9	26	0	1	2	28	5	22	0	1
Carpenter, Bubba, Prince William*	.317	68	240	41	76	110	15	2	5	41	1	6	1	35	2	44	4	4
Carroll, Kevin, Prince William	.131	68	176	8	23	26	0	0	1	10	5	1	0	13	0	69	0	0
Coss, Mike, Frederick	.158	68	177	14	28	33	2	0	1	8	4	0	2	11	0	43	1	2
Cotton, John, Kinston*	.200	103	360	67	72	118	7	3	11	39	1	2	2	48	1	106	23	7
Crowley, Jim, Lynchburg	.255	119	392	62	100	158	20	1	12	59	1	3	2	34	1	75	2	1
Cuevas, Johnny, Durham	.197	34	61	2	12	12	0	0	0	4	3	0	0	4	0	17	1	0
Cummings, Midre, Salem†	.305	113	420	55	128	200	20	5	14	75	0	3	4	35	2	67	23	9
Cunningham, Earl, Winston-Salem	.108	25	83	8	9	18	3	0	2	9	0	2	4	3	0	54	0	0
Donahue, Tim, Kinston†	.225	66	204	29	46	56	4	0	2	25	3	1	3	20	0	36	5	4
Edge, Tim, Salem	.181	68	216	18	39	64	5	1	6	26	0	1	5	21	0	55	3	2
Eierman, John, Lynchburg*	.221	119	408	36	90	128	19	2	5	41	2	2	1	37	4	93	5	8
Erdman, Brad, Winston-Salem	.192	65	219	29	42	55	4	0	3	14	4	1	4	12	0	53	1	5
Everett, Carl, Prince William*	.318	6	22	7	7	19	0	0	4	9	0	0	0	5	0	7	1	0
Fernandez, Rolando, Winston-Salem*	.202	74	173	19	35	44	6	0	1	13	0	3	0	28	2	28	1	1
Figga, Michael, Prince William	.200	3	10	0	2	3	1	0	0	0	0	0	0	0	0	3	0	1
Flowers, Doug, Frederick*	.000	7	8	0	0	0	0	0	0	1	0	0	0	2	0	1	0	0
Fox, Andy, Prince William*	.239	125	473	75	113	158	18	3	7	42	4	0	6	54	1	81	28	14
Friedman, Jason, Lynchburg*	.267	135	495	68	132	202	26	1	14	68	1	2	4	46	5	61	5	4
Furcal, Manuel, Peninsula*	.000	6	1	0	0	0	0	0	0	0	0	0	0	0	0	0	0	0
Gabbani, Mike, Winston-Salem	.209	16	43	2	9	11	0	1	0	3	1	1	0	3	0	17	1	0
Garland, Tim, Prince William	.234	43	128	13	30	42	4	4	0	18	2	2	2	14	0	33	10	2
Giles, Brian, Kinston*	.264	42	140	28	37	53	5	1	3	18	0	0	1	30	1	21	3	5
Gillis, Tim, Durham	.239	137	482	63	115	206	22	3	21	84	2	5	3	64	2	128	3	10
Glanville, Doug, Winston-Salem	.258	120	485	72	125	163	18	4	4	36	9	2	4	40	0	78	32	9
Godin, Steve, Frederick	.216	71	236	30	51	72	9	0	4	24	5	5	4	16	0	41	9	2
Gomez, Rudy, Winston-Salem	.231	112	363	43	84	102	13	1	1	25	7	2	4	28	0	60	8	6
Graham, Tim, Lynchburg*	.170	91	276	33	47	62	9	3	0	14	6	0	1	34	3	70	6	5
Green, Tom, Salem	.270	34	122	16	33	62	6	1	7	23	1	1	1	10	0	26	4	2
Hanel, Marcus, Salem	.186	75	231	12	43	60	8	0	3	17	6	1	2	11	0	53	4	0
Hankins, Mike, Prince William†	.278	46	169	31	47	54	3	2	0	11	3	1	1	31	0	27	2	3
Hardtke, Jason, Kinston†	.211	6	19	3	4	4	0	0	0	1	0	0	0	4	0	4	0	0
Hartung, Andy, Winston-Salem	.278	132	496	76	138	240	25	4	23	94	2	5	8	47	1	91	10	5
Harvey, Ray, Kinston*	.284	97	331	35	94	118	18	0	2	45	1	2	4	36	4	43	2	1
Heath, Lee, Durham†	.277	129	473	71	131	186	22	6	7	47	20	2	1	26	1	99	50	18
Houston, Tyler, Durham*	.226	117	402	39	91	131	17	1	7	38	3	5	1	20	0	89	5	6
Hughes, Troy, Durham	.245	128	449	64	110	187	21	4	16	53	2	6	1	49	3	97	12	7
Hunter, Greg, Peninsula*	.181	50	149	15	27	38	5	0	2	10	1	0	2	13	0	24	1	0
Jimenez, Ramon, Prince William*	.234	136	431	64	101	172	25	5	12	59	1	8	0	66	2	116	6	6
Johnson, Andre, Durham	.235	18	51	4	12	16	1	0	1	2	0	0	0	3	0	22	0	1
Jones, Chipper, Durham†	.277	70	264	43	73	109	22	1	4	31	1	3	2	31	1	34	10	8
Jordan, Kevin, Prince William	.311	112	438	67	136	205	29	8	8	63	1	5	3	27	3	54	6	4
Juday, Rick, Winston-Salem	.220	108	381	47	84	113	16	5	1	32	10	3	0	32	0	56	4	3
Kapano, Corey, Winston-Salem	.318	93	314	63	100	175	27	3	14	65	0	1	5	54	1	52	14	12
Karcher, Rick, Durham*	.205	79	200	16	41	53	6	0	2	19	1	1	0	14	2	64	0	1
Keeline, Jason, Durham	.235	69	213	17	50	53	3	0	0	5	8	0	1	14	0	35	2	2
Kostich, Bill, Peninsula*	.000	35	1	0	0	0	0	0	0	0	0	0	0	0	0	0	0	0
Kowitz, Brian, Durham*	.301	105	382	53	115	164	14	7	7	64	6	7	2	44	4	53	22	11
Krevokuch, Jim, Salem	.304	51	158	30	48	73	13	0	4	20	1	1	4	20	1	13	1	1
Leach, Jalal, Prince William*	.264	128	462	61	122	173	22	7	5	65	3	5	0	47	2	114	18	9
Lewis, T.R., Frederick	.307	84	313	58	96	156	27	6	7	54	0	5	2	36	0	46	5	2
Little, Mike, Winston-Salem	.240	47	154	13	37	54	8	0	3	16	3	0	2	15	0	42	2	1
Livesey, Steve, Prince William	.146	38	103	6	15	18	3	0	0	5	2	1	2	2	0	20	0	1
Lohry, Adin, Prince William*	.259	57	135	19	35	36	1	0	0	14	7	2	0	35	1	27	3	2
Lorms, John, Kinston†	.209	51	134	18	28	33	2	0	1	18	0	2	0	26	2	29	0	0
Magalanes, Bob, Peninsula	.185	41	108	7	20	26	3	0	1	10	1	2	1	5	0	17	1	2
Malzone, John, Lynchburg*	.306	117	386	49	118	166	24	6	4	52	2	2	2	29	0	53	1	2
Marin, Jose, Lynchburg	.132	46	106	12	14	17	3	0	0	6	6	1	0	12	0	41	1	0
Martindale, Ryan, Kinston	.227	99	331	38	75	100	8	1	5	40	1	2	12	25	1	74	8	2
Martinez, Ramon, Salem	.289	131	533	73	154	204	17	12	3	30	5	2	2	29	0	139	35	17
McConathy, Doug, Frederick*	.288	99	316	43	91	128	20	1	5	50	4	7	8	42	2	53	0	0
McKeel, Walt, Lynchburg	.222	96	288	33	64	111	11	0	12	33	5	1	3	22	0	77	2	1
Millares, Jose, Frederick	.217	129	452	48	98	151	21	1	10	68	3	10	9	25	2	79	8	5
Moore, Boo, Lynchburg	.240	106	371	50	89	168	16	3	19	58	0	5	3	31	6	107	3	3
Morales, Jorge, Peninsula	.242	67	165	20	40	46	6	0	0	16	2	0	2	7	0	28	6	5
Morrison, Jim, Lynchburg	.281	92	253	48	71	100	16	2	3	21	4	2	1	27	2	65	17	6
Motuzas, Jeff, Prince William	.177	63	203	21	36	64	13	0	5	20	5	2	3	14	0	74	1	1
Mouton, Lyle, Prince William	.265	50	189	28	50	84	14	1	6	34	0	4	0	17	1	42	4	2
Nava, Lipso, Peninsula	.225	102	346	32	78	107	16	2	3	35	4	1	8	18	1	56	7	3
Neff, Marty, Salem	.279	59	219	32	61	122	16	0	15	37	1	3	2	6	0	44	3	0
Nieves, Melvin, Durham†	.302	31	106	18	32	67	9	1	8	32	0	4	2	17	3	33	4	2
O'Connor, Kevin, Durham*	.281	122	438	79	123	162	17	2	6	35	5	2	3	48	4	49	31	17

Player, Team	Avg.	G	AB	R	H	TB	2B	3B	HR	RBI	SH	SF	HP	BB	Int. BB	SO	SB	CS
Odor, Rouglas, Kinston	.269	71	219	24	59	72	6	2	1	17	8	1	6	22	0	36	11	6
Olmeda, Jose, Durham†	.258	24	89	17	23	37	6	1	2	9	1	0	0	14	0	14	7	4
Ortiz, Basilo, Frederick	.275	54	182	26	50	67	11	3	0	19	2	1	3	18	0	40	7	3
Ortiz, Luis, Lynchburg	.290	94	355	43	103	162	27	1	10	61	0	5	2	22	3	55	4	2
Perry, Herbert, Kinston	.278	121	449	74	125	200	16	1	19	77	4	4	12	46	1	89	12	0
Pezzoni, Ron, Peninsula	.300	25	100	6	30	35	3	1	0	11	1	0	0	2	0	8	5	1
Pough, Clyde, Kinston	.226	114	411	59	93	151	23	1	11	58	4	5	6	50	1	98	12	3
Ramirez, Dan, Frederick	.229	107	363	40	83	102	12	2	1	23	4	3	12	27	3	70	1	7
Ramirez, Manny, Kinston	.278	81	291	52	81	146	18	4	13	63	1	3	4	45	3	74	1	3
Ramirez, Omar, Kinston	.299	110	411	73	123	192	20	5	13	49	8	2	3	38	1	53	19	12
Rappoli, Paul, Lynchburg*	.267	111	344	47	92	131	17	2	6	42	4	3	6	48	1	66	11	13
Relaford, Desi, Peninsula†	.216	130	445	53	96	125	18	1	3	34	4	6	1	39	1	88	27	7
Ripplemeyer, Brad, Durham	.227	115	392	38	89	164	16	1	19	48	6	6	4	25	1	134	2	5
Roa, Hector, Durham	.279	110	377	52	105	170	27	7	8	46	6	2	2	16	2	55	14	4
Robertson, Jason, Prince William*	.240	68	254	34	61	90	6	4	5	34	1	3	1	31	0	55	14	6
Rodarte, Raul, Peninsula	.248	94	290	37	72	98	8	6	2	22	3	2	1	35	2	37	15	10
Rodriguez, Tony, Lynchburg	.223	128	516	59	115	140	14	4	1	27	7	3	3	25	0	84	11	6
Ronca, Joe, Salem	.230	47	152	11	35	53	6	0	4	17	1	2	1	6	0	39	3	1
Roso, Jimmy, Frederick	.220	66	191	22	42	59	11	0	2	18	3	0	4	26	0	61	0	0
Salcedo, Edwin, Prince William	.250	44	132	15	33	62	6	1	7	29	1	1	3	8	0	47	1	1
Sanchez, Ozzie, Durham*	.234	61	171	25	40	75	10	2	7	21	2	0	1	14	0	43	1	4
Santana, Ruben, Peninsula	.294	113	401	54	118	169	19	4	8	61	6	1	9	21	0	54	17	16
Schreiber, Bruce, Salem	.187	33	107	9	20	37	3	4	2	8	1	0	1	10	1	21	1	1
Schroeder, Todd, Salem*	.258	59	155	10	40	48	8	0	0	13	1	2	4	10	1	35	0	0
Seitzer, Brad, Frederick	.248	129	459	59	114	183	21	3	14	61	4	3	7	38	2	111	2	4
Smith, Bubba, Peninsula	.261	137	482	70	126	246	22	1	32	93	0	5	5	65	7	138	4	10
Smith, Shad, Prince William	.000	36	1	0	0	0	0	0	0	0	0	0	0	0	0	1	0	0
Sondrini, Joe, Salem	.223	107	372	40	83	104	14	2	1	31	1	1	14	25	0	59	9	2
Soto, Rafael, Winston-Salem	.235	93	264	38	62	67	2	0	1	18	9	1	3	23	0	33	5	4
Speakman, Willie, Peninsula†	.167	31	60	6	10	12	2	0	0	4	0	1	1	1	0	20	0	0
Strickland, Ricky, Prince William†	.220	52	150	22	33	42	9	0	0	12	3	1	0	20	0	31	14	3
Sullivan, Dan, Peninsula	.000	33	1	0	0	0	0	0	0	0	0	0	0	0	0	1	0	0
Swail, Steve, Durham	.286	9	7	2	2	2	0	0	0	1	0	0	0	1	0	2	0	0
Taylor, Scott, Winston-Salem	.220	75	241	20	53	76	12	1	3	24	10	1	5	22	1	37	1	2
Taylor, Will, Peninsula†	.223	64	211	36	47	55	2	3	0	10	1	1	2	42	0	44	39	15
Terrell, James, Peninsula	.192	101	313	36	60	82	5	1	5	21	5	0	3	17	0	51	2	9
Thomas, Keith, Salem†	.277	104	372	54	103	191	24	8	16	51	1	6	5	18	2	90	30	7
Timmons, Ozzie, Winston-Salem	.282	86	305	64	86	158	18	0	18	56	4	4	2	58	3	46	11	0
Torres, Jessie, Salem	.298	25	57	7	17	22	2	0	1	9	0	0	1	7	0	7	2	0
Torres, Paul, Winston-Salem	.238	134	458	55	109	178	15	6	14	78	2	7	5	60	2	114	4	4
Twitty, Sean, Peninsula	.157	33	102	16	16	21	5	0	0	3	2	1	2	5	0	32	3	0
Tyler, Brad, Frederick*	.254	54	185	34	47	71	11	2	3	22	1	4	2	43	2	34	9	3
Van Tiger, Tom, Kinston*	.233	25	60	4	14	15	1	0	0	3	2	1	0	5	0	13	1	1
Viera, John, Prince William*	.247	52	174	30	43	73	6	3	6	29	1	0	2	33	0	35	6	5
Vierra, Jose, Winston-Salem	.274	117	405	55	111	197	32	0	18	58	4	6	1	39	2	72	3	3
Waldenberger, Dave, Peninsula†	.182	6	11	1	2	2	0	0	0	2	0	0	0	3	0	2	0	0
Wawruck, Jim, Frederick*	.309	102	350	61	108	158	18	4	8	46	1	5	2	47	2	69	11	8
Welch, Doug, Winston-Salem	.250	14	40	7	10	17	1	0	2	9	1	0	4	4	0	5	0	0
Whitmore, Darrell, Kinston*	.280	121	443	71	124	180	22	2	10	52	0	5	5	56	5	92	17	9
Wilder, Willie, Peninsula	.245	110	322	51	79	111	18	1	4	32	3	1	4	34	0	52	14	8
Wilson, Craig, Peninsula	.195	36	123	11	24	39	9	0	2	14	2	2	1	11	0	17	1	0
Zaun, Gregg, Frederick*	.251	108	383	54	96	144	18	6	6	52	1	7	3	42	0	45	3	5

The following pitchers, listed alphabetically by club, with games in parentheses, had no plate appearances, primarily through use of designated hitters:

DURHAM—Chiles, Barry (31); Hailey, Roger (34); Hostetler, Mike (13); Leahy, Tom (23); Lomon, Kevin (27); Potts, Mike (30); Reyes, Carlos (21); Ritter, Darren (30); Ryder, Scott (42); Sparma, Blase (21); Steinmetz, Earl (26); Vasquez, Marcos (15); Williams, Dave (53); Woodall, Brad (24).

FREDERICK—Anderson, Matt (19); Blumberg, Bob (1); Borowski, Joe (48); Brimhall, Brad (2); Dedrick, Jim (38); Farrar, Terry (28); Jones, Stacy (7); Krivda, Rick (9); Paveloff, Dave (51); Pennington, Brad (8); Plaster, Allen (27); Polasek, John (14); Ricci, Chuck (1); Ryan, Kevin (27); Sackinsky, Brian (5); Taylor, Tom (27); Tippitt, Brad (27).

KINSTON—Allen, Chad (10); Brown, Clarence (4); Bryant, Shawn (27); Cofer, Brian (24); Curtis, Mike (18); Embree, Alan (15); Garcia, Apolinar (10); Gibbs, Paul (3); Hernandez, Fernando (8); Johnson, Carl (11); Kovach, Ty (35); Lopez, Al (10); McCarthy, Greg (23); Morgan, Scott (12); Ogea, Chad (21); Rivera, Roberto (24); Stone, Eric (25); Sweeney, Mark (28); Tatterson, Gary (6); Winiarski, Ron (43).

LYNCHBURG—Bailey, Cory (49); Caruso, Joe (49); Davis, Chris (10); Dennison, Jim (28); Estrada, Peter (28); Klvac, Dave (46); Konopki, Mark (34); Plantenberg, Erik (21); Renko, Steve (6); Rodriguez, Francisco (25); Rush, Andrew (15); Sele, Aaron (20); Vanegmond, Tim (28); Young, Brian (13).

PENINSULA—Bicknell, Greg (28); Cummings, John (27); Darwin, Jeff (32); Fitzer, Doug (26); Holman, Brad (13); O'Donnell, Erik (30); Perkins, Paul (3); Pitcher, Scott (15); Rees, Sean (27); Russell, Lee (27); Wiley, Chuck (43); Youngblood, Todd (21).

PRINCE WILLIAM—Dunbar, Matt (44); Frazier, Ron (16); Gilbert, Brent (3); Greer, Ken (13); Hines, Rich (25); Hodges, Darren (9); Malone, Todd (32); Manon, Ramon (17); Polak, Rich (25); Prybylinski, Bruce (26); Quirico, Rafael (23); Ralph, Curtis (32); Rumer, Tim (23); Seiler, Keith (16); Short, Ben (4).

SALEM—Alvarez, Jose (28); Christiansen, Jason (38); Evans, Sean (15); Harrah, Doug (32); Hope, John (27); Hunter, Bob (19); Jones, Dan (13); McCurry, Jeff (30); Mooney, Troy (11); Parkinson, Eric (24); Robertson, Rich (6); Ruebel, Matt (13); Rychel, Kevin (37); Sosa, Jose (4); Tellers, Dave (32); Watson, Dave (30); White, Rich (18).

WINSTON-SALEM—Alicano, Pedro (13); Bradford, Troy (6); Budrewicz, Tim (16); Burlingame, Ben (31); Cheetham, Sean (7); Correa, Amilcar (34); Delgado, Tim (28); Doss, Jason (14); Kenny, Brian (7); Kirk, Chuck (48); Krahenbuhl, Ken (11); Kutzler, Jerry (6); Perez, Pedro (24); Szczepanski, Joe (60); Taylor, Aaron (62); Tidwell, Mike (4); Weiss, Scott (35).

GRAND SLAMS—Cameron, Jimenez, Martindale, Perry, 2 each; Bragg, Carroll, Glanville, Hartung, Krevokuch, Leach, Malzone, Millares, Motuzas, Robertson, Rappoli, Salcedo, C. Smith, Timmons, P. Torres, Viera, 1 each.

AWARDED FIRST BASE ON CATCHER'S INTERFERENCE—Houston 3 (Bradbury, McKeel, Motuzas); Carpenter (Houston); Cotton (Salcedo); Erdman (Morales); Friedman (Lohry); Gillis (Bradbury); Godin (Carroll); Hankins (Roso); Lorms (Salcedo); Morales (Salcedo); L. Ortiz (Salcedo); O. Ramirez (Lohry); Relaford (Bradbury); Soto (Morales).

PITCHING

TEAM

Team	ERA	G	CG	ShO	Sv.	IP	H	R	ER	HR	HB	BB	Int. BB	SO	WP	Bk.
Peninsula	3.23	138	14	15	34	1206.1	1120	566	433	80	49	447	35	946	59	25
Lynchburg	3.52	135	6	10	49	1194.0	1087	568	467	85	58	474	7	956	96	11
Prince William	3.60	140	8	3	38	1198.0	1098	632	479	91	51	452	19	931	49	21
Frederick	3.69	140	16	12	35	1210.2	1111	607	497	91	40	499	18	982	65	16
Durham	3.79	140	11	11	33	1220.1	1144	621	514	92	48	516	27	941	90	23
Winston-Salem	3.95	139	10	4	27	1194.1	1231	626	524	120	45	416	18	800	55	4
Kinston	4.01	136	20	10	24	1186.0	1117	627	528	84	44	479	8	980	100	23
Salem	4.05	140	15	7	29	1216.2	1149	645	547	133	60	438	19	842	84	20

INDIVIDUAL

(Leading qualifiers for earned-run average leadership—112 or more innings)

*Throws lefthanded.

Pitcher, Team	W	L	Pct.	ERA	G	GS	CG	GF	ShO	Sv.	IP	H	R	ER	HR	HB	BB	Int. BB	SO	WP
Caruso, Lynchburg	6	4	.600	1.98	49	0	0	27	0	15	118.0	68	36	26	5	3	40	3	133	8
Cummings, Peninsula*	16	6	.727	2.57	27	27	4	0	1	0	168.1	149	71	48	11	10	63	6	144	4
Plaster, Frederick	9	12	.429	2.87	27	26	3	0	1	0	150.1	113	70	48	6	6	75	1	129	8
Sele, Lynchburg	13	5	.722	2.91	20	19	2	0	1	0	127.0	104	51	41	5	14	46	0	112	5
Prybylinski, Prince William	12	10	.545	3.01	26	26	2	0	0	0	164.2	141	67	55	18	4	27	0	105	0
Rodriguez, Lynchburg	12	7	.632	3.09	25	25	1	0	0	0	148.2	125	56	51	11	6	65	0	129	6
Bicknell, Peninsula	10	7	.588	3.12	28	28	3	0	2	0	179.0	170	80	62	11	3	53	1	140	5
Russell, Peninsula	7	10	.412	3.15	27	26	2	1	1	0	157.1	132	76	55	4	8	59	4	130	5
Quirico, Prince William*	6	11	.353	3.17	23	23	2	0	0	0	130.2	128	84	46	11	1	50	1	123	7
Darwin, Peninsula	5	11	.313	3.35	32	20	4	9	2	3	139.2	132	58	52	13	4	40	5	122	6

Departmental leaders: G—A. Taylor, 62; W—Cummings, 16; L—Several pitchers tied with 12; Pct.—Ogea, .813; GS—Bicknell, Farrar, 28; CG—Farrar, Ogea, White, 5; GF—A. Taylor, 51; ShO—Bicknell, Darwin, Hostetler, Ogea, 2; Sv.—C. Bailey, 23; IP—Farrar, 182.1; H—Ryan, 175; R—Parkinson, 89; ER—Ryan, 78; HR—Perez, 23; HB—Sele, 14; BB—Plaster, 75; IBB—Wiley, 8; SO—Cummings, 144; WP—Vanegmond, 18.

(All pitchers—listed alphabetically)

Pitcher, Team	W	L	Pct.	ERA	G	GS	CG	GF	ShO	Sv.	IP	H	R	ER	HR	HB	BB	Int. BB	SO	WP
Alicano, Winston-Salem*	2	1	.667	4.50	13	0	0	5	0	0	16.0	20	8	8	1	0	7	0	11	0
Allen, Kinston	5	2	.714	2.51	10	10	2	0	1	0	61.0	54	22	17	3	0	13	0	28	4
Alvarez, Salem	4	5	.444	3.65	28	0	0	12	0	1	61.2	60	33	25	9	2	17	2	27	3
Anderson, Frederick*	7	7	.500	4.36	19	18	3	0	1	0	109.1	110	65	53	16	4	41	1	103	4
Bailey, Lynchburg	5	7	.417	2.44	49	0	0	43	0	23	66.1	43	20	18	3	2	30	2	87	5
Bailey, Salem	0	0	.000	18.00	1	0	0	1	0	0	1.0	1	2	2	0	1	2	0	0	0
Beasley, Salem	0	0	.000	12.00	2	0	0	2	0	0	3.0	5	4	4	2	0	1	0	2	0
Bicknell, Peninsula	10	7	.588	3.12	28	28	3	0	2	0	179.0	170	80	62	11	3	53	1	140	5
Blumberg, Frederick*	0	0	.000	4.50	1	1	0	0	0	0	4.0	2	2	2	0	0	6	0	1	0
Borowski, Frederick	5	6	.455	3.70	48	0	0	36	0	10	80.1	71	40	33	3	3	50	3	85	2
Bradbury, Peninsula	0	0	.000	0.00	1	0	0	0	0	0	1.0	0	0	0	0	1	0	0	1	0
Bradford, Winston-Salem	2	4	.333	6.75	6	4	1	0	0	0	26.2	25	21	20	3	1	14	0	7	2
Bragg, Peninsula	0	0	.000	0.00	1	0	0	1	0	0	3.0	1	0	0	0	1	0	0	3	0
Brimhall, Frederick	0	0	.000	5.06	2	0	0	1	0	0	5.1	4	3	3	0	0	3	0	4	1
Brown, Kinston	0	0	.000	8.56	4	1	0	1	0	0	13.2	16	15	13	2	0	7	0	7	0
Bryant, Kinston*	10	8	.556	3.81	27	27	3	0	1	0	167.2	152	85	71	8	5	69	0	121	15
Budrewicz, Winston-Salem	0	4	.000	3.67	16	6	0	4	0	0	41.2	41	21	17	2	1	19	0	24	3
Burlingame, Winston-Salem	8	12	.400	3.64	31	25	3	2	0	0	160.2	164	79	65	13	3	44	1	82	3
Caruso, Lynchburg	6	4	.600	1.98	49	0	0	27	0	15	118.0	68	36	26	5	3	40	3	133	8
Cheetham, Winston-Salem	0	4	.000	9.76	7	7	0	0	0	0	27.2	40	32	30	5	4	23	2	15	1
Chiles, Durham	6	8	.429	3.81	31	14	2	8	1	1	111.0	117	56	47	11	1	33	4	64	6
Christiansen, Salem*	3	1	.750	3.24	38	0	0	15	0	2	50.0	47	20	18	7	1	22	2	59	0
Cofer, Kinston	1	5	.167	3.58	24	0	0	17	0	1	37.2	33	17	15	0	0	23	1	38	2
Correa, Winston-Salem	1	0	1.000	4.88	34	0	0	10	0	0	59.0	59	41	32	5	1	31	0	43	5
Cuevas, Durham	0	0	.000	20.25	1	0	0	0	0	0	1.1	2	3	3	0	1	0	0	1	0
Cummings, Peninsula*	16	6	.727	2.57	27	27	4	0	1	0	168.1	149	71	48	11	10	63	6	144	4
Curtis, Kinston*	1	2	.333	3.86	18	0	0	12	0	2	23.1	16	11	10	1	2	10	1	24	2
Darwin, Peninsula	5	11	.313	3.35	32	20	4	9	2	3	139.2	132	58	52	13	4	40	5	122	6
Davis, Lynchburg	2	1	.667	3.24	10	4	0	4	0	0	33.1	26	13	12	2	2	16	0	15	4
Dedrick, Frederick	8	4	.667	3.06	38	5	1	19	0	3	108.2	94	41	37	5	5	42	4	86	4
Delgado, Winston-Salem	8	10	.444	3.41	28	20	3	1	0	1	145.1	144	68	55	16	8	38	2	114	1
Dennison, Lynchburg*	4	8	.333	4.34	28	14	0	4	0	1	95.1	92	53	46	12	1	41	0	74	6
Doss, Winston-Salem	4	4	.500	5.09	14	14	1	0	0	0	76.0	80	48	43	9	4	42	1	67	6
Dunbar, Prince William*	5	4	.556	2.87	44	0	0	21	0	2	81.2	68	37	26	5	6	33	2	68	7
Embree, Kinston*	10	5	.667	3.30	15	15	1	0	0	0	101.0	89	48	37	10	2	32	0	115	6
Estrada, Lynchburg	6	5	.545	3.53	28	11	1	7	0	3	107.0	87	49	42	6	5	45	0	47	8
Evans, Salem	4	4	.500	5.79	15	10	0	2	0	1	60.2	68	42	39	8	5	25	0	37	6
Farrar, Frederick*	11	10	.524	3.50	28	28	5	0	1	0	182.1	160	88	71	14	5	65	0	122	11
Fitzer, Peninsula*	3	1	.750	1.35	26	0	0	14	0	6	33.1	21	10	5	1	1	18	1	28	3
Frazier, Prince William	4	3	.571	3.20	16	7	0	4	0	0	56.1	51	27	20	10	5	11	0	52	2
Furcal, Peninsula*	0	1	.000	6.48	6	0	0	3	0	1	8.1	12	6	6	3	0	1	0	7	0
Garcia, Kinston	1	5	.167	3.95	10	10	1	0	1	0	57.0	51	30	25	8	3	17	0	61	4
Garland, Prince William	0	0	.000	18.00	1	0	0	1	0	0	1.0	2	2	2	0	0	2	0	0	0
Gibbs, Kinston	0	0	.000	11.25	3	0	0	2	0	0	4.0	7	5	5	1	0	2	0	9	0
Gilbert, Prince William	0	1	.000	15.43	3	0	0	0	0	0	7.0	13	13	12	3	1	4	0	6	0
Graham, Lynchburg	0	0	.000	6.00	2	0	0	2	0	0	3.0	5	3	2	0	0	2	0	0	0
Greer, Prince William	1	2	.333	3.67	13	0	0	6	0	1	27.0	25	11	11	1	1	9	0	30	1
Hailey, Durham*	2	2	.500	3.51	34	0	0	13	0	0	51.1	48	27	20	2	6	36	1	49	4
Harrah, Peninsula	8	8	.500	3.80	32	16	1	9	0	3	137.1	133	73	58	10	8	43	0	90	11
Harvey, Kinston*	0	0	.000	0.00	1	0	0	0	0	0	1.0	2	1	0	0	0	0	0	1	0
Hernandez, Kinston	1	3	.250	4.54	18	8	1	0	0	0	41.2	36	23	21	2	1	22	0	32	3
Hines, Prince William*	11	7	.611	3.60	25	24	0	1	0	0	140.0	131	75	56	12	7	61	3	84	10

Pitcher, Team	W	L	Pct.	ERA	G	GS	CG	GF	ShO	Sv.	IP	H	R	ER	HR	HB	BB	Int. BB	SO	WP
Hodges, Prince William	4	4	.500	2.60	9	9	1	0	0	0	52.0	42	26	15	2	3	20	0	28	3
Holman, Peninsula	1	1	.500	3.06	13	0	0	12	0	5	17.2	15	8	6	0	0	4	1	19	2
Hope, Salem	11	8	.579	3.47	27	27	4	0	0	0	176.1	169	75	68	13	10	46	0	106	10
Hostetler, Durham	9	3	.750	2.15	13	13	3	0	2	0	88.0	75	25	21	2	2	19	3	88	2
Hunter, Salem	2	0	1.000	1.52	19	1	0	7	0	2	29.2	24	6	5	0	3	12	0	25	3
Johnson, Kinston	3	5	.375	4.72	11	11	0	0	0	0	55.1	60	40	29	6	1	30	0	32	7
Jones, Salem	4	5	.444	3.71	13	13	2	0	0	0	63.0	52	31	26	5	2	25	0	52	3
Jones, Frederick	2	1	.667	3.21	7	6	0	0	0	0	33.2	32	15	12	3	1	4	0	30	0
Kapano, Winston-Salem	0	0	.000	0.00	1	0	0	1	0	0	1.0	0	0	0	0	0	0	0	0	0
Karcher, Durham*	0	0	.000	10.13	2	0	0	0	0	0	2.2	4	3	3	0	0	6	0	3	1
Kenny, Winston-Salem	1	2	.333	5.75	7	6	0	0	0	0	36.0	43	25	23	8	4	6	0	19	2
Kirk, Winston-Salem	10	6	.625	3.95	48	10	1	14	0	2	127.2	142	65	56	7	8	43	2	74	6
Klvac, Lynchburg*	7	4	.636	4.29	46	2	0	12	0	0	50.1	60	34	24	2	0	28	0	40	5
Konopki, Lynchburg	5	4	.556	4.72	34	9	0	15	0	5	87.2	95	51	46	8	4	34	1	44	9
Kostich, Peninsula*	2	2	.500	4.19	33	0	0	12	0	2	58.0	61	37	27	3	3	22	1	45	4
Kovach, Kinston	3	11	.214	5.95	35	15	2	10	1	1	107.1	107	80	71	15	5	62	0	84	15
Krahenbuhl, Winston-Salem	0	2	.000	3.90	11	3	0	3	0	0	27.2	30	16	12	3	1	9	0	19	2
Krivda, Frederick*	5	1	.833	2.98	9	9	1	0	1	0	57.1	51	23	19	7	1	15	0	64	1
Kutzler, Winston-Salem	4	0	1.000	3.38	6	6	1	0	1	0	37.1	41	14	14	3	0	6	0	21	0
Leahy, Durham	1	1	.500	7.36	23	0	0	8	0	1	33.0	38	28	27	5	4	21	2	14	2
Lomon, Durham	8	9	.471	4.93	27	27	0	0	0	0	135.0	147	83	74	13	11	63	1	113	16
Lopez, Kinston	5	2	.714	3.52	10	10	1	0	1	0	64.0	56	28	25	5	1	26	1	44	4
Lorms, Kinston	0	0	.000	0.00	2	0	0	1	0	0	2.0	0	0	0	0	0	1	0	0	0
Malone, Prince William*	5	5	.500	6.10	32	9	1	10	0	4	87.0	74	68	59	7	3	71	3	87	7
Malzone, Lynchburg	0	0	.000	0.00	1	0	0	0	0	0	1.0	0	0	0	0	0	0	0	0	0
Manon, Prince William	5	8	.385	4.89	17	17	1	0	1	0	92.0	96	59	50	3	3	34	1	78	6
McCarthy, Kinston*	3	0	1.000	0.00	23	0	0	21	0	12	27.1	14	0	0	0	5	9	0	37	8
McCurry, Salem	6	2	.750	2.87	30	0	0	15	0	3	62.2	49	22	20	3	3	24	3	52	7
Millares, Frederick	0	1	.000	27.00	1	0	0	1	0	0	1.0	4	3	3	0	0	1	0	0	0
Mooney, Salem	1	3	.250	5.91	11	6	0	2	0	0	32.0	26	26	21	3	2	21	1	18	5
Morgan, Kinston	1	0	1.000	4.50	12	0	0	5	0	1	18.0	16	9	9	0	0	11	0	14	1
O'Donnell, Peninsula	1	3	.250	4.31	30	3	0	15	0	0	71.0	80	42	34	8	1	22	2	41	5
Ogea, Kinston	13	3	.813	3.49	21	21	0	0	2	0	139.1	135	61	54	6	5	29	0	123	7
Parkinson, Salem	4	10	.286	6.06	24	17	2	2	1	0	108.1	107	89	73	17	3	40	1	82	12
Paveloff, Frederick	2	1	.667	2.40	51	0	0	37	0	16	82.1	62	28	22	3	1	31	2	54	5
Pennington, Frederick*	1	0	1.000	2.00	8	0	0	6	0	2	9.0	5	3	2	0	1	4	0	16	1
Perez, Winston-Salem	6	8	.429	4.20	24	23	0	1	0	0	128.2	139	74	60	23	3	39	2	93	11
Perkins, Peninsula	0	1	.000	3.86	3	0	0	1	0	0	4.2	2	2	2	0	1	1	0	2	0
Pitcher, Peninsula	3	0	1.000	0.69	15	0	0	8	0	2	26.0	18	4	2	1	2	11	1	24	0
Plantenberg, Lynchburg*	2	3	.400	5.18	21	12	0	4	0	0	81.2	112	69	47	7	5	36	0	62	6
Plaster, Frederick	9	12	.429	2.87	27	26	3	0	1	0	150.1	113	70	48	6	6	75	1	129	8
Polak, Prince William	2	2	.500	1.46	52	0	0	40	0	22	67.2	37	17	11	2	4	29	4	62	0
Polasek, Frederick*	2	3	.400	0.81	14	0	0	10	0	2	22.1	8	4	2	0	1	8	1	28	1
Potts, Durham*	6	8	.429	4.02	30	21	0	2	0	1	127.2	104	75	57	4	1	71	5	123	14
Prybylinski, Prince William	12	10	.545	3.01	26	26	2	0	1	0	164.2	141	67	55	18	4	27	0	105	0
Quirico, Prince William*	6	11	.353	3.17	23	23	2	0	0	0	130.2	128	84	46	11	1	50	1	123	7
Ralph, Prince William	3	2	.600	3.20	32	0	0	22	0	4	59.0	54	22	21	3	4	16	2	37	3
Ramirez, Frederick	0	0	.000	0.00	2	0	0	2	0	0	2.0	2	5	0	0	1	0	1	0	0
Rees, Peninsula*	10	12	.455	4.02	27	27	1	0	0	0	154.1	158	88	69	13	6	53	0	126	6
Renko, Lynchburg	1	1	.500	3.93	6	6	0	0	0	0	34.1	39	18	15	6	0	14	0	23	6
Reyes, Durham	2	1	.667	2.43	21	0	0	12	0	5	40.2	31	11	11	1	0	10	0	33	2
Ricci, Frederick	0	0	.000	0.00	1	0	0	0	0	0	2.1	2	1	0	0	0	1	0	2	0
Ritter, Durham	10	8	.556	3.48	30	26	3	1	1	1	157.2	157	78	61	8	6	58	2	90	14
Rivera, Kinston*	3	5	.375	3.25	24	8	4	5	1	1	88.2	83	35	32	7	3	11	3	56	4
Robertson, Salem*	3	0	1.000	3.41	6	6	0	0	0	0	37.0	29	18	14	6	1	10	0	27	1
Rodriguez, Lynchburg	12	7	.632	3.09	25	25	1	0	0	0	148.2	125	56	51	11	6	65	0	129	6
Ruebel, Salem*	1	6	.143	4.71	13	13	1	0	0	0	78.1	77	49	41	13	3	43	0	46	6
Rumer, Prince William*	10	7	.588	3.59	23	23	1	0	0	0	128.0	122	61	51	8	5	34	2	105	0
Rush, Lynchburg	0	3	.000	5.14	15	6	0	3	0	0	42.0	47	31	24	4	5	15	0	33	6
Russell, Peninsula	7	10	.412	3.15	27	26	2	1	1	0	157.1	132	76	55	4	8	59	4	130	5
Ryan, Frederick	7	12	.368	4.72	27	25	2	1	0	0	148.2	175	88	78	11	2	63	1	103	16
Rychel, Salem	2	3	.400	3.89	37	0	0	25	0	1	39.1	37	22	17	4	4	27	3	35	9
Ryder, Durham	6	8	.429	3.73	42	1	0	17	0	5	91.2	83	48	38	9	1	38	3	91	7
Sackinsky, Frederick	0	3	.000	13.06	5	3	0	0	0	0	10.1	20	15	15	3	0	6	0	10	4
Seiler, Prince William*	0	2	.000	6.35	16	0	0	13	0	5	17.0	21	13	12	1	0	11	0	11	2
Sele, Lynchburg	13	5	.722	2.91	20	19	2	0	1	0	127.0	104	51	41	5	14	46	2	112	5
Short, Prince William	0	0	.000	0.00	4	0	0	2	0	0	6.0	4	4	0	1	1	2	0	1	0
Smith, Peninsula	0	0	.000	27.00	1	0	0	0	0	0	1.0	2	5	3	1	0	2	0	1	0
Smith, Prince William	1	3	.250	3.56	36	2	0	12	0	0	81.0	89	46	32	4	3	38	1	54	1
Sosa, Salem	0	2	.000	6.63	4	3	0	1	0	0	19.0	20	15	14	4	0	13	0	9	2
Sparma, Durham	3	8	.273	4.77	21	21	3	0	0	0	120.2	114	73	64	16	9	53	2	76	12
Steinmetz, Durham	2	5	.286	5.03	26	8	0	5	0	0	73.1	70	48	41	11	2	36	0	49	4
Stone, Kinston	0	3	.000	4.05	25	0	0	11	0	4	40.0	37	21	18	1	0	28	1	53	7
Sullivan, Peninsula	2	1	.667	2.57	32	1	0	13	0	6	56.0	47	22	16	3	3	30	2	32	10
Sweeney, Kinston	0	4	.000	5.47	28	0	0	11	0	0	51.0	69	37	31	2	3	25	0	36	6
Szczepanski, Winston-Salem*	3	2	.600	2.82	60	1	0	20	0	1	76.2	77	32	24	5	0	30	2	43	5
Tatterson, Kinston	0	2	.000	5.23	6	0	0	2	0	1	10.1	13	10	6	1	2	5	0	10	0
Taylor, Winston-Salem	10	7	.588	2.21	62	0	0	51	0	20	85.2	74	29	21	4	2	17	1	59	5
Taylor, Frederick	4	8	.333	4.18	27	14	1	3	1	0	118.1	116	63	55	9	7	48	3	84	6
Tellers, Salem	3	7	.300	3.65	32	5	0	24	0	10	74.0	72	32	30	9	2	14	4	63	0
Tidwell, Winston-Salem*	0	0	.000	0.00	4	0	0	0	0	0	3.2	1	0	0	0	1	0	0	4	0
Tippitt, Frederick	6	2	.750	4.66	27	5	0	8	0	2	83.0	80	50	43	10	3	35	2	59	1
Vanegmond, Lynchburg	12	4	.750	3.42	28	27	2	0	1	0	173.2	161	73	66	12	8	52	0	140	18
Vazquez, Durham	5	0	1.000	2.17	15	9	0	2	0	0	74.2	53	24	18	5	2	32	1	53	4
Watson, Salem*	1	3	.250	3.16	30	5	0	8	0	0	62.2	57	28	22	5	5	29	2	42	1
Weiss, Winston-Salem	7	7	.500	3.38	35	14	0	17	0	3	117.0	111	53	44	13	5	47	5	105	3
White, Salem	7	9	.438	3.80	18	18	5	0	0	0	120.2	116	58	51	15	5	24	1	70	5
Wiley, Peninsula	7	5	.583	3.23	43	1	0	28	0	8	75.1	74	32	27	4	3	40	8	43	5
Williams, Durham	9	7	.563	2.86	53	0	0	45	0	15	69.1	71	28	22	1	2	28	1	43	1
Winiarski, Kinston	5	6	.455	4.94	43	0	0	17	0	1	74.2	71	49	41	6	6	47	1	55	5
Woodall, Durham*	1	2	.333	2.13	24	0	0	16	0	4	42.1	30	11	10	3	1	11	1	51	1
Young, Lynchburg	2	2	.500	3.28	13	0	0	7	0	2	24.2	23	11	9	2	3	10	1	17	4
Youngblood, Peninsula	7	3	.700	3.27	21	5	0	8	0	1	52.1	46	25	19	4	4	26	3	40	3

BALKS—Rees, 15; Bryant, 8; Quirico, 7; Alvarez, Darwin, 5 each; Ogea, Plaster, 4 each; Chiles, Dedrick, Dennison, Embree, Evans, Farrar, Hope, Hostetler, Lomon, Malone, Ralph, Rodriguez, Ryan, Ryder, Sele, S. Smith, Steinmetz, 3 each; Delgado, Kovach, Parkinson, Ritter, Vasquez, Watson, Winiarski, Woodall, 2 each; Brown, Christiansen, Cummings, Davis, Dunbar, Frazier, Hailey, Harrah, D. Jones, Kostich, Krivda, Manon, Morgan, Perez, Pitcher, Prybylinski, Robertson, Ruebel, Rumer, Russell, Sparma, Stone, Tatterson, T. Taylor, Tippitt, Vanegmond, Weiss, Youngblood, 1 each.

COMBINATION SHUTOUTS—Chiles-Reyes, Hostetler-Chiles-Potts-Williams, Hostetler-Williams, Lomon-Vasquez, Lomon-Williams, Ritter-Chiles, Vasquez-Ryder, Durham; Farrar-Borowski, Farrar-Dedrick, Farrar-Paveloff, Jones-Polasek, Krivda-Borowski, Krivda-Paveloff, Ryan-Paveloff, Frederick; Embree-McCarthy, Johnson-McCarthy-Cofer, Kinston; Estrada-Caruso-Bailey, Rodriguez-Bailey, Rodriguez-Caruso, Rodriguez-Estrada, Rodriguez-Konopki, Sele-Konopki, Sele-Konopki-Klvac-Caruso, Vanegmond-Caruso, Lynchburg; Bicknell-Fitzer, Bicknell-Kostich, Bicknell-Wiley, Cummings-Darwin, Cummings-Wiley, Darwin-Wiley-Fitzer, Rees-O'Donnell-Holman, Russell-Sullivan-Furcal, Youngblood-Sullivan, Peninsula; Malone-Ralph, Quirico-Polak, Prince William; Evans-McCurry, Hope-Tellers, Parkinson-Rychel-Christiansen, Robertson-Hunter-Tellers, Tellers-Evans-McCurry-Rychel, Watson-McCurry, Salem; Doss-Budrewicz, Kirk-Taylor, Kutzler-Szczepanski, Winston-Salem.

NO-HIT GAMES—Bicknell-Wiley, Peninsula, defeated Salem, 1-0, April 9; Hostetler-Chiles-Potts-Williams, Durham, defeated Peninsula, 9-0, April 13; Rodriguez-Caruso, Lynchburg, defeated Winston-Salem, 3-0, April 30; Vanegmond, Lynchburg, defeated Prince William, 2-0, June 1.

FIELDING

TEAM

Team	Pct.	G	PO	A	E	DP	PB	Team	Pct.	G	PO	A	E	DP	PB
Durham	.969	140	3661	1553	166	121	24	Prince William	.962	140	3594	1533	200	104	40
Lynchburg	.968	135	3582	1477	165	104	33	Kinston	.961	136	3558	1469	205	119	25
Salem	.965	140	3650	1657	194	119	16	Peninsula	.960	138	3619	1532	212	94	9
Winston-Salem	.965	139	3583	1529	188	121	16	Frederick	.959	140	3632	1455	216	111	14

Triple plays—Frederick, Lynchburg, Prince William, Salem.

INDIVIDUAL

FIRST BASEMEN

*Throws lefthanded.

Player, Team	Pct.	G	PO	A	E	DP
Aude, Salem	.992	113	1120	57	10	75
Berni, Lynchburg	1.000	13	83	6	0	8
Bonifay, Salem	1.000	11	96	3	0	7
Bradbury, Peninsula	.985	15	116	14	2	13
Campusano, Salem	1.000	1	2	0	0	0
Cuevas, Durham	.000	1	0	0	1	0
Fernandez, Winston-Salem*	.889	2	8	0	1	0
Flowers, Frederick	.952	3	17	3	1	1
FRIEDMAN, Lynchburg*	.995	127	1121	77	6	81
Gabbani, Winston-Salem	1.000	1	3	0	0	0
Gillis, Durham	1.000	13	72	5	0	5
Gomez, Winston-Salem	1.000	2	5	0	0	0
Hartung, Winston-Salem	.985	130	1152	104	19	97
Harvey, Kinston*	.990	22	184	14	2	13
Houston, Durham	1.000	6	34	0	0	2
Hunter, Peninsula	.988	10	79	3	1	3
Jimenez, Prince William*	.984	136	1144	79	20	86
Karcher, Durham*	.983	57	430	20	8	31
Livesey, Prince William	.958	16	129	7	6	11
Magallanes, Peninsula	.958	9	20	3	1	3
McConathy, Frederick	.982	94	789	33	15	53
Millares, Frederick	.981	39	241	12	5	22
Morales, Peninsula	1.000	2	2	0	0	1
O'Connor, Durham	.986	69	527	48	8	53
Perry, Kinston	.993	30	262	24	2	28
Pough, Kinston	.986	89	747	75	12	59
Ripplemeyer, Durham	1.000	4	31	2	0	0
Ronca, Salem	1.000	1	4	0	0	0
Roso, Frederick	.984	26	174	16	3	12
Sanchez, Durham*	.978	21	167	9	4	11
Schroeder, Salem*	.986	24	199	10	3	21
Smith, Kinston	.981	95	823	63	17	49
Speakman, Peninsula	.972	13	64	6	2	5
Sullivan, Peninsula	.500	1	1	0	1	0
Taylor, Winston-Salem	1.000	4	33	3	0	6
Terrell, Peninsula	1.000	1	1	0	0	0
Torres, Winston-Salem	.972	4	33	2	1	3
Waldenberger, Peninsula	1.000	1	2	0	0	0
Wilson, Peninsula	.976	14	118	3	3	9

Triple plays—Aude, Friedman, Jimenez, Millares.

SECOND BASEMEN

Player, Team	Pct.	G	PO	A	E	DP
Albornoz, Prince William	.946	23	40	65	6	11
Anderson, Prince William	.978	10	19	25	1	5
Beasley, Salem	.966	35	74	125	7	26
Biasucci, Winston-Salem	.968	25	48	74	4	11
Brittain, Durham	.952	35	48	52	5	13
Coss, Frederick	.944	15	13	21	2	7
Cotton, Kinston	.933	97	173	231	29	45
Crowley, Lynchburg	.972	78	123	195	9	39
Donahue, Kinston	.955	38	73	95	8	24
Gomez, Winston-Salem	.968	22	37	55	3	17
Hankins, Prince William	1.000	9	23	18	0	3

Player, Team	Pct.	G	PO	A	E	DP
Hardtke, Kinston	1.000	1	0	1	0	0
Jordan, Prince William	.960	100	186	274	19	53
Juday, Winston-Salem	.964	102	221	281	19	50
Keeline, Durham	1.000	1	0	1	0	0
Krevokuch, Salem	1.000	1	1	1	0	1
Malzone, Lynchburg	.956	72	118	164	13	28
Millares, Frederick	.957	79	154	223	17	39
Morales, Peninsula	1.000	2	0	2	0	1
O'Connor, Durham	.943	10	11	22	2	3
Odor, Kinston	1.000	6	7	11	0	3
Olmeda, Durham	.967	24	50	69	4	8
Roa, Durham	.977	92	195	266	11	59
Rodarte, Peninsula	.951	43	76	98	9	16
Santana, Peninsula	.964	102	204	285	18	37
SONDRINI, Salem	.972	107	201	380	17	61
Tyler, Frederick	.946	54	109	152	15	32
Waldenberger, Peninsula	1.000	4	4	6	0	1

Triple plays—Jordan, Malzone, Sondrini.

THIRD BASEMEN

Player, Team	Pct.	G	PO	A	E	DP
Albornoz, Prince William	1.000	7	2	11	0	1
Arace, Salem	1.000	1	0	1	0	0
Aude, Salem	1.000	1	0	1	0	0
Beasley, Salem	.900	24	12	51	7	4
Bell, Kinston	.946	121	83	264	20	19
Biasucci, Winston-Salem	1.000	3	3	4	0	0
Bonifay, Salem	.927	30	20	56	6	7
Brittain, Durham	.875	6	2	5	1	2
Coss, Frederick	.909	11	3	7	1	1
Crowley, Lynchburg	.893	36	30	78	13	5
Donahue, Kinston	.600	3	1	2	2	0
Fox, Prince William	.936	123	96	302	27	22
GILLIS, Durham	.950	128	86	216	16	27
Gomez, Winston-Salem	.899	30	28	34	7	1
Houston, Durham	.778	8	3	11	4	1
Hunter, Peninsula	1.000	3	0	3	0	0
Jordan, Prince William	.952	7	6	14	1	1
Keeline, Durham	.833	2	0	5	1	0
Krevokuch, Salem	.938	46	28	107	9	12
Livesey, Prince William	.654	12	10	7	9	1
Magallanes, Peninsula	.933	23	18	38	4	2
Malzone, Lynchburg	.880	29	14	52	9	4
Marin, Lynchburg	.908	24	18	51	7	4
Millares, Frederick	.943	13	13	20	2	3
Morales, Peninsula	1.000	2	1	0	0	0
Nava, Peninsula	.934	88	66	160	16	18
Odor, Kinston	.971	8	6	27	1	4
Ortiz, Lynchburg	.870	57	37	97	20	10
Perry, Kinston	.964	9	12	15	1	3
Roa, Durham	.963	11	5	21	1	2
Rodarte, Peninsula	.875	39	19	65	12	3
Ronca, Salem	.750	14	8	19	9	1
Schreiber, Salem	.906	33	21	56	8	2
Seitzer, Frederick	.898	128	91	304	45	29
Torres, Salem	.600	2	2	1	2	0
Vierra, Winston-Salem	.895	114	84	181	31	20

Triple plays—Bonifay, Crowley, Fox.

SHORTSTOPS

Player, Team	Pct.	G	PO	A	E	DP
Albornoz, Prince William	.853	6	7	22	5	0
Anderson, Prince William	1.000	2	2	5	0	0
Bates, Kinston	.890	82	124	200	40	34
Beasley, Salem	.865	11	10	22	5	1
Brittain, Durham	.857	1	2	4	1	0
BURNETT, Prince William	.951	101	132	279	21	45
Coss, Frederick	.925	42	40	84	10	14
Donahue, Kinston	.938	4	3	12	1	1
Fox, Prince William	1.000	1	1	2	0	1
Gillis, Durham	1.000	2	1	0	0	0
Gomez, Winston-Salem	.945	62	102	171	16	37
Hankins, Prince William	.933	33	40	99	10	19
Hardtke, Kinston	.909	5	6	4	1	0
Hunter, Peninsula	1.000	1	0	2	0	1
Jones, Durham	.956	70	106	200	14	35
Keeline, Durham	.958	67	81	217	13	28
Krevokuch, Salem	.909	3	2	8	1	1
Marin, Lynchburg	.941	17	20	28	3	6
Martinez, Salem	.917	130	194	359	50	62
Nava, Peninsula	.923	15	16	44	5	7
Odor, Kinston	.938	53	71	142	14	38
Ramirez, Frederick	.927	105	153	268	33	43
Relaford, Peninsula	.913	127	167	382	52	46
Roa, Durham	1.000	9	4	11	0	1
Rodarte, Peninsula	1.000	2	1	7	0	1
Rodriguez, Lynchburg	.950	123	196	370	30	63
Soto, Winston-Salem	.931	89	117	258	28	42

Triple play—Ramirez.

OUTFIELDERS

Player, Team	Pct.	G	PO	A	E	DP
Albrecht, Prince William	.974	30	36	1	1	0
Alstead, Frederick	.982	73	166	2	3	2
Arace, Salem	.971	62	95	4	3	1
Audley, Frederick*	1.000	40	68	1	0	1
Bailey, Salem	.981	78	146	9	3	2
Bonifay, Salem	.947	13	17	1	1	1
Bragg, Peninsula	.986	131	262	11	4	2
Cameron, Frederick	.971	124	219	15	7	0
Carpenter, Prince William*	.964	67	100	7	4	0
Cummings, Salem	.964	97	151	10	6	1
Cunningham, Winston-Salem	.919	20	33	1	3	0
Eierman, Lynchburg	.982	116	208	9	4	4
Everett, Prince William	1.000	6	12	1	0	0
Fernandez, Winston-Salem*	1.000	18	20	0	0	0
Garland, Prince William	.982	32	54	1	1	0
Giles, Kinston*	.987	42	74	3	1	1
Glanville, Winston-Salem	.978	120	293	12	7	4
Godin, Frederick	.969	65	118	7	4	1
Graham, Lynchburg	.981	84	152	3	3	0
Green, Salem	.939	34	60	2	4	0
Harvey, Kinston*	.978	54	87	4	2	1
Heath, Durham	.946	123	217	12	13	6
Hughes, Durham	.949	120	197	7	11	1
Hunter, Peninsula	.958	15	23	0	1	0
Johnson, Durham	1.000	7	8	0	0	0
Kapano, Winston-Salem	.927	64	72	4	6	0
Karcher, Durham*	1.000	1	0	1	0	0
KOWITZ, Durham*	.991	105	205	6	2	3
Leach, Prince William*	.974	117	249	9	7	3
Little, Winston-Salem	.962	30	50	1	2	0
Moore, Lynchburg	.964	63	104	2	4	0
Morrison, Lynchburg	.979	74	134	6	3	0
Mouton, Prince William	.931	41	49	5	4	2
Neff, Salem	.957	57	78	11	4	0
Nieves, Durham	.970	30	61	4	2	0
O'Connor, Durham	.959	54	66	4	3	1
Ortiz, Frederick	.969	42	87	8	3	2
Perry, Kinston	.920	14	23	0	2	0
Pezzoni, Peninsula	.951	20	37	2	2	0
M. Ramirez, Kinston	.956	81	128	3	6	0
O. Ramirez, Kinston	.980	110	236	13	5	4
Rappoli, Lynchburg	.986	105	202	8	3	2
Robertson, Prince William*	.991	67	113	1	1	0
Ronca, Salem	.947	18	18	0	1	0
Sanchez, Durham*	1.000	23	25	1	0	0
Schreiber, Salem	1.000	1	1	0	0	0
Schroeder, Salem*	1.000	1	1	0	0	0
Speakman, Peninsula	1.000	3	1	0	0	0
Strickland, Prince William	.917	21	31	2	3	0
Taylor, Peninsula	.956	52	80	6	4	0
Terrell, Peninsula	.973	94	170	12	5	2
Thomas, Salem	.958	85	175	9	8	1
Timmons, Winston-Salem	.990	51	90	7	1	1
Torres, Winston-Salem	.969	126	205	17	7	3
Twitty, Peninsula	.974	28	37	0	1	0
Van Tiger, Kinston	1.000	12	15	1	0	0
Viera, Prince William*	.959	52	116	2	5	0
Wawruck, Frederick*	.954	95	118	7	6	0
Welch, Winston-Salem	.917	8	21	1	2	0
Whitmore, Kinston	.960	120	184	6	8	1
Wilder, Peninsula	.931	99	150	13	12	3
Wilson, Peninsula	.500	1	1	0	1	0

Triple play—Eierman.

CATCHERS

Player, Team	Pct.	G	PO	A	E	DP	PB
Berni, Lynchburg	1.000	9	33	8	0	0	1
BRADBURY, Peninsula	.994	83	578	64	4	9	5
Carroll, Lynchburg	.980	64	383	48	9	3	10
Cuevas, Durham	.992	31	109	21	1	0	4
Donahue, Kinston	1.000	1	1	0	0	0	0
Edge, Salem	.993	62	359	62	3	4	7
Erdman, Winston-Salem	.991	63	367	61	4	4	6
Figga, Prince William	1.000	3	27	1	0	0	0
Gabbani, Winston-Salem	.973	12	62	9	2	0	4
Hanel, Salem	.989	73	407	60	5	6	7
Houston, Durham	.979	71	456	54	11	3	12
Lohry, Prince William	.971	52	309	27	10	0	11
Lorms, Kinston	.980	49	310	32	7	4	9
Martindale, Kinston	.983	99	673	90	13	8	16
McKeel, Lynchburg	.973	86	525	90	17	8	22
Morales, Peninsula	.972	55	315	33	10	3	2
Motuzas, Prince William	.988	58	371	41	5	3	15
Ripplemeyer, Durham	.993	56	361	46	3	7	8
Rodarte, Peninsula	1.000	3	1	0	0	0	0
Roso, Frederick	.982	41	257	22	5	4	8
Salcedo, Prince William	.950	38	227	18	13	0	14
Speakman, Peninsula	1.000	6	10	0	0	0	1
Swail, Durham	1.000	7	13	1	0	1	0
Taylor, Winston-Salem	.982	70	391	53	8	5	6
Torres, Salem	.981	17	92	9	2	2	2
Wilson, Peninsula	.964	10	71	10	3	1	1
Zaun, Frederick	.979	105	746	91	18	10	6

PITCHERS

Player, Team	Pct.	G	PO	A	E	DP
Alicano, Winston-Salem*	1.000	13	1	6	0	1
Allen, Kinston	1.000	10	4	10	0	1
Alvarez, Salem	.842	28	2	14	3	2
Anderson, Frederick*	.880	19	5	17	3	2
Bailey, Lynchburg	1.000	49	4	15	0	2
Bicknell, Peninsula	.850	28	14	20	6	1
Borowski, Frederick	1.000	48	2	9	0	0
Bradford, Winston-Salem	1.000	6	3	6	0	2
Brimhall, Frederick	1.000	2	1	1	0	0
Brown, Kinston	1.000	4	2	1	0	0
Bryant, Kinston*	.900	27	5	31	4	0
Budrewicz, Winston-Salem	.933	16	3	11	1	0
Burlingame, Winston-Salem	.952	31	14	26	2	3
Caruso, Lynchburg	.960	49	6	18	1	1
Cheetham, Winston-Salem	.818	7	3	6	2	1
Chiles, Durham	.880	31	8	14	3	1
Christiansen, Salem*	1.000	38	3	5	0	0
Cofer, Kinston	.765	24	3	10	4	1
Correa, Winston-Salem	1.000	34	6	7	0	1
Cummings, Peninsula*	.913	27	11	31	4	3
Curtis, Kinston*	.833	18	2	3	1	1
Darwin, Peninsula	.917	32	11	11	2	1
Davis, Lynchburg	.714	10	1	4	2	0
Dedrick, Frederick	.897	38	4	31	4	3
Delgado, Winston-Salem	.969	28	11	20	1	1
Dennison, Lynchburg*	.857	28	6	12	3	1
Doss, Winston-Salem	.947	14	7	11	1	2
Dunbar, Prince William*	.933	44	4	24	2	1
Embree, Kinston*	.955	15	2	19	1	1
Estrada, Lynchburg	.946	28	12	23	2	2
Evans, Salem	1.000	15	2	8	0	2
Farrar, Frederick*	.907	28	7	32	4	0
Fitzer, Peninsula*	1.000	26	1	6	0	0
Frazier, Prince William	.722	16	3	10	5	0
Furcal, Peninsula*	1.000	6	1	0	0	0
Garcia, Kinston	.833	10	3	7	2	1
Gilbert, Prince William	.000	3	0	0	1	0
Greer, Prince William	1.000	13	3	5	0	0
Hailey, Durham*	.786	34	5	6	3	0
Harrah, Salem	.946	32	12	23	2	2
Hernandez, Kinston	.875	8	1	6	1	0
Hines, Prince William*	.931	25	8	19	2	2
Hodges, Prince William	.909	9	3	7	1	0
Holman, Peninsula	.600	13	1	2	2	0
Hope, Salem	.977	27	10	32	1	4
Hostetler, Durham	.933	13	6	8	1	2
Hunter, Salem	1.000	19	0	5	0	0
Johnson, Kinston	.789	11	4	11	4	0
Jones, Salem	1.000	13	3	9	0	0
Jones, Frederick	.900	7	4	5	1	1
Kenny, Winston-Salem	1.000	7	2	9	0	1
Kirk, Winston-Salem	.949	48	12	25	2	3
Klvac, Lynchburg*	.900	46	4	5	1	1
Konopki, Lynchburg	1.000	34	6	13	0	2
Kostich, Peninsula*	1.000	33	6	18	0	1
Kovach, Kinston	.939	35	12	19	2	2

Player, Team	Pct.	G	PO	A	E	DP
Krahenbuhl, Winston-Salem	.750	11	0	3	1	0
Krivda, Frederick*	.833	9	2	3	1	0
Kutzler, Winston-Salem	1.000	6	2	4	0	0
Leahy, Durham	1.000	23	2	5	0	0
Lomon, Durham	.900	27	11	25	4	2
Lopez, Kinston	.867	10	5	8	2	0
Malone, Prince William*	1.000	32	1	6	0	0
Manon, Prince William	.971	17	9	24	1	1
McCarthy, Kinston*	1.000	23	2	2	0	1
McCurry, Salem	.944	30	5	12	1	2
Mooney, Salem	.944	11	1	16	1	1
Morgan, Kinston	1.000	12	2	5	0	0
O'Donnell, Peninsula	.938	30	10	5	1	0
Ogea, Kinston	.872	21	8	26	5	2
Parkinson, Salem	.885	24	5	18	3	3
Paveloff, Frederick	1.000	51	10	7	0	0
Pennington, Frederick*	.000	8	0	0	3	0
Perez, Winston-Salem	.900	24	12	15	3	0
Pitcher, Peninsula	1.000	15	4	3	0	0
Plantenberg, Lynchburg*	1.000	21	5	13	0	0
Plaster, Frederick	.885	27	7	16	3	1
Polak, Prince William	1.000	52	3	18	0	0
Polasek, Frederick*	1.000	14	4	5	0	0
Potts, Durham*	.949	30	8	29	2	2
Prybylinski, Prince William	.958	26	11	12	1	1
Quirico, Prince William*	.853	23	5	24	5	1
Ralph, Prince William	1.000	32	4	20	0	2
Rees, Peninsula*	.972	27	6	29	1	1
Renko, Lynchburg	.833	6	2	3	1	0
Reyes, Durham	1.000	21	2	10	0	0
Ritter, Durham	.912	30	8	23	3	3
Rivera, Kinston*	.920	24	6	17	2	1
Robertson, Salem*	.833	6	2	8	2	1
Rodriguez, Lynchburg	.971	25	9	24	1	2
Ruebel, Salem*	.895	13	1	16	2	0
Rumer, Prince William*	.935	23	4	25	2	1
Rush, Lynchburg	1.000	15	2	3	0	0
Russell, Peninsula	.926	27	11	39	4	2
Ryan, Frederick	.929	27	8	18	2	0
Rychel, Salem	.833	37	0	5	1	0
Ryder, Durham	1.000	42	7	19	0	0
Seiler, Prince William*	1.000	16	1	5	0	0
SELE, Lynchburg	1.000	20	9	23	0	0
Short, Prince William	1.000	4	1	2	0	0
Smith, Prince William	.909	36	3	7	1	0
Sosa, Salem	1.000	4	1	6	0	0
Sparma, Durham	.860	21	12	25	6	1
Steinmetz, Durham	.944	26	7	10	1	3
Stone, Kinston	1.000	25	3	10	0	1
Sullivan, Peninsula	1.000	32	3	9	0	1
Sweeney, Kinston	1.000	28	5	5	0	1
Szczepanski, Winston-Salem*	.958	60	8	15	1	3
Tatterson, Kinston	1.000	6	0	2	0	0
Taylor, Winston-Salem	.875	62	8	13	3	1
Taylor, Frederick	1.000	27	2	8	0	0
Tellers, Salem	1.000	32	0	12	0	2
Tippitt, Frederick	1.000	27	0	7	0	0
Vanegmond, Lynchburg	.973	28	11	25	1	0
Vasquez, Durham	1.000	15	8	13	0	0
Watson, Salem*	.933	30	2	12	1	0
WEISS, Winston-Salem	1.000	35	13	19	0	1
White, Salem	.906	18	7	22	3	3
Wiley, Peninsula	1.000	43	4	18	0	0
Williams, Durham	.917	53	3	19	2	1
Winiarski, Kinston	1.000	43	6	8	0	0
Woodall, Durham*	.875	24	1	6	1	1
Young, Lynchburg	1.000	13	4	4	0	0
Youngblood, Peninsula	.800	21	2	6	2	0

The following players did not have any fielding statistics at the positions indicated or appeared only as a designated hitter, pinch-hitter or pinch-runner: R. Bailey, p; Beasley, p; Blumberg, p; Bradbury, 3b, p; Bragg, 2b, p; Brittain, of; Carey, dh; Cuevas, p; Donahue, of; Garland, p; Gibbs, p; Graham, p; Harvey, p; Kapano, p; Karcher, p; Kostich, of; Lewis, dh; Lorms, of, p; Malzone, p; Marin, 2b; Millares, p; Morales, of; O'Connor, 3b; Perkins, p; D. Ramirez, p; Ricci, p; Ripplemeyer, of; Sackinsky, p; C. Smith, of, p; Strickland, 2b; Swail, 1b; W. Taylor, ss; Tidwell, p; Twitty, 3b; Waldenberger, 3b; Wilson, 2b; Zaun, 2b.

LEAGUE CHAMPIONS

Year	Team	Pct.	Year	Team	Pct.	Year	Team	Pct.
1945—	Danville	.681	1963—	Kinston§	.538	1977—	Lynchburg	.591
1946—	Greensboro	.599		Greensboro§	.590		Peninsula‡	.556
	Raleigh (2nd)+	.563		Wilson (2nd)+	.535	1978—	Peninsula	.696
1947—	Burlington	.613	1964—	Kinston§	.572		Lynchburg‡	.614
	Raleigh (3rd)+	.574		Winston-Salem§+	.590	1979—	Winston-Salem a	.607
1948—	Raleigh	.592	1965—	Peninsula§	.597	1980—	Peninsula‡	.714
	Martinsville (2nd)+	.570		Durham§	.580		Durham	.600
1949—	Danville	.601		Tidewater+	.528	1981—	Peninsula	.522
	Burlington (4th)+	.500	1966—	Kinston§	.547		Hagerstown‡	.507
1950—	Winston-Salem*	.693		Winston-Salem§	.586	1982—	Alexandria‡	.597
1951—	Durham	.600		Rocky Mount+	.533		Durham	.588
	Wins-Salem (2nd)+	.583	1967—	Durham x (West.)	.536	1983—	Lynchburg	.691
1952—	Raleigh	.581		Raleigh (East.)	.542		Winston-Salem	.529
	Reidsville (4th)+	.536	1968—	Salem (West.)	.607	1984—	Lynchburg‡	.645
1953—	Raleigh	.593		Ral-Dur (East.)	.597		Durham	.486
	Danville (2nd)+	.572		HP-Thom. y (W.)	.493	1985—	Lynchburg	.679
1954—	Fayetteville*	.628	1969—	Rocky M (East.)	.569		Winston-Salem‡	.417
1955—	HP-Thomasville	.580		Salem (West.)	.542	1986—	Hagerstown	.655
	Danville (2nd)+	.533		Ral-Dur z (East.)	.560		Winston-Salem‡	.594
1956—	HP-Thomasville	.591	1970—	Winston-Salem‡	.586	1987—	Salem‡	.576
	Fayetteville (4th)§	.523		Burlington	.597		Kinston	.536
1957—	Durham	.632	1971—	Peninsula‡	.647	1988—	Kinston§	.629
	HP-Thomasville	.622		Kinston	.623		Lynchburg	.486
1958—	Danville	.576	1972—	Salem‡	.657	1989—	Durham	.609
	Burlington (4th)+	.511		Burlington	.632		Prince William‡	.522
1959—	Raleigh	.600	1973—	Lynchburg	.588	1990—	Kinston	.652
	Wilson (2nd)+	.550		Winston-Salem‡	.557		Frederick‡	.544
1960—	Greensboro‡	.636	1974—	Salem	.671	1991—	Kinston‡	.645
	Burlington	.586		Salem	.582		Lynchburg	.482
1961—	Wilson	.594	1975—	Rocky Mount	.667	1992—	Lynchburg	.570
1962—	Durham	.636		Rocky Mount	.614		Peninsula‡	.536
	Wilson	.600	1976—	Winston-Salem	.618			
	Kinston (2nd)+	.593		Winston-Salem	.551			

*Won championship and four-club playoff. +Won four-club playoff. ‡Won split-season playoff. §League was divided into Eastern, Western divisions. xWon eight-club, two-division playoff. yWon eight-club, two-division playoff against Raleigh-Durham. zWon eight-club, two-division playoff against Burlington. aWon both halves of split season (no playoffs).

FLORIDA STATE LEAGUE

FINAL STANDINGS

FIRST HALF

EAST DIVISION

Team	W	L	T	Pct.	GB
West Palm Beach (Expos)	39	30	0	.565	......
St. Lucie (Mets)	35	34	0	.507	4
Fort Lauderdale (Yankees)	31	37	0	.456	7½
Vero Beach (Dodgers)	29	38	0	.433	9

CENTRAL DIVISION

Team	W	L	T	Pct.	GB
Osceola (Astros)	42	26	0	.618	......
Baseball City (Royals)	38	31	0	.551	4½
Lakeland (Tigers)	35	34	0	.507	7½
Winter Haven (Red Sox)	22	47	0	.319	20½

WEST DIVISION

Team	W	L	T	Pct.	GB
Sarasota (White Sox)	50	19	0	.725	......
Clearwater (Phillies)	38	31	0	.551	12
Charlotte (Rangers)	38	32	0	.543	12½
Dunedin (Blue Jays)	36	34	0	.514	14½
St. Petersburg (Cardinals)	27	42	0	.391	23
Miracle (Independent)	22	47	0	.319	28

SECOND HALF

EAST DIVISION

Team	W	L	T	Pct.	GB
St. Lucie (Mets)	39	28	0	.582	......
West Palm Beach (Expos)	37	31	0	.544	2½
Fort Lauderdale (Yankees)	28	39	0	.418	11
Vero Beach (Dodgers)	24	44	0	.353	15½

CENTRAL DIVISION

Team	W	L	T	Pct.	GB
Lakeland (Tigers)	35	28	0	.556	......
Baseball City (Royals)	33	29	0	.532	1½
Osceola (Astros)	30	36	0	.455	6½
Winter Haven (Red Sox)	29	39	0	.426	8½

WEST DIVISION

Team	W	L	T	Pct.	GB
Dunedin (Blue Jays)	42	25	0	.627	......
Clearwater (Phillies)	37	28	0	.569	4
Sarasota (White Sox)	35	29	0	.547	5½
Charlotte (Rangers)	35	30	0	.538	6
St. Petersburg (Cardinals)	30	34	0	.469	10½
Miracle (Independent)	24	38	0	.387	15½

COMPOSITE

Team	Sar.	Dun.	Clw.	WPB	StL	B.C.	Char.	Osc.	Lak.	Ft.L	St.P	V.B.	W.H.	Mir.	W	L	T	Pct.	GB
Sarasota (White Sox)	....	11	11	5	7	2	6	1	3	5	6	6	8	14	85	48	0	.639	......
Dunedin (Blue Jays)	5	....	6	1	5	5	9	3	5	4	12	7	5	11	78	59	0	.569	9
Clearwater (Phillies)	5	8	....	5	8	3	6	5	4	4	8	7	4	8	75	59	0	.560	10½
West Palm Beach (Expos)	3	7	3	....	8	5	3	4	2	11	8	13	3	6	76	61	0	.555	11
St. Lucie (Mets)	1	2	0	10	....	4	6	6	2	13	4	15	6	5	74	62	0	.544	12½
Baseball City (Royals)	2	3	5	3	4	....	3	13	13	5	0	3	12	5	71	60	0	.542	13
Charlotte (Rangers)	5	7	10	5	2	4	....	3	5	7	11	3	5	6	73	62	0	.541	13
Osceola (Astros)	6	5	3	4	2	7	5	....	9	4	6	4	13	4	72	62	0	.537	13½
Lakeland (Tigers)	5	2	2	6	5	7	1	11	....	4	4	5	12	6	70	62	0	.530	14½
Fort Lauderdale (Yankees)	3	4	4	9	7	2	1	4	3	....	2	10	4	6	59	76	0	.437	27
St. Petersburg (Cardinals)	9	4	5	0	4	6	4	2	4	6	....	4	3	6	57	76	0	.429	28
Vero Beach (Dodgers)	2	1	1	7	5	5	5	2	4	7	4	....	4	7	53	82	0	.393	33
Winter Haven (Red Sox)	0	2	3	4	2	8	3	7	8	2	5	4	....	3	51	86	0	.372	36
Miracle (Independent)	2	3	6	2	3	2	10	1	1	4	6	1	5	....	46	85	0	.351	38

Charlotte played home games in Port Charlotte, Fla.

Miracle played home games in Fort Myers, Fla.

Osceola played home games in Kissimmee, Fla.

Major league affiliations in parentheses.

Playoffs—Baseball City defeated Sarasota, two games to none; Clearwater defeated Dunedin, two games to none; Lakeland defeated West Palm Beach, two games to none; Osceola defeated St. Lucie, two games to one; Baseball City defeated Osceola, two games to one; Lakeland defeated Clearwater, two games to none; Lakeland defeated Baseball City, two games to none, to win league championship.

Regular-season attendance—Baseball City, 17,406; Charlotte, 92,996; Clearwater, 91,834; Dunedin, 74,983; Fort Lauderdale, 111,909; Lakeland, 56,951; Miracle, 105,578; Osceola, 49,857; St. Lucie, 66,899; St. Petersburg, 121,763; Sarasota, 91,574; Vero Beach, 79,555; West Palm Beach, 121,614; Winter Haven, 16,082. Total, 1,099,001. Playoffs (16 games), 6,096. All-Star Game, 5,047.

Managers—Baseball City, Ron Johnson; Charlotte, Bump Wills; Clearwater, Bill Dancy; Dunedin, Dennis Holmberg; Fort Lauderdale, Brian Butterfield; Lakeland, John Lipon; Miracle, Dan Rohn; Osceola, Sal Butera; St. Lucie, John Tamargo; St. Petersburg, Dave Bialas; Sarasota, Rick Patterson; Vero Beach, Glenn Hoffman; West Palm Beach, Dave Jauss; Winter Haven, Felix Maldonado.

All-Star team: 1B—Roberto Petagine, Osceola; 2B—Fernando Vina, St. Lucie; 3B—Howard Battle, Dunedin; SS—Brandon Wilson, Sarasota; LF—Rondell White, West Palm Beach; CF—Rob Butler, Dunedin; RF—Anthony Lewis, St. Petersburg; C—Carlos Delgado, Dunedin, and Lance Jennings, Baseball City; DH—Jay Kirkpatrick, Vero Beach; RHP—Tavo Alvarez, West Palm Beach; Steve Schrenk, Sarasota; LHP—Chris Hill, Osceola; Brien Taylor, Fort Lauderdale; Relievers—John Kelly, St. Petersburg; Jim Dougherty, Osceola; Most Valuable Player—Carlos Delgado, Dunedin; Manager—Rick Patterson, Sarasota.

BATTING

TEAM

Team	Avg.	G	AB	R	OR	H	TB	2B	3B	HR	RBI	SH	SF	HP	BB	Int. BB	SO	SB	CS	LOB
Dunedin	.263	137	4621	627	574	1214	1708	196	32	78	550	63	30	47	399	29	846	123	77	938
Sarasota	.258	133	4319	607	467	1114	1506	184	38	44	512	75	40	79	467	22	776	215	124	902
Osceola	.257	134	4448	602	591	1144	1639	207	51	62	533	35	38	55	389	18	876	162	77	876
Baseball City	.256	131	4248	532	464	1087	1459	147	36	51	459	55	32	51	414	16	880	120	89	901

Team	Avg.	G	AB	R	OR	H	TB	2B	3B	HR	RBI	SH	SF	HP	BB	Int. BB	SO	SB	CS	LOB
St. Lucie	.255	136	4369	520	507	1113	1511	174	31	54	460	25	39	41	341	21	655	142	91	809
West Palm Beach	.250	137	4554	574	456	1140	1589	183	52	54	492	42	51	65	514	34	949	130	83	998
Lakeland	.247	132	4190	527	449	1034	1436	183	33	51	462	52	53	57	411	19	664	112	67	866
Vero Beach	.245	135	4237	442	525	1037	1423	172	20	58	377	37	35	33	315	20	864	123	78	806
Charlotte	.239	135	4464	476	419	1044	1502	216	37	56	424	40	27	41	402	20	855	119	76	907
Fort Lauderdale	.236	135	4422	463	556	1044	1377	162	24	41	396	39	30	43	360	18	910	135	72	882
Clearwater	.235	134	4369	493	463	1028	1421	167	44	46	433	56	35	44	388	17	829	108	90	860
St. Petersburg	.235	133	4271	408	499	1004	1328	143	26	43	362	29	38	38	411	13	838	122	81	907
Miracle	.232	131	4284	396	547	992	1277	161	23	26	339	29	22	41	309	10	821	80	68	845
Winter Haven	.227	137	4353	435	585	986	1338	147	29	49	381	60	28	57	410	9	945	60	43	947

INDIVIDUAL

(Leading qualifiers for batting championship—378 or more plate appearances)

*Bats lefthanded.   †Switch-hitter.

Player, Team	Avg.	G	AB	R	H	TB	2B	3B	HR	RBI	SH	SF	HP	BB	Int. BB	SO	SB	CS
Butler, Rob, Dunedin*	.358	92	391	67	140	179	13	7	4	41	2	1	2	22	2	36	19	14
Delgado, Carlos, Dunedin*	.324	133	485	83	157	281	30	2	30	100	0	2	6	59	11	91	2	5
White, Rondell, West Palm Beach	.316	111	450	80	142	188	10	12	4	41	3	1	5	46	4	78	42	16
Hunter, Brian, Osceola	.299	131	489	62	146	185	18	9	1	62	6	4	5	31	0	76	39	19
Wilson, Brandon, Sarasota*	.296	103	399	68	118	164	22	6	4	54	5	2	4	45	2	64	30	16
Vina, Fernando, St. Lucie*	.295	111	421	61	124	152	15	5	1	42	4	2	3	32	2	26	36	17
Raabe, Brian, Miracle	.288	102	361	52	104	130	16	2	2	32	1	3	8	48	1	17	7	6
Wilstead, Randy, West Palm Beach*	.285	129	449	56	128	185	27	3	8	71	0	4	3	47	8	68	7	7
Vitiello, Joe, Baseball City	.283	115	400	52	113	155	16	1	8	65	0	8	7	46	1	101	0	5
Castillo, Ben, Charlotte	.282	105	347	46	98	150	25	3	7	55	1	3	2	45	0	67	6	7

Departmental leaders: G—H. Battle, 136; AB—Bowers, Davis, 524; R—Mouton, 110; H—C. Delgado, 157; TB—C. Delgado, 281; 2B—M. Burton, C. Delgado, Mouton, 30; 3B—White, 12; HR—C. Delgado, 30; RBI—C. Delgado, 100; SH—Dotel, 19; SF—Several players tied with 8; HP—Pemberton, D. Walker, 13; BB—Murray, 75; IBB—C. Delgado, 11; SO—Murray, 150; SB—Mouton, 51; CS—Donald, 21.

(All players—listed alphabetically)

Player, Team	Avg.	G	AB	R	H	TB	2B	3B	HR	RBI	SH	SF	HP	BB	Int. BB	SO	SB	CS
Abreu, Frank, St. Petersburg	.266	98	331	32	88	106	13	1	1	31	4	3	1	42	1	61	5	5
Adriana, Sharnol, Dunedin	.276	69	210	25	58	70	6	3	0	18	4	0	0	31	1	43	9	4
Albright, Eric, Lakeland	.157	25	70	4	11	17	3	0	1	7	0	1	2	6	0	16	0	0
Alder, Jimmy, Lakeland	.250	100	292	36	73	119	18	2	8	34	1	5	6	28	0	87	2	3
Alfonzo, Edgardo, St. Lucie	.000	4	5	0	0	0	0	0	0	0	0	0	0	0	0	0	0	0
Andujar, Juan, St. Petersburg	.270	104	359	37	97	132	11	9	2	29	6	3	3	20	0	77	14	12
Austin, James, West Palm Beach	.235	103	345	30	81	116	13	8	2	36	3	3	2	36	3	67	8	12
Aversa, Joe, St. Petersburg†	.159	25	44	4	7	8	1	0	0	3	0	1	0	8	0	8	0	1
Baez, Diogenes, Winter Haven*	.191	68	225	21	43	56	5	4	0	18	3	1	2	13	0	43	6	5
Barry, Jeff, St. Lucie†	.333	3	9	0	3	5	2	0	0	1	0	0	0	0	0	0	0	0
Battle, Allen, St. Petersburg	.320	60	222	34	71	87	9	2	1	15	4	2	4	35	2	38	21	11
Battle, Howard, Dunedin	.254	136	520	76	132	216	27	3	17	85	1	5	5	49	3	89	6	8
Beals, Greg, St. Lucie	.219	14	32	7	7	10	3	0	0	2	2	0	0	8	0	6	0	1
Beasley, Andy, St. Petersburg*	.180	68	200	10	36	42	6	0	0	14	0	1	0	26	1	37	0	0
Bell, Derek, Dunedin	.240	7	25	7	6	8	2	0	0	4	0	1	0	4	0	4	3	0
Bennett, Al, Clearwater	.172	44	134	9	23	38	5	2	2	13	3	2	1	5	0	38	2	1
Bethke, Jamie, Charlotte†	.133	5	15	1	2	3	1	0	0	1	0	0	0	1	0	4	0	0
Bieser, Steve, Clearwater†	.286	73	203	33	58	74	6	5	0	10	8	0	9	39	3	28	8	8
Bowers, Brent, Dunedin*	.254	128	524	74	133	158	10	3	3	46	8	1	3	34	0	99	31	15
Boyzuick, Mike, Vero Beach	.241	62	195	22	47	69	8	1	4	20	1	3	5	17	0	41	1	5
Brady, Doug, Sarasota*	.272	56	184	21	50	62	6	0	2	27	6	2	3	25	1	33	5	7
Brady, Pat, Clearwater*	.268	65	209	34	56	95	7	1	10	39	1	4	3	38	2	28	7	4
Bridges, Tony, Baseball City†	.207	43	111	17	23	27	2	1	0	8	5	0	1	16	0	28	9	2
Bright, Brian, Winter Haven	.227	52	176	16	40	53	4	0	3	16	1	1	1	8	0	32	0	2
Brito, Luis, Clearwater†	.218	65	188	18	41	45	4	0	0	11	6	1	1	5	0	21	4	7
Brooks, Eric, Dunedin	.232	30	82	7	19	25	3	0	1	6	0	0	1	6	1	16	0	0
Brown, Bryan, Winter Haven	.239	57	213	22	51	69	7	1	3	17	1	1	2	13	0	37	0	2
Brown, Mike, Vero Beach	.000	5	8	0	0	0	0	0	0	0	0	0	0	0	0	0	0	0
Brown, Randy, Winter Haven	.235	121	430	39	101	129	18	2	2	24	8	4	6	28	0	115	8	9
Bruce, Andy, St. Petersburg	.173	89	295	28	51	96	6	0	13	35	2	7	3	19	0	102	0	0
Buchanan, Shawn, Sarasota	.218	57	133	19	29	40	6	1	1	17	1	2	5	14	0	34	2	2
Buckley, Troy, Miracle	.256	121	434	26	111	134	20	0	1	44	1	6	3	29	1	59	1	2
Burbank, Dennis, Fort Lauderdale	.500	17	2	0	1	1	0	0	0	0	0	0	0	0	0	1	0	0
Burns, Michael, Osceola	.239	78	238	31	57	90	17	2	4	29	0	2	2	18	0	62	1	2
Burton, Darren, Baseball City†	.246	123	431	54	106	145	15	6	4	36	4	3	6	49	7	93	16	14
Burton, Mike, Charlotte	.260	109	396	48	103	158	30	2	7	57	0	3	3	43	2	80	4	2
Butler, Rob, Dunedin*	.358	92	391	67	140	179	13	7	4	41	2	1	2	22	2	36	19	14
Byrd, Jim, Winter Haven	.268	18	71	12	19	23	2	1	0	1	1	0	0	5	0	7	4	0
Cairo, Miguel, Vero Beach	.224	36	125	7	28	28	0	0	0	7	3	1	0	11	0	12	5	3
Calderon, Ivan, West Palm Beach	.115	9	26	2	3	3	0	0	0	2	0	0	0	4	0	6	0	0
Campbell, Don, St. Petersburg*	.160	22	50	6	8	12	2	1	0	5	0	0	1	8	0	12	4	0
Campbell, Scott, West Palm Beach*	.231	112	334	30	77	97	12	4	0	30	4	4	6	41	2	58	2	6
Cantu, Mike, St. Petersburg	.271	93	332	24	90	119	16	2	3	31	3	1	2	72	0	72	0	0
Capellan, Carlos, Baseball City	.263	11	38	7	10	10	0	0	0	2	1	0	0	7	0	3	2	0
Caple, Kyle, Miracle	.200	8	25	1	5	5	0	0	0	2	0	0	1	0	0	6	0	0
Caraballo, Gary, Baseball City	.289	67	239	30	69	98	9	4	4	40	3	4	6	24	1	43	6	3
Carbajal, Nilson, West Palm Beach	.000	1	1	0	0	0	0	0	0	0	0	0	0	0	0	1	0	0
Carvajal, Jovino, Fort Lauderdale†	.230	113	435	53	100	112	7	1	1	29	3	4	1	30	0	63	40	14
Cassels, Chris, West Palm Beach	.200	27	85	8	17	29	3	0	3	12	0	3	1	8	0	19	0	0
Castellano, Miguel, Charlotte	.247	120	442	38	109	145	25	1	3	42	3	2	2	21	3	55	3	7
Castillo, Alberto, St. Lucie	.204	60	162	11	33	48	6	0	3	17	3	2	2	16	0	37	0	0
Castillo, Ben, Charlotte	.282	105	347	46	98	150	25	3	7	55	1	3	2	45	0	67	6	7
Castleberry, Kevin, Sarasota*	.286	24	98	16	28	32	4	0	0	10	1	1	2	14	0	12	8	3
Cholowsky, Dan, St. Petersburg	.284	59	201	19	57	68	4	0	1	17	1	4	2	33	0	31	14	10
Christopherson, Gary, Osceola	.196	40	112	11	22	37	6	0	3	14	0	2	2	13	0	18	1	1

Player, Team	Avg.	G	AB	R	H	TB	2B	3B	HR	RBI	SH	SF	HP	BB	Int. BB	SO	SB	CS
Clem, Bradford, Miracle*	.135	21	52	4	7	8	1	0	0	0	1	0	1	1	0	18	0	0
Clinton, Jim, Charlotte	.176	92	239	27	42	54	5	2	1	15	9	0	2	19	0	64	9	2
Cole, Butch, Baseball City	.298	90	292	43	87	109	16	0	2	38	1	4	4	13	2	33	10	6
Coleman, Ken, Sarasota†	.261	100	299	52	78	108	16	4	2	31	10	3	10	35	1	41	14	7
Coleman, Paul, St. Petersburg	.271	21	70	10	19	23	1	0	1	7	0	1	2	2	0	14	3	0
Coleman, Vince, St. Lucie†	.364	6	22	4	8	8	0	0	0	2	0	0	0	2	0	6	3	0
Collier, Anthony, Vero Beach*	.323	67	232	26	75	111	16	4	4	35	1	1	1	17	2	37	3	1
Colon, Felix, Winter Haven	.245	97	339	33	83	118	14	3	5	40	0	1	5	36	2	75	1	1
Corbin, Ted, Miracle†	.201	62	179	18	36	41	5	0	0	11	5	1	5	16	0	30	1	3
Coughlin, Kevin, Sarasota*	.271	81	291	39	79	91	7	1	1	28	8	1	2	22	1	51	14	4
Crispin, Carlos, Osceola†	.000	3	2	0	0	0	0	0	0	0	0	0	0	1	0	1	0	0
Cruz, Ruben, Osceola	.247	108	369	24	91	104	8	1	1	47	2	5	6	23	4	41	5	4
Damon, Johnny, Baseball City*	.000	1	1	0	0	0	0	0	0	0	0	0	0	0	0	0	0	0
Dando, Pat, Baseball City*	.281	94	260	31	73	115	12	3	8	32	1	0	1	16	2	48	2	2
Daniel, Mike, West Palm Beach	.215	72	237	28	51	78	13	1	4	27	1	6	4	24	0	53	3	3
Davis, Jay, St. Lucie*	.281	134	524	56	147	179	15	7	1	36	2	3	6	7	0	70	21	17
DeLeon, Huascar, Baseball City	.200	2	5	0	1	1	0	0	0	1	0	0	0	0	0	1	0	0
DeLeon, Yabanne, Baseball City	.077	16	39	1	3	3	0	0	0	2	0	0	0	1	0	14	0	0
Delgado, Alex, Winter Haven	.210	56	167	11	35	43	2	0	2	12	4	1	1	16	0	11	1	1
Delgado, Carlos, Dunedin*	.324	133	485	83	157	281	30	2	30	100	0	2	6	59	11	91	2	5
Deller, Robert, Fort Lauderdale*	.254	52	177	23	45	66	10	4	1	19	0	0	0	12	1	41	3	5
Demerson, Tim, Fort Lauderdale	.182	51	165	17	30	36	4	1	0	4	1	1	3	14	0	38	7	4
Demus, Joe, Winter Haven†	.200	4	10	1	2	2	0	0	0	1	0	0	0	0	0	4	0	0
Difelice, Mike, St. Petersburg	.226	17	53	0	12	15	3	0	0	4	0	0	2	0	0	11	0	0
Dimare, Gino, Winter Haven*	.267	22	30	8	8	8	0	0	0	1	0	0	4	5	0	5	2	1
DiSarcina, Glenn, Sarasota*	.000	1	4	0	0	0	0	0	0	0	0	0	0	0	0	1	0	0
Donald, Tremayne, St. Petersburg†	.228	112	372	41	85	95	6	2	0	22	2	1	3	38	1	63	34	21
Dotel, Mariano, Dunedin†	.191	116	372	48	71	84	8	1	1	19	19	1	1	26	0	99	7	4
Dunn, Brian, St. Lucie	.000	2	5	0	0	0	0	0	0	0	0	0	0	0	0	3	0	0
Durham, Ray, Sarasota*	.272	57	202	37	55	67	6	3	0	7	5	0	10	32	0	36	28	8
Durkin, Marty, Winter Haven†	.247	72	219	19	54	70	10	0	2	18	5	2	0	16	0	48	3	2
Durso, Joe, Dunedin	.250	4	8	0	2	2	0	0	0	1	0	0	0	0	0	2	0	0
Ealy, Tom, Lakeland	.283	77	251	31	71	117	14	1	10	37	0	3	2	25	3	58	0	1
Eatinger, Mike, Sarasota	.244	71	225	28	55	68	7	0	2	20	5	4	2	29	0	32	6	5
Eenhoorn, Robert, Fort Lauderdale	.305	57	203	23	62	83	5	2	4	33	2	4	4	19	2	25	6	2
Eldridge, Rod, St. Petersburg	.221	30	86	8	19	27	2	0	2	6	0	0	2	5	0	23	0	0
Ellis, Paul, St. Petersburg*	.218	84	308	22	67	90	17	0	2	29	0	4	3	26	1	22	0	1
Erickson, Greg, Fort Lauderdale	.260	74	258	27	67	76	7	1	0	26	0	4	4	24	0	48	9	6
Estevez, Carlos, Miracle*	.241	56	158	13	38	58	12	1	2	22	1	1	1	10	3	40	0	0
Evangelista, George, Miracle	.231	100	303	34	70	94	12	3	2	23	2	1	3	32	0	61	4	4
Evans, Tim, Osceola*	.245	75	253	44	62	82	8	6	0	20	7	2	0	26	0	47	8	6
Everett, Carl, Fort Lauderdale†	.230	46	183	30	42	60	8	2	2	14	0	1	4	12	1	40	11	3
Farmer, Mike, Clearwater†	.241	94	303	37	73	93	10	2	2	32	2	3	2	15	0	61	12	7
Farrish, Keoki, Vero Beach	.190	74	211	17	40	43	3	0	1	8	1	0	2	11	0	59	5	3
Ferreira, Tony, Winter Haven†	.228	95	250	25	57	69	6	3	0	17	9	1	2	50	0	48	6	7
Figga, Mike, Fort Lauderdale	.177	80	249	12	44	60	13	0	1	15	3	0	2	13	1	78	3	1
Fisk, Carlton, Sarasota	.120	7	25	3	3	7	1	0	1	2	0	0	1	3	0	6	1	0
Fitzpatrick, Rob, West Palm Beach	.256	96	336	42	86	129	19	0	8	37	1	0	2	37	1	81	4	3
Flannelly, Tim, Fort Lauderdale*	.295	62	224	31	66	84	9	3	1	18	0	2	4	21	2	25	6	1
Floyd, Cliff, West Palm Beach*	.000	1	4	0	0	0	0	0	0	1	0	0	0	0	0	1	0	0
Fraraccio, Dan, Sarasota	.333	1	3	0	1	1	0	0	0	0	0	0	0	0	0	1	0	0
Fully, Ed, St. Lucie	.252	127	397	58	100	142	20	2	6	36	5	3	4	29	1	76	14	15
Gallardo, Luis, Fort Lauderdale	.178	69	242	16	43	57	5	0	3	23	1	3	4	13	1	67	3	2
Gallego, Mike, Fort Lauderdale	.200	3	10	0	2	3	1	0	0	2	0	0	0	1	0	4	1	0
Geisler, Phil, Clearwater*	.218	120	400	39	87	121	10	3	6	33	1	2	4	41	1	88	4	9
Geren, Bob, Winter Haven	.304	7	23	3	7	10	0	0	1	2	0	0	0	1	1	5	0	0
Gilliam, Bo, Fort Lauderdale	.220	97	350	36	77	132	16	0	13	50	0	3	6	4	1	83	6	5
Gilmore, Tony, Osceola	.207	80	266	26	55	65	7	0	1	21	1	1	4	17	2	46	1	5
Givens, Jim, Lakeland†	.241	124	456	51	110	131	15	3	0	29	12	3	1	27	2	50	18	13
Gonzalez, Freddy, Vero Beach	.248	90	303	32	75	121	14	1	10	31	1	1	1	14	1	87	13	7
Gonzalez, Pedro, Lakeland	.296	32	81	15	24	34	7	0	1	13	1	0	2	19	0	9	1	0
Gray, Dan, Vero Beach	.242	10	33	4	8	11	1	1	0	5	2	0	0	2	0	2	0	0
Green, Shawn, Dunedin*	.273	114	417	44	114	164	21	3	1	49	5	8	4	28	0	66	22	9
Griffin, Tim, Vero Beach	.254	45	134	21	34	48	6	1	2	14	1	1	1	21	0	39	1	4
Grifol, Pedro, Miracle	.228	94	333	24	76	103	13	1	4	32	3	1	2	17	1	38	1	0
Groppuso, Mike, Osceola	.217	115	369	53	80	113	19	1	4	37	3	3	9	43	2	98	6	3
Gumpf, John, Miracle	.247	78	223	21	55	69	6	1	2	9	0	0	0	18	2	79	2	4
Haase, Dean, Sarasota*	.213	30	47	6	10	10	0	0	0	5	0	0	0	6	2	5	1	0
Hajek, Dave, Osceola	.111	5	18	3	2	3	1	0	0	1	0	0	0	1	0	1	0	0
Halter, Shane, Baseball City	.239	44	117	11	28	32	1	0	1	14	5	4	0	24	0	31	5	5
Hamelin, Bob, Baseball City*	.273	11	44	7	12	17	0	1	1	6	0	0	0	2	0	11	0	0
Hankins, Mike, Fort Lauderdale†	.301	75	259	35	78	83	5	0	0	15	5	1	2	40	1	27	6	3
Hanlon, Larry, Charlotte	.245	102	347	33	85	114	24	1	1	25	6	5	3	32	0	67	11	10
Hansen, Elston, Fort Lauderdale	.241	45	162	16	39	49	10	0	0	15	2	0	4	14	1	33	0	1
Hardge, Mike, West Palm Beach	.333	4	15	3	5	6	1	0	0	0	0	0	2	0	0	5	2	0
Harmes, Kris, Dunedin*	.275	21	51	7	14	19	2	0	1	6	2	0	3	7	0	13	0	0
Harris, James, St. Lucie	.202	83	252	22	51	72	9	0	4	25	0	4	2	28	1	32	2	0
Hatcher, Chris, Osceola	.281	97	367	49	103	185	19	6	17	68	0	5	5	20	1	97	11	0
Hawkins, Craig, Miracle†	.266	34	124	18	33	37	4	0	0	9	0	0	1	14	0	21	15	7
Hecker, Doug, Winter Haven	.239	59	209	22	50	80	12	0	6	32	2	1	3	18	0	47	0	0
Henderson, Pedro, Miracle	.111	13	36	2	4	5	1	0	0	2	0	0	0	6	0	16	1	0
Henderson, Ramon, Clearwater	.154	5	13	1	2	3	1	0	0	3	0	0	0	2	0	4	0	0
Hernandez, Kiki, Fort Lauderdale	.111	3	9	1	1	1	0	0	0	1	0	0	0	2	0	2	0	0
Herrera, Edgar, Miracle	.129	12	31	0	4	4	0	0	0	1	0	0	0	0	0	11	0	0
Herrera, Ezequiel, St. Petersburg	.200	63	165	11	33	37	4	0	0	11	0	1	1	20	0	23	1	2
Hodge, Tim, Dunedin*	.231	83	238	29	55	92	13	0	8	36	3	0	7	24	2	68	5	5
Holland, Sid, Charlotte	.175	80	228	18	40	49	3	3	0	15	5	0	2	18	1	67	4	2
Hood, Randy, Sarasota	.225	67	138	19	31	38	5	1	0	12	6	1	5	18	0	28	0	1
Howard, Dave, Baseball City†	.444	3	9	3	4	5	1	0	0	1	0	0	0	2	0	0	5	0
Howard, Ron, Lakeland†	.241	100	344	61	83	110	13	4	2	21	7	1	3	50	0	53	14	7
Howell, David, St. Petersburg*	.277	31	101	10	28	33	3	0	0	6	1	1	2	11	0	9	1	0
Huckaby, Ken, Vero Beach	.241	73	261	14	63	72	9	0	0	21	2	2	1	7	0	42	1	1
Hunter, Brian, Osceola	.299	131	489	62	146	185	18	9	1	62	6	4	5	31	0	76	39	19
Huskey, Butch, St. Lucie	.254	134	493	65	125	198	17	1	18	75	0	5	3	33	6	74	7	3
Hyde, Mickey, Clearwater	.302	46	139	21	42	61	10	3	1	21	0	1	0	7	1	18	4	5

— 426 —

Player, Team	Avg.	G	AB	R	H	TB	2B	3B	HR	RBI	SH	SF	HP	BB	Int. BB	SO	SB	CS
Hyers, Tim, Dunedin*	.246	124	464	54	114	168	24	3	8	59	2	5	3	41	4	54	2	1
Jackson, Jeff, Clearwater	.242	79	297	35	72	105	11	2	6	36	0	2	4	23	2	78	6	6
Jacobs, Frank, St. Lucie*	.249	123	434	55	108	173	23	3	12	55	0	5	4	35	2	78	3	3
Jenkins, Brett, West Palm Beach	.262	99	362	39	95	132	21	2	4	45	1	1	5	22	3	45	8	5
Jennings, Lance, Baseball City	.259	51	174	16	45	73	7	0	7	24	1	1	2	15	0	44	0	0
Johnson, Mark, Baseball City*	.277	27	94	15	26	36	2	4	0	9	0	0	1	10	0	7	3	1
Jose, Felix, St. Petersburg†	.444	6	18	2	8	11	1	1	0	2	0	0	0	1	0	2	1	0
Keighley, Steve, West Palm Beach	.240	46	121	20	29	37	6	1	0	16	6	1	0	16	1	24	0	1
Kennedy, Darryl, Charlotte	.464	13	28	3	13	17	4	0	0	6	0	0	0	3	0	3	0	1
King, Jason, St. Lucie†	.295	51	122	20	36	43	5	1	0	10	2	1	1	22	1	11	8	2
Kirkpatrick, Jay, Vero Beach*	.281	114	385	32	108	152	22	2	6	50	1	6	4	31	4	82	2	2
Kliafas, Stephen, Vero Beach	.250	15	52	7	13	14	1	0	0	3	1	0	1	2	0	9	4	0
Krause, Ron, West Palm Beach*	.250	108	360	40	90	120	8	8	2	35	8	3	9	42	2	74	11	8
Lambert, Layne, Osceola*	.258	71	217	22	56	74	9	3	1	24	1	2	2	28	2	37	4	8
Landinez, Carlos, St. Petersburg	.214	21	42	7	9	10	1	0	0	2	1	0	0	4	0	11	0	2
Lane, Nolan, Miracle	.215	94	326	38	70	102	11	3	5	29	4	4	2	34	0	65	23	14
Ledesma, Aaron, St. Lucie	.263	134	456	51	120	147	17	2	2	50	2	7	11	46	1	66	20	12
Levangie, Dana, Winter Haven	.192	76	245	21	47	55	5	0	1	22	1	3	2	20	0	49	1	2
Lewis, Anthony, St. Petersburg*	.222	128	454	50	101	168	18	2	15	55	1	4	5	46	6	105	2	4
Loeb, Marc, Dunedin	.222	4	9	3	2	2	0	0	0	0	0	0	0	5	0	1	0	0
Lott, Billy, Vero Beach	.246	126	435	42	107	141	17	4	3	35	2	5	3	22	3	107	11	5
Lowery, David, Charlotte†	.277	125	459	66	127	170	22	9	1	32	3	5	53	6	45	24	15
Luce, Roger, Charlotte	.231	91	303	18	70	82	9	0	1	20	1	2	3	19	1	77	3	4
Luis, Joe, Winter Haven*	.250	1	4	0	1	1	0	0	0	0	0	0	0	0	0	1	0	0
Lund, Ed, Vero Beach	.246	60	167	17	41	57	7	0	3	14	4	1	4	15	1	22	1	3
Madril, Bill, Winter Haven	.240	16	50	2	12	15	3	0	0	5	0	0	0	5	0	11	0	1
Mahay, Ron, Winter Haven*	.254	19	63	6	16	20	2	1	0	4	1	0	0	2	0	19	0	1
Malave, Jose, Winter Haven	.160	8	25	1	4	4	0	0	0	0	0	0	0	0	0	11	0	0
Malinoski, Chris, West Palm Beach	.276	66	228	31	63	72	9	0	0	30	2	7	3	22	0	39	3	2
Martinez, Angel, Dunedin	.200	4	15	4	3	10	1	0	2	4	0	0	1	0	0	3	0	0
Martinez, Ernie, Osceola*	.091	6	22	1	2	3	1	0	0	0	0	0	0	0	0	2	0	0
Martinez, Hector, Dunedin	.333	2	6	1	2	2	0	0	0	1	1	0	0	0	0	0	0	0
Martinez, Sandy, Vero Beach†	.214	5	14	3	3	3	0	0	0	0	0	0	0	0	0	3	0	0
McClinton, Tim, St. Lucie	.172	86	250	24	43	65	7	3	3	32	0	2	1	32	4	76	10	12
McDonald, Chad, West Palm Beach	.200	40	130	11	26	37	3	1	2	6	1	1	5	18	2	20	0	1
McKamie, Sean, Vero Beach	.229	43	118	14	27	29	0	1	0	11	3	0	0	6	0	21	11	5
McNamara, Denny, Lakeland	.232	98	293	32	68	87	9	2	2	36	4	8	6	37	4	57	11	6
Medina, Facaner, Sarasota†	.286	11	14	0	4	5	1	0	0	2	0	0	0	0	0	5	0	0
Mejia, Roberto, Vero Beach	.248	96	330	42	82	137	17	1	12	40	0	5	2	37	4	60	14	10
Meyer, Rick, Clearwater	.219	98	301	18	66	80	9	1	1	22	6	2	0	18	1	77	6	6
Millan, Bernie, St. Lucie†	.271	77	262	26	71	86	8	2	1	23	1	0	0	12	2	24	1	2
Miller, Scott, Dunedin	.250	35	104	15	24	31	5	1	0	9	1	1	2	9	0	32	7	5
Miranda, Geovany, 7 BC- 18 Sar -43 Mir ...	.276	68	185	20	51	58	3	2	0	13	3	1	2	9	0	32	7	5
Moore, Kerwin, Baseball City†	.238	66	248	39	59	66	2	1	1	10	4	1	2	40	1	67	26	9
Morillo, Cesar, Baseball City†	.167	35	102	8	17	24	7	0	0	7	3	1	1	10	0	23	1	0
Morrow, Timmie, Charlotte	.232	108	384	48	89	143	11	5	11	40	3	1	8	23	2	64	17	10
Mota, Willie, Miracle†	.273	106	384	40	105	136	15	2	4	40	2	1	2	25	2	36	1	2
Mouton, James, Osceola	.282	133	507	110	143	218	30	6	11	62	9	5	8	71	3	78	51	11
Mulville, Duane, Clearwater	.257	57	179	20	46	61	12	0	1	14	0	0	0	10	0	28	3	1
Murphy, Shaun, West Palm Beach	.205	86	249	28	51	61	6	2	0	21	0	1	4	32	4	83	2	5
Murray, Glenn, West Palm Beach	.232	119	414	79	96	159	14	5	13	41	2	1	4	75	3	150	26	11
Nagashima, Kazushige, Vero Beach	.235	79	226	25	53	88	10	2	7	26	2	2	0	26	2	60	1	1
Nevers, Tom, Osceola	.251	125	455	49	114	174	24	6	8	55	2	1	3	22	1	124	6	2
Newkirk, Craig, Charlotte	.209	123	368	34	77	99	16	0	2	24	5	1	5	50	3	57	13	6
Noriega, Rey, Fort Lauderdale†	.222	99	338	41	75	121	19	6	5	38	1	1	1	41	5	86	12	2
Nunez, Alex, Miracle*	.122	34	82	6	10	11	1	0	0	3	0	0	0	3	0	25	3	0
Nunez, Rogelio, Sarasota†	.216	101	282	24	61	70	3	0	2	32	5	1	1	23	0	68	19	13
O'Donnell, Steve, Vero Beach	.170	36	106	11	18	28	4	0	2	6	1	0	1	7	0	24	0	2
O'Neal, Kelley, Lakeland*	.256	103	340	48	87	113	11	3	3	20	6	2	6	21	0	61	21	7
Ollison, Scott, Clearwater	.120	25	75	6	9	9	0	0	0	3	4	0	0	8	0	16	3	0
Otanez, Willis, Vero Beach	.221	117	390	27	86	113	18	0	3	27	5	3	4	24	0	60	2	4
Otero, Ricky, St. Lucie†	.318	40	151	20	48	64	8	4	0	19	3	2	2	9	1	11	10	5
Ozuna, Mateo, St. Petersburg	.172	50	169	12	29	32	3	0	0	8	3	0	3	12	0	23	18	7
Pagliarulo, Mike, Miracle*	.200	6	20	2	4	6	2	0	0	2	0	0	0	4	0	2	1	0
Pemberton, Rudy, Lakeland	.265	104	343	41	91	126	16	5	3	43	2	3	13	21	2	37	25	10
Perona, Joe, Lakeland	.220	94	286	28	63	81	6	4	0	37	6	4	5	24	0	27	2	2
Petagine, Roberto, Osceola*	.293	86	307	52	90	141	22	4	7	49	0	4	1	47	3	47	3	1
Pickett, Bobby, Winter Haven	.224	31	107	11	24	35	6	1	1	9	0	1	0	9	0	31	1	1
Pineda, Jose, Fort Lauderdale	.250	9	32	1	8	9	1	0	0	6	1	0	1	12	2	30	11	5
Pinkney, Alton, Vero Beach*	.179	40	95	16	17	18	1	0	0	6	0	0	2	28	4	47	13	9
Pledger, Kinnis, Sarasota*	.323	59	217	42	70	106	11	3	7	38	0	1	3	28	4	47	3	3
Plemmons, Ron, Sarasota*	.233	95	317	49	74	105	15	2	4	52	3	8	2	46	3	38	11	10
Ponte, Ed, Osceola	.000	7	1	0	0	0	0	0	0	0	1	0	0	1	0	0	0	0
Quintell, John, Fort Lauderdale*	.200	25	60	3	12	12	0	0	0	2	0	0	7	0	11	0	0
Raabe, Brian, Miracle	.288	102	361	52	104	130	16	2	2	32	1	3	8	48	1	17	7	6
Radziewicz, Doug, St. Petersburg*	.233	21	73	10	17	28	4	2	1	9	0	0	1	10	0	15	0	3
Randa, Joe, Baseball City	.275	51	189	22	52	62	7	0	1	18	0	1	0	12	0	21	4	3
Reams, Ron, Dunedin	.201	58	174	21	35	45	7	0	1	18	6	0	1	8	1	32	7	1
Reed, Darren, West Palm Beach	.250	10	40	6	10	20	4	0	2	12	0	1	4	1	0	14	0	0
Rendina, Mike, Lakeland*	.267	121	397	48	106	158	23	1	9	69	1	7	2	46	5	59	2	2
Reyes, Roberto, West Palm Beach	.000	9	13	0	0	0	0	0	0	0	1	0	1	0	0	3	0	0
Roberts, Bryan, Miracle	.201	46	134	7	27	32	5	0	0	8	1	1	0	6	0	47	0	1
Robertson, Mike, Sarasota*	.251	106	395	50	99	156	21	3	10	59	1	3	7	50	3	55	5	7
Rodriguez, Andres, Fort Lauderdale* ...	.255	65	165	21	42	48	4	1	0	18	4	1	0	10	1	59	5	4
Rodriguez, Ernesto, Dunedin†	.236	79	250	24	59	81	11	4	1	23	0	2	2	18	1	59	5	4
Rodriguez, Steve, Winter Haven*	.172	32	81	10	14	18	0	0	0	3	4	0	0	9	0	17	4	1
Roebuck, Joe, Charlotte	.198	108	339	36	67	119	14	4	10	36	0	4	4	36	2	95	10	3
Rolls, David, Charlotte	.294	77	211	39	62	108	15	2	9	33	0	0	5	22	0	42	1	5
Roman, Vince, Osceola	.283	86	254	35	72	99	11	5	2	35	4	1	3	16	0	52	18	13
Romano, Scott, Fort Lauderdale	.240	106	358	30	86	116	17	2	3	24	4	1	7	0	62	11	6
Romay, Willie, Vero Beach*	.199	39	141	11	28	41	5	2	1	13	0	0	0	13	0	35	2	5
Rosario, Gabriel, Dunedin	.263	54	186	24	49	58	7	1	0	18	6	1	5	14	1	27	2	3
Rudolph, Greg, St. Petersburg	.188	57	160	17	30	44	1	3	2	8	1	2	0	11	0	51	5	3
Rudolph, Mason, St. Lucie	.263	48	137	17	36	56	11	0	3	18	2	2	7	0	27	3	1
Ruff, Dan, Lakeland*	.225	96	280	34	63	100	13	6	4	41	2	5	1	20	1	41	1	1

Player, Team	Avg.	G	AB	R	H	TB	2B	3B	HR	RBI	SH	SF	HP	BB	Int. BB	SO	SB	CS
Rumsey, Derrell, Miracle	.215	66	205	20	44	63	10	0	3	14	0	1	2	7	0	50	6	7
Rusk, Troy, Clearwater*	.238	68	240	23	57	89	12	1	6	33	1	1	2	24	0	52	1	0
Saltzgaber, Brian, Lakeland	.243	106	334	42	81	108	17	2	2	28	10	4	5	48	1	47	9	10
Sanchez, Gordon, Fort Lauderdale*	.143	3	7	1	1	1	0	0	0	0	0	0	0	1	0	4	0	0
Sandy, Tim, St. Lucie*	.227	61	154	16	35	43	6	1	0	11	1	1	0	18	0	21	1	1
Savinon, Odalis, St. Petersburg	.253	54	166	14	42	47	3	1	0	7	1	0	0	13	0	28	0	1
Sawkiw, Warren, Lakeland†	.243	118	423	56	103	135	18	4	2	47	0	7	3	39	1	62	6	7
Schall, Gene, Clearwater	.248	40	133	16	33	53	4	2	4	19	1	3	4	14	0	29	1	2
Schmidt, David, Winter Haven†	.220	110	328	38	72	104	12	7	2	33	3	2	12	56	2	85	3	0
Scott, Kevin, Osceola	.242	63	186	27	45	58	6	2	1	6	0	1	1	12	0	44	7	2
Shields, Doug, Baseball City	.250	12	20	4	5	6	1	0	0	3	0	0	0	4	0	5	0	2
Shirley, Mike, Miracle	.210	97	310	28	65	82	11	3	0	23	3	1	5	11	0	83	5	5
Sirak, Ken, Clearwater*	.245	69	208	28	51	64	6	2	1	24	6	3	1	13	1	30	5	1
Smith, Tom, Baseball City†	.234	101	351	36	82	112	7	4	5	39	2	2	6	18	1	87	8	10
Soto, Emison, Winter Haven	.242	28	66	9	16	28	3	0	3	5	1	0	0	5	0	21	0	1
Spearman, Vernon, Vero Beach*	.304	73	276	50	84	99	13	1	0	16	3	1	1	26	1	25	33	14
Steffens, Mark, Clearwater*	.171	48	123	8	21	28	5	1	0	8	1	2	0	4	0	30	0	1
Stewart, Andy, Baseball City	.258	94	283	31	73	100	13	1	4	38	4	1	2	21	1	45	3	8
Stewart, Brady, Baseball City	.181	62	204	26	37	43	4	1	0	5	5	0	0	19	0	57	7	2
Stocker, Kevin, Clearwater†	.283	63	244	43	69	93	13	4	1	33	5	3	4	27	2	31	15	9
Strange, Keith, Sarasota	.225	60	160	17	36	47	8	0	1	18	2	1	3	27	1	39	4	4
Tatarian, Dean, Baseball City	.292	84	295	37	86	100	12	1	0	37	13	0	3	41	0	40	6	8
Tavarez, Hector, Dunedin†	.278	26	90	14	25	33	6	1	0	8	0	1	0	9	1	19	2	0
Tena, Jose, Miracle	.182	10	33	2	6	6	0	0	0	1	0	1	0	1	0	9	1	0
Tewell, Terrance, Clearwater	.208	52	159	11	33	47	11	0	1	11	3	0	1	12	0	52	0	1
Thomas, Corey, Clearwater	.223	105	386	46	86	118	16	8	0	27	6	4	3	48	0	78	16	9
Tijerina, Anthony, St. Lucie†	.222	32	81	7	18	20	2	0	0	6	0	0	2	5	0	14	0	0
Tokheim, David, Clearwater*	.235	106	396	40	93	129	12	6	4	41	2	2	5	30	4	40	10	12
Torres, Jaime, Fort Lauderdale	.333	3	12	1	4	7	3	0	0	1	0	0	0	1	0	4	0	0
Tosar, Miguel, West Palm Beach*	.260	31	96	11	25	36	7	2	0	9	6	2	0	14	0	13	0	2
Trevino, Tony, Clearwater	.256	18	39	6	10	15	3	1	0	0	0	0	0	5	0	4	1	1
Turco, Frank, Charlotte	.227	93	264	29	60	91	12	5	3	23	3	3	1	18	0	68	14	2
Turner, Brian, Fort Lauderdale*	.236	127	454	39	107	146	16	1	7	54	5	5	0	46	2	103	3	8
Twitty, Sean, Fort Lauderdale	.179	8	28	1	5	5	0	0	0	2	0	0	2	0	1	10	1	1
Urcioli, John, Miracle	.199	47	156	13	31	42	7	2	0	13	0	0	3	11	0	28	2	6
Valrie, Kerry, Sarasota	.236	51	174	13	41	53	9	0	1	23	0	2	1	14	0	42	13	1
Villalobos, Gary, Winter Haven	.235	50	183	17	43	60	8	3	1	16	4	3	2	6	0	22	3	0
Vina, Fernando, St. Lucie*	.295	111	421	61	124	152	15	5	1	42	4	2	3	32	2	26	36	17
Vinyard, Derek, Winter Haven*	.249	60	205	20	51	58	3	2	0	12	7	0	1	29	0	58	15	3
Vitiello, Joe, Baseball City	.283	115	400	52	113	155	16	1	8	65	0	8	7	46	1	101	0	5
Walker, Dennis, Sarasota	.239	118	339	51	81	112	12	5	3	32	6	5	13	25	0	81	15	11
Walker, Hugh, Baseball City*	.259	78	278	38	72	116	15	7	5	31	0	2	7	22	0	71	11	8
Walker, Larry, Fort Lauderdale	.175	14	40	5	7	9	2	0	0	2	1	0	1	5	0	13	2	0
Wallin, Les, Winter Haven*	.213	115	371	43	79	130	8	0	11	55	1	5	9	39	3	74	0	1
Weimerskirch, Mike, West Palm Beach	.241	78	203	23	49	60	6	1	1	13	3	0	8	20	1	32	10	0
White, Rondell, West Palm Beach	.316	111	450	80	142	188	10	12	4	41	3	1	5	46	4	78	42	16
Wilson, Brandon, Sarasota	.296	103	399	68	118	164	22	6	4	54	5	2	4	45	2	64	30	16
Wilstead, Randy, West Palm Beach*	.285	129	449	56	128	185	27	3	8	71	0	4	3	47	8	68	7	7
Winslow, Bryant, Osceola	.250	10	16	3	4	8	1	0	1	3	0	0	0	0	0	6	0	0
Wiseman, Greg, Miracle*	.216	93	255	17	55	75	9	4	1	10	2	0	1	9	0	59	2	1
Wolak, Jerry, Sarasota	.289	90	332	47	96	144	23	5	5	39	9	2	5	14	4	54	17	14
Woods, Tyrone, West Palm Beach	.286	15	56	7	16	24	1	2	1	7	0	1	1	6	0	15	2	1
Zambrano, Jose, Winter Haven	.218	77	257	22	56	80	7	1	5	17	3	1	4	22	1	69	2	2

The following pitchers, listed alphabetically by club, with games in parentheses, had no plate appearances, primarily through use of designated hitters:

BASEBALL CITY—Centala, Scott (5); Chrisman, Jim (32); Clark, Dera (3) Fyhrie, Mike (26); Gordon, Anthony (9); Gross, John (26); Harris, Doug (7); Harvey, Greg (11); Kobetitsch, Kevin (31); Landress, Roger (22); Lieber, Jonathan (7); Long, Tony (20); Perez, Dario (28); Perez, Vladimir (20); Peters, Doug (45); Pittsley, Jim (11); Pollard, Damon (50); Sanchez, Alex (15); Sanchez, Jose (3); Santos, Juan (3); Shaw, Kevin (40); Smith, Jeff (2); Stevens, Scott (6); Wiley, Warren (10).

CHARLOTTE—Alberro, Jose (28); Anderson, Mike (5); Arner, Mike (7); Barfield, John (3); Bickhardt, Eric (3); Bouton, Tony (40); Brownholtz, Joe (14); Burrows, Terry (14); Chiamparino, Scott (3); Dreyer, Steve (26); Fajardo, Hector (4); Felix, Nicholas (2); Geeve, Dave (25); Gies, Chris (11); Goetz, Barry (33); Helling, Ricky (3); Hurst, Jim (32); Leon, Danny (4); Martin, Jerry (5); Miller, Kurt (12); Oliver, Darren (8); Perez, David (13); Sadecki, Steve (16); Shaw, Shelby (29); Shiflett, Chris (4); Starr, Chris (5); Vlcek, Jim (2).

CLEARWATER—Adamson, Joel (15); Allen, Ron (15); Brown, Dan (6); Carter, Andrew (16); Elli, Rocky (5); Elliott, Don (3); Gaddy, Bob (44); Gilmore, Joel (5); Goedhart, Darrell (8); Goergen, Todd (23); Gray, Elliott (34); Hassinger, Brad (12); Hill, Eric (5); Langley, Wesley (48); Lindsey, Darrell (40); Munoz, Jarrod (33); Patterson, Jeff (30); Randall, Mark (33); Sepeda, Jamie (6); Sullivan, Mike (24); Wells, Bob (9).

DUNEDIN—Brow, Scott (25); Carrara, Giovanni (5); Duey, Kyle (48); Flener, Greg (41); Ganote, Joe (23); Garcia, Raphael (14); Grove, Scott (45); Hotchkiss, Tom (37); Jordan, Ricardo (45); Karsay, Steve (16); Ogliaruso, Mike (11); Rich, Bart (4); Singer, Tom (27); Steed, Ricky (20); Stieb, Dave (2); Timlin, Mike (6); Ware, Jeff (12).

FORT LAUDERDALE—Anderson, Allan (1); Carter, Tom (10); Faw, Brian (24); Gogolewski, Doug (37); Haller, Jim (41); Hillegas, Shawn (1); Jean, Domingo (23); Johnston, Dan (14); Kamieniecki, Scott (1); Long, Joe (2); Mmahat, Kevin (2); Morphy, Pat (37); Perez, Cesar (33); Ralph, Curtis (12); Rhodes, Ricky (16); Rivera, Mariano (10); Seiler, Keith (9); Sullivan, Grant (12); Taylor, Brien (27); Taylor, Wade (1); Wiley, Jim (11).

LAKELAND—Ahearne, Pat (1); Bauer, Matt (7); Bergman, Sean (13); Blomdahl, Ben (10); Coppeta, Greg (17); Drell, Tom (10); Guilfoyle, Mike (45); Haeger, Greg (8); Henry, Jim (10); Kosenski, John (27); Lima, Jose (25); Lira, Felipe (32); Pfaff, Jason (21); Raley, Dan (4); Reid, John (3); Rodriguez, Eddy (21); Schwarber, Tom (1); Stidham, Phil (45); Torres, Leonardo (8); Undorf, Bob (39); Wiggs, Johnny (14).

MIRACLE—Belcher, Jim (9); Best, Jayson (44); Diaz, Sandy (11); Garcia, Apolinar (14); Giberti, Dave (24); Hoppe, Dennis (37); Kohl, Jim (57); Lipson, Marc (22); Misuraca, Mike (28); Nedin, Tim (1); Persing, Tim (13); Peterson, Bart (7); Ringkamp, Mark (39); Schuermann, Lance (52); Swope, Mark (19); Washington, Tyrone (5).

OSCEOLA—Costello, Fred (10); Dougherty, Jim (57); Dovey, Troy (17); Fesh, Sean (3); Gallaher, Kevin (1); Gonzales, Ben (60); Gutierrez, Tony (29); Hernandez, Javier (16); Hill, Chris (30); Ketchen, Doug (34); Lane, Kevin (53); LaRose, Steve (12); Lewis, Jim (13); Linehan, Andrew (1); Luckham, Ken (8); Mercedes, Fernando (7); Purvis, Brian (4); Small, Mark (22); Wall, Donnell (7); Wheeler, Ken (5).

SARASOTA—Baldwin, Jim (6); Bere, Jason (18); Campos, Frank (22); Caridad, Rolando (32); Fritz, Greg (6); Gay, Chris (1); Gordon, Anthony (30); Hooper, Troy (5); Johnson, Earnie (12); Keating, Dave (19); Levine, Alan (3); Locklear, Dean (41); Matznick, Dan (2); Olsen, Steve (13); Perigny, Don (52); Person, Bob (19); Pierce, Jeff (1); Ruffcorn, Scott (25); Ruffin, Johnny (23); Schrenk, Steve (25); Soto, Juan (1); Starks, Fred (4); Stowell, Steve (3); Thomas, Larry (9).

ST. LUCIE—Carpenter, Bob (26); Castillo, Juan (24); Crawford, Joe (25); Dorn, Chris (8); Freitas, Mike (45); Guzik, Bob (9); Harriger, Dennis (27); Jacome, Jason (17); Keller, Clyde (14); Martinez, Jose (17); McCann, Joe (32); Proctor, Dave (11); Rees, Bob (3); Roa, Joe (26); Rogers, Bryan (17); Shanahan, Chris (25); Smith, Ottis (11).

ST. PETERSBURG—Anderson, Paul (5); Bailey, Roy (54); Baker, Ernie (12); Baker, Scott (24); Barber, Brian (19); Beltran, Rigoberto (2);

Botkin, Alan (40); Creek, Doug (13); Eversgerd, Bryan (57); Fanning, Steve (1); Fletcher, Dennis (57); Kelly, John (56); Magrane, Joe (3); Mc-Garity, Jeremy (23); Nielsen, Kevin (14); Salvior, Troy (16); Watson, Allen (14); Weber, Ron (24).

VERO BEACH—Bene, Bill (18); Bobb, Jason (2); Brosnan, Jason (18); Daspit, Jim (26); Delahoya, Javier (14); Duran, Roberto (2); Gutierrez, Rafael (6); Hamilton, Ken (25); Howell, Jay (5); Jones, Keith (5); Kerr, Jason (37); Mintz, Steve (43); Piotrowicz, Brian (24); Sinacori, Chris (42); Stryker, Ed (37); Van Ryn, Ben (26); Weaver, Eric (19); Wengert, Bill (5); Wray, Jim (47).

WEST PALM BEACH—Alvarez, Octavio (19); Batista, Miguel (24); Baxter, Bob (42); Brewer, Bill (28); Diaz, Rafael (24); Eddy, Jim (4); Eischen, Joe (27); Foster, Kevin (16); Grewal, Ranbir (42); LaRosa, Mark (22); Long, Steve (26); McDonald, Kevin (12); Moya, Felix (29); Myers, Chris (1); Powell, Corey (25); Schmidt, Curt (3); Tuss, Jeff (30).

WINTER HAVEN—Allen, Ron (1); Amos, Chad (9); Bakkum, Scott (5); Bennett, Joel (26); Ciccarelli, Joe (38); Davis, Chris C. (7); Davis, Chris L. (6); Donovan, Bret (5); Dzafic, Bernhard (25); Gonzalez, Melvin (6); Henkel, Bob (19); Lynch, Mike (11); MacNeil, Doug (2); Maloney, Ryan (28); Mejia, Jorge (3); Miller, Todd (29); Mitchelson, Mark (10); Niles, Tom (1); Owen, Dave (8); Parkins, Bob (10); Powell, Terry (21); Renko, Steve (10); Santamaria, Silverio (16); Schoenvogel, Chad (14); Young, Brian (20).

GRAND SLAMS—Jacobs, 2; D. Brady, M. Burton, Daniel, Gilliam, P. Gonzalez, Groppuso, Hatcher, Hecker, Hunter, Hyers, Morrow, Mouton, Radziewicz, M. Rudolph, Ruff, Rusk, A. Stewart, 1 each.

AWARDED FIRST BASE ON CATCHER'S INTERFERENCE—Hankins 3 (Grifol, R. Nunez, M. Rudolph); Romano 2 (Mulville, Rolls); Weimerskirch 2 (C. Delgado, R. Nunez); Abreu (Strange); Baez (P. Gonzalez); Burns (Perona); M. Burton (Tijerina); Cantu (Luce); Gumpf (Brooks); Hyers (Grifol); Murray (Tijerina); Rumsey (Rolls); Tokheim (Grifol); Wallin (Buckley); White (Tijerina).

PITCHING

TEAM

Team	ERA	G	CG	ShO	Sv.	IP	H	R	ER	HR	HB	BB	Int. BB	SO	WP	Bk.
Charlotte	2.67	135	12	18	38	1175.1	1044	419	349	55	62	333	18	860	40	20
West Palm Beach	2.77	137	19	18	33	1226.2	1035	456	378	32	55	409	23	893	49	14
Sarasota	2.83	133	12	16	42	1175.1	981	467	369	46	45	442	28	975	80	16
Baseball City	2.94	131	14	13	28	1125.0	989	464	367	52	60	376	20	697	54	20
St. Lucie	2.98	136	23	12	40	1168.1	1133	507	387	55	48	244	16	673	48	25
Clearwater	2.99	134	4	15	46	1184.2	1046	463	393	47	49	311	22	807	52	17
Lakeland	3.03	132	18	15	33	1128.0	1067	449	380	51	48	278	10	829	52	19
St. Petersburg	3.04	133	3	8	40	1150.2	1070	499	389	36	29	432	19	809	61	20
Fort Lauderdale	3.37	135	12	11	32	1175.1	1056	556	440	44	49	466	21	946	70	23
Dunedin	3.43	137	15	12	39	1208.0	1105	574	461	62	56	480	26	868	94	18
Miracle	3.50	131	11	11	29	1126.2	1121	547	438	54	45	406	9	752	53	13
Osceola	3.55	134	3	8	47	1168.2	1115	591	461	46	55	474	21	856	83	16
Vero Beach	3.57	135	12	12	28	1125.0	1047	525	446	77	45	433	18	896	79	15
Winter Haven	3.77	137	20	10	27	1157.0	1172	585	485	56	46	446	15	847	77	19

PITCHING

INDIVIDUAL

(Leading qualifiers for earned-run average leadership—112 or more innings)

*Throws lefthanded.

Pitcher, Team	W	L	Pct.	ERA	G	GS	CG	GF	ShO	Sv.	IP	H	R	ER	HR	HB	BB	Int. BB	SO	WP
Alvarez, West Palm Beach	13	4	.765	1.49	19	19	7	0	4	0	139.0	124	30	23	0	3	24	0	83	2
S. Baker, St. Petersburg*	10	9	.526	1.96	24	24	0	0	0	0	151.2	123	48	33	3	5	54	0	125	11
Schrenk, Sarasota	15	2	.882	2.05	25	22	4	2	2	1	154.0	130	48	35	1	7	40	2	113	7
Martinez, St. Lucie	6	5	.545	2.05	17	17	4	0	1	0	123.0	107	44	28	6	0	11	0	114	4
Pfaff, Lakeland	7	7	.500	2.14	21	21	1	0	0	0	134.1	112	39	32	5	8	33	1	79	5
Diaz, West Palm Beach	8	4	.667	2.18	24	12	3	5	2	2	119.2	88	34	29	5	3	24	0	77	2
Ruffcorn, Sarasota	14	5	.737	2.19	25	24	2	0	0	0	160.1	122	53	39	7	3	39	0	140	3
Flener, Dunedin*	7	3	.700	2.24	41	8	0	19	0	8	112.1	70	35	28	4	7	50	2	93	2
Dreyer, Charlotte	11	7	.611	2.40	26	26	4	0	3	0	168.2	164	54	45	8	6	37	2	111	4
Bere, Sarasota	7	2	.778	2.41	18	18	1	0	1	0	116.0	84	35	31	3	1	34	3	106	6

Departmental leaders: G—Gonzales, 60; W—C. Hill, 16; L—Swope, 15; Pct.—Olsen, .917; GS—Misuraca, 28; CG—Alvarez, Castillo, 7; GF—Dougherty, Kelly, 52; ShO—Alvarez, 4; Sv.—Kelly, 38; IP—Brow, 170.2; H—Roa, 176; R—Bennett, 86; ER—Bennett, 76; HR—Lima, 14; HB—Dovey, 12; BB—Eischen, 83; IBB—Duey, Grove, 7; SO—B. Taylor, 187; WP—Dovey, 19.

(All pitchers—listed alphabetically)

Pitcher, Team	W	L	Pct.	ERA	G	GS	CG	GF	ShO	Sv.	IP	H	R	ER	HR	HB	BB	Int. BB	SO	WP
Adamson, Clearwater*	5	6	.455	3.41	15	15	1	0	1	0	89.2	90	35	34	4	7	19	0	52	0
Ahearne, Lakeland	0	0	.000	1.93	1	1	0	0	0	0	4.2	4	2	1	0	0	4	0	4	0
Alberro, Charlotte	1	1	.500	1.20	28	0	0	20	0	15	45.0	37	10	6	0	3	9	0	29	1
Allen, Winter Haven*	0	0	.000	0.00	1	0	0	1	0	0	0.2	0	0	0	0	0	1	0	1	0
Allen, Clearwater	6	6	.500	2.86	15	15	1	0	1	0	91.1	87	36	29	6	1	24	0	49	1
Alvarez, West Palm Beach	13	4	.765	1.49	19	19	7	0	4	0	139.0	124	30	23	0	3	24	0	83	2
Amos, Winter Haven	1	1	.500	3.95	9	0	0	6	0	2	13.2	16	8	6	0	1	4	1	10	2
Anderson, Fort Lauderdale*	1	0	1.000	6.00	1	1	0	0	0	0	6.0	10	4	4	0	0	1	0	5	1
Anderson, Charlotte	0	0	.000	1.64	5	0	0	3	0	1	11.0	4	4	2	0	4	0	5	0
Anderson, St. Petersburg	2	0	.000	2.81	5	2	0	0	0	0	16.0	13	9	5	1	1	5	0	4	2
Arner, Charlotte	1	1	.500	2.20	7	0	0	3	0	0	16.1	13	4	4	1	2	0	16	0
Aversa, St. Petersburg	0	0	.000	12.00	3	0	0	0	0	0	3.0	3	4	4	1	0	2	0	1	1
Bailey, St. Petersburg	5	7	.417	3.82	54	0	0	13	0	0	70.2	75	35	30	5	0	26	5	28	2
E. Baker, St. Petersburg	1	0	1.000	3.15	12	1	0	3	0	0	34.1	46	21	12	1	1	14	0	15	0
S. Baker, St. Petersburg*	10	9	.526	1.96	24	24	0	0	0	0	151.2	123	48	33	3	5	54	0	125	11
Bakkum, Winter Haven	1	3	.250	2.93	5	4	0	0	0	0	27.2	19	9	9	1	1	10	0	10	0
Baldwin, Sarasota	2	2	.333	2.87	6	6	1	0	0	0	37.2	31	13	12	2	1	7	0	39	1
Barber, St. Petersburg	5	5	.500	3.26	19	19	1	0	0	0	113.1	99	51	41	7	5	46	0	102	4
Barfield, Charlotte*	1	0	.000	7.71	3	0	0	2	0	0	7.0	10	7	6	0	0	1	0	4	0
Batista, West Palm Beach	7	7	.500	3.79	24	24	1	0	0	0	135.1	130	69	57	3	6	54	1	92	9
Bauer, Lakeland*	1	2	.333	10.61	7	0	0	2	0	0	9.1	15	13	11	0	1	3	0	12	0
Baxter, West Palm Beach*	2	6	.750	1.41	42	0	0	27	0	3	63.2	46	12	10	1	0	9	1	54	2
Belcher, Miracle	1	0	1.000	6.97	10	0	0	5	0	0	10.1	14	13	8	1	6	1	3	1
Beltran, St. Petersburg*	0	0	.000	0.00	2	2	0	0	0	0	8.0	6	0	0	0	0	5	0	9	5
Bene, Vero Beach	2	2	.500	2.00	18	0	0	12	0	0	18.0	11	4	4	0	1	16	0	30	5
Bennett, Winter Haven	7	11	.389	4.23	26	26	4	0	0	0	161.2	161	86	76	7	7	55	2	154	7

Pitcher, Team	W	L	Pct.	ERA	G	GS	CG	GF	ShO	Sv.	IP	H	R	ER	HR	HB	BB	Int. BB	SO	WP
Bere, Sarasota	7	2	.778	2.41	18	18	1	0	1	0	116.0	84	35	31	3	1	34	3	106	6
Bergman, Lakeland	5	2	.714	2.49	13	13	0	0	0	0	83.0	61	28	23	2	2	14	0	67	2
Best, Miracle	0	6	.000	4.09	44	0	0	40	0	18	50.2	50	30	23	4	2	25	0	50	3
Bickhardt, Charlotte	0	1	.000	9.00	3	0	0	1	0	0	6.0	10	6	6	2	1	4	0	7	2
Blomdahl, Lakeland	5	3	.625	4.65	10	10	2	0	0	0	62.0	77	35	32	3	3	5	0	41	2
Bobb, Vero Beach	0	0	.000	17.36	2	1	0	0	0	0	4.2	7	9	9	1	1	5	0	1	0
Botkin, St. Petersburg*	2	4	.333	3.15	40	3	0	9	0	0	80.0	67	36	28	2	2	40	2	58	6
Bouton, Charlotte	5	4	.556	3.54	40	0	0	19	0	2	61.0	52	32	24	2	6	30	4	67	3
Brewer, West Palm Beach*	2	2	.500	1.73	28	0	0	20	0	8	36.1	27	10	7	0	2	14	1	37	2
Bridges, Baseball City	0	0	.000	0.00	1	0	0	1	0	0	2.0	0	0	0	0	0	0	0	1	0
Brosnan, Vero Beach*	3	4	.429	4.66	18	8	2	3	0	0	58.0	69	32	30	2	2	26	2	51	11
Brow, Dunedin	14	2	.875	2.43	25	25	3	0	1	0	170.2	143	53	46	8	7	44	2	107	3
Brown, Clearwater	0	1	.000	2.57	6	0	0	2	0	0	7.0	5	2	2	0	1	3	0	4	0
Brownholtz, Charlotte	6	5	.545	3.11	14	12	1	2	0	0	72.1	73	30	25	9	4	19	2	46	0
Burbank, Fort Lauderdale	3	1	.750	3.48	16	1	0	10	0	0	33.2	35	14	13	2	0	16	1	28	1
Burns, Osceola	0	0	.000	0.00	1	0	0	0	0	0	0.0	2	4	4	0	1	3	0	0	0
Burrows, Charlotte*	4	2	.667	2.03	14	14	0	0	0	0	80.0	71	22	18	2	4	25	1	66	5
Campos, Sarasota	1	2	.333	1.80	22	0	0	16	0	10	30.0	20	11	6	0	1	10	0	23	5
Caridad, Sarasota	4	3	.571	2.76	32	0	0	16	0	3	45.2	39	20	14	3	8	28	4	30	10
Carpentier, St. Lucie	1	3	.250	4.84	26	2	1	10	1	0	57.2	74	39	31	3	5	14	2	25	4
Carrara, Dunedin	0	1	.000	4.63	5	4	0	1	0	0	23.1	22	13	12	1	2	11	0	16	4
Carter, Clearwater*	3	4	.429	1.86	16	13	1	1	1	0	87.0	60	30	18	2	4	13	1	68	9
Carter, Fort Lauderdale*	3	5	.375	5.45	10	8	0	1	0	0	36.1	35	32	22	1	1	30	0	23	9
Castillo, St. Lucie	11	8	.579	2.58	24	24	7	0	3	0	153.2	135	53	44	9	10	27	1	80	9
Centala, Baseball City	2	3	.400	2.61	5	5	2	0	0	0	31.0	24	13	9	4	1	4	0	25	0
Chiamparino, Charlotte	1	1	.500	2.31	2	2	0	0	0	0	11.2	6	3	3	0	4	3	0	10	0
Chrisman, Baseball City	3	1	.750	3.63	32	3	0	11	0	0	67.0	56	31	27	3	6	28	1	40	2
Ciccarella, Winter Haven*	2	1	.667	2.66	38	0	0	30	0	12	40.2	35	13	12	2	0	26	1	45	0
Clark, Baseball City	2	0	1.000	1.69	3	3	0	0	0	0	16.0	15	3	3	0	0	3	0	7	0
Cole, Baseball City	0	0	.000	0.00	1	0	0	1	0	0	1.0	0	0	0	0	0	1	0	1	0
Coppeta, Lakeland*	7	3	.700	2.36	17	7	0	1	0	0	61.0	53	19	16	2	3	9	0	38	4
Costello, Osceola	1	2	.333	2.70	10	0	0	2	0	1	13.1	14	7	4	0	0	2	0	10	0
Crawford, St. Lucie*	3	3	.500	2.06	25	1	0	16	0	3	43.2	29	18	10	1	0	15	3	32	1
Creek, St. Petersburg*	5	4	.556	2.82	13	13	0	0	0	0	73.1	57	31	23	5	1	37	1	63	4
Daspit, Vero Beach	6	12	.333	3.44	26	25	0	0	0	0	149.1	135	67	57	10	7	57	1	109	7
C.C. Davis, Winter Haven	3	2	.600	3.52	7	6	1	1	1	0	38.1	31	16	15	2	3	12	0	21	2
C.L. Davis, Winter Haven	0	4	.000	5.01	6	6	0	0	0	0	32.1	36	23	18	3	1	19	0	21	5
Delahoya, Vero Beach	4	5	.444	2.81	14	14	2	0	2	0	80.0	68	25	25	4	4	26	0	92	2
Diaz, West Palm Beach	8	4	.667	2.18	24	12	3	5	2	2	119.2	88	34	29	5	3	24	0	77	2
Diaz, Miracle	2	4	.333	4.08	11	11	1	0	0	0	53.0	56	29	24	3	1	21	0	39	3
Donovan, Winter Haven*	1	2	.333	7.11	5	5	0	0	0	0	25.1	38	20	20	4	2	5	0	20	0
Dorn, St. Lucie	2	1	.667	2.84	8	0	0	5	0	1	12.2	14	6	4	1	0	4	1	11	0
Dougherty, Osceola	5	2	.714	1.56	57	0	0	52	0	31	81.0	66	21	14	1	2	22	4	77	0
Dovey, Osceola	2	7	.222	7.31	17	11	0	4	0	1	56.2	59	54	46	2	12	47	0	57	19
Drell, Lakeland	1	0	1.000	0.53	10	1	0	2	0	0	17.0	10	2	1	0	1	11	0	12	1
Dreyer, Charlotte	11	7	.611	2.40	26	26	4	0	3	0	168.2	164	54	45	8	6	37	2	111	4
Duey, Dunedin	7	3	.700	2.57	48	0	0	21	0	7	77.0	84	31	22	4	1	33	7	51	17
Duran, Vero Beach*	0	0	.000	9.00	2	1	0	0	0	0	5.0	6	5	5	1		4	0	5	1
Dzafic, Winter Haven	3	6	.333	2.83	25	2	0	13	0	0	76.1	80	26	24	1	1	12	2	43	4
Eatinger, Sarasota	0	0	.000	9.00	1	0	0	1	0	0	2.0	2	2	2	0	0	3	0	0	0
Eddy, West Palm Beach	1	0	1.000	0.00	4	0	0	2	0	1	10.2	10	0	0	0	0	3	0	9	0
Eischen, West Palm Beach*	9	8	.529	3.08	27	26	3	0	2	0	169.2	128	68	58	5	8	83	2	167	6
Elli, Clearwater*	1	1	.500	3.67	5	5	0	0	0	0	27.0	24	13	11	3	3	8	0	23	2
Elliott, Clearwater	1	1	.500	3.00	3	3	0	0	0	0	18.0	12	6	6	1	0	8	0	12	2
Eversgerd, St. Petersburg*	3	2	.600	2.68	57	1	0	13	0	14	74.0	65	25	22	0	2	25	4	57	1
Fajardo, Charlotte	2	2	.500	2.78	4	4	0	0	0	0	22.2	22	9	7	0	1	8	0	12	0
Farmer, Clearwater*	3	3	.500	1.87	11	9	1	2	1	0	53.0	33	16	11	1	1	13	1	41	2
Faw, Fort Lauderdale	5	9	.357	4.21	24	17	0	4	0	2	119.2	129	72	56	6	1	38	0	74	3
Felix, Charlotte*	0	1	.000	3.71	8	1	0	7	0	0	17.0	21	9	7	1	1	5	0	18	1
Fesh, Osceola*	0	1	.000	1.69	3	0	0	2	0	0	5.1	5	3	1	0	0	1	0	5	3
Flener, Dunedin*	7	3	.700	2.24	41	8	0	19	0	8	112.1	70	35	28	4	7	50	2	93	2
Fletcher, St. Petersburg	6	5	.545	2.45	57	0	0	29	0	2	62.1	57	18	17	1	0	16	1	52	3
Foster, West Palm Beach	7	2	.778	1.95	16	11	0	2	0	0	69.1	45	19	15	4	3	31	1	66	1
Freitas, St. Lucie	6	3	.667	1.25	45	0	0	39	0	24	57.2	51	17	8	2	4	9	1	30	0
Fritz, Sarasota*	2	3	.400	3.79	6	6	0	0	0	0	35.2	40	20	15	2	3	14	0	10	3
Fyhrie, Baseball City	7	13	.350	2.50	26	26	2	0	0	0	162.0	148	65	45	6	7	37	1	92	4
Gaddy, Clearwater*	5	5	.500	3.52	44	0	0	17	0	4	64.0	58	30	25	3	5	21	2	54	4
Gallaher, Osceola	0	1	.000	2.84	1	1	0	0	0	0	6.1	2	2	2	1	0	2	0	5	1
Ganote, Dunedin	6	10	.375	3.97	23	21	4	0	1	0	140.2	148	72	62	10	10	40	1	101	9
Garcia, Miracle	2	6	.250	3.48	14	14	1	0	0	0	82.2	85	36	32	9	4	16	0	78	4
Garcia, Dunedin	0	1	.000	6.25	14	0	0	4	0	0	31.2	40	28	22	3	0	13	0	24	1
Gay, Sarasota*	0	1	.000	12.71	1	1	0	0	0	0	5.1	8	8	8	0	0	3	1	5	1
Geeve, Charlotte	8	8	.500	3.36	25	24	0	1	0	0	139.1	138	61	52	8	6	22	1	97	6
Giberti, Miracle*	7	9	.438	3.26	24	24	2	0	1	0	135.1	120	53	49	6	5	42	0	90	6
Gies, Charlotte	7	2	.778	1.94	11	11	3	0	2	0	79.0	69	19	17	5	4	16	0	35	0
Gilmore, Clearwater	2	1	.667	3.42	5	5	0	0	0	0	26.1	25	11	10	3	1	9	0	22	0
Goedhart, Clearwater	4	3	.571	3.10	8	8	0	0	0	0	40.2	39	15	14	2	1	10	0	32	1
Goergen, Clearwater	7	7	.500	3.19	23	23	0	0	0	0	129.2	123	51	46	3	4	17	0	61	3
Goetz, Charlotte	4	5	.444	2.70	33	0	0	28	0	11	33.1	21	10	10	1	1	19	0	38	1
Gogolewski, Fort Lauderdale	0	5	.000	3.52	37	0	0	33	0	17	46.0	36	21	18	1	4	18	4	32	2
Gonzales, Osceola	7	2	.778	2.06	60	0	0	18	0	3	109.1	87	36	25	1	7	41	4	80	6
Gonzalez, Winter Haven	0	2	.000	1.13	6	1	0	1	0	0	16.0	12	2	2	0	1	8	1	7	1
Gordon, 9 B.C.-30 Sar.*	2	2	.500	4.60	39	3	0	10	0	2	60.2	61	43	31	3	1	41	3	60	8
Gray, Clearwater	9	4	.692	4.49	34	15	0	3	0	1	108.1	111	60	54	6	4	39	3	66	2
Grewal, West Palm Beach	3	6	.333	3.86	42	0	0	18	0	4	49.0	40	25	21	3	3	32	6	33	5
Gross, Baseball City	2	6	.250	2.85	26	26	3	0	2	0	151.2	138	61	48	9	11	45	1	96	9
Grove, Dunedin	10	6	.625	3.23	45	0	0	24	0	16	78.0	71	33	28	4	0	29	7	52	3
Guilfoyle, Lakeland*	4	1	.800	3.18	45	0	0	31	0	11	51.0	48	23	18	1	1	16	1	32	2
Gumpf, Miracle	0	0	.000	0.00	2	0	0	0	0	0	1.1	2	0	0	0	0	0	0	0	0
Gutierrez, Osceola*	4	8	.333	6.80	29	18	0	5	0	0	96.2	114	85	73	3	8	74	1	85	12
Gutierrez, Vero Beach	0	5	.000	4.00	6	6	1	0	0	0	27.0	29	19	12	3	1	13	0	17	3
Guzik, St. Lucie	4	2	.667	3.98	9	9	1	0	0	0	43.0	47	22	19	0	3	8	0	16	3
Haeger, Lakeland*	1	2	.333	5.92	8	4	0	0	0	0	24.1	30	18	16	1	1	15	1	20	3
Hajek, Osceola	1	0	1.000	0.00	1	0	0	1	0	0	2.0	1	0	0	0	1	1	0	1	0
Haller, Fort Lauderdale*	4	4	.500	3.06	41	0	0	16	0	2	64.2	52	25	22	1	2	40	4	50	13

Pitcher, Team	W	L	Pct.	ERA	G	GS	CG	GF	ShO	Sv.	IP	H	R	ER	HR	HB	BB	Int. BB	SO	WP
Hamilton, Vero Beach	6	11	.353	3.97	25	20	4	1	0	0	131.1	127	65	58	8	8	39	2	75	4
Harriger, St. Lucie	7	3	.700	2.24	27	10	0	9	0	3	88.1	89	30	22	1	3	14	1	65	5
Harris, Baseball City	0	2	.000	2.15	7	7	0	0	0	0	29.1	25	11	7	3	2	6	0	22	2
Harvey, Baseball City	3	4	.429	5.04	11	9	1	2	0	0	55.1	60	38	31	4	7	24	1	24	2
Hassinger, Clearwater	6	1	.857	2.54	12	10	0	0	0	0	63.2	63	22	18	0	3	10	0	29	1
Helling, Charlotte	1	1	.500	2.29	3	3	0	0	0	0	19.2	13	5	5	1	2	4	0	20	1
Henkel, Winter Haven	5	7	.417	3.32	19	19	3	0	2	0	116.2	110	48	43	5	10	37	3	102	18
Henry, Lakeland*	6	3	.667	1.09	10	10	3	0	2	0	66.0	43	11	8	0	2	19	0	48	4
Hernandez, Osceola	1	1	.500	5.27	16	0	0	8	0	2	41.0	54	29	24	2	2	15	0	24	1
Hill, Osceola*	16	7	.696	2.93	30	26	1	0	1	0	159.2	154	73	52	4	5	58	1	126	11
Hill, Clearwater	4	1	.800	3.25	5	5	0	0	0	0	27.2	26	13	10	3	0	7	0	18	0
Hillegas, Fort Lauderdale	1	0	1.000	0.00	1	1	0	0	0	0	6.0	3	0	0	0	0	1	0	2	0
Hooper, Sarasota	0	1	.000	3.86	3	0	0	1	0	0	2.1	4	2	1	0	0	4	1	1	0
Hoppe, Miracle	1	8	.111	3.73	37	4	0	10	0	1	91.2	93	46	38	9	3	26	0	77	4
Hotchkiss, Dunedin	4	6	.400	4.09	37	2	1	11	0	0	81.1	88	52	37	4	2	33	2	45	12
Howell, Vero Beach	0	0	.000	8.10	5	0	0	0	0	0	6.2	9	6	6	2	1	3	0	4	0
Hurst, Charlotte*	3	2	.600	3.81	32	1	0	11	0	1	54.1	60	29	23	2	2	12	0	49	3
Jacome, St. Lucie*	6	7	.462	2.83	17	17	5	0	1	0	114.1	98	45	36	7	3	30	0	66	6
Jean, Fort Lauderdale	6	11	.353	2.61	23	23	5	0	1	0	158.2	118	57	46	3	6	49	1	172	4
Johnson, Sarasota*	1	2	.333	3.71	12	1	0	7	0	3	26.2	26	13	11	2	2	7	2	26	2
Johnston, Fort Lauderdale	5	3	.625	3.99	41	2	0	17	0	3	70.0	70	38	31	4	2	26	5	40	5
Jones, Vero Beach	0	3	.000	5.51	5	5	0	0	0	0	16.1	19	12	10	2	2	11	0	11	0
Jordan, Dunedin*	0	5	.000	3.83	45	0	0	32	0	15	47.0	44	26	20	3	2	28	3	49	7
Kamieniecki, Fort Lauderdale	1	0	1.000	1.29	1	1	0	0	0	0	7.0	8	1	1	0	0	0	0	3	0
Karsay, Dunedin	6	3	.667	2.73	16	16	3	0	2	0	85.2	56	32	26	6	4	29	0	87	2
Keating, Sarasota*	0	1	.000	5.00	19	0	0	8	0	0	27.0	25	17	15	2	0	17	0	18	2
Keller, St. Lucie	1	0	1.000	5.79	14	0	0	10	0	4	18.2	19	12	12	1	1	11	1	11	1
Kelly, St. Petersburg	4	4	.500	2.03	56	0	0	52	0	38	62.0	47	15	14	1	1	13	2	59	3
Kerr, Vero Beach*	3	2	.600	4.15	37	0	0	14	0	0	43.1	35	21	20	2	2	24	3	39	4
Ketchen, Osceola	8	3	.727	2.79	34	12	0	9	0	5	116.0	121	43	36	6	1	28	4	72	9
Kobetitsch, Baseball City*	3	0	1.000	1.26	31	0	0	11	0	4	35.2	19	6	5	1	3	9	2	21	3
Kohl, Miracle	7	4	.636	2.55	57	0	0	24	0	2	99.0	95	33	28	3	2	34	3	50	3
Kosenski, Lakeland	5	8	.385	4.10	27	20	4	2	2	0	120.2	135	61	55	4	7	31	0	67	7
Landress, Baseball City	2	2	.500	3.29	22	2	0	8	0	0	27.1	29	13	10	0	2	13	2	9	0
Lane, Osceola	4	5	.444	3.38	53	0	0	16	0	3	96.0	80	47	36	3	3	47	4	64	7
Langley, Clearwater*	7	4	.636	2.70	48	1	0	9	0	0	80.0	63	27	24	2	2	37	3	71	9
Larosa, W.P. Beach*	1	2	.333	3.34	22	0	0	11	0	5	35.0	32	13	13	1	0	10	1	37	5
LaRose, Osceola	5	3	.625	3.82	12	11	0	0	0	0	63.2	63	31	27	4	4	16	0	32	0
Leon, Charlotte	0	0	.000	1.93	4	0	0	0	0	0	9.1	5	2	2	0	1	2	0	7	0
Levine, Sarasota	0	2	.000	4.02	3	2	0	0	0	0	15.2	17	11	7	1	0	5	1	11	0
Lewis, Osceola	5	1	.833	1.12	13	13	1	0	0	0	80.1	54	18	10	0	2	32	0	65	5
Lieber, Baseball City	3	3	.500	4.65	7	6	0	1	0	0	31.0	45	20	16	2	1	8	0	19	0
Lima, Lakeland	5	11	.313	3.16	25	25	4	0	2	0	151.0	132	57	53	14	5	21	2	137	3
Lindsey, Clearwater	3	2	.600	3.39	40	1	0	12	0	0	79.2	66	35	30	5	3	25	2	62	3
Linehan, Osceola*	0	1	.000	7.20	1	1	0	0	0	0	5.0	4	4	4	2	0	4	0	2	2
Lipson, Miracle	1	2	.333	1.50	22	0	0	7	0	4	54.0	33	11	9	0	1	13	1	41	0
Lira, Lakeland	11	5	.688	2.39	32	8	2	2	1	1	109.0	95	36	29	6	7	16	1	84	4
Locklear, Sarasota*	7	3	.700	3.15	41	0	0	15	0	4	60.0	52	28	21	3	4	21	5	43	2
Long, Fort Lauderdale	0	0	.000	14.29	2	1	0	0	0	0	5.2	13	10	9	1	0	2	0	3	1
Long, West Palm Beach	9	7	.563	2.44	26	23	4	0	0	0	151.1	121	53	41	2	7	42	3	67	7
Long, Baseball City*	3	3	.500	1.83	20	4	1	6	0	1	44.1	38	11	9	2	2	9	2	29	3
Luckham, Osceola	0	4	.000	5.28	8	7	0	0	0	0	29.0	26	23	17	3	3	10	0	14	0
Lund, Vero Beach	0	0	.000	9.00	1	0	0	1	0	0	1.0	3	1	1	0	0	0	0	0	0
Lynch, Winter Haven	0	1	.000	6.50	11	0	0	6	0	0	18.0	19	16	13	0	1	22	1	6	8
MacNeil, Winter Haven	1	1	.500	4.09	2	2	0	0	0	0	11.0	14	7	5	3	0	2	0	6	0
Magrane, St. Petersburg*	0	1	.000	1.50	3	3	0	0	0	0	18.0	14	4	3	0	1	5	0	15	2
Maloney, Winter Haven*	8	4	.667	3.69	28	10	2	7	0	0	90.1	124	53	37	5	2	38	0	46	8
Martin, Charlotte	1	1	.500	3.24	5	2	1	1	0	1	16.2	16	6	6	3	1	4	0	12	0
Martinez, St. Lucie	6	5	.545	2.05	17	17	4	0	1	0	123.0	107	44	28	6	0	11	0	114	4
Matznick, Sarasota	2	0	1.000	1.29	2	2	0	0	0	0	14.0	7	2	2	0	0	4	0	18	2
McCann, St. Lucie	5	1	.833	2.15	32	1	0	12	0	3	50.1	41	15	12	1	1	11	1	27	2
McDonald, West Palm Beach	3	2	.600	3.05	12	5	1	4	1	1	41.1	29	16	14	0	3	21	2	27	3
McGarity, St. Petersburg	3	12	.200	5.42	23	22	0	1	0	0	106.1	123	81	64	3	4	58	0	48	10
Mejia, Winter Haven	0	1	.000	6.00	3	2	0	0	0	0	9.0	11	6	6	1	0	8	0	7	0
Mercedes, Osceola	2	0	1.000	0.75	9	0	0	5	0	1	12.0	7	1	1	0	0	2	0	11	0
Miller, Charlotte	5	4	.556	2.39	12	12	0	0	0	0	75.1	51	23	20	2	2	29	0	58	5
Miller, Winter Haven	3	5	.375	2.53	29	0	0	15	0	3	64.0	59	23	18	1	0	30	2	38	5
Mintz, Vero Beach	3	6	.333	3.13	43	2	0	21	0	6	77.2	66	29	27	7	3	30	2	66	4
Misuraca, Miracle	7	14	.333	3.61	28	28	3	0	1	0	157.0	163	84	63	7	0	63	1	107	4
Mitchelson, Winter Haven*	0	1	.000	3.95	10	0	0	6	0	2	13.2	16	8	6	1	2	2	0	8	0
Mmahat, Fort Lauderdale	1	0	1.000	1.13	2	2	1	0	1	0	8.0	4	1	1	0	2	2	0	7	0
Morphy, Fort Lauderdale	4	5	.444	2.64	37	6	0	12	0	4	81.2	63	33	24	5	4	42	2	78	5
Moya, West Palm Beach	2	5	.286	3.90	29	1	0	7	0	0	55.1	56	29	24	3	5	12	4	34	2
Munoz, Clearwater*	2	3	.400	2.22	32	0	0	19	0	6	44.2	34	13	11	2	1	12	3	34	3
Murphy, West Palm Beach	0	0	.000	0.00	1	0	0	1	0	0	0.2	0	0	0	0	0	0	0	0	1
Myers, West Palm Beach*	0	0	.000	6.75	1	1	0	0	0	0	4.0	6	3	3	0	0	2	0	4	0
Nedin, Miracle*	0	0	.000	0.00	1	0	0	0	0	0	4.0	2	0	0	0	1	2	0	5	0
Nielsen, St. Petersburg*	1	8	.111	4.64	14	12	0	1	0	0	66.0	71	40	34	4	2	17	1	40	0
Niles, Winter Haven	0	0	.000	12.00	1	0	0	1	0	0	3.0	7	5	4	0	1	0	0	1	0
Ogliaruso, Dunedin	0	3	.000	14.09	11	2	0	7	0	0	15.1	22	24	24	1	3	29	1	9	6
Oliver, Charlotte*	1	0	1.000	0.72	8	2	1	2	1	2	25.0	11	2	2	0	2	10	2	33	3
Olsen, Sarasota	11	1	.917	1.94	13	13	3	0	1	0	88.0	68	22	19	4	3	32	0	85	3
Owen, Winter Haven*	0	2	.000	3.40	8	7	0	0	0	0	45.0	36	22	17	0	4	25	0	27	1
Parkins, Winter Haven	0	3	.000	1.53	10	3	1	1	0	0	35.1	22	15	6	2	2	13	0	28	1
Patterson, Clearwater	2	1	.667	1.98	30	0	0	22	0	14	36.1	29	11	8	0	2	11	2	33	3
Perez, Fort Lauderdale	4	2	.667	2.70	33	1	0	15	0	2	56.2	44	25	21	1	3	30	4	79	1
Dario Perez, Baseball City	8	4	.667	3.05	28	16	2	4	1	0	118.0	107	46	40	7	9	36	0	82	8
Perez, Charlotte	5	2	.714	2.12	13	7	1	5	1	3	59.1	44	14	14	3	1	15	2	31	2
V. Perez, Baseball City	3	3	.500	1.98	20	0	0	17	0	4	36.1	33	14	8	1	0	17	4	23	0
Perigny, Sarasota	6	1	.857	0.76	52	0	0	35	0	20	70.2	55	10	6	0	4	23	6	59	3
Persing, Miracle	4	4	.500	3.32	13	12	1	0	0	0	81.1	88	38	30	3	4	28	0	37	8
Person, Sarasota	5	7	.417	3.59	19	18	1	0	1	0	105.1	90	48	42	7	1	62	1	85	7
Peters, Baseball City	0	2	.000	4.02	4	4	0	0	0	0	15.2	19	8	7	1	1	10	0	11	0
Peterson, Miracle	1	2	.333	4.42	7	7	0	0	0	0	36.2	41	18	18	1	1	13	1	15	0
Pfaff, Lakeland	7	7	.500	2.14	21	21	1	0	0	0	134.1	112	39	32	5	8	33	1	79	5

Pitcher, Team	W	L	Pct.	ERA	G	GS	CG	GF	ShO	Sv.	IP	H	R	ER	HR	HB	BB	Int. BB	SO	WP
Pierce, Sarasota	0	0	.000	0.00	1	0	0	1	0	0	0.2	0	0	0	0	1	0	0	1	0
Piotrowicz, Vero Beach	3	1	.750	1.89	24	1	0	12	0	7	47.2	37	13	10	1	1	7	1	40	0
Pittsley, Baseball City	0	0	.000	0.00	1	1	0	0	0	0	3.0	2	0	0	0	0	1	0	4	0
Pollard, Baseball City	4	3	.571	2.66	49	0	0	35	0	13	71.0	46	30	21	2	1	43	3	51	6
Ponte, Osceola	1	1	.500	7.30	7	0	0	4	0	0	12.1	15	11	10	2	0	6	1	12	0
Powell, West Palm Beach	3	7	.300	4.26	25	15	0	5	0	0	99.1	100	56	47	3	9	30	0	72	1
Powers, Winter Haven	5	10	.333	4.51	21	21	4	0	1	0	133.2	129	72	67	4	1	62	1	105	4
Proctor, St. Lucie	3	6	.333	4.03	11	11	1	0	0	0	67.0	74	39	30	2	3	20	0	34	5
Purvis, Osceola*	1	1	.500	2.92	4	2	0	1	0	0	12.1	18	8	4	0	2	4	1	6	0
Raley, Lakeland	0	0	.000	7.71	4	0	0	4	0	0	4.2	8	4	4	1	0	2	0	1	1
Ralph, Fort Lauderdale	1	2	.333	2.45	12	0	0	6	0	1	22.0	23	10	6	2	3	7	1	22	1
Randall, Clearwater	0	2	.000	2.88	33	0	0	14	0	6	40.2	39	16	13	1	4	8	2	16	3
Rees, St. Lucie	1	1	.500	4.63	3	3	0	0	0	0	11.2	15	10	6	0	2	4	0	6	0
Reid, Lakeland	0	0	.000	4.50	3	1	0	0	0	0	6.0	9	4	3	0	0	2	0	4	1
Rendina, Lakeland*	0	0	.000	0.00	1	0	0	1	0	0	1.0	1	0	0	0	0	0	0	1	0
Renko, Winter Haven	3	5	.375	3.96	10	10	1	0	0	0	61.1	65	33	27	7	2	16	0	56	2
Rhodes, Fort Lauderdale	2	6	.250	5.50	16	12	0	3	0	1	68.2	75	51	42	3	2	41	1	38	6
Rich, Dunedin	0	1	.000	12.27	4	0	0	1	0	1	3.2	4	5	5	0	1	3	1	6	0
Ringkamp, Miracle	6	2	.750	2.94	39	1	0	17	0	2	64.1	64	27	21	1	3	16	1	40	1
Rivera, Fort Lauderdale	5	3	.625	2.28	10	10	3	0	1	0	59.1	40	17	15	5	0	5	0	42	0
Roa, St. Lucie	9	7	.563	3.63	26	24	2	0	1	0	156.1	176	80	63	9	6	15	1	61	0
Rodriguez, Lakeland*	4	4	.500	3.57	21	1	0	3	0	0	80.2	85	40	32	8	2	33	0	63	1
Rogers, St. Lucie	2	4	.333	2.93	17	0	0	6	0	2	30.2	24	12	10	1	2	7	2	17	1
Roman, Osceola	0	0	.000	0.00	1	0	0	1	0	0	2.0	2	0	0	0	0	1	0	1	0
Ruff, Lakeland	0	1	.000	13.50	1	0	0	1	0	0	2.0	2	3	3	1	0	0	0	0	0
Ruffcorn, Sarasota	14	5	.737	2.19	25	24	2	0	0	0	160.1	122	53	39	7	3	39	0	140	3
Ruffin, Sarasota	3	7	.300	5.89	23	8	0	6	0	0	62.2	56	46	41	5	4	61	0	61	10
Sadecki, Charlotte	5	7	.417	1.86	16	12	1	1	0	0	72.2	61	24	15	1	0	20	0	49	0
Saltzgaber, Lakeland	0	0	.000	9.00	1	0	0	0	0	0	1.0	2	1	1	0	0	1	0	0	2
Salvior, St. Petersburg	3	1	.750	1.61	16	0	0	4	0	2	22.1	15	5	4	0	1	7	1	8	1
A. Sanchez, Baseball City	6	5	.545	3.43	15	13	3	0	2	0	78.2	61	33	30	2	4	41	0	42	5
J. Sanchez, Baseball City	1	0	1.000	4.50	3	0	0	2	0	0	4.0	6	2	2	0	0	1	0	6	1
Santamaria, Winter Haven	0	0	.000	4.26	16	0	0	10	0	2	12.2	18	15	6	2	1	9	1	13	2
Santos, Baseball City*	0	0	.000	1.23	3	2	0	0	0	0	7.1	6	1	1	0	0	4	0	5	0
Schmidt, West Palm Beach	0	0	.000	0.00	3	0	0	2	0	0	5.0	3	0	0	0	0	1	0	3	0
Schoenvogel, Winter Haven	3	7	.300	5.09	14	13	2	0	0	0	74.1	86	46	42	3	3	15	0	42	3
Schrenk, Sarasota	15	2	.882	2.05	25	22	4	2	2	1	154.0	130	48	35	1	7	40	2	113	7
Schuermann, Miracle*	4	7	.364	4.69	51	5	0	17	0	2	86.1	87	51	45	1	2	56	1	68	7
Schwarber, Lakeland	0	0	.000	0.00	1	0	0	0	0	0	2.0	1	0	0	0	0	2	1	4	0
Scott, Osceola	0	0	.000	9.00	1	0	0	1	0	0	1.0	1	1	1	0	1	1	0	2	0
Seiler, Fort Lauderdale*	0	0	.000	1.80	9	0	0	6	0	0	15.0	19	7	3	1	0	6	0	4	0
Sepeda, Clearwater	2	3	.400	3.60	6	6	0	0	0	0	35.0	33	14	14	0	1	12	0	27	1
Shanahan, St. Lucie*	3	2	.600	3.31	25	6	0	5	0	0	73.1	74	29	27	5	2	25	2	38	4
Shaw, Baseball City	8	3	.727	2.83	40	2	0	9	0	3	86.0	77	35	27	5	4	21	0	35	1
Shaw, Charlotte	2	2	.500	4.23	29	1	0	13	0	1	55.1	57	29	26	4	3	23	4	31	2
Shiflett, Charlotte	0	0	.000	0.00	4	1	0	1	0	0	9.1	3	0	0	0	0	4	0	4	0
Sinacori, Vero Beach	5	4	.556	3.22	42	3	1	28	0	10	67.0	62	30	24	2	5	32	2	48	8
Singer, Dunedin*	10	7	.588	4.00	26	25	1	0	1	0	139.1	127	80	62	9	3	62	0	104	9
Small, Osceola	5	9	.357	3.86	22	20	1	2	0	0	105.0	97	56	45	8	0	38	0	69	5
Smith, Baseball City	0	1	.000	6.43	2	2	0	0	0	0	7.0	10	6	5	0	0	1	0	6	0
Smith, St. Lucie*	4	5	.444	3.17	11	11	2	0	1	0	65.1	63	33	23	6	3	20	0	39	3
Soto, Sarasota	0	1	.000	6.75	1	1	0	0	0	0	4.0	1	3	3	0	1	2	0	4	0
Starks, Sarasota	0	1	.000	10.50	4	0	0	4	0	0	6.0	6	7	7	0	0	9	0	6	6
Starr, Charlotte	0	0	.000	0.00	5	0	0	1	0	0	6.0	7	1	0	0	5	2	0	5	0
Steed, Dunedin	6	6	.500	3.81	20	19	2	1	0	0	104.0	106	56	44	4	9	40	0	57	11
Stevens, Baseball City	0	0	.000	2.19	6	0	0	1	0	0	12.1	7	4	3	0	0	8	0	7	1
Stidham, Lakeland	2	7	.222	3.69	45	0	0	27	0	6	53.2	61	28	22	3	3	28	2	47	4
Stieb, Dunedin	1	1	.500	2.13	2	2	0	0	0	0	12.2	7	6	3	0	2	4	0	11	0
Stowell, Sarasota*	0	0	.000	0.00	3	0	0	1	0	0	3.2	3	0	0	0	0	1	0	2	0
Stryker, Vero Beach	1	3	.250	2.79	37	1	0	13	0	2	84.0	76	36	26	9	1	9	1	59	3
Sullivan, Fort Lauderdale*	3	7	.300	4.02	12	11	0	0	0	0	69.1	83	37	31	1	5	27	0	27	5
Sullivan, Clearwater	2	0	1.000	1.05	24	0	0	21	0	10	25.2	16	3	3	0	1	2	1	24	0
Swope, Miracle	1	15	.063	3.87	19	19	3	0	0	0	97.2	101	58	42	6	5	35	0	51	6
B. Taylor, Fort Lauderdale*	8	6	.429	2.57	27	27	0	0	0	0	161.1	121	60	46	3	11	66	0	187	12
W. Taylor, Fort Lauderdale	0	1	.000	0.00	1	1	0	0	0	0	4.0	1	2	0	0	1	0	1	0	0
Thomas, Sarasota*	5	0	1.000	1.62	8	8	0	0	0	0	55.2	44	14	10	1	0	7	1	50	2
Tijerina, St. Lucie	0	1	.000	27.00	1	0	0	0	0	0	1.0	3	3	3	0	0	1	0	1	0
Timlin, Dunedin	0	0	.000	0.90	6	1	0	1	0	1	10.0	9	2	1	0	0	2	1	7	1
Torres, Lakeland	2	1	.667	3.52	8	0	0	3	0	0	7.2	7	4	3	0	0	1	0	7	2
Tuss, West Palm Beach	2	3	.400	3.43	30	0	0	14	0	3	44.0	50	19	16	2	3	15	1	31	1
Undorf, Lakeland	3	1	.750	2.28	39	0	0	24	0	11	59.1	60	18	15	0	0	8	0	37	3
Van Ryn, Vero Beach*	10	7	.588	3.20	26	25	1	0	1	0	137.2	125	58	49	4	2	54	1	108	4
Vlcek, Charlotte	0	1	.000	18.00	2	0	0	2	0	0	2.0	4	4	4	0	0	1	0	2	0
Wall, Osceola	3	1	.750	2.63	7	7	0	0	0	0	41.0	37	13	12	1	2	8	0	30	2
Wallin, Winter Haven*	0	0	.000	4.50	2	0	0	2	0	0	2.0	1	1	1	0	0	1	0	1	0
Ware, Dunedin	5	3	.625	2.63	12	12	1	0	1	0	75.1	64	26	22	1	3	30	0	49	7
Washington, Miracle	2	2	.500	3.05	5	5	0	0	0	0	20.2	25	14	7	0	1	7	0	11	1
Watson, St. Petersburg*	5	4	.556	1.91	14	14	2	0	0	0	89.2	81	31	19	0	2	18	2	80	1
Weaver, Vero Beach	4	11	.267	4.12	19	18	1	0	0	0	89.2	73	52	41	7	1	57	0	73	17
Weber, St. Petersburg*	4	8	.333	3.25	24	17	0	2	0	0	99.2	108	45	36	2	1	47	0	52	10
Wells, Clearwater	1	0	1.000	3.86	9	0	0	8	0	5	9.1	10	4	4	0	3	2	0	9	3
Wengert, Vero Beach	1	0	1.000	5.16	5	5	0	0	0	0	22.2	31	14	13	5	1	6	0	15	2
Wheeler, Osceola*	1	2	.333	6.23	5	5	0	0	0	0	21.2	32	21	15	3	0	10	0	7	0
Wiggs, Lakeland*	1	1	.500	2.00	14	1	0	3	0	0	18.0	15	5	4	1	0	8	1	24	1
Wiley, Fort Lauderdale	4	4	.500	4.19	11	10	2	0	0	0	62.1	74	39	29	4	3	18	0	23	2
Wiley, Baseball City	3	1	.750	2.08	10	0	0	7	0	2	17.1	15	4	4	1	0	3	1	18	0
Wiseman, Miracle*	0	0	.000	81.00	1	0	0	0	0	0	0.2	3	6	6	0	0	3	0	0	2
Wray, Vero Beach*	2	6	.250	2.95	47	0	0	18	0	3	58.0	59	27	19	7	1	14	0	53	1
Young, Winter Haven	5	4	.556	1.57	20	0	0	18	0	6	34.1	22	6	6	1	0	14	0	26	3

BALKS—B. Taylor, 10; S. Baker, 8; Castillo, 7; Fyhrie, Schrenk, 6 each; Farmer, Van Ryn, 5 each; Batista, Burrows, Kosenski, Lima, Linehan, Dario Perez, O. Smith, 4 each; Allen (Clearwater), Bailey, Bennett, Brow, Crawford, Giberti, Goergen, Gross, A. Gutierrez, Henkel, Karsay, Lipson, S. Long, McDonald, McGarity, Mintz, Parkins, C. Perez, Ware, 3 each; Bergman, Coppeta, Dovey, Elli, Faw, Freitas, Grove, Henry, Hernandez, Johnston, Jordan, Leon, K. Miller, Mitchelson, Morphy, Olsen, Owen, Piotrowicz, Proctor, Ralph, Ringkamp, Ruffin, Sadecki, Schuerman, Shanahan, Shiflett, Washington, Weaver, 2 each; Adamson, Alberro, Bouton, Brosnan, Brownholtz, Burbank, Caridad, Chrisman, Creek, Daspit, C.L. Davis, R. Diaz,

Donovan, Dorn, Dougherty, Eversgerd, Flener, Fletcher, Foster, Ganote, Goetz, Gray, Grewal, Guilfoyle, R. Gutierrez, Guzik, Harriger, Helling, C. Hill, E. Hill, Hotchkiss, Jean, Johnson, Kelly, Landress, Lane, Levine, Locklear, A. Long, Luckham, MacNeil, Maloney, Martin, McCann, Nielsen, Patterson, David Perez, Perigny, Pfaff, Pollard, Powell, Roa, Rodriguez, Ruffcorn, A. Sanchez, Schoenvogel, K. Shaw, S. Shaw, Small, Steed, Stevens, Stidham, Stieb, Swope, Torres, Weber, Young, 1 each.

COMBINATION SHUTOUTS—Fyhrie-Landress, Fyhrie-Pollard, Gross-Lieber, Gross-Long-Pollard, Harris-Perez-Long, Landress-Kobetitsch-Wiley, Pittsley-D. Perez-Landress-Wiley, Santos-Shaw-Kobetitsch, Baseball City; Brownholtz-Shaw, Burrows-Arner, Burrows-Perez, Dreyer-Goetz, Geeve-Alberro, Geeve-Bouton, Helling-Bouton-Shaw, Miller-Felix, Oliver-Alberro-Hurst, Perez-Hurst, Perez-Hurst-Goetz, Charlotte; Adamson-Munoz, Adamson-Patterson, Allen-Munoz, Elli-Gaddy-Patterson, Farmer-Randall-Sullivan, Goedhart-Patterson, Goergen-Lindsey-Sullivan, Gray-Langley-Patterson, Gray-Patterson, Gray-Patterson, Hassinger-Randall, Hill-Gaddy-Patterson, Clearwater; Brow-Flener 2, Brow-Duey-Jordan, Flener-Jordan, Karsay-Steed, Singer-Duey-Flener, Dunedin; Faw-Gogolewski, Faw-Ralph, Jean-Morphy, Morphy-Haller-Gogolewski, Perez-Morphy, Taylor-Burbank, Taylor-Johnston-Gogolewski, Taylor-Morphy-Johnston, Fort Lauderdale; Bergman-Stidham, Bergman-Wiggs, Drell-Lira-Undorf, Haeger-Undorf, Henry-Stidham, Lima-Undorf, Pfaff-Stidham-Undorf, Pfaff-Undorf, Lakeland; Diaz-Kohl-Best, Giberti-Hoppe, Giberti-Kohl, Giberti-Schuermann, Misuraca-Kohl, Misuraca-Ringkamp-Schuermann, Nedin-Schuermann-Hoppe-Best, Persing-Best, Schuermann-Best, Miracle; Hill-Gonzales, Hill-Lane, Ketchen-Dougherty, Ketchen-Gonzales-Dougherty, Ketchen-Lane-Dougherty, Lewis-Gonzales, Wall-Gonzales-Dougherty, Osceola; Ruffcorn-Perigny 2, Bere-Gordon, Olsen-Campos, Olsen-Campos-Perigny, Olsen-Gordon, Person-Caridad-Gordon, Ruffcorn-Keating-Caridad, Ruffcorn-Locklear, Ruffcorn-Locklear-Perigny, Ruffin-Gordon-Caridad-Perigny, Schrenk-Keating-Locklear-Perigny, Sarasota; Castillo-Rogers-Crawford, Guzik-Freitas, Roa-Freitas, Roa-Harriger-Freitas, St. Lucie; S. Baker-Fletcher-Kelly, S. Baker-Kelly, Barber-Fletcher-Kelly, Barber-Kelly, Creek-Fletcher-Kelly, Magrane-Fletcher-Kelly, Watson-Eversgerd-Fletcher, Watson-Fletcher-Kelly, St. Petersburg; Delahoya-Piotrowicz 2, Hamilton-Mintz, Jones-Hamilton-Sinacori, Mintz-Wray-Piotrowicz, Van Ryn-Mintz, Van Ryn-Stryker, Weaver-Mintz, Wengert-Piotrowicz-Wray, Vero Beach; Alvarez-Baxter, Alvarez-Grewal, Eischen-Baxter-Schmidt, Eischen-Brewer-Grewal, Eischen-Tuss, Foster-Tuss, Long-Baxter, Long-Brewer, Powell-Long-Tuss, West Palm Beach; Bennett-Dzafic, C.C. Davis-Amos, Maloney-Ciccarella, Powers-Young, Renko-Ciccarella, Schoenvogel-Miller, Winter Haven.

NO-HIT GAMES—Singer, Dunedin, defeated Miracle, 2-0, May 5; Eischen, West Palm Beach, defeated Vero Beach, 5-0 (first game), June 16; Weaver, Vero Beach, defeated Fort Lauderdale, 2-1 (first game), July 17; Carter, Clearwater, defeated Winter Haven, 1-0, August 23; Bakkum, Winter Haven, lost to Clearwater, 1-0, August 23.

FIELDING

TEAM

Team	Pct.	G	PO	A	E	DP	PB
Lakeland	.975	132	3384	1389	122	87	14
West Palm Beach	.972	137	3680	1535	148	105	19
Clearwater	.970	134	3554	1484	154	110	30
St. Petersburg	.970	133	3452	1429	152	113	16
Charlotte	.969	135	3526	1453	158	123	16
Baseball City	.965	131	3375	1357	170	106	14
Vero Beach	.965	135	3375	1370	173	102	18
Winter Haven	.965	137	3471	1467	181	120	22
Sarasota	.965	133	3526	1434	182	101	31
Miracle	.964	131	3380	1463	179	116	15
Dunedin	.964	137	3624	1575	194	106	27
Fort Lauderdale	.962	135	3526	1484	196	120	40
St. Lucie	.962	136	3505	1643	205	139	12
Osceola	.958	134	3506	1410	218	104	28

Triple plays—Baseball City, West Palm Beach.

INDIVIDUAL

FIRST BASEMEN

*Throws lefthanded.

Player, Team	Pct.	G	PO	A	E	DP
Adriana, Dunedin	.976	4	37	3	1	2
Boyzuick, Vero Beach	.982	8	48	6	1	3
Brady, Clearwater	1.000	12	89	9	0	12
Bruce, St. Petersburg	.959	17	113	5	5	6
Buckley, Miracle	.978	33	249	19	6	15
Burns, Osceola	.983	39	277	15	5	21
Burton, Charlotte	.987	107	965	76	14	76
Cantu, St. Petersburg	.989	68	599	42	7	44
Castellano, Charlotte	1.000	16	117	4	0	9
Christopherson, Osceola	1.000	3	16	1	0	1
Clinton, Charlotte	.988	22	157	12	2	21
Cole, Baseball City	.951	4	36	3	2	1
Coleman, Sarasota	.989	19	161	16	2	12
Colon, Winter Haven	1.000	11	72	9	0	5
Coughlin, Sarasota*	1.000	9	59	6	0	4
Dando, Baseball City*	.986	23	128	9	2	14
Daniel, West Palm Beach	.992	18	111	7	1	9
Demus, Winter Haven	1.000	1	9	1	0	0
Durkin, Winter Haven	1.000	1	1	0	0	0
Eatinger, Sarasota	1.000	1	12	0	0	2
Eldridge, St. Petersburg	.946	13	87	1	5	11
Ellis, St. Petersburg	1.000	3	24	1	0	6
Estevez, Miracle	.958	15	84	8	4	6
Evans, Osceola*	.991	19	104	10	1	6
Gallardo, Fort Lauderdale	.975	9	75	3	2	6
Geisler, Clearwater*	.991	109	965	58	9	76
Gilliam, Fort Lauderdale	.900	3	26	1	3	1
Gonzalez, Vero Beach	.984	8	60	2	1	8
Griffin, Vero Beach	1.000	10	72	5	0	3
Hamelin, Baseball City*	.864	3	18	1	3	3
Harmes, Dunedin	1.000	2	19	4	0	1
Harris, St. Lucie	.984	66	572	43	10	47
Hecker, Winter Haven	.976	39	296	25	8	30
Howell, St. Petersburg*	.992	27	238	17	2	21
Hyde, St. Petersburg	1.000	1	1	0	0	0
Hyers, Dunedin*	.993	123	1149	102	9	93
Jacobs, St. Lucie*	.988	79	702	54	9	76
Keighley, West Palm Beach	.952	2	19	1	1	2
Kirkpatrick, Vero Beach	.988	104	778	78	10	67
Lewis, St. Petersburg*	.970	3	30	2	1	2
Madril, Winter Haven	1.000	4	26	0	0	2
McDonald, West Palm Beach	1.000	5	38	3	0	1
Meyer, Clearwater	1.000	2	14	0	0	0
Millan, St. Lucie	.955	2	21	0	1	2
Miller, Dunedin	.988	8	76	4	1	3
Mota, Miracle	.980	92	768	48	17	74

Player, Team	Pct.	G	PO	A	E	DP
Mulville, Clearwater	1.000	3	5	0	0	1
O'Donnell, Vero Beach	.991	12	93	12	1	10
Perona, Lakeland	1.000	1	8	0	0	1
Petagine, Osceola	.987	84	701	74	10	58
Radziewicz, St. Petersburg*	.984	15	105	15	2	6
RENDINA, Lakeland*	.998	115	977	84	2	62
Roberts, Miracle	.953	5	37	4	2	8
Robertson, Sarasota*	.991	104	870	112	9	66
Rolls, Charlotte	.875	1	7	0	1	1
Ruff, Lakeland	.993	17	121	13	1	11
Rusk, Clearwater	.992	14	115	8	1	6
Saltzgaber, Lakeland	.976	11	78	4	2	5
Scott, Osceola	1.000	1	2	0	0	0
Steffens, Clearwater*	.988	13	81	4	1	6
Stewart, Baseball City	1.000	2	8	2	0	1
Strange, Sarasota	1.000	13	71	4	0	7
Trevino, Clearwater	.989	125	1076	89	13	96
Turner, Fort Lauderdale*	.986	101	879	44	13	68
Vitiello, Baseball City	1.000	2	8	1	0	0
Walker, Sarasota	.989	89	745	69	9	66
Wallin, Winter Haven*	1.000	1	1	0	0	0
Weimerskirch, West Palm Beach	.989	127	1103	115	13	87
Wilstead, West Palm Beach*	.968	9	58	2	2	6
Winslow, Osceola	1.000	1	3	0	0	0
Wiseman, Miracle*						

Triple plays—Vitiello, Wilstead.

SECOND BASEMEN

Player, Team	Pct.	G	PO	A	E	DP
Abreu, St. Petersburg	.948	19	24	49	4	9
Adriana, Dunedin	.959	45	101	108	9	22
Alfonzo, St. Lucie	1.000	1	1	3	0	0
Aversa, St. Petersburg	1.000	12	10	13	0	4
Bieser, Clearwater	.952	7	8	12	1	4
Brady, Sarasota	.957	13	14	31	2	2
Bridges, Baseball City	1.000	12	32	36	0	4
Byrd, Winter Haven	1.000	1	0	3	0	1
Cairo, Vero Beach	.921	19	38	32	6	10
Campbell, West Palm Beach	1.000	5	4	1	0	0
Capellan, Baseball City	.930	10	22	31	4	5
Castleberry, Sarasota	.967	24	42	77	4	15
Cholowsky, St. Petersburg	.963	47	88	120	8	18
Christopherson, Osceola	1.000	4	2	6	0	1
Clinton, Charlotte	.982	16	18	37	1	4
Coleman, Sarasota	.970	51	95	134	7	25
Durham, Sarasota	.945	45	66	107	10	17
Durkin, Winter Haven	1.000	9	20	20	0	6
Eatinger, Sarasota	.875	4	5	9	2	0

— 433 —

Player, Team	Pct.	G	PO	A	E	DP
Erickson, Fort Lauderdale	1.000	2	3	7	0	1
Evangelista, Miracle	.974	40	85	106	5	18
Ferreira, Winter Haven	.977	81	156	231	9	42
Gallardo, Fort Lauderdale	.933	3	12	2	1	0
Griffin, Vero Beach	.985	16	24	42	1	8
Hajek, Osceola	1.000	2	6	8	0	3
Hankins, Fort Lauderdale	.964	75	136	208	13	46
Hansen, Fort Lauderdale	.959	43	89	97	8	23
Hardge, West Palm Beach	1.000	4	2	13	0	0
Henderson, Clearwater	1.000	3	4	11	0	1
Howard, Lakeland	.975	51	76	122	5	25
Jenkins, West Palm Beach	.964	94	174	260	16	48
Johnson, Baseball City	.966	27	33	82	4	12
King, St. Lucie	.966	23	31	53	3	11
Kliafas, Vero Beach	.938	4	6	9	1	1
Lambert, Osceola	.926	5	12	13	2	6
Landinez, St. Petersburg	1.000	7	17	20	0	1
Lowery, Charlotte	.941	16	16	32	3	8
Malinoski, West Palm Beach	.964	12	22	31	2	4
Martinez, Vero Beach	.909	2	5	5	1	1
McKamie, Vero Beach	.909	16	26	34	6	6
Mejia, Vero Beach	.960	88	148	212	15	35
Millan, St. Lucie	.935	13	16	27	3	7
Miller, Dunedin	.992	24	47	71	1	18
Miranda, 6 B.C. - 11 Sar.	.972	17	33	37	2	5
Morillo, Baseball City	1.000	2	3	2	0	0
Mouton, Osceola	.934	126	288	294	41	61
Newkirk, Charlotte	.984	114	169	308	8	64
Noriega, Fort Lauderdale	.964	7	10	17	1	6
O'Donnell, Vero Beach	1.000	2	1	2	0	0
O'Neal, Lakeland	.964	96	166	231	15	37
Ollison, Clearwater	.964	24	49	59	4	14
Ozuna, St. Petersburg	.963	38	62	93	6	28
RAABE, Miracle	.991	101	231	300	5	72
Reyes, West Palm Beach	1.000	3	3	5	0	0
Rodriguez, Fort Lauderdale	.979	9	15	31	1	3
Rodriguez, Dunedin	.903	36	58	100	17	16
Rodriguez, Winter Haven	.946	26	44	78	7	20
Rosario, Dunedin	.956	26	33	75	5	13
Rudolph, St. Petersburg	.955	24	40	66	5	17
Schmidt, Winter Haven	.972	32	63	77	4	14
Sirak, Clearwater	.917	4	5	6	1	3
Stewart, Baseball City	.972	31	71	102	5	24
Tatarian, Baseball City	.965	48	91	129	8	25
Tavarez, Dunedin	.909	15	28	42	7	5
Thomas, Clearwater	.965	105	208	283	18	52
Tosar, West Palm Beach	1.000	29	42	78	0	10
Turco, Charlotte	1.000	5	1	0	0	0
Vina, St. Lucie	.971	106	219	360	17	85

THIRD BASEMEN

Player, Team	Pct.	G	PO	A	E	DP
Abreu, St. Petersburg	.966	52	36	105	5	11
Adriana, Dunedin	1.000	3	1	2	0	0
Alder, Lakeland	.894	92	66	153	26	6
Aversa, St. Petersburg	.900	4	2	7	1	0
Battle, Dunedin	.914	123	58	292	33	15
Boyzuick, Vero Beach	.945	44	37	67	6	7
Brady, Clearwater	.927	13	13	25	3	3
Bruce, St. Petersburg	.908	68	46	131	18	9
Buckley, Miracle	.909	9	5	15	2	1
Burns, Osceola	1.000	8	2	11	0	1
Campbell, West Palm Beach	.903	89	49	164	23	11
Caraballo, Baseball City	.907	65	49	146	20	13
Castellano, Charlotte	.925	107	66	194	21	20
Christopherson, Osceola	.667	7	3	5	4	1
Clinton, Charlotte	.922	16	8	39	4	3
Cole, Baseball City	.909	4	4	6	1	1
Coleman, Sarasota	.800	11	4	12	4	3
Colon, Winter Haven	.875	24	6	36	6	5
Durkin, Winter Haven	.714	2	1	4	2	0
Eatinger, Sarasota	.738	23	11	34	16	1
Erickson, Fort Lauderdale	1.000	1	0	2	0	0
Estevez, Miracle	.944	33	25	42	4	5
Evangelista, Miracle	.929	25	9	43	4	2
Ferreira, Winter Haven	1.000	5	1	0	0	0
Gallardo, Fort Lauderdale	.919	16	12	45	5	4
Griffin, Vero Beach	.867	13	8	18	4	1
Groppuso, Osceola	.906	114	77	240	33	15
Henderson, Clearwater	1.000	1	2	2	0	0
Howard, Lakeland	.958	42	22	70	4	5
Huskey, St. Lucie	.917	128	108	310	38	28
King, St. Lucie	.500	3	0	1	1	0
Krause, West Palm Beach	1.000	1	0	4	0	1
Lambert, Osceola	.919	15	10	24	3	1
Landinez, St. Petersburg	.870	11	6	14	3	1
Lowery, Charlotte	.800	5	4	8	3	0
Malinoski, West Palm Beach	.925	28	8	41	4	0
McDonald, West Palm Beach	.953	36	27	55	4	1
Meyer, Clearwater	.939	92	70	162	15	9
Millan, St. Lucie	.783	7	8	10	5	0
Miranda,	.932	31	20	49	5	4
Nagashima, Vero Beach	.913	53	26	79	10	2
Newkirk, Charlotte	.727	4	0	8	3	1

Player, Team	Pct.	G	PO	A	E	DP
O'Donnell, Vero Beach	.889	19	7	33	5	4
O'Neal, Lakeland	1.000	1	0	4	0	0
Otanez, Vero Beach	.893	13	8	17	3	1
Pagliarulo, Miracle	.895	6	3	14	2	2
Randa, Baseball City	.965	49	40	98	5	7
Reyes, West Palm Beach	1.000	4	0	1	0	0
Rodriguez, Fort Lauderdale	.953	19	12	29	2	4
Rolls, Charlotte	.867	15	4	22	4	2
Romano, Fort Lauderdale	.930	102	63	228	22	14
Rosario, Dunedin	.964	11	5	22	1	2
Rudolph, St. Petersburg	.929	17	7	32	3	4
Saltzgaber, Lakeland	1.000	3	2	5	0	1
Sawkiw, Lakeland	1.000	8	2	13	0	0
Schmidt, Winter Haven	.891	72	43	104	18	6
Sirak, Clearwater	.945	44	45	93	8	9
Stewart, Baseball City	1.000	2	3	4	0	0
Strange, Sarasota	.000	2	0	0	1	0
Tatarian, Baseball City	.979	14	19	28	1	3
Tavarez, Dunedin	1.000	1	1	3	0	0
Tena, Dunedin	.929	10	6	20	2	1
Trevino, Clearwater	1.000	1	1	2	0	0
Turco, Charlotte	.778	3	2	5	2	1
Urcioli, Miracle	.948	43	26	83	6	6
Villalobos, Winter Haven	.919	46	24	89	10	8
WALKER, Sarasota	.953	115	79	182	13	14
Weimerskirch, West Palm Beach	1.000	6	3	3	0	0

SHORTSTOPS

Player, Team	Pct.	G	PO	A	E	DP
Abreu, St. Petersburg	.969	28	40	87	4	15
Adriana, Dunedin	1.000	5	6	6	0	0
Andujar, St. Petersburg	.933	102	128	274	29	48
Aversa, St. Petersburg	.938	7	11	19	2	5
Brady, Sarasota	.922	29	41	65	9	13
Bridges, Baseball City	.964	23	46	62	4	12
Brito, Clearwater	.928	65	72	184	20	25
Brown, Winter Haven	.936	120	187	352	37	75
Byrd, Winter Haven	.934	14	34	37	5	5
Cairo, Vero Beach	.949	18	31	44	4	6
Campbell, West Palm Beach	.976	11	21	20	1	5
Caraballo, Baseball City	1.000	2	4	7	0	2
Castleberry, Sarasota	.750	1	0	3	1	0
Christopherson, Osceola	.857	4	6	12	3	2
Clinton, Charlotte	.929	43	75	107	14	23
Corbin, Miracle	.951	62	93	157	13	30
Crispin, Osceola	1.000	3	0	2	0	0
Dotel, Dunedin	.938	116	203	344	36	65
Eenhoorn, Fort Lauderdale	.925	51	60	138	16	18
Erickson, Fort Lauderdale	.937	70	97	202	20	46
Evangelista, Miracle	.884	37	48	97	19	18
Ferreira, Winter Haven	1.000	4	4	9	0	3
Fraraccio, Sarasota	1.000	1	0	5	0	1
Gallego, Fort Lauderdale	1.000	3	3	5	0	1
GIVENS, Lakeland	.969	123	176	385	18	58
Groppuso, Osceola	.875	3	0	7	1	0
Hajek, Osceola	.923	2	5	7	1	1
Halter, Baseball City	.969	44	70	115	6	17
Hanlon, Charlotte	.963	102	151	261	16	56
Howard, Baseball City	.909	3	3	7	1	0
Howard, Lakeland	.954	14	22	40	3	4
King, St. Lucie	.924	18	17	56	6	10
Kliafas, Vero Beach	.966	8	13	15	1	4
Krause, West Palm Beach	.951	105	166	276	23	48
Lambert, Osceola	.862	8	8	17	4	2
Ledesma, St. Lucie	.930	122	185	411	45	79
Malinoski, West Palm Beach	.965	32	46	93	5	15
Martinez, Vero Beach	.917	2	2	9	1	1
McDonald, West Palm Beach	1.000	1	1	0	0	0
McKamie, Vero Beach	.930	15	20	46	5	5
Meyer, Clearwater	1.000	1	1	0	0	0
Miranda, 8 Sar. - 15 Mir.	.965	23	32	50	3	9
Morillo, Baseball City	.892	32	49	67	14	20
Nevers, Osceola	.918	123	199	347	49	63
Nunez, Osceola	.902	30	40	70	12	14
Ollison, Clearwater	1.000	2	2	4	0	2
Otanez, Vero Beach	.936	95	152	288	30	56
Randa, Baseball City	.909	2	3	7	1	1
Reyes, West Palm Beach	.750	1	1	2	1	0
Rodriguez, Fort Lauderdale	.933	23	37	60	7	10
Rosario, Dunedin	.947	15	24	30	3	3
Sirak, Clearwater	.926	16	20	43	5	11
Stewart, Baseball City	.884	29	39	68	14	9
Stocker, Clearwater	.953	62	102	220	16	32
Tatarian, Baseball City	.800	3	6	6	3	0
Tavarez, Dunedin	.923	8	11	25	3	6
Tosar, West Palm Beach	.909	3	5	5	1	1
Turco, Charlotte	.786	10	3	8	3	3
Urcioli, Miracle	1.000	4	1	5	0	0
Villalobos, Winter Haven	1.000	1	3	3	0	0
Wilson, Sarasota	.929	101	151	278	33	46

Triple plays—Campbell, Halter.

OUTFIELDERS

Player, Team	Pct.	G	PO	A	E	DP
Austin, West Palm Beach	.980	82	137	7	3	0
Baez, Winter Haven	.964	67	129	5	5	1
Battle, St. Petersburg	.988	60	165	3	2	1
Bell, Dunedin	.867	7	13	0	2	0
Bennett, Clearwater	.967	42	83	5	3	1
Bieser, Clearwater	.978	21	43	1	1	0
Bowers, Dunedin	.988	123	247	7	3	0
Brady, Clearwater	1.000	13	19	2	0	0
Bridges, Baseball City	1.000	6	3	0	0	0
Bright, Winter Haven	.976	45	77	5	2	1
Brown, Winter Haven	.975	41	75	3	2	2
Buchanan, Sarasota	.940	48	73	5	5	1
Burton, Baseball City	.983	123	282	16	5	6
Butler, Dunedin*	.975	87	186	8	5	2
Calderon, West Palm Beach	1.000	8	9	0	0	0
Campbell, St. Petersburg*	1.000	8	11	0	0	0
Carvajal, Fort Lauderdale	.947	113	237	14	14	3
Castellano, Charlotte	1.000	4	1	0	0	0
Castillo, Charlotte	.982	96	157	6	3	1
Clem, Miracle*	.933	13	14	0	1	0
Cole, Baseball City	.951	57	113	3	6	0
Coleman, St. Petersburg	.969	21	30	1	1	0
Coleman, St. Lucie	1.000	6	9	0	0	0
Collier, Vero Beach*	.974	51	75	0	2	0
Colon, Winter Haven	.941	13	15	1	1	0
Coughlin, Sarasota*	.993	73	141	5	1	0
Cruz, Osceola*	.980	83	136	8	3	2
Davis, St. Lucie*	.956	133	306	19	15	3
Deller, Fort Lauderdale	.985	37	62	3	1	1
Demerson, Fort Lauderdale	.966	49	81	5	3	2
Donald, St. Petersburg	.971	90	167	2	5	0
Dotel, Dunedin	1.000	1	4	0	0	0
Durkin, Winter Haven	.957	59	88	0	4	0
Ealy, Lakeland*	1.000	8	8	1	0	0
Evans, Osceola*	.951	54	75	3	4	1
Everett, Fort Lauderdale	.975	46	111	5	3	3
Farmer, Clearwater*	.964	77	160	3	6	0
Farrish, Vero Beach	.971	56	98	4	3	2
Floyd, West Palm Beach*	1.000	1	2	0	0	0
Fully, St. Lucie	.957	125	209	13	10	1
Gallardo, Fort Lauderdale	1.000	5	4	1	0	0
Geisler, Clearwater*	1.000	6	5	0	0	0
Gilliam, Fort Lauderdale	.989	62	84	2	1	1
Gonzalez, Vero Beach	.948	69	103	6	6	0
Green, Dunedin	.974	106	182	3	5	1
Gumpf, Baseball City	.943	56	80	2	5	0
Hatcher, Osceola	.967	90	139	8	5	0
Hawkins, Miracle	.953	32	59	2	3	0
Henderson, Miracle	.923	11	12	0	1	0
Herrera, Miracle	1.000	6	7	0	0	0
Herrera, St. Petersburg	.965	57	104	5	4	1
Hodge, Dunedin	.959	50	69	2	3	1
Holland, Charlotte	.977	69	82	2	2	0
Hood, Sarasota	1.000	59	77	3	0	1
Howard, Lakeland	1.000	3	5	1	0	0
Hunter, Osceola	.971	130	295	10	9	3
Hyde, Clearwater	.971	21	34	0	1	0
Jackson, Clearwater	.993	77	141	6	1	1
Jose, St. Petersburg	1.000	5	6	0	0	0
Lane, Miracle	.982	92	218	4	4	1
Lewis, St. Petersburg*	.974	119	183	8	5	2
Lott, Vero Beach	.987	118	214	21	3	3
Mahay, Winter Haven*	.972	18	33	2	1	1
Malave, Winter Haven	.889	7	8	0	1	0
Malinoski, West Palm Beach	1.000	1	1	0	0	0
McClinton, St. Lucie	.972	79	99	6	3	1
McNamara, Lakeland	.980	93	146	2	3	1
Moore, Baseball City	.974	66	148	3	4	1
Morrow, Charlotte	.982	108	262	13	5	1
Murphy, West Palm Beach	.980	83	134	15	3	3
Murray, West Palm Beach	.996	108	229	11	1	1
Noriega, Fort Lauderdale	.946	93	144	15	9	1
Otero, St. Lucie	.990	40	94	6	1	3
Ozuna, St. Petersburg	1.000	7	9	2	0	0
Pemberton, Lakeland	.982	99	147	17	3	3
Pickett, Winter Haven	.970	29	63	2	2	0
Pinkney, Vero Beach	.957	14	18	4	1	0
Pledger, Sarasota	.935	55	96	4	7	0
Plemmons, Sarasota	.970	64	93	5	3	1
Radziewicz, St. Petersburg*	1.000	4	1	0	0	0
Reams, Dunedin	.968	58	87	3	3	0
Reed, West Palm Beach	1.000	9	20	1	0	0
Roberts, Miracle	.931	18	27	0	2	0
Roebuck, Charlotte	.994	90	147	14	1	4
Roman, Osceola	.963	66	122	8	5	3
Romay, Vero Beach	.978	39	81	7	2	2
Rudolph, St. Petersburg	1.000	1	1	0	0	0
Ruff, Lakeland	.987	45	75	3	1	0
Rumsey, Miracle	.954	60	119	6	6	1
Saltzgaber, Lakeland	.986	90	211	3	3	0
Sandy, St. Lucie	1.000	53	92	6	0	0
Savinon, St. Petersburg	.985	53	129	2	2	0
Sawkiw, Lakeland	.961	84	119	4	5	0
Schall, Clearwater	.966	40	56	1	2	0
Shields, Baseball City	1.000	8	18	0	0	0
Shirley, Miracle	.962	92	164	14	7	4
Smith, Baseball City	.957	87	149	7	7	0
Soto, Winter Haven	.944	20	28	6	2	0
Spearman, Vero Beach*	.950	69	148	4	8	2
Steffens, Clearwater*	1.000	29	32	2	0	0
TOKHEIM, Clearwater*	1.000	102	213	8	0	2
Turco, Charlotte	.965	75	130	6	5	2
Twitty, Fort Lauderdale	1.000	8	18	0	0	0
Valrie, Sarasota	.959	51	92	2	4	0
Vinyard, Winter Haven	.992	59	126	2	1	1
Walker, Sarasota	.500	1	1	0	1	0
Walker, Baseball City	.967	64	141	4	5	1
Wallin, Winter Haven*	1.000	1	1	0	0	0
Weimerskirch, West Palm Beach	.974	41	68	6	2	0
White, West Palm Beach	.984	89	187	2	3	0
Wiseman, Miracle*	.928	56	86	4	7	0
Wolak, Sarasota	.974	89	178	8	5	1
Woods, West Palm Beach	.938	13	28	2	2	0
Zambrano, Winter Haven	.981	76	151	4	3	0

CATCHERS

Player, Team	Pct.	G	PO	A	E	DP	PB
Albright, Lakeland	.988	25	154	16	2	2	0
Beals, St. Lucie	1.000	14	63	15	0	0	0
Beasley, St. Petersburg	.993	67	353	47	3	6	13
Bethke, Charlotte	1.000	5	35	1	0	0	0
Bieser, Clearwater	.966	42	232	26	9	0	9
Brooks, Dunedin	.981	26	130	26	3	2	5
Brown, Vero Beach	1.000	5	21	0	0	0	0
Buckley, Miracle	.988	44	214	30	3	4	6
Burns, Osceola	.967	6	23	6	1	0	1
Caple, Miracle	1.000	8	39	7	0	0	3
Castillo, St. Lucie	.967	60	317	40	12	4	6
Daniel, West Palm Beach	.988	38	217	31	3	2	4
H. DeLeon, Baseball City	1.000	2	14	3	0	0	0
Y. DeLeon, Baseball City	.959	16	62	8	3	1	3
Delgado, Winter Haven	.981	56	356	66	8	4	8
Delgado, Dunedin	.986	108	684	89	11	5	18
Demus, Winter Haven	1.000	3	8	0	0	0	0
DiFelice, St. Petersburg	.977	16	73	11	2	1	0
Dunn, St. Lucie	1.000	2	8	1	0	1	0
Durso, Dunedin	.955	4	19	2	1	0	0
Ellis, St. Petersburg	.996	63	423	43	2	6	3
Figga, Fort Lauderdale	.982	80	568	71	12	4	15
Fisk, Sarasota	1.000	4	31	3	0	2	2
Fitzpatrick, West Palm Beach	.987	81	509	83	8	4	12
Gallardo, Fort Lauderdale	1.000	19	143	7	0	1	6
Geren, Winter Haven	.958	5	19	4	1	1	0
Gilmore, Osceola	.98976	80	512	68	6	7	18
Gonzalez, Lakeland	.978	31	165	17	4	1	1
Gray, Vero Beach	1.000	9	72	3	0	0	2
Grifol, Miracle	.984	85	526	96	10	8	5
Haase, Dunedin	1.000	13	45	1	0	1	1
Harmes, Dunedin	1.000	2	9	1	0	0	0
Harris, St. Lucie	1.000	1	1	0	0	0	0
Hernandez, Fort Lauderdale	.917	2	11	0	1	0	0
Huckaby, Vero Beach	.982	67	442	56	9	3	10
Jennings, Baseball City	.997	50	280	45	1	3	3
Keighley, West Palm Beach	.972	32	182	23	6	1	3
Kennedy, Charlotte	.972	11	62	8	2	0	1
Levangie, Winter Haven	.973	70	413	61	13	9	12
Loeb, Dunedin	.938	4	14	1	1	0	1
LUCE, Charlotte	.99006	90	532	66	6	5	5
Luis, Winter Haven	1.000	1	6	1	0	0	0
Lund, Vero Beach	.987	58	408	44	6	6	6
Madril, Winter Haven	.938	9	56	4	4	1	2
A. Martinez, Dunedin	.929	3	11	2	1	0	3
H. Martinez, Dunedin	1.000	2	15	2	0	0	0
Mulville, Clearwater	.973	38	221	31	7	3	7
Nunez, Sarasota	.973	100	651	72	20	9	20
Perona, Lakeland	.981	83	536	40	11	3	13
Pineda, Fort Lauderdale	.971	9	57	9	2	2	3
Quintell, Fort Lauderdale	.982	22	101	7	2	1	12
Roberts, Miracle	1.000	3	2	1	0	0	0
Rolls, Charlotte	.981	48	275	30	6	3	10
Rudolph, St. Lucie	.987	48	201	29	3	2	4
Rusk, Clearwater	.982	21	99	13	2	0	4
Saltzgaber, Lakeland	.957	5	22	0	1	0	0
Sanchez, Fort Lauderdale	.769	3	9	1	3	0	2
Scott, Osceola	.992	59	346	46	3	2	9
Stewart, Baseball City	.979	75	364	56	9	4	8
Strange, Sarasota	.990	47	273	22	3	3	8
Tewell, Clearwater	.987	46	270	26	4	2	10
Tijerina, St. Lucie	.957	28	128	6	6	2	0
Torres, Fort Lauderdale	.960	3	23	1	1	0	0
Walker, Fort Lauderdale	.986	9	67	3	1	0	2

PITCHERS

Player, Team	Pct.	G	PO	A	E	DP
Adamson, Clearwater*	1.000	15	2	14	0	0
Alberro, Charlotte	.909	28	5	5	1	1
Allen, Clearwater	.957	15	4	18	1	3

Player, Team	Pct.	G	PO	A	E	DP
Alvarez, West Palm Beach	.978	19	19	26	1	6
Amos, Winter Haven	1.000	9	0	1	0	0
Anderson, Fort Lauderdale*	1.000	1	0	1	0	0
Anderson, St. Petersburg	.800	5	3	5	2	1
Arner, Charlotte	1.000	7	4	2	0	0
Aversa, St. Petersburg	1.000	3	1	0	0	0
Bailey, St. Petersburg	.944	54	8	9	1	3
E. Baker, St. Petersburg	1.000	12	5	4	0	0
S. Baker, St. Petersburg*	.932	24	4	37	3	2
Bakkum, Winter Haven	1.000	5	2	4	0	0
Baldwin, Sarasota	1.000	6	5	10	0	0
Barber, St. Petersburg	.889	19	8	8	2	1
Barfield, Charlotte*	1.000	3	0	1	0	1
Batista, West Palm Beach	.923	24	16	20	3	3
Bauer, Lakeland*	1.000	7	0	1	0	0
Baxter, West Palm Beach*	.917	42	8	14	2	3
Belcher, Miracle	1.000	9	1	1	0	0
Beltran, St. Petersburg*	1.000	2	2	1	0	0
Bene, Vero Beach	1.000	18	2	0	0	0
Bennett, Winter Haven	.926	26	9	16	2	0
Bere, Sarasota	.976	18	24	16	1	3
Bergman, Lakeland	.893	13	5	20	3	2
Best, Miracle	1.000	44	2	7	0	1
Blomdahl, Lakeland	1.000	10	5	7	0	0
Bobb, Vero Beach	1.000	2	0	1	0	0
Botkin, St. Petersburg	.952	40	7	13	1	0
Bouton, Charlotte	.900	40	2	7	1	0
Brewer, West Palm Beach*	1.000	28	1	6	0	1
Brosnan, Vero Beach*	.895	18	3	14	2	0
Brow, Dunedin	.923	25	11	25	3	2
Brown, Clearwater	1.000	6	0	2	0	0
Brownholtz, Charlotte*	.900	14	5	13	2	1
Burbank, Fort Lauderdale	.750	16	1	5	2	1
Burrows, Charlotte*	.900	14	8	10	2	1
Campos, Sarasota	.909	22	4	6	1	2
Caridad, Sarasota	.909	32	2	8	1	1
Carpentier, St. Lucie	1.000	26	3	8	0	2
Carrara, Dunedin	1.000	5	1	3	0	1
Carter, Clearwater*	1.000	16	5	12	0	0
Carter, Fort Lauderdale*	.750	10	1	2	1	1
Castillo, St. Lucie	.905	24	14	24	4	2
Centala, Baseball City	1.000	5	1	1	0	0
Chiamparino, Charlotte	.800	2	2	2	1	0
Chrisman, Baseball City	.833	32	4	6	2	0
Ciccarella, Winter Haven*	1.000	38	2	6	0	0
Cole, Baseball City	.000	1	0	0	1	0
Coppeta, Lakeland*	1.000	17	2	12	0	1
Costello, Osceola	1.000	10	1	1	0	0
Crawford, St. Lucie*	1.000	25	3	4	0	0
Creek, St. Petersburg*	1.000	13	2	16	0	2
Daspit, Vero Beach	.925	26	11	26	3	0
C.C. Davis, Winter Haven	1.000	7	1	4	0	0
C.L. Davis, Winter Haven	.857	6	3	3	1	0
Delahoya, Vero Beach	.947	14	9	9	1	1
Diaz, West Palm Beach	.970	24	10	22	1	0
Diaz, Miracle	.909	11	2	8	1	0
Donovan, Winter Haven*	.833	5	2	3	1	0
Dorn, St. Lucie	1.000	8	2	0	0	0
Dougherty, Osceola	1.000	57	5	16	0	1
Dovey, Osceola	.667	17	2	2	2	0
Drell, Lakeland	.857	10	2	4	1	0
Dreyer, Charlotte	.940	26	12	35	3	5
Duey, Dunedin	.941	48	6	10	1	0
Duran, Vero Beach*	1.000	2	0	1	0	1
Dzafic, Winter Haven	1.000	25	8	13	0	2
Eddy, West Palm Beach	1.000	4	0	7	0	0
Eischen, West Palm Beach*	.833	27	10	20	6	1
Elli, Clearwater*	1.000	5	1	4	0	0
Eversgerd, St. Petersburg*	.800	57	6	6	3	1
Fajardo, Charlotte	.750	4	2	4	2	0
Farmer, Clearwater*	.875	11	3	4	1	0
Faw, Fort Lauderdale	.926	24	7	18	2	2
Felix, Charlotte*	.667	8	1	1	1	0
Fesh, Osceola*	1.000	3	0	1	0	0
Flener, Dunedin*	.892	41	12	21	4	3
Fletcher, St. Petersburg	1.000	57	6	11	0	0
Foster, West Palm Beach	1.000	16	2	5	0	0
Freitas, St. Lucie	.929	45	2	11	1	0
Fritz, Sarasota	.889	6	0	8	1	0
Fyhrie, Baseball City	.974	26	10	27	1	0
Gaddy, Clearwater*	.957	44	2	20	1	2
Gallaher, Osceola	1.000	1	1	0	0	0
Ganote, Dunedin	.946	23	11	24	2	0
Garcia, Miracle	.952	14	5	15	1	0
Garcia, Dunedin	1.000	14	4	1	0	0
Geeve, Charlotte	.919	25	10	24	3	1
Giberti, Miracle*	.895	24	5	29	4	0
Gies, Charlotte	.917	11	8	14	2	0
Gilmore, Clearwater	.333	5	0	1	2	0
Goedhart, Lakeland	.800	8	4	4	2	1
Goergen, Clearwater	1.000	23	12	12	0	1
Goetz, Charlotte	.750	33	3	0	1	0
Gogolewski, Fort Lauderdale	1.000	37	2	6	0	0
GONZALES, Osceola	1.000	60	9	22	0	1
Gonzalez, Winter Haven	1.000	6	0	1	0	0
Gordon, 9 B.C.-30 Sar.*	.929	39	6	7	1	0

Player, Team	Pct.	G	PO	A	E	DP
Gray, Clearwater	.929	34	6	7	1	0
Grewal, West Palm Beach	1.000	42	1	2	0	1
Gross, Baseball City	.885	26	6	17	3	1
Grove, Dunedin	.967	45	7	22	1	0
Guilfoyle, Lakeland*	1.000	45	3	3	0	0
Gutierrez, Osceola	.789	29	4	11	4	1
Gutierrez, Vero Beach	.800	6	3	5	2	0
Guzik, St. Lucie	1.000	9	11	9	0	1
Haeger, Lakeland*	1.000	8	1	2	0	1
Haller, Fort Lauderdale*	.957	41	9	13	1	1
Hamilton, Vero Beach	.941	25	15	17	2	1
Harriger, St. Lucie	1.000	27	7	21	0	3
Harris, Baseball City	.667	7	2	0	1	0
Harvey, Baseball City	.889	11	3	5	1	0
Hassinger, Clearwater	.867	12	6	7	2	0
Helling, Charlotte	.333	3	0	1	2	0
Henkel, Winter Haven	.906	19	7	22	3	2
Henry, Lakeland*	.905	10	5	14	2	1
Hernandez, Osceola	.889	16	5	3	1	0
Hill, Clearwater	.833	5	2	3	1	2
Hill, Osceola*	.914	30	7	25	3	2
Hillegas, Fort Lauderdale	1.000	1	1	0	0	0
Hooper, Sarasota	.000	3	0	0	1	0
Hoppe, Miracle	.714	37	1	4	2	0
Hotchkiss, Dunedin	.833	37	5	15	4	0
Howell, Vero Beach	1.000	5	1	1	0	0
Hurst, Charlotte*	.938	32	2	13	1	1
Jacome, St. Lucie*	.923	17	5	19	2	0
Jean, Fort Lauderdale	.903	23	7	21	3	1
Johnson, Sarasota	1.000	12	1	6	0	0
Johnston, Fort Lauderdale	.885	41	9	14	3	2
Jones, Vero Beach	1.000	5	3	0	0	0
Jordan, Dunedin*	1.000	45	6	8	0	1
Kamieniecki, Fort Lauderdale	.800	1	2	2	1	0
Karsay, Dunedin	.850	16	5	12	3	2
Keating, Sarasota*	1.000	19	5	8	0	0
Keller, St. Lucie	1.000	14	1	3	0	1
Kelly, St. Petersburg	1.000	56	5	8	0	1
Kerr, Vero Beach*	.950	37	7	12	1	1
Ketchen, Osceola	.971	34	12	21	1	1
Kobetitsch, Baseball City*	.833	31	1	4	1	0
Kohl, Miracle	.923	57	5	19	2	3
Kosenski, Lakeland	.958	27	9	14	1	1
Landress, Baseball City	.857	22	0	6	1	0
Lane, Osceola	.833	53	2	13	3	0
Langley, Clearwater*	.900	48	4	14	2	0
Larosa, West Palm Beach*	.778	22	2	5	2	0
LaRose, Osceola	1.000	12	5	9	0	3
Leon, Charlotte	.667	4	0	2	1	0
Levine, Sarasota	1.000	3	1	3	0	0
Lewis, Osceola	.895	13	10	7	2	0
Lieber, Baseball City	1.000	7	1	4	0	0
Lima, Lakeland	.969	25	18	13	1	2
Lindsey, Clearwater	.952	40	9	11	1	0
Linehan, Osceola*	1.000	1	0	1	0	0
Lipson, Miracle	.944	22	3	14	1	0
Lira, Lakeland	.955	32	4	17	1	0
Locklear, Sarasota*	.923	41	3	9	1	2
Long, Fort Lauderdale	.500	2	0	1	1	1
Long, West Palm Beach	.949	26	15	22	2	2
Long, Baseball City*	1.000	20	2	8	0	1
Luckham, Osceola	1.000	8	5	6	0	0
Lynch, Winter Haven	1.000	11	4	4	0	0
MacNeil, Winter Haven	.667	2	0	2	1	0
Magrane, St. Petersburg*	1.000	3	3	4	0	0
Maloney, Winter Haven*	.931	28	7	20	2	3
Martin, Charlotte	1.000	5	2	2	0	0
Martinez, St. Lucie	.912	17	11	20	3	5
Matznick, Sarasota	1.000	2	2	2	0	0
McCann, St. Lucie	1.000	32	6	8	0	1
McDonald, West Palm Beach	1.000	12	4	4	0	0
McGarity, St. Petersburg	.967	23	9	20	1	1
Miller, Charlotte	.875	12	2	12	2	0
Miller, Winter Haven	.941	29	7	9	1	0
Mintz, Vero Beach	1.000	43	2	7	0	1
Misuraca, Miracle	.946	28	15	20	2	0
Mitchelson, Winter Haven*	1.000	10	1	3	0	0
Mmahat, Fort Lauderdale*	1.000	2	1	0	0	0
Morphy, Fort Lauderdale	.824	37	7	7	3	1
Moya, West Palm Beach	1.000	29	6	5	0	0
Munoz, Clearwater	.938	32	2	13	1	0
Murphy, West Palm Beach	1.000	1	2	0	0	0
Myers, Miracle*	1.000	1	1	1	0	0
Nedin, Miracle	1.000	1	1	0	0	0
Nielsen, St. Petersburg*	.909	14	3	17	2	0
Ogliaruso, Dunedin	1.000	11	1	1	0	0
Oliver, Charlotte*	.909	8	3	7	1	1
Olsen, Sarasota	.947	13	10	8	1	0
Owen, Winter Haven*	.833	8	1	9	2	0
Parkins, Winter Haven	.900	10	6	3	1	0
Patterson, Clearwater	.909	30	3	7	1	1
Perez, Fort Lauderdale	.917	33	3	8	1	2
Perez, Charlotte	1.000	13	3	8	0	0
D. Perez, Baseball City	.929	28	4	9	1	0
V. Perez, Baseball City	1.000	20	2	5	0	0
Perigny, Sarasota	.929	52	2	11	1	1

Player, Team	Pct.	G	PO	A	E	DP		Player, Team	Pct.	G	PO	A	E	DP
Persing, Miracle	.857	13	1	5	1	0		Shaw, Baseball City	.867	40	4	9	2	2
Person, Sarasota	.929	19	12	14	2	1		Shaw, Charlotte	1.000	29	3	9	0	0
Peters, Baseball City	1.000	4	3	4	0	1		Shiflett, Charlotte	.000	4	0	0	1	0
Peterson, Miracle	1.000	7	3	4	0	0		Sinacori, Vero Beach	.889	42	3	13	2	1
Pfaff, Lakeland	.939	21	9	22	2	0		Singer, Dunedin*	.838	27	8	23	6	0
Piotrowicz, Vero Beach	1.000	24	3	6	0	2		Small, Osceola	.833	22	5	10	3	0
Pollard, Baseball City	.923	49	5	7	1	0		Smith, Baseball City	1.000	2	0	1	0	0
Ponte, Osceola	.667	7	1	1	1	0		Smith, St. Lucie*	.941	11	4	12	1	1
Powell, West Palm Beach	.815	25	10	12	5	0		Soto, Sarasota	1.000	1	1	0	0	0
Powers, Winter Haven	1.000	21	8	11	0	1		Starks, Sarasota	1.000	4	1	1	0	0
Proctor, St. Lucie	.850	11	8	9	3	0		Steed, Dunedin	.842	20	13	19	6	0
Purvis, Osceola*	1.000	4	2	2	0	0		Stevens, Baseball City	1.000	6	1	0	0	0
Raley, Lakeland	1.000	4	0	1	0	0		Stidham, Lakeland	.929	45	4	9	1	0
Ralph, Fort Lauderdale	.750	12	1	2	1	0		Stieb, Dunedin	1.000	2	3	2	0	0
Randall, Clearwater	1.000	33	3	9	0	0		Stowell, Sarasota*	1.000	3	0	2	0	0
Reid, Lakeland	1.000	3	0	1	0	0		Stryker, Vero Beach	.952	37	4	16	1	2
Renko, Winter Haven	1.000	10	5	4	0	0		Sullivan, Fort Lauderdale*	.895	12	2	15	2	1
Rhodes, Fort Lauderdale	1.000	16	7	5	0	0		Sullivan, Clearwater	1.000	24	1	5	0	0
Rich, Dunedin	1.000	4	1	0	0	0		Swope, Miracle	.912	19	6	25	3	1
Ringkamp, Miracle	.875	39	3	11	2	2		B. Taylor, Fort Lauderdale*	.850	27	12	22	6	0
Rivera, Fort Lauderdale	1.000	10	3	13	0	1		Thomas, Sarasota*	1.000	8	6	9	0	0
Roa, St. Lucie	.931	26	11	16	2	2		Torres, Lakeland	1.000	8	0	1	0	0
Rodriguez, Lakeland*	1.000	21	3	4	0	1		Tuss, West Palm Beach	1.000	30	3	2	0	0
Rogers, St. Lucie	.875	17	4	3	1	0		Undorf, Lakeland	.957	39	10	12	1	1
Ruffcorn, Sarasota	.973	25	10	26	1	2		Van Ryn, Vero Beach*	.889	26	7	17	3	0
Ruffin, Sarasota	.867	23	6	3	2	0		Wall, Osceola	.909	7	5	5	1	2
Sadecki, Charlotte	.895	16	3	14	2	0		Ware, Dunedin	1.000	12	3	10	0	1
Salvior, St. Petersburg	1.000	16	3	4	0	2		Washington, Miracle	1.000	5	2	8	0	1
A. Sanchez, Baseball City	.864	15	4	15	3	1		Watson, St. Petersburg*	1.000	14	6	11	0	0
Santamaria, Winter Haven	1.000	16	1	2	0	0		Weaver, Vero Beach	.920	19	10	13	2	2
Santos, Baseball City*	1.000	3	0	1	0	0		Weber, St. Petersburg*	.955	24	3	18	1	0
Schmidt, West Palm Beach	1.000	3	2	3	0	0		Wells, Clearwater	.667	9	1	1	1	1
Schoenvogel, Winter Haven	.950	14	7	12	1	0		Wengert, Vero Beach	.833	5	3	2	1	0
Schrenk, Sarasota	.982	25	16	40	1	0		Wheeler, Osceola	.600	5	1	2	2	1
Schuermann, Miracle*	.857	52	7	11	3	0		Wiggs, Lakeland*	1.000	14	0	3	0	0
Schwarber, Lakeland	1.000	1	0	1	0	0		Wiley, Fort Lauderdale	.952	11	5	15	1	1
Seiler, Fort Lauderdale*	.857	9	0	6	1	0		Wiley, Baseball City	1.000	10	0	1	0	0
Sepeda, Clearwater	1.000	6	3	5	0	1		Wray, Vero Beach*	.900	47	6	3	1	0
Shanahan, St. Lucie*	1.000	25	6	7	0	1		Young, Winter Haven	.833	20	3	2	1	0

The following players did not have any fielding statistics at the positions indicated or appeared only as a designated hitter, pinch-hitter or pinch-runner: Ahearne, p; Alfonzo, ss; R. Allen (Winter Haven), p; M. Anderson, p; Austin, 3b; Barry, dh; Bickhardt, p; Bridges, p; Burns, of, p; Carbajal, ph; Cassels, dh, ph; Clark, p; Clinton, c; K. Coleman, ss; Damon, of; Dimare, dh, ph, pr; DiSarcina, dh; Eatinger, p; Elliott, p; Estevez, c; Evangelista, of; Fitzpatrick, 3b, of; Flannelly, dh, ph; Gay, p; Gumpf, p; Haase, 3b; Hajek, p; Lund, p; E. Martinez, dh, ph; Medina, of; J. Mejia, p; Mercedes, p; Niles, p; O'Donnell, of; Pierce, p; Pittsley, p; Rees, p; Rendina, p; Roman, p; Ruff, p; Saltzgaber, p; J. Sanchez, p; Scott, p; E. Soto, c; Starr, p; Tatarian, of; W. Taylor, p; C. Thomas, ss; Tijerina, p; Timlin, p; Trevino, of; Vlcek, p; L. Walker, of; Wallin, p; Weimerskirch, 2b; Wiseman, p.

LEAGUE CHAMPIONS

Year	Team	Pct.		Year	Team	Pct.		Year	Team	Pct.
1919—	Sanford*	.605		1953—	Daytona Beach†	.657		1973—	St. Petersburg d	.575
	Orlando*	.703			DeLand	.703			West Palm Beach	.580
1920—	Tampa	.654		1954—	Jacksonville Beach	.629		1974—	West Palm Beach d	.598
	Tampa	.722			Lakeland†	.594			Fort Lauderdale	.626
1921—	Orlando	.635		1955—	Orlando	.671		1975—	St. Petersburg d	.652
1922—	St. Petersburg	.503			Orlando	.643			Miami	.581
	St. Petersburg	.618		1956—	Cocoa	.614		1976—	Tampa	.559
1923—	Orlando	.667			Cocoa	.671			Lakeland d	.536
	Orlando	.678		1957—	Palatka	.629		1977—	Lakeland d	.616
1924—	Lakeland	.695			Tampa†	.681			West Palm Beach	.583
	Lakeland	.683		1958—	St. Petersburg	.732		1978—	Lakeland	.565
1925—	St. Petersburg	.667			St. Petersburg	.681			Miami§	.539
	Tampa†	.696		1959—	Tampa	.591		1979—	Fort Lauderdale	.643
1926—	Sanford	.647			St. Petersburg†	.612			Winter Haven e	.577
	Sanford	.623		1960—	Lakeland	.731		1980—	Daytona Beach	.628
1927—	Orlando†	.600			Palatka†	.614			Fort Lauderdale d	.606
	Miami	.661		1961—	Tampa†	.710		1981—	Fort Myers	.554
1928-35—Did not operate.					Sarasota	.696			Daytona Beach f	.504
1936—	Gainesville	.542		1962—	Sarasota	.689		1982—	Fort Lauderdale f	.621
	St. Augustine (4th)†	.492			Fort Lauderdale†	.623			Tampa	.546
1937—	Gainesville§	.616		1963—	Sarasota	.645		1983—	Daytona Beach	.634
1938—	Leesburg	.626			Sarasota	.667			Vero Beach f	.515
	Gainesville (2nd)‡	.615		1964—	Fort Lauderdale†	.629		1984—	Tampa	.532
1939—	Sanford§	.787			St. Petersburg	.594			Fort Lauderdale f	.521
1940—	Daytona Beach	.619		1965—	Fort Lauderdale	.627		1985—	Fort Myers g	.590
	Orlando (4th)‡	.507			Fort Lauderdale	.634			Fort Lauderdale	.550
1941—	St. Augustine	.659		1966—	Leesburg†	.781		1986—	St. Petersburg g	.647
	Leesburg (4th)‡	.488			St. Petersburg	.700			West Palm Beach	.593
1942-45—Did not operate.				1967—	St. Petersburg y	.691		1987—	Fort Lauderdale g	.616
1946—	Orlando§	.681			Orlando	.638			Osceola	.576
1947—	St. Augustine	.625		1968—	Miami	.613		1988—	Osceola	.606
	Gainesville (2nd)‡	.584			Orlando z	.579			St. Lucie h	.532
1948—	Orlando	.643		1969—	Miami a	.606		1989—	Port Charlotte h	.540
	Daytona Beach (2nd)‡	.616			Orlando	.606			St. Petersburg	.540
1949—	Gainesville	.635		1970—	Miami b	.662		1990—	West Palm Beach	.697
	St. Augustine (3rd)‡	.556			St. Petersburg	.600			Vero Beach h	.585
1950—	Orlando	.629		1971—	Miami b	.667		1991—	Clearwater	.623
	DeLand (3rd)‡	.590			Daytona Beach	.586			West Palm Beach h	.550
1951—	DeLand§	.643		1972—	Miami c	.562		1992—	Sarasota	.639
1952—	DeLand x	.704			Daytona Beach	.606			Lakeland i	.530
	Palatka (3rd)‡	.569								

*Split-season playoff abandoned after each team won three games. †Won split-season playoff. ‡Won four-club playoff. §Won championship and four-club playoff. xWon both halves of split season. yLeague divided into Eastern and Western divisions with split season. St. Petersburg and Orlando won both halves of split season; St. Petersburg won playoff. zLeague divided into Eastern and Western divisions. Miami won regular-season pennant on basis of highest won-lost percentage. Orlando won four-club playoff involving first two teams in each division. aLeague divided into Southern and Central divisions. Miami won playoff between division leaders. (NOTE—Pennant awarded to playoff winner in 1936.) bLeague divided into Eastern and Western divisions. Miami won regular-season pennant on basis of highest won-loss percentage, and also won four-club playoff involving first two teams in each division. cLeague divided into Eastern and Western divisions. Won four-club playoff involving first two teams in each division. dLeague divided into Northern and Southern divisions. Won four-club playoff involving first two teams in each division. eLeague divided into Northern and Southern divisions. Same two clubs won both halves; won playoffs. fWon split-season playoff. gLeague divided into Western, Central and Southern divisions. Won four-club playoff. hLeague divided into Eastern, Western and Central divisions; played split-season. Won six-club playoff. iLeague divided into Eastern, Western and Central divisions; played split-season. Won eight-club playoff.

MIDWEST LEAGUE

FIRST HALF

NORTHERN DIVISION

Team	W	L	T	Pct.	GB
Appleton (Royals)	41	23	0	.641	......
Beloit (Brewers)	37	29	0	.561	5
South Bend (White Sox)	35	33	1	.515	8
Madison (Athletics)	33	35	0	.485	10
Rockford (Expos)	33	36	0	.478	10 ½
Kenosha (Twins)	29	38	1	.433	13 ½
Kane County (Orioles)	29	39	0	.426	14

SOUTHERN DIVISION

Team	W	L	T	Pct.	GB
Cedar Rapids (Reds)	44	24	0	.647	......
Quad City (Angels)	43	25	0	.632	1
Springfield (Cardinals)	42	28	0	.600	3
Clinton (Giants)	30	39	0	.435	14 ½
Peoria (Cubs)	28	39	0	.418	15 ½
Waterloo (Padres)	28	41	0	.406	16 ½
Burlington (Astros)	22	45	0	.328	21 ½

SECOND HALF

NORTHERN DIVISION

Team	W	L	T	Pct.	GB
Beloit (Brewers)	40	29	0	.580	......
South Bend (White Sox)	38	31	0	.551	2
Kenosha (Twins)	34	32	0	.515	4 ½
Rockford (Expos)	33	34	0	.493	6
Kane County (Orioles)	32	37	0	.464	8
Appleton (Royals)	29	39	0	.426	10 ½
Madison (Athletics)	26	40	0	.394	12 ½

SOUTHERN DIVISION

Team	W	L	T	Pct.	GB
Quad City (Angels)	48	21	0	.696	......
Springfield (Cardinals)	42	28	0	.600	6 ½
Cedar Rapids (Reds)	38	32	0	.543	10 ½
Peoria (Cubs)	34	35	0	.493	14
Waterloo (Padres)	31	37	0	.456	16 ½
Clinton (Giants)	29	40	0	.420	19
Burlington (Astros)	25	44	0	.362	23

COMPOSITE

Team	Q.C.	Spr.	C.R.	Bel.	S.B.	App.	Rock.	Ken.	Peo.	K.C.	Mad.	Wat.	Cln.	Burl.	W	L	T	Pct.	GB
Quad City (Angels)	...	10	8	6	5	5	5	4	9	7	4	8	10	10	91	46	0	.664	......
Springfield (Cardinals)	4	...	11	5	3	5	5	5	6	7	6	8	9	10	84	56	0	.600	8 ½
Cedar Rapids (Reds)	6	3	...	2	6	5	2	5	10	7	8	10	11	8	82	56	0	.594	9 ½
Beloit (Brewers)	2	3	4	...	7	9	11	5	6	5	8	6	3	8	77	58	0	.570	13
South Bend (White Sox)	3	5	2	7	...	6	8	9	5	6	7	6	6	3	73	64	1	.533	18
Appleton (Royals)	3	3	3	4	7	...	6	12	3	10	10	4	3	2	70	62	0	.530	18 ½
Rockford (Expos)	2	3	6	5	6	6	...	6	4	10	5	5	3	5	66	70	0	.485	24 ½
Kenosha (Twins)	2	3	3	7	4	4	6	...	6	6	7	4	6	5	63	70	1	.474	26
Peoria (Cubs)	5	8	4	2	2	3	4	2	...	5	5	5	12	6	62	74	0	.456	28 ½
Kane County (Orioles)	1	1	1	9	6	4	6	8	3	...	6	7	5	4	61	76	0	.445	30
Madison (Athletics)	4	2	1	5	9	4	7	6	2	5	...	4	5	5	59	75	0	.440	30 ½
Waterloo (Padres)	6	6	6	2	2	3	2	4	9	1	4	...	7	7	59	78	0	.431	32
Clinton (Giants)	4	5	4	2	2	5	5	2	9	3	3	6	...	7	59	79	0	.428	32 ½
Burlington (Astros)	4	4	3	0	5	3	3	2	4	3	7	7	...		47	89	0	.346	43 ½

Kane County's home games played in Geneva, Ill.

Quad City's home games played in Davenport, Ia.

Major league affiliations in parentheses.

Playoffs—Cedar Rapids defeated Quad City, two games to none; Beloit defeated Appleton, two games to one; Cedar Rapids defeated Beloit, three games to two, to win league championship.

Regular-season attendance—Appleton, 46,576; Beloit, 60,999; Burlington, 69,679; Cedar Rapids, 133,899; Clinton, 79,374; Kane County, 323,769; Kenosha, 45,349; Madison, 95,046; Peoria, 172,560; Quad City, 250,745; Rockford, 50,900; South Bend, 213,951; Springfield, 152,942; Waterloo, 48,074. Total, 1,743,863. Playoffs (10 games), 13,136. All-Star Game— 3,755.

Managers—Appleton, Tom Poquette; Beloit, Wayne Krenchicki; Burlington, Steve Curry; Cedar Rapids, Mark Berry; Clinton, Bill Stein; Kane County, Joel Youngblood; Kenosha, Jim Dwyer; Madison, Dickie Scott; Peoria, Steve Roadcap; Quad City, Mitch Seoane; Rockford, Rob Leary; South Bend, Terry Francona; Springfield, Rick Colbert; Waterloo, Keith Champion.

All-Star team: 1B—Chris Pritchett, Quad City; 2B—Jason Hardtke, Waterloo; 3B—Dmitri Young, Springfield; SS—Shane Halter, Appleton; OF—Steve Gibralter, Cedar Rapids; Orlando Palmeiro, Quad City; Alex Ochoa, Kane County; C—Damian Miller, Kenosha; DH—Andre Keene, Clinton; LHP—Tyrone Hill, Beloit; RHP—James Baldwin, South Bend; LH Reliever—Ken Grundt, Clinton; RH Reliever—Jerry Santos, Springfield; Most Valuable Player—Steve Gibralter, Cedar Rapids; Manager of the Year—Tom Poquette, Appleton.

BATTING

TEAM

Team	Avg.	G	AB	R	OR	H	TB	2B	3B	HR	RBI	SH	SF	HP	BB	Int. BB	SO	SB	CS	LOB
Beloit	.265	135	4357	668	596	1155	1662	207	33	78	595	57	34	39	585	18	1053	155	108	960
Cedar Rapids	.259	138	4571	724	559	1183	1871	242	34	126	641	29	31	58	528	18	1074	163	79	927
Springfield	.254	140	4644	653	528	1179	1748	224	39	89	570	18	41	60	485	12	849	106	85	949
Appleton	.254	132	4353	618	581	1104	1555	202	30	63	552	39	60	35	483	10	824	145	72	925
Quad City	.253	138	4328	648	490	1093	1523	191	25	63	554	111	54	59	597	22	860	150	78	988
Kenosha	.246	134	4260	550	503	1050	1445	198	25	49	476	41	43	52	490	9	895	156	72	915
Kane County	.245	137	4511	547	636	1106	1461	174	26	43	476	78	28	45	484	19	1030	170	85	997
Rockford	.242	136	4418	542	528	1071	1544	210	28	69	478	25	38	47	348	14	1025	215	90	830
Peoria	.242	136	4447	611	625	1075	1478	213	23	48	513	78	33	97	485	18	966	105	57	983
Waterloo	.242	137	4497	593	739	1087	1546	201	27	68	518	35	31	47	460	15	982	149	63	963
Clinton	.236	138	4513	574	705	1066	1452	172	23	56	490	34	27	69	524	9	1142	193	92	963
South Bend	.236	138	4564	567	535	1078	1489	203	32	48	472	38	35	49	511	22	1018	198	104	951
Burlington	.233	136	4459	526	718	1041	1433	188	27	50	447	29	34	41	451	10	1120	154	75	921
Madison	.232	134	4362	544	622	1013	1412	164	26	61	457	80	32	74	572	15	1114	98	59	1072

(Leading qualifiers for batting championship—378 or more plate appearances)

*Bats lefthanded.   †Switch-hitter.

Player, Team	Avg.	G	AB	R	H	TB	2B	3B	HR	RBI	SH	SF	HP	BB	Int. BB	SO	SB	CS
Palmeiro, Orlando, Quad City*	.317	127	451	83	143	173	22	4	0	41	19	7	5	56	3	41	31	13
Young, Dmitri, Springfield†	.310	135	493	74	153	243	36	6	14	72	0	4	5	51	3	94	14	13
Gibralter, Steve, Cedar Rapids	.306	137	529	92	162	257	32	3	19	99	1	3	12	51	4	99	12	9
Hardtke, Jason, Waterloo†	.304	110	411	75	125	184	27	4	8	47	1	5	5	38	3	33	9	7
Cirillo, Jeff, Beloit	.304	126	444	65	135	195	27	3	9	71	5	6	6	84	6	85	21	12
Williams, George, Madison†	.304	115	349	56	106	143	18	2	5	42	5	1	8	76	6	53	9	5
Ochoa, Alex, Kane County	.295	133	499	65	147	186	22	7	1	59	5	7	7	58	5	55	31	17
Miller, Damian, Kenosha	.292	115	377	53	110	156	27	2	5	56	2	4	7	53	1	66	6	1
Woods, Tyrone, Rockford	.291	101	374	54	109	173	22	3	12	47	0	6	1	34	4	83	15	6
Fairman, Andy, Beloit*	.291	113	395	59	115	174	28	5	7	72	0	6	2	54	4	55	2	2

Departmental leaders: G—Gibralter, Pugh, 137; AB—Goodwin, 542; R—Gibralter, 92; H—Gibralter, 162; TB—Gibralter, 257; 2B—Young, 36; 3B—Wachter, 9; HR—Gibralter, 19; RBI—Gibralter, 99; SH—Forbes, 24; SF—Hinton, 10; HP—Wolff, 23; BB—Riggs, 97; IBB—Cirillo, C. Pritchett, Williams, 6; SO—Swinton, 182; SB—Burton, 65; CS—Burton, 23.

(All players—listed alphabetically)

Player, Team	Avg.	G	AB	R	H	TB	2B	3B	HR	RBI	SH	SF	HP	BB	Int. BB	SO	SB	CS
Abell, Scott, Appleton	.192	12	26	4	5	6	1	0	0	2	0	0	1	2	0	5	1	0
Abercrombie, John, Waterloo	.243	110	358	42	87	138	20	2	9	45	1	3	3	19	1	81	18	3
Adams, Dave, Waterloo*	.230	80	196	22	45	63	9	3	1	23	1	0	1	31	2	43	2	0
Adams, Derek, Kane County	.173	81	179	20	31	40	7	1	0	19	7	0	4	28	0	52	1	2
Albert, Tim, Beloit*	.238	82	168	28	40	41	1	0	0	14	5	3	1	23	0	44	11	7
Alimena, Charles, Clinton*	.218	119	399	39	87	125	12	1	8	51	2	3	2	42	2	105	5	8
Aracena, Luinis, Madison	.167	92	257	24	43	53	6	2	0	18	9	2	6	24	1	64	8	0
Arnold, Ken, Peoria	.210	91	271	41	57	70	4	3	1	22	4	1	3	42	0	65	11	4
Aurila, Brad, Rockford*	.000	1	3	0	0	0	0	0	0	0	0	0	0	1	0	2	0	0
Austin, Corey, South Bend*	.169	68	183	17	31	48	3	1	4	23	1	0	4	13	0	48	6	6
Babbitt, Troy, Appleton*	.192	64	182	25	35	53	6	3	2	18	3	2	0	28	1	27	0	1
Baber, LaRue, Beloit	.204	71	191	32	39	57	7	1	3	21	4	0	1	32	1	61	9	12
Battle, Allen, Springfield	.302	67	235	49	71	101	10	4	4	24	1	2	10	41	0	34	22	12
Beck, Wynn, Beloit*	.313	8	16	1	5	6	1	0	0	1	0	0	0	2	0	2	0	0
Bellomo, Kevin, Clinton	.181	23	94	12	17	30	4	0	3	13	0	0	1	6	0	12	2	0
Benhardt, Chris, Waterloo*	.000	20	1	0	0	0	0	0	0	0	0	0	0	0	0	1	0	0
Berry, Perry, Burlington	.220	102	313	50	69	111	17	2	7	27	1	1	4	38	0	78	5	6
Bertucci, Joseph, Quad City	.000	3	5	0	0	0	0	0	0	0	0	0	0	1	0	3	0	0
Biasucci, Joe, Peoria	.261	74	268	51	70	112	25	1	5	32	5	2	5	32	1	61	9	1
Black, Keith, Springfield	.277	27	47	11	13	27	2	4	1	11	0	1	0	12	0	10	1	0
Blakeman, Todd, Kenosha*	.212	35	104	14	22	33	3	1	2	19	2	2	0	12	0	29	0	1
Blanton, Garrett, Springfield	.178	45	107	11	19	20	1	0	0	6	3	1	2	4	0	30	3	1
Bobo, Elgin, Quad City	.240	27	96	6	23	28	3	1	0	6	0	0	1	6	0	19	0	1
Booker, Eric, Madison	.265	55	196	33	52	77	8	1	5	29	1	1	2	43	0	53	7	2
Boykin, Tyrone, Quad City	.227	119	383	77	87	128	18	1	7	43	2	6	4	93	1	108	20	12
Brady, Doug, South Bend†	.293	24	92	12	27	34	5	1	0	7	2	1	0	17	1	13	16	3
Brakebill, Mark, Quad City	.286	60	199	27	57	79	4	0	6	29	0	1	3	20	0	53	2	3
Bream, Scott, Waterloo	.230	124	392	50	90	114	9	6	1	29	4	0	2	33	0	126	17	9
Brede, Brent, Kenosha*	.242	110	363	44	88	103	15	0	0	29	4	3	4	53	1	77	10	12
Brewer, Matt, Clinton*	.254	18	67	6	17	24	7	0	0	15	0	0	1	3	0	13	3	2
Brown, Brant, Peoria*	.274	70	248	28	68	91	6	0	3	27	3	5	1	24	2	49	3	4
Buchanan, Shawn, South Bend	.248	30	117	15	29	35	3	0	1	12	2	0	0	17	2	25	8	5
Burgos, Carlos, Appleton	.206	22	68	3	14	15	1	0	0	7	0	1	2	3	1	6	0	1
Burton, Essex, South Bend†	.253	122	459	78	116	128	6	3	0	29	9	1	3	67	0	109	65	23
Byrd, Anthony, Kenosha	.233	46	150	15	35	46	5	3	0	10	3	0	0	12	0	35	7	1
Byrne, Clayton, Kane County	.225	109	347	42	78	100	14	1	2	35	6	1	3	13	0	74	12	5
Calcagno, Danny, Clinton	.230	32	87	14	20	20	0	0	0	5	5	0	2	10	0	15	4	1
Cameron, Mike, South Bend	.228	35	114	19	26	39	8	1	1	9	3	1	4	10	0	37	2	3
Campillo, Rob, Rockford	.135	16	37	4	5	7	2	0	0	3	1	0	1	4	0	7	0	0
Caple, Kyle, Kenosha	.195	30	87	3	17	20	3	0	0	6	1	0	0	9	0	26	0	0
Cappuccio, Carmine, South Bend*	.291	49	182	23	53	66	9	2	0	19	1	1	1	21	1	21	2	3
Castaldo, Gregg, Kane County	.162	19	37	2	6	6	0	0	0	3	0	0	2	3	0	6	2	3
Castenada, Hector, Kane County*	.154	5	13	1	2	3	1	0	0	0	0	0	0	0	0	4	0	0
Cerio, Steve, Springfield	.242	120	392	49	95	141	20	1	8	47	1	5	8	28	1	69	1	1
Charles, Frank, Clinton	.000	2	5	1	0	0	0	0	0	0	0	0	0	0	0	3	0	0
Christopher, Terry, Beloit	1.000	30	1	0	1	1	0	0	0	0	0	0	0	0	0	0	0	0
Cirillo, Jeff, Beloit	.304	126	444	65	135	195	27	3	9	71	5	6	6	84	6	85	21	12
Clarke, Jeff, Appleton†	.250	5	8	2	2	2	0	0	0	0	0	0	0	0	0	2	0	0
Claus, Marc, Kenosha	.250	72	224	32	56	68	6	0	2	24	7	1	10	25	0	38	4	1
Claus, Todd, Quad City†	.205	87	234	35	48	62	4	2	2	21	16	1	7	36	2	51	18	6
Coachman, Pete, Quad City	.366	10	41	4	15	16	1	0	0	7	1	0	1	4	0	5	5	0
Colon, Dennis, Burlington*	.253	123	458	54	116	175	27	7	6	63	2	6	2	32	1	50	4	7
Cookson, Brent, Clinton	.214	46	145	30	31	62	5	1	8	20	1	1	3	22	0	48	9	3
Couture, Mike, Beloit	.348	56	187	46	65	98	7	1	8	32	4	0	3	27	1	49	22	12
Craig, Mo, Peoria*	.251	54	175	32	44	56	9	0	1	14	4	0	4	16	1	38	4	5
Cunningham, Earl, Peoria	.227	72	238	30	54	92	10	2	8	34	1	2	12	16	0	98	3	3
Curtis, Craig, Burlington*	.225	58	178	18	40	53	5	1	2	18	2	1	2	20	1	47	16	1
Dana, Derek, Clinton	.182	53	143	15	26	29	3	0	0	8	0	0	2	24	0	40	6	2
Deak, Darrel, Springfield†	.285	126	428	84	122	212	28	7	16	79	2	5	7	65	2	71	12	2
DeBerry, Joe, Cedar Rapids*	.240	127	455	58	109	184	22	4	15	68	0	3	2	43	1	102	3	3
Dehdashtion, Derek, Rockford	.265	60	162	18	43	65	13	0	3	24	1	2	6	19	1	41	1	2
Delaney, Sean, Appleton	.214	22	56	2	12	15	3	0	0	4	0	1	1	2	0	13	0	1
DeLeon, Yabanne, Appleton	.040	9	25	3	1	1	0	0	0	0	1	0	0	2	0	7	0	0
Delgado, Eugene, Kane County	.191	34	89	5	17	19	2	0	0	6	1	0	0	17	0	18	2	2
Delgado, Robert, Clinton	.286	4	7	0	2	2	0	0	0	0	0	0	0	0	0	3	0	0
Dennison, Scott, Rockford	.172	54	134	16	23	28	5	0	0	11	2	0	3	17	0	25	8	6
Diaz, German, Peoria*	.217	26	83	10	18	23	3	1	0	6	0	0	1	5	0	26	2	1
DiSarcina, Glenn, South Bend*	.263	126	467	60	123	167	29	6	1	50	3	6	0	44	4	105	12	5
Dobrolsky, Bill, Beloit	.286	48	133	13	38	52	5	0	3	19	1	1	1	14	0	28	3	2
Dotolo, C.L., Clinton	.246	66	199	15	49	56	7	0	0	13	1	0	2	18	0	55	2	3
Dreifort, Todd, Rockford*	.250	1	4	2	1	2	1	0	0	0	0	0	0	1	0	1	1	0

Player, Team	Avg.	G	AB	R	H	TB	2B	3B	HR	RBI	SH	SF	HP	BB	Int. BB	SO	SB	CS
Dreisbach, Billy, Cedar Rapids	.188	26	69	6	13	18	2	0	1	4	0	1	0	4	0	21	2	2
Dufault, Monty, Kenosha	.138	38	87	8	12	15	1	1	0	5	2	1	1	11	0	24	10	1
Duncan, Jeff, Madison*	.200	96	245	23	49	76	9	3	4	31	2	4	2	38	1	82	5	3
Ealy, Tracey, Appleton†	.284	40	148	22	42	60	6	0	4	13	1	1	1	10	1	32	16	5
Eicher, Mike, Springfield	.252	89	250	36	63	83	11	0	3	23	2	2	2	33	0	64	4	6
Eldridge, Rodney, Springfield	.000	1	1	0	0	0	0	0	0	0	0	0	0	0	0	0	0	0
Enriquez, Graciano, Beloit†	.243	110	358	58	87	141	27	3	7	43	5	3	7	49	2	84	19	10
Estep, Chris, Cedar Rapids	.293	22	75	13	22	47	4	3	5	16	0	2	0	5	0	21	2	1
Estevez, Carlos, Kenosha*	.322	40	121	16	39	55	7	0	3	22	0	3	0	9	0	16	0	1
Evans, Glenn, Kenosha†	.206	23	68	8	14	19	5	0	0	5	1	0	1	9	0	13	6	2
Everly, David, Beloit	.000	8	12	0	0	0	0	0	0	0	2	0	1	4	0	7	0	1
Fairman, Andy, Beloit*	.291	113	395	59	115	174	28	5	7	72	0	6	2	54	4	55	2	2
Falco, Chris, Rockford	.224	69	183	17	41	62	9	0	4	22	3	4	8	11	0	41	2	0
Farlow, Kevin, Waterloo	.223	128	408	43	91	117	15	1	3	48	3	3	8	58	1	83	3	2
Feist, Ken, Clinton	.262	87	298	37	78	97	12	2	1	25	1	2	3	23	0	82	12	4
Felix, Lauro, Madison	.211	53	199	29	42	46	4	0	0	13	8	0	3	29	0	41	7	6
Fernandez, Mike, Kenosha	.266	81	271	36	72	112	13	3	7	31	1	1	4	22	0	69	2	2
Filosa, Brian, South Bend	.154	20	39	6	6	8	2	0	0	0	1	0	0	16	0	12	3	0
Filotei, Bobby, Cedar Rapids	.125	10	32	3	4	5	1	0	0	1	0	0	0	4	0	9	1	0
Fisk, Carlton, South Bend	.500	1	2	1	1	4	0	0	1	3	0	0	0	1	0	0	0	0
Florez, Tim, Clinton	.233	81	292	39	68	90	12	2	2	25	0	2	3	30	2	53	20	5
Forbes, P.J., Quad City	.282	105	376	53	106	138	16	5	2	46	24	5	2	44	1	51	15	6
Francisco, David, Madison	.195	43	133	9	26	33	5	1	0	11	7	0	2	16	0	32	3	1
Francisco, Vicente, Madison†	.214	118	355	34	76	83	3	2	0	20	17	2	3	23	0	89	4	5
Freitag, Brandt, Rockford	.194	26	62	6	12	17	0	1	1	6	0	0	1	5	0	21	0	0
Fryman, Troy, South Bend*	.174	129	432	45	75	129	26	2	8	34	3	2	5	60	5	130	7	2
Fuller, Jon, Cedar Rapids	.213	83	267	33	57	98	19	2	6	28	1	0	5	38	0	68	2	2
Gardner, Willie, Peoria	.184	104	358	53	66	104	16	5	4	36	3	1	4	39	1	99	12	3
Garrow, David, Kenosha	.237	119	397	41	94	130	22	4	2	44	7	3	3	20	0	70	12	6
Gerald, Ed, Appleton†	.248	123	420	55	104	169	13	8	12	62	2	4	1	45	2	127	17	3
Gibralter, Steve, Cedar Rapids	.306	137	529	92	162	257	32	3	19	99	1	3	12	51	4	99	12	9
Giegling, Matt, Cedar Rapids*	.207	54	140	18	29	41	6	0	2	12	3	1	2	11	1	35	0	1
Gilbert, Don, Kane County*	.249	113	293	32	73	97	13	1	3	44	2	2	0	55	5	80	3	1
Goins, Tim, Waterloo	.197	55	127	11	25	28	3	0	0	9	2	2	2	11	0	33	0	0
Gonzalez, David, Appleton	.203	21	74	10	15	22	2	1	1	10	1	2	0	2	0	13	2	0
Gonzalez, Jim, Burlington	.176	91	301	32	53	78	13	0	4	21	0	0	1	34	0	119	0	3
Gonzalez, Raul, Appleton	.256	119	449	82	115	176	32	1	9	51	4	6	2	57	1	58	13	5
Goodwin, Curtis, Kane County*	.282	134	542	85	153	173	7	5	1	42	14	0	2	38	0	106	52	18
Gordon, Keith, Cedar Rapids	.251	114	375	59	94	155	19	3	12	63	1	4	3	43	2	135	21	10
Greene, Willie, Cedar Rapids*	.283	34	120	26	34	82	8	2	12	40	0	2	2	18	0	27	3	4
Gresham, Kris, Kane County	.195	38	113	10	22	32	4	0	2	17	2	0	0	4	0	21	0	0
Grudzielanek, Mark, Rockford	.246	128	496	64	122	159	12	5	5	54	0	0	5	22	1	59	25	4
Gubanich, Creighton, Madison	.248	121	404	46	100	152	19	3	9	55	8	1	16	41	1	102	0	7
Guzman, Ramon, South Bend	.080	9	25	1	2	2	0	0	0	2	0	1	1	1	0	7	0	0
Haase, Dean, South Bend*	.135	14	37	2	5	5	0	0	0	1	0	0	1	9	0	4	1	0
Hagy, Gary, Quad City	.202	121	371	53	75	102	13	1	4	44	9	6	2	44	0	86	6	3
Halter, Shane, Appleton	.265	80	313	50	83	120	22	3	3	33	5	3	1	41	1	54	21	6
Hardge, Mike, Rockford	.217	127	448	63	97	158	21	2	12	49	4	2	3	47	0	141	44	13
Hardtke, Jason, Waterloo†	.304	110	411	75	125	184	27	4	8	47	1	5	5	38	3	33	9	7
Harley, Al, Burlington†	.265	83	279	33	74	93	12	2	1	19	6	0	4	23	1	65	13	6
Hart, Shelby, Clinton	.211	13	38	3	8	12	4	0	0	9	0	0	1	6	0	15	1	0
Havens, Tom, Madison	.209	93	234	30	49	81	6	1	8	37	2	5	11	44	0	57	4	4
Hazlett, Steve, Kenosha	.265	107	362	68	96	145	23	4	6	32	2	4	7	52	0	77	20	9
Heather, Brian, Kenosha	.130	24	54	9	7	8	1	0	0	1	1	1	1	13	0	12	0	0
Henry, Harold, South Bend	.261	114	387	53	101	150	16	3	9	43	1	4	8	31	2	116	18	8
Hinton, Steve, Appleton*	.270	118	419	67	113	161	25	1	7	63	2	10	5	54	1	71	5	6
Hodge, Roy, Kane County	.250	25	52	3	13	14	1	0	0	7	0	0	0	9	0	12	5	4
Horne, Tyrone, Rockford*	.279	129	480	71	134	205	27	4	12	48	2	2	1	62	5	141	23	13
House, Trini, Beloit*	.274	110	343	56	94	138	19	2	7	44	3	2	1	42	0	89	12	12
Huff, Mike, South Bend	.375	12	40	7	15	22	2	1	1	5	0	0	0	11	1	7	2	3
Hust, Gary, Madison	.194	114	387	41	75	124	13	3	10	45	1	4	6	36	1	163	5	2
Huyler, Mike, Beloit	.257	107	350	43	90	116	15	1	3	39	4	2	4	37	1	78	7	7
Imperial, Jason, Beloit	.178	32	90	7	16	22	3	0	1	15	0	1	1	9	0	37	1	2
Indriago, Juan, Appleton†	.238	74	185	19	44	47	3	0	0	18	5	0	1	35	1	38	7	14
Jackson, Ray, Clinton	.200	122	434	52	87	119	16	5	2	33	3	4	18	37	0	125	23	14
Jenkins, Bernie, Cedar Rapids	.287	71	258	53	74	118	16	2	8	32	1	0	5	31	0	60	26	9
Jensen, Marcus, Clinton†	.235	86	264	35	62	88	14	0	4	33	1	2	4	54	3	87	4	2
Johnson, Drew, Kane County	.254	110	335	28	85	108	15	1	2	30	1	0	6	16	0	73	2	4
Johnson, Greg, Kenosha	.225	114	391	50	88	108	10	2	2	32	5	3	3	30	1	64	26	6
Johnson, Mark, Appleton*	.306	66	258	51	79	115	17	5	3	27	3	1	1	27	0	26	12	4
Jones, Brian, Madison†	.141	23	71	6	10	12	2	0	0	3	1	0	1	2	0	27	0	0
Jones, Butter, Clinton	.200	14	60	5	12	16	1	0	1	7	0	0	0	4	0	22	4	1
Jones, Dax, Clinton	.298	79	295	45	88	111	12	4	1	42	1	1	1	21	0	32	18	5
Jones, Keith, Springfield*	.274	107	343	51	94	119	15	5	0	24	0	4	4	36	0	65	24	20
Jones, Mike, Cedar Rapids	.204	68	206	35	42	65	11	0	4	21	1	1	1	19	1	40	3	2
Keene, Andre, Clinton*	.272	128	438	67	119	186	19	3	14	70	0	0	9	77	1	100	28	13
Kessinger, Keith, Cedar Rapids†	.237	95	308	41	73	102	15	1	4	38	5	1	1	36	2	57	2	0
Koelling, Brian, Cedar Rapids	.263	129	460	81	121	168	18	7	5	43	9	2	1	49	0	137	47	16
Kontorinis, Andrew, Kenosha*	.282	75	273	26	77	104	12	0	5	44	0	5	4	28	2	39	2	4
Kuehl, John, Madison†	.208	13	48	5	10	12	2	0	0	3	0	1	1	3	0	14	1	2
Lane, Tom, Burlington	.265	38	113	14	30	32	2	0	0	13	2	1	1	6	0	25	1	0
Lanfranco, Raphel, Burlington	.197	26	66	3	13	16	1	1	0	5	0	2	1	6	0	18	0	0
Larregui, Ed, Peoria	.287	129	478	62	137	180	24	2	5	71	9	4	4	30	1	68	15	6
Leary, Rob, Madison*	.255	116	365	47	93	129	18	3	4	48	3	3	4	66	4	64	3	3
Lewis, T.R., Kane County	.299	45	134	26	40	56	10	0	2	22	1	4	3	13	0	22	5	4
Loftin, Bo, Cedar Rapids	.167	5	6	0	1	1	0	0	0	0	0	0	0	1	0	3	0	0
Mabry, John, Springfield*	.263	115	438	63	115	173	13	6	11	57	1	1	0	24	2	39	2	8
Mader, Chris, South Bend	.143	27	91	8	13	18	2	0	1	11	1	1	1	14	0	25	0	0
Manning, Henry, South Bend	.282	66	213	26	60	72	9	0	1	30	0	1	5	14	1	22	4	2
Markiewicz, Brandon, Quad City	.194	98	319	33	62	103	24	1	5	42	9	4	4	39	0	74	12	3
Marshall, David, Appleton	.237	37	114	10	27	34	2	1	1	12	3	3	1	3	0	29	0	1
Martinez, Eric, Burlington*	.216	59	199	21	43	72	14	0	5	28	0	3	0	28	1	28	1	0
Martinez, Jacen, Kane County†	.263	19	57	5	15	17	0	1	0	4	3	0	1	7	0	10	2	0
Martorana, David, South Bend	.229	53	166	12	38	51	7	0	2	23	0	2	0	15	0	35	1	2
Matos, Domingo, Rockford	.244	129	492	45	120	174	34	1	6	65	0	8	4	15	0	118	1	5

Player. Team	Avg.	G	AB	R	H	TB	2B	3B	HR	RBI	SH	SF	HP	BB	Int. BB	SO	SB	CS
McCaffery, Dennis, Quad City	.214	67	210	25	45	52	7	0	0	19	13	1	6	19	0	45	2	4
McClain, Scott, Kane County	.266	96	316	43	84	109	12	2	3	30	6	1	6	48	1	62	7	4
McGee, Brian, Peoria	.181	46	94	18	17	21	2	1	0	9	3	1	2	6	0	25	1	0
McGlone, Brian, Burlington*	.226	113	332	39	75	82	7	0	0	20	9	2	1	31	0	114	4	4
McGonnigal, Brett, Clinton†	.256	45	176	18	45	55	7	0	1	12	2	1	1	15	0	44	8	3
McGuire, Bill, Peoria	.200	8	20	1	4	5	1	0	0	1	1	0	0	2	0	4	1	0
McKoy, Keith, Waterloo*	.206	81	228	32	47	64	4	2	3	22	5	1	0	24	0	51	20	6
McNabb, Buck, Burlington*	.259	123	456	82	118	139	12	3	1	34	3	2	10	60	0	80	56	19
McNabb, Glen, Appleton	.154	15	39	1	6	8	0	1	0	3	0	1	2	3	0	3	0	0
Medina, Ricardo, Peoria	.263	125	457	47	120	164	27	1	5	67	3	4	2	60	1	58	5	7
Mendez, Ricardo, Madison	.081	16	37	2	3	6	1	1	0	2	3	0	0	3	0	10	1	0
Mendoza, Francisco, Beloit†	.223	53	139	22	31	38	1	3	0	17	3	0	0	20	0	33	3	2
Mercedes, Feliciano, Kane County†	.241	53	166	23	40	46	4	1	0	10	8	1	2	18	0	38	9	9
Meza, Larry, Springfield*	.205	99	215	20	44	63	9	2	2	15	0	2	2	25	0	45	4	2
Miller, Damian, Kenosha	.292	115	377	53	110	156	27	2	5	56	2	4	7	53	1	66	6	1
Miranda, Geovany, South Bend	.000	2	3	0	0	0	0	0	0	0	0	0	0	0	0	1	0	0
Montero, Alberto, Burlington	.235	27	102	9	24	37	8	1	1	17	0	0	1	4	0	28	0	0
Montgomery, Don, Clinton	.162	24	74	7	12	17	2	0	1	11	1	1	0	15	0	20	1	1
Monzon, Dan, South Bend	.333	2	3	0	1	2	1	0	0	1	0	0	1	0	0	2	0	1
Moock, Chris, Peoria	.272	53	184	22	50	71	8	2	3	15	2	0	1	10	3	45	1	0
Moore, Tim H., Kenosha†	.272	112	382	76	104	170	26	2	12	52	2	5	4	68	3	99	40	20
Moore, Tim J., Peoria	.242	89	289	41	70	85	10	1	1	27	11	0	12	30	1	59	5	7
Mulligan, Sean, Waterloo	.252	79	278	24	70	100	13	1	5	43	2	4	5	20	0	62	1	0
Mumma, Bob, South Bend	.159	15	44	6	7	13	3	0	1	8	0	0	0	14	0	13	0	0
Myers, Rod, Appleton*	.220	71	218	31	48	74	10	2	4	30	4	4	2	39	1	67	25	6
Nava, Marlo, Kenosha	.198	39	126	13	25	30	5	0	0	10	1	3	1	12	0	18	1	3
Newhouse, Andre, Appleton	.211	50	161	26	34	46	7	1	1	22	2	3	1	18	0	59	5	2
Norman, Jeff, Appleton	.083	8	24	2	2	2	0	0	0	1	0	0	1	2	0	6	1	0
Norman, Kenny, Kenosha†	.059	20	51	2	3	3	0	0	0	3	0	0	0	5	0	15	1	0
Norman, Les, Appleton	.376	59	218	38	82	113	17	1	4	47	2	3	1	22	0	18	8	6
Norris, Joe, Rockford	.000	27	2	0	0	0	0	0	0	0	0	0	0	0	0	0	0	0
O'Brien, John, Springfield	.243	92	333	52	81	130	16	0	11	54	0	5	5	36	0	72	0	2
O'Neill, Tom, Clinton	.255	40	141	24	36	42	6	0	0	14	2	1	7	29	0	37	12	6
Ochoa, Alex, Kane County	.295	133	499	65	147	186	22	7	1	59	5	7	7	58	5	55	31	17
Ochoa, Rafael, South Bend	.162	12	37	6	6	8	2	0	0	1	1	0	0	4	1	17	0	0
Ogden, Jamie, Kenosha*	.245	108	372	36	91	120	14	3	3	51	0	4	2	52	1	108	9	2
Ogden, Jason, South Bend	.243	21	37	4	9	10	1	0	0	6	0	1	0	7	0	9	2	2
Ortega, Hector, Rockford	.247	125	405	50	100	126	17	3	1	44	3	5	5	38	1	93	28	10
Owens, Billy, Kane County†	.254	73	283	23	72	94	16	0	2	33	2	4	0	26	1	63	4	3
Palmeiro, Orlando, Quad City*	.317	127	451	83	143	173	22	4	0	41	19	7	5	56	3	41	31	13
Parker, Brad, Madison	.238	66	261	29	62	87	10	0	5	36	0	2	3	16	0	51	5	1
Pearce, Jeff, Waterloo*	.271	118	373	56	101	167	19	4	13	52	1	2	2	30	2	82	24	10
Pimentel, Wander, Springfield	.183	123	372	25	68	94	15	1	3	23	10	0	2	6	0	82	1	4
Poe, Charles, South Bend	.180	67	228	26	41	65	9	3	3	26	2	3	2	23	0	64	4	1
Postiff, James, Peoria	.204	92	240	24	49	65	12	2	0	25	15	2	14	31	0	52	7	6
Powell, Gordon, Beloit	.285	78	253	42	72	95	11	3	2	27	8	1	4	18	0	67	12	8
Pritchett, Chris, Quad City*	.290	128	448	79	130	190	19	1	13	72	2	5	5	71	6	88	9	4
Pritchett, Tony, South Bend	.000	4	13	0	0	0	0	0	0	0	0	0	0	0	0	4	1	0
Pueschner, Craig, Cedar Rapids	.245	47	139	25	34	60	9	1	5	21	1	0	9	11	0	44	9	1
Pugh, Scott, Waterloo*	.241	137	522	62	126	170	26	0	6	44	4	2	3	33	3	84	1	1
Radziewicz, Doug, Springfield*	.303	55	165	25	50	72	12	2	2	33	0	3	4	26	1	17	2	1
Raffo, Tom, Cedar Rapids	.302	76	248	36	75	120	18	0	9	38	1	1	7	27	0	59	2	1
Randa, Joe, Appleton	.301	72	266	55	80	108	13	0	5	43	0	6	6	34	0	37	6	2
Reid, Greg, Madison†	.259	60	189	27	49	68	9	2	2	16	5	0	4	28	0	56	8	3
Reyes, Jimmy, South Bend†	.271	26	70	14	19	20	1	0	0	4	1	0	0	19	0	17	4	3
Reyes, Roberto, Rockford	.083	4	12	0	1	1	0	0	0	0	1	0	0	0	0	4	0	0
Riggs, Kevin, Cedar Rapids*	.289	126	457	87	132	170	24	4	2	44	4	5	5	97	3	63	23	15
Rijo, Rafael, Rockford	.262	105	309	41	81	97	10	3	0	20	5	2	1	11	0	63	32	19
Robertson, Shawn, Waterloo	.272	127	404	65	110	161	23	2	8	63	2	3	10	77	2	106	16	10
Robledo, Nilson, South Bend	.291	32	117	14	34	55	11	2	2	14	2	1	0	7	0	38	0	1
Rodriguez, Ahmed, Springfield†	.000	7	2	1	0	0	0	0	0	0	0	1	1	0	0	1	0	0
Rodriguez, Albert, Clinton	.217	33	92	1	20	22	0	1	0	7	1	1	0	6	0	9	1	0
Ronan, Marc, Springfield*	.215	110	376	45	81	122	19	2	6	48	0	4	1	23	2	58	4	5
Ruiz, Stewart, Kane County†	.195	77	210	22	41	45	2	1	0	14	5	3	2	10	0	41	6	1
Saenz, Olmedo, South Bend	.245	132	493	66	121	176	26	4	7	59	2	3	11	36	4	52	16	13
Salazar, Julian, Beloit	.296	13	27	1	8	8	0	0	0	2	0	0	0	4	0	3	2	1
Samples, Todd, Rockford	.239	117	410	52	98	140	21	6	3	34	2	3	7	25	2	83	29	10
Santana, Raul, Rockford	.208	121	404	39	84	130	16	0	10	51	1	4	1	36	0	102	6	2
Schmidt, Keith, Kane County*	.256	112	317	48	81	130	19	3	8	36	0	0	1	54	5	116	20	6
Schulte, Rich, Burlington*	.247	112	369	35	91	121	15	3	3	25	2	1	4	31	2	69	15	7
Servello, Dan, Appleton	.127	27	79	7	10	13	0	0	1	5	0	1	1	10	0	32	1	0
Sheldon, Scott, Madison	.272	74	279	41	76	110	16	0	6	24	3	4	1	32	1	78	5	4
Simpson, Jay, Quad City	.238	51	181	21	43	59	7	3	1	21	0	3	5	8	0	50	5	5
Sisco, Steve, Appleton	.250	1	4	1	1	1	0	0	0	0	0	0	0	0	0	1	0	0
Smith, Lance, Burlington	.227	105	357	32	81	115	16	0	6	45	0	4	3	24	1	75	0	1
Spiers, Bill, Beloit*	.236	16	55	9	13	16	3	0	0	7	0	1	0	7	0	7	4	0
Staydohar, Dave, Quad City	.163	16	49	3	8	11	3	0	0	7	0	1	1	2	0	14	0	0
Stefan, Todd, Peoria	.230	43	126	18	29	36	5	1	0	9	2	1	2	23	0	16	6	2
Stefanski, Michael, Beloit	.273	116	385	66	105	129	12	0	4	45	3	3	4	55	1	81	9	4
Stela, Jose, Quad City	.251	60	211	18	53	65	12	0	0	27	4	3	1	22	1	22	2	0
Stewart, Brady, Appleton	.289	14	45	4	13	14	1	0	0	2	1	0	0	6	0	8	1	2
Strickland, Chad, Appleton	.255	112	396	29	101	125	16	1	2	49	0	0	5	12	0	37	2	5
Sutch, Ray, Madison	.000	50	1	0	0	0	0	0	0	0	0	0	0	0	0	0	0	0
Sutton, Larry, Appleton*	.000	1	2	1	0	0	0	0	0	0	0	0	0	2	0	1	0	1
Sweeney, Mark, Quad City*	.271	120	424	65	115	187	20	5	14	76	6	5	4	47	3	85	15	11
Swinton, Jermaine, Burlington	.201	101	338	37	68	121	14	0	13	45	0	2	5	41	2	182	3	2
Tahan, Kevin, Springfield	.268	95	250	29	67	100	14	2	5	41	1	4	1	32	0	48	2	1
Talanoa, Scott, Beloit	.230	106	357	57	82	139	18	0	13	56	3	2	2	49	1	109	7	4
Tallman, Troy, Kane County	.175	75	189	25	33	60	7	1	6	18	12	3	2	33	0	83	4	0
Tamarez, Andres, Clinton	.229	102	306	43	70	78	6	1	0	19	12	2	4	29	0	63	16	14
Taylor, Gene, Cedar Rapids	.227	36	110	16	25	49	4	1	6	20	0	3	2	12	1	33	0	1
Terilli, Joey, Peoria*	.286	114	370	71	106	137	20	1	3	55	4	6	2	71	3	74	15	3
Thielen, D.J., Clinton	.244	128	459	66	112	171	23	3	10	58	1	4	8	50	1	159	14	5
Thomsen, Chris, Madison	.108	27	65	6	7	9	2	0	0	1	1	0	0	8	0	21	0	1
Thurston, Jerrey, Waterloo	.141	96	263	20	37	44	7	0	0	14	6	2	2	12	0	73	1	0

Player, Team	Avg.	G	AB	R	H	TB	2B	3B	HR	RBI	SH	SF	HP	BB	Int. BB	SO	SB	CS
Tillman, Darren, Peoria	.225	33	71	11	16	18	2	0	0	3	2	0	5	8	0	21	0	0
Trujillo, Jose, Peoria	.200	14	35	5	7	8	1	0	0	2	0	0	1	6	0	9	1	0
Tunison, Rich, Appleton†	.231	44	156	18	36	55	5	1	4	28	1	2	2	21	0	49	2	1
Turner, Chris, Quad City	.252	109	330	66	83	130	18	1	9	53	6	6	8	85	5	65	8	7
Valdez, Pedro, Peoria*	.232	33	112	8	26	33	7	0	0	20	0	4	0	7	3	32	0	0
Valrie, Kerry, South Bend	.258	79	314	34	81	112	12	2	5	37	0	4	1	16	0	53	22	15
Vasquez, Chris, Cedar Rapids*	.259	102	317	42	82	131	14	1	11	53	1	2	1	28	3	61	5	2
Vaughn, Derek, Waterloo	.253	120	400	65	101	137	19	1	5	49	3	3	4	50	1	99	35	13
Vinas, Julio, South Bend	.170	33	94	7	16	19	3	0	0	10	0	2	1	9	0	17	1	3
Vlasis, Chris, Springfield*	.218	84	197	28	43	48	3	1	0	13	0	3	3	27	1	50	10	7
Vogel, Mike, South Bend†	.328	22	64	5	21	30	7	1	0	9	0	0	0	14	0	15	1	0
Wachter, Derek, Beloit	.270	111	363	53	98	163	17	9	10	61	5	3	1	43	1	113	6	5
Walker, Dane, Madison*	.296	82	287	56	85	111	13	2	3	23	4	2	1	42	0	57	23	10
Wallace, David, Burlington	.175	84	228	28	40	45	5	0	0	20	1	3	0	35	0	58	19	6
Waszgis, B.J., Kane County	.215	111	340	39	73	126	18	1	11	47	3	2	4	54	2	94	3	2
Whalen, Shawn, Waterloo*	.235	41	136	26	32	59	7	1	6	30	0	1	0	24	0	25	2	2
White, Gabe, Rockford*	.000	27	1	0	0	0	0	0	0	0	0	0	0	0	0	0	0	0
White, Jimmy, Burlington*	.286	102	370	49	106	143	20	7	1	47	1	6	2	38	0	84	17	13
Whitford, Eric, Beloit	.233	27	90	10	21	33	5	2	1	9	2	0	0	14	0	21	5	5
Williams, George, Madison†	.304	115	349	56	106	143	18	2	5	42	5	1	8	76	6	53	9	5
Wolff, James, Peoria	.203	107	330	38	67	107	13	0	9	37	6	0	23	26	1	67	4	5
Woodfin, Chris, South Bend	1.000	36	1	0	1	1	0	0	0	0	0	0	0	0	0	0	0	0
Woods, Tyrone, Rockford	.291	101	374	54	109	173	22	3	12	47	0	6	1	34	4	83	15	6
Young, Dmitri, Springfield†	.310	135	493	74	153	243	36	6	14	72	0	4	5	51	3	94	14	13

The following pitchers, listed alphabetically by club, with games in parentheses, had no plate appearances, primarily through use of designated hitters:

APPLETON—Baez, Francisco (38); Berumen, Andres (46); Bevil, Brian (26); Bovee, Mike (28); Connolly, Chris (20); Dickens, John (18); Haas, Jeff (12); Harrison, Brian (16); Kobetitsch, Kevin (11); Landress, Roger (17); Lee, Anthony (24); Miceli, Dan (23); Pruitt, Jason (10); Rea, Shayne (38); Smith, Jeff (24); Toth, Bob (23).

BELOIT—Boze, Marshall (26); Browne, Byron (25); Cofer, Brian (12); Criminger, John (26); Dennison, Brian (10); England, Dave (7); Fetty, Pat (52); Froning, Tom (10); Grammig, Mike (3); Hardwick, Bill (17); Higuera, Ted (2); Hill, Tyrone (20); Kloek, Kevin (15); Knox, Kerry (14); Mattson, Bob (8); McKeon, Brian (3); O'Laughlin, Chuck (4); Pruitt, Don (8); Rutter, Sam (4); Souza, Brian (9); Trisler, John (26); Vonderlieth, Scott (11); Zurn, Ricky (7).

BURLINGTON—Biehl, Rodney (36); Bottoms, Derrick (7); Evans, Jim (15); Gallaher, Kevin (20); Hernandez, Javier (7); Holliday, Brian (21); Mercedes, Fernando (18); Miller, Jeff (50); Murphy, Pat (50); Ponte, Ed (30); Powers, Steve (55); Quijada, Ed (18); Reed, Dennis (18); Rose, Heath (27); Scott, Tyrone (16); Sewell, Joe (9); Waring, Jim (20).

CEDAR RAPIDS—Culberson, Calvain (28); Dodd, Scott (21); Doty, Sean (37); Duff, Scott (43); Edwards, Ryan (31); Ferry, Mike (25); Griffen, Leonard (36); Hook, Chris (26); Hrusovsky, John (25); Jarvis, Kevin (1); Kilgo, Ray (25); Leslie, Reginald (22); Luebbers, Larry (14); Margheim, Greg (5); Plemmons, Scott (3); Quinones, Rene (11); Ray, John (11); Spradlin, Jerry (1); Steph, Rod (27); Zastoupil, Rich (9).

CLINTON—Ayres, Lenny (38); Benavides, Alvaro (30); Boker, Mike (33); Castillo, Mariano (13); Gambs, Chris (26); Grundt, Ken (40); Henrikson, Dan (3); Huffman, Rodney (6); Hyde, Rich (8); Juelsgaard, Jarod (35); Locklear, Jeff (30); Lowery, John (20); McLain, Mike (18); Myers, Mike (7); Ortiz, Angel (38); Peltzer, Kurt (7); Stonecipher, Eric (8); Stroth, Scott (3); Szczechowski, Dennis (6); Vanderweele, Doug (9); Van Landingham, Bill (10); Wanke, Chuck (26).

KANE COUNTY—Benavides, Alvaro (14); Benge, Brett (2); Brimhall, Brad (14); Chouinard, Bob (26); Firsich, Steve (44); Forney, Ritchard (20); Haynes, Jimmy (24); Jarvis, Matt (34); Klingenbeck, Scott (11); Krivda, Rich (18); Lemp, Chris (58); Marquez, Ihosvany (18); Mercedes, Jose (8); Mercedes, Juan (40); O'Connell, Shawn (22); Pomeranz, Mike (5); Sanders, Matt (49); Smith, Mark (11).

KENOSHA—Carlson, Bob (1); Diaz, Sandy (22); Garcia, Luis (55); Gavaghan, Sean (20); Guardado, Ed (18); Johnson, Frank (12); Konieczki, Dominic (49); Mansur, Jeff (11); Naulty, Dan (6); Radke, Brad (26); Roberts, Brett (7); Saccavino, Paul (6); Sartain, Dave (24); Schwartz, Dave (5); Sweeney, Dennis (31); Taylor, Kerry (27); Watkins, Scott (27); Wissler, Bill (21).

MADISON—Ariola, Tony (3); Cusey, Lee (39); Fermin, Ramon (14); Foster, Clifton (10); Jiminez, Miguel (26); Millay, Keith (7); Minik, Tim (18); Misa, Joe (4); Myers, Tom (39); Pierce, Bob (34); Rose, Scott (8); Rossiter, Mike (27); Scharff, Tony (42); Shoemaker, Steve (22); Smock, Greg (8); Stowell, Brad (29); Thees, Mike (16); Wengert, Don (7).

PEORIA—Adams, Terry (25); Bliss, Bill (41); Bradford, Troy (6); Elsbecker, Andy (9); Godfrey, Tyson (18); Guerra, Esmili (20); Harkey, Mike (2); Kenny, Brian (39); Krahenbuhl, Ken (19); Meyer, Jay (35); Pacheco, Jose (11); Patterson, Ken (2); Phillips, Jim (4); Sanchez, Adrian (35); Schramm, Carl (32); Steenstra, Ken (12); Talemaco, Amaury (2); Tidwell, Mike (60); Wallace, Derek (3).

QUAD CITY—Bennett, Erik (8); Blanchette, Bill (13); Burgos, John (4); Castillo, Roberto (18); Fritz, John (27); Gledhill, Chance (28); Heredia, Julian (29); Mammola, Mark (13); Martinez, Eric (5); Mitchell, Glenn (16); Mitchelson, Mark (15); Musset, Jose (41); Perez, Beban (12); Ratekin, Mark (23); Sebach, Kyle (13); Silverio, Victor (13); Watson, Ron (40); Williams, Shad (27).

ROCKFORD—Aucoin, Derek (39); Fultz, Vince (7); Galart, Kevin (33); Gerstein, Ron (33); Haynes, Heath (45); Kilgo, Ray (4); Kotch, Darrin (42); Looney, Brian (17); Martinez, Williams (10); McDonald, Kevin (12); Morrison, Keith (15); Perez, Carlos (7); Rueter, Kirk (26); Thomas, Mike (28); Whitehead, Steve (19); Wynne, Jim (2).

SOUTH BEND—Andujar, Luis (32); Baldwin, Jim (21); Bertotti, Mike (11); Boehringer, Brian (15); Brincks, Mark (1); Caridad, Rolando (11); Culberson, Don (35); Ellis, Bob (18); Heathcott, Mike (15); Herrholz, John (4); Hooper, Mike (2); Jenkins, Jonathan (5); Johnson, Barry (16); Levine, Alan (23); Pierce, Jeff (52); Soto, Juan (7); Tagle, Henry (26); Tolar, Kevin (18); Worrell, Steve (14).

SPRINGFIELD—Badorek, Mike (29); Barber, Brian (8); Cimorelli, Frank (65); Creek, Doug (6); Dillman, Jeff (16); Konemann, Troy (29); Martinez, Francisco (18); Nielsen, Kevin (9); Romanoli, Paul (62); Santos, Gerald (63); Simmons, Scott (27); Slininger, Dennis (27); Smith, Mark (17); Speek, Frank (58); Tranbarger, Mark (42).

WATERLOO—Altaffer, Todd (30); Baker, Jared (2); Beckett, Bob (24); Bensching, Bruce (50); Brown, Jeff (24); Cairncross, Cameron (24); Davila, Jose (23); Hoeme, Steve (22); Huber, Jeff (3); Hyson, Cole (17); Ivie, Ryan (12); Johnson, Bill (7); Martin, Tom (39); Moody, Kyle (1); Paskievitch, Tom (49); Silcox, Russ (6); Waldron, Joe (49).

GRAND SLAMS—Gordon, Sweeney, 2 each; Buchanan, Couture, Cunningham, DeBerry, Gilbert, Gubanich, Havens, Keene, Kontorinis, Mabry, O'Brien, Parker, Pearce, C. Pritchett, Raffo, Schmidt, Smith, Swinton, Thielen, Turner, Vasquez, Vaughn, 1 each.

AWARDED FIRST BASE ON CATCHER'S INTERFERENCE—Medina 6 (Fuller 2, Burgos, Giegling, Jensen, Waszgis); Mabry 3 (Calcagno, Dreisbach, Giegling); Feist 2 (Robledo, Tallman); O'Brien 2 (Stela, Williams); Pearce 2 (Calcagno 2); Burton (Turner); Cerio (Vogel); Cunningham (Jensen); Fairman (Freitag); Kessinger (Turner); Markiewicz (DeLeon); Samples (Jensen); Vlasis (Calcagno); Vogel (Santana); Walker (J. Gonzalez); Young (Burgos).

PITCHING

TEAM

Team	ERA	G	CG	ShO	Sv.	IP	H	R	ER	HR	HB	BB	Int. BB	SO	WP	Bk.
South Bend	2.83	138	12	8	41	1234.1	1069	535	388	51	55	462	3	1082	93	19
Kenosha	3.03	134	11	11	29	1135.1	1054	503	382	55	45	366	9	1014	63	26
Springfield	3.15	140	3	7	48	1230.1	1095	528	430	78	53	386	6	1113	72	17
Quad City	3.16	137	18	12	32	1191.0	1017	490	418	58	49	442	7	1014	92	29
Rockford	3.18	136	17	10	29	1165.2	1042	528	412	40	47	472	12	1069	90	30

Team	ERA	G	CG	ShO	Sv.	IP	H	R	ER	HR	HB	BB	Int. BB	SO	WP	Bk.
Cedar Rapids	3.44	138	12	9	29	1198.2	1070	559	458	71	55	464	13	1040	81	22
Kane County	3.49	137	21	9	34	1196.1	1128	636	464	49	45	546	30	975	109	37
Beloit	3.65	135	14	8	38	1158.0	1050	596	470	56	67	579	20	936	105	40
Appleton	3.67	132	11	11	28	1143.2	1090	581	466	83	32	401	13	882	60	17
Madison	3.71	134	9	8	33	1158.1	1045	622	478	69	59	560	15	925	111	31
Peoria	3.98	136	17	8	24	1181.2	1177	625	523	81	57	478	15	895	75	21
Clinton	4.18	138	5	4	33	1201.2	1157	705	558	54	71	561	23	966	109	23
Burlington	4.36	136	7	5	24	1169.2	1131	718	567	95	70	623	19	945	119	21
Waterloo	4.52	137	7	9	39	1165.0	1176	739	585	71	67	663	26	1096	115	30

INDIVIDUAL

(Leading qualifiers for earned-run average leadership—112 or more innings)

*Throws lefthanded.

Pitcher, Team	W	L	Pct.	ERA	G	GS	CG	GF	ShO	Sv.	IP	H	R	ER	HR	HB	BB	Int. BB	SO	WP
Chouinard, Kane County	10	14	.417	2.08	26	26	9	0	2	0	181.2	151	60	42	4	6	38	3	112	13
Waring, Burlington	11	7	.611	2.21	20	20	2	0	0	0	122.0	100	42	30	9	4	19	0	104	5
Ellis, South Bend	6	5	.545	2.34	18	18	1	0	1	0	123.0	90	46	32	3	4	35	0	97	7
Locklear, Clinton*	8	5	.615	2.35	30	13	1	6	0	0	126.1	117	45	33	1	2	42	1	69	3
Baldwin, South Bend	9	5	.643	2.42	21	21	1	0	1	0	137.2	118	53	37	6	3	45	0	137	8
Forney, Kane County	3	6	.333	2.48	20	18	2	0	1	0	123.1	114	40	34	4	9	26	1	104	9
Haynes, Kane County	7	11	.389	2.56	24	24	4	0	0	0	144.0	131	66	41	2	4	45	0	141	12
Rueter, Rockford*	11	9	.550	2.58	26	26	6	0	2	0	174.1	150	68	50	5	1	36	2	153	4
Ferry, Cedar Rapids	13	4	.765	2.71	25	25	6	0	0	0	162.2	134	57	49	6	9	40	1	143	10
Hook, Cedar Rapids	14	8	.636	2.72	26	25	1	1	0	0	159.0	138	59	48	2	10	53	0	144	5
Sartain, Kenosha*	7	13	.350	2.72	24	24	1	0	1	0	132.1	103	55	40	3	2	59	1	125	9

Departmental leaders: G—Cimorelli, 65; W—Fritz, 20; L—Norris, H. Rose, 15; Pct.—Kloek, .909; GS—Badorek, 28; CG—Chouinard, 9; GF—Santos, 58; ShO—Several pitchers tied with 2; Sv.—Santos, 35; IP—Badorek, 187.1; H—Badorek, 175; R—Gambs, 101; ER—Gambs, 84; HR—Slininger, 19; HB—Sanchez, 16; BB—Beckett, 140; IBB—Sanders, 8; SO—White, 176; WP—Browne, 24.

(All pitchers—listed alphabetically)

Pitcher, Team	W	L	Pct.	ERA	G	GS	CG	GF	ShO	Sv.	IP	H	R	ER	HR	HB	BB	Int. BB	SO	WP
Adams, Kane County	0	0	.000	4.35	10	0	0	7	0	0	10.1	8	7	5	0	0	4	0	8	3
Adams, Peoria	7	12	.368	4.41	25	25	3	0	1	0	157.0	144	95	77	7	9	86	0	96	13
Albert, Beloit	0	0	.000	0.00	2	0	0	2	0	0	1.2	0	0	0	0	0	0	0	1	0
Altaffer, Waterloo*	4	12	.250	4.90	30	20	1	4	0	2	128.2	122	93	70	8	8	73	2	101	21
Andujar, South Bend	6	5	.545	2.92	32	15	1	11	1	3	120.1	109	49	39	5	6	47	0	91	5
Aracena, Madison	0	0	.000	4.15	3	0	0	3	0	0	4.1	3	2	2	1	1	1	0	4	2
Ariola, Madison*	1	0	1.000	2.20	3	3	0	0	0	0	16.1	15	4	4	1	0	2	0	11	0
Aucoin, Rockford	3	2	.600	3.00	39	2	0	17	0	3	69.0	48	32	23	2	4	34	2	65	6
Ayres, Clinton	4	6	.400	5.38	38	10	0	12	0	0	100.1	115	72	60	9	10	42	3	72	6
Babbitt, Appleton	0	1	.000	4.91	5	0	0	5	0	0	3.2	1	2	2	0	2	4	0	1	0
Badorek, Springfield	17	8	.680	2.93	29	28	1	0	0	0	187.1	175	74	61	6	9	39	1	119	10
Baez, Appleton	5	5	.500	2.90	38	1	0	14	0	4	62.0	49	29	20	3	2	27	3	37	3
Baker, Waterloo	0	2	.000	4.50	2	2	0	0	0	0	12.0	10	7	6	2	1	7	0	19	1
Baldwin, South Bend	9	5	.643	2.42	21	21	1	0	1	0	137.2	118	53	37	6	3	45	0	137	8
Barber, Springfield	3	4	.429	3.73	8	8	0	0	0	0	50.2	39	21	21	7	1	24	0	56	2
Beckett, Waterloo*	4	10	.286	4.77	24	24	1	0	1	0	120.2	77	88	64	4	6	140	0	147	20
Benavides, 30 Cln. - 14 K.C.	1	6	.143	4.31	44	0	0	21	0	4	56.1	57	29	27	6	7	18	7	43	2
Benge, Kane County	1	0	1.000	0.00	2	0	0	2	0	0	3.0	1	2	0	0	1	4	0	1	0
Benhardt, Waterloo*	1	5	.167	5.19	19	11	0	2	0	0	76.1	92	51	44	5	0	41	0	64	8
Bennett, Quad City	3	3	.500	2.67	8	8	1	0	1	0	57.1	46	20	17	0	4	22	0	59	3
Bensching, Waterloo	4	8	.333	2.14	50	0	0	34	0	18	63.0	50	25	15	4	3	26	5	69	5
Berry, Burlington	0	0	.000	0.00	1	0	0	1	0	0	1.0	1	0	0	0	0	1	0	1	0
Bertotti, South Bend*	0	3	.000	3.72	11	0	0	5	0	1	19.1	12	8	8	1	1	22	0	17	1
Berumen, Appleton	5	2	.714	2.65	46	0	0	38	0	13	57.2	50	25	17	3	1	23	2	52	3
Bevil, Appleton	9	7	.563	3.40	26	26	4	0	2	0	156.0	129	67	59	17	5	63	0	168	9
Biehl, Burlington*	3	6	.333	6.04	36	12	0	7	0	1	89.1	80	70	60	13	5	80	3	95	10
Blanchette, Quad City*	0	0	.000	3.00	13	1	0	7	0	0	18.0	18	8	6	0	2	7	0	7	1
Bliss, Peoria	6	7	.462	4.03	41	12	1	26	1	3	102.2	114	51	46	9	3	58	0	89	6
Boehringer, South Bend	6	7	.462	4.38	15	15	2	0	0	0	86.1	87	52	42	5	6	40	0	59	6
Boker, Clinton	6	8	.429	3.37	33	15	1	6	0	0	125.2	115	65	47	4	9	69	0	85	16
Bottoms, Burlington*	0	3	.000	14.34	7	3	0	0	0	0	10.2	14	18	17	2	1	19	0	4	5
Bovee, Appleton	9	10	.474	3.56	28	24	1	0	0	0	149.1	143	85	59	8	3	41	1	120	13
Boze, Beloit	13	7	.650	2.83	26	22	4	4	1	0	146.1	117	59	46	6	12	82	4	126	18
Bradford, Peoria	2	2	.500	2.97	6	6	0	0	0	0	39.1	33	19	13	1	0	20	0	31	4
Brimhall, Kane County	1	2	.333	6.16	14	1	0	3	0	0	19.0	24	20	13	0	1	15	0	9	9
Brincks, South Bend	0	0	.000	3.86	1	0	0	0	0	0	2.1	2	1	1	0	0	1	0	1	0
Brown, Waterloo*	7	6	.538	4.67	24	24	0	0	0	0	146.1	172	91	76	4	10	60	1	103	9
Browne, Beloit	9	8	.529	5.08	25	25	2	0	0	0	134.2	109	84	76	8	11	114	0	111	24
Burgos, Quad City*	0	0	.000	2.45	4	0	0	3	0	0	7.1	9	2	2	0	0	3	0	7	1
Cairncross, Waterloo*	8	8	.500	3.61	24	24	1	0	1	0	137.0	127	68	55	14	14	61	2	138	7
Calcagno, Clinton	0	0	.000	0.00	1	0	0	1	0	0	1.0	0	0	0	0	0	1	0	0	0
Caridad, South Bend	1	3	.250	2.37	11	0	0	6	0	0	19.0	10	11	5	0	0	12	1	22	2
Carlson, Kenosha	0	0	.000	18.00	1	0	0	0	0	0	1.0	2	2	2	1	0	1	0	1	0
Castillo, Clinton	1	3	.250	6.05	13	0	0	5	0	1	19.1	23	15	13	1	2	5	1	15	1
Castillo, Quad City	2	1	.667	3.35	18	3	0	8	0	1	43.0	48	18	16	2	1	10	0	39	5
Chouinard, Kane County	10	14	.417	2.08	26	26	9	0	2	0	181.2	151	60	42	4	6	38	3	112	13
Christopher, Beloit	6	2	.750	4.18	30	0	0	7	0	1	47.1	49	29	22	1	6	24	1	43	5
Cimorelli, Springfield	4	2	.667	1.73	65	0	0	25	0	9	72.2	48	22	14	2	2	22	1	66	1
Cofer, Beloit	1	2	.333	5.09	12	0	0	5	0	0	17.2	25	14	10	0	1	4	0	12	2
Connolly, Appleton*	0	0	.000	5.16	20	0	0	5	0	0	22.2	28	16	13	0	2	14	0	12	1
Creek, Springfield*	4	1	.800	2.58	6	6	0	0	0	0	38.1	32	11	11	4	0	13	1	43	0
Criminger, Beloit	1	3	.250	3.33	26	0	0	15	0	4	48.2	46	24	18	2	4	18	0	36	2
Culberson, Cedar Rapids	5	4	.556	2.80	28	20	2	5	0	2	125.1	102	50	39	7	1	52	0	93	4
Culberson, South Bend	2	3	.400	2.78	35	1	0	16	0	0	64.2	56	32	20	3	4	39	0	60	11
Cusey, Madison	1	3	.250	2.68	39	0	0	25	0	12	50.1	42	24	15	3	1	11	1	53	1
Dana, Clinton	0	0	.000	0.00	1	0	0	1	0	0	1.0	1	0	0	0	2	0	0	1	0
Davila, Waterloo	0	2	.000	8.46	23	2	0	12	0	0	50.0	66	57	47	10	3	55	0	46	11
Dennison, Beloit*	2	1	.667	2.55	10	8	1	0	1	0	49.1	44	15	14	0	2	24	2	22	1

Pitcher, Team	W	L	Pct.	ERA	G	GS	CG	GF	ShO	Sv.	IP	H	R	ER	HR	HB	BB	Int. BB	SO	WP
Diaz, Kenosha	1	2	.333	5.01	22	1	0	6	0	1	41.1	35	30	23	1	4	23	1	33	8
Dickens, Appleton*	0	1	.000	7.23	18	0	0	5	0	0	23.2	37	23	19	2	0	15	0	17	0
Dillman, Springfield	2	1	.667	5.48	16	1	0	0	0	0	23.0	21	16	14	3	6	22	0	19	1
Dodd, Cedar Rapids	6	8	.429	4.34	21	14	1	1	0	0	95.1	82	56	46	6	3	52	0	84	11
Dotolo, Clinton	0	0	.000	6.75	3	0	0	2	0	0	4.0	6	3	3	1	0	1	0	1	0
Doty, Cedar Rapids	3	3	.500	5.05	37	0	0	23	0	2	46.1	46	28	26	5	1	24	1	52	2
Duff, Cedar Rapids*	4	1	.800	4.09	43	0	0	10	0	1	44.0	43	26	20	1	3	40	3	41	6
Duncan, Madison	0	0	.000	1.69	3	0	0	2	0	0	5.1	2	1	1	1	2	3	0	1	3
Edwards, Cedar Rapids	2	4	.333	5.05	31	0	0	14	0	1	35.2	42	27	20	3	1	16	0	39	8
Ellis, South Bend	6	5	.545	2.34	18	18	1	0	1	0	123.0	90	46	32	3	4	35	0	97	7
Elsbecker, Peoria	0	0	.000	4.09	9	0	0	1	0	0	11.0	13	5	5	0	1	10	2	6	2
England, Beloit	1	4	.200	3.58	7	5	0	2	0	1	37.2	36	19	15	4	3	13	1	29	3
Evans, Burlington	4	6	.400	4.74	15	15	1	0	0	0	87.1	85	53	46	11	2	40	0	65	5
Farlow, Waterloo	0	0	.000	6.75	6	0	0	6	0	0	8.0	9	6	6	0	0	2	0	3	1
Fermin, Madison	5	5	.500	2.43	14	14	1	0	0	0	77.2	66	33	21	2	1	35	0	37	6
Ferry, Cedar Rapids	13	4	.765	2.71	25	25	6	0	0	0	162.2	134	57	49	6	9	40	1	143	10
Fetty, Beloit	3	3	.500	2.39	52	0	0	48	0	27	60.1	58	24	16	1	3	27	4	57	5
Firsich, Kane County	1	5	.167	6.93	44	5	0	11	0	4	62.1	63	52	48	2	2	53	2	51	7
Forney, Kane County	3	6	.333	2.48	20	18	2	0	1	0	123.1	114	40	34	4	9	26	1	104	9
Foster, Madison	5	4	.556	2.83	10	10	1	0	0	0	60.1	53	25	19	6	3	25	0	51	7
Fritz, Quad City	20	4	.833	3.03	27	25	6	0	1	0	172.1	129	65	58	10	3	69	1	143	16
Froning, Beloit*	1	1	.500	9.00	10	2	0	5	0	0	21.0	33	28	21	3	1	8	0	13	1
Fultz, Rockford	1	1	.500	0.00	7	0	0	5	0	1	12.0	10	2	0	0	0	3	0	14	1
Galart, Rockford	1	0	1.000	2.25	3	0	0	2	0	0	4.0	4	1	1	0	1	0	0	5	1
Gallaher, Burlington	6	10	.375	3.85	20	20	1	0	0	0	117.0	108	70	50	5	9	80	0	89	9
Gambs, Clinton	5	10	.333	5.63	26	26	0	0	0	0	134.1	119	101	84	7	8	101	1	98	18
Garcia, Kenosha	4	4	.500	3.09	54	1	0	36	0	11	67.0	71	31	23	7	0	11	2	57	7
Gavaghan, Kenosha	2	3	.400	2.05	20	6	0	8	0	1	57.0	63	22	13	2	2	18	1	39	3
Gerstein, Rockford*	4	8	.333	5.65	33	5	0	17	0	5	51.0	62	37	32	2	1	28	1	40	5
Gilbert, Kane County	0	0	.000	12.00	3	0	0	3	0	0	3.0	5	5	4	1	1	4	0	3	0
Gledhill, Quad City	13	5	.722	3.43	28	22	2	3	1	1	168.0	166	67	64	9	8	30	0	115	6
Godfrey, Peoria	0	1	.000	4.62	18	5	0	6	0	0	39.0	55	25	20	3	3	12	0	28	6
Grammig, Beloit	0	1	.000	2.08	3	0	0	2	0	0	4.1	2	2	1	1	0	2	0	1	0
Griffen, Cedar Rapids	2	2	.500	3.97	36	5	0	5	0	2	88.1	89	50	39	12	6	22	3	67	5
Grundt, Clinton*	5	3	.625	0.62	40	0	0	28	0	16	57.2	39	11	4	2	1	11	2	59	1
Guardado, Kenosha*	5	10	.333	4.37	18	18	2	0	1	0	101.0	106	57	49	5	4	30	0	103	2
Guerra, Peoria	1	0	1.000	4.28	20	0	0	7	0	0	33.2	35	17	16	3	1	9	0	24	2
Haas, Appleton*	6	4	.600	4.06	12	12	2	0	0	0	77.2	80	38	35	9	2	16	0	49	0
Hardwick, Beloit*	3	2	.600	1.34	17	4	2	3	1	0	47.0	26	10	7	0	2	13	1	42	2
Harkey, Peoria	1	0	1.000	3.00	2	2	0	0	0	0	12.0	15	6	4	2	1	3	0	17	1
Harrison, Appleton	5	6	.455	3.65	16	15	1	0	0	0	98.2	114	47	40	5	1	16	0	54	2
Havens, Madison	0	0	.000	0.00	1	0	0	1	0	0	1.0	0	0	0	0	0	0	0	0	0
Haynes, Rockford	3	1	.750	1.89	45	0	0	36	0	15	57.0	49	19	12	0	4	15	3	78	1
Haynes, Kane County	7	11	.389	2.56	24	24	4	0	0	0	144.1	131	66	41	2	4	45	0	141	12
Hazlett, Kenosha	0	0	.000	0.00	1	0	0	1	0	0	1.0	1	0	0	0	0	1	0	0	0
Heathcott, South Bend	9	5	.643	1.54	15	14	0	1	0	0	82.0	67	28	14	3	0	32	0	49	8
Henrikson, Clinton*	1	0	1.000	2.13	3	2	0	0	0	0	12.2	12	3	3	1	1	2	0	8	0
Heredia, Quad City	6	1	.857	1.66	29	0	0	25	0	10	43.1	27	8	8	0	0	11	1	45	3
Hernandez, Burlington	2	2	.500	4.21	7	6	0	0	0	0	36.1	44	18	17	3	0	12	0	23	3
Herrholz, South Bend	0	1	.000	16.20	4	0	0	2	0	0	5.0	9	9	9	2	0	10	0	5	3
Higuera, Beloit*	1	0	1.000	3.27	2	2	0	0	0	0	11.0	13	4	4	2	0	1	0	11	0
Hill, Beloit*	9	5	.643	3.25	20	19	1	1	0	0	113.2	76	51	41	4	3	74	0	133	12
Hoeme, Waterloo	1	1	.500	2.36	22	0	0	4	0	1	34.1	27	11	9	1	1	9	0	43	4
Holliday, Burlington	3	10	.231	5.52	21	19	0	0	0	0	93.0	111	71	57	6	12	43	0	57	12
Hook, Cedar Rapids	14	8	.636	2.72	26	25	1	1	0	0	159.0	138	59	48	2	10	53	0	144	5
Hooper, South Bend	0	0	.000	10.50	2	0	0	0	0	0	6.0	9	7	7	2	0	3	0	4	0
Hrusovsky, Cedar Rapids	2	3	.400	2.93	25	0	0	25	0	7	30.2	18	14	10	3	1	16	0	52	5
Huber, Waterloo*	1	2	.333	2.40	9	0	0	6	0	1	15.0	15	4	4	0	2	6	0	13	0
Huffman, Clinton	0	0	.000	5.68	6	0	0	3	0	1	6.1	8	5	4	0	2	3	1	4	0
Hyde, Clinton	0	0	.000	0.00	8	0	0	7	0	3	7.0	3	0	0	0	0	1	0	1	0
Hyson, Waterloo	0	1	.000	3.18	17	0	0	16	0	13	22.2	18	10	8	0	3	12	2	25	3
Ivie, Waterloo*	6	3	.667	5.01	12	11	1	1	1	0	59.1	75	39	33	2	2	30	0	39	0
Jarvis, Cedar Rapids	0	0	.000	0.00	1	0	0	0	0	0	1.0	1	0	0	0	0	0	0	0	0
Jarvis, Kane County*	4	4	.500	4.54	34	7	0	8	0	0	71.1	84	53	36	3	1	35	2	43	7
Jenkins, South Bend	0	0	.000	0.00	5	0	0	1	0	0	13.0	5	1	0	0	2	1	0	17	1
Jiminez, Madison	7	7	.500	2.92	26	19	2	0	1	0	120.1	78	48	39	3	8	78	1	135	12
Johnson, Kenosha*	0	0	.000	5.50	12	0	0	7	0	0	18.0	27	12	11	1	1	7	0	11	3
Johnson, South Bend	7	5	.583	3.79	16	16	5	0	1	0	109.1	111	56	46	5	6	23	0	74	8
Johnson, Waterloo	0	0	.000	8.71	7	0	0	5	0	0	10.1	14	15	10	0	1	12	0	12	0
Juelsgaard, Clinton	6	9	.400	5.28	35	9	1	11	0	2	76.2	86	58	45	2	3	52	6	60	12
Kenny, Peoria	9	7	.563	2.88	39	9	2	20	1	5	100.0	81	41	32	6	4	28	1	75	5
Kilgo, 4 Rock. - 25 C.R.*	3	0	1.000	0.64	29	0	0	23	0	11	42.1	21	4	3	0	1	6	0	42	2
Klingenbeck, Kane County	3	4	.429	2.63	11	11	0	0	0	0	68.1	50	31	20	3	1	28	1	64	4
Kloek, Beloit	10	1	.909	2.11	15	14	2	0	1	0	94.0	79	32	22	7	4	27	1	76	5
Knox, Beloit*	0	0	.000	3.77	14	1	0	5	0	4	31.0	30	20	13	3	1	8	0	27	1
Kobetitsch, Appleton*	0	1	.000	1.62	11	0	0	3	0	1	16.2	16	4	3	0	0	6	1	9	0
Konemann, Springfield	4	5	.444	4.05	29	14	0	6	0	0	97.2	110	51	44	3	5	35	0	76	7
Konieczki, Kenosha*	5	3	.625	1.76	49	0	0	31	0	13	56.1	44	14	11	2	0	19	2	79	3
Kotch, Rockford*	4	4	.500	3.43	42	0	0	13	0	0	65.2	66	31	25	0	1	35	1	61	11
Krahenbuhl, Peoria	7	7	.500	3.35	19	17	1	0	0	0	113.0	110	57	42	5	4	42	0	92	5
Krivda, Kane County*	12	5	.706	3.03	18	18	2	0	0	0	121.2	108	53	41	6	1	41	0	124	5
Landress, Appleton	2	2	.500	1.86	17	0	0	5	0	0	29.0	18	9	6	1	3	10	2	21	3
Leary, Madison*	0	0	.000	27.00	1	0	0	1	0	0	1.0	2	3	3	0	0	2	0	0	1
Lee, Appleton	3	5	.375	5.45	24	10	1	2	0	0	71.0	82	54	43	7	3	36	0	39	8
Lemp, Kane County	2	3	.400	3.46	58	1	0	46	0	26	65.0	41	27	25	6	0	49	5	74	10
Leslie, Cedar Rapids	2	3	.400	3.93	22	0	0	11	0	1	34.1	26	16	15	1	1	18	4	32	3
Levine, South Bend	9	5	.643	2.81	23	23	2	0	0	0	156.2	151	67	49	6	8	36	1	131	9
Locklear, Clinton*	8	5	.615	2.35	30	13	1	6	0	0	126.1	117	45	33	1	2	42	1	69	3
Looney, Rockford*	3	1	.750	3.16	17	0	0	5	0	0	31.1	28	13	11	0	1	23	0	34	1
Lowery, Clinton*	1	2	.333	5.61	20	0	0	6	0	0	33.2	43	22	21	2	1	10	0	20	6
Luebbers, Cedar Rapids	7	0	1.000	2.62	14	14	1	0	0	0	82.1	71	33	24	2	8	33	0	56	1
Mammola, Quad City*	0	1	.000	4.62	13	0	0	2	0	1	25.1	30	15	13	1	0	9	0	21	1
Mansur, Kenosha*	6	3	.667	2.89	11	10	1	0	0	0	65.1	69	27	21	6	1	8	1	46	1
Margheim, Cedar Rapids*	0	1	.000	11.57	5	0	0	3	0	0	4.2	10	7	6	0	2	1	0	3	0
Marquez, Kane County	1	2	.333	5.19	18	5	0	3	0	0	34.2	32	28	20	2	1	40	0	39	6

Pitcher, Team	W	L	Pct.	ERA	G	GS	CG	GF	ShO	Sv.	IP	H	R	ER	HR	HB	BB	Int. BB	SO	WP
Martin, Waterloo*	2	6	.250	4.25	39	2	0	11	0	3	55.0	62	38	26	3	4	22	4	57	5
Martinez, Rockford	2	1	.667	2.66	10	7	0	0	0	0	40.2	36	15	12	0	1	24	0	29	5
Martinez, Quad City	0	0	.000	7.50	5	4	0	0	0	0	12.0	19	10	10	0	0	8	0	7	1
Martinez, Springfield	1	3	.250	3.19	18	3	0	7	0	0	31.0	28	18	11	0	0	12	0	22	6
Mattson, Beloit	1	0	1.000	4.15	8	1	0	2	0	0	17.1	15	8	8	1	0	7	1	16	0
McDonald, Rockford	3	3	.500	2.56	11	8	0	2	0	0	59.2	50	24	17	1	1	23	1	49	3
McKeon, Beloit	1	1	.500	4.50	3	1	0	0	0	0	12.0	10	8	6	2	0	2	0	8	0
McLain, Clinton	1	2	.333	3.42	18	0	0	12	0	5	23.2	19	10	9	0	3	10	0	29	1
Mercedes, Burlington	0	3	.000	9.38	18	0	0	11	0	4	24.0	37	30	25	3	0	19	4	14	0
Jo. Mercedes, Kane County	3	2	.600	2.66	8	8	2	0	2	0	47.1	40	26	14	1	0	15	0	45	6
Ju. Mercedes, Kane County*	3	6	.333	6.09	40	3	0	11	0	1	57.2	74	47	39	3	2	48	3	35	1
Meyer, Peoria*	7	9	.438	4.30	35	14	1	7	0	0	121.1	116	63	58	5	2	58	3	91	4
Miceli, Appleton	1	1	.500	1.93	23	0	0	22	0	9	23.1	12	6	5	0	1	4	1	44	1
Millay, Madison	2	2	.500	3.64	7	6	0	0	0	0	42.0	28	22	17	3	7	20	0	28	6
Miller, Burlington	4	4	.500	3.60	50	0	0	23	0	1	80.0	62	38	32	4	11	47	1	82	20
Minik, Madison	0	0	.000	2.93	18	0	0	7	0	1	30.2	24	16	10	0	6	12	1	18	6
Misa, Madison	0	0	.000	0.00	4	0	0	1	0	1	5.2	6	5	0	0	0	3	0	8	0
Mitchell, Quad City	0	0	.000	6.29	16	0	0	10	0	1	24.1	23	19	17	3	1	15	0	27	5
Mitchelson, Quad City*	2	1	.667	2.11	15	0	0	4	0	1	21.1	16	7	5	1	1	10	2	13	3
Morrison, Rockford	1	2	.333	5.14	15	3	0	7	0	0	35.0	46	24	20	2	1	7	0	29	2
Murphy, Burlington	0	4	.000	4.54	50	0	0	16	0	2	83.1	80	60	42	7	4	49	0	67	10
Musset, Quad City	8	2	.800	2.39	41	0	0	22	0	6	71.2	41	19	19	3	3	25	0	104	5
Myers, Clinton*	1	2	.333	1.19	7	7	0	0	0	0	37.2	28	11	5	0	2	8	0	32	4
Myers, Madison*	3	1	.750	2.93	39	0	0	12	0	3	43.0	39	17	14	3	0	21	2	42	6
Naulty, Kenosha	0	1	.000	5.50	6	2	0	1	0	0	18.0	22	12	11	3	1	7	0	14	1
Nielsen, Springfield*	3	4	.429	6.21	9	8	0	0	0	0	37.2	56	30	26	4	1	8	0	29	1
Norris, Rockford	5	15	.250	3.75	27	27	1	0	0	0	163.0	160	88	68	5	10	79	2	143	21
O'Connell, Kane County	1	0	1.000	9.71	22	0	0	6	0	0	29.2	47	42	32	7	2	19	1	18	4
O'Laughlin, Beloit*	2	0	1.000	5.01	4	4	0	0	0	0	23.1	24	16	13	2	2	13	0	10	5
Ortiz, Clinton*	3	5	.375	4.92	37	4	0	13	0	1	82.1	86	55	45	4	2	44	2	100	12
Pacheco, Peoria	1	4	.200	9.84	11	5	0	1	0	0	32.0	53	41	35	5	2	9	0	23	1
Paskievitch, Waterloo	11	8	.579	4.91	49	0	1	14	0	0	102.2	105	65	56	5	7	67	7	122	10
Patterson, Peoria*	0	0	.000	12.00	2	0	0	1	0	0	3.0	5	4	4	0	0	2	0	5	0
Peltzer, Clinton*	1	0	1.000	1.46	7	0	0	1	0	0	12.1	5	2	2	1	1	4	0	13	0
Perez, Quad City*	3	0	1.000	4.50	12	3	0	6	0	1	28.0	28	17	14	0	0	14	0	18	2
Perez, Rockford*	0	1	.000	5.79	7	1	0	2	0	1	9.1	12	7	6	3	1	5	0	8	1
Phillips, Peoria	0	1	.000	18.00	4	1	0	3	0	0	5.0	13	10	10	0	1	7	0	3	1
Pierce, South Bend	3	5	.375	2.07	52	0	0	46	0	30	69.2	46	22	16	1	6	18	0	88	8
Pierce, Madison	2	3	.400	4.42	34	0	0	19	0	5	59.0	62	33	29	3	3	30	2	56	4
Plemmons, Cedar Rapids	0	0	.000	1.29	3	0	0	2	0	0	7.0	3	1	1	0	1	2	0	4	0
Pomeranz, Kane County*	0	0	.000	3.38	5	0	0	0	0	0	2.2	6	5	1	0	0	3	0	1	2
Ponte, Burlington	2	4	.333	1.79	30	1	0	27	0	10	40.1	29	16	8	2	4	19	4	54	3
Powers, Burlington*	5	5	.500	4.18	55	0	0	18	0	2	71.0	70	42	33	5	2	42	5	72	9
Pruitt, Beloit	3	3	.500	4.08	8	8	0	0	0	0	39.2	43	21	18	1	2	15	1	20	3
Pruitt, Appleton	3	5	.375	6.32	10	10	0	0	0	0	52.2	58	41	37	5	1	31	0	28	4
Quijada, Burlington	2	2	.500	4.26	18	9	0	1	0	0	57.0	51	36	27	4	2	32	1	43	11
Quinones, Cedar Rapids*	0	1	.000	4.43	11	2	0	3	0	1	20.1	19	13	10	0	1	15	1	11	3
Radke, Kenosha	10	10	.500	2.93	26	25	4	1	1	0	165.2	149	70	54	8	6	47	1	127	4
Ratekin, Quad City	5	6	.455	3.85	23	19	1	4	0	0	110.0	104	57	47	6	5	35	0	62	9
Ray, Cedar Rapids	5	3	.625	2.96	11	6	0	2	0	1	48.2	47	18	16	1	2	11	0	30	2
Rea, Appleton	9	3	.750	2.61	38	2	0	17	0	1	89.2	83	39	26	6	0	33	3	74	5
Reed, Burlington	0	2	.000	2.75	18	0	0	9	0	1	36.0	28	15	11	3	0	13	0	25	1
Roberts, Kenosha	1	1	.500	5.56	7	6	0	1	0	0	22.2	23	18	14	4	0	15	0	23	1
Romanoli, Springfield*	5	2	.714	1.48	62	0	0	11	0	2	79.0	46	21	13	4	11	17	0	112	5
Rose, Burlington*	4	15	.211	3.81	27	21	3	0	0	0	139.1	133	74	59	11	7	58	0	93	10
Rose, Madison	2	2	.500	4.25	8	8	1	0	0	0	36.0	35	22	17	2	2	10	0	15	3
Rossiter, Madison	8	14	.364	3.96	27	27	2	0	0	0	154.2	135	83	68	17	4	68	1	135	4
Rueter, Rockford*	11	9	.550	2.58	26	26	6	0	2	0	174.1	150	68	50	5	1	36	2	153	4
Rutter, Beloit	2	7	.222	4.96	14	4	1	5	0	0	49.0	59	37	27	1	2	22	1	30	3
Saccavino, Kenosha	4	1	.800	1.72	6	6	0	0	0	0	36.2	31	11	7	2	1	7	0	28	1
Sanchez, Peoria	5	11	.313	4.66	35	15	3	11	0	2	135.1	147	82	70	17	16	39	4	77	4
Sanders, Kane County	6	7	.462	3.46	49	0	0	8	0	3	67.2	61	43	26	1	3	57	8	54	9
Santos, Springfield	4	4	.500	2.08	63	1	0	58	0	35	69.1	40	20	16	1	5	26	1	107	7
Sartain, Kenosha*	7	13	.350	2.72	24	24	1	0	1	0	132.1	103	55	40	3	2	59	1	125	9
Scharff, Madison	7	9	.438	4.68	42	9	0	10	0	1	109.2	106	73	57	4	9	69	4	81	14
Schramm, Peoria	5	7	.417	4.14	32	12	2	8	1	1	117.1	117	62	54	13	5	40	2	94	9
Schulte, Burlington	0	0	.000	0.00	1	0	0	1	0	0	0.2	1	0	0	0	0	0	0	1	0
Schwartz, Kenosha	1	0	1.000	1.64	5	1	0	1	0	0	11.0	14	5	2	1	2	6	0	4	1
Scott, Burlington*	1	6	.143	6.42	16	8	1	0	0	0	54.2	65	47	39	4	6	40	0	32	3
Sebach, Quad City	3	4	.429	3.96	13	13	0	0	0	0	61.1	52	31	27	5	8	40	0	50	8
Sewell, Burlington	0	0	.000	3.94	9	0	0	3	0	3	16.0	18	8	7	2	0	3	1	11	0
Shoemaker, Madison	2	5	.286	5.08	22	11	0	2	3	0	83.1	98	56	47	5	2	18	0	56	5
Silcox, Waterloo	3	1	.750	1.24	6	6	0	0	0	0	29.0	22	8	4	0	2	13	0	22	2
Silverio, Quad City	5	2	.714	2.53	13	13	1	0	1	0	78.1	57	26	22	2	2	37	0	76	3
Simmons, Springfield*	15	7	.682	2.80	27	27	2	0	1	0	170.1	160	63	53	10	2	39	0	116	10
Slininger, Springfield	11	10	.524	3.90	27	27	0	0	0	0	163.2	157	87	71	19	2	56	1	125	15
Smith, Appleton	6	3	.667	3.81	24	10	0	4	0	0	82.2	79	38	35	8	1	27	0	58	3
Smith, Appleton	0	0	.000	5.91	8	0	0	7	0	0	10.2	14	10	7	1	1	7	0	13	3
Smith, 17 Spr. - 10 K.C.	11	7	.611	3.85	27	27	2	0	1	0	149.2	158	73	64	12	10	48	1	95	3
Smock, Madison*	1	0	1.000	0.60	18	0	0	5	0	1	15.0	14	9	1	2	0	6	1	8	2
Soto, South Bend	3	0	1.000	3.99	7	5	0	2	0	0	29.1	28	15	13	2	3	12	0	13	2
Souza, Beloit	1	2	.333	4.66	9	0	0	4	0	0	19.1	20	14	10	1	1	17	0	18	1
Speek, Springfield	2	1	.667	1.07	58	0	0	13	0	0	76.0	45	13	9	1	3	14	1	126	3
Spradlin, Cedar Rapids	1	0	1.000	7.71	1	0	0	0	0	0	2.1	5	2	2	0	0	0	0	4	0
Steenstra, Peoria	6	3	.667	2.11	12	12	4	0	2	0	89.2	79	29	21	5	3	21	1	68	4
Steph, Cedar Rapids	12	9	.571	4.32	27	27	1	0	1	0	154.1	157	86	74	18	6	54	0	136	11
Stonecipher, Clinton	2	3	.400	5.28	8	7	1	0	0	0	44.1	39	32	26	2	2	19	0	32	3
Stowell, Madison	5	7	.417	4.83	29	18	0	2	0	0	108.0	105	69	58	7	4	73	0	85	16
Stroth, Clinton	0	0	.000	15.00	3	0	0	2	0	0	3.0	4	6	5	1	1	4	0	5	1
Sutch, Madison	4	6	.400	4.11	49	0	0	25	0	7	70.0	67	40	32	4	4	43	2	54	9
Sweeney, Kenosha*	1	2	.333	3.40	31	0	0	16	0	2	50.1	50	23	19	2	5	9	0	49	2
Szczechowski, Clinton	1	0	1.000	4.88	6	5	0	1	0	0	24.0	27	16	13	2	0	14	0	14	0
Tagle, South Bend*	2	0	1.000	3.58	26	0	0	6	0	0	27.2	33	15	11	1	0	11	0	33	3
Talemaco, Peoria	0	1	.000	7.94	2	1	0	0	0	0	5.2	9	5	5	0	1	5	0	5	0
Tallman, Kane County	0	0	.000	0.00	2	0	0	2	0	0	2.0	1	0	0	0	0	1	0	1	0

Pitcher, Team	W	L	Pct.	ERA	G	GS	CG	GF	ShO	Sv.	IP	H	R	ER	HR	HB	BB	Int. BB	SO	WP
Taylor, Kenosha	10	9	.526	2.75	27	27	2	0	1	0	170.1	150	71	52	3	10	68	0	158	11
Thees, Madison	1	3	.250	5.32	16	1	0	8	0	1	23.2	22	16	14	0	0	12	0	18	1
Thomas, Rockford*	5	9	.357	3.58	28	17	1	8	0	2	113.0	98	52	45	8	6	51	0	108	5
Thomsen, Madison*	0	0	.000	9.00	1	0	0	1	0	0	1.0	1	1	1	0	0	1	0	0	0
Tidwell, Peoria*	5	1	.833	1.48	60	0	0	27	0	13	61.0	35	11	10	0	1	28	2	69	3
Tolar, South Bend*	6	5	.545	2.88	18	10	0	6	0	0	81.1	59	34	26	5	2	41	0	81	5
Toth, Appleton	7	6	.538	3.39	23	22	2	1	0	0	127.1	111	58	48	9	5	34	0	100	3
Tranbarger, Springfield*	1	0	1.000	3.62	42	0	0	17	0	2	49.2	47	27	20	4	3	24	0	38	2
Trisler, Beloit	7	1	.875	3.55	26	8	1	5	0	0	91.1	77	41	36	4	6	40	2	67	7
Vanderweele, Clinton	3	3	.500	4.94	9	9	0	0	0	0	51.0	61	33	28	5	2	24	1	39	7
Van Landingham, Clinton	0	4	.000	5.67	10	10	0	0	0	0	54.0	49	40	34	1	5	29	0	59	6
Vonderlieth, Beloit*	0	0	.000	6.23	11	0	0	6	0	0	13.0	23	16	9	0	0	12	0	5	1
Waldron, Waterloo*	7	3	.700	4.94	49	2	0	15	0	1	94.2	113	63	52	9	2	32	3	73	7
Wallace, Peoria	0	1	.000	4.91	2	0	0	1	0	0	3.2	3	2	2	0	0	1	0	2	0
Wanke, Clinton*	9	10	.474	4.10	26	21	1	1	0	0	123.0	115	81	56	4	9	62	1	118	11
Waring, Burlington	11	7	.611	2.21	20	20	2	0	0	0	122.0	100	42	30	9	4	19	0	104	5
Watkins, Kenosha*	2	5	.286	3.69	27	0	0	11	0	1	46.1	43	21	19	4	3	14	0	58	1
Watson, Quad City	8	5	.615	1.29	40	0	0	25	0	10	70.0	43	20	10	2	4	42	3	69	11
Wengert, Madison	3	4	.429	3.38	7	7	0	0	0	0	40.0	42	20	15	2	2	17	0	29	1
White, Rockford	14	8	.636	2.84	27	27	7	0	0	0	187.0	148	73	59	10	11	61	0	176	9
Whitehead, Rockford	6	4	.600	3.45	19	12	2	3	0	1	78.1	65	37	30	2	4	43	0	65	12
Williams, Quad City	13	11	.542	3.26	27	26	7	0	0	0	179.1	161	81	65	14	7	55	0	152	9
Wissler, Kenosha	4	3	.571	1.34	21	7	1	3	1	0	74.0	52	22	11	0	3	16	0	59	5
Woodfin, South Bend	3	6	.333	2.73	36	0	0	19	0	5	59.1	53	27	18	1	4	27	1	82	6
Worrell, South Bend*	1	1	.500	0.00	14	0	0	5	0	2	22.1	17	2	0	0	0	7	0	21	0
Wynne, Rockford	0	1	.000	2.70	2	1	0	0	0	0	6.2	7	5	2	0	0	4	0	4	2
Zastoupil, Cedar Rapids	1	2	.333	3.97	9	0	0	2	0	1	22.2	18	12	10	4	0	9	0	15	3
Zurn, Beloit	2	2	.500	5.60	7	7	0	0	0	0	27.1	35	20	17	2	1	12	1	22	4

BALKS—Jiminez, 14; Cairncross, M. Smith, White, 9 each; Holliday, Klingenbeck, 8 each; Guardado, J. Haynes, Kloek, 7 each; Browne, Hook, Wissler, 6 each; R. Castillo, Chouinard, Gledhill, 5 each; Ayres, Beckett, Benhardt, Boehringer, Brown, Fritz, Guerra, Hill, O'Laughlin, D. Pruitt, Silverio, Thomas, Trisler, 4 each; Aucoin, Bovee, C. Culberson, Dodd, Gavaghan, Gerstein, H. Haynes, Hernandez, M. Jarvis, Norris, Pacheco, Paskievitch, Rea, Rossiter, J. Smith, Steenstra, Stonecipher, Stowell, Tagel, Vanderweele, Waring, 3 each; Baez, Baldwin, Bliss, Boker, D. Culberson, Davila, Dickens, Duff, Ellis, England, Fermin, Forney, Foster, Garcia, Hardwick, F. Johnson, Kenny, Konemann, Lee, Locklear, Lowery, Mansur, Mattson, J. Mercedes, B. Perez, Sanders, Santos, Schramm, Shoemaker, Simmons, Slininger, Steph, Van Landingham, Waldron, Wallace, Wanke, 2 each; T. Adams, Altaffer, Andujar, Aracena, Ariola, Barber, Bennett, Bertotti, Blanchette, Boze, Brimhall, Creek, Dennison, Dillman, Doty, Ferry, Froning, Gallaher, Griffen, Harrison, Henrikson, Heredia, Hoeme, Hrusovsky, Jenkins, B. Johnson, Juelsgaard, Kobetitsch, Kotch, Krahenbuhl, Krivda, Levine, Luebbers, Marquez, F. Martinez, McDonald, McLain, Meyer, Miller, Mitchell, Mitchelson, Morrison, T. Myers, Naulty, R. Pierce, Plemmons, Ponte, Quijada, Ratekin, H. Rose, S. Rose, Rueter, Rutter, Sartain, Scott, Sebach, Sewell, Sweeney, Taylor, Tolar, Tranbarger, Watson, Whitehead, Williams, Zurn, 1 each.

COMBINATION SHUTOUTS—Bevil-Smith-Berumen, Bovee-Baez-Rea-Miceli, Bovee-Miceli, Bovee-Landress-Miceli, Bovee-Rea, Pruitt-Smith, Rea-Baez-Berumen, Smith-Kobetitsch, Toth-Berumen, Appleton; Boze-Criminger, Boze-Fetty, Hardwick-Fetty, Kloek-Christopher-Fetty, Beloit; Evans-Powers-Miller, Gallaher-Ponte, Holliday-Murphy-Powers-Miller, Quijada-Murphy-Biehl-Ponte, Waring-Ponte, Burlington; Dodd-Hrusovsky, Ferry-Griffen-Kilgo, Hook-Duff, Hook-Edwards-Hrusovsky, Hook-Leslie-Doty, Hook-Ray-Culberson, Luebbers-Leslie-Kilgo, Steph-Hrusovsky, Cedar Rapids; Ayres-Benavides, Gambs-Boker-Peltzer-Hyde, Locklear-Grundt, Wanke-Benavides, Clinton; Chouinard-Lemp, Klingenbeck-Benavides, Smith-Sanders, Kane County; Guardado-Roberts, Sartain-Garcia-Konieczki, Radke-Diaz, Saccavino-Gavaghan, Saccavino-Konieczki, Wissler-Garcia, Kenosha; Jiminez-Myers, Jiminez-Pierce, Jiminez-Scharf-Sutch, Jiminez-Shoemaker, Rossiter-Cusey, Stowell-Sutch, Madison; Krahenbuhl-Tidwell, Sanchez-Kenny-Bliss, Peoria; Gledhill-Musset-Jarvis, Fritz-Blanchette, Fritz-Mammola-Heredia, Fritz-Mitchelson-Watson, Rankin-Burgos-Watson, Sebach-Heredia, Silverio-Mitchelson-Watson, Quad City; Aucoin-Fultz, Martinez-Haynes, Thomas-Gerstein-Haynes, McDonald-Kotch-Haynes, Norris-Kotch-Aucoin, Rueter-Kotch-Haynes, White-Gerstein, White-Gerstein-Haynes, Rockford; Heathcott-Culberson-Tagle-Tolar, Heathcott-Worrell-Woodfin, Levine-Worrell-Pierce, Tolar-Woodfin, South Bend; Simmons-Santos 2, Badorek-Conemann, Santos-Romanoli-Speek-Konemann, Simmons-Speek-Romanoli-Cimorelli, Smith-Romanoli-Cimorelli-Santos, Springfield; Beckett-Martin-Paskievitch, Martin-Paskievitch-Bensching, Paskievitch-Hoeme, Silcox-Benhardt, Waterloo.

NO-HIT GAMES—Wanke, Clinton, defeated Peoria, 5-3, May 14; Sartain, Kenosha, defeated Clinton, 1-0 (second game), August 13.

FIELDING

TEAM

Team	Pct.	G	PO	A	E	DP	PB	Player, Team	Pct.	G	PO	A	E	DP	PB
Quad City	.972	137	3573	1463	145	92	23	Beloit	.959	135	3474	1464	212	92	18
Peoria	.964	136	3545	1434	186	132	17	Waterloo	.958	137	3495	1359	211	94	31
Springfield	.964	140	3691	1447	193	108	23	South Bend	.958	138	3703	1517	229	115	32
Appleton	.964	138	3431	1372	181	115	19	Madison	.957	134	3475	1497	221	105	45
Rockford	.961	136	3497	1322	194	101	23	Clinton	.956	138	3605	1498	236	127	30
Cedar Rapids	.960	138	3596	1356	204	102	17	Burlington	.953	136	3509	1493	248	119	24
Kenosha	.959	134	3406	1362	203	90	26	Kane County	.950	137	3589	1464	265	114	34

Triple plays—Appleton 2, Beloit, Cedar Rapids, Quad City, Springfield.

INDIVIDUAL

*Throws lefthanded.

FIRST BASEMEN

Player, Team	Pct.	G	PO	A	E	DP		Player, Team	Pct.	G	PO	A	E	DP
Adams, Waterloo	1.000	9	26	1	0	0		Dana, Clinton	.966	18	105	7	4	12
Albert, Beloit	.950	9	17	2	1	1		DeBerry, Cedar Rapids*	.986	106	852	58	13	73
Alimena, Clinton*	.986	117	990	68	15	82		Dehdashtion, Rockford	1.000	4	21	1	0	0
Aurila, Rockford*	.800	1	7	1	2	0		Diaz, Peoria	.964	13	102	6	4	8
Babbitt, Appleton	1.000	13	105	9	0	6		Dobrolsky, Beloit	1.000	1	3	0	0	0
Blakeman, Kenosha	.987	34	282	26	4	16		Duncan, Madison	1.000	1	2	0	0	0
Blanton, Springfield	1.000	1	4	0	0	1		Estevez, Kenosha	.974	15	101	12	3	4
Bobo, Quad City	1.000	1	10	1	0	0		Fairman, Beloit*	.985	72	615	34	10	38
Brakebill, Quad City	.976	18	149	11	4	10		Falco, Rockford	.969	14	91	3	3	6
Brede, Kenosha*	.988	14	78	7	1	8		Filosa, South Bend	.933	3	14	0	1	1
Brown, Peoria*	.990	68	582	39	6	50		Fryman, South Bend	.9886	128	1055	75	13	88
Burgos, Appleton	.983	8	58	1	1	6		Giegling, Cedar Rapids	1.000	3	8	0	0	1
Cerio, Springfield	1.000	1	1	0	0	0		Gilbert, Kane County	.983	56	359	41	7	24
Colon, Burlington	.976	33	271	19	7	21		Goins, Waterloo	1.000	7	22	0	0	3
Curtis, Burlington*	.980	56	464	24	10	43		Gresham, Kane County	1.000	3	3	3	0	0
								Gubanich, Madison	.968	20	133	16	5	5
								Hinton, Appleton*	.983	104	855	62	16	78
								Huff, South Bend	1.000	1	8	0	0	1

Player, Team	Pct.	G	PO	A	E	DP
Jensen, Clinton	1.000	2	15	0	0	3
Johnson, Kane County	1.000	2	1	0	0	0
Johnson, Kenosha	1.000	10	68	6	0	4
Keene, Clinton*	.961	10	71	3	3	5
Kessinger, Cedar Rapids	1.000	8	60	9	0	3
Kontorinis, Kenosha	.990	72	574	48	6	39
Leary, Madison*	.981	102	878	69	18	67
Mader, South Bend	1.000	2	11	0	0	1
Martinez, Burlington*	.986	57	477	20	7	36
Martorana, South Bend	.977	15	116	13	3	8
Matos, Rockford	.984	124	918	81	16	76
McGee, Peoria	1.000	5	28	1	0	3
Medina, Peoria	.988	45	396	25	5	42
Montgomery, Clinton	.980	7	43	7	1	7
Norman, Appleton	1.000	7	39	2	0	4
O'Brien, Springfield	.983	73	645	32	12	44
Owens, Kane County	.979	71	616	40	14	46
Parker, Madison	1.000	11	44	5	0	0
Postiff, Peoria	1.000	16	68	5	0	2
PRITCHETT, Quad City	.9887	123	1059	84	13	75
Pugh, Waterloo*	.982	136	970	87	19	78
Radziewicz, Springfield*	.996	31	226	19	1	11
Raffo, Cedar Rapids*	.978	34	212	9	5	9
Reid, Madison	1.000	1	1	0	0	0
Saenz, South Bend	1.000	1	9	0	0	1
Salazar, Beloit	1.000	1	3	0	0	0
Santana, Rockford	.667	1	1	1	1	0
Sheldon, Madison	1.000	1	2	0	0	0
Smith, Burlington	1.000	3	24	0	0	2
Stefan, Peoria	1.000	1	5	0	0	1
Stefanski, Beloit	1.000	4	7	1	0	3
Tahan, Springfield	.983	48	373	24	7	33
Talanoa, Beloit	.974	66	598	31	17	44
Terilli, Peoria*	1.000	3	22	1	0	2
Thielen, Clinton	1.000	2	9	0	0	0
Thomsen, Madison*	1.000	21	140	12	0	12
Tunison, Appleton	.958	9	65	4	3	7
Turner, Quad City	1.000	1	10	2	0	1
Valdez, Peoria*	1.000	1	1	0	0	1
Vinas, South Bend	.960	3	23	1	1	0
Vogel, South Bend	1.000	1	1	0	0	0
Waszgis, Kane County	.968	23	132	18	5	14

Triple plays—DeBerry, Hinton, Pritchett, Talanoa, Tunison.

SECOND BASEMEN

Player, Team	Pct.	G	PO	A	E	DP
Adams, Kane County	.933	14	29	27	4	2
Adams, Waterloo	.800	2	3	1	1	1
Babbitt, Appleton	1.000	7	8	14	0	2
Berry, Burlington	.942	57	108	152	16	32
Biasucci, Peoria	.952	62	101	174	14	28
Black, Springfield	.923	10	7	5	1	1
Brady, South Bend	.957	18	24	42	3	7
Bream, Waterloo	1.000	2	3	1	0	0
Burton, South Bend	.947	115	219	284	28	62
Cirillo, Beloit	.971	15	30	37	2	11
Clarke, Appleton	.909	4	6	4	1	0
Claus, Kenosha	.958	71	123	170	13	31
Claus, Quad City	.971	55	93	145	7	24
Coachman, Quad City	.952	4	9	11	1	4
Colon, Burlington	1.000	2	1	4	0	0
Craig, Peoria	.956	26	46	41	4	11
Deak, Springfield	.965	121	199	291	18	58
Delgado, Kane County	.971	20	47	52	3	11
Dennison, Rockford	.977	16	24	19	1	5
Diaz, Peoria	1.000	2	0	1	0	0
DiSarcina, South Bend	1.000	1	1	1	0	0
Dotolo, Clinton	.946	24	36	52	5	11
Dufault, Kenosha	.925	20	29	45	6	11
Duncan, Madison	.976	11	20	21	1	6
Farlow, Waterloo	.980	30	48	52	2	12
Felix, Madison	.953	51	89	155	12	24
Filotei, Cedar Rapids	.900	4	2	7	1	1
Florez, Clinton	.967	80	156	254	14	49
Forbes, Quad City	.973	83	131	233	10	39
Francisco, Madison	.937	54	65	112	12	18
Goins, Waterloo	1.000	1	2	2	0	0
Hardge, Rockford	.961	123	254	261	21	56
HARDTKE, Waterloo	.970	110	225	256	15	52
Harley, Burlington	.945	82	150	229	22	49
Hazlett, Kenosha	.875	2	1	6	1	1
Heather, Kenosha	.800	2	2	2	1	1
Huyler, Beloit	1.000	1	1	0	0	0
Indriago, Appleton	.966	53	85	114	7	23
Johnson, Kane County	.954	49	79	87	8	25
Johnson, Kenosha	.935	13	23	20	3	0
Johnson, Appleton	.966	62	106	177	10	42
Jones, Cedar Rapids	.909	5	6	14	2	0
Kessinger, Cedar Rapids	.986	17	33	35	1	12
Lane, Burlington	.889	5	7	9	2	0
Markiewicz, Quad City	.800	1	2	2	1	0
Martinez, Kane County	.906	18	36	41	8	4
Martorana, South Bend	1.000	2	0	1	0	0
McGlone, Burlington	.917	3	5	6	1	0
McNabb, Appleton	.933	10	14	14	2	1
Mendez, Madison	.961	15	19	30	2	2
Mendoza, Beloit	.943	42	64	86	9	12
Mercedes, Kane County	.890	39	47	66	14	18
Meza, Springfield	.971	27	42	58	3	12
Monzon, South Bend	1.000	1	0	2	0	0
Moock, Peoria	1.000	3	2	3	0	1
Moore, Peoria	.960	51	93	121	9	26
Nava, Kenosha	.950	37	56	76	7	9
O'Neill, Clinton	.950	36	69	84	8	16
Parker, Madison	.960	24	48	49	4	10
Postiff, Peoria	.963	7	9	17	1	3
Powell, Beloit	.955	71	139	179	15	32
Reyes, South Bend	.909	10	5	15	2	2
Reyes, Rockford	.933	4	5	9	1	1
Riggs, Cedar Rapids	.958	121	215	285	22	51
Rodriguez, Springfield	1.000	1	1	1	0	0
Rodriguez, Clinton	.941	6	10	6	1	3
Ruiz, Kane County	.981	21	41	62	2	15
Salazar, Beloit	1.000	1	2	2	0	0
Sisco, Appleton	1.000	1	0	1	0	0
Stewart, Appleton	.925	11	16	33	4	6
Trujillo, Peoria	.909	7	7	13	2	1
Whitford, Beloit	.962	23	43	58	4	10

Triple plays—Deak, Forbes, Indriago.

THIRD BASEMEN

Player, Team	Pct.	G	PO	A	E	DP
Abell, Appleton	1.000	3	2	3	0	0
Abercrombie, Waterloo	.849	42	20	59	14	5
Adams, Kane County	1.000	1	0	3	0	0
Adams, Waterloo	.853	44	20	61	14	6
Babbitt, Appleton	.876	43	25	74	14	10
Berry, Burlington	.750	9	9	9	6	0
Biasucci, Peoria	.750	3	3	3	2	0
Black, Springfield	.938	7	4	11	1	0
Brakebill, Quad City	.900	25	12	42	6	5
Calcagno, Clinton	.818	8	2	7	2	1
Cirillo, Beloit	.930	112	85	232	24	11
Colon, Burlington	.923	90	65	176	20	24
Couture, Beloit	1.000	1	0	1	0	0
Craig, Peoria	.877	22	23	41	9	5
Dennison, Rockford	1.000	4	2	3	0	0
Dotolo, Clinton	.889	11	4	12	2	0
Dufault, Kenosha	.944	9	5	12	1	0
Duncan, Madison	.846	66	40	103	26	10
Estevez, Kenosha	.833	5	2	8	2	0
Falco, Rockford	.917	37	30	58	8	6
Farlow, Waterloo	.902	81	53	131	20	14
Fernandez, Kenosha	.865	69	46	108	24	13
Filosa, South Bend	1.000	7	1	13	0	0
Filotei, Cedar Rapids	.875	4	2	12	2	1
Forbes, Quad City	.962	20	14	36	2	6
Francisco, Madison	.000	1	0	0	1	0
Fryman, South Bend	1.000	1	2	0	0	0
Gonzalez, Appleton	.909	9	8	12	2	0
Gordon, Cedar Rapids	1.000	4	1	5	0	0
Greene, Cedar Rapids	.901	30	13	60	8	3
Gubanich, Madison	.867	7	0	13	2	0
Hagy, Quad City	1.000	1	1	0	0	0
Havens, Madison	.857	34	12	36	8	3
Heather, Kenosha	.903	12	11	17	3	1
Huff, South Bend	1.000	1	1	1	0	0
Imperial, Beloit	.899	28	18	44	7	6
Indriago, Appleton	.870	16	6	14	3	1
Johnson, Kane County	.907	58	35	130	17	6
Johnson, Kenosha	.883	54	27	94	16	8
Jones, Cedar Rapids	.857	58	26	112	23	19
Kessinger, Cedar Rapids	.921	60	32	107	12	3
Kuehl, Madison	.870	12	6	14	3	0
Lane, Burlington	.935	17	6	37	3	3
Mader, South Bend	1.000	2	2	3	0	0
MARKIEWICZ, Quad City	.943	95	48	169	13	8
Martorana, South Bend	.909	9	1	9	1	1
McClain, Kane County	.917	83	78	143	20	20
McGlone, Burlington	1.000	2	2	2	0	3
McNabb, Appleton	1.000	3	1	3	0	0
Medina, Peoria	.922	77	50	128	15	21
Meza, Springfield	.950	23	14	24	2	3
Miranda, South Bend	1.000	1	0	2	0	0
Montero, Burlington	.897	26	20	58	9	6
Moody, Waterloo	.000	1	0	0	1	0
Moore, Peoria	.864	20	11	40	8	4
Norman, Appleton	.846	7	1	10	2	0
Ortega, Rockford	.910	106	68	154	22	14
Parker, Madison	.884	41	19	80	13	4
Postiff, Peoria	.950	19	11	27	2	6
Powell, Beloit	.917	5	2	9	1	0
Randa, Appleton	.941	70	53	137	12	14
Reyes, South Bend	.750	5	0	6	2	0
Rodriguez, Clinton	.750	5	0	3	1	1
Ruiz, Kane County	1.000	3	0	5	0	0
Saenz, South Bend	.892	127	104	294	48	26
Salazar, Beloit	1.000	2	1	1	0	0

Player, Team	Pct.	G	PO	A	E	DP
Stefan, Peoria	.889	8	7	9	2	1
Thielen, Clinton	.898	128	120	267	44	32
Wallace, Burlington	.571	4	3	5	6	1
Young, Springfield	.879	126	66	239	42	16

Triple play—Young.

SHORTSTOPS

Player, Team	Pct.	G	PO	A	E	DP
Adams, Kane County	.884	58	74	116	25	22
Arnold, Peoria	.950	90	138	261	21	44
Berry, Burlington	.851	35	36	67	18	14
Biasucci, Peoria	.917	4	2	9	1	1
Black, Springfield	.333	3	1	0	2	0
Brady, South Bend	1.000	1	0	2	0	1
Brakebill, Quad City	1.000	3	4	5	0	1
Bream, Waterloo	.929	121	157	272	33	51
Castaldo, Kane County	.851	15	17	23	7	7
Claus, Kenosha	1.000	1	0	3	0	0
Claus, Quad City	.897	21	32	38	8	10
Craig, Peoria	1.000	1	1	1	0	1
Delgado, Kane County	.889	14	16	32	6	6
Dennison, Rockford	.963	16	19	33	2	11
DiSarcina, South Bend	.945	122	182	313	29	61
Dotolo, Kenosha	.919	25	37	87	11	19
Dufault, Kenosha	.933	10	10	18	2	1
Everly, Beloit	.872	8	8	26	5	3
Farlow, Waterloo	.896	32	38	74	13	12
Felix, Madison	1.000	4	6	11	0	2
Filosa, South Bend	.917	10	14	19	3	4
Filotei, Cedar Rapids	1.000	1	2	2	0	0
Francisco, Madison	.964	64	108	186	11	32
Garrow, Kenosha	.913	119	166	284	43	47
Gonzalez, Appleton	.917	14	16	28	4	4
Grudzielanek, Rockford	.919	124	173	290	41	46
Hagy, Quad City	.943	120	158	321	29	50
Halter, Appleton	.959	80	150	227	16	64
Hazlett, Kenosha	1.000	1	1	2	0	0
Heather, Kenosha	.938	10	8	22	2	7
Huyler, Beloit	.939	106	125	307	28	41
Indriago, Appleton	.857	4	8	10	3	0
Kessinger, Cedar Rapids	.986	16	22	51	1	7
Koelling, Cedar Rapids	.926	127	196	280	38	50
Lane, Burlington	.809	17	11	27	9	4
Marshall, Appleton	.929	37	47	97	11	13
McClain, Kane County	.919	13	19	49	6	10
McGlone, Burlington	.941	110	141	272	26	47
Mendoza, Beloit	.811	16	12	18	7	2
Mercedes, Kane County	.831	17	13	41	11	6
Meza, Springfield	.885	52	41	75	15	21
Moore, Beloit	.905	10	9	10	2	2
PIMENTEL, Springfield	.953	123	134	337	23	51
Postiff, Peoria	.871	8	12	15	4	5
Reyes, South Bend	.889	11	12	28	5	3
Rodriguez, Springfield	.800	5	1	3	1	2
Rodriguez, Clinton	.911	18	14	37	5	6
Ruiz, Kane County	.927	54	54	111	13	12
Salazar, Beloit	.920	10	7	16	2	2
Sheldon, Madison	.928	73	105	217	25	33
Spiers, Beloit	.930	12	12	28	3	1
Stefan, Peoria	.926	33	41	71	9	13
Stewart, Appleton	.875	3	2	5	1	0
Tamarez, Clinton	.937	100	136	251	26	42
Trujillo, Peoria	.815	7	9	13	5	3
Whitford, Beloit	.875	6	7	14	3	4

Triple plays—Hagy, Halter, Huyler, Koelling, Marshall.

OUTFIELDERS

Player, Team	Pct.	G	PO	A	E	DP
Abercrombie, Waterloo	.940	42	61	2	4	0
Albert, Beloit	.926	63	71	4	6	1
Alimena, Clinton*	1.000	6	4	2	0	0
Aracena, Madison	.974	85	134	13	4	4
Austin, South Bend	.937	46	55	4	4	0
Baber, Beloit	.969	65	86	9	3	1
Battle, Springfield	.972	67	136	3	4	0
Bellomo, Clinton*	.978	23	41	3	1	1
Blanton, Springfield	.946	33	31	4	2	0
Booker, Madison	.986	35	67	6	1	3
Boykin, Quad City	.978	78	129	4	3	0
Brede, Kenosha*	.966	98	158	12	6	3
Brewer, Clinton	1.000	16	35	3	0	1
Buchanan, South Bend	.952	30	55	5	3	2
Byrd, Kenosha	.937	41	71	3	5	0
Byrne, Kane County	.956	104	158	16	8	1
Cameron, South Bend	.957	34	67	0	3	0
Cappuccio, South Bend	.975	49	72	6	2	0
Cerio, Springfield	1.000	6	6	0	0	0
Cookson, Clinton	.972	45	65	5	2	1
Couture, Beloit	.925	38	37	0	3	0
Craig, Peoria	.923	7	12	0	1	0
Cunningham, Peoria	.981	33	51	0	1	0
Diaz, Peoria	.895	13	15	2	2	2
Dotolo, Clinton	1.000	1	1	0	0	0
Dreifort, Rockford	1.000	1	1	0	0	0
Ealy, Appleton	.860	29	36	1	6	1
Eicher, Springfield	.955	71	103	2	5	0
Enriquez, Beloit	.972	106	202	8	6	2
Estep, Cedar Rapids	.951	20	37	2	2	0
Evans, Kenosha	1.000	14	18	0	0	0
Fairman, Beloit*	.500	1	1	0	1	0
Falco, Rockford	1.000	1	2	0	0	0
Feist, Clinton	.938	80	118	3	8	1
Francisco, Madison	.989	43	85	1	1	1
Gardner, Peoria	.961	66	117	7	5	0
Gerald, Appleton	.983	114	231	4	4	0
Gibralter, Cedar Rapids	.978	137	311	7	7	4
Goins, Waterloo	1.000	6	7	0	0	0
Gonzalez, Appleton	.981	118	248	10	5	2
Goodwin, Kane County*	.966	133	301	15	11	7
Gordon, Cedar Rapids	.956	106	146	5	7	1
Guzman, South Bend	1.000	4	3	1	0	1
Hardge, Rockford	1.000	1	1	0	0	0
Hart, Clinton	1.000	13	18	1	0	1
Havens, Madison	.978	30	43	1	1	0
Hazlett, Kenosha	.977	94	166	6	4	2
Henry, South Bend	.968	112	228	11	8	4
Hodge, Kane County	.960	24	23	1	1	0
Horne, Rockford	.966	105	169	4	6	0
House, Beloit*	.933	89	110	2	8	0
Huff, South Bend	.875	6	6	1	1	0
Hust, Madison	.955	112	206	5	10	4
Indriago, Appleton	1.000	2	1	0	0	0
Jackson, Clinton	.961	120	210	9	9	1
Jenkins, Cedar Rapids	.940	66	105	4	7	1
Johnson, Kenosha	1.000	4	2	0	0	0
Johnson, Appleton	1.000	4	7	1	0	0
Jones, Madison	.966	20	26	2	1	0
Dax Jones, Clinton	.956	78	159	13	8	4
De. Jones, Clinton	.947	11	17	1	1	0
Jones, Springfield*	.955	103	162	7	8	2
Keene, Clinton*	1.000	4	7	0	0	0
Kuehl, Madison	1.000	2	4	0	0	0
Larregui, Peoria	.975	125	224	7	6	3
Mabry, Springfield	.969	113	171	14	6	2
McCaffery, Quad City	.975	63	108	10	3	0
McGonnigal, Clinton*	.947	44	70	1	4	0
McKoy, Waterloo	.976	67	115	7	3	0
McNabb, Burlington	.962	119	213	14	9	4
Meza, Springfield	1.000	1	1	0	0	0
Moock, Peoria	.977	51	121	6	3	1
Moore, Kenosha*	.949	79	124	7	7	3
Myers, Appleton*	.932	61	132	5	10	0
Newhouse, Appleton	.974	22	37	1	1	1
Norman, Kenosha	.917	12	10	1	1	0
Norman, Appleton	.989	50	79	8	1	1
Ochoa, Kane County	.953	133	225	17	12	6
Ochoa, South Bend	.900	7	8	1	1	1
Ogden, Kenosha*	.957	81	126	7	6	1
Ogden, South Bend	.957	19	22	0	1	0
Ortega, Rockford	.968	19	26	4	1	0
Palmeiro, Quad City	.973	122	211	9	6	1
Pearce, Waterloo*	.958	105	175	9	8	1
Poe, South Bend	.914	54	91	5	9	0
Postiff, Peoria	1.000	8	9	0	0	0
Powell, Beloit	1.000	2	1	2	0	0
Pritchett, South Bend	1.000	1	2	0	0	0
Pueschner, Cedar Rapids	.951	24	38	1	2	0
Radziewicz, Springfield*	1.000	20	20	2	0	0
Reid, Madison	.985	48	62	3	1	1
Rijo, Rockford	.960	83	115	6	5	1
Robertson, Waterloo	.953	117	151	10	8	2
Samples, Rockford	.956	116	244	15	12	6
Schmidt, Kane County	.904	56	91	3	10	0
SCHULTE, Burlington	.994	107	166	6	1	1
Servello, Appleton	.966	13	25	3	1	0
Simpson, Clinton	.957	29	43	2	2	0
Staydohar, Quad City	.933	16	27	1	2	0
Stefanski, Beloit	1.000	2	3	0	0	0
Sweeney, Quad City*	.981	118	205	5	4	1
Swinton, Burlington	.899	41	56	6	7	0
Taylor, Cedar Rapids	.952	10	19	1	1	1
Terilli, Peoria*	.986	97	135	8	2	2
Tillman, Peoria	.962	28	50	1	2	0
Tunison, Appleton	1.000	1	1	0	0	0
Valdez, Peoria*	.971	22	32	1	1	0
Valrie, South Bend	.965	76	134	4	5	2
Vasquez, Cedar Rapids	.946	72	114	8	7	1
Vaughn, Waterloo	.963	110	221	10	9	0
Vlasis, Springfield	1.000	74	107	6	0	1
Wachter, Beloit	.946	103	139	1	8	0
Walker, Madison	.966	64	108	7	4	1
Wallace, Burlington	.937	66	86	3	6	0
Whalen, Waterloo*	1.000	4	6	0	0	0
White, Burlington	.964	100	170	17	7	5
Williams, Madison	1.000	5	3	0	0	0
Woods, Rockford	.946	100	166	9	10	1

Triple play—Baber.

CATCHERS

Player, Team	Pct.	G	PO	A	E	DP	PB
Abell, Appleton	1.000	6	18	4	0	0	0
Abercrombie, Waterloo	.977	28	109	16	3	3	9
Beck, Beloit	.889	2	8	0	1	0	0
Bertucci, Quad City	1.000	2	8	0	0	0	0
Bobo, Quad City	.974	10	69	7	2	1	2
Burgos, Appleton	.956	8	37	6	2	1	2
Calcagno, Clinton	.967	25	184	23	7	0	7
Campillo, Rockford	1.000	13	76	6	0	0	4
Caple, Kenosha	.981	30	234	24	5	2	5
Castenada, Kane County	1.000	5	22	2	0	0	0
Cerio, Springfield	.975	35	248	26	7	3	5
Charles, Clinton	1.000	2	14	0	0	0	0
Couture, Beloit	1.000	5	6	0	0	0	0
Dana, Peoria	.969	34	191	25	7	3	7
Dehdashtion, Rockford	.982	18	98	9	2	3	2
Delaney, Appleton	.960	20	85	12	4	0	5
DeLeon, Appleton	.931	9	49	5	4	0	3
Delgado, Clinton	1.000	4	25	2	0	0	2
Dobrolsky, Beloit	.981	41	234	29	5	1	8
Dotolo, Clinton	1.000	1	1	0	0	0	0
Dreisbach, Cedar Rapids	.970	26	175	21	6	1	1
Estevez, Kenosha	.960	4	22	2	1	0	0
Fisk, South Bend	.800	1	4	0	1	0	0
Freitag, Rockford	.972	18	94	12	3	1	3
Fuller, Cedar Rapids	.987	81	619	57	9	8	6
Giegling, Cedar Rapids	.977	47	269	25	7	0	9
Gilbert, Kane County	.889	3	7	1	1	0	0
Goins, Waterloo	1.000	23	72	4	0	0	2
Gonzalez, Burlington	.975	75	479	70	14	6	15
Gresham, Kane County	.984	27	162	25	3	3	4
Gubanich, Madison	.976	74	476	84	14	6	25
Haase, South Bend	.967	6	57	2	2	0	1
Jensen, Clinton	.982	76	478	68	10	4	14
Johnson, Kenosha	.939	16	82	11	6	0	7
Jones, Cedar Rapids	1.000	3	7	0	0	0	1
Lanfranco, Burlington	1.000	16	88	13	0	0	1
Loftin, Cedar Rapids	.750	2	3	0	1	0	0
Mader, South Bend	1.000	3	21	0	0	1	0
Manning, South Bend	.991	57	383	42	4	3	9
McGee, Peoria	1.000	25	87	4	0	1	2
McGuire, Peoria	1.000	8	48	3	0	1	0
Miller, Kenosha	.989	99	696	89	9	9	14
Montgomery, Clinton	.988	14	73	9	1	3	0
Mulligan, Waterloo	.984	34	231	18	4	0	5
Mumma, South Bend	.982	14	106	4	2	0	7
Postiff, Peoria	.969	20	119	8	4	1	3
Robledo, South Bend	.966	23	170	27	7	1	6
Ronan, Springfield	.988	110	818	90	11	11	14
Santana, Rockford	.986	108	817	85	13	8	14
Smith, Burlington	.973	53	398	68	13	2	8
Stefanski, Beloit	.984	106	714	94	13	8	10
Stela, Quad City	.988	37	231	26	3	2	6
Strickland, Appleton	.977	107	702	109	19	9	9
Tahan, Springfield	.984	18	60	3	1	0	4
Tallman, Kane County	.983	65	415	45	8	5	14
Thurston, Waterloo	.977	96	708	72	18	2	15
Turner, Quad City	.989	98	717	96	9	1	15
Vinas, Clinton	.982	29	197	19	4	1	3
Vogel, South Bend	.987	18	133	16	2	1	6
Waszgis, Kane County	.980	58	385	53	9	6	18
Williams, Madison	.966	69	452	57	18	8	20
WOLFF, Peoria	.991	107	684	97	7	13	12

Triple play—Fuller.

PITCHERS

Player, Team	Pct.	G	PO	A	E	DP
Adams, Kane County	1.000	10	0	2	0	0
Adams, Peoria	.800	25	10	30	10	5
Altaffer, Waterloo	.852	30	3	20	4	2
Andujar, South Bend	.854	32	11	24	6	0
Ariola, Madison*	1.000	3	2	2	0	0
Aucoin, Rockford	.900	39	9	9	2	2
Ayres, Clinton	.913	38	10	11	2	0
Badorek, Springfield	.887	29	18	29	6	1
Baez, Appleton*	1.000	38	1	13	0	0
Baker, Waterloo	1.000	2	0	2	0	0
Baldwin, South Bend	.868	21	7	26	5	2
Barber, Springfield	1.000	8	3	6	0	0
Beckett, Waterloo*	.857	24	1	17	3	0
Benavides, 30 Cln. - 14 K.C.	1.000	44	4	10	0	0
Benge, Kane County	1.000	2	0	1	0	0
Benhardt, Waterloo*	1.000	19	4	10	0	0
Bennett, Quad City	.875	8	5	16	3	1
Bensching, Waterloo	1.000	50	6	7	0	1
Bertotti, South Bend*	.800	11	0	4	1	0
Berumen, Appleton	1.000	46	6	2	0	0
Bevil, Appleton	.964	26	5	22	1	1
Biehl, Burlington*	.900	36	1	17	2	1
Blanchette, Quad City*	1.000	13	3	3	0	0
Bliss, Peoria	.846	41	3	8	2	2
Boehringer, South Bend	.852	15	8	15	4	1
Boker, Clinton	.930	33	7	33	3	2
Bottoms, Burlington*	1.000	7	1	2	0	0

Player, Team	Pct.	G	PO	A	E	DP
Bovee, Appleton	.810	28	7	10	4	0
Boze, Beloit	.917	26	3	19	2	0
Bradford, Peoria	.900	6	1	8	1	1
Brimhall, Kane County	.500	14	1	0	1	0
Brown, Waterloo*	.926	24	4	46	4	0
Browne, Beloit	.960	25	8	16	1	1
Burgos, Quad City*	1.000	4	0	1	0	0
Cairncross, Waterloo*	.946	24	5	30	2	1
Caridad, South Bend	1.000	11	0	6	0	0
Castillo, Clinton	1.000	13	0	1	0	0
Castillo, Quad City	1.000	18	10	5	0	0
Chouinard, Kane County	.943	26	16	34	3	3
Christopher, Beloit	.938	30	3	12	1	0
Cimorelli, Springfield	1.000	65	3	15	0	0
Cofer, Beloit	.875	12	1	6	1	2
Connolly, Appleton*	1.000	20	1	4	0	0
Creek, Springfield*	.833	6	1	4	1	0
Criminger, Beloit	.917	26	3	8	1	0
Culberson, Cedar Rapids	.893	28	5	20	3	1
Culberson, South Bend	.929	35	7	6	1	1
Cusey, Madison	.857	39	5	7	2	0
Davila, Waterloo	1.000	23	2	3	0	0
Dennison, Beloit*	.864	10	1	18	3	0
Diaz, Kenosha	1.000	22	2	8	0	0
Dickens, Appleton*	1.000	18	2	1	0	0
Dillman, Springfield	1.000	16	0	2	0	0
Dodd, Cedar Rapids*	.889	21	4	20	3	2
Doty, Cedar Rapids	1.000	37	4	3	0	0
Duff, Cedar Rapids*	.941	43	4	12	1	1
Edwards, Cedar Rapids	1.000	31	0	6	0	0
Ellis, South Bend	.958	18	8	38	2	1
Elsbecker, Peoria	1.000	9	0	1	0	0
England, Beloit	1.000	7	4	6	0	1
Evans, Burlington	.923	15	3	9	1	1
Farlow, Waterloo	1.000	6	4	0	0	0
Fermin, Madison	1.000	14	3	13	0	1
Ferry, Cedar Rapids	.919	25	11	23	3	2
Fetty, Beloit	1.000	52	3	5	0	0
Firsich, Kane County	.933	44	4	10	1	1
Forney, Kane County	.886	20	14	17	4	4
Foster, Madison	.733	10	3	8	4	1
Fritz, Quad City	.955	27	14	28	2	0
Froning, Beloit*	.714	10	0	5	2	1
Fultz, Rockford	1.000	7	2	1	0	0
Gallaher, Burlington	.857	20	3	21	4	1
Gambs, Clinton	.966	26	10	18	1	2
Garcia, Kenosha	.941	55	3	13	1	0
Gavaghan, Kenosha	.944	20	4	13	1	1
Gerstein, Rockford*	1.000	33	4	10	0	0
Gilbert, Kane County	1.000	3	1	1	0	0
Gledhill, Quad City	.961	28	15	34	2	1
Godfrey, Peoria	1.000	18	1	1	0	0
Grammig, Beloit	1.000	3	1	3	0	0
Griffen, Cedar Rapids	.933	36	5	9	1	0
Grundt, Clinton	.895	40	4	13	2	0
Guardado, Kenosha*	.974	18	8	29	1	3
Guerra, Peoria*	1.000	20	1	7	0	0
Haas, Appleton*	1.000	12	8	20	0	0
Hardwick, Beloit*	1.000	17	4	5	0	0
Harkey, Peoria	.500	2	0	2	2	0
Harrison, Appleton	1.000	16	9	17	0	0
Haynes, Rockford	.900	45	2	7	1	0
Haynes, Kane County	.857	24	13	17	5	2
Heathcott, South Bend	.933	15	9	19	2	1
Henrikson, Clinton*	1.000	3	0	1	0	0
Heredia, Quad City	.867	29	2	11	2	0
Hernandez, Burlington	1.000	7	4	2	0	0
Herrholz, South Bend	1.000	4	0	2	0	0
Higuera, Beloit*	1.000	2	0	1	0	0
Hill, Beloit*	.933	20	6	22	2	1
Hoeme, Waterloo	1.000	22	0	5	0	0
Holliday, Burlington	.900	21	8	19	3	1
Hook, Cedar Rapids	.929	26	14	25	3	1
Hooper, South Bend	1.000	2	0	1	0	0
Hrusovsky, Cedar Rapids	1.000	25	1	1	0	0
Huber, Waterloo*	.917	9	2	9	1	1
Huffman, Clinton	1.000	6	0	1	0	0
Hyde, Clinton	1.000	8	1	3	0	0
Hyson, Waterloo	.800	17	1	3	1	0
Ivie, Waterloo*	.938	12	3	12	1	0
Jarvis, Kane County*	.952	34	6	14	1	1
Jenkins, South Bend	1.000	5	3	1	0	0
Jiminez, Madison	.923	26	5	19	2	0
Johnson, South Bend	.900	16	5	22	3	0
Johnson, Kenosha*	1.000	12	1	2	0	0
Johnson, Waterloo	1.000	7	0	2	0	1
Juelsgaard, Clinton	.676	35	9	14	11	1
Kenny, Peoria	.970	39	6	26	1	4
Kilgo, 4 Rock. -25 C.R.*	1.000	29	1	12	0	1
Klingenbeck, Kane County	1.000	11	5	9	0	0
Kloek, Beloit	.950	15	5	14	1	1
Knox, Beloit*	1.000	14	1	4	0	0
Kobetitsch, Appleton*	.667	11	0	2	1	0
Konemann, Springfield	.923	29	5	7	1	1
Konieczki, Kenosha*	1.000	49	2	11	0	0
Kotch, Rockford*	1.000	42	6	22	0	1

Player, Team	Pct.	G	PO	A	E	DP
Krahenbuhl, Peoria	.905	19	3	16	2	0
Krivda, Kane County*	.882	18	5	25	4	1
Landress, Appleton	.750	17	1	2	1	0
Lee, Appleton	.929	24	7	6	1	0
Lemp, Kane County	.889	58	3	5	1	2
Leslie, Cedar Rapids	.889	22	3	5	1	2
Levine, South Bend	.979	23	12	35	1	4
Locklear, Madison*	.971	30	11	23	1	4
Looney, Rockford*	1.000	17	5	5	0	0
Lowery, Clinton*	.857	20	1	5	1	1
Luebbers, Cedar Rapids	.909	14	5	15	2	1
Mammola, Quad City*	1.000	13	1	5	0	0
Mansur, Kenosha*	.929	11	4	9	1	0
Marquez, Kane County	.769	18	4	6	3	0
Martin, Waterloo*	1.000	39	2	8	0	0
Martinez, Quad City	1.000	5	1	0	0	0
Martinez, Springfield	.824	18	5	9	3	0
Martinez, Rockford	1.000	10	3	8	0	0
Mattson, Beloit	1.000	8	1	3	0	0
McDonald, Rockford	.933	12	8	6	1	0
McKeon, Beloit	1.000	3	1	5	0	1
McLain, Clinton	1.000	18	0	1	0	0
Mercedes, Burlington	.889	18	1	7	1	0
Jo. Mercedes, Kane County	.769	8	5	5	3	0
Ju. Mercedes, Kane County*	1.000	40	6	7	0	0
Meyer, Peoria*	1.000	35	4	23	0	0
Miceli, Appleton	.750	23	1	2	1	0
Millay, Madison	1.000	7	3	10	0	0
Miller, Burlington	.800	50	1	19	5	2
Minik, Madison	1.000	18	6	4	0	0
Misa, Madison	1.000	4	0	2	0	0
Mitchell, Quad City	1.000	16	0	3	0	0
Mitchelson, Quad City*	1.000	15	6	5	0	0
Morrison, Rockford	1.000	15	4	9	0	0
Murphy, Burlington	.810	50	5	12	4	1
Musset, Quad City	1.000	41	3	5	0	0
Myers, Clinton*	.929	7	4	9	1	0
Myers, Madison*	1.000	39	4	11	0	0
Naulty, Kenosha	.667	6	4	0	2	0
Nielsen, Springfield*	1.000	9	0	5	0	1
Norris, Rockford	.894	27	5	37	5	1
O'Connell, Kane County	.867	22	5	8	2	1
O'Laughlin, Beloit*	.800	4	0	4	1	0
Ortiz, Clinton*	.750	38	1	8	3	0
Pacheco, Peoria	1.000	11	2	5	0	0
Paskievitch, Waterloo	.923	49	6	18	2	2
Peltzer, Clinton*	1.000	7	1	2	0	0
Perez, Quad City*	1.000	12	2	5	0	0
Perez, Rockford*	1.000	7	0	2	0	0
Pierce, South Bend	.900	52	4	5	1	0
Pierce, Madison	1.000	34	4	7	0	0
Plemmons, Cedar Rapids	1.000	3	1	2	0	0
Pomeranz, Kane County*	.667	5	0	2	1	0
Ponte, Burlington	.833	30	0	5	1	0
Powers, Burlington*	1.000	55	5	4	0	0
Pruitt, Beloit	1.000	8	3	8	0	1
Pruitt, Appleton	.929	10	2	11	1	0
Quijada, Burlington	.700	18	3	4	3	0
Quinones, Cedar Rapids*	.875	11	0	7	1	1
RADKE, Kenosha	1.000	26	21	36	0	3
Ratekin, Quad City	.929	23	10	29	3	0
Ray, Cedar Rapids	.500	11	1	0	1	0
Rea, Appleton	1.000	38	8	12	0	0
Reed, Burlington	1.000	18	2	5	0	0
Roberts, Kenosha	1.000	7	1	3	0	0

Player, Team	Pct.	G	PO	A	E	DP
Romanoli, Springfield*	.857	62	2	10	2	0
Rose, Burlington*	.972	27	4	31	1	1
Rose, Madison	.714	8	2	3	2	0
Rossiter, Madison	.967	27	7	22	1	3
Rueter, Rockford*	.983	26	7	50	1	2
Rutter, Beloit	1.000	14	6	9	0	0
Saccavino, Kenosha	.909	6	1	9	1	1
Sanchez, Peoria	.978	35	15	29	1	0
Sanders, Kane County	.875	49	8	13	3	1
Santos, Springfield	.889	63	1	7	1	0
Sartain, Kenosha*	.970	24	3	29	1	1
Scharff, Madison	.871	42	6	21	4	1
Schramm, Peoria	.857	32	8	28	6	0
Schwartz, Kenosha	.667	5	0	2	1	0
Scott, Burlington*	.600	16	0	3	2	0
Sebach, Quad City	1.000	13	3	14	0	0
Sewell, Burlington	1.000	9	0	1	0	0
Shoemaker, Madison	.875	22	8	13	3	0
Silcox, Waterloo	.929	6	4	9	1	1
Silverio, Quad City	.750	13	3	9	4	1
Simmons, Springfield*	.962	27	6	45	2	4
Slininger, Springfield	.914	27	15	17	3	1
Smith, Burlington	.818	24	1	8	2	0
Smith, 17 Spr. - 10 K.C.	.973	27	14	22	1	2
Smock, Madison*	.800	8	1	3	1	0
Soto, South Bend	.900	7	3	6	1	0
Souza, Beloit	.600	9	1	2	2	0
Speek, Springfield	.857	58	2	4	1	1
Steenstra, Peoria	.926	12	7	18	2	0
Steph, Cedar Rapids	.970	27	11	21	1	1
Stonecipher, Clinton	1.000	8	6	8	0	0
Stowell, Madison	.917	29	4	18	2	3
Sutch, Madison	.941	49	4	12	1	2
Sweeney, Kenosha*	1.000	31	4	4	0	0
Szczechowski, Clinton	1.000	6	2	2	0	1
Tagle, South Bend*	.909	26	2	8	1	0
Talemaco, Peoria	1.000	2	1	0	0	0
Taylor, Kenosha	.920	27	14	32	4	2
Thees, Madison	1.000	16	0	5	0	0
Thomas, Rockford*	.958	28	5	18	1	2
Tidwell, Peoria*	1.000	60	0	10	0	0
Tolar, South Bend*	1.000	18	4	13	0	1
Toth, Appleton	1.000	23	8	16	0	0
Tranbarger, Springfield*	1.000	42	2	3	0	0
Trisler, Beloit	.882	26	3	12	2	0
Vanderweele, Clinton	.778	9	2	5	2	0
Van Landingham, Clinton	.889	10	1	7	1	0
Vonderlieth, Beloit*	1.000	11	1	2	0	1
Waldron, Waterloo*	.857	49	5	13	3	1
Wallace, Peoria	1.000	3	0	3	0	0
Wanke, Clinton*	.704	26	3	16	8	0
Waring, Burlington	.939	20	12	19	2	1
Watkins, Kenosha*	.909	27	3	7	1	1
Watson, Quad City	1.000	40	3	8	0	0
Wengert, Madison	.933	7	5	9	1	0
White, Rockford*	.900	27	12	42	6	3
Whitehead, Rockford	.818	19	3	24	6	1
Williams, Quad City	.971	27	12	22	1	0
Wissler, Kenosha	.941	21	9	7	1	0
Woodfin, South Bend	.818	36	1	8	2	0
Worrell, South Bend*	.857	14	0	6	1	0
Wynne, Rockford	.667	2	0	2	1	0
Zastoupil, Cedar Rapids	1.000	9	1	4	0	0
Zurn, Beloit	.800	7	4	0	1	0

Triple play—Hook.

The following players did not have any fielding statistics at the positions indicated or appeared only as a designated hitter, pinch-hitter or pinch-runner: Da. Adams, ss, of; De. Adams, of; Albert, p; Aracena, p; Babbitt, of, p; Beck, of; Berry, p; Brede, 3b; Brincks, p; Calcagno, p; Campillo, 3b; Carlson, p; Cerio, 3b; Clarke, 3b; Coachman, 3b; Curtis, of; Dana, p; E. Delgado, of; Dotolo, p; Duncan, p; Eldridge, ph; Enriquez, 2b, 3b; Falco, ss; Galart, p; Harley, of; Havens, c, p; Hazlett, p; Hust, 1b, 3b; Imperial, 2b; K. Jarvis, p; Leary, p; Lewis, 1b; Margheim, p; Patterson, p; Phillips, p; Schulte, p; L. Smith, p; M. Smith, of; Spradlin, p; Stroth, p; Sutton, dh; Tahan, p; Tallman, of; Thielen, of; Thomsen, p; Trujillo, 3b; Walker, 2b; G. Williams, 2b, 3b.

LEAGUE CHAMPIONS

Year	Team	Pct.	Year	Team	Pct.	Year	Team	Pct.
1947—	Belleville	.667		Clinton	.623	1966—	Fox Cities z	.689
	Belleville	.672	1958—	Michigan City	.623		Cedar Rapids	.762
1948—	West Frankfort*	.708		Waterloo z	.613	1967—	Wisconsin Rapids	.685
1949—	Centralia	.627	1959—	Waterloo	.613		Appleton z	.587
	Paducah (4th)†	.454		Waterloo	.613	1968—	Decatur	.656
1950—	Centralia‡	.675	1960—	Waterloo	.629		Quad Cities z	.648
1951—	Paris§	.700		Waterloo	.677	1969—	Appleton	.648
	Danville (4th)†	.432	1961—	Waterloo	.613		Appleton	.690
1952—	Danville x	.685		Quincy	.594	1970—	Quincy z	.691
	Decatur (3rd)†	.584	1962—	Dubuque z	.667		Quad Cities	.581
1953—	Decatur*	.576		Waterloo	.625	1971—	Appleton	.642
1954—	Decatur	.587	1963—	Clinton	.710		Quad Cities a	.548
	Danville (2nd)‡	.528		Clinton	.629	1972—	Appleton	.598
1955—	Dubuque*	.587	1964—	Clinton	.667		Danville a	.584
1956—	Paris y	.656		Fox Cities z	.667	1973—	Wisconsin Rapids a	.562
	Dubuque	.603	1965—	Burlington	.667		Danville	.537
1957—	Decatur y	.683		Burlington	.677	1974—	Appleton	.593

Year	Team	Pct.	Year	Team	Pct.	Year	Team	Pct.
	Danville a	.517	1981—	Wausau a	.636		Kenosha b	.586
1975—	Waterloo a	.727		Quad Cities	.570	1988—	Cedar Rapids a	.621
	Quad Cities	.624	1982—	Madison	.626		Kenosha	.579
1976—	Waterloo a	.600		Appleton b	.579	1989—	South Bend a	.644
	Cedar Rapids	.595	1983—	Appleton c	.635		Springfield	.541
1977—	Waterloo	.580		Springfield	.576	1990—	Cedar Rapids	.657
	Burlington a	.511	1984—	Appleton c	.640		Quad City a	.579
1978—	Appleton a	.708		Springfield	.504	1991—	Clinton a	.583
	Burlington	.500	1985—	Kenosha b	.568		Madison	.558
1979—	Waterloo	.600		Peoria	.536	1992—	Quad City	.664
	Quad Cities a	.579	1986—	Springfield	.621		Cedar Rapids a	.594
1980—	Waterloo a	.610		Waterloo b	.557			
	Quad Cities	.532	1987—	Springfield	.671			

*Won championship and four-club playoff. †Won four-club playoff. ‡Playoff finals canceled because of bad weather. §Won both halves of split season. xWon first half of split season and tied Paris for second-half title. yWon first-half title and four-team playoff. zWon split season playoff. aLeague divided into Northern and Southern divisions and played split season. Playoff winner. bLeague divided into Northern, Central and Southern divisions. Playoff winner. cLeague divided into Northern, Central and Southern divisions; regular-season and playoff winner. (NOTE— Known as Illinois State League in 1947-48 and Mississippi-Ohio Valley League from 1949 through 1955.)

NEW YORK-PENN LEAGUE

FINAL STANDINGS

McNAMARA DIVISION

Team	W	L	T	Pct.	GB
Utica (White Sox)	42	32	0	.568	......
Pittsfield (Mets)	37	37	0	.500	5
Oneonta (Yankees)	37	38	0	.493	5½
Watertown (Indians)	37	39	0	.487	6

PINCKNEY DIVISION

Team	W	L	T	Pct.	GB
Geneva (Cubs)	41	34	0	.547	......
Batavia (Phillies)	36	34	0	.514	2½
Auburn (Astros)	32	41	0	.438	8
Elmira (Red Sox)	31	44	0	.413	10

STEDLER DIVISION

Team	W	L	T	Pct.	GB
Hamilton (Cardinals)	56	20	0	.737	......
Erie (Marlins)	40	37	0	.519	16½
Niagara Falls (Tigers)	39	39	0	.500	18
Jamestown (Expos)	34	43	0	.442	22½
St. Catharines (Blue Jays)	33	42	0	.440	22½
Welland (Pirates)	31	46	0	.403	25½

COMPOSITE

Team	Ham.	Uti.	Gen.	Erie	Bat.	Pit.	N.F.	One.	Wat.	Jam.	St.C.	Aub.	Elm.	Wel.	W	L	T	Pct.	GB
Hamilton (Cardinals)	...	3	2	7	3	8	6	3	2	4	10	4	3	6	56	20	0	.737	......
Utica (White Sox)	1	...	3	2	2	7	1	7	7	3	1	2	3	3	42	32	0	.568	13
Geneva (Cubs)	2	1	...	1	6	2	2	3	2	4	2	8	4	4	41	34	0	.547	14½
Erie (Marlins)	1	2	3	...	1	1	3	1	4	8	7	2	3	4	40	37	0	.519	16½
Batavia (Phillies)	0	2	6	2	...	0	3	0	2	1	3	5	9	3	36	34	0	.514	17
Pittsfield (Mets)	1	5	2	3	2	...	3	6	7	3	1	1	2	1	37	37	0	.500	18
Niagara Falls (Tigers)	2	3	2	5	1	1	...	3	0	3	5	2	2	10	39	39	0	.500	18
Oneonta (Yankees)	1	5	0	3	3	7	1	...	5	2	1	2	4	3	37	38	0	.493	18½
Watertown (Indians)	2	6	2	0	2	5	4	7	...	1	1	2	3	2	37	39	0	.487	19
Jamestown (Expos)	4	1	0	6	3	1	5	2	3	...	3	1	3	3	34	43	0	.442	22½
St. Catharines (Blue Jays)	3	3	2	1	0	2	3	3	3	5	...	2	3	3	33	42	0	.440	22½
Auburn (Astros)	0	0	4	2	7	3	2	2	1	2	2	...	6	1	32	41	0	.438	22½
Elmira (Red Sox)	1	0	8	1	3	2	2	0	1	3	1	6	...	3	31	44	0	.413	24½
Welland (Pirates)	2	1	0	4	1	3	4	1	2	4	5	3	1	...	31	46	0	.403	25½

Major league affiliations in parentheses.

Playoffs—Erie defeated Hamilton, one game to none; Geneva defeated Utica, one game to none; Geneva defeated Erie, two games to none, to win league championship.

Regular-season attendance—Auburn, 21,200; Batavia, 39,385; Elmira, 63,473; Erie, 79,245; Geneva, 32,075; Hamilton, 65,717; Jamestown, 40,269; Niagara Falls, 48,698; Oneonta, 50,534; Pittsfield, 52,967; St. Catharines, 36,066; Utica, 73,464; Watertown, 42,762; Welland, 38,209. Total—684,064. Playoffs (4 games)—5,462.

Managers—Auburn, Steve Dillard; Batavia, Ramon Aviles; Elmira, Dave Holt; Erie, Fredi Gonzales; Geneva, Greg Mahlberg; Hamilton, Chris Maloney; Jamestown, Q.V. Lowe; Niagara Falls, Larry Parrish; Oneonta, Jack Gillis; Pittsfield, Jim Thrift; St. Catharines, J.J. Cannon; Utica, Fred Kendall; Watertown, Shawn Pender; Welland, Trent Jewett.

All-Star team: 1B—Todd Pridy, Erie; 2B—Chad Tredaway, Geneva; 3B—Louis Lucca, Erie; SS—Edgardo Alfonzo, Pittsfield; OF—Jose Malave, Elmira; Robin Jennings, Geneva; Scott McCloughan, St. Catharines; Byron Mathews, Utica; C—(tie) Don Leshnock, Oneonta, and Jeff Murphy, Hamilton; DH—Dave Duplessis, Watertown; RHP—Tim Crabtree, St. Catharines; Jamie Cochran, Hamilton; LHP—David Oehrlein, Hamilton, and Bill Pulsipher, Pittsfield; Manager of the Year—Chris Maloney, Hamilton.

BATTING

TEAM

Team	Avg.	G	AB	R	OR	H	TB	2B	3B	HR	RBI	SH	SF	HP	BB	Int. BB	SO	SB	CS	LOB
Geneva	.252	75	2440	310	267	616	841	102	12	33	271	36	20	46	226	10	507	70	54	525
Hamilton	.250	76	2428	363	253	606	902	109	20	49	308	12	24	26	300	11	579	95	39	519
Utica	.247	74	2386	345	307	590	815	96	30	23	292	12	32	25	269	9	561	110	48	487
Batavia	.246	70	2290	338	326	564	806	86	21	38	274	42	14	40	218	7	470	106	32	465
Oneonta	.245	75	2470	321	296	604	799	97	19	20	263	19	19	30	288	8	549	81	31	574
Pittsfield	.240	74	2465	340	313	592	808	98	26	22	277	13	27	30	266	6	544	98	53	508
Erie	.240	77	2497	366	341	599	893	108	9	56	317	9	17	32	318	6	557	89	33	544
Niagara Falls	.238	78	2464	335	302	586	824	101	22	31	275	27	17	41	284	9	603	124	71	518
Jamestown	.235	77	2504	349	333	588	891	101	23	52	300	13	12	32	232	5	613	144	41	477
Auburn	.233	73	2384	312	369	555	771	86	20	30	261	18	17	27	234	11	462	114	41	477
Watertown	.231	76	2460	342	351	569	808	107	12	36	292	13	22	32	245	7	640	110	43	488
Elmira	.231	75	2536	319	394	585	852	104	8	49	269	29	12	42	221	14	619	43	33	521
St. Catharines	.218	75	2386	259	320	519	706	80	7	31	210	22	17	29	237	13	603	108	51	495
Welland	.216	77	2509	274	401	541	780	93	22	34	221	9	17	21	201	6	569	87	47	457

INDIVIDUAL

(Leading qualifiers for batting championship—211 or more plate appearances)

*Bats lefthanded.   †Switch-hitter.

Player, Team	Avg.	G	AB	R	H	TB	2B	3B	HR	RBI	SH	SF	HP	BB	Int. BB	SO	SB	CS
Alfonzo, Edgardo, Pittsfield	.356	74	298	41	106	132	13	5	1	44	2	4	0	18	1	31	7	5
Malave, Jose, Elmira	.325	65	268	44	87	134	9	1	12	46	0	1	3	14	3	48	8	3
Pridy, Todd, Erie*	.310	75	274	42	85	144	15	1	14	60	0	1	5	28	4	66	2	0
Owens, Brad, Hamilton	.304	56	181	40	55	82	9	3	4	24	0	2	4	30	0	31	17	2
Tredaway, Chad, Geneva†	.300	73	270	39	81	119	19	2	5	31	3	5	3	24	1	24	6	4
Jennings, Robin, Geneva*	.298	72	275	39	82	119	12	2	7	47	0	0	2	20	5	43	10	3
Taylor, Jamie, Watertown*	.293	60	208	25	61	79	13	1	1	35	0	3	1	30	1	36	4	0
Higginson, Robert, Niagara Falls*	.293	70	232	35	68	99	17	4	2	37	2	0	1	33	0	47	12	8

— 453 —

Player, Team	Avg.	G	AB	R	H	TB	2B	3B	HR	RBI	SH	SF	HP	BB	Int. BB	SO	SB	CS
Duplessis, Dave, Watertown*	.292	61	212	37	62	97	14	0	7	30	0	2	8	18	1	68	6	3
Mitchell, Donovan, Auburn*	.291	70	292	44	85	102	8	3	1	18	3	0	1	13	0	32	25	8

Departmental leaders: G—Raleigh, 77; AB—Alfonzo, 298; R—Wills, 53; H—Alfonzo, 106; TB—Pridy, 144; 2B—Tredaway, 19; 3B—Luke, 7; HR—Pridy, 14; RBI—Pridy, 60; SH—Peterson, 9; SF—Knowles, 6; HP—Madsen, 12; BB—Snopek, 52; IBB—Selby, 6; SO—Kimsey, 106; SB—Mathews, 42; CS—Mathews, De. Smith, 15.

(All players—listed alphabetically)

Player, Team	Avg.	G	AB	R	H	TB	2B	3B	HR	RBI	SH	SF	HP	BB	Int. BB	SO	SB	CS
Alfonzo, Edgardo, Pittsfield	.356	74	298	41	106	132	13	5	1	44	2	4	0	18	1	31	7	5
Allen, Matt, Jamestown	.179	58	168	17	30	53	11	0	4	16	0	1	4	10	0	64	1	1
Arntzen, Brian, Watertown	.207	36	116	12	24	30	3	0	1	10	0	0	1	7	0	33	0	1
Aubel, Mike, Auburn*	.242	62	215	38	52	77	7	3	4	24	2	4	5	25	0	33	7	5
Aurila, Brad, Jamestown*	.236	52	161	22	38	43	5	0	0	17	1	2	0	17	0	24	12	6
Austin, Jacob, Welland†	.364	9	33	4	12	14	2	0	0	4	0	1	0	1	0	2	3	1
Bauer, Matt, Niagara Falls*	.000	32	0	0	0	0	0	0	0	0	0	0	0	1	0	0	0	0
Beamon, Trey, Welland*	.290	19	69	15	20	34	5	0	3	9	0	0	8	0	9	4	3
Bell, Curt, Niagara Falls	.211	53	142	24	30	48	9	0	3	8	3	0	5	16	0	45	5	0
Bellum, Donnie, Hamilton	.269	73	279	51	75	117	14	2	8	29	1	3	0	30	1	54	11	3
Benbow, Lou, St. Catharines	.170	50	171	8	29	39	10	0	0	5	2	1	1	11	0	43	1	0
Benefiel, Doug, Jamestown	.159	39	107	11	17	25	3	1	1	15	1	0	1	8	0	31	3	2
Benitez, Yamil, Jamestown	.272	44	162	24	44	71	6	6	3	23	1	0	2	14	0	52	19	1
Bennett, Gary, Batavia	.205	47	146	22	30	32	2	0	0	12	3	0	2	15	0	27	2	1
Black, Keith, Hamilton	.294	18	51	9	15	22	2	1	1	12	2	1	0	4	0	15	4	0
Blanton, Garrett, Hamilton	.111	5	18	2	2	2	0	0	0	0	0	0	0	3	0	6	0	0
Boehlow, Jason, Geneva	.222	20	45	5	10	14	4	0	0	3	0	0	2	11	1	16	4	3
Bogan, Victor, Welland	.207	57	193	23	40	63	4	2	5	12	1	0	2	19	0	50	9	6
Boka, Ben, Welland	.229	19	48	2	11	12	1	0	0	6	2	0	0	1	0	19	0	0
Boston, D.J., St. Catharines*	.234	72	256	25	60	84	7	1	5	36	0	3	2	36	4	41	20	3
Bowrosen, Ricky, Utica	.232	53	177	23	41	55	8	0	2	24	0	1	2	21	0	61	3	1
Bradley, London, Geneva	.261	48	165	20	43	54	8	0	1	17	1	2	2	18	0	44	2	2
Brown, Willie, Erie*	.200	72	245	34	49	85	7	1	9	32	0	1	2	22	0	94	7	4
Bryant, Pat, Watertown	.264	63	220	41	58	94	13	1	7	30	1	1	5	33	1	61	35	8
Burke, Alan, Batavia	.276	61	217	29	60	88	16	0	4	29	0	2	4	21	1	21	2	2
Cameron, Mike, Utica	.276	28	87	15	24	39	1	4	2	12	1	1	0	11	0	26	3	7
Campbell, Keiver, St. Catharines	.172	43	128	14	22	33	2	0	3	10	0	1	4	23	0	56	7	4
Campillo, Rob, Jamestown	.261	18	46	9	12	18	3	0	1	7	1	0	2	3	0	12	0	0
Cannaday, Aaron, Welland	.229	26	83	9	19	27	3	1	1	5	0	0	3	8	0	21	0	0
Canton, Michael, Elmira	.195	42	113	19	22	40	6	0	4	13	0	0	4	18	0	45	3	2
Cappuccio, Carmine, Utica*	.276	22	87	15	24	32	4	2	0	13	0	1	1	6	0	10	5	0
Cardenas, Epi, Watertown	.231	59	234	29	54	74	9	1	3	27	4	4	1	10	1	45	5	2
Carey, Tim, Elmira	.125	5	16	0	2	2	0	0	0	0	0	0	0	2	0	8	0	0
Carey, Todd, Elmira*	.203	54	197	18	40	51	7	2	0	19	1	3	0	9	1	40	0	4
Cervantes, Ray, Erie	.188	37	101	13	19	21	2	0	0	7	0	0	2	22	0	21	3	2
Chandler, Chris, St. Catharines	.241	35	116	10	28	30	0	1	0	4	3	0	1	10	0	31	5	3
Cherry, Lamar, Batavia	.249	51	177	28	44	74	10	1	6	27	0	1	0	20	2	52	11	2
Chisum, Dave, Watertown*	.210	26	62	9	13	19	1	1	1	8	1	0	1	11	0	27	3	0
Choate, Mark, St. Catharines	.226	68	239	44	54	83	17	0	4	39	1	1	9	35	4	62	8	9
Clark, Tony, Niagara Falls†	.306	27	85	12	26	50	9	0	5	17	0	0	9	34	1	0
Clem, Bradford, Erie*	.197	23	66	4	13	16	3	0	0	2	0	0	3	0	12	3	1
Coleman, Ronnie, Watertown	.167	19	36	9	6	9	3	0	0	5	1	1	2	11	0	12	1	3
Collier, Dan, Elmira	.176	59	193	26	34	69	8	0	9	24	2	1	10	9	0	86	2	2
Colon, Angel, Welland	.080	9	25	2	2	3	0	0	0	3	0	0	0	1	0	2	0	0
Coolbaugh, Mike, St. Catharines	.286	15	49	3	14	17	1	1	0	2	0	0	3	0	12	0	2
Cordova, Luis, Erie*	.221	53	181	16	40	53	7	0	2	23	0	2	0	10	1	31	2	2
Craig, Mo, Geneva*	.252	36	127	15	32	41	4	1	1	19	2	1	4	7	0	31	2	3
Cranford, John, Welland	.256	60	223	22	57	78	9	6	0	27	0	2	0	14	1	58	7	7
Crimmins, John, Elmira	.205	40	127	12	26	42	4	0	4	12	1	0	3	9	0	44	0	0
Crouwel, Matt, Batavia	.159	19	44	3	7	11	1	2	0	6	0	1	0	11	0	22	1	0
Cruz, J.J., Batavia	.071	6	14	2	1	1	0	0	0	0	0	0	1	3	0	2	0	0
Cumberbatch, Abdiel, Oneonta†	.179	8	28	3	5	5	0	0	0	1	0	0	0	7	0	7	4	0
Daubach, Brian, Pittsfield*	.242	72	260	26	63	88	15	2	2	40	1	4	3	30	2	61	2	0
Davis, Gerald, Elmira	.261	20	92	9	24	28	4	0	0	5	0	1	1	0	19	2	0
DeJesus, Malvin, Niagara Falls	.216	67	194	23	42	49	3	2	0	20	4	5	4	27	1	33	16	12
Delafield, Glenn, Oneonta	.292	7	24	2	7	9	0	1	0	2	1	0	0	2	0	4	1	2
Delos Santos, Reynaldo, Batavia*	.260	44	150	21	39	62	8	3	3	14	2	0	2	18	1	30	7	1
Delvecchio, Nick, Oneonta*	.274	68	241	43	66	116	12	1	12	35	1	0	8	35	3	76	0	1
Demoss, David, Geneva*	.177	41	130	13	23	36	5	1	2	6	3	1	1	10	0	32	0	1
Diaz, Cesar, Pittsfield	.208	66	226	32	47	79	9	4	5	25	0	4	4	27	2	86	4	1
Diaz, German, Geneva*	.266	16	64	7	17	21	4	0	0	7	0	0	2	0	14	2	1
Dickerson, Bobby, Niagara Falls*	.200	23	45	6	9	10	1	0	0	1	0	0	0	7	0	12	4	3
DiFelice, Mike, Hamilton	.345	18	58	11	20	29	3	0	2	9	1	0	1	4	1	7	2	0
DiGiacomo, Kevin, Watertown	.111	38	126	10	14	25	5	0	2	13	0	1	1	11	0	37	1	0
Doucette, Darren, Hamilton*	.217	57	175	27	38	77	7	1	10	35	0	1	3	32	2	73	0	2
Doyle, Tom, Jamestown*	.167	2	6	1	1	1	0	0	0	0	0	0	0	0	3	0	0
Dreifort, Todd, Jamestown*	.223	67	211	21	47	59	5	2	1	9	0	0	2	31	3	49	3	5
Duplessis, Dave, Watertown*	.292	61	212	37	62	97	14	0	7	30	0	2	8	18	1	68	6	3
Eggert, David, Watertown	.000	30	1	0	0	0	0	0	0	0	0	0	0	0	0	0	0	0
Elliott, Greg, Auburn*	.184	58	174	23	32	44	6	0	2	18	2	0	1	34	1	35	5	1
Epps, Scott, Oneonta	.167	16	36	3	6	7	1	0	0	1	0	0	1	6	0	8	0	0
Espinosa, Ramon, Welland	.269	60	208	27	56	90	12	5	4	22	0	2	0	23	10	5
Evans, Jason, Utica†	.267	32	120	15	32	42	5	1	1	22	0	1	2	13	2	17	4	1
Evans, Matthew, Niagara Falls*	.205	29	73	4	15	21	3	0	1	13	0	1	0	27	1	0
Fairly, Pat, Geneva	.223	34	94	7	21	30	0	0	3	13	3	0	3	11	0	29	1	0
Farrell, Mike, Pittsfield	.000	2	6	0	0	0	0	0	0	0	0	0	0	0	4	0	0
Feeley, Peter, Niagara Falls	.253	74	257	35	65	79	6	4	0	14	0	1	38	0	47	11	5
Feno, Quinn, Elmira	.207	45	140	17	29	36	4	0	1	10	2	1	2	16	0	31	3	0
Fermin, Carlos, Niagara Falls	.169	29	71	9	12	16	2	0	0	7	1	0	2	9	0	13	3	3
Filosa, Brian, Utica	.190	59	168	20	32	35	3	0	0	20	1	2	1	36	1	3	1
Fisher, David, Batavia	.338	21	80	10	27	36	4	1	1	14	2	0	4	0	8	3	0
Fleming, Carlton, Oneonta†	.182	3	11	2	2	2	0	0	0	2	0	1	0	0	5	1	0
Flores, Joe, Pittsfield	.115	19	52	4	6	6	0	0	0	4	0	1	0	3	0	17	1	0
Freehling, Rick, Erie†	.246	37	130	17	32	40	5	0	1	9	5	0	1	18	0	32	4	4

Player, Team	Avg.	G	AB	R	H	TB	2B	3B	HR	RBI	SH	SF	HP	BB	Int. BB	SO	SB	CS
French, Ronnie, Hamilton	.241	54	170	25	41	63	14	1	2	24	0	1	4	23	0	48	13	2
Gamble, Freddie, Erie*	.206	49	165	21	34	53	8	1	3	15	3	2	1	19	0	24	3	3
Garcia, Guillermo, Pittsfield	.199	73	272	36	54	73	11	1	2	26	0	3	2	20	0	52	3	4
George, Chris, Pittsfield*	.000	18	2	0	0	0	0	0	0	0	0	0	0	0	0	1	0	0
George, Curt, Watertown	.189	63	217	27	41	48	5	1	0	16	0	2	3	10	0	60	7	6
Gholston, Rico, Welland	.176	52	165	13	29	38	3	0	2	13	0	2	4	8	0	51	3	1
Gilligan, Larry, Hamilton	.215	49	130	11	28	35	2	1	1	13	2	2	1	10	1	19	2	1
Gomez, Mike, Batavia	.271	59	221	38	60	70	6	2	0	16	8	3	6	16	0	23	12	3
Gousha, Sean, Erie	.242	20	62	4	15	17	2	0	0	6	0	1	0	5	0	19	3	0
Greene, Bart, Niagara Falls	.247	30	81	12	20	21	1	0	0	9	2	1	2	7	0	15	11	0
Gulan, Mike, Hamilton	.273	62	242	33	66	103	8	4	7	36	0	4	1	23	0	53	12	4
Hacopian, Derek, Watertown	.231	7	26	1	6	7	1	0	0	3	0	0	0	3	0	10	0	1
Hairston, Rodd, Watertown	.118	6	17	2	2	2	0	0	0	0	1	0	1	4	0	3	0	0
Hand, Janseen, Welland	.125	17	40	4	5	5	0	0	0	2	0	0	1	4	0	8	1	2
Harmes, Kris, St. Catharines*	.245	66	229	20	56	78	7	0	5	25	1	3	0	23	2	41	0	4
Harris, Marc, Utica	.191	27	68	8	13	16	1	1	0	4	0	0	1	15	0	21	3	1
Hawkins, Kraig, Oneonta	.220	70	227	24	50	51	1	0	0	18	7	0	1	26	0	67	14	5
Hence, Sam, Watertown	.289	53	194	32	56	83	16	1	3	25	1	1	1	4	0	27	12	3
Henderson, Jim, Jamestown	.333	1	3	2	1	2	1	0	0	3	0	0	0	1	0	0	0	0
Henderson, Todd, Hamilton	.197	24	61	4	12	20	2	0	2	6	0	1	0	7	0	20	5	1
Henry, Santiago, St. Catharines	.190	70	232	23	44	54	4	3	0	12	7	1	2	7	0	54	7	4
Hernandez, Rafael, Pittsfield	.161	36	112	12	18	25	3	2	0	5	3	0	3	7	0	27	2	0
Higginbotham, Robin, Niagara Falls*	.238	7	21	3	5	6	1	0	0	0	0	0	2	2	0	5	3	1
Higginson, Robert, Niagara Falls*	.293	70	232	35	68	99	17	4	2	37	2	0	1	33	0	47	12	8
Hinds, Robert, Oneonta	.288	69	264	40	76	88	8	2	0	11	0	0	7	34	0	51	21	9
Hines, Keith, St. Catharines	.114	14	44	3	5	6	1	0	0	3	0	0	0	6	1	10	0	1
Hopp, Dean, Batavia	.223	30	94	8	21	32	2	0	3	12	6	0	0	6	0	20	0	1
Hubbard, Mike, Geneva	.240	50	183	25	44	65	4	4	3	25	4	4	3	7	0	29	6	4
Hughes, Vinny, Erie	.300	9	20	2	6	12	1	1	1	4	0	0	0	2	0	3	0	0
Humes, Terryll, Hamilton	.136	31	88	7	12	16	2	1	0	5	2	0	0	12	0	18	9	3
Hunt, Riegal, Welland*	.188	47	154	17	29	46	6	1	3	14	0	1	0	18	0	43	5	1
Hurst, Jimmy, Utica	.227	68	220	31	50	86	8	5	6	35	2	5	4	27	1	78	11	3
Jennings, Robin, Geneva*	.298	72	275	39	82	119	12	2	7	47	0	2	2	20	5	43	10	3
Johns, Keith, Hamilton	.284	70	275	36	78	94	11	1	1	28	1	3	1	27	0	42	15	10
Johnson, J.J., Elmira	.228	30	114	8	26	34	3	1	1	12	4	1	1	4	0	32	8	0
Johnson, Wayne, Batavia†	.135	23	37	9	5	7	0	1	0	2	1	1	1	5	0	13	2	1
Johnston, Tom, Welland	.278	6	18	0	5	6	1	0	0	0	0	0	1	2	0	8	0	1
Jones, Matt, Welland*	.200	6	20	3	4	4	0	0	0	2	0	0	0	1	0	6	1	0
Jordan, Tim, Hamilton*	.233	64	180	24	42	61	9	2	2	19	1	2	0	21	0	52	4	4
Juday, Robert, Elmira†	.278	69	241	46	67	82	12	0	1	24	4	1	4	47	4	33	4	5
Kantor, Brad, Watertown	.211	19	71	6	15	25	4	0	2	14	0	1	0	1	0	21	2	1
Keister, Tripp, Pittsfield*	.245	68	245	46	60	68	4	2	0	15	3	1	3	42	0	39	23	8
Kelley, Erskine, Welland	.154	39	143	9	22	33	3	1	2	10	0	0	1	1	0	35	3	0
Kessinger, Kevin, Geneva	.000	2	2	0	0	0	0	0	0	0	0	0	0	0	0	2	0	0
Killen, Brent, Niagara Falls*	.216	76	236	32	51	73	13	0	3	29	1	2	3	42	4	44	1	5
Kimsey, Keith, Niagara Falls	.224	73	281	35	63	118	7	6	12	46	0	1	3	9	0	106	14	6
Knowles, Eric, Oneonta	.179	58	196	22	35	48	6	2	1	22	3	6	2	29	0	66	2	1
Kostrzewa, Mike, Watertown	.286	2	7	3	2	2	0	0	0	1	0	0	0	2	0	0	0	1
Kozeniewski, Blaise, Oneonta	.267	74	285	41	76	100	18	3	0	36	1	3	1	18	1	45	9	5
Kratz, Ron, Batavia*	.208	55	159	24	33	63	6	0	8	25	6	1	2	15	0	55	1	0
Ladd, Jeff, St. Catharines	.209	34	115	13	24	36	3	0	3	13	1	0	3	9	0	37	1	1
Lane, Dan, Jamestown	.269	56	182	36	49	87	16	2	6	27	1	0	2	16	0	32	3	1
Larson, Kirk, Auburn	.160	27	75	7	12	16	2	1	0	9	2	0	0	6	0	21	1	0
Lee, Charles, Jamestown	.291	47	151	24	44	65	5	2	4	19	3	1	3	8	0	37	17	2
Leshnock, Donnie, Oneonta*	.222	62	212	24	47	58	8	0	1	17	0	1	0	26	1	58	5	2
Lidle, Kevin, Niagara Falls	.243	58	140	21	34	47	6	2	1	18	6	3	1	8	0	42	3	2
Lockhart, Mike, Watertown*	.200	26	70	11	14	19	2	0	1	6	0	0	0	19	1	18	3	3
Long, R.D., Oneonta†	.255	42	153	26	39	50	9	1	0	15	0	2	0	24	0	31	13	3
Lucca, Louis, Erie	.281	76	263	51	74	131	16	1	13	44	0	2	5	33	0	40	6	3
Luke, Matt, Oneonta*	.247	69	271	30	67	98	11	7	2	34	0	3	2	19	3	32	4	1
Lussier, Pat, Welland	.199	53	166	16	33	41	3	1	1	7	0	0	1	13	0	37	3	2
Lynch, John, Erie	.000	8	2	0	0	0	0	0	0	0	0	0	0	0	0	0	0	0
Lynch, Ty, Utica	.238	51	151	21	36	41	5	0	0	13	3	4	0	16	1	40	5	3
Machado, Robert, Utica	.273	45	161	16	44	65	13	1	2	20	0	1	0	5	0	26	1	5
Madsen, Dan, Geneva*	.243	70	235	33	57	79	8	1	4	31	3	2	12	42	0	65	12	13
Maize, Dave, Welland†	.185	42	119	12	22	32	4	0	2	13	1	2	0	6	1	20	7	2
Malave, Jose, Elmira	.325	65	268	44	87	134	9	1	12	46	0	1	3	14	3	48	8	3
Martin, Andy, Hamilton*	.223	51	139	22	31	48	6	1	3	24	0	2	1	23	2	40	0	1
Martin, Jeff, Elmira	.158	12	38	4	6	12	0	0	2	5	2	1	1	3	0	16	0	0
Martinez, Ernie, Auburn*	.219	50	178	17	39	55	2	1	4	24	1	1	2	11	1	32	0	1
Martinez, Rick, Niagara Falls	.239	37	67	11	16	19	3	0	0	6	1	1	1	10	0	23	2	3
Mathews, Byron, Utica†	.264	66	269	49	71	95	9	6	1	19	1	3	2	27	0	32	42	15
Mayberry, Germaine, Watertown	.193	40	114	14	22	27	2	0	1	4	2	0	5	14	0	35	6	2
McCloughan, Scot, St. Catharines*	.281	58	203	17	57	76	10	0	3	23	0	4	2	18	1	35	3	6
McCubbin, Shane, Jamestown	.196	17	46	4	9	17	3	1	1	3	0	0	0	4	0	17	1	0
McDonald, Andy, Utica	.140	14	43	4	6	8	0	1	0	3	0	0	0	4	0	14	0	1
Milne, Blaine, Hamilton	.203	25	69	14	14	17	3	0	0	7	1	1	3	15	0	14	1	1
Minnich, Tom, Auburn*	.201	49	149	12	30	46	6	2	2	14	0	1	1	17	1	40	2	0
Mitchell, Donovan, Auburn*	.291	70	292	44	85	102	8	3	1	18	3	0	1	13	0	32	25	8
Moore, Andy, Elmira	.212	59	203	28	43	61	6	0	4	22	1	0	2	21	0	66	5	4
Moore, Mike, Watertown	.188	15	48	3	9	10	1	0	0	2	1	1	0	4	0	14	0	0
Mora, Frankie, Pittsfield	.195	38	118	13	23	31	3	1	1	15	2	1	4	14	1	26	4	4
Morales, Francisco, Geneva	.224	19	49	3	11	13	2	0	0	0	0	0	0	7	1	21	0	0
Mrowka, Jim, Pittsfield†	.000	1	1	0	0	0	0	0	0	0	0	0	0	2	0	0	0	0
Mumma, Bob, Utica	.000	1	4	0	0	0	0	0	0	0	0	0	0	0	0	3	0	0
Murphy, Jeff, Hamilton†	.264	57	201	27	53	87	14	1	6	27	0	0	3	21	3	53	1	2
Murphy, Mike, Batavia	.254	63	228	32	58	74	6	2	2	27	4	0	4	21	0	48	15	4
North, Tim, Erie†	.149	22	47	7	7	8	1	0	0	1	1	0	1	10	0	11	5	0
Northrup, Kevin, Jamestown	.292	18	72	14	21	39	4	1	4	15	0	0	3	8	0	17	4	1
Norton, Chris, 1 Wat.-60 Jam.	.199	61	211	16	42	60	4	1	4	27	0	2	2	15	0	66	3	0
Nunnally, Jon, Watertown	.240	69	246	39	59	92	10	4	5	43	0	4	1	32	2	55	12	3
Nutting, Robert, Geneva*	.241	23	79	7	19	23	4	0	0	4	3	0	0	13	1	11	1	1
O'Donnell, T.J., Elmira	.208	37	130	13	27	35	6	1	0	8	1	1	2	5	0	12	1	3
Ogden, Jason, Utica	.136	10	22	5	3	5	0	1	0	1	0	0	0	6	0	6	2	0

Player, Team	Avg.	G	AB	R	H	TB	2B	3B	HR	RBI	SH	SF	HP	BB	Int. BB	SO	SB	CS
Ollison, Scott, Batavia	.140	19	50	5	7	7	0	0	0	4	1	0	2	6	0	14	6	0
Ortiz, Nicolas, Elmira	.179	9	28	2	5	8	3	0	0	1	0	0	0	5	0	13	0	0
Owens, Brad, Hamilton	.304	56	181	40	55	82	9	3	4	24	0	2	4	34	0	31	17	2
Pagano, Scott, Niagara Falls†	.244	67	193	17	47	63	9	2	1	22	3	2	4	14	1	27	6	10
Parker, Corey, Niagara Falls*	.091	23	44	6	4	5	1	0	0	3	0	0	3	7	0	10	0	1
Penn, Shannon, Niagara Falls†	.273	70	253	47	69	91	9	2	3	25	3	1	6	28	2	53	31	10
Peterson, Chris, Geneva	.225	71	244	36	55	66	8	0	1	23	9	2	4	32	0	69	11	7
Poe, Charles, Utica	.299	47	164	27	49	74	8	1	5	29	0	2	2	18	0	39	10	2
Polidor, Wil, Utica†	.333	16	42	5	14	15	1	0	0	5	2	0	0	1	0	2	2	1
Pridy, Todd, Erie*	.310	75	274	42	85	144	15	1	14	60	0	1	5	28	4	66	2	0
Probst, Alan, Auburn	.237	66	224	24	53	84	14	1	5	34	1	2	3	23	1	48	1	0
Querecuto, Juan, St. Catharines	.215	42	135	16	29	41	6	0	2	12	1	0	1	11	0	23	0	0
Quillin, Ty, Pittsfield*	.216	15	37	1	8	10	2	0	0	2	0	0	0	3	0	9	1	1
Raleigh, Matthew, Jamestown	.218	77	261	41	57	108	14	2	11	44	0	2	0	45	2	101	14	2
Rhein, Jeff, Auburn	.231	63	199	32	46	66	5	3	3	24	1	3	2	23	2	54	23	8
Rich, Ted, Utica	.221	48	145	11	32	44	7	1	1	12	0	2	4	13	0	54	1	0
Ritz, Trey, Hamilton*	.212	38	113	14	24	29	1	2	0	7	2	0	0	8	1	30	6	3
Roberts, Lonell, St. Catharines	.205	62	244	37	50	55	3	1	0	11	4	0	3	19	1	75	33	13
Robertson, Stan, Jamestown	.156	41	96	13	15	23	4	2	0	9	1	1	2	6	0	35	7	1
Robinson, Alan, Hamilton	.140	42	86	13	12	16	4	0	0	8	1	2	6	15	0	22	2	3
Robinson, Dan, Erie*	.296	8	27	5	8	14	3	0	1	8	0	0	0	7	0	8	1	0
Robson, David, Niagara Falls	.500	2	4	2	2	2	0	0	0	0	0	0	0	3	0	1	0	0
Rossler, Brett, Pittsfield	.250	35	96	9	24	28	4	0	0	9	0	0	0	7	0	37	5	2
Rundels, Matthew, Jamestown	.256	75	277	43	71	99	6	2	6	28	2	3	5	25	0	43	32	11
Sallee, Andy, Batavia*	.249	68	241	26	60	87	5	5	4	38	0	3	3	22	2	58	3	4
Samuels, Scott, Erie*	.203	43	128	17	26	35	7	1	0	14	0	0	2	19	0	39	7	3
Sanchez, Gordon, Oneonta*	.143	4	14	3	2	2	0	0	0	1	0	0	1	2	0	3	0	0
Sanford, Chance, Welland*	.285	59	214	36	61	93	11	3	5	21	0	3	0	35	4	39	13	4
Santana, Jose, Auburn†	.198	64	212	17	42	47	5	0	0	17	3	2	2	18	0	34	2	3
Saunders, Chris, Pittsfield	.252	72	254	34	64	85	11	2	2	32	1	5	1	34	0	50	5	2
Scott, George, Elmira	.250	56	204	19	51	69	13	1	1	20	1	0	2	13	0	28	3	4
Secrist, Reed, Welland*	.214	42	117	16	25	34	6	0	1	13	2	1	2	19	0	36	4	3
Selby, Bill, Elmira*	.262	73	275	38	72	120	16	1	10	41	2	2	2	31	6	53	4	4
Senkowitz, Mark, Elmira	.146	31	82	7	12	14	2	0	0	6	0	0	4	7	0	17	0	0
Sheff, Chris, Erie	.238	57	193	29	46	67	8	2	3	16	1	1	1	32	1	47	15	2
Shelton, Derek, Oneonta	.382	23	68	4	26	30	4	0	0	13	3	1	1	13	0	15	0	0
Shotton, Craig, Welland	.160	10	25	5	4	7	1	1	0	0	0	0	2	1	0	8	1	0
Skeels, Mark, Erie†	.232	68	237	40	55	84	8	0	7	41	0	0	2	42	0	42	4	1
Smith, Dan, Geneva	.200	3	10	2	2	3	1	0	0	1	0	0	0	1	0	4	0	0
Smith, Demond, Pittsfield†	.249	66	233	39	58	79	10	4	1	24	1	3	7	23	0	42	21	15
Smith, Jason, Elmira	.160	30	75	9	12	15	1	1	0	3	0	0	1	7	0	28	0	1
Smith, John, Pittsfield	.240	68	254	46	61	104	13	3	8	35	0	1	3	36	0	66	18	11
Snopek, Chris, Utica	.282	73	245	49	69	92	15	1	2	29	1	4	2	52	4	44	14	4
Solomon, Steve, Batavia*	.393	10	28	5	11	13	2	0	0	3	0	0	0	0	0	7	4	0
Stahlhoefer, Larry, Welland	.234	28	94	12	22	34	3	0	3	14	1	2	2	12	0	12	3	1
Steele, Mike, Jamestown	.500	13	2	0	1	1	0	0	0	0	0	0	0	0	0	0	0	0
Steverson, Todd, St. Catharines	.209	65	225	26	47	74	9	0	6	24	0	3	1	26	0	83	23	7
Stojsavljevic, Paul, Geneva	.293	12	41	4	12	18	1	1	1	6	0	0	0	4	0	8	0	1
Sullivan, Brian, Niagara Falls*	.000	1	4	1	0	0	0	0	0	0	0	0	0	1	0	0	0	0
Suplee, Ray, Oneonta	.224	63	232	32	52	73	11	2	2	28	0	3	4	23	0	62	6	2
Sylvestri, Tony, Erie†	.233	42	159	28	37	43	6	0	0	11	1	2	5	21	0	26	9	3
Taylor, Jamie, Watertown*	.293	60	208	25	61	79	13	1	1	35	0	3	1	30	1	36	4	0
Taylor, Mike, Erie	.175	21	40	5	7	13	0	0	2	8	0	2	2	5	0	16	2	0
Thomas, Chris, Auburn*	.246	64	228	32	56	68	4	1	2	21	0	1	2	11	2	44	28	6
Thompson, Brian, Auburn	.303	27	89	19	27	42	6	3	1	21	1	2	1	21	0	19	4	3
Tillman, Darren, Geneva	.223	34	103	19	23	27	4	0	0	9	3	1	3	7	0	16	5	3
Timko, John, Niagara Falls	.195	24	41	0	8	9	1	0	0	4	0	0	1	1	0	19	0	0
Tooch, Chuck, Welland	.144	31	104	11	15	25	7	0	1	6	0	0	1	8	0	26	1	3
Torres, Tony, Erie	.293	40	157	31	46	57	9	1	0	16	0	2	4	20	0	26	13	5
Tovar, Edgar, Jamestown	.267	72	281	38	75	96	7	1	4	31	2	0	3	10	0	14	13	9
Tredaway, Chad, Geneva†	.300	73	270	39	81	119	19	2	5	31	3	5	3	24	1	24	6	4
Tremie, Chris, Utica	.063	6	16	1	1	1	0	0	0	0	0	0	0	0	0	5	0	0
Trujillo, Jose, Geneva	.214	25	70	9	15	19	4	0	0	5	0	0	4	7	0	16	4	3
Tucker, Kelly, Watertown	.135	17	52	6	7	16	3	0	2	7	0	0	0	5	0	30	0	0
Valdez, Pedro, Geneva*	.272	66	254	27	69	94	10	0	5	24	2	2	3	3	1	33	4	5
Ventura, Efrain, Utica	.261	19	46	8	12	19	2	1	1	7	0	0	3	0	0	14	0	1
Vilet, Tom, Batavia	.221	26	77	9	17	22	3	1	0	6	5	1	2	4	0	19	5	0
Vinas, Julio, Utica	.245	47	151	22	37	51	6	4	0	24	1	5	2	11	0	29	1	2
White, Johnny, Jamestown	.219	20	64	14	14	24	4	0	2	7	0	0	1	10	0	18	4	2
Wills, Shawn, Batavia	.226	63	239	53	54	82	9	2	5	18	4	0	6	20	0	43	31	6
Wiltz, Stan, Welland	.228	45	136	8	31	40	6	0	1	13	0	1	0	7	0	29	0	1
Winslow, Bryant, Auburn	.237	28	97	12	23	40	5	0	4	9	0	0	1	3	0	26	0	1
Winston, Todd, Auburn	.247	65	223	30	55	78	13	2	2	27	2	1	4	25	3	40	16	5
Wuerch, Jason, Oneonta*	.174	6	23	1	4	4	0	0	0	3	0	0	0	4	0	6	0	0
Wyngarden, Brett, Auburn	.103	10	29	5	3	6	3	0	0	1	0	0	2	4	0	4	0	0
Yaroshuk, Ernie, Oneonta*	.238	51	185	21	44	58	8	0	2	24	1	0	1	21	0	18	1	2
Zapata, Ramon, Welland	.208	8	24	1	5	6	1	0	0	0	0	0	1	2	0	9	0	1
Zollars, Mike, Watertown	.244	52	180	25	44	50	2	2	0	14	1	1	1	16	0	46	13	4
Zuber, Jon, Batavia*	.341	22	88	14	30	45	6	3	1	21	0	1	1	9	1	11	1	1

The following pitchers, listed alphabetically by club, with games in parentheses, had no plate appearances, primarily through use of designated hitters:

AUBURN—Bjornson, Craig (5); Bottoms, Derrick (9); Correa, Jorge (6); Cupit, John (19); Dawson, Dwayne (17); Guerry, Kyle (19); Holleday, Juan (6); Holt, Chris (14); Krislock, Zak (26); Mlicki, Dave (14); Rapaglia, Stephan (20); Rhine, Kendall (8); Tenbarge, Jeff (14); Walker, Jim (15); Westbrook, Destry (12).

BATAVIA—Agostinelli, Pete (4); Anderson, Chad (15); Bojcun, Pat (6); Boldt, Sean (9); Doolan, Blake (19); Edwards, Sam (3); Heisler, Larry (3); Herrmann, Gary (11); Irwin, Tom (18); McIntyre, Joe (21); McWilliams, Ryan (22); Mejias, Fernando (2); Mitchell, Larry (10); Nevill, Glenn (12); Page, Thane (3); Sepeda, Jamie (5); Smith, Eric (16); Tranberg, Mark (11).

ELMIRA—Bush, Craig (15); Davis, Tim (1); Donovan, Bret (19); Faino, Jeff (20); Glaze, Gettys (18); Hansen, Brent (13); Hudson, Joe (19); Lawrence, Randy (15); MacNeil, Doug (9); Martinez, Cesar (17); McKinley, Leif (23); Niles, Tom (21).

ERIE—Donahue, Mathew (15); Englehart, Scott (7); Frazier, Brad (21); Kendrena, Ken (22); Leahy, Pat (26); Lemon, Don (17); Mendoza, Reynol (15); Patterson, Jim (18); Petersen, Matt (14); Pettit, Doug (22); Roman, Dan (4); Sample, Deron (5); Stafford, Gerald (13); Whitman, Ryan (20); Whitten, Mike (11).

GENEVA—Daniel, Charles (18); Dark, Dave (7); Dreyer, Darren (13); Edwards, Todd (25); Gardner, Scott (10); Gustavson, Dan (6); Hassel, Jay (1); Jarolimek, Jonathan (23); Kerley, Collin (23); Latimer, Bill (6); Morones, Eugenio (11); Rodriguez, Cristobal (14); Schulhofer, Adam (14); Steenstra, Ken (3); Trinidad, Hector (15).

HAMILTON—Beavers, Al (2); Blake, Todd (1); Boone, Antonio (4); Britt, Ken (19); Brumley, Duff (9); Bullinger, Kirk (35); Cochran, Jamie (37); Corry, Delynn (9); Degrasse, Tim (24); Hurst, Bill (3); Jones, Steve (33); Lowe, Sean (5); Mathews, Tim (14); Milius, Dennis (7); Miller, Eric (1); Oehrlein, Dave (13); Smith, Chad (13); Smith, Mike (12).

JAMESTOWN—Falteisek, Steve (15); Ferguson, Jim (23); Gentile, Scott (13); Harrison, Bob (14); Henderson, Rodney (1); Hostetler, Jeff (1); Kermode, Al (4); Pacheco, Alex (16); Pisciotta, Scott (14); Rushworth, Jim (20); Schmidt, Curt (29); Stull, Everett (14).

NIAGARA FALLS—Adams, Art (9); Ban, Yoshitaro (5); Berlin, Mike (6); Carlyle, Ken (1); Crombie, Kevin (30); Durussel, Scott (33); Lopez, Mike (14); Magrini, Paul (1); Martin, Doug (8); Mendenhall, Casey (14); Munoz, Riccardo (21); Mysel, Dave (13); Navarro, Rich (13); Raffo, Greg (26); Verduzco, Dave (15); Whiteside, Sean (15); Yamazaki, Kazu (5).

ONEONTA—Antolick, Jeff (14); Brown, Tibor (9); Buddie, Mike (13); Cindrich, Jeff (2); DeJean, Michel (20); Ferguson, Howard (13); Ferguson, Shane (4); Inman, Bert (14); Karp, Ryan (14); Santiago, Sandi (23); Sutherland, John (4); Thibert, John (21); Thomforde, Jim (1); Turrentine, Rich (1); Underwood, Bill (24); Wallace, Kent (14).

PITTSFIELD—Beckerman, Todd (21); Fuller, Mark (26); Hokanson, Mark (13); Jones, Cliff (20); Lyons, Steve (10); Petcka, Joe (12); Popoff, Jim (1); Pulsipher, Bill (14); Seymour, Steve (3); Stark, Greg (15); Teske, Dave (11); Watson, Shaun (8).

ST. CATHARINES—Adkins, Bob (14); Brandow, Derek (22); Cornett, Brad (25); Crabtree, Tim (12); Daniels, Lee (17); Darley, Ned (16); Doman, Roger (15); Jersild, Aaron (22); Largusa, Levon (10); Mallory, Trevor (11); Meinershagen, Adam (11); Miller, Gary (19).

UTICA—Bertotti, Mike (17); Elsbernd, Dave (3); Gajkowski, Steve (29); Gay, Chris (4); Herrholz, John (15); Johnston, Sean (14); Lindemann, Wayne (17); McDermott, Jim (19); McGraw, Doug (13); Moore, Tim (14); Pierson, Jason (15); Starks, Fred (10); Watkins, Jason (26); Worrell, Steve (4).

WATERTOWN—Blake, Ben (13); Buzard, Brian (3); Carter, John (13); Fronio, Jason (5); Gibbs, Paul (29); Jewell, Mike (5); Johnson, Joel (2); Key, Denny (10); Koller, Rodney (15); Matthews, Mike (2); Najera, Noe (15); Neilson, Mike (5); Resendez, Oscar (15); Rideau, Greg (7); Sharts, Scott (22); Sides, Craig (3); Smith, Fred (33); Williams, Matt (6); York, Chuck (13).

WELLAND—Bonilla, Miguel (30); Carter, John (13); Fairfax, Ken (7); Ford, John (2); Garcia-Luna, Francisco (15); Klamm, Ed (12); Konuszewski, Dennis (2); LaPlante, Michel (11); Lawrence, Sean (15); Mesewicz, Marc (29); Nuttle, Jamie (18); Perez, Gil (21); Pontbriant, Matt (4); Teich, Mike (4); Townsend, Rich (28); Wilkins, Marc (6); Wilson, Gary (13).

GRAND SLAMS—Kimsey, 2; Brown, Cardenas, Doucette, Lucca, Northrup, Steverson, 1 each.

AWARDED FIRST BASE ON CATCHER'S INTERFERENCE—Clem 2 (Allen, Milne); Trujillo 2 (Harmes, Stahlhoefer); Duplessis (Leshnock); Greene (Querecuto); Hawkins (Machado); Hurst (Garcia); Leshnock (Vinas); Lussier (Ladd); McCloughan (Machado); Minnich (Stahlhoefer); Raleigh (Machado).

PITCHING

TEAM

Team	ERA	G	CG	ShO	Sv.	IP	H	R	ER	HR	HB	BB	Int. BB	SO	WP	Bk.
Geneva	2.64	75	10	5	25	648.0	525	190	190	30	32	161	9	521	35	8
Hamilton	2.81	76	6	6	33	654.0	510	253	204	38	29	247	6	670	38	13
Oneonta	3.07	75	5	8	20	645.2	569	296	220	19	15	228	2	623	35	13
Niagara Falls	3.07	78	5	7	17	660.1	543	302	225	29	35	245	22	613	63	26
Utica	3.14	74	5	5	23	636.1	593	307	222	32	18	201	8	538	47	10
Pittsfield	3.33	74	10	4	16	650.2	624	313	241	24	25	243	3	525	54	16
St. Catharines	3.47	75	2	3	21	641.0	554	320	247	41	32	281	0	555	56	20
Erie	3.47	77	4	5	22	655.2	569	341	253	53	44	279	5	532	41	35
Batavia	3.68	70	4	4	11	604.1	591	326	247	65	27	215	15	508	43	17
Jamestown	3.69	77	8	8	17	655.1	548	333	269	24	39	320	11	617	68	24
Watertown	3.73	76	5	5	16	645.0	610	351	267	35	30	317	6	521	46	19
Welland	3.90	77	2	3	13	666.1	606	401	289	36	45	269	15	581	73	19
Elmira	4.35	75	6	7	16	660.0	658	394	319	37	37	245	10	534	41	19
Auburn	4.40	73	1	2	12	626.1	614	369	306	41	45	288	9	535	65	16

INDIVIDUAL

(Leading qualifiers for earned-run average leadership—62 or more innings)

*Throws lefthanded.

Pitcher, Team	W	L	Pct.	ERA	G	GS	CG	GF	ShO	Sv.	IP	H	R	ER	HR	HB	BB	Int. BB	SO	WP
Crabtree, St. Catharines	6	3	.667	1.57	12	12	2	0	0	0	69.0	45	19	12	1	7	22	0	47	6
Antolick, Oneonta	4	2	.667	2.13	14	14	0	0	0	0	71.2	60	29	17	1	0	31	0	68	8
Mathews, Hamilton	10	1	.909	2.18	14	14	1	0	0	0	86.2	70	25	21	4	2	30	0	89	4
Donovan, Elmira*	5	4	.556	2.21	19	10	2	5	1	1	85.1	52	24	21	8	6	33	0	82	2
Pierson, Utica*	8	2	.800	2.38	15	15	1	0	1	0	87.0	90	34	23	5	1	18	2	62	1
Trinidad, Geneva	8	6	.571	2.40	15	15	2	0	0	0	93.2	78	33	25	6	4	13	2	70	1
Whiteside, Niagara Falls*	8	4	.667	2.45	15	11	0	0	0	0	69.2	54	26	19	2	0	24	0	72	7
Daniel, Geneva	5	5	.500	2.51	18	11	1	4	0	0	86.0	80	43	24	5	3	13	0	53	5
Inman, Oneonta	6	5	.545	2.52	15	15	2	0	1	0	93.0	69	32	26	3	2	28	0	81	2
Wallace, Oneonta	8	4	.667	2.55	14	14	1	0	1	0	81.1	76	32	23	2	0	11	0	55	3

Departmental leaders: G—Cochran, 37; W—Mathews, Oehrlein, 10; L—Falteisek, 8; Pct.—Mathews, Oehrlein, .909; GS—Several pitchers tied with 15; CG—Pisciotta, 4; GF—Cochran, 34; ShO—Pisciotta, 4; Sv.—Cochran, 24; IP—Falteisek, 96.0; H—Martinez, 97; R—Garcia-Luna, 56; ER—S. Lawrence, 43; HR—Anderson, 14; HB—Mendoza, Stafford, 8; BB—Stull, 61; IBB—Crombie, McIntyre, 5; SO—Oehrlein, 99; WP—Stull, 18.

(All pitchers—listed alphabetically)

Pitcher, Team	W	L	Pct.	ERA	G	GS	CG	GF	ShO	Sv.	IP	H	R	ER	HR	HB	BB	Int. BB	SO	WP
Adams, Niagara Falls	3	0	1.000	2.83	8	8	1	0	1	0	35.0	25	11	11	1	5	12	1	27	5
Adkins, St. Catharines	0	0	.000	6.67	14	0	0	7	0	1	28.1	17	24	21	1	5	35	0	28	5
Agostinelli, Batavia*	0	1	.000	6.75	4	0	0	2	0	0	4.0	4	3	3	0	0	3	0	3	0
Anderson, Batavia	7	6	.538	3.12	15	15	3	0	0	0	95.1	82	49	33	14	4	29	2	71	2
Antolick, Oneonta	4	2	.667	2.13	14	14	0	0	0	0	71.2	60	29	17	1	0	31	0	68	8
Ban, Niagara Falls	0	1	.000	6.75	5	1	0	2	0	0	9.1	10	7	7	3	0	5	1	8	0
Bauer, Niagara Falls*	0	0	.000	2.18	31	0	0	10	0	2	33.0	22	18	8	1	2	18	4	33	4
Beavers, Hamilton	0	3	.000	2.70	2	0	0	0	0	0	3.1	1	5	1	1	2	2	0	7	3
Beckerman, Pittsfield	1	0	.000	1.38	21	0	0	17	0	5	32.2	21	8	5	2	0	12	1	31	3
Berlin, Niagara Falls	1	2	.333	1.59	6	5	0	1	0	0	34.0	19	13	6	2	1	9	1	34	1
Bertotti, Utica*	2	2	.500	6.21	17	1	0	5	0	0	33.1	36	28	23	2	2	31	0	23	7
Bjornson, Auburn*	2	0	1.000	1.93	5	1	0	3	0	0	23.1	17	7	5	1	0	10	0	15	3
Blake, Watertown	3	3	.500	3.92	13	5	0	0	0	0	39.0	43	27	17	4	3	16	1	35	0

— 457 —

Pitcher, Team	W	L	Pct.	ERA	G	GS	CG	GF	ShO	Sv.	IP	H	R	ER	HR	HB	BB	Int. BB	SO	WP
Blake, Hamilton*	1	0	1.000	1.42	1	1	0	0	0	0	6.1	6	1	1	0	0	3	0	0	0
Bojcun, Batavia	1	0	1.000	5.59	6	0	0	5	0	1	9.2	13	7	6	0	0	3	1	12	0
Boldt, Batavia	2	0	1.000	5.74	9	0	0	5	0	1	15.2	20	13	10	3	1	4	1	25	2
Bonilla, Welland	3	3	.500	3.42	30	2	0	12	0	3	50.0	53	32	19	5	6	10	1	37	3
Boone, Oneonta	0	1	.000	7.94	4	1	0	3	0	1	5.2	5	5	5	0	0	6	0	1	0
Bottoms, Auburn*	3	1	.750	4.24	9	7	1	2	0	1	40.1	41	24	19	3	3	21	0	35	1
Brandow, St. Catharines	5	2	.714	2.47	22	2	0	9	0	3	58.1	51	23	16	6	2	26	0	74	5
Britt, Hamilton	1	1	.500	3.96	19	2	0	3	0	1	36.1	34	23	16	4	2	21	1	30	2
Brown, Oneonta*	0	0	.000	3.75	9	0	0	5	0	0	12.0	8	8	5	0	1	15	0	10	2
Brumley, Hamilton	6	0	1.000	2.72	9	9	2	0	0	0	59.2	38	19	18	3	2	21	0	83	0
Buddie, Oneonta	1	4	.200	3.88	13	13	1	0	0	0	67.1	69	36	29	3	3	34	0	87	7
Bullinger, Hamilton	2	2	.500	1.11	35	0	0	7	0	2	48.2	24	7	6	0	2	15	4	61	3
Bush, Elmira	1	4	.200	5.37	15	8	0	5	0	0	55.1	72	44	33	4	3	20	2	21	5
Buzard, Watertown*	0	0	.000	3.00	3	0	0	2	0	0	3.0	1	1	1	0	0	5	0	2	0
Canton, Elmira	0	0	.000	0.00	1	0	0	0	0	0	0.1	1	0	0	0	0	0	0	0	0
Cardenas, Watertown	0	0	.000	18.00	1	0	0	1	0	0	1.0	2	2	2	0	0	0	0	0	0
Carlyle, Niagara Falls	1	0	1.000	1.50	1	1	0	0	0	0	6.0	6	1	1	0	0	1	0	9	1
Carter, 3 Wel.- 13 Wat.	4	7	.364	4.00	16	14	3	0	0	0	78.2	67	47	35	4	3	39	0	54	5
Cindrich, Oneonta	0	1	.000	9.82	2	0	0	1	0	0	3.2	6	5	4	0	0	1	0	3	0
Cochran, Hamilton	5	0	1.000	1.04	37	0	0	34	0	24	43.1	24	6	5	1	1	8	1	55	1
Cornett, St. Catharines	4	1	.800	3.60	25	0	0	13	0	1	60.0	54	30	24	6	3	10	0	64	5
Correa, Auburn	1	0	1.000	20.65	6	0	0	2	0	0	5.2	11	13	13	1	0	14	0	4	2
Corry, Hamilton	1	2	.333	4.43	9	9	1	0	0	0	40.2	54	24	20	2	2	15	0	22	3
Crabtree, St. Catharines	6	3	.667	1.57	12	12	2	0	0	0	69.0	45	19	12	1	7	22	0	47	6
Crombie, Niagara Falls	1	1	.500	2.54	30	0	0	21	0	6	39.0	19	14	11	1	1	17	5	61	1
Cupit, Auburn	3	1	.750	3.16	19	1	0	10	0	0	37.0	38	16	13	2	1	17	1	25	0
Daniel, Geneva	5	5	.500	2.51	18	11	1	4	0	0	86.0	80	43	24	5	3	13	0	53	5
Daniels, St. Catharines	3	6	.333	4.34	17	4	0	5	0	0	58.0	61	34	28	4	2	20	0	37	6
Dark, Geneva*	1	1	.500	7.27	7	0	0	1	0	0	8.2	13	7	7	0	2	3	0	6	2
Darley, St. Catharines	4	5	.444	2.94	16	14	0	1	0	0	82.2	66	35	27	5	2	46	0	70	0
Dawson, Auburn	6	2	.750	2.77	17	6	0	5	0	0	65.0	63	23	20	2	6	18	0	47	4
DeGrasse, Hamilton	6	5	.545	4.85	24	4	1	3	1	0	55.2	57	31	30	7	0	15	0	56	2
DeJean, Oneonta	0	0	.000	0.44	20	0	0	19	0	16	20.2	12	3	1	1	0	3	0	20	0
Doman, St. Catharines	2	7	.222	4.59	15	14	0	1	0	0	68.2	70	47	35	3	2	47	0	53	12
Donahue, Erie	4	6	.400	4.31	15	15	1	0	0	0	62.2	58	38	30	7	5	19	0	49	2
Donovan, Elmira*	5	4	.556	2.21	19	10	2	5	1	1	85.1	52	24	21	8	6	33	0	82	2
Doolan, Batavia	6	2	.750	2.85	19	9	3	2	1	1	85.1	78	33	27	8	3	25	0	62	6
Dreyer, Geneva	7	4	.636	3.09	13	13	3	0	1	0	81.2	67	35	28	4	4	12	0	87	1
Durussel, Niagara Falls	5	3	.625	2.95	33	2	0	6	0	0	55.0	38	23	18	0	5	35	4	50	6
Edwards, Batavia	0	1	.000	8.00	3	2	0	0	0	0	9.0	15	8	8	2	0	4	0	9	0
Edwards, Geneva*	1	1	.500	1.17	25	0	0	15	0	7	38.1	25	8	5	0	1	14	2	34	2
Eggert, Jamestown*	4	2	.667	2.08	30	0	0	22	0	8	47.2	33	14	11	1	1	18	0	72	3
Elsbernd, Utica	1	1	.500	9.00	3	3	0	0	0	0	10.0	9	10	10	2	0	6	0	8	0
Englehart, Erie	0	1	.000	9.00	7	0	0	2	0	0	12.0	16	14	12	2	0	20	0	5	2
Evans, Niagara Falls*	0	0	.000	9.00	1	0	0	1	0	0	1.0	0	1	1	0	0	4	0	0	0
Faino, Elmira*	1	5	.167	5.06	20	1	0	10	0	2	42.2	44	33	24	1	3	18	4	36	3
Fairfax, Welland	1	4	.200	5.01	7	7	1	0	1	0	32.1	25	28	18	2	2	20	0	27	6
Falteisek, Jamestown	3	8	.273	3.56	15	15	2	0	0	0	96.0	84	47	38	5	5	31	2	82	9
Feno, Elmira	0	0	.000	22.50	2	0	0	1	0	0	2.0	6	6	5	0	0	4	0	1	0
H. Ferguson, Oneonta	2	0	1.000	3.29	13	3	0	2	0	0	27.1	20	10	10	1	1	16	0	29	0
Ferguson, Jamestown	3	3	.500	4.66	23	6	0	10	0	5	48.1	46	28	25	2	3	23	0	41	2
S. Ferguson, Oneonta	0	0	.000	5.40	4	0	0	2	0	0	3.1	6	5	2	0	1	0	0	4	0
Ford, Welland*	0	0	.000	10.80	2	0	0	1	0	0	1.2	6	2	2	1	0	3	0	1	0
Frazier, Erie*	1	3	.250	5.23	21	0	0	9	0	0	31.0	28	23	18	3	0	19	0	37	3
Fronio, Watertown	1	2	.333	4.50	5	0	0	1	0	0	10.0	8	5	5	1	0	4	1	13	0
Fuller, Pittsfield	2	1	.667	1.62	26	0	0	18	0	6	50.0	39	15	9	0	3	10	0	44	4
Gajkowski, Utica	3	2	.600	1.34	29	0	0	26	0	14	47.0	33	14	7	1	1	10	1	38	6
Garcia-Luna, Welland	2	7	.222	4.29	15	15	0	0	0	0	79.2	89	56	38	3	7	20	0	49	6
Gardner, Geneva	2	1	.667	2.70	10	2	0	1	0	0	20.0	19	11	6	0	1	6	0	20	1
Gay, Utica*	0	1	.000	6.39	4	2	0	0	0	0	12.2	16	11	9	0	0	3	0	7	3
Gentile, Jamestown	4	4	.500	3.88	13	13	0	0	0	0	62.2	59	32	27	3	6	34	0	44	5
George, Pittsfield*	6	3	.667	2.23	18	1	0	7	0	0	48.1	39	18	12	1	1	21	0	66	7
Gibbs, Watertown	4	3	.571	1.38	29	0	0	13	0	4	58.2	39	18	9	4	5	15	0	78	2
Glaze, Elmira	6	4	.600	3.35	18	11	1	5	1	0	83.1	77	40	31	2	4	19	1	88	3
Greene, Niagara Falls	0	0	.000	0.00	1	1	0	0	0	0	2.0	0	0	0	0	0	1	0	0	0
Guerry, Auburn*	1	3	.250	4.76	19	1	0	7	0	0	34.0	37	23	18	0	2	21	1	29	1
Gustavson, Geneva	2	0	1.000	1.32	6	0	0	3	0	0	13.2	12	2	2	0	2	2	0	7	1
Hansen, Elmira	3	5	.375	4.27	13	11	1	1	1	0	59.0	59	33	28	3	3	21	0	65	4
Harrison, Jamestown	2	1	.667	4.59	14	1	0	4	0	1	33.1	27	23	17	2	6	19	0	37	6
Hassel, Geneva	0	0	.000	1.29	1	0	0	1	0	0	7.0	4	1	1	0	1	0	0	6	1
Heisler, Batavia	1	0	1.000	3.52	3	1	0	1	0	0	7.2	9	3	3	0	0	3	0	3	1
Henderson, Jamestown	0	0	.000	6.00	1	1	0	0	0	0	3.0	2	3	2	0	0	5	0	2	0
Henderson, Hamilton	0	0	.000	0.00	1	0	0	1	0	0	2.0	1	0	0	0	0	1	0	2	0
Herrholz, Elmira	2	1	.667	1.74	15	0	0	6	0	0	20.2	14	9	4	1	3	16	0	22	3
Herrmann, Batavia*	1	3	.250	4.89	11	6	0	1	0	0	38.2	41	30	21	2	3	16	0	35	3
Hokanson, Pittsfield	2	5	.286	6.41	13	9	1	2	0	0	53.1	72	48	38	2	1	21	2	29	4
Holleday, Auburn	0	1	.000	9.58	6	0	0	4	0	1	10.1	12	16	11	2	0	5	0	8	4
Holt, Auburn	2	5	.286	4.45	14	14	0	0	0	0	83.0	75	48	41	9	7	24	0	81	11
Hostetler, Jamestown*	1	0	1.000	0.00	1	1	0	0	0	0	7.0	2	0	0	0	0	4	0	10	0
Hudson, Elmira	3	3	.500	4.38	19	7	0	6	0	0	72.0	76	46	35	2	2	33	0	38	4
Hurst, Hamilton	0	1	.000	3.68	3	3	0	0	0	0	14.2	11	7	6	1	3	4	0	9	3
Inman, Oneonta	6	5	.545	2.52	15	15	2	0	1	0	93.0	69	32	26	3	2	28	0	81	2
Irwin, Batavia	1	5	.167	5.06	18	10	0	5	0	0	53.1	67	40	30	11	2	21	1	30	5
Jarolimek, Geneva	1	5	.167	3.20	23	1	0	17	0	8	45.0	35	20	16	5	0	11	2	26	4
Jersild, St. Catharines*	0	1	.000	2.04	22	0	0	17	0	1	35.1	26	11	8	0	1	8	0	36	1
Jewell, Watertown	0	0	.000	3.48	5	0	0	1	0	0	10.1	10	4	4	0	2	2	0	12	1
Johnson, Watertown	0	2	.000	11.25	2	2	0	0	0	0	8.0	16	11	10	2	0	3	0	8	2
Johnston, Utica*	4	4	.500	2.79	14	14	1	0	0	0	80.2	78	44	25	4	2	12	0	56	4
Jones, Pittsfield*	3	1	.750	1.53	19	0	0	13	0	4	35.1	20	10	6	0	2	18	0	39	4
Jones, Hamilton	4	0	1.000	0.41	33	0	0	13	0	5	43.2	20	5	2	1	4	12	2	57	3
Karp, Oneonta*	6	4	.600	4.09	14	13	1	0	1	0	70.1	66	38	32	2	3	30	0	58	2
Kendrena, Erie	5	4	.556	3.79	22	0	0	10	0	3	54.2	47	33	23	5	5	12	2	61	2
Kerley, Geneva	3	1	.750	2.05	23	2	1	16	0	6	48.1	37	13	11	2	1	15	1	46	4
Kermode, Jamestown	0	2	.000	4.86	4	4	0	0	0	0	16.2	22	9	9	3	0	1	1	16	1
Key, Watertown	3	4	.429	3.28	10	7	0	1	0	0	46.2	51	22	17	2	0	10	1	19	3

Pitcher, Team	W	L	Pct.	ERA	G	GS	CG	GF	ShO	Sv.	IP	H	R	ER	HR	HB	BB	Int. BB	SO	WP
Killen, Niagara Falls	0	0	.000	18.00	1	0	0	0	0	0	1.0	2	2	2	0	1	0	0	0	0
Klamm, Welland*	2	1	.667	2.79	12	8	0	0	1	0	48.1	32	19	15	2	0	25	1	33	3
Koller, Watertown	3	7	.300	5.13	15	7	0	3	0	1	52.2	71	35	30	1	2	14	0	24	2
Konuszewski, Welland	0	0	.000	1.29	2	2	0	0	0	0	7.0	6	1	1	0	0	4	0	4	1
Krislock, Auburn	3	4	.429	3.10	26	0	0	21	0	9	40.2	41	19	14	1	3	22	4	50	5
LaPlante, Welland	1	5	.167	3.13	11	11	1	0	1	0	69.0	54	34	24	1	5	13	1	75	4
Largusa, St. Catharines*	5	2	.714	3.29	10	10	0	0	0	0	52.0	42	24	19	4	1	21	0	45	4
Latimer, Geneva	0	0	.000	0.00	6	0	0	2	0	1	11.0	5	2	0	0	0	2	0	11	0
Lawrence, Elmira	3	2	.600	6.86	15	4	0	4	0	1	42.0	42	37	32	5	0	35	0	24	4
Lawrence, Welland*	3	6	.333	5.23	15	15	0	0	0	0	74.0	75	55	43	10	2	34	1	71	6
Leahy, Erie	2	0	1.000	1.70	26	0	0	18	0	5	37.0	37	11	7	3	2	12	0	27	3
Lemon, Erie	6	3	.667	2.85	17	11	1	4	1	2	72.2	60	27	23	4	2	28	1	55	5
Lindemann, Utica*	5	3	.625	3.09	17	12	1	2	0	1	81.2	72	29	28	3	1	14	1	75	1
Lopez, Niagara Falls	3	4	.429	2.76	14	12	0	0	0	0	65.1	64	27	20	2	2	23	2	38	5
Lowe, Hamilton	2	0	1.000	1.61	5	5	0	0	0	0	28.0	14	8	5	0	1	14	0	22	1
Lynch, Erie	0	3	.000	2.15	7	7	0	0	0	0	29.1	24	15	7	1	2	17	0	16	0
Lyons, Pittsfield	4	5	.444	3.80	10	0	3	0	0	0	68.2	73	34	29	3	5	16	0	41	4
MacNeil, Elmira	3	1	.750	5.68	9	6	0	2	0	0	38.0	37	24	24	5	1	11	0	37	1
Magrini, Niagara Falls	0	1	.000	1.29	1	1	0	0	0	0	7.0	8	1	1	0	1	2	0	5	0
Mallory, St. Catharines	1	5	.167	4.71	11	11	0	0	0	0	57.1	60	40	30	5	4	19	0	33	3
Martin, Hamilton	0	0	.000	0.00	1	0	0	0	0	0	5.0	0	0	0	0	1	0	1	0	
Martin, Niagara Falls	0	0	.000	12.60	7	0	0	4	0	2	5.0	7	9	7	0	2	2	0	5	1
Martinez, Elmira*	3	7	.300	4.11	17	13	2	1	0	1	87.2	97	51	40	3	7	25	2	56	5
Mathews, Hamilton	10	1	.909	2.18	14	14	1	0	0	0	86.2	70	25	21	4	2	30	0	89	4
Matthews, Watertown*	1	0	1.000	3.27	2	2	0	0	0	0	11.0	10	4	4	0	0	8	0	5	1
McDermott, Utica	2	2	.500	4.05	19	1	0	6	0	2	33.1	39	17	15	1	1	5	1	30	2
McGraw, Utica	6	5	.545	3.46	13	13	2	0	1	0	78.0	66	38	30	4	2	27	0	64	4
McIntyre, Batavia*	6	3	.667	1.88	21	0	0	13	0	2	28.2	18	9	6	2	2	20	5	34	3
McKinley, Elmira	1	5	.167	5.17	23	1	0	16	0	5	47.0	53	32	27	2	2	11	0	31	3
McWilliams, Batavia	0	1	.000	4.04	22	0	0	11	0	1	42.1	46	22	19	3	4	14	3	38	5
Meinershagen, St. Catharines	0	1	.125	4.47	11	8	0	1	0	1	44.1	44	24	22	6	3	20	0	36	8
Mejias, Batavia	0	0	.000	2.70	2	0	0	1	0	0	3.1	3	1	1	0	0	3	0	5	0
Mendenhall, Niagara Falls	5	5	.500	4.06	14	14	2	0	0	0	82.0	83	42	37	5	5	17	2	59	5
Mendoza, Erie	3	6	.333	4.65	15	15	1	0	1	0	69.2	70	46	36	5	8	25	0	59	6
Mesewicz, Welland*	5	3	.625	2.47	29	0	0	17	0	5	47.1	43	19	13	1	1	16	2	55	5
Milius, Hamilton*	0	2	.000	8.22	7	1	0	2	0	0	7.2	9	11	7	1	0	9	0	8	2
Miller, Hamilton	0	0	.000	0.00	1	0	0	0	0	0	1.0	0	0	0	0	0	0	0	0	0
Miller, St. Catharines	2	3	.400	1.67	19	0	0	19	0	8	27.0	18	9	5	0	0	7	0	32	1
Mitchell, Batavia	7	2	.778	2.63	10	10	3	0	1	0	65.0	63	25	19	6	1	11	0	58	4
Milcki, Auburn	1	6	.143	2.99	14	13	0	0	0	0	81.1	50	35	27	4	6	30	0	83	9
Moore, Utica	6	5	.545	3.19	14	13	0	0	0	0	84.2	82	46	30	7	3	21	0	66	8
Morones, Geneva	1	0	1.000	0.73	11	0	0	8	0	3	12.1	8	5	1	0	0	10	1	7	1
Munoz, Niagara Falls	2	3	.400	2.80	21	0	0	14	0	5	35.1	27	13	11	1	2	7	1	30	3
Mysel, Niagara Falls	2	2	.500	1.71	12	6	1	0	1	0	47.1	33	14	9	1	3	13	1	40	4
Najera, Watertown	2	4	.333	4.25	15	8	2	0	0	0	55.0	46	33	26	1	7	41	0	48	5
Navarro, Niagara Falls*	3	4	.429	3.50	13	13	1	0	1	0	64.1	63	34	25	2	2	19	0	60	4
Neilson, Watertown*	1	0	1.000	3.80	5	4	0	0	0	0	21.1	17	12	9	1	1	11	0	26	0
Nevill, Batavia*	1	1	.500	1.90	12	1	0	6	0	3	23.2	21	9	5	1	0	8	0	24	2
Niles, Elmira	2	4	.333	3.97	21	3	0	13	0	6	45.1	42	24	20	2	6	15	1	55	6
Nuttle, Welland	0	0	.000	7.33	18	0	0	7	0	0	23.1	26	25	19	0	5	20	0	29	9
Oehrlein, Hamilton*	10	1	.909	2.61	13	13	1	0	1	0	76.0	48	24	22	7	0	28	0	99	2
Pacheco, Jamestown	3	3	.500	5.54	16	5	0	4	0	0	50.1	53	36	31	5	3	29	1	32	2
Pagano, Niagara Falls	0	0	.000	3.00	2	0	0	1	0	0	3.0	4	1	1	0	0	1	0	2	0
Page, Batavia	1	2	.333	11.00	3	3	0	0	0	0	9.0	14	14	11	2	0	8	0	5	1
Patterson, Erie	1	0	1.000	3.10	18	3	0	2	0	1	52.1	38	23	18	3	6	24	0	39	3
Perez, Welland	3	5	.375	6.07	21	7	0	6	0	0	56.1	60	45	38	5	7	24	2	35	6
Petcka, Pittsfield	2	5	.286	5.00	12	12	1	0	0	0	63.0	69	41	35	4	2	44	0	56	5
Petersen, Erie	5	1	.833	2.68	14	14	1	0	0	0	80.2	56	28	24	7	2	29	0	44	2
Pettit, Erie	2	2	.500	3.13	22	2	0	19	0	11	31.2	29	14	11	3	1	6	0	28	1
Pierson, Utica*	8	2	.800	2.38	15	15	1	0	1	0	87.0	90	34	23	5	1	18	2	62	4
Pisciotta, Jamestown	6	3	.667	2.84	14	14	4	0	4	0	85.2	61	39	27	1	5	35	2	77	9
Pontbriant, Welland*	0	1	.000	3.09	4	2	0	0	0	0	11.2	4	4	4	0	0	9	0	4	0
Pool, Oneonta*	3	6	.333	2.84	25	0	0	11	0	2	44.1	46	23	14	0	0	3	0	43	0
Popoff, Pittsfield	2	2	.500	1.91	4	4	0	0	0	0	28.1	23	9	6	1	0	6	0	43	1
Pulsipher, Pittsfield*	6	3	.667	2.84	14	14	0	0	0	0	95.0	88	40	30	3	3	56	0	83	16
Raffo, Niagara Falls	4	5	.444	3.74	26	4	0	9	0	1	53.0	46	34	22	6	3	26	0	62	10
Rapaglia, Auburn	5	3	.625	3.62	20	0	0	8	0	1	32.1	32	14	13	1	0	8	2	22	3
Resendez, Watertown	6	2	.750	3.79	15	15	2	0	0	0	73.2	77	42	31	6	2	58	0	62	7
Rhine, Auburn	0	3	.000	4.94	8	8	0	0	0	0	31.0	34	21	17	2	2	31	0	21	8
Rideau, Watertown	0	0	.000	5.84	7	0	0	2	0	0	12.1	10	12	8	2	0	8	0	8	1
Robinson, Hamilton	0	1	.000	16.88	2	0	0	1	0	0	2.2	4	5	5	1	0	6	0	3	0
Rodriguez, Geneva	4	6	.400	3.68	14	14	0	0	0	0	80.2	60	41	33	5	7	28	0	67	6
Roman, Erie*	0	3	.000	9.72	4	4	0	0	0	0	8.1	13	20	9	2	0	12	0	7	1
Rushworth, Jamestown	1	6	.143	2.06	20	2	1	6	0	1	52.1	39	16	12	1	2	20	1	54	6
Sample, Erie	1	1	.500	2.79	5	0	0	1	0	0	9.2	4	3	3	2	0	2	0	10	0
Santiago, Oneonta	1	2	.333	5.18	23	0	0	14	0	1	24.1	31	19	14	2	0	13	0	27	0
Schmidt, Jamestown	3	4	.429	2.70	29	1	1	19	0	2	63.1	42	21	19	1	5	29	2	61	6
Schulhofer, Geneva	3	4	.429	3.20	14	14	2	0	0	0	81.2	71	42	29	6	8	29	1	69	6
Secrist, Welland	0	0	.000	0.00	2	0	0	2	0	0	2.1	1	0	0	0	0	0	0	0	0
Sepeda, Batavia	0	0	.000	1.11	5	5	0	0	0	0	32.1	22	7	4	0	1	9	0	31	0
Seymour, Pittsfield	0	3	.000	5.82	3	3	0	0	0	0	17.0	20	12	11	0	2	11	0	9	1
Sharts, Watertown	3	4	.429	4.34	22	4	0	7	0	0	66.1	69	37	32	5	2	30	0	50	8
Shotton, Welland	0	0	.000	27.00	1	0	0	0	0	0	0.2	1	2	2	0	0	3	0	2	0
Sides, Watertown	0	1	.000	5.14	3	3	0	0	0	0	14.0	13	11	8	1	1	10	0	7	2
C. Smith, Hamilton	4	3	.571	3.72	13	13	0	0	0	0	67.2	70	38	28	4	6	27	0	43	7
Smith, Batavia	2	5	.286	4.18	16	8	0	3	0	0	60.1	52	33	28	5	4	17	1	37	6
Smith, Watertown	3	1	.750	1.51	33	0	0	30	0	11	35.2	26	10	6	0	0	25	3	24	5
M. Smith, Hamilton	4	0	1.000	2.79	12	1	0	2	0	0	19.1	20	9	6	1	2	8	1	22	2
Stafford, Erie*	3	2	.600	2.49	13	6	0	1	0	0	43.1	39	20	12	1	8	19	0	41	3
Stark, Pittsfield	6	3	.667	2.99	15	13	3	1	0	0	93.1	82	39	31	6	3	18	0	31	2
Starks, Utica	1	1	.000	2.51	10	0	0	5	0	1	14.1	10	8	4	0	0	11	0	20	1
Steele, Jamestown	1	2	.333	4.56	13	0	0	4	0	0	25.2	26	16	13	0	0	11	2	25	1
Steenstra, Geneva	3	0	1.000	0.90	3	3	1	0	0	0	20.0	11	4	2	0	0	6	0	18	0
Stull, Jamestown	3	5	.375	5.40	14	14	0	0	0	0	63.1	52	49	38	2	3	61	0	64	18
Sutherland, Oneonta	3	0	1.000	1.15	4	1	0	1	0	0	15.2	10	2	2	1	0	2	0	16	0

Pitcher, Team	W	L	Pct.	ERA	G	GS	CG	GF	ShO	Sv.	IP	H	R	ER	HR	HB	BB	Int. BB	SO	WP
Teich, Welland*	0	0	.000	0.00	4	0	0	0	0	0	8.0	5	2	0	0	0	6	0	11	0
Tenbarge, Auburn	1	3	.250	7.30	14	6	0	3	0	0	40.2	43	38	33	4	5	27	1	28	4
Teske, Pittsfield*	1	0	1.000	4.34	11	0	0	6	0	1	18.2	27	17	9	1	1	3	0	14	0
Thibert, Oneonta	0	4	.000	3.60	21	0	0	7	0	1	50.0	43	24	20	0	3	19	0	48	7
Thomforde, Oneonta	0	0	.000	13.50	1	0	0	0	0	0	0.2	3	4	1	0	0	1	0	2	2
Townsend, Welland*	4	4	.500	1.57	28	0	0	17	0	4	51.2	35	17	9	1	4	17	3	52	6
Tranberg, Batavia	0	2	.000	8.10	11	0	0	4	0	0	20.0	23	20	18	5	2	15	1	25	4
Trinidad, Geneva	8	6	.571	2.40	15	15	2	0	0	0	93.2	78	33	25	6	4	13	2	70	1
Turrentine, Oneonta	0	0	.000	0.00	1	0	0	0	0	0	0.0	1	2	0	0	0	1	0	0	0
Underwood, Oneonta	3	6	.333	2.70	24	2	0	8	0	0	60.0	43	24	18	3	2	19	2	72	2
Verduzco, Niagara Falls	0	0	.000	2.25	5	0	0	2	0	1	8.0	4	4	2	0	0	6	0	13	2
Walker, Auburn*	4	6	.400	3.13	15	14	0	0	0	0	83.1	75	35	29	4	6	21	0	67	4
Wallace, Oneonta	8	4	.667	2.55	14	14	1	0	1	0	81.1	76	32	23	2	0	11	0	55	3
Watkins, Utica	2	3	.400	2.09	26	0	0	17	0	3	43.0	37	14	10	2	1	16	1	57	3
Watson, Pittsfield	3	3	.500	3.83	8	8	1	0	1	0	47.0	45	22	20	2	1	7	0	42	3
Westbrook, Auburn	0	3	.000	15.35	12	2	0	5	0	0	17.0	29	33	29	5	4	19	0	19	6
Whiteside, Niagara Falls*	8	4	.667	2.45	15	11	0	0	0	0	69.2	54	26	19	2	2	20	0	72	7
Whitman, Erie	6	2	.750	1.81	20	0	0	4	0	0	44.2	33	13	9	3	2	20	0	41	3
Whitten, Erie*	1	0	1.000	6.19	11	0	0	3	0	0	16.0	17	13	11	2	1	15	0	13	5
Wilkins, Welland	4	2	.667	7.29	28	1	0	8	0	1	42.0	49	38	34	2	4	24	3	42	12
Williams, Watertown*	1	0	1.000	2.20	6	6	0	0	0	0	32.2	22	15	8	2	3	9	0	29	1
Wilson, Welland	3	2	.600	1.06	13	4	0	5	0	0	42.1	27	9	5	0	0	13	1	40	1
Wiltz, Welland	0	0	.000	3.00	2	0	0	1	0	0	3.0	5	2	1	0	0	1	0	1	0
Winston, Auburn	0	0	.000	0.00	1	0	0	1	0	0	0.1	0	0	0	0	0	0	0	1	0
Worrell, Utica*	1	0	1.000	3.60	4	0	0	2	0	1	10.0	11	5	4	0	0	2	0	10	3
Wyngarden, Auburn	0	0	.000	36.00	1	0	0	1	0	0	1.0	6	4	4	0	0	0	0	1	0
Yamazaki, Niagara Falls	1	1	.500	10.80	5	0	0	1	0	0	5.0	9	7	6	0	0	5	0	2	1
York, Watertown*	2	2	.500	3.23	13	2	0	5	0	0	30.2	24	14	11	1	1	16	0	32	2
Zuber, Batavia*	0	0	.000	0.00	1	0	0	1	0	0	1.0	0	0	0	0	0	2	0	1	0

BALKS—Donahue, 12; Faltesiek, 10; Crombie, Meinershagen, Petersen, 6 each; Buddie, Carter, Mendenhall, Whiteside, 5 each; Daniel, Daniels, Holt, Klamm, Pierson, Rushworth, Sepeda, Stark, Stull, 4 each; Anderson, Doolan, Faino, Koller, S. Lawrence, Lynch, Mysel, Patterson, Perez, Potcka, Pettit, Pisciotta, F. Smith, 3 each; Antolick, Beavers, Bonilla, Bottoms, Britt, Bush, Darley, Feno, Fuller, Glaze, Hansen, Hudson, LaPlante, Largusa, MacNeil, D. Martin, Mathews, McWilliams, G. Miller, Micki, Pool, Resendez, Rhine, E. Smith, Stafford, Tenbarge, Underwood, Verduzco, Watson, Westbrook, Williams, York, 2 each; Bertotti, B. Blake, Brandow, Brumley, Bullinger, Carlyle, Cochran, Dawson, Doman, Donovan, Englehart, Fairfax, S. Ferguson, George, Gibbs, Harrison, Herrmann, Hokanson, Hurst, Inman, Jersild, C. Jones, Kendrena, Kerley, Key, Konuszewski, R. Lawrence, Leahy, Lemon, Lindemann, Lopez, Lowe, Mallory, Martinez, McDermott, McGraw, Mendoza, Mitchell, Moore, Munoz, Niles, Oehrlein, Pacheco, Pontbriant, Popoff, Pulsipher, Rodriguez, Roman, Schmidt, Schulhofer, M. Smith, Starks, Steenstra, Tranberg, Walker, Wilkins, 1 each.

COMBINATION SHUTOUTS—Dawson-Guerry, Walker-Krislock, Auburn; Mitchell-McIntyre, Batavia; Donovan-Niles, Hansen-McKinley, Hudson-Faino, Hudson-Martinez, Elmira; Donahue-Patterson, Patterson-Frazier-Pettit, Petersen-Whitman-Leahy, Erie; Daniel-Edwards, Dreyer-Jarolimek-Edwards, Rodriguez-Latimer, Trinidad-Gardner-Jarolimek, Geneva; Brumley-Bullinger-Cochran, Brumley-Cochran, Oehrlein-Smith-Jones-Cochran, Smith-Cochran, Hamilton; Gentile-Eggert, Gentile-Harrison-Schmidt, Hostetler-Harrison, Jamestown; Adams-Durussel-Munoz-Crombie, Mendenhall-Bauer, Navarro-Durussel-Bauer, Whiteside-Durussel-Bauer, Niagara Falls; Antolick-Underwood-Brown-DeJean, Antolick-Underwood-DeJean, Inman-Santiago-Ferguson, Karp-Thibert, Sutherland-Thibert-Santiago, Oneonta; Petcka-Fuller, Popoff-Jones, Pulsipher-Beckerman-Teske, Pittsfield; Crabtree-Jersild, Crabtree-Miller, Largusa-Brandow, St. Catharines; Johnston-Bertotti, Lindemann-McDermott-Watkins, Pierson-Starks, Utica; Carter-Sharts, Key-Gibbs-Smith, Najera-Sharts, Resendez-Blake, Resendez-Gibbs-Smith, Watertown; Lawrence-Mesewicz, Welland.

NO-HIT GAMES—Oehrlein, Hamilton, defeated Auburn, 7-0 (five innings), August 10.

FIELDING

TEAM

Team	Pct.	G	PO	A	E	DP	PB	Team	Pct.	G	PO	A	E	DP	PB
Hamilton	.966	76	1962	771	95	56	16	Niagara Falls	.956	78	1981	818	128	59	26
Elmira	.960	75	1980	796	115	48	14	Erie	.955	77	1967	824	131	71	21
St. Catharines	.959	75	1923	788	116	61	27	Watertown	.954	76	1935	754	130	56	16
Oneonta	.959	75	1937	806	118	54	14	Batavia	.953	75	1813	791	127	61	13
Jamestown	.959	77	1966	799	119	52	29	Geneva	.953	75	1944	845	137	56	17
Auburn	.959	73	1879	758	114	50	16	Utica	.952	74	1909	770	136	55	16
Pittsfield	.957	74	1952	842	125	52	21	Welland	.945	77	1999	806	162	47	32

INDIVIDUAL

*Throws lefthanded.

FIRST BASEMEN

Player, Team	Pct.	G	PO	A	E	DP
Allen, Jamestown	.944	2	16	1	1	1
Aurila, Jamestown*	.978	32	245	23	6	9
Bell, Niagara Falls	1.000	3	10	1	0	0
Benefiel, Jamestown	1.000	26	220	13	0	16
Boehlow, Geneva	.955	9	61	2	3	6
Boston, St. Catharines*	.979	72	646	40	15	50
Bowrosen, Utica	.982	44	348	30	7	29
Burke, Batavia	1.000	17	170	7	0	8
Carey, Elmira	1.000	3	20	4	0	2
Cherry, Batavia	.875	1	7	0	1	0
Crimmins, Elmira	.933	1	14	0	1	0
Crouwel, Batavia	1.000	5	41	3	0	6
Cruz, Batavia	.938	4	14	1	1	0
Daubach, Pittsfield	.982	67	609	44	12	42
Delvecchio, Oneonta	.984	53	445	44	8	31
Diaz, Geneva	.950	9	71	5	4	6
DiFelice, Batavia	1.000	1	6	0	0	0
DiGiacomo, Watertown	.991	30	222	7	2	17
Doucette, Hamilton*	.984	37	290	13	5	17
Doyle, Jamestown	1.000	1	6	0	0	2
Duplessis, Watertown*	.976	42	347	25	9	32

Player, Team	Pct.	G	PO	A	E	DP
Evans, Niagara Falls*	1.000	3	11	0	0	2
Fairly, Geneva	.985	25	248	10	4	15
Feeley, Niagara Falls	1.000	1	5	3	0	1
Feno, Elmira	1.000	10	65	7	0	7
Garcia, Pittsfield	.981	11	94	11	2	8
Gholston, Welland	.974	48	395	23	11	22
Gilligan, Hamilton	1.000	2	16	0	0	0
Gulan, Hamilton	1.000	2	8	0	0	1
Hairston, Watertown	1.000	6	51	9	0	3
Harmes, St. Catharines	1.000	2	18	1	0	1
Jones, Welland*	.951	5	37	2	2	5
KILLEN, Niagara Falls	.98998	68	552	35	6	37
Luke, Oneonta*	.978	22	170	12	4	11
Malave, Elmira	.992	28	245	17	2	14
Martin, Hamilton	.986	26	209	7	3	19
Martinez, Niagara Falls	.833	2	5	0	1	1
Martinez, Auburn	.979	20	183	4	4	15
Moore, Elmira	.992	40	328	27	3	19
Murphy, Hamilton	.978	16	121	5	0	12
Norton, Jamestown	.978	25	213	7	5	18
Nutting, Geneva	.987	22	216	12	3	12
Parker, Niagara Falls*	.990	17	93	9	1	7
Pridy, Erie*	.98996	75	652	38	7	56
Probst, Hamilton	.967	17	142	5	5	5
Querecuto, St. Catharines	1.000	2	9	0	0	2

Player, Team	Pct.	G	PO	A	E	DP
Rich, Utica	.971	23	186	14	6	15
Sallee, Batavia	.988	37	313	24	4	28
Taylor, Erie	1.000	8	40	1	0	2
Valdez, Geneva*	.982	17	156	7	3	10
Vinas, Utica	.978	10	85	5	2	6
Wiltz, Welland	.990	35	278	14	3	17
Winslow, Auburn	1.000	24	173	22	0	12
Winston, Auburn	.965	16	133	6	5	10
Zuber, Batavia*	.980	14	132	16	3	12

SECOND BASEMEN

Player, Team	Pct.	G	PO	A	E	DP
Black, Hamilton	.979	11	18	29	1	4
Cardenas, Watertown	.935	59	111	148	18	26
Cervantes, Erie	.900	2	2	7	1	2
Choate, St. Catharines	.917	6	8	14	2	3
Colon, Welland	.769	5	3	7	3	1
Craig, Geneva	1.000	2	1	2	0	0
DeJesus, Niagara Falls	.969	17	26	37	2	4
Espinosa, Welland	1.000	3	4	10	0	0
Evans, Utica	.896	26	50	71	14	13
Farrell, Pittsfield	.900	2	3	6	1	2
Fleming, Oneonta	1.000	3	8	7	0	1
Flores, Pittsfield	.904	14	20	27	5	3
Gamble, Erie	.930	30	46	74	9	12
Garcia, Pittsfield	.967	29	58	89	5	13
Gilligan, Hamilton	1.000	2	8	5	0	4
Gomez, Batavia	.948	59	105	185	16	31
Hand, Welland	.952	4	10	10	1	2
Henry, St. Catharines	.958	70	136	181	14	37
Hernandez, Pittsfield	.939	34	59	94	10	16
HINDS, Oneonta	.978	65	143	163	7	33
Humes, Welland	.900	8	10	26	4	2
Johnston, Welland	.875	6	10	11	3	3
Juday, Elmira	.981	29	68	85	3	20
Kostrzewa, Watertown	.750	1	0	3	1	0
Kratz, Batavia	.939	11	20	26	3	8
Lane, Jamestown	.964	32	47	86	5	9
Larson, Auburn	.952	6	10	10	1	2
Long, Oneonta	.959	10	18	29	2	4
Lynch, Utica	.943	38	68	80	9	18
Martinez, Niagara Falls	.833	6	4	6	2	4
McDonald, Utica	.959	14	22	25	2	8
Mitchell, Auburn	.976	68	125	199	8	34
Moore, Elmira	.692	2	5	4	4	1
North, Erie	.813	3	4	9	3	3
O'Donnell, Elmira	.980	32	53	93	3	8
Ollison, Batavia	.800	1	0	4	1	0
Owens, Hamilton	.951	41	56	98	8	16
Penn, Niagara Falls	.947	67	107	160	15	27
Peterson, Geneva	.800	1	2	6	2	1
Ritz, Hamilton	.992	26	42	75	1	13
Rundels, Jamestown	.929	50	76	106	14	22
Sanford, Welland	.950	51	65	142	11	24
Selby, Elmira	.963	14	36	41	3	9
Sylvestri, Erie	.957	9	17	27	2	7
Torres, Erie	.963	36	74	109	7	28
Tovar, Jamestown	1.000	2	5	3	0	0
Tredaway, Geneva	.956	52	67	170	11	32
Trujillo, Geneva	.912	22	34	59	9	9
Zapata, Welland	.900	5	11	7	2	3
Zollars, Watertown	.948	16	25	48	4	5

THIRD BASEMEN

Player, Team	Pct.	G	PO	A	E	DP
Austin, Welland	.944	8	4	13	1	0
Bowrosen, Utica	.846	7	2	9	2	0
Bradley, Geneva	.847	48	29	76	19	6
Burke, Batavia	.810	27	17	51	16	4
Cervantes, Erie	1.000	4	0	2	0	0
Chandler, St. Catharines	1.000	3	1	0	0	0
Cherry, Batavia	.862	11	11	14	4	1
Choate, St. Catharines	.913	63	42	116	15	11
Colon, Welland	.667	2	0	2	1	0
Coolbaugh, St. Catharines	.846	8	7	15	4	3
Craig, Geneva	.724	8	4	17	8	0
Cranford, Welland	.895	24	14	54	8	5
Crouwel, Batavia	.833	3	2	8	2	0
Diaz, Geneva	.737	6	2	12	5	0
Elliott, Auburn	.885	54	27	89	15	8
Feeley, Niagara Falls	.893	71	42	158	24	5
Fermin, Niagara Falls	.500	1	1	0	1	0
Gilligan, Hamilton	.886	20	8	23	4	0
Gulan, Hamilton	.934	60	43	113	11	7
Hand, Welland	.800	5	1	7	2	0
Hernandez, Pittsfield	1.000	3	3	5	0	0
Hughes, Erie	1.000	1	1	1	0	0
Humes, Erie	.375	3	1	2	5	1
Juday, Elmira	.806	13	7	22	7	3

Player, Team	Pct.	G	PO	A	E	DP
Kantor, Watertown	.917	10	9	13	2	0
Killen, Niagara Falls	1.000	4	0	6	0	0
Kozeniewski, Oneonta	.890	74	51	143	24	14
Kratz, Batavia	.896	22	19	41	7	6
Lane, Jamestown	.913	7	4	17	2	0
Larson, Auburn	.636	3	3	4	4	0
Long, Oneonta	.500	1	0	1	1	0
Lucca, Erie	.906	75	56	175	24	17
Lynch, Utica	.875	6	2	5	1	0
Maize, Welland	.000	1	0	0	1	0
Martinez, Niagara Falls	.750	7	6	12	6	1
Martinez, Auburn	.911	19	13	28	4	1
McCloughan, St. Catharines	.800	3	3	1	1	0
Moore, Elmira	.813	10	6	20	6	2
North, Erie	.833	4	1	4	1	0
Nutting, Geneva	1.000	2	0	4	0	2
Ortiz, Elmira	1.000	3	4	4	0	0
Querecuto, St. Catharines	.833	3	1	4	1	0
Raleigh, Jamestown	.918	72	55	124	16	8
Sallee, Batavia	.868	15	12	21	5	5
Saunders, Pittsfield	.921	72	56	130	16	7
Secrist, Welland	.894	34	30	54	10	3
Selby, Elmira	.913	51	39	97	13	8
Snopek, Utica	.944	67	46	140	11	18
TAYLOR, Watertown	.947	53	41	84	7	4
Tooch, Welland	.828	9	9	15	5	2
Tredaway, Geneva	.775	12	10	21	9	0
Zollars, Watertown	.857	14	13	23	6	1

SHORTSTOPS

Player, Team	Pct.	G	PO	A	E	DP
Alfonzo, Pittsfield	.933	71	126	237	26	39
Benbow, St. Catharines	.950	49	70	140	11	23
Carey, Elmira	.897	51	62	130	22	12
Cervantes, Erie	.921	31	53	75	11	21
Chandler, St. Catharines	.897	26	29	75	12	9
Colon, Welland	.778	1	3	4	2	2
Cranford, Welland	.860	25	33	65	16	9
DeJesus, Niagara Falls	.933	52	70	124	14	31
Evans, Utica	.800	2	5	3	2	2
Fermin, Niagara Falls	.955	28	32	53	4	10
Filosa, Utica	.899	59	65	149	24	21
Fisher, Batavia	.940	21	18	61	5	10
Flores, Pittsfield	1.000	2	2	4	0	0
Garcia, Pittsfield	1.000	2	1	5	0	0
George, Watertown	.921	63	100	168	23	34
Gilligan, Hamilton	1.000	1	0	2	0	0
Hand, Welland	.923	5	8	16	2	2
Humes, Welland	.907	18	15	34	5	4
Johns, Hamilton	.929	69	106	183	22	32
Juday, Elmira	.944	20	28	56	5	10
Knowles, Oneonta	.907	58	75	159	24	21
Kratz, Batavia	.892	19	22	36	7	5
Lane, Jamestown	.949	11	14	23	2	8
Larson, Auburn	.892	11	13	20	4	4
Long, Oneonta	.906	19	29	48	8	4
Martinez, Niagara Falls	.762	10	5	11	5	1
North, Erie	.895	11	12	39	6	4
O'Donnell, Elmira	1.000	1	1	1	0	1
Ollison, Batavia	.908	18	20	59	8	7
Ortiz, Elmira	.950	5	8	11	1	3
PETERSON, Geneva	.960	70	117	218	14	36
Polidor, Utica	.947	16	18	36	3	7
Raleigh, Jamestown	1.000	1	0	1	0	0
Ritz, Hamilton	.848	9	11	17	5	4
Sallee, Batavia	.904	19	34	51	9	8
Sanford, Welland	.875	8	5	23	4	1
Santana, Auburn	.924	62	78	166	20	28
Smith, Geneva	1.000	1	1	2	0	0
Snopek, Utica	1.000	8	2	11	0	5
Sylvestri, Erie	.911	35	44	79	12	16
Tooch, Welland	.886	24	42	51	12	11
Torres, Erie	.700	3	8	6	6	0
Tovar, Jamestown	.931	69	94	175	20	26
Tredaway, Geneva	.864	4	4	15	3	2
Zapata, Welland	.923	4	4	8	1	2
Zollars, Watertown	.895	14	21	30	6	4

OUTFIELDERS

Player, Team	Pct.	G	PO	A	E	DP
Aubel, Auburn*	.951	57	91	6	5	0
Beamon, Welland	1.000	19	38	1	0	0
Bellum, Hamilton	.975	73	115	4	3	0
Benefiel, Jamestown	1.000	2	3	0	0	0
Benitez, Jamestown	.984	37	61	2	1	1
Black, Hamilton	1.000	2	2	1	0	1
Blanton, Hamilton	.875	5	6	1	1	1
Bogan, Welland	.966	52	84	2	3	0
Brown, Erie	.952	72	116	4	6	1
Bryant, Watertown	.919	62	72	7	7	2
Zuber, Batavia*	1.000	8	16	1	0	0

Player, Team	Pct.	G	PO	A	E	DP
Cameron, Utica	1.000	27	60	3	0	0
Campbell, St. Catharines	.946	37	35	0	2	0
Canton, Elmira	.952	30	40	0	2	0
Cappuccio, Utica	.971	21	31	2	1	1
Chandler, St. Catharines	1.000	1	1	0	0	0
Chisum, Watertown	1.000	22	24	1	0	0
Clark, Niagara Falls	1.000	15	18	1	0	0
Clem, Erie*	1.000	15	24	1	0	1
Coleman, Watertown	.944	14	15	2	1	1
Collier, Elmira	.907	50	86	2	9	1
Coolbaugh, St. Catharines	1.000	5	9	1	0	0
Cordova, Erie*	.968	45	57	4	2	1
Cumberbatch, Oneonta	1.000	8	13	1	0	0
Davis, Elmira	.944	20	34	0	2	0
Delafield, Oneonta	1.000	7	11	1	0	0
Delos Santos, Batavia	.924	43	56	5	5	2
Demoss, Geneva*	.962	31	50	1	2	1
Dickerson, Niagara Falls*	.900	11	9	0	1	0
Dreifort, Jamestown	.951	62	72	6	4	1
Epps, Oneonta	1.000	5	5	0	0	0
Espinosa, Welland	.950	56	113	4	6	0
Feeley, Niagara Falls	1.000	2	1	0	0	0
Feno, Elmira	.944	20	31	3	2	0
Freehling, Erie*	1.000	15	19	4	0	0
French, Hamilton	.934	54	66	5	5	0
Gamble, Erie	1.000	7	10	1	0	0
Greene, Niagara Falls	.917	25	30	3	3	0
Hacopian, Watertown	1.000	4	4	1	0	0
Harris, Utica	1.000	8	13	0	0	0
Hawkins, Oneonta	.928	70	125	4	10	1
Hence, Watertown	.929	43	73	6	6	0
Henderson, Hamilton	.933	22	25	3	2	2
Higginbotham, Niagara Falls*	1.000	7	10	0	0	0
Higginson, Niagara Falls	.983	67	109	5	2	1
Hines, St. Catharines	.857	14	17	1	3	0
Hunt, Welland	.955	33	38	4	2	0
Hurst, Utica	.935	52	81	6	6	0
Jennings, Geneva*	.963	68	96	9	4	2
Johnson, Elmira	.938	29	44	1	3	0
Johnson, Batavia	1.000	11	15	0	0	0
Jordan, Hamilton	.981	67	100	5	2	2
Keister, Pittsfield*	.978	30	41	4	1	1
Kelley, Welland	1.000	2	2	1	0	1
Kessinger, Geneva	.933	70	93	4	7	1
Kimsey, Niagara Falls	1.000	2	2	0	0	0
Ladd, St. Catharines	.938	41	57	3	4	1
Lee, Jamestown	.750	3	2	1	1	0
Long, Oneonta*	.955	43	60	4	3	0
Luke, Oneonta*	.984	41	60	2	1	0
Lussier, Welland	.984	70	123	3	2	0
Madsen, Geneva*	.957	35	61	5	3	0
Malave, Elmira	.750	7	3	0	1	0
Martinez, Niagara Falls	.968	65	149	3	5	1
Mathews, Utica	.988	37	78	2	1	0
Mayberry, Watertown	.975	47	76	2	2	0
McCloughan, St. Catharines	.923	30	35	1	3	1
Minnich, Auburn*	.932	27	37	4	3	0
Mora, Pittsfield	.950	62	92	3	5	0
Murphy, Batavia	.946	17	31	4	2	1
Northrup, Jamestown	1.000	16	8	2	0	0
Norton, Jamestown	.949	64	146	2	8	1
Nunnally, Watertown	1.000	2	3	0	0	0
O'Donnell, Elmira	1.000	8	14	0	0	0
Ogden, Utica	.944	57	80	5	5	1
Pagano, Niagara Falls	.943	40	64	2	4	0
Poe, Utica	.933	13	13	1	1	0
Querecuto, St. Catharines	1.000	12	16	0	0	0
Quillin, Pittsfield	.979	62	138	4	3	2
Rhein, Auburn*	1.000	1	1	0	0	0
Ritz, Hamilton	.981	62	94	7	2	2
Roberts, St. Catharines	1.000	32	36	3	0	1
Robertson, Jamestown	.977	39	42	1	1	0
Robinson, Hamilton	1.000	4	7	0	0	0
Robinson, Erie	1.000	4	6	0	0	0
Rossler, Pittsfield	.857	30	24	0	4	0
Rundels, Jamestown	.965	28	52	3	2	1
Samuels, Erie	.990	52	96	1	1	0
Scott, Elmira	.989	57	92	2	1	0
Sheff, Erie	1.000	8	10	1	0	1
Shotton, Welland	.925	56	73	1	6	0
D. Smith, Pittsfield	.992	65	115	2	1	0
J. Smith, Pittsfield	1.000	7	9	1	0	1
Solomon, Batavia*	.962	56	94	7	4	2
Steverson, St. Catharines	1.000	63	83	8	0	2
SUPLEE, Oneonta	.945	57	99	5	6	0
Thomas, Auburn*	.929	18	25	1	2	0
Thompson, Auburn	1.000	19	24	1	0	0
Tillman, Geneva	.902	40	54	1	6	0
Valdez, Geneva*	.867	9	12	1	2	0
Ventura, Utica	.949	24	33	4	2	2
Vilet, Batavia	.962	19	22	3	1	0
White, Jamestown	.990	61	100	1	1	0
Wills, Batavia	.909	7	8	2	1	0
Winston, Auburn	.974	31	35	2	1	0
Yaroshuk, Oneonta	1.000	1	1	0	0	0
Zollars, Watertown						

CATCHERS

Player, Team	Pct.	G	PO	A	E	DP	PB
Allen, Jamestown	.978	50	352	52	9	1	15
Arntzen, Watertown	.993	36	248	23	2	1	9
Bell, Niagara Falls	.984	24	156	24	3	1	10
Benefiel, Jamestown	1.000	2	9	1	0	0	3
BENNETT, Batavia	.994	44	292	42	2	2	8
Boka, Welland	.982	18	102	8	2	0	8
Campillo, Jamestown	1.000	14	98	7	0	2	4
Cannaday, Welland	.975	15	110	8	3	1	1
Carey, Elmira	.923	2	9	3	1	0	0
Crimmins, Elmira	.989	27	170	12	2	2	5
Crouwel, Batavia	1.000	3	16	1	0	0	2
Cruz, Batavia	.895	2	15	2	2	0	0
Diaz, Pittsfield	.969	55	354	56	13	1	11
DiFelice, Hamilton	.967	15	129	19	5	3	3
Epps, Oneonta	1.000	3	4	0	0	0	0
Fairly, Geneva	.929	7	36	3	3	0	1
Garcia, Pittsfield	.964	23	170	20	7	0	10
Gousha, Erie	.979	20	164	26	4	1	5
Harmes, St. Catharines	.981	36	279	28	6	1	7
Hopp, Batavia	.985	26	173	26	3	3	3
Hubbard, Geneva	.986	47	325	27	5	2	7
Ladd, St. Catharines	.975	24	166	29	5	1	12
Leshnock, Oneonta	.980	51	395	53	9	5	8
Lidle, Niagara Falls	.979	56	350	64	9	7	6
Lockhart, Watertown	.966	20	128	15	5	1	4
Machado, Utica	.963	40	279	30	12	2	10
Maize, Welland	.972	31	189	16	6	3	11
Martin, Elmira	.980	12	84	16	2	2	3
McCubbin, Jamestown	.946	6	44	9	3	0	2
Milne, Hamilton	.991	23	198	22	2	3	5
Moore, Watertown	.989	13	82	10	1	1	1
Morales, Geneva	.993	19	116	19	1	1	8
Murphy, Hamilton	.990	40	330	51	4	1	8
Norton, Jamestown	.992	18	111	18	1	1	5
Probst, Auburn	.996	37	254	30	1	1	7
Querecuto, St. Catharines	.985	19	113	21	2	2	8
Robson, Niagara Falls	1.000	2	11	5	0	0	2
Sanchez, Oneonta	.925	4	31	6	3	0	1
Senkowitz, Elmira	.992	24	118	14	1	0	6
Shelton, Oneonta	.980	22	175	24	4	1	6
Skeels, Erie	.986	57	374	40	6	3	15
Smith, Elmira	.985	30	170	21	3	0	5
Stahlhoefer, Welland	.986	25	190	22	3	0	12
Stojsavljevic, Geneva	.965	9	52	3	2	1	1
Taylor, Erie	1.000	5	11	0	0	0	1
Timko, Niagara Falls	.990	20	92	5	1	0	8
Tremie, Utica	.977	6	37	5	1	0	1
Tucker, Watertown	.954	16	90	14	5	1	2
Vinas, Utica	.974	35	235	32	7	2	5
Winston, Auburn	.979	31	248	34	6	3	2
Wyngarden, Auburn	1.000	7	43	10	0	1	7

PITCHERS

Player, Team	Pct.	G	PO	A	E	DP
Adams, Niagara Falls	1.000	8	3	7	0	0
Adkins, St. Catharines	.667	14	0	2	1	0
Anderson, Batavia	.909	14	5	5	2	0
Antolick, Oneonta	1.000	14	10	16	0	0
Ban, Niagara Falls	1.000	5	1	2	0	0
Bauer, Niagara Falls*	.867	31	3	10	2	0
Beckerman, Pittsfield	1.000	21	3	7	0	1
Berlin, Niagara Falls	1.000	6	6	2	0	0
Bertotti, Utica*	.786	17	2	9	3	0
Bjornson, Auburn*	.750	5	1	2	1	0
Blake, Hamilton*	1.000	1	1	0	0	0
Blake, Watertown	.900	13	2	7	1	2
Bojcun, Batavia	1.000	6	1	2	0	0
Boldt, Batavia	1.000	9	0	3	0	1
Bonilla, Welland	.813	30	3	10	3	0
Boone, Hamilton	1.000	4	0	2	0	0
Bottoms, Auburn*	.900	9	2	7	1	0
Brandow, St. Catharines	1.000	22	4	9	0	1
Britt, Hamilton	.875	19	2	5	1	1
Brown, Oneonta*	1.000	9	0	1	0	0
Brumley, Hamilton	1.000	9	3	5	0	0
Buddie, Oneonta	.895	13	5	12	2	0
Bullinger, Hamilton	.833	35	3	12	3	0
Bush, Elmira	.667	15	4	4	4	0
Buzard, Watertown*	1.000	3	0	1	0	0
Carlyle, Niagara Falls	1.000	1	0	1	0	0
Carter, 3 Wel. - 13 Wat.	.931	16	8	19	2	1
Cindrich, Oneonta	.500	2	0	1	1	0
Cochran, Hamilton	1.000	37	0	2	0	0
Cornett, St. Catharines	1.000	25	3	6	0	0
Correa, Auburn	1.000	6	1	1	0	0
Corry, Hamilton	.778	9	2	5	2	0
Crabtree, St. Catharines	.903	12	7	21	3	0
Crombie, Niagara Falls	1.000	30	2	4	0	1
Cupit, Auburn	.875	19	0	7	1	0
Daniel, Geneva	.969	18	6	25	1	3
Daniels, St. Catharines	.857	17	6	6	2	2
Dark, Geneva*	.800	7	0	4	1	0
Darley, St. Catharines	.931	16	10	17	2	2

Player, Team	Pct.	G	PO	A	E	DP
Dawson, Auburn	.800	17	2	10	3	1
DeGrasse, Hamilton	1.000	24	3	5	0	0
DeJean, Oneonta	1.000	20	2	0	0	0
Doman, St. Catharines	.944	15	6	11	1	1
Donahue, Erie	.700	15	4	3	3	0
Donovan, Elmira*	1.000	19	3	15	0	0
Doolan, Batavia	.846	19	6	16	4	1
Dreyer, Geneva	1.000	13	6	10	0	0
Durussel, Niagara Falls	.882	33	6	9	2	1
Edwards, Geneva*	.857	25	2	4	1	0
Edwards, Batavia	1.000	3	0	2	0	0
Eggert, Jamestown*	1.000	30	3	9	0	0
Elsbernd, Oneonta	1.000	3	1	0	0	0
Englehart, Erie	.667	7	1	1	1	0
Faino, Elmira*	.875	20	4	3	1	0
Fairfax, Welland	1.000	7	2	5	0	0
Falteisek, Jamestown	.853	15	8	21	5	0
H. Ferguson, Oneonta	1.000	13	3	2	0	0
Ferguson, Jamestown	.800	23	1	3	1	0
Frazier, Erie	.875	21	3	4	1	1
Fronio, Watertown	1.000	5	2	0	0	0
Fuller, Pittsfield	.700	26	3	4	3	0
Gajkowski, Utica	.923	29	2	10	1	0
Garcia-Luna, Welland	.875	15	2	26	4	1
Gardner, Geneva	.500	10	2	1	3	0
Gay, Utica*	.800	4	2	2	1	0
Gentile, Jamestown	1.000	13	3	6	0	0
George, Pittsfield*	.857	18	2	4	1	0
Gibbs, Watertown	.875	29	1	6	1	0
Glaze, Elmira	.920	18	8	15	2	0
Guerry, Auburn*	.700	19	4	3	3	0
Gustavson, Geneva	1.000	6	1	3	0	0
Hansen, Elmira	.882	13	7	8	2	0
Harrison, Jamestown	.933	14	4	10	1	1
Hassel, Geneva	1.000	1	0	3	0	0
Heisler, Batavia	1.000	3	0	2	0	0
Henderson, Jamestown	1.000	1	0	1	0	1
Herrholz, Utica	.889	15	2	6	1	0
Herrmann, Batavia*	1.000	11	2	11	0	1
Hokanson, Pittsfield	.850	13	5	12	3	0
Holleday, Auburn	.667	6	0	2	1	0
Holt, Auburn	.957	14	7	15	1	3
Hostetler, Jamestown*	.000	1	0	0	1	0
Hudson, Elmira	1.000	19	5	19	0	1
Hurst, Hamilton	1.000	3	1	2	0	0
Inman, Oneonta	.917	15	11	11	2	2
Irwin, Batavia	.850	18	6	11	3	2
Jarolimek, Geneva	1.000	23	3	14	0	1
Jersild, St. Catharines*	.778	22	3	4	2	1
Jewell, Watertown	.750	5	1	2	1	0
Johnson, Watertown	1.000	2	1	0	0	0
Johnston, Utica*	1.000	14	3	13	0	0
Jones, Pittsfield*	.750	20	2	1	1	0
Jones, Hamilton	.833	33	0	5	1	1
Karp, Oneonta*	.955	14	3	18	1	0
Kendrena, Erie	1.000	22	3	14	0	0
Kerley, Geneva	.947	23	4	14	1	0
Key, Watertown	.923	10	3	9	1	0
Klamm, Welland*	1.000	12	4	2	0	0
Koller, Watertown	.900	15	1	8	1	1
Konuszewski, Welland	1.000	2	0	4	0	0
Krislock, Auburn	.800	26	2	6	2	0
LaPlante, Welland	.909	11	4	16	2	0
Largusa, St. Catharines*	1.000	10	2	13	0	0
Latimer, Geneva	.667	6	0	2	1	0
Lawrence, Elmira	.929	15	4	9	1	0
Lawrence, Welland*	.778	15	1	13	4	0
Leahy, Erie	.900	26	1	8	1	0
Lemon, Erie	.933	17	3	11	1	2
Lindemann, Utica*	.963	17	8	18	1	4
Lopez, Niagara Falls	.917	14	6	5	1	0
Lowe, Hamilton	.833	5	1	4	1	0
Lynch, Erie	1.000	7	1	7	0	0
Lyons, Pittsfield	.941	10	8	8	1	1
MacNeil, Erie	1.000	9	0	4	0	0
Magrini, Niagara Falls	1.000	1	1	0	0	0
Mallory, St. Catharines	1.000	11	6	9	0	1
Martin, Niagara Falls	1.000	7	1	0	0	0
Martinez, Elmira*	.941	17	4	12	1	0
Mathews, Hamilton	.955	14	6	15	1	1
Matthews, Watertown*	1.000	2	1	3	0	1
McDermott, Utica	.857	19	2	4	1	0
McGraw, Utica	.889	13	4	12	2	0
McIntyre, Batavia*	.833	21	1	4	1	0
McKinley, Elmira	1.000	23	4	5	0	0
McWilliams, Batavia	.750	22	3	3	2	0
Meinershagen, St. Catharines	.833	11	5	5	2	0
Mendenhall, Niagara Falls	.947	14	6	12	1	0
Mendoza, Erie	.778	15	3	11	4	1
Mesewicz, Welland*	1.000	29	2	13	0	0
Milius, Hamilton*	1.000	7	0	2	0	0
Miller, St. Catharines	.750	19	2	1	1	0
Mitchell, Batavia	.923	10	4	8	1	0
Mlicki, Auburn	.957	14	8	14	1	0
Moore, Utica	.923	14	3	9	1	1
Morones, Geneva	.857	11	0	6	1	0
Munoz, Niagara Falls	.933	21	6	8	1	0
Mysel, Niagara Falls	.917	12	1	10	1	1
Najera, Watertown*	.923	15	1	11	1	0
Navarro, Niagara Falls*	.889	13	2	6	1	1
Neilson, Watertown*	.833	5	1	4	1	1
Nevill, Batavia*	1.000	12	0	4	0	0
Niles, Elmira	1.000	21	2	5	0	0
Nuttle, Welland	.000	18	0	0	2	0
Oehrlein, Hamilton*	1.000	13	2	7	0	0
Pacheco, Jamestown	.818	16	3	6	2	0
Page, Batavia	1.000	3	1	3	0	0
Patterson, Erie	.917	18	3	8	1	0
Perez, Welland	1.000	21	2	12	0	1
Petcka, Pittsfield	.733	12	2	9	4	0
Petersen, Erie	.867	14	3	10	2	3
Pettit, Erie	.000	22	0	0	2	0
Pierson, Utica*	.905	15	4	15	2	0
Pisciotta, Jamestown	.857	14	8	16	4	1
Pontbriant, Welland*	1.000	4	0	4	0	0
Pool, Oneonta*	1.000	25	2	7	0	0
Popoff, Pittsfield	1.000	4	1	2	0	0
Pulsipher, Pittsfield*	.944	14	8	26	2	2
Raffo, Niagara Falls	.400	26	0	2	3	0
Rapaglia, Auburn	1.000	20	4	10	0	1
Resendez, Watertown	.850	15	5	12	3	2
Rhine, Auburn	1.000	8	2	3	0	0
Rideau, Watertown	.750	7	1	2	1	0
Rodriguez, Geneva	1.000	14	3	12	0	0
Roman, Erie*	.167	4	1	0	5	0
Rushworth, Jamestown	1.000	20	6	9	0	0
Sample, Erie	1.000	5	2	0	0	0
Santiago, Oneonta	1.000	23	5	2	0	0
Schmidt, Jamestown	.900	29	1	17	2	1
Schulhofer, Geneva	.870	14	7	13	3	1
Sepeda, Batavia	1.000	5	2	7	0	2
Seymour, Pittsfield	.833	3	1	4	1	0
Sharts, Watertown	.929	22	4	9	1	1
Shotton, Welland	1.000	1	0	1	0	0
Sides, Watertown	1.000	3	0	1	0	0
C. Smith, Hamilton	.905	13	5	14	2	3
Smith, Batavia	.867	16	7	6	2	0
Smith, Watertown	.929	33	4	9	1	2
M. Smith, Hamilton	.857	12	1	5	1	0
Stafford, Erie*	1.000	13	1	8	0	0
STARK, Pittsfield	1.000	15	13	17	0	0
Starks, Utica	1.000	10	1	3	0	0
Steele, Jamestown	1.000	13	1	2	0	0
Steenstra, Geneva	.778	3	2	5	2	0
Stull, Jamestown	.833	14	5	10	3	0
Sutherland, Oneonta	.500	4	1	0	1	0
Teich, Welland*	1.000	4	0	1	0	0
Tenbarge, Auburn	.933	14	2	12	1	0
Teske, Pittsfield*	1.000	11	0	2	0	0
Thibert, Oneonta	1.000	21	5	8	0	0
Townsend, Welland*	.923	28	3	9	1	0
Tranberg, Batavia	1.000	11	1	0	0	0
Trinidad, Geneva	.968	15	7	23	1	3
Underwood, Oneonta	1.000	24	6	8	0	1
Verduzco, Niagara Falls	.500	5	1	1	2	0
Walker, Auburn*	.952	15	2	18	1	0
Wallace, Oneonta	.889	14	6	10	2	0
Watkins, Utica	.714	26	1	4	2	0
Watson, Pittsfield	1.000	8	2	6	0	0
Westbrook, Auburn	.750	12	1	2	1	0
Whiteside, Niagara Falls*	1.000	15	5	5	0	0
Whitman, Erie	1.000	20	2	6	0	1
Whitten, Erie*	1.000	11	0	2	0	0
Wilkins, Welland	.824	28	4	10	3	1
Williams, Watertown*	1.000	6	0	10	0	0
Wilson, Welland	.923	13	3	9	1	1
Worrell, Utica*	1.000	1	0	3	0	0
Yamazaki, Niagara Falls	.500	5	0	1	1	1
York, Watertown*	.500	13	0	1	1	1

The following players did not have any fielding statistics at the positions indicated or appeared only as a designated hitter, pinch-hitter or pinch-runner: Agostinelli, p; Allen, of; Beavers, p; Benefiel, 3b; Canton, p; Cardenas, p; Chisum, 2b, 3b; T. Davis, pr; DeJesus, 3b; Epps, 3b; M. Evans, p; Feno, p; S. Ferguson, p; Ford, p; Greene, p; J. Henderson, dh; T. Henderson, p; W. Johnson, 2b; Juday, 1b; Kermode, p; Killen, p; A. Martin, p; Mejias, p; E. Miller, p; Mrowka, 2b; Mumma, dh; Pagano, p; Penn, 3b, ss; Pettit, p; Rich, ss; A. Robinson, p; Santana, 3b; Secrist, of, p; Sullivan, of; Thomforde, p; Tooch, 2b; Turrentine, p; Wiltz, p; Winston, p; Wuerch, of; Wyngarden, p; Zuber, p.

LEAGUE CHAMPIONS

Year	Team	Pct.	Year	Team	Pct.	Year	Team	Pct.
1939—	Olean*	.631	1960—	Erie	.643	1979—	Geneva	.725
1940—	Olean*	.625		Wellsville (2nd)†	.535		Oneonta z	.618
1941—	Jamestown	.618	1961—	Geneva	.616	1980—	Oneonta y	.662
	Bradford (2nd)†	.549		Olean (4th)†	.512		Geneva	.649
1942—	Jamestown*	.672	1962—	Jamestown	.580	1981—	Oneonta y	.658
1943—	Lockport	.591		Auburn (3rd)†	.521		Jamestown	.649
	Wellsville (3rd)†	.532	1963—	Auburn	.585	1982—	Oneonta	.566
1944—	Lockport	.608		Batavia (3rd)†	.485		Niagara Falls y	.553
	Jamestown (2nd)†	.565	1964—	Auburn§	.622	1983—	Utica y	.649
1945—	Batavia*	.677	1965—	Binghamton	.677		Newark	.649
1946—	Jamestown‡	.672		Binghamton	.607	1984—	Newark	.622
	Batavia‡	.672	1966—	Auburn x	.620		Little Falls y	.587
1947—	Jamestown*	.690		Binghamton	.646	1985—	Oneonta*	.705
1948—	Lockport*	.603	1967—	Auburn	.667		Auburn	.603
1949—	Bradford*	.635	1968—	Auburn	.645	1986—	Oneonta	.766
1950—	Hornell	.653		Oneonta (2nd)*	.558		St. Catharines z	.632
	Olean (2nd)†	.568	1969—	Oneonta	.662	1987—	Geneva y	.632
1951—	Olean	.622	1970—	Auburn	.623		Watertown	.579
	Hornell (3rd)†	.568	1971—	Oneonta	.662	1988—	Oneonta y	.632
1952—	Hamilton	.659	1972—	Niagara Falls	.686		Jamestown	.618
	Jamestown (2nd)†	.643	1973—	Auburn	.667	1989—	Pittsfield	.697
1953—	Jamestown*	.704	1974—	Oneonta	.768		Jamestown y	.579
1954—	Corning*	.621	1975—	Newark	.688	1990—	Oneonta a	.667
1955—	Hamilton*	.656		Newark	.714		Geneva	.662
1956—	Wellsville*	.617	1976—	Elmira	.727	1991—	Pittsfield	.662
1957—	Wellsville	.632		Elmira	.703		Jamestown a	.654
	Erie (2nd)†	.598	1977—	Oneonta y	.671	1992—	Hamilton	.737
1958—	Wellsville	.556		Batavia	.600		Geneva b	.547
	Geneva (2nd)†	.548	1978—	Oneonta	.729			
1959—	Wellsville†	.635		Geneva z	.718			

*Won championship and four-club playoff. †Won four-club playoff. ‡Jamestown and Batavia declared co-champions; Batavia defeated Jamestown in final of four-club playoff. §Won championship and two-club playoff. xWon split-season playoff. yLeague divided into Eastern and Western Divisions; won playoff. zLeague divided into Wrigley and Yawkey Divisions; won playoff. aLeague divided into Eastern, Western and Stedler divisions; won playoff. bLeague divided into McNamara, Pinckney and Stedler divisions; won playoff. (NOTE—Known as Pennsylvania-Ontario-New York League from 1939 through 1956.)

NORTHWEST LEAGUE

FINAL STANDINGS

NORTHERN DIVISION

Team	W	L	T	Pct.	GB
Bellingham (Mariners)	43	33	0	.566	....
Yakima (Dodgers)	36	40	0	.474	7
Everett (Giants)	35	41	0	.461	8
Spokane (Padres)	32	44	0	.421	11

SOUTHERN DIVISION

Team	W	L	T	Pct.	GB
Bend (Rockies)	43	33	0	.566	....
Boise (Angels)	40	36	0	.526	3
Southern Oregon (Athletics)	39	37	0	.513	4
Eugene (Royals)	36	40	0	.474	7

COMPOSITE

Team	Bend	Bel.	Boi.	S.O.	Yak.	Eug.	Ever.	Spo.	W	L	T	Pct.	GB
Bend (Rockies)	...	4	8	9	5	6	6	5	43	33	0	.566	....
Bellingham (Mariners)	6	...	3	5	8	7	7	7	43	33	0	.566	....
Boise (Angels)	4	7	...	7	6	6	4	6	40	36	0	.526	3
Southern Oregon (Athletics)	3	5	5	...	4	7	8	7	39	37	0	.513	4
Yakima (Dodgers)	5	4	4	6	...	3	7	7	36	40	0	.474	7
Eugene (Royals)	6	3	6	5	7	...	4	5	36	40	0	.474	7
Everett (Giants)	4	5	6	2	5	6	...	7	35	41	0	.461	8
Spokane (Padres)	5	5	4	3	5	5	5	...	32	44	0	.421	11

Southern Oregon played home games in Medford and Cline Falls.

Major league affiliations in parentheses.

Playoffs—Bellingham defeated Bend, two games to none, to win league championship.

Regular-season attendance—Bellingham, 68,928; Bend, 58,777; Boise, 145,138; Eugene, 109,163; Everett, 85,936; Southern Oregon, 77,098; Spokane, 111,607; Yakima, 65,684. Total—722,331. Playoffs (2 games)—3,105.

Managers—Bellingham, Dave Myers; Bend, Gene Glynn; Boise, Tom Kotchman; Eugene, Bobby Meacham; Everett, Norm Sherry; Southern Oregon, Chris Pittaro; Spokane, Ed Romero; Yakima, Joe Vavra.

All-Star team: 1B—Larry Sutton, Eugene; 2B—Steve Sisco, Eugene; 3B—Mark Sobolewski, Southern Oregon; SS—Jason Bates, Bend; OF—Terrence Frazier, Southern Oregon; Papo Ramos, Everett; Bill Robbs, Spokane; C—Chris Abbe, Yakima; DH—Fred McNair, Bellingham; LHP—Mike Butler, Boise; RHP—Mark Thompson, Bend; LH Reliever—Chris Eddy, Eugene; RH Reliever—John Pricher, Boise; Most Valuable Player—Larry Sutton, Eugene; Manager of the Year—Tom Kotchman, Boise.

BATTING

TEAM

Team	Avg.	G	AB	R	OR	H	TB	2B	3B	HR	RBI	SH	SF	HP	BB	Int. BB	SO	SB	CS	LOB
Southern Oregon	.267	76	2555	401	363	683	1007	134	11	56	345	11	19	34	317	11	607	72	52	578
Bend	.262	76	2538	402	321	666	966	126	12	50	329	16	23	28	340	8	587	102	41	559
Everett	.259	76	2613	422	408	676	906	117	10	31	350	23	18	44	337	15	562	136	67	606
Yakima	.259	76	2583	393	427	668	950	120	18	42	317	19	27	57	270	15	626	81	36	576
Eugene	.251	76	2563	362	398	644	905	113	17	38	296	18	15	34	283	11	548	118	58	523
Bellingham	.247	76	2534	386	346	627	885	92	11	48	325	10	16	38	313	15	683	161	61	537
Boise	.246	76	2537	374	390	623	857	101	20	31	310	18	25	47	288	4	567	51	34	570
Spokane	.244	76	2513	316	403	612	844	115	18	27	272	27	26	28	247	12	605	80	44	516

INDIVIDUAL

(Leading qualifiers for batting championship—205 or more plate appearances)

*Bats lefthanded.   †Switch-hitter.

Player, Team	Avg.	G	AB	R	H	TB	2B	3B	HR	RBI	SH	SF	HP	BB	Int. BB	SO	SB	CS
Martinez, Sandy, Yakima†	.333	62	216	34	72	89	12	1	1	33	5	4	2	7	1	22	9	2
Sisco, Steve, Eugene	.330	67	261	41	86	95	7	1	0	30	2	2	4	26	0	32	22	12
McNair, Fred, Bellingham	.329	69	255	41	84	121	9	2	8	54	0	0	4	21	4	69	13	10
Sutton, Larry, Eugene*	.311	70	238	45	74	142	17	3	15	58	0	2	5	48	5	33	3	6
Ramos, Papo, Everett	.306	66	232	45	71	92	11	2	2	34	2	2	6	44	3	33	11	10
Robbs, Bill, Spokane	.305	68	233	33	71	91	10	2	2	28	0	4	6	31	2	42	7	4
Anderson, Chris, Boise	.304	58	217	35	66	84	9	3	1	23	4	2	3	18	0	23	0	4
Newhouse, Andre, Eugene	.303	57	211	33	64	88	12	0	4	26	1	2	5	24	2	49	20	4
Filson, Matt, Yakima*	.303	53	175	25	53	80	9	0	6	34	0	2	9	20	0	56	2	1
Abbe, Chris, Yakima	.302	52	192	25	58	94	9	0	9	37	0	0	7	17	2	43	0	0

Departmental leaders: G—Chapman, Freeburg, 71; AB—King, 264; R—Bates, 57; H—Sisco, 86; TB—Sutton, 142; 2B—Sobolewski, 18; 3B—Chapman, Teeters, 5; HR—Sutton, 15; RBI—Sutton, 58; SH—McCracken, 7; SF—Drinkwater, 6; HP—Bobo, 11; BB—Lawson, 60; IBB—Roach, 6; SO—Kerns, 99; SB—Bullock, 40; CS—Woods, 17.

(All players—listed alphabetically)

Player, Team	Avg.	G	AB	R	H	TB	2B	3B	HR	RBI	SH	SF	HP	BB	Int. BB	SO	SB	CS
Abbe, Chris, Yakima	.302	52	192	25	58	94	9	0	9	37	0	0	7	17	2	43	0	0
Abell, Scott, Eugene	.417	4	12	2	5	9	1	0	1	3	0	0	0	2	0	3	0	0
Anderson, Chris, Boise	.304	58	217	35	66	84	9	3	1	23	4	2	3	18	0	23	0	4
Anderson, Cliff, Yakima*	.218	51	147	24	31	55	11	2	3	18	2	4	4	24	2	29	2	4
Antoon, Jeff, Eugene	.276	57	196	23	54	80	11	0	5	27	0	0	1	19	1	32	0	2
Barwick, Lyall, Boise	.158	8	19	4	3	3	0	0	0	0	0	0	0	2	0	3	3	1
Bates, Jason, Bend†	.286	70	255	57	73	107	10	3	6	31	2	4	5	56	1	55	18	4
Benard, Marvin, Everett*	.236	64	161	31	38	55	10	2	1	17	1	0	6	24	0	39	17	3
Biley, Greg, Boise	.063	8	16	1	1	1	0	0	0	0	0	0	0	3	0	7	0	1
Bobo, Elgin, Boise	.270	43	141	31	38	50	7	1	1	17	0	3	11	21	0	21	0	1
Bond, Michael, Bellingham	.223	54	175	22	39	45	3	0	1	22	2	1	3	9	0	31	17	3

— 465 —

Player, Team	Avg.	G	AB	R	H	TB	2B	3B	HR	RBI	SH	SF	HP	BB	Int. BB	SO	SB	CS
Bonds, Bobby, Spokane	.179	25	84	15	15	21	2	2	0	5	2	0	0	13	0	37	13	2
Bonnici, James, Bellingham	.262	53	168	13	44	64	6	1	4	20	1	0	2	22	2	54	5	2
Brooks, Ramy, Eugene	.256	50	160	20	41	64	10	2	3	18	0	2	0	20	0	34	1	5
Brown, Mike, Yakima	.000	7	9	0	0	0	0	0	0	0	0	0	0	0	1	0	4	0	0
Bullock, Renaldo, Bellingham	.199	64	206	46	41	52	3	1	2	8	1	1	9	22	1	74	40	8
Burgos, Carlos, Eugene	.176	31	102	6	18	20	2	0	0	12	1	1	0	8	0	18	1	2
Callihan, John, Yakima	.119	26	67	8	8	13	5	0	0	4	0	2	2	9	1	25	0	1
Calvi, Mark, Bellingham	.154	26	52	3	8	8	0	0	0	5	1	0	0	6	0	8	0	0
Carrion, German, Spokane†	.251	53	199	35	50	71	8	2	3	21	4	0	4	14	0	36	8	5
Case, Mike, Bend	.253	49	170	30	43	70	10	1	5	20	0	1	2	22	0	48	10	2
Cavanagh, Mike, Everett	.173	33	75	7	13	19	3	0	1	8	1	0	2	4	0	16	1	2
Chapman, Ken, Yakima†	.269	71	253	40	68	105	15	5	4	30	1	3	0	31	4	65	5	4
Clifford, Jim, Bellingham*	.138	23	65	5	9	12	0	0	1	7	0	0	2	8	1	26	1	2
Connell, Lino, Boise†	.217	56	152	19	33	36	1	1	0	17	0	2	2	17	1	49	4	4
Constantino, Kraig, Spokane	.250	46	132	16	33	52	7	0	4	17	0	0	1	11	0	38	2	5
Cornell, David, Eugene*	.235	65	226	37	53	60	7	0	0	22	4	2	0	26	1	40	16	2
Counsell, Craig, Bend*	.246	18	61	11	15	23	6	1	0	8	1	0	1	9	1	10	1	2
Cromer, David, Southern Oregon*	.208	50	168	17	35	54	7	0	4	26	1	2	1	13	1	34	4	3
Cruz, Juan, Spokane	.217	60	166	13	36	49	8	1	1	11	3	1	1	4	1	55	9	0
DeJesus, Anito, Spokane	.361	24	97	13	35	48	8	1	1	15	0	0	0	5	0	24	1	1
De La Cruz, Marcelino, Spokane	.267	52	180	26	48	60	8	2	0	11	5	1	1	9	0	44	3	4
DeLeon, Roberto, Spokane	.210	42	119	10	25	34	4	1	1	7	2	1	1	9	0	25	7	4
Drinkwater, Sean, Spokane	.301	66	256	35	77	105	12	2	4	41	1	6	0	25	0	27	7	4
Dunckel, Bill, Boise	.263	68	247	32	65	84	11	1	2	40	1	5	4	30	1	50	5	1
Ealy, Tracey, Eugene†	.279	17	61	11	17	25	3	1	1	12	1	1	2	9	0	19	8	1
Echevarria, Angel, Bend	.224	57	205	24	46	67	4	1	5	30	0	0	2	19	1	54	8	1
Ehmann, Kurt, Everett	.265	64	215	25	57	72	9	0	2	20	4	0	4	31	0	51	6	3
Eldridge, Brian, Southern Oregon	.302	17	53	8	16	22	3	0	1	7	1	0	0	3	0	6	3	1
Endebrock, Kurt, Southern Oregon	.203	30	64	9	13	13	0	0	0	2	1	0	1	9	0	26	1	1
Erhard, Barney, Bellingham	.144	40	111	10	16	22	3	0	1	4	0	1	0	13	0	42	7	5
Felix, Lauro, Southern Oregon	.417	11	24	5	10	14	1	0	1	3	0	1	0	8	0	5	2	1
Filson, Matt, Yakima*	.303	53	175	25	53	80	9	0	6	34	0	2	9	20	1	56	2	1
Fonville, Chad, Everett†	.273	63	260	56	71	85	9	1	1	33	1	0	3	31	1	39	36	14
Frazier, Terance, Southern Oregon	.294	62	238	49	70	85	8	2	1	26	1	0	9	20	0	39	24	5
Freeburg, Ryan, Bend	.242	71	252	35	61	95	13	0	7	36	0	5	5	32	1	86	2	5
Gagliano, Manny, Spokane	.178	50	157	10	28	35	7	0	0	20	0	4	2	22	2	29	4	3
Galligani, Marcel, Southern Oregon	.200	47	120	20	24	33	6	0	1	18	1	2	0	30	1	33	6	5
Garcia, Marcelino, Spokane*	.231	40	117	13	27	32	5	0	0	15	4	2	0	14	1	19	1	2
Garcia, Marcos, Boise	.136	12	22	4	3	5	0	1	0	0	0	0	0	2	0	8	0	0
Geis, Jason, Southern Oregon	.311	44	148	23	46	68	10	0	4	15	0	0	2	15	0	48	2	1
Giambi, Jason, Southern Oregon*	.317	13	41	9	13	25	3	0	3	13	0	0	0	9	1	6	1	1
Gonzalez, Mauricio, Bend*	.111	9	18	3	2	2	0	0	0	1	0	0	0	3	0	2	0	0
Gorman, Paul, Boise	.214	12	14	1	3	3	0	0	0	3	0	0	0	3	0	2	0	0
Gray, Dan, Yakima	.280	33	107	14	30	43	7	0	2	17	1	2	3	13	0	20	3	0
Griffey, Craig, Bellingham	.250	63	220	30	55	66	6	1	1	21	2	2	3	22	0	35	15	8
Hamm, Stacy, Spokane†	.222	22	45	7	10	14	1	0	1	3	0	0	1	5	0	16	1	2
Hardwick, Joe, Boise	.222	37	108	14	24	27	3	0	0	11	1	0	2	17	1	29	7	3
Hart, Shelby, Everett	.263	14	38	3	10	14	1	0	1	8	0	1	3	5	1	11	0	0
Henderson, Dave, Bellingham	.173	25	81	7	14	18	1	0	1	7	0	0	2	10	0	26	3	2
Hernandez, A.J., Boise*	.000	2	4	0	0	0	0	0	0	0	0	0	0	0	0	2	0	0
Hickey, Mike, Bellingham†	.246	15	57	8	14	16	2	0	0	11	0	0	0	4	0	14	3	0
Hunt, Chris, Boise*	.271	45	140	12	38	43	2	0	1	13	0	1	3	14	0	15	0	1
Johnson, Herman, Southern Oregon	.243	25	70	11	17	26	6	0	1	15	0	1	0	11	1	18	1	0
Johnson, Keith, Yakima	.203	57	197	27	40	49	6	0	1	17	1	1	10	16	0	37	5	1
Johnson, Reggie, Yakima	.300	54	203	32	61	72	3	4	0	17	7	3	3	11	0	53	5	1
Jones, Butter, Everett	.276	37	87	25	24	40	2	1	4	14	0	2	4	12	0	16	19	2
Kerns, Mickey, Boise	.234	69	256	34	60	109	14	4	9	49	0	2	2	16	0	99	7	5
Kessler, David, Boise	.111	4	9	0	1	2	1	0	0	0	0	0	0	2	0	5	0	0
Killeen, Tim, Southern Oregon*	.235	39	119	20	28	44	7	0	3	12	0	0	2	17	1	30	5	3
King, Clay, Everett	.292	69	264	37	77	100	15	1	2	31	5	2	2	15	1	37	3	2
Krenke, Keith, Bend	.213	47	141	18	30	45	6	0	3	15	0	3	0	11	0	39	1	0
Landrum, Tito, Yakima	.252	62	226	36	57	91	7	3	7	34	0	2	4	24	0	63	6	4
Lawson, Brian, Bellingham*	.243	64	189	56	46	86	11	1	9	24	0	1	1	60	1	74	20	4
Lesher, Brian, Southern Oregon	.191	46	136	21	26	44	7	1	3	18	0	1	2	12	0	35	3	7
Llanos, Aurelio, Bellingham†	.225	31	89	15	20	29	2	2	1	9	0	0	1	11	0	31	1	1
Long, Ryan, Eugene	.230	54	183	19	42	51	5	2	0	18	2	1	4	3	0	33	7	5
Loomis, Geoffrey, Southern Oregon	.254	61	228	35	58	82	7	1	5	26	0	3	2	28	2	37	4	6
Marshall, Jason, Eugene	.281	10	32	5	9	10	1	0	0	1	0	1	0	7	1	0	7	0	0
Martinez, Javier, Boise†	.227	26	44	6	10	10	0	0	0	3	2	0	1	7	0	8	0	0
Martinez, Sandy, Yakima†	.333	62	216	34	72	89	12	1	1	33	5	4	2	7	1	22	9	2
Mayes, Craig, Everett*	.345	38	110	17	38	41	3	0	0	10	0	0	0	10	1	13	3	3
McAllister, Troy, Bend*	.108	35	74	10	8	8	0	0	0	2	1	0	0	14	0	30	1	3
McCracken, Quinton, Bend	.280	67	232	37	65	82	13	2	0	27	7	2	0	25	0	39	18	6
McMillin, Darrell, Eugene	.171	45	140	22	24	31	7	0	0	6	1	0	6	20	1	29	2	2
McNair, Fred, Bellingham	.329	69	255	41	84	121	9	2	8	54	0	4	4	21	4	69	13	10
Mee, Corey, Yakima†	.125	8	24	4	3	3	0	0	0	1	0	0	0	4	0	4	0	0
Mendez, Ricardo, Southern Oregon	.220	38	109	14	24	31	3	2	0	11	1	1	1	16	0	26	2	4
Minchk, Kevin, Spokane*	.237	54	139	12	33	39	6	0	0	12	2	0	2	23	2	32	1	0
Miran, Tory, Yakima	.244	34	86	15	21	31	4	0	2	10	0	0	2	11	1	15	2	2
Montgomery, Don, Everett	.289	53	187	28	54	80	9	1	5	38	1	4	1	28	1	39	2	1
Moore, Mark, Southern Oregon	.331	41	118	17	39	59	11	0	3	18	1	0	1	11	0	22	1	1
Moore, Mike, Boise	.207	18	58	12	12	19	1	0	2	6	0	0	0	9	1	25	3	2
Morillo, Cesar, Eugene†	.244	51	180	28	44	58	9	1	1	17	3	0	1	21	0	40	6	4
Newhouse, Andre, Eugene	.303	57	211	33	64	88	12	0	4	26	1	2	5	24	2	49	20	4
Norton, Rick, Southern Oregon*	.276	9	29	1	8	10	2	0	0	5	0	0	2	1	0	11	0	1
O'Neill, Tom, Everett	.118	9	17	2	2	3	1	0	0	0	0	0	0	3	0	7	0	0
Oakland, John, Bend	.287	68	237	34	68	87	7	0	4	32	0	1	2	40	3	50	3	1
Partrick, Dave, Boise	.000	21	1	0	0	0	0	0	0	0	0	0	0	0	0	0	1	0
Penix, Troy, Southern Oregon*	.287	56	209	25	60	94	9	2	7	38	0	1	1	21	1	52	4	4
Perez, Ralph, Spokane*	.242	48	132	17	32	41	5	2	0	8	2	2	0	16	1	29	7	2
Pineiro, Michael, Boise	.263	62	217	31	57	83	9	1	5	33	2	3	4	20	0	39	1	1
Pinkney, Alton, Yakima*	.292	68	250	42	73	92	12	2	1	29	1	2	3	31	3	47	27	9
Pozo, Arquimedez, Bellingham	.322	39	149	37	48	81	12	0	7	21	1	1	2	20	0	24	9	5
Ramirez, Roberto, Southern Oregon	.455	5	22	8	10	21	3	1	2	4	0	0	0	1	0	4	0	0
Ramos, Papo, Everett	.306	66	232	45	71	92	11	2	2	34	2	2	6	44	3	33	11	10

Player, Team	Avg.	G	AB	R	H	TB	2B	3B	HR	RBI	SH	SF	HP	BB	Int. BB	SO	SB	CS
Reed, Pat, Yakima	.202	50	114	19	23	33	5	1	1	8	1	1	2	13	0	47	6	1
Riley, Marquis, Boise	.239	52	201	47	48	62	12	1	0	12	2	0	2	37	0	29	7	4
Roach, Petie, Everett*	.212	70	250	35	53	76	14	0	3	37	1	1	2	34	6	73	7	3
Robbs, Bill, Spokane	.305	68	233	33	71	91	10	2	2	28	0	4	6	31	2	42	7	4
Rogers, Lamarr, Bend	.290	66	231	41	67	92	13	3	2	21	3	2	2	53	0	31	22	7
Rosario, Mel, Spokane†	.228	66	237	38	54	99	13	1	10	40	0	4	4	20	2	62	5	3
Saugstad, Mark, Everett	.216	60	199	21	43	65	11	1	3	32	3	3	1	15	0	60	2	3
Scalzitti, Will, Bend	.287	62	230	35	66	103	16	0	7	40	2	1	1	20	0	40	0	2
Scheibe, Britton, Spokane†	.167	52	114	11	19	28	7	1	0	13	0	1	0	13	0	46	2	2
Schmidt, Tom, Bend	.257	68	249	39	64	100	13	1	7	27	0	1	4	24	1	78	17	3
Scott, Sean, Southern Oregon*	.243	50	140	23	34	49	6	0	3	11	2	1	3	30	2	47	3	3
Scott, Tim, Bend	.256	54	156	21	40	55	9	0	2	28	1	3	1	17	0	26	1	4
Serbalik, Mike, Yakima	.160	35	94	5	15	20	5	0	0	8	0	0	1	10	0	18	1	1
Serrano, Nandy, Boise	.195	13	41	1	8	10	2	0	0	6	1	1	1	4	0	9	0	0
Shockey, Greg, Bellingham*	.289	62	232	31	67	86	11	1	2	36	1	2	1	27	3	34	3	3
Shrum, Dennis, Eugene	.333	5	12	0	4	4	0	0	0	1	0	0	0	0	0	1	0	0
Sievers, Jason, Everett	.139	19	36	3	5	5	0	0	0	3	1	0	0	6	0	8	0	0
Simmons, Mark, Boise†	.225	63	191	26	43	50	3	2	0	10	4	0	2	18	0	65	9	2
Simonton, Benji, Everett	.244	68	225	37	55	83	10	0	6	34	2	3	3	39	0	78	9	4
Simpson, Jay, Boise	.261	6	23	4	6	8	0	1	0	1	0	0	0	2	0	8	1	0
Sisco, Steve, Eugene	.330	67	261	41	86	95	7	1	0	30	2	2	4	26	0	32	22	12
Smith, Chris, Boise	.217	53	189	20	41	62	12	3	1	27	0	4	2	16	0	25	2	1
Smith, Frank, Yakima	.224	15	49	7	11	22	2	0	3	6	0	0	2	3	0	15	1	0
Smith, Joel, Boise	.257	9	35	2	9	12	3	0	0	6	0	0	2	3	0	11	1	0
Sobolewski, Mark, Southern Oregon	.290	68	262	44	76	115	18	0	7	38	1	3	3	33	0	52	2	4
Strittmatter, Mark, Bend	.257	35	101	17	26	38	6	0	2	13	0	0	3	12	0	28	0	4
Subero, Carlos, Eugene†	.227	7	22	3	5	7	0	1	0	1	0	0	0	3	0	3	0	0
Sutton, Larry, Eugene*	.311	70	238	45	74	142	17	3	15	58	0	2	5	48	5	33	3	6
Sweeney, Mike, Eugene	.221	59	199	17	44	70	12	1	4	28	1	2	4	13	0	54	3	3
Tacgere, Rich, Boise	.000	1	1	0	0	0	0	0	0	0	0	0	0	0	0	1	0	0
Teeters, Brian, Eugene*	.205	64	254	40	52	83	9	5	4	14	1	0	1	30	1	91	26	7
Thomsen, Chris, Southern Oregon	.280	7	25	4	7	13	1	1	1	5	0	0	0	1	0	9	0	0
Urso, Joe, Boise	.000	2	5	1	0	0	0	0	0	0	1	0	0	4	0	1	0	0
Wallace, Brian, Bellingham	.279	69	247	25	69	96	15	0	4	39	0	0	2	6	24	2	73	14	5
Warren, Derrick, Bellingham*	.139	28	72	9	10	14	1	0	1	7	1	0	1	12	1	32	2	2
White, Jason, Southern Oregon	.297	66	232	38	69	105	16	1	6	34	1	3	4	28	1	67	4	1
White, Kyle, Spokane	.179	40	106	12	19	25	4	1	0	5	2	0	5	13	1	44	2	1
Widger, Chris, Bellingham	.259	51	166	28	43	69	7	2	5	30	0	5	1	22	0	36	8	1
Wittig, Paul, Yakima	.250	3	12	3	3	4	1	0	0	2	0	0	0	2	0	5	0	0
Wolff, Mike, Boise	.270	68	244	49	66	113	12	1	11	39	1	2	6	32	1	60	5	5
Woods, Kenny, Everett	.253	64	257	50	65	76	9	1	0	31	1	0	7	35	1	46	20	17
Zahner, Kevin, Yakima	.314	24	51	9	16	19	3	0	0	5	0	1	2	8	0	14	0	0
Zammarchi, Erik, Yakima	.224	17	58	12	13	16	3	0	0	1	0	1	6	0	19	4	3	

The following pitchers, listed alphabetically by club, with games in parentheses, had no plate appearances, primarily through use of designated hitters:

BELLINGHAM—Aschoff, Jerry (14); Cody, Ron (23); Cudjo, Lavell (1); Deal, Jamon (16); Doughty, Brian (11); Estes, Shawn (15); Graham, Rich (27); Harikkala, Tim (15); Hartman, Kelly (16); Lowe, Derek (14); Mountain, Joe (12); Nickell, Julian (1); Rivera, Oscar (13); Schooler, Mike (2); Smith, Ryan (9); Stock, Kevin (21); Wolcott, Bob (9); Worley, Bob (18).

BEND—Acevedo, Juan (1); Alston, Garvin (14); Bailey, Roger (11); Burke, John (10); Eiffert, Mike (17); Henderson, Chris (12); Holland, Jay (20); Hovey, Jim (27); Hutchins, Jason (34); Kotarski, Mike (25); Metzinger, Bill (2); Peever, Lloyd (11); Thompson, Mark (16); Voisard, Mark (26).

BOISE—Blanchette, Bill (5); Briley, Paxton (2); Butler, Mike (17); Chavez, Tony (14); Hingle, Larry (15); Jose, Grabiel (2); Mitchell, Glenn (7); Perez, Beban (13); Pricher, John (32); Rinehart, Dallas (26); Schmidt, Jeff (11); Sebach, Kyle (13); Simas, Bill (14); Sutton, Daron (10); Valencia, Max (7); White, Steve (13); Wylie, John (24).

EUGENE—Bladow, Dave (13); Bunch, Mel (10); Clinkscales, Sherard (12); Currier, Bryan (3); Dickens, John (3); Dorlarque, Aaron (32); Eddy, Chris (23); Evans, Bart (13); Fletcher, Paul (16); Haas, Jeff (3); Heming, Tom (25); Hodgson, Jim (4); Lieber, Jonathan (5); Pruitt, Jason (16); Sheehan, Chris (19); Weglarz, John (19).

EVERETT—Baine, Dave (17); Brewington, Jamie (15); Gorham, Bob (11); Hanneman, Blair (24); Heckman, Andy (22); Henderson, Ken (12); Hicks, Chuck (21); Luther, Tim (17); Martin, Jeff (1); McLain, Mike (6); Myers, Jeff (15); Peterson, Mark (20); Richey, Jeff (24); Riley, Jim (15); Stroth, Scott (16); Szczechowski, Dennis (7); Valdez, Carlos (3).

SOUTHERN OREGON—Banks, Jim (24); Bennett, Bob (7); Bojan, Tim (15); Byerly, Jim (20); Caruso, Gene (12); Foster, Clifton (4); Gienger, Craig (14); Griffin, Steve (8); Haught, Gary (19); King, Rich (15); Lemke, Steve (21); MacCauley, John (16); Payne, Stan (8); Post, Jeff (7); Wengert, Don (6).

SPOKANE—Baker, Jared (13); Dale, Ron (17); Eggleston, Scott (11); Erdos, Todd (2); Grzelaczyk, Ken (19); Hermanson, Mike (14); Hollinger, Adrian (21); Kindler, Tom (12); Maffett, Chris (16); Marshall, Todd (22); Murphy, Chris (15); Ploeger, Tim (15); Schmitt, Todd (29); Valdez, Rafael (8); Vazquez, Art (15); Wechsberg, Von (6).

YAKIMA—Barbeln, Joe (4); Bennett, Doug (2); Colson, Brent (15); Graves, Jon (7); Gutierrez, Rafael (16); Herges, Matt (27); Lavalley, Todd (16); Minear, Clint (18); Rizzo, Todd (15); Salcedo, Jose (16); Thomas, Carlos (15); Troutman, Mike (26); Watts, Burgess (24); White, Brandon (12).

GRAND SLAMS—Cromer, Cruz, Filson, Pineiro, Scalzitti, T. Scott, Wolff, 1 each.

AWARDED FIRST BASE ON CATCHER'S INTERFERENCE—Griffey 3 (Hunt, Killeen, Rosario); Chapman (Montgomery); Cornell (Montgomery); Felix (Sweeney); McCracken (Sweeney); Serbalik (DeJesus); Simmons (Rosario); Simonton (Widger).

PITCHING

TEAM

Team	ERA	G	CG	ShO	Sv.	IP	H	R	ER	HR	HB	BB	Int. BB	SO	WP	Bk.
Bellingham	3.43	76	3	8	26	668.1	631	346	255	32	40	273	6	523	55	28
Bend	3.47	76	5	4	24	667.1	579	321	257	33	44	346	9	706	53	23
Southern Oregon	3.75	76	4	4	18	653.0	657	363	272	38	31	222	5	569	37	21
Boise	3.84	76	1	3	30	658.2	671	390	281	40	33	250	18	559	57	23
Eugene	3.97	76	0	1	22	675.1	673	398	298	49	32	271	5	652	66	37
Spokane	4.18	76	2	2	18	662.2	653	403	308	37	33	340	23	570	79	20
Yakima	4.44	76	0	1	18	661.0	674	427	326	46	51	313	11	590	52	32
Everett	4.61	76	3	4	13	667.2	661	408	342	48	46	380	14	616	70	37

(Leading qualifiers for earned-run average leadership—61 or more innings)

*Throws lefthanded.

Pitcher, Team	W	L	Pct.	ERA	G	GS	CG	GF	ShO	Sv.	IP	H	R	ER	HR	HB	BB	Int. BB	SO	WP
Thompson, Bend	8	4	.667	1.95	16	16	4	0	0	0	106.1	81	32	23	2	4	31	1	102	8
Haught, Southern Oregon	8	2	.800	1.98	19	4	0	9	0	2	68.1	58	18	15	3	2	14	0	69	1
Grzelaczyk, Spokane	5	5	.500	2.02	19	8	2	6	1	0	75.2	67	31	17	2	1	16	3	86	4
Bailey, Bend	5	2	.714	2.20	11	11	1	0	0	0	65.1	48	19	16	4	4	30	0	81	2
Butler, Boise*	9	5	.643	2.42	17	15	1	0	0	0	104.1	85	38	28	11	2	24	1	91	3
Lowe, Bellingham	7	3	.700	2.42	14	13	2	1	1	0	85.2	69	34	23	2	4	22	0	66	5
Wylie, Boise	4	0	1.000	2.69	24	4	0	7	0	0	70.1	67	32	21	3	2	21	4	36	2
Bunch, Eugene	5	3	.625	2.78	10	10	0	0	0	0	64.2	62	23	20	5	1	13	0	69	2
Baker, Spokane	6	3	.667	2.82	13	11	0	0	0	0	67.0	56	32	21	2	2	32	0	56	4
Myers, Everett*	5	5	.500	3.19	15	15	2	0	0	0	93.0	75	39	33	2	4	50	0	90	7

Departmental leaders: G—Hutchins, 34; W—Butler, 9; L—Pruitt, Thomas, 8; Pct.—Aschoff, Schmitt, .857; GS—Gutierrez, Thompson, 16; CG—Thompson, 4; GF—Dorlarque, 31; ShO—Five pitchers tied with 1; Sv.—Pricher, 23; IP—Thompson, 106.1; H—Gutierrez, 97; R—Thomas, 64; ER—Gutierrez, 52; HR—Butler, 11; HB—Thomas, 13; BB—Myers, Thomas, 50; IBB—Schmitt, 5; SO—Thompson, 102; WP—Luther, 15.

(All pitchers—listed alphabetically)

Pitcher, Team	W	L	Pct.	ERA	G	GS	CG	GF	ShO	Sv.	IP	H	R	ER	HR	HB	BB	Int. BB	SO	WP
Acevedo, Bend	0	0	.000	13.50	1	0	0	0	0	0	2.0	4	3	3	0	1	1	0	3	0
Alston, Bend	5	4	.556	3.95	14	12	0	0	0	0	73.0	71	40	32	1	9	29	0	73	7
Aschoff, Bellingham*	6	1	.857	2.13	14	7	0	4	0	0	50.2	48	22	12	2	1	19	1	50	0
Bailey, Bend	5	2	.714	2.20	11	11	1	0	0	0	65.1	48	19	16	4	4	30	0	81	2
Baine, Everett*	4	4	.500	6.02	17	9	0	1	0	0	55.1	61	39	37	8	2	39	0	55	2
Baker, Spokane	6	3	.667	2.82	13	11	0	0	0	0	67.0	56	32	21	2	2	32	0	56	4
Banks, Southern Oregon	3	2	.600	2.83	24	0	0	22	0	8	28.2	20	11	9	1	1	17	0	40	3
Barbeln, Yakima	0	0	.000	2.08	4	0	0	1	0	0	4.1	4	1	1	1	2	3	0	6	1
Bennett, Yakima	1	0	1.000	2.61	2	2	0	0	0	0	10.1	11	5	3	1	2	3	0	6	1
Bennett, Southern Oregon	2	6	.250	5.81	17	6	0	3	0	2	48.0	60	41	31	4	2	20	0	41	4
Bladow, Eugene	4	5	.444	3.94	13	12	0	1	0	0	75.1	78	43	33	5	3	24	0	55	6
Blanchette, Boise*	2	1	.667	4.15	5	3	0	1	0	1	21.2	21	10	10	2	1	2	0	16	0
Bojan, Southern Oregon	2	3	.400	3.76	15	15	2	0	1	0	83.2	88	54	35	7	3	27	0	69	2
Brewington, Everett	5	2	.714	4.33	15	11	1	1	1	0	68.2	65	40	33	2	5	47	2	63	9
Briley, Boise	0	1	.000	8.22	2	2	0	0	0	0	7.2	11	11	7	0	0	2	0	2	1
Bunch, Eugene	5	3	.625	2.78	10	10	0	0	0	0	64.2	62	23	20	5	1	13	0	69	2
Burke, Bend	2	0	1.000	2.41	10	10	0	0	0	0	41.0	38	13	11	3	0	18	0	32	0
Butler, Boise*	9	5	.643	2.42	17	15	1	0	0	0	104.1	85	38	28	11	2	24	1	91	3
Byerly, Southern Oregon	0	0	.000	3.62	20	0	0	13	0	4	37.1	31	21	15	0	2	16	0	29	2
Calvi, Bellingham	0	0	.000	0.00	1	0	0	1	0	0	0.2	2	0	0	0	0	1	0	2	0
Caruso, Southern Oregon*	2	0	1.000	0.42	12	0	0	6	0	1	21.1	15	3	1	0	3	18	1	27	1
Chavez, Boise	1	1	.500	3.94	14	0	0	2	0	0	16.0	22	13	7	0	0	4	2	21	3
Clinkscales, Eugene	2	3	.400	6.15	12	11	0	0	0	0	52.2	54	47	36	5	5	36	0	58	8
Cody, Bellingham	3	2	.600	3.86	23	1	0	5	0	2	49.0	45	22	21	0	5	16	1	33	4
Colson, Yakima*	3	6	.333	4.72	15	14	0	0	0	0	74.1	82	55	39	5	3	38	0	54	7
Cudjo, Bellingham	0	0	.000	0.00	1	0	0	1	0	0	1.0	1	0	0	0	0	0	0	2	1
Currier, Eugene	0	3	.000	8.18	3	3	0	0	0	0	11.0	13	11	10	2	1	5	0	13	3
Dale, Spokane	1	1	.500	4.78	17	0	0	8	0	0	26.1	26	15	14	1	0	18	2	20	2
Deal, Bellingham	2	4	.333	2.50	16	2	0	3	0	1	39.2	30	19	11	0	4	25	1	28	6
Dickens, Eugene*	0	0	.000	1.69	3	0	0	0	0	1	5.1	6	1	1	0	1	2	0	5	1
Dorlarque, Eugene	1	2	.333	1.79	32	0	0	31	0	13	40.1	30	12	8	0	1	10	2	46	2
Doughty, Bellingham	3	1	.750	2.56	11	0	0	3	1	0	38.2	32	16	11	2	1	9	0	27	3
Eddy, Eugene*	4	2	.667	1.59	23	0	0	11	0	5	45.1	25	13	8	1	6	23	1	63	3
Eggleston, Spokane	2	2	.500	3.24	11	0	0	2	0	0	41.2	33	20	15	3	3	14	0	41	3
Eiffert, Bend*	5	2	.714	2.78	17	4	0	3	0	0	55.0	46	27	17	3	3	36	0	66	5
Erdos, Spokane	1	0	1.000	0.69	2	2	0	0	0	0	13.0	9	2	1	0	1	5	0	11	0
Estes, Bellingham*	3	3	.500	4.32	15	15	0	0	0	0	77.0	84	55	37	6	3	45	0	77	10
Evans, Everett	1	1	.500	6.23	13	1	0	4	0	0	26.0	17	20	18	1	4	23	0	58	3
Fletcher, Eugene*	2	6	.250	4.34	16	9	0	2	0	0	64.1	81	45	31	7	4	23	0	58	3
Foster, Southern Oregon	0	0	.000	1.38	4	4	0	0	0	0	13.0	7	4	2	0	2	6	0	14	1
Galligani, Southern Oregon	0	0	.000	9.00	1	0	0	1	0	0	2.0	4	2	2	0	0	2	0	4	0
Gienger, Southern Oregon	5	4	.556	4.48	14	13	0	0	0	0	66.1	77	45	33	3	3	22	1	42	4
Gorham, Everett	1	2	.333	6.40	11	0	0	3	0	0	32.1	30	28	23	2	6	25	0	18	9
Graham, Bellingham	1	2	.333	2.63	27	0	0	22	0	12	41.0	33	14	12	3	3	13	2	42	5
Graves, Yakima	1	3	.250	7.20	7	4	0	1	0	0	20.0	24	16	16	1	1	12	0	12	1
Griffin, Southern Oregon	0	0	.000	2.75	8	0	0	4	0	0	19.2	14	9	6	2	1	11	1	20	1
Grzelaczyk, Spokane	5	5	.500	2.02	19	8	2	6	1	0	75.2	67	31	17	2	1	16	3	86	4
Gutierrez, Yakima	7	5	.583	5.18	16	16	0	0	0	0	90.1	97	63	52	6	5	47	0	70	14
Haas, Eugene*	2	0	1.000	3.38	3	3	0	0	0	0	16.0	17	10	6	2	0	3	0	9	0
Hanneman, Everett	3	3	.500	3.31	24	0	0	15	0	1	32.2	26	16	12	2	3	28	3	27	6
Harikkala, Bellingham	2	0	1.000	2.70	15	2	0	2	0	1	33.1	37	15	10	2	0	16	0	18	1
Hartman, Bellingham*	2	1	.667	4.97	16	0	0	9	0	0	25.1	20	16	14	1	1	21	0	31	0
Haught, Southern Oregon	8	2	.800	1.98	19	4	0	9	0	2	68.1	58	18	15	3	2	14	0	69	1
Heckman, Everett*	2	3	.400	2.68	22	2	0	12	0	2	40.1	26	12	12	6	2	14	2	41	1
Heming, Eugene*	4	1	.800	5.55	25	0	0	12	0	0	48.2	56	40	30	7	2	17	1	54	7
Henderson, Bend	2	6	.250	7.74	12	11	0	0	0	0	47.2	49	47	41	3	5	48	0	28	11
Henderson, Everett*	0	0	.000	4.02	12	0	0	4	0	0	15.2	13	12	7	1	2	18	0	17	2
Herges, Yakima	2	3	.400	3.22	27	0	0	23	0	9	44.2	33	21	16	2	3	24	1	57	2
Hermanson, Spokane	2	5	.286	4.69	14	13	0	0	0	0	63.1	69	42	33	5	2	32	1	34	6
Hicks, Everett	3	3	.500	6.52	21	0	0	4	0	1	48.1	64	37	35	6	5	25	2	29	2
Hingle, Boise*	6	4	.600	3.91	15	15	0	0	0	0	76.0	83	52	33	6	1	29	1	56	9
Hodgson, Eugene	0	0	.000	5.23	4	0	0	2	0	0	10.1	9	6	6	1	0	7	1	5	0
Holland, Bend	2	3	.400	6.89	12	0	0	10	0	1	31.1	32	29	24	3	1	22	0	36	4
Hollinger, Spokane	0	6	.000	6.20	21	2	0	4	0	1	53.2	61	43	37	4	4	29	1	39	8
Hovey, Bend*	3	4	.429	2.74	27	0	0	14	0	2	46.0	39	19	14	1	0	30	2	37	5
Hutchins, Bend	0	3	.000	2.59	34	0	0	26	0	18	41.2	24	15	12	4	6	24	2	65	3
Jose, Boise	0	1	.000	5.40	2	2	0	0	0	0	1.2	2	1	1	0	0	2	0	1	0
Kindler, Spokane	2	3	.400	5.49	12	0	0	8	0	0	39.1	44	28	24	4	1	14	1	27	12
King, Southern Oregon	3	7	.300	6.00	15	14	0	0	0	0	69.0	81	52	46	6	5	22	0	71	10
Kotarski, Bend*	3	1	.750	3.72	25	3	0	9	0	0	55.2	48	30	23	1	6	36	2	65	1
Lavalley, Yakima	4	3	.571	4.39	16	5	0	2	0	0	55.1	55	32	27	3	3	26	1	47	1
Lemke, Southern Oregon	5	5	.500	3.99	21	0	0	6	0	1	49.2	63	35	22	1	1	9	1	41	1

Pitcher, Team	W	L	Pct.	ERA	G	GS	CG	GF	ShO	Sv.	IP	H	R	ER	HR	HB	BB	Int. BB	SO	WP
Lieber, Eugene	3	0	1.000	1.16	5	5	0	0	0	0	31.0	26	6	4	1	0	2	0	23	0
Lowe, Bellingham	7	3	.700	2.42	14	13	2	1	1	0	85.2	69	34	23	2	4	22	0	66	5
Luther, Everett	3	3	.500	4.76	17	6	0	3	0	0	51.0	49	31	27	1	1	36	0	49	15
MacCauley, Southern Oregon	4	5	.444	3.65	16	8	0	3	0	0	69.0	64	39	28	4	3	21	1	42	5
Maffett, Spokane	0	1	.000	7.54	16	0	0	2	0	1	22.2	24	22	19	0	1	25	1	19	4
Marshall, Spokane	0	1	.000	5.52	22	0	0	9	0	1	31.0	37	25	19	0	3	30	4	24	3
Martin, Everett	0	1	.000	27.00	1	1	0	0	0	0	2.1	6	8	7	0	1	2	0	1	2
McLain, Everett	0	0	.000	5.00	6	0	0	1	0	0	9.0	10	6	5	0	1	4	0	7	1
Metzinger, Bend	0	0	.000	1.50	2	0	0	2	0	1	6.0	4	1	1	1	0	2	0	5	0
Minear, Yakima*	1	1	.500	5.63	18	1	0	4	0	1	38.1	54	39	24	5	1	17	1	35	4
Miran, Yakima*	1	1	.500	1.88	7	5	0	2	0	0	28.2	28	12	6	1	1	4	0	31	0
Mitchell, Boise	1	0	1.000	2.16	7	0	0	3	0	0	8.1	6	3	2	0	0	5	0	8	3
Mountain, Bellingham	0	2	.000	3.45	12	0	0	11	0	6	15.2	12	8	6	2	1	1	0	11	1
Murphy, Spokane	0	1	.000	11.34	15	0	0	8	0	0	16.2	22	24	21	4	1	17	1	15	3
Myers, Everett*	5	5	.500	3.19	15	15	2	0	0	0	93.0	75	39	33	2	4	50	0	90	7
Nickell, Bellingham	0	1	.000	7.20	1	1	0	0	0	0	5.0	5	4	4	1	1	1	0	3	0
Partrick, Boise	1	0	1.000	3.86	20	0	0	3	0	0	32.2	28	20	14	3	3	17	1	31	3
Payne, Southern Oregon*	2	0	1.000	4.33	8	7	0	0	0	0	27.0	25	13	13	3	0	6	0	32	1
Peever, Bend	3	2	.600	2.91	11	8	0	2	0	1	43.1	44	18	14	2	2	10	0	48	3
Perez, Boise*	0	2	.000	7.79	13	2	0	1	0	0	17.1	25	17	15	0	3	7	0	18	4
Peterson, Everett*	3	2	.600	3.23	20	5	0	7	0	2	53.0	58	23	19	5	1	17	1	47	0
Ploeger, Everett	4	7	.364	3.59	15	15	0	0	0	0	82.2	85	43	33	5	2	29	3	61	12
Post, Southern Oregon	1	3	.250	5.54	7	0	0	5	0	0	13.0	18	10	8	2	2	3	1	7	0
Pricher, Boise	2	1	.667	1.05	32	0	0	30	0	23	43.0	34	8	5	1	0	8	3	65	1
Pruitt, Eugene	4	8	.333	5.09	16	14	0	0	0	0	70.2	81	59	40	4	3	39	0	47	8
Richey, Everett	2	1	.667	3.38	24	0	0	17	0	7	37.1	30	18	14	4	4	21	2	48	3
Riley, Everett	2	5	.286	4.35	15	8	0	2	0	0	51.2	60	35	25	2	1	10	0	53	1
Rinehart, Boise	5	3	.625	3.13	26	4	0	6	0	1	60.1	54	28	21	5	3	25	3	51	7
Rivera, Bellingham	8	3	.727	4.43	13	13	0	0	0	0	67.0	73	38	33	3	5	20	0	40	3
Rizzo, Yakima*	2	0	1.000	4.50	15	0	0	8	0	0	26.0	21	13	13	3	2	24	0	26	5
Salcedo, Yakima	2	4	.333	3.78	16	7	0	3	0	1	64.1	64	36	27	6	1	21	1	63	3
Schmidt, Boise	1	6	.143	4.47	11	11	0	0	0	0	52.1	55	41	26	4	4	18	1	41	3
Schmitt, Spokane	6	1	.857	1.18	29	0	0	29	0	15	38.0	23	7	5	1	2	23	5	48	3
Schooler, Bellingham	0	0	.000	0.00	2	1	0	0	0	0	3.0	1	2	0	0	0	4	0	1	0
Sebach, Boise	1	5	.167	7.52	13	8	0	3	0	1	40.2	50	42	34	0	8	34	0	41	9
Sheehan, Eugene	2	3	.400	4.18	19	4	0	7	0	2	56.0	67	36	26	5	1	14	0	38	7
Simas, Boise	6	5	.545	3.95	14	12	0	1	0	1	70.2	82	44	31	0	3	29	2	39	4
Smith, Bellingham	4	3	.571	3.31	9	9	0	0	0	0	49.0	48	26	18	2	5	19	0	34	5
Stock, Bellingham*	1	1	.500	1.77	21	0	0	7	0	3	35.2	35	14	7	0	1	9	0	19	1
Stroth, Everett	2	4	.333	7.58	16	9	0	0	0	0	57.0	69	52	48	8	5	30	1	47	9
Sutton, Boise	0	0	.000	10.97	10	0	0	7	0	0	10.2	16	14	13	2	1	10	0	13	3
Szczechowski, Everett	0	1	.000	5.27	7	0	0	1	0	0	13.2	15	10	8	1	1	7	1	18	0
Thomas, Yakima	3	8	.273	5.10	15	15	0	0	0	0	83.0	72	64	47	8	13	50	0	59	5
Thompson, Bend	8	4	.667	1.95	16	16	4	0	0	0	106.1	81	32	23	2	4	31	1	102	8
Troutman, Yakima	4	1	.800	3.38	26	0	0	19	0	3	37.1	33	19	14	2	1	15	3	43	2
Valdez, Everett	0	1	.000	1.42	3	0	0	2	0	0	6.1	4	2	1	0	2	7	0	6	1
Valdez, Spokane	1	4	.200	4.15	8	8	0	0	0	0	34.2	41	22	16	2	4	19	0	34	3
Valencia, Boise	1	1	.500	6.35	7	0	0	3	0	1	11.1	16	10	8	1	0	7	0	13	0
Vazquez, Spokane	0	2	.000	6.87	15	1	0	5	0	0	36.2	38	39	28	4	5	30	0	41	9
Voisard, Bend	5	2	.714	4.42	26	1	0	5	0	2	53.0	51	28	26	5	3	29	2	65	4
Watts, Yakima	4	2	.667	3.58	24	1	0	11	0	4	50.1	59	25	20	0	5	16	2	44	0
Wechsberg, Spokane	2	2	.500	2.21	6	2	0	1	0	0	20.1	18	8	5	0	1	7	1	14	3
Weglarz, Eugene	2	3	.400	3.28	19	4	0	3	0	1	57.2	51	26	21	3	0	22	0	70	2
Wengert, Southern Oregon	2	0	1.000	1.46	6	5	1	0	0	0	37.0	32	6	6	1	1	7	0	29	1
White, Yakima	1	3	.250	5.61	12	6	0	2	0	0	33.2	37	26	21	3	4	10	1	31	0
White, Yakima	0	0	.000	3.29	13	0	0	7	0	0	13.2	14	6	5	0	2	6	0	16	2
Wolcott, Bellingham	0	1	1.000	6.85	9	7	0	2	0	0	22.1	25	18	17	4	2	19	0	17	3
Worley, Bellingham	1	5	.167	5.97	18	0	0	6	0	1	28.2	31	23	19	3	3	17	1	20	3
Wylie, Boise	4	0	1.000	2.69	24	4	0	7	0	0	70.1	67	32	21	3	2	21	4	36	2

BALKS—Bladow, 11; Gorham, 10; Clinkscales, 9; Alston, 8; Hingle, Sheehan, 7 each; Myers, 6; Cody, Colson, King, Ploeger, Riley, Thomas, 5 each; Bojan, Grzelaczyk, Kindler, Lowe, Peterson, Pricher, Rivera, Schmidt, Thompson, 4 each; Burke, Eddy, Estes, Graves, Gutierrez, Hanneman, Herges, Hutchins, Lavalley, Luther, Perez, 3 each; Aschoff, Deal, Graham, Haas, Harikkala, Haught, C. Henderson, Hermanson, MacCauley, Minear, Miran, Salcedo, Stroth, Troutman, Wolcott, 2 each; Bailey, Baker, D. Bennett, R. Bennett, Brewington, Briley, Bunch, Butler, Byerly, Caruso, Currier, Dorlarque, Eggleston, Fletcher, Foster, Gienger, Griffin, Hicks, Holland, Hollinger, Hovey, Lieber, Maffett, Marshall, McLain, Nickell, Post, Richey, Sebach, Simas, Watts, Wengert, Worley, Wylie, 1 each.

COMBINATION SHUTOUTS—Aschoff-Cody, Doughty-Cody-Graham, Lowe-Mountain, Rivera-Harikkala, Smith-Stock-Graham, Wolcott-Stock-Cody, Bellingham; Alston-Hovey, Burke-Hovey-Voisard, Henderson-Eiffert, Kotarski-Voisard-Hutchins, Bend; Butler-Pricher, Hingle-Wylie-Chavez, Schmidt-Blanchette-Rinehart-Pricher, Boise; Lieber-Clinkscales-Eddy, Eugene; Brewington-Richey, Luther-Henderson-Baine, Riley-Richey, Everett; Foster-Lemke-Banks, MacCauley-Banks, Payne-Haught-Byerly, Southern Oregon; Grzelaczyk-Maffett-Schmitt, Spokane; White-Troutman-Herges, Yakima.

NO-HIT GAMES—None.

FIELDING

TEAM

Team	Pct.	G	PO	A	E	DP	PB	Team	Pct.	G	PO	A	E	DP	PB
Bend	.966	76	2002	787	98	53	23	Spokane	.948	76	1988	815	155	60	31
Everett	.956	76	2003	754	127	52	17	Yakima	.947	76	1983	812	156	68	28
Southern Oregon	.953	76	1959	819	137	62	17	Eugene	.945	76	2026	822	165	60	26
Bellingham	.951	76	2005	890	150	67	19	Boise	.943	76	1976	813	169	75	13

INDIVIDUAL

FIRST BASEMEN

*Throws lefthanded.

Player, Team	Pct.	G	PO	A	E	DP
Antoon, Eugene	.980	13	97	3	2	9
Bobo, Boise	.969	37	297	17	10	28
Bonnici, Bellingham	.979	10	91	2	2	6

Player, Team	Pct.	G	PO	A	E	DP
Brooks, Eugene	1.000	1	3	0	0	0
Burgos, Eugene	.982	6	49	6	1	4
Callihan, Yakima	1.000	16	87	5	0	11
Calvi, Bellingham	1.000	1	1	0	0	0
Case, Bend	1.000	3	11	0	0	1
Chapman, Yakima*	.976	70	555	46	15	49

Player, Team	Pct.	G	PO	A	E	DP
Clifford, Bellingham*	1.000	7	42	1	0	2
Constantino, Spokane	.969	16	118	9	4	10
DeJesus, Spokane	.981	16	143	8	3	8
Dunckel, Boise	.929	3	26	0	2	5
Hart, Everett	.786	1	11	0	3	0
Hernandez, Boise*	1.000	1	9	0	0	1
Kerns, Boise	.990	25	193	7	2	18
Lesher, Southern Oregon*	1.000	3	11	1	0	0
Llanos, Bellingham	1.000	2	11	0	0	2
Long, Eugene	1.000	1	1	0	0	0
McMillin, Eugene	1.000	1	3	0	0	0
McNair, Bellingham	.990	66	575	43	6	50
Minchk, Spokane*	.980	37	277	12	6	21
Montgomery, Everett	1.000	6	31	2	0	4
OAKLAND, Bend	.993	67	544	39	4	37
Penix, Southern Oregon*	.961	7	49	0	2	4
Roach, Everett*	.982	62	470	16	9	38
Saugstad, Everett	.990	16	94	3	1	5
Scott, Bend	1.000	14	70	5	0	6
Sutton, Eugene*	.975	61	517	29	14	42
Thomsen, Southern Oregon*	1.000	7	49	4	0	1
White, Southern Oregon*	.992	66	558	41	5	47
White, Spokane	.979	17	134	7	3	13
Wolff, Boise	.993	16	145	1	1	16

SECOND BASEMEN

Player, Team	Pct.	G	PO	A	E	DP
Anderson, Boise	.963	25	39	66	4	11
Anderson, Yakima	.929	29	30	75	8	16
Bond, Bellingham	.842	6	6	10	3	0
Carrion, Spokane	.936	52	101	133	16	24
Connell, Boise	.940	53	99	136	15	38
Counsell, Bend	.981	12	20	31	1	8
De La Cruz, Spokane	.960	9	10	14	1	6
DeLeon, Spokane	.967	21	38	51	3	8
Eldridge, Southern Oregon	.951	10	16	23	2	3
Erhard, Bellingham	.926	26	45	68	9	13
Felix, Southern Oregon	.929	4	5	8	1	1
Fonville, Everett	.939	59	131	132	17	30
Gonzalez, Bend	.000	1	0	0	1	0
Hickey, Bellingham	.884	14	29	32	8	6
Kerns, Boise	.907	9	16	23	4	4
Loomis, Southern Oregon	.949	51	81	142	12	26
Martinez, Boise	1.000	2	2	3	0	1
Martinez, Yakima	.924	33	60	85	12	16
McAllister, Eugene	.927	9	10	28	3	6
McCracken, Bend	.929	49	92	129	17	23
Mendez, Southern Oregon	.904	16	24	42	7	9
Morillo, Eugene	1.000	2	3	7	0	2
O'Neill, Everett	.917	6	5	6	1	1
Pozo, Bellingham	.955	38	85	129	10	24
Saugstad, Everett	.889	6	10	6	2	2
Scott, Bend	.953	21	28	54	4	10
Serbalik, Yakima	.957	27	39	49	4	12
Shrum, Eugene	.909	3	5	5	1	0
SISCO, Eugene	.962	65	113	190	12	31
Urso, Boise	1.000	1	3	4	0	2
Woods, Everett	.864	13	29	22	8	7

THIRD BASEMEN

Player, Team	Pct.	G	PO	A	E	DP
Anderson, Yakima	.956	16	9	34	2	5
Antoon, Eugene	.787	32	13	61	20	6
Bond, Bellingham	.857	4	1	5	1	0
Bonnici, Bellingham	.909	7	2	8	1	1
Callihan, Bend	.909	5	1	9	1	0
De La Cruz, Spokane	.970	30	14	51	2	2
DeLeon, Spokane	.765	3	3	10	4	0
Gagliano, Spokane	.934	48	42	85	9	7
Giambi, Southern Oregon	.962	11	5	20	1	1
Gorman, Boise	.750	7	1	5	2	0
K. Johnson, Yakima	.857	2	2	4	1	0
R. Johnson, Yakima	.894	53	27	99	15	7
Kerns, Boise	.887	20	9	46	7	4
King, Everett	.924	55	40	118	13	6
Llanos, Bellingham	.500	3	1	0	1	0
Long, Eugene	.810	43	28	74	24	5
Loomis, Southern Oregon	.913	11	4	17	2	2
Marshall, Eugene	1.000	1	0	3	0	1
McAllister, Eugene	.667	2	3	1	2	0
McMillin, Eugene	1.000	3	2	4	0	0
Mee, Yakima	.923	7	4	8	1	1
O'Neill, Everett	.857	3	1	5	1	0
Saugstad, Everett	.939	22	24	38	4	3
Schmidt, Bend	.899	66	40	111	17	10
Scott, Bend	1.000	12	5	20	0	2
Serrano, Boise	.958	11	7	16	1	1
Simmons, Boise	.877	54	27	108	19	9
SOBOLEWSKI, Southern Oregon	.929	58	50	108	12	10
Wallace, Bellingham	.900	68	34	164	22	13
Woods, Everett	1.000	1	0	1	0	0

SHORTSTOPS

Player, Team	Pct.	G	PO	A	E	DP
Anderson, Boise	.878	20	34	45	11	12
Anderson, Yakima	1.000	6	7	9	0	4
BATES, Bend	.936	66	72	176	17	28
Biley, Boise	.733	4	2	9	4	1
Bond, Bellingham	.918	43	61	129	17	28
Counsell, Bend	.889	5	3	5	1	1
De La Cruz, Spokane	.500	2	3	0	3	1
DeLeon, Spokane	.930	16	23	43	5	10
Drinkwater, Spokane	.896	61	96	179	32	33
Ehmann, Everett	.926	64	92	171	21	23
Eldridge, Southern Oregon	.963	8	13	13	1	1
Erhard, Bellingham	.897	10	27	34	7	7
Felix, Southern Oregon	.960	7	8	16	1	3
Fonville, Everett	.923	2	3	9	1	1
Galligani, Southern Oregon	.819	43	50	95	32	19
Gonzalez, Bend	.882	7	4	11	2	2
Henderson, Bellingham	.890	25	27	62	11	5
Johnson, Yakima	.886	55	69	141	27	26
Long, Eugene	.750	2	0	3	1	0
Marshall, Eugene	.923	9	18	30	4	8
Martinez, Boise	.818	15	10	26	8	4
Martinez, Yakima	.963	22	32	72	4	12
McAllister, Eugene	.905	16	19	48	7	9
Mendez, Southern Oregon	.926	18	29	46	6	7
Morillo, Eugene	.910	48	71	132	20	24
Saugstad, Everett	1.000	1	0	1	0	0
Scott, Bend	.923	7	10	14	2	3
Serbalik, Yakima	.600	3	1	2	2	0
Smith, Boise	.900	49	58	140	22	27
Sobolewski, Southern Oregon	.875	10	14	35	7	8
Subero, Eugene	.957	6	8	14	1	4
Wallace, Bellingham	1.000	2	1	4	0	0
Woods, Everett	.967	14	25	34	2	3

OUTFIELDERS

Player, Team	Pct.	G	PO	A	E	DP
Anderson, Boise	.926	14	23	2	2	0
Barwick, Boise	1.000	5	4	0	0	0
Benard, Everett*	.970	53	90	8	3	1
Bonds, Spokane	.977	24	42	0	1	0
Bullock, Bellingham	.964	61	105	2	4	0
Case, Bend	1.000	36	61	6	0	0
Clifford, Bellingham*	1.000	1	1	0	0	0
Connell, Boise	1.000	1	1	0	0	0
Cornell, Eugene*	.955	60	104	1	5	0
Cromer, Southern Oregon*	.931	48	61	6	5	2
Cruz, Spokane	.945	58	96	8	6	1
DeLeon, Spokane	1.000	1	2	0	0	0
Dunckel, Boise	.950	53	92	3	5	0
Ealy, Eugene	1.000	16	15	0	0	0
Echevarria, Bend	1.000	37	65	7	0	1
Endebrock, Southern Oregon	.969	23	28	3	1	0
Filson, Yakima	1.000	37	54	5	0	2
Frazier, Southern Oregon	.954	60	116	8	6	1
Freeburg, Bend	.931	66	53	1	4	0
Garcia, Boise	1.000	8	6	0	0	0
Geis, Southern Oregon	.907	31	38	1	4	0
Griffey, Bellingham	.949	63	87	6	5	1
Hamm, Spokane	.909	19	16	4	2	0
Hardwick, Boise	.978	17	40	4	1	1
Jones, Everett	1.000	31	48	4	0	0
Kerns, Boise	.933	26	36	6	3	2
Krenke, Bend	.952	37	55	4	3	0
Landrum, Yakima	.915	59	111	7	11	3
Lawson, Bellingham*	.938	52	70	5	5	1
Lesher, Southern Oregon*	.931	37	52	2	4	1
Llanos, Bellingham	.903	15	26	2	3	0
Long, Eugene	1.000	2	3	0	0	0
McCracken, Bend	1.000	3	6	0	0	0
McMillin, Eugene	.972	38	65	5	2	0
Minchk, Spokane*	.000	1	0	0	1	0
Miran, Yakima*	.949	22	55	1	3	1
Moore, Yakima	.931	15	27	0	2	0
Newhouse, Eugene	.957	56	63	4	3	0
Partrick, Boise	.000	1	0	0	1	0
Perez, Spokane	.948	45	67	6	4	1
Pinkney, Yakima	.948	44	50	5	3	1
Ramirez, Southern Oregon	1.000	5	12	1	0	0
Ramos, Everett	.927	60	95	6	8	1
Reed, Yakima	.965	43	82	0	3	0
RILEY, Boise	.980	51	95	1	2	0
Roach, Everett*	1.000	9	10	0	0	0
Robbs, Spokane	.941	63	88	8	6	0
Rogers, Bend	.978	62	88	1	2	0
Scalzitti, Bend	1.000	1	1	0	0	0
Scheibe, Spokane	.959	49	47	0	2	0
Scott, Southern Oregon	.910	47	60	1	6	0
Shockey, Bellingham*	.989	45	81	5	1	0
Simmons, Boise	1.000	6	8	0	0	0
Simonton, Everett	.948	64	89	3	5	1
Simpson, Boise	1.000	6	11	0	0	0
Smith, Boise	1.000	1	0	2	0	0

Player, Team	Pct.	G	PO	A	E	DP
Smith, Yakima	.833	14	16	4	4	1
Teeters, Eugene*	.970	62	123	5	4	1
Warren, Bellingham*	.833	15	15	0	3	0
White, Spokane	.950	17	17	2	1	0
Wolff, Boise	.924	50	87	10	8	2
Woods, Everett	.939	40	71	6	5	0
Zammarchi, Yakima	.971	16	33	1	1	0

CATCHERS

Player, Team	Pct.	G	PO	A	E	DP	PB
Abbe, Yakima	.973	36	252	31	8	4	10
Bobo, Boise	1.000	6	40	4	0	0	0
Bonnici, Bellingham	.985	33	181	21	3	0	6
Brooks, Eugene	.968	25	186	23	7	3	5
Brown, Yakima	1.000	5	17	0	0	0	1
Burgos, Eugene	.991	14	101	9	1	1	7
Calvi, Bellingham	.960	20	90	5	4	0	3
Cavanagh, Everett	.971	32	175	25	6	2	6
DeJesus, Spokane	.846	2	10	1	2	0	0
Garcia, Spokane	.976	32	258	32	7	1	14
Gray, Yakima	.980	25	181	14	4	3	6
Hunt, Boise	.969	41	285	26	10	4	8
Johnson, Southern Oregon	.969	19	142	16	5	1	4
Kessler, Spokane	.966	4	21	7	1	0	0
Killeen, Southern Oregon	.975	35	238	35	7	*2	6
Mayes, Everett	.989	30	167	19	2	2	8
Montgomery, Everett	.980	25	187	14	4	1	1
Moore, Southern Oregon	1.000	22	144	13	0	1	4
Norton, Southern Oregon	1.000	7	57	9	0	1	3
Pineiro, Boise	.975	34	222	16	6	1	5
Rosario, Spokane	.955	45	313	67	18	6	17
Scalzitti, Bend	.975	51	454	45	13	3	20
Sievers, Everett	.980	18	91	9	2	0	2
Strittmatter, Bend	.993	34	269	36	2	2	3
Sweeney, Eugene	.967	44	367	42	14	1	14
WIDGER, Bellingham	.987	40	266	39	4	3	10
Wittig, Yakima	.960	3	20	4	1	0	1
Zahner, Yakima	.972	23	128	9	4	0	10

PITCHERS

Player, Team	Pct.	G	PO	A	E	DP
Alston, Bend	.846	14	5	6	2	0
Aschoff, Bellingham*	.923	14	1	11	1	2
Bailey, Bend	1.000	11	5	9	0	0
Baine, Everett*	1.000	11	7	8	0	0
Baker, Spokane	.933	13	5	9	1	1
Banks, Southern Oregon	1.000	24	1	4	0	0
Barbeln, Yakima	1.000	4	0	1	0	0
Bennett, Yakima	.750	2	1	2	1	0
Bennett, Southern Oregon	1.000	17	5	4	0	1
Bladow, Eugene	.882	13	7	8	2	0
Blanchette, Boise*	1.000	5	0	1	0	0
Bojan, Southern Oregon	.857	15	9	9	3	1
Brewington, Everett	.900	15	1	8	1	0
Bunch, Eugene	.769	10	3	7	3	0
Burke, Bend	1.000	10	6	6	0	0
Butler, Boise*	.958	17	6	17	1	0
Byerly, Southern Oregon	1.000	20	3	10	0	0
Caruso, Southern Oregon*	1.000	12	0	3	0	0
Chavez, Boise	.667	14	0	2	1	0
Clinkscales, Eugene	.625	12	1	4	3	0
Cody, Bellingham	1.000	23	1	9	0	0
Colson, Yakima*	.926	15	3	22	2	0
Dale, Spokane	.667	17	0	2	1	0
Deal, Bellingham	.700	16	3	4	3	0
Dickens, Eugene*	1.000	3	0	1	0	0
Dorlarque, Eugene	.923	32	3	9	1	0
Doughty, Bellingham	1.000	11	1	6	0	0
Eddy, Eugene*	.889	23	1	7	1	1
Eggleston, Spokane	1.000	11	0	5	0	1
Eiffert, Bend*	1.000	17	4	10	0	1
Erdos, Spokane	1.000	2	0	3	0	1
Estes, Bellingham*	.789	15	4	11	4	1
Evans, Eugene	1.000	13	3	0	0	0
Fletcher, Eugene*	.786	16	0	11	3	0
Foster, Southern Oregon	.833	4	3	2	1	1
Gienger, Southern Oregon	1.000	14	8	7	0	2
Gorham, Everett	.500	11	1	1	2	0
Graham, Bellingham	.800	27	2	10	3	1
Graves, Yakima	1.000	7	0	3	0	0
Griffin, Southern Oregon	1.000	8	2	2	0	0
Grzelaczyk, Spokane	.962	19	4	21	1	0
Gutierrez, Yakima	.833	16	10	10	4	0
Haas, Eugene*	.000	3	0	0	1	0
Hanneman, Everett	1.000	24	1	8	0	0
Harikkala, Bellingham	.750	15	2	4	2	0
Hartman, Bellingham*	1.000	16	2	4	0	0
Haught, Southern Oregon	.889	19	6	10	2	1
Heckman, Everett*	1.000	22	1	5	0	0
Heming, Eugene*	.933	25	6	8	1	0
Henderson, Bend	.833	12	3	7	2	1
Henderson, Everett*	.500	12	0	1	1	0
Herges, Yakima	.714	27	2	8	4	0
Hermanson, Spokane	.778	14	3	4	2	0
Hicks, Everett	.933	21	3	11	1	0
Hingle, Boise*	.833	15	2	13	3	0
Hodgson, Eugene	1.000	4	1	1	0	0
Holland, Bend	1.000	20	2	2	0	0
Hollinger, Spokane	.889	21	1	7	1	0
Hovey, Bend*	1.000	27	5	6	0	0
Hutchins, Bend	1.000	34	1	5	0	0
Kindler, Spokane	.667	12	1	5	3	0
King, Southern Oregon	1.000	15	2	13	0	0
Kotarski, Bend*	1.000	25	1	11	0	2
Lavalley, Yakima*	1.000	16	2	9	0	1
LEMKE, Southern Oregon	1.000	21	1	17	0	3
Lieber, Eugene	1.000	5	2	8	0	1
Lowe, Bellingham	1.000	14	5	12	0	2
Luther, Everett	.857	17	1	5	1	0
MacCauley, Southern Oregon	1.000	16	4	11	0	0
Maffett, Spokane	1.000	16	1	4	0	0
Marshall, Spokane	.714	22	4	1	2	0
McLain, Everett	1.000	6	0	3	0	0
Minear, Yakima*	1.000	18	1	4	0	0
Miran, Yakima*	1.000	7	0	5	0	0
Mitchell, Boise	.000	7	0	0	2	0
Mountain, Bellingham	.500	12	1	0	1	0
Murphy, Spokane	.667	15	1	1	1	0
Myers, Everett*	1.000	15	0	10	0	1
Nickell, Bellingham	1.000	1	0	2	0	0
Partrick, Boise	1.000	20	3	7	0	0
Payne, Southern Oregon*	1.000	8	0	7	0	0
Peever, Bend	.846	11	2	9	2	1
Perez, Boise*	1.000	13	1	1	0	0
Peterson, Everett*	1.000	20	4	11	0	0
Ploeger, Spokane	1.000	15	4	9	0	0
Post, Southern Oregon	.667	7	0	2	1	0
Pricher, Boise	1.000	32	1	4	0	0
Pruitt, Eugene	.818	16	5	4	2	0
Richey, Everett	1.000	24	1	8	0	0
Riley, Everett	1.000	15	1	10	0	0
Rinehart, Boise	.909	26	1	9	1	1
Rivera, Bellingham	.889	13	7	9	2	0
Rizzo, Yakima*	1.000	15	0	2	0	0
Salcedo, Yakima	.875	16	1	6	1	1
Schmidt, Boise	.533	11	3	5	7	0
Schmitt, Spokane	.833	29	1	4	1	0
Schooler, Bellingham	1.000	2	0	1	0	0
Sebach, Boise	1.000	13	2	1	0	0
Sheehan, Eugene	1.000	19	4	9	0	0
Simas, Spokane	.769	14	3	7	3	1
Smith, Bellingham	1.000	9	8	9	0	2
STOCK, Bellingham*	1.000	21	5	13	0	4
Stroth, Everett	.778	16	0	7	2	0
Sutton, Boise	1.000	10	2	1	0	0
Szczechowski, Everett	.000	7	0	0	1	0
Thomas, Yakima	.733	15	6	5	4	0
Thompson, Bend	.923	16	9	15	2	3
Troutman, Yakima	.500	26	2	0	2	0
Valdez, Spokane	1.000	8	2	3	0	1
Vazquez, Spokane	.667	15	1	1	1	0
Voisard, Bend	1.000	26	8	6	0	1
Watts, Yakima	.895	24	6	11	2	3
Wechsberg, Spokane	1.000	6	2	6	0	2
WEGLARZ, Eugene	1.000	19	0	18	0	1
Wengert, Southern Oregon	.929	6	1	12	1	2
White, Yakima	1.000	12	0	5	0	0
White, Boise	1.000	13	0	2	0	0
Wolcott, Bellingham	.800	9	1	3	1	0
Worley, Bellingham	.700	18	1	6	3	0
Wylie, Boise	1.000	24	4	10	0	0

The following players did not have any fielding statistics at the positions indicated or appeared only as a designated hitter, pinch-hitter or pinch-runner: Abell, dh, ph; Acevedo, p; Cl. Anderson, of; Biley, 2b, 3b; Briley, p; Calvi, p; Carrion, 3b; Constantino, 3b, of, c; Cudjo, p; Currier, p; Endebrock, ss; Galligani, p; Jose, p; Martin, p; J. Martinez, 3b; Mendez, 3b; Metzinger, p; Shrum, ss; Simmons, 2b; J. Smith, dh; Tacgere, ph; C. Valdez, p; Valencia, p.

Year	Team	Pct.
1901—	Portland	.675
1902—	Butte	.608
1903—	Butte	.578
1904—	Boise	.625
1905—	Vancouver	.586
	Everett*	.667
1906—	Tacoma	.600
1907—	Aberdeen	.625
1908—	Vancouver	.578
1909—	Seattle	.653
1910—	Spokane	.596
1911—	Vancouver	.628
1912—	Seattle	.600
1913—	Vancouver	.600
1914—	Vancouver	.632
1915—	Seattle	.564
1916—	Spokane	.622
1917—	Great Falls	.592
1918—	Seattle	.588
1919—	Seattle	.590
1920—	Victoria	.600
1921—	Yakima	.710
	Yakima	.660
1922—	Calgary†	.600
1923-36—	Did not operate.	
1937—	Wenatchee	.603
	Tacoma*	.627
1938—	Yakima	.583
	Bellingham (2nd)†	.511
1939—	Wenatchee	.601
	Tacoma (2nd)†	.533
1940—	Spokane	.587
	Tacoma (4th)†	.500
1941—	Spokane	.669
1942—	Vancouver	.594
1943-45—	Did not operate.	
1946—	Wenatchee	.622
1947—	Vancouver	.566
1948—	Spokane	.614
1949—	Yakima	.660
	Vancouver (2nd)†	.615
1950—	Yakima	.613
1951—	Spokane	.655
1952—	Victoria	.631
1953—	Salem	.635
	Spokane*	.590
1954—	Vancouver*	.636
	Lewiston	.629
1955—	Salem	.646
	Eugene*	.639
1956—	Yakima	.691
	Yakima	.619
1957—	Eugene	.576
	Wenatchee*	.647
1958—	Lewiston	.621
	Yakima*	.594
1959—	Salem	.623
	Yakima*	.563
1960—	Yakima	.638
	Yakima	.562
1961—	Lewiston*	.621
	Yakima	.600
1962—	Wenatchee*	.574
	Tri-City	.580
1963—	Lewiston	.594
	Yakima*	.613
1964—	Eugene	.636
	Yakima*	.611
1965—	Lewiston	.667
	Tri-City*	.681
1966—	Tri-City	.679
1967—	Medford	.607
1968—	Tri-City	.600
1969—	Rogue Valley	.633
1970—	Lewiston a	.538
	Coos Bay-No. Bend	.563
1971—	Tri-City a	.625
	Bend	.538
1972—	Lewiston a	.675
	Walla Walla	.513
1973—	Walla Walla b	.638
	Portland	.563
1974—	Bellingham	.619
	Eugene c	.571
1975—	Portland	.545
	Eugene d	.684
1976—	Portland	.556
	Walla Walla d	.639
1977—	Bellingham e	.618
	Portland	.667
1978—	Grays Harbor f	.671
	Eugene	.514
1979—	Central Oregon d	.606
	Walla Walla	.571
1980—	Bellingham g	.643
	Eugene g	.529
1981—	Medford d	.600
	Bellingham	.557
1982—	Medford	.757
	Salem d	.486
1983—	Medford h	.735
	Bellingham	.588
1984—	Tri-Cities h	.622
	Medford	.608
1985—	Everett h	.541
	Eugene	.541
1986—	Bellingham h	.608
	Eugene	.608
1987—	Spokane c	.711
	Everett	.653
1988—	Southern Oregon	.605
	Spokane d	.553
1989—	Southern Oregon	.600
	Spokane d	.547
1990—	Boise	.697
	Spokane d	.645
1991—	Boise d	.658
	Yakima	.579
1992—	Bellingham d	.566
	Bend	.566

*Won split-season playoff. †Won four-club playoff. §League disbanded June 18. aLeague divided into Northern and Southern divisions, declared champion under league rules. bLeague divided into Eastern and Western divisions, declared champion under league rules. cLeague divided into Eastern and Western divisions; won two-team playoff. dLeague divided into Northern and Southern divisions; won two-team playoff. eLeague divided into Affiliate and Independent divisions; won two-team playoff. fDeclared league champion after winning one-game playoff. Balance of playoff canceled due to rain and wet grounds. gDeclared co-champion after winning one game. Balance of playoff canceled due to rain and wet grounds. hLeague divided into Washington and Oregon divisions; won two-team playoff. (NOTE—Known as Pacific Northwest League 1901-02, Pacific National League 1903-04, Northwestern League 1905-18, Pacific Coast International League 1919-22 and Western International League 1937-54.)

SOUTH ATLANTIC LEAGUE

FINAL STANDINGS

FIRST HALF

NORTHERN DIVISION

Team	W	L	T	Pct.	GB
Charleston (W.Va.)(Reds)	45	26	0	.634	......
Columbia (Mets)	42	27	0	.609	2
Greensboro (Yankees)	40	32	0	.556	5½
Asheville (Astros)	38	32	0	.543	6½
Fayetteville (Tigers)	38	33	0	.535	7
Gastonia (Rangers)	30	34	0	.469	11½
Spartanburg (Phillies)	31	38	0	.449	13

SOUTHERN DIVISION

Team	W	L	T	Pct.	GB
Columbus (Indians)	40	32	0	.556	......
Savannah (Cardinals)	35	36	0	.493	4½
Augusta (Pirates)	35	36	0	.493	4½
Myrtle Beach (Blue Jays)	32	37	0	.464	6½
Albany (Expos)	32	40	0	.444	8
Macon (Braves)	27	42	0	.391	11½
Charleston (SC)(Padres)	25	45	0	.357	14

SECOND HALF

NORTHERN DIVISION

Team	W	L	T	Pct.	GB
Spartanburg (Phillies)	39	30	0	.565	......
Columbia (Mets)	37	32	0	.536	2
Fayetteville (Tigers)	36	34	0	.514	3½
Asheville (Astros)	36	34	0	.514	3½
Gastonia (Rangers)	36	36	0	.500	4½
Greensboro (Yankees)	34	35	0	.493	5
Charleston (W.Va.)(Reds)	32	38	0	.457	7½

SOUTHERN DIVISION

Team	W	L	T	Pct.	GB
Myrtle Beach (Blue Jays)	39	28	0	.582	......
Albany (Expos)	40	30	0	.571	½
Columbus (Indians)	37	30	0	.552	2
Augusta (Pirates)	32	38	0	.457	8½
Macon (Braves)	31	39	0	.443	9½
Charleston (SC)(Padres)	30	40	0	.429	10½
Savannah (Cardinals)	27	42	0	.391	13

COMPOSITE

Team	C'ia	C'us	CWV	Ash.	Gbr.	Fay.	M.B.	Spar.	Alb.	Gas.	Aug.	Sav.	Mac.	CSC	W	L	T	Pct.	GB
Columbia (Mets)	....	2	8	6	9	7	4	8	6	9	6	5	4	5	79	59	0	.572	......
Columbus (Indians)	6	....	4	5	4	7	6	3	6	5	9	6	9	7	77	62	0	.554	2½
Charleston (W.Va.)(Reds)	6	4	....	8	7	5	3	9	4	8	6	5	6	6	77	64	0	.546	3½
Asheville (Astros)	7	3	10	....	8	10	2	7	4	7	2	7	3	4	74	66	0	.529	6
Greensboro (Yankees)	5	4	7	5	....	9	7	7	6	6	3	4	5	6	74	67	0	.525	6½
Fayetteville (Tigers)	7	1	9	4	9	....	5	3	6	6	7	5	6	6	74	67	0	.525	6½
Myrtle Beach (Blue Jays)	4	4	3	6	1	2	....	2	9	5	7	8	8	12	71	65	0	.522	7
Spartanburg (Phillies)	6	5	5	7	6	9	6	....	4	5	4	5	8	6	70	68	0	.507	9
Albany (Expos)	1	12	3	4	2	2	5	4	....	4	9	8	9	9	72	70	0	.507	9
Gastonia (Rangers)	3	3	6	6	8	8	3	10	4	....	3	4	2	6	66	70	0	.485	12
Augusta (Pirates)	5	5	2	6	4	1	7	4	5	5	....	7	5	11	67	74	0	.475	13½
Savannah (Cardinals)	2	8	3	0	4	3	6	2	6	4	9	....	12	5	62	78	0	.443	18
Macon (Braves)	4	5	2	5	3	2	5	5	4	9	5	6	....	6	58	81	0	.417	21½
Charleston (SC)(Padres)	3	6	2	4	2	2	6	5	5	2	2	8	7	....	55	85	0	.393	25

Playoffs—Myrtle Beach defeated Columbus, two games to none; Charleston (W.Va.) defeated Spartanburg, two games to none; Myrtle Beach defeated Charleston (W.Va.), three games to none, to win league championship.

Regular-season attendance—Albany, 97,810; Asheville, 119,040; Augusta, 83,248; Charleston (S.C.), 103,881; Charleston (W.Va.), 135,010; Columbia, 124,448; Columbus, 118,238; Fayetteville, 100,226; Gastonia, 32,931; Greensboro, 156,387; Macon, 88,833; Myrtle Beach, 61,120; Savannah, 79,538; Spartanburg, 47,274. Total—1,347,984. Playoffs (7 games)—9,591. All-Star Game—2,323.

Managers—Albany, Lorenzo Bundy; Asheville, Tim Tolman; Augusta, Scott Little; Charleston (S.C.), Dave Trembley; Charleston (W.Va.), P.J. Carey; Columbia, Tim Blackwell; Columbus, Mike Brown; Fayetteville, Gerry Groninger; Gastonia, Walt Williams; Greensboro, Trey Hillman; Macon, Brian Snitker; Myrtle Beach, Doug Ault; Savannah, Mike Ramsey; Spartanburg, Roy Majtyka.

All-Star team: 1B—Jamie Dismuke, Charleston (W.Va.); 2B—Quilvio Veras, Columbia; 3B—Shane Andrews, Albany; SS—Benji Gil, Gastonia; OF—Gary Mota, Asheville; Cliff Floyd, Albany; Willie Canate, Columbus; DH—Antonio Mitchell, Columbus; C—Tommy Eason, Spartanburg; RHP—Ron Blazier, Spartanburg; LHP—Paul Spoljaric, Myrtle Beach; Most Valuable Player—Gary Mota, Asheville; Most Outstanding Pitcher—Paul Spoljaric, Myrtle Beach; Manager—Mike Brown, Columbus.

BATTING

TEAM

Team	Avg.	G	AB	R	OR	H	TB	2B	3B	HR	RBI	SH	SF	HP	BB	Int. BB	SO	SB	CS	LOB
Columbus	.262	139	4742	681	542	1242	1786	209	40	85	586	51	44	68	488	25	844	97	61	1030
Greensboro	.259	141	4715	703	672	1222	1785	200	39	95	608	10	42	49	596	9	1230	126	88	1036
Asheville	.253	140	4499	601	645	1139	1634	210	24	79	528	13	35	53	464	18	961	134	74	927
Charleston (W.Va.)	.253	141	4614	606	522	1166	1724	224	32	90	529	31	38	69	472	19	1027	163	87	973
Columbia	.252	141	4401	626	559	1107	1534	207	38	43	518	43	48	45	547	15	950	290	144	928
Myrtle Beach	.244	136	4369	590	515	1068	1534	192	23	76	479	49	39	66	429	21	868	136	100	905
Spartanburg	.242	138	4510	573	526	1092	1520	223	26	51	496	40	28	40	501	13	898	125	87	952
Fayetteville	.240	141	4527	592	533	1088	1428	166	33	36	493	61	35	58	553	12	859	169	120	945
Albany	.239	142	4654	601	555	1113	1597	193	45	67	520	19	32	58	561	20	1116	221	93	1008
Macon	.238	139	4533	493	576	1079	1515	182	34	62	417	36	28	50	412	13	1035	164	96	911
Gastonia	.236	136	4321	497	501	1021	1485	160	20	88	434	25	33	41	487	9	1019	124	112	859
Augusta	.235	141	4578	591	606	1077	1507	164	49	56	487	37	37	58	522	23	990	216	118	930
Savannah	.232	140	4483	510	637	1042	1429	153	33	56	411	37	39	51	490	10	953	224	126	923
Charleston (S.C.)	.227	140	4423	478	713	1003	1358	146	25	53	403	25	32	48	434	13	1023	115	103	911

INDIVIDUAL

(Leading qualifiers for batting championship—389 or more plate appearances)

*Bats lefthanded.   †Switch-hitter.

Player, Team	Avg.	G	AB	R	H	TB	2B	3B	HR	RBI	SH	SF	HP	BB	Int. BB	SO	SB	CS
Veras, Quilvio, Columbia†	.319	117	414	97	132	182	24	10	2	40	5	3	9	84	3	52	66	35
Canate, Bill, Columbus	.316	133	528	110	167	235	37	8	5	63	3	6	10	56	3	66	25	9

Player, Team	Avg.	G	AB	R	H	TB	2B	3B	HR	RBI	SH	SF	HP	BB	Int. BB	SO	SB	CS
Hill, Lew, Greensboro†	.313	98	374	75	117	192	12	9	15	52	0	3	11	30	0	89	24	17
Marini, Marc, Columbus*	.307	132	488	78	150	214	30	5	8	70	1	9	4	86	5	63	7	3
Floyd, Cliff, Albany*	.304	134	516	83	157	261	24	16	16	97	0	3	9	45	9	75	32	11
Perna, Bobby, Charleston (W.Va.)†	.301	129	499	73	150	214	27	2	11	71	4	5	0	44	3	77	14	9
Otero, Ricky, Columbia†	.300	96	353	57	106	162	24	4	8	60	4	3	8	38	0	53	39	13
Lis, Joe, Myrtle Beach	.300	125	434	70	130	194	25	0	13	79	2	7	7	68	5	54	5	11
Curtis, Randy, Columbia*	.295	102	353	53	104	128	11	5	1	56	3	3	5	62	2	80	33	16
Mitchell, Tony, 66 Aug.-55 C'bus†	.295	121	421	70	124	219	16	5	23	83	0	1	0	51	4	114	7	9

Departmental leaders: G—Seefried, 141; AB—Ozoria, 551; R—Canate, 110; H—Canate, 167; TB—Floyd, 261; 2B—Canate, 37; 3B—Floyd, 16; HR—Andrews, 25; RBI—Floyd, 97; SH—Stynes, 14; SF—O. Garcia, 11; HP—Mediavilla, 17; BB—Andrews, 107; IBB—Floyd, 9; SO—Andrews, 174; SB—Veras, 66; CS—Veras, 35.

(All players—listed alphabetically)

Player, Team	Avg.	G	AB	R	H	TB	2B	3B	HR	RBI	SH	SF	HP	BB	Int. BB	SO	SB	CS
Abreu, Bob, Asheville*	.292	135	480	81	140	193	21	4	8	48	0	3	3	63	1	79	15	11
Allen, Matt, Albany	.196	16	51	6	10	12	2	0	0	2	0	0	1	5	0	17	0	0
Anderson, Steve, Greensboro*	.292	77	250	44	73	95	12	5	0	31	1	5	3	21	0	42	8	8
Andrews, Shane, Albany	.230	136	453	76	104	199	18	1	25	87	0	3	7	107	4	174	8	3
Anthony, Mark, Charleston (S.C.)*	.236	116	402	45	95	122	13	4	2	32	0	2	3	53	0	80	16	12
Arias, Amador, Charleston (W.Va.)†	.242	58	149	17	36	40	4	0	0	7	2	2	1	9	0	37	7	6
Austin, Jacob, Augusta†	.231	62	221	19	51	69	9	3	1	23	0	2	5	22	3	44	4	1
Ayala, Adan, Charleston (S.C.)	.196	43	102	9	20	27	2	1	1	9	1	1	0	14	0	33	1	1
Ayrault, Joe, Macon	.259	90	297	24	77	107	12	0	6	24	2	1	4	24	0	68	1	1
Bautista, Danny, Fayetteville	.269	121	453	59	122	159	22	0	5	52	4	2	5	29	0	76	18	20
Beals, Greg, Columbia	.285	64	200	31	57	66	4	1	1	19	6	1	0	38	1	26	9	5
Beck, Brian, Augusta*	.171	32	105	8	18	34	5	1	3	13	0	1	0	8	0	39	1	0
Benitez, Yamil, Albany	.165	23	79	6	13	23	3	2	1	6	0	0	0	5	1	49	0	2
Bennett, Al, Spartanburg	.271	65	225	16	61	92	11	4	4	32	1	2	2	9	1	55	9	7
Beuerlein, Ed, Asheville	.264	22	72	6	19	26	1	0	2	8	0	1	1	10	0	15	1	3
Bigler, Jeff, Spartanburg*	.269	125	438	50	118	169	32	2	5	53	1	1	4	49	2	67	4	4
Billeci, Craig, Spartanburg	.230	43	122	13	28	37	6	0	1	11	0	1	1	11	0	34	0	0
Bohrofen, Brent, Savannah	.218	63	179	8	39	47	5	0	1	16	0	5	1	6	0	41	1	0
Bonifay, Ken, Augusta	.255	15	47	8	12	20	2	0	2	9	0	2	2	11	2	10	2	0
Briggs, Stoney, Myrtle Beach	.239	136	514	75	123	184	18	5	11	41	6	2	8	43	0	156	33	14
Brito, Luis, Spartanburg†	.219	34	105	11	23	26	1	1	0	9	1	0	0	4	0	17	7	8
Brock, Tarrik, Fayetteville*	.218	100	271	35	59	72	5	4	0	17	5	1	4	31	1	69	15	10
Brophy, E.J., Spartanburg	.235	25	81	3	19	19	0	0	0	6	4	0	3	2	0	14	0	2
Brown, Mike, Augusta*	.255	102	322	34	82	117	11	9	2	33	4	5	1	37	5	69	11	5
Bryant, Pat, Columbus	.219	49	151	36	33	57	14	2	2	19	2	0	7	30	2	52	10	2
Bullock, Craig, Columbia	.201	95	298	44	60	91	19	0	4	32	2	3	3	42	1	96	4	8
Burguillos, Carlos, Fayetteville	.224	106	352	59	79	95	6	5	0	38	6	2	2	36	0	33	13	12
Burton, Steve, Gastonia	.235	113	332	34	78	103	7	0	6	35	4	2	1	44	2	80	2	3
Bush, Homer, Charleston (S.C.)	.234	108	367	37	86	106	10	5	0	18	0	2	3	13	0	85	14	11
Bush, Ricky, Spartanburg	.175	19	63	6	11	15	4	0	0	7	1	1	0	6	0	17	0	0
Butler, Rich, Myrtle Beach*	.227	130	441	43	100	122	14	1	2	43	6	0	7	37	1	90	11	15
Cabrera, Jolbert, Albany	.228	118	377	44	86	99	9	2	0	23	6	0	1	34	0	77	22	11
Cabrera, Miguel, Asheville	.159	22	63	7	10	17	2	1	1	7	0	2	0	5	1	17	0	0
Cacini, Ron, Asheville	.157	68	172	16	27	32	3	1	0	11	1	2	4	17	0	75	8	6
Calder, Joe, Augusta	.235	84	272	29	64	100	9	3	7	31	0	1	4	19	0	80	11	3
Calzado, Johnny, Savannah	.222	6	18	0	4	4	0	0	0	0	0	0	0	1	0	7	0	0
Canate, Bill, Columbus	.316	133	528	110	167	235	37	8	5	63	3	6	10	56	3	66	25	9
Carabba, Robbie, Albany	.224	69	183	19	41	50	7	1	0	18	3	2	1	32	0	37	3	7
Cardenas, Epi, Columbus	.000	1	1	0	0	0	0	0	0	0	0	0	0	1	0	0	0	0
Carlsen, Bobby, Charleston (W.Va.)*	.225	103	333	42	75	91	8	1	2	25	0	4	0	59	0	62	13	7
Carrion, German, Charleston (S.C.)†	.191	45	115	10	22	28	3	0	1	8	1	0	0	5	0	27	1	1
Casanova, Raul, Columbia	.167	5	18	2	3	3	0	0	0	1	0	0	0	1	0	4	0	0
Cavazzoni, Ken, Charleston (W.Va.)	.120	10	25	2	3	4	1	0	0	1	0	0	0	1	0	5	0	0
Centeno, Henri, Asheville†	.249	126	461	62	115	135	15	1	1	24	6	2	16	37	0	65	14	7
Charbonnet, Mark, Columbus*	.276	122	416	55	115	180	14	6	13	64	7	1	4	14	2	86	10	4
Chavez, Raul, Asheville	.284	95	348	37	99	129	22	1	2	40	1	4	4	16	1	39	1	0
Cherry, Lamar, Spartanburg	.216	35	102	16	22	30	8	0	0	10	1	1	0	21	0	32	1	1
Cholowsky, Dan, Savannah	.328	69	232	44	76	114	6	4	8	34	0	2	3	51	2	48	34	16
Coates, Tom, Macon	.271	38	129	12	35	46	5	0	2	14	1	3	3	12	0	39	8	3
Colon, Angel, Augusta	.000	6	16	1	0	0	0	0	0	0	0	0	1	1	0	8	1	0
Conger, Jeff, Augusta*	.244	98	303	56	74	116	12	6	6	36	2	1	3	44	2	93	36	13
Conley, Greg, Columbus	.150	15	40	3	6	6	0	0	0	5	1	1	0	0	0	11	1	0
Cooper, Tim, Greensboro	.254	105	327	45	83	111	15	2	3	27	0	6	3	51	0	75	9	8
Cora, Manny, Charleston (S.C.)†	.243	121	452	45	110	120	4	3	0	19	4	4	4	29	0	65	12	17
Crespo, Felipe, Myrtle Beach†	.281	81	263	43	74	97	14	3	1	29	2	5	4	58	2	38	7	7
Crespo, Mike, Gastonia†	.166	85	217	20	36	62	6	1	6	20	2	3	0	39	0	68	5	1
Crosby, Mike, Columbus*	.168	53	149	14	25	28	3	0	0	13	2	2	4	6	0	32	0	1
Crosnoe, Cory, Macon	.178	29	73	10	13	18	2	0	1	3	1	0	1	6	0	14	0	0
Cruz, Juan, Charleston (S.C.)	.111	4	9	1	1	1	0	0	0	0	0	0	0	0	0	4	1	0
Cumberbatch, Abdiel, Greensboro†	.252	54	202	29	51	64	4	3	1	18	2	2	1	20	0	40	19	4
Curtis, Craig, Asheville*	.248	59	214	36	53	86	11	2	6	22	0	0	3	28	0	54	13	4
Curtis, Randy, Columbia*	.295	102	353	53	104	128	11	5	1	56	3	3	5	62	2	80	33	16
Dallas, Gershon, Columbus	.219	34	128	13	28	41	2	1	3	18	0	2	2	4	0	22	2	1
De La Cruz, Marcelino, Char.(S.C.)	.091	5	11	0	1	1	0	0	0	1	0	0	0	5	0	3	0	0
Demerson, Tim, Greensboro	.800	2	5	5	4	6	2	0	0	0	0	0	0	1	0	0	1	0
Dempsey, John, Savannah*	.100	7	20	3	2	2	0	0	0	3	0	1	0	2	0	2	0	0
Diaz, Cesar, Columbia	.194	16	62	4	12	12	0	0	0	6	0	0	0	2	0	21	2	0
Dismuke, Jamie, Charleston (W.Va.)*	.284	134	475	77	135	208	22	0	17	71	3	5	15	67	5	71	3	4
DuBose, Brian, Fayetteville*	.228	122	404	49	92	158	20	5	12	73	2	4	4	64	1	100	19	12
Dunn, Brian, Columbia	.297	24	74	9	22	33	5	0	2	10	1	0	1	6	0	9	2	3
Duran, Felipe, Columbus	.236	93	314	35	74	100	10	2	4	33	12	3	8	17	1	63	10	5
Duran, Iggy, Savannah	.215	116	396	48	85	123	14	0	8	39	0	3	3	26	0	91	6	5
Durkin, Chris, Asheville*	.255	100	314	59	80	129	21	2	8	55	0	2	3	67	5	89	27	17
Eason, Tommy, Spartanburg	.298	73	262	41	78	121	20	1	7	37	1	2	2	24	1	21	2	1
Edwards, Jerome, Spartanburg	.223	101	367	46	82	100	11	2	1	35	4	1	3	37	0	59	29	18
Edwards, Mike, Gastonia	.240	109	375	39	90	133	10	0	11	48	1	3	1	43	0	72	7	11
Ellsworth, Ben, Savannah†	.193	62	150	16	29	36	3	2	0	7	4	1	1	12	0	28	2	4
Encarnacion, Angelo, Augusta	.255	94	314	39	80	103	14	3	1	29	4	2	1	25	1	37	2	4
Evans, Stan, Spartanburg*	.278	52	205	36	57	71	10	2	0	12	3	0	2	30	0	33	22	14

Player, Team	Avg.	G	AB	R	H	TB	2B	3B	HR	RBI	SH	SF	HP	BB	Int. BB	SO	SB	CS
Farmer, Randy, Columbia	.248	68	214	24	53	71	11	2	1	23	3	5	2	15	0	48	24	12
Farrell, Jon, Augusta	.222	92	320	44	71	116	11	5	8	48	1	6	4	39	2	93	8	7
Fayne, Jeff, Savannah*	.125	6	16	1	2	2	0	0	0	1	0	0	0	3	0	6	0	1
Fiegel, Todd, Columbia*	.000	26	2	0	0	0	0	0	0	0	0	0	0	0	0	2	0	0
Filotei, Bobby, Charleston (W.Va.)	.174	7	23	4	4	4	0	0	0	1	0	0	0	4	0	6	0	1
Flannelly, Tim, Greensboro*	.273	57	220	26	60	77	9	1	2	29	0	2	1	20	1	34	2	1
Fleming, Carlton, Greensboro†	.331	68	236	35	78	81	1	1	0	24	1	0	0	31	0	20	9	7
Flores, Joe, Columbia	.175	20	63	10	11	16	2	0	1	7	1	1	0	9	0	18	0	1
Flores, Jose, Asheville†	.267	121	457	54	122	150	15	2	3	47	1	5	0	53	0	48	15	6
Flores, Juan, Albany*	.149	28	74	7	11	14	3	0	0	6	1	0	2	9	0	16	0	0
Floyd, Cliff, Albany*	.304	134	516	83	157	261	24	16	16	97	0	3	9	45	9	75	32	11
Franklin, Jay, Gastonia	.000	23	1	0	0	0	0	0	0	0	0	0	0	0	0	1	0	0
Frye, Dan, Charleston (W.Va.)	.192	8	26	0	5	5	0	0	0	0	0	0	0	8	0	10	1	2
Garces, Jesus, Spartanburg†	.056	12	36	5	2	2	0	0	0	1	1	0	0	9	0	2	2	0
Garcia, Anastacio, Myrtle Beach	.196	34	51	2	10	11	1	0	0	2	0	0	2	2	0	9	0	0
Garcia, Omar, Columbia	.290	126	469	66	136	173	18	5	3	70	0	11	1	55	1	37	35	11
Garvey, Don, Augusta	.230	67	183	19	42	48	3	0	1	12	1	3	4	17	0	30	4	6
Gennaro, Brad, Charleston (S.C.)*	.245	78	274	30	67	111	11	3	9	42	2	5	2	18	2	58	6	5
Gil, Benji, Gastonia	.274	132	482	75	132	182	21	1	9	55	3	4	3	50	0	106	26	13
Gillum, K.C., Charleston (W.Va.)*	.254	135	493	61	125	216	34	6	15	63	0	2	10	43	5	139	16	13
Gomez, Mike, Spartanburg	.250	1	4	1	1	2	1	0	0	0	0	0	0	0	0	0	0	0
Gonzalez, Alex, Myrtle Beach	.271	134	535	83	145	215	22	9	10	62	3	2	3	38	2	119	26	14
Gonzalez, Pedro, Fayetteville	.227	42	110	17	25	30	5	0	0	19	1	3	6	38	0	23	5	2
Grable, Rob, 24 Fay.-77 Spar.	.253	101	356	45	90	127	19	3	4	43	3	4	4	59	0	70	9	10
Graffagnino, Tony, Macon	.240	112	400	50	96	151	15	5	10	31	4	4	8	50	1	84	9	6
Graham, Derrick, Charleston (W.Va.)	.280	9	25	2	7	10	0	0	1	3	0	0	1	3	0	10	1	1
Greene, Charlie, Charleston (S.C.)	.185	98	298	22	55	69	9	1	1	24	3	2	5	11	0	60	1	2
Grijak, Kevin, Macon*	.261	47	157	20	41	69	13	0	5	21	0	2	3	15	2	16	3	0
Grissom, Antonio, Albany	.269	136	490	89	132	175	21	5	4	47	3	4	5	79	1	87	62	20
Hall, Tim, Charleston (S.C.)	.199	62	181	16	36	63	7	1	6	22	0	1	2	16	0	66	1	1
Hamlin, Jonas, Savannah	.237	128	455	48	108	172	19	3	13	71	0	6	3	46	1	105	5	6
Hamm, Stacey, Charleston (S.C.)†	.138	25	58	13	8	9	1	0	0	3	2	0	4	7	0	24	2	1
Hammargren, Tucker, Char.(W.Va.)*	.183	70	213	24	39	77	8	0	10	26	0	0	7	26	2	73	2	2
Hammond, Greg, Charleston (W.Va.)	.239	33	88	6	21	26	5	0	0	9	3	0	5	6	0	22	3	0
Hansen, Elston, Greensboro	.273	11	33	8	9	11	2	0	0	2	0	0	0	10	0	6	0	0
Harris, Eric, Columbia	.000	4	11	2	0	0	0	0	0	0	0	0	1	1	0	3	0	0
Harrison, Mike, Charleston (W.Va.)	.241	117	395	38	95	147	20	1	10	51	4	6	8	33	0	122	5	2
Hawks, Larry, Charleston (S.C.)	.168	29	95	12	16	23	4	0	1	6	0	0	1	12	0	25	0	2
Hayden, David, Spartanburg	.223	125	394	46	88	103	11	2	0	29	9	3	3	35	1	66	7	1
Hence, Sam, Columbus	.224	43	161	17	36	52	6	2	2	24	0	1	3	3	0	26	1	5
Hernandez, Ramon, Char.(W.Va.)	.000	1	3	1	0	0	0	0	0	0	0	0	0	0	0	1	0	0
Hill, Lew, Greensboro†	.313	98	374	75	117	192	12	9	15	52	0	3	11	30	0	89	24	17
Hines, Keith, Myrtle Beach	.207	41	111	10	23	29	4	1	0	8	0	1	2	10	0	24	4	5
Hmielewski, Chris, Albany*	.204	129	452	38	92	131	24	0	5	51	0	2	1	53	4	135	0	1
Hobson, Todd, Asheville	.209	90	282	26	59	78	9	2	2	17	2	0	1	21	0	107	8	7
Holbert, Aaron, Savannah	.267	119	438	53	117	145	17	4	1	34	6	3	8	40	0	57	62	25
Holifield, Rick, Myrtle Beach*	.199	93	281	32	56	99	15	2	8	27	3	3	5	23	1	81	6	5
Hopp, Dean, Spartanburg	.125	4	8	0	1	1	0	0	0	1	0	0	3	0	2	0	0
Hubbard, Mark, Greensboro*	.246	87	329	55	81	120	13	1	8	41	0	3	9	43	2	91	10	4
Hurtault, Roosevelt, Albany†	.000	2	3	1	0	0	0	0	0	0	0	0	0	0	0	0	0	0
Hymel, Gary, Albany	.189	87	286	29	54	79	11	1	4	23	1	1	6	31	0	97	2	4
Jelinek, Joe, Spartanburg†	.118	7	17	1	2	2	0	0	0	1	0	0	0	3	0	3	0	1
Jesperson, Bob, Charleston (W.Va.)	.199	99	271	30	54	76	9	2	3	23	3	2	4	29	1	86	7	5
Jeter, Derek, Greensboro	.243	11	37	4	9	12	0	0	1	4	0	0	1	7	0	16	0	1
Jimenez, Manny, Macon	.219	117	401	25	88	106	9	3	1	32	4	2	8	16	1	106	13	15
Johnson, Andre, Macon	.227	20	66	10	15	27	0	0	4	9	0	0	0	7	1	22	3	0
Jones, Motorboat, Charleston (W.Va.)	.268	132	515	75	138	201	29	8	6	54	3	1	0	47	2	81	37	17
Josephina, Mike, Macon*	.232	52	151	21	35	60	5	1	6	12	0	0	1	12	0	42	5	2
Keeline, Jason, Macon	.267	31	90	10	24	28	4	0	0	6	2	0	1	9	0	20	2	3
Kennedy, Darryl, Gastonia	.091	13	33	2	3	4	1	0	0	2	0	1	1	6	1	6	0	2
King, Jason, Columbia†	.100	4	10	1	1	1	0	0	0	1	0	2	0	2	0	3	0	0
Krevokuch, Jim, Augusta	.285	65	239	32	68	92	13	1	3	39	2	2	4	20	0	19	10	2
Kupsey, John, Spartanburg	.246	94	313	41	77	109	16	2	4	30	4	5	4	36	2	80	8	3
Lachance, Vince, Albany*	.100	3	10	0	1	1	0	0	0	0	0	0	1	0	0	1	0	1
Ladell, Cleveland, Charleston (W.Va.)	.200	8	30	3	6	6	0	0	0	0	0	0	3	0	14	3	1
Lantrip, Rick, Greensboro	.253	119	447	66	113	177	19	0	15	68	0	2	2	69	2	150	8	9
Larson, Danny, Spartanburg*	.216	59	185	26	40	62	7	0	5	22	2	2	0	18	2	49	9	5
Leatherman, Jeff, Augusta†	.179	27	78	11	14	16	2	0	0	9	0	0	3	21	0	13	5	3
Lebak, David, Charleston (S.C.)	.238	122	383	38	91	117	15	1	3	25	2	0	7	28	0	105	14	11
Leonhardt, Dave, Fayetteville	.243	110	391	50	95	113	9	0	3	47	3	3	5	48	0	65	12	7
Linares, Mario, Asheville	.241	73	237	28	57	80	20	0	1	37	1	1	6	7	0	22	0	0
Lindsay, Tim, Myrtle Beach	.000	33	1	0	0	0	0	0	0	0	0	0	0	0	0	0	0	0
Lis, Joe, Myrtle Beach	.300	125	434	70	130	194	25	0	13	79	2	7	7	68	5	54	5	11
List, Paul, Gastonia	.352	51	182	32	64	105	11	3	8	40	0	1	4	23	0	26	5	9
Lutz, Brent, Myrtle Beach	.167	49	90	10	15	23	2	0	2	10	2	1	4	13	0	31	2	1
Maguire, Kevin, Augusta	.209	17	43	6	9	10	1	0	0	5	1	0	0	3	0	12	0	0
Mallee, John, Spartanburg*	.188	76	192	34	36	44	2	3	0	14	4	0	3	26	0	49	3	4
Marchan, Jose, Fayetteville*	.100	7	20	2	2	5	1	1	0	4	1	0	1	1	0	6	1	1
Marini, Marc, Columbus*	.307	132	488	78	150	214	30	5	8	70	1	9	4	86	5	63	7	3
Marks, Lance, Macon	.229	125	467	55	107	168	24	2	11	54	2	6	6	24	2	105	12	6
Martinez, Eric, Asheville*	.263	70	251	27	66	86	13	2	1	27	0	4	1	21	3	28	1	0
Marx, Tim, Augusta	.217	44	138	20	30	37	7	0	0	9	3	0	1	23	0	16	0	1
Mashore, Justin, Fayetteville	.239	120	401	54	96	132	18	3	4	43	9	1	3	36	2	117	31	8
Matachun, Paul, Gastonia*	.227	107	344	44	78	100	10	0	4	22	3	3	0	64	3	83	14	11
Matos, Malvin, Gastonia	.219	108	384	37	84	118	10	6	4	23	1	2	1	18	1	87	12	10
Maxwell, Pat, Columbus*	.263	81	270	31	71	81	7	0	1	25	4	1	2	19	1	19	7	2
McCall, Rod, Columbus*	.240	116	404	55	97	172	15	0	20	80	0	6	4	68	4	121	1	1
McClinton, Tim, Columbia	.221	36	145	18	32	46	6	1	2	14	0	0	2	8	0	39	2	1
McCollough, Mike, Gastonia	.149	17	47	3	7	10	1	1	0	1	0	0	0	5	0	17	2	0
McConnell, Tim, Fayetteville	.244	53	176	21	43	67	6	3	4	22	6	3	3	19	1	28	0	0
McCoy, Trey, Gastonia	.354	32	99	17	35	65	6	0	8	30	0	2	7	23	0	19	3	0
Meade, Paul, Columbus†	.267	94	352	47	94	127	15	3	4	31	2	2	3	25	1	77	4	3
Mediavilla, Rick, Savannah	.257	130	490	71	126	165	18	6	3	31	6	1	17	39	1	61	48	21
Merriweather, James, Fayetteville	.219	82	265	27	58	66	6	1	0	17	5	2	0	21	0	34	3	6
Miller, Kevin, Fayetteville	.220	91	277	34	61	90	16	2	3	27	2	2	3	27	0	73	6	2

Player, Team	Avg.	G	AB	R	H	TB	2B	3B	HR	RBI	SH	SF	HP	BB	Int. BB	SO	SB	CS
Milne, Darren, Fayetteville	.226	46	137	16	31	42	5	0	2	18	4	1	6	20	1	34	9	5
Mitchell, Tony, 66 Aug.-55 C'bus†	.295	121	421	70	124	219	16	5	23	83	0	1	0	51	4	114	7	9
Mompres, Danilo, Columbia	.214	108	370	43	79	104	19	3	0	36	5	3	1	29	2	90	31	9
Moody, Kyle, Charleston (S.C.)	.221	115	394	38	87	101	12	1	0	33	5	2	2	36	1	52	10	10
Moore, Mike, Columbus	.182	10	22	5	4	7	1	1	0	1	0	1	1	8	0	2	0	1
Moore, Vince, Macon†	.227	123	436	52	99	142	15	5	6	48	4	3	1	48	2	118	25	11
Mora, Frankie, Columbia	.333	14	48	6	16	19	3	0	0	4	1	0	1	6	0	9	1	0
Moreno, Juan, Columbia	.226	100	318	45	72	107	16	2	5	27	3	2	4	38	1	92	19	12
Morgan, Kevin, Fayetteville	.227	123	466	55	106	129	19	2	0	37	6	4	6	49	2	61	15	19
Morland, Michael, Myrtle Beach	.170	104	265	21	45	66	9	0	4	26	1	4	2	29	0	60	2	1
Mota, Gary, Asheville	.291	137	484	92	141	241	21	5	23	89	0	6	3	58	5	131	22	10
Mowry, Dave, Charleston (S.C.) *	.233	128	430	51	100	159	20	3	11	59	0	6	4	48	4	114	5	3
Mucerino, Greg, Charleston (S.C.) *	.250	65	168	16	42	51	6	0	1	19	1	2	2	15	1	26	1	2
Neff, Marty, Augusta	.272	63	232	29	63	100	9	2	8	37	1	2	2	8	5	48	5	4
O'Neill, Doug, Albany	.250	11	36	3	9	12	3	0	0	3	0	0	0	6	0	13	1	1
Ostermeyer, Bill, Charleston (S.C.)	.273	79	245	43	67	119	13	0	13	43	0	0	4	47	4	79	1	2
Otero, Ricky, Columbia†	.300	96	353	57	106	162	24	4	8	60	4	6	3	38	0	53	39	13
Ozoria, Claudio, Albany	.261	136	551	93	144	207	27	9	6	47	1	3	10	51	1	115	41	12
Ozuna, Mateo, Savannah	.271	51	207	29	56	73	9	1	2	15	4	5	3	18	1	20	26	15
Pages, Javier, Albany	.191	70	246	24	47	64	5	0	4	24	1	1	3	20	0	87	2	1
Parnell, Mark, Charleston (W.Va.)	.000	19	1	0	0	0	0	0	0	0	0	0	0	0	0	0	0	0
Parra, Franklin, Gastonia†	.210	45	157	15	33	45	7	1	1	7	3	1	3	9	0	40	13	6
Patrizi, Mike, Columbia	.217	73	254	35	55	79	13	1	3	27	1	4	3	16	1	66	7	4
Paulino, Dario, Macon	.193	37	114	10	22	29	1	3	0	6	0	0	0	10	0	28	2	2
Perna, Bobby, Charleston (W.Va.)†	.301	129	499	73	150	214	27	2	11	71	4	5	0	44	3	77	14	9
Perozo, Ed, Columbia†	.229	55	179	15	41	56	9	0	2	22	2	2	4	18	2	49	1	3
Phillips, Steve, Greensboro *	.247	129	461	63	114	167	26	3	7	67	2	2	7	71	2	146	6	7
Pineda, Jose, Greensboro	.203	25	69	4	14	15	1	0	0	4	0	0	2	0	0	22	0	2
Polcovich, Kevin, Augusta	.261	46	153	24	40	50	6	2	0	10	3	0	8	18	0	30	7	7
Posada, Jorge, Greensboro†	.277	101	339	60	94	160	22	4	12	58	0	3	6	58	2	87	11	6
Powell, Ken, Gastonia	.232	118	397	50	92	155	13	1	16	56	2	3	6	41	0	117	15	11
Pratte, Evan, Fayetteville†	.284	131	465	73	132	170	17	6	3	43	4	4	5	82	4	80	13	6
Quinones, Eliezer, Charleston (W.Va.)	.239	99	330	49	79	122	15	5	6	34	2	2	10	36	1	51	25	6
Ragland, Trace, Augusta *	.267	52	180	22	48	64	11	1	1	27	2	1	2	19	0	35	5	2
Ramos, Eddie, Asheville	.222	110	379	43	84	153	18	0	17	61	0	2	5	28	1	125	2	0
Reams, Ron, Myrtle Beach	.225	43	138	6	31	37	6	0	0	14	3	3	1	3	0	26	6	3
Reese, Pokey, Charleston (W.Va.)	.268	106	380	50	102	145	19	3	6	53	4	7	5	24	0	75	19	8
Roberts, John, Charleston (S.C.)	.251	84	295	36	74	99	12	2	3	29	0	3	5	44	0	85	20	14
Robertson, Stan, Albany	.239	44	159	11	38	45	5	1	0	11	0	1	3	6	0	36	8	5
Robinson, Don, Macon *	.246	113	399	42	98	122	17	2	1	41	6	3	5	28	0	118	20	10
Robinson, Dwight, Columbia *	.195	79	221	27	43	62	8	1	3	23	4	3	1	36	1	59	8	7
Ronca, Joe, Augusta	.208	27	96	5	20	24	4	0	0	10	1	0	0	9	0	21	6	0
Rosario, Gabriel, Myrtle Beach	.182	23	33	2	6	8	2	0	0	1	0	0	0	1	1	5	2	0
Rose, Pete, Columbus *	.253	131	510	67	129	192	24	6	9	54	8	3	6	48	2	53	4	3
Rusk, Troy, Spartanburg *	.269	52	182	25	49	82	12	0	7	37	0	2	1	21	0	44	1	1
Ruth, Pat, Spartanburg	.201	69	229	27	46	69	18	1	1	20	1	0	2	30	2	71	5	4
Sanford, Chance, Augusta *	.109	14	46	3	5	6	1	0	0	2	0	0	1	3	0	10	0	2
Schall, Gene, Spartanburg	.268	77	276	44	74	113	13	1	8	41	2	2	3	29	0	52	3	2
Schroeder, Todd, Augusta *	.250	5	12	2	3	4	1	0	0	0	0	0	0	0	0	3	0	1
Schulte, John, Augusta *	.193	92	264	30	51	63	4	4	0	17	2	4	1	34	1	63	31	13
Sealy, Scot, Gastonia	.240	56	175	16	42	59	8	0	3	16	0	2	0	14	0	46	1	2
Seefried, Tate, Greensboro *	.242	141	532	73	129	222	23	5	20	90	1	3	2	51	0	166	8	8
Shotton, Craig, Augusta	.204	33	93	13	19	23	2	1	0	8	1	0	5	13	1	23	1	3
Simons, Mitch, Albany	.283	130	481	57	136	175	26	5	1	61	2	10	7	60	0	47	34	12
Smith, Mike, Gastonia	.202	81	302	30	61	94	15	3	4	23	2	4	1	37	0	48	3	11
Smith, Robbie, Columbus	.193	60	145	21	28	30	2	0	0	7	1	2	3	19	0	38	5	4
Spencer, Shane, Greensboro *	.287	83	258	43	74	97	10	2	3	27	1	2	3	33	0	37	8	2
Stanley, Derek, Savannah†	.182	22	44	2	8	10	2	0	0	3	1	0	0	13	0	14	1	2
Steffens, Mark, Spartanburg *	.247	32	97	15	24	36	5	2	1	10	0	0	1	10	1	14	2	2
Stewart, Reggie, Charleston (S.C.)	.235	6	17	2	4	5	1	0	0	4	1	0	0	0	0	3	2	1
Stovall, Darond, Savannah†	.204	135	450	51	92	140	13	7	7	40	1	1	0	63	0	138	20	14
Stynes, Chris, Myrtle Beach	.284	127	489	67	139	196	36	0	7	46	14	4	8	16	1	43	28	14
Sued, Nick, Columbus	.270	84	281	37	76	106	14	2	4	34	4	3	2	47	0	43	2	3
Sullivan, Brian, Fayetteville *	.250	4	12	2	3	3	0	0	0	2	0	0	0	2	0	3	1	0
Swail, Steve, Macon	.400	5	5	2	2	2	0	0	0	2	0	0	1	0	0	1	0	0
Taylor, Gary, Savannah *	.217	53	129	20	28	39	3	1	2	16	1	0	0	42	0	48	1	2
Taylor, Gene, Charleston (W.Va.)	.205	45	151	21	31	53	10	3	2	9	1	1	2	4	0	45	2	1
Tejada, Francisco, Spartanburg	.187	31	91	6	17	24	7	0	0	8	0	1	0	8	0	22	0	0
Texidor, Jose, Gastonia	.280	118	410	45	115	151	23	2	3	32	4	0	1	24	0	65	6	13
Therrien, Dominic, Macon *	.227	66	229	17	52	70	8	2	2	15	3	0	3	11	1	42	3	4
Tolliver, Jerome, Columbia	.222	94	325	37	72	106	15	2	5	41	1	1	4	41	0	94	7	3
Tomasello, John, Gastonia *	.172	61	174	17	30	41	5	3	0	12	0	2	7	27	2	69	2	3
Tosar, Mike, Albany *	.191	19	47	5	9	13	2	1	0	6	1	0	0	7	0	7	1	0
Toth, David, Macon	.258	87	310	32	80	108	15	2	3	41	0	2	4	21	0	44	3	3
Tsoukalas, John, Myrtle Beach *	.230	91	265	23	61	84	8	0	5	28	3	2	7	18	1	43	0	1
Turrentine, Rich, Greensboro	.179	59	201	18	36	55	9	2	2	17	1	1	1	8	0	81	1	3
Turvey, Joe, Savannah	.158	35	95	6	15	18	3	0	0	7	2	0	0	10	0	31	0	1
Ugueto, Jesus, Savannah	.000	4	9	0	0	0	0	0	0	0	0	0	0	0	0	5	0	0
Underwood, Curt, Savannah *	.195	78	241	22	47	69	7	0	5	30	0	3	5	41	1	56	4	2
Van Tiger, Tom, Columbus *	.278	56	180	21	50	57	7	0	0	9	4	1	4	15	1	16	7	8
Vazquetelles, Darren, Macon	.259	11	27	7	7	8	1	0	0	3	2	1	0	5	0	5	0	0
Velez, Jose, Savannah†	.272	93	316	32	86	100	12	1	0	25	4	2	2	18	0	56	8	5
Veras, Quilvio, Columbia *	.319	117	414	97	132	182	24	10	2	40	5	3	9	84	3	52	66	35
Vilet, Tom, Spartanburg	.258	11	31	4	8	9	1	0	0	1	0	0	3	3	0	10	2	1
Virgilio, George, Macon†	.227	112	370	30	84	114	17	5	1	34	3	2	1	44	2	59	18	17
Warner, Mike, Macon *	.278	50	180	40	50	64	7	2	1	8	3	0	0	34	0	28	21	4
Warner, Ron, Savannah	.219	85	242	30	53	63	8	1	0	12	5	2	1	29	2	63	2	3
Webb, Kevin, Asheville	.193	69	202	15	39	57	12	0	2	21	1	1	3	26	0	52	2	3
Weinke, Chris, Myrtle Beach *	.240	135	458	61	110	169	16	2	13	63	4	5	6	70	7	89	4	9
Wentz, Lenny, 54 Ch (WV) -40 Ch (SC)	.266	94	305	44	81	105	16	1	2	35	5	3	1	58	1	67	12	9
White, Jimmy, Asheville *	.337	24	83	12	28	42	6	1	2	14	0	0	0	7	1	15	5	0
White, John, Macon	.181	46	160	10	29	37	3	1	1	8	0	2	2	10	0	47	5	2
Wilkerson, Wayne, Char. (W.Va.) *	.091	5	11	1	1	1	0	0	0	0	0	0	0	0	0	2	0	0
Williams, Eddie, Savannah†	.194	110	356	26	69	107	14	3	6	27	3	4	3	31	2	80	4	4
Williams, Juan, Macon *	.233	67	232	24	54	76	12	2	2	14	0	0	0	25	1	77	16	6

Player, Team	Avg.	G	AB	R	H	TB	2B	3B	HR	RBI	SH	SF	HP	BB	Int. BB	SO	SB	CS
Williams, Lanny, Gastonia	.191	57	141	13	27	42	4	1	3	10	0	0	5	11	0	53	5	5
Wilson, Tom, Greensboro	.210	117	395	50	83	123	22	0	6	48	1	8	3	68	0	128	2	1
Womack, Tony, Augusta*	.245	102	380	62	93	107	8	3	0	18	4	2	5	41	0	59	50	25
Woodall, Kevin, Gastonia	.203	24	69	8	14	16	2	0	0	2	0	0	0	9	0	16	3	1
Yelton, Rob, Fayetteville	.252	79	250	30	63	69	6	0	0	24	0	2	3	38	0	41	5	6
Zapata, Ramon, Augusta	.182	99	302	41	55	70	11	2	0	22	5	2	1	54	0	75	10	13
Zuber, Jon, Spartanburg*	.286	54	206	24	59	83	13	1	3	36	0	1	1	33	1	31	3	1

The following pitchers, listed alphabetically by club, with games in parentheses, had no plate appearances, primarily through use of designated hitters:

ALBANY—Clelland, Rich (27); Conley, Matt (34); DaSilva, Fernando (1); DeHart, Rick (38); Ferguson, Jim (8); Fultz, Vince (11); Kermode, Al (22); Larosa, Mark (33); Looney, Brian (11); Morrison, Keith (15); Paxton, Darrin (33); Pedraza, Rodney (27); Respondek, Mark (33); Reyes, Alberto (27); Urbina, Ugueth (24); Wynne, Jim (27).

ASHEVILLE—Anderson, Tom (25); Bjornson, Craig (22); Brown, Duane (44); Carrasco, Hector (49); Evans, Jim (21); Loughlin, Mark (24); Morman, Al (58); Nieto, Roy (38); Scott, Tyrone (8); Smith, Chuck (28); Waring, Jim (3); West, Eric (8); White, Chris (41); Young, Dan (20).

AUGUSTA—Backlund, Brett (5); Carter, John (1); Christiansen, Jason (10); Coombs, Glenn (5); Danner, Deon (25); DeLosSantos, Mariano (52); Doorneweerd, Dave (25); Evans, Sean (7); Konuszewski, Dennis (17); LaPlante, Michael (3); Loaiza, Esteban (26); Martin, Jim (28); Mc-Curry, Jeff (19); Pisciotta, Marc (20); Pontbriant, Matt (6); Ruebel, Matt (12); Rychel, Kevin (13); Sosa, Jose (29); Sparks, Shane (40); Teich, Mike (17); Wilson, Gary (7).

CHARLESTON (S.C.)—Anthony, Greg (23); Barnes, Jonathan (27); Burns, Jerry (32); Ciocca, Eric (39); Compton, Clint (30); D'Amato, Brian (48); Eggleston, Scott (12); Florie, Bryce (1); Grohs, Mike (38); Hamilton, Joe (7); Hanson, Craig (28); Huber, Jeff (46); Loiselle, Rich (19); Soltero, Saul (19); Wechsberg, Von (19).

CHARLESTON (W.Va.)—Balentine, Bryant (3); Courtright, John (27); Doty, Sean (8); Garcia, Fermin (10); Harvey, Greg (8); Hrusovsky, John (19); Jarvis, Kevin (28); Kendall, Phil (30); Langford, Rich (8); Maberry, Louis (2); McClain, Chuck (31); Miller, Jim (6); Morales, Armando (18); Nieves, Ernesto (37); Nix, Jim (2); Quinones, Rene (5); Robinson, Scott (13); Stewart, Carl (27); Tuttle, Dave (17); Zastoupil, Rich (32).

COLUMBIA—Anaya, Mike (1); George, Chris (1); Guzik, Bob (19); Jacome, Jason (8); Lindsay, Darian (40); Manfred, Jim (32); McCready, Jim (35); Miller, Pat (7); Popoff, Jim (11); Ramirez, Hector (17); Rees, Bob (16); Reichenbach, Eric (30); Schorr, Brad (27); Shaffer, Travis (2); Shanahan, Chris (3); Smith, Ottis (18); Thomas, Steve (42).

COLUMBUS—Baker, Andy (19); Baker, Sam (27); Brown, Clarence (29); Buzard, Brian (6); Crawford, Carlos (28); Doyle, Ian (53); Fleet, Joe (31); Fronio, Jason (20); Harris, Hernando (18); Hernandez, Fernando (11); Johnson, Joel (2); Key, Denny (4); Logsdon, Keith (19); Lopez, Al (16); Resendez, Oscar (5); Shuey, Paul (14); Sweeney, Mark (12); Walden, Alan (40); Welch, Dave (23).

FAYETTEVILLE—Adams, Art (13); Berlin, Mike (4); Blomdahl, Ben (17); Bussa, Todd (44); Carlyle, Ken (14); Cedeno, Blas (2); Durussel, Scott (4); Edmondson, Brian (28); Haeger, Greg (27); Kelley, Rich (28); Lemay, Bob (38); Nowak, Steve (9); Reid, John (14); Schwarber, Tom (53); Thompson, Justin (20); Verduzco, David (7); Waite, Steve (17); Walsh, Dennis (35); Withem, Shannon (22).

GASTONIA—Alberro, Jose (17); Brownholtz, Joe (11); Curtis, Chris (24); Dettmer, John (15); Gandolph, Dave (30); Gerhart, Bert (2); Hampton, Mark (36); Henderson, Daryl (25); Heredia, Wilson (39); Lacy, Kerry (49); Magee, Dan (27); Moody, Ritchie (21); Patterson, Dan (23); Sa-decki, Steve (21); Vaughn, Heath (30).

GREENSBORO—Burbank, Dennis (28); Carter, Tom (13); Coleman, Bill (56); Croghan, Andy (33); Garagozzo, Keith (28); Gietzen, Pete (16); Gully, Scott (61); Inman, Bert (13); Janzen, Martin (2); Laviano, Frank (4); Munda, Steve (46); Pettitte, Andrew (27); Short, Ben (44); Smith, Sean (25); Sullivan, Grant (14); Sutherland, John (14); Thibert, John (6).

MACON—Blair, Dirk (41); Brown, Terry (3); Burgess, Kirk (51); Butler, Jason (24); Clontz, Brad (17); Dunlap, Travis (38); Francis, Scott (27); Koller, Jerome (21); Nelson, Earl (7); Place, Mike (32); Reyes, Carlos (23); Saulter, Kevin (37); Schmidt, Jason (7); Seelbach, Chris (27); Sparma, Blase (5); Steinmetz, Earl (6); Wilder, John (26).

MYRTLE BEACH—Adkins, Bob (11); Baptist, Travis (19); Carrara, Giovanni (22); Garcia, Raphael (18); Gray, Dennis (28); Heble, Kurt (8); Kotes, Chris (25); Mallory, Trevor (12); Martin, Gregg (39); Montoya, Al (42); Nolan, Darin (8); Robinson, Ken (20); Spoljaric, Paul (26); Taylor, Mike (6); Weber, Ben (41).

SAVANNAH—Beltran, Rigoberto (14); Brumley, Duff (6); Busby, Mike (28); Davis, Clint (51); Frascatore, John (50); Fusco, Tom (44); Hammond, Allan (26); Hisey, Jason (28); Johnson, Steve (23); Jolley, Mike (32); Knowles, Greg (39); Lucchetti, Larry (18); Lucero, Kevin (32); Spiller, Derron (23).

SPARTANBURG—Alger, Kevin (1); Blazier, Ron (30); Bottalico, Rich (42); Brown, Dan (16); Brown, Greg (17); DeSantis, Dominic (32); Gilmore, Joel (10); Grace, Mike (6); Hassinger, Brad (20); Holman, Craig (25); Humphry, Trevor (2); Hurst, Charles (31); Juhl, Mike (41); Manicchia, Bryan (25); McIntyre, Joe (3); Nevill, Glenn (11); Randall, Mark (20); Whisenant, Matt (27).

GRAND SLAMS—Mitchell, 3; Ramos, Seefried, 2 each; Andrews, Bigler, Calder, Conger, Dallas, Farrell, Gil, Harrison, Hill, Leonhardt, List, Marks, McCall, McCoy, Ostermeyer, Perna, Phillips, Roberts, Rusk, Sued, Underwood, Weinke, Wilson, 1 each.

AWARDED FIRST BASE ON CATCHER'S INTERFERENCE—Hawks 3 (Ayrault 2, Tejada); Phillips 3 (Encarnacion, Harrison, Turvey); Underwood 3 (Maguire, Pages, Sued); Mucerino 2 (Conley, Morland); Tolliver 2 (Chavez, Wilson); Anderson (Beals); Bonifay (Diaz); Bullock (Pages); Charbonnet (P. Gonzalez); Cooper (M. Crespo); Cora (Morland); Hmielewski (Marx); Johnson (Crosby); Mitchell (Miller); Roberts (Hammargren); Stanley (Hammond); Zuber (Beals).

PITCHING

TEAM

Team	ERA	G	CG	ShO	Sv.	IP	H	R	ER	HR	HB	BB	Int. BB	SO	WP	Bk.
Gastonia	2.99	136	9	13	42	1178.2	985	501	391	47	50	505	22	1042	87	54
Albany	3.09	142	17	13	31	1239.1	1087	555	426	67	43	484	14	1000	95	23
Charleston (W.Va.)	3.13	141	15	17	30	1225.2	1054	522	426	37	48	553	29	1069	103	35
Myrtle Beach	3.15	136	4	16	47	1170.1	970	515	410	66	54	502	11	1025	93	20
Fayetteville	3.16	141	11	18	38	1237.0	1107	533	435	79	57	506	5	1044	82	36
Spartanburg	3.18	138	14	10	34	1201.1	1088	526	425	77	46	396	10	1073	72	14
Columbus	3.23	139	8	18	40	1237.1	1037	542	444	66	49	625	30	1009	101	30
Macon	3.34	139	10	10	30	1210.2	1145	576	449	76	52	436	17	982	87	24
Columbia	3.44	138	9	12	41	1188.0	1102	559	454	71	60	398	3	833	84	21
Augusta	3.45	141	7	8	33	1234.0	1199	606	473	55	80	517	10	1002	96	26
Savannah	3.55	140	12	6	31	1211.2	1081	637	478	68	55	473	15	1057	130	39
Greensboro	3.62	141	9	6	33	1229.1	1218	672	495	69	48	522	9	938	128	13
Asheville	3.98	140	8	8	37	1178.2	1188	645	521	89	58	521	22	882	90	38
Charleston (S.C.)	4.34	140	4	8	29	1175.0	1198	713	566	70	54	518	23	817	96	30

INDIVIDUAL

(Leading qualifiers for earned-run average leadership—115 or more innings)

*Throws lefthanded.

Pitcher, Team	W	L	Pct.	ERA	G	GS	CG	GF	ShO	Sv.	IP	H	R	ER	HR	HB	BB	Int. BB	SO	WP
Baptist, Myrtle Beach*	11	2	.846	1.45	19	2	0	1	0	1	118.0	81	24	19	2	4	22	0	97	5
Pettitte, Greensboro*	10	4	.714	2.20	27	27	2	0	1	0	168.0	141	53	41	4	5	55	0	130	11
Magee, Gastonia*	7	9	.438	2.26	27	24	1	0	1	0	151.0	113	49	38	6	2	82	2	109	13

— 477 —

Pitcher, Team	W	L	Pct.	ERA	G	GS	CG	GF	ShO	Sv.	IP	H	R	ER	HR	HB	BB	Int. BB	SO	WP
Koller, Macon	10	5	.667	2.37	21	21	2	0	0	0	133.0	104	41	35	8	5	31	0	114	8
Bottalico, Spartanburg	5	10	.333	2.41	42	11	1	24	0	13	119.2	94	41	32	6	3	56	0	118	5
DeHart, Albany*	9	6	.600	2.46	38	10	1	15	1	3	117.0	91	42	32	11	4	40	1	133	5
Courtright, Charleston (W.Va.)*.	10	5	.667	2.50	27	26	1	0	1	0	173.0	147	64	48	5	7	55	2	147	9
Curtis, Gastonia	8	11	.421	2.63	24	24	1	0	1	0	147.0	117	60	43	3	6	54	0	107	6
Blazier, Spartanburg	14	7	.667	2.65	30	21	2	6	0	0	159.2	141	55	47	10	5	32	0	149	4
Desantis, Spartanburg	6	9	.400	2.71	32	17	4	8	1	0	133.0	123	53	40	9	8	29	0	100	5

Departmental leaders: G—Gully, 61; W—Blazier, Garagozzo, 14; L—Several pitchers tied with 13; Pct.—Dettmer, .909; GS—Five pitchers tied with 28; CG—Crawford, S. Robinson, 6; GF—Schwarber, 48; ShO—Crawford, S. Robinson, 3; Sv.—G. Martin, 27; IP—Crawford, Hisey, 188.1; H—Pedraza, 187; R—Busby, Schorr, 96; ER—Schorr, 85; HR—Several pitchers tied with 15; HB—Busby, 17; BB—Gray, 93; IBB—Carrasco, Davis, Nieves, 6; SO—Hisey, 182; WP—Hammond, 27.

(All pitchers—listed alphabetically)

Pitcher, Team	W	L	Pct.	ERA	G	GS	CG	GF	ShO	Sv.	IP	H	R	ER	HR	HB	BB	Int. BB	SO	WP
Adams, Fayetteville	0	1	.000	4.70	12	0	0	5	0	0	23.0	31	13	12	2	3	14	0	20	1
Adkins, Myrtle Beach	0	1	.000	10.64	11	0	0	5	0	0	11.0	1	16	13	0	5	23	0	16	6
Alberro, Gastonia	1	0	1.000	3.48	17	0	0	6	0	1	20.2	18	8	8	2	1	4	0	26	1
Alger, Spartanburg*	0	0	.000	0.00	1	0	0	0	0	0	3.0	2	1	0	0	0	1	0	4	0
Anaya, Columbia	0	0	.000	3.00	1	0	0	1	0	1	3.0	1	1	1	0	0	2	0	3	0
Anderson, Greensboro	0	0	.000	6.00	2	0	0	2	0	0	3.0	3	3	2	0	0	1	0	0	0
Anderson, Asheville	11	5	.688	3.52	25	25	2	0	2	0	156.0	130	69	61	10	13	59	0	114	20
Anthony, Charleston (S.C.)	6	10	.375	4.22	23	23	0	0	0	0	119.1	131	64	56	11	4	46	0	60	2
Backlund, Augusta	3	0	1.000	0.36	5	4	0	1	0	0	25.0	10	3	1	1	0	4	0	31	1
A. Baker, Columbus	9	4	.692	4.36	19	13	0	1	0	0	86.2	82	48	42	3	5	44	1	68	15
S. Baker, Columbus	4	4	.200	4.26	27	0	0	15	0	3	44.1	40	21	21	3	1	19	3	33	3
Balentine, Charleston (W.Va.)* .	0	1	.000	4.50	3	0	0	1	0	0	6.0	9	4	3	0	0	6	0	7	0
Baptist, Myrtle Beach*	11	2	.846	1.45	19	19	2	0	1	0	118.0	81	24	19	2	4	22	0	97	5
Barnes, Charleston (S.C.)	6	11	.353	4.51	27	27	1	0	0	0	131.2	146	85	66	7	4	58	1	80	21
Beltran, Savannah*	6	1	.857	2.17	13	13	2	0	1	0	83.0	38	20	20	4	4	40	0	106	8
Berlin, Fayetteville	1	1	.500	3.00	4	3	0	0	0	0	18.0	11	8	6	2	0	16	0	17	2
Bjornson, Asheville*	4	8	.333	3.70	22	16	1	4	0	0	104.2	122	62	43	5	2	28	1	53	6
Blair, Macon	2	1	.667	2.27	41	0	0	22	0	9	67.1	66	25	17	1	2	12	1	60	2
Blazier, Spartanburg	14	7	.667	2.65	30	21	2	6	0	0	159.2	141	55	47	10	5	32	0	149	4
Blomdahl, Fayetteville	10	4	.714	2.70	17	17	2	0	2	0	103.1	94	46	31	5	4	26	0	65	6
Bottalico, Spartanburg	5	10	.333	2.41	42	11	1	24	0	13	119.2	94	41	32	6	3	56	0	118	5
D. Brown, Spartanburg	2	0	.000	2.40	16	0	0	4	0	1	30.0	26	16	8	1	3	30	1	30	1
Brown, Columbus	8	3	.727	2.36	29	3	0	5	0	0	80.0	60	25	21	3	3	49	4	65	7
Brown, Asheville	5	3	.625	3.45	44	2	0	11	0	0	94.0	104	49	36	8	7	35	1	68	10
G. Brown, Spartanburg	6	5	.545	4.20	17	17	1	0	0	0	98.2	107	60	46	8	3	35	0	66	8
Brown, Macon	0	2	.000	5.06	3	3	0	0	0	0	10.2	17	7	6	0	0	3	0	8	0
Brownholtz, Gastonia*	6	2	.750	2.12	11	11	0	0	0	0	72.1	60	20	17	3	5	11	0	58	0
Brumley, Savannah	2	1	.667	1.74	5	5	0	0	0	0	31.0	17	9	6	1	0	14	0	46	2
Burbank, Greensboro	1	2	.333	5.72	27	0	0	10	0	0	45.2	55	34	29	2	1	17	0	38	9
Burgess, Macon*	3	6	.333	2.93	51	0	0	20	0	6	70.2	66	34	23	3	4	19	4	65	8
Burns, Charleston (S.C.)	5	12	.294	4.52	32	19	1	5	0	1	125.1	123	78	63	11	2	48	0	117	8
Busby, Savannah	4	13	.235	3.67	28	28	1	0	0	0	149.2	145	96	61	11	17	67	0	84	16
Bussa, Fayetteville	2	9	.182	3.88	44	0	0	24	0	4	67.1	65	37	29	3	9	30	1	52	3
Butler, Macon*	5	12	.294	4.32	24	24	1	0	0	0	131.1	118	83	63	15	5	68	1	85	17
Buzard, Columbus*	1	1	.500	13.50	6	0	0	2	0	0	8.2	9	15	13	1	0	19	2	6	2
Carlyle, Fayetteville	8	4	.667	1.92	14	14	1	0	1	0	79.2	64	21	17	3	4	24	0	59	6
Carrara, Myrtle Beach	11	7	.611	3.14	22	16	1	2	1	0	100.1	86	40	35	12	4	36	0	100	9
Carrasco, Asheville	5	5	.500	2.99	49	0	0	30	0	8	78.1	66	30	26	5	3	47	6	67	11
Carter, Augusta	0	0	.000	0.00	1	0	0	0	0	0	5.0	3	0	0	0	2	1	0	4	0
Carter, Greensboro*	3	3	.500	4.22	13	13	0	0	0	0	74.2	77	41	35	2	3	29	0	59	13
Cedeno, Fayetteville	0	1	.000	3.00	2	1	1	0	0	0	9.0	3	3	3	0	0	0	0	12	0
Christiansen, Augusta*	1	0	1.000	1.80	10	0	0	4	0	2	20.0	12	4	4	0	0	8	0	21	1
Ciocca, Charleston (S.C.)	3	4	.429	5.59	39	1	0	15	0	1	83.2	91	58	52	4	4	44	4	54	7
Clelland, Albany	10	12	.455	3.96	27	27	2	0	1	0	166.0	149	86	73	9	6	88	0	107	24
Clontz, Macon	2	1	.667	3.91	17	0	0	14	0	2	23.0	19	14	10	2	3	10	0	18	1
Coleman, Greensboro	3	5	.375	3.33	56	0	0	25	0	7	73.0	59	39	27	4	6	52	3	67	14
Compton, Charleston (S.C.)	5	13	.278	5.48	30	20	0	3	0	0	116.2	114	84	71	6	8	69	2	85	11
Conley, Albany	2	3	.400	4.74	34	5	1	14	0	3	81.2	82	46	43	4	2	39	1	56	9
Coombs, Augusta	0	3	.000	14.54	5	5	0	0	0	0	13.0	24	25	21	1	1	24	0	10	4
Courtright, Charleston (W.Va.)*.	10	5	.667	2.50	27	26	1	0	1	0	173.0	147	64	48	5	7	55	2	147	9
Crawford, Columbus	10	11	.476	2.92	28	28	6	0	3	0	188.1	167	78	61	7	12	85	4	127	3
Croghan, Greensboro	10	8	.556	4.49	33	19	1	3	0	0	122.1	128	78	61	11	3	57	0	98	9
Curtis, Gastonia	8	11	.421	2.63	24	24	1	0	1	0	147.0	117	60	43	3	6	54	0	107	6
D'Amato, Charleston (S.C.)	2	5	.286	3.87	48	1	0	31	0	10	93.0	100	48	40	3	9	38	4	42	6
Danner, Augusta*	7	6	.538	3.95	25	23	1	0	0	0	141.1	165	84	62	8	14	45	0	57	8
DaSilva, Albany	1	0	1.000	1.13	1	1	0	0	0	0	8.0	4	1	1	0	1	0	1	9	0
Davis, Savannah	4	2	.667	2.22	51	0	0	23	0	1	65.0	49	24	16	0	4	21	6	61	3
DeHart, Albany*	9	6	.600	2.46	38	10	1	15	1	3	117.0	91	42	32	11	4	40	1	133	5
DeLosSantos, Augusta	7	8	.467	2.25	52	1	0	28	0	12	96.0	75	33	24	2	6	38	2	103	4
Desantis, Spartanburg	6	9	.400	2.71	32	17	4	8	1	0	133.0	123	53	40	9	8	29	0	100	5
Dettmer, Gastonia	10	1	.909	2.02	15	15	3	0	1	0	98.0	74	25	22	1	2	17	0	102	2
Doorneweerd, Augusta	9	13	.409	3.04	25	24	1	0	0	0	148.0	129	66	50	13	6	58	0	152	15
Doty, Charleston (W.Va.)	0	3	.000	4.38	8	0	0	6	0	0	12.1	10	6	6	0	2	8	1	4	2
Doyle, Columbus	4	5	.444	3.31	53	0	0	44	0	26	68.0	55	31	25	3	3	25	3	55	4
Dunlap, Macon	3	5	.375	3.61	38	0	0	22	0	7	82.1	83	35	33	5	4	29	2	62	8
Durussel, Fayetteville	0	0	.000	3.00	4	0	0	1	0	0	9.0	5	3	3	0	1	4	0	10	0
Edmondson, Fayetteville	10	6	.625	3.36	28	27	3	0	1	0	155.1	145	69	58	10	6	67	0	125	6
Eggleston, Charleston (S.C.)	1	2	.333	5.75	12	4	0	5	0	0	36.0	33	27	23	5	2	25	0	28	6
Evans, Asheville	2	2	.500	5.23	21	0	0	9	0	0	31.0	28	20	18	5	2	18	1	27	1
Evans, Augusta	1	2	.333	2.23	7	7	0	0	0	0	40.1	25	14	10	0	2	18	0	32	2
Ferguson, Albany	1	0	1.000	10.45	8	0	0	2	0	0	10.1	13	12	12	0	1	8	1	7	4
Fiegel, Columbia*	5	6	.455	3.85	26	18	1	6	0	2	128.2	118	80	55	6	6	55	0	83	14
Fleet, Columbus	7	3	.700	3.15	31	14	0	7	0	2	111.1	87	46	39	6	6	66	2	78	16
Florie, Charleston (S.C.)	0	1	.000	1.80	1	1	0	0	0	0	5.0	5	3	1	1	0	0	0	5	0
Francis, Macon	2	3	.400	3.48	27	0	0	16	0	3	41.1	41	24	16	3	0	16	3	40	3
Franklin, Columbus	2	3	.400	3.26	22	1	0	16	0	2	38.2	33	17	14	0	7	13	1	28	3
Frascatore, Savannah	5	7	.417	3.84	50	0	0	44	0	23	58.2	49	32	25	4	3	29	2	56	4
Fronio, Columbus	3	1	.750	0.84	20	0	0	15	0	4	32.1	11	7	3	2	1	5	1	40	1
Fultz, Albany	0	0	.000	2.65	11	0	0	2	0	0	17.0	20	6	5	1	1	5	1	12	1

Pitcher, Team	W	L	Pct.	ERA	G	GS	CG	GF	ShO	Sv.	IP	H	R	ER	HR	HB	BB	Int. BB	SO	WP
Fusco, Savannah*	4	2	.667	5.14	44	1	0	13	0	1	56.0	54	46	32	5	0	42	1	58	7
Gandolph, Gastonia*	4	2	.667	2.24	30	2	0	7	0	2	52.1	32	18	13	0	0	34	1	52	12
Garagozzo, Greensboro*	14	8	.636	2.84	28	28	2	0	0	0	174.0	153	77	55	15	1	70	0	137	11
Garcia, Charleston (W.Va.)	0	1	.000	2.00	10	0	0	7	0	0	18.0	20	8	4	0	1	7	0	12	3
Garcia, Myrtle Beach	4	2	.667	3.55	18	5	0	6	0	0	50.2	43	21	20	0	2	24	0	35	5
Garvey, Augusta	0	0	.000	9.00	1	0	0	1	0	0	1.0	3	1	1	0	0	1	0	1	0
George, Columbia*	0	0	.000	0.00	1	0	0	1	0	0	1.0	0	0	0	0	0	1	0	1	0
Gerhart, Gastonia	0	1	.000	2.25	2	2	0	0	0	0	8.0	7	6	2	0	0	4	0	7	0
Gietzen, Greensboro*	0	1	.000	4.00	16	0	0	4	0	0	18.0	18	12	8	2	1	11	0	16	2
Gilmore, Spartanburg	2	4	.333	2.64	10	9	1	0	0	0	61.1	47	21	18	3	2	17	1	60	2
Grace, Spartanburg	0	1	.000	4.94	6	6	0	0	0	0	27.1	25	16	15	3	1	8	0	21	2
Gray, Myrtle Beach*	11	12	.478	3.82	28	28	0	0	0	0	155.1	122	82	66	8	6	93	0	141	13
Grijak, Macon	0	0	.000	0.00	2	0	0	2	0	0	1.2	2	0	0	0	0	0	0	0	0
Grohs, Charleston (S.C.)	6	2	.750	6.78	38	1	0	13	0	2	66.1	77	57	50	5	6	44	4	53	9
Gully, Greensboro	7	9	.438	3.61	61	0	0	29	0	4	82.1	83	57	33	3	5	35	5	55	11
Guzik, Columbia	6	6	.500	3.12	19	14	0	2	0	0	98.0	98	43	34	4	7	25	0	47	6
Haeger, Fayetteville*	4	2	.667	3.97	27	0	0	12	0	2	47.2	41	24	21	3	4	39	1	46	4
Hamilton, Charleston (S.C.)	2	2	.500	3.38	7	7	0	0	0	0	34.2	37	24	13	2	0	4	0	35	6
Hammond, Savannah	6	12	.333	3.41	26	25	2	0	0	0	153.0	139	78	58	8	2	66	0	109	27
Hampton, Gastonia	4	9	.308	4.91	36	5	0	13	0	3	80.2	82	54	44	3	8	47	4	59	7
Hanson, Charleston (S.C.)	2	10	.167	3.28	28	17	0	4	0	0	118.0	115	60	43	7	5	49	4	75	7
Harris, Columbus	7	4	.636	3.67	18	17	0	0	0	0	90.2	88	51	37	10	2	51	1	57	11
Harvey, Charleston (W.Va.)	2	0	1.000	5.12	8	2	0	2	0	1	19.1	20	13	11	0	2	14	0	11	8
Hassinger, Spartanburg	4	1	.800	1.35	20	2	0	14	0	5	46.2	38	9	7	1	1	11	2	34	5
Heble, Myrtle Beach	0	0	.000	3.72	8	0	0	5	0	1	9.2	7	5	4	0	0	7	0	13	3
Henderson, Gastonia*	9	9	.500	2.87	25	25	1	0	0	0	156.2	128	67	50	10	2	62	2	138	8
Heredia, Gastonia	1	2	.333	5.12	39	1	0	22	0	5	63.1	71	45	36	4	5	30	2	64	11
Hernandez, Columbus	4	5	.444	1.57	11	11	1	0	1	0	68.2	42	16	12	4	6	33	1	70	4
Hisey, Savannah	13	7	.650	2.87	28	28	5	0	2	0	188.1	157	79	60	13	4	42	0	182	15
Holman, Spartanburg	9	6	.600	3.70	25	24	3	1	0	0	143.1	153	72	59	9	4	39	0	129	10
Hrusovsky, Charleston (W.Va.)	1	0	1.000	0.83	19	0	0	16	0	9	21.2	13	3	2	0	0	9	1	27	0
Huber, Charleston (S.C.)*	8	3	.727	2.91	46	0	0	30	0	9	77.1	66	31	25	3	4	21	2	59	6
Humphry, Spartanburg	0	0	.000	0.00	2	0	0	2	0	2	2.0	0	0	0	0	0	0	0	1	0
Hurst, Spartanburg	4	5	.444	3.48	31	3	0	15	0	2	62.0	62	26	24	5	0	16	0	47	4
Inman, Greensboro	1	6	.143	6.08	13	13	0	0	0	0	60.2	82	52	41	5	2	32	0	31	6
Jacome, Columbia*	4	1	.800	1.03	8	8	1	0	0	0	52.2	40	7	6	2	0	15	0	49	4
Janzen, Greensboro	0	0	.000	3.60	2	0	0	2	0	1	5.0	5	2	2	0	0	1	0	5	2
Jarvis, Charleston (W.Va.)	6	8	.429	3.11	28	18	2	3	1	0	133.0	123	59	46	3	1	37	1	131	9
Johnson, Columbus	0	1	.000	20.25	2	0	0	1	0	0	1.1	3	3	3	1	0	1	0	1	0
Johnson, Savannah	7	8	.467	3.19	23	17	1	3	0	1	124.0	115	54	44	8	3	24	0	90	4
Jolley, Savannah	2	6	.250	5.17	32	8	1	3	0	1	92.1	89	61	53	6	3	38	0	83	20
Juhl, Spartanburg*	5	5	.500	3.52	41	0	0	18	0	1	64.0	54	28	25	3	1	15	0	83	6
Kelley, Fayetteville*	13	5	.722	2.82	28	26	2	0	0	0	162.2	140	62	51	15	6	63	0	117	12
Kendall, Charleston (W.Va.)	2	1	.667	2.01	30	0	0	20	0	2	49.1	36	15	11	1	2	23	4	43	5
Kermode, Albany*	0	3	.000	2.08	22	0	0	21	0	12	26.0	19	7	6	1	0	8	1	29	2
Key, Columbus	1	1	.500	13.50	4	0	0	2	0	0	6.2	13	10	10	2	0	5	0	6	1
Knowles, Savannah	6	4	.600	3.07	39	0	0	23	0	3	44.0	37	17	15	1	2	15	3	30	1
Koller, Macon	10	5	.667	2.37	21	21	2	0	0	0	133.0	104	41	35	8	5	31	0	114	8
Konuszewski, Augusta	3	3	.500	2.31	17	8	0	4	0	1	62.1	50	19	16	1	5	19	0	45	2
Kotes, Myrtle Beach	12	5	.706	3.54	25	25	0	0	0	0	132.1	110	63	52	11	4	68	1	100	7
Lacy, Gastonia	3	7	.300	3.88	49	1	0	32	0	17	55.2	55	35	24	2	1	42	2	57	9
Langford, Charleston (W.Va.)	3	4	.429	5.17	8	8	1	0	0	0	38.1	35	26	22	2	0	30	0	43	4
LaPlante, Augusta	1	1	.500	3.44	3	3	0	0	0	0	18.1	20	7	7	1	0	6	0	7	1
Larosa, Albany*	1	2	.333	1.69	33	0	0	27	0	7	37.1	21	9	7	0	1	14	1	37	1
Laviano, Greensboro	0	0	.000	8.31	4	0	0	2	0	0	8.2	8	9	8	0	1	6	0	7	2
Lemay, Fayetteville*	6	7	.462	4.20	38	0	0	11	0	1	85.2	81	43	40	5	2	34	1	91	5
Lindsay, Columbia*	9	2	.818	2.54	40	0	0	26	0	7	56.2	48	20	16	5	4	12	1	54	3
Lindsay, Myrtle Beach	1	6	.143	3.56	33	6	0	16	0	1	86.0	96	47	34	5	5	24	3	65	9
Loaiza, Augusta	10	8	.556	3.89	26	25	3	1	0	0	143.1	134	72	62	7	10	60	0	123	7
Logsdon, Columbus*	6	5	.545	2.94	19	18	0	0	0	0	113.1	104	43	37	1	5	48	0	86	9
Loiselle, Charleston (S.C.)	4	8	.333	3.71	19	19	2	0	2	0	97.0	93	51	40	2	3	42	0	64	2
Looney, Albany*	3	2	.600	2.14	11	11	0	0	1	0	67.1	51	22	16	1	0	30	0	56	4
Lopez, Columbus	7	2	.778	2.88	16	16	1	0	0	0	97.0	80	41	31	4	2	33	0	117	9
Loughlin, Asheville*	6	8	.429	5.94	24	23	0	1	0	0	119.2	146	89	79	15	11	50	0	85	10
Lucchetti, Savannah	0	2	.000	7.32	18	2	0	5	0	0	35.2	55	39	29	2	3	21	0	31	6
Lucero, Savannah*	3	5	.375	5.23	32	0	0	13	0	1	41.1	44	25	24	2	4	27	2	47	7
Maberry, Charleston (W.Va.)	0	1	.000	5.40	2	0	0	1	0	0	3.1	3	2	2	0	0	1	0	5	0
Magee, Gastonia*	7	9	.438	2.26	27	24	1	0	1	0	151.0	113	49	38	6	2	82	2	109	13
Mallory, Myrtle Beach	0	7	.000	7.35	12	8	0	1	0	0	45.1	60	47	37	5	1	29	0	17	5
Manfred, Columbia	3	4	.429	3.54	32	1	0	19	0	6	53.1	46	23	21	3	2	26	0	40	8
Manicchia, Spartanburg	2	1	.667	5.66	25	1	0	6	0	0	49.1	61	36	31	6	3	21	0	28	7
Martin, Myrtle Beach	2	1	.667	1.02	39	0	0	36	0	27	44.1	19	7	5	2	1	11	0	57	2
Martin, Augusta*	1	2	.333	1.39	28	0	0	16	0	5	51.2	44	10	8	2	2	22	1	47	5
Matachun, Gastonia	0	0	.000	0.00	1	0	0	1	0	0	1.0	1	0	0	0	0	1	0	0	0
McClain, Charleston (W.Va.)	12	6	.667	3.74	31	19	2	5	1	1	139.2	108	67	58	3	15	76	2	120	14
McCready, Columbia	5	3	.625	2.47	35	9	1	17	1	5	87.1	85	35	24	3	5	23	0	54	4
McCurry, Augusta	2	1	.667	3.30	19	0	0	13	0	7	30.0	36	14	11	1	3	15	1	34	4
McIntyre, Spartanburg*	0	0	.000	13.50	3	0	0	1	0	0	4.0	6	6	6	1	1	3	0	4	0
Miller, Charleston (W.Va.)	0	1	.000	3.68	6	1	0	3	0	0	14.2	10	6	6	0	3	11	0	11	2
Miller, Columbia	1	0	1.000	2.31	7	0	0	7	0	2	11.2	13	3	3	0	0	3	0	10	0
Montoya, Myrtle Beach*	4	4	.500	2.82	42	2	0	21	0	10	99.0	96	36	31	7	4	33	4	99	5
Moody, Charleston (S.C.)	0	0	.000	0.00	1	0	0	1	0	0	1.0	1	0	0	0	2	0	0	0	0
Moody, Gastonia*	0	2	.000	0.34	21	0	0	15	0	11	26.1	9	7	1	0	0	16	0	29	4
Morales, Charleston (W.Va.)	8	3	.727	3.39	18	12	2	4	2	0	71.2	57	34	27	3	0	41	2	56	6
Morman, Asheville*	8	0	1.000	1.55	57	0	0	37	0	15	75.1	60	17	13	3	3	26	2	70	2
Morrison, Albany	8	4	.667	2.43	15	15	2	0	1	0	111.0	113	46	30	2	3	28	1	85	3
Munda, Greensboro	8	0	1.000	3.70	46	0	0	8	0	4	90.0	97	54	37	9	8	36	0	73	10
Nelson, Macon*	0	5	.000	5.19	7	7	0	0	0	0	34.2	34	24	20	1	4	15	0	24	2
Nevill, Spartanburg*	2	1	.667	4.24	11	0	0	6	0	0	17.0	20	9	8	1	1	9	1	16	2
Nieto, Asheville	6	9	.400	4.71	38	16	3	7	1	2	126.0	139	75	66	12	6	53	5	77	3
Nieves, Charleston (W.Va.)	11	6	.647	3.74	37	0	0	14	0	1	74.2	71	37	31	5	1	38	6	35	5
Nix, Charleston (W.Va.)	0	0	.000	0.00	2	0	0	1	0	0	3.1	3	0	0	0	1	1		5	2
Nolan, Myrtle Beach	0	3	.000	5.00	8	0	0	6	0	1	9.0	16	9	5	1	2	6	0	9	1
Nowak, Fayetteville	0	0	.000	11.45	9	0	0	2	0	0	11.0	19	14	14	0	2	8	0	10	0
Parnell, Charleston (W.Va.)	0	3	.000	2.01	19	0	0	16	0	8	31.1	28	9	7	0	4	12	2	36	2

Pitcher, Team	W	L	Pct.	ERA	G	GS	CG	GF	ShO	Sv.	IP	H	R	ER	HR	HB	BB	Int. BB	SO	WP
Patterson, Gastonia	4	6	.400	3.59	23	21	3	0	1	0	105.1	106	47	42	9	4	33	3	84	5
Paxton, Albany*	6	9	.400	2.99	33	15	2	5	1	0	129.1	102	56	43	8	1	62	4	120	9
Pedraza, Albany	13	8	.619	3.26	27	26	2	0	0	0	176.2	187	90	64	7	9	30	0	106	10
Pettitte, Greensboro*	10	4	.714	2.20	27	27	2	0	1	0	168.0	141	53	41	4	5	55	0	130	11
Pisciotta, Augusta	4	5	.444	4.54	20	12	1	5	0	1	79.1	91	51	40	4	10	43	2	54	12
Place, Macon	2	7	.222	3.91	32	8	1	5	0	0	92.0	105	59	40	5	3	35	2	54	12
Pontbriant, Augusta*	1	2	.333	5.64	6	5	0	0	0	0	30.1	36	22	19	1	1	16	0	15	6
Popoff, Columbia	4	3	.571	4.34	11	6	0	5	0	0	45.2	48	23	22	5	2	16	0	29	1
Quinones, Charleston (W.Va.)*	0	1	.000	5.00	5	0	0	3	0	0	9.0	9	6	5	0	2	0	6	0
Ramirez, Columbia	5	4	.556	3.61	17	17	1	0	0	0	94.2	93	50	38	5	3	33	1	53	4
Randall, Spartanburg	0	4	.000	1.82	20	0	0	19	0	10	29.2	15	8	6	2	0	9	3	32	1
Rees, Columbia	4	4	.500	2.96	16	8	1	4	1	2	67.0	64	29	22	3	5	21	0	36	3
Reichenbach, Columbia	8	9	.471	3.94	30	16	1	8	0	2	132.1	125	68	58	9	7	45	1	86	10
Reid, Fayetteville	4	6	.400	2.75	14	14	1	0	0	0	85.0	74	28	26	5	2	24	0	78	3
Resendez, Columbus	0	1	.000	1.54	5	1	0	2	0	0	11.2	9	2	2	0	0	7	0	13	1
Respondek, Albany*	3	2	.600	1.90	33	0	0	11	0	0	47.1	43	20	10	1	3	24	2	39	5
Reyes, Albany	0	2	.000	3.95	27	0	0	18	0	4	27.1	24	14	12	0	3	13	0	29	4
Reyes, Macon	2	3	.400	2.10	23	0	0	7	0	2	60.0	57	16	14	2	5	11	1	57	2
Robinson, Myrtle Beach	1	0	1.000	2.82	20	0	0	9	0	1	38.1	25	12	12	2	3	30	0	45	4
Robinson, Charleston (W.Va.)	8	2	.800	1.72	13	13	6	0	3	0	99.1	73	28	19	3	0	25	2	80	1
Ruebel, Augusta*	5	2	.714	2.78	12	10	1	1	0	0	64.2	53	26	20	1	5	19	0	65	2
Rychel, Augusta	1	3	.250	4.50	13	0	0	8	0	2	16.0	12	12	8	0	0	12	1	16	0
Sadecki, Gastonia	4	3	.571	4.43	21	3	0	4	0	1	42.2	42	23	21	1	3	25	4	49	2
Saulter, Macon	4	3	.571	3.23	37	0	0	21	0	1	61.1	68	33	22	2	4	21	3	54	7
Schmidt, Macon	0	3	.000	4.01	7	7	0	0	0	0	24.2	31	18	11	2	1	19	0	33	2
Schorr, Columbia	12	6	.667	4.78	27	27	2	0	1	0	160.0	169	96	85	13	10	48	0	106	16
Schwarber, Fayetteville	2	6	.250	1.53	53	0	0	48	0	24	76.2	60	22	13	3	2	17	1	87	4
Scott, Asheville*	0	1	.000	4.30	8	1	0	6	0	0	14.2	10	7	7	1	1	11	0	10	0
Seelbach, Macon	9	11	.450	3.32	27	27	1	0	0	0	157.1	134	65	58	11	9	68	0	144	5
Shaffer, Columbia	0	1	.000	19.29	2	1	0	0	0	0	2.1	5	5	5	0	2	3	0	2	2
Shanahan, Columbia*	1	0	1.000	0.00	2	1	0	0	0	0	10.0	7	0	0	0	1	0	0	5	1
Short, Greensboro	1	4	.200	3.02	44	0	0	39	0	16	47.2	54	25	16	3	0	23	1	67	3
Shuey, Columbus	5	5	.500	3.35	14	14	0	0	0	0	78.0	62	35	29	2	3	47	2	73	5
Smith, Asheville	9	9	.500	5.18	28	20	1	3	0	1	132.0	128	93	76	14	4	78	1	117	4
Smith, Columbia*	6	6	.500	3.02	18	12	1	4	0	2	95.1	75	39	32	5	3	38	0	94	6
Smith, Greensboro	9	9	.500	3.97	25	25	1	0	0	0	131.1	128	76	58	3	8	57	0	63	12
Soltero, Charleston (S.C.)	2	2	.500	2.76	19	0	0	18	0	4	29.1	21	13	9	1	1	9	1	25	1
Sosa, Augusta	2	5	.286	3.18	29	6	0	8	0	0	70.2	84	38	25	2	1	22	3	52	11
Sparks, Augusta	2	3	.400	5.50	40	0	0	20	0	1	72.0	85	50	44	5	9	37	0	50	4
Sparma, Macon	2	0	1.000	4.74	5	5	0	0	0	0	24.2	21	15	13	4	1	11	0	19	5
Spencer, Greensboro	0	0	.000	0.00	1	0	0	1	0	0	1.0	2	1	0	0	0	1	0	1	0
Spiller, Savannah*	0	8	.000	3.51	23	13	0	1	0	0	89.2	93	57	35	3	6	27	1	74	10
Spoljaric, Myrtle Beach*	10	8	.556	2.82	26	26	1	0	0	0	162.2	111	68	51	7	5	58	0	161	7
Steinmetz, Macon	2	2	.500	3.60	6	6	0	0	0	0	35.0	37	16	14	0	0	10	0	17	1
Stewart, Charleston (W.Va.)	6	10	.375	3.55	27	26	1	1	0	0	164.2	147	76	65	6	6	84	1	167	25
Sullivan, Greensboro*	4	6	.400	2.19	13	13	3	0	0	0	82.1	87	35	20	3	3	21	0	53	7
Sutherland, Greensboro	3	2	.600	3.97	14	3	0	1	0	0	34.0	29	17	15	2	1	12	0	27	3
Sweeney, Columbus	0	2	.000	4.50	12	0	0	4	0	0	26.0	21	14	13	3	2	18	3	21	1
Taylor, Myrtle Beach*	0	0	.000	7.45	6	0	0	2	0	0	9.2	14	11	8	3	1	9	0	9	0
Teich, Augusta	5	4	.556	3.66	41	0	0	23	0	1	64.0	65	33	26	3	0	42	0	56	6
Thibert, Greensboro	0	0	.000	8.22	6	0	0	6	0	1	7.2	9	7	7	1	0	6	0	11	3
Thomas, Columbia	6	4	.600	3.26	42	0	0	29	0	12	88.1	67	37	32	5	3	31	0	81	2
Thompson, Fayetteville*	4	4	.500	2.18	20	19	0	1	0	0	95.0	79	32	23	6	1	40	0	88	7
Tuttle, Charleston (W.Va.)	3	5	.375	3.88	17	16	0	0	0	0	97.1	87	46	42	5	1	53	1	93	4
Urbina, Albany	7	13	.350	3.22	24	24	5	0	2	0	142.1	111	68	51	14	4	54	0	100	4
Vaughn, Gastonia	3	3	.500	2.44	30	1	0	11	0	0	59.0	37	20	16	3	4	31	1	73	4
Verduzco, Fayetteville	0	3	.000	3.91	7	5	1	1	0	0	25.1	26	20	11	0	2	15	0	17	3
Waite, Fayetteville	1	0	1.000	5.70	17	0	0	6	0	0	23.2	31	15	15	1	2	20	0	15	1
Walden, Columbus	4	3	.571	4.21	40	0	0	21	0	2	72.2	66	40	34	7	5	42	1	55	9
Walsh, Fayetteville*	8	5	.615	3.11	35	13	0	10	0	4	121.2	98	50	42	13	3	41	1	101	10
Waring, Asheville	1	1	.500	0.45	3	3	1	0	0	0	20.0	11	2	1	0	1	4	0	20	1
Webb, Asheville	0	0	.000	0.00	1	0	0	1	0	0	1.0	1	0	0	0	0	0	0	1	0
Weber, Myrtle Beach	4	7	.364	1.64	41	1	0	23	0	6	98.2	83	27	18	1	7	29	3	65	7
Wechsberg, Charleston (S.C.)	3	0	1.000	4.08	19	0	0	10	0	2	39.2	45	30	18	2	1	19	1	35	4
Welch, Columbus*	0	1	.000	1.92	23	4	0	12	0	3	51.2	38	16	11	1	0	22	2	38	0
Wentz, Charleston (S.C.)	0	0	.000	0.00	1	0	0	1	0	0	1.0	0	0	0	0	0	0	0	0	0
West, Asheville	1	1	.500	3.86	8	1	0	1	0	0	14.0	15	16	6	2	0	13	0	7	3
Whisenant, Spartanburg*	11	7	.611	3.23	27	27	2	0	0	0	150.2	117	69	54	9	10	85	0	151	10
White, Asheville	13	4	.765	3.38	41	13	0	22	0	8	117.1	122	51	44	4	3	29	3	103	7
Wilder, Macon	10	12	.455	3.04	26	26	4	0	2	0	159.2	142	67	54	12	2	58	0	128	4
Wilson, Augusta	2	3	.400	3.67	7	7	0	0	0	0	41.2	43	22	17	2	3	7	0	27	1
Withem, Fayetteville	1	3	.250	4.74	22	2	0	8	0	2	38.0	40	23	20	3	4	20	0	34	9
Wynne, Albany	8	4	.667	2.53	27	8	1	7	1	1	74.2	58	29	21	1	3	40	1	75	10
Young, Asheville*	3	10	.231	4.28	20	20	0	0	0	0	94.2	106	65	45	5	2	70	1	64	11
Zastoupil, Charleston (W.Va.)	5	3	.625	2.17	32	0	0	23	0	7	45.2	45	13	11	1	2	20	3	30	4

BALKS—McClain, 16; Patterson, 13; Kelley, 9; Walsh, 8; Anthony, Compton, Curtis, Heredia, S. Johnson, Konuszewski, Lopez, C. Smith, 7 each; Beltran, Bjornson, DeHart, Hisey, Whisenant, 6 each; Barnes, Brownholtz, Courtright, Frascatore, Huber, Loughlin, Pedraza, Place, Shuey, Welch, White, 5 each; Baptist, Gray, Hamilton, Hampton, Loaiza, Reichenbach, O. Smith, Urbina, 4 each; Blomdahl, Burgess, Butler, Carrara, Carrasco, DeLosSantos, Fusco, Guzik, Henderson, Logsdon, Magee, Montoya, Munda, Nieves, Paxton, Ramirez, Spiller, Thompson, Vaughn, Wilder, Young, 3 each; Adkins, T. Anderson, A. Baker, S. Baker, Du. Brown, G. Brown, Brumley, Crawford, Danner, Dettmer, Edmonson, Ferguson, Fiegel, Garagozza, F. Garcia, Holman, Inman, Jarvis, Jolley, Kendall, Koller, Lacy, Lemay, Morales, Nieto, Pettitte, Pisciotta, Sadecki, Saulter, Schmidt, Schorr, Short, Withem, Zastoupil, 2 each; Adams, Backlund, Balentine, Blair, Da. Brown, Burns, Busby, Carlyle, J. Carter, Coleman, Conley, DeSantis, Doorneweerd, Doyle, Durussel, Franklin, Fronio, Gandolph, R. Garcia, Hammond, Hernandez, Hurst, Jacome, Key, Knowles, Kotes, T. Lindsay, Lucchetti, Lucero, Manicchia, J. Martin, McCurry, R. Moody, Morrison, Popoff, Reid, A. Reyes, Ruebel, Schwarber, Scott, Seelbach, Soltero, Sparks, Sparma, Spoljaric, Steinmetz, Sullivan, Thomas, Verduzco, Waite, Webb, West, Wilson, 1 each.

COMBINATION SHUTOUTS—DeHart-Respondek-Kermode, Pedraza-Fultz-Larosa, Pedraza-Reyes, Urbina-Conley-DeHart, Wynne-Kermode, Albany; White-Morman 2, Bjornson-Morman, Loughlin-Carrasco-Morman, White-Carrasco, Asheville; Backlund-DeLosSantos-Sparks, Danner-Backlund, Doorneweerd-Martin-Teich, Evans-Christiansen, Evans-Christiansen-DeLosSantos, Konuszewski-DeLosSantos-Teich, Loaiza-Christiansen-Rychel, Pisciotta-Konuszewski-DeLosSantos, Augusta; Anthony-Huber 2, Barnes-Eggleston-Ciocca-Wechsberg, Compton-Ciocca, Hamilton-Huber, Hanson-Soltero, Charleston (S.C.); Stewart-Hrusovsky 3, Courtright-Nieves-Hrusovsky, McClain-Kendall, McClain-Zastoupil, Stewart-McClain-Zastoupil, Tuttle-Kendall, Tuttle-Kendall-Nieves, Charleston (W.Va.); Guzik-McCready, Guzik-Thomas, Jacome-Manfred, Jacome-McCready, McCready-Fiegel, Ramirez-Smith, Schorr-Lindsay-Thomas, Shanahan-McCready-Lindsay-Rees, Smith-Manfred, Columbia; Baker-Welch, Fleet-Doyle, Fleet-Walden-Fronio, Harris-Fleet, Hernandez-Fleet, Hernandez-Sweeney, Logsdon-Brown-Walden-Baker, Logsdon-Resendez, Logsdon-Walden-Fronio, Logsdon-Welch, Lopez-Welch, Resendez-Baker-Fleet, Shuey-Baker-Walden, Shuey-Welch, Columbus;

Berlin-Walsh, Blomdahl-Haeger-Schwarber, Carlyle-Cedeno, Carlyle-Lemay-Bussa-Schwarber, Carlyle-Withem-Walsh, Edmondson-Haeger-Schwarber, Kelley-Adams-Schwarber, Kelley-Schwarber, Kelley-Thompson, Reid-Lemay-Bussa, Reed-Lemay-Durussel, Reed-Walsh-Haeger-Schwarber, Thompson-Bussa-Walsh, Walsh-Edmondson-Bussa, Fayetteville; Brownholtz-Sadecki-Lacy, Curtis-Alberro, Curtis-Vaughn, Dettmer-Franklin, Dettmer-Lacy, Gandolph-Vaughn-Moody, Henderson-Alberro-Lacy, Henderson-Lacy-Moody, Magee-Lacy, Gastonia; Garagozzo-Short, Pettitte-Coleman, Pettitte-Gully-Coleman, Pettitte-Short, Sullivan-Croghan-Gietzen, Greensboro; Koller-Burgess, Koller-Burgess-Blair, Koller-Francis, Seelbach-Clontz, Seelbach-Reyes-Dunlap, Steinmetz-Dunlap, Wilder-Blair, Wilder-Place-Burgess, Macon; Spoljaric-Martin 2, Baptist-Lindsay, Baptist-Robinson, Baptist-Weber-Mallory-Martin, Carrara-Martin, Carrara-Montoya, Garcia-Montoya, Gray-Lindsay-Heble, Gray-Martin, Gray-Robinson-Martin, Kotes-Montoya-Carrara-Martin, Montoya-Martin, Spoljaric-Weber, Myrtle Beach; Hammond-Frascatore 2, Hisey-Knowles-Frascatore, Savannah; Blazier-DeSantis-Juhl, Blazier-Humphry, Blazier-Juhl, Bottalico-Hassinger, Holman-Humphry, Whisenhunt-Hurst, Whisenant-Hurst-Hassinger, Whisenant-Hurst-Randall, Spartanburg.

PERFECT GAME—Blomdahl, Fayetteville, defeated Spartanburg, 1-0 (second game), June 4.

NO-HIT GAME—McCready-Fiegel, Columbia, defeated Fayetteville, 6-0, July 24.

FIELDING

TEAM

Team	Pct.	G	PO	A	E	DP	PB	Player, Team	Pct.	G	PO	A	E	DP	PB
Fayetteville	.967	141	3711	1414	177	90	19	Albany	.961	142	3718	1480	213	119	16
Columbia	.967	138	3564	1485	175	107	21	Myrtle Beach	.960	136	3511	1442	206	97	21
Columbus	.966	139	3712	1660	187	135	26	Augusta	.960	141	3702	1519	219	126	15
Charleston (W.Va.)	.966	141	3677	1481	183	108	27	Greensboro	.958	141	3688	1537	227	93	34
Spartanburg	.964	138	3604	1337	183	85	22	Asheville	.958	140	3536	1627	225	139	27
Macon	.961	139	3632	1342	200	121	13	Savannah	.957	140	3635	1485	230	96	30
Gastonia	.961	136	3536	1521	206	88	32	Charleston (S.C.)	.954	140	3525	1584	244	117	31

Triple plays—Augusta, Columbus.

INDIVIDUAL

FIRST BASEMEN

*Throws lefthanded.

Player, Team	Pct.	G	PO	A	E	DP
Allen, Albany	1.000	6	40	2	0	7
Anderson, Greensboro	1.000	4	12	0	0	0
Andrews, Albany	1.000	4	27	1	0	3
Beuerlein, Asheville	.983	11	109	5	2	12
Bigler, Spartanburg*	.983	124	956	74	18	53
Billeci, Spartanburg	.985	10	64	3	1	7
Bohrofen, Savannah	1.000	2	4	0	0	0
Bonifay, Augusta	.965	9	50	5	2	3
Brown, Augusta*	.981	77	626	38	13	54
Bullock, Columbia	1.000	2	11	0	0	0
Burton, Gastonia	.990	92	764	54	8	44
Bush, Spartanburg	.750	1	6	0	2	3
Calder, Augusta	.977	47	347	37	9	31
Cavazzoni, Charleston (W.Va.)	.950	7	35	3	2	5
Charbonnet, Columbus*	.971	46	424	17	13	43
Cherry, Spartanburg	1.000	1	9	0	0	0
Crosnoe, Macon	1.000	1	7	0	0	1
Curtis, Asheville*	.991	56	496	28	5	53
Dismuke, Charleston (W.Va.)	.980	131	1055	99	24	88
DuBose, Fayetteville	.986	117	871	110	14	62
Flores, Columbia	1.000	1	1	1	0	0
Flores, Albany	.975	12	75	3	2	9
Floyd, Albany*	.981	23	184	19	4	12
Garcia, Columbia	.987	124	1114	78	16	82
Garvey, Augusta	.972	10	66	4	2	6
Graham, Charleston (W.Va.)	1.000	1	1	0	0	0
Grijak, Macon	.993	20	139	10	1	14
Hamlin, Savannah	.978	95	829	75	20	54
Hammargren, Char. (W.Va.)	.968	8	58	2	2	2
Harris, Columbia	1.000	1	11	0	0	1
Hmielewski, Albany*	.985	108	827	83	14	73
Jones, Charleston (W.Va.)	1.000	1	2	0	0	0
Kupsey, Spartanburg	1.000	1	0	1	0	0
Leatherman, Augusta	.983	10	52	6	1	4
Leonhardt, Fayetteville	1.000	5	32	3	0	0
Linares, Asheville	.987	7	72	5	1	2
Marks, Macon	.980	122	938	61	20	76
Martinez, Asheville*	.986	65	606	42	9	50
Matachun, Gastonia	1.000	5	28	2	0	1
McCall, Columbus*	.986	99	912	62	14	81
McCoy, Gastonia	.963	5	45	7	2	4
Merriweather, Fayetteville	1.000	1	1	0	0	0
Miller, Fayetteville	1.000	10	57	7	0	3
Mowry, Charleston (S.C.)*	.989	118	1079	75	13	87
Mucerino, Charleston (S.C.)*	.974	26	171	17	5	12
Neff, Augusta	.875	2	13	1	2	2
Ostermeyer, Charleston (S.C.)	.947	8	53	1	3	3
Paulino, Macon	1.000	1	7	1	0	2
Perozo, Columbia	1.000	9	80	10	0	8
Robinson, Columbia	1.000	6	45	2	0	4
Rusk, Spartanburg	.988	12	77	3	1	6
Schroeder, Augusta*	.969	5	29	2	1	0
SEEFRIED, Greensboro	.991	141	1257	118	13	86
Tejada, Spartanburg	.000	1	0	0	1	0
Tomasello, Gastonia*	.974	43	350	21	10	28
Tsoukalas, Myrtle Beach	1.000	5	19	4	0	3

Player, Team	Pct.	G	PO	A	E	DP
Underwood, Savannah*	.974	46	415	37	12	26
Webb, Asheville	.953	5	41	0	2	7
Weinke, Myrtle Beach*	.979	134	1141	85	26	79
Williams, Gastonia	1.000	10	54	6	0	5
Yelton, Fayetteville	.974	20	127	22	4	8
Zuber, Spartanburg*	1.000	1	10	1	0	2

Triple play—McCall.

SECOND BASEMEN

Player, Team	Pct.	G	PO	A	E	DP
Anderson, Greensboro	.952	17	35	44	4	8
Arias, Charleston (W.Va.)	.955	31	53	52	5	15
Brito, Spartanburg	1.000	6	6	16	0	2
Burton, Gastonia	.750	1	2	1	1	0
Bush, Charleston (S.C.)	.935	102	199	287	34	57
Cacini, Columbus	.955	17	23	41	3	6
Carabba, Albany	.982	14	30	24	1	5
Cardenas, Columbus	.800	1	2	2	1	1
Carlsen, Charleston (W.Va.)	.979	91	161	209	8	37
Carrion, Charleston (S.C.)	.959	18	24	46	3	9
Centeno, Asheville	.951	126	243	379	32	90
Cholowsky, Savannah	.942	64	103	175	17	24
Crespo, Myrtle Beach	.934	71	161	149	22	32
Ellsworth, Savannah	.919	31	41	61	9	9
Farmer, Columbia	.981	24	38	66	2	12
Filotei, Charleston (W.Va.)	.970	6	14	18	1	2
Fleming, Greensboro	.955	68	139	159	14	31
Flores, Asheville	1.000	3	5	7	0	4
Flores, Columbia	.955	10	20	22	2	4
Garces, Spartanburg	.974	12	16	22	1	3
Garvey, Augusta	.973	22	36	35	2	6
Gomez, Spartanburg	.600	1	2	1	2	1
Graffagnino, Macon	.961	85	178	239	17	54
Hansen, Greensboro	.000	1	0	0	1	0
Hayden, Spartanburg	.955	111	184	278	22	38
Jelinek, Spartanburg	.933	6	4	10	1	1
Keeline, Macon	1.000	9	14	22	0	2
King, Columbia	1.000	2	3	3	0	0
Krevokuch, Augusta	.971	21	22	46	2	6
Lis, Myrtle Beach	.982	61	112	162	5	28
Mallee, Spartanburg	.880	20	23	43	9	5
Matachun, Gastonia	.982	16	22	33	1	8
Maxwell, Columbus	.960	69	128	210	14	36
Meade, Columbus	.975	69	148	209	9	50
Merriweather, Fayetteville	.975	69	106	129	6	20
Moody, Charleston (S.C.)	.928	23	45	58	8	8
Ozoria, Albany	1.000	1	0	1	0	0
Ozuna, Savannah	.965	20	27	55	3	9
Parra, Gastonia	.955	44	86	103	9	19
Polcovich, Augusta	1.000	3	3	10	0	3
Pratte, Fayetteville	.978	83	156	196	8	38
Rosario, Myrtle Beach	1.000	7	7	10	0	3
Sanford, Columbus	.967	13	24	34	2	7
SIMONS, Albany	.979	124	248	362	13	74
Smith, Gastonia	.956	80	113	236	16	38
Smith, Columbus	.952	11	14	26	2	3
Stynes, Myrtle Beach	1.000	11	2	1	0	0

Player, Team	Pct.	G	PO	A	E	DP
Tosar, Albany	.979	7	24	23	1	5
Turrentine, Greensboro	.935	58	102	144	17	27
Ugueto, Savannah	.333	2	1	0	2	0
Vazquetelles, Macon	.917	10	18	15	3	5
Veras, Columbia	.963	107	208	313	20	51
Virgilio, Macon	.967	40	55	91	5	14
Warner, Savannah	.963	36	66	89	6	19
Wentz, Ch.W.Va.-Ch.S.C.	.982	29	47	64	2	12
Womack, Augusta	.958	16	27	41	3	5
Woodall, Gastonia	1.000	1	0	1	0	0
Zapata, Augusta	.979	87	178	200	8	44

Triple plays—Maxwell, Zapata.

THIRD BASEMEN

Player, Team	Pct.	G	PO	A	E	DP
Allen, Albany	.500	1	0	2	2	0
Anderson, Greensboro	.954	37	19	84	5	10
Andrews, Albany	.922	121	98	211	26	16
Austin, Augusta	.868	50	25	74	15	3
Bonifay, Augusta	1.000	7	7	11	0	1
Bullock, Columbia	.945	84	60	146	12	10
Burton, Gastonia	.750	2	1	2	1	0
Cacini, Asheville	.000	3	0	0	1	0
Carabba, Albany	.844	18	10	28	7	1
Carrion, Charleston (S.C.)	.830	18	9	30	8	5
Cherry, Spartanburg	.918	29	20	47	6	6
Cholowsky, Savannah	1.000	1	0	3	0	0
Cooper, Greensboro	.899	88	66	193	29	17
Crosnoe, Macon	.860	26	12	37	8	4
De La Cruz, Charleston (S.C.)	.800	3	1	3	1	0
Duran, Savannah	.928	106	82	213	23	15
Edwards, Gastonia	.932	93	60	160	16	14
Ellsworth, Savannah	.786	19	4	18	6	1
Farmer, Columbia	.944	9	3	14	1	1
Frye, Charleston (W.Va.)	1.000	3	4	3	0	0
Garvey, Augusta	.894	22	15	27	5	4
Grable, 13 Fay.-74 Spar.	.935	87	81	148	16	14
Graham, Charleston (W.Va.)	1.000	2	0	3	0	0
Greene, Charleston (S.C.)	.500	1	0	1	1	0
Hansen, Greensboro	.821	10	10	22	7	2
Harrison, Charleston (W.Va.)	.800	6	3	9	3	1
Hawks, Charleston (S.C.)	.902	14	18	19	4	2
Krevokuch, Augusta	.967	53	33	85	4	8
Kupsey, Spartanburg	.923	38	24	60	7	4
Lantrip, Greensboro	1.000	9	5	13	0	0
Leatherman, Augusta	.939	18	8	23	2	2
Lebak, Charleston (S.C.)	.833	4	4	6	2	0
Leonhardt, Fayetteville	.933	99	73	150	16	12
Lis, Myrtle Beach	.923	29	25	47	6	6
Matachun, Gastonia	.927	40	18	83	8	3
McConnell, Fayetteville	1.000	2	1	2	0	0
Meade, Columbus	.926	8	5	20	2	4
Moody, Charleston (S.C.)	.902	72	51	142	21	13
Neff, Augusta	.909	5	4	6	1	1
PERNA, Charleston (W.Va.)	.977	128	85	252	8	30
Polcovich, Augusta	1.000	2	1	2	0	0
Posada, Greensboro	.750	5	4	8	4	0
Pratte, Fayetteville	.948	33	40	51	5	3
Ramos, Asheville	.885	83	68	156	29	15
Robinson, Columbia	.924	59	32	101	11	7
Rosario, Myrtle Beach	1.000	1	0	1	0	0
Rose, Columbus	.949	131	90	282	20	24
Sealy, Gastonia	1.000	2	1	7	0	1
Smith, Columbus	.667	4	1	1	1	0
Stynes, Myrtle Beach	.919	106	86	208	26	13
Tejada, Spartanburg	1.000	1	0	4	0	0
Therrien, Macon	.950	63	44	88	7	11
Tosar, Albany	1.000	6	4	15	0	1
Toth, Macon	1.000	2	0	1	0	0
Tsoukalas, Myrtle Beach	1.000	2	0	7	0	1
Virgilio, Macon	.893	58	37	80	14	6
Warner, Savannah	.892	22	22	36	7	4
Webb, Asheville	.873	60	29	122	22	9
Wentz, 4 Ch.W.Va.-35 Ch.S.C.	.926	39	26	86	9	3
Woodall, Gastonia	1.000	4	4	6	0	1

SHORTSTOPS

Player, Team	Pct.	G	PO	A	E	DP
Anderson, Greensboro	.938	19	30	45	5	5
Arias, Charleston (W.Va.)	.949	17	28	47	4	5
Brito, Spartanburg	.950	28	42	53	5	9
Cabrera, Albany	.927	115	169	277	35	59
Cacini, Asheville	.898	29	44	62	12	8
Carabba, Albany	.886	30	39	78	15	15
Carrion, Charleston (S.C.)	.923	6	4	8	1	0
Colon, Augusta	.885	6	11	12	3	4
Cooper, Greensboro	.931	7	11	16	2	2
Cora, Charleston (S.C.)	.913	120	191	366	53	63
De La Cruz, Charleston (S.C.)	.875	2	1	6	1	2
Duran, Columbus	.945	91	154	290	26	47
Farmer, Columbia	.919	31	46	101	13	23
Filotei, Charleston (W.Va.)	.833	1	2	3	1	1

Player, Team	Pct.	G	PO	A	E	DP
Flores, Asheville	.940	119	181	403	37	86
Flores, Columbia	1.000	8	12	23	0	2
Frye, Charleston (W.Va.)	1.000	6	8	9	0	1
Garvey, Augusta	1.000	12	18	19	0	5
Gil, Gastonia	.931	128	226	384	45	58
Gonzalez, Myrtle Beach	.932	134	248	406	48	63
Hayden, Spartanburg	.983	18	27	31	1	5
Hernandez, Charleston (W.Va.)	1.000	1	1	6	0	0
Holbert, Savannah	.915	117	190	314	47	52
Jelinek, Spartanburg	1.000	1	3	5	0	3
Jeter, Greensboro	.813	11	14	25	9	3
JIMENEZ, Macon	.951	117	215	313	27	70
Keeline, Macon	.929	22	30	49	6	9
King, Columbia	1.000	2	4	5	0	0
Kupsey, Spartanburg	.941	53	70	106	11	17
Lantrip, Greensboro	.918	110	178	303	43	43
Lis, Myrtle Beach	1.000	2	1	6	0	1
Mallee, Spartanburg	.921	56	61	125	16	16
Matachun, Gastonia	.938	9	12	18	2	0
Meade, Columbus	.938	19	34	57	6	14
Merriweather, Fayetteville	1.000	2	3	4	0	1
Mompres, Columbia	.936	104	145	294	30	40
Moody, Charleston (S.C.)	.947	21	36	54	5	8
Morgan, Fayetteville	.904	123	158	295	48	48
Polcovich, Augusta	.953	40	74	107	9	23
Pratte, Fayetteville	.968	17	30	31	2	5
Reese, Charleston (W.Va.)	.932	103	181	287	34	51
Rosario, Myrtle Beach	1.000	1	1	3	0	1
Smith, Columbus	.939	40	52	102	10	21
Tosar, Albany	.833	4	4	6	2	1
Ugueto, Savannah	.857	2	4	2	1	0
Virgilio, Macon	.810	5	4	13	4	3
Warner, Savannah	.930	22	32	61	7	10
Wentz, Charleston (W.Va.)	.970	18	26	39	2	10
Womack, Augusta	.917	86	159	250	37	49
Woodall, Gastonia	1.000	4	3	11	0	2
Zapata, Augusta	.863	13	13	31	7	6

Triple play—Duran.

OUTFIELDERS

Player, Team	Pct.	G	PO	A	E	DP
Abreu, Asheville	.943	127	167	15	11	0
Anthony, Charleston (S.C.)	.969	115	182	7	6	1
Arias, Charleston (W.Va.)	1.000	2	2	0	0	0
Austin, Augusta	1.000	8	13	0	0	0
Bautista, Fayetteville	.974	117	210	17	6	5
Beck, Augusta*	.946	20	33	2	2	2
Benitez, Albany	.968	16	30	0	1	0
Bennett, Spartanburg	.986	62	134	10	2	2
Billeci, Spartanburg	1.000	1	1	2	0	0
Bohrofen, Savannah	.929	47	48	4	4	0
Briggs, Myrtle Beach	.945	134	174	14	11	2
Brock, Fayetteville*	.977	85	160	9	4	0
Bryant, Columbus	.937	40	69	5	5	1
Burguillos, Fayetteville	.970	84	158	6	5	3
Burton, Gastonia	.933	12	14	0	1	0
Butler, Myrtle Beach	.960	125	186	4	8	0
Cabrera, Albany	1.000	4	2	0	0	0
Cabrera, Asheville	1.000	8	3	0	0	0
Calzado, Savannah	1.000	3	6	0	0	0
Canate, Columbus	.976	129	185	15	5	5
Cavazzoni, Charleston (W.Va.)	1.000	1	1	0	0	0
Charbonnet, Columbus*	.963	49	76	2	3	0
Coates, Macon	.982	32	55	0	1	0
Conger, Augusta*	.966	83	165	3	6	0
Cooper, Greensboro	1.000	9	9	0	0	0
Cruz, Charleston (S.C.)	.000	4	0	0	1	0
Cumberbatch, Greensboro	.964	53	126	7	5	0
Curtis, Asheville*	1.000	4	5	1	0	0
Curtis, Columbia*	.960	92	180	12	8	1
Demerson, Greensboro	1.000	2	1	0	0	0
Durkin, Asheville*	.941	97	164	10	11	0
Edwards, Spartanburg	.954	101	180	5	9	1
Evans, Spartanburg	.963	52	121	8	5	0
Farrell, Augusta	.967	82	168	8	6	2
Floyd, Albany*	.950	102	239	10	13	3
Garvey, Augusta	1.000	4	2	0	0	0
Gennaro, Charleston (S.C.)*	.976	77	116	5	3	1
Gillum, Charleston (W.Va.)	.967	126	196	12	7	1
Grijak, Macon	1.000	1	1	0	0	0
Grissom, Albany	.966	102	190	7	7	2
Hamm, Charleston (S.C.)	.955	20	19	2	1	0
Hawks, Charleston (S.C.)	.923	7	12	0	1	0
Hence, Columbus	.966	35	55	2	2	0
Hill, Greensboro	.962	93	172	7	7	0
Hines, Myrtle Beach	.978	31	41	4	1	0
Hmielewski, Albany*	.939	19	29	2	2	0
Hobson, Asheville	.967	45	56	2	2	0
Holifield, Myrtle Beach*	.936	84	157	4	11	0
Hubbard, Greensboro*	.955	85	157	14	8	3
Hurtault, Albany	1.000	1	3	0	0	0
Jesperson, Charleston (W.Va.)	.978	91	177	3	4	0
Johnson, Macon	.857	13	24	0	4	0
Jones, Charleston (W.Va.)	.964	129	226	17	9	1

Player, Team	Pct.	G	PO	A	E	DP
Josephina, Macon*	.971	22	30	3	1	0
Lachance, Albany	1.000	3	3	0	0	0
Ladell, Charleston (W.Va.)	1.000	8	27	1	0	0
Larson, Spartanburg*	.984	42	59	3	1	0
LEBAK, Charleston (S.C.)	.982	113	201	19	4	2
List, Gastonia	.922	50	79	4	7	0
Marchan, Fayetteville*	1.000	6	7	2	0	0
Marini, Columbus*	.978	116	161	17	4	3
Mashore, Fayetteville	.975	113	259	14	7	5
Matachun, Gastonia	1.000	7	6	0	0	0
Matos, Gastonia	.949	102	180	8	10	0
McClinton, Columbia	.986	35	65	3	1	0
McCollough, Gastonia	.778	12	6	1	2	0
McCoy, Gastonia	1.000	1	2	0	0	0
Mediavilla, Savannah	.976	120	189	17	5	6
Miller, Fayetteville	.889	4	8	0	1	0
Milne, Fayetteville	.951	31	56	2	3	0
Mitchell, 45 Aug.-32 C'bus	.955	77	138	10	7	1
Moore, Macon*	.975	116	266	8	7	1
Mora, Columbia	.960	14	24	0	1	0
Moreno, Columbia	.950	97	179	11	10	0
Mota, Asheville	.963	129	166	14	7	2
Mucerino, Charleston (S.C.)*	1.000	21	20	1	0	0
Neff, Augusta	.960	57	86	9	4	1
O'Neill, Albany	.957	8	21	1	1	1
Otero, Columbia	.956	94	203	15	10	1
Ozoria, Albany	.946	103	185	6	11	0
Ozuna, Savannah	1.000	29	24	0	0	0
Paulino, Macon	.945	25	50	2	3	1
Perozo, Columbia	1.000	32	45	5	0	1
Phillips, Greensboro*	.960	123	189	5	8	1
Powell, Gastonia	.963	105	149	5	6	1
Quinones, Charleston (W.Va.)	.938	62	74	1	5	1
Ragland, Augusta	.900	36	42	3	5	1
Reams, Myrtle Beach	.982	37	55	0	1	0
Roberts, Charleston (S.C.)	.928	80	114	14	10	4
Robertson, Albany	.985	37	62	5	1	0
Robinson, Macon	.951	110	226	7	12	1
Ronca, Augusta	.959	27	46	1	2	1
Ruth, Spartanburg	.935	54	78	8	6	2
Schall, Spartanburg	.980	59	89	9	2	1
Schulte, Augusta	.929	74	95	9	8	2
Shotton, Augusta	.960	14	24	0	1	0
Simons, Albany	1.000	3	8	0	0	0
Spencer, Greensboro	1.000	76	135	5	0	1
Stanley, Savannah	.920	19	18	5	2	0
Steffens, Spartanburg*	.952	27	38	2	2	1
Stewart, Charleston (S.C.)	1.000	5	11	0	0	0
Stovall, Savannah*	.956	133	250	8	12	1
Sullivan, Fayetteville*	.667	2	2	0	1	0
Taylor, Savannah	.966	20	27	1	1	0
Taylor, Charleston (W.Va.)	.960	22	24	0	1	0
Texidor, Gastonia	.918	116	163	16	16	2
Tolliver, Columbia	.960	61	96	1	4	1
Tomasello, Gastonia*	.800	6	4	0	1	0
Tsoukalas, Myrtle Beach	.875	9	6	1	1	0
Van Tiger, Columbus	.977	30	40	2	1	0
Velez, Savannah*	.968	78	118	4	4	1
Vilet, Spartanburg	1.000	10	21	1	0	0
Warner, Macon*	.974	49	108	3	3	0
White, Asheville	.967	24	54	4	2	0
White, Albany	.965	44	73	9	3	1
Wilkerson, Charleston (W.Va.)*	1.000	5	7	0	0	0
Williams, Macon	.965	64	108	1	4	1
Williams, Gastonia	.909	26	27	3	3	0
Wilson, Greensboro	1.000	5	6	0	0	0
Woodall, Gastonia	1.000	1	1	0	0	0
Zuber, Spartanburg*	.978	29	44	0	1	0

CATCHERS

Player, Team	Pct.	G	PO	A	E	DP	PB
Allen, Albany	.960	5	19	5	1	0	1
Ayala, Charleston (S.C.)	.981	28	134	17	3	3	9
Ayrault, Macon	.973	83	584	101	19	5	6
Beals, Columbia	.988	50	299	33	4	1	6
Beuerlein, Asheville	.969	9	54	9	2	0	0
Brophy, Spartanburg	.986	25	189	25	3	1	4
Bush, Spartanburg	.977	18	116	13	3	0	1
Casanova, Columbia	1.000	4	29	1	0	0	3
Chavez, Asheville	.976	77	456	77	13	5	22
Conley, Columbus	.988	15	72	7	1	0	1
CRESPO, Gastonia	.987	76	520	72	8	4	15
Crosby, Columbus	.987	52	334	48	5	3	9
Dempsey, Savannah	.966	7	53	3	2	0	4
Diaz, Columbia	.933	13	84	13	7	0	4
Dunn, Columbia	.978	8	41	3	1	0	1
Eason, Spartanburg	.990	70	546	64	6	4	8
Encarnacion, Augusta	.973	93	676	121	22	15	7
Flores, Albany	1.000	6	22	1	0	0	0
Garcia, Myrtle Beach	.980	32	132	15	3	2	4
Gonzalez, Fayetteville	.989	40	315	46	4	2	8
Greene, Charleston (S.C.)	.981	95	561	118	13	8	17
Hall, Charleston (S.C.)	.974	36	160	28	5	1	5
Hammargren, Char. (W.Va.)	.970	49	344	38	12	2	4

Player, Team	Pct.	G	PO	A	E	DP	PB
Hammond, Char. (W.Va.)	.989	31	223	50	3	5	9
Harrison, Charleston (W.Va.)	.978	70	523	61	13	2	14
Hopp, Spartanburg	.967	4	25	4	1	1	1
Hymel, Albany	.972	79	556	72	18	8	10
Kennedy, Gastonia	1.000	13	95	10	0	0	1
Linares, Asheville	.994	63	417	42	3	7	5
Lutz, Myrtle Beach	.983	47	255	33	5	5	5
Maguire, Augusta	.966	16	104	8	4	1	4
Marx, Augusta	.973	39	261	32	8	10	4
McConnell, Fayetteville	.993	34	242	29	2	5	4
Miller, Fayetteville	.982	43	248	22	5	2	5
Moore, Columbus	1.000	6	36	4	0	0	1
Morland, Myrtle Beach	.983	104	643	109	13	5	14
Pages, Albany	.979	60	402	74	10	5	5
Patrizi, Columbia	.985	66	400	47	7	6	7
Pineda, Greensboro	.986	23	126	17	2	0	5
Posada, Greensboro	.976	41	259	31	7	1	6
Rusk, Spartanburg	1.000	4	28	4	0	0	0
Sealy, Gastonia	.984	53	377	63	7	2	14
Sued, Columbus	.984	83	595	78	11	2	15
Swail, Macon	1.000	5	8	2	0	0	1
Tejada, Spartanburg	.982	27	192	29	4	4	8
Toth, Macon	.973	62	416	52	13	5	6
Turvey, Savannah	.974	35	234	25	7	3	4
Williams, Savannah	.985	109	763	107	13	8	25
Williams, Gastonia	.966	7	47	10	2	0	2
Wilson, Greensboro	.984	89	541	76	10	1	23
Yelton, Fayetteville	.983	40	266	30	5	2	2

PITCHERS

Player, Team	Pct.	G	PO	A	E	DP
Adams, Fayetteville	1.000	12	4	2	0	0
Adkins, Myrtle Beach	1.000	11	0	1	0	0
Alberro, Gastonia	1.000	17	1	1	0	0
Anaya, Columbia	1.000	1	0	1	0	0
Anderson, Greensboro	1.000	2	1	1	0	0
Anderson, Asheville	.957	25	13	31	2	2
Anthony, Charleston (S.C.)	.867	23	6	7	2	0
Backlund, Augusta	1.000	5	2	1	0	0
A. Baker, Columbus	.967	19	6	23	1	1
S. Baker, Columbus	.909	27	4	6	1	0
Balentine, Charleston (W.Va.)*	.000	3	0	0	1	0
Baptist, Myrtle Beach*	.962	19	8	17	1	0
Barnes, Charleston (S.C.)	.800	27	7	21	7	1
Beltran, Savannah*	1.000	14	5	18	0	1
Berlin, Fayetteville	1.000	4	0	3	0	0
Bjornson, Asheville*	.944	22	5	29	2	1
Blair, Macon	.857	41	1	5	1	1
Blazier, Spartanburg	.958	30	9	14	1	1
Blomdahl, Fayetteville	.967	17	10	19	1	2
Bottalico, Spartanburg	.867	42	6	7	2	1
Brown, Asheville	.864	44	6	13	3	1
Brown, Columbus	.857	29	9	3	2	1
D. Brown, Spartanburg	1.000	16	1	8	0	0
G. Brown, Spartanburg	1.000	17	5	11	0	0
Brown, Macon	1.000	3	3	4	0	1
Brownholtz, Gastonia*	1.000	11	4	14	0	0
Brumley, Savannah	.750	5	1	2	1	0
Burbank, Greensboro	1.000	27	4	1	0	0
Burgess, Macon*	1.000	51	4	10	0	2
Burns, Charleston (S.C.)	.909	32	9	21	3	4
Busby, Savannah	.941	28	7	25	2	2
Bussa, Fayetteville	.913	44	7	14	2	1
Butler, Macon*	.857	24	3	21	4	0
Buzard, Columbus*	.750	6	1	2	1	0
Carlyle, Fayetteville	1.000	14	10	12	0	0
Carrara, Myrtle Beach	1.000	22	3	10	0	0
Carrasco, Asheville	1.000	49	2	15	0	0
Carter, Augusta	1.000	1	1	2	0	0
Carter, Greensboro*	.857	13	2	4	1	0
Cedeno, Fayetteville	1.000	2	2	2	0	0
Christiansen, Augusta*	1.000	10	0	3	0	0
Ciocca, Charleston (S.C.)	.944	39	5	12	1	1
Clelland, Albany	.906	27	10	19	3	3
Clontz, Macon	.667	17	0	4	2	0
Coleman, Greensboro	1.000	56	6	11	0	1
Compton, Charleston (S.C.)	.952	30	7	13	1	1
Conley, Albany	.846	34	2	9	2	0
Coombs, Columbus	.800	5	1	3	1	1
Courtright, Charleston (W.Va.)*	.955	27	6	36	2	0
Crawford, Columbus	.852	28	11	41	9	5
Croghan, Greensboro	.857	33	7	17	4	0
Curtis, Gastonia	.907	24	9	40	5	2
D'Amato, Charleston (S.C.)	.960	48	12	12	1	2
Danner, Albany*	.962	25	8	42	2	2
Davis, Savannah	.964	51	6	21	1	0
DeHart, Albany*	1.000	38	5	10	0	0
DeLosSantos, Augusta	.875	52	3	11	2	0
DeSantis, Spartanburg	.900	32	4	14	2	1
Dettmer, Gastonia	.920	15	8	15	2	0
Doorneweerd, Augusta	.909	25	3	17	2	0
Doty, Charleston (W.Va.)	1.000	8	1	4	0	0
Doyle, Columbus	.944	53	8	9	1	2
Dunlap, Macon	.867	38	4	9	2	0

Player, Team	Pct.	G	PO	A	E	DP	Player, Team	Pct.	G	PO	A	E	DP
Durussel, Fayetteville	.833	4	2	3	1	0	Moody, Gastonia	.857	21	2	4	1	0
Edmondson, Fayetteville	.884	28	19	19	5	0	Morales, Charleston (W.Va.)	.917	18	5	6	1	0
Eggleston, Charleston (S.C.)	1.000	12	3	3	0	0	Morman, Asheville*	.952	57	4	16	1	1
Evans, Asheville	1.000	21	2	4	0	0	Morrison, Albany	.917	15	15	18	3	1
Evans, Augusta	1.000	7	2	3	0	0	Munda, Greensboro	.828	46	9	15	5	0
Ferguson, Albany	.500	8	0	1	1	0	Nelson, Macon*	.875	7	0	7	1	0
Fiegel, Columbia*	.879	26	9	20	4	1	Nevill, Spartanburg*	1.000	11	2	0	0	0
Fleet, Columbus	.800	31	8	12	5	1	NIETO, Asheville	1.000	38	15	25	0	4
Florie, Charleston (S.C.)	.667	1	0	2	1	0	Nieves, Charleston (W.Va.)	.840	37	7	14	4	2
Francis, Macon	.867	27	6	7	2	2	Nix, Charleston (W.Va.)	.000	2	0	0	1	0
Franklin, Gastonia	1.000	22	5	3	0	0	Nolan, Myrtle Beach	.667	8	1	1	1	0
Frascatore, Savannah	.778	50	4	10	4	0	Nowak, Fayetteville	1.000	9	1	3	0	0
Fronio, Columbus	1.000	20	1	4	0	0	Parnell, Charleston (W.Va.)	.875	19	4	3	1	1
Fultz, Albany	.714	11	5	0	2	1	Patterson, Gastonia	.880	23	9	13	3	1
Fusco, Savannah*	.727	44	2	6	3	0	Paxton, Albany*	.960	33	5	19	1	0
Gandolph, Gastonia	.900	30	0	9	1	0	Pedraza, Albany	.911	27	21	30	5	3
Garagozzo, Greensboro*	.980	28	12	38	1	0	Pettitte, Greensboro*	.963	27	7	45	2	1
Garcia, Charleston (W.Va.)	1.000	10	4	4	0	1	Pisciotta, Augusta	.929	20	1	12	1	0
Garcia, Myrtle Beach	.917	18	6	5	1	0	Place, Macon	.941	32	3	13	1	1
Gietzen, Greensboro*	.833	16	0	5	1	0	Pontbriant, Augusta*	1.000	6	3	5	0	1
Gilmore, Spartanburg	1.000	10	4	7	0	0	Popoff, Columbia	1.000	11	5	4	0	1
Grace, Spartanburg	.500	6	1	1	2	0	Quinones, Charleston (W.Va.)*	1.000	5	0	2	0	0
Gray, Myrtle Beach*	.839	28	2	24	5	2	Ramirez, Columbia	.905	17	7	12	2	2
Grijak, Macon	1.000	2	0	1	0	0	Randall, Spartanburg	1.000	20	1	5	0	0
Grohs, Charleston (S.C.)	.917	38	4	7	1	1	Rees, Columbia	.941	16	5	11	1	0
Gully, Greensboro	.852	61	4	19	4	1	Reichenbach, Columbia	.919	30	16	18	3	5
Guzik, Columbia	.957	19	5	17	1	1	Reid, Fayetteville	.926	14	13	12	2	1
Haeger, Fayetteville*	.958	27	9	14	1	0	Resendez, Columbus	1.000	5	0	1	0	0
Hamilton, Charleston (S.C.)	.833	7	4	6	2	0	Respondek, Albany*	.923	33	6	6	1	0
Hammond, Savannah	.973	26	22	14	1	1	Reyes, Macon	1.000	23	3	6	0	1
Hampton, Gastonia	.826	36	7	12	4	2	Reyes, Albany	1.000	27	3	1	0	0
Hanson, Charleston (S.C.)	.952	28	4	16	1	2	Robinson, Myrtle Beach	1.000	20	1	5	0	1
Harris, Columbus	.889	18	8	8	2	0	Robinson, Charleston (W.Va.)	.968	13	11	19	1	2
Harvey, Charleston (W.Va.)	.900	8	5	4	1	1	Ruebel, Augusta*	1.000	12	4	5	0	0
Hassinger, Spartanburg	.875	20	5	9	2	2	Rychel, Augusta	1.000	13	1	4	0	0
Heble, Myrtle Beach	.667	8	1	1	1	0	Sadecki, Gastonia	1.000	21	2	4	0	0
Henderson, Gastonia*	.930	25	7	33	3	0	Saulter, Macon	1.000	37	5	6	0	0
Heredia, Gastonia	1.000	39	3	5	0	0	Schmidt, Macon	.600	7	1	2	2	0
Hernandez, Columbus	.933	11	2	12	1	0	Schorr, Columbia	1.000	27	11	27	0	3
Hisey, Savannah	.903	28	9	19	3	0	Schwarber, Fayetteville	1.000	53	3	11	0	1
Holman, Spartanburg	.875	25	10	18	4	2	Scott, Asheville*	.800	8	1	3	1	0
Hrusovsky, Charleston (W.Va.)	.667	19	2	0	1	0	Seelbach, Macon	.889	27	7	17	3	2
Huber, Charleston (S.C.)*	.967	46	5	24	1	1	Shanahan, Columbia*	1.000	2	1	0	0	0
Hurst, Spartanburg	1.000	31	2	8	0	1	Short, Greensboro	1.000	44	6	3	0	0
Inman, Greensboro	.867	13	7	6	2	1	Shuey, Columbus	.913	14	4	17	2	0
Jacome, Columbia*	1.000	8	0	9	0	0	Smith, Asheville	.915	28	14	29	4	1
Jarvis, Charleston (W.Va.)	.833	28	11	19	6	0	Smith, Greensboro	.879	25	11	18	4	1
Johnson, Savannah	.964	23	5	22	1	0	Smith, Columbia*	.957	18	11	11	1	0
Jolley, Macon	1.000	32	8	7	0	0	Soltero, Charleston (S.C.)	.833	19	1	4	1	0
Juhl, Spartanburg*	1.000	41	5	7	0	0	Sosa, Augusta	1.000	29	3	19	0	1
Kelley, Fayetteville*	.852	28	11	41	9	0	Sparks, Augusta	.947	40	4	14	1	2
Kendall, Charleston (W.Va.)	.867	30	1	12	2	0	Sparma, Macon	1.000	5	2	2	0	1
Kermode, Albany	1.000	22	0	2	0	0	Spencer, Greensboro	1.000	1	0	1	0	0
Knowles, Savannah	.933	39	7	7	1	1	Spiller, Savannah*	.900	23	6	12	2	1
Koller, Macon	.938	21	7	8	1	1	Spoljaric, Myrtle Beach*	.930	26	10	30	3	1
Konuszewski, Augusta	.913	17	6	15	2	2	Steinmetz, Macon	1.000	6	0	3	0	0
Kotes, Myrtle Beach	.935	25	7	22	2	0	Stewart, Charleston (W.Va.)	.953	27	14	27	2	1
Lacy, Gastonia	.929	49	3	10	1	0	Sullivan, Greensboro*	.900	14	5	13	2	0
Langford, Charleston (W.Va.)	.625	8	3	2	3	0	Sutherland, Greensboro	.857	14	3	3	1	0
LaPlante, Augusta	.667	3	1	1	1	1	Sweeney, Columbus	1.000	12	0	3	0	0
Larosa, Albany*	.909	33	1	9	1	0	Taylor, Myrtle Beach*	1.000	6	1	1	0	0
Laviano, Greensboro	1.000	4	0	1	0	0	Teich, Augusta*	1.000	41	3	7	0	0
Lemay, Fayetteville*	.885	38	7	16	3	2	Thibert, Greensboro	1.000	6	1	0	0	0
Lindsay, Columbia*	1.000	40	0	4	0	0	Thomas, Columbia	.917	42	3	8	1	1
Lindsay, Myrtle Beach	.938	33	3	12	1	1	Thompson, Fayetteville*	1.000	20	4	21	0	0
Loaiza, Augusta	.929	26	7	19	2	0	Tuttle, Charleston (W.Va.)	.938	17	6	9	1	1
Logsdon, Columbus*	1.000	19	4	28	0	1	Urbina, Albany	.909	24	10	10	2	0
Loiselle, Charleston (S.C.)	.880	19	9	13	3	1	Vaughn, Gastonia	.950	30	7	12	1	3
Looney, Albany*	1.000	11	6	11	0	2	Verduzco, Fayetteville	.818	7	1	8	2	0
Lopez, Columbus	.933	16	1	13	1	2	Waite, Fayetteville	.500	17	0	1	1	0
Loughlin, Asheville*	.905	24	5	14	2	2	Walden, Columbus	.875	40	0	7	1	2
Lucchetti, Savannah	1.000	18	2	2	0	1	Walsh, Fayetteville*	.960	35	8	16	1	2
Lucero, Savannah*	.889	32	1	7	1	0	Waring, Asheville	1.000	3	1	5	0	1
Maberry, Charleston (W.Va.)	1.000	2	0	1	0	0	Weber, Myrtle Beach	.905	41	5	14	2	2
Magee, Gastonia*	.906	27	10	19	3	1	Wechsberg, Charleston (S.C.)	1.000	19	4	3	0	0
Mallory, Myrtle Beach	.929	12	5	8	1	0	Welch, Columbus*	.857	23	3	9	2	0
Manfred, Columbia	1.000	32	10	5	0	0	West, Asheville	.500	8	1	1	2	0
Manicchia, Spartanburg	1.000	25	3	5	0	1	Whisenant, Spartanburg*	.821	27	12	20	7	2
Martin, Myrtle Beach	1.000	39	4	4	0	0	White, Macon	1.000	41	5	7	0	2
Martin, Augusta*	.944	28	3	14	1	1	Wilder, Macon	.931	26	9	18	2	0
McClain, Charleston (W.Va.)	.878	31	9	27	5	1	Wilson, Augusta	1.000	7	5	7	0	2
McCready, Columbia	.900	35	3	15	2	3	Withem, Fayetteville	.875	22	2	5	1	0
McCurry, Augusta	.818	19	2	7	2	1	Wynne, Albany	.875	27	6	8	2	2
Miller, Charleston (W.Va.)	1.000	6	0	1	0	0	Young, Charleston (W.Va.)	.875	20	3	11	2	0
Montoya, Myrtle Beach*	.941	42	2	14	1	0	Zastoupil, Charleston (W.Va.)	.900	32	3	6	1	0
Moody, Charleston (S.C.)*	1.000	1	0	1	0	0							

The following players did not have any fielding statistics at the positions indicated or appeared only as a designated hitter, pinch-hitter or pinch-runner: Alger, p; Ayala, of; Burbank, 1b; Cherry, of; Crespo, 3b; Dallas, dh, ph; DaSilva, p; Ellsworth, ss; Fayne, of; Flannelly, dh, ph; J. Flores, 3b; Garvey, p; George, p; Gerhart, p; Gil, of; Humphry, p; Janzen, p; Jesperson, 3b; J. Johnson, p; Key, p; Kupsey, of; Mashore, 3b; Matachun, p; McIntyre, p; P. Miller, p; Mompres, of; K. Moody, of; D. Robinson, 2b; Shaffer, p; R. Smith, of; Tosar, of; Vazquetelles, 3b; R. Warner, 1b; Webb, p; Wentz, p.

LEAGUE CHAMPIONS

Year	Team	Pct.
1948—	Lincolnton*	.627
1949—	Newton-Conover	.667
	Ruth'ford Co. (2nd)†	.627
1950—	Newton-Conover	.627
	Lenoir (2nd)†	.626
1951—	Morganton	.645
	Shelby (2nd)†	.604
1952—	Lincolnton	.649
	Shelby (2nd)†	.645
1953-59—	League inactive.	
1960—	Lexington	.707
	Salisbury (2nd)†	.650
1961—	Salisbury	.627
	Shelby (4th)†	.481
1962—	Statesville	.563
	Statesville	.700
1963—	Greenville+	.576
	Salisbury	.631
1964—	Rock Hill	.672
	Salisbury‡	.631
1965—	Salisbury	.641
	Rock Hill‡	.603
1966—	Spartanburg	.682
	Spartanburg	.767
1967—	Spartanburg	.730
	Spartanburg	.567

Year	Team	Pct.
1968—	Spartanburg	.597
	Greenwood‡	.597
1969—	Greenwood‡	.587
	Shelby	.565
1970—	Greenville	.576
	Greenville	.619
1971—	Greenwood	.631
	Greenwood	.759
1972—	Spartanburg‡	.788
	Greenville	.652
1973—	Spartanburg‡	.646
	Gastonia	.619
1974—	Gastonia	.606
	Gastonia	.672
1975—	Spartanburg	.543
	Spartanburg	.614
1976—	Asheville	.544
	Greenwood‡	.600
1977—	Greenwood	.557
	Gastonia‡	.590
1978—	Greenwood	.614
	Greenwood	.565
1979—	Greenwood‡	.565
	Spartanburg	.525
1980—	Greensboro	.590
	Charleston	.561

Year	Team	Pct.
1981—	Greensboro‡	.695
	Greenwood	.549
1982—	Greensboro‡	.681
	Florence	.546
1983—	Columbia	.620
	Florence	.587
1984—	Charleston	.549
	Asheville‡	.510
1985—	Florence‡	.599
	Greensboro	.540
1986—	Columbia‡	.682
	Asheville	.643
1987—	Asheville	.655
	Myrtle Beach‡	.597
1988—	Charleston (S.C.)	.616
	Spartanburg‡	.500
1989—	Gastonia	.657
	Augusta‡	.535
1990—	Columbia	.580
	Charleston (W.Va.)‡	.538
1991—	Charleston (W.Va.)	.648
	Columbia‡	.614
1992—	Columbia	.572
	Myrtle Beach‡	.522

*Won championship and four-club playoff. †Won four-club playoff. ‡Won split-season playoff. (NOTE—Known as Western Carolina League from 1948 through 1962 and known as Western Carolinas League through 1979.)

APPALACHIAN LEAGUE

FINAL STANDINGS

NORTHERN DIVISION

Team	W	L	T	Pct.	GB
Bluefield (Orioles)	37	25	0	.597	....
Burlington (Indians)	35	31	0	.530	4
Princton (Reds)	34	31	0	.523	4 ½
Huntington (Cubs)	28	34	0	.452	9
Martinsville (Phillies)	22	43	0	.338	16 ½

SOUTHERN DIVISION

Team	W	L	T	Pct.	GB
Elizabethton (Twins)	49	17	0	.742	....
Johnson City (Cardinals)	33	32	0	.508	15 ½
Bristol (Tigers)	33	35	0	.485	17
Kingsport (Mets)	27	35	0	.435	20
Pulaski (Braves)	23	38	0	.377	23 ½

COMPOSITE

Team	Eliz.	Blu.	Burl.	Prn.	J.C.	Bri.	Hun.	Kng.	Pul.	Mar.	W	L	T	Pct.	GB
Elizabethton (Twins)	....	0	2	7	10	10	1	8	11	0	49	17	0	.742	....
Bluefield (Orioles)	1	....	5	5	2	0	7	7	2	8	37	25	0	.597	10
Burlington (Indians)	0	7	....	8	0	5	7	1	1	6	35	31	0	.530	14
Princeton (Reds)	5	7	4	....	1	1	6	1	0	9	34	31	0	.523	14 ½
Johnson City (Cardinals)	2	0	2	0	....	8	2	7	5	7	33	32	0	.508	15 ½
Bristol (Tigers)	2	2	7	1	4	....	0	6	9	2	33	35	0	.485	17
Huntington (Cubs)	1	1	5	5	0	2	....	1	4	9	28	34	0	.452	19
Kingsport (Mets)	4	4	0	1	5	6	0	....	6	1	27	35	0	.435	20
Pulaski (Braves)	1	0	0	1	5	3	8	4	....	1	23	38	0	.377	23 ½
Martinsville (Phillies)	1	4	6	3	5	0	3	0	0	....	22	43	0	.338	26 ½

Major league affiliations in parentheses.

Playoffs—Bluefield defeated Elizabethton, two games to one, to win league championship.

Regular-season attendance—Bluefield, 39,339; Bristol, 29,158; Burlington, 67,276; Elizabethton, 15,451; Huntington, 42,129; Johnson City, 42,868; Kingsport, 23,786; Martinsville, 66,695; Princeton, 18,652; Pulaski, 16,993. Total—362,347. Playoffs (3 games)—1,383.

Managers—Bluefield, Mike O'Berry; Bristol, Mark Wagner; Burlington, Minnie Mendoza; Elizabethton, Ray Smith; Huntington, Phil Hannon; Johnson City, Steve Turco; Kingsport, Andre David; Martinsville, Roly DeArmas; Princeton, Sam Mejias; Pulaski, Randy Ingle.

All-Star team: 1B—Ken Tirpack, Elizabethton; 2B—Marlon Nava, Elizabethton; 3B—Dan Frye, Princeton; SS—David Fisher, Martinsville; OF—Derek Hacopian, Burlington; Roy Hodge, Bluefield; Basil Shabazz, Johnson City; C—Marco Manrique, Bluefield; DH—Aldo Pecorilli, Johnson City; RHP—Mike D'Andrea, Pulaski; LHP—Mike Mathews, Burlington; Relief Pitcher—Gus Gandarillas, Elizabethton; Most Valuable Player—Dan Frye, Princeton; Manager of the Year—Ray Smith, Elizabethton.

BATTING

TEAM

Team	Avg.	G	AB	R	OR	H	TB	2B	3B	HR	RBI	SH	SF	HP	BB	Int. BB	SO	SB	CS	LOB
Bluefield	.272	62	2119	404	386	577	798	95	9	36	316	17	19	23	274	9	482	70	34	439
Elizabethton	.271	66	2185	429	274	593	866	99	12	50	361	8	33	29	308	12	439	39	30	483
Pulaski	.253	61	2024	286	373	512	743	89	23	32	243	8	13	24	219	6	457	122	42	410
Huntington	.251	62	2054	333	316	516	675	75	15	18	273	28	14	38	273	3	442	96	46	456
Martinsville	.250	65	2218	306	414	554	777	105	11	32	266	16	17	29	244	9	443	49	25	500
Princeton	.247	65	2175	356	378	538	796	82	22	44	291	12	12	27	247	4	557	100	37	455
Bristol	.246	68	2254	309	309	554	732	94	15	18	256	9	19	28	296	8	537	81	39	516
Kingsport	.240	62	2025	311	319	486	707	92	6	39	259	10	14	31	296	6	474	79	36	450
Burlington	.238	66	2177	326	271	518	710	82	7	32	265	33	22	28	314	7	515	78	30	522
Johnson City	.234	65	2195	311	331	513	736	104	13	31	256	19	21	16	302	13	495	138	48	478

INDIVIDUAL

(Leading qualifiers for batting championship—184 or more plate appearances)

*Bats lefthanded.   Switch-hitter.

Player, Team	Avg.	G	AB	R	H	TB	2B	3B	HR	RBI	SH	SF	HP	BB	Int. BB	SO	SB	CS
Stutheit, Tim, Huntington	.338	49	154	30	52	61	7	1	0	21	6	1	7	33	1	29	11	3
Tirpack, Ken, Elizabethton*	.333	61	228	42	76	120	13	2	9	42	0	5	5	31	2	36	1	2
Nava, Marlon, Elizabethton	.326	46	175	37	57	74	14	0	1	20	1	1	1	17	1	22	1	0
Frye, Dan, Princeton	.325	65	243	50	79	140	10	3	15	59	2	1	1	42	0	60	19	5
Pecorilli, Aldo, Johnson City	.323	54	201	36	65	101	14	2	6	41	0	2	2	25	1	21	6	2
Hacopian, Derek, Bristol+	.322	50	171	39	55	93	11	0	9	43	0	3	2	38	1	32	1	3
Whitehurst, Todd, Bristol+	.316	51	174	25	55	73	8	2	2	17	0	1	4	25	4	54	1	0
Newman, Rob, Pulaski	.308	49	169	30	52	82	6	3	6	31	0	2	1	25	0	29	5	2
Fisher, David, Martinsville	.303	50	188	31	57	82	14	1	3	42	1	1	0	30	2	27	6	1
White, Don, Kingsport	.303	55	221	37	67	91	10	1	4	27	2	4	3	21	0	38	25	9

Departmental leaders: G—Frye, 65; AB—Frye, 243; R—Ashton, Frye, 50; H—Frye, 79; TB—Frye, 140; 2B—Swann, 18; 3B—R. Hernandez, A. Johnson, 6; HR—Frye, 15; RBI—Frye, 59; SH—Whitaker, 7; SF—Anderson, 6; HP—T. Thomas, 9; BB—Ashton, 50; IBB—Metcalf, Whitehurst, 4; SO—Harris, 76; SB—Shabazz, 43; CS—Rojas, Shabazz, 11.

(All players—listed alphabetically)

Player, Team	Avg.	G	AB	R	H	TB	2B	3B	HR	RBI	SH	SF	HP	BB	Int. BB	SO	SB	CS
Anderson, Charlie, Johnson City	.195	45	154	17	30	43	2	1	3	15	2	6	1	14	1	32	4	3
Ashton, Jeff, Princeton	.241	53	170	50	41	61	9	1	3	21	1	1	5	50	0	50	16	7
Ayala, Moises, Bristol	.118	10	17	3	2	3	1	0	0	0	0	0	0	1	0	6	0	0
Baker, Jason, Elizabethton*	.217	22	60	12	13	19	3	0	1	5	0	1	0	8	0	14	1	0
Ballara, Juan, Johnson City	.185	26	81	9	15	27	5	2	1	11	1	1	0	11	0	27	0	1
Barton, Scott, Huntington*	.162	14	37	1	6	6	0	0	0	1	1	0	0	3	0	9	1	0
Bell, Brent, Martinsville	.199	46	161	16	32	51	8	1	3	11	2	0	1	19	0	43	2	2
Beltre, Eddy, Kingsport	.222	32	99	15	22	25	3	0	0	8	2	0	0	9	0	15	9	4
Bess, John, Princeton+	.208	48	173	22	36	53	9	1	2	21	1	0	4	15	2	55	3	2
Blanco, Pedro, Elizabethton+	.299	32	87	13	26	28	2	0	0	14	1	1	1	7	0	21	0	3

Player, Team	Avg.	G	AB	R	H	TB	2B	3B	HR	RBI	SH	SF	HP	BB	Int. BB	SO	SB	CS
Boehlow, Jason, Huntington	.176	17	51	5	9	9	0	0	0	4	0	1	1	5	1	7	0	0
Booker, Kevin, Huntington	.241	37	133	18	32	41	4	1	1	8	1	0	3	11	0	24	6	1
Bradley, Ken, Kingsport	.118	6	17	1	2	3	1	0	0	1	0	0	0	2	0	5	0	1
Brophy, E.J., Martinsville	.330	35	109	11	36	46	7	0	1	17	3	2	4	11	0	11	0	0
Burrough, Butch, Elizabethton	.229	43	140	41	32	73	8	0	11	28	0	1	0	39	0	32	2	0
Bush, Ricky, Martinsville	.235	5	17	2	4	8	1	0	1	6	0	1	0	1	0	2	0	0
Cabrera, Jose, Bristol	.000	13	1	0	0	0	0	0	0	0	0	0	0	0	0	0	0	0
Carmona, William, Martinsville	.196	59	224	27	44	81	7	0	10	39	1	3	4	16	1	65	3	2
Casanova, Raul, Kingsport	.270	42	137	25	37	60	9	1	4	27	0	0	4	26	2	25	3	1
Castaldo, Gregg, Bluefield*	.310	12	29	7	9	9	0	0	0	2	0	1	1	5	0	5	0	1
Catalanotto, Frank, Bristol*	.200	21	50	6	10	12	2	0	0	4	0	0	0	8	0	8	0	1
Chambers, Mark, Pulaski	.207	55	193	28	40	48	4	2	0	15	0	0	2	25	0	34	32	6
Chavez, Eric, Bluefield	.297	56	192	35	57	100	14	1	9	32	1	1	4	34	0	48	2	2
Chisum, Dave, Bristol*	.190	17	42	1	8	14	3	0	1	8	0	0	5	0	0	20	1	0
Claudio, Patricio, Bristol	.261	48	165	31	43	53	4	0	2	12	4	1	1	20	0	43	20	7
Coates, Tom, Pulaski	.238	10	42	9	10	19	3	0	2	6	0	0	0	4	0	8	2	1
Coleman, Ronnie, Bristol	.176	7	17	3	3	3	0	0	0	2	1	1	0	1	0	9	0	1
Colon, Hector, Johnson City	.183	38	93	18	17	20	3	0	0	8	2	0	1	16	3	14	15	2
Colon, Roque, Huntington	.136	19	44	14	6	14	2	0	2	6	0	0	2	11	0	16	0	0
Cornish, Tim, Martinsville	.255	22	55	4	14	15	1	0	0	5	0	0	2	5	0	16	2	1
Costic, Tim, Elizabethton*	.235	55	196	39	46	68	4	0	6	31	2	0	6	22	1	50	3	3
Crouwel, Mike, Martinsville	.286	5	14	3	4	4	0	0	0	1	0	0	1	2	0	6	0	0
Delarosa, Maximo, Bristol	.243	62	222	27	54	64	5	1	1	30	3	0	1	24	0	52	4	3
Diaz, Einar, Bristol	.208	52	178	19	37	43	3	0	1	14	2	2	3	20	0	9	2	3
Dicken, Rongie, Johnson City	.136	23	59	7	8	9	1	0	0	3	1	0	0	7	0	20	5	2
Dickerson, Bobby, Bristol*	.119	20	59	6	7	12	2	0	1	8	0	2	2	7	1	19	1	1
Dudek, Steve, Johnson City*	.257	46	140	19	36	50	8	0	2	21	1	0	1	13	1	28	3	4
Duncan, Enrique, Princeton	.200	5	15	2	3	5	0	1	0	1	0	0	1	0	0	4	0	0
Eaddy, Keith, Kingsport	.274	50	175	42	48	75	7	1	6	31	3	2	4	34	1	47	10	5
Evans, Glenn, Elizabethton†	.235	30	98	16	23	26	3	0	0	12	0	0	1	13	2	27	1	4
Evans, Matt, Bristol*	.291	35	117	19	34	53	7	0	4	19	0	2	1	21	1	24	0	1
Evans, Stan, Martinsville*	.415	14	53	12	22	31	7	1	0	10	1	1	0	6	0	3	5	0
Fisher, David, Martinsville	.303	50	188	31	57	82	14	1	3	42	1	1	0	30	2	27	6	1
Flores, Joe, Kingsport	.429	2	7	1	3	3	0	0	0	3	0	0	0	0	0	2	0	0
Freeberger, George, Bluefield	.214	19	42	8	9	10	1	0	0	2	0	0	0	4	0	14	1	0
Frye, Dan, Princeton	.325	65	243	50	79	140	10	3	15	59	2	1	1	42	0	60	19	5
Garcia, Adrian, Pulaski	.231	45	143	18	33	48	9	0	2	15	1	1	2	13	0	53	4	1
Genao, Huascar, Bristol*	.226	41	146	23	33	46	2	1	3	24	0	2	5	11	0	25	0	1
Graham, Derrick, Princeton	.218	16	55	7	12	20	2	0	2	10	0	1	0	5	0	22	0	1
Greene, Bart, Bristol	.300	23	80	15	24	29	3	1	0	9	2	1	1	9	0	14	13	4
Grijak, Kevin, Pulaski*	.355	10	31	1	11	14	3	0	0	6	0	0	0	6	0	2	2	2
Hacopian, Derek, Bristol	.322	50	171	39	55	93	11	0	9	43	0	3	2	38	1	32	1	3
Harris, Eric, Kingsport	.244	59	209	36	51	96	12	0	11	45	0	2	4	35	0	76	0	3
Hawkins, Craig, Elizabethton†	.330	24	97	31	32	57	7	3	4	29	1	1	1	16	2	11	8	2
Haws, Scott, Martinsville*	.211	36	128	20	27	30	3	0	0	9	0	0	1	18	2	12	0	0
Henry, Antoine, Johnson City	.239	46	142	34	34	47	6	2	1	17	0	1	1	39	0	35	19	4
Hernandez, Luis, Bristol	.160	7	25	1	4	5	1	0	0	0	0	0	0	3	0	7	1	1
Hernandez, Ramon, Princeton	.244	54	205	30	50	82	8	6	4	30	3	2	2	6	1	47	5	3
Hobbs, Shane, Martinsville	.300	16	40	4	12	15	3	0	0	3	0	0	0	1	0	9	0	1
Hodge, Roy, Bluefield	.295	58	241	41	71	89	13	1	1	46	0	0	2	22	1	32	2	3
Horincewich, Tom, Elizabethton*	.284	44	169	33	48	63	9	0	2	23	0	5	0	12	0	15	2	5
Horn, Jeff, Elizabethton*	.243	41	144	20	35	44	6	0	1	26	0	2	4	25	1	25	2	0
Houston, Maceo, Huntington*	.274	30	106	12	29	41	5	2	1	12	0	0	0	5	0	31	1	1
Ignash, Reggie, Bristol	.093	17	43	6	4	4	0	0	0	5	1	0	0	7	0	23	0	0
Jackson, Damian, Bristol	.248	62	226	32	56	70	12	1	0	23	6	3	6	32	0	31	29	5
Jelinek, Joe, Martinsville†	.222	33	126	15	28	32	4	0	0	11	1	0	1	16	1	20	6	4
Johnson, Art, Bristol	.256	61	223	31	57	72	3	6	0	27	2	4	4	26	0	47	15	2
Johnson, Marcel, Pulaski	.235	9	34	1	8	9	1	0	0	6	1	1	0	3	0	10	0	0
Jones, Paul, Bluefield*	.213	42	127	18	27	39	6	0	2	12	2	1	0	7	0	34	0	1
Keenan, Bradley, Princeton	.239	22	67	13	16	18	2	0	0	6	0	0	4	10	0	19	0	2
Kendall, Jeremey, Martinsville	.275	49	204	37	56	77	8	2	3	23	0	3	5	13	0	42	14	5
Kiraly, Jeff, Kingsport*	.206	55	199	29	41	75	13	0	7	37	0	3	2	31	2	62	1	2
Kopriva, Dan, Princeton	.258	24	89	11	23	35	3	0	3	11	0	0	1	10	0	13	3	1
Kostrzewa, Mike, Bristol	.190	23	42	8	8	14	3	0	1	6	2	1	0	6	0	11	0	0
Lackey, Steve, Kingsport	.176	38	148	16	26	28	2	0	0	10	0	0	3	17	0	22	3	4
Ladell, Cleveland, Princeton	.266	64	241	37	64	90	6	4	4	32	2	2	1	13	0	45	24	3
Lamar, Johnny, Bristol*	.264	61	220	29	58	75	11	0	2	29	0	1	1	22	1	44	0	1
LeGree, Keith, Elizabethton*	.260	44	173	34	45	79	10	3	6	43	1	5	1	22	0	42	1	3
Lewandowski, John, Bristol	.172	29	93	11	16	19	0	0	1	9	1	2	0	10	0	23	0	1
Manrique, Marco, Bluefield	.301	58	183	28	55	66	8	0	1	18	2	0	2	18	1	33	3	2
Manship, Jeff, Princeton	.256	11	39	8	10	20	1	0	3	6	0	0	1	3	0	15	0	1
Marine, Del, Bristol†	.252	50	163	18	41	55	8	0	2	23	0	2	3	26	0	42	2	0
Marrero, Kenny, Bristol	.258	29	89	10	23	31	5	0	1	11	0	1	0	6	0	21	0	1
Martinez, Ben, Martinsville	.333	14	24	8	8	9	1	0	0	4	0	0	2	0	0	3	1	0
Mayberry, Germaine, Bristol	.000	5	10	1	0	0	0	0	0	0	0	0	0	0	0	2	2	0
McMullen, Jon, Martinsville*	.258	27	89	8	23	38	9	0	2	14	0	1	1	24	1	17	0	0
Meluskey, Mitchell, Bristol†	.230	43	126	23	29	45	7	0	3	16	0	2	0	29	0	36	3	0
Mercedes, Feliciano, Bluefield†	.272	43	158	42	43	56	5	4	0	13	2	2	2	29	0	43	14	4
Metcalf, Scott, Bluefield*	.298	57	215	38	64	77	8	1	1	39	0	0	2	19	4	37	2	1
Miller, Joey, Elizabethton	.329	28	73	13	24	28	1	0	1	12	0	3	1	13	1	18	3	3
Miller, Terry, Bristol	.115	21	52	3	6	10	4	0	0	3	2	0	2	3	1	19	2	0
Milne, Darren, Bristol	.273	15	55	7	15	18	3	0	0	5	0	0	1	7	0	11	0	1
Montero, Danny, Huntington	.302	32	86	16	26	36	3	2	1	7	1	0	3	8	0	17	5	1
Moon, Ray, Princeton	.278	38	126	24	35	36	1	0	0	4	0	0	1	13	0	17	7	4
Moore, Charlton, Martinsville	.189	58	206	22	39	52	8	1	1	17	1	3	6	21	1	46	0	2
Morales, Francisco, Huntington	.179	13	39	4	7	11	1	0	1	9	1	0	1	10	0	13	1	2
Moreno, Jorge, Bristol†	.288	51	156	23	45	55	5	1	1	15	0	1	1	21	0	45	6	2
Morris, Rossi, Princeton	.189	20	37	6	7	10	3	0	0	5	0	1	0	3	0	14	1	1
Mota, Santo, Johnson City†	.258	20	66	12	17	18	1	0	0	9	3	0	0	14	0	12	16	5
Moyle, Mike, Bristol	.220	18	41	4	9	10	1	0	0	2	0	0	0	13	0	12	0	0
Mrowka, Jim, Kingsport†	.241	43	133	10	32	38	6	0	0	7	2	1	3	27	1	18	5	1
Nava, Marlon, Elizabethton	.326	46	175	37	57	74	14	0	1	20	1	1	1	17	1	22	1	0
Nelson, Andre, Huntington	.294	37	119	17	35	47	7	1	1	20	2	0	1	7	0	23	12	5
Newman, Rob, Pulaski	.308	49	169	30	52	82	6	3	6	31	0	2	2	25	0	29	5	2
Norman, Kenny, Elizabethton†	.248	35	129	32	32	44	4	1	2	11	1	2	4	10	1	30	8	3

Player, Team	Avg.	G	AB	R	H	TB	2B	3B	HR	RBI	SH	SF	HP	BB	Int. BB	SO	SB	CS
Norton, Chris, Bristol	.250	4	12	2	3	3	0	0	0	2	0	1	0	1	0	4	0	0
Nunez, Ramon, Pulaski	.252	59	218	28	55	83	9	2	5	32	0	3	14	1	0	57	8	3
Nutting, Robert, Huntington*	.283	35	127	22	36	49	10	0	1	25	1	0	3	28	1	18	3	3
Ollison, Scott, Martinsville	.255	15	51	6	13	16	0	0	1	7	2	0	0	3	0	7	1	2
Ortega, Roberto, Bristol*	.173	23	75	3	13	16	3	0	0	5	0	0	6	0	0	16	0	0
Osentowski, Jared, Kingsport	.249	59	213	33	53	67	11	0	1	21	1	0	6	26	0	48	6	2
Oyas, Dan, Princeton	.266	49	192	18	51	63	7	1	1	20	1	2	0	12	1	48	4	1
Paragin, Billy, Pulaski	.139	31	72	7	10	12	2	0	0	7	1	0	4	12	0	25	0	1
Parker, Corey, Bristol*	.248	35	129	13	32	46	5	0	3	23	0	1	0	15	1	31	1	2
Parker, Don, Kingsport	.209	38	129	19	27	41	4	2	2	14	0	0	1	27	0	30	8	1
Paulino, Nelson, Pulaski†	.276	56	225	31	62	77	7	4	0	14	1	0	2	22	0	31	21	7
Pecorilli, Aldo, Johnson City	.323	54	201	36	65	101	14	2	6	41	0	2	2	25	1	21	6	2
Perez, Richard, Huntington	.289	51	190	33	55	68	7	3	0	22	4	3	4	17	0	25	5	3
Pico, Brandon, Huntington*	.220	32	109	18	24	34	3	2	1	16	2	0	0	13	0	24	4	5
Plonk, Chris, Huntington	.227	22	66	12	15	22	2	1	1	10	0	1	1	11	0	21	2	0
Quillin, Ty, Kingsport*	.261	20	69	5	18	22	4	0	0	6	0	1	0	11	1	17	0	0
Reeves, Mickey, Huntington	.167	26	72	5	12	16	1	0	1	6	1	1	1	6	0	21	6	3
Riemer, Matt, Bluefield	.274	47	146	29	40	49	6	0	1	23	4	3	2	24	0	47	6	1
Robinson, Eli, Princeton	.205	40	127	22	26	42	5	1	3	14	0	0	0	15	0	33	2	1
Rojas, Roberto, Bristol*	.285	57	214	38	61	75	8	3	0	11	1	0	0	27	2	46	32	11
Romero, Phil, Martinsville	.297	58	239	37	71	94	11	3	2	22	2	1	2	18	1	20	6	5
Root, Mitch, Huntington	.336	32	116	15	39	46	2	1	1	24	0	1	1	15	0	23	6	2
Roper, Chad, Elizabethton	.286	39	147	20	42	51	4	1	1	25	0	2	1	12	0	29	0	1
St. Claire, Mark, Pulaski	.210	27	81	5	17	22	2	0	1	6	0	0	0	3	0	23	1	1
Sanchez, Yuri, Bristol*	.176	36	102	11	18	24	2	2	0	5	1	0	0	21	0	41	5	3
Sanders, Rodriguez, Princeton	.219	25	73	9	16	20	1	0	1	7	0	0	0	4	0	19	4	1
Serra, Jose, Bluefield	.256	55	219	37	56	63	7	0	0	30	3	3	2	26	1	25	19	9
Shabazz, Basil, Johnson City	.229	56	223	33	51	71	7	2	3	20	1	2	0	28	1	75	43	11
Shipman, Mike, Martinsville	.269	14	26	6	7	7	0	0	0	0	1	0	0	5	0	9	0	0
Shirley, Al, Kingsport	.313	29	99	26	31	57	3	1	7	22	0	0	1	26	0	37	9	2
Silvia, Brian, Princeton	.303	36	122	19	37	46	4	1	1	23	1	1	1	18	0	23	2	1
Simmons, Josh, Huntington	.247	29	89	19	22	26	4	0	0	13	1	1	5	14	0	15	4	3
Slattery, Don, Johnson City*	.191	44	141	18	27	42	3	0	4	15	0	1	3	22	2	30	1	2
Sly, Kian, Pulaski*	.208	48	144	18	30	50	5	3	3	11	1	2	0	11	0	60	13	2
Smith, Coleman, Huntington	.191	41	115	26	22	24	2	0	0	13	1	3	1	37	0	27	7	5
Smith, Dan, Huntington	.254	30	114	17	29	40	8	0	1	19	1	1	0	7	0	19	6	0
Spetter, Bryan, Pulaski*	.263	50	171	27	45	64	9	2	2	19	1	4	1	17	1	23	5	2
Stanley, Derek, Johnson City†	.320	8	25	6	8	11	1	1	0	4	1	0	0	4	0	6	1	0
Steele, Steve, Kingsport	.188	21	69	10	13	19	3	0	1	2	0	0	0	11	0	14	1	1
Stojsavljevic, Paul, Huntington	.184	22	76	10	14	18	2	1	0	5	0	0	1	9	0	19	0	2
Stutheit, Tim, Bluefield	.338	49	154	30	52	61	7	1	0	21	6	1	7	33	1	29	11	3
Stutz, John, Johnson City	.290	53	183	21	53	81	14	1	4	27	0	1	3	29	2	47	2	2
Sumner, Chad, Johnson City	.228	57	215	22	49	65	13	0	1	21	2	0	1	26	1	48	4	2
Sutey, John, Bristol	.178	32	90	10	16	24	1	1	0	12	0	1	3	4	0	26	0	2
Swann, Pedro, Pulaski*	.300	59	203	36	61	96	18	1	5	34	0	1	7	32	3	33	13	6
Taylor, Todd A., Elizabethton*	.264	45	129	25	34	58	5	2	5	29	0	1	2	46	1	33	0	1
Thomas, Duane, Bluefield	.203	43	138	33	28	69	8	0	11	31	0	2	1	22	0	65	6	1
Thomas, Mike, Bluefield	.301	43	163	26	49	66	9	1	2	29	0	1	2	12	1	28	2	3
Thomas, Rod, Princeton	.182	48	159	23	29	49	10	2	2	19	1	1	3	19	0	57	9	3
Thomas, Tim, Bristol	.290	63	210	41	61	80	7	0	4	36	0	3	9	46	2	48	2	4
Thompson, Leroy, Bristol*	.250	16	40	6	10	16	3	0	1	6	0	0	0	6	0	15	0	2
Thompson, Mike, Martinsville	.204	50	167	20	34	56	8	1	4	19	0	1	2	22	0	54	1	0
Tirpack, Ken, Elizabethton*	.333	61	228	42	76	120	13	2	9	42	0	5	5	31	2	36	1	2
Towle, Justin, Princeton	.071	19	42	5	3	6	1	1	0	2	0	0	2	9	0	16	1	0
Townsend, Charles, Bristol*	.271	44	133	19	36	65	8	0	7	26	3	1	2	15	1	31	0	0
Ugueto, Jesus, Johnson City	.209	47	163	14	34	45	6	1	1	15	1	2	0	9	0	27	3	3
Urbanek, Jason, Martinsville	.237	28	97	17	23	33	5	1	1	6	1	0	1	11	0	31	2	1
Valdez, Ken, Bristol	.148	27	61	5	9	15	4	1	0	5	0	0	2	5	0	25	0	0
Valette, Ramon, Bristol	.200	44	140	21	28	34	6	0	0	11	1	3	1	15	0	34	6	0
Vaske, Terry, Huntington*	.220	15	50	4	11	13	2	0	0	5	1	0	0	7	0	14	0	1
Vazquez, Jose, Johnson City	.261	55	188	32	49	71	14	1	2	19	3	3	3	27	0	30	15	5
Velandia, George, Bristol	.202	45	119	20	24	32	6	1	0	15	0	0	0	15	0	16	3	2
Vivenzio, Augie, Pulaski*	.333	5	9	2	3	5	0	0	0	0	0	0	0	2	0	1	0	1
Walker, Steve, Huntington†	.217	52	161	35	35	53	3	0	5	27	4	2	4	16	0	47	16	6
Whitaker, Jeff, Bristol	.184	57	147	27	27	32	3	1	0	12	7	1	2	28	0	42	9	4
White, Andre, Bristol*	.333	8	36	8	12	15	1	1	0	3	0	0	0	2	0	4	3	0
White, Don, Kingsport	.303	55	221	37	67	91	10	1	4	27	2	4	3	21	0	38	25	9
White, Eric, Bristol	.233	19	60	8	14	18	4	0	0	2	1	1	0	10	0	18	1	1
Whitehurst, Todd, Bristol†	.316	51	174	25	55	73	8	2	2	17	0	1	4	25	4	54	1	0
Williams, Juan, Pulaski*	.278	47	169	26	47	79	6	4	6	31	1	1	0	13	1	46	9	3
Williams, Mark, Johnson City	.165	41	121	13	20	35	6	0	3	10	1	2	0	18	1	43	1	0
Williams, Terrell, Kingsport†	.203	20	59	9	12	19	4	0	1	12	1	0	2	9	0	26	3	2
Winget, Jeremy, Bluefield*	.213	18	61	12	13	19	3	0	1	2	0	0	0	11	0	16	2	1
Wipf, Mark, Kingsport†	.235	57	217	29	51	63	7	1	1	17	2	2	2	18	0	39	6	3
Yeske, Kyle, Bluefield	.267	17	30	8	8	11	0	0	1	6	0	1	1	7	0	7	0	0
Zimmerman, Phil, Pulaski	.233	39	120	18	28	35	5	1	0	10	1	0	3	17	0	24	7	5

The following pitchers, listed alphabetically by club, with games in parentheses, had no plate appearances, primarily through use of designated hitters:

BLUEFIELD—Benitez, Armando (25); Chatterton, Chris (25); Chavez, Carlos (15); Devereux, Chuck (4); Emerson, Scott (14); Fregoso, Dan (9); Knott, Shawn (13); Lane, Aaron (14); Lantrip, Joe (6); Marquez, Ihosvany (15); Porter, Mike (13); Sackinsky, Brian (5); Saneaux, Francisco (4); Shenk, Larry (21); Stephenson, Garrett (12).

BRISTOL—Augustine, Bob (18); Ban, Yoshitaro (9); Berlin, Mike (4); Cedeno, Blas (13); Grimm, John (20); Jones, Tim (4); Magrini, Paul (13); Maxcy, Dave (14); McFarland, Toby (12); Miller, Trever (12); Munoz, Riccardo (4); Reincke, Corey (11); Rodriguez, Dave (19); Rosengren, John (14); Santos, Henry (12); Sodowski, Clint (15); Yamazaki, Kazu (9).

BURLINGTON—Bluhm, Brandon (17); Gallagher, Allen (16); Garza, Roberto (23); Holter, Brian (17); Koller, Rodney (1); Leyva, Damian (15); Maffett, Chris (5); Matthews, Mike (10); Rideau, Greg (3); Sides, Craig (11); Sinner, Greg (11); Tavarez, Julian (14); Zubiri, Jon (14).

ELIZABETHTON—Caridad, Ron (12); Correa, Jose (22); DeJesus, Guido (2); Gandarillas, Gustavo (29); Hawkins, Latroy (5); Legault, Kevin (17); Lidle, Cory (19); Linebarger, Keith (11); Miller, Shawn (6); Moten, Scott (13); Pina, Rafael (11); Saccavino, Paul (6); Taylor, Todd (7).

HUNTINGTON—Childress, Bill (3); Elsbecker, Andy (10); Garcia, Mario (11); Gavlick, Daryle (13); Guerra, Esmili (17); Gustavson, Dan (12); Hassel, Jay (13); Kendrick, Pat (19); Latimer, Bill (6); Lawrence, Matt (9); Lopez, Orlando (4); Matos, Luis (3); Pacheco, Jose (12); Phillips, Jim (9); Talemaoc, Amaury (12); Waite, Jon (5).

JOHNSON CITY—Blake, Todd (13); Carrillo, Joe (10); Goodman, Doug (23); Guyton, Duffy (16); Larson, Joe (19); Lopez, Jose (17);

Marchesi, Jim (23); Matranga, Jeff (19); Matulevich, Jeff (13); Meek, Darryl (12); Miller, Eric (27); Pittman, Chuck (21).

KINGSPORT—Bellman, Bill (10); Belmonte, Pedro (11); Berg, Chris (12); Collier, Ervin (10); Cotner, Andy (6); Grennan, Steve (16); Hiljus, Erik (12); Isringhausen, Jason (7); Kroon, Marc (12); McDill, Allen (1); Pinson, Tom (16); Seymour, Steve (2); Shaffer, Travis (15); Swanson, Dave (12); Williams, Scott (3).

MARTINSVILLE—Alger, Kevin (15); Boldt, Sean (13); Coleman, Scott (17); Costa, Tim (12); Edwards, Sam (11); Fiore, Tony (17); Humphry, Trevor (16); Kirkland, Kris (4); Mejias, Fernando (11); Mitchell, Bob (14); Mitchell, Larry (3); Nutt, Steve (13); Page, Thane (12); Pugh, Tim (12).

PRINCETON—Balentine, Bryant (2); Brunson, Bill (13); Concepcion, Yamil (12); Cullop, Glen (11); Etheridge, Roger (17); Etler, Todd (12); Fox, Chad (15); Fussell, Denny (20); Lyons, Curt (11); Maberry, Louis (21); Miller, Jim (10); Mullins, Chris (13); Nix, Jim (27); Rhodriguez, Rory (2); Ruyak, Todd (12).

PULASKI—Avery, John (17); Clontz, Brad (4); D'Andrea, Mike (11); Hassan, Ted (23); Havens, Bill (17); Kempfer, Jason (13); Martineau, Yves (17); Roeder, Steve (15); Schmidt, Jason (11); Shafer, Bill (17); Smoot, Chris (5); Turnier, Aaron (6); Weeks, Ben (14); Wendt, Jason (6).

GRAND SLAMS—Harris, 2; Burrough, Carmona, Casanova, Frye, Hawkins, Kiraly, LeGree, Morales, Nelson, D. Thomas, J. Williams, 1 each.

AWARDED FIRST BASE ON CATCHER'S INTERFERENCE—Hodge (Meluskey); Ladell (Lewandowski); Meluskey (Harris); St. Claire (Freeberger).

PITCHING

TEAM

Team	ERA	G	CG	ShO	Sv.	IP	H	R	ER	HR	HB	BB	Int. BB	SO	WP	Bk.
Elizabethton	3.14	66	5	6	24	567.0	488	274	198	16	24	223	5	499	42	9
Burlington	3.22	66	4	3	17	579.1	485	271	207	30	36	212	6	483	41	15
Kingsport	3.74	62	4	1	13	534.2	508	319	222	37	17	251	15	445	54	10
Bristol	3.79	68	8	4	14	591.2	504	309	249	32	25	312	6	560	58	10
Huntington	3.79	62	12	4	6	536.2	513	316	226	29	13	215	6	546	43	13
Johnson City	4.17	65	0	2	17	586.2	573	331	272	43	29	275	17	477	51	8
Princeton	4.21	65	0	4	19	557.1	567	378	261	37	32	267	7	436	66	7
Bluefield	4.64	62	2	1	14	541.0	535	386	279	46	28	322	4	479	67	14
Martinsville	5.18	65	2	1	11	561.2	636	414	323	29	25	340	6	496	73	11
Pulaski	5.38	61	0	2	12	524.0	552	373	313	33	44	356	5	420	77	11

INDIVIDUAL

(Leading qualifiers for earned-run average leadership—54 or more innings)

*Throws lefthanded.

Pitcher, Team	W	L	Pct.	ERA	G	GS	CG	GF	ShO	Sv.	IP	H	R	ER	HR	HB	BB	Int. BB	SO	WP
Matthews, Bristol*	7	0	1.000	1.01	10	10	0	0	0	0	62.1	33	13	7	1	3	27	0	55	3
Cabrera, Bristol	8	3	.727	1.75	13	13	1	0	0	0	92.1	74	27	18	6	2	18	0	79	3
Pacheco, Huntington	5	4	.556	2.00	12	12	5	0	1	0	90.0	87	42	20	3	3	10	1	84	1
Cedeno, Bristol	8	2	.800	2.01	13	13	3	0	2	0	80.2	64	21	18	2	5	41	0	77	6
Legault, Elizabethton	7	0	1.000	2.10	17	2	0	6	0	2	55.2	38	20	13	0	2	11	0	53	1
Hassel, Huntington	4	1	.800	2.39	13	11	1	1	1	1	75.1	64	31	20	0	0	32	1	92	5
Moten, Elizabethton	8	1	.889	2.40	13	12	1	0	1	0	78.2	60	31	21	1	6	32	0	71	2
Tavarez, Bristol	6	3	.667	2.68	14	14	2	0	2	0	87.1	86	41	26	3	10	12	0	69	5
Lyons, Princeton	5	3	.625	2.77	11	11	0	0	0	0	55.1	61	36	17	4	4	17	0	33	6
D'Andrea, Pulaski	8	1	.889	2.79	11	11	0	0	0	0	61.1	39	20	19	3	0	28	0	79	3

Departmental leaders: G—Gandarillas, 29; W—Cabrera, Cedeno, D'Andrea, Moten, 8; L—Humphry, T. Miller, 8; Pct.—Legault, Matthews, 1.000; GS—Tavarez, 14; CG—Pacheco, 5; GF—Gandarillas, 29; ShO—Cedeno, Gavlick, Maxcy, Tavarez, 2; Sv.—Gandarillas, E. Miller, Nix, 13; IP—Cabrera, 92.1; H—Pacheco, 87; R—Kempfer, 62; ER—R. Mitchell, 50; HR—Carrillo, 8; HB—Tavarez, 10; BB—Kempfer, Kroon, 57; IBB—Pinson, 5; SO—Talemaco, 93; WP—Mullins, 19.

(All pitchers—listed alphabetically)

Pitcher, Team	W	L	Pct.	ERA	G	GS	CG	GF	ShO	Sv.	IP	H	R	ER	HR	HB	BB	Int. BB	SO	WP
Alger, Martinsville*	3	0	1.000	4.10	15	1	0	6	0	3	37.1	33	19	17	3	1	31	1	51	9
Augustine, Bristol	2	2	.500	4.80	18	2	0	3	0	0	30.0	27	19	16	1	1	22	1	24	4
Avery, Pulaski*	1	2	.333	4.33	17	0	0	7	0	1	35.1	31	18	17	2	4	25	2	25	6
Balentine, Princeton*	0	0	.000	4.91	2	0	0	1	0	0	3.2	4	2	2	0	1	2	0	5	1
Ban, Bristol	0	0	.000	3.38	9	2	0	3	0	1	21.1	15	8	8	1	0	6	0	20	2
Bellman, Kingsport	1	5	.167	4.71	10	3	0	4	0	1	28.2	35	23	15	4	1	10	0	15	0
Belmonte, Kingsport	1	1	.500	2.76	11	0	0	7	0	2	29.1	33	22	9	2	1	11	2	14	5
Benitez, Bluefield	1	2	.333	4.31	25	0	0	18	0	5	31.1	35	31	15	1	3	23	0	37	7
Berg, Kingsport	0	0	.000	1.96	21	0	0	18	0	10	23.0	16	5	5	0	1	9	2	21	0
Berlin, Bristol	1	1	.500	3.09	4	1	0	0	0	0	11.2	11	4	4	0	0	5	1	10	0
Blake, Johnson City*	4	3	.571	4.38	13	13	0	0	0	0	74.0	74	40	36	4	5	34	0	63	6
Bluhm, Bristol*	2	2	.500	4.75	17	1	0	11	0	2	30.1	33	18	16	2	3	14	0	25	1
Boldt, Martinsville	2	1	.667	1.16	13	0	0	8	0	2	38.2	28	6	5	1	0	19	1	39	2
Brunson, Princeton*	5	5	.500	3.59	13	13	0	0	0	0	72.2	68	34	29	6	3	28	0	48	2
Cabrera, Bristol	8	3	.727	1.75	13	13	1	0	0	0	92.1	74	27	18	6	2	18	0	79	3
Caridad, Elizabethton	5	3	.625	4.08	12	11	0	1	0	0	64.0	56	35	29	0	7	35	0	53	13
Carrillo, Johnson City*	3	3	.500	4.62	10	10	0	0	0	0	50.2	40	30	26	8	3	22	0	42	8
Cedeno, Bristol	8	2	.800	2.01	13	13	3	0	2	0	80.2	64	21	18	2	5	41	0	77	6
Chatterton, Bluefield	5	1	.833	2.58	25	0	0	19	0	6	45.1	50	24	13	3	1	18	0	36	5
Chavez, Bluefield	1	2	.333	6.90	15	7	0	3	0	1	45.2	49	42	35	5	1	34	0	44	10
Childress, Huntington*	0	0	.000	3.38	3	0	0	2	0	0	2.2	3	2	1	0	0	3	0	3	0
Clontz, Pulaski	0	0	.000	1.59	4	0	0	3	0	1	5.2	5	1	1	0	2	2	0	7	1
Coleman, Martinsville*	2	2	.500	6.37	17	0	0	7	0	1	35.1	40	30	25	2	1	19	0	25	8
Collier, Kingsport	4	6	.400	3.47	10	10	2	0	0	0	57.0	68	35	22	6	1	11	0	31	0
Concepcion, Princeton	0	1	.000	9.82	12	0	0	9	0	0	18.1	34	27	20	0	1	11	0	8	3
Correa, Elizabethton	7	2	.778	2.25	22	0	0	13	0	3	44.0	27	13	11	2	0	18	0	50	3
Costa, Martinsville	0	4	.000	9.12	12	4	0	6	0	1	24.2	44	40	25	3	2	13	0	21	5
Cotner, Kingsport*	1	1	.500	3.38	6	0	0	3	0	0	10.2	14	8	4	0	0	7	1	10	1
Cullop, Princeton	0	1	.000	2.22	11	1	0	3	0	2	28.1	33	15	7	1	0	7	0	23	1
D'Andrea, Pulaski	8	1	.889	2.79	11	11	0	0	0	0	61.1	39	20	19	3	0	28	0	79	3
DeJesus, Elizabethton*	0	0	.000	7.71	2	0	0	0	0	0	2.1	3	3	2	0	0	3	0	3	1
Devereux, Bluefield	0	1	.000	2.89	4	1	0	1	0	0	9.1	5	5	3	2	1	3	0	12	1
Edwards, Martinsville	1	5	.167	5.31	11	11	1	0	0	0	57.2	77	45	34	3	0	22	0	40	4
Elsbecker, Huntington	0	1	.000	7.91	10	1	0	3	0	0	19.1	29	19	17	2	2	12	0	13	3

Pitcher, Team	W	L	Pct.	ERA	G	GS	CG	GF	ShO	Sv.	IP	H	R	ER	HR	HB	BB	Int. BB	SO	WP
Emerson, Bluefield*	4	3	.571	2.87	14	11	0	0	0	0	69.0	72	31	22	5	3	35	0	41	6
Etheridge, Princeton*	1	1	.500	6.88	17	5	0	5	0	1	35.1	37	33	27	3	1	25	1	35	5
Etler, Princeton	4	4	.500	4.85	12	10	0	0	0	0	52.0	62	40	28	3	4	21	0	29	5
Fiore, Martinsville	2	3	.400	4.18	17	2	0	9	0	0	32.1	32	20	15	0	3	31	1	30	11
Fox, Princeton	4	2	.667	4.74	15	8	0	4	0	0	49.1	55	43	26	2	2	34	1	37	6
Fregoso, Bluefield	2	4	.333	4.65	9	9	1	0	0	0	50.1	40	34	26	6	2	33	0	41	11
Fussell, Princeton*	3	2	.600	7.29	20	0	0	13	0	1	33.1	36	36	27	6	5	25	1	29	5
Gallagher, Bristol	2	2	.500	4.74	16	2	0	7	0	3	38.0	33	23	20	0	2	13	3	21	4
Gandarillas, Elizabethton	1	2	.333	3.00	29	0	0	29	0	13	36.0	24	14	12	1	3	10	2	34	4
Garcia, Huntington	0	3	.000	8.56	11	0	0	5	0	0	13.2	14	13	13	1	0	14	1	18	4
Garza, Bristol	0	0	.000	1.86	23	0	0	21	0	11	29.0	21	6	6	3	1	7	1	36	2
Gavlick, Huntington*	6	4	.600	3.05	13	12	4	0	2	0	82.2	73	38	28	7	0	23	0	75	5
Goodman, Johnson City	2	2	.500	4.84	23	1	0	6	0	1	35.1	38	21	19	2	2	25	0	32	5
Grennan, Kingsport*	2	1	.667	3.58	16	0	0	8	0	0	37.2	28	16	15	2	3	30	0	48	8
Grimm, Bristol	1	3	.250	4.45	20	0	0	15	0	6	30.1	33	18	15	5	2	14	2	42	8
Guerra, Huntington*	3	3	.500	3.82	17	1	0	10	0	0	30.2	28	18	13	3	0	10	0	31	5
Gustavson, Huntington	1	2	.333	6.31	12	1	0	2	0	0	25.2	39	25	18	3	2	9	0	20	0
Guyton, Johnson City	1	6	.143	6.23	16	7	0	5	0	1	43.1	50	37	30	7	0	26	3	25	3
Hassan, Pulaski	2	3	.400	5.91	22	2	0	10	0	3	45.2	57	36	30	3	1	37	0	39	10
Hassel, Huntington	4	1	.800	2.39	13	11	1	1	1	1	75.1	64	31	20	0	0	32	1	92	5
Havens, Pulaski	2	5	.286	5.98	17	1	0	9	0	1	40.2	46	30	27	2	6	34	1	29	6
Hawkins, Elizabethton	0	1	.000	3.38	5	5	1	0	0	0	26.2	21	12	10	2	0	11	0	36	0
Hiljus, Kingsport	3	6	.333	5.09	12	11	0	1	0	0	70.2	66	49	40	5	2	40	0	63	7
Holter, Bristol	0	3	.000	3.94	17	0	0	5	0	0	29.2	27	21	13	1	2	17	1	24	1
Humphry, Martinsville	1	8	.111	4.78	16	9	0	5	0	1	64.0	74	44	34	3	4	42	2	61	8
Isringhausen, Kingsport	4	1	.800	3.25	7	6	1	0	1	0	36.0	32	22	13	2	1	12	1	24	2
Jones, Bluefield*	0	0	.000	18.00	1	0	0	1	0	0	2.0	3	4	4	0	1	3	0	2	0
Jones, Bristol	1	0	1.000	2.57	4	0	0	2	0	0	7.0	4	2	2	0	0	6	0	9	1
Kempfer, Pulaski	2	7	.222	6.82	13	13	0	0	0	0	64.2	78	62	49	6	7	57	1	51	14
Kendrick, Huntington	1	3	.250	4.15	19	0	0	12	0	4	30.1	25	18	14	1	1	20	3	39	4
Kirkland, Martinsville	0	0	.000	4.50	4	0	0	4	0	0	8.0	10	5	4	1	0	3	0	4	1
Knott, Bluefield	2	0	1.000	6.20	13	0	0	5	0	0	24.2	35	24	17	3	3	15	0	8	2
Koller, Bristol	0	1	.000	12.00	1	1	0	0	0	0	3.0	3	4	4	0	0	3	0	2	2
Kroon, Kingsport	3	5	.375	4.10	12	12	0	0	0	0	68.0	52	41	31	3	1	57	0	60	13
Lane, Bluefield*	5	1	.833	3.00	14	7	0	1	0	0	45.0	36	24	15	7	0	24	0	39	3
Lantrip, Bluefield*	1	2	.333	8.44	6	5	0	0	0	0	21.1	22	23	20	5	1	13	0	18	2
Larson, Johnson City*	5	3	.625	3.30	19	6	0	4	0	0	62.2	59	25	23	7	5	28	3	47	1
Latimer, Huntington	0	3	.000	4.73	6	2	0	3	0	0	13.1	13	8	7	0	0	8	0	11	3
Lawrence, Huntington	3	2	.600	4.46	9	9	0	0	0	0	42.1	33	28	21	1	2	32	0	32	5
Legault, Elizabethton	7	0	1.000	2.10	17	2	0	6	0	2	55.2	38	20	13	0	2	11	0	53	1
Leyva, Bristol*	1	2	.333	3.86	15	0	0	3	0	0	23.1	19	13	10	1	4	13	0	28	3
Lidle, Elizabethton	2	1	.667	3.71	19	2	0	11	0	6	43.2	40	29	18	2	0	21	0	32	3
Linebarger, Elizabethton	4	2	.667	2.92	11	8	1	0	0	0	52.1	47	25	17	3	4	26	0	41	6
Lopez, Johnson City	1	0	1.000	3.22	17	1	0	2	0	0	36.1	28	20	13	2	3	21	1	27	3
Lopez, Huntington*	1	0	1.000	2.45	4	0	0	2	0	1	3.2	3	2	1	0	0	2	0	2	0
Lyons, Princeton	5	3	.625	2.77	11	11	0	0	0	0	55.1	61	36	17	4	4	17	0	33	6
Maberry, Princeton	4	0	1.000	2.14	21	0	0	6	0	2	42.0	26	13	10	4	4	16	1	51	1
Maffett, Bristol	0	1	.000	3.52	5	0	0	1	0	0	7.2	5	3	3	0	0	5	0	9	0
Magrini, Bristol	4	3	.571	3.34	13	12	2	0	0	0	89.0	69	39	33	1	5	40	0	84	3
Marchesi, Johnson City	3	4	.429	3.89	23	1	0	9	0	0	34.2	36	20	15	1	2	19	2	25	4
Marquez, Bluefield	3	1	.750	5.56	15	12	1	0	0	0	69.2	65	58	43	2	4	56	0	69	0
Martineau, Pulaski	2	1	.667	3.57	17	0	0	12	0	4	22.2	22	12	9	0	2	8	0	15	3
Matos, Huntington	0	0	.000	4.91	3	0	0	3	0	0	3.2	1	2	2	0	0	1	0	3	0
Matranga, Johnson City	3	0	1.000	2.97	19	1	0	12	0	2	36.1	34	17	12	1	3	13	1	47	3
Matthews, Bristol*	7	0	1.000	1.01	10	10	0	0	0	0	62.1	33	13	7	1	3	27	0	55	3
Matulevich, Johnson City	3	4	.429	3.79	13	13	0	0	0	0	71.1	77	41	30	2	2	31	2	46	7
Maxcy, Bristol	4	2	.667	3.47	14	7	2	7	2	3	49.1	41	24	19	4	0	17	1	43	3
McDill, Kingsport*	0	0	.000	0.00	1	0	0	0	0	0	0.1	0	0	0	0	0	2	0	0	0
McFarland, Bristol*	4	4	.500	5.08	12	12	0	0	0	0	56.2	53	38	32	4	4	40	0	43	4
Meek, Johnson City	5	6	.455	4.62	12	12	0	0	0	0	62.1	58	41	32	6	3	25	0	47	9
Mejias, Martinsville	0	3	.000	3.04	11	0	0	8	0	0	23.2	18	10	8	0	1	11	0	32	3
Miller, Johnson City	2	0	1.000	2.33	27	0	0	20	0	13	38.2	29	11	10	0	1	19	2	51	1
Miller, Princeton	1	0	1.000	3.68	10	0	0	2	0	0	22.0	18	11	9	1	4	13	1	23	6
Miller, Elizabethton	2	2	.500	3.97	6	6	0	0	0	0	34.0	44	19	15	1	0	6	0	19	1
Miller, Bristol*	3	8	.273	4.93	12	12	1	0	0	0	69.1	75	45	38	4	1	27	0	64	4
L. Mitchell, Martinsville	1	0	1.000	1.42	3	3	0	0	0	0	19.0	17	8	3	0	1	6	0	18	0
R. Mitchell, Martinsville	1	5	.167	6.59	14	13	0	1	0	0	68.1	70	58	50	3	4	50	0	53	13
Moten, Elizabethton	8	1	.889	2.40	13	12	1	0	1	0	78.2	60	31	21	1	6	32	0	71	2
Mullins, Princeton	6	5	.545	4.62	13	13	0	0	0	0	76.0	70	51	39	3	3	35	0	43	19
Munoz, Bristol	0	0	.000	0.00	4	0	0	2	0	2	14.1	5	0	0	0	0	4	0	12	0
Newman, Pulaski	0	0	.000	0.00	2	0	0	2	0	1	1.2	0	0	0	0	0	1	0	0	1
Nix, Princeton	0	4	.000	2.86	27	0	0	24	0	13	34.2	27	16	11	0	0	13	2	44	4
Nunez, Pulaski	0	0	.000	0.00	1	0	0	1	0	0	1.0	1	0	0	0	0	2	0	0	0
Nutt, Martinsville*	3	7	.300	5.32	13	11	0	1	0	0	67.2	83	51	40	6	6	36	0	50	1
Pacheco, Huntington	5	4	.556	2.00	12	12	5	0	1	0	90.0	87	42	20	3	3	10	1	84	1
Page, Martinsville	5	5	.500	6.25	12	11	1	1	0	0	59.0	75	48	41	2	1	43	0	43	5
Paragin, Pulaski	0	1	.000	19.29	2	0	0	0	0	0	2.1	8	6	5	0	1	3	0	1	0
Phillips, Huntington	0	1	.000	5.68	9	0	0	2	0	0	12.2	14	12	8	0	0	10	0	11	1
Pina, Elizabethton	6	2	.750	3.68	11	10	0	0	0	0	66.0	68	39	27	2	2	22	0	43	7
Pinson, Kingsport*	1	2	.333	4.79	16	0	0	6	0	0	35.2	46	25	19	4	1	9	5	29	2
Pittman, Johnson City	1	1	.500	5.71	21	0	0	7	0	0	41.0	50	28	26	3	0	12	3	25	1
Porter, Bluefield	1	3	.250	9.00	13	1	0	2	0	0	20.0	16	24	20	3	2	30	1	17	11
Pugh, Martinsville*	1	0	1.000	7.62	12	0	0	7	0	3	26.0	35	30	22	2	1	24	1	29	3
Reeves, Huntington	1	0	1.000	7.36	3	0	0	1	0	0	7.1	8	6	6	2	0	8	0	8	0
Reincke, Bristol	2	1	.667	3.63	11	0	0	2	0	1	22.1	17	12	9	1	2	11	0	25	5
Rhodriguez, Princeton*	0	0	.000	2.70	2	0	0	0	0	0	3.1	1	1	1	0	0	5	0	2	1
Rideau, Bristol	0	0	.000	0.00	3	0	0	3	0	1	1.1	0	0	0	0	0	1	0	1	0
Rodriguez, Bristol	1	4	.200	3.86	19	0	0	11	0	0	25.2	26	16	11	0	2	23	2	20	3
Roeder, Bristol	1	3	.250	5.26	15	6	0	6	0	0	51.1	52	37	30	4	6	42	0	36	10
Rosengren, Bristol*	0	3	.000	7.83	14	3	0	3	0	0	23.0	16	21	20	2	0	30	0	28	6
Ruyak, Princeton*	1	3	.250	2.32	12	4	0	1	0	0	31.0	35	20	8	1	0	15	0	26	2
Saccavino, Elizabethton	4	0	1.000	3.27	6	6	1	0	0	0	33.0	29	17	12	2	0	9	0	32	0
Sackinsky, Bluefield	2	2	.500	3.58	5	5	0	0	0	0	27.2	30	15	11	0	2	9	0	33	2
Saneaux, Bluefield	2	0	1.000	6.75	4	1	0	0	0	0	8.0	7	6	6	0	1	7	0	7	6
Santos, Bristol*	0	1	.000	6.60	12	0	0	7	0	0	15.0	17	18	11	3	0	12	0	16	4

Pitcher, Team	W	L	Pct.	ERA	G	GS	CG	GF	ShO	Sv.	IP	H	R	ER	HR	HB	BB	Int. BB	SO	WP
Schmidt, Pulaski	3	4	.429	4.01	11	11	0	0	0	0	58.1	55	38	26	4	3	31	0	56	3
Seymour, Kingsport	1	0	1.000	4.35	2	2	0	0	0	0	10.1	7	8	5	0	2	7	0	12	1
Shafer, Pulaski	0	3	.000	7.43	17	0	0	5	0	1	36.1	35	36	30	3	5	35	1	23	3
Shaffer, Kingsport	2	3	.400	1.98	15	4	1	10	0	0	41.0	33	16	9	3	1	18	4	35	4
Shenk, Bluefield	5	2	.714	2.75	21	0	0	10	0	1	39.1	35	19	12	0	2	12	3	45	3
Sides, Bristol	4	5	.444	4.28	11	11	0	0	0	0	61.0	54	34	29	3	5	28	0	55	7
Sinner, Bristol	1	6	.143	4.91	11	11	0	0	0	0	58.2	47	39	32	7	2	27	0	35	2
Sly, Pulaski	0	0	.000	0.00	1	0	0	1	0	0	1.0	1	0	0	0	0	0	0	1	0
Smoot, Pulaski*	0	2	.000	6.35	5	5	0	0	0	0	17.0	20	13	12	1	1	8	0	6	1
Sodowsky, Bristol	2	2	.500	3.54	15	6	0	2	0	0	56.0	46	35	22	3	4	29	0	48	6
Stephenson, Bluefield	3	1	.750	4.73	12	3	0	0	0	0	32.1	35	22	17	4	1	7	0	30	4
Swanson, Kingsport*	4	2	.667	3.09	12	12	0	0	0	0	75.2	64	38	26	6	2	22	0	77	10
Talemaco, Huntington	3	5	.375	4.01	12	12	2	0	0	0	76.1	71	45	34	6	2	17	0	93	7
Tavarez, Bristol	6	3	.667	2.68	14	14	2	0	2	0	87.1	86	41	26	3	10	12	0	69	5
Taylor, Elizabethton*	3	1	.750	3.23	7	4	0	1	0	0	30.2	31	17	11	0	0	19	0	32	1
Turnier, Pulaski*	0	1	.000	3.24	6	4	0	0	0	0	16.2	17	8	6	2	1	10	0	15	1
Waite, Pulaski*	0	1	.000	3.86	5	1	0	4	0	0	7.0	8	7	3	0	1	4	0	11	0
Weeks, Pulaski	2	3	.400	6.75	14	7	0	4	0	1	50.2	60	41	38	3	3	30	0	31	14
Wendt, Pulaski	0	2	.000	10.80	6	1	0	1	0	0	11.2	27	15	14	0	2	2	0	6	1
Williams, Kingsport	0	2	.000	7.59	3	2	0	1	0	0	10.2	14	11	9	0	0	6	0	6	1
Yamazaki, Bristol	2	1	.667	3.15	9	0	0	6	0	2	20.0	12	8	7	2	0	9	0	19	3
Zubiri, Bristol	2	1	.667	2.55	14	1	0	8	0	0	24.2	22	10	7	2	1	5	0	20	3

BALKS—Chavez, 6; Hassel, 5; Gallagher, 4; Costa, Goodman, Hassan, Rodriguez, Sides, 3 each; Berg, Concepcion, D'Andrea, Edwards, Fox, Fregoso, Hiljus, Kroon, Lantrip, Leyva, Matos, Mejias, Moten, Rosengren, 2 each; Avery, Bellman, Blake, Boldt, Cabrera, Caridad, Carrillo, Chatterton, Collier, Cotner, Elsbecker, Etheridge, Gandarillas, Garza, Gustavson, Hawkins, Holter, Humphry, Isringhausen, Kempfer, Kendrick, Kirkland, Lane, Lidle, J. Lopez, O. Lopez, Lyons, Magrini, Marchesi, Martineau, Matthews, Maxcy, E. Miller, T. Miller, R. Mitchell, Munoz, Nix, Phillips, Pina, Saccavino, Saneaux, Shafer, Sinner, Smoot, Sodowsky, Stephenson, Tavarez, Taylor, Waite, Weeks, 1 each.

COMBINATION SHUTOUTS—Stephenson-Chatterton, Bluefield; Matthews-Maffett-Garza, Burlington; Caridad-Gandarillas 2, Legault-Lidle-Gandarillas, Linebarger-Legault, Moten-Correa, Elizabethton; Carrillo-Miller, Meek-Miller, Johnson City; Page-Coleman, Martinsville; Brunson-Nix, Lyons-Cullop-Maberry, Lyons-Etheridge, Lyons-Nix-Fussell, Princeton; D'Andrea-Martineau 2, Pulaski.

NO-HIT GAMES—None.

FIELDING

TEAM

Team	Pct.	G	PO	A	E	DP	PB	Team	Pct.	G	PO	A	E	DP	PB
Burlington	.964	66	1738	764	93	65	27	Elizabethton	.951	66	1701	760	127	49	22
Bristol	.962	68	1775	719	98	51	15	Bluefield	.947	62	1623	675	129	55	32
Johnson City	.956	65	1760	662	112	53	16	Kingsport	.945	62	1604	596	129	35	18
Pulaski	.953	61	1572	680	110	70	16	Huntington	.942	62	1610	594	135	35	27
Martinsville	.952	65	1685	742	122	52	25	Princeton	.933	65	1672	711	172	46	18

INDIVIDUAL

FIRST BASEMEN

*Throws lefthanded.

Player, Team	Pct.	G	PO	A	E	DP
Bell, Martinsville	1.000	5	40	2	0	5
Bess, Princeton	.938	7	42	3	3	3
Boehlow, Huntington	1.000	13	98	9	0	7
Bush, Martinsville	1.000	1	6	1	0	1
Carmona, Martinsville	.986	38	324	29	5	28
Chavez, Bluefield	.978	6	41	3	1	6
Colon, Johnson City	1.000	1	2	0	0	1
Costic, Elizabethton*	1.000	7	48	0	0	2
Crouwel, Martinsville	1.000	3	23	3	0	0
Dicken, Johnson City	1.000	1	1	0	0	0
Dudek, Johnson City*	1.000	3	14	0	0	3
Evans, Bristol*	.976	27	226	17	6	21
Frye, Princeton	.986	9	64	6	1	2
Genao, Burlington*	.992	29	250	10	2	26
Harris, Kingsport	1.000	20	179	13	0	9
Haws, Martinsville	.985	8	63	3	1	6
Houston, Huntington*	.968	14	85	5	3	1
Johnson, Pulaski	1.000	9	83	6	0	11
Jones, Bluefield*	.992	17	115	9	1	9
Keenan, Princeton	.989	20	170	15	2	15
Kiraly, Kingsport*	.989	42	345	25	4	23
Manrique, Bluefield	1.000	1	10	1	0	2
Marrero, Bristol	1.000	1	1	0	0	0
McMullen, Martinsville	1.000	11	116	5	0	5
Metcalf, Bluefield	.988	32	298	20	4	24
Newman, Pulaski	.967	43	349	28	13	41
Norton, Burlington	1.000	2	14	2	0	1
Nunez, Pulaski	1.000	1	7	3	0	1
Nutting, Huntington	.984	7	59	3	1	5
Ortega, Bristol*	.985	16	117	11	2	6
Parker, Bristol*	.985	29	250	20	4	20
Parker, Kingsport	1.000	2	11	0	0	0
Pecorilli, Johnson City	1.000	2	7	1	0	0
Plonk, Huntington	.975	10	75	3	2	4
Robinson, Princeton	.977	33	282	16	7	20
Root, Huntington	.986	10	69	4	1	4
Slattery, Johnson City	.982	28	259	20	5	14
Sly, Pulaski	1.000	10	74	8	0	8
Stutheit, Huntington	1.000	1	3	0	0	0
Stutz, Johnson City	.985	36	323	7	5	31
TIRPACK, Elizabethton	.985	61	551	44	9	45
Townsend, Burlington*	.989	30	252	15	3	20
Urbanek, Martinsville	1.000	1	1	0	0	0
Vaske, Huntington	.966	14	109	3	4	8
Whitehurst, Burlington	1.000	14	135	10	0	12
Winget, Bluefield*	1.000	10	94	4	0	9
Zimmerman, Pulaski	1.000	2	1	0	0	1

SECOND BASEMEN

Player, Team	Pct.	G	PO	A	E	DP
Anderson, Johnson City	.944	36	61	91	9	19
Ashton, Princeton	.925	51	92	129	18	24
Beltre, Kingsport	.975	12	9	30	1	3
Blanco, Elizabethton	.867	6	5	8	2	3
Castaldo, Bluefield	.900	3	4	5	1	1
Catalanotto, Bristol	.875	9	8	6	2	2
Colon, Johnson City	.938	13	8	22	2	4
Dicken, Johnson City	.922	21	41	53	8	8
Duncan, Princeton	.750	2	0	6	2	0
Flores, Kingsport	1.000	2	1	5	0	2
Horincewich, Elizabethton	.978	16	37	53	2	10
Jelinek, Martinsville	.974	6	20	17	1	3
Kostrzewa, Burlington	.947	12	17	19	2	5
LeGree, Elizabethton	1.000	1	2	0	0	0
Mercedes, Bluefield	.950	7	17	21	2	5
Mrowka, Kingsport	.925	43	52	108	13	14
Nava, Elizabethton	.950	45	104	123	12	24
Paulino, Pulaski	.944	52	121	150	16	40
Perez, Huntington	.942	19	24	57	5	11
Romero, Martinsville	.959	55	114	145	11	28
Sanders, Princeton	.887	20	40	46	11	5
Serra, Bluefield	.947	55	119	133	14	29
Simmons, Huntington	.980	12	20	29	1	6
Smith, Huntington	1.000	2	4	0	0	0
Spetter, Pulaski	.951	10	18	21	2	6
Stutheit, Huntington	.923	31	47	85	11	7
THOMAS, Bristol	.983	60	116	166	5	34
Ugueto, Johnson City	.875	5	6	15	3	2
Urbanek, Martinsville	.938	5	4	11	1	1
Velandia, Bristol	.947	6	9	9	1	2
Whitaker, Burlington	.952	57	107	133	12	34
White, Burlington	.891	13	12	29	5	4
Williams, Kingsport	.839	8	9	17	5	3

THIRD BASEMEN

Player, Team	Pct.	G	PO	A	E	DP
Anderson, Johnson City	.800	3	1	3	1	0
Bell, Martinsville	.868	42	22	70	14	3
Blanco, Elizabethton	.824	21	10	46	12	2
Bradley, Kingsport	1.000	1	1	2	0	0
Bush, Martinsville	.750	1	1	2	1	0
Castaldo, Bluefield	1.000	1	0	1	0	0
Chavez, Bluefield	.931	51	34	114	11	15
Colon, Johnson City	1.000	1	3	0	0	0
DIAZ, Burlington	.959	49	17	125	6	11
Duncan, Princeton	1.000	1	1	1	0	0
Fisher, Martinsville	1.000	1	1	0	0	0
Frye, Princeton	.821	37	28	64	20	5
Graham, Princeton	.852	8	7	16	4	1
Hernandez, Bristol	.783	7	6	12	5	1
Jelinek, Martinsville	.901	24	16	57	8	6
Johnson, Bristol	.906	60	29	115	15	9
Keenan, Princeton	1.000	1	1	0	0	0
Kopriva, Princeton	.897	21	20	41	7	0
Kostrzewa, Burlington	1.000	2	2	2	0	0
LeGree, Elizabethton	.675	10	5	22	13	2
Marine, Bristol	1.000	2	2	1	0	0
Mercedes, Bluefield	.905	13	12	26	4	2
Montero, Huntington	.750	1	3	0	1	0
Newman, Pulaski	1.000	2	4	2	0	1
Nunez, Pulaski	.908	51	62	86	15	14
Nutting, Huntington	.831	28	14	40	11	1
Osentowski, Kingsport	.883	59	56	102	21	7
Paragin, Pulaski	1.000	2	1	1	0	0
Paulino, Pulaski	1.000	1	1	0	0	0
Plonk, Huntington	.700	4	4	3	3	1
Riemer, Bluefield	1.000	2	1	2	0	0
Root, Huntington	.741	11	9	11	7	0
Roper, Elizabethton	.877	38	26	67	13	6
Smith, Huntington	.891	19	11	30	5	3
Spetter, Pulaski	.889	5	1	7	1	1
Stutheit, Huntington	.800	4	2	6	2	0
Stutz, Johnson City	.962	11	9	16	1	0
Sumner, Johnson City	.891	52	49	98	18	6
Thomas, Bristol	1.000	1	0	1	0	0
Ugueto, Johnson City	1.000	1	2	1	0	0
White, Burlington	1.000	5	2	10	0	0
Whitehurst, Burlington	.892	18	7	26	4	1
Williams, Kingsport	.750	4	1	8	3	0
Zimmerman, Pulaski	.875	6	7	7	2	1

SHORTSTOPS

Player, Team	Pct.	G	PO	A	E	DP
Beltre, Kingsport	.841	19	20	33	10	6
Blanco, Elizabethton	1.000	1	0	1	0	0
Bradley, Kingsport	.773	5	7	10	5	1
Castaldo, Bluefield	.905	7	5	14	2	3
Colon, Johnson City	.917	12	20	35	5	4
Diaz, Burlington	.957	5	10	12	1	4
Fisher, Martinsville	.925	49	67	169	19	26
Frye, Princeton	.931	17	22	45	5	5
Hernandez, Princeton	.887	51	78	150	29	26
Horincewich, Elizabethton	.931	26	31	90	9	12
JACKSON, Burlington	.933	60	102	217	23	45
Jelinek, Martinsville	.909	3	5	5	1	1
Kostrzewa, Burlington	.917	4	3	8	1	0
Lackey, Kingsport	.877	38	56	101	22	14
Mercedes, Bluefield	.943	14	17	33	3	4
Mota, Johnson City	.910	18	28	53	8	9
Nunez, Pulaski	1.000	3	3	8	0	3
Ollison, Martinsville	.882	15	21	39	8	7
Perez, Huntington	.916	34	49	82	12	11
Riemer, Bluefield	.858	46	59	134	32	24
Sanchez, Bristol	.874	36	41	70	16	7
Simmons, Huntington	.909	16	19	31	5	8
Smith, Huntington	.889	9	16	24	5	5
Spetter, Pulaski	.950	33	41	91	7	20
Stutheit, Huntington	.958	9	8	15	1	4
Thomas, Bristol	1.000	4	5	13	0	2
Ugueto, Johnson City	.920	40	70	125	17	26
Valdez, Bristol	1.000	1	0	1	0	1
Valette, Elizabethton	.921	44	42	134	15	20
Velandia, Bristol	.919	39	45	79	11	19
Williams, Kingsport	.846	4	2	9	2	2
Zimmerman, Pulaski	.941	29	59	100	10	24

OUTFIELDERS

Player, Team	Pct.	G	PO	A	E	DP
Anderson, Johnson City	1.000	1	2	1	0	0
Baker, Elizabethton*	1.000	10	7	1	0	0
Booker, Huntington	.896	36	68	1	8	0
Burrough, Elizabethton	.962	39	74	2	3	0
Carmona, Martinsville	.931	20	22	5	2	0
Chambers, Pulaski	.948	52	87	4	5	0
Chisum, Burlington	1.000	15	18	0	0	0

Player, Team	Pct.	G	PO	A	E	DP
Claudio, Burlington	.954	45	61	1	3	0
Coates, Pulaski	1.000	8	12	0	0	0
Coleman, Burlington	1.000	7	5	4	0	0
Colon, Johnson City	.909	8	10	0	1	0
Colon, Huntington	1.000	13	21	1	0	0
Cornish, Martinsville	.896	19	39	4	5	1
Costic, Elizabethton*	.976	49	78	2	2	0
Delarosa, Burlington	.963	58	100	3	4	0
Dickerson, Bristol*	.923	8	12	0	1	0
Dudek, Johnson City*	.969	31	29	2	1	0
Eaddy, Bluefield	.875	50	51	5	8	0
Evans, Elizabethton	.939	23	29	2	2	1
Evans, Martinsville	.909	13	19	1	2	0
Genao, Burlington*	.900	6	7	2	1	0
Greene, Bristol	.966	20	26	2	1	0
Grijak, Pulaski	1.000	4	6	0	0	0
Hacopian, Burlington	.950	37	36	2	2	1
Hawkins, Elizabethton	.979	19	45	2	1	0
Henry, Johnson City	.949	44	91	2	5	0
Hodge, Elizabethton	.922	57	100	7	9	2
Ignash, Burlington	.955	17	21	0	1	0
Jones, Bluefield*	1.000	1	1	0	0	0
Kendall, Martinsville	.947	47	68	4	4	1
Ladell, Princeton	.975	64	147	8	4	1
Lamar, Bristol	.952	42	57	2	3	0
LeGree, Elizabethton	1.000	25	26	1	0	0
Manship, Princeton	.900	6	8	1	1	0
Mayberry, Burlington	1.000	5	4	0	0	0
Mercedes, Bluefield	.750	4	6	0	2	0
Metcalf, Bluefield	1.000	15	20	0	0	0
Miller, Elizabethton	1.000	10	6	1	0	0
Miller, Burlington	.941	20	16	0	1	0
Milne, Bristol	.963	15	25	1	1	0
Moon, Princeton	.925	30	47	2	4	0
Moore, Martinsville	.971	55	93	6	3	2
Moreno, Bristol	.973	47	66	7	2	0
Morris, Princeton	.917	12	10	1	1	0
Nava, Elizabethton	1.000	1	2	1	0	0
Nelson, Huntington	.857	27	22	2	4	0
Norman, Elizabethton	.938	31	41	4	3	1
Nunez, Pulaski	1.000	1	1	0	0	0
Oyas, Princeton	.968	47	56	4	2	0
Parker, Bristol*	1.000	7	14	0	0	0
Parker, Huntington	.966	31	53	3	2	0
Pecorilli, Johnson City	1.000	6	11	0	0	0
Pico, Huntington*	.960	16	22	2	1	0
Quillin, Kingsport	.979	20	43	3	1	0
Reeves, Huntington	1.000	23	35	2	0	1
Rojas, Bristol*	.972	54	97	6	3	0
Shabazz, Johnson City	.955	55	102	3	5	1
Shirley, Kingsport	.968	28	60	1	2	0
Sly, Pulaski	.977	29	41	1	1	0
Smith, Huntington	.969	38	62	0	2	0
Stanley, Johnson City	1.000	6	7	2	0	0
Sutey, Bristol	.962	18	24	1	1	0
Swann, Pulaski	.912	54	73	10	8	0
D. Thomas, Bluefield	.818	28	34	2	8	1
M. Thomas, Bluefield	.975	41	71	7	2	3
Thomas, Princeton	.896	47	81	5	10	3
Thompson, Burlington*	.900	7	8	1	1	0
Thompson, Martinsville*	.882	49	55	5	8	0
Valdez, Bristol	.923	10	11	1	1	0
Vazquez, Johnson City	.968	55	86	4	3	0
Walker, Huntington	.952	47	95	4	5	1
White, Burlington*	1.000	7	12	1	0	0
WHITE, Kingsport	.982	53	107	4	2	0
Williams, Pulaski	.955	43	59	5	3	1
Williams, Kingsport	1.000	3	3	0	0	0
Wipf, Kingsport	.942	56	94	3	6	1

CATCHERS

Player, Team	Pct.	G	PO	A	E	DP	PB
Ayala, Bristol	1.000	7	18	0	0	0	1
Ballara, Johnson City	.980	25	175	18	4	1	8
Barton, Huntington	.959	13	84	9	4	0	8
Bess, Princeton	.981	29	180	29	4	2	9
Brophy, Martinsville	.989	35	233	42	3	4	7
Bush, Martinsville	1.000	1	9	2	0	1	0
Casanova, Kingsport	.982	41	286	34	6	2	10
Crouwel, Martinsville	1.000	2	11	2	0	1	0
Freeberger, Bluefield	.981	17	103	2	2	1	6
Garcia, Pulaski	.983	40	247	34	5	1	8
Harris, Kingsport	.977	6	40	2	1	0	5
Haws, Martinsville	.978	26	188	34	5	3	10
Hobbs, Martinsville	.944	12	59	9	4	2	3
Horn, Elizabethton	.989	41	321	44	4	2	5
Lewandowski, Burlington	.995	25	195	11	1	0	13
Manrique, Bluefield	.984	56	381	51	7	4	26
Marine, Bristol	.988	46	335	63	5	2	11
Marrero, Bristol	.981	26	194	16	4	1	3
Melusky, Burlington	.985	42	227	29	4	2	10
Montero, Huntington	.981	28	188	21	4	2	9
Morales, Huntington	.942	13	88	9	6	3	3
Moyle, Burlington	.987	9	69	7	1	1	4

Player, Team	Pct.	G	PO	A	E	DP	PB
Paragin, Pulaski	.973	17	90	19	3	0	3
Pecorilli, Johnson City	1.000	7	53	10	0	1	2
St. Claire, Pulaski	.955	14	74	10	4	3	5
Shipman, Martinsville	1.000	4	15	0	0	0	4
Silvia, Princeton	.960	26	171	21	8	0	5
Steele, Kingsport	.966	18	131	9	5	0	3
Stojsavljevic, Huntington	.965	20	173	20	7	0	5
Taylor, Elizabethton	.970	26	175	16	6	1	17
Towle, Princeton	.964	16	93	14	4	1	4
Vivenzio, Pulaski	.889	4	12	4	2	1	0
WILLIAMS, Johnson City	.990	39	264	27	3	3	6

PITCHERS

Player, Team	Pct.	G	PO	A	E	DP
Alger, Martinsville*	.857	15	1	5	1	1
Augustine, Burlington	.714	18	0	5	2	0
Avery, Pulaski*	.929	17	2	11	1	1
Balentine, Princeton*	1.000	2	1	0	0	0
Ban, Bristol	.833	9	1	4	1	0
Bellman, Kingsport	.714	10	2	3	2	0
Belmonte, Kingsport	1.000	11	1	2	0	0
Benitez, Bluefield	1.000	25	0	5	0	0
Berg, Kingsport	1.000	21	4	7	0	0
Berlin, Bristol	1.000	4	1	3	0	0
Blake, Johnson City*	.667	13	1	3	2	0
Bluhm, Burlington*	1.000	17	2	4	0	0
Boldt, Martinsville	1.000	13	1	6	0	1
Brunson, Princeton*	.800	13	6	18	6	0
Cabrera, Burlington	.947	13	4	14	1	1
Caridad, Elizabethton	.967	12	5	24	1	2
Carrillo, Johnson City*	1.000	10	5	6	0	0
Cedeno, Bristol	1.000	13	6	6	0	1
Chatterton, Bluefield	.938	25	7	8	1	2
Chavez, Bluefield	.727	15	3	5	3	0
Childress, Huntington*	1.000	3	0	1	0	0
Clontz, Pulaski	1.000	4	0	2	0	0
Coleman, Martinsville*	1.000	17	0	1	0	0
Collier, Kingsport	.882	10	3	12	2	0
Concepcion, Princeton	.429	12	1	2	4	0
Correa, Elizabethton	.818	22	5	4	2	0
Costa, Martinsville	.667	12	2	2	2	0
Cullop, Princeton	.857	11	1	5	1	1
D'Andrea, Pulaski	1.000	11	4	9	0	1
DeJesus, Elizabethton*	1.000	2	0	2	0	0
Devereux, Bluefield	1.000	4	1	1	0	0
Edwards, Martinsville	.727	11	3	5	3	0
Elsbecker, Huntington	.875	10	2	5	1	0
Emerson, Bluefield*	.955	14	0	21	1	1
Etheridge, Princeton*	.800	17	1	3	1	0
Etler, Princeton	1.000	12	6	4	0	0
Fiore, Martinsville	.857	17	4	8	2	0
Fox, Bluefield	.700	15	3	4	3	0
Fregoso, Bluefield	.750	9	2	4	2	0
Fussell, Princeton*	.857	20	0	6	1	0
Gallagher, Burlington	.889	16	1	7	1	1
Gandarillas, Elizabethton	.667	29	1	3	2	0
Garcia, Huntington	1.000	11	0	2	0	0
Garza, Burlington	1.000	23	0	5	0	0
Gavlick, Huntington*	.867	13	1	12	2	0
Goodman, Johnson City	1.000	23	1	5	0	1
Grennan, Kingsport*	.923	16	5	7	1	0
Grimm, Bristol	.800	20	4	4	2	1
Guerra, Huntington*	1.000	17	0	4	0	0
Gustavson, Huntington	1.000	12	2	6	0	2
Guyton, Johnson City	1.000	16	4	2	0	0
Hassan, Pulaski	.733	22	5	6	4	0
Hassel, Huntington	.786	13	2	9	3	0
Havens, Pulaski	.929	17	4	9	1	1
Hawkins, Elizabethton	.875	5	2	5	1	0
Hiljus, Kingsport	.889	12	5	11	2	1
Holter, Burlington	.500	17	0	1	1	0
Humphry, Martinsville	1.000	16	5	6	0	0
Isringhausen, Kingsport	.714	7	0	5	2	0
Jones, Bristol	.000	4	0	0	1	0
Kempfer, Pulaski	.750	13	4	5	3	0
Kendrick, Huntington	.800	19	2	6	2	0
Kirkland, Martinsville	.000	4	0	0	1	0

Player, Team	Pct.	G	PO	A	E	DP
Knott, Bluefield	1.000	13	1	2	0	0
Koller, Burlington	1.000	1	1	0	0	0
Kroon, Kingsport	.667	12	3	3	3	0
Lane, Bluefield*	.923	14	1	11	1	0
Lantrip, Bluefield*	1.000	6	1	2	0	0
Larson, Johnson City*	.714	19	2	3	2	0
Latimer, Huntington	1.000	6	0	1	0	0
Lawrence, Huntington	.778	9	3	4	2	0
Legault, Elizabethton	.875	17	3	4	1	0
Leyva, Burlington*	.800	15	0	4	1	0
Lidle, Elizabethton	.846	19	3	8	2	0
Linebarger, Elizabethton	1.000	11	3	7	0	0
Lopez, Johnson City	.714	17	0	5	2	0
Lopez, Huntington*	1.000	4	0	2	0	0
Lyons, Princeton	.833	11	1	9	2	1
Maberry, Princeton	.875	21	4	3	1	0
MAGRINI, Bristol	1.000	13	10	14	0	0
Marchesi, Johnson City	1.000	23	2	2	0	1
Marquez, Bluefield	.722	15	5	8	5	0
Martineau, Pulaski	.833	17	3	2	1	0
Matos, Huntington	1.000	3	1	1	0	0
Matranga, Johnson City	1.000	19	2	3	0	0
Matthews, Burlington*	.833	10	4	11	3	1
Matulevich, Johnson City	1.000	13	3	3	0	0
Maxcy, Bristol	1.000	14	5	12	0	1
McFarland, Huntington*	1.000	12	2	9	0	0
Meek, Johnson City	1.000	12	4	7	0	0
Mejias, Martinsville	1.000	11	2	4	0	0
Miller, Johnson City	.909	27	0	10	1	1
Miller, Princeton	.833	10	3	2	1	1
Miller, Elizabethton	.667	6	0	8	4	0
Miller, Bristol*	.960	14	5	19	1	1
L. Mitchell, Martinsville	1.000	3	1	0	0	0
R. Mitchell, Martinsville	.789	14	5	10	4	0
Moten, Elizabethton	.842	13	8	8	3	1
Mullins, Princeton	.833	13	3	12	3	0
Munoz, Bristol	1.000	4	1	1	0	0
Nix, Princeton	1.000	27	0	6	0	1
Nutt, Martinsville*	.929	13	2	11	1	0
Pacheco, Huntington	.920	12	7	16	2	1
Page, Martinsville	.875	12	3	11	2	0
Phillips, Huntington	1.000	9	0	1	0	0
Pina, Elizabethton	.947	11	6	12	1	0
Pinson, Kingsport*	1.000	16	6	7	0	0
Pittman, Johnson City	.857	21	2	4	1	0
Porter, Bluefield	.667	13	1	1	1	0
Pugh, Martinsville*	1.000	3	0	1	0	0
Reeves, Huntington	1.000	11	2	3	0	0
Reincke, Bristol	1.000	11	2	3	0	0
Rhodriguez, Princeton	.500	2	0	1	1	0
Rodriguez, Bristol	.818	19	0	9	2	0
Roeder, Pulaski	.846	15	3	8	2	1
Rosengren, Bristol*	1.000	14	0	2	0	0
Ruyak, Princeton*	.938	12	2	13	1	0
Saccavino, Elizabethton	.857	6	0	6	1	0
Sackinsky, Bluefield	.889	5	3	5	1	0
Saneaux, Bluefield	1.000	4	0	3	0	0
Santos, Bristol*	1.000	12	1	1	0	0
Schmidt, Pulaski	.917	11	3	8	1	2
Seymour, Kingsport	.500	2	1	0	1	0
Shafer, Pulaski	1.000	17	1	1	0	0
Shaffer, Kingsport	.750	15	3	6	3	0
Shenk, Bluefield	.750	21	1	2	1	0
Sides, Burlington	.900	11	1	8	1	1
Sinner, Burlington	.769	11	5	5	3	1
Smoot, Pulaski*	1.000	5	2	3	0	2
Sodowsky, Bristol	.929	15	3	10	1	1
Stephenson, Bluefield	1.000	12	4	3	0	0
Swanson, Kingsport*	.875	12	5	9	2	0
Talemaco, Huntington	.867	12	4	9	2	0
Tavarez, Burlington	.939	14	11	20	2	1
Taylor, Elizabethton*	.833	7	0	5	1	0
Turnier, Pulaski*	1.000	6	0	3	0	0
Waite, Huntington*	1.000	5	0	3	0	0
Weeks, Pulaski	1.000	14	5	5	0	0
Wendt, Pulaski	1.000	6	2	3	0	0
Williams, Kingsport	1.000	3	0	2	0	1
Yamazaki, Bristol	.667	9	0	2	1	0
Zubiri, Burlington	1.000	14	0	1	0	0

The following players did not have any fielding statistics at the positions indicated or appeared only as a designated hitter, pinch-hitter or pinch-runner: Ballara, of; Catalanotto, 1b; Claudio, 3b; Cotner, p; M. Evans, of; A. Johnson, 2b; P. Jones, p; Maffett, p; Martinez, of; McDill, p; Montero, 2b; Newman, p; Nunez, p; Nutting, c; Paragin, 1b, p; Paulino, ss; Rideau, p; Slattery, 2b, c; Sly, p; Sumner, 1b, of; D. Thomas, ss; Yeske, dh, ph, pr.

Year	Team	Pct.	Year	Team	Pct.	Year	Team	Pct.
1921—	Greenville	.608	1951—	Kingsport‡	.659	1975—	Marion	.515
	Johnson City*	.627	1952—	Johnson City	.595		Johnson City a	.603
1922—	Bristol	.557		Welch (3rd)†	.509	1976—	Johnson City a	.714
1923—	Knoxville	.635	1953—	Welch*	.705		Bluefield	.600
1924—	Knoxville*	.642		Johnson City	.672	1977—	Kingsport	.623
	Bristol	.607	1954—	Bluefield‡	.619	1978—	Elizabethton	.594
1925—	Greenville	.667	1955—	Salem**	.689	1979—	Paintsville	.800
1926-36—Did not operate.			1956—Did not operate.			1980—	Paintsville	.657
1937—	Elizabethton	.559	1957—	Bluefield	.701	1981—	Paintsville	.657
	Pennington Gap*	.580	1958—	Johnson City	.662	1982—	Bluefield a	.681
1938—	Elizabethton	.664	1959—	Morristown	.603		Johnson City	.478
	Greenville (3rd)†	.571	1960—	Wytheville	.614	1983—	Paintsville	.653
1939—	Elizabethton‡	.597	1961—	Middlesboro	.591	1984—	Elizabethton b	.580
1940—	Johnson City§	.726	1962—	Bluefield	.671		Pulaski	.536
	Elizabethton	.750	1963—	Bluefield	.652	1985—	Bristol c	.638
1941—	Johnson City	.614	1964—	Johnson City	.662	1986—	Johnson City	.667
	Elizabethton*	.661	1965—	Salem	.614		Pulaski b	.621
1942—	Bristol	.667	1966—	Marion	.623	1987—	Burlington b	.729
	Bristol x	.660	1967—	Bluefield	.627		Johnson City	.609
1943—	Bristol	.755	1968—	Marion	.583	1988—	Kingsport b	.644
	Bristol y	.617	1969—	Pulaski a	.576		Burlington	.529
1944—	Kingsport‡	.575		Johnson City	.544	1989—	Elizabethton b	.691
1945—	Kingsport‡	.670	1970—	Bluefield	.638		Pulaski	.618
1946—	New River‡	.675	1971—	Bluefield a	.609	1990—	Elizabethton	.761
1947—	Pulaski	.648		Kingsport	.559	1991—	Pulaski b	.662
	New River (3rd)†	.516	1972—	Bristol a	.588		Burlington	.597
1948—	Pulaski‡	.680		Covington	.586	1992—	Elizabethton	.742
1949—	Bluefield‡	.721	1973—	Kingsport	.757		Bluefield b	.597
1950—	Bluefield	.600	1974—	Bristol a	.754			
	Bluefield z	.745		Bluefield	.536			

*Won split-season playoff. +Won four-team playoff. ‡Won championship and four-team playoff. §Johnson City, first-half winner, won playoff involving six clubs. xWon both halves and defeated second-place Elizabethton in playoff. yWon both halves, but Erwin won four-team playoff. zWon both halves, but Bristol won two-club playoff. **Salem and Johnson City declared playoff co-champions when weather forced cancellation of final series. aLeague was divided into Northern, Southern divisions; declared league champion, based on highest won-lost percentage. bLeague was divided into Northern, Southern divisions; won playoff for league championship. cBristol declared league champion based on regular-season record.

ARIZONA LEAGUE

FINAL STANDINGS

Team	Ath.	Mar.	Gia.	Brw.	Ang.	Car.	Pad.	R-C	W	L	T	Pct.	GB
Athletics	...	5	4	5	5	5	6	4	34	22	0	.607	—
Mariners	3	....	3	5	6	4	6	5	32	24	0	.571	2
Giants	4	5	....	3	5	4	5	6	32	24	0	.571	2
Brewers	3	3	5	....	4	4	6	6	31	25	0	.554	3
Angels	3	2	3	4	....	7	4	6	29	27	0	.518	5
Cardinals	3	4	4	4	1	....	6	6	28	28	0	.500	6
Padres	2	2	3	2	4	2	....	5	20	36	0	.357	14
Rockies/Cubs	4	3	2	2	2	2	3	....	18	38	0	.321	16

Games played in Mesa, Peoria, Scottsdale and Tempe.

Club names are major league affiliations.

Playoffs—No playoffs scheduled.

Regular-season attendance—No total official attendance figures reported.

Managers—Angels, Bill Lachemann; Athletics, Bruce Hines; Brewers, Tommy Jones; Giants, Alan Bannister; Cardinals, Joe Cunningham III; Mariners, Carlos Lezcano; Padres, Ken Berry; Rockies/Cubs, Paul Zuvella.

All-Star team: 1B—Greg Boyd, Rockies/Cubs; 2B—Enrique Atencio, Mariners; 3B—Brian Guzik, Angels; SS—Brian Rupp, Cardinals; OF—Joe McEwing, Cardinals; Byron Thomas, Mariners; Vince Zarate, Brewers; C—Juan Moreno, Brewers; LHP—John Vanhof, Mariners; RHP—(tie) Todd Erdos, Padres, and Miguel Fermin, Angels; LH Reliever—Brendan House, Athletics; RH Reliever—Marcial Gomez, Giants; Most Valuable Player—Brian Rupp, Cardinals; Manager of the Year—Tommy Jones, Brewers.

BATTING

TEAM

Team	Avg.	G	AB	R	OR	H	TB	2B	3B	HR	RBI	SH	SF	HP	BB	Int. BB	SO	SB	CS	LOB
Mariners	.275	56	1961	322	274	539	694	91	17	10	254	11	24	38	165	9	310	80	42	415
Athletics	.258	56	1886	310	249	487	620	79	18	6	236	23	22	39	240	8	410	59	25	455
Brewers	.249	56	1863	312	273	464	596	73	16	9	247	38	21	38	228	8	367	93	39	426
Giants	.249	56	1868	285	234	465	622	74	28	9	225	11	22	23	230	6	468	82	29	431
Angels	.249	56	1840	326	274	458	605	75	27	6	252	28	18	29	260	5	426	62	35	399
Cardinals	.248	56	1830	254	246	453	543	62	11	2	192	9	21	21	155	6	326	65	44	350
Rockies/Cubs	.243	56	1884	263	396	457	592	61	25	8	195	8	18	38	146	4	472	51	32	370
Padres	.219	56	1803	213	339	395	487	43	20	3	144	13	14	23	170	1	497	124	45	353

INDIVIDUAL

(Leading qualifiers for batting championship—151 or more plate appearances)

*Bats lefthanded.   †Switch-hitter.

Player, Team	Avg.	G	AB	R	H	TB	2B	3B	HR	RBI	SH	SF	HP	BB	Int. BB	SO	SB	CS
Rupp, Brian, Cardinals	.386	56	207	34	80	102	20	1	0	40	0	7	1	21	5	16	10	7
Gonzalez, Mauricio, Rockies/Cubs*	.345	35	148	19	51	65	4	5	0	14	0	1	0	6	0	19	3	4
McEwing, Joe, Cardinals	.336	55	211	55	71	79	4	2	0	13	1	1	5	24	0	18	23	7
Jones, John, Athletics	.318	44	148	23	47	57	7	0	1	16	0	1	1	9	0	31	0	5
Rivera, Bolivar, Giants	.315	52	222	40	70	87	11	3	0	25	2	1	1	9	0	30	30	8
Furtado, Tim, Mariners	.313	41	134	25	42	53	6	1	1	20	0	2	4	16	1	9	1	2
Sturdivant, Marcus, Mariners*	.312	42	141	27	44	52	6	1	0	14	0	3	1	12	3	14	7	5
Zarate, Vince, Brewers	.308	51	201	33	62	71	5	2	0	31	7	4	2	16	0	32	12	7
Lantigua, Pablo, Athletics	.307	43	153	30	47	57	6	2	0	15	1	3	1	11	1	25	7	2
Hause, Brendan, Athletics*	.303	45	145	23	44	59	13	1	0	17	1	3	3	13	3	32	0	0

Departmental leaders: G—Rupp, 56; AB—B. Rivera, 222; R—McEwing, 55; H—Rupp, 80; TB—Rupp, 102; 2B—Rupp, 20; 3B—Keel, Stafford, 6; HR—Five players with 3; RBI—Rupp, 40; SH—Cephas, 7; SF—Rupp, Stafford, 7; HP—Jo. Jones, 11; BB—Dilone, 39; IBB—Rupp, 5; SO—Malekovic, 57; SB—B. Rivera, 30; CS—B. Rivera, 8.

(All players—listed alphabetically)

Player, Team	Avg.	G	AB	R	H	TB	2B	3B	HR	RBI	SH	SF	HP	BB	Int. BB	SO	SB	CS
Aguirre, Jose, Angels	.000	3	1	0	0	0	0	0	0	0	0	0	0	0	0	1	0	0
Anderson, Armond, Giants	.266	37	124	17	33	36	3	0	0	14	1	1	0	15	0	27	9	2
Aquino, Pedro, Mariners	.279	34	111	12	31	39	5	0	1	15	0	1	2	7	0	14	2	2
Arendt, Jamie, Rockies/Cubs	.239	34	117	12	28	38	4	3	0	14	0	2	0	5	0	19	3	1
Arredondo, Paul, Brewers	.202	44	114	23	23	33	5	1	1	13	3	1	3	21	1	29	10	4
Atencio, Enrique, Mariners	.303	43	175	25	53	73	13	2	1	31	1	2	1	10	1	28	4	5
Barnes, Keith, Rockies/Cubs*	.000	13	1	0	0	0	0	0	0	0	0	0	0	0	0	1	0	0
Batista, Dario, Mariners	.206	18	63	10	13	15	2	0	0	3	0	0	2	6	0	10	4	2
Batista, Tony, Athletics	.246	45	167	32	41	51	6	2	0	22	5	0	2	15	0	29	1	0
Bautista, Juan, Cardinals	.264	46	174	25	46	56	4	3	0	23	0	3	1	5	0	37	11	5
Bertucci, Joseph, Angels	.224	50	170	38	38	61	12	4	1	21	1	2	1	27	1	50	5	2
Blomeyer, Mike, Giants	.173	24	81	14	14	25	6	1	1	12	0	1	0	14	0	26	3	0
Bogatyrev, Ilya, Angels	.196	19	46	6	9	12	1	1	0	3	2	0	1	6	0	14	4	3
Bonds, Bobby, Padres	.317	12	41	10	13	19	2	2	0	2	0	0	0	7	0	11	5	0
Borzello, Mike, Cardinals	.088	13	34	2	3	3	0	0	0	1	0	0	1	7	0	6	0	0
Bowden, Joseph, Padres	.234	24	77	9	18	20	2	0	0	2	0	0	5	0	26	8	0
Bowen, Jae, Cardinals	.205	34	83	11	17	26	2	2	1	9	2	0	2	13	0	37	2	5
Boyd, Greg, Rockies/Cubs*	.297	54	192	35	57	90	16	4	3	31	0	2	5	27	3	49	4	3
Cabrera, Alex, Rockies/Cubs	.207	41	135	18	28	35	4	0	1	19	0	2	6	9	0	48	1	1
Cabrera, Antonio, Mariners*	.317	29	101	14	32	47	8	2	1	22	0	3	2	6	0	29	1	3
Cantrell, Derrick, Brewers	.209	17	43	5	9	12	0	0	1	4	0	0	2	4	0	13	4	2
Castro, Antonio, Angels	.206	50	160	31	33	36	3	0	0	22	5	1	3	21	0	38	3	4
Cedeno, Juan, Rockies/Cubs	.187	32	91	7	17	29	7	1	1	11	0	2	1	3	0	22	0	2

Player, Team	Avg.	G	AB	R	H	TB	2B	3B	HR	RBI	SH	SF	HP	BB	Int. BB	SO	SB	CS
Cephas, Ruben, Brewers	.231	42	108	27	25	30	3	1	0	13	7	1	2	16	0	22	20	3
Christopher, Carlos, Rockies/Cubs*	.115	29	61	9	7	7	0	0	0	3	0	1	3	7	1	16	7	0
Corps, Erick, Padres	.214	36	126	19	27	30	3	0	0	4	1	1	4	20	0	20	10	2
Cox, Steve, Athletics*	.234	52	184	30	43	52	4	1	1	35	0	2	3	27	1	51	2	1
Creer, Jerry, Padres*	.257	24	70	10	18	20	0	1	0	5	1	0	1	2	0	25	9	5
Cruz, Javier, Mariners	.198	22	86	10	17	21	2	1	0	8	0	2	1	4	1	9	1	0
Cuevas, Eduardo, Padres	.267	33	116	20	31	41	4	3	0	15	6	2	0	7	0	17	14	4
Daniels, Morisse, Brewers	.283	40	152	33	43	62	6	5	1	22	2	1	0	20	0	32	12	6
Darwin, Brian, Athletics	.140	43	107	14	15	20	3	1	0	9	1	1	6	19	0	34	4	2
Davis, Stacey, Mariners	.292	25	72	8	21	26	5	0	0	14	1	0	2	12	0	20	1	1
DeJesus, Anito, Padres	.325	19	77	7	25	29	4	0	0	11	0	0	0	4	1	6	3	0
DeLeon, Jose, Mariners	.284	26	81	18	23	33	5	1	1	14	0	1	4	4	0	18	1	1
Delgado, Robert, Giants	.258	39	128	14	33	41	4	2	0	19	1	1	0	9	0	13	3	0
Diaz, Freddie, Angels	.270	14	37	6	10	13	3	0	0	4	2	1	0	5	0	7	3	1
Dilone, Juan, Athletics	.232	48	151	30	35	40	5	0	0	13	2	3	0	39	0	42	12	3
Donati, John, Angels	.279	47	140	38	39	55	6	5	0	20	3	0	6	33	0	39	1	1
Donohue, Pat, Cardinals*	.225	49	173	22	39	46	5	1	0	17	2	3	0	17	0	31	4	4
Dumas, Mike, Brewers	.311	31	103	32	32	38	4	1	0	13	4	2	3	21	0	9	10	3
Edwards, Randy, Rockies/Cubs	.268	39	138	29	37	48	6	1	1	14	1	0	3	19	0	31	3	0
Fantauzzi, John, Padres*	.310	16	58	9	18	26	0	1	2	14	0	0	0	9	0	9	3	0
Figueroa, Danny, Rockies/Cubs	.281	33	114	21	32	39	5	1	0	11	1	0	5	9	0	27	4	3
Francisco, David, Athletics	.378	10	37	12	14	20	1	1	1	8	0	0	4	5	0	6	6	2
Frazier, Julian, Giants	.198	42	126	15	25	34	5	2	0	10	3	1	4	8	1	40	4	5
Furtado, Tim, Brewers	.313	41	134	25	42	53	6	1	1	20	0	2	4	16	1	9	1	2
Garcia, Marcos, Angels	.303	25	109	16	33	45	6	3	0	18	1	2	2	2	0	12	2	0
Garcia, Tony, Mariners	.091	4	11	0	1	1	0	0	0	0	0	0	0	1	0	4	0	0
Garcia, Wendel, Rockies/Cubs	.200	25	65	5	13	19	2	2	0	8	1	3	2	4	0	23	0	1
Gay, Brad, Brewers	.256	35	90	15	23	33	7	0	1	15	1	3	0	13	1	28	1	0
Gillis, Troy, Padres	.194	32	98	9	19	20	1	0	0	9	2	0	2	8	0	26	5	5
Gipson, Charles, Mariners	.315	39	124	30	39	41	2	0	0	14	2	1	6	13	1	19	11	5
Goebel, Matt, Padres	.140	18	50	3	7	7	0	0	0	7	0	0	0	5	0	17	0	0
Gonzalez, Mauricio, Rockies/Cubs*	.345	35	148	19	51	65	4	5	0	14	0	0	1	6	0	19	3	4
Gorman, Paul, Angels	.571	3	7	3	4	5	1	0	0	3	0	1	0	6	0	0	0	0
Guillen, Jose, Athletics	.244	11	41	6	10	11	1	0	0	9	1	0	0	4	0	7	3	1
Guzik, Brian, Angels	.278	36	126	16	35	54	6	2	3	23	0	0	4	6	0	35	4	1
Hannah, Tim, Giants	.000	3	2	0	0	0	0	0	0	0	0	0	0	1	0	1	0	0
Harris, Todd, Giants	.268	48	153	33	41	51	2	4	0	21	1	4	4	28	1	29	5	2
Hart, Shelby, Giants	.301	23	83	7	25	29	4	0	0	8	0	3	5	10	2	1	1
Hatfield, Rick, Rockies/Cubs*	.308	35	104	14	32	39	3	2	0	22	2	1	1	10	0	15	1	2
Hause, Brendan, Athletics*	.303	45	145	23	44	59	13	1	0	17	1	3	3	13	3	32	0	0
Hernandez, Pedro, Rockies/Cubs*	.273	31	77	13	21	29	1	2	1	7	0	0	0	9	0	25	8	5
Herrick, Jason, Angels*	.400	8	30	7	12	15	3	0	0	6	0	0	1	5	0	4	2	1
Hunter, Lanier, Rockies/Cubs	.176	24	51	10	9	9	0	0	0	2	1	0	3	0	15	4	0
Ibanez, Raul, Mariners*	.308	33	120	25	37	52	8	2	1	16	0	0	2	9	1	18	1	2
Imperial, Jason, Brewers	.318	13	44	13	14	29	4	1	3	8	0	0	2	10	0	6	1	1
Jimenez, Jose A., Angels*	.286	14	42	8	12	12	0	0	0	3	2	0	0	11	1	11	1	1
Jimenez, Jose G., Angels	.188	18	64	12	12	14	2	0	0	7	4	1	0	9	0	12	2	0
Johnson, Earl, Padres	.168	35	101	20	17	18	1	0	0	1	0	0	1	10	0	28	19	5
Johnson, Juan, Giants	.215	45	135	33	29	31	0	1	0	7	1	1	4	28	0	48	6	6
Jones, Brian, Athletics	.348	19	66	12	23	33	2	1	2	13	0	0	0	8	0	8	4	1
Jones, John, Athletics	.318	44	148	23	47	57	7	0	1	16	0	1	11	9	0	31	0	5
Keel, Chris, Athletics*	.272	50	191	34	52	74	10	6	0	24	0	1	2	20	0	39	1	1
Kim, Bobby, Angels	.183	23	82	12	15	22	5	1	0	14	0	2	1	10	2	13	4	3
Lantigua, Pablo, Athletics*	.307	43	153	30	47	57	6	2	0	15	1	3	1	11	1	25	7	2
Llanos, Victor, Cardinals	.283	54	205	27	58	73	12	0	1	31	0	2	0	12	0	36	5	2
Lloyd, John, Brewers	.000	11	2	0	0	0	0	0	0	0	0	0	0	0	0	1	0	0
Luckett, Zaven, Padres	.149	22	67	7	10	11	1	0	0	5	0	1	0	10	0	20	5	3
Machado, Mike, Rockies/Cubs	.233	25	86	15	20	27	1	3	0	9	0	1	0	6	0	28	4	4
Malekovic, Brett, Padres	.240	36	129	16	31	38	3	2	0	8	0	0	4	12	0	57	3	2
Marquez, Jesus, Mariners*	.270	40	148	20	40	56	4	3	2	21	1	0	1	14	1	21	9	3
Martin, Ron, Angels	.247	43	154	13	38	45	3	2	0	19	1	1	1	13	0	48	6	5
Martinez, Eduard, Mariners	.234	36	128	15	30	44	5	3	1	19	3	3	5	10	0	26	4	4
Martinez, Esteban, Brewers	.183	29	93	11	17	21	2	1	0	8	4	2	4	5	0	28	4	2
Martinez, Gabby, Padres	.176	26	68	6	12	12	0	0	0	4	0	1	0	7	0	23	2	1
Martinez, Gabriel, Brewers	.261	48	165	29	43	54	7	2	0	24	2	2	3	12	0	19	7	5
Matos, Alberto, Padres	.119	20	59	6	7	11	0	2	0	3	0	0	2	3	0	18	5	2
Maxwell, Trent, Mariners	.214	11	28	3	6	9	3	0	0	4	0	0	2	0	0	8	0	0
McArn, Brian, Athletics*	.225	24	71	9	16	17	1	0	0	6	4	2	3	11	1	17	3	0
McCoy, Marcus, Padres	.167	19	60	3	10	13	1	1	0	3	0	1	0	11	0	11	3	2
McEwing, Joe, Cardinals	.336	55	211	55	71	79	4	2	0	13	1	1	5	24	0	18	23	7
McKinnon, Tom, Cardinals*	.240	7	25	2	6	6	0	0	0	1	0	0	0	1	0	3	0	0
Mercedes, Juan, Rockies/Cubs	.263	40	137	12	36	39	1	1	0	9	0	0	2	6	0	28	1	2
Mesa, Luis, Brewers	.286	3	7	2	2	3	1	0	0	0	0	0	0	0	0	0	0	0
Millan, Jorge, Cardinals	.202	32	104	11	21	25	2	1	0	3	0	1	3	5	0	14	0	1
Miller, Kumandae, Giants	.160	35	100	6	16	20	1	0	1	9	0	1	2	6	0	39	2	0
Minton, Rusty, Cardinals	.100	24	40	6	4	4	0	0	0	2	1	0	4	6	0	18	1	3
Moncion, Manuel, Athletics	.180	23	61	6	11	14	3	0	0	2	1	1	0	3	0	13	0	0
Monday, Mike, Angels	.268	26	71	9	19	26	7	0	0	8	1	2	1	9	0	19	2	0
Morel, Plinio, Cardinals	.242	53	182	16	44	54	8	1	0	21	0	1	0	11	0	12	2	0
Moreno, Juan, Brewers	.291	50	148	24	43	63	10	2	2	22	0	0	6	16	2	23	1	1
Myers, Matt, Angels	.667	18	3	0	2	2	0	0	0	1	0	0	0	0	0	1	0	0
Nunez, Francisco, Brewers	.224	47	143	22	32	41	9	0	0	23	1	1	3	24	3	23	3	3
Pellot, Victor, Cardinals	.150	38	120	10	18	19	1	0	0	7	1	2	1	3	0	26	1	1
Pena, Juan, Brewers	.286	4	7	0	2	3	1	0	0	1	0	0	0	2	0	4	0	0
Perez, Susano, Padres	.183	22	71	2	13	20	3	2	0	8	0	0	0	5	0	25	1	0
Perez, Tony, Giants	.135	25	74	9	10	13	1	1	0	2	1	0	0	5	0	33	1	1
Phillips, Gary, Giants	.376	29	109	14	41	55	14	0	0	21	0	2	0	9	0	22	2	2
Pomierski, Joe, Mariners*	.233	32	103	19	24	30	4	1	0	13	2	0	2	14	0	26	2	1
Pooschke, Mark, Giants	.200	44	150	21	30	50	7	2	3	23	0	1	4	24	2	43	3	1
Powers, Robert, Brewers	.238	27	63	13	15	17	0	1	0	8	2	1	1	16	0	18	7	0
Poyner, Jim, Giants	.225	27	89	10	20	32	6	3	0	7	0	1	0	15	1	37	0	0
Pozo, Yohel, Rockies/Cubs	.220	36	100	10	22	23	1	0	0	6	1	0	1	1	0	26	1	1
Pridgen, Tony, Brewers	.211	51	175	18	37	50	5	4	0	23	1	0	2	10	0	44	6	5
Puchkov, Evgeni, Angels*	.245	33	106	17	26	27	1	0	0	10	1	1	3	10	0	16	3	3
Ramirez, Hiram, Giants	.273	42	143	23	39	58	4	3	3	21	0	0	1	16	1	36	2	0

Player, Team	Avg.	G	AB	R	H	TB	2B	3B	HR	RBI	SH	SF	HP	BB	Int. BB	SO	SB	CS
Razhigaev, Rudy, Angels	.000	6	1	0	0	0	0	0	0	0	0	0	0	0	0	1	0	0
Reyes, Juan, Mariners	.157	32	83	12	13	20	4	0	1	6	0	3	3	10	0	8	0	1
Rivera, Alex, Padres	.217	19	60	9	13	17	4	0	0	2	0	2	2	7	0	20	3	2
Rivera, Bolivar, Giants	.315	52	222	40	70	87	11	3	0	25	2	1	1	9	0	30	30	8
Rodriguez, Nelson, Padres	.226	18	62	5	14	17	3	0	0	0	0	0	0	5	0	14	2	0
Roques, Aaron, Padres	.183	20	71	5	13	18	1	2	0	4	0	1	0	2	0	17	4	0
Rubiera, Jose, Angels	.222	3	9	0	2	2	0	0	0	1	0	0	1	0	0	1	0	0
Rupp, Brian, Cardinals	.386	56	207	34	80	102	20	1	0	40	0	7	1	21	5	16	10	7
Salazar, Mal, Rockies/Cubs	.219	22	64	9	14	17	3	0	0	6	1	1	1	6	0	23	0	2
Salvador, Felix, Athletics	.302	46	149	29	45	62	8	3	1	22	4	3	2	30	0	15	14	6
Salzano, Jerry, Brewers	.243	51	177	18	43	48	5	0	0	20	2	3	4	23	0	31	1	3
Sanchez, Juan, Rockies/Cubs	.295	14	44	8	13	15	2	0	0	1	0	0	0	2	0	10	2	0
Sanderfer, Shawn, Athletics	.263	25	57	8	15	18	3	0	0	9	1	0	0	5	0	16	1	0
Sanders, Mike, Padres	.077	6	13	0	1	1	0	0	0	0	0	0	0	5	0	4	2	1
Smith, Brandon, Athletics	.263	11	19	1	5	6	1	0	0	4	1	0	0	1	0	1	0	0
Sosa, Francisco, Mariners	.303	18	76	13	23	26	3	0	0	5	0	1	0	5	0	10	7	1
Stadler, Mike, Padres	.077	26	65	0	5	5	0	0	0	3	3	2	1	8	0	36	1	3
Stafford, Keith, Giants*	.262	46	149	29	39	60	6	6	1	26	1	7	0	37	0	34	10	1
Stewart, Reggie, Padres	.329	28	76	15	25	31	2	2	0	9	0	1	3	5	0	18	13	4
Strehlow, Robert, Cardinals	.122	28	49	8	6	7	1	0	0	2	0	0	0	5	0	18	1	3
Sturdivant, Marcus, Mariners*	.312	42	141	27	44	52	6	1	0	14	0	3	1	12	3	14	7	5
Talbott, Richard, Padres	.235	33	119	13	28	38	5	1	1	19	0	1	3	16	0	34	0	3
Tatrow, Dan, Cardinals	.125	23	72	3	9	10	1	0	0	2	1	1	0	9	0	22	1	2
Thomas, Byron, Mariners	.284	46	176	36	50	56	6	0	0	15	1	2	0	10	0	19	24	4
Thompson, Paul, Padres*	.000	1	1	0	0	0	0	0	0	0	0	0	0	0	0	0	0	0
Thurmond, Travis, Angels	.000	8	1	0	0	0	0	0	0	0	0	0	0	0	0	0	0	0
Torres, Ismael, Brewers*	.186	45	113	19	21	23	2	0	0	12	4	1	0	15	0	30	2	0
Tucker, Robert, Angels	.252	38	127	25	32	40	4	2	0	17	1	0	0	21	0	29	2	3
Ugueto, Hector, Cardinals	.205	44	151	22	31	33	2	0	0	18	1	0	3	16	0	32	4	4
Valdez, Jose, Rockies/Cubs	.108	32	93	13	10	14	1	0	1	6	0	1	6	10	0	27	4	1
Valencia, Max, Angels	1.000	19	1	1	1	1	0	0	0	1	0	0	0	1	0	0	0	0
Vallejo, Jose, Angels	.204	17	49	2	10	10	0	0	0	2	0	1	0	10	1	11	1	1
Ventura, Leonardo, Athletics	.156	32	77	8	12	15	3	0	0	5	0	1	1	14	0	25	0	1
Vizcaino, Julian, Angels	.221	45	149	32	33	46	6	2	1	27	2	3	4	27	0	31	5	2
Walton, Marco, Rockies/Cubs	.152	22	66	4	10	10	0	0	0	2	1	0	1	4	0	20	1	0
Warren, Deshawn, Angels	.000	11	1	0	0	0	0	0	0	0	0	0	0	0	0	1	0	0
Wyatt, Dwight, Padres	.294	21	68	10	20	25	3	1	0	6	0	1	0	7	0	15	5	1
Wyss, David, Brewers	.304	21	69	8	21	27	3	0	1	9	0	1	1	4	1	8	4	0
Yots, Adrian, Athletics	.194	21	62	3	12	14	2	0	0	7	1	1	1	6	2	19	1	0
Zarate, Vince, Brewers	.308	51	201	33	62	71	5	2	0	31	7	4	2	16	0	32	12	7

The following pitchers, listed alphabetically by club, with games in parentheses, had no plate appearances, primarily through use of designated hitters:

ANGELS—Carrasco, Jose (16); Dafun, Kekoa (14); Fermin, Miguel (12); Holcomb, Shawn (4); Snyder, John (15); Williard, Brian (6).

ATHLETICS—Belliard, Carlos (13); Caruso, Gene (7); Domenico, Brian (17); Griffin, Steve (6); Grigsby, Mike (3); Hollins, Stacy (15); Martinez, Julio (12); Montgomery, Trent (11); Post, Jeff (14); Sawyer, Zachary (10); Urbina, Bill (12).

BREWERS—Alexander, Mark (3); Arias, Wagner (7); Demyan, Kirk (23); Gaskill, Derek (11); Gold, Steve (13); Gonzalez, Francisco (12); Hardwick, Billy (4); Krause, Kevin (16); MacNeill, Randy (2); Maltagliati, Steve (10); O'Laughlin, Chuck (1); Ortiz, Dan (16); Rhoda, Gary (16); Rodriguez, Francisco (9); Sadler, Aldren (7); Salmon, Fabian (11); Snure, Jeremy (7); Werner, Rich (10).

CARDINALS—Bledsoe, Randy (17); Burley, Travis (19); Charles, Domingo (11); Davis, Ray (11); Grasser, Craig (17); Lair, Scott (8); Raggio, Brady (14); Ruiz, Diego (12); Sailors, Jim (11); Stanton, Ed (23); Stoppello, Jason (15); Wagner, Dale (19).

GIANTS—Baxter, Herbert (14); Brown, Kevin (15); Collins, Doug (4); Fultz, Aaron (14); Gomez, Marcial (20); Israel, Kurt (16); Martin, Jeff (13); Mitchell, Kendrick (17); Murray, Jim (6); Perez, Hector (2); Pinder, Chris (18); Rosenbohm, Jim (14); Towns, Vince (13); Valdez, Carlos (6); Vazquez, Jorge (15).

MARINERS—Alcantara, Milciades (1); Cope, Robin (16); Dessellier, Chris (13); Golden, Chuck (3); Hinchliffe, Brett (24); Jenkins, Kevin (2); Klomp, Brian (6); Mantei, Matt (3); Montane, Ivan (13); Ortega, Oscar (19); Soto, Fernando (21); Theron, Greg (12); Thompson, John (14); Vanhof, John (10); Wallace, Reese (12).

PADRES—Arroyo, Luis (17); Baron, Jim (14); Dunckel, Keith (19); Erdos, Todd (12); Estrella, Alejandro (14); Fargas, Hector (13); Fjeld, Randy (6); Jones, Jeff (5); Jumonville, Joe (16); McClain, Brian (12); Santiago, Rafael (3); Severino, Blas (7); Singleton, Scott (11); White, Darell (15); Winchester, Martin (13).

ROCKIES/CUBS—Blanco, Rosmel (6); Garrett, Neil (11); Gonzalez, Geremis (14); Goodrich, Jonathan (7); Luckert, Gabriel (13); Matos, Jose (17); Matos, Luis (3); Metzinger, Bill (14); Morris, Marc (14); Neier, Chris (14); Sabino, Miguel (16); Sobkoviak, Jeff (16); Tafoya, Greg (10).

GRAND SLAMS—Atencio, Bowen, 1 each.

AWARDED FIRST BASE ON CATCHER'S INTERFERENCE—Cox (Delgado); Gipson (Borzello); Guzik (G. Martinez, Padres); J. Jones (G. Martinez, Padres).

PITCHING

TEAM

Team	ERA	G	CG	ShO	Sv.	IP	H	R	ER	HR	HB	BB	Int. BB	SO	WP	Bk.
Giants	2.87	56	1	5	14	483.1	423	234	154	0	23	197	8	421	64	22
Cardinals	3.19	56	7	5	12	477.1	456	246	169	5	25	163	2	396	42	11
Mariners	3.30	56	3	5	7	491.1	440	274	180	8	36	220	13	429	75	15
Athletics	3.37	56	5	4	8	486.0	438	249	182	15	18	151	4	435	41	27
Angels	3.50	56	7	4	12	486.1	465	274	189	8	36	200	5	438	57	17
Brewers	3.54	56	2	5	11	486.0	460	273	191	9	35	168	3	434	41	30
Padres	4.45	56	1	1	8	477.2	470	339	236	3	29	260	8	419	77	41
Rockies/Cubs	5.43	56	3	0	6	478.2	566	396	289	5	46	235	4	304	67	18

INDIVIDUAL

(Leading qualifiers for earned-run average leadership—45 or more innings)

*Throws lefthanded.

Pitcher, Team	W	L	Pct.	ERA	G	GS	CG	GF	ShO	Sv.	IP	H	R	ER	HR	HB	BB	Int. BB	SO	WP
Rodriguez, Brewers	3	1	.750	1.10	9	7	0	0	0	0	49.0	35	9	6	1	1	14	0	37	1
Theron, Mariners	4	1	.800	1.26	12	8	1	0	1	0	57.0	40	16	8	0	3	17	1	44	2
Vanhof, Mariners*	3	1	.750	1.29	10	7	0	0	0	0	49.0	27	13	7	0	5	24	2	35	7
Fermin, Angels	6	2	.750	1.69	12	12	4	0	1	0	85.1	76	25	16	2	2	9	0	67	4

Pitcher, Team	W	L	Pct.	ERA	G	GS	CG	GF	ShO	Sv.	IP	H	R	ER	HR	HB	BB	Int. BB	SO	WP
Fultz, Giants*	3	2	.600	2.13	14	14	0	0	0	0	67.2	51	24	16	0	4	33	0	72	7
Neier, Rockies/Cubs	5	1	.833	2.24	14	6	1	2	0	0	56.1	53	23	14	0	3	7	0	49	2
Davis, Cardinals	5	4	.556	2.49	11	11	4	0	4	0	76.0	75	30	21	1	1	22	0	74	3
Werner, Brewers	5	1	.833	2.56	10	8	1	0	1	0	45.2	43	17	13	0	2	11	0	38	1
Cope, Mariners	1	1	.500	2.57	16	5	1	1	0	0	56.0	64	31	16	1	5	13	0	50	5
Urbina, Athletics	7	1	.875	2.58	12	8	0	2	0	0	59.1	51	21	17	2	0	12	0	45	4

Departmental leaders: G—Hinchliffe, 24; W—Martin, Urbina, 7; L—J. Matos, Rosenbohm, Winchester, 7; Pct.—Urbina, .875; GS—Baxter, Fultz, Hollins, Rosenbohm, 14; CG—Davis, Fermin, 4; GF—Demyan, 21; ShO—Davis, 4; Sv.—Demyan, 11; IP—Hollins, 93.0; H—Hollins, 89; R—G. Gonzalez, 59; ER—J. Matos, 46; HR—Carrasco, Martinez, Salmon, 3; HB—G. Gonzalez, 10; BB—Montane, 41; IBB—Soto, 5; SO—Hollins, 93; WP—Montane, 18.

(All pitchers—listed alphabetically)

Pitcher, Team	W	L	Pct.	ERA	G	GS	CG	GF	ShO	Sv.	IP	H	R	ER	HR	HB	BB	Int. BB	SO	WP
Aguirre, Angels*	1	0	1.000	0.63	3	1	0	0	0	0	14.1	8	4	1	0	1	6	0	20	1
Alcantara, Mariners	0	0	.000	0.00	2	0	0	1	0	0	2.0	1	1	0	0	0	1	0	4	0
Alexander, Brewers	1	2	.333	4.82	3	1	0	0	0	0	9.1	6	9	5	0	0	6	0	5	0
Arias, Brewers	1	1	.500	1.15	7	2	0	2	0	0	15.2	16	9	2	1	0	5	0	11	1
Arroyo, Padres*	4	4	.500	4.21	17	9	0	3	0	0	57.2	65	45	27	0	2	21	0	55	4
Barnes, Rockies/Cubs*	2	2	.500	3.15	12	8	0	1	0	0	45.2	47	27	16	1	4	19	0	21	5
Baron, Padres*	2	0	1.000	8.28	14	0	0	3	0	0	25.0	24	28	23	0	1	25	0	18	10
Baxter, Giants*	1	3	.250	3.75	14	14	0	0	0	0	57.2	62	40	24	0	1	28	0	60	10
Belliard, Athletics*	1	2	.333	2.93	13	5	1	5	0	0	46.0	36	19	15	0	2	27	0	55	4
Blanco, Rockies/Cubs*	0	0	.000	70.88	6	0	0	2	0	0	2.2	6	22	21	0	1	18	0	1	5
Bledsoe, Cardinals	1	0	1.000	5.20	17	1	0	4	0	0	27.2	31	21	16	0	2	16	0	21	4
Brown, Giants	4	1	.800	1.62	15	1	0	2	0	0	33.1	24	11	6	0	1	10	0	22	3
Burley, Cardinals	3	2	.600	1.30	19	0	0	17	0	9	27.2	12	6	4	0	2	13	0	27	1
Carrasco, Angels	5	1	.833	4.57	16	0	0	5	0	1	43.1	52	30	22	3	3	8	0	41	7
Caruso, Athletics*	1	1	.500	4.76	7	1	0	4	0	1	17.0	15	14	9	1	1	12	0	22	1
Charles, Cardinals	5	2	.714	3.02	11	11	0	0	0	0	56.2	58	28	19	1	3	13	0	52	1
Collins, Giants	0	2	.000	6.75	4	0	0	1	0	0	4.0	5	6	3	0	0	4	0	1	3
Cope, Mariners	1	1	.500	2.57	16	5	1	1	0	0	56.0	64	31	16	1	5	13	0	50	5
Cruz, Mariners	0	0	.000	0.00	1	0	0	0	0	0	0.2	1	0	0	0	0	0	0	0	1
Dafun, Angels	2	2	.500	5.27	13	7	0	4	0	1	42.2	41	29	25	0	6	32	0	40	7
Davis, Cardinals	5	4	.556	2.49	11	11	4	0	4	0	76.0	75	30	21	1	1	22	0	74	3
Demyan, Brewers	2	4	.333	2.61	23	0	0	21	0	11	38.0	32	15	11	0	5	9	2	40	4
Dessellier, Mariners	2	0	1.000	6.14	13	3	0	5	0	1	22.0	20	26	15	1	2	20	0	28	4
Domenico, Athletics	2	4	.333	4.32	11	0	0	9	0	2	41.2	38	31	20	0	3	29	1	35	12
Dunckel, Padres	1	2	.333	4.43	19	0	0	16	0	5	22.1	19	15	11	0	3	15	2	22	5
Erdos, Padres	3	4	.429	2.65	12	9	1	2	0	0	57.2	36	28	17	1	3	18	0	61	8
Estrella, Padres	3	1	.750	2.96	14	0	0	4	0	0	24.1	27	12	8	0	1	7	2	18	4
Fargas, Padres	0	3	.000	6.28	13	4	0	1	0	0	38.2	45	34	27	0	5	22	1	33	3
Fermin, Angels	6	2	.750	1.69	12	12	4	0	1	0	85.1	76	25	16	2	2	9	0	67	4
Fjeld, Padres	0	1	.000	1.98	6	1	0	1	0	0	13.2	15	3	3	0	5	1	8	2	2
Fultz, Giants*	3	2	.600	2.13	14	14	0	0	0	0	67.2	51	24	16	0	4	33	0	72	7
Garrett, Rockies/Cubs	3	3	.500	3.93	11	10	1	0	0	0	52.2	60	36	23	1	4	16	0	23	12
Gaskill, Brewers	0	0	.000	5.29	11	1	0	4	0	0	17.0	22	18	10	0	1	9	0	16	3
Goebel, Padres	0	0	.000	4.91	4	0	0	2	0	0	3.2	3	3	2	0	0	0	0	2	2
Gold, Brewers	2	0	1.000	2.37	13	1	0	1	0	0	19.0	17	11	5	0	0	5	0	21	2
Golden, Mariners	0	0	.000	0.00	3	0	0	1	0	0	3.0	2	2	0	0	0	1	0	6	0
Gomez, Giants	5	0	1.000	0.30	20	0	0	17	0	7	29.2	23	8	1	0	0	3	1	31	2
Gonzalez, Brewers	0	4	.000	9.87	12	4	0	3	0	0	31.0	40	37	34	2	7	19	1	16	3
Gonzalez, Rockies/Cubs	0	5	.000	7.80	14	7	0	1	0	0	45.0	65	59	39	0	10	22	0	39	11
Goodrich, Rockies/Cubs	4	1	.800	3.45	21	0	0	19	0	3	31.1	28	16	12	1	3	12	0	25	4
Grasser, Cardinals	1	0	1.000	0.65	17	0	0	8	0	2	27.2	19	4	2	0	2	4	0	18	1
Griffin, Athletics	0	1	.000	0.87	6	0	0	6	0	0	10.1	5	1	1	0	0	3	0	11	1
Grigsby, Athletics	1	1	.500	1.64	3	3	0	0	0	0	11.0	4	2	2	2	0	1	0	7	0
Hardwick, Brewers*	0	0	.000	2.45	4	0	0	3	0	0	7.1	6	2	2	0	1	1	0	9	0
Hause, Athletics*	1	0	1.000	2.66	14	0	0	13	0	2	20.1	18	10	6	1	0	5	2	30	4
Hinchliffe, Mariners	5	4	.556	2.31	24	0	0	20	0	3	35.0	42	17	9	0	3	9	0	26	1
Holcomb, Angels	0	0	.000	5.68	4	0	0	1	0	0	12.2	15	11	8	0	0	4	0	15	1
Hollins, Athletics	6	3	.667	3.39	15	14	3	0	2	0	93.0	89	47	35	0	4	19	0	93	5
Israel, Giants	1	2	.333	2.78	16	0	0	4	0	1	22.2	19	10	7	0	2	7	1	15	2
Jenkins, Mariners	0	0	.000	9.00	2	0	0	1	0	0	4.0	9	5	4	0	0	2	0	2	1
Jones, Padres	0	0	.000	9.00	5	0	0	3	0	1	5.0	5	5	5	0	0	7	0	2	2
Jumonville, Padres	3	3	.500	3.08	16	3	0	6	0	1	52.2	46	22	18	0	4	15	0	45	4
Klomp, Mariners	0	0	.000	4.76	6	0	0	4	0	0	5.2	2	3	3	0	4	8	0	2	2
Krause, Brewers	4	0	1.000	2.77	16	1	0	6	0	0	26.0	18	9	8	0	1	15	0	27	3
Lair, Cardinals	1	3	.250	6.41	8	6	0	0	0	0	26.2	37	21	19	1	2	14	0	19	7
Lloyd, Angels	4	3	.571	3.05	11	11	2	0	1	0	62.0	58	29	21	0	8	20	0	54	6
Luckert, Rockies/Cubs	0	4	.000	5.91	13	8	0	1	0	0	45.2	51	38	30	0	7	29	1	23	2
MacNeill, Brewers	0	1	.000	10.80	2	1	0	1	0	0	5.0	9	8	6	0	0	0	0	3	1
Maltagliati, Brewers	2	1	.667	2.87	10	7	0	0	0	0	47.0	41	18	15	2	0	6	0	42	6
Mantei, Mariners	1	1	.500	5.63	3	3	0	0	0	0	16.0	18	10	10	1	0	5	0	19	0
Martin, Giants	7	3	.700	3.13	13	13	1	0	1	0	72.0	65	31	25	0	2	13	0	64	6
Martinez, Athletics	3	3	.500	3.36	10	8	0	1	0	0	59.0	57	28	22	3	4	12	0	37	2
Matos, Padres	0	0	.000	0.00	2	0	0	2	0	0	3.1	2	0	0	0	0	3	0	3	0
J. Matos, Rockies/Cubs	1	7	.125	7.86	17	8	0	0	0	0	52.2	70	53	46	1	1	28	0	24	7
L. Matos, Rockies/Cubs	0	1	.000	4.50	3	1	0	0	0	0	6.0	7	4	3	0	1	4	0	2	2
McClain, Padres	1	4	.200	2.94	11	11	0	0	0	0	49.0	42	22	16	2	3	26	1	40	3
Metzinger, Rockies/Cubs	2	3	.400	3.41	14	2	0	10	0	3	29.0	33	14	11	0	0	13	1	31	2
Mitchell, Giants	1	0	1.000	5.10	17	0	0	5	0	0	30.0	36	26	17	0	4	22	1	26	5
Moncion, Athletics	0	0	.000	0.00	1	0	0	0	0	0	1.0	0	0	0	0	0	0	0	0	0
Montane, Mariners	1	3	.250	5.67	13	11	0	1	0	0	46.0	44	39	29	0	3	41	0	48	18
Montgomery, Athletics	2	2	.500	4.03	11	2	0	3	0	1	29.0	26	20	13	2	2	17	1	17	3
Morel, Cardinals	0	0	.000	9.00	1	0	0	1	0	0	2.0	3	2	2	0	0	1	0	2	1
Morris, Rockies/Cubs	0	2	.000	8.38	14	0	0	3	0	0	19.1	29	21	18	1	4	23	0	15	2
Murray, Giants*	1	1	.500	1.23	6	0	0	3	0	0	7.1	5	1	1	0	1	4	2	10	1
Myers, Angels	3	2	.600	2.93	18	2	1	9	0	1	58.1	55	31	19	2	6	23	1	58	11
Neier, Rockies/Cubs	5	1	.833	2.24	14	6	1	2	0	0	56.1	53	23	14	0	3	7	0	49	2
O'Laughlin, Brewers*	0	2	.000	11.57	1	1	0	0	0	0	2.1	4	4	3	0	0	2	0	2	3
Ortega, Mariners*	1	4	.200	4.67	19	0	0	8	0	0	34.2	43	23	18	0	2	10	4	28	2
Ortiz, Brewers*	2	1	.333	3.10	16	3	0	4	0	0	40.2	26	22	14	0	5	30	1	46	3
Perez, Giants	0	0	.000	0.00	2	0	0	1	0	0	3.1	2	0	0	0	0	1	0	1	0

ZONA LEA

Pitcher, Team	W	L	Pct.	ERA	G	GS	CG	GF	ShO	Sv.	IP	H	R	ER	HR	HB	BB	Int. BB	SO	WP
Pinder, Giants	3	0	1.000	2.37	18	0	0	5	0	1	30.1	29	9	8	0	3	11	0	19	11
Post, Athletics	5	0	1.000	3.60	14	0	0	7	0	1	30.0	25	15	12	2	1	3	0	28	2
Raggio, Cardinals	4	3	.571	3.54	14	6	3	4	0	1	48.1	51	26	19	1	3	7	1	48	5
Razhigaev, Angels*	0	1	.000	4.91	6	1	0	3	0	0	7.1	12	10	4	0	0	9	0	1	1
Rhoda, Brewers	1	3	.250	8.67	16	3	0	5	0	0	27.0	40	31	26	0	2	11	0	15	2
Rodriguez, Brewers	3	1	.750	1.10	9	7	0	0	0	0	49.0	35	9	6	1	1	14	0	37	1
Rosenbohm, Giants	2	7	.222	4.38	14	14	0	0	0	0	63.2	63	45	31	0	4	30	1	53	6
Ruiz, Cardinals*	3	4	.429	3.09	12	10	0	1	0	0	64.0	71	36	22	0	2	11	0	42	3
Sabino, Rockies/Cubs	0	3	.000	6.48	16	0	0	8	0	0	25.0	40	28	18	0	4	16	1	10	7
Sadler, Brewers	2	2	.500	2.10	7	5	0	0	0	0	30.0	32	12	7	0	0	6	0	33	3
Sailors, Cardinals*	1	4	.200	4.22	11	9	0	0	0	0	42.2	53	40	20	1	2	19	0	27	3
Salmon, Brewers	6	2	.750	3.32	11	10	1	0	1	0	59.2	55	32	22	3	7	16	0	58	2
Santiago, Padres*	0	0	.000	9.00	3	0	0	0	0	0	4.0	8	8	4	0	0	4	0	2	0
Sawyer, Athletics	5	4	.556	3.95	10	10	1	0	1	0	68.1	74	38	30	2	1	11	0	54	3
Severino, Padres	1	2	.333	8.76	7	1	0	3	0	0	12.1	23	17	12	0	2	7	0	13	3
Singleton, Padres*	0	0	.000	12.46	11	0	0	4	0	0	13.0	24	24	18	0	1	14	0	13	1
Snure, Brewers*	1	1	.500	1.74	7	1	0	2	0	0	10.1	9	3	2	0	2	2	0	12	2
Snyder, Angels	2	4	.333	3.27	15	0	0	7	0	3	44.0	40	27	16	0	3	16	1	38	1
Sobkoviak, Rockies/Cubs	1	6	.143	4.58	16	6	1	3	0	0	53.0	58	37	27	0	3	21	1	35	3
Soto, Mariners	5	3	.625	3.29	21	0	0	13	0	1	38.1	36	27	14	2	2	12	5	37	6
Stanton, Cardinals	3	4	.429	3.22	23	2	0	6	0	0	36.1	26	16	13	0	1	21	1	27	7
Stoppello, Cardinals*	0	0	.000	2.76	15	0	0	4	0	0	16.1	14	5	5	0	0	5	0	12	2
Tafoya, Rockies/Cubs*	0	0	.000	6.91	10	0	0	3	0	0	14.1	19	18	11	0	1	7	0	7	3
Theron, Mariners	4	1	.800	1.26	12	8	1	0	1	0	57.0	40	16	8	0	3	17	1	44	2
Thompson, Mariners	6	3	.667	3.69	14	11	1	1	1	0	70.2	54	35	29	1	2	32	1	65	13
Thurmond, Angels	0	2	.000	4.78	8	5	0	2	0	0	26.1	28	18	14	0	1	21	2	18	6
Torres, Brewers*	0	0	.000	3.00	2	0	0	2	0	0	6.0	4	3	2	0	1	1	0	3	1
Towns, Cardinals	0	1	1.000	5.31	13	0	0	7	0	0	20.1	17	17	12	0	1	11	0	12	4
Urbina, Athletics	7	1	.875	2.58	12	8	0	2	0	0	59.1	51	21	17	2	0	12	0	45	4
Valdez, Giants	3	1	.750	0.00	6	0	0	3	0	0	14.2	7	2	0	0	0	5	0	14	1
Valencia, Angels	2	5	.286	3.18	19	0	0	19	0	7	22.2	23	13	8	0	1	4	1	16	1
Vanhof, Mariners*	3	1	.750	1.29	10	7	0	0	0	0	49.0	27	13	7	0	5	24	2	35	7
Vazquez, Giants	1	1	.500	1.01	15	0	0	11	0	5	26.2	15	4	3	0	0	6	2	21	3
Wagner, Cardinals	1	1	.500	2.49	19	0	0	4	0	0	25.1	24	11	7	0	5	17	0	17	4
Wallace, Mariners	3	3	.500	3.16	12	7	0	2	0	2	51.1	37	26	18	0	6	25	0	45	13
Warren, Angels*	2	4	.333	4.29	10	9	0	0	0	0	35.2	24	22	17	1	4	30	0	50	8
Werner, Brewers	5	1	.833	2.56	10	8	1	0	1	0	45.2	43	17	13	0	2	11	0	38	1
White, Padres	0	5	.000	5.08	15	5	0	5	0	1	44.1	40	32	25	0	0	40	1	36	14
Williard, Angels	2	1	.667	5.12	6	4	0	0	0	0	31.2	33	25	18	0	1	18	0	20	3
Winchester, Padres*	1	7	.125	3.35	13	13	0	0	0	0	51.0	48	33	19	0	4	27	0	48	12
Wyatt, Padres	0	0	.000	0.00	1	0	0	0	0	0	0.0	2	2	1	0	0	1	0	0	0

BALKS—Arroyo, Baxter, 12 each; Domenico, J. Matos, 8 each; Baron, Estrella, Gaskill, Rosenbohm, 6 each; Salmon, 5; Lair, Montane, Snyder, Thompson, White, 4 each; Belliard, Carrasco, Caruso, Erdos, Hollins, Krause, MacNeill, Montgomery, Post, Severino, Singleton, Thurmond, Torres, Warren, 3 each; Blanco, Bledsoe, Brown, Cope, Fargas, Lloyd, Neier, Ortega, Ortiz, Rhoda, Sawyer, Sobkoviak, Stoppello, 2 each; Arias, Charles, Dafun, Davis, Dunckel, Garrett, Gold, G. Gonzalez, Griffin, Hardwick, Hinchliffe, Maltagliati, Martin, L. Matos, Morris, Sadler, Sailors, Soto, Theron, Urbina, Vazquez, Werner, Williard, Winchester, 1 each.

COMBINATION SHUTOUTS—Fermin-Thurmond-Valencia, Angels; Martinez-Domenico, Athletics; Maltagliati-Krause, Rodriguez-Demyan, Salmon-Krause, Brewers; Charles-Burley, Cardinals; Fultz-Israel-Towns, Martin-Brown-Gomez, Martin-Pinder, Rosenbohm-Towns, Giants; Montane-Soto-Dessellier, Vanhof-Ortega-Dessellier, Wallace-Hinchliffe, Mariners; McClain-Dunckel, Padres.

NO-HIT GAMES—None.

FIELDING

TEAM

Team	Pct.	G	PO	A	E	DP	PB	Team	Pct.	G	PO	A	E	DP	PB
Athletics	.950	56	1458	637	110	41	11	Angels	.940	56	1457	567	130	36	18
Cardinals	.948	56	1432	663	114	45	19	Mariners	.934	56	1474	634	150	53	8
Giants	.948	56	1450	646	116	48	18	Padres	.933	56	1433	594	146	32	22
Brewers	.942	56	1458	601	127	33	15	Rockies/Cubs	.928	56	1436	636	161	42	11

Triple play—Athletics.

INDIVIDUAL

FIRST BASEMEN

*Throws lefthanded.

Player, Team	Pct.	G	PO	A	E	DP
Aquino, Mariners	.985	33	252	18	4	21
BOYD, Rockies/Cubs	.979	39	346	25	8	26
Cabrera, Rockies/Cubs	.973	21	170	10	5	14
Cox, Athletics*	.975	46	407	28	11	35
Davis, Mariners	.984	18	126	1	2	8
Donati, Angels	.966	47	353	20	13	22
Fantauzzi, Padres*	.929	14	105	12	9	8
Furtado, Mariners	.986	10	64	5	1	2
Hart, Mariners	.985	20	178	15	3	6
Hause, Athletics*	.991	15	108	8	1	5
Ibanez, Mariners	.945	6	49	3	3	11
Kim, Angels	.959	12	89	4	4	5
Llanos, Cardinals	.975	54	509	34	14	36
Malekovic, Padres	.969	32	264	20	9	11
Monday, Angels	.923	2	11	1	1	0
Nunez, Brewers	.957	27	182	16	9	15
Perez, Giants	.985	17	121	7	2	5
Perez, Padres	.952	13	92	8	5	9
Pomierski, Mariners	.917	2	11	0	1	2
Poyner, Giants	.986	8	66	3	1	8
Ramirez, Giants	.982	18	157	8	3	22
Salazar, Rockies/Cubs	1.000	1	3	0	0	0

Player, Team	Pct.	G	PO	A	E	DP
Salzano, Brewers	1.000	12	87	1	0	5
Tatrow, Cardinals	.852	4	22	1	4	1
Torres, Brewers*	.978	33	210	15	5	9

Triple play—Cox.

SECOND BASEMEN

Player, Team	Pct.	G	PO	A	E	DP
Anderson, Giants	.879	10	15	14	4	4
Arredondo, Brewers	.954	35	67	78	7	11
Atencio, Mariners	.919	39	85	130	19	30
Batista, Athletics	.970	28	52	77	4	12
Bogatyrev, Angels	.867	5	8	5	2	1
Cabrera, Mariners	.957	5	11	11	1	0
Castro, Angels	1.000	2	1	3	0	1
Cedeno, Rockies/Cubs	.902	18	31	43	8	8
Corps, Padres	.941	11	17	31	3	6
Cristopher, Rockies/Cubs	.913	25	50	55	10	15
Cruz, Mariners	.906	13	26	32	6	7
Cuevas, Padres	.935	28	49	67	8	7
Diaz, Mariners	.980	11	16	32	1	5
Dilone, Athletics	.967	21	42	47	3	8
Dumas, Brewers	.957	13	20	25	2	5
Figueroa, Rockies/Cubs	.955	5	14	7	1	2
Gillis, Padres	.899	22	34	37	8	6

Player, Team	Pct.	G	PO	A	E	DP
Gonzalez, Rockies/Cubs	.958	4	5	18	1	4
Guillen, Athletics	.964	11	18	36	2	10
Hunter, Rockies/Cubs	.918	18	33	34	6	6
Jimenez, Angels	.923	10	21	27	4	3
Johnson, Giants	1.000	2	4	5	0	2
Jones, Athletics	.875	4	4	3	1	1
Martinez, Mariners	1.000	1	2	0	0	1
Mercedes, Rockies/Cubs	.500	1	1	0	1	0
Mesa, Brewers	1.000	3	2	6	0	1
Millan, Cardinals	.941	25	37	59	6	10
Perez, Giants	1.000	3	3	1	0	0
Powers, Brewers	.886	11	21	18	5	3
Puchkov, Angels	1.000	1	0	2	0	0
Rivera, Giants	.919	7	15	19	3	5
STAFFORD, Giants	.954	39	71	96	8	29
Ugueto, Cardinals	.936	36	61	99	11	15
Vizcaino, Angels	.947	31	75	68	8	11
Zarate, Brewers	.800	6	0	8	2	0

THIRD BASEMEN

Player, Team	Pct.	G	PO	A	E	DP
Anderson, Giants	.833	1	1	4	1	0
Arendt, Rockies/Cubs	.667	1	0	2	1	1
Bertucci, Angels	.500	1	2	2	4	0
Bowden, Padres	.837	20	10	31	8	1
Cabrera, Rockies/Cubs	.826	6	8	11	4	1
Cabrera, Mariners	1.000	4	1	9	0	0
Castro, Angels	1.000	10	6	16	0	1
Cedeno, Rockies/Cubs	.850	16	6	28	6	1
Cristopher, Rockies/Cubs	.000	1	0	0	1	0
Cruz, Mariners	1.000	2	1	0	0	0
Dilone, Athletics	.798	22	14	53	17	5
DONOHUE, Cardinals	.849	41	31	70	18	5
Dumas, Brewers	.778	11	5	23	8	2
Gonzalez, Rockies/Cubs	1.000	6	7	11	0	1
Gorman, Angels	.833	3	0	5	1	1
Guzik, Angels	.855	29	23	42	11	6
Imperial, Brewers	.810	5	3	14	4	0
J. Jones, Athletics	.772	21	11	33	13	1
Martinez, Brewers	1.000	1	1	0	0	0
Martinez, Mariners	.862	34	26	80	17	4
Mercedes, Rockies/Cubs	.773	5	5	12	5	0
Morel, Cardinals	.978	12	12	32	1	1
Perez, Giants	1.000	2	2	1	0	0
Phillips, Giants	.880	20	12	54	9	1
Pomierski, Mariners	.792	21	8	30	10	4
Pooschke, Giants	.847	35	22	89	20	7
Powers, Brewers	.917	13	9	13	2	2
Puchkov, Angels	.907	20	17	32	5	1
Rivera, Padres	.778	5	4	10	4	2
Salzano, Brewers	.792	38	14	47	16	2
Talbott, Padres	.865	32	27	56	13	1
Ugueto, Cardinals	.880	7	6	16	3	3
Valdez, Rockies/Cubs	.808	32	21	42	15	3
Vizcaino, Angels	1.000	1	2	2	0	0
Yots, Athletics	.814	17	7	28	8	2

SHORTSTOPS

Player, Team	Pct.	G	PO	A	E	DP
Anderson, Giants	.848	13	10	29	7	5
Arredondo, Brewers	.933	4	7	7	1	1
Batista, Athletics	.939	18	15	47	4	7
Bogatyrev, Angels	.759	11	4	18	7	2
Bowden, Padres	.833	2	3	7	2	2
Cabrera, Mariners	.908	17	24	55	8	11
Castro, Angels	.917	41	60	94	14	13
Corps, Padres	.908	24	40	69	11	12
Cristopher, Rockies/Cubs	1.000	2	2	3	0	0
Cruz, Mariners	.875	7	9	19	4	3
Cuevas, Padres	.917	5	6	16	2	0
Dumas, Brewers	.941	12	12	20	2	3
Gillis, Padres	.804	10	14	27	10	5
Gipson, Mariners	.876	36	49	114	23	16
Gonzalez, Rockies/Cubs	.913	26	30	96	12	14
Johnson, Giants	.925	41	67	129	16	23
Martinez, Brewers	.899	47	58	129	21	18
McEwing, Cardinals	1.000	2	0	1	0	0
Mercedes, Rockies/Cubs	.869	32	47	92	21	19
Perez, Giants	.941	5	5	11	1	1
Phillips, Giants	1.000	1	2	1	0	0
Rodriguez, Padres	.926	18	22	66	7	6
Rupp, Cardinals	.918	56	85	173	23	28
SALVADOR, Athletics	.934	44	52	133	13	15
Salzano, Brewers	1.000	1	1	1	0	1
Stafford, Giants	1.000	2	0	5	0	0
Vizcaino, Angels	1.000	15	10	41	0	7
Zarate, Brewers	.000	1	0	0	1	0

Triple play—Salvador.

OUTFIELDERS

Player, Team	Pct.	G	PO	A	E	DP
Arendt, Rockies/Cubs	.979	27	44	3	1	0
Batista, Mariners	1.000	17	29	1	0	0
Bautista, Cardinals	.910	39	65	6	7	1
Bertucci, Angels	.857	7	6	0	1	0
Blomeyer, Giants	.974	23	37	1	1	0
Bonds, Padres	1.000	8	12	1	0	0
Cabrera, Rockies/Cubs	.933	11	24	4	2	0
Cantrell, Brewers	.815	14	21	1	5	0
Castro, Angels	.833	3	5	0	1	0
Cephas, Brewers	.968	33	57	4	2	2
Creer, Padres	.867	12	13	0	2	0
Daniels, Angels	.924	38	85	0	7	0
Darwin, Athletics	.923	39	36	0	3	0
Davis, Mariners	1.000	2	1	0	0	0
DeLeon, Mariners	.917	24	33	0	3	0
Dilone, Athletics	.500	2	2	0	2	0
Edwards, Rockies/Cubs	.925	37	72	2	6	0
Figueroa, Rockies/Cubs	.927	26	49	2	4	0
Francisco, Athletics	1.000	9	18	2	0	1
Frazier, Giants	.969	41	59	4	2	0
Garcia, Angels	1.000	22	28	1	0	0
Goebel, Padres	.810	8	16	1	4	0
Guzik, Angels	1.000	4	3	0	0	0
Harris, Giants	.985	45	58	8	1	1
Hause, Athletics*	.923	10	12	0	1	0
Hernandez, Rockies/Cubs*	.912	22	29	2	3	0
Herrick, Angels*	1.000	8	9	1	0	1
Jose A. Jimenez, Angels	.909	3	8	10	0	1
Jose G. Jimenez, Angels	.897	14	26	0	3	0
Johnson, Padres	1.000	28	60	5	0	3
B. Jones, Athletics	.971	16	33	1	1	0
Keel, Athletics	.970	40	63	1	2	0
Kim, Angels	.929	11	11	2	1	0
Lantigua, Athletics	.938	39	59	2	4	0
Luckett, Padres	1.000	15	15	2	0	0
Machado, Rockies/Cubs	.941	21	28	4	2	0
Marquez, Mariners*	.978	37	43	2	1	1
Martin, Angels	.930	43	65	1	5	0
Martinez, Brewers	.930	28	51	2	4	0
Matos, Padres	1.000	16	30	2	0	0
McArn, Athletics*	.953	22	40	1	2	0
McCoy, Padres	1.000	16	23	0	0	0
McEWING, Cardinals	.991	55	94	11	1	4
Miller, Giants	1.000	29	27	1	0	0
Minton, Cardinals	.923	17	12	0	1	0
Monday, Angels	1.000	4	5	0	0	0
Morel, Cardinals	.929	18	22	4	2	1
Moreno, Brewers	.882	12	15	0	2	0
Pellot, Cardinals	.951	36	39	0	2	0
Pena, Brewers	1.000	3	2	1	0	0
Phillips, Giants	1.000	1	1	1	0	0
Pridgen, Brewers*	.986	50	71	0	1	0
Rivera, Padres	.968	14	29	1	1	0
Rivera, Giants	.923	44	82	2	7	0
Roques, Padres	.875	18	19	2	3	0
Rubiera, Angels	1.000	3	5	0	0	0
Salazar, Rockies/Cubs	.941	13	14	2	1	0
Sanchez, Rockies/Cubs	.893	13	25	0	3	0
Sanders, Padres	.778	6	6	1	2	0
Sosa, Mariners	.917	16	31	2	3	1
Stewart, Padres	.974	22	36	2	1	0
Strehlow, Cardinals	.750	21	17	1	6	0
Sturdivant, Mariners*	.944	38	58	9	4	2
Thomas, Mariners	.927	44	72	4	6	1
Torres, Brewers*	.889	6	6	2	1	0
Tucker, Padres	.750	5	3	0	1	0
Vallejo, Angels	.968	16	27	3	1	1
Walton, Rockies/Cubs	1.000	19	22	4	0	0
Wyatt, Padres	.912	15	28	3	3	1
Zarate, Brewers	.938	48	72	3	5	1

CATCHERS

Player, Team	Pct.	G	PO	A	E	DP	PB
Bertucci, Angels	.969	28	194	26	7	2	11
Borzello, Cardinals	1.000	11	79	10	0	1	3
Bowen, Cardinals	.980	33	168	25	4	1	14
DeJesus, Padres	.959	16	105	13	5	1	3
Delgado, Giants	.965	37	212	33	9	3	9
Furtado, Mariners	.982	27	198	15	4	1	2
Garcia, Mariners	1.000	1	3	0	0	0	0
Garcia, Rockies/Cubs	.846	13	30	3	6	0	1
Gay, Brewers	.984	35	214	34	4	2	8
Hatfield, Rockies/Cubs	.963	28	133	22	6	0	6
Ibanez, Mariners	.667	2	2	0	1	0	0
Kim, Angels	1.000	1	1	0	0	0	0
Martinez, Padres	.953	26	193	10	10	0	7
Maxwell, Mariners	.984	10	57	5	1	1	1
Moncion, Athletics	.980	22	128	16	3	0	2
Monday, Angels	.961	19	109	13	5	0	3
Morel, Cardinals	1.000	26	150	24	0	1	2
Moreno, Brewers	.984	22	107	13	2	2	3
Poyner, Giants	.976	10	75	7	2	1	6

Player, Team	Pct.	G	PO	A	E	DP	PB
Pozo, Rockies/Cubs	.974	34	156	32	5	0	2
Ramirez, Giants	.968	21	130	22	5	1	3
Reyes, Mariners	.961	31	175	20	8	3	5
Sanderfer, Athletics	.982	21	103	7	2	1	4
Smith, Athletics	.960	11	43	5	2	0	0
Stadler, Padres	.988	24	133	25	2	0	12
Tucker, Angels	.994	17	139	20	1	4	4
VENTURA, Athletics	.990	30	163	26	2	0	5
Wyss, Brewers	.978	16	118	15	3	0	4

PITCHERS

Player, Team	Pct.	G	PO	A	E	DP
Aguirre, Angels*	.800	3	0	4	1	0
Alcantara, Mariners	.000	1	0	0	1	0
Alexander, Brewers	.833	3	3	2	1	0
Arias, Brewers	.667	7	0	2	1	0
Arroyo, Padres*	1.000	17	4	11	0	1
Barnes, Rockies/Cubs*	.938	12	7	8	1	1
Baron, Padres*	1.000	14	1	5	0	0
Baxter, Giants*	.824	14	2	12	3	0
Belliard, Athletics*	1.000	13	5	12	0	0
Bledsoe, Cardinals	1.000	17	0	4	0	0
Brown, Giants	1.000	15	3	6	0	1
Burley, Cardinals	1.000	19	1	2	0	0
Carrasco, Angels	.800	16	3	9	3	0
Caruso, Athletics*	1.000	7	1	5	0	0
Charles, Cardinals	1.000	11	3	15	0	1
Collins, Giants	.500	4	0	1	1	0
Cope, Mariners	.786	16	4	7	3	0
Dafun, Angels	.700	13	2	5	3	0
Davis, Cardinals	.813	11	3	10	3	0
Demyan, Brewers	.917	23	1	10	1	1
Dessellier, Mariners	.857	13	2	4	1	0
Domenico, Athletics	.875	17	2	5	1	0
Dunckel, Padres	1.000	19	2	3	0	0
Erdos, Padres	.867	12	4	9	2	0
Estrella, Padres	.833	14	2	3	1	0
Fargas, Padres	.667	13	4	2	3	0
FERMIN, Angels	1.000	12	5	15	0	1
Fjeld, Padres	1.000	6	0	4	0	0
Fultz, Giants*	.960	14	3	21	1	0
Garrett, Rockies/Cubs	.813	11	3	10	3	0
Gaskill, Brewers	1.000	11	0	1	0	0
Goebel, Padres	1.000	4	1	0	0	0
Gold, Brewers	1.000	13	0	3	0	1
Golden, Mariners	.000	3	0	0	3	0
Gomez, Giants	1.000	20	2	5	0	0
Gonzalez, Brewers	1.000	12	1	11	0	0
Gonzalez, Rockies/Cubs	.750	14	5	4	3	0
Goodrich, Rockies/Cubs	1.000	21	2	2	0	0
Grasser, Cardinals	1.000	17	2	2	0	0
Griffin, Athletics	1.000	6	1	1	0	0
Grigsby, Athletics	1.000	3	2	2	0	0
Hause, Athletics*	1.000	14	1	3	0	0
Hinchliffe, Mariners	.750	24	1	2	1	0
Holcomb, Angels	1.000	4	3	0	0	0
Hollins, Athletics	.824	15	5	9	3	1
Israel, Giants	1.000	16	0	3	0	0
Jones, Padres	1.000	5	1	2	0	0
Jumonville, Padres	1.000	16	3	7	0	0
Klomp, Mariners	1.000	6	0	2	0	0
Krause, Brewers	.818	16	3	6	2	0

Player, Team	Pct.	G	PO	A	E	DP
Lair, Cardinals	.900	8	0	9	1	0
Lloyd, Angels	.737	11	4	10	5	0
Luckert, Rockies/Cubs	.800	13	1	7	2	0
MacNeill, Brewers	1.000	2	0	2	0	0
Maltagliati, Brewers	.824	10	1	13	3	0
Mantei, Mariners	1.000	3	2	5	0	1
Martin, Giants	1.000	13	0	8	0	1
Martinez, Athletics	.909	10	2	8	1	0
J. Matos, Rockies/Cubs	1.000	17	1	4	0	0
L. Matos, Rockies/Cubs	.667	3	0	2	1	0
McClain, Padres	.833	12	3	7	2	1
Metzinger, Rockies/Cubs	.800	14	1	3	1	0
Mitchell, Giants	1.000	17	0	2	0	0
Montane, Mariners	1.000	13	1	6	0	1
Montgomery, Athletics	.900	11	1	8	1	0
Morris, Rockies/Cubs	.750	14	0	3	1	0
Murray, Giants*	1.000	6	0	1	0	0
Myers, Angels	.875	18	0	7	1	0
Neier, Rockies/Cubs	.889	14	9	7	2	1
Ortega, Mariners*	.769	19	4	6	3	1
Ortiz, Brewers*	.813	16	1	12	3	1
Perez, Giants	.000	2	0	0	1	0
Pinder, Giants	.857	18	0	6	1	0
Post, Athletics	1.000	14	1	5	0	0
Raggio, Cardinals	.864	14	4	15	3	4
Razhigaev, Angels*	.600	6	1	2	2	1
Rhoda, Brewers	1.000	16	2	1	0	0
Rodriguez, Brewers	.875	9	4	10	2	1
Rosenbohm, Giants	.909	14	4	6	1	0
Ruiz, Cardinals	.923	12	6	18	2	1
Sabino, Rockies/Cubs	.500	16	0	1	1	0
Sadler, Brewers	1.000	7	0	2	0	0
Sailors, Cardinals*	.857	11	2	4	1	0
Salmon, Brewers	1.000	11	5	13	0	0
Santiago, Padres*	1.000	3	0	1	0	0
Sawyer, Athletics	.857	10	3	15	3	0
Severino, Padres	.600	7	0	3	2	0
Singleton, Padres	1.000	11	0	1	0	0
Snure, Brewers*	1.000	7	0	4	0	0
Snyder, Angels	.941	15	4	12	1	0
Sobkoviak, Rockies/Cubs	.889	16	1	15	2	0
Soto, Mariners	.857	21	1	5	1	0
Stanton, Cardinals	.909	23	1	9	1	1
Stoppello, Cardinals*	1.000	15	1	4	0	0
Tafoya, Rockies/Cubs*	1.000	10	1	1	0	0
Theron, Mariners	.875	12	5	9	2	0
Thompson, Mariners	1.000	14	2	3	0	0
Thurmond, Angels	.818	8	3	6	2	0
Torres, Brewers*	1.000	2	0	2	0	0
Towns, Giants	.714	13	3	2	2	0
Urbina, Athletics	1.000	12	4	10	0	0
Valdez, Giants	.750	6	1	2	1	0
Valencia, Angels	.857	19	0	6	1	0
Vanhof, Mariners*	.765	10	3	10	4	0
Vazquez, Giants	1.000	15	0	1	0	0
Wagner, Cardinals	1.000	19	0	5	0	0
Wallace, Brewers	.929	12	3	10	1	0
Warren, Angels*	.857	10	1	5	1	0
Werner, Brewers	1.000	10	4	11	0	0
White, Padres	.625	15	0	5	3	0
Williard, Angels	.875	6	2	5	1	0
Winchester, Padres*	.900	13	3	6	1	0

Triple play—Hause.

The following players did not have any fielding statistics at the positions indicated or appeared only as a designated hitter, pinch-hitter or pinch-runner: Barnes, of; T. Batista, of; Blanco, p; Cruz, p; Hardwick, p; Hart, of; Hunter, 3b; Ibanez, of; Jenkins, p; B. Jones, 3b; Jo. Jones, of; Keel, 1b; A. Matos, p; McKinnon, dh; Minton, ss; Moncion, p; Morel, p; O'Laughlin, p; Powers, ss; P. Thompson, ph; Vizcaino, of; Wyatt, p; Wyss, of; Yots, ss.

LEAGUE CHAMPIONS

Year	Team	Pct.
1988—	Peoria Brewers	.690
1989—	Peoria Brewers	.732
1990—	Peoria Brewers	.679

Year	Team	Pct.
1991—	Scottsdale A's	.650
1992—	Scottsdale A's	.607

DOMINICAN SUMMER LEAGUE

FINAL STANDINGS

SANTO DOMINGO WEST DIVISION

Team	W	L	T	Pct.	GB
Oakland	47	24	0	.662	....
Yankees/San Diego	43	27	0	.614	3½
Pittsburgh	38	31	0	.555	8
New York Mets	39	32	0	.549	8
Montreal	31	40	0	.437	16
Toronto West	28	42	0	.400	18½
Detroit/St. Louis	21	51	0	.292	26½

SAN PEDRO DE MACORIS DIVISION

Team	W	L	T	Pct.	GB
Atlanta	49	20	0	.710	....
San Francisco	44	25	0	.638	5
Baltimore/White Sox	42	26	0	.618	6½
Houston	28	40	0	.412	20½
Texas/Florida	22	47	0	.319	27
California	21	48	0	.304	28

SANTO DOMINGO EAST DIVISION

Team	W	L	T	Pct.	GB
Toronto East	68	2	0	.971	....
Los Angeles I	31	38	0	.449	36½
Seattle	23	46	0	.333	44½
Milwaukee	17	53	0	.243	51

CIBAO DIVISION

Team	W	L	T	Pct.	GB
Los Angeles II	53	19	0	.736	....
Co-op II	40	31	0	.563	12½
Cleveland	34	38	0	.472	19
Co-op I	16	55	0	.225	36½

Club names are major league affiliations.

Co-op I represents Chicago White Sox, California Angels, Cleveland Indians, Kansas City Royals and Seattle Mariners.

Co-op II represents Kansas City Royals, Chicago Cubs and Colorado Rockies.

Playoffs—Oakland defeated Toronto East, two games to none; Los Angeles II defeated Atlanta, two games to one; Los Angeles II defeated Oakland, two games to none, to win league championship.

Managers—Atlanta, Jose Salado; Baltimore/White Sox, Juan R. Benhardt; California, Juan Mercedes and Miguel Rodriguez; Cleveland, Alejandro Taveras; Co-op I, Jose Gomez; Co-op II, Julio Alcala; Detroit/St. Louis, Felix Nivar; Houston, Ramon Garcia; Los Angeles I, Teodoro Martinez; Los Angeles II, Antonio Bautista; Milwaukee, Cesar Prebox; Montreal, Hilario Soriano; New York Mets, Roberto Marte; Oakland, Luis Martinez; Pittsburgh, Hall Dyer; San Francisco, Mateo Rojas Alou; Seattle, Ramon de los Santos; Texas/Florida, Rodolfo Rosario; Toronto East, Ramon Webster; Toronto West, Julio Cesar Paula; Yankees/San Diego, Victor Mata.

BATTING

TEAM

Team	Avg.	G	AB	R	OR	H	TB	2B	3B	HR	RBI	SH	SF	HP	BB	Int. BB	SO	SB	CS	LOB
Toronto East	.307	70	2319	571	165	712	1024	108	33	46	483	13	41	28	406	9	312	135	44	.....
Atlanta	.305	69	2468	502	237	752	979	126	31	13	398	29	28	40	370	14	335	153	72	.....
Montreal	.292	71	2322	415	440	679	926	99	11	42	333	13	21	29	301	3	374	129	63	.....
Toronto West	.289	70	2269	400	436	655	858	105	16	22	311	15	29	42	330	7	287	166	100	.....
Los Angeles II	.284	72	2517	480	259	714	922	91	45	9	374	55	31	25	405	18	339	96	51	.....
Baltimore/White Sox	.276	68	2345	445	415	647	821	103	16	13	325	25	42	325	11	345	146	77		.....
Yankees/San Diego	.271	71	2249	450	343	610	824	85	24	27	350	5	37	27	432	10	361	143	82	.....
Pittsburgh	.268	70	2275	368	346	610	769	78	15	17	273	33	24	58	288	8	282	166	101	.....
New York Mets	.266	71	2138	451	384	569	810	71	13	48	363	22	30	40	429	8	350	149	85	.....
Cleveland	.264	72	2469	354	323	652	869	107	19	24	297	21	23	32	249	23	376	115	64	.....
Los Angeles I	.249	70	2160	303	369	538	705	73	20	18	240	47	26	28	299	7	372	101	62	.....
San Francisco	.249	69	2253	399	341	562	738	78	22	18	324	11	30	29	425	21	362	167	60	.....
California	.247	69	2195	344	458	543	688	84	17	9	245	9	15	50	375	7	363	165	121	.....
Co-op II	.240	71	2322	383	373	558	738	70	22	22	289	36	15	59	316	13	442	136	102	.....
Detroit/St. Louis	.239	72	2285	285	515	546	700	88	9	16	242	8	15	26	220	4	359	71	56	.....
Oakland	.238	70	2269	410	314	540	706	90	11	18	320	14	34	66	394	11	356	109	47	.....
Houston	.237	68	2195	340	433	520	635	63	11	10	251	16	14	50	329	19	403	139	53	.....
Seattle	.228	70	2177	277	405	496	669	88	14	19	216	11	15	46	324	2	586	129	75	.....
Milwaukee	.226	70	2176	275	486	491	609	71	13	7	217	29	12	37	333	5	422	73	38	.....
Texas/Florida	.224	69	2114	282	443	474	592	67	9	11	202	17	24	50	320	13	337	130	68	.....
Co-op I	.219	64	2005	262	558	440	566	66	12	12	207	32	10	33	316	5	417	90	69	.....

INDIVIDUAL

(Leading qualifiers for batting championship)

Player, Team	Avg.	G	AB	R	H	TB	2B	3B	HR	RBI	SH	SF	HP	BB	Int. BB	SO	SB	CS
Campos, Jesus, Montreal	.403	59	236	42	95	115	13	2	1	48	0	1	0	20	0	10	25	7
Guerrero, Wilton, Los Angeles II	.387	61	225	52	87	102	7	4	0	38	7	2	2	34	1	21	15	10
Valdez, Guillermo, Atlanta	.386	57	207	55	80	118	8	12	2	44	1	2	0	41	3	19	23	8
Henson, Eugene, Atlanta	.374	59	238	53	89	111	15	2	1	28	1	2	5	27	1	24	18	5
Mosquera, Julio, Toronto West	.362	67	235	47	85	108	12	1	3	39	1	1	5	17	2	20	17	6
Rojas, Freddy, New York Mets	.362	71	229	59	83	134	11	2	12	63	1	3	2	52	3	35	11	7
Perez, Eduardo, Atlanta	.359	41	153	50	55	55	6	0	0	13	2	2	3	39	0	17	22	8
Castro, Francisco, Los Angeles II	.358	72	279	74	100	135	11	9	2	49	6	3	3	73	3	27	35	10
DeLaCruz, Lorenzo, Toronto East	.353	68	258	67	91	141	8	2	14	80	0	8	2	50	0	46	12	3
Portes, Miguel, Yankees/San Diego	.353	69	249	61	88	119	9	5	4	48	1	2	3	34	0	18	24	13

Departmental leaders: G—F. Castro, A. Hernandez, Ozorio, 72; AB—Acencio, 293; R—Debrand, 89; H—F. Castro, 100; TB—L. DeLaCruz, 141; 2B—J. Vargas, 21; 3B—G. Valdez, 12; HR—L. DeLaCruz, 14; RBI—L. DeLaCruz, 80; SH—Cesar, Payano, 10; SF—J.J. Espinal, 13; HP—F. Soriano, 19; BB—Debrand, 86; IBB—I. Devers, Mi. Garcia (Clev.), 5; SO—A. DeLosSantos, 64; SB—Ozorio, 62; CS—Payano, 22.

(All players—listed alphabetically)

Player, Team	Avg.	G	AB	R	H	TB	2B	3B	HR	RBI	SH	SF	HP	BB	Int. BB	SO	SB	CS
Abad, Irvin, Toronto West	.227	57	150	28	34	50	7	3	1	21	2	3	2	45	1	16	12	6
Abea, Marlon, Toronto East	.291	67	237	52	69	86	17	0	0	42	2	7	6	31	1	14	2	5
Abreu, Junior, Milwaukee	.311	61	190	45	59	87	13	6	1	29	2	0	4	45	1	21	10	4

Player, Team	Avg.	G	AB	R	H	TB	2B	3B	HR	RBI	SH	SF	HP	BB	Int. BB	SO	SB	CS
Acencio, Alexander, Los Angeles II	.287	69	293	54	84	115	11	10	0	44	6	4	2	32	1	29	6	3
Alvarado, Basilio, Montreal	.293	49	167	20	49	63	8	0	2	21	1	1	2	12	1	22	0	1
Alvarez, Luis, Baltimore/White Sox	.000	12	0	1	0	0	0	0	0	0	0	0	0	0	0	0	0	0
Alvino, Eleazar, Los Angeles II	.263	34	38	9	10	13	1	1	0	4	2	0	0	7	0	10	3	2
Arias, Francisco, Oakland	.170	48	241	22	41	48	4	0	1	28	2	2	4	26	2	15	5	2
Arias, Georgie, Cleveland	.206	49	141	21	29	37	8	0	0	12	2	0	2	27	0	29	3	3
Arias, Jose, New York Mets	.231	47	108	17	25	37	2	2	2	13	0	1	3	12	0	20	2	1
Arias, Wagner, Milwaukee	.000	1	1	0	0	0	0	0	0	0	0	0	0	1	0	1	0	0
Arvelo, Luis A., Milwaukee	.214	32	103	16	22	30	5	0	1	7	0	0	0	15	0	28	2	0
Asencio, Hector, California	.216	48	116	20	25	34	2	2	1	9	1	2	3	26	0	25	6	9
Asencio, Jose, Los Angeles I	.256	30	82	7	21	29	3	1	1	8	0	0	2	8	0	17	6	4
Asencio, Juan, San Francisco	.216	38	88	13	19	19	0	0	0	8	2	0	0	13	0	18	15	1
Aybar, Manuel, Detroit/St. Louis	.203	55	153	18	31	39	5	0	1	11	0	0	3	10	0	27	2	5
Azuaje, Jesus, Cleveland	.281	66	235	36	66	85	10	0	3	27	0	2	6	28	1	23	14	5
Baez, Victor, Los Angeles II	.215	40	79	12	17	17	0	0	0	9	2	0	2	14	2	9	0	2
Balcazar, Carlos, California	.188	39	80	14	15	18	3	0	0	9	0	0	0	15	0	20	2	2
Barazarte, Wilfred, Los Angeles I	.294	61	197	29	58	84	13	2	3	23	8	0	3	18	0	36	6	3
Bautista, Juan, Baltimore/White Sox	.256	54	176	34	45	55	7	0	1	16	1	3	7	28	0	20	4	10
Bautista, Perfecto, Detroit/St. Louis	.234	49	137	11	32	35	0	0	1	16	0	3	0	3	0	23	5	3
Beato, Hector, Houston	.262	64	210	49	55	63	3	1	1	27	0	1	5	65	1	25	26	5
Beltre, Juan, Atlanta	.241	32	108	11	26	32	4	1	0	14	1	1	0	10	0	19	3	3
Bido, Jorge, Houston	.248	65	218	31	54	73	11	1	2	29	2	0	6	26	2	54	9	3
Bonilla, Danny, Co-op I	.375	5	8	0	3	4	1	0	0	2	0	0	0	2	0	1	0	0
Bonilla, Ramon, Oakland	.198	41	111	18	22	30	8	0	0	15	0	3	2	12	1	15	0	3
Borges, Andry, Co-op II	.269	44	160	16	43	52	7	1	0	28	5	0	7	8	2	31	7	6
Brea, Juan, New York Mets	.250	24	64	7	16	21	2	0	1	8	1	0	1	10	0	3	3	4
Brito, Edgar, Toronto East	.216	28	88	7	19	23	2	1	0	11	0	2	3	7	0	16	4	1
Brito, Hernan, Milwaukee	.160	22	50	5	8	9	1	0	0	5	2	0	0	13	0	22	1	0
Brito, Vicente, Toronto West	.264	33	72	10	19	24	3	1	0	8	2	1	0	7	0	11	2	2
Brown, Alfonso, Los Angeles I	.272	63	206	35	56	94	11	3	7	35	4	4	3	34	2	38	12	6
Bryan, Leonardo, California	.293	52	188	30	55	76	8	2	3	22	0	1	1	30	0	41	10	10
Cabrera, Carlos, Toronto East	.297	67	165	39	49	66	7	2	2	31	4	1	2	20	0	13	13	0
Cabrera, Jairo, Cleveland	.230	49	165	18	38	41	3	0	0	6	0	1	3	11	2	18	1	3
Campos, Jesus, Montreal	.403	59	236	42	95	115	13	2	1	48	0	1	0	20	0	10	25	7
Campusano, Anito, Los Angeles I	.219	38	105	10	23	28	1	2	0	8	4	2	1	2	0	16	4	2
Carizosa, Alejandro, Los Angeles I	.276	45	170	18	47	57	7	0	1	16	0	1	1	9	0	23	6	1
Carrasquel, Domingo, Toronto West	.277	55	177	28	49	59	7	0	1	21	2	2	3	21	0	6	7	9
Castillo, Amaury, Houston	.235	25	98	9	23	26	3	0	0	11	0	0	0	7	3	22	1	1
Castillo, Edwin, San Francisco	.263	33	95	13	25	33	2	0	2	16	0	2	1	9	0	15	1	0
Castillo, Guillermo, Oakland	.242	50	157	33	38	53	7	1	2	23	0	2	5	37	3	33	10	2
Castillo, Juan, Milwaukee	.231	63	208	34	48	55	3	2	0	25	0	2	3	51	0	16	21	5
Castillo, Santos, Seattle	.295	23	61	4	18	23	0	1	1	4	0	0	3	8	0	16	4	4
Castro, Francisco, Los Angeles II	.358	72	279	74	100	135	11	9	2	49	6	3	3	73	3	27	35	10
Castro, Jose, Baltimore/White Sox	.225	51	142	30	32	44	7	1	1	17	2	3	0	27	1	26	13	7
Cedeno, Efrain, Cleveland	.246	47	134	19	33	43	8	1	0	10	1	1	0	15	1	23	2	3
Cedeno, Jose, Co-op II	.273	42	132	26	36	47	0	1	3	24	0	2	3	23	1	23	4	5
Cesar, Angel, Los Angeles II	.281	67	278	49	78	105	9	9	0	50	10	3	0	39	1	27	7	4
Collins, Richard, Oakland	.200	17	45	3	9	9	0	0	0	2	0	1	1	4	0	7	0	0
Colmenares, Carlos, Toronto East	.400	2	5	1	2	2	0	0	0	2	0	0	1	3	0	1	1	1
Colmenarez, Ivan, Balt./White Sox	.193	48	135	28	26	35	5	2	0	10	4	0	1	37	1	17	11	4
Colon, Daniel, Milwaukee	.244	18	45	5	11	14	1	1	0	4	0	0	0	3	0	13	2	0
Concepcion, Enrique, San Francisco	.264	50	163	32	43	48	5	0	0	19	3	3	3	21	1	16	10	6
Contrera, Jorge M., Balt./White Sox	.113	24	53	6	6	6	0	0	0	2	0	0	1	4	0	19	1	2
Contreras, Franklin, Houston	.125	8	16	2	2	2	0	0	0	2	0	0	0	1	0	3	0	0
Contreras, Julio, Montreal	.235	6	17	1	4	5	1	0	0	1	0	0	2	1	0	2	0	1
Cordero, Pablo, San Francisco	.235	45	183	31	43	58	8	2	1	24	0	1	4	23	1	38	10	4
Crisotomo, Danny, Seattle	.229	48	153	19	35	42	7	0	0	13	2	0	3	13	0	37	6	8
Cruz, Francisco, Yankees/San Diego	.273	40	121	25	33	47	5	0	3	11	0	1	2	20	0	35	5	6
Cruz, Miguel, Detroit/St. Louis	.244	51	135	18	33	37	4	0	0	14	1	1	3	23	1	43	6	4
Dalis, Jamie, Seattle	.272	37	92	9	25	29	2	1	0	7	0	1	2	8	0	35	9	4
Davis, Melvin, San Francisco	.234	54	201	37	47	67	5	3	3	36	0	3	1	48	2	34	14	7
Debrand, Rafael, Toronto East	.315	70	241	89	76	121	16	7	5	49	1	4	3	86	3	15	24	6
DeJesus Diaz, Victor, New York Mets	.185	34	81	11	15	18	3	0	0	12	0	1	0	12	0	15	2	0
DeLaCruz, Francisco, Houston	.149	50	114	12	17	19	2	0	0	11	2	2	7	16	1	29	0	0
DeLaCruz, Henry, Atlanta	.220	16	41	5	9	10	1	0	0	4	0	0	0	6	0	5	2	0
DeLaCruz, Jesus, California	.192	49	130	15	25	29	2	1	0	8	2	0	3	21	0	12	11	11
DeLaCruz, Joselin, Co-op II	.283	24	46	11	13	14	1	0	0	4	0	0	1	15	0	16	1	3
DeLaCruz, Juan, Montreal	.260	28	77	13	20	31	2	0	3	7	0	0	1	4	0	25	4	1
DeLaCruz, Kelvin, Toronto East	.183	45	109	12	20	24	4	0	0	11	1	0	0	18	0	12	2	4
DeLaCruz, Lorenzo, Toronto East	.353	68	258	67	91	141	8	4	14	80	0	8	2	50	0	46	12	3
DeLaCruz, Roberto, Atlanta	.227	37	110	15	25	35	5	1	1	13	0	2	4	20	0	34	9	2
DeLaCruz, Roberto, California	.000	4	1	0	0	0	0	0	0	0	0	0	0	0	0	0	0	0
DeLaRosa, Dario, Houston	.231	26	13	0	3	3	0	0	0	1	0	0	1	0	0	5	1	0
DeLaRosa, Luis, Pittsburgh	.203	49	128	15	26	30	4	0	0	7	3	1	1	13	2	33	5	4
DeLeon, Felix, Yankees/San Diego	.288	54	163	34	47	51	4	0	0	24	1	2	0	36	0	5	13	7
DeLeon, Santos, Seattle	.286	64	217	45	62	76	9	1	1	18	3	2	4	47	0	52	48	15
DeLosSantos, Alex, Texas/Florida	.190	59	163	20	31	39	2	0	2	10	1	1	2	25	0	64	13	4
DeLosSantos, Esteban, Oakland	.278	52	126	24	35	44	6	0	1	17	1	2	2	32	1	15	3	4
DeLosSantos, Miguel, Co-op I	.192	41	99	14	19	25	0	0	2	8	0	0	2	24	0	37	6	3
DeRotal, Francisco, Yankees/S.D.	.206	48	155	21	32	51	6	2	3	23	2	4	4	20	0	35	6	3
Devers, Iran, Baltimore/White Sox	.328	62	241	46	79	120	16	5	5	66	0	3	4	28	5	20	18	5
Devers, Jose, Co-op I	.256	26	78	12	20	22	2	0	0	7	0	0	3	8	0	16	6	3
Diaz, Alexis, Seattle	.248	37	105	10	26	41	8	2	1	7	1	0	1	28	1	24	1	6
Diaz, Javier, Co-op II	.183	32	93	11	17	18	1	0	0	7	2	0	3	7	1	19	2	3
Diaz, Juan, Houston	.250	10	24	3	6	7	1	0	0	3	0	0	0	4	0	3	0	0
Diaz, Victor Anselmo, New York Mets	.259	45	116	30	30	52	4	0	6	31	3	4	0	31	1	24	7	0
Diaz S., Jacobo, California	.243	54	202	27	49	53	2	1	0	14	1	0	4	20	0	9	18	15
Duncan, Jason, Oakland	.188	54	149	28	28	31	1	1	0	12	2	1	3	30	0	39	13	6
Duval, Aristides, Oakland	.118	14	34	5	4	4	0	0	0	2	0	0	0	11	0	11	2	0
Espinal, Felix, Houston	.116	37	95	6	11	11	0	0	0	3	3	0	1	5	0	28	1	1
Espinal, Juan Jose, Yankees/S.D.	.201	62	189	35	38	58	6	1	4	44	0	13	4	53	2	30	10	1
Espinosa, Jose, Co-op I	.204	51	137	12	28	32	4	0	0	13	4	1	2	17	1	24	4	1
Estevez, Luis, Co-op I	.133	48	105	9	14	21	4	0	1	10	1	1	3	24	0	43	2	1
Evangelista, German, Cleveland	.241	60	195	26	47	63	7	3	1	25	2	1	4	26	4	41	11	10

Player, Team	Avg.	G	AB	R	H	TB	2B	3B	HR	RBI	SH	SF	HP	BB	Int. BB	SO	SB	CS
Faneyte, Reynaldo, Seattle	.207	45	145	16	30	43	4	3	1	17	1	1	1	17	0	33	3	2
Fantause, Yran, Texas/Florida	.219	56	160	22	35	45	7	0	1	13	0	1	3	27	0	28	13	1
Feliz, Julio, Texas/Florida	.270	66	226	31	61	75	11	0	1	20	2	1	7	30	2	13	8	7
Feliz, Sony, Co-op II	.197	60	223	27	44	64	5	3	3	24	0	1	0	15	0	34	5	10
Fermin, Juan, Co-op I	.000	11	1	0	0	0	0	0	0	0	0	0	0	0	0	0	0	0
Fernandez, Juan, Atlanta	.279	34	129	15	36	48	6	0	2	24	3	2	2	6	0	27	4	2
Fernandez, Nelson, Cleveland	.273	54	165	23	45	61	6	2	2	23	1	3	1	15	2	35	3	3
Fernandez, Randy, Detroit/St. Louis	.276	59	152	30	42	58	12	2	0	16	0	1	0	30	0	21	14	8
Fernandez, Reyes, Co-op II	.195	37	128	13	25	36	3	1	2	13	1	0	1	10	0	31	0	4
Ferreras, Ramon, Houston	.213	61	202	19	43	57	7	2	1	27	1	2	6	14	1	55	6	2
Figuereo, Roberto, Atlanta	.545	11	11	3	6	9	1	1	0	1	0	0	1	0	2	1	1	
Figueroa, Walter, Atlanta	.183	55	191	17	35	48	6	2	1	10	3	1	1	12	1	48	1	0
Florian, Hipolito, Toronto East	.306	55	186	40	57	63	2	2	0	25	1	3	0	31	0	12	17	5
Forsythe, Alvaro, Los Angeles I	.339	45	109	17	37	41	4	0	0	11	3	0	3	20	0	20	8	5
Galan, Manolo, Baltimore/White Sox	.250	38	132	12	33	34	1	0	0	17	1	4	1	13	2	14	0	0
Garcia, Edward, Co-op II	.140	58	186	22	26	38	6	0	2	15	5	0	2	31	0	63	4	5
Garcia, Fidel, Cleveland	.250	3	4	1	1	1	0	0	0	0	0	0	0	1	0	1	0	1
Garcia, Franklin, Milwaukee	.271	66	251	36	68	83	10	1	1	30	2	3	0	35	0	32	19	7
Garcia, Freddy, Toronto East	.293	70	249	56	73	126	13	2	12	62	2	2	2	61	3	52	5	4
Garcia, Julio, Houston	.276	68	232	46	64	71	5	1	0	25	1	2	5	44	3	25	19	8
Garcia, Luis, Atlanta	.328	43	177	41	58	73	9	3	0	25	2	3	4	5	0	16	13	4
Garcia, Marcos, Co-op I	.219	45	128	17	28	37	7	1	0	11	0	3	2	19	0	22	3	3
Garcia, Miguel, Cleveland	.271	53	170	24	46	60	8	3	0	24	2	3	3	21	5	23	7	3
Garcia, Miguel, Los Angeles II	.250	68	236	50	59	70	6	1	1	20	5	1	1	50	0	59	11	4
German, Juan Pablo, Oakland	.251	60	195	38	49	69	6	4	0	36	1	5	15	31	1	21	4	4
German, Rigoberto, Detroit/St. Louis	.260	53	150	15	39	50	9	1	0	21	0	2	3	15	0	18	5	3
German, Ruben, Yankees/San Diego	.282	69	241	48	68	88	9	1	3	45	0	3	2	48	1	31	19	8
German, Santos, California	.243	41	74	6	18	18	0	0	0	5	0	1	2	10	0	14	6	7
Gomez, Agustin, Baltimore/White Sox	.000	13	1	0	0	0	0	0	0	0	0	0	0	0	0	0	0	0
Gomez, Luis, Oakland	.163	41	92	12	15	19	4	0	0	16	3	1	0	15	0	19	0	1
Gonzales, Marino, Atlanta	.291	56	203	37	59	81	12	2	2	36	2	2	1	35	3	27	9	5
Gonzalez, Jesus, San Francisco	.246	53	175	22	43	51	4	2	0	19	1	3	0	33	3	24	16	9
Gonzalez, Juan E., Milwaukee	.250	2	4	1	1	2	1	0	0	0	1	0	0	1	0	2	0	0
Gonzalez, Singuerton, Los Angeles II	.241	68	241	45	58	68	8	1	0	24	5	4	1	47	3	46	6	5
Gonzalez, Wodiklenman, Pittsburgh	.253	63	190	20	48	65	6	1	3	33	1	3	4	22	1	12	4	1
Guerrero, Ramon, California	.211	61	185	29	39	50	7	2	0	22	1	2	5	33	0	52	14	6
Guerrero, Wilton, Los Angeles II	.387	61	225	52	87	102	7	4	0	38	7	2	2	34	1	21	15	10
Guevara, Antonio, Seattle	.313	45	163	30	51	75	13	4	1	24	1	1	4	19	0	30	14	2
Guillermo, Henry, Texas/Florida	.240	56	175	21	42	54	4	1	2	22	1	4	10	19	3	25	6	4
Gumbs, Edwin, San Francisco	.209	27	91	9	19	25	4	1	0	6	0	2	2	4	0	20	4	0
Guzman, Ismael, Detroit/St. Louis	.203	59	197	25	40	54	6	1	2	19	1	1	1	14	1	23	4	3
Henriquez, Fabio, Milwaukee	.207	8	29	3	6	7	1	0	0	6	0	0	0	6	0	3	0	1
Henriquez, Ramon, Detroit/St. Louis	.285	69	253	40	72	93	10	1	3	27	1	1	4	22	1	23	17	6
Henson, Eugene, Atlanta	.374	59	238	53	89	111	15	2	1	28	1	2	5	27	1	24	18	5
Herdosia, Harold, California	.297	65	219	34	65	93	15	2	3	34	1	2	6	36	2	21	12	8
Heredia, Confesor, Montreal	.347	51	190	31	66	100	8	1	8	40	1	1	2	20	0	15	3	5
Hernandez, Andres, Detroit/St. Louis	.228	72	259	22	59	83	15	0	3	26	0	3	4	7	0	43	1	0
Hernandez, Carlos, California	.244	21	41	4	10	10	0	0	0	0	0	0	1	6	1	10	0	1
Hernandez, Jose, New York Mets	.288	35	80	17	23	33	1	0	3	19	1	2	4	14	0	13	2	2
Hernandez, Raul, Los Angeles I	.206	52	165	24	34	38	4	0	0	13	2	2	2	11	0	31	10	2
Hernandez, Renny, Atlanta	.257	37	136	18	35	45	8	1	0	31	1	2	4	10	0	13	8	3
Hidalgo, Benardino, Detroit/St. Louis	.232	44	142	16	33	40	4	0	1	10	2	0	0	9	0	23	2	7
Hurtado, Rafael, Los Angeles II	.000	0	0	0	0	0	0	0	0	0	0	0	0	0	0	0	0	0
Jaime, Wilson, Co-op II	.175	31	97	9	17	24	3	2	0	10	2	0	4	11	0	23	0	5
Jasson, Thomas, California	.206	48	126	16	26	32	6	0	0	12	1	2	3	16	0	39	8	4
Javier, Jesus, San Francisco	.160	28	75	16	12	15	1	1	0	8	0	1	1	22	0	20	2	0
Jimenez, Daniel, New York Mets	.176	23	34	6	6	13	1	0	2	7	0	0	0	5	0	11	2	0
Jimenez, Jose, Cleveland	.206	17	34	6	7	10	3	0	0	3	0	0	1	14	0	6	0	2
Jimenez, Luis, San Francisco	.196	47	143	11	28	33	5	0	0	12	1	2	2	15	0	33	1	0
Jimenez, Ramon, Detroit/St. Louis	.122	37	82	11	10	14	1	0	1	3	0	0	1	13	0	25	1	1
Jose, David, New York Mets	.270	34	122	18	33	42	4	1	1	18	0	0	5	7	0	16	8	3
Liriano, Moises, Toronto West	.292	66	219	29	64	84	13	2	1	33	0	2	2	36	2	21	7	13
Liriano, Ramon, Milwaukee	.226	51	168	21	38	48	7	0	1	16	1	0	0	16	0	44	5	2
Lopez, Jose Louis, Los Angeles I	.214	19	56	6	12	15	3	0	0	4	1	0	0	10	0	12	2	2
Lopez, Mendy, Co-op II	.276	49	145	22	40	44	1	0	1	23	2	3	2	22	1	15	7	3
Luis, Ramon, Oakland	.224	20	49	7	11	11	0	0	0	4	0	0	2	0	0	11	2	0
Luna, Alexis, Toronto West	.250	3	12	2	3	4	1	0	0	2	0	0	0	1	0	3	2	0
Macias, Jose, Montreal	.293	61	198	58	58	71	5	1	2	23	1	3	5	60	0	11	41	18
Marcelo, Alfredo, Milwaukee	.242	70	244	18	59	69	7	0	1	31	3	0	8	35	2	41	0	4
Marquez, Felix, Seattle	.159	32	82	8	13	14	1	0	0	5	1	0	5	11	0	41	2	4
Martinez, Aristides, Atlanta	.351	48	168	31	59	79	10	2	2	40	3	1	3	30	2	14	7	3
Martinez, Carlos, San Francisco	.241	51	158	27	38	58	9	1	3	33	0	3	5	33	4	39	18	7
Martinez, Edward, Detroit/St. Louis	.196	42	92	10	18	22	4	0	0	6	3	0	2	9	0	19	2	4
Martinez, Jesus, Toronto East	.217	50	152	31	33	56	6	1	5	35	0	2	1	31	1	38	2	0
Martinez, Jonny, Cleveland	.000	19	1	0	0	0	0	0	0	0	0	0	0	0	0	1	0	0
Martinez, Jose R., Seattle	.134	35	112	11	15	16	1	0	0	4	0	0	5	26	0	49	0	4
Martinez, Juan, Toronto East	.319	54	191	47	61	94	14	5	3	39	0	5	2	22	0	42	7	3
Martinez, Leonardo, Yankees/S.D.	.224	61	192	35	43	53	5	1	1	17	0	2	0	28	0	26	12	6
Martinez, Rafael, Los Angeles II	.209	68	263	26	55	69	10	2	0	37	4	3	5	18	2	30	2	2
Martinez, Victor, Seattle	.187	49	134	12	25	41	7	0	3	14	0	4	3	15	0	22	0	1
Mata, Alexander, Los Angeles I	.236	52	174	23	41	46	5	0	0	27	4	4	3	26	0	15	9	5
Mateo, Jose, Yankees/San Diego	.290	25	62	22	18	27	2	2	1	13	0	1	0	25	0	9	9	6
Matos, Pascual, Atlanta	.328	19	58	6	19	28	4	1	1	14	0	0	1	6	0	12	0	0
Matthews, Michael, Cleveland	.257	56	183	26	47	68	9	3	1	20	0	1	2	13	4	45	11	5
Mazara, Hommy, California	.290	68	224	39	65	85	11	3	1	40	0	2	8	39	2	31	24	11
Medina, Aloer, Seattle	.181	38	94	24	17	19	0	1	0	3	1	0	4	21	1	13	21	6
Mega, Pedro, Los Angeles II	.228	47	136	34	31	37	2	2	0	13	7	1	6	25	1	32	1	2
Mejia, Fausto, Milwaukee	.000	2	2	0	0	0	0	0	0	0	0	0	0	0	0	1	0	0
Mejia, Miguel, Baltimore/White Sox	.337	51	187	42	63	77	11	0	1	31	1	3	3	30	1	19	30	10
Mejia, Ronny, Baltimore/White Sox	.303	31	89	19	27	40	8	1	1	20	0	0	1	14	0	21	0	2
Melendez, Osmin, Balt./White Sox	.325	48	123	35	40	42	2	0	0	14	5	2	2	25	0	15	9	3
Melendez, Pastor, Pittsburgh	.234	54	137	33	32	33	1	0	0	12	3	0	5	34	0	24	19	6
Mendez, Andres William, Milwaukee	.000	2	3	0	0	0	0	0	0	0	0	0	0	0	0	2	0	0
Mendez, Julio Cesar, Yankees/S.D.	.232	38	99	11	23	32	6	0	1	6	0	1	3	9	0	27	0	1

Player, Team	Avg.	G	AB	R	H	TB	2B	3B	HR	RBI	SH	SF	HP	BB	Int. BB	SO	SB	CS
Mendez, Sergio, Pittsburgh	.321	46	190	21	61	88	10	1	5	42	0	4	5	10	3	13	9	5
Mendoza, Francisco, Co-op II	.336	42	149	27	50	74	9	3	3	33	0	4	4	23	2	15	4	3
Mendoza, Jesus, Co-op I	.247	40	97	12	24	26	2	0	0	15	5	0	1	12	1	8	4	1
Meran, Jorge, Montreal	.275	48	178	24	49	77	10	0	6	30	0	1	2	12	1	42	5	1
Minaya, Alexis, Pittsburgh	.366	21	41	8	15	16	1	0	0	3	1	1	3	11	0	2	3	2
Mohamed, Edwin, Yankees/San Diego..	.297	58	209	61	62	73	7	2	0	20	1	2	0	45	3	31	17	17
Mojica, Francis, Oakland	.000	7	2	3	0	0	0	0	0	0	0	0	0	1	0	1	2
Montano, Justo, Oakland	.120	26	50	6	6	6	0	0	0	1	3	0	0	6	0	5	3	1
Montero, Cesar, Texas/Florida	.186	61	188	23	35	38	3	0	0	19	2	2	2	37	0	49	7	7
Montilla, Jose, Toronto West	.250	41	136	21	34	44	6	2	0	20	0	2	2	24	0	23	5	5
Morales, Jose, Atlanta	.261	27	92	16	24	32	8	0	0	13	1	0	0	20	0	28	3	3
Morel, Jose, Pittsburgh	.000	1	1	0	0	0	0	0	0	0	0	0	0	0	0	1	0	0
Morizo, Pablo, Co-op I	.188	36	96	12	18	26	3	1	1	13	0	0	3	16	0	29	2	2
Mosquera, Julio, Toronto West	.362	67	235	47	85	108	12	1	3	39	1	1	5	17	2	20	17	6
Mota, Alfonso, California	.315	61	200	48	63	87	16	4	0	29	0	1	1	58	2	16	27	12
Mota, Gleyde, New York Mets	.280	63	157	39	44	62	10	1	2	28	3	1	2	57	2	35	8	10
Mota, Guillermo, New York Mets	.298	70	228	49	68	102	10	3	6	40	1	5	6	28	0	40	10	11
Munoz, Juan, Pittsburgh	.269	60	130	20	35	49	8	0	2	12	3	2	10	10	0	8	4	1
Navarro, Allan, Los Angeles I	.222	59	180	25	40	52	6	3	0	16	4	5	1	30	4	26	8	6
Navas, Jose, Oakland	.189	45	122	23	23	28	1	2	0	17	0	1	0	26	1	17	2	3
Nieves, Cesar, Oakland	.190	10	21	2	4	4	0	0	0	4	0	0	1	4	0	5	0	0
Nieves, Jose Miguel, Milwaukee	.333	8	15	2	5	8	0	0	1	3	0	0	2	4	0	4	0	0
Nunez, Colacito, Co-op I	.280	37	100	17	28	32	4	0	0	16	1	3	1	20	1	19	4	3
Nunez, Isaias, Detroit/St. Louis	.208	66	245	20	51	57	4	1	0	25	0	1	4	25	0	25	4	6
Nunez, Jose, Seattle	.146	49	123	11	18	22	4	0	0	6	0	0	3	12	0	36	4	5
Nunez, Julio C., Toronto West	.000	2	2	0	0	0	0	0	0	0	0	0	0	0	0	0	0	0
Nunez, Maximo, Toronto West	.306	69	245	40	75	103	14	1	4	37	4	6	5	31	0	35	16	13
Nunez, Sergio, Co-op II	.302	62	202	49	61	75	4	5	0	30	2	2	4	31	1	21	29	11
Oliva, Carlos, San Francisco	.275	47	193	32	53	70	7	2	2	32	1	3	1	18	0	16	9	4
Oliveros, Hector, Seattle	.204	35	108	6	22	27	2	0	1	13	0	1	4	6	0	41	4	2
Ortiz, Amparo, Pittsburgh	.218	40	55	9	12	13	1	0	0	4	0	0	1	8	0	3	0	0
Oviedo, Igor, Texas/Florida	.235	58	204	22	48	57	6	0	1	24	1	2	3	26	0	26	19	7
Ozorio, Yudith, New York Mets	.257	72	241	57	62	72	6	2	0	20	3	3	7	38	0	28	62	15
Ozuna, Roberto, San Francisco	.289	36	152	34	44	54	4	3	0	13	0	1	0	30	4	6	16	6
Padilla, Rafael, Baltimore/White Sox	.268	37	138	23	37	53	11	1	1	20	0	0	1	7	0	25	1	0
Padilla, Valentin, Montreal	.128	15	39	3	5	5	0	0	0	1	0	0	0	6	0	14	0	1
Pascual, Rufino, Yankees/San Diego	.154	6	13	3	2	2	0	0	0	0	0	0	1	0	0	5	0	0
Payano, Adolfo, Co-op II	.338	59	213	51	72	92	9	4	1	27	10	1	12	34	2	22	37	22
Pedra, Carlos, Los Angeles I	.155	25	58	10	9	9	0	0	0	4	1	1	1	12	0	21	1	0
Pemberton, Juan, Montreal	.327	34	104	21	34	49	4	1	3	8	0	0	0	14	0	23	1	1
Pena, Alejandro, Cleveland	.328	67	271	49	89	117	12	2	4	32	5	2	3	21	0	23	33	13
Pena, Elvio, Co-op I	.258	46	97	17	25	35	3	2	1	12	0	0	0	33	0	14	17	12
Pena, Jesus, Montreal	.284	26	74	9	21	24	0	0	1	9	2	0	0	3	0	6	5	0
Perez, Cesar, Co-op II	.158	9	19	2	3	3	0	0	0	0	0	0	0	1	0	2	0	0
Perez, Eduardo, Atlanta	.359	41	153	50	55	61	6	0	0	13	2	2	3	39	0	17	22	8
Perez, Edward, Co-op II	.182	3	11	3	2	3	1	0	0	1	0	0	0	1	0	1	0	0
Perez, Franklin, Oakland	.118	18	34	2	4	5	1	0	0	2	0	1	3	5	0	9	0	0
Perez, Julio Cesar, Yankees/San Diego	.299	61	204	37	61	92	8	4	5	44	0	3	4	49	4	39	15	7
Perez, Luis, California	.130	14	23	2	3	3	0	0	0	0	0	0	2	0	0	6	2	0
Perez, Pablo, Yankees/San Diego	.300	46	160	30	48	67	8	4	1	29	0	2	2	17	0	24	8	2
Perez, Tomas, Montreal	.305	44	151	35	46	56	7	0	1	19	1	2	1	27	0	20	12	5
Perozo, Alberto, Atlanta	.264	45	121	26	32	41	4	1	1	13	0	1	6	24	0	16	4	5
Piters, Moises, California	.264	41	72	13	19	23	1	0	1	13	0	0	3	17	0	8	7	2
Polanco, Enohel, New York Mets	.154	31	52	9	8	12	1	0	1	4	0	0	1	9	0	6	5	3
Polanco, Felipe, Pittsburgh	.355	44	110	27	39	42	1	1	0	14	2	2	5	19	0	12	27	6
Polanco, Marino, San Francisco	.237	46	156	36	37	68	10	3	5	33	1	2	5	43	1	33	15	6
Polanco, Pedro, Co-op I	.220	51	141	17	31	37	4	1	0	8	3	0	3	16	0	22	8	8
Portes, Miguel, Yankees/San Diego	.353	69	249	61	88	119	9	5	4	48	1	2	3	34	0	18	24	13
Prensi, Dagoberto, Toronto West	.293	68	229	43	67	89	11	1	3	24	0	1	10	19	1	37	16	11
Puello, Kervin, Los Angeles I	.252	60	206	34	52	62	4	3	0	16	9	1	2	24	0	23	10	12
Puente, Roberto, Seattle	.174	43	132	16	23	33	4	0	2	12	0	2	0	21	0	54	3	1
Pulido, Francisco, Balt./White Sox	.167	10	36	2	6	6	0	0	0	3	0	1	2	1	0	7	0	0
Quintana, Eddy, Oakland	.242	49	157	26	38	56	6	0	4	20	2	3	2	26	0	30	3	1
Rafael, Ruan, Montreal	.293	53	198	28	58	95	16	0	7	41	0	3	4	9	1	49	7	3
Ramirez, Alex, Cleveland	.290	69	272	28	79	122	13	3	8	48	1	4	0	13	2	34	17	7
Ramirez, Angel, Toronto East	.325	70	283	64	92	134	14	11	2	59	0	4	5	17	1	34	10	4
Ramirez, Daniel, New York Mets	.214	62	168	24	36	44	5	0	1	26	1	4	2	24	1	32	2	9
Ramirez, Jose Luis, Pittsburgh	.256	52	168	20	43	60	8	0	3	18	1	1	2	26	1	33	4	5
Ramirez, Juan, Milwaukee	.259	45	108	12	28	33	5	0	0	16	4	1	3	15	0	12	0	0
Ramirez, Juan, New York Mets	.229	62	157	40	36	50	2	0	4	22	3	1	2	59	0	32	13	9
Ramos, Jose, Houston	.030	15	33	5	1	1	0	0	0	2	0	0	1	6	0	9	1	1
Ramos, Juan, Houston	.279	59	197	42	55	70	6	3	1	13	1	0	3	45	2	29	36	8
Ramos, Quintino, Montreal	.182	38	110	15	20	24	4	0	0	11	1	1	1	16	0	28	0	1
Restitullo, Helpy, California	.203	57	148	14	30	36	6	0	0	11	2	3	2	6	0	32	5	5
Reyes, Henry, Atlanta	.209	18	43	2	9	10	1	0	0	11	1	3	0	6	0	4	0	4
Reyes, Jose, Los Angeles I	.225	44	129	16	29	37	2	0	2	15	2	0	1	19	0	20	4	1
Reyes, Pablo, Cleveland	.300	60	233	36	70	82	8	2	0	26	2	0	0	20	0	31	8	4
Reyes, Winston, Co-op I	.198	52	162	22	32	50	3	3	3	17	0	0	3	17	0	38	8	3
Rincones, Wagner, Co-op I	.232	51	138	21	32	46	8	0	2	21	3	1	0	20	0	20	3	3
Rios, Eduardo, Los Angeles II	.310	47	184	42	57	91	13	3	5	36	0	4	1	34	1	14	6	4
Rivera, Maximo, Pittsburgh	.329	66	252	55	83	119	17	8	1	45	3	3	5	30	0	26	32	16
Rivera, Santos, Yankees/San Diego	.175	20	57	7	10	12	2	0	0	5	0	0	1	12	0	17	1	1
Robles, Rafael, Detroit/St. Louis	.310	66	213	40	66	91	13	3	2	33	0	1	1	33	1	36	7	6
Robles, Trinidad, Los Angeles I	.218	44	124	26	27	37	5	1	1	16	0	3	4	39	0	26	10	3
Rodriguez, Enrique, Houston	.222	66	239	46	53	66	5	1	2	21	5	2	4	34	3	46	12	4
Rodriguez, Fernando, Texas/Florida	.215	63	181	33	39	47	6	1	0	21	2	4	6	36	3	26	13	10
Rodriguez, Francisco, Co-op I	.318	60	170	29	54	71	5	3	2	21	2	0	5	22	0	27	3	5
Rodriguez, Juan, Texas/Florida	.221	41	104	11	23	26	3	0	0	9	3	2	0	22	0	20	5	2
Rodriguez, Luis, Los Angeles I	.261	63	199	23	52	76	5	5	3	28	5	1	1	37	1	48	5	10
Rodriguez, Orlando, Montreal	.258	31	97	17	25	33	2	0	2	15	1	1	2	11	0	17	1	1
Rodriguez, Ricardo, Co-op I	.200	19	10	0	2	2	0	0	0	0	0	0	0	0	0	4	0	1
Rojas, Freddy, New York Mets	.362	71	229	59	83	134	11	2	12	63	1	3	2	52	3	35	11	7
Rojas, Jose, Montreal	.272	52	151	39	41	54	5	1	2	14	4	2	1	31	0	17	13	7
Rojas, Roberto, Pittsburgh	.208	26	48	5	10	16	1	1	1	13	0	0	2	8	0	14	0	1

Player, Team	Avg.	G	AB	R	H	TB	2B	3B	HR	RBI	SH	SF	HP	BB	Int. BB	SO	SB	CS
Romano, Manuel, Baltimore/White Sox.	.057	21	35	2	2	3	1	0	0	0	0	0	0	2	0	12	0	0
Rondon, Alexander, Oakland	.283	33	99	14	28	35	4	0	1	17	1	1	0	17	0	13	1	1
Rosario, Felix, Toronto West	.304	70	260	67	79	116	13	3	6	40	1	3	8	38	0	40	47	10
Rosario, Juan, Houston	.253	67	229	38	58	66	6	1	0	26	1	3	8	20	0	16	13	11
Rosario, Juan, Texas/Florida	.240	67	221	29	53	68	10	1	1	23	3	1	5	37	2	16	18	14
Rosario, Manuel, Detroit/St. Louis	.258	14	31	5	8	9	1	0	0	3	0	0	0	1	0	5	0	0
Rosario, Reynaldo, Texas/Florida	.218	62	225	31	49	64	7	4	0	17	1	0	3	31	0	33	13	8
Rosario, Soltero, Milwaukee	.200	64	220	18	44	51	7	0	0	16	3	2	4	10	0	53	1	3
Ruiz, Cesar, Detroit/St. Louis	.273	18	44	4	12	18	0	0	2	12	0	1	0	6	0	5	1	0
Salazar, Elias, San Francisco	.262	45	145	29	38	45	3	2	0	21	1	2	2	49	1	24	9	4
Salazar, Tomas, Baltimore/White Sox ..	.297	25	64	6	19	19	0	0	0	8	0	0	0	13	0	10	1	0
Salcedo, Elias, Co-op II	.217	56	203	40	44	71	10	1	5	26	1	2	2	32	2	44	11	7
Salomon, Domingo, Atlanta	.239	30	88	22	21	22	1	0	0	11	3	1	3	18	0	15	4	6
Salvador, Diego, Los Angeles II	.268	19	71	10	19	30	6	1	1	13	0	2	0	2	0	10	2	0
Salvador, Freddy, Balt./White Sox	.261	45	134	20	35	41	6	0	0	18	1	2	1	21	0	17	0	1
Sanchez, Carlos, Pittsburgh	.202	54	124	18	25	27	2	0	0	10	3	1	1	12	0	21	10	7
Sanchez, Daniel, California	.667	2	3	1	2	2	0	0	0	1	0	0	1	1	0	0	1	2
Sanchez, Marcos, Yankees/San Diego..	.261	43	111	16	29	44	8	2	1	19	0	1	1	28	0	26	3	4
Sanchez, Nelson, Toronto West	.282	36	71	15	20	22	2	0	0	5	0	3	0	20	0	12	2	4
Santa, Milciades, Toronto West	.267	49	135	22	36	43	5	1	0	18	1	3	1	24	0	19	9	8
Santana, Angel, San Francisco	.361	14	36	5	13	16	3	0	0	6	1	0	0	7	0	4	9	2
Santana, Francisco, Co-op II	.241	52	162	24	39	54	9	0	2	17	1	0	7	25	0	61	2	5
Santana, Francisco, Oakland	.123	30	73	13	9	11	2	0	0	8	0	2	4	21	0	30	1	2
Santana, Francisco, Pittsburgh	.318	64	214	50	68	75	3	2	0	15	6	0	5	35	0	8	31	21
Santana, Julio, Texas/Florida	.229	17	48	7	11	19	2	0	0	2	0	0	1	11	0	8	0	2
Santana, Junior, California	.235	36	68	11	16	20	4	0	0	6	0	0	3	8	0	14	3	2
Santana, Miguel, Pittsburgh	.144	47	104	18	15	16	1	0	0	4	1	0	2	13	0	21	6	5
Santana, Ramon, Houston	.267	68	258	28	69	94	14	1	3	48	0	2	3	34	3	52	12	8
Santos, Geovanny, Cleveland	.111	31	72	10	8	9	1	0	0	8	3	0	0	4	1	3	3	2
Segura, Juan, Pittsburgh	.241	60	220	25	53	61	5	0	1	25	2	3	2	18	0	31	6	10
Selmo, Feliberto, Atlanta	.316	35	136	46	43	55	7	1	1	24	4	0	5	22	0	4	18	2
Serrano, Nestor, Seattle	.258	62	217	29	56	84	16	0	4	36	0	1	1	24	1	25	10	5
Sierra, Hector, Montreal	.235	17	34	6	8	9	1	0	0	7	0	1	0	13	0	10	0	1
Sierra, Roberto, Houston	.353	9	17	4	6	6	0	0	0	2	0	0	1	5	0	1	0	1
Sierra, Santos, Montreal	.254	45	142	28	36	59	7	2	4	22	0	2	4	33	0	43	6	3
Simon, Randal, California	.279	11	43	7	12	20	4	2	0	7	0	1	1	5	1	6	1	0
Solano, Fausto, Toronto East	.338	65	260	75	88	110	9	2	3	44	3	1	0	45	0	28	38	11
Soriano, Carlos Juan, New York Mets ..	.309	69	181	45	56	87	6	2	7	39	3	4	2	39	1	22	8	4
Soriano, Freddy, Oakland	.288	65	208	63	60	82	8	1	4	25	0	2	19	57	2	31	30	9
Soriano, Jose, Oakland	.316	60	209	42	66	83	12	1	1	41	1	5	5	29	0	37	17	6
Soriano, Juan Carlos, New York Mets	.233	50	120	23	28	31	3	0	0	13	2	1	3	32	0	18	4	4
Sosa, Ramon, Cleveland	.242	63	198	32	48	74	11	0	5	33	2	5	7	21	1	42	2	1
Soto, Manuel, Baltimore/White Sox	.318	63	245	64	78	93	7	4	0	31	3	0	8	37	0	35	27	13
Soto, Marcos, Detroit/St. Louis	.000	1	0	0	0	0	0	0	0	0	0	0	0	0	0	0	0	0
Soto, Wilson, Milwaukee	.123	34	65	8	8	8	0	0	0	6	3	2	0	10	0	15	3	3
Suero, Jose, Milwaukee	.000	5	9	0	0	0	0	0	0	1	0	0	0	3	0	7	0	0
Suero, Miguel, Milwaukee	.200	43	95	21	19	19	0	0	0	9	2	0	2	33	0	15	4	6
Tapia, Leonard, Co-op I	.130	44	100	6	13	14	1	0	0	2	6	0	1	15	0	27	6	5
Tatis, Adriano, Atlanta	.167	22	54	10	9	9	0	0	0	2	3	0	0	7	0	14	0	2
Tatis, Milton, Yankees/San Diego	.348	9	23	4	8	8	0	0	0	2	0	0	0	7	0	3	1	0
Thomas, Juan, San Francisco	.302	63	199	52	60	78	8	2	2	38	0	2	2	57	4	22	18	4
Tinoco, Luis, Seattle	.266	59	184	23	49	72	9	1	4	24	0	2	1	39	0	52	8	6
Torrez, Derrick, Milwaukee	.183	57	175	18	32	38	4	1	0	10	4	3	6	22	1	42	4	1
Tremols, Johnny, Pittsburgh	.260	35	50	5	13	14	1	0	0	4	2	0	1	5	1	1	0	3
Trinidad, Manuel, Co-op I	.209	40	86	18	18	21	3	0	0	7	3	1	1	18	0	16	5	4
Tunon, Roque, Baltimore/White Sox	.291	43	117	19	34	42	5	0	1	16	1	1	3	17	1	27	8	8
Ulises, Pedro, Baltimore/White Sox......	.287	43	129	28	37	54	7	2	2	22	1	2	3	11	0	33	15	5
Uribe, Dilone, Los Angeles II	.304	58	194	23	59	70	7	2	0	37	1	4	2	30	3	25	2	3
Valdespino, Jose, Toronto West	.263	47	114	16	30	35	2	0	1	7	1	1	0	16	0	7	4	3
Valdez, Dario, Co-op II	.153	23	59	6	9	10	1	0	0	4	4	1	2	6	0	8	2	4
Valdez, Guillermo, Atlanta	.386	57	207	55	80	118	8	12	2	44	1	2	0	41	3	19	23	8
Valdez, Sencion, Toronto West	.314	46	169	25	53	67	8	0	2	32	0	3	0	23	1	22	16	8
Vargas, Cesar, Toronto West	.163	36	43	7	7	10	1	1	0	4	1	1	1	8	0	15	4	2
Vargas, Franklin, California	.190	39	84	19	16	17	1	0	0	10	0	0	4	28	0	13	9	9
Vargas, Julio, Oakland	.320	65	244	54	78	109	21	2	2	42	0	3	1	34	0	32	25	6
Vasquez, Diomedes, Toronto East	.000	2	1	2	0	0	0	0	0	0	0	0	0	1	0	1	0	0
Vasquez, Leepergey, Atlanta	.304	38	148	32	45	59	12	1	0	30	0	1	0	31	4	18	4	5
Vasquez, Pedro, Yankees/San Diego	.000	1	1	0	0	0	0	0	0	0	0	0	0	0	0	0	0	0
Veras, Gabriel, Co-op I	.217	53	143	15	31	41	8	1	0	13	3	0	3	14	2	38	7	7
Vicioso, Francisco, Texas/Florida	.215	65	219	32	47	60	6	2	1	22	1	6	8	19	3	29	15	2
Villalona, Kadill, Toronto East	.667	2	3	1	2	2	0	0	0	4	0	0	2	0	1	0	0	1
Vizcaino, Julian, California	.182	4	11	2	2	2	0	0	0	0	0	0	0	3	0	0	1	0
Wilson, Hipolito, Pittsburgh	.283	42	113	19	32	45	8	1	1	12	2	2	2	14	0	19	6	6
Zapata, Jose, Montreal	.277	47	159	25	44	56	6	3	0	16	1	2	2	9	0	20	6	6
Zerpa, Mauro, Baltimore/White Sox	.286	49	168	28	48	57	9	0	0	16	2	1	4	20	0	15	8	6

PITCHING

TEAM

Team	ERA	G	CG	ShO	Sv.	IP	H	R	ER	HR	HB	BB	Int. BB	SO	WP	Bk.
Toronto East	1.78	70	5	12	27	601.0	411	165	119	16	22	282	3	551	42	4
Atlanta	2.05	69	12	7	18	623.2	490	237	142	4	27	271	22	383	28	27
Los Angeles II	2.68	72	0	1	15	654.1	488	259	195	22	45	350	16	510	36	4
Cleveland	3.06	72	13	4	10	634.1	577	323	216	10	37	277	13	364	42	11
Co-op II	3.33	71	2	2	25	631.2	585	373	234	15	17	350	17	420	57	4
San Francisco	3.39	69	17	2	14	605.1	576	341	228	10	35	301	11	389	42	17
Oakland	3.55	70	18	5	14	580.1	567	314	230	17	33	271	3	333	50	9
Pittsburgh	3.76	70	7	2	15	605.0	599	346	253	19	23	302	7	332	40	21
Yankees/San Diego	4.03	71	13	3	17	598.0	567	343	268	16	33	306	2	358	37	7
Los Angeles I	4.09	70	5	6	15	588.1	571	369	268	18	41	361	0	483	71	3
California	4.11	69	5	0	5	594.0	580	458	271	4	35	398	23	297	56	36

Team	ERA	G	CG	ShO	Sv.	IP	H	R	ER	HR	HB	BB	Int. BB	SO	WP	Bk.
Baltimore/White Sox	4.49	68	4	0	19	606.0	561	415	302	34	66	425	15	443	78	37
New York Mets	4.61	71	10	3	11	575.2	597	384	295	22	56	434	8	363	61	12
Seattle	4.75	70	2	2	10	583.1	593	405	308	28	36	399	17	317	58	9
Houston	4.77	68	6	3	13	584.2	661	433	310	9	38	338	8	252	41	29
Texas/Florida	4.78	69	13	0	4	572.2	623	443	304	12	57	362	3	349	65	37
Toronto West	4.84	70	6	2	10	587.0	603	436	316	16	40	409	4	283	43	8
Montreal	4.93	70	12	3	13	578.0	566	440	315	38	76	428	8	345	83	20
Detroit/St. Louis	5.21	72	15	5	5	595.1	710	515	355	21	41	377	19	354	63	8
Milwaukee	5.21	70	12	1	7	571.2	661	486	331	28	38	325	3	345	73	8
Co-op I	5.31	71	8	1	5	595.0	769	558	351	25	53	334	14	340	80	8

INDIVIDUAL

(Leading qualifiers for earned-run average leadership)

Pitcher, Team	W	L	Pct.	ERA	G	GS	CG	GF	ShO	Sv.	IP	H	R	ER	HR	HB	BB	Int. BB	SO	WP
Veras, Dario, Los Angeles II	7	1	.875	0.89	26	0	0	23	0	7	61.0	34	11	6	0	3	15	7	54	1
Perez, Erick, Toronto East	6	0	1.000	0.97	20	3	0	13	0	5	64.2	39	8	7	1	3	25	0	51	2
Lopez, Freddy, Toronto East	9	1	.900	1.20	13	13	1	0	0	0	74.2	51	17	10	2	0	38	0	58	7
Yan, Esteban, Atlanta	12	3	.800	1.32	16	16	7	0	4	0	115.2	85	37	17	1	2	23	2	86	3
Hurtado, Edwin, Toronto East	11	0	1.000	1.36	16	15	2	1	1	0	92.1	65	17	14	2	1	37	0	110	2
Rodriguez, Jose, Atlanta	9	1	.900	1.43	16	16	2	0	1	0	107.0	77	38	17	0	1	26	1	86	1
Mendoza, Marcos, Los Angeles II.	9	2	.818	1.51	15	5	0	2	0	0	59.2	38	17	10	3	2	28	2	81	5
Delgado, Jesus, Toronto East	10	1	.909	1.63	16	13	2	0	2	1	88.0	63	27	16	3	4	38	0	85	5
Avila, Edwin, California	6	2	.750	1.63	16	9	2	5	0	0	71.2	43	25	13	0	5	31	3	45	1
Urena, Bernardo, San Francisco..	12	4	.750	1.77	18	15	8	3	1	0	122.0	100	30	24	2	0	15	2	56	3
Rosado, Jose, Atlanta	7	3	.700	1.77	16	15	2	1	2	1	101.2	79	35	20	0	2	31	3	51	1

Departmental leaders: G—J.S. Aybar, 36; W—Sandy Castillo, Urena, E. Yan, 12; L—Mesa, Sabino, 10; Pct.—Hurtado, 1.000; GS—Taveras, 17; CG—Acosta, 9; GF—A. Lopez, 29; ShO—E. Yan, 4; Sv.—A. Lopez, 20; IP—Taveras, 131.0; H—A. Alvarez, 132; R—A. Alvarez, 94; ER—A. Alvarez, 59; HR—Sanchez, 14; HB—Zayas, 16; BB—Oreposa, 83; IBB—F. Cruz, D. Veras, Leger, 7; SO—Hurtado, 110; WP—J. Gomez, 21.

(All pitchers—listed alphabetically)

Pitcher, Team	W	L	Pct.	ERA	G	GS	CG	GF	ShO	Sv.	IP	H	R	ER	HR	HB	BB	Int. BB	SO	WP
Abreu, Pedro, Pittsburgh	7	4	.636	2.01	16	10	2	3	0	0	71.2	58	24	16	3	1	19	1	45	4
Acevedo, Milton, Co-op II	5	2	.714	2.08	10	10	0	0	0	0	56.1	39	20	13	2	1	41	0	59	5
Acosta, Roberto, Oakland	11	3	.786	1.84	16	15	9	1	1	0	117.1	100	34	24	1	5	18	0	66	1
Adames, Jaime, Montreal	1	1	.500	6.11	7	1	0	3	0	0	17.2	14	17	12	0	3	22	0	13	4
Agromonte, Freddy, L.A. II	2	2	.500	4.73	12	9	0	1	0	0	45.2	42	29	24	1	6	39	0	23	2
Albino, Eleazar, Los Angeles II	0	0	.000	2.70	13	0	0	5	0	0	16.2	16	5	5	0	2	6	2	9	1
Alcantara, Miguel, Co-op II	3	2	.600	6.27	15	0	0	5	0	1	33.0	45	28	23	1	0	23	5	14	2
Alexis, Julio, Det./St. Louis	3	5	.375	3.24	21	8	2	10	1	1	77.2	79	47	28	4	7	29	4	28	3
Almanzar, Carlos, Toronto East..	10	0	1.000	2.01	13	11	2	1	1	1	67.0	45	26	15	2	3	31	0	60	8
Almonte, Elvio, Cleveland	0	1	.000	7.97	12	1	0	5	0	0	20.1	29	19	18	0	1	15	0	5	0
Almonte, Romulo, Houston	0	0	.000	5.93	17	3	0	8	0	0	44.0	59	39	29	1	2	34	0	11	5
Altagracia, Jose, New York Mets.	0	0	.000	36.00	3	0	0	1	0	0	1.0	1	9	4	0	3	6	0	1	1
Alvarez, Angelo, Co-op I	2	7	.222	6.81	21	12	1	6	1	0	78.0	132	94	59	4	7	45	0	20	10
Alvarez, Luis, Balt./White Sox..	0	0	.000	9.74	12	0	0	4	0	0	20.1	29	33	22	5	1	17	0	8	4
Alvarez, Marcos, Det./St. Louis..	1	3	.250	5.24	19	3	1	11	0	1	52.1	69	53	34	4	5	43	1	36	5
Aquino, Juan, Montreal	0	2	.000	2.57	2	2	0	0	0	0	7.0	4	6	2	0	0	4	0	3	0
Aquino, Julio, Los Angeles II	9	0	1.000	2.07	14	11	0	1	0	0	69.2	56	23	16	2	4	26	0	39	2
Arias, Alfredo, Toronto East	1	0	1.000	6.75	4	2	0	0	0	0	10.2	4	8	8	1	0	22	0	8	4
Arias, Wadner, Milwaukee	1	6	.143	5.00	8	8	1	0	0	0	45.0	52	33	25	4	2	30	1	39	15
Ariaz, Alejandro, Texas/Florida..	5	8	.385	4.30	15	9	2	4	0	0	83.2	87	61	40	0	6	34	1	41	6
Arvelo, Luis Antonio, Milw.	1	3	.250	6.07	16	4	2	7	0	0	40.0	53	49	27	2	5	35	0	20	7
Astacio, Lermon, New York Mets.	0	1	.000	18.00	1	1	0	0	0	0	1.0	4	2	2	0	0	0	0	0	0
Avila, Edwin, California	6	2	.750	1.63	16	9	2	5	0	0	71.2	43	25	13	0	5	31	3	45	1
Ayala, Fernando, Los Angeles I..	5	6	.455	4.33	17	16	2	0	0	0	89.1	94	53	43	0	3	40	0	77	15
Aybar, Jose Soriano, NYM	7	5	.583	3.28	36	0	0	24	0	5	71.1	67	35	26	7	5	44	3	47	13
Aybar, Manuel, Det./St. Louis	1	0	1.000	0.00	1	0	0	0	0	0	3.0	1	0	0	0	0	3	1	1	0
Baez, Homer, Pittsburgh	1	1	.500	6.56	14	0	0	5	0	1	19.2	15	14	14	1	2	11	0	12	0
Balbuena, Roberto, S. Francisco..	6	6	.500	3.63	23	11	5	8	0	4	91.2	99	63	37	6	10	46	1	57	12
Barrera, Enrique, California	2	3	.400	6.12	13	2	0	7	0	0	32.1	54	34	22	0	1	19	3	17	1
Batista, Mario, Pittsburgh	0	0	.000	7.50	8	4	0	0	0	0	12.2	18	15	10	0	2	5	0	7	1
Batista, Onesimo, Yankees/S.D...	0	2	.000	7.10	4	4	0	0	0	0	6.0	7	9	5	1	0	12	0	6	4
Bautista, Jorge, Los Angeles I ...	6	3	.667	2.92	15	13	1	2	1	1	77.0	58	32	25	3	3	36	0	68	4
Bautista, Juan, Atlanta	1	0	1.000	0.77	7	0	0	3	0	1	11.2	7	2	1	0	0	7	0	10	0
Bele, Roble, Texas/Florida	1	7	.125	5.92	13	11	2	0	0	0	65.1	90	52	43	2	4	27	0	18	3
Belioso, Chester, Yankees/S.D. ..	5	3	.625	3.96	14	14	4	0	0	0	81.2	77	41	36	1	3	44	0	44	5
Betancourt, Damaso, L.A. I	1	3	.250	5.26	26	0	0	21	0	6	41.0	33	26	24	1	3	40	0	44	5
Bonilla, Danny, Co-op I	0	0	.000	15.75	1	0	0	1	0	0	4.0	13	11	7	1	2	1	0	2	0
Bonilla, Denny Brito, Seattle	5	4	.556	2.77	15	9	0	2	0	1	68.0	60	27	21	2	3	24	0	28	2
Brazoban, Delfin, Toronto West ..	2	5	.286	7.52	25	0	0	12	0	0	61.0	65	61	51	4	3	66	0	33	6
Brazoban, Omar, Oakland	0	1	.000	16.89	2	0	0	0	0	0	5.1	6	11	10	1	1	6	0	3	2
Brito, Herman, Milwaukee	0	0	.000	0.00	1	0	0	1	0	0	1.0	1	0	0	0	1	1	0	0	0
Brito, Jose, Milwaukee	2	8	.200	3.57	12	11	9	0	3	0	78.0	86	51	31	3	0	43	0	52	7
Caminero, Jose, Co-op II	3	1	.750	1.78	7	6	1	0	0	0	35.1	26	17	7	0	8	20	2	20	6
Cardona, Isbel, Toronto West	4	3	.571	4.02	14	14	0	0	0	0	69.1	56	41	31	0	3	58	0	31	4
Carmona, Roberto, Seattle	3	4	.429	7.07	16	9	0	3	0	0	54.2	67	50	43	3	6	46	0	33	1
Carrasquel, Domingo, Tor. West..	0	1	.000	36.00	2	0	0	0	0	0	1.0	3	4	4	0	0	3	0	0	1
Carrion, Jose, Montreal	2	4	.333	9.08	15	5	0	3	0	0	34.2	43	52	35	3	5	46	0	20	6
Carrion, Jose, Texas/Florida	2	3	.400	5.01	15	3	1	8	0	1	46.2	58	43	26	3	2	31	0	12	3
Castillo, Jose, Texas/Florida	1	1	.500	11.90	7	2	0	2	0	0	15.0	17	18	17	1	1	20	0	5	2
Castillo, Miguel, Balt./White Sox.	7	2	.778	3.58	14	9	0	1	0	0	60.1	40	41	24	3	11	52	0	59	12
Castillo, Sandy, Atlanta	12	1	.923	1.85	15	15	1	0	0	0	87.2	86	24	18	3	3	32	0	33	3
Castillo, Santo, Toronto West	3	2	.600	2.41	12	9	4	1	1	0	59.2	59	26	16	0	2	19	1	29	4
Castro, Daniel, Seattle	2	5	.286	4.73	13	13	1	0	0	0	64.2	62	46	34	8	6	35	1	28	2
Catedral, Raul, New York Mets	0	0	.000	16.17	1	0	0	0	0	0	1.2	3	3	3	0	0	2	0	2	1
Chalas, Basilio, Toronto West	2	4	.333	3.42	16	13	0	2	0	0	68.1	49	39	26	1	1	64	0	50	5
Charles, Israel, Co-op II	1	6	.143	3.91	16	14	0	0	0	0	71.1	70	50	31	0	4	42	0	35	5
Chevalier, Marino, Cleveland	1	2	.333	4.65	23	1	0	13	0	2	40.2	33	28	21	1	4	34	3	18	10
Colomet, Jesus, Co-op II	8	5	.615	3.93	29	0	0	10	0	2	66.1	65	41	29	1	0	29	4	30	3

Pitcher, Team	W	L	Pct.	ERA	G	GS	CG	GF	ShO	Sv.	IP	H	R	ER	HR	HB	BB	Int. BB	SO	WP
Colon, Daniel, Milwaukee	3	5	.375	5.06	33	5	0	17	0	1	87.0	104	68	49	0	9	51	0	69	19
Contrera, Jorge M., Balt/WS	0	2	.000	3.00	6	0	0	3	0	1	12.0	11	8	4	1	0	7	0	4	2
Cordoba, Luis, Yankees/S.D.	2	6	.250	5.84	13	12	1	1	0	0	57.0	60	54	37	2	5	50	0	32	3
Coronado, Osvaldo, NY Mets	4	6	.400	4.67	13	11	2	1	0	0	67.1	82	49	35	7	4	26	0	40	4
Cruz, Fermin, Seattle	2	3	.400	2.52	27	0	0	23	0	4	46.1	29	19	13	0	1	30	7	32	2
Cruz, Juan C., Atlanta	0	0	.000	3.00	2	0	0	2	0	0	3.0	4	1	1	0	0	0	0	1	1
Cruz, Miguel, Det./St. Louis	0	0	.000	0.00	1	0	0	0	0	0	0.0	0	0	0	0	0	1	0	0	0
DeJesus Perez, Jose, Y/SD	3	1	.750	4.23	17	5	0	6	0	1	51.0	47	26	24	1	3	34	1	25	1
DeLaCruz, Juan, Montreal	0	0	.000	0.00	1	0	0	1	0	0	1.1	0	0	0	0	0	4	0	1	0
DeLaCruz, Juan, Pittsburgh	4	5	.444	3.54	15	9	1	3	0	2	68.1	66	31	23	1	3	34	0	28	3
DeLaCruz, Kelvin, Co-op I	1	1	.500	2.31	5	1	0	3	0	0	11.2	13	6	3	0	0	8	0	9	1
DeLaCruz, Roberto, Calif.	0	0	.000	5.10	15	2	0	7	0	0	30.0	24	20	17	0	1	24	0	16	5
DeLaCruz S., Juan, Houston	1	9	.100	4.48	13	11	2	0	0	0	76.1	100	48	38	3	2	24	0	29	5
DeLanoy, Angelo, Oakland	1	2	.333	8.77	12	0	0	6	0	2	13.1	16	13	13	0	2	15	0	7	6
DeLaRosa, Dario, Houston	4	0	1.000	3.06	22	0	0	13	0	2	47.0	53	30	16	1	2	26	1	20	2
DeLeon, Andres, Cleveland	0	2	.000	4.27	8	0	0	7	0	2	6.1	10	7	3	0	0	4	1	2	0
DeLeon, Andres, Houston	0	0	.000	6.57	15	0	0	10	0	0	38.1	48	41	28	0	5	22	1	12	6
DeLeon, Ercilio, Pittsburgh	0	1	.000	4.20	3	3	0	0	0	0	15.0	15	9	7	0	1	7	0	9	2
DeLeon, Javier, Toronto West	0	5	.000	7.56	10	9	0	0	0	0	33.1	41	40	28	1	1	40	0	17	6
DeLeon, Nicanor, Atlanta	0	0	.000	3.00	3	0	0	2	1	0	3.0	2	1	1	0	1	4	0	1	2
Delgado, Jesus, Toronto East	10	1	.909	1.63	16	13	0	2	0	1	88.0	63	27	16	3	4	38	0	85	5
DeLosSantos, Alex, Tex/Fla	0	0	.000	0.00	2	0	0	2	0	0	1.2	1	0	0	0	0	1	0	2	0
DeLosSantos, Prosculo, T.W.	6	0	1.000	2.66	27	0	0	15	0	4	50.2	48	21	15	2	2	20	1	31	4
DeLosSantos, Salomon, Cal.	1	7	.125	3.99	20	9	0	5	0	0	70.0	49	47	31	0	2	51	3	36	2
Devers, Jose, Co-op I	0	0	.000	3.86	3	0	0	2	0	0	7.0	7	3	3	1	0	4	0	3	0
Diaz, Dionicio, Toronto East	4	0	1.000	2.90	18	1	0	8	0	2	43.1	31	16	14	0	4	17	0	38	2
Diaz, Javier, Co-op II	0	0	.000	0.00	1	0	0	1	0	0	0.1	0	0	0	0	0	1	0	0	0
Doval, Eliezer, Atlanta	1	0	1.000	2.18	15	0	0	9	1	4	20.2	23	11	5	0	0	9	0	12	4
D'Anda, Alfredo, California	0	3	.000	6.88	7	4	0	1	0	0	17.0	20	18	13	0	1	14	0	4	3
Encarnacion, Eliel, Los Angeles II	0	0	.000	6.26	13	1	0	3	0	0	23.0	17	18	16	1	3	32	0	20	4
Escalante, Juan, Los Angeles I	0	2	.000	3.43	10	0	0	4	0	0	18.1	21	15	7	1	1	11	0	8	0
Escobar, Elvin, Seattle	0	2	.000	3.04	8	3	0	2	0	0	23.2	21	17	8	2	1	15	0	16	6
Falcon, Dehan, Montreal	5	4	.556	4.66	12	12	2	0	0	0	63.2	78	40	33	2	7	26	1	32	6
Febles, Narciso, San Francisco	3	1	.750	4.29	19	4	0	4	0	0	58.2	48	44	28	0	4	57	0	49	9
Fereiras, Marcos, Balt./W. Sox	3	3	.500	5.19	11	8	0	1	0	0	43.1	45	37	25	3	2	28	0	23	5
Fermin, Juan, Co-op I	1	3	.250	3.69	13	0	0	11	0	2	39.0	48	29	16	2	3	14	3	26	0
Figuereo, Leonardo, Mont.	2	1	.667	4.06	16	5	0	7	0	0	55.1	46	33	25	5	7	42	0	33	11
Figueroa, Antonio, Montreal	0	1	.000	8.27	9	0	0	4	0	1	16.1	16	15	15	2	5	15	2	7	3
Figueroa, Julio, Montreal	1	8	.111	6.10	25	3	0	20	0	10	56.0	56	46	38	4	6	46	4	42	6
Figueroa, Walter, Milwaukee	0	0	.000	0.00	3	0	0	2	0	0	4.0	1	0	0	0	0	2	0	2	0
Franco, Wander, Balt./White Sox	5	3	.625	4.18	14	11	0	2	0	0	66.2	61	45	31	2	7	52	4	63	5
Garcia, Alberto, New York Mets	1	0	1.000	6.20	14	1	0	6	0	0	24.2	22	20	17	2	4	23	0	9	3
Garcia, Eusebio, Texas/Florida	2	7	.222	6.31	15	14	0	1	0	0	61.1	68	60	43	2	7	45	0	34	9
Garcia, Jose, Los Angeles II	3	1	.750	1.05	29	0	0	23	0	6	43.0	31	7	5	0	2	11	1	37	1
Garcia, Marcos, Co-op I	0	0	.000	2.84	1	0	0	1	0	0	6.1	6	2	2	0	1	2	0	2	0
Garcia, Ramon, Pittsburgh	7	2	.778	3.35	16	15	1	1	0	0	94.0	94	48	35	1	6	48	0	46	4
Garibay, Daniel, Los Angeles I	2	3	.400	3.37	10	5	1	4	1	2	32.0	20	15	12	2	5	23	0	36	1
Genao, Ramon, Pittsburgh	7	1	.875	2.31	27	4	3	21	0	7	81.2	75	28	21	0	1	15	2	48	2
Gerardo, Antonio, Toronto West	3	2	.600	1.67	6	5	0	0	0	0	37.2	25	12	7	0	3	21	0	11	5
German, Rigoberto, Det/StL	0	0	.000	3.86	4	0	0	4	0	1	2.1	2	1	1	0	0	0	0	1	0
German, Santo, California	0	0	.000	18.00	1	0	0	0	0	0	1.0	2	2	2	0	0	2	0	0	0
Giron, Emiliano, Toronto East	9	0	1.000	1.65	13	12	0	0	0	0	70.2	39	16	13	2	4	40	0	67	5
Giron, Juan, Toronto West	0	3	.000	9.31	17	2	0	10	0	0	31.0	49	43	31	0	5	35	1	12	6
Gomez, Agustin, Balt./White Sox	1	2	.333	3.00	15	0	0	10	0	5	33.0	34	12	11	1	0	23	5	28	4
Gomez, Alex, California	2	3	.400	4.67	8	5	0	2	0	0	34.2	33	23	18	0	3	17	0	22	4
Gomez, Erick, New York Mets	0	1	.000	3.64	11	0	0	9	0	1	12.1	5	5	5	0	0	12	1	8	6
Gomez, Juan, Co-op I	0	5	.000	14.69	14	7	0	3	0	0	22.2	21	44	37	0	3	53	0	14	21
Gomez, Miguel, Toronto West	2	8	.200	7.33	12	12	0	0	0	0	61.1	81	66	50	3	5	30	0	30	1
Gonzalez, Christian, Clev.	2	1	.667	3.69	15	3	0	3	0	1	39.0	35	25	16	1	1	19	0	31	4
Gonzalez, Juan, Milwaukee	4	9	.308	5.58	17	14	0	0	0	0	77.1	86	81	48	4	11	61	0	43	10
Gonzalez, Maximo, Oakland	1	0	1.000	3.28	15	4	1	6	1	3	38.1	38	26	14	0	3	27	0	12	3
Gonzalez, Teddoro, Yankees/SD	4	3	.571	3.93	21	4	0	14	0	4	68.2	64	37	30	2	3	29	1	36	2
Guerrero, Domingo, Balt/WS	4	1	.800	5.85	10	9	0	0	0	0	47.2	46	34	31	6	7	41	0	28	3
Guerrero, Edward, Pitts.	0	1	.000	15.30	9	1	0	1	0	0	10.0	15	21	17	3	0	16	0	3	0
Guilamo, Osvaldo, Texas/Florida	0	6	.000	7.68	10	6	1	2	0	0	41.0	55	52	35	2	12	34	0	13	9
Guzman, Carlos, Montreal	4	4	.500	2.97	9	7	0	0	0	0	45.1	45	29	15	0	7	17	0	17	2
Herdosia, Donald, California	1	9	.100	5.44	18	2	0	7	0	1	39.2	45	40	24	1	6	42	2	11	5
Herminio, Toribio, Los Angeles II	4	2	.667	3.17	16	6	0	4	0	0	48.1	34	23	17	3	3	31	0	29	3
Hernandez, Alvaro, Los Angeles I	6	8	.429	3.14	17	9	1	3	0	2	63.0	66	45	22	2	5	32	0	58	5
Hernandez, Etanislao, Calif.	2	4	.333	4.42	18	5	0	7	0	0	53.0	46	38	26	0	6	43	2	19	4
Hernandez, Julio, California	0	5	.000	9.42	16	5	0	4	0	0	28.2	49	53	30	1	2	48	3	12	14
Hernandez, Rafael, Oakland	0	0	.000	18.91	3	0	0	1	0	0	3.1	5	7	7	1	0	9	0	1	1
Herrera, Henry, Co-op I	1	2	.333	4.03	9	2	0	4	0	1	29.0	29	25	13	2	3	20	1	29	5
Hinetrosa, Wilfredo, Pitts.	0	0	.000	0.00	1	0	0	0	0	0	1.0	0	0	0	0	0	2	0	1	0
Hurtado, Edwin, Toronto East	11	0	1.000	1.36	16	15	2	1	1	0	92.1	65	17	14	2	1	37	0	110	2
Jimenez, Jose, Det./St. Louis	3	2	.600	6.10	18	2	0	11	0	0	48.2	68	43	33	0	2	23	1	21	4
Leger, Francisco, Atlanta	1	4	.200	4.08	17	1	0	8	1	4	39.2	37	25	18	0	2	35	7	17	1
Leonardo, Ricardo, S. Francisco	9	3	.750	2.86	16	10	2	2	0	0	85.0	91	45	27	0	2	32	6	46	5
Linares, Juan Ramon, NYM	7	3	.700	5.07	18	12	1	2	0	0	76.1	73	46	43	5	4	51	0	63	3
Linares, Roman, New York Mets	5	5	.500	4.03	15	15	5	0	2	0	84.2	92	47	38	6	2	18	1	40	3
Liquet, Wilton, Los Angeles II	7	2	.778	1.85	13	12	0	0	0	0	82.2	51	25	17	3	9	21	1	60	2
Lopez, Andres, Co-op II	2	1	.667	1.16	33	0	0	29	0	20	46.2	39	13	6	0	4	17	2	49	4
Lopez, Freddy, Toronto East	9	1	.900	1.20	13	13	1	0	0	0	74.2	51	17	10	2	0	38	0	58	7
Maldonado, Rosendo, Hou.	6	5	.545	3.92	14	14	1	0	1	0	75.2	68	43	33	1	4	45	0	35	6
Malena, Juan, Cleveland	4	5	.444	3.12	17	11	0	3	0	0	75.0	65	41	26	2	7	39	2	50	3
Manon, Julio, Det./St. Louis	0	5	.000	7.58	20	6	1	5	0	1	59.1	85	88	50	2	4	66	1	40	13
Marmolejos, Julio, Seattle	0	1	.000	9.58	12	1	0	4	0	0	20.2	35	28	22	1	7	23	0	11	5
Marte, Francis, Houston	1	1	.500	5.68	5	4	0	0	0	0	19.0	20	15	12	0	2	10	0	10	1
Martinez, Fausto, Co-op I	3	7	.300	5.29	20	12	1	5	0	1	83.1	106	70	49	3	3	41	1	41	6
Martinez, Gustavo, Los Angeles I.	5	3	.625	2.29	18	10	0	5	0	2	82.1	78	43	21	1	3	34	0	63	6
Martinez, Johnny, Cleveland	7	3	.700	2.25	19	16	3	2	2	0	108.0	98	46	27	2	7	51	2	92	5
Martinez, Julio, Pittsburgh	1	4	.200	7.36	22	3	0	10	0	2	33.0	42	30	27	0	1	38	2	10	6
Martinez, Osvaldo, Det/StL	0	2	.000	5.40	6	1	0	3	0	1	15.0	18	14	9	0	0	10	1	7	1
Mateo, Francisco, Milw.	0	2	.000	10.80	4	3	0	1	0	0	8.1	15	13	10	0	2	5	1	5	0

Pitcher, Team	W	L	Pct.	ERA	G	GS	CG	GF	ShO	Sv.	IP	H	R	ER	HR	HB	BB	Int. BB	SO	WP
Matos, Jorge, Co-op II	0	1	.000	4.50	1	1	0	0	0	0	4.0	6	6	2	0	0	3	0	4	0
Mejia, Fausto, Milwaukee	0	7	.000	8.24	11	7	1	4	0	1	45.1	66	49	40	6	1	17	0	19	2
Mejia, Jhovanny, Seattle	2	3	.400	4.05	24	0	0	10	0	5	57.2	67	34	26	4	2	15	5	33	4
Mejia, Juan P., California	1	5	.167	2.89	16	9	1	5	0	3	56.0	52	38	18	0	2	33	2	50	7
Mena, Jose, Co-op I	1	9	.100	4.08	15	11	2	3	0	0	79.1	103	69	36	6	9	29	3	38	6
Mendez, William, Milwaukee	2	8	.200	4.68	14	14	2	0	1	0	82.2	89	57	43	4	2	36	0	46	5
Mendoza, Jesus, Co-op I	0	0	.000	5.39	1	0	0	0	0	0	1.2	3	2	1	0	1	1	0	2	1
Mendoza, Juan, Atlanta	1	1	.500	4.09	15	6	0	5	2	0	33.0	18	16	15	0	13	31	0	24	4
Mendoza, Marcos, Los Angeles II.	9	2	.818	1.51	15	5	0	2	0	0	59.2	38	17	10	3	2	28	2	81	5
Mendoza, Ramiro, Yankees/S.D.	10	2	.833	2.29	15	15	5	0	0	0	109.2	93	37	28	3	3	28	0	79	3
Mercedes, Hector, Houston	6	3	.667	2.83	23	0	0	22	2	9	41.1	38	22	13	0	4	20	4	35	2
Mercedes, Roberto, S. Francisco	1	1	.500	11.70	7	4	0	2	0	0	12.1	11	28	16	1	2	32	0	5	2
Mesa, Rafael, Cleveland	4	10	.286	3.96	19	14	3	4	0	0	100.0	96	61	44	2	6	33	1	56	6
Millan, Alejandro, Balt./W. Sox	0	1	.000	80.60	1	1	0	0	0	0	0.2	3	6	6	0	0	4	0	0	3
Miranda, Walter, Texas/Florida	0	1	.000	5.94	8	3	0	3	0	1	16.2	14	14	11	0	5	10	0	9	4
Mohamed, Edwin, Yankees/S.D.	0	0	.000	0.00	1	0	0	1	0	0	0.2	0	0	0	0	0	1	0	1	0
Mojica, Francis, Oakland	3	1	.750	1.36	18	1	0	11	0	4	26.1	14	11	4	1	1	22	2	21	6
Mojica, Jorge, New York Mets	0	0	.000	3.17	5	0	0	2	0	0	5.2	5	2	2	1	1	1	0	5	0
Montano, Lenny, Atlanta	1	3	.250	3.29	16	0	0	6	2	1	27.1	22	14	10	1	2	22	1	21	1
Montero, Olmedo, Co-op II	1	3	.250	7.67	16	2	0	8	0	0	27.0	36	35	23	2	0	32	2	11	8
Mora, Nelson, Seattle	2	5	.286	6.39	15	4	0	3	0	0	43.2	59	36	31	3	2	39	3	15	2
Morales, Nicolas, Atlanta	3	4	.429	2.35	22	0	0	16	1	6	46.0	36	17	12	1	2	20	6	20	4
Morel, Jose, Pittsburgh	3	3	.500	3.60	16	1	0	4	0	0	25.0	25	20	10	1	2	16	0	14	2
Morel, Rafael, Oakland	6	1	.857	2.22	11	10	1	1	0	0	61.0	60	24	15	0	2	21	1	37	2
Morel, Ramon, Pittsburgh	2	0	1.000	1.06	3	3	0	0	0	0	17.0	12	2	2	0	0	7	0	9	2
Naveda, Richard, Balt./W. Sox	0	0	.000	6.88	12	0	0	7	0	0	17.0	19	13	13	2	2	7	0	4	1
Neris, Jose, Seattle	0	0	.000	7.41	14	0	0	11	0	0	17.0	19	17	14	0	1	17	0	10	3
Newton, Geronimo, Seattle	5	6	.455	3.37	16	14	1	1	0	0	74.2	63	40	28	0	1	44	1	47	8
Nixon, Luis, Los Angeles II	2	6	.250	4.45	13	13	0	0	0	0	62.2	58	41	31	4	2	53	2	54	1
Nunez, Colacito, Co-op I	0	0	.000	0.00	1	0	0	1	0	0	1.0	0	0	0	0	0	1	0	0	0
Nunez, Julio C., Toronto West	6	2	.750	2.20	29	0	0	25	0	7	45.0	37	14	11	0	0	20	1	28	5
Nunez, Manuel, San Francisco	4	4	.500	4.06	11	11	1	0	0	0	71.0	64	40	32	0	9	32	1	60	4
Nunez, Ramon, Texas/Florida	0	0	.000	2.63	5	0	0	3	0	0	13.2	11	6	4	0	2	10	0	17	6
Oliva, Carlos, San Francisco	0	0	.000	0.00	1	1	0	0	0	0	2.0	1	0	0	0	0	3	0	1	0
Olivier, Richart, Yankees/S.D.	4	5	.444	3.83	16	8	0	7	0	1	65.2	69	43	28	0	2	34	0	31	7
Oropesa, Igor, Texas/Florida	5	5	.500	3.87	14	14	4	0	0	0	81.1	70	50	35	1	11	83	1	88	7
Ortega, Franklin, Balt./W. Sox	3	2	.600	4.07	16	2	0	7	0	1	42.0	34	23	19	1	6	35	0	29	5
Pacencia, Leonardo, Clev.	1	2	.333	2.63	19	2	0	3	0	1	37.2	30	14	11	0	1	25	1	21	4
Padilla, Valentin, Montreal	0	1	.000	3.70	7	1	0	5	0	0	17.0	18	16	7	1	1	12	0	10	3
Paniagua, Felix, Yankees/S.D.	6	1	.857	4.66	18	1	0	9	0	3	44.1	45	25	23	1	0	17	0	32	1
Paniagua, Jose L., Montreal	3	7	.300	4.15	13	13	3	0	1	0	73.2	69	50	34	5	11	46	1	60	11
Pascual, Rufino, Yankees/S.D.	0	0	.000	9.34	5	0	0	3	0	0	8.2	9	9	9	0	3	5	0	5	0
Paulino, Mario, Los Angeles II	4	2	.667	3.80	22	1	0	4	0	0	47.1	40	26	20	1	1	27	1	32	9
Peguero, Juan, San Francisco	2	0	1.000	3.00	6	6	0	0	0	0	24.0	15	9	8	0	1	22	0	23	2
Peguero, Pablo, San Francisco	5	2	.714	3.95	21	2	0	10	1	1	54.2	57	33	24	0	6	33	1	25	1
Pelaez, Sabdy, Oakland	0	0	.000	3.86	5	3	0	1	0	0	7.0	7	4	3	1	1	9	0	5	0
Pena, Andres, Pittsburgh	1	1	.500	6.15	8	3	0	4	0	0	26.1	32	25	18	3	0	15	0	8	4
Pena, Elvio, Co-op I	0	1	.000	9.00	2	0	0	1	0	0	3.0	5	5	3	0	0	1	0	1	0
Pena, Moises, New York Mets	2	1	.667	0.64	14	0	0	1	0	0	25.2	31	24	18	3	3	21	1	16	6
Perez, Angel B., California	3	5	.375	2.65	18	8	2	6	0	1	74.2	67	47	22	1	1	24	1	33	4
Perez, Bernando, New York Mets	2	1	.667	8.64	18	0	0	11	0	5	25.0	41	29	24	7	3	5	0	11	1
Perez, Edward, Co-op II	7	3	.700	2.40	18	13	0	2	0	0	90.0	80	42	24	3	3	35	1	47	8
Perez, Erick, Toronto East	6	0	1.000	0.97	20	3	0	13	0	5	64.2	39	8	7	1	3	25	0	51	2
Perez, Juan, Oakland	6	2	.750	3.17	15	6	0	6	0	2	68.0	70	30	24	3	2	28	0	43	5
Perez, Luis, California	1	0	1.000	4.66	15	2	0	5	0	0	29.0	38	28	15	1	1	12	0	12	1
Pierret, Juan, Los Angeles II	3	1	.750	2.84	12	7	0	2	0	1	44.1	34	16	14	3	4	27	0	26	2
Pimentel, Robert, Co-op II	2	3	.400	3.26	15	10	0	1	0	0	49.2	46	31	18	1	1	34	0	59	7
Polanco, Pedro, Co-op I	0	0	.000	8.31	2	0	0	2	0	0	4.1	7	4	4	0	0	1	0	2	1
Portillo, Alex, San Francisco	1	3	.250	3.95	28	1	0	20	0	8	54.2	60	35	24	1	0	21	0	32	3
Primera, Dario, Pittsburgh	5	5	.500	2.69	15	11	0	3	0	1	76.2	72	38	23	3	0	27	2	53	2
Pulido, Francisco, Balt./W. Sox	0	0	.000	0.00	1	0	0	1	0	0	1.0	0	0	0	0	0	0	0	2	0
Quiroz, Diego, Oakland	0	0	.000	1.29	4	0	0	0	0	0	7.0	7	2	1	0	2	2	0	4	1
Ramirez, Francisco, Co-op II	2	0	1.000	3.96	14	0	0	6	0	0	36.1	33	20	16	1	2	13	0	12	1
Ramirez, Jose, Balt./White Sox	0	0	.000	6.46	8	0	0	3	0	1	15.1	17	15	11	3	2	13	0	6	2
Ramirez, Juan, Milwaukee	0	0	.000	5.05	5	0	0	5	0	0	12.2	13	10	8	0	0	3	0	9	1
Ramirez, Rafael, Det./St. Louis	5	6	.455	5.03	14	14	4	0	0	0	89.1	121	66	50	2	6	20	2	41	7
Ramos, Ambiorix, Texas/Florida.	6	8	.429	2.91	29	6	3	21	0	2	105.0	106	59	34	1	4	39	1	93	11
Ramos, Cesar, Cleveland	9	6	.600	2.28	18	16	6	1	1	0	122.1	110	55	31	2	5	26	1	47	6
Rascon, Julio, Los Angeles I	1	0	1.000	3.60	11	1	0	4	0	1	25.0	23	10	10	0	2	11	0	17	7
Regalado, Alejandro, Hou.	3	4	.429	5.59	15	4	0	8	1	2	46.2	40	41	29	0	2	40	1	20	3
Regalado, Victor, Yankees/S.D.	0	1	.000	27.00	1	0	0	0	0	0	1.0	3	3	3	0	0	2	0	1	0
Reyes, Dany, Houston	0	3	.000	5.83	10	9	0	0	0	0	41.2	58	38	27	1	0	28	0	15	0
Reyes, Jose, Los Angeles I	0	0	.000	9.00	1	0	0	1	0	0	1.0	2	1	1	0	1	0	0	0	0
Reyes, Luis, Oakland	6	2	.750	4.05	14	4	0	7	0	1	46.2	45	23	21	4	2	19	0	28	6
Reynaldo G., Angel, Balt/WS	6	0	1.000	3.15	15	1	0	10	0	4	40.0	37	16	14	4	2	23	1	18	9
Reynoso, Gabriel, Toronto West	1	0	1.000	1.80	1	1	0	0	0	0	5.0	1	2	1	0	2	7	0	2	1
Rijo, Julio, California	2	2	.500	3.25	17	7	0	3	0	0	55.1	56	42	20	0	4	37	4	20	5
Rincones, Wagner, Co-op I	0	0	.000	0.00	1	0	0	1	0	1	0.1	0	0	0	0	0	0	0	0	0
Rivera, Santo, Yankees/S.D.	1	0	1.000	9.00	2	1	0	0	0	0	7.0	10	7	7	0	0	3	0	3	0
Roberts, Willy, Det./St. Louis	0	6	.000	8.22	12	7	1	2	0	0	35.0	43	49	32	1	4	46	1	17	5
Rodriguez, Alan, Houston	3	3	.500	7.38	15	5	0	1	0	0	50.0	64	60	41	1	6	42	0	21	7
Rodriguez, Jose, Atlanta	9	1	.900	1.43	16	16	2	0	1	0	107.0	77	38	17	0	1	26	1	86	1
Rodriguez, Juan, Texas/Florida	0	0	.000	6.75	1	0	0	1	0	0	4.0	10	8	3	0	0	5	0	0	1
Rodriguez, Julio, Los Angeles I	0	1	.000	5.48	11	0	0	7	0	0	21.1	24	19	13	0	2	17	0	17	5
Rodriguez, Ricardo, Co-op I	0	2	.000	7.00	12	0	0	9	0	0	27.0	47	26	21	1	2	4	0	15	0
Rojas, Ronald, Toronto West	5	6	.455	4.55	26	5	2	12	0	1	104.2	122	74	53	4	11	39	1	33	0
Romano, Manuel, Balt./W. Sox	2	0	1.000	6.03	15	3	0	8	0	2	40.1	32	32	27	1	10	35	0	18	7
Romero, Ramon, Det./St. Louis	2	6	.250	3.40	16	11	1	5	0	0	79.1	76	43	30	4	2	36	2	76	7
Romo, Guillermo, Los Angeles I	0	2	.000	3.09	8	4	0	1	0	1	20.1	10	10	7	1	3	19	0	9	5
Rosa, Roberto, Los Angeles I	1	1	.500	7.04	13	0	0	3	0	0	23.0	26	19	18	0	1	21	0	16	4
Rosado, Jose, Atlanta	7	3	.700	1.77	16	15	2	1	2	1	101.2	79	35	20	0	2	31	3	51	1
Rosario, Juan, Texas/Florida	0	0	.000	3.10	11	0	0	7	0	0	29.0	28	15	10	0	2	17	0	12	3
Rosario, Manuel, Det./St. Louis	0	0	.000	81.82	1	0	0	0	0	0	0.1	2	3	3	0	0	2	0	0	0
Rosario, Michael, Cleveland	3	4	.429	2.10	18	7	1	6	1	1	60.0	56	19	14	0	2	20	2	26	2

Pitcher, Team	W	L	Pct.	ERA	G	GS	CG	GF	ShO	Sv.	IP	H	R	ER	HR	HB	BB	Int. BB	SO	WP
Rosario, Soterio, Milwaukee........	0	1	.000	8.58	5	1	0	4	0	0	14.2	18	15	14	3	0	10	1	6	0
Ruiz, Mauricio, Balt./White Sox ..	5	3	.625	2.76	15	13	1	2	0	1	78.1	70	42	24	1	8	36	0	67	9
Ruiz, Wilmer, Los Angeles I.........	1	0	1.000	7.78	16	0	0	10	0	0	39.1	58	45	34	2	6	40	0	28	11
Sabino, Jose, Det./St. Louis.......	1	10	.091	6.78	15	8	1	4	0	0	61.0	76	62	46	2	6	48	4	30	8
Salcedo, Mateo, Pittsburgh........	0	2	.000	5.15	12	5	0	2	0	1	36.2	40	28	21	2	6	27	0	23	4
Saldana, Roberto, Cleveland.......	3	2	.600	1.80	16	1	0	12	0	3	25.0	15	8	5	0	3	11	0	16	2
Samboy, Alvaro, Milwaukee........	4	1	.800	3.62	10	6	3	3	0	2	44.2	38	27	18	6	4	25	0	33	8
Samboy, Javier, New York Mets ..	3	1	.750	2.15	15	4	1	0	0	0	46.0	38	18	11	2	1	20	1	25	4
Sanchez, Jesus, New York Mets ..	5	5	.500	4.18	15	15	1	0	0	0	81.2	86	52	38	14	4	38	1	72	9
Santa, Milciades, Toronto West....	0	1	.000	7.88	4	0	0	2	0	1	8.0	15	11	7	1	3	4	0	4	0
Santana, Domingo, Houston	4	8	.333	3.08	13	13	3	0	2	0	79.0	80	38	27	0	6	37	1	34	4
Santana, Julio, Texas/Florida	0	1	.000	3.24	4	1	0	2	0	0	8.1	8	5	3	0	1	7	0	5	1
Santana, Junior, California	0	0	.000	0.00	1	0	0	1	0	0	1.0	2	3	0	0	1	1	0	0	0
Santana, Kelvin, Seattle..............	0	0	.000	6.75	3	0	0	1	0	0	5.1	7	8	4	1	3	7	0	1	0
Santana, Manuel, Pittsburgh.......	0	2	.000	4.05	4	2	0	2	0	1	13.1	15	9	6	0	0	1	0	11	1
Santana, Marino, Co-op I............	6	9	.400	2.38	18	16	4	0	0	0	106.0	109	59	28	3	1	37	3	91	15
Santive, Antonio, Oakland	1	1	.500	5.91	10	1	0	5	0	1	21.1	28	22	14	2	5	13	0	8	0
Santos, Jose, Montreal	0	2	.000	10.50	18	1	0	9	0	0	24.0	23	36	28	5	2	45	0	6	13
Severino, Jose, Det./St. Louis......	5	6	.455	4.87	15	12	4	2	2	0	72.0	70	46	39	2	5	50	1	56	10
Severino, Ramon, New York Mets	1	0	1.000	4.01	8	6	0	1	0	0	24.2	19	18	11	4	3	17	0	10	5
Soriano, Modesto, Pittsburgh	0	0	.000	7.44	8	0	0	2	0	0	9.2	16	10	8	0	0	7	0	6	0
Sosa, Helpy, Oakland	4	5	.444	6.40	15	13	3	0	1	0	70.1	90	67	50	3	5	25	0	34	11
Suero, Jose, Milwaukee	4	4	.500	4.28	24	3	1	17	0	5	75.2	77	60	36	2	6	32	0	35	7
Suriel, Rosendo, New York Mets ..	2	3	.400	5.92	13	6	0	3	0	0	27.1	29	26	18	4	2	22	0	14	2
Tapia, Leonardo, Co-op I	0	1	.000	5.90	3	0	0	1	0	0	10.2	5	8	7	0	2	9	0	6	2
Tavarez, Jose, Co-op I................	1	8	.111	7.36	21	10	0	4	0	0	66.0	91	88	54	1	14	59	2	34	11
Taveras, Roberto, Montreal	11	3	.786	2.12	19	17	7	1	2	1	131.0	117	46	31	6	5	50	0	82	8
Tejada, Juan, Houston	0	1	.000	5.09	7	4	0	0	0	0	23.0	25	14	13	1	2	9	0	9	0
Tejeda, Manuel, Balt./White Sox..	6	7	.462	3.78	18	11	3	6	0	4	88.0	81	54	37	1	8	48	5	86	7
Torres, Dilson, Toronto East........	2	0	1.000	1.61	25	0	0	25	0	14	39.0	26	9	7	1	1	14	2	43	3
Torres, Jackson, Los Angeles II ...	0	0	.000	5.84	6	1	0	3	0	1	12.1	10	9	8	0	3	17	0	12	2
Tovar, Paul, Seattle....................	0	2	.000	1.59	3	3	0	0	0	0	17.0	14	6	3	0	1	6	0	10	0
Trinidad, Manuel, Co-op I............	0	0	.000	3.75	4	0	0	4	0	0	12.0	16	7	5	0	1	4	1	4	1
Uceta, Victor, Oakland	0	0	.000	5.51	10	1	0	3	0	0	16.1	15	15	10	0	1	16	0	3	2
Umanzor, Kenny, Atlanta	1	0	1.000	2.31	14	0	0	5	1	1	27.1	14	13	7	1	1	31	2	21	3
Urbina, Jose, Co-op II	0	2	.000	3.86	11	0	0	7	0	2	25.2	31	18	11	1	1	13	3	17	3
Urena, Bernardo, San Francisco...	12	4	.750	1.77	18	15	8	3	1	0	122.0	100	30	24	2	0	15	2	56	3
Urvina, Dan, Los Angeles I..........	3	6	.333	5.04	12	12	0	0	0	0	55.1	58	36	31	5	3	37	0	42	3
Valdez, Carlos, San Francisco	1	1	.500	2.45	5	4	1	1	0	1	29.1	30	14	8	0	1	8	0	35	1
Valdez, Ismael, Los Angeles II	3	0	1.000	1.42	6	6	0	0	0	0	38.0	27	9	6	1	1	17	0	34	1
Valdez, Ruben, Oakland	8	5	.615	2.29	15	12	4	2	0	1	78.2	66	25	20	0	1	31	0	61	4
Vallejo, Julio, Seattle..................	0	4	.000	7.86	21	1	0	7	0	0	42.1	41	44	37	3	0	54	0	26	14
Vargas, Cesar, Toronto West.......	0	0	.000	0.00	1	0	0	0	0	0	1.2	0	0	0	0	1	1	0	2	0
Vasquez, Leonel, Co-op II...........	6	2	.750	3.12	16	15	1	0	0	0	89.1	69	52	31	3	1	59	0	63	9
Vasquez, Pedro, Yankees/S.D.	4	2	.667	2.95	21	1	0	14	0	6	45.2	34	19	15	0	5	29	0	29	6
Veras, Dario, Los Angeles II	7	1	.875	0.89	26	0	0	23	0	7	61.0	34	11	6	0	3	15	7	54	1
Veras, Gabriel, Co-op I................	0	0	.000	10.11	2	0	0	1	0	0	2.2	6	3	3	1	1	0	0	1	0
Vincentino, Andy, Seattle............	2	7	.222	4.53	15	13	0	1	0	0	47.2	19	33	24	1	2	44	0	27	9
Yan, Esteban, Atlanta	12	3	.800	1.32	16	16	7	0	4	0	115.2	85	37	17	1	2	23	2	86	3
Yan, Manolo, Houston	0	1	.000	13.48	1	1	0	0	0	0	2.2	8	4	4	0	1	1	0	1	0
Zayas, Evelio, Montreal	1	2	.333	10.20	19	3	0	5	0	1	35.0	37	54	40	5	16	53	0	19	10
Zerpa, Mauro, Balt./White Sox	0	0	.000	....	1	0	0	0	0	0	0.0	2	4	3	0	0	4	0	0	0

FIELDING

TEAM

Team	Pct.	G	PO	A	E	DP	PB	Team	Pct.	G	PO	A	E	DP	PB
New York Mets	.962	71	1727	775	153	60	9	Cleveland.....................	.937	72	1903	893	188	69	9
Toronto East	.962	70	1803	685	99	51	6	Toronto West.................	.936	70	1761	856	179	60	13
Los Angeles II	.950	72	1957	947	154	71	7	Montreal	.934	71	1734	824	180	61	16
Atlanta	.947	69	1869	865	154	69	16	San Francisco	.931	69	1779	793	190	76	18
Seattle	.943	70	1750	795	153	90	20	Milwaukee	.929	70	1715	787	192	53	28
Yankees/San Diego	.943	71	1794	786	157	77	25	Co-op II	.928	71	1895	896	218	70	25
Houston	.942	68	1740	885	163	59	15	Texas/Florida	.925	69	1659	761	196	52	12
Oakland	.942	71	1741	736	153	71	10	Detroit/St. Louis............	.924	72	1786	765	210	56	8
Pittsburgh	.942	70	1815	809	162	68	7	California	.908	69	1716	845	261	37	11
Los Angeles I	.938	70	1765	777	169	59	12	Co-op I.........................	.905	71	1781	744	266	78	11
Baltimore/White Sox	.937	68	1813	786	176	74	18								

INDIVIDUAL

Player, Team	Pos.	Pct.	PO	A	E	DP	PB	Player, Team	Pos.	Pct.	PO	A	E	DP	PB
Abad, Tor. West	INF	.891	105	165	33	14	0	Altagracia, N.Y. Mets .	P	.000	0	0	1	0	0
Abea, Tor. East	C	.996	489	64	2	1	6	Alvarado, Mont.	C	.961	233	65	12	0	12
Abreu, Milw.	INF	.916	83	168	23	8	0	Alvarez, Co-op I...........	P	.857	1	11	2	0	0
Abreu, Pitts.	P	.933	0	14	1	0	0	Alvarez, Balt./W.S......	P	.833	1	4	1	1	0
Acencio, L.A. II...........	OF	.950	103	10	6	4	0	Alvino, L.A. II...............	P/OF	.720	15	3	7	0	0
Acevedo, Co-op II	P	.813	2	11	3	1	0	Amaparo, Pitts.............	C	.943	98	18	7	0	2
Acosta, Oak.	P	.935	8	21	2	3	0	Angel, L.A. II...............	2B	.930	104	147	19	6	0
Adames, Mont.	P	1.000	0	1	0	0	0	Anselmo Diaz, N.Y.M. .	INF	.965	222	25	9	1	0
Adolfo, Co-op II...........	OF	.976	117	4	3	2	0	Aquino, Mont.	P	.750	1	2	1	0	0
Agramonte, L.A. II......	P	.789	1	14	4	0	0	Aquino, L.A. II	P	.857	4	14	3	1	0
Alcantara, Co-op II......	P	1.000	1	5	0	0	0	Arias, Tor. East...........	P	1.000	1	3	0	0	0
Alexis, Det./St. L.	P	.882	6	9	2	0	0	Arias, Oak.	INF	.827	17	50	14	2	0
Almanzar, Tor. East....	P	.813	2	11	3	0	0	Arias, Clev.	1B	.975	374	11	10	0	0
Almonte, Clev.	P	1.000	2	1	0	0	0	Arias, N.Y. Mets	OF	.971	34	0	1	0	0
Almonte, Hou.	P	.778	1	6	2	0	0	Arias, Milw.	P	1.000	0	5	0	0	0

Player, Team	Pos.	Pct.	PO	A	E	DP	PB
Ariaz, Tex./Fla.	P	.913	5	16	2	2	0
Arvelo, Milw.	P/C/IF	.921	110	29	12	1	2
Asencio, Calif.	INF	.879	33	76	15	0	0
Asencio, L.A. I	C	.989	147	29	2	0	7
Asencio, San Fran.	OF/INF	.911	43	29	7	3	0
Astacio, N.Y. Mets	P	.000	0	0	0	0	0
Avila, Calif.	P	.875	10	11	3	0	0
Ayala, L.A. I	P	.760	1	18	6	1	0
Aybar, Det./St. L.	INF/P	.906	53	131	19	9	0
Azuaje, Clev.	2B	.976	192	177	9	19	0
Baez, L.A. II	C	.972	139	32	5	0	3
Baez, Pitts.	P	1.000	0	3	0	0	0
Balbuena, San Fran.	P	.923	6	18	2	0	0
Balcarzar, Calif.	C	.966	137	31	6	1	0
Barazar, L.A. I	INF	.888	115	92	26	8	0
Barrera, Calif.	P	.933	10	4	1	0	0
Batista, Pitts.	P	.750	1	2	1	1	0
Batista, Yan./S.D.	P	1.000	0	3	0	0	0
Bautista, L.A. I	P	.905	4	15	2	1	0
Bautista, Atl.	P	1.000	0	1	0	0	0
Bautista, Balt./W.S.	INF	.875	79	167	35	12	0
Bautista, Det./St. L.	OF	.914	49	4	5	0	0
Beato, Hou.	OF	.938	111	11	8	0	0
Bele, Tex./Fla.	P	.913	10	11	2	0	0
Belioso, Yan./S.D.	P	.857	3	15	3	0	0
Beltre, Atl.	INF	.974	163	25	5	1	0
Bernardo, San Fran.	P	.917	14	19	3	0	0
Betancourt, L.A. I	P	1.000	0	14	0	1	0
Bido, Hou.	OF	.964	103	5	4	2	0
Bonilla, Co-op I	C	1.000	12	3	0	0	1
Bonilla, Sea.	P	.875	0	7	1	0	0
Bonilla, Oak.	C	.987	134	18	2	0	3
Brayan, Calif.	OF	.947	118	7	7	3	0
Brazoban, Tor. West	P	.769	4	6	3	0	0
Brazoban, Oak.	P	1.000	0	1	0	0	0
Brea, N.Y. Mets	C	.953	105	17	6	0	2
Brito, Tor. East	INF	1.000	1	0	0	0	0
H. Brito, Milw.	C/P	.968	51	10	2	0	8
J. Brito, Milw.	P	.850	3	14	3	1	0
Brito, Tor. West	INF	.922	31	64	8	8	0
Brown, L.A. I	OF	.941	84	11	6	2	0
Cabrera, Tor. East	INF	.928	56	72	10	10	0
Cabrera, Clev.	C/3B	.934	165	77	17	5	2
Caminero, Co-op II	P	.929	0	13	1	0	0
Campos, Mont.	OF	.948	120	8	7	2	0
Campusano, L.A. I	OF	.912	27	4	3	0	0
Cardona, Tor. West	P	.824	4	10	3	0	0
Carizosa, L.A. I	OF	.897	48	4	6	1	0
Carmona, Sea.	P	.875	1	6	1	0	0
Carrasquel, Tor. West	INF/P	.939	100	117	14	14	0
Carrion, Mont.	P	.375	0	3	5	0	0
Carrion, Tex./Fla.	P	1.000	3	7	0	0	0
Castillo, Hou.	INF	.879	21	59	11	6	0
Castillo, San Fran.	C	.980	123	27	3	2	6
Castillo, Oak.	OF	.973	72	1	2	0	0
Castillo, Tex./Fla.	P	1.000	2	3	0	0	0
Castillo, Milw.	INF	.912	128	70	19	10	0
Castillo, Balt./W.S.	P	.667	0	4	2	1	0
Castillo, Atl.	P	1.000	3	20	0	1	0
Castillo, Sea.	OF	.882	15	0	2	0	0
Castillo, Tor. West	P	.889	3	5	1	0	0
Castro, Sea.	P	1.000	2	5	0	1	0
Castro, L.A. II	OF	.969	119	6	4	2	0
Castro, Balt./W.S.	INF	.912	32	51	8	5	0
Catedral, N.Y. Mets	P	.000	0	0	0	0	0
Cedeno, Clev.	SS	.884	44	86	17	7	0
Cedeno, Co-op II	3B/1B	.946	238	27	15	2	0
Chalas, Tor. West	P	.933	1	13	1	0	0
Charles, Co-op II	P	.964	5	22	1	0	0
Chevalier, Clev.	P	1.000	1	6	0	0	0
Collins, Oak.	C	.917	9	2	1	0	1
Colmenares, Tor. East	INF	.000	0	0	0	0	0
Colmenares, Balt/WS.	OF	.938	69	7	5	1	0
Colome, Co-op II	P	.765	4	9	4	0	0
Colon, Milw.	P/O/I	.933	13	15	2	1	0
Concepcion, S.F.	INF	.970	337	21	11	2	0
Contreras, Hou.	C	1.000	13	1	0	0	0
Contreras, Balt./W.S..	INF/OF	.926	24	1	2	0	0
Contreras, Mont.	INF	.800	8	4	3	0	0
Cordero, San Fran.	OF	.872	77	5	12	1	0
Cordoba, Yan./S.D.	P	.769	2	8	3	0	0
Coronado, N.Y. Mets	P	1.000	3	10	0	0	0
Crisotomo, Sea.	INF	.918	64	115	16	18	0
Cruz, Sea.	P	.714	2	8	4	1	0
Cruz, Yan./S.D.	OF	.951	53	5	3	2	0
Cruz, Co-op II	OF	.912	31	0	3	0	0
Cruz, Atl.	P	.000	0	0	0	0	0
Cruz, Det./St. L.	OF/P	.850	47	4	9	1	0
Dalis, Sea.	OF	.913	40	2	4	0	0
D'Anda, Calif.	P	1.000	1	1	0	0	0
David, San Fran.	OF	.930	71	9	6	3	0
Debrano, Tor. East	OF	.987	149	8	2	1	0
DeJesus Diaz, N.Y.M.	C	.972	145	29	5	0	6
DeJesus P., NYY/SD	P	.533	2	6	7	0	0
DeLaCruz, Hou.	C	.974	150	39	5	1	10
H. DeLaCruz, Atl.	C	1.000	57	5	0	0	3
J. DeLaCruz, Calif.	INF	.920	72	77	13	0	0
DeLaCruz, Mont.	OF/P	.881	36	1	5	0	0
DeLaCruz, Pitts.	P	.846	4	18	4	1	0
DeLaCruz, Co-op I	2B	.922	82	83	14	5	0
DeLaCruz, Tor. East	OF	.973	96	13	3	9	0
R. DeLaCruz, Atl.	OF	.953	55	6	3	3	0
R. DeLaCruz, Calif.	P	1.000	7	3	0	0	0
DeLaCruz S., Hou.	P	1.000	5	27	0	1	0
DeLanoy, Oak.	P	1.000	0	1	0	0	0
DeLaRosa, Pitts.	OF	.944	60	7	4	2	0
DeLaRosa, Hou.	INF/P	.958	17	29	2	3	0
DeLeon, Clev.	P	.750	1	2	1	0	0
DeLeon, Hou.	P	.714	1	4	2	0	0
DeLeon, Pitts.	P	1.000	1	6	0	0	0
DeLeon, Yan./S.D.	INF	.975	134	99	6	6	0
DeLeon, Tor. West	P	.667	2	4	3	0	0
DeLeon, Atl.	P	1.000	0	1	0	0	0
DeLeon, Sea.	OF	.964	150	12	6	2	0
Delgado, Tor. East	P	.833	1	14	3	1	0
DeLosSantos, Tx/Fl	OF/INF	.913	62	1	6	2	0
DeLosSantos, Oak.	INF/OF	.931	60	34	7	5	0
DeLosSantos, Co-op I	3B	.890	59	14	9	3	0
DeLosSantos, Tor. E...	P	1.000	2	6	0	1	0
DeLosSantos, Calif.	P	1.000	10	4	0	0	0
DeRotal, Yan./S.D.	OF	.940	74	4	5	0	0
Devers, Balt./W.S.	INF	.978	374	27	9	2	0
Devers, Co-op I	SS	.794	25	56	21	7	0
Diaz, Sea.	INF	.971	255	12	8	1	0
Diaz, Tor. East	P	1.000	0	2	0	1	0
Diaz, Calif.	OF	.891	92	6	12	1	0
Diaz, Hou.	C	.818	24	3	6	0	0
Doval, Atl.	P	1.000	1	5	0	0	0
Duncan, Sea.	INF	.961	138	111	10	15	0
Duval, Oak.	P	1.000	8	1	0	0	0
Encarnacion, L.A. II	P	1.000	2	2	0	0	0
Escalante, L.A. I	P	.667	0	2	1	0	0
Escobar, Sea.	P	.667	1	3	2	0	0
Espinal, Hou.	C	.963	93	37	5	0	5
Espinal, Yan./S.D.	INF	.975	393	34	11	4	0
Espinosa, Co-op I	OF	.961	110	12	5	2	0
Estevez, Co-op I	1B	.954	339	15	17	2	0
Evangelista, Clev.	OF	.848	51	5	10	1	0
Falcon, Mont.	P	.923	0	12	1	1	0
Faneyte, Sea.	INF	.896	60	87	17	8	0
Fantause, Tex./Fla.	OF	.972	33	2	1	0	0
Febles, San Fran.	P	.950	6	13	1	0	0
Feliz, Tex./Fla.	OF/INF	.977	315	24	8	4	0
Fereiras, Balt./W.S.	P	.875	2	5	1	0	0
Fermin, Co-op I	SS	.929	2	11	1	0	0
Fernandez, Atl.	OF	1.000	12	0	0	0	0
Fernandez, Clev.	3B	.822	35	53	19	3	0
Fernandez, Det./St. L.	OF	.963	127	2	5	1	0
Ferreras, Hou.	INF	.981	200	7	4	1	0
Figuereo, Mont.	P	.625	0	5	3	0	0
Figuereo, Atl.	INF	.950	8	11	1	1	0
A. Figueroa, Mont.	P	1.000	0	2	0	1	0
J. Figueroa, Mont.	P	1.000	1	10	0	0	0
Figueroa, Milw.	OF/P	.938	185	11	13	3	0
Florian, Tor. East	INF	.975	113	86	5	8	0
Forsythe, L.A. I	INF	.929	55	36	7	4	0
Franco, Balt./W.S.	P	.905	2	17	2	2	0
Galan, Balt./W.S.	C	.996	190	44	1	2	1
Galvez, Balt./W.S.	P	.909	4	6	1	0	0
Garcia, N.Y. Mets	P	.000	0	0	1	0	0
Garcia, Co-op II.	OF	.950	127	6	7	3	0
Garcia, Tex./Fla.	P	.909	9	11	2	1	0
Garcia, Milw.	INF	.967	158	136	10	11	0
Garcia, Tor. East.	INF	.870	68	146	32	5	0

DOMINICAN SUMMER LEAGUE
SUMMER CLASS A
DOMINICAN SUMMER LEAGUE

Player, Team	Pos.	Pct.	PO	A	E	DP	PB
J. Garcia, L.A. II	P	.850	4	13	3	0	0
Garcia, Hou.	INF	.983	487	38	9	4	0
L. Garcia, Atl.	INF	.918	55	102	14	13	0
Garcia, Clev.	OF/1B	.981	295	19	6	1	0
M. Garcia, L.A. II	OF	.940	69	10	5	2	0
Garcia, Pitts.	P	.923	4	8	1	0	0
Garibay, L.A. I	P	.889	0	8	1	0	0
Genao, Pitts.	P	.833	6	9	3	0	0
Gerardo, Tor. West	P	1.000	1	4	0	0	0
German, Oak.	OF	.931	116	5	9	0	0
German, Det./St. L.	OF/P	.885	52	2	7	0	0
German, Yan./S.D.	OF	.940	162	11	11	5	0
S. German, Calif.	INF	.857	34	62	16	2	0
Giron, Tor. East	P	.813	3	10	3	0	0
Giron, Tor. West	P	1.000	0	2	0	0	0
Gomez, Balt./W.S.	P	.667	2	2	2	1	0
Gomez, Calif.	P	1.000	2	1	0	0	0
Gomez, N.Y. Mets	P	1.000	0	2	0	0	0
Gomez, Co-op I	P	.714	2	3	2	0	0
Gomez, Oak.	C	.964	131	32	6	1	0
Gomez, Tor. West	P	.750	2	13	5	1	0
Gonzalez, Clev.	P	1.000	0	3	0	0	0
Gonzalez, San Fran.	INF	.895	151	70	26	18	0
Gonzalez, Milw.	P	.895	3	14	2	1	0
Gonzalez, Atl.	INF/OF	.955	160	10	8	1	0
Gonzalez, Oak.	P	.750	2	7	3	0	0
Gonzalez, L.A. II	3B	.885	55	177	30	10	0
Gonzalez, Yan./S.D.	P	.938	2	13	1	0	0
Gonzalez, Pitts.	C	.969	244	42	9	2	2
Guerrero, Balt./W.S.	P	.867	3	10	2	1	0
Guerrero, Pitts.	P	.429	2	1	4	1	0
Guerrero, Calif.	OF	.903	124	16	15	3	0
Guerrero, L.A. II	SS	.938	104	215	21	23	0
Guevara, Sea.	INF	.933	37	103	10	15	0
Guilamo, Tex./Fla.	P	.750	2	4	2	0	0
Guillermo, Tex./Fla.	INF	.858	139	109	41	13	0
Gumbs, San Fran.	OF	.848	27	1	5	0	0
Guzman, Mont.	P	.750	1	8	3	1	0
Guzman, Det./St. L.	OF	.964	95	12	4	4	0
Henriquez, Milw.	OF	.966	25	3	1	1	0
Henriquez, Det./St. L.	INF	.922	133	115	21	7	0
Henson, Atl.	INF	.945	163	181	20	15	0
D. Herdosia, Calif.	P	.727	2	6	3	0	0
H. Herdosia, Calif.	INF	.965	440	26	17	7	0
Heredia, Mont.	INF	.981	440	24	9	2	0
Hernandez, Atl.	C/INF	1.000	80	7	0	0	0
A. Hernandez, L.A. I	P	.882	7	8	2	1	0
Hernandez, Det./St. L.	C	.937	372	88	31	4	8
C. Hernandez, Calif.	C	.934	51	6	4	1	0
E. Hernandez, Calif.	P	.818	3	6	2	0	0
Hernandez, N.Y. Mets	C	.994	125	42	1	1	1
J. Hernandez, Calif.	P	.750	2	1	1	0	0
R. Hernandez, L.A. I	OF	.982	50	5	1	0	0
Herrera, Co-op I	P	.714	2	3	2	1	0
Hidalgo, Det./St. L.	OF	.914	72	2	7	1	0
Hinetrosa, Pitts.	P	.000	0	0	0	0	0
Hurtado, Tor. East	P	.947	8	10	1	0	0
Jasson, Calif.	INF	.768	36	90	38	0	0
Javier, Co-op II	SS/2B	.864	25	64	14	4	0
Javier, San Fran.	INF/C	.875	26	44	10	5	0
Jimenez, N.Y. Mets	INF	.833	7	28	7	3	0
Jimenez, Clev.	C	.943	56	10	4	1	0
J. Jimenez, Det./St. L.	P	.900	3	6	1	0	0
Jimenez, San Fran.	C	.963	236	73	12	2	12
R. Jimenez, Det./St. L.	INF	.873	28	34	9	1	0
Jose, N.Y. Mets	OF	.944	30	4	2	0	0
Leger, Atl.	P	.875	2	5	1	0	0
J.R. Linares, N.Y.M.	P	.875	2	19	3	1	0
R. Linares, N.Y. Mets	P	.929	2	11	1	0	0
Liquet, L.A. II	P	.950	8	11	1	2	0
Liriano, Tor. West	INF	.933	106	130	17	11	0
Liriano, Milw.	OF	.963	304	6	12	2	0
A. Lopez, Co-op II	P	1.000	3	9	0	1	0
Lopez, Tor. East	P	.882	3	12	2	1	0
Lopez, L.A. I	INF	.925	19	43	5	4	0
M. Lopez, Co-op II	SS	.901	81	155	26	23	0
Luis, Oak.	C	.950	60	16	4	0	2
Luna, Tor. West	INF	.000	0	0	0	0	0
Macias, Mont.	OF	.942	73	41	7	2	0
Maldonado, Hou.	P	.750	2	10	4	0	0
Malena, Clev.	P	.917	3	19	2	1	0
Manon, Det./St. L.	P	.733	2	9	4	1	0

Player, Team	Pos.	Pct.	PO	A	E	DP	PB
Marcelo, Milw.	C	.955	262	59	15	0	18
Marcos, Co-op I	OF	.964	74	7	3	1	0
Marmolejos, Sea.	P	1.000	0	2	0	1	0
Marquez, Sea.	C	.967	75	13	3	0	6
Marte, Hou.	P	1.000	1	3	0	1	0
Martinez, Atl.	INF	.990	384	16	4	1	0
Martinez, San Fran.	INF/OF	.960	299	15	13	1	0
E. Martinez, Det/StL	INF	.858	43	102	24	8	0
Martinez, Co-op I	P	.833	4	11	3	0	0
Martinez, L.A. I	P	.905	6	13	2	0	0
Je. Martinez, Tor. E.	INF	.986	198	17	3	0	0
Martinez, Clev.	P	.811	4	26	7	1	0
J. Martinez, Sea.	OF	.926	49	1	4	0	0
Ju. Martinez, Tor. E.	INF	.986	408	20	6	0	0
Martinez, Pitts.	P	.941	8	8	1	0	0
Martinez, Yan./S.D.	INF	.907	82	173	26	24	0
O. Martinez, Det/StL	P	1.000	0	3	0	0	0
Martinez, L.A. II	1B	.989	674	26	8	2	0
V. Martinez, Sea.	C	.965	210	38	9	0	7
Mata, L.A. I	INF	.955	162	95	12	4	0
Matco, Milw.	P	.000	0	0	2	0	0
Mateo, Yan./S.D.	INF	.841	16	21	7	3	0
Mathews, Clev.	OF	.875	74	3	11	0	0
Matos, Co-op II	P	.500	0	1	1	0	0
Matos, Atl.	C	.976	105	15	3	0	4
Mazara, Calif.	OF/INF	.843	78	147	42	7	0
Medina, Co-op II	1B	.971	259	12	8	2	0
Mega, L.A. II	2B	.887	20	27	6	4	0
Mejia, Milw.	P	.813	2	11	3	0	0
Mejia, Sea.	P	.800	1	15	4	0	0
Mejia, Calif.	P	.800	7	5	3	0	0
M. Mejia, Balt./W.S.	OF	.882	93	12	14	5	0
R. Mejia, Balt./W.S.	OF	.875	18	3	3	0	0
Melendes, Balt./W.S.	INF	.912	78	87	16	10	0
Melendez, Pitts.	OF/INF	.942	60	53	7	2	0
Mena, Co-op I	P	.677	2	19	10	0	0
Mendez, Yan./S.D.	C	.947	166	29	11	2	14
Mendez, Pitts.	C/INF	.966	210	45	9	3	0
Mendez, Milw.	P	.929	2	11	1	1	0
Mendoza, Co-op II	3B	.871	39	103	21	4	0
Mendoza, Co-op I	2B	.950	91	79	9	7	0
Mendoza, Atl.	P	.875	2	5	1	0	0
Mendoza, L.A. II	P	.846	3	8	2	0	0
Mendoza, Yan./S.D.	P	.964	5	22	1	0	0
Meran, Mont.	OF	.955	57	6	3	1	0
Mercedes, Hou.	P	1.000	1	11	0	0	0
Mercedes, San Fran.	P	.818	2	7	2	0	0
Mesa, Clev.	P	.977	11	31	1	1	0
Millan, Balt./W.S.	P	1.000	0	1	0	0	0
Minaya, Pitts.	INF	1.000	18	3	0	1	0
Miranda, Tex./Fla.	P/INF	.917	4	7	1	0	0
Mohamed, N.Y.Y./S.D.	INF/P	.957	104	116	10	10	0
Mojica, Oak.	INF/P	1.000	3	6	0	0	0
Mojica, N.Y. Mets	P	1.000	0	3	0	0	0
Montano, Oak.	OF	.957	19	3	1	3	0
Montano, Atl.	P	.833	2	3	1	0	0
Montero, Tex./Fla.	INF	.937	102	134	16	10	0
Montero, Co-op II	P	.600	1	2	2	0	0
Montilla, Tor. West	INF	.901	68	78	16	4	0
Mora, Sea.	P	1.000	5	11	0	1	0
J. Morales, Atl.	OF	.842	31	1	6	0	0
N. Morales, Atl.	P	.909	3	7	1	1	0
J. Morel, Pitts.	P/OF	.500	0	1	1	0	0
Morel, Oak.	P	.833	2	8	2	2	0
R. Morel, Pitts.	P	1.000	0	5	0	1	0
Morizo, Co-op I	C	.960	183	9	8	0	4
Mosquera, Tor. West	C	.956	207	94	14	1	7
Mota, Calif.	OF/INF	.958	87	49	6	5	0
Gl. Mota, N.Y. Mets	OF	.967	80	8	3	3	0
Gu. Mota, N.Y. Mets	INF	.927	133	173	24	15	0
Munoz, Pitts.	INF	.980	317	25	7	3	0
Navarro, L.A. I	INF	.981	441	24	9	2	0
Navas, Oak.	INF	.867	26	91	18	9	0
Neris, Sea.	P	.000	0	0	1	0	0
Nevada, Balt./W.S.	P	1.000	1	0	0	0	0
Newton, Sea.	P	.875	7	14	3	1	0
Nieves, Oak.	OF	.941	15	1	1	0	0
Nieves, Milw.	INF	.815	9	13	5	2	0
Nixon, L.A. II	P	.789	3	12	4	0	0
Nunez, Co-op I	OF	.958	64	5	3	1	0
Nunez, Det./St. L.	INF	.972	560	23	17	3	0
Nunez, Sea.	C/INF	.960	104	88	8	10	0

Player, Team	Pos.	Pct.	PO	A	E	DP	PB
J. Nunez, Tor. West.....	P	1.000	0	5	0	0	0
Nunez, San Fran.	P	.818	2	7	2	0	0
M. Nunez, Tor. West ...	OF	.958	125	11	6	1	0
Nunez, Tex./Fla.	P	1.000	0	2	0	0	0
Nunez, Co-op II	2B/SS	.924	123	169	24	9	0
Oliva, San Fran.	INF	.888	58	132	24	14	0
Oliveros, Sea.	C	.960	64	8	3	0	7
Olivier, Yan./S.D.	P	.714	0	10	4	0	0
Orpesa, Tex./Fla.	P	.773	7	10	5	0	0
Ortega, Balt./W.S.	P	1.000	2	6	0	0	0
Oviedo, Tex./Fla.	OF	.921	150	13	14	3	0
Ozorio, N.Y. Mets	INF	.919	105	89	17	7	0
Ozuna, San Fran.	INF	.943	107	92	12	8	0
Padilla, Balt./W.S.	OF	.911	35	6	4	0	0
Padilla, Mont.	INF/P	.977	82	2	2	1	0
Paniagua, Mont.	P	.895	6	11	2	1	0
Paniagua, N.Y.Y./S.D.	P	1.000	0	5	0	1	0
Pascual, Yan./S.D.	OF/P	1.000	4	0	0	0	0
Paulino, L.A. II..........	P	1.000	3	9	0	0	0
Pedra, L.A. I	C	.987	130	26	2	1	4
J. Peguero, San Fran. ..	P	.900	2	7	1	0	0
P. Peguero, San Fran..	P	1.000	3	9	0	0	0
Pelaez, Oak.	P	.667	0	2	1	1	0
Pemberton, Mont.	C	.970	150	11	5	0	2
Pena, Clev.	OF	.932	120	17	10	2	0
Pena, Pitts.	P	.800	1	4	1	1	0
Pena, Co-op I	OF	.944	77	7	5	2	0
Pena, Mont.	OF	.963	47	5	2	0	0
Pena, N.Y. Mets	P	.667	3	1	2	0	0
A. Perez, Calif.	P	.917	6	5	1	0	0
Perez, N.Y. Mets	P	.667	0	2	1	0	0
C. Perez, Co-op II	2B	.960	21	3	1	0	0
Perez, Atl.	OF	.919	56	1	5	0	0
E. Perez, Co-op II	2B/P	.837	11	30	8	1	0
Perez, Tor. East	P	1.000	1	11	0	0	0
F. Perez, Oak.	C	.927	29	9	3	1	3
J. Perez, Yan./S.D.....	P	.500	0	1	1	0	0
J. Perez, ...	P	1.000	3	13	0	0	0
J.C. Perez, Yan./S.D.....	OF	.981	147	10	3	2	0
L. Perez, Calif.	INF/P	.872	28	6	5	0	0
P. Perez, Yan./S.D.......	C/INF	.972	62	8	2	0	2
Perez, Mont.	INF	.954	112	138	12	15	0
Perozo, Atl.	OF	.935	82	4	6	1	0
Pierret, L.A. II..........	P	.857	4	2	1	0	0
Pimentel, Co-op II	P	.400	1	1	3	0	0
Piters, Calif.	C	.935	74	26	7	0	11
Placencia, Clev.	P	1.000	1	4	0	0	0
Polanco, N.Y. Mets......	INF	.917	17	60	7	9	0
Polanco, Pitts..............	INF	.957	68	21	4	0	0
Polanco, San Fran.	OF	.976	73	8	2	4	0
Polanco, Co-op I	OF	.838	48	9	11	0	0
Portes, Yan./S.D.........	INF	.869	65	134	30	14	0
Portillo, San Fran.......	P	.941	5	11	1	0	0
Prensi, Tor. West	OF	.841	84	11	18	1	0
Primera, Pitts............	P	1.000	4	14	0	2	0
Puello, L.A. I	OF	.925	116	7	10	1	0
Puente, Sea...............	OF	.947	69	2	4	2	0
Pulido, Balt./W.S.	IF	.853	16	13	5	1	0
Quintana, Oak.	INF	.968	372	19	13	2	0
Quiroz, Oak...............	P	1.000	1	1	0	0	0
Ramirez, Clev.	OF	.948	136	9	8	2	0
Ramirez, Tor. East	OF	.965	103	6	4	0	0
D. Ramirez, N.Y. Mets .	OF	.924	100	10	9	2	0
Ramirez, Co-op II	P	.941	2	14	1	0	0
Ramirez, Balt./W.S.	P	.500	0	1	1	0	0
Ramirez, Pitts............	OF	.960	89	7	4	0	0
J. Ramirez, Milw.	INF/P	.879	81	57	19	3	0
J. Ramirez, N.Y. Mets..	OF	.957	106	4	5	2	0
Ramirez, Det./St.L.	P	1.000	6	6	0	0	0
Ramos, Tex./Fla.........	P	.850	6	11	3	2	0
Ramos, Clev.	P	.625	1	19	12	2	0
Jo. Ramos, Hou.	INF	.935	14	29	3	0	0
Ju. Ramos, Hou.	OF	.941	120	7	8	2	0
Ramos, Mont.	INF	.890	47	118	20	9	0
Rascon, L.A. I............	P	1.000	1	4	0	0	0
Regalado, Hou.	P	.765	2	11	4	0	0
Regalado, Yan./S.D.....	P	.000	0	0	0	0	0
Restitullo, Calif.	OF	.831	45	4	10	0	0
Reyes, Hou.	P	.875	3	4	1	0	0
Reyes, Co-op II...........	2B	.934	48	65	8	6	0
Reyes, Atl.	INF	.904	15	32	5	0	0
Reyes, L.A. I	C/INF	.962	202	50	10	1	1

Player, Team	Pos.	Pct.	PO	A	E	DP	PB
Reyes, Oak.	P	1.000	2	3	0	0	0
Reyes, Clev.	SS	.935	93	197	20	15	0
Reyes, Co-op I...........	3B	.823	37	79	25	11	0
Reynoso, Tor. West.....	P	1.000	0	1	0	0	0
Ricardo, San Fran......	P	.846	6	16	4	0	0
Rijo, Calif.	P	.929	7	6	1	0	0
Rincones, Co-op I	3B	.845	34	64	18	7	0
Rios, L.A. II...............	2B	.964	86	100	7	6	0
Rivera, Pitts.	INF	.926	136	150	23	13	0
Rivera, Yan./S.D.........	INF	.975	141	16	4	4	0
Roberts, Det./St.L.	P	.800	2	6	2	2	0
Roble, L.A. I	INF	.918	69	99	15	13	0
Robles, Det./St.L.	INF	.915	108	140	23	9	0
A. Rodriguez, Hou.	P	.813	3	10	3	0	0
E. Rodriguez, Hou.	INF	.911	99	208	30	25	0
F. Rodriguez, Tx/Fl.....	OF	.917	108	14	11	2	0
F. Rodriguez, Co-op I...	C	.960	298	66	15	1	2
Rodriguez, Atl.	P	.917	9	13	2	0	0
J. Rodriguez, Tx/Fl.....	C/I/P	.924	64	21	7	0	5
J. Rodriguez, L.A. I.....	P	.750	1	2	1	0	0
L. Rodriguez, L.A. I.....	INF	.865	77	153	36	13	0
Rodriguez, Mont.........	INF	.862	34	66	16	5	0
R. Rodriguez, Co-op I...	2B	1.000	30	21	0	1	4
Rojas, N.Y. Mets.........	INF/OF	.983	378	21	7	2	0
Rojas, Mont.	INF	.927	102	125	18	6	0
Rojas, Pitts.	OF	.952	19	1	1	0	0
Rojas, Tor. West	P	.900	2	16	2	1	0
Romano, Balt./W.S.	INF	.969	78	17	3	1	0
Romero, Det./St.L.	P	1.000	0	9	0	1	0
Romo, L.A. I	P	1.000	1	0	0	0	0
Rondon, Oak..............	INF/C	.979	30	16	1	2	1
Rosa, L.A. I	P	.667	1	1	1	0	0
Rosado, Atl.	P	.920	5	18	2	2	0
Rosario, Tor. West	OF	.966	159	13	6	1	0
Rosario, Hou..............	INF	.952	163	193	18	9	0
J. Rosario, Tx/Fl.........	C/I/P	.965	314	70	14	0	7
Rosario, Det./St.L.	INF/P	.850	10	24	6	3	0
Rosario, Clev.	P	1.000	5	16	0	1	0
R. Rosario, Tex./Fla. ..	INF	.872	90	128	32	10	0
Rosario, Milw.	OF/P	.908	126	52	18	1	0
Ruan, Mont.	OF	.929	13	0	1	0	0
Ruiz, Det./St.L.	INF	.955	12	9	1	1	0
Ruiz, Balt./W.S.	P	.952	0	20	1	1	0
Ruiz, L.A. I	P	.667	0	2	1	0	0
Sabino, Det./St.L.	P	.750	3	9	4	0	0
Salazar, San Fran.......	INF	.924	74	96	14	4	0
Salazar, Balt./W.S.......	C	.959	60	10	3	0	2
Salcedo, Co-op II	3B/1B	.916	130	66	18	3	0
Salcedo, Pitts............	P	1.000	2	2	0	0	0
Saldana, Clev.	P	.889	1	7	1	0	0
Salomon, Atl.	INF	.894	53	74	15	12	0
Salvador, L.A. II.........	1B	.968	56	4	2	0	0
Salvador, Balt./W.S. ..	C	.982	269	51	6	0	15
Samboy, Yan./S.D.......	P	.846	2	9	2	0	0
Samboy, N.Y. Mets......	P	.667	0	10	5	1	0
Sanchez, Pitts.	OF	.935	96	4	7	1	0
Sanchez, Calif.	INF	1.000	1	6	0	0	0
Sanchez, N.Y. Mets	P	1.000	2	7	0	0	0
Sanchez, Yan./S.D......	C	.969	134	20	5	0	9
Sanchez, Tor. West.....	INF	.898	55	24	9	1	0
Santa, Tor. West........	INF/P	.961	173	23	8	1	0
Santana, San Fran......	INF	.893	11	39	6	6	0
D. Santana, Hou.	P	.889	4	20	3	1	0
Santana, Co-op II.......	C	.970	282	39	10	1	20
Santana, Oak.	INF	.974	219	10	6	0	0
F. Santana, Pitts.	INF/OF	.940	66	107	11	10	0
J. Santana, Tx/Fl........	O/I/P	.929	50	2	4	0	0
J. Santana, Calif.	C	.910	101	20	12	0	0
M. Santana, Sea.	P	1.000	1	1	0	0	0
M. Santana, Pitts.	P	1.000	2	1	0	0	0
Santana, Co-op I........	P/C	.879	7	22	4	1	0
M. Santana, Pitts.	OF	.921	64	6	6	1	0
R. Santana, Hou.	INF/OF	.868	102	102	31	4	0
Santive, Oak..............	P	.500	0	1	1	0	0
Santos, Clev.	SS	.840	38	41	15	4	0
Santos, Mont.	P	.714	3	2	2	0	0
Segura, Pitts.	INF	.874	87	177	38	19	0
Selmo, Atl.	INF	.908	63	104	17	7	0
Serrano, Sea.	INF	.949	202	98	16	13	0
Severino, Det./St.L.	P	.667	3	11	7	0	0
Severino, N.Y. Mets.....	P	.857	1	5	1	0	0
H. Sierra, Mont.	C	.957	48	18	3	0	2

Player, Team	Pos.	Pct.	PO	A	E	DP	PB
Sierra, Hou.	INF	1.000	0	3	0	0	0
S. Sierra, Mont.	OF	.900	50	4	6	0	0
Simon, Atl.	C	.979	146	40	4	0	8
Solano, Tor. East	INF	.931	98	172	20	13	0
Sony, Co-op II	OF	.907	80	8	9	2	0
C.J. Soriano, N.Y.M.	INF	.878	46	113	22	9	0
F. Soriano, Oak.	INF	.962	155	176	13	16	0
J. Soriano, N.Y. Mets	P	.800	2	10	3	1	0
J. Soriano, Oak.	OF	.985	127	5	2	4	0
J.C. Soriano, N.Y.M.	INF	.943	77	72	9	3	0
Soriano, Pitts.	P	1.000	1	1	0	0	0
Sosa, Oak.	P	.889	6	10	2	0	0
Sosa, Clev.	C	.969	200	54	8	3	7
Soto, Balt./W.S.	INF	.962	166	134	12	20	0
Soto, Det./St. L.	P	.714	0	5	2	0	0
Soto, Milw.	INF	.875	36	55	13	3	0
J. Suero, Milw.	P	1.000	2	12	0	0	0
M. Suero, Milw.	INF	.884	48	28	10	3	0
Suriel, N.Y. Mets	P	.667	2	0	1	0	0
Tapia, Co-op I	2B	.850	76	88	29	7	0
Tatis, Atl.	C	.980	77	23	2	0	1
Tatis, Yan./S.D.	C	1.000	40	5	0	0	0
Tavarez, Co-op I	C	.682	3	12	7	0	0
Taveras, Mont.	P	.914	9	23	3	1	0
Tejada, Hou.	P	1.000	0	7	0	0	0
Tejada, Balt./W.S.	P	.824	2	12	3	0	0
Thomas, San Fran.	INF	.787	17	20	10	3	0
Tinoco, Sea.	OF/INF	.950	195	15	11	0	0
Toribio, L.A. II	P	.833	2	8	2	2	0
Torres, Tor. East	P	1.000	0	5	0	0	0
Torres, L.A. II	P	1.000	1	2	0	0	0
Torrez, Milw.	OF	.929	84	8	7	1	0
Tovar, Sea.	P	.750	0	3	1	0	0
Tremols, Pitts.	C	.978	75	12	2	0	3
Trinidad, Co-op I	OF	.860	43	6	8	3	0
Tunon, Balt./W.S.	OF	.923	44	4	4	0	0
Uceta, Oak.	P	.750	1	2	1	0	0
Ulises, Balt./W.S.	OF	.887	52	3	7	0	0
Umanzor, Atl.	P	.800	0	4	1	0	0
Urbina, Co-op II	P	.500	0	5	5	1	0
Uribe, L.A. II	C	.976	369	79	11	7	4
Urvina, L.A. I	P	.867	1	12	2	1	0
Valdespino, Tor. West	C	.984	97	29	2	0	6
Valdez, San Fran.	P	.889	3	5	1	0	0
Valdez, Co-op II	OF	.967	84	5	3	1	0
Valdez, Atl.	OF	.909	44	6	5	1	0
Valdez, L.A. II	P	.923	5	7	1	0	0
Valdez, Oak.	P	.824	3	11	3	0	0
Valdez, Tor. West	INF	.989	421	18	5	1	0
Vallejo, Sea.	P	.667	2	4	3	0	0
Vargas, Tor. West	OF	.688	11	0	5	0	0
Vargas, Calif.	INF	.925	11	26	3	2	0
Vargas, Oak.	INF	.886	111	160	35	20	0
Vasquez, Tor. East	INF	1.000	1	0	0	0	0
Vasquez, Atl.	INF	.864	21	100	19	8	0
Vasquez, Co-op II	P	.875	1	27	4	4	0
Vasquez, Yan./S.D.	P	.909	1	9	1	0	0
Veras, L.A. II	P	.867	4	9	2	0	0
Veras, Co-op I	SS	.750	76	29	35	16	0
Vicioso, Tex./Fla.	INF	.932	183	161	25	3	0
Villalona, Tor. East	OF	.000	0	0	0	0	0
Vincentino, Sea.	P	.857	1	11	2	1	0
Vizcaino, Calif.	INF	.857	4	8	2	0	0
Vorges, Co-op II	OF	.917	40	4	4	0	0
Wilson, Pitts.	INF/OF	.947	73	34	6	4	0
Wilson, Co-op II	C	.934	139	17	11	0	5
Yan, Atl.	P	.914	12	20	3	1	0
Yan, Hou.	P	1.000	0	1	0	0	0
Zapata, Mont.	INF	.861	61	112	28	13	0
Zayas, Mont.	P	.000	0	0	1	0	0
Zerpa, Balt./W.S.	INF	.886	117	61	23	8	0

GULF COAST LEAGUE

FINAL STANDINGS

SOUTHERN DIVISION

Team	W	L	T	Pct.	GB
Blue Jays	35	24	0	.593	....
Yankees	31	28	1	.525	4
Twins	30	28	0	.517	4½
White Sox	30	29	1	.508	5
Orioles	29	29	0	.500	5½
Rangers	28	31	0	.475	7

CENTRAL DIVISION

Team	W	L	T	Pct.	GB
Royals	41	18	0	.695	....
Marlins	33	27	0	.550	8½
Astros	27	33	0	.450	14½
Red Sox	18	41	0	.305	23
Pirates	23	37	0	.383	18½

EASTERN DIVISION

Team	W	L	T	Pct.	GB
Expos	35	24	0	.593	....
Dodgers	32	27	0	.542	3
Mets	29	30	0	.492	6
Braves	22	37	0	.373	13

COMPOSITE

Team	Ryl.	Exp.	B.J.	Mrl.	Dod.	Yan.	Twi.	W.S.	Orl.	Mets	Rng.	Ast.	Pir.	Brv.	R.S.	W	L	T	Pct.	GB
Royals	...	0	0	13	0	0	0	0	0	0	0	13	0	0	15	41	18	0	.695	....
Expos	0	0	0	0	12	0	0	0	0	10	0	0	13	0	0	35	24	0	.593	6
Blue Jays	0	0	...	0	0	7	5	7	4	0	5	0	7	0	0	35	24	0	.593	6
Marlins	7	0	0	...	0	0	0	0	0	0	0	11	0	0	15	33	27	0	.550	8½
Dodgers	0	8	0	0	...	0	0	0	0	11	0	0	13	0	0	32	27	0	.542	9
Yankees	0	0	3	0	0	...	5	5	6	0	6	0	6	0	0	31	28	1	.525	10
Twins	0	0	5	0	0	5	...	3	3	0	6	0	8	0	0	30	28	0	.517	10½
White Sox	0	0	3	0	0	5	6	...	6	0	4	0	6	0	0	30	29	1	.508	11
Orioles	0	0	5	0	0	4	6	4	...	0	5	0	5	0	0	29	29	0	.500	11½
Mets	0	9	0	0	9	0	0	0	0	...	0	0	0	11	0	29	30	0	.492	12
Rangers	0	0	5	0	0	3	4	6	5	0	...	0	5	0	0	28	31	0	.475	13
Astros	7	0	0	9	0	0	0	0	0	0	0	...	0	0	11	27	33	0	.450	14½
Pirates	0	0	3	0	0	4	2	4	5	0	5	0	...	0	0	23	37	0	.383	18½
Braves	0	7	0	0	6	0	0	0	0	9	0	0	0	...	0	22	37	0	.373	19
Red Sox	4	0	0	5	0	0	0	0	0	0	0	9	0	0	...	18	41	0	.305	23

Games played in Bradenton and Sarasota, Fla.

Club names are major league affiliations.

Playoffs—Expos defeated Blue Jays, one game to none; Royals defeated Expos, two games to one, to win league championship.

Regular-season attendance—No official attendance figures reported.

Managers—Astros, Julio Linares; Blue Jays, Omar Malave; Braves, Jim Saul; Dodgers, John Shoemaker; Expos, Nelson Norman; Marlins, Carlos Tosca; Mets, Junior Roman; Orioles, Phil Wellman; Pirates, Woody Huyke; Rangers, Chino Cadahia; Red Sox, Frank White; Royals, Mike Jirschele; Twins, Jim Lemon; White Sox, Mike Rojas; Yankees, Gary Denbo.

All-Star team: 1B—Chris Burr, Rangers; 2B—Jose Vidro, Expos; 3B—Tilson Brito, Blue Jays; SS—Brandon Cromer, Blue Jays; OF—Danny Clyburn, Pirates; Johnny Damon, Royals; Edgar Herrera, Twins; C—Jaime Torres, Yankees; Starting Pitcher—Fernando DaSilva, Expos; Relief Pitcher—Bart Rich, Blue Jays; Manager of the Year—Mike Jirschele, Royals.

BATTING

TEAM

Team	Avg.	G	AB	R	OR	H	TB	2B	3B	HR	RBI	SH	SF	HP	BB	Int. BB	SO	SB	CS	LOB
Royals	.274	59	2023	359	226	554	768	99	29	19	297	20	21	30	234	7	361	82	48	430
White Sox	.253	60	2004	272	231	508	669	89	15	14	220	9	21	30	179	1	421	117	56	410
Pirates	.247	60	1949	229	315	481	612	66	19	9	189	5	11	17	151	3	429	76	32	389
Marlins	.246	60	1967	248	266	484	613	77	20	4	211	21	17	29	272	4	412	74	34	468
Twins	.242	58	1918	286	330	464	625	77	21	14	219	12	26	50	218	4	406	57	18	441
Expos	.241	59	1917	243	209	462	597	76	10	13	207	12	16	21	164	9	461	50	31	380
Astros	.241	60	1906	212	236	459	577	74	16	4	179	19	21	27	189	3	346	100	57	389
Blue Jays	.240	59	1872	253	227	449	590	66	24	9	193	22	17	34	167	3	389	94	57	368
Orioles	.239	58	1787	238	251	427	557	71	25	3	192	18	17	19	187	4	413	80	44	351
Yankees	.237	60	1907	258	196	452	587	75	15	10	209	6	13	30	226	1	395	53	21	447
Dodgers	.236	59	1810	244	208	428	604	90	28	10	169	24	19	40	184	1	423	88	33	376
Red Sox	.231	59	2010	223	314	465	608	70	20	11	191	16	17	34	233	1	450	27	27	500
Rangers	.222	59	1783	238	224	395	523	74	15	8	186	4	24	47	210	1	341	106	38	371
Mets	.216	59	1821	233	287	394	508	66	15	6	189	13	25	26	217	3	386	62	26	394
Braves	.206	59	1884	205	221	388	496	57	9	11	146	15	11	19	215	3	479	75	36	386

INDIVIDUAL

(Leading qualifiers for batting championship—162 or more plate appearances)

*Bats lefthanded.   †Switch-hitter.

Player, Team	Avg.	G	AB	R	H	TB	2B	3B	HR	RBI	SH	SF	HP	BB	Int. BB	SO	SB	CS
Damon, Johnny, Royals*	.349	50	192	58	67	109	12	9	4	24	4	0	4	31	1	21	23	6
Herrera, Edgar, Twins*	.347	44	173	25	60	90	10	4	4	41	0	3	1	10	0	19	2	1
Burr, Chris, Rangers	.340	59	206	29	70	106	18	0	6	47	0	10	6	16	0	26	3	2
Robinson, Dan, Marlins*	.335	55	197	30	66	90	8	8	0	26	0	2	3	35	3	23	7	2
Vidro, Jose, Expos†	.330	54	200	29	66	88	6	2	4	31	1	2	0	16	1	31	10	1
Vasquez, Diomedes, Blue Jays†	.311	47	164	29	51	71	9	4	1	15	2	0	4	6	0	34	10	7
Hidalgo, Richard, Astros	.310	51	184	20	57	73	7	3	1	27	1	3	3	13	0	27	14	5
Brito, Tilson, Blue Jays	.307	54	189	36	58	85	10	4	3	36	0	5	6	22	1	22	16	8
Mendez, Carlos, Royals	.305	49	200	34	61	88	16	1	3	33	0	3	2	8	2	13	2	1
Jimenez, Oscar, Royals	.299	49	167	34	50	61	6	1	1	23	2	1	2	34	0	32	8	8

Departmental leaders: G—Wuerch, 60; AB—Alcantara, 224; R—Damon, 58; H—Burr, 70; TB—Damon, 109; 2B—Burr, 18; 3B—Damon, 9; HR—Burr, Thomas, 6; RBI—Burr, 47; SH—James, 7; SF—Burr, 10; HP—K. Pearson, 12; BB—Clapinski, 49; IBB—Alcantara, 4; SO—Thomas, 76; SB—Stewart, 32; CS—Walls, 11.

(All players—listed alphabetically)

Player, Team	Avg.	G	AB	R	H	TB	2B	3B	HR	RBI	SH	SF	HP	BB	Int. BB	SO	SB	CS
Acevedo, Jesus, Twins	.152	24	66	11	10	12	2	0	0	3	1	0	4	5	0	13	0	0
Aguado, Victor, Red Sox	.212	41	118	11	25	27	2	0	0	7	1	1	1	5	0	16	2	1
Albaladejo, Randy, Astros	.258	32	93	6	24	31	7	0	0	8	1	1	1	8	0	13	1	0
Albornoz, Rodolfo, Yankees	.316	17	57	7	18	20	2	0	0	3	0	1	0	3	0	5	0	1
Alcantara, Isreal, Expos	.277	59	224	29	62	89	14	2	3	37	0	2	1	17	4	35	6	5
Alfonzo, Julius, Royals	.071	5	14	2	1	1	0	0	0	1	1	0	1	0	0	3	0	0
Allen, John, Pirates	.170	24	53	4	9	10	1	0	0	2	1	0	1	4	0	18	1	2
Alonso, Marcelino, Orioles	.230	34	113	15	26	30	2	1	0	11	2	1	0	5	0	25	2	1
Ansley, Willie, Astros	.371	10	35	9	13	16	3	0	0	7	0	2	0	7	0	6	5	0
Antigua, Jose, White Sox	.375	14	24	7	9	16	2	1	1	5	1	0	0	1	0	5	1	0
Aquino, Geronimo, Orioles	.125	15	40	2	5	5	0	0	0	2	0	0	0	3	0	9	2	0
Aranzamendi, Alex, Marlins	.186	33	102	10	19	24	5	0	0	7	1	1	0	13	1	13	2	0
Arvelo, Tomas, Mets	.238	46	147	31	35	38	3	0	0	14	3	4	1	25	0	31	18	4
Baker, Keivi, Orioles†	.206	38	97	11	20	25	3	1	0	9	0	0	1	16	0	28	7	5
Barnden, Myles, Orioles*	.240	49	171	24	41	52	5	3	0	18	1	1	3	21	0	36	8	9
Barry, Jeff, Mets†	.174	8	23	5	4	5	1	0	0	2	0	0	0	6	1	2	2	0
Basey, Marsalis, Astros	.267	41	150	18	40	49	7	1	0	16	6	1	2	13	0	7	10	6
Baucom, Chad, Twins	.234	40	137	16	32	39	4	0	1	18	1	2	3	13	0	26	1	1
Baugh, Gavin, Marlins	.249	50	169	17	42	51	7	1	0	10	4	1	0	16	0	41	1	2
Beamon, Trey, Pirates*	.308	13	39	9	12	16	1	0	1	6	0	0	0	4	1	0	0	1
Beason, Samuel, Yankees	.180	34	111	10	20	23	1	1	0	6	0	0	3	11	0	34	1	0
Becker, David, Blue Jays	.212	31	85	7	18	25	3	2	0	4	1	1	1	6	0	22	1	4
Benitez, Fernando, Braves	.139	18	36	3	5	8	0	0	1	4	1	0	2	5	0	13	0	0
Bennett, Ricky, White Sox	.000	20	1	0	0	0	0	0	0	0	0	0	0	0	0	1	0	0
Blackburn, Tyres, White Sox	.207	41	140	22	29	40	8	0	1	11	1	2	1	16	0	43	14	1
Bogan, Victor, Pirates	.250	3	12	0	3	4	1	0	0	0	0	0	0	0	0	4	1	0
Boka, Ben, Pirates	.149	15	47	1	7	10	1	1	0	3	0	0	0	0	0	15	0	0
Bonifazio, Tony, Marlins	.237	55	215	30	51	67	11	1	1	28	0	2	6	18	0	49	4	2
Borrero, Richie, Red Sox	.182	34	99	9	18	30	5	2	1	12	1	1	1	14	0	24	2	1
Bostic, Dwain, Dodgers	.203	35	118	10	24	33	2	2	1	13	1	1	3	5	0	28	10	1
Bowers, Ray, Astros	.161	21	62	3	10	10	0	0	0	3	0	0	0	10	0	15	1	2
Bowles, John, Red Sox*	.189	30	95	10	18	21	1	1	0	4	1	1	0	22	0	29	0	2
Bradley, Ken, Mets	.128	21	78	9	10	15	5	0	0	7	0	0	0	8	0	22	3	1
Brady, Doug, White Sox†	.125	3	8	1	1	1	0	0	0	2	0	2	0	1	0	1	0	0
Brandon, Jelani, Royals	.244	30	82	14	20	26	4	1	0	8	0	1	0	11	1	24	6	3
Brea, Vincente, Orioles	.217	29	69	10	15	20	5	0	0	9	1	0	0	10	0	34	2	0
Brennan, Shawn, Braves	.165	41	133	14	22	23	1	0	0	7	0	0	0	14	0	26	4	0
Bright, Brian, Red Sox	.303	9	33	5	10	17	2	1	1	7	0	1	0	5	0	7	1	0
Brito, Tilson, Blue Jays	.307	54	189	36	58	85	10	4	3	36	0	5	6	22	1	22	16	8
Brown, Adrian, Pirates	.256	39	121	11	31	37	2	2	0	12	0	0	2	0	0	12	8	4
Brown, Armann, Twins	.273	20	77	13	21	22	1	0	0	4	0	0	0	12	0	11	4	1
Brown, DeShon, Rangers†	.119	23	67	6	8	14	2	2	0	3	0	1	2	4	0	29	2	1
Bumgardner, Rusty, Marlins	.080	9	25	0	2	2	0	0	0	4	0	0	0	3	0	12	0	0
Burr, Chris, Rangers	.340	59	206	29	70	106	18	0	6	47	0	10	6	16	0	26	3	2
Burton, Adam, Orioles	.176	37	108	19	19	29	5	1	1	11	1	1	1	13	0	29	9	2
Cairo, Miguel, Dodgers	.303	21	76	10	23	32	5	2	0	9	2	1	2	2	0	6	1	0
Calcaterra, Jeff, Yankees	.625	7	8	1	5	7	2	0	0	1	0	0	1	3	0	0	0	0
Candelaria, Ben, Blue Jays*	.156	29	77	10	12	16	2	1	0	3	1	1	0	6	0	16	4	3
Carbajal, Nilson, Expos	.274	23	62	4	17	22	5	0	0	9	0	0	1	10	1	21	0	0
Cardona, Claudio, Marlins	.176	11	17	0	3	3	0	0	0	0	0	0	0	0	0	8	0	0
Carey, Tim, Red Sox*	.278	39	115	15	32	33	1	0	0	21	3	2	2	21	0	17	0	1
Cassels, Chris, Expos	.233	13	43	4	10	13	3	0	0	7	0	0	2	4	0	11	0	0
Castenada, Hector, Orioles*	.287	42	122	18	35	44	9	0	0	14	0	0	3	27	1	23	2	1
Cedeno, Eduardo, Astros	.209	47	153	18	32	44	10	1	0	12	0	0	0	12	0	35	13	6
Chancey, Robert, Orioles	.291	43	141	22	41	53	3	3	1	23	0	2	0	7	0	50	13	4
Christian, Eddie, Marlins†	.279	59	219	33	61	77	10	3	0	29	0	3	1	31	2	35	14	5
Clapinski, Chris, Marlins†	.241	59	212	36	51	64	8	1	1	15	3	2	4	49	2	42	5	6
Clark, Howard, Orioles*	.239	43	138	12	33	42	7	1	0	6	1	0	2	12	2	21	1	2
Clarke, Jeff, Royals†	.179	8	28	2	5	7	2	0	0	7	0	0	0	2	0	2	0	0
Clyburn, Danny, Pirates	.342	39	149	26	51	72	9	0	4	25	0	2	1	5	0	20	7	3
Conner, Jamie, Orioles	.252	43	147	26	37	41	4	0	0	4	3	0	1	20	0	32	17	6
Corporan, Roberto, Twins	.259	31	108	10	28	35	5	1	0	14	0	0	1	5	0	12	2	1
Correa, Dalphie, Expos†	.111	25	63	12	7	7	0	0	0	3	1	0	1	11	1	16	1	1
Coughlin, Kevin, White Sox*	.333	4	15	1	5	5	0	0	0	2	0	0	0	2	0	1	0	0
Crick, Jeff, Twins	.135	31	89	13	12	21	4	1	1	5	0	0	0	25	0	41	2	2
Crispin, Carlos, Astros†	.201	52	164	20	33	34	1	0	0	11	6	1	1	15	0	36	4	5
Cromer, Brandon, Blue Jays*	.283	49	180	26	51	72	12	3	1	21	2	2	5	14	0	26	7	8
Cruz, Hiram, Twins	.161	32	87	11	14	16	2	0	0	9	2	1	5	19	0	32	3	0
Curran, Shawn, Orioles	.273	3	11	2	3	6	3	0	0	1	0	0	0	1	0	1	0	0
Daly, Rob, Mets	.271	50	181	17	49	61	8	2	0	18	1	2	1	12	0	12	1	0
Damon, Johnny, Royals*	.349	50	192	58	67	109	12	9	4	24	4	0	4	31	1	21	23	6
Davis, Tim, Red Sox	.297	36	128	23	38	53	4	4	1	12	3	1	3	21	0	12	2	2
Delafield, Glenn, Yankees	.253	51	182	28	46	56	7	0	1	23	0	2	1	26	0	38	6	4
Delgado, Eugene, Orioles	.372	13	43	8	16	20	2	1	0	4	1	0	0	7	0	6	3	1
Delgado, Pablo, Marlins	.000	3	8	0	0	0	0	0	0	0	0	0	0	1	0	3	0	0
DePastino, Joey, Red Sox	.261	40	157	13	41	52	6	1	1	16	0	2	3	7	1	25	1	1
Diaz, Alejandro, Pirates	.200	3	10	0	2	2	0	0	0	0	0	0	0	0	0	3	0	0
Diaz, Jenny, Red Sox	.204	25	54	6	11	17	4	1	0	3	0	0	5	0	0	18	1	3
Diieso, Tony, Braves†	.173	30	104	12	18	29	3	1	2	5	2	1	1	7	1	39	3	0
Dimare, Gino, Red Sox*	.143	3	7	1	1	1	0	0	0	1	0	0	0	0	0	0	0	0
Doezie, Troy, Twins	.196	20	51	5	10	12	0	1	0	6	0	1	0	6	0	14	0	0
Domingo, Tyrone, Braves	.154	22	65	3	10	10	0	0	0	4	0	0	2	3	0	21	5	1
Doval, Ruben, Braves	.236	27	89	9	21	26	3	1	0	12	2	2	2	9	0	22	2	1
Durham, Ray, White Sox†	.538	5	13	3	7	9	2	0	0	2	0	0	0	3	0	1	1	0
Durso, Joe, Blue Jays	.299	25	67	6	20	25	3	1	0	10	1	0	0	11	0	9	0	1
Eaglin, Michael, Braves	.244	14	45	4	11	12	1	0	0	3	2	1	0	4	0	8	3	1
Edmondson, Gavin, Dodgers	.230	28	87	10	20	27	3	2	0	8	1	1	2	0	0	15	2	0
Epperson, Chad, Mets†	.165	37	97	7	16	21	2	0	1	12	0	3	3	12	0	20	1	1

Player, Team	Avg.	G	AB	R	H	TB	2B	3B	HR	RBI	SH	SF	HP	BB	Int. BB	SO	SB	CS
Espinoza, Jose, Mets	.131	32	99	10	13	15	0	1	0	5	0	1	5	8	0	43	0	1
Faggett, Ethan, Red Sox*	.175	34	103	9	18	24	1	1	1	9	0	2	2	10	0	37	1	2
Faircloth, Eugene, White Sox	.236	22	55	5	13	15	2	0	0	5	0	1	1	5	0	13	1	2
Farrell, Mike, Mets	.230	34	126	17	29	33	4	0	0	3	0	0	1	6	0	29	2	0
Flagg, Paul, Dodgers*	.118	20	51	4	6	6	0	0	0	1	0	1	1	8	0	14	0	0
Fraraccio, Dan, White Sox	.208	52	149	19	31	38	5	1	0	8	1	1	4	5	0	18	5	7
Frazier, Jason, Marlins†	.067	15	30	1	2	2	0	0	0	3	0	0	2	0	0	6	0	0
Frias, Hanley, Rangers	.244	58	205	37	50	63	9	2	0	28	2	2	2	27	0	30	28	6
Garcia, Eduardo, Dodgers	.202	52	183	30	37	69	11	6	3	25	0	2	2	18	0	37	6	1
Garcia, Jose, Orioles	.000	3	4	0	0	0	0	0	0	0	0	0	0	1	0	1	0	0
Garcia, Luis, Rangers†	.164	53	146	21	24	28	2	1	0	8	1	3	1	12	0	30	17	4
Gerald, Dwayne, Royals	.200	46	160	25	32	48	5	1	3	21	2	3	0	16	0	49	11	2
Gipner, Marcus, Yankees†	.198	35	111	14	22	28	6	0	0	10	1	0	2	10	0	23	1	0
Gomez, Paul, Twins	.122	28	82	8	10	15	3	1	0	5	0	0	1	8	0	24	0	0
Gonzalez, Carlos, Expos	.269	53	186	27	50	62	7	1	1	26	0	1	3	16	0	41	1	1
Gonzalez, Mario, Rangers†	.222	58	198	35	44	54	8	1	0	15	0	1	4	40	0	28	11	6
Gordon, Adrian, Twins	.301	29	103	15	31	40	7	1	0	11	0	2	3	5	0	25	3	0
Grapenthien, Dan, Astros	.229	43	144	10	33	43	8	1	0	14	0	3	3	4	0	35	2	5
Griffin, Ryan, Blue Jays	.182	25	55	6	10	14	0	2	0	2	1	0	1	9	0	21	2	1
Guerrero, Rafael, Mets	.278	56	209	36	58	86	11	7	1	36	0	3	1	15	0	16	10	6
Haggas, Josh, Mets	.153	26	72	7	11	12	1	0	0	7	0	0	2	14	1	13	3	1
Hairston, Jeff, Pirates	.136	30	81	6	11	13	0	1	0	5	0	0	4	5	0	30	4	3
Halbruner, Rich, Blue Jays*	.184	48	158	11	29	38	6	0	1	18	0	1	4	13	0	49	1	0
Haley, Rich, Dodgers*	.357	20	70	12	25	35	8	1	0	10	0	0	3	8	0	13	0	0
Hamilton, Joe, Red Sox*	.215	23	65	6	14	16	2	0	0	6	1	0	0	8	0	18	2	0
Hammell, Alfred, Mets	.222	33	81	3	18	21	3	0	0	8	2	0	0	14	1	20	2	1
Hand, Janseen, Pirates	.302	18	63	11	19	27	2	3	0	8	1	0	0	2	0	9	2	0
Harris, Ghainbria, Pirates	.300	44	150	18	45	55	10	0	0	20	0	0	7	0	16	4	0
Harris, Marc, Pirates	.247	27	89	12	22	30	1	2	1	16	0	1	2	5	0	19	7	3
Hauswirth, Trenton, Royals	.267	46	146	23	39	49	8	1	0	20	0	1	6	25	0	22	1	4
Heaps, Chris, Yankees	.172	32	99	12	17	22	5	0	0	6	1	1	1	6	0	22	4	1
Hecker, Doug, Red Sox	.214	8	28	1	6	7	1	0	0	1	0	0	0	5	0	3	0	0
Heidelberg, Khary, Expos*	.172	30	93	9	16	20	1	0	1	8	0	0	6	1	38	3	3
Hernaiz, Juan, Dodgers	.125	35	104	10	13	16	3	0	0	4	2	1	2	4	0	41	3	2
Herrera, Edgar, Twins	.347	44	173	25	60	90	10	4	4	41	0	3	1	10	0	19	2	1
Hidalgo, Richard, Astros	.310	51	184	20	57	73	7	3	1	27	1	3	3	13	0	27	14	5
Hightower, Aaron, Blue Jays	.250	29	92	10	23	29	2	2	0	6	0	1	4	5	0	20	1	1
Hiraldo, Jerry, Mets	.212	31	85	16	18	21	1	1	0	9	0	1	1	15	0	17	2	1
Hollins, Damon, Braves	.229	49	179	35	41	58	12	1	1	15	2	0	2	30	0	22	15	2
Hollrah, Scot, White Sox*	.278	49	162	23	45	55	6	2	0	15	0	4	1	9	0	22	15	7
Humes, Terryll, Pirates	.186	18	70	6	13	18	1	2	0	8	0	0	0	5	0	22	7	1
Hurtault, Roosevelt, Expos†	.197	53	183	23	36	47	7	2	0	12	6	0	1	9	0	42	7	4
Izquierdo, Nelson, White Sox	.268	55	198	20	53	64	11	0	0	18	2	0	0	19	0	36	5	3
Jackson, Vince, Dodgers	.321	11	28	3	9	10	1	0	0	1	1	0	0	6	0	5	2	2
James, Greg, Marlins	.242	49	161	22	39	49	7	0	1	18	7	2	3	21	4	43	11	2
Jeffery, Scott, Blue Jays*	1.000	15	1	1	1	1	0	0	0	1	0	0	0	0	0	0	0	0
Jeter, Derek, Yankees	.202	47	173	19	35	54	10	0	3	25	0	2	5	19	0	36	2	2
Jimenez, Manuel, Astros	.164	22	55	5	9	11	2	0	0	3	1	0	1	5	0	10	1	1
Jimenez, Oscar, Royals	.299	49	167	36	50	61	6	1	1	23	2	1	2	34	0	32	8	8
Johnston, Tom, Pirates	.240	52	150	21	36	42	4	1	0	14	1	0	3	22	0	34	2	3
Jones, Ben, Twins	.251	50	187	33	47	58	7	2	0	10	3	2	5	15	0	21	12	5
Jones, Donny, Red Sox	.245	48	163	15	40	53	3	2	2	12	2	1	5	5	0	37	1	1
Jones, Matt, Pirates*	.229	9	35	3	8	12	1	0	1	5	0	0	2	0	4	1	0
Jose, David, Mets	.154	17	52	4	8	8	0	0	0	2	1	0	0	6	0	15	0	0
Keefe, Jim, Pirates	.190	33	100	12	19	21	0	1	0	8	0	0	1	11	0	23	5	3
Kendall, Jason, Pirates	.261	33	111	7	29	31	2	0	0	10	0	2	2	8	1	9	2	2
Kern, Mike, Royals	.180	32	100	11	18	22	4	0	0	9	0	0	1	8	0	30	3	3
Kingman, Brendan, Marlins	.231	42	121	8	28	32	2	1	0	13	2	0	2	22	0	29	2	2
Knauss, Tom, Twins	.251	55	191	25	48	77	14	3	3	26	1	5	0	29	1	36	3	1
Koeyers, Ramsey, Expos	.168	42	125	7	21	23	2	0	0	16	0	6	0	8	1	28	1	0
Kraut, Jim, Astros	.250	33	116	11	29	40	5	3	0	3	2	0	0	11	0	21	3	3
Kuhn, Alex, Braves	.333	1	6	2	2	2	0	0	0	0	0	0	0	0	0	1	0	0
Lachance, Vince, Expos*	.283	46	166	34	47	54	5	1	0	12	0	1	4	19	0	39	3	1
Lackey, Steve, Mets	.191	12	47	6	9	10	1	0	0	3	1	0	1	3	0	7	0	1
Lantigua, Eduardo, Dodgers	.314	20	70	11	22	38	7	3	1	15	1	3	1	1	0	24	1	0
Latham, Chris, Dodgers†	.229	14	48	4	11	13	2	0	0	2	1	1	0	5	1	17	2	3
Lawton, Matt, Twins*	.260	53	173	39	45	65	8	3	2	26	1	7	9	27	0	27	20	1
Lebron, Ruben, Red Sox†	.111	10	9	1	1	2	1	0	0	1	0	0	1	0	0	2	0	0
Ledee, Ricky, Yankees*	.229	52	179	25	41	60	9	2	2	23	0	1	1	24	1	47	1	4
Lee, Charles, Expos	.375	4	16	4	6	9	3	0	0	3	0	0	1	1	0	4	3	1
Leger, Tim, Pirates	.211	27	90	6	19	22	1	1	0	7	0	1	3	8	0	24	7	2
Levias, Andres, White Sox†	.360	37	100	20	36	42	4	1	0	7	3	1	3	7	0	17	11	6
Lewis, Brian, Yankees*	.229	46	157	17	36	45	3	3	0	10	1	1	0	14	0	30	2	1
Lewis, Tyrone, Dodgers	.248	49	161	24	40	53	8	1	1	9	5	1	2	15	0	29	13	5
Livsey, Shawn, Astros†	.274	38	117	20	32	42	3	2	1	14	0	3	4	29	0	12	10	5
Lloyd, Ron, Braves*	.164	28	73	7	12	17	3	1	0	0	0	0	9	0	16	7	2
Lopez, Miguel, Royals†	.200	9	30	4	6	8	2	0	0	1	1	0	0	2	0	5	0	0
Lopez, Orangel, Yankees	.220	32	100	13	22	26	4	0	0	11	0	1	3	3	0	16	3	1
Lorenzo, Odalis, Red Sox	.032	14	31	2	1	1	0	0	0	1	0	0	1	4	0	5	1	1
Mackert, Jamie, Pirates	.000	3	8	0	0	0	0	0	0	0	0	0	0	0	0	4	0	0
Mader, Chris, White Sox	.300	15	40	5	12	15	1	1	0	2	0	0	2	4	0	4	3	0
Madera, Remberto, Royals	.174	6	23	1	4	4	0	0	0	0	0	0	0	2	0	1	0	0
Maness, Dwight, Dodgers	.252	44	139	24	35	47	6	3	0	12	3	3	8	14	0	36	18	9
Maple, Marcus, Rangers	.156	12	32	4	5	7	0	1	0	3	0	0	2	4	0	8	0	0
Martin, Jeff, Red Sox	.291	40	117	15	34	50	9	2	1	12	0	0	5	22	0	32	0	1
Martinez, Hector, Blue Jays	.197	34	127	11	25	34	7	1	0	16	1	2	0	1	0	20	1	3
Martinez, Luis, Expos	.179	12	28	2	5	6	1	0	0	4	0	1	0	1	0	7	0	1
Martinez, Ramon, Astros	.233	47	146	18	34	44	5	1	1	13	2	1	1	13	0	37	8	3
Matos, Pasqual, Braves	.152	13	33	3	5	6	1	0	0	1	0	0	0	3	0	12	0	1
McDonald, Andy, White Sox	.319	27	69	12	22	36	4	2	2	15	0	2	1	9	0	10	6	0
McDonald, Bob, Expos	.000	11	2	0	0	0	0	0	0	0	1	0	0	0	0	1	0	0
Melendez, Jorge, Rangers	.231	27	78	7	18	21	1	1	0	9	0	1	5	19	0	17	1	1
Mendez, Carlos, Royals	.305	49	200	34	61	88	16	1	3	33	0	3	2	8	2	13	2	1
Mendez, Roberto, Pirates	.147	14	34	3	5	8	1	1	0	1	0	1	0	4	0	9	0	0

Player, Team	Avg.	G	AB	R	H	TB	2B	3B	HR	RBI	SH	SF	HP	BB	Int. BB	SO	SB	CS
Mendez, Sergio, Pirates	.269	15	52	6	14	15	1	0	0	5	0	1	0	1	0	8	3	0
Mendoza, Francisco, Royals	.287	26	94	14	27	36	4	1	1	14	0	1	2	12	2	14	1	1
Mercedes, Guillermo, Rangers	.216	49	176	30	38	42	4	0	0	7	0	0	4	18	0	26	18	6
Miley, Scott, Orioles	.255	45	149	18	38	58	7	5	1	21	1	2	6	9	0	32	4	2
Milligan, Ricky, Red Sox	.227	49	163	23	37	56	9	2	2	20	1	1	3	23	0	43	4	3
Montilla, Julio, Royals	.375	21	80	17	30	46	1	3	3	17	1	1	0	3	0	6	1	1
Mora, Melvin, Astros	.222	49	144	28	32	35	3	0	0	8	0	1	5	18	0	16	16	3
Morales, Heriberto, Mets†	.109	26	64	4	7	8	1	0	0	6	1	1	2	8	0	15	0	1
Moultrie, Pat, Blue Jays*	.232	47	125	12	29	32	3	0	0	12	4	0	0	20	0	35	7	8
Mumma, Bob, White Sox	.235	9	17	3	4	4	0	0	0	1	0	0	0	2	0	5	0	0
Nelson, Trey, Yankees	.163	33	104	12	17	26	3	3	0	13	0	0	0	19	0	41	1	0
Niethammer, Marc, Expos*	.113	23	80	8	9	20	2	0	3	6	0	1	3	7	0	40	0	0
Noel, Jason, Braves	.118	9	34	2	4	5	1	0	0	2	0	0	0	3	0	11	1	1
Nolan, Sean, Pirates	.228	37	127	20	29	40	6	1	1	9	1	2	0	8	0	28	8	3
Norman, Jeff, Royals	.280	8	25	3	7	8	1	0	0	4	0	0	0	4	0	9	0	1
Norman, Tyrone, Red Sox	.220	21	41	4	9	13	1	0	1	2	0	0	3	4	0	6	2	2
Nunez, Clemente, Marlins	.000	12	2	0	0	0	0	0	0	0	0	0	0	0	0	2	0	0
O'Donnell, T.J., Red Sox	.344	10	32	4	11	12	1	0	0	6	0	1	0	2	0	2	1	1
O'Neill, Doug, Expos	.200	3	10	0	2	2	0	0	0	0	0	0	0	2	0	3	1	1
Ordonez, Magglio, White Sox	.180	38	111	17	20	37	10	2	1	14	0	1	2	13	0	26	6	4
Ortiz, Nick, Red Sox	.264	50	163	25	43	58	9	3	0	15	2	1	0	28	0	36	3	2
Oster, Paul, Yankees†	.222	7	27	3	6	9	0	0	1	4	1	0	1	3	0	3	0	0
Pagan, Angel, Orioles	.197	41	127	14	25	29	4	0	0	16	1	4	1	4	0	23	2	3
Palmer, Travis, Pirates	.317	28	82	6	26	32	6	0	0	6	0	1	0	5	0	24	1	2
Patton, Scott, White Sox	.237	44	131	18	31	40	7	1	0	16	0	0	3	20	0	39	10	3
Patzke, Jeff, Blue Jays†	.095	6	21	3	2	2	0	0	0	1	0	0	0	3	0	2	0	1
Pearson, Cory, Yankees	.172	54	151	19	26	31	3	1	0	15	0	1	9	21	0	33	11	4
Pearson, Eddie, White Sox*	.235	28	102	10	24	29	5	0	0	12	0	1	2	9	1	17	1	3
Pearson, Kevin, Twins	.211	45	142	20	30	36	1	1	1	12	2	1	12	14	0	57	0	1
Perez, Ed, Braves	.333	2	6	1	2	2	0	0	0	1	0	0	0	2	0	2	1	0
Pichardo, Sandy, Mets†	.296	44	142	26	42	55	7	3	0	12	2	0	2	26	0	31	14	5
Pitts, Jon, Rangers	.212	35	113	13	24	32	8	0	0	7	0	0	3	12	0	14	1	2
Polidor, Wil, White Sox†	.282	27	78	3	22	24	2	0	0	4	0	0	0	2	0	8	1	3
Prater, Andrew, Marlins	.208	54	144	14	30	44	7	2	1	25	1	2	6	30	1	41	7	2
Pulido, Francisco, White Sox	.200	5	5	0	1	1	0	0	0	0	0	0	0	0	0	0	1	0
Randle, Mike, White Sox	.333	11	24	3	8	11	3	0	0	5	0	0	0	2	0	6	1	0
Reese, Terling, Braves*	.300	13	40	3	12	16	1	0	1	7	0	0	2	0	0	7	1	0
Rennhack, Mike, Astros†	.206	35	126	11	26	36	2	4	0	16	0	1	0	14	2	18	6	4
Rennspies, Dustin, Dodgers†	.100	3	10	2	1	1	0	0	0	0	0	0	0	2	0	2	0	0
Renteria, Dave, Yankees	.230	20	61	6	14	15	1	0	0	7	0	0	0	6	0	14	0	0
Renteria, Edgar, Marlins	.288	43	163	25	47	57	8	1	0	9	2	0	2	8	0	29	10	6
Reyes, Angel, Yankees*	.000	1	0	1	0	0	0	0	0	0	0	0	0	1	0	0	0	0
Reyes, Roberto, Expos	.258	45	178	27	46	61	11	2	0	11	1	1	1	14	0	33	7	6
Richardson, Brian, Dodgers	.213	37	122	8	26	36	6	2	0	15	0	2	0	11	0	27	3	0
Richardson, Eric, White Sox	.283	43	113	18	32	33	1	0	0	14	0	4	0	17	0	10	18	6
Richmond, Clarence, Dodgers†	.259	37	85	12	22	27	1	2	0	2	2	0	3	8	0	21	8	1
Riggs, Anthony, Rangers	.211	56	175	23	37	54	10	2	1	16	1	1	7	14	0	48	7	3
Rivera, Ruben, Yankees	.273	53	194	37	53	72	10	3	1	20	2	0	6	42	0	49	21	6
Rivers, Jon, Blue Jays	.222	32	72	12	16	24	2	0	2	9	0	0	2	4	0	20	5	1
Robinson, Dan, Marlins*	.335	55	197	30	66	90	8	8	0	26	0	2	3	35	3	23	7	2
Robledo, Nilson, White Sox	.129	10	31	0	4	5	1	0	0	3	0	0	0	0	0	7	1	0
Rodriguez, Anthony, Dodgers	.279	17	43	10	12	16	4	0	0	5	0	0	3	6	0	15	2	1
Rodriguez, Jose, Braves	.500	2	6	0	3	3	0	0	0	0	0	0	0	0	0	1	0	0
Rodriguez, Nerio, White Sox	.270	41	122	18	33	49	8	1	2	13	1	3	1	10	0	31	1	5
Rodriguez, Noel, Astros	.313	37	134	8	42	52	7	0	1	16	0	3	1	4	1	22	3	6
Roper, Chad, Twins	.329	20	76	16	25	39	5	3	1	11	0	1	1	5	1	16	1	0
Ross, Tony, Astros	.200	3	10	0	2	2	0	0	0	1	0	0	0	1	0	3	2	1
Rounsifer, Aaron, Red Sox	.100	17	40	6	4	4	0	0	0	1	0	0	4	8	0	11	1	1
Ruoff, Matt, Yankees*	.000	2	4	0	0	0	0	0	0	0	0	0	0	0	0	0	0	0
Saffer, Jon, Expos*	.273	36	139	18	38	40	2	0	0	11	2	1	1	11	0	23	7	5
Santiago, Carlos, Blue Jays	.173	23	52	8	9	11	2	0	0	3	0	0	4	1	0	11	0	0
Seesz, Brian, Rangers*	.227	52	176	10	40	56	7	3	1	25	0	4	1	15	1	38	1	2
Selmo, Feliberto, Braves	.278	21	79	8	22	27	3	1	0	5	0	0	0	12	0	17	3	3
Sheffield, Tony, Red Sox*	.190	48	153	11	29	35	6	0	0	14	2	3	1	13	0	50	2	2
Shelley, Jason, Braves	.125	13	40	3	5	5	0	0	0	2	0	0	1	6	0	20	0	1
Shrum, Dennis, Royals	.237	39	131	25	31	46	10	1	1	13	2	3	2	15	0	10	1	2
Smith, Bobby, Braves	.235	57	217	31	51	71	9	1	3	28	0	2	3	17	1	55	5	6
Smith, James, Marlins	.094	13	32	1	3	4	1	0	0	1	1	0	0	3	0	12	0	1
Smith, Jerrod, Royals*	.250	41	128	19	32	49	7	5	0	20	1	1	4	13	1	43	1	4
Smith, Sean, Braves*	.287	27	87	13	25	29	4	0	0	8	1	1	1	12	0	14	2	1
Stewart, Shannon, Blue Jays	.233	50	172	44	40	44	1	0	1	11	4	2	3	24	0	27	32	5
Strickland, Erick, Marlins*	.267	44	150	21	40	47	3	2	0	23	0	2	2	20	0	26	11	4
Stutts, Jim, Marlins	.172	31	93	13	16	21	2	0	1	6	1	2	1	13	0	34	6	3
Subero, Carlos, Royals†	.289	40	152	27	44	58	8	3	0	30	5	4	1	12	0	15	6	0
Tackett, Tim, Red Sox	.246	25	61	6	15	17	2	0	0	5	1	1	1	2	0	12	0	0
Tatro, Glenn, Orioles*	.204	17	49	7	10	14	2	1	0	3	0	0	0	4	0	7	0	2
Tena, Dario, Pirates†	.313	6	16	5	5	5	0	0	0	3	0	0	0	4	0	1	3	1
Thomas, Juan, White Sox	.222	55	189	30	42	68	6	1	6	29	0	2	3	18	0	76	6	1
Thorsteinson, Jason, Expos*	.202	39	119	6	24	34	7	0	1	15	0	1	0	12	0	48	0	1
Torres, Jaime, Yankees	.347	33	121	21	42	60	8	2	2	23	0	2	3	6	0	12	0	0
Turlais, John, Pirates*	.177	32	96	14	17	22	3	1	0	8	1	0	0	6	0	29	1	0
Urena, Fausto, Dodgers*	.277	36	112	20	31	49	9	3	1	16	1	0	1	22	0	22	4	2
Valera, Antonio, Orioles†	.174	22	46	5	8	10	0	1	0	7	4	1	0	5	0	14	0	1
Vaninetti, Gene, Blue Jays	.176	38	91	8	16	18	2	0	0	7	3	1	2	9	0	31	3	0
Vasquez, Diomedes, Blue Jays†	.311	47	164	29	51	71	9	4	1	15	2	0	4	12	1	19	10	7
Vasquez, Lipergey, Braves	.190	19	63	3	12	14	2	0	0	7	1	1	0	6	0	18	0	2
Vaught, Craig, Blue Jays	.271	45	144	13	39	49	2	4	0	18	2	1	2	10	0	24	4	5
Vazquetelles, Darren, Braves	.208	8	24	2	5	5	0	0	0	0	0	0	0	6	0	1	1	1
Ventura, Efrain, White Sox	.111	6	18	2	2	2	0	0	0	0	0	0	0	0	0	5	1	1
Vidro, Jose, Expos*	.330	54	200	29	66	88	6	2	4	31	1	2	0	16	1	31	10	1
Vindivich, Paul, Royals	.309	32	94	13	29	45	6	2	2	25	0	2	6	9	0	28	2	1
Vinyard, Derek, Red Sox*	.269	6	26	1	7	7	0	0	0	1	0	0	0	2	0	4	0	0
Vizcaino, Romulo, Twins†	.197	39	132	14	26	32	1	1	1	10	0	1	0	16	1	28	1	4
Walker, Shon, Pirates*	.295	47	156	27	46	66	10	2	2	15	0	1	0	30	1	50	8	2

Player, Team	Avg.	G	AB	R	H	TB	2B	3B	HR	RBI	SH	SF	HP	BB	Int. BB	SO	SB	CS
Walls, Eric, Royals*	.288	51	177	31	51	57	3	0	1	25	1	1	0	31	0	34	16	11
Walton, Carlo, Dodgers	.105	6	19	0	2	2	0	0	0	1	2	0	1	0	0	0	1	0
Warner, Ken, Braves	.203	45	148	18	30	38	6	1	0	8	1	1	1	27	0	49	9	3
Warner, Randy, Mets	.260	56	200	23	52	77	16	0	3	38	2	8	2	13	0	38	3	2
Warren, Mel, Dodgers	.200	21	60	11	12	15	3	0	0	3	0	0	0	14	0	20	6	3
Washington, Lamann, Orioles	.170	37	94	12	16	23	3	2	0	6	1	2	1	13	0	29	5	3
Watts, Craig, Dodgers	.163	14	43	4	7	14	1	0	2	3	1	0	1	6	0	15	0	0
Wieser, Mike, Braves	.194	48	175	10	34	47	5	1	2	19	2	0	4	10	0	42	2	3
Williams, Ray, Rangers	.183	24	60	4	11	15	2	1	0	3	0	0	1	8	0	14	6	2
Williams, Richard, Braves+	.183	33	109	6	20	22	2	0	0	6	0	0	1	9	1	28	5	4
Wilson, Enrique, Twins+	.341	13	44	12	15	16	1	0	0	8	0	1	4	4	0	4	3	0
Wingate, Ervan, Dodgers	.286	37	126	22	36	49	8	1	1	11	1	2	1	18	0	19	3	2
Winget, Jeremy, Orioles*	.331	31	118	13	39	56	7	5	0	27	1	3	0	11	0	13	3	2
Witt, Joe, Astros*	.151	27	73	7	11	15	4	0	0	7	0	1	5	12	0	33	1	2
Wittig, Paul, Dodgers	.255	23	55	3	14	16	2	0	0	4	0	0	5	8	0	17	3	1
Wolf, Brian, Pirates*	.258	30	97	7	25	32	3	2	0	9	0	0	0	9	0	33	1	0
Wuerch, Jason, Yankees*	.265	60	219	32	58	64	4	1	0	24	0	2	3	30	0	25	11	1
Young, Ty, Mets*	.127	44	118	12	15	22	2	1	1	7	0	2	4	26	0	55	1	1
Zambrano, Jose, Red Sox	.222	2	9	1	2	2	0	0	0	0	0	0	0	0	0	4	0	0

The following pitchers, listed alphabetically by club, with games in parentheses, had no plate appearances, primarily through use of designated hitters:

ASTROS—Billingsley, Marv (12); Dault, Don (8); Fesh, Sean (18); Grzanich, Mike (17); Holleday, Juan (14); Linehan, Andy (9); Lopez, Johann (17); Lugo, Arquimedes (13); Mercado, Hector (13); Narcisse, Tyrone (11); Rapaglia, Stephan (8); Runyan, Sean (10); Spring, Joshua (18); Valdez, Victor (11).

BLUE JAYS—Adkins, Tim (11); Arias, Alfredo (9); Cheek, Jeff (12); Geraldo, Tony (8); Kennedy, Scott (9); Leystra, Jeff (20); Maldonado, Jason (9); Meiners, Doug (7); Patterson, Bob (3); Pearlman, Dave (21); Rich, Bart (27); Silva, Jose (12); Sinclair, Steve (5); Stefanoff, Mike (9); Taylor, Mike (1).

BRAVES—Arnold, Jim (7); Blaine, Jim (17); Christmas, Maurice (11); Church, Chris (22); Gagnon, Clint (14); Jacobs, Ryan (12); May, Darrell (12); Paige, Carey (13); Robinson, Raul (10); Rondon, Silverio (15); Smoot, Chris (6); Teran, Dan (15).

DODGERS—Bobb, Jason (12); Cook, Kenny (13); Costello, Chris (7); Duran, Roberto (9); Hendricks, Kacy (11); Jacobson, Joe (6); Kenady, Jason (16); Linares, Rich (7); Markham, Dan (9); Martinez, Jesus (7); Perez, Jayson (12); Rizzo, Todd (3); Sarmiento, Dan (7); Smith, Kevin (16); Stephens, Bill (17); Watts, Brandon (4); White, Brandon (5).

EXPOS—Alfonseca, Tony (12); Cuda, John (18); DaSilva, Fernando (12); Encarnacion, Alex (9); Fultz, Vince (2); Galart, Kevin (14); Hostetler, Jeff (11); Hylton, Jim (14); McDonald, Kevin (9); Mellor, Jon (15); Randall, Derrick (6); Steele, Mike (1); Vializ, Arce (11).

MARLINS—Bavousett, Brian (18); Campbell, Todd (14); Darensbourg, Victor (8); Gomez, Phil (12); Harms, Mike (7); Ireland, Rich (10); Johnson, Scott (16); Larkin, Andy (14); Moore, Kendrick (10); Reeder, Greg (20); Saunders, Tony (24); Tidwell, Jason (11); Veneziale, Mike (7).

METS—Baker, Derek (11); Carr, Bob (16); Harris, John (10); Hayward, Brent (15); Hokanson, Mark (11); Isringhausen, Jason (6); Knott, Jim (6); Krablin, Justin (12); McDill, Allen (10); McGinn, Mark (7); Roque, Antonio (20); Sherman, Tyril (16); Spang, Bob (6); Tatis, Ramon (11); Trumpour, Andy (8).

ORIOLES—Alfonseca, Yhonny (21); Andujar, Guillermo (19); Brown, Cory (11); Conner, Scott (12); Florentino, Ramon (15); Hale, Shane (2); Lee, Calvin (1); Maduro, Calvin (13); McCarthy, John (9); Mercedes, Jose (8); Percibal, Bill (16); Price, Tobias (9); Smith, Byrond (11).

PIRATES—Beck, Brian (8); Davidson, Rodney (12); Del Toro, Miguel (11); DeLeon, Elcidio (18); Dillinger, John (13); Fairfax, Ken (7); Ford, John (16); Johnson, Jason (5); Lambert, Ryan (2); Morel, Ramon (14); Nuttle, Jamie (7); Pelka, Brian (7); Phillips, Jason (4); Santana, Manuel (13); Taylor, Mike (15).

RANGERS—Anderson, Mike (12); Andrews, Dave (1); Ayala, Jason (1); Chiamparino, Scott (1); Delzine, Domingo (13); Dunivan, Kevin (12); Fajardo, Hector (1); Henson, Mickey (8); Manning, Dave (5); Martin, Jerry (9); Martinez, Ramiro (10); McCray, Eric (2); Perez, Leopardo (17); Perez, Luis (16); Reinozo, Querbin (11); Runion, Jeff (13); Seaton, Bill (14); Seip, Rodney (17); Starr, Chris (1); Ubiera, Miguel (10); Vallot, Joe (1).

RED SOX—Allen, Ron (13); Amos, Chad (11); Anacki, Paul (2); Bakkum, Scott (4); Becker, Kevin (13); Berryman, Bob (5); Brooks, Wes (14); Cormier, Eric (13); Craig, Ricky (14); Davis, Chris C. (6); Davis, Chris L. (1); Gonzalez, Mel (2); Hansen, Brent (3); Mejia, Jorge (13); Perez, Hilario (11); Pinango, Simon (14); Renfroe, Chad (1); Schoenvogel, Chris (1); Tyrrell, Jim (7).

ROYALS—Adam, Justin (13); Bacon, Rich (18); Bennett, Matt (10); Bunch, Mel (5); Burley, Rich (15); Campusano, Anibal (3); Centala, Scott (3); Clark, Dera (2); Fitzpatrick, Ken (11); Hodges, Kevin (11); Hodgson, Jim (7); Pittsley, Jim (9); Sanchez, Jose (23); Santos, Juan (14); Solomon, Ray (21); Towns, Ryan (9).

TWINS—Alvarado, Luis (16); Belcher, Jim (18); Bermudez, Carlos (11); Cobb, Trevor (11); Debrino, Bob (15); Fidge, Darren (14); Gourdin, Tom (13); Hawkins, Latroy (6); Herrera, Raul (12); Pina, Pedro (15); Serafini, Dan (8); Sosa, Alex (8); Stevens, Neil (12); Tatar, Jason (17); Tejada, Antonio (3).

WHITE SOX—Bell, Jason (3); Boehringer, Brian (2); Brincks, Mark (9); Donnelly, Brendan (9); Ellis, Bob (1); Elsbernd, Dave (4); Ford, Yusef (7); Fritz, Greg (6); Gay, Chris (9); Howard, Chris (1); Jackson, Mike (2); Jenkins, Jonathan (1); Johnson, Earnie (1); Kubicki, Marc (8); Lehman, Toby (9); Malaver, Johnny (20); McKinion, Mickey (8); Soto, Juan (8); Starks, Fred (5); Theodile, Bob (4); Worrell, Steve (2).

YANKEES—Brown, Chuck (12); Brown, Tibor (2); Christopher, Tyron (16); Cindrich, Jeff (12); Ferguson, Howard (4); Ferguson, Shane (19); Gordon, Mike (11); Janzen, Martin (12); Kiper, Joe (15); Long, Joe (7); McDermott, Randy (3); Mmahat, Kevin (4); Parra, Luis (10); Plonk, Chadwick (15); Ramirez, Luis (13); Taylor, Wade (3); Thomforde, Jim (5); Turrentine, Rich (2); Wiley, Jim (4); Witt, Mike (3).

GRAND SLAMS—Ledee, Seesz, Vindivich, 1 each.

AWARDED FIRST BASE ON CATCHER'S INTERFERENCE—Ledee 3 (Baucom, Boka, H. Martinez); G. Harris 2 (Acevedo, Ne. Rodriguez); Heaps 2 (Acevedo, Ne. Rodriguez); Barnden (Kendall); L. Garcia (Torres); Gipner (Pitts); Grapenthien (Prater); Hidalgo (Prater); D. Jones (Prater); Strickland (Kraut); Torres (Ne. Rodriguez); Witt (Martin).

PITCHING

TEAM

Team	ERA	G	CG	ShO	Sv.	IP	H	R	ER	HR	HB	BB	Int. BB	SO	WP	Bk.
Yankees	2.30	60	2	4	15	498.0	390	196	127	5	34	170	4	506	31	20
Expos	2.61	59	12	13	9	507.1	369	209	147	5	30	207	0	429	41	9
Dodgers	2.66	59	5	7	14	488.0	395	208	144	12	21	203	5	462	44	13
Braves	2.86	59	3	5	10	512.1	416	221	163	8	24	186	5	442	31	12
White Sox	2.89	60	5	9	15	520.2	458	231	167	9	33	169	3	403	42	16
Blue Jays	2.92	59	1	3	20	501.2	445	227	163	9	22	155	0	435	38	12
Astros	2.95	60	0	3	16	519.0	463	236	170	7	37	200	4	431	55	22
Rangers	3.11	59	2	1	17	485.2	429	224	168	13	25	159	5	346	28	15
Royals	3.26	59	1	6	15	524.1	457	226	190	8	33	241	1	428	40	9
Orioles	3.37	58	10	5	5	478.2	438	251	179	10	30	210	3	386	58	17
Marlins	3.63	60	3	5	15	530.1	498	266	214	12	27	234	8	322	39	15
Mets	3.91	59	2	5	16	489.2	492	287	213	15	31	184	6	416	66	14

Team	ERA	G	CG	ShO	Sv.	IP	H	R	ER	HR	HB	BB	Int. BB	SO	WP	Bk.
Red Sox	4.04	59	1	2	10	521.0	544	314	234	11	23	253	11	388	44	21
Twins	4.24	58	3	3	19	499.0	491	330	235	14	44	248	0	334	31	17
Pirates	4.34	60	4	1	8	499.2	525	315	241	7	39	227	0	384	46	24

INDIVIDUAL

(Leading qualifiers for earned-run average leadership—48 or more innings)

*Throws lefthanded.

Pitcher, Team	W	L	Pct.	ERA	G	GS	CG	GF	ShO	Sv.	IP	H	R	ER	HR	HB	BB	Int. BB	SO	WP
Cindrich, Yankees	8	3	.727	0.80	12	11	2	0	1	0	67.2	39	17	6	0	2	19	0	87	3
Hostetler, Expos*	6	2	.750	0.98	11	11	2	0	1	0	73.1	45	13	8	0	4	35	0	64	8
Valdez, Astros*	5	2	.714	1.28	11	11	0	0	1	0	63.1	51	17	9	0	1	8	0	36	5
Gay, White Sox*	5	3	.625	1.32	9	9	0	0	0	0	61.1	52	13	9	2	2	9	0	37	0
May, Braves*	4	3	.571	1.36	12	7	0	4	0	1	53.0	34	13	8	0	2	13	0	61	2
DaSilva, Expos	10	1	.909	1.42	12	12	8	0	4	0	95.0	59	16	15	1	5	10	0	86	2
Adkins, Blue Jays*	6	2	.750	1.72	11	10	0	1	0	0	57.2	50	15	11	2	1	11	0	49	3
Bennett, White Sox	2	2	.500	1.85	20	1	0	12	0	4	48.2	30	12	10	0	3	10	0	42	2
Conner, Orioles	4	5	.444	1.93	12	11	3	0	1	0	70.0	56	29	15	2	5	31	0	39	4
Smith, Orioles	4	3	.571	1.95	11	10	2	1	2	0	60.0	37	20	13	0	7	18	0	54	4

Departmental leaders: G—Rich, 27; W—DaSilva, 10; L—Rondon, 8; Pct.—DaSilva, .909; GS—Several pitchers tied with 12; CG—DaSilva, 8; GF—Rich, 26; ShO—DaSilva, 4; Sv.—Rich, 16; IP—DaSilva, 95.0; H—Renfroe, 81; R—Renfroe, 49; ER—Renfroe, 42; HR—Bobb, 5; HB—Santana, 10; BB—Stevens, 44; IBB—Allen, 3; SO—Cindrich, 87; WP—Florentino, 13.

(All pitchers—listed alphabetically)

Pitcher, Team	W	L	Pct.	ERA	G	GS	CG	GF	ShO	Sv.	IP	H	R	ER	HR	HB	BB	Int. BB	SO	WP
Adam, Royals	0	1	.000	7.15	13	1	0	2	0	0	22.2	24	22	18	1	2	29	0	18	4
Adkins, Blue Jays*	6	2	.750	1.72	11	10	0	1	0	0	57.2	50	15	11	2	1	11	0	49	3
Alfonseca, Expos	3	4	.429	3.68	12	10	1	0	1	0	66.0	55	31	27	0	3	35	0	62	8
Alfonseca, Orioles	6	1	.857	2.63	21	1	1	14	0	2	41.0	45	18	12	0	1	13	1	46	2
Allen, Red Sox*	0	2	.000	3.81	13	2	0	6	0	2	28.1	20	15	12	0	5	34	3	21	7
Alvarado, Twins	2	2	.500	6.83	16	1	0	8	0	2	29.0	42	30	22	2	3	8	0	18	2
Amos, Red Sox	4	0	1.000	4.86	11	0	0	10	0	2	16.2	23	10	9	0	4	2	0	18	2
Anacki, Red Sox	1	0	1.000	9.82	9	0	0	0	0	0	3.2	1	4	4	0	1	7	0	2	0
Anderson, Rangers	0	3	.000	5.79	12	0	0	8	0	4	18.2	24	14	12	0	2	7	2	14	2
Andrews, Rangers	0	0	.000	0.00	1	0	0	0	0	0	1.0	2	1	0	0	0	0	0	0	0
Andujar, Orioles	5	1	.833	3.60	19	1	0	14	0	3	40.0	26	17	16	0	1	23	1	37	0
Arias, Blue Jays	1	1	.500	8.79	9	1	0	2	0	0	14.1	28	27	14	1	1	20	0	9	5
Arnold, Braves	0	1	.000	4.05	7	5	0	2	0	0	20.0	26	16	9	0	4	6	0	22	0
Ayala, Rangers	0	1	.000	20.25	1	1	0	0	0	0	1.1	3	3	3	0	0	3	0	1	0
Bacon, Royals	3	1	.750	2.23	18	0	0	4	0	1	36.1	27	14	9	1	0	24	0	41	9
Baker, Mets	4	2	.667	2.45	11	10	2	1	0	0	58.2	53	21	16	1	2	16	0	40	4
Bakkum, Red Sox	0	1	.000	9.00	4	1	0	2	0	0	11.0	19	11	11	0	0	5	0	8	0
Bavousett, Marlins	2	2	.500	3.86	18	1	0	8	0	3	28.0	31	17	12	1	6	14	1	8	5
Beck, Pirates*	1	0	1.000	2.08	7	0	0	2	0	0	13.0	10	6	3	0	3	7	0	6	4
Becker, Red Sox	0	3	.000	6.17	13	1	0	10	0	2	23.1	24	19	16	3	4	21	2	18	6
Belcher, Twins	2	3	.400	2.48	18	0	0	16	0	7	29.0	27	13	8	0	2	11	0	17	1
Bell, White Sox	0	0	.000	12.27	3	0	0	1	0	0	3.2	5	5	5	0	1	5	0	1	1
Bennett, Royals	3	2	.600	3.49	10	10	0	0	0	0	49.0	41	21	19	0	2	29	0	34	4
Bennett, White Sox	2	2	.500	1.85	20	1	0	12	0	4	48.2	30	12	10	0	3	10	0	42	2
Bermudez, Twins	3	2	.600	2.40	11	9	0	0	0	0	48.2	40	22	13	0	5	34	0	27	4
Berryman, Red Sox	0	3	.000	5.29	5	2	0	2	0	0	17.0	16	11	10	0	1	12	0	16	0
Billingsley, Astros*	3	1	.750	2.57	12	3	0	3	0	0	28.0	28	10	8	1	2	18	0	26	2
Blaine, Braves	0	3	.000	1.71	17	3	0	4	0	1	42.0	27	10	8	1	2	15	0	23	5
Bobb, Dodgers	6	1	.857	3.55	12	12	1	0	0	0	71.0	73	42	28	5	0	18	1	67	4
Boehringer, White Sox	1	1	.500	1.50	2	2	0	0	0	0	12.0	9	3	2	0	1	2	0	8	0
Brincks, White Sox	2	3	.400	3.29	9	4	0	2	0	0	41.0	39	17	15	1	1	5	0	32	2
Brooks, Red Sox	3	5	.375	3.53	14	11	1	1	0	0	71.1	78	40	28	1	2	21	0	57	1
C. Brown, Yankees	2	1	.667	3.20	12	7	0	0	0	0	45.0	45	20	16	1	2	14	0	34	3
Brown, Orioles	3	2	.600	3.60	11	7	1	0	1	0	50.0	47	27	20	2	4	20	0	43	4
T. Brown, Yankees*	0	0	.000	3.00	2	0	0	1	0	1	3.0	1	2	1	0	2	2	1	2	1
Bunch, Royals	2	1	.667	1.50	5	4	0	1	0	0	24.0	11	6	4	2	1	3	0	26	0
Burley, Royals*	4	3	.571	3.79	15	8	0	3	0	1	54.2	59	31	23	1	5	26	0	51	3
Calcaterra, Yankees	0	0	.000	0.00	2	0	0	0	0	0	4.0	0	0	0	0	1	0	0	6	0
Campbell, Marlins	0	2	.000	7.20	14	2	0	4	0	0	25.0	26	22	20	1	0	16	0	19	1
Campusano, Royals	0	0	.000	1.50	3	1	0	2	0	0	6.0	2	1	1	0	2	0	1	1	0
Carr, Mets*	5	0	1.000	1.99	16	2	0	9	0	2	40.2	30	14	9	3	0	11	1	40	0
Centala, Royals	2	0	1.000	0.00	3	3	0	0	0	0	15.0	8	0	0	0	0	3	0	14	0
Cheek, Blue Jays	4	4	.500	2.30	12	7	1	2	0	0	54.2	52	24	14	0	5	14	0	40	5
Chiamparino, Rangers	0	1	.000	0.00	1	1	0	0	0	0	7.0	4	2	0	0	0	0	0	5	1
Christmas, Braves	3	4	.429	2.49	11	10	0	0	0	0	50.2	42	21	14	0	1	14	0	30	0
Christopher, Yankees	2	2	.500	1.73	16	0	0	11	0	2	26.0	26	8	5	0	4	9	0	28	1
Church, Braves*	2	5	.286	1.76	22	0	0	19	0	5	41.0	27	11	8	1	1	10	1	34	1
Cindrich, Yankees	8	3	.727	0.80	12	11	2	0	1	0	67.2	39	17	6	0	2	19	0	87	3
Clark, Royals	0	0	.000	2.08	2	1	0	0	0	0	8.2	7	4	2	0	0	2	0	13	2
Cobb, Twins*	3	3	.500	3.62	11	11	1	0	0	0	59.2	54	34	24	1	0	17	0	40	5
Conner, Orioles	4	5	.444	1.93	12	11	3	0	1	0	70.0	56	29	15	2	5	31	0	39	4
Cook, Dodgers	0	1	.000	3.50	13	0	0	11	0	5	18.0	18	8	7	1	2	9	1	19	1
Cormier, Red Sox	4	3	.571	2.09	13	9	0	1	0	0	64.2	50	23	15	2	0	33	0	54	7
Costello, Dodgers	3	0	1.000	2.77	7	7	0	0	0	0	39.0	30	14	12	0	2	13	0	40	4
Craig, Red Sox	1	4	.200	4.64	14	1	0	4	0	0	36.1	37	18	17	0	2	29	1	17	4
Cuda, Expos	4	1	.800	2.23	18	0	0	12	0	3	36.1	19	19	9	0	0	2	0	34	4
Darensbourg, Marlins*	2	1	.667	0.64	8	4	0	2	0	1	42.0	28	5	3	1	3	11	2	37	0
DaSilva, Expos	10	1	.909	1.42	12	12	8	0	4	0	95.0	59	16	15	1	5	10	0	86	2
Dault, Astros	0	1	.000	3.60	8	4	0	1	0	0	25.0	20	13	10	1	2	10	0	25	3
Davidson, Pirates*	0	2	.000	5.06	12	8	1	2	0	0	42.2	49	28	24	0	0	32	0	32	7
C.C. Davis, Red Sox	2	2	.500	2.45	6	3	0	0	0	0	25.2	25	15	7	1	0	6	1	17	0
C.L. Davis, Red Sox	0	0	.000	0.00	1	0	0	0	0	0	3.0	3	0	0	0	0	0	0	0	0
Debrino, Twins	0	2	.000	4.50	15	4	0	9	0	6	30.0	33	15	15	2	5	16	0	23	0
Del Toro, Pirates	2	5	.286	3.43	11	10	1	1	0	1	60.1	64	30	23	0	4	21	0	42	5

Pitcher, Team	W	L	Pct.	ERA	G	GS	CG	GF	ShO	Sv.	IP	H	R	ER	HR	HB	BB	Int. BB	SO	WP
DeLeon, Pirates	1	4	.200	5.73	18	0	0	14	0	3	33.0	45	26	21	1	3	11	0	40	4
Delgado, Orioles	0	0	.000	0.00	1	0	0	1	0	0	2.0	1	0	0	0	0	1	0	2	0
Delzine, Rangers	2	2	.500	1.88	13	0	0	4	0	1	28.2	26	8	6	0	0	3	0	16	0
Dillinger, Pirates	3	3	.500	3.44	13	10	0	1	0	1	52.1	43	37	20	1	6	42	0	45	6
Donnelly, White Sox	0	3	.000	3.67	9	7	0	1	0	1	41.2	41	25	17	0	8	21	0	31	6
Dunivan, Rangers	2	4	.333	8.20	12	6	0	0	0	0	26.1	25	28	24	3	3	24	0	19	5
Duran, Dodgers*	4	3	.571	2.79	9	8	0	0	0	0	38.2	22	17	12	1	2	31	0	57	8
Ellis, White Sox	1	0	1.000	10.80	1	1	0	0	0	0	5.0	10	6	6	0	0	1	0	4	0
Elsbernd, White Sox	1	1	.667	4.76	4	3	0	0	0	0	17.0	23	9	9	0	1	2	0	16	1
Encarnacion, Expos	0	2	.000	0.91	9	4	0	0	0	0	29.2	14	13	3	1	3	11	0	30	3
Fairfax, Pirates	1	5	.167	5.25	7	7	1	0	0	0	36.0	43	28	21	1	6	13	0	19	1
Fajardo, Rangers	0	1	.000	5.68	1	1	0	0	0	0	6.1	5	4	4	0	1	2	0	9	1
H. Ferguson, Yankees	0	0	.000	6.43	3	1	0	1	0	0	7.0	11	5	5	0	0	1	0	7	0
S. Ferguson, Yankees	1	1	.000	1.66	19	0	0	19	0	8	21.2	17	9	4	0	0	10	1	24	1
Fesh, Astros*	1	0	1.000	1.73	18	0	0	12	0	6	36.1	25	7	7	0	4	8	0	35	4
Fidge, Twins	3	4	.429	4.74	14	8	1	2	1	1	57.0	59	38	30	1	7	12	0	24	1
Fitzpatrick, Royals	3	0	1.000	2.65	11	3	0	2	0	0	37.1	27	13	11	1	2	16	0	28	2
Florentino, Orioles	1	2	.333	6.59	15	2	0	2	0	0	28.2	33	25	21	1	1	27	1	10	13
Ford, Pirates*	1	2	.333	6.75	16	0	0	11	0	2	28.0	41	26	21	0	0	9	0	32	0
Ford, White Sox*	0	1	.000	4.70	7	2	0	2	0	1	15.1	16	13	8	1	0	10	0	9	2
Fritz, White Sox*	3	1	.750	2.06	6	6	3	0	1	0	39.1	26	14	9	0	1	12	0	23	3
Fultz, Expos	0	0	.000	3.00	2	1	0	0	0	0	3.0	2	1	1	0	0	1	0	3	1
Gagnon, Braves	2	1	.667	1.33	14	0	0	7	0	1	27.0	14	5	4	0	2	9	0	23	0
Galart, Expos	6	4	.600	1.55	14	3	1	10	0	1	40.2	37	18	7	1	4	12	0	28	1
Gay, White Sox*	5	3	.625	1.32	9	9	0	0	0	0	61.1	52	13	9	2	2	9	0	37	0
Geraldo, Blue Jays	1	3	.250	6.75	8	7	0	0	0	0	28.0	30	25	21	1	4	15	0	12	5
Gomez, Marlins	2	3	.400	2.47	12	10	0	0	0	0	62.0	60	24	17	1	0	19	1	34	4
Gonzalez, Red Sox	0	2	.000	1.00	2	2	0	0	0	0	9.0	9	8	1	0	1	0	0	6	1
Gordon, Yankees	3	4	.429	3.04	11	10	0	1	0	0	53.1	33	21	18	1	5	33	0	55	5
Gourdin, Twins	3	1	.750	6.04	13	0	0	4	0	0	22.1	26	22	15	0	4	9	0	3	3
Grzanich, Astros	2	5	.286	4.54	17	3	0	9	0	3	33.2	38	21	17	0	6	14	0	29	1
Hale, Orioles*	0	1	.000	9.00	2	0	0	1	0	0	2.0	2	2	2	0	1	3	0	4	0
Hansen, Red Sox	0	0	.000	0.90	3	2	0	1	0	0	10.0	4	1	1	0	1	4	0	5	0
Harms, Marlins	2	0	1.000	6.94	7	0	0	4	0	0	11.2	20	13	9	0	0	3	1	4	1
Harris, Mets	1	0	1.000	3.22	10	3	0	2	0	0	22.1	21	10	8	0	0	16	0	29	9
Hawkins, Twins	3	2	.600	3.22	6	6	1	0	0	0	36.1	36	19	13	1	3	10	0	35	3
Hayward, Mets	1	2	.333	4.78	15	1	0	7	0	2	37.2	54	32	20	0	2	13	0	35	10
Hendricks, Dodgers*	2	1	.667	1.50	11	0	0	3	0	1	24.0	17	5	4	0	0	4	0	16	0
Henson, Rangers	0	0	.000	3.00	8	0	0	5	0	0	18.0	17	14	6	0	1	9	0	11	2
Herrera, Twins	2	2	.500	6.53	12	2	0	2	0	0	20.2	19	21	15	0	0	24	0	16	1
Hodges, Royals	5	3	.625	4.71	11	9	0	0	0	0	49.2	60	30	26	1	4	25	0	24	1
Hodgson, Royals	1	0	1.000	1.65	7	0	0	3	0	1	27.1	19	6	5	0	2	7	0	17	0
Hokanson, Mets	0	0	.000	5.40	1	0	0	0	0	0	3.1	2	3	2	0	0	0	0	3	1
Holleday, Astros	1	4	.200	3.38	14	0	0	7	0	0	18.2	18	12	7	0	2	7	0	15	2
Hostetler, Expos*	6	2	.750	0.98	11	11	2	0	1	0	73.1	45	13	8	0	4	35	0	64	8
Howard, White Sox*	0	0	.000	4.50	1	0	0	0	0	0	2.0	3	1	1	0	0	0	0	3	0
Hurtault, Expos	0	0	.000	0.00	2	0	0	2	0	1	1.2	0	0	0	0	0	0	1	1	0
Hylton, Expos	3	4	.429	5.46	14	2	0	8	0	2	29.2	26	26	18	0	3	16	0	32	4
Ireland, Marlins*	4	3	.571	4.57	10	10	0	0	0	0	43.1	42	28	22	2	1	28	0	26	2
Isringhausen, Mets	2	4	.333	4.34	6	6	0	0	0	0	29.0	26	19	14	0	3	17	1	25	2
Jackson, White Sox	4	1	.800	5.11	18	1	0	11	0	1	37.0	41	23	21	1	4	19	1	29	5
Jacobs, Braves*	1	3	.250	2.57	12	2	0	6	0	1	35.0	30	18	10	1	1	8	2	40	2
Jacobson, Dodgers	1	1	.500	1.73	6	3	0	2	0	0	26.0	17	7	5	0	0	6	0	25	2
Janzen, Yankees	7	2	.778	2.36	12	11	0	0	0	0	68.2	55	21	18	0	5	15	0	73	3
Jeffery, Blue Jays*	2	1	.667	5.06	15	1	0	3	0	1	32.0	32	23	18	0	0	7	0	31	3
Jenkins, White Sox	0	0	.000	0.00	1	0	0	1	0	0	2.0	0	0	0	0	0	0	0	4	0
Johnson, White Sox*	0	0	.000	0.00	1	0	0	0	0	0	2.0	1	0	0	0	0	0	0	5	0
Johnson, Pirates	2	0	1.000	3.68	5	0	0	4	0	0	7.1	3	3	3	0	0	6	0	3	1
Johnson, Marlins	1	1	.500	9.38	16	0	0	6	0	1	24.0	44	26	25	1	0	10	0	22	3
Kenady, Dodgers*	2	2	.500	1.90	16	0	0	11	0	3	23.2	22	11	5	0	3	6	0	26	3
Kennedy, Blue Jays	1	2	.333	6.15	9	8	0	0	0	0	33.2	38	24	23	1	3	13	0	32	4
Kiper, Yankees	1	4	.200	1.61	15	0	0	5	0	0	22.1	17	14	4	0	2	16	0	21	1
Knott, Mets	1	1	.500	6.97	6	0	0	5	0	1	10.1	18	9	8	0	1	4	0	8	4
Krablin, Mets	2	3	.400	5.93	12	2	0	7	0	1	30.1	39	23	20	2	1	9	1	13	5
Kubicki, White Sox	0	3	.000	10.00	8	0	0	5	0	0	9.0	14	12	10	0	3	8	0	12	4
Lambert, Pirates	0	0	.000	5.40	2	0	0	2	0	0	3.1	6	2	2	0	1	1	0	4	0
Larkin, Marlins	1	2	.333	5.23	14	4	0	2	0	2	41.1	41	26	24	0	7	19	0	20	4
Lee, Orioles	0	0	.000	27.00	1	0	0	0	0	0	0.1	1	2	1	0	0	1	0	0	1
Lehman, White Sox	4	1	.800	0.95	9	7	0	1	0	1	38.0	19	11	4	0	3	18	0	38	4
Leystra, Blue Jays	6	1	.857	1.15	20	1	0	5	0	1	47.0	38	13	6	0	2	7	0	48	1
Linares, Dodgers	1	2	.333	0.77	7	0	0	6	0	1	11.2	8	2	1	0	1	3	1	14	0
Linehan, Astros*	1	3	.250	1.94	9	9	0	0	0	0	46.1	42	14	10	0	4	20	0	47	1
Lloyd, Braves*	0	1	.000	6.30	6	0	0	4	0	0	10.0	13	9	7	0	0	9	0	2	3
Long, Yankees	1	3	.250	2.62	7	4	0	1	0	0	34.1	39	20	10	0	4	2	0	27	3
Lopez, Astros	1	1	.500	4.50	17	0	0	4	0	0	34.0	42	28	17	1	3	13	0	19	7
Lugo, Astros	3	5	.375	2.43	13	10	0	2	0	0	66.2	60	27	18	1	4	9	0	43	2
Maduro, Orioles	1	4	.200	2.27	13	12	1	1	1	0	71.1	56	29	18	2	1	26	0	66	4
Malaver, White Sox	3	0	1.000	2.60	20	2	0	14	0	4	45.0	50	21	13	0	1	12	1	30	3
Maldonado, Blue Jays	0	0	.000	0.00	9	0	0	3	0	0	15.2	10	2	0	0	1	7	0	10	2
Manning, Rangers	1	1	.500	6.06	5	3	0	0	0	0	16.1	22	13	11	0	1	4	0	9	1
Markham, Dodgers*	0	2	.000	4.85	9	0	0	2	0	0	13.0	13	7	7	0	0	10	0	17	3
Martin, Rangers	3	0	1.000	2.58	9	6	0	1	0	0	38.1	31	12	11	0	3	8	0	26	1
Martinez, Dodgers*	1	4	.200	3.29	7	7	1	0	0	0	41.0	38	19	15	1	1	11	0	39	5
Martinez, Rangers*	4	1	.800	1.18	10	10	1	0	1	0	45.2	28	15	6	0	4	22	0	52	3
May, Braves*	4	3	.571	1.36	12	7	0	4	0	1	53.0	34	13	8	0	2	13	0	61	2
McCarthy, Orioles	0	1	.000	5.63	9	1	0	4	0	0	16.0	21	13	10	1	4	3	0	10	2
McCray, Rangers*	0	0	.000	0.00	2	0	0	1	0	0	3.0	0	0	0	0	0	1	0	3	0
McDermott, Yankees	0	0	.000	4.91	3	0	0	2	0	0	3.2	4	2	2	0	0	5	0	5	2
McDill, Mets*	3	4	.429	2.70	10	9	0	0	0	0	53.1	36	23	16	3	4	15	0	60	3
K. McDonald, Expos	0	0	.000	0.00	1	1	0	0	0	0	2.0	1	0	0	0	0	1	0	2	0
R. McDonald, Expos*	1	0	1.000	4.87	9	0	0	3	0	0	20.1	19	11	11	1	0	11	0	24	1
McGinn, Mets	0	1	.000	15.12	7	1	0	1	0	0	8.1	9	18	14	0	1	18	0	4	6
McKinion, White Sox	1	4	.200	4.66	8	6	0	1	0	1	29.0	34	26	15	1	4	7	1	13	5
Meiners, Blue Jays	1	2	.333	2.25	7	7	0	0	0	0	28.0	20	10	7	0	1	9	0	17	2

Pitcher, Team	W	L	Pct.	ERA	G	GS	CG	GF	ShO	Sv.	IP	H	R	ER	HR	HB	BB	Int. BB	SO	WP
Mejia, Red Sox	0	2	.000	4.56	13	7	0	1	0	1	53.1	65	32	27	1	0	16	0	40	3
Mellor, Expos	1	2	.333	2.28	15	0	0	9	0	2	23.2	14	9	6	0	2	6	0	16	2
Mercado, Astros*	1	2	.333	4.20	13	3	0	4	0	0	30.0	22	17	14	0	3	25	0	36	7
Mercedes, Orioles	2	3	.400	1.78	8	5	2	1	0	0	35.1	31	12	7	0	1	13	0	21	5
Mmahat, Yankees*	0	0	.000	3.00	4	3	0	0	0	0	15.0	9	5	5	0	1	5	0	29	0
Moore, Marlins*	0	0	.000	7.30	10	0	0	5	0	0	12.1	12	15	10	0	1	19	0	9	4
Morel, Pirates	2	2	.500	4.34	14	2	1	7	1	0	45.2	49	26	22	0	1	11	0	29	4
Narcisse, Astros	3	2	.600	4.93	11	6	0	2	0	0	34.2	31	25	19	0	2	24	0	32	5
Norman, Red Sox	0	1	.000	5.40	1	0	0	1	0	0	1.2	4	1	1	0	0	1	0	0	1
Nunez, Marlins	5	5	.500	2.78	12	12	3	0	2	0	71.1	55	24	22	2	2	25	0	26	3
Nuttle, Pirates	2	0	1.000	1.32	7	0	0	5	0	1	13.2	11	3	2	0	1	6	0	14	1
Paige, Braves	0	3	.000	3.83	13	7	0	1	0	0	40.0	32	19	17	1	3	17	0	39	5
Parra, Yankees	1	0	1.000	1.59	10	0	0	2	0	0	17.0	8	4	3	0	1	4	0	9	2
Patterson, Blue Jays*	1	0	1.000	5.40	3	0	0	0	0	0	6.2	6	4	4	1	0	6	0	8	0
Pearlman, Blue Jays	2	1	.667	2.30	21	0	0	11	0	0	43.0	32	13	11	0	1	11	0	22	2
Pelka, Pirates	3	2	.600	2.88	7	7	0	0	0	0	34.1	30	17	11	2	2	9	0	26	2
Percibal, Orioles	2	1	.667	8.10	16	0	0	9	0	0	26.2	42	26	24	0	1	7	0	25	6
Perez, Red Sox	0	2	.000	4.28	14	2	0	7	0	1	33.2	36	27	16	1	0	10	1	22	2
Perez, Dodgers	2	5	.286	2.44	12	7	1	2	0	0	48.0	41	28	13	1	0	20	1	45	4
Le. Perez, Rangers	0	1	.000	4.39	17	0	0	7	0	0	26.2	30	18	13	1	1	9	0	12	4
Lu. Perez, Rangers	1	0	1.000	0.65	16	0	0	12	0	6	27.2	15	2	2	0	1	2	0	24	0
Phillips, Pirates	1	2	.333	8.47	4	4	0	0	0	0	17.0	21	21	16	0	0	13	0	10	4
Pina, Twins	2	1	.667	5.17	15	0	0	4	0	1	31.1	30	21	18	3	3	14	0	27	1
Pinango, Red Sox*	0	3	.000	3.57	14	1	0	9	0	0	22.2	23	14	9	0	2	23	1	13	5
Pittsley, Royals	4	1	.800	3.32	9	9	0	0	0	0	43.1	27	16	16	0	5	15	0	47	2
Plonk, Yankees	3	3	.500	3.06	15	2	0	6	0	1	32.1	21	19	11	1	3	19	2	30	3
Price, Orioles*	1	5	.167	5.09	9	8	0	1	0	0	35.1	40	31	20	2	3	24	0	29	7
Ramirez, Yankees	0	4	.000	4.08	13	1	0	6	0	2	28.2	34	21	13	1	3	11	1	14	2
Randall, Expos	0	1	.000	7.00	6	3	0	2	0	0	18.0	18	20	14	0	1	20	0	8	1
Rapaglia, Astros	0	1	.000	1.00	8	0	0	7	0	3	9.0	3	1	1	0	0	1	0	11	0
Reeder, Marlins	7	2	.778	2.79	20	0	0	10	0	0	38.2	35	16	12	0	2	20	1	22	1
Reese, Braves	0	0	.000	9.00	1	0	0	1	0	0	2.0	2	2	2	0	0	2	0	0	0
Reinozo, Rangers	7	2	.778	2.10	11	11	0	0	0	0	60.0	53	17	14	3	0	7	0	36	1
Renfroe, Red Sox	2	7	.222	5.67	14	10	0	1	0	0	66.2	81	49	42	1	2	26	0	59	3
Rich, Blue Jays	3	1	.750	1.22	27	0	0	26	0	16	37.0	28	5	5	0	1	4	0	43	4
Rizzo, Dodgers*	0	1	.000	3.86	3	1	0	1	0	0	7.0	4	4	3	0	1	8	0	7	0
Robinson, Braves	4	1	.800	4.35	10	5	1	0	0	0	41.1	41	29	20	1	2	23	0	41	7
Rondon, Braves	1	8	.111	3.82	15	12	1	2	1	0	77.2	72	39	33	1	2	24	1	62	8
Roque, Mets*	3	1	.750	2.14	20	0	0	18	0	8	33.2	28	13	8	0	1	16	2	33	3
Runion, Rangers	6	2	.750	3.02	13	12	0	0	0	0	56.2	49	21	19	2	1	17	1	42	3
Runyan, Astros*	3	3	.500	3.20	10	10	0	0	0	0	45.0	54	19	16	0	5	16	0	30	8
Sanchez, Royals	3	3	.500	3.38	23	0	0	16	0	4	40.0	41	19	15	0	4	21	1	40	4
Santana, Pirates	1	7	.125	3.89	13	9	0	2	0	0	69.1	77	37	30	1	10	16	0	37	2
Santos, Royals*	6	2	.750	3.61	14	8	1	2	0	1	52.1	54	22	21	0	0	19	0	34	4
Sarmiento, Dodgers*	3	1	.750	1.85	7	6	0	0	0	0	34.0	22	9	7	3	3	21	1	21	2
Saunders, Marlins*	4	1	.800	1.18	24	0	0	16	0	7	45.2	29	10	6	0	1	13	2	37	4
Schoenvogel, Red Sox	0	0	.000	0.00	1	0	0	1	0	0	3.0	2	0	0	0	0	0	0	4	0
Seaton, Rangers	0	2	.000	3.12	14	0	0	3	0	0	26.0	21	11	9	2	3	7	1	19	2
Seip, Rangers	1	3	.250	2.76	17	1	0	13	0	4	29.1	26	16	9	1	1	12	1	20	2
Serafini, Twins*	1	0	1.000	3.64	8	0	0	6	0	0	29.2	27	16	12	0	1	15	0	33	3
Sherman, Mets	3	3	.500	3.09	16	7	0	7	0	2	55.1	56	29	19	1	9	22	0	52	6
Silva, Blue Jays	6	4	.600	2.28	12	12	0	0	0	0	59.1	42	23	15	1	2	18	0	78	1
Sinclair, Blue Jays*	1	2	.333	2.74	5	4	0	0	0	0	23.0	23	10	7	2	0	5	0	18	1
Smith, Orioles	4	3	.571	1.95	11	10	1	0	0	0	60.0	37	20	13	0	7	18	0	54	8
Smith, Dodgers*	1	2	.333	2.35	16	2	1	5	0	1	30.2	29	13	8	1	3	17	0	25	0
Smoot, Braves*	1	0	1.000	1.76	6	0	0	1	0	0	15.1	12	3	3	0	0	4	0	10	0
Solomon, Royals	4	0	1.000	1.45	21	0	0	19	0	5	31.0	24	5	5	0	3	7	0	16	0
Sosa, Twins	0	0	.000	7.15	9	0	0	1	0	0	11.1	7	13	9	2	5	16	0	7	0
Soto, White Sox	3	2	.600	2.42	8	8	2	0	1	0	48.1	34	19	13	3	1	24	0	35	1
Spang, Mets	1	3	.250	3.94	6	6	0	0	0	0	32.0	31	16	14	2	2	7	1	26	2
Spring, Astros	3	3	.500	3.17	18	1	0	9	0	3	48.1	37	22	17	4	1	30	0	50	5
Starks, White Sox	0	0	.000	0.00	5	0	0	1	0	0	7.1	3	0	0	0	0	4	0	10	1
Starr, Rangers	0	0	.000	0.00	1	0	0	0	0	0	1.0	0	0	0	0	0	0	0	1	0
Steele, Expos	0	0	.000	0.00	1	0	0	1	0	0	2.0	0	0	0	0	0	1	0	0	0
Stefanoff, Blue Jays	0	0	.000	3.57	9	0	0	5	0	0	17.2	14	9	7	0	0	11	0	15	0
Stephens, Dodgers	3	0	1.000	2.01	17	2	0	9	0	2	31.1	22	10	7	1	3	17	0	15	1
Stevens, Twins	3	4	.429	4.63	12	8	0	1	0	0	46.2	50	40	24	0	6	44	0	36	3
Tatar, Twins	3	2	.600	2.68	17	3	0	6	0	2	43.2	31	19	13	2	0	17	0	26	4
Tatis, Mets*	1	3	.250	8.50	11	5	0	0	0	0	36.0	56	40	34	2	4	15	0	25	7
Taylor, Pirates*	3	3	.500	4.75	15	3	0	6	0	0	41.2	30	25	22	1	2	29	0	43	5
Taylor, Blue Jays*	0	0	.000	0.00	1	1	0	0	0	0	4.0	2	0	0	0	0	3	0	3	0
Taylor, Yankees	0	0	.000	1.50	3	0	0	1	0	0	6.0	5	1	1	0	0	1	0	2	0
Tejada, Twins	0	0	.000	9.82	3	0	0	2	0	0	3.2	10	7	4	0	0	1	0	2	0
Teran, Braves*	4	3	.571	3.11	15	8	2	3	1	1	55.0	50	29	19	2	4	27	1	51	1
Theodile, White Sox	2	0	1.000	0.69	4	1	0	0	0	0	13.0	7	1	1	0	0	4	0	12	2
Thomforde, Yankees	0	0	.000	1.50	3	1	0	0	0	0	6.0	4	1	1	0	1	6	0	6	0
Tidwell, Marlins	2	4	.333	3.79	11	11	0	0	0	0	57.0	52	29	24	2	4	28	0	43	4
Towns, Royals	1	1	.500	5.00	9	2	0	4	0	1	27.0	26	16	15	1	2	16	0	29	4
Trumpour, Mets	2	3	.400	2.56	8	7	0	0	0	0	38.2	33	17	11	1	1	5	0	23	3
Turlais, Pirates	0	0	.000	0.00	1	0	0	1	0	0	2.0	0	0	0	0	0	1	0	2	0
Turrentine, Royals	0	0	.000	0.00	2	0	0	2	0	1	2.0	0	0	0	0	0	0	0	6	0
Tyrrell, Red Sox*	1	1	.500	3.09	7	5	0	1	0	0	23.1	24	16	8	1	2	10	0	19	3
Ubiera, Yankees	1	6	.143	3.28	10	8	0	2	0	1	46.2	44	22	17	1	1	21	0	26	0
Valdez, Astros	5	2	.714	1.28	11	11	0	0	0	0	63.1	51	17	9	0	1	8	0	36	5
Vallot, Rangers	0	0	.000	18.00	1	0	0	1	0	0	1.0	2	2	2	0	2	1	0	1	0
Veneziale, Marlins	1	1	.500	2.57	7	6	0	0	0	0	28.0	23	11	8	1	0	9	0	15	3
Vializ, Expos	1	3	.250	3.82	11	11	0	0	0	0	66.0	60	32	28	1	3	20	0	38	5
Watts, Dodgers*	2	1	.667	3.00	4	4	1	0	1	0	24.0	15	9	8	1	0	8	0	19	3
White, Dodgers	1	0	1.000	2.57	5	0	0	2	0	1	7.0	4	3	2	0	0	1	0	10	1
Wiley, Yankees	2	1	.667	1.61	4	3	0	1	0	0	22.1	15	5	4	0	2	4	0	21	0
Williams, Braves	0	1	.000	3.86	1	0	0	0	0	0	2.1	4	1	1	0	0	2	0	1	0
Witt, Yankees	1	0	1.000	0.00	3	3	0	0	0	0	12.0	7	1	0	0	0	2	0	13	2
Worrell, White Sox*	0	0	.000	0.00	2	0	0	2	0	2	3.0	1	0	0	0	0	0	0	5	0

BALKS—Mercado, Sherman, 6 each; Del Toro, McCarthy, Pelka, Reinozo, Valdez, 5 each; S. Bennett, Galart, Gordon, Lopez, Mejia, H. Perez, J. Perez, Phillips, 4 each; Bavousett, Geraldo, Herrera, Jackson, Janzen, Maduro, Nunez, B. Smith, Tidwell, Tyrrell, 3 each; Adam, A. Alfonseca, Amos, Arnold, Baker, Becker, Bermudez, Blaine, Brooks, Ch. Brown, Cheek, Christopher, Dault, DeLeon, Dillinger, Gagnon, Gay, Harms, Hawkins, Jacobson, Kennedy, Kiper, Long, Markham, Martin, Morel, Percibal, Pittsley, Ramirez, Santana, Silva, Sosa, Stephens, Stevens, Tatar, Ubiera, Vializ, 2 each; Adkins, Andujar, Bacon, Bakkum, Bell, M. Bennett, Campbell, Church, Cindrich, Cobb, Cormier, Costello, Debrino, Dunivan, Elsbernd, S. Ferguson, Fidge, Florentino, J. Ford, Gonzalez, Hayward, Hendricks, Henson, Hodges, Hodgson, Holleday, Howard, S. Johnson, Lehman, Linares, Linehan, Malaver, R. Martinez, May, McGinn, McKinion, Meiners, Mellor, Mercedes, Narcisse, L. Perez, Pinango, Plonk, Price, Reeder, Reese, Rich, Robinson, Roque, Runion, Runyan, Seip, Serafini, Smoot, Solomon, Soto, Spang, Spring, Tatis, M.W. Taylor, Teran, Trumpour, Veneziale, 1 each.

COMBINATION SHUTOUTS—Lugo-Rapaglia, Narcisse-Holleday-Fesh, Valdez-Holleday-Billingsley, Astros; Adkins-Pearlman, Meiners-Cheek-Rich, Silva-Pearlman-Rich, Blue Jays; Christmas-Gagnon, Christmas-Teran-Rondon-Church, May-Blaine, Braves; Costello-Kenady, Costello-Stephens, Duran-Perez-Cook-Kenady, Jacobson-Linares, Perez-Linares, Sarmiento-Smith-Cook, Dodgers; DaSilva-Mellor-Cuda, Galart-McDonald-Hylton, Hostetler-Cuda, Hostetler-Galart, Hostetler-Hylton, Vializ-Hylton, Expos; Campbell-Harms, Darensbourg-Saunders, Harris-Roque, Ireland-Saunders, Marlins; Isringhausen-Roque, McDill-Knott, McDill-Roque, Sherman-Carr, Mets; Cormier-Schoenvogel, Renfroe-Craig-Mejia, Red Sox; Burley-Sanchez-Adam, Centala-Bunch, Centala-Sanchez-Bacon, Hodges-Bacon-Adam-Solomon, Hodges-Bacon-Sanchez, Pittsley-Towns, Royals; Bermudez-Belcher-Pina, Bermudez-Serafini-Fidge, Twins; Gay-Malaver 2, Elsbernd-Bennett, Ford-Bennett-Worrell, Gay-Jackson-Worrell, Gay-Starks-Malaver, Lehman-Malaver, White Sox; Cindrich-Ferguson, Gordon-Christopher, Witt-Wiley, Yankees.

NO-HIT GAMES—Smith, Orioles, defeated Blue Jays, 3-0 (first game), August 10; DaSilva, Expos, defeated Braves, 2-0, August 14; Cindrich, Yankees, defeated Rangers, 2-0 (first game), August 24.

FIELDING

TEAM

Team	Pct.	G	PO	A	E	DP	PB
Royals	.962	59	1573	717	90	70	24
Expos	.959	59	1522	628	91	36	21
Rangers	.957	59	1457	654	96	46	20
Dodgers	.956	59	1464	568	93	36	20
Red Sox	.955	59	1563	688	107	58	14
Marlins	.954	60	1591	747	113	55	21
Braves	.954	59	1537	623	105	38	23

Team	Pct.	G	PO	A	E	DP	PB
Blue Jays	.950	59	1505	626	112	42	20
Astros	.949	60	1557	668	119	33	13
White Sox	.947	60	1562	673	124	54	10
Pirates	.947	60	1499	599	117	44	31
Mets	.947	59	1469	540	113	38	23
Orioles	.947	58	1436	583	114	44	21
Yankees	.940	60	1494	636	136	29	12
Twins	.934	58	1497	642	151	37	24

Triple plays—Dodgers, Royals.

INDIVIDUAL

*Throws lefthanded.

FIRST BASEMEN

Player, Team	Pct.	G	PO	A	E	DP
Aguado, Red Sox	1.000	2	6	0	0	0
Antigua, White Sox	1.000	1	7	0	0	1
Baucom, Twins	.978	25	211	14	5	16
Beason, Yankees	.945	34	278	15	17	16
Becker, Blue Jays	1.000	4	14	1	0	0
Brown, Pirates	1.000	1	4	2	0	1
Bumgardner, Marlins	.917	6	50	5	5	3
Burr, Rangers	.980	59	519	23	11	43
Carbajal, Expos	1.000	1	1	0	0	0
Cardona, Marlins	1.000	2	11	0	0	1
Carey, Red Sox	.991	14	106	8	1	8
Clark, Orioles	1.000	2	5	1	0	0
Daly, Mets	.976	50	413	27	11	29
DePastino, Red Sox	.997	32	267	21	1	29
Diaz, Pirates	1.000	3	30	2	0	2
Doval, Braves	.988	27	226	19	3	11
Durso, Blue Jays	1.000	1	3	0	0	0
Epperson, Mets	.967	7	54	4	2	6
Faircloth, White Sox	1.000	4	17	0	0	2
Gerald, Royals	.968	7	55	5	2	7
Gipner, Yankees	1.000	1	3	1	0	0
Gonzalez, Expos	.984	31	297	13	5	20
Grapenthien, Astros	.976	39	350	13	9	14
Griffin, Blue Jays	.833	2	5	0	1	0
Halbruner, Blue Jays*	.979	47	407	19	9	29
Haley, Dodgers*	.976	9	74	9	2	6
Harris, White Sox	1.000	1	5	0	0	0
Harris, Pirates	.973	41	306	22	9	23
Hecker, Red Sox	1.000	7	73	4	0	9
Jones, Pirates*	1.000	3	20	1	0	3
Kingman, Marlins	.933	1	14	0	1	0
Koeyers, Expos	1.000	1	11	0	0	0
Lloyd, Braves*	1.000	3	26	5	0	0
Lorenzo, Red Sox	.977	6	40	3	1	2
Mader, White Sox	.981	9	50	2	1	3
Madera, Royals	1.000	6	66	6	0	5
McDonald, White Sox	1.000	1	3	1	0	0
Mendez, Royals	1.000	27	255	18	0	27
Miley, Orioles	.987	32	217	14	3	18
Mumma, White Sox	.952	4	18	2	1	2
Oster, Yankees*	1.000	6	52	3	0	1
Pearson, Twins	.963	35	294	19	12	18
Pulido, White Sox	1.000	2	13	2	0	0
Richmond, Dodgers	1.000	2	3	0	0	1
ROBINSON, Marlins	.987	54	515	31	7	48
Rodriguez, Dodgers	1.000	1	6	0	0	0
Ruoff, White Sox	1.000	2	12	0	0	1
Santiago, Blue Jays	1.000	2	9	0	0	1
Shelley, Braves	.925	4	33	4	3	1
Smith, Royals	.966	26	193	7	7	26
Stutts, Braves	1.000	1	4	1	0	0
Tackett, Red Sox	.870	8	42	5	7	0
Thomas, White Sox	.970	53	453	32	15	40

Player, Team	Pct.	G	PO	A	E	DP
Thorsteinson, Expos	.984	29	248	5	4	12
Turlais, Pirates	.987	10	71	4	1	4
Urena, Dodgers*	.967	36	269	23	10	18
Vasquez, Braves	.984	11	113	9	2	8
Vaught, Blue Jays	.954	13	96	7	5	6
Watts, Dodgers	.989	14	85	5	1	9
Weiser, Braves	.974	15	138	13	4	13
Wingate, Dodgers	1.000	4	18	1	0	0
Winget, Orioles*	.988	26	241	7	3	17
Witt, Astros	.977	26	207	9	5	17
Wolf, Pirates*	.984	8	61	2	1	1
Wuerch, Yankees	.989	20	168	10	2	7
Young, Mets	1.000	3	13	4	0	1

Triple plays—Gerald, Haley.

SECOND BASEMEN

Player, Team	Pct.	G	PO	A	E	DP
Aguado, Red Sox	.986	21	31	40	1	10
Albornoz, Yankees	1.000	3	2	7	0	0
Alcantara, Expos	.800	3	2	2	1	0
Alfonzo, Royals	.944	5	6	11	1	1
Allen, Pirates	.875	9	11	10	3	2
Arvelo, Mets	.600	2	0	3	2	0
Basey, Astros	.981	31	65	87	3	11
Baugh, Marlins	.944	4	13	4	1	0
Brito, Blue Jays	.952	17	30	49	4	12
Burton, Orioles	.962	30	65	60	5	17
Cedeno, Astros	1.000	1	1	7	0	0
Clapinski, Marlins	.970	58	156	167	10	40
Clark, Orioles	.961	23	55	44	4	7
Clarke, Royals	1.000	3	5	7	0	1
Correa, Expos	1.000	3	6	6	0	1
Crick, Twins	1.000	4	2	7	0	1
Crispin, Astros	.949	20	41	34	4	4
Cruz, Twins	.976	9	21	19	1	2
Davis, Twins	.979	28	72	68	3	18
Delgado, Orioles	1.000	1	6	2	0	1
Diaz, Red Sox	.600	3	1	2	2	0
Domingo, Braves	.905	6	10	9	2	1
Durham, White Sox	1.000	1	4	3	0	1
Eaglin, Braves	.923	7	9	15	2	3
Farrell, Mets	.938	21	38	53	6	13
Fraraccio, White Sox	1.000	3	4	3	0	0
Frias, Rangers	.961	45	78	118	8	24
Gonzalez, Rangers	.983	18	20	39	1	7
Hand, Pirates	.956	11	25	18	2	3
Heaps, Yankees	.934	29	55	73	9	11
Hollrah, White Sox	.947	47	78	102	10	26
Humes, Pirates	.923	11	26	34	5	5
Johnston, Pirates	.968	36	84	69	5	16
Kingman, Marlins	1.000	1	1	0	0	0
Latham, Dodgers	1.000	9	21	12	0	3
Lawton, Twins	.958	50	129	142	12	20

Player, Team	Pct.	G	PO	A	E	DP
Lewis, Dodgers	.964	39	62	70	5	14
Lopez, Royals	.921	9	17	18	3	7
Lopez, Yankees	.917	19	20	46	6	2
McDonald, White Sox	.952	12	18	22	2	5
Montilla, Royals	.978	8	20	25	1	9
Mora, Astros	.933	12	20	22	3	3
Norman, Red Sox	.951	10	16	23	2	3
O'Donnell, Red Sox	1.000	7	12	11	0	2
Ortiz, Red Sox	.947	7	17	19	2	5
Pichardo, Mets	.953	37	77	85	8	14
Randle, White Sox	.870	9	8	12	3	3
Renteria, Yankees	.872	12	14	27	6	2
Reyes, Expos	1.000	2	4	6	0	1
Shrum, Royals	.953	31	65	97	8	30
Subero, Royals	1.000	6	9	11	0	3
Valera, Orioles	.914	9	15	17	3	3
Vasquez, Blue Jays	.928	47	72	108	14	17
Vaught, Blue Jays	1.000	1	0	3	0	0
Vazquetelles, Braves	.976	8	11	30	1	1
VIDRO, Expos	.982	54	114	107	4	18
Vindivich, Royals	.762	5	6	10	5	4
Warner, Braves	.929	40	58	100	12	14
Wingate, Dodgers	.971	15	23	44	2	6

THIRD BASEMEN

Player, Team	Pct.	G	PO	A	E	DP
Aguado, Red Sox	.952	11	10	10	1	3
Albornoz, Yankees	.813	6	2	11	3	0
Alcantara, Expos	.932	57	50	128	13	8
Aranzamendi, Marlins	.897	11	6	20	3	1
Barnden, Orioles	.910	48	43	88	13	7
Basey, Astros	.852	8	2	21	4	1
Baugh, Marlins	.890	40	25	104	16	5
Bowles, Red Sox	.877	29	21	43	9	3
Brandon, Royals	.700	3	2	5	3	1
Brennan, Braves	.500	1	0	1	1	0
Brito, Blue Jays	.874	30	20	63	12	7
Cairo, Dodgers	.800	1	1	3	1	0
Carbajal, Expos	.571	2	2	2	3	0
Cedeno, Astros	.871	41	36	106	21	7
Clark, Orioles	.885	10	7	16	3	1
Clarke, Royals	1.000	1	2	2	0	0
Crick, Twins	.831	22	20	39	12	4
Delgado, Orioles	.875	3	1	6	1	2
Espinoza, Mets	.831	32	19	40	12	2
Farrell, Mets	.931	9	11	16	2	3
Fraraccio, White Sox	1.000	5	1	3	0	1
Gerald, Royals	.907	25	16	52	7	9
GONZALEZ, Rangers	.941	42	28	116	9	10
Haggas, Mets	.962	22	11	39	2	3
Hamilton, Red Sox	.955	19	15	27	2	1
Hand, Pirates	1.000	9	3	13	0	1
Harris, White Sox	1.000	1	1	1	0	0
Hauswirth, Royals	.917	5	3	8	1	0
Izquierdo, White Sox	.829	49	24	83	22	7
Jimenez, Astros	1.000	1	0	1	0	0
Johnston, Pirates	.857	3	1	5	1	0
Kingman, Marlins	.817	21	15	34	11	3
Knauss, Twins	.885	18	16	38	7	2
Kraut, Astros	.979	14	10	36	1	2
Lantigua, Dodgers	.935	14	12	31	3	1
Latham, Dodgers	.667	1	1	1	1	0
Leger, Pirates	1.000	1	0	3	0	0
Lopez, Yankees	.690	13	8	12	9	0
Lorenzo, Red Sox	.889	6	2	6	1	1
Mackert, Pirates	.750	3	1	2	1	0
McDonald, White Sox	1.000	10	4	24	0	0
Mendez, Pirates	.826	7	1	18	4	0
Mendoza, Royals	.955	22	11	52	3	4
Mora, Astros	1.000	1	1	2	0	0
Nolan, Pirates	.881	37	21	68	12	3
Norman, Royals	1.000	3	0	2	0	0
O'Donnell, Red Sox	1.000	2	1	3	0	0
Palmer, Pirates	.941	4	5	11	1	1
Pearson, White Sox	.588	6	3	7	7	0
Renteria, Yankees	.800	4	0	4	1	0
Richardson, Dodgers	.840	34	25	54	15	5
Roper, Twins	.878	19	24	41	9	3
Rounsifer, Red Sox	.818	5	4	5	2	1
Shrum, Royals	1.000	4	3	6	0	0
Smith, Marlins	.600	1	1	2	2	0
Smith, Braves	.910	52	37	115	15	8
Vaninetti, Blue Jays	.868	30	13	46	9	3
Vasquez, Braves	.900	4	5	4	1	0
Vaught, Blue Jays	.839	14	8	18	5	0
Vindivich, Royals	1.000	1	0	4	0	0
Weiser, Braves	.800	3	1	3	1	1
Williams, Rangers	.871	22	17	44	9	5
Wingate, Dodgers	.900	11	11	16	3	2
Wuerch, Yankees	.826	42	20	80	21	3

SHORTSTOPS

Player, Team	Pct.	G	PO	A	E	DP
Aguado, Red Sox	.946	13	16	37	3	6
Albornoz, Yankees	.870	8	10	30	6	5
Alcantara, Expos	1.000	1	3	7	0	2
Allen, Pirates	.829	15	9	25	7	2
Aranzamendi, Marlins	.889	13	20	36	7	8
Arvelo, Mets	.862	35	46	66	18	12
Baugh, Marlins	.930	11	7	33	3	3
Bostic, Dodgers	.939	35	44	80	8	8
Bradley, Mets	.819	16	29	39	15	10
Brito, Blue Jays	.955	5	6	15	1	0
Cairo, Dodgers	.963	20	25	53	3	6
Cedeno, Astros	.913	6	3	18	2	2
Correa, Expos	.931	20	25	56	6	9
Crick, Twins	.714	2	1	4	2	0
Crispin, Astros	.877	32	46	89	19	10
Cromer, Blue Jays	.932	48	65	127	14	22
Cruz, Twins	.838	22	30	37	13	5
Delgado, Orioles	.926	9	15	35	4	5
Domingo, Braves	.889	6	5	11	2	0
Eaglin, Braves	1.000	4	4	7	0	3
Fraraccio, White Sox	.941	44	68	124	12	24
Frias, Rangers	.925	12	12	25	3	3
Gerald, Royals	.890	14	21	44	8	6
Heaps, Yankees	.714	3	6	4	4	0
Humes, Pirates	.909	6	5	15	2	2
Jeter, Yankees	.943	46	67	132	12	17
Johnston, Pirates	.907	16	16	33	5	5
Keefe, Pirates	.904	33	54	88	15	17
Knauss, Twins	.877	28	33	81	16	12
Lackey, Mets	.914	9	10	22	3	3
Latham, Dodgers	1.000	2	4	1	0	1
Lebron, Red Sox	.875	5	3	4	1	0
Livesey, Astros	.863	28	38	63	16	4
Lopez, Yankees	.667	2	1	3	2	0
MERCEDES, Rangers	.961	49	87	161	10	24
Montilla, Royals	.922	10	11	36	4	8
Norman, Red Sox	1.000	4	1	1	0	0
Ortiz, Red Sox	.921	45	57	141	17	25
Pagan, Orioles	.895	40	61	109	20	15
Patzke, Blue Jays	.926	5	12	13	2	1
Polidor, White Sox	.940	27	33	61	6	9
Pulido, White Sox	1.000	2	2	2	0	0
Renteria, Yankees	.900	4	4	5	1	0
Renteria, Marlins	.897	41	56	152	24	25
Reyes, Expos	.922	40	57	133	16	14
Rounsifer, Red Sox	.918	12	13	32	4	6
Selmo, Braves	.922	21	31	63	8	9
Shrum, Royals	1.000	5	14	20	0	3
Subero, Royals	.935	35	61	125	13	30
Valera, Orioles	.867	11	14	25	6	5
Vaught, Blue Jays	1.000	4	8	3	0	2
Weiser, Braves	.886	29	50	74	16	8
Wilson, Twins	.897	11	9	26	4	2
Wingate, Dodgers	.939	7	17	14	2	4

Triple plays—Cairo, Subero.

OUTFIELDERS

Player, Team	Pct.	G	PO	A	E	DP
Acevedo, Twins	1.000	1	1	0	0	0
Alonso, Orioles	.945	33	48	4	3	1
Ansley, Astros	1.000	7	15	0	0	0
Aquino, Orioles	1.000	11	8	0	0	0
Arvelo, Mets	1.000	1	4	0	0	0
Baker, Orioles	.897	30	34	1	4	0
Beamon, Pirates	.926	10	25	0	2	0
Blackburn, White Sox	.970	35	63	1	2	0
Bogan, Pirates	1.000	2	3	0	0	0
BONIFAZIO, Marlins	1.000	52	81	1	0	0
Borrero, Red Sox	1.000	1	0	1	0	0
Bowers, Astros	.833	16	15	0	3	0
Brandon, Royals	1.000	15	17	0	0	0
Brennan, Braves	.984	37	59	4	1	0
Bright, Red Sox	1.000	9	14	0	0	0
Brown, Pirates	.983	33	56	2	1	0
Brown, Twins	.868	19	32	1	5	0
Brown, Rangers	.923	22	23	1	2	0
Candelaria, Blue Jays	.950	28	17	2	1	0
Chancey, Orioles	.915	39	70	5	7	1
Christian, Marlins*	.994	59	148	10	1	2
Clyburn, Pirates	.932	30	41	0	3	0
Conner, Orioles	.966	39	81	3	3	1
Corporan, Twins	.935	18	28	1	2	0
Coughlin, White Sox*	.889	4	7	1	1	1
Damon, Royals*	.988	49	77	7	1	1
Delafield, Yankees	.934	42	57	0	4	1
Delgado, Marlins	1.000	1	2	0	0	0
DePastino, Red Sox	.947	10	15	3	1	2
Diaz, Red Sox	.933	17	24	4	2	0

Player, Team	Pct.	G	PO	A	E	DP
Diieso, Braves	.950	23	38	0	2	0
Faggett, Red Sox*	.946	25	31	4	2	0
Flagg, Dodgers*	1.000	3	2	0	0	0
Garcia, Dodgers	.967	49	85	3	3	0
Garcia, Rangers	.978	53	77	10	2	2
Gonzalez, Expos	.917	16	19	3	2	1
Gordon, Twins	.864	16	19	0	3	0
Griffin, Blue Jays	.885	17	23	0	3	0
Guerrero, Mets	.952	53	112	6	6	0
Hairston, Pirates	.975	24	39	0	1	0
Harris, White Sox	.977	23	40	2	1	0
Heidelberg, Expos	.955	27	41	1	2	0
Hernaiz, Dodgers	.976	35	39	1	1	0
Herrera, Twins	.986	40	67	5	1	1
Hidalgo, Astros	1.000	46	67	6	0	3
Hightower, Blue Jays	.967	29	27	2	1	1
Hiraldo, Mets	.959	26	47	0	2	0
Hollins, Braves*	.989	45	83	6	1	3
Hurtault, Expos	.934	52	78	7	6	1
Jackson, Dodgers	.929	11	13	0	1	0
James, Marlins	.937	33	55	4	4	0
Jimenez, Royals	.957	44	60	6	3	0
Jones, Twins	.965	50	104	5	4	2
Jones, Red Sox	.938	46	55	5	4	0
Jose, Mets	1.000	17	26	2	0	0
Kern, Royals	.967	23	28	1	1	1
Lachance, Expos	.985	46	63	2	1	0
Ledee, Yankees*	.971	41	62	4	2	0
Lee, Expos	.917	4	11	0	1	0
Leger, Pirates	.967	26	57	1	2	0
Levias, White Sox	.977	28	38	4	1	0
Lewis, Yankees	1.000	25	28	3	0	1
Lloyd, Braves*	1.000	15	24	0	0	0
Maness, Dodgers	.944	43	64	4	4	0
Maple, Rangers*	.895	11	17	0	2	0
Martinez, Astros	.958	45	64	5	3	1
McDonald, White Sox	1.000	1	1	0	0	0
McDonald, Expos*	1.000	2	2	0	0	0
Mendez, Pirates*	1.000	13	12	2	0	0
Milligan, Red Sox	.967	44	85	2	3	0
Mora, Astros	.981	32	50	3	1	0
Moultrie, Blue Jays*	1.000	46	69	3	0	2
Nelson, Yankees	1.000	27	28	2	0	0
Noel, Braves	1.000	9	20	0	0	0
O'Neill, Expos	1.000	3	4	0	0	0
Odrozez, White Sox	1.000	28	26	2	0	0
Oster, Yankees*	1.000	1	1	0	0	0
Palmer, Pirates	1.000	11	7	0	0	0
Patton, White Sox	.966	39	52	4	2	0
Pearson, Rangers	.954	51	97	7	5	1
Pearson, Twins	.875	7	7	0	1	0
Perez, Braves	1.000	2	2	0	0	0
Rennhack, Astros	.953	24	41	0	2	0
Richardson, White Sox	1.000	42	72	3	0	0
Richmond, Dodgers	1.000	30	39	4	0	0
Riggs, Rangers	.940	55	81	13	6	4
Rivera, Yankees	.951	45	67	10	4	0
Rivers, Blue Jays	1.000	28	25	0	0	0
Rodriguez, Astros	.967	24	27	2	1	0
Ross, Astros	1.000	2	7	0	0	0
Saffer, Expos	.946	32	52	1	3	0
Santiago, Blue Jays	.920	18	22	1	2	0
Sheffield, Red Sox*	.986	44	70	1	1	0
Shelley, Braves	1.000	9	11	1	0	0
Smith, Royals	.957	11	21	1	1	0
Stewart, Blue Jays	.988	48	81	1	1	0
Strickland, Marlins	.971	37	64	3	2	1
Stutts, Braves	.893	19	24	1	3	0
Tatro, Orioles*	1.000	12	13	0	0	0
Tena, Pirates	1.000	5	9	2	0	0
Ventura, White Sox	1.000	5	7	1	0	1
Vinyard, Red Sox	.857	6	10	2	2	1
Vizcaino, Twins	.921	32	65	5	6	0
Walker, Pirates*	.926	41	58	5	5	1
Walls, Royals*	.955	49	80	4	4	2
Warner, Mets	.988	56	74	9	1	2
Warren, Dodgers	.971	20	33	1	1	0
Washington, Orioles	.912	25	28	3	3	2
Williams, Braves	.974	25	37	1	1	0
Wolf, Pirates*	1.000	14	14	1	0	0
Young, Mets	.976	31	39	1	1	0
Zambrano, Red Sox	1.000	2	5	1	0	0

CATCHERS

Player, Team	Pct.	G	PO	A	E	DP	PB
Acevedo, Twins	.976	22	106	17	3	0	9
Albaladejo, Astros	.991	27	187	30	2	0	7
Antigua, White Sox	.951	12	38	1	2	1	1
Baucom, Twins	.933	13	72	25	7	0	4
Becker, Blue Jays	.975	18	105	13	3	2	6
Benitez, Braves	.954	18	75	8	4	1	6
Boka, Pirates	.927	15	77	12	7	1	7
Borrero, Red Sox	.969	28	163	23	6	2	10

Player, Team	Pct.	G	PO	A	E	DP	PB
Brea, Orioles	.981	27	128	24	3	0	6
Calcaterra, Yankees	1.000	4	23	3	0	0	0
Carbajal, Expos	.982	18	90	19	2	0	8
Cardona, Marlins	1.000	4	5	0	0	0	0
Carey, Red Sox	.964	9	50	4	2	0	0
Castenada, Orioles	.983	37	241	41	5	1	12
Curran, Orioles	.944	3	13	4	1	2	3
Doezie, Twins	.969	11	54	9	2	0	2
Durso, Blue Jays	.978	21	116	16	3	1	2
Edmondson, Dodgers	.979	28	201	33	5	2	8
Epperson, Mets	.965	17	75	8	3	0	5
Faircloth, White Sox	.981	19	87	17	2	1	2
Frazier, Marlins	1.000	8	12	3	0	0	7
Garcia, Orioles	1.000	1	2	0	0	0	0
Gipner, Yankees	.975	32	247	24	7	0	10
Gomez, Twins	.947	23	122	22	8	1	9
Hammell, Mets	.983	33	207	24	4	3	8
HAUSWIRTH, Royals	1.000	39	241	32	0	1	6
Humes, Pirates	1.000	1	4	1	0	0	0
Jimenez, Astros	.992	21	116	16	1	0	2
Kendall, Pirates	.978	30	182	36	5	3	13
Koeyers, Expos	.966	37	226	31	9	3	2
Kraut, Astros	.968	19	130	23	5	0	4
Kuhn, Braves	1.000	1	9	0	0	0	0
Mader, White Sox	.900	2	8	1	1	1	0
Martin, Red Sox	.969	26	152	35	6	3	3
Martinez, Blue Jays	.981	31	224	34	5	1	12
Martinez, Expos	.955	11	69	15	4	1	5
Matos, Braves	1.000	12	97	11	0	0	2
Melendez, Rangers	.977	7	37	5	1	1	1
Mendez, Royals	.987	21	130	17	2	0	7
Mendez, Pirates	.953	8	44	17	3	1	5
Morales, Mets	.975	26	138	18	4	0	10
Mumma, White Sox	.952	4	20	0	1	0	1
Niethammer, Expos	.950	5	30	8	2	0	6
Pitts, Rangers	.971	33	218	13	7	0	10
Prater, Marlins	.984	54	245	56	5	1	9
Reese, Braves	.924	12	78	7	7	0	6
Rennspies, Dodgers	1.000	1	8	0	0	0	0
Robledo, White Sox	.824	2	13	1	3	0	0
Rodriguez, Dodgers	.975	16	106	12	3	1	4
Rodriguez, Braves	1.000	2	19	1	0	0	0
Rodriguez, White Sox	.962	40	257	43	12	4	6
Seesz, Rangers	.971	20	121	14	4	1	9
Smith, Marlins	.984	12	52	8	1	1	5
Smith, Braves	.967	27	158	18	6	0	9
Tackett, Red Sox	.974	8	34	4	1	1	1
Torres, Yankees	.982	29	235	37	5	1	2
Turlais, Pirates	.989	16	79	9	1	0	6
Vindivich, Royals	.981	12	44	9	1	0	11
Wittig, Dodgers	.971	23	146	21	5	0	8

PITCHERS

Player, Team	Pct.	G	PO	A	E	DP
Adam, Royals	.000	13	0	0	1	0
Adkins, Blue Jays*	.929	11	3	10	1	0
Alfonseca, Expos	1.000	12	3	8	0	0
Alfonseca, Orioles	.833	21	7	8	3	1
Allen, Red Sox*	.889	13	2	6	1	1
Alvarado, Twins	.857	16	3	3	1	0
Amos, Red Sox	.857	11	1	5	1	0
Anacki, Red Sox	1.000	4	2	1	0	0
Anderson, Rangers	1.000	12	0	4	0	1
Andrews, Rangers	.000	1	0	0	1	0
Andujar, Orioles	1.000	19	2	1	0	0
Arias, Blue Jays	.333	9	0	1	2	0
Arnold, Braves	.889	7	2	6	1	0
Ayala, Rangers	1.000	1	0	1	0	0
Bacon, Royals	.769	18	4	6	3	0
Baker, Mets	.917	11	5	6	1	0
Bakkum, Red Sox	1.000	4	1	1	0	0
Bavousett, Marlins	.800	18	2	2	1	0
Beck, Pirates*	1.000	7	2	1	0	0
Becker, Red Sox	1.000	18	3	1	0	0
Belcher, Twins	.833	18	1	4	1	1
Belcher, Twins	.833	18	1	4	1	1
Bennett, Royals	.818	10	3	6	2	0
Bennett, White Sox	1.000	20	0	8	0	0
Bermudez, Twins	.889	11	4	4	1	0
Berryman, Red Sox	.667	5	1	1	1	0
Billingsley, Astros*	.750	12	2	1	1	0
Blaine, Braves	1.000	17	3	9	0	0
Bobb, Dodgers	1.000	12	4	7	0	0
Boehringer, White Sox	1.000	2	0	5	0	0
Brincks, White Sox	1.000	9	2	7	0	0
Brooks, Red Sox	.900	14	6	12	2	2
Brown, Yankees	1.000	12	3	6	0	0
Brown, Orioles	1.000	11	1	6	0	0
Bunch, Royals	1.000	5	2	4	0	0
Burley, Royals*	1.000	15	4	6	0	0
Calcaterra, Yankees	1.000	2	1	0	0	0
Campbell, Marlins	.667	14	1	1	1	0
Campusano, Royals	1.000	3	1	0	0	0
Carr, Mets*	.900	16	2	7	1	0

Player, Team	Pct.	G	PO	A	E	DP
Centala, Royals	.667	3	1	1	1	0
Cheek, Blue Jays	.929	12	2	11	1	0
Chiamparino, Rangers	1.000	1	0	1	0	0
Christmas, Braves	1.000	11	3	10	0	0
Christopher, Yankees	.909	16	2	8	1	0
Church, Braves*	.909	22	5	5	1	0
Cindrich, Yankees	.846	12	4	7	2	0
Clark, Royals	1.000	2	0	1	0	0
Cobb, Twins*	.903	11	4	24	3	1
Conner, Orioles	.828	12	4	20	5	1
Cook, Dodgers	1.000	13	0	1	0	0
Cormier, Red Sox	.750	13	2	7	3	0
Costello, Dodgers	.889	7	2	6	1	1
Craig, Red Sox	1.000	14	3	2	0	0
Cuda, Expos	1.000	18	0	6	0	0
Darensbourg, Marlins*	1.000	8	3	7	0	1
DaSilva, Expos	.950	12	3	16	1	1
Dault, Astros	.556	8	1	4	4	0
Davidson, Pirates*	1.000	12	2	5	0	0
C.C. Davis, Red Sox	.500	6	0	1	1	0
C.L. Davis, Red Sox	1.000	1	1	1	0	0
Debrino, Twins	1.000	15	1	7	0	0
Del Toro, Pirates	.941	11	7	9	1	2
DeLeon, Pirates	.750	18	0	3	1	0
Delzine, Rangers	1.000	13	0	4	0	0
Dillinger, Pirates	.833	13	1	4	1	0
Donnelly, White Sox	.923	9	3	9	1	0
Dunivan, Rangers	.750	12	2	4	2	0
Duran, Dodgers*	.000	9	0	0	1	0
Ellis, White Sox	1.000	1	1	1	0	0
Elsbernd, White Sox	1.000	4	1	4	0	2
Encarnacion, Expos	.800	9	1	3	1	0
Fairfax, Pirates	.833	7	4	6	2	0
H. Ferguson, Yankees	1.000	3	0	1	0	0
S. Ferguson, Yankees	.778	19	2	5	2	0
Fesh, Astros*	1.000	18	1	8	0	0
Fidge, Twins	1.000	14	1	8	0	0
Fitzpatrick, Royals	1.000	11	3	4	0	0
Florentino, Orioles	.667	15	2	0	1	0
Ford, Pirates*	.800	16	1	3	1	0
Ford, White Sox	.857	7	1	5	1	1
Fritz, White Sox*	.800	6	1	7	2	0
Fultz, Expos	1.000	2	1	2	0	0
Gagnon, Braves	1.000	14	1	6	0	0
Galart, Expos	.875	14	1	6	1	1
Gay, White Sox*	.857	9	5	13	3	1
Geraldo, Blue Jays	.667	8	2	4	3	0
Gomez, Marlins	.938	12	8	7	1	0
Gonzalez, Red Sox	1.000	2	1	2	0	0
Gordon, Yankees	.800	11	2	10	3	0
Gourdin, Twins	1.000	13	3	4	0	0
Grzanich, Astros	1.000	17	0	6	0	1
Hansen, Red Sox	1.000	3	1	1	0	0
Harms, Marlins	1.000	7	2	2	0	0
Harris, Mets	1.000	10	0	4	0	0
Hawkins, Twins	.857	6	4	8	2	0
Hayward, Mets	.700	15	5	2	3	0
Hendricks, Dodgers*	1.000	11	4	8	0	0
Henson, Rangers	.800	8	2	2	1	0
Herrera, Twins	1.000	12	0	4	0	0
Hodges, Royals	1.000	11	5	8	0	0
Hodgson, Royals	1.000	7	1	3	0	0
Holleday, Astros	1.000	14	0	2	0	0
Hostetler, Expos*	.867	11	2	11	2	1
Hylton, Expos	1.000	14	1	6	0	0
Ireland, Marlins*	.875	10	1	6	1	0
Isringhausen, Mets	1.000	6	0	5	0	0
Jackson, White Sox	1.000	18	2	8	0	0
Jacobs, Braves*	1.000	12	0	3	0	0
Jacobson, Dodgers	1.000	6	2	3	0	0
JANZEN, Yankees*	1.000	12	3	14	0	0
Jeffery, Blue Jays*	.875	15	0	7	1	0
Johnson, Pirates	1.000	5	1	3	0	0
Johnson, Marlins	.667	16	2	0	1	0
Kenady, Dodgers*	.667	16	1	3	2	1
Kennedy, Blue Jays	.889	9	0	8	1	0
Kiper, Yankees	.750	15	0	6	2	1
Knott, Mets	1.000	6	0	3	0	0
Krablin, Mets	.900	12	4	5	1	0
Lambert, Pirates	1.000	2	1	0	0	0
Larkin, Marlins	1.000	14	2	6	0	0
Lee, Orioles	1.000	1	0	1	0	0
Lehman, White Sox	.714	9	0	5	2	0
Leystra, Blue Jays	.500	20	0	2	2	0
Linares, Dodgers	1.000	7	1	0	0	0
Linehan, Astros*	1.000	9	2	4	0	0
Long, Yankees	.750	7	2	4	2	0
Lopez, Astros	.600	17	0	6	4	0
Lugo, Astros	1.000	13	3	10	0	0
Maduro, Orioles	.789	13	4	11	4	2
Malaver, White Sox	.769	20	2	8	3	1
Maldonado, Blue Jays	1.000	9	3	5	0	0
Manning, Rangers	1.000	5	0	2	0	0
Markham, Dodgers*	.800	9	0	4	1	0
Martin, Rangers	.818	9	4	5	2	0
Martinez, Dodgers*	1.000	7	3	7	0	0
Martinez, Rangers*	.800	10	0	4	1	0
May, Braves*	1.000	12	3	11	0	0
McCarthy, Orioles	1.000	9	1	1	0	0
McCray, Rangers*	1.000	2	0	1	0	0
McDermott, Yankees	1.000	3	1	1	0	0
McDill, Mets*	1.000	10	4	12	0	0
McDonald, Expos*	1.000	9	0	1	0	0
McGinn, Mets	.000	7	0	0	1	0
McKinion, White Sox	.800	8	1	3	1	0
Meiners, Blue Jays	1.000	7	6	3	0	0
Mejia, Red Sox	.875	13	1	6	1	0
Mellor, Expos	1.000	15	2	4	0	0
Mercado, Astros*	.714	13	0	5	2	0
Mercedes, Orioles	.857	8	4	8	2	1
Mmahat, Yankees*	1.000	4	0	4	0	0
Moore, Marlins*	.000	10	0	0	1	0
Morel, Pirates	.929	14	3	10	1	1
Narcisse, Astros	1.000	11	0	4	0	0
Nunez, Marlins	.900	12	6	12	2	0
Nuttle, Rangers	.833	7	2	3	1	1
Paige, Braves	.857	13	3	3	1	2
Parra, Yankees	.800	10	0	4	1	1
Patterson, Blue Jays*	1.000	3	0	1	0	0
Pearlman, Blue Jays	.882	21	5	10	2	0
Pelka, Pirates	1.000	7	3	0	0	0
Percibal, Orioles	1.000	16	0	3	0	0
Perez, Red Sox	.700	14	3	4	3	0
Perez, Dodgers	.769	12	3	7	3	0
Le. Perez, Rangers	.625	17	3	2	3	0
Lu. Perez, Rangers	.750	16	0	3	1	0
Phillips, Pirates	.800	4	0	4	1	0
Pina, Twins	1.000	15	2	2	0	0
Pinango, Red Sox*	1.000	14	2	8	0	0
Pittsley, Royals	1.000	9	2	7	0	0
Plonk, Yankees	.875	15	2	5	1	0
Price, Orioles*	.375	9	0	3	5	0
Ramirez, Yankees	1.000	13	0	7	0	0
Randall, Expos	.600	6	0	3	2	0
Rapaglia, Astros	1.000	8	1	2	0	0
Reeder, Marlins	1.000	20	4	11	0	0
Reese, Braves	1.000	1	1	0	0	0
Reinozo, Rangers	1.000	11	3	10	0	0
Renfroe, Red Sox	.947	14	2	16	1	1
Rich, Blue Jays	1.000	27	1	4	0	0
Rizzo, Dodgers*	.000	9	0	0	1	0
Robinson, Braves	.833	10	2	3	1	0
Rondon, Braves	.913	15	11	10	2	0
Roque, Mets*	1.000	20	2	5	0	0
Runion, Rangers	.813	13	7	6	3	0
Runyan, Astros*	.900	10	3	6	1	1
Sanchez, Royals	.769	23	1	9	3	1
Santana, Pirates	.900	13	9	9	2	1
Santos, Royals*	.900	14	6	3	1	0
Sarmiento, Dodgers*	1.000	7	2	9	0	3
Saunders, Marlins*	.833	24	0	5	1	0
Schoenvogel, Red Sox	1.000	1	1	0	0	0
Seaton, Rangers	.800	14	1	3	1	0
Seip, Rangers	.857	17	1	5	1	0
Serafini, Twins*	1.000	8	0	2	0	0
Sherman, Mets	.786	16	0	11	3	0
Silva, Blue Jays	.857	12	2	10	2	1
Sinclair, Blue Jays*	.857	5	3	3	1	1
Smith, Orioles	1.000	11	2	10	0	0
Smith, Dodgers*	.857	16	0	6	1	0
Smoot, Braves*	1.000	6	0	2	0	0
Solomon, Royals	1.000	21	0	8	0	0
Sosa, Twins	.800	8	1	3	1	0
Soto, White Sox	.750	8	5	7	4	2
Spang, Mets	1.000	6	0	3	0	0
Spring, Astros	.889	18	0	8	1	0
Starks, White Sox	1.000	5	1	2	0	0
Stefanoff, Blue Jays	.750	9	1	2	1	0
Stephens, Dodgers	.800	17	5	3	2	2
Stevens, Twins	.600	12	2	7	6	0
Tatar, Twins	.900	17	4	5	1	0
Tatis, Mets*	.889	11	3	5	1	0
Taylor, Blue Jays*	1.000	1	0	1	0	0
Taylor, Pirates*	.800	15	2	6	2	0
Taylor, Rangers	1.000	3	0	2	0	0
Teran, Braves*	.957	15	8	14	1	0
Theodile, White Sox	1.000	4	1	1	0	0
Thomforde, Yankees	.000	3	0	0	1	0
Tidwell, Marlins	.938	11	6	9	1	1
Towns, Royals	1.000	9	1	3	0	0
Trumpour, Mets	1.000	8	1	6	0	0
Tyrrell, Red Sox*	.727	7	2	6	3	0
Ubiera, Rangers	1.000	10	2	8	0	0
Valdez, Astros	.933	11	5	9	1	0
Veneziale, Marlins	1.000	7	0	6	0	0
Vializ, Expos	1.000	11	3	10	0	1
Watts, Dodgers*	.857	4	0	6	1	0
White, Dodgers	.667	5	0	2	1	0
Wiley, Yankees	1.000	4	0	2	0	0
Witt, Yankees	1.000	3	1	2	0	0
Worrell, White Sox*	1.000	2	0	1	0	0

The following players did not have any fielding statistics at the positions indicated or appeared only as a designated hitter, pinch-hitter or pinch-runner: Arvelo, 3b; Barry, dh; Bell, p; Brennan, ss; T. Brown, p; Cassels, dh; Corporan, c; Correa, of; Crick, 1b; E. Delgado, p; DePastino, 3b; Di-mare, of; Fajardo, p; Halbruner, 3b; Hale, p; Hamilton, 2b; Hokanson, p; Howard, p; Hurtault, p; Jenkins, p; E. Johnson, p; Knauss, of; Kubicki, p; Lloyd, p; K. McDonald, p; C. Mendez, 3b; Mendoza, ss; T. Norman, of, p; O'Donnell, of; Pulido, 3b; A. Reyes, of; Starr, p; Steele, p; Tejada, p; Thorsteinson, 3b; Turlais, p; Turrentine, p; Vallot, p; Vindivich, of; Ri. Williams, p.

LEAGUE CHAMPIONS

Year	Team	Pct.	Year	Team	Pct.	Year	Team	Pct.
1964—	Sarasota Braves	.610	1977—	Chicago AL	.731	1987—	Dodgers b	.683
1965—	Bradenton Astros	.632	1978—	Texas	.600		Royals	.635
1966—	New York AL	.667	1979—	Houston	.635	1988—	Yankees b	.714
1967—	Kansas City	.614	1980—	Kansas City-Blue	.635		Royals	.619
1968—	Oakland	.650	1981—	Kansas City-Gold	.688	1989—	Yankees c	.651
1969—	Montreal	.585	1982—	New York AL	.667		Dodgers	.635
1970—	Chicago AL	.600	1983—	Texas	.645	1990—	Expos	.635
1971—	Kansas City	.755		Los Angeles b	.617		Dodgers c	.603
1972—	Chicago NL a	.651	1984—	White Sox	.651	1991—	Orioles	.593
	Kansas City a	.651		Rangers b	.571		Expos e	.533
1973—	Texas	.732	1985—	Yankees d	.705	1992—	Royals f	.695
1974—	Chicago NL	.702		Rangers	.532		Expos	.593
1975—	Texas	.774	1986—	Reds	.548			
1976—	Texas	.704		Dodgers b	.541			

(Note—Known as Sarasota Rookie League in 1964 and Florida Rookie League in 1965.) aDeclared co-champions; no playoff. bLeague divided into Northern and Southern divisions; won one-game playoff for league championship. cLeague divided into Northern and Southern divisions; won best-of-three playoff for league championship. dYankees declared champion based on winning percentage when one-game playoff against Rangers was rained out. eLeague divided into Northern, Southern and Central divisions; won best-of-three playoff for league championship. fLeague divided into Eastern, Central and Western divisions; won three-team playoff.

PIONEER LEAGUE

FINAL STANDINGS

NORTHERN DIVISION

Team	W	L	T	Pct.	GB
Billings (Reds)	53	23	0	.697	......
Great Falls (Dodgers)	38	35	0	.521	13½
Lethbridge (Independent)	24	50	0	.324	28
Medicine Hat (Blue Jays)	23	52	0	.307	29½

SOUTHERN DIVISION

Team	W	L	T	Pct.	GB
Salt Lake (Independent)	53	23	0	.697	......
Helena (Brewers)	50	26	0	.658	3
Butte (Rangers)	33	43	0	.434	20
Idaho Falls (Braves)	27	49	0	.355	26

COMPOSITE

Team	S.L.	Bil	Hel.	G.F.	But.	I.F.	Leth.	M.H.	W	L	T	Pct.	GB
Salt Lake (Independent)	....	3	5	5	10	17	6	7	53	23	0	.697	......
Billings (Reds)	4	....	4	10	5	7	11	12	53	23	0	.697	......
Helena (Brewers)	9	3	....	5	13	8	7	5	50	26	0	.658	3
Great Falls (Dodgers)	2	8	4	....	2	6	7	9	38	35	0	.521	13½
Butte (Rangers)	4	2	7	5	....	8	2	5	33	43	0	.434	20
Idaho Falls (Braves)	3	2	4	1	6	...	6	5	27	49	0	.355	26
Lethbridge (Independent)	1	3	0	5	5	1	...	9	24	50	0	.324	28
Medicine Hat (Blue Jays)	0	2	2	4	2	2	11	...	23	52	0	.307	29½

Major league affiliations in parentheses.

Playoffs—Billings defeated Salt Lake, two games to none, to win league championship.

Regular-season attendance—Billings, 100,788; Butte, 24,530; Great Falls, 70,411; Helena, 49,015; Idaho Falls, 46,104; Lethbridge, 21,669; Medicine Hat, 16,827; Salt Lake, 217,263. Total, 546,607. Playoffs (2 games), 4,695.

Managers—Billings, Donnie Scott; Butte, Victor Ramirez; Great Falls, Jon Debus; Helena, Harry Dunlop; Idaho Falls, Dave Hilton; Lethbridge, Larry Milbourne; Medicine Hat, Jim Nettles; Salt Lake, Nick Belmonte.

All-Star team: 1B—Tim Belk, Billings; 2B—Demetrish Jenkins, Billings; 3B—Tim Unroe, Helena; SS—Wesley Weger, Helena; OF—Roger Cedeno, Great Falls; Tim Clark, Salt Lake; Miguel Correa, Idaho Falls; C—Brian Hostetler, Helena; DH—Micah Franklin, Billings; RHP—Jason Kummerfeldt, Billings; LHP—Scott Karl, Helena; Relief Pitcher—Bo Loftin, Billings; Manager of the Year—Donnie Scott, Billings.

BATTING

TEAM

Team	Avg.	G	AB	R	OR	H	TB	2B	3B	HR	RBI	SH	SF	HP	BB	Int. BB	SO	SB	CS	LOB
Salt Lake	.295	76	2603	488	336	768	1068	143	14	43	413	25	37	58	384	7	439	81	48	651
Helena	.280	76	2648	524	418	742	1144	118	22	80	455	19	27	45	337	8	621	93	35	576
Billings	.279	76	2615	483	394	729	1116	133	22	70	408	14	22	47	318	10	505	121	56	575
Idaho Falls	.274	76	2591	411	502	709	963	105	25	33	344	14	19	36	229	4	569	97	47	524
Butte	.271	76	2538	428	485	687	969	123	27	35	365	12	23	26	341	4	545	92	60	550
Great Falls	.267	73	2476	424	371	660	906	99	36	25	329	24	23	41	317	5	545	134	61	553
Lethbridge	.239	74	2451	328	432	587	785	99	15	23	260	23	13	44	273	9	591	98	43	554
Medicine Hat	.226	75	2366	297	445	535	714	86	6	27	249	26	9	32	298	4	595	86	36	519

INDIVIDUAL

(Leading qualifiers for batting championship—205 or more plate appearances)

*Bats lefthanded.   †Switch-hitter.

Player. Team	Avg.	G	AB	R	H	TB	2B	3B	HR	RBI	SH	SF	HP	BB	Int. BB	SO	SB	CS
Clark, Tim, Salt Lake City*	.357	69	272	57	97	159	25	2	11	53	1	4	3	28	1	36	1	2
Ramirez, J.D., Salt Lake City	.347	44	173	46	60	79	9	2	2	24	2	2	4	32	0	18	2	6
Aurilia, Richard, Butte	.337	59	202	37	68	94	11	3	3	30	5	2	0	42	0	18	13	9
Franklin, Micah, Billings†	.335	75	251	58	84	134	13	2	11	60	0	3	15	53	3	65	18	17
Jenkins, Demetrish, Billings*	.335	72	281	52	94	118	17	2	1	38	1	4	3	34	3	49	9	5
Wilson, Pookie, Salt Lake City*	.332	66	241	57	80	89	5	2	0	20	2	2	4	26	0	24	24	12
McMullan, Kevin, Salt Lake City	.328	67	238	51	78	137	22	2	11	60	0	4	16	41	3	59	5	5
Wilson, Desi, Butte*	.320	72	253	45	81	113	9	4	5	42	0	0	1	31	1	45	13	11
Vosik, Bill, Salt Lake City	.317	73	243	38	77	92	13	1	0	46	3	3	7	36	0	22	3	1
Cedeno, Roger, Great Falls†	.316	69	256	60	81	103	6	5	2	27	4	2	2	51	3	53	40	9

Departmental leaders: G—Franklin, E. Gonzalez, Malone, Welch, 75; AB—Parra, 300; R—Rodriques, 63; H—Clark, 97; TB—Clark, 159; 2B—Clark, 25; 3B—J. Martin, Welch, 7; HR—Unroe, 16; RBI—Welch, 62; SH—Good, 7; SF—Malone, 7; HP—House, 17; BB—Welch, 62; IBB—Five players tied with 3; SO—Felder, 102; SB—Cedeno, 40; CS—Franklin, 17.

(All players—listed alphabetically)

Player. Team	Avg.	G	AB	R	H	TB	2B	3B	HR	RBI	SH	SF	HP	BB	Int. BB	SO	SB	CS
Aurilia, Richard, Butte	.337	59	202	37	68	94	11	3	3	30	5	2	0	42	0	18	13	9
Babki, Blake, Lethbridge*	.189	56	169	27	32	54	7	0	5	22	0	0	6	40	1	59	6	2
Baker, George, Salt Lake City*	.211	46	123	17	26	35	7	1	0	20	0	3	3	21	1	16	0	0
Behr, George, Helena	.270	54	196	29	53	83	9	0	7	39	1	2	2	13	1	56	1	0
Belk, Tim, Billings	.286	73	273	60	78	127	13	0	12	56	0	6	4	35	0	33	15	2
Benjamin, Bobby, Salt Lake City*	.186	23	70	7	13	23	1	0	3	16	1	0	1	16	1	28	1	0
Bethke, Jamie, Butte†	.257	60	237	27	61	78	12	1	1	30	0	0	15	0	60	0	1	
Bills, Walter, Medicine Hat	.000	21	1	0	0	0	0	0	0	0	0	0	0	0	0	1	0	0
Bingham, David, Idaho Falls	.289	51	180	36	52	79	10	4	3	38	1	3	8	20	0	41	11	3
Brown, Mike, Great Falls	.257	12	35	8	9	10	1	0	0	3	0	1	0	6	0	7	0	2
Calarco, John, Salt Lake City	.194	14	31	2	6	7	1	0	0	2	0	1	2	3	0	4	0	1
Campbell, John, Lethbridge	.208	17	53	9	11	14	3	0	0	7	0	0	0	7	0	13	0	1
Cardona, James, Lethbridge*	.231	7	26	6	6	7	1	0	0	2	0	0	0	2	0	3	1	2
Carew, Jeff, Butte	.000	15	0	0	0	0	0	0	0	0	0	0	0	2	0	0	0	0

Player, Team	Avg.	G	AB	R	H	TB	2B	3B	HR	RBI	SH	SF	HP	BB	Int. BB	SO	SB	CS
Cedeno, Roger, Great Falls†	.316	69	256	60	81	103	6	5	2	27	4	2	2	51	3	53	40	9
Clark, Tim, Salt Lake City*	.357	69	272	57	97	159	25	2	11	53	1	4	3	28	1	36	1	2
Collins, Mike, Billings	.172	19	29	2	5	5	0	0	0	1	2	1	1	6	0	12	0	1
Colmenares, Carlos, Medicine Hat	.167	36	96	11	16	18	2	0	0	8	2	0	2	13	0	30	1	0
Correa, Miguel, Idaho Falls	.297	66	266	43	79	105	7	5	3	28	0	4	14	0	49	14	10
Cradle, Rickey, Medicine Hat	.226	65	217	38	49	84	8	0	9	36	1	2	6	42	0	69	16	2
Cunningham, O'Brian, Lethbridge	.211	45	152	13	32	55	8	0	5	21	0	1	3	6	0	59	2	2
Dobrolsky, Bill, Helena	.241	11	29	4	7	10	3	0	0	4	0	0	0	5	0	8	0	1
Dolson, Andy, Medicine Hat*	.000	16	1	0	0	0	0	0	0	0	0	0	0	0	0	1	0	0
Dreisbach, Billy, Billings	.100	6	10	0	1	1	0	0	0	2	0	2	0	0	0	3	0	0
Dumas, Mike, Helena	.229	14	48	5	11	14	3	0	0	5	2	0	2	0	6	5	1
Dunn, Nathan, Great Falls	.266	37	109	24	29	37	6	1	0	20	3	1	2	6	0	14	5	1
Edmondson, Chris, Lethbridge	.239	64	238	25	57	79	12	2	2	30	1	3	4	23	0	40	1	3
Eggleston, Wayne, Butte	.235	59	200	24	47	62	7	1	2	23	0	2	2	18	1	61	9	6
Evans, Tom, Medicine Hat	.217	52	166	17	36	42	3	0	1	21	1	1	1	33	0	29	4	3
Felder, Ken, Helena	.217	74	276	58	60	115	8	1	15	48	0	4	16	35	0	102	11	2
Folger, Ken, Salt Lake City	.283	30	46	9	13	18	5	0	0	5	1	2	0	7	0	15	0	1
Franklin, Micah, Billings†	.335	75	251	58	84	134	13	2	11	60	0	3	15	53	3	65	18	17
Garr, Ralph, Idaho Falls	.235	57	200	25	47	71	5	5	3	24	1	0	1	13	0	57	10	5
Gates, Todd, Butte†	.000	4	4	2	0	0	0	0	0	0	0	0	2	1	0	4	0	1
Gonzalez, Efrain, Butte*	.246	75	276	44	68	100	12	4	4	33	1	2	2	17	0	52	7	7
Gonzalez, German, Great Falls	.255	36	102	17	26	39	5	1	2	16	1	0	1	21	1	26	0	2
Good, Thomas, Lethbridge*	.207	57	208	26	43	51	4	2	0	13	7	3	1	16	0	34	21	6
Graham, Derrick, Billings	.247	22	77	18	19	29	5	1	1	5	0	0	2	6	1	22	2	1
Guild, David, Salt Lake City	.250	5	8	0	2	2	0	0	0	0	0	0	0	1	0	3	0	0
Haley, Rich, Great Falls*	.225	32	111	11	25	38	2	1	3	10	0	1	1	6	0	36	0	1
Hayes, Emanuel, Medicine Hat	.202	36	94	16	19	19	0	0	0	1	4	1	5	24	0	26	8	5
Hearn, Sean, Medicine Hat*	.217	35	106	10	23	31	5	0	1	5	0	0	0	14	0	39	5	2
Herrera, Jose, Medicine Hat*	.272	72	265	45	72	85	9	2	0	21	7	0	6	32	1	62	32	8
Hieb, Dave, Butte	.247	58	190	36	47	75	9	2	5	29	1	2	0	34	0	42	4	4
Holub, Sean, Helena	.000	2	5	0	0	0	0	0	0	0	0	0	0	0	0	5	0	0
Hostetler, Brian, Helena *	.313	60	195	34	61	98	13	0	8	56	0	4	3	29	1	25	1	1
House, Mitch, Lethbridge	.242	73	264	45	64	100	13	1	7	35	0	1	17	28	2	74	11	3
Hudson, Todd, Lethbridge	.125	3	8	1	1	1	0	0	0	1	0	0	0	1	0	2	0	0
Hughes, Bobby, Helena	.175	11	40	5	7	10	1	1	0	6	0	0	2	4	0	14	0	0
Hughes, Dana, Helena	.317	33	120	29	38	48	5	1	1	22	0	1	2	17	0	38	2	0
Hughes, Vinny, Salt Lake City	.214	19	28	0	6	6	0	0	0	2	0	1	1	4	0	9	0	1
Jackson, Andrew, Salt Lake City	.280	13	25	3	7	8	1	0	0	4	1	0	1	9	0	6	3	1
Jackson, Vince, Great Falls	.226	12	31	1	7	7	0	0	0	4	0	0	0	2	0	11	2	1
Jaime, Angel, Great Falls	.271	62	236	38	64	79	8	2	1	34	4	1	1	32	0	58	21	7
Jenkins, Demetrish, Billings*	.335	72	281	52	94	118	17	2	1	38	1	4	3	34	3	49	9	5
Jennette, Les, Salt Lake City	.233	12	30	4	7	9	2	0	0	3	1	1	1	5	0	5	0	0
Johnson, Andre, Idaho Falls	.265	9	34	3	9	11	2	0	0	5	0	0	0	3	0	13	3	1
Johnson, Matthew, Medicine Hat	.256	67	234	33	60	80	10	2	2	28	3	2	6	38	0	36	6	4
Johnson, Reggie, Great Falls	.235	15	51	12	12	18	2	2	0	8	0	1	0	11	0	15	1	2
Keenan, Bradley, Billings	.174	9	23	3	4	4	0	0	0	0	0	0	1	3	1	12	0	0
Kimball, Doug, Great Falls	.056	8	18	2	1	2	1	0	0	1	0	1	0	3	0	5	0	0
Kimler, Mike, Lethbridge	.250	2	8	0	2	2	0	0	0	2	0	0	0	0	0	1	0	0
Kingston, Mark, Helena†	.262	39	122	21	32	44	7	1	1	14	1	1	1	12	0	32	0	0
Koeper, Chris, Salt Lake City	.150	7	20	3	3	3	0	0	0	3	1	1	1	1	0	3	2	1
Kopriva, Dan, Billings	.306	51	196	37	60	112	15	2	11	38	0	0	3	21	0	23	5	2
Kuhn, Alex, Idaho Falls	.181	28	83	9	15	18	3	0	0	7	2	2	1	10	0	20	0	1
Lampkin, Steve, Lethbridge	.255	27	94	5	24	28	4	0	0	14	0	0	0	5	0	30	1	1
Lantigua, Eduardo, Great Falls	.275	25	91	17	25	39	5	3	1	14	1	1	3	10	0	21	3	2
Latham, Chris, Great Falls†	.324	17	37	8	12	14	2	0	0	3	0	0	0	8	1	1	1	1
Lavigne, Ben, Idaho Falls*	.357	6	14	0	5	5	0	0	0	2	0	0	0	1	0	2	0	0
Lay, Shane, Helena*	.274	37	106	24	29	38	6	0	1	14	1	2	2	14	1	16	1	1
Lee, Thomas, Lethbridge	.000	22	1	0	0	0	0	0	0	0	0	0	0	0	0	1	0	0
Luna, Alexis, Medicine Hat	.140	52	157	19	22	29	4	0	1	8	1	0	1	23	1	54	1	3
Luzinski, Ryan, Great Falls	.251	61	227	26	57	91	14	4	4	29	0	1	2	22	2	47	2	1
Malloy, Marty, Idaho Falls*	.315	62	251	45	79	105	18	1	2	28	0	1	2	11	0	43	8	4
Malone, Scott, Butte*	.278	75	241	33	67	96	20	0	3	42	0	7	1	39	0	49	1	3
Manship, Jeff, Billings	.059	9	17	2	1	1	0	0	0	2	0	0	1	1	0	9	0	0
Martin, Jim, Great Falls	.309	56	204	37	63	97	5	7	5	30	0	3	7	28	2	52	8	2
Martin, Matt, Billings†	.243	30	70	10	17	19	2	0	0	11	1	0	0	9	0	19	5	4
Martinez, Angel, Medicine Hat	.252	57	206	27	52	79	15	0	4	39	0	2	1	14	0	62	0	0
McMullan, Kevin, Salt Lake City	.328	67	238	51	78	137	22	2	11	60	0	4	16	41	3	59	5	5
Meggers, Mike, Billings	.268	73	257	47	69	127	16	3	12	48	1	2	3	48	1	72	10	7
Mendoza, Francisco, Helena†	.276	22	58	8	16	16	0	0	0	8	2	0	1	3	0	22	1	2
Merrick, Tim, Salt Lake City	.355	34	76	24	27	34	4	0	1	8	3	2	4	9	0	9	9	2
Miller, Scott, Medicine Hat	.500	1	2	0	1	1	0	0	0	0	0	0	0	0	0	1	0	0
Montgomery, Damon, Billings	.000	1	2	0	0	0	0	0	0	0	0	0	0	0	0	1	0	0
Mottola, Chad, Billings	.286	57	213	53	61	111	8	3	12	37	0	0	0	25	0	43	12	3
Nagy, Jeff, Billings	.172	29	64	10	11	14	3	0	0	7	4	0	4	14	0	24	5	1
Nalepka, Keith, Butte	.244	45	119	27	29	42	4	0	3	20	0	0	5	34	0	32	2	1
Nalls, Kevin, Idaho Falls	.284	51	190	34	54	61	5	1	0	18	1	1	5	9	0	17	2	1
Newcomb, Chris, Butte	.000	22	1	0	0	0	0	0	0	0	0	0	0	0	0	0	0	0
Newman, Rob, Idaho Falls	.308	8	26	3	8	9	1	0	0	4	0	1	0	3	0	7	0	0
Norris, Wade, Medicine Hat	.257	48	175	17	45	54	6	0	1	16	0	0	2	12	0	22	1	0
Ortega, Eddie, Salt Lake City *	.191	26	47	5	9	9	0	0	0	5	1	1	1	3	0	5	1	1
Owens, Eric, Billings	.301	67	239	41	72	97	10	3	3	26	3	0	0	23	0	22	15	4
Palumbo, Richard, Salt Lake City	.277	61	166	28	46	66	6	1	4	25	0	2	0	32	0	31	5	7
Parra, Franklin, Butte†	.277	73	300	58	83	113	16	4	2	27	4	1	5	23	1	67	24	9
Patterson, Rob, Medicine Hat*	.000	19	5	0	0	0	0	0	0	0	0	0	0	0	0	2	0	0
Patzke, Jeff, Medicine Hat†	.218	59	193	19	42	52	4	0	2	17	3	0	0	17	0	42	3	1
Payne, Jake, Lethbridge†	.400	2	5	1	2	3	1	0	0	0	0	0	0	1	0	2	0	0
Perez, Dan, Helena	.212	33	104	12	22	28	3	0	1	13	1	0	1	10	0	17	3	0
Polis, Pete, Medicine Hat	.232	45	151	14	35	59	9	0	5	20	1	0	1	12	1	64	0	1
Ponder, Marcus, Lethbridge	.274	56	197	29	54	76	9	5	1	26	1	0	0	14	0	50	13	0
Post, David, Great Falls	.290	41	138	23	40	51	8	0	1	25	3	2	4	23	0	16	10	5
Powers, Robert, Helena	.235	8	17	3	4	4	0	0	0	0	0	0	0	5	0	5	0	1
Pratt, John, Salt Lake City	.167	10	12	1	2	2	0	0	0	2	0	0	0	0	0	3	0	0
Ragland, Trace, Lethbridge*	.361	11	36	8	13	20	4	0	1	10	0	1	1	9	0	3	2	1
Ramey, Jeff, Billings	.242	18	62	7	15	23	5	0	1	2	0	0	0	8	0	8	4	1

Player, Team	Avg.	G	AB	R	H	TB	2B	3B	HR	RBI	SH	SF	HP	BB	Int. BB	SO	SB	CS
Ramirez, J.D., Salt Lake City	.347	44	173	46	60	79	9	2	2	24	2	2	4	32	0	18	2	6
Rea, Clarke, Lethbridge*	.210	50	157	19	33	41	5	0	1	14	2	1	1	26	1	29	3	2
Rennspies, Dustin, Great Falls†	.000	2	5	0	0	0	0	0	0	0	0	0	0	3	0	1	0	0
Richardson, Scott, Helena	.287	69	289	58	83	109	10	5	2	36	1	0	4	35	1	43	22	5
Rigsby, Tim, Salt Lake City	.304	42	148	30	45	56	6	1	1	16	0	0	0	17	0	23	11	8
Rodrigues, Cecil, Helena	.305	72	279	63	85	150	17	6	12	49	1	3	4	30	2	62	23	7
Rodriguez, Eddy, Great Falls	.237	58	186	24	44	60	8	4	0	19	2	2	4	24	0	46	11	13
Rodriguez, Felix, Great Falls	.291	32	110	20	32	46	8	0	2	20	1	1	1	0	0	16	2	0
Rosenthal, Todd, Salt Lake City*	.305	70	262	46	80	95	11	2	0	41	4	2	1	36	1	24	5	0
Ross, Jackie, Helena†	.299	60	211	44	63	96	4	4	7	36	2	4	2	32	1	33	11	6
Ruhl, Dan, Lethbridge	.275	64	204	27	56	75	8	4	1	17	1	1	7	31	0	56	5	3
Rumfield, Toby, Billings	.269	66	253	34	68	101	15	3	4	50	0	4	4	7	0	34	5	2
Samson, Fred, Salt Lake City	.253	52	178	32	45	84	12	0	9	39	0	4	5	33	0	52	4	0
Saturnino, Sherton, Idaho Falls	.240	51	167	19	40	48	4	2	0	13	1	0	6	7	1	49	5	4
Scales, Matthew, Lethbridge*	.252	48	155	19	39	47	8	0	0	15	2	0	0	23	0	51	3	3
Schula, Kevin, Idaho Falls	.178	16	45	3	8	12	1	0	1	6	0	2	0	7	0	25	0	1
Shook, Wesley, Butte	.242	11	33	4	8	13	3	1	0	3	0	1	0	1	0	3	0	0
Silvia, Brian, Billings	.154	5	13	4	2	2	0	0	0	1	0	0	0	4	0	7	0	0
Smith, Craig, Helena	.286	21	63	12	18	21	3	0	0	1	1	0	0	9	0	15	1	1
Smith, Frank, Great Falls	.217	22	69	9	15	22	0	2	1	7	1	0	1	7	0	16	1	1
Smith, Willie, Salt Lake City	.500	3	2	1	1	1	0	0	0	1	0	0	0	0	0	1	0	0
Snyder, Randy, Salt Lake City†	.232	54	164	27	38	54	13	0	1	20	4	3	3	24	0	42	5	0
Soto, Miguel, Idaho Falls	.291	58	203	31	59	72	5	1	2	29	0	3	1	17	0	19	1	0
Stefanik, Robert, Lethbridge*	.271	73	291	49	79	91	10	1	0	25	5	2	2	32	1	50	21	9
Sullivan, Charlie, Butte*	.080	9	25	3	2	2	0	0	0	2	0	0	0	2	0	11	0	0
Sweeney, Roger, Great Falls*	.267	45	116	20	31	33	2	0	0	11	1	2	3	20	0	29	9	2
Tena, Dario, Lethbridge†	.282	20	71	11	20	21	1	0	0	5	3	0	0	7	0	9	8	2
Thomas, Chris, Helena	.133	13	30	8	4	7	0	0	1	4	0	0	1	5	0	9	1	0
Torian, Van, Idaho Falls	.253	21	75	9	19	23	2	1	0	7	2	1	0	6	0	21	9	4
Towle, Justin, Billings	.364	7	11	1	4	5	1	0	0	1	0	0	0	3	0	4	0	0
Trevino, Gerald, Idaho Falls*	.243	56	185	29	45	60	7	1	2	26	3	1	0	36	3	56	9	1
Triplett, Al, Butte	.254	20	63	10	16	19	3	0	0	7	1	1	1	5	0	14	0	0
Unroe, Tim, Helena	.278	74	266	61	74	139	14	3	16	58	1	1	4	47	1	91	3	4
Villalona, Kadir, Medicine Hat*	.210	70	257	22	54	67	9	2	0	24	3	1	1	17	1	45	6	3
Vosik, Bill, Salt Lake City†	.317	73	243	38	77	92	13	1	0	46	3	3	7	36	0	22	3	1
Waldrop, Tom, Idaho Falls*	.311	65	244	51	76	125	16	3	9	45	0	2	1	31	1	63	5	3
Warner, Mike, Idaho Falls*	.273	10	33	4	9	15	3	0	1	6	0	0	0	3	0	5	1	0
Watts, Craig, Great Falls	.321	34	112	17	36	51	10	1	1	24	0	3	4	10	1	22	0	0
Weger, Wesley, Helena	.429	36	133	36	57	83	9	1	5	31	2	5	0	22	0	9	7	2
Welch, Mike, Butte*	.298	75	258	59	77	123	11	7	7	62	0	5	4	62	1	59	9	7
Wilke, Matt, Medicine Hat*	.225	12	40	9	9	14	2	0	1	5	0	0	0	7	0	13	1	2
Wilkerson, Wayne, Billings*	.234	67	274	44	64	86	10	3	2	23	2	0	5	18	1	43	16	6
Williams, Rod, Lethbridge	.167	34	114	7	19	20	1	0	0	5	1	0	2	3	0	27	0	3
Willman, David, Helena	.295	22	61	10	18	31	4	0	3	11	2	0	0	8	0	13	0	1
Wilson, Desi, Butte*	.320	72	253	45	81	113	9	4	5	42	0	0	1	31	1	45	13	11
Wilson, Pookie, Salt Lake City*	.332	66	241	57	80	89	5	2	0	20	2	2	4	26	0	24	24	12
Winicki, Dennis, Great Falls	.247	51	170	36	42	53	6	1	1	18	3	2	4	27	0	37	12	7
Wollenburg, Doug, Idaho Falls	.304	69	257	43	78	102	10	1	4	43	1	2	4	24	1	29	11	5
Woodall, Kevin, Idaho Falls	.243	44	136	17	33	39	6	0	0	14	0	0	3	15	0	28	10	1
Woods, Byron, Idaho Falls	.196	44	138	24	27	42	6	0	3	16	2	0	3	14	0	53	8	4
Zammarchi, Erik, Great Falls	.145	26	62	14	9	16	0	2	1	6	0	1	2	13	0	18	6	2

The following pitchers, listed alphabetically by club, with games in parentheses, had no plate appearances, primarily through use of designated hitters:

BILLINGS—Angel, Jason (15); Burke, Gordon (9); Garcia, Fermin (31); Kummerfeldt, Jason (13); Langford, Rich (15); Lister, Martin (26); Loftin, Bill (33); Morales, Armando (8); Murphy, Jeff (21); Pickett, Cecil (20); Reed, Chris (10); Sullivan, Bill (24); Tobin, Dan (9).

BUTTE—Brandenburg, Mark (24); Chavarria, Dave (13); Evans, Brent (2); Eyre, Scott (15); Kelley, Chris (18); Kimel, Jack (16); Lesch, Paul (16); Madrigal, Victor (17); Manning, Dave (8); Mascia, Dan (17); O'Brien, Mark (8); Rosenkranz, Terry (14); Wiley, Chad (18).

GREAT FALLS—Butcher, Jason (3); Cope, Gary (19); Costello, Chris (7); Fitzpatrick, Dave (21); Groot, Fransiscus (16); Henderson, Ryan (11); Iglesias, Mike (12); Jacobson, Joe (6); Linares, Rich (19); Martinez, Jesus (6); Pincavitch, Kevin (26); Pyc, Dave (25); Smith, Joe (5); Spykstra, Dave (8); Vogelgesang, Joe (9); Watts, Brandon (13); Zerbe, Chad (15).

HELENA—Demyan, Kirk (3); Droll, Jeff (9); England, Dave (3); Hardwick, Billy (5); Jones, Bob (14); Karl, Scott (9); Kyslinger, Dan (4); Maltagliati, Steve (2); Marshall, Terry (18); Paul, Andrew (13); Petrocella, Chris (27); Rico, Ron (4); Roberson, Sidney (9); Rodriguez, Francisco (6); Rutter, Sam (15); Sadler, Aldren (4); Schenbeck, Tommy (32); Torrez, Rafael (17); Winter, Rich (13).

IDAHO FALLS—Behrens, Scott (7); Bradshaw, Craig (24); Brock, Chris (15); Cromer, Burke (18); Ford, Stewart (27); Giard, Ken (11); Lairsey, Eric (17); Maitland, Bill (24); Martineau, Yves (6); Pike, Dave (24); Rusciano, Chris (20); Simmons, John (27); Stoecklin, Tony (16); Wade, Terrell (13).

LETHBRIDGE—Acevedo, Milt (5); Aronetz, Cameron (14); Ballance, Dale (15); Campusano, Anibal (11); Coleman, Pete (19); Cudjo, Lavell (20); Jenkins, Kevin (16); Matthews, Ron (25); Myers, Rodney (15); Polanco, Giovanni (9); Urshan, Ross (12); West, Paul (16).

MEDICINE HAT—Beltran, Alonso (15); Brown, Chad (21); Crema, Pat (21); Herrera, Pasqual (4); Muir, Harry (17); O'Halloran, Mike (13); Phillips, Randall (16); Reynoso, Gabriel (14); Sinclair, Steve (9); Taylor, Mike (11).

SALT LAKE—Canestro, Art (5); Dempsey, Steve (2); DeVaughn, Todd (12); Gilligan, John (28); Guidi, Jim (23); Harden, Jonathan (5); Huie, Brian (2); Jones, Shannon (3); Kerfut, George (16); Licursi, Rico (18); Mammola, Mark (10); Marcon, Dave (11); Nettnin, Rodney (4); Parisotto, Barry (14); Pettiford, Cecil (14); Ryan, Bob (7); Schultea, Chris (24); Thoden, John (15).

GRAND SLAMS—Behr, Correa, Franklin, Jaime, Rodriques, Ross, Samson, Soto, Unroe, Welch, 1 each.

AWARDED FIRST BASE ON CATCHER'S INTERFERENCE—Cunningham 3 (Luzinski, Martinez, Snyder); Baker (Ramey); Jennette (Schula); Nalepka (Snyder); Ponder (McMullan).

PITCHING

TEAM

Team	ERA	G	CG	ShO	Sv.	IP	H	R	ER	HR	HB	BB	Int. BB	SO	WP	Bk.
Salt Lake	3.57	76	7	5	16	671.0	704	336	266	30	43	188	8	574	35	7
Great Falls	4.00	73	3	7	18	637.1	599	371	283	28	42	297	11	583	72	14
Billings	4.10	76	1	5	22	667.1	600	394	304	32	50	345	9	609	97	14
Helena	4.37	76	5	5	16	669.1	710	418	325	50	36	298	1	544	92	17
Medicine Hat	4.75	75	7	2	8	625.1	699	445	330	52	41	250	4	427	79	14

Team	ERA	G	CG	ShO	Sv.	IP	H	R	ER	HR	HB	BB	Int. BB	SO	WP	Bk.
Lethbridge	4.79	74	9	4	15	628.0	665	432	334	45	33	346	12	470	99	27
Butte	5.32	76	4	2	10	648.0	740	485	383	59	41	300	6	618	60	22
Idaho Falls	5.65	76	2	3	11	642.1	700	502	403	40	43	473	2	585	108	39

INDIVIDUAL

(Leading qualifiers for earned-run average leadership—61 or more innings)

*Throws lefthanded.

Pitcher, Team	W	L	Pct.	ERA	G	GS	CG	GF	ShO	Sv.	IP	H	R	ER	HR	HB	BB	Int. BB	SO	WP
Karl, Helena*	7	0	1.000	1.46	9	9	1	0	1	0	61.2	54	13	10	2	2	16	0	57	5
Thoden, Salt Lake City	9	3	.750	1.79	15	15	3	0	2	0	100.1	87	35	20	2	3	16	0	78	2
Zerbe, Great Falls*	8	3	.727	2.14	15	15	1	0	2	0	92.1	75	27	22	2	5	26	0	70	5
Brock, Idaho Falls	6	4	.600	2.31	15	15	1	0	0	0	78.0	61	27	20	3	3	48	0	72	12
Kummerfeldt, Billings	8	0	1.000	2.38	13	13	1	0	1	0	87.0	65	32	23	1	5	26	1	75	6
Parisotto, Salt Lake City	7	4	.636	2.47	14	14	1	0	1	0	91.0	97	41	25	2	6	26	1	89	6
Eyre, Butte*	7	3	.700	2.90	15	14	2	0	1	0	80.2	71	30	26	6	4	39	0	94	6
Pettiford, Salt Lake City	5	2	.714	2.96	14	12	1	1	0	0	79.0	73	32	26	3	9	19	0	61	6
Marcon, Salt Lake City*	6	2	.750	2.97	11	10	1	0	0	0	63.2	83	27	21	3	1	17	1	51	1
Beltran, Medicine Hat	4	5	.444	3.14	15	15	1	0	0	0	91.2	78	46	32	7	7	25	0	66	4

Departmental leaders: G—Loftin, 33; W—Kerfut, 10; L—Kelley, Myers, Reynoso, 8; Pct.—Karl, Kummerfeldt, 1.000; GS—Torrez, 16; CG—Myers, 5; GF—Loftin, 31; ShO—Thoden, 2; Sv.—Loftin, 17; IP—Myers, 103.1; H—Torrez, 108; R—Torrez, 60; ER—Lee, Torrez, 48; HR—Campusano, Phillips, 9; HB—Langford, 10; BB—Lairsey, 71; IBB—Pyc, 5; SO—Langford, 95; WP—Langford, 20.

(All pitchers—listed alphabetically)

Pitcher, Team	W	L	Pct.	ERA	G	GS	CG	GF	ShO	Sv.	IP	H	R	ER	HR	HB	BB	Int. BB	SO	WP
Acevedo, Lethbridge*	0	1	.000	9.45	5	0	0	1	0	0	6.2	8	7	7	1	0	9	0	7	3
Angel, Billings	8	3	.727	4.37	15	15	0	0	0	0	82.1	83	52	40	7	6	39	0	48	9
Aronetz, Lethbridge*	6	7	.462	4.54	14	14	1	0	0	0	83.1	96	48	42	5	1	35	0	57	8
Ballance, Lethbridge*	0	4	.000	4.70	15	7	0	2	0	0	46.0	50	32	24	3	2	29	1	32	8
Behrens, Idaho Falls	3	3	.500	5.63	7	7	0	0	0	0	40.0	48	31	25	1	3	14	0	34	8
Beltran, Medicine Hat	4	5	.444	3.14	15	15	1	0	0	0	91.2	78	46	32	7	7	25	0	66	4
Bills, Medicine Hat	3	4	.429	5.26	20	0	0	13	0	1	37.2	47	33	22	2	3	20	2	16	5
Bradshaw, Idaho Falls*	0	2	.000	10.47	24	1	0	7	0	1	38.2	59	51	45	5	2	28	0	37	10
Brandenburg, Butte	7	1	.875	4.06	24	1	0	16	0	2	62.0	70	32	28	3	5	14	1	78	1
Brock, Idaho Falls	6	4	.600	2.31	15	15	1	0	0	0	78.0	61	27	20	3	3	48	0	72	12
Brown, Medicine Hat*	3	3	.500	4.38	21	0	0	9	0	1	37.0	46	28	18	4	1	21	1	28	7
Burke, Billings	1	0	1.000	6.75	9	0	0	4	0	0	16.0	16	14	12	1	1	10	0	19	1
Butcher, Great Falls*	0	0	.000	4.15	3	1	0	1	0	0	4.1	5	4	2	0	1	3	0	7	0
Campusano, Lethbridge	1	5	.167	6.75	11	11	0	0	0	0	57.1	78	53	43	9	2	14	0	43	8
Canestro, Salt Lake City*	1	1	.500	4.79	5	5	0	0	0	0	20.2	24	15	11	0	1	8	0	17	2
Carew, Butte	1	1	.500	5.28	15	0	0	10	0	0	30.2	27	19	18	2	1	15	0	35	2
Chavarria, Butte	2	7	.222	6.27	13	12	0	0	0	0	47.1	54	44	33	0	2	30	0	33	6
Coleman, Lethbridge	3	3	.500	2.91	19	4	1	8	1	1	43.1	37	21	14	7	2	12	1	37	3
Colmenares, Medicine Hat	0	0	.000	0.00	1	0	0	1	0	0	1.0	1	0	0	0	0	2	0	0	0
Cope, Great Falls*	2	1	.667	4.11	19	0	0	5	0	0	35.0	31	21	16	2	1	26	1	30	4
Costello, Great Falls	1	1	.500	2.97	7	3	0	2	0	0	30.1	26	13	10	1	2	9	0	28	2
Crema, Medicine Hat	1	4	.200	4.67	21	0	0	16	0	4	27.0	26	15	14	3	1	9	0	28	7
Cromer, Idaho Falls	4	4	.500	5.44	18	8	0	3	0	0	51.1	63	38	31	5	2	32	0	45	6
Cudjo, Lethbridge	2	1	.667	2.63	20	0	0	16	0	11	27.1	22	10	8	1	4	13	1	23	3
Dempsey, Salt Lake City	0	0	.000	13.50	2	0	0	2	0	0	2.0	6	3	3	0	0	1	0	3	0
Demyan, Helena	1	0	1.000	6.00	3	0	0	2	0	0	6.0	5	4	4	0	1	4	0	5	1
Devaughn, Salt Lake City	0	1	.000	8.04	12	0	0	6	0	2	15.2	13	18	14	2	2	12	0	9	1
Dolson, Medicine Hat*	2	6	.250	4.80	16	10	1	4	0	1	75.0	82	49	40	4	3	21	0	62	6
Dreisbach, Billings	0	0	.000	9.00	1	0	0	1	0	0	1.0	1	1	1	0	0	0	0	2	0
Droll, Helena	0	1	.000	14.21	9	0	0	2	0	0	12.2	20	24	20	1	1	18	0	8	5
Edmondson, Lethbridge	0	0	.000	9.00	1	0	0	1	0	0	1.0	3	1	1	0	1	0	0	0	0
Evans, Butte*	0	0	.000	7.36	2	0	0	0	0	0	3.2	5	3	3	1	0	3	1	2	0
Eyre, Butte*	7	3	.700	2.90	15	14	2	0	1	0	80.2	71	30	26	6	4	39	0	94	6
Fitzpatrick, Great Falls	2	3	.400	5.16	21	2	0	11	0	3	45.1	49	30	26	1	5	20	4	46	8
Ford, Idaho Falls*	0	3	.000	6.18	27	0	0	10	0	3	43.2	49	43	30	0	7	48	0	41	11
Garcia, Billings	3	2	.600	2.44	31	1	0	11	0	2	55.1	44	22	15	1	2	19	1	62	4
Giard, Idaho Falls	0	3	.000	3.88	11	10	0	0	0	0	51.0	49	29	22	1	2	35	0	36	0
Gilligan, Salt Lake City	7	2	.778	2.25	28	0	0	26	0	9	36.0	28	12	9	4	4	8	3	49	3
Groot, Great Falls	4	1	.800	3.38	16	9	0	1	0	0	58.2	56	28	22	1	2	29	0	48	12
Guidi, Salt Lake City	3	1	.750	4.70	23	2	0	6	0	1	46.0	48	27	24	3	3	16	2	34	3
Harden, Salt Lake City*	1	0	1.000	4.26	5	0	0	3	0	0	6.1	9	3	3	0	0	3	0	5	0
Hardwick, Helena*	0	0	.000	0.00	5	0	0	5	0	4	8.0	1	0	0	0	2	3	0	6	0
Henderson, Great Falls	5	1	.833	2.13	11	11	1	0	1	0	55.0	37	22	13	2	2	25	0	54	5
Herrera, Medicine Hat	0	2	.000	3.45	4	3	0	0	0	0	15.2	15	15	6	2	2	4	0	12	2
Huie, Salt Lake City*	0	0	.000	31.50	2	0	0	1	0	0	2.0	6	7	7	0	0	2	0	1	1
Iglesias, Great Falls	3	6	.333	6.11	12	12	0	0	0	0	56.0	69	56	38	4	4	26	0	37	10
Jacobson, Great Falls	2	2	.500	5.29	6	6	1	0	0	0	32.1	37	22	19	2	1	9	0	24	3
Jenkins, Lethbridge	1	1	.500	5.00	16	0	0	7	0	0	27.0	35	21	15	2	0	14	1	14	1
Jones, Helena*	5	4	.556	4.36	14	13	1	0	0	0	76.1	93	51	37	7	1	23	0	53	6
Jones, Salt Lake City	0	0	.000	10.57	3	2	0	0	0	0	7.2	11	10	9	0	2	3	0	5	0
Karl, Helena*	7	0	1.000	1.46	9	9	1	0	1	0	61.2	54	13	10	2	2	16	0	57	5
Kelley, Butte	0	8	.000	8.16	18	7	0	6	0	1	43.0	59	47	39	8	3	22	2	36	3
Kerfut, Salt Lake City	10	2	.833	3.91	15	15	0	0	0	0	96.2	95	45	42	8	6	27	1	81	5
Kimel, Great Falls	5	4	.556	4.06	15	10	2	4	0	1	71.0	69	42	32	7	7	14	0	83	4
Kummerfeldt, Billings	8	0	1.000	2.38	13	13	1	0	1	0	87.0	65	32	23	1	5	26	1	75	6
Kyslinger, Helena	0	0	.000	4.70	4	0	0	2	0	0	7.2	6	4	4	0	1	5	0	13	2
Lairsey, Idaho Falls*	0	6	.000	9.29	17	6	1	3	0	0	41.2	40	49	43	1	5	71	0	32	11
Langford, Billings	7	3	.700	3.43	15	15	0	0	0	0	86.2	73	51	33	4	10	54	1	95	20
Lee, Lethbridge	1	6	.143	5.61	21	10	1	8	0	0	77.0	85	58	48	3	3	42	1	66	18
Lesch, Butte	1	2	.333	7.28	16	2	0	2	0	0	38.1	56	38	31	4	3	22	0	30	9
Licursi, Salt Lake City	2	0	1.000	3.47	18	1	0	7	0	1	36.1	34	16	14	0	2	19	0	38	3
Linares, Great Falls	3	1	.750	2.45	19	0	0	6	0	3	47.2	32	22	13	4	6	11	0	53	2

Pitcher, Team	W	L	Pct.	ERA	G	GS	CG	GF	ShO	Sv.	IP	H	R	ER	HR	HB	BB	Int. BB	SO	WP
Lister, Billings*	3	1	.750	7.86	26	2	0	3	0	1	34.1	36	33	30	2	3	37	1	39	11
Loftin, Billings	7	2	.778	2.31	33	0	0	31	0	17	46.2	28	14	12	1	2	20	1	51	6
Madrigal, Butte	0	3	.000	7.27	16	2	0	2	0	0	34.2	41	36	28	7	2	27	1	36	6
Maitland, Idaho Falls	3	7	.300	6.11	24	7	0	17	0	3	56.0	79	47	38	5	1	35	2	60	6
Maltagliati, Helena	1	0	1.000	5.54	2	2	0	0	0	0	13.0	15	9	8	3	0	4	0	3	1
Mammola, Salt Lake City*	0	1	.000	7.45	10	0	0	3	0	0	9.2	11	8	8	1	0	1	0	10	0
Manning, Butte	0	4	.000	11.01	8	7	0	0	0	0	25.1	50	41	31	4	3	15	0	13	6
Marcon, Salt Lake City*	6	2	.750	2.97	11	10	1	0	0	0	63.2	83	27	21	3	1	17	1	51	1
Marshall, Helena	3	2	.600	5.55	18	0	0	13	0	1	24.1	30	21	15	4	0	16	0	17	2
Martin, Billings	0	0	.000	3.00	4	0	0	4	0	0	3.0	2	2	1	0	0	2	0	2	0
Martineau, Idaho Falls	0	0	.000	8.49	6	0	0	2	0	0	11.2	16	12	11	2	0	5	0	3	0
Martinez, Great Falls*	0	3	.000	13.25	6	6	0	0	0	0	18.1	36	30	27	4	2	21	0	23	9
Mascia, Butte	2	2	.500	4.50	17	4	0	4	0	0	46.0	51	30	23	2	3	33	0	31	5
Matthews, Lethbridge	2	4	.333	5.13	24	1	0	13	0	2	54.1	49	31	31	4	4	28	3	43	6
Morales, Billings	6	1	.857	2.19	8	8	0	0	0	0	53.1	46	23	13	2	1	9	0	62	1
Muir, Medicine Hat	0	3	.000	10.86	17	4	0	10	0	0	29.0	41	36	35	7	4	15	0	17	6
Murphy, Billings	2	1	.667	7.36	21	2	0	9	0	0	33.0	38	33	27	2	5	28	1	33	11
Myers, Lethbridge	5	8	.385	4.01	15	15	5	0	0	0	103.1	93	57	46	3	5	61	1	76	14
Nalls, Idaho Falls	0	0	.000	0.00	1	0	0	1	0	0	1.0	0	0	0	0	0	2	0	0	0
Nettnin, Salt Lake City*	0	0	.000	19.64	4	0	0	0	0	0	3.2	11	8	8	1	0	3	0	4	0
Newcomb, Butte	2	4	.333	2.79	22	2	0	16	0	5	38.2	38	25	12	1	3	15	1	30	2
O'Brien, Butte*	2	3	.400	7.44	8	8	0	0	0	0	32.2	46	32	27	6	2	11	0	26	2
O'Halloran, Medicine Hat	0	4	.000	7.04	13	2	0	4	0	0	30.2	49	36	24	1	2	25	0	14	12
Parisotto, Salt Lake City	7	4	.636	2.47	14	14	1	0	1	0	91.0	97	41	25	2	6	26	1	89	6
Patterson, Medicine Hat*	0	1	.000	5.86	17	0	0	7	0	0	27.2	41	26	18	4	1	15	1	24	8
Paul, Helena	3	0	1.000	7.24	13	4	0	3	0	1	32.1	45	31	26	3	2	21	0	41	7
Petrocella, Helena	3	0	1.000	6.28	27	0	0	8	0	1	43.0	43	37	30	3	4	25	0	44	9
Pettiford, Salt Lake City	5	2	.714	2.96	14	12	1	1	0	0	79.0	73	32	26	3	9	19	0	61	6
Phillips, Medicine Hat	2	4	.333	3.36	15	13	1	0	0	0	91.0	88	48	34	9	9	25	0	69	4
Pickett, Billings*	1	2	.333	2.35	20	4	0	4	0	2	53.2	35	21	14	2	5	28	0	41	3
Pike, Idaho Falls	4	3	.571	4.74	24	2	0	6	0	0	43.2	45	27	23	2	4	25	0	42	11
Pincavitch, Great Falls	2	2	.500	1.95	26	0	0	9	0	1	50.2	36	16	11	1	4	26	1	65	4
Polanco, Lethbridge	0	1	.000	5.40	9	0	0	3	0	1	11.2	13	16	7	1	0	16	0	8	5
Pyc, Great Falls*	2	3	.400	2.86	25	0	0	19	0	9	34.2	32	15	11	0	1	16	5	34	1
Reed, Billings	6	3	.667	5.06	10	10	0	0	0	0	48.0	46	30	27	2	3	32	0	39	5
Reynoso, Medicine Hat*	4	8	.333	5.48	14	14	0	1	0	0	67.1	79	55	41	4	5	33	0	47	10
Rico, Helena*	0	0	.000	2.70	4	0	0	2	0	0	3.1	2	2	1	0	0	4	0	0	0
Roberson, Helena*	4	4	.500	3.46	9	8	1	1	0	0	65.0	68	32	25	8	2	18	0	65	4
Rodriguez, Helena	1	1	.500	2.53	6	1	0	2	0	0	10.2	14	6	3	1	1	3	0	3	3
Rosenkranz, Butte*	0	0	.000	5.74	14	0	0	8	0	0	26.2	34	22	17	4	1	12	0	23	2
Ross, Helena	0	1	.000	27.00	1	0	0	1	0	0	0.1	1	1	1	0	1	0	0	0	0
Rusciano, Idaho Falls	3	5	.375	6.00	20	7	0	3	0	0	63.0	57	47	42	6	6	54	0	60	14
Rutter, Helena	6	3	.667	3.44	15	15	2	0	0	0	96.2	96	50	37	3	9	41	0	70	10
Ryan, Salt Lake City*	1	2	.333	4.38	7	0	0	5	0	0	12.1	14	7	6	1	1	3	0	9	1
Sadler, Helena	1	1	.500	2.74	4	3	0	1	0	0	23.0	19	10	7	1	3	7	0	19	3
Schenbeck, Helena	6	3	.667	2.33	32	1	0	27	0	9	54.0	42	21	14	1	3	25	1	48	12
Schultea, Salt Lake City	1	2	.333	3.43	24	0	0	11	0	3	42.0	54	22	16	0	3	4	0	31	1
Simmons, Idaho Falls*	3	1	.750	3.57	27	0	0	17	0	3	40.1	40	25	16	2	1	13	0	44	4
Sinclair, Medicine Hat*	2	3	.400	4.60	9	7	0	1	0	0	43.0	54	25	22	2	2	12	0	28	3
Smith, Great Falls*	0	0	.000	14.54	5	0	0	4	0	0	4.1	7	7	7	1	0	4	0	1	1
Spykstra, Great Falls	0	6	.000	9.62	8	8	0	0	0	0	24.1	34	35	26	4	3	23	0	17	5
Stoecklin, Idaho Falls*	0	4	.000	6.10	16	2	0	4	0	1	31.0	35	30	21	2	5	20	0	25	10
Sullivan, Helena	1	1	.500	8.05	24	0	0	7	0	0	34.2	44	32	31	3	3	24	2	23	10
Taylor, Medicine Hat	2	5	.286	4.18	11	7	2	3	1	1	51.2	52	33	24	3	2	23	0	16	5
Thoden, Salt Lake City	9	3	.750	1.79	15	15	3	0	2	0	100.1	87	35	20	2	3	16	0	78	2
Tobin, Billings	0	4	.000	6.96	9	6	0	1	0	0	32.1	43	34	25	4	4	17	1	20	10
Torrez, Helena	6	5	.545	4.97	17	16	0	1	0	0	87.0	108	60	48	7	1	31	0	54	4
Trevino, Idaho Falls	0	0	.000	0.00	1	0	0	1	0	0	1.0	0	0	0	0	0	1	0	0	0
Urshan, Lethbridge	0	6	.000	4.94	12	10	0	2	0	0	58.1	71	48	32	4	8	37	1	37	14
Vogelgesang, Great Falls	3	1	.750	3.07	9	0	0	5	0	1	29.1	25	12	10	1	2	8	0	30	0
Wade, Idaho Falls*	1	4	.200	6.44	13	11	0	1	0	0	50.1	59	46	36	5	2	42	0	54	5
Watts, Great Falls*	1	1	.500	5.09	13	0	0	6	0	1	17.2	12	11	10	0	1	14	0	15	1
Welch, Butte*	0	0	.000	0.00	1	0	0	1	0	0	1.0	3	0	0	0	0	0	0	0	0
West, Lethbridge	3	3	.500	4.60	16	2	0	4	0	0	31.1	25	29	16	1	2	35	2	27	8
Wiley, Butte	4	1	.800	4.75	18	7	0	3	0	1	66.1	66	44	35	5	7	28	0	68	6
Winter, Helena	1	0	1.000	9.21	13	1	0	3	0	0	28.1	34	36	29	5	1	32	0	23	12
Zammarchi, Great Falls	0	0	.000	0.00	1	0	0	1	0	0	1.0	0	0	0	0	0	1	0	1	0
Zerbe, Great Falls*	8	3	.727	2.14	15	15	1	0	1	0	92.1	75	27	22	2	5	26	0	70	5

BALKS—Stoecklin, 9; Brock, 8; Ballance, Henderson, 6 each; R. Jones, Maitland, Manning, 5 each; Behrens, Reynoso, Urshan, 4 each; Aronetz, Campusano, Chavarria, Lairsey, Lister, Marcon, Newcomb, Paul, Phillips, 3 each; Angel, Beltran, Bradshaw, Crema, Cromer, Fitzpatrick, Kelley, Kimel, Kummerfeldt, Lee, Madrigal, Matthews, Myers, Petrocella, Rusciano, Simmons, Tobin, Vogelgesang, West, 2 each; Acevedo, Brown, Butcher, Dreisbach, Droll, England, Eyre, Giard, Gilligan, Groot, Hardwick, Huie, Iglesias, Jenkins, Karl, Linares, Loftin, Marshall, Mascia, Muir, O'Brien, Parisotto, Patterson, Pickett, Pike, Polanco, Reed, Roberson, Rosenkranz, Schultea, Sullivan, Torrez, Wiley, 1 each.

COMBINATION SHUTOUTS—Angel-Murphy, Garcia-Murphy, Morales-Loftin, Reed-Murphy, Billings; Wiley-Brandenburg, Butte; Groot-Linares-Pyc, Henderson-Pincavitch, Henderson-Vogelgesang, Iglesias-Pincavitch-Pyc, Great Falls; Jones-Hardwick, Sadler-Schenbeck, Torrez-Roberson, Helena; Brock-Pike-Bradshaw, Brock-Rusciano-Simmons, Pike-Ford, Idaho Falls; Aronetz-Cudjo 2, Aronetz-West, Lethbridge; Pettiford-Gilligan, Thoden-Gilligan, Salt Lake.

NO-HIT GAMES—None.

FIELDING

TEAM

Team	Pct.	G	PO	A	E	DP	PB	Team	Pct.	G	PO	A	E	DP	PB
Salt Lake	.963	76	2013	784	106	57	15	Lethbridge	.950	74	1884	814	143	59	18
Helena	.956	76	2008	870	131	75	20	Great Falls	.948	73	1912	756	146	57	14
Billings	.950	76	2002	772	145	66	13	Idaho Falls	.948	76	1927	727	147	75	15
Butte	.950	76	1944	781	144	47	13	Medicine Hat	.942	75	1876	772	164	58	27

Triple play—Helena.

*Throws lefthanded.

FIRST BASEMEN

, Team	Pct.	G	PO	A	E	DP
Helena	.975	49	447	29	12	38
Billings	.982	73	608	40	12	53
am, Idaho Falls	1.000	4	24	5	0	1
co, Salt Lake City	1.000	3	18	2	0	1
alez, Great Falls	.965	34	234	12	9	18
, Great Falls*	.963	31	248	15	10	22
e, Lethbridge	.973	73	655	33	19	48
es, Billings	1.000	2	16	1	0	1
ette, Salt Lake City	.989	10	82	5	1	5
an, Billings	.974	7	35	3	1	5
all, Great Falls	1.000	2	17	0	0	0
ton, Helena	.989	32	243	16	3	26
Medicine Hat	.972	44	332	19	10	28
ne, Butte	.989	54	411	30	5	20
n, Billings	1.000	1	3	0	0	0
ullan, Salt Lake City	.885	3	22	1	3	1
ka, Butte	.996	31	218	16	1	21
Idaho Falls	.982	22	156	5	3	18
nan, Idaho Falls	.983	7	50	9	1	5
s, Medicine Hat	.982	32	259	18	5	22
rson, Medicine Hat*	1.000	2	10	3	0	1
Medicine Hat	1.000	1	0	1	0	0
y, Billings	1.000	1	12	0	0	0
NTHAL, Salt Lake City*	.992	52	446	25	4	39
nino, Idaho Falls	1.000	2	1	0	0	1
s, Lethbridge	1.000	2	14	2	0	1
a, Idaho Falls	1.000	3	23	1	0	1
tt, Butte	1.000	1	2	1	0	0
e, Helena	.889	3	8	0	1	3
, Salt Lake City	.989	13	83	3	1	7
rop, Idaho Falls*	.982	41	300	27	6	39
s, Great Falls	.966	16	156	14	6	9

Triple play—Behr.

SECOND BASEMEN

, Team	Pct.	G	PO	A	E	DP
s, Billings	.871	13	16	11	4	2
Great Falls	.913	10	13	29	4	4
ston, Butte	.886	53	74	113	24	17
r, Salt Lake City	.894	15	19	23	5	8
s, Medicine Hat	.867	17	23	42	10	11
INS, Billings	.966	71	126	191	11	32
son, Medicine Hat	.962	62	106	124	9	25
m, Great Falls	.872	14	17	24	6	4
y, Idaho Falls	.969	45	86	99	6	23
n, Billings	.923	3	3	9	1	3
oza, Helena	.898	10	21	23	5	9
a, Salt Lake City	.984	25	28	34	1	8
nbo, Salt Lake City	1.000	2	1	1	0	0
, Butte	.931	6	9	18	2	2
Great Falls	.951	40	65	110	9	19
rs, Billings	1.000	4	7	13	0	2
ez, Salt Lake City	.962	43	70	132	8	19
rdson, Helena	.954	62	145	188	16	41
on, Salt Lake City	.957	8	20	24	2	6
s, Lethbridge	1.000	1	0	5	0	0
, Helena	1.000	1	1	0	0	0
nik, Lethbridge	.955	73	134	184	15	35
n, Idaho Falls	.975	6	18	21	1	4
no, Idaho Falls	.965	16	43	39	3	7
tt, Butte	.833	6	7	8	3	1
, Salt Lake City	.800	3	2	2	1	0
r, Helena	1.000	1	0	1	0	0
ki, Idaho Falls	.905	16	23	34	6	4
nburg, Idaho Falls	.922	12	23	24	4	8
all, Butte	.952	19	27	33	3	10

Triple play—Richardson.

THIRD BASEMEN

r, Team	Pct.	G	PO	A	E	DP
r, Salt Lake City	.917	8	2	9	1	1
co, Salt Lake City	.833	7	4	11	3	0
enares, Medicine Hat	.917	5	3	8	1	0
, Great Falls	.941	13	13	19	2	2
ndson, Lethbridge	.921	64	56	119	15	12
ston, Butte	.750	2	1	2	1	0
s, Medicine Hat	.894	52	53	115	20	13
am, Billings	.833	22	17	48	13	5
Butte	.000	2	0	0	1	0
o, Helena	1.000	2	0	1	0	0
es, Salt Lake City	.875	7	1	6	1	2
ette, Salt Lake City	1.000	1	3	0	0	1

(continued — right column)

Player, Team	Pct.	G	PO	A	E	DP
Johnson, Medicine Hat	1.000	3	2	5	0	0
Johnson, Great Falls	.863	15	10	34	7	1
Kimball, Great Falls	1.000	5	2	1	0	0
Kingston, Helena	1.000	2	0	1	0	0
Kopriva, Billings	.862	51	31	106	22	8
Lantigua, Great Falls	.902	25	22	52	8	3
Luna, Medicine Hat	.692	3	3	6	4	0
Martin, Billings	.750	6	0	3	1	0
Mendoza, Helena	1.000	2	0	2	0	0
Nalls, Idaho Falls	.892	24	15	43	7	7
Newman, Idaho Falls	.000	1	0	0	1	0
Owens, Billings	.900	4	2	7	1	1
Parra, Butte	.886	51	40	108	19	5
Powers, Helena	1.000	3	0	2	0	1
Rodrigues, Helena	1.000	1	1	0	0	0
Samson, Salt Lake City	.958	11	10	13	1	2
Scales, Lethbridge	.852	13	10	13	4	1
Smith, Helena	.800	3	3	1	1	0
Soto, Idaho Falls	.938	4	6	9	1	1
Sullivan, Butte	.800	3	1	3	1	0
Torian, Idaho Falls	.857	3	1	5	1	0
Trevino, Idaho Falls	.838	36	24	59	16	7
Triplett, Butte	.846	8	1	10	2	0
Unroe, Helena	.919	74	62	155	19	16
VOSIK, Salt Lake City	.931	59	39	96	10	10
Wilke, Medicine Hat	.789	12	10	20	8	2
Winicki, Great Falls	.863	20	15	29	7	5
Wollenburg, Idaho Falls	.857	9	8	16	4	1
Woodall, Butte	.822	16	13	24	8	1

SHORTSTOPS

Player, Team	Pct.	G	PO	A	E	DP
AURILIA, Butte	.943	56	78	154	14	24
Collins, Billings	.667	4	1	5	3	0
Colmenares, Medicine Hat	.815	13	20	24	10	6
Dumas, Helena	.905	14	22	45	7	9
Dunn, Great Falls	.933	8	5	9	1	1
Folger, Salt Lake City	1.000	12	4	11	0	2
Hayes, Medicine Hat	.690	6	7	13	9	3
Jaime, Great Falls	.909	60	98	173	27	33
Malloy, Idaho Falls	.885	17	41	44	11	11
Martin, Billings	.980	16	20	29	1	6
Mendoza, Helena	.920	7	12	11	2	5
Owens, Billings	.894	61	80	157	28	32
Parra, Butte	.965	17	47	35	3	7
Patzke, Medicine Hat	.925	59	117	180	24	28
Powers, Helena	1.000	2	0	4	0	0
Richardson, Helena	.861	7	12	19	5	5
Rigsby, Salt Lake City	.921	42	61	114	15	20
Ruhl, Lethbridge	.921	64	117	209	28	32
Samson, Salt Lake City	.922	36	59	107	14	15
Scales, Lethbridge	.926	13	24	26	4	5
Smith, Helena	.859	17	19	42	10	6
Torian, Idaho Falls	.937	12	22	37	4	7
Weger, Helena	.957	34	46	133	8	21
Winicki, Great Falls	.923	12	17	19	3	2
Wollenburg, Idaho Falls	.891	48	85	103	23	29
Woodall, Butte	.897	10	6	20	3	1

OUTFIELDERS

Player, Team	Pct.	G	PO	A	E	DP
Babki, Lethbridge	.956	48	82	4	4	2
Behr, Helena	1.000	2	3	0	0	0
Benjamin, Salt Lake City	.929	19	25	1	2	0
Bingham, Idaho Falls	.911	27	35	6	4	2
Cardona, Lethbridge	.000	1	0	0	1	0
Cedeno, Great Falls	.937	69	113	6	8	1
Clark, Salt Lake City*	.982	69	106	6	2	1
Colmenares, Medicine Hat	1.000	13	15	0	0	0
Correa, Idaho Falls	.962	62	121	5	5	1
Cradle, Medicine Hat	.978	60	129	5	3	1
Cunningham, Lethbridge	.906	22	27	2	3	0
Felder, Helena	.934	57	94	5	7	0
Franklin, Billings	.957	28	42	3	2	0
Garr, Idaho Falls	.938	44	71	5	5	0
Gates, Butte	1.000	2	2	0	0	0
Gonzalez, Butte	.962	75	141	12	6	4
Good, Lethbridge*	.967	56	81	8	3	0
Guild, Salt Lake City	.800	4	4	0	1	0
Hayes, Medicine Hat	1.000	2	3	0	0	0
Hearn, Medicine Hat*	.808	15	20	1	5	0
Herrera, Medicine Hat*	.931	72	132	3	10	0
Hughes, Helena	.972	23	31	4	1	0
Jackson, Salt Lake City	1.000	10	8	0	0	0
Jackson, Great Falls*	1.000	11	10	1	0	0
Johnson, Idaho Falls	1.000	6	10	0	0	0

Player, Team	Pct.	G	PO	A	E	DP
Koeper, Salt Lake City	.500	4	2	0	2	0
Lay, Helena*	1.000	10	13	0	0	0
Malone, Butte	1.000	20	20	1	0	0
Manship, Billings	1.000	7	6	0	0	0
Martin, Great Falls*	.891	38	39	2	5	0
MEGGERS, Billings	.985	62	60	6	1	0
Merrick, Salt Lake City	.914	30	30	2	3	0
Montgomery, Billings	1.000	1	1	0	0	0
Mottola, Billings	.970	54	89	9	3	1
Nagy, Billings	.981	27	51	0	1	0
Palumbo, Salt Lake City	.975	57	75	3	2	0
Perez, Helena	.982	28	50	5	1	0
Ponder, Lethbridge	.944	41	63	4	4	2
Pratt, Salt Lake City	1.000	8	5	0	0	0
Ragland, Lethbridge	.933	11	11	3	1	0
Richardson, Helena	1.000	1	3	0	0	0
Rodrigues, Helena	.944	71	93	9	6	3
E. Rodriguez, Great Falls	.953	55	92	9	5	0
F. Rodriguez, Great Falls	1.000	1	3	0	0	0
Rosenthal, Salt Lake City*	1.000	11	23	1	0	0
Ross, Helena	.957	49	84	5	4	0
Saturnino, Idaho Falls	.947	33	47	7	3	2
Shook, Butte	1.000	6	6	0	0	0
Smith, Great Falls	1.000	17	13	0	0	1
Sweeney, Great Falls*	.971	33	31	2	1	2
Tena, Lethbridge	.975	20	39	0	1	0
Triplett, Butte	1.000	2	1	0	0	0
Villalona, Medicine Hat*	.963	69	146	8	6	1
Waldrop, Idaho Falls*	.872	19	32	2	5	0
Warner, Idaho Falls*	.944	10	17	0	1	0
Welch, Butte*	.948	67	88	3	5	0
Wilkerson, Billings*	.971	67	129	4	4	2
Williams, Lethbridge	.961	33	48	1	2	0
Wilson, Butte*	.916	71	90	8	9	0
Wilson, Salt Lake City*	.977	63	120	5	3	0
Woods, Idaho Falls	.925	36	45	4	4	1
Zammarchi, Great Falls	.962	20	23	2	1	0

Triple play—Ross.

CATCHERS

Player, Team	Pct.	G	PO	A	E	DP	PB
Baker, Salt Lake City	.989	34	172	14	2	0	9
Bethke, Butte	.974	41	298	33	9	1	3
Brown, Great Falls	1.000	12	80	2	0	0	5
Campbell, Lethbridge	.938	2	14	1	1	0	0
Dobrolsky, Helena	.983	11	50	8	1	0	1
Dreisbach, Billings	1.000	5	29	6	0	0	0
Hieb, Butte	.980	40	331	54	8	1	10
HOSTETLER, Helena	.994	48	292	26	2	1	12
Hughes, Helena	1.000	5	33	5	0	0	0
Kimler, Lethbridge	.933	2	10	4	1	0	0
Kuhn, Idaho Falls	.986	27	194	24	3	0	2
Lampkin, Lethbridge	.974	25	159	32	5	3	9
Lavigne, Idaho Falls*	1.000	6	25	2	0	0	2
Luzinski, Great Falls	.987	40	278	26	4	1	7
Martinez, Medicine Hat	.985	47	275	58	5	2	24
McMullan, Salt Lake City	.931	6	25	2	2	0	1
Norris, Medicine Hat	.929	2	11	2	1	1	0
Payne, Lethbridge	.923	1	11	1	1	1	0
Polis, Medicine Hat	.974	31	157	32	5	2	3
Ramey, Billings	.956	10	59	6	3	0	3
Rea, Lethbridge	.977	49	295	48	8	1	9
Rennspies, Great Falls	1.000	2	21	1	0	0	0
Rodriguez, Great Falls	.992	28	218	33	2	4	1
Rumfield, Billings	.985	60	474	37	8	1	8
Schula, Idaho Falls	.958	4	22	1	1	0	1
Silvia, Billings	.976	4	40	1	1	0	2
Smith, Salt Lake City	1.000	3	7	1	0	0	0
Snyder, Salt Lake City	.979	54	383	41	9	1	5
Soto, Idaho Falls	.983	49	335	60	7	6	10
Thomas, Helena	.988	13	71	11	1	2	3
Towle, Billings	1.000	7	25	4	0	0	0
Watts, Great Falls	1.000	3	2	0	0	0	1
Willman, Helena	.991	19	103	12	1	1	4

PITCHERS

Player, Team	Pct.	G	PO	A	E	DP
Acevedo, Lethbridge*	1.000	5	0	3	0	0
Angel, Billings	.828	15	11	13	5	2
Aronetz, Lethbridge*	.808	14	5	16	5	3
Ballance, Lethbridge*	.923	15	3	9	1	0
Behrens, Idaho Falls	.714	7	3	2	2	0
Beltran, Medicine Hat	.950	15	8	11	1	0
Bills, Medicine Hat	.636	20	3	4	4	0
Bradshaw, Idaho Falls*	1.000	24	2	5	0	0
Brandenburg, Butte	.917	24	3	8	1	0
Brock, Idaho Falls	.778	15	4	10	4	0
Brown, Medicine Hat*	1.000	21	5	3	0	0

Player, Team	Pct.	G	PO	A	E	DP
Burke, Billings	1.000	9	1	2	0	0
Campusano, Lethbridge	.818	11	3	6	2	0
Canestro, Salt Lake City*	.500	5	0	3	3	0
Carew, Butte	1.000	15	5	2	0	0
Chavarria, Butte	.933	13	6	8	1	0
Coleman, Lethbridge	.889	19	1	7	1	0
Colmenares, Medicine Hat	1.000	1	0	1	0	0
Cope, Great Falls*	1.000	19	3	6	0	0
Costello, Great Falls	.800	7	1	3	1	0
Crema, Medicine Hat	1.000	21	1	2	0	0
Cromer, Idaho Falls	.857	18	6	6	2	0
Cudjo, Lethbridge	1.000	20	1	5	0	0
Demyan, Helena	1.000	3	1	1	0	0
Devaughan, Salt Lake City	1.000	12	0	1	0	0
Dolson, Medicine Hat*	.813	16	6	7	3	1
Droll, Helena	1.000	9	0	1	0	0
England, Helena	1.000	3	3	2	0	1
Evans, Butte*	1.000	2	0	2	0	0
Eyre, Butte*	.833	15	3	12	3	1
Fitzpatrick, Great Falls	.889	21	2	6	1	0
Ford, Idaho Falls*	1.000	27	3	2	0	1
Garcia, Billings	.857	31	3	9	2	1
Giard, Idaho Falls	1.000	11	2	6	0	0
Gilligan, Salt Lake City	1.000	28	2	4	0	0
Groot, Great Falls	.909	16	5	5	1	0
Guidi, Salt Lake City	1.000	23	1	5	0	0
Harden, Salt Lake City*	1.000	5	1	3	0	1
Hardwick, Helena*	1.000	5	0	2	0	0
Henderson, Great Falls	1.000	11	4	14	0	1
Herrera, Medicine Hat	.500	4	0	1	1	0
Huie, Salt Lake City*	1.000	2	1	0	0	0
Iglesias, Great Falls	.900	12	1	8	1	1
Jacobson, Great Falls	.900	6	2	7	1	0
Jenkins, Lethbridge	1.000	16	2	4	0	1
Jones, Helena*	.895	14	4	13	2	2
Jones, Salt Lake City	1.000	3	0	3	0	1
Karl, Helena*	.900	9	7	11	2	2
Kelley, Butte	.750	18	1	5	2	0
Kerfut, Salt Lake City	.947	15	3	15	1	1
Kimel, Butte*	.850	15	2	15	3	0
Kummerfeldt, Billings	.842	13	4	12	3	1
Lairsey, Idaho Falls*	.833	17	3	7	2	0
Langford, Billings	.833	15	9	6	3	1
Lee, Lethbridge	.882	21	4	11	2	0
Lesch, Butte	.667	16	1	3	2	0
Licursi, Salt Lake City	1.000	18	2	2	0	1
Linares, Great Falls	.800	19	5	3	2	0
Lister, Billings*	.714	26	1	4	2	0
Loftin, Billings	1.000	33	5	10	0	1
Madrigal, Butte	1.000	16	1	8	0	0
Maitland, Idaho Falls	.933	24	8	6	1	1
Maltagliati, Helena	1.000	2	1	1	0	0
Manning, Butte	.857	8	0	6	1	0
Marcon, Salt Lake City*	1.000	11	4	12	0	0
Marshall, Helena	1.000	18	1	2	0	0
Martineau, Idaho Falls	1.000	6	1	1	0	1
Martinez, Great Falls*	1.000	6	0	2	0	0
Mascia, Butte	1.000	17	2	6	0	1
Matthews, Lethbridge	1.000	24	2	4	0	0
Morales, Billings	1.000	8	3	4	0	0
Muir, Medicine Hat	1.000	17	3	7	0	0
Murphy, Billings	.500	21	0	1	1	0
Myers, Lethbridge	.824	15	10	32	9	2
Nettnin, Salt Lake City*	1.000	4	0	1	0	0
Newcomb, Butte	1.000	22	1	5	0	0
O'Brien, Butte*	.889	8	2	6	1	0
O'Halloran, Medicine Hat	.500	13	1	3	4	0
Parisotto, Salt Lake City	1.000	14	8	11	0	1
Patterson, Medicine Hat*	.900	17	2	7	1	0
Paul, Helena	1.000	13	1	5	0	0
Petrocella, Helena	.714	27	0	5	2	1
Pettiford, Salt Lake City	1.000	14	6	8	0	0
Phillips, Medicine Hat	1.000	15	2	10	0	1
Pickett, Billings*	.778	20	2	5	2	1
Pike, Idaho Falls	.778	24	3	4	2	1
Pincavitch, Great Falls	.667	26	3	5	4	0
Polanco, Lethbridge	1.000	9	0	4	0	0
Pyc, Great Falls*	.917	25	1	10	1	0
Reed, Billings	.769	10	1	9	3	2
Reynoso, Medicine Hat*	.786	14	4	7	3	0
Rico, Helena*	.500	4	0	1	1	0
Roberson, Helena*	.900	9	4	14	2	1
Rodriguez, Helena	1.000	6	0	2	0	0
Rosenkranz, Butte*	.750	14	2	1	1	0
Rusciano, Idaho Falls	.917	20	4	7	1	2
Rutter, Helena	.882	15	5	10	2	1
Ryan, Salt Lake City*	1.000	7	0	2	0	0
Sadler, Butte	.833	4	1	4	1	0
Schenbeck, Helena	.700	32	2	5	3	0
Schultea, Salt Lake City	1.000	24	2	5	0	0
Simmons, Idaho Falls*	1.000	27	2	5	0	1
Sinclair, Medicine Hat*	.867	9	5	8	2	0
Smith, Great Falls*	1.000	5	1	1	0	0
Spykstra, Great Falls	.333	8	0	1	2	1
Stoecklin, Idaho Falls*	.857	16	3	3	1	0
Sullivan, Billings	.818	24	2	7	2	1

ɔr. Team	Pct.	G	PO	A	E	DP	Player, Team	Pct.	G	PO	A	E	DP
or, Medicine Hat*	1.000	11	3	14	0	2	Watts, Great Falls*	.750	13	0	3	1	0
den, Salt Lake City	.875	15	8	13	3	1	West, Lethbridge	.714	16	0	5	2	0
n, Billings	.857	9	1	5	1	0	Wiley, Butte	.846	18	3	8	2	1
ez, Helena	.850	17	6	11	3	0	Winter, Helena	1.000	13	3	4	0	0
an, Lethbridge	.923	12	3	9	1	1	Zammarchi, Great Falls	1.000	1	0	1	0	0
lgesang, Great Falls	1.000	9	0	1	0	0	ZERBE, Great Falls*	1.000	15	6	19	0	1
e, Idaho Falls*	.800	13	3	5	2	0							

The following players did not have any fielding statistics at the positions indicated or appeared only as a designated hitter, pinch-hitter or
-runner: Butcher, p; Colmenares, 1b; Dempsey, p; Dreisbach, p; Dunn, of; Edmondson, p; Gates, 2b; G. Gonzalez, c; Hudson, dh, ph; Kyslinger, p;
mola, p; M. Martin, p; A. Martinez, 1b, ss; Mendoza, of; Miller, of; Nalepka, 3b; Nalls, p; Payne, 3b; Polis, 2b, of; Ponder, 1b; Rodrigues, 2b; Ross,
Shook, c; Trevino, p; Triplett, ss; Unroe, 2b; Welch, p; Willman, of; Winicki, of.

LEAGUE CHAMPIONS

Year	Team	Pct.	Year	Team	Pct.	Year	Team	Pct.
	— Twin Falls*	.581	1957	— Salt Lake City	.650	1979	— Helena	.623
	— Salt Lake City	.608		Billings†	.582		Lethbridge y	.559
	Ogden (4th)*	.492	1958	— Great Falls	.582	1980	— Lethbridge y	.743
	— Boise	.623		Boise†	.615		Billings	.629
	Ogden (2nd)*	.598	1959	— Boise	.633	1981	— Calgary	.657
	— Pocatello†	.690		Billings (2nd)*	.523		Butte y	.557
	Boise	.683	1960	— Boise†	.686	1982	— Medicine Hat y	.629
-44-45—Did not operate.				Idaho Falls	.650		Idaho Falls	.600
	— Twin Falls‡	.585	1961	— Boise	.638	1983	— Billings y	.614
	Salt Lake City†	.585		Great Falls*	.571		Calgary	.600
	— Salt Lake City	.618	1962	— Boise§	.565	1984	— Billings	.691
	Twin Falls†	.600		Billings†	.706		Helena y	.647
	— Pocatello	.611	1963	— Idaho Falls	.702	1985	— Great Falls	.771
	Twin Falls (2nd)*	.595		Magic Valley†	.643		Salt Lake City y	.657
	— Twin Falls	.624	1964	— Treasure Valley	.615	1986	— Salt Lake City z	.643
	Pocatello (3rd)*	.595	1965	— Treasure Valley	.530		Great Falls	.571
	— Pocatello	.635	1966	— Ogden	.591	1987	— Salt Lake City z	.700
	Billings (3rd)*	.571	1967	— Ogden	.621		Helena	.657
	— Salt Lake City	.618	1968	— Ogden	.609	1988	— Great Falls z	.754
	Great Falls (3rd)*	.559	1969	— Ogden	.620		Butte	.629
	— Pocatello	.595	1970	— Idaho Falls	.629	1989	— Great Falls z	.791
	Idaho Falls (2nd)*	.573	1971	— Great Falls	.643		Butte	.621
	— Ogden	.679	1972	— Billings	.694	1990	— Great Falls z	.706
	Salt Lake City (4th)*	.527	1973	— Billings	.629		Salt Lake	.618
	— Salt Lake City	.595	1974	— Idaho Falls	.569	1991	— Salt Lake City z	.700
	Great Falls (4th)*	.530	1975	— Great Falls	.577		Great Falls	.657
	— Boise	.588	1976	— Great Falls	.577	1992	— Salt Lake	.697
	Magic Valley (4th)*	.489	1977	— Lethbridge	.629		Billings z	.697
	— Boise	.561	1978	— Billings x	.735			

*Won four-club playoff. †Won split-season playoff. ‡Ended first half in tie with Salt Lake City and won one-game playoff. §Ended first half in
th Billings and Great Falls and won playoff. xBillings (first place) defeated Idaho Falls (second place) in First Place-Second Place playoff.
gue divided into Northern and Southern divisions; won two-club playoff. zWon two-club playoff.

MINOR LEAGUE INDEX